NCAA FOOTBALL

THE OFFICIAL 1996 COLLEGE FOOTBALL RECORDS BOOK

NATIONAL COLLEGIATE ATHLETIC ASSOCIATION

THE NATIONAL COLLEGIATE ATHLETIC ASSOCIATION
6201 College Boulevard, Overland Park, Kansas 66211-2422
913/339-1906
http://www.ncaa.org

July 1996

Compiled By:
Richard M. Campbell, *Assistant Statistics Coordinator.*
John D. Painter, *Assistant Statistics Coordinator.*
Sean W. Straziscar, *Assistant Statistics Coordinator.*

Edited By:
J. Gregory Summers, *Assistant Director of Publishing.*

Typesetting/Production By:
Karen S. Larsen, *Typesetter.*
Teresa S. Wolfgang, *Publishing Production Assistant.*

Cover Design By:
Wayne O. Davis, *Assistant Publishing Production Coordinator.*

Cover Photograph By:
Young Company, Kansas City, Missouri.

Distributed to sports information directors and conference publicity directors.

Printed in the United States of America.

ISSN 0735-5475
NCAA 11069-7/96

Contents

Division I-A Records

Individual Records

Under a three-division reorganization plan adopted by the special NCAA Convention of August 1973, teams classified major-college in football on August 1, 1973, were placed in Division I. College-division teams were divided into Division II and Division III. At the NCAA Convention of January 1978, Division I was divided into Division I-A and Division I-AA for football only.

From 1937, when official national statistics rankings began, through 1969, individual rankings were by totals. Beginning in 1970, most season individual rankings were by per-game averages. In total offense, rushing and scoring, it is yards or points per game; in receiving, catches per game and yards per game; in interceptions, catches per game; and in punt and kickoff returns, yards per return. Punting always has been by average, and all team rankings have been per game. Beginning in 1979, passers were rated in all divisions on "efficiency rating points," which are derived from a formula that compares passers to the national averages for 14 seasons of two-platoon Division I football starting with the 1965 season. One hundred points equals the 14-year averages for all players in Division I. Those averages break down to 6.29 yards per attempt, 47.14 percent completions, 3.97 percent touchdown passes and 6.54 percent interceptions. The formula assumes that touchdowns are as good as interceptions are bad; therefore, these two figures offset each other for the average player. To determine efficiency rating points, multiply a passer's yards per attempt by 8.4, add his completion percentage, add his touchdown percentage times 3.3, then subtract his interception percentage times two.

Passers must have a minimum of 15 attempts per game to determine rating points because fewer attempts could allow a player to win the championship with fewer than 100 attempts in a season. A passer must play in at least 75 percent of his team's games to qualify for the rankings (e.g., a player on a team with a nine-game season could qualify by playing in seven games); thus, a passer with 105 attempts could qualify for the national rankings.

A pass efficiency rating comparison for each year since 1979 has been added to the passing section of all-time leaders.

All individual and team records and rankings include regular-season games only. Career records of players include only those years in which they competed in Division I-A.

Statistics in some team categories were not tabulated until the advent of the computerized statistics program in 1966. The records listed in those categories begin with the 1966 season and are so indicated.

In 1954, the regular-season schedule was limited to a maximum of 10 games, and in 1970, to a limit of 11 games, excluding postseason competition.

A player whose career includes statistics for parts of five seasons (or an active player who will play in five seasons) because he was granted an additional season of competition for reasons of hardship or a freshman redshirt are denoted by "$."

COLLEGIATE RECORDS

Individual collegiate records are determined by comparing the best records in all four divisions (I-A, I-AA, II and III) in comparable categories. Included are career records of players who played parts of their careers in different divisions (such as Dennis Shaw of San Diego State, Howard Stevens of Randolph-Macon and Louisville, and Doug Williams of Grambling). For individual collegiate career leaders, see page 187.

Total Offense

(Rushing Plus Passing)

MOST PLAYS

Quarter
36—Rusty LaRue, Wake Forest vs. Duke, Oct. 28, 1995 (4th; 35 passes, 1 rush)

Half
57—Rusty LaRue, Wake Forest vs. Duke, Oct. 28, 1995 (2nd; 56 passes, 1 rush)

Game
94—Matt Vogler, Texas Christian vs. Houston, Nov. 3, 1990 (696 yards)

Season
704—David Klingler, Houston, 1990 (5,221 yards)

2 Yrs
1,293—David Klingler, Houston, 1990-91 (8,447 yards)

3 Yrs
1,610—Ty Detmer, Brigham Young, 1989-91 (13,456 yards)

Career
(4 yrs.) 1,795—Ty Detmer, Brigham Young, 1988-91 (14,665 yards)

MOST PLAYS PER GAME

Season
64.0—David Klingler, Houston, 1990 (704 in 11)

2 Yrs
61.6—David Klingler, Houston, 1990-91 (1,293 in 21)

Career
48.5—Doug Gaynor, Long Beach St., 1984-85 (1,067 in 22)

MOST PLAYS BY A FRESHMAN

Game
76—Sandy Schwab, Northwestern vs. Michigan, Oct. 23, 1982 (431 yards)

Season
504—Sandy Schwab, Northwestern, 1982 (2,555 yards)
Also holds per-game record at 45.8 (504 in 11)

MOST YARDS GAINED

Quarter
347—Jason Davis, UNLV vs. Idaho, Sept. 17, 1994 (4th)

Half
510—Andre Ware, Houston vs. Southern Methodist, Oct. 21, 1989 (1st)

Game
732—David Klingler, Houston vs. Arizona St., Dec. 2, 1990 (16 rushing, 716 passing)

Season
5,221—David Klingler, Houston, 1990 (81 rushing, 5,140 passing)

2 Yrs
9,455—Ty Detmer, Brigham Young, 1989-90 (-293 rushing, 9,748 passing)

3 Yrs
13,456—Ty Detmer, Brigham Young, 1989-91 (-323 rushing, 13,779 passing)

Career
(4 yrs.) 14,665—Ty Detmer, Brigham Young, 1988-91 (-366 rushing, 15,031 passing)

MOST YARDS GAINED PER GAME

Season
474.6—David Klingler, Houston, 1990 (5,221 in 11)

2 Yrs
402.2—David Klingler, Houston, 1990-91 (8,447 in 21)

Career
320.9—Chris Vargas, Nevada, 1992-93 (6,417 in 20)

MOST YARDS GAINED, FIRST TWO SEASONS

6,710—Doug Gaynor, Long Beach St., 1984-85
Also holds per-game record at 305.0

MOST SEASONS GAINING 4,000 YARDS OR MORE

3—Ty Detmer, Brigham Young, 1989-91

MOST SEASONS GAINING 3,000 YARDS OR MORE

3—Ty Detmer, Brigham Young, 1989-91

MOST SEASONS GAINING 2,500 YARDS OR MORE

3—Stoney Case, New Mexico, 1992-94; Shane Matthews, Florida, 1990-92; Ty Detmer, Brigham Young, 1989-91; Shawn Moore, Virginia, 1988-90; Erik Wilhelm, Oregon St., 1986-88; Brian McClure, Bowling Green, 1983-85; Randall Cunningham, UNLV, 1982-84; Doug Flutie, Boston College, 1982-84; John Elway, Stanford, 1980-82

MOST YARDS GAINED BY A FRESHMAN

Game
458—Bob Hoernschemeyer, Indiana vs. Nebraska, Oct. 9, 1943 (37 plays)

Season
2,975—Todd Ellis, South Caro., 1986 (436 plays)
Also holds per-game record at 270.5

MOST YARDS GAINED BY A SOPHOMORE

Game
625—Scott Mitchell, Utah vs. Air Force, Oct. 15, 1988 (-6 rushing, 631 passing)

Season
4,433—Ty Detmer, Brigham Young, 1989 (12 games, 497 plays)
Per-game record—390.8, Scott Mitchell, Utah, 1988

MOST YARDS GAINED IN FIRST GAME OF CAREER

483—Billy Stevens, UTEP vs. North Texas, Sept. 18, 1965

MOST YARDS GAINED IN TWO, THREE AND FOUR CONSECUTIVE GAMES

2 Games
1,310—David Klingler, Houston, 1990 (578 vs. Eastern Wash., Nov. 17; 732 vs. Arizona St., Dec. 2)

3 Games
1,651—David Klingler, Houston, 1990 (341 vs. Texas, Nov. 10; 578 vs. Eastern Wash., Nov. 17; 732 vs. Arizona St., Dec. 2)

4 Games
2,276—David Klingler, Houston, 1990 (625 vs. Texas Christian, Nov. 3; 341 vs. Texas, Nov. 10; 578 vs. Eastern Wash., Nov. 17; 732 vs. Arizona St., Dec. 2)

MOST GAMES GAINING 300 YARDS OR MORE

Season
12—Ty Detmer, Brigham Young, 1990

Career
33—Ty Detmer, Brigham Young, 1988-91

MOST CONSECUTIVE GAMES GAINING 300 YARDS OR MORE

Season
12—Ty Detmer, Brigham Young, 1990

Career
19—Ty Detmer, Brigham Young, 1989-90

MOST GAMES GAINING 400 YARDS OR MORE

Season
9—David Klingler, Houston, 1990

Career
13—Ty Detmer, Brigham Young, 1988-91

MOST CONSECUTIVE GAMES GAINING 400 YARDS OR MORE

Season
5—Ty Detmer, Brigham Young, 1990
Also holds career record at 5

MOST YARDS GAINED AGAINST ONE OPPONENT
Career
1,483—Ty Detmer, Brigham Young vs. San Diego St., 1988-91

MOST YARDS GAINED PER GAME AGAINST ONE OPPONENT
Career
(Min. 3 games) 399.0—Cody Ledbetter, New Mexico St. vs. UNLV, 1993-95 (1,197 yards)
(Min. 4 games) 370.8—Ty Detmer, Brigham Young vs. San Diego St., 1988-91 (1,483 yards)

MOST YARDS GAINED BY TWO OPPOSING PLAYERS
Game
1,321—Matt Vogler, Texas Christian (696) & David Klingler, Houston (625), Nov. 3, 1990

GAINING 1,000 YARDS RUSHING AND 1,000 YARDS PASSING
Season
Beau Morgan (QB), Air Force, 1995 (1,285 rushing, 1,165 passing); Michael Carter (QB), Hawaii, 1991 (1,092 rushing, 1,172 passing); Brian Mitchell (QB), Southwestern La., 1989 (1,311 rushing, 1,966 passing); Dee Dowis (QB), Air Force, 1989 (1,286 rushing, 1,285 passing); Darian Hagan (QB), Colorado, 1989 (1,004 rushing, 1,002 passing); Bart Weiss (QB), Air Force, 1985 (1,032 rushing, 1,449 passing); Reggie Collier (QB), Southern Miss., 1981 (1,005 rushing, 1,004 passing); Johnny Bright (HB), Drake, 1950 (1,232 rushing, 1,168 passing)

A QUARTERBACK GAINING 2,000 YARDS RUSHING AND 4,000 YARDS PASSING
Career
Major Harris, West Va., 1987-89 (2,030 rushing, 4,834 passing); Brian Mitchell, Southwestern La., 1986-89 (3,335 rushing, 5,447 passing); Rickey Foggie, Minnesota, 1984-87 (2,038 rushing, 4,903 passing); John Bond, Mississippi St., 1980-83 (2,280 rushing, 4,621 passing); Prince McJunkins, Wichita St., 1979-82 (2,047 rushing, 4,544 passing)

A QUARTERBACK GAINING 300 YARDS PASSING AND 100 YARDS RUSHING
Game
Donald Douglas, Houston vs. Southern Methodist, Oct. 19, 1991 (103 rushing, 319 passing); Randy Welniak, Wyoming vs. Air Force, Sept. 24, 1988 (108 rushing, 359 passing); Ned James, New Mexico vs. Wyoming, Nov. 1, 1986 (118 rushing, 406 passing)

A QUARTERBACK GAINING 200 YARDS RUSHING AND 200 YARDS PASSING
Game
Brian Mitchell, Southwestern La. vs. Colorado St., Nov. 21, 1987 (271 rushing, 205 passing); Steve Gage, Tulsa vs. New Mexico, Nov. 8, 1986 (212 rushing, 209 passing); Reds Bagnell, Pennsylvania vs. Dartmouth, Oct. 14, 1950 (214 rushing, 276 passing)

TEAMS HAVING A 3,000-YARD PASSER, 1,000-YARD RUSHER AND 1,000-YARD RECEIVER IN THE SAME YEAR
11 teams. Most recent: Nevada, 1995 (Mike Maxwell [3,611 passer], Alex Van Dyke [1,854 receiver] and Kim Minor [1,052 rusher]); New Mexico St., 1995 (Cody Ledbetter [3,501 passer], Denvis Manns [1,120 rusher] and Lucious Davis [1,018 receiver]); Ohio St., 1995 (Bobby Hoying [3,023 passer], Eddie George [1,826 rusher] and Terry Glenn [1,316 receiver]); San Diego St., 1995 (Billy Blanton [3,300 passer], George Jones [1,842 rusher], Will Blackwell [1,207 receiver] and Az Hakim [1,022 receiver]); Nevada, 1994 (Mike Maxwell [3,537 passer], Alex Van Dyke [1,246 receiver] and Marcellus Chrishon [1,076 rusher])

TEAMS HAVING A 2,000-YARD RUSHER AND 2,000-YARD PASSER IN THE SAME YEAR
2—Colorado, 1994 (Rashaan Salaam [2,055 rusher] and Kordell Stewart [2,071 passer]); Oklahoma St., 1988 (Barry Sanders [2,628 rusher] and Mike Gundy [2,163 passer])

HIGHEST AVERAGE GAIN PER PLAY
Game
(Min. 37-62 plays) 12.8—Chris Vargas, Nevada vs. UNLV, Oct. 2, 1993 (42 for 537)
(Min. 63 plays) 9.9—David Klingler, Houston vs. Texas Christian, Nov. 3, 1990 (63 for 625)
Season
(Min. 3,000 yards) 8.9—Ty Detmer, Brigham Young, 1989 (497 for 4,433)
Career
(Min. 7,500 yards) 8.2—Ty Detmer, Brigham Young, 1988-91 (1,795 for 14,665)

MOST TOUCHDOWNS RESPONSIBLE FOR (TDs Scored and Passed For)
Game
11—David Klingler, Houston vs. Eastern Wash., Nov. 17, 1990 (passed for 11)
Season
55—David Klingler, Houston, 1990 (scored 1, passed for 54)
2 Yrs
85—David Klingler, Houston, 1990-91 (scored 2, passed for 83)
3 Yrs
122—Ty Detmer, Brigham Young, 1989-91 (scored 14, passed for 108)
Career
135—Ty Detmer, Brigham Young, 1988-91 (scored 14, passed for 121)

MOST TOUCHDOWNS RESPONSIBLE FOR PER GAME
Season
5.0—David Klingler, Houston, 1990 (55 in 11)
2 Yrs
4.0—David Klingler, Houston, 1990-91 (85 in 21)
3 Yrs
3.4—Ty Detmer, Brigham Young, 1989-91 (122 in 36)
Career
2.9—Ty Detmer, Brigham Young, 1988-91 (135 in 46)
Collegiate record—3.6, Dennis Shaw, San Diego St., 1968-69 (72 in 20)

MOST POINTS RESPONSIBLE FOR (Points Scored and Passed For)
Game
66—David Klingler, Houston vs. Eastern Wash., Nov. 17, 1990 (passed for 11 TDs)
Season
334—David Klingler, Houston, 1990 (scored 1 TD, passed for 54 TDs, accounted for 2 two-point conversions)
2 Yrs
514—David Klingler, Houston, 1990-91 (scored 2 TDs, passed for 83 TDs, accounted for 2 two-point conversions)
3 Yrs
582—Ty Detmer, Brigham Young, 1988-90 (scored 10 TDs, passed for 86 TDs, accounted for 3 two-point conversions)
Career
820—Ty Detmer, Brigham Young, 1988-91 (scored 14 TDs, passed for 121 TDs, accounted for 5 two-point conversions)

MOST POINTS RESPONSIBLE FOR PER GAME
Season
30.4—David Klingler, Houston, 1990 (334 in 11)
2 Yrs
22.8—Jim McMahon, Brigham Young, 1980-81 (502 in 22)
3 Yrs
17.1—Ty Detmer, Brigham Young, 1988-90 (582 in 34)
Career
17.8—Ty Detmer, Brigham Young, 1988-91 (820 in 46)
Collegiate record—21.6, Dennis Shaw, San Diego St., 1968-69 (432 in 20)

SCORING 200 POINTS AND PASSING FOR 200 POINTS
Career
Rick Leach, Michigan, 1975-78 (scored 204, passed for 270)

Rushing

MOST RUSHES
Quarter
22—Alex Smith, Indiana vs. Michigan St., Nov. 11, 1995 (1st, 114 yards)
Half
34—Tony Sands, Kansas vs. Missouri, Nov. 23, 1991 (2nd, 240 yards)
Game
58—Tony Sands, Kansas vs. Missouri, Nov. 23, 1991 (396 yards)
Season
403—Marcus Allen, Southern Cal, 1981 (2,342 yards)
2 Yrs
757—Marcus Allen, Southern Cal, 1980-81 (3,905 yards)
Career
(3 yrs.) 994—Herschel Walker, Georgia, 1980-82 (5,259 yards)
(4 yrs.) 1,215—Steve Bartalo, Colorado St., 1983-86 (4,813 yards)

MOST RUSHES PER GAME
Season
39.6—Ed Marinaro, Cornell, 1971 (356 in 9)
2 Yrs
36.0—Marcus Allen, Southern Cal, 1980-81 (757 in 21)
Career
34.0—Ed Marinaro, Cornell, 1969-71 (918 in 27)

MOST RUSHES BY A FRESHMAN
Game
45—James McDougal, Wake Forest vs. Clemson, Oct. 9, 1976 (249 yards)
Season
292—Steve Bartalo, Colorado St., 1983 (1,113 yards)

MOST RUSHES PER GAME BY A FRESHMAN
Season
29.2—Steve Bartalo, Colorado St., 1983 (292 in 10)

MOST CONSECUTIVE RUSHES BY SAME PLAYER
Game
16—William Howard, Tennessee vs. Mississippi, Nov. 15, 1986 (during two possessions)

MOST RUSHES IN TWO CONSECUTIVE GAMES
Season
102—Lorenzo White, Michigan St., 1985 (53 vs. Purdue, Oct. 26; 49 vs. Minnesota, Nov. 2)

MOST YARDS GAINED
Quarter
214—Andre Herrera, Southern Ill. vs. Northern Ill., Oct. 23, 1976 (1st, 17 rushes)
Half
287—Stacey Robinson, Northern Ill. vs. Fresno St., Oct. 6, 1990 (1st; 114 in first quarter, 173 in second quarter; 20 rushes)
Game
396—Tony Sands, Kansas vs. Missouri, Nov. 23, 1991 (58 rushes) (240 yards on 34 carries, second half)
Season
2,628—Barry Sanders, Oklahoma St., 1988 (344 rushes, 11 games)
2 Yrs
3,905—Marcus Allen, Southern Cal, 1980-81 (757 rushes)
Career
(3 yrs.) 5,259—Herschel Walker, Georgia, 1980-82 (994 rushes)
(4 yrs.) 6,082—Tony Dorsett, Pittsburgh, 1973-76 (1,074 rushes)

MOST YARDS GAINED PER GAME
Season
238.9—Barry Sanders, Oklahoma St., 1988 (2,628 in 11)
2 Yrs
186.0—Marcus Allen, Southern Cal, 1980-81 (3,905 in 21)
Career
174.6—Ed Marinaro, Cornell, 1969-71 (4,715 in 27)

MOST YARDS GAINED BY A FRESHMAN
Game
386—Marshall Faulk, San Diego St. vs. Pacific (Cal.), Sept. 14, 1991 (37 rushes)

Season
1,616—Herschel Walker, Georgia, 1980 (274 rushes)
Per-game record—158.8, Marshall Faulk, San Diego St., 1991 (1,429 in 9)

MOST YARDS GAINED BY A SOPHOMORE
Game
342—Charlie Davis, Colorado vs. Oklahoma St., Nov. 13, 1971 (34 rushes)
Season
2,010—Troy Davis, Iowa St., 1995 (345 rushes)
Also holds per-game record at 182.7 (2,010 in 11)

FRESHMEN GAINING 1,000 YARDS OR MORE
Season
By 40 players (see chart after Annual Rushing Champions). Most recent: Denvis Manns, New Mexico St., 1995 (1,120); Silas Massey, Central Mich., 1995 (1,089); Ahman Green, Nebraska, 1995 (1,086); Alex Smith, Indiana, 1994 (1,475); Astron Whatley, Kent, 1994 (1,003)

TWO FRESHMEN, SAME TEAM, GAINING 1,000 YARDS OR MORE
Season
Mike Smith (1,062) & Gwain Durden (1,049), Tenn.-Chatt., 1977

EARLIEST GAME A FRESHMAN REACHED 1,000 YARDS
Season
7—Marshall Faulk, San Diego St., 1991 (1,157 vs. Colorado St., Nov. 9); Emmitt Smith, Florida, 1987 (1,011 vs. Temple, Oct. 17)

FIRST PLAYER TO GAIN 1,000 YARDS OR MORE
Season
Byron "Whizzer" White, Colorado, 1937 (1,121)
(Note: Before NCAA records began in 1937, Morley Drury of Southern Cal gained 1,163 yards in 1927)

EARLIEST GAME GAINING 1,000 YARDS OR MORE
Season
5—Marcus Allen, Southern Cal, 1981 (1,136); Ernest Anderson, Oklahoma St., 1982 (1,042); Ed Marinaro, Cornell, 1971 (1,026); Ricky Bell, Southern Cal, 1976 (1,008); Barry Sanders, Oklahoma St., 1988 (1,002)

MOST YARDS GAINED BY A QUARTERBACK
Game
308—Stacey Robinson, Northern Ill. vs. Fresno St., Oct. 6, 1990 (22 rushes)
Season
1,443—Stacey Robinson, Northern Ill., 1989 (223 rushes)
Also holds per-game record at 131.2 (1,443 in 11)
Career
3,612—Dee Dowis, Air Force, 1986-89 (543 rushes)
Per-game record—109.1, Stacey Robinson, Northern Ill., 1988-90 (2,727 in 25)

LONGEST GAIN BY A QUARTERBACK
Game
98—Mark Malone, Arizona St. vs. Utah St., Oct. 27, 1979 (TD)

MOST GAMES GAINING 100 YARDS OR MORE
Season
11—By 12 players. Most recent: Wasean Tait, Toledo, 1995; Darnell Autry, Northwestern, 1995
Career
33—Tony Dorsett, Pittsburgh, 1973-76 (43 games); Archie Griffin, Ohio St., 1972-75 (42 games)

MOST GAMES GAINING 100 YARDS OR MORE BY A FRESHMAN
Season
9—Tony Dorsett, Pittsburgh, 1973; Ron "Po" James, New Mexico St., 1968
James holds consecutive record at 8

MOST CONSECUTIVE GAMES GAINING 100 YARDS OR MORE
Career
31—Archie Griffin, Ohio St. Began Sept. 15, 1973 (vs. Minnesota), ended Nov. 22, 1975 (vs. Michigan)

MOST GAMES GAINING 200 YARDS OR MORE
Season
8—Marcus Allen, Southern Cal, 1981
Career
11—Marcus Allen, Southern Cal, 1978-81 (in 21 games during 1980-81)

MOST GAMES GAINING 200 YARDS OR MORE BY A FRESHMAN
Season
4—Herschel Walker, Georgia, 1980

MOST CONSECUTIVE GAMES GAINING 200 YARDS OR MORE
Season
5—Barry Sanders, Oklahoma St., 1988 (320 vs. Kansas St., Oct. 29; 215 vs. Oklahoma, Nov. 5; 312 vs. Kansas, Nov. 12; 293 vs. Iowa St., Nov. 19; 332 vs. Texas Tech, Dec. 3); Marcus Allen, Southern Cal, 1981 (210 vs. Tennessee, Sept. 12; 274 vs. Indiana, Sept. 19; 208 vs. Oklahoma, Sept. 26; 233 vs. Oregon St., Oct. 3; 211 vs. Arizona, Oct. 10)

MOST GAMES GAINING 300 YARDS OR MORE
Season
4—Barry Sanders, Oklahoma St., 1988
Also holds career record at 4

MOST YARDS GAINED IN TWO, THREE, FOUR AND FIVE CONSECUTIVE GAMES
2 Games
626—Mike Pringle, Cal St. Fullerton, 1989 (357 vs. New Mexico St., Nov. 4; 269 vs. Long Beach St., Nov. 11)
3 Games
937—Barry Sanders, Oklahoma St., 1988 (312 vs. Kansas, Nov. 12; 293 vs. Iowa St., Nov. 19; 332 vs. Texas Tech, Dec. 3)
4 Games
1,152—Barry Sanders, Oklahoma St., 1988 (215 vs. Oklahoma, Nov. 5; 312 vs. Kansas, Nov. 12; 293 vs. Iowa St., Nov. 19; 332 vs. Texas Tech, Dec. 3)
5 Games
1,472—Barry Sanders, Oklahoma St., 1988 (320 vs. Kansas St., Oct. 29; 215 vs. Oklahoma, Nov. 5; 312 vs. Kansas, Nov. 12; 293 vs. Iowa St., Nov. 19; 332 vs. Texas Tech, Dec. 3)

MOST SEASONS GAINING 1,500 YARDS OR MORE
Career
3—Herschel Walker, Georgia, 1980-82; Tony Dorsett, Pittsburgh, 1973, 1975-76

MOST SEASONS GAINING 1,000 YARDS OR MORE
Career
4—Amos Lawrence, North Caro., 1977-80; Tony Dorsett, Pittsburgh, 1973-76
Collegiate record tied by Howard Stevens, Randolph-Macon, 1968-69, Louisville, 1971-72

TWO PLAYERS, SAME TEAM, EACH GAINING 1,000 YARDS OR MORE
Season
22 times. Most recent: North Caro., 1993—Curtis Johnson (1,034) & Leon Johnson (1,012)

TWO PLAYERS, SAME TEAM, EACH GAINING 200 YARDS OR MORE
Game
Gordon Brown, 214 (23 rushes) & Steve Gage (QB), 206 (26 rushes), Tulsa vs. Wichita St., Nov. 2, 1985

TWO OPPOSING I-A PLAYERS EACH GAINING 200 YARDS OR MORE
Game
Barry Sanders, Oklahoma St. (215) & Mike Gaddis, Oklahoma (213), Nov. 5, 1988; George Swarn, Miami (Ohio) (239) & Otis Cheathem, Western Mich. (219), Sept. 8, 1984

MOST YARDS GAINED BY TWO OPPOSING PLAYERS
Game
553—Marshall Faulk, San Diego St. (386) & Ryan Benjamin, Pacific (Cal.) (167), Sept. 14, 1991

MOST YARDS GAINED BY TWO PLAYERS, SAME TEAM
Game
476—Tony Sands (396) & Chip Hilleary (80), Kansas vs. Missouri, Nov. 23, 1991
Season
2,997—Barry Sanders (2,628) & Gerald Hudson (Sanders' backup, 369), Oklahoma St., 1988
Also hold per-game record at 272.5
Career
8,193—Eric Dickerson (4,450) & Craig James (3,743), Southern Methodist, 1979-82 (alternated at the same position during the last 36 games)

MOST YARDS GAINED IN FIRST GAME OF CAREER
273—Chris McCoy (Soph.), Navy vs. Southern Methodist, Sept. 9, 1995

MOST YARDS GAINED BY A FRESHMAN IN FIRST GAME OF CAREER
212—Greg Hill, Texas A&M vs. LSU, Sept. 14, 1991 (30 carries)

LONGEST RUSH BY A FRESHMAN IN FIRST GAME OF CAREER
98—Jerald Sowell, Tulane vs. Alabama, Sept. 4, 1993

MOST YARDS GAINED IN OPENING GAME OF SEASON
343—Tony Jeffery, Texas Christian vs. Tulane, Sept. 13, 1986 (16 rushes)

MOST YARDS GAINED AGAINST ONE OPPONENT
Career
(3 yrs.) 690—Mike Gaddis, Oklahoma vs. Oklahoma St., 1988-89, 1991 (82 rushes)
(4 yrs.) 754—Tony Dorsett, Pittsburgh vs. Notre Dame, 1973-76 (96 rushes)

MOST YARDS GAINED PER GAME AGAINST ONE OPPONENT
Career
(Min. 2 games) 256.0—Marshall Faulk, San Diego St. vs. Hawaii, 1991-92 (512 yards, 65 rushes)
(Min. 3 games) 230.0—Mike Gaddis, Oklahoma vs. Oklahoma St., 1988-89, 1991 (690 yards, 82 rushes)

HIGHEST AVERAGE GAIN PER RUSH
Game
(Min. 8-14 rushes) 30.2—Kevin Lowe, Wyoming vs. South Dak. St., Nov. 10, 1984 (10 for 302)
(Min. 15-25 rushes) 21.4—Tony Jeffery, Texas Christian vs. Tulane, Sept. 13, 1986 (16 for 343)
(Min. 26 rushes) 13.7—Eddie Lee Ivery, Georgia Tech vs. Air Force, Nov. 11, 1978 (26 for 356)
Season
(Min. 75-100 rushes) 11.5—Glenn Davis, Army, 1945 (82 for 944)
(Min. 101-213 rushes) 9.6—Chuck Weatherspoon, Houston, 1989 (119 for 1,146)
(Min. 214-281 rushes) 7.8—Mike Rozier, Nebraska, 1983 (275 for 2,148)
(Min. 282 rushes) 7.6—Barry Sanders, Oklahoma St., 1988 (344 for 2,628)
Career
(Min. 300-413 rushes) 8.3—Glenn Davis, Army, 1943-46 (358 for 2,957)
(Min. 414-780 rushes) 7.2—Mike Rozier, Nebraska, 1981-83 (668 for 4,780)
(Min. 781 rushes) 6.1—Archie Griffin, Ohio St., 1972-75 (845 for 5,177)

MOST TOUCHDOWNS SCORED BY RUSHING
Game
8—Howard Griffith, Illinois vs. Southern Ill., Sept. 22, 1990 (5, 51, 7, 41, 5, 18, 5, 3 yards; Griffith scored three touchdowns [51, 7, 41] on consecutive carries and scored four touchdowns in the third quarter)
Season
37—Barry Sanders, Oklahoma St., 1988 (11 games)
Also holds per-game record at 3.4 (37 in 11)
Career
64—Anthony Thompson, Indiana, 1986-89

MOST GAMES SCORING TWO OR MORE TOUCHDOWNS BY RUSHING
Season
11—Barry Sanders, Oklahoma St., 1988

MOST CONSECUTIVE GAMES SCORING TWO OR MORE TOUCHDOWNS BY RUSHING
Career
12—Barry Sanders, Oklahoma St. (last game of 1987, all 11 in 1988)

MOST TOUCHDOWNS SCORED BY RUSHING BY A FRESHMAN
Game
7—Marshall Faulk, San Diego St. vs. Pacific (Cal.), Sept. 14, 1991
Season
21—Marshall Faulk, San Diego St., 1991
Also holds per-game record at 2.3 (21 in 9)

MOST RUSHING TOUCHDOWNS SCORED BY A QUARTERBACK
Game
6—Dee Dowis, Air Force vs. San Diego St., Sept. 1, 1989 (55, 28, 12, 16, 60, 17 yards; 249 yards rushing on 13 carries)
Season
19—Beau Morgan, Air Force, 1995; Stacey Robinson, Northern Ill., 1990, 1989; Brian Mitchell, Southwestern La., 1989; Fred Solomon, Tampa, 1974
Career
47—Brian Mitchell, Southwestern La., 1986-89 (in 43 games)

MOST TOUCHDOWNS SCORED IN ONE QUARTER
4—Howard Griffith, Illinois vs. Southern Ill., Sept. 22, 1990 (all rushing, 3rd quarter); Dick Felt, Brigham Young vs. San Jose St., Nov. 8, 1952 (all rushing, 4th quarter)

MOST RUSHING TOUCHDOWNS SCORED BY A QUARTERBACK IN TWO CONSECUTIVE SEASONS
38—Stacey Robinson, Northern Ill., 1989-90 (19 and 19)

MOST YARDS GAINED BY TWO BROTHERS
Season
3,690—Barry Sanders, Oklahoma St. (2,628) & Byron Sanders, Northwestern (1,062), 1988

Passing

HIGHEST PASSING EFFICIENCY RATING POINTS
Game
(Min. 12-24 atts.) 403.4—Tim Clifford, Indiana vs. Colorado, Sept. 26, 1980 (14 attempts, 11 completions, 0 interceptions, 345 yards, 5 TD passes)
(Min. 25-49 atts.) 273.8—Tom Tunnicliffe, Arizona vs. Pacific (Cal.), Oct. 23, 1982 (28 attempts, 21 completions, 0 interceptions, 427 yards, 6 TD passes)
(Min. 50 atts.) 197.8—David Klingler, Houston vs. Eastern Wash., Nov. 17, 1990 (58 attempts, 41 completions, 2 interceptions, 572 yards, 11 TD passes)
Season
(Min. 15 atts. per game) 178.4—Danny Wuerffel, Florida, 1995 (325 attempts, 210 completions, 10 interceptions, 3,266 yards, 35 TD passes)
Career
(Min. 200 comps.) 162.7—Ty Detmer, Brigham Young, 1988-91 (1,530 attempts, 958 completions, 65 interceptions, 15,031 yards, 121 TD passes)

HIGHEST PASSING EFFICIENCY RATING POINTS BY A FRESHMAN
Season
(Min. 15 atts. per game) 162.3—Donovan McNabb, Syracuse, 1995 (207 attempts, 128 completions, 6 interceptions, 1,991 yards, 16 TD passes)

MOST PASSES ATTEMPTED
Quarter
41—Jason Davis, UNLV vs. Idaho, Sept. 17, 1994 (4th, completed 28)
Half
56—Rusty LaRue, Wake Forest vs. Duke, Oct. 28, 1995 (2nd, completed 41)
Game
79—Matt Vogler, Texas Christian vs. Houston, Nov. 3, 1990 (completed 44)
Season
643—David Klingler, Houston, 1990 (11 games, completed 374)
2 Yrs
1,140—David Klingler, Houston, 1990-91 (completed 652)
3 Yrs
1,377—Ty Detmer, Brigham Young, 1989-91 (completed 875)
Career
(4 yrs.) 1,530—Ty Detmer, Brigham Young, 1988-91 (completed 958)

MOST PASSES ATTEMPTED PER GAME
Season
58.5—David Klingler, Houston, 1990 (643 in 11)
Career
39.6—Mike Perez, San Jose St., 1986-87 (792 in 20)

MOST PASSES ATTEMPTED BY A FRESHMAN
Game
71—Sandy Schwab, Northwestern vs. Michigan, Oct. 23, 1982 (completed 45)
Season
503—Mike Romo, Southern Methodist, 1989 (completed 282)

MOST PASSES COMPLETED
Quarter
28—Jason Davis, UNLV vs. Idaho, Sept. 17, 1994 (4th, attempted 41)
Half
41—Rusty LaRue, Wake Forest vs. Duke, Oct. 28, 1995 (2nd, attempted 56)
Game
55—Rusty LaRue, Wake Forest vs. Duke, Oct. 28, 1995 (attempted 78)
Season
374—David Klingler, Houston, 1990 (11 games, attempted 643)
2 Yrs
652—David Klingler, Houston, 1990-91 (attempted 1,140)
Also holds per-game record at 31.0 (652 in 21)
3 Yrs
875—Ty Detmer, Brigham Young, 1989-91 (attempted 1,377)
Per-game record—24.8, David Klingler, Houston, 1989-91 (720 in 29)
Career
(4 yrs.) 958—Ty Detmer, Brigham Young, 1988-91 (attempted 1,530)

MOST PASSES COMPLETED PER GAME
Season
34.0—David Klingler, Houston, 1990 (374 in 11)
Career
25.9—Doug Gaynor, Long Beach St., 1984-85 (569 in 22)

MOST PASSES COMPLETED BY A FRESHMAN
Game
45—Sandy Schwab, Northwestern vs. Michigan, Oct. 23, 1982 (attempted 71)
Season
282—Mike Romo, Southern Methodist, 1989 (attempted 503)
Also holds per-game record at 25.6 (282 in 11)

MOST CONSECUTIVE PASSES COMPLETED
Game
22—Chuck Long, Iowa vs. Indiana, Oct. 27, 1984
Season
23—Rob Johnson, Southern Cal, 1994 (completed last 15 attempts vs. Arizona, Nov. 12, and first 8 vs. UCLA, Nov. 19); Scott Milanovich, Maryland, 1994 (completed last 4 attempts vs. Tulane, Oct. 29, and first 19 vs. North Caro. St., Nov. 5)

MOST PASSES COMPLETED IN TWO, THREE AND FOUR CONSECUTIVE GAMES
2 Games
96—Rusty LaRue, Wake Forest, 1995 (55 vs. Duke, Oct. 28; 41 vs. Georgia Tech, Nov. 4)
3 Games
146—Rusty LaRue, Wake Forest, 1995 (55 vs. Duke, Oct. 28; 41 vs. Georgia Tech, Nov. 4; 50 vs. North Caro. St., Nov. 18)
4 Games
157—Rusty LaRue, Wake Forest, 1995 (11 vs. North Caro., Oct. 21; 55 vs. Duke, Oct. 28; 41 vs. Georgia Tech, Nov. 4; 50 vs. North Caro. St., Nov. 18)

HIGHEST PERCENTAGE OF PASSES COMPLETED
Game
(Min. 20-29 comps.) 92.6%—Rick Neuheisel, UCLA vs. Washington, Oct. 29, 1983 (25 of 27)
(Min. 30-39 comps.) 91.2%—Steve Sarkisian, Brigham Young vs. Fresno St., Nov. 25, 1995 (31 of 34)
(Min. 40 comps.) 81.1%—Rich Campbell, California vs. Florida, Sept. 13, 1980 (43 of 53)
Season
(Min. 150 atts.) 71.3%—Steve Young, Brigham Young, 1983 (306 of 429)
Career
(Min. 875-999 atts.) 66.2%—Scott Milanovich, Maryland, 1992-95 (650 of 982)
(Min. 1,000-1,099 atts.) 64.6%—$Chuck Long, Iowa, 1981-85 (692 of 1,072)
(Min. 1,100 atts.) 63.9%—Jack Trudeau, Illinois, 1981, 1983-85 (736 of 1,151)

$ *See page 6 for explanation.*

HIGHEST PERCENTAGE OF PASSES COMPLETED BY A FRESHMAN
Season
(Min. 200 atts.) 66.2%—Grady Benton, Arizona St., 1992 (149 of 225)

MOST PASSES HAD INTERCEPTED
Game
9—John Reaves, Florida vs. Auburn, Nov. 1, 1969 (attempted 66)
Season
34—John Eckman, Wichita St., 1966 (attempted 458)
Also holds per-game record at 3.4 (34 in 10)
Career
(3 yrs.) 68—Zeke Bratkowski, Georgia, 1951-53 (attempted 734)
(4 yrs.) 73—Mark Herrmann, Purdue, 1977-80 (attempted 1,218)
Per-game record—2.3, Steve Ramsey, North Texas, 1967-69 (67 in 29)

LOWEST PERCENTAGE OF PASSES HAD INTERCEPTED
Season
(Min. 150-349 atts.) 0.0%—Matt Blundin, Virginia, 1991 (0 of 224)
(Min. 350 atts.) 1.1%—Peyton Manning, Tennessee, 1995 (4 of 380); Charlie Ward, Florida St., 1993 (4 of 380)
Career
(Min. 600-799 atts.) 1.7%—Damon Allen, Cal St. Fullerton, 1981-84 (11 of 629)
(Min. 800-1,049 atts.) 2.3%—Anthony Calvillo, Utah St., 1992-93 (19 of 829)
(Min. 1,050 atts.) 2.6%—Eric Zeier, Georgia, 1991-94 (37 of 1,402)

MOST PASSES ATTEMPTED WITHOUT AN INTERCEPTION
Game
68—David Klingler, Houston vs. Baylor, Oct. 6, 1990 (completed 35)
Entire Season
224—Matt Blundin, Virginia, 1991 (completed 135)

MOST CONSECUTIVE PASSES ATTEMPTED WITHOUT AN INTERCEPTION
Season
271—Trent Dilfer, Fresno St., 1993
Also holds career record at 271

MOST CONSECUTIVE PASSES ATTEMPTED WITH JUST ONE INTERCEPTION
Career
329—Damon Allen, Cal St. Fullerton, 1983-84 (during 16 games; began Oct. 8, 1983, vs. Nevada, ended Nov. 3, 1984, vs. Fresno St. Interception occurred vs. Idaho, Sept. 15, 1984)

MOST CONSECUTIVE PASSES ATTEMPTED WITHOUT AN INTERCEPTION AT THE START OF A CAREER BY A FRESHMAN
138—Mike Gundy, Oklahoma St., 1986 (during 8 games)

MOST CONSECUTIVE PASSES ATTEMPTED WITHOUT AN INTERCEPTION AT THE START OF A DIVISION I-A CAREER
202—Brad Otton, Southern Cal, 1994-95 (played 1993 at I-AA Weber St.)

MOST YARDS GAINED
Quarter
347—Jason Davis, UNLV vs. Idaho, Sept. 17, 1994 (4th)

Half
517—Andre Ware, Houston vs. Southern Methodist, Oct. 21, 1989 (1st, completed 25 of 41)
Game
716—David Klingler, Houston vs. Arizona St., Dec. 2, 1990 (completed 41 of 70)
Season
(11 games) 5,140—David Klingler, Houston, 1990 (completed 374 of 643)
(12 games) 5,188—Ty Detmer, Brigham Young, 1990 (completed 361 of 562)
2 Yrs
9,748—Ty Detmer, Brigham Young, 1989-90 (completed 626 of 974)
3 Yrs
13,779—Ty Detmer, Brigham Young, 1989-91 (completed 875 of 1,377)
Career
(4 yrs.) 15,031—Ty Detmer, Brigham Young, 1988-91 (completed 958 of 1,530)

MOST YARDS GAINED PER GAME
Season
467.3—David Klingler, Houston, 1990 (5,140 in 11)
2 Yrs
406.2—Ty Detmer, Brigham Young, 1989-90 (9,748 in 24)
3 Yrs
382.8—Ty Detmer, Brigham Young, 1989-91 (13,779 in 36)
Career
326.8—Ty Detmer, Brigham Young, 1988-91 (15,031 in 46)

MOST YARDS GAINED BY A FRESHMAN
Game
469—Ben Bennett, Duke vs. Wake Forest, Nov. 8, 1980
Season
3,020—Todd Ellis, South Caro., 1986
Also holds per-game record at 274.5 (3,020 in 11)

MOST YARDS GAINED BY A SOPHOMORE
Game
631—Scott Mitchell, Utah vs. Air Force, Oct. 15, 1988
Season
4,560—Ty Detmer, Brigham Young, 1989
Per-game record—392.9, Scott Mitchell, Utah, 1988 (4,322 in 11)

MOST SEASONS GAINING 2,000 YARDS OR MORE
Career
4—Glenn Foley, Boston College, 1990-93 (2,189—2,225—2,231—3,397); Alex Van Pelt, Pittsburgh, 1989-92 (2,527—2,427—2,796—3,163); T. J. Rubley, Tulsa, 1987-89, 1991 (2,058—2,497—2,292—2,054); Tom Hodson, LSU, 1986-89 (2,261—2,125—2,074—2,655); Todd Santos, San Diego St., 1984-87 (2,063—2,877—2,553—3,932); Kevin Sweeney, Fresno St., 1983-86 (2,359—3,259—2,604—2,363)

MOST YARDS GAINED IN TWO, THREE AND FOUR CONSECUTIVE GAMES
2 Games
1,288—David Klingler, Houston, 1990 (572 vs. Eastern Wash., Nov. 17; 716 vs. Arizona St., Dec. 2)
3 Games
1,798—David Klingler, Houston, 1990-91 (572 vs. Eastern Wash., Nov. 17, 1990; 716 vs. Arizona St., Dec. 2, 1990; 510 vs. Louisiana Tech, Aug. 31, 1991)
4 Games
2,150—David Klingler, Houston, 1990 (563 vs. Texas Christian, Nov. 3; 299 vs. Texas, Nov. 10; 572 vs. Eastern Wash., Nov. 17; 716 vs. Arizona St., Dec. 2)

MOST GAMES GAINING 200 YARDS OR MORE
Season
12—Ty Detmer, Brigham Young, 1990, 1989; Robbie Bosco, Brigham Young, 1985, 1984
Career
38—Ty Detmer, Brigham Young, 1988-91

MOST CONSECUTIVE GAMES GAINING 200 YARDS OR MORE
Season
12—Ty Detmer, Brigham Young, 1990, 1989; Robbie Bosco, Brigham Young, 1984
Career
27—Ty Detmer, Brigham Young (from Sept. 2, 1989, to Sept. 21, 1991)

MOST GAMES GAINING 300 YARDS OR MORE
Season
12—Ty Detmer, Brigham Young, 1990, 1989
Career
33—Ty Detmer, Brigham Young, 1988-91

MOST CONSECUTIVE GAMES GAINING 300 YARDS OR MORE
Season
12—Ty Detmer, Brigham Young, 1990, 1989
Career
24—Ty Detmer, Brigham Young (from Sept. 2, 1989, to Dec. 1, 1990)

MOST GAMES GAINING 400 YARDS OR MORE
Season
9—David Klingler, Houston, 1990
Career
12—Ty Detmer, Brigham Young, 1988-91

MOST YARDS GAINED BY TWO OPPOSING PLAYERS
Game
1,253—Matt Vogler, Texas Christian (690) & David Klingler, Houston (563), Nov. 3, 1990

TWO PLAYERS, SAME TEAM, EACH PASSING FOR 250 YARDS OR MORE
Game
Jason Davis (381) & Jared Brown (254), UNLV vs. Idaho, Sept. 17, 1994; Andre Ware (517) & David Klingler (254), Houston vs. Southern Methodist, Oct. 21, 1989; Steve Cottrell (311) & John Elway (270), Stanford vs. Arizona St., Oct. 24, 1981

MOST YARDS GAINED IN OPENING GAME OF SEASON
511—Scott Mitchell, Utah vs. Idaho St., Sept. 10, 1988

MOST YARDS GAINED AGAINST ONE OPPONENT
Career
1,495—Ty Detmer, Brigham Young vs. New Mexico, 1988-91

MOST YARDS GAINED PER GAME AGAINST ONE OPPONENT
Career
(Min. 3 games) 410.7—Gary Schofield, Wake Forest vs. Maryland, 1981-83 (1,232 yards)
(Min. 4 games) 373.8—Ty Detmer, Brigham Young vs. New Mexico, 1988-91 (1,495 yards)

MOST YARDS GAINED PER ATTEMPT
Game
(Min. 25-39 atts.) 15.8—Koy Detmer, Colorado vs. Northeast La., Sept. 16, 1995 (27 for 426)
(Min. 40-59 atts.) 14.1—John Walsh, Brigham Young vs. Utah St., Oct. 30, 1993 (44 for 619)
(Min. 60 atts.) 10.5—Scott Mitchell, Utah vs. Air Force, Oct. 15, 1988 (60 for 631)
Season
(Min. 412 atts.) 11.1—Ty Detmer, Brigham Young, 1989 (412 for 4,560)
Career
(Min. 1,000 atts.) 9.8—Ty Detmer, Brigham Young, 1988-91 (1,530 for 15,031)

MOST YARDS GAINED PER COMPLETION
Game
(Min. 22-41 comps.) 22.9—John Walsh, Brigham Young vs. Utah St., Oct. 30, 1993 (27 for 619)
(Min. 42 comps.) 15.7—Matt Vogler, Texas Christian vs. Houston, Nov. 3, 1990 (44 for 690)
Season
(Min. 109-204 comps.) 18.2—Doug Williams, Grambling, 1977 (181 for 3,286)
(Min. 205 comps.) 17.2—Ty Detmer, Brigham Young, 1989 (265 for 4,560)
Career
(Min. 275-399 comps.) 17.3—J. J. Joe, Baylor, 1990-93 (347 for 5,995)
(Min. 400 comps.) 15.7—Shawn Moore, Virginia, 1987-90 (421 for 6,629)

MOST TOUCHDOWN PASSES
Quarter
6—David Klingler, Houston vs. Louisiana Tech, Aug. 31, 1991 (2nd)
Half
7—Terry Dean, Florida vs. New Mexico St., Sept. 3, 1994 (1st); Dennis Shaw, San Diego St. vs. New Mexico St., Nov. 15, 1969 (1st)
Game
11—David Klingler, Houston vs. Eastern Wash., Nov. 17, 1990
Season
54—David Klingler, Houston, 1990 (11 games)
2 Yrs
83—David Klingler, Houston, 1990-91
Also holds per-game record at 4.0 (83 in 21)
3 Yrs
108—Ty Detmer, Brigham Young, 1989-91
Career
121—Ty Detmer, Brigham Young, 1988-91

MOST TOUCHDOWN PASSES PER GAME
Season
4.9—David Klingler, Houston, 1990 (54 in 11)
Career
2.8—David Klingler, Houston, 1988-91 (91 in 32)
Collegiate record—2.9, Dennis Shaw, San Diego St., 1968-69 (58 in 20)

HIGHEST PERCENTAGE OF PASSES FOR TOUCHDOWNS
Season
(Min. 175-374 atts.) 11.6%—Dennis Shaw, San Diego St., 1969 (39 of 335)
(Min. 375 atts.) 10.6%—Jim McMahon, Brigham Young, 1980 (47 of 445)
Career
(Min. 400-499 atts.) 9.7%—Rick Leach, Michigan, 1975-78 (45 of 462)
(Min. 500 atts.) 9.1%—Danny White, Arizona St., 1971-73 (59 of 649)

MOST CONSECUTIVE GAMES THROWING A TOUCHDOWN PASS
Career
35—Ty Detmer, Brigham Young (from Sept. 7, 1989, to Nov. 23, 1991)

MOST CONSECUTIVE PASSES COMPLETED FOR TOUCHDOWNS
Game
6—Brooks Dawson, UTEP vs. New Mexico, Oct. 28, 1967 (first six completions of the game)

MOST TOUCHDOWN PASSES IN FIRST GAME OF CAREER
5—John Reaves, Florida vs. Houston, Sept. 20, 1969

MOST TOUCHDOWN PASSES BY A FRESHMAN
Game
6—Bob Hoernschemeyer, Indiana vs. Nebraska, Oct. 9, 1943
Season
22—Danny Wuerffel, Florida, 1993

MOST TOUCHDOWN PASSES IN FRESHMAN AND SOPHOMORE SEASONS
45—Ty Detmer, Brigham Young, 1988 (13) & 1989 (32)

MOST TOUCHDOWN PASSES BY A SOPHOMORE
32—Jimmy Klingler, Houston, 1992; Ty Detmer, Brigham Young, 1989

MOST TOUCHDOWN PASSES AT CONCLUSION OF JUNIOR YEAR
86—Ty Detmer, Brigham Young, 1988 (13), 1989 (32) & 1990 (41)

MOST TOUCHDOWN PASSES, SAME PASSER AND RECEIVER
Season
19—Elvis Grbac to Desmond Howard, Michigan, 1991; Andre Ware to Manny Hazard, Houston, 1989
Career
33—Troy Kopp to Aaron Turner, Pacific (Cal.), 1989-92

MOST PASSES ATTEMPTED WITHOUT A TOUCHDOWN PASS
Season
266—Stu Rayburn, Kent, 1984 (completed 125)

FEWEST TIMES SACKED ATTEMPTING TO PASS
Season
(Min. 300 atts.) 4—Steve Walsh, Miami (Fla.), 1988, in 390 attempts. Last 4 games of the season: Tulsa, 1 for -8 yards; LSU, 1 for -2; Arkansas, 1 for -12; Brigham Young, 1 for-9.

Receiving

MOST PASSES CAUGHT
Game
23—Randy Gatewood, UNLV vs. Idaho, Sept. 17, 1994 (363 yards)
Season
142—Manny Hazard, Houston, 1989 (1,689 yards)
Career
(2 yrs.) 227—Alex Van Dyke, Nevada, 1994-95 (3,100 yards)
(3 yrs.) 261—Howard Twilley, Tulsa, 1963-65 (3,343 yards)
(4 yrs.) 266—Aaron Turner, Pacific (Cal.), 1989-92 (4,345 yards)

MOST PASSES CAUGHT PER GAME
Season
13.4—Howard Twilley, Tulsa, 1965 (134 in 10)
Career
10.5—Manny Hazard, Houston, 1989-90 (220 in 21)

MOST PASSES CAUGHT BY TWO PLAYERS, SAME TEAM
Season
212—Howard Twilley (134) & Neal Sweeney (78), Tulsa, 1965 (2,662 yards, 24 TDs)
Career
453—Mark Templeton (262) & Charles Lockett (191), Long Beach St., 1983-86 (4,871 yards, 30 TDs)

MOST PASSES CAUGHT IN CONSECUTIVE GAMES
38—Manny Hazard, Houston, 1989 (19 vs. Texas Christian, Nov. 4; 19 vs. Texas, Nov. 11)

MOST CONSECUTIVE GAMES CATCHING A PASS
Career
46—Carl Winston, New Mexico, 1990-93 (every game)

MOST PASSES CAUGHT BY A TIGHT END
Game
17—Jon Harvey, Northwestern vs. Michigan, Oct. 23, 1982 (208 yards); Emilio Vallez, New Mexico vs. UTEP, Oct. 27, 1967 (257 yards)
Season
73—Dennis Smith, Utah, 1989 (1,089 yards)
Career
190—Pete Mitchell, Boston College, 1991-94 (2,389 yards)

MOST PASSES CAUGHT PER GAME BY A TIGHT END
Season
6.4—Jamie Asher, Louisville, 1994 (70 in 11); Mark Dowdell, Bowling Green, 1983 (70 in 11); Chuck Scott, Vanderbilt, 1983 (70 in 11)
Career
5.4—Gordon Hudson, Brigham Young, 1980-83 (178 in 33)

MOST PASSES CAUGHT BY A RUNNING BACK
Game
18—Mark Templeton, Long Beach St. vs. Utah St., Nov. 1, 1986 (173 yards)
Season
99—Mark Templeton, Long Beach St., 1986 (688 yards)
Career
262—Mark Templeton, Long Beach St., 1983-86 (1,969 yards)

MOST PASSES CAUGHT BY A FRESHMAN
Game
18—Richard Woodley (WR), Texas Christian vs. Texas Tech, Nov. 10, 1990 (180 yards)
Season
75—Brandon Stokley, Southwestern La., 1995 (1,121 yards)
Also holds per-game record at 6.8

CATCHING AT LEAST 50 PASSES AND GAINING AT LEAST 1,000 YARDS RUSHING
Season
By 10 players. Most recent: Ryan Benjamin, Pacific (Cal.), 1991 (51 catches and 1,581 yards rushing)
Darrin Nelson, Stanford, holds record for most seasons at 3 (1977-78, 1981)

CATCHING AT LEAST 60 PASSES AND GAINING AT LEAST 1,000 YARDS RUSHING
Johnny Johnson, San Jose St., 1988 (61 catches and 1,219 yards rushing); Brad Muster, Stanford, 1986 (61 catches and 1,053 yards rushing); Darrin Nelson, Stanford, 1981 (67 catches and 1,014 yards rushing)

MOST YARDS GAINED
Game
363—Randy Gatewood, UNLV vs. Idaho, Sept. 17, 1994 (caught 23)
Season
1,854—Alex Van Dyke, Nevada, 1995 (caught 129)
Career
4,357—Ryan Yarborough, Wyoming, 1990-93 (caught 229)

MOST YARDS GAINED PER GAME
Season
177.9—Howard Twilley, Tulsa, 1965 (1,779 in 10)
Career
140.9—Alex Van Dyke, Nevada, 1994-95 (3,100 in 22)

MOST YARDS GAINED BY A TIGHT END
Game
259—Gordon Hudson, Brigham Young vs. Utah, Nov. 21, 1981 (caught 13)
Season
1,156—Chris Smith, Brigham Young, 1990 (caught 68)
Career
2,484—Gordon Hudson, Brigham Young, 1980-83 (caught 178)

MOST YARDS GAINED PER GAME BY A TIGHT END
Season
102.0—Mike Moore, Grambling, 1977 (1,122 in 11)
Career
75.3—Gordon Hudson, Brigham Young, 1980-83 (2,484 in 33)

MOST YARDS GAINED BY A FRESHMAN
Game
243—Darnay Scott, San Diego St. vs. Brigham Young, Nov. 16, 1991 (caught 8)
Season
1,121—Brandon Stokley, Southwestern La., 1995 (caught 75)
Also holds per-game record at 101.9

MOST GAMES GAINING 100 YARDS OR MORE
Season
11—Aaron Turner, Pacific (Cal.), 1991
Also holds consecutive record at 11
Career
23—Aaron Turner, Pacific (Cal.), 1989-92 (in 44 games played)
Consecutive record: 11, Keyshawn Johnson, Southern Cal, 1994-95 (over two seasons), and Aaron Turner, Pacific (Cal.), 1991 (all one season)

MOST GAMES GAINING 200 YARDS OR MORE
Season
5—Howard Twilley, Tulsa, 1965
Also holds consecutive record at 3

MOST YARDS GAINED BY TWO PLAYERS, SAME TEAM
Game
640—Rick Eber (322) & Harry Wood (318), Tulsa vs. Idaho St., Oct. 7, 1967 (caught 33, 6 TDs)
Season
2,732—Alex Van Dyke (1,854) & Steve McHenry (878), Nevada, 1995

TWO PLAYERS, SAME TEAM, EACH GAINING 1,000 YARDS
Chris Doering (1,045; 70 catches) & Ike Hilliard (1,008; 57 catches), Florida, 1995; E. G. Green (1,007; 60 catches) & Andre Cooper (1,002; 71 catches), Florida St., 1995; Will Blackwell (1,207; 86 catches) & Az Hakim (1,022; 57 catches), San Diego St., 1995; Bryan Reeves (1,362; 91 catches) & Michael Stephens (1,062; 80 catches), Nevada, 1993; Charles Johnson (1,149; 57 catches) & Michael Westbrook (1,060; 76 catches), Colorado, 1992; Andy Boyce (1,241; 79 catches) & Chris Smith (1,156; 68 catches), Brigham Young, 1990; Patrick Rowe (1,392; 71 catches) & Dennis Arey (1,118; 68 catches), San Diego St., 1990; Jason Phillips (1,444; 108 catches) & James Dixon (1,103; 102 catches), Houston, 1988

TWO PLAYERS, SAME TEAM, RANKED NO. 1 & NO. 2 IN FINAL RECEIVING RANKINGS
Season
Jason Phillips (No. 1, 9.8 catches per game) & James Dixon (No. 2, 9.3 catches per game), Houston, 1988

THREE PLAYERS, SAME TEAM, EACH CATCHING 60 PASSES OR MORE
Patrick Rowe (71), Dennis Arey (68) & Jimmy Raye (62), San Diego St., 1990

MOST 1,000-YARD RECEIVING SEASONS
3—Ryan Yarborough, Wyoming, 1991-93 (1,081 in 1991; 1,351 in 1992; 1,512 in 1993); Aaron Turner, Pacific (Cal.), 1990-92 (1,264 in 1990; 1,604 in 1991; 1,171 in 1992); Clarkston Hines, Duke, 1987-89 (1,084 in 1987; 1,067 in 1988; 1,149 in 1989); Marc Zeno, Tulane, 1985-87 (1,137 in 1985; 1,033 in 1986; 1,206 in 1987)

HIGHEST AVERAGE GAIN PER RECEPTION
Game
(Min. 3-4 receps.) 72.7—Terry Gallaher, East Caro. vs. Appalachian St., Sept. 13, 1975 (3 for 218; 82, 77, 59 yards)
(Min. 5-9 receps.) 52.6—Alexander Wright, Auburn vs. Pacific (Cal.), Sept. 9, 1989 (5 for 263; 78, 60, 41, 73, 11 yards)
(Min. 10 receps.) 34.9—Chuck Hughes, UTEP vs. North Texas, Sept. 18, 1965 (10 for 349)
Season
(Min. 30-49 receps.) 27.9—Elmo Wright, Houston, 1968 (43 for 1,198)
(Min. 50 receps.) 24.4—Henry Ellard, Fresno St., 1982 (62 for 1,510)
Career
(Min. 75-104 receps.) 25.7—Wesley Walker, California, 1973-76 (86 for 2,206)

Photo from Nevada sports information

Nevada wide receiver Alex Van Dyke set a Division I-A record with 1,854 yards receiving in 1995. He also set the career mark for most yards gained per game (140.9).

(Min. 105 receps.) 22.0—Herman Moore, Virginia, 1988-90 (114 for 2,504)

HIGHEST AVERAGE GAIN PER RECEPTION BY A TIGHT END

Season

(Min. 30 receps.) 22.6—Jay Novacek, Wyoming, 1984 (33 for 745)

Career

(Min. 75 receps.) 19.2—Clay Brown, Brigham Young, 1978-80 (88 for 1,691)

MOST TOUCHDOWN PASSES CAUGHT

Game

6—Tim Delaney, San Diego St. vs. New Mexico St., Nov. 15, 1969 (16 receptions)

Season

22—Manny Hazard, Houston, 1989 (142 receptions)

Per-game record—2.3, Tom Reynolds, San Diego St., 1969 (18 in 8)

Career

43—Aaron Turner, Pacific (Cal.), 1989-92 (266 receptions)

MOST GAMES CATCHING A TOUCHDOWN PASS

Season

11—Chris Doering, Florida, 1995

Career

27—Ryan Yarborough, Wyoming, 1990-93 (caught a total of 42 in 46 games)

MOST CONSECUTIVE GAMES CATCHING A TOUCHDOWN PASS

Season

10—Desmond Howard, Michigan, 1991

Career

12—Desmond Howard, Michigan (last two games of 1990 and first 10 games of 1991); Aaron Turner, Pacific (Cal.) (last three games of 1990 and first nine games of 1991)

MOST TOUCHDOWN PASSES CAUGHT BY A TIGHT END

Season

18—Dennis Smith, Utah, 1989 (73 receptions)

Career

24—Dennis Smith, Utah, 1987-89 (156 receptions); Dave Young, Purdue, 1977-80 (172 receptions)

HIGHEST PERCENTAGE OF PASSES CAUGHT FOR TOUCHDOWNS

Season

(Min. 10 TDs) 58.8%—Kevin Williams, Southern Cal, 1978 (10 of 17)

Career

(Min. 20 TDs) 35.3%—Kevin Williams, Southern Cal, 1977-80 (24 of 68)

HIGHEST AVERAGE YARDS PER TOUCHDOWN PASS

Season

(Min. 10) 56.1—Elmo Wright, Houston, 1968 (11 for 617 yards; 87, 50, 75, 2, 80, 79, 13, 67, 61, 43, 60 yards)

Career

(Min. 15) 46.5—Charles Johnson, Colorado, 1990-93 (15 for 697 yards)

MOST TOUCHDOWN PASSES CAUGHT, 50 YARDS OR MORE

Season

8—Henry Ellard, Fresno St., 1982 (68, 51, 80, 61, 67, 72, 80, 72 yards); Elmo Wright, Houston, 1968 (87, 50, 75, 80, 79, 67, 61, 60 yards)

MOST CONSECUTIVE PASSES CAUGHT FOR TOUCHDOWNS

6—Gerald Armstrong, Nebraska, 1992 (1 vs. Utah, Sept. 5; 1 vs. Arizona St., Sept. 26; 1 vs. Oklahoma St., Oct. 10; 1 vs. Colorado, Oct. 31; 2 vs. Kansas, Nov. 7); Carlos Carson, LSU, 1977 (5 vs. Rice, Sept. 24; 1 vs. Florida, Oct. 1; first receptions of his career)

MOST TOUCHDOWN PASSES CAUGHT BY A FRESHMAN

Season

10—Dwight Collins, Pittsburgh, 1980

Punting

MOST PUNTS

Game

36—Charlie Calhoun, Texas Tech vs. Centenary (La.), Nov. 11, 1939 (1,318 yards; 20 were returned, 8 went out of bounds, 6 were downed, 1 was blocked [blocked kicks counted against the punter until 1955] and 1 went into the end zone for a touchback. Thirty-three of the punts occurred on first down during a heavy downpour in the game played at Shreveport, Louisiana)

Season

101—Jim Bailey, Va. Military, 1969 (3,507 yards)

Career

(3 yrs.) 276—Jim Bailey, Va. Military, 1969-71 (10,127 yards)

(4 yrs.) 320—Cameron Young, Texas Christian, 1976-79 (12,947 yards)

HIGHEST AVERAGE PER PUNT

Game

(Min. 5-9 punts) 60.4—Lee Johnson, Brigham Young vs. Wyoming, Oct. 8, 1983 (5 for 302; 53, 44, 63, 62, 80 yards)

(Min. 10 punts) 53.6—Jim Benien, Oklahoma St. vs. Colorado, Nov. 13, 1971 (10 for 536)

Season

(Min. 40-49 punts) 49.8—Reggie Roby, Iowa, 1981 (44 for 2,193)

(Min. 50-74 punts) 48.4—Todd Sauerbrun, West Va., 1994 (72 for 3,486)

(Min. 75 punts) 45.8—Bucky Scribner, Kansas, 1982 (76 for 3,478)

Career

(Min. 150-199 punts) 46.3—Todd Sauerbrun, West Va., 1991-94 (167 for 7,733)

(Min. 200-249 punts) 44.7—Ray Guy, Southern Miss., 1970-72 (200 for 8,934)

(Min. 250 punts) 44.3—Bill Smith, Mississippi, 1983-86 (254 for 11,260)

HIGHEST AVERAGE PER PUNT BY A FRESHMAN

Season

(Min. 40 punts) 47.0—Tom Tupa, Ohio St., 1984 (41 for 1,927)

MOST YARDS ON PUNTS

Game

1,318—Charlie Calhoun, Texas Tech vs. Centenary (La.), Nov. 11, 1939 (36 punts)

Season

4,138—Johnny Pingel, Michigan St., 1938 (99 punts)

Career

12,947—Cameron Young, Texas Christian, 1976-79 (320 punts)

MOST GAMES WITH A 40-YARD AVERAGE OR MORE

Career

(Min. 4 punts) 36—Bill Smith, Mississippi, 1983-86 (punted in 44 games)

MOST PUNTS, 50 YARDS OR MORE

Season

32—Todd Sauerbrun, West Va., 1994 (72 punts)

Career

(2 yrs.) 51—Marv Bateman, Utah, 1970-71 (133 punts)

(3 yrs.) 61—Russ Henderson, Virginia, 1976-78 (226 punts)

(4 yrs.) 88—Bill Smith, Mississippi, 1983-86 (254 punts)

MOST CONSECUTIVE GAMES WITH AT LEAST ONE PUNT OF 50 YARDS OR MORE

Career

32—Bill Smith, Mississippi, 1983-86

MOST PUNTS IN A CAREER WITHOUT HAVING ONE BLOCKED

300—Tony DeLeone, Kent, 1981-84

Also holds consecutive record at 300

LONGEST PUNT

99—Pat Brady, Nevada vs. Loyola Marymount, Oct. 28, 1950

RANKING IN TOP 12 IN BOTH PUNTING AND FIELD GOALS

Daron Alcorn, Akron, 1992 (No. 11 in punting, 43.6-yard average and tied for No. 9 in field goals, 1.64 per game); Dan Eichloff, Kansas, 1991 (No. 12 in punting, 42.3-yard average and No. 3 in field goals, 1.64 per game); Chris Gardocki, Clemson, 1990 (No. 4 in punting, 44.3-yard average and No. 4 in field goals, 1.73 per game), 1989 (No. 10 in punting, 42.7-yard average and No. 6 in field goals, 1.82 per game); Rob Keen, California, 1988 (No. 11 in punting, 42.6-yard average and No. 3 in field goals, 1.91 per game); Steve Little, Arkansas, 1977 (No. 4 in punting, 44.3-yard average and No. 2 in field goals, 1.73 per game)

Interceptions

MOST PASSES INTERCEPTED

Game

5—Dan Rebsch, Miami (Ohio) vs. Western Mich., Nov. 4, 1972 (88 yards); Byron Beaver, Houston vs. Baylor, Sept. 22, 1962 (18 yards); Walt Pastuszak, Brown vs. Rhode Island, Oct. 8, 1949 (47 yards); Lee Cook, Oklahoma St. vs. Detroit, Nov. 28, 1942 (15 yards)

Season

14—Al Worley, Washington, 1968 (130 yards)

Career

29—Al Brosky, Illinois, 1950-52 (356 yards)

MOST PASSES INTERCEPTED PER GAME

Season

1.4—Al Worley, Washington, 1968 (14 in 10)

Career

1.1—Al Brosky, Illinois, 1950-52 (29 in 27)

MOST PASSES INTERCEPTED BY A LINEBACKER

Season

9—Bill Sibley, Texas A&M, 1941 (57 yards)

MOST PASSES INTERCEPTED BY A FRESHMAN

Game

3—Torey Hunter, Washington St. vs. Arizona St., Oct. 19, 1991 (22 yards); Shawn Simms, Bowling Green vs. Toledo, Oct. 24, 1981 (46 yards)

Season

13—George Shaw, Oregon, 1951 (136 yards)

Also holds per-game record at 1.3 (13 in 10)

MOST YARDS ON INTERCEPTION RETURNS

Game

182—Ashley Lee, Virginia Tech vs. Vanderbilt, Nov. 12, 1983 (2 interceptions)

Season

302—Charles Phillips, Southern Cal, 1974 (7 interceptions)

Career

501—Terrell Buckley, Florida St., 1989-91 (21 interceptions)

MOST TOUCHDOWNS SCORED ON INTERCEPTION RETURNS

Game

3—Johnny Jackson, Houston vs. Texas, Nov. 7, 1987 (31, 53, 97 yards)

Season

3—By many players. Most recent: Reggie Tongue, Oregon St., 1994 (5 interceptions)

Career

5—Ken Thomas, San Jose St., 1979-82 (14 interceptions); Jackie Walker, Tennessee, 1969-71 (11 interceptions)

MOST TOUCHDOWNS SCORED ON INTERCEPTION RETURNS BY A LINEBACKER

Game

2—Randy Neal, Virginia vs. Virginia Tech, Nov. 21, 1992 (37, 30 yards)

Season

2—Randy Neal, Virginia, 1994, 1992

Career

4—Randy Neal, Virginia, 1991-94 (37, 30, 77, 28 yards)

HIGHEST AVERAGE GAIN PER INTERCEPTION

Game

(Min. 2 ints.) 91.0—Ashley Lee, Virginia Tech vs. Vanderbilt, Nov. 12, 1983 (2 for 182)

Season
(Min. 5 ints.) 50.6—Norm Thompson, Utah, 1969 (5 for 253)
Career
(Min. 15 ints.) 26.5—Tom Pridemore, West Va., 1975-77 (15 for 398)

MOST CONSECUTIVE GAMES INTERCEPTING A PASS
15—Al Brosky, Illinois, began Nov. 11, 1950 (vs. Iowa), ended Oct. 18, 1952 (vs. Minnesota)

Punt Returns

MOST PUNT RETURNS
Game
20—Milton Hill, Texas Tech vs. Centenary (La.), Nov. 11, 1939 (110 yards)
Season
55—Dick Adams, Miami (Ohio), 1970 (578 yards)
Also holds per-game record at 5.5
Career
153—Vai Sikahema, Brigham Young, 1980-81, 1984-85 (1,312 yards)

MOST YARDS ON PUNT RETURNS
Game
225—Chris McCranie, Georgia vs. South Caro., Sept. 2, 1995 (5 returns)
Season
791—Lee Nalley, Vanderbilt, 1948 (43 returns)
Also holds per-game record at 79.1
Career
1,695—Lee Nalley, Vanderbilt, 1947-49 (109 returns)

HIGHEST AVERAGE GAIN PER RETURN
Game
(Min. 3-4 rets.) 59.7—Chip Hough, Air Force vs. Southern Methodist, Oct. 9, 1971 (3 for 179)
(Min. 5 rets.) 45.0—Chris McCranie, Georgia vs. South Caro., Sept. 2, 1995 (5 for 225)
Season
(Min. 1.2 rets. per game) 25.9—Bill Blackstock, Tennessee, 1951 (12 for 311)
(Min. 1.5 rets. per game) 25.0—George Sims, Baylor, 1948 (15 for 375)
Career
(Min. 1.2 rets. per game) 23.6—Jack Mitchell, Oklahoma, 1946-48 (39 for 922)
(Min. 1.5 rets. per game) 20.5—Gene Gibson, Cincinnati, 1949-50 (37 for 760)

MOST TOUCHDOWNS SCORED ON PUNT RETURNS
Game
2—By many players. Most recent: Andre Parvis, North Caro. vs. Tulane, Nov. 13, 1993 (fell on two blocked punts in end zone); Jeff Sweitzer, Akron vs. Northern Ariz., Nov. 4, 1989 (53 and 70 yards in first and second quarters)
Season
4—James Henry, Southern Miss., 1987; Golden Richards, Brigham Young, 1971; Cliff Branch, Colorado, 1971
Career
7—Johnny Rodgers, Nebraska, 1970-72 (2 in 1970, 3 in 1971, 2 in 1972); Jack Mitchell, Oklahoma, 1946-48 (3 in 1946, 1 in 1947, 3 in 1948)

Kickoff Returns

MOST KICKOFF RETURNS
Game
11—Reidel Anthony, Florida vs. Tennessee, Sept. 16, 1995 (123 yards); Trevor Cobb, Rice vs. Houston, Dec. 2, 1989 (166 yards)
Season
46—Cedric Johnson, UTEP, 1995 (1,039 yards)
Career
114—Joe Redding, Southwestern La., 1985-88 (2,642 yards)

MOST RETURNS PER GAME
Season
4.6—Dwayne Owens, Oregon St., 1990 (41 in 9)
Career
3.0—Steve Odom, Utah, 1971-73 (99 in 33)

MOST YARDS ON KICKOFF RETURNS
Game
241—Jerry Blitz, Harvard vs. Princeton, Nov. 8, 1952 (7 returns)
Season
1,065—Tijan Redmon, Duke, 1995 (45 returns)
Career
2,642—Joe Redding, Southwestern La., 1985-88 (114 returns)

MOST YARDS RETURNED PER GAME
Season
112.7—Dwayne Owens, Oregon St., 1990 (1,014 in 9)
Career
78.2—Steve Odom, Utah, 1971-73 (2,582 in 33)

HIGHEST AVERAGE GAIN PER RETURN
Game
(Min. 3 rets.) 72.7—Anthony Davis, Southern Cal vs. Notre Dame, Dec. 2, 1972 (3 for 218)
Season
(Min. 1.2 rets. per game) 40.1—Paul Allen, Brigham Young, 1961 (12 for 481)
(Min. 1.5 rets. per game) 38.2—Forrest Hall, San Francisco, 1946 (15 for 573)
Career
(Min. *1.2 rets. per game)* 36.2—Forrest Hall, San Francisco, 1946-47 (22 for 796)
(Min. 1.5 rets. per game) 31.0—Overton Curtis, Utah St., 1957-58 (32 for 991)

MOST TOUCHDOWNS SCORED ON KICKOFF RETURNS
Game
2—Leeland McElroy, Texas A&M vs. Rice, Oct. 23, 1993 (93 & 88 yards); Stacey Corley, Brigham Young vs. Air Force, Nov. 11, 1989 (99 & 85 yards); *Raghib Ismail, Notre Dame vs. Michigan, Sept. 16, 1989 (88 & 92 yards); Raghib Ismail, Notre Dame vs. Rice, Nov. 5, 1988 (87 & 83 yards); Anthony Davis, Southern Cal vs. Notre Dame, Dec. 2, 1972 (97 & 96 yards); Ollie Matson, San Francisco vs. Fordham, Oct. 20, 1951 (94 & 90 yards); Ron Horwath, Detroit vs. Hillsdale, Sept. 22, 1950 (96 & 96 yards); Paul Copoulos, Marquette vs. Iowa Pre-Flight, Nov. 6, 1943 (85 & 82 yards)
Season
3—Leeland McElroy, Texas A&M, 1993; Terance Mathis, New Mexico, 1989; Willie Gault, Tennessee, 1980; Anthony Davis, Southern Cal, 1974; Stan Brown, Purdue, 1970; Forrest Hall, San Francisco, 1946
Career
6—Anthony Davis, Southern Cal, 1972-74

**Ismail is the only player in history to score twice in two games.*

SCORING A TOUCHDOWN ON TEAM'S OPENING KICKOFF OF TWO SEASONS
Season
Barry Sanders, Oklahoma St., 1988 (100 yards vs. Miami, Ohio, Sept. 10) & 1987 (100 yards vs. Tulsa, Sept. 5)

Total Kick Returns

(Combined Punt and Kickoff Returns)

MOST KICK RETURNS
Game
20—Milton Hill, Texas Tech vs. Centenary, Nov. 11, 1939 (20 punts, 110 yards)
Season
70—Keith Stephens, Louisville, 1986 (28 punts, 42 kickoffs, 1,162 yards); Dick Adams, Miami (Ohio), 1970 (55 punts, 15 kickoffs, 944 yards)
Career
199—Thomas Bailey, Auburn, 1991-94 (125 punts, 74 kickoffs, 2,690 yards); Tony James, Mississippi St., 1989-92 (121 punts, 78 kickoffs, 3,194 yards)

MOST YARDS ON KICK RETURNS
Game
247—Tyrone Hughes, Nebraska vs. Kansas St., Oct. 6, 1991 (8 returns); Golden Richards, Brigham Young vs. North Texas, Sept. 10, 1971 (7 returns)
Season
1,228—Steve Odom, Utah, 1972
Per-game record—116.2, Dion Johnson, East Caro., 1990 (1,046 yards, with 167 on punt returns and 879 on kickoff returns in 9 games)
Career
3,194—Tony James, Mississippi St., 1989-92 (1,332 on punts, 1,862 on kickoffs)

GAINING 1,000 YARDS ON PUNT RETURNS AND 1,000 YARDS ON KICKOFF RETURNS
Career
Thomas Bailey, Auburn, 1991-94 (1,170 & 1,520); Tony James, Mississippi St., 1989-92 (1,332 & 1,862); Willie Drewrey, West Va., 1981-84 (1,072 & 1,302); Anthony Carter, Michigan, 1979-82 (1,095 & 1,504); Devon Ford, Appalachian St., 1973-76 (1,197 & 1,761); Troy Slade, Duke, 1973-75 (1,021 & 1,757)

HIGHEST AVERAGE PER KICK RETURN (Min. 1.2 Punt Returns and 1.2 Kickoff Returns Per Game)
Season
27.2—Erroll Tucker, Utah, 1985 (40 for 1,087; 16 for 389 on punt returns, 24 for 698 on kickoff returns)

HIGHEST AVERAGE PER KICK RETURN (Min. 1.3 Punt Returns and 1.3 Kickoff Returns Per Game)
Career
22.0—Erroll Tucker, Utah, 1984-85 (79 for 1,741; 38 for 650 on punt returns, 41 for 1,091 on kickoff returns)

AVERAGING 20 YARDS EACH ON PUNT RETURNS AND KICKOFF RETURNS (Min. 1.2 Returns Per Game Each)
Season
By 7 players. Most recent: Lee Gissendaner, Northwestern, 1992 (21.8 on punt returns, 15 for 327; 22.4 on kickoff returns, 17 for 381)

MOST TOUCHDOWNS SCORED ON KICK RETURNS (Must Have at Least One Punt Return and One Kickoff Return)
Game
2—By 5 players. Most recent: Eric Blount, North Caro. vs. William & Mary, Oct. 5, 1991 (1 punt, 1 kickoff)
Season
5—Robert Woods, Grambling, 1977 (3 punts, 2 kickoffs); Pinky Rohm, LSU, 1937 (3 punts, 2 kickoffs)
Career
8—Johnny Rodgers, Nebraska, 1970-72 (7 punts, 1 kickoff); Cliff Branch, Colorado, 1970-71 (6 punts, 2 kickoffs)

WINNING BOTH PUNT RETURN AND KICKOFF RETURN CHAMPIONSHIPS
Season
Erroll Tucker, Utah, 1985
Career
Erroll Tucker, Utah, 1985; Ira Matthews, Wisconsin, kickoff returns (1976) and punt returns (1978)

All Runbacks

(Combined Interceptions, Punt Returns and Kickoff Returns)

SCORING MORE THAN ONE TOUCHDOWN IN EACH CATEGORY
Season
Erroll Tucker, Utah, 1985 (3 interceptions, 2 punt returns, 2 kickoff returns)

SCORING ONE TOUCHDOWN IN EACH CATEGORY
Season
Joe Crocker, Virginia, 1994; Scott Thomas, Air Force, 1985; Mark Haynes, Arizona St., 1974; Dick Harris, South Caro., 1970

HIGHEST AVERAGE PER RUNBACK
Season
(Min. 40 rets.) 28.3—Erroll Tucker, Utah, 1985 (6 for 216 on interceptions, 16 for 389 on punt returns, 24 for 698 on kickoff returns; total 46 for 1,303)

HIGHEST AVERAGE PER RUNBACK
(At Least 7 Interceptions and Min. 1.3 Punt Returns and 1.3 Kickoff Returns Per Game)
Career
22.6—Erroll Tucker, Utah, 1984-85 (8 for 224 on interceptions, 38 for 650 on punt returns, 41 for 1,091 on kickoff returns; total 87 for 1,965)

MOST TOUCHDOWNS ON INTERCEPTIONS, PUNT RETURNS AND KICKOFF RETURNS
(Must Have at Least One Touchdown in Each Category)
Season
7—Erroll Tucker, Utah, 1985 (3 interceptions, 2 punt returns, 2 kickoff returns)
Career
8—Erroll Tucker, Utah, 1984-85 (3 interceptions, 3 punt returns, 2 kickoff returns)

Opponent's Kicks Blocked

MOST OPPONENT'S PUNTS BLOCKED BY
Game
4—Ken Irvin, Memphis vs. Arkansas, Sept. 26, 1992 (4 punts)
Season
8—James Francis (LB), Baylor, 1989 (11 games); Jimmy Lisko, Arkansas St., 1975 (11 games)

MOST OPPONENT'S PAT KICKS BLOCKED BY
Season
5—Ray Farmer, Duke, 1993
Career
8—Ray Farmer, Duke, 1992-95

MOST OPPONENT'S TOTAL KICKS BLOCKED BY (Includes Punts, PAT Attempts, FG Attempts)
Game
4—Ken Irvin, Memphis vs. Arkansas, Sept. 26, 1992 (4 punts)
Career
19—James Ferebee, New Mexico St., 1978-81 (8 FG attempts, 6 PAT attempts, 5 punts)

MOST TOUCHDOWNS SCORED ON BLOCKED PUNTS
Season
3—Joe Wessel, Florida St., 1984

MOST FIELD GOAL ATTEMPTS BLOCKED BY
Quarter
2—Pat Larson, Wyoming vs. Fresno St., Nov. 18, 1995 (2nd quarter); Jerald Henry, Southern Cal vs. California, Oct. 22, 1994 (1st quarter, returned first one 60 yards for touchdown)

All-Purpose Yards

(Yardage Gained From Rushing, Receiving and All Runbacks)

MOST PLAYS
Game
58—Tony Sands, Kansas vs. Missouri, Nov. 23, 1991 (58 rushes)
Season
432—Marcus Allen, Southern Cal, 1981 (403 rushes, 29 receptions)
Career
(3 yrs.) 1,034—Herschel Walker, Georgia, 1980-82 (994 rushes, 26 receptions, 14 kickoff returns)
(4 yrs.) 1,347—Steve Bartalo, Colorado St., 1983-86 (1,215 rushes, 132 receptions)

MOST YARDS GAINED
Game
435—Brian Pruitt, Central Mich. vs. Toledo, Nov. 5, 1994 (356 rushing, 79 kickoff returns)
Season
3,250—Barry Sanders, Oklahoma St., 1988 (2,628 rushing, 106 receiving, 95 punt returns, 421 kickoff returns; 11 games)
Career
(3 yrs.) 5,749—Herschel Walker, Georgia, 1980-82 (5,259 rushing, 243 receiving, 247 kickoff returns; 1,034 plays)
(4 yrs.) 7,172—$Napoleon McCallum, Navy, 1981-85 (4,179 rushing, 796 receiving, 858 punt returns, 1,339 kickoff returns; 1,138 plays)
$ See page 6 for explanation.

MOST YARDS GAINED PER GAME
Season
295.5—Barry Sanders, Oklahoma St., 1988 (3,250 in 11 games)
Career
237.8—Ryan Benjamin, Pacific (Cal.), 1990-92 (5,706 in 24 games; 3,119 rushing, 1,063 receiving, 100 punt returns, 1,424 kickoff returns)

MOST YARDS GAINED BY A FRESHMAN
Game
422—Marshall Faulk, San Diego St. vs. Pacific (Cal.), Sept. 14, 1991 (386 rushing, 11 receiving, 25 kickoff returns)
Season
2,026—Terrell Willis, Rutgers, 1993 (1,261 rushing, 61 receiving, 704 kickoff returns; 234 plays)
Per-game record—184.8, Marshall Faulk, San Diego St., 1991 (1,663 in 9)

MOST SEASONS WITH 2,000 OR MORE YARDS
2—Ryan Benjamin, Pacific (Cal.), 1991 (2,995) & 1992 (2,597); Glyn Milburn, Stanford, 1990 (2,222) & 1992 (2,121); Sheldon Canley, San Jose St., 1989 (2,513) & 1990 (2,213); Chuck Weatherspoon, Houston, 1989 (2,391) & 1990 (2,038); Napoleon McCallum, Navy, 1983 (2,385) & 1985 (2,330); Howard Stevens, Randolph-Macon, 1968 (2,115) & Louisville, 1972 (2,132)

HIGHEST AVERAGE GAIN PER PLAY
Game
(Min. 300 yards, 25 plays) 16.8—Randy Gatewood, UNLV vs. Idaho, Sept. 17, 1994 (419 on 25)
Season
(Min. 1,500 yards, 100-124 plays) 18.5—Henry Bailey, UNLV, 1992 (1,883 on 102)
(Min. 1,500 yards, 125 plays) 15.7—Terance Mathis, New Mexico, 1989 (2,138 on 136)
Career
(Min. 5,000 yards, 275-374 plays) 17.4—Anthony Carter, Michigan, 1979-82 (5,197 on 298)
(Min. 5,000 yards, 375 plays) 14.6—Terance Mathis, New Mexico, 1985-87, 1989 (6,691 on 457)

MOST YARDS GAINED BY TWO PLAYERS, SAME TEAM
Career
10,253—Marshall Faulk (5,595) & Darnay Scott (4,658), San Diego St., 1991-93

Scoring

MOST POINTS SCORED (By Non-Kickers)
Game
48—Howard Griffith, Illinois vs. Southern Ill., Sept. 22, 1990 (8 TDs on runs of 5, 51, 7, 41, 5, 18, 5, 3 yards)
Game vs. Major-College Opponent
44—Marshall Faulk, San Diego St. vs. Pacific (Cal.), Sept. 14, 1991 (7 TDs, 1 two-point conversion)
Season
234—Barry Sanders, Oklahoma St., 1988 (39 TDs in 11 games)
2 Yrs
312—Barry Sanders, Oklahoma St., 1987-88 (52 TDs in 22 games)
Career
(3 yrs.) 376—Marshall Faulk, San Diego St., 1991-93 (62 TDs, 2 two-point conversions)
(4 yrs.) 394—Anthony Thompson, Indiana, 1986-89 (65 TDs, 4 PATs)

MOST POINTS SCORED PER GAME
Season
21.3—Barry Sanders, Oklahoma St., 1988 (234 in 11)
2 Yrs
14.2—Barry Sanders, Oklahoma St., 1987-88 (312 in 22)
Career
12.1—Marshall Faulk, San Diego St., 1991-93 (376 in 31)

MOST POINTS SCORED BY A FRESHMAN
Game
44—Marshall Faulk, San Diego St. vs. Pacific (Cal.), Sept. 14, 1991 (7 TDs, 1 two-point conversion)
Season
140—Marshall Faulk, San Diego St., 1991 (23 TDs, 1 two-point conversion)
Also holds per-game record at 15.6 (140 in 9)

MOST TOUCHDOWNS SCORED
Game
8—Howard Griffith, Illinois vs. Southern Ill., Sept. 22, 1990 (all 8 by rushing on runs of 5, 51, 7, 41, 5, 18, 5, 3 yards)
Game vs. Major-College Opponent
7—Marshall Faulk, San Diego St. vs. Pacific (Cal.), Sept. 14, 1991; Arnold "Showboat" Boykin, Mississippi vs. Mississippi St., Dec. 1, 1951
Season
39—Barry Sanders, Oklahoma St., 1988 (11 games)
Also holds per-game record at 3.5 (39 in 11)
2 Yrs
52—Barry Sanders, Oklahoma St., 1987-88 (22 games)
Also holds per-game record at 2.4 (52 in 22)
Career
(3 yrs.) 62—Marshall Faulk, San Diego St., 1991-93 (57 rushing, 5 pass receptions)
Also holds per-game record at 2.0 (62 in 31)
(4 yrs.) 65—Anthony Thompson, Indiana, 1986-89 (64 rushing, 1 pass reception)

MOST TOUCHDOWNS SCORED IN TWO AND THREE CONSECUTIVE GAMES
2 Games
11—Kelvin Bryant, North Caro., 1981 (6 vs. East Caro., Sept. 12; 5 vs. Miami, Ohio, Sept. 19)
3 Games
15—Kelvin Bryant, North Caro., 1981 (6 vs. East Caro., Sept. 12; 5 vs. Miami, Ohio, Sept. 19; 4 vs. Boston College, Sept. 26)

MOST TOUCHDOWNS SCORED BY A FRESHMAN
Game
7—Marshall Faulk, San Diego St. vs. Pacific (Cal.), Sept. 14, 1991 (all by rushing)
Season
23—Marshall Faulk, San Diego St., 1991 (21 rushing, 2 pass receptions)
Also holds per-game record at 2.6 (23 in 9)

MOST CONSECUTIVE GAMES SCORING A TOUCHDOWN
Career
23—Bill Burnett, Arkansas (from Oct. 5, 1968, through Oct. 31, 1970; 47 touchdowns)

MOST GAMES SCORING A TOUCHDOWN
Season
11—By many players. Most recent: Chris Doering, Florida, 1995
Career
31—Ted Brown, North Caro. St., 1975-78; Tony Dorsett, Pittsburgh, 1973-76; Glenn Davis, Army, 1943-46

MOST GAMES SCORING TWO OR MORE TOUCHDOWNS
Season
11—Barry Sanders, Oklahoma St., 1988
Career
17—Tony Dorsett, Pittsburgh, 1973-76; Steve Owens, Oklahoma, 1967-69; Glenn Davis, Army, 1943-46

MOST CONSECUTIVE GAMES SCORING TWO OR MORE TOUCHDOWNS
Season
11—Barry Sanders, Oklahoma St., 1988
Career
13—Barry Sanders, Oklahoma St. (from Nov. 14, 1987, through 1988)

MOST GAMES SCORING THREE OR MORE TOUCHDOWNS
Season
9—Barry Sanders, Oklahoma St., 1988

MOST CONSECUTIVE GAMES SCORING THREE OR MORE TOUCHDOWNS
Season
5—Barry Sanders, Oklahoma St., 1988 (from Sept. 10

through Oct. 15); Paul Hewitt, San Diego St., 1987 (from Oct. 10 through Nov. 7)

MOST TOUCHDOWNS AND POINTS SCORED BY TWO PLAYERS, SAME TEAM
Season
54 and 324—Barry Sanders (39-234) & Hart Lee Dykes (15-90), Oklahoma St., 1988
Career
97 and 585—Glenn Davis (59-354) & Doc Blanchard (38-231), Army, 1943-46

PASSING FOR A TOUCHDOWN AND SCORING TOUCHDOWNS BY RUSHING AND RECEIVING
Game
By many players. Most recent: Keith Byars, Ohio St. vs. Iowa, Sept. 22, 1984

PASSING FOR A TOUCHDOWN AND SCORING ON A PASS RECEPTION AND PUNT RETURN
Game
By many players. Most recent: Scott Schwedes, Syracuse vs. Temple, Oct. 26, 1985

MOST EXTRA POINTS ATTEMPTED BY KICKING
Game
14—Terry Leiweke, Houston vs. Tulsa, Nov. 23, 1968 (13 made)
Season
71—Scott Bentley, Florida St., 1995 (67 made); Bart Edmiston, Florida, 1995 (71 made); Kurt Gunther, Brigham Young, 1980 (64 made)
Career
222—Derek Mahoney, Fresno St., 1990-93 (216 made)

MOST EXTRA POINTS MADE BY KICKING
Game
13—Derek Mahoney, Fresno St. vs. New Mexico, Oct. 5, 1991 (13 attempts); Terry Leiweke, Houston vs. Tulsa, Nov. 23, 1968 (14 attempts)
Season
71—Bart Edmiston, Florida, 1995 (71 attempts)
Per-game record—6.1, Scott Bentley, Florida St., 1995, and Cary Blanchard, Oklahoma St., 1988 (67 in 11)
Career
216—Derek Mahoney, Fresno St., 1990-93 (222 attempts)
Per-game record—5.2, Al Limahelu, San Diego St., 1969-70 (103 in 20)

BEST PERFECT RECORD OF EXTRA POINTS MADE
Season
71 of 71—Bart Edmiston, Florida, 1995

HIGHEST PERCENTAGE OF EXTRA POINTS MADE
Career
(Min. 100 atts.) 100%—John Becksvoort, Tennessee, 1991-94 (161 of 161); David Browndyke, LSU, 1986-89 (109 of 109); Pete Stoyanovich, Indiana, 1985-88 (101 of 101); Van Tiffin, Alabama, 1983-86 (135 of 135)

MOST CONSECUTIVE EXTRA POINTS MADE
Game
13—Derek Mahoney, Fresno St. vs. New Mexico, Oct. 5, 1991 (13 attempts)
Season
71—Bart Edmiston, Florida, 1995 (71 attempts)
Career
161—John Becksvoort, Tennessee, 1991-94

MOST POINTS SCORED BY KICKING
Game
24—Mike Prindle, Western Mich. vs. Marshall, Sept. 29, 1984 (7 FGs, 3 PATs)
Season
131—Roman Anderson, Houston, 1989 (22 FGs, 65 PATs)
Also holds per-game record at 11.9 (131 in 11)
Career
423—Roman Anderson, Houston, 1988-91 (70 FGs, 213 PATs)
Also holds per-game record at 9.6 (423 in 44)

HIGHEST PERCENTAGE OF EXTRA POINTS AND FIELD GOALS MADE
Season
(Min. 30 PATs and 15 FGs made) 98.3%—Chuck Nelson, Washington, 1982 (34 of 34 PATs, 25 of 26 FGs)
(Min. 40 PATs and 20 FGs made) 97.3%—Chris Jacke, UTEP, 1988 (48 of 48 PATs, 25 of 27 FGs)
Career
(Min. 100 PATs and 50 FGs made) 93.3%—John Lee, UCLA, 1982-85 (116 of 117 PATs, 79 of 92 FGs)

MOST TWO-POINT ATTEMPTS MADE
Game
6—Jim Pilot, New Mexico St. vs. Hardin-Simmons, Nov. 25, 1961 (all by running, attempted 7)
Season
6—Howard Twilley, Tulsa, 1964 (all on pass receptions); Jim Pilot, New Mexico St., 1961 (all by running); Pat McCarthy, Holy Cross, 1960 (all by running)
Career
13—Pat McCarthy, Holy Cross, 1960-62 (all by running)

MOST SUCCESSFUL TWO-POINT PASSES
Season
12—John Hangartner, Arizona St., 1958 (attempted 21)
Career
19—Pat McCarthy, Holy Cross, 1960-62 (attempted 33)

Defensive Extra Points

MOST DEFENSIVE EXTRA POINTS SCORED
Game
1—By 34 players
Season
1—By 34 players

LONGEST RETURN OF A DEFENSIVE EXTRA-POINT ATTEMPT
Game
100—Joe Crocker (CB), Virginia vs. North Caro. St., Nov. 25, 1994 (intercepted pass five yards deep in North Caro. St. end zone); William Price (CB), Kansas St. vs. Indiana St., Sept. 7, 1991 (intercepted pass three yards deep in Indiana St. end zone); Curt Newton (LB), Washington St. vs. Oregon St., Oct. 20, 1990 (returned conversion pass attempt from Washington St. goal line); Quintin Parker (DB), Illinois vs. Wisconsin, Oct. 28, 1989 (returned kick from Illinois goal line); Lee Ozmint (SS), Alabama vs. LSU, Nov. 11, 1989 (intercepted pass at Alabama goal line)

FIRST DEFENSIVE EXTRA-POINT ATTEMPT
Season
Thomas King (S), Southwestern La. vs. Cal St. Fullerton, Sept. 3, 1988 (returned blocked kick 6 yards)

MOST DEFENSIVE EXTRA-POINT KICKS BLOCKED
Game
2—Nigel Codrington (DB), Rice vs. Notre Dame, Nov. 5, 1988 (1 resulted in a score)
Also holds season record at 2

Fumble Returns

(Since 1992)

MOST FUMBLE RETURNS
Game
1—By many players

Field Goals

MOST FIELD GOALS ATTEMPTED
Game
9—Mike Prindle, Western Mich. vs. Marshall, Sept. 29, 1984 (7 made)
Season
38—Jerry DePoyster, Wyoming, 1966 (13 made)
Also holds per-game record at 3.8
Career
(3 yrs.) 93—Jerry DePoyster, Wyoming, 1965-67 (36 made)
Also holds per-game record at 3.1 (93 in 30)
(4 yrs.) 105—Philip Doyle, Alabama, 1987-90 (78 made); Luis Zendejas, Arizona St., 1981-84 (78 made)
Doyle holds per-game record at 2.4 (105 in 43)

MOST FIELD GOALS MADE
Quarter
4—By 4 players. Most recent: David Hardy, Texas A&M vs. Texas-Arlington, Sept. 18, 1982 (2nd)
Half
5—Dat Ly, New Mexico St. vs. Kansas, Oct. 1, 1988 (1st); Dale Klein, Nebraska vs. Missouri, Oct. 19, 1985 (1st)
Game
7—Dale Klein, Nebraska vs. Missouri, Oct. 19, 1985 (32, 22, 43, 44, 29, 43, 43 yards), 7 attempts; Mike Prindle, Western Mich. vs. Marshall, Sept. 29, 1984 (32, 44, 42, 23, 48, 41, 27 yards), 9 attempts
Season
29—John Lee, UCLA, 1984 (33 attempts)
2 Yrs
50—John Lee, UCLA, 1984-85 (57 attempts)
Career
80—Jeff Jaeger, Washington, 1983-86 (99 attempts)

MOST FIELD GOALS MADE PER GAME
Season
2.6—John Lee, UCLA, 1984 (29 in 11)
Career
1.8—John Lee, UCLA, 1982-85 (79 in 43)

BEST PERFECT RECORD OF FIELD GOALS MADE
Game
7 of 7—Dale Klein, Nebraska vs. Missouri, Oct. 19, 1985

MOST FIELD GOALS MADE BY A FRESHMAN
Game
6—*Mickey Thomas, Virginia Tech vs. Vanderbilt, Nov. 4, 1989 (6 attempts)
Season
23—Collin Mackie, South Caro., 1987 (30 attempts)

**Conventional-style kicker.*

HIGHEST PERCENTAGE OF FIELD GOALS MADE
Season
(Min. 15 atts.) 96.2%—Chuck Nelson, Washington, 1982 (25 of 26)
Career
(Min. 45-54 atts.) 87.8%—Bobby Raymond, Florida, 1983-84 (43 of 49)
(Min. 55 atts.) 85.9%—John Lee, UCLA, 1982-85 (79 of 92)

MOST CONSECUTIVE FIELD GOALS MADE
Season
25—Chuck Nelson, Washington, 1982 (first 25, missed last attempt of season vs. Washington St., Nov. 20)

Florida sports information photo by Jason R. Davis

Florida kicker Bart Edmiston had more success kicking extra points in 1995 than any kicker in Division I-A history. His 71 extra points set an all-time record, and his 71-for-71 mark was the best perfect season.

Career
30—Chuck Nelson, Washington, 1981-82 (last 5 in 1981, from Southern Cal, Nov. 14, and first 25 in 1982, ending with last attempt vs. Washington St., Nov. 20)

MOST GAMES KICKING A FIELD GOAL
Career
40—Gary Gussman, Miami (Ohio), 1984-87 (in 44 games played)

MOST CONSECUTIVE GAMES KICKING A FIELD GOAL
19—Gary Gussman, Miami (Ohio), 1986-87; Larry Roach, Oklahoma St., 1983-84

MOST FIELD GOALS MADE, 60 YARDS OR MORE
Game
2—Tony Franklin, Texas A&M vs. Baylor, Oct. 16, 1976 (65 & 64 yards)
Season
3—Russell Erxleben, Texas, 1977 (67 vs. Rice, Oct. 1; 64 vs. Baylor, Oct. 16; 60 vs. Texas Tech, Oct. 29) (4 attempts)
Career
3—Russell Erxleben, Texas, 1975-78 (see Season Record above)

MOST FIELD GOALS ATTEMPTED, 60 YARDS OR MORE
Season
5—Tony Franklin, Texas A&M, 1976 (2 made)
Career
11—Tony Franklin, Texas A&M, 1975-78 (2 made)

MOST FIELD GOALS MADE, 50 YARDS OR MORE
Game
3—Sergio Lopez-Chavero, Wichita St. vs. Drake, Oct. 27, 1984 (54, 54, 51 yards); Jerry DePoyster, Wyoming vs. Utah, Oct. 8, 1966 (54, 54, 52 yards)
Season
8—Fuad Reveiz, Tennessee, 1982 (10 attempts)
Career
20—Jason Hanson, Washington St., 1988-91 (35 attempts)

MOST FIELD GOALS ATTEMPTED, 50 YARDS OR MORE
Season
17—Jerry DePoyster, Wyoming, 1966 (5 made)
Career
38—Tony Franklin, Texas A&M, 1975-78 (16 made)

HIGHEST PERCENTAGE OF FIELD GOALS MADE, 50 YARDS OR MORE
Season
(Min. 10 atts.) 80.0%—Fuad Reveiz, Tennessee, 1982 (8 of 10)
Career
(Min. 15 atts.) 60.9%—Max Zendejas, Arizona, 1982-85 (14 of 23)

MOST FIELD GOALS MADE, 40 YARDS OR MORE
Game
5—Alan Smith, Texas A&M vs. Arkansas St., Sept. 17, 1983 (44, 45, 42, 59, 57 yards)
Season
14—Chris Jacke, UTEP, 1988 (16 attempts)
Career
39—Jason Hanson, Washington St., 1988-91 (66 attempts) (19 of 31, 40-49 yards; 20 of 35, 50 or more yards)

MOST FIELD GOALS ATTEMPTED, 40 YARDS OR MORE
Season
25—Jerry DePoyster, Wyoming, 1966 (6 made)
Career
66—Jason Hanson, Washington St., 1988-91 (39 made)

HIGHEST PERCENTAGE OF FIELD GOALS MADE, 40 YARDS OR MORE
Season
(Min. 10 made) 90.9%—John Carney, Notre Dame, 1984 (10 of 11)
Career
(Min. 20 made) 69.4%—John Lee, UCLA, 1982-85 (25 of 36)

HIGHEST PERCENTAGE OF FIELD GOALS MADE, 40-49 YARDS
Season
(Min. 10 made) 100%—John Carney, Notre Dame, 1984 (10 of 10)
Career
(Min. 15 made) 82.6%—Jeff Jaeger, Washington, 1983-86 (19 of 23)

MOST CONSECUTIVE FIELD GOALS MADE, 40-49 YARDS
Career
12—John Carney, Notre Dame, 1984-85

HIGHEST PERCENTAGE OF FIELD GOALS MADE, UNDER 40 YARDS
Season
(Min. 16 made) 100%—Philip Doyle, Alabama, 1989 (19 of 19); Scott Slater, Texas A&M, 1986 (16 of 16); Bobby Raymond, Florida, 1984 (18 of 18); John Lee, UCLA, 1984 (16 of 16); Randy Pratt, California, 1983 (16 of 16); Paul Woodside, West Va., 1982 (23 of 23)
Career
(Min. 30-39 made) 97.0%—Bobby Raymond, Florida, 1983-84 (32 of 33)
(Min. 40 made) 96.4%—John Lee, UCLA, 1982-85 (54 of 56)

LONGEST AVERAGE DISTANCE FIELD GOALS MADE
Game
(Min. 4 made) 49.5—Jeff Heath, East Caro. vs. Texas-Arlington, Nov. 6, 1982 (58, 53, 42, 45 yards)
Season
(Min. 10 made) 50.9—Jason Hanson, Washington St., 1991 (10 made)
Career
(Min. 25 made) 42.4—Russell Erxleben, Texas, 1975-78 (49 made)

LONGEST AVERAGE DISTANCE FIELD GOALS ATTEMPTED
Season
(Min. 20 atts.) 51.2—Jason Hanson, Washington St., 1991 (22 attempts)
Career
(Min. 40 atts.) 44.7—Russell Erxleben, Texas, 1975-78 (78 attempts)

MOST TIMES KICKING TWO OR MORE FIELD GOALS IN A GAME
Season
10—Paul Woodside, West Va., 1982
Career
27—Kevin Butler, Georgia, 1981-84

MOST TIMES KICKING THREE OR MORE FIELD GOALS IN A GAME
Season
6—Joe Allison, Memphis, 1992; Luis Zendejas, Arizona St., 1983
Career
13—Luis Zendejas, Arizona St., 1981-84

MOST TIMES KICKING FOUR FIELD GOALS IN A GAME
Season
4—Matt Bahr, Penn St., 1978
Career
6—John Lee, UCLA, 1982-85
Also holds career record for most times kicking four or more field goals in a game at 8

LONGEST FIELD GOAL MADE
67—Joe Williams, Wichita St. vs. Southern Ill., Oct. 21, 1978; Steve Little, Arkansas vs. Texas, Oct. 15, 1977; Russell Erxleben, Texas vs. Rice, Oct. 1, 1977

LONGEST INDOOR FIELD GOAL MADE
62—Chip Lohmiller, Minnesota vs. Iowa, Nov. 22, 1986 (in Minnesota's Metrodome)

LONGEST FIELD GOAL MADE WITHOUT USE OF A KICKING TEE
62—Jason Hanson, Washington St. vs. UNLV, Sept. 28, 1991

LONGEST FIELD GOAL MADE BY A FRESHMAN
61—Kyle Bryant, Texas A&M vs. Southern Miss., Sept. 24, 1994

LONGEST FIELD GOAL MADE ON FIRST ATTEMPT OF CAREER
61—Ralf Mojsiejenko, Michigan St. vs. Illinois, Sept. 11, 1982

MOST FIELD GOALS MADE IN FIRST GAME OF CAREER
5—Jose Oceguera, Long Beach St. vs. Kansas St., Sept. 3, 1983 (5 attempts); Nathan Ritter, North Caro. St. vs. East Caro., Sept. 9, 1978 (6 attempts); Joe Liljenquist, Brigham Young vs. Colorado St., Sept. 20, 1969 (6 attempts)

MOST GAMES IN WHICH FIELD GOAL(S) PROVIDED THE WINNING MARGIN
Season
6—Henrik Mike-Mayer, Drake, 1981
Career
10—Jeff Ward, Texas, 1983-86; John Lee, UCLA, 1982-85; Dan Miller, Miami (Fla.), 1978-81

Team Records

SINGLE GAME—Offense

Total Offense

MOST PLAYS
112—Montana vs. Montana St., Nov. 1, 1952 (475 yards)

MOST PLAYS, BOTH TEAMS
196—San Diego St. (99) & North Texas (97), Dec. 4, 1971 (851 yards)

FEWEST PLAYS
12—Texas Tech vs. Centenary (La.), Nov. 11, 1939 (10 rushes, 2 passes, -1 yard)

FEWEST PLAYS, BOTH TEAMS
33—Texas Tech (12) & Centenary (La.) (21), Nov. 11, 1939 (28 rushes, 5 passes, 30 yards)

MOST YARDS GAINED
1,021—Houston vs. Southern Methodist, Oct. 21, 1989 (250 rushing, 771 passing, 86 plays)

MOST YARDS GAINED, BOTH TEAMS
1,563—Houston (827) & Texas Christian (736), Nov. 3, 1990 (187 plays)

FEWEST YARDS GAINED
Minus 47—Syracuse vs. Penn St., Oct. 18, 1947 (-107 rushing, gained 60 passing, 49 plays)

FEWEST YARDS GAINED, BOTH TEAMS
30—Texas Tech (-1) & Centenary (La.) (31), Nov. 11, 1939 (33 plays)

MOST YARDS GAINED BY A LOSING TEAM
736—Texas Christian vs. Houston, Nov. 3, 1990 (lost 56-35)

BOTH TEAMS GAINING 600 YARDS OR MORE
In 14 games. Most recent: Nevada (727) & Louisiana Tech (607), Oct. 21, 1995 (180 plays); Idaho (707) & UNLV (614), Sept. 17, 1994 (181 plays); Houston (684) & Texas Tech (636), Nov. 30, 1991 (182 plays); Brigham Young (767) & San Diego St. (695), Nov. 16, 1991 (168 plays); San Jose St. (616) & Pacific (Cal.) (603), Oct. 19, 1991 (157 plays)

FEWEST YARDS GAINED BY A WINNING TEAM
10—North Caro. St. vs. Virginia, Sept. 30, 1944 (won 13-0)

HIGHEST AVERAGE GAIN PER PLAY (Min. 75 Plays)
11.9—Houston vs. Southern Methodist, Oct. 21, 1989 (86 for 1,021)

MOST TOUCHDOWNS SCORED BY RUSHING AND PASSING
15—Wyoming vs. Northern Colo., Nov. 5, 1949 (9 rushing, 6 passing)

Rushing

MOST RUSHES
99—Missouri vs. Colorado, Oct. 12, 1968 (421 yards)

MOST RUSHES, BOTH TEAMS
141—Colgate (82) & Bucknell (59), Nov. 6, 1971 (440 yards)

FEWEST RUSHES
5—Houston vs. Texas Tech, Nov. 25, 1989 (36 yards)

FEWEST RUSHES, BOTH TEAMS
28—Texas Tech (10) & Centenary (La.) (18), Nov. 11, 1939 (23 yards)

MOST YARDS GAINED
768—Oklahoma vs. Kansas St., Oct. 15, 1988 (72 rushes)

MOST YARDS GAINED, BOTH TEAMS
1,039—Lenoir-Rhyne (837) & Davidson (202), Oct. 11, 1975 (111 rushes)

MOST YARDS GAINED, BOTH TEAMS, MAJOR-COLLEGE OPPONENTS
956—Oklahoma (711) & Kansas St. (245), Oct. 23, 1971 (111 rushes)

FEWEST YARDS GAINED
Minus 109—Northern Ill. vs. Toledo, Nov. 11, 1967 (33 rushes)

FEWEST YARDS GAINED, BOTH TEAMS
Minus 24—San Jose St. (-102) & UTEP (78), Oct. 22, 1966 (75 rushes)

MOST YARDS GAINED WITHOUT LOSS
677—Nebraska vs. New Mexico St., Sept. 18, 1982 (78 rushes)

MOST YARDS GAINED BY A LOSING TEAM
525—Air Force vs. New Mexico, Nov. 2, 1991 (70 rushes, lost 34-32)

HIGHEST AVERAGE GAIN PER RUSH (Min. 50 Rushes)
11.9—Alabama vs. Virginia Tech, Oct. 27, 1973 (63 for 748)

MOST PLAYERS ON ONE TEAM EACH GAINING 100 YARDS OR MORE
4—Army vs. Montana, Nov. 17, 1984 (Doug Black 183, Nate Sassaman 155, Clarence Jones 130, Jarvis Hollingsworth 124); Alabama vs. Virginia Tech, Oct. 27, 1973 (Jimmy Taylor 142, Wilbur Jackson 138, Calvin Culliver 127, Richard Todd 102); Texas vs. Southern Methodist, Nov. 1, 1969 (Jim Bertelsen 137, Steve Worster 137, James Street 121, Ted Koy 111); Arizona St. vs. Arizona, Nov. 10, 1951 (Bob Tarwater 140, Harley Cooper 123, Duane Morrison 118, Buzz Walker 113)

MOST TOUCHDOWNS SCORED BY RUSHING
12—UTEP vs. New Mexico St., Nov. 25, 1948

Passing

MOST PASSES ATTEMPTED
81—Houston vs. Southern Methodist, Oct. 20, 1990 (completed 53)

MOST PASSES ATTEMPTED, BOTH TEAMS
135—Texas Christian (79) & Houston (56), Nov. 3, 1990 (completed 81)

FEWEST PASSES ATTEMPTED
0—By many teams. Most recent: Baylor vs. Southern Methodist, Oct. 9, 1993 (91 rushes)

FEWEST PASSES ATTEMPTED, BOTH TEAMS
1—Michigan St. (0) & Maryland (1), Oct. 20, 1944 (not completed)

MOST PASSES ATTEMPTED WITHOUT COMPLETION
18—West Va. vs. Temple, Oct. 18, 1946

MOST PASSES ATTEMPTED WITHOUT INTERCEPTION
72—Houston vs. Texas Christian, Nov. 4, 1989 (completed 47)

MOST PASSES ATTEMPTED WITHOUT INTERCEPTION, BOTH TEAMS
114—Illinois (67) & Purdue (47), Oct. 12, 1985 (completed 67)

MOST CONSECUTIVE PASSES ATTEMPTED WITHOUT A RUSHING PLAY
32—North Caro. St. vs. Duke, Nov. 11, 1989 (3rd & 4th quarters, completed 16)

MOST PASSES COMPLETED
55—Wake Forest vs. Duke, Oct. 28, 1995 (attempted 78)

MOST PASSES COMPLETED, BOTH TEAMS
81—Texas Christian (44) & Houston (37), Nov. 3, 1990 (attempted 135)

BEST PERFECT GAME (1.000 Pct.)
11 of 11—North Caro. vs. William & Mary, Oct. 5, 1991; Air Force vs. Northwestern, Sept. 17, 1988; Oregon St. vs. UCLA, Oct. 2, 1971; Southern Cal vs. Washington, Oct. 9, 1965

HIGHEST PERCENTAGE OF PASSES COMPLETED
(Min. 15-24 comps.) 95.0%—Mississippi vs. Tulane, Nov. 6, 1982 (19 of 20)
(Min. 25-34 comps.) 92.6%—UCLA vs. Washington, Oct. 29, 1983 (25 of 27)
(Min. 35 comps.) 87.0%—South Caro. vs. Mississippi St., Oct. 14, 1995 (40 of 46)

HIGHEST PERCENTAGE OF PASSES COMPLETED, BOTH TEAMS (Min. 40 Completions)
84.6%—UCLA & Washington, Oct. 29, 1983 (44 of 52)

MOST PASSES HAD INTERCEPTED
10—California vs. UCLA, Oct. 21, 1978 (52 attempts); Detroit vs. Oklahoma St., Nov. 28, 1942

MOST YARDS GAINED
771—Houston vs. Southern Methodist, Oct. 21, 1989 (completed 40 of 61)

MOST YARDS GAINED, BOTH TEAMS
1,253—Texas Christian (690) & Houston (563), Nov. 3, 1990 (135 attempts)

FEWEST YARDS GAINED, BOTH TEAMS
Minus 13—North Caro. (-7 on 1 of 3 attempts) & Pennsylvania (-6 on 2 of 12 attempts), Nov. 13, 1943

MOST YARDS GAINED PER ATTEMPT
(Min. 30-39 atts.) 15.5—Mississippi St. vs. Tulane, Oct. 22, 1994 (30 for 466)
(Min. 40 atts.) 15.9—UTEP vs. North Texas, Sept. 18, 1965 (40 for 634)

MOST YARDS GAINED PER COMPLETION
(Min. 15-24 comps.) 31.9—UTEP vs. New Mexico, Oct. 28, 1967 (16 for 510)
(Min. 25 comps.) 25.4—UTEP vs. North Texas, Sept. 18, 1965 (25 for 634)

MOST TOUCHDOWN PASSES
11—Houston vs. Eastern Wash., Nov. 17, 1990

MOST TOUCHDOWN PASSES, MAJOR-COLLEGE OPPONENTS
10—Houston vs. Southern Methodist, Oct. 21, 1989; San Diego St. vs. New Mexico St., Nov. 15, 1969

MOST TOUCHDOWN PASSES, BOTH TEAMS
14—Houston (11) & Eastern Wash. (3), Nov. 17, 1990

MOST TOUCHDOWN PASSES, BOTH TEAMS, MAJOR-COLLEGE OPPONENTS
13—San Diego St. (10) & New Mexico St. (3), Nov. 15, 1969

Punting

MOST PUNTS
39—Texas Tech vs. Centenary (La.), Nov. 11, 1939 (1,377 yards)
38—Centenary (La.) vs. Texas Tech, Nov. 11, 1939 (1,248 yards)

MOST PUNTS, BOTH TEAMS
77—Texas Tech (39) & Centenary (La.) (38), Nov. 11, 1939 (2,625 yards) (The game was played in a heavy downpour in Shreveport, Louisiana. Forty-two punts were returned, 19 went out of bounds, 10 were downed, 1 went into the end zone for a touchback, 4 were blocked and 1 was fair caught. Sixty-seven punts [34 by Texas Tech and 33 by Centenary] occurred on first-down plays, including 22 consecutively in the third and fourth quarters. The game was a scoreless tie.)

FEWEST PUNTS
0—By many teams. Most recent: Ohio St. vs. Illinois, Nov. 11, 1995 (won 41-3); Nebraska vs. Iowa St., Nov. 4, 1995 (won 73-14); Syracuse vs. Minnesota, Sept. 23, 1995 (won 27-17)

FEWEST PUNTS BY A LOSING TEAM
0—By many teams. Most recent: New Mexico St. vs. UTEP, Sept. 14, 1991 (lost 22-21)

HIGHEST AVERAGE PER PUNT
(Min. 5-9 punts) 60.4—Brigham Young vs. Wyoming, Oct. 8, 1983 (5 for 302)
(Min. 10 punts) 53.6—Oklahoma St. vs. Colorado, Nov. 13, 1971 (10 for 536)

HIGHEST AVERAGE PER PUNT, BOTH TEAMS (Min. 10 Punts)
55.3—Brigham Young & Wyoming, Oct. 8, 1983 (11 for 608)

Punt Returns

MOST PUNT RETURNS
22—Texas Tech vs. Centenary (La.), Nov. 11, 1939 (112 yards)

MOST PUNT RETURNS, BOTH TEAMS
42—Texas Tech (22) & Centenary (La.) (20), Nov. 11, 1939 (233 yards)

MOST YARDS ON PUNT RETURNS
319—Texas A&M vs. North Texas, Sept. 21, 1946 (10 returns)

HIGHEST AVERAGE GAIN PER RETURN (Min. 5 Returns)
45.0—Georgia vs. South Caro., Sept. 2, 1995 (5 for 225)

MOST TOUCHDOWNS SCORED ON PUNT RETURNS
3—Holy Cross vs. Brown, Sept. 21, 1974; LSU vs. Mississippi, Dec. 5, 1970; Wichita St. vs. Northern St., Oct. 22, 1949; Wisconsin vs. Iowa, Nov. 8, 1947

Kickoff Returns

MOST KICKOFF RETURNS
14—Arizona St. vs. Nevada, Oct. 12, 1946 (290 yards)

MOST YARDS ON KICKOFF RETURNS
295—Cincinnati vs. Memphis, Oct. 30, 1971 (8 returns)

HIGHEST AVERAGE GAIN PER RETURN (Min. 6 Returns)
46.2—Southern Cal vs. Washington St., Nov. 7, 1970 (6 for 277)

MOST TOUCHDOWNS SCORED ON KICKOFF RETURNS
2—By many teams. Most recent: Texas A&M vs. Rice, Oct. 23, 1993; Brigham Young vs. Air Force, Nov. 11, 1989; Notre Dame vs. Michigan, Sept. 16, 1989; New Mexico St. vs. Drake, Oct. 15, 1983 (consecutive returns)

TOUCHDOWNS SCORED ON BACK-TO-BACK KICKOFF RETURNS, BOTH TEAMS
2—By many teams. Most recent: Wisconsin & Northern Ill., Sept. 14, 1985

Total Kick Returns

(Combined Punt and Kickoff Returns)

MOST YARDS ON KICK RETURNS
376—Florida St. vs. Virginia Tech, Nov. 16, 1974 (9 returns)

HIGHEST AVERAGE GAIN PER RETURN (Min. 7 Returns)
41.8—Florida St. vs. Virginia Tech, Nov. 16, 1974 (9 for 376)

Scoring

MOST POINTS SCORED
103—Wyoming vs. Northern Colo. (0), Nov. 5, 1949 (15 TDs, 13 PATs)

MOST POINTS SCORED AGAINST A MAJOR-COLLEGE OPPONENT
100—Houston vs. Tulsa (6), Nov. 23, 1968 (14 TDs, 13 PATs, 1 FG)

MOST POINTS SCORED, BOTH TEAMS
124—Oklahoma (82) & Colorado (42), Oct. 4, 1980

MOST POINTS SCORED BY A LOSING TEAM
56—Purdue vs. Minnesota (59), Oct. 9, 1993

MOST POINTS, BOTH TEAMS IN A TIE GAME
104—Brigham Young (52) & San Diego St. (52), Nov. 16, 1991

MOST POINTS SCORED IN ONE QUARTER
49—Fresno St. vs. New Mexico, Oct. 5, 1991 (2nd quarter); Davidson vs. Furman, Sept. 27, 1969 (2nd quarter); Houston vs. Tulsa, Nov. 23, 1968 (4th quarter)

MOST POINTS SCORED IN ONE HALF
76—Houston vs. Tulsa, Nov. 23, 1968 (2nd half)

MOST TOUCHDOWNS SCORED
15—Wyoming vs. Northern Colo., Nov. 5, 1949 (9 rushing, 6 passing)

MOST TOUCHDOWNS SCORED, BOTH TEAMS
18—Oklahoma (12) & Colorado (6), Oct. 4, 1980

MOST EXTRA POINTS MADE BY KICKING
13—Fresno St. vs. New Mexico, Oct. 5, 1991 (attempted 13); Houston vs. Tulsa, Nov. 23, 1968 (attempted 14); Wyoming vs. Northern Colo., Nov. 5, 1949 (attempted 15)

MOST TWO-POINT ATTEMPTS SCORED
7—Pacific (Cal.) vs. San Diego St., Nov. 22, 1958 (attempted 9)

MOST DEFENSIVE EXTRA-POINT ATTEMPTS
2—Northern Ill. vs. Akron, Nov. 3, 1990 (2 interception returns); Rice vs. Notre Dame, Nov. 5, 1988 (2 kick returns; 1 scored)

MOST DEFENSIVE EXTRA POINTS SCORED
1—By many teams

MOST FIELD GOALS MADE
7—Nebraska vs. Missouri, Oct. 19, 1985 (attempted 7); Western Mich. vs. Marshall, Sept. 29, 1984 (attempted 9)

MOST FIELD GOALS MADE, BOTH TEAMS
9—Southwestern La. (5) & Central Mich. (4), Sept. 9, 1989 (attempted 11)

MOST FIELD GOALS ATTEMPTED
9—Western Mich. vs. Marshall, Sept. 29, 1984 (made 7)

MOST FIELD GOALS ATTEMPTED, BOTH TEAMS
12—Clemson (6) & Georgia (6), Sept. 17, 1983 (made 6)

MOST FIELD GOALS MISSED
7—LSU vs. Florida, Nov. 25, 1972 (attempted 8)

First Downs

MOST FIRST DOWNS
44—Nebraska vs. Utah St., Sept. 7, 1991 (33 rush, 10 pass, 1 penalty)

MOST FIRST DOWNS, BOTH TEAMS
72—New Mexico (37) & San Diego St. (35), Sept. 27, 1986

FEWEST FIRST DOWNS BY A WINNING TEAM
0—Michigan vs. Ohio St., Nov. 25, 1950 (won 9-3); North Caro. St. vs. Virginia, Sept. 30, 1944 (won 13-0)

MOST FIRST DOWNS BY RUSHING
36—Nebraska vs. New Mexico St., Sept. 18, 1982

MOST FIRST DOWNS BY PASSING
30—Brigham Young vs. Colorado St., Nov. 7, 1981; Tulsa vs. Idaho St., Oct. 7, 1967

Fumbles

MOST FUMBLES
17—Wichita St. vs. Florida St., Sept. 20, 1969 (lost 10)

MOST FUMBLES, BOTH TEAMS
27—Wichita St. (17) & Florida St. (10), Sept. 20, 1969 (lost 17)

MOST FUMBLES LOST
10—Wichita St. vs. Florida St., Sept. 20, 1969 (17 fumbles)

MOST FUMBLES LOST, BOTH TEAMS
17—Wichita St. (10) & Florida St. (7), Sept. 20, 1969 (27 fumbles)

MOST FUMBLES LOST IN A QUARTER
5—San Diego St. vs. California, Sept. 18, 1982 (1st quarter); East Caro. vs. Southwestern La., Sept. 13, 1980 (3rd quarter on 5 consecutive possessions)

Penalties

MOST PENALTIES AGAINST
24—San Jose St. vs. Fresno St., Oct. 4, 1986 (199 yards)

MOST PENALTIES, BOTH TEAMS
36—San Jose St. (24) & Fresno St. (12), Oct. 4, 1986 (317 yards)

FEWEST PENALTIES, BOTH TEAMS
0—By many teams. Most recent: Army & Navy, Dec. 6, 1986

MOST YARDS PENALIZED
238—Arizona St. vs. UTEP, Nov. 11, 1961 (13 penalties)

MOST YARDS PENALIZED, BOTH TEAMS
421—Grambling (16 for 216 yards) & Texas Southern (17 for 205 yards), Oct. 29, 1977

Turnovers

(Number of Times Losing the Ball on Interceptions and Fumbles)

MOST TURNOVERS LOST
13—Georgia vs. Georgia Tech, Dec. 1, 1951 (8 interceptions, 5 fumbles)

MOST TURNOVERS, BOTH TEAMS
20—Wichita St. (12) & Florida St. (8), Sept. 20, 1969 (17 fumbles, 3 interceptions)

MOST TOTAL PLAYS WITHOUT A TURNOVER (Rushes, Passes, All Runbacks)
110—Baylor vs. Rice, Nov. 13, 1976; California vs. San Jose St., Oct. 5, 1968 (also did not fumble)

MOST TOTAL PLAYS WITHOUT A TURNOVER, BOTH TEAMS
184—Arkansas (93) & Texas A&M (91), Nov. 2, 1968

MOST TOTAL PLAYS WITHOUT A TURNOVER OR A FUMBLE, BOTH TEAMS
158—Stanford (88) & Oregon (70), Nov. 2, 1957

MOST TURNOVERS BY A WINNING TEAM
11—Purdue vs. Illinois, Oct. 2, 1943 (9 fumbles, 2 interceptions; won 40-21)

MOST PASSES HAD INTERCEPTED BY A WINNING TEAM
7—Florida vs. Kentucky, Sept. 11, 1993 (52 attempts; won 24-20); Pittsburgh vs. Army, Nov. 15, 1980 (54 attempts; won 45-7)

MOST FUMBLES LOST BY A WINNING TEAM
9—Arizona St. vs. Utah, Oct. 14, 1972 (10 fumbles; won 59-48); Purdue vs. Illinois, Oct. 2, 1943 (10 fumbles; won 40-21)

SINGLE GAME—Defense

Total Defense

FEWEST PLAYS ALLOWED
12—Centenary (La.) vs. Texas Tech, Nov. 11, 1939 (10 rushes, 2 passes; -1 yard)

FEWEST YARDS ALLOWED
Minus 47—Penn St. vs. Syracuse, Oct. 18, 1947 (-107 rushing, 60 passing; 49 plays)

MOST YARDS ALLOWED
1,021—Southern Methodist vs. Houston, Oct. 21, 1989 (250 rushing, 771 passing)

Rushing Defense

FEWEST RUSHES ALLOWED
5—Texas Tech vs. Houston, Nov. 25, 1989 (36 yards)

FEWEST RUSHING YARDS ALLOWED
Minus 109—Toledo vs. Northern Ill., Nov. 11, 1967 (33 rushes)

Pass Defense

FEWEST ATTEMPTS ALLOWED
0—By many teams. Most recent: Colorado vs. Oklahoma, Nov. 15, 1986

FEWEST COMPLETIONS ALLOWED
0—By many teams. Most recent: UCLA vs. Oregon St., Oct. 15, 1994 (4 attempts)

LOWEST COMPLETION PERCENTAGE ALLOWED (Min. 10 Attempts)
.000—San Jose St. vs. Cal St. Fullerton, Oct. 10, 1992 (0 of 11 attempts); Temple vs. West Va., Oct. 18, 1946 (0 of 18 attempts)

FEWEST YARDS ALLOWED
Minus 16—Va. Military vs. Richmond, Oct. 5, 1957 (2 completions)

MOST PASSES INTERCEPTED BY
11—Brown vs. Rhode Island, Oct. 8, 1949 (136 yards)

MOST PASSES INTERCEPTED BY AGAINST A MAJOR-COLLEGE OPPONENT
10—UCLA vs. California, Oct. 21, 1978; Oklahoma St. vs. Detroit, Nov. 28, 1942

MOST PASSES INTERCEPTED BY A LOSING TEAM
7—Kentucky vs. Florida, Sept. 11, 1993 (52 attempts)

MOST YARDS ON INTERCEPTION RETURNS
240—Kentucky vs. Mississippi, Oct. 1, 1949 (6 returns)

MOST TOUCHDOWNS ON INTERCEPTION RETURNS
4—Houston vs. Texas, Nov. 7, 1987 (198 yards; 3 TDs in the fourth quarter)

First Downs

FEWEST FIRST DOWNS ALLOWED
0—By many teams. Most recent: North Caro. St. vs. Western Caro., Sept. 1, 1990

Opponent's Kicks Blocked

MOST OPPONENT'S PUNTS BLOCKED
4—Memphis vs. Arkansas, Sept. 26, 1992 (10 attempts); Michigan vs. Ohio St., Nov. 25, 1950; Southern Methodist vs. Texas-Arlington, Sept. 30, 1944

MOST OPPONENT'S PUNTS BLOCKED, ONE QUARTER
3—Purdue vs. Northwestern, Nov. 11, 1989 (4 attempts)

MOST OPPONENT'S FIELD GOALS BLOCKED, ONE QUARTER
2—Southern Cal vs. California, Oct. 22, 1994

Turnovers Gained

(Number of Times Gaining the Ball on Interceptions and Fumbles)

MOST TURNOVERS GAINED
13—Georgia Tech vs. Georgia, Dec. 1, 1951 (8 interceptions, 5 fumbles)

MOST CONSECUTIVE OPPONENT'S SERIES RESULTING IN TURNOVERS
7—Florida vs. Florida St., Oct. 7, 1972 (3 interceptions, 4 fumbles lost; first seven series of the game)

Fumble Returns

(Since 1992)

MOST TOUCHDOWNS ON FUMBLE RETURNS
2—Iowa vs. Minnesota, Nov. 19, 1994; Arizona vs. Illinois, Sept. 18, 1993; Toledo vs. Arkansas St., Sept. 5, 1992

LONGEST RETURN OF A FUMBLE
100—Rutgers vs. Pittsburgh, Oct. 28, 1995

Defensive Extra Points

MOST DEFENSIVE EXTRA POINTS SCORED AGAINST
1—By many teams. Most recent: Nevada vs. Utah St., Nov. 4, 1995 (interception return)

MOST DEFENSIVE EXTRA-POINT ATTEMPTS AGAINST
2—Akron vs. Northern Ill., Nov. 3, 1990 (2 interception returns); Notre Dame vs. Rice, Nov. 5, 1988 (2 blocked kick returns, 1 scored)

SEASON—Offense

Total Offense

MOST YARDS GAINED PER GAME
624.9—Houston, 1989 (6,874 in 11)

MOST YARDS GAINED
6,874—Houston, 1989 (11 games)

HIGHEST AVERAGE GAIN PER PLAY
7.9—Army, 1945 (526 for 4,164)

GAINING 300 YARDS OR MORE PER GAME RUSHING AND 200 YARDS OR MORE PER GAME PASSING
Arizona St., 1973 (310.2 rushing, 255.3 passing); Houston, 1968 (361.7 rushing, 200.3 passing)

MOST PLAYS PER GAME
92.4—Notre Dame, 1970 (924 in 10)

MOST TOUCHDOWNS RUSHING AND PASSING
84—Nebraska, 1983
Also holds per-game record at 7.0

Rushing

MOST YARDS GAINED PER GAME
472.4—Oklahoma, 1971 (5,196 in 11)

HIGHEST AVERAGE GAIN PER RUSH
7.6—Army, 1945 (424 for 3,238)

HIGHEST AVERAGE GAIN PER RUSH (Min. 500 Rushes)
7.0—Nebraska, 1995 (627 for 4,398)

MOST RUSHES PER GAME
73.9—Oklahoma, 1974 (813 in 11)

MOST TOUCHDOWNS RUSHING PER GAME
5.1—Texas, 1970, 1969; Oklahoma, 1956 (each 51 in 10)

Passing

MOST YARDS GAINED PER GAME
511.3—Houston, 1989 (5,624 in 11)

MOST YARDS GAINED
5,624—Houston, 1989 (11 games)

HIGHEST AVERAGE GAIN PER ATTEMPT (Min. 350 Attempts)
10.9—Brigham Young, 1989 (433 for 4,732)

HIGHEST AVERAGE GAIN PER COMPLETION
(Min. 100-174 comps.) 19.1—Houston, 1968 (105 for 2,003)
(Min. 175-224 comps.) 18.0—Grambling, 1977 (187 for 3,360)
(Min. 225 comps.) 17.0—Brigham Young, 1989 (279 for 4,732)

MOST PASSES ATTEMPTED PER GAME
63.1—Houston, 1989 (694 in 11)

MOST PASSES COMPLETED PER GAME
39.4—Houston, 1989 (434 in 11)

HIGHEST PERCENTAGE COMPLETED (Min. 150 Attempts)
70.8%—Long Beach St., 1985 (323 of 456)

LOWEST PERCENTAGE HAD INTERCEPTED
(Min. 300-399 atts.) 1.0%—Tennessee, 1995 (4 of 391)
(Min. 400 atts.) 1.2%—Southern Cal, 1993 (5 of 432)

MOST TOUCHDOWN PASSES PER GAME
5.0—Houston, 1989 (55 in 11)

MOST TOUCHDOWN PASSES
55—Houston, 1989 (11 games)

FEWEST TOUCHDOWN PASSES
0—By 6 teams since 1975. Most recent: Vanderbilt, 1993 (11 games, 157 attempts)

HIGHEST PASSING EFFICIENCY RATING POINTS (Min. 150 Attempts)
174.5—Brigham Young, 1989 (433 attempts, 279 completions, 15 interceptions, 4,732 yards, 33 TD passes)

A TEAM WITH A 3,000-YARD PASSER, 1,000-YARD RECEIVER AND 1,000-YARD RUSHER
11 teams. Most recent: Nevada, 1995 (Mike Maxwell [3,611 passer], Alex Van Dyke [1,854 receiver] and Kim Minor [1,052 rusher]); New Mexico St., 1995 (Cody Ledbetter [3,501 passer], Lucious Davis [1,018 receiver] and Denvis Manns [1,120 rusher]); Ohio St., 1995 (Bobby Hoying [3,023 passer], Terry Glenn [1,316 receiver] and Eddie George [1,826 rusher]); San Diego St., 1995 (Billy Blanton [3,300 passer], Will Blackwell [1,207 receiver], Az Hakim [1,022 receiver] and George Jones [1,842 rusher]); Nevada, 1994 (Mike Maxwell [3,537 passer], Alex Van Dyke [1,246 receiver] and Marcellus Chrishon [1,076 rusher]); Wyoming, 1993 (Joe Hughes [3,135 passer], Ryan Yarborough [1,512 receiver] and Ryan Christopherson [1,014 rusher]); San Diego St., 1993 (Tim Gutierrez [3,033 passer], Darnay Scott [1,262 receiver] and Marshall Faulk [1,530 rusher])

A TEAM WITH TWO 1,000-YARD RECEIVERS
Florida, 1995 (Chris Doering 1,045 & Ike Hilliard 1,008); Florida St., 1995 (E. G. Green 1,007 & Andre Cooper 1,002); San Diego St., 1995 (Will Blackwell 1,207 & Az Hakim 1,022); Nevada, 1993 (Bryan Reeves 1,362 & Michael Stephens 1,062); Colorado, 1992 (Charles Johnson 1,149 & Michael Westbrook 1,060); San Diego St., 1990 (Patrick Rowe 1,392 & Dennis Arey 1,118); Brigham Young, 1990 (Andy Boyce 1,241 & Chris Smith 1,156); Houston, 1988 (Jason Phillips 1,444 & James Dixon 1,103)

A TEAM WITH THE NO. 1 & NO. 2 RECEIVERS
Houston, 1988 (Jason Phillips, No. 1, 9.82 catches per game & James Dixon, No. 2, 9.27 catches per game)

MOST 100-YARD RECEIVING GAMES IN A SEASON, ONE TEAM
19—San Diego St., 1990 (Patrick Rowe 9, Dennis Arey 8 & Jimmy Raye 2)

Punting

MOST PUNTS PER GAME
13.9—Tennessee, 1937 (139 in 10)

FEWEST PUNTS PER GAME
2.0—Nevada, 1948 (18 in 9)

HIGHEST PUNTING AVERAGE
50.6—Brigham Young, 1983 (24 for 1,215 yards)

HIGHEST PUNTING AVERAGE (Min. 40 Punts)
47.6—Vanderbilt, 1984 (59 for 2,810)

HIGHEST NET PUNTING AVERAGE
45.0—Brigham Young, 1983 (24 for 1,215 yards, 134 yards in punts returned)

HIGHEST NET PUNTING AVERAGE (Min. 40 Punts)
44.4—Colorado St., 1976 (72 for 3,323, 123 yards in punts returned)

Punt Returns

MOST PUNT RETURNS PER GAME
6.9—Texas A&M, 1943 (69 in 10)

FEWEST PUNT RETURNS PER GAME
0.5—Iowa, 1971 (6 in 11)

MOST PUNT-RETURN YARDS PER GAME
114.5—Colgate, 1941 (916 in 8)

HEST AVERAGE GAIN PER RETURN
(Min. 15-29 rets.) 25.2—Arizona St., 1952 (18 for 454 yards)
(Min. 30 rets.) 22.4—Oklahoma, 1948 (43 for 963)

MOST TOUCHDOWNS SCORED ON PUNT RETURNS (Since 1966)
7—Southern Miss., 1987 (on 46 returns)

Kickoff Returns

MOST KICKOFF RETURNS PER GAME
7.3—Cal St. Fullerton, 1990 (80 in 11)

FEWEST KICKOFF RETURNS PER GAME
0.7—Boston College, 1939 (7 in 10)

MOST KICKOFF-RETURN YARDS PER GAME
134.7—Virginia Tech, 1973 (1,482 in 11)

HIGHEST AVERAGE GAIN PER RETURN
(Min. 25-34 rets.) 30.3—Florida St., 1992 (27 for 819)
(Min. 35 rets.) 27.5—Rice, 1973 (39 for 1,074)

MOST TOUCHDOWNS SCORED ON KICKOFF RETURNS (Since 1966)
4—Dayton, 1974 (on 44 returns)

Scoring

MOST POINTS PER GAME
56.0—Army, 1944 (504 in 9)

MOST POINTS SCORED
624—Nebraska, 1983 (12 games)

HIGHEST SCORING MARGIN
52.1—Army, 1944 (scored 504 points for 56.0 average and allowed 35 points for 3.9 average in 9 games)

MOST POINTS SCORED, TWO CONSECUTIVE GAMES
177—Houston, 1968 (77-3 vs. Idaho, Nov. 16, and 100-6 vs. Tulsa, Nov. 23)

MOST TOUCHDOWNS PER GAME
8.2—Army, 1944 (74 in 9)

MOST TOUCHDOWNS
89—Nebraska, 1983 (12 games)

MOST EXTRA POINTS MADE BY KICKING
77—Nebraska, 1983 (77 in 12, attempted 85)
Also holds per-game record at 6.4

MOST CONSECUTIVE EXTRA POINTS MADE BY KICKING
71—Florida, 1995 (attempted 71)

MOST TWO-POINT ATTEMPTS MADE PER GAME
2.2—Rutgers, 1958 (20 in 9, attempted 31)

MOST DEFENSIVE EXTRA-POINT ATTEMPTS
3—Rice, 1988 (1 vs. Southwestern La., Sept. 24, blocked kick return; 2 vs. Notre Dame, Nov. 5, 2 blocked kick returns, 1 scored)

MOST DEFENSIVE EXTRA POINTS SCORED
1—By 34 teams. Most recent: Utah St., 1995 (interception return vs. Nevada, Nov. 4)

MOST FIELD GOALS PER GAME
2.6—UCLA, 1984 (29 in 11)

First Downs

MOST FIRST DOWNS PER GAME
30.9—Brigham Young, 1983 (340 in 11)

MOST RUSHING FIRST DOWNS PER GAME
21.4—Oklahoma, 1974 (235 in 11)

MOST PASSING FIRST DOWNS PER GAME
19.8—Nevada, 1995 (218 in 11)

Fumbles

MOST FUMBLES
73—Cal St. Fullerton, 1992 (lost 41)

MOST FUMBLES LOST
41—Cal St. Fullerton, 1992 (fumbled 73 times)

FEWEST OWN FUMBLES LOST
2—Clemson, 1994; Bowling Green, 1993; Dayton, 1968; UCLA, 1952; Tulsa, 1942; Washington, 1941

MOST CONSECUTIVE FUMBLES LOST
14—Oklahoma, 1983 (during 5 games, Oct. 8-Nov. 5)

Penalties

MOST PENALTIES PER GAME
12.9—Grambling, 1977 (142 in 11, 1,476 yards)

MOST YARDS PENALIZED PER GAME
134.2—Grambling, 1977 (1,476 in 11, 142 penalties)

Turnovers (Giveaways)

(Passes Had Intercepted and Fumbles Lost)

FEWEST TURNOVERS
8—Miami (Ohio), 1966 (4 interceptions, 4 fumbles lost); Clemson, 1940 (6 interceptions, 2 fumbles lost)

FEWEST TURNOVERS PER GAME
0.8—Miami (Ohio), 1966 (8 in 10 games)

MOST TURNOVERS
61—Tulsa, 1976 (24 interceptions, 37 fumbles lost); North Texas, 1971 (33 interceptions, 28 fumbles lost)

MOST TURNOVERS PER GAME
6.1—Mississippi St., 1949 (55 in 9 games; 25 interceptions, 30 fumbles lost)

SEASON—Defense

Total Defense

FEWEST YARDS ALLOWED PER GAME
69.9—Santa Clara, 1937 (559 in 8)

FEWEST RUSHING AND PASSING TOUCHDOWNS ALLOWED PER GAME
0.0—Tennessee, 1939; Duke, 1938

LOWEST AVERAGE YARDS ALLOWED PER PLAY
1.7—Texas A&M, 1939 (447 for 763)

LOWEST AVERAGE YARDS ALLOWED PER PLAY
(Min. 600-699 plays) 2.5—Nebraska, 1967 (627 for 1,576)
(Min. 700 plays) 2.7—Toledo, 1971 (734 for 1,795)

MOST YARDS ALLOWED PER GAME
553.0—Maryland, 1993 (6,083 in 11)

Rushing Defense

FEWEST YARDS ALLOWED PER GAME
17.0—Penn St., 1947 (153 in 9)

MOST YARDS LOST BY OPPONENTS PER GAME
70.1—Wyoming, 1968 (701 in 10, 458 rushes)

LOWEST AVERAGE YARDS ALLOWED PER RUSH
(Min. 240-399 rushes) 0.6—Penn St., 1947 (240 for 153)
(Min. 400-499 rushes) 1.3—North Texas, 1966 (408 for 513)
(Min. 500 rushes) 2.1—Nebraska, 1971 (500 for 1,031)

Pass Defense

FEWEST YARDS ALLOWED PER GAME
13.1—Penn St., 1938 (105 in 8)

FEWEST YARDS ALLOWED PER ATTEMPT
(Min. 200-299 atts.) 3.4—Toledo, 1970 (251 for 856)
(Min. 300 atts.) 3.8—Notre Dame, 1967 (306 for 1,158)

FEWEST YARDS ALLOWED PER COMPLETION
(Min. 100-149 comps.) 9.4—Oklahoma, 1986 (128 for 1,198)
(Min. 150 comps.) 9.5—Notre Dame, 1993 (263 for 2,502)

LOWEST COMPLETION PERCENTAGE ALLOWED
(Min. 150-199 atts.) 31.1%—Virginia, 1952 (50 of 161)
(Min. 200 atts.) 33.3%—Notre Dame, 1967 (102 of 306)

FEWEST TOUCHDOWNS ALLOWED BY PASSING
0—By many teams. Most recent: LSU, 1959; North Texas, 1959

LOWEST PASS EFFICIENCY DEFENSIVE RATING (Since 1990)
75.0—Texas A&M, 1993 (292 attempts, 116 completions, 13 interceptions, 1,339 yards, 5 TDs)

MOST PASSES INTERCEPTED BY PER GAME
4.1—Pennsylvania, 1940 (33 in 8)

HIGHEST PERCENTAGE INTERCEPTED BY (Min. 200 Attempts)
17.9%—Army, 1944 (36 of 201)

MOST YARDS GAINED ON INTERCEPTION RETURNS
782—Tennessee, 1971 (25 interceptions)

MOST INTERCEPTION YARDS PER GAME
72.5—Texas, 1943 (580 in 8)

HIGHEST AVERAGE PER INTERCEPTION RETURN
(Min. 10-14 ints.) 36.3—Oregon St., 1959 (12 for 436)
(Min. 15 ints.) 31.3—Tennessee, 1971 (25 for 782)

MOST TOUCHDOWNS ON INTERCEPTION RETURNS
7—Tennessee, 1971 (25 interceptions; 287 pass attempts against)

Punting

MOST OPPONENT'S PUNTS BLOCKED BY
11—Arkansas St., 1975 (11 games, 95 punts against)

Punt Returns

FEWEST RETURNS ALLOWED
5—Nebraska, 1995 (12 yards); Notre Dame, 1968 (52 yards)

FEWEST YARDS ALLOWED
2—Miami (Fla.), 1989 (12 returns)

LOWEST AVERAGE YARDS ALLOWED PER PUNT RETURN
0.2—Miami (Fla.), 1989 (12 for 2 yards)

Kickoff Returns

LOWEST AVERAGE YARDS ALLOWED PER KICKOFF RETURN
8.3—Richmond, 1951 (23 for 192 yards)

Opponent's Kicks Blocked

MOST PAT KICKS BLOCKED
Season
6—Duke, 1993

Scoring

FEWEST POINTS ALLOWED PER GAME
0.0—Tennessee, 1939 (10 games); Duke, 1938 (9 games)

MOST POINTS ALLOWED AND POINTS ALLOWED PER GAME
544 and 49.5—UTEP, 1973 (11 games)

Fumbles

MOST OPPONENT'S FUMBLES RECOVERED
36—Brigham Young, 1977; North Texas, 1972

MOST TOUCHDOWNS SCORED ON FUMBLE RETURNS
4—Alabama, 1994

Turnovers (Takeaways)

(Opponent's Passes Intercepted and Fumbles Recovered)

MOST OPPONENT'S TURNOVERS
57—Tennessee, 1970 (36 interceptions, 21 fumbles lost)

MOST OPPONENT'S TURNOVERS PER GAME
5.4—UCLA, 1954 (49 in 9); UCLA, 1952 (49 in 9); Pennsylvania, 1950 (49 in 9); Wyoming, 1950 (49 in 9)

HIGHEST MARGIN OF TURNOVERS PER GAME OVER OPPONENTS
4.0—UCLA, 1952 (36 in 9; 13 giveaways vs. 49 takeaways)
Also holds total-margin record at 36

HIGHEST MARGIN OF TURNOVERS PER GAME BY OPPONENTS
3.1—Southern Miss., 1969 (31 in 10; 45 giveaways vs. 14 takeaways)

Defensive Extra Points

MOST DEFENSIVE EXTRA-POINT ATTEMPTS AGAINST
2—Oklahoma, 1992 (2 kick returns, 2 scored); Akron, 1990 (2 interception returns, none scored); Notre Dame, 1988 (2 kick returns, 1 scored); Southwestern La., 1988 (2 kick returns, none scored)

MOST DEFENSIVE EXTRA POINTS SCORED AGAINST
2—Oklahoma, 1992 (vs. Texas Tech, Sept. 3, and vs. Oklahoma St., Nov. 14)

Consecutive Records

MOST CONSECUTIVE VICTORIES
47—Oklahoma, 1953-57

MOST CONSECUTIVE GAMES WITHOUT DEFEAT
48—Oklahoma, 1953-57 (1 tie)

MOST CONSECUTIVE LOSSES
34—Northwestern, from Sept. 22, 1979, vs. Syracuse through Sept. 18, 1982, vs. Miami (Ohio) (ended with 31-6 victory over Northern Ill., Sept. 25, 1982)

MOST CONSECUTIVE GAMES WITHOUT A VICTORY ON THE ROAD
46—Northwestern (including one tie), from Nov. 23, 1974, through Oct. 30, 1982

MOST CONSECUTIVE GAMES WITHOUT A TIE (Includes Bowl Games)
333—Miami (Fla.) (current), from Nov. 11, 1968

MOST CONSECUTIVE GAMES WITHOUT BEING SHUT OUT
260—Brigham Young (current), from Oct. 3, 1975

MOST CONSECUTIVE SHUTOUTS (Regular Season)
17—Tennessee, from Nov. 5, 1938, through Oct. 12, 1940

MOST CONSECUTIVE QUARTERS OPPONENTS HELD SCORELESS (Regular Season)
71—Tennessee, from 2nd quarter vs. LSU, Oct. 29, 1938, to 2nd quarter vs. Alabama, Oct. 19, 1940

MOST CONSECUTIVE VICTORIES AT HOME
58—Miami (Fla.) (Orange Bowl), from Oct. 12, 1985, to Sept. 24, 1994 (lost to Washington, 38-20)

MOST CONSECUTIVE WINNING SEASONS (All-Time)
42—Notre Dame, 1889-1932 (no teams in 1890 & 1891) (see list on page 79)

MOST CONSECUTIVE WINNING SEASONS (Current)
34—Nebraska, from 1962

MOST CONSECUTIVE NON-LOSING SEASONS
49—Penn St., 1939-1987

MOST CONSECUTIVE NON-WINNING SEASONS
28—Rice, 1964-91

MOST CONSECUTIVE SEASONS WINNING NINE OR MORE GAMES
27—Nebraska (current), from 1969

MOST CONSECUTIVE SEASONS PLAYING IN A BOWL GAME
27—Nebraska (current), from 1969

MOST CONSECUTIVE GAMES SCORING ON A PASS
53—Brigham Young, from Sept. 7, 1989, through Sept. 18, 1993

MOST CONSECUTIVE GAMES PASSING FOR 200 YARDS OR MORE
64—Brigham Young, from Sept. 13, 1980, through Oct. 19, 1985

MOST CONSECUTIVE GAMES INTERCEPTING A PASS (Includes Bowl Games)
29—Virginia (current), from Nov. 6, 1993

MOST CONSECUTIVE GAMES WITHOUT POSTING A SHUTOUT
223—New Mexico St. (current), from Sept. 21, 1974

MOST CONSECUTIVE EXTRA POINTS MADE
262—Syracuse, from Nov. 18, 1978, to Sept. 9, 1989. (By the following kickers: Dave Jacobs, last PAT of 1978; Gary Anderson, 72 from 1979 through 1981; Russ Carpentieri, 17 in 1982; Don McAulay, 62 from 1983 through 1985; Tim Vesling, 71 in 1986 and 1987; Kevin Greene, 37 in 1988; John Biskup, 2 in 1989.)

MOST CONSECUTIVE STADIUM SELLOUTS
207—Nebraska (current), from 1962

Additional Records

HIGHEST-SCORING TIE GAME
52-52—Brigham Young & San Diego St., Nov. 16, 1991

MOST TIE GAMES IN A SEASON
4—Central Mich., 1991 (11 games); UCLA, 1939 (10 games); Temple, 1937 (9 games)

MOST SCORELESS TIE GAMES IN A SEASON
4—Temple, 1937 (9 games)

MOST CONSECUTIVE SCORELESS TIE GAMES
2—Alabama, 1954, vs. Georgia, Oct. 30 & vs. Tulane, Nov. 6; Georgia Tech, 1938, vs. Florida, Nov. 19 & vs. Georgia, Nov. 26

LAST SCORELESS TIE GAME
Nov. 19, 1983—Oregon & Oregon St.

MOST POINTS OVERCOME TO WIN A GAME (Between Division I-A Teams)
31—Ohio St. (41) vs. Minnesota (37), Oct. 28, 1989 (trailed 31-0 with 4:29 remaining in 2nd quarter); Maryland (42) vs. Miami (Fla.) (40), Nov. 10, 1984 (trailed 31-0 with 12:35 remaining in 3rd quarter)
30—California (42) vs. Oregon (41), Oct. 2, 1993 (trailed 30-0 in 2nd quarter)

MOST POINTS SCORED IN FOURTH QUARTER TO WIN OR TIE A GAME
28—Florida St. (31) vs. Florida (31), Nov. 26, 1994 (trailed 31-3 beginning fourth quarter); Washington St. (49) vs. Stanford (42), Oct. 20, 1984 (trailed 42-14 with 5:38 remaining in third quarter and scored 35 consecutive points); Utah (28) vs. Arizona (27), Nov. 4, 1972 (trailed 27-0 beginning fourth quarter)

MOST POINTS SCORED IN A BRIEF PERIOD OF TIME
41 in 2:55 of possession time during six drives—Nebraska vs. Colorado, Oct. 15, 1983 (6 TDs, 5 PATs in 3rd quarter. Drives occurred during 9:10 of total playing time in the period)
21 in 1:24 of total playing time—San Jose St. (42) vs. Fresno St. (7), Nov. 17, 1990 (3 TDs, 3 PATs in second quarter; 1:17 of possession time on two drives and one intercepted pass returned for a TD)
15 in :10 of total playing time—Utah (22) vs. Air Force (21), Oct. 21, 1995 (2 TDs, 2-point conversion, 1 PAT. Drives occurred during :41of final quarter)

MOST IMPROVED WON-LOST RECORD
8 games—Purdue, 1943 (9-0) from 1942 (1-8); Stanford, 1940 (10-0, including a bowl win) from 1939 (1-7-1)

MOST IMPROVED WON-LOST RECORD AFTER WINLESS SEASON
7 games—Florida, 1980 (8-4-0, including a bowl win) from 1979 (0-10-1)

File photos

A combination of dominating backs (such as Mike Rozier, left) and devastating offensive linemen (such as Dave Rimington, right) has enabled Nebraska to post 34 straight winning seasons, the longest current streak in Division I-A.

Photo from New Mexico State sports information

New Mexico State quarterback Cody Ledbetter's per-game average of 338.6 yards in total offense in 1995 ranks 13th on the all-time Division I-A list.

Annual Champions, All-Time Leaders

Total Offense

CAREER YARDS PER GAME

(Minimum 5,500 yards)

Player, Team	Years	G	Plays	Yards	TDR‡	Yd. PG
Chris Vargas, Nevada	1992-93	20	872	6,417	48	*320.9
Ty Detmer, Brigham Young	1988-91	46	*1,795	*14,665	*135	318.8
Mike Perez, San Jose St.	1986-87	20	875	6,182	37	309.1
Doug Gaynor, Long Beach St.	1984-85	22	1,067	6,710	45	305.0
Tony Eason, Illinois	1981-82	22	1,016	6,589	43	299.5
David Klingler, Houston	1988-91	32	1,439	9,363	93	292.6
Steve Young, Brigham Young	1981-83	31	1,177	8,817	74	284.4
Doug Flutie, Boston College	1981-84	42	1,558	11,317	74	269.5
Brent Snyder, Utah St.	1987-88	22	1,040	5,916	43	268.9
Scott Mitchell, Utah	1987-89	33	1,306	8,836	71	267.8
Mike Maxwell, Nevada	1993-95	27	946	7,226	66	267.6
Anthony Calvillo, Utah St.	1992-93	22	983	5,838	43	265.4
Shane Matthews, Florida	1989-92	35	1,397	9,241	82	264.0
Joe Hughes, Wyoming	1992-93	23	911	6,007	49	261.2
Larry Egger, Utah	1985-86	22	903	5,651	42	256.9
Jim Plunkett, Stanford	1968-70	31	1,174	7,887	62	254.4
Stoney Case, New Mexico	1991-94	42	1,673	10,651	98	253.6
Troy Kopp, Pacific (Cal.)	1989-92	40	1,595	10,037	90	250.9
Randall Cunningham, UNLV	1982-84	33	1,330	8,224	67	249.2
Eric Zeier, Georgia	1991-94	44	1,560	10,841	71	246.4
Erik Wilhelm, Oregon St.	1985-88	37	1,689	9,062	55	244.9
Todd Dillon, Long Beach St.	1982-83	23	1,031	5,588	38	243.0
Bernie Kosar, Miami (Fla.)	1983-84	23	847	5,585	48	242.8
Alex Van Pelt, Pittsburgh	1989-92	45	1,570	10,814	58	240.3
Steve Stenstrom, Stanford	1991-94	41	1,550	9,825	75	239.6
Jack Trudeau, Illinois	1981, 83-85	34	1,318	8,096	56	238.1
Chuck Hixson, Southern Methodist	1968-70	29	1,358	6,884	50	237.4
Robbie Bosco, Brigham Young	1983-85	35	1,159	8,299	72	237.1
Dan McGwire, Iowa/San Diego St.	1986-87, 89-90	32	1,067	7,557	50	236.2
Johnny Bright, Drake	1949-51	25	825	5,903	64	236.1
Jeff Garcia, San Jose St.	1991-93	31	1,146	7,274	63	234.6
Cody Ledbetter, New Mexico St.	1991, 93-95	35	1,362	8,207	68	234.5
Brian McClure, Bowling Green	1982-85	42	1,630	9,774	67	232.7
Marc Wilson, Brigham Young	1977-79	33	1,183	7,602	68	230.4
Todd Santos, San Diego St.	1984-87	46	1,722	10,513	71	228.5
Pat Sullivan, Auburn	1969-71	30	970	6,844	71	228.1
John Reaves, Florida	1969-71	32	1,258	7,283	58	227.6

**Record. ‡Touchdowns-responsible-for are player's TDs scored and passed for.*

SEASON YARDS PER GAME

Player, Team	Year	G	Plays	Yards	TDR‡	Yd. PG
David Klingler, Houston	†1990	11	*704	*5,221	*55	*474.6
Andre Ware, Houston	†1989	11	628	4,661	49	423.7
Ty Detmer, Brigham Young	1990	12	635	5,022	45	418.5
Mike Maxwell, Nevada	†1995	9	443	3,623	34	402.6
Steve Young, Brigham Young	†1983	11	531	4,346	41	395.1
Chris Vargas, Nevada	†1993	11	535	4,332	35	393.8
Scott Mitchell, Utah	†1988	11	589	4,299	29	390.8
Jim McMahon, Brigham Young	†1980	12	540	4,627	53	385.6
Ty Detmer, Brigham Young	1989	12	497	4,433	38	369.4
Troy Kopp, Pacific (Cal.)	1990	9	485	3,276	32	364.0
Jim McMahon, Brigham Young	†1981	10	487	3,458	30	345.8
Jimmy Klingler, Houston	†1992	11	544	3,768	34	342.5
Cody Ledbetter, New Mexico St.	1995	11	543	3,724	32	338.6
Anthony Dilweg, Duke	1988	11	539	3,713	26	337.6
Bill Anderson, Tulsa	†1965	10	580	3,343	35	334.3
Ty Detmer, Brigham Young	†1991	12	478	4,001	39	333.4
Dan McGwire, San Diego St.	1990	11	484	3,664	28	333.1
Mike McCoy, Utah	1993	12	529	3,969	21	330.8
Mike Perez, San Jose St.	†1986	9	425	2,969	14	329.9
Robbie Bosco, Brigham Young	†1984	12	543	3,932	35	327.7
Doug Flutie, Boston College	1984	11	448	3,603	30	327.5
Jim Everett, Purdue	†1985	11	518	3,589	24	326.3
Todd Dillon, Long Beach St.	†1982	11	585	3,587	23	326.1
Marc Wilson, Brigham Young	†1979	11	488	3,580	32	325.5

**Record. †National champion. ‡Touchdowns-responsible-for are player's TDs scored and passed for.*

CAREER YARDS

			Yards			
Player, Team	Years	Plays	Rush	Pass	Total	Avg.
Ty Detmer, Brigham Young	1988-91	*1,795	-366	*15,031	*14,665	#8.17
Doug Flutie, Boston College	1981-84	1,558	738	10,579	11,317	7.26
Eric Zeier, Georgia	1991-94	1,560	-312	11,153	10,841	6.95
Alex Van Pelt, Pittsburgh	1989-92	1,570	-99	10,913	10,814	6.89
Stoney Case, New Mexico	1991-94	1,673	1,191	9,460	10,651	6.37

Player, Team	Years	Plays	Yards Rush	Yards Pass	Total	Avg.
Todd Santos, San Diego St.	1984-87	1,722	-912	11,425	10,513	6.11
Kevin Sweeney, Fresno St.	$1982-86	1,700	-371	10,623	10,252	6.03
Troy Kopp, Pacific (Cal.)	1989-92	1,595	-221	10,258	10,037	6.29
Steve Stenstrom, Stanford	1991-94	1,550	-706	10,531	9,825	6.34
Brian McClure, Bowling Green	1982-85	1,630	-506	10,280	9,774	6.00
Jim McMahon, Brigham Young	1977-78, 80-81	1,325	187	9,536	9,723	7.34
Glenn Foley, Boston College	1990-93	1,440	-340	10,042	9,702	6.74
Terrence Jones, Tulane	1985-88	1,620	1,761	7,684	9,445	5.83
David Klingler, Houston	1988-91	1,439	-103	9,466	9,363	6.51
Shawn Jones, Georgia Tech	1989-92	1,609	855	8,441	9,296	5.78
Shane Matthews, Florida	1989-92	1,397	-46	9,287	9,241	6.61
Spence Fischer, Duke	1992-95	1,612	89	9,021	9,110	5.65
T. J. Rubley, Tulsa	1987-89, 91	1,541	-244	9,324	9,080	5.89
Brad Tayles, Western Mich.	1989-92	1,675	354	8,717	9,071	5.42
John Elway, Stanford	1979-82	1,505	-279	9,349	9,070	6.03
Erik Wilhelm, Oregon St.	1985-88	1,689	-331	9,393	9,062	5.37
Ben Bennett, Duke	1980-83	1,582	-553	9,614	9,061	5.73
Chuck Long, Iowa	$1981-85	1,410	-176	9,210	9,034	6.41
Todd Ellis, South Caro.	1986-89	1,517	-497	9,519	9,022	5.95
Tom Hodson, LSU	1986-89	1,307	-177	9,115	8,938	6.84
Scott Mitchell, Utah	1987-89	1,306	-145	8,981	8,836	6.77
Steve Young, Brigham Young	1981-83	1,177	1,084	7,733	8,817	7.49
Brian Mitchell, Southwestern La.	1986-89	1,521	3,335	5,447	8,782	5.77
Marvin Graves, Syracuse	1990-93	1,373	286	8,466	8,752	6.37
Jeremy Leach, New Mexico	1988-91	1,695	-762	9,382	8,620	5.09
Robert Hall, Texas Tech	1990-93	1,341	581	7,908	8,489	6.33
Mark Herrmann, Purdue	1977-80	1,354	-744	9,188	8,444	6.24
Mike McCoy, Long Beach St./Utah	1991, 92-94	1,315	97	8,342	8,439	6.42
Robbie Bosco, Brigham Young	1983-85	1,158	-101	8,400	8,299	7.17
Cody Ledbetter, New Mexico St.	1991, 93-95	1,362	727	7,480	8,207	6.03
Troy Taylor, California	1986-89	1,490	110	8,126	8,236	5.53
Randall Cunningham, UNLV	1982-84	1,330	204	8,020	8,224	6.18
Steve Taneyhill, South Caro.	1992-95	1,423	-392	8,555	8,163	5.74
Steve Slayden, Duke	1984-87	1,546	125	8,004	8,129	5.26
Jack Trudeau, Illinois	1981, 83-85	1,318	-50	8,146	8,096	6.14
Mark Barsotti, Fresno St.	1988-91	1,192	768	7,321	8,089	6.79
Gene Swick, Toledo	1972-75	1,579	807	7,267	8,074	5.11
Andre Ware, Houston	1987-89	1,194	-144	8,202	8,058	6.75
Len Williams, Northwestern	1990-93	1,614	542	7,486	8,028	4.97
Joe Adams, Tennessee St.	1977-80	1,256	-677	8,649	7,972	6.35
Rodney Peete, Southern Cal	1985-88	1,226	309	7,640	7,949	6.48
Stan White, Auburn	1990-93	1,481	-96	8,016	7,920	5.35
Shawn Moore, Virginia	1987-90	1,177	1,268	6,629	7,897	6.71
Jim Plunkett, Stanford	1968-70	1,174	343	7,544	7,887	6.72
Art Schlichter, Ohio St.	1978-81	1,316	1,285	6,584	7,869	5.98
Mike Gundy, Oklahoma St.	1986-89	1,275	-248	8,072	7,824	6.14
John Holman, Northeast La.	1979-82	1,376	-25	7,827	7,802	5.67
Gino Torretta, Miami (Fla.)	1989-92	1,101	32	7,690	7,722	7.01
John Walsh, Brigham Young	1991-94	1,152	-654	8,375	7,721	6.70
Jack Thompson, Washington St.	1975-78	1,345	-120	7,818	7,698	5.72
Dan Marino, Pittsburgh	1979-82	1,185	-270	7,905	7,635	6.44
Brett Favre, Southern Miss.	1987-90	1,362	-89	7,695	7,606	5.58
Marc Wilson, Brigham Young	1977-79	1,183	-35	7,637	7,602	6.43

*Record. $See page 6 for explanation. #Record for minimum of 7,500 yards. (Note: Chris Vargas of Nevada competed two years in Division I-A and two years in Division I-AA. Four-year total: 8,184 yards.)

Photo from South Carolina sports information

Steve Taneyhill finished his illustrious career at South Carolina last season with 8,163 yards in total offense, which ranks 38th in Division I-A history.

CAREER YARDS RECORD PROGRESSION

(Record Yards—Player, Team, Seasons Played)

3,481—Davey O'Brien, Texas Christian, 1936-38; **3,882**—Paul Christman, Missouri, 1938-40; **4,602**—Frank Sinkwich, Georgia, 1940-42; **4,627**—Bob Fenimore, Oklahoma St., 1943-46; **4,871**—Charlie Justice, North Caro., 1946-49; **5,903**—Johnny Bright, Drake, 1949-51; **6,354**—Virgil Carter, Brigham Young, 1964-66; **6,568**—Steve Ramsey, North Texas, 1967-69; **7,887**—Jim Plunkett, Stanford, 1968-70; **8,074**—Gene Swick, Toledo, 1972-75; **8,444**—Mark Herrmann, Purdue, 1977-80; **9,723**—Jim McMahon, Brigham Young, 1977-78, 1980-81; **11,317**—Doug Flutie, Boston College, 1981-84; **14,665**—Ty Detmer, Brigham Young, 1988-91.

SEASON YARDS

Player, Team	Year	G	Plays	Yards Rush	Yards Pass	Total	Avg.
David Klingler, Houston	†1990	11	*704	81	5,140	*5,221	7.42
Ty Detmer, Brigham Young	1990	12	635	-106	*5,188	5,022	7.91
Andre Ware, Houston	†1989	11	628	-38	4,699	4,661	7.42
Jim McMahon, Brigham Young	†1980	12	540	56	4,571	4,627	8.57
Ty Detmer, Brigham Young	1989	12	497	-127	4,560	4,433	@8.92
Steve Young, Brigham Young	†1983	11	531	444	3,902	4,346	8.18
Chris Vargas, Nevada	†1993	11	535	67	4,265	4,332	8.10
Scott Mitchell, Utah	†1988	11	589	-23	4,322	4,299	7.30
Robbie Bosco, Brigham Young	1985	13	578	-132	4,273	4,141	7.16
Ty Detmer, Brigham Young	†1991	12	478	-30	4,031	4,001	8.37
Mike McCoy, Utah	1993	12	529	109	3,860	3,969	7.50
Robbie Bosco, Brigham Young	†1984	12	543	57	3,875	3,932	7.24
Jimmy Klingler, Houston	†1992	11	544	-50	3,818	3,768	6.93
Cody Ledbetter, New Mexico St.	1995	11	543	223	3,501	3,724	6.86
Anthony Dilweg, Duke	1988	11	539	-111	3,824	3,713	6.89
Todd Santos, San Diego St.	†1987	12	562	-244	3,932	3,688	6.56
Troy Kopp, Pacific (Cal.)	1991	12	496	-81	3,767	3,686	7.43

Photo from Houston sports information

Quarterback David Klingler gained 519 or more yards in total offense five times during his career at Houston, including a collegiate record of 732 on December 2, 1990, against Arizona State.

Player, Team	Year	G	Plays	Yards Rush	Yards Pass	Yards Total	Avg.
Dan McGwire, San Diego St.	1990	11	484	-169	3,833	3,664	7.57
Stoney Case, New Mexico	1994	12	549	532	3,117	3,649	6.65
Mike Maxwell, Nevada	†1995	9	443	12	3,611	3,623	8.18
Doug Flutie, Boston College	1984	11	448	149	3,454	3,603	8.04
Jim Everett, Purdue	†1985	11	518	-62	3,651	3,589	6.93
Todd Dillon, Long Beach St.	†1982	11	585	70	3,517	3,587	6.13
Marc Wilson, Brigham Young	†1979	11	488	-140	3,720	3,580	7.34
Sam King, UNLV	1981	12	507	-216	3,778	3,562	7.03
Matt Kofler, San Diego St.	1981	11	594	191	3,337	3,528	5.94
Steve Young, Brigham Young	1982	11	481	407	3,100	3,507	7.29
Mike Maxwell, Nevada	†1994	11	477	-39	3,537	3,498	7.33
Eric Zeier, Georgia	1993	11	484	-43	3,525	3,482	7.19
John Walsh, Brigham Young	1994	12	540	-239	3,712	3,473	6.43
John Kaleo, Maryland	1992	11	588	80	3,392	3,472	5.90
Doug Gaynor, Long Beach St.	1985	12	589	-96	3,563	3,467	5.89
Jim McMahon, Brigham Young	1981	10	487	-97	3,555	3,458	7.10

**Record. †National champion. @ Record for minimum of 3,000 yards.*

SINGLE-GAME YARDS

Yds.	Rush	Pass	Player, Team (Opponent)	Date
732	16	716	David Klingler, Houston (Arizona St.)	Dec. 2, 1990
696	6	690	Matt Vogler, Texas Christian (Houston)	Nov. 3, 1990
625	62	563	David Klingler, Houston (Texas Christian)	Nov. 3, 1990
625	-6	631	Scott Mitchell, Utah (Air Force)	Oct. 15, 1988
612	-1	613	Jimmy Klingler, Houston (Rice)	Nov. 28, 1992
603	4	599	Ty Detmer, Brigham Young (San Diego St.)	Nov. 16, 1991
601	37	564	Troy Kopp, Pacific, Cal. (New Mexico St.)	Oct. 20, 1990
599	86	513	Virgil Carter, Brigham Young (UTEP)	Nov. 5, 1966
597	-22	619	John Walsh, Brigham Young (Utah St.)	Oct. 30, 1993
594	-28	622	Jeremy Leach, New Mexico (Utah)	Nov. 11, 1989
585	-36	621	Dave Wilson, Illinois (Ohio St.)	Nov. 8, 1980
582	11	571	Marc Wilson, Brigham Young (Utah)	Nov. 5, 1977
578	6	572	David Klingler, Houston (Eastern Wash.)	Nov. 17, 1990
562	25	537	Ty Detmer, Brigham Young (Washington St.)	Sept. 7, 1989
559	13	546	Cody Ledbetter, New Mexico St. (UNLV)	Nov. 18, 1995
554	9	545	Rusty LaRue, Wake Forest (North Caro. St.)	Nov. 18, 1995
552	-13	565	Jim McMahon, Brigham Young (Utah)	Nov. 21, 1981
548	12	536	Dave Telford, Fresno St. (Pacific, Cal.)	Oct. 24, 1987
543	-9	552	Mike Maxwell, Nevada (UNLV)	Oct. 28, 1995
541	6	535	Mike Maxwell, Nevada (Louisiana Tech)	Oct. 21, 1995
540	-45	585	Robbie Bosco, Brigham Young (New Mexico)	Oct. 19, 1985
540	104	436	Archie Manning, Mississippi (Alabama)	Oct. 4, 1969
539	1	538	Jim McMahon, Brigham Young (Colorado St.)	Nov. 7, 1981
537	65	472	Anthony Calvillo, Utah St. (Brigham Young)	Oct. 30, 1993
537	-1	538	Chris Vargas, Nevada (UNLV)	Oct. 2, 1993
537	2	535	Shane Montgomery, North Caro. St. (Duke)	Nov. 11, 1989
537	-24	561	Tony Adams, Utah St. (Utah)	Nov. 11, 1972
536	58	478	Tim Schade, Minnesota (Penn St.)	Sept. 4, 1993
536	28	508	Mike Perez, San Jose St. (Pacific, Cal.)	Oct. 25, 1986
532	0	532	Jeff Van Raaphorst, Arizona St. (Florida St.)	Nov. 3, 1984
531	13	518	Jeff Graham, Long Beach St. (Hawaii)	Oct. 29, 1988
528	-40	568	David Lowery, San Diego St. (Brigham Young)	Nov. 16, 1991
528	-2	530	Dan McGwire, San Diego St. (New Mexico)	Nov. 17, 1990
527	-17	544	Eric Zeier, Georgia (Southern Miss.)	Oct. 9, 1993
527	17	510	David Klingler, Houston (Louisiana Tech)	Aug. 31, 1991
525	-29	554	Greg Cook, Cincinnati (Ohio)	Nov. 16, 1968
524	118	406	Ned James, New Mexico (Wyoming)	Nov. 1, 1986
521	-39	560	Ty Detmer, Brigham Young (Utah St.)	Nov. 24, 1990
521	57	464	Whit Taylor, Vanderbilt (Tennessee)	Nov. 28, 1981
519	-14	533	David Klingler, Houston (Texas Tech)	Nov. 30, 1991
517	45	472	Doug Flutie, Boston College (Miami, Fla.)	Nov. 23, 1984
517	73	444	Matt Kofler, San Diego St. (Iowa St.)	Oct. 10, 1981

ANNUAL CHAMPIONS

Year	Player, Team	Class	Plays	Yards Rush	Yards Pass	Yards Total
1937	Byron "Whizzer" White, Colorado	Sr.	224	1,121	475	1,596
1938	Davey O'Brien, Texas Christian	Sr.	291	390	1,457	1,847
1939	Kenny Washington, UCLA	Sr.	259	811	559	1,370
1940	Johnny Knolla, Creighton	Sr.	298	813	607	1,420
1941	Bud Schwenk, Washington (Mo.)	Sr.	354	471	1,457	1,928
1942	Frank Sinkwich, Georgia	Sr.	341	795	1,392	2,187
1943	Bob Hoernschemeyer, Indiana	Fr.	355	515	1,133	1,648
1944	Bob Fenimore, Oklahoma St.	So.	241	897	861	1,758
1945	Bob Fenimore, Oklahoma St.	Jr.	203	1,048	593	1,641
1946	Travis Tidwell, Auburn	Fr.	339	772	943	1,715
1947	Fred Enke, Arizona	So.	329	535	1,406	1,941
1948	Stan Heath, Nevada	Sr.	233	-13	2,005	1,992
1949	Johnny Bright, Drake	So.	275	975	975	1,950
1950	Johnny Bright, Drake	Jr.	320	1,232	1,168	2,400
1951	Dick Kazmaier, Princeton	Sr.	272	861	966	1,827
1952	Ted Marchibroda, Detroit	Sr.	305	176	1,637	1,813
1953	Paul Larson, California	Jr.	262	141	1,431	1,572
1954	George Shaw, Oregon	Sr.	276	178	1,358	1,536

Year	Player, Team	Class	Plays	Yards Rush	Pass	Total
1955	George Welsh, Navy	Sr.	203	29	1,319	1,348
1956	John Brodie, Stanford	Sr.	295	9	1,633	1,642
1957	Bob Newman, Washington St.	Jr.	263	53	1,391	1,444
1958	Dick Bass, Pacific (Cal.)	Jr.	218	1,361	79	1,440
1959	Dick Norman, Stanford	Jr.	319	55	1,963	2,018
1960	Bill Kilmer, UCLA	Sr.	292	803	1,086	1,889
1961	Dave Hoppmann, Iowa St.	Jr.	320	920	718	1,638
1962	Terry Baker, Oregon St.	Sr.	318	538	1,738	2,276
1963	George Mira, Miami (Fla.)	Sr.	394	163	2,155	2,318
1964	Jerry Rhome, Tulsa	Sr.	470	258	2,870	3,128
1965	Bill Anderson, Tulsa	Sr.	580	-121	3,464	3,343
1966	Virgil Carter, Brigham Young	Sr.	388	363	2,182	2,545
1967	Sal Olivas, New Mexico St.	Sr.	368	-41	2,225	2,184
1968	Greg Cook, Cincinnati	Sr.	507	-62	3,272	3,210
1969	Dennis Shaw, San Diego St.	Sr.	388	12	3,185	3,197

Beginning in 1970, ranked on per-game (instead of total) yards

Year	Player, Team	Class	G	Plays	Yards Rush	Pass	Total	Avg.
1970	Pat Sullivan, Auburn	Jr.	10	333	270	2,586	2,856	285.6
1971	Gary Huff, Florida St.	Jr.	11	386	-83	2,736	2,653	241.2
1972	Don Strock, Virginia Tech	Sr.	11	480	-73	3,243	3,170	288.2
1973	Jesse Freitas, San Diego St.	Sr.	11	410	-92	2,993	2,901	263.7
1974	Steve Joachim, Temple	Sr.	10	331	277	1,950	2,227	222.7
1975	Gene Swick, Toledo	Sr.	11	490	219	2,487	2,706	246.0
1976	Tommy Kramer, Rice	Sr.	11	562	-45	3,317	3,272	297.5
1977	Doug Williams, Grambling	Sr.	11	377	-57	3,286	3,229	293.5
1978	Mike Ford, Southern Methodist	So.	11	459	-50	3,007	2,957	268.8
1979	Marc Wilson, Brigham Young	Sr.	11	488	-140	3,720	3,580	325.5
1980	Jim McMahon, Brigham Young	Jr.	12	540	56	4,571	4,627	385.6
1981	Jim McMahon, Brigham Young	Sr.	10	487	-97	3,555	3,458	345.8
1982	Todd Dillon, Long Beach St.	Jr.	11	585	70	3,517	3,587	326.1
1983	Steve Young, Brigham Young	Sr.	11	531	444	3,902	4,346	395.1
1984	Robbie Bosco, Brigham Young	Jr.	12	543	57	3,875	3,932	327.7
1985	Jim Everett, Purdue	Sr.	11	518	-62	3,651	3,589	326.3
1986	Mike Perez, San Jose St.	Jr.	9	425	35	2,934	2,969	329.9
1987	Todd Santos, San Diego St.	Sr.	12	562	-244	3,932	3,688	307.3
1988	Scott Mitchell, Utah	So.	11	589	-23	4,322	4,299	390.8
1989	Andre Ware, Houston	Jr.	11	628	-38	4,699	4,661	423.7
1990	David Klingler, Houston	Jr.	11	*704	81	5,140	*5,221	*474.6
1991	Ty Detmer, Brigham Young	Sr.	12	478	-30	4,031	4,001	333.4
1992	Jimmy Klingler, Houston	So.	11	544	-50	3,818	3,768	342.5
1993	Chris Vargas, Nevada	Sr.	11	535	67	4,265	4,332	393.8
1994	Mike Maxwell, Nevada	Jr.	11	477	-39	3,537	3,498	318.0
1995	Mike Maxwell, Nevada	Sr.	9	443	12	3,611	3,623	402.6

*Record.

File photo

Auburn quarterback Pat Sullivan was the major-college leader in total offense in 1970 with an average of 285.6 yards per game.

Rushing

CAREER YARDS PER GAME

(Minimum 2,500 yards)

Player, Team	Years	G	Plays	Yards	TD	Yd. PG
Ed Marinaro, Cornell	1969-71	27	918	4,715	50	*174.6
O. J. Simpson, Southern Cal	1967-68	19	621	3,124	33	164.4
Herschel Walker, Georgia	1980-82	33	994	5,259	49	159.4
LeShon Johnson, Northern Ill.	1992-93	22	592	3,314	18	150.6
Marshall Faulk, San Diego St.	1991-93	31	766	4,589	57	148.0
Tony Dorsett, Pittsburgh	1973-76	43	1,074	*6,082	55	141.4
Mike Rozier, Nebraska	1981-83	35	668	4,780	50	136.6
Howard Stevens, Louisville	1971-72	20	509	2,723	25	136.2
Jerome Persell, Western Mich.	1976-78	31	842	4,190	39	135.2
Rudy Mobley, Hardin-Simmons	1942,46	19	414	2,543	32	133.8
Vaughn Dunbar, Indiana	1990-91	22	565	2,842	24	129.2
Steve Owens, Oklahoma	1967-69	30	905	3,867	56	128.9
Charles White, Southern Cal	1976-79	44	1,023	5,598	46	127.2
Johnny Bright, Drake	1949-51	25	513	3,134	39	125.4
Woody Green, Arizona St.	1971-73	30	601	3,754	33	125.1
Archie Griffin, Ohio St.	1972-75	42	845	5,177	25	123.3
Anthony Thompson, Indiana	1986-89	41	1,089	4,965	*64	121.1
Mark Kellar, Northern Ill.	1971-73	31	743	3,745	32	120.8
Paul Gipson, Houston	1966-68	23	447	2,769	25	120.4
John Cappelletti, Penn St.	‡1972-73	22	519	2,639	29	120.0
Brian Pruitt, Central Mich.	1992-94	31	671	3,693	31	119.1
Steve Bartalo, Colorado St.	1983-86	41	*1,215	4,813	46	117.4
Louie Giammona, Utah St.	1973-75	30	756	3,499	21	116.6
Paul Palmer, Temple	1983-86	42	948	4,895	39	116.5
Bill Marek, Wisconsin	1972-75	32	719	3,709	44	115.9
Toraino Singleton, UTEP	1994-95	23	560	2,635	19	114.6
Darren Lewis, Texas A&M	1987-90	44	909	5,012	44	113.9
Dick Jauron, Yale	1970-72	26	515	2,947	27	113.3
Bo Jackson, Auburn	1982-85	38	650	4,303	43	113.2
Rashaan Salaam, Colorado	1992-94	27	486	3,057	33	113.2
Joe Morris, Syracuse	1978-81	38	813	4,299	25	113.1
Eugene "Mercury" Morris, West Tex. A&M	1966-68	30	541	3,388	34	112.9

*Record. ‡Defensive back in 1971.

SEASON YARDS PER GAME

Player, Team	Year	G	Plays	Yards	TD	Yd. PG
Barry Sanders, Oklahoma St.	†1988	11	344	*2,628	*37	*238.9
Marcus Allen, Southern Cal	†1981	11	*403	2,342	22	212.9
Ed Marinaro, Cornell	†1971	9	356	1,881	24	209.0
Rashaan Salaam, Colorado	†1994	11	298	2,055	24	186.8
Troy Davis, Iowa St.	†1995	11	345	2,010	15	182.7
Charles White, Southern Cal	†1979	10	293	1,803	18	180.3
LeShon Johnson, Northern Ill.	†1993	11	327	1,976	12	179.6
Mike Rozier, Nebraska	†1983	12	275	2,148	29	179.0
Tony Dorsett, Pittsburgh	†1976	11	338	1,948	21	177.1
Ollie Matson, San Francisco	†1951	9	245	1,566	20	174.0
Lorenzo White, Michigan St.	†1985	11	386	1,908	17	173.5
Wasean Tait, Toledo	1995	11	357	1,905	20	173.2
Herschel Walker, Georgia	1981	11	385	1,891	18	171.9
Brian Pruitt, Central Mich.	1994	11	292	1,890	20	171.8
O. J. Simpson, Southern Cal	†1968	10	355	1,709	22	170.9
Ernest Anderson, Oklahoma St.	†1982	11	353	1,877	8	170.6
Ricky Bell, Southern Cal	†1975	11	357	1,875	13	170.5

*Record. †National champion.

CAREER YARDS

Player, Team	Years	Plays	Yards	Avg.	Long
Tony Dorsett, Pittsburgh	1973-76	1,074	*6,082	5.66	73
Charles White, Southern Cal	1976-79	1,023	5,598	5.47	79
Herschel Walker, Georgia	1980-82	994	5,259	5.29	76
Archie Griffin, Ohio St.	1972-75	845	5,177	††6.13	75
Darren Lewis, Texas A&M	1987-90	909	5,012	5.51	84

Player, Team	Years	Plays	Yards	Avg.	Long
Anthony Thompson, Indiana	1986-89	1,089	4,965	4.56	52
George Rogers, South Caro.	1977-80	902	4,958	5.50	80
Trevor Cobb, Rice	1989-92	1,091	4,948	4.54	79
Paul Palmer, Temple	1983-86	948	4,895	5.16	78
Steve Bartalo, Colorado St.	1983-86	*1,215	4,813	3.96	39
Mike Rozier, Nebraska	1981-83	668	4,780	#7.16	93
Ed Marinaro, Cornell	1969-71	918	4,715	5.14	79
Marcus Allen, Southern Cal	1978-81	893	4,682	5.24	45
Ted Brown, North Caro. St.	1975-78	860	4,602	5.35	95
Thurman Thomas, Oklahoma St.	1984-87	898	4,595	5.12	66
Marshall Faulk, San Diego St.	1991-93	766	4,589	5.99	71
Terry Miller, Oklahoma St.	1974-77	847	4,582	5.41	81
Darrell Thompson, Minnesota	1986-89	911	4,518	4.96	98
Lorenzo White, Michigan St.	1984-87	991	4,513	4.55	73
Eric Dickerson, Southern Methodist	1979-82	790	4,450	5.63	80
Earl Campbell, Texas	1974-77	765	4,443	5.81	‡‡83
Amos Lawrence, North Caro.	1977-80	881	4,391	4.98	62
Deland McCullough, Miami (Ohio)	1992-95	949	4,368	4.60	51
Bo Jackson, Auburn	1982-85	650	4,303	6.62	80
Joe Morris, Syracuse	1978-81	813	4,299	5.29	75
Reggie Taylor, Cincinnati	1983-86	876	4,242	4.48	‡‡68
Mike Mayweather, Army	1987-90	832	4,212	5.06	52
Jerome Persell, Western Mich.	1976-78	842	4,190	4.98	86
Napoleon McCallum, Navy	$1981-85	908	4,179	4.60	60
Tico Duckett, Michigan St.	1989-92	824	4,176	5.07	88
George Swarn, Miami (Ohio)	1983-86	881	4,172	4.74	98
Errict Rhett, Florida	$1989-93	873	4,163	4.77	49
Curtis Adams, Central Mich.	1981-84	761	4,162	5.47	87
Allen Pinkett, Notre Dame	1982-85	889	4,131	4.65	76
James Gray, Texas Tech	1986-89	742	4,066	5.48	72
Robert Lavette, Georgia Tech	1981-84	914	4,066	4.45	83
Stump Mitchell, Citadel	1977-80	756	4,062	5.37	77
Dalton Hilliard, LSU	1982-85	882	4,050	4.59	66
Napoleon Kaufman, Washington	1991-94	710	4,041	5.69	91
Charles Alexander, LSU	1975-78	855	4,035	4.72	64
Darrin Nelson, Stanford	1977-78, 80-81	703	4,033	5.74	80
Joe Washington, Oklahoma	1972-75	656	3,995	6.09	71
Mike Voight, North Caro.	1973-76	826	3,971	4.81	84
Jamie Morris, Michigan	1984-87	742	3,944	5.32	74
Eric Bieniemy, Colorado	1987-90	699	3,940	5.64	69
Emmitt Smith, Florida	1987-89	700	3,928	5.61	96
Ron "Po" James, New Mexico St.	1968-71	818	3,884	4.75	69
Steve Owens, Oklahoma	1967-69	905	3,867	4.27	‡‡49
Mike Williams, New Mexico	1975-78	857	3,862	4.51	36
Sonny Collins, Kentucky	1972-75	777	3,835	4.94	66
Eric Wilkerson, Kent	1985-88	735	3,830	5.21	74
Billy Sims, Oklahoma	$1975-79	538	3,813	7.09	‡‡71
James McDougald, Wake Forest	1976-79	880	3,811	4.33	62
Tony Sands, Kansas	1988-91	778	3,788	4.87	66

**Record. $See page 6 for explanation. ‡‡Did not score. ††Record for minimum 781 carries. #Record for minimum 414 carries.*

CAREER YARDS RECORD PROGRESSION

(Record Yards—Player, Team, Seasons Played)

1,961—Marshall Goldberg, Pittsburgh, 1936-38; **2,105**—Tom Harmon, Michigan, 1938-40; **2,271**—Frank Sinkwich, Georgia, 1940-42; **2,301**—Bill Daley, Minnesota, 1940-42, Michigan, 1943; **2,957**—Glenn Davis, Army, 1943-46; **3,095**—Eddie Price, Tulane, 1946-49; **3,238**—John Papit, Virginia, 1947-50; **3,381**—Art Luppino, Arizona, 1953-56; **3,388**—Eugene "Mercury" Morris, West Tex. A&M, 1966-68; **3,867**—Steve Owens, Oklahoma, 1967-69; **4,715**—Ed Marinaro, Cornell, 1969-71; **5,177**—Archie Griffin, Ohio St., 1972-75; **6,082**—Tony Dorsett, Pittsburgh, 1973-76.

CAREER RUSHING TOUCHDOWNS

Player, Team	Years	G	TDs
Anthony Thompson, Indiana	1986-89	41	*64
Marshall Faulk, San Diego St.	1991-93	31	57
Steve Owens, Oklahoma	1967-69	30	56
Tony Dorsett, Pittsburgh	1973-76	43	55
Mike Rozier, Nebraska	1982-83	35	50
Billy Sims, Oklahoma	1975, 77-79	42	50
Ed Marinaro, Cornell	1969-71	27	50
Allen Pinkett, Notre Dame	1982-85	44	49
Herschel Walker, Georgia	1980-82	33	49
Ted Brown, North Caro. St.	1975-78	43	49
Barry Sanders, Oklahoma St.	1986-88	30	47
Eric Dickerson, Southern Methodist	1979-82	42	47
Steve Bartalo, Colorado St.	1983-86	41	46
Charles White, Southern Cal	1976-79	44	46
James Gray, Texas Tech	1986-89	44	45
Keith Byars, Ohio St.	1982-85	33	45
Robert Lavette, Georgia Tech	1981-84	43	45
Marcus Allen, Southern Cal	1978-81	44	45
Terry Miller, Oklahoma St.	1974-77	41	45

**Record. (Note: Howard Stevens of Louisville played two years at college division Randolph-Macon, 1968-69, with 33 touchdowns and two years at Louisville, 1971-72, with 25 touchdowns, scoring a total of 58 touchdowns in four years.)*

SEASON YARDS

Player, Team	Year	G	Plays	Yards	Avg.
Barry Sanders, Oklahoma St.	†1988	11	344	*2,628	‡7.64
Marcus Allen, Southern Cal	†1981	11	*403	2,342	5.81
Mike Rozier, Nebraska	†1983	12	275	2,148	#7.81
Rashaan Salaam, Colorado	†1994	11	298	2,055	6.90
Troy Davis, Iowa St.	†1995	11	345	2,010	5.83
LeShon Johnson, Northern Ill.	†1993	11	327	1,976	6.04
Tony Dorsett, Pittsburgh	†1976	11	338	1,948	5.76
Lorenzo White, Michigan St.	†1985	11	386	1,908	4.94
Wasean Tait, Toledo	1995	11	357	1,905	5.34
Herschel Walker, Georgia	1981	11	385	1,891	4.91
Brian Pruitt, Central Mich.	1994	11	292	1,890	6.47
Ed Marinaro, Cornell	†1971	9	356	1,881	5.28
Ernest Anderson, Oklahoma St.	†1982	11	353	1,877	5.32
Ricky Bell, Southern Cal	†1975	11	357	1,875	5.25
Paul Palmer, Temple	†1986	11	346	1,866	5.39
George Jones, San Diego St.	1995	12	305	1,842	6.04
Eddie George, Ohio St.	1995	12	303	1,826	6.03
Charles White, Southern Cal	†1979	10	293	1,803	6.15
Anthony Thompson, Indiana	†1989	11	358	1,793	5.01
Obie Graves, Cal St. Fullerton	1978	12	275	1,789	6.51
Bo Jackson, Auburn	1985	11	278	1,786	6.42
George Rogers, South Caro.	†1980	11	297	1,781	6.00
Billy Sims, Oklahoma	†1978	11	231	1,762	7.63
Charles White, Southern Cal	1978	12	342	1,760	5.15
Robert Newhouse, Houston	1971	11	277	1,757	6.34
Byron Morris, Texas Tech	1993	11	298	1,752	5.88
Herschel Walker, Georgia	1982	11	335	1,752	5.23
Earl Campbell, Texas	†1977	11	267	1,744	6.53
Mike Pringle, Cal St. Fullerton	1989	11	296	1,727	5.83
Tim Biakabutuka, Michigan	1995	12	279	1,724	6.18
Lawrence Phillips, Nebraska	1994	12	286	1,722	6.02
Don McCauley, North Caro.	1970	11	324	1,720	5.31

**Record. †National champion. ‡Record for minimum 282 carries. #Record for minimum 214 carries.*

SINGLE-GAME YARDS

Yds.	Player, Team (Opponent)	Date
396	Tony Sands, Kansas (Missouri)	Nov. 23, 1991
386	Marshall Faulk, San Diego St. (Pacific, Cal.)	Sept. 14, 1991
377	Anthony Thompson, Indiana (Wisconsin)	Nov. 11, 1989
357	Mike Pringle, Cal St. Fullerton (New Mexico St.)	Nov. 4, 1989
357	Rueben Mayes, Washington St. (Oregon)	Oct. 27, 1984
356	Brian Pruitt, Central Mich. (Toledo)	Nov. 5, 1994
356	Eddie Lee Ivery, Georgia Tech (Air Force)	Nov. 11, 1978
350	Eric Allen, Michigan St. (Purdue)	Oct. 30, 1971
349	Paul Palmer, Temple (East Caro.)	Oct. 11, 1986
347	Ricky Bell, Southern Cal (Washington St.)	Oct. 9, 1976
347	Ron Johnson, Michigan (Wisconsin)	Nov. 16, 1968
343	Tony Jeffery, Texas Christian (Tulane)	Sept. 13, 1986
342	Roosevelt Leaks, Texas (Southern Methodist)	Nov. 3, 1973
342	Charlie Davis, Colorado (Oklahoma St.)	Nov. 13, 1971
340	Eugene "Mercury" Morris, West Tex. A&M (Montana St.)	Oct. 5, 1968
332	Barry Sanders, Oklahoma St. (Texas Tech)	Dec. 3, 1988
329	John Leach, Wake Forest (Maryland)	Nov. 20, 1993
328	Derrick Fenner, North Caro. (Virginia)	Nov. 15, 1986
326	George Swarn, Miami, Ohio (Eastern Mich.)	Nov. 16, 1985
326	Fred Wendt, UTEP (New Mexico St.)	Nov. 25, 1948
325	Andre Davis, Texas Christian (New Mexico)	Sept. 10, 1994
322	LeShon Johnson, Northern Ill. (Southern Ill.)	Oct. 2, 1993
322	Greg Allen, Florida St. (Western Caro.)	Oct. 31, 1981
321	Frank Mordica, Vanderbilt (Air Force)	Nov. 18, 1978
320	Barry Sanders, Oklahoma St. (Kansas St.)	Oct. 29, 1988
319	Andre Herrera, Southern Ill. (Northern Ill.)	Oct. 23, 1976
319	Jim Pilot, New Mexico St. (Hardin-Simmons)	Nov. 25, 1961
317	Rashaan Salaam, Colorado (Texas)	Oct. 1, 1994
316	Emmitt Smith, Florida (New Mexico)	Oct. 21, 1989
316	Mike Adamle, Northwestern (Wisconsin)	Oct. 18, 1969
314	Eddie George, Ohio St. (Illinois)	Nov. 11, 1995
313	Tim Biakabutuka, Michigan (Ohio St.)	Nov. 25, 1995
312	Mark Brus, Tulsa (New Mexico St.)	Oct. 27, 1990
312	Barry Sanders, Oklahoma St. (Kansas)	Nov. 12, 1988
310	Tony Alford, Colorado St. (Utah)	Oct. 28, 1989
310	Mitchell True, Pacific, Cal. (UC Davis)	Nov. 18, 1972
308	Stacey Robinson (QB), Northern Ill. (Fresno St.)	Oct. 6, 1990
307	Curtis Kuykendall, Auburn (Miami, Fla.)	Nov. 24, 1944
306	LeShon Johnson, Northern Ill. (Iowa)	Nov. 6, 1993
304	Casey McBeth, Toledo (Akron)	Oct. 22, 1994
304	Barry Sanders, Oklahoma St. (Tulsa)	Oct. 1, 1988
304	Sam Dejarnette, Southern Miss. (Florida St.)	Sept. 25, 1982
304	Bill Marek, Wisconsin (Minnesota)	Nov. 23, 1974

Yds.	Player, Team (Opponent)	Date
303	Tony Dorsett, Pittsburgh (Notre Dame)	Nov. 15, 1975
302	Troy Davis, Iowa St. (UNLV)	Sept. 23, 1995
302	Jason Davis, Louisiana Tech (Southwestern La.)	Sept. 29, 1990
302	Kevin Lowe, Wyoming (South Dak. St.)	Nov. 10, 1984
300	Marshall Faulk, San Diego St. (Hawaii)	Nov. 14, 1992

ANNUAL CHAMPIONS

Year	Player, Team	Class	Plays	Yards
1937	Byron "Whizzer" White, Colorado	Sr.	181	1,121
1938	Len Eshmont, Fordham	So.	132	831
1939	John Polanski, Wake Forest	So.	137	882
1940	Al Ghesquiere, Detroit	Sr.	146	957
1941	Frank Sinkwich, Georgia	Jr.	209	1,103
1942	Rudy Mobley, Hardin-Simmons	So.	187	1,281
1943	Creighton Miller, Notre Dame	Sr.	151	911
1944	Wayne "Red" Williams, Minnesota	Jr.	136	911
1945	Bob Fenimore, Oklahoma St.	Jr.	142	1,048
1946	Rudy Mobley, Hardin-Simmons	Sr.	227	1,262
1947	Wilton Davis, Hardin-Simmons	So.	193	1,173
1948	Fred Wendt, UTEP	Sr.	184	1,570
1949	John Dottley, Mississippi	Jr.	208	1,312
1950	Wilford White, Arizona St.	Sr.	199	1,502
1951	Ollie Matson, San Francisco	Sr.	245	1,566
1952	Howie Waugh, Tulsa	Sr.	164	1,372
1953	J. C. Caroline, Illinois	So.	194	1,256
1954	Art Luppino, Arizona	So.	179	1,359
1955	Art Luppino, Arizona	Jr.	209	1,313
1956	Jim Crawford, Wyoming	Sr.	200	1,104
1957	Leon Burton, Arizona St.	Sr.	117	1,126
1958	Dick Bass, Pacific (Cal.)	Jr.	205	1,361
1959	Pervis Atkins, New Mexico St.	Jr.	130	971
1960	Bob Gaiters, New Mexico St.	Sr.	197	1,338
1961	Jim Pilot, New Mexico St.	So.	191	1,278
1962	Jim Pilot, New Mexico St.	Jr.	208	1,247
1[illegible]	[illegible] Memphis	Sr.	219	1,016
[illegible]	[illegible]	[illegible]	[illegible]52	1,044
[illegible]	[illegible]	[illegible]	[illegible]67	1,440
[illegible]	[illegible]	[illegible]	[illegible]59	1,329
[illegible]	[illegible]	[illegible]	[illegible]66	1,415
[illegible]	[illegible]	[illegible]	[illegible]55	1,709
[illegible]	[illegible]	[illegible]	[illegible]58	1,523

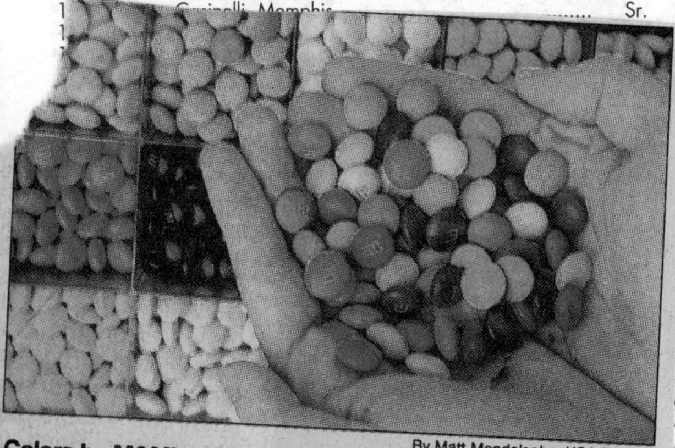

[illegible]	[illegible]	…rds	Avg.
[illegible]	[illegible]	[illegible]425	158.3
[illegible]	[illegible]	[illegible]881	209.0
[illegible]	[illegible]	[illegible]386	138.6
[illegible]	[illegible]	[illegible]719	156.3
[illegible]	[illegible]	[illegible]534	153.4
[illegible]	[illegible]	[illegible],875	170.5
[illegible]	[illegible]	[illegible],948	177.1
[illegible]	[illegible]	[illegible],744	158.5
[illegible]	[illegible]	[illegible],762	160.2
[illegible]	[illegible]	[illegible],803	180.3
[illegible]	[illegible]	[illegible],781	161.9
[illegible]	[illegible]	[illegible],342	212.9
[illegible]	[illegible]	[illegible],877	170.6
[illegible]	[illegible]	[illegible],148	179.0
[illegible]	[illegible]	[illegible],655	150.5
[illegible]	[illegible]	[illegible],908	173.5
[illegible]	[illegible]	[illegible],866	169.6
[illegible]	[illegible]	[illegible],658	150.7
[illegible]	[illegible]	2,628	*238.9
[illegible]	[illegible]	1,793	163.0
[illegible]	[illegible]	1,642	149.3
[illegible]	[illegible]	1,429	158.8
[illegible]	[illegible]	1,630	163.0
[illegible]	[illegible]	1,976	179.6
[illegible]	[illegible]	2,055	186.8
1995	Troy Davis, [illegible]	2,010	182.7

*Record.

By Matt Mendelsohn, USA TODAY

Colors by M&M's: Twenty-four new hues are unveiled Friday, including dark pink and aqua, available in specialty stores.

CHANGING COLORS: There's a new color scheme in the world of M&M's. Starting Friday, 24 new hues will be introduced — including navy blue, light purple, teal green, dark pink, aqua and light orange. But don't look for M&M's Colorworks in your favorite candy store or vending machine — they'll be sold in specialty stores only and cost $5-$7 a pound, compared with $2.79 a pound for the classic five-color combo. Sorry, peanut fanciers, they're available only in plain. For stores in your area, call 800-766-[illegible]327, 9 a.m.-6 p.m. ET/6 a.m.-3 p.m. PT.

FRESHMAN 1,000-YARD RUSHERS

Player, Team	Year	Yards
Ron "Po" James, New Mexico St.	1968	1,291
Tony Dorsett, Pittsburgh	1973	1,586
James McDougald, Wake Forest	1976	1,018
Mike Harkrader, Indiana	1976	1,003
Amos Lawrence, North Caro.	1977	1,211
Darrin Nelson, Stanford	1977	1,069
Mike Smith, Tenn.-Chatt.	1977	1,062
Gwain Durden, Tenn.-Chatt.	1977	1,049
Allen Ross, Northern Ill.	1977	1,036
Allen Harvin, Cincinnati	1978	1,238
Joe Morris, Syracuse	1978	1,001
Ron Lear, Marshall	1979	1,162
Herschel Walker, Georgia	1980	*1,616
Kerwin Bell, Kansas	1980	1,114
Joe McIntosh, North Caro. St.	1981	1,190
Steve Bartalo, Colorado St.	1983	1,113
Spencer Tillman, Oklahoma	1983	1,047
D. J. Dozier, Penn St.	1983	1,002
Eddie Johnson, Utah	1984	1,021
Darrell Thompson, Minnesota	1986	1,240
Emmitt Smith, Florida	1987	1,341
Reggie Cobb, Tennessee	1987	1,197
Bernie Parmalee, Ball St.	1987	1,064
Curvin Richards, Pittsburgh	1988	1,228
Chuck Webb, Tennessee	1989	1,236
Robert Smith, Ohio St.	1990	1,064
Marshall Faulk, San Diego St.	1991	1,429
Greg Hill, Texas A&M	1991	1,216
David Small, Cincinnati	1991	1,004
Winslow Oliver, New Mexico	1992	1,063
Deland McCullough, Miami (Ohio)	1992	1,026
Terrell Willis, Rutgers	1993	1,261
Charles Henley, Kansas	1993	1,127
Marquis Williams, Arkansas St.	1993	1,060
Leon Johnson, North Caro.	1993	1,012
Alex Smith, Indiana	1994	1,475
Astron Whatley, Kent	1994	1,003
Denvis Manns, New Mexico St.	1995	1,120
Silas Massey, Central Mich.	1995	1,089
Ahman Green, Nebraska	1995	1,086

*Record for freshman.

Quarterback Rushing

SEASON YARDS

Player, Team	Year	G	Plays	Yards	TD	Avg.
Stacey Robinson, Northern Ill.	1989	11	223	*1,443	*19	6.47
Dee Dowis, Air Force	1987	12	194	1,315	10	6.78
Brian Mitchell, Southwestern La.	1989	11	237	1,311	*19	5.53
Fred Solomon, Tampa	1974	11	193	1,300	*19	6.74
Dee Dowis, Air Force	1989	12	172	1,286	18	*7.48
Beau Morgan, Air Force	1995	12	229	1,285	*19	5.61
Stacey Robinson, Northern Ill.	1990	11	193	1,238	*19	6.41
Rob Perez, Air Force	1991	12	233	1,157	10	4.97
Jack Mildren, Oklahoma	1971	11	193	1,140	17	5.91
Nolan Cromwell, Kansas	1975	11	218	1,124	9	5.16
Michael Carter, Hawaii	1991	12	221	1,092	16	4.94
Tory Crawford, Army	1986	11	*244	1,075	15	4.41
Bart Weiss, Air Force	1985	12	180	1,032	12	5.73
Jimmy Sidle, Auburn	1963	10	185	1,006	10	5.44
Reggie Collier, Southern Miss.	1981	11	153	1,005	12	6.57
Darian Hagan, Colorado	1989	11	186	1,004	17	5.40

*Record.

CAREER YARDS

Player, Team	Years	G	Plays	Yards	TD	Avg.
Dee Dowis, Air Force	1986-89	47	543	*3,612	41	76.9
Brian Mitchell, Southwestern La.	1986-89	43	678	3,335	*47	77.6
Fred Solomon, Tampa	1971-74	43	557	3,299	39	76.7
Stacey Robinson, Northern Ill.	1988-90	25	429	2,727	38	*109.1
Jamelle Holieway, Oklahoma	1985-88	38	505	2,699	30	71.0
Bill Hurley, Syracuse	1975-79	46	*685	2,551	19	55.5
Michael Carter, Hawaii	1990-93	46	574	2,534	39	55.1
Bill Deery, William & Mary	1972-74	33	443	2,401	19	72.8
Reggie Collier, Southern Miss.	1979-82	39	446	2,304	26	59.1
John Bond, Mississippi St.	1980-83	44	572	2,280	24	51.8
Tory Crawford, Army	1984-87	31	495	2,255	34	72.7
Tom Parr, Colgate	1971-73	30	435	2,221	31	74.0
Alton Grizzard, Navy	1987-90	38	599	2,174	15	57.2
Gary Wood, Cornell	1961-63	27	433	2,156	19	79.9
Roy DeWalt, Texas-Arlington	1975, 77-79	38	468	2,136	27	56.2
Steve Taylor, Nebraska	1985-88	37	431	2,125	32	57.4
Bucky Richardson, Texas A&M	1987-88, 90-91	41	370	2,095	30	51.1
Rocky Long, New Mexico	1969-71	31	469	2,071	21	66.8
Steve Davis, Oklahoma	1973-75	33	515	2,069	33	62.7
Rick Leach, Michigan	1975-78	43	440	2,053	34	47.7
Prince McJunkins, Wichita St.	1979-82	44	613	2,047	27	46.5
Rickey Foggie, Minnesota	1984-87	41	510	2,038	24	49.7
Major Harris, West Va.	1987-89	33	386	2,030	18	51.5
Steve Gage, Tulsa	1983-84, 86	33	522	2,029	30	61.5
Harry Gilmer, Alabama	1944-47	40	390	2,025	19	50.6
Darian Hagan, Colorado	1988-91	41	489	2,007	27	49.0

*Record.

Photo from Wisconsin sports information

Darrell Bevell finished his four-year career at Wisconsin with a passing efficiency rating of 135.0, which ranks 28th on the all-time Division I-A list.

Passing

SAMPLE COMPILATION OF NCAA PASSING EFFICIENCY RATING

Player	G	Att.	Cmp.	Yds.	TD	Int.
Ty Detmer, Brigham Young	46	1,530	958	15,031	121	65

Completion Percentage:	62.61
Yards Per Attempted Pass:	9.82
Percent of Passes for TDs:	7.91
Percent of Passes Intercepted:	4.25

ADD the first three factors:

			Rating Points
Completion Percentage:	62.61		62.61
Yards Per Attempted Pass:	9.82	times 8.4	82.49
Percent of Passes for TDs:	7.91	times 3.3	26.10
			171.20

SUBTRACT the last factor:

Percent of Passes Intercepted:	4.25	times 2	-8.50
		Round off to:	**162.7**

DIVISION I-A PASSING EFFICIENCY RATING COMPARISON
1979-95

Passing statistics in Division I-A have increased dramatically since 1979, the first year that the NCAA official national statistics used the passing efficiency formula to rank passers in all divisions. Because passers have become more proficient every year, the average passing efficiency rating (based on final regular-season trends) also has risen at a similar rate. For historical purposes, the average passing efficiency rating for the division by year is presented below to show how any individual or team might rank in a particular season.

Year	Pass Effic. Rating	Year	Pass Effic. Rating
1979	104.49	1989	118.35
1980	106.63	1990	117.39
1981	107.00	1991	117.94
1982	110.77	1992	114.50
1983	113.56	1993	122.43
1984	113.02	1994	120.59
1985	114.58	1995	120.17
1986	115.00		
1987	112.67		
1988	114.32		

CAREER PASSING EFFICIENCY
(Minimum 500 Completions)

Player, Team	Years	Att.	Cmp.	Int.	Pct.	Yds.	TD	Pts.
Ty Detmer, Brigham Young	1988-91	*1,530	*958	65	.626	*15,031	*121	*162.7
Jim McMahon, Brigham Young	1977-78, 80-81	1,060	653	34	.616	9,536	84	156.9
Steve Young, Brigham Young	1981-83	908	592	33	.652	7,733	56	149.8
Robbie Bosco, Brigham Young	1983-85	997	638	36	.640	8,400	66	149.4
Mike Maxwell, Nevada	1993-95	881	560	33	.636	7,256	62	148.5
Chuck Long, Iowa	$1981-85	1,072	692	46	‡.646	9,210	64	147.8
John Walsh, Brigham Young	1991-94	973	587	35	.603	8,375	66	147.8
Rob Johnson, Southern Cal	1991-94	963	623	24	.647	7,743	52	145.1
Andre Ware, Houston	1987-89	1,074	660	28	.615	8,202	75	143.3
Steve Stenstrom, Stanford	1991-94	1,320	833	36	.631	10,531	72	142.7
Marvin Graves, Syracuse	1990-93	943	563	45	.597	8,466	48	142.4
Doug Gaynor, Long Beach St.	1984-85	837	569	35	.680	6,793	35	141.6
Danny Kanell, Florida St.	1992-95	851	529	26	.622	6,372	57	141.1
Dan McGwire, Iowa/San Diego St.	1986-87, 89-90	973	575	30	.591	8,164	49	140.0
Chris Vargas, Nevada	1992-93	806	502	34	.623	6,359	47	139.4
John Elway, Stanford	1979-82	1,246	774	39	.621	9,349	77	139.3
Mike McCoy, Long Beach St./Utah	1991, 92-94	1,069	650	26	.608	8,342	56	138.8
David Klingler, Houston	1988-91	1,268	732	38	.577	9,466	91	138.1
Scott Milanovich, Maryland	1992-95	982	650	35	**.662	7,301	49	138.0
Scott Mitchell, Utah	1987-89	1,165	669	38	.574	8,981	68	137.7
Shane Matthews, Florida	1989-92	1,202	722	46	.601	9,287	74	137.6
Marc Wilson, Brigham Young	1977-79	937	535	46	.571	7,637	61	137.2
Eric Zeier, Georgia	1991-94	1,402	838	37	.598	11,153	67	137.1
Randall Cunningham, UNLV	1982-84	1,029	597	29	.580	8,020	59	136.8
Kerwin Bell, Florida	1984-87	953	549	35	.576	7,585	56	136.5
Tom Hodson, LSU	1986-89	1,163	674	41	.580	9,115	69	136.3
Rodney Peete, Southern Cal	1985-88	972	571	32	.587	7,640	52	135.8
Darrell Bevell, Wisconsin	1992-95	1,012	625	37	.618	7,429	58	135.0
Troy Kopp, Pacific (Cal.)	1989-92	1,374	798	47	.581	10,258	87	134.9
Joe Adams, Tennessee St.	1977-80	1,100	604	60	.549	8,649	81	134.4
Mike Gundy, Oklahoma St.	1986-89	1,037	606	37	.584	8,072	54	133.9
Todd Santos, San Diego St.	1984-87	1,484	910	57	.613	11,425	70	133.9
Tony Eason, Illinois	1981-82	856	526	29	.615	6,608	37	133.8
Danny McCoin, Cincinnati	1984-87	899	544	26	.605	6,801	39	132.6
Rich Campbell, California	1977-80	891	574	42	.644	6,933	33	132.6
Jim Everett, Purdue	$1981-85	923	550	30	.596	7,158	40	132.5
Matt Rodgers, Iowa	1988-91	844	516	30	.611	6,308	40	132.5
Doug Flutie, Boston College	1981-84	1,270	677	54	.533	10,579	67	132.2
Gino Torretta, Miami (Fla.)	1989-92	991	555	24	.560	7,690	47	132.0
Robert Hall, Texas Tech	1990-93	997	548	28	.550	7,908	48	131.9

Player, Team	Years	Att.	Cmp.	Int.	Pct.	Yds.	TD	Pts.
Jack Trudeau, Illinois	1981, 83-85	1,151	736	38	†.639	8,146	51	131.4
Kevin Sweeney, Fresno St.	$1982-86	1,336	731	48	.547	10,623	66	130.6
Bill Musgrave, Oregon	1987-90	1,018	582	38	.572	7,631	55	130.6
Stoney Case, New Mexico	1991-94	1,237	677	39	.547	9,460	67	130.5
Glenn Foley, Boston College	1990-93	1,275	703	60	.551	10,042	72	130.5
Gene Swick, Toledo	1972-75	938	556	45	.593	7,267	44	130.3
Steve Taneyhill, South Caro.	1992-95	1,209	727	37	.601	8,555	61	130.1
Jason Verduzco, Illinois	1989-92	986	622	29	.631	6,974	40	130.0
Brian McClure, Bowling Green	1982-85	1,427	900	58	.631	10,280	63	130.0

(400-499 Completions)

Player, Team	Years	Att.	Cmp.	Int.	Pct.	Yds.	TD	Pts.
Vinny Testaverde, Miami (Fla.)	1982, 84-86	674	413	25	.613	6,058	48	152.9
Trent Dilfer, Fresno St.	1991-93	774	461	21	.596	6,944	51	151.2
Troy Aikman, Oklahoma/UCLA	1984-85, 87-88	637	401	18	.630	5,436	40	149.7
Chuck Hartlieb, Iowa	1985-88	716	461	17	.643	6,269	34	148.9
Elvis Grbac, Michigan	1989-92	754	477	29	.633	5,859	64	148.9
Bobby Hoying, Ohio St.	1992-95	782	463	33	.592	6,751	54	146.1
Gifford Nielsen, Brigham Young	1975-77	708	415	29	.586	5,833	55	145.3
Tom Ramsey, UCLA	1979-82	691	411	33	.595	5,844	48	143.9
Shawn Moore, Virginia	1987-90	762	421	32	.552	6,629	55	143.8
Jerry Rhome, Southern Methodist/Tulsa	1961, 63-64	713	448	23	.628	5,472	47	142.6
Charlie Ward, Florida St.	1989, 91-93	759	474	21	.625	5,747	49	141.8
Bernie Kosar, Miami (Fla.)	1983-84	743	463	29	.623	5,971	40	139.8
Craig Erickson, Miami (Fla.)	1987-90	752	420	22	.559	6,056	46	137.8
Dave Yarema, Michigan St.	$1982-86	727	447	29	.615	5,569	41	136.5
Gary Huff, Florida St.	1970-72	796	436	42	.548	6,378	52	133.1
Joe Hughes, Wyoming	1992-93	744	424	25	.570	5,841	38	133.1
Jeff Francis, Tennessee	1985-88	768	476	26	.620	5,867	31	132.7
Mike Perez, San Jose St.	1986-87	792	471	30	.595	6,194	36	132.6
Cale Gundy, Oklahoma	1990-93	751	420	31	.559	6,142	36	132.2

(325-399 Completions)

Player, Team	Years	Att.	Cmp.	Int.	Pct.	Yds.	TD	Pts.
Jim Harbaugh, Michigan	1983-86	582	368	19	.632	5,215	31	149.6
Danny White, Arizona St.	1971-73	649	345	36	.532	5,932	59	148.9
Tim Gutierrez, San Diego St.	1992-94	580	357	19	.616	4,740	36	144.1
Jim Karsatos, Ohio St.	1983-86	573	330	19	.576	4,698	36	140.6
Jerry Tagge, Nebraska	1969-71	581	348	19	.599	4,704	33	140.1
Garrett Gabriel, Hawaii	1987-90	661	356	31	.539	5,631	47	139.5
Rick Mirer, Notre Dame	1989-92	698	377	23	.540	5,996	41	139.0
Gary Sheide, Brigham Young	1973-74	594	358	31	.603	4,524	45	138.8
Dan Speltz, Cal St. Fullerton	1988-89	583	350	19	.600	4,595	33	138.4
Don McPherson, Syracuse	$1983-87	687	367	29	.534	5,812	46	138.1
Joe Youngblood, Central Mich.	1990-93	572	331	28	.579	4,718	35	137.6
Kerry Collins, Penn St.	1991-94	657	370	21	.563	5,304	39	137.3
Sam King, UNLV	1979-81	625	360	29	.576	5,393	30	136.6
J. J. Joe, Baylor	1990-93	665	347	28	.522	5,995	31	134.9
Jesse Freitas, Stanford/San Diego St.	1970, 72-73	547	338	33	.618	4,408	28	134.3
Jeff Blake, East Caro.	1988-91	667	360	20	.540	5,133	43	133.9

**Record. $See page 6 for explanation. **Record for minimum 875 attempts. ‡Record for minimum 1,000 attempts. †Record for minimum 1,100 attempts.*

SEASON PASSING EFFICIENCY

(Minimum 15 Attempts Per Game)

Player, Team	Year	G	Att.	Cmp.	Int.	Pct.	Yds.	TD	Pts.
Danny Wuerffel, Florida	†1995	11	325	210	10	.646	3,266	35	*178.4
Jim McMahon, Brigham Young	#†1980	12	445	284	18	.638	4,571	47	176.9
Ty Detmer, Brigham Young	†1989	12	412	265	15	.643	4,560	32	175.6
Trent Dilfer, Fresno St.	†1993	11	333	217	4	.652	3,276	28	173.1
Kerry Collins, Penn St.	†1994	11	264	176	7	.667	2,679	21	172.9
Jerry Rhome, Tulsa	#†1964	10	326	224	4	.687	2,870	32	172.6
Bobby Hoying, Ohio St.	1995	12	303	192	11	.634	3,023	28	170.4
Elvis Grbac, Michigan	†1991	11	228	152	5	.667	1,955	24	169.0
Ty Detmer, Brigham Young	#1991	12	403	249	12	.618	4,031	35	168.5
Steve Young, Brigham Young	#†1983	11	429	306	10	*.713	3,902	33	168.5
Vinny Testaverde, Miami (Fla.)	†1986	10	276	175	9	.634	2,557	26	165.8
Brian Dowling, Yale	1968	9	160	92	10	.575	1,554	19	165.8
Dave Barr, California	1993	11	275	187	12	.680	2,619	21	164.5
Don McPherson, Syracuse	†1987	11	229	129	11	.563	2,341	22	164.3
Dave Wilson, Ball St.	1977	11	177	115	7	.650	1,589	17	164.2
Bob Berry, Oregon	1963	10	171	101	7	.591	1,675	16	164.0
Jim Harbaugh, Michigan	†1985	11	212	139	6	.656	1,913	18	163.7
Troy Aikman, UCLA	1987	11	243	159	6	.654	2,354	16	163.6
Turk Schonert, Stanford	†1979	11	221	148	6	.670	1,922	19	163.0
Donovan McNabb, Syracuse	1995	11	207	128	6	.618	1,991	16	162.3
Brian Broomell, Temple	1979	11	214	120	11	.561	2,103	22	162.3
Dennis Shaw, San Diego St.	†1969	10	335	199	26	.594	3,185	39	162.2
Timm Rosenbach, Washington St.	†1988	11	302	199	10	.659	2,791	23	162.0
Davey O'Brien, Texas Christian	¢#†1938	10	167	93	4	.557	1,457	19	161.7
Chuck Hartlieb, Iowa	1987	12	299	196	8	.656	2,855	19	161.4
Darrell Bevell, Wisconsin	1993	11	256	177	10	.691	2,294	19	161.1
David Brown, Duke	1989	9	163	104	6	.638	1,479	14	161.0
Shawn Moore, Virginia	†1990	10	241	144	8	.598	2,262	21	160.7

Photo from Fresno State sports information

Fresno State quarterback Trent Dilfer's career passing efficiency rating of 151.2 ranks second among Division I-A passers with 400-499 completions.

Kansas State sports information photo by Peter G. Aiken

Kansas State's Matt Miller completed 64.2 percent of his passes in 1995, which helped him earn a passing efficiency rating of 157.3.

Player, Team	Year	G	Att.	Cmp.	Int.	Pct.	Yds.	TD	Pts.
Chuck Long, Iowa	1983	10	236	144	8	.610	2,434	14	160.4
Mike Maxwell, Nevada	#1995	9	409	277	17	.677	3,611	33	160.2
Jeff Garcia, San Jose St.	1991	9	160	99	5	.619	1,519	12	160.1
Matt Blundin, Virginia	1991	9	224	135	0	.603	1,902	19	159.6
Kerwin Bell, Florida	1985	11	288	180	8	.625	2,687	21	159.4
Mike Gundy, Oklahoma St.	1988	11	236	153	12	.648	2,163	19	158.2
Charlie Ward, Florida St.	1993	11	380	264	4	.695	3,032	27	157.8
Maurice DeShazo, Virginia Tech	1993	11	230	129	7	.561	2,080	22	157.5
Danny White, Arizona St.	1973	11	265	146	12	.551	2,609	23	157.4
Matt Miller, Kansas St.	1995	11	240	154	11	.642	2,059	22	157.3
Heath Shuler, Tennessee	1993	11	285	184	8	.646	2,354	25	157.3
Stan Heath, Nevada	#†1948	9	222	126	9	.568	2,005	22	157.2
Glenn Foley, Boston College	1993	11	363	222	10	.612	3,397	25	157.0
Jim Harbaugh, Michigan	1986	11	254	167	8	.658	2,557	10	157.0
Chris Vargas, Nevada	#1993	11	490	331	18	.676	4,265	34	156.2
Shawn Moore, Virginia	1989	11	221	125	7	.566	2,078	18	156.1
Dan Speltz, Cal St. Fullerton	1989	11	309	214	11	.693	2,671	20	156.1
John Walsh, Brigham Young	1993	11	397	244	15	.615	3,727	28	156.0
Ty Detmer, Brigham Young	1990	12	562	361	28	.642	*5,188	41	155.9
Terry Dean, Florida	1994	10	180	109	10	.606	1,492	20	155.7
Rob Johnson, Southern Cal	1993	12	405	278	5	.686	3,285	26	155.5
Doug Williams, Grambling	#1977	11	352	181	18	.514	3,286	38	155.2
John Huarte, Notre Dame	1964	10	205	114	11	.556	2,062	16	155.1
Jim McMahon, Brigham Young	#†1981	10	423	272	7	.643	3,555	30	155.0
Elvis Grbac, Michigan	†1992	9	169	112	12	.663	1,465	15	154.2
Steve Taneyhill, South Caro.	1995	11	389	261	9	.671	3,094	29	153.9
Steve Sloan, Alabama	1965	10	160	97	3	.606	1,453	10	153.8
Tom Ramsey, UCLA	†1982	11	311	191	10	.614	2,824	21	153.5
Martin Vaughn, Pennsylvania	1973	9	206	114	8	.553	1,926	17	153.3
Dick Doheny, Fordham	1949	8	140	87	5	.621	1,127	13	153.3

**Record. †National pass-efficiency champion. #National total-offense champion. ¢Available records before 1946 do not include TD passes except for O'Brien and relatively few other passers; thus, passing efficiency points cannot be compiled for those players without TD passes.*

ANNUAL PASSING EFFICIENCY LEADERS

(% Minimum 11 Attempts Per Game)

1946—Bill Mackrides, Nevada, 176.9; **1947**—Bobby Layne, Texas, 138.9; **1948**—Stan Heath, Nevada, 157.2 (#); **1949**—Bob Williams, Notre Dame, 159.1; **1950**—Claude Arnold, Oklahoma, 157.3; **1951**—Dick Kazmaier, Princeton, 155.3 (#); **1952**—Ron Morris, Tulsa, 177.4; **1953**—Bob Garrett, Stanford, 142.2; **1954**—Pete Vann, Army, 166.5; **1955**—George Welsh, Navy, 146.1 (#); **1956**—Tom Flores, Pacific (Cal.), 147.5; **1957**—Lee Grosscup, Utah, 175.5; **1958**—John Hangartner, Arizona St., 150.1; **1959**—Charley Johnson, New Mexico St., 135.7; **1960**—Eddie Wilson, Arizona, 140.8; **1961**—Ron DiGravio, Purdue, 140.1; **1962**—John Jacobs, Arizona St., 153.9; **1963**—Bob Berry, Oregon, 164.0; **1964**—Jerry Rhome, Tulsa, 172.6 (#).

(Minimum 15 Attempts Per Game)

1946—Ben Raimondi, Indiana, 117.0; **1947**—Charley Conerly, Mississippi, 125.8; **1948**—Stan Heath, Nevada, 157.2 (#); **1949**—Dick Doheny, Fordham, 153.3; **1950**—Dick Doheny, Fordham, 149.5; **1951**—Babe Parilli, Kentucky, 130.8; **1952**—Gene Rossi, Cincinnati, 149.7; **1953**—Bob Garrett, Stanford, 142.2; **1954**—Len Dawson, Purdue, 145.8; **1955**—George Welsh, Navy, 146.1 (#); **1956**—Bob Reinhart, San Jose St., 121.3; **1957**—Bob Newman, Washington St., 126.5 (#); **1958**—Randy Duncan, Iowa, 135.1; **1959**—Charley Johnson, New Mexico St., 135.7; **1960**—Charley Johnson, New Mexico St., 134.1; **1961**—Eddie Wilson, Arizona, 134.2; **1962**—Terry Baker, Oregon St., 146.5 (#); **1963**—Bob Berry, Oregon, 164.0; **1964**—Jerry Rhome, Tulsa, 172.6 (#).

(Minimum 15 Attempts Per Game)

Year	Player, Team	G	Att.	Cmp.	Int.	Pct.	Yds.	TD	Pts.
1965	Steve Sloan, Alabama	10	160	97	3	.606	1,453	10	153.8
1966	Dewey Warren, Tennessee	10	229	136	7	.594	1,716	18	142.2
1967	Bill Andrejko, Villanova	10	187	114	6	.610	1,405	13	140.6
1968	Brian Dowling, Yale	9	160	92	10	.575	1,554	19	165.8
1969	#Dennis Shaw, San Diego St.	10	335	199	26	.594	3,185	39	162.2
1970	Jerry Tagge, Nebraska	11	165	104	7	.630	1,383	12	149.0
1971	Jerry Tagge, Nebraska	12	239	143	4	.598	2,019	17	150.9
1972	John Hufnagel, Penn St.	11	216	115	8	.532	2,039	15	148.0
1973	Danny White, Arizona St.	11	265	146	12	.551	2,609	23	157.4
1974	#Steve Joachim, Temple	10	221	128	13	.579	1,950	20	150.1
1975	James Kubacki, Harvard	8	137	77	9	.562	1,273	11	147.6
1976	Steve Haynes, Louisiana Tech	10	216	120	11	.556	1,981	16	146.9
1977	Dave Wilson, Ball St.	11	177	115	7	.650	1,589	17	164.2
1978	Paul McDonald, Southern Cal	11	194	111	7	.572	1,667	18	152.8

(See page 35 for annual leaders beginning in 1979)

#National total-offense champion. %In many seasons during 1946-64, only a few passers threw as many as 15 passes per game; thus, a lower minimum was used.

CAREER YARDS

Player, Team	Years	Att.	Cmp.	Int.	Pct.	Yds.	TD	Long
Ty Detmer, Brigham Young	1988-91	*1,530	*958	65	.626	*15,031	*121	76
Todd Santos, San Diego St.	1984-87	1,484	910	57	.613	11,425	70	84
Eric Zeier, Georgia	1991-94	1,402	838	37	.598	11,153	67	80
Alex Van Pelt, Pittsburgh	1989-92	1,463	845	59	.578	10,913	64	91
Kevin Sweeney, Fresno St.	$1982-86	1,336	731	48	.547	10,623	66	95
Doug Flutie, Boston College	1981-84	1,270	677	54	.533	10,579	67	80
Steve Stenstrom, Stanford	1991-94	1,320	833	36	.631	10,531	72	92
Brian McClure, Bowling Green	1982-85	1,427	900	58	.631	10,280	63	90
Troy Kopp, Pacific (Cal.)	1989-92	1,374	798	47	.581	10,258	87	80
Glenn Foley, Boston College	1990-93	1,275	703	60	.551	10,042	72	78

Player, Team	Years	Att.	Cmp.	Int.	Pct.	Yds.	TD	Long
Ben Bennett, Duke	1980-83	1,375	820	57	.596	9,614	55	88
Jim McMahon, Brigham Young	1977-78, 80-81	1,060	653	34	.616	9,536	84	80
Todd Ellis, South Caro.	1986-89	1,266	704	66	.556	9,519	49	97
David Klingler, Houston	1988-91	1,268	732	38	.577	9,466	91	95
Stoney Case, New Mexico	1991-94	1,237	677	39	.547	9,460	67	79
Erik Wilhelm, Oregon St.	1985-88	1,480	870	61	.588	9,393	52	‡74
Jeremy Leach, New Mexico	1988-91	1,432	735	62	.513	9,382	50	82
John Elway, Stanford	1979-82	1,246	774	39	.621	9,349	77	70
T. J. Rubley, Tulsa	1987-89, 91	1,336	682	54	.510	9,324	73	75
Shane Matthews, Florida	1989-92	1,202	722	46	.601	9,287	74	70
Chuck Long, Iowa	$1981-85	1,072	692	46	‡‡.646	9,210	64	89
Mark Herrmann, Purdue	1977-80	1,218	717	*73	.589	9,188	62	75
Tom Hodson, LSU	1986-89	1,163	674	41	.580	9,115	69	80
Spence Fischer, Duke	1992-95	1,369	786	46	.574	9,021	48	80
Scott Mitchell, Utah	1987-89	1,165	669	38	.574	8,981	68	72
Brad Tayles, Western Mich.	1989-92	1,370	663	67	.484	8,717	49	84
Joe Adams, Tennessee St.	1977-80	1,100	604	60	.549	8,649	81	71
Steve Taneyhill, South Caro.	1992-95	1,209	727	37	.601	8,555	61	93
Marvin Graves, Syracuse	1990-93	943	563	45	.597	8,466	48	84
Shawn Jones, Georgia Tech	1989-92	1,217	652	50	.536	8,441	51	82
Robbie Bosco, Brigham Young	1983-85	997	638	36	.640	8,400	66	‡89
John Walsh, Brigham Young	1991-94	973	587	35	.603	8,375	66	93
Mike McCoy, Long Beach St./Utah	1991, 92-94	1,069	650	26	.608	8,342	56	87
Andre Ware, Houston	1987-89	1,074	660	28	.615	8,202	75	87
Dan McGwire, Iowa/San Diego St.	1986-87, 89-90	973	575	30	.591	8,164	49	71
Jack Trudeau, Illinois	1981, 83-85	1,151	736	38	†.639	8,146	51	83
Troy Taylor, California	1986-89	1,162	683	46	.588	8,126	51	79
Mike Gundy, Oklahoma St.	1986-89	1,037	606	37	.584	8,072	54	‡84
Jeff Graham, Long Beach St.	1985-88	1,175	664	42	.565	8,063	42	85
Randall Cunningham, UNLV	1982-84	1,029	597	29	.580	8,020	59	69
Stan White, Auburn	1990-93	1,231	659	52	.535	8,016	40	78
Steve Slayden, Duke	1984-87	1,204	699	53	.581	8,004	48	73
Robert Hall, Texas Tech	1990-93	997	548	28	.550	7,908	48	95
Dan Marino, Pittsburgh	1979-82	1,084	626	64	.577	7,905	74	65
John Holman, Northeast La.	1979-82	1,201	593	54	.494	7,827	51	85
Jack Thompson, Washington St.	1975-78	1,086	601	49	.553	7,818	53	80
Bobby Fuller, Appalachian St./South Caro.	1987-88, 90-91	1,061	596	32	.562	7,746	52	79
Rob Johnson, Southern Cal	1991-94	963	623	24	.647	7,743	52	72
Steve Young, Brigham Young	1981-83	908	592	33	.652	7,733	56	63
Brett Favre, Southern Miss.	1987-90	1,169	613	34	.524	7,695	52	80
Gino Torretta, Miami (Fla.)	1989-92	991	555	24	.560	7,690	47	99
Terrence Jones, Tulane	1985-88	1,042	570	41	.547	7,684	46	76
John Paye, Stanford	1983-86	1,198	715	44	.597	7,669	38	80
Rodney Peete, Southern Cal	1985-88	972	571	32	.587	7,640	52	‡68

**Record. $See page 6 for explanation. ‡Did not score. †Record for minimum 1,100 attempts. ‡‡Record for minimum 1,000 attempts.*

Photo from Duke sports information

Duke quarterback Spence Fischer finished his career last season 24th in Division I-A career passing yardage with 9,021.

CAREER YARDS RECORD PROGRESSION

(Record Yards—Player, Team, Seasons Played)

3,075—Billy Patterson, Baylor, 1936-38; **3,777**—Bud Schwenk, Washington (Mo.), 1939-41; **4,004**—Johnny Rauch, Georgia, 1945-48; **4,736**—John Ford, Hardin-Simmons, 1947-50; **4,863**—Zeke Bratkowski, Georgia, 1951-53; **5,472**—Jerry Rhome, Southern Methodist, 1961, Tulsa, 1963-64; **6,495**—Billy Stevens, UTEP, 1965-67; **7,076**—Steve Ramsey, North Texas, 1967-69; **7,544**—Jim Plunkett, Stanford, 1968-70; **7,549**—John Reaves, Florida, 1969-71; **7,818**—Jack Thompson, Washington St., 1975-78; **9,188**—Mark Herrmann, Purdue, 1977-80; **9,536**—Jim McMahon, BrighamYoung, 1977-78, 1980-81; **9,614**—Ben Bennett, Duke, 1980-83; **10,579**—Doug Flutie, Boston College, 1981-84; **10,623**—Kevin Sweeney, Fresno St., $1982-86; **11,425**—Todd Santos, San Diego St., 1984-87; **15,031**—Ty Detmer, Brigham Young, 1988-91.

$See page 6 for explanation.

CAREER YARDS PER GAME

(Minimum 5,000 yards)

Player, Team	Years	G	Att.	Cmp.	Int.	Pct.	Yds.	TD	Yd.PG
Ty Detmer, Brigham Young	1988-91	46	*1,530	*958	65	.626	*15,031	*121	*326.8
Chris Vargas, Nevada	1992-93	20	806	502	34	.623	6,359	47	318.0
Mike Perez, San Jose St.	1986-87	20	792	471	30	.595	6,194	36	309.7
Doug Gaynor, Long Beach St.	1984-85	22	837	569	35	.680	6,793	35	308.8
Tony Eason, Illinois	1981-82	22	856	526	29	.614	6,608	37	300.4
David Klingler, Houston	1988-91	32	1,268	732	38	.577	9,466	91	295.8
Brent Snyder, Utah St.	1987-88	22	875	472	36	.539	6,105	39	277.5
Mike Maxwell, Nevada	1993-95	27	881	560	33	.636	7,256	62	268.7
Shane Matthews, Florida	1989-92	35	1,202	722	46	.601	9,287	74	265.3
Larry Egger, Utah	1985-86	22	799	470	31	.588	5,749	39	261.3
Bernie Kosar, Miami (Fla.)	1983-84	23	743	463	29	.623	5,971	40	259.6

**Record.*

CAREER TOUCHDOWN PASSES

Player, Team	Years	G	TD Passes
Ty Detmer, Brigham Young	1988-91	46	*121
David Klingler, Houston	1988-91	32	91
Troy Kopp, Pacific (Cal.)	1989-92	40	87
Jim McMahon, Brigham Young	1977-78, 80-81	44	84
Joe Adams, Tennessee St.	1977-80	41	81

Photo from Florida sports information

Florida's Danny Wuerffel is tied for seventh in Division I-A career touchdown passes with 75.

Player, Team	Years	G	TD Passes
John Elway, Stanford	1979-82	43	77
¢Danny Wuerffel, Florida	1993-95	34	75
Andre Ware, Houston	1987-89	29	75
Shane Matthews, Florida	1989-92	35	74
Dan Marino, Pittsburgh	1979-82	40	74
T. J. Rubley, Tulsa	1987-89, 91	47	73
Steve Stenstrom, Stanford	1991-94	41	72
Glenn Foley, Boston College	1990-93	44	72
Todd Santos, San Diego St.	1984-87	46	70
Tom Hodson, LSU	1986-89	44	69
Steve Ramsey, North Texas	1967-69	29	69
Scott Mitchell, Utah	1987-89	33	68
Stoney Case, New Mexico	1991-94	42	67
Eric Zeier, Georgia	1991-94	44	67
Doug Flutie, Boston College	1981-84	42	67
John Walsh, Brigham Young	1991-94	35	66
Kevin Sweeney, Fresno St.	1983-86	47	66
Robbie Bosco, Brigham Young	1983-85	35	66
Elvis Grbac, Michigan	1989-92	41	64
Alex Van Pelt, Pittsburgh	1989-92	45	64
Chuck Long, Iowa	$1981-85	45	64

¢Active player.
*Record. $See page 6 for explanation.

SEASON YARDS

Player, Team	Year	G	Att.	Cmp.	Int.	Pct.	Yards	TD	Long
Ty Detmer, Brigham Young	1990	12	562	361	28	.642	*5,188	41	69
David Klingler, Houston	1990	11	*643	*374	20	.582	5,140	*54	95
Andre Ware, Houston	1989	11	578	365	15	.631	4,699	46	87
Jim McMahon, Brigham Young	†1980	12	445	284	18	.638	4,571	47	80
Ty Detmer, Brigham Young	†1989	12	412	265	15	.643	4,560	32	67
Scott Mitchell, Utah	1988	11	533	323	15	.606	4,322	29	72
Robbie Bosco, Brigham Young	1985	13	511	338	24	.661	4,273	30	‡89
Chris Vargas, Nevada	1993	11	490	331	18	.676	4,265	34	78
Ty Detmer, Brigham Young	1991	12	403	249	12	.618	4,031	35	97
Todd Santos, San Diego St.	1987	12	492	306	15	.622	3,932	26	74
Steve Young, Brigham Young	†1983	11	429	306	10	*.713	3,902	33	63
Robbie Bosco, Brigham Young	1984	12	458	283	11	.618	3,875	33	54
Mike McCoy, Utah	1993	12	430	276	10	.642	3,860	21	87
Dan McGwire, San Diego St.	1990	11	449	270	7	.601	3,833	27	71
Anthony Dilweg, Duke	1988	11	484	287	18	.593	3,824	24	65
Jimmy Klingler, Houston	1992	11	504	303	18	.601	3,818	32	82
Sam King, UNLV	1981	12	433	255	19	.589	3,778	18	71
Troy Kopp, Pacific (Cal.)	1991	12	449	275	16	.612	3,767	37	68
John Walsh, Brigham Young	1993	11	397	244	15	.615	3,727	28	69
Marc Wilson, Brigham Young	1979	12	427	250	15	.585	3,720	29	‡76
John Walsh, Brigham Young	1994	12	463	284	14	.613	3,712	29	93
Dan McGwire, San Diego St.	1989	12	440	258	19	.586	3,651	16	57
Jim Everett, Purdue	1985	11	450	285	11	.633	3,651	23	70
Bernie Kosar, Miami (Fla.)	1984	12	416	262	16	.630	3,642	25	85
Steve Stenstrom, Stanford	1993	11	455	300	14	.659	3,627	27	91
Mike Maxwell, Nevada	1995	9	409	277	17	.677	3,611	33	87
Jeremy Leach, New Mexico	1989	12	511	282	20	.552	3,573	22	82
Doug Gaynor, Long Beach St.	1985	12	452	321	18	.710	3,563	19	57
Jim McMahon, Brigham Young	†1981	10	423	272	7	.643	3,555	30	‡67
Mike Maxwell, Nevada	1994	11	447	271	15	.606	3,537	29	80
Eric Zeier, Georgia	1993	11	425	269	7	.633	3,525	24	80
Todd Dillon, Long Beach St.	1982	11	504	289	21	.573	3,517	19	‡73

*Record. †National pass-efficiency champion. ‡Did not score.

SEASON YARDS PER GAME

Player, Team	Year	G	Att.	Cmp.	Int.	Pct.	Yards	TD	Yd.PG
David Klingler, Houston	1990	11	*643	*374	20	.582	5,140	*54	*467.3
Ty Detmer, Brigham Young	1990	12	562	361	28	.642	*5,188	41	432.3
Andre Ware, Houston	1989	11	578	365	15	.631	4,699	46	427.2
Mike Maxwell, Nevada	1995	9	409	277	17	.677	3,611	33	401.2
Scott Mitchell, Utah	1988	11	533	323	15	.606	4,322	29	392.9
Chris Vargas, Nevada	1993	11	490	331	18	.676	4,265	34	387.7
Jim McMahon, Brigham Young	†1980	12	445	284	18	.638	4,571	47	380.9
Ty Detmer, Brigham Young	†1989	12	412	265	15	.643	4,560	32	380.0
Troy Kopp, Pacific (Cal.)	1990	9	428	243	14	.568	3,311	31	367.9
Jim McMahon, Brigham Young	†1981	10	423	272	7	.643	3,555	30	355.5
Steve Young, Brigham Young	†1983	11	429	306	10	*.713	3,902	33	354.7
Dan McGwire, San Diego St.	1990	11	449	270	7	.601	3,833	27	348.5
Anthony Dilweg, Duke	1988	11	484	287	18	.593	3,824	24	347.6
Jimmy Klingler, Houston	1992	11	504	303	18	.601	3,818	32	347.1
Bill Anderson, Tulsa	†1965	10	509	296	14	.582	3,464	30	346.4
David Klingler, Houston	1991	10	497	278	17	.559	3,388	29	338.8
Marc Wilson, Brigham Young	1979	12	427	250	15	.585	3,720	29	338.2

*Record. †National pass-efficiency champion.

SEASON TOUCHDOWN PASSES

Player, Team	Year	G	TD Passes
David Klingler, Houston	1990	11	*54
Jim McMahon, Brigham Young	1980	12	47
Andre Ware, Houston	1989	11	46
Ty Detmer, Brigham Young	1990	12	41
Dennis Shaw, San Diego St.	1969	10	39
Doug Williams, Grambling	1977	11	38
Troy Kopp, Pacific (Cal.)	1991	12	37
Danny Wuerffel, Florida	1995	11	35
Ty Detmer, Brigham Young	1991	12	35
Chris Vargas, Nevada	1993	11	34
Dan Marino, Pittsburgh	1981	11	34
Mike Maxwell, Nevada	1995	9	33
Robbie Bosco, Brigham Young	1984	12	33
Steve Young, Brigham Young	1983	11	33
Danny Kanell, Florida St.	1995	11	32
Jimmy Klingler, Houston	1992	11	32
Ty Detmer, Brigham Young	1989	12	32
Jerry Rhome, Tulsa	1964	10	32
Troy Kopp, Pacific (Cal.)	1990	9	31

**Record.*

CAREER YARDS PER ATTEMPT

(Minimum 900 Attempts)

Player, Team	Years	Att.	Cmp.	Pct.	Yards	Yards Per Cmp.	Yards Per Att.
Ty Detmer, Brigham Young	1988-91	*1,530	*958	.626	*15,031	*15.69	*9.82
Jim McMahon, Brigham Young	1977-78, 80-81	1,060	653	.616	9,536	14.60	9.00
Marvin Graves, Syracuse	1990-93	943	563	.597	8,466	15.04	8.98
John Walsh, Brigham Young	1991-94	973	587	.603	8,375	14.27	8.61
Chuck Long, Iowa	$1981-85	1,072	692	#.646	9,210	13.31	8.59
Steve Young, Brigham Young	1981-83	908	592	.652	7,733	13.06	8.52
Robbie Bosco, Brigham Young	1983-85	997	638	.640	8,400	13.17	8.43
Dan McGwire, Iowa/San Diego St.	1986-87, 89-90	973	575	.591	8,164	14.20	8.39
Doug Flutie, Boston College	1981-84	1,270	677	.533	10,579	15.63	8.33
Marc Wilson, Brigham Young	1977-79	937	535	.571	7,637	14.27	8.15
Rob Johnson, Southern Cal	1991-94	963	623	.647	7,743	12.43	8.04
Steve Stenstrom, Stanford	1991-94	1,320	833	.631	10,531	12.64	7.98
Kerwin Bell, Florida	1984-87	953	549	.576	7,585	13.82	7.96
Eric Zeier, Georgia	1991-94	1,402	838	.598	11,153	13.31	7.96
Kevin Sweeney, Fresno St.	$1982-86	1,336	731	.547	10,623	14.53	7.95
Robert Hall, Texas Tech	1990-93	997	548	.550	7,908	14.43	7.93
Glenn Foley, Boston College	1990-93	1,275	703	.551	10,042	14.28	7.88
Joe Adams, Tennessee St.	1977-80	1,100	604	.549	8,649	14.32	7.86
Rodney Peete, Southern Cal	1985-88	972	571	.587	7,640	13.38	7.86
Tom Hodson, LSU	1986-89	1,163	674	.580	9,115	13.52	7.84
Jim Plunkett, Stanford	1968-70	962	530	.551	7,544	14.23	7.84

**Record. $See page 6 for explanation. #Record for minimum 1,000 attempts.*

SINGLE-GAME YARDS

Yds.	Player, Team (Opponent)	Date
716	David Klingler, Houston (Arizona St.)	Dec. 2, 1990
690	Matt Vogler, Texas Christian (Houston)	Nov. 3, 1990
631	Scott Mitchell, Utah (Air Force)	Oct. 15, 1988
622	Jeremy Leach, New Mexico (Utah)	Nov. 11, 1989
621	Dave Wilson, Illinois (Ohio St.)	Nov. 8, 1980
619	John Walsh, Brigham Young (Utah St.)	Oct. 30, 1993
613	Jimmy Klingler, Houston (Rice)	Nov. 28, 1992
599	Ty Detmer, Brigham Young (San Diego St.)	Nov. 16, 1991
585	Robbie Bosco, Brigham Young (New Mexico)	Oct. 19, 1985
572	David Klingler, Houston (Eastern Wash.)	Nov. 17, 1990
571	Marc Wilson, Brigham Young (Utah)	Nov. 5, 1977
568	David Lowery, San Diego St. (Brigham Young)	Nov. 16, 1991
565	Jim McMahon, Brigham Young (Utah)	Nov. 21, 1981
564	Troy Kopp, Pacific, Cal. (New Mexico St.)	Oct. 20, 1990
563	David Klingler, Houston (Texas Christian)	Nov. 3, 1990
561	Tony Adams, Utah St. (Utah)	Nov. 11, 1972
560	Ty Detmer, Brigham Young (Utah St.)	Nov. 24, 1990
558	Chuck Hartlieb, Iowa (Indiana)	Oct. 29, 1988
554	Greg Cook, Cincinnati (Ohio)	Nov. 16, 1968
552	Mike Maxwell, Nevada (UNLV)	Oct. 28, 1995
546	Cody Ledbetter, New Mexico St. (UNLV)	Nov. 18, 1995
545	Rusty LaRue, Wake Forest (North Caro. St.)	Nov. 18, 1995
544	Eric Zeier, Georgia (Southern Miss.)	Oct. 9, 1993
538	Chris Vargas, Nevada (UNLV)	Oct. 2, 1993
538	Jim McMahon, Brigham Young (Colorado St.)	Nov. 7, 1981
537	Ty Detmer, Brigham Young (Washington St.)	Sept. 7, 1989
536	Dave Telford, Fresno St. (Pacific, Cal.)	Oct. 24, 1987
536	Todd Santos, San Diego St. (Stanford)	Oct. 17, 1987
536	David Spriggs, New Mexico St. (Southern Ill.)	Sept. 30, 1978
535	Mike Maxwell, Nevada (Louisiana Tech)	Oct. 21, 1995
535	Shane Montgomery, North Caro. St. (Duke)	Nov. 11, 1989
534	Paul Justin, Arizona St. (Washington St.)	Oct. 28, 1989
533	David Klingler, Houston (Texas Tech)	Nov. 30, 1991
532	Jeff Van Raaphorst, Arizona St. (Florida St.)	Nov. 3, 1984

File photo

Although four seasons of high-octane offense have passed since he finished his collegiate career, Brigham Young's Ty Detmer still holds Division I-A career records for passing attempts (1,530), completions (958), yards (15,031), and yards per completion (15.7) and attempt (9.8).

Photo from Maryland sports information

In a November 18, 1995, game against Florida State, Maryland quarterback Scott Milanovich completed 46 passes, the fourth highest total in Division I-A history.

SINGLE-GAME ATTEMPTS

No.	Player, Team (Opponent)	Date
79	Matt Vogler, Texas Christian (Houston)	Nov. 3, 1990
78	Rusty LaRue, Wake Forest (Duke)	Oct. 28, 1995
76	David Klingler, Houston (Southern Methodist)	Oct. 20, 1990
75	Chris Vargas, Nevada (McNeese St.)	Sept. 19, 1992
73	Jeff Handy, Missouri (Oklahoma St.)	Oct. 17, 1992
73	Troy Kopp, Pacific, Cal. (Hawaii)	Oct. 27, 1990
73	Shane Montgomery, North Caro. St. (Duke)	Nov. 11, 1989
72	Matt Vogler, Texas Christian (Texas Tech)	Nov. 10, 1990
71	Jimmy Klingler, Houston (Rice)	Nov. 28, 1992
71	Sandy Schwab, Northwestern (Michigan)	Oct. 23, 1982
70	David Klingler, Houston (Texas Tech)	Nov. 30, 1991
70	David Klingler, Houston (Arizona St.)	Dec. 2, 1990
70	Dave Telford, Fresno St. (Utah St.)	Nov. 14, 1987
69	Dave Wilson, Illinois (Ohio St.)	Nov. 8, 1980
69	Chuck Hixson, Southern Methodist (Ohio St.)	Sept. 28, 1968
68	David Klingler, Houston (Baylor)	Oct. 6, 1990
68	Jeremy Leach, New Mexico (Utah)	Nov. 11, 1989
68	Steve Smith, Stanford (Notre Dame)	Oct. 7, 1989
68	Andre Ware, Houston (Arizona St.)	Sept. 23, 1989
67	Rusty LaRue, Wake Forest (North Caro. St.)	Nov. 18, 1995
67	Danny Kanell, Florida St. (Virginia)	Nov. 2, 1995
67	Mike Hohensee, Minnesota (Ohio St.)	Nov. 7, 1981
66	Chuck Clements, Houston (Cincinnati)	Nov. 13, 1993
66	Tim Schade, Minnesota (Penn St.)	Sept. 4, 1993
66	Drew Bledsoe, Washington St. (Montana)	Sept. 5, 1992
66	Jack Trudeau, Illinois (Purdue)	Oct. 12, 1985
66	John Reaves, Florida (Auburn)	Nov. 1, 1969
65	Rusty LaRue, Wake Forest (Georgia Tech)	Nov. 4, 1995
65	Jason Martin, Louisiana Tech (Nevada)	Oct. 21, 1995
65	Eric Zeier, Georgia (Florida)	Oct. 30, 1993
65	Jimmy Klingler, Houston (Texas Christian)	Oct. 31, 1992
65	Scott Mitchell, Utah (UTEP)	Oct. 1, 1988
65	Mike Bates, Miami, Ohio (Toledo)	Oct. 24, 1987
65	Craig Burnett, Wyoming (San Diego St.)	Nov. 15, 1986
65	Gary Schofield, Wake Forest (Maryland)	Oct. 16, 1982
65	Jim McMahon, Brigham Young (Colorado St.)	Nov. 7, 1981
65	Brooks Dawson, UTEP (UC Santa Barb.)	Sept. 14, 1968
65	Bill Anderson, Tulsa (Southern Ill.)	Oct. 30, 1965
65	Bill Anderson, Tulsa (Memphis)	Oct. 9, 1965

SINGLE-GAME COMPLETIONS

No.	Player, Team (Opponent)	Date
55	Rusty LaRue, Wake Forest (Duke)	Oct. 28, 1995
50	Rusty LaRue, Wake Forest (North Caro. St.)	Nov. 18, 1995
48	David Klingler, Houston (Southern Methodist)	Oct. 20, 1990
46	Scott Milanovich, Maryland (Florida St.)	Nov. 18, 1995
46	Jimmy Klingler, Houston (Rice)	Nov. 28, 1992
45	Sandy Schwab, Northwestern (Michigan)	Oct. 23, 1982
44	Matt Vogler, Texas Christian (Houston)	Nov. 3, 1990
44	Chuck Hartlieb, Iowa (Indiana)	Oct. 29, 1988
44	Jim McMahon, Brigham Young (Colorado St.)	Nov. 7, 1981
43	Jeff Handy, Missouri (Oklahoma St.)	Oct. 17, 1992
43	Chris Vargas, Nevada (McNeese St.)	Sept. 19, 1992
43	Gary Schofield, Wake Forest (Maryland)	Oct. 17, 1981
43	Dave Wilson, Illinois (Ohio St.)	Nov. 8, 1980
43	Rich Campbell, California (Florida)	Sept. 13, 1980
42	Jimmy Klingler, Houston (Texas Christian)	Oct. 31, 1992
42	Troy Kopp, Pacific, Cal. (Hawaii)	Oct. 27, 1990
42	Andre Ware, Houston (Texas Christian)	Nov. 4, 1989
42	Dan Speltz, Cal St. Fullerton (Utah St.)	Oct. 7, 1989
42	Robbie Bosco, Brigham Young (New Mexico)	Oct. 19, 1985
42	Bill Anderson, Tulsa (Southern Ill.)	Oct. 30, 1965
41	Rusty LaRue, Wake Forest (Georgia Tech)	Nov. 4, 1995
41	Mike Maxwell, Nevada (UNLV)	Oct. 28, 1995
41	Danny Kanell, Florida St. (Georgia Tech)	Oct. 21, 1995
41	David Klingler, Houston (Texas Tech)	Nov. 30, 1991
41	David Klingler, Houston (Arizona St.)	Dec. 2, 1990
41	David Klingler, Houston (Eastern Wash.)	Nov. 17, 1990
41	Jeremy Leach, New Mexico (Utah)	Nov. 11, 1989
41	Scott Mitchell, Utah (UTEP)	Oct. 1, 1988
41	Doug Gaynor, Long Beach St. (Utah St.)	Sept. 7, 1985
40	Danny Kanell, Florida St. (Florida)	Nov. 26, 1994
40	Mike Romo, Southern Methodist (Rice)	Nov. 10, 1990
40	Andre Ware, Houston (Arizona St.)	Sept. 23, 1989
40	Dave Telford, Fresno St. (Utah St.)	Nov. 14, 1987
40	Todd Santos, San Diego St. (Stanford)	Oct. 17, 1987
40	Larry Egger, Utah (UTEP)	Nov. 29, 1986
40	John Paye, Stanford (San Diego St.)	Oct. 5, 1985
40	Gary Schofield, Wake Forest (Maryland)	Oct. 16, 1982
40	Jim McMahon, Brigham Young (North Texas)	Nov. 8, 1980

ANNUAL CHAMPIONS

Year	Player, Team	Class	Att.	Cmp.	Int.	Pct.	Yds.	TD
1937	Davey O'Brien, Texas Christian	Jr.	234	94	18	.402	969	—
1938	Davey O'Brien, Texas Christian	Sr.	167	93	4	.557	1,457	—
1939	Kay Eakin, Arkansas	Sr.	193	78	18	.404	962	—
1940	Billy Sewell, Washington St.	Sr.	174	86	17	.494	1,023	—
1941	Bud Schwenk, Washington (Mo.)	Sr.	234	114	19	.487	1,457	—
1942	Ray Evans, Kansas	Jr.	200	101	9	.505	1,117	—
1943	Johnny Cook, Georgia	Fr.	157	73	20	.465	1,007	—
1944	Paul Rickards, Pittsburgh	So.	178	84	20	.472	997	—
1945	Al Dekdebrun, Cornell	Sr.	194	90	15	.464	1,227	—
1946	Travis Tidwell, Auburn	Fr.	158	79	10	.500	943	5
1947	Charlie Conerly, Mississippi	Sr.	233	133	7	.571	1,367	18
1948	Stan Heath, Nevada	Sr.	222	126	9	.568	2,005	22
1949	Adrian Burk, Baylor	Sr.	191	110	6	.576	1,428	14
1950	Don Heinrich, Washington	Jr.	221	134	9	.606	1,846	14
1951	Don Klosterman, Loyola Marymount	Sr.	315	159	21	.505	1,843	9
1952	Don Heinrich, Washington	Sr.	270	137	17	.507	1,647	13
1953	Bob Garrett, Stanford	Sr.	205	118	10	.576	1,637	17
1954	Paul Larson, California	Sr.	195	125	8	.641	1,537	10
1955	George Welsh, Navy	Sr.	150	94	6	.627	1,319	8
1956	John Brodie, Stanford	Sr.	240	139	14	.579	1,633	12
1957	Ken Ford, Hardin-Simmons	Sr.	205	115	11	.561	1,254	14
1958	Buddy Humphrey, Baylor	Sr.	195	112	8	.574	1,316	7
1959	Dick Norman, Stanford	Jr.	263	152	12	.578	1,963	11
1960	Harold Stephens, Hardin-Simmons	Sr.	256	145	14	.566	1,254	3
1961	Chon Gallegos, San Jose St.	Sr.	197	117	13	.594	1,480	14
1962	Don Trull, Baylor	Jr.	229	125	12	.546	1,627	11
1963	Don Trull, Baylor	Sr.	308	174	12	.565	2,157	12
1964	Jerry Rhome, Tulsa	Sr.	326	224	4	.687	2,870	32
1965	Bill Anderson, Tulsa	Sr.	509	296	14	.582	3,464	30
1966	John Eckman, Wichita St.	Jr.	458	195	*34	.426	2,339	7
1967	Terry Stone, New Mexico	Jr.	336	160	19	.476	1,946	9
1968	Chuck Hixson, Southern Methodist	So.	468	265	23	.566	3,103	21
1969	John Reaves, Florida	So.	396	222	19	.561	2,896	24

Beginning in 1970, ranked on per-game (instead of total) completions

Year	Player, Team	Class	G	Att.	Cmp.	Avg.	Int.	Pct.	Yds.	TD
1970	Sonny Sixkiller, Washington	So.	10	362	186	18.6	22	.514	2,303	15
1971	Brian Sipe, San Diego St.	Sr.	11	369	196	17.8	21	.531	2,532	17
1972	Don Strock, Virginia Tech	Sr.	11	427	228	20.7	27	.534	3,243	16
1973	Jesse Freitas, San Diego St.	Sr.	11	347	227	20.6	17	.654	2,993	21
1974	Steve Bartkowski, California	Sr.	11	325	182	16.5	7	.560	2,580	12
1975	Craig Penrose, San Diego St.	Sr.	11	349	198	18.0	24	.567	2,660	15
1976	Tommy Kramer, Rice	Sr.	11	501	269	24.5	19	.537	3,317	21
1977	Guy Benjamin, Stanford	Sr.	10	330	208	20.8	15	.630	2,521	19
1978	Steve Dils, Stanford	Sr.	11	391	247	22.5	15	.632	2,943	22

Beginning in 1979, ranked on passing efficiency rating points (instead of per-game completions)

Year	Player, Team	Class	G	Att.	Cmp.	Int.	Pct.	Yds.	TD	Pts.
1979	Turk Schonert, Stanford	Sr.	11	221	148	6	.670	1,922	19	163.0
1980	Jim McMahon, Brigham Young	Jr.	12	445	284	18	.638	4,571	47	176.9
1981	Jim McMahon, Brigham Young	Sr.	10	423	272	7	.643	3,555	30	155.0
1982	Tom Ramsey, UCLA	Sr.	11	311	191	10	.614	2,824	21	153.5
1983	Steve Young, Brigham Young	Sr.	11	429	306	10	*.713	3,902	33	168.5
1984	Doug Flutie, Boston College	Sr.	11	386	233	11	.604	3,454	27	152.9
1985	Jim Harbaugh, Michigan	Jr.	11	212	139	6	.656	1,913	18	163.7
1986	Vinny Testaverde, Miami (Fla.)	Sr.	10	276	175	9	.634	2,557	26	165.8
1987	Don McPherson, Syracuse	Sr.	11	229	129	11	.563	2,341	22	164.3
1988	Timm Rosenbach, Washington St.	Jr.	11	302	199	10	.659	2,791	23	162.0
1989	Ty Detmer, Brigham Young	So.	12	412	265	15	.643	4,560	32	175.6
1990	Shawn Moore, Virginia	Sr.	10	241	144	8	.598	2,262	21	160.7
1991	Elvis Grbac, Michigan	Jr.	11	228	152	5	.667	1,955	24	169.0
1992	Elvis Grbac, Michigan	Sr.	9	169	112	12	.663	1,465	15	154.2
1993	Trent Dilfer, Fresno St.	Jr.	11	333	217	4	.652	3,276	28	173.1
1994	Kerry Collins, Penn St.	Sr.	11	264	176	7	.667	2,679	21	172.9
1995	Danny Wuerffel, Florida	Jr.	11	325	210	10	.646	3,266	35	*178.4

**Record.*

Photo from Southern California sports information

Keyshawn Johnson's two-year collegiate career went by much too fast for Southern California fans. The standout receiver played in just 21 regular-season games for the Trojans but averaged 7.1 receptions and 112.3 yards per game.

Receiving

CAREER RECEPTIONS PER GAME

(Minimum 125 Receptions)

Player, Team	Years	G	Rec.	Yards	TD	Rec.PG
Manny Hazard, Houston	1989-90	21	220	2,635	31	*10.5
Alex Van Dyke, Nevada	1994-95	22	227	3,100	26	10.3
Howard Twilley, Tulsa	1963-65	26	261	3,343	32	10.0
Jason Phillips, Houston	1987-88	22	207	2,319	18	9.4
Bryan Reeves, Nevada	1992-93	21	172	2,476	27	8.2
David Williams, Illinois	1983-85	33	245	3,195	22	7.4
James Dixon, Houston	1987-88	22	161	1,762	14	7.3
John Love, North Texas	1965-66	20	144	2,124	17	7.2
Fred Gilbert, UCLA/Houston	1989, 91-92	22	158	1,672	14	7.2
Ron Sellers, Florida St.	1966-68	30	212	3,598	23	7.1
Keyshawn Johnson, Southern Cal	1994-95	21	148	2,358	12	7.1
Barry Moore, North Texas	1968-69	20	140	2,183	12	7.0
Mike Kelly, Davidson	1967-69	23	156	2,114	17	6.8
Guy Liggins, San Jose St.	1986-87	22	149	2,191	16	6.8
Dave Petzke, Northern Ill.	1977-78	22	148	1,960	16	6.7
Loren Richey, Utah	1985-86	21	140	1,746	13	6.7
Chris Penn, Tulsa	1991, 93	22	142	2,370	17	6.5
Tim Delaney, San Diego St.	1968-70	29	180	2,535	22	6.2
Larry Willis, Fresno St.	1983-84	23	142	2,260	14	6.2
Phil Odle, Brigham Young	1965-67	30	183	2,548	25	6.1

Player, Team	Years	G	Rec.	Yards	TD	Rec.PG
Randy Gatewood, UNLV	1993-94	21	128	1,832	13	6.1
Aaron Turner, Pacific (Cal.)	1989-92	44	*266	4,345	*43	6.0
Mike Mikolayunas, Davidson	1968-70	29	175	1,768	14	6.0
Terance Mathis, New Mexico	1985-87, 89	44	263	4,254	36	6.0
Michael Stephens, Nevada	1992-93	21	125	1,712	15	6.0

*Record.

SEASON RECEPTIONS PER GAME

Player, Team	Year	G	Rec.	Yards	TD	Rec.PG
Howard Twilley, Tulsa	†1965	10	134	1,779	16	*13.4
Manny Hazard, Houston	†1989	11	*142	1,689	*22	12.9
Alex Van Dyke, Nevada	†1995	11	129	*1,854	16	11.7
Jason Phillips, Houston	†1988	11	108	1,444	15	9.8
Fred Gilbert, Houston	†1991	11	106	957	7	9.6
Chris Penn, Tulsa	†1993	11	105	1,578	12	9.5
Jerry Hendren, Idaho	†1969	10	95	1,452	12	9.5
Howard Twilley, Tulsa	†1964	10	95	1,178	13	9.5
Sherman Smith, Houston	†1992	11	103	923	6	9.4
James Dixon, Houston	1988	11	102	1,103	11	9.3
David Williams, Illinois	†1984	11	101	1,278	8	9.2
Bryan Reeves, Nevada	1993	10	91	1,362	17	9.1
Glenn Meltzer, Wichita St.	†1966	10	91	1,115	4	9.1
Jay Miller, Brigham Young	†1973	11	100	1,181	8	9.1

*Record. †National champion.

CAREER RECEPTIONS

Player, Team	Years	Rec.	Yards	Avg.	TD
Aaron Turner, Pacific (Cal.)	1989-92	*266	4,345	16.3	*43
Terance Mathis, New Mexico	1985-87, 89	263	4,254	16.2	36
Mark Templeton, Long Beach St. (RB)	1983-86	262	1,969	7.5	11
Howard Twilley, Tulsa	1963-65	261	3,343	12.8	32
David Williams, Illinois	1983-85	245	3,195	13.0	22
Marc Zeno, Tulane	1984-87	236	3,725	15.8	25
Jason Wolf, Southern Methodist	1989-92	235	2,232	9.5	17
Ryan Yarborough, Wyoming	1990-93	229	*4,357	‡19.0	42
Alex Van Dyke, Nevada	1994-95	227	3,100	13.7	26
Manny Hazard, Houston	1989-90	220	2,635	12.0	31
Darrin Nelson, Stanford (RB)	1977-78, 80-81	214	2,368	11.1	16
Ron Sellers, Florida St.	1966-68	212	3,598	17.0	23
Jason Phillips, Houston	1987-88	207	2,319	11.2	18
Hart Lee Dykes, Oklahoma St.	1985-88	203	3,171	15.6	29
Carl Winston, New Mexico	1990-93	202	2,972	14.7	14
Keith Edwards, Vanderbilt	1980, 82-84	200	1,757	8.8	3
Bobby Slaughter, Louisiana Tech	1987-90	198	2,544	12.9	14
Richard Buchanan, Northwestern	1987-90	197	2,474	12.6	22
Gerald Harp, Western Caro.	1977-80	197	3,305	16.8	26
Matt Bellini, Brigham Young (RB)	1987-90	196	2,544	13.0	13
Brad Muster, Stanford (FB)	1984-87	196	1,669	8.5	6
Jermaine Lewis, Maryland	1992-95	193	2,932	15.2	21
Greg Primus, Colorado St.	1989-92	192	3,200	16.7	16
Charles Lockett, Long Beach St.	1983-86	191	2,902	15.1	19
Pete Mitchell, Boston College (TE)	1991-94	190	2,389	12.6	20
Kez McCorvey, Florida St.	1991-94	189	2,660	14.1	16
Lloyd Hill, Texas Tech	1990-93	189	3,059	16.2	20
Clarkston Hines, Duke	1986-89	189	3,318	17.6	38
Wil Ursin, Tulane	1990-93	188	2,466	13.1	17
Ricky Proehl, Wake Forest	1986-89	188	2,949	15.7	25
Boo Mitchell, Vanderbilt	1985-88	188	2,964	15.8	9
Monty Gilbreath, San Diego St.	1986-89	187	2,241	12.0	8
Mick Rossley, Southern Methodist	1991-94	186	1,911	10.3	10
Eric Henley, Rice	1988-91	186	2,200	11.8	16
Johnnie Morton, Southern Cal	1990-93	185	2,957	16.0	21
Jeff Champine, Colorado St.	1980-83	184	2,811	15.3	21
Wendell Davis, LSU	1984-85	183	2,708	14.8	19
Phil Odle, Brigham Young	1965-67	183	2,548	13.9	25
Brice Hunter, Georgia	1992-95	182	2,373	13.0	19
Mark Szlachcic, Bowling Green	1989-92	182	2,507	13.8	18
Charlie Jones, Fresno St.	1992-95	181	3,260	18.0	25
Kelly Blackwell, Texas Christian (TE)	1988-91	181	2,155	11.9	13
Tim Delaney, San Diego St.	1968-70	180	2,535	14.1	22
Michael Smith, Kansas St.	1988-91	179	2,457	13.7	11
Darnay Scott, San Diego St.	1991-93	178	3,139	17.6	25
Walter Murray, Hawaii	1982-85	178	2,865	16.1	20
Gordon Hudson, Brigham Young (TE)	1980-83	178	2,484	14.0	22
Rick Beasley, Appalachian St.	1978-80	178	3,124	17.6	23
Bryan Rowley, Utah	$1989-93	177	3,143	17.8	25

*Record. $See page 6 for explanation. ‡Record for minimum of 200 catches.

SEASON RECEPTIONS

Player, Team	Year	G	Rec.	Yards	TD
Manny Hazard, Houston	†1989	11	*142	1,689	*22
Howard Twilley, Tulsa	†1965	10	134	1,779	16
Alex Van Dyke, Nevada	†1995	11	129	*1,854	16
Jason Phillips, Houston	†1988	11	108	1,444	15
Fred Gilbert, Houston	†1991	11	106	957	7
Chris Penn, Tulsa	†1993	11	105	1,578	12
Sherman Smith, Houston	†1992	11	103	923	6
James Dixon, Houston	1988	11	102	1,103	11
David Williams, Illinois	†1984	11	101	1,278	8
Jay Miller, Brigham Young	†1973	11	100	1,181	8
Jason Phillips, Houston	†1987	11	99	875	3
Mark Templeton, Long Beach St. (RB)	†1986	11	99	688	2
Alex Van Dyke, Nevada	†1994	11	98	1,246	10
Rodney Carter, Purdue	†1985	11	98	1,099	4
Keith Edwards, Vanderbilt	†1983	11	97	909	0
Jerry Hendren, Idaho	†1969	10	95	1,452	12
Howard Twilley, Tulsa	†1964	10	95	1,178	13
Richard Buchanan, Northwestern	1989	11	94	1,115	9
Kevin Alexander, Utah St.	1995	11	92	1,400	6
Aaron Turner, Pacific (Cal.)	1991	11	92	1,604	18
Bryan Reeves, Nevada	1993	10	91	1,362	17
Dave Petzke, Northern Ill.	†1978	11	91	1,217	11
Glenn Meltzer, Wichita St.	†1966	10	91	1,115	4

*Record. †National champion.

SEASON TOUCHDOWN RECEPTIONS

Player, Team	Year	G	TD
Manny Hazard, Houston	1989	11	*22
Desmond Howard, Michigan	1991	11	19
Aaron Turner, Pacific (Cal.)	1991	11	18
Dennis Smith, Utah	1989	12	18
Tom Reynolds, San Diego St.	1971	10	18
Terry Glenn, Ohio St.	1995	11	17
Chris Doering, Florida	1995	12	17
Bryan Reeves, Nevada	1993	10	17
J. J. Stokes, UCLA	1993	11	17
Mario Bailey, Washington	1991	11	17
Clarkston Hines, Duke	1989	11	17
Alex Van Dyke, Nevada	1995	11	16
Ryan Yarborough, Wyoming	1993	11	16
Dan Bitson, Tulsa	1989	11	16
Howard Twilley, Tulsa	1965	10	16
Andre Cooper, Florida St.	1995	11	15
Ike Hilliard, Florida	1995	11	15
Jack Jackson, Florida	1994	12	15
Jason Phillips, Houston	1988	11	15
Henry Ellard, Fresno St.	1982	11	15

*Record.

SINGLE-GAME RECEPTIONS

Rec.	Player, Team (Opponent)	Date
23	Randy Gatewood, UNLV (Idaho)	Sept. 17, 1994
22	Jay Miller, Brigham Young (New Mexico)	Nov. 3, 1973
20	Rick Eber, Tulsa (Idaho St.)	Oct. 7, 1967
19	Manny Hazard, Houston (Texas)	Nov. 11, 1989
19	Manny Hazard, Houston (Texas Christian)	Nov. 4, 1989
19	Ron Fair, Arizona St. (Washington St.)	Oct. 28, 1989
19	Howard Twilley, Tulsa (Colorado St.)	Nov. 27, 1965
18	Alex Van Dyke, Nevada (UNLV)	Oct. 28, 1995
18	Alex Van Dyke, Nevada (Toledo)	Sept. 23, 1995
18	Richard Woodley, Texas Christian (Texas Tech)	Nov. 10, 1990
18	Mark Templeton (RB), Long Beach St. (Utah St.)	Nov. 1, 1986
18	Howard Twilley, Tulsa (Southern Ill.)	Oct. 30, 1965
17	Willie Gosha, Auburn (Arkansas)	Oct. 28, 1995
17	Chad Mackey, Louisiana Tech (Nevada)	Oct. 21, 1995
17	Curtis Shearer, San Diego St. (Air Force)	Oct. 1, 1994
17	Loren Richey, Utah (UTEP)	Nov. 29, 1986
17	Keith Edwards, Vanderbilt (Georgia)	Oct. 15, 1983
17	Jon Harvey, Northwestern (Michigan)	Oct. 23, 1982
17	Don Roberts, San Diego St. (California)	Sept. 18, 1982
17	Tom Reynolds, San Diego St. (Utah St.)	Oct. 22, 1971
17	Mike Mikolayunas, Davidson (Richmond)	Oct. 11, 1969
17	Jerry Hendren, Idaho (Southern Miss.)	Oct. 4, 1969
17	Emilio Vallez, New Mexico (New Mexico St.)	Oct. 27, 1967
17	Chuck Hughes, UTEP (Arizona St.)	Oct. 30, 1965

CAREER YARDS

Player, Team	Years	Rec.	Yards	Avg.	TD
Ryan Yarborough, Wyoming	1990-93	229	*4,357	#19.0	42
Aaron Turner, Pacific (Cal.)	1989-92	*266	4,345	16.3	*43
Terance Mathis, New Mexico	1985-87, 89	263	4,254	16.2	36
Marc Zeno, Tulane	1984-87	236	3,725	15.8	25
Ron Sellers, Florida St.	1966-68	212	3,598	17.0	23
Elmo Wright, Houston	1968-70	153	3,347	21.9	34
Howard Twilley, Tulsa	1963-65	261	3,343	12.8	32
Clarkston Hines, Duke	1986-89	189	3,318	17.6	38

Player, Team	Years	Rec.	Yards	Avg.	TD
Gerald Harp, Western Caro.	1977-80	197	3,305	16.8	26
Dan Bitson, Tulsa	1987-89, 91	163	3,300	20.2	29
Charlie Jones, Fresno St.	1992-95	181	3,260	18.0	25
Greg Primus, Colorado St.	1989-92	192	3,200	16.7	16
David Williams, Illinois	1983-85	245	3,195	13.0	22
Hart Lee Dykes, Oklahoma St.	1985-88	203	3,171	15.6	29
Bryan Rowley, Utah	$1989-93	177	3,143	17.8	25
Darnay Scott, San Diego St.	1991-93	178	3,139	17.6	25
Rick Beasley, Appalachian St.	1978-80	178	3,124	17.6	23
Alex Van Dyke, Nevada	1994-95	227	3,100	13.7	26
Eric Drage, Brigham Young	1990-93	162	3,065	18.9	29
Lloyd Hill, Texas Tech	1990-93	189	3,059	16.2	20
Bobby Engram, Penn St.	1991, 93-95	167	3,026	18.1	31
Carl Winston, New Mexico	1990-93	202	2,972	14.7	14
Johnnie Morton, Southern Cal	1990-93	185	2,957	16.0	21
Ricky Proehl, Wake Forest	1986-89	188	2,949	15.7	25
Henry Ellard, Fresno St.	1979-82	138	2,947	21.4	25
Kendal Smith, Utah St.	1985-88	169	2,943	17.4	25
Jermaine Lewis, Maryland	1992-95	193	2,932	15.2	21
Charles Lockett, Long Beach St.	1983-86	191	2,902	15.1	19
Chuck Hughes, UTEP	1964-66	162	2,882	17.8	19
Walter Murray, Hawaii	1982-85	178	2,865	16.1	20

Record. $See page 6 for explanation. #Record for minimum 200 catches.

CAREER YARDS PER GAME
(Minimum 2,200 Yards)

Player, Team	Years	G	Yards	Yd.PG
Alex Van Dyke, Nevada	1994-95	22	3,100	*140.9
Manny Hazard, Houston	1989-90	21	2,635	125.5
Ron Sellers, Florida St.	1966-68	30	3,598	119.9
Bryan Reeves, Nevada	1992-93	21	2,476	117.9
Keyshawn Johnson, Southern Cal	1994-95	21	2,358	112.3
Elmo Wright, Houston	1968-70	30	3,347	111.6
Howard Twilley, Tulsa	1963-65	30	3,343	111.4
Chris Penn, Tulsa	1991, 93	22	2,370	107.7
Jason Phillips, Houston	1987-88	22	2,319	105.4
Aaron Turner, Pacific (Cal.)	1989-92	44	4,345	98.8
Rick Beasley, Appalachian St.	†1977-80	32	3,124	97.6
David Williams, Illinois	1982-85	33	3,195	96.8
Terance Mathis, New Mexico	1985-87, 89	44	4,254	96.7
Ryan Yarborough, Wyoming	1990-93	46	*4,357	94.7
Darnay Scott, San Diego St.	1991-93	34	3,139	92.3
Lloyd Hill, Texas Tech	1990-93	34	3,059	90.0
Marc Zeno, Tulane	1984-87	44	3,725	84.7
Tim Delaney, San Diego St.	1968-70	30	2,535	84.5

Record. †Played defensive back in 1977.

CAREER TOUCHDOWN RECEPTIONS

Player, Team	Years	G	TD
Aaron Turner, Pacific (Cal.)	1989-92	44	*43
Ryan Yarborough, Wyoming	1990-93	46	42
Clarkston Hines, Duke	1986-89	44	38
Terance Mathis, New Mexico	1985-87, 89	44	36
Elmo Wright, Houston	1968-70	30	34
Steve Largent, Tulsa	1973-75	30	32
Howard Twilley, Tulsa	1963-65	30	32
Chris Doering, Florida	1992-95	40	31
Lucious Davis, New Mexico St.	1992-95	42	31
Bobby Engram, Penn St.	1991, 93-95	42	31
Manny Hazard, Houston	1989-90	21	31
Sean Dawkins, California	1990-92	33	30
Desmond Howard, Michigan	1989-91	33	30
Jade Butcher, Indiana	1967-69	30	30
Jack Jackson, Florida	1992-94	34	29
Eric Drage, Brigham Young	1990-93	46	29
Dan Bitson, Tulsa	1987-89, 91	44	29
Hart Lee Dykes, Oklahoma St.	1985-88	41	29

Record.

SEASON YARDS

Player, Team	Year	Rec.	Yards	Avg.	TD
Alex Van Dyke, Nevada	†1995	129	*1,854	14.4	16
Howard Twilley, Tulsa	1965	134	1,779	13.3	16
Manny Hazard, Houston	1989	*142	1,689	11.9	*22
Aaron Turner, Pacific (Cal.)	†1991	92	1,604	17.4	18
Chris Penn, Tulsa	†1993	105	1,578	15.0	12
Chuck Hughes, UTEP	1965	80	1,519	19.0	12
Ryan Yarborough, Wyoming	1993	67	1,512	22.6	16
Henry Ellard, Fresno St.	1982	62	1,510	††24.4	15
Ron Sellers, Florida St.	1968	86	1,496	17.4	12
Jerry Hendren, Idaho	1969	95	1,452	15.3	12
Jason Phillips, Houston	1988	108	1,444	13.4	15

Record. †National champion. ††Record for minimum 50 catches.

SINGLE-GAME YARDS

Yds.	Player, Team (Opponent)	Date
363	Randy Gatewood, UNLV (Idaho)	Sept. 17, 1994
349	Chuck Hughes, UTEP (North Texas)	Sept. 18, 1965
322	Rick Eber, Tulsa (Idaho St.)	Oct. 7, 1967
318	Harry Wood, Tulsa (Idaho St.)	Oct. 7, 1967
316	Jeff Evans, New Mexico St. (Southern Ill.)	Sept. 30, 1978
314	Alex Van Dyke, Nevada (San Jose St.)	Nov. 18, 1995
297	Brian Oliver, Ball St. (Toledo)	Oct. 9, 1993
290	Tom Reynolds, San Diego St. (Utah St.)	Oct. 22, 1971
289	Wesley Walker, California (San Jose St.)	Oct. 2, 1976
288	Mike Siani, Villanova (Xavier, Ohio)	Oct. 30, 1971
285	Thomas Lewis, Indiana (Penn St.)	Nov. 6, 1993
284	Don Clune, Pennsylvania (Harvard)	Oct. 30, 1971
283	Chris Castor, Duke (Wake Forest)	Nov. 6, 1982
282	Larry Willis, Fresno St. (Montana St.)	Nov. 17, 1984
278	Derek Graham, Princeton (Yale)	Nov. 14, 1981

ANNUAL CHAMPIONS

Year	Player, Team	Class	Rec.	Yards	TD
1937	Jim Benton, Arkansas	Sr.	48	814	7
1938	Sam Boyd, Baylor	Sr.	32	537	—
1939	Ken Kavanaugh, LSU	Sr.	30	467	—
1940	Eddie Bryant, Virginia	So.	30	222	2
1941	Hank Stanton, Arizona	Sr.	50	820	—
1942	Bill Rogers, Texas A&M	Sr.	39	432	—
1943	Neil Armstrong, Oklahoma St.	Fr.	39	317	—
1944	Reid Moseley, Georgia	So.	32	506	—
1945	Reid Moseley, Georgia	Jr.	31	662	—
1946	Neil Armstrong, Oklahoma St.	Sr.	32	479	1
1947	Barney Poole, Mississippi	Jr.	52	513	8
1948	Johnny "Red" O'Quinn, Wake Forest	Jr.	39	605	7
1949	Art Weiner, North Caro.	Sr.	52	762	7
1950	Gordon Cooper, Denver	Jr.	46	569	8
1951	Dewey McConnell, Wyoming	Sr.	47	725	9
1952	Ed Brown, Fordham	Sr.	57	774	6
1953	John Carson, Georgia	Sr.	45	663	4
1954	Jim Hanifan, California	Sr.	44	569	7
1955	Hank Burnine, Missouri	Sr.	44	594	2
1956	Art Powell, San Jose St.	So.	40	583	5
1957	Stuart Vaughan, Utah	Sr.	53	756	5
1958	Dave Hibbert, Arizona	Jr.	61	606	4
1959	Chris Burford, Stanford	Sr.	61	756	6
1960	Hugh Campbell, Washington St.	So.	66	881	10
1961	Hugh Campbell, Washington St.	Jr.	53	723	5
1962	Vern Burke, Oregon St.	Jr.	69	1,007	10
1963	Lawrence Elkins, Baylor	Jr.	70	873	8
1964	Howard Twilley, Tulsa	Jr.	95	1,178	13
1965	Howard Twilley, Tulsa	Sr.	134	1,779	16
1966	Glenn Meltzer, Wichita St.	So.	91	1,115	4
1967	Bob Goodridge, Vanderbilt	Sr.	79	1,114	6
1968	Ron Sellers, Florida St.	Sr.	86	1,496	12
1969	Jerry Hendren, Idaho	Sr.	95	1,452	12

Beginning in 1970, ranked on per-game (instead of total) catches

Year	Player, Team	Class	G	Rec.	Avg.	Yards	TD
1970	Mike Mikolayunas, Davidson	Sr.	10	87	8.7	1,128	8
1971	Tom Reynolds, San Diego St.	Sr.	10	67	6.7	1,070	7
1972	Tom Forzani, Utah St.	Sr.	11	85	7.7	1,169	8
1973	Jay Miller, Brigham Young	So.	11	100	9.1	1,181	8
1974	Dwight McDonald, San Diego St.	Sr.	11	86	7.8	1,157	7
1975	Bob Farnham, Brown	Jr.	9	56	6.2	701	2
1976	Billy Ryckman, Louisiana Tech	Sr.	11	77	7.0	1,382	10
1977	Wayne Tolleson, Western Caro.	Sr.	11	73	6.6	1,101	7
1978	Dave Petzke, Northern Ill.	Sr.	11	91	8.3	1,217	11
1979	Rick Beasley, Appalachian St.	Jr.	11	74	6.7	1,205	12
1980	Dave Young, Purdue	Sr.	11	67	6.1	917	8
1981	Pete Harvey, North Texas	Sr.	9	57	6.3	743	3
1982	Vincent White, Stanford	Sr.	10	68	6.8	677	8
1983	Keith Edwards, Vanderbilt	Jr.	11	97	8.8	909	8
1984	David Williams, Illinois	Jr.	11	101	9.2	1,278	8
1985	Rodney Carter, Purdue	Sr.	11	98	8.9	1,099	4
1986	Mark Templeton, Long Beach St. (RB)	Sr.	11	99	9.0	688	2
1987	Jason Phillips, Houston	Jr.	11	99	9.0	875	3
1988	Jason Phillips, Houston	Sr.	11	108	9.8	1,444	15
1989	Manny Hazard, Houston	Jr.	11	*142	12.9	1,689	*22

Beginning in 1990, ranked on both per-game catches and yards per game

PER-GAME CATCHES

Year	Player, Team	Class	G	Rec.	Avg.	Yards	TD
1990	Manny Hazard, Houston	Sr.	10	78	7.8	946	9
1991	Fred Gilbert, Houston	Jr.	11	106	9.6	957	7
1992	Sherman Smith, Houston	Jr.	11	103	9.4	923	6
1993	Chris Penn, Tulsa	Sr.	11	105	9.6	1,578	12
1994	Alex Van Dyke, Nevada	Jr.	11	98	8.9	1,246	10
1995	Alex Van Dyke, Nevada	Sr.	11	129	11.7	*1,854	16

YARDS PER GAME

Year	Player, Team	Class	G	Rec.	Yards	Avg.	TD
1990	Patrick Rowe, San Diego St.	Jr.	11	71	1,392	126.6	8
1991	Aaron Turner, Pacific (Cal.)	Jr.	11	92	1,604	145.8	18
1992	Lloyd Hill, Texas Tech	Jr.	11	76	1,261	114.6	12
1993	Chris Penn, Tulsa	Sr.	11	105	1,578	143.5	12
1994	Marcus Harris, Wyoming	So.	12	71	1,431	119.3	11
1995	Alex Van Dyke, Nevada	Sr.	11	129	*1,854	168.6	16

*Record.

Scoring

CAREER POINTS PER GAME
(Minimum 225 Points)

Player, Team	Years	G	TD	XPt.	FG	Pts.	Pt.PG
Marshall Faulk, San Diego St.	1991-93	31	‡62	4	0	‡376	*12.1
Ed Marinaro, Cornell	1969-71	27	52	6	0	318	11.8
Bill Burnett, Arkansas	1968-70	26	49	0	0	294	11.3
Steve Owens, Oklahoma	1967-69	30	56	0	0	336	11.2
Eddie Talboom, Wyoming	1948-50	28	34	99	0	303	10.8
Howard Twilley, Tulsa	1963-65	26	32	67	0	259	10.0
Tom Harmon, Michigan	1938-40	24	33	33	2	237	9.9
Roman Anderson, Houston	1988-91	44	0	213	70	*423	9.6
Anthony Thompson, Indiana	1986-89	41	*65	4	0	394	9.6
Johnny Bright, Drake	1949-51	25	40	0	0	240	9.6
Glenn Davis, Army	1943-46	37	59	0	0	354	9.6
Stacey Robinson, Northern Ill. (QB)	1988-90	25	38	6	0	234	9.4
Floyd Little, Syracuse	1964-66	30	46	2	0	278	9.3
Felix "Doc" Blanchard, Army	1944-46	25	38	3	0	231	9.2
Anthony Davis, Southern Cal	1972-74	33	50	2	0	302	9.2

*Record. ‡Three-year totals record.

SEASON POINTS PER GAME

Player, Team	Year	G	TD	XPt.	FG	Pts.	Pt.PG
Barry Sanders, Oklahoma St.	†1988	11	*39	0	0	*234	*21.3
Bobby Reynolds, Nebraska	†1950	9	22	25	0	157	17.4
Art Luppino, Arizona	†1954	10	24	22	0	166	16.6
Ed Marinaro, Cornell	†1971	9	24	4	0	148	16.4
Lydell Mitchell, Penn St.	1971	11	29	0	0	174	15.8
Marshall Faulk, San Diego St.	†1991	9	23	2	0	140	15.6
Byron "Whizzer" White, Colorado	†1937	8	16	23	1	122	15.3

*Record. †National champion.

CAREER POINTS
(Non-Kickers)

Player, Team	Years	TD	XPt.	FG	Pts.
Anthony Thompson, Indiana	1986-89	*65	4	0	*394
Marshall Faulk, San Diego St.	1991-93	‡62	4	0	‡376
Tony Dorsett, Pittsburgh	1973-76	59	2	0	356
Glenn Davis, Army	1943-46	59	0	0	354
Art Luppino, Arizona	1953-56	48	49	0	337
Steve Owens, Oklahoma	1967-69	56	0	0	336
Wilford White, Arizona St.	1947-50	48	27	4	327
Barry Sanders, Oklahoma St.	1986-88	54	0	0	324
Allen Pinkett, Notre Dame	1982-85	53	2	0	320
Pete Johnson, Ohio St.	1973-76	53	0	0	318
Ed Marinaro, Cornell	1969-71	52	6	0	318
Herschel Walker, Georgia	1980-82	52	2	0	314
James Gray, Texas Tech	1986-89	52	0	0	312
Mike Rozier, Nebraska	1981-83	52	0	0	312
Ted Brown, North Caro. St.	1975-78	51	6	0	312
John Harvey, UTEP	1985-88	51	0	0	306
Eddie Talboom, Wyoming	1948-50	34	99	0	303
Anthony Davis, Southern Cal	1972-74	50	2	0	302
Dalton Hilliard, LSU	1982-85	50	0	0	300
Billy Sims, Oklahoma	$1975-79	50	0	0	300
Charles White, Southern Cal	1976-79	49	2	0	296
Nolan Jones, Arizona St.	1958-61	30	77	13	296
Steve Bartalo, Colorado St.	1983-86	49	0	0	294
Bill Burnett, Arkansas	1968-70	49	0	0	294
Brian Mitchell, Southwestern La.	1986-89	47	4	0	286
Rick Badanjek, Maryland	1982-85	46	10	0	286
Keith Byars, Ohio St.	1982-85	48	0	0	286

*Record. $See page 6 for explanation. ‡Three-year totals record.

CAREER POINTS
(Kickers)

Player, Team	Years	PAT	PAT Att.	FG	FG Att.	Pts.
Roman Anderson, Houston	1988-91	213	217	70	101	*423
Carlos Huerta, Miami (Fla.)	1988-91	178	181	73	91	397
Jason Elam, Hawaii	$1988-92	158	161	79	100	395
Derek Schmidt, Florida St.	1984-87	174	178	73	102	393
Luis Zendejas, Arizona St.	1981-84	134	135	78	*105	368
Jeff Jaeger, Washington	1983-86	118	123	*80	99	358
John Lee, UCLA	1982-85	116	117	79	92	353
Max Zendejas, Arizona	1982-85	122	124	77	104	353
Kevin Butler, Georgia	1981-84	122	125	77	98	353
Derek Mahoney, Fresno St.	1990-93	*216	*222	45	63	351
Philip Doyle, Alabama	1987-90	105	108	78	*105	†345
Andy Trakas, San Diego St.	1989-92	170	178	56	82	338
Michael Proctor, Alabama	1992-95	131	132	65	91	326
Barry Belli, Fresno St.	1984-87	116	123	70	99	326
Jason Hanson, Washington St.	1988-91	136	141	62	95	322
R. D. Lashar, Oklahoma	1987-90	194	200	42	60	320
Collin Mackie, South Caro.	1987-90	112	113	69	95	319
John Becksvoort, Tennessee	1991-94	161	161	52	75	317
Cary Blanchard, Oklahoma St.	1987-90	150	151	54	73	#314
Fuad Reveiz, Tennessee	1981-84	101	103	71	95	314
Sean Fleming, Wyoming	1988-91	150	155	54	92	312
Van Tiffin, Alabama	1983-86	135	135	59	87	312
Jess Atkinson, Maryland	1981-84	128	131	60	82	308
Gary Gussman, Miami (Ohio)	1984-87	102	104	68	94	306
Greg Cox, Miami (Fla.)	1984-87	162	169	47	64	303
Dan Eichloff, Kansas	1990-93	116	119	62	87	302
Scott Sisson, Georgia Tech	1989-92	119	121	60	88	299
Rusty Hanna, Toledo	1989-92	94	99	68	99	298
Tim Lashar, Oklahoma	1983-86	168	170	43	65	297
John Biskup, Syracuse	1989-92	125	132	57	78	296
Quin Rodriguez, Southern Cal	1987-90	139	146	52	68	295

*Record. $See page 6 for explanation. †Includes one TD reception. #Includes one two-point conversion.

SEASON POINTS

Player, Team	Year	TD	XPt.	FG	Pts.
Barry Sanders, Oklahoma St.	†1988	*39	0	0	*234
Mike Rozier, Nebraska	†1983	29	0	0	174
Lydell Mitchell, Penn St.	1971	29	0	0	174
Art Luppino, Arizona	†1954	24	22	0	166
Bobby Reynolds, Nebraska	†1950	22	25	0	157
Anthony Thompson, Indiana	†1989	25	4	0	154
Fred Wendt, UTEP	†1948	20	32	0	152
Pete Johnson, Ohio St.	†1975	25	0	0	150

*Record. †National champion.

SINGLE-GAME POINTS

No.	Player, Team (Opponent)	Date
48	Howard Griffith, Illinois (Southern Ill.)	Sept. 22, 1990
44	Marshall Faulk, San Diego St. (Pacific, Cal.)	Sept. 14, 1991
43	Jim Brown, Syracuse (Colgate)	Nov. 17, 1956
42	Arnold "Showboat" Boykin, Mississippi (Mississippi St.)	Dec. 1, 1951
42	Fred Wendt, UTEP (New Mexico St.)	Nov. 25, 1948
38	Dick Bass, Pacific, Cal. (San Diego St.)	Nov. 22, 1958
37	Jimmy Nutter, Wichita St. (Northern St.)	Oct. 22, 1949
36	Madre Hill, Arkansas (South Caro.)	Sept. 9, 1995
36	Calvin Jones, Nebraska (Kansas)	Nov. 9, 1991
36	Blake Ezor, Michigan St. (Northwestern)	Nov. 18, 1989
36	Dee Dowis, Air Force (San Diego St.)	Sept. 2, 1989
36	Kelvin Bryant, North Caro. (East Caro.)	Sept. 12, 1981
36	Andre Herrera, Southern Ill. (Northern Ill.)	Oct. 23, 1976
36	Anthony Davis, Southern Cal (Notre Dame)	Dec. 2, 1972
36	Tim Delaney, San Diego St. (New Mexico St.)	Nov. 15, 1969
36	Tom Francisco, Virginia Tech (Va. Military)	Nov. 24, 1966
36	Howard Twilley, Tulsa (Louisville)	Nov. 6, 1965
36	Pete Pedro, West Tex. A&M (UTEP)	Sept. 30, 1961
36	Tom Powers, Duke (Richmond)	Oct. 21, 1950

ANNUAL CHAMPIONS

Year	Player, Team	Class	TD	XPt.	FG	Pts.
1937	Byron "Whizzer" White, Colorado	Sr.	16	23	1	122
1938	Parker Hall, Mississippi	Sr.	11	7	0	73
1939	Tom Harmon, Michigan	Jr.	14	15	1	102
1940	Tom Harmon, Michigan	Sr.	16	18	1	117
1941	Bill Dudley, Virginia	Sr.	18	23	1	134
1942	Bob Steuber, Missouri	Sr.	18	13	0	121
1943	Steve Van Buren, LSU	Sr.	14	14	0	98
1944	Glenn Davis, Army	So.	20	0	0	120
1945	Felix "Doc" Blanchard, Army	Jr.	19	1	0	115
1946	Gene Roberts, Tenn.-Chatt.	Sr.	18	9	0	117
1947	Lou Gambino, Maryland	Jr.	16	0	0	96
1948	Fred Wendt, UTEP	Sr.	20	32	0	152
1949	George Thomas, Oklahoma	Sr.	19	3	0	117

Year	Player, Team	Class	TD	XPt.	FG	Pts.
1950	Bobby Reynolds, Nebraska	So.	22	25	0	157
1951	Ollie Matson, San Francisco	Sr.	21	0	0	126
1952	Jackie Parker, Mississippi St.	Jr.	16	24	0	120
1953	Earl Lindley, Utah St.	Sr.	13	3	0	81
1954	Art Luppino, Arizona	So.	24	22	0	166
1955	Jim Swink, Texas Christian	Jr.	20	5	0	125
1956	Clendon Thomas, Oklahoma	Jr.	18	0	0	108
1957	Leon Burton, Arizona St.	Jr.	16	0	0	96
1958	Dick Bass, Pacific (Cal.)	Jr.	18	8	0	116
1959	Pervis Atkins, New Mexico St.	Jr.	17	5	0	107
1960	Bob Gaiters, New Mexico St.	Sr.	23	7	0	145
1961	Jim Pilot, New Mexico St.	So.	21	12	0	138
1962	Jerry Logan, West Tex. A&M	Sr.	13	32	0	110
1963	Cosmo Iacavazzi, Princeton	Jr.	14	0	0	84
	Dave Casinelli, Memphis	Sr.	14	0	0	84
1964	Brian Piccolo, Wake Forest	Sr.	17	9	0	111
1965	Howard Twilley, Tulsa	Sr.	16	31	0	127
1966	Ken Hebert, Houston	Jr.	11	41	2	113
1967	Leroy Keyes, Purdue	Jr.	19	0	0	114
1968	Jim O'Brien, Cincinnati	Jr.	12	31	13	142
1969	Steve Owens, Oklahoma	Sr.	23	0	0	138

Beginning in 1970, ranked on per-game (instead of total) points

Year	Player, Team	Class	G	TD	XPt.	FG	Pts.	Avg.
1970	Brian Bream, Air Force	Jr.	10	20	0	0	120	12.0
	Gary Kosins, Dayton	Jr.	9	18	0	0	108	12.0
1971	Ed Marinaro, Cornell	Sr.	9	24	4	0	148	16.4
1972	Harold Henson, Ohio St.	So.	10	20	0	0	120	12.0
1973	Jim Jennings, Rutgers	Sr.	11	21	2	0	128	11.6
1974	Bill Marek, Wisconsin	Jr.	9	19	0	0	114	12.7
1975	Pete Johnson, Ohio St.	Jr.	11	25	0	0	150	13.6
1976	Tony Dorsett, Pittsburgh	Sr.	11	22	2	0	134	12.2
1977	Earl Campbell, Texas	Sr.	11	19	0	0	114	10.4
1978	Billy Sims, Oklahoma	Jr.	11	20	0	0	120	10.9
1979	Billy Sims, Oklahoma	Sr.	11	22	0	0	132	12.0
1980	Sammy Winder, Southern Miss.	Jr.	11	20	0	0	120	10.9
1981	Marcus Allen, Southern Cal	Sr.	11	23	0	0	138	12.5
1982	Greg Allen, Florida St.	So.	11	21	0	0	126	11.5
1983	Mike Rozier, Nebraska	Sr.	12	29	0	0	174	14.5
1984	Keith Byars, Ohio St.	Jr.	11	24	0	0	144	13.1
1985	Bernard White, Bowling Green	Sr.	11	19	0	0	114	10.4
1986	Steve Bartalo, Colorado St.	Sr.	11	19	0	0	114	10.4
1987	Paul Hewitt, San Diego St.	Jr.	12	24	0	0	144	12.0
1988	Barry Sanders, Oklahoma St.	Jr.	11	*39	0	0	*234	*21.3
1989	Anthony Thompson, Indiana	Sr.	11	25	4	0	154	14.0
1990	Stacey Robinson, Northern Ill. (QB)	Sr.	11	19	6	0	120	10.9
1991	Marshall Faulk, San Diego St.	Fr.	9	23	2	0	140	15.6
1992	Garrison Hearst, Georgia	Jr.	11	21	0	0	126	11.5
1993	Byron Morris, Texas Tech	Jr.	11	22	2	0	134	12.2
1994	Rashaan Salaam, Colorado	Jr.	11	24	0	0	144	13.1
1995	Eddie George, Ohio St.	Sr.	12	24	0	0	144	12.0

*Record.

Interceptions

CAREER INTERCEPTIONS

Player, Team	Years	No.	Yards	Avg.
Al Brosky, Illinois	1950-52	*29	356	12.3
Martin Bayless, Bowling Green	1980-83	27	266	9.9
John Provost, Holy Cross	1972-74	27	470	17.4
Tracy Saul, Texas Tech	1989-92	25	425	17.0
Tony Thurman, Boston College	1981-84	25	221	8.8
Tom Curtis, Michigan	1967-69	25	440	17.6
Jeff Nixon, Richmond	1975-78	23	377	16.4
Bennie Blades, Miami (Fla.)	1984-87	22	355	16.1
Jim Bolding, East Caro.	1973-76	22	143	6.5
Terrell Buckley, Florida St.	1989-91	21	*501	23.9
Chuck Cecil, Arizona	1984-87	21	241	11.5
Barry Hill, Iowa St.	1972-74	21	202	9.6
Mike Sensibaugh, Ohio St.	1968-70	21	226	10.8
Kevin Smith, Texas A&M	1988-91	20	289	14.5
Mark Collins, Cal St. Fullerton	1982-85	20	193	9.7
Anthony Young, Temple	1981-84	20	230	11.5
Chris Williams, LSU	1977-80	20	91	4.6
Charles Jefferson, McNeese St.	1975-78	20	95	4.8
Artimus Parker, Southern Cal	1971-73	20	268	13.4
Dave Atkinson, Brigham Young	1971-73	20	222	11.1
Jackie Wallace, Arizona	1970-72	20	250	12.5
Tom Wilson, Colgate	1964-66	20	215	10.8
Lynn Chandnois, Michigan St.	1946-49	20	410	20.5
Bobby Wilson, Mississippi	1946-49	20	369	18.5

*Record.

SEASON INTERCEPTIONS

Player, Team	Year	No.	Yards
Al Worley, Washington	†1968	*14	130
George Shaw, Oregon	†1951	13	136
Terrell Buckley, Florida St.	†1991	12	238
Cornelius Price, Houston	†1989	12	187
Bob Navarro, Eastern Mich.	†1989	12	73
Tony Thurman, Boston College	†1984	12	99
Terry Hoage, Georgia	†1982	12	51
Frank Polito, Villanova	†1971	12	261
Bill Albrecht, Washington	1951	12	140
Hank Rich, Arizona St.	†1950	12	135

*Record. †National champion.

ANNUAL CHAMPIONS

Year	Player, Team	Class	No.	Yards
1938	Elmer Tarbox, Texas Tech	Sr.	11	89
1939	Harold Van Every, Minnesota	Sr.	8	59
1940	Dick Morgan, Tulsa	Jr.	7	210
1941	Bobby Robertson, Southern Cal	Sr.	9	126
1942	Ray Evans, Kansas	Jr.	10	76
1943	Jay Stoves, Washington	Sr.	7	139
1944	Jim Hardy, Southern Cal	Sr.	8	73
1945	Jake Leicht, Oregon	So.	9	195
1946	Larry Hatch, Washington	So.	8	114
1947	John Bruce, William & Mary	Jr.	9	78
1948	Jay Van Noy, Utah St.	Jr.	8	228
1949	Bobby Wilson, Mississippi	Sr.	10	70
1950	Hank Rich, Arizona St.	Sr.	12	135
1951	George Shaw, Oregon	Fr.	13	136
1952	Cecil Ingram, Alabama	Jr.	10	163
1953	Bob Garrett, Stanford	Sr.	9	80
1954	Gary Glick, Colorado St.	Jr.	8	168
1955	Sam Wesley, Oregon St.	Jr.	7	61
1956	Jack Hill, Utah St.	Sr.	7	132
1957	Ray Toole, North Texas	Sr.	7	133
1958	Jim Norton, Idaho	Jr.	9	222
1959	Bud Whitehead, Florida St.	Jr.	6	111
1960	Bob O'Billovich, Montana	Jr.	7	71
1961	Joe Zuger, Arizona St.	Sr.	10	121
1962	Byron Beaver, Houston	Sr.	10	56
1963	Dick Kern, William & Mary	Sr.	8	116
1964	Tony Carey, Notre Dame	Jr.	8	121
1965	Bob Sullivan, Maryland	Sr.	10	61
1966	Henry King, Utah St.	Sr.	11	180
1967	Steve Haterius, West Tex. A&M	Sr.	11	90
1968	Al Worley, Washington	Sr.	*14	130
1969	Seth Miller, Arizona St.	Sr.	11	63

Beginning in 1970, ranked on per-game (instead of total) number

Year	Player, Team	Class	G	No.	Avg.	Yards
1970	Mike Sensibaugh, Ohio St.	Sr.	8	8	1.00	40
1971	Frank Polito, Villanova	So.	10	12	1.20	261
1972	Mike Townsend, Notre Dame	Jr.	10	10	1.00	39
1973	Mike Gow, Illinois	Jr.	11	10	0.91	142
1974	Mike Haynes, Arizona St.	Jr.	11	10	0.91	115
1975	Jim Bolding, East Caro.	Jr.	10	10	1.00	51
1976	Anthony Francis, Houston	Jr.	11	10	0.91	118
1977	Paul Lawler, Colgate	Sr.	9	7	0.78	53
1978	Pete Harris, Penn St.	Jr.	11	10	0.91	155
1979	Joe Callan, Ohio	Sr.	9	9	1.00	110
1980	Ronnie Lott, Southern Cal	Sr.	11	8	0.73	166
	Steve McNamee, William & Mary	Sr.	11	8	0.73	125
	Greg Benton, Drake	Sr.	11	8	0.73	119
	Jeff Hipp, Georgia	Sr.	11	8	0.73	104
	Mike Richardson, Arizona St.	So.	11	8	0.73	89
	Vann McElroy, Baylor	Jr.	11	8	0.73	73
1981	Sam Shaffer, Temple	Sr.	10	9	0.90	76
1982	Terry Hoage, Georgia	Jr.	10	12	1.20	51
1983	Martin Bayless, Bowling Green	Sr.	11	10	0.91	64
1984	Tony Thurman, Boston College	Sr.	11	12	1.09	99
1985	Chris White, Tennessee	Sr.	11	9	0.82	168
	Kevin Walker, East Caro.	Sr.	11	9	0.82	155
1986	Bennie Blades, Miami (Fla.)	Jr.	11	10	0.91	128
1987	Keith McMeans, Virginia	Fr.	10	9	0.90	35
1988	Kurt Larson, Michigan St. (LB)	Sr.	11	8	0.73	78
	Andy Logan, Kent	Sr.	11	8	0.73	54
1989	Cornelius Price, Houston	Jr.	11	12	1.09	187
	Bob Navarro, Eastern Mich.	Jr.	11	12	1.09	73
1990	Jerry Parks, Houston	Jr.	11	8	0.73	124
1991	Terrell Buckley, Florida St.	Jr.	12	12	1.00	238
1992	Carlton McDonald, Air Force	Sr.	11	8	0.73	109
1993	Orlanda Thomas, Southwestern La.	Jr.	11	9	0.82	84
1994	Aaron Beasley, West Va.	Jr.	12	10	0.83	133
1995	Willie Smith, Louisiana Tech	Jr.	10	8	0.80	65

*Record.

Punting

CAREER AVERAGE

(Minimum 250 Punts)

Player, Team	Years	No.	Yards	Avg.	Long
Bill Smith, Mississippi	1983-86	254	11,260	*44.3	92
Jim Arnold, Vanderbilt	1979-82	277	12,171	43.9	79
Ralf Mojsiejenko, Michigan St.	1981-84	275	11,997	43.6	72
Jim Miller, Mississippi	1976-79	266	11,549	43.4	82
Russ Henderson, Virginia	1975-78	276	11,957	43.3	74
Maury Buford, Texas Tech	1978-81	293	12,670	43.2	75
Chris Becker, Texas Christian	1985-88	265	11,407	43.0	77
Ron Keller, New Mexico	1983-86	252	10,737	42.6	77
James Gargus, Texas Christian	1981-84	255	10,862	42.6	74

(Minimum 150-249 Punts)

Player, Team	Years	No.	Yards	Avg.	Long
Todd Sauerbrun, West Va.	1991-94	167	7,733	*46.3	90
Reggie Roby, Iowa	1979-82	172	7,849	45.6	69
Greg Montgomery, Michigan St.	1985-87	170	7,721	45.4	86
Tom Tupa, Ohio St.	1984-87	196	8,854	45.2	75
Barry Helton, Colorado	1984-87	153	6,873	44.9	68
Ray Guy, Southern Miss.	1970-72	200	8,934	44.7	93
Bucky Scribner, Kansas	1980-82	217	9,670	44.6	70
Terry Daniel, Auburn	1992-94	169	7,522	44.5	71
Greg Horne, Arkansas	1983-86	180	8,002	44.5	72
Ray Criswell, Florida	1982-85	161	7,153	44.4	73
Russell Erxleben, Texas	1975-78	214	9,467	44.2	80
Mark Simon, Air Force	1984-86	156	6,898	44.2	64
Johnny Evans, North Caro. St.	1974-77	185	8,143	44.0	81
Chuck Ramsey, Wake Forest	1971-73	205	9,010	44.0	70
Jimmy Colquitt, Tennessee	1981-84	201	8,816	43.9	70
John Teltschik, Texas	1982-85	217	9,496	43.8	81

**Record.*

SEASON AVERAGE

(Qualifiers for Championship)

Player, Team	Year	No.	Yards	Avg.
Reggie Roby, Iowa	†1981	44	2,193	*49.8
Kirk Wilson, UCLA	†1956	30	1,479	49.3
Todd Sauerbrun, West Va.	†1994	72	3,486	‡48.4
Zack Jordan, Colorado	†1950	38	1,830	48.2
Ricky Anderson, Vanderbilt	†1984	58	2,793	48.2
Reggie Roby, Iowa	†1982	52	2,501	48.1
Marv Bateman, Utah	†1971	68	3,269	48.1
Owen Price, UTEP	†1940	30	1,440	48.0
Jack Jacobs, Oklahoma	1940	31	1,483	47.8
Bill Smith, Mississippi	1984	44	2,099	47.7
Ed Bunn, UTEP	†1992	41	1,955	47.7

**Record. †National champion. ‡Record for minimum 50 punts.*

ANNUAL CHAMPIONS

Year	Player, Team	Class	No.	Yards	Avg.
1937	Johnny Pingel, Michigan St.	Jr.	49	2,101	42.9
1938	Jerry Dowd, St. Mary's (Cal.)	Sr.	62	2,711	43.7
1939	Harry Dunkle, North Caro.	So.	37	1,725	46.6
1940	Owen Price, UTEP	Jr.	30	1,440	48.0
1941	Owen Price, UTEP	Sr.	40	1,813	45.3
1942	Bobby Cifers, Tennessee	Jr.	37	1,586	42.9
1943	Harold Cox, Arkansas	Fr.	37	1,518	41.0
1944	Bob Waterfield, UCLA	Sr.	60	2,575	42.9
1945	Howard Maley, Southern Methodist	Sr.	59	2,458	41.7
1946	Johnny Galvin, Purdue	Sr.	30	1,286	42.9
1947	Leslie Palmer, North Caro. St.	Sr.	65	2,816	43.3
1948	Charlie Justice, North Caro.	Jr.	62	2,728	44.0
1949	Paul Stombaugh, Furman	Sr.	57	2,550	44.7
1950	Zack Jordan, Colorado	So.	38	1,830	48.2
1951	Chuck Spaulding, Wyoming	Jr.	37	1,610	43.5
1952	Des Koch, Southern Cal	Jr.	47	2,043	43.5
1953	Zeke Bratkowski, Georgia (QB)	Sr.	50	2,132	42.6
1954	A. L. Terpening, New Mexico	Sr.	41	1,869	45.6
1955	Don Chandler, Florida	Sr.	22	975	44.3
1956	Kirk Wilson, UCLA	So.	30	1,479	49.3
1957	Dave Sherer, Southern Methodist	Jr.	36	1,620	45.0
1958	Bobby Walden, Georgia	So.	44	1,991	45.3
1959	John Hadl, Kansas	So.	43	1,960	45.6
1960	Dick Fitzsimmons, Denver	So.	25	1,106	44.2
1961	Joe Zuger, Arizona St.	Sr.	31	1,305	42.1
1962	Joe Don Looney, Oklahoma	Jr.	34	1,474	43.4
1963	Danny Thomas, Southern Methodist	Jr.	48	2,110	44.0
1964	Frank Lambert, Mississippi	Sr.	50	2,205	44.1
1965	Dave Lewis, Stanford	Jr.	29	1,302	44.9
1966	Ron Widby, Tennessee	Sr.	48	2,104	43.8
1967	Zenon Andrusyshyn, UCLA	So.	34	1,502	44.2
1968	Dany Pitcock, Wichita St.	Sr.	71	3,068	43.2
1969	Ed Marsh, Baylor	Jr.	68	2,965	43.6
1970	Marv Bateman, Utah	Jr.	65	2,968	45.7
1971	Marv Bateman, Utah	Sr.	68	3,269	48.1
1972	Ray Guy, Southern Miss.	Sr.	58	2,680	46.2
1973	Chuck Ramsey, Wake Forest	Sr.	87	3,896	44.8
1974	Joe Parker, Appalachian St.	So.	63	2,788	44.3
1975	Tom Skladany, Ohio St.	Jr.	36	1,682	46.7
1976	Russell Erxleben, Texas	So.	61	2,842	46.6
1977	Jim Miller, Mississippi	So.	66	3,029	45.9
1978	Maury Buford, Texas Tech	Fr.	71	3,131	44.1
1979	Clay Brown, Brigham Young	Jr.	43	1,950	45.3

Beginning in 1980, ranked on minimum 3.6 punts per game

Year	Player, Team	Class	No.	Yards	Long	Avg.
1980	Steve Cox, Arkansas	Sr.	47	2,186	86	46.5
1981	Reggie Roby, Iowa	Jr.	44	2,193	68	*49.8
1982	Reggie Roby, Iowa	Sr.	52	2,501	66	48.1
1983	Jack Weil, Wyoming	Sr.	52	2,369	86	45.6
1984	Ricky Anderson, Vanderbilt	Sr.	58	2,793	82	48.2
1985	Mark Simon, Air Force	Jr.	53	2,506	71	47.3
1986	Greg Horne, Arkansas	Sr.	49	2,313	65	47.2
1987	Tom Tupa, Ohio St. (QB)	Sr.	63	2,963	72	47.0
1988	Keith English, Colorado	Sr.	51	2,297	77	45.0
1989	Tom Rouen, Colorado	So.	36	1,651	63	45.8
1990	Cris Shale, Bowling Green	Sr.	66	3,087	81	46.8
1991	Mark Bounds, Texas Tech	Sr.	53	2,481	78	46.8
1992	Ed Bunn, UTEP	Sr.	41	1,955	73	47.7
1993	Chris MacInnis, Air Force	Sr.	49	2,303	74	47.0
1994	Todd Sauerbrun West Va.	Sr.	72	3,486	90	‡48.4
1995	Brad Maynard, Ball St.	Jr.	66	3,071	67	46.5

**Record. ‡Record for minimum of 50 punts.*

Punt Returns

CAREER AVERAGE

(Minimum 1.2 Returns Per Game; Minimum 30 Returns)

Player, Team	Years	No.	Yards	TD	Long	Avg.
Jack Mitchell, Oklahoma	1946-48	39	922	**7	70	*23.6
Gene Gibson, Cincinnati	1949-50	37	760	4	75	‡20.5
Eddie Macon, Pacific (Cal.)	1949-51	48	907	4	**100	18.9
Jackie Robinson, UCLA	1939-40	37	694	2	89	18.8
Mike Fuller, Auburn	1972-74	50	883	3	63	17.7
Bobby Dillon, Texas	1949-51	47	830	1	84	17.7
Erroll Tucker, Utah	1984-85	38	650	3	89	17.1
George Hoey, Michigan	1966-68	31	529	1	60	17.1
Jack Christiansen, Colorado St.	1948-50	37	626	2	89	16.9
Henry Pryor, Rutgers	1948-49	37	625	1	85	16.9
Adolph Bellizeare, Pennsylvania	1972-74	33	557	3	73	16.9
Ken Hatfield, Arkansas	1962-64	70	1,135	5	95	16.2
Gene Rossides, Columbia	1945-48	53	851	3	70	16.1
Bill Hillenbrand, Indiana	1941-42	65	1,042	2	88	16.0

**Record. **Record tied. ‡Record for minimum 1.5 returns per game.*

SEASON AVERAGE

(Minimum 1.2 Returns Per Game)

Player, Team	Year	No.	Yards	Avg.
Bill Blackstock, Tennessee	1951	12	311	*25.9
George Sims, Baylor	1948	15	375	25.0
Gene Derricotte, Michigan	1947	14	347	24.8
Erroll Tucker, Utah	†1985	16	389	24.3
George Hoey, Michigan	1967	12	291	24.3
Floyd Little, Syracuse	1965	18	423	23.5

**Record. †National champion. ‡Ranked for minimum 1.5 returns per game.*

ANNUAL CHAMPIONS
(Ranked on Total Yards Until 1970)

Year	Player, Team	Class	No.	Yards	Avg.
1939	Bosh Pritchard, Va. Military	So.	42	583	13.9
1940	Junie Hovious, Mississippi	Sr.	33	498	15.1
1941	Bill Geyer, Colgate	Sr.	33	616	18.7
1942	Bill Hillenbrand, Indiana	Jr.	23	481	20.9
1943	Marion Flanagan, Texas A&M	Jr.	49	475	9.7
1944	Joe Stuart, California	Jr.	39	372	9.5
1945	Jake Leicht, Oregon	So.	28	395	14.1
1946	Harry Gilmer, Alabama	Jr.	37	436	11.8
1947	Lindy Berry, Texas Christian	So.	42	493	11.7
1948	Lee Nalley, Vanderbilt	Jr.	43	*791	18.4
1949	Lee Nalley, Vanderbilt	Sr.	35	498	14.2
1950	Dave Waters, Wash. & Lee	Jr.	30	445	14.8
1951	Tom Murphy, Holy Cross	So.	25	533	21.3
1952	Horton Nesrsta, Rice	Jr.	44	536	12.2
1953	Paul Giel, Minnesota	Sr.	17	288	16.9
1954	Dicky Maegle, Rice	Sr.	15	293	19.5
1955	Mike Sommer, Geo. Washington	So.	24	330	13.8
1956	Bill Stacy, Mississippi St.	Jr.	24	290	12.1
1957	Bobby Mulgado, Arizona St.	Sr.	14	267	19.1
1958	Howard Cook, Colorado	Sr.	24	242	10.1
1959	Pervis Atkins, New Mexico St.	Jr.	16	241	15.1
1960	Lance Alworth, Arkansas	Jr.	18	307	17.1
1961	Lance Alworth, Arkansas	Sr.	28	336	12.0
1962	Darrell Roberts, Utah St.	Sr.	16	333	20.8
1963	Ken Hatfield, Arkansas	Jr.	21	350	16.7
1964	Ken Hatfield, Arkansas	Sr.	31	518	16.7
1965	Nick Rassas, Notre Dame	Sr.	24	459	19.1
1966	Vic Washington, Wyoming	Jr.	34	443	13.0
1967	Mike Battle, Southern Cal	Jr.	47	570	12.1
1968	Roger Wehrli, Missouri	Sr.	41	478	11.7
1969	Chris Farasopoulous, Brigham Young	Jr.	35	527	15.1

Beginning in 1970, ranked on average per return (instead of total yards)‡

Year	Player, Team	Class	No.	Yards	TD	Long	Avg.
1970	Steve Holden, Arizona St.	So.	17	327	2	94	19.2
1971	Golden Richards, Brigham Young	Jr.	33	624	**4	87	18.9
1972	Randy Rhino, Georgia Tech	So.	25	441	1	96	17.6
1973	Gary Hayman, Penn St.	Sr.	23	442	1	83	19.2
1974	John Provost, Holy Cross	Sr.	13	238	2	85	18.3
1975	Donnie Ross, New Mexico St.	Sr.	21	338	1	#81	16.1
1976	Henry Jenkins, Rutgers	Sr.	30	449	0	#40	15.0
1977	Robert Woods, Grambling	Sr.	††11	279	3	72	25.4
1978	Ira Matthews, Wisconsin	Sr.	16	270	3	78	16.9
1979	Jeffrey Shockley, Tennessee St.	Sr.	27	456	1	79	16.9
1980	Scott Woerner, Georgia	Sr.	31	488	1	67	15.7
1981	Glen Young, Mississippi St.	Jr.	19	307	2	87	16.2
1982	Lionel James, Auburn	Jr.	25	394	0	#63	15.8
1983	Jim Sandusky, San Diego St.	Sr.	20	381	1	90	19.0
1984	Ricky Nattiel, Florida	So.	22	346	1	67	15.7
1985	Erroll Tucker, Utah	Sr.	16	389	2	89	24.3
1986	Rod Smith, Nebraska	Jr.	‡‡12	227	1	63	18.9
1987	Alan Grant, Stanford	Jr.	27	446	2	77	16.5
1988	Deion Sanders, Florida St.	Sr.	33	503	1	76	15.2
1989	Larry Hargrove, Ohio	Sr.	17	309	2	83	18.2
1990	Dave McCloughan, Colorado	Sr.	32	524	2	90	16.4
1991	Bo Campbell, Virginia Tech	Jr.	15	273	0	45	18.2
1992	Lee Gissendaner, Northwestern	Jr.	15	327	1	72	21.8
1993	Aaron Glenn, Texas A&M	Sr.	17	339	2	76	19.9
1994	Steve Clay, Eastern Mich.	Jr.	14	278	1	65	19.9
1995	James Dye, Brigham Young	Jr.	20	438	2	90	21.9

**Record. **Record tied. #Did not score. ‡Ranked on minimum 1.5 returns per game, 1970-73; 1.2 from 1974. ††Declared champion; with three more returns (making 1.3 per game) for zero yards still would have highest average. ‡‡Declared champion; with two more returns (making 1.2 per game) for zero yards still would have highest average.*

ANNUAL PUNT RETURN LEADERS (1939-69) BASED ON AVERAGE PER RETURN
(Minimum 1.2 Returns Per Game)

1939—Jackie Robinson, UCLA, 20.0; **1940**—Jackie Robinson, UCLA, 21.0; **1941**—Walt Slater, Tennessee, 20.4; **1942**—Billy Hillenbrand, Indiana, 20.9; **1943**—Otto Graham, Northwestern, 19.7; **1944**—Glenn Davis, Army, 18.4; **1945**—Jake Leicht, Oregon, 14.8; **1946**—Harold Griffin, Florida, 20.1; **1947**—Gene Derricotte, Michigan, 24.8; **1948**—George Sims, Baylor, ‡25.0; **1949**—Gene Evans, Wisconsin, 21.8; **1950**—Lindy Hanson, Boston U., 22.5; **1951**—Bill Blackstock, Tennessee, *25.9; **1952**—Gil Reich, Kansas, 17.2; **1953**—Bobby Lee, New Mexico, 19.4; **1954**—Dicky Maegle, Rice, 19.5; **1955**—Ron Lind, Drake, 21.1; **1956**—Ron Lind, Drake, 19.1; **1957**—Bobby Mulgado, Arizona St., 19.1; **1958**—Herb Hallas, Yale, 23.4; **1959**—Jacque MacKinnon, Colgate, 17.5; **1960**—Pat Fischer, Nebraska, 21.2; **1961**—Tom Larscheid, Utah St., 23.4; **1962**—Darrell Roberts, Utah St., 20.8; **1963**—Rickie Harris, Arizona, 17.4; **1964**—Ken Hatfield, Arkansas, 16.7; **1965**—Floyd Little, Syracuse, 23.5; **1966**—Don Bean, Houston, 20.2; **1967**—George Hoey, Michigan, 24.3; **1968**—Rob Bordley, Princeton, 20.5; **1969**—George Hannen, Davidson, 22.4.

**Record. ‡Record for minimum 1.5 returns per game.*

Kickoff Returns

CAREER AVERAGE
(Minimum 1.2 Returns Per Game; Minimum 30 Returns)

Player, Team	Years	No.	Yards	Avg.
Anthony Davis, Southern Cal	1972-74	37	1,299	*35.1
Overton Curtis, Utah St.	1957-58	32	991	‡31.0
Fred Montgomery, New Mexico St.	1991-92	39	1,191	30.5
Altie Taylor, Utah St.	1966-68	40	1,170	29.3
Stan Brown, Purdue	1968-70	49	1,412	28.8
Henry White, Colgate	1974-77	41	1,180	28.8
Paul Loughran, Temple	1970-72	40	1,123	28.1
Jim Krieg, Washington	1970-71	31	860	27.7

**Record. ‡Record for minimum 1.5 returns per game.*

SEASON AVERAGE
(Minimum 1.2 Returns Per Game)

Player, Team	Year	No.	Yards	Avg.
Paul Allen, Brigham Young	1961	12	481	*40.1
Leeland McElroy, Texas A&M	†1993	15	590	39.3
Forrest Hall, San Francisco	†1946	15	573	‡38.2
Tony Ball, Tenn.-Chatt.	†1977	13	473	36.4
George Marinkov, North Caro. St.	1954	13	465	35.8
Bob Baker, Cornell	1964	11	386	35.1

**Record. †National champion. ‡Record for minimum 1.5 returns per game.*

ANNUAL CHAMPIONS
(Ranked on Total Yards Until 1970)

Year	Player, Team	Class	No.	Yards	Avg.
1939	Nile Kinnick, Iowa	Sr.	15	377	25.1
1940	Jack Emigh, Montana	Sr.	18	395	21.9
1941	Earl Ray, Wyoming	So.	23	496	21.6
1942	Frank Porto, California	Sr.	17	483	28.4
1943	Paul Copoulos, Marquette	So.	11	384	34.9
1944	Paul Copoulos, Marquette	Jr.	14	337	24.1
1945	Al Dekdebrun, Cornell	Sr.	14	321	22.9
1946	Forrest Hall, San Francisco	Jr.	15	573	**38.2
1947	Doak Walker, Southern Methodist	So.	10	387	38.7
1948	Bill Gregus, Wake Forest	Jr.	19	503	26.5
1949	Johnny Subda, Nevada	Sr.	18	444	24.7
1950	Chuck Hill, New Mexico	Jr.	27	729	27.0
1951	Chuck Hill, New Mexico	Sr.	17	504	29.6
1952	Curly Powell, Va. Military	Sr.	27	517	19.1
1953	Max McGee, Tulane	Sr.	17	371	21.8
1954	Art Luppino, Arizona	So.	20	632	31.6
1955	Sam Woolwine, Va. Military	Jr.	22	471	21.4
1956	Sam Woolwine, Va. Military	Sr.	18	503	27.9
1957	Overton Curtis, Utah St.	Jr.	23	695	30.2
1958	Sonny Randle, Virginia	Sr.	21	506	24.1
1959	Don Perkins, New Mexico	Sr.	15	520	34.7
1960	Bruce Samples, Brigham Young	Sr.	23	577	25.1
1961	Dick Mooney, Idaho	Sr.	23	494	21.5
1962	Donnie Frederick, Wake Forest	Sr.	29	660	22.8
1963	Gary Wood, Cornell	Sr.	19	618	32.5
1964	Dan Bland, Mississippi St.	Jr.	20	558	27.9
1965	Eric Crabtree, Pittsburgh	Sr.	25	636	25.4
1966	Marcus Rhoden, Mississippi St.	Sr.	26	572	22.0
1967	Joe Casas, New Mexico	Sr.	23	602	26.2
1968	Mike Adamle, Northwestern	So.	34	732	21.5
1969	Stan Brown, Purdue	Jr.	26	698	26.8

Beginning in 1970, ranked on average per return (instead of total yards)‡

Year	Player, Team	Class	No.	Yards	Avg.
1970	Stan Brown, Purdue	Sr.	19	638	33.6
1971	Paul Loughran, Temple	Jr.	15	502	33.5
1972	Larry Williams, Texas Tech	So.	16	493	30.8
1973	Steve Odom, Utah	Sr.	21	618	29.4
1974	Anthony Davis, Southern Cal	Sr.	††11	467	42.5
1975	John Schultz, Maryland	Sr.	13	403	31.0
1976	Ira Matthews, Wisconsin	So.	14	415	29.6
1977	Tony Ball, Tenn.-Chatt.	Fr.	13	473	36.4
1978	Drew Hill, Georgia Tech	Sr.	19	570	30.0
1979	Stevie Nelson, Ball St.	Fr.	18	565	31.4
1980	Mike Fox, San Diego St.	So.	†11	361	32.8
1981	Frank Minnifield, Louisville	Jr.	11	334	30.4
1982	Carl Monroe, Utah	Sr.	14	421	30.1
1983	Henry Williams, East Caro.	Jr.	19	591	31.1
1984	Keith Henderson, Texas Tech	Fr.	13	376	28.9

Year	Player, Team	Class	No.	Yards	Avg.
1985	Erroll Tucker, Utah	Sr.	24	698	29.1
1986	Terrance Roulhac, Clemson	Sr.	17	561	33.0
1987	Barry Sanders, Oklahoma St.	So.	14	442	31.6
1988	Raghib Ismail, Notre Dame	Fr.	#12	433	36.1
1989	Tony Smith, Southern Miss.	So.	14	455	32.5
1990	Dale Carter, Tennessee	Jr.	17	507	29.8
1991	Fred Montgomery, New Mexico St.	Jr.	25	734	29.4
1992	Fred Montgomery, New Mexico St.	Sr.	14	457	32.6
1993	Leeland McElroy, Texas A&M	Fr.	15	590	39.3
1994	Eric Moulds, Mississippi St.	Jr.	†13	426	32.8
1995	Robert Tate, Cincinnati	Jr.	15	515	34.3

***Record for minimum 1.5 returns per game. #Declared champion; with two more returns (making 1.3 per game) for zero yards still would have highest average. †Declared champion; with one more return (making 1.2 per game) for zero yards still would have highest average. ††Declared champion; with three more returns (making 1.3 per game) for zero yards still would have highest average. ‡Ranked on minimum 1.5 returns per game, 1970-73; 1.2 from 1974.*

ANNUAL KICKOFF RETURN LEADERS (1939-69) BASED ON AVERAGE PER RETURN

(Minimum 1.2 Returns Per Game)

1939—Nile Kinnick, Iowa, 25.1; **1940**—Bill Geyer, Colgate, 27.0; **1941**—Vern Lockard, Colorado, 24.4; **1942-45**—Not compiled; **1946**—Forrest Hall, San Francisco, ‡38.2; **1947**—Skippy Minisi, Pennsylvania, 28.8; **1948**—Jerry Williams, Washington St., 29.9; **1949**—Billy Conn, Georgetown, 31.1; **1950**—Johnny Turco, Holy Cross, 27.4; **1951**—Bob Mischak, Army, 31.3; **1952**—Carroll Hardy, Colorado, 32.2; **1953**—Carl Bolt, Wash. & Lee, 27.1; **1954**—George Marinkov, North Caro. St., 35.8; **1955**—Jim Brown, Syracuse, 32.0; **1956**—Paul Hornung, Notre Dame, 31.0; **1957**—Overton Curtis, Utah St., 30.2; **1958**—Marshall Starks, Illinois, 26.3; **1959**—Don Perkins, New Mexico, 34.7; **1960**—Tom Hennessey, Holy Cross, 33.4; **1961**—Paul Allen, Brigham Young, *40.1; **1962**—Larry Coyer, Marshall, 30.2; **1963**—Gary Wood, Cornell, 32.5; **1964**—Bob Baker, Cornell, 35.1; **1965**—Tom Barrington, Ohio St., 34.3; **1966**—Frank Moore, Louisville, 27.9; **1967**—Altie Taylor, Utah St., 31.9; **1968**—Kerry Reardon, Iowa, 32.1; **1969**—Chris Farasopoulous, Brigham Young, 32.2.

**Record. ‡Record for minimum 1.5 returns per game.*

Iowa State sports information photo by John W. Matila

Iowa State running back Troy Davis averaged 224.2 all-purpose yards per game as a sophomore in 1995. Only nine players in major-college history have averaged more yards in a single season.

All-Purpose Yards

CAREER YARDS PER GAME

(Minimum 3,500 Yards)

Player, Team	Years	Rush	Rcv.	Int.	PR	KOR	Yds.	Yd.PG
Ryan Benjamin, Pacific (Cal.)	1990-92	3,119	1,063	0	100	1,424	5,706	*237.8
Sheldon Canley, San Jose St.	1988-90	2,513	828	0	5	1,800	5,146	205.8
Howard Stevens, Louisville	1971-72	2,723	389	0	401	360	3,873	193.7
O. J. Simpson, Southern Cal	1967-68	3,124	235	0	0	307	3,666	192.9
Alex Van Dyke, Nevada	1994-95	7	3,100	0	5	1,034	4,146	188.5
Ed Marinaro, Cornell	1969-71	4,715	225	0	0	0	4,940	183.0
Marshall Faulk, San Diego St.	1991-93	4,589	973	0	0	33	5,595	180.5
Herschel Walker, Georgia	1980-82	5,259	243	0	0	247	5,749	174.2
Louie Giammona, Utah St.	1973-75	3,499	171	0	188	1,345	5,203	173.4

**Record.*

SEASON YARDS PER GAME

Player, Team	Year	Rush	Rcv.	Int.	PR	KOR	Yds.	Yd.PG
Barry Sanders, Oklahoma St.	†1988	*2,628	106	0	95	421	*3,250	*295.5
Ryan Benjamin, Pacific (Cal.)	†1991	1,581	612	0	4	798	2,995	249.6
Byron "Whizzer" White, Colorado	†1937	1,121	0	103	587	159	1,970	246.3
Mike Pringle, Cal St. Fullerton	†1989	1,727	249	0	0	714	2,690	244.6
Paul Palmer, Temple	†1986	1,866	110	0	0	657	2,633	239.4
Ryan Benjamin, Pacific (Cal.)	†1992	1,441	434	0	96	626	2,597	236.1
Marcus Allen, Southern Cal	†1981	2,342	217	0	0	0	2,559	232.6
Sheldon Canley, San Jose St.	1989	1,201	353	0	0	959	2,513	228.5
Ollie Matson, San Francisco	†1951	1,566	58	18	115	280	2,037	226.3
Troy Davis, Iowa St.	†1995	2,010	159	0	0	297	2,466	224.2
Alex Van Dyke, Nevada	1995	6	*1,854	0	0	583	2,443	222.1
Art Luppino, Arizona	†1954	1,359	50	84	68	632	2,193	219.3
Chuck Weatherspoon, Houston	1989	1,146	735	0	715	95	2,391	217.4
Anthony Thompson, Indiana	1989	1,793	201	0	0	394	2,388	217.1
Napoleon McCallum, Navy	†1983	1,587	166	0	272	360	2,385	216.8
Ed Marinaro, Cornell	†1971	1,881	51	0	0	0	1,932	214.7
Rashaan Salaam, Colorado	†1994	2,055	294	0	0	0	2,349	213.6
Howard Stevens, Louisville	†1972	1,294	221	0	337	240	2,132	213.2
Napoleon McCallum, Navy	†1985	1,327	358	0	157	488	2,330	211.8
Brian Pruitt, Central Mich.	1994	1,890	69	0	0	330	2,289	208.1
Keith Byars, Ohio St.	†1984	1,655	453	0	0	176	2,284	207.6
Mike Rozier, Nebraska	1983	2,148	106	0	0	232	2,486	207.2

**Record. †National champion.*

CAREER YARDS

Player, Team	Years	Rush	Rcv.	Int.	PR	KOR	Yds.	Yd.PP
Napoleon McCallum, Navy	$1981-85	4,179	796	0	858	1,339	*7,172	6.3
Darrin Nelson, Stanford	1977-78, 80-81	4,033	2,368	0	471	13	6,885	7.1
Terance Mathis, New Mexico	1985-87, 89	329	4,254	0	115	1,993	6,691	**14.6
Tony Dorsett, Pittsburgh	1973-76	*6,082	406	0	0	127	6,615	5.9
Paul Palmer, Temple	1983-86	4,895	705	0	12	997	6,609	6.1
Charles White, Southern Cal	1976-79	5,598	507	0	0	440	6,545	6.0
Trevor Cobb, Rice	1989-92	4,948	892	0	21	651	6,512	5.3
Glyn Milburn, Oklahoma/Stanford	1988, 90-92	2,302	1,495	0	1,145	1,246	6,188	8.1
Anthony Thompson, Indiana	1986-89	4,965	713	0	0	412	6,090	5.1
Archie Griffin, Ohio St.	1972-75	5,177	286	0	0	540	6,003	6.7
Ron "Po" James, New Mexico St.	1968-71	3,884	217	0	8	1,870	5,979	6.5
Eric Wilkerson, Kent	1985-88	3,830	506	0	0	1,638	5,974	7.0
Steve Bartalo, Colorado St.	1983-86	4,813	1,079	0	0	0	5,892	4.4
Wilford White, Arizona St.	1947-50	3,173	892	212	798	791	5,866	9.2
Joe Washington, Oklahoma	1972-75	3,995	253	0	807	726	5,781	7.3

Player, Team	Years	Rush	Rcv.	Int.	PR	KOR	Yds.	Yd.PP
Herschel Walker, Georgia	1980-82	5,259	243	0	0	247	‡5,749	5.6
George Swarn, Miami (Ohio)	1983-86	4,172	1,057	0	0	498	5,727	5.6
Chuck Weatherspoon, Houston	1987-90	3,247	1,375	0	611	482	5,715	9.7
Ryan Benjamin, Pacific (Cal.)	1990-92	3,119	1,063	0	100	1,424	‡5,706	8.8
Eric Metcalf, Texas	1985-88	2,661	1,394	0	1,076	574	5,705	6.7
George Rogers, South Caro.	1977-80	4,958	371	0	0	339	5,668	5.9
Napoleon Kaufman, Washington	1991-94	4,041	424	0	368	825	5,658	6.7
Jamie Morris, Michigan	1984-87	3,944	703	0	0	984	5,631	6.4
Joe Morris, Syracuse	1978-81	4,299	278	0	0	1,023	5,600	6.3
James Brooks, Auburn	1977-80	3,523	219	0	128	1,726	5,596	7.6
Marshall Faulk, San Diego St.	1991-93	4,589	973	0	0	33	‡5,595	6.6
Johnny Rodgers, Nebraska	1970-72	745	2,479	0	1,515	847	‡5,586	13.8
Thurman Thomas, Oklahoma St.	1984-87	4,595	551	0	143	237	5,526	5.5
Mike Rozier, Nebraska	1981-83	4,780	216	0	0	449	‡5,445	7.7

**Record. $See page 6 for explanation. ‡Three-year totals. **Record for minimum 375 plays*

Kentucky sports information photo by David Coyle

Moe Williams' total of 429 all-purpose yards against South Carolina last season was just six yards shy of the Division I-A single-game mark.

SEASON YARDS

Player, Team	Year	Rush	Rcv.	Int.	PR	KOR	Yds.	Yd.PP
Barry Sanders, Oklahoma St.	†1988	*2,628	106	0	95	421	*3,250	8.3
Ryan Benjamin, Pacific (Cal.)	†1991	1,581	612	0	4	798	2,995	9.6
Mike Pringle, Cal St. Fullerton	†1989	1,727	249	0	0	714	2,690	7.6
Paul Palmer, Temple	†1986	1,866	110	0	0	657	2,633	6.8
Ryan Benjamin, Pacific (Cal.)	†1992	1,441	434	0	96	626	2,597	8.1
Marcus Allen, Southern Cal	†1981	2,342	217	0	0	0	2,559	5.9
Sheldon Canley, San Jose St.	1989	1,201	353	0	0	959	2,513	7.4
Mike Rozier, Nebraska	1983	2,148	106	0	0	232	2,486	8.4
Troy Davis, Iowa St.	†1995	2,010	159	0	0	297	2,466	6.7
Alex Van Dyke, Nevada	1995	6	*1,854	0	0	583	2,443	15.7
Chuck Weatherspoon, Houston	1989	1,146	735	0	415	95	2,391	10.7
Anthony Thompson, Indiana	1989	1,793	201	0	0	394	2,388	5.8
Napoleon McCallum, Navy	†1983	1,587	166	0	272	360	2,385	6.1
Rashaan Salaam, Colorado	†1994	2,055	294	0	0	0	2,349	7.3
Napoleon McCallum, Navy	†1985	1,327	358	0	157	488	2,330	6.3
Brian Pruitt, Central Mich.	1994	1,890	69	0	0	330	2,289	7.3
Keith Byars, Ohio St.	†1984	1,655	453	0	0	176	2,284	6.4
Eddie George, Ohio St.	1995	1,826	399	0	0	0	2,225	6.4
Glyn Milburn, Stanford	†1990	729	632	0	267	594	2,222	8.4
Vaughn Dunbar, Indiana	1991	1,699	252	0	0	262	2,213	5.9
Sheldon Canley, San Jose St.	1990	1,248	386	0	5	574	2,213	6.3
Johnny Johnson, San Jose St.	1988	1,219	668	0	0	315	2,202	7.1
Art Luppino, Arizona	†1954	1,359	50	84	68	632	2,193	10.4
Rick Calhoun, Cal St. Fullerton	1986	1,398	125	0	138	522	2,183	7.0
Marshall Faulk, San Diego St.	1993	1,530	644	0	0	0	2,174	6.3
Terance Mathis, New Mexico	1989	38	1,315	0	0	785	2,138	‡15.7
Howard Stevens, Louisville	†1972	1,294	221	0	377	240	2,132	6.4

**Record. †National champion. ‡Record for minimum 125 plays.*

ALL-PURPOSE SINGLE-GAME HIGHS

Yds.	Player, Team (Opponent)	Date
435	Brian Pruitt, Central Mich. (Toledo)	Nov. 5, 1994
429	Moe Williams, Kentucky (South Caro.)	Sept. 23, 1995
422	Marshall Faulk, San Diego St. (Pacific, Cal.)	Sept. 14, 1991
419	Randy Gatewood, UNLV (Idaho)	Sept. 17, 1994
417	Paul Palmer, Temple (East Caro.)	Nov. 10, 1986
417	Greg Allen, Florida St. (Western Caro.)	Oct. 31, 1981
416	Anthony Thompson, Indiana (Wisconsin)	Nov. 11, 1989
411	John Leach, Wake Forest (Maryland)	Nov. 20, 1993
402	Ryan Benjamin, Pacific, Cal. (Utah St.)	Nov. 21, 1992
401	Chuck Hughes, UTEP (North Texas)	Sept. 18, 1965
397	Eric Allen, Michigan St. (Purdue)	Oct. 30, 1971
388	Ryan Benjamin, Pacific, Cal. (Cal St. Fullerton)	Oct. 5, 1991
387	Kendal Smith, Utah St. (San Jose St.)	Oct. 22, 1988
387	Ron Johnson, Michigan (Wisconsin)	Nov. 16, 1968
386	Barry Sanders, Oklahoma St. (Kansas)	Nov. 12, 1988
379	Glyn Milburn, Stanford (California)	Nov. 17, 1990
375	Alex Van Dyke, Nevada (Toledo)	Sept. 23, 1995
375	Rueben Mayes, Washington St. (Oregon St.)	Nov. 3, 1984
374	Tony Dorsett, Pittsburgh (Penn St.)	Nov. 22, 1975
373	Barry Sanders, Oklahoma St. (Oklahoma)	Nov. 5, 1988
372	Chuck Weatherspoon, Houston (Eastern Wash.)	Nov. 17, 1990

ANNUAL CHAMPIONS

Year	Player, Team	Class	Rush	Rcv.	Int.	PR	KOR	Yds.	Yd.PG
1937	Byron "Whizzer" White, Colorado	Sr.	1,121	0	103	587	159	1,970	246.3
1938	Parker Hall, Mississippi	Sr.	698	0	128	0	594	1,420	129.1
1939	Tom Harmon, Michigan	Jr.	868	110	98	0	132	1,208	151.0
1940	Tom Harmon, Michigan	Sr.	844	0	20	244	204	1,312	164.0
1941	Bill Dudley, Virginia	Sr.	968	60	76	481	89	1,674	186.0
1942	records not available	—	—	—	—	—	—	—	—
1943	Stan Koslowski, Holy Cross	Fr.	784	63	50	438	76	1,411	176.4
1944	Red Williams, Minnesota	Jr.	911	0	0	242	314	1,467	163.0
1945	Bob Fenimore, Oklahoma St.	Jr.	1,048	12	129	157	231	1,577	197.1
1946	Rudy Mobley, Hardin-Simmons	Sr.	1,262	13	79	273	138	1,765	176.5

Photo from Alabama sports information

Alabama kicker Michael Proctor's total of 65 field goals is tied for 18th on the Division I-A career list.

Year	Player, Team	Class	Rush	Rcv.	Int.	PR	KOR	Yds.	Yd.PG
1947	Wilton Davis, Hardin-Simmons	So.	1,173	79	0	295	251	1,798	179.8
1948	Lou Kusserow, Columbia	Sr.	766	463	19	130	359	1,737	193.0
1949	Johnny Papit, Virginia	Jr.	1,214	0	0	0	397	1,611	179.0
1950	Wilford White, Arizona St.	Sr.	1,502	225	0	64	274	2,065	206.5
1951	Ollie Matson, San Francisco	Sr.	1,566	58	18	115	280	2,037	226.3
1952	Billy Vessels, Oklahoma	Sr.	1,072	165	10	120	145	1,512	151.2
1953	J. C. Caroline, Illinois	So.	1,256	52	0	129	33	1,470	163.3
1954	Art Luppino, Arizona	So.	1,359	50	84	68	632	2,193	219.3
1955	Jim Swink, Texas Christian	Jr.	1,283	111	46	64	198	1,702	170.2
	Art Luppino, Arizona	Jr.	1,313	74	0	62	253	1,702	170.2
1956	Jack Hill, Utah St.	Sr.	920	215	132	21	403	1,691	169.1
1957	Overton Curtis, Utah St.	Jr.	616	193	60	44	695	1,608	160.8
1958	Dick Bass, Pacific (Cal.)	Jr.	1,361	121	5	164	227	1,878	187.8
1959	Pervis Atkins, New Mexico St.	Jr.	971	301	23	241	264	1,800	180.0
1960	Pervis Atkins, New Mexico St.	Sr.	611	468	23	218	293	1,613	161.3
1961	Jim Pilot, New Mexico St.	So.	1,278	20	0	161	147	1,606	160.6
1962	Gary Wood, Cornell	Jr.	889	7	0	69	430	1,395	155.0
1963	Gary Wood, Cornell	Sr.	818	15	0	57	618	1,508	167.6
1964	Donny Anderson, Texas Tech	Jr.	966	396	0	28	320	1,710	171.0
1965	Floyd Little, Syracuse	Jr.	1,065	248	0	423	254	1,990	199.0
1966	Frank Quayle, Virginia	So.	727	420	0	30	439	1,616	161.6
1967	O. J. Simpson, Southern Cal	Jr.	1,415	109	0	0	176	1,700	188.9
1968	O. J. Simpson, Southern Cal	Sr.	1,709	126	0	0	131	1,966	196.6
1969	Lynn Moore, Army	Sr.	983	44	0	223	545	1,795	179.5
1970	Don McCauley, North Caro.	Sr.	1,720	235	0	0	66	2,021	183.7
1971	Ed Marinaro, Cornell	Sr.	1,881	51	0	0	0	1,932	214.7
1972	Howard Stevens, Louisville	Sr.	1,294	221	0	377	240	2,132	213.2
1973	Willard Harrell, Pacific (Cal.)	Jr.	1,319	18	0	88	352	1,777	177.7
1974	Louie Giammona, Utah St.	Jr.	1,534	79	0	16	355	1,984	198.4
1975	Louie Giammona, Utah St.	Sr.	1,454	33	0	124	434	2,045	185.9
1976	Tony Dorsett, Pittsburgh	Sr.	1,948	73	0	0	0	2,021	183.7
1977	Earl Campbell, Texas	Sr.	1,744	111	0	0	0	1,855	168.6
1978	Charles White, Southern Cal	Jr.	1,760	191	0	0	145	2,096	174.7
1979	Charles White, Southern Cal	Sr.	1,803	138	0	0	0	1,941	194.1
1980	Marcus Allen, Southern Cal	Jr.	1,563	231	0	0	0	1,794	179.4
1981	Marcus Allen, Southern Cal	Sr.	2,342	217	0	0	0	2,559	232.6
1982	Carl Monroe, Utah	Sr.	1,507	108	0	0	421	2,036	185.1
1983	Napoleon McCallum, Navy	Jr.	1,587	166	0	272	360	2,385	216.8
1984	Keith Byars, Ohio St.	Jr.	1,655	453	0	0	176	2,284	207.6
1985	Napoleon McCallum, Navy	Sr.	1,327	358	0	157	488	2,330	211.8
1986	Paul Palmer, Temple	Sr.	1,866	110	0	0	657	2,633	239.4
1987	Eric Wilkerson, Kent	Jr.	1,221	269	0	0	584	2,074	188.6
1988	Barry Sanders, Oklahoma St.	Jr.	*2,628	106	0	95	421	*3,250	*295.5
1989	Mike Pringle, Cal St. Fullerton	Sr.	1,727	249	0	0	714	2,690	244.6
1990	Glyn Milburn, Stanford	So.	729	632	0	267	594	2,222	202.0
1991	Ryan Benjamin, Pacific (Cal.)	Jr.	1,581	612	0	4	798	2,995	249.6
1992	Ryan Benjamin, Pacific (Cal.)	Sr.	1,441	434	0	96	626	2,597	236.1
1993	LeShon Johnson, Northern Ill.	Sr.	1,976	106	0	0	0	2,082	189.3
1994	Rashaan Salaam, Colorado	Jr.	2,055	294	0	0	0	2,349	213.6
1995	Troy Davis, Iowa St.	So.	2,010	159	0	0	297	2,466	224.2

**Record.*

Field Goals

CAREER FIELD GOALS

(One-inch tees were permitted in 1949, two-inch tees were permitted in 1965, and use of tees was eliminated in 1989. The goal posts were widened from 18 feet, 6 inches to 23 feet, 4 inches in 1959 and were narrowed back to 18 feet, 6 inches in 1991. In 1993, the hash marks were moved 6 feet, 8 inches closer to the center of the field, to 60 feet from each sideline.)

Player, Team	Years	Total	Pct.	Under 40 Yds.	40 Plus	Long	‡Won
Jeff Jaeger, Washington (S)	1983-86	*80-99	.808	59-68	21-31	52	5
John Lee, UCLA (S)	1982-85	79-92	@.859	54-56	25-36	52	**10
Jason Elam, Hawaii (S)	$1988-92	79-100	.790	50-55	29-45	56	3
Philip Doyle, Alabama (S)	1987-90	78-*105	.743	57-61	21-44	53	6
Luis Zendejas, Arizona St. (S)	1981-84	78-*105	.743	53-59	25-46	55	1
Kevin Butler, Georgia (S)	1981-84	77-98	.786	50-56	27-42	60	7
Max Zendejas, Arizona (S)	1982-85	77-104	.740	47-53	30-51	57	7
Carlos Huerta, Miami (Fla.) (S)	1988-91	73-91	.802	56-60	17-31	52	3
Derek Schmidt, Florida St. (S)	1984-87	73-104	.702	44-55	29-49	54	1
Fuad Reveiz, Tennessee (S)	1981-84	71-95	.747	45-53	26-42	60	7
Barry Belli, Fresno St. (S)	1984-87	70-99	.707	47-53	23-46	55	5
Nelson Welch, Clemson (S)	1991-94	70-100	.700	49-64	21-36	53	7
Roman Anderson, Houston (S)	1988-91	70-101	.693	*61-*72	9-29	53	3
Collin Mackie, South Caro. (S)	1987-90	69-95	.726	48-57	21-38	52	5
Gary Gusman, Miami (Ohio) (S)	1984-87	68-94	.723	50-57	18-37	53	2
Rusty Hanna, Toledo (S)	1989-92	68-99	.687	51-58	17-41	51	3
Larry Roach, Oklahoma St. (S)	1981-84	68-101	.673	46-54	22-47	56	5
Paul Woodside, West Va. (S)	1981-84	65-81	.802	45-49	20-32	55	5
Michael Proctor, Alabama (S)	1992-95	65-91	.714	48-64	17-27	53	5
John Diettrich, Ball St. (S)	1983-86	63-90	.700	42-50	21-40	62	5

Player, Team	Years	Total	Pct.	Under 40 Yds.	40 Plus	Long	‡Won
Jason Hanson, Washington St. (S)	1988-91	63-96	.656	24-30	*39-*66	62	4
Dan Eichloff, Kansas (S)	1990-93	62-87	.713	40-50	22-37	61	5
Kenny Stucker, Ball St. (S)	1988-91	62-87	.713	45-51	17-36	52	4
David Browndyke, LSU (S)	1986-89	61-75	.813	49-53	12-22	52	3
Todd Gregoire, Wisconsin (S)	1984-87	61-81	.753	48-56	13-25	54	6
Kanon Parkman, Georgia (S)	1991, 93-95	61-85	.718	52-61	9-24	48	1
Todd Wright, Arkansas (S)	1989-92	60-79	.759	41-47	19-32	50	2
Jess Atkinson, Maryland (S)	1981-84	60-82	.732	40-48	20-34	50	5
Scott Sisson, Georgia Tech (S)	1989-92	60-88	.682	45-53	15-35	51	6
Obed Ariri, Clemson (S)	1977-80	60-92	.652	47-55	13-37	57	5
Chuck Nelson, Washington (S)	1980-82	59-72	.819	47-53	12-19	51	5
Van Tiffin, Alabama (S)	1983-86	59-87	.678	32-38	27-49	57	5
John Hopkins, Stanford (S)	1987-90	59-88	.670	43-50	16-38	54	4
Jeff Ward, Texas (S)	1983-86	58-78	.744	36-41	22-37	57	**10
Jeff Shudak, Iowa St. (S)	1987-90	58-79	.734	38-45	20-34	55	5

*Record. $See page 6 for explanation. **Record tied. @Record for minimum 55 attempts. ‡Number of games in which his field goal(s) provided the winning margin. (S) Soccer-style kicker.

Photo from UCLA sports information

UCLA's John Lee (#25) kicked a Division I-A single-season record 29 field goals in 1984.

SEASON FIELD GOALS

Player, Team	Year	Total	Pct.	Under 40 Yds.	40 Plus	Long	‡Won
John Lee, UCLA (S)	†1984	*29-33	.879	16-16	13-17	51	5
Paul Woodside, West Va. (S)	†1982	28-31	.903	23-23	5-8	45	2
Luis Zendejas, Arizona St. (S)	†1983	28-37	.757	19-22	9-15	52	1
Fuad Reveiz, Tennessee (S)	1982	27-31	.871	14-14	13-17	60	2
Chuck Nelson, Washington (S)	1982	25-26	*.962	22-23	3-3	49	1
Chris Jacke, UTEP (S)	1988	25-27	.926	11-11	*14-16	52	2
John Diettrich, Ball St. (S)	†1985	25-29	.862	16-17	9-12	54	2
Kendall Trainor, Arkansas (S)	†1988	24-27	.889	14-15	10-12	58	4
Carlos Reveiz, Tennessee (S)	1985	24-28	.857	12-14	12-14	52	2
Chris White, Illinois (S)	1984	24-28	.857	16-17	8-11	52	1
Remy Hamilton, Michigan (S)	†1994	24-29	.828	23-27	1-2	42	2
Philip Doyle, Alabama (S)	†1990	24-29	.828	16-17	8-12	47	2
Bruce Kallmeyer, Kansas (S)	1983	24-29	.828	13-14	11-15	57	1
Mike Prindle, Western Mich. (S)	1984	24-30	.800	17-20	7-10	56	1
Michael Reeder, Texas Christian (S)	†1995	23-25	.920	19-19	4-6	47	3
Joe Allison, Memphis (S)	†1992	23-25	.920	13-14	10-11	51	1
Bobby Raymond, Florida (S)	1984	23-26	.885	18-18	5-8	51	1
Mike Bass, Illinois (S)	1982	23-26	.885	12-13	11-13	53	1
Kevin Butler, Georgia (S)	1984	23-28	.821	12-14	11-14	60	2
Steve McLaughlin, Arizona (S)	1994	23-29	.793	11-13	12-16	54	4
Collin Mackie, South Caro. (S)	†1987	23-30	.767	17-21	6-9	49	0
Obed Ariri, Clemson (S)	†1980	23-30	.767	18-19	5-11	52	3
Derek Schmidt, Florida St. (S)	†1987	23-31	.742	16-21	7-10	53	0

*Record. †National champion. ‡Number of games in which his field goal(s) provided the winning margin. (S) Soccer-style kicker.

SINGLE-GAME FIELD GOALS

No.	Player, Team (Opponent)	Date
7	Dale Klein, Nebraska (Missouri)	Oct. 19, 1985
7	Mike Prindle, Western Mich. (Marshall)	Sept. 29, 1984
6	Rusty Hanna, Toledo (Northern Ill.)	Nov. 21, 1992
6	Philip Doyle, Alabama (Southwestern La.)	Oct. 6, 1990
6	Sean Fleming, Wyoming (Arkansas St.)	Sept. 15, 1990
6	Bobby Raymond, Florida (Kentucky)	Nov. 17, 1984
6	John Lee, UCLA (San Diego St.)	Sept. 8, 1984
6	Bobby Raymond, Florida (Florida St.)	Dec. 3, 1983
6	Alan Smith, Texas A&M (Arkansas St.)	Sept. 17, 1983
6	Al Del Greco, Auburn (Kentucky)	Oct. 9, 1982
6	Vince Fusco, Duke (Clemson)	Oct. 16, 1976
6	Frank Nester, West Va. (Villanova)	Sept. 9, 1972
6	Charley Gogolak, Princeton (Rutgers)	Sept. 25, 1965

ANNUAL CHAMPIONS

(From 1959-90, goal posts were 23 feet, 4 inches; and from 1991, narrowed to 18 feet, 6 inches)

Year	Player, Team	Total	PG	Pct.	Under 40 Yds.	40 Plus	Long	‡Won
1959	Karl Holzwarth, Wisconsin (C)	7-8	0.8	.875	7-8	0-0	29	4
1960	Ed Dyas, Auburn (C)	13-18	1.3	.722	13-17	0-1	37	2
1961	Greg Mather, Navy (C)	11-15	1.1	.733	9-12	2-3	45	1
1962	Bob Jencks, Miami (Ohio) (C)	8-11	0.8	.727	7-9	1-2	52	3
	Al Woodall, Auburn (C)	8-20	0.8	.400	8-13	0-7	35	0
1963	Billy Lothridge, Georgia Tech (C)	12-16	1.2	.750	10-14	2-2	41	3
1964	Doug Moreau, LSU (C)	13-20	1.3	.650	13-20	0-0	36	0
1965	Charley Gogolak, Princeton (S)	16-23	1.8	.696	7-10	9-13	54	0
1966	Jerry DePoyster, Wyoming (C)	13-*38	1.3	.342	7-13	6-*25	54	1
1967	Gerald Warren, North Caro. St. (C)	17-22	1.7	.773	13-14	4-8	47	1
1968	Bob Jacobs, Wyoming (C)	14-29	1.4	.483	10-15	4-14	51	2
1969	Bob Jacobs, Wyoming (C)	18-27	1.8	.667	13-16	5-11	43	2

Photo from Texas Christian sports information

Michael Reeder of Texas Christian led Division I-A kickers with an average of 2.1 field goals per game in 1995. He was perfect on 19 tries of less than 40 yards.

Beginning in 1970, ranked on per-game (instead of total) made

Year	Player, Team	Total	PG	Pct.	Under 40 Yds.	40 Plus	Long	‡Won
1970	Kim Braswell, Georgia (C)	13-17	1.3	.765	11-14	2-3	43	0
1971	Nick Mike-Mayer, Temple (S)	12-17	1.3	.706	8-10	4-7	48	1
1972	Nick Mike-Mayer, Temple (S)	13-20	1.4	.650	10-11	3-9	44	3
1973	Rod Garcia, Stanford (S)	18-29	1.6	.621	10-14	8-15	59	2
1974	Dave Lawson, Air Force (C)	19-31	1.7	.613	13-14	6-17	60	1
1975	Don Bitterlich, Temple (S)	21-31	1.9	.677	13-14	8-17	56	0
1976	Tony Franklin, Texas A&M (S)	17-26	1.6	.654	9-12	8-14	65	0
1977	Paul Marchese, Kent (S)	18-27	1.8	.667	13-15	5-12	51	2
1978	Matt Bahr, Penn St. (S)	22-27	2.0	.815	19-20	3-7	50	3
1979	Ish Ordonez, Arkansas (S)	18-22	1.6	.818	12-14	6-8	50	2
1980	Obed Ariri, Clemson (S)	23-30	2.1	.767	18-19	5-11	52	3
1981	Bruce Lahay, Arkansas (S)	19-24	1.7	.792	12-15	7-9	49	4
	Kevin Butler, Georgia (S)	19-26	1.7	.731	11-14	8-12	52	0
	Larry Roach, Oklahoma St. (S)	19-28	1.7	.679	12-14	7-14	56	3
1982	Paul Woodside, West Va. (S)	28-31	2.6	.903	23-23	5-8	45	2
1983	Luis Zendejas, Arizona St. (S)	28-37	2.6	.757	19-22	9-15	52	1
1984	John Lee, UCLA (S)	*29-33	*2.6	.879	16-16	13-17	51	5
1985	John Diettrich, Ball St. (S)	25-29	2.3	.862	16-17	9-12	54	2
1986	Chris Kinzer, Virginia Tech (C)	22-27	2.0	.815	14-17	8-10	50	5
1987	Collin Mackie, South Caro. (S)	23-30	2.1	.767	17-21	6-9	49	0
	Derek Schmidt, Florida St. (S)	23-31	2.1	.742	16-21	7-10	53	0
1988	Kendall Trainor, Arkansas (S)	24-27	2.2	.889	14-15	10-12	58	4
1989	Philip Doyle, Alabama (S)	22-25	2.0	.880	19-19	3-6	44	2
	Gregg McCallum, Oregon (S)	22-29	2.0	.759	15-15	7-14	47	2
	Roman Anderson, Houston (S)	22-34	2.0	.647	17-20	5-14	51	0
1990	Philip Doyle, Alabama (S)	24-29	2.2	.828	16-17	8-12	47	2
1991	Doug Brien, California (S)	19-28	1.7	.679	15-20	4-8	50	2
1992	Joe Allison, Memphis (S)	23-25	2.1	.920	13-14	10-11	51	1
1993	Michael Proctor, Alabama (S)	22-29	1.8	.759	15-20	7-9	53	0
1994	Remy Hamilton, Michigan (S)	24-29	2.2	.828	23-27	1-2	42	2
1995	Michael Reeder, Texas Christian (S)	23-25	2.1	.920	19-19	4-6	47	3

**Record.* ‡*Number of games in which his field goal(s) provided the winning margin.* (C) *Conventional kicker.* (S) *Soccer-style kicker.*

All-Time Longest Plays

Since 1941, official maximum length of all plays fixed at 100 yards.

RUSHING

Yds.	Player, Team (Opponent)	Year
99	Kelsey Finch, Tennessee (Florida)	1977
99	Ralph Thompson, West Tex. A&M (Wichita St.)	1970
99	Max Anderson, Arizona St. (Wyoming)	1967
99	Gale Sayers, Kansas (Nebraska)	1963
98	Jerald Sowell, Tulane (Alabama)	1993
98	Darrell Thompson, Minnesota (Michigan)	1987
98	George Swarn, Miami, Ohio (Western Mich.)	1984
98	Mark Malone, Arizona St. (Utah St.)	1979
98	Stanley Howell, Mississippi St. (Southern Miss.)	1979
98	Steve Atkins, Maryland (Clemson)	1978
98	Granville Amos, Va. Military (William & Mary)	1964
98	Jim Thacker, Davidson (Geo. Washington)	1952
98	Bill Powell, California (Oregon St.)	1951
98	Al Yannelli, Bucknell (Delaware)	1946
98	Meredith Warner, Iowa St. (Iowa Pre-Flight)	1943

PASSING

Yds.	Passer-Receiver, Team (Opponent)	Year
99	John Paci-Thomas Lewis, Indiana (Penn St.)	1993
99	Gino Torretta-Horace Copeland, Miami, Fla. (Arkansas)	1991
99	Scott Ankrom-James Maness, Texas Christian (Rice)	1984
99	Cris Collinsworth-Derrick Gaffney, Florida (Rice)	1977
99	Terry Peel-Robert Ford, Houston (San Diego St.)	1972
99	Terry Peel-Robert Ford, Houston (Syracuse)	1970
99	Colin Clapton-Eddie Jenkins, Holy Cross (Boston U.)	1970
99	Bo Burris-Warren McVea, Houston (Washington St.)	1966
99	Fred Owens-Jack Ford, Portland (St. Mary's, Cal.)	1947
98	Mike Neu-Brian Oliver, Ball St. (Toledo)	1993
98	Tom Dubs-Richard Hill, Ohio (Kent)	1991
98	Paul Oates-Sean Foster, Long Beach St. (San Diego St.)	1989
98	Barry Garrison-Al Owens, New Mexico (Brigham Young)	1987
98	Kelly Donohoe-Willie Vaughn, Kansas (Colorado)	1987
98	Jeff Martin-Mark Flaker, Drake (New Mexico St.)	1976
98	Pete Woods-Joe Stewart, Missouri (Nebraska)	1976
98	Dan Hagemann-Jack Steptoe, Utah (New Mexico)	1976
98	Bruce Shaw-Pat Kenney, North Caro. St. (Penn St.)	1972
98	Jerry Rhome-Jeff Jordan, Tulsa (Wichita St.)	1963
98	Bob Dean-Norman Dawson, Cornell (Navy)	1947

INTERCEPTION RETURNS

Since 1941, 63 players have returned interceptions 100 yards. The most recent:

Yds.	Player, Team (Opponent)	Year
100	Reggie Love, North Caro. (Tulane)	1994
100	Harold Lusk, Utah (Colorado St.)	1994
100	Marlon Kerner, Ohio St. (Purdue)	1993
100	Ray Jackson, Colorado St. (UTEP)	1993
100	John Hardy, California (Wisconsin)	1990
100	Ed Givens, Army (Lafayette)	1990

PUNT RETURNS

Yds.	Player, Team (Opponent)	Year
100	Eddie Kennison, LSU (Mississippi St.)	1994
100‡	Richie Luzzi, Clemson (Georgia)	1968
100‡	Don Guest, California (Washington St.)	1966
100	Jimmy Campagna, Georgia (Vanderbilt)	1952
100	Hugh McElhenny, Washington (Southern Cal)	1951
100	Frank Brady, Navy (Maryland)	1951
100	Bert Rechichar, Tennessee (Wash. & Lee)	1950
100	Eddie Macon, Pacific, Cal. (Boston U.)	1950

‡*Return of field goal attempt.*

KICKOFF RETURNS

Since 1941, 178 players have returned kickoffs 100 yards. The most recent:

Yds.	Player, Team (Opponent)	Year
100	Jason Jacoby, Tulsa (Brigham Young)	1995
100	Aaron Stecker, Wisconsin (Minnesota)	1995
100	Leeland McElroy, Texas A&M (Southern Miss.)	1994
100	Jason Jacoby, Tulsa (UNLV)	1994
100	Seth Smith, Michigan (Wisconsin)	1994
100	Derrick Mason, Michigan St. (Penn St.)	1994
100	Madre Hill, Arkansas (LSU)	1994
100	Clint Johnson, Notre Dame (Stanford)	1993
100	Leroy Gallman, Duke (Tennessee)	1993
100	Jack Jackson, Florida (Mississippi St.)	1993
100	Charles Henley, Kansas (Colorado)	1993
100	Leeland McElroy, Texas A&M (Texas)	1993

PUNTS

Yds.	Player, Team (Opponent)	Year
99	Pat Brady, Nevada (Loyola Marymount)	1950
96	George O'Brien, Wisconsin (Iowa)	1952
94	John Hadl, Kansas (Oklahoma)	1959
94	Carl Knox, Texas Christian (Oklahoma St.)	1947
94	Preston Johnson, Southern Methodist (Pittsburgh)	1940

FUMBLE RETURNS

(Since 1992)

Yds.	Player, Team (Opponent)	Year
100	Paul Rivers, Rutgers (Pittsburgh)	1995
97	Chris Martin, Northwestern (Air Force)	1994
97	Mike Collins, West Va. (Missouri)	1993
97	Ernie Lewis, East Caro. (West Va.)	1992
96	Jeff Arneson, Illinois (Ohio St.)	1992
95	Ben Hanks, Florida (Arkansas)	1995
93	Parrish Foster, New Mexico St. (Nevada)	1993
92	Marcus Coleman, Texas Tech (New Mexico)	1995
92	Gerald Nickelberry, Northern Ill. (Arkansas St.)	1993
92	David Thomas, Miami, Ohio (Akron)	1993
91	Michael Barber, Clemson (Tenn.-Chatt.)	1992
91	Cassius Ware, Mississippi (Auburn)	1992

FIELD GOALS

Yds.	Player, Team (Opponent)	Year
67	Joe Williams, Wichita St. (Southern Ill.)	1978
67	Steve Little, Arkansas (Texas)	1977
67	Russell Erxleben, Texas (Rice)	1977
65	Tony Franklin, Texas A&M (Baylor)	1976
64	Russell Erxleben, Texas (Oklahoma)	1977
64	Tony Franklin, Texas A&M (Baylor)	1976
63	Morten Andersen, Michigan St. (Ohio St.)	1981
63	Clark Kemble, Colorado St. (Arizona)	1975
62†	Jason Hanson, Washington St. (UNLV)	1991
62	John Diettrich, Ball St. (Ohio)	1986
62#	Chip Lohmiller, Minnesota (Iowa)	1986
62	Tom Whelihan, Missouri (Colorado)	1986
62	Dan Christopulos, Wyoming (Colorado St.)	1977
62	Iseed Khoury, North Texas (Richmond)	1977
62	Dave Lawson, Air Force (Iowa St.)	1975
61$	Kyle Bryant, Texas A&M (Southern Miss.)	1994
61	Dan Eichloff, Kansas (Ball St.)	1992
61	Mark Porter, Kansas St. (Nebraska)	1988
61	Ralf Mojsiejenko, Michigan St. (Illinois)	1982
61	Steve Little, Arkansas (Tulsa)	1976
61	Wayne Latimer, Virginia Tech (Florida St.)	1975
61	Ray Guy, Southern Miss. (Utah St.)	1972
60	Derek Schorejs, Bowling Green (Toledo)	1995
60	John Hall, Wisconsin (Minnesota)	1995
60	Joe Nedney, San Jose St. (Wyoming)	1992
60	Don Shafer, Southern Cal (Notre Dame)	1986
60	Steve DeLine, Colorado St. (Air Force)	1985
60	Kevin Butler, Georgia (Clemson)	1984
60	Chris Perkins, Florida (Tulane)	1984
60	Fuad Reveiz, Tennessee (Georgia Tech)	1982
60	Russell Erxleben, Texas (Texas Tech)	1977
60	Bubba Hicks, Baylor (Rice)	1975
60	Dave Lawson, Air Force (Colorado)	1974
60	Tony Di Rienzo, Oklahoma (Kansas)	1973
60	Bill McClard, Arkansas (Southern Methodist)	1970

†Longest collegiate field goal without use of a kicking tee; all kicks after 1988 season were without the use of a tee. Also longest field goal with narrower (18'6'') goal posts. $Longest field goal made by a freshman. #Longest field goal made indoors.

Team Champions

Annual Offense Champions

TOTAL OFFENSE

Year	Team	Avg.
1937	Colorado	375.4
1938	Fordham	341.6
1939	Ohio St.	309.3
1940	Lafayette	368.2
1941	Duke	372.2
1942	Georgia	429.5
1943	Notre Dame	418.0
1944	Tulsa	434.7
1945	Army	462.7
1946	Notre Dame	441.3
1947	Michigan	412.7
1948	Nevada	487.0
1949	Notre Dame	434.8
1950	Arizona St.	470.4
1951	Tulsa	480.1
1952	Tulsa	466.6
1953	Cincinnati	409.5
1954	Army	448.7
1955	Oklahoma	410.7
1956	Oklahoma	481.7
1957	Arizona St.	444.9
1958	Iowa	405.9
1959	Syracuse	451.5
1960	New Mexico St.	419.6
1961	Mississippi	418.7
1962	Arizona St.	384.4
1963	Utah St.	395.3
1964	Tulsa	461.8
1965	Tulsa	427.8
1966	Houston	437.2
1967	Houston	427.9
1968	Houston	562.0
1969	San Diego St.	532.2
1970	Arizona St.	514.5
1971	Oklahoma	566.5
1972	Arizona St.	516.5
1973	Arizona St.	565.5
1974	Oklahoma	507.7
1975	California	458.5
1976	Michigan	448.1
1977	Colgate	486.1
1978	Nebraska	501.4
1979	Brigham Young	521.4
1980	Brigham Young	535.0
1981	Arizona St.	498.7
1982	Nebraska	518.6
1983	Brigham Young	584.2
1984	Brigham Young	486.5
1985	Brigham Young	500.2
1986	San Jose St.	481.4
1987	Oklahoma	499.7
1988	Utah	526.8
1989	Houston	*624.9
1990	Houston	586.8
1991	Fresno St.	541.9
1992	Houston	519.5
1993	Nevada	569.1
1994	Penn St.	520.2
1995	Nevada	569.4

**Record.*

RUSHING OFFENSE

Year	Team	Avg.
1937	Colorado	310.0
1938	Fordham	297.1
1939	Wake Forest	290.3
1940	Lafayette	306.4
1941	Missouri	307.7
1942	Hardin-Simmons	307.4
1943	Notre Dame	313.7
1944	Army	298.6
1945	Army	359.8
1946	Notre Dame	340.1
1947	Detroit	319.7
1948	UTEP	378.3
1949	UTEP	333.2
1950	Arizona St.	347.0
1951	Arizona St.	334.8
1952	Tulsa	321.5
1953	Oklahoma	306.9
1954	Army	322.0
1955	Oklahoma	328.9
1956	Oklahoma	391.0
1957	Colorado	322.4
1958	Pacific (Cal.)	259.6
1959	Syracuse	313.6
1960	Utah St.	312.0
1961	New Mexico St.	299.1
1962	Ohio St.	278.9
1963	Nebraska	262.6
1964	Syracuse	251.0
1965	Nebraska	290.0
1966	Harvard	269.0
1967	Houston	270.9
1968	Houston	361.7
1969	Texas	363.0
1970	Texas	374.5
1971	Oklahoma	*472.4
1972	Oklahoma	368.8
1973	UCLA	400.3
1974	Oklahoma	438.8
1975	Arkansas St.	340.5
1976	Michigan	362.6
1977	Oklahoma	328.9
1978	Oklahoma	427.5
1979	East Caro.	368.5
1980	Nebraska	378.3
1981	Oklahoma	334.3
1982	Nebraska	394.3
1983	Nebraska	401.7
1984	Army	345.3
1985	Nebraska	374.3
1986	Oklahoma	404.7
1987	Oklahoma	428.8
1988	Nebraska	382.3
1989	Nebraska	375.3
1990	Northern Ill.	344.6
1991	Nebraska	353.2
1992	Nebraska	328.2
1993	Army	298.5
1994	Nebraska	340.0
1995	Nebraska	399.8

**Record.*

PASSING OFFENSE

Year	Team	Avg.
1937	Arkansas	185.0
1938	Texas Christian	164.1
1939	Texas Christian	148.5
1940	Cornell	186.3
1941	Arizona	177.7
1942	Tulsa	233.9
1943	Brown	133.1
1944	Tulsa	206.3
1945	St. Mary's (Cal.)	161.3
1946	Nevada	198.1
1947	Michigan	173.9
1948	Nevada	255.0
1949	Fordham	183.4
1950	Southern Methodist	214.6
1951	Loyola Marymount	210.6

Year	Team	Avg.
1952	Fordham	225.8
1953	Stanford	179.5
1954	Purdue	177.3
1955	Navy	185.1
1956	Washington St.	206.8
1957	Utah	195.2
1958	Army	172.2
1959	Stanford	227.8
1960	Washington St.	185.5
1961	Wisconsin	188.4
1962	Tulsa	199.3
1963	Tulsa	244.8
1964	Tulsa	317.9
1965	Tulsa	346.4
1966	Tulsa	272.0
1967	UTEP	301.1
1968	Cincinnati	335.8
1969	San Diego St.	374.2
1970	Auburn	288.5
1971	San Diego St.	251.4
1972	Virginia Tech	304.4
1973	San Diego St.	305.0
1974	Colorado St.	261.8
1975	San Diego St.	291.3
1976	Brigham Young	307.8
1977	Brigham Young	341.6
1978	Southern Methodist	276.2
1979	Brigham Young	368.3
1980	Brigham Young	409.8
1981	Brigham Young	356.9
1982	Long Beach St.	326.8
1983	Brigham Young	381.2
1984	Brigham Young	346.2
1985	Brigham Young	354.5
1986	San Jose St.	312.5
1987	San Jose St.	338.1
1988	Utah	395.9
1989	Houston	*511.3
1990	Houston	473.9
1991	Houston	372.8
1992	Houston	407.1
1993	Nevada	397.5
1994	Georgia	338.3
1995	Nevada	416.3

**Record.*

SCORING OFFENSE

Year	Team	Avg.
1937	Colorado	31.0
1938	Dartmouth	28.2
1939	Utah	28.4
1940	Boston College	32.0
1941	Texas	33.8
1942	Tulsa	42.7
1943	Duke	37.2
1944	Army	*56.0
1945	Army	45.8
1946	Georgia	37.2
1947	Michigan	38.3
1948	Nevada	44.4
1949	Army	39.3
1950	Princeton	38.8
1951	Maryland	39.2
1952	Oklahoma	40.7
1953	Texas Tech	38.9
1954	UCLA	40.8
1955	Oklahoma	36.5
1956	Oklahoma	46.6
1957	Arizona St.	39.7
1958	Rutgers	33.4
1959	Syracuse	39.0
1960	New Mexico St.	37.4
1961	Utah St.	38.7
1962	Wisconsin	31.7
1963	Utah St.	31.7
1964	Tulsa	38.4
1965	Arkansas	32.4
1966	Notre Dame	36.2
1967	UTEP	35.9
1968	Houston	42.5
1969	San Diego St.	46.4
1970	Texas	41.2
1971	Oklahoma	44.9
1972	Arizona St.	46.6
1973	Arizona St.	44.6
1974	Oklahoma	43.0
1975	Ohio St.	34.0
1976	Michigan	38.7
1977	Grambling	42.0
1978	Oklahoma	40.0
1979	Brigham Young	40.6
1980	Brigham Young	46.7
1981	Brigham Young	38.7
1982	Nebraska	41.1
1983	Nebraska	52.0
1984	Boston College	36.7
1985	Fresno St.	39.1
1986	Oklahoma	42.4
1987	Oklahoma	43.5
1988	Oklahoma St.	47.5
1989	Houston	53.5
1990	Houston	46.5
1991	Fresno St.	44.2
1992	Fresno St.	40.5
1993	Florida St.	43.2
1994	Penn St.	47.8
1995	Nebraska	52.4

**Record.*

Annual Defense Champions

TOTAL DEFENSE

Year	Team	Avg.
1937	Santa Clara	*69.9
1938	Alabama	77.9
1939	Texas A&M	76.3
1940	Navy	96.0
1941	Duquesne	110.6
1942	Texas	117.3
1943	Duke	121.7
1944	Virginia	96.8
1945	Alabama	109.9
1946	Notre Dame	141.7
1947	Penn St.	76.8
1948	Georgia Tech	151.3
1949	Kentucky	153.8
1950	Wake Forest	163.2
1951	Wisconsin	154.8
1952	Tennessee	166.7
1953	Cincinnati	184.3
1954	Mississippi	172.3
1955	Army	160.7
1956	Miami (Fla.)	189.4
1957	Auburn	133.0
1958	Auburn	157.5
1959	Syracuse	96.2
1960	Wyoming	149.6
1961	Alabama	132.6
1962	Mississippi	142.2
1963	Southern Miss.	131.2
1964	Auburn	164.7
1965	Southern Miss.	161.1
1966	Southern Miss.	163.7
1967	Nebraska	157.6
1968	Wyoming	206.8
1969	Toledo	209.1
1970	Toledo	185.8
1971	Toledo	179.5
1972	Louisville	202.5
1973	Miami (Ohio)	177.4
1974	Notre Dame	195.2
1975	Texas A&M	183.8
1976	Rutgers	179.2
1977	Jackson St.	207.0
1978	Penn St.	203.9
1979	Yale	175.4
1980	Pittsburgh	205.5
1981	Pittsburgh	224.8
1982	Arizona St.	228.9
1983	Texas	212.0
1984	Nebraska	203.3
1985	Oklahoma	193.5
1986	Oklahoma	169.6
1987	Oklahoma	208.1
1988	Auburn	218.1
1989	Miami (Fla.)	216.5
1990	Clemson	216.9
1991	Texas A&M	222.4
1992	Alabama	194.2
1993	Mississippi	234.5
1994	Miami (Fla.)	220.9
1995	Kansas St.	250.8

**Record.*

RUSHING DEFENSE

Year	Team	Avg.
1937	Santa Clara	25.3
1938	Oklahoma	43.3
1939	Texas A&M	41.5
1940	Texas A&M	44.3
1941	Duquesne	56.0
1942	Boston College	48.9
1943	Duke	39.4
1944	Navy	53.8
1945	Alabama	33.9
1946	Oklahoma	58.0
1947	Penn St.	*17.0
1948	Georgia Tech	74.9
1949	Oklahoma	55.6
1950	Ohio St.	64.0
1951	San Francisco	51.6
1952	Michigan St.	83.9
1953	Maryland	83.9
1954	UCLA	73.2
1955	Maryland	75.9
1956	Miami (Fla.)	106.9
1957	Auburn	67.4
1958	Auburn	79.6
1959	Syracuse	19.3
1960	Wyoming	82.4
1961	Utah St.	50.8
1962	Minnesota	52.2
1963	Mississippi	77.3
1964	Washington	61.3
1965	Michigan St.	45.6
1966	Wyoming	38.5
1967	Wyoming	42.3
1968	Arizona St.	57.0
1969	LSU	38.9
1970	LSU	52.2
1971	Michigan	63.3
1972	Louisville	82.1
1973	Miami (Ohio)	77.0
1974	Notre Dame	102.8
1975	Texas A&M	80.3
1976	Rutgers	83.9
1977	Jackson St.	67.8
1978	Penn St.	54.5
1979	Yale	75.0
1980	Pittsburgh	65.3
1981	Pittsburgh	62.4
1982	Virginia Tech	49.5
1983	Virginia Tech	69.4
1984	Oklahoma	68.8
1985	UCLA	70.3
1986	Oklahoma	60.7
1987	Michigan St.	61.5
1988	Auburn	63.2
1989	Southern Cal	61.5
1990	Washington	66.8
1991	Clemson	53.4
1992	Alabama	55.0
1993	Arizona	30.1
1994	Virginia	63.6
1995	Virginia Tech	77.4

**Record.*

PASSING DEFENSE

Year	Team	$Avg.
1937	Harvard	31.0
1938	Penn St.	*13.1
1939	Kansas	34.1
1940	Harvard	33.3
1941	Purdue	27.1
1942	Harvard	45.4
1943	North Caro.	36.5
1944	Michigan St.	26.7

Year	Team	$Avg.
1945	Holy Cross	37.7
1946	Holy Cross	53.7
1947	North Caro. St.	39.3
1948	Northwestern	54.1
1949	Miami (Fla.)	54.7
1950	Tennessee	67.5
1951	Wash. & Lee	67.9
1952	Virginia	50.3
1953	Richmond	40.3
1954	Alabama	45.8
1955	Florida	42.0
1956	Villanova	43.8
1957	Georgia Tech	33.4
1958	Iowa St.	39.0
1959	Alabama	45.7
1960	Iowa St.	30.2
1961	Pennsylvania	56.9
1962	New Mexico	56.8
1963	UTEP	43.8
1964	Kent	53.6
1965	Toledo	69.8
1966	Toledo	70.4
1967	Nebraska	90.1
1968	Kent	107.6
1969	Dayton	90.0
1970	Toledo	77.8
1971	Texas Tech	60.1
1972	Vanderbilt	80.3
1973	Nebraska	39.9
1974	Iowa	65.7
1975	Va. Military	51.1
1976	Western Mich.	78.5
1977	Tennessee St.	67.9
1978	Boston College	65.1
1979	Western Caro.	77.5
1980	Kansas St.	91.4
1981	Nebraska	100.1
1982	Missouri	123.5
1983	Ohio	115.3
1984	Texas Tech	114.8
1985	Oklahoma	103.6
1986	Oklahoma	108.9
1987	Oklahoma	102.4
1988	Baylor	117.8
1989	Kansas St.	129.3
1990	Alabama	82.5
1991	Texas	77.4
1992	Western Mich.	83.2
1993	Texas A&M	75.0
1994	Miami (Fla.)	81.3
1995	Miami (Ohio)	85.5

**Record. $Beginning in 1990, ranked on passing-efficiency defense rating points instead of per-game yardage allowed.*

SCORING DEFENSE

Year	Team	Avg.
1937	Santa Clara	1.1
1938	Duke	**0.0
1939	Tennessee	**0.0
1940	Tennessee	2.6
1941	Duquesne	2.9
1942	Tulsa	3.2
1943	Duke	3.8
1944	Army	3.9
1945	St. Mary's (Cal.)	4.0
1946	Notre Dame	2.7
1947	Penn St.	3.0
1948	Michigan	4.9
1949	Kentucky	4.8
1950	Army	4.4
1951	Wisconsin	5.9
1952	Southern Cal	4.7
1953	Maryland	3.1
1954	UCLA	4.4
1955	Georgia Tech	4.6
1956	Georgia Tech	3.3
1957	Auburn	2.8
1958	Oklahoma	4.9
1959	Mississippi	2.1
1960	LSU	5.0
1961	Alabama	2.2
1962	LSU	3.4
1963	Mississippi	3.7
1964	Arkansas	5.7
1965	Michigan St.	6.2
1966	Alabama	3.7
1967	Oklahoma	6.8
1968	Georgia	9.8
1969	Arkansas	7.6
1970	Dartmouth	4.7
1971	Michigan	6.4
1972	Michigan	5.2
1973	Ohio St.	4.3
1974	Michigan	6.8
1975	Alabama	6.0
1976	Michigan	7.4
	Rutgers	7.4
1977	North Caro.	7.4
1978	Ball St.	7.5
1979	Alabama	5.3
1980	Florida St.	7.7
1981	Southern Miss.	8.1
1982	Arkansas	10.5
1983	Virginia Tech	8.3
1984	Nebraska	9.5
1985	Michigan	6.8
1986	Oklahoma	6.6
1987	Oklahoma	7.5
1988	Auburn	7.2
1989	Miami (Fla.)	9.3
1990	Central Mich.	8.9
1991	Miami (Fla.)	9.1
1992	Arizona	8.9
1993	Florida St.	9.4
1994	Miami (Fla.)	10.8
1995	Northwestern	12.7

***Record tied.*

Other Annual Team Champions

PUNTING

Year	Team	#Avg.
1937	Iowa	43.0
1938	Arkansas	41.6
1939	Auburn	43.3
1940	Auburn	42.3
1941	Clemson	42.3
1942	Tulsa	41.3
1943	Michigan	39.2
1944	UCLA	43.0
1945	Miami (Fla.)	39.9
1946	UTEP	41.2
1947	Duke	41.9
1948	North Caro.	44.0
1949	Furman	44.7
1950	Colorado	45.1
1951	Alabama	41.8
1952	Colorado	43.3
1953	Georgia	41.2
1954	New Mexico	42.6
1955	Michigan St.	41.2
1956	Colorado St.	42.2
1957	Utah St.	40.1
1958	Georgia	41.9
1959	Brigham Young	43.2
1960	Georgia	43.7
1961	Arizona St.	42.1
1962	Wyoming	42.6
1963	Southern Methodist	41.4
1964	Mississippi	44.1
1965	Arizona St.	44.0
1966	Tennessee	43.4
1967	Houston	44.4
1968	Wichita St.	43.2
1969	Georgia	43.5
1970	Utah	45.0
1971	Utah	46.7
1972	Southern Miss.	45.1
1973	Wake Forest	44.1
1974	Ohio St.	44.9
1975	Ohio St.	44.1
1976	Colorado St.	**44.4
1977	Mississippi	43.4
1978	Texas	41.7
1979	Mississippi	42.4
1980	Florida St.	42.6
1981	Michigan	43.1
1982	Vanderbilt	42.1
1983	Brigham Young	*45.0
1984	Ohio St.	44.0
1985	Colorado	43.6
1986	Michigan	43.1
1987	Ohio St.	40.7
1988	Brigham Young	42.9
1989	Colorado	43.8
1990	Pittsburgh	41.2
1991	Texas Tech	40.6
1992	Nebraska	41.7
1993	New Mexico	41.8
1994	Ball St.	42.2
1995	Ball St.	41.3

*#Beginning in 1975, ranked on net punting average. *Record for net punting average. **Record for net punting average, minimum 40 punts.*

PUNT RETURNS

Year	Team	Avg.
1937	—	—
1938	—	—
1939	UCLA	16.3
1940	UCLA	16.2
1941	Colgate	18.7
1942	—	—
1943	Columbia	20.9
1944	New York U.	22.0
1945	—	—
1946	Columbia	16.8
1947	Florida	19.7
1948	Oklahoma	*22.4
1949	Wichita St.	18.3
1950	Texas A&M	17.6
1951	Holy Cross	18.1
1952	Arizona St.	**25.2
1953	Kansas St.	23.8
1954	Miami (Fla.)	19.7
1955	North Caro.	22.5
1956	Cincinnati	17.7
1957	North Texas	17.5
1958	Notre Dame	17.6
1959	Wyoming	16.6
1960	Arizona	17.7
1961	Memphis	17.4
1962	West Tex. A&M	18.4
1963	Army	18.1
1964	UTEP	16.9
1965	Georgia Tech	23.0
1966	Brown	21.0
1967	Memphis	16.3
1968	Army	17.4
1969	Davidson	21.3
1970	Wichita St.	28.5
1971	Mississippi St.	20.8
1972	Georgia Tech	17.3
1973	Utah	23.4
1974	Auburn	16.6
1975	New Mexico St.	15.3
1976	Wichita St.	15.0
1977	Grambling	16.9
1978	McNeese St.	15.7
1979	Tennessee St.	16.9
1980	Georgia	16.5
1981	North Caro. St.	13.4
1982	Auburn	15.8
1983	San Diego St.	17.0
1984	Florida	13.8
1985	Utah	20.7
1986	Arizona St.	17.9
1987	Stanford	15.4
1988	Florida St.	15.5
1989	Ohio	18.2
1990	Michigan	15.6
1991	Alabama	16.9
1992	Northwestern	21.8
1993	Texas A&M	17.9
1994	Ball St.	19.9
1995	Eastern Mich.	20.8

**Record for minimum 30 punt returns. **Record for minimum 15 punt returns.*

KICKOFF RETURNS

Year	Team	Avg.
1937	—	—
1938	—	—
1939	Wake Forest	32.9
1940	Minnesota	36.4
1941	Tulane	32.1
1942	—	—
1943	Navy	28.8
1944	—	—
1945	—	—
1946	William & Mary	31.7
1947	Southern Methodist	31.4
1948	Wyoming	27.4
1949	Army	34.1
1950	Wyoming	29.3
1951	Marquette	25.0
1952	Wake Forest	25.1
1953	Texas Tech	23.8
1954	Arizona	26.1
1955	Southern Cal	25.8
1956	Georgia Tech	24.6
1957	Notre Dame	27.6
1958	Tulsa	25.8
1959	Auburn	25.8
1960	Yale	26.7
1961	Harvard	25.9
1962	Alabama	28.9
1963	Memphis	27.7
1964	Cornell	27.1
1965	Dartmouth	28.7
1966	Notre Dame	29.6
1967	Air Force	25.3
1968	Louisville	25.7
1969	Brigham Young	28.7
1970	South Caro.	26.5
1971	Miami (Fla.)	24.1
1972	Michigan	26.9
1973	Rice	*27.5
1974	Southern Cal	25.7
1975	Maryland	**29.5
1976	South Caro.	27.0
1977	Miami (Ohio)	24.6
1978	Utah St.	26.7
1979	Brigham Young	26.3
1980	Oklahoma	33.2
1981	Iowa	29.1
1982	Utah	25.5
1983	Tennessee	28.8
1984	Texas Tech	25.2
1985	Air Force	27.0
1986	Clemson	26.1
1987	Oklahoma St.	23.7
1988	Notre Dame	24.2
1989	Colorado	26.1
1990	Nebraska	27.8
1991	New Mexico St.	25.2
1992	Florida St.	30.3
1993	Texas A&M	31.2
1994	Texas A&M	27.8
1995	New Mexico	27.1

**Record for minimum 35 kickoff returns. **Record for minimum 25 kickoff returns.*

Toughest-Schedule Annual Leaders

The NCAA's toughest-schedule program (which began in 1977) is based on what all Division I-A opponents did against other Division I-A teams when not playing the team in question. Games against non-I-A teams are deleted, and nine intradivision games are required to qualify. (Bowl games are not included.) The leaders:

Year	Team (†Record)	¢Opponents' Record W	L	T	Pct.
1977	Miami (Fla.) (3-8-0)	66	42	2	.609
	Penn St. (10-1-0)	61	39	2	.608
1978	Notre Dame (8-3-0)	77	31	2	.709
	Southern Cal (11-1-0)	79	40	1	.663
1979	UCLA (5-6-0)	71	37	2	.655
	South Caro. (8-3-0)	69	38	2	.642
1980	Florida St. (10-1-0)	70	34	0	.673
	Miami (Fla.) (8-3-0)	64	33	1	.658
1981	Penn St. (9-2-0)	71	33	2	.679
	Temple (5-5-0)	71	33	2	.669
1982	Penn St. (10-1-0)	63	34	2	.646
	Kentucky (0-10-1)	63	34	5	.642
1983	Auburn (10-1-0)	70	31	3	.688
	UCLA (6-4-1)	68	37	5	.641
1984	Penn St. (6-5-0)	58	36	3	.613
	Georgia (7-4-0)	60	39	4	.602
1985	Notre Dame (5-6-0)	72	29	3	.707
	Alabama (8-2-1)	65	32	5	.662
1986	Florida (6-5-0)	64	29	3	.682
	LSU (9-2-0)	67	36	2	.648
1987	Notre Dame (8-3-0)	71	34	2	.673
	Florida St. (10-1-0)	60	29	4	.667
1988	Virginia Tech (3-8-0)	74	36	0	.673
	Arizona (7-4-0)	70	37	3	.650
1989	Notre Dame (11-1-0)	74	38	4	.655
	LSU (4-7-0)	67	41	1	.619
1990	Colorado (10-1-1)	72	42	3	.628
	Stanford (5-6-0)	67	39	4	.627

†Not including bowl games. ¢When not playing the team listed.

Top 10 Toughest-Schedule Leaders for 1991-95

1991

	Team	¢Opp. Record	Pct.
1.	South Caro.	57-31-2	.644
2.	Florida	66-37-1	.639
3.	LSU	60-38-0	.612
4.	Florida St.	64-40-3	.612
5.	Maryland	62-39-3	.611
6.	Southern Cal	67-43-0	.609
7.	Oklahoma St.	62-40-3	.605
8.	Northern Ill.	44-30-4	.590
9.	Tennessee	63-44-0	.589
10.	Houston	61-43-2	.585

1992

	Team	¢Opp. Record	Pct.
1.	Southern Cal	68-38-4	.636
2.	Stanford	73-43-4	.625
3.	Florida	72-46-1	.609
4.	Northwestern	64-41-7	.603
5.	Arizona	64-43-1	.597
6.	Missouri	55-37-5	.593
7.	Arkansas	58-40-0	.592
8.	Oregon St.	65-46-0	.586
	LSU	64-45-2	.586
10.	Iowa	65-46-7	.581

1993

	Team	¢Opp. Record	Pct.
1.	LSU	67-38-5	.632
2.	Purdue	66-38-3	.631
3.	Miami (Fla.)	62-36-2	.630
4.	Maryland	68-40-0	.630
5.	Florida	72-42-5	.626
6.	Pittsburgh	65-39-3	.621
7.	Southern Cal	73-46-1	.613
8.	Northwestern	65-41-2	.611
9.	UCLA	67-43-0	.609
10.	Florida St.	71-46-0	.607

1994

	Team	¢Opp. Record	Pct.
1.	Michigan	67-38-6	.631
2.	Oklahoma	66-39-4	.624
3.	Florida St.	64-40-1	.614
4.	Southern Cal	67-42-1	.614
5.	Southern Miss.	58-38-2	.602
6.	Michigan St.	61-42-7	.586
7.	Tennessee	64-45-2	.586
8.	Florida	66-49-2	.573
9.	Alabama	60-45-3	.569
10.	Miami (Fla.)	56-42-3	.569

1995

	Team	¢Opp. Record	Pct.
1.	Notre Dame	67-37-5	.638
2.	Illinois	69-40-2	.631
3.	Minnesota	64-38-5	.621
4.	Cincinnati	66-40-2	.620
5.	Vanderbilt	68-42-1	.617
6.	Indiana	66-41-3	.614
7.	Washington	64-40-2	.613
8.	Purdue	67-42-2	.613
9.	Houston	66-42-3	.608
	Northwestern	65-41-5	.608

†Not including bowl games. ¢When not playing the team listed.

Annual Most-Improved Teams

Year	Team	$Games Improved	From		To		Coach
1937	California	4½	1936	6-5-0	1937	*10-0-1	Stub Allison
	Syracuse	4½	1936	1-7-0	1937	5-2-1	#Ossie Solem
1938	Texas Christian	5½	1937	4-4-2	1938	*11-0-0	Dutch Meyer
1939	Texas A&M	5½	1938	4-4-1	1939	*11-0-0	Homer Norton
1940	Stanford	8	1939	1-7-1	1940	*10-0-0	#Clark Shaughnessy
1941	Vanderbilt	4½	1940	3-6-1	1941	8-2-0	Red Sanders
1942	Utah St.	5½	1941	0-8-0	1942	6-3-1	Dick Romney
1943	Purdue	8	1942	1-8-0	1943	9-0-0	Elmer Burnham
1944	Ohio St.	6	1943	3-6-0	1944	9-0-0	#Carroll Widdoes
1945	Miami (Fla.)	7	1944	1-7-1	1945	*9-1-1	Jack Harding
1946	Illinois	5	1945	2-6-1	1946	*8-2-0	Ray Eliot
	Kentucky	5	1945	2-8-0	1946	7-3-0	#Paul "Bear" Bryant
1947	California	6½	1946	2-7-0	1947	9-1-0	#Lynn "Pappy" Waldorf
1948	Clemson	6	1947	4-5-0	1948	*11-0-0	Frank Howard
1949	Tulsa	5	1948	0-9-1	1949	5-4-1	J. O. Brothers
1950	Brigham Young	5	1949	0-11-0	1950	4-5-1	Chick Atkinson
	Texas A&M	5	1949	1-8-1	1950	*7-4-0	Harry Stiteler
1951	Georgia Tech	6	1950	5-6-0	1951	*11-0-1	Bobby Dodd
1952	Alabama	4½	1951	5-6-0	1952	*10-2-0	Harold "Red" Drew
1953	Texas Tech	7	1952	3-7-1	1953	*11-1-0	DeWitt Weaver
1954	Denver	5	1953	3-5-2	1954	9-1-0	Bob Blackman
1955	Texas A&M	6½	1954	1-9-0	1955	7-2-1	Paul "Bear" Bryant
1956	Iowa	5	1955	3-5-1	1956	*9-1-0	Forest Evashevski
1957	Notre Dame	5	1956	2-8-0	1957	7-3-0	Terry Brennan
	Texas	5	1956	1-9-0	1957	†6-4-1	#Darrell Royal
1958	Air Force	6	1957	3-6-1	1958	‡9-0-1	#Ben Martin
1959	Washington	6½	1958	3-7-0	1959	*10-1-0	Jim Owens
1960	Minnesota	5½	1959	2-7-0	1960	†8-2-0	Murray Warmath
	North Caro. St.	5½	1959	1-9-0	1960	6-3-1	Earle Edwards
1961	Villanova	6	1960	2-8-0	1961	*8-2-0	Alex Bell
1962	Southern Cal	6	1961	4-5-1	1962	*11-0-0	John McKay
1963	Illinois	6	1962	2-7-0	1963	*8-1-1	Pete Elliott
1964	Notre Dame	6½	1963	2-7-0	1964	9-1-0	#Ara Parseghian
1965	UTEP	6½	1964	0-8-2	1965	*8-3-0	#Bobby Dobbs
1966	Dayton	6½	1965	1-8-1	1966	8-2-0	John McVay
1967	Indiana	7	1966	1-8-1	1967	†9-2-0	John Pont
1968	Arkansas	5	1967	4-5-1	1968	*10-1-0	Frank Broyles
1969	UCLA	5½	1968	3-7-0	1969	8-1-1	Tommy Prothro
1970	Tulsa	5	1969	1-9-0	1970	6-4-0	#Claude Gibson
1971	Army	5	1970	1-9-1	1971	6-4-0	Tom Cahill
	Georgia	5	1970	5-5-0	1971	*11-1-0	Vince Dooley
1972	Pacific (Cal.)	5	1971	3-8-0	1972	8-3-0	Chester Caddas
	Southern Cal	5	1971	6-4-1	1972	*12-0-0	John McKay
	UCLA	5	1971	2-7-1	1972	8-3-0	Pepper Rodgers
1973	Pittsburgh	5	1972	1-10-0	1973	†6-5-1	#Johnny Majors
1974	Baylor	5½	1973	2-9-0	1974	†8-4-0	Grant Teaff
1975	Arizona St.	5	1974	7-5-0	1975	*12-0-0	Frank Kush
1976	Houston	7	1975	2-8-0	1976	*10-2-0	Bill Yeoman
1977	Miami (Ohio)	7	1976	3-8-0	1977	10-1-0	Dick Crum
1978	Tulsa	6	1977	3-8-0	1978	9-2-0	John Cooper
1979	Wake Forest	6½	1978	1-10-0	1979	†8-4-0	John Mackovic
1980	Florida	7	1979	0-10-1	1980	*8-4-0	Charley Pell
1981	Clemson	5½	1980	6-5-0	1981	*12-0-0	Danny Ford
1982	New Mexico	6	1981	4-7-1	1982	10-1-0	Joe Morrison
	Southwestern La.	6	1981	1-9-1	1982	7-3-1	Sam Robertson
1983	Kentucky	5½	1982	0-10-1	1983	†6-5-1	Jerry Claiborne
	Memphis	5½	1982	1-10-0	1983	6-4-1	Rex Dockery
1984	Army	6	1983	2-9-0	1984	*8-3-1	Jim Young
1985	Colorado	5½	1984	1-10-0	1985	†7-5-0	Bill McCartney
	Fresno St.	5½	1984	6-6-0	1985	*11-0-1	Jim Sweeney
1986	San Jose St.	7	1985	2-8-1	1986	*10-2-0	Claude Gilbert
1987	Syracuse	6	1986	5-6-0	1987	‡11-0-1	Dick MacPherson
1988	West Va.	5	1987	6-6-0	1988	†11-1-0	Don Nehlen
	Washington St.	5	1987	3-7-1	1988	*9-3-0	Dennis Erickson
1989	Tennessee	5½	1988	5-6-0	1989	*11-1-0	Johnny Majors
1990	Temple	6	1989	1-10-0	1990	7-4-0	Jerry Berndt
1991	Tulsa	6½	1990	3-8-0	1991	*10-2-0	Dave Rader
1992	Hawaii	6	1991	4-7-1	1992	*11-2-0	Bob Wagner
1993	Southwestern La.	6	1992	2-9-0	1993	8-3-0	Nelson Stokley
	Virginia Tech	6	1992	2-8-1	1993	*9-3-0	Frank Beamer
1994	Colorado St.	4½	1993	5-6-0	1994	†10-2-0	Sonny Lubick
	Duke	4½	1993	3-8-0	1994	†8-4-0	#Fred Goldsmith
	East Caro.	4½	1993	2-9-0	1994	†7-5-0	Steve Logan
1995	Northwestern	6	1994	3-7-1	1995	†10-2-0	Gary Barnett

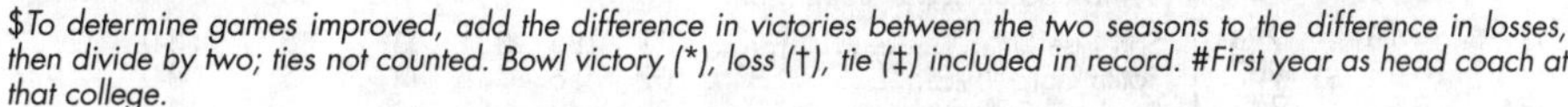

$To determine games improved, add the difference in victories between the two seasons to the difference in losses, then divide by two; ties not counted. Bowl victory (*), loss (†), tie (‡) included in record. #First year as head coach at that college.

Photo from Northwestern media services

Coach Gary Barnett's surprising Northwestern Wildcats were Division I-A's most-improved team last season, finishing with a 10-2 record after going 3-7-1 in 1994.

All-Time Most-Improved Teams

Games	Team (Year)	Games	Team (Year)
8	Purdue (1943)	6½	Tulsa (1991)
8	Stanford (1940)	6½	Wake Forest (1979)
7	San Jose St. (1986)	6½	Toledo (1967)
7	Florida (1980)	6½	Dayton (1966)
7	Miami (Ohio) (1977)	6½	UTEP (1965)
7	Houston (1976)	6½	Notre Dame (1964)
7	Indiana (1967)	6½	Washington (1959)
7	Texas Tech (1953)	6½	Texas A&M (1955)
7	Miami (Fla.) (1945)	6½	California (1947)

1995 Most-Improved Teams

College (Coach)	1995	1994	$Games Improved
Northwestern (Gary Barnett)	10-2-0	3-7-1	+6
Arkansas St. (John Bobo)	6-5-0	1-10-0	+5
Georgia Tech (George O'Leary)	6-5-0	1-10-0	+5
Toledo (Gary Pinkel)	11-0-1	6-4-1	+4½
Cincinnati (Rick Minter)	6-5-0	2-8-1	+3½
Kansas (Glen Mason)	10-2-0	6-5-0	+3½
San Diego St. (Ted Tollner)	8-4-0	4-7-0	+3½
Stanford (Tyrone Willingham)	7-4-1	3-7-1	+3½
Arizona St. (Bruce Snyder)	6-5-0	3-8-0	+3
Arkansas (Danny Ford)	8-5-0	4-7-0	+3
Kentucky (Bill Curry)	4-7-0	1-10-0	+3
LSU (Gerry DiNardo)	7-4-1	4-7-0	+3
Miami (Ohio) (Randy Walker)	8-2-1	5-5-1	+3
Tennessee (Phillip Fulmer)	11-1-0	8-4-0	+3
Texas Tech (Spike Dykes)	9-3-0	6-6-0	+3
Clemson (Tommy West)	8-4-0	5-6-0	+2½
Iowa St. (Dan McCarney)	3-8-0	0-10-1	+2½
Notre Dame (Lou Holtz)	9-3-0	6-5-1	+2½
Ohio (Jim Grobe)	2-8-1	0-11-0	+2½
East Caro. (Steve Logan)	9-3-0	7-5-0	+2
Iowa (Hayden Fry)	8-4-0	5-5-1	+2
Louisiana Tech (Joe Raymond Peace)	5-6-0	3-8-0	+2
Maryland (Mark Duffner)	6-5-0	4-7-0	+2
Mississippi (Tommy Tuberville)	6-5-0	4-7-0	+2
Navy (Charlie Weatherbie)	5-6-0	3-8-0	+2
Ohio St. (John Cooper)	11-2-0	9-4-0	+2
Texas (John Mackovic)	10-2-1	8-4-0	+2
Virginia Tech (Frank Beamer)	10-2-0	8-4-0	+2

$To determine games improved, add the difference in victories between the two seasons to the difference in losses, then divide by two; ties not counted. Includes bowl games.

All-Time Team Won-Lost Records

Classified as Division I-A for the last 10 years. Won-lost-tied record includes bowl games.

PERCENTAGE (TOP 25)

Team	Yrs.	Won	Lost	Tied	Pct.†	*Bowls W-L-T	Total Games
Notre Dame#	107	738	219	42	.760	13-8-0	999
Michigan	116	756	250	36	.743	13-14-0	1,042
Alabama√	101	703	250	43	.727	27-17-3	996
Oklahoma	101	670	251	53	.715	20-11-1	974
Texas	103	705	279	33	.709	17-17-2	1,017
Ohio St.	106	679	271	53	.703	12-16-0	1,003
Southern Cal	103	647	259	54	.702	25-13-0	960
Nebraska$	106	698	290	40	.698	16-18-0	1,028
Penn St.	109	695	294	41	.695	20-10-2	1,030
Tennessee√	99	656	281	52	.690	20-16-0	989
Florida St.√	49	336	179	17	.648	16-7-2	532
Central Mich.	95	493	265	36	.644	3-2-0	794
Washington√	105	569	314	49	.637	12-8-1	932
Miami (Ohio)	107	559	315	44	.633	5-2-0	918
Army	106	597	339	51	.631	2-1-0	987
Georgia	102	601	343	54	.629	15-14-3	998
LSU√	102	584	336	47	.628	12-16-1	967
Arizona St.	83	453	268	24	.624	9-5-1	745
Auburn√	103	575	340	47	.622	12-10-2	962
Colorado	106	578	351	36	.618	8-12-0	965
Miami (Fla.)	69	429	265	19	.615	10-11-0	713
Bowling Green	77	403	250	52	.609	2-3-0	705
Michigan St.	99	532	339	44	.605	5-7-0	915
Texas A&M	101	568	364	48	.604	11-10-0	980
UCLA	77	449	291	37	.602	10-9-1	777

ALPHABETICAL LISTING

Team	Yrs.	Won	Lost	Tied	Pct.†	*Bowls W-L-T	Total Games
Air Force	40	226	206	13	.522	6-6-1	445
Alabama√	101	703	250	43	.727	27-17-3	996
Arizona	91	473	322	33	.591	3-7-1	828
Arizona St.	83	453	268	24	.624	9-5-1	745
Arkansas√	102	563	372	40	.598	9-16-3	975
Army	106	597	339	51	.631	2-1-0	987
Auburn√	103	575	340	47	.622	12-10-2	962
Ball St.	71	336	267	32	.554	0-2-0	635
Baylor	93	482	411	43	.538	8-8-0	936
Boston College	97	508	363	36	.580	5-5-0	907
Bowling Green	77	403	250	52	.609	2-3-0	705
Brigham Young	71	387	315	26	.549	6-12-1	728
California	100	537	394	51	.573	5-6-1	982
Central Mich.	95	493	265	36	.644	3-2-0	794
Cincinnati	108	453	469	52	.492	1-1-0	974
Clemson	100	539	366	45	.591	12-8-0	950
Colorado	106	578	351	36	.618	8-12-0	965
Colorado St.	97	375	440	33	.462	1-3-0	848
Duke	83	425	333	31	.558	3-5-0	789
East Caro.	60	298	277	12	.518	3-1-0	587
Eastern Mich.	103	379	390	46	.493	1-0-0	815
Florida	89	513	335	40	.600	10-13-0	888
Florida St.√	49	336	179	17	.648	16-7-2	532
Fresno St.	74	441	294	29	.596	7-2-0	764
Georgia	102	601	343	54	.629	15-14-3	998
Georgia Tech	103	562	384	43	.590	17-8-0	989
Hawaii	80	421	303	26	.579	1-1-0	750
Houston	50	285	237	15	.545	7-5-1	537
Illinois	105	508	417	50	.547	5-6-0	975
Indiana	108	390	502	44	.440	3-5-0	936
Iowa	107	478	441	39	.519	7-6-1	958
Iowa St.	104	424	478	46	.472	0-4-0	948
Kansas	106	493	460	58	.516	3-5-0	1,011
Kansas St.√	100	345	542	42	.394	2-2-0	929
Kent	73	260	377	28	.412	0-1-0	665
Kentucky√	105	495	462	44	.516	5-3-0	1,001
LSU√	102	584	336	47	.628	12-16-1	967
Louisville√	77	338	358	17	.486	3-1-1	713
Maryland	103	515	450	42	.532	6-9-2	1,007
Memphis√	80	364	360	32	.503	1-0-0	756
Miami (Fla.)	69	429	265	19	.615	10-11-0	713
Miami (Ohio)	107	559	315	44	.633	5-2-0	918
Michigan	116	756	250	36	.743	13-14-0	1,042
Michigan St.	99	532	339	44	.605	5-7-0	915
Minnesota	112	561	375	43	.595	2-3-0	979
Mississippi√	101	524	391	35	.570	14-11-0	950
Mississippi St.√	96	418	440	39	.488	4-5-0	897
Missouri	105	513	441	52	.536	8-11-0	1,006
Navy	115	554	439	57	.555	3-4-1	1,050
Nebraska$	106	698	290	40	.698	16-18-0	1,028
UNLV	28	171	136	4	.556	2-0-0	311
New Mexico	97	370	433	31	.462	2-2-1	834
New Mexico St.	100	370	443	32	.457	2-0-1	845
North Caro.	105	563	404	54	.578	8-12-0	1,021
North Caro. St.	104	446	444	55	.501	8-8-1	945
Northern Ill.	94	425	368	51	.534	1-0-0	844
Northwestern	108	384	532	43	.423	1-1-0	959
Notre Dame%	107	738	219	42	.760	13-8-0	999
Ohio	100	423	426	48	.498	0-2-0	897
Ohio St.	106	679	271	53	.703	12-16-0	1,003
Oklahoma	101	670	251	53	.715	20-11-1	974
Oklahoma St.	94	417	442	48	.486	9-3-0	907
Oregon	100	451	412	46	.521	3-8-0	909
Oregon St.	99	397	458	50	.466	2-2-0	905
Penn St.	109	695	294	41	.695	20-10-2	1,030
Pittsburgh	106	572	401	42	.584	8-10-0	1,015
Purdue	108	479	418	48	.532	4-1-0	945
Rice√	84	358	456	32	.442	4-3-0	846
Rutgers	126	539	495	42	.520	0-1-0	1,076
San Diego St.	73	412	284	32	.588	2-3-0	728
San Jose St.	77	385	331	38	.536	4-3-0	754
South Caro.√	102	456	446	44	.505	1-8-0	946
Southern Cal	103	647	259	54	.702	25-13-0	960
Southern Methodist@	79	393	373	54	.512	4-6-1	820
Southern Miss.√	79	429	297	26	.588	2-6-0	752
Southwestern La.	88	418	396	32	.513	0-1-0	846
Stanford	89	490	340	49	.585	8-8-1	879

Team	Yrs.	Won	Lost	Tied	Pct.†	*Bowls W-L-T	Total Games
Syracuse	106	599	390	49	.601	9-6-1	1,038
Temple	97	370	410	52	.476	1-1-0	832
Tennessee√	99	656	281	52	.690	20-16-0	989
Texas	103	705	279	33	.709	17-17-2	1,017
UTEP	78	296	416	30	.419	5-3-0	742
Texas A&M	101	568	364	48	.604	11-10-0	980
Texas Christian	99	453	456	56	.498	4-10-1	965
Texas Tech	71	400	330	32	.546	5-15-1	762
Toledo	75	362	326	24	.525	5-1-0	712
Tulane√	102	422	476	38	.471	2-6-0	936
Tulsa	91	481	334	27	.587	4-7-0	842
UCLA	77	449	291	37	.602	10-9-1	777
Utah	102	490	370	31	.567	3-1-0	891
Utah St.	98	424	380	31	.526	1-4-0	835
Vanderbilt√	106	510	442	50	.534	1-1-1	1,002
Virginia	106	519	466	48	.526	4-4-0	1,033
Virginia Tech	102	531	386	46	.575	3-6-0	963
Wake Forest	94	330	506	23	.398	2-2-0	859
Washington√	105	569	314	49	.637	12-8-1	932
Washington St.	99	412	410	45	.501	4-2-0	867
West Va.	103	569	391	45	.589	8-9-0	1,005
Western Mich.	90	427	317	24	.572	0-1-0	768
Wisconsin	106	489	410	53	.541	3-5-0	952
Wyoming	99	410	419	28	.495	4-6-0	857

The following are not listed above because of reclassification to Division I-A (year joined I-A):

Team	Yrs.	Won	Lost	Tied	Pct.†	*Bowls W-L-T	Total Games
Akron (1987)	95	417	379	36	.523	2-3-0	832
Ala.-Birmingham (1996)	5	32	18	2	.635	0-0-0	52
Arkansas St. (1992)	81	354	338	37	.511	0-0-0	729
Central Fla. (1996)	17	95	86	1	.525	2-2-0	182
Louisiana Tech (1989)√	92	462	328	37	.581	0-0-1	827
Nevada (1992)	85	406	338	32	.544	0-2-0	776
North Texas (1995)	80	411	334	33	.549	0-0-0	778
Northeast La. (1994)	45	210	250	8	.457	0-0-0	468

BY VICTORIES

Team	Wins
Michigan	.756
Notre Dame%	.738
Texas	.705
Alabama√	.703
Nebraska$	.698
Penn St.	.695
Ohio St.	.679
Oklahoma	.670
Tennessee√	.656
Southern Cal	.647
Georgia	.601
Syracuse	.599
Army	.597
LSU√	.584
Colorado	.578
Auburn√	.575
Pittsburgh	.572
Washington√	.569
West Va.	.569
Texas A&M	.568
Arkansas√	.563
North Caro.	.563
Georgia Tech	.562
Minnesota	.561
Miami (Ohio)	.559
Navy	.554
Clemson	.539
Rutgers	.539
California	.537
Michigan St.	.532
Virginia Tech	.531
Mississippi√	.524
Virginia	.519
Maryland	.515
Florida	.513
Missouri	.513
Vanderbilt√	.510
Boston College	.508
Illinois	.508
Kentucky√	.495
Central Mich.	.493
Kansas	.493
Stanford	.490

Team	Wins
Utah	.490
Wisconsin	.489
Baylor	.482
Tulsa	.481
Purdue	.479
Iowa	.478
Arizona	.473
South Caro.√	.456
Arizona St.	.453
Cincinnati	.453
Texas Christian	.453
Oregon	.451
UCLA	.449
North Caro. St.	.446
Fresno St.	.441
Miami (Fla.)	.429
Southern Miss.√	.429
Western Mich.	.427
Duke	.425
Northern Ill.	.425
Iowa St.	.424
Utah St.	.424
Ohio	.423
Tulane√	.422
Hawaii	.421
Mississippi St.√	.418
Southwestern La.	.418
Oklahoma St.	.417
San Diego St.	.412
Washington St.	.412
Wyoming	.410
Bowling Green	.403
Texas Tech	.400
Oregon St.	.397
Southern Methodist@	.393
Indiana	.390
Brigham Young	.387
San Jose St.	.385
Northwestern	.384
Eastern Mich.	.379
Colorado St.	.375
New Mexico	.370

Team	Wins
New Mexico St.	.370
Temple	.370
Memphis√	.364
Toledo	.362
Rice√	.358
Kansas St.√	.345
Louisville√	.338
Ball St.	.336

Team	Wins
Florida St.√	.336
Wake Forest	.330
East Caro.	.298
UTEP	.296
Houston	.285
Kent	.260
Air Force	.226
UNLV	.171

The following are not listed above because of reclassification to Division I-A:

Team	Wins
Louisiana Tech	.462
Akron	.417
North Texas	.411
Nevada	.406
Arkansas St.	.354
Northeast La.	.210
Central Fla.	.95
Ala.-Birmingham	.32

*†Ties computed as half won and half lost. *Record in a major bowl game only (i.e., a team's opponent was classified as a major-college team that season or it was classified as a major-college team at the time.) #Leader since 1948. Notre Dame displaced all-time leader Yale, .8082 to .8081, after the 1947 season. $Record adjusted in 1989 (8 less victories, 1 less defeat). @ Football program suspended 1987-88. √Includes games forfeited or changed by action of the NCAA Council and/or Committee on Infractions.*

Records in the 1990s

(1990-91-92-93-94-95, Including Bowls and Playoffs)

PERCENTAGE

Team	W-L-T	Pct.†
Florida St.	64-9-1	.872
Nebraska	63-9-1	.870
Miami (Fla.)	60-11-0	.845
Texas A&M	60-11-2	.836
Florida	61-13-1	.820
Colorado	57-12-4	.808
Penn St.	58-15-0	.795
Tennessee#	56-15-2	.781
Nevada**	57-17-0	.770
Notre Dame	55-16-2	.767
Washington	52-17-1	.750
Michigan	53-17-3	.747
Ohio St.	53-18-3	.736
Syracuse	49-19-3	.711
Alabama@	52-22-0	.703
Auburn	46-19-3	.699
Bowling Green	44-19-4	.687
Virginia	48-23-1	.674
North Caro.	47-23-1	.669
Brigham Young	49-24-2	.667
Clemson	46-23-1	.664
Toledo	43-21-3	.664
Kansas St.	45-23-1	.659
Texas	44-24-2	.643
Central Fla.$	44-25-0	.638
Western Mich.	41-23-2	.636
Ala.-Birmingham$	32-18-2	.635
Oklahoma	42-24-3	.630
Fresno St.	45-26-2	.630
North Caro. St.	44-27-1	.618
Iowa	42-27-2	.606
Southern Cal	42-27-4	.603
Air Force	44-30-0	.595
Arizona	41-28-1	.593
Baylor	40-28-1	.587
Georgia	40-28-1	.587
Virginia Tech	40-28-1	.587
Central Mich.	37-26-5	.581
Louisville	39-28-1	.581
UCLA	40-29-0	.580
Utah	41-30-0	.577
Mississippi#	39-29-0	.574
East Caro.	39-30-0	.565
West Va.	38-29-2	.565
Colorado St.	40-31-0	.563
Oregon	40-31-0	.563
Kansas	38-30-1	.558
Ball St.	38-27-2	.557
Miami (Ohio)	34-27-5	.553
Northeast La.**	38-31-1	.550
Illinois	37-31-2	.543
San Diego St.	37-31-2	.543
Stanford	37-31-2	.543

Team	W-L-T	Pct.†
Wyoming	38-32-1	.542
California	37-32-1	.536
Georgia Tech	36-32-0	.529
Boston College	36-32-2	.529
Texas Tech	36-33-0	.522
Southern Miss.#	34-32-1	.515
Indiana	34-33-2	.507
Mississippi St.#	34-33-2	.507
Louisiana Tech#	32-32-3	.500
Wisconsin	32-32-4	.500
Hawaii	35-36-2	.493
Michigan St.	33-34-2	.493
Washington St.	32-36-0	.471
Texas Christian	31-35-1	.470
Arizona St.	31-35-0	.470
South Caro.#	30-34-3	.470
San Jose St.	30-35-2	.463
Army	30-35-1	.462
Memphis	30-35-1	.462
Arkansas#	30-37-2	.449
Rutgers	29-36-1	.447
Southwestern La.	29-36-1	.447
Utah St.	29-37-1	.440
Rice	28-37-1	.432
LSU	28-38-1	.425
Tulsa	28-38-1	.425
North Texas**	26-39-0	.400
UNLV	26-41-0	.388
Cincinnati	24-41-1	.371
Duke	24-42-1	.366
Akron	23-41-2	.364
Northern Ill.	24-42-0	.364
Maryland	23-43-1	.351
Northwestern	23-43-1	.351
Houston	22-43-1	.341
New Mexico	23-46-0	.333
Vanderbilt#	22-44-0	.333
Kentucky	22-45-0	.328
Eastern Mich.	21-44-1	.326
New Mexico St.	21-45-0	.318
Purdue	19-44-3	.311
Missouri	19-45-3	.306
Pittsburgh	20-46-1	.306
Minnesota	20-46-0	.303
Wake Forest	20-47-0	.299
Oklahoma St.	18-46-3	.291
Navy	19-47-0	.288
Iowa St.	17-46-3	.280
Arkansas St.**	14-49-2	.231
UTEP	14-53-2	.217
Temple	14-52-0	.212
Tulane#	14-53-0	.209

Team	W-L-T	Pct.†	Team	W-L-T	Pct.†
Oregon St.	12-53-1	.189	Ohio	10-53-3	.174
Southern Methodist	11-52-3	.189	Kent	8-57-1	.129

BY VICTORIES

(Minimum 45 Victories)

Team	Wins	Team	Wins
Florida St.	64	Ohio St.	53
Nebraska	63	Alabama@	52
Florida	61	Washington	52
Miami (Fla.)	60	Brigham Young	49
Texas A&M	60	Syracuse	49
Penn St.	58	Virginia	48
Colorado	57	North Caro.	47
Nevada**	57	Auburn	46
Tennessee#	56	Clemson	46
Notre Dame	55	Fresno St.	45
Michigan	53	Kansas St.	45

*†Ties counted as half won and half lost. @ Alabama forfeited eight victories and one tie from 1993 by order of NCAA Committee on Infractions. # Includes forfeit win over Alabama in 1993 by order of NCAA Committee on Infractions. **Joined I-A as follows: Arkansas St. (1992); Nevada (1992); Northeast La. (1994) and North Texas (1995). $ Joined I-A in 1996.*

Winningest Teams by Decade

(By Percentage; Bowls and Playoffs Included, Unless Noted)

1980-89

Rank	Team	W-L-T	Pct.†	Rank	Team	W-L-T	Pct.†
1.	Nebraska	103-20-0	.837	11.	Alabama	85-32-2	.723
2.	Miami (Fla.)	98-20-0	.831		Arkansas	85-32-2	.723
3.	Brigham Young	102-26-0	.797	13.	UCLA	81-30-6	.718
4.	Oklahoma	91-25-2	.780	14.	Washington	83-33-1	.714
5.	Clemson	86-25-4	.765	15.	Fresno St.	80-34-1	.700
6.	Penn St.	89-27-2	.763	16.	Ohio St.	82-35-2	.697
7.	Georgia	88-27-4	.756	17.	Southern Meth.	63-28-1	.690
8.	Florida St.	87-28-3	.750	18.	Southern Cal	78-35-3	.685
	Michigan	89-29-2	.750	19.	Florida	76-37-3	.668
10.	Auburn	86-31-1	.733	20.	Arizona St.	73-36-4	.664

1970-79

Rank	Team	W-L-T	Pct.†	Rank	Team	W-L-T	Pct.†
1.	Oklahoma	102-13-3	.877	11.	Arizona St.	90-28-0	.763
2.	Alabama	103-16-1	.863	12.	Yale@	67-21-2	.756
3.	Michigan	96-16-3	.848	13.	San Diego St.	82-26-2	.755
4.	Tennessee St.*	85-17-2	.827	14.	Miami (Ohio)	80-26-2	.750
5.	Nebraska	98-20-4	.820	15.	Central Mich.#	80-27-3	.741
6.	Penn St.	96-22-0	.814	16.	Arkansas	79-31-5	.709
7.	Ohio St.	91-20-3	.811	17.	Houston	80-33-2	.704
8.	Notre Dame	91-22-0	.805	18.	Louisiana Tech#	77-34-2	.690
9.	Southern Cal	93-21-5	.803	19.	McNeese St.#	75-33-4	.688
10.	Texas	88-26-1	.770	20.	Dartmouth@	60-27-3	.683

1960-69

(By Percentage; Bowls and Playoffs Not Included)

Rank	Team	W-L-T	Pct.†	Rank	Team	W-L-T	Pct.†
1.	Alabama	85-12-3	.865	11.	Memphis	70-25-1	.734
2.	Texas	80-18-2	.810	12.	Arizona St.	72-26-1	.732
3.	Arkansas	80-19-1	.805	13.	LSU	70-25-5	.725
4.	Mississippi	72-20-6	.765		Nebraska	72-27-1	.725
5.	Bowling Green	71-22-2	.758	15.	Wyoming	69-26-4	.717
6.	Dartmouth@	68-22-0	.756	16.	Princeton@	64-26-0	.711
	Ohio St.	67-21-2	.756	17.	Utah St.	68-29-3	.695
8.	Missouri	72-22-6	.750	18.	Purdue	64-28-3	.689
	Southern Cal	73-23-4	.750	19.	Syracuse	68-31-0	.687
10.	Penn St.	73-26-0	.737	20.	Florida	66-30-4	.680
					Miami (Ohio)	66-30-4	.680
					Tennessee	65-29-6	.680

1950-59

Rank	Team	W-L-T	Pct.†	Rank	Team	W-L-T	Pct.†
1.	Oklahoma	93-10-2	.895	11.	Syracuse	62-29-2	.677
2.	Mississippi	80-21-5	.778	12.	Army	58-27-5	.672
3.	Michigan St.	70-21-1	.766	13.	Cincinnati	64-30-7	.668
4.	Princeton@	67-22-1	.750	14.	Notre Dame	64-31-4	.667
5.	Georgia Tech	79-26-6	.739	15.	Clemson	64-32-5	.658
6.	UCLA	68-26-3	.716	16.	Wisconsin	57-28-7	.658
7.	Ohio St.	63-24-5	.712	17.	Colorado	62-33-6	.644
8.	Tennessee	71-31-4	.692	18.	Duke	62-33-7	.642
9.	Penn St.	62-28-4	.681	19.	Navy	55-30-8	.634
10.	Maryland	67-31-3	.678	20.	Yale@	54-30-6	.633

*†Ties computed as half won and half lost. *In I-A less than 8 years, now a member of I-AA. @Now a member of I-AA. #A member of I-A less than 8 years.*

Major Selectors With Most Active Seasons

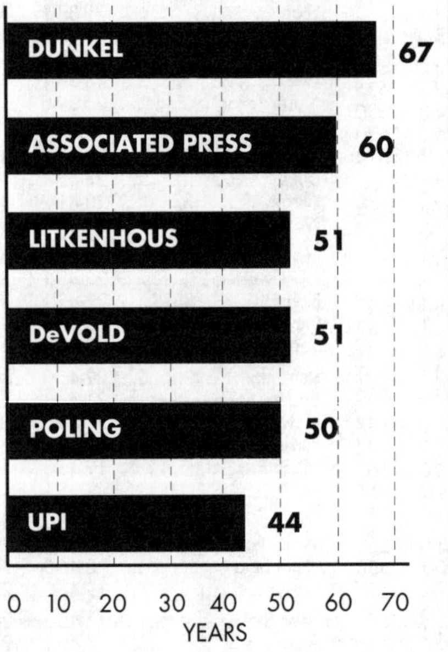

Selector	Years
DUNKEL	67
ASSOCIATED PRESS	60
LITKENHOUS	51
DeVOLD	51
POLING	50
UPI	44

0 10 20 30 40 50 60 70
YEARS

National Poll Rankings

National Champion Major Selectors (1869 to Present)

Selector	Selection Format	Active Seasons First	Last	Total	Predated Seasons	Total Rankings
Frank Dickinson	Math	1926	1940	15	1924-25	17
Deke Houlgate	Math	1927	1958	32	1885-1926	72
Dick Dunkel	Math	1929	1995	67		67
William Boand	Math	1930	1960	31	1919-29	42
Paul Williamson	Math	1932	1963	32		32
Parke Davis	Research	1933	1933	1	1869-1932	65
Edward Litkenhous	Math	1934	1984	51		51
Richard Poling	Math	1935	1984	50	1924-34	61
Associated Press	Poll	1936	1995	60		60
Helms Athletic Foundation	Poll	1941	1982	42	1883-1940	100
Harry DeVold	Math	1945	1995	51	1939-44	57
United Press International	Poll	1950	1995	44		44
International News Service	Poll	1952	1957	6		6
Football Writers Association	Poll	1954	1995	42		42
Football News	Poll	1958	1995	38		38
National Football Foundation	Poll	1959	1995	33		33
Billingsley	Math	1960	1995	36	1869-70, 1872-1959	126
Herman Matthews	Math	1966	1995	29		29
FACT	Math	1968	1995	28		28
Sporting News	Poll	1975	1995	21		21
Sagarin	Math	1978	1995	18	1938, 56-77	41
New York Times	Math	1979	1995	17		17
National Championship Foundation	Poll	1980	1995	16	1869-70, 1872-1979	126
College Football Researchers Association	Poll	1982	1992	11	1919-81	74
USA Today/CNN	Poll	1982	1995	14		14
Berryman	Math	1990	1995	6	1940-89	56
UPI/National Football Foundation	Poll	1991	1992	2		2
USA Today/National Football Foundation	Poll	1993	1994	2		2
Alderson	Math	1994	1995	2		2

POLL SYSTEMS HISTORY

Alderson System (1994-present), a mathematical rating system based strictly on a point value system reflecting competition as well as won-lost record. Developed by Bob Alderson of Muldrow, Oklahoma.

Associated Press (1936-present), the first major nationwide poll for ranking college football teams was voted on by sportswriters and broadcasters. It continues to this day and is probably the most well-known and widely circulated among all of history's polls. The Associated Press annual national champions were awarded the Williams Trophy and the Reverend J. Hugh O'Donnell Trophy. In 1947, Notre Dame retired the Williams Trophy (named after Henry L. Williams, Minnesota coach, and sponsored by the M Club of Minnesota). In 1956, Oklahoma retired the O'Donnell Trophy (named for Notre Dame's president and sponsored by Notre Dame alumni). Beginning with the 1957 season, the award was known as the AP Trophy, and since 1983 the award has been known as the Paul "Bear" Bryant Trophy.

Berryman (QPRS) (1990-present), a mathematical rating system based on a quality point rating formula developed by Clyde P. Berryman of Washington, D.C. Predated national champions from 1940-1989.

Billingsley Report (1960-present), a mathematically based power rating system developed by Richard Billingsley of Nashville, Tennessee. His work is published annually as the Billingsley Report through his own company, the College Football Research Center. In 1996, he finished his three-year research project ranking the national champions from 1869-95. Predated national champions from 1869-1959.

Boand System (1930-60), known as the Azzi Ratem System developed by William Boand of Tucson, Arizona. He moved to Chicago in 1932. Appeared in many newspapers as well as Illustrated Football Annual (1932-42) and weekly in Football News (1942-44, 1951-60). Predated national champions from 1919-29.

College Football Researchers Association (1982-92), founded by Anthony Cusher of Reeder, North Dakota, and Robert Kirlin of Spokane, Washington. Announced its champion in its monthly bulletin and No. 1 team determined by top-10 vote of membership on a point system. Predated national champions from 1919-81, conducted on a poll by Harry Carson Frye.

DeVold System (1945-present), a mathematical rating system developed by Harry DeVold from Minneapolis, Minnesota, a former football player at Cornell. He eventually settled in the Detroit, Michigan, area and worked in the real estate business. The ratings have appeared in The Football News since 1962. Predated national champions from 1939-44.

Dickinson System (1926-40), a mathematical point system devised by Frank Dickinson, a professor of economics at Illinois. The annual Dickinson ratings were emblematic of the national championship and the basis for awarding the Rissman National Trophy and the Knute K. Rockne Intercollegiate Memorial Trophy. Notre Dame gained permanent possession of the Rissman Trophy (named for Jack F. Rissman, a Chicago clothing manufacturer) after its third victory in 1930. Minnesota retired the Rockne Trophy (named in honor of the famous Notre Dame coach) after winning it for a third time in 1940.

Dunkel System (1929-present), a power index system devised by Dick Dunkel Sr. (1929-71); from 1972 by Dick Dunkel Jr. of the Daytona (Fla.) Beach News-Journal.

FACT (1968-present), a computerized mathematical ranking system developed by David Rothman of Hawthorne, California. FACT is the Foundation for the Analysis of Competitions and Tournaments, which began selecting a national champion in 1968. Rothman is a semiretired defense and aerospace statistician and was cochair of the Committee on Statistics in Sports and Competition of the American Statistical Association in the 1970s.

Football News (1958-present), weekly poll of its staff writers has named a national champion since 1958.

Football Writers Association of America (1954-present), the No. 1 team of the year is determined by a five-person panel representing the nation's football writers. The national championship team named receives the Grantland Rice Award.

Helms Athletic Foundation (1941-82), originally known by this name from 1936-69 and established by the founding sponsor, Paul H. Helms, Los Angeles sportsman and philanthropist. After Helms' death in 1957, United Savings & Loan Association became its benefactor during 1970-72. A merger of United Savings and Citizen Savings was completed in 1973, and the Athletic Foundation became known as Citizens Savings Athletic Foundation. In 1982, First Interstate Bank assumed sponsorship for its final rankings. In 1941, Bill Schroeder, managing director of the Helms Athletic Foundation, retroactively selected the national football champions for the period beginning in 1883 (the first year of a scoring system) through 1940. Thereafter, Schroeder, who died in 1988, then chose, with the assistance of a Hall Board, the annual national champion after the bowl games.

Houlgate System (1927-58), a mathematical rating system developed by Deke Houlgate of Los Angeles, California. His ratings were syndicated in newspapers and published in Illustrated Football and the Football Thesaurus (1946-58).

International News Service (1952-57), a poll conducted for six years by members of the International News Service (INS) before merger with United Press in 1958.

Litkenhous (1934-84), a difference-by-score formula developed by Edward E. Litkenhous, a professor of chemical engineering at Vanderbilt, and his brother, Frank.

Matthews Grid Ratings (1966-present), a mathematical rating system developed by college mathematics professor Herman Matthews of Middlesboro, Kentucky. Has appeared in newspapers and The Football News.

National Championship Foundation (1980-present), established by Mike Riter of Germantown, New York. Issues annual report. Predated national champions from 1869-1979.

National Football Foundation (1959-1990, 1995), the National Football Foundation and Hall of Fame named its first national champion in 1959. Headquartered in Larchmont, New York, the present National Football Foundation was established in 1947 to promote amateur athletics in America. The national champion was awarded the MacArthur Bowl from 1959-90. In 1991 and 1992, the NFF/HOF joined with UPI to award the MacArthur Bowl, and in 1993 and 1994 the NFF/HOF joined with USA Today to award the MacArthur Bowl.

New York Times (1979-present), a mathematical rating system introduced by this major newspaper.

Parke Davis (1933), a noted college football historian, Parke H. Davis went back and named the championship teams from 1869 through the 1932 season. He also named a national champion at the conclusion of the 1933 season. Interestingly, the years 1869-75 were identified by Davis as the Pioneer Period; the years 1876-93 were called the Period of the American Intercollegiate Football Association, and the years 1894-1933 were referred to as the Period of Rules Committees and Conferences.

Poling System (1935-84), a mathematical rating system for college football teams developed by Richard Poling from Mansfield, Ohio, a former football player at Ohio Wesleyan. Poling's football ratings were published annually in the Football Review Supplement and in various newspapers. Predated national champions from 1924-34.

Sagarin Ratings (1978-present), a mathematical rating system developed by Jeff Sagarin of Bloomington, Indiana, a 1970 MIT mathematics graduate. Runs annually in USA Today newspaper. Predated national champions from 1938 and 1956-1977.

Sporting News (1975-present), voted on annually by the staff of this St. Louis-based nationally circulated sports publication.

United Press International (1950-90, 1993-present), in 1950, the United Press news service began its poll of football coaches (replaced as coaches' poll after 1990 season). When the United Press merged with the International News Service in 1958, it became known as United Press International. The weekly UPI rankings were featured in newspapers and on radio and television nationwide. UPI and the National Football Foundation formed a coalition for 1991 and 1992 to name the MacArthur Bowl national champion. Returned to single poll in 1994.

USA Today/Cable News Network (1982-present), introduced a weekly poll of sportswriters in 1982 and ranked the top 25 teams in the nation with a point system. The poll results are featured in USA Today, a national newspaper, and on the Cable News Network, a national cable television network. Took over as the coaches' poll in 1991. USA Today also formed a coalition with the National Football Foundation in 1993 to name the MacArthur Bowl national champion.

Williamson System (1932-63), a power rating system chosen by Paul Williamson of New Orleans, Louisiana, a geologist and member of the Sugar Bowl committee.

Thanks from the NCAA Statistics Service to Robert A. Rosiek of Dearborn, Michigan, who researched much of the former polls' history.

National Poll Champions

Over the last 126 years, there have been nearly 30 selectors of national champions using polls, historical research and mathematical rating systems. Beginning in 1936, The Associated Press began the best-known and most widely circulated poll of sportswriters and broadcasters. Before 1936, national champions were determined by historical research and retroactive ratings and polls.

*Note: * indicates selectors that chose multiple schools. The national champion was selected before bowl games as follows: AP (1936-64 and 1966-67); UP-UPI (1950-73); FWAA (1954); NFF-HOF (1959-70). In all other latter-day polls, champions were selected after bowl games.*

1869
Princeton: Billingsley, National Championship Foundation, Parke Davis*
Rutgers: Parke Davis*

1870
Princeton: Billingsley, National Championship Foundation, Parke Davis

1871
No national champions selected.

1872
Princeton: Billingsley, National Championship Foundation, Parke Davis*
Yale: Parke Davis*

1873
Princeton: Billingsley, National Championship Foundation, Parke Davis

1874
Harvard: Parke Davis*
Princeton: Billingsley, Parke Davis*
Yale: National Championship Foundation, Parke Davis*

1875
Colgate: Parke Davis*
Harvard: National Championship Foundation, Parke Davis*
Princeton: Billingsley, Parke Davis*

1876
Yale: Billingsley, National Championship Foundation, Parke Davis

1877
Princeton: Parke Davis*
Yale: Billingsley, National Championship Foundation, Parke Davis*

1878
Princeton: Billingsley, National Championship Foundation, Parke Davis

1879
Princeton: Billingsley, National Championship Foundation, Parke Davis*
Yale: Parke Davis*

1880
Princeton: National Championship Foundation*, Parke Davis*
Yale: Billingsley, National Championship Foundation*, Parke Davis*

1881
Princeton: Billingsley, Parke Davis*
Yale: National Championship Foundation, Parke Davis*

1882
Yale: Billingsley, National Championship Foundation, Parke Davis

1883
Yale: Billingsley, Helms, National Championship Foundation, Parke Davis

1884
Princeton: Parke Davis*
Yale: Billingsley, Helms, National Championship Foundation, Parke Davis*

1885
Princeton: Billingsley, Helms, Houlgate, National Championship Foundation, Parke Davis

1886
Princeton: Parke Davis*
Yale: Billingsley, Helms, National Championship Foundation, Parke Davis*

1887
Yale: Billingsley, Helms, Houlgate, National Championship Foundation, Parke Davis

1888
Yale: Billingsley, Helms, Houlgate, National Championship Foundation, Parke Davis

1889
Princeton: Billingsley, Helms, Houlgate, National Championship Foundation, Parke Davis

1890
Harvard: Billingsley, Helms, Houlgate, National Championship Foundation, Parke Davis

1891
Yale: Billingsley, Helms, Houlgate, National Championship Foundation, Parke Davis

1892
Yale: Billingsley, Helms, Houlgate, National Championship Foundation, Parke Davis

1893
Princeton: Billingsley, Helms, Houlgate, National Championship Foundation
Yale: Parke Davis

1894
Pennsylvania: Parke Davis*
Princeton: Houlgate
Yale: Billingsley, Helms, National Championship Foundation, Parke Davis*

1895
Pennsylvania: Billingsley, Helms, Houlgate, National Championship Foundation, Parke Davis*
Yale: Parke Davis*

1896
Lafayette: National Championship Foundation*, Parke Davis*
Princeton: Billingsley, Helms, Houlgate, National Championship Foundation*, Parke Davis*

1897
Pennsylvania: Billingsley, Helms, Houlgate, National Championship Foundation, Parke Davis*
Yale: Parke Davis*

1898
Harvard: Billingsley, Helms, Houlgate, National Championship Foundation
Princeton: Parke Davis

1899
Harvard: Billingsley, Helms, Houlgate, National Championship Foundation
Princeton: Parke Davis

1900
Yale: Billingsley, Helms, Houlgate, National Championship Foundation, Parke Davis

1901
Michigan: Billingsley, Helms, Houlgate, National Championship Foundation
Yale: Parke Davis

1902
Michigan: Billingsley, Helms, Houlgate, National Championship Foundation, Parke Davis*
Yale: Parke Davis*

1903
Michigan: Billingsley, National Championship Foundation*
Princeton: Helms, Houlgate, National Championship Foundation*, Parke Davis

1904
Michigan: Billingsley, National Championship Foundation*
Pennsylvania: Helms, Houlgate, National Championship Foundation*, Parke Davis

1905
Chicago: Billingsley, Helms, Houlgate, National Championship Foundation
Yale: Parke Davis

1906
Princeton: Helms, National Championship Foundation
Vanderbilt: Billingsley
Yale: Parke Davis

1907
Pennsylvania: Billingsley
Yale: Helms, Houlgate, National Championship Foundation, Parke Davis

1908
LSU: National Championship Foundation*
Pennsylvania: Billingsley, Helms, Houlgate, National Championship Foundation*, Parke Davis

1909
Yale: Billingsley, Helms, Houlgate, National Championship Foundation, Parke Davis

1910
Auburn: Billingsley
Harvard: Helms, Houlgate, National Championship Foundation*
Pittsburgh: National Championship Foundation*

1911
Penn St.: National Championship Foundation*
Princeton: Helms, Houlgate, National Championship Foundation*, Parke Davis
Vanderbilt: Billingsley

1912
Harvard: Helms, Houlgate, National Championship Foundation*, Parke Davis
Penn St.: National Championship Foundation*
Wisconsin: Billingsley

1913
Chicago: Billingsley, Parke Davis*
Harvard: Helms, Houlgate, National Championship Foundation, Parke Davis*

1914
Army: Helms, Houlgate, National Championship Foundation, Parke Davis*
Illinois: Billingsley, Parke Davis*

1915
Cornell: Helms, Houlgate, National Championship Foundation, Parke Davis*
Nebraska: Billingsley
Pittsburgh: Parke Davis*

1916
Army: Parke Davis*
Pittsburgh: Billingsley, Helms, Houlgate, National Championship Foundation, Parke Davis*

1917
Georgia Tech: Billingsley, Helms, Houlgate, National Championship Foundation

1918
Michigan: Billingsley, National Championship Foundation*
Pittsburgh: Helms, Houlgate, National Championship Foundation*

1919
Harvard: Football Research*, Helms, Houlgate, National Championship Foundation*, Parke Davis*
Illinois: Billingsley, Boand, Football Research*, Parke Davis*
Notre Dame: National Championship Foundation*, Parke Davis*

1920
California: Billingsley, Football Research, Helms, Houlgate, National Championship Foundation
Harvard: Boand*
Notre Dame: Parke Davis*
Princeton: Boand*, Parke Davis*

1921
California: Boand*, Football Research
Cornell: Helms, Houlgate, National Championship Foundation, Parke Davis*
Iowa: Billingsley, Parke Davis*
Lafayette: Boand*, Parke Davis*
Wash. & Jeff.: Boand*

1922
California: Houlgate, National Championship Foundation*
Cornell: Helms, Parke Davis*
Iowa: Billingsley
Princeton: Boand, Football Research, National Championship Foundation*, Parke Davis*

1923
California: Houlgate
Illinois: Boand, Football Research, Helms, National Championship Foundation*, Parke Davis
Michigan: Billingsley, National Championship Foundation*

1924
Notre Dame: Billingsley, Boand, Dickinson, Football Research, Helms, Houlgate, National Championship Foundation, Poling
Pennsylvania: Parke Davis

1925
Alabama: Billingsley, Boand, Football Research, Helms, Houlgate, National Championship Foundation, Poling
Dartmouth: Dickinson, Parke Davis

1926
Alabama: Billingsley, Football Research, Helms*, National Championship Foundation*, Poling
Lafayette: Parke Davis
Navy: Boand, Houlgate
Stanford: Dickinson, Helms*, National Championship Foundation*

1927
Georgia: Boand, Poling
Illinois: Billingsley, Dickinson, Helms, National Championship Foundation, Parke Davis
Notre Dame: Houlgate
Yale: Football Research

1928
Detroit: Parke Davis*
Georgia Tech: Billingsley, Boand, Football Research, Helms, Houlgate, National Championship Foundation, Parke Davis*, Poling
Southern Cal: Dickinson

1929
Notre Dame: Billingsley, Boand, Dickinson, Dunkel, Football Research, Helms, National Championship Foundation, Poling
Pittsburgh: Parke Davis
Southern Cal: Houlgate

1930
Alabama: Football Research, Parke Davis*
Notre Dame: Billingsley, Boand, Dickinson, Dunkel, Helms, Houlgate, National Championship Foundation, Parke Davis*, Poling

1931
Pittsburgh: Parke Davis*
Purdue: Parke Davis*
Southern Cal: Billingsley, Boand, Dickinson, Dunkel, Helms, Houlgate, Football Research, National Championship Foundation, Poling, Williamson

1932
Colgate: Parke Davis*
Michigan: Dickinson, Parke Davis*
Southern Cal: Billingsley, Boand, Dunkel, Football Research, Helms, Houlgate, National Championship Foundation, Parke Davis*, Poling, Williamson

1933
Michigan: Billingsley, Boand, Dickinson, Helms, Houlgate, Football Research, National Championship Foundation, Parke Davis*, Poling
Ohio St.: Dunkel
Princeton: Parke Davis*
Southern Cal: Williamson

1934
Alabama: Billingsley, Dunkel, Houlgate, Poling, Williamson
Minnesota: Boand, Dickinson, Football Research, Helms, Litkenhous, National Championship Foundation

1935
LSU: Williamson*
Minnesota: Billingsley, Boand, Football Research, Helms, Litkenhous, National Championship Foundation, Poling
Princeton: Dunkel
Southern Methodist: Dickinson, Houlgate
Texas Christian: Williamson*

1936
LSU: Williamson
Minnesota: AP, Billingsley, Dickinson, Dunkel, Helms, Litkenhous, National Championship Foundation, Poling
Pittsburgh: Boand, Football Research, Houlgate

1937
California: Dunkel, Helms
Pittsburgh: AP, Billingsley, Boand, Dickinson, Football Research, Houlgate, Litkenhous, National Championship Foundation, Poling, Williamson

1938
Notre Dame: Dickinson
Tennessee: Billingsley, Boand, Dunkel, Football Research, Houlgate, Litkenhous, Poling, Sagarin
Texas Christian: AP, Helms, National Championship Foundation, Williamson

1939
Cornell: Litkenhous
Southern Cal: Dickinson
Texas A&M: AP, Billingsley, Boand, DeVold, Dunkel, Football Research, Helms, Houlgate, National Championship Foundation, Poling, Williamson

1940
Minnesota: AP, Berryman, Billingsley, Boand, DeVold, Dickinson, Football Research, Houlgate, Litkenhous, National Championship Foundation
Stanford: Helms, Poling
Tennessee: Dunkel, Williamson

1941
Alabama: Houlgate
Minnesota: AP, Billingsley, Boand, DeVold, Dunkel, Football Research, Helms, Litkenhous, National Championship Foundation, Poling
Texas: Berryman, Williamson

1942
Georgia: Berryman, DeVold, Houlgate, Litkenhous, Poling, Williamson
Ohio St.: AP, Billingsley, Boand, Dunkel, Football Research, National Championship Foundation
Wisconsin: Helms

1943
Notre Dame: AP, Berryman, Billingsley, Boand, DeVold, Dunkel, Football Research, Helms, Houlgate, Litkenhous, National Championship Foundation, Poling, Williamson

1944
Army: AP, Berryman, Billingsley, Boand, DeVold, Dunkel, Football Research, Helms, Houlgate, Litkenhous, National Championship Foundation*, Poling, Williamson
Ohio St.: National Championship Foundation*

1945
Alabama: National Championship Foundation*
Army: AP, Berryman, Billingsley, Boand, DeVold, Dunkel, Football Research, Helms, Houlgate, Litkenhous, National Championship Foundation*, Poling, Williamson

1946
Army: Boand*, Football Research, Helms*, Houlgate, Poling*
Georgia: Williamson
Notre Dame: AP, Berryman, Billingsley, Boand*, DeVold, Dunkel, Helms*, Litkenhous, National Championship Foundation, Poling*

1947
Michigan: Berryman, Billingsley, Boand, DeVold, Dunkel, Football Research, Helms*, Houlgate, Litkenhous, National Championship Foundation, Poling
Notre Dame: AP, Helms*, Williamson

1948
Michigan: AP, Berryman, Billingsley, Boand, DeVold, Dunkel, Football Research, Helms, Houlgate, Litkenhous, National Championship Foundation, Poling, Williamson

1949
Notre Dame: AP, Berryman, Boand, DeVold, Dunkel, Helms, Houlgate, Litkenhous, National Championship Foundation, Poling, Williamson
Oklahoma: Billingsley, Football Research

1950
Oklahoma: AP, Berryman, Helms, Litkenhous, UPI, Williamson
Princeton: Boand, Poling
Tennessee: Billingsley, DeVold, Dunkel, Football Research, National Championship Foundation

1951
Georgia Tech: Berryman, Boand*
Illinois: Boand*
Maryland: Billingsley, DeVold, Dunkel, Football Research, National Championship Foundation
Michigan St.: Helms, Poling
Tennessee: AP, Litkenhous, UPI, Williamson

1952
Georgia Tech: Berryman, INS, Poling
Michigan St.: AP, Billingsley, Boand, DeVold, Dunkel, Football Research, Helms, Litkenhous, National Championship Foundation, UPI, Williamson

1953
Maryland: AP, INS, UPI
Notre Dame: Billingsley, Boand, DeVold, Dunkel, Helms, Litkenhous, National Championship Foundation, Poling, Williamson
Oklahoma: Berryman, Football Research

1954
Ohio St.: AP, Berryman, Boand, DeVold, Football Research*, Helms*, INS, National Championship Foundation*, Poling, Williamson
UCLA: Billingsley, Dunkel, Football Research*, FW, Helms*, Litkenhous, National Championship Foundation*, UPI

1955
Michigan St.: Boand
Oklahoma: AP, Berryman, Billingsley, DeVold, Dunkel, Football Research, FW, Helms, INS, Litkenhous, National Championship Foundation, Poling, UPI, Williamson

1956
Georgia Tech: Berryman
Iowa: Football Research
Oklahoma: AP, Billingsley, Boand, DeVold, Dunkel, FW, Helms, INS, Litkenhous, National Championship Foundation, Sagarin, UPI, Williamson

1957
Auburn: AP, Football Research, Helms, National Championship Foundation, Poling, Williamson
Michigan St.: Billingsley, Dunkel, Sagarin
Ohio St.: Boand, DeVold, FW, INS, Litkenhous, UPI
Oklahoma: Berryman

1958
Iowa: FW, Sagarin
LSU: AP, Berryman, Billingsley, Boand, DeVold, Dunkel, FB News, Football Research, Helms, Litkenhous, National Championship Foundation, Poling, UPI, Williamson

1959
Mississippi: Berryman, Billingsley, Dunkel, Sagarin
Syracuse: AP, Boand, DeVold, FB News, Football Research, FW, Helms, Litkenhous, National Championship Foundation, NFF, Poling, UPI, Williamson

1960
Iowa: Berryman, Billingsley, Boand, Litkenhous, Sagarin
Minnesota: AP, FB News, NFF, UPI
Mississippi: DeVold, Dunkel, Football Research, FW, National Championship Foundation, Williamson
Missouri: Poling
Washington: Helms

1961
Alabama: AP, Berryman, Billingsley, DeVold, Dunkel, FB News, Football Research, Helms, Litkenhous, National Championship Foundation, NFF, UPI, Williamson
Ohio St.: FW, Poling
Texas: Sagarin

1962
Alabama: Billingsley, Sagarin
LSU: Berryman*
Southern Cal: AP, Berryman*, DeVold, Dunkel, FB News, Football Research, FW, Helms, National Championship Foundation, NFF, Poling, UPI, Williamson
Texas: Litkenhous

1963
Texas: AP, Berryman, Billingsley, DeVold, Dunkel, FB News, Football Research, FW, Helms, Litkenhous, National Championship Foundation, NFF, Poling, Sagarin, UPI, Williamson

1964
Alabama: AP, Berryman, Litkenhous, UPI
Arkansas: Billingsley, Football Research, FW, Helms, National Championship Foundation, Poling
Michigan: Dunkel
Notre Dame: DeVold, FB News, NFF, Sagarin

1965
Alabama: AP, Billingsley, Football Research, FW*, National Championship Foundation
Michigan St.: Berryman, DeVold, Dunkel, FB News, FW*, Helms, Litkenhous, NFF, Poling, Sagarin, UPI

1966
Alabama: Berryman
Michigan St.: Football Research, Helms*, NFF*, Poling*
Notre Dame: AP, Billingsley, DeVold, Dunkel, FB News, FW, Helms*, Litkenhous, Matthews, National Championship Foundation, NFF*, Poling*, Sagarin, UPI

1967
Notre Dame: Dunkel
Oklahoma: Poling
Southern Cal: AP, Berryman, Billingsley, DeVold, FB News, Football Research, FW, Helms, Matthews, National Championship Foundation, NFF, Sagarin, UPI
Tennessee: Litkenhous

1968
Georgia: Litkenhous
Ohio St.: AP, Berryman, Billingsley, Dunkel, FACT, FB News, Football Research, FW, Helms, National Championship Foundation, NFF, Poling, UPI
Texas: DeVold, Matthews, Sagarin

1969
Ohio St.: Matthews
Penn St.: FACT*
Texas: AP, Berryman, Billingsley, DeVold, Dunkel, FACT*, FB News, Football Research, FW, Helms, Litkenhous,

National Championship Foundation, NFF, Poling, Sagarin, UPI

1970
Arizona St.: Poling
Nebraska: AP, Billingsley, DeVold, Dunkel, FACT*, FB News, Football Research, FW, Helms, National Championship Foundation
Notre Dame: FACT*, Matthews, Sagarin
Ohio St.: NFF*
Texas: Berryman, FACT*, Litkenhous, NFF*, UPI

1971
Nebraska: AP, Berryman, Billingsley, DeVold, Dunkel, FACT, FB News, Football Research, FW, Helms, Litkenhous, Matthews, National Championship Foundation, NFF, Poling, Sagarin, UPI

1972
Southern Cal: AP, Berryman, Billingsley, DeVold, Dunkel, FACT, FB News, Football Research, FW, Helms, Litkenhous, Matthews, National Championship Foundation, NFF, Poling, Sagarin, UPI

1973
Alabama: Berryman, UPI
Michigan: National Championship Foundation*, Poling*
Notre Dame: AP, FB News, FW, Helms, National Championship Foundation*, NFF
Ohio St.: FACT, National Championship Foundation*, Poling*, Sagarin
Oklahoma: Billingsley, DeVold, Dunkel, Football Research

1974
Ohio St.: Matthews
Oklahoma: AP, Berryman, Billingsley, DeVold, Dunkel, FACT, FB News, Football Research, Helms*, Litkenhous, National Championship Foundation, Poling, Sagarin
Southern Cal: FW, Helms*, NFF, UPI

1975
Alabama: Matthews*
Arizona St.: National Championship Foundation*, Sporting News
Ohio St.: Berryman, FACT*, Helms*, Matthews*, Poling
Oklahoma: AP, Billingsley, DeVold, Dunkel, FACT*, FB News, Football Research, FW, Helms*, National Championship Foundation*, NFF, Sagarin, UPI

1976
Pittsburgh: AP, FACT, FB News, FW, Helms, National Championship Foundation, NFF, Poling, Sagarin, Sporting News, UPI
Southern Cal: Berryman, Billingsley, DeVold, Dunkel, Football Research, Matthews

1977
Alabama: Football Research*
Arkansas: FACT*
Notre Dame: AP, Billingsley, DeVold, Dunkel, FACT*, FB News, Football Research*, FW, Helms, Matthews, National Championship Foundation, NFF, Poling, Sagarin, Sporting News, UPI
Texas: Berryman, FACT*

1978
Alabama: AP, FACT*, Football Research, FW, Helms*, National Championship Foundation, NFF
Oklahoma: Billingsley, DeVold, Dunkel, FACT*, Helms*, Litkenhous, Matthews, Poling, Sagarin
Southern Cal: Berryman, FACT*, FB News, Helms*, Sporting News, UPI

1979
Alabama: AP, Berryman, Billingsley, DeVold, Dunkel, FACT, FB News, FW, Helms, Matthews, National Championship Foundation, NFF, NY Times, Poling, Sagarin, Sporting News, UPI
Southern Cal: Football Research

1980
Florida St.: FACT*
Georgia: AP, Berryman, FACT*, FB News, FW, Helms, National Championship Foundation, NFF, Poling, Sporting News, UPI
Nebraska: FACT*, Sagarin
Oklahoma: Billingsley, Dunkel, Matthews
Pittsburgh: DeVold, FACT*, Football Research, NY Times

1981
Clemson: AP, Berryman, Billingsley, DeVold, FACT, FB News, Football Research, FW, Helms, Litkenhous, Matthews, National Championship Foundation*, NFF, NY Times, Poling, Sporting News, UPI
Nebraska: National Championship Foundation*
Penn St.: Dunkel, Sagarin
Pittsburgh: National Championship Foundation*
Texas: National Championship Foundation*

1982
Nebraska: Berryman
Penn St.: AP, Billingsley, DeVold, Dunkel, FACT, FB News, Football Research, FW, Helms*, Litkenhous, Matthews, National Championship Foundation, NFF, NY Times, Poling, Sagarin, Sporting News, UPI, USA/CNN
Southern Methodist: Helms*

1983
Auburn: FACT*, Football Research, NY Times
Miami (Fla.): AP, Billingsley, Dunkel, FB News, FW, National Championship Foundation, NFF, Sporting News, UPI, USA/CNN
Nebraska: Berryman, DeVold, FACT*, Litkenhous, Matthews, Poling, Sagarin

1984
Brigham Young: AP, Football Research, FW, National Championship Foundation, NFF, Poling, UPI, USA/CNN
Florida: Billingsley, DeVold, Dunkel, FACT, Matthews, NY Times, Sagarin, Sporting News
Nebraska: Litkenhous
Washington: Berryman, FB News

1985
Michigan: Matthews, Sagarin
Oklahoma: AP, Berryman, Billingsley, DeVold, Dunkel, FACT, FB News, Football Research, FW, National Championship Foundation, NFF, NY Times, Sporting News, UPI, USA/CNN

1986
Miami (Fla.): FACT*
Oklahoma: Berryman, Billingsley, DeVold, Dunkel, Football Research, NY Times, Sagarin
Penn St.: AP, FACT*, FB News, FW, Matthews, National Championship Foundation, NFF, Sporting News, UPI, USA/CNN

1987
Florida St.: Berryman, Sagarin
Miami (Fla.): AP, Billingsley, DeVold, Dunkel, FACT, FB News, Football Research, FW, Matthews, National Championship Foundation, NFF, NY Times, Sporting News, UPI, USA/CNN

1988
Miami (Fla.): Berryman, Sagarin
Notre Dame: AP, Billingsley, DeVold, Dunkel, FACT, FB News, Football Research, FW, Matthews, National Championship Foundation, NFF, NY Times, Sporting News, UPI, USA/CNN

1989
Florida St.: Billingsley
Miami (Fla.): AP, DeVold, Dunkel, FACT*, FB News, Football Research, FW, Matthews, National Championship Foundation, NFF, NY Times, Sporting News, UPI, USA/CNN
Notre Dame: Berryman, FACT*, Sagarin

1990
Colorado: AP, Berryman, DeVold, FACT*, FB News, Football Research, FW, Matthews, National Championship Foundation*, NFF, Sporting News, USA/CNN
Georgia Tech: Dunkel, FACT*, National Championship Foundation*, UPI
Miami (Fla.): Billingsley, FACT*, NY Times, Sagarin
Washington: FACT*

1991
Miami (Fla.): AP, Football Research, National Championship Foundation*, NY Times, Sporting News
Washington: Berryman, Billingsley, DeVold, Dunkel, FACT, FB News, FW, Matthews, National Championship Foundation*, Sagarin, UPI/NFF, USA/CNN

1992
Alabama: AP, Berryman, Billingsley, DeVold, Dunkel, FACT, FB News, Football Research, FW, Matthews, National Championship Foundation, NY Times, Sporting News, UPI/NFF, USA/CNN
Florida St.: Sagarin

1993
Auburn: National Championship Foundation*
Florida St.: AP, Berryman, Billingsley, DeVold, Dunkel, FACT, FB News, FW, National Championship Foundation*, NY Times, Sagarin, Sporting News, UPI, USA/CNN, USA/NFF
Nebraska: National Championship Foundation*
Notre Dame: Matthews, National Championship Foundation*

1994
Florida St.: Dunkel
Nebraska: Alderson, AP, Berryman, FACT*, FB News, FW, National Championship Foundation*, Sporting News, UPI, USA/CNN, USA/NFF
Penn St.: Billingsley, DeVold, FACT*, Matthews, National Championship Foundation*, NY Times, Sagarin

1995
Nebraska: Alderson, AP, Berryman, Billingsley, DeVold, Dunkel, FACT, FB News, FW, Matthews, National Championship Foundation, NFF, NY Times, Sagarin, Sporting News, UPI, USA/CNN

(**Legend of Present Major Selectors:** Associated Press (AP) from 1936-present; United Press International (UPI) from 1950-90, United Press, 1950-57, UPI from 1958 after merger with International News Service; Football Writers Association of America (FW) from 1954-present; National Football Foundation and Hall of Fame (NFF) from 1959-90 and 1995; USA Today/Cable News Network (USA/CNN) from 1982-present; United Press International/National Football Foundation and Hall of Fame (UPI/NFF) from 1991-92; USA Today/National Football Foundation and Hall of Fame (USA/NFF) from 1993-94. The Associated Press has been the designated media poll since 1936. United Press International served as the coaches' poll from 1950 to 1991 when it was taken over by USA Today/Cable News Network. In 1991-92, the No. 1 team in the final UPI/NFF ratings received the MacArthur Bowl as the national champion by the NFF. In 1993-94, the No. 1 team in the USA Today/NFF final poll received the MacArthur Bowl.)

Major Selectors Since 1936

Year	ASSOCIATED PRESS Team	Record	UNITED PRESS INT'L Team	Record	USA TODAY/CNN Team	Record	FOOTBALL WRITERS' Team	Record
1936	Minnesota	7-1-0						
1937	Pittsburgh	9-0-1						
1938	Texas Christian	11-0-0						
1939	Texas A&M	11-0-0						
1940	Minnesota	8-0-0						
1941	Minnesota	8-0-0						
1942	Ohio St.	9-1-0						
1943	Notre Dame	9-1-0						
1944	Army	9-0-0						
1945	Army	9-0-0						
1946	Notre Dame	8-0-1						
1947	Notre Dame	9-0-0						
1948	Michigan	9-0-0						
1949	Notre Dame	10-0-0						
1950	Oklahoma	10-1-0	Oklahoma	10-1-0				
1951	Tennessee	10-0-0	Tennessee	10-0-0				
1952	Michigan St.	9-0-0	Michigan St.	9-0-0				
1953	Maryland	10-1-0	Maryland	10-1-0				
1954	Ohio St.	10-0-0	UCLA	9-0-0			UCLA	9-0-0
1955	Oklahoma	11-0-0	Oklahoma	11-0-0			Oklahoma	11-0-0
1956	Oklahoma	10-0-0	Oklahoma	10-0-0			Oklahoma	10-0-0
1957	Auburn	10-0-0	Ohio St.	9-1-0			Ohio St.	9-1-0
1958	LSU	11-0-0	LSU	11-0-0			Iowa	8-1-1
1959	Syracuse	11-0-0	Syracuse	11-0-0			Syracuse	11-0-0
1960	Minnesota	8-2-0	Minnesota	8-2-0			Mississippi	10-0-1
1961	Alabama	11-0-0	Alabama	11-0-0			Ohio St.	8-0-1
1962	Southern Cal	11-0-0	Southern Cal	11-0-0			Southern Cal	11-0-0
1963	Texas	11-0-0	Texas	11-0-0			Texas	11-0-0
1964	Alabama	10-1-0	Alabama	10-1-0			Arkansas	11-0-0
1965	Alabama	9-1-1	Michigan St.	10-1-0			Alabama	9-1-1
							Michigan St.	10-1-0
1966	Notre Dame	9-0-1	Notre Dame	9-0-1			Notre Dame	9-0-1
1967	Southern Cal	10-1-0	Southern Cal	10-1-0			Southern Cal	10-1-0
1968	Ohio St.	10-0-0	Ohio St.	10-0-0			Ohio St.	10-0-0
1969	Texas	11-0-0	Texas	11-0-0			Texas	11-0-0
1970	Nebraska	11-0-1	Texas	10-1-0			Nebraska	11-0-1
1971	Nebraska	13-0-0	Nebraska	13-0-0			Nebraska	13-0-0
1972	Southern Cal	12-0-0	Southern Cal	12-0-0			Southern Cal	12-0-0
1973	Notre Dame	11-0-0	Alabama	11-1-0			Notre Dame	11-0-0
1974	Oklahoma	11-0-0	Southern Cal	10-1-1			Southern Cal	10-1-1
1975	Oklahoma	11-1-0	Oklahoma	11-1-0			Oklahoma	11-1-0
1976	Pittsburgh	12-0-0	Pittsburgh	12-0-0			Pittsburgh	12-0-0
1977	Notre Dame	11-1-0	Notre Dame	11-1-0			Notre Dame	11-1-0
1978	Alabama	11-1-0	Southern Cal	12-1-0			Alabama	11-1-0
1979	Alabama	12-0-0	Alabama	12-0-0			Alabama	12-0-0
1980	Georgia	12-0-0	Georgia	12-0-0			Georgia	12-0-0
1981	Clemson	12-0-0	Clemson	12-0-0			Clemson	12-0-0
1982	Penn St.	11-1-0	Penn St.	11-1-0	Penn St.	11-1-0	Penn St.	11-1-0
1983	Miami (Fla.)	11-1-0	Miami (Fla.)	11-1-0	Miami (Fla.)	11-1-0	Miami (Fla.)	11-1-0
1984	Brigham Young	13-0-0	Brigham Young	13-0-0	Brigham Young	13-0-0	Brigham Young	13-0-0
1985	Oklahoma	11-1-0	Oklahoma	11-1-0	Oklahoma	11-1-0	Oklahoma	11-1-0
1986	Penn St.	12-0-0	Penn St.	12-0-0	Penn St.	12-0-0	Penn St.	12-0-0
1987	Miami (Fla.)	12-0-0	Miami (Fla.)	12-0-0	Miami (Fla.)	12-0-0	Miami (Fla.)	12-0-0
1988	Notre Dame	12-0-0	Notre Dame	12-0-0	Notre Dame	12-0-0	Notre Dame	12-0-0
1989	Miami (Fla.)	11-1-0	Miami (Fla.)	11-1-0	Miami (Fla.)	11-1-0	Miami (Fla.)	11-1-0
1990	Colorado	11-1-1	Georgia Tech	11-0-1	Colorado	11-1-1	Colorado	11-1-1
1991	Miami (Fla.)	12-0-0	Washington (UPI/NFF)	12-0-0	Washington	12-0-0	Washington	12-0-0
1992	Alabama	13-0-0	Alabama (UPI/NFF)	13-0-0	Alabama	13-0-0	Alabama	13-0-0
1993	Florida St.	12-1-0	Florida St.	12-1-0	Florida St.	12-1-0	Florida St.	12-1-0
1994	Nebraska	13-0-0	Nebraska	13-0-0	Nebraska	13-0-0	Nebraska	13-0-0
1995	Nebraska	12-0-0	Nebraska	12-0-0	Nebraska	12-0-0	Nebraska	12-0-0

National Champions in Bowl Games

Before 1936, teams listed are those deemed either eastern champion or national champion to reflect historical reality at the time.

Year	Team	Coach (Years†)	Record	Bowl (Result)
1900	Yale	Malcolm McBride	12-0-0	None
1901	Michigan	Fielding Yost	11-0-0	Rose (beat Stanford, 49-0)
	Harvard	William Reid	12-0-0	None
1902	Michigan	Fielding Yost	11-0-0	None
	Yale	Joseph Swan	11-0-1	None
1903	Princeton	Art Hillebrand	11-0-0	None
1904	Pennsylvania	Carl Williams	12-0-0	None

File photo

Bruce Smith played left halfback on Minnesota's consensus national champion teams of 1940 and 1941, helping the Gophers to a 16-0 mark over the two seasons. He earned all-America honors in 1941.

Year	Team	Coach (Years†)	Record	Bowl (Result)
1905	Chicago	Amos Alonzo Stagg	11-0-0	None
	Yale	J. E. Owsley	10-0-0	None
1906	Princeton	Bill Roper	9-0-1	None
	Yale	Foster Rockwell	9-0-1	None
1907	Yale	William Knox	9-0-1	None
1908	Pennsylvania	Sol Metzer	11-0-1	None
	Harvard	Percy Haughton	9-0-1	None
1909	Yale	Howard Jones	10-0-0	None
1910	Harvard	Percy Haughton	8-0-1	None
1911	Princeton	Bill Roper	8-0-2	None
1912	Harvard	Percy Haughton	9-0-0	None
1913	Harvard	Percy Haughton	9-0-0	None
1914	Army	Charley Daly	9-0-0	None
	Harvard	Percy Haughton	7-0-2	None
1915	Cornell	Al Sharpe	9-0-0	None
1916	Pittsburgh	Glenn "Pop" Warner	8-0-0	None
1917	Georgia Tech	John Heisman	9-0-0	None
1918	Pittsburgh	Glenn "Pop" Warner	4-1-0	None
1919	Harvard	Robert Fisher	9-0-1	Rose (beat Oregon, 7-6)
	Penn St.	Hugo Bezdek	7-1-0	None
1920	California	Andy Smith	9-0-0	Rose (beat Ohio St., 28-0)
	Princeton	Bill Roper	6-0-1	None
1921	Cornell	Gil Dobie	8-0-0	None
	Penn St.	Hugo Bezdek	8-0-2	None
1922	Cornell	Gil Dobie	8-0-0	None
	Princeton	Bill Roper	8-0-0	None
1923	Illinois	Robert Zuppke	8-0-0	None
1924	Notre Dame	Knute Rockne	10-0-0	Rose (beat Stanford, 27-10)
1925	Alabama	Wallace Wade	10-0-0	Rose (beat Washington, 20-19)
	Dartmouth	Jesse Hawley	8-0-0	None
1926	Alabama	Wallace Wade	9-0-1	Rose (tied Stanford, 7-7)
	Stanford	Glenn "Pop" Warner	10-0-1	Rose (tied Alabama, 7-7)
1927	Illinois	Robert Zuppke	7-0-1	None
1928	Georgia Tech	Bill Alexander	10-0-0	Rose (beat California, 8-7)
	Southern Cal	Howard Jones	9-0-1	None
1929	Notre Dame	Knute Rockne	9-0-0	None
1930	Notre Dame	Knute Rockne	10-0-0	None
1931	Southern Cal	Howard Jones	10-1-0	Rose (beat Tulane, 21-12)
1932	Michigan	Harry Kipke	8-0-0	None
	Southern Cal	Howard Jones	10-0-0	Rose (beat Pittsburgh, 35-0)
1933	Michigan	Harry Kipke	7-0-1	None
1934	Minnesota	Bernie Bierman	8-0-0	None
1935	Minnesota	Bernie Bierman	8-0-0	None
	Southern Methodist	Matty Bell	12-1-0	Rose (lost to Stanford, 7-0)
1936	Minnesota	Bernie Bierman (5-15)	7-1-0	None
1937	Pittsburgh	Jock Sutherland (13-18)	9-0-1	None
1938	Texas Christian	Dutch Meyer (5-5)	11-0-0	Sugar (beat Carnegie Mellon, 15-7)
1939	Texas A&M	Homer Norton (6-16)	11-0-0	Sugar (beat Tulane, 14-13)
1940	Minnesota	Bernie Bierman (9-19)	8-0-0	None
1941	Minnesota	Bernie Bierman (10-20)	8-0-0	None
1942	Ohio St.	Paul Brown (2-2)	9-1-0	None
1943	Notre Dame	Frank Leahy (3-5)	9-1-0	None
1944	Army	Earl "Red" Blaik (4-11)	9-0-0	None
1945	Army	Earl "Red" Blaik (5-12)	9-0-0	None
1946	Notre Dame	Frank Leahy (4-6)	8-0-1	None
1947	Notre Dame	Frank Leahy (5-7)	9-0-0	None
1948	Michigan	Bennie Oosterbaan (1-1)	9-0-0	None
1949	Notre Dame	Frank Leahy (7-9)	10-0-0	None
1950	Oklahoma	Bud Wilkinson (4-4)	10-1-0	Sugar (lost to Kentucky, 13-7)
1951	Tennessee	Robert Neyland (20-20)	10-0-0	Sugar (lost to Maryland, 28-13)
1952	Michigan St.	Clarence "Biggie" Munn (6-9)	9-0-0	None
1953	Maryland	Jim Tatum (7-9)	10-1-0	Orange (lost to Oklahoma, 7-0)
1954	Ohio St.	Woody Hayes (4-9)	10-0-0	Rose (beat Southern Cal, 20-7)
	UCLA	Red Sanders (6-12)	9-0-0	None
1955	Oklahoma	Bud Wilkinson (9-9)	11-0-0	Orange (beat Maryland, 20-6)
1956	Oklahoma	Bud Wilkinson (10-10)	10-0-0	None
1957	Auburn	Ralph "Shug" Jordan (7-7)	10-0-0	None
	Ohio St.	Woody Hayes (7-12)	9-1-0	Rose (beat Oregon, 10-7)
1958	LSU	Paul Dietzel (4-4)	11-0-0	Sugar (beat Clemson, 7-0)
	Iowa	Forest Evashevski (5-8)	8-1-1	Rose (beat California, 38-12)
1959	Syracuse	Ben Schwartzwalder (11-14)	11-0-0	Cotton (beat Texas, 23-14)
1960	Minnesota	Murray Warmath (7-9)	8-2-0	Rose (lost to Washington, 17-7)
	Mississippi	Johnny Vaught (14-14)	10-0-1	Sugar (beat Rice, 14-6)
1961	Alabama	Paul "Bear" Bryant (4-17)	11-0-0	Sugar (beat Arkansas, 10-3)
	Ohio St.	Woody Hayes (11-16)	8-0-1	None
1962	Southern Cal	John McKay (3-3)	11-0-0	Rose (beat Wisconsin, 42-37)
1963	Texas	Darrell Royal (7-10)	11-0-0	Cotton (beat Navy, 28-6)
1964	Alabama	Paul "Bear" Bryant (7-20)	10-1-0	Orange (lost to Texas, 21-17)
	Arkansas	Frank Broyles (3-4)	11-0-0	Cotton (beat Nebraska, 10-7)
	Notre Dame	Ara Parseghian (1-14)	9-1-0	None
1965	Alabama	Paul "Bear" Bryant (8-21)	9-1-1	Orange (beat Nebraska, 39-28)
	Michigan St.	Duffy Daugherty (12-12)	10-1-0	Rose (lost to UCLA, 14-12)
1966	Michigan St.	Duffy Daugherty (13-13)	9-0-1	None
	Notre Dame	Ara Parseghian (3-17)	9-0-1	None
1967	Southern Cal	John McKay (8-8)	10-1-0	Rose (beat Indiana, 14-3)

Year	Team	Coach (Years†)	Record	Bowl (Result)
1968	Ohio St.	Woody Hayes (18-23)	10-0-0	Rose (beat Southern Cal, 27-16)
1969	Texas	Darrell Royal (13-16)	11-0-0	Cotton (beat Notre Dame, 21-17)
1970	Nebraska	Bob Devaney (9-14)	11-0-1	Orange (beat LSU, 17-12)
	Ohio St.	Woody Hayes (20-25)	9-1-0	Rose (lost to Stanford, 27-17)
	Texas	Darrell Royal (14-17)	10-1-0	Cotton (lost to Notre Dame, 24-11)
1971	Nebraska	Bob Devaney (10-15)	13-0-0	Orange (beat Alabama, 38-6)
1972	Southern Cal	John McKay (13-13)	12-0-0	Rose (beat Ohio St., 42-17)
1973	Alabama	Paul "Bear" Bryant (16-29)	11-1-0	Sugar (lost to Notre Dame, 24-23)
	Notre Dame	Ara Parseghian (10-23)	11-0-0	Sugar (beat Alabama, 24-23)
1974	Oklahoma	Barry Switzer (2-2)	11-0-0	None
	Southern Cal	John McKay (15-15)	10-1-1	Rose (beat Ohio St., 18-17)
1975	Oklahoma	Barry Switzer (3-3)	11-1-0	Orange (beat Michigan, 14-6)
1976	Pittsburgh	Johnny Majors (4-9)	12-0-0	Sugar (beat Georgia, 27-3)
1977	Notre Dame	Dan Devine (3-19)	11-1-0	Cotton (beat Texas, 38-10)
1978	Alabama	Paul "Bear" Bryant (21-34)	11-1-0	Sugar (beat Penn St., 14-7)
	Southern Cal	John Robinson (3-3)	12-1-0	Rose (beat Michigan, 17-10)
1979	Alabama	Paul "Bear" Bryant (22-35)	12-0-0	Sugar (beat Arkansas, 24-9)
1980	Georgia	Vince Dooley (17-17)	12-0-0	Sugar (beat Notre Dame, 17-10)
1981	Clemson	Danny Ford (4-4#)	12-0-0	Orange (beat Nebraska, 22-15)
1982	Penn St.	Joe Paterno (17-17)	11-1-0	Sugar (beat Georgia, 27-23)
1983	Miami (Fla.)	Howard Schnellenberger (5-5)	11-1-0	Orange (beat Nebraska, 31-30)
1984	Brigham Young	LaVell Edwards (13-13)	13-0-0	Holiday (beat Michigan, 24-17)
1985	Oklahoma	Barry Switzer (13-13)	11-1-0	Orange (beat Penn St., 25-10)
1986	Penn St.	Joe Paterno (21-21)	12-0-0	Fiesta (beat Miami, Fla., 14-10)
1987	Miami (Fla.)	Jimmy Johnson (3-9)	12-0-0	Orange (beat Oklahoma, 20-14)
1988	Notre Dame	Lou Holtz (3-19)	12-0-0	Fiesta (beat West Va., 34-21)
1989	Miami (Fla.)	Dennis Erickson (1-8)	11-1-0	Sugar (beat Alabama, 33-25)
1990	Colorado	Bill McCartney (9-9)	11-1-1	Orange (beat Notre Dame, 10-9)
	Georgia Tech	Bobby Ross (4-14)	11-0-1	Fla. Citrus (beat Nebraska, 45-21)
1991	Miami (Fla.)	Dennis Erickson (3-10)	12-0-0	Orange (beat Nebraska, 22-0)
	Washington	Don James (17-21)	12-0-0	Rose (beat Michigan, 34-14)
1992	Alabama	Gene Stallings (3-10)	13-0-0	Sugar (beat Miami, Fla., 34-13)
1993	Florida St.	Bobby Bowden (18-28)	12-1-0	Orange (beat Nebraska, 18-16)
1994	Nebraska	Tom Osborne (22-22)	13-0-0	Orange (beat Miami, Fla., 24-17)
1995	Nebraska	Tom Osborne (23-23)	12-0-0	Fiesta (beat Florida, 62-24)

†Years head coach at that college and total years at four-year colleges. #Includes last game of 1978 season.

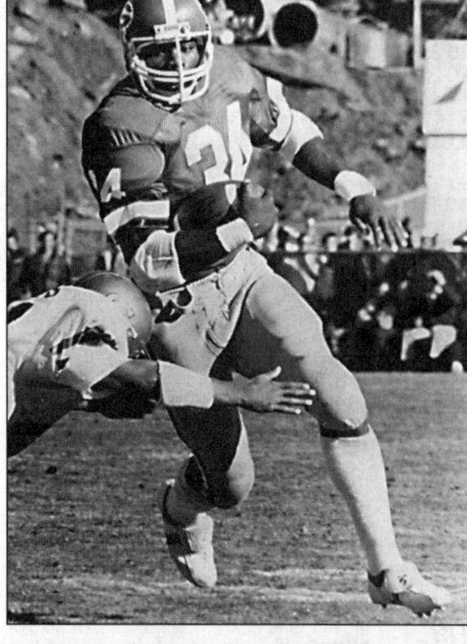

File photo

Freshman sensation Herschel Walker rushed for 1,616 yards and 15 touchdowns to lead Georgia to a perfect 11-0 regular-season record in 1980. The Bulldogs defeated Notre Dame, 17-10, in the Sugar Bowl to earn the mythical national championship.

Associated Press Weekly Poll Leaders

The weekly dates are for Tuesday, the most frequent release date of the poll, except when the final poll was taken after January 1-2 bowl games. A team's record includes its last game before the weekly poll. A new weekly leader's rank the previous week is indicated in parentheses after its record. Final poll leaders (annual champions) are in bold face. (Note: Only 10 teams were ranked in the weekly polls during 1962, 1963, 1964, 1965, 1966 and 1967; 20 were ranked in all other seasons until 1989, when 25 were ranked.)

1936

Date	Team	Record
10-20	Minnesota	(3-0-0)
10-27	Minnesota	(4-0-0)
11-3	Northwestern	(5-0-0) (3)
11-10	Northwestern	(6-0-0)
11-17	Northwestern	(7-0-0)
11-24	Minnesota	(7-1-0) (2)
12-1	**Minnesota**	**(7-1-0)**

1937

Date	Team	Record
10-20	California	(5-0-0)
10-27	California	(6-0-0)
11-2	California	(7-0-0)
11-9	Pittsburgh	(6-0-1) (3)
11-16	Pittsburgh	(7-0-1)
11-23	Pittsburgh	(8-0-1)
11-30	**Pittsburgh**	**(9-0-1)**

1938

Date	Team	Record
10-18	Pittsburgh	(4-0-0)
10-25	Pittsburgh	(5-0-0)
11-1	Pittsburgh	(6-0-0)
11-8	Texas Christian	(7-0-0) (2)
11-15	Notre Dame	(7-0-0) (2)
11-22	Notre Dame	(8-0-0)
11-29	Notre Dame	(8-0-0)
12-6	**Texas Christian**	**(10-0-0) (2)**

1939

Date	Team	Record
10-17	Pittsburgh	(3-0-0)
10-24	Tennessee	(4-0-0) (5)
10-31	Tennessee	(5-0-0)
11-7	Tennessee	(6-0-0)
11-14	Tennessee	(7-0-0)
11-21	Texas A&M	(9-0-0) (2)
11-28	(tie) Texas A&M	(9-0-0)
	(tie) Southern Cal	(6-0-1) (4)
12-5	Texas A&M	(10-0-0)
12-12	**Texas A&M**	**(10-0-0)**

1940

Date	Team	Record
10-15	Cornell	(2-0-0)
10-22	Cornell	(3-0-0)
10-29	Cornell	(4-0-0)
11-5	Cornell	(5-0-0)
11-12	Minnesota	(6-0-0) (2)
11-19	Minnesota	(7-0-0)
11-26	Minnesota	(8-0-0)
12-3	**Minnesota**	**(8-0-0)**

1941

Date	Team	Record
10-14	Minnesota	(2-0-0)
10-21	Minnesota	(3-0-0)
10-28	(tie) Minnesota	(4-0-0)
	(tie) Texas	(5-0-0) (2)
11-4	Texas	(6-0-0)
11-11	Minnesota	(6-0-0) (2)
11-18	Minnesota	(7-0-0)
11-25	Minnesota	(8-0-0)
12-2	**Minnesota**	**(8-0-0)**

1942

Date	Team	Record
10-13	Ohio St.	(3-0-0)
10-20	Ohio St.	(4-0-0)
10-27	Ohio St.	(5-0-0)
11-3	Georgia	(7-0-0) (2)
11-10	Georgia	(8-0-0)
11-17	Georgia	(9-0-0)
11-24	Boston College	(8-0-0) (3)
12-1	**Ohio St.**	**(9-1-0) (3)**

1943

Date	Team	Record
10-5	Notre Dame	(2-0-0)
10-12	Notre Dame	(3-0-0)
10-19	Notre Dame	(4-0-0)
10-26	Notre Dame	(5-0-0)
11-2	Notre Dame	(6-0-0)
11-9	Notre Dame	(7-0-0)
11-16	Notre Dame	(8-0-0)
11-23	Notre Dame	(9-0-0)
11-30	**Notre Dame**	**(9-1-0)**

1944

Date	Team	Record
10-10	Notre Dame	(2-0-0)
10-17	Notre Dame	(3-0-0)
10-24	Notre Dame	(4-0-0)
10-31	Army	(5-0-0) (2)
11-7	Army	(6-0-0)
11-14	Army	(7-0-0)
11-21	Army	(8-0-0)
11-28	Army	(8-0-0)
12-5	**Army**	**(9-0-0)**

1945

Date	Team	Record
10-9	Army	(2-0-0)
10-16	Army	(3-0-0)
10-23	Army	(4-0-0)
10-30	Army	(5-0-0)
11-6	Army	(6-0-0)
11-13	Army	(7-0-0)
11-20	Army	(8-0-0)
11-27	Army	(8-0-0)
12-4	**Army**	**(9-0-0)**

1946

Date	Team	Record
10-8	Texas	(3-0-0)
10-15	Army	(4-0-0) (2)
10-22	Army	(5-0-0)
10-29	Army	(6-0-0)
11-5	Army	(7-0-0)
11-12	Army	(7-0-1)
11-19	Army	(8-0-1)
11-26	Army	(8-0-1)
12-3	**Notre Dame**	**(8-0-1) (2)**

1947*

10-7 Notre Dame (1-0-0)
10-14 Michigan (3-0-0) (2)
10-21 Michigan (4-0-0)
10-28 Notre Dame (4-0-0) (2)
11-4 Notre Dame (5-0-0)
11-11 Notre Dame (6-0-0)
11-18 Michigan (8-0-0) (2)
11-25 Notre Dame (8-0-0) (2)
12-2 Notre Dame (8-0-0)
12-9 Notre Dame (9-0-0)

1948

10-5 Notre Dame (2-0-0)
10-12 North Caro. (3-0-0) (2)
10-19 Michigan (4-0-0) (4)
10-26 Michigan (5-0-0)
11-2 Notre Dame (6-0-0) (2)
11-9 Michigan (7-0-0) (2)
11-16 Michigan (8-0-0)
11-23 Michigan (9-0-0)
11-30 Michigan (9-0-0)

1949

10-4 Michigan (2-0-0)
10-11 Notre Dame (3-0-0) (2)
10-18 Notre Dame (4-0-0)
10-25 Notre Dame (4-0-0)
11-1 Notre Dame (5-0-0)
11-8 Notre Dame (6-0-0)
11-15 Notre Dame (7-0-0)
11-22 Notre Dame (8-0-0)
11-29 Notre Dame (9-0-0)

1950

10-3 Notre Dame (1-0-0)
10-10 Army (2-0-0) (4)
10-17 Army (3-0-0)
10-24 Southern Methodist (5-0-0) (3)
10-31 Southern Methodist (5-0-0)
11-7 Army (6-0-0) (2)
11-14 Ohio St. (6-1-0) (2)
11-21 Oklahoma (8-0-0) (2)
11-28 Oklahoma (9-0-0)

1951

10-2 Michigan St. (2-0-0)
10-9 Michigan St. (3-0-0)
10-16 California (4-0-0) (2)
10-23 Tennessee (4-0-0) (2)
10-30 Tennessee (5-0-0)
11-6 Tennessee (6-0-0)
11-13 Michigan St. (7-0-0)(5)
11-20 Tennessee (8-0-0) (2)
11-27 Tennessee (9-0-0)
12-4 Tennessee (10-0-0)

1952

9-30 Michigan St. (1-0-0)
10-7 Wisconsin (2-0-0) (8)
10-14 Michigan St. (3-0-0)(2)
10-21 Michigan St. (4-0-0)
10-28 Michigan St. (5-0-0)
11-4 Michigan St. (6-0-0)
11-11 Michigan St. (7-0-0)
11-18 Michigan St. (8-0-0)
11-25 Michigan St. (9-0-0)
12-1 Michigan St. (9-0-0)

1953

9-29 Notre Dame (1-0-0)
10-6 Notre Dame (2-0-0)
10-13 Notre Dame (2-0-0)
10-20 Notre Dame (3-0-0)
10-27 Notre Dame (4-0-0)
11-3 Notre Dame (5-0-0)
11-10 Notre Dame (6-0-0)
11-17 Notre Dame (7-0-0)
11-24 Maryland (10-0-0) (2)
12-1 Maryland (10-0-0)

1954

9-21 Oklahoma (1-0-0)
9-28 Notre Dame (1-0-0) (2)
10-5 Oklahoma (2-0-0) (2)
10-12 Oklahoma (3-0-0)
10-19 Oklahoma (4-0-0)
10-26 Ohio St. (5-0-0) (4)
11-2 UCLA (7-0-0) (3)
11-9 UCLA (8-0-0)
11-16 Ohio St. (8-0-0) (2)
11-23 Ohio St. (9-0-0)
11-30 Ohio St. (9-0-0)

1955

9-20 UCLA (1-0-0)
9-27 Maryland (2-0-0) (5)
10-4 Maryland (3-0-0)
10-11 Michigan (3-0-0) (2)
10-18 Michigan (4-0-0)
10-25 Maryland (6-0-0) (2)
11-1 Maryland (7-0-0)
11-8 Oklahoma (7-0-0) (2)
11-15 Oklahoma (8-0-0)
11-22 Oklahoma (9-0-0)
11-29 Oklahoma (10-0-0)

1956

9-25 Oklahoma (0-0-0)
10-2 Oklahoma (1-0-0)
10-9 Oklahoma (2-0-0)
10-16 Oklahoma (3-0-0)
10-23 Michigan St. (4-0-0) (2)
10-30 Oklahoma (5-0-0) (2)
11-6 Oklahoma (6-0-0)
11-13 Tennessee (7-0-0) (3)
11-20 Oklahoma (8-0-0) (2)
11-27 Oklahoma (9-0-0)
12-4 Oklahoma (10-0-0)

1957

9-24 Oklahoma (1-0-0)
10-1 Oklahoma (1-0-0)
10-8 Oklahoma (2-0-0)
10-15 Michigan St. (3-0-0) (2)
10-22 Oklahoma (4-0-0) (2)
10-29 Texas A&M (6-0-0) (2)
11-5 Texas A&M (7-0-0)
11-12 Texas A&M (8-0-0)
11-19 Michigan St. (7-1-0)(4)
11-26 Auburn (9-0-0) (2)
12-3 Auburn (10-0-0)

1958

9-23 Ohio St. (0-0-0)
9-30 Oklahoma (1-0-0) (2)
10-7 Auburn (2-0-0) (2)
10-14 Army (3-0-0) (3)
10-21 Army (4-0-0)
10-28 LSU (6-0-0) (3)
11-4 LSU (7-0-0)
11-11 LSU (8-0-0)
11-18 LSU (9-0-0)
11-25 LSU (10-0-0)
12-2 LSU (10-0-0)

1959

9-22 LSU (1-0-0)
9-29 LSU (2-0-0)
10-6 LSU (3-0-0)
10-13 LSU (4-0-0)
10-20 LSU (5-0-0)
10-27 LSU (6-0-0)
11-3 LSU (7-0-0)
11-10 Syracuse (7-0-0) (4)
11-17 Syracuse (8-0-0)
11-24 Syracuse (9-0-0)
12-1 Syracuse (9-0-0)
12-8 Syracuse (10-0-0)

1960

9-20 Mississippi (1-0-0)
9-27 Mississippi (2-0-0)
10-4 Syracuse (2-0-0) (2)
10-11 Mississippi (4-0-0) (2)
10-18 Iowa (4-0-0) (2)
10-25 Iowa (5-0-0)
11-1 Iowa (6-0-0)
11-8 Minnesota (7-0-0) (3)
11-15 Missouri (9-0-0) (2)
11-22 Minnesota (8-1-0) (4)
11-29 Minnesota (8-1-0)

1961

9-26 Iowa (0-0-0)
10-3 Iowa (1-0-0)
10-10 Mississippi (3-0-0) (2)
10-17 Michigan St. (3-0-0) (5)
10-24 Michigan St. (4-0-0)
10-31 Michigan St. (5-0-0)
11-7 Texas (7-0-0) (3)
11-14 Texas (8-0-0)
11-21 Alabama (9-0-0) (2)
11-28 Alabama (9-0-0)
12-5 Alabama (10-0-0)

1962

9-25 Alabama (1-0-0)
10-2 Ohio St. (1-0-0) (2)
10-9 Alabama (3-0-0) (2)
10-16 Texas (4-0-0) (2)
10-23 Texas (5-0-0)
10-30 Northwestern (5-0-0) (3)
11-6 Northwestern (6-0-0)
11-13 Alabama (8-0-0) (3)
11-20 Southern Cal (8-0-0) (2)
11-27 Southern Cal (9-0-0)
12-4 Southern Cal (10-0-0)

1963

9-24 Southern Cal (1-0-0)
10-1 Oklahoma (1-0-0) (3)
10-8 Oklahoma (2-0-0)
10-15 Texas (4-0-0) (3)
10-22 Texas (5-0-0)
10-29 Texas (6-0-0)
11-5 Texas (7-0-0)
11-12 Texas (8-0-0)
11-19 Texas (9-0-0)
11-26 Texas (9-0-0)
12-3 Texas (10-0-0)
12-10 Texas (10-0-0)

1964

9-29 Texas (2-0-0)
10-6 Texas (3-0-0)
10-13 Texas (4-0-0)
10-20 Ohio St. (4-0-0)(2)
10-27 Ohio St. (5-0-0)
11-3 Notre Dame (6-0-0)(2)
11-10 Notre Dame (7-0-0)
11-17 Notre Dame (8-0-0)
11-24 Notre Dame (9-0-0)
12-1 Alabama (10-0-0) (2)

1965

9-21 Notre Dame (1-0-0)
9-28 Texas (2-0-0) (3)
10-5 Texas (3-0-0)
10-12 Texas (4-0-0)
10-19 Arkansas (5-0-0) (3)
10-26 Michigan St. (6-0-0) (2)
11-2 Michigan St. (7-0-0)
11-9 Michigan St. (8-0-0)
11-16 Michigan St. (9-0-0)
11-23 Michigan St. (10-0-0)
11-30 Michigan St. (10-0-0)
1-4 Alabama (9-1-1) (4)

1966

9-20 Michigan St. (1-0-0)
9-27 Michigan St. (2-0-0)
10-4 Michigan St. (3-0-0)
10-11 Michigan St. (4-0-0)
10-18 Notre Dame (4-0-0) (2)
10-25 Notre Dame (5-0-0)
11-1 Notre Dame (6-0-0)
11-8 Notre Dame (7-0-0)
11-15 Notre Dame (8-0-0)
11-22 Notre Dame (8-0-1)
11-29 Notre Dame (9-0-1)
12-5 Notre Dame (9-0-1)

1967

9-19 Notre Dame (0-0-0)
9-26 Notre Dame (1-0-0)
10-3 Southern Cal (3-0-0) (2)
10-10 Southern Cal (4-0-0)
10-17 Southern Cal (5-0-0)
10-24 Southern Cal (6-0-0)
10-31 Southern Cal (7-0-0)
11-7 Southern Cal (8-0-0)
11-14 UCLA (7-0-1) (2)
11-21 Southern Cal (9-1-0) (4)
11-28 Southern Cal (9-1-0)

1968

9-17 Purdue (0-0-0)
9-24 Purdue (1-0-0)

Date	Team	Record
10-1	Purdue	(2-0-0)
10-8	Purdue	(3-0-0)
10-15	Southern Cal	(4-0-0) (2)
10-22	Southern Cal	(5-0-0)
10-29	Southern Cal	(5-0-0)
11-5	Southern Cal	(6-0-0)
11-12	Southern Cal	(7-0-0)
11-19	Southern Cal	(8-0-0)
11-26	Ohio St.	(9-0-0) (2)
12-2	Ohio St.	(9-0-0)
12-9	**Ohio St.**	**(10-0-0)**

1969

Date	Team	Record
9-23	Ohio St.	(0-0-0)
9-30	Ohio St.	(1-0-0)
10-7	Ohio St.	(2-0-0)
10-14	Ohio St.	(3-0-0)
10-21	Ohio St.	(4-0-0)
10-28	Ohio St.	(5-0-0)
11-4	Ohio St.	(6-0-0)
11-11	Ohio St.	(7-0-0)
11-18	Ohio St.	(8-0-0)
11-25	Texas	(8-0-0) (2)
12-2	Texas	(9-0-0)
12-9	Texas	(10-0-0)
1-4	**Texas**	**(11-0-0)**

1970

Date	Team	Record
9-15	Ohio St.	(0-0-0)
9-22	Ohio St.	(0-0-0)
9-29	Ohio St.	(1-0-0)
10-6	Ohio St.	(2-0-0)
10-13	Ohio St.	(3-0-0)
10-20	Ohio St.	(4-0-0)
10-27	Texas	(5-0-0) (2)
11-3	Texas	(6-0-0)
11-10	Texas	(7-0-0)
11-17	Texas	(8-0-0)
11-24	Texas	(8-0-0)
12-1	Texas	(9-0-0)
12-8	Texas	(10-0-0)
1-6	**Nebraska**	**(11-0-1) (3)**

1971

Date	Team	Record
9-14	Nebraska	(1-0-0)
9-21	Nebraska	(2-0-0)
9-28	Nebraska	(3-0-0)
10-5	Nebraska	(4-0-0)
10-12	Nebraska	(5-0-0)
10-19	Nebraska	(6-0-0)
10-26	Nebraska	(7-0-0)
11-2	Nebraska	(8-0-0)
11-9	Nebraska	(9-0-0)
11-16	Nebraska	(10-0-0)
11-23	Nebraska	(10-0-0)
11-30	Nebraska	(11-0-0)
12-7	Nebraska	(12-0-0)
1-4	**Nebraska**	**(13-0-0)**

1972

Date	Team	Record
9-12	Southern Cal	(1-0-0)
9-19	Southern Cal	(2-0-0)
9-26	Southern Cal	(3-0-0)
10-3	Southern Cal	(4-0-0)
10-10	Southern Cal	(5-0-0)
10-17	Southern Cal	(6-0-0)
10-24	Southern Cal	(7-0-0)
10-31	Southern Cal	(8-0-0)
11-7	Southern Cal	(9-0-0)
11-14	Southern Cal	(9-0-0)
11-21	Southern Cal	(10-0-0)
11-28	Southern Cal	(10-0-0)
12-5	Southern Cal	(11-0-0)
1-3	**Southern Cal**	**(12-0-0)**

1973

Date	Team	Record
9-11	Southern Cal	(0-0-0)
9-18	Southern Cal	(1-0-0)
9-25	Southern Cal	(2-0-0)
10-2	Ohio St.	(2-0-0) (3)
10-9	Ohio St.	(3-0-0)
10-16	Ohio St.	(4-0-0)
10-23	Ohio St.	(5-0-0)
10-30	Ohio St.	(6-0-0)
11-6	Ohio St.	(7-0-0)
11-13	Ohio St.	(8-0-0)
11-20	Ohio St.	(9-0-0)
11-27	Alabama	(10-0-0) (2)
12-4	Alabama	(11-0-0)
1-3	**Notre Dame**	**(11-0-0) (3)**

1974

Date	Team	Record
9-10	Oklahoma	(0-0-0)
9-17	Notre Dame	(1-0-0) (2)
9-24	Ohio St.	(2-0-0) (2)
10-1	Ohio St.	(3-0-0)
10-8	Ohio St.	(4-0-0)
10-15	Ohio St.	(5-0-0)
10-22	Ohio St.	(6-0-0)
10-29	Ohio St.	(7-0-0)
11-5	Ohio St.	(8-0-0)
11-12	Oklahoma	(8-0-0) (2)
11-19	Oklahoma	(9-0-0)
11-26	Oklahoma	(10-0-0)
12-3	Oklahoma	(11-0-0)
1-3	**Oklahoma**	**(11-0-0)**

1975

Date	Team	Record
9-9	Oklahoma	(0-0-0)
9-16	Oklahoma	(1-0-0)
9-23	Oklahoma	(2-0-0)
9-30	Oklahoma	(3-0-0)
10-7	Ohio St.	(4-0-0) (2)
10-14	Ohio St.	(5-0-0)
10-21	Ohio St.	(6-0-0)
10-28	Ohio St.	(7-0-0)
11-4	Ohio St.	(8-0-0)
11-11	Ohio St.	(9-0-0)
11-18	Ohio St.	(10-0-0)
11-25	Ohio St.	(11-0-0)
12-2	Ohio St.	(11-0-0)
1-3	**Oklahoma**	**(11-1-0) (3)**

1976

Date	Team	Record
9-14	Michigan	(1-0-0)
9-21	Michigan	(2-0-0)
9-28	Michigan	(3-0-0)
10-5	Michigan	(4-0-0)
10-12	Michigan	(5-0-0)
10-19	Michigan	(6-0-0)
10-26	Michigan	(7-0-0)
11-2	Michigan	(8-0-0)
11-9	Pittsburgh	(9-0-0) (2)
11-16	Pittsburgh	(10-0-0)
11-23	Pittsburgh	(10-0-0)
11-30	Pittsburgh	(11-0-0)
1-5	**Pittsburgh**	**(12-0-0)**

1977

Date	Team	Record
9-13	Michigan	(1-0-0)
9-20	Michigan	(2-0-0)
9-27	Oklahoma	(3-0-0) (3)
10-4	Southern Cal	(4-0-0) (2)
10-11	Michigan	(5-0-0) (3)
10-18	Michigan	(6-0-0)
10-25	Texas	(6-0-0) (2)
11-1	Texas	(7-0-0)
11-8	Texas	(8-0-0)
11-15	Texas	(9-0-0)
11-22	Texas	(10-0-0)
11-29	Texas	(11-0-0)
1-4	**Notre Dame**	**(11-1-0) (5)**

1978

Date	Team	Record
9-12	Alabama	(1-0-0)
9-19	Alabama	(2-0-0)
9-26	Oklahoma	(3-0-0) (tie 3
10-3	Oklahoma	(4-0-0)
10-10	Oklahoma	(5-0-0)
10-17	Oklahoma	(6-0-0)
10-24	Oklahoma	(7-0-0)
10-31	Oklahoma	(8-0-0)
11-7	Oklahoma	(9-0-0)
11-14	Penn St.	(10-0-0) (2)
11-21	Penn St.	(10-0-0)
11-28	Penn St.	(11-0-0)
12-5	Penn St.	(11-0-0)
1-4	**Alabama**	**(11-1-0) (2)**

1979

Date	Team	Record
9-11	Southern Cal	(1-0-0)
9-18	Southern Cal	(2-0-0)
9-25	Southern Cal	(3-0-0)
10-2	Southern Cal	(4-0-0)
10-9	Southern Cal	(5-0-0)
10-16	Alabama	(5-0-0) (2)
10-23	Alabama	(6-0-0)
10-30	Alabama	(7-0-0)
11-6	Alabama	(8-0-0)
11-13	Alabama	(9-0-0)
11-20	Alabama	(10-0-0)
11-27	Alabama	(10-0-0)
12-4	Ohio St.	(11-0-0) (3)
1-3	**Alabama**	**(12-0-0) (2)**

1980

Date	Team	Record
9-9	Ohio St.	(0-0-0)
9-16	Alabama	(1-0-0) (2)
9-23	Alabama	(2-0-0)
9-30	Alabama	(3-0-0)
10-7	Alabama	(4-0-0)
10-14	Alabama	(5-0-0)
10-21	Alabama	(6-0-0)
10-28	Alabama	(7-0-0)
11-4	Notre Dame	(7-0-0) (3)
11-11	Georgia	(9-0-0) (2)
11-18	Georgia	(10-0-0)
11-25	Georgia	(10-0-0)
12-2	Georgia	(11-0-0)
12-9	Georgia	(11-0-0)
1-4	**Georgia**	**(12-0-0)**

1981

Date	Team	Record
9-8	Michigan	(0-0-0)
9-15	Notre Dame	(1-0-0) (4)
9-22	Southern Cal	(2-0-0) (2)
9-29	Southern Cal	(3-0-0)
10-6	Southern Cal	(4-0-0)
10-13	Texas	(4-0-0) (3)
10-20	Penn St.	(5-0-0) (2)
10-27	Penn St.	(6-0-0)
11-3	Pittsburgh	(7-0-0) (2)
11-10	Pittsburgh	(8-0-0)
11-17	Pittsburgh	(9-0-0)
11-24	Pittsburgh	(10-0-0)
12-1	Clemson	(11-0-0) (2)
1-3	**Clemson**	**(12-0-0)**

1982

Date	Team	Record
9-7	Pittsburgh	(0-0-0)
9-14	Washington	(1-0-0) (2)
9-21	Washington	(2-0-0)
9-28	Washington	(3-0-0)
10-5	Washington	(4-0-0)
10-12	Washington	(5-0-0)
10-19	Washington	(6-0-0)
10-26	Pittsburgh	(6-0-0) (2)
11-2	Pittsburgh	(7-0-0)
11-9	Georgia	(9-0-0) (3)
11-16	Georgia	(10-0-0)
11-23	Georgia	(10-0-0)
11-30	Georgia	(11-0-0)
12-7	Georgia	(11-0-0)
1-3	**Penn St.**	**(11-1-0) (2)**

1983

Date	Team	Record
9-6	Nebraska	(1-0-0)
9-13	Nebraska	(2-0-0)
9-20	Nebraska	(3-0-0)
9-27	Nebraska	(4-0-0)
10-4	Nebraska	(5-0-0)
10-11	Nebraska	(6-0-0)
10-18	Nebraska	(7-0-0)
10-25	Nebraska	(8-0-0)
11-1	Nebraska	(9-0-0)
11-8	Nebraska	(10-0-0)
11-15	Nebraska	(11-0-0)
11-22	Nebraska	(11-0-0)
11-29	Nebraska	(12-0-0)
12-6	Nebraska	(12-0-0)
1-3	**Miami (Fla.)**	**(11-1-0) (5)**

1984

Date	Team	Record
9-4	Miami (Fla.)	(2-0-0)
9-11	Nebraska	(1-0-0) (2)
9-18	Nebraska	(2-0-0)
9-25	Nebraska	(3-0-0)
10-2	Texas	(2-0-0) (2)
10-9	Texas	(3-0-0)
10-16	Washington	(6-0-0) (2)
10-23	Washington	(7-0-0)
10-30	Washington	(8-0-0)
11-6	Washington	(9-0-0)
11-13	Nebraska	(9-1-0) (2)
11-20	Brigham Young	(11-0-0) (3)
11-27	Brigham Young	(12-0-0)
12-4	Brigham Young	(12-0-0)
1-3	**Brigham Young**	**(13-0-0)**

1985

Date	Team	Record
9-3	Oklahoma	(0-0-0)
9-10	Auburn	(1-0-0) (2)
9-17	Auburn	(2-0-0)

Date	Team	Record
9-24	Auburn	(2-0-0)
10-1	Iowa	(3-0-0) (3)
10-8	Iowa	(4-0-0)
10-15	Iowa	(5-0-0)
10-22	Iowa	(6-0-0)
10-29	Iowa	(7-0-0)
11-5	Florida	(7-0-1) (2)
11-12	Penn St.	(9-0-0) (2)
11-19	Penn St.	(10-0-0)
11-26	Penn St.	(11-0-0)
12-3	Penn St.	(11-0-0)
1-3	**Oklahoma**	**(11-1-0) (4)**

1986

Date	Team	Record
9-9	Oklahoma	(1-0-0)
9-16	Oklahoma	(1-0-0)
9-23	Oklahoma	(2-0-0)
9-30	Miami (Fla.)	(4-0-0) (2)
10-7	Miami (Fla.)	(5-0-0)
10-14	Miami (Fla.)	(6-0-0)
10-21	Miami (Fla.)	(7-0-0)
10-28	Miami (Fla.)	(7-0-0)
11-4	Miami (Fla.)	(8-0-0)
11-11	Miami (Fla.)	(9-0-0)
11-18	Miami (Fla.)	(10-0-0)
11-25	Miami (Fla.)	(10-0-0)
12-2	Miami (Fla.)	(11-0-0)
1-4	**Penn St.**	**(12-0-0) (2)**

1987

Date	Team	Record
9-8	Oklahoma	(1-0-0)
9-15	Oklahoma	(2-0-0)
9-22	Oklahoma	(2-0-0)
9-29	Oklahoma	(3-0-0)
10-6	Oklahoma	(4-0-0)
10-13	Oklahoma	(5-0-0)
10-20	Oklahoma	(6-0-0)
10-27	Oklahoma	(7-0-0)
11-3	Oklahoma	(8-0-0)
11-10	Oklahoma	(9-0-0)
11-17	Nebraska	(9-0-0) (2)
11-24	Oklahoma	(11-0-0) (2)
12-1	Oklahoma	(11-0-0)
12-8	Oklahoma	(11-0-0)
1-3	**Miami (Fla.)**	**(12-0-0) (2)**

1988

Date	Team	Record
9-6	Miami (Fla.)	(1-0-0)
9-13	Miami (Fla.)	(1-0-0)
9-20	Miami (Fla.)	(2-0-0)
9-27	Miami (Fla.)	(3-0-0)
10-4	Miami (Fla.)	(4-0-0)
10-11	Miami (Fla.)	(4-0-0)
10-18	UCLA	(6-0-0) (2)
10-25	UCLA	(7-0-0)
11-1	Notre Dame	(8-0-0) (2)
11-8	Notre Dame	(9-0-0)
11-15	Notre Dame	(9-0-0)
11-22	Notre Dame	(10-0-0)
11-29	Notre Dame	(11-0-0)
12-6	Notre Dame	(11-0-0)
1-3	**Notre Dame**	**(12-0-0)**

1989

Date	Team	Record
9-5	Notre Dame	(1-0-0)
9-12	Notre Dame	(1-0-0)
9-19	Notre Dame	(2-0-0)
9-26	Notre Dame	(3-0-0)
10-3	Notre Dame	(4-0-0)
10-10	Notre Dame	(5-0-0)
10-17	Notre Dame	(6-0-0)
10-24	Notre Dame	(7-0-0)
10-31	Notre Dame	(8-0-0)
11-7	Notre Dame	(9-0-0)
11-14	Notre Dame	(10-0-0)
11-21	Notre Dame	(11-0-0)
11-28	Colorado	(11-0-0) (2)
12-5	Colorado	(11-0-0)
1-2	**Miami (Fla.)**	**(11-1-0) (2)**

1990

Date	Team	Record
9-4	Miami (Fla.)	(0-0-0)
9-11	Notre Dame	(0-0-0) (2)
9-18	Notre Dame	(1-0-0)
9-25	Notre Dame	(2-0-0)
10-2	Notre Dame	(3-0-0)
10-9	Michigan	(3-1-0) (3)
10-16	Virginia	(6-0-0) (2)
10-23	Virginia	(7-0-0)
10-30	Virginia	(7-0-0)
11-6	Notre Dame	(7-1-0) (2)
11-13	Notre Dame	(8-1-0)
11-20	Colorado	(10-1-1) (2)
11-27	Colorado	(10-1-1)
12-4	Colorado	(10-1-1)
1-2	**Colorado**	**(11-1-1)**

1991

Date	Team	Record
9-3	Florida St.	(1-0-0)
9-10	Florida St.	(2-0-0)
9-17	Florida St.	(3-0-0)
9-23	Florida St.	(3-0-0)
9-30	Florida St.	(4-0-0)
10-7	Florida St.	(5-0-0)
10-14	Florida St.	(6-0-0)
10-21	Florida St.	(7-0-0)
10-28	Florida St.	(8-0-0)
11-4	Florida St.	(9-0-0)
11-11	Florida St.	(10-0-0)
11-18	Miami (Fla.)	(9-0-0) (2)
11-25	Miami (Fla.)	(10-0-0)
12-2	Miami (Fla.)	(11-0-0)
1-2	**Miami (Fla.)**	**(12-0-0)**

1992

Date	Team	Record
9-8	Miami (Fla.)	(1-0-0)
9-15	Miami (Fla.)	(1-0-0)
9-22	Miami (Fla.)	(2-0-0)
9-29	Washington	(3-0-0) (2)
10-6	Washington	(4-0-0)
10-13	Washington	(5-0-0)
10-20	Miami (Fla.)†	(6-0-0) (2)
10-27	Miami (Fla.)	(7-0-0)
11-3	Washington	(8-0-0) (2)
11-10	Miami (Fla.)	(8-0-0) (2)
11-17	Miami (Fla.)	(9-0-0)
11-24	Miami (Fla.)	(10-0-0)
12-1	Miami (Fla.)	(11-0-0)
12-8	Miami (Fla.)	(11-0-0)
1-2	**Alabama**	**(13-0-0) (2)**

1993

Date	Team	Record
8-31	Florida St.	(1-0-0)
9-7	Florida St.	(2-0-0)
9-14	Florida St.	(3-0-0)
9-21	Florida St.	(4-0-0)
9-28	Florida St.	(4-0-0)
10-5	Florida St.	(5-0-0)
10-12	Florida St.	(6-0-0)
10-19	Florida St.	(7-0-0)
10-26	Florida St.	(7-0-0)
11-2	Florida St.	(8-0-0)
11-9	Florida St.	(9-0-0)
11-16	Notre Dame	(10-0-0) (2)
11-23	Florida St.	(10-1-0) (2)
11-30	Florida St.	(11-1-0)
12-7	Florida St.	(11-1-0)
1-3	**Florida St.**	**(12-1-0)**

1994

Date	Team	Record
8-31	Florida	(0-0-0)
9-6	Nebraska	(1-0-0) (2)
9-13	Florida	(2-0-0) (2)
9-20	Florida	(3-0-0)
9-27	Florida	(3-0-0)
10-4	Florida	(4-0-0)
10-11	Florida	(5-0-0)
10-18	Penn St.	(6-0-0) (3)
10-25	Penn St.	(6-0-0)
11-1	Nebraska	(9-0-0) (3)
11-8	Nebraska	(10-0-0)
11-15	Nebraska	(11-0-0)
11-22	Nebraska	(11-0-0)
11-29	Nebraska	(12-0-0)
12-6	Nebraska	(12-0-0)
1-3	**Nebraska**	**(13-0-0)**

1995

Date	Team	Record
8-29	Florida St.	(0-0-0)
9-5	Florida St.	(1-0-0)
9-12	Florida St.	(2-0-0)
9-19	Florida St.	(3-0-0)
9-26	Florida St.	(4-0-0)
10-3	Florida St.	(4-0-0)
10-10	Florida St.	(5-0-0)
10-17	Florida St.	(6-0-0)
10-24	Florida St.	(7-0-0)
10-31	Nebraska	(8-0-0) (2)
11-7	Nebraska	(9-0-0)
11-14	Nebraska	(10-0-0)
11-21	Nebraska	(10-0-0)
11-28	Nebraska	(11-0-0)
12-5	Nebraska	(11-0-0)
1-3	**Nebraska**	**(12-0-0)**

**On January 6, 1948, in a special postseason poll after the Rose Bowl, The Associated Press voted Michigan No. 1 and Notre Dame No. 2. However, the postseason poll did not supersede the final regular-season poll of December 9, 1947. †Miami (Fla.) and Washington actually tied for first place in The Associated Press poll for the first time in 51 years, but Miami (Fla.) had one more first-place vote, 31-30, than Washington.*

1995 Associated Press Week-By-Week Polls

Preseason (8-11)	8-29	9-5	9-12	9-19	9-26	10-3	10-10	10-17	10-24	10-31	11-7	11-14	11-21	11-28	12-5	1-3
1. Florida St.	1	1	1	1	1	1	1	1	1	2	6	6	6	8	8	4
2. Nebraska	2	2	2	2	2	2	2	2	2	1	1	1	1	1	1	1
3. Texas A&M	3	3	3	3	9	8	22	22	19	17	18	18	15	16	19	15
4. Penn St.	4	4	7	6	6	12	20	19	16	12	19	19	14	15	15	13
5. Florida	5	5	4	4	3	3	3	3	3	3	3	3	3	2	2	2
6. Auburn	6	6	5	14	13	11	7	13	11	21	20	21	16	17	16	22
7. Southern Cal	7	7	6	5	5	5T	5	5	13	14	12	11	17	18	17	12
8. Tennessee	8	8	8	15	12	10	6	6	5	5	4	4	5	4	4T	3
9. Notre Dame	9	25	24	21	15	23	17	17	12	8	8	8	7	6	6	11
10. Alabama	11	13	13	23	20	16	12	21	18	16	16	17	21	21	21	21
11. Miami (Fla.)	12	19	19	17	NR	NR	NR	NR	NR	NR	NR	25	25	22	22	20
12. Ohio St.	10	9	10	8	7	5T	4	4	4	4	2	2	2	5	4T	6
13. Colorado	14	10	9	7	4	4	9	9	7	10	9	9	8	7	7	5
14. Michigan	13	11	11	9	8	7	11	10	9	7	13	12	18	14	14	17
15. Oklahoma	16	14	14	10	10	14	13	15	23	25	NR	NR	NR	NR	NR	NR

Preseason (8-11)	8-28	9-5	9-12	9-19	9-26	10-3	10-10	10-17	10-24	10-31	11-7	11-14	11-21	11-28	12-5	1-3
16. UCLA	15	12	12	16	NR	NR	NR	NR	24	22	NR	NR	NR	NR	NR	NR
17. Virginia	17	16	16	11	11	9	19	14	20	24	14	13	19	19	18	16
18. Texas	18	15	15	13	21	20	18	16	15	13	11	10	9	9	9	14
19. Arizona	19	17	17	25	NR	NR	NR	NR	NR	NR	NR	NR	NR	NR	NR	NR
20. North Caro.	20	NR	NR	NR	NR	NR	NR	NR	NR	NR	NR	NR	NR	NR	NR	NR
21. Wisconsin	21	NR	NR	NR	NR	22	21	24	NR	NR	NR	NR	NR	NR	NR	NR
22. Boston College	NR	NR	NR	NR	NR	NR	NR	NR	NR	NR	NR	NR	NR	NR	NR	NR
23. West Va.	23	NR	NR	NR	NR	NR	NR	NR	NR	NR	NR	NR	NR	NR	NR	NR
24. Virginia Tech	24	20	NR	NR	NR	NR	NR	NR	NR	NR	21	20	13	13	13	10
Washington	22	18	18	22	18	15	24	20	17	15	22	22	20	20	20	NR
NR Illinois	25	NR	NR	NR	NR	NR	NR	NR	NR	NR	NR	NR	NR	NR	NR	NR
NR Kansas St.	NR	21	22	19	16	13	8	8	14	9	7	7	10	10	10	7
NR Syracuse	NR	22	NR	NR	NR	NR	NR	NR	21	20	23	23	22	NR	NR	19
NR North Caro. St.	NR	23	NR	NR	NR	NR	NR	NR	NR	NR	NR	NR	NR	NR	NR	NR
NR Oregon	NR	24	20	12	19	17	15	12	10	19	17	16	12	12	12	18
NR Air Force	NR	NR	21	NR	NR	NR	NR	NR	NR	NR	NR	NR	NR	NR	NR	NR
NR Georgia	NR	NR	23	NR	NR	NR	NR	NR	NR	NR	NR	NR	NR	NR	NR	NR
NR Northwestern	NR	NR	25	NR	NR	25	14	11	8	6	5	5	4	3	3	8
NR LSU	NR	NR	NR	18	14	21	NR	NR	NR	NR	NR	NR	NR	NR	NR	NR
NR Georgia	NR	NR	NR	20	NR	NR	NR	NR	NR	NR	NR	NR	NR	NR	NR	NR
NR Maryland	NR	NR	NR	24	17	NR	NR	NR	NR	NR	NR	NR	NR	NR	NR	NR
NR Stanford	NR	NR	NR	NR	22	19	16	23	NR	NR	NR	NR	NR	NR	NR	NR
NR Arkansas	NR	NR	NR	NR	23	18	NR	NR	NR	18	15	14	23	23	24	NR
NR Texas Tech	NR	NR	NR	NR	24	NR	25	25	22	23	NR	NR	NR	NR	NR	23
NR Kansas	NR	NR	NR	NR	25	24	10	7	6	11	10	15	11	11	11	9
NR Iowa	NR	NR	NR	NR	NR	NR	23	18	25	NR	NR	NR	NR	NR	NR	25
NR Clemson	NR	NR	NR	NR	NR	NR	NR	NR	NR	NR	24	24	24	24	23	NR
NR San Diego St.	NR	NR	NR	NR	NR	NR	NR	NR	NR	NR	25	NR	NR	NR	NR	NR
NR Toledo	NR	NR	NR	NR	NR	NR	NR	NR	NR	NR	NR	NR	NR	25	25	24

No. 1 vs. No. 2

The No. 1 and No. 2 teams in The Associated Press poll (begun in 1936) have faced each other 30 times (19 in regular-season games and 11 in bowl games). The No. 1 team has won 18, with two games ending in ties.

Date	Score	Stadium (Site)
10-9-43	No. 1 Notre Dame 35, No. 2 Michigan 12	Michigan Stadium (Ann Arbor)
11-20-43	No. 1 Notre Dame 14, No. 2 Iowa Pre-Flight 13	Notre Dame (South Bend)
12-2-44	No. 1 Army 23, No. 2 Navy 7	Municipal (Baltimore)
11-10-45	No. 1 Army 48, No. 2 Notre Dame 0	Yankee (New York)
12-1-45	No. 1 Army 32, No. 2 Navy 13	Municipal (Philadelphia)
11-9-46	No. 1 Army 0, No. 2 Notre Dame 0 (tie)	Yankee (New York)
1-1-63	No. 1 Southern Cal 42, No. 2 Wisconsin 37 (Rose Bowl)	Rose Bowl (Pasadena)
10-12-63	No. 2 Texas 28, No. 1 Oklahoma 7	Cotton Bowl (Dallas)
1-1-64	No. 1 Texas 28, No. 2 Navy 6 (Cotton Bowl)	Cotton Bowl (Dallas)
11-19-66	No. 1 Notre Dame 10, No. 2 Michigan St. 10 (tie)	Spartan (East Lansing)
9-28-68	No. 1 Purdue 37, No. 2 Notre Dame 22	Notre Dame (South Bend)
1-1-69	No. 1 Ohio St. 27, No. 2 Southern Cal 16 (Rose Bowl)	Rose Bowl (Pasadena)
12-6-69	No. 1 Texas 15, No. 2 Arkansas 14	Razorback (Fayetteville)
11-25-71	No. 1 Nebraska 35, No. 2 Oklahoma 31	Owen Field (Norman)
1-1-72	No. 1 Nebraska 38, No. 2 Alabama 6 (Orange Bowl)	Orange Bowl (Miami)
1-1-79	No. 2 Alabama 14, No. 1 Penn St. 7 (Sugar Bowl)	Sugar Bowl (New Orleans)
9-26-81	No. 1 Southern Cal 28, No. 2 Oklahoma 24	Coliseum (Los Angeles)
1-1-83	No. 2 Penn St. 27, No. 1 Georgia 23 (Sugar Bowl)	Sugar Bowl (New Orleans)
10-19-85	No. 1 Iowa 12, No. 2 Michigan 10	Kinnick (Iowa City)
9-27-86	No. 2 Miami (Fla.) 28, No. 1 Oklahoma 16	Orange Bowl (Miami)
1-2-87	No. 2 Penn St. 14, No. 1 Miami (Fla.) 10 (Fiesta Bowl)	Sun Devil (Tempe)
11-21-87	No. 2 Oklahoma 17, No. 1 Nebraska 7	Memorial (Lincoln)
1-1-88	No. 2 Miami (Fla.) 20, No. 1 Oklahoma 14 (Orange Bowl)	Orange Bowl (Miami)
11-26-88	No. 1 Notre Dame 27, No. 2 Southern Cal 10	Coliseum (Los Angeles)
9-16-89	No. 1 Notre Dame 24, No. 2 Michigan 19	Michigan (Ann Arbor)
11-16-91	No. 2 Miami (Fla.) 17, No. 1 Florida St. 16	Doak Campbell (Tallahassee)
1-1-93	No. 2 Alabama 34, No. 1 Miami (Fla.) 13 (Sugar Bowl)	Superdome (New Orleans)
11-13-93	No. 2 Notre Dame 31, No. 1 Florida St. 24	Notre Dame (South Bend)
1-1-94	No. 1 Florida St. 18, No. 2 Nebraska 16 (Orange Bowl)	Orange Bowl (Miami)
1-2-96	No. 1 Nebraska 62, No. 2 Florida 24 (Fiesta Bowl)	Sun Devil (Tempe)

Nebraska sports information photo by Joe Mixan

Quarterback Tommie Frazier rushed for 199 yards and two touchdowns to help top-ranked Nebraska cruise to a 62-24 victory over Florida in the 1996 Fiesta Bowl. It was the third time in four seasons that the top two teams in The Associated Press poll squared off in a bowl game.

Games in Which a No. 1-Ranked Team Was Defeated or Tied

Listed here are 106 games in which the No. 1-ranked team in The Associated Press poll was defeated or tied. An asterisk (*) indicates the home team, an (N) a neutral site. In parentheses after the winning or tying team is its rank in the previous week's poll (NR indicates it was not ranked), its won-lost record entering the game and its score. The defeated or tied No. 1-ranked team follows with its score, and in parentheses is its rank in the poll the following week. Before 1965, the polls were final before bowl games. (Note: Only 10 teams were ranked in the weekly polls during 1962, 1963, 1964, 1965, 1966 and 1967; 20 teams all other seasons until 1989, when 25 teams were ranked.)

10-31-36 *Northwestern (3, 4-0-0) 6, Minnesota 0 (2)
11-21-36 *Notre Dame (11, 5-2-0) 26, Northwestern 6 (7)
10-30-37 (Tie) Washington (NR, 3-2-1) 0, *California 0 (2)
10-29-38 Carnegie Mellon (T19, 4-1-0) 20, *Pittsburgh 10 (3)
12-2-38 *Southern Cal (8, 7-2-0) 13, Notre Dame 0 (5)

10-14-39 Duquesne (NR, 3-0-0) 21, *Pittsburgh 13 (18)
11-8-41 (Tie) Baylor (NR, 3-4-0) 7, *Texas 7 (2)
10-31-42 *Wisconsin (6, 5-0-1) 17, Ohio St. 7 (6)
11-21-42 (N) Auburn (NR, 4-4-1) 27, Georgia 13 (5)
11-28-42 Holy Cross (NR, 4-4-1) 55, *Boston College 12 (8)

11-27-43 *Great Lakes NTS (NR, 9-2-0) 19, Notre Dame 14 (1)
11-9-46 (Tie) (N) Notre Dame (2, 5-0-0) 0, Army 0 (1)
10-8-49 Army (7, 2-0-0) 21, *Michigan 7 (7)
10-7-50 Purdue (NR, 0-1-0) 28, *Notre Dame 14 (10)
11-4-50 *Texas (7, 4-1-0) 23, Southern Methodist 20 (7)

11-18-50 *Illinois (10, 6-1-0) 14, Ohio St. 7 (8)
1-1-51 (Sugar Bowl) Kentucky (7, 10-1-0) 13, Oklahoma 7 (1)
10-20-51 Southern Cal (11, 4-1-0) 21, *California 14 (9)
1-1-52 (Sugar Bowl) Maryland (3, 9-0-0) 28, Tennessee 13 (1)
10-11-52 *Ohio St. (NR, 1-1-0) 23, Wisconsin 14 (12)

11-21-53 (Tie) Iowa (20, 5-3-0) 14, *Notre Dame 14 (2)
1-1-54 (Orange Bowl) Oklahoma (4, 8-1-1) 7, Maryland 0 (1)
10-2-54 Purdue (19, 1-0-0) 27, *Notre Dame 14 (8)
9-24-55 *Maryland (5, 1-0-0) 7, UCLA 0 (7)
10-27-56 *Illinois (NR, 1-3-0) 20, Michigan St. 13 (4)

10-19-57 Purdue (NR, 0-3-0) 20, *Michigan St. 13 (8)
11-16-57 *Rice (20, 4-3-0) 7, Texas A&M 6 (4)
10-25-58 (Tie) *Pittsburgh (NR, 4-1-0) 14, Army 14 (3)
11-7-59 *Tennessee (13, 4-1-1) 14, LSU 13 (3)
11-5-60 *Minnesota (3, 6-0-0) 27, Iowa 10 (5)

11-12-60 Purdue (NR, 2-4-1) 23, *Minnesota 14 (4)
11-19-60 Kansas (NR, 6-2-1) 23, *Missouri 7 (5)
1-1-61 (Rose Bowl) Washington (6, 9-1-0) 17, Minnesota 7 (1)
11-4-61 *Minnesota (NR, 4-1-0) 13, Michigan St. 0 (6)
11-18-61 Texas Christian (NR, 2-4-1) 6, *Texas 0 (5)

10-6-62 *UCLA (NR, 0-0-0) 9, Ohio St. 7 (10)
10-27-62 (Tie) *Rice (NR, 0-3-1) 14, Texas 14 (5)
11-10-62 *Wisconsin (8, 5-1-0) 37, Northwestern 6 (9)
11-17-62 *Georgia Tech (NR, 5-2-1) 7, Alabama 6 (6)
9-28-63 Oklahoma (3, 1-0-0) 17, *Southern Cal 12 (8)

10-12-63 (N) Texas (2, 3-0-0) 28, Oklahoma 7 (6)
10-17-64 Arkansas (8, 4-0-0) 14, *Texas 13 (6)
11-28-64 *Southern Cal (NR, 6-3-0) 20, Notre Dame 17 (3)
1-1-65 (Orange Bowl) Texas (5, 9-1-0) 21, Alabama 17 (1)
9-25-65 *Purdue (6, 1-0-0) 25, Notre Dame 21 (8)

10-16-65 *Arkansas (3, 4-0-0) 27, Texas 24 (5)
1-1-66 (Rose Bowl) UCLA (5, 7-2-1) 14, Michigan St. 12 (2)
11-19-66 (Tie) *Michigan St. (2, 9-0-0) 10, Notre Dame 10 (1)
9-30-67 *Purdue (10, 1-0-0) 28, Notre Dame 21 (6)
11-11-67 *Oregon St. (NR, 5-2-1) 3, Southern Cal 0 (4)

11-18-67 *Southern Cal (4, 8-1-0) 21, UCLA 20 (4)
10-12-68 *Ohio St. (4, 2-0-0) 13, Purdue 0 (5)
11-22-69 *Michigan (12, 7-2-0) 24, Ohio St. 12 (4)
1-1-71 (Cotton Bowl) Notre Dame (6, 8-1-1) 24, Texas 11 (3)
9-29-73 (Tie) Oklahoma (8, 1-0-0) 7, *Southern Cal 7 (4)

11-24-73 (Tie) *Michigan (4, 10-0-0) 10, Ohio St. 10 (3)
12-31-73 (Sugar Bowl) Notre Dame (3, 10-0-0) 24, Alabama 23 (4)
11-9-74 *Michigan St. (NR, 4-3-1) 16, Ohio St. 13 (4)
1-1-76 (Rose Bowl) UCLA (11, 8-2-1) 23, Ohio St. 10 (4)
11-6-76 *Purdue (NR, 3-5-0) 16, Michigan 14 (4)

10-8-77 Alabama (T7, 3-1-0) 21, *Southern Cal 20 (6)
10-22-77 *Minnesota (NR, 4-2-0) 16, Michigan 0 (6)
1-2-78 (Cotton Bowl) Notre Dame (5, 10-1-0) 38, Texas 10 (4)
9-23-78 (N) Southern Cal (7, 2-0-0) 24, Alabama 14 (3)
11-11-78 *Nebraska (4, 8-1-0) 17, Oklahoma 14 (4)

1-1-79 (Sugar Bowl) Alabama (2, 10-1-0) 14, Penn St. 7 (4)
10-13-79 (Tie) Stanford (NR, 3-2-0) 21, *Southern Cal 21 (4)
1-1-80 (Rose Bowl) Southern Cal (3, 10-0-1) 17, Ohio St. 16 (4)
11-1-80 (N) Mississippi St. (NR, 6-2-0) 6, Alabama 3 (6)
11-8-80 (Tie) *Georgia Tech (NR, 1-7-0) 3, Notre Dame 3 (6)

9-12-81 *Wisconsin (NR, 0-0-0) 21, Michigan 14 (11)
9-19-81 *Michigan (11, 0-1-0) 25, Notre Dame 7 (13)
10-10-81 Arizona (NR, 2-2-0) 13, *Southern Cal 10 (7)
10-17-81 *Arkansas (NR, 4-1-0) 42, Texas 11 (10)
10-31-81 *Miami (Fla.) (NR, 4-2-0) 17, Penn St. 14 (5)

11-28-81 Penn St. (11, 8-2-0) 48, *Pittsburgh 14 (10)
11-6-82 Notre Dame (NR, 5-1-1) 31, *Pittsburgh 16 (8)
1-1-83 (Sugar Bowl) Penn St. (2, 10-1-0) 27, Georgia 23 (4)
1-2-84 (Orange Bowl) Miami (Fla.) (5, 10-1-0) 31, Nebraska 30 (4)
9-8-84 *Michigan (14, 0-0-0) 22, Miami (Fla.) 14 (5)

9-29-84 *Syracuse (NR, 2-1-0) 17, Nebraska 9 (8)
10-13-84 (N) (Tie) Oklahoma (3, 4-0-0) 15, Texas 15 (3)
11-10-84 *Southern Cal (12, 7-1-0) 16, Washington 7 (5)
11-17-84 Oklahoma (6, 7-1-1) 17, *Nebraska 7 (7)
9-28-85 *Tennessee (NR, 0-0-1) 38, Auburn 20 (14)

11-2-85 *Ohio St. (7, 6-1-0) 22, Iowa 13 (6)
11-9-85 (N) Georgia (17, 6-1-1) 24, Florida 3 (11)
1-1-86 (Orange Bowl) Oklahoma (4, 9-1-0) 25, Penn St. 10 (3)
9-27-86 *Miami (Fla.) (2, 3-0-0) 28, Oklahoma 16 (6)
1-2-87 (Fiesta Bowl) Penn St. (2, 11-0-0) 14, Miami (Fla.) 10 (2)

11-21-87 Oklahoma (2, 11-0-0) 17, *Nebraska 7 (5)
1-1-88 (Orange Bowl) Miami (Fla.) (2, 11-1-0) 20, Oklahoma 14 (3)
10-15-88 *Notre Dame (4, 5-0-0) 31, Miami (Fla.) 30 (4)
10-29-88 Washington St. (NR, 4-3-0) 34, *UCLA 30 (6)
11-25-89 *Miami (Fla.) (7, 9-1-0) 27, Notre Dame 10 (5)

1-1-90 (Orange Bowl) Notre Dame (4, 11-1-0) 21, Colorado 6 (4)
9-8-90 *Brigham Young (16, 1-0-0) 28, Miami (Fla.) 21 (10)
10-6-90 Stanford (NR, 1-3-0) 36, *Notre Dame 31 (8)
10-13-90 Michigan St. (NR, 1-2-1) 28, *Michigan 27 (10)
11-3-90 Georgia Tech (16, 6-0-1) 41, *Virginia 38 (11)

11-17-90 Penn St. (18, 7-2-0) 24, *Notre Dame 21 (7)
11-16-91 Miami (Fla.) (2, 8-0-0) 17, *Florida St. 16 (3)
11-7-92 *Arizona (12, 5-2-1) 16, Washington 3 (6)
1-1-93 (Sugar Bowl) Alabama (2, 12-0) 34, Miami (Fla.) 13 (3)
11-13-93 *Notre Dame (2, 9-0-0) 31, Florida St. 24 (2)

10-15-94 Auburn (6, 6-0-0) 36, *Florida 33 (5)

Associated Press (Writers and Broadcasters) Final Polls

1936
Team
1. Minnesota
2. LSU
3. Pittsburgh
4. Alabama
5. Washington
6. Santa Clara
7. Northwestern
8. Notre Dame
9. Nebraska
10. Pennsylvania
11. Duke
12. Yale
13. Dartmouth
14. Duquesne
15. Fordham
16. Texas Christian
17. Tennessee
18. Arkansas
    Navy
20. Marquette

1937
Team
1. Pittsburgh
2. California
3. Fordham
4. Alabama
5. Minnesota
6. Villanova
7. Dartmouth
8. LSU
9. Notre Dame
   Santa Clara
11. Nebraska
12. Yale
13. Ohio St.
14. Holy Cross
    Arkansas
16. Texas Christian
17. Colorado
18. Rice
19. North Caro.
20. Duke

1938
Team
1. Texas Christian
2. Tennessee
3. Duke
4. Oklahoma
5. Notre Dame
6. Carnegie Mellon
7. Southern Cal
8. Pittsburgh
9. Holy Cross
10. Minnesota
11. Texas Tech
12. Cornell
13. Alabama
14. California
15. Fordham
16. Michigan
17. Northwestern
18. Villanova
19. Tulane
20. Dartmouth

1939
Team
1. Texas A&M
2. Tennessee
3. Southern Cal
4. Cornell
5. Tulane
6. Missouri
7. UCLA
8. Duke
9. Iowa
10. Duquesne
11. Boston College
12. Clemson
13. Notre Dame
14. Santa Clara
15. Ohio St.
16. Georgia Tech
17. Fordham
18. Nebraska
19. Oklahoma
20. Michigan

1940
Team
1. Minnesota
2. Stanford
3. Michigan
4. Tennessee
5. Boston College
6. Texas A&M
7. Nebraska
8. Northwestern
9. Mississippi St.
10. Washington
11. Santa Clara
12. Fordham
13. Georgetown
14. Pennsylvania
15. Cornell
16. Southern Methodist
17. Hardin-Simmons
18. Duke
19. Lafayette

1941
Team
1. Minnesota
2. Duke
3. Notre Dame
4. Texas
5. Michigan
6. Fordham
7. Missouri
8. Duquesne
9. Texas A&M
10. Navy
11. Northwestern
12. Oregon St.
13. Ohio St.
14. Georgia
15. Pennsylvania
16. Mississippi St.
17. Mississippi
18. Tennessee
19. Washington St.
20. Alabama

1942
Team
1. Ohio St.
2. Georgia
3. Wisconsin
4. Tulsa
5. Georgia Tech
6. Notre Dame
7. Tennessee
8. Boston College
9. Michigan
10. Alabama
11. Texas
12. Stanford
13. UCLA
14. William & Mary
15. Santa Clara
16. Auburn
17. Washington St.
18. Mississippi St.
19. Minnesota
    Holy Cross
    Penn St.

1943
Team
1. Notre Dame
2. Iowa Pre-Flight
3. Michigan
4. Navy
5. Purdue
6. Great Lakes
7. Duke
8. Del Monte P-F
9. Northwestern
10. March Field
11. Army
12. Washington
13. Georgia Tech
14. Texas
15. Tulsa
16. Dartmouth
17. Bainbridge NTS
18. Colorado Col.
19. Pacific (Cal.)
20. Pennsylvania

1944
Team
1. Army
2. Ohio St.
3. Randolph Field
4. Navy
5. Bainbridge NTS
6. Iowa Pre-Flight
7. Southern Cal
8. Michigan
9. Notre Dame
10. March Field
11. Duke
12. Tennessee
13. Georgia Tech
    Norman Pre-Flight
15. Illinois
16. El Toro Marines
17. Great Lakes
18. Fort Pierce
19. St. Mary's Pre-Flight
20. Second Air Force

1945
Team
1. Army
2. Alabama
3. Navy
4. Indiana
5. Oklahoma St.
6. Michigan
7. St. Mary's (Cal.)
8. Pennsylvania
9. Notre Dame
10. Texas
11. Southern Cal
12. Ohio St.
13. Duke
14. Tennessee
15. LSU
16. Holy Cross
17. Tulsa
18. Georgia
19. Wake Forest
20. Columbia

1946
Team
1. Notre Dame
2. Army
3. Georgia
4. UCLA
5. Illinois
6. Michigan
7. Tennessee
8. LSU
9. North Caro.
10. Rice
11. Georgia Tech
12. Yale
13. Pennsylvania
14. Oklahoma
15. Texas
16. Arkansas
17. Tulsa
18. North Caro. St.
19. Delaware
20. Indiana

*1947
Team
1. Notre Dame
2. Michigan
3. Southern Methodist
4. Penn St.
5. Texas
6. Alabama
7. Pennsylvania
8. Southern Cal
9. North Caro.
10. Georgia Tech
11. Army
12. Kansas
13. Mississippi
14. William & Mary
15. California
16. Oklahoma
17. North Caro. St.
18. Rice
19. Duke
20. Columbia

1948
Team
1. Michigan
2. Notre Dame
3. North Caro.
4. California
5. Oklahoma
6. Army
7. Northwestern
8. Georgia
9. Oregon
10. Southern Methodist
11. Clemson
12. Vanderbilt
13. Tulane
14. Michigan St.
15. Mississippi
16. Minnesota
17. William & Mary
18. Penn St.
19. Cornell
20. Wake Forest

1949
Team
1. Notre Dame
2. Oklahoma
3. California
4. Army
5. Rice
6. Ohio St.
7. Michigan
8. Minnesota
9. LSU
10. Pacific (Cal.)
11. Kentucky
12. Cornell
13. Villanova
14. Maryland
15. Santa Clara
16. North Caro.
17. Tennessee
18. Princeton
19. Michigan St.
20. Missouri
    Baylor

1950
Team
1. Oklahoma
2. Army
3. Texas
4. Tennessee
5. California
6. Princeton
7. Kentucky
8. Michigan St.
9. Michigan
10. Clemson
11. Washington
12. Wyoming
13. Illinois
14. Ohio St.
15. Miami (Fla.)
16. Alabama
17. Nebraska
18. Wash. & Lee
19. Tulsa
20. Tulane

1951
Team
1. Tennessee
2. Michigan St.
3. Maryland
4. Illinois
5. Georgia Tech
6. Princeton
7. Stanford
8. Wisconsin
9. Baylor
10. Oklahoma
11. Texas Christian
12. California
13. Virginia
14. San Francisco
15. Kentucky
16. Boston U.
17. UCLA
18. Washington St.
19. Holy Cross
20. Clemson

1952
Team
1. Michigan St.
2. Georgia Tech
3. Notre Dame
4. Oklahoma
5. Southern Cal
6. UCLA
7. Mississippi
8. Tennessee
9. Alabama
10. Texas
11. Wisconsin
12. Tulsa
13. Maryland
14. Syracuse
15. Florida
16. Duke
17. Ohio St.
18. Purdue
19. Princeton
20. Kentucky

1953
Team
1. Maryland
2. Notre Dame
3. Michigan St.
4. Oklahoma
5. UCLA
6. Rice
7. Illinois
8. Georgia Tech
9. Iowa
10. West Va.
11. Texas
12. Texas Tech
13. Alabama
14. Army
15. Wisconsin
16. Kentucky
17. Auburn
18. Duke
19. Stanford
20. Michigan

1954
Team
1. Ohio St.
2. UCLA
3. Oklahoma
4. Notre Dame
5. Navy
6. Mississippi
7. Army
8. Maryland
9. Wisconsin
10. Arkansas
11. Miami (Fla.)
12. West Va.
13. Auburn
14. Duke
15. Michigan
16. Virginia Tech
17. Southern Cal
18. Baylor
19. Rice
20. Penn St.

1955
Team
1. Oklahoma
2. Michigan St.
3. Maryland
4. UCLA
5. Ohio St.
6. Texas Christian
7. Georgia Tech
8. Auburn
9. Notre Dame
10. Mississippi
11. Pittsburgh
12. Michigan
13. Southern Cal
14. Miami (Fla.)
15. Miami (Ohio)
16. Stanford
17. Texas A&M
18. Navy
19. West Va.
20. Army

1956
Team
1. Oklahoma
2. Tennessee
3. Iowa
4. Georgia Tech
5. Texas A&M
6. Miami (Fla.)
7. Michigan
8. Syracuse
9. Michigan St.
10. Oregon St.
11. Baylor
12. Minnesota
13. Pittsburgh
14. Texas Christian
15. Ohio St.
16. Navy
17. Geo. Washington
18. Southern Cal
19. Clemson
20. Colorado

1957
Team
1. Auburn
2. Ohio St.
3. Michigan St.
4. Oklahoma
5. Navy
6. Iowa
7. Mississippi
8. Rice
9. Texas A&M
10. Notre Dame
11. Texas
12. Arizona St.
13. Tennessee
14. Mississippi St.
15. North Caro. St.
16. Duke
17. Florida
18. Army
19. Wisconsin
20. Va. Military

1958
Team
1. LSU
2. Iowa
3. Army
4. Auburn
5. Oklahoma
6. Air Force
7. Wisconsin
8. Ohio St.
9. Syracuse
10. Texas Christian
11. Mississippi
12. Clemson
13. Purdue
14. Florida
15. South Caro.
16. California
17. Notre Dame
18. Southern Methodist
19. Oklahoma St.
20. Rutgers

1959
Team
1. Syracuse
2. Mississippi
3. LSU
4. Texas
5. Georgia
6. Wisconsin
7. Texas Christian
8. Washington
9. Arkansas
10. Alabama
11. Clemson
12. Penn St.
13. Illinois
14. Southern Cal
15. Oklahoma
16. Wyoming
17. Notre Dame
18. Missouri
19. Florida
20. Pittsburgh

1960
Team
1. Minnesota
2. Mississippi
3. Iowa
4. Navy
5. Missouri
6. Washington
7. Arkansas
8. Ohio St.
9. Alabama
10. Duke
11. Kansas
12. Baylor
13. Auburn
14. Yale
15. Michigan St.
16. Penn St.
17. New Mexico St.
18. Florida
19. Syracuse
   Purdue

1961
Team
1. Alabama
2. Ohio St.
3. Texas
4. LSU
5. Mississippi
6. Minnesota
7. Colorado
8. Michigan St.
9. Arkansas
10. Utah St.
11. Missouri
12. Purdue
13. Georgia Tech
14. Syracuse
15. Rutgers
16. UCLA
17. Rice
   Penn St.
   Arizona
20. Duke

1962
Team
1. Southern Cal
2. Wisconsin
3. Mississippi
4. Texas
5. Alabama
6. Arkansas
7. LSU
8. Oklahoma
9. Penn St.
10. Minnesota

Only 10 ranked

1963
Team
1. Texas
2. Navy
3. Illinois
4. Pittsburgh
5. Auburn
6. Nebraska
7. Mississippi
8. Alabama
9. Oklahoma
10. Michigan St.

Only 10 ranked

1964
Team
1. Alabama
2. Arkansas
3. Notre Dame
4. Michigan
5. Texas
6. Nebraska
7. LSU
8. Oregon St.
9. Ohio St.
10. Southern Cal

Only 10 ranked

1965
Team
1. Alabama
2. Michigan St.
3. Arkansas
4. UCLA
5. Nebraska
6. Missouri
7. Tennessee
8. LSU
9. Notre Dame
10. Southern Cal

Only 10 ranked

1966
Team
1. Notre Dame
2. Michigan St.
3. Alabama
4. Georgia
5. UCLA
6. Nebraska
7. Purdue
8. Georgia Tech
9. Miami (Fla.)
10. Southern Methodist

Only 10 ranked

1967
Team
1. Southern Cal
2. Tennessee
3. Oklahoma
4. Indiana
5. Notre Dame
6. Wyoming
7. Oregon St.
8. Alabama
9. Purdue
10. Penn St.

Only 10 ranked

1968
Team
1. Ohio St.
2. Penn St.
3. Texas
4. Southern Cal
5. Notre Dame
6. Arkansas
7. Kansas
8. Georgia
9. Missouri
10. Purdue
11. Oklahoma
12. Michigan
13. Tennessee
14. Southern Methodist
15. Oregon St.
16. Auburn
17. Alabama
18. Houston
19. LSU
20. Ohio

1969
Team
1. Texas
2. Penn St.
3. Southern Cal
4. Ohio St.
5. Notre Dame
6. Missouri
7. Arkansas
8. Mississippi
9. Michigan
10. LSU
11. Nebraska
12. Houston
13. UCLA
14. Florida
15. Tennessee
16. Colorado
17. West Va.
18. Purdue
19. Stanford
20. Auburn

1970
Team
1. Nebraska
2. Notre Dame
3. Texas
4. Tennessee
5. Ohio St.
6. Arizona St.
7. LSU
8. Stanford
9. Michigan
10. Auburn
11. Arkansas
12. Toledo
13. Georgia Tech
14. Dartmouth
15. Southern Cal
16. Air Force
17. Tulane
18. Penn St.
19. Houston
20. Oklahoma
   Mississippi

1971
Team
1. Nebraska
2. Oklahoma
3. Colorado
4. Alabama
5. Penn St.
6. Michigan
7. Georgia
8. Arizona St.
9. Tennessee
10. Stanford
11. LSU
12. Auburn
13. Notre Dame
14. Toledo
15. Mississippi
16. Arkansas
17. Houston
18. Texas
19. Washington
20. Southern Cal

1972

Team

1. Southern Cal
2. Oklahoma
3. Texas
4. Nebraska
5. Auburn
6. Michigan
7. Alabama
8. Tennessee
9. Ohio St.
10. Penn St.
11. LSU
12. North Caro.
13. Arizona St.
14. Notre Dame
15. UCLA
16. Colorado
17. North Caro. St.
18. Louisville
19. Washington St.
20. Georgia Tech

1973

Team

1. Notre Dame
2. Ohio St.
3. Oklahoma
4. Alabama
5. Penn St.
6. Michigan
7. Nebraska
8. Southern Cal
9. Arizona St.
   Houston
11. Texas Tech
12. UCLA
13. LSU
14. Texas
15. Miami (Ohio)
16. North Caro. St.
17. Missouri
18. Kansas
19. Tennessee
20. Maryland
    Tulane

1974

Team

1. Oklahoma
2. Southern Cal
3. Michigan
4. Ohio St.
5. Alabama
6. Notre Dame
7. Penn St.
8. Auburn
9. Nebraska
10. Miami (Ohio)
11. North Caro. St.
12. Michigan St.
13. Maryland
14. Baylor
15. Florida
16. Texas A&M
17. Mississippi St.
    Texas
19. Houston
20. Tennessee

1975

Team

1. Oklahoma
2. Arizona St.
3. Alabama
4. Ohio St.
5. UCLA
6. Texas
7. Arkansas
8. Michigan
9. Nebraska
10. Penn St.
11. Texas A&M
12. Miami (Ohio)
13. Maryland
14. California
15. Pittsburgh
16. Colorado
17. Southern Cal
18. Arizona
19. Georgia
20. West Va.

1976

Team

1. Pittsburgh
2. Southern Cal
3. Michigan
4. Houston
5. Oklahoma
6. Ohio St.
7. Texas A&M
8. Maryland
9. Nebraska
10. Georgia
11. Alabama
12. Notre Dame
13. Texas Tech
14. Oklahoma St.
15. UCLA
16. Colorado
17. Rutgers
18. Kentucky
19. Iowa St.
20. Mississippi St.

1977

Team

1. Notre Dame
2. Alabama
3. Arkansas
4. Texas
5. Penn St.
6. Kentucky
7. Oklahoma
8. Pittsburgh
9. Michigan
10. Washington
11. Ohio St.
12. Nebraska
13. Southern Cal
14. Florida St.
15. Stanford
16. San Diego St.
17. North Caro.
18. Arizona St.
19. Clemson
20. Brigham Young

1978

Team

1. Alabama
2. Southern Cal
3. Oklahoma
4. Penn St.
5. Michigan
6. Clemson
7. Notre Dame
8. Nebraska
9. Texas
10. Houston
11. Arkansas
12. Michigan St.
13. Purdue
14. UCLA
15. Missouri
16. Georgia
17. Stanford
18. North Caro. St.
19. Texas A&M
20. Maryland

1979

Team

1. Alabama
2. Southern Cal
3. Oklahoma
4. Ohio St.
5. Houston
6. Florida St.
7. Pittsburgh
8. Arkansas
9. Nebraska
10. Purdue
11. Washington
12. Texas
13. Brigham Young
14. Baylor
15. North Caro.
16. Auburn
17. Temple
18. Michigan
19. Indiana
20. Penn St.

1980

Team

1. Georgia
2. Pittsburgh
3. Oklahoma
4. Michigan
5. Florida St.
6. Alabama
7. Nebraska
8. Penn St.
9. Notre Dame
10. North Caro.
11. Southern Cal
12. Brigham Young
13. UCLA
14. Baylor
15. Ohio St.
16. Washington
17. Purdue
18. Miami (Fla.)
19. Mississippi St.
20. Southern Methodist

1981

Team

1. Clemson
2. Texas
3. Penn St.
4. Pittsburgh
5. Southern Methodist
6. Georgia
7. Alabama
8. Miami (Fla.)
9. North Caro.
10. Washington
11. Nebraska
12. Michigan
13. Brigham Young
14. Southern Cal
15. Ohio St.
16. Arizona St.
17. West Va.
18. Iowa
19. Missouri
20. Oklahoma

1982

Team

1. Penn St.
2. Southern Methodist
3. Nebraska
4. Georgia
5. UCLA
6. Arizona St.
7. Washington
8. Clemson
9. Arkansas
10. Pittsburgh
11. LSU
12. Ohio St.
13. Florida St.
14. Auburn
15. Southern Cal
16. Oklahoma
17. Texas
18. North Caro.
19. West Va.
20. Maryland

1983

Team

1. Miami (Fla.)
2. Nebraska
3. Auburn
4. Georgia
5. Texas
6. Florida
7. Brigham Young
8. Michigan
9. Ohio St.
10. Illinois
11. Clemson
12. Southern Methodist
13. Air Force
14. Iowa
15. Alabama
16. West Va.
17. UCLA
18. Pittsburgh
19. Boston College
20. East Caro.

1984

Team

1. Brigham Young
2. Washington
3. Florida
4. Nebraska
5. Boston College
6. Oklahoma
7. Oklahoma St.
8. Southern Methodist
9. UCLA
10. Southern Cal
11. South Caro.
12. Maryland
13. Ohio St.
14. Auburn
15. LSU
16. Iowa
17. Florida St.
18. Miami (Fla.)
19. Kentucky
20. Virginia

1985

Team

1. Oklahoma
2. Michigan
3. Penn St.
4. Tennessee
5. Florida
6. Texas A&M
7. UCLA
8. Air Force
9. Miami (Fla.)
10. Iowa
11. Nebraska
12. Arkansas
13. Alabama
14. Ohio St.
15. Florida St.
16. Brigham Young
17. Baylor
18. Maryland
19. Georgia Tech
20. LSU

1986

Team

1. Penn St.
2. Miami (Fla.)
3. Oklahoma
4. Arizona St.
5. Nebraska
6. Auburn
7. Ohio St.
8. Michigan
9. Alabama
10. LSU
11. Arizona
12. Baylor
13. Texas A&M
14. UCLA
15. Arkansas
16. Iowa
17. Clemson
18. Washington
19. Boston College
20. Virginia Tech

1987

Team

1. Miami (Fla.)
2. Florida St.
3. Oklahoma
4. Syracuse
5. LSU
6. Nebraska
7. Auburn
8. Michigan St.
9. UCLA
10. Texas A&M
11. Oklahoma St.
12. Clemson
13. Georgia
14. Tennessee
15. South Caro.
16. Iowa
17. Notre Dame
18. Southern Cal
19. Michigan
20. Arizona St.

1988

Team

1. Notre Dame
2. Miami (Fla.)
3. Florida St.
4. Michigan
5. West Va.
6. UCLA
7. Southern Cal
8. Auburn
9. Clemson
10. Nebraska
11. Oklahoma St.
12. Arkansas
13. Syracuse
14. Oklahoma
15. Georgia
16. Washington St.
17. Alabama
18. Houston
19. LSU
20. Indiana

†1989

Team

1. Miami (Fla.)
2. Notre Dame
3. Florida St.
4. Colorado
5. Tennessee
6. Auburn
7. Michigan
8. Southern Cal
9. Alabama
10. Illinois
11. Nebraska
12. Clemson
13. Arkansas
14. Houston
15. Penn St.
16. Michigan St.
17. Pittsburgh
18. Virginia
19. Texas Tech
20. Texas A&M
21. West Va.
22. Brigham Young
23. Washington
24. Ohio St.
25. Arizona

1990

Team
1. Colorado
2. Georgia Tech
3. Miami (Fla.)
4. Florida St.
5. Washington
6. Notre Dame
7. Michigan
8. Tennessee
9. Clemson
10. Houston
11. Penn St.
12. Texas
13. Florida
14. Louisville
15. Texas A&M
16. Michigan St.
17. Oklahoma
18. Iowa
19. Auburn
20. Southern Cal
21. Mississippi
22. Brigham Young
23. Virginia
24. Nebraska
25. Illinois

1991

Team
1. Miami (Fla.)
2. Washington
3. Penn St.
4. Florida St.
5. Alabama
6. Michigan
7. Florida
8. California
9. East Caro.
10. Iowa
11. Syracuse
12. Texas A&M
13. Notre Dame
14. Tennessee
15. Nebraska
16. Oklahoma
17. Georgia
18. Clemson
19. UCLA
20. Colorado
21. Tulsa
22. Stanford
23. Brigham Young
24. North Caro. St.
25. Air Force

1992

Team
1. Alabama
2. Florida St.
3. Miami (Fla.)
4. Notre Dame
5. Michigan
6. Syracuse
7. Texas A&M
8. Georgia
9. Stanford
10. Florida
11. Washington
12. Tennessee
13. Colorado
14. Nebraska
15. Washington St.
16. Mississippi
17. North Caro. St.
18. Ohio St.
19. North Caro.
20. Hawaii
21. Boston College
22. Kansas
23. Mississippi St.
24. Fresno St.
25. Wake Forest

1993

Team
1. Florida St.
2. Notre Dame
3. Nebraska
4. Auburn
5. Florida
6. Wisconsin
7. West Va.
8. Penn St.
9. Texas A&M
10. Arizona
11. Ohio St.
12. Tennessee
13. Boston College
14. Alabama
15. Miami (Fla.)
16. Colorado
17. Oklahoma
18. UCLA
19. North Caro.
20. Kansas St.
21. Michigan
22. Virginia Tech
23. Clemson
24. Louisville
25. California

1994

Team
1. Nebraska
2. Penn St.
3. Colorado
4. Florida St.
5. Alabama
6. Miami (Fla.)
7. Florida
8. Texas A&M
9. Auburn
10. Utah
11. Oregon
12. Michigan
13. Southern Cal
14. Ohio St.
15. Virginia
16. Colorado St.
17. North Caro. St.
18. Brigham Young
19. Kansas St.
20. Arizona
21. Washington St.
22. Tennessee
23. Boston College
24. Mississippi St.
25. Texas

1995

Team
1. Nebraska
2. Florida
3. Tennessee
4. Florida St.
5. Colorado
6. Ohio St.
7. Kansas St.
8. Northwestern
9. Kansas
10. Virginia Tech
11. Notre Dame
12. Southern Cal
13. Penn St.
14. Texas
15. Texas A&M
16. Virginia
17. Michigan
18. Oregon
19. Syracuse
20. Miami (Fla.)
21. Alabama
22. Auburn
23. Texas Tech
24. Toledo
25. Iowa

**On January 6, 1948, in a special postseason poll after the Rose Bowl, the Associated Press voted Michigan No. 1 and Notre Dame No. 2. However, the postseason poll did not supersede the final regular-season poll of December 6, 1947. †Beginning in 1989 season, AP selected top 25 teams instead of 20.*

Photo from Michigan sports information

Michigan receiver Mercury Hayes got the 1995 college football season off to a thrilling start by catching a 15-yard pass from Scott Dreisbach in the corner of the end zone on the game's final play to give the Wolverines an 18-17 victory over Virginia in the season-opening Pigskin Classic.

United Press International Weekly Poll Leaders

1994

Date	Team	Record
9-6	Nebraska	(1-0-0)
9-13	Florida	(2-0-0) (2)
9-20	Florida	(3-0-0)
9-27	Florida	(3-0-0)
10-4	Florida	(4-0-0)
10-11	Florida	(5-0-0)
10-18	Penn St.	(6-0-0) (3)
10-25	Penn St.	(6-0-0)
11-1	Penn St.	(7-0-0)
11-8	Nebraska	(10-0-0) (2)
11-15	Nebraska	(11-0-0)
11-22	Nebraska	(11-0-0)
11-29	Nebraska	(12-0-0)
12-6	Nebraska	(12-0-0)
1-3	**Nebraska**	**(13-0-0)**

1995

Date	Team	Record
9-5	Florida St.	(1-0-0)
9-12	Florida St.	(2-0-0)
9-19	Florida St.	(3-0-0)
9-26	Florida St.	(4-0-0)
10-3	Florida St.	(4-0-0)
10-10	Florida St.	(5-0-0)
10-17	Florida St.	(6-0-0)
10-24	Florida St.	(7-0-0)
10-31	Nebraska	(8-0-0) (2)
11-7	Nebraska	(9-0-0)
11-14	Nebraska	(10-0-0)
11-21	Nebraska	(10-0-0)
11-28	Nebraska	(11-0-0)
12-5	Nebraska	(11-0-0)
1-3	**Nebraska**	**(12-0-0)**

United Press International Final Polls

United Press (UP), 1950-57; United Press International (UPI) from 1958 after merger with International News Service (INS). Served as the coaches' poll until 1991, when it was taken over by USA Today/Cable News Network (CNN) poll.

1950
Team
1. Oklahoma
2. Texas
3. Tennessee
4. California
5. Army
6. Michigan
7. Kentucky
8. Princeton
9. Michigan St.
10. Ohio St.
11. Illinois
12. Clemson
13. Miami (Fla.)
14. Wyoming
15. Washington
    Baylor
17. Alabama
18. Wash. & Lee
19. Navy
20. Nebraska
    Wisconsin
    Cornell

1951
Team
1. Tennessee
2. Michigan St.
3. Illinois
4. Maryland
5. Georgia Tech
6. Princeton
7. Stanford
8. Wisconsin
9. Baylor
10. Texas Christian
11. Oklahoma
12. California
13. Notre Dame
14. San Francisco
    Purdue
    Washington St.
17. Holy Cross
    UCLA
    Kentucky
20. Kansas

1952
Team
1. Michigan St.
2. Georgia Tech
3. Notre Dame
4. Oklahoma
    Southern Cal
6. UCLA
7. Mississippi
8. Tennessee
9. Alabama
10. Wisconsin
11. Texas
12. Purdue
13. Maryland
14. Princeton
15. Ohio St.
    Pittsburgh
17. Navy
18. Duke
19. Houston
    Kentucky

1953
Team
1. Maryland
2. Notre Dame
3. Michigan St.
4. UCLA
5. Oklahoma
6. Rice
7. Illinois
8. Texas
9. Georgia Tech
10. Iowa
11. Alabama
12. Texas Tech
13. West Va.
14. Wisconsin
15. Kentucky
16. Army
17. Stanford
18. Duke
19. Michigan
20. Ohio St.

1954
Team
1. UCLA
2. Ohio St.
3. Oklahoma
4. Notre Dame
5. Navy
6. Mississippi
7. Army
8. Arkansas
9. Miami (Fla.)
10. Wisconsin
11. Southern Cal
    Maryland
    Georgia Tech
14. Duke
15. Michigan
16. Penn St.
17. Southern Methodist
18. Denver
19. Rice
20. Minnesota

1955
Team
1. Oklahoma
2. Michigan St.
3. Maryland
4. UCLA
5. Ohio St.
6. Texas Christian
7. Georgia Tech
8. Auburn
9. Mississippi
10. Notre Dame
11. Pittsburgh
12. Southern Cal
13. Michigan
14. Texas A&M
15. Army
16. Duke
17. West Va.
18. Miami (Fla.)
19. Iowa
20. Navy
    Stanford
    Miami (Ohio)

1956
Team
1. Oklahoma
2. Tennessee
3. Iowa
4. Georgia Tech
5. Texas A&M
6. Miami (Fla.)
7. Michigan
8. Syracuse
9. Minnesota
10. Michigan St.
11. Baylor
12. Pittsburgh
13. Oregon St.
14. Texas Christian
15. Southern Cal
16. Wyoming
17. Yale
18. Colorado
19. Navy
20. Duke

1957
Team
1. Ohio St.
2. Auburn
3. Michigan St.
4. Oklahoma
5. Iowa
6. Navy
7. Rice
8. Mississippi
9. Notre Dame
10. Texas A&M
11. Texas
12. Arizona St.
13. Army
14. Duke
    Wisconsin
16. Tennessee
17. Oregon
18. Clemson
    UCLA
20. North Caro. St.

1958
Team
1. LSU
2. Iowa
3. Army
4. Auburn
5. Oklahoma
6. Wisconsin
7. Ohio St.
8. Air Force
9. Texas Christian
10. Syracuse
11. Purdue
12. Mississippi
13. Clemson
14. Notre Dame
15. Florida
16. California
17. Northwestern
18. Southern Methodist

(Only 18 teams received votes)

1959
Team
1. Syracuse
2. Mississippi
3. LSU
4. Texas
5. Georgia
6. Wisconsin
7. Washington
8. Texas Christian
9. Arkansas
10. Penn St.
11. Clemson
12. Illinois
13. Alabama
    Southern Cal
15. Auburn
16. Michigan St.
17. Oklahoma
18. Notre Dame
19. Pittsburgh
    Missouri
    Florida

1960
Team
1. Minnesota
2. Iowa
3. Mississippi
4. Missouri
5. Wisconsin
6. Navy
7. Arkansas
8. Ohio St.
9. Kansas
10. Alabama
11. Duke
    Baylor
    Michigan St.
14. Auburn
15. Purdue
16. Florida
17. Texas
18. Yale
19. New Mexico St.
    Tennessee

1961
Team
1. Alabama
2. Ohio St.
3. LSU
4. Texas
5. Mississippi
6. Minnesota
7. Colorado
8. Arkansas
9. Michigan St.
10. Utah St.
11. Purdue
    Missouri
13. Georgia Tech
14. Duke
15. Kansas
16. Syracuse
17. Wyoming
18. Wisconsin
19. Miami (Fla.)
    Penn St.

1962
Team
1. Southern Cal
2. Wisconsin
3. Mississippi
4. Texas
5. Alabama
6. Arkansas
7. Oklahoma
8. LSU
9. Penn St.
10. Minnesota
11. Georgia Tech
12. Missouri
13. Ohio St.
14. Duke
    Washington
16. Northwestern
    Oregon St.
18. Arizona St.
    Illinois
    Miami (Fla.)

1963
Team
1. Texas
2. Navy
3. Pittsburgh
4. Illinois
5. Nebraska
6. Auburn
7. Mississippi
8. Oklahoma
9. Alabama
10. Michigan St.
11. Mississippi St.
12. Syracuse
13. Arizona St.
14. Memphis
15. Washington
16. Penn St.
    Southern Cal
    Missouri
19. North Caro.
20. Baylor

1964
Team
1. Alabama
2. Arkansas
3. Notre Dame
4. Michigan
5. Texas
6. Nebraska
7. LSU
8. Oregon St.
9. Ohio St.
10. Southern Cal
11. Florida St.
12. Syracuse
13. Princeton
14. Penn St.
    Utah
16. Illinois
    New Mexico
18. Tulsa
    Missouri
20. Mississippi
    Michigan St.

1965
Team
1. Michigan St.
2. Arkansas
3. Nebraska
4. Alabama
5. UCLA
6. Missouri
7. Tennessee
8. Notre Dame
9. Southern Cal
10. Texas Tech
11. Ohio St.
12. Florida
13. Purdue
14. LSU
15. Georgia
16. Tulsa
17. Mississippi
18. Kentucky
19. Syracuse
20. Colorado

1966
Team
1. Notre Dame
2. Michigan St.
3. Alabama
4. Georgia
5. UCLA
6. Purdue
7. Nebraska
8. Georgia Tech
9. Southern Methodist
10. Miami (Fla.)
11. Florida
12. Mississippi
13. Arkansas
14. Tennessee
15. Wyoming
16. Syracuse
17. Houston
18. Southern Cal
19. Oregon St.
20. Virginia Tech

1967
Team
1. Southern Cal
2. Tennessee
3. Oklahoma
4. Notre Dame
5. Wyoming
6. Indiana
7. Alabama
8. Oregon St.
9. Purdue
10. UCLA
11. Penn St.
12. Syracuse
13. Colorado
14. Minnesota
15. Florida St.
16. Miami (Fla.)
17. North Caro. St.
18. Georgia
19. Houston
20. Arizona St.

1968
Team
1. Ohio St.
2. Southern Cal
3. Penn St.
4. Georgia
5. Texas
6. Kansas
7. Tennessee
8. Notre Dame
9. Arkansas
10. Oklahoma
11. Purdue
12. Alabama
13. Oregon St.
14. Florida St.
15. Michigan
16. Southern Methodist
17. Missouri
18. Ohio
Minnesota
20. Houston
Stanford

1969
Team
1. Texas
2. Penn St.
3. Arkansas
4. Southern Cal
5. Ohio St.
6. Missouri
7. LSU
8. Michigan
9. Notre Dame
10. UCLA
11. Tennessee
12. Nebraska
13. Mississippi
14. Stanford
15. Auburn
16. Houston
17. Florida
18. Purdue
San Diego St.
West Va.

1970
Team
1. Texas
2. Ohio St.
3. Nebraska
4. Tennessee
5. Notre Dame
6. LSU
7. Michigan
8. Arizona St.
9. Auburn
10. Stanford
11. Air Force
12. Arkansas
13. Houston
Dartmouth
15. Oklahoma
16. Colorado
17. Georgia Tech
Toledo
19. Penn St.
Southern Cal

1971
Team
1. Nebraska
2. Alabama
3. Oklahoma
4. Michigan
5. Auburn
6. Arizona St.
7. Colorado
8. Georgia
9. Tennessee
10. LSU
11. Penn St.
12. Texas
13. Toledo
14. Houston
15. Notre Dame
16. Stanford
17. Iowa St.
18. North Caro.
19. Florida St.
20. Arkansas
Mississippi

1972
Team
1. Southern Cal
2. Oklahoma
3. Ohio St.
4. Alabama
5. Texas
6. Michigan
7. Auburn
8. Penn St.
9. Nebraska
10. LSU
11. Tennessee
12. Notre Dame
13. Arizona St.
14. Colorado
North Caro.
16. Louisville
17. UCLA
Washington St.
19. Utah St.
20. San Diego St.

1973
Team
1. Alabama
2. Oklahoma
3. Ohio St.
4. Notre Dame
5. Penn St.
6. Michigan
7. Southern Cal
8. Texas
9. UCLA
10. Arizona St.
11. Nebraska
Texas Tech
13. Houston
14. LSU
15. Kansas
Tulane
17. Miami (Ohio)
18. Maryland
19. San Diego St.
Florida

*1974
Team
1. Southern Cal
2. Alabama
3. Ohio St.
4. Notre Dame
5. Michigan
6. Auburn
7. Penn St.
8. Nebraska
9. North Caro. St.
10. Miami (Ohio)
11. Houston
12. Florida
13. Maryland
14. Baylor
15. Texas A&M
Tennessee
17. Mississippi St.
18. Michigan St.
19. Tulsa

1975
Team
1. Oklahoma
2. Arizona St.
3. Alabama
4. Ohio St.
5. UCLA
6. Arkansas
7. Texas
8. Michigan
9. Nebraska
10. Penn St.
11. Maryland
12. Texas A&M
13. Arizona
Pittsburgh
15. California
16. Miami (Ohio)
17. Notre Dame
West Va.
19. Georgia
Southern Cal

1976
Team
1. Pittsburgh
2. Southern Cal
3. Michigan
4. Houston
5. Ohio St.
6. Oklahoma
7. Nebraska
8. Texas A&M
9. Alabama
10. Georgia
11. Maryland
12. Notre Dame
13. Texas Tech
14. Oklahoma St.
15. UCLA
16. Colorado
17. Rutgers
18. Iowa St.
19. Baylor
Kentucky

1977
Team
1. Notre Dame
2. Alabama
3. Arkansas
4. Penn St.
5. Texas
6. Oklahoma
7. Pittsburgh
8. Michigan
9. Washington
10. Nebraska
11. Florida St.
12. Ohio St.
Southern Cal
14. North Caro.
15. Stanford
16. North Texas
Brigham Young
18. Arizona St.
19. San Diego St.
North Caro. St.

1978
Team
1. Southern Cal
2. Alabama
3. Oklahoma
4. Penn St.
5. Michigan
6. Notre Dame
7. Clemson
8. Nebraska
9. Texas
10. Arkansas
11. Houston
12. UCLA
13. Purdue
14. Missouri
15. Georgia
16. Stanford
17. Navy
18. Texas A&M
19. Arizona St.
North Caro. St.

1979
Team
1. Alabama
2. Southern Cal
3. Oklahoma
4. Ohio St.
5. Houston
6. Pittsburgh
7. Nebraska
8. Florida St.
9. Arkansas
10. Purdue
11. Washington
12. Brigham Young
13. Texas
14. North Caro.
15. Baylor
16. Indiana
17. Temple
18. Penn St.
19. Michigan
20. Missouri

1980
Team
1. Georgia
2. Pittsburgh
3. Oklahoma
4. Michigan
5. Florida St.
6. Alabama
7. Nebraska
8. Penn St.
9. North Caro.
10. Notre Dame
11. Brigham Young
12. Southern Cal
13. Baylor
14. UCLA
15. Ohio St.
16. Purdue
17. Washington
18. Miami (Fla.)
19. Florida
20. Southern Methodist

1981
Team
1. Clemson
2. Pittsburgh
3. Penn St.
4. Texas
5. Georgia
6. Alabama
7. Washington
8. North Caro.
9. Nebraska
10. Michigan
11. Brigham Young
12. Ohio St.
13. Southern Cal
14. Oklahoma
15. Iowa
16. Arkansas
17. Mississippi St.
18. West Va.
19. Southern Miss.
20. Missouri

1982
Team
1. Penn St.
2. Southern Methodist
3. Nebraska
4. Georgia
5. UCLA
6. Arizona St.
7. Washington
8. Arkansas
9. Pittsburgh
10. Florida St.
11. LSU
12. Ohio St.
13. North Caro.
14. Auburn
15. Michigan
16. Oklahoma
17. Alabama
18. Texas
19. West Va.
20. Maryland

1983
Team
1. Miami (Fla.)
2. Nebraska
3. Auburn
4. Georgia
5. Texas
6. Florida
7. Brigham Young
8. Ohio St.
9. Michigan
10. Illinois
11. Southern Methodist
12. Alabama
13. UCLA
14. Iowa
15. Air Force
16. West Va.
17. Penn St.
18. Oklahoma St.
19. Pittsburgh
20. Boston College

1984
Team
1. Brigham Young
2. Washington
3. Nebraska
4. Boston College
5. Oklahoma St.
6. Oklahoma
7. Florida
8. Southern Methodist
9. Southern Cal
10. UCLA
11. Maryland
12. Ohio St.
13. South Caro.
14. Auburn
15. Iowa
16. LSU
17. Virginia
18. West Va.
19. Kentucky
Florida St.

1985
Team
1. Oklahoma
2. Michigan
3. Penn St.
4. Tennessee
5. Air Force
6. UCLA
7. Texas A&M
8. Miami (Fla.)
9. Iowa
10. Nebraska
11. Ohio St.
12. Arkansas
13. Florida St.
14. Alabama
15. Baylor
16. Fresno St.
17. Brigham Young
18. Georgia Tech
19. Maryland
20. LSU

1986
Team
1. Penn St.
2. Miami (Fla.)
3. Oklahoma
4. Nebraska
5. Arizona St.
6. Ohio St.
7. Michigan
8. Auburn
9. Alabama
10. Arizona
11. LSU
12. Texas A&M
13. Baylor
14. UCLA
15. Iowa
16. Arkansas
17. Washington
18. Boston College
19. Clemson
20. Florida St.

1987
Team
1. Miami (Fla.)
2. Florida St.
3. Oklahoma
4. Syracuse
5. LSU
6. Nebraska
7. Auburn
8. Michigan St.
9. Texas A&M
10. Clemson
11. UCLA
12. Oklahoma St.
13. Tennessee
14. Georgia
15. South Caro.
16. Iowa
17. Southern Cal
18. Michigan
19. Texas
20. Indiana

1988
Team
1. Notre Dame
2. Miami (Fla.)
3. Florida St.
4. Michigan
5. West Va.
6. UCLA
7. Auburn
8. Clemson
9. Southern Cal
10. Nebraska
11. Oklahoma St.
12. Syracuse
13. Arkansas
14. Oklahoma
15. Georgia
16. Washington St.
17. North Caro. St.
    Alabama
19. Indiana
20. Wyoming

1989
Team
1. Miami (Fla.)
2. Florida St.
3. Notre Dame
4. Colorado
5. Tennessee
6. Auburn
7. Alabama
8. Michigan
9. Southern Cal
10. Illinois
11. Clemson
12. Nebraska
13. Arkansas
14. Penn St.
15. Virginia
16. Texas Tech
    Michigan St.
18. Brigham Young
19. Pittsburgh
20. Washington

#1990
Team
1. Georgia Tech
2. Colorado
3. Miami (Fla.)
4. Florida St.
5. Washington
6. Notre Dame
7. Tennessee
8. Michigan
9. Clemson
10. Penn St.
11. Texas
12. Louisville
13. Texas A&M
14. Michigan St.
15. Virginia
16. Iowa
17. Brigham Young
    Nebraska
19. Auburn
20. San Jose St.
21. Syracuse
22. Southern Cal
23. Mississippi
24. Illinois
25. Virginia Tech

¢1991
Team
1. Washington
2. Miami (Fla.)
3. Penn St.
4. Florida St.
5. Alabama
6. Michigan
7. Florida
8. California
9. East Caro.
10. Iowa
11. Syracuse
12. Notre Dame
13. Texas A&M
14. Tennessee
15. Nebraska
16. Oklahoma
17. Clemson
18. Colorado
19. UCLA
20. Georgia
21. Tulsa
22. Stanford
23. North Caro. St.
24. Brigham Young
25. Ohio St.

1992
Team
1. Alabama
2. Florida St.
3. Miami (Fla.)
4. Notre Dame
5. Michigan
6. Syracuse
7. Texas A&M
8. Georgia
9. Stanford
10. Florida
11. Washington
12. Tennessee
13. Colorado
14. Nebraska
15. Washington St.
16. Mississippi
17. North Caro. St.
18. North Caro.
19. Ohio St.
20. Hawaii
21. Boston College
22. Kansas
23. Fresno St.
24. Penn St.
25. Mississippi St.

1993
Team
1. Florida St.
2. Notre Dame
3. Nebraska
4. Florida
5. Wisconsin
6. Texas A&M
7. Penn St.
8. West Va.
9. Ohio St.
10. Arizona
11. Boston College
12. Tennessee
13. Alabama
14. Miami (Fla.)
15. Oklahoma
16. Colorado
17. UCLA
18. Kansas St.
19. Michigan
20. North Caro.
21. Virginia Tech
22. Louisville
23. Clemson
24. California
25. Southern Cal

1994
Team
1. Nebraska
2. Penn St.
3. Colorado
4. Florida St.
5. Alabama
6. Miami (Fla.)
7. Florida
8. Utah
9. Michigan
10. Ohio St.
11. Oregon
12. Brigham Young
13. Southern Cal
14. Colorado St.
15. Virginia
16. Kansas St.
17. North Caro. St.
18. Tennessee
19. Washington St.
20. Arizona
21. North Caro.
22. Boston College
23. Texas
24. Virginia Tech
25. Mississippi St.

1995
Team
1. Nebraska
2. Florida
3. Tennessee
4. Colorado
5. Florida St.
6. Ohio St.
7. Kansas St.
8. Northwestern
9. Virginia Tech
10. Kansas
11. Southern Cal
12. Penn St.
13. Notre Dame
14. Texas A&M
15. Texas
16. Virginia
17. Syracuse
18. Oregon
19. Michigan
20. Texas Tech
21. Auburn
22. Toledo
23. Iowa
24. East Caro.
25. LSU

**Beginning in 1974, by agreement with the American Football Coaches Association, teams on probation by the NCAA were ineligible for ranking and national championship consideration by the UPI Board of Coaches. #Beginning in 1990 season, UPI selected top 25 teams instead of 20. ¢In 1991-92, the No. 1 team in the final UPI/NFF poll received the MacArthur Bowl, awarded by the NFF since 1959 to recognize its national champion. Beginning in 1993, the No. 1 team in the USA Today/Hall of Fame poll was awarded the MacArthur Bowl. The National Football Foundation and Hall of Fame MacArthur Bowl national champions before 1991 are listed in national polls section.*

USA Today/Cable News Network (Coaches) Weekly Poll Leaders

1992

Date	Team	Record
9-8	Miami (Fla.)	(1-0-0)
9-15	Miami (Fla.)	(1-0-0)
9-22	Miami (Fla.)	(2-0-0)
9-29	Washington	(3-0-0) (2)
10-6	Washington	(4-0-0)
10-13	Miami (Fla.)	(5-0-0) (2)
10-20	Miami (Fla.)	(6-0-0)
10-27	Miami (Fla.)	(7-0-0)
11-3	Miami (Fla.)	(8-0-0)
11-10	Miami (Fla.)	(8-0-0)
11-17	Miami (Fla.)	(9-0-0)
11-24	Miami (Fla.)	(10-0-0)
12-1	Miami (Fla.)	(11-0-0)
12-8	Miami (Fla.)	(11-0-0)
1-2	**Alabama**	**(13-0-0) (2)**

1993

Date	Team	Record
8-31	Florida St.	(1-0-0)
9-7	Florida St.	(2-0-0)
9-14	Florida St.	(3-0-0)
9-21	Florida St.	(4-0-0)
9-28	Florida St.	(4-0-0)
10-5	Florida St.	(5-0-0)
10-12	Florida St.	(6-0-0)
10-19	Florida St.	(7-0-0)
10-26	Florida St.	(7-0-0)
11-2	Florida St.	(8-0-0)
11-9	Florida St.	(9-0-0)
11-16	Notre Dame	(10-0-0) (2)
11-23	Nebraska	(10-0-0) (2)
11-30	Nebraska	(11-0-0)
12-7	Nebraska	(11-0-0)
1-3	**Florida St.**	**(12-1-0) (3)**

1994

Date	Team	Record
9-6	Nebraska	(1-0-0)
9-13	Nebraska	(2-0-0)
9-20	Nebraska	(3-0-0)
9-27	Nebraska	(4-0-0)
10-4	Florida	(4-0-0) (2)
10-11	Florida	(5-0-0)
10-18	Penn St.	(6-0-0) (3)
10-25	Penn St.	(6-0-0)
11-1	Penn St.	(7-0-0)
11-8	Nebraska	(10-0-0) (2)
11-15	Nebraska	(11-0-0)
11-22	Nebraska	(11-0-0)
11-29	Nebraska	(12-0-0)
12-6	Nebraska	(12-0-0)
1-3	**Nebraska**	**(13-0-0)**

1995

9-5	Florida St.	(1-0-0)
9-12	Florida St.	(2-0-0)
9-19	Florida St.	(3-0-0)
9-26	Florida St.	(4-0-0)
10-3	Florida St.	(4-0-0)
10-10	Florida St.	(5-0-0)
10-17	Florida St.	(6-0-0)
10-24	Florida St.	(7-0-0)
10-31	Nebraska	(8-0-0) (2)
11-7	Nebraska	(9-0-0)
11-14	Nebraska	(10-0-0)
11-21	Nebraska	(10-0-0)
11-28	Nebraska	(11-0-0)
12-5	Nebraska	(11-0-0)
1-3	**Nebraska**	**(12-0-0)**

1995 USA Today/Cable News Network Week-by-Week Polls

Preseason (8-11)	9-5	9-12	9-19	9-26	10-3	10-10	10-17	10-24	10-31	11-7	11-14	11-21	11-28	12-5	1-3
1. Florida St.	1	1	1	1	1	1	1	1	2	6	6	6	8	8	5
2. Nebraska	2	2	2	2	2	2	2	2	1	1	1	1	1	1	1
3. Texas A&M	3	3	3	10	8	18	19	18	16	14	15	13	13	18	15
4. Penn St.	4	7	6	7	12	20	18	16	13	21	21	16	17	16	12
5. Florida	5	4	4	3	3	3	3	3	3	3	3	3	2	2	3
6. Southern Cal	7	5	5	4	4	5	5	10	11	10T	11	17	18	17	11
7. Auburn	6	6	12	12	10	6	13	11	23	20	20	15	16	15	21
8. Notre Dame	NR	24	21	14	23	21	22	15	10	9	10	9	9	9	13
9. Miami (Fla.)	21	20	17	NR	NR	NR	NR	NR	NR	NR	NR	25	21	NR	NR
10. Ohio St.	8	8	7	6	5	4	4	4	4	2	2	2	5	5	8
11. Tennessee	11	12	16	13	11	7	6	5	5	4	4	5	4	4	2
12. Michigan	9	9	9	8	7	11	10	9	7	15	14	20	15	14	19
13. Colorado	10	10	8	5	6	10	9	7	12	10T	9	8	7	7	4
14. Alabama	16	18	23	21	17	14	24	22	22	18	19	23	23	NR	NR
15. UCLA	12	11	15	25	25	NR	NR	24	21	24	NR	NR	NR	24	NR
16. Virginia	18	17	14	11	9	16	15	20	20	13	12	19	19	19	17
17. Oklahoma	14	14	11	9	14	12	14	21	25	NR	NR	NR	NR	NR	NR
18. Texas	13	13	10	19	16	13	16	13	9	8	8	7	6	6	14
19. Arizona	15	16	24	NR	NR	NR	NR	NR	NR	NR	NR	NR	NR	NR	NR
20. North Caro.	NR	NR	NR	NR	NR	NR	NR	NR	NR	NR	NR	NR	NR	NR	NR
21. Washington	17	15	22	18	15	NR	23	19	17	23	23	21	20	20	NR
22. Wisconsin	NR	NR	NR	NR	NR	25	NR	NR	NR	NR	NR	NR	NR	NR	NR
23. Boston College	NR	25	NR	NR	NR	NR	NR	NR	NR	NR	NR	NR	NR	NR	NR
24. Illinois	NR	NR	NR	NR	NR	NR	NR	NR	NR	NR	NR	NR	NR	NR	NR
25. North Caro. St.	19	NR	NR	NR	NR	NR	NR	NR	NR	NR	NR	NR	NR	NR	NR
NR Syracuse	20	NR	NR	NR	NR	24	20	17	15	22	22	18	25	22	16
NR Virginia Tech	22	NR	NR	NR	NR	NR	NR	NR	NR	19	18	11	11	11	9
NR Kansas St.	23	21	19	15	13	8	8	14	8	7	7	10	10	10	6
NR Georgia	24	23	18	NR	NR	NR	NR	NR	NR	NR	NR	NR	NR	NR	NR
NR Air Force	25	19	NR	NR	NR	NR	NR	NR	NR	NR	NR	NR	NR	NR	NR
NR Oregon	NR	22	13	20	18	15	12	12	19	17	16	12	12	12	18
NR LSU	NR	NR	20	16	22	NR	NR	NR	NR	NR	NR	NR	NR	NR	25
NR Maryland	NR	NR	25	17	NR	NR	NR	NR	NR	NR	NR	NR	NR	NR	NR
NR Kansas	NR	NR	NR	22	19	9	7	6	14	12	17	14	14	13	10
NR Stanford	NR	NR	NR	23	20	19	25	NR	NR	NR	NR	NR	NR	NR	NR
NR Arkansas	NR	NR	NR	24	21	NR	NR	NR	18	16	13	24	24	23	NR
NR Baylor	NR	NR	NR	NR	24	23	21	NR	NR	NR	NR	NR	NR	NR	NR
NR Northwestern	NR	NR	NR	NR	NR	17	11	8	6	5	5	4	3	3	7
NR Iowa	NR	NR	NR	NR	NR	22	17	23	NR	NR	NR	NR	NR	NR	22
NR Texas Tech	NR	NR	NR	NR	NR	NR	NR	25	24	NR	NR	NR	NR	25	20
NR Clemson	NR	NR	NR	NR	NR	NR	NR	NR	NR	NR	22	22	21	NR	
NR Brigham Young	NR	NR	NR	NR	NR	NR	NR	NR	NR	NR	25	NR	NR	NR	NR
NR East Caro.	NR	NR	NR	NR	NR	NR	NR	NR	NR	NR	NR	NR	NR	NR	23
NR Toledo	NR	NR	NR	NR	NR	NR	NR	NR	NR	NR	NR	NR	NR	NR	24

USA Today/Cable News Network Final Polls (Coaches)

Took over as coaches poll in 1991.

1982
Team
1. Penn St.
2. Southern Methodist
3. Nebraska
4. Georgia
5. UCLA
6. Arizona St.
7. Pittsburgh
8. Arkansas
9. Clemson
10. Washington
11. LSU
12. Florida St.
13. Ohio St.
14. Southern Cal
15. Oklahoma
16. Auburn
17. West Va.
18. Maryland
19. North Caro.
20. Texas
21. Michigan
22. Alabama
23. Tulsa
24. Iowa
25. Florida

1983
Team
1. Miami (Fla.)
2. Auburn
3. Nebraska
4. Georgia
5. Texas
6. Brigham Young
7. Michigan
8. Ohio St.
9. Florida
10. Clemson
11. Illinois
12. Southern Methodist
13. Alabama
14. Air Force
15. West Va.
16. Iowa
17. Tennessee
18. UCLA
19. Pittsburgh
20. Penn St.
21. Oklahoma
22. Boston College
23. Oklahoma St.
24. Maryland
25. East Caro.

1984
Team
1. Brigham Young
2. Washington
3. Florida
4. Nebraska
5. Oklahoma
6. Boston College
7. Oklahoma St.
8. Southern Methodist
9. Maryland
10. South Caro.
11. Southern Cal
12. UCLA
13. LSU
14. Ohio St.
15. Auburn
16. Miami (Fla.)
17. Florida St.
18. Virginia
19. Kentucky
20. Iowa
21. West Va.
22. Army
23. Georgia
24. Air Force
25. Notre Dame

1985
Team
1. Oklahoma
2. Penn St.
3. Michigan
4. Tennessee
5. Florida
6. Miami (Fla.)
7. Air Force
8. Texas A&M
9. UCLA
10. Iowa
11. Nebraska
12. Alabama
13. Ohio St.
14. Florida St.
15. Arkansas
16. Brigham Young
17. Maryland
18. Georgia Tech
19. Baylor
20. Auburn
21. LSU
22. Army
23. Fresno St.
24. Georgia
25. Oklahoma St.

1986
Team
1. Penn St.
2. Miami (Fla.)
3. Oklahoma
4. Nebraska
5. Arizona St.
6. Ohio St.
7. Auburn
8. Michigan
9. Alabama
10. LSU
11. Arizona
12. Texas A&M
13. UCLA
14. Baylor
15. Boston College
16. Iowa
17. Arkansas
18. Clemson
19. Washington
20. Virginia Tech
21. Florida St.
22. Stanford
23. Georgia
24. North Caro. St.
25. San Diego St.

1987
Team
1. Miami (Fla.)
2. Florida St.
3. Oklahoma
4. Syracuse
5. Nebraska
6. LSU
7. Auburn
8. Michigan St.
9. Texas A&M
10. UCLA
11. Clemson
12. Oklahoma St.
13. Georgia
14. Tennessee
15. Iowa
16. Notre Dame
17. Southern Cal
18. South Caro.
19. Michigan
20. Texas
21. Pittsburgh
22. Indiana
23. Penn St.
24. Ohio St.
25. Alabama

1988
Team
1. Notre Dame
2. Miami (Fla.)
3. Florida St.
4. UCLA
5. Michigan
6. West Va.
7. Southern Cal
8. Nebraska
9. Auburn
10. Clemson
11. Oklahoma St.
12. Syracuse
13. Oklahoma
14. Arkansas
15. Washington St.
16. Georgia
17. Alabama
18. North Caro. St.
19. Houston
20. Indiana
21. Wyoming
22. LSU
23. Colorado
24. Southern Miss.
25. Brigham Young

1989
Team
1. Miami (Fla.)
2. Notre Dame
3. Florida St.
4. Colorado
5. Tennessee
6. Auburn
7. Southern Cal
8. Michigan
9. Alabama
10. Illinois
11. Nebraska
12. Clemson
13. Arkansas
14. Houston
15. Penn St.
16. Virginia
17. Michigan St.
18. Texas Tech
19. Pittsburgh
20. Texas A&M
21. West Va.
22. Brigham Young
23. Syracuse
24. Ohio St.
25. Washington

1990
Team
1. Colorado
2. Georgia Tech
3. Miami (Fla.)
4. Florida St.
5. Washington
6. Notre Dame
7. Tennessee
8. Michigan
9. Clemson
10. Texas
11. Penn St.
12. Houston
13. Florida
14. Louisville
15. Michigan St.
16. Texas A&M
17. Oklahoma
18. Iowa
19. Auburn
20. Brigham Young
21. Mississippi
22. Southern Cal
23. Nebraska
24. Illinois
25. Virginia

1991
Team
1. Washington
2. Miami (Fla.)
3. Penn St.
4. Florida St.
5. Alabama
6. Michigan
7. California
8. Florida
9. East Caro.
10. Iowa
11. Syracuse
12. Notre Dame
13. Texas A&M
14. Oklahoma
15. Tennessee
16. Nebraska
17. Clemson
18. UCLA
19. Georgia
20. Colorado
21. Tulsa
22. Stanford
23. Brigham Young
24. Air Force
25. North Caro. St.

1992
Team
1. Alabama
2. Florida St.
3. Miami (Fla.)
4. Notre Dame
5. Michigan
6. Texas A&M
7. Syracuse
8. Georgia
9. Stanford
10. Washington
11. Florida
12. Tennessee
13. Colorado
14. Nebraska
15. North Caro. St.
16. Mississippi
17. Washington St.
18. North Caro.
19. Ohio St.
20. Hawaii
21. Boston College
22. Fresno St.
23. Kansas
24. Penn St.
25. Wake Forest

1993
Team
1. Florida St.
2. Notre Dame
3. Nebraska
4. Florida
5. Wisconsin
6. West Va.
7. Penn St.
8. Texas A&M
9. Arizona
10. Ohio St.
11. Tennessee
12. Boston College
13. Alabama
14. Oklahoma
15. Miami (Fla.)
16. Colorado
17. UCLA
18. Kansas St.
19. Michigan
20. Virginia Tech
21. North Caro.
22. Clemson
23. Louisville
24. California
25. Southern Cal

1994
Team
1. Nebraska
2. Penn St.
3. Colorado
4. Alabama
5. Florida St.
6. Miami (Fla.)
7. Florida
8. Utah
9. Ohio St.
10. Brigham Young
11. Oregon
12. Michigan
13. Virginia
14. Colorado St.
15. Southern Cal
16. Kansas St.
17. North Caro. St.
18. Tennessee
19. Washington St.
20. Arizona
21. North Caro.
22. Boston College
23. Texas
24. Virginia Tech
25. Mississippi St.

1995
Team
1. Nebraska
2. Tennessee
3. Florida
4. Colorado
5. Florida St.
6. Kansas St.
7. Northwestern
8. Ohio St.
9. Virginia Tech
10. Kansas
11. Southern Cal
12. Penn St.
13. Notre Dame
14. Texas
15. Texas A&M
16. Syracuse
17. Virginia
18. Oregon
19. Michigan
20. Texas Tech
21. Auburn
22. Iowa
23. East Caro.
24. Toledo
25. LSU

National Football Foundation and College Hall of Fame Final Polls (MacArthur Bowl)

The 62 voters are members of the National Football Foundation and College Hall of Fame, Inc. They include former players and coaches as well as current athletics administrators and sports journalists. Beginning in 1993, the winner of the poll's national championship receives the MacArthur Bowl, given by the National Football Foundation since 1959.

1993

Team

1. Florida St.
2. Notre Dame
3. Nebraska
4. Florida
5. Wisconsin
6. Penn St.
7. West Va.
8. Arizona
9. Texas A&M
10. Ohio St.
11. Tennessee
12. Boston College
13. Alabama
14. Miami (Fla.)
15. Oklahoma
16. UCLA
17. Colorado
18. Michigan
19. Kansas St.
20. North Caro.
21. Virginia Tech
22. Louisville
23. Clemson
24. California
25. Southern Cal

1994

Team

1. Nebraska
2. Penn St.
3. Alabama
4. Colorado
5. Florida St.
6. Miami (Fla.)
7. Florida
8. Utah
9. Oregon
10. Ohio St.
11. Virginia
12. Colorado St.
13. Kansas St.
14. Southern Cal
15. Brigham Young
16. Michigan
17. North Caro. St.
18. Arizona
19. Tennessee
20. Washington St.
21. Boston College
22. Mississippi St.
23. North Caro.
24. Virginia Tech
25. Texas

1995

Team

1. Nebraska
2. Florida
3. Tennessee
4. Florida St.
5. Colorado
6. Northwestern
7. Ohio St.
8. Kansas St.
9. Virginia Tech
10. Kansas
11. Southern Cal
12. Penn St.
13. Notre Dame
14. Texas
15. Texas A&M
16. Virginia
17. Syracuse
18. Oregon
19. Michigan
20. Auburn
21. Texas Tech
22. Iowa
23. East Caro.
24. Toledo
25. Washington

College Football Bowl Alliance Final Polls

Combined point totals of the final regular-season Associated Press (media) and USA Today/CNN (coaches) polls to help determine bowl matchups.

1993

Team

1. Nebraska
2. Florida St.
3. West Va.
4. Notre Dame
5. Auburn*
6. Tennessee
7. Texas A&M
8. Florida
9. Wisconsin
10. Miami (Fla.)
11. Ohio St.
12. North Caro.
13. Penn St.
14. UCLA
15. Boston College
16. Arizona
17. Colorado
18. Alabama
19. Oklahoma
20. Kansas St.
21. Indiana
22. Virginia Tech
23. Michigan
24. Clemson
25. Fresno St.

1994

Team

1. Nebraska
2. Penn St.
3. Miami (Fla.)
4. Colorado
5. Florida
6. Alabama
7. Florida St.
8. Texas A&M*
9. Auburn*
10. Kansas St.
11. Oregon
12. Colorado St.
13. Ohio St.
14. Utah
15. Arizona
16. Virginia Tech
17. North Caro.
18. Mississippi St.
19. Virginia
20. Michigan
21. Brigham Young
22. Southern Cal
23. North Caro. St.
24. Duke
25. Washington St.

1995

Team

1. Nebraska
2. Florida
3. Northwestern
4. Tennessee
5. Ohio St.
6. Texas
7. Colorado
8. Notre Dame
9. Florida St.
10. Kansas St.
11. Virginia Tech
12. Oregon
13. Kansas
14. Michigan
15. Penn St.
16. Auburn
17. Southern Cal
18. Texas A&M
19. Virginia
20. Washington
21. Alabama*
22. Miami (Fla.)*
23. Clemson
24. Syracuse
25. Arkansas

**Ineligible for bowl participation because of NCAA sanctions.*

Undefeated, Untied Teams

(Regular-Season Games Only)

Minimum of five games played against opponents above the high-school level. Subsequent bowl win is indicated by (†), loss (‡) and tie ($). Unscored-on teams are indicated by (•).

(*Note:* Following are undefeated, untied teams in regular-season games not included with major colleges at the time—Centre, 1919 & 1921; Lafayette, 1921, 1926 & 1937; Wash. & Jeff., 1921; Marquette, 1923; Louisville, 1925; Centenary (La.), 1927; Memphis, 1938; San Jose St., 1939; Hardin-Simmons, 1940; Arizona, 1945; Pacific [Cal.], 1949; Fresno St., 1961; and San Diego St., 1966.)

Year	College	Wins
1878	Princeton	6
1882	Yale	8
1883	Yale	8
1885	Princeton	9
1887	Yale	9
1888	Yale	•13
1889	Princeton	10
1890	Harvard	11
1891	Yale	•13
1892	Minnesota	5
	Purdue	8
	Yale	•13
1893	Minnesota	6
	Princeton	11
1894	Pennsylvania	12
	Va. Military	5
	Yale	16
1895	Pennsylvania	14
1896	LSU	6
1897	Pennsylvania	15
1898	Harvard	11
	Kentucky	•7
	Michigan	10
	North Caro.	9
1899	Kansas	10
	Sewanee	12
1900	Clemson	6
	Texas	6
	Tulane	•5
	Yale	12
1901	Harvard	12
	Michigan	†•10
	Wisconsin	9
1902	Arizona	•5
	California	8
	Michigan	11
	Nebraska	•9
1903	Nebraska	10
	Princeton	11
1904	Auburn	5
	Michigan	10
	Minnesota	13
	Pennsylvania	12
	Pittsburgh	10
	Vanderbilt	9
1905	Chicago	10
	Stanford	8
	Yale	10
1906	New Mexico St.	5
	Washington St.	•6
	Wisconsin	5
1907	Oregon St.	•6
1908	Kansas	9
	LSU	10
1909	Arkansas	7
	Colorado	•6
	Washington	7
	Yale	•10
1910	Colorado	6
	Illinois	•7
	Pittsburgh	•9
	Washington	6
1911	Colorado	6
	Oklahoma	8
	Utah St.	•5
	Washington	7
1912	Harvard	9
	Notre Dame	7
	Penn St.	8
	Washington	6
	Wisconsin	7
1913	Auburn	8
	Chicago	7
	Harvard	9
	Michigan St.	7
	Nebraska	8
	Notre Dame	7
	Washington	7
1914	Army	9
	Illinois	7
	Tennessee	9
	Texas	8
	Wash. & Lee	9
1915	Colorado St.	7
	Columbia	5
	Cornell	9
	Nebraska	8
	Oklahoma	10
	Pittsburgh	8
	Washington	7
	Washington St.	†6
1916	Army	9
	Ohio St.	7
	Pittsburgh	8
	Tulsa	10
1917	Denver	9
	Georgia Tech	9
	Pittsburgh	9
	Texas A&M	•8
	Washington St.	6
1918	Michigan	5
	Oklahoma	6
	Texas	9
	Virginia Tech	7
	Washington (Mo.)	6
1919	Notre Dame	9
	Texas A&M	•10
1920	Boston College	8
	California	†8
	Notre Dame	9
	Ohio St.	‡7
	Southern Cal	6
	Texas	9
	Va. Military	9
1921	California	$9
	Cornell	8
	Iowa	7
1922	California	9
	Cornell	8
	Drake	7
	Iowa	7
	Princeton	8
	Tulsa	7
1923	Colorado	9
	Cornell	8
	Illinois	8
	Michigan	8
	Southern Methodist	9
	Yale	8

Year	College	Wins
1924	Notre Dame	†9
1925	Alabama	†9
	Dartmouth	8
1926	Alabama	$9
	Stanford	$10
	Utah	7
1927	(None)	
1928	Boston College	9
	Detroit	9
	Georgia Tech	†9
1929	Notre Dame	9
	Pittsburgh	‡9
	Purdue	8
	Tulane	9
	Utah	7
1930	Alabama	†9
	Notre Dame	10
	Utah	8
	Washington St.	‡9
1931	Tulane	‡11
1932	Colgate	•9
	Michigan	8
	Southern Cal	†9
1933	Princeton	9
1934	Alabama	†9
	Minnesota	8
1935	Minnesota	8
	Princeton	9
	Southern Methodist	‡12
1936	(None)	
1937	Alabama	‡9
	Colorado	‡8
	Santa Clara	†8
1938	Duke	‡•9
	Georgetown	8
	Oklahoma	‡10
	Tennessee	†10
	Texas Christian	†10
	Texas Tech	‡10
1939	Cornell	8
	Tennessee	‡•10
	Texas A&M	†10
1940	Boston College	†10
	Lafayette	9
	Minnesota	8
	Stanford	†9
	Tennessee	‡10
1941	Duke	‡9
	Duquesne	8
	Minnesota	8
1942	Tulsa	‡10
1943	Purdue	9
1944	Army	9
	Ohio St.	9
1945	Alabama	†9
	Army	9
	Oklahoma St.	†8
1946	Georgia	†10
	Hardin-Simmons	†10
	UCLA	‡10
1947	Michigan	†9
	Notre Dame	9
	Penn St.	$9
1948	California	‡10
	Clemson	†10
	Michigan	9
1949	Army	9
	California	‡10
	Notre Dame	10
	Oklahoma	†10
1950	Oklahoma	‡10
	Princeton	9
	Wyoming	†9
1951	Maryland	†9
	Michigan St.	9
	Princeton	9
	San Francisco	9
	Tennessee	‡10
1952	Georgia Tech	†11
	Michigan St.	9
1953	Maryland	‡10
1954	Ohio St.	†9
	Oklahoma	10
	UCLA	9
1955	Maryland	‡10
	Oklahoma	†10
1956	Oklahoma	10
	Tennessee	‡10
	Wyoming	10
1957	Arizona St.	10
	Auburn	10
1958	LSU	†10
1959	Syracuse	‡10
1960	New Mexico St.	†10
	Yale	9
1961	Alabama	†10
	Rutgers	9
1962	Dartmouth	9
	Mississippi	†9
	Southern Cal	†10
1963	Texas	†10
1964	Alabama	‡10
	Arkansas	‡10
	Princeton	9
1965	Arkansas	‡10
	Dartmouth	9
	Michigan St.	‡10
	Nebraska	‡10
1966	Alabama	†10
1967	Wyoming	‡10
1968	Ohio	‡10
	Ohio St.	†9
	Penn St.	†10
1969	Penn St.	†10
	San Diego St.	†10
	Texas	†10
	Toledo	†10
1970	Arizona St.	†10
	Dartmouth	9
	Ohio St.	‡9
	Texas	‡10
	Toledo	†11
1971	Alabama	‡11
	Michigan	‡11
	Nebraska	†12
	Toledo	†11
1972	Southern Cal	†11
1973	Alabama	‡11
	Miami (Ohio)	†10
	Notre Dame	†10
	Penn St.	†11
1974	Alabama	‡11
	Oklahoma	11
1975	Arizona St.	†11
	Arkansas St.	11
	Ohio St.	‡11
1976	Maryland	‡11
	Pittsburgh	†11
	Rutgers	11
1977	Texas	‡11
1978	Penn St.	‡11
1979	Alabama	†11
	Brigham Young	‡11
	Florida St.	‡11
	McNeese St.	‡11
	Ohio St.	‡11
1980	Georgia	†11
1981	Clemson	†11
1982	Georgia	‡11
1983	Nebraska	‡12
	Texas	‡11
1984	Brigham Young	†12
1985	Bowling Green	‡11
	Penn St.	‡11
1986	Miami (Fla.)	‡11
	Penn St.	†11
1987	Miami (Fla.)	†11
	Oklahoma	‡11
	Syracuse	$11
1988	Notre Dame	†11
	West Va.	‡11
1989	Colorado	‡11
1990	(None)	
1991	Miami (Fla.)	†11
	Washington	†11
1992	Alabama	†12
	Miami (Fla.)	‡11
	Texas A&M	‡12
1993	Auburn	11
	Nebraska	‡11
	West Va.	‡11
1994	Nebraska	†12
	Penn St.	†11
1995	Florida	‡12
	Nebraska	†11

DIVISION I-A

The Spoilers

(From 1937 Season)

Following is a list of the spoilers of major-college teams that lost their perfect (undefeated, untied) record in their **final** game of the season, including a bowl game (in parentheses). Confrontations of two undefeated, untied teams at the time are in bold face. An asterisk (*) indicates the home team in a regular-season game, a dagger (†) indicates a neutral site.

Date	Spoiler	Victim	Score
1-1-38	California	Alabama (Rose)	13-0
1-1-38	Rice	Colorado (Cotton)	28-14
12-3-38	*Southern Cal	Notre Dame	13-0
1-2-39	Southern Cal	Duke (Rose)	7-3
1-2-39	**Tennessee**	**Oklahoma (Orange)**	17-0
1-2-39	St. Mary's (Cal.)	Texas Tech (Cotton)	20-13
12-2-39	*Duquesne	Detroit	tie 10-10
1-1-40	Southern Cal	Tennessee (Rose)	14-0
1-1-41	**Boston College**	**Tennessee (Sugar)**	19-13
1-1-42	Oregon St.	Duke (Rose)	20-16
11-27-43	*Great Lakes	Notre Dame	19-14
1-1-44	Southern Cal	Washington (Rose)	29-0
11-25-44	*Virginia	Yale	tie 6-6
1-1-47	Illinois	UCLA (Rose)	45-14
1-1-48	Southern Methodist	Penn St. (Cotton)	tie 13-13
11-27-48	†Navy	Army	tie 21-21
12-2-48	*Southern Cal	Notre Dame	tie 14-14
1-1-49	Northwestern	California (Rose)	20-14
1-2-50	Ohio St.	California (Rose)	17-14
12-2-50	†Navy	Army	14-2
1-1-51	Kentucky	Oklahoma (Sugar)	13-7
1-1-52	**Maryland**	**Tennessee (Sugar)**	28-13
11-22-52	Southern Cal	*UCLA	14-12
1-1-54	Oklahoma	Maryland (Orange)	7-0
1-2-56	**Oklahoma**	**Maryland (Orange)**	20-6
1-1-57	Baylor	Tennessee (Sugar)	13-7
11-28-64	*Southern Cal	Notre Dame	20-17
1-1-65	Texas	Alabama (Orange)	21-17
11-20-65	**Dartmouth**	***Princeton**	28-14
1-1-66	UCLA	Michigan St. (Rose)	14-12
1-1-66	Alabama	Nebraska (Orange)	39-28
1-1-66	LSU	Arkansas (Cotton)	14-7
11-19-66	**Notre Dame**	***Michigan St.**	tie 10-10
1-1-68	LSU	Wyoming (Sugar)	20-13
11-23-68	***Harvard**	**Yale**	tie 29-29

Date	Spoiler	Victim	Score
12-27-68	Richmond	Ohio (Tangerine)	49-42
11-22-69	*Michigan	Ohio St.	24-12
11-22-69	*Princeton	Dartmouth	35-7
11-21-70	***Ohio St.**	**Michigan**	20-9
1-1-71	Stanford	Ohio St. (Rose)	27-17
1-1-71	Notre Dame	Texas (Cotton)	24-11
1-1-72	Stanford	Michigan (Rose)	13-12
1-1-72	**Nebraska**	**Alabama (Orange)**	38-6
11-25-72	*Ohio St.	Michigan	14-11
11-24-73	**Ohio St.**	***Michigan**	tie 10-10
12-31-73	**Notre Dame**	**Alabama (Sugar)**	24-23
11-23-74	*Ohio St.	Michigan	12-10
11-23-74	*Harvard	Yale	21-16
1-1-75	Notre Dame	Alabama (Orange)	13-11
1-1-76	UCLA	Ohio St. (Rose)	23-10
1-1-77	Houston	Maryland (Cotton)	30-21
11-19-77	*Delaware	Colgate	21-3
1-2-78	Notre Dame	Texas (Cotton)	38-10
1-1-79	Alabama	Penn St. (Sugar)	14-7
11-17-79	Harvard	*Yale	22-7
12-15-79	Syracuse	McNeese St. (Independence)	31-7
12-21-79	Indiana	Brigham Young (Holiday)	38-37
1-1-80	Southern Cal	Ohio St. (Rose)	17-16
1-1-80	Oklahoma	Florida St. (Orange)	24-7
1-1-83	Penn St.	Georgia (Sugar)	27-23
1-2-84	Georgia	Texas (Cotton)	10-9
1-2-84	Miami (Fla.)	Nebraska (Orange)	31-30
12-14-85	Fresno St.	Bowling Green (California)	51-7
1-1-86	Oklahoma	Penn St. (Orange)	25-10
1-2-87	**Penn St.**	**Miami (Fla.) (Fiesta)**	14-10
1-1-88	Auburn	Syracuse (Sugar)	tie 16-16
1-1-88	**Miami (Fla.)**	**Oklahoma (Orange)**	20-14
1-2-89	**Notre Dame**	**West Va. (Fiesta)**	34-21
1-1-90	Notre Dame	Colorado (Orange)	21-6
1-1-93	Notre Dame	Texas A&M (Cotton)	28-3
1-1-93	**Alabama**	**Miami (Fla.) (Sugar)**	34-13
1-1-94	Florida St.	Nebraska (Orange)	18-16
1-1-94	Florida	West Va. (Sugar)	41-7
1-2-96	**Nebraska**	**Florida (Fiesta)**	62-24

Streaks and Rivalries

Longest Winning Streaks

(Includes Bowl Games)

Wins	Team	Years	Ended by	Score
47	Oklahoma	1953-57	Notre Dame	7-0
39	Washington	1908-14	Oregon St.	0-0
37	Yale	1890-93	Princeton	6-0
37	Yale	1887-89	Princeton	10-0
35	Toledo	1969-71	Tampa	21-0
34	Pennsylvania	1894-96	Lafayette	6-4
31	Oklahoma	1948-50	Kentucky	*13-7
31	Pittsburgh	1914-18	Cleveland Naval Reserve	10-9
31	Pennsylvania	1896-98	Harvard	10-0
30	Texas	1968-70	Notre Dame	*24-11
29	Miami (Fla.)	1990-93	Alabama	*34-13
29	Michigan	1901-03	Minnesota	6-6
28	Alabama	1991-93	Tennessee	17-17
28	Alabama	1978-80	Mississippi St.	6-3
28	Oklahoma	1973-75	Kansas	23-3
28	Michigan St.	1950-53	Purdue	6-0
26	Cornell	1921-24	Williams	14-7
26	Michigan	1903-05	Chicago	2-0
25	Nebraska	1994-95	Current	
25	Brigham Young	1983-85	UCLA	27-24
25	San Diego St.	1965-67	Utah St.	31-25
25	Michigan	1946-49	Army	21-7
25	Army	1944-46	Notre Dame	0-0
25	Southern Cal	1931-33	Oregon St.	0-0
24	Princeton	1949-52	Pennsylvania	13-7
24	Minnesota	1903-05	Wisconsin	16-12
24	Nebraska	1901-04	Colorado	6-0
24	Yale	1894-95	Boston AC	0-0
24	Harvard	1890-91	Yale	10-0
24	Yale	1882-84	Princeton	0-0
23	Alabama	1991-92	#	
23	Notre Dame	1988-89	Miami (Fla.)	27-10
23	Nebraska	1970-71	UCLA	20-17
23	Penn St.	1968-70	Colorado	41-13
23	Tennessee	1937-39	Southern Cal	*14-0
23	Harvard	1901-02	Yale	23-0
22	Washington	1990-92	Arizona	16-3
22	Nebraska	1982-83	Miami (Fla.)	*31-30
22	Ohio St.	1967-69	Michigan	24-12
22	Arkansas	1963-65	LSU	*14-7
22	UCLA	1953-56	Southern Cal	10-7
22	Harvard	1912-14	Penn St.	13-13
22	Yale	1904-06	Princeton	0-0
21	Arizona St.	1969-71	Oregon St.	24-18
21	San Diego St.	1968-70	Long Beach St.	27-11
21	Notre Dame	1946-48	Southern Cal	14-14
21	Minnesota	1933-36	Northwestern	6-0
21	Colorado	1908-12	Colorado St.	21-0
21	Pennsylvania	1903-05	Lafayette	6-6
21	Yale	1900-01	Army	5-5
21	Harvard	1898-99	Yale	0-0
20	Auburn	1993-94	Georgia	23-23
20	Oklahoma	1986-87	Miami (Fla.)	*20-14
20	Tennessee	1950-51	Maryland	*28-13
20	Texas A&M	1938-40	Texas	7-0
20	Notre Dame	1929-31	Northwestern	0-0
20	Alabama	1924-26	Stanford	*7-7
20	Iowa	1920-23	Illinois	9-6
20	Notre Dame	1919-21	Iowa	10-7

Streak ended in bowl game. #Eight victories and one tie in 1993 forfeited by action of the NCAA Committee on Infractions.

Longest Unbeaten Streaks

(Includes Bowl Games; May Include Ties)

No.	Wins	Ties	Team	Years	Ended by	Score
63	59	4	Washington	1907-17	California	27-0
56	55	1	Michigan	1901-05	Chicago	2-0
50	46	4	California	1920-25	Olympic Club	15-0
48	47	1	Oklahoma	1953-57	Notre Dame	7-0
48	47	1	Yale	1885-89	Princeton	10-0
47	42	5	Yale	1879-85	Princeton	6-5
44	42	2	Yale	1894-96	Princeton	24-6
42	39	3	Yale	1904-08	Harvard	4-0
39	37	2	Notre Dame	1946-50	Purdue	28-14
37	37	0	Yale	1890-93	Princeton	6-0
37	36	1	Oklahoma	1972-75	Kansas	23-3
35	35	0	Toledo	1969-71	Tampa	21-0
35	34	1	Minnesota	1903-05	Wisconsin	16-12
34	34	0	Pennsylvania	1894-96	Lafayette	6-4
34	33	1	Nebraska	1912-16	Kansas	7-3
34	32	2	Princeton	1884-87	Harvard	12-0
34	29	5	Princeton	1877-82	Harvard	1-0
33	31	2	Georgia Tech	1914-18	Pittsburgh	32-0
33	30	3	Tennessee	1926-30	Alabama	18-6
33	30	3	Harvard	1911-15	Cornell	10-0
32	31	1	Nebraska	1969-71	UCLA	20-17
32	31	1	Harvard	1898-00	Yale	28-0
32	30	2	Army	1944-47	Columbia	21-20
31	31	0	Oklahoma	1948-50	Kentucky	13-7
31	31	0	Pittsburgh	1914-18	Cleveland Naval	10-9
31	31	0	Pennsylvania	1896-98	Harvard	10-0
31	30	1	Penn St.	1967-70	Colorado	41-13
31	30	1	San Diego St.	1967-70	Long Beach St.	27-11
31	29	2	Georgia Tech	1950-53	Notre Dame	27-14
30	30	0	Texas	1968-70	Notre Dame	24-11
30	28	2	Pennsylvania	1903-06	Swarthmore	4-0
30	25	5	Penn St.	1919-22	Navy	14-0
29	29	0	Miami (Fla.)	1990-93	Alabama	34-13
28	28	0	Alabama	1978-80	Mississippi St.	6-3
28	28	0	Michigan St.	1950-53	Purdue	6-0
28	26	2	Southern Cal	1978-80	Washington	20-10
28	26	2	Army	1947-50	Navy	14-2
28	26	2	Tennessee	1930-33	Duke	10-2
28	24	4	Minnesota	1933-36	Northwestern	6-0
27	26	1	Southern Cal	1931-33	Stanford	13-7
27	24	3	Notre Dame	1910-14	Yale	28-0

Longest Home Winning Streaks

(Includes Bowl Games)

Wins	Team	Years	Ended by	Score
58	Miami (Fla.)	1985-94	Washington	38-20
57	Alabama	1963-82	Southern Miss.	38-29
56	Harvard	1890-95	Boston AA	0-0
50	Michigan	1901-07	Pennsylvania	6-0
42	Texas	1968-76	Houston	30-0
40	Notre Dame	1907-18	Great Lakes	7-7
38	Notre Dame	1919-27	Minnesota	7-7
37	Yale	1904-08	Brown	10-10
37	Yale	1900-03	Princeton	11-6
33	Nebraska	1901-06	Iowa St.	14-2
33	Harvard	1900-03	Amherst	5-0
31	Texas A&M	1990-95	Texas	16-6
31	Yale	1890-93	Princeton	6-0
30	Nebraska	1991-95	Current	
30	Auburn	1952-61	Kentucky	14-12
30	Tennessee	1928-33	Alabama	12-6
29	Yale	1885-89	Princeton	10-0
28	Michigan	1969-73	Ohio St.	0-0
28	Notre Dame	1942-50	Purdue	28-14
27	Vanderbilt	1903-07	Michigan	8-0
26	Utah	1928-34	Oregon	8-7
26	California	1919-23	Nevada	0-0
25	Ohio St.	1972-76	Missouri	22-21
25	Oklahoma	1947-53	Notre Dame	28-21
25	Wisconsin	1900-03	Chicago	15-6
24	Georgia	1980-83	Auburn	13-7
24	Georgia Tech	1916-19	Wash. & Lee	3-0
24	Virginia	1899-04	Navy	5-0
23	Florida St.	1992-95	Current	
23	Florida	1990-93	Florida St.	33-21
23	Tulane	1929-32	Vanderbilt	6-6
23	Michigan St.	1904-08	Michigan	0-0
23	Michigan	1897-00	Ohio St.	0-0
23	Harvard	1887-89	Princeton	41-15
22	Wyoming	1965-70	Air Force	41-17
22	Navy	1953-64	Syracuse	14-6
22	Minnesota	1933-37	Notre Dame	7-6
22	LSU	1907-12	Mississippi	10-7
22	Notre Dame	1901-05	Wabash	5-0
21	Arizona St.	1969-72	Air Force	39-31
21	Mississippi	1952-60	LSU	6-6
21	Oklahoma	1953-57	Notre Dame	7-0
21	Miami (Ohio)	1942-48	Xavier (Ohio)	27-19
21	North Caro.	1893-00	Virginia Tech	0-0
20	Fresno St.	1987-90	Utah St.	24-24
20	Rutgers	1974-78	Colgate	14-9
20	Mississippi St.	1939-45	Mississippi	7-6
20	Missouri	1938-43	Oklahoma	20-13
20	Southern Cal	1927-29	California	15-7
20	Southern Cal	1919-23	California	13-7
20	Iowa	1918-23	Illinois	9-6
20	Harvard	1912-14	Penn St.	13-13

Longest Losing Streaks

Losses	Team	Years	Ended by	Score
34	Northwestern	1979-82	Northern Ill.	31-6
28	Virginia	1958-61	William & Mary	21-6
28	Kansas St.	1944-48	Arkansas St.	37-6
27	New Mexico St.	1988-90	Cal St. Fullerton	43-9
27	Eastern Mich.	1980-82	Kent	9-7
26	Colorado St.	1960-63	Pacific (Cal.)	20-0
21	Kent	1981-83	Eastern Mich.	37-13
21	New Mexico	1967-69	Kansas	16-7
20	Texas Christian	1974-75	Rice	28-21
20	Florida St.	1972-74	Miami (Fla.)	21-14
18	Rice	1987-89	Southern Methodist	35-6
18	Wisconsin	1967-69	Iowa	23-17
18	Wake Forest	1962-63	South Caro.	20-19
17	Kent	1992-94	Akron	32-16
17	Kent	1989-90	Ohio	44-15
17	Memphis	1981-82	Arkansas St.	12-0
17	Tulane	1961-63	South Caro.	20-7
17	Alabama	1954-56	Mississippi St.	13-12
17	Kansas	1953-55	Washington St.	13-0
16	Indiana	1983-85	Louisville	41-28
16	Vanderbilt	1961-62	Tulane	20-0
16	Iowa St.	1929-31	Simpson	6-0

Most Consecutive Winning Seasons

(All-Time and Current)

No.	School	Years
42	Notre Dame	1889-1932#
38	Alabama	1911-50†
34	Nebraska	1962-95*
29	Oklahoma	1966-94
28	Virginia	1888-1915
27	Michigan	1892-1918
26	Penn St.	1939-64
21	Ohio St.	1967-87
21	Southern Cal	1962-82
21	Vanderbilt	1915-35
19	Florida St.	1977-95*
19	Washington	1977-95*
19	Ohio St.	1899-1917
19	Wisconsin	1891-1909
18	Nebraska	1920-37
17	San Diego St.	1961-77
16	Miami (Fla.)	1980-95*
16	LSU	1958-73
16	Texas A&M	1914-29
15	Bowling Green	1955-69
15	Syracuse	1913-27
15	Georgia Tech	1908-22
14	Kentucky	1903-16
13	Arkansas	1977-89
13	Georgia	1964-76
13	Wyoming	1949-61
12	Auburn	1953-64
12	Colorado	1950-61
12	Ohio St.	1928-39
12	Tulane	1928-39
12	Texas Christian	1925-36
12	West Va.	1914-26@

**Current streak. #No teams in 1890 and 1891. †No teams in 1918 and 1943. @No team in 1918.*

Most-Played Rivalries

(Ongoing Unless Indicated)

Games	Opponents (Series leader listed first)	Rivalry Record	First Game
105	Minnesota-Wisconsin	57-40-8	1890
104	Missouri-Kansas	48-47-9	1891
103	Baylor-Texas Christian	49-47-7	1899
102	Nebraska-Kansas	78-21-3	1892
102	Texas-Texas A&M	65-32-5	1894
100	Miami (Ohio)-Cincinnati	54-39-7	1888
100	North Caro.-Virginia	53-43-4	1892
99	Auburn-Georgia	47-44-8	1892
99	Oregon-Oregon St.	49-40-10	1894
98	Purdue-Indiana	59-33-6	1891
98	Stanford-California	48-39-11	1892
96	Army-Navy	46-43-7	1890
93	Utah-Utah St.	62-27-4	1892
93	Clemson-South Caro.	55-34-4	1896
93	Kansas-Kansas St.	61-27-5	1902
93	Oklahoma-Kansas	62-25-6	1903
92	North Caro.-Wake Forest	61-29-2	1888
92	$Penn St.-Pittsburgh	47-41-4	1893
92	LSU-Tulane	*63-22-7	1893
92	Michigan-Ohio St.	52-34-6	1897
92	Mississippi-Mississippi St.	53-33-6	1901
91	Tennessee-Kentucky	59-23-9	1893
90	#Auburn-Georgia Tech	47-39-4	1892
90	Georgia-Georgia Tech	50-35-5	1893
90	Nebraska-Iowa St.	74-14-2	1896
90	Texas-Oklahoma	52-33-5	1900
90	Oklahoma-Oklahoma St.	71-12-7	1904
89	Illinois-Northwestern	47-37-5	1892
89	Nebraska-Missouri	54-32-3	1892
89	Tennessee-Vanderbilt	58-26-5	1892
89	North Caro. St.-Wake Forest	54-29-6	1895
88	Pittsburgh-West Va.	55-30-3	1895
88	Michigan-Michigan St.	57-26-5	1898
88	Washington-Washington St.	56-26-6	1900

*$Have not met since 1992. *Disputed series record: Tulane claims 23-61-7 record; LSU and Tulane have not met since 1994. #Have not met since 1989.*

Additional Records

Longest Uninterrupted Series (Must have played every year)
93 games—Kansas-Oklahoma (from 1903)
90 games—Kansas-Nebraska (from 1906)
89 games—Minnesota-Wisconsin (from 1907)
87 games—Clemson-South Caro. (from 1909)
86 games—Wake Forest-North Caro. St. (from 1910)

85 games—Kansas-Kansas St. (from 1911)
84 games—North Caro.-Virginia (from 1910)*
82 games—Illinois-Ohio St. (from 1914)
80 games—Southern Methodist-Baylor (from 1916)
78 games—Michigan-Ohio St. (from 1918)

77 games—Kansas-Missouri (from 1919)
77 games—Missouri-Iowa St. (from 1919)
77 games—Missouri-Oklahoma (from 1919)
76 games—Tulane-LSU (1919-1994)
76 games—Indiana-Purdue (from 1920)

76 games—Southern Methodist-Texas A&M (from 1920)
75 games—Southern Methodist-Texas Christian (from 1921)
74 games—Missouri-Nebraska (from 1922)
74 games—North Caro.-Duke (from 1922)
72 games—Michigan-Illinois (from 1924)

72 games—Southern Methodist-Texas (from 1924)

**Neither school fielded a team in 1917-18 due to World War I.*

Most Consecutive Wins Over a Major Opponent in an Uninterrupted Series (Must have played in consecutive years)
32—Notre Dame over Navy, 1964-95 (current)
32—Oklahoma over Kansas St., 1937-68
28—Texas over Rice, 1966-93
27—Nebraska over Kansas, 1969-95 (current)
27—Nebraska over Kansas St., 1969-95 (current)

26—Syracuse over Hobart, 1906-31
25—Penn St. over West Va., 1959-83
22—Arkansas over Texas Christian, 1959-80
22—Alabama over Mississippi St., 1958-79
20—Purdue over Iowa, 1961-80

17—New Mexico over UTEP, 1970-86
17—Arizona St. over UTEP, 1957-73
17—LSU over Tulane, 1956-72
16—Michigan over Illinois, 1967-82
16—North Caro. over Wake Forest, 1908-23

15—Southern Methodist over Texas Christian, 1972-86

Most Consecutive Wins Over a Major Opponent in a Nonconsecutive Series (Did not play in consecutive years)
29—Clemson over Virginia, 1955-90 (over 36-year period)
22—Southern Cal over Oregon St., 1968-95 (28-year period)
19—Michigan over Northwestern, 1966-92 (27-year period)
19—Vanderbilt over Mississippi, 1894-1938 (45-year period)
17—Tulsa over Drake, 1939-85 (47-year period)

17—Mississippi over Memphis, 1921-62 (42-year period)

Most Consecutive Current Wins Over a Major Opponent in a Series (Must have played every year)
32—Notre Dame over Navy, 1964-95 (59-9-1 in rivalry)
27—Nebraska over Kansas, 1969-95 (78-21-3 in rivalry)
27—Nebraska over Kansas St., 1969-95 (68-10-2 in rivalry)
13—Iowa over Iowa St., 1983-95 (31-12-0 in rivalry)
12—Colorado over Iowa St., 1984-95 (38-11-1 in rivalry)

12—San Diego St. over New Mexico, 1984-95 (17-5-0 in rivalry)
12—Virginia over Wake Forest, 1984-95 (26-11-0 in rivalry)

Most Consecutive Games Without a Loss Against a Major Opponent
34—Oklahoma over Kansas St., 1935-68 (1 tie)

"Heartbreak Kids"

Div. I-A Teams With Most Losses on Final Play (Since 1971)

(5 losses)
Stanford

(4 losses)
California, Michigan

(3 losses)
Cincinnati, Louisville, Southwestern La., Virginia, Wisconsin

Cliffhangers

Regular-season Division I-A games won on the final play (since 1971, when first recorded). The extra point is listed when it provided the margin of victory after the winning touchdown on the game's final play.

Date	Opponents, Score	Game-Winning Play
9-25-71	Marshall 15, Xavier (Ohio) 13	Terry Gardner 13 pass from Reggie Oliver
10-9-71	California 30, Oregon St. 27	Steve Sweeney 7 pass from Jay Cruze
10-23-71	Washington St. 24, Stanford 23	Don Sweet 27 FG
11-6-71	Kentucky 14, Vanderbilt 7	Darryl Bishop 43 interception return
11-4-72	LSU 17, Mississippi 16	Brad Davis 10 pass from Bert Jones (Rusty Jackson kick)
11-18-72	California 24, Stanford 21	Steve Sweeney 7 pass from Vince Ferragamo
9-15-73	Lamar 21, Howard Payne 17	Larry Spears 14 pass from Jabo Leonard
9-22-73	Hawaii 13, Fresno St. 10	Reinhold Stuprich 29 FG
11-17-73	New Mexico 23, Wyoming 21	Bob Berg 43 FG
11-23-74	Stanford 22, California 20	Mike Langford 50 FG
9-20-75	Indiana St. 23, Southern Ill. 21	Dave Vandercook 50 FG
10-18-75	Cal St. Fullerton 32, UC Riverside 31	John Choukair 52 FG
11-8-75	West Va. 17, Pittsburgh 14	Bill McKenzie 38 FG
11-8-75	Stanford 13, Southern Cal 10	Mike Langford 37 FG
11-15-75	North Caro. 17, Tulane 15	Tom Biddle 40 FG
11-6-76	Eastern Mich. 30, Central Mich. 27	Ken Dudal 38 FG
9-30-78	Virginia Tech 22, William & Mary 19	Ron Zollicoffer 50 pass from David Lamie
10-21-78	Arkansas St. 6, McNeese St. 3	Doug Dobbs 42 FG
11-9-78	San Jose St. 33, Pacific (Cal.) 31	Rick Parma 5 pass from Ed Luther
10-6-79	Stanford 27, UCLA 24	Ken Naber 56 FG
10-20-79	UNLV 43, Utah 41	Todd Peterson 49 FG
10-27-79	Michigan 27, Indiana 21	Anthony Carter 45 pass from John Wangler
11-10-79	Penn St. 9, North Caro. St. 7	Herb Menhardt 54 FG
11-17-79	Air Force 30, Vanderbilt 29	Andy Bark 14 pass from Dave Ziebart
11-24-79	Arizona 27, Arizona St. 24	Brett Weber 27 FG
9-13-80	Southern Cal 20, Tennessee 17	Eric Hipp 47 FG
9-13-80	Illinois 20, Michigan St. 17	Mike Bass 38 FG
9-20-80	Notre Dame 29, Michigan 27	Harry Oliver 51 FG
9-27-80	Tulane 26, Mississippi 24	Vince Manalla 29 FG
10-18-80	Connecticut 18, Holy Cross 17	Ken Miller 4 pass from Ken Sweitzer (Keith Hugger pass from Sweitzer)
10-18-80	Washington 27, Stanford 24	Chuck Nelson 25 FG
11-1-80	Tulane 24, Kentucky 22	Vince Manalla 22 FG
11-15-80	Florida 17, Kentucky 15	Brian Clark 34 FG
10-16-82	Arizona 16, Notre Dame 13	Max Zendejas 48 FG
10-23-82	Illinois 29, Wisconsin 28	Mike Bass 46 FG
11-20-82	California 25, Stanford 20	57 (5 laterals) kickoff return involving, in order: Kevin Moen, Richard Rodgers, Dwight Garner, Rodgers, Mariet Ford and Moen
10-8-83	Iowa St. 38, Kansas 35	Marc Bachrodt 47 FG
10-29-83	Bowling Green 15, Central Mich. 14	Stan Hunter 8 pass from Brian McClure

Date	Opponents, Score	Game-Winning Play
11-5-83	Baylor 24, Arkansas 21	Marty Jimmerson 24 FG
11-12-83	Pacific (Cal.) 30, San Jose St. 26	Ron Woods 85 pass from Mike Pitz
11-12-83	Miami (Fla.) 17, Florida St. 16	Jeff Davis 19 FG
11-26-83	Arizona 17, Arizona St. 15	Max Zendejas 45 FG
9-8-84	Southwestern La. 17, Louisiana Tech 16	Patrick Broussard 21 FG
9-15-84	Syracuse 13, Northwestern 12	Jim Tait 2 pass from Todd Norley (Don McAulay kick)
10-13-84	UCLA 27, Washington St. 24	John Lee 47 FG
11-17-84	Southwestern La. 18, Tulsa 17	Patrick Broussard 45 FG
11-17-84	Temple 19, West Va. 17	Jim Cooper 36 FG
11-23-84	Boston College 47, Miami (Fla.) 45	Gerard Phelan 48 pass from Doug Flutie
9-14-85	Clemson 20, Virginia Tech 17	David Treadwell 36 FG
9-14-85	Oregon St. 23, California 20	Jim Nielsen 20 FG
9-14-85	Utah 29, Hawaii 27	Andre Guardi 19 FG
9-21-85	New Mexico St. 22, UTEP 20	Andy Weiler 32 FG
10-5-85	Mississippi St. 31, Memphis 28	Artie Cosby 54 FG
10-5-85	Illinois 31, Ohio St. 28	Chris White 38 FG
10-12-85	Tulsa 37, Long Beach St. 35	Jason Staurovsky 46 FG
10-19-85	Northwestern 17, Wisconsin 14	John Duvic 42 FG
10-19-85	Iowa 12, Michigan 10	Rob Houghtlin 29 FG
10-19-85	Utah 39, San Diego St. 37	Andre Guardi 42 FG
11-30-85	Alabama 25, Auburn 23	Van Tiffin 52 FG
9-13-86	Oregon 32, Colorado 30	Matt MacLeod 35 FG
9-13-86	Wyoming 23, Pacific (Cal.) 20	Greg Worker 38 FG
9-20-86	Clemson 31, Georgia 28	David Treadwell 46 FG
9-20-86	Southern Cal 17, Baylor 14	Don Shafer 32 FG
10-18-86	Michigan 20, Iowa 17	Mike Gillette 34 FG
10-25-86	Syracuse 27, Temple 24	Tim Vesling 32 FG
11-1-86	North Caro. St. 23, South Caro. 22	Danny Peebles 33 pass from Erik Kramer
11-1-86	North Caro. 32, Maryland 30	Lee Gliarmis 28 FG
11-8-86	Southern Miss. 23, East Caro. 21	Rex Banks 31 FG
11-15-86	Minnesota 20, Michigan 17	Chip Lohmiller 30 FG
11-29-86	Notre Dame 38, Southern Cal 37	John Carney 19 FG
9-12-87	Youngstown St. 20, Bowling Green 17	John Dowling 36 FG
9-19-87	Utah 31, Wisconsin 28	Scott Lieber 39 FG
10-10-87	Marshall 34, Louisville 31	Keith Baxter 31 pass from Tony Petersen
10-17-87	Texas 16, Arkansas 14	Tony Jones 18 pass from Bret Stafford
11-12-88	New Mexico 24, Colorado St. 23	Tony Jones 28 pass from Jeremy Leach
9-16-89	Southern Methodist 31, Connecticut 30	Mike Bowen 4 pass from Mike Romo
9-30-89	Kansas St. 20, North Texas 17	Frank Hernandez 12 pass from Carl Straw
10-7-89	Florida 16, LSU 13	Arden Czyzewski 41 FG
10-14-89	Southern Miss. 16, Louisville 10	Darryl Tillman 79 pass from Brett Favre
10-28-89	Virginia 16, Louisville 15	Jake McInerney 37 FG
11-4-89	Toledo 19, Western Mich. 18	Romauldo Brown 9 pass from Kevin Meger
11-4-89	Northern Ill. 23, Southwestern La. 20	Stacey Robinson 7 run
9-8-90	Utah 35, Minnesota 29	Lavon Edwards 91 run of blocked FG
9-29-90	North Caro. St. 12, North Caro. 9	Damon Hartman 56 FG
10-6-90	Colorado 33, Missouri 31	Charles S. Johnson 1 run
10-20-90	Alabama 9, Tennessee 6	Philip Doyle 47 FG
11-3-90	Southern Miss. 14, Southwestern La. 13	Michael Welch 11 pass from Brett Favre (Jim Taylor kick)
11-17-90	Stanford 27, California 25	John Hopkins 39 FG
11-24-90	Michigan 16, Ohio St. 13	J. D. Carlson 37 FG
9-7-91	Central Mich. 27, Southwestern La. 24	L. J. Muddy 2 pass from Jeff Bender
9-21-91	California 23, Arizona 21	Doug Brien 33 FG
9-21-91	Georgia Tech 24, Virginia 21	Scott Sisson 33 FG
9-21-91	Louisiana Tech 17, Eastern Mich. 14	Chris Bonoil 54 FG
10-12-91	Ball St. 10, Eastern Mich. 8	Kenny Stucker 41 FG
11-2-91	Kentucky 20, Cincinnati 17	Doug Pelphrey 53 FG
11-2-91	Tulsa 13, Southern Miss. 10	Eric Lange 24 FG
9-5-92	Louisiana Tech 10, Baylor 9	Chris Bonoil 30 FG
9-19-92	Miami (Ohio) 17, Cincinnati 14	Chad Seitz 21 FG
9-19-92	Southern Miss. 16, Louisiana Tech 13	Johnny Lomoro 46 FG
10-3-92	Texas A&M 19, Texas Tech 17	Terry Venetoulias 21 FG
10-3-92	Georgia Tech 16, North Caro. St. 13	Scott Sisson 29 FG
10-3-92	San Jose St. 26, Wyoming 24	Joe Nedney 60 FG
10-24-92	Maryland 27, Duke 25	Marcus Badgett 38 pass from John Kaleo
10-31-92	Rutgers 50, Virginia Tech 49	Chris Brantley 15 pass from Bryan Fortay
11-14-92	UCLA 9, Oregon 6	Louis Perez 40 FG
10-2-93	Tulane 27, Navy 25	Bart Baldwin 43 FG
10-9-93	Ball St. 31, Toledo 30	Eric McCray 6 pass from Mike Neu (Matt Swart kick)
10-9-93	North Caro. St. 36, Texas Tech 34	Gary Downs 11 pass from Robert Hinton
10-16-93	Arizona 27, Stanford 24	Steve McLaughlin 27 FG
10-30-93	Missouri 37, Iowa St. 34	Kyle Pooler 40 FG
11-20-93	Maryland 33, Wake Forest 32	Russ Weaver 8 pass from Scott Milanovich (John Milligan kick)
11-20-93	Boston College 41, Notre Dame 39	David Gordon 41 FG
11-20-93	Arkansas St. 23, Nevada 21	Reginald Murphy 30 pass from Johnny Covington
9-10-94	Tulane 15, Rice 13	Bart Baldwin 47 FG
9-10-94	San Diego St. 22, California 20	Peter Holt 32 FG
9-24-94	Colorado 27, Michigan 26	Michael Westbrook 64 pass from Kordell Stewart
10-22-94	Central Mich. 32, Miami (Ohio) 30	Terrance McMillan 19 pass from Erik Timpf
10-22-94	Army 25, Citadel 24	Kurt Heiss 24 FG
11-19-94	Eastern Mich. 40, Toledo 37	Ontario Pryor 16 pass from Charlie Batch
8-26-95	Michigan18, Virginia 17	Mercury Hayes 15 pass from Scott Dreisbach
9-9-95	Kansas St. 23, Cincinnati 21	Kevin Lockett 22 pass from Matt Miller
10-21-95	Texas 17, Virginia 16	Phil Dawson 50 FG
10-28-95	East Caro. 36, Southern Miss. 34	Chad Holcomb 29 FG

Photo from Texas sports information

Phil Dawson kicked a 50-yard field goal as time expired to give Texas a 17-16 victory over Virginia on October 21, 1995. It was the Cavaliers' second final-play loss of the season.

"CARDIAC SEASONS"

(From 1937; Won-Lost Record in Parentheses)

Games Decided by Two Points or Less

6—Kansas, 1973 (3-2-1): Tennessee 27-28, Nebraska 9-10, Iowa St. 22-20, Oklahoma St. 10-10, Colorado 17-15, Missouri 14-13 (season record: 7-3-1)

5—Illinois, 1992 (2-2-1): Minnesota 17-18, Ohio St. 18-16, Northwestern 26-27, Wisconsin 13-12, Michigan 22-22 (season record: 6-4-1)

5—Columbia, 1971 (4-1-0): Princeton 22-20, Harvard 19-21, Yale 15-14, Rutgers 17-16, Dartmouth 31-29 (season record: 6-3-0)

5—Missouri, 1957 (2-2-1): Vanderbilt 7-7, Southern Methodist 7-6, Nebraska 14-13, Kansas St. 21-23, Kansas 7-9 (season record: 5-4-1)

Games Decided by Three Points or Less

7—Bowling Green, 1980 (2-5-0): Ohio 20-21, Ball St. 24-21, Western Mich. 17-14, Kentucky 20-21, Long Beach St. 21-23, Eastern Mich. 16-18, Richmond 17-20 (season record: 4-7-0)

7—Columbia, 1971 (4-3-0): Lafayette 0-3, Princeton 22-20, Harvard 19-21, Yale 15-14, Rutgers 17-16, Cornell 21-24, Dartmouth 31-29 (season record: 6-3-0)

6—Illinois, 1992 (3-2-1): Minnesota 17-18, Ohio St. 18-16, Northwestern 26-27, Wisconsin 13-12, Purdue 20-17, Michigan 22-22 (season record: 6-4-1)

6—Central Mich., 1991 (2-0-4): Ohio 17-17, Southwestern La. 27-24, Akron 31-29, Toledo 16-16, Miami (Ohio) 10-10, Eastern Mich. 14-14 (season record: 6-1-4)

6—Kansas, 1973 (3-2-1): Tennessee 27-28, Nebraska 9-10, Iowa St. 22-20, Oklahoma St. 10-10, Colorado 17-15, Missouri 14-13 (season record: 7-3-1)

6—Air Force, 1967 (2-2-2): Oklahoma St. 0-0, California 12-14, North Caro. 10-8, Tulane 13-10, Colorado St. 17-17, Army 7-10 (season record: 2-6-2)

6—Missouri, 1957 (3-2-1): Vanderbilt 7-7, Southern Methodist 7-6, Nebraska 14-13, Colorado 9-6, Kansas St. 21-23, Kansas 7-9 (season record: 5-4-1)

Division I-A Stadiums

STADIUMS LISTED ALPHABETICALLY

School	Stadium	Conference	Year Built	Cap.	Surface* (Year)
Air Force	Falcon	Western Ath.-P	1962	52,480	Grass
Akron	^Rubber Bowl	Mid-American	1940	35,202	AstroTurf (83)
Alabama	^Legion Field	Southeastern-W	1927	83,091	Grass (S95)
	Bryant-Denny	Southeastern-W	1929	70,123	PAT (S91)
Ala.-Birmingham	^Legion Field	Independent	1927	83,091	Grass (S95)
Arizona	Arizona	Pacific-10	1929	57,803	Grass
Arizona St.	Sun Devil	Pacific-10	1959	73,656	Grass
Arkansas	^War Memorial	Southeastern-W	1948	53,727	Grass (S94)
	Razorback	Southeastern-W	1938	50,019	Grass (S95)
Arkansas St.	Indian	Independent	1974	33,410	Grass
Army	Michie	Independent	1924	39,929	AstroTurf (92)
Auburn	Jordan-Hare	Southeastern-W	1939	85,214	Grass
Ball St.	Ball St.	Mid-American	1967	18,159	Grass
Baylor	Floyd Casey	Big 12-S	1950	50,000	All-Pro Turf (90)
Boston College	Alumni	Big East	1957	44,500	PolyknitTurf
Bowling Green	Doyt Perry	Mid-American	1966	30,599	Grass
Brigham Young	Cougar	Western Ath.-M	1964	65,000	Grass
California	Memorial	Pacific-10	1923	75,662	Grass (S95)
Central Fla.	^Florida Citrus	Independent	1936	70,188	Grass
Central Mich.	Kelly/Shorts	Mid-American	1972	20,086	AstroTurf (83)
Cincinnati	Nippert	Conference USA	1916	35,000	AstroTurf-8 (92)
Clemson	Memorial	Atlantic Coast	1942	81,474	Grass
Colorado	Folsom Field	Big 12-N	1924	51,808	AstroTurf-8 (89)
Colorado St.	Hughes	Western Ath.-P	1968	30,000	Grass
Duke	Wallace Wade	Atlantic Coast	1929	33,941	Grass
East Caro.	Dowdy-Ficklen	Independent	1963	35,000	Grass
Eastern Mich.	Rynearson	Mid-American	1969	30,200	StadiaTurf (91)
Florida	Florida Field	Southeastern-E	1930	83,000	Grass (S90)
Florida St.	Doak Campbell	Atlantic Coast	1950	77,500	PAT (88)
Fresno St.	Bulldog	Western Ath.-P	1980	41,031	Grass
Georgia	Sanford	Southeastern-E	1929	86,117	Grass
Georgia Tech	Dodd/Grant	Atlantic Coast	1913	46,000	Grass (S95)
Hawaii	^Aloha	Western Ath.-P	1975	50,000	AstroTurf (85)
Houston	^Astrodome@	Conference USA	1965	60,000	AstroTurf
	Robertson	Conference USA	1941	22,000	Grass
Illinois	Memorial	Big Ten	1923	70,904	AstroTurf (89)
Indiana	Memorial	Big Ten	1960	52,354	AstroTurf (86)
Iowa	Kinnick	Big Ten	1929	70,397	PAT (S89)
Iowa St.	Cyclone-Jack Trice	Big 12-N	1975	50,000	Grass (S96)
Kansas	Memorial	Big 12-N	1921	50,250	AstroTurf (90)
Kansas St.	KSU	Big 12-N	1968	42,000	AstroTurf-8 (91)
Kent	Dix	Mid-American	1969	30,520	Grass
Kentucky	Commonwealth	Southeastern-E	1973	57,800	Grass
LSU	Tiger	Southeastern-W	1924	79,940	Grass
Louisiana Tech	Joe Aillet	Independent	1968	30,600	Grass
Louisville	^Cardinal	Conference USA	1956	35,500	AstroTurf (89)
Maryland	Byrd	Atlantic Coast	1950	48,000	Grass
Memphis	^Liberty Bowl	Conference USA	1965	62,380	PAT (87)
Miami (Fla.)	^Orange Bowl	Big East	1935	74,476	PAT (S77)
Miami (Ohio)	Fred Yager	Mid-American	1983	30,000	Grass
Michigan	Michigan	Big Ten	1927	102,501	PAT (S91)
Michigan St.	Spartan	Big Ten	1957	76,000	AstroTurf (83)
Minnesota	^Metrodome@	Big Ten	1982	63,669	AstroTurf-8
Mississippi	Vaught-Hemingway	Southeastern-W	1941	42,577	Grass
Mississippi St.	Scott Field	Southeastern-W	1915	40,656	PAT (86)
Missouri	Faurot Field	Big 12-N	1926	62,000	Grass (S95)
Navy	Navy-MC	Independent	1959	30,000	Grass
Nebraska	Memorial	Big 12-N	1923	72,700	AstroTurf-8 (92)
UNLV	^Sam Boyd	Western Ath.-P	1971	32,000	MonsantoTurf (85)
Nevada	Mackay	Big West	1965	31,545	Grass
New Mexico	University	Western Ath.-M	1960	31,218	Grass
New Mexico St.	Aggie Memorial	Big West	1978	30,343	Grass
North Caro.	Kenan Memorial	Atlantic Coast	1927	52,000	Grass
North Caro. St.	Carter-Finley	Atlantic Coast	1966	47,000	Grass
North Texas	Fouts Field	Big West	1952	30,500	All-Pro Turf
Northeast La.	Malone	Independent	1978	30,427	Grass
Northern Ill.	Huskie	Independent	1965	30,998	AstroTurf (89)
Northwestern	Dyche	Big Ten	1926	49,256	AstroTurf (94)
Notre Dame	Notre Dame	Independent	1930	59,075	Grass
Ohio	Peden	Mid-American	1929	20,000	Grass
Ohio St.	Ohio	Big Ten	1922	91,470	PAT (S90)
Oklahoma	Memorial	Big 12-S	1923	75,004	Grass (S94)
Oklahoma St.	Lewis	Big 12-S	1920	50,614	AstroTurf (87)
Oregon	Autzen	Pacific-10	1967	41,678	Omni-Turf (91)
Oregon St.	Parker	Pacific-10	1953	35,362	All-Pro Turf (84)
Penn St.	Beaver	Big Ten	1960	93,967	Grass
Pittsburgh	Pitt	Big East	1925	56,500	AstroTurf (90)
Purdue	Ross-Ade	Big Ten	1924	67,861	PAT (75)
Rice	Rice	Western Ath.-M	1950	70,000	All-Pro Turf (84)
Rutgers	Rutgers	Big East	1994	42,500	Grass
San Diego St.	^Jack Murphy	Western Ath.-P	1967	61,121	Grass
San Jose St.	Spartan	Western Ath.-P	1933	31,218	Grass
South Caro.	Williams-Brice	Southeastern-E	1934	80,250	Grass
Southern Cal	^LA Mem. Coliseum	Pacific-10	1923	92,000	Grass
Southern Meth.	Cotton Bowl	Western Ath.-M	1930	68,252	Grass (S93)
Southern Miss.	Roberts	Conference USA	1976	33,000	Grass
Southwestern La.	Cajun Field	Independent	1971	31,000	Grass
Stanford	Stanford	Pacific-10	1921	85,500	Grass
Syracuse	Carrier Dome@	Big East	1980	50,000	AstroTurf
Temple	Veterans	Big East	1971	66,592	AstroTurf-8
Tennessee	Neyland	Southeastern-E	1921	102,485	Grass (S94)
Texas	Memorial	Big 12-S	1924	75,512	PAT (S96)
UTEP	^Sun Bowl	Western Ath.-M	1963	51,270	AstroTurf (83)
Texas A&M	Kyle Field	Big 12-S	1925	70,210	Grass (S96)
Texas Christian	Amon Carter	Western Ath.-M	1929	46,000	Grass (S92)
Texas Tech	Jones	Big 12-S	1947	50,500	AstroTurf-8 (88)
Toledo	Glass Bowl	Mid-American	1937	26,248	AstroTurf (90)
Tulane	^Superdome@	Conference USA	1975	70,892	AstroTurf
Tulsa	Skelly	Western Ath.-M	1930	40,385	Stadia Turf (91)
UCLA	^Rose Bowl	Pacific-10	1922	100,089	Grass
Utah	Robert Rice	Western Ath.-M	1927	32,500	Grass (S95)
Utah St.	E. L. Romney	Big West	1968	30,257	Grass
Vanderbilt	Vanderbilt	Southeastern-E	1922	41,600	AstroTurf (81)
Virginia	Scott	Atlantic Coast	1931	40,000	PAT (S95)
Virginia Tech	Lane	Big East	1965	50,000	Grass
Wake Forest	Groves	Atlantic Coast	1968	31,500	Grass
Washington	Husky	Pacific-10	1920	72,500	AstroTurf (95)
Washington St.	Martin	Pacific-10	1972	37,600	Omni-Turf (90)
West Va.	Mountaineer	Big East	1980	63,500	Omni-Turf (88)
Western Mich.	Waldo	Mid-American	1939	30,200	PAT (92)
Wisconsin	Camp Randall	Big Ten	1917	76,129	AstroTurf (90)
Wyoming	War Memorial	Western Ath.-P	1950	33,500	Grass

STADIUMS LISTED BY CAPACITY (Top 25)

School	Stadium	Surface* (Year)	Capacity
Michigan	Michigan	PAT (S91)	102,501
Tennessee	Neyland	Grass (S94)	102,485
UCLA	^Rose Bowl	Grass	100,089
Penn St.	Beaver	Grass	93,967
Southern Cal	^LA Mem. Coliseum	Grass	92,000
Ohio St.	Ohio	PAT (S90)	91,470
Georgia	Sanford	Grass	86,117
Stanford	Stanford	Grass	85,500
Auburn	Jordan-Hare	Grass	85,214
Alabama	^Legion Field	Grass (S95)	83,091
Ala.-Birmingham	^Legion Field	Grass (S95)	83,091
Florida	Florida Field	Grass (S90)	83,000
Clemson	Memorial	Grass	81,474
South Caro.	Williams-Brice	Grass	80,250
LSU	Tiger	Grass	79,940
Florida St.	Doak Campbell	PAT (88)	77,500
Wisconsin	Camp Randall	AstroTurf (90)	76,129
Michigan St.	Spartan	AstroTurf (83)	76,000
California	Memorial	Grass (S95)	75,662
Texas	Memorial	PAT (S96)	75,512
Oklahoma	Memorial	Grass (S94)	75,004
Miami (Fla.)	^Orange Bowl	PAT (S77)	74,476
Arizona St.	Sun Devil	Grass	73,656
Nebraska	Memorial	AstroTurf-8(92)	72,700
Washington	Husky	AstroTurf (95)	72,500

^Not located on campus. @ Indoor facility. S=switch to grass or vice-versa and year switched.

Surface Notes: **This column indicates the type of surface (either artificial or natural grass) present this year in the stadium. The brand name of the artificial turf, if known, is listed as well as the year the last installation occurred. The "S" preceding the year indicates that the school has switched either from natural grass to artificial turf or vice-versa. Legend: Turf—Any of several types of artificial turfs (name brands include AstroTurf, All-Pro, Omni-Turf, SuperTurf, etc.); Grass—Natural grass surface; PAT—Prescription Athletic Turf (a "natural-artificial" surface featuring a network of pipes connected to pumps capable of sucking water from the natural turf or watering it. The pipes are located 18 inches from the surface and covered with a mixture of sand and filler. The turf also is lined with heating coils to keep it from freezing in temperatures below 32 degrees).*

Division I-A Stadium Facts: *Houston and Tulsa claim to be the first college football teams to play in an indoor stadium (the Astrodome on September 11, 1965). But actually, Utah and West Virginia met December 19, 1964, in the Liberty Bowl in the Atlantic City Convention Hall. Technically, the Astrodome was the first indoor stadium built specially for football and baseball. The first major-college football game ever played on artificial turf was between Houston and Washington State on September 23, 1966.*

Famous Major-College Dynasties

The following are singled out because of their historical significance, and all represent an outstanding record as well as at least one national championship.

NOTRE DAME (1919-30)

Under Knute Rockne, the Fighting Irish posted an overall record of 101-11-3 (.891 winning percentage) and captured three national titles during this 12-year period. Rockne, who died in an airplane crash in 1931, did not accomplish this by himself, with athletes like George Gipp and the legendary Four Horsemen (Harry Stuhldreher, Elmer Layden, Jim Crowley and Don Miller) around. The longest unbeaten streak was 22 games, which began in 1918 under Gipp, but the South Benders had three other streaks of at least 15 games in the period.

MINNESOTA (1933-41)

Bernie Bierman, known as "The Silver Fox" for his prematurely gray hair, led the Golden Gophers through their best era. In the nine-year span, Minnesota posted a 58-9-5 (.840) record and won five national titles (1934, 1936, 1940 and 1941 outright and 1935 shared). Bierman oversaw five undefeated teams in the span, and the longest unbeaten streak was 28 games. Defense was a trademark of the Gophers, who notched 23 shutouts in the 72 games. The top offensive player was 1941 Heisman Trophy winner Bruce Smith.

NOTRE DAME (1946-53)

Under head coach Frank Leahy, Notre Dame began another streak almost as successful as the Rockne era. Leahy led the Irish to a national title in 1943, and beginning in 1946, Notre Dame set off on a 63-8-6 (.857) journey that yielded three more national championships (1946, 1947 and 1949) in four years. The longest unbeaten streak stretched to 39 games. The top players were Heisman Trophy winners Johnny Lujack (1947), Leon Hart (1949) and John Lattner (1953).

OKLAHOMA (1948-58)

Many felt this particular span featured the greatest accomplishment in modern-day collegiate football—Oklahoma's Bud Wilkinson-led 47-game winning streak from 1953-57. The Sooners posted a 107-8-2 (.923) mark during the 11-year stretch that included three consensus national titles (1950, 1955 and 1956). Halfback Billy Vessels, the 1952 Heisman winner, was the outstanding individual player in the streak, but Wilkinson's teams were typified by overall speed and quickness.

ALABAMA (1959-67)

Paul "Bear" Bryant's return to his alma mater started a chain of events that eventually yielded one of the greatest dynasties in history. During the nine-year span, Bryant's teams fashioned an 83-10-6 (.869) record and captured three national prizes (1961, 1964 and 1965). His players included Joe Namath, Ken Stabler, Pat Trammell, Ray Perkins, Steve Sloan and Lee Roy Jordan, an eclectic group that featured no Heisman winners. All his players knew how to do was win football games, and the 1963-67 teams never lost a home game.

SOUTHERN CAL (1967-79)

Two coaches—John McKay and John Robinson—shared this dynasty, which posted a 122-23-7 (.826) record and four national titles (1967, 1972 and 1974 under McKay and 1978 under Robinson). The longest unbeaten streak was 28 games. Southern Cal had two Heisman winners—O. J. Simpson (1968) and Charles White (1979)—and 18 consensus all-Americans in the 13-year period.

ALABAMA (1971-80)

This was the second great run for the Crimson Tide under Bryant. Alabama reeled off a 28-game unbeaten streak and posted a 107-13-0 (.892) record during the 10-year span, including national championships in 1973, 1978 and 1979. Again, there were no Heisman winners for Bryant, but he had a list of players like John Hannah, Steadman Shealy, Jeff Rutledge, Tony Nathan and Major Ogilvie. Bryant died in 1983 as the winningest college coach.

OKLAHOMA (1971-80)

Barry Switzer led the Sooner dynasty to a 102-14-2 (.873) record that included a 37-game unbeaten string and 10 Big Eight championships. Back-to-back national titles in 1974 and 1975 were the result of enormous talent and Switzer's coaching. Some of the Sooner all-Americans during the 10-year period included Jack Mildren, Greg Pruitt, Lucious Selmon, Rod Shoate, Tinker Owens, Dewey Selmon, Lee Roy Selmon, Joe Washington, Billy Brooks and George Cumby. Heisman Trophy winner Billy Sims (1978) was the biggest name in a Sooner rushing attack that was virtually unstoppable.

MIAMI (FLA.) (1983-92)

The loss to Alabama in the 1993 Sugar Bowl ended a real streak for the Hurricanes, going for a fifth national title since 1983. Few would argue that during the 1980s under three different coaches—Howard Schnellenberger, Jimmy Johnson and Dennis Erickson—the Hurricanes were the most successful team in America. With a 107-13-0 (.892) record that included national titles in 1983, 1987, 1989 and 1991, the Hurricanes served notice that an undefeated season was a possibility every year.

FLORIDA ST. (1987-95)

Under Bobby Bowden, Florida State fashioned one of the most remarkable regular-season and postseason records over this nine-year period. The Seminoles did what no other Division I school ever accomplished—win at least 10 games in all nine seasons. In fact, Florida State posted a 76-13-1 mark during the streak, which also includes an unprecedented 11 straight bowl victories. Bowden led teams that finished in the top five of The Associated Press poll for nine consecutive years. Florida State captured Bowden's first national title in 1993.

NEBRASKA (1988-95)

Some suggest that Nebraska under Tom Osborne was on a 23-year dynasty streak, beginning with the fact that every one of his first 23 teams posted at least nine victories. But that aside, these eight years were a remarkable run for the Cornhuskers, with an 84-13-1 (.862) record including back-to-back national championships in 1994 and 1995. The Huskers' 25-game win streak was the nation's longest in 1995, and the 27-year consecutive bowl string was a collegiate record. Actually, the Huskers were just a last-second field goal away from three straight national titles, losing to Florida State, 18-16, in the 1994 FedEx Orange Bowl.

Other College Football Dynasties

(Listed Because of Their Historical Significance)

School (Years)	W-L-T	Pct.	Duration	Titles*
Yale (1876-1909)	315-14-18	.934	34 years	19
Princeton (1877-1903)	233-21-11	.900	27 years	12
Pennsylvania (1894-1908)	168-21-7	.875	15 years	4
Michigan (1901-09)	75-6-2	.916	9 years	2
Harvard (1908-15)	64-4-5	.911	8 years	5
Pittsburgh (1913-20)	55-5-4	.891	8 years	3
Southern Cal (1919-33)	129-18-3	.870	15 years	2
Tennessee (1938-46)#	72-9-2	.880	9 years	2
Michigan (1940-48)	68-13-2	.831	9 years	2
Army (1943-50)	64-5-5	.899	8 years	3
Michigan St. (1950-66)	117-37-4	.753	17 years	4
Ohio St. (1954-61)	56-14-4	.784	8 years	3
Texas (1961-72)	107-21-2	.831	12 years	3
Nebraska (1969-76)	79-14-4	.835	8 years	2
Penn St. (1980-87)	76-19-1	.797	8 years	2

**Some titles were shared. No team in 1943 due to World War II.*
(Special thanks to Bob Kirlin of Spokane, Wash., for his compilations.)

Major-College Statistics Trends†

(Average Per Game, Both Teams)

Year	Rushing Plays	Rushing Yds.	Rushing Avg.	Passing Att.	Passing Cmp.	Passing Pct.	Passing Yds.	Passing Av. Att.	Total Offense Plays	Total Offense Yds.	Total Offense Avg.	Scoring TD	Scoring FG	Scoring Pts.
1937	—	267.6	—	26.0	9.9	.381	129.0	4.96	—	396.8	—	—	—	20.2
1938	81.6	280.2	3.43	28.0	10.4	.371	140.2	5.01	109.6	420.4	3.85	3.50	0.12	23.5
1939	81.6	271.8	3.33	27.6	10.3	.374	132.8	4.81	109.2	404.6	3.70	3.32	0.18	22.7
1940	83.8	281.0	3.35	29.6	11.5	.386	156.0	5.26	113.4	437.0	3.85	3.94	0.16	26.6
1941	84.4	282.4	3.35	30.0	11.7	.392	161.2	5.38	114.4	443.6	3.88	4.06	0.12	27.5
1946	84.6	304.8	3.60	31.0	12.1	.389	176.6	5.69	115.6	481.4	4.16	4.78	0.08	32.1
1947	84.6	317.4	3.75	30.5	12.6	.414	180.2	5.91	115.1	497.6	4.32	4.73	0.07	31.8
1948	87.4	324.4	3.71	31.7	13.4	.423	188.4	5.95	119.0	513.0	4.31	5.04	0.09	34.2
1949	94.4	361.2	3.83	35.3	15.1	.431	220.1	6.24	129.7	581.3	4.48	5.71	0.08	38.8
1950	94.0	360.3	3.83	35.0	15.3	.438	216.9	6.19	129.0	577.2	4.47	5.58	0.07	37.8
1951	97.1	365.0	3.76	37.7	16.8	.446	227.1	6.02	134.9	592.1	4.39	5.72	0.09	38.8
1952	96.6	352.7	3.65	36.7	16.2	.441	223.6	6.09	133.4	576.3	4.32	5.36	0.14	36.7
1953	90.1	353.1	3.92	30.4	13.0	.428	183.4	6.03	120.5	536.4	4.45	5.07	0.09	34.2
1954	90.9	368.1	*4.05	29.7	13.0	.437	182.2	6.14	120.6	550.2	4.56	5.17	0.09	34.7
1955	92.1	353.3	3.83	27.1	11.8	.435	169.3	6.24	119.2	522.6	4.38	4.74	0.10	32.1
1956	98.3	386.2	3.93	28.2	12.3	.437	171.8	6.09	126.5	558.0	4.41	4.90	0.09	33.0
1957	98.5	355.0	3.60	28.8	12.8	.444	171.0	5.94	127.2	526.0	4.14	4.61	0.11	31.1
1958	94.2	341.4	3.62	32.2	14.7	.458	195.3	6.06	126.4	536.7	4.24	4.61	0.18	32.0
1959	92.4	332.0	3.59	33.0	14.9	.451	197.0	5.96	125.4	529.0	4.21	4.50	0.34	31.7
1960	90.6	339.7	3.75	31.5	14.3	.454	187.1	5.94	122.1	526.8	4.31	4.37	0.38	31.1
1961	91.1	333.3	3.66	31.8	14.3	.448	189.4	5.95	122.9	522.7	4.25	4.46	0.47	32.0
1962	90.5	328.0	3.63	34.4	15.9	.463	209.9	6.10	124.9	537.9	4.31	4.59	0.42	32.7
1963	88.2	320.0	3.63	35.2	16.2	.461	210.5	5.98	123.4	530.6	4.30	4.38	0.53	31.6
1964	87.4	299.3	3.43	35.8	16.9	.472	219.9	6.14	123.2	519.2	4.21	4.13	0.59	30.1
1965	90.2	298.7	3.31	41.5	19.3	.464	246.4	5.93	131.7	545.0	4.14	4.51	0.83	33.3
1966	88.5	297.3	3.36	43.9	20.6	.470	266.3	6.07	132.3	563.6	4.26	4.70	0.84	34.9
1967	94.6	309.3	3.27	45.8	21.4	.467	279.6	6.10	140.4	588.9	4.19	4.95	0.91	36.8
1968	99.4	341.5	3.44	50.7	24.1	.474	315.4	6.22	*150.1	657.0	4.38	5.77	0.92	42.4
1969	98.9	343.6	3.47	50.9	24.0	.471	314.1	6.17	149.8	657.7	4.39	5.80	1.08	43.2
1970	98.5	351.3	3.57	49.9	23.3	.467	305.3	6.12	148.4	656.6	4.42	5.66	1.13	42.6
1971	99.3	364.3	3.67	43.4	20.1	.463	264.6	6.10	142.6	628.9	4.41	5.38	1.08	40.4
1972	99.6	369.0	3.70	43.9	20.3	.462	273.7	6.24	143.5	642.7	4.48	5.42	1.22	41.1
1973	100.2	385.5	3.85	40.8	19.2	.472	261.7	6.41	141.0	647.2	4.59	5.50	1.29	41.9
1974	103.7	403.6	3.89	37.6	17.8	.474	244.6	6.50	141.3	648.2	4.59	5.27	1.26	40.3
1975	*103.8	*408.9	3.94	36.7	17.3	.473	239.2	6.52	140.5	648.1	4.61	5.14	1.48	40.1
1976	102.7	397.5	3.87	38.1	18.1	.474	246.9	6.49	140.8	644.4	4.58	5.13	1.49	40.0
1977	102.5	389.2	3.80	40.3	19.5	.483	269.0	6.67	142.9	658.2	4.61	5.34	1.46	41.5
1978	101.7	385.2	3.79	42.4	20.6	.486	277.7	6.55	144.1	662.9	4.60	5.28	1.51	41.1
1979	98.1	375.8	3.83	43.1	21.2	.491	278.6	6.47	141.2	654.4	4.63	5.09	1.53	39.9
1980	95.3	356.6	3.74	46.6	23.3	.500	303.7	6.52	141.9	660.3	4.65	5.22	1.61	41.0
1981	92.6	338.8	3.66	50.6	25.4	.502	329.4	6.51	143.2	668.2	4.67	5.14	1.73	41.0
1982	90.2	338.5	3.75	55.2	28.9	.522	364.8	6.61	145.4	703.3	4.84	5.42	2.04	43.8
1983	89.2	338.9	3.80	53.9	28.8	.536	365.5	6.79	143.1	704.5	4.92	5.45	2.11	44.2
1984	89.4	336.2	3.76	53.5	28.2	.527	362.2	6.77	142.9	698.4	4.89	5.32	2.30	44.1
1985	89.1	338.3	3.80	54.5	29.3	.537	372.2	6.82	143.6	710.5	4.95	5.48	2.18	44.7
1986	88.4	335.8	3.80	54.4	29.2	.537	370.2	6.81	142.8	706.0	4.95	5.59	2.14	45.4
1987	88.8	348.4	3.92	54.1	28.5	.526	367.1	6.78	142.9	715.5	5.01	5.65	2.25	46.1
1988	88.0	349.1	3.97	54.1	28.6	.529	371.5	6.87	142.1	720.6	5.07	5.82	*2.31	47.5
1989	85.4	332.8	3.90	57.0	30.8	.540	401.8	7.05	142.4	734.6	5.16	5.94	2.26	48.2
1990	86.1	335.3	3.90	56.6	30.2	.534	394.3	6.96	142.7	729.6	5.11	6.07	2.16	48.8
1991	86.6	339.4	3.91	54.4	29.1	.535	379.2	6.98	141.0	718.7	5.10	5.90	1.77	46.2
1992	85.3	331.2	3.89	56.2	29.8	.530	380.9	6.77	141.5	712.1	5.03	5.67	2.08	45.8
1993	83.5	332.6	3.98	57.4	31.7	*.551	409.7	*7.13	141.0	742.3	*5.27	6.18	1.93	48.8
1994	83.6	333.6	3.99	57.0	31.2	.547	396.6	6.96	140.6	730.2	5.19	6.21	1.98	49.1
1995	83.0	334.6	4.03	*59.4	*32.5	.547	*410.9	6.92	142.4	*745.5	5.24	*6.41	1.85	*50.2

Record. †Records not compiled in 1942-45 except for Scoring Points Per Game: 1942 (31.3); 1943 (31.3); 1944 (32.6); 1945 (32.2).

Additional Major-College Statistics Trends†

Rules changes and statistics changes affecting trends: PUNTING—Beginning in 1965, 20 yards not deducted from a punt into the end zone for a touchback. INTERCEPTIONS—Interception yards not compiled, 1958-65. KICKOFF RETURNS—During 1937-45, if a kickoff went out of bounds, the receiving team put the ball in play on its 35-yard line instead of a second kickoff; in 1984 (rescinded in 1985), a 30-yard-line touchback for kickoffs crossing the goal line in flight and first touching the ground out of the end zone; in 1986, kickoffs from the 35-yard line. PUNT RETURNS—In 1967, interior linemen restricted from leaving until the ball is kicked.

(Average Per Game, Both Teams)

Year	Punting No.	Punting Avg.	Punting Net Avg.	Interceptions No.	Interceptions Avg. Ret.	Interceptions Yds.	Punt Returns No.	Punt Returns Avg. Ret.	Punt Returns Yds.	Kickoff Returns No.	Kickoff Returns Avg. Ret.	Kickoff Returns Yds.	Kickoff Returns Pct. Ret'd
1937	18.4	36.3	—	3.36	—	—	—	—	—	—	—	—	—
1938	18.6	37.2	—	3.40	9.19	31.6	—	—	—	—	—	—	—
1939	*18.7	36.7	—	3.34	9.84	33.0	*8.84	9.40	83.2	4.28	19.3	82.6	.764
1940	18.1	36.6	—	3.58	10.05	36.0	8.41	10.58	89.0	4.64	*20.4	95.0	.753
1941	17.7	36.1	—	*3.62	11.28	40.8	8.54	11.10	*94.8	4.82	20.2	97.2	.768
1946	14.6	35.7	—	3.50	11.79	41.2	7.40	11.32	83.8	6.02	18.9	113.8	.870
1947	13.4	36.4	30.3	3.21	11.93	38.3	6.94	11.73	81.4	6.07	18.9	114.5	.884
1948	12.6	36.3	30.2	3.20	12.59	40.3	6.18	*12.16	75.1	6.34	18.5	117.2	.873
1949	12.5	36.6	30.3	3.37	*13.23	*44.6	6.41	12.13	77.7	7.02	17.9	125.5	.885
1950	12.0	36.3	30.8	3.21	11.99	38.5	6.07	10.72	65.1	6.92	16.6	114.8	.889
1951	12.8	35.9	30.7	3.34	12.00	40.1	6.20	10.58	65.6	7.06	17.0	119.7	.884
1952	12.5	36.4	31.6	3.19	11.60	37.0	6.13	9.95	61.0	6.89	17.6	121.4	.908

(Average Per Game, Both Teams)

Year	Punting No.	Punting Avg.	Punting Net Avg.	Interceptions No.	Interceptions Avg. Ret.	Interceptions Yds.	Punt Returns No.	Punt Returns Avg. Ret.	Punt Returns Yds.	Kickoff Returns No.	Kickoff Returns Avg. Ret.	Kickoff Returns Yds.	Kickoff Returns Pct. Ret'd
1953	10.4	34.9	29.7	2.74	12.12	33.2	5.13	10.66	54.7	6.54	17.8	116.4	.903
1954	9.7	34.9	29.4	2.71	12.48	33.8	4.84	11.16	54.0	6.64	18.4	122.0	*.910
1955	9.8	34.9	29.8	2.52	12.96	33.5	4.78	10.54	50.4	6.17	18.5	114.4	.892
1956	10.1	35.1	30.1	2.57	12.86	33.1	4.97	10.07	50.1	6.37	18.0	114.8	.906
1957	10.6	34.8	30.2	2.52	11.95	30.1	5.06	9.57	48.4	6.09	18.7	114.1	.897
1958	11.1	35.4	30.9	2.65	—	—	5.13	9.70	49.8	6.03	18.9	113.9	.880
1959	11.0	35.9	31.5	2.66	—	—	5.34	9.06	48.4	6.18	18.7	115.6	.892
1960	10.2	36.0	31.4	2.48	—	—	4.78	9.73	46.5	6.09	18.8	114.6	.890
1961	10.3	35.5	31.1	2.44	—	—	4.85	9.44	45.8	6.12	18.3	112.2	.873
1962	10.4	35.7	31.3	2.50	—	—	4.72	9.66	45.6	6.20	19.6	121.4	.876
1963	10.3	36.3	32.5	2.38	—	—	4.68	9.71	45.4	6.15	20.1	123.7	.880
1964	10.6	36.4	32.5	2.39	—	—	4.65	8.99	41.8	5.86	19.6	114.6	.862
1965	11.7	38.5	33.9	2.84	—	—	5.46	9.99	54.5	6.30	18.8	118.6	.849
1966	11.8	37.5	33.5	3.00	12.07	36.2	5.26	8.82	46.4	6.48	18.7	121.6	.849
1967	12.9	36.8	31.6	3.04	11.39	34.6	6.83	9.92	67.7	6.61	18.7	123.3	.831
1968	13.3	37.4	33.3	3.22	11.51	37.1	6.01	8.95	53.8	7.27	19.1	139.1	.829
1969	13.1	37.5	33.4	3.39	11.07	37.5	6.00	9.00	54.0	7.34	18.9	138.7	.818
1970	12.6	37.4	33.2	3.32	11.65	38.7	5.78	9.28	53.7	7.37	19.0	140.2	.828
1971	12.3	37.6	33.4	2.97	11.75	34.9	5.78	9.04	52.3	7.14	19.2	137.2	.834
1972	12.1	37.2	33.4	3.07	11.54	35.4	5.44	8.61	46.8	6.99	19.0	132.8	.803
1973	11.6	37.8	34.1	2.72	11.30	30.8	5.03	8.65	43.5	7.08	19.6	138.4	.797
1974	11.2	37.6	34.2	2.46	11.30	27.8	4.80	7.92	38.0	6.75	19.1	128.5	.784
1975	10.8	38.1	35.0	2.42	11.26	27.2	4.77	7.19	34.3	6.39	19.3	123.3	.733
1976	11.3	38.0	35.1	2.45	11.44	28.0	4.83	6.83	33.0	6.28	18.3	114.7	.722
1977	11.5	38.0	35.0	2.51	11.05	27.8	4.89	7.10	34.6	6.32	18.4	116.1	.711
1978	12.0	38.0	34.9	2.68	10.83	29.0	5.02	7.39	37.1	6.36	18.7	119.1	.665
1979	11.6	37.7	34.8	2.62	10.66	27.9	4.76	7.09	33.8	6.03	18.8	113.7	.637
1980	11.6	38.3	35.4	2.74	10.85	29.7	4.88	7.01	34.2	5.81	19.0	110.2	.651
1981	11.9	38.9	35.9	2.76	10.22	28.2	4.90	7.22	35.4	5.72	18.8	107.8	.636
1982	11.7	*39.8	*36.5	2.78	10.70	29.7	4.79	8.00	38.3	5.37	19.3	103.7	.561
1983	11.0	39.5	35.9	2.74	10.43	28.6	4.94	7.95	39.3	5.29	19.2	101.6	.549
1984	11.1	39.7	36.3	2.61	10.07	26.3	4.94	7.61	37.6	6.05	18.6	112.3	.621
1985	11.0	39.6	36.1	2.59	10.47	27.1	4.89	7.92	38.8	5.88	19.4	114.0	.603
1986	10.7	39.2	35.4	2.59	10.99	28.5	5.01	8.23	41.3	7.55	19.8	149.2	.770
1987	10.7	38.6	34.7	2.64	10.82	28.6	4.95	8.31	41.1	7.78	19.1	149.0	.780
1988	10.4	38.4	34.7	2.47	11.17	28.0	4.78	7.96	38.1	*7.94	19.4	154.2	.778
1989	10.4	38.5	34.3	2.56	10.75	27.6	4.72	8.46	39.9	7.83	19.7	*154.3	.776
1990	10.6	38.6	34.3	2.46	11.40	28.0	4.89	9.33	45.7	7.58	19.6	148.9	.738
1991	10.5	38.4	34.3	2.35	11.30	26.6	5.00	8.74	43.7	6.86	19.4	133.1	.741
1992	11.2	39.0	34.9	2.39	11.00	26.3	5.25	9.04	47.5	6.60	20.1	132.7	.732
1993	10.3	38.8	35.1	2.27	11.00	24.9	4.56	8.28	37.7	6.86	20.0	137.3	.679
1994	10.6	39.2	35.3	2.19	12.10	26.5	4.75	8.64	41.0	6.99	20.0	139.5	.714
1995	10.5	38.7	34.9	2.24	11.67	26.2	4.45	8.98	39.9	7.13	19.5	139.4	.848

*Record. †Records not compiled in 1942-45.

Field Goal Trends (1938-1968)

Year	Made	Year	Made	Year	Made	Atts.	Pct.
1938	47	1951	53	1961	277		
1939	80	1952	83	1962	261		
1940	84	1953	50	1963	314		
1941	59	1954	48	1964	368		
1942-45	*	1955	57	1965	484	1,035	.468
1946	44	1956	53	1966	522	1,125	.464
1947	38	1957	64	1967	555	1,266	.438
1948	53	1958	103	1968	566	1,287	.440
1949	46	1959	†199				
1950	46	1960	224				

*Records not compiled. †Goal posts widened from 18 feet, 6 inches to 23 feet, 4 inches in 1959.

Field Goal Trends (From 1969)

(Includes Field Goal Attempts by Divisions I-AA, II and III Opponents)

Year	Totals Made	Totals Atts.	Totals Pct.	16-39	Pct.	16-49	Pct.	40-49	Pct.	50 Plus	Pct.	60 Plus
1969	669	1,402	.477	538-872	.617	654-1,267	.516	116-395	.294	15-135	.111	0-8
1970	754	1,548	.487	614-990	.620	740-1,380	.536	126-390	.323	14-168	.083	1-9
1971	780	1,625	.480	607-1,022	.594	760-1,466	.518	153-444	.345	20-159	.126	0-11
1972	876	1,828	.479	705-1,150	.613	855-1,641	.521	150-491	.305	21-187	.112	1-12
1973	958	1,920	.499	728-1,139	.639	914-1,670	.547	186-531	.350	44-250	.176	1-21
1974	947	1,905	.497	706-1,096	.644	906-1,655	.547	200-559	.358	41-250	.164	1-17
1975	1,164	2,237	.520	849-1,255	.676	1,088-1,896	.574	239-641	.373	76-341	.223	4-32
1976	1,187	2,330	.509	854-1,301	.656	1,131-1,997	.566	277-696	.398	56-333	.168	3-24
1977	1,238	2,514	.492	882-1,315	.671	1,160-2,088	.556	278-773	.360	78-426	.183	6-40
1978	1,229	2,113	.582	938-1,361	.689	1,193-1,982	.602	255-621	.411	36-131	.275	1-4

Year	Totals Made	Totals Atts.	Totals Pct.	Under 20	Pct.	20-29	Pct.	30-39	Pct.	40-49	Pct.	50-59	Pct.	60 Plus	Pct.
1979	1,241	2,129	.583	34-43	.791	455-601	.757	425-706	.602	286-600	.477	41-173	.237	0-6	.000
1980	1,245	2,128	.585	31-39	.795	408-529	.771	452-696	.649	317-682	.465	37-175	.211	0-7	.000

Year	Totals Made	Atts.	Pct.	Breakdown by Distances Under 20	Pct.	20-29	Pct.	30-39	Pct.	40-49	Pct.	50-59	Pct.	60 Plus	Pct.
1981	1,368	2,254	.607	42-48	.875	471-598	.788	461-731	.631	335-698	.480	58-169	.343	1-10	.100
1982	1,224	1,915	.639	31-34	.912	384-475	.808	415-597	.695	319-604	.528	73-190	.384	2-15	.133
1983	1,329	2,025	.656	34-37	.919	417-508	.821	477-636	.750	329-628	.524	72-201	.358	0-15	.000
1984	1,442	2,112	.683	44-49	.898	450-532	.846	503-681	.739	363-630	.576	80-206	.388	2-14	.143
1985	1,360	2,106	.646	40-47	.851	416-511	.814	478-657	.728	341-647	.527	84-227	.370	1-17	.059
1986	1,326	2,034	.652	45-48	.938	445-525	.848	448-641	.699	340-629	.541	44-182	.242	4-9	.444
1987	1,381	2,058	.671	45-48	.938	484-559	.866	469-638	.735	311-604	.515	72-200	.360	0-9	.000
1988	1,421	2,110	.673	33-35	.943	487-573	.850	495-664	.745	337-610	.552	68-217	.313	1-11	.091
1989#	1,389	2,006	*.692	50-53	.943	497-565	.880	471-655	.719	319-573	.557	52-154	.338	0-6	.000
1990	1,348	2,011	.670	39-42	.929	477-546	.874	454-626	.725	319-625	.510	59-167	.353	0-5	.000
1991$	1,092	1,831	.596	31-32	.969	395-519	.761	366-612	.598	254-531	.478	45-132	.341	1-5	.200
1992	1,288	1,986	.649	32-38	.842	464-569	.815	447-673	.664	294-577	.510	49-126	.389	2-3	.667
1993§	1,182	1,832	.645	23-25	.920	490-599	.818	407-617	.660	224-488	.459	38-98	.388	0-5	.000
1994	1,220	1,877	.650	39-40	.975	458-528	.867	419-626	.669	263-547	.481	40-128	.313	1-8	.125
1995	1,150	1,759	.654	32-32	1.000	468-549	.852	373-587	.635	244-489	.499	31-100	.310	2-2	1.000

**Record. #First year after kicking tee became illegal. $First year after goal-post width narrowed back to 18′6″ from 23′4″. §First year after hash marks narrowed to 60 feet from each sideline.*

Field Goal Trends by Soccer-Style and Conventional Kickers

(Division I-A Kickers Only)

(Pete Gogolak of Cornell was documented as the first soccer-style kicker in college football history. The Hungarian-born kicker played at Cornell from 1961 through 1963. He set a national major-college record of 44 consecutive extra-point conversions and finished 54 of 55 for his career. His younger brother, Charley, also a soccer-styler, kicked at Princeton from 1963 through 1965.)

SOCCER-STYLE

Year	†No.	Totals Made	Atts.	Pct.	Breakdown by Distances 16-39	Pct.	16-49	Pct.	40-49	Pct.	50 Plus	Pct.	60 Plus
1975	70	528	1,012	.522	370-540	.685	479-816	.587	109-276	.395	49-196	.250	1-17
1976	84	517	1,019	.507	350-517	.677	477-831	.574	127-314	.404	40-188	.213	3-16
1977	96	665	1,317	.505	450-649	.693	615-1,047	.587	165-398	.415	50-270	.185	2-27
1978	98	731	1,244	.588	540-768	.703	703-1,148	.612	163-380	.429	28-96	.292	1-3

Year	†No.	Totals Made	Atts.	Pct.	Breakdown by Distances Under 20	20-29	30-39	40-49	50-59	60 Plus
1979	116	839	1,413	.594	23-28	288-380	282-455	214-419	32-126	0-5
1980	121	988	1,657	.596	26-32	327-416	342-522	261-540	32-147	0-5
1981	138	1,108	1,787	.620	32-36	377-476	376-576	279-551	43-142	1-6
1982	105	1,026	1,548	.663	26-27	317-375	346-482	273-495	62-156	2-13
1983	110	1,139	1,724	.661	29-31	345-416	403-541	294-543	68-179	0-14
1984	127	1,316	1,898	*.694	43-47	414-480	438-589	341-572	78-197	2-13
1985	133	1,198	1,838	.652	35-41	369-452	415-578	306-560	72-191	1-16
1986	128	1,201	1,829	.657	37-40	398-467	410-575	313-576	39-162	4-9
1987	122	1,275	1,892	.674	40-43	458-523	424-574	290-566	63-177	0-9
1988	140	1,317	1,947	.676	31-33	445-521	468-630	311-562	61-201	1-11
1989	138	1,313	1,897	.692	49-52	462-526	441-612	310-551	51-150	0-6
1990	135	1,282	1,890	.678	36-38	450-515	432-589	308-590	56-154	0-4
1991	132	1,048	1,763	.594	30-31	381-500	349-589	243-512	44-130	1-1
1992	135	1,244	1,926	.646	31-37	447-554	429-647	288-561	47-124	2-3
1993	132	1,153	1,776	.649	23-25	475-578	398-600	219-475	38-93	0-5
1994	138	1,203	1,856	.648	38-39	452-522	410-617	263-543	39-127	1-8
1995	148	1,150	1,759	.654	32-32	468-549	373-587	244-489	31-100	2-2

CONVENTIONAL

Year	†No.	Totals Made	Atts.	Pct.	Breakdown by Distances 16-39	Pct.	16-49	Pct.	40-49	Pct.	50 Plus	Pct.	60 Plus
1975	116	564	1,085	.520	427-640	.667	541-959	.564	114-319	.357	23-126	.183	3-13
1976	101	608	1,192	.510	460-720	.639	594-1,065	.558	134-345	.388	14-127	.110	0-7
1977	98	513	1,054	.487	384-586	.655	487-916	.532	103-330	.312	26-138	.188	4-14
1978	86	440	761	.578	352-516	.682	434-729	.595	82-213	.385	6-32	.188	0-0

Year	†No.	Totals Made	Atts.	Pct.	Breakdown by Distances Under 20	20-29	30-39	40-49	50-59	60 Plus
1979	70	333	585	.569	10-14	140-185	111-198	63-150	9-37	0-1
1980	62	258	471	.548	5-7	81-113	110-174	56-142	6-33	0-2
1981	50	195	367	.531	8-9	70-97	69-126	41-112	7-22	0-1
1982	25	103	195	.528	3-4	36-50	34-62	25-59	5-18	0-2
1983	23	112	181	.619	4-5	40-55	46-58	22-50	0-12	0-1
1984	10	44	76	.579	0-1	17-26	20-33	7-15	0-1	0-0
1985	12	81	138	.587	3-4	22-29	29-40	19-44	8-20	0-1
1986	8	58	89	.652	4-4	21-28	17-27	14-24	2-6	0-0
1987	4	35	50	.700	4-4	10-14	14-16	6-9	1-7	0-0
1988	5	26	40	.650	0-0	17-21	5-7	4-10	0-2	0-0
1989	2	37	47	.787	1-1	19-20	12-16	5-9	0-1	0-0
1990	2	23	38	.605	1-1	8-10	8-9	4-13	2-5	0-0
1991	2	16	24	.667	0-0	5-9	6-7	5-7	0-1	0-0
1992	1	12	18	.667	0-0	5-6	6-8	1-4	0-0	0-0
1993	1	6	11	.545	0-0	4-5	2-3	0-3	0-0	0-0
1994	1	17	21	*.810	1-1	6-6	9-9	0-4	1-1	0-0
1995	0	0	0	.000	0-0	0-0	0-0	0-0	0-0	0-0

**Record. †Number of kickers attempting at least one field goal.*

Average Yardage of Field Goals

(Division I-A Kickers Only)

	Soccer-Style			Conventional			Nation		
Year	**Made**	**Missed**	**Total**	**Made**	**Missed**	**Total**	**Made**	**Missed**	**Total**
1975	35.1	43.2	39.0	33.1	41.3	37.0	34.1	42.2	37.9
1976	35.0	43.1	39.0	33.2	40.7	36.9	34.0	41.8	37.9
1977	34.7	44.3	39.5	33.3	41.9	37.7	34.1	43.2	38.7
1978	34.0	39.9	36.4	31.9	38.3	34.6	33.2	39.3	35.7
1979	33.7	39.9	36.2	31.9	38.0	34.5	33.2	39.3	35.7
1980	34.0	40.7	36.7	33.4	39.6	36.2	33.8	40.4	36.6
1981	33.9	40.1	36.2	33.2	38.6	35.7	33.8	39.8	36.1
1982	34.8	41.8	37.2	34.0	39.8	36.7	34.7	41.5	37.1
1983	34.7	42.1	37.2	32.3	40.5	35.5	34.5	41.9	37.0
1984	34.4	41.8	36.7	32.3	34.9	33.4	34.3	41.5	36.5
1985	34.5	41.3	36.8	35.4	41.7	38.0	34.5	41.3	36.9
1986	33.9	41.6	36.6	32.5	38.6	34.7	33.9	41.4	36.5
1987	33.5	41.8	36.2	32.3	41.4	35.1	33.5	41.8	36.2
1988	33.9	41.7	36.4	30.0	37.6	32.7	32.0	39.3	34.4
1989	33.5	41.2	35.9	30.5	39.6	32.4	33.4	41.2	35.8
1990	33.4	41.3	36.0	33.4	42.0	36.7	33.4	41.3	36.0
1991	33.2	40.7	35.8	28.6	31.9	40.7	35.9	40.4	36.1
1992	34.1	41.2	36.7	30.1	37.8	32.7	37.2	41.3	37.8
1993	32.4	38.9	34.7	26.8	38.0	31.9	32.3	38.9	34.6
1994	32.9	40.6	35.6	31.4	45.5	34.0	32.9	40.7	35.6
1995	32.4	40.1	35.0	—	—	—	32.4	40.1	35.0

Division I-A Extra-Point Trends

(From Start of Two-Point Attempts)

		Percent Total Tries		Kick Attempts			Two-Point Attempts		
Year	**Games**	**Kick**	**2-Pt.**	**Atts.**	**Made**	**Pct.**	**Atts.**	**Made**	**Pct.**
1958	578	#.486	*.514	1,295	889	.686	*1,371	*613	.447
1959	578	.598	.402	1,552	1,170	.754	1,045	421	.403
1960	596	.701	.299	1,849	1,448	.783	790	345	.437
1961	574	.723	.277	1,842	1,473	.800	706	312	.442
1962	602	.724	.276	1,987	1,549	.780	757	341	.450
1963	605	.776	.224	2,057	1,659	.807	595	256	.430
1964	613	.814	.186	2,053	1,704	.830	469	189	.403
1965	619	.881	.119	2,460	2,083	.847	331	134	.405
1966	626	.861	.139	2,530	2,167	.857	410	165	.402
1967	611	.869	.131	2,629	2,252	.857	397	160	.403
1968	615	.871	.129	3,090	2,629	.851	456	181	.397
1969	621	.880	.120	3,168	2,781	.878	432	170	.394
1970	667	.862	.138	3,255	2,875	.883	522	246	*.471
1971	726	.889	.111	3,466	3,081	.889	433	173	.400
1972	720	.872	.128	3,390	3,018	.890	497	219	.441
1973	741	.893	.107	3,637	3,258	.896	435	180	.414
1974	749	.885	.115	3,490	3,146	.901	455	211	.464
1975	785	.891	.109	3,598	3,266	.908	440	171	.389
1976	796	.877	.123	3,579	3,241	.906	502	203	.404
1977	849	.891	.109	*4,041	*3,668	.908	495	209	.422
1978	816	.884	.116	3,808	3,490	.916	498	208	.418
1979	811	.897	.103	3,702	3,418	.923	424	176	.415
1980	810	.895	.105	3,785	3,480	.919	442	170	.384
1981	788	.901	.099	3,655	3,387	.927	403	172	.427
1982	599	.901	.099	2,920	2,761	.946	320	120	.375
1983	631	.896	.104	3,080	2,886	.937	356	151	.424
1984	626	.889	.111	2,962	2,789	.942	370	173	.468
1985	623	.899	.101	3,068	2,911	.949	345	121	.351
1986	619	.905	.095	3,132	2,999	.958	330	131	.397
1987	615	.892	.108	3,094	2,935	.949	375	163	.435
1988	616	.899	.101	3,215	3,074	.956	363	156	.430
1989	614	.888	.112	3,233	3,090	.956	409	179	.438
1990	623	.911	.089	3,429	3,291	*.960	335	138	.412
1991	617	.906	.094	3,279	3,016	.920	342	128	.374
1992	619	.899	.101	3,156	2,967	.940	353	159	.450
1993	613	*.912	#.088	3,455	3,251	.941	333	143	.429
1994	617	.897	.103	3,433	3,207	.934	395	163	.413
1995	622	.902	.098	3,594	3,354	.933	389	173	.445

**Record high. #Record low.*

Division I-A Extra-Point Kick Attempts (1938-1957)

Year	Pct. Made	Year	Pct. Made	Year	Pct. Made	Year	Pct. Made
1938	.608	1946	.657	1951	.711	1956	.666
1939	.625	1947	.657	1952	.744	1957	.653
1940	.607	1948	.708	1953	.650		
1941	.638	1949	.738	1954	.656		
1942-45	*	1950	.713	1955	.669		

**Not compiled.*

All-Divisions Defensive Extra-Point Trends

In 1988, the NCAA Football Rules Committee adopted a rule that gave defensive teams an opportunity to score two points on point-after-touchdown tries. The two points were awarded for returning an interception or advancing a blocked kick for a touchdown on point-after tries.

DIVISION I-A

Year	Games	Kick Ret./TDs	Int. Ret./TDs	Total Ret./TDs
1988	616	8/2	6/0	14/2
1989	614	12/3	9/2	21/5
1990	623	9/3	5/2	14/5
1991	617	9/3	10/3	19/6
1992	619	8/5	1/0	9/5
1993	613	5/2	6/1	11/3
1994	617	4/0	8/3	12/3
1995	622	12/5	5/3	17/8

DIVISION I-AA

Year	Games	Kick Ret./TDs	Int. Ret./TDs	Total Ret./TDs
1988	553	4/1	7/1	11/2
1989	554	11/4	4/2	15/6
1990	548	7/3	4/2	11/5
1991	560	12/3	9/2	21/5
1992	553	9/5	8/5	17/10
1993	725	11/5	19/3	30/8
1994	733	4/1	5/1	9/2
1995	736	9/2	9/4	18/6

DIVISION II

Year	Games	Kick Ret./TDs	Int. Ret./TDs	Total Ret./TDs
1988	580	19/4	9/0	28/4
1989	590	18/8	11/3	29/11
1990	596	9/3	2/2	11/5
1991	575	10/3	8/2	18/5
1992	580	9/4	7/3	16/7
1993	694	16/6	9/5	25/11
1994	663	15/8	6/4	21/12
1995	681	16/3	14/2	30/5

DIVISION III

Year	Games	Kick Ret./TDs	Int. Ret./TDs	Total Ret./TDs
1988	994	29/8	25/3	54/11
1989	1,012	16/5	13/4	29/9
1990	1,020	25/10	16/6	41/16
1991	1,006	18/7	14/5	32/12
1992	1,028	14/6	17/7	31/13
1993	997	17/5	18/6	35/11
1994	1,002	25/8	17/7	42/15
1995	948	37/12	15/7	52/19

ALL DIVISIONS—NATIONWIDE

Year	Games	Kick Ret./TDs	Int. Ret./TDs	Total Ret./TDs
1988	2,743	60/15	47/4	107/19
1989	2,770	57/20	37/11	94/31
1990	2,787	50/19	27/12	77/31
1991	2,758	49/16	41/12	90/28
1992	2,780	40/20	33/15	73/35
1993	3,029	49/18	52/15	101/33
1994	3,015	48/17	36/15	84/32
1995	2,987	74/22	43/16	117/38

All-Divisions Fumble-Recovery Returns

In 1990, the NCAA Football Rules Committee adopted a rule that gave the defense an opportunity to advance fumbles that occur beyond the neutral zone (or line of scrimmage). In 1992, the rule was changed to allow defenses to advance any fumble regardless of position behind or beyond the line of scrimmage. Here are the number of fumble recoveries by division that were advanced, and the number that resulted in a score.

DIVISION I-A

Year	Games	Fumble Rec./TDs
1990	623	51/17
1991	617	60/16
1992	619	126/34
1993	613	117/24
1994	617	131/43
1995	622	148/49

DIVISION I-AA

Year	Games	Fumble Rec./TDs
1990	548	34/16
1991	560	42/13
1992	553	96/42
1993	725	86/25
1994	733	99/23
1995	736	164/58

DIVISION II

Year	Games	Fumble Rec./TDs
1990	596	46/25
1991	575	43/19
1992	580	77/39
1993	694	110/41
1994	663	92/38
1995	681	108/47

DIVISION III

Year	Games	Fumble Rec./TDs
1990	1,020	55/19
1991	1,006	62/22
1992	1,028	94/47
1993	997	88/33
1994	1,002	108/54
1995	948	117/60

ALL DIVISIONS—NATIONWIDE

Year	Games	Fumble Rec./TDs
1990	2,787	186/77
1991	2,758	207/70
1992	2,780	393/162
1993	3,029	401/123
1994	3,015	430/158
1995	2,987	537/214

Major-College Tie Games

The record for most tie games in a single week is six—on October 27, 1962; September 28, 1963; and October 9, 1982.

Year	No.	Games	Pct.	Scoreless
1954	15	551	2.72	2
1955	22	536	4.10	1
1956	28	558	5.02	2
1957	24	570	4.21	4
1958*	19	578	3.29	2
1959	13	578	2.25	4
1960	23	596	3.86	4
1961	11	574	1.92	1
1962	20	602	3.32	2
1963	25	605	4.13	4
1964	19	613	3.10	2
1965	19	619	3.07	4
1966	13	626	2.08	0
1967	14	611	2.29	1
1968	17	615	2.76	1
1969	9	621	1.45	0
1970	7	667	1.05	0
1971	12	726	1.65	1
1972	14	720	1.94	1
1973	18	741	2.43	2
1974	18	749	2.40	0
1975	16	785	2.04	0
1976	13	796	1.63	1
1977	16	849	1.88	1
1978	16	816	1.96	1
1979	17	811	2.10	1
1980	12	810	1.48	0
1981	17	788	2.16	0
1982	14	599	2.34	0
1983	13	631	2.06	†1
1984	15	626	2.40	0
1985	13	623	2.09	0
1986	10	619	1.62	0
1987	13	615	2.11	0
1988	12	616	1.95	0
1989	15	614	2.44	0
1990	15	623	2.41	0
1991	14	617	2.27	0
1992	13	619	2.10	0
1993	11	613	1.79	0
1994	13	617	2.11	0
1995	9	622	1.45	0

**First year of two-point conversion rule. †Last scoreless tie game: Nov. 19, 1983, Oregon vs. Oregon St.*

Highest-Scoring Tie Games

(Home Team Listed First; Both Teams Classified Major-College or Division I-A at Time)

Score	Date	Opponents
52-52	11-16-91	San Diego St.-Brigham Young
48-48	9-8-79	San Jose St.-Utah St.
43-43	11-12-88	Duke-North Caro. St.
41-41	9-10-94	Northwestern-Stanford
41-41	9-23-89	San Diego St.-Cal St. Fullerton
40-40	11-8-75	Idaho-Weber St.
39-39	11-7-82	Texas Tech-Texas Christian
37-37	9-23-67	*Alabama-Florida St.
36-36	9-30-72	Georgia Tech-Rice
35-35	9-23-95	Michigan St.-Purdue
35-35	11-16-91	San Jose St.-Hawaii
35-35	12-9-89	Hawaii-Air Force
35-35	9-23-89	Colorado St.-Eastern Mich.
35-35	10-7-78	Ohio St.-Southern Methodist
35-35	10-19-74	Idaho-Montana
35-35	10-9-71	New Mexico-New Mexico St.
35-35	9-27-69	Minnesota-Ohio
35-35	9-21-68	Washington-Rice
35-35	11-18-67	Navy-Vanderbilt
35-35	12-11-48	†Pacific (Cal.)—Hardin-Simmons
34-34	10-6-90	Iowa St.-Kansas
33-33	10-1-83	California-Arizona
33-33	9-24-49	Texas Christian-Oklahoma St.
33-33	10-31-31	Yale-Dartmouth

**At Birmingham. †Grape Bowl, Lodi, Calif.*

Home-Field Records

(Includes Host Teams at Neutral-Site Games)

Year	Games	Home Team Won	Lost	Tied	Pct.
1966	626	365	248	13	.594
1967	611	333	264	14	.557
1968	615	348	250	17	.580
1969	621	366	246	9	.596
1970	667	399	261	7	.603
1971	726	416	298	12	.581
1972	720	441	265	14	.622
1973	741	439	284	18	.605
1974	749	457	274	18	.622
1975	785	434	335	16	.563
1976	796	463	320	13	.590
1977	849	501	332	16	.600
1978	816	482	318	16	.601
1979	811	460	334	17	.578
1980	809	471	327	12	.589
1981	788	457	314	17	.591
1982	599	368	217	14	.626
1983	631	364	254	13	.587
1984	626	371	240	15	.605
1985	623	371	239	13	.606
1986	619	363	246	10	.595
1987	615	387	215	13	*.640
1988	616	370	234	12	.610
1989	614	365	234	15	.607
1990	623	373	235	15	.611
1991	617	362	241	14	.598
1992	619	388	218	13	.637
1993	613	375	227	11	.621
1994	617	357	247	13	.589
1995	622	354	259	9	.576

** Record.*

College Football Rules Changes

The Ball

1869—Round, rubber Association ball.
1875—Egg-shaped, leather-covered Rugby ball.
1896—Prolate spheroid, without specific measurements.
1912—28-28 1/2 inches around ends, 22 1/2-23 inches around middle, weight 14-15 ounces.
1929—28-28 1/2 inches around ends, 22-22 1/2 inches around middle, weight 14-15 ounces.
1934—28-28 1/2 inches around ends, 21 1/4-21 1/2 inches around middle, weight 14-15 ounces.
1941—For night games, a white ball or other colored ball with two black stripes around the ball may be used at the discretion of the referee.
1952—Ball may be inclined no more than 45 degrees by snapper.
1956—Rubber-covered ball permitted.
1973—Teams allowed to use ball of their choice while in possession.
1978—Ball may not be altered, and new or nearly new balls added.
1982—10 7/8 to 11 7/16 inches long, 20 3/4 to 21 1/4 inches around middle, and 27 3/4 to 28 1/2 inches long-axis circumference.
1993—Rubber or composition ball ruled illegal.

The Field

1869—120 yards by 75 yards; uprights 24 feet apart.
1871—166 2/3 yards by 100 yards.
1872—133 1/3 yards by 83 1/3 yards.
1873—Uprights 25 feet apart.
1876—110 yards by 53 1/3 yards. Uprights 18 1/2 feet apart; crossbar 10 feet high.
1882—Field marked with transverse lines every five yards. This distance to be gained in three downs to retain possession.
1912—Field 120 yards by 53 1/3 yards, including two 10-yard end zones.
1927—Goal posts moved back 10 yards, to end line.
1957—Team area at 35-yard lines.
1959—Uprights widened to 23 feet, 4 inches apart.
1966—Pylons placed in corners of end zone and at goal lines mandatory in 1974.
1991—Uprights moved back to 18 feet, 6 inches apart.
1993—Hash marks moved six feet, eight inches closer to center of field to 60 feet from each sideline (40 feet apart).

Scoring

1869—All goals count 1 each.
1883—Safety 1, touchdown 4, goal after TD 4, goal from field 5.
1884—Safety 2, touchdown 4, goal from field 5.
1897—Touchdown 6, field goal 5, touchdown failing goal 5, safety 2.
1902—Teams change goals after every try at goal following a touchdown, after every goal from the field and also at the beginning of the half.
1904—Goal from field 4.
1909—Goal from field 3.
1912—Touchdown 6.
1921—Ball put in play at 30-yard line after a safety, 20-yard line after a touchback.
1922—Try-for-point by scrimmage play from 5-yard line.
1924—Try-for-point by scrimmage play from 3-yard line.
1927—Goal posts placed on end lines.
1929—Try-for-point by scrimmage play from 2-yard line.
1958—One-point & two-point conversion (from 3-yard line). One-point safety added.
1974—Ball must go between the uprights for a successful field goal, over the uprights previously scored.
1976—Forfeit score changed from 1-0 to score at time of forfeit if the offended team is ahead at time of forfeit.
1984—Try may be eliminated at end of game if both captains agree.
1995—Try at end of game mandatory unless team behind in score leaves field.

Players

1869—Each team consisted of 25 players.
1873—Each team consisted of 20 players.
1876—Each team consisted of 15 players.
1880—Each team consisted of 11 players.
1895—Only one man in motion forward before the snap. No more than three players behind the line. One player permitted in motion toward own goal line.
1910—Seven players required on line.
1911—Illegal to conceal ball beneath a player's clothing.
1947—All players urged to be numbered in a uniform manner. Ends to wear numbers in the 80s; tackles, 70s; guards, 60s; centers, 50s; and backs, 10-49.
1966—Mandatory numbering of five players on the line 50-79.
1970—All players numbered 1-99.

Equipment

1894—No one wearing projecting nails or iron plates on his shoes, or any metal substance upon his person, is allowed to play. No greasy or sticky substance shall be used on the person of players.
1903—If head protectors are worn, there can be no sole leather or other hard or unyielding substances in their construction. Leather cleats on shoes allowed.
1908—First documented jersey numbers used by Washington & Jefferson.
1915—Numbering of players recommended.
1927—Rubber cleats allowed, but under no conditions are cleats to be dangerously sharp.
1930—No player shall wear equipment that endangers players. The committee forbids the use of head protectors or jerseys that are so similar in color to the ball that they give the wearer an unfair and unsportsmanlike advantage over the opponent. Stripes may be used to break up the solid colors.
1933—Head protectors or helmets recommended to be worn by all players.
1937—All players must wear minimum 6-inch Arabic numerals on the front and minimum 8-inch Arabic numerals on the back of jerseys.
1939—All players must wear helmets.
1946—All players must wear minimum 8-inch Arabic numerals on front (changed from 6 inches) and minimum 10-inch Arabic numerals on back of jerseys (changed from 8 inches), of a single color which must be in sharp contrast with the color of the jerseys.
1948—One-inch kicking tees permitted.
1951—Any circular or ring cleat prohibited unless it has rounded edges and a wall at least 3/16-inch thick. Any face mask—unless it is made of nonbreakable, molded plastic with rounded edges or of rubber-covered wire—prohibited.
1962—All players recommended to wear properly fitted mouth protectors.
1965—Two-inch kicking tees permitted.
1966—Players prohibited from wearing equipment with electronic, mechanical or other signal devices for the purpose of communicating with any source.
1968—Metal face masks having surfaces with material as resilient as rubber are allowed.
1970—Shoe cleats more than one-half inch in length (changed from three-quarters inch) prohibited.
1972—All players must wear mouth protectors, beginning with 1973 season.
1973—All players shall wear head protectors with a secured chin strap.
1974—All players shall wear shoulder pads.
1976—All players shall wear hip pads and thigh guards.
1979—Beginning in 1981, one team shall wear white jerseys.
1982—Tearaway jersey eliminated by charging a timeout.
1983—Mandatory white jersey for visiting teams.
1986—Therapeutic or preventive knee braces must be worn under the pants.
1989—Kicking tees eliminated for field goals and extra-point attempts.
1991—Rib and back pad covering mandatory.
1994—Standards established to limit glove stickiness. Jerseys that extend below the top of the pants must be tucked into the pants.
1995—Home team may wear white jerseys if both teams agree before the season.
1996—Cleats limited to one-half inch in length (see 1970). Violators disqualified for remainder of game and entire next game. Rule a dead ball when a ball carrier's helmet comes completely off, with the ball belonging to runner's team at that spot. Jerseys must extend to top of pants and must be tucked in if longer.

Substitutions

1876—Fifteen players to a team and few if any substitutions.
1882—Replacements for disqualified or injured players.
1897—Substitutions may enter the game any time at discretion of captains.
1922—Players withdrawn during the first half may be returned during the second half. A player withdrawn in the second half may not return.
1941—A player may substitute any time but may not be withdrawn or the outgoing player returned to the game until one play had intervened. Platoon football made possible.
1948—Unlimited substitution on change of team possession.
1953—Two-platoon abolished and players allowed to enter the game only once in each quarter.
1954-64—Changes each year toward more liberalize substitution rule and platoon football.
1965—Platoon football returns. Unlimited substitutions between periods, after a score or try.
1974—Substitutes must be in for one play and replaced players out for one play.
1993—Players who are bleeding or whose uniforms are saturated with blood must come out of the game until their return has been approved by medical personnel.

Passing Game

1906—One forward pass legalized behind the line if made five yards right or left of center. Ball went to opponents if it failed to touch a player of either side before touching the ground. Either team could recover a pass touched by an opponent. One pass each scrimmage down.
1910—Pass interference does not apply 20 yards beyond the line of scrimmage. Passer must be five yards behind the line of scrimmage. One forward pass permitted during each down.
1914—Roughing the passer added.
1923—Handing the ball forward is an illegal forward pass and receivers going out of bounds and returning prohibited.
1934—Three changes encourage use of pass. (1) First forward pass in series of downs can be incomplete in the end zone without loss of ball except on fourth down. (2) Circumference of ball reduced, making it easier to throw. (3) Five-yard penalty for more than one incomplete pass in same series of downs eliminated.
1941—Fourth-down forward pass incomplete in end zone no longer a touchback. Ball goes to opponent at spot where put in play.
1945—Forward pass may be thrown from anywhere behind the line, encouraging use of modern T formation.
1966—Compulsory numbering system makes only players numbered other than 50-79 eligible forward-pass receivers.
1976—Offensive blocking changed to provide half extension of arms to assist pass blocking.
1980—Retreat blocking added with full arm extension to assist pass blocking, and illegal use of hands reduced to five yards.
1982—Pass interference only on a catchable forward pass. Forward pass intentionally grounded to conserve time permitted.
1983—First down added to roughing the passer.
1985—Retreat block deleted and open hands and extended arms permitted anywhere on the field.
1990—Pass thrown immediately to the ground to conserve time legal.
1994—Ball must be catchable for offensive player to be charged with pass interference.
1996—Principle of "reasonable opportunity to catch the pass" applied to intentional grounding situations.

General Changes

1876—Holding and carrying the ball permitted.
1880—Eleven players on a side and a scrimmage line established.
1882—Downs and yards to gain enter the rules.
1883—Scoring system established.
1906—Forward passes permitted. Ten yards for first down.
1920—Clipping defined.
1922—Try-for-point introduced. Ball brought out five yards from goal line for scrimmage, allowing try for extra point by place kick, drop kick, run or forward pass.
1925—Kickoff returned to 40-yard line. Clipping made a violation, with penalty of 25 yards.
1927—One-second pause imposed on shift. Thirty seconds allowed for putting ball in play. Huddle limited to 15 seconds. To encourage use of lateral pass, missed backward pass other than from center declared dead ball when it hits the ground and cannot be recovered by opponents.
1929—All fumbles ruled dead at point of recovery.
1932—Most far-reaching changes in nearly a quarter of a century set up safeguards against hazards of game. (1) Ball declared dead when any portion of player in possession, except his hands or feet, touches ground. (2) Use of flying block and flying tackle barred under penalty of five yards. (3) Players on defense forbidden to strike opponents on head, neck or face. (4) Hard and dangerous equipment must be covered with padding.
1941—Legal to hand ball forward behind the neutral zone.

1949—Blockers required to keep hands against their chest.
1951—Fair catch restored.
1952—Penalty for striking with forearm, elbow or locked hands, or for flagrantly rough play or unsportsmanlike conduct, changed from 15 yards to mandatory suspension.
1957—Penalty for grabbing face mask.
1959—Distance penalties limited to one-half distance to offending team's goal line.
1967—Coaching from sideline permitted.
1971—Crack-back block (blocking below waist) illegal.
1972—Freshman eligibility restored.
1977—Clock started on snap after a penalty.
1978—Unsuccessful field goal returned to the previous spot.
1983—Offensive encroachment changed...no offensive player permitted in or beyond the neutral zone after snapper touches ball.
1985—One or both feet on ground required for blocking below waist foul.
1986—Kickoff from the 35-yard line.
1988—Defensive team allowed to score two points on return of blocked extra-point kick attempt or interception of extra-point pass attempt.
1990—Defense allowed to advance fumbles that occur beyond the neutral zone.
1991—Width between goal-post uprights reduced from 23 feet, 4 inches to 18 feet, 6 inches. Kickoffs out of bounds allow receiving team to elect to take ball 30 yards beyond yard line where kickoff occurred.
1992—Defense allowed to advance fumbles regardless of where they occur. Changes ruling of 1990 fumble advancement.
1993—Guard-around or "fumblerooski" play ruled illegal.
1994—Players involved in a fight after half time disqualified for first half of next game; substitutes and coaches who participate in a fight in their team area or leave the team area to join a fight disqualified for entire next game; squad members and coaches involved in a fight during half time disqualified for first half of next game.
1995—Defense penalized five yards for entering neutral zone before snap and causing offensive player to react immediately. Players prohibited from removing helmets on the field. Players disqualified after second unsportsmanlike-conduct foul in one game. Fight suspensions allowed to carry over to next season.
1996—NCAA tiebreaker system to be used in all games tied after four periods.

Division I-AA Records

Individual Records

Total Offense

(Rushing Plus Passing)

MOST PLAYS

Quarter

31—Mike Hanlin, Morehead St. vs. Austin Peay, Oct. 10, 1981 (4th)

Half

48—John Witkowski, Columbia vs. Dartmouth, Nov. 6, 1982 (2nd)

Game

89—Thomas Leonard, Mississippi Val. vs. Texas Southern, Oct. 25, 1986 (440 yards)

Season

649—Steve McNair, Alcorn St., 1994 (5,799 yards)

Career

2,055—Steve McNair, Alcorn St., 1991-94 (16,823 yards)

MOST PLAYS PER GAME

Season

59.0—Steve McNair, Alcorn St., 1994 (649 in 11)

Career

49.5—Tom Proudian, Iona, 1993-95 (1,337 in 27)

MOST PLAYS BY A FRESHMAN

Game

79—Adrian Breen, Morehead St. vs. Austin Peay, Oct. 8, 1983 (206 yards)

Season

462—Greg Wyatt, Northern Ariz., 1986 (2,695 yards)

Per-game record—44.7, Jason Whitmer, Idaho St., 1987 (402 in 9)

MOST YARDS GAINED

Quarter

278—Willie Totten, Mississippi Val. vs. Kentucky St., Sept. 1, 1984 (2nd)

Half

404—Todd Hammel, Stephen F. Austin vs. Northeast La., Nov. 11, 1989 (1st)

Game

649—Steve McNair, Alcorn St. vs. Samford, Oct. 29, 1994 (587 passing, 62 rushing)

Season

5,799—Steve McNair, Alcorn St., 1994 (4,863 passing, 936 rushing)

2 Yrs

9,629—Steve McNair, Alcorn St., 1993-94 (8,060 passing, 1,569 rushing)

3 Yrs

13,686—Steve McNair, Alcorn St., 1992-94 (11,601 passing, 2,085 rushing)

Career

(4 yrs.) 16,823—Steve McNair, Alcorn St., 1991-94 (14,496 passing, 2,327 rushing)

MOST YARDS GAINED PER GAME

Season

527.2—Steve McNair, Alcorn St., 1994 (5,799 in 11)

Career

400.5—Steve McNair, Alcorn St., 1991-94 (16,823 in 42)

MOST SEASONS GAINING 3,000 YARDS OR MORE

4—Steve McNair, Alcorn St., 1991-94

MOST YARDS GAINED BY A FRESHMAN

Game

536—Brad Otton, Weber St. vs. Northern Ariz., Nov. 6, 1993 (48 plays)

Season

3,137—Steve McNair, Alcorn St., 1991

Also holds per-game record at 313.7

MOST YARDS GAINED IN TWO, THREE AND FOUR CONSECUTIVE GAMES

2 Games

1,280—Steve McNair, Alcorn St., 1994 (633 vs. Grambling, Sept. 3; 647 vs. Tenn.-Chatt., Sept. 10)

3 Games

1,859—Steve McNair, Alcorn St., 1994 (649 vs. Samford, Oct. 29; 624 vs. Mississippi Val., Nov. 5; 586 vs. Troy St., Nov. 12)

4 Games

2,423—Steve McNair, Alcorn St., 1994 (649 vs. Samford, Oct. 29; 624 vs. Mississippi Val., Nov. 5; 586 vs. Troy St., Nov. 12; 564 vs. Jackson St., Nov. 19)

MOST GAMES GAINING 300 YARDS OR MORE

Season

11—Steve McNair, Alcorn St., 1994

Career

32—Steve McNair, Alcorn St., 1991-94

MOST CONSECUTIVE GAMES GAINING 300 YARDS OR MORE

Season

11—Steve McNair, Alcorn St., 1994

Career

13—Steve McNair, Alcorn St., 1992-93; Willie Totten, Mississippi Val., 1984-85; Neil Lomax, Portland St., 1979-80

MOST GAMES GAINING 400 YARDS OR MORE

Season

9—Steve McNair, Alcorn St., 1994

Career

15—Steve McNair, Alcorn St., 1991-94

MOST CONSECUTIVE GAMES GAINING 400 YARDS OR MORE

Season

5—Steve McNair, Alcorn St., 1994; Willie Totten, Mississippi Val., 1984

MOST GAMES GAINING 500 YARDS OR MORE

Season

6—Steve McNair, Alcorn St., 1994

Career

9—Steve McNair, Alcorn St., 1991-94

MOST YARDS GAINED AGAINST ONE OPPONENT

Career

1,772—Steve McNair, Alcorn St. vs. Jackson St., 1991-94

Also holds per-game record at 443.0 (1,772 in 4)

GAINING 1,000 YARDS RUSHING AND 1,000 YARDS PASSING

Season

Alcede Surtain (QB), Alabama St., 1995 (1,024 rushing, 1,224 passing); Tracy Ham (QB), Ga. Southern, 1986 (1,048 rushing, 1,772 passing)

GAINING 2,000 YARDS RUSHING AND 4,000 YARDS PASSING

Career

Steve McNair (QB), Alcorn St., 1991-94 (2,327 rushing, 14,496 passing); Bill Vergantino (QB), Delaware, 1989-92 (2,287 rushing, 6,177 passing); Tracy Ham (QB), Ga. Southern, 1984-86 (2,506 rushing, 4,871 passing)

HIGHEST AVERAGE GAIN PER PLAY

Game

(Min. 39-49 plays) 12.4—John Whitcomb, Ala.-Birmingham vs. Prairie View, Nov. 19, 1994 (43 for 533)

(Min. 50-59 plays) 11.4—Steve McNair, Alcorn St. vs. Tenn.-Chatt., Sept. 10, 1994 (57 for 647)

(Min. 60 plays) 9.7—Steve McNair, Alcorn St. vs. Grambling, Sept. 3, 1994 (65 for 633)

Season

(Min. 2,500-3,299 yards) 9.6—Frank Baur, Lafayette, 1988 (285 for 2,727)

(Min. 3,300 yards) 8.9—Steve McNair, Alcorn St., 1994 (649 for 5,799)

Career

(Min. 4,000-4,999 yards) 7.5—Reggie Lewis, Sam Houston St., 1986-87 (653 for 4,929)

(Min. 5,000 yards) 8.2—Steve McNair, Alcorn St., 1991-94 (2,055 for 16,823)

MOST TOUCHDOWNS RESPONSIBLE FOR (TDs Scored and Passed For)

Game

9—Willie Totten, Mississippi Val. vs. Prairie View, Oct. 27, 1984 (passed for 8, scored 1) & vs. Kentucky St., Sept. 1, 1984 (passed for 9); Neil Lomax, Portland St. vs. Delaware St., Nov. 8, 1980 (passed for 8, scored 1)

Season

61—Willie Totten, Mississippi Val., 1984 (passed for 56, scored 5)

Also holds per-game record at 6.1 (61 in 10)

Career

157—Willie Totten, Mississippi Val., 1982-85 (passed for 139, scored 18)

Also holds per-game record at 3.9 (157 in 40)

MOST POINTS RESPONSIBLE FOR (Points Scored and Passed For)

Game

56—Willie Totten, Mississippi Val. vs. Kentucky St., Sept. 1, 1984 (passed for 9 TDs and 1 two-point conversion)

Season

368—Willie Totten, Mississippi Val., 1984 (passed for 56 TDs, scored 5 TDs and passed for 1 two-point conversion)

Also holds per-game record at 36.8 (368 in 10)

Career

946—Willie Totten, Mississippi Val., 1982-85 (passed for 139 TDs, scored 18 TDs and passed for 1 two-point conversion)

Also holds per-game record at 23.7 (946 in 40)

Rushing

MOST RUSHES

Quarter

20—Arnold Mickens, Butler vs. Dayton, Oct. 15, 1994 (4th)

Half

32—Arnold Mickens, Butler vs. Valparaiso, Oct. 8, 1994 (1st); David Clark, Dartmouth vs. Pennsylvania, Nov. 18, 1989 (2nd)

Game

56—Arnold Mickens, Butler vs. Valparaiso, Oct. 8, 1994 (295 yards)

Season

409—Arnold Mickens, Butler, 1994 (2,255 yards)

Career

1,027—Erik Marsh, Lafayette, 1991-94 (4,834 yards)

MOST RUSHES PER GAME

Season

40.9—Arnold Mickens, Butler, 1994 (409 in 10)

Career

38.2—Arnold Mickens, Butler, 1994-95 (763 in 20)

MOST RUSHES IN TWO CONSECUTIVE GAMES

110—Arnold Mickens, Butler, 1994 (56 vs. Valparaiso, Oct. 8; 54 vs. Dayton, Oct. 15)

MOST CONSECUTIVE CARRIES BY SAME PLAYER

Game

26—Arnold Mickens, Butler vs. Valparaiso, Oct. 8, 1994 (during 6 series)

MOST YARDS GAINED

Quarter

194—Otto Kelly, Nevada vs. Idaho, Nov. 12, 1983 (3rd, 8 rushes)

Half

272—Tony Vinson, Towson St. vs. Morgan St., Nov. 20, 1993 (1st, 26 rushes)

Game

364—Tony Vinson, Towson St. vs. Bucknell, Nov. 13, 1993 (33 rushes)

Season

2,255—Arnold Mickens, Butler, 1994 (409 rushes)

Career

5,333—Frank Hawkins, Nevada, 1977-80 (945 rushes)

MOST YARDS GAINED PER GAME

Season

225.5—Arnold Mickens, Butler, 1994 (2,255 in 10)

Career

(2 yrs.) 190.7—Arnold Mickens, Butler, 1994-95 (3,813 in 20)

(3 yrs.) 140.3—Keith Elias, Princeton, 1991-93 (4,208 in 30)

(4 yrs.) 124.3—Kenny Gamble, Colgate, 1984-87 (5,220 in 42)

MOST YARDS GAINED BY A FRESHMAN
Game
304—Tony Citizen, McNeese St. vs. Prairie View, Sept. 6, 1986 (30 rushes)
Season
1,620—Markus Thomas, Eastern Ky., 1989 (232 rushes)

MOST YARDS GAINED PER GAME BY A FRESHMAN
Season
147.3—Markus Thomas, Eastern Ky., 1989 (1,620 in 11)

MOST YARDS GAINED BY A QUARTERBACK
Game
309—Eddie Thompson, Western Ky. vs. Southern Ill., Oct. 31, 1992 (28 rushes)
Season
1,201—Marvin Marshall, South Caro. St., 1994 (160 rushes)
Also holds per-game record at 109.2
Career
3,674—Jack Douglas, Citadel, 1989-92 (832 rushes)

MOST GAMES GAINING 100 YARDS OR MORE
Season
11—Rich Lemon, Bucknell, 1994; Frank Hawkins, Nevada, 1980
Career
29—Kenny Gamble, Colgate, 1984-87 (42 games); Frank Hawkins, Nevada, 1977-80 (43 games)

MOST CONSECUTIVE GAMES GAINING 100 YARDS OR MORE
Season
11—Rich Lemon, Bucknell, 1994; Frank Hawkins, Nevada, 1980
Career
20—Frank Hawkins, Nevada, 1979-80

MOST GAMES GAINING 100 YARDS OR MORE BY A FRESHMAN
8—David Wright, Indiana St., 1992; Markus Thomas, Eastern Ky., 1989

MOST GAMES GAINING 200 YARDS OR MORE
Season
8—Arnold Mickens, Butler, 1994
Career
10—Arnold Mickens, Butler, 1994-95

MOST CONSECUTIVE GAMES GAINING 200 YARDS OR MORE
Season
8—Arnold Mickens, Butler, 1994

MOST YARDS GAINED IN TWO, THREE AND FOUR CONSECUTIVE GAMES
2 Games
691—Tony Vinson, Towson St., 1993 (364 vs. Bucknell, Nov. 13; 327 vs. Morgan St., Nov. 20)
3 Games
876—Arnold Mickens, Butler, 1994 (288 vs. Wis.-Stevens Point, Sept. 24; 293 vs. Drake, Oct. 1; 295 vs. Valparaiso, Oct. 8)
4 Games
1,109—Arnold Mickens, Butler, 1994 (233 vs. Georgetown, Ky., Sept. 17; 288 vs. Wis.-Stevens Point, Sept. 24; 293 vs. Drake, Oct. 1; 295 vs. Valparaiso, Oct. 8)

MOST SEASONS GAINING 1,000 YARDS OR MORE
Career
3—By 19 players. Most recent: Rich Lemon, Bucknell, 1993-95; Kelvin Anderson, Southeast Mo. St., 1992-94; Sherriden May, Idaho, 1992-94; Eric Gant, Grambling, 1991-93; Markus Thomas, Eastern Ky., 1989, 1991-92

TWO PLAYERS, SAME TEAM, EACH GAINING 1,000 YARDS OR MORE
Massachusetts, 1995—Frank Alessio (1,276) & Rene Ingoglia (1,178); South Caro. St., 1994—Michael Hicks (1,368) & Marvin Marshall (1,201); Eastern Ky., 1993—Mike Penman (1,139) & Leon Brown (1,046); Northeast La., 1992—Greg Robinson (1,011) & Roosevelt Potts (1,004); Yale, 1991—Chris Kouri (1,101) & Nick Crawford (1,024); William & Mary, 1990—Robert Green (1,185) & Tyrone Shelton (1,020); Citadel, 1988—Adrian Johnson (1,091) & Gene Brown (1,006); Eastern Ky., 1986—Elroy Harris (1,152) & James Crawford (1,070); Eastern Ky., 1985—James Crawford (1,282) & Elroy Harris (1,134); Nevada, 1983—Otto Kelly (1,090) & Tony Corley (1,006); Jackson St., 1978—Perry Harrington (1,105) & Jeffrey Moore (1,094)

MOST YARDS GAINED BY TWO PLAYERS, SAME TEAM
Game
445—Joe Delaney (299) & Brett Knecht (146), Northwestern St. vs. Nicholls St., Oct. 28, 1978
Season
2,569—Michael Hicks (1,368) & Marvin Marshall (1,201), South Caro. St., 1994

EARLIEST GAME GAINING 1,000 YARDS OR MORE
Season
5—Arnold Mickens, Butler, 1994 (1,106)

MOST YARDS GAINED IN OPENING GAME OF SEASON
304—Tony Citizen, McNeese St. vs. Prairie View, Sept. 6, 1986 (30 rushes)

MOST YARDS GAINED IN FIRST GAME OF CAREER
304—Tony Citizen, McNeese St. vs. Prairie View, Sept. 6, 1986 (30 rushes)

HIGHEST AVERAGE GAIN PER RUSH
Game
(Min. 15-19 rushes) 19.1—Gene Brown, Citadel vs. Va. Military, Nov. 12, 1988 (15 for 286)
(Min. 20 rushes) 17.3—Russell Davis, Idaho vs. Portland St., Oct. 3, 1981 (20 for 345)
Season
(Min. 150-199 rushes) 8.7—Tim Hall, Robert Morris, 1994 (154 for 1,336)
(Min. 200 rushes) 7.3—Mike Clark, Akron, 1986 (245 for 1,786)
Career
(Min. 350-599 rushes) 7.4—Tim Hall, Robert Morris, 1994-95 (393 for 2,908)
(Min. 600 rushes) 6.6—Markus Thomas, Eastern Ky., 1989-92 (784 for 5,149)

MOST TOUCHDOWNS SCORED BY RUSHING
Game
6—Gene Lake, Delaware St. vs. Howard, Nov. 3, 1984; Gill Fenerty, Holy Cross vs. Columbia, Oct. 29, 1983; Henry Odom, South Caro. St. vs. Morgan St., Oct. 18, 1980
Season
24—Geoff Mitchell, Weber St., 1991
Career
55—Kenny Gamble, Colgate, 1984-87

MOST TOUCHDOWNS SCORED PER GAME BY RUSHING
Season
2.3—Tony Vinson, Towson St., 1993 (23 in 10)
Career
1.6—Keith Elias, Princeton, 1991-93 (49 in 30)

MOST TOUCHDOWNS SCORED BY RUSHING BY A QUARTERBACK
Season
21—Alcede Surtain, Alabama St., 1995
Career
48—Jack Douglas, Citadel, 1989-92
Also holds per-game record at 1.1 (48 in 44)

LONGEST PLAY
99—Jim Varick, Monmouth (N.J.) vs. Sacred Heart, Oct. 29, 1994; Phillip Collins, Southwest Mo. St. vs. Western Ill., Sept. 16, 1989; Pedro Bacon, Western Ky. vs. West Ala., Sept. 13, 1986 (only rush of the game); Hubert Owens, Mississippi Val. vs. Ark.-Pine Bluff, Sept. 20, 1980

Passing

HIGHEST PASSING EFFICIENCY RATING POINTS
Game
(Min. 15-24 atts.) 368.5—Rich Green, New Hampshire vs. Rhode Island, Nov. 13, 1993 (15 attempts, 12 completions, 0 interceptions, 358 yards, 4 TD passes)
(Min. 25-44 atts.) 283.3—Mike Smith, Northern Iowa vs. McNeese St., Nov. 8, 1986 (27 attempts, 22 completions, 0 interceptions, 413 yards, 6 TD passes)
(Min. 45 atts.) 220.8—Todd Hammel, Stephen F. Austin vs. Northeast La., Nov. 11, 1989 (45 attempts, 31 completions, 3 interceptions, 571 yards, 8 TD passes)
Season
(Min. 15 atts. per game) 204.6—Shawn Knight, William & Mary, 1993 (177 attempts, 125 completions, 4 interceptions, 2,055 yards, 22 TD passes)
Career
(Min. 300-399 comps.) 170.8—Shawn Knight, William & Mary, 1991-94 (558 attempts, 367 completions, 15 interceptions, 5,527 yards, 46 TD passes)
(Min. 400 comps.) 166.3—Dave Dickenson, Montana, 1992-95 (1,208 attempts, 813 completions, 26 interceptions, 11,080 yards, 96 TD passes)

MOST PASSES ATTEMPTED
Quarter
28—Paul Peterson, Idaho St. vs. Cal Poly SLO, Oct. 22, 1983 (4th)
Half
42—Doug Pederson, Northeast La. vs. Stephen F. Austin, Nov. 11, 1989 (1st, completed 27); Mike Machurek, Idaho St. vs. Weber St., Sept. 20, 1980 (2nd, completed 18)
Game
77—Neil Lomax, Portland St. vs. Northern Colo., Oct. 20, 1979 (completed 44)
Season
530—Steve McNair, Alcorn St., 1994 (completed 304)
Per-game record—51.8, Willie Totten, Mississippi Val., 1984 (518 in 10)
Career
1,680—Steve McNair, Alcorn St., 1991-94 (completed 929)
Per-game record—42.9, Stan Greene, Boston U., 1989-90 (944 in 22)

MOST PASSES ATTEMPTED BY A FRESHMAN
Game
66—Chris Swartz, Morehead St. vs. Tennessee Tech, Oct. 17, 1987 (completed 35)
Season
392—Greg Wyatt, Northern Ariz., 1986 (completed 250)
Per-game record—37.8, Jason Whitmer, Idaho St., 1987 (340 in 9)

MOST PASSES COMPLETED
Quarter
18—Kirk Schulz, Villanova vs. Central Conn. St., Oct. 10, 1987 (3rd); Willie Totten, Mississippi Val. vs. Grambling, Oct. 31, 1984 (2nd) & vs. Kentucky St., Sept. 1, 1984 (2nd)
Half
27—Doug Pederson, Northeast La. vs. Stephen F. Austin, Nov. 11, 1989 (1st, attempted 42)
Game
48—Clayton Millis, Cal St. Northridge vs. St. Mary's (Cal.), Nov. 11, 1995 (attempted 65)
Season
324—Willie Totten, Mississippi Val., 1984 (attempted 518)
Also holds per-game record at 32.4
Career
934—Jamie Martin, Weber St., 1989-92 (attempted 1,544)
Per-game record—24.3—Tom Proudian, Iona, 1993-95 (656 in 27)

MOST PASSES COMPLETED BY A FRESHMAN
Game
35—Chris Swartz, Morehead St. vs. Tennessee Tech, Oct. 17, 1987 (attempted 66)
Season
250—Greg Wyatt, Northern Ariz., 1986 (attempted 392)
Also holds per-game record at 22.7 (250 in 11)

MOST PASSES COMPLETED IN FRESHMAN AND SOPHOMORE SEASONS

518—Greg Wyatt, Northern Ariz., 1986-87 (attempted 804)

MOST CONSECUTIVE PASSES COMPLETED

Game

19—Kirk Schulz, Villanova vs. Central Conn. St., Oct. 10, 1987

MOST CONSECUTIVE PASS COMPLETIONS TO START GAME

18—Jeff Lewis, Northern Ariz. vs. Cal St. Northridge, Sept. 23, 1995; Scott Auchenbach, Bucknell vs. Colgate, Nov. 11, 1989

HIGHEST PERCENTAGE OF PASSES COMPLETED

Game

(Min. 20-29 comps.) 95.7%—Butch Mosby, Murray St. vs. Tenn.-Martin, Oct. 2, 1993 (22 of 23)

(Min. 30 comps.) 81.6%—Eric Beavers, Nevada vs. Idaho St., Nov. 17, 1984 (31 of 38)

Season

(Min. 200 atts.) 68.2%—Jason Garrett, Princeton, 1988 (204 of 299)

Career

(Min. 750 atts.) 67.3%—Dave Dickenson, Montana, 1992-95 (813 of 1,208)

MOST PASSES HAD INTERCEPTED

Game

7—Dan Crowley, Towson St. vs. Maine, Nov. 16, 1991 (53 attempts); Carlton Jenkins, Mississippi Val. vs. Prairie View, Oct. 31, 1987 (34 attempts); Charles Hebert, Southeastern La. vs. Northwestern St., Nov. 12, 1983 (23 attempts); Mick Spoon, Idaho St. vs. Montana, Oct. 21, 1978 (attempted 35)

Season

29—Willie Totten, Mississippi Val., 1985 (492 attempts)
Also holds per-game record at 2.6 (29 in 11)

Career

75—Willie Totten, Mississippi Val., 1982-85
Per-game record—2.0, John Witkowski, Columbia, 1981-83 (60 in 30)

LOWEST PERCENTAGE OF PASSES HAD INTERCEPTED

Season

(Min. 175-324 atts.) 0.6%—Kharon Brown, Hofstra, 1995 (2 of 320)

(Min. 325 atts.) 1.2%—Bill Lazor, Cornell, 1992 (4 of 328)

Career

(Min. 500-749 atts.) 1.8%—Jason Garrett, Princeton, 1987-88 (10 of 550)

(Min. 750 atts.) 1.8%—Jeff Lewis, Northern Ariz., 1992-95 (24 of 1,315)

MOST PASSES ATTEMPTED WITHOUT INTERCEPTION

Game

68—Tony Petersen, Marshall vs. Western Caro., Nov. 14, 1987 (completed 34)

MOST CONSECUTIVE PASSES ATTEMPTED WITHOUT INTERCEPTION

Season

176—Jason Garrett, Princeton, 1988 (in 7 games, from Sept. 17 through Oct. 29)

Career

199—Thomas Debow, Tennessee Tech, began Sept. 17, 1988, ended Oct. 14, 1989

MOST YARDS GAINED

Quarter

278—Willie Totten, Mississippi Val. vs. Kentucky St., Sept. 1, 1984 (2nd)

Half

383—Michael Payton, Marshall vs. Va. Military, Nov. 16, 1991 (1st)

Game

624—Jamie Martin, Weber St. vs. Idaho St., Nov. 23, 1991

Season

4,863—Steve McNair, Alcorn St., 1994

Career

14,496—Steve McNair, Alcorn St., 1991-94

MOST YARDS GAINED PER GAME

Season

455.7—Willie Totten, Mississippi Val., 1984 (4,557 in 10)

Career

350.0—Neil Lomax, Portland St., 1978-80 (11,550 in 33)

MOST YARDS GAINED BY A FRESHMAN

Game

540—Brad Otton, Weber St. vs. Northern Ariz., Nov. 6, 1993

Season

2,895—Steve McNair, Alcorn St., 1991
Also holds per-game record at 289.5 (2,895 in 10)

MOST YARDS GAINED IN FRESHMAN AND SOPHOMORE SEASONS

6,436—Steve McNair, Alcorn St., 1991-92

MOST YARDS GAINED IN TWO, THREE AND FOUR CONSECUTIVE GAMES

2 Games

1,150—Steve McNair, Alcorn St., 1994 (587 vs. Samford, Oct. 29; 563 vs. Mississippi Val., Nov. 5)

3 Games

1,626—Steve McNair, Alcorn St., 1994 (587 vs. Samford, Oct. 29; 563 vs. Mississippi Val., Nov. 5; 476 vs. Troy St., Nov. 12)

4 Games

2,159—Steve McNair, Alcorn St., 1994 (587 vs. Samford, Oct. 29; 563 vs. Mississippi Val., Nov. 5; 476 vs. Troy St., Nov. 12; 533 vs. Jackson St., Nov. 19)

MOST GAMES GAINING 200 YARDS OR MORE

Season

11—By 13 players. Most recent: Steve McNair, Alcorn St., 1994; Chris Hakel, William & Mary, 1991; Jamie Martin, Weber St., 1991

Career

41—Steve McNair, Alcorn St., 1991-94 (42 games)

MOST CONSECUTIVE GAMES GAINING 200 YARDS OR MORE

Season

11—By 11 players. Most recent: Steve McNair, Alcorn St., 1994; Chris Hakel, William & Mary, 1991; Jamie Martin, Weber St., 1991

Career

28—Steve McNair, Alcorn St., 1991-93; Neil Lomax, Portland St., 1978-80

MOST GAMES GAINING 300 YARDS OR MORE

Season

10—Steve McNair, Alcorn St., 1994; John Friesz, Idaho, 1989; Willie Totten, Mississippi Val., 1984

Career

28—Neil Lomax, Portland St., 1978-80

MOST CONSECUTIVE GAMES GAINING 300 YARDS OR MORE

Season

10—John Friesz, Idaho, 1989; Willie Totten, Mississippi Val., 1984

Career

13—Neil Lomax, Portland St., 1979-80

MOST YARDS GAINED AGAINST ONE OPPONENT

Career

1,675—Willie Totten, Mississippi Val. vs. Prairie View, 1982-85
Also holds per-game record at 418.8 (1,675 in 4)

MOST YARDS PER ATTEMPT

Game

(Min. 30-44 atts.) 16.1—Gilbert Renfroe, Tennessee St. vs. Dist. Columbia, Nov. 5, 1983 (30 for 484)

(Min. 45 atts.) 12.7—Todd Hammel, Stephen F. Austin vs. Northeast La., Nov. 11, 1989 (45 for 571)

Season

(Min. 250-324 atts.) 10.3—Mike Smith, Northern Iowa, 1986 (303 for 3,125)

(Min. 325 atts.) 9.5—John Friesz, Idaho, 1989 (425 for 4,041)

Career

(Min. 500-999 atts.) 9.5—Jay Johnson, Northern Iowa, 1989-92 (744 for 7,049)

(Min. 1,000 atts.) 9.2—Dave Dickenson, Montana, 1992-95 (1,208 for 11,080)

MOST YARDS GAINED PER COMPLETION

Game

(Min. 15-19 comps.) 28.5—Kendrick Nord, Grambling vs. Alcorn St., Sept. 3, 1994 (17 for 485)

(Min. 20 comps.) 22.5—Michael Payton, Marshall vs. Va. Military, Nov. 16, 1991 (22 for 496)

Season

(Min. 200 comps.) 16.4—Todd Hammel, Stephen F. Austin, 1989 (238 for 3,914)

Career

(Min. 350-399 comps.) 17.8—Jay Johnson, Northern Iowa, 1989-92 (397 for 7,049)

(Min. 400 comps.) 15.6—Steve McNair, Alcorn St., 1991-94 (929 for 14,496)

MOST TOUCHDOWN PASSES

Quarter

7—Neil Lomax, Portland St. vs. Delaware St., Nov. 8, 1980 (1st)

Half

7—Neil Lomax, Portland St. vs. Delaware St., Nov. 8, 1980 (1st)

Game

9—Willie Totten, Mississippi Val. vs. Kentucky St., Sept. 1, 1984

Season

56—Willie Totten, Mississippi Val., 1984
Also holds per-game record at 5.6 (56 in 10)

Career

139—Willie Totten, Mississippi Val., 1982-85
Also holds per-game record at 3.5 (139 in 40)

MOST CONSECUTIVE GAMES THROWING A TOUCHDOWN PASS

Career

36—Steve McNair, Alcorn St., 1991-94

MOST TOUCHDOWN PASSES, SAME PASSER AND RECEIVER

Season

27—Willie Totten to Jerry Rice, Mississippi Val., 1984

Career

47—Willie Totten to Jerry Rice, Mississippi Val., 1982-84

HIGHEST PERCENTAGE OF PASSES FOR TOUCHDOWNS

Season

(Min. 200-299 atts.) 11.7%—Mike Williams, Grambling, 1980 (28 of 239)

(Min. 300 atts.) 10.9%—Doug Nussmeier, Idaho, 1993 (33 of 304)

Career

(Min. 500-749 atts.) 8.5%—Mike Williams, Grambling, 1977-80 (44 of 520)

(Min. 750 atts.) 7.9%—Dave Dickenson, Montana, 1992-95 (96 of 1,208)

Receiving

MOST PASSES CAUGHT

Game

24—Jerry Rice, Mississippi Val. vs. Southern-B.R., Oct. 1, 1983 (219 yards)

Season

115—Brian Forster, Rhode Island, 1985 (1,617 yards)

Career

301—Jerry Rice, Mississippi Val., 1981-84 (4,693 yards)

MOST PASSES CAUGHT PER GAME

Season

11.5—Brian Forster, Rhode Island, 1985 (115 in 10)

Career

7.3—Jerry Rice, Mississippi Val., 1981-84 (301 in 41)

MOST PASSES CAUGHT BY A TIGHT END

Game

18—Brian Forster, Rhode Island vs. Brown, Sept. 28, 1985 (327 yards)

Season

115—Brian Forster, Rhode Island, 1985 (1,617 yards)
Also holds per-game record at 11.5 (115 in 10)

Career

245—Brian Forster, Rhode Island, 1983-85, 1987 (3,410 yards)

MOST PASSES CAUGHT BY A RUNNING BACK
Game
21—David Pandt, Montana St. vs. Eastern Wash., Sept. 21, 1985 (169 yards)
Season
78—Gordie Lockbaum, Holy Cross, 1987 (1,152 yards)
2 Yrs
135—Gordie Lockbaum, Holy Cross, 1986-87 (2,012 yards)
Also holds per-game record at 6.1 (135 in 22)
Career
182—Merril Hoge, Idaho St., 1983-86 (1,734 yards)

MOST PASSES CAUGHT BY A FRESHMAN
Game
15—Emerson Foster, Rhode Island vs. Northeastern, Nov. 9, 1985 (205 yards)
Season
61—Blake Tuffli, St. Mary's (Cal.), 1993 (929 yards)

MOST PASSES CAUGHT BY TWO PLAYERS, SAME TEAM
Season
183—Jerry Rice (103 for 1,682 yards and 27 TDs) & Joe Thomas (80 for 1,119 yards and 11 TDs), Mississippi Val., 1984
Career
420—Darrell Colbert (217 for 3,177 yards and 33 TDs) & Donald Narcisse (203 for 2,429 yards and 26 TDs), Texas Southern, 1983-86

MOST YARDS GAINED
Game
370—Michael Lerch, Princeton vs. Brown, Oct. 12, 1991 (caught 9)
Season
1,682—Jerry Rice, Mississippi Val., 1984 (caught 103)
Career
4,693—Jerry Rice, Mississippi Val., 1981-84 (caught 301)

MOST YARDS GAINED PER GAME
Season
168.2—Jerry Rice, Mississippi Val., 1984 (1,682 in 10)
Career
(Min. 2,000-2,999 yds.) 116.9—Derrick Ingram, Ala.-Birmingham, 1993-94 (2,572 in 22)
(Min. 3,000 yds.) 114.5—Jerry Rice, Mississippi Val., 1981-84 (4,693 in 41)

MOST YARDS GAINED BY A TIGHT END
Game
327—Brian Forster, Rhode Island vs. Brown, Sept. 28, 1985 (caught 18)
Season
1,617—Brian Forster, Rhode Island, 1985 (caught 115)
Also holds per-game record at 161.7 (1,617 in 10)
Career
3,410—Brian Forster, Rhode Island, 1983-85, 1987 (caught 245)

MOST YARDS GAINED BY A RUNNING BACK
Game
220—Alvin Atkinson, Davidson vs. Furman, Nov. 3, 1979 (caught 9)
Season
1,152—Gordie Lockbaum, Holy Cross, 1987 (caught 78)
Also holds per-game record at 104.7 (1,152 in 11)

MOST YARDS GAINED BY A FRESHMAN
Game
223—George Delaney, Colgate vs. Virginia, Oct. 8, 1988 (10 catches)
Season
929—Blake Tuffli, St. Mary's (Cal.), 1993 (61 catches)

MOST YARDS GAINED BY TWO PLAYERS, SAME TEAM
Season
2,801—Jerry Rice (1,682, 103 caught and 27 TDs) & Joe Thomas (1,119, 80 caught and 11 TDs), Mississippi Val., 1984
Career
5,806—Roy Banks (3,177, 184 caught and 38 TDs) & Cal Pierce (2,629, 163 caught and 13 TDs), Eastern Ill., 1983-86

HIGHEST AVERAGE GAIN PER RECEPTION
Game
(Min. 5-9 receps.) 44.6—John Taylor, Delaware St. vs. St. Paul's, Sept. 21, 1985 (5 for 223)
(Min. 10 receps.) 29.0—Jason Cristino, Lehigh vs. Lafayette, Nov. 21, 1992 (11 for 319)
Season
(Min. 30-59 receps.) 26.5—Dedric Ward, Northern Iowa, 1995 (44 for 1,164)
(Min. 60 receps.) 20.7—Golden Tate, Tennessee St., 1983 (63 for 1,307)
Career
(Min. 90-124 receps.) 24.3—John Taylor, Delaware St., 1982-85 (100 for 2,426)
(Min. 125 receps.) 20.1—Reggie Barlow, Alabama St., 1992-95 (133 for 2,672)

MOST GAMES GAINING 100 YARDS OR MORE
Career
23—Jerry Rice, Mississippi Val., 1981-84 (in 41 games played)

MOST TOUCHDOWN PASSES CAUGHT
Game
5—Rod Marshall, Northern Ariz. vs. Abilene Christian, Sept. 16, 1995 (154 yards); Wayne Chrebet, Hofstra vs. Delaware, Nov. 12, 1994 (245 yards); Rennie Benn, Lehigh vs. Indiana (Pa.), Sept. 14, 1985 (266 yards); Jerry Rice, Mississippi Val. vs. Prairie View, Oct. 27, 1984 & vs. Kentucky St., Sept. 1, 1984
Season
27—Jerry Rice, Mississippi Val., 1984
Career
50—Jerry Rice, Mississippi Val., 1981-84

MOST TOUCHDOWN PASSES CAUGHT BY A FRESHMAN
Season
9—Mike Guerrino, Bucknell, 1987

MOST TOUCHDOWN PASSES CAUGHT PER GAME
Season
2.7—Jerry Rice, Mississippi Val., 1984 (27 in 10)
Career
1.2—Jerry Rice, Mississippi Val., 1981-84 (50 in 41)

MOST GAMES CATCHING A TOUCHDOWN PASS
Season
10—Jerry Rice, Mississippi Val., 1984
Also holds consecutive record at 10 (1984)
Career
26—Jerry Rice, Mississippi Val., 1981-84
Also holds consecutive record at 17 (1983-84)

Punting

MOST PUNTS
Game
16—Matt Stover, Louisiana Tech vs. Northeast La., Nov. 18, 1988 (567 yards)
Season
98—Barry Hickingbotham, Louisiana Tech, 1987 (3,821 yards)
Career
301—Barry Bowman, Louisiana Tech, 1983-86 (11,441 yards)

HIGHEST AVERAGE PER PUNT
Game
(Min. 5-9 punts) 55.7—Harold Alexander, Appalachian St. vs. Citadel, Oct. 3, 1992 (6 for 334); Jody Farmer, Montana vs. Nevada, Oct. 1, 1988 (9 for 501)
(Min. 10 punts) 52.2—Stuart Dodds, Montana St. vs. Northern Ariz., Oct. 20, 1979 (10 for 522)
Season
(Min. 60 punts) 47.0—Harold Alexander, Appalachian St., 1991 (64 for 3,009)
Career
(Min. 150 punts) 44.4—Pumpy Tudors, Tenn.-Chatt., 1989-91 (181 for 8,041)

LONGEST PUNT
91—Bart Helsley, North Texas vs. Northeast La., Nov. 17, 1990

Interceptions

MOST PASSES INTERCEPTED
Game
5—Mark Cordes, Eastern Wash. vs. Boise St., Sept. 6, 1986 (48 yards); Michael Richardson, Northwestern St. vs. Southeastern La., Nov. 12, 1983 (128 yards); Karl Johnson, Jackson St. vs. Grambling, Oct. 23, 1982 (29 yards)
Season
12—Dean Cain, Princeton, 1987 (98 yards)
Also holds per-game record at 1.2 (12 in 10)
Career
28—Dave Murphy, Holy Cross, 1986-89 (309 yards)
Per-game record—0.7, Dean Cain, Princeton, 1985-87 (22 in 30)

MOST YARDS ON INTERCEPTION RETURNS
Game
216—Keiron Bigby, Brown vs. Yale, Sept. 29, 1984 (3 interceptions) (first career game)
Season
280—William Hampton, Murray St., 1995 (8 interceptions)
Career
452—Rick Harris, East Tenn. St., 1986-88 (20 interceptions)

MOST TOUCHDOWNS SCORED ON INTERCEPTION RETURNS
Game
2—By seven players. Most recent: William Hampton, Murray St. vs. Tenn.-Martin, Oct. 7, 1995; Jimmy Conner, Southern-B.R. vs. Grambling, Nov. 26, 1994
Season
4—William Hampton, Murray St., 1995 (8 interceptions, 280 yards); Joseph Vaughn, Cal St. Northridge, 1994 (9 interceptions, 265 yards); Robert Turner, Jackson St., 1990 (9 interceptions, 212 yards)
Career
5—¢William Hampton, Murray St., 1993-95 (16 interceptions)
¢*Active player.*

HIGHEST AVERAGE GAIN PER INTERCEPTION
Game
(Min. 3 ints.) 72.0—Keiron Bigby, Brown vs. Yale, Sept. 29, 1984 (3 for 216)
Season
(Min. 3 ints.) 72.0—Keiron Bigby, Brown, 1984 (3 for 216)
Career
(Min. 12 ints.) 24.9—Roger Robinson, Tennessee St., 1981-84 (12 for 299)

Punt Returns

MOST PUNT RETURNS
Game
9—By 14 players. Most recent: Tim Hilton, Cal St. Northridge vs. Menlo, Sept. 9, 1995 (148 yards)
Season
55—Tommy Houk, Murray St., 1980 (442 yards)
Also holds per-game record at 5.0 (55 in 11)
Career
123—Chuck Calhoun, Southwest Mo. St., 1990-93 (978 yards)
Per-game record—3.8, Tommy Houk, Murray St., 1979-80 (84 in 22)

MOST YARDS ON PUNT RETURNS
Game
216—Gary Harrell, Howard vs. Morgan St., Nov. 3, 1990 (7 returns); Willie Ware, Mississippi Val. vs. Washburn, Sept. 15, 1984 (7 returns)
Season
563—Dewayne Harper, Tenn.-Martin, 1994 (45 returns)
Also holds per-game record at 51.2 (563 in 11)

Career
1,230—David McCrary, Tenn.-Chatt., 1982-85 (117 returns)

HIGHEST AVERAGE GAIN PER RETURN
Game
(Min. 5 rets.) 40.0—Aaron Fix, Canisius vs. Siena, Sept. 24, 1994 (5 for 200)
Season
(Min. 1.2 rets. per game) 23.0—Tim Egerton, Delaware St., 1988 (16 for 368)
Career
(Min. 1.2 rets. per game) 16.4—Willie Ware, Mississippi Val., 1982-85 (61 for 1,003)

MOST TOUCHDOWNS SCORED ON PUNT RETURNS
Game
3—Aaron Fix, Canisius vs. Siena, Sept. 24, 1994 (5 returns)
Season
4—Aaron Fix, Canisius, 1994 (34 returns); Kenny Shedd, Northern Iowa, 1992 (27 returns); Howard Huckaby, Florida A&M, 1988 (26 returns)
Career
7—Kenny Shedd, Northern Iowa, 1989-92

LONGEST PUNT RETURN
98—Barney Bussey, South Caro. St. vs. Johnson Smith, Oct. 10, 1981

MOST CONSECUTIVE GAMES RETURNING PUNT FOR TOUCHDOWN
3—Troy Jones, McNeese St., 1989 (vs. Mississippi Col., Sept. 2; vs. Samford, Sept. 9; vs. Northeast La., Sept. 16)

Kickoff Returns

MOST KICKOFF RETURNS
Game
10—Ryan Steen, Cal Poly SLO vs. Eastern Wash., Sept. 10, 1994 (203 yards); Merril Hoge, Idaho St. vs. Weber St., Oct. 25, 1986 (179 yards)
Season
50—David Primus, Samford, 1989 (1,411 yards)
Career
118—Clarence Alexander, Mississippi Val., 1986-89 (2,439 yards)

MOST KICKOFF RETURNS PER GAME
Season
4.5—David Primus, Samford, 1989 (50 in 11)
Career
3.0—Lorenza Rivers, Tennessee Tech, 1985, 1987 (62 in 21)

MOST YARDS ON KICKOFF RETURNS
Game
262—Herman Hunter, Tennessee St. vs. Mississippi Val., Nov. 13, 1982 (6 returns)
Season
1,411—David Primus, Samford, 1989 (50 returns)
Career
2,439—Clarence Alexander, Mississippi Val., 1986-89 (118 returns)

MOST YARDS PER GAME ON KICKOFF RETURNS
Season
128.3—David Primus, Samford, 1989 (1,411 in 11)
Career
61.0—Clarence Alexander, Mississippi Val., 1986-89 (2,439 in 40)

HIGHEST AVERAGE GAIN PER RETURN
Game
(Min. 5 rets.) 45.6—Jerome Stelly, Western Ill. vs. Youngstown St., Nov. 7, 1981 (5 for 228)
Season
(Min. 1.2 rets. per game) 37.3—David Fraterrigo, Canisius, 1993 (13 for 485)
Career
(Min. 1.2 Returns Per Game)
(Min. 30-44 rets.) 29.7—Troy Brown, Marshall, 1991-92 (32 for 950)
(Min. 45 rets.) 29.3—Charles Swann, Indiana St., 1989-91 (45 for 1,319)

MOST TOUCHDOWNS SCORED ON KICKOFF RETURNS
Game
2—Rory Lee, Western Ill. vs. St. Ambrose, Nov. 13, 1993; Kerry Hayes, Western Caro. vs. Va. Military, Oct. 10, 1992 (90 & 94 yards); Paul Ashby, Alabama St. vs. Grambling, Nov. 9, 1991 (97 & 94 yards); David Lucas, Florida A&M vs. North Caro. A&T, Oct. 12, 1991 (99 & 93 yards); Jerome Stelly, Western Ill. vs. Youngstown St., Nov. 7, 1981 (99 & 97 yards)
Season
3—Todd Cleveland, Central Fla., 1994; Kerry Hayes, Western Caro., 1993; Troy Brown, Marshall, 1991; David Lucas, Florida A&M, 1991
Career
5—Kerry Hayes, Western Caro., 1991-94

Total Kick Returns

(Combined Punt and Kickoff Returns)

MOST KICK RETURNS
Game
12—Craig Hodge, Tennessee St. vs. Morgan St., Oct. 24, 1987 (8 punts, 4 kickoffs; 319 yards)
Season
64—Joe Markus, Connecticut, 1981 (34 punts, 30 kickoffs; 939 yards)
Career
199—Herman Hunter, Tennessee St., 1981-84 (103 punts, 96 kickoffs; 3,232 yards)

MOST YARDS ON KICK RETURNS
Game
319—Craig Hodge, Tennessee St. vs. Morgan St., Oct. 24, 1987 (12 returns, 206 on punts, 113 on kickoffs)
Season
1,469—David Primus, Samford, 1989 (1,411 on kickoffs, 58 on punts)
Also holds per-game record at 133.5 (1,469 in 11)
Career
3,232—Herman Hunter, Tennessee St., 1981-84 (974 on punts, 2,258 on kickoffs)
Also holds per-game record at 75.2 (3,232 in 43)

GAINING 1,000 YARDS ON PUNT RETURNS AND 1,000 YARDS ON KICKOFF RETURNS
Career
Kenny Shedd, Northern Iowa, 1989-92 (1,081 on punts and 1,359 on kickoffs); Joe Markus, Connecticut, 1979-82 (1,012 on punts and 1,185 on kickoffs)

HIGHEST AVERAGE PER KICK RETURN
Game
(Min. 6 rets.) 42.3—Herman Hunter, Tennessee St. vs. Mississippi Val., Nov. 13, 1982 (7 for 296)
Season
(Min. 40 rets.) 26.7—David Primus, Samford, 1989 (55 for 1,469)
Career
(Min. 60 rets.) 20.9—Bill LaFreniere, Northeastern, 1978-81 (112 for 2,336)

MOST TOUCHDOWNS SCORED ON KICK RETURNS
Game
3—Aaron Fix, Canisius vs. Siena, Sept. 24, 1994 (1 kickoff and 5 punt returns, 3 touchdowns)
Season
4—Andrew McFadden, Liberty, 1995 (2 kickoffs and 2 punts); Aaron Fix, Canisius, 1994 (4 punts); Troy Brown, Marshall, 1991 (3 kickoffs and 1 punt); Howard Huckaby, Florida A&M, 1988 (4 punts); Willie Ware, Mississippi Val., 1985 (2 punts and 2 kickoffs)
Career
7—Kerry Hayes, Western Caro., 1991-94 (2 punts and 5 kickoffs); Kenny Shedd, Northern Iowa, 1989-92 (7 punts); Willie Ware, Mississippi Val., 1982-85 (5 punts and 2 kickoffs)

All-Purpose Yards

(Yardage Gained From Rushing, Receiving and All Runbacks; Must Have One Attempt From at Least Two Categories)

MOST PLAYS
Game
54—Ron Darby, Marshall vs. Western Caro., Nov. 12, 1988 (47 rushes, 4 receptions, 3 kickoff returns; 329 yards)
(Note: 56—Arnold Mickens, Butler vs. Valparaiso, Oct. 8, 1994; all rushes)
Season
411—Arnold Mickens, Butler, 1994 (409 rushes, 2 receptions; 2,262 yards)
Career
1,110—Erik Marsh, Lafayette, 1991-94 (1,027 rushes, 50 receptions, 6 punt returns, 27 kickoff returns; 5,783 yards)

MOST YARDS GAINED
Game
467—Joey Stockton, Western Ky. vs. Austin Peay, Sept. 16, 1995 (29 rushing, 276 receiving, 18 punt returns, 144 kickoff returns; 14 plays)
Season
2,425—Kenny Gamble, Colgate, 1986 (1,816 rushing, 178 receiving, 40 punt returns, 391 kickoff returns; 343 plays)
Career
7,623—Kenny Gamble, Colgate, 1984-87 (5,220 rushing, 53 receiving, 104 punt returns, 1,763 kickoff returns; 1,096 plays)

MOST YARDS GAINED PER GAME
Season
226.2—Arnold Mickens, Butler, 1994 (2,262 in 10)
Career
197.4—Arnold Mickens, Butler, 1994-95 (3,947 in 20)

MOST YARDS GAINED BY A FRESHMAN
Season
2,014—David Wright, Indiana St., 1992 (1,313 rushing, 108 receiving, 593 kickoff returns; 254 plays)

HIGHEST AVERAGE GAIN PER PLAY
Game
(Min. 20 plays) 20.6—Herman Hunter, Tennessee St. vs. Mississippi Val., Nov. 13, 1982 (453 on 22)
Season
(Min. 1,000 yards, 100 plays) 19.7—Otis Washington, Western Caro., 1988 (2,086 on 106)
Career
(Min. 4,000 yards, 350 plays) 14.8—Pete Mandley, Northern Ariz., 1979-80, 1982-83 (5,925 on 401)

Scoring

MOST POINTS SCORED
Game
36—By six players. Most recent: Derrick Cullors, Murray St. vs. Morehead St., Oct. 14, 1995 (6 TDs)
Season
170—Geoff Mitchell, Weber St., 1991 (28 TDs, 2 PATs)
Career
385—Marty Zendejas, Nevada, 1984-87 (72 FGs, 169 PATs)

MOST POINTS SCORED PER GAME
Season
16.2—Jerry Rice, Mississippi Val., 1984 (162 in 10)
Career
(Min. 200-299 pts.) 10.9—Tim Hall, Robert Morris, 1994-95 (208 in 19)
(Min. 300 pts.) 10.7—Keith Elias, Princeton, 1991-93 (320 in 30)

MOST TOUCHDOWNS SCORED
Game
6—By six players. Most recent: Derrick Cullors, Murray St. vs. Morehead St., Oct. 14, 1995
Season
28—Geoff Mitchell, Weber St., 1991
Career
61—Sherriden May, Idaho, 1992-94

MOST TOUCHDOWNS SCORED PER GAME
Season
2.7—Jerry Rice, Mississippi Val., 1984 (27 in 10)
Career
(Min. 18-29 games) 1.8—Tim Hall, Robert Morris, 1994-95 (34 in 19)
(Min. 30 games) 1.7—Keith Elias, Princeton, 1991-93 (52 in 30)

MOST TOUCHDOWNS SCORED BY A FRESHMAN
Season
18—Charvez Foger, Nevada, 1985
Also holds per-game record at 1.8 (18 in 10)

MOST EXTRA POINTS ATTEMPTED BY KICKING
Game
15—John Kincheloe, Portland St. vs. Delaware St., Nov. 8, 1980 (15 made)
Season
74—John Kincheloe, Portland St., 1980 (70 made)
Per-game record—7.2, Jonathan Stokes, Mississippi Val., 1984 (72 in 10)
Career
194—Gilad Landau, Grambling, 1991-94 (181 made)

MOST EXTRA POINTS MADE BY KICKING
Game
15—John Kincheloe, Portland St. vs. Delaware St., Nov. 8, 1980 (15 attempts)
Season
70—John Kincheloe, Portland St., 1980 (74 attempts)
Per-game record—6.8, Jonathan Stokes, Mississippi Val., 1984 (68 in 10)
Career
181—Gilad Landau, Grambling, 1991-94 (194 attempts)
Also holds per-game record at 4.1 (181 in 44)

BEST PERFECT RECORD OF EXTRA POINTS MADE
Season
68 of 68—Mike Hollis, Idaho, 1993

HIGHEST PERCENTAGE OF EXTRA POINTS MADE
Career
(Min. 100-119 atts.) 100%—Anders Larsson, Montana St., 1985-88 (101 of 101)
(Min. 120 atts.) 99.2%—Brian Mitchell, Marshall/Northern Iowa, 1987, 1989-91 (130 of 131)

MOST CONSECUTIVE EXTRA POINTS MADE
Game
15—John Kincheloe, Portland St. vs. Delaware St., Nov. 8, 1980
Season
68—Mike Hollis, Idaho, 1993
Career
121—Brian Mitchell, Marshall/Northern Iowa, 1987, 1989-91

MOST POINTS SCORED BY KICKING
Game
24—Goran Lingmerth, Northern Ariz. vs. Idaho, Oct. 25, 1986 (8 FGs)
Season
109—Brian Mitchell, Northern Iowa, 1990 (26 FGs, 31 PATs)
Career
385—Marty Zendejas, Nevada, 1984-87 (72 FGs, 169 PATs)

MOST POINTS SCORED BY KICKING PER GAME
Season
9.9—Brian Mitchell, Northern Iowa, 1990 (109 in 11)
Career
9.1—Tony Zendejas, Nevada, 1981-83 (300 in 33)

MOST DEFENSIVE EXTRA-POINT RETURNS, ONE GAME, SINGLE PLAYER
2—Joe Lee Johnson, Western Ky. vs. Indiana St., Nov. 10, 1990 (both kick returns, scored on neither)

MOST DEFENSIVE EXTRA POINTS SCORED
Game
1—By many players
Season
2—Jackie Kellogg, Eastern Wash. vs. Weber St., Oct. 6, 1990 (90-yard interception return) & vs. Portland St., Oct. 27, 1990 (94-yard interception return)

LONGEST RETURN OF A DEFENSIVE EXTRA POINT
100—Rich Kinsman (DB), William & Mary vs. Lehigh, Nov. 14, 1992; Morgan Ryan (DB), Montana St. vs. Sam Houston St., Sept. 7, 1991 (interception return)

FIRST DEFENSIVE EXTRA-POINT ATTEMPTS
Mike Rogers (DB), Davidson vs. Lehigh, Sept. 10, 1988 (30-yard interception return); Dave Benna (LB), Towson St. vs. Northeastern, Sept. 10, 1988 (35-yard interception return)

MOST TWO-POINT ATTEMPTS
Season
11—Jamie Martin, Weber St., 1990; Brent Woods, Princeton, 1982

MOST SUCCESSFUL TWO-POINT PASSES
Game
3—Brent Woods, Princeton vs. Lafayette, Nov. 6, 1982 (attempted 3)
Season
7—Jamie Martin, Weber St., 1992 (attempted 7)
Career
15—Jamie Martin, Weber St., 1989-92 (attempted 28)

Kick Blocks

MOST KICKS BLOCKED
Game
3—Adrian Hardy, Northwestern St. vs. Arkansas St., Oct. 3, 1992 (2 PATs, 1 FG)
Season
5—Mario Wilson, Marist, 1994 (3 FGs, 2 punts)
Career
9—Adrian Hardy, Northwestern St., 1989-92 (3 PATs, 6 FGs)

Field Goals

MOST FIELD GOALS ATTEMPTED
Game
8—Goran Lingmerth, Northern Ariz. vs. Idaho, Oct. 25, 1986 (made 8)
Season
33—David Ettinger, Hofstra, 1995 (made 22); Tony Zendejas, Nevada, 1982 (made 26)
Career
102—Kirk Roach, Western Caro., 1984-87 (made 71)

MOST FIELD GOALS MADE
Quarter
4—Ryan Weeks, Tennessee Tech vs. Tenn.-Chatt., Sept. 9, 1989 (3rd); Tony Zendejas, Nevada vs. Northern Ariz., Oct. 16, 1982 (4th)
Half
5—Ryan Weeks, Tennessee Tech vs. Tenn.-Chatt., Sept. 9, 1989 (2nd); Tony Zendejas, Nevada vs. Northern Ariz., Oct. 16, 1982 (2nd); Dean Biasucci, Western Caro. vs. Mars Hill, Sept. 18, 1982 (1st)
Game
8—Goran Lingmerth, Northern Ariz. vs. Idaho, Oct. 25, 1986 (39, 18, 20, 33, 46, 27, 22, 35 yards; by quarters—1, 3, 2, 2), 8 attempts
Season
26—Brian Mitchell, Northern Iowa, 1990 (27 attempts); Tony Zendejas, Nevada, 1982 (33 attempts)
Career
72—Marty Zendejas, Nevada, 1984-87 (90 attempts)

MOST FIELD GOALS MADE PER GAME
Season
2.4—Brian Mitchell, Northern Iowa, 1990 (26 in 11); Tony Zendejas, Nevada, 1982 (26 in 11)
Career
2.1—Tony Zendejas, Nevada, 1981-83 (70 in 33)

HIGHEST PERCENTAGE OF FIELD GOALS MADE
Season
(Min. 20 atts.) 96.3%—Brian Mitchell, Northern Iowa, 1990 (26 of 27)
Career
(Min. 50 atts.) 81.4%—Tony Zendejas, Nevada, 1981-83 (70 of 86)

BEST PERFECT RECORD OF FIELD GOALS MADE
Season
100.0%—John Coursey, James Madison, 1995 (14 of 14)

MOST CONSECUTIVE FIELD GOALS MADE
Game
8—Goran Lingmerth, Northern Ariz. vs. Idaho, Oct. 25, 1986
Season
21—Brian Mitchell, Northern Iowa, 1990
Career
26—Brian Mitchell, Northern Iowa, 1990-91

MOST CONSECUTIVE GAMES KICKING A FIELD GOAL
Career
33—Tony Zendejas, Nevada, 1981-83 (at least one in every game played)

MOST FIELD GOALS MADE, 50 YARDS OR MORE
Game
3—Terry Belden, Northern Ariz. vs. Cal St. Northridge, Sept. 18, 1993 (60, 50, 54 yards); Jesse Garcia, Northeast La. vs. McNeese St., Oct. 29, 1983 (52, 56, 53 yards)
Season
7—Kirk Roach, Western Caro., 1987 (12 attempts); Jesse Garcia, Northeast La., 1983 (12 attempts)
Career
11—Kirk Roach, Western Caro., 1984-87 (26 attempts)

HIGHEST PERCENTAGE OF FIELD GOALS MADE, 50 YARDS OR MORE
Season
(Min. 6 atts.) 83.3%—Tim Foley, Ga. Southern, 1987 (5 of 6)
Career
(Min. 10 atts.) 90.9%—Tim Foley, Ga. Southern, 1984-87 (10 of 11)

MOST FIELD GOALS MADE, 40 YARDS OR MORE
Season
12—Marty Zendejas, Nevada, 1985 (15 attempts)
Career
30—Marty Zendejas, Nevada, 1984-87 (45 attempts)

HIGHEST PERCENTAGE OF FIELD GOALS MADE, 40 YARDS OR MORE
Season
(Min. 8 made) 100.0%—Tim Foley, Ga. Southern, 1985 (8 of 8)

Photo from Northern Iowa sports information

Brian Mitchell made 26 of 27 field goal attempts for Northern Iowa in 1990, tying a Division I-AA record for most field goals in a season and setting a record for best field goal percentage (96.3).

Career
(Min. 15 made) 72.0%—Tim Foley, Ga. Southern, 1984-87 (18 of 25)

HIGHEST PERCENTAGE OF FIELD GOALS MADE, 40-49 YARDS
Season
(Min. 8 made) 90.0%—Marty Zendejas, Nevada, 1985 (9 of 10)
Career
(Min. 12 made) 72.0%—Tony Zendejas, Nevada, 1981-83 (18 of 25)

HIGHEST PERCENTAGE OF FIELD GOALS MADE, UNDER 40 YARDS
Season
(Min. 15 made) 100.0%—Brian Mitchell, Northern Iowa, 1990 (23 of 23); Kirk Roach, Western Caro., 1986 (17 of 17); Matt Stover, Louisiana Tech, 1986 (15 of 15)
Career
(Min. 25 made) 93.3%—Marty Zendejas, Nevada, 1984-87 (42 of 45)

MOST TIMES KICKING TWO OR MORE FIELD GOALS IN A GAME
Season
10—Brian Mitchell, Northern Iowa, 1991
Career
25—Kirk Roach, Western Caro., 1984-87

MOST TIMES KICKING THREE OR MORE FIELD GOALS IN A GAME
Season
7—Brian Mitchell, Northern Iowa, 1991
Career
11—Brian Mitchell, Marshall/Northern Iowa, 1987, 1989-91

MOST CONSECUTIVE QUARTERS KICKING A FIELD GOAL
Season
7—Scott Roper, Arkansas St., 1986 (last 3 vs. McNeese St., Oct. 25; all 4 vs. North Texas, Nov. 1)

LONGEST AVERAGE DISTANCE FIELD GOALS MADE
Game
(Min. 3 made) 54.7—Terry Belden, Northern Ariz. vs. Cal St. Northridge, Sept. 18, 1993 (60, 50, 54 yards)
Season
(Min. 14 made) 45.0—Jesse Garcia, Northeast La., 1983 (15 made)
Career
(Min. 35 made) 37.5—Roger Ruzek, Weber St., 1979-82 (46 made)

LONGEST AVERAGE DISTANCE FIELD GOALS ATTEMPTED
Season
(Min. 20 atts.) 45.9—Jesse Garcia, Northeast La., 1983 (26 attempts)
Career
(Min. 60 atts.) 40.5—Kirk Roach, Western Caro., 1984-87 (102 attempts)

LONGEST FIELD GOAL MADE
63—Scott Roper, Arkansas St. vs. North Texas, Nov. 7, 1987; Tim Foley, Ga. Southern vs. James Madison, Nov. 7, 1987

LONGEST FIELD GOAL MADE BY A FRESHMAN
60—David Cool, Ga. Southern vs. James Madison, Nov. 5, 1988

MOST FIELD GOALS MADE BY A FRESHMAN
Game
5—Chuck Rawlinson, Stephen F. Austin vs. Prairie View, Sept. 10, 1988 (5 attempts); Marty Zendejas, Nevada vs. Idaho St., Nov. 17, 1984 (5 attempts); Mike Powers, Colgate vs. Army, Sept. 10, 1983 (6 attempts)
Season
22—Marty Zendejas, Nevada, 1984 (27 attempts)

MOST FIELD GOALS MADE IN FIRST GAME OF CAREER
5—Mike Powers, Colgate vs. Army, Sept. 10, 1983 (6 attempts)

MOST GAMES IN WHICH FIELD GOAL(S) PROVIDED WINNING MARGIN
Career
11—John Dowling, Youngstown St., 1984-87

LONGEST RETURN OF A MISSED FIELD GOAL
89—Pat Bayers, Western Ill. vs. Youngstown St., Nov. 6, 1982 (TD)

Team Records

SINGLE GAME—Offense

Total Offense

MOST PLAYS
113—Villanova vs. Connecticut, Oct. 7, 1989 (553 yards)

MOST PLAYS, BOTH TEAMS
196—Villanova (113) & Connecticut (83), Oct. 7, 1989 (904 yards)

MOST YARDS GAINED
876—Weber St. vs. Idaho St., Nov. 23, 1991 (252 rushing, 624 passing)

MOST YARDS GAINED, BOTH TEAMS
1,418—Howard (740) & Bethune-Cookman (678), Sept. 19, 1987 (161 plays)

MOST YARDS GAINED BY A LOSING TEAM
756—Alcorn St. vs. Grambling, Sept. 3, 1994 (lost 62-56)

FEWEST YARDS GAINED BY A WINNING TEAM
31—Middle Tenn. St. vs. Murray St., Oct. 17, 1981 (won 14-9)

HIGHEST AVERAGE GAIN PER PLAY (Min. 55 Plays)
12.7—Marshall vs. Va. Military, Nov. 16, 1991 (62 for 789)

MOST TOUCHDOWNS SCORED BY RUSHING AND PASSING
14—Portland St. vs. Delaware St., Nov. 8, 1980 (10 passing, 4 rushing)

Rushing

MOST RUSHES
90—Va. Military vs. East Tenn. St., Nov. 17, 1990 (311 yards)

MOST RUSHES, BOTH TEAMS
125—Austin Peay (81) & Murray St. (44), Nov. 17, 1990 (443 yards); Southwest Mo. St. (71) & Northern Ill. (54), Oct. 17, 1987 (375 yards)

FEWEST RUSHES
11—Western Ill. vs. Northern Iowa, Oct. 24, 1987 (-11 yards); Mississippi Val. vs. Kentucky St., Sept. 1, 1984 (17 yards)

MOST YARDS GAINED
681—Southwest Mo. St. vs. Mo. Southern St., Sept. 10, 1988 (83 rushes)

MOST YARDS GAINED, BOTH TEAMS
762—Arkansas St. (604) & East Tex. St. (158), Sept. 26, 1987 (102 rushes)

MOST YARDS GAINED BY A LOSING TEAM
448—Western Ky. vs. Southern Ill., Nov. 4, 1995 (lost 30-28)

HIGHEST AVERAGE GAIN PER RUSH (Min. 45 Rushes)
11.2—Southwest Mo. St. vs. Truman St., Oct. 5, 1985 (45 for 505)

MOST TOUCHDOWNS SCORED BY RUSHING
10—Arkansas St. vs. East Tex. St., Sept. 26, 1987

Passing

MOST PASSES ATTEMPTED
77—Portland St. vs. Northern Colo., Oct. 20, 1979 (completed 44 for 499 yards)

MOST PASSES ATTEMPTED, BOTH TEAMS
122—Idaho (62) & Idaho St. (60), Sept. 24, 1983 (completed 48 for 639 yards)

FEWEST PASSES ATTEMPTED
1—By many teams. Most recent: Northeastern vs. Towson St., Sept. 9, 1989 (completed 1)

FEWEST PASSES ATTEMPTED, BOTH TEAMS
11—Citadel (3) & Ga. Southern (8), Nov. 19, 1994 (completed 6); North Caro. A&T (5) & Western Ky. (6), Nov. 19, 1988 (completed 2); Memphis (3) & Arkansas St. (8), Nov. 27, 1982 (completed 6)

MOST PASSES ATTEMPTED WITHOUT INTERCEPTION
72—Marshall vs. Western Caro., Nov. 14, 1987 (completed 35)

MOST PASSES COMPLETED
50—Mississippi Val. vs. Prairie View, Oct. 27, 1984 (attempted 66 for 642 yards); Mississippi Val. vs. Southern-B.R., Sept. 29, 1984 (attempted 70 for 633 yards)

MOST PASSES COMPLETED, BOTH TEAMS I-AA
77—Northeast La. (46) & Stephen F. Austin (31), Nov. 11, 1989 (attempted 116 for 1,190 yards)

MOST PASSES COMPLETED, BOTH TEAMS
80—Hofstra (50) & Fordham (30), Oct. 19, 1991 (attempted 120 for 987 yards)

FEWEST PASSES COMPLETED
0—By many teams. Most recent: Ga. Southern vs. Liberty, Nov. 11, 1995; Citadel vs. East Tenn. St., Sept. 19, 1992

FEWEST PASSES COMPLETED, BOTH TEAMS
2—North Caro. A&T (0) & Western Ky. (2), Nov. 19, 1988 (attempted 11)

HIGHEST PERCENTAGE COMPLETED
(Min. 30-44 atts.) 81.6%—Nevada vs. Idaho St., Nov. 17, 1984 (31 of 38)
(Min. 45 atts.) 79.2%—Montana vs. Weber St., Oct. 7, 1995 (38 of 48)

LOWEST PERCENTAGE COMPLETED (Min. 20 Attempts)
9.5%—Florida A&M vs. Central St., Oct. 11, 1986 (2 of 21)

MOST PASSES HAD INTERCEPTED
10—Boise St. vs. Montana, Oct. 28, 1989 (55 attempts); Mississippi Val. vs. Grambling, Oct. 17, 1987 (47 attempts)

MOST YARDS GAINED
699—Mississippi Val. vs. Kentucky St., Sept. 1, 1984

MOST YARDS GAINED, BOTH TEAMS
1,190—Northeast La. (619) & Stephen F. Austin (571), Nov. 11, 1989

MOST YARDS GAINED PER ATTEMPT (Min. 25 Attempts)
17.4—Marshall vs. Va. Military, Nov. 16, 1991 (37 for 642)

MOST YARDS GAINED PER COMPLETION
(Min. 10-24 comps.) 33.0—Jackson St. vs. Southern-B.R., Oct. 13, 1990 (14 for 462)
(Min. 25 comps.) 22.9—Marshall vs. Va. Military, Nov. 16, 1991 (28 for 642)

MOST TOUCHDOWN PASSES
11—Mississippi Val. vs. Kentucky St., Sept. 1, 1984

MOST TOUCHDOWN PASSES, BOTH TEAMS
14—Mississippi Val. (8) & Texas Southern (6), Oct. 26, 1985

Punting

MOST PUNTS
16—Louisiana Tech vs. Northeast La., Nov. 19, 1988 (567 yards)

HIGHEST AVERAGE PER PUNT
(Min. 5-9 punts) 55.7—Appalachian St. vs. Citadel, Oct. 3, 1992 (6 for 334); Montana vs. Nevada, Oct. 1, 1988 (9 for 501)
(Min. 10 punts) 52.2—Montana St. vs. Northern Ariz., Oct. 20, 1979 (10 for 522)

FEWEST PUNTS
0—By many teams. Most recent: Central Fla. vs. Buffalo, Nov. 19, 1994; Western Ill. vs. Murray St., Nov. 19, 1994

FEWEST PUNTS, BOTH TEAMS
0—Ga. Southern & James Madison, Nov. 15, 1986

MOST OPPONENT'S PUNTS BLOCKED BY
4—Middle Tenn. St. vs. Mississippi Val., Oct. 8, 1988 (7 punts); Montana vs. Montana St., Oct. 31, 1987 (13 punts)

Punt Returns

MOST PUNT RETURNS
12—Northern Iowa vs. Youngstown St., Oct. 20, 1984 (83 yards)

MOST YARDS ON PUNT RETURNS
221—Howard vs. Morgan St., Nov. 3, 1990 (8 returns)

HIGHEST AVERAGE GAIN PER RETURN (Min. 6 Returns)
30.9—Mississippi Val. vs. Washburn, Sept. 15, 1984 (7 for 216, 2 TDs)

MOST TOUCHDOWNS SCORED ON PUNT RETURNS
3—Canisius vs. Siena, Sept. 24, 1994

Kickoff Returns

MOST KICKOFF RETURNS
15—Delaware St. vs. Portland St., Nov. 8, 1980 (209 yards)

MOST YARDS ON KICKOFF RETURNS
277—Idaho St. vs. Tex. A&M-Kingsville, Sept. 12, 1987 (10 returns)

HIGHEST AVERAGE GAIN PER RETURN
(Min. 3-5 rets.) 50.5—Eastern Ky. vs. Murray St., Oct. 28, 1978 (4 for 202)
(Min. 6 rets.) 46.3—Western Caro. vs. Va. Military, Oct. 10, 1992 (6 for 278)

MOST TOUCHDOWNS SCORED ON KICKOFF RETURNS
2—Western Ill. vs. St. Ambrose, Nov. 13, 1993; Western Caro. vs. Va. Military, Oct. 10, 1992; Western Ill. vs. Youngstown St., Nov. 7, 1981

Total Kick Returns

(Combined Punt and Kickoff Returns)

MOST YARDS ON KICK RETURNS
318—Tennessee St. vs. Morgan St., Oct. 24, 1987 (12 returns)

HIGHEST AVERAGE GAIN PER RETURN (Min. 6 Returns)
46.8—Connecticut vs. Yale, Sept. 24, 1983 (6 for 281)

Scoring

MOST POINTS SCORED
105—Portland St. vs. Delaware St., Nov. 8, 1980 (15 TDs, 15 PATs)

MOST POINTS SCORED, BOTH TEAMS
122—Weber St. (63) & Eastern Wash. (59), Sept. 28, 1991 (17 TDs, 14 PATs, 2 FGs)

MOST POINTS SCORED BY A LOSING TEAM
59—Eastern Wash. vs. Weber St. (63), Sept. 28, 1991

MOST POINTS SCORED EACH QUARTER
1st: 49—Portland St. vs. Delaware St., Nov. 8, 1980
2nd: 50—Alabama St. vs. Prairie View, Oct. 26, 1991
3rd: 35—Northeast La. vs. Arkansas St., Nov. 6, 1993; Portland St. vs. Delaware St., Nov. 8, 1980
4th: 39—Montana vs. South Dak. St., Sept. 4, 1993

MOST POINTS SCORED EACH HALF
1st: 73—Montana St. vs. Eastern Ore. St., Sept. 14, 1985
2nd: 56—Brown vs. Columbia, Nov. 19, 1994

MOST TOUCHDOWNS SCORED
15—Portland St. vs. Delaware St., Nov. 8, 1980

MOST TOUCHDOWNS SCORED, BOTH TEAMS
17—Grambling (9) & Alcorn St. (8), Sept. 3, 1994; Weber St. (9) & Eastern Wash. (8), Sept. 28, 1991; Furman (9) & Davidson (8), Nov. 3, 1979

MOST EXTRA POINTS MADE BY KICKING
15—Portland St. vs. Delaware St., Nov. 8, 1980 (15 attempts)

MOST TWO-POINT ATTEMPTS MADE
5—Weber St. vs. Eastern Wash., Oct. 6, 1990 (5 passes attempted)

MOST FIELD GOALS MADE
8—Northern Ariz. vs. Idaho, Oct. 25, 1986 (8 attempts)

MOST FIELD GOALS ATTEMPTED
8—Northern Ariz. vs. Idaho, Oct. 25, 1986 (made 8)

MOST FIELD GOALS MADE, BOTH TEAMS
9—Nevada (5) & Weber St. (4), Nov. 6, 1982 (11 attempts, 3 OT); Nevada (5) & Northern Ariz. (4), Oct. 9, 1982 (12 attempts)

MOST SAFETIES SCORED
3—Alabama St. vs. Albany St. (Ga.), Oct. 15, 1988

MOST DEFENSIVE EXTRA POINTS SCORED
2—Va. Military vs. Davidson, Nov. 4, 1989 (Jeff Barnes, 95-yard interception return, and Wayne Purcell, 90-yard interception return)

MOST DEFENSIVE EXTRA-POINT ATTEMPTS
2—Western Ky. vs. Indiana St., Nov. 10, 1990 (2 interception returns); Va. Military vs. Davidson, Nov. 4, 1989 (2 interception returns)

First Downs

MOST FIRST DOWNS
46—Weber St. vs. Idaho St., Nov. 23, 1991 (12 rushing, 31 passing, 3 penalty)

MOST FIRST DOWNS, BOTH TEAMS
72—Bethune-Cookman (40) & Howard (32), Sept. 19, 1987

MOST FIRST DOWNS BY RUSHING
29—By six teams. Most recent: Arkansas St. vs. Southern Ill., Nov. 5, 1988; Southwest Mo. St. vs. Mo. Southern St., Sept. 10, 1988

MOST FIRST DOWNS BY PASSING
31—Weber St. vs. Idaho St., Nov. 23, 1991

MOST FIRST DOWNS BY PENALTY
11—Towson St. vs. Liberty, Oct. 21, 1990

Fumbles

MOST FUMBLES
16—Delaware St. vs. Portland St., Nov. 8, 1980 (lost 6)

MOST FUMBLES, BOTH TEAMS
21—North Caro. A&T (15) & Lane (6), Nov. 11, 1995 (lost 12)

MOST FUMBLES LOST
9—North Caro. A&T vs. Lane, Nov. 11, 1995 (15 fumbles)

MOST FUMBLES LOST, BOTH TEAMS
12—North Caro. A&T (9) & Lane (3), Nov. 11, 1995 (21 fumbles); Austin Peay (8) & Mars Hill (4), Nov. 17, 1979 (18 fumbles); Virginia St. (7) & Howard (5), Oct. 13, 1979 (16 fumbles)

Penalties

MOST PENALTIES AGAINST
23—Idaho vs. Idaho St., Oct. 10, 1992 (204 yards)

MOST PENALTIES, BOTH TEAMS
39—In four games. Most recent: Jackson St. (22) & Grambling (17), Oct. 24, 1987 (370 yards)

MOST YARDS PENALIZED
260—Southern-B.R. vs. Howard, Nov. 4, 1978 (22 penalties)

MOST YARDS PENALIZED, BOTH TEAMS
423—Southern-B.R. (260) & Howard (163), Nov. 4, 1978 (37 penalties)

Turnovers

(Passes Had Intercepted and Fumbles Lost)

MOST TURNOVERS
12—Texas Southern vs. Lamar, Sept. 6, 1980 (4 interceptions, 8 fumbles lost)

MOST TURNOVERS, BOTH TEAMS
15—Stephen F. Austin (8) & Nicholls St. (7), Sept. 22, 1990 (8 interceptions, 7 fumbles lost); Bucknell (8) & Hofstra (7), Sept. 8, 1990 (10 interceptions, 5 fumbles lost)

SINGLE GAME—Defense

Total Defense

FEWEST PLAYS ALLOWED
31—Howard vs. Dist. Columbia, Sept. 2, 1989 (32 yards)

FEWEST YARDS ALLOWED
Minus 12—Eastern Ill. vs. Kentucky St., Nov. 13, 1982 (-67 rushing, 55 passing)

Rushing Defense

FEWEST RUSHES ALLOWED
10—Ga. Southern vs. Valdosta St., Sept. 12, 1992 (21 yards)

FEWEST RUSHING YARDS ALLOWED
Minus 88—Austin Peay vs. Morehead St., Oct. 8, 1983 (31 rushes)

Pass Defense

FEWEST ATTEMPTS ALLOWED
1—By five teams. Most recent: Towson St. vs. Northeastern, Sept. 9, 1989 (1 completed)

FEWEST COMPLETIONS ALLOWED
0—By many teams. Most recent: Colgate vs. Army, Nov. 18, 1989 (2 attempts); Illinois St. vs. Arkansas St., Nov. 11, 1989 (3 attempts); Marshall vs. Va. Military, Oct. 28, 1989 (4 attempts)

LOWEST COMPLETION PERCENTAGE ALLOWED (Min. 30 Attempts)
11.8%—Southern-B.R. vs. Nicholls St., Oct. 11, 1980 (4 of 34)

FEWEST YARDS ALLOWED
Minus 2—Florida A&M vs. Albany St. (Ga.), Oct. 16, 1982

MOST PASSES INTERCEPTED BY
10—Montana vs. Boise St., Oct. 28, 1989 (55 attempts); Grambling vs. Mississippi Val., Oct. 17, 1987 (47 attempts)

MOST TIMES OPPONENT TACKLED FOR LOSS ATTEMPTING TO PASS
13—Austin Peay vs. Morehead St., Oct. 8, 1983 (110 yards)

MOST INTERCEPTIONS RETURNED FOR TOUCHDOWNS
3—Canisius vs. Siena, Sept. 16, 1995 (6 for 120 yards); Delaware St. vs. Akron, Oct. 17, 1987 (5 for 124 yards); Montana vs. Eastern Wash., Nov. 12, 1983 (4 for 134 yards); Tenn.-Chatt. vs. Southwestern La., Sept. 17, 1983 (4 for 122 yards)

Kick Blocks

MOST KICKS BLOCKED
3—Northwestern St. vs. Arkansas St., Oct. 3, 1992 (2 PATs, 1 FG)

MOST PUNTS BLOCKED
4—Middle Tenn. St. vs. Mississippi Val., Oct. 8, 1988 (7 punts); Montana vs. Montana St., Oct. 31, 1987 (13 punts)

Fumble Returns

(Since 1992)

MOST FUMBLES RETURNED FOR TOUCHDOWNS
2—Idaho vs. Weber St., Nov. 12, 1994; Marshall vs. Va. Military, Oct. 9, 1993

SEASON—Offense

Total Offense

MOST YARDS GAINED PER GAME
640.1—Mississippi Val., 1984 (6,401 in 10)

HIGHEST AVERAGE GAIN PER PLAY
7.8—Alcorn St., 1994 (848 for 6,577)

MOST PLAYS PER GAME
89.6—Weber St., 1991 (986 in 11)

MOST TOUCHDOWNS BY RUSHING AND PASSING PER GAME
8.4—Mississippi Val., 1984 (84 in 10)

Rushing

MOST YARDS GAINED PER GAME
382.0—Citadel, 1994 (4,202 in 11)

HIGHEST AVERAGE GAIN PER RUSH
6.6—Citadel, 1994 (633 for 4,202)

MOST RUSHES PER GAME
69.8—Northeastern, 1986 (698 in 10)

MOST TOUCHDOWNS BY RUSHING PER GAME
4.5—Howard, 1987 (45 in 10)

Passing

MOST YARDS GAINED PER GAME
496.8—Mississippi Val., 1984 (4,968 in 10)

HIGHEST AVERAGE GAIN PER ATTEMPT
(Min. 250-399 atts.) 10.5—Northern Iowa, 1995 (250 for 2,616)
(Min. 400 atts.) 9.3—Idaho, 1989 (445 for 4,117)

HIGHEST AVERAGE GAIN PER COMPLETION
(Min. 125-199 comps.) 19.3—Jackson St., 1990 (156 for 3,006)
(Min. 200 comps.) 16.6—Stephen F. Austin, 1989 (240 for 3,985)

MOST PASSES ATTEMPTED PER GAME
55.8—Mississippi Val., 1984 (558 in 10)

MOST PASSES COMPLETED PER GAME
35.1—Mississippi Val., 1984 (351 in 10)

HIGHEST PERCENTAGE COMPLETED
(Min. 200-449 atts.) 69.4%—William & Mary, 1993 (161 of 232)
(Min. 450 atts.) 67.2%—Montana, 1995 (336 of 500)

LOWEST PERCENTAGE HAD INTERCEPTED
(Min. 200-399 atts.) 0.9%—Hofstra, 1995 (3 of 336)
(Min. 400 atts.) 1.2%—Lamar, 1988 (5 of 411)

MOST CONSECUTIVE PASSES ATTEMPTED WITHOUT AN INTERCEPTION
275—Lamar, 1988 (during 8 games, Sept. 3 to Oct. 29)

MOST TOUCHDOWN PASSES PER GAME
6.4—Mississippi Val., 1984 (64 in 10)

HIGHEST PASSING EFFICIENCY RATING POINTS
190.6—William & Mary, 1993 (232 attempts, 161 completions, 4 interceptions, 2,499 yards, 24 TDs)

Punting

MOST PUNTS PER GAME
9.6—Louisiana Tech, 1987 (106 in 11)

FEWEST PUNTS PER GAME
2.2—Alcorn St., 1994 (24 in 11)

HIGHEST PUNTING AVERAGE
47.0—Appalachian St., 1991 (64 for 3,009)

HIGHEST NET PUNTING AVERAGE
42.9—Marshall, 1994 (27 for 1,226; 69 yards returned)

MOST PUNTS HAD BLOCKED
8—Western Ky., 1982

Punt Returns

MOST PUNT RETURNS PER GAME
5.4—Murray St., 1980 (59 in 11)

FEWEST PUNT RETURNS PER GAME
0.6—Southern Ill., 1991 (7 in 11); Prairie View, 1991 (7 in 11); Youngstown St., 1990 (7 in 11)

MOST PUNT-RETURN YARDS PER GAME
56.1—South Caro. St., 1981 (617 in 11)

HIGHEST AVERAGE GAIN PER PUNT RETURN
(Min. 20-29 rets.) 19.5—Towson St., 1994 (27 for 526)
(Min. 30 rets.) 18.1—Mississippi Val., 1985 (31 for 561)

MOST TOUCHDOWNS SCORED ON PUNT RETURNS
5—Southern Ill., 1985

Kickoff Returns

MOST KICKOFF RETURNS PER GAME
7.7—Morehead St., 1994 (85 in 11; 1,582 yards)

FEWEST KICKOFF RETURNS PER GAME
1.4—North Texas, 1983 (15 in 11)

MOST KICKOFF-RETURN YARDS PER GAME
143.8—Morehead St., 1994 (1,582 in 11; 85 returns)

HIGHEST AVERAGE GAIN PER KICKOFF RETURN (Min. 20 Returns)
29.5—Eastern Ky., 1986 (34 for 1,022)

Combined Returns

(Interceptions, Punt Returns and Kickoff Returns)

MOST TOUCHDOWNS SCORED
9—Delaware St., 1987 (5 interceptions, 3 punt returns, 1 kickoff return)

Scoring

MOST POINTS PER GAME
60.9—Mississippi Val., 1984 (609 in 10)

MOST TOUCHDOWNS PER GAME
8.7—Mississippi Val., 1984 (87 in 10)

MOST EXTRA POINTS MADE BY KICKING PER GAME
7.7—Mississippi Val., 1984 (77 in 10)

MOST CONSECUTIVE EXTRA POINTS MADE BY KICKING
56—Murray St., 1995

MOST TWO-POINT ATTEMPTS MADE
9—Weber St., 1992 (11 attempts)

MOST DEFENSIVE EXTRA-POINT ATTEMPTS
2—Western Ky., 1990; Eastern Wash., 1990; Va. Military, 1989

MOST DEFENSIVE EXTRA POINTS SCORED
2—Eastern Wash., 1990 (2 interception returns); Va. Military, 1989 (2 interception returns)

MOST FIELD GOALS MADE PER GAME
2.4—Northern Iowa, 1990 (26 in 11); Nevada, 1982 (26 in 11)

MOST SAFETIES SCORED
5—Jackson St., 1986

First Downs

MOST FIRST DOWNS PER GAME
31.7—Mississippi Val., 1984 (317 in 10)

MOST RUSHING FIRST DOWNS PER GAME
18.1—Citadel, 1994 (199 in 11)

MOST PASSING FIRST DOWNS PER GAME
21.4—Mississippi Val., 1984 (214 in 10)

MOST FIRST DOWNS BY PENALTY PER GAME
3.7—Texas Southern, 1987 (41 in 11; 134 penalties by opponents); Alabama St., 1984 (41 in 11; 109 penalties by opponents)

Fumbles

MOST FUMBLES PER GAME
5.3—Prairie View, 1984 (58 in 11)

MOST FUMBLES LOST PER GAME
3.1—Delaware St., 1980 (31 in 10); Idaho, 1978 (31 in 10)

FEWEST OWN FUMBLES LOST
2—Brown, 1994 (13 fumbles)

Penalties

MOST PENALTIES PER GAME
13.7—Grambling, 1984 (151 in 11; 1,206 yards)

MOST YARDS PENALIZED PER GAME
125.5—Tennessee St., 1982 (1,255 in 10; 132 penalties)

Turnovers

FEWEST TURNOVERS
9—Hofstra, 1995 (6 fumbles, 3 interceptions)

MOST TURNOVERS
59—Texas Southern, 1980 (27 fumbles, 32 interceptions)

HIGHEST TURNOVER MARGIN PER GAME OVER OPPONENTS
2.5—Appalachian St., 1985; Florida A&M, 1981

SEASON—Defense

Total Defense

FEWEST YARDS ALLOWED PER GAME
149.9—Florida A&M, 1978 (1,649 in 11)

FEWEST RUSHING AND PASSING TOUCHDOWNS ALLOWED PER GAME
0.7—Western Mich., 1982 (8 in 11)

LOWEST AVERAGE YARDS ALLOWED PER PLAY
2.4—South Caro. St., 1978 (719 for 1,736)

Rushing Defense

FEWEST YARDS ALLOWED PER GAME
44.5—Grambling, 1984 (489 in 11)

LOWEST AVERAGE YARDS ALLOWED PER RUSH
1.3—Florida A&M, 1978 (419 for 535)

FEWEST RUSHING TOUCHDOWNS ALLOWED PER GAME
0.3—Florida A&M, 1978 (3 in 11)

Pass Defense

FEWEST YARDS ALLOWED PER GAME
59.9—Bethune-Cookman, 1981 (659 in 11)

FEWEST YARDS ALLOWED PER ATTEMPT (Min. 200 Attempts)
4.0—Middle Tenn. St., 1988 (251 for 999)

FEWEST YARDS ALLOWED PER COMPLETION (Min. 100 Completions)
9.1—Middle Tenn. St., 1988 (110 for 999)

LOWEST COMPLETION PERCENTAGE ALLOWED
(Min. 200-299 atts.) 32.3%—Alcorn St., 1979 (76 of 235)
(Min. 300 atts.) 34.2%—Tennessee St., 1986 (107 of 313)

FEWEST TOUCHDOWNS ALLOWED BY PASSING
1—Pennsylvania, 1994; Middle Tenn. St., 1990; Nevada, 1978

LOWEST PASSING EFFICIENCY DEFENSE RATING (Since 1990)
63.1—Pennsylvania, 1994 (235 attempts, 90 completions, 15 interceptions, 1,013 yards, 1 TD)

MOST PASSES INTERCEPTED BY, PER GAME
3.2—Florida A&M, 1981 (35 in 11)

HIGHEST PERCENTAGE INTERCEPTED BY
13.4%—Florida A&M, 1981 (35 of 262)

MOST YARDS GAINED ON INTERCEPTIONS
498—Jackson St., 1985 (28 interceptions)

MOST YARDS GAINED PER GAME ON INTERCEPTIONS
49.8—Jackson St., 1985 (498 in 10)

HIGHEST AVERAGE PER INTERCEPTION RETURN (Min. 15 Returns)
23.7—Cal St. Northridge, 1994 (18 for 426)

MOST TOUCHDOWNS ON INTERCEPTION RETURNS
7—Jackson St., 1985

Punting

MOST OPPONENT'S PUNTS BLOCKED BY
9—Middle Tenn. St., 1988 (73 punts)

Punt Returns

LOWEST AVERAGE YARDS ALLOWED PER PUNT RETURN
1.0—Yale, 1988 (24 for 23)

FEWEST RETURNS ALLOWED
7—Furman, 1984 (11 games, 8 yards)

Kickoff Returns

LOWEST AVERAGE YARDS ALLOWED PER KICKOFF RETURN
11.0—Lafayette, 1980 (20 for 220)

Scoring

FEWEST POINTS ALLOWED PER GAME
6.5—South Caro. St., 1978 (72 in 11)

Fumbles

MOST OPPONENT'S FUMBLES RECOVERED
29—Western Ky., 1982 (43 fumbles)

Fumble Returns

(Since 1992)

MOST FUMBLES RETURNED FOR TOUCHDOWNS
2—Marshall, 1993 (both vs. Va. Military, Oct. 9); Citadel, 1992 (vs. Arkansas, Sept. 5 & vs. Western Caro., Oct. 24)

Turnovers

MOST OPPONENT'S TURNOVERS PER GAME
4.8—Grambling, 1985 (53 in 11)

Additional Records

MOST CONSECUTIVE VICTORIES
24—Pennsylvania, from Nov. 14, 1992, through Sept. 30, 1995 (ended Oct. 7, 1995, with 24-14 loss to Columbia)

MOST CONSECUTIVE HOME VICTORIES
38—Ga. Southern, from Oct. 5, 1985, through Sept. 22, 1990 (includes 10 I-AA playoff games)

MOST CONSECUTIVE LOSSES
57—Prairie View, from Nov. 4, 1989, through Nov. 11, 1995 (current)

MOST CONSECUTIVE GAMES WITHOUT A WIN
57—Prairie View, from Nov. 4, 1989, through Nov. 11, 1995 (current)

MOST CONSECUTIVE GAMES WITHOUT BEING SHUT OUT
193—Boise St., from Sept. 21, 1968, through Nov. 10, 1984
(Note: Dayton currently has a 225-game streak without being shut out but has been a I-AA member only since 1993)

MOST SHUTOUTS IN A SEASON
5—South Caro. St., 1978

MOST CONSECUTIVE QUARTERS HOLDING OPPONENTS SCORELESS
14—McNeese St., 1985; Bucknell, 1979

MOST CONSECUTIVE GAMES WITHOUT A TIE
343—Richmond, from Nov. 2, 1963, to Oct. 14, 1995 (ended Oct. 21, 1995, with 3-3 tie with Fordham)

LAST SCORELESS-TIE GAME
Oct. 26, 1985—McNeese St. & North Texas

HIGHEST-SCORING TIE GAME
51-51—Villanova vs. William & Mary, Oct. 23, 1993

MOST CONSECUTIVE PASSES ATTEMPTED WITHOUT AN INTERCEPTION
297—Lamar (in 9 games from Nov. 21, 1987, to Oct. 29, 1988)

MOST POINTS OVERCOME IN SECOND HALF TO WIN A GAME
35—Nevada (55) vs. Weber St. (49), Nov. 2, 1991 (trailed 49-14 with 12:16 remaining in 3rd quarter)
32—Morehead St. (36) vs. Wichita St. (35), Sept. 20, 1986 (trailed 35-3 with 9:03 remaining in 3rd quarter)
31—Montana (52) vs. South Dak. St. (48), Sept. 4, 1993 (trailed 38-7 with 8:12 remaining in 3rd quarter)

MOST POINTS OVERCOME IN FOURTH QUARTER TO WIN A GAME
28—Delaware St. (38) vs. Liberty (37), Oct. 6, 1990 (trailed 37-9 with 13:00 remaining in 4th quarter)

MOST POINTS SCORED IN FOURTH QUARTER TO WIN A GAME
39—Montana (52) vs. South Dak. St. (48), Sept. 4, 1993 (trailed 38-13 to begin 4th quarter)
33—Southwest Mo. St. (40) vs. Illinois St. (28), Oct. 9, 1993 (trailed 21-7 with 11:30 remaining in 4th quarter)

MOST OVERTIME PERIODS IN A GAME
6—Villanova vs. Connecticut, Oct. 7, 1989 (score after regulation time was 21-21; Villanova won, 41-35)

Score by Periods

				Regulation			
Connecticut			0	14	0	7—21	
Villanova			0	0	14	7—21	
				Overtime			
Connecticut	0	0	7	0	7	0—35	
Villanova	0	0	7	0	7	6—41	

There were 11 TDs, 10 PATs. Game time was 3:40. Villanova's Jeff Johnson scored the winning TD on a 3-yard run (his third TD of the game).

6—Rhode Island vs. Maine, Sept. 18, 1982 (score after regulation time was 21-21; Rhode Island won, 58-55)

Score by Periods

				Regulation		
Rhode Island			7	7	0	7—21
Maine			0	7	0	14—21
				Overtime		
Rhode Island	7	7	3	7	7	6—58
Maine	7	7	3	7	7	3—55

There were 15 TDs, 14 PATs, 3 FGs. Game time was 3:46, including 51 minutes of overtime. Rhode Island's T. J. Del Santo scored the winning TD on a 2-yard run (his fourth TD of the game) after Maine kicked a field goal in the sixth overtime.

MOST CONSECUTIVE OVERTIME GAMES PLAYED
2—Connecticut, 1989 (Villanova 41, Connecticut 35, 6 OT, Oct. 7; and Connecticut 39, Massachusetts 33, 1 OT, Oct. 14); Maine, 1982 (Rhode Island 58, Maine 55, 6 OT, Sept. 18; and Boston U. 48, Maine 45, 4 OT, Sept. 25)

MOST CONSECUTIVE EXTRA-POINT KICKS MADE
134—Boise St. (began Oct. 27, 1984; ended Nov. 12, 1988)

MOST CONSECUTIVE WINNING SEASONS
27—Grambling (1960-86)

MOST IMPROVED WON-LOST RECORD
9 1/2 games—Montana St., 1984 (12-2-0, including 3 Division I-AA playoff games) from 1983 (1-10-0)

Annual Champions, All-Time Leaders

Total Offense

CAREER YARDS PER GAME
(Minimum 5,500 Yards)

Player, Team	Years	G	Plays	Yards	TDR‡	Yd. PG
Steve McNair, Alcorn St.	1991-94	42	*2,055	*16,823	152	*400.5
Neil Lomax, Portland St.	1978-80	33	1,680	11,647	100	352.9
Dave Dickenson, Montana	1992-95	35	1,539	11,523	116	329.2
Willie Totten, Mississippi Val.	1982-85	40	1,812	13,007	*157	325.2
Tom Ehrhardt, Rhode Island	1984-85	21	1,010	6,492	66	309.1
Doug Nussmeier, Idaho	1990-93	39	1,556	12,054	109	309.1
Jamie Martin, Weber St.	1989-92	41	1,838	12,287	93	299.7
Tom Proudian, Iona	1993-95	27	1,337	7,939	61	294.0
Robert Dougherty, Boston U.	1993-94	21	918	6,135	56	292.1
Stan Greene, Boston U.	1989-90	22	1,167	6,408	49	291.3
John Friesz, Idaho	1986-89	35	1,459	10,187	79	291.1
Grady Bennett, Montana	1988-90	31	1,389	8,304	69	267.9
Sean Payton, Eastern Ill.	1983-86	39	1,690	10,298	91	264.1
John Whitcomb, Ala.-Birmingham	1993-94	22	800	5,683	43	258.3
John Witkowski, Columbia	1981-83	30	1,330	7,748	58	258.3
Ken Hobart, Idaho	1980-83	44	1,847	11,127	105	252.9
Jeff Wiley, Holy Cross	1985-88	40	1,428	9,877	76	246.9
Doug Butler, Princeton	1983-85	29	1,137	7,157	52	246.8
Tom Ciaccio, Holy Cross	1988-91	37	1,283	9,066	87	245.0
Greg Wyatt, Northern Ariz.	1986-89	42	1,753	10,277	75	244.7
Jeff Lewis, Northern Ariz.	1992-95	40	1,654	9,769	82	244.2
Jay Fiedler, Dartmouth	1991-93	30	1,063	7,249	73	241.6
Chris Hakel, William & Mary	1988-91	28	915	6,458	56	239.2
Bob Jean, New Hampshire	1985-88	32	1,287	7,621	59	238.2
Michael Proctor, Murray St.	1986-89	43	1,577	9,886	66	230.0
Fred Gatlin, Nevada	1989-91	32	1,109	7,329	61	229.0
Mike Cawley, James Madison	1993-95	32	1,199	7,249	64	226.5
Frank Baur, Lafayette	1985, 87-89	38	1,312	8,579	72	225.8
Eric Beavers, Nevada	1983-86	40	1,307	9,025	85	225.6

**Record. ‡Touchdowns-responsible-for are player's TDs scored and passed for.*

SEASON YARDS PER GAME

Player, Team	Year	G	Plays	Yards	TDR‡	Yd. PG
Steve McNair, Alcorn St.	†1994	11	*649	*5,799	53	*527.2
Willie Totten, Mississippi Val.	†1984	10	564	4,572	*61	457.2
Steve McNair, Alcorn St.	†1992	10	519	4,057	39	405.7
Jamie Martin, Weber St.	†1991	11	591	4,337	37	394.3
Dave Dickenson, Montana	†1995	11	544	4,209	41	382.6
Neil Lomax, Portland St.	†1980	11	550	4,157	42	377.9
Dave Dickenson, Montana	†1993	11	530	3,978	46	361.6
Neil Lomax, Portland St.	†1979	11	611	3,966	31	360.5
John Friesz, Idaho	†1989	11	464	3,853	31	350.3
Steve McNair, Alcorn St.	1993	11	493	3,830	30	348.2
Todd Hammel, Stephen F. Austin	1989	11	487	3,822	38	347.5
Tom Ehrhardt, Rhode Island	†1985	10	529	3,460	35	346.0
Ken Hobart, Idaho	†1983	11	578	3,800	37	345.5
Dave Dickenson, Montana	1994	9	431	3,108	27	345.3
Dave Stireman, Weber St.	1985	11	502	3,759	33	341.7
Willie Totten, Mississippi Val.	1985	11	561	3,742	43	340.2
Jeff Wiley, Holy Cross	†1987	11	445	3,722	34	338.4
Jamie Martin, Weber St.	†1990	11	508	3,713	25	337.6
Sean Payton, Eastern Ill.	1984	11	584	3,661	31	332.8
Tod Mayfield, West Tex. A&M	1985	10	526	3,328	21	332.8
Tom Proudian, Iona	1993	10	521	3,322	30	332.2

**Record. †National champion. ‡Touchdowns-responsible-for are player's TDs scored and passed for.*

CAREER YARDS

Player, Team	Years	Plays	Yards	Avg.
Steve McNair, Alcorn St.	1991-94	*2,055	*16,823	*8.19
Willie Totten, Mississippi Val.	1982-85	1,812	13,007	7.18
Jamie Martin, Weber St.	1989-92	1,838	12,287	6.68
Doug Nussmeier, Idaho	1990-93	1,556	12,054	7.75
Neil Lomax, Portland St.	1978-80	1,680	11,647	6.93
Dave Dickenson, Montana	1992-95	1,539	11,523	7.49
Ken Hobart, Idaho	1980-83	1,847	11,127	6.02
Sean Payton, Eastern Ill.	1983-86	1,690	10,298	6.09
Greg Wyatt, Northern Ariz.	1986-89	1,753	10,277	5.86
John Friesz, Idaho	1986-89	1,459	10,187	6.98
Michael Proctor, Murray St.	1986-89	1,577	9,886	6.27
Jeff Wiley, Holy Cross	1985-88	1,428	9,877	6.92
Jeff Lewis, Northern Ariz.	1992-95	1,654	9,769	5.91
Matt DeGennaro, Connecticut	1987-90	1,619	9,269	5.73
Tom Ciaccio, Holy Cross	1988-91	1,283	9,066	7.07
Eric Beavers, Nevada	1983-86	1,307	9,025	6.91
Marty Horn, Lehigh	1982-85	1,612	8,956	5.56
Kirk Schulz, Villanova	1986-89	1,534	8,900	5.80
Darin Hinshaw, Central Fla.	1991-94	1,266	8,841	6.98
Robbie Justino, Liberty	1989-92	1,469	8,803	5.99
Dan Crowley, Towson St.	1991-94	1,263	8,797	6.97
Mitch Maher, North Texas	1991-94	1,417	8,735	6.16
Chris Swartz, Morehead St.	1987-90	1,559	8,648	5.55
Frank Baur, Lafayette	1985, 87-89	1,312	8,579	6.54
Steve Calabria, Colgate	1981-84	1,342	8,532	6.36
Mike Buck, Maine	1986-89	1,288	8,457	6.57
Jason Whitmer, Idaho St.	1987-90	1,618	8,449	5.22
Scott Davis, North Texas	1987-90	1,548	8,436	5.45
Grady Bennett, Montana	1988-90	1,389	8,304	5.98
Bill Vergantino, Delaware	1989-92	1,459	8,225	5.64
Stan Yagiello, William & Mary	$1981-85	1,492	8,168	5.47
Mike Smith, Northern Iowa	1984-87	1,163	8,145	7.00
Eric Randall, Southern-B.R.	1992-95	1,383	7,991	5.78
Bob Bleier, Richmond	1983-86	1,313	7,991	6.09
Tom Proudian, Iona	1993-95	1,337	7,939	5.94
Alan Hooker, North Caro. A&T	1984-87	1,476	7,787	5.28
John Witkowski, Columbia	1981-83	1,330	7,748	5.83
Michael Payton, Marshall	1989-92	1,106	7,744	7.00
Kelly Bradley, Montana St.	1983-86	1,547	7,740	5.00
Jeff Cesarone, Western Ky.	1984-87	1,502	7,694	5.12

**Record. $See page 6 for explanation.*

SEASON YARDS

Player, Team	Year	G	Plays	Yards	Avg.
Steve McNair, Alcorn St.	†1994	11	*649	*5,799	*8.94
Willie Totten, Mississippi Val.	†1984	10	564	4,572	8.11
Jamie Martin, Weber St.	†1991	11	591	4,337	7.34
Dave Dickenson, Montana	†1995	11	544	4,209	7.74
Neil Lomax, Portland St.	†1980	11	550	4,157	7.56
Steve McNair, Alcorn St.	†1992	10	519	4,057	7.82
Dave Dickenson, Montana	†1993	11	530	3,978	7.51
Neil Lomax, Portland St.	†1979	11	611	3,966	6.49
John Friesz, Idaho	†1989	11	464	3,853	8.30
Steve McNair, Alcorn St.	1993	11	493	3,830	7.77
Todd Hammel, Stephen F. Austin	1989	11	487	3,822	7.85
Ken Hobart, Idaho	†1983	11	578	3,800	6.57
Dave Stireman, Weber St.	1985	11	502	3,759	7.49
Willie Totten, Mississippi Val.	1985	11	561	3,742	6.67
Jeff Wiley, Holy Cross	†1987	11	445	3,722	8.36
Jamie Martin, Weber St.	†1990	11	508	3,713	7.31
Sean Payton, Eastern Ill.	1984	11	584	3,661	6.27
Todd Brunner, Lehigh	1989	11	504	3,639	7.22
Scott Semptimphelter, Lehigh	1993	11	515	3,528	6.85
Neil Lomax, Portland St.	†1978	11	519	3,524	6.79
Doug Nussmeier, Idaho	1993	11	400	3,514	8.79
Glenn Kempa, Lehigh	1991	11	513	3,511	6.84
John Friesz, Idaho	1987	11	543	3,489	6.43
Jay Walker, Howard	1993	11	466	3,469	7.44
Doug Nussmeier, Idaho	1991	11	472	3,460	7.33
Tom Ehrhardt, Rhode Island	†1985	10	529	3,460	6.54

**Record. †National champion.*

SINGLE-GAME YARDS

Yds.	Player, Team (Opponent)	Date
649	Steve McNair, Alcorn St. (Southern-B.R.)	Oct. 22, 1994
647	Steve McNair, Alcorn St. (Tenn.-Chatt.)	Sept. 10, 1994
643	Jamie Martin, Weber St. (Idaho St.)	Nov. 23, 1991
633	Steve McNair, Alcorn St. (Grambling)	Sept. 3, 1994
624	Steve McNair, Alcorn St. (Samford)	Oct. 29, 1994
621	Willie Totten, Mississippi Val. (Prairie View)	Oct. 27, 1984
614	Bryan Martin, Weber St. (Cal Poly SLO)	Sept. 23, 1995
604	Steve McNair, Alcorn St. (Jackson St.)	Nov. 21, 1992
595	Doug Pederson, Northeast La. (Stephen F. Austin)	Nov. 11, 1989
587	Vern Harris, Idaho St. (Montana)	Oct. 12, 1985
586	Steve McNair, Alcorn St. (Troy St.)	Nov. 12, 1994
574	Dave Dickenson, Montana (Idaho)	Oct. 21, 1995
570	Steve McNair, Alcorn St. (Texas Southern)	Sept. 11, 1993
566	Tom Ehrhardt, Rhode Island (Connecticut)	Nov. 16, 1985
564	Steve McNair, Alcorn St. (Jackson St.)	Nov. 19, 1994
562	Todd Hammel, Stephen F. Austin (Northeast La.)	Nov. 11, 1989
561	Willie Totten, Mississippi Val. (Southern-B.R.)	Sept. 29, 1984
549	Steve McNair, Alcorn St. (Jacksonville St.)	Oct. 31, 1992
547	Tod Mayfield, West Tex. A&M (New Mexico St.)	Nov. 16, 1985
546	Dave Stireman, Weber St. (Montana)	Nov. 2, 1985

Yds.	Player, Team (Opponent)	Date
543	Ken Hobart, Idaho (Southern Colo.)	Sept. 10, 1983
539	Dave Dickenson, Montana (Idaho)	Nov. 6, 1993
539	Jamie Martin, Weber St. (Montana St.)	Sept. 26, 1992
536	Brad Otten, Weber St. (Northern Ariz.)	Nov. 6, 1993
536	Willie Totten, Mississippi Val. (Kentucky St.)	Sept. 1, 1984
533	John Whitcomb, Ala.-Birmingham (Prairie View)	Nov. 19, 1994
527	Willie Totten, Mississippi Val. (Grambling)	Oct. 13, 1984
519	Bernard Hawk, Bethune-Cookman (Ga. Southern)	Oct. 6, 1984

ANNUAL CHAMPIONS

Year	Player, Team	Class	G	Plays	Yards	Avg.
1978	Neil Lomax, Portland St.	So.	11	519	3,524	320.4
1979	Neil Lomax, Portland St.	Jr.	11	611	3,966	360.5
1980	Neil Lomax, Portland St.	Sr.	11	550	4,157	377.9
1981	Mike Machurek, Idaho St.	Sr.	9	363	2,645	293.9
1982	Brent Woods, Princeton	Sr.	10	577	3,079	307.9
1983	Ken Hobart, Idaho	Sr.	11	578	3,800	345.5
1984	Willie Totten, Mississippi Val.	Jr.	10	564	4,572	457.2
1985	Tom Ehrhardt, Rhode Island	Sr.	10	529	3,460	346.0
1986	Brent Pease, Montana	Sr.	10	499	3,094	309.4
1987	Jeff Wiley, Holy Cross	Jr.	11	445	3,722	338.4
1988	John Friesz, Idaho	Jr.	10	424	2,751	275.1
1989	John Friesz, Idaho	Sr.	11	464	3,853	350.3
1990	Jamie Martin, Weber St.	So.	11	508	3,713	337.6
1991	Jamie Martin, Weber St.	Jr.	11	591	4,337	394.3
1992	Steve McNair, Alcorn St.	So.	10	519	4,057	405.7
1993	Dave Dickenson, Montana	So.	11	530	3,978	361.6
1994	Steve McNair, Alcorn St.	Sr.	11	*649	*5,799	*527.2
1995	Dave Dickenson, Montana	Sr.	11	544	4,209	382.6

*Record.

Rushing

CAREER YARDS PER GAME

(Minimum 2,500 Yards)

Player, Team	Years	G	Plays	Yards	TD	Yd. PG
Arnold Mickens, Butler	1994-95	20	763	3,813	29	*190.7
Tim Hall, Robert Morris	1994-95	19	393	2,908	27	153.1
Keith Elias, Princeton	1991-93	30	736	4,208	49	140.3
Mike Clark, Akron	1984-86	32	804	4,257	24	133.0
Michael Hicks, South Caro. St.	1993-95	32	701	4,093	51	127.9
Rich Erenberg, Colgate	1982-83	21	464	2,618	22	124.7
Kenny Gamble, Colgate	1984-87	42	963	5,220	*55	124.3
Frank Hawkins, Nevada	1977-80	43	945	*5,333	39	124.0
Elroy Harris, Eastern Ky.	1985, 87-88	31	648	3,829	47	123.5
Gill Fenerty, Holy Cross	1983-85	30	622	3,618	26	120.6
Markus Thomas, Eastern Ky.	1989-92	43	784	5,149	51	119.7
Marquette Smith, Central Fla.	1994-95	22	467	2,569	19	116.8
Erik Marsh, Lafayette	1991-94	42	*1,027	4,834	35	115.1
Sherriden May, Idaho	1992-94	33	689	3,748	50	113.6
Rene Ingoglia, Massachusetts	1992-95	41	905	4,623	54	112.8
Willie High, Eastern Ill.	1992-95	38	913	4,231	37	111.3
Derrick Harmon, Cornell	1981-83	28	545	3,074	26	109.8
Paul Lewis, Boston U.	1982-84	37	878	3,995	50	108.0
Eric Gant, Grambling	1990-93	34	617	3,667	32	107.9
Derrick Franklin, Indiana St.	1989-91	30	710	3,231	23	107.7
Charvez Foger, Nevada	1985-88	42	864	4,484	52	106.8
James Crawford, Eastern Ky.	1985-87	32	661	3,404	22	106.4
Bryan Keys, Pennsylvania	1987-89	30	609	3,137	34	104.6
Judd Garrett, Princeton	1987-89	30	687	3,109	32	103.6

*Record.

SEASON YARDS PER GAME

Player, Team	Year	G	Plays	Yards	TD	Yd. PG
Arnold Mickens, Butler	†1994	10	*409	*2,255	18	*225.5
Tony Vinson, Towson St.	†1993	10	293	2,016	23	201.6
Keith Elias, Princeton	1993	10	305	1,731	19	173.1
Gene Lake, Delaware St.	†1984	10	238	1,722	20	172.2
Rich Erenberg, Colgate	†1983	11	302	1,883	20	171.2
Kenny Gamble, Colgate	†1986	11	307	1,816	21	165.1
Mike Clark, Akron	1986	11	245	1,786	8	162.4
Reggie Greene, Siena	†1995	9	273	1,461	11	162.3
Derrick Cullors, Murray St.	1995	11	269	1,765	16	160.5
Keith Elias, Princeton	†1992	10	245	1,575	18	157.5
Tim Hall, Robert Morris	1995	10	239	1,572	16	157.2
Frank Hawkins, Nevada	†1980	11	307	1,719	9	156.3
Arnold Mickens, Butler	1995	10	354	1,558	11	155.8
Brad Baxter, Alabama St.	1986	11	302	1,705	13	155.0
Elroy Harris, Eastern Ky.	1988	10	277	1,543	21	154.3
Richard Johnson, Butler	1993	10	322	1,535	10	153.5
Frank Hawkins, Nevada	†1979	11	293	1,683	13	153.0
Carl Smith, Maine	†1989	11	305	1,680	20	152.7
Harvey Reed, Howard	†1987	10	211	1,512	20	151.2
John Settle, Appalachian St.	1986	11	317	1,661	20	151.0
Tim Hall, Robert Morris	1994	9	154	1,336	11	148.4
Garry Pearson, Massachusetts	†1982	11	312	1,631	13	148.3
Lorenzo Bouier, Maine	1980	11	349	1,622	9	147.5

*Record. †National champion.

CAREER YARDS

Player, Team	Years	Plays	Yards	Avg.	Long
Frank Hawkins, Nevada	1977-80	945	*5,333	5.64	50
Kenny Gamble, Colgate	1984-87	963	5,220	5.42	91
Markus Thomas, Eastern Ky.	1989-92	784	5,149	‡6.57	90
Erik Marsh, Lafayette	1991-94	*1,027	4,834	4.71	62
Rene Ingoglia, Massachusetts	1992-95	905	4,623	5.11	84
Chris Parker, Marshall	1992-95	780	4,571	5.86	89
Cedric Minter, Boise St.	1977-80	752	4,475	5.95	77
John Settle, Appalachian St.	1983-86	891	4,409	4.95	88
Mike Clark, Akron	1984-86	804	4,257	5.29	†65
Willie High, Eastern Ill.	1992-95	913	4,231	4.63	55
Keith Elias, Princeton	1991-93	736	4,208	5.72	69
David Wright, Indiana St.	1992-95	784	4,181	5.33	75
Warren Marshall, James Madison	$1982-86	737	4,168	5.66	59
Carl Tremble, Furman	1989-92	696	4,149	5.96	65
Harvey Reed, Howard	1984-87	635	4,142	6.52	85
Michael Hicks, South Caro. St.	1993-95	701	4,093	5.84	82
Paul Lewis, Boston U.	1981-84	878	3,995	4.55	80
¢Rich Lemon, Bucknell	1993-95	787	3,944	5.01	83
Daryl Brown, Delaware	1991-94	678	3,932	5.80	71
Joe Ross, Ga. Southern	1987-90	687	3,876	5.64	75
Garry Pearson, Massachusetts	1979-82	808	3,859	4.78	71
Elroy Harris, Eastern Ky.	1985, 87-88	648	3,829	5.91	64
Lorenzo Bouier, Maine	1979-82	879	3,827	4.35	77
Lewis Tillman, Jackson St.	$1984-88	779	3,824	4.91	39
Joe Campbell, Middle Tenn. St.	1988-91	638	3,823	5.99	81
Carl Smith, Maine	1988-91	759	3,815	5.03	89
Arnold Mickens, Butler	1994-95	763	3,813	5.00	70
Sherriden May, Idaho	1992-94	689	3,748	5.44	68
Derek Fitzgerald, William & Mary	1992-95	720	3,744	5.20	66
Brad Baxter, Alabama St.	1985-88	773	3,732	4.83	71
Toby Davis, Illinois St.	1989-92	825	3,702	4.49	34
Eric Gant, Grambling	1990-93	617	3,667	5.94	49
Gill Fenerty, Holy Cross	1983-85	622	3,618	5.82	76

*Record. †Did not score. $See page 6 for explanation. ¢Active player. ‡Record for minimum 600 carries.

DIVISION I-AA

CAREER RUSHING TOUCHDOWNS

Player, Team	Years	G	TDs
Kenny Gamble, Colgate	1984-87	42	*55
Rene Ingoglia, Massachusetts	1992-95	41	54
Charvez Foger, Nevada	1985-88	42	52
Michael Hicks, South Caro. St.	1993-95	32	51
Markus Thomas, Eastern Ky.	1989-92	43	51
Sherriden May, Idaho	1992-94	33	50
Paul Lewis, Boston U.	1981-84	37	50
Chris Parker, Marshall	1992-95	45	49
Keith Elias, Princeton	1991-93	30	49
Elroy Harris, Eastern Ky.	1985, 87-88	31	47
Harvey Reed, Howard	1984-87	41	47

*Record. (Note: Anthony Russo of St. John's, N.Y., scored 16 TDs in 1993 at I-AA level but had 57 total touchdowns during 1990-94.)

SEASON YARDS

Player, Team	Year	G	Plays	Yards	Avg.
Arnold Mickens, Butler	†1994	10	*409	*2,255	5.51
Tony Vinson, Towson St.	†1993	10	293	2,016	6.89
Rich Erenberg, Colgate	†1983	11	302	1,883	6.24
Kenny Gamble, Colgate	†1986	11	307	1,816	5.92
Mike Clark, Akron	1986	11	245	1,786	‡7.29
Derrick Cullors, Murray St.	1995	11	269	1,765	6.56
Keith Elias, Princeton	1993	10	305	1,731	5.68
Gene Lake, Delaware St.	†1984	10	238	1,722	7.24
Frank Hawkins, Nevada	†1980	11	307	1,719	5.60
Brad Baxter, Alabama St.	1986	11	302	1,705	5.65
Frank Hawkins, Nevada	†1979	11	293	1,683	5.74
Carl Smith, Maine	†1989	11	305	1,680	5.51
John Settle, Appalachian St.	1986	11	317	1,661	5.24
Garry Pearson, Massachusetts	†1982	11	312	1,631	5.23
Lorenzo Bouier, Maine	1980	11	349	1,622	4.65
Markus Thomas, Eastern Ky.	1989	11	232	1,620	6.98
Keith Elias, Princeton	†1992	10	245	1,575	6.43
Tim Hall, Robert Morris	1995	10	239	1,572	6.58

Player, Team	Year	G	Plays	Yards	Avg.
Don Wilkerson, Southwest Tex. St.	1994	11	302	1,569	5.20
James Black, Akron	1983	11	351	1,568	4.47
Irving Spikes, Northeast La.	1993	11	246	1,563	6.35
Toby Davis, Illinois St.	1992	11	341	1,561	4.58
Arnold Mickens, Butler	1995	10	354	1,558	4.40
Anthony Russo, St. John's (N.Y.)	1993	11	311	1,558	5.01
Carl Tremble, Furman	1992	11	228	1,555	6.82
Thomas Haskins, Va. Military	1995	11	248	1,548	6.24
Burton Murchison, Lamar	†1985	11	265	1,547	5.84
Jerome Bledsoe, Massachusetts	†1991	11	264	1,545	5.85

**Record. †National champion. ‡Record for minimum of 200 carries.*

SINGLE-GAME YARDS

Yds.	Player, Team (Opponent)	Date
364	Tony Vinson, Towson St. (Bucknell)	Nov. 13, 1993
346	William Arnold, Jackson St. (Texas Southern)	Nov. 6, 1993
345	Russell Davis, Idaho (Portland St.)	Oct. 3, 1981
337	Frank Alessio, Massachusetts (Boston U.)	Nov. 11, 1995
337	Gill Fenerty, Holy Cross (Columbia)	Oct. 29, 1983
336	Gene Lake, Delaware St. (Liberty)	Nov. 10, 1984
327	Tony Vinson, Towson St. (Morgan St.)	Nov. 20, 1993
324	Robert Vaughn, Alabama St. (Tuskegee)	Nov. 24, 1994
323	Matt Johnson, Harvard (Brown)	Nov. 9, 1991
313	Rene Ingoglia, Massachusetts (Rhode Island)	Oct. 1, 1994
312	Surkano Edwards, Samford (Tenn.-Martin)	Nov. 14, 1992
309	Eddie Thompson, Western Ky. (Southern Ill.)	Oct. 29, 1992
305	Lawrence Worthington, Liberty (Charleston So.)	Nov. 19, 1994
305	Lucius Floyd, Nevada (Montana St.)	Sept. 27, 1986
304	Tony Citizen, McNeese St. (Prairie View)	Sept. 6, 1986
302	Lorenzo Bouier, Maine (Northeastern)	Nov. 1, 1980
301	Jovan Rhodes, Marist (Siena)	Nov. 12, 1994
300	Markus Thomas, Eastern Ky. (Marshall)	Oct. 21, 1989
299	Keith Elias, Princeton (Lafayette)	Sept. 26, 1992
299	Joe Delaney, Northwestern St. (Nicholls St.)	Oct. 28, 1978
295	Arnold Mickens, Butler (Valparaiso)	Oct. 8, 1994

ANNUAL CHAMPIONS

Year	Player, Team	Class	G	Plays	Yards	Avg.
1978	Frank Hawkins, Nevada	So.	10	259	1,445	144.5
1979	Frank Hawkins, Nevada	Jr.	11	293	1,683	153.0
1980	Frank Hawkins, Nevada	Sr.	11	307	1,719	156.3
1981	Gregg Drew, Boston U.	Jr.	10	309	1,257	125.7
1982	Garry Pearson, Massachusetts	Sr.	11	312	1,631	148.3
1983	Rich Erenberg, Colgate	Sr.	11	302	1,883	171.2
1984	Gene Lake, Delaware St.	Jr.	10	238	1,722	172.2
1985	Burton Murchison, Lamar	So.	11	265	1,547	140.6
1986	Kenny Gamble, Colgate	Jr.	11	307	1,816	165.1
1987	Harvey Reed, Howard	Sr.	10	211	1,512	151.2
1988	Elroy Harris, Eastern Ky.	Jr.	10	277	1,543	154.3
1989	Carl Smith, Maine	So.	11	305	1,680	152.7
1990	Walter Dean, Grambling	Sr.	11	221	1,401	127.4
1991	Al Rosier, Dartmouth	Sr.	10	258	1,432	143.2
1992	Keith Elias, Princeton	Jr.	10	245	1,575	157.5
1993	Tony Vinson, Towson St.	Sr.	10	293	2,016	201.6
1994	Arnold Mickens, Butler	Jr.	10	*409	*2,255	*225.5
1995	Reggie Greene, Siena	So.	9	273	1,461	162.3

**Record.*

Quarterback Rushing

CAREER YARDS
(Since 1978)

Player, Team	Years	G	Plays	Yards	TD	Yd.PG
Jack Douglas, Citadel	1989-92	44	*832	*3,674	*48	83.5
Tracy Ham, Ga. Southern	1984-86	33	511	2,506	32	75.9
Tony Scales, Va. Military	1989-92	44	561	2,475	19	56.3
Eddie Thompson, Western Ky.	1991-93	27	387	2,349	19	*87.0
Steve McNair, Alcorn St.	1991-94	42	375	2,327	33	55.4
Eriq Williams, James Madison	1989-92	43	642	2,321	32	54.0
Raymond Gross, Ga. Southern	1987-90	42	695	2,290	20	54.5
Bill Vergantino, Delaware	1989-92	44	656	2,287	34	52.0
Dwane Brown, Arkansas St.	1984-87	42	595	2,192	33	52.2
Roy Johnson, Arkansas St.	1988-91	43	558	2,182	22	50.7
DeAndre Smith, Southwest Mo. St.	1987-90	42	558	2,140	36	50.9
Ken Hobart, Idaho	1980-83	44	628	1,827	26	41.5
Darin Kehler, Yale	1987-90	28	402	1,643	13	58.7

**Record.*

SEASON YARDS
(Since 1978)

Player, Team	Year	G	Plays	Yards	TD	Avg.
Marvin Marshall, South Caro. St.	1994	11	160	*1,201	10	7.51
Jack Douglas, Citadel	1991	11	*266	1,152	13	4.33
Tony Scales, Va. Military	1991	11	185	1,105	8	5.97
Tracy Ham, Ga. Southern	1986	11	207	1,048	18	5.06
Alcede Surtain, Alabama St.	1995	11	178	1,024	*21	5.75
Nick Crawford, Yale	1991	10	210	1,024	8	4.98
Gene Brown, Citadel	1988	9	152	1,006	13	6.62
Kharon Brown, Hofstra	1995	11	151	977	7	6.47
Corey Thomas, Nicholls St.	1994	11	158	962	8	6.09
Steve McNair, Alcorn St.	1994	11	119	936	9	*7.87
Jack Douglas, Citadel	1992	11	178	926	13	5.20
Roy Johnson, Arkansas St.	1989	11	193	925	6	4.79
Darin Kehler, Yale	1989	10	210	903	6	4.30
Jim O'Leary, Northeastern	1986	10	195	884	10	4.53
Earl Easley, Arkansas St.	1988	11	196	861	11	4.39
Brad Brown, Northwestern St.	1990	11	192	843	8	4.39
DeAndre Smith, Southwest Mo. St.	1989	11	176	841	12	4.78
Eddie Thompson, Western Ky.	1992	9	113	837	9	7.41
Gilbert Price, Southwest Tex. St.	1991	11	244	837	8	3.43
Jack Douglas, Citadel	1990	11	211	836	13	3.96

**Record.*

Photo from Northern Arizona sports information

Northern Arizona quarterback Jeff Lewis' career passing efficiency rating of 134.4 ranks 28th in Division I-AA history.

Passing

CAREER PASSING EFFICIENCY
(Minimum 300 Completions)

Player, Team	Years	Att.	Cmp.	Int.	Pct.	Yards	TD	Pts.
Shawn Knight, William & Mary	1991-94	558	367	15	.658	5,527	46	*170.8
Dave Dickenson, Montana	1992-95	1,208	813	26	*.673	11,080	96	166.3
Doug Nussmeier, Idaho	1990-93	1,225	746	32	.609	10,824	91	154.4
Jay Johnson, Northern Iowa	1989-92	744	397	25	.534	7,049	51	148.9
Michael Payton, Marshall	1989-92	876	542	32	.619	7,530	57	148.2
Bryan Martin, Weber St.	1992-95	606	365	14	.602	5,211	37	148.0
Willie Totten, Mississippi Val.	1982-85	1,555	907	*75	.583	12,711	*139	146.8
Kenneth Biggles, Tennessee St.	1981-84	701	397	28	.566	5,933	57	146.6
Steve McNair, Alcorn St.	1991-94	*1,680	929	58	.553	*14,496	119	144.3
Mike Smith, Northern Iowa	1984-87	943	557	43	.591	8,219	58	143.5
Tom Ciaccio, Holy Cross	1988-91	1,073	658	46	.613	8,603	72	142.2
Jim Zaccheo, Nevada	1987-88	554	326	27	.588	4,750	35	142.0
Todd Donnan, Marshall	1991-94	712	425	25	.597	5,566	51	142.0
Eric Beavers, Nevada	1983-86	1,094	646	37	.591	8,626	77	141.8
Scott Semptimphelter, Lehigh	1990-93	823	493	27	.599	6,668	50	141.5
John Whitcomb, Ala.-Birmingham	1993-94	738	448	28	.607	6,043	43	141.1
Jason Garrett, Princeton	1987-88	550	368	10	.669	4,274	20	140.6
Neil Lomax, Portland St.	1978-80	1,425	836	50	.587	11,550	88	140.1

Player, Team	Years	Att.	Cmp.	Int.	Pct.	Yards	TD	Pts.
Jamie Martin, Weber St.	1989-92	1,544	*934	56	.605	12,207	87	138.2
Darin Hinshaw, Central Fla.	1991-94	1,113	614	52	.552	9,000	82	138.1
Ricky Jones, Alabama St.	1988-91	644	324	30	.503	5,472	49	137.5
Jeff Carlson, Weber St.	1984, 86-88	723	384	33	.531	6,147	47	136.9
Chris Hakel, William & Mary	1988-91	812	489	26	.602	6,447	40	136.7
Jeff Wiley, Holy Cross	1985-88	1,208	723	63	.599	9,698	71	136.3
Robert Dougherty, Boston U.	1993-94	705	405	26	.574	5,608	41	136.1
Eriq Williams, James Madison	1989-92	617	326	35	.528	5,356	40	135.8
Tom Ehrhardt, Rhode Island	1984-85	919	526	35	.572	6,722	66	134.8
Jeff Lewis, Northern Ariz.	1992-95	1,316	785	24	.597	9,655	67	134.4
Tom Kirchoff, Lafayette	1989-92	878	510	36	.581	6,721	53	134.1
Mike Buck, Maine	1986-89	1,134	637	41	.562	8,721	68	133.4
Frankie DeBusk, Furman	1987-90	634	333	29	.525	5,414	35	133.3
Frank Novak, Lafayette	1981-83	834	478	36	.573	6,378	51	133.1
Robbie Justino, Liberty	1989-92	1,267	769	51	.607	9,548	64	132.6
Rick Worman, Eastern Wash.	1984-85	672	381	23	.567	5,004	41	132.5
Glenn Kempa, Lehigh	1989-91	901	520	27	.577	6,722	49	132.3
Jay Walker, Howard	1991-93	718	377	23	.525	5,671	42	131.8
James Ritchey, Stephen F. Austin	1992-95	613	325	25	.530	4,766	40	131.7
Gilbert Renfroe, Tennessee St.	1982-85	721	370	23	.513	5,556	48	131.6
Tracy Ham, Ga. Southern	1984-86	568	301	31	.530	4,881	29	131.1
Matt DeGennaro, Connecticut	1987-90	1,319	803	49	.609	9,288	73	130.9
Lonnie Galloway, Western Caro.	1990-93	639	355	43	.556	5,545	30	130.5
Dan Crowley, Towson St.	1991-94	1,170	617	54	.527	8,900	81	130.3
Ken Hobart, Idaho	1980-83	1,219	629	42	.516	9,300	79	130.2

**Record. $See page 6 for explanation.*

SEASON PASSING EFFICIENCY

(Minimum 15 Attempts Per Game)

Player, Team	Year	G	Att.	Cmp.	Int.	Pct.	Yards	TD	Pts.
Shawn Knight, William & Mary	†1993	10	177	125	4	.706	2,055	22	*204.6
Michael Payton, Marshall	†1991	9	216	143	5	.622	2,333	19	181.3
Doug Nussmeier, Idaho	1993	11	304	185	5	.609	2,960	33	175.2
Brian Kadel, Dayton	†1995	11	183	115	6	.628	1,880	18	175.0
Kelvin Simmons, Troy St.	1993	11	224	143	6	.638	2,144	23	172.8
Frank Baur, Lafayette	†1988	10	256	164	11	.641	2,621	23	171.1
Bobby Lamb, Furman	†1985	11	181	106	6	.586	1,856	18	170.9
Jay Fiedler, Dartmouth	†1992	10	273	175	13	.641	2,748	25	169.4
Dave Dickenson, Montana	1995	11	455	309	9	.679	4,176	38	168.6
Mike Smith, Northern Iowa	†1986	11	303	190	16	.627	3,125	27	168.2
Dave Dickenson, Montana	1993	11	390	262	9	.672	3.640	32	168.0
Willie Totten, Mississippi Val.	†1983	9	279	174	9	.624	2,566	29	167.5
Lonnie Galloway, Western Caro.	1992	11	211	128	12	.607	2,181	20	167.4
Leo Hamlett, Delaware	1995	11	174	95	6	.546	1,849	15	165.4
Eriq Williams, James Madison	1991	11	192	107	7	.557	1,914	19	164.8
Dave Dickenson, Montana	†1994	9	336	229	6	.682	3,053	24	164.5
Willie Totten, Mississippi Val.	†1984	10	518	*324	22	.626	4,557	*56	163.6
Jeff Wiley, Holy Cross	†1987	11	400	265	17	.663	3,677	34	163.0
Todd Hammel, Stephen F. Austin	†1989	11	401	238	13	.594	3,914	34	162.8
Mike Williams, Grambling	†1980	11	239	127	5	.531	2,116	28	162.0
Dan Crowley, Towson St.	1993	10	217	125	4	.576	1,882	23	161.7
John Friesz, Idaho	1989	11	425	260	8	.612	4,041	31	161.4
Wendal Lowrey, Northeast La.	1992	11	227	147	9	.648	2,190	16	161.1
Donny Simmons, Western Ill.	1992	11	281	182	11	.648	2,496	25	160.9
Chris Berg, Northern Iowa	1995	10	206	113	6	.549	2,144	15	160.5
David Charpia, Furman	1983	9	155	99	4	.635	1,419	12	160.1
Todd Donnan, Marshall	1994	11	288	182	8	.632	2,403	28	159.8
Joe Aliotti, Boise St.	†1979	11	219	144	7	.658	1,870	19	159.7
Gilbert Renfroe, Tennessee St.	1984	11	165	95	5	.576	1,458	17	159.7
Mike Buck, Maine	1989	11	264	170	3	.644	2,315	19	159.5
Bobby Lamb, Furman	1984	11	191	106	7	.555	1,781	19	159.3
Kenneth Biggles, Tennessee St.	1984	11	258	157	7	.609	2,242	24	159.1
Michael Payton, Marshall	1992	11	313	200	11	.639	2,788	26	159.1

**Record. †National champion.*

CAREER YARDS

Player, Team	Years	Att.	Cmp.	Int.	Pct.	Yards	TD
Steve McNair, Alcorn St.	1991-94	*1,680	929	58	.553	*14,496	119
Willie Totten, Mississippi Val.	1982-85	1,555	907	*75	.583	12,711	*139
Jamie Martin, Weber St.	1989-92	1,544	*934	56	.605	12,207	87
Neil Lomax, Portland St.	1978-80	1,425	836	50	.587	11,550	88
Dave Dickenson, Montana	1992-95	1,208	813	26	*.673	11,080	96
Doug Nussmeier, Idaho	1990-93	1,225	746	32	.609	10,824	91
John Friesz, Idaho	1986-89	1,350	801	40	.593	10,697	77
Greg Wyatt, Northern Ariz.	1986-89	1,510	926	49	.613	10,697	70
Sean Payton, Eastern Ill.	1983-86	1,408	756	55	.537	10,655	75
Jeff Wiley, Holy Cross	1985-88	1,208	723	63	.599	9,698	71
Jeff Lewis, Northern Ariz.	1992-95	1,316	785	24	.597	9,655	67
Robbie Justino, Liberty	1989-92	1,267	769	51	.607	9,548	64
Kirk Schulz, Villanova	1986-89	1,297	774	70	.597	9,305	70
Ken Hobart, Idaho	1980-83	1,219	629	42	.516	9,300	79
Matt DeGennaro, Connecticut	1987-90	1,319	803	49	.609	9,288	73

Photo from Dayton sports information

Dayton quarterback Brian Kadel's passing efficiency rating of 175.0 in 1995 was the fourth best in Division I-AA history among passers with 15 or more attempts per game.

Delaware sports information photo by Max Gretsch

Fifteen touchdown passes and only six interceptions helped Delaware quarterback Leo Hamlett's passing efficiency rating reach 165.4 last season, a mark that only 13 Division I-AA passers have exceeded.

Player, Team	Years	Att.	Cmp.	Int.	Pct.	Yards	TD
Marty Horn, Lehigh	1982-85	1,390	744	64	.535	9,120	62
Jason Whitmer, Idaho St.	1987-90	1,349	721	53	.534	9,081	55
Chris Swartz, Morehead St.	1987-90	1,408	774	47	.550	9,027	56
Darin Hinshaw, Central Fla.	1991-94	1,114	614	52	.551	9,000	82
Dan Crowley, Towson St.	1991-94	1,170	617	54	.527	8,900	81
Michael Proctor, Murray St.	1986-89	1,148	578	45	.503	8,682	52
Eric Beavers, Nevada	1983-86	1,094	646	37	.590	8,626	77
Tom Ciaccio, Holy Cross	1988-91	1,073	658	46	.613	8,603	72
Steve Calabria, Colgate	1981-84	1,143	626	68	.548	8,555	54
Mike Buck, Maine	1986-89	1,102	619	39	.562	8,491	67
Jeff Cesarone, Western Ky.	1984-87	1,339	714	39	.533	8,404	45
Frank Baur, Lafayette	1985, 87-89	1,103	636	46	.577	8,399	62
Mitch Maher, North Texas	1991-94	1,100	610	47	.555	8,252	66
Stan Yagiello, William & Mary	$1981-85	1,247	737	36	.591	8,249	51
Mike Smith, Northern Iowa	1984-87	943	557	43	.591	8,219	58
Kelly Bradley, Montana St.	1983-86	1,238	714	45	.577	8,152	60
Tom Proudian, Iona	1993-95	1,134	656	48	.578	8,088	58
Bob Bleier, Richmond	1983-86	1,169	672	56	.575	8,057	54
Chris Goetz, Towson St.	1987-90	1,172	648	51	.553	7,882	42
Paul Singer, Western Ill.	1985-88	1,171	646	43	.552	7,850	61
John Witkowski, Columbia	1981-83	1,176	613	60	.521	7,849	56
Grady Bennett, Montana	1987-90	1,097	641	42	.584	7,778	55
Bernard Hawk, Bethune-Cookman	1982-85	1,120	554	51	.495	7,737	56
Bob Jean, New Hampshire	1985-88	1,126	567	49	.504	7,704	51

**Record. $See page 6 for explanation.*

CAREER YARDS PER GAME

(Minimum 5,000 Yards)

Player, Team	Years	G	Att.	Cmp.	Yards	TD	Yd.PG
Neil Lomax, Portland St.	1978-80	33	1,425	836	11,550	88	*350.0
Steve McNair, Alcorn St.	1991-94	42	*1,680	929	*14,496	119	345.1
Willie Totten, Mississippi Val.	1982-85	40	1,555	907	12,711	*139	317.8
Dave Dickenson, Montana	1992-95	35	1,208	813	11,080	96	316.6
John Friesz, Idaho	1986-89	35	1,350	801	10,697	77	305.6
Tom Proudian, Iona	1993-95	27	1,134	656	8,088	58	299.6
Jamie Martin, Weber St.	1989-92	41	1,544	*934	12,207	87	297.7
Sean Payton, Eastern Ill.	1983-86	37	1,408	756	10,655	75	288.0
Doug Nussmeier, Idaho	1990-93	39	1,225	746	10,824	91	277.5
Robert Dougherty, Boston U.	1993-94	21	705	405	5,608	41	267.0
Scott Semptimphelter, Lehigh	1990-93	26	823	493	6,668	50	256.5
Greg Wyatt, Northern Ariz.	1986-89	42	1,510	926	10,697	70	254.7

**Record.*

CAREER TOUCHDOWN PASSES

Player, Team	Years	G	TD Passes
Willie Totten, Mississippi Val.	1982-85	40	*139
Steve McNair, Alcorn St.	1991-94	42	119
Dave Dickenson, Montana	1992-95	35	96
Doug Nussmeier, Idaho	1990-93	39	91
Neil Lomax, Portland St.	1978-80	33	88
Jamie Martin, Weber St.	1989-92	41	87
Darin Hinshaw, Central Fla.	1991-94	40	82
Dan Crowley, Towson St.	1991-94	40	81
Ken Hobart, Idaho	1980-83	44	79
John Friesz, Idaho	1986-89	35	77
Eric Beavers, Nevada	1983-86	40	77
Sean Payton, Eastern Ill.	1983-86	39	75
Matt DeGennaro, Connecticut	1987-90	43	73
Tom Ciaccio, Holy Cross	1988-91	37	72
Jeff Wiley, Holy Cross	1985-88	41	71
Kirk Schulz, Villanova	1986-89	42	70
Greg Wyatt, Northern Ariz.	1986-89	42	70

**Record.*

SEASON YARDS

Player, Team	Year	G	Att.	Cmp.	Int.	Pct.	Yards	TD
Steve McNair, Alcorn St.	1994	11	*530	304	17	.574	*4,863	44
Willie Totten, Mississippi Val.	†1984	10	518	*324	22	.626	4,557	*56
Dave Dickenson, Montana	1995	11	455	309	9	.679	4,176	38
Jamie Martin, Weber St.	1991	11	500	310	17	.620	4,125	35
Neil Lomax, Portland St.	1980	11	473	296	12	.626	4,094	37
John Friesz, Idaho	1989	11	425	260	8	.612	4,041	31
Neil Lomax, Portland St.	1979	11	516	299	16	.579	3,950	26
Todd Hammel, Stephen F. Austin	†1989	11	401	238	13	.594	3,914	34
Sean Payton, Eastern Ill.	1984	11	473	270	15	.571	3,843	28
Jamie Martin, Weber St.	1990	11	428	256	15	.598	3,700	23
Willie Totten, Mississippi Val.	1985	11	492	295	*29	.600	3,698	39
Jeff Wiley, Holy Cross	†1987	11	400	265	17	.663	3,677	34
John Friesz, Idaho	1987	11	502	311	14	.620	3,677	28
Dave Dickenson, Montana	1993	11	390	262	9	.672	3,640	32
Ken Hobart, Idaho	1983	11	477	268	19	.562	3,618	32

Player, Team	Year	G	Att.	Cmp.	Int.	Pct.	Yards	TD
Glenn Kempa, Lehigh	1991	11	474	286	15	.603	3,565	31
Tom Ehrhardt, Rhode Island	1985	10	497	283	19	.569	3,542	35
Steve McNair, Alcorn St.	1992	10	427	231	11	.541	3,541	29
Tony Petersen, Marshall	1987	11	466	251	25	.539	3,529	22
Todd Brunner, Lehigh	1989	11	450	273	19	.607	3,516	26
Kelly Bradley, Montana St.	1984	11	499	289	20	.579	3,508	30
Neil Lomax, Portland St.	†1978	11	436	241	22	.553	3,506	25

**Record. †National pass-efficiency champion.*

SEASON YARDS PER GAME

Player, Team	Year	G	Att.	Cmp.	Int.	Pct.	Yards	TD	Yd.PG
Willie Totten, Mississippi Val.	†1984	10	518	*324	22	.626	4,557	*56	*455.7
Steve McNair, Alcorn St.	1994	11	*530	304	17	.574	*4,863	44	442.1
Dave Dickenson, Montana	1995	11	455	309	9	.679	4,176	38	379.6
Jamie Martin, Weber St.	1991	11	500	310	17	.620	4,125	35	375.0
Neil Lomax, Portland St.	1980	11	473	296	12	.626	4,094	37	372.2
John Friesz, Idaho	1989	11	425	260	8	.612	4,041	31	367.4
Neil Lomax, Portland St.	1979	11	516	299	16	.579	3,950	26	359.1
Todd Hammel, Stephen F. Austin	†1989	11	401	238	13	.594	3,914	34	355.8
Tom Ehrhardt, Rhode Island	1985	10	497	283	19	.569	3,542	35	354.2
Steve McNair, Alcorn St.	1992	10	427	231	11	.541	3,541	29	354.1
Sean Payton, Eastern Ill.	1984	11	473	270	15	.571	3,843	28	349.4
Dave Dickenson, Montana	†1994	9	336	229	6	.682	3,053	24	339.2
Tom Proudian, Iona	1993	10	440	262	13	.595	3,368	29	336.8
Jamie Martin, Weber St.	1990	11	428	256	15	.598	3,700	23	336.4
Willie Totten, Mississippi Val.	1985	11	492	295	*29	.600	3,698	39	336.2

**Record. †National pass-efficiency champion.*

SEASON TOUCHDOWN PASSES

Player, Team	Year	G	TD Passes
Willie Totten, Mississippi Val.	1984	10	*56
Steve McNair, Alcorn St.	1994	11	44
Willie Totten, Mississippi Val.	1985	11	39
Dave Dickenson, Montana	1995	11	38
Neil Lomax, Portland St.	1980	11	37
Jamie Martin, Weber St.	1991	11	35
Tom Ehrhardt, Rhode Island	1985	10	35
Todd Hammel, Stephen F. Austin	1989	11	34
Jeff Wiley, Holy Cross	1987	11	34
Doug Nussmeier, Idaho	1993	11	33
Dave Dickenson, Montana	1993	11	32
Doug Hudson, Nicholls St.	1986	11	32
Ken Hobart, Idaho	1983	11	32
Glenn Kempa, Lehigh	1991	11	31
John Friesz, Idaho	1989	11	31
Scott Semptimphelter, Lehigh	1993	11	30
Brent Pease, Montana	1986	11	30
Kelly Bradley, Montana St.	1984	11	30

**Record.*

SINGLE-GAME YARDS

Yds.	Player, Team (Opponent)	Date
624	Jamie Martin, Weber St. (Idaho St.)	Nov. 23, 1991
619	Doug Pederson, Northeast La. (Stephen F. Austin)	Nov. 11, 1989
599	Willie Totten, Mississippi Val. (Prairie View)	Oct. 27, 1984
589	Vern Harris, Idaho St. (Montana)	Oct. 12, 1985
587	Steve McNair, Alcorn St. (Southern-B.R.)	Oct. 22, 1994
571	Todd Hammel, Stephen F. Austin (Northeast La.)	Nov. 11, 1989
566	Tom Ehrhardt, Rhode Island (Connecticut)	Nov. 16, 1985
563	Steve McNair, Alcorn St. (Samford)	Oct. 29, 1994
558	Dave Dickenson, Montana (Idaho)	Oct. 21, 1995
553	Willie Totten, Mississippi Val. (Southern-B.R.)	Sept. 29, 1984
547	Jamie Martin, Weber St. (Montana St.)	Sept. 26, 1992
545	Willie Totten, Mississippi Val. (Grambling)	Oct. 13, 1984
540	Brad Otten, Weber St. (Northern Ariz.)	Nov. 6, 1993
539	John Whitcomb, Ala.-Birmingham (Prairie View)	Nov. 19, 1994
537	Tod Mayfield, West Tex. A&M (New Mexico St.)	Nov. 16, 1985
536	Willie Totten, Mississippi Val. (Kentucky St.)	Sept. 1, 1984
534	Steve McNair, Alcorn St. (Grambling)	Sept. 3, 1994
534	Todd Hammel, Stephen F. Austin (Sam Houston St.)	Nov. 4, 1989
533	Steve McNair, Alcorn St. (Jackson St.)	Nov. 19, 1994
527	Bernard Hawk, Bethune-Cookman (Ga. Southern)	Oct. 6, 1984
527	Ken Hobart, Idaho (Southern Colo.)	Sept. 1, 1983
526	Willie Totten, Mississippi Val. (Jackson St.)	Sept. 22, 1984

SINGLE-GAME ATTEMPTS

No.	Player, Team (Opponent)	Date
77	Neil Lomax, Portland St. (Northern Colo.)	Oct. 20, 1979
74	Paul Peterson, Idaho St. (Nevada)	Oct. 1, 1983
72	Dave Dickenson, Montana (Idaho)	Oct. 21, 1995
71	Doug Pederson, Northeast La. (Stephen F. Austin)	Nov. 11, 1989
70	Greg Farland, Rhode Island (Boston U.)	Oct. 18, 1986

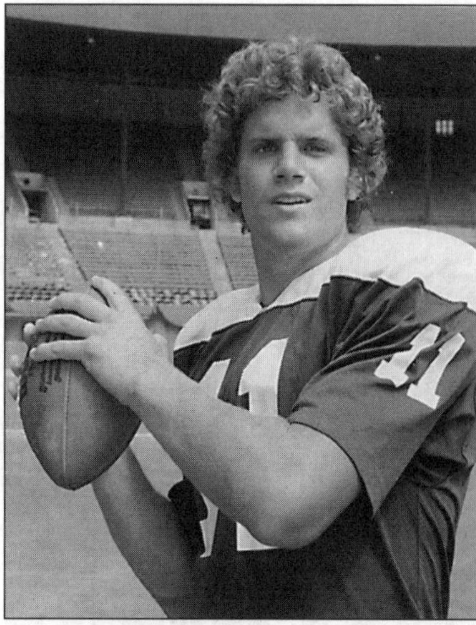

File photo

Portland State's Neil Lomax was the first Division I-AA quarterback to average more than 350 passing yards per game in two separate seasons. His 1979 average of 359.1 yards per game was a record at the time, and he broke it the following season with a mark of 372.2.

Photo from Cal State Northridge sports information

Cal State Northridge quarterback Clayton Millis completed 48 passes, a Division I-AA record, in a game last season against St. Mary's (California).

No.	Player, Team (Opponent)	Date
69	Steve McNair, Alcorn St. (Jacksonville St.)	Oct. 31, 1992
68	Tony Petersen, Marshall (Western Caro.)	Nov. 14, 1987
67	Tom Proudian, Iona (Siena)	Oct. 1, 1994
67	Michael Payton, Marshall (Western Caro.)	Oct. 31, 1992
67	Vern Harris, Idaho St. (Montana)	Oct. 12, 1985
67	Rick Worman, Eastern Wash. (Nevada)	Oct. 12, 1985
67	Tod Mayfield, West Tex. A&M (Indiana St.)	Oct. 5, 1985
67	Tom Ehrhardt, Rhode Island (Brown)	Sept. 28, 1985
66	Chris Swartz, Morehead St. (Tennessee Tech)	Oct. 17, 1987
66	Sean Cook, Texas Southern (Tex. A&M-Kingsville)	Sept. 6, 1986
66	Kelly Bradley, Montana St. (Eastern Wash.)	Sept. 21, 1985
66	Bernard Hawk, Bethune-Cookman (Ga. Southern)	Oct. 6, 1984
66	Willie Totten, Mississippi Val. (Southern-B.R.)	Sept. 29, 1984
66	Paul Peterson, Idaho St. (Cal Poly SLO)	Oct. 22, 1983

SINGLE-GAME COMPLETIONS

No.	Player, Team (Opponent)	Date
48	Clayton Millis, Cal St. Northridge (St. Mary's, Cal.)	Nov. 11, 1995
47	Jamie Martin, Weber St. (Idaho St.)	Nov. 23, 1991
46	Doug Pederson, Northeast La. (Stephen F. Austin)	Nov. 11, 1989
46	Willie Totten, Mississippi Val. (Southern-B.R.)	Sept. 29, 1984
45	Willie Totten, Mississippi Val. (Prairie View)	Oct. 27, 1984
44	Neil Lomax, Portland St. (Northern Colo.)	Oct. 20, 1979
43	Dave Dickenson, Montana (Idaho)	Oct. 21, 1995
42	Tod Mayfield, West Tex. A&M (Indiana St.)	Oct. 5, 1985
42	Kelly Bradley, Montana St. (Eastern Wash.)	Sept. 21, 1985
42	Rusty Hill, North Texas (Tulsa)	Nov. 20, 1982

ANNUAL CHAMPIONS

Year	Player, Team	Class	G	Att.	Cmp.	Avg.	Int.	Pct.	Yds.	TD
1978	Neil Lomax, Portland St.	So.	11	436	241	21.9	22	.553	3,506	25

Beginning in 1979, ranked on passing efficiency rating points (instead of per-game completions)

Year	Player, Team	Class	G	Att.	Cmp.	Int.	Pct.	Yds.	TD	Pts.
1979	Joe Aliotti, Boise St.	Jr.	11	219	144	7	.658	1,870	19	159.7
1980	Mike Williams, Grambling	Sr.	11	239	127	5	.531	2,116	28	162.0
1981	Mike Machurek, Idaho St.	Sr.	9	313	188	11	.601	2,752	22	150.1
1982	Frank Novak, Lafayette	Jr.	10	257	154	12	.599	2,257	20	150.0
1983	Willie Totten, Mississippi Val.	So.	9	279	174	9	.624	2,566	29	167.5
1984	Willie Totten, Mississippi Val.	Jr.	10	518	*324	22	.626	4,557	*56	163.6
1985	Bobby Lamb, Furman	Sr.	11	181	106	6	.586	1,856	18	170.9
1986	Mike Smith, Northern Iowa	Jr.	11	303	190	16	.627	3,125	27	168.2
1987	Jeff Wiley, Holy Cross	Jr.	11	400	265	17	.663	3,677	34	163.0
1988	Frank Baur, Lafayette	Jr.	10	256	164	11	.641	2,621	23	171.1
1989	Todd Hammel, Stephen F. Austin	Sr.	11	401	238	13	.594	3,914	34	162.8
1990	Connell Maynor, North Caro. A&T	Jr.	11	191	123	10	.644	1,699	16	156.3
1991	Michael Payton, Marshall	Jr.	9	216	143	5	.662	2,333	19	181.3
1992	Jay Fiedler, Dartmouth	Jr.	10	273	175	13	.641	2,748	25	169.4
1993	Shawn Knight, William & Mary	Jr.	10	177	125	4	.706	2,055	22	*204.6
1994	Dave Dickenson, Montana	Jr.	9	336	229	6	.682	3,053	24	164.5
1995	Brian Kadel, Dayton	Sr.	11	183	115	6	.628	1,880	18	175.0

**Record.*

Receiving

CAREER RECEPTIONS PER GAME

(Minimum 125 Receptions)

Player, Team	Years	G	Rec.	Yards	TD	Rec.PG
Jerry Rice, Mississippi Val.	1981-84	41	*301	*4,693	*50	*7.3
Derrick Ingram, Ala.-Birmingham	1993-94	22	159	2,572	21	7.2
Jeff Johnson, East Tenn. St.	1993-94	20	142	1,772	19	7.1
Miles Macik, Pennsylvania	1993-95	29	200	2,364	26	6.9
Kevin Guthrie, Princeton	1981-83	28	193	2,645	16	6.9
Eric Yarber, Idaho	1984-85	19	129	1,920	17	6.8
Brian Forster, Rhode Island (TE)	1983-85, 87	38	245	3,410	31	6.5
Kasey Dunn, Idaho	1988-91	42	268	3,847	25	6.4
Gordie Lockbaum, Holy Cross (RB)	‡1986-87	22	135	2,012	17	6.1
Derek Graham, Princeton	1981, 83-84	29	176	2,819	19	6.1
Stuart Gaussoin, Portland St.	1978-80	23	135	1,909	14	5.9
Don Lewis, Columbia	1981-83	30	176	2,207	11	5.9
Mike Barber, Marshall	1985-88	36	209	3,520	20	5.8
Rennie Benn, Lehigh	1982-85	41	237	3,662	44	5.8
Daren Altieri, Boston U.	1987-90	39	225	2,518	15	5.8
Bill Reggio, Columbia	1981-83	30	170	2,384	26	5.7

**Record. ‡Defensive back in 1984-85.*

SEASON RECEPTIONS PER GAME

Player, Team	Year	G	Rec.	Yards	TD	Rec.PG
Brian Forster, Rhode Island (TE)	†1985	10	*115	1,617	12	*11.5
Jerry Rice, Mississippi Val.	†1984	10	103	*1,682	*27	10.3
Jerry Rice, Mississippi Val.	†1983	10	102	1,450	14	10.2
Stuart Gaussoin, Portland St.	†1979	9	90	1,132	8	10.0
Kevin Guthrie, Princeton	1983	10	88	1,259	9	8.8
Alfred Pupunu, Weber St. (TE)	†1991	11	93	1,204	12	8.5
Derek Graham, Princeton	1983	10	84	1,363	11	8.4
Don Lewis, Columbia	†1982	10	84	1,000	6	8.4
Peter Macon, Weber St.	†1989	11	92	1,047	6	8.4
Marvin Walker, North Texas	1982	11	91	934	11	8.3

**Record. †National champion.*

CAREER RECEPTIONS

Player, Team	Years	Rec.	Yards	Avg.	TD
Jerry Rice, Mississippi Val.	1981-84	*301	*4,693	15.6	*50
Kasey Dunn, Idaho	1988-91	268	3,847	14.4	25
Brian Forster, Rhode Island	1983-85, 87	245	3,410	13.9	31
Mark Didio, Connecticut	1988-91	239	3,535	14.8	21
Rennie Benn, Lehigh	1982-85	237	3,662	15.5	44
Daren Altieri, Boston U.	1987-90	225	2,518	11.2	15
Darrell Colbert, Texas Southern	1983-86	217	3,177	14.6	33
David Rhodes, Central Fla.	1991-94	213	3,618	17.0	29
Mike Barber, Marshall	1985-88	209	3,520	16.8	20
Trevor Shaw, Weber St.	1989-90, 92-93	206	2,383	11.6	17

Player, Team	Years	Rec.	Yards	Avg.	TD
William Brooks, Boston U.	1982-85	204	3,154	15.5	26
Donald Narcisse, Texas Southern	1983-86	203	2,429	12.0	26
Alex Davis, Connecticut	1989-92	202	2,567	12.7	24
Shawn Collins, Northern Ariz.	1985-88	201	2,764	13.8	24
Miles Macik, Pennsylvania	1993-95	200	2,364	11.8	26
Leland Melvin, Richmond	1982-85	198	2,669	13.5	16
Mike Wilson, Boise St.	1990-93	196	3,017	15.4	13
Curtis Olds, New Hampshire	1985-88	193	3,028	15.7	23
Kevin Guthrie, Princeton	1981-83	193	2,645	13.7	16
Matt Wells, Montana	1992-95	189	2,733	14.5	19
Sergio Hebra, Maine	1984-87	189	2,612	13.8	17
John Perry, New Hampshire	1989-92	186	2,798	15.0	19
Glenn Antrum, Connecticut	1985-88	186	2,552	13.7	14
Joe Thomas, Mississippi Val.	1982-85	186	2,816	15.1	36
Gary Harrell, Howard	1990-93	184	2,619	14.2	19
Roy Banks, Eastern Ill.	1983-86	184	3,177	17.3	38
Merril Hoge, Idaho St. (RB)	1983-86	182	1,734	9.5	13
George Delaney, Colgate	1988-91	181	2,938	16.2	25
Robert Brady, Villanova	1986-89	180	2,725	15.1	28
Cisco Richard, Northeast La.	1987-90	179	1,874	10.5	12
David Gamble, New Hampshire	1990-93	178	2,990	16.8	23

*Record.

SEASON RECEPTIONS

Player, Team	Year	G	Rec.	Yards	TD
Brian Forster, Rhode Island (TE)	†1985	10	*115	1,617	12
Jerry Rice, Mississippi Val.	†1984	10	103	*1,682	*27
Jerry Rice, Mississippi Val.	†1983	10	102	1,450	14
Alfred Pupunu, Weber St. (TE)	†1991	11	93	1,204	12
Peter Macon, Weber St.	†1989	11	92	1,047	6
Marvin Walker, North Texas	1982	11	91	934	11
Stuart Gaussoin, Portland St.	†1979	9	90	1,132	8
Dave Cecchini, Lehigh	†1993	11	88	1,318	16
Mark Didio, Connecticut	1991	11	88	1,354	8
Kasey Dunn, Idaho	†1990	11	88	1,164	7
Donald Narcisse, Texas Southern	†1986	11	88	1,074	15
Kevin Guthrie, Princeton	1983	10	88	1,259	9
Kasey Dunn, Idaho	1991	11	85	1,263	6
Derek Graham, Princeton	1983	10	84	1,363	11
Don Lewis, Columbia	†1982	10	84	1,000	6

*Record. †National champion.

SEASON TOUCHDOWN RECEPTIONS

Player, Team	Year	G	TD
Jerry Rice, Mississippi Val.	1984	10	*27
Mark Carrier, Nicholls St.	1986	11	17
Dameon Reilly, Rhode Island	1985	11	17
Joe Thomas, Mississippi Val.	1985	11	17
Roy Banks, Eastern Ill.	1984	11	17
Wayne Chrebet, Hofstra	1994	10	16
Dave Cecchini, Lehigh	1993	11	16
Donald Narcisse, Texas Southern	1986	11	15
Rennie Benn, Lehigh	1983	11	15
Rennie Benn, Lehigh	1985	11	14
Jerry Rice, Mississippi Val.	1983	10	14
Bill Reggio, Columbia	1982	10	14

*Record.

SINGLE-GAME CATCHES

No.	Player, Team (Opponent)	Date
24	Jerry Rice, Mississippi Val. (Southern-B.R.)	Oct. 1, 1983
22	Marvin Walker, North Texas (Tulsa)	Nov. 20, 1982
21	David Pandt, Montana St. (Eastern Wash.)	Sept. 21, 1985
20	Tim Hilton, Cal St. Northridge (St. Mary's, Cal.)	Nov. 11, 1995
18	Jerome Williams, Morehead St. (Eastern Ky.)	Nov. 18, 1989
18	Brian Forster, Rhode Island (Brown)	Sept. 28, 1985
17	Elliot Miller, St. Francis, Pa. (Central Conn. St.)	Oct. 2, 1993
17	Lifford Jackson, Louisiana Tech (Kansas St.)	Oct. 1, 1988
17	Brian Forster, Rhode Island (Lehigh)	Oct. 12, 1985
17	Jerry Rice, Mississippi Val. (Southern-B.R.)	Sept. 29, 1984
17	Jerry Rice, Mississippi Val. (Kentucky St.)	Sept. 1, 1984

CAREER YARDS

Player, Team	Years	Rec.	Yards	Avg.	TD
Jerry Rice, Mississippi Val.	1981-84	*301	*4,693	15.6	*50
Kasey Dunn, Idaho	1988-91	268	3,847	14.4	25
Rennie Benn, Lehigh	1982-85	237	3,662	15.5	44
David Rhodes, Central Fla.	1991-94	213	3,618	17.0	29
Mark Didio, Connecticut	1988-91	239	3,535	14.8	21
Mike Barber, Marshall	1985-88	209	3,520	16.8	20
Brian Forster, Rhode Island (TE)	1983-85, 87	245	3,410	13.9	31
Tracy Singleton, Howard	1979-82	159	3,187	20.0	16
Roy Banks, Eastern Ill.	1983-86	184	3,177	17.3	38
Darrell Colbert, Texas Southern	1983-86	217	3,177	14.6	33
William Brooks, Boston U.	1982-85	204	3,154	15.5	26

*Record.

CAREER YARDS PER GAME
(Minimum 2,000 Yards)

Player, Team	Years	G	Yards	Yds.PG
Derrick Ingram, Ala.-Birmingham	1993-94	22	2,572	*116.9
Jerry Rice, Mississippi Val.	1981-84	41	*4,693	114.5
Derek Graham, Princeton	1981, 83-84	29	2,819	97.2
Kevin Guthrie, Princeton	1981-83	28	2,645	94.5
Tracy Singleton, Howard	1979-82	34	3,187	93.7
David Rhodes, Central Fla.	1991-94	39	3,618	92.8
Kasey Dunn, Idaho	1988-91	42	3,847	91.6
Gordie Lockbaum, Holy Cross	‡1986-87	22	2,012	91.5
Bryan Calder, Nevada	1984-86	28	2,559	91.4
Mike Barber, Marshall	1985-88	36	3,250	90.3
Brian Forster, Rhode Island	1983-85, 87	38	3,410	89.7

*Record. ‡Defensive back in 1984-85.

CAREER TOUCHDOWN RECEPTIONS

Player, Team	Years	G	TD
Jerry Rice, Mississippi Val.	1981-84	41	*50
Rennie Benn, Lehigh	1982-85	41	44
Roy Banks, Eastern Ill.	1983-86	38	38
Mike Jones, Tennessee St.	1979-82	42	38
Joe Thomas, Mississippi Val.	1982-85	41	36
Dameon Reilly, Rhode Island	1983-85	32	35
Darrell Colbert, Texas Southern	1983-86	43	33
John Taylor, Delaware St.	1982-85	43	33
Trumaine Johnson, Grambling	1979-82	44	32
Brian Forster, Rhode Island	1983-85, 87	38	31
David Rhodes, Central Fla.	1991-94	39	29
Tom Stenglein, Colgate	1983-85	32	29

*Record.

SEASON YARDS

Player, Team	Year	Rec.	Yards	Avg.	TD
Jerry Rice, Mississippi Val.	1984	103	*1,682	16.3	*27
Brian Forster, Rhode Island	1985	*115	1,617	14.1	12
Derrick Ingram, Ala.-Birmingham	1994	83	1,457	17.6	13
Jerry Rice, Mississippi Val.	1983	102	1,450	14.2	14
Derek Graham, Princeton	1983	84	1,363	16.2	11
Mark Didio, Connecticut	†1991	88	1,354	15.4	8
Dave Cecchini, Lehigh	†1993	88	1,318	15.0	16
Golden Tate, Tennessee St.	1983	63	1,307	20.7	13

*Record. †National champion.

SINGLE-GAME YARDS

Yds.	Player, Team (Opponent)	Date
370	Michael Lerch, Princeton (Brown)	Oct. 12, 1991
330	Nate Singleton, Grambling (Virginia Union)	Sept. 14, 1991
327	Brian Forster, Rhode Island (Brown)	Sept. 28, 1985
319	Jason Cristino, Lehigh (Lafayette)	Nov. 21, 1992
316	Marcus Hinton, Alcorn St. (Tenn.-Chatt.)	Sept. 10, 1994
299	Treamelle Taylor, Nevada (Montana)	Oct. 14, 1989
299	Brian Forster, Rhode Island (Lehigh)	Oct. 12, 1985
294	Jerry Rice, Mississippi Val. (Kentucky St.)	Sept. 1, 1984
289	Derrick Ingram, Ala.-Birmingham (Prairie View)	Nov. 19, 1994
285	Jerry Rice, Mississippi Val. (Jackson St.)	Sept. 22, 1984
279	Jerry Rice, Mississippi Val. (Southern-B.R.)	Oct. 1, 1983
276	Joey Stockton, Western Ky. (Austin Peay)	Sept. 16, 1995
266	Mark Orlando, Towson St. (American Int'l)	Oct. 22, 1994
266	Rennie Benn, Lehigh (Indiana, Pa.)	Sept. 14, 1985
264	Jason Anderson, Eastern Wash. (Montana)	Sept. 17, 1994
263	Mark Stock, Va. Military (East Tenn. St.)	Nov. 22, 1986
262	Andre Motley, Marshall (Tenn.-Chatt.)	Oct. 20, 1990
262	Kenneth Gilstrap, Tennessee Tech (Morehead St.)	Oct. 17, 1987
261	Joel Pelagio-Williams, Weber St. (Cal Poly SLO)	Sept. 23, 1995
260	Reggie Barlow, Alabama St. (Grambling)	Nov. 5, 1994
254	Kamil Loud, Cal Poly SLO (Cal St. Sacramento)	Oct. 21, 1995
253	Chris Johnson, Indiana St. (Illinois St.)	Oct. 18, 1986
252	Jeff Sanders, William & Mary (Miami, Ohio)	Sept. 11, 1982
251	Lifford Jackson, Louisiana Tech (Kansas St.)	Oct. 1, 1988

ANNUAL CHAMPIONS

Year	Player, Team	Class	G	Rec.	Avg.	Yards	TD
1978	Dan Ross, Northeastern	Sr.	11	68	6.2	988	7
1979	Stuart Gaussoin, Portland St.	Jr.	9	90	10.0	1,132	8
1980	Kenny Johnson, Portland St.	So.	11	72	6.5	1,011	11

Year	Player, Team	Class	G	Rec.	Avg.	Yards	TD
1981	Ken Harvey, Northern Iowa	Sr.	11	78	7.1	1,161	15
1982	Don Lewis, Columbia	Jr.	10	84	8.4	1,000	6
1983	Jerry Rice, Mississippi Val.	Jr.	10	102	10.2	1,450	14
1984	Jerry Rice, Mississippi Val.	Sr.	10	103	10.3	*1,682	*27
1985	Brian Forster, Rhode Island (TE)	Jr.	10	*115	*11.5	1,617	12
1986	Donald Narcisse, Texas Southern	Sr.	11	88	8.0	1,074	15
1987	Mike Barber, Marshall	Jr.	11	78	7.1	1,237	7
	Gordie Lockbaum, Holy Cross (RB)	Sr.	11	78	7.1	1,152	9
1988	Glenn Antrum, Connecticut	Sr.	11	77	7.0	1,130	7
1989	Peter Macon, Weber St.	Sr.	11	92	8.4	1,047	6

Beginning in 1990, ranked on both per-game catches and yards per game

PER-GAME CATCHES

Year	Player, Team	Class	G	Rec.	Avg.	Yards	TD
1990	Kasey Dunn, Idaho	Jr.	11	88	8.0	1,164	7
1991	Alfred Pupunu, Weber St. (TE)	Sr.	11	93	8.5	1,204	12
1992	Glenn Krupa, Southeast Mo. St.	Sr.	11	77	7.0	773	4
1993	Dave Cecchini, Lehigh	Sr.	11	88	8.0	1,318	16
1994	Jeff Johnson, East Tenn. St.	Sr.	9	73	8.1	857	8
1995	Ed Mantie, Boston U.	Sr.	11	81	7.4	943	1

YARDS PER GAME

Year	Player, Team	Class	G	Rec.	Yards	Avg.	TD
1990	Kasey Dunn, Idaho	Jr.	11	88	1,164	105.8	7
1991	Mark Didio, Connecticut	Sr.	11	88	1,354	123.1	8
1992	Jason Cristino, Lehigh	Sr.	11	65	1,282	116.5	9
1993	Dave Cecchini, Lehigh	Sr.	11	88	1,318	119.8	16
1994	Mark Orlando, Towson St.	Sr.	9	55	1,223	135.9	12
1995	Dedric Ward, Northern Iowa	Jr.	10	44	1,164	116.4	12

*Record.

Scoring

CAREER POINTS PER GAME

(Minimum 225 Points)

Player, Team	Years	G	TD	XPt.	FG	Pts.	Pt.PG
Keith Elias, Princeton	1991-93	30	52	8	0	320	*10.7
Michael Hicks, South Caro. St.	1993-95	32	52	4	0	316	9.9
Elroy Harris, Eastern Ky.	1985, 87-88	31	47	6	0	288	9.3
Joel Sigel, Portland St.	1978-80	30	46	2	0	278	9.3
Tony Zendejas, Nevada	1981-83	33	0	90	70	300	9.1
Gerald Harris, Ga. Southern	1984-86	31	45	2	0	272	8.8
Marty Zendejas, Nevada	1984-87	44	0	169	*72	*385	8.8
Charvez Foger, Nevada	1985-88	42	60	2	0	362	8.6
Paul Lewis, Boston U.	1981-84	37	51	2	0	308	8.3
Sherriden May, Idaho	1991-94	44	*61	0	0	366	8.3
Judd Garrett, Princeton	1987-89	30	41	1	0	248	8.3
Andre Garron, New Hampshire	1982-85	30	41	0	0	246	8.2
Kenny Gamble, Colgate	1984-87	42	57	0	0	342	8.1
Rene Ingoglia, Massachusetts	1992-95	41	55	2	0	332	8.1
Barry Bourassa, New Hampshire	1989-92	39	51	0	0	306	7.8
Markus Thomas, Eastern Ky.	1989-92	43	53	4	0	322	7.5
Jerry Rice, Mississippi Val.	1981-84	41	50	2	0	302	7.4
Brian Mitchell, Marshall/ Northern Iowa	1987, 89-91	44	0	130	64	322	7.3
Harvey Reed, Howard	1984-87	41	48	6	0	294	7.2
Thayne Doyle, Idaho	1988-91	43	0	160	49	307	7.1
Chris Parker, Marshall	1992-95	44	52	2	0	314	7.1

*Record.

SEASON POINTS PER GAME

Player, Team	Year	G	TD	XPt.	FG	Pts.	Pt.PG
Jerry Rice, Mississippi Val.	†1984	10	27	0	0	162	*16.2
Geoff Mitchell, Weber St.	†1991	11	*28	1	0	*170	15.5
Tony Vinson, Towson St.	†1993	10	24	0	0	144	14.4
Sherriden May, Idaho	†1992	11	25	0	0	150	13.6
Keith Elias, Princeton	1993	10	21	4	0	130	13.0
Elroy Harris, Eastern Ky.	†1988	10	21	2	0	128	12.8
Sean Sanders, Weber St.	†1987	10	21	0	0	126	12.6
Rich Erenberg, Colgate	†1983	11	21	10	0	136	12.4
Harvey Reed, Howard	1987	10	20	2	0	122	12.2
Paul Lewis, Boston U.	1983	10	20	2	0	122	12.2
Alcede Surtain, Alabama St.	†1995	11	21	6	0	132	12.0
Tim Hall, Robert Morris	†1995	10	20	0	0	120	12.0
Michael Hicks, South Caro. St.	†1994	11	22	0	0	132	12.0
Sherriden May, Idaho	1993	11	22	0	0	132	12.0
Gordie Lockbaum, Holy Cross	1987	11	22	0	0	132	12.0
Gordie Lockbaum, Holy Cross	†1986	11	22	0	0	132	12.0
Gene Lake, Delaware St.	1984	10	20	0	0	120	12.0
Ernest Thompson, Ga. Southern	1988	10	19	2	0	116	11.6
Barry Bourassa, New Hampshire	1991	11	21	0	0	126	11.5
Kenny Gamble, Colgate	1986	11	21	0	0	126	11.5

Player, Team	Year	G	TD	XPt.	FG	Pts.	Pt.PG
Gerald Harris, Ga. Southern	1984	9	17	0	0	102	11.3
Richard Howell, Davidson	1993	10	18	2	0	110	11.0
Keith Elias, Princeton	1992	10	18	2	0	110	11.0
Harvey Reed, Howard	1986	10	18	2	0	110	11.0
Derrick Cullors, Murray St.	1995	11	20	0	0	120	10.9
Rupert Grant, Howard	1993	11	20	0	0	120	10.9
Toby Davis, Illinois St.	1992	11	20	0	0	120	10.9
Carl Smith, Maine	†1989	11	20	0	0	120	10.9
Joe Segreti, Holy Cross	1988	11	20	0	0	120	10.9
Luther Turner, Sam Houston St.	1987	11	20	0	0	120	10.9
John Settle, Appalachian St.	1986	11	20	0	0	120	10.9

*Record. †National champion.

CAREER POINTS

(Non-Kickers)

Player, Team	Years	TD	XPt.	Pts.
Sherriden May, Idaho	1991-94	*61	0	366
Charvez Foger, Nevada	1985-88	60	2	362
Kenny Gamble, Colgate	1984-87	57	0	342
Rene Ingoglia, Massachusetts	1992-95	55	2	332
Markus Thomas, Eastern Ky.	1989-92	53	4	322
Keith Elias, Princeton	1991-93	52	8	320
Michael Hicks, South Caro. St.	1993-95	52	4	316
Chris Parker, Marshall	1992-95	52	2	314
Paul Lewis, Boston U.	1981-84	51	2	308
Barry Bourassa, New Hampshire	1989-92	51	0	306
Erick Torain, Lehigh	1987-90	50	6	306
Jerry Rice, Mississippi Val.	1981-84	50	2	302
Harvey Reed, Howard	1984-87	48	6	294
Jack Douglas, Citadel (QB)	1989-92	48	0	288
Elroy Harris, Eastern Ky.	1985, 87-88	47	6	288
Joel Sigel, Portland St.	1978-80	46	2	278
Joe Campbell, Middle Tenn. St.	1988-91	45	2	272
Gerald Harris, Ga. Southern	1984-86	45	2	272
Carl Tremble, Furman	1989-92	45	0	270
Norm Ford, New Hampshire	1986-89	45	0	270
John Settle, Appalachian St.	1983-86	44	4	268
Ernest Thompson, Ga. Southern	1985, 87-89	44	2	266
Rennie Benn, Lehigh	1982-85	44	2	266
Joe Segreti, Holy Cross	1987-90	44	0	264
Gordie Lockbaum, Holy Cross	1984-87	44	0	264
Frank Hawkins, Nevada	1977-80	44	0	264

*Record.

CAREER POINTS

(Kickers)

Player, Team	Years	PAT	PAT Att.	FG	FG Att.	Pts.
Marty Zendejas, Nevada	1984-87	169	175	*72	90	*385
Brian Mitchell, Marshall/ Northern Iowa	1987, 89-91	130	131	64	81	322
Thayne Doyle, Idaho	1988-91	160	174	49	75	307
Jose Larios, McNeese St.	1992-95	133	136	57	89	304
Kirk Roach, Western Caro.	1984-87	89	91	71	*102	302
Tim Foley, Ga. Southern	1984-87	151	156	50	62	301
Dewey Klein, Marshall	1988-91	156	165	48	66	300
Tony Zendejas, Nevada	1981-83	90	96	70	86	300
Jeff Wilkins, Youngstown St.	1990-93	134	136	50	73	286
Garth Petrilli, Middle Tenn. St.	1991-94	166	170	38	60	280
Steve Christie, William & Mary	1986-89	108	116	57	83	279
Franco Grilla, Central Fla.	1989-92	141	147	45	69	278
Gilad Landau, Grambling	1991-94	*181	*194	32	50	277
Mike Black, Boise St.	1988-91	122	127	51	75	275
Kirk Duce, Montana	1988-91	131	141	47	78	272
Paul Hickert, Murray St.	1984-87	116	121	49	79	263
Dean Biasucci, Western Caro.	1980-83	101	106	54	80	263
Kelly Potter, Middle Tenn. St.	1981-84	105	109	52	78	261
Steve Largent, Eastern Ill.	1992-95	122	126	46	73	260
Billy Hayes, Sam Houston St.	1985-88	117	120	47	71	258
Michael O'Neal, Samford	1989-92	142	152	38	60	256
Jason McLaughlin, Lafayette	1991-94	131	138	41	74	254
Jim Hodson, Lafayette	1987-90	134	140	40	66	254
Dave Parkinson, Delaware St.	1985-88	134	143	40	77	254
Chuck Rawlinson, Stephen F. Austin	1988-91	106	110	49	69	253
Paul Politi, Illinois St.	1983-86	101	103	50	78	251
Teddy Garcia, Northeast La.	1984-87	78	81	56	88	246
Paul McFadden, Youngstown St.	1980-83	87	90	52	90	243

*Record.

SEASON POINTS

Player, Team	Year	TD	XPt.	FG	Pts.
Geoff Mitchell, Weber St.	†1991	*28	2	0	*170
Jerry Rice, Mississippi Val.	†1984	27	0	0	162

Player, Team	Year	TD	XPt.	FG	Pts.
Sherriden May, Idaho	†1992	25	0	0	150
Tony Vinson, Towson St.	†1993	24	0	0	144
Rich Erenberg, Colgate	†1983	21	10	0	136
Alcede Surtain, Alabama St.	†1995	21	6	0	132
Michael Hicks, South Caro. St.	†1994	22	0	0	132
Sherriden May, Idaho	1993	22	0	0	132
Gordie Lockbaum, Holy Cross	1987	22	0	0	132
Gordie Lockbaum, Holy Cross	†1986	22	0	0	132
Keith Elias, Princeton	1993	21	4	0	130
Elroy Harris, Eastern Ky.	†1988	21	1	0	128
Barry Bourassa, New Hampshire	1991	21	0	0	126
Sean Sanders, Weber St.	†1987	21	0	0	126
Kenny Gamble, Colgate	1986	21	0	0	126
Harvey Reed, Howard	1987	20	2	0	122
Paul Lewis, Boston U.	1983	20	2	0	122
Tim Hall, Robert Morris	†1995	20	0	0	120
Derrick Cullors, Murray St.	1995	20	0	0	120
Rupert Grant, Howard	1993	20	0	0	120
Toby Davis, Illinois St.	1992	20	0	0	120
Carl Smith, Maine	†1989	20	0	0	120
Joe Segreti, Holy Cross	1988	20	0	0	120
Luther Turner, Sam Houston St.	1987	20	0	0	120
John Settle, Appalachian St.	1986	20	0	0	120
Gene Lake, Delaware St.	1984	20	0	0	120

*Record. †National champion.

ANNUAL CHAMPIONS

Year	Player, Team	Class	G	TD	XPt.	FG	Pts.	Avg.
1978	Frank Hawkins, Nevada	So.	10	17	0	0	102	10.2
1979	Joel Sigel, Portland St.	Jr.	10	16	0	0	96	9.6
1980	Ken Jenkins, Bucknell	Jr.	10	16	0	0	96	9.6
1981	Paris Wicks, Youngstown St.	Jr.	11	17	2	0	104	9.5
1982	Paul Lewis, Boston U.	So.	10	18	0	0	108	10.8
1983	Rich Erenberg, Colgate	Sr.	11	21	10	0	136	12.4
1984	Jerry Rice, Mississippi Val.	Sr.	10	27	0	0	162	*16.2
1985	Charvez Foger, Nevada	Fr.	10	18	0	0	108	10.8
1986	Gordie Lockbaum, Holy Cross	Jr.	11	22	0	0	132	12.0
1987	Sean Sanders, Weber St.	Sr.	10	21	0	0	126	12.6
1988	Elroy Harris, Eastern Ky.	Jr.	10	21	1	0	128	12.8
1989	Carl Smith, Maine	So.	11	20	0	0	120	10.9
1990	Barry Bourassa, New Hampshire	So.	9	16	0	0	96	10.7
1991	Geoff Mitchell, Weber St.	Sr.	11	*28	1	0	*170	15.5
1992	Sherriden May, Idaho	So.	11	25	0	0	150	13.6
1993	Tony Vinson, Towson St.	Sr.	10	24	0	0	144	14.4
1994	Michael Hicks, South Caro. St.	Jr.	11	22	0	0	132	12.0
1995	Alcede Surtain, Alabama St.	Sr.	11	21	6	0	132	12.0
	Tim Hall, Robert Morris	Sr.	10	20	0	0	120	12.0

*Record.

Interceptions

CAREER INTERCEPTIONS

Player, Team	Years	No.	Yards	Avg.
Dave Murphy, Holy Cross	1986-89	*28	309	11.0
Cedric Walker, Stephen F. Austin	1990-93	25	230	9.2
Issiac Holt, Alcorn St.	1981-84	24	319	13.3
Bill McGovern, Holy Cross	1981-84	24	168	7.0
Adrion Smith, Southwest Mo. St.	1990-93	23	219	9.5
William Carroll, Florida A&M	1989-92	23	328	14.3
Kevin Smith, Rhode Island	1987-90	23	287	12.5
Mike Prior, Illinois St.	1981-84	23	211	9.2
Chris Helon, Boston U.	1991-94	22	110	5.0
Morgan Ryan, Montana St.	1990-93	22	245	11.1
Dave Roberts, Youngstown St.	1989-92	22	131	6.0
Frank Robinson, Boise St.	1988-91	22	203	9.2
Dean Cain, Princeton	1985-87	22	203	9.2
Brian Randall, Delaware St.	1990-93	21	367	17.4
Kevin Dent, Jackson St.	1985-88	21	280	13.3
Mark Seals, Boston U.	1985-88	21	169	8.0
Jeff Smith, Illinois St.	1985-88	21	152	7.2
Chris Demarest, Northeastern	1984-87	21	255	12.1
Greg Greely, Nicholls St.	1981-84	21	218	10.4
George Floyd, Eastern Ky.	1978-81	21	318	15.1
Rick Harris, East Tenn. St.	1986-88	20	*452	22.6
Mark Kelso, William & Mary	1981-84	20	171	8.6
Leslie Frazier, Alcorn St.	1977-80	20	269	13.5
Bob Jordan, New Hampshire	1990-93	19	96	5.1
Ricky Thomas, South Caro. St.	1988-91	19	374	19.7
Dwayne Harper, South Caro. St.	1984-87	19	163	8.6
Joe Burton, Delaware St.	1983-86	19	248	13.1
Michael Richardson, Northwestern St.	1981-84	19	344	18.1
Mike Genetti, Northeastern	1980-83	19	296	15.6
George Schmitt, Delaware	1980-82	19	280	14.7

*Record.

SEASON INTERCEPTIONS

Player, Team	Year	No.	Yards
Dean Cain, Princeton	†1987	*12	98
Aeneas Williams, Southern-B.R.	‡1990	11	173
Claude Pettaway, Maine	‡1990	11	161
Bill McGovern, Holy Cross	†1984	11	102
Everson Walls, Grambling	†1980	11	145
Anthony Young, Jackson St.	†1978	11	108
Chris Helon, Boston U.	†1993	10	42
Cedric Walker, Stephen F. Austin	1990	10	11
Chris Demarest, Northeastern	1987	10	129
Kevin Dent, Jackson St.	‡1986	10	192
Eric Thompson, New Hampshire	‡1986	10	94
Anthony Anderson, Grambling	†1986	10	37
Mike Armentrout, Southwest Mo. St.	†1983	10	42
George Schmitt, Delaware	†1982	10	186
Mike Genetti, Northeastern	†1981	10	144
Bob Mahr, Lafayette	1981	10	48
Neale Henderson, Southern-B.R.	†1979	10	151

*Record. †National champion. ‡National championship shared.

ANNUAL CHAMPIONS
(Ranked on Per-Game Average)

Year	Player, Team	Class	G	No.	Avg.	Yards
1978	Anthony Young, Jackson St.	Sr.	11	11	1.00	108
1979	Neale Henderson, Southern-B.R.	Sr.	11	10	0.91	151
1980	Everson Walls, Grambling	Sr.	11	11	1.00	145
1981	Mike Genetti, Northeastern	So.	10	10	1.00	144
1982	George Schmitt, Delaware	Sr.	11	10	0.91	186
1983	Mike Armentrout, Southwest Mo. St.	Jr.	11	10	0.91	42
1984	Bill McGovern, Holy Cross	Sr.	11	11	1.00	102
1985	Mike Cassidy, Rhode Island	Sr.	10	9	0.90	169
	George Duarte, Northern Ariz.	Jr.	10	9	0.90	150
1986	Kevin Dent, Jackson St.	So.	11	10	0.91	192
	Eric Thompson, New Hampshire	Sr.	11	10	0.91	94
	Anthony Anderson, Grambling	Sr.	11	10	0.91	37
1987	Dean Cain, Princeton	Sr.	10	*12	*1.20	98
1988	Kevin Smith, Rhode Island	So.	10	9	0.90	94
1989	Mike Babb, Weber St.	Sr.	11	9	0.82	90
1990	Aeneas Williams, Southern-B.R.	Sr.	11	11	1.00	173
	Claude Pettaway, Maine	Sr.	11	11	1.00	161
1991	Warren McIntire, Delaware	Jr.	11	9	0.82	208
1992	Dave Roberts, Youngstown St.	Sr.	11	9	0.82	39
1993	Chris Helon, Boston U.	Jr.	11	10	0.91	42
1994	Joseph Vaughn, Cal St. Northridge	Sr.	10	9	0.90	265
	Brian Clark, Hofstra	Jr.	10	9	0.90	56
1995	Picasso Nelson, Jackson St.	Sr.	9	8	0.89	101

*Record.

Punting

CAREER AVERAGE
(Minimum 150 Punts)

Player, Team	Years	No.	Yards	Long	Avg.
Pumpy Tudors, Tenn.-Chatt.	1989-91	181	8,041	79	*44.4
Case de Bruijn, Idaho St.	1978-81	256	11,184	76	43.7
Terry Belden, Northern Ariz.	1990-93	225	9,760	76	43.4
George Cimadevilla, East Tenn. St.	1983-86	225	9,676	72	43.0
Harold Alexander, Appalachian St.	1989-92	259	11,100	78	42.9
John Christopher, Morehead St.	1979-82	298	12,633	62	42.4
Colin Godfrey, Tennessee St.	1989-92	213	9,012	69	42.3
Bret Wright, Southeastern La.	1981-83	165	6,963	66	42.2
Jeff Kaiser, Idaho St.	1982-84	156	6,571	88	42.1
Greg Davis, Citadel	1983-86	263	11,076	81	42.1
Mark Royals, Appalachian St.	1983-85	223	9,372	67	42.0

*Record.

SEASON AVERAGE
(Qualifiers for Championship)

Player, Team	Year	No.	Yards	Avg.
Harold Alexander, Appalachian St.	†1991	64	3,009	*47.0
Terry Belden, Northern Ariz.	†1993	59	2,712	46.0
Case de Bruijn, Idaho St.	†1981	42	1,928	45.9
Colin Godfrey, Tennessee St.	†1990	57	2,614	45.9
Stuart Dodds, Montana St.	†1979	59	2,689	45.6

Player, Team	Year	No.	Yards	Avg.
Pumpy Tudors, Tenn.-Chatt.	1991	53	2,414	45.5
Paul Asbury, Southwest Tex. St.	1990	39	1,749	44.9
Tom Sugg, Idaho	1991	53	2,371	44.7
Mike Rice, Montana	†1985	62	2,771	44.7
Case de Bruijn, Idaho St.	1979	73	3,261	44.7
George Cimadevilla, East Tenn. St.	1985	66	2,948	44.7
Greg Davis, Citadel	†1986	61	2,723	44.6
Pumpy Tudors, Tenn.-Chatt.	1990	63	2,810	44.6
Pat Velarde, Marshall	†1983	64	2,852	44.6
Bart Bradley, Sam Houston St.	1986	44	1,957	44.5
Harold Alexander, Appalachian St.	†1992	55	2,445	44.5
Curtis Moody, Texas Southern	1985	64	2,844	44.4
Terry Belden, Northern Ariz.	1991	43	1,908	44.4
Terry Belden, Northern Ariz.	1992	59	2,614	44.3
Bret Wright, Southeastern La.	1983	66	2,923	44.3
George Cimadevilla, East Tenn. St.	1986	65	2,876	44.2
Case de Bruijn, Idaho St.	†1980	67	2,945	44.0

**Record. †National champion.*

ANNUAL CHAMPIONS

Year	Player, Team	Class	No.	Yards	Avg.
1978	Nick Pavich, Nevada	So.	47	1,939	41.3
1979	Stuart Dodds, Montana St.	Sr.	59	2,689	45.6
1980	Case de Bruijn, Idaho St.	Jr.	67	2,945	44.0
1981	Case de Bruijn, Idaho St.	Sr.	42	1,928	45.9
1982	John Christopher, Morehead St.	Sr.	93	4,084	43.9
1983	Pat Velarde, Marshall	Sr.	64	2,852	44.6
1984	Steve Kornegay, Western Caro.	Jr.	49	2,127	43.4
1985	Mike Rice, Montana	Jr.	62	2,771	44.7
1986	Greg Davis, Citadel	Sr.	61	2,723	44.6
1987	Eric Stein, Eastern Wash.	Sr.	74	3,193	43.2
1988	Mike McCabe, Illinois St.	Sr.	69	3,042	44.1
1989	Pumpy Tudors, Tenn.-Chatt.	So.	65	2,817	43.3
1990	Colin Godfrey, Tennessee St.	So.	57	2,614	45.9
1991	Harold Alexander, Appalachian St.	Jr.	64	3,009	*47.0
1992	Harold Alexander, Appalachian St.	Sr.	55	2,445	44.5
1993	Terry Belden, Northern Ariz.	Sr.	59	2,712	46.0
1994	Scott Holmes, Samford	Jr.	49	2,099	42.8
1995	Kevin O'Leary, Northern Ariz.	Sr.	44	1,881	42.8

**Record.*

Punt Returns

CAREER AVERAGE

(Minimum 1.2 Returns Per Game; Minimum 30 Returns)

Player, Team	Years	No.	Yards	Avg.
Willie Ware, Mississippi Val.	1982-85	61	1,003	*16.4
Buck Phillips, Western Ill.	1994-95	40	656	16.4
Tim Egerton, Delaware St.	1986-89	59	951	16.1
Mark Orlando, Towson St.	1991-94	41	644	15.7
John Armstrong, Richmond	1984-85	31	449	14.5
Kenny Shedd, Northern Iowa	1989-92	79	1,081	13.7
Dione Tyler, Southeast Mo. St.	1994-95	39	523	13.5
Reggie Barlow, Alabama St.	1992-95	49	645	13.2
Joe Fuller, Northern Iowa	1982-85	69	888	12.9
Eric Yarber, Idaho	1984-85	32	406	12.7
Troy Brown, Marshall	1991-92	36	455	12.6
Kerry Hayes, Western Caro.	1991-94	70	876	12.5
Trumaine Johnson, Grambling	1979-82	53	662	12.5
Tony Merriwether, North Texas	1982-83	41	507	12.4
Eric Alden, Idaho St.	1992-93	31	383	12.4
Thaylen Armstead, Grambling	1989-91	44	540	12.3
Barney Bussey, South Caro. St.	1980-83	47	573	12.2
Cornell Johnson, Southern-B.R.	1990-92	40	482	12.1
John Taylor, Delaware St.	1982-85	48	576	12.0

**Record.*

SEASON AVERAGE

(Minimum 1.2 Returns Per Game and Qualifiers for Championship)

Player, Team	Year	No.	Yards	Avg.
Tim Egerton, Delaware St.	†1988	16	368	*23.0
Ryan Priest, Lafayette	†1982	12	271	22.6
Craig Hodge, Tennessee St.	†1987	19	398	21.0
Reggie Barlow, Alabama St.	†1995	12	249	20.8
John Armstrong, Richmond	†1985	19	391	20.6
Mark Orlando, Towson St.	†1994	19	377	19.8
Willie Ware, Mississippi Val.	†1984	19	374	19.7
Buck Phillips, Western Ill.	1994	24	464	19.3
Mark Hurt, Alabama St.	1988	10	185	18.5
Howard Huckaby, Florida A&M	1988	26	478	18.4
Ashley Ambrose, Mississippi Val.	†1991	28	514	18.4
Quincy Miller, South Caro. St.	†1992	17	311	18.3
Barney Bussey, South Caro. St.	†1981	14	255	18.2
Chris Darrington, Weber St.	†1986	16	290	18.1
Willie Ware, Mississippi Val.	1985	31	*561	18.1
Kerry Lawyer, Boise St.	1992	18	325	18.1
Kenny Shedd, Northern Iowa	1992	27	477	17.7
Claude Mathis, Southwest Tex. St.	1995	20	352	17.6
Clarence Alexander, Mississippi Val.	1986	22	380	17.3
Henry Richard, Northeast La.	†1989	15	258	17.2
Ray Marshall, St. Peter's	†1993	10	171	17.1
Carl Williams, Texas Southern	1981	16	269	16.8
Jerome Bledsoe, Massachusetts	1988	17	285	16.8

**Record. †National champion.*

ANNUAL CHAMPIONS

Year	Player, Team	Class	No.	Yards	Avg.
1978	Ray Smith, Northern Ariz.	Sr.	13	181	13.9
1979	Joseph Markus, Connecticut	Fr.	17	219	12.9
1980	Trumaine Johnson, Grambling	So.	††13	226	17.4
1981	Barney Bussey, South Caro. St.	So.	14	255	18.2
1982	Ryan Priest, Lafayette	Fr.	12	271	22.6
1983	Joe Fuller, Northern Iowa	So.	22	344	15.6
1984	Willie Ware, Mississippi Val.	Jr.	19	374	19.7
1985	John Armstrong, Richmond	Sr.	19	391	20.6
1986	Chris Darrington, Weber St.	Sr.	16	290	18.1
1987	Craig Hodge, Tennessee St.	Sr.	19	398	21.0
1988	Tim Egerton, Delaware St.	Jr.	16	368	*23.0
1989	Henry Richard, Northeast La.	Jr.	15	258	17.2
1990	Gary Harrell, Howard	Fr.	26	417	16.0
1991	Ashley Ambrose, Mississippi Val.	Sr.	28	514	18.4
1992	Quincy Miller, South Caro. St.	Jr.	17	311	18.3
1993	Ray Marshall, St. Peter's	Jr.	10	171	17.1
1994	Mark Orlando, Towson St.	Sr.	19	377	19.8
1995	Reggie Barlow, Alabama St.	Sr.	12	249	20.8

**Record. ††Declared champion; with one more return (making 1.3 per game) for zero yards, still would have highest average.*

Kickoff Returns

CAREER AVERAGE

(Minimum 1.2 Returns Per Game; Minimum 30 Returns)

Player, Team	Years	No.	Yards	Avg.
Troy Brown, Marshall	1991-92	32	950	*29.7
Charles Swann, Indiana St.	1989-91	45	1,319	29.3
Craig Richardson, Eastern Wash.	1983-86	71	2,021	28.5
Kenyatta Sparks, Southern-B.R.	1992-95	39	1,100	28.2
Kerry Hayes, Western Caro.	1991-94	73	2,058	28.2
Daryl Holcombe, Eastern Ill.	1986-89	49	1,379	28.1
Dwight Robinson, James Madison	1990-93	51	1,434	28.1
Curtis Chappell, Howard	1984-87	42	1,177	28.0
Leon Brown, Eastern Ky.	1990-93	44	1,230	28.0
Marcus Durgin, Samford	1990-93	44	1,218	27.7
Cornelius Turner, Mississippi Val.	1992-94	50	1,379	27.6
Anthony Taylor, Northern Iowa	1992-95	30	821	27.4
Jerry Parrish, Eastern Ky.	1978-81	61	1,668	27.3
Tony James, Eastern Ky.	1982-84	57	1,552	27.2
Frank Selto, Idaho St.	1986-87	30	803	26.8
Chris Hickman, Northeast La.	1991-92	30	798	26.6
Chris Pollard, Dartmouth	1986-88	52	1,376	26.5
John Jarvis, Howard	1986-88	39	1,031	26.4
Ronald Scott, Southern-B.R.	1982-85	38	1,003	26.4
Rob Tesch, Montana St.	1989-92	50	1,317	26.3
Vernon Williams, Eastern Wash.	1986-88	40	1,052	26.3
Steve Ortman, Pennsylvania	1982-84	31	808	26.1
John Armstrong, Richmond	1984-85	32	826	25.8
Renard Coleman, Montana	1985-88	57	1,465	25.7
Michael Haynes, Northern Ariz.	1986-87	36	925	25.7
Kevin Gainer, Bethune-Cookman	1988-90	42	1,070	25.5
Archie Herring, Youngstown St.	1987-90	79	2,005	25.4
Kenny Shedd, Northern Iowa	1989-92	54	1,359	25.2
Damon Boddie, Montana	1993-94	49	1,232	25.1
Michael High, North Texas	1991-93	47	1,171	24.9
Jerome Stelly, Western Ill.	1981-82	42	1,024	24.4
Chris Pierce, Rhode Island	1989-92	63	1,521	24.1
Albert Brown, Western Ill.	1985-86	30	723	24.1
Sylvester Stamps, Jackson St.	1980, 82-83	42	1,012	24.1
Sean Hill, Montana St.	1991-93	44	1,060	24.1

**Record.*

SEASON AVERAGE
(Minimum 1.2 Returns Per Game and Qualifiers for Championship)

Player, Team	Year	No.	Yards	Avg.
David Fraterrigo, Canisius	†1993	13	485	*37.3
Kerry Hayes, Western Caro.	1993	16	584	36.5
Craig Richardson, Eastern Wash.	†1984	21	729	34.7
Errin Hatwood, St. John's (N.Y.)	†1994	12	401	33.4
Marcus Durgin, Samford	†1992	15	499	33.3
Rory Lee, Western Ill.	1993	16	527	32.9
Dave Meggett, Towson St.	†1988	13	418	32.2
Josh Cole, Furman	†1995	17	546	32.1
Charles Swann, Indiana St.	†1990	20	642	32.1
Archie Herring, Youngstown St.	1990	18	575	31.9
Dwight Robinson, James Madison	1994	16	510	31.9
Davlin Mullen, Western Ky.	†1982	18	574	31.9
Todd Cleveland, Central Fla.	1994	15	476	31.7
Naylon Albritton, South Caro. St.	1993	15	475	31.7
Jermine Sharp, Southern-B.R.	1995	16	504	31.5
Ozzie Young, Valparaiso	1994	17	533	31.4
Danny Copeland, Eastern Ky.	†1986	26	812	31.2
Chris Chappell, Howard	1986	17	528	31.1
Thomas Haskins, Va. Military	1994	15	464	30.9
Dave Loehle, New Hampshire	†1978	15	460	30.7
Paul Ashby, Alabama St.	†1991	17	520	30.6
Juan Jackson, North Caro. A&T	1986	16	487	30.4
Kevin Gainer, Bethune-Cookman	1990	21	635	30.2
Howard Huckaby, Florida A&M	†1987	20	602	30.1
Tony James, Eastern Ky.	†1983	17	511	30.1
Anthony Brown, Southern Utah	1994	18	539	29.9
Kenny Bynum, South Caro. St.	1995	13	389	29.9
Robert Johnson, Idaho St.	1992	14	416	29.7
Jerry Parrish, Eastern Ky.	†1981	18	534	29.7
John Armstrong, Richmond	1984	18	531	29.5
Clarence Matthews, Northwestern St.	1994	19	560	29.5
Claude Mathis, Southwest Tex. St.	1994	26	765	29.4
Renard Coleman, Montana	1987	20	588	29.4

**Record. †National champion.*

ANNUAL CHAMPIONS

Year	Player, Team	Class	No.	Yards	Avg.
1978	Dave Loehle, New Hampshire	Jr.	15	460	30.7
1979	Garry Pearson, Massachusetts	Fr.	12	348	29.0
1980	Danny Thomas, North Caro. A&T	Fr.	15	381	25.4
1981	Jerry Parrish, Eastern Ky.	Sr.	18	534	29.7
1982	Davlin Mullen, Western Ky.	Sr.	18	574	31.9
1983	Tony James, Eastern Ky.	Jr.	17	511	30.1
1984	Craig Richardson, Eastern Wash.	So.	21	729	34.7
1985	Rodney Payne, Murray St.	Fr.	16	464	29.0
1986	Danny Copeland, Eastern Ky.	Jr.	26	812	31.2
1987	Howard Huckaby, Florida A&M	So.	20	602	30.1
1988	Dave Meggett, Towson St.	Sr.	13	418	32.2
1989	Scott Thomas, Liberty	Fr.	13	373	28.7
1990	Charles Swann, Indiana St.	Jr.	20	642	32.1
1991	Paul Ashby, Alabama St.	Jr.	17	520	30.6
1992	Marcus Durgin, Samford	Jr.	15	499	33.3
1993	David Fraterrigo, Canisius	Sr.	13	485	*37.3
1994	Errin Hatwood, St. John's (N.Y.)	Sr.	12	401	33.4
1995	Josh Cole, Furman	Jr.	17	546	32.1

**Record.*

DIVISION I-AA

All-Purpose Yards

CAREER YARDS PER GAME
(Minimum 3,200 Yards)

Player, Team	Years	Rush	Rcv.	Int.	PR	KOR	Yds.	Yd.PG
Arnold Mickens, Butler	1994-95	3,813	47	0	0	87	3,947	*197.4
Tim Hall, Robert Morris	1994-95	2,908	793	0	0	0	3,701	194.8
Dave Meggett, Towson St.	1987-88	1,658	788	0	212	745	3,403	189.1
Kenny Gamble, Colgate	1984-87	5,220	536	0	104	1,763	*7,623	181.5
Rich Erenberg, Colgate	1982-83	2,618	423	0	268	315	3,624	172.6
Ozzie Young, Valparaiso	1993-95	1,576	1,123	0	418	1,728	4,845	167.1
Fine Unga, Weber St.	1987-88	2,298	391	0	7	967	3,663	166.5
Gill Fenerty, Holy Cross	1983-85	3,618	477	0	1	731	4,827	160.9
Keith Elias, Princeton	1991-93	4,208	508	0	0	25	4,741	158.0
Don Wilkerson, Southwest Tex. St.	1993-94	2,356	255	0	83	757	3,451	156.9
Kito Lockwood, Wagner	1993-95	2,576	891	0	0	420	3,887	155.5
Barry Bourassa, New Hampshire	1989-92	2,960	1,307	0	306	1,370	5,943	152.4
Judd Garrett, Princeton	1987-89	3,109	1,385	0	0	10	4,510	150.3
Treamelle Taylor, Nevada	1987-90	0	1,926	0	662	687	3,275	148.9
Troy Brown, Marshall	1991-92	138	1,716	0	455	950	3,259	148.1
Andre Garron, New Hampshire	1982-85	2,901	809	0	8	651	4,369	145.6
Carl Boyd, Northern Iowa	1983, 85-87	2,735	1,987	0	0	183	4,905	144.3
Merril Hoge, Idaho St.	1983-86	2,713	1,734	0	1	1,005	5,453	139.8
Pete Mandley, Northern Ariz.	1979-80, 82-83	436	2,598	11	901	1,979	5,925	137.8
Erik Marsh, Lafayette	1991-94	4,834	383	0	76	490	5,783	137.7
Kerry Hayes, Western Caro.	1991-94	75	2,594	0	876	2,058	5,603	136.7
Frank Hawkins, Nevada	1977-80	*5,333	519	0	0	0	5,852	136.1
Derrick Harmon, Cornell	1981-83	3,074	679	0	5	42	3,800	135.7
Dorron Hunter, Morehead St.	1977-80	1,336	1,320	0	510	1,970	5,136	135.2

**Record.*

SEASON YARDS PER GAME

Player, Team	Year	Rush	Rcv.	Int.	PR	KOR	Yds.	Yd.PG
Arnold Mickens, Butler	†1994	*2,255	7	0	0	0	2,262	*226.2
Kenny Gamble, Colgate	†1986	1,816	178	0	40	391	*2,425	220.5
Reggie Greene, Siena	†1995	1,461	77	0	53	363	1,954	217.1
Michael Clemons, William & Mary	1986	1,065	516	0	330	423	2,334	212.2
Tony Vinson, Towson St.	†1993	2,016	57	0	0	0	2,073	207.3
Derrick Cullors, Murray St.	1995	1,765	312	0	0	201	2,278	207.1
Clarence Matthews, Northwestern St.	1995	1,384	194	0	145	554	2,277	207.0
Claude Mathis, Southwest Tex. St.	1995	1,286	315	0	352	308	2,261	205.6
Anthony Jordan, Samford	1994	924	400	0	169	767	2,260	205.5
Rich Erenberg, Colgate	†1983	1,883	214	0	126	18	2,241	203.7
Tim Hall, Robert Morris	1994	1,336	460	0	0	0	1,796	199.6
Joey Stockton, Western Ky.	1995	46	863	0	147	934	1,990	199.0
Dave Meggett, Towson St.	†1987	814	572	0	78	327	1,791	199.0
Gordie Lockbaum, Holy Cross	1986	827	860	34	0	452	2,173	197.6
Gill Fenerty, Holy Cross	†1985	1,368	187	0	1	414	1,970	197.0

Photo from Robert Morris sports information

Running back Tim Hall averaged more than 190 all-purpose yards per game in each of his two seasons at Robert Morris. His career average of 194.8 yards per game is second in Division I-AA history.

Northwestern State sports information photo by Don Sepulvado

Northwestern State running back Clarence Matthews gained 2,277 all-purpose yards in 1995, the fourth best single-season total in Division I-AA history.

Player, Team	Year	Rush	Rcv.	Int.	PR	KOR	Yds.	Yd.PG
Barry Bourassa, New Hampshire	†1991	1,130	426	0	0	596	2,152	195.6
Thomas Haskins, Va. Military	1995	1,548	33	0	0	553	2,134	194.0
Keith Elias, Princeton	1993	1,731	193	0	0	15	1,939	193.9
Barry Bourassa, New Hampshire	†1990	957	276	0	133	368	1,734	192.7
Merril Hoge, Idaho St.	1985	1,041	708	0	0	364	2,113	192.1
Andre Garron, New Hampshire	1983	1,009	539	0	0	359	1,907	190.7
Kenny Gamble, Colgate	1987	1,411	151	0	64	471	2,097	190.6
Tim Hall, Robert Morris	1995	1,572	333	0	0	0	1,905	190.5
Kito Lockwood, Wagner	1995	1,018	187	0	0	127	1,332	190.3
Otis Washington, Western Caro.	†1988	64	907	0	0	1,113	2,086	189.6
Ken Jenkins, Bucknell	†1980	1,270	293	0	65	256	1,884	188.4
Don Wilkerson, Southwest Tex. St.	1994	1,569	131	0	21	327	2,048	186.2
Kenny Gamble, Colgate	1985	1,361	162	0	0	520	2,043	185.7
Gordie Lockbaum, Holy Cross	1987	403	1,152	0	209	277	2,041	185.6
Ozzie Young, Valparaiso	1994	606	426	0	96	533	1,661	184.6
Thomas Haskins, Va. Military	1994	1,509	50	0	0	464	2,023	183.9
Dominic Corr, Eastern Wash.	†1989	796	52	0	0	807	1,655	183.9
Al Rosier, Dartmouth	1991	1,432	113	0	0	290	1,835	183.5
Jerome Bledsoe, Massachusetts	1991	1,545	178	0	0	293	2,016	183.3
David Wright, Indiana St.	†1992	1,313	108	0	0	593	2,014	183.1
Mark Stock, Va. Military	1988	90	1,161	0	260	500	2,011	182.8
Jamie Jones, Eastern Ill.	1991	1,403	299	0	0	305	2,007	182.5

**Record. †National champion.*

CAREER YARDS

Player, Team	Years	Rush	Rcv.	Int.	PR	KOR	Yds.	Yd.PP
Kenny Gamble, Colgate	1984-87	5,220	536	0	104	1,763	*7,623	7.0
Barry Bourassa, New Hampshire	1989-92	2,960	1,307	0	306	1,370	5,943	7.5
Pete Mandley, Northern Ariz.	1979-80, 82-83	436	2,598	11	901	1,979	5,925	14.8
Frank Hawkins, Nevada	1977-80	*5,333	519	0	0	0	5,852	5.8
Erik Marsh, Lafayette	1991-94	4,834	383	0	76	490	5,783	5.2
Kerry Hayes, Western Caro.	1991-94	5	2,594	0	876	2,058	5,603	*19.1
Jamie Jones, Eastern Ill.	1988-91	3,466	816	0	66	1,235	5,583	6.2
Chris Parker, Marshall	1992-95	4,571	838	0	0	133	5,542	6.5
Sherriden May, Idaho	1991-94	3,748	926	0	153	646	5,473	6.9
Merril Hoge, Idaho St.	1983-86	2,713	1,734	0	1	1,005	5,453	6.6
Herman Hunter, Tennessee St.	1981-84	1,049	1,129	0	974	*2,258	5,410	10.5
David Wright, Indiana St.	1992-95	4,181	255	0	0	904	5,340	6.2
Cedric Minter, Boise St.	1977-80	4,475	525	0	49	267	5,316	6.5
Charvez Foger, Nevada	1985-88	4,484	821	0	0	0	5,305	5.7
Garry Pearson, Massachusetts	1979-82	3,859	466	0	0	952	5,277	5.9
John Settle, Appalachian St.	1983-86	4,409	526	0	0	319	5,254	5.3
Dorron Hunter, Morehead St.	1977-80	1,336	1,320	0	510	1,970	5,136	9.6

**Record.*

SEASON YARDS

Player, Team	Year	Rush	Rcv.	Int.	PR	KOR	Yds.	Yd.PP
Kenny Gamble, Colgate	†1986	1,816	178	0	40	391	*2,425	7.1
Michael Clemons, William & Mary	1986	1,065	516	0	330	423	2,334	6.7
Derrick Cullors, Murray St.	1995	1,765	312	0	0	201	2,278	7.6
Clarence Matthews, Northwestern St.	1995	1,384	194	0	145	554	2,277	7.7
Arnold Mickens, Butler	†1994	*2,255	7	0	0	0	2,262	5.5
Claude Mathis, Southwest Tex. St.	1995	1,286	315	0	352	308	2,261	7.3
Anthony Jordan, Samford	1994	924	400	0	169	767	2,260	10.8
Rich Erenberg, Colgate	†1983	1,883	214	0	126	18	2,241	6.7
Gordie Lockbaum, Holy Cross	1986	827	860	34	0	452	2,173	9.7
Barry Bourassa, New Hampshire	†1991	1,130	426	0	0	596	2,152	7.5
Thomas Haskins, Va. Military	1995	1,548	33	0	0	553	2,134	7.6
Merril Hoge, Idaho St.	1985	1,041	708	0	0	364	2,113	7.4
Kenny Gamble, Colgate	1987	1,411	151	0	64	471	2,097	6.5
Otis Washington, Western Caro.	†1988	66	907	0	0	1,113	2,086	*19.7
Tony Vinson, Towson St.	†1993	2,016	57	0	0	0	2,073	6.8
Don Wilkerson, Southwest Tex. St.	1994	1,569	131	0	21	327	2,048	6.2
Kenny Gamble, Colgate	1985	1,361	162	0	0	520	2,043	7.3
Gordie Lockbaum, Holy Cross	1987	403	1,152	0	209	277	2,041	10.4
Thomas Haskins, Va. Military	1994	1,509	50	0	0	464	2,023	7.2
Jerome Bledsoe, Massachusetts	1991	1,545	178	0	0	293	2,016	6.7
David Wright, Indiana St.	†1992	1,313	108	0	0	593	2,014	7.9
Mark Stock, Va. Military	1988	90	1,161	0	260	500	2,011	14.0
Jamie Jones, Eastern Ill.	1991	1,403	299	0	0	305	2,007	7.2

**Record. †National champion.*

ALL-PURPOSE SINGLE-GAME HIGHS

Yds.	Player, Team (Opponent)	Date
467	Joey Stockton, Western Ky. (Austin Peay)	Sept. 16, 1995
463	Michael Lerch, Princeton (Brown)	Oct. 12, 1991
453	Herman Hunter, Tennessee St. (Mississippi Val.)	Nov. 13, 1982
395	Scott Oliaro, Cornell (Yale)	Nov. 3, 1990
386	Gill Fenerty, Holy Cross (Columbia)	Oct. 29, 1983
378	Joe Delaney, Northwestern St. (Nicholls St.)	Oct. 28, 1978
373	William Arnold, Jackson St. (Texas Southern)	Nov. 6, 1993
372	Gary Harrell, Howard (Morgan St.)	Nov. 3, 1990

Yds.	Player, Team (Opponent)	Date
372	Treamelle Taylor, Nevada (Montana)	Oct. 14, 1989
369	Flip Johnson, McNeese St. (Southwestern La.)	Nov. 15, 1986
367	Chris Darrington, Weber St. (Idaho St.)	Oct. 25, 1986
365	Erwin Matthews, Richmond (Delaware)	Sept. 26, 1987
361	Patrick Robinson, Tennessee St. (Jackson St.)	Sept. 12, 1992
358	Claude Mathis, Southwest Tex. St. (Eastern Wash.)	Sept. 7, 1995
357	Tony Vinson, Towson St. (Bucknell)	Nov. 13, 1993
352	Jason Anderson, Eastern Wash. (Montana)	Sept. 17, 1994
352	Andre Garron, New Hampshire (Lehigh)	Oct. 15, 1983
347	Tony Vinson, Towson St. (Morgan St.)	Nov. 20, 1993
345	Russell Davis, Idaho (Weber St.)	Oct. 2, 1982
343	Richardo Sarille, Wagner (St. Peter's)	Sept. 29, 1995
341	Barry Bourassa, New Hampshire (Delaware)	Oct. 5, 1991
340	Reggie Greene, Siena (St. John's, N.Y.)	Oct. 28, 1995
340	Gene Lake, Delaware St. (Liberty)	Nov. 10, 1984
335	Judd Garrett, Princeton (Harvard)	Oct. 22, 1988

ANNUAL CHAMPIONS

Year	Player, Team	Class	Rush	Rcv.	Int.	PR	KOR	Yds.	Yd.PG
1978	Frank Hawkins, Nevada	So.	1,445	211	0	0	0	1,656	165.6
1979	Frank Hawkins, Nevada	Jr.	1,683	123	0	0	0	1,806	164.2
1980	Ken Jenkins, Bucknell	Jr.	1,270	293	0	65	256	1,884	188.4
1981	Garry Pearson, Massachusetts	Jr.	1,026	105	0	0	450	1,581	175.7
1982	Pete Mandley, Northern Ariz.	Jr.	36	1,067	0	344	532	1,979	179.9
1983	Rich Erenberg, Colgate	Sr.	1,883	214	0	126	18	2,241	203.7
1984	Gene Lake, Delaware St.	Jr.	1,722	37	0	0	0	1,759	175.9
1985	Gill Fenerty, Holy Cross	Sr.	1,368	187	0	1	414	1,970	197.0
1986	Kenny Gamble, Colgate	Jr.	1,816	178	0	40	391	*2,425	220.5
1987	Dave Meggett, Towson St.	Jr.	814	572	0	78	327	1,791	199.0
1988	Otis Washington, Western Caro.	Sr.	66	907	0	0	1,113	2,086	189.6
1989	Dominic Corr, Eastern Wash.	Sr.	796	52	0	0	807	1,655	183.9
1990	Barry Bourassa, New Hampshire	So.	957	276	0	133	368	1,734	192.7
1991	Barry Bourassa, New Hampshire	Jr.	1,130	426	0	0	596	2,152	195.6
1992	David Wright, Indiana St.	Fr.	1,313	108	0	0	593	2,014	183.1
1993	Tony Vinson, Towson St.	Sr.	2,016	57	0	0	0	2,073	207.3
1994	Arnold Mickens, Butler	Jr.	*2,255	7	0	0	0	2,262	*226.2
1995	Reggie Greene, Siena	So.	1,461	77	0	53	363	1,954	217.1

*Record.

File photo

Despite the fact that he had no return yardage, Nevada running back Frank Hawkins (#27) led Division I-AA in all-purpose yards in 1978 and 1979, the first two years that the division existed.

DIVISION I-AA

Field Goals

CAREER FIELD GOALS

Player, Team	Years	Total	Pct.	Under 40 Yds.	40 Plus	Long
Marty Zendejas, Nevada (S)	1984-87	*72-90	.800	42-45	30-45	54
Kirk Roach, Western Caro. (S)	1984-87	71-*102	.696	45-49	26-53	57
Tony Zendejas, Nevada (S)	1981-83	70-86	*.814	45-49	25-37	58
Brian Mitchell, Marshall/Northern Iowa (S)	1987, 89-91	64-81	.790	48-55	16-26	57
Jose Larios, McNeese St. (S)	1992-95	57-89	.640	47-57	10-32	47
Steve Christie, William & Mary (S)	1986-89	57-83	.686	39-49	18-34	53
Teddy Garcia, Northeast La. (S)	1984-87	56-88	.636	35-43	21-45	55
Bjorn Nittmo, Appalachian St. (S)	1985-88	55-74	.743	35-40	20-34	54
Kelly Potter, Middle Tenn. St. (S)	1981-84	52-78	.667	37-49	15-29	57
Paul McFadden, Youngstown St. (S)	1980-83	52-90	.578	28-42	24-48	54
Mike Black, Boise St. (S)	1988-91	51-75	.680	35-43	16-32	48
Jeff Wilkins, Youngstown St. (S)	1990-93	50-73	.685	33-38	17-35	54
Tim Foley, Ga. Southern (S)	1984-87	50-62	.806	32-37	18-25	**63
Paul Politi, Illinois St. (S)	1983-86	50-78	.641	34-48	16-30	50
Chuck Rawlinson, Stephen F. Austin (S)	1988-91	49-69	.710	34-43	15-26	58
Thayne Doyle, Idaho (S)	1988-91	49-75	.653	35-51	14-24	52
Matt Stover, Louisiana Tech (S)	1986-88	49-68	.721	29-34	20-34	57
Scott Roper, Texas-Arlington/Arkansas St. (S)	1985, 86-87	49-75	.653	35-43	14-32	**63
Paul Hickert, Murray St. (S)	1984-87	49-79	.620	34-48	15-31	62
Dewey Klein, Marshall (S)	1988-91	48-66	.727	37-47	11-19	54
John Dowling, Youngstown St. (S)	1984-87	48-76	.632	36-44	12-32	49
Kirk Duce, Montana (S)	1988-91	47-78	.603	37-51	10-27	51
Billy Hayes, Sam Houston St. (S)	1985-88	47-71	.662	37-55	10-16	54
Steve Largent, Eastern Ill. (S)	1992-95	46-73	.630	30-38	16-35	53
Roger Ruzek, Weber St. (S)	1979-82	46-78	.590	28-37	18-41	51

*Record. **Record tied. (S) Soccer-style kicker.

SEASON FIELD GOALS

Player, Team	Year	Total	Pct.	Under 40 Yds.	40 Plus	Long
Brian Mitchell, Northern Iowa (S)	†1990	**26-27	*.963	23-23	3-4	45
Tony Zendejas, Nevada (S)	†1982	**26-**33	.788	18-20	8-13	52
Kirk Roach, Western Caro. (S)	†1986	24-28	.857	17-17	7-11	52
George Benyola, Louisiana Tech (S)	†1985	24-31	.774	15-18	9-13	53
Goran Lingmerth, Northern Ariz. (S)	1986	23-29	.793	16-19	7-10	55
Tony Zendejas, Nevada (S)	†1983	23-29	.793	14-15	9-14	58
David Ettinger, Hofstra (S)	†1995	22-**33	.667	17-22	5-11	54
Jose Larios, McNeese St. (S)	†1993	22-28	.786	19-21	3-7	47
Mike Dodd, Boise St. (S)	†1992	22-31	.710	16-21	6-10	50
Marty Zendejas, Nevada (S)	†1984	22-27	.815	12-13	10-14	52

Hofstra sports information photo by Brian Ballweg

Hofstra's David Ettinger was the Division I-AA leader in field goals in 1995 with an average of 2.0 per game (22 in 11 games).

Player, Team	Year	Total	Pct.	Under 40 Yds.	40 Plus	Long
Kevin McKelvie, Nevada (S)	1990	21-24	.875	16-17	5-7	52
Matt Stover, Louisiana Tech (S)	1986	21-25	.840	15-15	6-10	53
Scott Roper, Arkansas St. (S)	1986	21-28	.750	15-17	6-11	50
Tony Zendejas, Nevada (S)	†1981	21-24	.875	13-14	8-10	55
Darren Goodman, Idaho St. (S)	1990	20-28	.714	12-14	8-14	53
Steve Christie, William & Mary (S)	†1989	20-29	.690	16-17	4-12	53
Teddy Garcia, Northeast La. (S)	1987	20-28	.714	10-11	10-17	55

**Record. **Record tied. †National champion. (S) Soccer-style kicker.*

ANNUAL CHAMPIONS

(Ranked on Per-Game Average)

Year	Player, Team	Total	PG	Pct.	Under 40 Yds.	40 Plus	Long
1978	Tom Sarette, Boise St. (S)	12-20	1.2	.600	8-10	4-10	47
1979	Wilfredo Rosales, Alcorn St. (S)	13-20	1.3	.650	10-11	3-9	45
	Sandro Vitiello, Massachusetts (S)	13-22	1.3	.591	10-12	3-10	47
1980	Scott Norwood, James Madison (S)	15-21	1.5	.714	10-11	5-10	48
1981	Tony Zendejas, Nevada (S)	21-24	1.9	.875	13-14	8-10	55
1982	Tony Zendejas, Nevada (S)	**26-**33	**2.4	.788	18-20	8-13	52
1983	Tony Zendejas, Nevada (S)	23-29	2.1	.793	14-15	9-14	58
1984	Marty Zendejas, Nevada (S)	22-27	2.0	.815	12-13	10-14	52
1985	George Benyola, Louisiana Tech (S)	24-31	2.2	.774	15-18	9-13	53
1986	Kirk Roach, Western Caro. (S)	24-28	2.2	.857	17-17	7-11	52
1987	Micky Penaflor, Northern Ariz. (S)	19-27	1.9	.704	12-16	7-11	51
1988	Chris Lutz, Princeton (S)	19-24	1.9	.792	19-21	0-3	39
1989	Steve Christie, William & Mary (S)	20-29	1.8	.690	16-17	4-12	53
1990	Brian Mitchell, Northern Iowa (S)	**26-27	**2.4	*.963	23-23	3-4	45
1991	Brian Mitchell, Northern Iowa (S)	19-24	1.7	.792	15-16	4-8	57
1992	Mike Dodd, Boise St. (S)	22-31	2.0	.710	16-21	6-10	50
1993	Jose Larios, McNeese St. (S)	22-28	2.0	.786	19-21	3-7	47
1994	Andy Glockner, Pennsylvania (S)	14-20	1.6	.700	10-14	4-6	44
1995	David Ettinger, Hofstra (S)	22-**33	2.0	.667	17-22	5-11	54

**Record. **Record tied. (S) Soccer-style kicker.*

All-Time Longest Plays

Since 1941, official maximum length of all plays fixed at 100 yards.

RUSHING

Yds.	Player, Team (Opponent)	Year
99	Jim Varick, Monmouth, N.J. (Sacred Heart)	1994
99	Phillip Collins, Southwest Mo. St. (Western Ill.)	1989
99	Pedro Bacon, Western Ky. (West Ala.)	1986
99	Hubert Owens, Mississippi Val. (Ark.-Pine Bluff)	1980
98	Johnny Gordon, Nevada (Montana St.)	1984
97	Pat Williams, Delaware (West Chester)	1995
97	Norman Bradford, Grambling (Prairie View)	1992
97	David Clark, Dartmouth (Harvard)	1989
97	David Clark, Dartmouth (Princeton)	1988
96	Kelvin Anderson, Southeast Mo. St. (Murray St.)	1992
96	Andre Lockhart, Tenn.-Chatt. (East Tenn. St.)	1986
95	Brett Chappell, Western Caro. (Elon)	1995
95	Tim Hall, Robert Morris (Gannon)	1994
95	Jeff Sawulski, Siena (Iona)	1993
95	Jerry Ellison, Tenn.-Chatt. (Boise St.)	1992
95	Joe Sparksman, James Madison (William & Mary)	1990
94	Mark Vigil, Idaho (Simon Fraser)	1980

PASSING

Yds.	Passer-Receiver, Team (Opponent)	Year
99	Todd Bennett-Jason Anderson, Eastern Wash. (Montana)	1994
99	Aaron Garcia-Greg Ochoa, Cal St. Sacramento (Cal Poly SLO)	1993
99	Todd Donnan-Troy Brown, Marshall (East Tenn. St.)	1991
99	Antoine Ezell-Tyrone Davis, Florida A&M (Bethune-Cookman)	1991
99	Jay Johnson-Kenny Shedd, Northern Iowa (Oklahoma St.)	1990
99	John Bonds-Hendricks Johnson, Northern Ariz. (Boise St.)	1990
99	Scott Stoker-Victor Robinson, Northwestern St. (Northeast La.)	1989
98	Derek Jensen-Jason Cannon, Southwest Mo. St. (Eastern Ill.)	1995
98	Jonathan Quinn-Dee Mostiller, Middle Tenn. St. (Tennessee Tech)	1995
98	Antoine Ezell-Tim Daniel, Florida A&M (Delaware St.)	1991
98	John Friesz-Lee Allen, Idaho (Northern Ariz.)	1989
98	Fred Gatlin-Treamelle Taylor, Nevada (Montana)	1989
98	Steve Monaco-Emerson Foster, Rhode Island (Holy Cross)	1988
98	Frank Baur-Maurice Caldwell, Lafayette (Columbia)	1988
98	David Gabianelli-Craig Morton, Dartmouth (Columbia)	1986
98	Joe Pizzo-Bryan Calder, Nevada (Eastern Wash.)	1984
98	Bobby Hebert-Randy Liles, Northwestern St. (Southeastern La.)	1980
97	Lester Anderson-Kevin Glenn, Illinois St. (Ball St.)	1993
97	Nate Harrison-Brian Thomas, Southern-B.R. (Dist. Columbia)	1989
97	Jerome Baker-John Taylor, Delaware St. (St. Paul's)	1985
97	John McKenzie-Chris Burkett, Jackson St. (Mississippi Val.)	1983
96	Chris Berg-Dedric Ward, Northern Iowa (Western Ill.)	1995
96	Damon Williams-Ryan Blakely, Alabama St. (Texas Southern)	1994
96	Greg Wyatt-Shawn Collins, Northern Ariz. (Montana St.)	1988
96	Rick Fahnestock-Albert Brown, Western Ill. (Northern Iowa)	1986
96	Jeff Cesarone-Keith Paskett, Western Ky. (Akron)	1985
96	Mike Williams-Trumaine Johnson, Grambling (Jackson St.)	1980

INTERCEPTION RETURNS

Yds.	Player, Team (Opponent)	Year
100	Derek Grier, Marshall (East Tenn. St.)	1991
100	Ricky Fields, Samford (Concord, W.Va.)	1990
100	Warren Smith, Stephen F. Austin (Nicholls St.)	1990
100	Rob Pouliot, Montana St. (Boise St.)	1988
100	Rick Harris, East Tenn. St. (Davidson)	1986
100	Bruce Alexander, Stephen F. Austin (Lamar)	1986
100	Guy Carbone, Rhode Island (Lafayette)	1985
100	Moses Aimable, Northern Iowa (Western Ill.)	1985
100	Kervin Fontennette, Southeastern La. (Nicholls St.)	1985
100	Jim Anderson, Princeton (Cornell)	1984
100	Keiron Bigby, Brown (Yale)	1984
100	Vencie Glenn, Indiana St. (Wayne St., Mich.)	1984
100	George Floyd, Eastern Ky. (Youngstown St.)	1980

PUNT RETURNS

Yds.	Player, Team (Opponent)	Year
98	Willie Ware, Mississippi Val. (Bishop)	1985
98	Barney Bussey, South Caro. St. (Johnson Smith)	1981
96	Carl Williams, Texas Southern (Grambling)	1981
95	Clarence Weathers, Delaware St. (Salisbury St.)	1980
93	Andrew McFadden, Liberty (Delaware St.)	1995
93	Patrick Plott, Jacksonville St. (Southwest Mo. St.)	1995
93	Joe Fuller, Northern Iowa (Wis.-Whitewater)	1984

KICKOFF RETURNS

Thirty-five players have returned kickoffs 100 yards. The most recent:

Yds.	Player, Team (Opponent)	Year
100	Joe Rosato, Duquesne (Robert Morris)	1995
100	Chris Watson, Eastern Ill. (Northern Iowa)	1995
100	Jason Anderson, Eastern Wash. (Cal Poly SLO)	1994

Yds.	Player, Team (Opponent)	Year
100	Todd Cleveland, Central Fla. (Bethune-Cookman)	1994
100	Montrel Williams, Idaho (Eastern Wash.)	1994
100	Len Raney, Northern Ariz. (Idaho St.)	1994
100	Leon Brown, Eastern Ky. (Western Ky.)	1992
100	Eddie Godfrey, Western Ky. (Louisville)	1990
100	Roman Carter, Idaho (Cal St. Chico)	1990
100	Dominic Corr, Eastern Wash. (Weber St.)	1989
100	Leon Brown, Eastern Ky. (Austin Peay)	1989

PUNTS

Yds.	Player, Team (Opponent)	Year
91	Bart Helsley, North Texas (Northeast La.)	1990
89	Jim Carriere, Connecticut (Maine)	1987
88	Jeff Kaiser, Idaho St. (UTEP)	1983
87	John Starnes, North Texas (Texas-Arlington)	1983
85	Don Alonzo, Nicholls St. (Northwestern St.)	1980
84	Billy Smith, Tenn.-Chatt. (Appalachian St.)	1988
83	Jason Harkins, Appalachian St. (Citadel)	1986
82	Tim Healy, Delaware (Boston U.)	1987
82	John Howell, Tenn.-Chatt. (Vanderbilt)	1982

FIELD GOALS

Yds.	Player, Team (Opponent)	Year
63	Scott Roper, Arkansas St. (North Texas)	1987
63	Tim Foley, Ga. Southern (James Madison)	1987
62	Paul Hickert, Murray St. (Eastern Ky.)	1986
60	Terry Belden, Northern Ariz. (Cal St. Northridge)	1993
58	Rich Emke, Eastern Ill. (Northern Iowa)	1986
58	Tony Zendejas, Nevada (Boise St.)	1983

DIVISION I-AA

Team Champions

Annual Offense Champions

TOTAL OFFENSE

Year	Team	Avg.
1978	Portland St.	477.4
1979	Portland St.	460.7
1980	Portland St.	504.3
1981	Idaho	438.8
1982	Drake	444.8
1983	Idaho	479.5
1984	Mississippi Val.	*640.1
1985	Weber St.	516.1
1986	Nevada	492.0
1987	Holy Cross	552.2
1988	Lehigh	485.6
1989	Idaho	495.9
1990	William & Mary	498.7
1991	Weber St.	581.4
1992	Alcorn St.	502.9
1993	Idaho	532.0
1994	Alcorn St.	597.9
1995	Montana	512.5

Record.

RUSHING OFFENSE

Year	Team	Avg.
1978	Jackson St.	314.5
1979	Jackson St.	288.4
1980	North Caro. A&T	322.1
1981	Idaho	266.3
1982	Delaware	258.4
1983	Furman	287.1
1984	Delaware St.	377.3
1985	Southwest Mo. St.	298.7
1986	Northeastern	336.0
1987	Howard	381.6
1988	Eastern Ky.	303.0
1989	Ga. Southern	329.2
1990	Delaware St.	298.7
1991	Va. Military	316.9
1992	Citadel	345.5
1993	Western Ky.	300.1
1994	Citadel	*382.0
1995	Massachusetts	302.5

Record.

PASSING OFFENSE

Year	Team	Avg.
1978	Portland St.	367.1
1979	Portland St.	368.9
1980	Portland St.	434.9
1981	Idaho St.	325.7
1982	West Tex. A&M	313.7
1983	Idaho	336.1
1984	Mississippi Val.	*496.8
1985	Rhode Island	384.3
1986	Eastern Ill.	326.1
1987	Holy Cross	358.4
1988	Lehigh	330.1
1989	Idaho	374.3
1990	Weber St.	342.2
1991	Weber St.	389.1
1992	Alcorn St.	360.5
1993	Montana	359.0
1994	Alcorn St.	442.3
1995	Montana	408.2

Record.

SCORING OFFENSE

Year	Team	Avg.
1978	Nevada	35.6
1979	Portland St.	34.3
1980	Portland St.	49.2
1981	Delaware	34.1
1982	Delaware	34.1
1983	Mississippi Val.	39.2
1984	Mississippi Val.	*60.9
1985	Mississippi Val.	41.5
1986	Nevada	39.4
1987	Holy Cross	46.5
1988	Lafayette	38.2
1989	Grambling	37.1
1990	Jackson St.	38.0
1991	Nevada	45.1
1992	Marshall	42.4
1993	Idaho	47.5
1994	Alcorn St.	45.7
1995	Montana	42.5

Record.

Annual Defense Champions

TOTAL DEFENSE

Year	Team	Avg.
1978	Florida A&M	*149.9
1979	Alcorn St.	166.3
1980	Massachusetts	193.5
1981	South Caro. St.	204.0
1982	South Caro. St.	191.4
1983	Grambling	206.0
1984	Tennessee St.	187.0
1985	Arkansas St.	258.8
1986	Tennessee St.	178.5
1987	Southern-B.R.	202.8
1988	Alcorn St.	215.4
1989	Howard	220.0
1990	Middle Tenn. St.	244.8
1991	South Caro. St.	208.9
1992	South Caro. St.	250.9
1993	McNeese St.	249.5
1994	Pennsylvania	218.9
1995	Georgetown	216.4

Record.

RUSHING DEFENSE

Year	Team	Avg.
1978	Florida A&M	48.6
1979	Alcorn St.	56.7
1980	South Caro. St.	61.8
1981	South Caro. St.	60.8
1982	South Caro. St.	59.4
1983	Jackson St.	79.2
1984	Grambling	*44.5
1985	Jackson St.	63.0
1986	Eastern Ky.	62.8
1987	Southern-B.R.	64.5
1988	Stephen F. Austin	83.5
1989	Montana	70.2
1990	Delaware St.	77.2
1991	Boise St.	84.4
1992	Villanova	77.8
1993	Wagner	87.0
1994	Idaho	65.3
1995	McNeese St.	60.9

Record.

PASSING DEFENSE

Year	Team	$Avg.
1978	Southern-B.R.	85.6
1979	Mississippi Val.	64.2
1980	Howard	93.8
1981	Bethune-Cookman	*59.9
1982	Northeastern	98.8
1983	Louisiana Tech	111.4
1984	Louisiana Tech	105.5
1985	Dartmouth	110.3
1986	Bethune-Cookman	99.8
1987	Alcorn St.	101.3
1988	Middle Tenn. St.	90.8
1989	Tenn.-Chatt.	104.4
1990	Middle Tenn. St.	78.83
1991	South Caro. St.	70.01
1992	Middle Tenn. St.	76.93
1993	Georgetown	76.92
1994	Pennsylvania	*63.15
1995	Canisius	69.13

Record. $Beginning in 1990, ranked on passing-efficiency defense rating points instead of per-game yardage allowed.

SCORING DEFENSE

Year	Team	Avg.
1978	South Caro. St.	*6.5
1979	Lehigh	7.2
1980	Murray St.	9.1
1981	Jackson St.	9.4
1982	Western Mich.	7.1
1983	Grambling	8.6
1984	Northwestern St.	9.0
1985	Appalachian St.	9.9
1986	Tennessee St.	8.3
1987	Holy Cross	10.0
1988	Furman	9.7
1989	Howard	10.5
1990	Middle Tenn. St.	9.2
1991	Villanova	12.0
1992	Citadel	13.0
1993	Marshall	11.2
1994	Pennsylvania	7.6
1995	McNeese St.	8.9

Record.

Western Kentucky sports information photo by Robbie Hammer

Despite facing the toughest schedule in Division I-AA, Western Kentucky wide receiver Joey Stockton averaged 199.0 all-purpose yards per game, fifth best in the division. The Hilltoppers went 2-8 against opponents that combined for a .648 winning percentage.

Toughest-Schedule Annual Leaders

The Division I-AA toughest-schedule program, which began in 1982, is based on what all Division I-AA opponents did against other Division I-AA and Division I-A teams when *not* playing the team in question. Games against non-I-AA and I-A teams are deleted. (Playoff or postseason games are not included.) The top two leaders by year:

		¢Opponents' Record			
Year	**Team (Record†)**	**W**	**L**	**T**	**Pct.**
1982	Massachusetts (5-6-0)	50	30	1	.623
	Lehigh (4-6-0)	44	31	0	.587
1983	Florida A&M (7-4-0)	42	23	3	.640
	Grambling (8-1-2)	49	31	0	.613
1984	North Texas (2-9-0)	55	35	2	.609
	Va. Military (1-9-0)	53	37	2	.587
1985	South Caro. St. (5-6-0)	43	20	1	.680
	Lehigh (5-6-0)	47	33	1	.586
1986	James Madison (5-5-1)	46	28	1	.620
	Bucknell (3-7-0)	43	27	0	.614
1987	Ga. Southern (8-3-0)	47	31	0	.603
	Northeastern (6-5-0)	50	37	0	.575
1988	Northwestern St. (9-2-0)	54	36	2	.598
	Ga. Southern (9-2-0)	43	31	1	.580
1989	Liberty (7-3-0)	39	22	2	.635
	Western Caro. (3-7-1)	46	34	2	.573
1990	Ga. Southern (8-3-0)	53	25	1	.677
	Western Ky. (2-8-0)	55	36	1	.603
1991	Bucknell (1-9-0)	53	29	1	.645
	William & Mary (5-6-0)	62	43	0	.590
1992	Va. Military (3-8-0)	46	36	0	.561
	Harvard (3-7-0)	51	40	0	.560
1993	Samford (5-6-0)	55	26	0	.679
	Delaware St. (6-5-0)	44	30	0	.595
1994	Montana (9-2-0)	46	30	1	.604
	McNeese St. (9-2-0)	44	29	5	.596
1995	Western Ky. (2-8-0)	59	32	0	.648
	Nicholls St. (0-11-0)	61	38	0	.616

†Not including playoff or postseason games. ¢When not playing the team listed.

Top 10 Toughest-Schedule Leaders for 1991-95†

1991

Team	¢Opp. Record	Pct.
1. Bucknell	53-29-1	.645
2. William & Mary	62-43-0	.590
3. North Texas	51-36-5	.582
4. Liberty	45-33-0	.577
5. Morgan St.	41-30-1	.576
6. Massachusetts	60-47-0	.561
7. Fordham	46-36-1	.560
8. Connecticut	59-47-0	.557
9. Idaho	48-39-0	.552
10. Ga. Southern	43-35-1	.551

1992

Team	¢Opp. Record	Pct.
1. Va. Military	46-36-0	.561
2. Harvard	51-40-0	.560
3. Florida A&M	47-37-0	.560
4. Appalachian St.	53-43-1	.552
5. McNeese St.	52-42-4	.551
6. Maine	50-41-2	.548
7. Massachusetts	51-42-2	.547
8. James Madison	45-37-3	.547
9. New Hampshire	56-47-0	.544
10. Delaware St.	40-34-1	.540

1993

Team	¢Opp. Record	Pct.
1. Samford	55-26-0	.679
2. Delaware St.	44-30-0	.595
3. Troy St.	47-32-1	.594
4. Eastern Wash.	46-32-0	.590
5. James Madison	52-37-0	.584
6. Illinois St.	58-42-2	.578
7. Nicholls St.	53-39-0	.576
8. Alcorn St.	44-32-4	.575
9. North Texas	53-41-0	.564
10. Idaho	56-44-0	.560

1994

Team	¢Opp. Record	Pct.
1. Montana	46-30-1	.604
2. McNeese St.	44-29-5	.596
3. Montana St.	44-30-2	.592
4. Idaho	55-38-2	.589
5. Buffalo	50-35-4	.584
6. Eastern Wash.	50-37-0	.575
7. Stephen F. Austin	46-35-0	.568
8. Pennsylvania	46-35-1	.567
9. Rhode Island	59-45-2	.566
10. Northeastern	60-47-1	.560

1995

Team	¢Opp. Record	Pct.
1. Western Ky.	59-32-0	.648
2. Nicholls St.	61-38-0	.616
3. William & Mary	65-43-1	.601
4. Northwestern St.	48-33-0	.593
5. Central Fla.	55-38-0	.591
6. East Tenn. St.	62-43-1	.590
7. Western Ill.	52-38-0	.578
8. Columbia	49-37-2	.568
9. Rhode Island	60-46-0	.566
10. Va. Military	58-46-1	.557

†Not including playoff or postseason games. ¢When not playing the team listed.

Annual Most-Improved Teams

Year	Team	$Games Improved	From		To		Coach
1978	Western Ky.	6½	1977	1-8-1	1978	8-2-0	Jimmy Feix
1979	Murray St.	5	1978	4-7-0	1979	*9-2-1	Mike Gottfried
1980	Idaho St.	6	1979	0-11-0	1980	6-5-0	#Dave Kragthorpe
1981	Lafayette	5½	1980	3-7-0	1981	9-2-0	#Bill Russo
1982	Pennsylvania	6	1981	1-9-0	1982	7-3-0	Jerry Berndt
1983	North Texas	5½	1982	2-9-0	1983	*8-4-0	Corky Nelson
	Southern Ill.	5½	1982	6-5-0	1983	*13-1-0	Rey Dempsey
1984	Montana St.	9½	1983	1-10-0	1984	*12-2-0	Dave Arnold
1985	Appalachian St.	4	1984	4-7-0	1985	8-3-0	Sparky Woods
	Massachusetts	4	1984	3-8-0	1985	7-4-0	Bob Stull
	West Tex. A&M	4	1984	3-8-0	1985	6-3-1	#Bill Kelly
1986	Morehead St.	6	1985	1-10-0	1986	7-4-0	Bill Baldridge
1987	Weber St.	6	1986	3-8-0	1987	*10-3-0	Mike Price
1988	Stephen F. Austin	5½	1987	3-7-1	1988	*10-3-0	Jim Hess
1989	Yale	4½	1988	3-6-1	1989	8-2-0	Carmen Cozza
1990	Nevada	4	1989	7-4-0	1990	*13-2-0	Chris Ault
	North Caro. A&T	4	1989	5-6-0	1990	9-2-0	Bill Hayes
1991	Alcorn St.	5	1990	2-7-0	1991	7-2-1	#Cardell Jones
	Austin Peay	5	1990	0-11-0	1991	5-6-0	#Roy Gregory
	Princeton	5	1990	3-7-0	1991	8-2-0	Steve Tosches
	Southern Ill.	5	1990	2-9-0	1991	7-4-0	Bob Smith
1992	Howard	5	1991	2-9-0	1992	7-4-0	Steve Wilson
	Pennsylvania	5	1991	2-8-0	1992	7-3-0	#Al Bagnoli
	Richmond	5	1991	2-9-0	1992	7-4-0	Jim Marshall
	Tennessee Tech	5	1991	2-9-0	1992	7-4-0	Jim Ragland
	Western Caro.	5	1991	2-9-0	1992	7-4-0	Steve Hodgin
1993	Boston U.	8	1992	3-8-0	1993	*12-1-0	Dan Allen
1994	Boise St.	8	1993	3-8-0	1994	*13-2-0	Pokey Allen
1995	Murray St.	5½	1994	5-6-0	1995	*11-1-0	Houston Nutt

*$To determine games improved, add the difference in victories between the two seasons to the difference in losses, then divide by two; ties not counted. *I-AA playoff included. #First year as head coach at that college.*

Photo from Murray State sports information

Led by running back Derrick Cullors, who finished second in Division I-AA in rushing (160.5 yards per game) and all-purpose yards (207.1 yards per game), Murray State was the division's most-improved team in 1995. The Racers finished the regular season with a perfect 11-0 record after going 5-6 in 1994.

DIVISION I-AA

ALL-TIME MOST-IMPROVED TEAMS

Games	Team (Year)
9½	Montana St. (1984)
8	Boise St. (1994)
8	Boston U. (1993)
6½	Western Ky. (1978)
6	Weber St. (1987)
6	Morehead St. (1986)
6	Pennsylvania (1982)
6	Idaho St. (1980)
5½	Murray St. (1995)
5½	Southern-B.R. (1993)
5½	Stephen F. Austin (1988)
5½	East Tenn. St. (1986)
5½	Holy Cross (1986)
5½	Yale (1984)
5½	North Texas (1983)
5½	Southern Ill. (1983)
5½	Lafayette (1981)

1995 MOST-IMPROVED TEAMS
(Includes Playoff Games)

College (Coach)	1995	1994	$Games Improved
Murray St. (Houston Nutt)	11-1-0	5-6-0	5½
Rhode Island (Floyd Keith)	7-4-0	2-9-0	5
Southern-B.R. (Pete Richardson)	11-1-0	6-5-0	4½
Richmond (#Jim Reid)	7-3-1	3-8-0	4½
Fordham (Nick Quartaro)	4-6-1	0-11-0	4½
Connecticut (Skip Holtz)	8-3-0	4-7-0	4
Southern Ill. (Shawn Watson)	5-6-0	1-10-0	4
Eastern Ill. (Bob Spoo)	10-2-0	6-5-0	3½
Dartmouth (John Lyons)	7-2-1	4-6-0	3½
Appalachian St. (Jerry Moore)	12-1-0	9-4-0	3
Stephen F. Austin (John Pearce)	11-2-0	6-3-2	3
Troy St. (Larry Blakeney)	11-1-0	8-4-0	3
Duquesne (Greg Gattuso)	9-1-0	6-4-0	3
Liberty (Sam Rutigliano)	8-3-0	5-6-0	3
Wagner (Walt Hameline)	8-1-0	6-5-0	3
Jacksonville St. (Bill Burgess)	7-4-0	4-7-0	3
Furman (Bobby Johnson)	6-5-0	3-8-0	3
Va. Military (Bill Stewart)	4-7-0	1-10-0	3

$To determine games improved, add the difference in victories between the two seasons to the difference in losses, then divide by two; ties not counted. #First year as head coach at that college.

All-Time Team Won-Lost Records

Includes records as a senior college only, minimum of 20 seasons of competition. Bowl and playoff games are included, and each tie game is computed as half won and half lost.

PERCENTAGE (TOP 23)

Team	Yrs.	Won	Lost	Tied	Pct.†	*Playoffs W-L-T	Total Games
Yale	123	781	276	55	.727	0-0-0	1,112
Grambling	53	402	149	15	.724	9-7-0	566
Tennessee St. @	68	430	166	30	.711	8-2-1	626
Florida A&M	63	435	176	18	.706	2-2-1	629
Princeton	126	721	293	50	.701	0-0-0	1,064
Harvard	121	707	336	50	.670	1-0-0	1,093
Fordham	97	675	355	53	.648	2-3-0	1,083
Jackson St.	50	320	175	13	.643	1-9-0	508
Dartmouth	114	602	332	46	.638	0-0-0	980
Eastern Ky.	72	437	247	27	.634	17-16-0	711
Pennsylvania	119	710	412	42	.628	0-1-0	1,164
South Caro. St.	68	376	220	27	.625	6-5-0	623
Southern-B.R.	74	431	254	25	.625	6-0-0	710
Ga. Southern	27	178	109	7	.617	22-4-0	294
Hofstra	55	314	194	11	.616	2-8-0	519
McNeese St.	45	287	179	14	.613	8-8-0	480
Appalachian St.	66	405	253	29	.611	5-11-0	687
Dayton	88	493	310	26	.610	16-11-0	829
Middle Tenn. St.	79	443	285	28	.605	8-9-0	756
Alcorn St.	72	356	229	39	.602	1-4-0	624
Delaware	104	525	352	43	.594	20-12-0	920
Butler	106	482	326	35	.593	0-3-0	843
Jacksonville St.#	63	339	229	27	.592	19-10-0	595

ALPHABETICAL LISTING

Team	Yrs.	Won	Lost	Tied	Pct.†	*Playoffs W-L-T	Total Games
Alabama St.	90	367	344	43	.515	1-0-0	754
Alcorn St.	72	356	229	39	.602	1-4-0	624
Appalachian St.	66	405	253	29	.611	5-11-0	687
Austin Peay	59	223	351	16	.392	0-0-0	590
Bethune-Cookman	57	303	208	22	.589	6-2-0	533
Boise St.	28	219	102	2	.681	10-7-0	323
Boston U.	76	313	351	28	.473	2-6-0	692
Brown	110	487	483	40	.502	0-1-0	1,010
Bucknell	110	488	453	51	.518	1-0-0	992
Buffalo	82	290	346	29	.458	0-0-0	665
Butler	106	482	326	35	.593	0-3-0	843
Cal Poly SLO	55	294	225	9	.565	4-3-0	528
Cal St. Northridge	34	150	196	4	.434	0-2-0	350
Cal St. Sacramento	42	190	224	8	.460	2-3-0	422
Canisius	50	213	178	24	.542	0-1-0	415
Central Conn. St.	57	211	247	22	.463	0-0-0	480
Citadel	88	397	413	32	.491	2-3-0	842
Colgate	105	483	392	50	.549	1-2-0	925
Columbia	105	321	515	43	.390	1-0-0	879
Connecticut	97	385	419	38	.480	0-0-0	842
Cornell	108	560	385	34	.589	0-0-0	979
Dartmouth	114	602	332	46	.638	0-0-0	980
Davidson	98	332	481	45	.413	0-1-0	858
Dayton	88	493	310	26	.610	16-11-0	829
Delaware	104	525	352	43	.594	20-12-0	920
Delaware St.	50	225	242	8	.482	1-0-0	475
Drake	102	459	425	29	.519	2-3-0	913
Duquesne	48	205	203	18	.502	1-0-0	426
East Tenn. St.	72	294	354	27	.456	1-0-0	675
Eastern Ill.	95	372	406	44	.479	8-7-0	822
Eastern Ky.	72	437	247	27	.634	17-16-0	711
Eastern Wash.	85	362	311	23	.537	2-3-0	696
Evansville	70	258	356	22	.423	1-1-0	636
Florida A&M	63	435	176	18	.706	2-2-1	629
Fordham	97	675	355	53	.648	2-3-0	1,083
Furman	82	443	350	37	.556	10-6-0	830
Georgetown	84	400	274	31	.589	0-2-0	705
Ga. Southern	27	178	109	7	.617	22-4-0	294
Grambling	53	402	149	15	.724	9-7-0	566
Hampton	94	415	321	34	.561	2-3-0	770
Harvard	121	707	336	50	.670	1-0-0	1,093
Hofstra	55	314	194	11	.616	2-8-0	519
Holy Cross	100	527	377	55	.578	0-2-0	959
Howard	99	399	320	42	.552	0-1-0	761
Idaho	98	375	435	25	.464	6-11-0	835
Idaho St.	91	389	346	20	.528	3-1-0	755
Illinois St.	96	361	420	65	.465	0-0-0	846
Indiana St.	79	306	341	20	.474	1-2-0	667
Jackson St.	50	320	175	13	.643	1-9-0	508
Jacksonville St.	63	339	229	27	.592	19-10-0	595
James Madison	23	138	109	3	.558	2-4-0	250
Lafayette	114	573	462	39	.552	0-0-0	1,074
Lehigh	112	522	508	45	.507	4-4-0	1,075
Liberty	23	114	115	4	.498	0-0-0	233
Maine	104	400	382	38	.511	0-3-0	820
Marshall	92	399	439	44	.477	20-6-0	882
Massachusetts	113	439	452	51	.493	2-5-0	942
McNeese St.	45	287	179	14	.613	8-8-0	480
Middle Tenn. St.	79	443	285	28	.605	8-9-0	756
Mississippi Val.	43	175	219	11	.446	0-1-0	405
Montana	96	372	427	26	.467	8-7-0	825
Montana St.	92	354	370	34	.489	7-1-2	758
Morehead St.	66	223	354	22	.391	0-0-0	599
Morgan St.	75	356	268	30	.567	1-2-0	654
Murray St.	71	367	294	34	.553	0-3-1	695
New Hampshire	99	413	357	54	.534	1-4-0	824
Nicholls St.	24	114	147	4	.438	1-1-0	265
North Caro. A&T	72	351	290	39	.545	1-6-0	680
Northeastern	60	221	275	17	.447	0-1-0	513
Northern Ariz.	71	306	318	22	.491	1-2-0	646
Northern Iowa	97	479	327	47	.589	6-9-0	853
Northwestern St.	87	406	330	33	.549	2-1-0	769
Pennsylvania	119	710	412	42	.628	0-1-0	1,164
Prairie View	69	327	329	31	.499	1-3-0	687
Princeton	126	721	293	50	.701	0-0-0	1,064
Rhode Island	95	326	423	41	.439	2-4-0	790
Richmond	112	396	526	53	.433	2-3-0	975
St. Francis (Pa.)	47	145	216	13	.405	0-0-0	374
St. John's (N.Y.)	27	141	104	7	.573	0-0-0	252
St. Mary's (Cal.)	67	333	232	20	.586	1-2-0	585
St. Peter's	24	50	138	1	.267	0-0-0	189
Sam Houston St.	80	359	357	34	.501	4-3-1	750
Samford	79	321	320	47	.501	2-2-0	688
San Diego	28	129	127	8	.504	0-0-0	264
South Caro. St.	68	376	220	27	.625	6-5-0	623
Southeast Mo. St.	83	355	348	37	.505	0-0-0	740
Southern-B.R.	74	431	254	25	.625	6-0-0	710
Southern Ill.	80	314	393	33	.447	3-0-0	740
Southern Utah	33	159	156	6	.505	0-0-0	321
Southwest Mo. St.	84	369	355	40	.509	1-5-0	764
Southwest Tex. St.	81	401	304	27	.566	6-1-0	732
Stephen F. Austin%	69	277	381	30	.424	7-4-0	688
Tenn.-Chatt.	88	423	385	33	.523	0-1-0	841
Tenn.-Martin	39	178	218	5	.450	1-0-0	401
Tennessee St.@	68	430	166	30	.711	8-2-1	626
Tennessee Tech	74	314	367	31	.463	0-3-0	712
Texas Southern	50	235	256	27	.480	1-0-0	518
Towson St.	27	155	118	4	.567	3-4-0	277
Troy St.	65	336	268	15	.555	11-4-0	619
Valparaiso	75	300	337	24	.472	0-1-0	661
Villanova	98	450	383	41	.538	2-5-1	874
Va. Military	105	423	497	43	.462	0-0-0	963
Wagner	65	291	242	17	.545	6-5-0	550
Weber St.	34	174	182	3	.489	1-2-0	359
Western Caro.	62	257	333	23	.438	3-2-0	613
Western Ill.	92	382	343	37	.526	1-4-0	762
Western Ky.	77	410	281	31	.589	7-4-0	722
William & Mary	100	439	446	37	.496	2-6-0	922
Wofford	87	370	401	36	.481	1-4-0	807
Yale	123	781	276	55	.727	0-0-0	1,112
Youngstown St.	55	313	219	17	.586	19-7-0	549
I-AA teams lacking 20 seasons:							
Charleston So.	5	9	42	0	.176	0-0-0	51
Iona	18	80	94	3	.460	0-1-0	177
Marist	18	66	95	3	.412	0-0-0	164
Monmouth (N.J.)	2	14	5	0	.737	0-0-0	19
Robert Morris	2	13	5	1	.711	0-0-0	19
Siena	8	13	60	0	.178	0-0-0	73

VICTORIES

Team	Wins
Yale	781
Princeton	721
Pennsylvania	710
Harvard	707
Fordham	675
Dartmouth	602
Lafayette	573
Cornell	560
Holy Cross	527
Delaware	525
Lehigh	522
Dayton	493
Bucknell	488
Brown	487
Colgate	483
Butler	482
Northern Iowa	479
Drake	459
Villanova	450
Furman	443
Middle Tenn. St.	443
Massachusetts	439
William & Mary	439
Eastern Ky.	437
Florida A&M	435
Southern-B.R.	431
Tennessee St.@	430
Tenn.-Chatt.	423
Va. Military	423
Hampton	415
New Hampshire	413
Western Ky.	410
Northwestern St.	406
Appalachian St.	405
Grambling	402
Southwest Tex. St.	401
Georgetown	400
Maine	400
Howard	399
Marshall	399
Citadel	397
Richmond	396
Idaho St.	389
Connecticut	385
Western Ill.	382
South Caro. St.	376
Idaho	375
Eastern Ill.	372
Montana	372
Wofford	370
Southwest Mo. St.	369
Alabama St.	367
Murray St.	367
Eastern Wash.	362
Illinois St.	361
Sam Houston St.	359
Alcorn St.	356
Morgan St.	356
Southeast Mo. St.	355
Montana St.	354
North Caro. A&T	351
Jacksonville St.	339
Troy St.	336
St. Mary's (Cal.)	333
Davidson	332
Prairie View	327
Rhode Island	326
Columbia	321
Samford	321
Jackson St.	320
Hofstra	314
Southern Ill.	314
Tennessee Tech	314
Boston U.	313
Youngstown St.	313
Indiana St.	306
Northern Ariz.	306
Bethune-Cookman	303
Valparaiso	300
Cal Poly SLO	294
East Tenn. St.	294
Wagner	291
Buffalo	290
McNeese St.	287

Team	Wins
Stephen F. Austin%	277
Evansville	258
Western Caro.	257
Texas Southern	235
Delaware St.	225
Austin Peay	223
Morehead St.	223
Northeastern	221
Boise St.	219
Canisius	213
Central Conn. St.	211
Duquesne	205
Cal St. Sacramento	190
Ga. Southern	178
Tenn.-Martin	178
Mississippi Val.	175
Weber St.	174
Southern Utah	159
Towson St.	155
Cal St. Northridge	150
St. Francis (Pa.)	145
St. John's (N.Y.)	141
James Madison	138
San Diego	129
Liberty	114
Nicholls St.	114
Iona	80
Marist	66
St. Peter's	50
Monmouth (N.J.)	14
Robert Morris	13
Siena	13
Charleston So.	9

**Also includes any participation in major bowl games. †Ties computed as half won and half lost. @Tennessee State's participation in 1981 and 1982 Division I-AA championships (1-2 record) voided. %Stephen F. Austin's participation in 1989 Division I-AA championship (3-1 record) voided.*

Records in the 1990s

(1990-91-92-93-94-95, Includes Playoffs)

PERCENTAGE

Team	W-L-T	Pct.†
Dayton^	60-8-0	.882
Youngstown St.	64-17-2	.783
Eastern Ky.	58-17-0	.773
Hofstra^	48-15-2	.754
Marshall	64-21-0	.753
Monmouth (N.J.)$	14-5-0	.737
Delaware	54-19-1	.736
Troy St.^	51-18-1	.736
Montana	54-20-0	.730
Northern Iowa	55-21-0	.724
McNeese St.	53-21-2	.711
Robert Morris$	13-5-1	.711
Princeton	42-17-1	.708
William & Mary	48-21-0	.696
Middle Tenn. St.	50-22-1	.692
Dartmouth	40-17-3	.692
Ga. Southern	51-23-0	.689
Idaho	50-23-0	.685
Hampton%	46-21-1	.684
Drake^	40-18-2	.683
Jacksonville St.%	47-23-1	.669
Alabama St.	42-20-4	.667
North Caro. A&T	45-23-0	.662
St. Mary's (Cal.)^	39-20-1	.658
Wagner^	40-21-0	.656
San Diego^	38-20-1	.653
Grambling	44-24-0	.647
New Hampshire	43-23-2	.647
Pennsylvania	38-21-0	.644
Appalachian St.	46-26-0	.639
South Caro. St.	42-24-0	.636
Samford	43-25-2	.629
Jackson St.	41-25-1	.619
Boise St.	45-28-0	.616
Delaware St.	40-25-0	.615
St. John's (N.Y.)^	38-24-0	.613
Southern-B.R.	41-27-0	.603
Marist^	35-23-2	.600
Lehigh	39-26-1	.598
Wofford%	40-27-1	.596
Massachusetts	38-26-1	.592
James Madison	42-29-0	.592
Florida A&M	40-28-0	.588
Alcorn St.	36-25-3	.586
Cornell	35-25-0	.583
Butler^	35-26-1	.573
Cal Poly SLO!	36-27-1	.570
Liberty	37-29-0	.561
Weber St.	37-30-0	.552
Iona^	32-26-1	.551
Citadel	38-31-0	.551
Southwest Mo. St.	36-30-1	.545
Howard	36-31-0	.537
Furman	36-31-1	.537
Cal St. Sacramento^	32-28-1	.533
Villanova	36-32-0	.529
Georgetown^	30-27-0	.526
Holy Cross	34-31-1	.523
Sam Houston St.	33-30-3	.523
Boston U.	36-33-0	.522
Northwestern St.	34-32-0	.515
Evansville^	30-29-0	.508
Lafayette	32-31-3	.508
Eastern Ill.	33-33-1	.500
Northern Ariz.	33-33-0	.500
Western Ill.	33-33-1	.500
Stephen F. Austin	32-34-3	.486
Connecticut	32-34-0	.485
Illinois St.	31-33-2	.485
Towson St.	30-32-0	.484
Eastern Wash.	31-34-0	.477
Tennessee Tech	31-35-0	.470
Yale	27-33-0	.450
Duquesne^	26-32-1	.449
Indiana St.	29-37-0	.439
Southern Utah^	28-36-2	.439
Southwest Tex. St.	28-37-1	.432
Bucknell	28-37-0	.431
Davidson^	24-32-1	.430
Mississippi Val.	25-34-3	.427
Tenn.-Martin¢	28-38-0	.424
Western Caro.	27-38-0	.415
Southeast Mo. St.&	27-39-0	.409
Murray St.	27-40-0	.403
Tenn.-Chatt.	26-40-0	.394
Tennessee St.	26-40-0	.394
Cal St. Northridge^	24-37-0	.393
St. Francis (Pa.)^	22-35-1	.388
Richmond	25-40-1	.386
Canisius^	22-36-1	.381
Western Ky.	24-39-0	.381
Montana St.	25-41-0	.379
Valparaiso^	22-38-1	.369
Rhode Island	24-42-0	.364
Bethune-Cookman	23-41-0	.359
Harvard	21-38-1	.358
Idaho St.	23-42-1	.356
East Tenn. St.	23-43-0	.348
Texas Southern	22-42-1	.346
St. Peter's^	17-34-0	.333
Colgate	21-44-1	.326
Maine	21-45-0	.318
Southern Ill.	21-45-0	.318
Brown	19-41-0	.317
Northeastern	18-47-1	.280
Central Conn. St.^	15-42-1	.267
Columbia	15-43-2	.267
Nicholls St.	17-48-1	.265
Morehead St.	17-48-0	.262
Va. Military	17-49-0	.258
Buffalo^	16-47-0	.254
Austin Peay	16-50-0	.242
Charleston So.*	9-42-0	.176
Morgan St.	10-55-0	.154
Fordham	9-53-1	.151
Siena^	8-46-0	.148
Prairie View@	0-55-0	.000

VICTORIES

(Minimum 40 Wins)

Team	Wins
Marshall	64
Youngstown St.	64
Dayton^	60
Eastern Ky.	58
Northern Iowa	55
Delaware	54
Montana	54
McNeese St.	53
Ga. Southern	51
Troy St.^	51
Idaho	50
Middle Tenn. St.	50
Hofstra^	48
William & Mary	48
Jacksonville St.%	47
Appalachian St.	46
Hampton%	46
Boise St.	45
North Caro. A&T	45
Grambling	44
New Hampshire	43
Samford	43
Alabama St.	42
James Madison	42
Princeton	42
South Caro. St.	42
Jackson St.	41
Southern-B.R.	41
Dartmouth	40
Delaware St.	40
Drake^	40
Florida A&M	40
Wagner^	40
Wofford%	40

*†Ties counted as half won and half lost. & Joined I-AA in 1991. ¢ Joined I-AA in 1992. ^ Joined I-AA in 1993. ! Joined I-AA in 1994. % Joined I-AA in 1995. * Began varsity program in 1991. $ Began varsity program in 1994. @ Did not play in 1990.*

Records in the 1980s

(Playoffs Included)

PERCENTAGE

Rank	Team	W-L-T	Pct.†
1	Eastern Ky.	88-24-2	.781
2	Furman	83-23-4	.773
3	Ga. Southern	68-22-1	*.753
4	Jackson St.	71-25-5	.728
5	Grambling	68-30-3	.688
6	Nevada	71-35-1	.668
7	Holy Cross	67-33-2	.667
8	Tennessee St.	64-32-4	.660
9	Eastern Ill.	70-36-1	.659
10	Idaho	69-36-0	.657
11	Delaware	68-36-0	.654
12	Middle Tenn. St.	65-36-0	.644
13	Boise St.	66-38-0	.635
14	Southwest Tex. St.	66-39-0	.629
15	Murray St.	61-36-2	.626
16	Northern Iowa	64-38-2	.625
17	Towson St.	60-36-2	.622
18	Alcorn St.	56-34-0	.622
19	Northeast La.	64-39-0	.621
20	South Caro. St.	55-34-1	.617

*†Ties counted as half won and half lost. *Includes two nonvarsity seasons and five varsity seasons; varsity record, 55-14-0 for .797.*

National Poll Rankings

Final Poll Leaders

(Released Before Division Championship Playoffs)

Year	Team, Record*	Coach	Record in Championship†
1978	Nevada (10-0-0)	Chris Ault	0-1 Lost in semifinals
1979	Grambling (8-2-0)	Eddie Robinson	Did not compete
1980	South Caro. St. (10-0-0)	Bill Davis	Did not compete
1981	Eastern Ky. (9-1-0)	Roy Kidd	2-1 Runner-up
1982	Eastern Ky. (10-0-0)	Roy Kidd	3-0 Champion
1983	Southern Ill. (10-1-0)	Rey Dempsey	3-0 Champion
1984	Alcorn St. (9-0-0)	Marino Casem	0-1 Lost in quarterfinals
1985	Middle Tenn. St. (11-0-0)	James Donnelly	0-1 Lost in quarterfinals
1986	Nevada (11-0-0)	Chris Ault	2-1 Lost in semifinals
1987	Holy Cross (11-0-0)	Mark Duffner	Did not compete
1988	Idaho (9-1-0)	Keith Gilbertson	2-1 Lost in semifinals
1989	Ga. Southern (11-0-0)	Erk Russell	4-0 Champion
1990	Middle Tenn. St. (10-1-0)	James Donnelly	1-1 Lost in quarterfinals
1991	Nevada (11-0-0)	Chris Ault	1-1 Lost in quarterfinals
1992	tie Citadel (10-1-0)	Charlie Taaffe	1-1 Lost in quarterfinals
	Northeast La. (9-2-0)	Dave Roberts	1-1 Lost in quarterfinals
1993	Troy St. (10-0-1)	Larry Blakeney	2-1 Lost in semifinals
1994	Youngstown St. (10-0-1)	Jim Tressel	4-0 Champion
1995	McNeese St. (11-0-0)	Bobby Keasler	2-1 Lost in semifinals

**Final poll record; in some cases, a team had one or two games remaining before the championship playoffs. †Number of teams in the championship: 4 (1978-80); 8 (1981); 12 (1982-85); 16 (1986-present).*

Final Regular-Season Polls

1982
Team
1. Eastern Ky.
2. Louisiana Tech
3. Delaware
4. Tennessee St.
5. Eastern Ill.
6. Furman
7. South Caro. St.
8. Jackson St.
9. Colgate
10. Grambling
11. Idaho
12. Northern Ill.
13. Holy Cross
14. Bowling Green
15. Boise St.
16. Western Mich.
17. Tenn.-Chatt.
18. Northwestern St.
19. Montana
20. Lafayette

1983
Team
1. Southern Ill.
2. Furman
3. Holy Cross
4. North Texas
5. Indiana St.
6. Eastern Ill.
7. Colgate
8. Eastern Ky.
9. Western Caro.
10. Grambling
11. Nevada
12. Idaho St.
13. Boston U.
    Northeast La.
15. Jackson St.
16. Middle Tenn. St.
17. Tennessee St.
18. South Caro. St.
19. Mississippi Val.
20. New Hampshire

1984
Team
1. Alcorn St.
2. Montana St.
   Rhode Island
4. Boston U.
5. Indiana St.
6. Middle Tenn. St.
   Mississippi Val.
8. Eastern Ky.
9. Louisiana Tech
10. Arkansas St.
11. New Hampshire
12. Richmond
13. Murray St.
14. Western Caro.
15. Holy Cross
16. Furman
17. Tenn.-Chatt.
18. Northern Iowa
19. Delaware
20. McNeese St.

1985
Team
1. Middle Tenn. St.
2. Furman
   Nevada
4. Northern Iowa
5. Idaho
6. Arkansas St.
7. Rhode Island
8. Grambling
9. Ga. Southern
10. Akron
11. Eastern Wash.
12. Appalachian St.
    Delaware St.
14. Louisiana Tech
15. Jackson St.
16. William & Mary
17. Murray St.
18. Richmond
19. Eastern Ky.
20. Alcorn St.

1986
Team
1. Nevada
2. Arkansas St.
3. Eastern Ill.
4. Ga. Southern
5. Holy Cross
6. Appalachian St.
7. Pennsylvania
8. William & Mary
9. Jackson St.
10. Eastern Ky.
11. Sam Houston St.
12. Nicholls St.
13. Delaware
14. Tennessee St.
15. Furman
16. Idaho
17. Southern Ill.
18. Murray St.
19. Connecticut
20. North Caro. A&T

1987
Team
1. Holy Cross
2. Appalachian St.
3. Northeast La.
4. Northern Iowa
5. Idaho
6. Ga. Southern
7. Eastern Ky.
8. James Madison
9. Jackson St.
10. Weber St.
11. Western Ky.
12. Arkansas St.
13. Maine
14. Marshall
15. Youngstown St.
16. North Texas
17. Richmond
18. Howard
19. Sam Houston St.
20. Delaware St.

1988
Team
1. Stephen F. Austin
2. Idaho
3. Ga. Southern
4. Western Ill.
5. Furman
6. Jackson St.
7. Marshall
8. Eastern Ky.
9. Citadel
10. Northwestern St.
11. Massachusetts
12. North Texas
13. Boise St.
14. Florida A&M
    Pennsylvania
16. Western Ky.
17. Connecticut
18. Grambling
19. Montana
20. New Hampshire

1989
Team
1. Ga. Southern
2. Furman
3. Stephen F. Austin
4. Holy Cross
   Idaho
6. Montana
7. Appalachian St.
8. Maine
9. Southwest Mo. St.
10. Middle Tenn. St.
    William & Mary
12. Eastern Ky.
13. Grambling
14. Youngstown St.
15. Eastern Ill.
16. Villanova
17. Jackson St.
18. Connecticut
19. Nevada
20. Northern Iowa

1990
Team
1. Middle Tenn. St.
2. Youngstown St.
3. Ga. Southern
4. Nevada
5. Eastern Ky.
6. Southwest Mo. St.
7. William & Mary
8. Holy Cross
9. Massachusetts
10. Boise St.
11. Northern Iowa
12. Furman
13. Idaho
14. Northeast La.
15. Citadel
16. Jackson St.
17. Dartmouth
18. Central Fla.
19. New Hampshire
    North Caro. A&T

1991
Team
1. Nevada
2. Eastern Ky.
3. Holy Cross
4. Northern Iowa
5. Alabama St.
6. Delaware
7. Villanova
8. Marshall
9. Middle Tenn. St.
10. Samford
11. New Hampshire
12. Sam Houston St.
13. Youngstown St.
14. Western Ill.
15. Weber St.
16. James Madison
17. Appalachian St.
18. Northeast La.
19. McNeese St.
20. Citadel
    Furman

1992
Team
1. Citadel
   Northeast La.
3. Northern Iowa
4. Middle Tenn. St.
5. Idaho
6. Marshall
7. Youngstown St.
8. Delaware
9. Samford
10. Villanova
11. McNeese St.
12. Eastern Ky.
13. William & Mary
14. Eastern Wash.
15. Florida A&M
16. Appalachian St.
17. North Caro. A&T
18. Alcorn St.
19. Liberty
20. Western Ill.

1993
Team
1. Troy St.
2. Ga. Southern
3. Montana
4. Northeast La.
5. McNeese St.
6. Boston U.
7. Youngstown St.
8. Howard
9. Marshall
10. William & Mary
11. Idaho
12. Central Fla.
13. Northern Iowa
14. Stephen F. Austin
15. Southern-B.R.
16. Pennsylvania
17. Eastern Ky.
18. Delaware
19. Western Ky.
20. Eastern Wash.
21. North Caro. A&T
22. Tennessee Tech
23. Alcorn St.
24. Towson St.
25. Massachusetts

1994
Team
1. Youngstown St.
2. Marshall
3. Boise St.
4. Eastern Ky.
5. McNeese St.
6. Idaho
7. Grambling
8. Montana
9. Boston U.
10. Troy St.
11. Northern Iowa
12. New Hampshire
13. James Madison
14. Pennsylvania
15. Alcorn St.
16. Middle Tenn. St.
17. Appalachian St.
18. North Texas
19. William & Mary
20. Central Fla.
21. Stephen F. Austin
22. South Caro. St.
23. Hofstra
24. Western Ill.
25. Northern Ariz.

1995
(By The Sports Network)

Team	Record*	Total Pts.	How Season Ended†
1. McNeese St.	11-0-0	2,069	Lost in I-AA semifinals
2. Appalachian St.	11-0-0	1,983	Lost in I-AA quarterfinals
3. Troy St.	11-0-0	1,900	Lost in I-AA first round
4. Murray St.	11-0-0	1,802	Lost in I-AA first round
5. Stephen F. Austin	9-1-0	1,724	Lost in I-AA semifinals
6. Marshall	9-2-0	1,666	Lost in I-AA championship
7. Delaware	10-1-0	1,558	Lost in I-AA quarterfinals
8. Montana	9-2-0	1,439	I-AA national champion
9. Hofstra	10-1-0	1,364	Lost in I-AA first round
10. Eastern Ky.	9-2-0	1,323	Lost in I-AA first round
11. Southern-B.R.	9-1-0	1,232	Won Heritage Bowl
12. Eastern Ill.	10-1-0	1,169	Lost in I-AA first round
13. James Madison	8-3-0	1,034	Lost in I-AA first round
14. Jackson St.	9-2-0	1,011	Lost in I-AA first round
15. Ga. Southern	8-3-0	886	Lost in I-AA quarterfinals
16. Florida A&M	8-2-0	871	Lost Heritage Bowl
17. Idaho	6-4-0	645	Lost in I-AA first round
18. Northern Iowa	7-4-0	630	Lost in I-AA quarterfinals
19. William & Mary	7-4-0	583	Not in postseason play
20. Richmond	7-3-1	375	Not in postseason play
21. Boise St.	7-4-0	374	Not in postseason play
22. Northern Ariz.	7-4-0	287	Not in postseason play
23. Connecticut	8-3-0	254	Not in postseason play
24. Indiana St.	7-4-0	235	Not in postseason play
25. Middle Tenn. St.	7-4-0	118	Not in postseason play

Regular-season record does not include postseason results. †Vote taken before Division I-AA playoffs.

Photo from McNeese State sports information

McNeese State finished the 1995 regular season as the top-ranked team in Division I-AA, thanks in large part to its defense. The opportunistic Cowboys forced 40 turnovers and led the division in rushing defense (60.9 yards per game) and scoring defense (8.9 points per game).

1995 Week-by-Week Polls by The Sports Network

Final Poll—11-21	11-14	11-7	10-31	10-24	10-17	10-10	10-3	9-26	9-19	9-12	9-5
1. McNeese St.	1	1	1	1	1	1	1	1	1	1	1
2. Appalachian St.	2	2	2	2	2	2	2	2	2	2	2
3. Troy St.	3	3	3	4	5	6	6	6	7	8	9
4. Murray St.	4	5	8	8	9	11	11	15	19	24	NR
5. Stephen F. Austin	5	6	6	3	4	4	4	4	5	5	8
6. Marshall	6	7	7	7	3	3	3	3	4	4	3
7. Delaware	8	4	4	5	7	8	9	10	11	11	12
8. Montana	9	9	10	10	6	5	5	5	6	7	4
9. Hofstra	7	8	9	9	11	14	15	19	25	NR	NR
10. Eastern Ky.	10	10	5	6	8	9	8	8	9	9	11
11. Southern-B.R.	11	11	12	12	13	10	10	9	10	10	10
12. Eastern Ill.	12	12	15	18	20	25	22	NR	NR	6	NR
13. James Madison	13	18	21	15	10	7	7	7	8	NR	7
14. Jackson St.	14	16	19	23	NR	NR	NR	NR	23	NR	NR
15. Ga. Southern	17	21	22	13	17	13	14	17	18	13	17
16. Florida A&M	15	20	14	17	18	21	23	23	NR	NR	25
17. Idaho	25	NR	NR	NR	NR	NR	24	13	13	16	14
18. Northern Iowa	22	15	11	11	14	18	21	22	22	21	23
19. William & Mary	20	25	18	20	12	17	17	18	20	19	16
20. Richmond	18	13	16	19	16	12	12	16	17	20	NR
21. Boise St.	16	23	24	25	NR	NR	19	11	3	3	5
22. Northern Ariz.	23	17	13	16	21	16	18	20	24	25	NR
23. Connecticut	NR	24	25	21	15	20	NR	NR	NR	NR	NR
24. Indiana St.	19	14	17	22	NR	23	NR	NR	NR	NR	NR
25. Middle Tenn. St.	24	NR	NR	NR	NR	NR	NR	NR	NR	NR	NR
Other Teams:											
Northwestern St.	21	19	20	14	19	24	NR	NR	NR	NR	NR
Rhode Island	NR	22	23	NR	NR	NR	NR	NR	NR	NR	NR
Jacksonville St.	NR	NR	NR	24	24	NR	NR	NR	NR	NR	NR
Idaho St.	NR	NR	NR	NR	22	15	16	24	NR	NR	NR
Montana St.	NR	NR	NR	NR	23	NR	NR	NR	NR	NR	NR
Dayton	NR	NR	NR	NR	25	NR	NR	NR	NR	NR	NR
Central Fla.	NR	NR	NR	NR	NR	19	20	12	12	14	21
Pennsylvania	NR	NR	NR	NR	NR	22	13	14	16	17	15
Boston U.	NR	NR	NR	NR	NR	NR	NR	21	15	18	22
Youngstown St.	NR	NR	NR	NR	NR	NR	NR	25	14	15	6
Western Ill.	NR	NR	NR	NR	NR	NR	NR	NR	21	23	24
Grambling	NR	NR	NR	NR	NR	NR	NR	NR	NR	12	13
New Hampshire	NR	NR	NR	NR	NR	NR	NR	NR	NR	22	18
Massachusetts	NR	NR	NR	NR	NR	NR	NR	NR	NR	NR	19
Liberty	NR	NR	NR	NR	NR	NR	NR	NR	NR	NR	20

NR=Not ranked

Undefeated, Untied Teams

Regular-season games only, from 1978. Subsequent loss in Division I-AA championship is indicated by (††).

Year	Team	Wins
1978	Nevada	††11
1979	(None)	
1980	(None)	
1981	(None)	
1982	*Eastern Ky.	10
1983	(None)	
1984	Tennessee St.	11
	Alcorn St.	††9
1985	Middle Tenn. St.	††11
1986	Nevada	††11
	Pennsylvania	10
1987	Holy Cross	11
1988	(None)	
1989	*Ga. Southern	11
1990	Youngstown St.	††11
1991	Holy Cross	11
	Nevada	††11
1992	(None)	
1993	Boston U.	††11
	Howard	††11
	Pennsylvania	10
1994	Pennsylvania	9
1995	Appalachian St.	††11
	McNeese St.	††11
	Murray St.	††11
	Troy St.	††11

**Won Division I-AA championship.*

The Spoilers

(From 1978 Season)

Following is a list of the spoilers of Division I-AA teams that lost their perfect (undefeated, untied) record in their **season-ending** game, including the Division I-AA championship playoffs. An asterisk (*) indicates a championship playoff game and a dagger (†) indicates the home team in a regular-season game.

Date	Spoiler	Victim	Score
12-9-78	*Massachusetts	Nevada	44-21
11-15-80	†Grambling	South Caro. St.	26-3
11-22-80	†Murray St.	Western Ky.	49-0
12-1-84	*Louisiana Tech	Alcorn St.	44-21
12-7-85	*Ga. Southern	Middle Tenn. St.	28-21
11-22-86	Boston College	†Holy Cross	56-26
12-19-86	*Ga. Southern	Nevada	48-38
11-19-88	*Cornell	Pennsylvania	19-6
11-24-90	*Central Fla.	Youngstown St.	20-17
12-7-91	*Youngstown St.	Nevada	30-28
11-27-93	*Marshall	Howard	28-14
12-4-93	*Idaho	Boston U.	21-14
11-25-95	*Ga. Southern	Troy St.	24-21
11-25-95	*Northern Iowa	Murray St.	35-34
12-2-95	*Stephen F. Austin	Appalachian St.	27-17
12-9-95	*Marshall	McNeese St.	25-13

Streaks and Rivalries

Because Division I-AA began in 1978, only those streaks from the period (1978-present) are listed. Only schools that have been I-AA members for five years are eligible for inclusion.

Longest Winning Streaks

(From 1978; Includes Playoff Games)

Wins	Team	Years	Ended by	Score
24	Pennsylvania	1992-95	Columbia	14-24
20	Holy Cross	1990-92	Army	7-17
18	Eastern Ky.	1982-83	Western Ky.	10-10
16	Ga. Southern	1989-90	Middle Tenn. St.	13-16
14	Youngstown St.	1994	Kent	14-17
14	Delaware	1979-80	Lehigh	20-27
13	McNeese St.	1995	Marshall	13-25
13	Holy Cross	1988-89	Army	9-45
13	Nevada	1986	Ga. Southern	38-48
13	Tennessee St.	1983-85	Western Ky.	17-22
13	Eastern Ill.	1978-79	Western Ill.	7-10
12	Appalachian St.	1995	Stephen F. Austin	17-27
12	Nevada	1989-90	Boise St.	14-30
12	Furman	1989	Stephen F. Austin	19-21
12	Holy Cross	1987-88	Army	3-23
12	Southern Ill.	1982-83	Wichita St.	6-28
12	Florida A&M	1978-79	Tennessee St.	3-20

Longest Unbeaten Streaks

(From 1978; Includes Playoff Games and Ties)

No.	Wins	Ties	Team	Years	Ended by
24	24	0	Pennsylvania	1992-95	Columbia
20	20	0	Holy Cross	1990-92	Army
20	19	1	Youngstown St.	1993-94	Kent
19	18	1	Eastern Ky.	1982-83	Murray St.
17	16	1	Alabama St.	1990-92	Alcorn St.
17	16	1	Grambling	1977-78	Florida A&M
16	16	0	Ga. Southern	1989-90	Middle Tenn. St.
15	14	1	Delaware	1994-95	Navy
14	14	0	Delaware	1979-80	Lehigh
13	13	0	McNeese St.	1995	Marshall
13	13	0	Holy Cross	1988-89	Army
13	13	0	Nevada	1986	Ga. Southern
13	13	0	Tennessee St.	1983-85	Western Ky.
13	13	0	Eastern Ill.	1978-79	Western Ill.
13	12	1	Mississippi Val.	1983-84	Alcorn St.
13	12	1	Eastern Ill.	1981-82	Tennessee St.
12	12	0	Appalachian St.	1995	Stephen F. Austin
12	12	0	Nevada	1989-90	Boise St.
12	12	0	Furman	1989	Stephen F. Austin
12	12-	0	Holy Cross	1987-88	Army
12	12	0	Southern Ill.	1982-83	Wichita St.
12	12	0	Florida A&M	1978-79	Tennessee St.
12	11	1	Tennessee St.	1985-86	Alabama St.
12	11	1	Tennessee St.	1981-83	Jackson St.
11	11	0	Pennsylvania	1985-87	Cornell
10	9	1	Stephen F. Austin	1989	Ga. Southern
10	9	1	Holy Cross	1983	Boston College
10	9	1	Jackson St.	1980	Grambling

Longest Home Winning Streaks

(From 1978; Includes Playoff Games)

Wins	Team	Years	Ended by
38	Ga. Southern	1985-90	Eastern Ky.
34	Eastern Ky.	1978-83	Western Ky.
31	Middle Tenn. St.	1987-94	Eastern Ky.
25	Northern Iowa	1989-92	Youngstown St.
23	Northern Iowa	1983-87	Montana
22	Nevada	1989-91	Youngstown St.
20	Arkansas St.	1984-87	Northwestern St.
18	Montana	1994-95	Current
16	Pennsylvania	1992-95	Princeton
16	Southwest Tex. St.	1981-83	Central St.
16	Citadel	1980-82	East Tenn. St.
15	Holy Cross	1987-89	Massachusetts
14	William & Mary	1991-94	Massachusetts
13	Youngstown St.	1992-93	Stephen F. Austin
13	William & Mary	1988-91	Delaware
13	Idaho	1987-89	Eastern Ill.
13	Sam Houston St.	1986-88	Stephen F. Austin
13	Delaware St.	1983-86	Northeastern
12	Rhode Island	1984-85	Towson St.
12	Eastern Ill.	1981-83	Indiana St.

Longest Losing Streaks

(From 1978; Can Include Playoff Games)

Losses	Team	Years	Ended by
57	Prairie View	1989-95	Current
44	Columbia	1983-88	Princeton
19	Charleston So.	1993-95	Morehead St.
19	Idaho St.	1978-80	Portland St.
17	Davidson	1985-87	Wofford
16	Middle Tenn. St.	1978-79	Tennessee Tech
14	Fordham	1993-95	Marist
13	Nicholls St.	1994-95	Current
12	Colgate	1994-95	Current
12	St. Francis (Pa.)	1994-95	Current
12	Siena	1994-95	Current
12	Fordham	1991-92	Bucknell
12	Central Fla.	1981-82	Elizabeth City St.

Most-Played Rivalries

(Ongoing Unless Indicated)

Games	Opponents (Series leader listed first)	Rivalry Record	First Game
131	Lafayette-Lehigh	71-55-5	1884
118	Yale-Princeton	64-44-10	1873
112	Yale-Harvard	61-43-8	1875
105	William & Mary-Richmond	53-47-5	1898
102	Pennsylvania-Cornell	58-39-5	1893
100	Yale-Brown	71-24-5	1880
99	Harvard-Dartmouth	51-43-5	1882
97	Western Ill.-Illinois St.	39-35-3	1904
95	Montana-Montana St.	58-32-5	1897
95	Harvard-Brown	68-25-2	1893
88	Princeton-Harvard	49-32-7	1877
87	Princeton-Pennsylvania	60-26-1	1876
86	Connecticut-Rhode Island	45-33-8	1897
84	Illinois St.-Eastern Ill.	40-35-9	1901
83	Maine-New Hampshire	37-38-8	1903
83	Cornell-Columbia	53-27-3	1889
79	#Cornell-Colgate	46-30-3	1896

#Teams have not met since 1993.

Additional Rivalry Records

LONGEST UNINTERRUPTED SERIES
(Must have played every year; current unless indicated)

106 games—Lafayette-Lehigh (from 1897)$
103 games—Cornell-Pennsylvania (from 1893)
77 games—Cornell-Dartmouth (from 1919)
70 games—Dartmouth-Yale (from 1926)
64 games—Brown-Yale (from 1932)
63 games—Dartmouth-Princeton (from 1933)
54 games—Columbia-Dartmouth (from 1942)
53 games—Columbia-Yale (from 1943)
52 games—Richmond-William & Mary (from 1944)
52 games—Va. Military-William & Mary (from 1944)
52 games—Dartmouth-Holy Cross (1942-93)
51 games—Brown-Harvard (from 1945)
51 games—Bucknell-Lafayette (from 1945)
51 games—Harvard-Yale (from 1945)
51 games—Princeton-Yale (from 1945)
51 games—Southwest Tex. St.-Tex. A&M-Kingsville (from 1946)√
50 games—Eastern Ky.-Western Ky. (from 1946)
50 games—Harvard-Princeton (from 1946)
50 games—Sam Houston St.-Southwest Tex. St. (from 1946)
50 games—Southwest Tex. St.-Stephen F. Austin (from 1946)

$Played twice in 1897-1901 and 1943-44. √Played twice in 1983.

MOST CONSECUTIVE WINS OVER AN OPPONENT IN AN UNINTERRUPTED SERIES
(Must have played in consecutive years)

20—Eastern Ky. over Tennessee Tech, 1976-95 (current)
19—Grambling over Prairie View, 1977-95 (current)
18—Eastern Ky. over Morehead St., 1972-89
18—Southeast Mo. St. over Lincoln (Mo.), 1972-89
17—Princeton over Columbia, 1954-70

16—Harvard over Columbia, 1979-94
16—Middle Tenn. St. over Morehead St., 1951-66
15—Delaware over West Chester, 1968-82
15—Dartmouth over Brown, 1960-74
14—Yale over Princeton, 1967-80
13—Evansville over Ky. Wesleyan, 1983-95 (current)
13—Marshall over Va. Military, 1983-95 (current)
13—Duquesne over St. Francis (Pa.), 1977-89
12—Dartmouth over Columbia, 1984-95 (current)
12—Western Ill. over Southern Ill., 1984-95 (current)
12—Idaho over Boise St., 1982-93
12—Cornell over Columbia, 1977-88
11—Wofford over Newberry, 1960-70
11—Tennessee Tech over Morehead St., 1951-61
11—William & Mary over Richmond, 1944-54

MOST CONSECUTIVE WINS OVER AN OPPONENT IN A SERIES
(Did not have to play in consecutive years)
46—Yale over Wesleyan (Conn.), 1875-1913
30—Harvard over Williams, 1883-1920
23—Harvard over Bates, 1899-1944
23—Brown over Rhode Island, 1909-34
21—Grambling over Mississippi Val., 1957-77
17—Harvard over Columbia, 1979-95
16—Yale over Connecticut, 1948-64
14—Delaware over Massachusetts, 1958-89
12—Yale over Pennsylvania, 1879-92
12—Idaho over Ricks College, 1919-33

MOST CONSECUTIVE CURRENT WINS OVER AN OPPONENT IN AN UNINTERRUPTED SERIES
(Must have played in consecutive years)
20—Eastern Ky. over Tennessee Tech, 1976-95
19—Grambling over Prairie View, 1977-95
13—Evansville over Ky. Wesleyan, 1983-95
13—Marshall over Va. Military, 1983-95
12—Dartmouth over Columbia, 1984-95
12—Western Ill. over Southern Ill., 1984-95

Cliffhangers

Regular-season Division I-AA games won on the final play in regulation time. The extra point is listed when it provided the margin of victory after the winning touchdown on the game's final play.

Date	Opponents, Score	Game-Winning Play
10-21-78	Western Ky. 17, Eastern Ky. 16	Kevin McGrath 25 FG
9-8-79	Northern Ariz. 22, Portland St. 21	Ken Fraser 15 pass from Brian Potter (Mike Jenkins pass from Potter)
11-15-80	Morris Brown 19, Bethune-Cookman 18	Ray Mills 1 run (Carlton Johnson kick)
9-26-81	Abilene Christian 41, Northwestern St. 38	David Russell 17 pass from Loyal Proffitt
10-10-81	LIU-C.W. Post 37, James Madison 36	Tom DeBona 10 pass from Tom Ehrhardt
11-13-82	Pennsylvania 23, Harvard 21	Dave Shulman 27 FG
10-1-83	Connecticut 9, New Hampshire 7	Larry Corn 7 run
9-8-84	Southwestern La. 17, Louisiana Tech 16	Patrick Broussard 21 FG
9-15-84	Lehigh 10, Connecticut 7	Dave Melick 45 FG
9-15-84	William & Mary 23, Delaware 21	Jeff Sanders 18 pass from Stan Yagiello
10-13-84	Lafayette 20, Connecticut 13	Ryan Priest 2 run
10-20-84	Central Fla. 28, Illinois St. 24	Jeff Farmer 30 punt return
10-27-84	Western Ky. 33, Morehead St. 31	Arnold Grier 50 pass from Jeff Cesarone
9-7-85	Central Fla. 39, Bethune-Cookman 37	Ed O'Brien 55 FG
10-26-85	Va. Military 39, William & Mary 38	Al Comer 3 run (James Wright run)
8-30-86	Texas Southern 38, Prairie View 35	Don Espinoza 23 FG
9-20-86	Delaware 33, West Chester 31	Fred Singleton 3 run
10-4-86	Northwestern St. 17, Northeast La. 14	Keith Hodnett 27 FG
10-11-86	Eastern Ill. 31, Northern Iowa 30	Rich Ehmke 58 FG
9-12-87	Youngstown St. 20, Bowling Green 17	John Dowling 36 FG
10-3-87	Northeast La. 33, Northwestern St. 31	Jackie Harris 48 pass from Stan Humphries
10-10-87	Marshall 34, Louisville 31	Keith Baxter 31 pass from Tony Petersen
10-17-87	Princeton 16, Lehigh 15	Rob Goodwin 38 FG
11-12-87	South Caro. St. 15, Grambling 13	William Wrighten 23 FG
9-24-88	Holy Cross 30, Princeton 26	70 kickoff return; Tim Donovan 55 on lateral from Darin Cromwell (15)
10-15-88	Weber St. 37, Nevada 31	Todd Beightol 57 pass from Jeff Carlson
10-29-88	Nicholls St. 13, Southwest Tex. St. 10	Jim Windham 33 FG
9-2-89	Alabama St. 16, Troy St. 13	Reggie Brown 28 pass from Antonius Smith
9-16-89	Western Caro. 26, Tenn.-Chatt. 20	Terrell Wagner 68 interception return
9-23-89	Northwestern St. 18, McNeese St. 17	Chris Hamler 25 FG
10-14-89	East Tenn. St. 24, Tenn.-Chatt. 23	George Searcy 1 run
9-29-90	Southwest Tex. St. 33, Nicholls St. 30	Robbie Roberson 32 FG
10-6-90	Grambling 27, Alabama A&M 20	Dexter Butcher 28 pass from Shawn Burras
11-2-91	Grambling 30, Texas Southern 27	Gilad Landau 37 FG
9-19-92	Eastern Ky. 26, Northeast La. 21	Sean Little recovered fumble in end zone
10-10-92	Appalachian St. 27, James Madison 21	Craig Styron 44 pass from D. J. Campbell
11-14-92	Towson St. 33, Northeastern 32	Mark Orlando 10 pass from Dan Crowley
9-4-93	Delaware St. 31, Fayetteville St. 28	Jon Jensen 17 FG
9-11-93	Connecticut 24, New Hampshire 23	Wilbur Gilliard 14 run (Nick Sosik kick)
10-16-93	Howard 44, Towson St. 41	Germaine Kohn 9 pass from Jay Walker
10-7-95	Valparaiso 44, Butler 42	Cameron Hatten 27 FG
10-14-95	Montana 24, Northern Ariz. 21	Andy Larson 29 FG
10-14-95	Connecticut 31, Maine 30	David DeArmas 38 FG
10-28-95	Northern Iowa 19, Southwest Mo. St. 17	Matt Waller 39 FG
10-28-95	William & Mary 18, Villanova 15	Brian Shallcross 49 FG

William and Mary sports information photo by Alan P. Owens

Brian Shallcross kicked a 49-yard field goal on the game's final play to lift William and Mary to an 18-15 victory over Villanova on October 28, 1995.

Regular-Season Overtime Games

In 1981, the NCAA Football Rules Committee approved an overtime tiebreaker system to decide a tie game for the purpose of determining a conference champion. The following conferences used the tiebreaker system to decide conference-only tie games. (Beginning in 1996, all college football games will use the tiebreaker if the score is tied after four periods.) In an overtime period, one end of the field is used and each team gets an offensive possession beginning at the 25-yard line. Each team shall have possession until it has scored, failed to gain a first down or lost possession. The team scoring the greater number of points after completion of both possessions is declared the winner. The periods continue until a winner is determined.

BIG SKY CONFERENCE

Date	Opponents, Score	No. OTs	Score, Reg.
10-31-81	‡Weber St. 24, Northern Ariz. 23	1	17-17
11-21-81	‡Idaho St. 33, Weber St. 30	3	23-23
10-2-82	‡Montana St. 30, Idaho St. 27	3	17-17
11-6-82	Nevada 46, ‡Weber St. 43	3	30-30
10-13-84	‡Montana St. 44, Nevada 41	4	21-21
9-17-88	Boise St. 24, ‡Northern Ariz. 21	2	14-14
10-15-88	‡Montana 33, Northern Ariz. 26	2	26-26
9-15-90	‡Weber St. 45, Idaho St. 38	2	31-31
9-29-90	‡Nevada 31, Idaho 28	1	28-28
11-3-90	Eastern Wash. 33, ‡Idaho St. 26	1	26-26
11-10-90	Montana St. 28, ‡Eastern Wash. 25	1	25-25
10-26-91	Eastern Wash. 34, ‡Idaho 31	2	24-24
11-16-91	Montana 35, ‡Idaho 34	1	28-28

GATEWAY CONFERENCE

Date	Opponents, Score	No. OTs	Score, Reg.
9-24-94	Western Ill. 31, ‡Southwest Mo. St. 24	1	24-24
9-30-95	Illinois St. 20, ‡Southwest Mo. St. 17	1	17-17
10-14-95	‡Southern Ill. 33, Southwest Mo. St. 30	1	30-30

MID-EASTERN ATHLETIC CONFERENCE

Date	Opponents, Score	No. OTs	Score, Reg.
11-1-86	‡North Caro. A&T 30, Bethune-Cookman 24	1	24-24
10-22-93	Howard 41, ‡North Caro. A&T 35	1	35-35
11-20-93	‡South Caro. St. 58, North Caro. A&T 52	1	52-52

OHIO VALLEY CONFERENCE

Date	Opponents, Score	No. OTs	Score, Reg.
10-13-84	Youngstown St. 17, ‡Austin Peay 13	1	10-10
11-3-84	‡Murray St. 20, Austin Peay 13	2	10-10
10-19-85	‡Middle Tenn. St. 31, Murray St. 24	2	17-17
11-2-85	‡Middle Tenn. St. 28, Youngstown St. 21	2	14-14
10-4-86	‡Austin Peay 7, Middle Tenn. St. 0	1	0-0
10-10-87	‡Austin Peay 20, Morehead St. 13	1	13-13
11-7-87	‡Youngstown St. 20, Murray St. 13	1	13-13
10-1-88	Tennessee Tech 16, ‡Murray St. 13	1	10-10
10-29-88	Eastern Ky. 31, ‡Murray St. 24	1	24-24
11-18-89	Eastern Ky. 38, ‡Morehead St. 31	3	24-24
11-10-90	‡Tennessee Tech 20, Austin Peay 14	1	14-14
11-17-90	Murray St. 31, ‡Austin Peay 24	3	24-24
11-7-92	‡Eastern Ky. 21, Murray St. 18	1	18-18
10-2-93	Murray St. 28, ‡Tenn.-Martin 21	1	21-21
11-20-93	Tenn.-Martin 39, ‡Austin Peay 33	2	26-26

PATRIOT LEAGUE

Date	Opponents, Score	No. OTs	Score, Reg.
11-11-95	Bucknell 21, ‡Colgate 14	1	14-14
11-11-95	‡Lafayette 24, Fordham 21	1	21-21

YANKEE CONFERENCE

Date	Opponents, Score	No. OTs	Score, Reg.
9-18-82	Rhode Island 58, ‡Maine 55	6	21-21
9-25-82	‡Boston U. 48, Maine 45	4	24-24
10-27-84	Maine 13, ‡Connecticut 10	1	10-10
9-13-86	New Hampshire 28, ‡Delaware 21	1	21-21
11-15-86	‡Connecticut 21, Rhode Island 14	1	14-14
9-19-87	‡Richmond 52, Massachusetts 51	4	28-28
9-19-87	New Hampshire 27, ‡Boston U. 20	3	17-17
10-31-87	Maine 59, ‡Delaware 56	2	49-49
11-21-87	‡Delaware 17, Boston U. 10	1	10-10
9-24-88	Villanova 31, ‡Boston U. 24	1	24-24
10-8-88	‡Richmond 23, New Hampshire 17	1	17-17
10-7-89	‡Villanova 41, Connecticut 35	6	21-21
11-16-91	Boston U. 29, ‡Connecticut 26	2	23-23
9-11-93	‡Connecticut 24, New Hampshire 23	1	17-17
10-16-93	Maine 26, ‡Rhode Island 23	2	17-17
9-17-94	Delaware 38, ‡Villanova 31	1	31-31
11-19-94	Northeastern 9, ‡James Madison 6	1	6-6
9-23-95	James Madison 28, ‡Villanova 27	1	21-21
10-7-95	‡Richmond 26, Northeastern 23	1	23-23
11-4-95	‡Maine 24, Massachusetts 21	1	21-21

‡*Home team.*

Division I-AA Stadiums

STADIUMS LISTED ALPHABETICALLY

School	Stadium	Conference	Year Built	Cap.	Surface*
Alabama St.	√ Cramton Bowl	SWAC	1922	24,600	Grass
Alcorn St.	Jack Spinks	SWAC	1992	25,000	Grass
Appalachian St.	Kidd Brewer	Southern	1962	18,000	AstroTurf
Austin Peay	Governors	Ohio Valley	1946	10,000	Stadia Turf
Bethune-Cookman	Municipal	MEAC	NA	10,000	Grass
Boise St.	Bronco	Big Sky	1970	22,600	Blue AstroTurf
Boston U.	Nickerson Field	Yankee	1930	17,369	AstroTurf
Brown	Brown	Ivy	1925	20,000	Grass
Bucknell	Christy Mathewson	Patriot	1924	13,100	Grass
Buffalo	UB Stadium	Independent	1992	16,500	Grass
Butler	Butler Bowl	Pioneer	1928	18,000	Grass
Cal Poly SLO	Mustang	Independent	1935	8,000	Grass
Cal St. Northridge	North Campus	Big Sky	#1944	6,000	Grass
Cal St. Sacramento	Hornet Field	Big Sky	%1969	23,000	Grass
Canisius	Demske	MAAC	1989	1,000	AstroTurf
Central Conn. St.	Arute Field	Northeast	1969	5,000	Grass
Charleston So.	CSU	Independent	1991	3,000	Grass
Citadel	Johnson Hagood	Southern	1948	22,500	Grass
Colgate	Andy Kerr	Patriot	1939	10,221	Grass
Columbia	Lawrence Wien	Ivy	1984	17,000	Grass
Connecticut	Memorial	Yankee	1953	16,200	Grass
Cornell	Schoellkopf Field	Ivy	1915	27,000	All-Pro Turf
Dartmouth	Memorial Field	Ivy	1923	20,416	Grass
Davidson	Richardson	Independent	1924	5,200	Grass
Dayton	Welcome	Pioneer	1949	11,000	AstroTurf
Delaware	Delaware	Yankee	1952	23,000	Grass
Delaware St.	Alumni Field	MEAC	1957	5,000	Grass
Drake	Drake	Pioneer	1925	18,000	Grass
Duquesne	Arthur Rooney Field	MAAC	1993	4,500	AstroTurf
East Tenn. St.	@ Memorial	Southern	1977	12,000	AstroTurf
Eastern Ill.	O'Brien	Ohio Valley	1970	10,000	Grass
Eastern Ky.	Roy Kidd	Ohio Valley	1969	20,000	Grass
Eastern Wash.	Woodward	Big Sky	1967	6,000	Grass
Evansville	Arad McCutchan	Pioneer	1984	3,000	Grass
Fairfield	Fairfield	MAAC	1980	3,000	Grass
Florida A&M	Bragg Memorial	MEAC	1957	25,500	Grass
Fordham	Jack Coffey Field	Patriot	1930	7,000	Grass
Furman	Paladin	Southern	1981	16,000	Grass
Georgetown	Kehoe Field	MAAC	NA	2,400	AstroTurf
Ga. Southern	Paulson	Southern	1984	18,000	PAT
Grambling	Robinson	SWAC	1983	19,600	Grass
Hampton	Armstrong Field	MEAC	1928	11,000	Grass
Harvard	Harvard	Ivy	1903	37,967	Grass
Hofstra	Hofstra	Independent	1963	15,000	AstroTurf
Holy Cross	Fitton Field	Patriot	1924	23,500	Grass
Howard	William H. Greene	MEAC	1986	12,500	AstroTurf
Idaho	@ Kibbie Dome	Big Sky	$1971	16,000	AstroTurf
Idaho St.	@ Holt Arena	Big Sky	1970	12,000	AstroTurf
Illinois St.	Hancock	Gateway	1967	15,000	AstroTurf
Indiana St.	Memorial	Gateway	!1924	20,500	All-Pro Turf
Iona	Mazzella Field	MAAC	1989	1,200	AstroTurf
Jackson St.	√ Miss. Veterans	SWAC	1949	62,512	Grass
Jacksonville St.	Paul Snow	Southland	1947	15,000	Grass
James Madison	Bridgeforth	Yankee	1974	12,500	AstroTurf
Lafayette	Fisher Field	Patriot	1926	13,750	Grass
Lehigh	Goodman	Patriot	1988	16,000	Grass
Liberty	Williams	Independent	1989	12,000	OmniTurf
Maine	Alumni	Yankee	1942	10,000	Grass
Marist	Leonidoff	MAAC	1965	2,500	Grass
Marshall	Marshall University	Southern	1991	30,000	PolyTurf
Massachusetts	McGuirk	Yankee	1965	16,000	Grass
McNeese St.	Cowboy	Southland	1965	17,500	Grass
Middle Tenn. St.	Johnny (Red) Floyd	Ohio Valley	!!1933	15,000	AstroTurf
Mississippi Val.	Magnolia	SWAC	1958	10,500	Grass
Monmouth (N.J.)	Kessler Field	Northeast	1993	4,600	Grass
Montana	Wash.-Grizzly	Big Sky	1986	18,845	Grass
Montana St.	Reno Sales	Big Sky	1973	15,197	Grass
Morehead St.	Jayne	Independent	1964	10,000	OmniTurf
Morgan St.	Hughes	MEAC	NA	10,000	Grass
Murray St.	Roy Stewart	Ohio Valley	1973	16,800	AstroTurf
New Hampshire	Cowell	Yankee	1936	9,571	Grass
Nicholls St.	John L. Guidry	Southland	1972	12,800	Grass
North Caro. A&T	Aggie	MEAC	1981	17,500	Grass
Northeastern	E. S. Parsons	Yankee	1932	7,000	AstroTurf
Northern Ariz.	@ Walkup Skydome	Big Sky	1977	15,300	AstroTurf
Northern Iowa	@ UNI-Dome	Gateway	1976	16,324	AstroTurf
Northwestern St.	Turpin	Southland	1976	15,971	AstroTurf
Pennsylvania	Franklin Field	Ivy	1895	60,546	AstroTurf
Prairie View	Blackshear	SWAC	1960	6,000	Grass
Princeton	Palmer	Ivy	1914	45,725	Grass
Rhode Island	Meade	Yankee	1933	8,000	Grass
Richmond	Richmond	Yankee	1929	22,611	SuperTurf
Robert Morris	Moon	Northeast	1950	7,000	Grass
St. Francis (Pa.)	Pine Bowl	Northeast	1979	1,500	Grass
St. John's (N.Y.)	Redmen Field	MAAC	1961	3,000	OmniTurf

School	Stadium	Conference	Year Built	Cap.	Surface*
St. Mary's (Cal.)	St. Mary's	Independent	1973	6,700	Grass
St. Peter's	JFK	MAAC	1990	4,000	Grass
Sam Houston St.	Bowers	Southland	1986	14,000	All-Pro Turf
Samford	Siebert	Independent	NA	6,700	Grass
San Diego	USD Torero	Pioneer	1955	4,000	Grass
Siena	Siena Field	MAAC	NA	500	Grass
South Caro. St.	Dawson Bulldog	MEAC	1955	22,000	Grass
Southeast Mo. St.	Houck	Ohio Valley	1930	10,000	Grass
Southern-B.R.	Mumford	SWAC	1928	24,000	Grass
Southern Ill.	McAndrew	Gateway	1975	17,324	OmniTurf
Southern Utah	Coliseum	Independent	1967	6,500	Grass
Southwest Mo. St.	Plaster Field	Gateway	1941	16,300	OmniTurf
Southwest Tex. St.	Bobcat	Southland	1981	14,104	Grass
Stephen F. Austin	Homer Bryce	Southland	1973	14,575	All-Pro Turf
Tenn.-Chatt.	Chamberlain	Southern	1947	10,501	Grass
Tenn.-Martin	Pacer	Ohio Valley	1964	7,500	Grass
Tennessee St.	W. J. Hale	Ohio Valley	1953	16,000	Grass
Tennessee Tech	Tucker	Ohio Valley	1966	16,500	Stadia Turf
Texas Southern	√ Robertson	SWAC	1965	25,000	Grass
Towson St.	Minnegan	Independent	1978	5,000	Grass
Troy St.	Memorial	Southland	1950	12,000	Grass
Valparaiso	Brown Field	Pioneer	1947	5,000	Grass
Villanova	Villanova	Yankee	1927	12,000	AstroTurf-8
Va. Military	Alumni Field	Southern	1962	10,000	Grass
Wagner	Fischer Memorial	Northeast	1967	5,000	Grass
Weber St.	Wildcat	Big Sky	1966	17,500	Grass
Western Caro.	E. J. Whitmire	Southern	1974	12,000	AstroTurf
Western Ill.	Hanson Field	Gateway	1950	15,000	Grass
Western Ky.	L. T. Smith	Independent	1968	17,500	Grass
William & Mary	Walter Zable	Yankee	1935	15,000	Grass
Wofford	Gibbs	Independent	1996	8,500	Grass
Yale	Yale Bowl	Ivy	1914	60,000	Grass
Youngstown St.	Stambaugh	Independent	1982	18,000	AstroTurf

STADIUMS LISTED BY CAPACITY (TOP 23)

School	Stadium	Surface	Capacity
Jackson St.	√ Miss. Veterans	Grass	62,512
Pennsylvania	Franklin Field	AstroTurf	60,546
Yale	Yale Bowl	Grass	60,000
Princeton	Palmer	Grass	45,725
Harvard	Harvard	Grass	37,967
Marshall	Marshall University	AstroTurf	30,000
Cornell	Schoellkopf Field	All-Pro Turf	27,000
Florida A&M	Bragg Memorial	Grass	25,500
Alcorn St.	Jack Spinks	Grass	25,000
Texas Southern	√ Robertson	Grass	25,000
Alabama St.	√ Cramton Bowl	Grass	24,600
Southern-B.R.	Mumford	Grass	24,000
Holy Cross	Fitton Field	Grass	23,500
Cal St. Sacramento	Hornet Field	Grass	23,000
Delaware	Delaware	Grass	23,000
Richmond	Richmond	SuperTurf	22,611
Boise St.	Bronco	Blue AstroTurf	22,600
Citadel	Johnson Hagood	Grass	22,500
South Caro. St.	Dawson Bulldog	Grass	22,000
Indiana St.	Memorial	All-Pro Turf	20,500
Dartmouth	Memorial Field	Grass	20,416
Brown	Brown	Grass	20,000
Eastern Ky.	Roy Kidd	Grass	20,000

*√Not located on campus. @ Indoor facility. *This column indicates the type of surface (either artificial or natural grass) present this year in the stadium. The brand name of the artificial turf, if known, is listed. #Built in 1944 as Devonshire Downs Race Track, refurbished in 1971 for football. %Originally built in 1969 with 6,000 capacity, renovated 1992 and increased to 23,000. $Built in 1971, roof added in 1975. !Built in 1924 as minor league baseball field, acquired by school in 1967 and renovated for football in 1967. !!Built in 1933, remodeled and expanded in 1953 and 1968.*

Division I-AA Statistics Trends

(Average Per Game, Both Teams)

	Rushing			Passing					Total Offense			Scoring		
Year	Plays	Yds.	Avg.	Att.	Cmp.	Pct.	Yds.	Av. Att.	Plays	Yds.	Avg.	TD	FG	Pts.
1978	*96.7	*343.5	3.55	41.4	19.1	46.2	258.6	6.24	138.1	602.1	4.36	5.20	1.03	39.0
1979	94.1	329.3	3.50	40.9	18.4	45.0	250.4	6.13	135.0	579.7	4.30	4.79	1.23	36.9
1980	90.3	329.6	3.65	44.8	20.8	46.5	288.8	6.45	135.1	618.4	4.58	5.15	1.18	39.2
1981	88.5	309.9	3.50	49.7	23.7	47.7	322.9	6.49	138.2	632.8	4.58	5.42	1.38	41.7
1982	88.8	313.1	3.53	52.2	25.6	48.9	332.0	6.35	141.0	645.1	4.57	5.24	1.59	41.0
1983	87.8	310.3	3.54	52.4	25.9	49.4	334.5	6.38	140.2	644.8	4.60	5.38	1.58	42.1
1984	85.7	305.1	3.56	55.7	27.9	50.0	361.9	6.49	141.4	666.9	4.72	5.59	1.60	43.6
1985	84.7	315.2	3.72	*57.7	*29.1	50.4	374.6	6.49	*142.4	689.8	4.84	5.67	1.61	44.2
1986	84.8	315.8	3.72	56.5	28.1	49.7	372.8	6.60	141.3	688.6	4.87	5.80	1.72	45.4
1987	86.2	317.2	3.68	54.2	27.1	50.1	351.1	6.48	140.4	668.3	4.76	5.55	1.81	44.0
1988	86.3	322.5	3.74	52.9	26.5	50.2	345.4	6.53	139.2	667.9	4.80	5.59	*1.81	44.2
1989	84.9	320.4	3.77	55.4	28.4	51.3	372.0	6.71	140.3	692.4	4.93	5.43	1.49	45.5
1990	85.3	323.0	3.79	55.6	28.1	50.6	374.0	6.73	140.9	697.0	4.95	5.96	1.67	46.4
1991	86.4	341.2	3.95	53.7	27.9	*51.9	369.3	6.87	140.1	*710.5	5.07	6.38	1.33	48.1
1992	86.0	342.8	*3.99	52.0	26.9	51.7	358.8	6.89	138.0	701.6	5.08	6.32	1.36	47.7
1993	84.7	336.6	3.97	54.0	28.0	51.8	372.8	*6.90	138.7	709.3	*5.11	*6.40	1.40	*48.4
1994	83.1	328.1	3.95	54.9	28.5	51.9	*376.1	6.85	138.0	704.2	5.10	6.35	1.40	48.1
1995	83.9	330.2	3.94	54.1	27.7	51.3	355.4	6.57	138.0	685.6	4.97	6.12	1.36	46.4

**Record.*

Additional Division I-AA Statistics Trends

(Average Per Game, Both Teams)

	Punting			Interceptions			Punt Returns			Kickoff Returns		
Year	No.	Avg.	Net Avg.	No.	Avg. Ret.	Yds.	No.	Avg. Ret.	Yds.	No.	Avg. Ret.	Yds.
1978	*12.2	36.5	33.6	2.84	11.92	33.9	4.78	7.49	35.8	6.45	18.4	118.4
1979	11.9	36.5	33.4	2.88	11.39	32.8	4.82	7.46	35.9	6.11	18.4	112.3
1980	11.6	37.0	33.7	2.74	10.06	27.6	4.87	7.94	38.7	6.17	17.4	107.4
1981	11.8	37.2	33.9	*3.19	10.63	*33.9	4.99	7.77	38.8	6.54	18.4	120.1
1982	12.0	37.1	34.0	2.99	10.15	30.3	4.88	7.63	37.2	6.15	19.0	116.8
1983	11.9	37.3	34.1	3.03	9.99	30.2	*5.17	7.58	39.2	6.11	18.6	113.8
1984	11.6	37.3	33.9	3.05	10.40	31.7	5.10	7.84	40.0	6.46	18.6	120.0
1985	11.4	37.6	*34.2	3.02	10.56	31.9	5.09	7.52	38.3	6.39	18.1	115.7
1986	11.2	*37.6	34.0	3.01	10.90	32.8	5.09	7.92	40.3	*8.04	19.4	*155.7
1987	11.2	36.8	33.4	2.80	10.57	29.7	4.96	7.51	37.3	7.91	19.0	149.1
1988	10.9	36.3	32.8	2.68	10.61	28.4	4.80	7.96	38.3	7.90	18.8	148.6
1989	11.0	36.1	32.8	2.62	10.40	27.3	4.63	7.93	36.7	7.92	18.9	149.4
1990	10.8	36.7	32.7	2.76	11.94	32.9	4.97	8.46	42.0	8.03	18.9	151.7
1991	10.6	36.6	32.6	2.70	10.81	29.1	4.92	8.57	42.2	7.68	19.1	146.7
1992	10.6	36.6	32.2	2.41	10.24	24.6	5.05	*9.35	*47.2	7.63	19.5	148.7
1993	10.4	36.0	32.3	2.45	10.79	26.4	4.70	8.26	38.9	7.44	19.3	143.4
1994	10.4	36.3	32.1	2.53	10.94	27.6	4.76	9.20	43.8	7.65	*19.9	152.0
1995	10.8	35.8	32.0	2.31	*12.20	28.2	4.72	8.57	40.4	7.46	18.6	138.7

**Record.*

Black College National Champions

Sheridan Poll

Selected by the Pittsburgh Courier, 1920-1980, and compiled by Collie Nicholson, former Grambling sports information director; William Nunn Jr., Pittsburgh Courier sports editor; and Eric "Ric" Roberts, Pittsburgh Courier sports writer and noted black college sports historian. Selected from 1981 by the Sheridan Broadcasting Network, 411 Seventh Ave., Suite 1500, Pittsburgh, Pa. 15219-1905. Records include postseason games.

Year	Team	Won	Lost	Tied	Coach
1920	Howard	7	0	0	Edward Morrison
	Talladega	5	0	1	Jubie Bragg
1921	Talladega	6	0	1	Jubie Bragg
	Wiley	7	0	1	Jason Grant
1922	Hampton	6	1	0	Gideon Smith
1923	Virginia Union	6	0	1	Harold Martin
1924	Tuskegee	9	0	1	Cleve Abbott
	Wiley	8	0	1	Fred Long
1925	Tuskegee	8	0	1	Cleve Abbott
	Howard	6	0	2	Louis Watson
1926	Tuskegee	10	0	0	Cleve Abbott
	Howard	7	0	0	Louis Watson
1927	Tuskegee	9	0	1	Cleve Abbott
	Bluefield St. (Va.)	8	0	1	Harry Jefferson
1928	Bluefield St. (Va.)	8	0	1	Harry Jefferson
	Wiley	8	0	1	Fred Long
1929	Tuskegee	10	0	0	Cleve Abbott
1930	Tuskegee	11	0	1	Cleve Abbott
1931	Wilberforce	9	0	0	Harry Graves
1932	Wiley	9	0	0	Fred Long
1933	Morgan St.	9	0	0	Edward Hurt
1934	Kentucky St.	9	0	0	Henry Kean
1935	Texas College	9	0	0	Arnett Mumford
1936	West Va. St.	8	0	0	Adolph Hamblin
	Virginia St.	7	0	2	Harry Jefferson
1937	Morgan St.	7	0	0	Edward Hurt
1938	Florida A&M	8	0	0	Bill Bell
1939	Langston	9	0	0	Felton "Zip" Gayles
1940	Morris Brown	9	1	0	Artis Graves
1941	Morris Brown	8	1	0	William Nicks
1942	Florida A&M	9	0	0	Bill Bell
1943	Morgan St.	5	0	0	Edward Hurt
1944	Morgan St.	6	1	0	Edward Hurt
1945	Wiley	10	0	0	Fred Long
1946	Tennessee St.	10	1	0	Henry Kean
	Morgan St.	8	0	0	Edward Hurt
1947	Tennessee St.	10	0	0	Henry Kean
	Shaw	10	0	0	Brutus Wilson
1948	Southern-B.R.	12	0	0	Arnett Mumford
1949	Southern-B.R.	10	0	1	Arnett Mumford
	Morgan St.	8	0	0	Edward Hurt
1950	Southern-B.R.	10	0	1	Arnett Mumford
	Florida A&M	8	1	1	Alonzo "Jake" Gaither
1951	Morris Brown	10	1	0	Edward "Ox" Clemons
1952	Florida A&M	8	2	0	Alonzo "Jake" Gaither
	Texas Southern	10	0	1	Alexander Durley
	Lincoln (Mo.)	8	0	1	Dwight Reed
	Virginia St.	8	1	0	Sylvester "Sal" Hall
1953	Prairie View	12	0	0	William Nicks
1954	Tennessee St.	10	1	0	Henry Kean
	Southern-B.R.	10	1	0	Arnett Mumford
	Florida A&M	8	1	0	Alonzo "Jake" Gaither
	Prairie View	10	1	0	William Nicks
1955	Grambling	10	0	0	Eddie Robinson
1956	Tennessee St.	10	0	0	Howard Gentry
1957	Florida A&M	9	0	0	Alonzo "Jake" Gaither
1958	Prairie View	10	0	1	William Nicks
1959	Florida A&M	10	0	0	Alonzo "Jake" Gaither
1960	Southern-B.R.	9	1	0	Arnett Mumford
1961	Florida A&M	10	0	0	Alonzo "Jake" Gaither
1962	Jackson St.	10	1	0	John Merritt
1963	Prairie View	10	1	0	William Nicks
1964	Prairie View	9	0	0	William Nicks
1965	Tennessee St.	9	0	1	John Merritt
1966	Tennessee St.	10	0	0	John Merritt
1967	Morgan St.	8	0	0	Earl Banks
	Grambling	9	1	0	Eddie Robinson
1968	Alcorn St.	9	1	0	Marino Casem
	North Caro. A&T	8	1	0	Hornsby Howell
1969	Alcorn St.	8	0	1	Marino Casem
1970	Tennessee St.	11	0	0	John Merritt
1971	Tennessee St.	9	1	0	John Merritt
1972	Grambling	11	2	0	Eddie Robinson
1973	Tennessee St.	10	0	0	John Merritt
1974	Grambling	11	1	0	Eddie Robinson
	Alcorn St.	9	2	0	Marino Casem
1975	Grambling	10	2	0	Eddie Robinson
1976	South Caro. St.	10	1	0	Willie Jeffries
1977	South Caro. St.	9	1	1	Willie Jeffries
	Grambling	10	1	0	Eddie Robinson
	Florida A&M	11	0	0	Rudy Hubbard
1978	Florida A&M	12	1	0	Rudy Hubbard
1979	Tennessee St.	8	3	0	John Merritt
1980	Grambling	10	2	0	Eddie Robinson
1981	South Caro. St.	10	3	0	Bill Davis
1982	* Tennessee St.	9	0	1	John Merritt
1983	Grambling	8	1	2	Eddie Robinson
1984	Alcorn St.	9	1	0	Marino Casem
1985	Jackson St.	8	3	0	W. C. Gorden
1986	Central St.	10	1	1	Billy Joe
1987	Central St.	10	1	1	Billy Joe
1988	Central St.	11	2	0	Billy Joe
1989	Central St.	10	2	0	Billy Joe
1990	# Central St.	11	1	0	Billy Joe
1991	Alabama St.	11	0	1	Houston Markham
1992	Grambling	10	2	0	Eddie Robinson
1993	Southern-B.R.	11	1	0	Pete Richardson
1994	Hampton	10	1	0	Joe Taylor
1995	Southern-B.R.	11	1	0	Pete Richardson

**Tennessee State's participation in the 1982 Division I-AA championship (1-1 record) voided. #NAIA Division I national champion.*

American Sports Wire

Selected by American Sports Wire and compiled by Dick Simpson, CEO. Selected from 1990 by the American Sports Wire, P.O. Box 802031, Santa Clarita, Calif. 91380-2031. Record includes postseason games.

Year	Team	Won	Lost	Tied	Coach
1990	North Caro. A&T	9	2	0	Bill Hayes
1991	Alabama St.	11	0	1	Houston Markham
1992	Grambling	10	2	0	Eddie Robinson
1993	Southern-B.R.	11	1	0	Pete Richardson
1994	Hampton	10	1	0	Joe Taylor
1995	Southern-B.R.	11	1	0	Pete Richardson

Heritage Bowl

The first bowl game matching historically black schools in Division I-AA . The champion of the Southwestern Athletic Conference meets the champion of the Mid-Eastern Athletic Conference.

Date	Score (Attendance)	Site
12-21-91	Alabama St. 36, North Caro. A&T 13 (7,724)	Miami, Fla.
1-2-93	Grambling 45, Florida A&M 15 (11,273)	Tallahassee, Fla.
1-1-94	Southern-B.R. 11, South Caro. St. 0 (36,128)	Atlanta, Ga.
12-30-94	South Caro. St. 31, Grambling 27 (22,179)	Atlanta, Ga.
12-29-95	Southern-B.R. 30, Florida A&M 25 (25,164)	Atlanta, Ga.

All-Time Black College Football Team

(Selected by the Sheridan Broadcasting Network in 1993)

OFFENSE

QB Doug Williams .... Grambling
RB Walter Payton .... Jackson St.
RB Tank Younger .... Grambling
WR Jerry Rice .... Mississippi Val.
WR John Stallworth .... Alabama A&M
WR Charlie Joiner .... Grambling
OL Art Shell .... Md.-East. Shore
OL Rayfield Wright .... Fort Valley St.
OL Jackie Slater .... Jackson St.
OL Larry Little .... Bethune-Cookman
OL Ernie Barnes .... N.C. Central

DEFENSE

DL Willie Davis .... Grambling
DL Ed "Too Tall" Jones .... Tennessee St.
DL Deacon Jones .... South Caro. St.
DL L. C. Greenwood .... Arkansas A&M
LB Robert Brazile .... Jackson St.
LB Harry Carson .... South Caro. St.
LB Willie Lanier .... Morgan St.
DB Mel Blount .... Southern-B.R.
DB Lem Barney .... Jackson St.
DB Donnie Shell .... South Caro. St.
DB Everson Walls .... Grambling

Division II Records

Individual Records

Official national statistics for all nonmajor four-year colleges began in 1946 with a limited postseason survey. In 1948, the service was expanded to include weekly individual and team statistics rankings in all categories except interceptions, field goals, punt returns and kickoff returns; these categories were added to official individual rankings and records in 1970. In 1992, statistics compilations for individual all-purpose yards and team net punting, punt returns, kickoff returns and turnover margin were begun.

From 1946, individual rankings were by totals. Beginning in 1970, most season individual rankings were by per-game averages. In total offense, receiving yards, all-purpose yards, rushing and scoring, yards or points per game determine rankings; in receiving and interceptions, catches per game; in punt and kickoff returns, yards per return; and in field goals, number made per game. Punting always has been by average, and all team rankings have been per game.

Beginning in 1979, passers were ranked in all divisions on efficiency rating points (see page 6 for explanation).

Before 1967, rankings and records included all four-year colleges that reported their statistics to the NCAA. Beginning with the 1967 season, rankings and records included only members of the NCAA.

In 1973, College Division teams were divided into Division II and Division III under a three-division reorganization plan adopted by the special NCAA Convention on August 1, 1973. Career records of players include only those years in which they competed in Division II.

Collegiate records for all NCAA divisions can be determined by comparing records for all four divisions.

All individual and team statistics rankings include regular-season games only.

Total Offense

(Rushing Plus Passing)

MOST PLAYS

Game

85—Jermaine Whitaker, N.M. Highlands vs. Adams St., Nov. 12, 1994 (486 yards); Dave Walter, Michigan Tech vs. Ferris St., Oct. 18, 1986 (457 yards)

Season

594—Chris Hegg, Truman St., 1985 (3,782 yards)

Per-game record—58.3, Dave Walter, Michigan Tech, 1986 (525 in 9)

Career

2,045—Earl Harvey, N.C. Central, 1985-88 (10,667 yards)

Also holds per-game record at 52.4 (2,045 in 39)

MOST PLAYS BY A FRESHMAN

Season

538—Earl Harvey, N.C. Central, 1985 (3,008 yards)

Also holds per-game record at 53.8 (538 in 10)

MOST YARDS GAINED

Game

623—Perry Klein, LIU-C.W. Post vs. Salisbury St., Nov. 6, 1993 (9 rushing, 614 passing)

Season

4,052—Perry Klein, LIU-C.W. Post, 1993 (295 rushing, 3,757 passing)

Per-game record—411.0, Grady Benton, West Tex. A&M, 1994 (3,699 in 9)

Career

11,227—Vernon Buck, Wingate, 1991-94 (1,343 rushing, 9,884 passing)

Per-game record—323.9, Grady Benton, West Tex. A&M, 1994-95 (5,831 in 18)

MOST SEASONS GAINING 3,000 YARDS OR MORE

2—Chris Hatcher, Valdosta St., 1993 (3,532) & 1994 (3,512); Pat Brennan, Franklin, 1983 (3,239) & 1984 (3,248)

MOST SEASONS GAINING 2,500 YARDS OR MORE

3—Bob McLaughlin, Lock Haven, 1993 (2,928), 1994 (2,996) & 1995 (3,092); Thad Trujillo, Fort Lewis, 1992 (3,047), 1993 (2,784) & 1994 (2,535); Jim Lindsey, Abilene Christian, 1968 (2,740), 1969 (2,646) & 1970 (2,654)

GAINING 2,500 YARDS RUSHING AND 3,000 YARDS PASSING

Career

Jeff Bentrim, North Dak. St., 1983-86 (2,946 rushing, 3,453 passing)

MOST YARDS GAINED BY A FRESHMAN

Game

482—Matt Montgomery, Hampton vs. Tuskegee, Oct. 26, 1991

Season

3,008—Earl Harvey, N.C. Central, 1985 (538 plays)

Per-game record—318.1, Shawn Dupris, Southwest St., 1993 (2,863 in 9)

MOST GAMES GAINING 300 YARDS OR MORE

Season

8—Chris Hegg, Truman St., 1985

Career

16—Thad Trujillo, Fort Lewis, 1991-94

HIGHEST AVERAGE GAIN PER PLAY

Season

(Min. 350 plays) 8.8—Brett Salisbury, Wayne St. (Neb.), 1993 (424 for 3,732)

Career

(Min. 950 plays) 7.4—Donald Smith, Langston, 1958-61 (998 for 7,376)

MOST TOUCHDOWNS RESPONSIBLE FOR (TDs Scored and Passed For)

Game

10—Bruce Swanson, North Park vs. North Central, Oct. 12, 1968 (passed for 10)

Also holds Most Points Responsible For record at 60

Season

50—Chris Hatcher, Valdosta St., 1994 (passed for 50)

Also holds Most Points Responsible For record at 300

Career

120—Chris Hatcher, Valdosta St., 1991-94 (scored 4, passed for 116)

Also holds Most Points Responsible For record at 722

Rushing

MOST RUSHES

Game

62—Nelson Edmonds, Northern Mich. vs. Wayne St. (Mich.), Oct. 26, 1991 (291 yards)

Season

385—Joe Gough, Wayne St. (Mich.), 1994 (1,593 yards)

Per-game record—38.6, Mark Perkins, Hobart, 1968 (309 in 8)

Career

1,072—Bernie Peeters, Luther, 1968-71 (4,435 yards)

Also holds per-game record at 29.8 (1,072 in 36)

MOST CONSECUTIVE RUSHES BY SAME PLAYER

Game

21—Roger Graham, New Haven vs. Knoxville, Oct. 29, 1994 (during six possessions)

MOST RUSHES BY A QUARTERBACK

Career

730—Shawn Graves, Wofford, 1989-92

MOST YARDS GAINED

Half

223—Albert Bland, Mo. Southern St. vs. Washburn, Oct. 29, 1994 (21 rushes)

Game

382—Kelly Ellis, Northern Iowa vs. Western Ill., Oct. 13, 1979 (40 rushes)

Season

2,011—Johnny Bailey, Tex. A&M-Kingsville, 1986 (271 rushes)

Per-game record—188.9, Richard Huntley, Winston-Salem, 1995 (1,889 in 10)

Career

6,320—Johnny Bailey, Tex. A&M-Kingsville, 1986-89 (885 rushes)

Also holds per-game record at 162.1 (6,320 in 39)

MOST YARDS GAINED BY A FRESHMAN

Game

370—Jim Hissam, Marietta vs. Bethany (W.Va.), Nov. 15, 1958 (22 rushes)

Season

2,011—Johnny Bailey, Tex. A&M-Kingsville, 1986 (271 rushes)

Also holds per-game record at 182.8 (2,011 in 11)

MOST YARDS GAINED IN FIRST GAME OF CAREER

238—Johnny Bailey, Tex. A&M-Kingsville vs. Texas Southern, Sept. 6, 1986

MOST YARDS GAINED BY TWO PLAYERS, SAME TEAM

Game

514—Thelbert Withers (333) & Derrick Ray (181), N.M. Highlands vs. Fort Lewis, Oct. 17, 1992

Season

3,526—Johnny Bailey (2,011) & Heath Sherman (1,515), Tex. A&M-Kingsville, 1986

Also hold per-game record at 320.5 (3,526 in 11)

Career

8,594—Johnny Bailey (5,051) & Heath Sherman (3,543), Tex. A&M-Kingsville, 1986-88 (1,317 rushes)

TWO PLAYERS, SAME TEAM, EACH GAINING 200 YARDS OR MORE

Game

Four times. Most recent: Ed Tillison (272) & Jeremy Wilson (204), Northwest Mo. St. vs. Neb.-Kearney, Nov. 11, 1990

TWO PLAYERS, SAME TEAM, EACH GAINING 1,000 YARDS OR MORE

Season

12 times. Most recent: Grand Valley St., 1994—Darnell Jamison (1,022) & Spencer Calhoun (1,018)

MOST GAMES GAINING 100 YARDS OR MORE

Season

11—Ronald Moore, Pittsburg St., 1992; Johnny Bailey, Tex. A&M-Kingsville, 1986

Bailey also holds freshman record at 11

Career

33—Roger Graham, New Haven, 1991-94 (40 games); Johnny Bailey, Tex. A&M-Kingsville, 1986-89 (39 games)

MOST CONSECUTIVE GAMES GAINING 100 YARDS OR MORE

Season

11—Ronald Moore, Pittsburg St., 1992; Johnny Bailey, Tex. A&M-Kingsville, 1986

Bailey also holds freshman record at 11

Career

25—Roger Graham, New Haven, 1992-94

MOST GAMES GAINING 200 YARDS OR MORE

Season

5—Johnny Bailey, Tex. A&M-Kingsville, 1986

Also holds freshman record at 5

Career

11—Johnny Bailey, Tex. A&M-Kingsville, 1986-89 (39 games)

MOST CONSECUTIVE GAMES GAINING 200 YARDS OR MORE
Season
4—Clifton Davis, Fayetteville St., 1993; Johnny Bailey, Tex. A&M-Kingsville, 1986 (first games of his career)

MOST YARDS GAINED BY A QUARTERBACK
Game
323—Shawn Graves, Wofford vs. Lenoir-Rhyne, Sept. 15, 1990 (23 rushes)
Season
1,483—Shawn Graves, Wofford, 1989 (241 rushes)
Career
5,128—Shawn Graves, Wofford, 1989-92 (730 rushes)

MOST SEASONS GAINING 1,000 YARDS OR MORE
Career
4—Jeremy Monroe, Michigan Tech, 1990-93; Johnny Bailey, Tex. A&M-Kingsville, 1986-89

HIGHEST AVERAGE GAIN PER RUSH
Game
(Min. 20 rushes) 17.5—Don Polkinghorne, Washington (Mo.) vs. Wash. & Lee, Nov. 23, 1957 (21 for 367)
Season
(Min. 140 rushes) 10.5—Billy Johnson, Widener, 1972 (148 for 1,556)
(Min. 200 rushes) 8.6—Roger Graham, New Haven, 1992 (200 for 1,717)
(Min. 250 rushes) 7.4—Johnny Bailey, Tex. A&M-Kingsville, 1986 (271 for 2,011)
Career
(Min. 500 rushes) 8.5—Bill Rhodes, Western St., 1953-56 (506 for 4,294)

MOST RUSHING TOUCHDOWNS SCORED
Game
8—Junior Wolf, Okla. Panhandle St. vs. St. Mary (Kan.), Nov. 8, 1958
Season
28—Terry Metcalf, Long Beach St., 1971
Career
72—Shawn Graves, Wofford, 1989-92
Per-game record—1.8, Jeff Bentrim, North Dak. St., 1983-86 (64 in 35)

MOST RUSHING TOUCHDOWNS SCORED BY A FRESHMAN
Season
24—Shawn Graves, Wofford, 1989
Also holds per-game record at 2.2 (24 in 11)

MOST RUSHING TOUCHDOWNS SCORED BY A QUARTERBACK
Season
24—Shawn Graves, Wofford, 1989
Per-game record—2.3, Jeff Bentrim, North Dak. St., 1986 (23 in 10)
Career
72—Shawn Graves, Wofford, 1989-92
Per-game record—1.8, Jeff Bentrim, North Dak. St., 1983-86 (64 in 35)

MOST RUSHING TOUCHDOWNS SCORED BY TWO PLAYERS, SAME TEAM
Season
41—Roger Graham (22) & A. J. Livingston (19), New Haven, 1992; Heath Sherman (23) & Johnny Bailey (18), Tex. A&M-Kingsville, 1986
Per-game record—4.1, Roger Graham & A. J. Livingston, New Haven, 1992 (41 in 10)
Career
106—Heath Sherman (55) & Johnny Bailey (51), Tex. A&M-Kingsville, 1985-88

LONGEST PLAY
99 yards—20 times. Most recent: Thelbert Withers, N.M. Highlands vs. Fort Lewis, Oct. 17, 1992

Passing

HIGHEST PASSING EFFICIENCY RATING POINTS
Season
(Min. 15 atts. per game) 210.1—Boyd Crawford, Col. of Idaho, 1953 (120 attempts, 72 completions, 6 interceptions, 1,462 yards, 21 TD passes)
(Min. 100 comps.) 189.0—Chuck Green, Wittenberg, 1963 (182 attempts, 114 completions, 8 interceptions, 2,181 yards, 19 TD passes)
(Min. 200 comps.) 179.0—Chris Hatcher, Valdosta St., 1994 (430 attempts, 321 completions, 9 interceptions, 3,591 yards, 50 TD passes)
Career
(Min. 375 comps.) 164.0—Chris Petersen, UC Davis, 1985-86 (553 attempts, 385 completions, 13 interceptions, 4,988 yards, 39 TD passes)
(Min. 750 comps.) 153.1—Chris Hatcher, Valdosta St., 1991-94 (1,451 attempts, 1,001 completions, 38 interceptions, 10,878 yards, 116 TD passes)

MOST PASSES ATTEMPTED
Game
74—Jermaine Whitaker, N.M. Highlands vs. Western St., Nov. 5, 1994 (completed 42)
Season
544—Lance Funderburk, Valdosta St., 1995 (completed 356)
Per-game record—50.5, Marty Washington, West Ala., 1993 (404 in 8)
Career
1,719—Bob McLaughlin, Lock Haven, 1992-95 (completed 910)
Per-game record—46.2, Tim Von Dulm, Portland St., 1969-70 (924 in 20)

MOST PASSES COMPLETED
Game
45—Chris Hatcher, Valdosta St. vs. Mississippi Col., Oct. 23, 1993 (attempted 56), and vs. West Ga., Oct. 16, 1993 (attempted 61)
Season
356—Lance Funderburk, Valdosta St., 1995 (attempted 544)
Also holds per-game record at 32.4 (356 in 11)
Career
1,001—Chris Hatcher, Valdosta St., 1991-94 (attempted 1,451)
Also holds per-game record at 25.7 (1,001 in 39)

MOST PASSES COMPLETED BY A FRESHMAN
Game
41—Neil Lomax, Portland St. vs. Montana St., Nov. 19, 1977 (attempted 59)

MOST CONSECUTIVE PASSES COMPLETED
Game
20—Chris Hatcher, Valdosta St. vs. New Haven, Oct. 8, 1994; Rod Bockwoldt, Weber St. vs. South Dak. St., Nov. 6, 1976
Season
23—Mike Ganey, Allegheny, 1967 (completed last 16 attempts vs. Carnegie Mellon, Oct. 9, and first 7 vs. Oberlin, Oct. 16)

HIGHEST PERCENTAGE OF PASSES COMPLETED
Game
(Min. 20 comps.) 90.9%—Rod Bockwoldt, Weber St. vs. South Dak. St., Nov. 6, 1976 (20 of 22)
(Min. 35 comps.) 88.6%—Chris Hatcher, Valdosta St. vs. New Haven, Oct. 8, 1994 (39 of 44)
Season
(Min. 225 atts.) 74.7%—Chris Hatcher, Valdosta St., 1994 (321 of 430)
Career
(Min. 500 atts.) 69.6%—Chris Petersen, UC Davis, 1985-86 (385 of 553)
(Min. 1,000 atts.) 69.0%—Chris Hatcher, Valdosta St., 1991-94 (1,001 of 1,451)

MOST PASSES HAD INTERCEPTED
Game
9—Pat Brennan, Franklin vs. Saginaw Valley, Sept. 24, 1983; Henry Schafer, Johns Hopkins vs. Haverford, Oct. 16, 1965
Season
32—Joe Stetser, Cal St. Chico, 1967 (attempted 464)
Career
88—Bob McLaughlin, Lock Haven, 1992-95 (attempted 1,719)

LOWEST PERCENTAGE OF PASSES HAD INTERCEPTED
Season
(Min. 200 atts.) 0.4%—James Weir, New Haven, 1993 (1 of 266)
(Min. 300 atts.) 1.9%—Matt Hoard, Northern Mich., 1995 (6 of 321)
Career
(Min. 500 atts.) 2.4%—Chris Petersen, UC Davis, 1985-86 (13 of 553)
(Min. 1,000 atts.) 2.6%—Chris Hatcher, Valdosta St., 1991-94 (38 of 1,451)

MOST PASSES ATTEMPTED WITHOUT INTERCEPTION
Game
70—Tim Von Dulm, Portland St. vs. Eastern Wash., Nov. 21, 1970
Season
113—Jeff Allen, New Hampshire, 1975

MOST CONSECUTIVE PASSES ATTEMPTED WITHOUT INTERCEPTION
Season
211—Ken Suhl, New Haven, during 10 games from Sept. 5 to Nov. 14, 1992

MOST YARDS GAINED
Game
614—Alfred Montez, Western N.M. vs. West Tex. A&M, Oct. 8, 1994; Perry Klein, LIU-C.W. Post vs. Salisbury St., Nov. 6, 1993
Season
3,757—Perry Klein, LIU-C.W. Post, 1993
Per-game record—393.4, Grady Benton, West Tex. A&M, 1994 (3,541 in 9)
Career
10,878—Chris Hatcher, Valdosta St., 1991-94
Per-game record—312.1, Grady Benton, West Tex. A&M, 1994-95 (5,618 in 18)

MOST YARDS GAINED BY A FRESHMAN
Game
469—Neil Lomax, Portland St. vs. Montana St., Nov. 19, 1977
Season
3,190—Earl Harvey, N.C. Central, 1985

MOST GAMES GAINING 200 YARDS OR MORE
Season
11—Five times. Most recent: Lance Funderburk, Valdosta St., 1995
Career
31—Chris Hatcher, Valdosta St., 1991-94

MOST CONSECUTIVE GAMES GAINING 200 YARDS OR MORE
Career
28—Chris Hatcher, Valdosta St., during last six games of 1992, all 11 games of 1993 and all 11 games of 1994

MOST GAMES GAINING 300 YARDS OR MORE
Season
10—Brett Salisbury, Wayne St. (Neb.), 1993
Career
16—Chris Hatcher, Valdosta St., 1991-94

MOST CONSECUTIVE GAMES GAINING 300 YARDS OR MORE
Season
10—Brett Salisbury, Wayne St. (Neb.), 1993

MOST YARDS GAINED PER ATTEMPT
Season
(Min. 300 atts.) 11.3—Jayson Merrill, Western St., 1991 (309 for 3,484)
Career
(Min. 500 atts.) 10.6—John Charles, Portland St., 1991-92 (510 for 5,389)
(Min. 700 atts.) 9.0—Bruce Upstill, Col. of Emporia, 1960-63 (769 for 6,935)

MOST YARDS GAINED PER COMPLETION
Season
(Min. 125 comps.) 18.7—Matt Cook, Mo. Southern St., 1991 (141 for 2,637)
(Min. 175 comps.) 17.9—Jayson Merrill, Western St., 1991 (195 for 3,484)
Career
(Min. 300 comps.) 17.8—Jayson Merrill, Western St., 1990-91 (328 for 5,830)
(Min. 600 comps.) 15.4—Earl Harvey, N.C. Central, 1985-88 (690 for 10,621)

MOST TOUCHDOWN PASSES
Quarter
5—Kevin Russell, Calif. (Pa.) vs. Frostburg St., Nov. 5, 1983 (2nd quarter)
Game
10—Bruce Swanson, North Park vs. North Central, Oct. 12, 1968
Season
50—Chris Hatcher, Valdosta St., 1994
Also holds per-game record at 4.5 (50 in 11)
Career
116—Chris Hatcher, Valdosta St., 1991-94
Also holds per-game record at 3.0 (116 in 39)

MOST TOUCHDOWN PASSES BY A FRESHMAN
Game
6—Earl Harvey, N.C. Central vs. Johnson Smith, Nov. 9, 1985
Season
28—Shawn Dupris, Southwest St., 1993

HIGHEST PERCENTAGE OF PASSES FOR TOUCHDOWNS
Season
(Min. 150 atts.) 16.0%—John Ford, Hardin-Simmons, 1949 (26 of 163)
(Min. 300 atts.) 11.6%—Chris Hatcher, Valdosta St., 1994 (50 of 430)
Career
(Min. 500 atts.) 12.2%—Al Niemela, West Chester, 1985-88 (73 of 600)

MOST CONSECUTIVE GAMES THROWING A TOUCHDOWN PASS
Career
24—Matt Cook, Mo. Southern St., 1990-93 (last 2 in 1990, all 11 in 1991, 1 in 1992, all 10 in 1993)

MOST GAMES THROWING A TOUCHDOWN PASS
Career
41—John Craven, Gardner-Webb, 1991-94 (played in 43 games)

LONGEST COMPLETION
99 yards—17 times. Most recent: Ken Collums to Jerome Davis, Central Ark. vs. Delta St., Oct. 1, 1994

Receiving

MOST PASSES CAUGHT
Game
23—Chris George, Glenville St. vs. West Va. Wesleyan, Oct. 15, 1994 (303 yards); Barry Wagner, Alabama A&M vs. Clark Atlanta, Nov. 4, 1989 (370 yards)
Season
119—Brad Bailey, West Tex. A&M, 1994 (1,552 yards)
Per-game record—11.7, Chris George, Glenville St., 1993 (117 in 10)
Career
261—Jon Spinosa, Lock Haven, 1992-95 (2,710 yards)
Per-game record—11.5, Chris George, Glenville St., 1993-94 (230 in 20)

MOST CONSECUTIVE GAMES CATCHING A PASS
Career
43—Jon Spinosa, Lock Haven, 1992-95 (43 of 43 games played)

MOST PASSES CAUGHT BY A TIGHT END
Game
15—By six players. Most recent: Mark Martin, Cal St. Chico vs. San Fran. St., Oct. 21, 1989 (223 yards)
Season
77—Bob Tucker, Bloomsburg, 1967 (1,325 yards)
Career
199—Barry Naone, Portland St., 1985-88 (2,237 yards)

MOST PASSES CAUGHT BY A RUNNING BACK
Season
94—Billy Joe Masters, Evansville, 1987 (960 yards)
Also holds per-game record at 9.4 (94 in 10)
Career
200—Mark Steinmeyer, Kutztown, 1988-91 (2,118 yards)
Per-game record—5.4, Mark Marana, Northern Mich., 1979-80 (107 in 20)

MOST PASSES CAUGHT BY A FRESHMAN
Season
94—Jarett Vito, Emporia St., 1995 (932 yards)

MOST PASSES CAUGHT BY TWO PLAYERS, SAME TEAM
Career
399—Jon Spinosa (218) & Bryan McGinty (181), Lock Haven, 1993-95 (4,615 yards)

MOST YARDS GAINED
Game
370—Barry Wagner, Alabama A&M vs. Clark Atlanta, Nov. 4, 1989 (caught 23)
Season
1,876—Chris George, Glenville St., 1993 (caught 117)
Also holds per-game record at 187.6 (1,876 in 10)
Career
4,468—James Roe, Norfolk St., 1992-95 (caught 239)
Per-game record—160.8, Chris George, Glenville St., 1993-94 (3,215 in 20)

MOST YARDS GAINED BY A TIGHT END
Game
290—Bob Tucker, Bloomsburg vs. Susquehanna, Oct. 7, 1967 (caught 15)
Season
1,325—Bob Tucker, Bloomsburg, 1967 (caught 77)
Career
2,494—Dan Anderson, Northwest Mo. St., 1982-85 (caught 186)

MOST YARDS GAINED BY A RUNNING BACK
Game
209—Don Lenhard, Bucknell vs. Delaware, Nov. 19, 1966 (caught 11)
Season
960—Billy Joe Masters, Evansville, 1987 (caught 94)
Also holds per-game record at 96.0 (960 in 10)
Career
2,118—Mark Steinmeyer, Kutztown, 1988-91 (caught 200)

MOST YARDS GAINED BY TWO PLAYERS, SAME TEAM
Career
6,528—Robert Clark (4,231) & Robert Green (2,297), N.C. Central, 1983-86 (caught 363)

HIGHEST AVERAGE GAIN PER RECEPTION
Season
(Min. 30 receps.) 32.5—Tyrone Johnson, Western St., 1991 (32 for 1,039)
(Min. 40 receps.) 27.6—Chris Harkness, Ashland, 1987 (41 for 1,131)
(Min. 55 receps.) 24.0—Rod Smith, Mo. Southern St., 1991 (60 for 1,439)
Career
(Min. 135 receps.) 22.8—Tyrone Johnson, Western St., 1990-93 (163 for 3,717)
(Min. 180 receps.) 20.1—Robert Clark, N.C. Central, 1983-86 (210 for 4,231)

HIGHEST AVERAGE GAIN PER RECEPTION BY A RUNNING BACK
Season
(Min. 40 receps.) 19.4—John Smith, Boise St., 1975 (45 for 854)
Career
(Min. 80 receps.) 18.1—John Smith, Boise St., 1972-75 (89 for 1,608)

MOST TOUCHDOWN PASSES CAUGHT
Game
8—Paul Zaeske, North Park vs. North Central, Oct. 12, 1968 (11 receptions)
Season
21—Chris Perry, Adams St., 1995 (88 receptions)
Also holds per-game record at 2.1 (21 in 10)
Career
49—Bruce Cerone, Yankton/Emporia St., 1965-66, 1968-69 (241 receptions)
Per-game record—1.6, Ed Bell, Idaho St., 1968-69 (30 in 19)

MOST TOUCHDOWN PASSES CAUGHT BY A TIGHT END
Game
5—Mike Palomino, Portland St. vs. Cal Poly SLO, Nov. 16, 1991; Alex Preuss, Grand Valley St. vs. Winona St., Sept. 17, 1988
Season
13—Bob Tucker, Bloomsburg, 1967

MOST TOUCHDOWN PASSES CAUGHT BY A RUNNING BACK
Season
11—John Smith, Boise St., 1975
Career
24—John Smith, Boise St., 1972-75

MOST TOUCHDOWN PASSES CAUGHT BY A FRESHMAN
Season
11—Charles Davis, Saginaw Valley, 1993; Douglas Grant, Savannah St., 1990; "Red" Roberts, Austin Peay, 1967

HIGHEST PERCENTAGE OF PASSES CAUGHT FOR TOUCHDOWNS
Season
(Min. 10 TDs) 68.8%—Jim Callahan, Temple, 1966 (11 of 16)
Career
(Min. 20 TDs) 30.0%—Bob Cherry, Wittenberg, 1960-63 (27 of 90)

MOST CONSECUTIVE PASSES CAUGHT FOR TOUCHDOWNS
Season
10—Jim Callahan, Temple, 1966 (first 5 games of career)

MOST CONSECUTIVE GAMES CATCHING A TOUCHDOWN PASS
Career
20—Brian Penecale, West Chester, from Oct. 30, 1993, through Oct. 7, 1995

MOST GAMES CATCHING A TOUCHDOWN PASS
Career
27—James Roe, Norfolk St., 1992-95 (in 41 games)

LONGEST RECEPTION
99 yards—17 times. Most recent: Jerome Davis from Ken Collums, Central Ark. vs. Delta St., Oct. 1, 1994

Punting

MOST PUNTS
Game
32—Jan Jones, Sam Houston St. vs. East Tex. St., Nov. 2, 1946 (1,203 yards)
Season
98—John Tassi, Lincoln (Mo.), 1981 (3,163 yards)
Career
328—Dan Brown, Nicholls St., 1976-79 (12,883 yards)

HIGHEST AVERAGE PER PUNT
Game
(Min. 5 punts) 57.5—Tim Baer, Colorado Mines vs. Fort Lewis, Oct. 25, 1986 (8 for 460)
Season
(Min. 20 punts) 49.1—Steve Ecker, Shippensburg, 1965 (32 for 1,570)
(Min. 40 punts) 46.3—Mark Bounds, West Tex. A&M, 1990 (69 for 3,198)
Career
(Min. 100 punts) 44.3—Tim Baer, Colorado Mines, 1986-89 (235 for 10,406)

LONGEST PUNT
97 yards—Earl Hurst, Emporia St. vs. Central Mo. St., Oct. 3, 1964

Interceptions

(From 1970)

MOST PASSES INTERCEPTED
Quarter
3—Anthony Devine, Millersville vs. Cheyney, Oct. 13, 1990 (3rd quarter; 90 yards); Mike McDonald,

Southwestern La. vs. Lamar, Oct. 24, 1970 (4th quarter; 25 yards)

Game

5—By five players. Most recent: Gary Evans, Truman St. vs. Mo.-Rolla, Oct. 18, 1975

Season

14—By five players. Most recent: Luther Howard, Delaware St., 1972 (99 yards); Eugene Hunter, Fort Valley St., 1972 (211 yards)

Per-game record—1.6, Luther Howard, Delaware St., 1972 (14 in 9); Eugene Hunter, Fort Valley St., 1972 (14 in 9); Tom Rezzuti, Northeastern, 1971 (14 in 9)

Career

37—Tom Collins, Indianapolis, 1982-85 (390 yards)

MOST CONSECUTIVE GAMES INTERCEPTING A PASS

Career

8—Darin Nix, Mo.-Rolla, 1993-94

MOST YARDS ON INTERCEPTION RETURNS

Game

152—Desmond Brown, Tuskegee vs. Morris Brown, Sept. 15, 1990 (2 interceptions)

Season

300—Mike Brim, Virginia Union, 1986 (8 interceptions)

Career

504—Anthony Leonard, Virginia Union, 1973-76 (17 interceptions)

HIGHEST AVERAGE GAIN PER INTERCEPTION

Season

(Min. 6 ints.) 40.0—Steve Smith, Bowie St., 1992 (6 for 240)

Career

(Min. 10 ints.) 37.4—Greg Anderson, Montana, 1974-76 (11 for 411)

(Min. 15 ints.) 29.6—Anthony Leonard, Virginia Union, 1973-76 (17 for 504)

MOST TOUCHDOWNS SCORED ON INTERCEPTIONS

Season

4—Clay Blalack, Tenn.-Martin, 1976 (8 interceptions)

LONGEST INTERCEPTION RETURN

100 yards—Many times. Most recent: Brian Oliver, New Haven vs. Bloomsburg, Sept. 2, 1995

Punt Returns

(From 1970)

MOST PUNT RETURNS

Game

12—David Nelson, Ferris St. vs. Northern Mich., Oct. 2, 1993 (240 yards)

Season

61—Armin Anderson, UC Davis, 1984 (516 yards)

Career

153—Armin Anderson, UC Davis, 1983-85 (1,207 yards)

MOST YARDS ON PUNT RETURNS

Game

265—Billy Johnson, Widener vs. St. John's (N.Y.), Sept. 23, 1972 (4 returns)

Season

604—David Nelson, Ferris St., 1993 (50 returns)

Career

1,207—Armin Anderson, UC Davis, 1983-85 (153 returns)

HIGHEST AVERAGE GAIN PER RETURN

Game

(Min. 4 rets.) 66.3—Billy Johnson, Widener vs. St. John's (N.Y.), Sept. 23, 1972 (4 for 265)

Season

(Min. 1.2 rets. per game) 34.1—Billy Johnson, Widener, 1972 (15 for 511)

Career

(Min. 1.2 rets. per game) 26.2—Billy Johnson, Widener, 1971-72 (29 for 759)

MOST TOUCHDOWNS SCORED ON PUNT RETURNS

Game

3—By four players. Most recent: Virgil Seay, Troy St. vs. West Ala., Sept. 29, 1979

Season

4—Michael Fields, Mississippi Col., 1984; Billy Johnson, Widener, 1972

Career

6—Billy Johnson, Widener, 1971-72

LONGEST PUNT RETURN

100 yards—Many times. Most recent: Randy Ladson, Fayetteville St. vs. St. Paul's, Sept. 19, 1987

Kickoff Returns

(From 1970)

MOST KICKOFF RETURNS

Game

12—Johnny Cox, Fort Lewis vs. Mesa St., Nov. 3, 1990

Season

47—Sean Tarrant, Lincoln (Mo.), 1986 (729 yards)

Career

116—Johnny Cox, Fort Lewis, 1990-93 (2,476 yards)

MOST YARDS ON KICKOFF RETURNS

Game

276—Matt Pericolosi, Central Conn. St. vs. Hofstra, Sept. 14, 1991 (6 returns); Tom Dufresne, Hamline vs. Minn.-Duluth, Sept. 30, 1972 (7 returns)

Season

1,002—Doug Parrish, San Fran. St., 1990 (35 returns)

Career

2,630—Dave Ludy, Winona St., 1991-94 (89 returns)

HIGHEST AVERAGE GAIN PER RETURN

Game

(Min. 3 rets.) 71.7—Clarence Martin, Cal Poly SLO vs. Cal Poly Pomona, Nov. 20, 1982 (3 for 215)

Season

(Min. 1.2 rets. per game) 39.4—LaVon Reis, Western St., 1993 (14 for 552)

Career

(Min. 1.2 rets. per game) 34.0—Glen Printers, Southern Colo., 1973-74 (25 for 851)

MOST TOUCHDOWNS SCORED ON KICKOFF RETURNS

Game

2—By four players. Most recent: Lamart Cooper, Wayne St. (Neb.) vs. Moorhead St., Oct. 29, 1994

Season

3—By six players. Most recent: Terry Guess, Gardner-Webb, 1994; Lamart Cooper, Wayne St. (Neb.), 1994; Bobby Felix, Western N.M., 1994

Career

8—Dave Ludy, Winona St., 1991-94

LONGEST KICKOFF RETURN

100 yards—Many times. Most recent: Jurome Lee, Angelo St. vs. West Tex. A&M, Sept. 30, 1995

Total Kick Returns

(Combined Punt and Kickoff Returns)

MOST KICK RETURNS

Season

63—Bobby Yates, Central Mo. St., 1990 (31 kickoffs, 32 punts, 840 yards)

MOST KICK-RETURN YARDS

Career

2,971—Johnny Cox, Fort Lewis, 1990-93 (157 returns, 495 on punt returns, 2,476 on kickoff returns)

MOST TOUCHDOWNS

Career

10—Anthony Leonard, Virginia Union, 1973-76 (6 punt returns, 4 kickoff returns)

MOST CONSECUTIVE TOUCHDOWNS ON KICK RETURNS

Game

2—Kendall James, Carson-Newman vs. Presbyterian, Nov. 13, 1993 (89- & 94-yard kickoff returns); Victor Barnes, Neb.-Omaha vs. Neb.-Kearney, Sept. 8, 1990 (94-yard kickoff return & 79-yard punt return)

All Runbacks

(Combined Interceptions, Punt Returns and Kickoff Returns)

MOST TOUCHDOWNS

Season

6—Terry Guess, Gardner-Webb, 1994 (3 punt returns, 3 kickoff returns); Anthony Leonard, Virginia Union, 1974 (2 interceptions, 2 punt returns, 2 kickoff returns)

Career

13—Anthony Leonard, Virginia Union, 1973-76 (3 interceptions, 6 punt returns, 4 kickoff returns)

LONGEST RETURN OF A MISSED FIELD GOAL

100—Kalvin Simmons, Clark Atlanta vs. Morris Brown, Sept. 5, 1987 (actually from 6 yards in end zone)

Opponent's Punts Blocked

Season

6—Tim Bowie, Northern Colo., 1995

All-Purpose Yards

(Yardage Gained From Rushing, Receiving and All Runbacks)

MOST PLAYS

Season

415—Steve Roberts, Butler, 1989 (325 rushes, 49 receptions, 21 punt returns, 20 kickoff returns; 2,669 yards)

Career

1,195—Steve Roberts, Butler, 1986-89 (1,026 rushes, 120 receptions, 21 punt returns, 28 kickoff returns)

MOST YARDS GAINED

Game

525—Andre Johnson, Ferris St. vs. Clarion, Sept. 16, 1989 (19 rushing, 235 receiving, 10 punt returns, 261 kickoff returns; 17 plays)

Season

2,669—Steve Roberts, Butler, 1989 (1,450 rushing, 532 receiving, 272 punt returns, 415 kickoff returns; 415 plays)

Also holds per-game record at 266.9 (2,669 in 10)

Career

7,803—Johnny Bailey, Tex. A&M-Kingsville, 1986-89 (6,302 rushing, 452 receiving, 20 punt returns, 1,011 kickoff returns)

Per-game record—234.0, Chris George, Glenville St., 1993-94 (4,679 in 20)

MOST YARDS GAINED BY A FRESHMAN

Season

2,425—Johnny Bailey, Tex. A&M-Kingsville, 1986 (2,011 rushing, 54 receiving, 20 punt returns, 340 kickoff returns; 296 plays)

Also holds per-game record at 220.5 (2,425 in 11)

MOST YARDS GAINED BY TWO PLAYERS, SAME TEAM

Season

4,076—Johnny Bailey (2,425) & Heath Sherman (1,651), Tex. A&M-Kingsville, 1986

Also hold per-game record at 370.5 (4,076 in 11)

HIGHEST AVERAGE GAIN PER PLAY

Game

(Min. 15 plays) 30.9—Andre Johnson, Ferris St. vs. Clarion, Sept. 16, 1989 (17 for 525)

Season

(Min. 150 plays, 1,500 yards) 12.9—Billy Johnson, Widener, 1972 (175 for 2,265)

Career

(Min. 300 plays, 4,000 yards) 15.2—Chris George, Glenville St., 1993-94 (307 for 4,679)

Scoring

MOST POINTS SCORED
Game
48—Paul Zaeske, North Park vs. North Central, Oct. 12, 1968 (8 TDs); Junior Wolf, Okla. Panhandle St. vs. St. Mary (Kan.), Nov. 8, 1958 (8 TDs)
Season
178—Terry Metcalf, Long Beach St., 1971 (29 TDs, 4 PATs)
Per-game record—21.0, Carl Herakovich, Rose-Hulman, 1958 (168 in 8)
Career
464—Walter Payton, Jackson St., 1971-74 (66 TDs, 53 PATs, 5 FGs)
Per-game record—13.4, Ole Gunderson, St. Olaf, 1969-71 (362 in 27)

MOST POINTS SCORED BY A FRESHMAN
Season
144—Shawn Graves, Wofford, 1989
Also holds per-game record at 13.1 (144 in 11)

MOST POINTS SCORED BY A QUARTERBACK
Season
144—Shawn Graves, Wofford, 1989
Per-game record—13.8, Jeff Bentrim, North Dak. St., 1986 (138 in 10)
Career
438—Shawn Graves, Wofford, 1989-92
Per-game record—11.0, Jeff Bentrim, North Dak. St., 1983-86 (386 in 35)

MOST POINTS SCORED BY TWO PLAYERS, SAME TEAM
Season
254—Heath Sherman (138) & Johnny Bailey (116), Tex. A&M-Kingsville, 1986
Career
666—Heath Sherman (336) & Johnny Bailey (330), Tex. A&M-Kingsville, 1986-88

MOST TOUCHDOWNS SCORED
Game
8—Paul Zaeske, North Park vs. North Central, Oct. 12, 1968 (all on pass receptions); Junior Wolf, Okla. Panhandle St. vs. St. Mary (Kan.), Nov. 8, 1958 (all by rushing)
Season
29—Terry Metcalf, Long Beach St., 1971
Per-game record—3.1, Carl Herakovich, Rose-Hulman, 1958 (25 in 8)
Career
72—Shawn Graves, Wofford, 1989-92
Per-game record—2.2, Ole Gunderson, St. Olaf, 1969-71 (60 in 27)

MOST TOUCHDOWNS SCORED BY A FRESHMAN
Season
24—Shawn Graves, Wofford, 1989
Also holds per-game record at 2.2 (24 in 11)

MOST TOUCHDOWNS SCORED BY A QUARTERBACK
Season
24—Shawn Graves, Wofford, 1989
Per-game record—2.3, Jeff Bentrim, North Dak. St., 1986 (23 in 10)
Career
72—Shawn Graves, Wofford, 1989-92
Per-game record—1.8, Jeff Bentrim, North Dak. St., 1983-86 (64 in 35)

MOST TOUCHDOWNS SCORED BY TWO PLAYERS, SAME TEAM
Season
42—Heath Sherman (23) & Johnny Bailey (19), Tex. A&M-Kingsville, 1986
Career
110—Heath Sherman (56) & Johnny Bailey (54), Tex. A&M-Kingsville, 1986-88

MOST CONSECUTIVE GAMES SCORING A TOUCHDOWN
Career
22—Billy Johnson, Widener, 1971-72

MOST EXTRA POINTS MADE BY KICKING
Game
14—Art Anderson, North Park vs. North Central, Oct. 12, 1968 (attempted 15); Matt Johnson, Connecticut vs. Newport Naval Training, Oct. 22, 1949 (attempted 17)
Season
71—John O'Riordan, New Haven, 1993 (attempted 78)
Career
163—Miguel Sagaro, Grand Valley St., 1989-92 (attempted 179)

MOST EXTRA POINTS ATTEMPTED BY KICKING
Game
17—Matt Johnson, Connecticut vs. Newport Naval Training, Oct. 22, 1949 (made 14)
Season
78—John O'Riordan, New Haven, 1993 (made 71)
Career
179—Miguel Sagaro, Grand Valley St., 1989-92 (made 163); James Jenkins, Pittsburg St., 1988-91 (made 156)

HIGHEST PERCENTAGE OF EXTRA POINTS MADE BY KICKING
Season
(Best perfect season) 100.0%—Bryan Thompson, Angelo St., 1989 (51 of 51)
Career
(Min. 90 atts.) 98.9%—Mark DeMoss, Liberty, 1980-83 (92 of 93)
(Min. 130 atts.) 93.7%—Billy Watkins, East Tex. St., 1990-93 (134 of 143)

MOST CONSECUTIVE EXTRA POINTS MADE BY KICKING
Season
51—Bryan Thompson, Angelo St., 1989 (entire season)
Career
82—Mark DeMoss, Liberty (from Sept. 13, 1980, to Oct. 1, 1983; ended with missed PAT vs. Central St., Oct. 1, 1983)

MOST POINTS SCORED BY KICKING
Game
20—Clarence Joseph, Central St. vs. Kentucky St., Oct. 16, 1982 (5 FGs, 5 PATs)
Season
93—Michael Geary, Indiana (Pa.), 1993 (15 FGs, 48 PATs)
Also holds per-game record at 9.3 (93 in 10)
Career
281—Billy Watkins, East Tex. St., 1990-93 (49 FGs, 134 PATs)
Per-game record *(min. 145 pts.)*—8.3, Dave Austinson, Truman St., 1981-82 (149 in 18)
Per-game record *(min. 200 pts.)*—6.7, Eddie Loretto, UC Davis, 1985-88 (266 in 40)

Defensive Extra Points

MOST DEFENSIVE EXTRA POINTS SCORED
Game and Season
1—Many times

LONGEST DEFENSIVE EXTRA POINT BLOCKED-KICK RETURN
99—Robert Fair (DB), Carson-Newman vs. Mars Hill, Oct. 15, 1994 (scored)

LONGEST DEFENSIVE EXTRA POINT FUMBLE RETURN
87—Rod Beauchamp (DB), Colorado Mines vs. Hastings, Sept. 3, 1988

LONGEST DEFENSIVE EXTRA POINT INTERCEPTION RETURN
100—Brian Muldrow (CB), St. Francis (Ill.) vs. Northwood, Oct. 8, 1994 (scored); Morice Mabry (DB), UC Davis vs. St. Mary's (Cal.), Sept. 28, 1991 (scored)

Fumble Returns

LONGEST FUMBLE RETURN
94—Ken Rose, Grand Valley St. vs. Ferris St., Oct. 1, 1994 (scored)

Field Goals

MOST FIELD GOALS MADE
Game
6—Steve Huff, Central Mo. St. vs. Southeast Mo. St., Nov. 2, 1985 (37, 45, 37, 24, 32, 27 yards; 6 attempts)
Season
20—Raul De la Flor, Humboldt St., 1993 (26 attempts); Pat Beaty, North Dak., 1988 (26 attempts); Tom Jurich, Northern Ariz., 1977 (29 attempts)
Per-game record—1.9, Dennis Hochman, Sonoma St., 1986 (19 in 10); Jaime Nunez, Weber St., 1971 (19 in 10)
Career
64—Mike Wood, Southeast Mo. St., 1974-77 (109 attempts)
Also holds per-game record at 1.5 (64 in 44)

MOST CONSECUTIVE FIELD GOALS MADE
Career
14—Keith Kasnic, Tenn.-Martin, 1982-83; Kurt Seibel, South Dak., 1982-83

MOST FIELD GOALS ATTEMPTED
Game
7—Jim Turcotte, Mississippi Col. vs. Troy St., Oct. 3, 1981 (made 2)
Season
35—Mike Wood, Southeast Mo. St., 1977 (made 16)
Per-game record—3.3, Skipper Butler, Texas-Arlington, 1968 (33 in 10)
Career
109—Mike Wood, Southeast Mo. St., 1974-77 (made 64)
Per-game record—2.7, Jaime Nunez, Weber St., 1969-71 (83 in 31)

HIGHEST PERCENTAGE OF FIELD GOALS MADE
Season
(Min. 15 atts.) 88.2%—Howie Guarini, Shippensburg, 1990 (15 of 17); Kurt Seibel, South Dak., 1983 (15 of 17)
(Min. 20 atts.) 86.4%—Dennis Hochman, Sonoma St., 1986 (19 of 22)
Career
(Min. 35 made) 80.0%—Bill May, Clarion, 1977-80 (48 of 60)

LONGEST FIELD GOAL
67 yards—Tom Odle, Fort Hays St. vs. Washburn, Nov. 5, 1988
Special reference: Ove Johannson, Abilene Christian (not an NCAA-member institution at the time), kicked a 69-yard field goal against East Tex. St., Oct. 16, 1976

Team Records

SINGLE GAME—Offense

Total Offense

MOST YARDS GAINED
910—Hanover vs. Franklin, Oct. 30, 1948 (426 rushing, 484 passing; 75 plays)

MOST PLAYS
117—Tex. A&M-Kingsville vs. Angelo St., Oct. 30, 1982 (96 rushes, 21 passes; 546 yards)

HIGHEST AVERAGE GAIN PER PLAY
12.1—Hanover vs. Franklin, Oct. 30, 1948 (75 for 910)

MOST TOUCHDOWNS SCORED BY RUSHING AND PASSING
15—North Park vs. North Central, Oct. 12, 1968 (4 by rushing, 11 by passing)

MOST TOUCHDOWNS SCORED BY RUSHING AND PASSING, BOTH TEAMS
20—North Park (15) & North Central (5), Oct. 12, 1968

MOST YARDS GAINED BY A LOSING TEAM
645—Tex. A&M-Kingsville vs. West Tex. A&M, Nov. 1, 1986 (lost 54-49)

Rushing

MOST YARDS GAINED
719—Coe vs. Beloit, Oct. 16, 1971 (73 rushes)

MOST RUSHES
97—Hobart vs. Union (N.Y.), Oct. 23, 1971 (444 yards)

HIGHEST AVERAGE GAIN PER RUSH (Min. 50 Rushes)
11.2—Wofford vs. Charleston So., Nov. 12, 1994 (53 for 595)

MOST TOUCHDOWNS SCORED BY RUSHING
12—Coe vs. Beloit, Oct. 16, 1971

MOST PLAYERS, ONE TEAM, EACH GAINING 100 YARDS OR MORE
5—South Dak. vs. St. Cloud St., Nov. 1, 1986 (James Hambrick 125, Darryl Colvin 123, Tony Higgins 118, Dave Elle 109, Joe Longueville [QB] 106; team gained 581)

Passing

MOST PASSES ATTEMPTED
85—West Tex. A&M vs. Eastern N.M., Nov. 5, 1994 (completed 47)

MOST PASSES ATTEMPTED, BOTH TEAMS
121—Franklin (68) & Saginaw Valley (53), Sept. 22, 1984 (completed 63)

MOST PASSES COMPLETED
49—West Ala. vs. Jacksonville St., Nov. 7, 1992 (attempted 84)

MOST PASSES COMPLETED, BOTH TEAMS
72—Western N.M. (39) & West Tex. A&M (33), Oct. 8, 1994 (attempted 111)

MOST PASSES HAD INTERCEPTED
11—Hamline vs. Concordia-M'head, Nov. 5, 1955; Rhode Island vs. Brown, Oct. 8, 1949

MOST PASSES ATTEMPTED WITHOUT INTERCEPTION
63—Hamline vs. St. John's (Minn.), Oct. 8, 1955 (completed 34)

HIGHEST PERCENTAGE OF PASSES COMPLETED (Min. 20 Attempts)
90.0%—Northwestern St. vs. Southwestern La., Nov. 12, 1966 (20 of 22)

MOST YARDS GAINED
678—Portland St. vs. Mont. St.-Billings, Nov. 20, 1976

MOST YARDS GAINED, BOTH TEAMS
1,065—Western N.M. (614) & West Tex. A&M (451), Oct. 8, 1994

MOST TOUCHDOWN PASSES
11—North Park vs. North Central, Oct. 12, 1968

MOST TOUCHDOWN PASSES, BOTH TEAMS
14—North Park (11) & North Central (3), Oct. 12, 1968

Punting

MOST PUNTS
32—Sam Houston St. vs. East Tex. St., Nov. 2, 1946 (1,203 yards)

MOST PUNTS, BOTH TEAMS
63—Sam Houston St. (32) & East Tex. St. (31), Nov. 2, 1946

HIGHEST AVERAGE PER PUNT (Min. 5 Punts)
57.5—Colorado Mines vs. Fort Lewis, Oct. 21, 1989 (8 for 460)

Punt Returns

MOST YARDS ON PUNT RETURNS
265—Widener vs. St. John's (N.Y.), Sept. 23, 1972 (4 returns)

MOST TOUCHDOWNS SCORED ON PUNT RETURNS
3—Troy St. vs. West Ala., Sept. 29, 1979; Widener vs. St. John's (N.Y.), Sept. 23, 1972

Scoring

MOST POINTS SCORED
125—Connecticut vs. Newport Naval Training, Oct. 22, 1949

MOST POINTS SCORED AGAINST A COLLEGE OPPONENT
106—Fort Valley St. vs. Knoxville, Oct. 11, 1969 (14 TDs, 2 PATs, 9 two-point conversions, 1 safety)

MOST POINTS SCORED BY A LOSING TEAM
60—New Haven vs. Southern Conn. St. (64), Oct. 25, 1991

MOST POINTS SCORED, BOTH TEAMS
136—North Park (104) & North Central (32), Oct. 12, 1968

MOST POINTS SCORED IN TWO CONSECUTIVE GAMES
172—Tuskegee, 1966 (93-0 vs. Morehouse, Oct. 14; 79-0 vs. Lane, Oct. 22)

MOST POINTS OVERCOME TO WIN A GAME
28—Ferris St. (46) vs. Saginaw Valley (42), Nov. 11, 1995 (trailed 28-0 with 11:17 remaining in 2nd quarter)

MOST POINTS SCORED IN A BRIEF PERIOD OF TIME
21 in 1:20—Winona St. vs. Bemidji St., Oct. 15, 1994 (turned 14-0 game into 35-0 in first quarter)

MOST TOUCHDOWNS SCORED
17—Connecticut vs. Newport Naval Training, Oct. 22, 1949

MOST TOUCHDOWNS SCORED AGAINST A COLLEGE OPPONENT
15—North Park vs. North Central, Oct. 12, 1968; Alcorn St. vs. Paul Quinn, Sept. 9, 1967; Iowa Wesleyan vs. William Penn, Oct. 31, 1953

MOST SAFETIES SCORED
3—Fort Valley St. vs. Miles, Oct. 16, 1993

MOST POINTS AFTER TOUCHDOWN MADE BY KICKING
14—North Park vs. North Central, Oct. 12, 1968 (attempted 15); Connecticut vs. Newport Naval Training, Oct. 22, 1949 (attempted 17)

MOST TWO-POINT ATTEMPTS
11—Fort Valley St. vs. Knoxville, Oct. 11, 1969 (made 9)

MOST TWO-POINT ATTEMPTS MADE
9—Fort Valley St. vs. Knoxville, Oct. 11, 1969 (attempted 11)

MOST FIELD GOALS MADE
6—Central Mo. St. vs. Southeast Mo. St., Nov. 2, 1985 (6 attempts)

MOST DEFENSIVE EXTRA POINTS SCORED
1—By many teams

MOST DEFENSIVE EXTRA-POINT OPPORTUNITIES
2—North Dak. St. vs. Augustana (S.D.), Sept. 24, 1988 (2 interceptions; none scored)

First Downs

MOST TOTAL FIRST DOWNS
42—Delaware vs. Baldwin-Wallace, Oct. 6, 1973

MOST FIRST DOWNS BY PENALTY
14—La Verne vs. Northern Ariz., Oct. 11, 1958

MOST TOTAL FIRST DOWNS, BOTH TEAMS
66—North Dak. (36) & Tex. A&M-Kingsville (30), Sept. 13, 1986; Ferris St. (33) & Northwood (33), Oct. 26, 1985

Penalties

MOST PENALTIES
28—Northern Ariz. vs. La Verne, Oct. 11, 1958 (155 yards)

MOST PENALTIES, BOTH TEAMS
42—N.C. Central (23) & St. Paul's (19), Sept. 13, 1986 (453 yards)

MOST YARDS PENALIZED
293—Cal Poly SLO vs. Portland St., Oct. 31, 1981 (26 penalties)

MOST YARDS PENALIZED, BOTH TEAMS
453—N.C. Central (256) & St. Paul's (197), Sept. 13, 1986 (42 penalties)

Fumbles

MOST FUMBLES
16—Carthage vs. North Park, Nov. 14, 1970 (lost 7)

SINGLE GAME—Defense

Total Defense

FEWEST TOTAL OFFENSE PLAYS ALLOWED
29—North Park vs. Concordia (Ill.), Sept. 26, 1964

FEWEST TOTAL OFFENSE YARDS ALLOWED
Minus 69—Fort Valley St. vs. Miles, Oct. 16, 1993 (39 plays)

FEWEST RUSHES ALLOWED
7—Indianapolis vs. Valparaiso, Oct. 30, 1982 (-57 yards)

FEWEST RUSHING YARDS ALLOWED
Minus 95—San Diego St. vs. U.S. Int'l, Nov. 27, 1965 (35 plays)

FEWEST PASS COMPLETIONS ALLOWED
0—By many teams. Most recent: Delta St. vs. Mississippi Col., Nov. 11, 1995 (attempted 4)

FEWEST PASSING YARDS ALLOWED
Minus 19—Ashland vs. Heidelberg, Sept. 25, 1948 (completed 4)

MOST QUARTERBACK SACKS
19—Southern Conn. St. vs. Albany (N.Y.), Oct. 6, 1984

Punting

MOST OPPONENT'S PUNTS BLOCKED BY
5—Winston-Salem vs. N.C. Central, Oct. 4, 1986; Southeastern La. vs. Troy St., Oct. 7, 1978 (holds record for most consecutive punts blocked with 4)

Interceptions

MOST PASSES INTERCEPTED BY
11—St. Cloud St. vs. Bemidji St., Oct. 31, 1970 (45 attempts); Concordia-M'head vs. Hamline, Nov. 5, 1955 (37 attempts)

MOST TOUCHDOWNS ON INTERCEPTION RETURNS
3—By many teams. Most recent: Fort Valley St. vs. North Ala., Oct. 12, 1991

SEASON—Offense

Total Offense

MOST YARDS GAINED
6,284—West Tex. A&M, 1994 (931 plays, 11 games)
Per-game record—624.1, Hanover, 1948 (4,993 in 8)

HIGHEST AVERAGE GAIN PER PLAY
(Min. 500 plays) 9.2—Hanover, 1948 (543 for 4,993)
(Min. 800 plays) 6.7—West Tex. A&M, 1994 (931 for 6,284)

MOST PLAYS PER GAME
88.7—Cal St. Chico, 1967 (887 in 10)

Rushing

MOST YARDS GAINED
4,347—Tex. A&M-Kingsville, 1986 (689 rushes, 11 games)
Per-game record—404.8, Col. of Emporia, 1954 (3,643 in 9)

HIGHEST AVERAGE GAIN PER RUSH
(Min. 300 rushes) 8.4—Hanover, 1948 (382 for 3,203)
(Min. 600 rushes) 6.3—Tex. A&M-Kingsville, 1986 (689 for 4,347)

MOST RUSHES PER GAME
78.9—Panhandle St., 1963 (789 in 10)

Passing

MOST YARDS GAINED
5,000—West Tex. A&M, 1994 (363 completions, 11 games)
Also holds per-game record at 454.5 (5,000 in 11)

HIGHEST AVERAGE GAIN PER ATTEMPT (Min. 175 Attempts)
10.8—Western St., 1991 (330 for 3,574)

HIGHEST AVERAGE GAIN PER COMPLETION
(Min. 100 comps.) 19.4—Calif. (Pa.), 1966 (116 for 2,255)
(Min. 200 comps.) 17.6—Western St., 1991 (203 for 3,574)

MOST PASSES ATTEMPTED
623—Emporia St., 1995 (completed 322)
Also holds per-game record at 56.6 (623 in 11)

MOST PASSES COMPLETED
373—Valdosta St., 1995 (attempted 570)
Also holds per-game record at 33.9 (373 in 11)

FEWEST PASSES COMPLETED PER GAME
0.4—Hobart, 1971 (4 in 9)

HIGHEST PERCENTAGE COMPLETED (Min. 200 Attempts)
70.8%—Valdosta St., 1993 (363 of 513)

LOWEST PERCENTAGE OF PASSES HAD INTERCEPTED (Min. 275 Attempts)
0.7%—New Haven, 1993 (2 of 296)

MOST TOUCHDOWN PASSES PER GAME
4.9—San Fran. St., 1967 (49 in 10)

HIGHEST PASSING EFFICIENCY RATING POINTS
(Min. 200 atts.) 183.8—Wittenberg, 1963 (216 attempts, 138 completions, 10 interceptions, 2,457 yards, 22 TDs)
(Min. 300 atts.) 180.2—Western St., 1991 (330 attempts, 203 completions, 12 interceptions, 3,574 yards, 35 TDs)

Punting

MOST PUNTS PER GAME
10.0—Wash. & Lee, 1968 (90 in 9)

FEWEST PUNTS PER GAME
1.9—Kent, 1954 (17 in 9)

HIGHEST PUNTING AVERAGE
48.0—Adams St., 1966 (36 for 1,728)

Punt Returns

MOST PUNT RETURNS
64—UC Davis, 1984 (557 yards)

MOST TOUCHDOWNS SCORED ON PUNT RETURNS
5—Northern Colo., 1995 (41 returns)

Kickoff Returns

MOST KICKOFF RETURNS
73—Lock Haven, 1995 (1,255 yards); Catawba, 1994 (1,368 yards); Lock Haven, 1993 (1,257 yards)

Scoring

MOST POINTS PER GAME
54.7—New Haven, 1993 (547 in 10)

MOST TOUCHDOWNS PER GAME
7.8—New Haven, 1993 (78 in 10)

MOST CONSECUTIVE EXTRA POINTS MADE BY KICKING
51—Angelo St., 1989 (entire season)

MOST CONSECUTIVE FIELD GOALS MADE
13—UC Davis, 1976

MOST TWO-POINT ATTEMPTS PER GAME
6.8—Florida A&M, 1961 (61 in 9, made 32)

MOST TWO-POINT ATTEMPTS MADE PER GAME
3.6—Florida A&M, 1961 (32 in 9, attempted 61)

MOST FIELD GOALS MADE
20—Humboldt St., 1993 (attempted 26); North Dak., 1988 (attempted 26); Northern Ariz., 1977 (attempted 29)

MOST DEFENSIVE EXTRA POINTS SCORED
2—UC Davis, 1991 (1 blocked kick return, 1 interception)

MOST DEFENSIVE EXTRA-POINT OPPORTUNITIES
3—UC Davis, 1991 (2 interceptions, 1 blocked kick return; two scored); Central Okla., 1989 (2 blocked kick returns, 1 interception; one scored); Northern Colo., 1988 (2 blocked kick returns, 1 interception; none scored)

Penalties

MOST PENALTIES AGAINST
146—Portland St., 1994 (1,340 yards); Gardner-Webb, 1992 (1,344 yards)
Per-game record—14.6, Portland St., 1994 (146 in 10)

MOST YARDS PENALIZED
1,356—Hampton, 1977 (124 penalties, 11 games)

Turnovers (Giveaways)

(From 1985)

FEWEST TURNOVERS
8—Lenoir-Rhyne, 1994 (4 interceptions, 4 fumbles lost)
Also holds per-game record at 0.8 (8 in 10)

MOST TURNOVERS
61—Cheyney, 1990 (36 interceptions, 25 fumbles lost)
Per-game record—5.8, Livingstone, 1986 (58 in 10)

FEWEST FUMBLES LOST
2—Michigan Tech, 1995 (9 fumbles)

SEASON—Defense

Total Defense

FEWEST YARDS ALLOWED PER GAME
44.4—John Carroll, 1962 (311 in 7)

LOWEST AVERAGE YARDS ALLOWED PER PLAY
(Min. 300 plays) 1.0—John Carroll, 1962 (310 for 311 yards)
(Min. 600 plays) 1.8—Alcorn St., 1976 (603 for 1,089)

Rushing Defense

FEWEST YARDS ALLOWED PER GAME
Minus 16.7—Tennessee St., 1967 (-150 in 9)

LOWEST AVERAGE YARDS ALLOWED PER RUSH
(Min. 250 rushes) Minus 0.5—Tennessee St., 1967 (296 for -150 yards)
(Min. 400 rushes) 1.3—Luther, 1971 (414 for 518)

Pass Defense

FEWEST YARDS ALLOWED PER GAME
10.1—Ashland, 1948 (91 in 9)

FEWEST YARDS ALLOWED PER ATTEMPT
(Min. 200 atts.) 3.1—Virginia St., 1971 (205 for 630)
(Min. 300 atts.) 3.2—Southwest Mo. St., 1966 (315 for 996)

FEWEST YARDS ALLOWED PER COMPLETION (Min. 100 Completions)
8.8—Long Beach St., 1965 (144 for 1,264)

LOWEST COMPLETION PERCENTAGE ALLOWED (Min. 250 Attempts)
24.1%—Southwest Mo. St., 1966 (76 of 315)

MOST PASSES INTERCEPTED BY PER GAME
3.9—Whitworth, 1959 (35 in 9); Delaware, 1946 (35 in 9)

FEWEST PASSES INTERCEPTED BY (Min. 150 Attempts)
1—Gettysburg, 1972 (175 attempts; 0 yards returned)

HIGHEST PERCENTAGE INTERCEPTED BY
(Min. 150 atts.) 21.7%—Stephen F. Austin, 1949 (35 of 161)
(Min. 275 atts.) 11.8%—Mo.-Rolla, 1978 (35 of 297)

MOST TOUCHDOWNS ON INTERCEPTION RETURNS
7—Gardner-Webb, 1992 (35 interceptions); Fort Valley St., 1991 (15 interceptions); Virginia Union, 1986 (31 interceptions)

LOWEST PASSING EFFICIENCY RATING ALLOWED (Min. 250 Attempts)
41.7—Fort Valley St., 1985 (allowed 283 attempts, 90 completions, 1,039 yards, 2 TDs and intercepted 33)

Blocked Kicks

MOST BLOCKED KICKS
27—Winston-Salem, 1986 (16 punts, 7 field goal attempts, 4 point-after-touchdown kicks)

Scoring

FEWEST POINTS ALLOWED PER GAME
0.0—Albany St. (Ga.), 1960 (0 in 9 games)

MOST POINTS ALLOWED PER GAME
64.5—Rose-Hulman, 1961 (516 in 8)

Turnovers (Takeaways)

(From 1985)

HIGHEST TURNOVER MARGIN PER GAME
2.7—Hillsdale, 1993 (plus 30 in 11; 11 giveaways vs. 41 takeaways)

MOST TAKEAWAYS
56—Gardner-Webb, 1992 (35 interceptions, 21 fumble recoveries)
Also holds per-game record at 5.1 (56 in 11)

Additional Records

MOST CONSECUTIVE VICTORIES
34—Hillsdale (from Oct. 2, 1954, to Nov. 16, 1957; ended with 27-26 loss to Pittsburg St., Dec. 21, 1957)

MOST CONSECUTIVE VICTORIES OVER DIVISION II OPPONENT
40—North Ala. (current, from Sept. 4, 1993)

MOST CONSECUTIVE HOME VICTORIES
28—North Dak. St. (from Sept. 12, 1964, to Nov. 1, 1969; ended with 14-14 tie vs. Eastern Mich., Sept. 12, 1970)

MOST CONSECUTIVE GAMES UNBEATEN
54—Morgan St. (from Nov. 5, 1931, to Nov. 18, 1938; ended with 15-0 loss to Virginia St., Nov. 30, 1938)

MOST CONSECUTIVE VICTORIES OVER ONE OPPONENT
40—West Chester vs. Millersville (from Nov. 18, 1922, to Oct. 5, 1974; ended with 17-12 loss Oct. 4, 1975)

MOST CONSECUTIVE VICTORIES OVER ONE OPPONENT IN AN UNINTERRUPTED SERIES (Must have played in consecutive years)
25—UC Davis vs. San Fran. St. (from Sept. 26, 1970, to Nov. 12, 1994; San Fran. St. dropped football program after 1994 season)

MOST CONSECUTIVE GAMES WITHOUT BEING SHUT OUT
178—North Dak. (from Oct. 7, 1967, to Nov. 10, 1984; ended with 41-0 loss to Northern Ariz., Aug. 31, 1985)

MOST CONSECUTIVE WINNING SEASONS
31—West Chester (from 1940-72; ended with 5-5-0 record in 1973)

MOST CONSECUTIVE NON-LOSING SEASONS
33—West Chester (from 1940-74; ended with 4-5-0 record in 1975)

MOST CONSECUTIVE LOSSES
39—St. Paul's (from Oct. 23, 1948, to Oct. 24, 1953; ended with 7-6 win over Delaware St., Oct. 31, 1953)

MOST CONSECUTIVE GAMES WITHOUT A VICTORY
49—Paine (1954-61, includes 1 tie)

MOST CONSECUTIVE GAMES WITHOUT A TIE
329—West Chester (from Oct. 26, 1945, to Oct. 31, 1980; ended with 24-24 tie vs. Cheyney, Nov. 8, 1980)

MOST TIE GAMES IN A SEASON
5—Wofford, 1948 (Sept. 25 to Oct. 23, consecutive)

HIGHEST-SCORING TIE GAME
54-54—Norfolk St. vs. Winston-Salem, Oct. 9, 1993

MOST CONSECUTIVE QUARTERS WITHOUT YIELDING A RUSHING TOUCHDOWN
51—Butler (from Sept. 25, 1982, to Oct. 15, 1983)

MOST CONSECUTIVE POINT-AFTER-TOUCHDOWN KICKS MADE
123—Liberty (from 1976 to Sept. 10, 1983; ended with missed PAT vs. Saginaw Valley, Sept. 10, 1983)

MOST IMPROVED WON-LOST RECORD
11 games—Northern Mich., 1975 (13-1, including three Division II playoff victories, from 0-10 in 1974)

Annual Champions, All-Time Leaders

Total Offense

CAREER YARDS PER GAME

(Minimum 5,000 Yards)

Player, Team	Years	G	Plays	Yards	Yd. PG
Grady Benton, West Tex. A&M	1994-95	18	844	5,831	*323.9
Marty Washington, West Ala.	1992-93	17	773	5,212	306.6
Scott Otis, Glenville St.	1994-95	20	755	5,911	295.6
Jayson Merrill, Western St.	1990-91	20	641	5,619	281.0
Jermaine Whitaker, N.M. Highlands	1992-94	31	1,374	8,650	279.0
Chris Petersen, UC Davis	1985-86	20	735	5,532	276.6
Tim Von Dulm, Portland St.	1969-70	20	989	5,501	275.1
Vernon Buck, Wingate	1991-94	41	1,761	*11,227	273.8
Chris Hatcher, Valdosta St.	1991-94	39	1,557	10,588	271.5
Chris Hegg, Truman St.	1984-85	20	930	5,418	270.9
June Jones, Portland St.	1975-76	21	760	5,590	266.2
Troy Mott, Wayne St. (Neb.)	1991-92	20	943	5,212	260.6
Earl Harvey, N.C. Central	1985-88	41	*2,045	10,667	260.2
Jim Zorn, Cal Poly Pomona	1973-74	21	946	5,364	255.4
Steve Wray, Franklin	1979, 81-82	26	1,178	6,564	252.5
Bob McLaughlin, Lock Haven	1992-95	44	2,007	11,041	250.9
Thad Trujillo, Fort Lewis	1991-94	41	1,787	10,209	249.0
Rob Tomlinson, Cal St. Chico	1988-91	40	1,656	9,921	248.0
Pat Brennan, Franklin	1981-84	30	1,286	7,316	243.9
Carl Wright, Virginia Union	1989-91	31	1,104	7,517	242.5
Dave MacDonald, West Chester	1991-94	36	1,257	8,453	234.8
Jim Lindsey, Abilene Christian	1967-70	36	1,510	8,385	232.9

*Record.

SEASON YARDS PER GAME

Player, Team	Year	G	Plays	Yards	Yd. PG
Grady Benton, West Tex. A&M	†1994	9	505	3,699	*411.0
Perry Klein, LIU-C.W. Post	†1993	10	499	*4,052	405.2
Marty Washington, West Ala.	1993	8	453	3,146	393.3
Brett Salisbury, Wayne St. (Neb.)	1993	10	424	3,732	373.2
Jed Drenning, Glenville St.	1993	10	473	3,593	359.3
Alfred Montez, Western N.M.	1994	6	244	2,130	355.0
Rob Tomlinson, Cal St. Chico	†1989	10	534	3,525	352.5
Chris Hegg, Truman St.	†1985	11	*594	3,782	343.8
Bob Toledo, San Fran. St.	†1967	10	409	3,407	340.7
Jayson Merrill, Western St.	†1991	10	337	3,400	340.0
John Charles, Portland St.	†1992	8	303	2,708	338.5
Aaron Sparrow, Norfolk St.	†1995	10	464	3,300	330.0
George Bork, Northern Ill.	†1963	9	413	2,945	327.2
Richard Strasser, San Fran. St.	1985	10	536	3,259	325.9
Pat Brennan, Franklin	†1984	10	583	3,248	324.8
Pat Brennan, Franklin	†1983	10	524	3,239	323.9
Kevin Vickers, Tarleton St.	1994	10	487	3,232	323.2
Lance Funderburk, Valdosta St.	1995	11	581	3,549	322.6
Jamie Pass, Mankato St.	1993	11	543	3,537	321.5
Tod Mayfield, West Tex. St.	†1986	11	555	3,533	321.2

*Record. †National champion.

CAREER YARDS

Player, Team	Years	Plays	Yards
Vernon Buck, Wingate	1991-94	1,761	*11,227
Bob McLaughlin, Lock Haven	1992-95	2,007	11,041
Earl Harvey, N.C. Central	1985-88	*2,045	10,667
Chris Hatcher, Valdosta St.	1991-94	1,557	10,588
Thad Trujillo, Fort Lewis	1991-94	1,787	10,209
Rob Tomlinson, Cal St. Chico	1988-91	1,656	9,921
John Craven, Gardner-Webb	1991-94	1,666	9,630
Sam Mannery, Calif. (Pa.)	1987-90	1,669	9,125
Andy Breault, Kutztown	1989-92	1,459	8,975
Jermaine Whitaker, N.M. Highlands	1992-94	1,374	8,650
Dave MacDonald, West Chester	1991-94	1,257	8,453
Jim Lindsey, Abilene Christian	1967-70	1,510	8,385
Dave Walter, Michigan Tech	1983-86	1,660	8,345
Maurice Heard, Tuskegee	1988-91	1,289	8,321
Aaron Sparrow, Norfolk St.	1992-95	1,345	8,301
Jack Hull, Grand Valley St.	1988-91	1,196	8,221
Dave DenBraber, Ferris St.	1984-87	1,522	8,115
Tracy Kendall, Alabama A&M	1988-91	1,480	8,112
Bill Bair, Mansfield	1989-92	1,352	8,101
Ned Cox, Angelo St.	1983-86	1,831	8,097
Matt Montgomery, Hampton	1991-94	1,220	8,091
Heath Rylance, Augustana (S.D.)	1991-94	1,667	7,883
Rex Lamberti, Abilene Christian	1984-86, 93	1,223	7,546
Carl Wright, Virginia Union	1989-91	1,104	7,517
John St. Jacques, Santa Clara	1988-89, 91-92	1,219	7,505

*Record.

SEASON YARDS

Player, Team	Year	G	Plays	Yards
Perry Klein, LIU-C.W. Post	†1993	10	499	*4,052
Chris Hegg, Truman St.	†1985	11	*594	3,782
Brett Salisbury, Wayne St. (Neb.)	1993	10	424	3,732
Grady Benton, West Tex. A&M	†1994	9	505	3,699
Jed Drenning, Glenville St.	1993	10	473	3,593
Lance Funderburk, Valdosta St.	1995	11	581	3,549
Jamie Pass, Mankato St.	1993	11	543	3,537
Tod Mayfield, West Tex. A&M	†1986	11	555	3,533
Chris Hatcher, Valdosta St.	1993	11	495	3,532
Rob Tomlinson, Cal St. Chico	†1989	10	534	3,525
Chris Hatcher, Valdosta St.	1994	11	452	3,512
June Jones, Portland St.	†1976	11	465	3,463
Bob Toledo, San Fran. St.	†1967	10	409	3,407
Jayson Merrill, Western St.	†1991	10	337	3,400
Gregory Clark, Virginia St.	1993	11	425	3,386
Vernon Buck, Wingate	1993	11	463	3,307
Aaron Sparrow, Norfolk St.	†1995	10	464	3,300
Dave MacDonald, West Chester	1994	11	512	3,286
Richard Strasser, San Fran. St.	1985	10	536	3,259
Pat Brennan, Franklin	†1984	10	583	3,248

*Record. †National champion.

SINGLE-GAME YARDS

Yds.	Player, Team (Opponent)	Date
623	Perry Klein, LIU-C.W. Post (Salisbury St.)	Nov. 6, 1993
614	Alfred Montez, Western N.M. (West Tex. A&M)	Oct. 8, 1994
591	Marty Washington, West Ala. (Nicholls St.)	Sept. 11, 1993
584	Tracy Kendall, Alabama A&M (Clark Atlanta)	Nov. 4, 1989
580	Grady Benton, West Tex. A&M (Howard Payne)	Sept. 17, 1994
575	Scott Otis, Glenville St. (West Va. Wesleyan)	Oct. 15, 1994
573	Pat Graham, Augustana, S.D. (Mankato St.)	Oct. 28, 1995
571	John Charles, Portland St. (Cal Poly SLO)	Nov. 16, 1991
569	Bob McLaughlin, Lock Haven (Calif., Pa.)	Oct. 29, 1994
562	Bob Toledo, San Fran. St. (Cal St. Hayward)	Oct. 21, 1967
555	A. J. Vaughn, Wayne St., Mich. (Wis.-Milwaukee)	Sept. 30, 1967
542	Perry Klein, LIU-C.W. Post (Gannon)	Oct. 9, 1993
536	Earl Harvey, N.C. Central (Jackson St.)	Aug. 30, 1986
528	Rob Tomlinson, Cal St. Chico (Southern Conn. St.)	Oct. 7, 1989
526	Dwayne Butler, Dist. Columbia (Central St.)	Nov. 20, 1982
526	Dennis Shaw, San Diego St. (Southern Miss.)	Nov. 9, 1968

ANNUAL CHAMPIONS

Year	Player, Team	Class	Plays	Yards
1946	Buster Dixon, Abilene Christian	Sr.	170	960
1947	Jim Peterson, Hanover	So.	108	1,449
1948	Jim Peterson, Hanover	Jr.	130	1,589
1949	Connie Callahan, Morningside	Sr.	311	2,006
1950	Bob Heimerdinger, Northern Ill.	Jr.	286	1,782
1951	Bob Heimerdinger, Northern Ill.	Sr.	292	1,775
1952	Don Gottlob, Sam Houston St.	Sr.	303	2,470
1953	Ralph Capitani, Northern Iowa	Jr.	317	1,755
1954	Bill Engelhardt, Neb.-Omaha	So.	243	1,645
1955	Jim Stehlin, Brandeis	Sr.	222	1,455
1956	Dick Jamieson, Bradley	So.	240	1,925
1957	Stan Jackson, Cal Poly Pomona	Jr.	301	2,145
1958	Stan Jackson, Cal Poly Pomona	Sr.	334	2,478
1959	Gary Campbell, Whittier	Sr.	309	2,383
1960	Charles Miller, Austin	Sr.	287	1,966
1961	Denny Spurlock, Whitworth	Sr.	224	1,684
1962	George Bork, Northern Ill.	Jr.	397	2,398
1963	George Bork, Northern Ill.	Sr.	413	2,945
1964	Jerry Bishop, Austin	Jr.	332	2,152
1965	Ron Christian, Northern Ill.	Sr.	377	2,307
1966	Joe Stetser, Cal St. Chico	Jr.	406	2,382
1967	Bob Toledo, San Fran. St.	Sr.	409	3,407
1968	Terry Bradshaw, Louisiana Tech	Jr.	426	2,987
1969	Tim Von Dulm, Portland St.	Jr.	462	2,736

Beginning in 1970, ranked on per-game (instead of total) yards

Year	Player, Team	Class	G	Plays	Yards	Avg.
1970	Jim Lindsey, Abilene Christian	Sr.	9	440	2,654	294.9
1971	Randy Mattingly, Evansville	Jr.	9	402	2,234	248.2
1972	Bob Biggs, UC Davis	Sr.	9	381	2,356	261.8
1973	Jim Zorn, Cal Poly Pomona	Jr.	11	499	3,000	272.7
1974	Jim McMillan, Boise St.	Sr.	10	403	3,101	310.1
1975	Lynn Hieber, Indiana (Pa.)	Sr.	10	402	2,503	250.3
1976	June Jones, Portland St.	Sr.	11	465	3,463	314.8
1977	Steve Mariucci, Northern Mich.	Sr.	8	270	1,780	222.5
1978	Charlie Thompson, Western St.	Jr.	9	304	2,138	237.6
1979	Phil Kessel, Northern Mich.	Jr.	9	368	2,164	240.4
1980	Curt Strasheim, Southwest St.	Jr.	10	501	2,565	256.5
1981	Steve Wray, Franklin	Jr.	10	488	2,726	272.6
1982	Steve Wray, Franklin	Sr.	8	382	2,114	264.3
1983	Pat Brennan, Franklin	Jr.	10	524	3,239	323.9
1984	Pat Brennan, Franklin	Sr.	10	583	3,248	324.8
1985	Chris Hegg, Truman St.	Sr.	11	*594	3,782	343.8
1986	Tod Mayfield, West Tex. A&M	Sr.	11	555	3,533	312.2
1987	Randy Hobson, Evansville	Sr.	10	457	2,964	296.4
1988	Mark Sedinger, Northern Colo.	Sr.	10	413	2,828	282.8
1989	Rob Tomlinson, Cal St. Chico	So.	10	534	3,525	352.5
1990	Andy Breault, Kutztown	Jr.	11	562	3,173	288.5
1991	Jayson Merrill, Western St.	Sr.	10	337	3,400	340.0
1992	John Charles, Portland St.	Sr.	8	303	2,708	338.5
1993	Perry Klein, LIU-C.W. Post	Sr.	10	499	*4,052	405.2
1994	Grady Benton, West Tex. A&M	Jr.	9	505	3,699	*411.0
1995	Aaron Sparrow, Norfolk St.	Sr.	10	464	3,300	330.0

*Record.

Rushing

CAREER YARDS PER GAME

(Minimum 2,500 Yards)

Player, Team	Years	G	Plays	Yards	Yd. PG
Johnny Bailey, Tex. A&M-Kingsville	1986-89	39	885	*6,320	*162.1
Ole Gunderson, St. Olaf	1969-71	27	639	4,060	150.4
Richard Huntley, Winston-Salem	1992-95	42	932	6,286	149.7
Roger Graham, New Haven	1991-94	40	821	5,953	148.8
Brad Hustad, Luther	1957-59	27	655	3,943	146.0
Quincy Tillmon, Emporia St.	1990-92, 94	29	790	4,141	142.8
Joe Iacone, West Chester	1960-62	27	565	3,767	139.5
Leonard Davis, Lenoir-Rhyne	$1990-94	35	839	4,853	138.7
Don Aleksiewicz, Hobart	1969-72	34	819	4,525	133.1
Jim VanWagner, Michigan Tech	1973-76	36	958	4,788	133.0
Steve Roberts, Butler	1986-89	35	1,026	4,623	132.1

*Record. $See page 6 for explanation.

SEASON YARDS PER GAME

Player, Team	Year	G	Plays	Yards	TD	Yd. PG
Richard Huntley, Winston-Salem	†1995	10	273	1,889	16	*188.9
Fred Lane, Lane	1995	10	273	1,833	19	183.3
Johnny Bailey, Tex. A&M-Kingsville	†1986	11	271	*2,011	18	182.8
Bob White, Western N.M.	†1951	9	202	1,643	20	182.6
Kevin Mitchell, Saginaw Valley	†1989	8	236	1,460	6	182.5
Don Aleksiewicz, Hobart	†1971	9	276	1,616	19	179.6
Jim Holder, Panhandle St.	†1963	10	275	1,775	9	177.5
Jim Baier, Wis.-River Falls	†1966	9	240	1,587	17	176.3
Keith Higdon, Cheyney	†1993	10	330	1,742	17	174.2
Leonard Davis, Lenoir-Rhyne	†1994	9	216	1,559	19	173.2
Billy Johnson, Widener	†1972	9	148	1,556	23	172.9
Hank Treesh, Hanover	†1948	8	100	1,383	17	172.9
Dave Kiarsis, Trinity (Conn.)	†1970	8	201	1,374	10	171.8
Roger Graham, New Haven	†1992	10	200	1,717	22	171.7

*Record. †National champion.

CAREER YARDS

Player, Team	Years	Plays	Yards	Avg.
Johnny Bailey, Tex. A&M-Kingsville	1986-89	885	*6,320	7.14
Richard Huntley, Winston-Salem	1992-95	932	6,286	6.74
Roger Graham, New Haven	1991-94	821	5,953	7.25
Shawn Graves, Wofford	1989-92	730	5,128	7.02
Chris Cobb, Eastern Ill.	1976-79	930	5,042	5.42
Harry Jackson, St. Cloud St.	1986-89	915	4,890	5.34
Leonard Davis, Lenoir-Rhyne	$1990-94	839	4,853	5.78
Jerry Linton, Okla. Panhandle St.	1959-62	648	4,839	7.47
Jim VanWagner, Michigan Tech	1973-76	958	4,788	5.00
Jeremy Monroe, Michigan Tech	1990-93	666	4,661	7.00
Heath Sherman, Tex. A&M-Kingsville	1985-88	804	4,654	5.79
Steve Roberts, Butler	1986-89	1,026	4,623	4.51
Don Aleksiewicz, Hobart	1969-72	819	4,525	5.53
Dale Mills, Truman St.	1957-60	751	4,502	5.99
Scott Schulte, Hillsdale	1990-93	879	4,495	5.11
Leo Lewis, Lincoln (Mo.)	1951-54	623	4,458	7.16
Bernie Peeters, Luther	1968-71	*1,072	4,435	4.14
Larry Schreiber, Tennessee Tech	1966-69	878	4,421	5.04
Brad Rowland, McMurry	1947-50	683	4,347	6.36
Ronald Moore, Pittsburg St.	1989-92	619	4,299	6.95
Bill Rhodes, Western St.	1953-56	506	4,294	*8.49
Lem Harkey, Col. of Emporia	1951-54	502	4,232	8.43
Shannon Burnell, North Dak.	1990-93	828	4,218	5.09
Joe Gough, Wayne St. (Mich.)	1991-94	996	4,204	4.22
Curtis Delgardo, Portland St.	1987-90	703	4,178	5.94

*Record. $See page 6 for explanation.

SEASON YARDS

Player, Team	Year	G	Plays	Yards	Avg.
Johnny Bailey, Tex. A&M-Kingsville	†1986	11	271	*2,011	‡7.42
Richard Huntley, Winston-Salem	†1995	10	273	1,889	6.92
Ronald Moore, Pittsburg St.	1992	11	239	1,864	7.80
Fred Lane, Lane	1995	10	273	1,833	6.71
Zed Robinson, Southern Utah	1991	11	254	1,828	7.20
Richard Huntley, Winston-Salem	1994	11	251	1,815	7.23
Fred Lane, Lane	1994	11	280	1,779	6.35
Jim Holder, Panhandle St.	†1963	10	275	1,775	6.45
Keith Higdon, Cheyney	†1993	10	330	1,742	5.28
Mike Thomas, UNLV	†1973	11	274	1,741	6.35
Roger Graham, New Haven	†1992	10	200	1,717	+8.59
Joe Simmons, N.C. Central	1993	11	249	1,699	6.82
Roger Graham, New Haven	1993	10	182	1,687	9.27
Terry Metcalf, Long Beach St.	1971	12	273	1,673	6.13
Troy Mills, Cal St. Sacramento	1991	10	223	1,668	7.48
Larry Jackson, Edinboro	1994	10	274	1,660	6.06
Leon Burns, Long Beach St.	†1969	11	350	1,659	4.74
Chad Guthrie, Truman St.	1991	11	302	1,649	5.46
Bob White, Western N.M.	†1951	9	202	1,643	8.13
Joe Aska, Central Okla.	1994	10	278	1,629	5.86

**Record. †National champion. ‡Record for minimum 250 rushes. +Record for minimum 200 rushes.*

SINGLE-GAME YARDS

Yds.	Player, Team (Opponent)	Date
382	Kelly Ellis, Northern Iowa (Western Ill.)	Oct. 13, 1979
373	Dallas Garber, Marietta (Wash. & Jeff.)	Nov. 7, 1959
370	Jim Baier, Wis.-River Falls (Wis.-Stevens Point)	Nov. 5, 1966
370	Jim Hissam, Marietta (Bethany, W.Va.)	Nov. 15, 1958
367	Don Polkinghorne, Washington, Mo. (Wash. & Lee)	Nov. 23, 1957
363	Richie Weaver, Widener (Moravian)	Oct. 17, 1970
361	Richard Huntley, Winston-Salem (Virginia Union)	Nov. 5, 1994
356	Ole Gunderson, St. Olaf (Monmouth, Ill.)	Oct. 11, 1969
350	Ricke Stonewall, Millersville (New Haven)	Nov. 13, 1982
343	Zed Robinson, Southern Utah (Santa Clara)	Oct. 12, 1991
343	Jesse Lakes, Central Mich. (Wis.-Milwaukee)	Sept. 27, 1969
342	Leonard Davis, Lenoir-Rhyne (Gardner-Webb)	Oct. 9, 1993
337	Harry Jackson, St. Cloud St. (South Dak.)	Nov. 4, 1989
333	Thelbert Withers, N.M. Highlands (Fort Lewis)	Oct. 17, 1992
329	Chris Pulliams, Ferris St. (Saginaw Valley)	Nov. 11, 1995

ANNUAL CHAMPIONS

Year	Player, Team	Class	Plays	Yards
1946	V. T. Smith, Abilene Christian	So.	99	733
1947	John Williams, Jacksonville St.	Jr.	150	931
1948	Hank Treesh, Hanover	Jr.	100	1,383
1949	Odie Posey, Southern-B.R.	Jr.	121	1,399
1950	Meriel Michelson, Eastern Wash.	Sr.	180	1,234
1951	Bob White, Western N.M.	Jr.	202	1,643
1952	Al Conway, William Jewell	Sr.	134	1,325
1953	Elroy Payne, McMurry	So.	183	1,274
1954	Lem Harkey, Col. of Emporia	Sr.	121	1,146
1955	Gene Scott, Centre	Sr.	107	1,138
1956	Bill Rhodes, Western St.	Sr.	130	1,200
1957	Brad Hustad, Luther	So.	219	1,401
1958	Dale Mills, Truman St.	So.	186	1,358
1959	Dale Mills, Truman St.	Jr.	248	1,385
1960	Joe Iacone, West Chester	So.	199	1,438
1961	Bobby Lisa, St. Mary (Kan.)	Jr.	156	1,082
1962	Jerry Linton, Okla. Panhandle St.	Sr.	272	1,483
1963	Jim Holder, Okla. Panhandle St.	Sr.	275	1,775
1964	Jim Allison, San Diego St.	Sr.	174	1,186
1965	Allen Smith, Findlay	Jr.	207	1,240
1966	Jim Baier, Wis.-River Falls	Sr.	240	1,587
1967	Dickie Moore, Western Ky.	Jr.	208	1,444
1968	Howard Stevens, Randolph-Macon	Fr.	191	1,468
1969	Leon Burns, Long Beach St.	Jr.	350	1,659

Beginning in 1970, ranked on per-game (instead of total) yards

Year	Player, Team	Class	G	Plays	Yards	Avg.
1970	Dave Kiarsis, Trinity (Conn.)	Sr.	8	201	1,374	171.8
1971	Don Aleksiewicz, Hobart	Jr.	9	276	1,616	179.6
1972	Billy Johnson, Widener	So.	9	148	1,556	172.9
1973	Mike Thomas, UNLV	Jr.	11	274	1,741	158.3
1974	Jim VanWagner, Michigan Tech	So.	9	246	1,453	161.4
1975	Jim VanWagner, Michigan Tech	Jr.	9	289	1,331	147.9
1976	Ted McKnight, Minn.-Duluth	Sr.	10	220	1,482	148.2
1977	Bill Burnham, New Hampshire	Sr.	10	281	1,422	142.2
1978	Mike Harris, Truman St.	Sr.	11	329	1,598	145.3
1979	Chris Cobb, Eastern Ill.	Sr.	11	293	1,609	146.3
1980	Louis Jackson, Cal Poly SLO	Sr.	10	287	1,424	142.4
1981	Rick Porter, Slippery Rock	Sr.	9	208	1,179	131.0
1982	Ricke Stonewall, Millersville	So.	10	191	1,387	138.7
1983	Mark Corbin, Central St.	So.	10	208	1,502	150.2
1984	Charles Sanders, Slippery Rock	Jr.	10	269	1,280	128.0
1985	Dan Sonnek, South Dak. St.	So.	11	303	1,518	138.0
1986	Johnny Bailey, Tex. A&M-Kingsville	Fr.	11	271	2,011	182.8
1987	Johnny Bailey, Tex. A&M-Kingsville	So.	10	217	1,598	159.8
1988	Johnny Bailey, Tex. A&M-Kingsville	Jr.	10	229	1,442	144.2
1989	Kevin Mitchell, Saginaw Valley	Jr.	8	236	1,460	182.5
1990	David Jones, Chadron St.	Sr.	10	225	1,570	157.0
1991	Quincy Tillmon, Emporia St.	So.	9	259	1,544	171.6
1992	Roger Graham, New Haven	So.	10	200	1,717	171.7
1993	Keith Higdon, Cheyney	Sr.	10	330	1,742	174.2
1994	Leonard Davis, Lenoir-Rhyne	Sr.	9	216	1,559	173.2
1995	Richard Huntley, Winston-Salem	Sr.	10	273	1,889	*188.9

**Record.*

DIVISION II

Passing

CAREER PASSING EFFICIENCY
(Minimum 375 Completions)

Player, Team	Years	Att.	Cmp.	Int.	Pct.	Yards	TD	Pts.
Chris Petersen, UC Davis	1985-86	553	385	13	*.696	4,988	39	*164.0
Chris Hatcher, Valdosta St.	1991-94	1,451	*1,001	38	‡.690	*10,878	*116	+153.1
Jim McMillan, Boise St.	1971-74	640	382	29	.597	5,508	58	152.8
Jack Hull, Grand Valley St.	1988-91	835	485	22	.581	7,120	64	149.7
Scott Otis, Glenville St.	1994-95	693	421	21	.608	5,563	56	148.8
Grady Benton, West Tex. A&M	1994-95	686	421	22	.614	5,618	49	147.3
Bruce Upstill, Col. of Emporia	1960-63	769	438	36	.570	6,935	48	144.0
George Bork, Northern Ill.	1960-63	902	577	33	.640	6,782	60	141.8
June Jones, Portland St.	1975-76	658	375	34	.570	5,798	41	141.2
Steve Mariucci, Northern Mich.	1974-77	678	380	33	.561	6,022	41	140.9
Scott Barry, UC Davis	1982-84	588	377	16	.641	4,421	33	140.4
Matt Cook, Mo. Southern St.	$1989-93	816	411	29	.504	6,715	63	137.9
Aaron Sparrow, Norfolk St.	1992-95	1,117	615	38	.551	8,758	79	137.5
Chris Crawford, Portland St.	1985-88	954	588	35	.616	7,543	48	137.3
Trevor Spradley, Southwest Baptist	1990-92	712	441	27	.619	5,881	29	137.2
Dan Miles, Southern Ore.	1964-67	871	577	56	.662	6,531	52	136.1
Al Niemela, West Chester	1985-88	1,063	600	36	.564	7,853	73	134.4
Jody Dickerson, Edinboro	1991-94	845	447	42	.529	6,787	60	133.9
Denny Spurlock, Whitworth	1958-61	723	388	48	.537	5,526	63	133.4
Jeff Tisdel, Nevada	1974-77	776	394	34	.508	6,098	59	133.1

**Record. ‡Record for minimum 1,000 attempts. +Record for minimum 750 completions. $See page 6 for explanation.*

Photo from Glenville State sports information

Glenville State quarterback Scott Otis' career passing efficiency rating of 148.8 is the fifth best in Division II history among passers with 375 or more completions.

Photo from West Texas A&M sports information

Quarterback Grady Benton averaged 312.1 passing yards per game, the best in Division II history, during his two years at West Texas A&M.

SEASON PASSING EFFICIENCY

(Minimum 15 Attempts Per Game)

Player, Team	Year	G	Att.	Cmp.	Int.	Pct.	Yards	TD	Pts.
Boyd Crawford, Col. of Idaho	†1953	8	120	72	6	.600	1,462	21	*210.1
Chuck Green, Wittenberg	†1963	9	182	114	8	.626	2,181	19	+189.0
Jayson Merrill, Western St.	†1991	10	309	195	11	.631	3,484	35	188.1
Jim Feely, Johns Hopkins	†1967	7	110	69	5	.627	1,264	12	186.2
John Charles, Portland St.	1991	11	247	147	7	.595	2,619	32	185.7
Steve Smith, Western St.	†1992	10	271	180	5	.664	2,719	30	183.5
Jim Peterson, Hanover	†1948	8	125	81	12	.648	1,571	12	182.9
John Wristen, Southern Colo.	†1982	8	121	68	2	.562	1,358	13	182.6
John Charles, Portland St.	1992	8	263	179	7	.681	2,770	24	181.3
Richard Basil, Savannah St.	†1989	9	211	120	7	.569	2,148	29	181.1
Chris Hatcher, Valdosta St.	†1994	11	430	321	9	*.747	3,591	*50	‡179.0
Jim Cahoon, Ripon	†1964	8	127	74	7	.583	1,206	19	176.4
Ken Suhl, New Haven	1992	10	239	148	5	.619	2,336	26	175.7
Tony Aliucci, Indiana (Pa.)	†1990	10	181	111	10	.613	1,801	21	172.2
James Weir, New Haven	†1993	10	266	161	1	.605	2,336	31	172.0
Shawn Behr, Fort Hays St.	†1995	11	318	191	6	.600	3,158	31	171.9
John Costello, Widener	†1956	9	149	74	10	.497	1,702	17	169.8
Kurt Coduti, Michigan Tech	1992	9	155	92	3	.594	1,518	15	169.7
Chris Petersen, UC Davis	†1985	10	242	167	6	.690	2,366	17	169.4
Mike Rieker, Lehigh	†1977	11	230	137	14	.596	2,431	23	169.2

Record. †National champion. +Record for minimum 100 completions. ‡Record for minimum 200 completions.

CAREER YARDS PER GAME

(Minimum 4,500 Yards)

Player, Team	Years	G	Att.	Cmp.	Int.	Pct.	Yards	TD	Avg.
Grady Benton, West Tex. A&M	1994-95	18	686	421	22	.614	5,618	49	*312.1
Tim Von Dulm, Portland St.	1969-70	20	924	500	41	.541	5,967	51	298.4
Marty Washington, West Ala.	1992-93	17	690	379	25	.549	5,018	40	295.2
Jayson Merrill, Western St.	1990-91	20	580	328	25	.566	5,830	56	291.5
John Charles, Portland St.	1991-92	19	510	326	14	.639	5,389	56	283.6
Chris Hatcher, Valdosta St.	1991-94	39	1,451	*1,001	38	‡.690	*10,878	*116	278.9
Scott Otis, Glenville St.	1994-95	20	693	421	21	.608	5,563	56	278.2
June Jones, Portland St.	1975-76	21	658	375	34	.570	5,798	41	276.1
Jermaine Whitaker, N.M. Highlands	1992-94	31	1,150	625	45	.543	8,532	71	275.2
Steve Wray, Franklin	1979, 81-82	26	1,070	511	40	.478	7,019	56	270.0
Earl Harvey, N.C. Central	1985-88	40	1,442	690	81	.479	10,621	86	265.5
Chris Hegg, Truman St.	1984-85	20	771	410	32	.532	5,306	44	265.3
Pat Brennan, Franklin	1981-84	30	1,123	535	62	.476	7,717	53	257.2
Jay McLucas, New Haven	1989-90	20	699	370	30	.529	5,139	37	257.0
Troy Mott, Wayne St. (Neb.)	1991-92	20	757	437	37	.577	5,003	25	250.2
Chris Petersen, UC Davis	1985-86	20	553	385	13	*.696	4,988	39	249.4
Rich Ingold, Indiana (Pa.)	1983-85	26	852	499	36	.586	6,454	48	248.2
Jeff Phillips, Central Mo. St.	1986-88	26	892	496	54	.556	6,294	46	242.1
Bob McLaughlin, Lock Haven	1992-95	44	*1,719	910	*88	.529	10,640	60	241.8
Vernon Buck, Wingate	1991-94	41	1,393	728	61	.523	9,884	72	241.1
Thad Trujillo, Fort Lewis	1991-94	41	1,455	760	57	.522	9,873	78	240.8
Joe Stetser, Cal St. Chico	1966-67	20	813	394	48	.485	4,803	40	240.2
Leonard Williams, Tenn.-Martin	1990-91	19	594	305	21	.513	4,518	40	237.8
Jim Lindsey, Abilene Christian	1967-70	36	1,237	642	69	.519	8,521	61	236.7

Record. ‡Record for minimum 1,000 attempts.

SEASON YARDS PER GAME

Player, Team	Year	G	Att.	Cmp.	Int.	Pct.	Yards	TD	Avg.
Grady Benton, West Tex. A&M	1994	9	409	258	13	.631	3,541	30	*393.4
Marty Washington, West Ala.	1993	8	404	221	13	.547	3,062	26	382.8
Perry Klein, LIU-C.W. Post	1993	10	407	248	18	.609	*3,757	38	375.7
Brett Salisbury, Wayne St. (Neb.)	1993	10	395	276	14	.699	3,729	29	372.9
Alfred Montez, Western N.M.	1994	6	231	133	7	.576	2,182	18	363.7
Bob Toledo, San Fran. St.	1967	10	396	211	24	.533	3,513	45	351.3
Pat Brennan, Franklin	1983	10	458	226	30	.493	3,491	25	349.1
Jayson Merrill, Western St.	†1991	10	309	195	11	.631	3,484	35	348.4
John Charles, Portland St.	1992	8	263	179	7	.681	2,770	24	346.3
Aaron Sparrow, Norfolk St.	1995	10	409	238	14	.581	3,434	32	343.4
George Bork, Northern Ill.	†1963	9	374	244	12	.652	3,077	32	341.9
Chris Hegg, Truman St.	†1985	11	503	284	20	.565	3,741	32	340.1
Jed Drenning, Glenville St.	1993	10	390	244	12	.626	3,391	25	339.1
Lance Funderburk, Valdosta St.	1995	11	*544	*356	12	.654	3,706	26	336.9
Pat Brennan, Franklin	1984	10	502	238	20	.474	3,340	18	334.0
Tod Mayfield, West Tex. A&M	1986	11	515	317	20	.615	3,664	31	333.1
Chris Hatcher, Valdosta St.	1993	11	471	335	11	.711	3,651	37	331.9
Richard Strasser, San Fran. St.	1985	10	452	250	19	.553	3,317	20	331.7
Shawn Dupris, Southwest St.	1993	9	373	220	14	.590	2,955	28	328.3
Chris Hatcher, Valdosta St.	†1994	11	430	321	9	*.747	3,591	*50	326.5

Record. †National champion.

CAREER YARDS

Player, Team	Years	Att.	Cmp.	Int.	Pct.	Yards	TD
Chris Hatcher, Valdosta St.	1991-94	1,451	*1,001	38	‡.690	*10,878	*116
Bob McLaughlin, Lock Haven	1992-95	*1,719	910	*88	.529	10,640	60
Earl Harvey, N.C. Central	1985-88	1,442	690	81	.479	10,621	86
John Craven, Gardner-Webb	1991-94	1,535	828	82	.539	9,934	80
Vernon Buck, Wingate	1991-94	1,393	728	61	.523	9,884	72
Thad Trujillo, Fort Lewis	1991-94	1,455	760	57	.522	9,873	78
Rob Tomlinson, Cal St. Chico	1988-91	1,328	748	43	.563	9,434	52
Andy Breault, Kutztown	1989-92	1,259	733	63	.582	9,086	86
Aaron Sparrow, Norfolk St.	1992-95	1,117	615	38	.551	8,758	79
Sam Mannery, Calif. (Pa.)	1987-90	1,283	649	68	.506	8,680	64
Dave DenBraber, Ferris St.	1984-87	1,254	661	45	.527	8,536	52
Jermaine Whitaker, N.M. Highlands	1992-94	1,150	625	45	.543	8,532	71
Jim Lindsey, Abilene Christian	1967-70	1,237	642	69	.519	8,521	61
Dave MacDonald, West Chester	1991-94	1,123	604	46	.538	8,449	82
Maurice Heard, Tuskegee	1988-91	1,134	556	54	.490	8,434	87
John St. Jacques, Santa Clara	1988-89, 91-92	1,060	543	36	.512	7,968	68
Rex Lamberti, Abilene Christian	1984-86, 93	1,133	595	44	.525	7,934	84
Al Niemela, West Chester	1985-88	1,063	600	36	.564	7,853	73
Ned Cox, Angelo St.	1983-86	1,205	589	58	.489	7,843	56
Matt Montgomery, Hampton	1991-94	1,036	545	34	.526	7,839	63
Loyal Proffitt, Abilene Christian	1981-84	1,157	550	80	.475	7,824	54
Pat Brennan, Franklin	1981-84	1,123	535	62	.476	7,717	53
Chris Crawford, Portland St.	1985-88	954	588	35	.616	7,543	48
Bill Bair, Mansfield	1989-92	1,041	617	44	.593	7,531	56
Chris Fagan, Millersville	1989-92	1,098	556	52	.506	7,362	48

**Record. ‡Record for minimum 1,000 attempts.*

SEASON YARDS

Player, Team	Year	G	Att.	Cmp.	Int.	Pct.	Yards	TD
Perry Klein, LIU-C.W. Post	1993	10	407	248	18	.609	*3,757	38
Chris Hegg, Truman St.	1985	11	503	284	20	.565	3,741	32
Brett Salisbury, Wayne St. (Neb.)	1993	10	395	276	14	.699	3,729	29
Lance Funderburk, Valdosta St.	1995	11	*544	*356	12	.654	3,706	26
Tod Mayfield, West Tex. A&M	1986	11	515	317	20	.616	3,664	31
Chris Hatcher, Valdosta St.	1993	11	471	335	11	.711	3,651	37
Chris Hatcher, Valdosta St.	†1994	11	430	321	9	*.747	3,591	*50
Grady Benton, West Tex. A&M	1994	9	409	258	13	.631	3,541	30
June Jones, Portland St.	†1976	11	423	238	24	.563	3,518	25
Bob Toledo, San Fran. St.	1967	10	396	211	24	.533	3,513	45
Pat Brennan, Franklin	1983	10	458	226	30	.493	3,491	25
Jayson Merrill, Western St.	†1991	10	309	195	11	.631	3,484	35
Gregory Clark, Virginia St.	1993	11	380	227	11	.597	3,437	38
Aaron Sparrow, Norfolk St.	1995	10	409	238	14	.581	3,434	32
Jed Drenning, Glenville St.	1993	10	390	244	12	.626	3,391	25
Pat Brennan, Franklin	1984	10	502	238	20	.474	3,340	18
Phil Basso, Liberty	1984	11	426	250	15	.587	3,326	24
John Craven, Gardner-Webb	1992	11	423	240	16	.567	3,320	32
Richard Strasser, San Fran. St.	1985	10	452	250	19	.553	3,317	20
Dave MacDonald, West Chester	1994	11	458	251	18	.548	3,308	35

**Record. †National champion.*

SINGLE-GAME YARDS

Yds.	Player, Team (Opponent)	Date
614	Alfred Montez, Western N.M. (West Tex. A&M)	Oct. 8, 1994
614	Perry Klein, LIU-C.W. Post (Salisbury St.)	Nov. 6, 1993
592	John Charles, Portland St. (Cal Poly SLO)	Nov. 16, 1991
568	Scott Otis, Glenville St. (West Va. Wesleyan)	Oct. 15, 1994
568	Bob Toledo, San Fran. St. (Cal St. Hayward)	Oct. 21, 1967
564	Pat Graham, Augustana, S.D. (Mankato St.)	Oct. 28, 1995
550	Earl Harvey, N.C. Central (Jackson St.)	Aug. 30, 1986
549	Matt LaTour, Northern Mich. (Ashland)	Nov. 5, 1994
541	Arnold Marcha, West Tex. A&M (Okla. Panhandle St.)	Nov. 12, 1994
539	Maurice Heard, Tuskegee (Alabama A&M)	Nov. 10, 1990
538	Grady Benton, West Tex. A&M (Howard Payne)	Sept. 17, 1994
525	Rob Tomlinson, Cal St. Chico (Southern Conn. St.)	Oct. 7, 1989
524	Dennis Shaw, San Diego St. (Southern Miss.)	Nov. 9, 1968
523	Marty Washington, West Ala. (Nicholls St.)	Sept. 11, 1993
520	Bob McLaughlin, Lock Haven (Calif., Pa.)	Oct. 29, 1994
520	Perry Klein, LIU-C.W. Post (Gannon)	Oct. 9, 1993

SINGLE-GAME ATTEMPTS

No.	Player, Team (Opponent)	Date
74	Jermaine Whitaker, N.M. Highlands (Western St.)	Nov. 5, 1994
72	Kurt Otto, North Dak. (Tex. A&M-Kingsville)	Sept. 13, 1986
72	Kaipo Spencer, Santa Clara (Portland St.)	Oct. 11, 1975
72	Joe Stetser, Cal St. Chico (Oregon Tech)	Sept. 23, 1967
71	Pat Brennan, Franklin (Ashland)	Nov. 3, 1984

Photo from Long Island-C.W. Post sports information

Long Island-C.W. Post quarterback Perry Klein passed for a Division II-record 3,757 yards in 1993.

Photo from Fort Hays State sports information

Shawn Behr of Fort Hays State led Division II quarterbacks with a passing efficiency rating of 171.9 in 1995.

SINGLE-GAME COMPLETIONS

No.	Player, Team (Opponent)	Date
45	Chris Hatcher, Valdosta St. (Mississippi Col.)	Oct. 23, 1993
45	Chris Hatcher, Valdosta St. (West Ga.)	Oct. 16, 1993
44	Tom Bonds, Cal Lutheran (St. Mary's, Cal.)	Nov. 22, 1986
43	George Bork, Northern Ill. (Central Mich.)	Nov. 9, 1963
42	Lance Funderburk, Valdosta St. (West Ga.)	Nov. 11, 1995
42	Jermaine Whitaker, N.M. Highlands (Western St.)	Nov. 5, 1994
42	Marty Washington, West Ala. (Jacksonville St.)	Nov. 7, 1992
42	Chris Teal, West Ga. (Valdosta St.)	Oct. 19, 1991
42	Tim Von Dulm, Portland St. (Eastern Wash.)	Nov. 21, 1970
41	Pat Graham, Augustana, S.D. (Mankato St.)	Oct. 28, 1995
41	Steve Lopez, Cal St. Chico (St. Mary's, Cal.)	Sept. 9, 1995
41	Chris Hatcher, Valdosta St. (West Ga.)	Oct. 15, 1994
41	Grady Benton, West Tex. A&M (Howard Payne)	Sept. 17, 1994
41	Kurt Otto, North Dak. (Tex. A&M-Kingsville)	Sept. 13, 1986
41	Neil Lomax, Portland St. (Montana St.)	Nov. 19, 1977

ANNUAL CHAMPIONS

Year	Player, Team	Class	Att.	Cmp.	Int.	Pct.	Yds.	TD
1946	Hank Caver, Presbyterian	Sr.	128	59	13	.461	790	7
1947	James Batchelor, East Tex. St.	Sr.	184	94	10	.511	1,114	9
1948	Sam Gary, Swarthmore	Jr.	153	93	11	.608	1,218	16
1949	Sam McGowan, New Mexico St.	Sr.	219	112	22	.511	1,712	12
1950	Andy MacDonald, Central Mich.	Jr.	200	109	12	.545	1,577	15
1951	Andy MacDonald, Central Mich.	Sr.	183	114	7	.623	1,560	12
1952	Wes Bair, Illinois St.	So.	242	135	18	.558	1,375	14
1953	Pence Dacus, Southwest Tex. St.	Sr.	207	113	10	.546	1,654	11
1954	Tommy Egan, Brandeis	Sr.	144	87	8	.604	1,050	11
1955	Jerry Foley, Hamline	Fr.	167	87	8	.521	1,034	6
1956	James Stehlin, Brandeis	Sr.	206	116	11	.563	1,155	6
1957	Jay Roelen, Pepperdine	Sr.	214	106	16	.495	1,428	13
1958	Stan Jackson, Cal Poly Pomona	Sr.	256	123	14	.480	1,994	16
1959	Gary Campbell, Whittier	Sr.	183	111	4	.607	1,717	12
1960	Denny Spurlock, Whitworth	Jr.	257	135	16	.525	1,892	14
1961	Tom Gryzwinski, Defiance	Jr.	258	127	17	.492	1,684	14
1962	George Bork, Northern Ill.	Jr.	356	232	11	.652	2,506	22
1963	George Bork, Northern Ill.	Sr.	374	244	12	.652	3,077	32
1964	Jerry Bishop, Austin	Jr.	300	182	16	.607	2,246	17
1965	Bob Caress, Bradley	Sr.	393	210	21	.534	2,167	24
1966	Paul Krause, Dubuque	Sr.	318	179	22	.563	2,210	16
1967	Joe Stetser, Cal St. Chico	Sr.	464	220	*32	.474	2,446	14
1968	Jim Lindsey, Abilene Christian	So.	396	204	19	.515	2,717	18
1969	Tim Von Dulm, Portland St.	Jr.	434	241	18	.555	2,926	26

Beginning in 1970, ranked on per-game (instead of total) completions

Year	Player, Team	Class	G	Att.	Cmp.	Avg.	Int.	Pct.	Yds.	TD
1970	Tim Von Dulm, Portland St.	Sr.	10	490	259	25.9	23	.529	3,041	25
1971	Bob Baron, Rensselaer	Sr.	9	302	168	18.7	13	.556	2,105	15
1972	Bob Biggs, UC Davis	Sr.	9	327	186	20.7	16	.569	2,291	15
1973	Kim McQuilken, Lehigh	Sr.	11	326	196	17.8	13	.601	2,603	19
1974	Jim McMillan, Boise St.	Sr.	10	313	192	19.2	15	.613	2,900	13
1975	Dan Hayes, UC Riverside	Sr.	10	316	171	17.1	20	.541	2,215	21
1976	June Jones, Portland St.	Sr.	11	423	238	21.6	24	.563	3,518	25
1977	Ed Schultz, Moorhead St.	Sr.	10	304	187	18.7	16	.615	1,943	21
1978	Jeff Knapple, Northern Colo.	Sr.	10	349	178	17.8	21	.510	2,191	16

Beginning in 1979, ranked on passing efficiency rating points (instead of per-game completions)

Year	Player, Team	Class	G	Att.	Cmp.	Int.	Pct.	Yds.	TD	Pts.
1979	Dave Alfaro, Santa Clara	Jr.	9	168	110	9	.655	1,721	13	166.3
1980	Willie Tullis, Troy St.	Sr.	10	203	108	8	.532	1,880	15	147.5
1981	Steve Michuta, Grand Valley St.	Sr.	8	173	114	11	.659	1,702	17	168.3
1982	John Wristen, Southern Colo.	Jr.	8	121	68	2	.562	1,358	13	182.6
1983	Kevin Parker, Fort Valley St.	Jr.	9	168	87	8	.518	1,539	18	154.6
1984	Brian Quinn, Northwest Mo. St.	Sr.	10	178	96	2	.539	1,561	14	151.3
1985	Chris Petersen, UC Davis	Jr.	10	242	167	6	.690	2,366	17	169.4
1986	Chris Petersen, UC Davis	Sr.	10	311	218	7	.701	2,622	22	159.7
1987	Dave Biondo, Ashland	Jr.	10	177	95	11	.537	1,828	14	154.1
1988	Al Niemela, West Chester	Sr.	10	217	138	9	.636	1,932	21	162.0
1989	Richard Basil, Savannah St.	Sr.	9	211	120	7	.569	2,148	29	181.1
1990	Tony Aliucci, Indiana (Pa.)	Jr.	10	181	111	10	.613	1,801	21	172.2
1991	Jayson Merrill, Western St.	Sr.	10	309	195	11	.631	3,484	35	188.1
1992	Steve Smith, Western St.	Sr.	10	271	180	5	.664	2,719	30	183.5
1993	James Weir, New Haven	Jr.	10	266	161	1	.605	2,336	31	172.0
1994	Chris Hatcher, Valdosta St.	Sr.	11	430	321	9	*.747	3,591	*50	‡179.0
1995	Shawn Behr, Fort Hays St.	Sr.	11	318	191	6	.600	3,158	31	171.9

**Record. ‡Record for minimum 200 completions.*

ANNUAL PASSING EFFICIENCY LEADERS BEFORE 1979

(Minimum 11 Attempts Per Game)

1948—Jim Peterson, Hanover, 182.9; **1949**—John Ford, Hardin-Simmons, 179.6; **1950**—Edward Ludorf, Trinity (Conn.), 167.8; **1951**—Vic Lesch, Western Ill., 182.4; **1952**—Jim Gray, East Tex. St., 205.5; **1953**—Boyd Crawford, Col. of Idaho, *210.1; **1954**—Bill Englehardt, Neb.-Omaha, 170.7; **1955**—Robert Alexander, Trinity (Conn.), 208.7; **1956**—John Costello, Widener, 169.8; **1957**—Doug Maison, Hillsdale, 200.0; **1958**—Kurt Duecker, Ripon, 161.7; **1959**—Fred Whitmire, Humboldt St., 188.7; **1960**—Larry Cline, Otterbein, 195.2.

(Minimum 15 Attempts Per Game)

Year	Player, Team	G	Att.	Cmp.	Int.	Pct.	Yds.	TD	Pts.
1961	Denny Spurlock, Whitworth	10	189	115	16	.608	1,708	26	165.2
1962	Roy Curry, Jackson St.	10	194	104	8	.536	1,862	15	151.5
1963	Chuck Green, Wittenberg	9	182	114	8	.626	2,181	19	+189.0
1964	Jim Cahoon, Ripon	8	127	74	7	.583	1,206	19	176.4
1965	Ed Buzzell, Ottawa	9	238	118	5	.496	2,170	31	165.0
1966	Jim Alcorn, Clarion	9	199	107	4	.538	1,714	24	161.9
1967	Jim Feely, Johns Hopkins	7	110	69	5	.627	1,264	12	186.2
1968	Larry Green, Doane	9	182	97	7	.533	1,592	22	159.0
1969	George Kaplan, Northern Colo.	9	155	92	5	.594	1,396	16	162.6
1970	Gary Wichard, LIU-C.W. Post	9	186	100	5	.538	1,527	12	138.6
1971	Peter Mackey, Middlebury	8	180	101	4	.561	1,597	19	161.0
1972	David Hamilton, Fort Valley St.	9	180	99	9	.550	1,571	24	162.3
1973	Jim McMillan, Boise St.	11	179	110	5	.615	1,525	17	158.8
1974	Jim McMillan, Boise St.	10	313	192	15	.613	2,900	33	164.4
1975	Joe Sterrett, Lehigh	11	228	135	13	.592	2,114	22	157.5
1976	Mike Makings, Western St.	10	179	90	6	.503	1,617	14	145.3
1977	Mike Rieker, Lehigh	11	230	137	14	.596	2,431	23	169.2
1978	Mike Moroski, UC Davis	10	205	119	9	.580	1,689	17	145.9

**Record. +Record for minimum 100 completions.*

(See page 142 for annual leaders beginning in 1979.)

Photo from Norfolk State sports information

Norfolk State wide receiver James Roe finished his collegiate career in 1995 as the all-time Division II leader in receiving yards (4,468) and fourth in career receptions (239).

Receiving

CAREER RECEPTIONS PER GAME

(Minimum 125 Receptions)

Player, Team	Years	G	Rec.	Yards	TD	Rec.PG
Chris George, Glenville St.	1993-94	20	230	3,215	30	*11.5
Ed Bell, Idaho St.	1968-69	19	163	2,608	30	8.6
Byron Chamberlain, Wayne St. (Neb.)	1993-94	19	161	1,941	14	8.3
Jerry Hendren, Idaho	1967-69	30	230	3,435	27	7.7
Gary Garrison, San Diego St.	1964-65	20	148	2,188	26	7.4
Brad Bailey, West Tex. A&M	1992-94	30	221	2,677	22	7.4
Chris Myers, Kenyon	1967-70	35	253	3,897	33	7.2

**Record.*

SEASON RECEPTIONS PER GAME

Player, Team	Year	G	Rec.	Yards	TD	Rec.PG
Chris George, Glenville St.	†1993	10	117	*1,876	15	*11.7
Chris George, Glenville St.	†1994	10	113	1,339	15	11.3
Brad Bailey, West Tex. A&M	1994	11	*119	1,552	16	10.8
Bruce Cerone, Emporia St.	1968	9	91	1,479	15	10.1
Mike Healey, Valparaiso	†1985	10	101	1,279	11	10.1
Sean Pender, Valdosta St.	†1995	11	111	983	2	10.1
Barry Wagner, Alabama A&M	†1989	11	106	1,812	17	9.6
Ed Bell, Idaho St.	†1969	10	96	1,522	20	9.6
Jerry Hendren, Idaho	1968	9	86	1,457	14	9.6
Dick Hewins, Drake	†1968	10	95	1,316	13	9.5
Jarett Vito, Emporia St.	1995	10	+94	932	7	9.4
Billy Joe Masters, Evansville	†1987	10	‡94	‡960	4	‡9.4
Joe Dittrich, Southwest St.	†1980	9	83	974	7	9.2
Manley Sarnowsky, Drake	†1966	10	92	1,114	7	9.2

**Record. †National champion. +Record for a freshman. ‡Record for a running back.*

CAREER RECEPTIONS

Player, Team	Years	Rec.	Yards	TD
Jon Spinosa, Lock Haven	1992-95	*261	2,710	12
Chris Myers, Kenyon	1967-70	253	3,897	33
Bruce Cerone, Yankton/Emporia St.	1965-66, 68-69	241	4,354	*49
James Roe, Norfolk St.	1992-95	239	*4,468	46
"Red" Roberts, Austin Peay	1967-70	232	3,005	31
Chris George, Glenville St.	1993-94	230	3,215	30
Jerry Hendren, Idaho	1967-69	230	3,435	27
Mike Healey, Valparaiso	1982-85	228	3,212	26
William Mackall, Tenn.-Martin	1985-88	224	2,488	16
Brad Bailey, West Tex. A&M	1992-94	221	2,677	22
Johnny Cox, Fort Lewis	1990-93	220	3,611	33
Greg Hopkins, Slippery Rock	1991-94	215	3,382	28
Robert Clark, N.C. Central	1983-86	210	4,231	38
Terry Fredenberg, Wis.-Milwaukee	1965-68	206	2,789	24
Dan Bogar, Valparaiso	1981-84	204	2,816	26
Rich Otte, Truman St.	1980-83	202	2,821	16
Mark Steinmeyer, Kutztown (RB)	1988-91	200	2,118	23
Barry Naone, Portland St. (TE)	1985-88	199	2,237	8
Tony Willis, New Haven	1990-93	194	3,420	38
Jon Braff, St. Mary's (Cal.) (TE)	1985-88	193	2,461	20
Shannon Sharpe, Savannah St.	1986-89	192	3,744	40
Bill Wick, Carroll (Wis.)	1966-69	190	2,967	20
Don Hutt, Boise St.	1971-73	187	2,716	30
Steve Hansley, Northwest Mo. St.	1983-85	186	2,898	24
Dan Anderson, Northwest Mo. St. (TE)	1982-85	186	2,494	16

**Record.*

SEASON RECEPTIONS

Player, Team	Year	G	Rec.	Yards	TD
Brad Bailey, West Tex. A&M	1994	11	*119	1,552	16
Chris George, Glenville St.	†1993	10	117	*1,876	15
Chris George, Glenville St.	†1994	10	113	1,339	15
Sean Pender, Valdosta St.	†1995	11	111	983	2
Barry Wagner, Alabama A&M	†1989	11	106	1,812	17
Mike Healey, Valparaiso	†1985	10	101	1,279	11
Ed Bell, Idaho St.	†1969	10	96	1,522	20
Dick Hewins, Drake	†1968	10	95	1,316	13
Jarett Vito, Emporia St.	1995	10	+94	932	7
Billy Joe Masters, Evansville	†1987	10	‡94	‡960	4
Stan Carraway, West Tex. A&M	†1986	11	94	1,175	9
Manley Sarnowsky, Drake	†1966	10	92	1,114	7
Rus Bailey, N.M. Highlands	1993	10	91	1,192	12
Bruce Cerone, Emporia St.	1968	9	91	1,479	15
Rodney Robinson, Gardner-Webb	1992	11	89	1,496	16
Chris Perry, Adams St.	1995	10	88	1,719	*21
Matt Carman, West Ala.	1993	10	88	1,085	14
Harvey Tanner, Murray St.	†1967	10	88	1,019	3

**Record. †National champion. +Record for a freshman. ‡Record for a running back.*

SINGLE-GAME RECEPTIONS

No.	Player, Team (Opponent)	Date
23	Chris George, Glenville St. (West Va. Wesleyan)	Oct. 15, 1994
23	Barry Wagner, Alabama A&M (Clark Atlanta)	Nov. 4, 1989
21	Jarett Vito, Emporia St. (Truman St.)	Nov. 4, 1995
20	Sean Pender, Valdosta St. (Mississippi Col.)	Nov. 4, 1995
20	Keylie Martin, N.M. Highlands (Western St.)	Nov. 5, 1994
20	"Red" Roberts, Austin Peay (Murray St.)	Nov. 8, 1969
19	Preston Cunningham, Southwest St. (Mo. Western St.)	Sept. 3, 1994
19	Matt Carman, West Ala. (Jacksonville St.)	Nov. 7, 1992
19	Aaron Marsh, Eastern Ky. (Northwood)	Oct. 14, 1967
19	George LaPorte, Union, N.Y. (Rensselaer)	Oct. 16, 1965

No.	Player, Team (Opponent)	Date
18	Brad Bailey, West Tex. A&M (Okla. Panhandle St.)	Nov. 12, 1994
18	Chris Pelczarski, Millersville (Bloomsburg)	Nov. 9, 1991
18	Carl Bruere, N.M. Highlands (Western St.)	Oct. 12, 1991
18	Billy Joe Masters, Evansville (Ashland)	Oct. 31, 1987
18	Bruce Cerone, Emporia St. (Washburn)	Nov. 9, 1968
18	Bill Delaney, American Int'l (Springfield)	Oct. 21, 1965
18	Dick Donlin, Hamline (St. John's, Minn.)	Oct. 8, 1955

CAREER YARDS PER GAME

(Minimum 2,200 yards)

Player, Team	Years	G	Rec.	Yards	Avg.
Chris George, Glenville St.	1993-94	20	230	3,215	*160.8
Ed Bell, Idaho St.	1968-69	19	163	2,608	137.3
Bruce Cerone, Yankton/Emporia St.	1965-66, 68-69	36	241	4,354	120.9
Jerry Hendren, Idaho	1967-69	30	230	3,435	114.5
Chris Myers, Kenyon	1967-70	35	253	3,897	111.3
James Roe, Norfolk St.	1992-95	41	239	*4,468	109.0

*Record.

CAREER YARDS

Player, Team	Years	Rec.	Yards	Avg.	TD
James Roe, Norfolk St.	1992-95	239	*4,468	18.7	46
Bruce Cerone, Yankton/Emporia St.	1965-66, 68-69	241	4,354	18.1	*49
Robert Clark, N.C. Central	1983-86	210	4,231	‡20.1	38
Chris Myers, Kenyon	1967-70	253	3,897	15.4	33
Shannon Sharpe, Savannah St.	1986-89	192	3,744	19.5	40
Tyrone Johnson, Western St.	1990-93	163	3,717	*22.8	35
Jeff Tiefenthaler, South Dak. St.	1983-86	173	3,621	20.9	31
Willie Richardson, Jackson St.	1959-62	166	3,616	21.8	36
Johnny Cox, Fort Lewis	1990-93	220	3,611	16.4	33

*Record. ‡Record for minimum 180 catches.

SEASON YARDS PER GAME

Player, Team	Years	G	Rec.	Yards	Avg.
Chris George, Glenville St.	†1993	10	117	*1,876	*187.6
Chris Perry, Adams St.	†1995	10	88	1,719	171.9
Barry Wagner, Alabama A&M	†1989	11	106	1,812	164.7
Bruce Cerone, Emporia St.	1968	9	91	1,479	164.3
Jerry Hendren, Idaho	†1969	9	86	1,457	161.9
Ed Bell, Idaho St.	†1969	10	96	1,522	152.2
James Roe, Norfolk St.	†1994	10	77	1,454	145.4
Dan Fulton, Neb.-Omaha	1976	11	67	1,581	143.7
Brad Bailey, West Tex. A&M	1994	11	*119	1,552	141.1

*Record. †National champion.

SEASON YARDS

Player, Team	Year	Rec.	Yards	Avg.	TD
Chris George, Glenville St.	†1993	117	*1,876	16.0	15
Barry Wagner, Alabama A&M	1989	106	1,812	17.1	17
Chris Perry, Adams St.	†1995	88	1,719	19.5	*21
Dan Fulton, Neb.-Omaha	1976	67	1,581	23.6	16
Brad Bailey, West Tex. A&M	1994	*119	1,552	13.0	16
Jeff Tiefenthaler, South Dak. St.	1986	73	1,534	21.0	11
Ed Bell, Idaho St.	1969	96	1,522	15.9	20
Rodney Robinson, Gardner-Webb	†1992	89	1,496	16.8	16
Bruce Cerone, Emporia St.	1968	91	1,479	16.3	15
Jerry Hendren, Idaho	1968	86	1,457	16.9	14

*Record. †National champion.

ANNUAL CHAMPIONS

Year	Player, Team	Class	Rec.	Yards	TD
1946	Hugh Taylor, Oklahoma City	Jr.	23	457	8
1947	Bill Klein, Hanover	So.	52	648	12
1948	Bill Klein, Hanover	Jr.	43	812	6
1949	Cliff Coggin, Southern Miss.	Sr.	53	1,087	9
1950	Jack Bighead, Pepperdine	Jr.	38	551	6
1951	Jim Stefoff, Kalamazoo	Jr.	45	680	5
1952	Jim McKinzie, Northern Ill.	Sr.	44	703	6
1953	Dick Beetsch, Northern Iowa	So.	54	837	9
1954	R. C. Owens, Col. of Idaho	Sr.	48	905	7
1955	Dick Donlin, Hamline	Sr.	41	480	2
1956	Tom Rychlec, American Int'l	Sr.	40	353	3
1957	Tom Whitaker, Nevada	Jr.	40	527	4
1958	Bruce Shenk, West Chester	Sr.	39	580	9
1959	Fred Tunnicliffe, UC Santa Barb.	So.	48	1,087	11
1960	Ken Gregory, Whittier	Sr.	74	1,018	4
1961	Marty Baumhower, Defiance	Jr.	57	708	4
1962	Hugh Rohrschneider, Northern Ill.	Jr.	76	795	5
1963	Hugh Rohrschneider, Northern Ill.	Sr.	75	1,036	14
1964	Steve Gilliatt, Parsons	So.	81	984	12
1965	George LaPorte, Union (N.Y.)	Sr.	74	724	5
1966	Manley Sarnowsky, Drake	Sr.	92	1,114	7
1967	Harvey Tanner, Murray St.	Jr.	88	1,019	3
1968	Dick Hewins, Drake	Sr.	95	1,316	13
1969	Ed Bell, Idaho St.	Sr.	96	1,522	20

Beginning in 1970, ranked on per-game (instead of total) catches

Year	Player, Team	Class	G	Rec.	Avg.	Yards	TD
1970	Steve Mahaffey, Wash. & Lee	Sr.	9	74	8.2	897	2
1971	Kalle Kontson, Rensselaer	Sr.	9	69	7.7	1,031	7
1972	Freddie Scott, Amherst	Jr.	8	66	8.3	936	12
1973	Ron Gustafson, North Dak.	Jr.	10	67	6.7	1,210	10
1974	Andy Sanchez, Cal Poly Pomona	Sr.	10	62	6.2	903	0
1975	Butch Johnson, UC Riverside	Sr.	8	67	8.4	1,027	8
1976	Bo Darden, Shaw	So.	9	57	6.3	863	4
1977	Jeff Tesch, Moorhead St.	Sr.	10	67	6.7	760	9
1978	Mike Chrobot, Butler	Sr.	10	55	5.5	628	5
	Tom Ferguson, Cal St. Hayward	Jr.	10	55	5.5	698	6
	Mark McDaniel, Northern Colo.	Sr.	10	55	5.5	761	6
1979	Robbie Ray, Franklin	Sr.	10	63	6.3	987	3
1980	Joe Dittrich, Southwest St.	Sr.	9	83	9.2	974	7
1981	Paul Choudek, Southwest St.	Sr.	10	70	7.0	747	5
1982	Jay Barnett, Evansville	Sr.	10	81	8.1	1,181	12
1983	Perry Kemp, Calif. (Pa.)	Sr.	10	74	7.4	1,101	9
1984	Dan Bogar, Valparaiso	Sr.	10	73	7.3	861	11
1985	Mike Healey, Valparaiso	Sr.	10	101	10.1	1,279	11
1986	Stan Carraway, West Tex. A&M	Sr.	11	94	8.5	1,175	9
1987	Billy Joe Masters, Evansville	Sr.	10	‡94	‡9.4	‡960	4
1988	Todd Smith, Morningside	Sr.	11	86	7.8	1,006	8
1989	Barry Wagner, Alabama A&M	Sr.	11	106	9.6	1,812	17

Beginning in 1990, ranked on both per-game catches and yards per game

PER-GAME RECEPTIONS

Year	Player, Team	Class	G	Rec.	Avg.	Yards	TD
1990	Mark Steinmeyer, Kutztown	Jr.	11	86	7.8	940	5
1991	Jesse Lopez, Cal St. Hayward	Sr.	10	86	8.6	861	4
1992	Randy Bartosh, Southwest Baptist	Sr.	8	65	8.1	860	2
1993	Chris George, Glenville St.	Jr.	10	117	*11.7	*1,876	15
1994	Chris George, Glenville St.	Sr.	10	113	11.3	1,339	15
1995	Sean Pender, Valdosta St.	Jr.	11	111	10.1	983	2

YARDS PER GAME

Year	Player, Team	Class	G	Rec.	Yards	Avg.	TD
1990	Ernest Priester, Edinboro	Sr.	8	45	1,060	132.5	14
1991	Rod Smith, Mo. Southern St.	Jr.	11	60	1,439	130.8	15
1992	Rodney Robinson, Gardner-Webb	Sr.	11	89	1,496	136.0	16
1993	Chris George, Glenville St.	Jr.	10	117	*1,876	*187.6	15
1994	James Roe, Norfolk St.	Jr.	10	77	1,454	145.4	17
1995	Chris Perry, Adams St.	Sr.	10	88	1,719	171.9	*21

*Record. ‡Record for a running back.

Scoring

CAREER POINTS PER GAME

(Minimum 225 Points)

Player, Team	Years	G	TD	XPt.	FG	Pts.	Pt.PG
Ole Gunderson, St. Olaf	1969-71	27	60	2	0	362	*13.4
Leon Burns, Long Beach St.	1969-70	22	47	2	0	284	12.9
Billy Johnson, Widener	1971-72	19	39	0	0	234	12.3
Dale Mills, Truman St.	1957-60	36	64	23	0	407	11.3
Walter Payton, Jackson St.	1971-74	42	66	53	5	*464	11.0
Steve Roberts, Butler	1986-89	35	63	4	0	386	11.0
Jeff Bentrim, North Dak. St.	1983-86	35	64	2	0	386	11.0
Shawn Graves, Wofford	1989-92	40	*72	3	0	438	11.0
Johnny Bailey, Tex. A&M-Kingsville	1986-89	39	70	3	0	426	10.9
Garney Henley, Huron	1956-59	37	63	16	0	394	10.6
Roger Graham, New Haven	1991-94	40	70	2	0	424	10.6

*Record.

SEASON POINTS PER GAME

Player, Team	Year	G	TD	XPt.	FG	Pts.	Pt.PG
Carl Herakovich, Rose-Hulman	†1958	8	25	18	0	168	*21.0
Jim Switzer, Col. of Emporia	†1963	9	28	0	0	168	18.7
Billy Johnson, Widener	†1972	9	27	0	0	162	18.0
Carl Garrett, N.M. Highlands	†1966	9	26	2	0	158	17.6
Ted Scown, Sul Ross St.	†1948	10	28	0	0	168	16.8

*Record. †National champion.

CAREER POINTS

Player, Team	Years	TD	XPt.	FG	Pts.
Walter Payton, Jackson St.	1971-74	66	53	5	*464
Shawn Graves, Wofford	1989-92	*72	3	0	438
Johnny Bailey, Tex. A&M-Kingsville	1986-89	70	3	0	426
Roger Graham, New Haven	1991-94	70	2	0	424
Dale Mills, Truman St.	1957-60	64	23	0	407

Player, Team	Years	TD	XPt.	FG	Pts.
Jeremy Monroe, Michigan Tech	1990-93	67	0	0	402
Garney Henley, Huron	1956-59	63	16	0	394
Steve Roberts, Butler	1986-89	63	4	0	386
Jeff Bentrim, North Dak. St.	1983-86	64	2	0	386
Leo Lewis, Lincoln (Mo.)	1951-54	64	0	0	384
Heath Sherman, Tex. A&M-Kingsville	1985-88	63	0	0	378
Tank Younger, Grambling	1945-48	60	9	0	369
Richard Huntley, Winston-Salem	1992-95	60	8	0	368
Bill Cooper, Muskingum	1957-60	54	37	1	364

**Record.*

SEASON POINTS

Player, Team	Year	TD	XPt.	FG	Pts.
Terry Metcalf, Long Beach St.	1971	*29	4	0	*178
Jim Switzer, Col. of Emporia	†1963	28	0	0	168
Carl Herakovich, Rose-Hulman	†1958	25	18	0	168
Ted Scown, Sul Ross St.	†1948	28	0	0	168
Ronald Moore, Pittsburg St.	1992	27	4	0	166
Leon Burns, Long Beach St.	†1969	27	2	0	164
Mike Deutsch, North Dak.	1972	27	0	0	162
Billy Johnson, Widener	†1972	27	0	0	162

**Record. †National champion.*

ANNUAL CHAMPIONS

Year	Player, Team	Class	TD	XPt.	FG	Pts.
1946	Joe Carter, Florida N&I	So.	21	26	0	152
1947	Darwin Horn, Pepperdine	Jr.	19	1	0	115
	Chuck Schoenherr, Wheaton (Ill.)	So.	19	1	0	115
1948	Ted Scown, Sul Ross St.	So.	28	0	0	168
1949	Sylvester Polk, Md.-East. Shore	Jr.	19	15	0	129
1950	Carl Taseff, John Carroll	Sr.	23	0	0	138
1951	Paul Yackey, Heidelberg	Jr.	22	0	0	132
1952	Al Conway, William Jewell	Sr.	22	1	0	133
1953	Leo Lewis, Lincoln (Mo.)	Jr.	22	0	0	132
1954	Jim Podoley, Central Mich.	Jr.	18	1	0	109
	Dick Nyers, Indianapolis	Sr.	16	13	0	109
1955	Nate Clark, Hillsdale	Jr.	24	0	0	144
1956	Larry Houdek, Kan. Wesleyan	Sr.	19	0	0	114
1957	Lenny Lyles, Louisville	Sr.	21	6	0	132
1958	Carl Herakovich, Rose-Hulman	Sr.	25	18	0	168
1959	Garney Henley, Huron	Sr.	22	9	0	141
1960	Bill Cooper, Muskingum	Sr.	23	14	0	152
1961	John Murio, Whitworth	Jr.	15	33	2	129
1962	Mike Goings, Bluffton	So.	22	0	0	132
1963	Jim Switzer, Col. of Emporia	Sr.	28	0	0	168
1964	Henry Dyer, Grambling	Jr.	17	2	0	104
	Dunn Marteen, Cal St. Los Angeles	Sr.	11	38	0	104
1965	Allen Smith, Findlay	Jr.	24	2	0	146
1966	Carl Garrett, N.M. Highlands	So.	26	2	0	158
1967	Bert Nye, West Chester	Jr.	19	13	0	127
1968	Howard Stevens, Randolph-Macon	Fr.	23	4	0	142
1969	Leon Burns, Long Beach St.	Jr.	27	2	0	164

Beginning in 1970, ranked on per-game (instead of total) points

Year	Player, Team	Class	G	TD	XPt.	FG	Pts.	Avg.
1970	Mike DiBlasi, Mount Union	Sr.	9	22	0	0	132	14.7
1971	Larry Ras, Michigan Tech	Sr.	9	24	0	0	144	16.0
1972	Billy Johnson, Widener	Jr.	9	27	0	0	162	18.0
1973	Walter Payton, Jackson St.	Jr.	11	24	13	1	160	14.5
1974	Walter Payton, Jackson St.	Sr.	10	19	6	1	123	12.3
1975	Dale Kasowski, North Dak.	Sr.	7	16	4	0	100	14.3
1976	Ted McKnight, Minn.-Duluth	Sr.	10	24	0	0	144	14.4
1977	Bill Burnham, New Hampshire	Sr.	10	22	0	0	132	13.2
1978	Marschell Brunfield, Youngstown St.	Sr.	9	14	0	0	84	9.3
	Charlie Thompson, Western St.	Sr.	9	14	0	0	84	9.3
1979	Robby Robson, Youngstown St.	Jr.	10	20	0	0	120	12.0
1980	Amory Bodin, Minn.-Duluth	Sr.	10	19	2	0	116	11.6
1981	George Works, Northern Mich.	Jr.	10	21	0	0	126	12.6
1982	George Works, Northern Mich.	Sr.	10	23	0	0	138	13.8
1983	Clarence Johnson, North Ala.	Jr.	10	16	0	0	96	9.6
1984	Jeff Bentrim, North Dak. St.	So.	9	14	0	0	84	9.3
1985	Jeff Bentrim, North Dak. St.	Jr.	8	18	2	0	110	††13.8
1986	Jeff Bentrim, North Dak. St.	Sr.	10	23	0	0	138	13.8
1987	Johnny Bailey, Tex. A&M-Kingsville	So.	10	20	0	0	120	12.0
1988	Steve Roberts, Butler	Jr.	10	23	4	0	142	14.2
1989	Jimmy Allen, St. Joseph's (Ind.)	Jr.	10	23	0	0	138	13.8
1990	Ernest Priester, Edinboro	Sr.	8	16	0	0	96	12.0
1991	Quincy Tillmon, Emporia St.	So.	9	19	0	0	114	12.7
1992	David McCartney, Chadron St.	Jr.	10	25	4	0	154	15.4
1993	Roger Graham, New Haven	Jr.	10	23	0	0	138	13.8
1994	Leonard Davis, Lenoir-Rhyne	Sr.	9	19	0	0	114	12.7
1995	Antonio Leroy, Albany St. (Ga.)	Jr.	11	24	0	0	144	13.1

††Declared champion; with one more game (to meet 75 percent of games played minimum) for zero points, still would have highest per-game average (12.2).

Interceptions

CAREER INTERCEPTIONS

Player, Team	Years	No.	Yards	Avg.
Tom Collins, Indianapolis	1982-85	*37	390	10.5
Dean Diaz, Humboldt St.	1980-83	31	328	10.6
Bill Grantham, Mo.-Rolla	1977-80	29	263	9.1
Jason Johnson, Shepherd	1991-94	28	321	11.5
Tony Woods, Bloomsburg	1982-85	26	105	4.0
Buster West, Gust. Adolphus	1967-70	26	192	7.4
Nate Gruber, Winona St.	1991-94	25	275	11.0
Gary Rubeling, Towson St.	1980-83	25	122	4.9
Greg Mercier, Ripon	1968-70	25	243	9.7

**Record.*

SEASON INTERCEPTIONS

Player, Team	Year	No.	Yards
Eugene Hunter, Fort Valley St.	†1972	**14	211
Luther Howard, Delaware St.	†1972	**14	99
Tom Rezzuti, Northeastern	†1971	**14	153
Jim Blackwell, Southern-B.R.	†1970	**14	196
Carl Ray Harris, Fresno St.	1970	**14	98

***Record tied. †National champion.*

ANNUAL CHAMPIONS

Year	Player, Team	Class	G	No.	Avg.	Yards
1970	Jim Blackwell, Southern-B.R.	Sr.	11	**14	1.27	196
1971	Tom Rezzuti, Northeastern	Jr.	9	**14	**1.56	153
1972	Eugene Hunter, Fort Valley St.	So.	9	**14	**1.56	211
	Luther Howard, Delaware St.	Sr.	9	**14	**1.56	99
1973	Mike Pierce, Northern Colo.	Sr.	7	7	1.00	158
	James Smith, Shaw	So.	8	8	1.00	94
1974	Terry Rusin, Wayne St. (Mich.)	Fr.	10	10	1.00	62
1975	Jim Poettgen, Cal Poly Pomona	Jr.	11	12	1.09	156
1976	Johnny Tucker, Tennessee Tech	Sr.	11	10	0.91	74
1977	Mike Ellis, Norfolk St.	So.	11	12	1.09	257
	Cornelius Washington, Winston-Salem	Sr.	11	12	1.09	128
1978	Bill Grantham, Mo.-Rolla	So.	11	11	1.00	109
1979	Jeff Huffman, Michigan Tech	Sr.	10	11	1.10	97
1980	Mike Lush, East Stroudsburg	Sr.	10	12	1.20	208
1981	Bobby Futrell, Elizabeth City St.	So.	9	11	1.22	159
1982	Greg Maack, Central Mo. St.	Sr.	10	11	1.10	192
1983	Matt Didio, Wayne St. (Mich.)	Sr.	10	13	1.30	131
1984	Bob Jahelka, LIU-C.W. Post	Sr.	8	9	1.13	83
1985	Duvaal Callaway, Fort Valley St.	Sr.	11	10	0.91	175
	Tony Woods, Bloomsburg	Sr.	11	10	0.91	10
1986	Doug Smart, Winona St.	Jr.	8	10	1.25	56
1987	Mike Petrich, Minn.-Duluth	Jr.	11	9	0.82	151
1988	Pete Jaros, Augustana (S.D.)	Jr.	11	13	1.18	120
1989	Jacque DeMatteo, Clarion	Jr.	8	6	0.75	21
1990	Eric Turner, East Tex. St.	So.	11	10	0.91	105
1991	Jeff Fickes, Shippensburg	Sr.	11	12	1.09	154
1992	Pat Williams, East Tex. St.	Sr.	11	13	1.18	145
1993	Troy Crissman, Ky. Wesleyan	So.	10	9	0.90	39
1994	Keith Hawkins, Humboldt St.	Sr.	10	11	1.10	159
	Elton Rhoades, Central Okla.	Sr.	10	11	1.10	126
1995	Chenelle Jones, Western N.M.	Sr.	8	7	0.88	61

***Record tied.*

Punting

CAREER AVERAGE
(Minimum 100 Punts)

Player, Team	Years	No.	Yards	Avg.
Tim Baer, Colorado Mines	1986-89	235	10,406	*44.3
Jeff Guy, Western St.	1983-85	113	4,967	44.0
Russ Pilcher, Carroll (Mont.)	1964-66	124	5,424	43.7
Russell Gonzales, Morris Brown	1976-77	111	4,833	43.5
Gerald Circo, Cal St. Chico	1964-65	103	4,470	43.4
Trent Morgan, Cal St. Northridge	1987-88	128	5,531	43.2
Bryan Wagner, Cal St. Northridge	1981-84	203	8,762	43.2
Tom Kolesar, Nevada	1973-74	140	6,032	43.1
Jimmy Morris, Angelo St.	1991-92	101	4,326	42.8
Don Geist, Northern Colo.	1981-84	263	11,247	42.8
Jan Chapman, San Diego	1958-60	106	4,533	42.8
Warner Robertson, Md.-East. Shore	1968-70	131	5,578	42.6

**Record.*

SEASON AVERAGE
(Qualifiers for Championship)

Player, Team	Year	No.	Yards	Avg.
Steve Ecker, Shippensburg	†1965	32	1,570	*49.1
Don Cockroft, Adams St.	†1966	36	1,728	48.0
Jack Patterson, William Jewell	1965	29	1,377	47.5
Art Calandrelli, Canisius	†1949	25	1,177	47.1
Grover Perkins, Southern-B.R.	†1961	22	1,034	47.0
Erskine Valrie, Alabama A&M	1966	36	1,673	46.5
Mark Bounds, West Tex. A&M	†1990	69	3,198	+46.3
Bruce Swanson, North Park	†1967	53	2,455	46.3
Lyle Johnston, Weber St.	1965	29	1,340	46.2

**Record. †National champion. +Record for minimum 40 punts.*

ANNUAL CHAMPIONS

Year	Player, Team	Class	No.	Yards	Avg.
1948	Arthur Teixeira, Central Mich.	Sr.	42	1,867	44.5
1949	Art Calandrelli, Canisius	Jr.	25	1,177	47.1
1950	Flavian Weidekamp, Butler	Sr.	41	1,762	43.0
1951	Curtiss Harris, Savannah St.	Sr.	42	1,854	44.1
1952	Virgil Stan, Western St.	Sr.	37	1,622	43.8
1953	Bill Bradshaw, Bowling Green	Jr.	50	2,199	44.0
1954	Bill Bradshaw, Bowling Green	Sr.	28	1,228	43.9
1955	Don Baker, North Texas	Sr.	30	1,349	45.0
1956	Marion Zody, Ashland	Jr.	34	1,475	43.4
1957	Lawson Persley, Mississippi Val.	Sr.	36	1,659	46.1
1958	Tom Lewis, Lake Forest	Jr.	24	1,089	45.4
1959	Buck Grover, Salem-Teikyo	Fr.	27	1,203	44.6
1960	Joe Roy, N.M. Highlands	So.	40	1,744	43.6
1961	Grover Perkins, Southern-B.R.	Fr.	22	1,034	47.0
1962	Ron Crouse, Catawba	Jr.	37	1,653	44.7
1963	Steve Bailey, Kentucky St.	Sr.	39	1,747	44.8
1964	Russ Pilcher, Carroll (Mont.)	So.	34	1,545	45.4
1965	Steve Ecker, Shippensburg	Sr.	32	1,570	*49.1
1966	Don Cockroft, Adams St.	Sr.	36	1,728	48.0
1967	Bruce Swanson, North Park	Jr.	53	2,455	46.3
1968	Warner Robertson, Md.-East. Shore	Fr.	61	2,699	44.2
1969	Warner Robertson, Md.-East. Shore	So.	37	1,629	44.0
1970	John Bonner, Tenn.-Chatt.	Sr.	73	3,243	44.4
1971	Ken Gamble, Fayetteville St.	Sr.	47	2,092	44.5
1972	Raymond Key, Jackson St.	Jr.	44	1,883	42.8
1973	Jerry Pope, Louisiana Tech	Fr.	48	2,064	43.0
1974	Mike Shawen, Middle Tenn. St.	Sr.	62	2,720	43.9
1975	Mike Wood, Southeast Mo. St.	Jr.	40	1,729	43.2
1976	Russell Gonzales, Morris Brown	So.	54	2,474	45.8
1977	Jeff Gossett, Eastern Ill.	Jr.	62	2,668	43.0
1978	Bill Moats, South Dak.	Sr.	77	3,377	43.9
1979	Bob Fletcher, Truman St.	Sr.	79	3,409	43.2
1980	Sean Landeta, Towson St.	So.	47	2,038	43.4
1981	Gregg Lowery, Jacksonville St.	Jr.	64	2,787	43.5
1982	Don Geist, Northern Colo.	So.	66	2,966	44.4
1983	Jeff Guy, Western St.	So.	39	1,734	44.5
1984	Jeff Guy, Western St.	Jr.	46	2,012	43.7
1985	Jeff Williams, Slippery Rock	Sr.	46	1,977	43.0
1986	Tim Baer, Colorado Mines	Fr.	62	2,797	45.1
1987	Jeff McComb, Southern Utah	Sr.	42	1,863	44.4
1988	Tim Baer, Colorado Mines	Jr.	65	2,880	43.9
1989	Tim Baer, Colorado Mines	Sr.	55	2,382	43.3
1990	Mark Bounds, West Tex. A&M	Jr.	69	3,198	+46.3
1991	Doug O'Neill, Cal Poly SLO	Sr.	42	1,895	45.1
1992	Jimmy Morris, Angelo St.	So.	45	2,001	44.5
1993	Chris Carter, Henderson St.	Sr.	53	2,305	43.5
1994	Pat Hogelin, Colorado Mines	Sr.	48	2,167	45.1
1995	Jon Mason, West Tex. A&M	Sr.	54	2,459	45.5

**Record. +Record for minimum 40 punts.*

Punt Returns

CAREER AVERAGE
(Minimum 1.2 Returns Per Game)

Player, Team	Years	No.	Yards	Avg.
Billy Johnson, Widener	1971-72	29	759	*26.2
Chuck Goehl, Monmouth (Ill.)	1970-72	48	911	19.0
Robbie Martin, Cal Poly SLO	1978-80	69	1,168	16.9
Roscoe Word, Jackson St.	1970-73	35	554	15.8
Darryl Skinner, Hampton	1983-86	53	835	15.8
Michael Fields, Mississippi Col.	1984-85	50	695	13.9

**Record.*

SEASON AVERAGE
(Minimum 1.2 Returns Per Game)

Player, Team	Year	No.	Yards	Avg.
Billy Johnson, Widener	†1972	15	511	*34.1
William Williams, Livingstone	†1976	16	453	28.3
Terry Egerdahl, Minn.-Duluth	†1975	13	360	27.7
Ennis Thomas, Bishop	†1971	18	450	25.0
Chuck Goehl, Monmouth (Ill.)	1972	17	416	24.5

**Record. †National champion.*

ANNUAL CHAMPIONS

Year	Player, Team	Class	No.	Yards	Avg.
1970	Kevin Downs, Ill. Benedictine	Jr.	11	255	23.2
1971	Ennis Thomas, Bishop	So.	18	450	25.0
1972	Billy Johnson, Widener	Jr.	15	511	*34.1
1973	Roscoe Word, Jackson St.	Sr.	19	316	16.6
1974	Greg Anderson, Montana	So.	13	263	20.2
1975	Terry Egerdahl, Minn.-Duluth	Sr.	13	360	27.7
1976	William Williams, Livingstone	So.	16	453	28.3
1977	Armando Olivieri, New York Tech	So.	14	270	19.3
1978	Dwight Walker, Nicholls St.	Fr.	16	284	17.8
1979	Ricky Eberhart, Morris Brown	Fr.	18	401	22.3
1980	Ron Bagby, Puget Sound	So.	16	242	15.1
1981	Ron Trammell, East Tex. St.	Jr.	29	467	16.1
1982	Darrel Green, Tex. A&M-Kingsville	Sr.	19	392	20.6
1983	Steve Carter, Albany St. (Ga.)	Sr.	27	511	18.9
1984	Michael Fields, Mississippi Col.	Jr.	23	487	21.2
1985	Darryl Skinner, Hampton	Jr.	19	426	22.4
1986	Ben Frazier, Cheyney	So.	14	246	17.6
1987	Ronald Day, Savannah St.	Sr.	12	229	19.1
1988	Donnie Morris, Norfolk St.	Jr.	12	283	23.6
1989	Dennis Mailhot, East Stroudsburg	Jr.	16	284	17.8
1990	Ron West, Pittsburg St.	Jr.	23	388	16.9
1991	Doug Grant, Savannah St.	So.	19	331	17.4
1992	Doug Grant, Savannah St.	Jr.	15	366	24.4
1993	Jerry Garrett, Wayne St. (Neb.)	Jr.	26	498	19.2
1994	Terry Guess, Gardner-Webb	So.	16	312	19.5
1995	Kevin Cannon, Millersville	Sr.	16	277	17.3

**Record.*

Kickoff Returns

CAREER AVERAGE
(Minimum 1.2 Returns Per Game)

Player, Team	Years	No.	Yards	Avg.
Glen Printers, Southern Colo.	1973-74	25	851	*34.0
Karl Evans, Mo. Southern St.	1991-92	32	959	30.0
Kevin Cannon, Millersville	1992-95	67	1,999	29.8
Dave Ludy, Winona St.	1991-94	89	*2,630	29.6
Doug Parrish, San Fran. St.	1990	35	1,002	28.6
Clarence Chapman, Eastern Mich.	1973-75	45	1,278	28.4
Greg Wilson, East Tenn. St.	1975-77	34	952	28.0
Bernie Rose, North Ala.	1974-76	62	1,681	27.1
Roscoe Word, Jackson St.	1970-73	74	1,980	26.8

**Record.*

SEASON AVERAGE
(Minimum 1.2 Returns Per Game)

Player, Team	Year	No.	Yards	Avg.
LaVon Reis, Western St.	†1993	14	552	*39.43
Danny Lee, Jacksonville St.	†1992	12	473	39.42
Fran DeFalco, Assumption	1993	12	461	38.4
Kendall James, Carson-Newman	1993	15	549	36.6
Roscoe Word, Jackson St.	†1973	18	650	36.1
Steve Levenseller, Puget Sound	†1978	17	610	35.9
Winston Horshaw, Shippensburg	†1991	15	536	35.7
Anthony Rivera, Western St.	1991	18	635	35.3
Dave Ludy, Winona St.	1992	25	881	35.2
Mike Scullin, Baldwin-Wallace	†1970	14	492	35.1
Rufus Smith, Eastern N.M.	†1985	11	386	35.1
Norman Miller, Tex. A&M-Kingsville	1995	12	405	33.8
Greg Anderson, Montana	†1974	10	335	33.5
Kevin Cannon, Millersville	1995	14	463	33.1
Kevin McDevitt, Butler	†1975	12	395	32.9

**Record. †National champion.*

ANNUAL CHAMPIONS

Year	Player, Team	Class	No.	Yards	Avg.
1970	Mike Scullin, Baldwin-Wallace	So.	14	492	35.1
1971	Joe Brockmeyer, Western Md.	Jr.	16	500	31.3
1972	Rick Murphy, Indiana St.	Jr.	22	707	32.1
1973	Roscoe Word, Jackson St.	Sr.	18	650	36.1
1974	Greg Anderson, Montana	So.	10	335	33.5
1975	Kevin McDevitt, Butler	Jr.	12	395	32.9
1976	Henry Vereen, UNLV	So.	20	628	31.4
1977	Dickie Johnson, Southern Colo.	Jr.	13	385	29.6
1978	Steve Levenseller, Puget Sound	Sr.	17	610	35.9
1979	Otha Hill, Central St.	Sr.	18	526	29.2
1980	Charlie Taylor, Southeast Mo. St.	Sr.	13	396	30.5
1981	Willie Canady, Fort Valley St.	Jr.	13	415	31.9
1982	Clarence Martin, Cal Poly SLO	So.	11	360	32.7
1983	David Anthony, Southern Ore.	Jr.	14	436	31.1
1984	Larry Winters, St. Paul's	Sr.	20	644	32.2
1985	Rufus Smith, Eastern N.M.	Fr.	11	386	35.1
1986	John Barron, Butler	So.	21	653	31.1
1987	Albert Fann, Cal St. Northridge	Fr.	16	468	29.3
1988	Pierre Fils, New Haven	So.	12	378	31.5
1989	Dennis Mailhot, East Stroudsburg	Jr.	11	359	32.6
1990	Alfred Banks, West Ala.	Sr.	17	529	31.1
1991	Winston Horshaw, Shippensburg	Jr.	15	536	35.7
1992	Danny Lee, Jacksonville St.	Sr.	12	473	39.4
1993	LaVon Reis, Western St.	Sr.	14	552	*39.4
1994	Darell Whitaker, Eastern N.M.	Sr.	20	642	32.1
1995	Melvin German, Southwest St.	Sr.	9	413	††45.9

**Record. ††Declared champion; with two more returns (to make 1.2 per game minimum) for zero yards, still would have highest average (37.5).*

All-Purpose Yards

CAREER YARDS PER GAME
(Minimum 3,500 Yards)

Player, Team	Years	G	Rush	Rcv.	Int.	PR	KOR	Yds.	Yd.PG
Chris George, Glenville St.	1993-94	20	23	3,215	0	391	1,050	4,679	*234.0
Howard Stevens, Randolph-Macon	1968-69	18	2,574	349	0	380	388	3,691	205.1
Johnny Bailey, Tex. A&M-Kingsville	1986-89	39	*6,320	452	0	20	1,011	*7,803	200.1
Steve Roberts, Butler	1986-89	35	4,623	1,201	0	272	578	6,674	190.7
Billy Johnson, Widener	1971-72	19	2,241	242	43	759	251	3,536	186.1

**Record.*

SEASON YARDS PER GAME

Player, Team	Year	G	Rush	Rcv.	Int.	PR	KOR	Yds.	Yd.PG
Steve Roberts, Butler	1989	10	1,450	532	0	272	415	*2,669	*266.9
Bobby Felix, Western N.M.	†1994	8	439	853	0	150	667	2,109	263.6
Chris George, Glenville St.	†1993	10	23	1,876	0	157	562	2,618	261.8
Billy Johnson, Widener	1972	9	1,556	40	43	511	115	2,265	251.7
Roger Graham, New Haven	1993	10	1,687	116	0	0	516	2,319	231.9
Larry Jackson, Edinboro	1994	10	1,660	237	0	0	387	2,284	228.4
Johnny Bailey, Tex. A&M-Kingsville	1986	11	*2,011	54	0	20	340	2,425	220.5
Johnny Cox, Fort Lewis	†1992	10	95	1,331	0	80	679	2,185	218.5
Steve Papin, Portland St.	†1995	11	1,619	525	0	1	252	2,397	217.9
Ronald Moore, Pittsburg St.	1992	11	1,864	141	0	0	388	2,393	217.6
Karl Evans, Mo. Southern St.	1992	10	1,586	10	0	0	571	2,167	216.7
Roger Graham, New Haven	1994	10	1,607	197	0	0	333	2,137	213.7
Dave Ludy, Winona St.	1994	11	1,553	153	0	0	568	2,274	206.7
Chris George, Glenville St.	1994	10	0	1,339	0	234	488	2,061	206.1
Fred Lane, Lane	1995	10	1,833	209	0	0	0	2,042	204.2
Johnny Cox, Fort Lewis	1993	10	9	1,032	0	247	733	2,021	202.1

**Record. †National champion.*

CAREER YARDS

Player, Team	Years	Rush	Rcv.	Int.	PR	KOR	Yds.
Johnny Bailey, Tex. A&M-Kingsville	1986-89	*6,320	452	0	20	1,011	*7,803
Roger Graham, New Haven	1991-94	5,953	393	0	0	870	7,216
Dave Ludy, Winona St.	1991-94	3,501	906	0	34	*2,630	7,071
Albert Fann, Cal St. Northridge	1987-90	4,090	803	0	0	2,141	7,032
Curtis Delgardo, Portland St.	$1986-90	4,178	1,258	0	318	1,188	6,942
Johnny Cox, Fort Lewis	1990-93	112	3,611	0	495	2,476	6,694
Steve Roberts, Butler	1986-89	4,623	1,201	0	272	578	6,674
Richard Huntley, Winston-Salem	1992-95	6,286	333	0	0	0	6,619
Chris Cobb, Eastern Ill.	1976-79	5,042	520	0	37	478	6,077
Don Aleksiewicz, Hobart	1969-72	4,525	470	0	320	748	6,063

**Record. $See page 6 for explanation.*

Photo from Winona State sports information

A Division II-record 2,630 career yards in kickoff returns helped Winona State's Dave Ludy rank third in division history in all-purpose yards (7,071).

DIVISION II

SEASON YARDS

Player, Team	Year	Rush	Rcv.	Int.	PR	KOR	Yds.
Steve Roberts, Butler	1989	1,450	532	0	272	415	*2,669
Chris George, Glenville St.	†1993	23	1,876	0	157	562	2,618
Johnny Bailey, Tex. A&M-Kingsville	1986	*2,011	54	0	20	340	2,425
Rick Wegher, South Dak. St.	1984	1,317	264	0	0	824	2,405
Steve Papin, Portland St.	†1995	1,619	525	0	1	252	2,397
Ronald Moore, Pittsburg St.	1992	1,864	141	0	0	388	2,393
Roger Graham, New Haven	1993	1,687	116	0	0	516	2,319
Larry Jackson, Edinboro	1994	1,660	237	0	0	387	2,284
Dave Ludy, Winona St.	1994	1,553	153	0	0	568	2,274
Billy Johnson, Widener	1972	1,556	40	43	511	115	2,265
Johnny Cox, Fort Lewis	†1992	95	1,331	0	80	679	2,185
Karl Evans, Mo. Southern St.	1992	1,586	10	0	0	571	2,167
Roger Graham, New Haven	1994	1,607	197	0	0	333	2,137
Bobby Felix, Western N.M.	†1994	439	853	0	150	667	2,109
Andre Johnson, Ferris St.	1989	32	1,010	0	120	938	2,100
Chris George, Glenville St.	1994	0	1,339	0	234	488	2,061
Fred Lane, Lane	1995	1,833	209	0	0	0	2,042
Johnny Cox, Fort Lewis	1993	9	1,032	0	247	733	2,021

**Record. †National champion.*

ANNUAL CHAMPIONS

Year	Player, Team	Cl.	G	Rush	Rcv.	Int.	PR	KOR	Yds.	Yd.PG
1992	Johnny Cox, Fort Lewis	Jr.	10	95	1,331	0	80	679	2,185	218.5
1993	Chris George, Glenville St.	Jr.	10	23	1,876	0	157	562	2,618	261.8
1994	Bobby Felix, Western N.M.	Jr.	8	439	853	0	150	667	2,109	263.6
1995	Steve Papin, Portland St.	Sr.	11	1,619	525	0	1	252	2,397	217.9

Field Goals

CAREER FIELD GOALS

Player, Team	Years	Made	Atts.	Pct.
Mike Wood, Southeast Mo. St. (S)	1974-77	*64	*109	.587
Pat Beaty, North Dak. (S)	1985-88	52	82	.634
Bob Gilbreath, Eastern N.M. (S)	1986-89	50	77	.649
Ed O'Brien, Central Fla. (S)	1984-87	50	77	.649
Billy Watkins, East Tex. St. (S)	1990-93	49	84	.583
Bill May, Clarion (C)	1977-80	48	60	*.800
Ed Detwiler, East Stroudsburg (S)	1989-92	48	87	.552
Steve Huff, Central Mo. St. (C)	1982-85	47	80	.588
Phil Brandt, Central Mo. St. (S)	1987-90	46	66	.697
Scott Doyle, Chadron St. (S)	1992-95	46	69	.667
Howie Guarini, Shippensburg (S)	1988-91	45	62	.726
James Knowles, North Ala. (C)	1982-85	45	77	.584
Ed Hotz, Southeast Mo. St. (S)	1978-81	45	77	.584
Kurt Seibel, South Dak. (C)	1980-83	44	62	.710
Jason Monday, Lenoir-Rhyne (S)	1989-92	44	64	.688
Pat Bolton, Montana St. (C)	1972-75	44	76	.579
Skipper Butler, Texas-Arlington (C)	1966-69	44	101	.436

**Record. (C) Conventional kicker. (S) Soccer-style kicker.*

SEASON FIELD GOALS

Player, Team	Year	Made	Atts.	Pct.
Raul De la Flor, Humboldt St. (S)	†1993	**20	26	.769
Pat Beaty, North Dak. (S)	†1988	**20	26	.769
Tom Jurich, Northern Ariz. (C)	†1977	**20	29	.690
Dennis Hochman, Sonoma St. (S)	†1986	19	22	+.864
Cory Solberg, North Dak. (S)	†1989	19	27	.704
Jaime Nunez, Weber St. (S)	†1971	19	32	.594
Jon Ruff, Indiana (Pa.) (S)	†1995	18	23	.783
Bernard Henderson, Albany St. (Ga.) (S)	†1985	18	26	.692
Ki Tok Chu, Tenn.-Martin (S)	1988	17	22	.773
Jack McTyre, Valdosta St. (S)	1990	17	23	.739
Dino Beligrinis, Winston-Salem (S)	1988	17	23	.739
David Dell, East Tex. St. (S)	1995	17	26	.654
Ed O'Brien, Central Fla. (S)	†1987	17	26	.654
Mike Wood, Southeast Mo. St. (S)	1976	17	33	.515

***Record tied. +Record for minimum 20 attempts. (C) Conventional kicker. (S) Soccer-style kicker.*

ANNUAL CHAMPIONS

Year	Player, Team	Class	Made	Atts.	Pct.	PG
1970	Chris Guerrieri, Alfred (S)	Sr.	11	21	.524	1.38
1971	Jaime Nunez, Weber St. (S)	Sr.	19	32	.594	**1.90
1972	Randy Walker, Northwestern St. (C)	Jr.	13	19	.684	1.30
1973	Reinhold Struprich, Hawaii (S)	Jr.	15	23	.652	1.36
1974	Mike Wood, Southeast Mo. St. (S)	Fr.	16	23	.696	1.45
1975	Wolfgang Taylor, Western St. (S)	Sr.	14	21	.667	1.56
1976	Rolf Benirschke, UC Davis (S)	Sr.	14	19	.737	1.56
1977	Tom Jurich, Northern Ariz. (C)	Sr.	**20	29	.690	1.81
1978	Frank Friedman, Cal St. Northridge (S)	Jr.	15	22	.682	1.50
1979	Bill May, Clarion (C)	Jr.	16	21	.762	1.60
1980	Nelson McMurain, North Ala. (S)	Jr.	14	22	.636	1.40
	Sean Landeta, Towson St. (S)	So.	14	28	.500	1.40
1981	Russ Meier, South Dak. St. (S)	Fr.	16	21	.762	1.60
1982	Joey Malone, Alabama A&M (C)	Fr.	15	21	.714	1.36
	Rick Ruszkiewicz, Edinboro (S)	Sr.	15	24	.625	1.36
1983	Mike Thomas, Angelo St. (S)	Sr.	16	22	.727	1.45
1984	Terry Godfrey, South Dak. (S)	Jr.	16	26	.615	1.60
1985	Bernard Henderson, Albany St. (Ga.) (S)	Sr.	18	26	.692	1.64
1986	Dennis Hochman, Sonoma St. (S)	Sr.	19	22	+.864	**1.90
1987	Ed O'Brien, Central Fla. (S)	Sr.	17	26	.654	1.70
1988	Pat Beaty, North Dak. (S)	Sr.	**20	26	.769	1.82
1989	Cory Solberg, North Dak. (S)	Jr.	19	27	.704	1.73
1990	Jack McTyre, Valdosta St. (S)	Sr.	17	23	.739	1.70
1991	Billy Watkins, East Tex. St. (S)	So.	15	24	.625	1.36
1992	Mike Estrella, St. Mary's (Cal.) (S)	Jr.	15	27	.556	1.67
1993	Raul De la Flor, Humboldt St. (S)	Sr.	**20	26	.769	1.82
1994	Matt Seagreaves, East Stroudsburg (S)	So.	15	26	.577	1.50
1995	Jon Ruff, Indiana (Pa.) (S)	Sr.	18	23	.783	1.64

***Record tied. +Record for minimum 20 attempts. (C) Conventional kicker. (S) Soccer-style kicker.*

All-Time Longest Plays

Since 1941, official maximum length of all plays fixed at 100 yards.

RUSHING

Rushing plays have covered 99 yards 20 times. The most recent:

Yds.	Player, Team (Opponent)	Year
99	Thelbert Withers, N.M. Highlands (Fort Lewis)	1992
99	Lester Frye, Edinboro (Calif., Pa.)	1991
99	Kelvin Minefee, Southern Utah (Mesa St.)	1988
99	Fred Deutsch, Springfield (Wagner)	1977
99	Sammy Croom, San Diego (Azusa Pacific)	1972
99	John Stenger, Swarthmore (Widener)	1970
99	Jed Knuttila, Hamline (St. Thomas, Minn.)	1968
99	Dave Lanoha, Colorado Col. (Texas Lutheran)	1967
99	Tom Pabst, UC Riverside (Cal Tech)	1965
99	George Phillips, Concord (Davis & Elkins)	1961

PASSING

Pass plays have resulted in 99-yard completions 17 times. The most recent:

Yds.	Passer-Receiver, Team (Opponent)	Year
99	Ken Collums-Jerome Davis, Central Ark. (Delta St.)	1994
99	Greg Younger-Marty Walsh, Hillsdale (St. Francis, Ill.)	1994
99	Ray Morrow-Jeff Williamson, Cal St. Hayward (Redlands)	1993
99	Bob McLaughlin-Eric Muldowney, Lock Haven (Mansfield)	1993
99	Rob Rayl-John Unger, Valparaiso (Hillsdale)	1992
99	Bret Comp-Ken Kopetchny, East Stroudsburg (Mansfield)	1990
99	Mike Turk-Titus Dixon, Troy St. (Nicholls St.)	1986
99	Keith Young-John Ragin, Dist. Columbia (Fayetteville St.)	1985
99	Nick Pannunzo-Herman Heard, Southern Colo. (Adams St.)	1982
99	Tim Ebersole-Ed Noon, Shippensburg (Indiana, Pa.)	1982

PUNTS

Yds.	Player, Team (Opponent)	Year
97	Earl Hurst, Emporia St. (Central Mo. St.)	1964
96	Alex Campbell, Morris Brown (Clark Atlanta)	1994
96	Gary Frens, Hope (Olivet)	1966
96	Jim Jarrett, North Dak. (South Dak.)	1957
93	Elliot Mills, Carleton (Monmouth, Ill.)	1970
93	Kaspar Fitins, Taylor (Georgetown, Ky.)	1966
93	Leeroy Sweeney, Pomona-Pitzer (UC Riverside)	1960

FIELD GOALS

Yds.	Player, Team (Opponent)	Year
67	Tom Odle, Fort Hays St. (Washburn)	1988
63	Joe Duren, Arkansas St. (McNeese St.)	1974
62	Mike Flater, Colorado Mines (Western St.)	1973
61	Duane Christian, Cameron (Southwestern Okla.)	1976
61	Mike Wood, Southeast Mo. St. (Lincoln, Mo.)	1975
61	Bill Shear, Cortland St. (Hobart)	1966
60	Mike Panasuk, Ferris St. (St. Joseph's, Ind.)	1990
60	Ed Beaulac, Sonoma St. (St. Mary's, Cal.)	1989
60	Roger McCoy, Grand Valley St. (Grand Rapids)	1976
60	Skipper Butler, Texas-Arlington (East Tex. St.)	1968

Since 1941, many players have returned interceptions, punts and kickoffs 100 yards. For the 1995 season leaders, see pages 414-415.

Team Champions

Annual Offense Champions

TOTAL OFFENSE

Year	Team	Avg.
1948	Hanover	*624.1
1949	Pacific (Cal.)	505.3
1950	West Tex. A&M	465.3
1951	Western Ill.	473.6
1952	Sam Houston St.	448.2
1953	Col. of Idaho	476.3
1954	Col. of Emporia	469.7
1955	Centre	431.0
1956	Florida A&M	475.0
1957	Denison	430.8
1958	Missouri Valley	449.6
1959	Whittier	461.3
1960	Muskingum	456.4
1961	Florida A&M	413.6
1962	Baker	438.4
1963	Col. of Emporia	517.1
1964	San Diego St.	422.6
1965	Long Beach St.	439.5
1966	Weber St.	460.1
1967	San Fran. St.	490.0
1968	Louisiana Tech	459.1
1969	Delaware	488.9
1970	Grambling	457.7
1971	Delaware	515.6
1972	Hobart	457.3
1973	Boise St.	466.5
1974	Boise St.	516.9
1975	Portland St.	472.4
1976	Portland St.	497.5
1977	Portland St.	506.7
1978	Western St.	487.0
1979	Delaware	450.5
1980	Southwest Tex. St.	423.0
1981	Southwest Tex. St.	482.3
1982	Northern Mich.	450.4
1983	Central St.	491.1
1984	North Dak. St.	455.3
1985	Truman St.	471.4
1986	Tex. A&M-Kingsville	542.6
1987	Tex. A&M-Kingsville	486.4
1988	Cal St. Sacramento	486.0
1989	Grand Valley St	480.8
1990	Chadron St.	479.6
1991	Western St.	549.8
1992	New Haven	587.7
1993	Wayne St. (Neb.)	581.5
1994	West Tex. A&M	571.3
1995	Portland St.	472.0

*Record.

RUSHING OFFENSE

Year	Team	Avg.
1948	Hanover	400.4
1949	Southern-B.R.	382.9
1950	St. Lawrence	356.1
1951	Western N.M.	379.2
1952	William Jewell	345.0
1953	McPherson	375.9
1954	Col. of Emporia	*404.8
1955	Centre	373.4
1956	Tufts	359.9
1957	Denison	372.1
1958	Huron	353.3
1959	Bemidji St.	326.6
1960	Muskingum	355.2
1961	Huron	313.1
1962	Northern St.	355.3
1963	Luther	356.0
1964	Cal St. Los Angeles	325.9
1965	Huron	303.3
1966	Neb.-Kearney	370.1
1967	North Dak. St.	299.6
1968	Delaware	315.8
1969	St. Olaf	369.1
1970	Delaware	385.9
1971	Delaware	371.2
1972	Hobart	380.7
1973	Bethune-Cookman	308.8
1974	Central Mich.	324.6
1975	North Dak.	344.4
1976	Montana St.	287.5
1977	South Caro. St.	321.5
1978	Western St.	320.2
1979	Mississippi Col.	314.5
1980	Minn.-Duluth	307.3
1981	Millersville	322.9
1982	Mississippi Col.	297.0
1983	Jamestown	297.7
1984	North Dak. St.	334.7
1985	Saginaw Valley	300.4
1986	Tex. A&M-Kingsville	395.2
1987	Tex. A&M-Kingsville	330.5
1988	North Dak. St.	373.1
1989	Wofford	373.7
1990	North Dak. St.	364.2
1991	Wofford	347.9
1992	Pittsburg St.	353.8
1993	North Ala.	371.5
1994	Moorhead St.	375.0
1995	Pittsburg St.	318.8

*Record.

PASSING OFFENSE

Year	Team	Avg.
1948	Hanover	223.8
1949	Baldwin-Wallace	196.9
1950	Northern Ill.	187.0
1951	Central Mich.	213.8
1952	Sam Houston St.	263.0
1953	Southern Conn. St.	193.5
1954	Northern Iowa	206.1
1955	Hamline	210.7
1956	Widener	207.7
1957	Cal Poly Pomona	236.0
1958	Cal Poly Pomona	217.6
1959	Whittier	199.3
1960	Whitworth	213.6
1961	Cal Poly Pomona	244.1
1962	Northern Ill.	285.6
1963	Northern Ill.	349.3
1964	Parsons	301.3
1965	Southern Ore. St.	268.9
1966	San Diego St.	268.1
1967	San Fran. St.	387.0
1968	Louisiana Tech	316.4
1969	Portland St.	308.6
1970	Portland St.	313.8
1971	LIU-C.W. Post	262.5
1972	Maryville (Tenn.)	277.8
1973	Lehigh	275.0
1974	Boise St.	334.5
1975	Portland St.	361.7
1976	Portland St.	404.1
1977	Portland St.	378.5
1978	Northern Mich.	242.3
1979	Northern Mich.	284.2
1980	Northern Mich.	269.6
1981	Franklin	306.5
1982	Evansville	313.0
1983	Franklin	358.0
1984	Franklin	334.0
1985	Truman St.	345.1
1986	West Tex. A&M	345.5
1987	Evansville	306.6
1988	Central Fla.	292.2
1989	Cal St. Chico	328.8
1990	New Haven	335.4
1991	Western St.	357.4
1992	Gardner-Webb	367.8
1993	LIU-C.W. Post	409.0
1994	West Tex. A&M	*454.5
1995	Norfolk St.	367.4

*Record.

SCORING OFFENSE

Year	Team	Avg.
1948	Sul Ross St.	43.1
1949	Pacific (Cal.)	50.0
1950	West Tex. A&M	37.2
1951	Western Ill.	42.1
1952	East Tex. St.	49.6
1953	Col. of Idaho	42.4
1954	Col. of Emporia	43.2
1955	Central Mich.	36.3
1956	Florida A&M	45.9
1957	Denison	38.6
1958	West Chester	51.4
1959	Florida A&M	42.6
1960	Florida A&M	52.8
1961	Florida A&M	54.7
1962	Florida A&M	42.0
1963	Col. of Emporia	42.4
1964	San Diego St.	42.3
1965	Ottawa	43.2
1966	N.M. Highlands	48.1
1967	Waynesburg	53.7
1968	Doane	52.9
1969	St. Olaf	45.2
1970	Wittenberg	40.0
1971	Michigan Tech	42.4
1972	Fort Valley St.	45.0
1973	Western Ky.	37.7
1974	Boise St.	44.6
1975	Bethune-Cookman	37.9
1976	Northern Mich.	43.0
1977	South Caro. St.	38.4
1978	Western St.	45.2
1979	Delaware	35.5
1980	Minn.-Duluth	35.4
1981	Southwest Tex. St.	37.5
1982	Truman St.	40.0
1983	Central St.	43.6
1984	North Dak. St.	39.0
1985	UC Davis	37.6
1986	Tex. A&M-Kingsville	43.1
1987	Central Fla.	34.5
	West Chester	34.5
1988	North Dak. St.	39.6
	Tex. A&M-Kingsville	39.6
1989	Grand Valley St.	44.5
1990	Indiana (Pa.)	44.2
1991	Western St.	46.1
1992	New Haven	50.5
1993	New Haven	*54.7
1994	Hampton	46.4
1995	Tex. A&M-Kingsville	40.1

*Record.

Annual Defense Champions

TOTAL DEFENSE

Year	Team	Avg.
1948	Morgan St.	104.4
1949	Southern Conn. St.	95.6
1950	Southern Conn. St.	93.6
1951	Southern Conn. St.	84.3
1952	West Chester	128.4
1953	Shippensburg	81.9
1954	Geneva	106.3
1955	Col. of Emporia	102.0
1956	Tennessee St.	118.9
1957	West Chester	90.2
1958	Rose-Hulman	95.8
1959	Md.-East. Shore	75.3
1960	Md.-East. Shore	104.8
1961	Florida A&M	85.3
1962	John Carroll	*44.4
1963	West Chester	100.8
1964	Morgan St.	126.4
1965	Morgan St.	91.5
1966	Tennessee St.	85.7
1967	Tennessee St.	61.6
1968	Alcorn St.	103.4
1969	Livingstone	148.5
1970	Delaware St.	103.5
1971	Hampden-Sydney	115.6
1972	Wis.-Whitewater	143.8
1973	Livingstone	114.9
1974	Livingstone	120.5

Year	Team	Avg.
1975	South Caro. St.	100.6
1976	Alcorn St.	108.9
1977	Virginia Union	160.3
1978	East Stroudsburg	153.8
1979	Virginia Union	138.2
1980	Concordia-M'head	191.7
1981	Fort Valley St.	148.3
1982	Jamestown	187.9
1983	Virginia Union	143.7
1984	Virginia St.	180.6
1985	Fort Valley St.	162.2
1986	Virginia Union	163.5
1987	Alabama A&M	167.1
1988	Alabama A&M	175.8
1989	Winston-Salem	185.7
1990	Sonoma St.	218.5
1991	Ashland	195.5
1992	Ashland	211.5
1993	Bentley	188.3
1994	Bentley	195.5
1995	Kentucky St.	205.1

*Record.

RUSHING DEFENSE

Year	Team	Avg.
1948	Morgan St.	44.8
1949	Hanover	43.5
1950	Lewis & Clark	50.3
1951	Southern Conn. St.	17.1
1952	East Tex. St.	48.5
1953	Shippensburg	53.6
1954	Tennessee St.	29.2
1955	Muskingum	52.5
1956	Hillsdale	51.1
1957	West Chester	27.9
1958	Ithaca	48.4
1959	Md.-East. Shore	36.3
1960	West Chester	41.4
1961	Florida A&M	20.1
1962	John Carroll	-1.0
1963	St. John's (Minn.)	12.9
1964	Fort Valley St.	39.7
1965	Morgan St.	15.0
1966	Tennessee St.	13.9
1967	Tennessee St.	*-16.7
1968	Alcorn St.	8.8
1969	Merchant Marine	16.2
1970	Delaware St.	-4.9
1971	Northern Colo.	27.5
1972	Alcorn St.	49.8
1973	Alcorn St.	45.9
1974	Livingstone	53.0
1975	Alcorn St.	15.9
1976	Alcorn St.	32.5
1977	Virginia Union	63.6
1978	East Stroudsburg	52.2
1979	Virginia Union	41.0
1980	Mo.-Rolla	34.6
1981	Fort Valley St.	46.9
1982	Butler	71.1
1983	Butler	38.2
1984	Norfolk St.	53.8
1985	Norfolk St.	50.9
1986	Central St.	44.5
1987	West Chester	67.2
1988	Cal Poly SLO	56.4
1989	Tex. A&M-Kingsville	60.7
1990	Sonoma St.	58.3
1991	Sonoma St.	63.6
1992	Ashland	64.4
1993	Albany St. (Ga.)	59.1
1994	Hampton	66.0
1995	North Ala.	56.8

*Record.

PASSING DEFENSE

Year	Team	$Avg.
1948	Ashland	*10.1
1949	Wilmington (Ohio)	39.8
1950	Vermont	34.4
1951	Alfred	52.0
1952	Cortland St.	45.9
1953	Shippensburg	28.3
1954	St. Augustine's	26.5
1955	Ithaca	15.5
1956	West Va. Tech	29.1
1957	Lake Forest	25.0
1958	Coast Guard	25.4
1959	Huron	21.9
1960	Susquehanna	27.3
1961	Westminster (Utah)	24.8
1962	Principia	27.8
1963	Western Caro.	39.3
1964	Mont. St.-Billings	44.1
1965	Minot St.	44.5
1966	Manchester	54.7
1967	Mount Union	61.4
1968	Bridgeport	47.6
1969	Wabash	72.0
1970	Hampden-Sydney	62.9
1971	Western Ky.	57.7
1972	Howard	48.8
1973	East Stroudsburg	37.6
1974	Tennessee St.	52.6
1975	N.C. Central	60.2
1976	Morris Brown	60.8
1977	Delaware St.	64.3
1978	Concordia-M'head	55.8
1979	Kentucky St.	62.3
1980	Norfolk St.	71.5
1981	Bowie St.	75.7
1982	Elizabeth City St.	49.0
1983	Elizabeth City St.	65.0
1984	Virginia St.	80.4
1985	Fort Valley St.	94.5
1986	Virginia Union	84.7
1987	Alabama A&M	72.5
1988	Alabama A&M	84.3
1989	Mo. Southern St.	93.0
1990	Angelo St.	65.4
1991	Carson-Newman	64.9
1992	East Tex. St.	61.8
1993	Alabama A&M	71.5
1994	Bentley	55.6
1995	Savannah St.	72.4

*Record. $Beginning in 1990, based on pass efficiency ranking instead of yards per game.

SCORING DEFENSE

Year	Team	Avg.
1959	Huron	2.1
1960	Albany St. (Ga.)	*0.0
1961	Florida A&M	2.8
1962	John Carroll	2.9
1963	Massachusetts	1.3
1964	Central (Iowa)	4.8
1965	St. John's (Minn.)	2.2
1966	Morgan St.	3.6
1967	Waynesburg	4.3
1968	Central Conn. St.	4.4
1969	Carthage	6.0
1970	Hampden-Sydney	2.8
1971	Hampden-Sydney	3.4
1972	Ashland	5.6
1973	Virginia Union	3.8
1974	Minn.-Duluth	5.5
1975	South Caro. St.	2.9
1976	South Caro. St.	3.4
1977	Minn.-Duluth	7.8
1978	Southwestern La.	7.1
1979	Virginia Union	6.1
1980	Minn.-Duluth	7.6
1981	Moorhead St.	5.0
1982	Jamestown	5.9
1983	Towson St.	5.8
1984	Cal Poly SLO	9.0
1985	Fort Valley St.	6.3
1986	North Dak. St.	6.8
1987	Tuskegee	9.1
1988	Alabama A&M	7.5
1989	Jacksonville St.	7.0
1990	Cal Poly SLO	11.3
1991	Butler	7.1
1992	Ferris St.	10.5
1993	Albany St. (Ga.)	8.7
1994	Bentley	6.0
1995	North Ala.	10.6

*Record.

Other Annual Team Champions

NET PUNTING

Year	Team	Avg.
1992	Fort Lewis	37.9
1993	North Ala.	39.5
1994	Colorado Mines	42.9
1995	New Haven	38.7

PUNT RETURNS

Year	Team	Avg.
1992	Savannah St.	21.2
1993	Wayne St. (Neb.)	19.1
1994	Adams St.	16.7
1995	Elizabeth City St.	23.1

KICKOFF RETURNS

Year	Team	Avg.
1992	Jacksonville St.	34.0
1993	Adams St.	27.5
1994	Western N.M.	31.8
1995	Millersville	26.0

TURNOVER MARGIN

Year	Team	Avg.
1992	Hillsdale	2.2
1993	Hillsdale	*2.7
1994	Lenoir-Rhyne	2.6
1995	Central Okla.	2.6

*Record.

All-Time Team Won-Lost Records

Includes records as a senior college only, minimum 20 seasons of competition since 1937. Postseason games are included, and each tie game is computed as half won and half lost.

PERCENTAGE (TOP 25)

Team	Yrs.	Won	Lost	Tied	Pct.
West Chester	67	431	181	17	.699
Tex. A&M-Kingsville	67	462	203	16	.690
Indiana (Pa.)	66	378	202	23	.646
Central Okla.	90	497	275	47	.636
Neb.-Kearney	72	404	226	27	.635
Grand Valley St.	25	161	92	3	.635
Pittsburg St.	88	506	284	48	.632
Minn.-Duluth	63	327	195	24	.621
Carson-Newman	72	412	249	30	.618
Northern St.	90	443	269	33	.617
Truman St.	88	455	278	35	.615
North Dak. St.	99	500	307	34	.615
Hillsdale	103	505	309	46	.614
Angelo St.	32	205	130	7	.610
Virginia St.	84	423	265	48	.607
East Stroudsburg	68	349	223	19	.607
Tuskegee	100	488	310	50	.605
North Ala.	47	286	187	16	.601
Virginia Union	95	429	278	47	.600
North Dak.	99	476	316	29	.597
Fort Valley St.	50	273	182	21	.596
LIU-C.W. Post	39	218	153	5	.586
Mesa St.	20	121	85	5	.585
Central Ark.	84	417	292	42	.583
Albany (N.Y.)	23	130	95	0	.578

ALPHABETICAL LISTING

(No Minimum Seasons of Competition)

Team	Yrs.	Won	Lost	Tied	Pct.
Abilene Christian	74	369	308	32	.543
Adams St.	61	266	240	17	.525
Alabama A&M	58	263	241	26	.521
Albany (N.Y.)	23	130	95	0	.578
Albany St. (Ga.)	50	239	210	21	.531
American Int'l	59	234	254	20	.480
Angelo St.	32	205	130	7	.610
Ashland	73	337	278	29	.546
Assumption	8	32	40	1	.445
Augustana (S.D.)	75	291	345	14	.458
Bemidji St.	70	222	333	23	.404
Bentley	8	59	14	1	.804
Bloomsburg	68	269	282	21	.489
Bowie St.	24	77	149	6	.345
UC Davis	77	369	297	33	.552
Calif. (Pa.)	66	243	290	19	.457
Cal St. Chico	72	290	333	24	.467
Carson-Newman	72	412	249	30	.618
Catawba	76	360	350	26	.507
Central Ark.	84	417	292	42	.583
Central Mo. St.	99	385	428	51	.475
Central Okla.	90	497	275	47	.636
Chadron St.	81	355	294	15	.546
Cheyney	42	82	287	5	.226
Clarion	67	309	239	17	.562
Clark Atlanta	57	182	272	23	.406
Colorado Mines	106	313	448	32	.415
Concord	71	313	295	27	.514
Delta St.	66	300	304	23	.497
East Stroudsburg	68	349	223	19	.607
East Tex. St.	78	411	302	31	.573
Eastern N.M.	52	259	245	15	.513
Edinboro	67	251	281	24	.473
Elizabeth City St.	54	236	234	18	.502
Elon	74	395	303	18	.564
Emporia St.	98	384	420	44	.479
Fairmont St.	82	351	291	44	.544
Fayetteville St.	50	167	269	26	.390
Ferris St.	67	249	288	34	.466
Fort Hays St.	74	334	343	49	.494
Fort Lewis	33	108	197	3	.356
Fort Valley St.	50	273	182	21	.596
Gannon	8	48	25	2	.653
Gardner-Webb	26	127	146	2	.465
Glenville St.	83	256	320	37	.448
Grand Valley St.	25	161	92	3	.635
Henderson St.	88	379	328	44	.534
Hillsdale	103	505	309	46	.614
Humboldt St.	68	310	261	20	.541
Indiana (Pa.)	66	378	202	23	.646
Indianapolis	58	239	268	23	.473
Johnson Smith	68	268	308	34	.467
Kentucky St.	67	282	337	26	.457
Ky. Wesleyan	35	105	145	16	.425
Kutztown	65	217	304	21	.420
Lane	72	190	335	26	.368
Lenoir-Rhyne	76	392	310	34	.556
Livingstone	47	181	239	15	.433
Lock Haven	67	248	333	25	.430
LIU-C.W. Post	39	218	153	5	.586
Mankato St.	70	305	278	27	.522
Mansfield	66	208	317	30	.402
Mars Hill	32	144	167	10	.464
Mass.-Lowell	16	70	79	2	.470
Mercyhurst	15	75	58	4	.562
Mesa St.	20	121	85	5	.585
Michigan Tech	73	258	250	17	.508
Miles	26	49	177	7	.225
Millersville	64	287	237	21	.546
Minn.-Duluth	63	327	195	24	.621
Minn.-Morris	34	164	156	10	.512
Mississippi Col.	83	393	305	37	.560
Mo.-Rolla	90	339	402	36	.459
Mo. Southern St.	28	153	124	7	.551
Mo. Western St.	26	121	142	9	.461
Moorhead St.	78	340	283	31	.544
Morehouse	96	333	348	49	.490
Morningside	94	331	427	37	.440
Morris Brown	70	309	293	37	.513
Neb.-Kearney	72	404	226	27	.635
Neb.-Omaha	79	321	337	30	.488
New Haven	23	127	97	5	.566
N.M. Highlands	69	237	307	27	.439
Newberry	82	302	443	33	.409
Norfolk St.	35	175	155	7	.530
North Ala.	47	286	187	16	.601
N.C. Central	65	328	252	24	.563
North Dak.	99	476	316	29	.597
North Dak. St.	99	500	307	34	.615
Northern Colo.	83	324	330	24	.496
Northern Mich.	82	340	254	26	.569
Northern St.	90	443	269	33	.617
Northwest Mo. St.	78	313	360	32	.467
Northwood	34	130	170	8	.435
Pace	18	64	105	2	.380
Pittsburg St.	88	506	284	48	.632
Portland St.	41	218	204	7	.516
Presbyterian	83	392	373	35	.512
Quincy	9	48	34	1	.584
Sacred Heart	5	14	32	0	.304
Saginaw Valley	21	109	106	3	.507
St. Cloud St.	68	316	255	21	.552
St. Francis (Ill.)	10	54	49	0	.524
St. Joseph's (Ind.)	76	234	305	24	.437
Savannah St.	43	170	214	15	.445
Shepherd	72	302	273	26	.524
Shippensburg	66	312	265	21	.539
Slippery Rock	68	329	246	28	.569
Sonoma St.	17	62	106	2	.371
South Dak.	100	426	396	34	.518
South Dak. St.	98	436	361	38	.545
Southern Conn. St.	48	251	185	11	.574
Southwest Baptist	13	42	83	2	.339
Southwest St.	28	107	164	5	.397
Stonehill	8	45	25	3	.637
Stony Brook	13	60	58	2	.508
Tarleton St.	35	143	203	3	.414
Tex. A&M-Kingsville	67	462	203	16	.690
Truman St.	88	455	278	35	.615
Tuskegee	100	488	310	50	.605
Valdosta St.	14	87	58	3	.598
Virginia St.	84	423	265	48	.607
Virginia Union	95	429	278	47	.600
Washburn	104	422	462	40	.478
Wayne St. (Mich.)	78	275	346	29	.445
Wayne St. (Neb.)	70	302	334	38	.476
West Ala.	54	207	274	15	.432

Team	Yrs.	Won	Lost	Tied	Pct.
West Chester	67	431	181	17	.699
West Ga.	17	78	96	0	.448
West Liberty St.	69	337	266	35	.556
West Tex. A&M	84	371	393	22	.486
West Va. Tech	76	263	327	35	.449
West Va. Wesleyan	90	334	387	30	.465
Western N.M.	59	221	274	15	.448
Western St.	73	304	306	14	.498
Wingate	10	41	59	0	.410
Winona St.	95	267	412	32	.398
Winston-Salem	52	269	212	22	.557

VICTORIES (TOP 25)

Team	Wins
Pittsburg St.	506
Hillsdale	505
North Dak. St.	500
Central Okla.	497
Tuskegee	488
North Dak.	476
Tex. A&M-Kingsville	462
Truman St.	455
Northern St.	443
South Dak. St.	436
West Chester	431
Virginia Union	429
South Dak.	426
Virginia St.	423
Washburn	422
Central Ark.	417
Carson-Newman	412
East Tex. St.	411
Neb.-Kearney	404
Elon	395
Mississippi Col.	393
Lenoir-Rhyne	392
Presbyterian	392
Central Mo. St.	385
Emporia St.	384

National Poll Rankings

Wire Service National Champions

(1958-74)

(For what was then known as College Division teams. Selections by United Press International from 1958 and Associated Press from 1960.)

Year	Team	Coach	Record*
1958	Southern Miss.	Thad "Pie" Vann	9-0-0
1959	Bowling Green	Doyt Perry	9-0-0
1960	Ohio	Bill Hess	10-0-0
1961	Pittsburg St.	Carnie Smith	9-0-0
1962	Southern Miss. (UPI)	Thad "Pie" Vann	9-1-0
	Florida A&M (AP)	Jake Gaither	9-0-0
1963	Delaware (UPI)	Dave Nelson	8-0-0
	Northern Ill. (AP)	Howard Fletcher	9-0-0
1964	Cal St. Los Angeles (UPI)	Homer Beatty	9-0-0
	Wittenberg (AP)	Bill Edwards	8-0-0
1965	North Dak. St.	Darrell Mudra	10-0-0
1966	San Diego St.	Don Coryell	10-0-0
1967	San Diego St.	Don Coryell	9-1-0
1968	San Diego St. (UPI)	Don Coryell	9-0-1
	North Dak. St. (AP)	Ron Erhardt	9-0-0
1969	North Dak. St.	Ron Erhardt	9-0-0
1970	Arkansas St.	Bennie Ellender	10-0-0
1971	Delaware	Harold "Tubby" Raymond	9-1-0
1972	Delaware	Harold "Tubby" Raymond	10-0-0
1973	Tennessee St.	John Merritt	10-0-0
1974	Louisiana Tech (UPI)	Maxie Lambright	10-0-0
	Central Mich. (AP)	Roy Kramer	9-1-0

Regular season.

Final Poll Leaders

(Released Before Division Championship Playoffs)

Year	Team (Record*)	Coach	Record in Championship†
1975	North Dak. (9-0-0)	Jerry Olson	0-1 Lost in first round
1976	Northern Mich. (10-0-0)	Gil Krueger	1-1 Lost in semifinals
1977	North Dak. St. (8-1-1)	Jim Wacker	1-1 Lost in semifinals
1978	Winston-Salem (10-0-0)	Bill Hayes	Did not compete
1979	Delaware (9-1-0)	Harold "Tubby" Raymond	3-0 Champion
1980	Eastern Ill. (8-2-0)	Darrell Mudra	2-1 Runner-up
1981	Southwest Tex. St. (9-0-0)	Jim Wacker	3-0 Champion
1982	Southwest Tex. St. (11-0-0)	Jim Wacker	3-0 Champion
1983	UC Davis (9-0-0)	Jim Sochor	1-1 Lost in semifinals
1984	North Dak. St. (9-1-0)	Don Morton	2-1 Runner-up
1985	UC Davis (9-1-0)	Jim Sochor	0-1 Lost in first round
1986	North Dak. St. (10-0-0)	Earle Solomonson	3-0 Champion
1987	Tex. A&M-Kingsville (9-1-0)	Ron Harms	Did not compete
1988	North Dak. St. (10-0-0)	Rocky Hager	4-0 Champion
1989	Tex. A&M-Kingsville (10-0-0)	Ron Harms	0-1 Lost in first round
1990	North Dak. St. (10-0-0)	Rocky Hager	4-0 Champion
1991	Indiana (Pa.) (10-0-0)	Frank Cignetti	2-1 Lost in semifinals
1992	Pittsburg St. (11-0-0)	Chuck Broyles	3-1 Runner-up
1993	North Ala. (10-0-0)	Bobby Wallace	4-0 Champion
1994	North Ala. (8-1-0)	Bobby Wallace	4-0 Champion
1995	North Ala. (9-0)	Bobby Wallace	4-0 Champion

**Final poll record; in some cases, a team had one game remaining before the championship playoffs. †Number of teams in the championship: 8 (1975-87); 16 (1988-present).*

Undefeated, Untied Teams

(Regular-Season Games Only)

In 1948, official national statistics rankings began to include all nonmajor four-year colleges. Until the 1967 season, rankings and records included all four-year colleges that reported their statistics to the NCAA. Beginning with the 1967 season, statistics (and won-lost records) included only members of the NCAA.

Since 1981, conference playoff games have been included in a team's regular-season statistics and won-lost record (previously, such games were considered postseason contests).

The regular-season list includes games in which a home team served as a predetermined, preseason host of a "bowl game" regardless of its record and games scheduled before the season, thus eliminating postseason designation for the Orange Blossom Classic, annually hosted by Florida A&M, and the Prairie View Bowl, annually hosted by Prairie View, for example.

Figures are regular-season wins only. A subsequent postseason win(s) is indicated by (*), a loss by (†) and a tie by (‡).

Year	College	Wins
1948	Alma	8
	Bloomsburg	9
	Denison	8
	Heidelberg	9
	Michigan Tech	7
	Missouri Valley	†‡9
	Occidental	*8
	Southern-B.R.	*11
	Sul Ross St.	‡10
	Wesleyan (Conn.)	8
1949	Ball St.	8
	Emory & Henry	*†10
	Gannon	8
	Hanover	†8
	Lewis	8
	Md.-East. Shore	8
	Morgan St.	8
	Pacific (Cal.)	11
	St. Ambrose	8
	St. Vincent	*9
	Trinity (Conn.)	8
	Wayne St. (Neb.)	9
	Wofford	11
1950	Abilene Christian	*10
	Canterbury	8
	Florida St.	8
	Frank. & Marsh.	9
	Lehigh	9
	Lewis & Clark	*8
	Md.-East. Shore	8
	Mission House	6
	New Hampshire	8
	St. Lawrence	8
	St. Norbert	7
	Thiel	7
	Valparaiso	†9
	West Liberty St.	*8
	Wis.-La Crosse	*9
	Wis.-Whitewater	6
1951	Bloomsburg	8
	Bucknell	9
	Col. of Emporia	8
	Ill. Wesleyan	8
	Lawrence	7
	Northern Ill.	9
	Principia	6
	St. Michael's	6
	South Dak. Tech	8
	Susquehanna	6
	Trenton St.	6
	Valparaiso	9
	Western Md.	8
1952	Beloit	8
	Clarion	*8
	East Tex. St.	*10
	Fairmont St.	6
	Idaho St.	8
	Lenoir-Rhyne	†8
	Northeastern St.	†9
	Peru St.	10
	Rochester	8
	St. Norbert	6
	Shippensburg	7
	West Chester	7
1953	Cal Poly SLO	9
	Col. of Emporia	8
	Col. of Idaho	†8

Year	College	Wins
	Defiance	8
	East Tex. St.	‡10
	Florida A&M	10
	Indianapolis	8
	Iowa Wesleyan	†9
	Juniata	7
	Northern St.	8
	Martin Luther	6
	Peru St.	8
	Prairie View	10
	St. Olaf	8
	Shippensburg	8
	Westminster (Pa.)	8
	Wis.-La Crosse	‡9
	Wis.-Platteville	6
1954	Ashland	7
	Carleton	8
	Central Conn. St.	6
	Col. of Emporia	†9
	Delta St.	8
	Hastings	*8
	Hobart	8
	Juniata	8
	Luther	9
	Miles	8
	Neb.-Omaha	*9
	Martin Luther	6
	Pomona-Pitzer	8
	Principia	7
	Southeastern La.	9
	Tennessee St.	†10
	Trinity (Conn.)	7
	Trinity (Tex.)	9
	Whitworth	8
	Widener	7
	Worcester Tech	6
1955	Alfred	8
	Centre	8
	Coe	8
	Col. of Emporia	9
	Drexel	8
	Grambling	10
	Heidelberg	9
	Hillsdale	9
	Juniata	‡8
	Md.-East. Shore	9
	Miami (Ohio)	9
	Muskingum	8
	Northern St.	†9
	Parsons	8
	Shepherd	8
	Southeast Mo. St.	9
	Trinity (Conn.)	7
	Whitworth	9
	Wis.-Stevens Point	8
1956	Alfred	7
	Central Mich.	9
	Hillsdale	9
	Lenoir-Rhyne	10
	Milton	6
	Montana St.	‡9
	Neb.-Kearney	9
	Redlands	9
	St. Thomas (Minn.)	8
	Sam Houston St.	*9
	Southern Conn. St.	9
	Tennessee St.	10
	Westminster (Pa.)	8
1957	Elon	6
	Fairmont St.	7
	Florida A&M	9
	Hillsdale	†9
	Hobart	6
	Idaho St.	9
	Jamestown	7
	Juniata	7
	Lock Haven	8
	Middle Tenn. St.	10
	Pittsburg St.	*10
	Ripon	8
	St. Norbert	8
	West Chester	9
1958	Calif. (Pa.)	8
	Chadron St.	8
	Gust. Adolphus	†8
	Missouri Valley	†8
	Neb.-Kearney	9
	Northeastern St.	**9
	Northern Ariz.	*†10
	Rochester	8
	Rose-Hulman	8
	St. Benedict's	†10
	Sewanee	8
	Southern Miss.	9
	Wheaton (Ill.)	8
1959	Bowling Green	9
	Butler	9
	Coe	8
	Fairmont St.	9
	Florida A&M	10
	Hofstra	9
	John Carroll	7
	Lenoir-Rhyne	*†9
	San Fran. St.	10
	Western Ill.	9
1960	Albright	9
	Arkansas Tech	†10
	Humboldt St.	*†10
	Langston	9
	Lenoir-Rhyne	*‡10
	Montclair St.	8
	Muskingum	9
	Northern Iowa	†9
	Ohio	10
	Ottawa	9
	Wagner	9
	West Chester	9
	Whitworth	9
	Willamette	8
1961	Albion	8
	Baldwin-Wallace	9
	Butler	9
	Central Okla.	9
	Florida A&M	10
	Fresno St.	*9
	Linfield	*†10
	Mayville St.	8
	Millikin	8
	Northern St.	9
	Ottawa	9
	Pittsburg St.	**9
	Wash. & Lee	9
	Wheaton (Ill.)	8
	Whittier	†9
1962	Carthage	8
	Central Okla.	**9
	Col. of Emporia	†10
	Earlham	8
	East Stroudsburg	†8
	John Carroll	7
	Kalamazoo	8
	Lenoir-Rhyne	*†10
	Northern St.	†9
	Parsons	9
	St. John's (Minn.)	9
	Susquehanna	9
	Wittenberg	9
1963	Alabama A&M	8
	Central Wash.	9
	Coast Guard	†8
	Col. of Emporia	10
	Delaware	8
	John Carroll	7
	Lewis & Clark	8
	Luther	9
	McNeese St.	8
	Neb.-Kearney	†9
	Northeastern	†8
	Northeastern St.	*10
	Northern Ill.	*9
	Prairie View	*†9
	Ripon	8
	St. John's (Minn.)	**8
	Sewanee	8
	Southwest Mo. St.	†9
	Southwest Tex. St.	10
	Wis.-Eau Claire	7
1964	Albion	8
	Amherst	8
	Cal St. Los Angeles	9
	Concordia-M'head	*‡9
	Frank. & Marsh.	8
	Montclair St.	7
	Prairie View	9
	Wagner	10
	Western St.	†9
	Westminster (Pa.)	8
	Wittenberg	8
1965	Ball St.	‡9
	East Stroudsburg	*9
	Fairmont St.	†8
	Georgetown (Ky.)	9
	Ill. Wesleyan	8
	Ithaca	8
	Middle Tenn. St.	10
	Morgan St.	9
	North Dak. St.	*10
	Northern Ill.	†9
	Ottawa	9
	St. John's (Minn.)	**9
	Springfield	9
	Sul Ross St.	†10
	Tennessee St.	‡9
1966	Central (Iowa)	†9
	Clarion	*9
	Defiance	9
	Morgan St.	*8
	Muskingum	†9
	Northwestern St.	9
	San Diego St.	*10
	Tennessee St.	*9
	Waynesburg	**9
	Wilkes	8
	Wis.-Whitewater	*†9

Beginning in 1967, NCAA members only.

Year	College	Wins
1967	Alma	8
	Central (Iowa)	9
	Doane	‡8
	Lawrence	8
	Morgan St.	8
	North Dak. St.	†9
	Northern Mich.	†9
	Wagner	9
	West Chester	*†9
	Wilkes	8
1968	Alma	8
	Doane	*9
	East Stroudsburg	‡8
	Indiana (Pa.)	†9
	North Dak. St.	*9
	Randolph-Macon	9
1969	Albion	8
	Carthage	9
	Defiance	9
	Doane	8
	Montana	†10
	North Dak. St.	*9
	Northern Colo.	10
	Wesleyan (Conn.)	8
	Wittenberg	*9
1970	Arkansas St.	*10
	Jacksonville St.	10
	Montana	†10
	St. Olaf	9
	Tennessee St.	*10
	Westminster (Pa.)	**8
	Wittenberg#	9
1971	Alfred	8
	Hampden-Sydney	†10
	Westminster (Pa.)	†‡8
1972	Ashland	11
	Bridgeport	*10
	Delaware	10
	Doane	†10
	Frank. & Marsh.	9
	Heidelberg	**9
	Louisiana Tech	*11
	Middlebury	8
	Monmouth (Ill.)	9
1973	Tennessee St.	10
	Western Ky.	**†10
1974	Louisiana Tech	*†10
	Michigan Tech	9
	UNLV	*†11
1975	East Stroudsburg	*9
	North Dak.	†9
1976	East Stroudsburg	‡9
1977	UC Davis	*†10
	Florida A&M	11
	Winston-Salem	†11
1978	Western St.	*†9
	Winston-Salem	*†10
1979	(None)	
1980	Minn.-Duluth	10
	Mo.-Rolla	10
1981	Northern Mich.	*†10
	Shippensburg	*†11
	Virginia Union	†11
1982	UC Davis	**†10

Year	College	Wins
	North Dak. St.	*†11
	Southwest Tex. St.	***11
1983	UC Davis	*†10
	Central St.	**†10
1984	(None)	
1985	Bloomsburg	*†11
1986	UC Davis	†10
	North Dak. St.	***10
	Virginia Union	†11
1987	(None)	
1988	North Dak. St.	****10
	St. Mary's (Cal.)	10
1989	Grand Valley St.	†11
	Jacksonville St.	***†10
	Pittsburg St.	*†11
	Tex. A&M-Kingsville	†10
1990	North Dak. St.	****10
	Pittsburg St.	**†10
1991	Carson-Newman	†10
	Indiana (Pa.)	**†10
	Jacksonville St.	***†9
1992	New Haven	**†10
	Pittsburg St.	***†11
1993	Albany St. (Ga.)	†11
	Bentley	10
	Hampton	*†11
	Indiana (Pa.)	***†10
	New Haven	*†10
	North Ala.	****10
	Quincy	9
1994	Bentley	*10
	Ferris St.	*†10
	Pittsburg St.	†10
1995	Ferris St.	**†10
	North Ala.	****10

#Later forfeited all games.

The Spoilers

Compiled since 1973, when the three-division reorganization plan was adopted by the special NCAA Convention. Following is a list of the spoilers of Division II teams that lost their perfect (undefeated, untied) record in their season-ending game, including the Division II championship playoffs. An asterisk (*) indicates an NCAA championship playoff game, a pound sign (#) indicates an NAIA championship playoff game, a dagger (†) indicates the home team in a regular-season game, and (@) indicates a neutral-site game. A game involving two undefeated, untied teams is in **bold** face.

Date	Spoiler	Victim	Score
12-15-73	*Louisiana Tech	Western Ky.	34-0
11-30-74	*Louisiana Tech	Western Caro.	10-7
11-15-75	†LIU-C.W. Post	American Int'l	21-0
11-15-75	Eastern N.M.	†Northern Colo.	16-14
11-29-75	*West Ala.	North Dak.	34-14
11-20-76	†Shippensburg	East Stroudsburg	tie 14-14
12-3-77	‡South Caro. St.	Winston-Salem	10-7
12-3-77	*Lehigh	UC Davis	39-30
12-2-78	*Delaware	Winston-Salem	41-0
11-28-81	*Shippensburg	Virginia Union	40-27
12-5-81	*North Dak. St.	Shippensburg	18-6
12-5-81	*Southwest Tex. St.	Northern Mich.	62-0
12-4-82	*UC Davis	North Dak. St.	19-14
12-11-82	***Southwest Tex. St.**	**UC Davis**	34-9
12-3-83	*North Dak. St.	UC Davis	26-17
12-10-83	*North Dak. St.	Central St.	41-21
12-7-85	*North Ala.	Bloomsburg	34-0
11-15-86	West Chester	†Millersville	7-3
11-29-86	*Troy St.	Virginia Union	31-7
11-29-86	*South Dak.	UC Davis	26-23
12-10-88	#Adams St.	Pittsburg St.	13-10
11-18-89	*Mississippi Col.	Tex. A&M-Kingsville	34-19
11-18-89	*Indiana (Pa.)	Grand Valley St.	34-24
11-25-89	*Angelo St.	Pittsburg St.	24-21
12-9-89	*Mississippi Col.	Jacksonville St.	3-0
12-1-90	***North Dak. St.**	**Pittsburg St.**	39-29
11-23-91	#Western St.	Carson-Newman	38-21
12-7-91	***Jacksonville St.**	**Indiana (Pa.)**	27-20
12-14-91	*Pittsburg St.	Jacksonville St.	23-6
11-14-92	@ Moorhead St.	Michigan Tech	36-35
12-5-92	*Jacksonville St.	New Haven	46-35
12-12-92	*Jacksonville St.	Pittsburg St.	17-13
11-13-93	@ Minn.-Duluth	Wayne St. (Neb.)	29-28
11-20-93	***Hampton**	**Albany St. (Ga.)**	33-7
11-27-93	***Indiana (Pa.)**	**New Haven**	38-35
11-27-93	***North Ala.**	**Hampton**	45-20
12-11-93	***North Ala.**	**Indiana (Pa.)**	41-34
11-19-94	*North Dak. St.	Pittsburg St.	(3 OT) 18-12
11-26-94	*Indiana (Pa.)	Ferris St.	21-17
12-2-95	***North Ala.**	**Ferris St.**	45-7

‡Gold Bowl.

Streaks and Rivalries

Longest Winning Streaks

(From 1931; Includes Postseason Games)

Wins	Team	Years
34	Hillsdale	1954-57
32	Wilkes	1965-69
31	Morgan St.	1965-68
31	Missouri Valley	1946-48
30	Bentley	1993-95
29	East Tex. St.	1951-53
27	Truman St.	1931-35
25	Pittsburg St.	1991-92
25	San Diego St.	1965-67
25	Peru St.	1951-54
25	Md.-East. Shore	1948-51
24	North Dak. St.	1964-66
24	Wesleyan (Conn.)	1945-48

Longest Unbeaten Streaks

(From 1931; Includes Postseason Games)

No.	Wins	Ties	Team	Years
54	47	7	Morgan St.	1931-38
38	36	2	Doane	1965-70
37	35	2	Southern-B.R.	1947-51
35	34	1	North Dak. St.	1968-71
34	34	0	Hillsdale	1954-57
32	32	0	Wilkes	1965-69
31	31	0	Morgan St.	1965-68
31	31	0	Missouri Valley	1946-48
31	29	2	St. Ambrose	1935-38
30	30	0	Bentley	1993-95
30	29	1	Wittenberg	1961-65
30	29	1	East Tex. St.	1951-53
28	27	1	Wesleyan (Conn.)	†1942-48
28	27	1	Case Reserve	1934-37
27	26	1	Pittsburg St.	1991-92
27	26	1	Juniata	1956-59
27	27	0	Truman St.	1931-35

†Did not field teams in 1943-44.

Most-Played Rivalries

Games	Opponents (Series leader listed first)	Series Record	First Game
102	North Dak.-North Dak. St.	56-43-3	1894
96	South Dak.-South Dak. St.	48-41-7	1889
88	Colorado Mines-Colorado Col.	46-37-5	1889
86	South Dak.-Morningside	53-28-5	1898
84	Tuskegee-Morehouse	51-25-8	1902
83	Virginia Union-Hampton	41-39-3	1906
82	North Dak. St.-South Dak. St.	43-34-5	1903

Cliffhangers

Regular-season Division II games won on the final play of the game (from 1973). The extra point is listed when it provided the margin of victory after the winning touchdown.

Date	Opponents, Score	Game-Winning Play
9-22-73	South Dak. 9, North Dak. St. 7	Kelly Higgins 5 pass from Mark Jenkins
10-12-74	Westminster (Pa.) 23, Indiana (Pa.) 20	Rick Voltz 20 FG
11-23-74	Arkansas St. 22, McNeese St. 20	Joe Duren 56 FG
10-11-75	Indiana (Pa.) 16, Westminster (Pa.) 14	Tom Alper 37 FG
10-18-75	Cal St. Fullerton 32, UC Riverside 31	John Choukair 52 FG
9-25-76	Portland St. 50, Montana 49	Dave Stief 2 pass from June Jones
10-30-76	South Dak. St. 16, Northern Iowa 13	Monte Mosiman 53 pass from Dick Weikert
10-27-77	Albany (N.Y.) 42, Maine 39	Larry Leibowitz 19 FG
10-6-79	Indiana (Pa.) 31, Shippensburg 24	Jeff Heath 4 run
10-20-79	North Dak. 23, South Dak. 22	Tom Biolo 6 run
9-6-80	Ferris St. 20, St. Joseph's (Ind.) 15	Greg Washington 17 pass from (holder) John Gibson (after bad snap on 34 FG attempt)
11-15-80	Morris Brown 19, Bethune-Cookman 18	Ray Mills 1 run (Carlton Jackson kick)
11-15-80	Tuskegee 23, Alabama A&M 21	Korda Joseph 45 FG
9-26-81	Abilene Christian 41, Northwestern St. 38	David Russell 17 pass from Loyal Proffitt
9-26-81	Cal St. Chico 10, Santa Clara 7	Mike Sullivan 46 FG
10-10-81	LIU-C.W. Post 37, James Madison 36	Tom DeBona 10 pass from Tom Ehrhardt (Ehrhardt run)
10-9-82	Grand Valley St. 38, Ferris St. 35	Randy Spangler 20 FG
10-9-82	Westminster (Pa.) 3, Indiana (Pa.) 0	Ron Bauer 35 FG
11-6-82	South Dak. 30, Augustana (S.D.) 28	Kurt Seibel 47 FG
9-17-83	Central Mo. St. 13, Sam Houston St. 10	Steve Huff 27 FG
9-22-84	Clarion 16, Shippensburg 13	Eric Fairbanks 26 FG
9-29-84	Angelo St. 18, Eastern N.M. 17	Ned Cox 3 run
10-13-84	UC Davis 16, Cal St. Chico 13	Ray Sullivan 48 FG
10-13-84	Northwest Mo. St. 35, Central Mo. St. 34	Pat Johnson 20 FG
11-3-84	Bloomsburg 34, West Chester 31	Curtis Still 50 pass from Jay Dedea
11-20-84	Central Fla. 28, Illinois St. 24	Jeff Farmer 30 punt return
9-7-85	Central Fla. 39, Bethune-Cookman 37	Ed O'Brien 55 FG
10-12-85	South Dak. 40, Morningside 38	Scott Jones 2 run
9-13-86	Michigan Tech 34, St. Norbert 30	Jim Wallace 41 pass from Dave Walter
9-20-86	Delaware 33, West Chester 31	Fred Singleton 3 run
10-18-86	Indianapolis 25, Evansville 24	Ken Bruce 18 FG
10-24-87	Indianapolis 27, Evansville 24	Doug Sabotin 2 pass from Tom Crowell
11-7-87	Central Mo. St. 35, Truman St. 33	Phil Brandt 25 FG
9-3-88	Alabama A&M 17, North Ala. 16	Edmond Allen 30 FG
9-17-88	Michigan Tech 17, Hope 14	Pete Weiss 22 FG
9-17-89	Morehouse 22, Fort Valley St. 21	David Boone 18 pass from Jimmie Davis
11-11-89	East Stroudsburg 22, Central Conn. St. 19	Frank Magolon 4 pass from Tom Taylor
10-13-90	East Stroudsburg 23, Bloomsburg 21	Ken Kopetchny 3 pass from Bret Comp
11-10-90	Southern Conn. St. 12, Central Conn. St. 10	Paul Boulanger 48 FG
9-21-91	West Ala. 22, Albany St. (Ga.) 21	Matt Carman 24 pass from Deon Timmons (Anthony Armstrong kick)
10-26-91	Central Mo. St. 38, Truman St. 37	Chris Pyatt 45 FG
10-26-91	Eastern N.M. 17, East Tex. St. 14	Jodie Peterson 35 FG
10-9-93	Delta St. 20, Henderson St. 19	Greg Walker 3 run (Stephen Coker kick)
11-6-93	Henderson St. 46, West Ala. 44	Craig Moses 44 FG
9-24-94	Mo.-Rolla 15, Emporia St. 14	Jason Politte 1 run
9-24-94	St. Cloud St. 18, North Dak. 17	Todd Bouman 1 run
9-30-95	Michigan Tech 37, Saginaw Valley 35	Matt Johnson 46 FG

Photo from Michigan Tech sports information

Matt Johnson's 46-yard field goal on the game's final play gave Michigan Tech a 37-35 victory over Saginaw Valley State on September 30, 1995. It was the longest game-winning field goal on the last play of a Division II game since 1990.

Division II Stadiums

STADIUMS LISTED ALPHABETICALLY

School	Stadium	Year Built	Capacity	Surface
Abilene Christian	Shotwell	1959	15,000	Grass
Adams St.	Rex Field	1949	2,800	Grass
Alabama A&M	Milton Frank	NA	10,000	Grass
Albany (N.Y.)	University Field	1967	10,000	Grass
Albany St. (Ga.)	Mills Memorial	1957	11,000	Grass
American Int'l	John Homer Miller	1964	5,000	Grass
Angelo St.	San Angelo	1962	17,500	Grass
Ashland	Community	1963	5,700	Grass
Assumption	Rocheleau Field	1961	1,200	Grass
Augustana (S.D.)	Howard Wood	1957	10,000	Grass
Bemidji St.	BSU	1937	4,000	Grass
Bentley	Bentley College	1990	1,500	Grass
Bloomsburg	Robert B. Redman	1974	5,000	Grass
Bowie St.	Bulldog	1992	6,000	Grass
UC Davis	Toomey Field	1949	10,111	Grass
Calif. (Pa.)	Adamson	1970	5,000	Grass
Cal St. Chico	University	1952	8,000	Grass
Carson-Newman	Burke-Tarr	1966	5,000	Grass
Catawba	Shuford Field	1926	4,000	Grass
Central Ark.	Estes	1939	7,000	Grass
Central Mo. St.	Vernon Kennedy	1995	10,000	Grass
Central Okla.	Wantland	1965	10,000	Grass
Chadron St.	Elliott Field	1930	2,500	Grass
Cheyney	O'Shield-Stevenson	NA	3,500	Grass
Clarion	Memorial Field	1965	5,000	Grass
Clark Atlanta	Georgia Dome#	1992	71,000	AstroTurf
Colorado Mines	Brooks Field	1922	5,000	Grass
Concord	Callahan	NA	5,000	Grass
Delta St.	Travis Parker Field	1970	8,000	Grass
East Stroudsburg	Eller-Martin	1969	6,000	Grass
East Tex. St.	Memorial	1950	10,000	Grass
Eastern N.M.	Greyhound	1969	6,500	Grass
Edinboro	Sox-Harrison	1965	5,000	Grass
Elizabeth City St.	Roebuck	NA	6,500	Grass
Elon	Burlington Memorial	1949	10,000	Grass

School	Stadium	Year Built	Capacity	Surface
Emporia St.	Welch	1937	7,000	Grass
Fairmont St.	Rosier Field	1929	6,000	Grass
Fayetteville St.	Jeralds Ath. Complex	1940	6,000	Grass
Ferris St.	Top Taggart Field	1957	9,100	Grass
Fort Hays St.	Lewis Field	1936	7,000	Turf
Fort Lewis	Ray Dennison Memorial	1958	4,000	Grass
Fort Valley St.	Wildcat	1957	7,500	Grass
Gannon	Erie Veterans Memorial	1958	10,500	AstroTurf
Gardner-Webb	Spangler	1969	5,000	Grass
Glenville St.	Pioneer	1977	5,000	Grass
Grand Valley St.	Arend D. Lubbers	1979	4,146	PAT
Henderson St.	Carpenter-Haygood	1968	9,600	Grass
Hillsdale	Frank Waters	1982	8,500	PAT
Humboldt St.	Redwood Bowl	1946	7,000	Grass
Indiana (Pa.)	George P. Miller	1962	6,500	AstroTurf
Indianapolis	Key	1970	5,500	Grass
Johnson Smith	The Bullpit	1992	5,000	Grass
Kentucky St.	Alumni Field	1978	6,000	Grass
Ky. Wesleyan	Apollo	1989	3,000	Grass
Kutztown	University Field	1987	5,600	Grass
Lane	Rothrock	1930	3,500	Grass
Lenoir-Rhyne	Moretz	1923	8,500	Grass
Livingstone	Alumni	NA	5,500	Grass
Lock Haven	Hubert Jack	NA	3,000	Turf
LIU-C.W. Post	Hickox Field	1966	5,000	Grass
Mankato St.	Blakeslee Field	1962	7,500	Grass
Mansfield	Van Norman Field	NA	5,000	Grass
Mars Hill	Meares	1965	5,000	Grass
Mass.-Lowell	Cawley Memorial	1934	7,000	Grass
Mercyhurst	Erie Veterans Memorial	1958	10,500	Grass
Mesa St.	Stocker	1949	8,000	Grass
Michigan Tech	Sherman Field	1954	3,000	Grass
Miles	Alumni	NA	3,400	Grass
Millersville	Biemesderfer Field	1970	6,500	Grass
Minn.-Duluth	Griggs Field	1966	4,000	SuperTurf II
Minn.-Morris	UMM Field	NA	5,000	Grass
Mississippi Col.	Robinson Field	1985	8,500	Grass
Mo.-Rolla	Jackling Field	1967	8,000	Grass
Mo. Southern St.	Fred G. Hughes	1975	7,000	Turf
Mo. Western St.	Spratt	1979	6,000	Grass
Moorhead St.	Alex Nemzek	1960	5,000	Grass
Morehouse	B. T. Harvey	1983	9,850	Grass
Morningside	Roberts	1939	9,000	Grass
Morris Brown	A. F. Herndon	NA	20,000	Grass
Neb.-Kearney	Foster Field	1929	8,000	Grass
Neb.-Omaha	Al F. Caniglia Field	1949	9,500	Turf
New Haven	Robert B. Dodds	NA	3,500	Grass
N.M. Highlands	Perkins	NA	5,000	Grass
Newberry	Setzler Field	1930	4,000	Grass
Norfolk St.	Foreman Field	1935	26,000	Turf
North Ala.	Braly Municipal	1940	13,000	PAT
N.C. Central	O'Kelly	NA	11,500	Grass
North Dak.	Memorial	1927	10,000	Turf
North Dak. St.	FargoDome#	1992	18,700	AstroTurf
Northern Colo.	Nottingham Field	1995	6,500	Grass
Northern Mich.	Superior Dome#	1991	8,000	Turf
Northern St.	Swisher	1975	6,000	Grass
Northwest Mo. St.	Rickenbrode	1917	7,500	Grass
Northwood	Louis Juillerat	1964	2,500	Grass
Pace	Finnerty Field	NA	1,200	Grass
Pittsburg St.	Carnie Smith	1924	5,600	Grass
Portland St.	Civic	1928	23,150	AstroTurf
Presbyterian	Bailey Memorial	NA	5,000	Grass
Quincy	QU Stadium	1938	2,500	Grass
Sacred Heart	Campus Field	1993	2,000	Turf
Saginaw Valley	Harvey R. Wickes	1975	4,028	PAT
St. Cloud St.	Selke Field	1937	4,000	Grass
St. Francis (Ill.)	Joliet Memorial	1951	10,000	Grass
St. Joseph's (Ind.)	Alumni Field	1947	4,000	Grass
Savannah St.	Ted Wright	1967	7,500	Grass
Shepherd	Ram	1959	3,000	Grass
Shippensburg	Grove	1972	7,700	Grass
Slippery Rock	N. Kerr Thompson	1974	10,000	Grass
Sonoma St.	Cossack	1961	3,000	Grass
South Dak.	DakotaDome#	1979	10,000	Monsanto
South Dak. St.	Coughlin-Alumni	1962	16,000	Grass
Southern Conn. St.	Jess Dow Field	1988	6,000	Turf
Southwest Baptist	Plaster	1986	2,500	Grass
Southwest St.	Mattke Field	1971	5,000	Grass
Stonehill	Chieftain	1980	1,200	Grass
Stony Brook	Seawolves Field	1978	2,000	Grass
Tarleton St.	Memorial	1976	5,284	Grass
Tex. A&M-Kingsville	Javelina	1950	15,000	Grass
Truman St.	Stokes	1962	4,000	Grass
Tuskegee	Alumni Bowl	1925	10,000	Grass
Valdosta St.	Cleveland Field	1922	11,500	Grass
Virginia St.	Rogers	1950	13,500	Grass
Virginia Union	Hovey Field	NA	10,000	Grass
Washburn	Moore Bowl	1928	7,200	Grass
Wayne St. (Mich.)	Wayne State	1968	6,000	Grass
Wayne St. (Neb.)	Memorial	1931	3,500	Grass
West Ala.	Tiger	1952	8,500	Grass
West Chester	Farrell	1970	7,500	Grass
West Ga.	Grisham	1966	6,500	Grass
West Liberty St.	Russek Field	1960	4,000	Grass
West Tex. A&M	Kimbrough	1959	20,000	Grass
West Va. Tech	Martin	NA	3,000	Turf
West Va. Wesleyan	Cebe Ross Field	1957	4,000	Grass
Western N.M.	Silver Sports Complex	1969	2,000	Grass
Western St.	Mountaineer Bowl	1950	2,400	Grass
Wingate	Walter Bickett	NA	5,000	Grass
Winona St.	Maxwell Field	NA	3,500	Grass
Winston-Salem	Bowman-Gray	1940	18,000	Grass

STADIUMS LISTED BY CAPACITY (TOP 15)

School	Stadium	Surface	Capacity
Clark Atlanta	Georgia Dome#	AstroTurf	71,000
Norfolk St.	Foreman Field	Turf	26,000
Portland St.	Civic	AstroTurf	23,150
Morris Brown	A. F. Herndon	Grass	20,000
West Tex. A&M	Kimbrough	Grass	20,000
North Dak. St.	FargoDome#	AstroTurf	18,700
Winston-Salem	Bowman-Gray	Grass	18,000
Angelo St.	San Angelo	Grass	17,500
South Dak. St.	Coughlin-Alumni	Grass	16,000
Abilene Christian	Shotwell	Grass	15,000
Tex. A&M-Kingsville	Javelina	Grass	15,000
Virginia St.	Rogers	Grass	13,500
North Ala.	Braly Municipal	PAT	13,000
N.C. Central	O'Kelly	Grass	11,500
Valdosta St.	Cleveland Field	Grass	11,500

#Indoor facility. PAT=Prescription Athletic Turf.

Division II Statistics Trends

For valid comparisons from 1973, when College Division teams were divided into Division II and Division III.

(Average Per Game, Both Teams)

	Rushing			Passing					Total Offense			Scoring		
Year	Plays	Yds.	Avg.	Att.	Cmp.	Pct.	Yds.	Av.Att.	Plays	Yds.	Avg.	TD	FG	Pts.
1973	95.1	339.1	3.57	40.0	17.6	.442	243.0	6.08	135.1	582.1	4.31	5.06	0.83	36.4
1974	95.1	312.6	3.29	38.9	17.3	.445	244.8	6.28	134.0	557.3	4.16	5.10	0.86	37.9
1975	94.6	337.1	3.56	38.9	17.4	.448	241.2	6.21	133.5	578.3	4.33	4.98	0.89	37.1
1976	94.7	331.4	3.50	39.8	18.2	.457	251.8	6.32	134.5	583.2	4.34	5.03	0.93	37.4
1977	*96.7	347.6	3.59	40.6	18.4	.453	252.4	6.21	137.3	599.9	4.37	5.16	0.91	38.2
1978	95.9	338.5	3.52	41.1	18.4	.448	248.5	6.05	137.0	587.0	4.29	5.11	0.98	38.6
1979	91.6	309.4	3.38	41.9	18.9	.450	251.6	6.00	133.4	560.9	4.20	4.73	1.03	35.8
1980	90.5	307.5	3.40	44.7	20.7	.463	275.2	6.16	135.2	582.6	4.31	5.02	1.04	37.8
1981	89.1	293.2	3.29	47.9	21.9	.457	291.7	6.09	137.0	584.9	4.27	4.95	1.08	37.4
1982	86.5	288.2	3.32	52.2	24.5	.469	322.0	6.17	138.6	610.2	4.40	5.25	1.24	39.6
1983	86.3	290.7	3.37	52.1	25.0	.479	329.0	6.31	138.4	619.7	4.48	5.27	1.23	39.2
1984	83.8	284.3	3.39	52.0	25.0	.481	329.5	6.33	135.8	613.8	4.52	5.25	1.23	38.7
1985	83.3	288.0	3.46	54.8	26.4	.483	341.2	6.23	138.1	629.2	4.56	5.46	1.30	41.8
1986	83.6	297.7	3.56	53.7	26.0	.484	336.8	6.27	137.3	634.5	4.62	5.78	1.27	43.9
1987	85.6	303.7	3.55	49.2	23.8	.483	311.0	6.31	134.9	614.7	4.56	5.29	1.28	40.4
1988	87.7	318.8	3.64	49.2	23.8	.484	319.5	6.49	136.9	638.3	4.66	5.83	1.29	44.2
1989	87.3	332.0	3.80	50.1	24.3	.485	323.0	6.45	137.4	655.0	4.77	5.94	1.24	45.1
1990	87.3	336.6	3.86	52.8	25.6	.485	346.6	6.57	140.0	683.2	4.88	6.19	1.29	46.7
1991	87.4	335.5	3.84	52.7	25.5	.484	344.8	6.54	140.0	680.3	4.86	6.09	*1.31	46.4
1992	88.1	335.1	3.80	51.2	24.8	.484	342.8	6.70	139.3	677.9	4.87	6.01	1.30	46.2
1993	85.4	334.5	3.92	*54.8	*27.1	.495	*360.3	6.11	*140.2	694.8	4.96	6.55	1.06	47.9
1994	85.1	*349.0	*4.10	52.5	26.4	*.503	356.0	*6.79	137.6	*705.0	*5.13	*6.84	1.07	*50.2
1995	83.1	327.9	3.95	53.5	26.8	.501	353.8	6.61	136.6	681.7	4.99	6.43	1.11	47.3

**Record.*

Division II Average Yards Per Offensive Play, 1985-1995

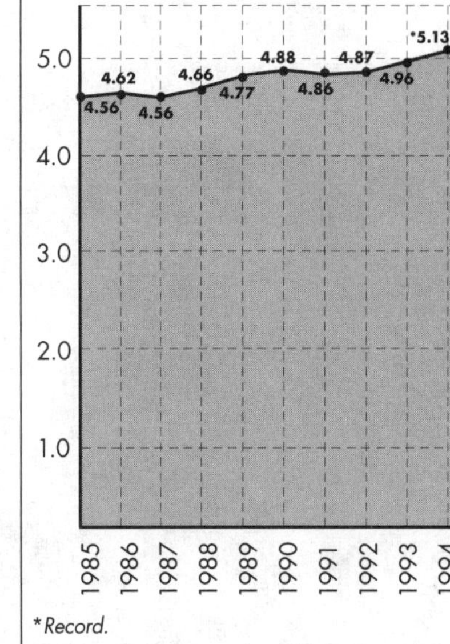

Additional Division II Statistics Trends

(Average Per Game, Both Teams)

			Punting		PAT Kick Attempts		Two-Point Attempts		Field Goals
Year	Teams†	Games	No.	Avg.	Pct. Made	Pct. of Total Tries	Pct. Made	Pct. of Total Tries	Pct. Made
1973	131	1,326	11.5	36.0	.833	.876	.419	.124	.439
1974	136	1,388	11.4	*36.8	.830	.859	.432	.141	.472
1975	126	1,282	11.0	36.3	.837	.874	.464	.126	.476
1976	122	1,244	11.6	36.2	.841	.878	.419	.122	.461
1977	124	1,267	11.7	36.1	.832	.874	.436	.126	.442
1978	91	921	11.9	35.9	.830	.880	.452	.120	.519
1979	99	1,016	12.1	35.2	.854	.861	.459	.139	.543
1980	103	1,040	11.7	35.6	.852	.864	.438	.136	.512
1981	113	1,138	*12.2	35.6	.856	.861	.440	.139	.531
1982	118	1,196	12.2	36.4	.862	.877	.431	.123	.560
1983	115	1,175	11.9	36.1	.866	.847	.428	.153	.564
1984	112	1,150	11.8	36.4	.876	.875	.448	.125	.567
1985	107	1,098	11.5	35.9	*.905	.864	.414	.136	.549
1986	109	1,124	11.1	36.5	.870	.865	.466	.135	*.576
1987	105	1,100	11.4	35.7	.857	.865	.435	.135	.547
1988	111	1,114	11.2	35.6	.886	.868	.399	.132	.555
1989	106	1,084	10.9	36.7	.873	.845	.376	.155	.567
1990	105	1,065	11.3	35.7	.876	*.885	*.474	.115	.568
1991	114	1,150	10.9	36.1	.882	.880	.426	.120	.572
1992	115	1,145	11.0	35.9	.888	.870	.442	.130	.575
1993	136	1,354	10.6	35.2	.839	.853	.438	.147	.528
1994	128	1,325	10.1	36.0	.850	.840	.439	.160	.559
1995	131	1,362	10.6	34.9	.835	.837	.473	*.163	.552

**Record. †Teams reporting statistics, not the total number of teams in the division.*

Division III Records

Individual Records

Division III football records are based on the performances of Division III teams since the three-division reorganization plan was adopted by the special NCAA Convention in August 1973.

Total Offense

(Rushing Plus Passing)

MOST PLAYS
Quarter
33—Aaron Keen, Washington (Mo.) vs. Trinity (Tex.), Oct. 3, 1992 (4th)
Half
59—Mike Wallace, Ohio Wesleyan vs. Denison, Oct. 3, 1981 (2nd)
Game
91—Jordan Poznick, Principia vs. Blackburn, Oct. 10, 1992 (81 passes, 10 rushes; 538 yards)
Season
614—Tim Peterson, Wis.-Stout, 1989 (3,244 yards)
Per-game record—64.9, Jordan Poznick, Principia, 1992 (519 in 8)
Career
2,007—Kirk Baumgartner, Wis.-Stevens Point, 1986-89 (12,767 yards)
Also holds per-game record at 49.0 (2,007 in 41)

MOST PLAYS BY A FRESHMAN
Season
491—Mark Novara, Lakeland, 1994 (2,572 yards)
Also holds per-game record at 54.6 (491 in 9)

MOST YARDS GAINED
Game
596—John Love, North Park vs. Elmhurst, Oct. 13, 1990 (533 passing, 63 rushing)
Season
3,981—Terry Peebles, Hanover, 1995 (460 rushing, 3,521 passing)
Also holds per-game record at 398.1 (3,981 in 10)
Career
12,767—Kirk Baumgartner, Wis.-Stevens Point, 1986-89 (-261 rushing, 13,028 passing)
Per-game record—333.6, Terry Peebles, Hanover, 1992-95 (7,672 in 23)

MOST YARDS GAINED BY A FRESHMAN
Season
2,572—Mark Novara, Lakeland, 1994 (491 plays)
Also holds per-game record at 285.8 (2,572 in 9)

MOST GAMES GAINING 300 YARDS OR MORE
Season
8—Kirk Baumgartner, Wis.-Stevens Point, 1989
Career
26—Kirk Baumgartner, Wis.-Stevens Point, 1986-89

MOST CONSECUTIVE GAMES GAINING 300 YARDS OR MORE
Season
6—Kirk Baumgartner, Wis.-Stevens Point, 1987

GAINING 4,000 YARDS RUSHING AND 2,000 YARDS PASSING
Career
Chris Spriggs, Denison, 1983-86 (4,248 rushing & 2,799 passing)
Also holds record for yards gained by a running back at 7,047

GAINING 3,000 YARDS RUSHING AND 3,000 YARDS PASSING
Career
Clay Sampson (TB), Denison, 1977-80 (3,726 rushing & 3,194 passing)

HIGHEST AVERAGE GAIN PER PLAY
Season
(Min. 2,500 yards) 10.1—Willie Seiler, St. John's (Minn.), 1993 (263 for 2,648)
Career
(Min. 6,000 yards) 7.9—Jim Ballard, Wilmington (Ohio)/Mount Union, 1990, 1991-93 (1,328 for 10,545)

MOST TOUCHDOWNS RESPONSIBLE FOR (TDs Scored and Passed For)
Career
123—Kirk Baumgartner, Wis.-Stevens Point, 1986-89 (110 passing, 13 rushing)
Per-game record—3.1, Jim Ballard, Wilmington (Ohio)/Mount Union, 1990, 1991-93 (122 in 40)

Rushing

MOST RUSHES
Game
58—Bill Kaiser, Wabash vs. DePauw, Nov. 9, 1985 (211 yards)
Season
380—Mike Birosak, Dickinson, 1989 (1,798 yards)
Also holds per-game record at 38.0 (380 in 10)
Career
1,112—Mike Birosak, Dickinson, 1986-89 (4,662 yards)
Per-game record—32.7, Chris Sizemore, Bridgewater (Va.), 1972-74 (851 in 26)

MOST RUSHES BY A QUARTERBACK
Season
231—Jeff Saueressig, Wis.-River Falls, 1988 (1,095 yards)
Also holds per-game record at 25.7 (231 in 9)

MOST CONSECUTIVE RUSHES BY THE SAME PLAYER
Game
46—Dan Walsh, Montclair St. vs. Ramapo, Sept. 30, 1989 (during 13 possessions)
Season
51—Dan Walsh, Montclair St., 1989 (Sept. 23 to Sept. 30)

MOST YARDS GAINED
Half
310—Leroy Horn, Montclair St. vs. Jersey City St., Nov. 9, 1985 (21 rushes)
Game
417—Carey Bender, Coe vs. Grinnell, Oct. 9, 1993 (33 rushes)
Season
2,243—Carey Bender, Coe, 1994 (295 rushes)
Also holds per-game record at 224.3 (2,243 in 10)
Career
6,125—Carey Bender, Coe, 1991-94 (926 rushes)
Per-game record—175.1, Ricky Gales, Simpson, 1988-89 (3,326 in 19)

MOST YARDS GAINED BY A FRESHMAN
Season
1,380—Fredrick Nanhed, Cal Lutheran, 1995 (242 rushes)
Also holds per-game record at 153.3 (1,380 in 9)

MOST RUSHING YARDS GAINED BY A QUARTERBACK
Game
235—Mark Cota, Wis.-River Falls vs. Minn.-Morris, Sept. 13, 1986 (27 rushes)
Season
1,279—Mark Cota, Wis.-River Falls, 1986 (227 rushes)
Also holds per-game record at 127.9 (1,279 in 10)
Career
3,252—Adam Kowles, Wis.-River Falls, 1992-95 (487 rushes)

LONGEST GAIN BY A QUARTERBACK
Game
98 yards—Jon Hinds, Principia vs. Illinois Col., Sept. 20, 1986 (TD)

MOST GAMES GAINING 100 YARDS OR MORE
Career
30—Joe Dudek, Plymouth St., 1982-85 (41 games)

MOST CONSECUTIVE GAMES GAINING 100 YARDS OR MORE
Career
18—Hank Wineman, Albion, 1990-91

MOST GAMES GAINING 200 YARDS OR MORE
Season
8—Ricky Gales, Simpson, 1989 (consecutive)
Career
11—Rob Marchitello, Maine Maritime, 1993-95; Ricky Gales, Simpson, 1988-89

MOST SEASONS GAINING 1,000 YARDS OR MORE
Career
4—Carey Bender, Coe, 1991-94; Steve Dixon, Beloit, 1990-93; Joe Dudek, Plymouth St., 1982-85; Rich Kowalski, Hobart, 1972-75

TWO PLAYERS, SAME TEAM, EACH GAINING 1,000 YARDS OR MORE
Season
By nine teams. Most recent: Thomas More, 1994—Ryan Reynolds (TB) 1,280 & Carlton Carter (FB) 1,014; Wis.-River Falls, 1994—Chris Guenterberg (FB) 1,047 & Adam Kowles (QB) 1,005

MOST YARDS GAINED RUSHING BY TWO PLAYERS, SAME TEAM
Game
519—Carey Bender 417 & Jason Whitaker 102, Coe vs. Grinnell, Oct. 9, 1993
Season
2,590—Jon Warga (TB) 1,836 & Jeff Stockdale (FB) 727, Wittenberg, 1990 (10 games)

HIGHEST AVERAGE GAIN PER RUSH
Game
(Min. 15 rushes) 19.1—Billy Johnson, Widener vs. Swarthmore, Nov. 10, 1973 (15 for 286)
(Min. 24 rushes) 15.9—Pete Baranek, Carthage vs. North Central, Oct. 5, 1985 (24 for 382)
Season
(Min. 140 rushes) 8.9—Billy Johnson, Widener, 1973 (168 for 1,494)
(Min. 195 rushes) 7.6—Carey Bender, Coe, 1994 (295 for 2,243)
Career
(Min. 500 rushes) 7.1—Joe Dudek, Plymouth St., 1982-85 (785 for 5,570)

MOST TOUCHDOWNS SCORED BY RUSHING
Game
8—Carey Bender, Coe vs. Beloit, Nov. 12, 1994
Season
29—Carey Bender, Coe, 1994
Per-game record—3.0, Stanley Drayton, Allegheny, 1991 (27 in 9)
Career
76—Joe Dudek, Plymouth St., 1982-85
Also holds per-game record at 1.9 (76 in 41)

MOST RUSHING TOUCHDOWNS SCORED BY A QUARTERBACK
Season
17—Mark Reed, Monmouth (Ill.), 1987
Also holds per-game record at 1.7 (17 in 10)

Passing

HIGHEST PASSING EFFICIENCY RATING POINTS
Season
(Min. 15 atts. per game) 225.0—Mike Simpson, Eureka, 1994 (158 attempts, 116 completions, 5 interceptions, 1,988 yards, 25 TDs)
(Min. 25 atts. per game) 193.2—Jim Ballard, Mount Union, 1993 (314 attempts, 229 completions, 11 interceptions, 3,304 yards, 37 TDs)
Career
(Min. 325 comps.) 159.8—Craig Kusick, Wis.-La Crosse, 1993-95 (537 attempts, 327 completions, 14 interceptions, 4,767 yards, 48 TDs)
(Min. 650 comps.) 159.5—Jim Ballard, Wilmington (Ohio)/Mount Union, 1990, 1991-93 (1,199 attempts, 743 completions, 41 interceptions, 10,379 yards, 115 TDs)

MOST PASSES ATTEMPTED
Quarter
31—Mike Wallace, Ohio Wesleyan vs. Denison, Oct. 3, 1981 (4th)
Half
57—Mike Wallace, Ohio Wesleyan vs. Denison, Oct. 3, 1981 (2nd)

Game
81—Jordan Poznick, Principia vs. Blackburn, Oct. 10, 1992 (completed 48)
Season
527—Kirk Baumgartner, Wis.-Stevens Point, 1988 (completed 276)
Per-game record—56.4, Jordan Poznick, Principia, 1992 (451 in 8)
Career
1,696—Kirk Baumgartner, Wis.-Stevens Point, 1986-89 (completed 883)
Per-game record—42.3, Keith Bishop, Ill. Wesleyan/Wheaton (Ill.), 1981, 1983-85 (1,311 in 31)

MOST PASSES ATTEMPTED BY A FRESHMAN
Season
384—Brad Hensley, Kenyon, 1991 (completed 198)
Per-game record—46.3, Jordan Poznick, Principia, 1990 (278 in 6)

MOST PASSES COMPLETED
Quarter
21—Rob Bristow, Pomona-Pitzer vs. Whittier, Oct. 19, 1985 (4th)
Half
36—Mike Wallace, Ohio Wesleyan vs. Denison, Oct. 3, 1981 (2nd)
Game
50—Tim Lynch, Hofstra vs. Fordham, Oct. 19, 1991 (attempted 69)
Season
283—Terry Peebles, Hanover, 1995 (attempted 488)
Per-game record—30.1, Jordan Poznick, Principia, 1992 (241 in 8)
Career
883—Kirk Baumgartner, Wis.-Stevens Point, 1986-89 (attempted 1,696)
Per-game record—24.9, Keith Bishop, Ill. Wesleyan/Wheaton (Ill.), 1981, 1983-85 (772 in 31)

MOST PASSES COMPLETED BY A FRESHMAN
Season
199—Luke Hanks, Otterbein, 1990 (attempted 370)
Per-game record—21.8, Jordan Poznick, Principia, 1990 (131 in 6)

HIGHEST PERCENTAGE OF PASSES COMPLETED
Game
(Min. 20 comps.) 91.3%—Chris Esterley, St. Thomas (Minn.) vs. St. Olaf, Sept. 23, 1995 (21 of 23)
(Min. 25 comps.) 83.3%—Scott Driggers, Colorado Col. vs. Neb. Wesleyan, Sept. 10, 1983 (35 of 42)
Season
(Min. 250 atts.) 72.9%—Jim Ballard, Mount Union, 1993 (229 of 314)
Career
(Min. 550 atts.) 62.2%—Brian Moore, Baldwin-Wallace, 1981-84 (437 of 703)
(Min. 750 atts.) 62.0%—Jim Ballard, Wilmington (Ohio)/Mount Union, 1990, 1991-93 (743 of 1,199)

MOST CONSECUTIVE PASSES COMPLETED
Game
17—Jim Ballard, Mount Union vs. Ill. Wesleyan, Nov. 28, 1992; William Snyder, Carnegie Mellon vs. Wooster, Oct. 20, 1990
Season
21—Kevin Keefe, Baldwin-Wallace vs. Moravian (16), Sept. 10, and vs. Heidelberg (5), Sept. 17, 1994

MOST CONSECUTIVE PASSES COMPLETED BY TWO PLAYERS, SAME TEAM
Game
20—Kevin Keefe (16) & David Skarupa (4), Baldwin-Wallace vs. Moravian, Sept. 10, 1994

MOST PASSES HAD INTERCEPTED
Game
8—Jason Clark, Ohio Northern vs. John Carroll, Nov. 9, 1991; Jim Higgins, Brockport St. vs. Buffalo St., Sept. 29, 1990; Dennis Bogacz, Wis.-Oshkosh vs. Wis.-Stevens Point, Oct. 29, 1988; Kevin Karwath, Canisius vs. Liberty, Nov. 19, 1979
Season
43—Steve Hendry, Wis.-Superior, 1982 (attempted 480)
Also holds per-game record at 3.9 (43 in 11)
Career
117—Steve Hendry, Wis.-Superior, 1980-83 (attempted 1,343)
Per-game record—3.2, Willie Martinez, Oberlin, 1973-74 (58 in 18)

LOWEST PERCENTAGE OF PASSES HAD INTERCEPTED
Season
(Min. 150 atts.) 0.9%—Brett Russ, Union (N.Y.), 1991 (2 of 224)
Career
(Min. 600 atts.) 1.9%—Mark Casale, Montclair St., 1980-83 (16 of 828)

MOST PASSES ATTEMPTED WITHOUT INTERCEPTION
Game
67—Brian Van Deusen, Western Md. vs. Frank. & Marsh., Oct. 23, 1993 (37 completions)
Season
124—Tim Tenhet, Sewanee, 1982

MOST CONSECUTIVE PASSES ATTEMPTED WITHOUT AN INTERCEPTION
Season
205—Kirk Baumgartner, Wis.-Stevens Point, 1989 (during 6 games; began Sept. 16 vs. Wis.-Platteville, ended Oct. 21 vs. Wis.-Whitewater)

MOST YARDS GAINED
Game
602—Tom Stallings, St. Thomas (Minn.) vs. Bethel (Minn.), Nov. 13, 1993
Season
3,828—Kirk Baumgartner, Wis.-Stevens Point, 1988
Also holds per-game record at 369.2 (3,692 in 10, 1989)
Career
13,028—Kirk Baumgartner, Wis.-Stevens Point, 1986-89
Also holds per-game record at 317.8 (13,028 in 41)

MOST YARDS GAINED BY A FRESHMAN
Season
2,520—Brad Hensley, Kenyon, 1991
Per-game record—268.8, Dennis Bogacz, Wis.-Oshkosh, 1988 (2,150 in 8)

MOST GAMES PASSING FOR 200 YARDS OR MORE
Season
10—Kirk Baumgartner, Wis.-Stevens Point, 1989, 1988, 1987
Career
32—Kirk Baumgartner, Wis.-Stevens Point, 1986-89

MOST CONSECUTIVE GAMES PASSING FOR 200 YARDS OR MORE
Season
10—Kirk Baumgartner, Wis.-Stevens Point, 1989 (entire season)
Career
27—Keith Bishop, Ill. Wesleyan/Wheaton (Ill.), 1981, 1983-85

MOST GAMES PASSING FOR 300 YARDS OR MORE
Season
9—Kirk Baumgartner, Wis.-Stevens Point, 1989
Career
24—Kirk Baumgartner, Wis.-Stevens Point, 1986-89

MOST CONSECUTIVE GAMES PASSING FOR 300 YARDS OR MORE
Season
9—Kirk Baumgartner, Wis.-Stevens Point, 1989 (began Sept. 9 vs. St. Norbert, through Nov. 4 vs. Wis.-Superior)
Career
13—Kirk Baumgartner, Wis.-Stevens Point, 1988-89 (began Oct. 22, 1988, vs. Wis.-Stout, through Nov. 4, 1989, vs. Wis.-Superior)

MOST YARDS GAINED BY TWO OPPOSING PLAYERS
Game
928—Brion Demski, Wis.-Stevens Point (477) & Steve Hendry, Wis.-Superior (451), Oct. 17, 1981 (completed 70 of 123)

MOST YARDS GAINED PER ATTEMPT
Season
(Min. 175 atts.) 12.9—Willie Seiler, St. John's (Minn.), 1993 (205 for 2,648)
(Min. 275 atts.) 10.5—Jim Ballard, Mount Union, 1993 (314 for 3,304)
Career
(Min. 600 atts.) 9.2—Joe Blake, Simpson, 1987-90 (672 for 6,183)
(Min. 950 atts.) 8.7—Jim Ballard, Wilmington (Ohio)/Mount Union, 1990, 1991-93 (1,199 for 10,379)

MOST YARDS GAINED PER COMPLETION
Season
(Min. 100 comps.) 19.7—David Parker, Bishop, 1981 (114 for 2,242)
(Min. 200 comps.) 16.1—John Furmaniak, Eureka, 1995 (210 for 3,372)
Career
(Min. 300 comps.) 18.3—David Parker, Bishop, 1981-84 (378 for 6,934)
(Min. 425 comps.) 15.1—Rob Light, Moravian, 1986-89 (438 for 6,624)

MOST TOUCHDOWN PASSES
Quarter
5—David Sullivan, Williams vs. Hamilton, Oct. 30, 1993 (2nd)
Game
8—John Koz, Baldwin-Wallace vs. Ohio Northern, Nov. 6, 1993; Steve Austin, Mass.-Boston vs. Framingham St., Nov. 14, 1992; Kirk Baumgartner, Wis.-Stevens Point vs. Wis.-Superior, Nov. 4, 1989
Season
39—Terry Peebles, Hanover, 1995; Kirk Baumgartner, Wis.-Stevens Point, 1989
Also hold per-game record at 3.9 (39 in 10)
Career
115—Jim Ballard, Wilmington (Ohio)/Mount Union, 1990, 1991-93
Also holds per-game record at 2.9 (115 in 40)

HIGHEST PERCENTAGE OF PASSES FOR TOUCHDOWNS
Season
(Min. 200 atts.) 16.1%—Willie Seiler, St. John's (Minn.), 1993 (33 of 205)
(Min. 300 atts.) 11.8%—Jim Ballard, Mount Union, 1993 (37 of 314)
Career
(Min. 625 atts.) 10.8%—Gary Collier, Emory & Henry, 1984-87 (80 of 738)
(Min. 800 atts.) 9.6%—Jim Ballard, Wilmington (Ohio)/Mount Union, 1990, 1991-93 (115 of 1,199)

MOST TOUCHDOWN PASSES BY A FRESHMAN
Season
26—Bill Borchert, Mount Union, 1994
Also holds per-game record at 2.6 (26 in 10)

MOST CONSECUTIVE GAMES THROWING A TOUCHDOWN PASS
Career
30—Dan Stewart, Union (N.Y.) (from Nov. 14, 1981, through Nov. 10, 1984)

Receiving

MOST PASSES CAUGHT
Game
23—Sean Munroe, Mass.-Boston vs. Mass. Maritime, Oct. 10, 1992 (332 yards)
Season
106—Theo Blanco (RB), Wis.-Stevens Point, 1987 (1,616 yards)
Per-game record—12.3, Matt Newton, Principia, 1992 (98 in 8)
Career
287—Matt Newton, Principia, 1990-93 (3,646 yards)
Also holds per-game record at 8.7 (287 in 33)

MOST PASSES CAUGHT BY A TIGHT END
Game
16—Shawn Graham, St. Thomas (Minn.) vs. Hamline, Nov. 13, 1982
Season
75—Ryan Davis, St. Thomas (Minn.), 1994 (1,164 yards)
Career
185—Hanz Hoag, Evansville, 1991-93 (2,173 yards)

MOST PASSES CAUGHT BY A RUNNING BACK
Game
17—Theo Blanco, Wis.-Stevens Point vs. Wis.-Oshkosh, Oct. 31, 1987 (271 yards); Tim Mowery, Wis.-Superior vs. Wis.-Stevens Point, Oct. 17, 1981 (154 yards)
Season
106—Theo Blanco, Wis.-Stevens Point, 1987 (1,616 yards)
Career
169—Mike Christman, Wis.-Stevens Point, 1983-86 (2,190 yards)

MOST PASSES CAUGHT BY A FRESHMAN
Season
71—Eric Nemec, Albright, 1995 (834 yards)

MOST PASSES CAUGHT BY TWO PLAYERS, SAME TEAM
Season
158—Theo Blanco (RB) 106 & Aatron Kenney (WR) 52, Wis.-Stevens Point, 1987 (2,713 yards, 24 TDs)

MOST PASSES CAUGHT BY THREE PLAYERS, SAME TEAM
Season
217—Theo Blanco (WR) 80, Don Moehling (TE) 72 & Jim Mares (RB) 65, Wis.-Stevens Point, 1988. Totaled 2,959 yards and 19 TDs (team totals: 285—3,924—26)

MOST CONSECUTIVE GAMES CATCHING A PASS
Career
37—Kendall Griffin, Loras, 1990-93

MOST YARDS GAINED
Game
332—Sean Munroe, Mass.-Boston vs. Mass. Maritime, Oct. 10, 1992 (caught 23)
Season
1,693—Sean Munroe, Mass.-Boston, 1992 (caught 95)
Also holds per-game record at 188.1 (1,693 in 9)
Career
3,846—Dale Amos, Frank. & Marsh., 1986-89 (caught 233)
Per-game record—110.5, Matt Newton, Principia, 1990-93 (3,646 in 33)

MOST YARDS GAINED BY A TIGHT END
Game
267—Tom Mullady, Rhodes vs. Rose-Hulman, Nov. 11, 1978 (caught 13)
Season
1,290—Don Moehling, Wis.-Stevens Point, 1988 (caught 72)
Career
2,663—Don Moehling, Wis.-Stevens Point, 1986-89 (caught 152)

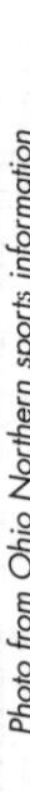
Photo from Ohio Northern sports information

Ohio Northern's LaVant King tied a Division III record by returning two punts for touchdowns in an October 7, 1995, game against Otterbein.

MOST YARDS GAINED BY A RUNNING BACK
Game
271—Theo Blanco, Wis.-Stevens Point vs. Wis.-Oshkosh, Oct. 31, 1987 (caught 17)
Season
1,616—Theo Blanco, Wis.-Stevens Point, 1987 (caught 106)
Career
2,190—Mike Christman, Wis.-Stevens Point, 1983-86 (caught 169)

MOST YARDS GAINED BY TWO PLAYERS, SAME TEAM
Season
2,713—Theo Blanco (RB) 1,616 & Aatron Kenney (WR) 1,097, Wis.-Stevens Point, 1987 (158 receptions, 24 TDs)

HIGHEST AVERAGE GAIN PER RECEPTION
Game
(Min. 3 receps.) 68.3—Paul Jaeckel, Elmhurst vs. Ill. Wesleyan, Oct. 8, 1983 (3 for 205)
(Min. 5 receps.) 56.8—Tom Casperson, Trenton St. vs. Ramapo, Nov. 15, 1980 (5 for 284)
Season
(Min. 35 receps.) 26.9—Marty Redlawsk, Concordia (Ill.), 1985 (38 for 1,022)
(Min. 50 receps.) 23.5—Evan Elkington, Worcester Tech, 1989 (52 for 1,220)
Career
(Min. 125 receps.) 20.6—Rodd Patten, Framingham St., 1990-93 (154 for 3,170)

HIGHEST AVERAGE GAIN PER RECEPTION BY A RUNNING BACK
Season
(Min. 50 receps.) 17.5—Barry Rose, Wis.-Stevens Point, 1989 (67 for 1,171)

MOST TOUCHDOWN PASSES CAUGHT
Game
5—By 12 players. Most recent: Burnell Roques, Claremont-M-S vs. Occidental, Oct. 21, 1995
Season
20—John Aromando, Trenton St., 1983
Also holds per-game record at 2.0 (20 in 10)
Career
55—Chris Bisaillon, Ill. Wesleyan, 1989-92 (223 receptions)
Also holds per-game record at 1.5 (55 in 36)

MOST TOUCHDOWN PASSES CAUGHT BY A FRESHMAN
Season
12—Chris Bisaillon, Ill. Wesleyan, 1989

HIGHEST PERCENTAGE OF PASSES CAUGHT FOR TOUCHDOWNS
Season
(Min. 12 TDs) 54.3%—Keith Gilliam, Randolph-Macon, 1984 (19 of 35)
Career
(Min. 20 TDs) 28.0%—Pat Schwanke, Lawrence, 1979-82 (28 of 100)

MOST CONSECUTIVE PASSES CAUGHT FOR TOUCHDOWNS
9—Keith Gilliam, Randolph-Macon, 1984 (during four games)

Punting

MOST PUNTS
Game
17—Jerry Williams, Frostburg St. vs. Salisbury St., Sept. 30, 1978
Season
106—Bob Blake, Wis.-Superior, 1977 (3,404 yards)
Per-game record—11.0, Mark Roedelbronn, FDU-Madison, 1990 (99 in 9)
Career
263—Chris Gardner, Loras, 1987-90 (9,394 yards)

HIGHEST AVERAGE PER PUNT
Season
(Min. 40 punts) 45.0—Jeff Shea, Cal Lutheran, 1995 (43 for 1,933)
Career
(Min. 100 punts) 42.1—Mike Manson, Ill. Benedictine, 1975-78 (120 for 5,056)

Interceptions

MOST PASSES INTERCEPTED
Game
5—By eight players. Most recent: Chris Butts, Worcester St. vs. Fitchburg St., Oct. 10, 1992
Season
15—Mark Dorner, Juniata, 1987 (202 yards)
Also holds per-game record at 1.5 (15 in 10)
Career
29—Ralph Gebhardt, Rochester, 1973-75 (384 yards)

MOST CONSECUTIVE GAMES INTERCEPTING A PASS
Season
9—Brent Sands, Cornell College, 1992
Also holds career record at 9

MOST YARDS ON INTERCEPTION RETURNS
Game
164—Rick Conner, Western Md. vs. Dickinson, Oct. 15, 1983 (89-yard interception and 75-yard lateral after an interception)
Season
358—Rod Pesek, Whittier, 1987 (10 interceptions)
Career
443—Mark Dorner, Juniata, 1984-87 (26 interceptions)

HIGHEST AVERAGE GAIN PER INTERCEPTION
Season
(Min. 7 ints.) 35.8—Rod Pesek, Whittier, 1987 (10 for 358)
Career
(Min. 20 ints.) 20.4—Todd Schoelzel, Wis.-Oshkosh, 1985-88 (22 for 448)

MOST TOUCHDOWNS SCORED ON INTERCEPTIONS
Game
3—Krumie Mabry, Alfred vs. Denison, Sept. 4, 1993
Season
3—By eight players. Most recent: Krumie Mabry, Alfred, 1993 (7 interceptions)

Punt Returns

MOST PUNT RETURNS
Game
10—Ellis Wangelin, Wis.-River Falls vs. Wis.-Platteville, Oct. 12, 1985 (87 yards)
Season
48—Rick Bealer, Lycoming, 1989 (492 yards)
Career
126—Mike Caterbone, Frank. & Marsh., 1980-83 (1,141 yards)

MOST YARDS ON PUNT RETURNS
Game
212—Melvin Dillard, Ferrum vs. Newport News App., Oct. 13, 1990 (6 returns)
Season
688—Melvin Dillard, Ferrum, 1990 (25 returns)
Career
1,198—Chuck Downey, Stony Brook, 1984-87 (59 returns)

HIGHEST AVERAGE GAIN PER RETURN
Season
(Min. 1.2 rets. per game) 31.2—Chuck Downey, Stony Brook, 1986 (17 for 530)
Career
(Min. 1.2 rets. per game) 22.9—Keith Winston, Knoxville, 1986-87 (30 for 686)
(Min. 50 rets.) 20.3—Chuck Downey, Stony Brook, 1984-87 (59 for 1,198)

MOST TOUCHDOWNS SCORED ON PUNT RETURNS
Game
2—By nine players. Most recent: LaVant King, Ohio Northern vs. Otterbein, Oct. 7, 1995 (50 & 73 yards)

Season

4—Chris Warren, Ferrum, 1989 (18 returns); Keith Winston, Knoxville, 1986 (14 returns); Chuck Downey, Stony Brook, 1986 (17 returns); Matt Pekarske, Wis.-La Crosse, 1986 (37 returns)

Career

7—Chuck Downey, Stony Brook, 1984-87 (59 returns)

Kickoff Returns

MOST KICKOFF RETURNS

Game

9—Larry Schurder, North Park vs. Elmhurst, Sept. 17, 1983 (229 yards)

Season

42—Phil Puryear, Wooster, 1990 (834 yards); Dirk Blood, Ohio Northern, 1987 (973 yards)

Career

104—Simeon Henderson, Elmhurst, 1991-94 (2,063 yards)

MOST YARDS ON KICKOFF RETURNS

Game

279—Chuck Downey, Stony Brook vs. Trenton St., Oct. 5, 1984 (7 returns)

Season

973—Dirk Blood, Ohio Northern, 1987 (42 returns)

Career

2,063—Simeon Henderson, Elmhurst, 1991-94 (104 returns)

HIGHEST AVERAGE GAIN PER RETURN

Game

(Min. 3 rets.) 68.0—Victor Johnson, Elmhurst vs. Wheaton (Ill.), Sept. 15, 1979 (3 for 204)

Season

(Min. 1.2 rets. per game) 42.2—Brandon Steinheim, Wesley, 1994 (10 for 422)

Career

(Min. 1.2 rets. per game) 29.2—Daryl Brown, Tufts, 1974-76 (38 for 1,111)

MOST TOUCHDOWNS SCORED ON KICKOFF RETURNS

Game

2—By many players. Most recent: Bill Nashwinter, Buffalo St. vs. Alfred, Oct. 27, 1990

Season

4—Byron Womack, Iona, 1989

Career

6—Byron Womack, Iona, 1988-91

Total Kick Returns

(Combined Punt and Kickoff Returns)

MOST YARDS ON KICK RETURNS

Game

354—Chuck Downey, Stony Brook vs. Trenton St., Oct. 5, 1984 (7 kickoff returns for 279 yards, 1 punt return for 75 yards)

GAINING 1,000 YARDS ON PUNT RETURNS AND 1,000 YARDS ON KICKOFF RETURNS

Career

LaVant King, Ohio Northern, 1991, 93-95 (1,298 on kickoff returns, 1,074 on punt returns); Chuck Downey, Stony Brook, 1984-87 (1,281 on kickoff returns, 1,198 on punt returns)

MOST TOUCHDOWNS ON KICK RETURNS

Game

3—Chuck Downey, Stony Brook vs. Trenton St., Oct. 5, 1984 (2 kickoff returns 98 & 95 yards, 1 punt return 75 yards)

Season

5—Charles Jordan, Occidental, 1993 (2 punt returns, 3 kickoff returns); Chris Warren, Ferrum, 1989 (4 punt returns, 1 kickoff return); Chuck Downey, Stony Brook, 1986 (4 punt returns, 1 kickoff return)

Career

10—Chuck Downey, Stony Brook, 1984-87 (7 punt returns, 3 kickoff returns)

HIGHEST AVERAGE PER KICK RETURN (Min. 1.2 Returns Per Game Each)

Career

23.6—Chuck Downey, Stony Brook, 1984-87 (59 for 1,198 on punt returns, 46 for 1,281 on kickoff returns)

AVERAGING 20 YARDS EACH ON PUNT RETURNS AND KICKOFF RETURNS (Min. 1.2 Returns Per Game Each)

Career

Chuck Downey, Stony Brook, 1984-87 (20.3 on punt returns, 59 for 1,198; 27.8 on kickoff returns, 46 for 1,281)

All Runbacks

(Combined Interceptions, Punt Returns and Kickoff Returns)

MOST TOUCHDOWNS ON INTERCEPTIONS, PUNT RETURNS AND KICKOFF RETURNS

Season

6—Chuck Downey, Stony Brook, 1986 (4 punt returns, 1 kickoff return, 1 interception return)

Career

11—Chuck Downey, Stony Brook, 1984-87 (7 punt returns, 3 kickoff returns, 1 interception return)

Punts Blocked By

MOST PUNTS BLOCKED BY

Game

3—Jim Perryman, Millikin vs. Carroll (Wis.), Nov. 1, 1980

Season

9—Jim Perryman, Millikin, 1980

Career

13—Frank Lyle, Millsaps, 1979-82

Note: Daryl Hobson, Ill. Benedictine DB, blocked 9 punts during 17 games in 1987-88

All-Purpose Yards

(Yardage Gained From Rushing, Receiving and All Runbacks)

MOST PLAYS

Season

383—Mike Birosak, Dickinson, 1989 (380 rushes, 3 receptions)

Career

1,158—Eric Frees, Western Md., 1988-91 (1,059 rushes, 34 receptions, 58 kickoff returns, 7 punt returns)

MOST YARDS GAINED

Game

509—Carey Bender, Coe vs. Grinnell, Oct. 9, 1993 (417 rushing, 92 receiving)

Season

2,656—Carey Bender, Coe, 1994 (2,243 rushing, 319 receiving, 7 punt returns, 87 kickoff returns; 320 plays)

Also holds per-game record at 265.6 (2,656 in 10)

Career

7,970—Carey Bender, Coe, 1991-94 (6,125 rushing, 1,751 receiving, 7 punt returns, 87 kickoff returns; 1,046 plays)

Per-game record—210.8, $Kirk Matthieu, Maine Maritime, 1989-93 (6,955 in 33)

$*See page 6 for explanation.*

HIGHEST AVERAGE GAIN PER PLAY

Season

(Min. 1,500 yards, 125 plays) 12.0—Darnell Morgan, Chapman, 1995 (1,602 in 134)

Career

(Min. 4,000 yards, 300 plays) 16.0—Chris Wiesehan, Wabash, 1990-93 (4,825 yards on 301)

Scoring

MOST POINTS SCORED

Game

48—Carey Bender, Coe vs. Beloit, Nov. 12, 1994

Season

194—Carey Bender, Coe, 1994 (32 TDs & 2 PATs)

Also holds per-game record at 19.4 (194 in 10)

Career

528—Carey Bender, Coe, 1991-94 (86 TDs & 12 PATs)

Per-game record—14.4, Ricky Gales, Simpson, 1988-89 (274 in 19)

TWO PLAYERS, SAME TEAM, EACH SCORING 100 POINTS OR MORE

Season

Steve Harris (122) & R. J. Hoppe (106), Carroll (Wis.), 1994; Denis McDermott (126) & Manny Tsantes (102), St. John's (N.Y.), 1989; Theo Blanco (102) & Aatron Kenney (102), Wis.-Stevens Point, 1987

MOST TOUCHDOWNS SCORED

Season

32—Carey Bender, Coe, 1994

Also holds per-game record at 3.2 (32 in 10)

Career

86—Carey Bender, Coe, 1991-94

Also holds per-game record at 2.2 (86 in 39)

MOST GAMES SCORING A TOUCHDOWN

Career

36—Carey Bender, Coe, 1991-94 (39 games)

MOST GAMES SCORING TWO OR MORE TOUCHDOWNS

Career

24—Joe Dudek, Plymouth St., 1982-85 (41 games)

MOST EXTRA POINTS ATTEMPTED BY KICKING

Game

14—Kurt Christenson, Concordia-M'head vs. Macalester, Sept. 24, 1977 (made 13)

Season

70—Greg Poulin, St. John's (Minn.), 1993 (made 63)

Career

194—Tim Mercer, Ferrum, 1987-90 (made 183)

MOST EXTRA POINTS MADE BY KICKING

Game

13—Kurt Christenson, Concordia-M'head vs. Macalester, Sept. 24, 1977 (attempted 14)

Season

63—Greg Poulin, St. John's (Minn.), 1993 (attempted 70)

Career

183—Tim Mercer, Ferrum, 1987-90 (attempted 194)

HIGHEST PERCENTAGE OF EXTRA POINTS MADE (Best Perfect Season)

100.0%—Mike Duvic, Dayton, 1989 (46 of 46)

HIGHEST PERCENTAGE OF EXTRA POINTS MADE

Career

(Min. 80 atts.) 100.0%—Mike Farrell, Adrian, 1983-85 (84 of 84)

(Min. 100 atts.) 98.5%—Rims Roof, Coe, 1982-85 (135 of 137)

MOST CONSECUTIVE EXTRA POINTS MADE BY KICKING

Game

13—Kurt Christenson, Concordia-M'head vs. Macalester, Sept. 24, 1977

Career

102—Rims Roof, Coe (from Sept. 24, 1983, through Nov. 9, 1985)

MOST POINTS SCORED BY KICKING

Game

20—Jim Hever, Rhodes vs. Millsaps, Sept. 22, 1984 (6 FGs, 2 PATs)

Season

102—Ken Edelman, Mount Union, 1990 (20 FGs, 42 PATs)

Also holds per-game record at 10.2 (102 in 10)

Career

274—Ken Edelman, Mount Union, 1987-90 (52 FGs, 118 PATs)

Also holds per-game record at 6.9 (274 in 40)

MOST SUCCESSFUL TWO-POINT PASS ATTEMPTS

Game

4—Rob Bristow, Pomona-Pitzer vs. Whittier, Oct. 19, 1985 (all in 4th quarter); Dave Geissler, Wis.-Stevens Point vs. Wis.-La Crosse, Sept. 21, 1985 (all in 4th quarter)

Season

7—Kirk Baumgartner, Wis.-Stevens Point, 1988 (8 attempts); Gary Collier, Emory & Henry, 1987 (11 attempts); Dave Geissler, Wis.-Stevens Point, 1985 (8 attempts)

Career

11—Dave Geissler, Wis.-Stevens Point, 1982-85 (14 attempts)

Note: Rob Bristow, Pomona-Pitzer, 1983-86, holds record for highest percentage of successful two-point pass attempts (best perfect record) at 9 of 9

MOST TWO-POINT PASSES CAUGHT

Season

4—Rob Brooks, Albright, 1992; Don Moehling, Wis.-Stevens Point, 1988; Mike Christman, Wis.-Stevens Point, 1985

Defensive Extra Points

MOST DEFENSIVE EXTRA POINTS SCORED

Game

1—By many players

Season

2—Dan Fichter, Brockport St., 1990 (2 blocked kick returns)

LONGEST DEFENSIVE EXTRA POINT BLOCKED KICK RETURN

97—Keith Mottram (CB), Colorado Col. vs. Austin, Oct. 10, 1992 (scored)

LONGEST DEFENSIVE EXTRA POINT INTERCEPTION

100—By four players. Most recent: Chris Schleeper (FS), Quincy vs. Ill. Wesleyan, Sept. 29, 1990 (scored)

FIRST DEFENSIVE EXTRA POINT SCORED

Steve Nieves (DB), St. John's (N.Y.) vs. Iona, Sept. 10, 1988 (83-yard blocked kick return)

Field Goals

MOST FIELD GOALS MADE

Game

6—Jim Hever, Rhodes vs. Millsaps, Sept. 22, 1984 (30, 24, 42, 44, 46, 30 yards; attempted 8)

Season

20—Ken Edelman, Mount Union, 1990 (attempted 27)

Also holds per-game record at 2.0 (20 in 10)

Career

52—Ken Edelman, Mount Union, 1987-90 (attempted 71)

Also holds per-game record *(Min. 30)* at 1.3 (52 in 40)

MOST FIELD GOALS ATTEMPTED

Game

8—Jim Hever, Rhodes vs. Millsaps, Sept. 22, 1984 (made 6)

Season

29—Scott Ryerson, Central Fla., 1981 (made 18)

Career

71—Ken Edelman, Mount Union, 1987-90 (made 52); Doug Hart, Grove City, 1985-88 (made 40)

HIGHEST PERCENTAGE OF FIELD GOALS MADE

Season

(Min. 15 atts.) 93.8%—Steve Graeca, John Carroll, 1988 (15 of 16)

Career

(Min. 50 atts.) *77.6%—Mike Duvic, Dayton, 1986-89 (38 of 49)

**Declared champion; with one more attempt (making 50), failed, still would have highest percentage (76.0).*

LONGEST FIELD GOAL MADE

62—Dom Antonini, Rowan vs. Salisbury St., Sept. 18, 1976

MOST FIELD GOALS ATTEMPTED WITHOUT SUCCESS

Season

11—Scott Perry, Moravian, 1986

Team Records

Single Game—Offense

Total Offense

MOST PLAYS

112—Gust. Adolphus vs. Bethel (Minn.), Nov. 2, 1985 (65 passes, 47 rushes; 493 yards)

MOST PLAYS, BOTH TEAMS

214—Gust. Adolphus (112) & Bethel (Minn.) (102), Nov. 2, 1985 (143 passes, 71 rushes; 930 yards)

MOST YARDS GAINED

774—Allegheny vs. Wooster, Oct. 29, 1994

MOST YARDS GAINED, BOTH TEAMS

1,395—Occidental (753) & Claremont-M-S (642), Oct. 30, 1993 (136 plays)

MOST TOUCHDOWNS SCORED BY RUSHING AND PASSING

14—Concordia-M'head vs. Macalester, Sept. 24, 1977 (12 rushing, 2 passing)

Rushing

MOST RUSHES

92—Wis.-River Falls vs. Wis.-Platteville, Oct. 21, 1989 (464 yards)

MOST YARDS GAINED RUSHING

642—Wis.-River Falls vs. Wis.-Superior, Oct. 14, 1989 (88 rushes)

MOST TOUCHDOWNS SCORED BY RUSHING

12—Concordia-M'head vs. Macalester, Sept. 24, 1977

Passing

MOST PASSES ATTEMPTED

81—Principia vs. Blackburn, Oct. 10, 1992 (completed 48)

MOST PASSES ATTEMPTED, BOTH TEAMS

143—Bethel (Minn.) (78) & Gust. Adolphus (65), Nov. 2, 1985 (completed 65)

MOST PASSES ATTEMPTED WITHOUT AN INTERCEPTION

68—Western Md. vs. Frank. & Marsh., Oct. 23, 1994 (completed 38)

MOST PASSES COMPLETED

50—Hofstra vs. Fordham, Oct. 19, 1991 (attempted 69)

MOST PASSES COMPLETED, BOTH TEAMS

72—Wis.-Superior (41) & Wis.-Stevens Point (31), Oct. 17, 1981 (attempted 131)

HIGHEST PERCENTAGE OF PASSES COMPLETED (Min. 35 Attempts)

78.9%—Wheaton (Ill.) vs. North Park, Oct. 8, 1983 (30 of 38)

MOST YARDS GAINED

602—St. Thomas (Minn.) vs. Bethel (Minn.), Nov. 13, 1993

MOST YARDS GAINED, BOTH TEAMS

1,100—St. Thomas (Minn.) (602) & Bethel (Minn.) (498), Nov. 13, 1993 (attempted 113, completed 69)

MOST TOUCHDOWN PASSES

8—Mass.-Boston vs. Framingham St., Nov. 14, 1992; Wis.-Stevens Point vs. Wis.-Superior, Nov. 4, 1989

MOST TOUCHDOWN PASSES, BOTH TEAMS

12—St. Thomas (Minn.) (6) & Bethel (Minn.) (6), Nov. 13, 1993

Punt Returns

MOST TOUCHDOWNS SCORED ON PUNT RETURNS

2—By many teams. Most recent: Ohio Northern vs. Otterbein, Oct. 7, 1995

Kickoff Returns

MOST YARDS ON KICKOFF RETURNS

283—Oberlin vs. Wittenberg, Oct. 30, 1993

Scoring

MOST POINTS SCORED

97—Concordia-M'head vs. Macalester, Sept. 24, 1977

MOST POINTS SCORED, BOTH TEAMS

111—Coe (63) & Beloit (48), Nov. 12, 1994; Carroll (Wis.) (58) & Ill. Wesleyan (53), Nov. 11, 1989

MOST POINTS SCORED BY A LOSING TEAM

53—Ill. Wesleyan vs. Carroll (Wis.) (58), Nov. 11, 1989

MOST POINTS OVERCOME TO WIN A GAME

33—Salisbury St. vs. Randolph-Macon, Sept. 15, 1984 (trailed 33-0 with 14:18 left in 2nd quarter; won 34-33); Wis.-Platteville vs. Wis.-Eau Claire, Nov. 8, 1980 (trailed 33-0 with 7:00 left in 2nd quarter; won 52-43)

MOST POINTS SCORED IN A BRIEF PERIOD OF TIME

21 in 1:58—Occidental vs. Claremont-M-S, Oct. 30, 1993 (turned 14-14 game into 35-20 in 2nd quarter; won 68-42)

32 in 4:04—Wis.-Stevens Point vs. Wis.-La Crosse, Sept. 21, 1985 (trailed 27-3 and 35-11 in 4th quarter; ended in 35-35 tie)

MOST POINTS SCORED IN FIRST VARSITY GAME

63—Bentley vs. Brooklyn (26), Sept. 24, 1988

MOST TOUCHDOWNS SCORED

14—Concordia-M'head vs. Macalester, Sept. 24, 1977

MOST EXTRA POINTS MADE BY KICKING

13—Concordia-M'head vs. Macalester, Sept. 24, 1977 (attempted 14)

MOST FIELD GOALS MADE

6—Rhodes vs. Millsaps, Sept. 22, 1984 (attempted 8)

MOST FIELD GOALS ATTEMPTED

8—Rhodes vs. Millsaps, Sept. 22, 1984 (made 6)

MOST DEFENSIVE EXTRA-POINT RETURNS SCORED

1—By many teams

MOST DEFENSIVE EXTRA-POINT OPPORTUNITIES

2—Frank. & Marsh. vs. Johns Hopkins, Nov. 7, 1992 (1 interception & 1 kick return; none scored); Wis.-River Falls vs. Wis.-La Crosse, Nov. 11, 1989 (2 kick returns; 1 scored); Wis.-Platteville vs. Wis.-Oshkosh, Oct. 15, 1988 (2 interceptions; none scored); Buffalo St. vs. Brockport St., Oct. 1, 1988 (1 interception & 1 kick return; none scored)

Turnovers

(Most Times Losing the Ball on Interceptions and Fumbles)

MOST TURNOVERS

13—St. Olaf vs. St. Thomas (Minn.), Oct. 12, 1985 (10 interceptions, 3 fumbles); Mercyhurst vs. Buffalo St., Oct. 23, 1982 (12 fumbles, 1 interception); Albany (N.Y.) vs. Rochester Inst., Oct. 1, 1977

MOST TURNOVERS, BOTH TEAMS

24—Albany (N.Y.) (13) & Rochester Inst. (11), Oct. 1, 1977

First Downs

MOST TOTAL FIRST DOWNS
40—Upper Iowa vs. Loras, Nov. 7, 1992 (19 rushing, 17 passing, 4 by penalty)

Penalties

MOST PENALTIES AGAINST
25—Norwich vs. Coast Guard, Sept. 29, 1985 (192 yards)

SINGLE GAME—Defense

Total Defense

FEWEST YARDS ALLOWED
Minus 50—Ithaca vs. Springfield, Oct. 11, 1975 (-94 rushing, 44 passing)

Rushing Defense

FEWEST RUSHES ALLOWED
10—Augustana (Ill.) vs. Ill. Wesleyan, Oct. 11, 1983 (28 yards); Wis.-Superior vs. Wis.-Stevens Point, Oct. 17, 1981 (-3 yards)

FEWEST YARDS ALLOWED
Minus 112—Coast Guard vs. Wesleyan (Conn.), Oct. 7, 1989 (23 plays)

Pass Defense

FEWEST ATTEMPTS ALLOWED
0—By many teams. Most recent: Concordia-M'head vs. Macalester, Oct. 12, 1991

FEWEST COMPLETIONS ALLOWED
0—By many teams. Most recent: Mass.-Boston vs. Maine Maritime, Oct. 21, 1995 (2 attempts)

FEWEST YARDS ALLOWED
Minus 6—Central (Iowa) vs. Simpson, Oct. 19, 1985 (1 completion)

MOST PASSES INTERCEPTED BY
10—St. Thomas (Minn.) vs. St. Olaf, Oct. 12, 1985 (91 yards; 50 attempts)

MOST PLAYERS INTERCEPTING A PASS
8—Samford vs. Anderson, Oct. 11, 1986 (8 interceptions in the game)

Punts Blocked By

MOST OPPONENT'S PUNTS BLOCKED BY
4—Ill. Benedictine vs. Olivet Nazarene, Oct. 22, & vs. Aurora, Oct. 29, 1988 (consecutive games, resulting in 4 TDs and 1 safety). Blocked 9 punts in three consecutive games, vs. MacMurray, Oct. 15, Olivet Nazarene and Aurora, resulting in 4 TDs and 2 safeties

First Downs

FEWEST FIRST DOWNS ALLOWED
0—Case Reserve vs. Wooster, Sept. 21, 1985

SEASON—Offense

Total Offense

MOST YARDS GAINED PER GAME
549.7—St. John's (Minn.), 1993 (5,497 in 10)

HIGHEST AVERAGE GAIN PER PLAY
8.1—Ferrum, 1990 (534 for 4,350)

MOST PLAYS PER GAME
85.6—Hampden-Sydney, 1978 (856 in 10)

MOST TOUCHDOWNS SCORED PER GAME BY RUSHING AND PASSING
8.4—St. John's (Minn.), 1993 (84 in 10; 44 rushing, 40 passing)

Rushing

MOST YARDS GAINED PER GAME
434.7—Ferrum, 1990 (3,912 in 9)

HIGHEST AVERAGE GAIN PER RUSH
8.3—Ferrum, 1990 (470 for 3,912)

MOST RUSHES PER GAME
71.4—Wis.-River Falls, 1988 (714 in 10)

MOST TOUCHDOWNS SCORED PER GAME BY RUSHING
5.4—Ferrum, 1990 (49 in 9)

Passing

MOST YARDS GAINED PER GAME
403.5—Hofstra, 1991 (4,035 in 10)

FEWEST YARDS GAINED PER GAME
18.4—Wis.-River Falls, 1983 (184 in 10)

HIGHEST AVERAGE GAIN PER ATTEMPT
(Min. 250 atts.) 11.1—St. John's (Minn.), 1993 (299 for 3,308)
(Min. 350 atts.) 8.7—Wheaton (Ill.), 1983 (393 for 3,424)

HIGHEST AVERAGE GAIN PER COMPLETION (Min. 200 Completions)
15.4—Wis.-Stevens Point, 1987 (249 for 3,836)

MOST PASSES ATTEMPTED PER GAME
58.5—Hofstra, 1991 (585 in 10)

FEWEST PASSES ATTEMPTED PER GAME
4.0—Wis.-River Falls, 1988 (40 in 10)

MOST PASSES COMPLETED PER GAME
34.4—Hofstra, 1991 (344 in 10)

FEWEST PASSES COMPLETED PER GAME
1.3—Wis.-River Falls, 1983 (13 in 10)

HIGHEST PERCENTAGE COMPLETED (Min. 200 Attempts)
70.7%—Mount Union, 1993 (244 of 345)

LOWEST PERCENTAGE OF PASSES HAD INTERCEPTED (Min. 150 Attempts)
0.7%—San Diego, 1990 (1 of 153)

MOST TOUCHDOWN PASSES PER GAME
4.0—St. John's (Minn.), 1993 (40 in 10); Samford, 1987 (40 in 10)

HIGHEST PASSING EFFICIENCY RATING POINTS
(Min. 15 atts. per game) 211.3—Eureka, 1994 (205 attempts, 142 completions, 8 interceptions, 2,478 yards, 30 TDs)
(Min. 300 atts.) 186.0—Mount Union, 1993 (345 attempts, 244 completions, 12 interceptions, 3,528 yards, 38 TDs)

Punting

MOST PUNTS PER GAME
11.0—FDU-Madison, 1990 (99 in 9)

FEWEST PUNTS PER GAME
2.4—Frostburg St., 1990 (24 in 10)

HIGHEST PUNTING AVERAGE
44.6—Occidental, 1982 (55 for 2,454)

Scoring

MOST POINTS PER GAME
61.5—St. John's (Minn.), 1993 (615 in 10)

MOST TOUCHDOWNS PER GAME
8.9—St. John's (Minn.), 1993 (89 in 10)

BEST PERFECT RECORD ON EXTRA POINTS MADE BY KICKING
49 of 49—Dayton, 1989

MOST TWO-POINT ATTEMPTS PER GAME
2.8—Martin Luther, 1990 (17 in 6)

MOST FIELD GOALS MADE PER GAME
2.0—Mount Union, 1990 (20 in 10)

HIGHEST SCORING MARGIN
51.8—St. John's (Minn.), 1993 (averaged 61.5 and allowed 9.7 in 10 games)

MOST TOUCHDOWNS ON BLOCKED PUNT RETURNS
5—Widener, 1990

MOST SAFETIES
4—Upper Iowa, 1995; Alfred, 1992; Central (Iowa), 1992; Westfield St., 1992; Wis.-Stevens Point, 1990

MOST DEFENSIVE EXTRA-POINT RETURNS SCORED
2—Eureka, 1991; Brockport St., 1990

MOST DEFENSIVE EXTRA POINT BLOCKED KICK RETURNS
3—Assumption, 1992 (1 scored); Ohio Wesleyan, 1991 (0 scored); Brockport St., 1990 (2 scored)

MOST DEFENSIVE EXTRA POINT INTERCEPTIONS
2—Swarthmore, 1989 (1 scored); Wis.-Platteville, 1988 (none scored)

Penalties

MOST PENALTIES PER GAME
13.3—Kean, 1990 (133 in 10, 1,155 yards)

MOST YARDS PENALIZED PER GAME
121.9—Hofstra, 1991 (1,219 in 10, 124 penalties)

Turnovers (Giveaways)

(Passes Had Intercepted and Fumbles Lost; From 1985)

FEWEST TURNOVERS
6—Mount Union, 1995 (4 interceptions, 2 fumbles lost)
Also holds per-game record at 0.6 (6 in 10)

MOST TURNOVERS
52—William Penn, 1985 (19 interceptions, 33 fumbles lost)
Also holds per-game record at 5.2 (52 in 10)

SEASON—Defense

Total Defense

FEWEST YARDS ALLOWED PER GAME
94.0—Knoxville, 1977 (940 in 10)

LOWEST AVERAGE YARDS ALLOWED PER PLAY
(Min. 500 plays) 1.8—Bowie St., 1978 (576 for 1,011)
(Min. 650 plays) 2.0—Plymouth St., 1987 (733 for 1,488)

FEWEST RUSHING AND PASSING TOUCHDOWNS ALLOWED PER GAME
0.3—Montclair St., 1984 (3 in 10)

Rushing Defense

FEWEST YARDS ALLOWED PER GAME
Minus 2.3—Knoxville, 1977 (-23 in 10 games)

LOWEST AVERAGE YARDS ALLOWED PER RUSH
(Min. 275 rushes) Minus 0.1—Knoxville, 1977 (333 for -23)
(Min. 400 rushes) 1.0—Lycoming, 1976 (400 for 399)

FEWEST TOUCHDOWNS BY RUSHING ALLOWED
0—Union (N.Y.), 1983 (9 games); New Haven, 1978 (9 games)

Pass Defense

FEWEST YARDS ALLOWED PER GAME
48.5—Mass. Maritime, 1976 (388 in 8)

FEWEST YARDS ALLOWED PER ATTEMPT
(Min. 150 atts.) 2.9—Plymouth St., 1982 (170 for 488)
(Min. 225 atts.) 3.3—Plymouth St., 1987 (281 for 919)

FEWEST YARDS ALLOWED PER COMPLETION (Min. 100 Completions)
8.6—Baldwin-Wallace, 1990 (151 for 1,305)

LOWEST COMPLETION PERCENTAGE ALLOWED
(Min. 150 atts.) 24.3%—Doane, 1973 (41 of 169)
(Min. 250 atts.) 33.5%—Plymouth St., 1987 (94 of 281)

HIGHEST PERCENTAGE INTERCEPTED BY (Min. 200 Attempts)
15.2%—Rose-Hulman, 1977 (32 of 210)

MOST PASSES INTERCEPTED BY
35—Plymouth St., 1987 (12 games, 281 attempts against, 348 yards returned)
Per-game record—3.4, Montclair St., 1981 (34 in 10)

FEWEST PASSES INTERCEPTED BY (Min. 125 Attempts)
1—Bates, 1987 (134 attempts against in 8 games, 0 yards returned)

MOST YARDS ON INTERCEPTION RETURNS
576—Emory & Henry, 1987 (31 interceptions)

MOST TOUCHDOWNS SCORED ON INTERCEPTIONS
6—Coe, 1992 (22 interceptions, 272 passes against); Augustana (Ill.), 1987 (23 interceptions, 229 passes against)

FEWEST TOUCHDOWN PASSES ALLOWED
0—By many teams. Most recent: Dayton, 1980 (11 games)

LOWEST PASSING EFFICIENCY RATING POINTS ALLOWED OPPONENTS
(Min. 150 atts.) 27.8—Plymouth St., 1982 (allowed 170 attempts, 53 completions, 488 yards, 1 TD & intercepted 25 passes)
(Min. 275 atts.) 43.1—Plymouth St., 1987 (allowed 281 attempts, 94 completions, 919 yards, 6 TDs & intercepted 35 passes)

Punting

MOST OPPONENT'S PUNTS BLOCKED BY
11—Ill. Benedictine, 1987 (78 punts against in 10 games). Blocked 17 punts in 18 games during 1987-88, resulting in 5 TDs and 3 safeties

Scoring

FEWEST POINTS ALLOWED PER GAME
3.4—Millsaps, 1980 (31 in 9)

FEWEST TOUCHDOWNS ALLOWED
4—Baldwin-Wallace, 1981 (10 games); Millsaps, 1980 (9 games); Bentley, 1990 (8 games)

MOST SHUTOUTS
6—Cortland St., 1989; Plymouth St., 1982 (consecutive)

MOST CONSECUTIVE SHUTOUTS
6—Plymouth St., 1982

MOST POINTS ALLOWED PER GAME
59.1—Macalester, 1977 (532 in 9; 76 TDs, 64 PATs, 4 FGs)

MOST DEFENSIVE EXTRA-POINT ATTEMPTS BY OPPONENTS
5—Norwich, 1992 (4 blocked kick returns, 1 interception; none scored)

Turnovers (Takeaways)

(Opponent's Passes Intercepted and Fumbles Recovered, From 1985)

HIGHEST MARGIN OF TURNOVERS PER GAME OVER OPPONENTS
2.9—Macalester, 1986 (29 in 10; 29 giveaways vs. 58 takeaways)

MOST TAKEAWAYS
58—Macalester, 1986 (28 interceptions, 30 fumbles gained)
Also holds per-game record at 5.8 (58 in 10)

Additional Records

MOST CONSECUTIVE VICTORIES
37—Augustana (Ill.) (from Sept. 17, 1983, through 1985 Division III playoffs; ended with 0-0 tie vs. Elmhurst, Sept. 13, 1986)

MOST CONSECUTIVE REGULAR-SEASON VICTORIES
49—Augustana (Ill.) (from Oct. 25, 1980, through 1985; ended with 0-0 tie vs. Elmhurst, Sept. 13, 1986)

MOST CONSECUTIVE GAMES WITHOUT DEFEAT
60—Augustana (Ill.), (from Sept. 17, 1983, through Nov. 22, 1987; ended with 38-36 loss to Dayton, Nov. 29, 1987, in Division III playoffs and included one tie)

MOST CONSECUTIVE REGULAR-SEASON GAMES WITHOUT DEFEAT
70—Augustana (Ill.) (from Oct. 25, 1980, through Oct. 1, 1988; ended with 24-21 loss to Carroll, Wis., Oct. 8, 1988)

MOST CONSECUTIVE WINNING SEASONS
34—Wittenberg (from 1955 through 1988; ended with 4-5 record in 1989)

MOST CONSECUTIVE GAMES WITHOUT BEING SHUT OUT
224—Carnegie Mellon (from Sept. 30, 1972, through Nov. 4, 1995; ended with 3-0 loss to Case Reserve, Nov. 11, 1995)

MOST CONSECUTIVE LOSSES
50—Macalester (from Oct. 5, 1974, to Nov. 10, 1979; ended with 17-14 win over Mount Senario, Sept. 6, 1980)

MOST CONSECUTIVE GAMES WITHOUT A TIE
371—Widener (from Oct. 29, 1949, to Nov. 11, 1989; ended with 14-14 tie against Gettysburg, Sept. 8, 1990)

HIGHEST-SCORING TIE GAME
40-40—Montclair St. & Wagner, Sept. 11, 1982

LAST SCORELESS TIE GAME
Oct. 4, 1986—Delaware Valley & Moravian

MOST CONSECUTIVE QUARTERS WITHOUT YIELDING A TOUCHDOWN BY RUSHING
61—Augustana (Ill.) (in 16 games from Sept. 27, 1986, to Nov. 7, 1987; 77 including four 1986 Division III playoff games); Union (N.Y.) (in 16 games from Oct. 23, 1982, to Sept. 29, 1984)

MOST CONSECUTIVE QUARTERS WITHOUT YIELDING A TOUCHDOWN BY PASSING
44—Swarthmore (from Oct. 31, 1981, to Nov. 13, 1982)

MOST IMPROVED WON-LOST RECORD (Including Postseason Games)
7 games—Catholic, 1994 (8-2-0) from 1993 (1-9-0); Susquehanna, 1986 (11-1-0) from 1985 (3-7-0); Maryville (Tenn.), 1976 (7-2-0) from 1975 (0-9-0)

Annual Champions, All-Time Leaders

Total Offense

CAREER YARDS PER GAME

Player, Team	Years	G	Plays	Yards	Yd. PG
Terry Peebles, Hanover	1992-95	23	1,140	7,672	*333.6
Kirk Baumgartner, Wis.-Stevens Point	1986-89	41	*2,007	*12,767	311.4
Willie Reyna, La Verne	1991-92	17	551	4,996	293.9
Keith Bishop, Ill. Wesleyan/ Wheaton (Ill.)	1981, 83-85	31	1,467	9,052	292.0
Jordan Poznick, Principia	1990-93	32	1,757	8,983	280.7
John Rooney, Ill. Wesleyan	1982-84	27	1,260	7,393	273.8
Tim Peterson, Wis.-Stout	1986-89	36	1,558	9,701	269.5
Jim Ballard, Wilmington (Ohio)/ Mount Union	1990, 91-93	40	1,328	10,545	263.6
Robert Farra, Claremont-M-S	1978-79	16	690	4,179	261.2
Chris Ings, Wabash	1992-95	37	1,532	9,608	259.7
Eric Noble, Wilmington (Ohio)	1992-95	38	1,513	9,731	256.0
Brian Van Deusen, Western Md.	1992-95	30	1,415	7,172	239.1
Dennis Bogacz, Wis.-Oshkosh/ Wis.-Whitewater	1988-89, 90-91	38	1,394	8,850	232.9
John Clark, Wis.-Eau Claire	1987-90	38	1,354	8,838	232.6
Ed Smith, Ill. Benedictine	1991-93	29	892	6,599	227.6
Tom Stallings, St. Thomas (Minn.)	1990-93	24	819	5,460	227.5
Mark Peterson, Neb. Wesleyan	1982-84	28	1,151	6,367	227.4
Scott Scesney, St. John's (N.Y.)	1986-89	32	1,048	7,196	224.9
Rob Bristow, Pomona-Pitzer	1983-86	29	1,290	6,465	222.9
Sean Keville, Moravian	1991-94	27	894	5,948	220.3
Dave Geissler, Wis.-Stevens Point	1982-85	42	1,695	8,990	214.0
Jeff Beer, Bethany (W.Va.)	1978-80	25	878	5,228	209.1
John Love, North Park	1988-90	27	1,182	5,613	207.9
Seamus Crotty, Hamilton	1982-85	31	1,225	6,402	206.5
Jeff Voris, DePauw	1986-89	28	993	5,754	205.5

**Record.*

SEASON YARDS PER GAME

Player, Team	Year	G	Plays	Yards	Yd. PG
Terry Peebles, Hanover	†1995	10	572	*3,981	*398.1
Keith Bishop, Wheaton (Ill.)	†1983	9	421	3,193	354.8
Kirk Baumgartner, Wis.-Stevens Point	†1989	10	530	3,540	354.0
John Furmaniak, Eureka	1995	10	414	3,503	350.3
Kirk Baumgartner, Wis.-Stevens Point	†1988	11	604	3,790	344.5
Terry Peebles, Hanover	†1994	10	520	3,441	344.1
Jordan Poznick, Principia	†1992	8	519	2,747	343.4
Eric Noble, Wilmington (Ohio)	1994	9	460	3,072	341.3
Jordan Poznick, Principia	†1993	8	488	2,705	338.1
Kirk Baumgartner, Wis.-Stevens Point	1987	11	561	3,712	337.5
Jim Ballard, Mount Union	1993	10	372	3,371	337.1
Steve Austin, Mass.-Boston	1992	9	466	3,003	333.7
Willie Reyna, La Verne	†1991	8	220	2,633	329.1
Keith Bishop, Wheaton (Ill.)	†1985	9	521	2,951	327.9
Tim Peterson, Wis.-Stout	1989	10	*614	3,244	324.4
John Shipp, Claremont-M-S	1994	9	442	2,871	319.0
Jon Nielsen, Claremont-M-S	1995	9	405	2,848	316.4
Tom Stallings, St. Thomas (Minn.)	1993	10	438	3,158	315.8
Scott Isphording, Hanover	1992	10	484	3,150	315.0
Keith Bishop, Wheaton (Ill.)	†1984	9	479	2,777	308.6
Rhory Moss, Hofstra	†1990	9	372	2,775	308.3
Bill Lech, Coe	1989	9	404	2,743	304.8
Robert Farra, Claremont-M-S	†1978	9	427	2,685	298.3
Rob Shippy, Concordia (Ill.)	1985	9	370	2,682	298.0
Brett Butler, Wabash	1989	9	449	2,666	296.2

*Record. †National champion.

CAREER YARDS

Player, Team	Years	Plays	Yards
Kirk Baumgartner, Wis.-Stevens Point	1986-89	*2,007	*12,767
Jim Ballard, Wilmington (Ohio)/Mount Union	1990, 91-93	1,328	10,545
Eric Noble, Wilmington (Ohio)	1992-95	1,513	9,731
Tim Peterson, Wis.-Stout	1986-89	1,558	9,701
Chris Ings, Wabash	1992-95	1,532	9,608
Keith Bishop, Ill. Wesleyan/Wheaton (Ill.)	1981, 83-85	1,467	9,052
Dave Geissler, Wis.-Stevens Point	1982-85	1,695	8,990
Jordan Poznick, Principia	1990-93	1,757	8,983
Dennis Bogacz, Wis.-Oshkosh/Wis.-Whitewater	1988-89, 90-91	1,394	8,850
John Clark, Wis.-Eau Claire	1987-90	1,354	8,838
Matt Jozokos, Plymouth St.	1987-90	1,234	8,188
Darryl Kosut, William Penn	1983-86	1,583	7,817
Luke Hanks, Otterbein	1990-93	1,503	7,686
Terry Peebles, Hanover	1992-95	1,140	7,672
Steve Osterberger, Drake	1987-90	1,263	7,520
David Parker, Bishop	1981-84	1,257	7,516
John Koz, Baldwin-Wallace	1990-93	1,171	7,511
John Rooney, Ill. Wesleyan	1982-84	1,260	7,393
Larry Barretta, Lycoming	1983-86	1,205	7,320
John Wortham, Earlham	1989-92	1,574	7,296
Shane Fulton, Heidelberg	1983-86	1,344	7,203
Scott Scesney, St. John's (N.Y.)	1986-89	1,048	7,196
Brian Van Deusen, Western Md.	1992-95	1,415	7,172
Ron Devorsky, Hiram	1984-87	1,178	7,059
Ed Dougherty, Lycoming	1988-91	1,320	7,055
Craig Solomon, Rhodes	1975-78	1,261	7,055

*Record.

SEASON YARDS

Player, Team	Year	G	Plays	Yards
Terry Peebles, Hanover	†1995	10	572	*3,981
Kirk Baumgartner, Wis.-Stevens Point	†1988	11	604	3,790
Kirk Baumgartner, Wis.-Stevens Point	1987	11	561	3,712
Kirk Baumgartner, Wis.-Stevens Point	†1989	10	530	3,540
John Furmaniak, Eureka	1995	10	414	3,503
Terry Peebles, Hanover	†1994	10	520	3,441
Jim Ballard, Mount Union	1993	10	372	3,371
Tim Peterson, Wis.-Stout	1989	10	*614	3,244
Keith Bishop, Wheaton (Ill.)	†1983	9	421	3,193
Tom Stallings, St. Thomas (Minn.)	1993	10	438	3,158
Scott Isphording, Hanover	1992	10	484	3,150
Eric Noble, Wilmington (Ohio)	1994	9	460	3,072
Tim Peterson, Wis.-Stout	1987	11	393	3,052
Steve Austin, Mass.-Boston	1992	9	466	3,003
Keith Bishop, Wheaton (Ill.)	†1985	9	521	2,951
Dennis Bogacz, Wis.-Oshkosh	1989	10	417	2,939
Brion Demski, Wis.-Stevens Point	†1981	10	503	2,895
Larry Barretta, Lycoming	†1986	10	453	2,875
John Shipp, Claremont-M-S	1994	9	442	2,871
Shane Fulton, Heidelberg	1985	10	485	2,858
Jon Nielsen, Claremont-M-S	1995	9	405	2,848
Mark Peterson, Neb. Wesleyan	1983	10	425	2,846
Sean Keville, Moravian	1994	10	416	2,829
Leroy Williams, Upsala	1992	10	476	2,822
Keith Bishop, Wheaton (Ill.)	†1984	9	479	2,777

*Record. †National champion.

SINGLE-GAME YARDS

Yds.	Player, Team (Opponent)	Date
596	John Love, North Park (Elmhurst)	Oct. 13, 1990
590	Tom Stallings, St. Thomas, Minn. (Bethel, Minn.)	Nov. 13, 1993
577	Eric Noble, Wilmington, Ohio (Urbana)	Nov. 5, 1994
567	Jim Newland, Heidelberg (Ohio Northern)	Nov. 12, 1994
564	Tim Lynch, Hofstra (Fordham)	Oct. 19, 1991
545	Terry Peebles, Hanover (Franklin)	Nov. 12, 1994
538	Jordan Poznick, Principia (Blackburn)	Oct. 10, 1992
534	Cliff Scott, Buffalo (New Haven)	Sept. 12, 1992
528	Scott Burre, Capital (Heidelberg)	Sept. 30, 1995
528	Steve Austin, Mass.-Boston (Mass. Maritime)	Oct. 10, 1992
527	Rob Shippy, Concordia, Ill. (Concordia, Wis.)	Oct. 5, 1985
515	Seamus Crotty, Hamilton (Middlebury)	Oct. 27, 1984
513	Terry Peebles, Hanover (DePauw)	Oct. 7, 1995
512	Bob Monroe, Knox (Cornell College)	Oct. 11, 1986
511	Kirk Baumgartner, Wis.-Stevens Point (Wis.-Superior)	Nov. 4, 1989
511	Kirk Baumgartner, Wis.-Stevens Point (Wis.-Stout)	Oct. 24, 1987
509	Michael Ferraro, LIU-C.W. Post (Alfred)	Nov. 14, 1992
509	Craig Solomon, Rhodes (Rose-Hulman)	Nov. 11, 1978
508	Eric Noble, Wilmington, Ohio (Geneva)	Oct. 22, 1994
507	George Beisel, Hofstra (LIU-C.W. Post)	Sept. 28, 1991

ANNUAL CHAMPIONS

Year	Player, Team	Class	G	Plays	Yards	Avg.
1973	Bob Dulich, San Diego	Jr.	11	340	2,543	231.2
1974	Larry Cenotto, Pomona-Pitzer	Sr.	9	436	2,127	236.3
1975	Ricky Haygood, Millsaps	Jr.	9	332	2,176	241.8
1976	Rollie Wiebers, Buena Vista	So.	9	353	2,198	244.2
1977	Tom Hamilton, Occidental	Sr.	9	358	2,050	227.8
1978	Robert Farra, Claremont-M-S	Jr.	9	427	2,685	298.3
1979	Clay Sampson, Denison	Jr.	9	412	2,255	250.6
1980	Jeff Beer, Bethany (W.Va.)	Sr.	9	372	2,331	259.0
1981	Brion Demski, Wis.-Stevens Point	Sr.	10	503	2,895	289.5
1982	Dave McCarrell, Wheaton (Ill.)	Sr.	9	387	2,503	278.1
1983	Keith Bishop, Wheaton (Ill.)	So.	9	421	3,193	354.8
1984	Keith Bishop, Wheaton (Ill.)	Jr.	9	479	2,777	308.6
1985	Keith Bishop, Wheaton (Ill.)	Sr.	9	521	2,951	327.9
1986	Larry Barretta, Lycoming	Sr.	10	453	2,875	287.5
1987	Todde Greenough, Willamette	Jr.	9	436	2,567	285.2
1988	Kirk Baumgartner, Wis.-Stevens Point	Jr.	11	604	3,790	344.5
1989	Kirk Baumgartner, Wis.-Stevens Point	Sr.	10	530	3,540	354.0
1990	Rhory Moss, Hofstra	Jr.	9	372	2,775	308.3
1991	Willie Reyna, La Verne	Jr.	8	220	2,633	329.1
1992	Jordan Poznick, Principia	Jr.	8	519	2,747	343.4
1993	Jordan Poznick, Principia	Sr.	8	488	2,705	338.1
1994	Terry Peebles, Hanover	Jr.	10	520	3,441	344.1
1995	Terry Peebles, Hanover	Sr.	10	572	*3,981	*398.1

*Record.

Rushing

CAREER YARDS PER GAME
(Minimum 2,200 Yards)

Player, Team	Years	G	Plays	Yards	Yd. PG
Ricky Gales, Simpson	1988-89	19	530	3,326	*175.1
Rob Marchitello, Maine Maritime	1993-95	26	879	4,300	165.4
Kelvin Gladney, Millsaps	1993-94	19	510	3,085	162.4
Carey Bender, Coe	1991-94	39	926	*6,125	157.1
Kirk Matthieu, Maine Maritime	$1989-93	33	964	5,107	154.8
Terry Underwood, Wagner	1985-88	33	742	5,010	151.8
Anthony Russo, St. John's (N.Y.)	1990-92	30	841	4,276	142.5
Joe Dudek, Plymouth St.	1982-85	41	785	5,570	135.9
Rich Kowalski, Hobart	1973-75	27	762	3,574	132.4
Eric Frees, Western Md.	1988-91	40	1,059	5,281	132.0
Tim Barrett, John Carroll	1973-74	19	457	2,469	129.9
Heath Butler, Martin Luther	1990-93	31	767	4,000	129.0
Scott Reppert, Lawrence	1979-82	33	757	4,211	127.6
Chris Babirad, Wash. & Jeff.	1989-92	35	683	4,419	126.3
Steve Dixon, Beloit	1990-93	38	986	4,792	126.1

*Record. $See page 6 for explanation.

DIVISION III

SEASON YARDS PER GAME

Player, Team	Year	G	Plays	Yards	TD	Yd. PG
Carey Bender, Coe	†1994	10	295	*2,243	*29	*224.3
Ricky Gales, Simpson	†1989	10	297	2,035	26	203.5
Terry Underwood, Wagner	†1988	9	245	1,809	21	201.0
Brad Olson, Lawrence	†1995	9	242	1,760	16	195.6
Kirk Matthieu, Maine Maritime	†1992	9	327	1,733	16	192.6
Kelvin Gladney, Millsaps	1994	10	307	1,882	19	188.2
Jon Warga, Wittenberg	†1990	10	254	1,836	15	183.6
Anthony Jones, La Verne	1995	8	200	1,453	19	181.6
Hank Wineman, Albion	†1991	9	307	1,629	14	181.0
Eric Grey, Hamilton	1991	8	217	1,439	13	179.9
Mike Birosak, Dickinson	1989	10	*380	1,798	18	179.8
Rob Marchitello, Maine Maritime	1995	8	292	1,413	19	176.6
Chris Babirad, Wash. & Jeff.	1992	9	243	1,589	22	176.6
Mark Kacmarynski, Central (Iowa)	1994	10	236	1,741	21	174.1
Carey Bender, Coe	†1993	10	261	1,718	15	171.8
Heath Butler, Martin Luther	1993	8	236	1,371	15	171.4
Spencer Johnson, Wis.-Whitewater	1994	10	290	1,697	18	169.7
Clay Sampson, Denison	†1979	9	323	1,517	13	168.6
Anthony Russo, St. John's (N.Y.)	1991	10	287	1,685	18	168.5
Chris Babirad, Wash. & Jeff.	1991	9	224	1,508	18	167.6
John Bernatavitz, Dickinson	1990	10	266	1,666	15	166.6
Billy Johnson, Widener	†1973	9	168	1,494	21	166.0
Scott Reppert, Lawrence	†1982	8	254	1,323	14	165.4
Chris Dabrow, Claremont-M-S	†1987	9	265	1,486	13	165.1
Jamall Pollock, Williams	1995	8	216	1,319	7	164.9

**Record. †National champion.*

CAREER YARDS

Player, Team	Years	Plays	Yards	Avg.
Carey Bender, Coe	1991-94	926	*6,125	6.61
Joe Dudek, Plymouth St.	1982-85	785	5,570	‡7.10
Eric Frees, Western Md.	1988-91	1,059	5,281	4.99
Kirk Matthieu, Maine Maritime	$1989-93	964	5,107	5.30
Terry Underwood, Wagner	1985-88	742	5,010	6.75
Steve Dixon, Beloit	1990-93	986	4,792	4.86
Mike Birosak, Dickinson	1986-89	*1,112	4,662	4.19
Jim Romagna, Loras	1989-92	983	4,493	4.57
Chris Babirad, Wash. & Jeff.	1989-92	683	4,419	6.47
Petie Davis, Wesley	1991-94	741	4,414	5.96
Tim Lightfoot, Westfield St.	1992-95	876	4,380	5.00
Willie Beers, John Carroll	1989-92	848	4,332	5.11
Rob Marchitello, Maine Maritime	1993-95	879	4,300	4.89
Bob Beatty, Wartburg	1991-94	875	4,292	4.91
Frank Baker, Chicago	1990-93	855	4,283	5.01
Anthony Russo, St. John's (N.Y.)	1990-92	841	4,276	5.08
Mark Kacmarynski, Central (Iowa)	1992-95	640	4,255	6.65
Remon Smith, Randolph-Macon	1984-87	737	4,249	5.77
Chris Spriggs, Denison	1983-86	787	4,248	5.40
Scott Reppert, Lawrence	1979-82	757	4,211	5.56
Alonzo Patterson, Wagner	1979-82	816	4,177	5.12
Von Cummings, Defiance	1989-92	810	4,131	5.10
Bryce Tuohy, Heidelberg	1986-89	905	4,067	4.49

**Record. $See page 6 for explanation. ‡Record for minimum 500 carries.*

SEASON YARDS

Player, Team	Year	G	Plays	Yards	Avg.
Carey Bender, Coe	†1994	10	295	*2,243	‡7.60
Ricky Gales, Simpson	†1989	10	297	2,035	6.85
Kelvin Gladney, Millsaps	1994	10	307	1,882	6.13
Jon Warga, Wittenberg	†1990	10	254	1,836	7.23
Terry Underwood, Wagner	†1988	9	245	1,809	6.75
Mike Birosak, Dickinson	1989	10	*380	1,798	4.73
Brad Olson, Lawrence	†1995	9	242	1,760	7.27
Mark Kacmarynski, Central (Iowa)	1994	10	236	1,741	7.38
Kirk Matthieu, Maine Maritime	†1992	9	327	1,733	5.30
Sandy Rogers, Emory & Henry	†1986	11	231	1,730	7.49
Carey Bender, Coe	†1993	10	261	1,718	6.58
Spencer Johnson, Wis.-Whitewater	1994	10	290	1,697	5.85
Anthony Russo, St. John's (N.Y.)	†1991	10	287	1,685	5.87
John Bernatavitz, Dickinson	1990	10	266	1,666	6.26
Hank Wineman, Albion	1991	9	307	1,629	5.31
Gary Trettel, St. Thomas (Minn.)	1990	10	293	1,620	5.53
Joe Dudek, Plymouth St.	†1985	11	216	1,615	7.48
Ronnie Howard, Bridgewater (Va.)	1993	10	281	1,610	5.73
Frank Baker, Chicago	1993	10	281	1,606	5.72
Eric Frees, Western Md.	1990	10	295	1,594	5.40
Chris Babirad, Wash. & Jeff.	1992	9	243	1,589	6.54
George Rainey, Wis.-Whitewater	1987	11	279	1,567	5.62
Rob Johnson, Western Md.	1992	10	330	1,560	4.73
Jimmy Henderson, Wis.-Stevens Point	1993	10	261	1,556	5.96
Eric Frees, Western Md.	1991	10	304	1,545	5.08

**Record. †National champion. ‡Record for minimum 195 carries.*

SINGLE-GAME YARDS

Yds.	Player, Team (Opponent)	Date
417	Carey Bender, Coe (Grinnell)	Oct. 9, 1993
382	Pete Baranek, Carthage (North Central)	Oct. 5, 1985
363	Terry Underwood, Wagner (Hofstra)	Oct. 15, 1988
354	Terry Underwood, Wagner (Western Conn. St.)	Oct. 3, 1986
348	Carey Bender, Coe (Beloit)	Nov. 12, 1994
347	Chuck Wotkowicz, Johns Hopkins (Georgetown)	Oct. 22, 1993
342	Dave Bednarek, Wis.-River Falls (Wis.-Stevens Point)	Oct. 29, 1983
337	Kirk Matthieu, Maine Maritime (Curry)	Oct. 27, 1990
337	Ted Helsel, St. Francis, Pa. (Gallaudet)	Nov. 3, 1979
334	Oliver Bridges, Stony Brook (Pace)	Nov. 16, 1991
333	Mike Leon, Maine Maritime (Mass.-Boston)	Oct. 21, 1995
331	Brad Olson, Lawrence (Eureka)	Sept. 16, 1995
329	Don Williams, Lowell (Colby)	Oct. 4, 1985
326	Mike Krueger, Tufts (Amherst)	Oct. 25, 1980
325	John Klasen, Lake Forest (St. Norbert)	Oct. 8, 1994
321	Jack Davis, Hobart (Brockport St.)	Nov. 5, 1977
320	Carey Bender, Coe (Lake Forest)	Oct. 1, 1994
317	Greg Novarro, Bentley (St. John's, N.Y.)	Nov. 14, 1992
314	Anthony Russo, St. John's, N.Y. (Georgetown)	Nov. 7, 1992
313	Fredrick Nanhed, Cal Lutheran (Claremont-M-S)	Oct. 14, 1995
313	Pedro Arruza, Wheaton, Ill. (North Central)	Oct. 30, 1993

ANNUAL CHAMPIONS

Year	Player, Team	Class	G	Plays	Yards	Avg.
1973	Billy Johnson, Widener	Sr.	9	168	1,494	166.0
1974	Tim Barrett, John Carroll	Sr.	9	256	1,409	156.6
1975	Ron Baker, Monmouth (Ill.)	Sr.	8	200	1,116	139.5
1976	Chuck Evans, Ferris St.	Jr.	10	224	1,509	150.9
1977	Don Taylor, Central (Iowa)	Sr.	9	267	1,329	147.7
1978	Dino Hall, Rowan	Sr.	10	239	1,330	133.0
1979	Clay Sampson, Denison	Jr.	9	323	1,517	168.6
1980	Scott Reppert, Lawrence	So.	8	223	1,223	152.9
1981	Scott Reppert, Lawrence	Jr.	9	250	1,410	156.7
1982	Scott Reppert, Lawrence	Sr.	8	254	1,323	165.4
1983	John Franco, Wagner	Sr.	8	175	1,166	145.8
1984	Gary Errico, Mass.-Lowell	Sr.	9	165	1,404	156.0
1985	Bruce Montella, Chicago	Sr.	9	265	1,372	152.4
1986	Sandy Rogers, Emory & Henry	Sr.	11	231	1,730	157.3
1987	Chris Dabrow, Claremont-M-S	Sr.	9	265	1,486	165.1
1988	Terry Underwood, Wagner	Sr.	9	245	1,809	201.0
1989	Ricky Gales, Simpson	Sr.	10	297	2,035	203.5
1990	Jon Warga, Wittenberg	Sr.	10	254	1,836	183.6
1991	Hank Wineman, Albion	Sr.	9	307	1,629	181.0
1992	Kirk Matthieu, Maine Maritime	Jr.	9	327	1,733	192.6
1993	Carey Bender, Coe	Jr.	10	261	1,718	171.8
1994	Carey Bender, Coe	Sr.	10	295	*2,243	*224.3
1995	Brad Olson, Lawrence	So.	9	242	1,760	195.6

**Record.*

Passing

CAREER PASSING EFFICIENCY
(Minimum 325 Completions)

Player, Team	Years	Att.	Cmp.	Int.	Pct.	Yards	TD	Pts.
Craig Kusick, Wis.-La Crosse	1993-95	537	327	14	.609	4,767	48	*159.8
Jim Ballard, Wilmington (Ohio)/Mount Union	1990, 91-93	1,199	743	41	‡.620	10,379	*115	¢159.5
Joe Blake, Simpson	1987-90	672	399	15	.594	6,183	43	153.3
Willie Reyna, La Verne	1991-92	542	346	19	.638	4,712	37	152.4
Gary Collier, Emory & Henry	1984-87	738	386	33	.523	6,103	80	148.6
John Koz, Baldwin-Wallace	1990-93	981	609	28	.621	7,724	71	146.4
Greg Heeres, Hope	1981-84	630	347	21	.537	5,120	53	144.4
Jeff Brown, Wheaton (Ill.)	1992-95	767	441	30	.575	6,219	60	143.6
Ed Hesson, Rowan	1990-93	895	504	26	.563	7,035	67	141.2
Bruce Crosthwaite, Adrian	1984-87	618	368	31	.596	4,959	45	141.0
Matt Jozokos, Plymouth St.	1987-90	1,003	527	39	.525	7,658	95	140.2
Joe Coviello, Frank. & Marsh.	1973-76	591	334	36	.565	4,651	52	139.5
Terry Peebles, Hanover	1992-95	969	550	29	.568	6,928	79	137.7
John Clark, Wis.-Eau Claire	1987-90	1,119	645	42	.576	9,196	63	137.7
Joe Shield, Trinity (Conn.)	1981-84	845	476	39	.563	6,646	52	133.5
Jim Connolley, Wesley	1992-94	747	437	18	.585	5,306	45	133.2
Larry Hutson, Thomas More	1992-95	647	346	22	.534	5,042	40	132.5
David Broecker, Wabash	1979-82	633	369	45	.583	4,895	45	132.5
Dick Puccio, Cortland St.	1988-91	727	451	34	.620	5,301	40	131.9
Mike Culver, Juniata	1983-86	756	406	41	.537	5,799	56	131.7
Robb Disbennett, Salisbury St.	1982-85	633	359	40	.567	5,023	40	131.6
Kirk Baumgartner, Wis.-Stevens Point	1986-89	*1,696	*883	57	.521	*13,028	110	131.3
Walter Briggs, Montclair St.	1983-86	832	417	36	.501	6,489	59	130.4
Brian Cox, Beloit	1988-91	620	337	43	.544	4,641	50	130.0
Randy Muetzel, St. Thomas (Minn.)	1979-82	613	339	20	.553	4,462	36	129.3
Larry Barretta, Lycoming	1983-86	732	361	26	.493	5,345	57	129.3

**Record. ‡Record for minimum 750 attempts. ¢Record for minimum 650 completions.*

Wheaton (Illinois) sports information photo by Michael Hudson

Wheaton (Illinois) quarterback Jeff Brown finished his collegiate career last season with a passing efficiency rating of 143.6, which ranks eighth on the all-time Division III career list.

SEASON PASSING EFFICIENCY
(Minimum 15 Attempts Per Game)

Player, Team	Year	G	Att.	Cmp.	Int.	Pct.	Yards	TD	Pts.
Mike Simpson, Eureka	†1994	10	158	116	5	.734	1,988	25	*225.0
Willie Seiler, St. John's (Minn.)	†1993	10	205	141	6	.687	2,648	33	224.6
Bill Borchert, Mount Union	†1995	10	225	160	4	.711	2,270	30	196.3
Jim Ballard, Mount Union	1993	10	314	229	11	*.729	3,304	37	‡193.2
Jason Baer, Wash. & Jeff.	1995	8	146	95	3	.650	1,536	19	192.3
Kurt Ramler, St. John's (Minn.)	1994	9	154	93	4	.603	1,560	22	187.4
Mike Bajakian, Williams	1994	8	141	92	1	.652	1,382	17	186.0
Mitch Sanders, Bridgeport	1973	10	151	84	7	.556	1,551	23	182.9
Pat Mayew, St. John's (Minn.)	†1991	9	247	154	4	.623	2,408	30	181.0
Guy Simons, Coe	1993	10	185	110	9	.594	1,979	21	177.1
Jimbo Fisher, Samford	†1987	10	252	139	5	.551	2,394	34	175.4
Gary Collier, Emory & Henry	1987	11	249	152	10	.610	2,317	33	174.8
Paul Bell, Allegheny	1994	10	215	142	2	.660	2,137	17	173.8
James Grant, Ramapo	1989	9	147	91	7	.619	1,441	17	172.7
Chris Adams, Gettysburg	1994	10	211	139	2	.658	1,977	19	172.4
Mike Donnelly, Wittenberg	1995	10	153	92	2	.601	1,480	15	171.1
Gary Urwiler, Eureka	1991	10	171	103	5	.602	1,656	18	170.3
Kyle Adamson, Allegheny	1995	10	209	142	8	.679	2,039	17	169.1
Kyle Klein, Albion	1994	9	146	87	4	.595	1,487	13	169.0
Steve Keller, Dayton	†1992	10	153	99	5	.647	1,350	17	168.9
Robb Disbennett, Salisbury St.	†1985	10	153	94	6	.614	1,462	16	168.4
Chris Conkling, Anderson (Ind.)	1993	10	185	127	3	.686	1,788	12	168.0
Scott Scesney, St. John's (N.Y.)	1989	10	244	131	9	.536	2,314	31	167.8
Jim Ballard, Mount Union	1992	10	292	186	8	.637	2,656	29	167.4
Chuck Hooker, Cornell College	1985	9	186	108	10	.581	1,818	21	166.7

**Record. †National champion. ‡Record for minimum 25 attempts per game.*

CAREER YARDS

Player, Team	Years	Att.	Cmp.	Int.	Pct.	Yards	TD
Kirk Baumgartner, Wis.-Stevens Point	1986-89	*1,696	*883	57	.521	*13,028	110
Jim Ballard, Wilmington (Ohio)/Mount Union	1990, 91-93	1,199	743	41	.620	10,379	*115
Keith Bishop, Ill. Wesleyan/Wheaton (Ill.)	1981, 83-85	1,311	772	65	.589	9,579	71
Dennis Bogacz, Wis.-Oshkosh/ Wis.-Whitewater	1988-89, 90-91	1,275	654	59	.513	9,536	66
Dave Geissler, Wis.-Stevens Point	1982-85	1,346	789	57	.586	9,518	65
Eric Noble, Wilmington (Ohio)	1992-95	1,264	682	62	.540	9,260	62
John Clark, Wis.-Eau Claire	1987-90	1,119	645	42	.576	9,196	63
Tim Peterson, Wis.-Stout	1986-89	1,185	653	62	.551	8,881	59
Jordan Poznick, Principia	1990-93	1,480	765	68	.517	8,485	55
Brad Hensley, Kenyon	1991-94	1,439	718	61	.499	8,154	65
John Koz, Baldwin-Wallace	1990-93	981	609	28	.621	7,724	71
Luke Hanks, Otterbein	1990-93	1,267	715	62	.564	7,718	47
Matt Jozokos, Plymouth St.	1987-90	1,003	527	39	.525	7,658	95
Chris Ings, Wabash	1992-95	1,087	569	43	.523	7,637	55
Bill Hyland, Iona	1989-92	1,017	511	55	.502	7,382	57
Shane Fulton, Heidelberg	1983-86	1,024	587	55	.573	7,372	50
Paul Brandenburg, Ripon	1984-87	1,181	607	66	.514	7,320	39

Western Maryland sports information photo by Marcy Dubroff

Quarterback Brian Van Deusen passed for 7,239 yards during his career at Western Maryland, good for 19th place on the Division III career yards list.

Player, Team	Years	Att.	Cmp.	Int.	Pct.	Yards	TD
Craig Solomon, Rhodes	1975-78	1,022	542	70	.530	7,314	71
Brian Van Deusen, Western Md.	1992-95	1,129	621	40	.550	7,239	51
Rob Bristow, Pomona-Pitzer	1983-86	1,155	628	60	.544	7,120	27
Ed Dougherty, Lycoming	1988-91	1,025	589	47	.575	7,108	69
Ed Hesson, Rowan	1990-93	895	504	26	.563	7,035	67
Steve Osterberger, Drake	1987-90	981	536	33	.546	7,021	53
Ron Devorsky, Hiram	1984-87	1,028	542	59	.527	7,012	50
Gary Walljasper, Wartburg	1981-84	974	521	50	.535	6,992	49

**Record.*

CAREER YARDS PER GAME

Player, Team	Years	G	Att.	Cmp.	Int.	Pct.	Yards	TD	Avg.
Kirk Baumgartner, Wis.-Stevens Point	1986-89	41	*1,696	*883	57	.521	*13,028	110	*317.8
Keith Bishop, Ill. Wesleyan/Wheaton (Ill.)	1981, 83-85	31	1,311	772	65	.589	9,579	71	309.0
Willie Reyna, La Verne	1991-92	17	542	346	19	.638	4,712	37	277.2
Robert Farra, Claremont-M-S	1978-79	16	579	313	24	.541	4,360	31	272.5
Jordan Poznick, Principia	1990-93	32	1,480	765	68	.517	8,485	55	265.2
Jim Ballard, Wilmington (Ohio)/ Mount Union	1990, 91-93	40	1,199	743	41	.620	10,379	*115	259.5
Dennis Bogacz, Wis.-Oshkosh/ Wis.-Whitewater	1988-89, 90-91	38	1,275	654	59	.513	9,536	66	250.9
Tim Peterson, Wis.-Stout	1986-89	36	1,185	653	62	.551	8,881	59	246.7
Rob Bristow, Pomona-Pitzer	1983-86	29	1,155	628	60	.544	7,120	27	245.5
Eric Noble, Wilmington (Ohio)	1992-95	38	1,264	682	62	.540	9,260	62	243.7
John Rooney, Ill. Wesleyan	1982-84	27	986	489	47	.496	6,576	55	243.6
John Clark, Wis.-Eau Claire	1987-90	38	1,119	645	42	.576	9,196	63	242.0
Brian Van Deusen, Western Md.	1992-95	30	1,129	621	40	.550	7,239	51	241.3
Tom Stallings, St. Thomas (Minn.)	1990-93	24	726	387	40	.533	5,608	44	233.7
Ed Smith, Ill. Benedictine	1991-93	29	862	456	41	.529	6,734	47	232.2
Dave Geissler, Wis.-Stevens Point	1982-85	42	1,346	789	57	.586	9,518	65	226.6
Scott Scesney, St. John's (N.Y.)	1986-89	32	945	463	44	.490	6,914	72	216.1
Jeff Voris, DePauw	1986-89	28	910	504	25	.554	6,035	56	215.5
Paul Brandenburg, Ripon	1984-87	34	1,181	607	66	.514	7,320	39	215.3

**Record.*

SEASON YARDS

Player, Team	Year	G	Att.	Cmp.	Int.	Pct.	Yards	TD
Kirk Baumgartner, Wis.-Stevens Point	1988	11	*527	276	16	.524	*3,828	25
Kirk Baumgartner, Wis.-Stevens Point	1987	11	466	243	22	.521	3,755	31
Kirk Baumgartner, Wis.-Stevens Point	1989	10	455	247	9	.542	3,692	*39
Terry Peebles, Hanover	1995	10	488	*283	10	.579	3,521	*39
John Furmaniak, Eureka	1995	10	361	210	11	.581	3,372	34
Jim Ballard, Mount Union	1993	10	314	229	11	*.729	3,304	37
Keith Bishop, Wheaton (Ill.)	1983	9	375	236	19	.629	3,274	24
Tom Stallings, St. Thomas (Minn.)	1993	10	395	219	20	.554	3,210	22
Terry Peebles, Hanover	1994	10	445	252	17	.566	3,197	37
Keith Bishop, Wheaton (Ill.)	1985	9	457	262	22	.573	3,171	25
Scott Isphording, Hanover	1992	10	359	207	19	.576	3,098	24
Eric Noble, Wilmington (Ohio)	1994	9	398	221	17	.555	3,058	22
Dennis Bogacz, Wis.-Oshkosh	1989	10	378	219	18	.579	3,051	18
Steve Austin, Mass.-Boston	1992	9	396	181	25	.457	2,991	29
Keith Bishop, Wheaton (Ill.)	1984	9	440	259	21	.589	2,968	21
Tim Peterson, Wis.-Stout	1989	10	445	256	15	.575	2,956	20
Brion Demski, Wis.-Stevens Point	1981	10	452	222	20	.491	2,889	16
Shane Fulton, Heidelberg	1985	10	393	222	24	.565	2,876	19
Tim Peterson, Wis.-Stout	1987	11	302	180	19	.596	2,871	18
Chris Creighton, Kenyon	1990	10	398	231	18	.580	2,843	29
Kevin Enterlein, Pace	1986	10	427	205	28	.480	2,829	20
Sean Keville, Moravian	1994	10	363	190	16	.523	2,819	24
John Clark, Wis.-Eau Claire	1989	10	344	199	14	.578	2,785	22
Ed Smith, Ill. Benedictine	1992	10	320	184	16	.575	2,770	25
Robert Farra, Claremont-M-S	†1978	9	359	196	15	.546	2,770	20

**Record. †National champion.*

SEASON YARDS PER GAME

Player, Team	Year	G	Att.	Cmp.	Int.	Pct.	Yards	TD	Avg.
Kirk Baumgartner, Wis.-Stevens Point	1989	10	455	247	9	.543	3,692	*39	*369.2
Keith Bishop, Wheaton (Ill.)	1983	9	375	236	19	.629	3,274	24	363.8
Keith Bishop, Wheaton (Ill.)	1985	9	457	262	22	.573	3,171	25	352.3
Terry Peebles, Hanover	1995	10	488	*283	10	.579	3,521	*39	352.1
Kirk Baumgartner, Wis.-Stevens Point	1988	11	*527	276	16	.524	*3,828	25	348.0
Kirk Baumgartner, Wis.-Stevens Point	1987	11	466	243	22	.521	3,755	31	341.4
Eric Noble, Wilmington (Ohio)	1994	9	398	221	17	.555	3,058	22	339.8
John Furmaniak, Eureka	1995	10	361	210	11	.581	3,372	34	337.2
Steve Austin, Mass.-Boston	1992	9	396	181	25	.457	2,991	29	332.3
Jim Ballard, Mount Union	1993	10	314	229	11	*.729	3,304	37	330.4
Keith Bishop, Wheaton (Ill.)	1984	9	440	259	21	.589	2,968	21	329.8
Jordan Poznick, Principia	1992	8	451	241	13	.534	2,618	21	327.3
Tom Stallings, St. Thomas (Minn.)	1993	10	395	219	20	.554	3,210	22	321.0
Terry Peebles, Hanover	1994	10	445	252	17	.566	3,197	37	319.7
Willie Reyna, La Verne	1991	8	267	170	6	.636	2,543	16	317.9
Scott Isphording, Hanover	1992	10	359	207	19	.576	3,098	24	309.8
Robert Farra, Claremont-M-S	†1978	9	359	196	15	.546	2,770	20	307.8
Dennis Bogacz, Wis.-Oshkosh	1989	10	378	219	18	.580	3,051	18	305.1

**Record. †National champion.*

SINGLE-GAME YARDS

Yds.	Player, Team (Opponent)	Date
602	Tom Stallings, St. Thomas, Minn. (Bethel, Minn.)	Nov. 13, 1993
585	Tim Lynch, Hofstra (Fordham)	Oct. 19, 1991
575	Eric Noble, Wilmington, Ohio (Urbana)	Nov. 5, 1994
533	John Love, North Park (Elmhurst)	Oct. 13, 1990
532	Bob Monroe, Knox (Cornell College)	Oct. 11, 1986
523	Kirk Baumgartner, Wis.-Stevens Point (Wis.-Stout)	Oct. 24, 1987
517	Jon Nielsen, Claremont-M-S (Occidental)	Oct. 21, 1995
513	Craig Solomon, Rhodes (Rose-Hulman)	Nov.11, 1978
510	Troy Dougherty, Grinnell (Lawrence)	Oct. 1, 1994
509	Bob Krepfle, Wis.-La Crosse (Wis.-River Falls)	Nov. 12, 1983
507	Eric Noble, Wilmington, Ohio (Geneva)	Oct. 22, 1994
507	George Beisel, Hofstra (LIU-C.W. Post)	Sept. 28, 1991
506	Keith Bishop, Wheaton, Ill. (Ill. Wesleyan)	Oct. 29, 1983
505	Kirk Baumgartner, Wis.-Stevens Point (Wis.-Superior)	Nov. 4, 1989
504	Jordan Poznick, Principia (Blackburn)	Oct. 10, 1992
504	Rob Shippy, Concordia, Ill. (Concordia, Wis.)	Oct. 5, 1985
503	Dave Detrick, Wis.-Superior (Wis.-Oshkosh)	Sept. 16, 1989
501	Keith Bishop, Wheaton, Ill. (North Park)	Oct. 12, 1985

SINGLE-GAME COMPLETIONS

Cmp.	Player, Team (Opponent)	Date
50	Tim Lynch, Hofstra (Fordham)	Oct. 19, 1991
48	Jordan Poznick, Principia (Blackburn)	Oct. 10, 1992
47	Mike Wallace, Ohio Wesleyan (Denison)	Oct. 3, 1981
43	Terry Peebles, Hanover (Franklin)	Nov. 12, 1994
42	Mark Novara, Lakeland (Concordia, Wis.)	Oct. 15, 1994
42	Tim Lynch, Hofstra (Towson St.)	Nov. 2, 1991
42	Keith Bishop, Wheaton, Ill. (Millikin)	Sept. 14, 1985
41	Troy Dougherty, Grinnell (Lawrence)	Oct. 1, 1994
41	Michael Doto, Hofstra (Central Conn. St.)	Sept. 14, 1991
41	Todd Monken, Knox (Cornell College)	Oct. 8, 1988
40	Dave Geissler, Wis.-Stevens Point (Wis.-Eau Claire)	Nov. 12, 1983
39	Rob Bristow, Pomona-Pitzer (La Verne)	Oct. 12, 1985
39	Steve Hendry, Wis.-Superior (Wis.-Stevens Point)	Oct. 17, 1981
38	Bill Nietzke, Alma (Kalamazoo)	Oct. 22, 1994
38	George Beisel, Hofstra (Southern Conn. St.)	Oct. 9, 1992
38	Jeff Voris, DePauw (Findlay)	Oct. 31, 1987
38	Todde Greenough, Willamette (Southern Ore. St.)	Sept. 26, 1987
38	Pat Moyer, Maryville, Tenn. (Cumberland)	Oct. 5, 1985

ANNUAL CHAMPIONS

Year	Player, Team	Class	G	Att.	Cmp.	Avg.	Int.	Pct.	Yds.	TD
1973	Pat Clements, Kenyon	Jr.	9	239	133	14.8	17	.556	1,738	12
1974	Larry Cenotto, Pomona-Pitzer	Sr.	9	294	147	16.3	23	.500	2,024	15
1975	Ron Miller, Elmhurst	Sr.	8	205	118	14.8	15	.576	1,398	7
1976	Tom Hamilton, Occidental	Jr.	8	235	131	16.4	10	.557	1,988	10
1977	Tom Hamilton, Occidental	Sr.	9	323	171	19.0	17	.529	2,132	13
1978	Robert Farra, Claremont-M-S	Jr.	9	359	196	21.8	15	.546	2,770	20

Beginning in 1979, ranked on passing efficiency rating points, minimum 15 attempts per game (instead of per-game completions)

Year	Player, Team	Class	G	Att.	Cmp.	Int.	Pct.	Yds.	TD	Pts.
1979	David Broecker, Wabash	Fr.	9	145	81	9	.559	1,311	13	149.0
1980	George Muller, Hofstra	Sr.	10	189	115	14	.608	1,983	15	160.4
1981	Larry Atwater, Coe	Sr.	9	172	92	10	.535	1,615	15	147.2
1982	Mike Bennett, Cornell College	Sr.	9	154	83	8	.539	1,436	17	158.3
1983	Joe Shield, Trinity (Conn.)	Jr.	8	238	135	13	.567	2,185	19	149.1
1984	Cody Dearing, Randolph-Macon	Sr.	10	226	125	12	.553	2,139	27	163.4
1985	Robb Disbennett, Salisbury St.	Sr.	10	153	94	6	.614	1,462	16	168.4
1986	Gary Collier, Emory & Henry	Jr.	11	171	88	6	.514	1,509	21	158.9
1987	Jimbo Fisher, Samford	Sr.	10	252	139	5	.551	2,394	34	175.4
1988	Steve Flynn, Central (Iowa)	Jr.	8	133	82	6	.616	1,190	10	152.5
1989	Joe Blake, Simpson	††Jr.	10	144	93	3	.645	1,705	19	203.3
1990	Dan Sharley, Dayton	†††Sr.	10	149	95	2	.637	1,377	12	165.1
1991	Pat Mayew, St. John's (Minn.)	Sr.	9	247	154	4	.623	2,408	30	181.0
1992	Steve Keller, Dayton	Sr.	10	153	99	5	.647	1,350	17	168.9
1993	Willie Seiler, St. John's (Minn.)	Sr.	10	205	141	6	.687	2,648	33	224.6
1994	Mike Simpson, Eureka	So.	10	158	116	5	.734	1,988	25	*225.0
1995	Bill Borchert, Mount Union	So.	10	225	160	4	.711	2,270	30	196.3

**Record. ††Declared champion; with six more pass attempts (making 15 per game), all interceptions, still would have highest efficiency (187.3). †††Declared champion; with one more attempt (making 15 per game), an interception, still would have highest efficiency (162.8).*

ANNUAL PASSING EFFICIENCY LEADERS BEFORE 1979

(Minimum 15 Attempts Per Game)

Year	Player, Team	G	Att.	Cmp.	Int.	Pct.	Yds.	TD	Pts.
1973	Mitch Sanders, Bridgeport	10	151	84	7	.556	1,551	23	182.9
1974	Tom McGuire, Ill. Benedictine	10	221	142	16	.643	2,206	16	157.5
1975	Jim Morrow, Wash. & Jeff.	9	137	82	7	.599	1,283	11	154.8
1976	Aaron Van Dyke, Cornell College	9	154	91	12	.591	1,611	14	161.4
1977	Matt Winslow, Middlebury	8	130	79	5	.608	919	17	155.6
1978	Matt Dillon, Cornell College	9	166	98	7	.590	1,567	16	161.7

Photo from Wilmington (Ohio) sports information

Eric Noble of Wilmington (Ohio) is one of only three quarterbacks in Division III history to pass for more than 500 yards in a game on two occasions. He broke the 500-yard barrier on October 22, 1994, against Geneva (507 yards) and again two weeks later against Urbana (575 yards).

Receiving

CAREER RECEPTIONS PER GAME

Player, Team	Years	G	Rec.	Yards	TD	Rec.PG
Matt Newton, Principia	1990-93	33	*287	3,646	32	*8.7
Bill Stromberg, Johns Hopkins	1978-81	36	258	3,776	39	7.2
Tim McNamara, Trinity (Conn.)	1981-84	21	146	2,313	19	7.0
Ron Severance, Otterbein	1989-91	30	207	2,378	17	6.9
Chuck Braun, Wis.-Stevens Point	1980-81	18	124	1,914	19	6.9
Jim Jorden, Wheaton (Ill.)	1982-85	33	225	3,022	22	6.8
Mike Whitehouse, St. Norbert	1986-89	35	230	3,480	37	6.6
Dan Daley, Pomona-Pitzer	1985-88	35	227	2,598	10	6.5
Rich Johnson, Pace	1985-87	29	188	2,614	8	6.5
Steve Wilkerson, Catholic	1993-94	19	120	1,966	17	6.3
Chris Bisaillon, Ill. Wesleyan	1989-92	36	223	3,670	*55	6.2
Rick Fry, Occidental	1974-77	33	200	3,073	18	6.1
Mike Funk, Wabash	1985, 87-89	38	228	2,858	33	6.0
Scott Faessler, Framingham St.	1989-92	34	201	2,121	8	5.9
Ted Taggart, Kenyon	1988-90	28	165	2,034	20	5.9
Pat McNamara, Trinity (Conn.)	1977-79	24	141	2,280	20	5.9
Theo Blanco, Wis.-Stevens Point	1985-88	38	223	3,139	18	5.9
Dale Amos, Frank. & Marsh.	1986-89	40	233	*3,846	35	5.8
Scott Fredrickson, Wis.-Stout	1986-89	40	233	3,390	23	5.8

*Record.

SEASON RECEPTIONS PER GAME

Player, Team	Year	G	Rec.	Yards	TD	Rec.PG
Matt Newton, Principia	†1992	8	98	1,487	14	*12.3
Matt Newton, Principia	†1993	8	96	1,080	11	12.0
Ben Fox, Hanover	†1995	9	95	1,087	15	10.6
Sean Munroe, Mass.-Boston	1992	9	95	*1,693	17	10.6
Scott Faessler, Framingham St.	†1990	9	92	916	5	10.2
Mike Funk, Wabash	†1989	9	87	1,169	12	9.7
Jim Jorden, Wheaton (Ill.)	†1985	9	87	1,011	8	9.7
Theo Blanco, Wis.-Stevens Point	1987	11	*106	1,616	8	9.6
Jason Tincher, Wilmington (Ohio)	†1994	9	85	1,298	9	9.4
Rick Fry, Occidental	†1976	8	74	1,214	8	9.3
Mike Cook, Claremont-M-S	1995	9	83	993	7	9.2
Ron Severance, Otterbein	1990	10	92	1,049	8	9.2
Rick Fry, Occidental	†1977	9	82	1,222	5	9.1
Jim Myers, Kenyon	†1974	9	82	1,483	12	9.1
Steve Wilkerson, Catholic	1994	10	90	1,457	13	9.0
Bob Glanville, Lewis & Clark	1985	9	80	1,054	9	8.9
Ed Brady, Ill. Wesleyan	†1983	9	80	873	7	8.9
John Tucci, Amherst	†1986	8	70	1,025	8	8.8
Greg Lehrer, Heidelberg	1993	10	87	1,202	8	8.7
Ted Taggart, Kenyon	1989	10	87	1,004	7	8.7

*Record. †National champion.

CAREER RECEPTIONS

Player, Team	Years	Rec.	Yards	TD
Matt Newton, Principia	1990-93	*287	3,646	32
Bill Stromberg, Johns Hopkins	1978-81	258	3,776	39
Dale Amos, Frank. & Marsh.	1986-89	233	*3,846	35
Scott Fredrickson, Wis.-Stout	1986-89	233	3,390	23
Mike Whitehouse, St. Norbert	1986-89	230	3,480	37
Mike Funk, Wabash	1985, 87-89	228	2,858	33
Dan Daley, Pomona-Pitzer	1985-88	227	2,598	10
Jim Jorden, Wheaton (Ill.)	1982-85	225	3,022	22
Chris Bisaillon, Ill. Wesleyan	1989-92	223	3,670	*55
Theo Blanco, Wis.-Stevens Point	1985-88	223	3,139	18
Ed Brady, Ill. Wesleyan	1981-84	220	2,907	22
Walter Kalinowski, Catholic	1983-86	219	2,430	16
Jim Bradford, Carleton	1988-91	212	3,719	32
Mike Cottle, Juniata	1985-88	212	2,607	36
John Ward, Cornell College	1979-82	211	3,085	30
Kendall Griffin, Loras	1990-93	208	3,036	26
Ron Severance, Otterbein	1989-91	207	2,378	17
Vince Dortch, Jersey City St.	1983-86	206	3,037	28
Chris Murphy, Georgetown	1989-92	205	2,817	26
Ben Fox, Hanover	1992-95	201	2,232	26
Scott Faessler, Framingham St.	1989-92	201	2,121	8
Rick Fry, Occidental	1974-77	200	3,073	18
Steve Endres, Wilkes	1990-93	198	2,901	11
Ted Brockman, Kenyon	1990-93	198	2,180	21
Todd Stoner, Kenyon	1981-84	197	3,191	31

*Record.

SEASON RECEPTIONS

Player, Team	Year	G	Rec.	Yards	TD
Theo Blanco, Wis.-Stevens Point	1987	11	*106	1,616	8
Matt Newton, Principia	†1992	8	98	1,487	14
Matt Newton, Principia	†1993	8	96	1,080	11
Ben Fox, Hanover	†1995	9	95	1,087	15
Sean Munroe, Mass.-Boston	1992	9	95	*1,693	17
Ron Severance, Otterbein	1990	10	92	1,049	8
Scott Faessler, Framingham St.	†1990	9	92	916	5
Steve Wilkerson, Catholic	1994	10	90	1,457	13
Greg Lehrer, Heidelberg	1993	10	87	1,202	8
Mike Funk, Wabash	†1989	9	87	1,169	12
Ted Taggart, Kenyon	1989	10	87	1,004	7
Jim Jorden, Wheaton (Ill.)	†1985	9	87	1,011	8
Jason Tincher, Wilmington (Ohio)	†1994	9	85	1,298	9
Ron Severance, Otterbein	†1991	10	85	929	4
Sam Williams, Defiance	1993	10	84	1,209	14
Mike Cook, Claremont-M-S	1995	9	83	993	7
Scott Fredrickson, Wis.-Stout	1989	10	83	1,102	7
Ryan Ditze, Albright	1994	10	82	1,023	5
Rick Fry, Occidental	†1977	9	82	1,222	5
Jim Myers, Kenyon	†1974	9	82	1,483	12
Wayne Morris, Hofstra	1991	10	80	890	7
Theo Blanco, Wis.-Stevens Point	†1988	10	80	1,009	7
Bob Glanville, Lewis & Clark	1985	9	80	1,054	9
Ed Brady, Ill. Wesleyan	†1983	9	80	873	7

*Record. †National champion.

SINGLE-GAME RECEPTIONS

No.	Player, Team (Opponent)	Date
23	Sean Munroe, Mass.-Boston (Mass. Maritime)	Oct. 10, 1992
20	Rich Johnson, Pace (Fordham)	Nov. 7, 1987
20	Pete Thompson, Carroll, Wis. (Augustana, Ill.)	Nov. 4, 1978
18	Craig Antonio, Waynesburg (Bethany, W.Va.)	Oct. 16, 1993
18	Ed Sullivan, Catholic (Carnegie Mellon)	Nov. 7, 1992
17	Eric Nemec, Albright (Widener)	Oct. 14, 1995
17	Ryan Ditze, Albright (Lycoming)	Sept. 9, 1995
17	Ben Fox, Hanover (Otterbein)	Sept. 9, 1995
17	Ryan Ditze, Albright (Widener)	Oct. 15, 1994
17	Chris Garrity, Wilmington, Ohio (Defiance)	Oct. 16, 1993
17	Matt Newton, Principia (Concordia, Ill.)	Nov. 7, 1992
17	Danny Cole, Lake Forest (Monmouth, Ill.)	Sept. 29, 1990
17	Dan Daley, Pomona-Pitzer (Occidental)	Oct. 15, 1988
17	Theo Blanco, Wis.-Stevens Point (Wis.-Oshkosh)	Oct. 31, 1987
17	Tim Mowery, Wis.-Superior (Wis.-Stevens Point)	Oct. 17, 1971

CAREER YARDS

Player, Team	Year	Rec.	Yards	Avg.	TD
Dale Amos, Frank. & Marsh	1986-89	233	*3,846	16.5	35
Bill Stromberg, Johns Hopkins	1978-81	258	3,776	14.6	39
Jim Bradford, Carleton	1988-91	212	3,719	17.5	32
Chris Bisaillon, Ill. Wesleyan	1989-92	223	3,670	16.5	*55
Matt Newton, Principia	1990-93	*287	3,646	12.7	32
Mike Whitehouse, St. Norbert	1986-89	230	3,480	15.1	37
Scott Fredrickson, Wis.-Stout	1986-89	233	3,390	14.5	23
John Aromando, Trenton St.	1981-84	165	3,197	19.4	39
Todd Stoner, Kenyon	1981-84	197	3,191	16.2	31
Rodd Patten, Framingham St.	1990-93	154	3,170	*20.6	38
Theo Blanco, Wis.-Stevens Point	1985-88	223	3,139	14.1	18
John Ward, Cornell College	1979-82	211	3,085	14.6	30
Rick Fry, Occidental	1974-77	200	3,073	15.4	18

*Record.

SEASON YARDS

Player, Team	Year	Rec.	Yards	Avg.	TD
Sean Munroe, Mass.-Boston	†1992	95	*1,693	17.8	17
Theo Blanco, Wis.-Stevens Point	1987	*106	1,616	15.2	8
Matt Newton, Principia	1992	98	1,487	15.2	14
Jim Myers, Kenyon	1974	82	1,483	18.1	12
Steve Wilkerson, Catholic	†1994	90	1,457	16.2	13
Beau Almodobar, Norwich	1984	71	1,375	19.4	10
Kurt Barth, Eureka	†1995	68	1,337	19.7	18
Chris Vogel, Knox	1987	78	1,326	17.0	15
Dale Amos, Frank. & Marsh.	1989	72	1,302	18.1	15
Jason Tincher, Wilmington (Ohio)	1994	85	1,298	15.3	9
Don Moehling, Wis.-Stevens Point	1988	72	1,290	17.9	7
Ed Bubonics, Mount Union	1993	74	1,286	17.4	10
Tom Buslee, St. Olaf	1993	75	1,281	17.1	10
Rob Lokerson, Muhlenberg	†1993	76	1,275	16.8	6
Mike Gundersdorf, Wilkes	1995	79	1,269	16.1	8

Player, Team	Year	Rec.	Yards	Avg.	TD
Jim Bradford, Carleton	1989	69	1,238	17.9	6
Rick Fry, Occidental	1977	82	1,222	14.9	5
Evan Elkington, Worcester Tech	1989	52	1,220	+23.5	16
Vic Moncato, FDU-Madison	1993	64	1,217	19.0	14
Rick Fry, Occidental	1976	74	1,214	16.4	8
Sam Williams, Defiance	1993	84	1,209	14.4	14
Mike Howey, Moravian	1989	61	1,203	19.7	7
Greg Lehrer, Heidelberg	1993	87	1,202	13.8	8
Jake Doran, FDU-Madison	1995	70	1,201	17.2	11
Chris Palmer, St. John's (Minn.)	1995	71	1,197	16.9	13

**Record. †National champion. +Record for minimum 50 receptions.*

SINGLE-GAME YARDS

Yds.	Player, Team (Opponent)	Date
332	Sean Munroe, Mass.-Boston (Mass. Maritime)	Oct. 10, 1992
309	Dale Amos, Frank. & Marsh. (Western Md.)	Oct. 24, 1987
303	Chuck Braun, Wis.-Stevens Point (Wis.-Superior)	Oct. 17, 1981
303	Rick Fry, Occidental (Claremont-M-S)	Oct. 30, 1976
301	Greg Holmes, Carroll, Wis. (North Central)	Nov. 7, 1981
296	Joe Richards, Johns Hopkins (Georgetown)	Oct. 26, 1991
296	Vince Hull, Minn.-Morris (Bemidji St.)	Oct. 10, 1981
295	Aatron Kenney, Wis.-Stevens Point (Wis.-Stout)	Oct. 24, 1987
293	Mike Stotz, Catholic (Bridgewater, Va.)	Nov. 15, 1980
292	Andy Steckel, Western Md. (Gettysburg)	Sept. 15, 1990
291	R. J. Letendre, Plymouth St. (Worcester Tech)	Nov. 12, 1994
289	Kurt Barth, Eureka (Lakeland)	Nov. 5, 1994
287	Matt Newton, Principia (Concordia, Wis.)	Nov. 7, 1992
287	Chris Bisaillon, Ill. Wesleyan (Carroll, Wis.)	Sept. 15, 1990
285	Jim Bradford, Carleton (Gust. Adolphus)	Oct. 20, 1990

ANNUAL CHAMPIONS

RECEPTIONS PER GAME

Year	Player, Team	Class	G	Rec.	Avg.	Yards	TD
1973	Ron Duckett, Trinity (Conn.)	Sr.	8	57	7.1	834	7
1974	Jim Myers, Kenyon	Sr.	9	82	9.1	1,483	12
1975	C. J. DeWitt, Bridgewater (Va.)	Sr.	9	64	7.1	836	2
1976	Rick Fry, Occidental	Jr.	8	74	9.3	1,214	8
1977	Rick Fry, Occidental	Sr.	9	82	9.1	1,222	5
1978	Pat McNamara, Trinity (Conn.)	Jr.	8	67	8.4	1,024	11
1979	Theodore Anderson, Fisk	Jr.	7	49	7.0	699	2
1980	Bill Stromberg, Johns Hopkins	Jr.	9	66	7.3	907	11
1981	Bill Stromberg, Johns Hopkins	Sr.	9	78	8.7	924	10
1982	Jim Gustafson, St. Thomas (Minn.)	Jr.	10	72	7.2	990	5
1983	Ed Brady, Ill. Wesleyan	Jr.	9	80	8.9	873	7
1984	Tim McNamara, Trinity (Conn.)	Sr.	8	67	8.4	1,004	10
1985	Jim Jorden, Wheaton (Ill.)	Sr.	9	87	9.7	1,011	8
1986	John Tucci, Amherst	Sr.	8	70	8.8	1,025	8
1987	Chris Vogel, Knox	So.	9	78	8.7	1,326	15
1988	Theo Blanco, Wis.-Stevens Point	Sr.	10	80	8.0	1,009	7
1989	Mike Funk, Wabash	Sr.	9	87	9.7	1,169	12
1990	Scott Faessler, Framingham St.	So.	9	92	10.2	916	5
1991	Ron Severance, Otterbein	Sr.	10	85	8.5	929	4
1992	Matt Newton, Principia	Jr.	8	98	*12.3	1,487	14
1993	Matt Newton, Principia	Sr.	8	96	12.0	1,080	11
1994	Jason Tincher, Wilmington (Ohio)	Sr.	9	85	9.4	1,298	9
1995	Ben Fox, Hanover	Sr.	9	95	10.6	1,087	15

YARDS PER GAME

Year	Player, Team	Class	G	Rec.	Yards	TD	Avg.
1990	Ray Shelley, Juniata	Sr.	10	54	1,147	12	114.7
1991	Rodd Patten, Framingham St.	So.	8	49	956	13	119.5
1992	Sean Munroe, Mass.-Boston	Sr.	9	95	*1,693	17	*188.1
1993	Rob Lokerson, Muhlenberg	Jr.	9	76	1,275	6	141.7
1994	Steve Wilkerson, Catholic	Sr.	10	90	1,457	13	145.7
1995	Kurt Barth, Eureka	So.	10	68	1,337	18	133.7

**Record.*

Scoring

CAREER POINTS PER GAME

Player, Team	Years	G	TD	XPt.	FG	Pts.	Pt.PG
Ricky Gales, Simpson	1988-89	19	44	10	0	274	*14.4
Rob Marchitello, Maine Maritime	1993-95	26	59	4	0	358	13.8
Carey Bender, Coe	1991-94	39	*86	12	0	*528	13.5
Joe Dudek, Plymouth St.	1982-85	41	79	0	0	474	11.6
Chris Babirad, Wash. & Jeff.	1989-92	35	62	2	0	374	10.7
Terry Underwood, Wagner	1985-88	33	58	0	0	348	10.5
Chris Bisaillon, Ill. Wesleyan	1989-92	36	61	12	0	378	10.5
Stanley Drayton, Allegheny	1989-92	32	56	0	0	336	10.5
Greg Novarro, Bentley	1990-92	24	42	0	0	252	10.5
Ryan Kolpin, Coe	1987-90	28	48	0	0	288	10.3
Trent Nauholz, Simpson	1990-93	31	49	4	0	298	9.6
Mark Kacmarynski, Central (Iowa)	1992-95	34	49	10	0	314	9.2
Jason Wooley, Worcester Tech	1990-93	37	55	8	0	338	9.1
A. J. Pagano, Wash. & Jeff.	1984-87	36	53	5	0	323	9.0
Heath Butler, Martin Luther	1990-93	31	44	14	0	278	9.0
Scott Tumilty, Augustana (Ill.)	1992-95	37	55	0	0	330	8.9
Matt Malmberg, St. John's (Minn.)	1991-94	31	44	12	0	276	8.9
Gary Trettel, St. Thomas (Minn.)	1988-90	29	43	0	0	258	8.9
Steve Harris, Carroll (Wis.)	1991-94	35	49	12	0	306	8.7
Vance Mueller, Occidental	1982-85	36	51	8	0	314	8.7
Jeff Norman, St. John's (Minn.)	1974-77	34	25	119	8	293	8.6
Denis McDermott, St. John's (N.Y.)	1987-89	30	43	0	0	258	8.6
Joe Thompson, Augustana (Ill.)	1973-76	34	48	4	0	292	8.6
Kirk Matthieu, Maine Maritime	$1989-93	33	47	0	0	282	8.5
Tim McDaniel, Centre	1988-91	38	54	0	0	324	8.5

**Record. $See page 6 for explanation.*

SEASON POINTS PER GAME

Player, Team	Year	G	TD	XPt.	FG	Pts.	Pt.PG
Carey Bender, Coe	†1994	10	*32	2	0	*194	*19.4
Rob Marchitello, Maine Maritime	1994	9	25	4	0	154	17.1
Stanley Drayton, Allegheny	†1991	10	28	0	0	168	16.8
Ricky Gales, Simpson	†1989	10	26	10	0	166	16.6
Matt Malmberg, St. John's (Minn.)	†1993	10	27	2	0	164	16.4
Chris Babirad, Wash. & Jeff.	†1992	9	24	0	0	144	16.0
Trent Nauholz, Simpson	†1992	8	21	2	0	128	16.0
Billy Johnson, Widener	†1973	9	23	0	0	138	15.3
Greg Novarro, Bentley	1992	10	25	0	0	150	15.0
Bruce Naszimento, Jersey City St.	1973	10	25	0	0	150	15.0
Chris Babirad, Wash. & Jeff.	1991	9	22	2	0	134	14.9
Anthony Jones, La Verne	†1995	8	19	4	0	118	14.8
Chris Hipsley, Cornell College	†1976	9	14	42	2	132	14.7
Carey Bender, Coe	1992	9	21	4	0	130	14.4
Rob Marchitello, Maine Maritime	1995	8	19	0	0	114	14.3
Michael Waithe, Curry	†1987	8	19	0	0	114	14.3
Kelvin Gladney, Millsaps	1993	9	21	2	0	128	14.2
Rick Bell, St. John's (Minn.)	†1982	9	21	2	0	128	14.2
Darnell Morgan, Chapman	1995	9	21	0	0	126	14.0
Terry Underwood, Wagner	†1988	9	21	0	0	126	14.0
Scott Barnyak, Carnegie Mellon	†1990	10	22	6	0	138	13.8
Ryan Kolpin, Coe	†1990	10	23	0	0	138	13.8
Kevin Weaver, Wash. & Lee	†1985	8	17	8	0	110	13.8
Joe Dudek, Plymouth St.	1985	11	25	0	0	150	13.6

** Record. †National champion.*

CAREER POINTS

Player, Team	Year	TD	XPt.	FG	Pts.
Carey Bender, Coe	1991-94	*86	12	0	*528
Joe Dudek, Plymouth St.	1982-85	79	0	0	474
Chris Bisaillon, Ill. Wesleyan	1989-92	61	12	0	378
Chris Babirad, Wash. & Jeff.	1989-92	62	2	0	374
Rob Marchitello, Maine Maritime	1993-95	59	4	0	358
Terry Underwood, Wagner	1985-88	58	0	0	348
Jim Romagna, Loras	1989-92	57	2	0	344
Jason Wooley, Worcester Tech	1990-93	55	8	0	338
Stanley Drayton, Allegheny	1989-92	56	0	0	336
Scott Tumilty, Augustana (Ill.)	1992-95	55	0	0	330
Cary Osborn, Wis.-Eau Claire	1987-90	55	0	0	330
Tim McDaniel, Centre	1988-91	54	0	0	324
A. J. Pagano, Wash. & Jeff.	1984-87	53	5	0	323
Mark Kacmarynski, Central (Iowa)	1992-95	49	10	0	314
Greg Corning, Wis.-River Falls	1984-87	52	2	0	314
Vance Mueller, Occidental	1982-85	51	8	0	314
Scott Barnyak, Carnegie Mellon	1987-90	49	14	0	308
Steve Harris, Carroll (Wis.)	1991-94	49	12	0	306
Prentes Wilson, Ill. Benedictine	1987-90	50	0	0	300
Trent Nauholz, Simpson	1990-93	49	4	0	298
Eric Frees, Western Md.	1988-91	49	4	0	298
Petie Davis, Wesley	1991-94	49	0	0	294
Michael Waithe, Curry	1984-87	49	0	0	294
Jeff Norman, St. John's (Minn.)	1974-77	25	119	8	293
Joe Thompson, Augustana (Ill.)	1973-76	48	4	0	292

**Record.*

SEASON POINTS

Player, Team	Year	TD	XPt.	FG	Pts.
Carey Bender, Coe	†1994	*32	2	0	*194
Stanley Drayton, Allegheny	†1991	28	0	0	168
Ricky Gales, Simpson	†1989	26	10	0	166
Matt Malmberg, St. John's (Minn.)	†1993	27	2	0	164
Rob Marchitello, Maine Maritime	1994	25	4	0	154
Greg Novarro, Bentley	1992	25	0	0	150
Joe Dudek, Plymouth St.	1985	25	0	0	150
Bruce Naszimento, Jersey City St.	1973	25	0	0	150

Player, Team	Year	TD	XPt.	FG	Pts.
Chris Babirad, Wash. & Jeff.	†1992	24	0	0	144
Scott Barnyak, Carnegie Mellon	†1990	22	6	0	138
Ryan Kolpin, Coe	†1990	23	0	0	138
Ron Corbett, Cornell College	1982	23	0	0	138
Billy Johnson, Widener	†1973	23	0	0	138
Matt Taylor, Catholic	1994	22	2	0	134
Chris Babirad, Wash. & Jeff.	1991	22	2	0	134
Thomas Lee, Anderson (Ind.)	1992	22	0	0	132
Tim McDaniel, Centre	1990	22	0	0	132
Chris Hipsley, Cornell College	†1976	14	42	2	132
Carey Bender, Coe	1993	21	4	0	130
Carey Bender, Coe	1992	21	4	0	130
Kelvin Gladney, Millsaps	1993	21	2	0	128
Trent Nauholz, Simpson	†1992	21	2	0	128
Karl Kohl, Catholic	1989	21	2	0	128

* Record. †National champion.

ANNUAL CHAMPIONS

Year	Player, Team	Class	G	TD	XPt.	FG	Pts.	Avg.
1973	Billy Johnson, Widener	Sr.	9	23	0	0	138	15.3
1974	Joe Thompson, Augustana (Ill.)	So.	9	17	0	0	102	11.3
1975	Ron Baker, Monmouth (Ill.)	Sr.	8	15	2	0	92	11.5
1976	Chris Hipsley, Cornell College	So.	9	14	42	2	132	14.7
1977	Chip Zawoiski, Widener	Sr.	9	18	0	0	108	12.0
1978	Roger Andrachik, Baldwin-Wallace	Sr.	8	16	0	0	96	12.0
1979	Jay Wessler, Illinois Col.	Jr.	8	16	4	0	100	12.5
1980	Daryl Johnson, Wabash	Jr.	9	20	0	0	120	13.3
1981	Scott Reppert, Lawrence	Jr.	9	15	0	0	90	10.0
	Daryl Johnson, Wabash	Sr.	9	15	0	0	90	10.0
1982	Rick Bell, St. John's (Minn.)	Sr.	9	21	2	0	128	14.2
1983	John Aromando, Trenton St.	Jr.	10	20	0	0	120	12.0
1984	Joe Dudek, Plymouth St.	Jr.	10	21	0	0	126	12.6
1985	Kevin Weaver, Wash. & Lee	Jr.	8	17	8	0	110	13.8
1986	Jim Korfonta, Hamilton	Sr.	8	16	0	0	96	12.0
	Russ Kring, Mount Union	Jr.	10	20	0	0	120	12.0
1987	Michael Waithe, Curry	Sr.	8	19	0	0	114	14.3
1988	Terry Underwood, Wagner	Sr.	9	21	0	0	126	14.0
1989	Ricky Gales, Simpson	Sr.	10	26	10	0	166	16.6
1990	Scott Barnyak, Carnegie Mellon	Sr.	10	22	6	0	138	13.8
	Ryan Kolpin, Coe	Sr.	10	23	0	0	138	13.8
1991	Stanley Drayton, Allegheny	Jr.	10	28	0	0	168	16.8
1992	Chris Babirad, Wash. & Jeff.	Sr.	9	24	0	0	144	16.0
	Trent Nauholz, Simpson	Jr.	8	21	2	0	128	16.0
1993	Matt Malmberg, St. John's (Minn.)	Jr.	10	27	2	0	164	16.4
1994	Carey Bender, Coe	Sr.	10	*32	2	0	*194	*19.4
1995	Anthony Jones, La Verne	Sr.	8	19	4	0	118	14.8

*Record.

Interceptions

CAREER INTERCEPTIONS

Player, Team	Years	No.	Yards	Avg.
Ralph Gebhardt, Rochester	1973-75	*29	384	13.2
Brian Fetterolf, Aurora	1986-89	28	390	13.9
Rick Bealer, Lycoming	1987-90	28	279	10.0
Andrew Ostrand, Carroll (Wis.)	1990-93	27	258	9.6
Tim Lennon, Curry	1986-89	27	190	7.0
Mike Hintz, Wis.-Platteville	1983-86	27	183	6.8
Scott Stanitous, Moravian	1985-88	27	178	6.6
Mark Dorner, Juniata	1984-87	26	*443	17.0
Cory Mabry, Susquehanna	1988-91	26	400	15.4
Jeff Hughes, Ripon	1975-78	26	333	12.8
Neal Guggemos, St. Thomas (Minn.)	1982-85	25	377	15.1
Dave Adams, Carleton	1984-87	25	327	13.1
Will Hill, Bishop	1983-86	25	261	10.4
Tom Devine, Juniata	1979-82	25	248	9.9
Gary Ellis, Rose-Hulman	1974-77	25	226	9.1

*Record.

SEASON INTERCEPTIONS

Player, Team	Year	No.	Yards
Mark Dorner, Juniata	†1987	*15	202
Steve Nappo, Buffalo	†1986	13	155
Antonio Moore, Widener	†1994	13	116
Chris McMahon, Catholic	†1984	13	105
Ralph Gebhardt, Rochester	†1973	13	105
Brian Barr, Gettysburg	†1985	12	144
John Bernard, Buffalo	†1983	12	143
Mick McConkey, Neb. Wesleyan	†1982	12	111
Chris Butts, Worcester St.	†1992	12	109
Tom Devine, Juniata	†1981	12	91

*Record. †National champion.

ANNUAL CHAMPIONS
(Ranked on Average Per Game)

Year	Player, Team	Class	G	No.	Avg.	Yards
1973	Ralph Gebhardt, Rochester	So.	9	13	1.44	105
1974	Kevin Birkholz, Carleton	Jr.	9	11	1.22	137
1975	Mark Persichetti, Wash. & Jeff.	So.	9	10	1.11	97
1976	Gary Jantzer, Southern Ore. St.	Sr.	9	10	1.11	63
1977	Greg Jones, FDU-Madison	So.	9	10	1.11	106
	Mike Jones, Norwich	So.	9	10	1.11	98
1978	Don Sutton, San Fran. St.	Fr.	8	10	1.25	43
1979	Greg Holland, Simpson	Fr.	9	11	1.22	150
1980	Tim White, Lawrence	Sr.	8	10	1.25	131
1981	Tom Devine, Juniata	Sr.	9	12	1.33	91
1982	Mick McConkey, Neb. Wesleyan	Sr.	9	12	1.33	111
1983	John Bernard, Buffalo	Sr.	10	12	1.20	143
1984	Chris McMahon, Catholic	Sr.	9	13	1.44	140
1985	Kim McManis, Lane	Sr.	9	11	1.22	165
1986	Steve Nappo, Buffalo	Sr.	11	13	1.18	155
1987	Mark Dorner, Juniata	Sr.	10	*15	*1.50	202
1988	Tim Lennon, Curry	Jr.	9	11	1.22	86
1989	Ron Davies, Coast Guard	So.	9	11	1.22	90
1990	Craig Garritano, FDU-Madison	Jr.	9	10	1.11	158
	Brad Bohn, Neb. Wesleyan	So.	9	10	1.11	90
	Frank Greer, Sewanee	So.	9	10	1.11	67
	Harold Krebs, Merchant Marine	Sr.	9	10	1.11	19
1991	Murray Meadows, Millsaps	Sr.	9	11	1.22	46
1992	Chris Butts, Worcester St.	Jr.	9	12	1.33	109
1993	Ricky Webb, Emory & Henry	Sr.	8	8	1.00	56
1994	Antonio Moore, Widener	So.	10	13	1.30	116
1995	Mike Susi, Lebanon Valley	Sr.	8	8	1.00	153
	LeMonde Zachary, St. Lawrence	Fr.	7	7	1.00	109

* Record.

Punting

CAREER AVERAGE
(Minimum 100 Punts)

Player, Team	Years	No.	Yards	Avg.
Mike Manson, Ill. Benedictine	1975-78	120	5,056	*42.1
Dan Osborn, Occidental	1981-83	157	6,528	41.6
Jim Allshouse, Adrian	1973-75	163	6,718	41.2
Thomas Murray, Catholic	1983-84	122	5,028	41.2
Ryan Haley, John Carroll	1991-94	151	6,208	41.1
Scott Lanz, Bethany (W.Va.)	1975-78	235	9,592	40.8
Mitch Holloway, Millsaps	1992-93	105	4,283	40.8

*Record.

SEASON AVERAGE
(Qualifiers for Championship)

Player, Team	Year	No.	Yards	Avg.
Jeff Shea, Cal Lutheran	†1995	43	1,933	*45.0
Bob Burwell, Rose-Hulman	†1978	61	2,740	44.9
Charles McPherson, Clark Atlanta	1978	50	2,237	44.7
Dan Osborn, Occidental	†1982	55	2,454	44.6
Mike Manson, Ill. Benedictine	†1976	36	1,587	44.1
Linc Welles, Bloomsburg	†1973	39	1,708	43.8
Kirk Seufert, Rhodes	†1983	44	1,921	43.7
Kelvin Albert, Knoxville	†1987	30	1,308	43.6

*Record. †National champion.

ANNUAL CHAMPIONS

Year	Player, Team	Class	No.	Yards	Avg.
1973	Linc Welles, Bloomsburg	Sr.	39	1,708	43.8
1974	Sylvester Cunningham, Fort Valley St.	So.	40	1,703	42.6
1975	Larry Hersh, Shepherd	Jr.	58	2,519	43.4
1976	Mike Manson, Ill. Benedictine	So.	36	1,587	44.1
1977	Scott Lanz, Bethany (W.Va.)	Jr.	78	3,349	42.9
1978	Bob Burwell, Rose-Hulman	Sr.	61	2,740	44.9
1979	Jay Lenstrom, Neb. Wesleyan	Sr.	64	2,641	41.3
1980	Duane Harrison, Bridgewater (Va.)	Sr.	43	1,792	41.7
1981	Dan Paro, Denison	Jr.	54	2,223	41.2
1982	Dan Osborn, Occidental	Jr.	55	2,454	44.6
1983	Kirk Seufert, Rhodes	Jr.	44	1,921	43.7
1984	Thomas Murray, Catholic	Sr.	59	2,550	43.2
1985	Dave Lewis, Muhlenberg	So.	55	2,290	41.6
	Mike Matzen, Coe	Sr.	55	2,290	41.6
1986	Darren Estes, Millsaps	Jr.	45	1,940	43.1
1987	Kelvin Albert, Knoxville	So.	30	1,308	43.6

Year	Player, Team	Class	No.	Yards	Avg.
1988	Bobby Graves, Sewanee	So.	57	2,445	42.9
1989	Paul Becker, Kenyon	Sr.	57	2,307	40.5
1990	Bill Nolan, Carroll (Wis.)	Sr.	33	1,322	40.1
1991	Jeff Stolte, Chicago	So.	54	2,295	42.5
1992	Robert Ray, San Diego	So.	44	1,860	42.3
1993	Mitch Holloway, Millsaps	Sr.	45	1,910	42.4
1994	Ryan Haley, John Carroll	Sr.	54	2,311	42.8
1995	Jeff Shea, Cal Lutheran	So.	43	1,933	*45.0

**Record.*

Punt Returns

CAREER AVERAGE

(Minimum 1.2 Returns Per Game)

Player, Team	Years	No.	Yards	Avg.
Keith Winston, Knoxville	1986-87	30	686	*22.9
Robert Middlebrook, Knoxville	1984-85	21	473	22.5
Kevin Doherty, Mass. Maritime	1976-78, 80	45	939	20.9
Chuck Downey, Stony Brook	1984-87	59	*1,198	+20.3
Mike Askew, Kean	1980-81	28	555	19.8
Willie Canady, Fort Valley St.	1979-82	41	772	18.8

**Record. +Record for minimum 50 returns.*

SEASON AVERAGE

(Minimum 1.2 Returns Per Game)

Player, Team	Year	No.	Yards	Avg.
Chuck Downey, Stony Brook	†1986	17	530	*31.2
Kevin Doherty, Mass. Maritime	†1976	11	332	30.2
Robert Middlebrook, Knoxville	†1984	9	260	28.9
Joe Troise, Kean	†1974	12	342	28.5
Melvin Dillard, Ferrum	†1990	25	*688	27.5
Eric Green, Ill. Benedictine	†1993	13	346	26.6
Chris Warren, Ferrum	†1989	18	421	23.4
Kevin Doherty, Mass. Maritime	1978	11	246	22.4

**Record. †National champion.*

ANNUAL CHAMPIONS

Year	Player, Team	Class	No.	Yards	‡Avg.
1973	Al Shepherd, Monmouth (Ill.)	Sr.	18	347	19.3
1974	Joe Troise, Kean	Fr.	12	342	28.5
1975	Mitch Brown, St. Lawrence	So.	25	430	17.2
1976	Kevin Doherty, Mass. Maritime	Fr.	11	332	30.2
1977	Charles Watkins, Knoxville	Sr.	15	278	18.5
1978	Dennis Robinson, Wesleyan (Conn.)	Sr.	††9	263	29.2
1979	Steve Moffett, Maryville (Tenn.)	Jr.	19	357	18.8
1980	Mike Askew, Kean	Jr.	16	304	19.0
1981	Mike Askew, Kean	Sr.	12	251	20.9
1982	Tom Southall, Colorado Col.	So.	13	281	21.6
1983	Edmond Donald, Millsaps	Jr.	15	320	21.3
1984	Robert Middlebrook, Knoxville	So.	9	260	28.9
1985	Dan Schone, Illinois Col.	Fr.	11	231	21.0
1986	Chuck Downey, Stony Brook	Jr.	17	530	*31.2
1987	Keith Winston, Knoxville	Sr.	16	343	21.4
1988	Dennis Tarr, Framingham St.	Jr.	9	178	19.8
1989	Chris Warren, Ferrum	Sr.	18	421	23.4
1990	Melvin Dillard, Ferrum	Sr.	25	*688	27.5
1991	Jordan Nixon, Augustana (Ill.)	Sr.	27	473	17.5
1992	Vic Moncato, FDU-Madison	So.	†††10	243	24.3
1993	Eric Green, Ill. Benedictine	Sr.	13	346	26.6
1994	Ariel Bell, Frostburg St.	Sr.	19	329	17.3
1995	Jim Wallace, Ripon	Jr.	17	305	17.9

**Record. ‡Ranked on minimum of 1.5 returns per game in 1973; 1.2 from 1974. ††Declared champion; with one more return (making 1.25 per game) for zero yards, still would have highest average (26.3). †††Declared champion; with one more return (making 1.22 per game) for zero yards, still would have highest average (22.1).*

Kickoff Returns

CAREER AVERAGE

(Minimum 1.2 Returns Per Game)

Player, Team	Years	No.	Yards	Avg.
Daryl Brown, Tufts	1974-76	38	1,111	*29.2
Mike Askew, Kean	1980-81	33	938	28.4
Chuck Downey, Stony Brook	1984-87	46	1,281	27.8
Ryan Reynolds, Thomas More	1991-94	49	1,311	26.8
LaVant King, Ohio Northern	1991, 93-95	50	1,298	26.0
Scott Reppert, Lawrence	1979-82	44	1,134	25.8
Rick Rosenfeld, Western Md.	1973-76	69	1,732	25.1

**Record.*

SEASON AVERAGE

(Minimum 1.2 Returns Per Game)

Player, Team	Year	No.	Yards	Avg.
Brandon Steinheim, Wesley	†1994	10	422	*42.2
Jason Martin, Coe	†1992	11	438	39.8
Nate Kirtman, Pomona-Pitzer	†1990	14	515	36.8
Tom Myers, Coe	†1983	11	401	36.5
Ron Scott, Occidental	1983	10	363	36.3
Alan Hill, DePauw	1980	12	434	36.2
Al White, Wm. Paterson	1990	12	427	35.6
Byron Womack, Iona	†1989	15	531	35.4
Derrick Brooms, Chicago	†1995	12	422	35.2
Darnell Marshall, Carroll (Wis.)	1989	17	586	34.5
Daryl Brown, Tufts	†1976	11	377	34.3
Rich Jinnette, Methodist	1992	15	514	34.3
Jeff Higgins, Ithaca	1995	12	407	33.9
Oscar Ford, Chapman	1995	11	373	33.9
Sean Healy, Coe	1989	11	372	33.8
Anthony Drakeford, Ferrum	†1987	15	507	33.8
Ryan Reynolds, Thomas More	1992	14	473	33.8
Glenn Koch, Tufts	†1986	14	472	33.7

**Record. †National champion.*

ANNUAL CHAMPIONS

Year	Player, Team	Class	No.	Yards	‡Avg.
1973	Greg Montgomery, Wis.-Whitewater	So.	17	518	30.5
1974	Tom Oleksa, Muhlenberg	Sr.	15	467	31.1
1975	Jeff Levant, Beloit	Jr.	15	434	28.9
1976	Daryl Brown, Tufts	Sr.	11	377	34.3
1977	Charlie Black, Marietta	Jr.	14	465	33.2
1978	Russ Atchison, Centre	So.	11	284	25.8
1979	Jim Iannone, Rochester	Jr.	13	411	31.6
1980	Mike Askew, Kean	So.	††10	415	41.5
1981	Gene Cote, Wesleyan (Conn.)	Sr.	16	521	32.6
1982	Jim Hachey, Bri'water (Mass.)	Jr.	16	477	29.8
1983	Tom Myers, Coe	So.	11	401	36.5
1984	Mike Doetsch, Trinity (Conn.)	Jr.	13	434	33.4
1985	Gary Newsom, Lane	So.	10	319	31.9
1986	Glenn Koch, Tufts	Sr.	14	472	33.7
1987	Anthony Drakeford, Ferrum	Sr.	15	507	33.8
1988	Harold Owens, Wis.-La Crosse	Jr.	10	508	29.9
1989	Byron Womack, Iona	Sr.	15	531	35.4
1990	Nate Kirtman, Pomona-Pitzer	Jr.	14	515	36.8
1991	Tom Reason, Albion	So.	13	423	32.5
1992	Jason Martin, Coe	So.	11	438	39.8
1993	Eric Green, Ill. Benedictine	Sr.	19	628	33.1
1994	Brandon Steinheim, Wesley	Fr.	10	422	*42.2
1995	Derrick Brooms, Chicago	Sr.	12	422	35.2

**Record. ‡Ranked on minimum of 1.5 returns per game in 1973; 1.2 from 1974. ††Declared champion; with one more return (making 1.2 per game) for zero yards, still would have highest average (37.7).*

Photo from Carleton sports information

Carleton running back Adam Henry ranks fifth on the all-time Division III career list with 6,108 all-purpose yards.

All-Purpose Yards

CAREER YARDS PER GAME
(Minimum 3,500 Yards)

Player, Team	Year	G	Rush	Rcv.	Int.	PR	KOR	Yds.	Yd.PG
Kirk Matthieu, Maine Maritime	$1989-93	33	5,107	315	0	254	1,279	6,955	*210.8
Carey Bender, Coe	1991-94	39	*6,125	1,751	0	7	87	*7,970	204.4
Gary Trettel, St. Thomas (Minn.)	1988-90	29	3,483	834	0	0	1,407	5,724	197.4

**Record. $See page 6 for explanation.*

SEASON YARDS PER GAME

Player, Team	Year	G	Rush	Rcv.	Int.	PR	KOR	Yds.	Yd.PG
Carey Bender, Coe	†1994	10	*2,243	319	0	7	87	*2,656	*265.6
Kirk Matthieu, Maine Maritime	†1992	9	1,733	91	0	56	308	2,188	243.1
Ricky Gales, Simpson	1989	10	2,035	102	0	0	248	2,385	238.5
Gary Trettel, St. Thomas (Minn.)	1989	10	1,502	337	0	0	496	2,335	233.5
Kirk Matthieu, Maine Maritime	1990	9	1,428	77	0	99	495	2,099	233.2
Gary Trettel, St. Thomas (Minn.)	1990	10	1,620	388	0	0	319	2,327	232.7
Carey Bender, Coe	†1993	10	1,718	601	0	0	0	2,319	231.9

**Record. †National champion.*

CAREER YARDS

Player, Team	Year	Rush	Rcv.	Int.	PR	KOR	Yds.
Carey Bender, Coe	1991-94	*6,125	1,751	0	7	87	*7,970
Kirk Matthieu, Maine Maritime	$1989-93	5,107	315	0	254	1,279	6,955
Eric Frees, Western Md.	1988-91	5,281	392	0	47	1,158	6,878
Joe Dudek, Plymouth St.	1982-85	5,570	348	0	0	243	6,509
Adam Henry, Carleton	1990-93	3,482	601	0	186	1,839	6,108
Gary Trettel, St. Thomas (Minn.)	1988-90	3,724	853	0	0	1,467	6,044

**Record. $See page 6 for explanation.*

SEASON YARDS

Player, Team	Year	Rush	Rcv.	Int.	PR	KOR	Yds.
Carey Bender, Coe	†1994	*2,243	319	0	7	87	*2,656
Theo Blanco, Wis.-Stevens Point	1987	454	1,616	0	245	103	2,418
Ricky Gales, Simpson	1989	2,035	102	0	0	248	2,385
Gary Trettel, St. Thomas (Minn.)	1989	1,502	337	0	0	496	2,335
Gary Trettel, St. Thomas (Minn.)	1990	1,620	388	0	0	319	2,327
Carey Bender, Coe	†1993	1,718	601	0	0	0	2,319

**Record. †National champion.*

ANNUAL CHAMPIONS

Year	Player, Team	Cl.	Rush	Rcv.	Int.	PR	KOR	Yds.	Yd.PG
1992	Kirk Matthieu, Maine Matime	Jr.	1,733	91	0	56	308	2,188	243.1
1993	Carey Bender, Coe	Jr.	1,718	601	0	0	0	2,319	231.9
1994	Carey Bender, Coe	Sr.	*2,243	319	0	7	87	*2,656	*265.6
1995	Brad Olson, Lawrence	So.	1,760	279	0	0	0	2,039	226.6

**Record.*

Field Goals

CAREER FIELD GOALS

Player, Team	Year	Made	Atts.	Pct.
Ken Edelman, Mount Union (S)	1987-90	*52	*71	.732
Ted Swan, Colorado Col. (S)	1973-76	43	57	.754
Jim Hever, Rhodes (S)	1982-85	42	66	.636
Manny Matsakis, Capital (C)	1980-83	40	66	.606
Doug Hart, Grove City (S)	1985-88	40	*71	.563
Mike Duvic, Dayton (S)	1986-89	38	49	$.776
Jeff Reitz, Lawrence (C)	1974-77	37	60	.617
Dan Deneher, Montclair St. (S)	1978-79, 81-82	37	65	.569
Jim Flynn, Gettysburg (S)	1982-85	37	68	.544

**Record. $Declared record; with one more attempt (making 50), failed, still would have highest percentage (.760). (C) Conventional kicker. (S) Soccer-style kicker.*

SEASON FIELD GOALS

Player, Team	Year	Made	Atts.	Pct.
Ken Edelman, Mount Union (S)	†1990	*20	27	.741
Scott Ryerson, Central Fla. (S)	†1981	18	*29	.621
Dennis Unger, Albright (S)	†1995	16	20	.800
Steve Graeca, John Carroll (S)	†1988	15	16	*.938
Ken Edelman, Mount Union (S)	1988	15	17	.882
Gary Potter, Hamline (C)	†1984	15	21	.714
Jeff Reitz, Lawrence (C)	†1975	15	26	.577

**Record. (C) Conventional kicker. (S) Soccer-style kicker. †National champion.*

ANNUAL CHAMPIONS

Year	Player, Team	Class	Made	Atts.	Pct.	PG
1973	Chuck Smeltz, Susquehanna (C)	Jr.	10	14	.714	1.11
1974	Ted Swan, Colorado Col. (S)	So.	13	15	.867	1.44
1975	Jeff Reitz, Lawrence (C)	So.	15	26	.577	1.67
1976	Mark Sniegocki, Bethany (W.Va.) (C)	So.	11	14	.786	1.22
1977	Bob Unruh, Wheaton (Ill.) (S)	Jr.	11	14	.786	1.22
1978	Craig Walker, Western Md. (C)	So.	13	24	.542	1.44
1979	Jeff Holter, Concordia-M'head (S)	Jr.	12	15	.800	1.33
1980	Jeff Holter, Concordia-M'head (S)	Sr.	13	19	.684	1.30
1981	Scott Ryerson, Central Fla. (S)	So.	18	*29	.621	1.80
1982	Manny Matsakis, Capital (C)	Jr.	13	20	.650	1.44
1983	Mike Farrell, Adrian (S)	So.	12	21	.571	1.33
1984	Gary Potter, Hamline (C)	Jr.	15	21	.714	1.50
1985	Joe Bevelhimer, Wabash (C)	Sr.	14	22	.636	1.40
	Jim Hever, Rhodes (S)	Sr.	14	23	.609	1.40
1986	Tim Dewberry, Occidental (C)	Sr.	13	21	.619	1.44
1987	Doug Dickason, John Carroll (S)	Sr.	13	21	.619	1.44
1988	Steve Graeca, John Carroll (S)	Fr.	15	16	*.938	1.67
1989	Dave Bergmann, San Diego (S)	So.	14	18	.778	1.56
	Rich Egal, Merchant Marine (S)	Fr.	14	22	.636	1.56
1990	Ken Edelman, Mount Union (S)	Sr.	*20	27	.741	*2.00
1991	Greg Harrison, Union (N.Y.) (S)	So.	12	16	.750	1.33
1992	Todd Holthaus, Rose-Hulman (S)	Jr.	13	19	.684	1.30
1993	Steve Milne, Brockport St. (S)	Sr.	13	16	.813	1.30
1994	Chris Kondik, Baldwin-Wallace (S)	Fr.	13	17	.765	1.30
1995	Dennis Unger, Albright (S)	So.	16	20	.800	1.60

**Record. (C) Conventional kicker. (S) Soccer-style kicker.*

All-Time Longest Plays

Since 1941, official maximum length of all plays fixed at 100 yards.

RUSHING

Yds.	Player, Team (Opponent)	Year
99	Bill Casey, Mass.-Dartmouth (Norwich)	1995
99	Arnie Boigner, Ohio Northern (Muskingum)	1992
99	Reese Wilson, MacMurray (Eureka)	1986
99	Don Patria, Rensselaer (Mass.-Lowell)	1981
99	Kevin Doherty, Mass. Maritime (New Haven)	1980
99	Sam Halliston, Albany, N.Y. (Norwich)	1977
98	Rich Vargas, Wis.-Stout (Wis.-Oshkosh)	1992
98	Ted Pretasky, Wis.-La Crosse (Wis.-River Falls)	1987
98	Jon Hinds, Principia (Illinois Col.)	1986
98	Alex Schmidt, Muhlenberg (Lebanon Valley)	1984
98	Eric Batt, Ohio Northern (Ohio Wesleyan)	1982
98	Mike Shannon, Centre (Sewanee)	1978

PASSING

Yds.	Passer-Receiver, Team (Opponent)	Year
99	Mike Schultz-R. J. Hoppe, Carroll, Wis. (Ripon)	1995
99	Mike Magistrelli-Jason Martin, Coe (Quincy)	1994
99	Jim Connolley-Duane Martin, Wesley (FDU-Madison)	1993
99	Marc Klausner-Eric Frink, Pace (Hobart)	1992
99	Carlos Nazario-Ray Marshall, St. Peter's (Georgetown)	1991
99	Mike Jones-Warren Tweedy, Frostburg St. (Waynesburg)	1990
99	Chris Etzler-Andy Nowlin, Bluffton (Urbana)	1990
99	John Clark-Pete Balistrieri, Wis.-Eau Claire (Minn.-Duluth)	1989
99	Kelly Sandidge-Mark Green, Centre (Sewanee)	1988
99	Mike Francis-John Winter, Carleton (Trinity, Tex.)	1983
99	Rich Boling-Lewis Borsellino, DePauw (Valparaiso)	1976
99	John Wicinski-Donnell Lipford, John Carroll (Allegheny)	1975
99	Jack Berry-Mercer West, Wash. & Lee (Hampden-Sydney)	1974
99	Gary Shope-Rick Rudolph, Juniata (Moravian)	1973

INTERCEPTION RETURNS

Twenty-five players have returned interceptions 100 yards. The most recent:

Yds.	Player, Team (Opponent)	Year
100	Dan Gilson, Curry (Stonehill)	1995
100	Tony Hinkle, Rose-Hulman (Millsaps)	1995
100	Mike Gerhart, Susquehanna (Moravian)	1994
100	Bruce Pritchett, Kean (Widener)	1994
100	Adam Smith, Heidelberg (Capital)	1994
100	Jason Pass, Hamline (St. John's, Minn.)	1994
100	Guy Nardulli, Elmhurst (North Central)	1994

PUNT RETURNS

Yds.	Player, Team (Opponent)	Year
99	Robert Middlebrook, Knoxville (Miles)	1985
98	Mark Griggs, Wooster (Oberlin)	1980
98	Ron Mabry, Emory & Henry (Maryville, Tenn.)	1973
97	Rob Allard, Nichols (Curry)	1991
96	Marvin Robbins, Salisbury St. (Wesley)	1987
96	Gary Martin, Muskingum (Wooster)	1976
95	Tyrone Croom, Susquehanna (Delaware Valley)	1993
95	Brian Sarver, William Penn (Dubuque)	1992
95	Stan Thompson, Knoxville (Livingstone)	1982

KICKOFF RETURNS

Forty players have returned kickoffs 100 yards. The most recent:

Yds.	Player, Team (Opponent)	Year
100	Eric Green, Ill. Benedictine (Carthage)	1992
100	Nate Kirtman, Pomona-Pitzer (Redlands)	1990
100	Phil Bryant, Wilmington, Ohio (Tiffin)	1990
100	Steve Burns, Mass.-Boston (Curry)	1989
100	Wayne Morris, Hofstra (Pace)	1989

PUNTS

Yds.	Player, Team (Opponent)	Year
90	Dan Heeren, Coe (Lawrence)	1974
86	David Anastasi, Buffalo (John Carroll)	1989
86	Dana Loucks, Buffalo (Frostburg St.)	1987
86	John Pavlik, Wabash (Centre)	1978
84	Rob Sarvis, Norwich (Western Conn. St.)	1995
83	Jeff Shooks, Albion (Alma)	1994
83	Geoff Hansen, Gust. Adolphus (Augustana, S.D.)	1992
82	John Massab, Albion (Adrian)	1982
82	Mike Manson, Ill. Benedictine (Monmouth, Ill.)	1976
81	Jason Berg, Mass. Maritime (Mass.-Lowell)	1990
81	Tom Illig, Ohio Wesleyan (Wittenberg)	1975

FIELD GOALS

Yds.	Player, Team (Opponent)	Year
62	Dom Antonini, Rowan (Salisbury St.)	1976
59	Chris Gustafson, Carroll, Wis. (North Park)	1985
59	Hartmut Strecker, Dayton (Iowa St.)	1977
57	Scott Fritz, Wartburg (Simpson)	1982
57	Kevin Shea, St. Mary's, Cal. (Oregon Tech)	1976

Team Champions

Annual Offense Champions

TOTAL OFFENSE

Year	Team	Avg.
1973	San Diego	441.0
1974	Ithaca	487.9
1975	Frank. & Marsh.	439.4
1976	St. John's (Minn.)	451.8
1977	St. John's (Minn.)	437.5
1978	Lawrence	432.6
1979	Norwich	465.2
1980	Widener	459.0
1981	Middlebury	446.5
1982	West Ga.	470.6
1983	Elmhurst	483.3
1984	Alma	465.1
1985	St. Thomas (Minn.)	446.9
1986	Mount Union	452.8
1987	Samford	523.1
1988	Wagner	465.9
1989	Simpson	514.0
1990	Hofstra	505.7
1991	St. John's (Minn.)	503.8
1992	Mount Union	463.7
1993	St. John's (Minn.)	*549.7
1994	Allegheny	543.8
1995	Mount Union	495.8

**Record.*

RUSHING OFFENSE

Year	Team	Avg.
1973	Widener	361.7
1974	Albany (N.Y.)	361.6
1975	Widener	345.8
1976	St. John's (Minn.)	348.9
1977	St. John's (Minn.)	315.3
1978	Ithaca	320.1
1979	Norwich	383.1
1980	Widener	317.5
1981	Augustana (Ill.)	313.6
1982	West Ga.	319.6
1983	Augustana (Ill.)	345.7
1984	Augustana (Ill.)	338.4
1985	Denison	351.0
1986	Wis.-River Falls	361.4
1987	Augustana (Ill.)	369.1
1988	Tufts	369.0
1989	Wis.-River Falls	388.5
1990	Ferrum	*434.7
1991	Ferrum	361.4
1992	Wis.-River Falls	315.6
1993	Chicago	324.8
1994	Wis.-River Falls	336.7
1995	Lawrence	344.0

**Record.*

PASSING OFFENSE

Year	Team	Avg.
1973	San Diego	231.7
1974	Ill. Benedictine	255.4
1975	St. Norbert	227.7
1976	Occidental	255.4
1977	Southwestern	257.8
1978	Claremont-M-S	331.7
1979	Claremont-M-S	250.1
1980	Occidental	255.9
1981	Wis.-Stevens Point	288.9
1982	Wheaton (Ill.)	308.7
1983	Wheaton (Ill.)	380.4
1984	Wheaton (Ill.)	351.6
1985	Wheaton (Ill.)	371.6
1986	Pace	286.9
1987	Wis.-Stout	314.6
1988	Wis.-Stevens Point	356.7
1989	Wis.-Stevens Point	380.4
1990	Hofstra	342.2
1991	St. John's (Minn.)	302.8
1992	Mass.-Boston	337.0
1993	Mount Union	352.8
1994	Hanover	351.3
1995	Hanover	362.8

SCORING OFFENSE

Year	Team	Avg.
1973	San Diego	40.1
1974	Frank. & Marsh.	45.1
1975	Frank. & Marsh.	38.2
1976	St. John's (Minn.)	42.5
1977	Lawrence	38.2
1978	Georgetown	36.5
1979	Wittenberg	39.7
1980	Widener	43.3

Year	Team	Avg.
1981	Lawrence	35.3
1982	West Ga.	42.1
1983	Elmhurst	38.1
1984	Hope	40.3
1985	Salisbury St.	39.5
1986	Dayton	40.8
1987	Samford	51.7
1988	Central (Iowa)	37.6
1989	Ferrum	46.7
1990	Ferrum	47.3
1991	Union (N.Y.)	46.1
1992	Coe	46.4
1993	St. John's (Minn.)	*61.5
1994	St. John's (Minn.)	47.1
1995	Chapman	47.2

**Record.*

Annual Defense Champions

TOTAL DEFENSE

Year	Team	Avg.
1973	Doane	144.3
1974	Alfred	153.6
1975	Lycoming	133.1
1976	Albion	129.9
1977	Knoxville	*94.0
1978	Bowie St.	112.3
1979	Catholic	116.9
1980	Maine Maritime	127.2
1981	Millsaps	147.6
1982	Plymouth St.	122.2
1983	Lycoming	154.5
1984	Swarthmore	159.2
1985	Augustana (Ill.)	149.1
1986	Augustana (Ill.)	136.2
1987	Plymouth St.	135.3
1988	Plymouth St.	143.6
1989	Frostburg St.	119.7
1990	Bentley	139.8
1991	Wash. & Jeff.	143.0
1992	Bentley	184.5
1993	Wash. & Jeff.	142.4
1994	Wash. & Jeff.	165.3
1995	Mass. Maritime	161.2

**Record.*

RUSHING DEFENSE

Year	Team	Avg.
1973	Oregon Col.	61.2
1974	Millersville	57.2
1975	Cal Lutheran	62.4
1976	Lycoming	44.3
1977	Knoxville	*-2.3
1978	Western Md.	43.4
1979	Catholic	46.4
1980	Maine Maritime	3.2
1981	Augustana (Ill.)	30.7
1982	Lycoming	34.2
1983	DePauw	41.6
1984	Swarthmore	40.0
1985	Augustana (Ill.)	35.1
1986	Dayton	13.5
1987	Lycoming	35.4
1988	Worcester St.	43.9
1989	Frostburg St.	49.7
1990	Ohio Wesleyan	18.9
1991	Wash. & Jeff.	64.6
1992	Bri'water (Mass.)	43.2
1993	Wash. & Jeff.	19.1
1994	Wash. & Jeff.	23.7
1995	Marietta	46.2

**Record.*

PASSING DEFENSE

Year	Team	$Avg.
1973	Nichols	53.0
1974	Findlay	49.2
1975	Wash. & Jeff.	56.0
1976	Mass. Maritime	*48.5
1977	Hofstra	49.4
1978	Bowie St.	64.7
1979	Wagner	59.5
1980	Williams	63.8
1981	Plymouth St.	66.9
1982	Plymouth St.	48.8
1983	Muhlenberg	76.4
1984	Bri'water (Mass.)	68.7
1985	Bri'water (Mass.)	77.3
1986	Knoxville	83.2
1987	Jersey City St.	67.0
1988	Colorado Col.	78.9
1989	Frostburg St.	70.0
1990	Bentley	47.4
1991	Wash. & Jeff.	50.3
1992	St. Peter's	51.7
1993	Worcester St.	50.0
1994	Worcester St.	69.2
1995	Union (N.Y.)	54.6

**Record. $Beginning in 1990, ranked on passing efficiency defense rating points instead of per-game yardage allowed.*

SCORING DEFENSE

Year	Team	Avg.
1973	Fisk	6.4
	Slippery Rock	6.4
1974	Central (Iowa)	6.9
	Rhodes	6.9
1975	Millsaps	5.0
1976	Albion	5.4
1977	Central (Iowa)	5.0
1978	Minn.-Morris	5.9
1979	Carnegie Mellon	4.9
1980	Millsaps	*3.4
1981	Baldwin-Wallace	3.9
1982	West Ga.	4.6
1983	Carnegie Mellon	5.3
1984	Union (N.Y.)	4.6
1985	Augustana (Ill.)	4.7
1986	Augustana (Ill.)	5.1
1987	Plymouth St.	6.2
1988	Plymouth St.	6.5
1989	Millikin	4.8
1990	Bentley	4.5
1991	Mass.-Lowell	5.4
1992	Dayton	6.7
1993	Wash. & Jeff.	6.1
1994	Trinity (Tex.)	6.2
1995	Wash. & Jeff.	5.6
	Williams	5.6

**Record.*

Other Annual Team Champions

NET PUNTING

Year	Team	Avg.
1992	San Diego	39.2
1993	Ill. Benedictine	38.9
1994	Redlands	37.9
1995	Hardin-Simmons	37.9

PUNT RETURNS

Year	Team	Avg.
1992	Occidental	18.7
1993	Curry	17.9
	Wheaton (Ill.)	17.9
1994	Frostburg St.	15.2
1995	Ohio Northern	16.5

KICKOFF RETURNS

Year	Team	Avg.
1992	Thomas More	27.7
1993	St. John's (Minn.)	28.9
1994	Buffalo St.	26.8
1995	Howard Payne	29.5

TURNOVER MARGIN

Year	Team	Avg.
1992	Illinois Col.	2.44
1993	Trinity (Conn.)	2.87
1994	Dickinson	2.70
1995	Thomas More	2.80

All-Time Team Won-Lost Records

Includes records as a senior college only, minimum 20 seasons of competition since 1937. Postseason games are included, and each tie game is computed as half won and half lost.

PERCENTAGE (TOP 25)

Team	Yrs.	Won	Lost	Tied	Pct.
Plymouth St.	26	174	68	7	.713
Wis.-La Crosse	71	434	179	40	.695
St. John's (Minn.)	85	421	198	24	.673
Ithaca	63	329	178	11	.646
Wittenberg	102	563	315	32	.636
Cal Lutheran	34	208	119	7	.633
Wis.-Whitewater	71	366	208	21	.633
Augustana (Ill.)	83	420	239	28	.632
Concordia-M'head	76	385	220	38	.628
Baldwin-Wallace	91	449	263	30	.625
Montclair St.	65	323	193	20	.621
Central (Iowa)	87	436	270	26	.613
Williams	110	523	325	47	.611
Millikin	90	442	278	28	.610
Gust. Adolphus	80	386	245	21	.608
Wash. & Jeff.	104	539	341	40	.608
Widener	115	536	345	38	.604
Wis.-River Falls	70	338	221	32	.599
St. Thomas (Minn.)	90	427	281	32	.599
Albion	109	482	319	43	.597
Lawrence	102	449	305	29	.592
Wabash	109	490	338	59	.586
Coe	103	457	320	38	.584
Trinity (Conn.)	111	443	315	42	.580
Frank. & Marsh.	108	515	374	47	.575

ALPHABETICAL LISTING

(No Minimum Seasons of Competition)

Team	Yrs.	Won	Lost	Tied	Pct.
Adrian	93	296	379	17	.440
Albion	109	482	319	43	.597

Team	Yrs.	Won	Lost	Tied	Pct.
Albright	83	333	386	22	.464
Alfred	97	378	294	45	.559
Allegheny	101	394	337	44	.537
Alma	99	396	335	27	.540
Amherst	116	503	374	54	.569
Anderson (Ind.)	49	219	210	12	.510
Augsburg	64	148	356	18	.301
Augustana (Ill.)	83	420	239	28	.632
Aurora	10	48	36	1	.571
Baldwin-Wallace	91	449	263	30	.625
Bates	100	278	418	46	.406
Beloit	105	359	418	47	.464
Bethany (W.Va.)	95	291	444	34	.401
Bethel (Minn.)	43	131	244	8	.352
Blackburn	7	16	43	0	.271
Bluffton	73	234	325	23	.422
Bowdoin	102	345	397	44	.467
Bri'water (Mass.)	36	151	153	6	.497
Bridgewater (Va.)	51	119	286	11	.299
Brockport St.	49	131	255	4	.341
Buena Vista	91	348	329	28	.513
Buffalo St.	15	68	72	0	.486
Cal Lutheran	34	208	119	7	.633
Capital	72	279	283	27	.497
Carleton	101	419	313	25	.570
Carnegie Mellon	86	399	303	29	.566
Carroll (Wis.)	92	364	274	38	.567
Carthage	99	354	347	42	.505
Case Reserve	26	92	143	4	.393
Catholic	50	197	207	13	.488
Central (Iowa)	87	436	270	26	.613
Centre	103	462	342	38	.571
Chapman	2	14	3	1	.806
Chicago	76	330	310	33	.515
Claremont-M-S	38	125	205	5	.381
Coast Guard	72	245	323	49	.437
Coe	103	457	320	38	.584
Colby	102	298	402	33	.429
Colorado Col.	110	430	384	35	.527
Concordia (Ill.)	57	168	263	19	.394
Concordia-M'head	76	385	220	38	.628
Cornell College	105	437	349	33	.554
Cortland St.	69	284	242	28	.538
Curry	31	98	159	6	.384
Defiance	73	291	303	20	.490
Delaware Valley	48	178	222	10	.446
Denison	106	463	371	57	.552
DePauw	108	435	417	41	.510
Dickinson	107	391	460	55	.462
Dubuque	73	263	318	25	.455
Earlham	105	313	455	23	.410
Elmhurst	76	235	366	24	.395
Emory & Henry	80	417	325	19	.560
Eureka	62	145	320	26	.322
FDU-Madison	22	62	129	1	.326
Ferrum	11	73	40	1	.645
Fitchburg St.	12	11	94	1	.108
Framingham St.	22	78	115	2	.405
Franklin	95	344	402	31	.463
Frank. & Marsh.	108	515	374	47	.575
Frostburg St.	35	159	163	8	.494
Gettysburg	103	476	396	42	.544
Grinnell	105	336	463	33	.424
Grove City	101	392	393	60	.499
Guilford	90	238	472	25	.341
Gust. Adolphus	80	386	245	21	.608
Hamilton	102	329	388	47	.461
Hamline	104	365	349	30	.511
Hampden-Sydney	101	420	368	28	.532
Hanover	103	357	349	29	.505
Hardin-Simmons	59	284	208	35	.572
Hartwick	24	55	117	11	.331
Heidelberg	100	399	393	41	.504
Hiram	97	239	473	32	.343
Hobart	102	356	417	40	.462
Hope	86	331	267	38	.550
Howard Payne	90	388	369	41	.512
Ill. Benedictine	74	241	285	24	.460
Illinois Col.	99	344	386	36	.473
Ill. Wesleyan	104	434	332	41	.563
Ithaca	63	329	178	11	.646
Jersey City St.	28	87	171	3	.339
John Carroll	73	335	258	37	.561
Johns Hopkins	111	359	422	57	.462
Juniata	73	305	277	22	.523
Kalamazoo	101	336	391	41	.464
Kean	24	99	124	9	.446
Kenyon	106	304	482	47	.393
King's (Pa.)	3	4	24	1	.155
Knox	102	350	438	43	.447
La Verne	70	273	293	18	.483
Lake Forest	103	341	384	55	.472
Lakeland	61	232	244	13	.488
Lawrence	102	449	305	29	.592
Lebanon Valley	95	342	426	36	.448
Loras	67	287	230	31	.552
Luther	82	355	288	21	.550
Lycoming	46	225	169	11	.569
Macalester	93	225	430	29	.350
MacMurray	11	43	61	1	.414
Maine Maritime	50	212	176	9	.545
Manchester	70	214	340	20	.391
Marietta	101	347	441	36	.443
Martin Luther	97	300	309	31	.493
Maryville (Tenn.)	98	378	398	35	.488
Mass.-Boston	8	21	50	1	.299
Mass.-Dartmouth	8	36	38	0	.486
MIT	8	23	38	1	.379
Mass. Maritime	23	116	89	1	.566
Menlo	10	33	55	2	.378
Merchant Marine	51	221	233	13	.487
Methodist	7	16	54	0	.229
Middlebury	99	332	347	42	.490
Millikin	90	442	278	28	.610
Millsaps	73	305	285	36	.516
Monmouth (Ill.)	103	418	393	39	.515
Montclair St.	65	323	193	20	.621
Moravian	62	266	245	21	.520
Mount Union	99	473	381	34	.552
Muhlenberg	96	386	422	42	.479
Muskingum	101	447	336	39	.568
Neb. Wesleyan	87	381	337	42	.529
Nichols	37	147	145	6	.503
North Central	91	314	361	36	.467
North Park	38	80	247	7	.250
Norwich	97	285	412	31	.413
Oberlin	105	351	460	39	.436
Occidental	94	391	325	26	.544
Ohio Northern	97	362	397	35	.478
Ohio Wesleyan	105	478	400	44	.542
Olivet	95	264	431	33	.385
Otterbein	106	337	491	43	.412
Plymouth St.	26	174	68	7	.713
Pomona-Pitzer	98	330	370	31	.473
Principia	62	178	291	16	.384
Randolph-Macon	108	396	385	57	.507
Redlands	86	376	349	28	.518
Rensselaer	106	292	477	46	.387
Rhodes	84	300	317	38	.487
Ripon	102	411	298	46	.575
Rochester	107	436	384	38	.530
Rose-Hulman	100	339	421	29	.448
Rowan	36	178	149	8	.543
St. John Fisher	8	34	41	0	.453
St. John's (Minn.)	85	421	198	24	.673
St. Lawrence	101	340	358	29	.488
St. Norbert	62	275	234	20	.539
St. Olaf	78	351	267	20	.566
St. Thomas (Minn.)	90	427	281	32	.599
Salisbury St.	24	128	100	4	.560
Salve Regina	3	18	6	0	.750
Sewanee	101	417	377	39	.524
Simpson	90	360	416	37	.466
Springfield	102	422	377	55	.526
Susquehanna	97	345	390	38	.471
Swarthmore	115	437	420	36	.510
Thiel	91	293	369	36	.446
Thomas More	6	47	13	0	.783
Trenton St.	71	255	264	32	.492
Trinity (Conn.)	111	443	315	42	.580
Trinity (Tex.)	91	326	406	49	.449
Tufts	114	436	434	46	.501
Union (N.Y.)	108	401	386	62	.509
Upper Iowa	93	286	366	25	.441
Ursinus	103	304	490	54	.390
Wabash	109	490	338	59	.586
Wartburg	60	247	257	12	.490
Washington (Mo.)	98	389	396	28	.496

Team	Yrs.	Won	Lost	Tied	Pct.
Wash. & Jeff.	104	539	341	40	.608
Wash. & Lee	102	393	430	39	.479
Waynesburg	92	346	322	37	.517
Wesley	10	47	47	1	.500
Wesleyan (Conn.)	114	435	426	42	.505
Western Conn. St.	24	76	148	3	.341
Western Md.	101	419	385	49	.520
Western New Eng.	15	48	84	1	.365
Westfield St.	14	60	71	1	.458
Wheaton (Ill.)	83	346	298	29	.536
Whittier	86	407	305	36	.568
Widener	115	536	345	38	.604
Wilkes	50	194	226	8	.463
Wm. Paterson	24	100	133	4	.430
William Penn	95	258	456	35	.368
Williams	110	523	325	47	.611
Wilmington (Ohio)	63	244	272	14	.474
Wis.-Eau Claire	77	283	305	34	.482
Wis.-La Crosse	71	434	179	40	.695
Wis.-Oshkosh	69	220	309	30	.420
Wis.-Platteville	87	298	292	31	.505
Wis.-River Falls	70	338	221	32	.599
Wis.-Stevens Point	96	372	309	43	.544
Wis.-Stout	76	205	386	33	.355
Wis.-Whitewater	71	366	208	21	.633
Wittenberg	102	563	315	32	.636
Wooster	97	401	368	41	.520
Worcester St.	11	54	44	0	.551
Worcester Tech	106	254	403	30	.392

VICTORIES

Team	Wins
Wittenberg	563
Wash. & Jeff.	539
Widener	536
Williams	523
Frank. & Marsh.	515
Amherst	503
Wabash	490
Albion	482
Ohio Wesleyan	478
Gettysburg	476
Mount Union	473
Denison	463
Centre	462

Team	Wins
Coe	457
Baldwin-Wallace	449
Lawrence	449
Muskingum	447
Trinity (Conn.)	443
Millikin	442
Cornell College	437
Swarthmore	437
Central (Iowa)	436
Rochester	436
Tufts	436
DePauw	435
Wesleyan (Conn.)	435

National Poll Rankings

Final Poll Leaders

(Released Before Division Championship Playoffs)

Year	Team, Record*	Coach	Record in Championship†
1975	Ithaca (8-0-0)	Jim Butterfield	2-1 Runner-up
1976	St. John's (Minn.) (7-0-1)	John Gagliardi	3-0 Champion
1977	Wittenberg (8-0-0)	Dave Maurer	Did not compete
1978	Minn.-Morris (9-0-0)	Al Molde	1-1 Lost in semifinals
1979	Wittenberg (8-0-0)	Dave Maurer	2-1 Runner-up
1980	Ithaca (10-0-0)	Jim Butterfield	2-1 Runner-up
1981	Widener (9-0-0)	Bill Manlove	3-0 Champion
1982	Baldwin-Wallace (10-0-0)	Bob Packard	0-1 Lost in first round
1983	Augustana (Ill.) (9-0-0)	Bob Reade	3-0 Champion
1984	Augustana (Ill.) (9-0-0)	Bob Reade	3-0 Champion
1985	Augustana (Ill.) (9-0-0)	Bob Reade	4-0 Champion
1986	Dayton (10-0-0)	Mike Kelly	0-1 Lost in first round
1987	Augustana (Ill.) (9-0-0)	Bob Reade	1-1 Lost in quarterfinals
1988	**East Region**		
	Cortland St. (9-0-0)	Dennis Kayser	1-1 Lost in quarterfinals
	North Region		
	Dayton (9-1-0)	Mike Kelly	0-1 Lost in first round
	South Region		
	Ferrum (9-0-0)	Hank Norton	2-1 Lost in semifinals
	West Region		
	Central (Iowa) (8-0-0)	Ron Schipper	3-1 Runner-up
1989	**East Region**		
	Union (N.Y.) (9-0-0)	Al Bagnoli	3-1 Runner-up
	North Region		
	Dayton (8-0-1)	Mike Kelly	4-0 Champion
	South Region		
	Rhodes (7-0-0)	Mike Clary	Did not compete
	West Region		
	Central (Iowa) (8-0-0)	Ron Schipper	1-1 Lost in quarterfinals
1990	**East Region**		
	Hofstra (9-0-0)	Joe Gardi	2-1 Lost in semifinals
	North Region		
	Dayton (9-0-0)	Mike Kelly	1-1 Lost in quarterfinals
	South Region		
	Ferrum (8-0-0)	Hank Norton	0-1 Lost in first round
	West Region		
	Wis.-Whitewater (9-0-0)	Bob Berezowitz	0-1 Lost in first round
1991	**East Region**		
	Ithaca (7-1-0)	Jim Butterfield	4-0 Champion
	North Region		
	Allegheny (10-0-0)	Ken O'Keefe	1-1 Lost in quarterfinals
	South Region		
	Lycoming (8-0-0)	Frank Girardi	1-1 Lost in quarterfinals
	West Region		
	St. John's (Minn.) (9-0-0)	John Gagliardi	2-1 Lost in semifinals
1992	**East Region**		
	Rowan (9-0-0)	John Bunting	2-1 Lost in semifinals
	North Region		
	Dayton (9-0-0)	Mike Kelly	0-1 Lost in first round
	South Region		
	Wash. & Jeff. (8-0-0)	John Luckhardt	3-1 Runner-up
	West Region		
	Central (Iowa) (9-0-0)	Ron Schipper	1-1 Lost in quarterfinals
1993	**East Region**		
	Rowan (7-1-0)	K. C. Keeler	3-1 Runner-up
	North Region		
	Mount Union (9-0-0)	Larry Kehres	4-0 Champion
	South Region		
	Wash. & Jeff. (8-0-0)	John Luckhardt	2-1 Lost in semifinals
	West Region		
	Wis.-La Crosse (9-0-0)	Roger Harring	1-1 Lost in quarterfinals
1994	**East Region**		
	Plymouth St. (8-0-0)	Don Brown	1-1 Lost in quarterfinals
	North Region		
	Allegheny (9-0-0)	Ken O'Keefe	0-1 Lost in first round
	South Region		
	Dickinson (9-0-0)	Darwin Breaux	0-1 Lost in first round
	West Region		
	Central (Iowa) (9-0-0)	Ron Schipper	0-1 Lost in first round
1995	**East Region**		
	Buffalo St. (8-1-0)	Jerry Boyes	0-1 Lost in first round
	North Region		
	Mount Union (9-0-0)	Larry Kehres	2-1 Lost in semifinals
	South Region		
	Wash. & Jeff. (7-0-0)	John Luckhardt	2-1 Lost in semifinals
	West Region		
	Wis.-La Crosse (9-0-0)	Roger Harring	4-0 Champion

**Final poll record.* †*Number of teams in the championship: 8 (1975-84); 16 (1985-present).*

Undefeated, Untied Teams

(Regular-Season Games Only)

Following is a list of undefeated and untied teams since 1973, when College Division teams were divided into Division II and Division III under a three-division reorganization plan adopted by the special NCAA Convention in August 1973. Since 1981, conference playoff games have been included in a team's won-lost record (previously, such games were considered postseason contests). Figures indicate the regular-season wins (minimum seven games against four-year varsity opponents). A subsequent postseason win(s) in the Division III championship or a conference playoff game (before 1981) is indicated by (*), a loss by (†) and a tie by (‡).

Year	College	Wins
1973	Fisk	9
	Wittenberg	***9
1974	Albany (N.Y.)	9
	Central (Iowa)	**9
	Frank. & Marsh.	9
	Ithaca	*†9
	Towson St.	10
1975	Cal Lutheran	*†9
	Ithaca	**†8
	Widener	*†9
	Wittenberg	†***9
1976	Albion	9
1977	Central (Iowa)	†9
	Cornell College	†8
	Wittenberg	†9
1978	Baldwin-Wallace	‡***8
	Illinois Col.	9
	Minn.-Morris	*†10
	Wittenberg	‡**†8
1979	Carnegie Mellon	*†9
	Dubuque	†9
	Jamestown	7
	Tufts	8
	Widener	*†9
	Wittenberg	***†8
1980	Adrian	9
	Baldwin-Wallace	†9
	Bethany (W.Va.)	†9
	Dayton	***11
	Ithaca	**†10
	Millsaps	9
	Widener	*†10
1981	Alfred	†10
	Augustana (Ill.)	†9
	Lawrence	*†9
	West Ga.	†9
	Widener	***10
1982	Augustana (Ill.)	**†9
	Baldwin-Wallace	†10
	Plymouth St.	10
	St. John's (Minn.)	9
	St. Lawrence	*†9
	Wabash	10
	West Ga.	***9
1983	Augustana (Ill.)	***9
	Carnegie Mellon	†9
	Hofstra	†10
	Worcester Tech	8
1984	Amherst	8
	Augustana (Ill.)	***9
	Case Reserve	9
	Central (Iowa)	**†9
	Dayton	†10
	Hope	9
	Occidental	†10
	Plymouth St.	†10
1985	Augustana (Ill.)	****9
	Carnegie Mellon	†8
	Central (Iowa)	**†9
	Denison	†10
	Lycoming	†10
	Mount Union	*†10
	Union (N.Y.)	†9
1986	Central (Iowa)	*†10
	Dayton	†10
	Ithaca	**†9
	Mount Union	*†10
	Salisbury St.	***†10
	Susquehanna	*†10
	Union (N.Y.)	†9
1987	Augustana (Ill.)	*†9
	Gust. Adolphus	†10
	Wash. & Jeff.	*†9
1988	Cortland St.	*†10
	Ferrum	**†9
1989	Central (Iowa)	*†9
	Millikin	*†9
	Union (N.Y.)	***†10
	Williams	8
1990	Carnegie Mellon	†10
	Dayton	*†10
	Hofstra	**†10
	Lycoming	***†9
	Mount Union	†10
	Wash. & Jeff.	*†9
	Williams	8
	Wis.-Whitewater	†10
1991	Allegheny	*†10
	Baldwin-Wallace	†10
	Dayton	***†10
	Dickinson	†10
	Eureka	10
	Lycoming	*†9
	Mass.-Lowell	†10
	St. John's (Minn.)	**†9
	Simpson	†10
	Thomas More	10
	Union (N.Y.)	*†9
1992	Aurora	†9
	Central (Iowa)	*†9
	Cornell College	10
	Dayton	†10
	Emory & Henry	*†10
	Ill. Wesleyan	*†9
	Mount Union	**†10
	Rowan	**†10
1993	Albion	*†9
	Anderson (Ind.)	†10
	Coe	†10
	Mount Union	****10
	St. John's (Minn.)	**†10
	Trinity (Conn.)	8
	Union (N.Y.)	†9
	Wash. & Jeff.	**†9
	Wilkes	†10
	Wis.-La Crosse	*†10
1994	Albion	****9
	Allegheny	†10
	Central (Iowa)	†10
	Dickinson	†10
	La Verne	†9
	Plymouth St.	*†9
	Trinity (Tex.)	†10
	Williams	8
1995	Central (Iowa)	†10
	Hanover	†10
	La Verne	9
	Mount Union	**†10
	Plymouth St.	†9
	Thomas More	10
	Wash. & Jeff.	**†8
	Wheaton (Ill.)	*†9
	Wis.-La Crosse	****10
	Wittenberg	†10

The Spoilers

(Since 1973, when the three-division reorganization plan was adopted by the special NCAA Convention, creating Divisions II and III.)

Following is a list of the spoilers of Division III teams that lost their perfect (undefeated, untied) record in their **season-ending** game, including the Division III championship playoffs. An asterisk (*) indicates a Division III championship playoff game and a dagger (†) indicates the home team in a regular-season game or a conference playoff. A game involving two undefeated, untied teams is in bold face.

Date	Spoiler	Victim	Score
11-17-73	†Williams	Amherst	30-14
12-7-74	*Central (Iowa)	Ithaca	10-8
11-8-75	Cornell College	†Lawrence	17-16
11-22-75	***Ithaca**	**Widener**	23-14
12-6-75	*Wittenberg	Ithaca	28-0
11-12-77	Norwich	†Middlebury	34-20
11-12-77	Ripon	†Cornell College	10-7
11-19-77	†Baldwin-Wallace	Wittenberg	14-7
11-19-77	*Widener	Central (Iowa)	19-0
11-25-78	*Wittenberg	Minn.-Morris	35-14
11-17-79	*Ithaca	Dubuque	27-7
11-17-79	‡Findlay	Jamestown	41-15
11-24-79	***Wittenberg**	**Widener**	17-14
11-24-79	*Ithaca	Carnegie Mellon	15-6
12-1-79	*Ithaca	Wittenberg	14-10
11-8-80	DePauw	†Wabash	tie 22-22
11-22-80	***Widener**	**Bethany (W.Va.)**	43-12
11-22-80	*Dayton	Baldwin-Wallace	34-0
11-29-80	*Dayton	Widener	28-24
12-6-80	#*Dayton	Ithaca	63-0
11-14-81	†DePauw	Wabash	21-14
11-14-81	†St. Mary's (Cal.)	San Diego	31-14
11-21-81	*Widener	West Ga.	10-3
11-21-81	*Dayton	Augustana (Ill.)	19-7
11-21-81	*Montclair St.	Alfred	13-12
11-28-81	*Dayton	Lawrence	38-0
11-13-82	†Widener	Swarthmore	24-7
11-20-82	‡Northwestern (Iowa)	St. John's (Minn.)	33-28
11-20-82	***Augustana (Ill.)**	**Baldwin-Wallace**	28-22
11-27-82	***Augustana (Ill.)**	**St. Lawrence**	14-0
12-4-82	***West Ga.**	**Augustana (Ill.)**	14-0
11-19-83	*Salisbury St.	Carnegie Mellon	16-14
11-19-83	*Union (N.Y.)	Hofstra	51-19
11-10-84	St. John's (N.Y.)	†Hofstra	19-16
11-10-84	†St. Olaf	Hamline	tie 7-7
11-17-84	*Union (N.Y.)	Plymouth St.	26-14
11-17-84	*Central (Iowa)	Occidental	23-22
11-17-84	*Augustana (Ill.)	Dayton	14-13
12-8-84	***Augustana (Ill.)**	**Central (Iowa)**	21-12
11-23-85	*Gettysburg	Lycoming	14-10
11-23-85	***Mount Union**	**Denison**	35-3
11-23-85	*Salisbury St.	Carnegie Mellon	35-22
11-23-85	*Ithaca	Union (N.Y.)	13-12
11-30-85	***Augustana (Ill.)**	**Mount Union**	21-14
12-7-85	***Augustana (Ill.)**	**Central (Iowa)**	14-7

Date	Spoiler	Victim	Score
11-15-86	†Lawrence	Coe	14-10
11-22-86	***Mount Union**	**Dayton**	42-36
11-22-86	***Ithaca**	**Union (N.Y.)**	OT 24-17
11-29-86	*Concordia-M'head	Central (Iowa)	17-14
11-29-86	***Salisbury St.**	**Susquehanna**	31-17
11-29-86	***Augustana (Ill.)**	**Mount Union**	16-7
12-6-86	***Salisbury St.**	**Ithaca**	44-40
12-13-86	***Augustana (Ill.)**	**Salisbury St.**	31-3
11-11-87	St. Norbert	†Monmouth (Ill.)	20-15
11-21-87	*St. John's (Minn.)	Gust. Adolphus	7-3
11-28-87	*Emory & Henry	Wash. & Jeff.	23-16
11-28-87	$*Dayton	Augustana (Ill.)	38-36
11-12-88	†St. Norbert	Monmouth (Ill.)	12-0
11-19-88	Coast Guard	†Plymouth St.	28-19
11-26-88	*Ithaca	Cortland St.	24-17
12-3-88	*Ithaca	Ferrum	62-28
11-11-89	†Baldwin-Wallace	John Carroll	25-19
11-11-89	**†Bri'water (Mass.)**	**Mass.-Lowell**	14-10
11-11-89	†Centre	Rhodes	13-10
11-18-89	†Alfred	Bri'water (Mass.)	30-27
11-25-89	*St. John's (Minn.)	Central (Iowa)	27-24
11-25-89	*Dayton	Millikin	28-16
12-9-89	*Dayton	Union (N.Y.)	17-7
11-10-90	Trenton St.	†Ramapo	9-0
11-10-90	†Waynesburg	Frostburg St.	28-18
11-17-90	*Allegheny	Mount Union	26-15
11-17-90	***Lycoming**	**Carnegie Mellon**	17-7
11-17-90	*St. Thomas (Minn.)	Wis.-Whitewater	24-23
11-24-90	*Allegheny	Dayton	31-23
11-24-90	***Lycoming**	**Wash. & Jeff.**	24-0
12-1-90	***Lycoming**	**Hofstra**	20-10
12-8-90	*Allegheny	Lycoming	OT 21-14
11-9-91	†Coe	Beloit	26-10
11-23-91	***Union (N.Y.)**	**Mass.-Lowell**	55-16
11-23-91	***Dayton**	**Baldwin-Wallace**	27-10
11-30-91	***Dayton**	**Allegheny**	OT 28-25
11-30-91	*Ithaca	Union (N.Y.)	35-23
11-30-91	*Susquehanna	Lycoming	31-24
12-7-91	***Dayton**	**St. John's (Minn.)**	19-7
12-14-91	*Ithaca	Dayton	34-20
11-7-92	Cornell College	†Coe	37-20
11-7-92	Union (N.Y.)	†Rochester	14-10
11-21-92	***Ill. Wesleyan**	**Aurora**	21-12
11-21-92	***Mount Union**	**Dayton**	27-10
11-28-92	***Mount Union**	**Ill. Wesleyan**	49-27
11-28-92	*Wash. & Jeff.	Emory & Henry	51-15
11-28-92	*Wis.-La Crosse	Central (Iowa)	34-9
12-5-92	*Wash. & Jeff.	Rowan	18-13
12-5-92	*Wis.-La Crosse	Mount Union	29-24
10-30-93	Mount Senario	†Martin Luther	21-20
11-13-93	Hastings	†Colorado Col.	22-21
11-20-93	***Albion**	**Anderson (Ind.)**	41-21
11-20-93	***St. John's (Minn.)**	**Coe**	32-14
11-20-93	*Frostburg St.	Wilkes	26-25
11-20-93	*Wm. Paterson	Union (N.Y.)	17-7
11-27-93	***Mount Union**	**Albion**	30-16
11-27-93	***St. John's (Minn.)**	**Wis.-La Crosse**	47-25
12-5-93	***Mount Union**	**St. John's (Minn.)**	56-8
12-5-93	*Rowan	Wash. & Jeff.	23-16
11-12-94	John Carroll	†Baldwin-Wallace	9-0
11-19-94	*Mount Union	Allegheny	28-19
11-19-94	*Wartburg	Central (Iowa)	22-21
11-19-94	*St. John's (Minn.)	La Verne	51-12
11-19-94	*Widener	Dickinson	14-0
11-19-94	*Wash. & Jeff.	Trinity (Tex.)	28-0
11-26-94	*Ithaca	Plymouth St.	22-7
11-11-95	Amherst	†Williams	0-0
11-18-95	***Mount Union**	**Hanover**	52-18
11-18-95	***Wheaton (Ill.)**	**Wittenberg**	63-41
11-18-95	*Wis.-River Falls	Central (Iowa)	10-7
11-18-95	*Union (N.Y.)	Plymouth St.	24-7
11-25-95	***Mount Union**	**Wheaton (Ill.)**	40-14
12-2-95	***Wis.-La Crosse**	**Mount Union**	20-17
12-2-95	*Rowan	Wash. & Jeff.	28-15

‡NAIA championship playoff game. #Defeated three consecutive perfect-record teams in the Division III championship playoffs. $Ended Augustana's (Illinois) 60-game undefeated streak.

Streaks and Rivalries

Longest Winning Streaks

(Minimum Two Seasons in Division III; Includes Postseason Games)

Wins	Team	Years
37	Augustana (Ill.)	1983-85
24	Allegheny	1990-91
23	Williams	1988-91
22	Dayton	1989-90
22	Augustana (Ill.)	1986-87
21	Dayton	1979-81
20	Plymouth St.	1987-88
19	Mount Union	1993-94
19	Wis.-La Crosse	1992-93
19	Plymouth St.	1981-82
18	Lawrence	1980-81
18	Ithaca	1979-80

Longest Unbeaten Streaks

(Minimum Two Seasons in Division III; Includes Postseason Games)

No.	Wins	Ties	Team	Years
60	59	1	Augustana (Ill.)	1983-87
25	24	1	Dayton	1989-90
24	24	0	Allegheny	1990-91
24	23	1	Wis.-La Crosse	1992-93
24	23	1	Wabash	1979-81
23	23	0	Williams	1988-91
22	21	1	Dayton	1979-81
21	20	1	Baldwin-Wallace	1977-79
20	20	0	Plymouth St.	1987-88
20	18	2	St. John's (Minn.)	1975-76

Longest Division III Series

Games	Opponents (Series leader listed first)	Series Record	First Game
110	Williams-Amherst	60-45-5	1884
109	Albion-Kalamazoo	71-34-4	1896
107	Bowdoin-Colby	60-38-9	1892
106	Monmouth (Ill.)-Knox	49-47-10	1891
105	Coe-Cornell College	56-45-4	1891
102	Wabash-DePauw	47-46-9	1890
101	Amherst-Wesleyan (Conn.)	52-40-9	1882
101	Williams-Wesleyan (Conn.)	61-35-5	1881
101	Hampden-Sydney—Randolph-Macon	51-39-11	1893
98	Colby-Bates	53-37-8	1893
97	Occidental—Pomona-Pitzer	52-42-3	1895
96*	Union (N.Y.)-Hamilton	46-38-12	1890

**Did not play in 1994-95.*

Cliffhangers

Regular-season Division III games won on the final play of the game in regulation time (from 1973). The extra point is listed when it provided the margin of victory after the winning touchdown.

Date	Opponents, Score	Game-Winning Play
9-22-73	Hofstra 21, Seton Hall 20	Tom Calder 15 pass from Steve Zimmer (Jim Hogan kick)
9-18-76	Ohio Wesleyan 23, DePauw 20	Tom Scurfield 48 pass from Bob Mauck
10-27-77	Albany (N.Y.) 42, Maine 39	Larry Leibowitz 19 FG
9-22-79	Augustana (Ill.) 19, Carthage 18	John Stockton 14 pass from Mark Schick
10-6-79	Carleton 17, Lake Forest 14	Tim Schoonmaker 46 FG
11-10-79	Dayton 24, St. Norbert 22	Jim Fullenkamp 21 FG
9-13-80	Cornell College 14, Lawrence 13	John Bryant 8 pass from Matt Dillon (Keith Koehler kick)
9-27-80	Muhlenberg 41, Johns Hopkins 38	Mickey Mottola 1 run
10-25-80	Mass.-Lowell 15, Marist 13	Ed Kulis 3 run
10-17-81	Carleton 22, Ripon 21	John Winter 23 pass from Billy Ford (Dave Grein kick)
10-2-82	Frostburg St. 10, Mercyhurst 7	Mike Lippold 34 FG
11-6-82	Williams 27, Wesleyan (Conn.) 24	Marc Hummon 33 pass from Robert Connolly
10-7-83	Johns Hopkins 19, Ursinus 17	John Tucker 10 pass from Mark Campbell
10-8-83	Susquehanna 17, Widener 14	Todd McCarthy 20 FG
10-29-83	Frank. & Marsh. 16, Swarthmore 15	Billy McLean 51 pass from Niall Rosenzweig
9-24-84	Muhlenberg 3, Frank. & Marsh. 0	Tom Mulroy 26 FG
10-26-85	Buffalo 13, Brockport St. 11	Dan Friedman 37 FG
11-9-85	Frank. & Marsh. 29, Johns Hopkins 28	Brad Ramsey 1 run (Ken Scalet pass from John Travagline)
9-18-86	Beloit 16, Lakeland 13	Sean Saturnio 38 pass from Ed Limon
9-20-86	Susquehanna 43, Lycoming 42	Rob Sochovka 40 pass from Todd Coolidge (Randy Pozsar kick)
10-18-86	Ill. Wesleyan 25, Elmhurst 23	Dave Anderson 11 pass from Doug Moews
9-5-87	Wash. & Jeff. 17, Ohio Wesleyan 16	John Ivory 28 FG
9-26-87	Gust. Adolphus 19, Macalester 17	Dave Fuecker 8 pass from Dean Kraus
10-3-87	Wis.-Whitewater 10, Wis.-Platteville 7	Dave Emond 25 FG
10-24-87	Geneva 9, St. Francis (Pa.) 7	John Moores 19 FG
10-1-88	Canisius 17, Rochester 14	Jim Ehrig 34 FG
10-1-88	Cortland St. 24, Western Conn. St. 21	Ted Nagengast 35 FG
10-8-88	UC Santa Barb. 20, Sonoma St. 18	Harry Konstantinopoulos 52 FG
10-8-88	Hamilton 13, Bowdoin 10	Nate O'Steen 19 FG
11-5-88	Colby 20, Middlebury 18	Eric Aulenback 1 run
11-12-88	Wis.-River Falls 24, Wis.-Stout 23	Andy Feil 45 FG
10-7-89	Moravian 13, Juniata 10	Mike Howey 75 pass from Rob Light
10-21-89	Western New Eng. 17, Bentley 14	Leo Coughlin 17 FG
10-21-89	Thiel 19, Carnegie Mellon 14	Bill Barber 4 pass from Jeff Sorenson
9-8-90	Emory & Henry 22, Wash. & Lee 21	Todd Woodall 26 pass from Pat Walker
9-15-90	Otterbein 20, Capital 17	Korey Brown 39 FG
10-27-90	Hamline 26, Gust. Adolphus 24	Mike Sunnarborg 2 pass from Bob Hackney
11-10-90	Colby 23, Bowdoin 20	Paul Baisley 10 pass from Bob Ward
9-7-91	Central (Iowa) 26, Gust. Adolphus 25	Brian Krob 1 pass from Shad Flynn
9-13-91	St. John's (N.Y.) 30, Iona 27	John Ledwith 42 FG
10-5-91	Trinity (Conn.) 30, Williams 27	John Mullaney 5 pass from James Lane
10-26-91	DePauw 12, Anderson (Ind.) 7	Steve Broderick 65 pass from Brian Goodman
9-19-92	Lake Forest 9, North Park 7	Dave Mills 2 pass from Jim DeLisa
10-17-92	Elmhurst 30, North Central 28	Eric Ekstrom 2 pass from Jack Lamb
10-16-93	Union (N.Y.) 16, Rensselaer 13	Greg Harrison 38 FG
10-16-93	North Central 24, Elmhurst 22	Bryce Cann 35 FG
10-23-93	Stony Brook 21, Merchant Marine 20	Brian Hughes 44 FG
10-30-93	Thomas More 24, Defiance 18	Greg Stofko 6 blocked field goal return
9-10-94	Colorado Col. 16, Buena Vista 14	Josh Vitt 4 run
9-8-95	FDU-Madison 20, Johns Hopkins 17	Jason Herrick 37 FG

Photo from Fairleigh Dickinson-Madison sports information

Jason Herrick kicked a 37-yard field goal on the game's final play to lift Fairleigh Dickinson-Madison to a 20-17 victory over Johns Hopkins on September 8, 1995.

Regular-Season Overtime Games

In 1981, the NCAA Football Rules Committee approved an overtime tiebreaker system to decide a tie game for the purpose of determining a conference champion. The following conferences used the tiebreaker system to decide conference-only tie games. (In 1996, the tiebreaker will be mandatory in all games tied after four periods.) The number of overtimes is indicated in parentheses.

EASTERN COLLEGIATE FOOTBALL CONFERENCE

Date	Opponents, Score
10-28-95	Western New Eng. 6, Nichols 0 (4 OT)

IOWA INTERCOLLEGIATE ATHLETIC CONFERENCE

Date	Opponents, Score
9-26-81	William Penn 24, Wartburg 21 (1 OT)
9-25-82	Dubuque 16, Buena Vista 13 (1 OT)
10-2-82	Luther 25, Dubuque 22 (1 OT)
10-30-82	Wartburg 27, Dubuque 24 (3 OT)
10-4-86	Luther 28, Wartburg 21 (1 OT)
9-26-87	William Penn 19, Upper Iowa 13 (2 OT)
11-7-87	William Penn 17, Loras 10 (1 OT)
10-10-92	Simpson 20, Loras 14 (1 OT)
11-14-92	Luther 17, Buena Vista 10 (1 OT)

MIDWEST CONFERENCE

Date	Opponents, Score
10-25-86	Lake Forest 30, Chicago 23 (1 OT)
10-26-86	Lawrence 7, Beloit 0 (1 OT)
9-30-89	Illinois Col. 26, Ripon 20 (3 OT)
10-27-90	Beloit 16, St. Norbert 10 (1 OT)
11-2-91	Monmouth (Ill.) 13, Knox 7 (1 OT)
10-14-95	Beloit 20, Carroll (Wis.) 14 (1 OT)

NEW ENGLAND FOOTBALL CONFERENCE
(From 1987)

Date	Opponents, Score
10-31-87	Nichols 21, Mass.-Lowell 20 (1 OT)
9-17-88	Mass.-Lowell 22, Worcester St. 19 (2 OT)
9-30-89	Worcester St. 23, Mass.-Dartmouth 20 (1 OT)
10-27-89	Westfield St. 3, Mass.-Dartmouth 0 (3 OT)
10-28-89	Worcester St. 27, Nichols 20 (1 OT)
11-7-92	Mass.-Dartmouth 21, Westfield St. 14 (3 OT)
9-25-93	Mass. Maritime 28, Mass.-Dartmouth 21 (1 OT)
11-5-94	Mass.-Dartmouth 21, Westfield St. 14 (1 OT)

SOUTHERN CALIFORNIA INTERCOLLEGIATE ATHLETIC CONFERENCE

Date	Opponents, Score
10-18-86	La Verne 53, Occidental 52 (1 OT)
9-26-87	Claremont-M-S 33, Occidental 30 (1 OT)
10-27-90	Occidental 47, Claremont-M-S 41 (1 OT)
10-17-92	Cal Lutheran 17, Occidental 14 (1 OT)
10-30-93	Redlands 23, Cal Lutheran 17 (2 OT)

Division III Stadiums

STADIUMS LISTED ALPHABETICALLY

School	Stadium	Year Built	Capacity	Surface
Adrian	Maple	1960	5,000	Grass
Albion	Sprankle-Sprandel	1976	5,010	Grass
Albright	Eugene L. Shirk	1925	7,000	Grass
Alfred	Merrill Field	1926	5,000	OmniTurf
Allegheny	Robertson Field	1948	5,000	Grass
Alma	Bahlke Field	1986	4,000	Turf
Amherst	Pratt Field	1891	8,000	Grass
Anderson (Ind.)	Macholtz	NA	4,200	Grass
Augsburg	Anderson-Nelson Field	1984	2,000	AstroTurf
Augustana (Ill.)	Ericson Field	1938	3,200	Grass
Aurora	Aurora Field	NA	1,500	Grass
Baldwin-Wallace	George Finnie	1971	8,100	StadiaTurf
Bates	Garcelon Field	1900	3,000	Grass
Beloit	Strong	1934	3,500	Grass
Bethany (W.Va.)	Bethany Field	1938	1,000	Grass
Bethel (Minn.)	Bremer Field	1972	3,000	Grass
Blackburn	Blackburn College	NA	1,500	Grass
Bluffton	Salzman	1993	3,000	Grass
Bowdoin	Whittier Field	NA	9,000	Grass
Bri'water (Mass.)	College	1974	3,000	Grass
Bridgewater (Va.)	Jopson Field	1971	3,000	Grass
Brockport St.	Special Olympics	1979	10,000	Grass
Buena Vista	J. Leslie Rollins	1980	3,500	Grass
Buffalo St.	Coyer Field	NA	3,000	Grass
Cal Lutheran	Mt. Clef	1962	2,000	Grass
Capital	Bernlohr	1928	2,000	Grass
Carleton	Laird	1926	7,500	Grass
Carnegie Mellon	Gesling	1990	3,500	Omni-Turf
Carroll (Wis.)	Van Male Field	1976	4,200	Grass
Carthage	Art Keller Field	1965	3,100	Grass
Case Reserve	E. L. Finningan Field	1968	3,000	Grass
Catholic	Cardinal Field	1985	3,500	Grass
Central (Iowa)	A. N. Kuyper	1977	5,000	Grass
Centre	Farris	1925	2,500	Grass
Chapman	Chapman	NA	3,000	Grass
Chicago	Stagg Field	1969	1,500	Grass
Claremont-M-S	Zinda Field	1955	3,000	Grass
Coast Guard	Cadet Memorial Field	1932	4,500	Grass
Coe	Clark Field	1989	1,100	Grass
Colby	Seaverns	1948	5,000	Grass
Colorado Col.	Washburn Field	1898	2,000	Grass
Concordia (Ill.)	Concordia	NA	1,500	Grass
Concordia-M'head	Jake Christiansen	NA	7,500	Grass
Cornell College	Ash Park Field	1922	2,500	Grass
Cortland St.	Davis Field	1959	5,000	Grass
Curry	D. Forbes Will Field	NA	1,500	Grass
Defiance	Justin F. Coressel	1994	4,000	Grass
Delaware Valley	James Work Memorial	1978	4,500	Grass
Denison	Deeds Field	1922	5,000	Grass
DePauw	Blackstock	1941	4,000	Grass
Dickinson	Biddle Field	1909	2,577	Grass
Dubuque	Chalmers Field	1942	2,800	PAT
Earlham	M. O. Ross Field	1975	1,500	Grass
Elmhurst	Langhorst Field	1920	2,500	Grass
Emory & Henry	Fullerton Field	NA	5,000	Grass
Eureka	McKinzie	1913	3,000	Grass
FDU-Madison	Jersey Devils	1973	4,000	Grass
Ferrum	W. B. Adams	1970	5,500	Grass
Fitchburg St.	Robert Elliot	1984	1,200	Grass
Framingham St.	Maple Street Field	NA	1,500	Grass
Franklin	Goodell Field	1889	2,000	Grass
Frank. & Marsh.	Sponaugle-Williamson Field	1920	4,000	Grass
Frostburg St.	Bobcat	1974	4,000	Grass
Gettysburg	Musselman	1965	6,176	Grass
Grinnell	Rosenbloom Field	1911	1,750	Grass
Grove City	Thorn Field	1981	3,500	Grass
Guilford	Armfield Athletic Center	1960	3,500	Grass
Gust. Adolphus	Hollingsworth Field	1929	5,500	Grass
Hamilton	Steuben Field	NA	2,500	Grass
Hamline	Norton	1921	2,000	Grass
Hampden-Sydney	Hundley	1964	2,400	Grass
Hanover	L. S. Ayers Field	1973	4,000	Grass
Hardin-Simmons	Shelton	1993	4,000	Grass
Hartwick	AstroTurf Field	1985	1,200	AstroTurf
Heidelberg	Columbian	1941	7,500	Grass
Hiram	Charles Henry Field	1958	3,000	Grass
Hobart	Boswell Field	1975	4,500	Grass
Hope	Holland Municipal	1979	5,322	Grass
Howard Payne	Gordon Wood	NA	7,600	Grass
Ill. Benedictine	Alumni	1951	3,000	Grass
Illinois Col.	England Field	1960	2,500	Grass
Ill. Wesleyan	Ill. Wesleyan	1893	3,500	Grass
Ithaca	Jim Butterfield	1958	5,000	Grass
Jersey City St.	Tidelands Ath. Complex	1986	2,500	Grass
John Carroll	Wasmer Field	1968	3,500	Turf
Johns Hopkins	Homewood Field	1906	4,000	Turf
Juniata	Chuck Knox	1988	3,000	Grass
Kalamazoo	Angell Field	1946	3,000	Grass
Kean	Zweidinger Field	NA	2,200	Grass
Kenyon	McBride Field	1962	2,500	Grass
King's (Pa.)	Monarch Field	NA	3,000	Grass
Knox	Knox Bowl	1968	6,000	Grass
La Verne	Ortmayer	1991	1,500	Grass
Lake Forest	Farwell Field	NA	2,000	Grass
Lakeland	John Taylor Field	1958	1,500	Grass
Lawrence	Banta Bowl	1965	5,255	Grass
Lebanon Valley	Arnold Field	1969	2,500	Grass
Loras	Rock Bowl	1945	3,000	Grass
Luther	Carlson	1966	5,000	Grass
Lycoming	Person Field	1962	2,500	Grass
Macalester	Macalester	1965	4,000	Grass
MacMurray	MacMurray Field	1984	5,000	Grass
Maine Maritime	Ritchie	1965	3,500	Turf
Manchester	Burt Memorial	NA	4,500	Grass
Marietta	Don Drumm Field	1935	7,000	Grass
Martin Luther	Northwestern	1953	2,000	Grass
Maryville (Tenn.)	Thornton-Honaker Field	1951	2,500	Grass
Mass.-Boston	Clark Ath. Center	1981	750	Grass
Mass.-Dartmouth	University	NA	1,850	Grass
MIT	Henry G. Steinbrenner	1980	1,600	Grass
Mass. Maritime	Edward Ellis Field	1972	3,000	Grass
Menlo	Conner Field	1972	1,000	Grass
Merchant Marine	Captain Tomb Field	1945	5,840	Grass
Methodist	Monarch Field	1989	1,500	Grass
Middlebury	Alumni	1991	3,500	Grass
Millikin	Frank M. Lindsay Field	1987	4,000	Grass
Millsaps	Alumni Field	NA	4,000	Grass
Monmouth (Ill.)	Bobby Woll Field	1981	3,000	Grass
Montclair St.	Sprague Field	1934	6,000	AstroTurf
Moravian	Steel Field	1932	2,200	Grass
Mount Union	Mount Union	1915	5,800	Grass
Muhlenberg	Muhlenberg Field	1928	4,000	Grass
Muskingum	McConagha	1925	5,000	Grass
Neb. Wesleyan	Abel	1986	2,000	Grass
Nichols	Bison Bowl	1961	3,000	Grass
North Central	Kroehler Field	NA	3,000	Grass
North Park	Hedstrand Field	1955	2,500	Grass
Norwich	Sabine Field	1921	5,000	Grass
Oberlin	Dill Field	1925	3,500	Grass
Occidental	Patterson Field	1900	4,000	Grass
Ohio Northern	Ada Memorial	1948	4,000	Grass
Ohio Wesleyan	Selby	1929	9,600	Grass
Olivet	Griswold Field	1972	3,500	Grass
Otterbein	Memorial	1946	4,000	Grass
Plymouth St.	Currier Memorial Field	1970	1,000	Grass
Pomona-Pitzer	Merritt Field	1991	2,000	Grass
Principia	Clark Field	1937	1,000	Grass
Randolph-Macon	Day Field	1953	5,000	Grass
Redlands	Ted Runner	1968	7,000	Grass
Rensselaer	86 Field	1912	3,000	Grass
Rhodes	Fargason Field	NA	5,000	Grass
Ripon	Ingalls Field	1888	2,500	Grass
Rochester	Edwin Fauver	1930	5,000	All-Pro Turf
Rose-Hulman	Phil Brown Field	NA	2,500	Grass
Rowan	John Page	1969	5,000	Grass
St. John Fisher	Cardinal Field	NA	1,000	Grass
St. John's (Minn.)	St. John's	1908	5,000	Grass

School	Stadium	Year Built	Capacity	Surface
St. Lawrence	Weeks Field	1906	3,000	Grass
St. Norbert	Minahan	1937	3,100	Grass
St. Olaf	Manitou Field	1930	5,000	Grass
St. Thomas (Minn.)	O'Shaughnessy	1948	5,025	Grass
Salisbury St.	Sea Gull	1980	2,500	Grass
Salve Regina	Toppa	NA	2,500	Grass
Sewanee	McGee Field	1935	1,500	Grass
Simpson	Simpson/Indianola Field	1990	5,000	Grass
Springfield	Benedum Field	1971	2,500	All-Pro Plus
Susquehanna	Amos Alonzo Stagg Field	1892	4,600	Grass
Swarthmore	Clothier	1950	2,000	Grass
Thiel	Stewart Field	1954	5,000	Grass
Thomas More	Lockland	1945	6,500	Grass
Trenton St.	Lions	1984	5,000	AstroTurf
Trinity (Conn.)	Dan Jessee Field	1900	6,500	Grass
Trinity (Tex.)	E. M. Stevens	1972	3,500	Grass
Tufts	Ellis Oval	1923	6,000	Grass
Union (N.Y.)	Frank Bailey Field	1981	2,000	AstroTurf
Upper Iowa	Eischeid	1993	3,500	Grass
Ursinus	Patterson Field	1923	2,500	Grass
Wabash	Little Giant	1967	4,200	Grass
Wartburg	Schield	1956	2,500	Grass
Washington (Mo.)	Francis Field	1904	4,000	Grass
Wash. & Jeff.	College Field	1958	5,000	Grass
Wash. & Lee	Wilson Field	1930	7,000	Grass
Waynesburg	College Field	1904	1,300	Grass
Wesley	Wolverine	1989	2,000	Grass
Wesleyan (Conn.)	Andrus Field	1881	8,000	Grass
Western Conn. St.	Midtown Campus Field	NA	2,500	Turf
Western Md.	Scott S. Bair	1981	4,000	Grass
Western New Eng.	WNEC	NA	1,500	Grass
Westfield St.	Alumni Field	1982	4,800	AstroTurf
Wheaton (Ill.)	McCully Field	1956	7,000	Grass
Whittier	Memorial	NA	7,000	Grass
Widener	Leslie C. Quick Jr.	1994	4,000	Grass
Wilkes	Ralston Field	1965	4,000	Grass
Wm. Paterson	Wrightman	NA	2,000	Grass
William Penn	Community	NA	5,000	Grass
Williams	Weston Field	1875	7,500	Grass
Wilmington (Ohio)	Williams	1983	3,250	Grass
Wis.-Eau Claire	Carson Park	NA	6,500	Grass
Wis.-La Crosse	Veterans Memorial	1924	4,349	Grass
Wis.-Oshkosh	Titan	1970	9,680	Grass
Wis.-Platteville	Ralph E. Davis Pioneer	1972	10,000	Grass
Wis.-River Falls	Ramer Field	1966	4,800	Grass
Wis.-Stevens Point	Goerke Field	1932	4,000	Grass
Wis.-Stout	Nelson Field	1936	5,000	Grass
Wis.-Whitewater	Warhawk	1970	11,000	Grass
Wittenberg	Edwards-Maurer	1995	2,400	StadiaTurf
Wooster	John P. Papp	1991	4,500	Grass
Worcester St.	John Coughlin Memorial	1976	2,500	Grass
Worcester Tech	Alumni Field	1916	2,800	Omni-Turf

STADIUMS LISTED BY CAPACITY (Top 35)

School	Stadium	Surface	Capacity
Wis.-Whitewater	Warhawk	Grass	11,000
Brockport St.	Special Olympics	Grass	10,000
Wis.-Platteville	Ralph E. Davis Pioneer	Grass	10,000
Wis.-Oshkosh	Titan	Grass	9,680
Ohio Wesleyan	Selby	Grass	9,600
Bowdoin	Whittier Field	Grass	9,000
Baldwin-Wallace	George Finnie	StadiaTurf	8,100
Amherst	Pratt Field	Grass	8,000
Wesleyan (Conn.)	Andrus Field	Grass	8,000
Howard Payne	Gordon Wood	Grass	7,600
Carleton	Laird	Grass	7,500
Concordia-M'head	Jake Christiansen	Grass	7,500
Heidelberg	Columbian	Grass	7,500
Williams	Weston Field	Grass	7,500
Albright	Eugene L. Shirk	Grass	7,000
Marietta	Don Drumm Field	Grass	7,000
Redlands	Ted Runner	Grass	7,000
Wash. & Lee	Wilson Field	Grass	7,000
Wheaton (Ill.)	McCully Field	Grass	7,000
Whittier	Memorial	Grass	7,000
Thomas More	Lockland	Grass	6,500
Trinity (Conn.)	Dan Jessee Field	Grass	6,500
Wis.-Eau Claire	Carson Park	Grass	6,500
Gettysburg	Musselman	Grass	6,176
Knox	Knox Bowl	Grass	6,000
Montclair St.	Sprague Field	AstroTurf	6,000
Tufts	Ellis Oval	Grass	6,000
Merchant Marine	Captain Tomb Field	Grass	5,840
Mount Union	Mount Union	Grass	5,800
Ferrum	W. B. Adams	Grass	5,500
Gust. Adolphus	Hollingsworth Field	Grass	5,500
Hope	Holland Municipal	Grass	5,322
Lawrence	Banta Bowl	Grass	5,255
St. Thomas (Minn.)	O'Shaughnessy Field	Grass	5,025
Albion	Sprankle-Sprandel	Grass	5,010

PAT=*Prescription Athletic Turf.*

Individual Collegiate Records

Photo from Alcorn State sports information

Alcorn State quarterback Steve McNair was far and away the most prolific offensive player in college football history. His marks for career total yards per game (400.5), season total yards per game (527.2 in 1994) and career total offense (16,823) are all collegiate records that surpass the next-highest figures by at least 10 percent.

Individual Collegiate Records

Individual collegiate records are determined by comparing the best records in all four divisions (I-A, I-AA, II and III) in comparable categories. Included are career records of players who played in two divisions (e.g., Dennis Shaw of San Diego St., Howard Stevens of Randolph-Macon and Louisville, and Tom Ehrhardt of LIU-C.W. Post and Rhode Island). Players who played seasons other than in the NCAA will have statistics only including NCAA seasons.

Total Offense

CAREER YARDS PER GAME
(Minimum 5,500 Yards)

Player, Team (Division[s])	Years	G	Plays	Yards	TDR‡	Yd. PG
Steve McNair, Alcorn St. (I-AA)	1991-94	42	*2,055	*16,823	152	*400.5
Terry Peebles, Hanover (III)	1992-95	23	1,140	7,672	89	333.6
Dave Dickenson, Montana (I-AA)	1992-95	35	1,539	11,523	116	329.2
Willie Totten, Mississippi Val. (I-AA)	1982-85	40	1,812	13,007	*157	325.2
Grady Benton, West Tex. A&M (II)	1994-95	18	844	5,831	55	323.9
Ty Detmer, Brigham Young (I-A)	1988-91	46	1,795	14,665	135	318.8
Neil Lomax, Portland St. (II; I-AA)	1977; 78-80	42	1,901	13,345	120	317.7
Kirk Baumgartner, Wis.-Stevens Point (III)	1986-89	41	2,007	12,767	110	311.4
Mike Perez, San Jose St. (I-A)	1986-87	20	875	6,182	37	309.1
Doug Nussmeier, Idaho (I-AA)	1990-93	39	1,556	12,054	109	309.1
Doug Gaynor, Long Beach St. (I-A)	1984-85	22	1,067	6,710	45	305.0
Tod Mayfield, West Tex. A&M (I-AA; II)	1984-85; 86	24	1,165	7,316	58	304.8
Jamie Martin, Weber St. (I-AA)	1989-92	41	1,838	12,287	93	299.7
Tony Eason, Illinois (I-A)	1981-82	22	1,016	6,589	43	299.5
Scott Otis, Glenville St. (II)	1994-95	20	755	5,911	66	295.6
Tom Proudian, Iona (I-AA)	1993-95	27	1,337	7,939	61	294.0
Robert Dougherty, Boston U. (I-AA)	1993-94	21	918	6,135	56	292.1
Keith Bishop, Ill. Wesleyan/Wheaton (Ill.) (III)	1981, 83-85	31	1,467	9,052	77	292.0
David Klingler, Houston (I-A)	1988-91	32	1,431	9,327	93	291.5
Stan Greene, Boston U. (I-AA)	1989-90	22	1,167	6,408	49	291.3
John Friesz, Idaho (I-AA)	1986-89	35	1,459	10,187	79	291.1
Steve Young, Brigham Young (I-A)	1981-83	31	1,177	8,817	74	284.4
Jayson Merrill, Western St. (II)	1990-91	20	641	5,619	57	281.0
Jordan Poznick, Principia (III)	1990-93	32	1,757	8,983	71	280.7
Jermaine Whitaker, N.M. Highlands (II)	1992-94	31	1,374	8,650	76	279.0
Andre Ware, Houston (I-A)	1987-89	29	1,194	8,058	81	277.9
Chris Petersen, UC Davis (II)	1985-86	20	735	5,532	52	276.6
Tim Von Dulm, Portland St. (II)	1969-70	20	989	5,501	51	275.1
Vernon Buck, Wingate (II)	1991-94	41	1,761	11,227	81	273.8
John Rooney, Ill. Wesleyan (III)	1982-84	27	1,260	7,363	71	272.2
Chris Hatcher, Valdosta St. (II)	1991-94	39	1,557	10,588	120	271.5
Tim Peterson, Wis.-Stout (III)	1986-89	36	1,558	9,701	59	269.5
Doug Flutie, Boston College (I-A)	1981-84	42	1,558	11,317	74	269.5

**Record. ‡Touchdowns-responsible-for are player's TDs scored and passed for.*

SEASON YARDS PER GAME

Player, Team (Division)	Year	G	Plays	Yards	TDR‡	Yd. PG
Steve McNair, Alcorn St. (I-AA)	†1994	11	649	*5,799	53	*527.2
David Klingler, Houston (I-A)	†1990	11	*704	5,221	55	474.6
Willie Totten, Mississippi Val. (I-AA)	†1984	10	564	4,572	*61	457.2
Andre Ware, Houston (I-A)	†1989	11	628	4,661	49	423.7
Ty Detmer, Brigham Young (I-A)	1990	12	635	5,022	45	418.5
Grady Benton, West Tex. A&M (II)	†1994	9	505	3,699	35	411.0
Steve McNair, Alcorn St. (I-AA)	†1992	10	519	4,057	39	405.7
Perry Klein, LIU-C.W. Post (II)	†1993	10	499	4,052	41	405.2
Mike Maxwell, Nevada (I-A)	†1995	9	443	3,623	34	402.6
Terry Peebles, Hanover (III)	†1995	10	572	3,981	43	398.1
Steve Young, Brigham Young (I-A)	†1983	11	531	4,346	41	395.1
Jamie Martin, Weber St. (I-AA)	†1991	11	591	4,337	37	394.3
Chris Vargas, Nevada (I-A)	†1993	11	535	4,332	35	393.8
Marty Washington, West Ala. (II)	1993	8	453	3,146	29	393.8
Scott Mitchell, Utah (I-A)	†1988	11	589	4,299	29	390.8
Jim McMahon, Brigham Young (I-A)	†1980	12	540	4,627	53	385.6
Dave Dickenson, Montana (I-AA)	†1995	11	544	4,209	41	382.6
Neil Lomax, Portland St. (I-AA)	†1980	11	550	4,157	42	377.9
Brett Salisbury, Wayne St. (Neb.) (II)	1993	10	424	3,732	32	373.2
Ty Detmer, Brigham Young (I-A)	1989	12	497	4,433	38	369.4
Troy Kopp, Pacific (Cal.) (I-A)	1990	9	485	3,276	32	364.0
Dave Dickenson, Montana (I-AA)	†1993	11	530	3,978	46	361.6
Neil Lomax, Portland St. (I-AA)	†1979	11	611	3,966	31	360.5
Jed Drenning, Glenville St. (II)	1993	10	473	3,593	32	359.3
Alfred Montez, Western N.M. (II)	1994	6	244	2,130	18	355.0
Keith Bishop, Wheaton (Ill.) (III)	†1983	9	421	3,193	24	354.8
Kirk Baumgartner, Wis.-Stevens Point (III)	†1989	10	530	3,540	39	354.0
Rob Tomlinson, Cal St. Chico (II)	†1989	10	534	3,525	26	352.5
John Furmaniak, Eureka (III)	1995	10	414	3,503	35	350.3
John Friesz, Idaho (I-AA)	†1989	11	464	3,853	31	350.3

Player, Team (Division)	Year	G	Plays	Yards	TDR‡	Yd. PG
Steve McNair, Alcorn St. (I-AA)	1993	11	493	3,830	30	348.2
Todd Hammel, Stephen F. Austin (I-AA)	1989	11	487	3,822	38	347.5
Tom Ehrhardt, Rhode Island (I-AA)	†1985	10	529	3,460	35	346.0
Jim McMahon, Brigham Young (I-A)	†1981	10	487	3,458	30	345.8
Ken Hobart, Idaho (I-AA)	†1983	11	578	3,800	37	345.5
Dave Dickenson, Montana (I-AA)	1994	9	431	3,108	27	345.3
Kirk Baumgartner, Wis.-Stevens Point (III)	†1988	11	604	3,790	27	344.5
Terry Peebles, Hanover (III)	†1994	10	520	3,441	42	344.1
Chris Hegg, Truman St. (II)	†1985	11	594	3,782	35	343.8
Jordan Poznick, Principia (III)	†1992	8	519	2,747	25	343.4

**Record. †National total-offense champion. ‡Touchdowns-responsible-for are player's TDs scored and passed for.*

CAREER YARDS

Player, Team (Division[s])	Years	Plays	Yards	Avg.
Steve McNair, Alcorn St. (I-AA)	1991-94	*2,055	*16,823	*8.19
Ty Detmer, Brigham Young (I-A)	1988-91	1,795	14,665	8.17
Neil Lomax, Portland St. (II; I-AA)	1977; 78-80	1,901	13,345	7.02
Willie Totten, Mississippi Val. (I-AA)	1982-85	1,812	13,007	7.18
Kirk Baumgartner, Wis.-Stevens Point (III)	1986-89	2,007	12,767	6.36
Jamie Martin, Weber St. (I-AA)	1989-92	1,838	12,287	6.68
Doug Nussmeier, Idaho (I-AA)	1990-93	1,556	12,054	7.75
Dave Dickenson, Montana (I-AA)	1992-95	1,539	11,523	7.49
Doug Flutie, Boston College (I-A)	1981-84	1,558	11,317	7.26
Vernon Buck, Wingate (II)	1991-94	1,761	11,227	6.38
Ken Hobart, Idaho (I-AA)	1980-83	1,847	11,127	6.02
Bob McLaughlin, Lock Haven (II)	1992-95	2,007	11,041	5.50
Eric Zeier, Georgia (I-A)	1991-94	1,560	10,841	6.95
Alex Van Pelt, Pittsburgh (I-A)	1989-92	1,570	10,814	6.89
Earl Harvey, N.C. Central (II)	1985-88	2,045	10,667	5.22
Stoney Case, New Mexico (I-A)	1991-94	1,673	10,651	6.37
Chris Hatcher, Valdosta St. (II)	1991-94	1,557	10,588	6.80
Jim Ballard, Wilmington (Ohio)/ Mount Union (III)	1990, 91-93	1,328	10,545	7.94
Todd Santos, San Diego St. (I-A)	1984-87	1,722	10,513	6.11
Sean Payton, Eastern Ill. (I-AA)	1983-86	1,690	10,298	6.09
Greg Wyatt, Northern Ariz. (I-AA)	1986-89	1,753	10,277	5.86
Kevin Sweeney, Fresno St. (I-A)	$1982-86	1,700	10,252	6.03
Thad Trujillo, Fort Lewis (II)	1991-94	1,787	10,209	5.71
John Friesz, Idaho (I-AA)	1986-89	1,459	10,187	6.98
Troy Kopp, Pacific (Cal.) (I-A)	1989-92	1,595	10,037	6.29
Rob Tomlinson, Cal St. Chico (II)	1988-91	1,656	9,921	5.99
Michael Proctor, Murray St. (I-AA)	1986-89	1,577	9,886	6.27
Jeff Wiley, Holy Cross (I-AA)	1985-88	1,428	9,877	6.92
Tom Ehrhardt, LIU-C.W. Post (II); Rhode Island (I-AA)	1981-82; 84-85	1,674	9,793	5.85
Brian McClure, Bowling Green (I-A)	1982-85	1,630	9,774	6.00
Jeff Lewis, Northern Ariz. (I-AA)	1992-95	1,654	9,769	5.91
Eric Noble, Wilmington (Ohio) (III)	1992-95	1,513	9,731	6.43
Jim McMahon, Brigham Young (I-A)	1977-78, 80-81	1,325	9,723	7.34
Glenn Foley, Boston College (I-A)	1990-93	1,440	9,702	6.74
Tim Peterson, Wis.-Stout (III)	1986-89	1,558	9,701	6.23
John Craven, Gardner-Webb (II)	1991-94	1,666	9,630	5.78
Chris Ings, Wabash (III)	1992-95	1,532	9,608	6.27
Terrence Jones, Tulane (I-A)	1985-88	1,620	9,445	5.83
David Klingler, Houston (I-A)	1988-91	1,431	9,327	6.52
Shawn Jones, Georgia Tech (I-A)	1989-92	1,609	9,296	5.78
Matt DeGennaro, Connecticut (I-AA)	1987-90	1,619	9,269	5.73
Shane Matthews, Florida (I-A)	1989-92	1,397	9,241	6.61
Sam Mannery, Calif. (Pa.) (II)	1987-90	1,669	9,125	5.47
Spence Fischer, Duke (I-A)	1992-95	1,612	9,110	5.65
T. J. Rubley, Tulsa (I-A)	1987-89, 91	1,541	9,080	5.89
Brad Tayles, Western Mich. (I-A)	1989-92	1,675	9,071	5.42
John Elway, Stanford (I-A)	1979-82	1,505	9,070	6.03
Tom Ciaccio, Holy Cross (I-AA)	1988-91	1,283	9,066	7.07
Erik Wilhelm, Oregon St. (I-A)	1985-88	1,689	9,062	5.37

**Record. $See page 6 for explanation.*

SEASON YARDS

Player, Team (Division)	Year	G	Plays	Yards	Avg.
Steve McNair, Alcorn St. (I-AA)	†1994	11	649	*5,799	@8.94
David Klingler, Houston (I-A)	†1990	11	*704	5,221	7.42
Ty Detmer, Brigham Young (I-A)	1990	12	635	5,022	7.91
Andre Ware, Houston (I-A)	†1989	11	628	4,661	7.42
Jim McMahon, Brigham Young (I-A)	†1980	12	540	4,627	8.57
Willie Totten, Mississippi Val. (I-AA)	†1984	10	564	4,572	8.11
Ty Detmer, Brigham Young (I-A)	1989	12	497	4,433	8.92
Steve Young, Brigham Young (I-A)	†1983	11	531	4,346	8.18
Jamie Martin, Weber St. (I-AA)	†1991	11	591	4,337	7.34
Chris Vargas, Nevada (I-A)	†1993	11	535	4,332	8.10
Scott Mitchell, Utah (I-A)	†1988	11	589	4,299	7.30
Dave Dickenson, Montana (I-AA)	†1995	11	544	4,209	7.74
Neil Lomax, Portland St. (I-AA)	†1980	11	550	4,157	7.56
Robbie Bosco, Brigham Young (I-A)	1985	13	578	4,141	7.16
Steve McNair, Alcorn St. (I-AA)	†1992	10	519	4,057	7.82
Perry Klein, LIU-C.W. Post (II)	†1993	10	499	4,052	8.12
Ty Detmer, Brigham Young (I-A)	†1991	12	478	4,001	8.37
Terry Peebles, Hanover (III)	†1995	10	572	3,981	6.96
Dave Dickenson, Montana (I-AA)	†1993	11	530	3,978	7.51
Neil Lomax, Portland St. (I-AA)	†1979	11	611	3,966	6.49
Robbie Bosco, Brigham Young (I-A)	†1984	12	543	3,932	7.24
Mike McCoy, Utah (I-A)	1993	12	529	3,860	7.50
John Friesz, Idaho (I-AA)	†1989	11	464	3,853	8.30
Steve McNair, Alcorn St. (I-AA)	1993	11	493	3,830	7.77
Todd Hammel, Stephen F. Austin (I-AA)	1989	11	487	3,822	7.85
Ken Hobart, Idaho (I-AA)	1983	11	578	3,800	6.57
Kirk Baumgartner, Wis.-Stevens Point (III)	†1988	11	604	3,790	6.27
Chris Hegg, Truman St. (II)	†1985	11	594	3,782	6.37
Jimmy Klingler, Houston (I-A)	†1992	11	544	3,768	6.93
Dave Stireman, Weber St. (I-AA)	1985	11	502	3,759	7.49
Willie Totten, Mississippi Val. (I-AA)	1985	11	561	3,742	6.67
Brett Salisbury, Wayne St. (Neb.) (II)	1993	10	424	3,732	8.80
Jeff Wiley, Holy Cross (I-AA)	†1987	11	445	3,722	8.36
Jamie Martin, Weber St. (I-AA)	1990	11	508	3,713	7.31
Anthony Dilweg, Duke (I-A)	1988	11	539	3,713	6.89
Kirk Baumgartner, Wis.-Stevens Point (III)	1987	11	561	3,712	6.62

**Record. †National total-offense champion. @ Record for minimum 3,000 yards.*

SINGLE-GAME YARDS

Yds.	Div.	Player, Team (Opponent)	Date
732	I-A	David Klingler, Houston (Arizona St.)	Dec. 2, 1990
696	I-A	Matt Vogler, Texas Christian (Houston)	Nov. 3, 1990
649	I-AA	Steve McNair, Alcorn St. (Southern-B.R.)	Oct. 22, 1994
647	I-AA	Steve McNair, Alcorn St. (Tenn.-Chatt.)	Sept. 10, 1994
643	I-AA	Jamie Martin, Weber St. (Idaho St.)	Nov. 23, 1991
633	I-AA	Steve McNair, Alcorn St. (Grambling)	Sept. 3, 1994
625	I-A	David Klingler, Houston (Texas Christian)	Nov. 3, 1990
625	I-A	Scott Mitchell, Utah (Air Force)	Oct. 15, 1988
624	I-AA	Steve McNair, Alcorn St. (Samford)	Oct. 29, 1994
623	II	Perry Klein, LIU-C.W. Post (Salisbury St.)	Nov. 6, 1993
621	I-AA	Willie Totten, Mississippi Val. (Prairie View)	Oct. 27, 1984
614	I-AA	Bryan Martin, Weber St. (Cal Poly SLO)	Sept. 23, 1995
614	II	Alfred Montez, Western N.M. (West Tex. A&M)	Oct. 8, 1994
612	I-A	Jimmy Klingler, Houston (Rice)	Nov. 28, 1992
604	I-AA	Steve McNair, Alcorn St. (Jackson St.)	Nov. 21, 1992
603	I-A	Ty Detmer, Brigham Young (San Diego St.)	Nov. 16, 1991
601	I-A	Troy Kopp, Pacific, Cal. (New Mexico St.)	Oct. 20, 1990
599	I-A	Virgil Carter, Brigham Young (UTEP)	Nov. 5, 1966
597	I-A	John Walsh, Brigham Young (Utah St.)	Oct. 30, 1993
596	III	John Love, North Park (Elmhurst)	Oct. 13, 1990
595	I-AA	Doug Pederson, Northeast La. (Stephen F. Austin)	Nov. 11, 1989
594	I-A	Jeremy Leach, New Mexico (Utah)	Nov. 11, 1989
591	II	Marty Washington, West Ala. (Nicholls St.)	Sept. 11, 1993
590	III	Tom Stallings, St. Thomas, Minn. (Bethel, Minn.)	Nov. 13, 1993
587	I-AA	Vern Harris, Idaho St. (Montana)	Oct. 12, 1985
586	I-AA	Steve McNair, Alcorn St. (Troy St.)	Nov. 12, 1994
585	I-A	Dave Wilson, Illinois (Ohio St.)	Nov. 8, 1980
584	II	Tracy Kendall, Alabama A&M (Clark Atlanta)	Nov. 4, 1989
582	I-A	Marc Wilson, Brigham Young (Utah)	Nov. 5, 1977
580	II	Grady Benton, West Tex. A&M (Howard Payne)	Sept. 17, 1994
578	I-A	David Klingler, Houston (Eastern Wash.)	Nov. 17, 1990
577	III	Eric Noble, Wilmington, Ohio (Urbana)	Nov. 5, 1994

Rushing

CAREER YARDS PER GAME

(Minimum 2,500 Yards)

Player, Team (Division[s])	Years	G	Plays	Yards	TD	Yd. PG
Arnold Mickens, Butler (I-AA)	1994-95	20	763	3,813	29	*190.7
Ed Marinaro, Cornell (I-A)	1969-71	27	918	4,715	50	174.6
Rob Marchitello, Maine Maritime (III)	1993-95	26	879	4,300	59	165.4
O. J. Simpson, Southern Cal (I-A)	1967-68	19	621	3,214	33	164.4
Kelvin Gladney, Millsaps (III)	1993-94	19	510	3,085	36	162.4
Johnny Bailey, Tex. A&M-Kingsville (II)	1986-89	39	885	*6,320	66	162.1
Herschel Walker, Georgia (I-A)	1980-82	33	994	5,259	49	159.4
Carey Bender, Coe (III)	1991-94	39	926	6,125	71	157.1
Kirk Matthieu, Maine Maritime (III)	$1989-93	33	964	5,107	41	154.8
Tim Hall, Robert Morris (I-AA)	1994-95	19	393	2,908	27	153.1
Terry Underwood, Wagner (III)	1985-88	33	742	5,010	52	151.8
LeShon Johnson, Northern Ill. (I-A)	1992-93	22	592	3,314	18	150.6
Ole Gunderson, St. Olaf (II)	1969-71	27	639	4,060	56	150.4
Richard Huntley, Winston-Salem (II)	1992-95	42	932	6,286	57	149.7
Roger Graham, New Haven (II)	1991-94	40	821	5,953	66	148.8
Marshall Faulk, San Diego St. (I-A)	1991-93	31	766	4,589	57	148.0
Brad Hustad, Luther (II)	1957-59	27	655	3,943	25	146.0
Quincy Tillmon, Emporia St. (II)	1990-92, 94	29	790	4,141	37	142.8
Anthony Russo, St. John's (N.Y.) (III)	1990-93	41	1,152	5,834	57	142.3
Tony Dorsett, Pittsburgh (I-A)	1973-76	43	1,074	6,082	55	141.4
Keith Elias, Princeton (I-AA)	1991-93	30	736	4,208	49	140.3
Joe Iacone, West Chester (II)	1960-62	27	565	3,767	40	139.5

*Record. $See page 6 for explanation.

SEASON YARDS PER GAME

Player, Team (Division)	Year	G	Plays	Yards	TD	Yd. PG
Barry Sanders, Oklahoma St. (I-A)	†1988	11	344	*2,628	*37	*238.9
Arnold Mickens, Butler (I-AA)	†1994	10	*409	2,255	18	225.5
Carey Bender, Coe (III)	†1994	10	295	2,243	29	224.3
Marcus Allen, Southern Cal (I-A)	†1981	11	403	2,342	22	212.9
Ed Marinaro, Cornell (I-A)	†1971	9	356	1,881	24	209.0
Ricky Gales, Simpson (III)	†1989	10	297	2,035	26	203.5
Tony Vinson, Towson St. (I-AA)	†1993	10	293	2,016	23	201.6
Terry Underwood, Wagner (III)	†1988	9	245	1,809	21	201.0
Brad Olson, Lawrence (III)	†1995	9	242	1,760	16	195.6
Kirk Matthieu, Maine Maritime (III)	†1992	9	327	1,733	16	192.6
Richard Huntley, Winston-Salem (II)	†1995	10	273	1,889	16	188.9
Kelvin Gladney, Millsaps (III)	1994	10	307	1,882	19	188.2
Rashaan Salaam, Colorado (I-A)	†1994	11	298	2,055	24	186.8
Jon Warga, Wittenberg (III)	†1990	10	254	1,836	15	183.6
Fred Lane, Lane (II)	1995	10	273	1,833	19	183.3
Johnny Bailey, Tex. A&M-Kingsville (II)	†1986	11	271	2,011	18	182.8
Troy Davis, Iowa St. (I-A)	†1995	11	345	2,010	15	182.7
Bob White, Western N.M. (II)	†1951	9	202	1,643	20	182.6
Kevin Mitchell, Saginaw Valley (II)	1989	8	236	1,460	6	182.5
Anthony Jones, La Verne (III)	1995	8	200	1,453	19	181.6
Hank Wineman, Albion (III)	†1991	9	307	1,629	14	181.0
Charles White, Southern Cal (I-A)	†1979	10	293	1,803	18	180.3
Eric Grey, Hamilton (III)	1991	8	217	1,439	13	179.9
Mike Birosak, Dickinson (III)	1989	10	380	1,798	18	179.8
LeShon Johnson, Northern Ill. (I-A)	†1993	11	327	1,976	12	179.6
Don Aleksiewicz, Hobart (II)	†1971	9	276	1,616	19	179.6
Mike Rozier, Nebraska (I-A)	†1983	12	275	2,148	29	179.0
Jim Holder, Okla. Panhandle St. (II)	†1963	10	275	1,775	9	177.5
Tony Dorsett, Pittsburgh (I-A)	†1976	11	338	1,948	21	177.1
Rob Marchitello, Maine Maritime (III)	1995	8	292	1,413	19	176.6
Chris Babirad, Wash. & Jeff. (III)	1992	9	243	1,589	22	176.6
Jim Baier, Wis.-River Falls (II)	†1966	9	240	1,587	17	176.3
Keith Higdon, Cheyney (II)	†1993	10	330	1,742	17	174.2
Mark Kacmarynski, Central (Iowa) (III)	1994	10	236	1,741	21	174.1
Ollie Matson, San Francisco (I-A)	†1951	9	245	1,566	20	174.0

*Record. †National champion.

CAREER YARDS

Player, Team (Division[s])	Years	Plays	Yards	Avg.
Johnny Bailey, Tex. A&M-Kingsville (II)	1986-89	885	*6,320	7.14
Richard Huntley, Winston-Salem (II)	1992-95	932	6,286	6.74
Carey Bender, Coe (III)	1991-94	926	6,125	6.61
Tony Dorsett, Pittsburgh (I-A)	1973-76	1,074	6,082	5.66
Roger Graham, New Haven (II)	1991-94	821	5,953	7.25
Anthony Russo, St. John's (N.Y.) (III)	1990-93	1,152	5,834	5.06
Charles White, Southern Cal (I-A)	1976-79	1,023	5,598	5.47
Joe Dudek, Plymouth St. (III)	1982-85	785	5,570	7.10
Frank Hawkins, Nevada (I-AA)	1977-80	945	5,333	5.64
Howard Stevens, Randolph-Macon (II); Louisville (I-A)	1968-69; 71-72	891	5,297	5.95
Eric Frees, Western Md. (III)	1988-91	1,059	5,281	4.99
Herschel Walker, Georgia (I-A)	1980-82	994	5,259	5.29
Kenny Gamble, Colgate (I-AA)	1984-87	963	5,220	5.42
Archie Griffin, Ohio St. (I-A)	1972-75	845	5,177	6.13
Markus Thomas, Eastern Ky. (I-AA)	1989-92	784	5,149	6.57
Shawn Graves, Wofford (QB) (II)	1989-92	730	5,128	7.02
Kirk Matthieu, Maine Maritime (III)	$1989-93	964	5,107	5.30
Chris Cobb, Eastern Ill. (II)	1976-79	930	5,042	5.42
Darren Lewis, Texas A&M (I-A)	1987-90	909	5,012	5.51
Terry Underwood, Wagner (III)	1985-88	742	5,010	6.75
Anthony Thompson, Indiana (I-A)	1986-89	1,089	4,965	4.56
George Rogers, South Caro. (I-A)	1977-80	902	4,958	5.50
Trevor Cobb, Rice (I-A)	1989-92	1,091	4,948	4.54
Paul Palmer, Temple (I-A)	1983-86	948	4,895	5.16
Harry Jackson, St. Cloud St. (II)	1986-89	915	4,890	5.34
Leonard Davis, Lenoir-Rhyne (II)	$1990-94	839	4,853	5.78
Jerry Linton, Okla. Panhandle St. (II)	1959-62	648	4,839	‡7.47
Erik Marsh, Lafayette (I-AA)	1991-94	1,027	4,834	4.71

*Record. ‡Record for minimum 600 carries. $See page 6 for explanation.

SEASON YARDS

Player, Team (Division)	Year	G	Plays	Yards	Avg.
Barry Sanders, Oklahoma St. (I-A)	†1988	11	344	*2,628	@7.64
Marcus Allen, Southern Cal (I-A)	†1981	11	403	2,342	5.81
Arnold Mickens, Butler (I-AA)	†1994	10	*409	2,255	5.51
Carey Bender, Coe (III)	†1994	10	295	2,243	7.60
Mike Rozier, Nebraska (I-A)	†1983	12	275	2,148	††7.81
Rashaan Salaam, Colorado (I-A)	†1994	11	298	2,055	6.90
Ricky Gales, Simpson (III)	†1989	10	297	2,035	6.85
Tony Vinson, Towson St. (I-AA)	†1993	10	293	2,016	6.89
Johnny Bailey, Tex. A&M-Kingsville (II)	†1986	11	271	2,011	7.42
Troy Davis, Iowa St. (I-A)	†1995	11	345	2,010	5.83
LeShon Johnson, Northern Ill. (I-A)	†1993	11	327	1,976	6.04
Tony Dorsett, Pittsburgh (I-A)	†1976	11	338	1,948	5.76
Lorenzo White, Michigan St. (I-A)	†1985	11	386	1,908	4.94
Wasean Tait, Toledo (I-A)	1995	11	357	1,905	5.34
Herschel Walker, Georgia (I-A)	†1981	11	385	1,891	4.91
Brian Pruitt, Central Mich. (I-A)	1994	11	292	1,890	6.47
Richard Huntley, Winston-Salem (II)	†1995	10	273	1,889	6.92
Rich Erenberg, Colgate (I-AA)	†1983	11	302	1,883	6.24
Kelvin Gladney, Millsaps (III)	1994	10	307	1,882	6.13
Ed Marinaro, Cornell (I-A)	†1971	9	356	1,881	5.28
Ernest Anderson, Oklahoma St. (I-A)	†1982	11	353	1,877	5.32
Ricky Bell, Southern Cal (I-A)	†1975	11	357	1,875	5.25
Paul Palmer, Temple (I-A)	†1986	11	346	1,866	5.39
Ronald Moore, Pittsburg St. (II)	1992	11	239	1,864	7.80
George Jones, San Diego St. (I-A)	1995	12	305	1,842	6.04
Jon Warga, Wittenberg (III)	†1990	10	254	1,836	7.23
Fred Lane, Lane (II)	1995	10	273	1,833	6.71
Zed Robinson, Southern Utah (II)	1991	11	254	1,828	7.20
Eddie George, Ohio St. (I-A)	1995	12	303	1,826	6.03
Kenny Gamble, Colgate (I-AA)	†1986	11	307	1,816	5.92
Richard Huntley, Winston-Salem (II)	1994	11	251	1,815	7.23
Terry Underwood, Wagner (III)	†1988	9	245	1,809	6.75
Charles White, Southern Cal (I-A)	†1979	10	293	1,803	6.15

*Record. †National champion. ††Record for minimum 214 carries. @ Record for minimum 282 carries.

SINGLE-GAME YARDS

Yds.	Div.	Player, Team (Opponent)	Date
417	III	Carey Bender, Coe (Grinnell)	Oct. 9, 1993
396	I-A	Tony Sands, Kansas (Missouri)	Nov. 23, 1991
386	I-A	Marshall Faulk, San Diego St. (Pacific, Cal.)	Sept. 14, 1991
382	III	Pete Baranek, Carthage (North Central)	Oct. 5, 1985
382	II	Kelly Ellis, Northern Iowa (Western Ill.)	Oct. 13, 1979
377	I-A	Anthony Thompson, Indiana (Wisconsin)	Nov. 11, 1989
373	II	Dallas Garber, Marietta (Wash. & Jeff.)	Nov. 7, 1959
370	II	Jim Baier, Wis.-River Falls (Wis.-Stevens Point)	Nov. 5, 1966
370	II	Jim Hissam, Marietta (Bethany, W.Va.)	Nov. 15, 1958
367	II	Don Polkinghorne, Washington, Mo. (Wash. & Lee)	Nov. 23, 1957
364	I-AA	Tony Vinson, Towson St. (Bucknell)	Nov. 13, 1993
363	III	Terry Underwood, Wagner (Hofstra)	Oct. 15, 1988
363	II	Richie Weaver, Widener (Moravian)	Oct. 17, 1970
361	II	Richard Huntley, Winston-Salem (Virginia Union)	Nov. 5, 1994
357	I-A	Mike Pringle, Cal St. Fullerton (New Mexico St.)	Nov. 4, 1989
357	I-A	Rueben Mayes, Washington St. (Oregon)	Oct. 27, 1984
356	I-A	Brian Pruitt, Central Mich. (Toledo)	Nov. 5, 1994
356	I-A	Eddie Lee Ivery, Georgia Tech (Air Force)	Nov. 11, 1978
356	II	Ole Gunderson, St. Olaf (Monmouth, Ill.)	Oct. 11, 1969
354	III	Terry Underwood, Wagner (Western Conn. St.)	Oct. 3, 1986
350	II	Ricke Stonewall, Millersville (New Haven)	Nov. 13, 1982
350	I-A	Eric Allen, Michigan St. (Purdue)	Oct. 30, 1971

Passing

CAREER PASSING EFFICIENCY

(Minimum 475 Completions)

Player, Team (Division[s])	Years	Att.	Cmp.	Int.	Pct.	Yds.	TD	Pts.
Dave Dickenson, Montana (I-AA)	1992-95	1,208	813	26	.673	11,080	96	*166.3
Ty Detmer, Brigham Young (I-A)	1988-91	1,530	958	65	.626	*15,031	121	162.7
Jim Ballard, Wilmington (Ohio)/ Mount Union (III)	1990, 91-93	1,199	743	41	.620	10,379	115	159.5
Jim McMahon, Brigham Young (I-A)	1977-78, 80-81	1,060	653	34	.616	9,536	84	156.9
Doug Nussmeier, Idaho (I-AA)	1990-93	1,225	746	32	.609	10,824	91	154.4
Chris Hatcher, Valdosta St. (II)	1991-94	1,451	*1,001	38	.690	10,878	116	153.1
Steve Young, Brigham Young (I-A)	1981-83	908	592	33	.652	7,733	56	149.8
Jack Hull, Grand Valley St. (II)	1988-91	835	485	22	.581	7,120	64	149.7
Robbie Bosco, Brigham Young (I-A)	1983-85	997	638	36	.640	8,400	66	149.4
Elvis Grbac, Michigan (I-A)	1989-92	754	477	29	.633	5,859	64	148.9
Mike Maxwell, Nevada (I-A)	1993-95	881	560	33	.636	7,256	62	148.5
Michael Payton, Marshall (I-AA)	1989-92	876	542	32	.619	7,530	57	148.2
Chuck Long, Iowa (I-A)	$1981-85	1,072	692	46	.646	9,210	64	147.8
John Walsh, Brigham Young (I-A)	1991-94	973	587	35	.603	8,375	66	147.8
Willie Totten, Mississippi Val. (I-AA)	1982-85	1,555	907	75	.583	12,711	*139	146.8
John Koz, Baldwin-Wallace (III)	1990-93	981	609	28	.621	7,724	71	146.4
Rob Johnson, Southern Cal (I-A)	1991-94	963	623	24	.647	7,743	52	145.1
Steve McNair, Alcorn St. (I-AA)	1991-94	1,680	929	58	.553	14,496	119	144.3
Mike Smith, Northern Iowa (I-AA)	1984-87	943	557	43	.591	8,219	58	143.5
Steve Stenstrom, Stanford (I-A)	1991-94	1,320	833	36	.631	10,531	72	142.7
Neil Lomax, Portland St. (II; I-AA)	1977; 78-80	1,606	938	55	.584	13,220	106	142.5
Marvin Graves, Syracuse (I-A)	1990-93	943	563	45	.597	8,466	48	142.4
Tom Ciaccio, Holy Cross (I-AA)	1988-91	1,073	658	46	.613	8,603	72	142.2
George Bork, Northern Ill. (II)	1960-63	902	577	33	.640	6,782	60	141.8
Eric Beavers, Nevada (I-AA)	1983-86	1,094	646	37	.591	8,626	77	141.8
Doug Gaynor, Long Beach St. (I-A)	1984-85	837	569	35	.680	6,793	35	141.6
Scott Semptimphelter, Lehigh (I-AA)	1990-93	823	493	27	.599	6,668	50	141.5
Ed Hesson, Rowan (III)	1990-93	895	504	26	.563	7,053	67	141.2
Danny Kanell, Florida St. (I-A)	1992-95	851	529	26	.622	6,372	57	141.1
Matt Jozokos, Plymouth St. (III)	1987-90	1,003	527	39	.525	7,658	95	140.2
Dan McGwire, Iowa/San Diego St. (I-A)	1986-87, 89-90	973	575	30	.591	8,164	49	140.0
Chris Vargas, Nevada (I-AA; I-A)	1990-91; 92-93	1,017	625	42	.615	8,130	60	139.8
John Elway, Stanford (I-A)	1979-82	1,246	774	39	.621	9,349	77	139.3
Mike McCoy, Long Beach St./Utah (I-A)	1991, 92-94	1,069	650	26	.608	8,342	56	138.8
Jamie Martin, Weber St. (I-AA)	1989-92	1,544	934	56	.605	12,207	87	138.2
David Klingler, Houston (I-A)	1988-91	1,261	726	38	.576	9,430	91	138.2

*Record. $See page 6 for explanation.

CAREER PASSING EFFICIENCY

(Minimum 325-474 Completions)

Player, Team (Division[s])	Years	Att.	Cmp.	Int.	Pct.	Yds.	TD	Pts.
John Charles, Portland St. (II)	1991-92	510	326	14	.639	5,389	56	*183.4
Shawn Knight, William & Mary (I-AA)	1991-94	558	367	15	.658	5,527	46	170.8
Tony Aliucci, Indiana (Pa.) (II)	1988-91	579	350	24	.604	5,655	53	164.4
Jayson Merrill, Western St. (II)	1990-91	580	328	25	.566	5,830	56	164.2
Chris Petersen, UC Davis (II)	1985-86	553	385	13	*.696	4,988	39	164.0
Craig Kusick, Wis.-La Crosse (III)	1993-95	537	327	14	.609	4,767	48	159.8
Dennis Shaw, San Diego St. (II; I-A)	1968; 69	575	333	41	.579	5,324	58	154.7
Joe Blake, Simpson (III)	1987-90	672	399	15	.594	6,183	43	153.3
Vinny Testaverde, Miami (Fla.) (I-A)	1982, 84-86	674	413	25	.613	6,058	48	152.9
Jim McMillan, Boise St. (II)	1971-74	640	382	29	.597	5,508	58	152.8
Willie Reyna, La Verne (III)	1991-92	542	346	19	.638	4,712	37	152.4
Trent Dilfer, Fresno St. (I-A)	1991-93	774	461	21	.596	6,944	51	151.2
Troy Aikman, Oklahoma/UCLA (I-A)	1984-85, 87-88	637	401	18	.630	5,436	40	149.7
Jim Harbaugh, Michigan (I-A)	1983-86	582	368	19	.632	5,215	31	149.6
Chuck Hartlieb, Iowa (I-A)	1985-88	716	461	17	.643	6,269	34	148.9
Jay Johnson, Northern Iowa (I-AA)	1989-92	744	397	25	.534	7,049	51	148.9
Danny White, Arizona St. (I-A)	1971-73	649	345	36	.532	5,932	59	148.9
Scott Otis, Glenville St. (II)	1994-95	693	421	21	.608	5,563	55	148.8
Gary Collier, Emory & Henry (III)	1984-87	738	386	33	.523	6,103	80	148.6
Bryan Martin, Weber St. (I-AA)	1992-95	606	365	14	.602	5,211	37	148.0
Grady Benton, West Tex. A&M (II)	1994-95	686	421	22	.614	5,618	49	147.3
Kenneth Biggles, Tennessee St. (I-AA)	1981-84	701	397	28	.566	5,933	57	146.6
Bobby Hoying, Ohio St. (I-A)	1992-95	782	463	33	.592	6,751	54	146.1
Gifford Nielsen, Brigham Young (I-A)	1975-77	708	415	29	.586	5,833	55	145.3
Greg Heeres, Hope (III)	1981-84	630	347	21	.537	5,120	53	144.4
Tim Gutierrez, San Diego St. (I-A)	1992-94	580	357	19	.616	4,740	36	144.1
Bruce Upstill, Col. of Emporia (II)	1960-63	769	438	36	.570	6,935	48	144.0
Tom Ramsey, UCLA (I-A)	1979-82	691	411	33	.595	5,844	48	143.9
Shawn Moore, Virginia (I-A)	1987-90	762	421	32	.552	6,629	55	143.8
Jeff Brown, Wheaton (Ill.) (III)	1992-95	767	441	30	.575	6,219	60	143.6
Jerry Rhome, Southern Methodist/Tulsa (I-A)	1961, 63-64	713	448	23	.628	5,472	47	142.6
Todd Donnan, Marshall (I-AA)	1991-94	712	425	25	.597	5,566	51	142.0
Jim Zaccheo, Nevada (I-AA)	1987-88	554	326	27	.588	4,750	35	142.0
Charlie Ward, Florida St. (I-A)	1989, 91-93	759	474	21	.625	5,747	49	141.8
Bruce Crosthwaite, Adrian (III)	1984-87	618	368	31	.596	4,959	45	141.0

*Record.

Jason Burfield/NCAA photos

Montana quarterback Dave Dickenson holds the collegiate record for career passing efficiency among passers with 475 or more completions (166.3).

Photo from Mount Union sports information

Mount Union quarterback Jim Ballard's passing efficiency rating of 193.2 in 1993 was the highest in collegiate history among passers who attempted 30 or more passes per game.

SEASON PASSING EFFICIENCY
(Minimum 30 Attempts Per Game)

Player, Team (Division)	Year	G	Att.	Cmp.	Int.	Pct.	Yds.	TD	Pts.
Jim Ballard, Mount Union (III)	1993	10	314	229	11	.729	3,304	37	*193.2
Jayson Merrill, Western St. (II)	†1991	10	309	195	11	.631	3,484	35	188.1
John Charles, Portland St. (II)	1992	8	263	179	7	.681	2,770	24	181.3
Chris Hatcher, Valdosta St. (II)	†1994	11	430	321	9	*.747	3,591	50	179.0
Jim McMahon, Brigham Young (I-A)	†1980	12	445	284	18	.638	4,571	47	176.9
Ty Detmer, Brigham Young (I-A)	†1989	12	412	265	15	.643	4,560	32	175.6
Trent Dilfer, Fresno St. (I-A)	†1993	11	333	217	4	.652	3,276	28	173.1
Jerry Rhome, Tulsa (I-A)	†1964	10	326	224	4	.687	2,870	32	172.6
Dave Dickenson, Montana (I-AA)	1995	11	455	309	9	.679	4,176	38	168.6
Ty Detmer, Brigham Young (I-A)	1991	12	403	249	12	.618	4,031	35	168.5
Steve Young, Brigham Young (I-A)	†1983	11	429	306	10	.713	3,902	33	168.5
Willie Totten, Mississippi Val. (I-AA)	†1983	9	279	174	9	.624	2,566	29	167.5
Dave Dickenson, Montana (I-AA)	†1994	9	336	229	6	.682	3,053	24	164.5
Jim McMillan, Boise St. (II)	†1974	10	313	192	15	.613	2,900	33	164.4
Willie Totten, Mississippi Val. (I-AA)	†1984	10	518	324	22	.626	4,557	*56	163.6
Jeff Wiley, Holy Cross (I-AA)	†1987	11	400	265	17	.663	3,677	34	163.0
Todd Hammel, Stephen F. Austin (I-AA)	†1989	11	401	238	13	.594	3,914	34	162.8
Dennis Shaw, San Diego St. (I-A)	†1969	10	335	199	26	.594	3,185	39	162.2
John Friesz, Idaho (I-AA)	1989	11	425	260	8	.612	4,041	31	161.4
Willie Reyna, La Verne (III)	1991	8	267	170	6	.636	2,543	16	158.8
Charlie Ward, Florida St. (I-A)	1993	11	380	264	4	.695	3,032	27	157.8
Glenn Foley, Boston College (I-A)	1993	11	363	222	10	.612	3,395	25	157.0
Chris Vargas, Nevada (I-A)	1993	11	490	331	18	.676	4,265	34	156.2
George Bork, Northern Ill. (II)	1963	9	374	244	12	.652	2,824	32	156.2
John Walsh, Brigham Young (I-A)	1993	11	397	244	15	.615	3,727	28	156.0
Neil Lomax, Portland St. (I-AA)	1980	11	473	296	12	.626	4,094	37	156.0
Ty Detmer, Brigham Young (I-A)	1990	12	562	361	28	.642	*5,188	41	155.9
Rob Johnson, Southern Cal (I-A)	1993	12	405	278	5	.686	3,285	26	155.5
Doug Williams, Grambling (I-A)	1977	11	352	181	18	.514	3,286	38	155.2
Jim McMahon, Brigham Young (I-A)	†1981	10	423	272	7	.643	3,555	30	155.0
Andy Breault, Kutztown (II)	1991	10	360	225	20	.625	2,927	37	153.4
Chuck Long, Iowa (I-A)	1985	11	351	231	15	.658	2,978	26	153.0
Doug Flutie, Boston College (I-A)	1984	11	386	233	11	.604	3,454	27	152.9

**Record. †National pass-efficiency champion.*

SEASON PASSING EFFICIENCY
(Minimum 15 Attempts Per Game)

Player, Team (Division)	Year	G	Att.	Cmp.	Int.	Pct.	Yds.	TD	Pts.
Mike Simpson, Eureka (III)	†1994	10	158	116	5	.734	1,988	25	*225.0
Willie Seiler, St. John's (Minn.) (III)	†1993	10	205	141	6	.687	2,648	33	224.6
Boyd Crawford, Col. of Idaho (II)	†1953	8	120	72	6	.600	1,462	21	210.1
Shawn Knight, William & Mary (I-AA)	†1993	10	177	125	4	.706	2,055	22	204.6
Bill Borchert, Mount Union (III)	†1995	10	225	160	4	.711	2,270	30	196.3
Jason Baer, Wash. & Jeff. (III)	1995	8	146	95	3	.650	1,536	19	192.3
Chuck Green, Wittenberg (II)	†1963	9	182	114	8	.626	2,181	19	189.0
Kurt Ramler, St. John's (Minn.) (III)	1994	9	154	93	4	.603	1,560	22	187.4
Jim Feeley, Johns Hopkins (II)	†1967	7	110	69	5	.627	1,264	12	186.2
Mike Bajakian, Williams (III)	1994	8	141	92	1	.652	1,382	17	186.0
John Charles, Portland St. (II)	1991	11	247	147	7	.595	2,619	32	185.7
Steve Smith, Western St. (II)	†1992	10	271	180	5	.664	2,719	30	183.5
Mitch Sanders, Bridgeport (III)	†1973	10	151	84	7	.556	1,551	23	182.9
Jim Peterson, Hanover (II)	†1948	8	125	81	12	.648	1,571	12	182.9
John Wristen, Southern Colo. (II)	†1982	8	121	68	2	.562	1,358	13	182.6
Michael Payton, Marshall (I-AA)	†1991	9	216	143	5	.622	2,333	19	181.3
Richard Basil, Savannah St. (II)	†1989	9	211	120	7	.568	2,148	29	181.1
Pat Mayew, St. John's (Minn.) (III)	†1991	9	247	154	4	.623	2,408	30	181.0
Danny Wuerffel, Florida (I-A)	†1995	11	325	210	10	.646	3,266	35	178.4
Guy Simons, Coe (III)	1993	10	185	110	9	.594	1,979	21	177.1
Jim Cahoon, Ripon (II)	†1964	8	127	74	7	.583	1,206	19	176.4
Ken Suhl, New Haven (II)	1992	10	239	148	5	.619	2,336	26	175.7
Jimbo Fisher, Samford (III)	†1987	10	252	139	5	.551	2,394	34	175.4
Doug Nussmeier, Idaho (I-AA)	1993	11	304	185	5	.609	2,960	33	175.2
Brian Kadel, Dayton (I-AA)	†1995	11	183	115	6	.628	1,880	18	175.0
Gary Collier, Emory & Henry (III)	1987	11	249	152	10	.610	2,317	33	174.8
Paul Bell, Allegheny (III)	1994	10	215	142	2	.660	2,137	17	173.8
Kerry Collins, Penn St. (I-A)	†1994	11	264	176	7	.667	2,679	21	172.9
Kelvin Simmons, Troy St. (I-AA)	1993	11	224	143	6	.638	2,144	23	172.8
James Grant, Ramapo (III)	1989	9	147	91	7	.619	1,441	17	172.7
Tony Aliucci, Indiana (Pa.) (II)	†1990	10	181	111	10	.613	1,801	21	172.7
Chris Adams, Gettysburg (III)	1994	10	211	139	2	.658	1,977	19	172.4
James Weir, New Haven (II)	†1993	10	266	161	1	.605	2,336	31	172.0
Shawn Behr, Fort Hays St. (II)	†1995	11	318	191	6	.600	3,158	31	171.9
Frank Baur, Lafayette (I-AA)	†1988	10	256	164	11	.641	2,621	23	171.1
Mike Donnelly, Wittenberg (III)	1995	10	153	92	2	.601	1,480	15	171.1
Bobby Lamb, Furman (I-AA)	†1985	11	181	106	6	.586	1,856	18	170.9
Bobby Hoying, Ohio St. (I-A)	1995	12	303	192	11	.634	3,023	28	170.4
Gary Urwiler, Eureka (III)	1991	10	171	103	5	.602	1,656	18	170.3

**Record. †National pass-efficiency champion.*

CAREER YARDS

Player, Team (Division[s])	Years	Att.	Cmp.	Int.	Pct.	Yds.	TD
Ty Detmer, Brigham Young (I-A)	1988-91	1,530	958	65	.626	*15,031	121
Steve McNair, Alcorn St. (I-AA)	1991-94	1,680	929	58	.553	14,496	119
Neil Lomax, Portland St. (II; I-AA)	1977; 78-80	1,606	938	55	.584	13,220	106
Kirk Baumgartner, Wis.-Stevens Point (III)	1986-89	1,696	883	57	.521	13,028	110
Willie Totten, Mississippi Val. (I-AA)	1982-85	1,555	907	75	.583	12,711	*139
Jamie Martin, Weber St. (I-AA)	1989-92	1,544	934	56	.605	12,207	87
Todd Santos, San Diego St. (I-A)	1984-87	1,484	910	57	.613	11,425	70
Eric Zeier, Georgia (I-A)	1991-94	1,402	838	37	.598	11,153	67
Dave Dickenson, Montana (I-AA)	1992-95	1,208	813	26	.673	11,080	96
Alex Van Pelt, Pittsburgh (I-A)	1989-92	1,463	845	59	.578	10,913	64
Chris Hatcher, Valdosta St. (II)	1991-94	1,451	*1,001	38	.690	10,878	116
Doug Nussmeier, Idaho (I-AA)	1990-93	1,225	746	32	.609	10,824	91
John Friesz, Idaho (I-AA)	1986-89	1,350	801	40	.593	10,697	77
Greg Wyatt, Northern Ariz. (I-AA)	1986-89	1,510	926	49	.613	10,697	70
Sean Payton, Eastern Ill. (I-AA)	1983-86	1,408	756	55	.537	10,655	75
Bob McLaughlin, Lock Haven (II)	1992-95	*1,719	910	*88	.529	10,640	60
Kevin Sweeney, Fresno St. (I-A)	$1982-86	1,336	731	48	.547	10,623	66
Earl Harvey, N.C. Central (II)	1985-88	1,442	690	81	.479	10,621	86
Doug Flutie, Boston College (I-A)	1981-84	1,270	677	54	.533	10,579	67
Jim Ballard, Wilmington (Ohio)/Mount Union (III)	1990, 91-93	1,199	743	41	.620	10,379	115
Tom Ehrhardt, LIU-C.W. Post (II); Rhode Island (I-AA)	1981-82; 84-85	1,489	833	63	.559	10,325	92
Brian McClure, Bowling Green (I-A)	1982-85	1,427	900	58	.631	10,280	63
Troy Kopp, Pacific (Cal.) (I-A)	1989-92	1,374	798	47	.581	10,258	87
Glenn Foley, Boston College (I-A)	1990-93	1,275	703	60	.551	10,042	72
John Craven, Gardner-Webb (II)	1991-94	1,535	828	82	.539	9,934	80
Vernon Buck, Wingate (II)	1991-94	1,393	728	61	.523	9,884	72
Thad Trujillo, Fort Lewis (II)	1991-94	1,455	760	57	.522	9,873	78
Jeff Wiley, Holy Cross (I-AA)	1985-88	1,208	723	63	.599	9,698	71
Jeff Lewis, Northern Ariz. (I-AA)	1992-95	1,316	785	24	.597	9,655	67
Ben Bennett, Duke (I-A)	1980-83	1,375	820	57	.596	9,614	53
Keith Bishop, Ill. Wesleyan/Wheaton (Ill.) (III)	1981, 83-85	1,311	772	65	.589	9,579	71
Robbie Justino, Liberty (I-AA)	1989-92	1,267	769	51	.607	9,548	64
Dennis Bogacz, Wis.-Oshkosh/Wis.-Whitewater (III)	1988-89, 90-91	1,275	654	59	.513	9,536	66
Jim McMahon, Brigham Young (I-A)	1977-78, 80-81	1,060	653	34	.616	9,536	84
Todd Ellis, South Caro. (I-A)	1986-89	1,266	704	66	.556	9,519	97
Dave Geissler, Wis.-Stevens Point (III)	1982-85	1,346	789	57	.586	9,518	65
Stoney Case, New Mexico (I-A)	1991-94	1,237	677	39	.547	9,460	67
Rob Tomlinson, Cal St. Chico (II)	1988-91	1,328	748	43	.563	9,434	52
David Klingler, Houston (I-A)	1988-91	1,261	726	38	.576	9,430	91
Erik Wilhelm, Oregon St. (I-A)	1985-88	1,480	870	61	.588	9,393	52
Jeremy Leach, New Mexico (I-A)	1988-91	1,432	735	62	.513	9,382	50
John Elway, Stanford (I-A)	1979-82	1,246	774	39	.621	9,349	77

**Record. $See page 6 for explanation.*

CAREER YARDS PER GAME

(Minimum 5,000 Yards)

Player, Team (Division[s])	Years	G	Att.	Cmp.	Int.	Pct.	Yds.	TD	Yd.PG
Steve McNair, Alcorn St. (I-AA)	1991-94	42	1,680	929	58	.553	14,496	119	*345.1
Ty Detmer, Brigham Young (I-A)	1988-91	46	1,530	958	65	.626	*15,031	121	326.8
Willie Totten, Mississippi Val. (I-AA)	1982-85	40	1,555	907	75	.583	12,711	*139	317.8
Kirk Baumgartner, Wis.-Stevens Point (III)	1986-89	41	1,696	883	57	.521	13,028	110	317.8
Dave Dickenson, Montana (I-AA)	1992-95	35	1,208	813	26	.673	11,080	96	316.6
Neil Lomax, Portland St. (II; I-AA)	1977; 78-80	42	1,606	938	55	.584	13,220	106	314.8
Grady Benton, West Tex. A&M (II)	1994-95	18	686	421	22	.614	5,618	49	312.1
Mike Perez, San Jose St. (I-A)	1986-87	20	792	471	30	.595	6,194	36	309.7
Keith Bishop, Ill. Wes./Wheaton (Ill.) (III)	1981, 83-85	31	1,311	772	65	.589	9,579	71	309.0
Doug Gaynor, Long Beach St. (I-A)	1984-85	22	837	569	35	.680	6,793	35	308.8
John Friesz, Idaho (I-AA)	1986-89	35	1,350	801	40	.593	10,697	77	305.6
Tony Eason, Illinois (I-A)	1981-82	22	856	526	29	.615	6,608	37	300.4

**Record.*

CAREER TOUCHDOWN PASSES

Player, Team (Division[s])	Years	Att.	Cmp.	Int.	Pct.	Yds.	TD
Willie Totten, Mississippi Val. (I-AA)	1982-85	1,555	907	75	.583	12,711	*139
Ty Detmer, Brigham Young (I-A)	1988-91	1,530	958	65	.626	*15,031	121
Steve McNair, Alcorn St. (I-AA)	1991-94	1,680	929	58	.553	14,496	119
Chris Hatcher, Valdosta St. (II)	1991-94	1,451	*1,001	38	.690	10,878	116
Jim Ballard, Wilmington (Ohio)/Mount Union (III)	1990, 91-93	1,199	743	41	.620	10,379	115
Kirk Baumgartner, Wis.-Stevens Point (III)	1986-89	1,696	883	57	.521	13,028	110
Neil Lomax, Portland St. (II; I-AA)	1977; 78-80	1,606	938	55	.584	13,220	106
Dave Dickenson, Montana (I-AA)	1992-95	1,208	813	26	.673	11,080	96
Matt Jozokos, Plymouth St. (III)	1987-90	1,003	527	39	.525	7,658	95
Doug Williams, Grambling (II; I-A)	1974-76; 77	1,009	484	52	.480	8,411	93
Tom Ehrhardt, LIU-C.W. Post (II); Rhode Island (I-AA)	1981-82; 84-85	1,489	833	63	.559	10,325	92
Doug Nussmeier, Idaho (I-AA)	1990-93	1,225	746	32	.609	10,824	91
David Klingler, Houston (I-A)	1988-91	1,261	726	38	.576	9,430	91
Troy Kopp, Pacific (Cal.) (I-A)	1989-92	1,374	798	47	.581	10,258	87
Jamie Martin, Weber St. (I-AA)	1989-92	1,544	934	56	.605	12,207	87
Andy Breault, Kutztown (II)	1989-92	1,259	733	63	.582	9,086	86
Earl Harvey, N.C. Central (II)	1985-88	1,442	690	81	.479	10,621	86

Photo from Georgia sports information

Georgia quarterback Eric Zeier ranks eighth in collegiate history with 11,153 career passing yards.

Photo from Valdosta State sports information

In addition to holding the collegiate record for career pass completions (1,001), Valdosta State quarterback Chris Hatcher ranks fourth on the all-time collegiate list with 116 touchdown passes.

Player, Team (Division[s])	Years	Att.	Cmp.	Int.	Pct.	Yds.	TD
Rex Lamberti, Abilene Christian (II)	1984-86, 93	1,133	595	44	.525	7,934	84
Jim McMahon, Brigham Young (I-A)	1977-78, 80-81	1,060	653	34	.616	9,536	84
Darin Hinshaw, Central Fla. (I-AA)	1991-94	1,113	614	52	.552	9,000	82
Dave MacDonald, West Chester (II)	1991-94	1,123	604	46	.538	8,449	82
Dan Crowley, Towson St. (I-AA)	1991-94	1,170	617	54	.527	8,900	81
Joe Adams, Tennessee St. (I-A)	1977-80	1,100	604	60	.549	8,649	81
John Craven, Gardner-Webb (II)	1991-94	1,535	828	82	.539	9,934	80
Gary Collier, Emory & Henry (III)	1984-87	738	386	33	.523	6,103	80
Terry Peebles, Hanover (III)	1992-95	969	550	29	.568	6,928	79
Aaron Sparrow, Norfolk St. (II)	1992-95	1,117	615	38	.551	8,758	79
Ken Hobart, Idaho (I-AA)	1980-83	1,219	629	42	.516	9,300	79

**Record.*

SEASON YARDS

Player, Team (Division)	Year	G	Att.	Cmp.	Int.	Pct.	Yds.	TD
Ty Detmer, Brigham Young (I-A)	†1990	12	562	361	28	.642	*5,188	41
David Klingler, Houston (I-A)	1990	11	*643	*374	20	.582	5,140	54
Steve McNair, Alcorn St. (I-AA)	1994	11	530	304	17	.574	4,863	44
Andre Ware, Houston (I-A)	†1989	11	578	365	15	.631	4,699	46
Jim McMahon, Brigham Young (I-A)	†1980	12	445	284	18	.638	4,571	47
Ty Detmer, Brigham Young (I-A)	1989	12	412	265	15	.643	4,560	32
Willie Totten, Mississippi Val. (I-AA)	†1984	10	518	324	22	.626	4,557	*56
Scott Mitchell, Utah (I-A)	1988	11	533	323	15	.606	4,322	29
Chris Vargas, Nevada (I-A)	1993	11	490	331	18	.676	4,265	34
Robbie Bosco, Brigham Young (I-A)	1985	13	511	338	24	.661	4,257	30
Dave Dickenson, Montana (I-AA)	1995	11	455	309	9	.679	4,176	38
Jamie Martin, Weber St. (I-AA)	1991	11	500	310	17	.620	4,125	35
Neil Lomax, Portland St. (I-AA)	1980	11	473	296	12	.626	4,094	37
John Friesz, Idaho (I-AA)	†1989	11	425	260	8	.612	4,041	31
Ty Detmer, Brigham Young (I-A)	1991	12	403	249	12	.618	4,031	35
Neil Lomax, Portland St. (I-AA)	1979	11	516	299	16	.579	3,950	26
Todd Santos, San Diego St. (I-A)	1987	12	492	306	15	.622	3,932	26
Todd Hammel, Stephen F. Austin (I-AA)	1989	11	401	238	13	.594	3,914	34
Steve Young, Brigham Young (I-A)	†1983	11	429	306	10	.713	3,902	33
Robbie Bosco, Brigham Young (I-A)	1984	12	458	283	11	.618	3,875	33
Mike McCoy, Utah (I-A)	1993	12	430	276	10	.642	3,860	21
Sean Payton, Eastern Ill. (I-AA)	1984	11	473	270	15	.571	3,843	28
Dan McGwire, San Diego St. (I-A)	1990	11	449	270	7	.601	3,833	27
Kirk Baumgartner, Wis.-Stevens Point (III)	1988	11	527	276	16	.524	3,828	25
Anthony Dilweg, Duke (I-A)	1988	11	484	287	18	.593	3,824	24
Jimmy Klingler, Houston (I-A)	1992	11	504	303	18	.601	3,818	32
Sam King, UNLV (I-A)	1981	12	433	255	19	.589	3,778	18
Troy Kopp, Pacific (Cal.) (I-A)	1991	12	449	275	16	.612	3,767	37
Perry Klein, LIU-C.W. Post (II)	1993	10	407	248	18	.609	3,757	38
Kirk Baumgartner, Wis.-Stevens Point (III)	1987	11	466	243	22	.521	3,755	31
Chris Hegg, Truman St. (II)	1985	11	503	284	20	.565	3,741	32
Brett Salisbury, Wayne St. (Neb.) (II)	1993	10	395	276	14	.699	3,729	29
John Walsh, Brigham Young (I-A)	1993	11	397	244	15	.615	3,727	28
Marc Wilson, Brigham Young (I-A)	1979	12	427	250	15	.585	3,720	29

**Record. †National pass-efficiency champion.*

SEASON YARDS PER GAME

Player, Team (Division)	Year	G	Att.	Cmp.	Int.	Pct.	Yds.	TD	Yd.PG
David Klingler, Houston (I-A)	1990	11	*643	*374	20	.582	5,140	54	*467.3
Willie Totten, Mississippi Val. (I-AA)	1984	10	518	324	22	.626	4,557	*56	455.7
Steve McNair, Alcorn St. (I-AA)	1994	11	530	304	17	.574	4,863	44	442.1
Ty Detmer, Brigham Young (I-A)	1990	12	562	361	28	.642	*5,188	41	432.3
Andre Ware, Houston (I-A)	1989	11	578	365	15	.631	4,699	46	427.2
Mike Maxwell, Nevada (I-A)	1995	9	409	277	17	.677	3,611	33	401.2
Grady Benton, West Tex. A&M (II)	1994	9	409	258	13	.631	3,541	30	393.4
Scott Mitchell, Utah (I-A)	1988	11	533	323	15	.606	4,322	29	392.9
Chris Vargas, Nevada (I-A)	1993	11	490	331	18	.676	4,265	34	387.7
Marty Washington, West Ala. (II)	1993	8	404	221	13	.547	3,062	26	382.8
Jim McMahon, Brigham Young (I-A)	1980	12	445	284	18	.638	4,571	47	380.9
Ty Detmer, Brigham Young (I-A)	1989	12	412	265	15	.643	4,560	32	380.0

**Record.*

SEASON TOUCHDOWN PASSES

Player, Team (Division)	Year	Att.	Cmp.	Int.	Pct.	Yds.	TD
Willie Totten, Mississippi Val. (I-AA)	1984	518	324	22	.626	4,557	*56
David Klingler, Houston (I-A)	1990	*643	*374	20	.582	5,140	54
Chris Hatcher, Valdosta St. (II)	†1994	430	321	9	*.747	3,591	50
Jim McMahon, Brigham Young (I-A)	1980	445	284	18	.638	4,571	47
Andre Ware, Houston (I-A)	1989	578	365	15	.631	4,699	46
Bob Toledo, San Fran. St. (II)	1967	396	211	24	.533	3,513	45
Steve McNair, Alcorn St. (I-AA)	1994	530	304	17	.574	4,863	44
Ty Detmer, Brigham Young (I-A)	1990	562	361	28	.642	*5,188	41
Terry Peebles, Hanover (III)	1995	488	283	10	.579	3,521	39
Kirk Baumgartner, Wis.-Stevens Point (III)	1989	455	247	9	.542	3,692	39
Willie Totten, Mississippi Val. (I-AA)	1985	492	295	29	.600	3,698	39
Dennis Shaw, San Diego St. (I-A)	1969	335	199	26	.594	3,185	39
Dave Dickenson, Montana (I-AA)	1995	455	309	9	.679	4,176	38
Perry Klein, LIU-C.W. Post (II)	1993	407	248	18	.609	3,757	38
Doug Williams, Grambling (I-A)	1977	352	181	18	.514	3,286	38
Terry Peebles, Hanover (III)	1994	445	252	17	.566	3,197	37
Jim Ballard, Mount Union (III)	1993	314	229	11	.729	3,304	37
Chris Hatcher, Valdosta St. (II)	1993	471	335	11	.711	3,651	37
Andy Breault, Kutztown (II)	1991	360	225	20	.625	2,927	37
Troy Kopp, Pacific (Cal.) (I-A)	1991	449	275	16	.613	3,767	37
Neil Lomax, Portland St. (I-AA)	1980	473	296	12	.626	4,094	37
Danny Wuerffel, Florida (I-A)	1995	325	210	10	.646	3,266	35
Jarrod Furgason, Fairmont St. (II)	1995	349	222	8	.636	2,696	35
Dave MacDonald, West Chester (II)	1994	458	251	18	.548	3,308	35
Jayson Merrill, Western St. (II)	1991	309	195	11	.631	3,484	35
Ty Detmer, Brigham Young (I-A)	1991	403	249	12	.618	4,031	35
Jamie Martin, Weber St. (I-AA)	1991	500	310	17	.620	4,125	35
Tom Ehrhardt, Rhode Island (I-AA)	1985	497	283	19	.569	3,542	35

**Record. †National pass-efficiency champion.*

SINGLE-GAME YARDS

Yds.	Div.	Player, Team (Opponent)	Date
716	I-A	David Klingler, Houston (Arizona St.)	Dec. 2, 1990
690	I-A	Matt Vogler, Texas Christian (Houston)	Nov. 3, 1990
631	I-A	Scott Mitchell, Utah (Air Force)	Oct. 15, 1988
624	I-AA	Jamie Martin, Weber St. (Idaho St.)	Nov. 23, 1991
622	I-A	Jeremy Leach, New Mexico (Utah)	Nov. 11, 1989
621	I-A	Dave Wilson, Illinois (Ohio St.)	Nov. 8, 1980
619	I-A	John Walsh, Brigham Young (Utah St.)	Oct. 30, 1993
619	I-AA	Doug Pederson, Northeast La. (Stephen F. Austin)	Nov. 11, 1989
614	II	Alfred Montez, Western N.M. (West Tex. A&M)	Oct. 8, 1994
614	II	Perry Klein, LIU-C.W. Post (Salisbury St.)	Nov. 6, 1993
613	I-A	Jimmy Klingler, Houston (Rice)	Nov. 28, 1992
602	III	Tom Stallings, St. Thomas, Minn. (Bethel, Minn.)	Nov. 13, 1993
599	I-A	Ty Detmer, Brigham Young (San Diego St.)	Nov. 16, 1991
599	I-AA	Willie Totten, Mississippi Val. (Prairie View)	Oct. 27, 1984
592	II	John Charles, Portland St. (Cal Poly SLO)	Nov. 16, 1991
589	I-AA	Vern Harris, Idaho St. (Montana)	Oct. 12, 1985
587	I-AA	Steve McNair, Alcorn St. (Southern-B.R.)	Oct. 22, 1994
585	III	Tim Lynch, Hofstra (Fordham)	Oct. 19, 1991
585	I-A	Robbie Bosco, Brigham Young (New Mexico)	Oct. 19, 1985
575	III	Eric Noble, Wilmington, Ohio (Urbana)	Nov. 5, 1994
572	I-A	David Klingler, Houston (Eastern Wash.)	Nov. 17, 1990
571	I-AA	Todd Hammel, Stephen F. Austin (Northeast La.)	Nov. 11, 1989
571	I-A	Marc Wilson, Brigham Young (Utah)	Nov. 5, 1977
568	II	Scott Otis, Glenville St. (West Va. Wesleyan)	Oct. 15, 1994
568	I-A	David Lowery, San Diego St. (Brigham Young)	Nov. 16, 1991
568	II	Bob Toledo, San Fran. St. (Cal St. Hayward)	Oct. 21, 1967
566	I-AA	Tom Ehrhardt, Rhode Island (Connecticut)	Nov. 16, 1985
565	I-A	Jim McMahon, Brigham Young (Utah)	Nov. 21, 1981
564	II	Pat Graham, Augustana, S.D. (Mankato St.)	Oct. 28, 1995
564	I-A	Troy Kopp, Pacific, Cal. (New Mexico St.)	Oct. 20, 1990
563	I-AA	Steve McNair, Alcorn St. (Samford)	Oct. 29, 1994
563	I-A	David Klingler, Houston (Texas Christian)	Nov. 3, 1990
561	I-A	Tony Adams, Utah St. (Utah)	Nov. 11, 1972

SINGLE-GAME ATTEMPTS

Atts.	Div.	Player, Team (Opponent)	Date
81	III	Jordan Poznick, Principia (Blackburn)	Oct. 10, 1992
79	I-A	Matt Vogler, Texas Christian (Houston)	Nov. 3, 1990
79	III	Mike Wallace, Ohio Wesleyan (Denison)	Oct. 3, 1981
78	I-A	Rusty LaRue, Wake Forest (Duke)	Oct. 28, 1995
77	I-AA	Neil Lomax, Portland St. (Northern Colo.)	Oct. 20, 1979
76	I-A	David Klingler, Houston (Southern Methodist)	Oct. 20, 1990
75	I-A	Chris Vargas, Nevada (McNeese St.)	Sept. 19, 1992
74	II	Jermaine Whitaker, N.M. Highlands (Western St.)	Nov. 5, 1994
74	I-AA	Paul Peterson, Idaho St. (Nevada)	Oct. 1, 1983
73	I-A	Jeff Handy, Missouri (Oklahoma St.)	Oct. 17, 1992
73	I-A	Troy Kopp, Pacific, Cal. (Hawaii)	Oct. 27, 1990
73	I-A	Shane Montgomery, North Caro. St. (Duke)	Nov. 11, 1989
72	I-AA	Dave Dickenson, Montana (Idaho)	Oct. 21, 1995
72	I-A	Matt Vogler, Texas Christian (Texas Tech)	Nov. 10, 1990
72	II	Kurt Otto, North Dak. (Tex. A&M-Kingsville)	Sept. 13, 1986
72	III	Bob Lockhart, Millikin (Franklin)	Nov. 12, 1977
72	II	Kaipo Spencer, Santa Clara (Portland St.)	Oct. 11, 1975
72	II	Joe Stetser, Cal St. Chico (Oregon Tech)	Sept. 23, 1967

SINGLE-GAME COMPLETIONS

Cmp.	Div.	Player, Team (Opponent)	Date
55	I-A	Rusty LaRue, Wake Forest (Duke)	Oct. 28, 1995
50	I-A	Rusty LaRue, Wake Forest (North Caro. St.)	Nov. 18, 1995
50	III	Tim Lynch, Hofstra (Fordham)	Oct. 19, 1991
48	I-AA	Clayton Millis, Cal St. Northridge (St. Mary's, Cal.)	Nov. 11, 1995
48	III	Jordan Poznick, Principia (Blackburn)	Oct. 10, 1992
48	I-A	David Klingler, Houston (Southern Methodist)	Oct. 20, 1990
47	I-AA	Jamie Martin, Weber St. (Idaho St.)	Nov. 23, 1991
47	III	Mike Wallace, Ohio Wesleyan (Denison)	Oct. 3, 1981
46	I-A	Scott Milanovich, Maryland (Florida St.)	Nov. 18, 1995
46	I-A	Jimmy Klingler, Houston (Rice)	Nov. 28, 1992
46	I-AA	Doug Pederson, Northeast La. (Stephen F. Austin)	Nov. 11, 1989
46	I-AA	Willie Totten, Mississippi Val. (Southern-B.R.)	Sept. 29, 1984
45	II	Chris Hatcher, Valdosta St. (Mississippi Col.)	Oct. 23, 1993
45	II	Chris Hatcher, Valdosta St. (West Ga.)	Oct. 16, 1993
45	I-AA	Willie Totten, Mississippi Val. (Prairie View)	Oct. 27, 1984
45	I-A	Sandy Schwab, Northwestern (Michigan)	Oct. 23, 1982
44	I-A	Matt Vogler, Texas Christian (Houston)	Nov. 3, 1990
44	I-A	Chuck Hartlieb, Iowa (Indiana)	Oct. 29, 1988
44	II	Tom Bonds, Cal Lutheran (St. Mary's, Cal.)	Nov. 22, 1986
44	I-A	Jim McMahon, Brigham Young (Colorado St.)	Nov. 7, 1981
44	I-AA	Neil Lomax, Portland St. (Northern Colo.)	Oct. 20, 1979
43	I-AA	Dave Dickenson, Montana (Idaho)	Oct. 21, 1995
43	III	Terry Peebles, Hanover (Franklin)	Nov. 12, 1994
43	I-A	Jeff Handy, Missouri (Oklahoma St.)	Oct. 17, 1992
43	I-A	Chris Vargas, Nevada (McNeese St.)	Sept. 19, 1992
43	I-A	Gary Schofield, Wake Forest (Maryland)	Oct. 17, 1981
43	I-A	Dave Wilson, Illinois (Ohio St.)	Nov. 8, 1980
43	I-A	Rich Campbell, California (Florida)	Sept. 13, 1980
43	II	George Bork, Northern Ill. (Central Mich.)	Nov. 9, 1963

Receiving

CAREER RECEPTIONS

Player, Team (Division[s])	Years	Rec.	Yards	Avg.	TD
Jerry Rice, Mississippi Val. (I-AA)	1981-84	*301	*4,693	15.6	50
Matt Newton, Principia (III)	1990-93	287	3,646	12.7	32
Kasey Dunn, Idaho (I-AA)	1988-91	268	3,847	14.4	25
Aaron Turner, Pacific (Cal.) (I-A)	1989-92	266	4,345	16.3	43
Terance Mathis, New Mexico (I-A)	1985-87, 89	263	4,254	16.2	36
Mark Templeton, Long Beach St. (I-A) (RB)	1983-86	¢262	1,969	7.5	11
Jon Spinosa, Lock Haven (II)	1992-95	261	2,710	10.4	12
Howard Twilley, Tulsa (I-A)	1963-65	261	3,343	12.8	32
Bill Stromberg, Johns Hopkins (III)	1978-81	258	3,776	14.6	39
Chris Myers, Kenyon (II)	1967-70	253	3,897	15.4	33
Brian Forster, Rhode Island (I-AA) (TE)	1983-85, 87	#245	#3,410	13.9	31
David Williams, Illinois (I-A)	1983-85	245	3,195	13.0	22
Bruce Cerone, Yankton/Emporia St. (II)	1965-66, 68-69	241	4,354	18.1	49
James Roe, Norfolk St. (II)	1992-95	239	4,468	18.7	46
Mark Didio, Connecticut (I-AA)	1988-91	239	3,535	14.8	21
Rennie Benn, Lehigh (I-AA)	1982-85	237	3,662	15.5	44
Marc Zeno, Tulane (I-A)	1984-87	236	3,725	15.8	25
Jason Wolf, Southern Methodist (I-A)	1989-92	235	2,232	9.5	17
Bryan Reeves, Nevada (I-AA; I-A)	1991; 92-93	234	3,407	14.6	32
Dale Amos, Frank. & Marsh. (III)	1986-89	233	3,846	16.5	35
Scott Fredrickson, Wis.-Stout (III)	1986-89	233	3,390	14.5	23
"Red" Roberts, Austin Peay (II)	1967-70	232	3,005	13.0	31
Chris George, Glenville St. (II)	1993-94	230	3,215	14.0	30
Mike Whitehouse, St. Norbert (III)	1986-89	230	3,480	15.1	37
Jerry Hendren, Idaho (II; I-A)	1967-68; 69	230	3,435	14.9	27

**Record. ¢Record for a running back. #Record for a tight end.*

CAREER RECEPTIONS PER GAME

(Minimum 125 Receptions)

Player, Team (Division[s])	Years	G	Rec.	Yards	TD	Rec.PG
Chris George, Glenville St. (II)	1993-94	20	230	3,215	30	*11.5
Manny Hazard, Houston (I-A)	1989-90	21	220	2,635	31	10.5
Alex Van Dyke, Nevada (I-A)	1994-95	22	227	3,100	26	10.3
Howard Twilley, Tulsa (I-A)	1963-65	26	261	3,343	32	10.0
Jason Phillips, Houston (I-A)	1987-88	22	207	2,319	18	9.4
Matt Newton, Principia (III)	1990-93	33	287	3,646	32	8.7
Ed Bell, Idaho St. (II)	1968-69	19	163	2,608	30	8.6
Byron Chamberlain, Wayne St. (Neb.) (II)	1993-94	19	161	1,941	14	8.3
Jerry Hendren, Idaho (II)	1967-69	30	230	3,435	27	7.7
Bryan Reeves, Nevada (I-AA; I-A)	1991; 92-93	31	234	3,407	32	7.6

Player, Team (Division[s])	Years	G	Rec.	Yards	TD	Rec.PG
David Williams, Illinois (I-A)	1983-85	33	245	3,195	22	7.4
Gary Garrison, San Diego St. (II)	1964-65	20	148	2,188	26	7.4
Brad Bailey, West Tex. A&M (II)	1992-94	30	221	2,677	22	7.4
Jerry Rice, Mississippi Val. (I-AA)	1981-84	41	*301	*4,693	50	7.3
James Dixon, Houston (I-A)	1987-88	22	161	1,762	14	7.3

*Record.

CAREER TOUCHDOWN RECEPTIONS

Player, Team (Division[s])	Years	G	TD
Chris Bisaillon, Ill. Wesleyan (III)	1989-92	36	*55
Jerry Rice, Mississippi Val. (I-AA)	1981-84	41	50
Bruce Cerone, Yankton/Emporia St. (II)	1965-66, 68-69	36	49
James Roe, Norfolk St. (II)	1992-95	41	46
Rennie Benn, Lehigh (I-AA)	1982-85	41	44
Aaron Turner, Pacific (Cal.) (I-A)	1989-92	44	43
Ryan Yarborough, Wyoming (I-A)	1990-93	46	42
Shannon Sharpe, Savannah St. (II)	1986-89	42	40
John Aromando, Trenton St. (III)	1981-84	40	39
Bill Stromberg, Johns Hopkins (III)	1978-81	40	39
Rodd Patten, Framingham St. (III)	1990-93	35	38
Tony Willis, New Haven (II)	1990-93	40	38
Clarkston Hines, Duke (I-A)	1986-89	44	38
Roy Banks, Eastern Ill. (I-AA)	1983-86	38	38
Robert Clark, N.C. Central (II)	1983-86	40	38
Mike Jones, Tennessee St. (I-AA)	1979-82	42	38
Chris Holder, Tuskegee (II)	1988-91	40	37
Mike Whitehouse, St. Norbert (III)	1986-89	38	37
Terance Mathis, New Mexico (I-A)	1985-87, 89	44	36
Mike Cottle, Juniata (III)	1985-88	37	36
Joe Thomas, Mississippi Val. (I-AA)	1982-85	41	36
Willie Richardson, Jackson St. (II)	1959-62	38	36

*Record.

SEASON RECEPTIONS

Player, Team (Division)	Year	G	Rec.	Yards	TD
Manny Hazard, Houston (I-A)	†1989	11	*142	1,689	22
Howard Twilley, Tulsa (I-A)	†1965	10	134	1,779	16
Alex Van Dyke, Nevada (I-A)	†1995	11	129	1,854	16
Brad Bailey, West Tex. A&M (II)	1994	11	119	1,552	16
Chris George, Glenville St. (II)	†1993	10	117	*1,876	15
Brian Forster, Rhode Island (I-AA) (TE)	†1985	10	115	1,617	12
Chris George, Glenville St. (II)	†1994	10	113	1,339	15
Sean Pender, Valdosta St. (II)	†1995	11	111	983	2
Fred Gilbert, Houston (I-A)	†1991	11	106	957	7
Barry Wagner, Alabama A&M (II)	†1989	11	106	1,812	17
Theo Blanco, Wis.-Stevens Point (III) (RB)	1987	11	#106	#1,616	8
Chris Penn, Tulsa (I-A)	†1993	11	105	1,578	12
Sherman Smith, Houston (I-A)	†1992	11	103	923	6
Jerry Rice, Mississippi Val. (I-AA)	†1984	10	103	1,682	*27
James Dixon, Houston (I-A)	1988	11	102	1,103	11
Jerry Rice, Mississippi Val. (I-AA)	†1983	10	102	1,450	14
Mike Healey, Valparaiso (II)	†1985	10	101	1,279	11
David Williams, Illinois (I-A)	†1984	11	101	1,278	8
Jay Miller, Brigham Young (I-A)	†1973	11	100	1,181	8
Jason Phillips, Houston (I-A)	†1987	11	99	875	3
Mark Templeton, Long Beach St. (I-A) (RB)	†1986	11	99	688	2
Alex Van Dyke, Nevada (I-A)	†1994	11	98	1,246	10
Matt Newton, Principia (III)	†1992	8	98	1,487	14
Rodney Carter, Purdue (I-A)	†1985	11	98	1,099	4
Keith Edwards, Vanderbilt (I-A)	†1983	11	97	909	0

*Record. †National champion. #Record for a running back.

SEASON RECEPTIONS PER GAME

Player, Team (Division)	Year	G	Rec.	Yards	TD	Rec.PG
Howard Twilley, Tulsa (I-A)	†1965	10	134	1,779	16	*13.4
Manny Hazard, Houston (I-A)	†1989	11	*142	1,689	22	12.9
Matt Newton, Principia (III)	†1992	8	98	1,487	14	12.3
Matt Newton, Principia (III)	†1993	8	96	1,080	11	12.0
Alex Van Dyke, Nevada (I-A)	†1995	11	129	1,854	16	11.7
Chris George, Glenville St. (II)	†1993	10	117	*1,876	15	11.7
Brian Forster, Rhode Island (I-AA) (TE)	†1985	10	115	1,617	12	11.5
Chris George, Glenville St. (II)	†1994	10	113	1,339	15	11.3
Brad Bailey, West Tex. A&M (II)	1994	11	119	1,552	16	10.8
Ben Fox, Hanover (III)	†1995	9	95	1,087	15	10.6
Sean Munroe, Mass.-Boston (III)	1992	9	95	1,693	17	10.6
Jerry Rice, Mississippi Val. (I-AA)	†1984	10	103	1,682	*27	10.3
Scott Faessler, Framingham St. (III)	†1990	9	92	916	5	10.2
Jerry Rice, Mississippi Val. (I-AA)	†1983	10	102	1,450	14	10.2
Bruce Cerone, Emporia St. (II)	†1968	9	91	1,479	15	10.1
Mike Healy, Valparaiso (II)	†1985	10	101	1,279	11	10.1
Sean Pender, Valdosta St. (II)	†1995	11	111	983	2	10.1
Stuart Gaussoin, Portland St. (I-AA)	†1979	9	90	1,132	8	10.0

*Record. †National champion.

SINGLE-GAME RECEPTIONS

No.	Div.	Player, Team (Opponent)	Date
24	I-AA	Jerry Rice, Mississippi Val. (Southern-B.R.)	Oct. 1, 1983
23	II	Chris George, Glenville St. (West Va. Wesleyan)	Oct. 15, 1994
23	I-A	Randy Gatewood, UNLV (Idaho)	Sept. 17, 1994
23	III	Sean Munroe, Mass.-Boston (Mass. Maritime)	Oct. 10, 1992
23	II	Barry Wagner, Alabama A&M (Clark Atlanta)	Nov. 4, 1989
22	I-AA	Marvin Walker, North Texas (Tulsa)	Nov. 20, 1982
22	I-A	Jay Miller, Brigham Young (New Mexico)	Nov. 3, 1973
21	II	Jarett Vito, Emporia St. (Truman St.)	Nov. 4, 1995
21#	I-AA	David Pandt, Montana St. (Eastern Wash.)	Sept. 21, 1985
20	I-AA	Tim Hilton, Cal St. Northridge (St. Mary's, Cal.)	Nov. 11, 1995
20	II	Sean Pender, Valdosta St. (Mississippi Col.)	Nov. 4, 1995
20	II	Keylie Martin, N.M. Highlands (Western St.)	Nov. 5, 1994
20	III	Rich Johnson, Pace (Fordham)	Nov. 7, 1987
20	III	Pete Thompson, Carroll, Wis. (Augustana, Ill.)	Nov. 4, 1978
20	II	Harold "Red" Roberts, Austin Peay (Murray St.)	Nov. 8, 1969
20	I-A	Rick Eber, Tulsa (Idaho St.)	Oct. 7, 1967

#Record for a running back.

CAREER YARDS

Player, Team (Division[s])	Years	Rec.	Yards	Avg.	TD
Jerry Rice, Mississippi Val. (I-AA)	1981-84	*301	*4,693	15.6	50
James Roe, Norfolk St. (II)	1992-95	239	4,468	18.7	46
Ryan Yarborough, Wyoming (I-A)	1990-93	229	4,357	19.0	42
Bruce Cerone, Yankton/Emporia St. (II)	1965-66, 68-69	241	4,354	18.1	49
Aaron Turner, Pacific (Cal.) (I-A)	1989-92	266	4,345	16.3	43
Terance Mathis, New Mexico (I-A)	1985-87, 89	263	4,254	16.2	36
Robert Clark, N.C. Central (II)	1983-86	210	4,231	‡20.1	38
Chris Myers, Kenyon (II)	1967-70	253	3,897	15.4	33
Kasey Dunn, Idaho (I-AA)	1988-91	268	3,847	14.4	25
Dale Amos, Frank. & Marsh. (III)	1986-89	233	3,846	16.5	35
Bill Stromberg, Johns Hopkins (III)	1978-81	258	3,776	14.6	39
Shannon Sharpe, Savannah St. (II)	1986-89	192	3,744	19.5	40
Marc Zeno, Tulane (I-A)	1984-87	236	3,725	15.8	25
Jim Bradford, Carleton (III)	1988-91	212	3,719	17.5	32
Tyrone Johnson, Western St. (II)	1990-93	163	3,717	22.8	35
Chris Bisaillon, Ill. Wesleyan (III)	1989-92	223	3,670	16.5	*55
Rennie Benn, Lehigh (I-AA)	1982-85	237	3,662	15.5	44
Matt Newton, Principia (III)	1990-93	287	3,646	12.7	32
Jeff Tiefenthaler, South Dak. St. (II)	1983-86	173	3,621	20.9	31
David Rhodes, Central Fla. (I-AA)	1991-94	213	3,618	17.0	29
Willie Richardson, Jackson St. (II)	1959-62	166	3,616	21.8	36
Johnny Cox, Fort Lewis (II)	1990-93	220	3,611	16.4	33
Ron Sellers, Florida St. (I-A)	1966-68	212	3,598	17.0	23

*Record. ‡Record for minimum 180 catches.

CAREER YARDS PER GAME

(Minimum 2,200 Yards)

Player, Team (Division[s])	Years	G	Yards	Yd.PG
Chris George, Glenville St. (II)	1993-94	20	3,215	*160.8
Alex Van Dyke, Nevada (I-A)	1994-95	22	3,100	140.9
Ed Bell, Idaho St. (II)	1968-69	19	2,608	137.3
Manny Hazard, Houston (I-A)	1989-90	21	2,635	125.5
Bruce Cerone, Yankton/Emporia St. (II)	1965-66, 68-69	36	4,354	120.9
Ron Sellers, Florida St. (I-A)	1966-68	30	3,598	119.9
Derrick Ingram, Ala.-Birmingham (I-AA)	1993-94	22	2,572	116.9
Jerry Rice, Mississippi Val. (I-AA)	1981-84	41	*4,693	114.5
Jerry Hendren, Idaho (II)	1967-69	30	3,435	114.5
Elmo Wright, Houston (I-A)	1968-70	30	3,347	111.6
Howard Twilley, Tulsa (I-A)	1963-65	30	3,343	111.4
Chris Myers, Kenyon (II)	1967-70	35	3,897	111.3
Matt Newton, Principia (III)	1990-93	33	3,646	110.5
Tim McNamara, Trinity (Conn.) (III)	1981-84	21	2,313	110.1
Bryan Reeves, Nevada (I-AA; I-A)	1991; 92-93	31	3,407	109.9
James Roe, Norfolk St. (II)	1992-95	41	4,468	109.0
Chris Penn, Tulsa (I-A)	1991, 93	22	2,370	107.7
Jason Phillips, Houston (I-A)	1987-88	22	2,319	105.4
Bill Stromberg, Johns Hopkins (III)	1978-81	36	3,776	104.9
Chris Bisaillon, Ill. Wesleyan (III)	1989-92	36	3,670	101.9

*Record.

SEASON YARDS

Player, Team (Division)	Year	Rec.	Yards	Avg.	TD
Chris George, Glenville St. (II)	†1993	117	*1,876	16.0	15
Alex Van Dyke, Nevada (I-A)	†1995	129	1,854	14.4	16
Barry Wagner, Alabama A&M (II)	†1989	106	1,812	17.1	17
Howard Twilley, Tulsa (I-A)	†1965	134	1,779	13.3	16
Chris Perry, Adams St. (II)	†1995	88	1,719	19.5	21
Sean Munroe, Mass.-Boston (III)	†1992	95	1,693	17.8	17
Manny Hazard, Houston (I-A)	†1989	*142	1,689	11.9	22
Jerry Rice, Mississippi Val. (I-AA)	†1984	103	1,682	16.3	*27
Brian Forster, Rhode Island (I-AA) (TE)	†1985	115	1,617	14.1	12
Theo Blanco, Wis.-Stevens Point (III) (RB)	1987	#106	#1,616	15.2	8

Player, Team (Division)	Year	Rec.	Yards	Avg.	TD
Aaron Turner, Pacific (Cal.) (I-A)	†1991	92	1,604	17.4	18
Dan Fulton, Neb.-Omaha (II)	1976	67	1,581	23.6	16
Chris Penn, Tulsa (I-A)	†1993	105	1,578	15.0	12
Brad Bailey, West Tex. A&M (II)	1994	119	1,552	13.0	16
Jeff Tiefenthaler, South Dak. St. (II)	1986	73	1,534	21.0	11
Ed Bell, Idaho St. (II)	†1969	96	1,522	15.9	20
Chuck Hughes, UTEP (I-A)	1965	80	1,519	19.0	12
Ryan Yarborough, Wyoming (I-A)	1993	67	1,512	22.6	16
Henry Ellard, Fresno St. (I-A)	1982	62	1,510	††24.4	15
Rodney Robinson, Gardner-Webb (II)	†1992	89	1,496	16.8	16
Ron Sellers, Florida St. (I-A)	†1968	86	1,496	17.4	12

**Record. †National champion. ††Record for minimum 55 catches. #Record for a running back.*

SEASON YARDS PER GAME

Player, Team (Division)	Year	G	Rec.	Yards	Yd. PG
Sean Munroe, Mass.-Boston (III)	†1992	9	95	1,693	*188.1
Chris George, Glenville St. (II)	†1993	10	117	*1,876	187.6
Matt Newton, Principia (III)	†1992	8	98	1,487	185.9
Howard Twilley, Tulsa (I-A)	†1965	10	134	1,779	177.9
Chris Perry, Adams St. (II)	†1995	10	88	1,719	171.9
Alex Van Dyke, Nevada (I-A)	†1995	11	129	1,854	168.5
Jerry Rice, Mississippi Val. (I-AA)	†1984	10	103	1,682	168.2
Barry Wagner, Alabama A&M (II)	†1989	11	106	1,812	164.7
Bruce Cerone, Emporia St. (II)	†1968	9	91	1,479	164.3
Brian Forster, Rhode Island (I-AA)	†1985	10	115	1,617	161.7

**Record. †National champion.*

SEASON TOUCHDOWN RECEPTIONS

Player, Team (Division)	Year	G	TD
Jerry Rice, Mississippi Val. (I-AA)	1984	10	*27
Manny Hazard, Houston (I-A)	1989	11	22
Chris Perry, Adams St. (II)	1995	10	21
John Aromando, Trenton St. (III)	1983	10	20
Ed Bell, Idaho St. (II)	1969	10	20
Stanley Flanders, Valdosta St. (II)	1994	11	19
Desmond Howard, Michigan (I-A)	1991	11	19
Kurt Barth, Eureka (III)	1995	10	18
Brian Penecale, West Chester (II)	1994	11	18
Aaron Turner, Pacific (Cal.) (I-A)	1991	11	18
Dennis Smith, Utah (I-A)	1989	12	18
Tom Reynolds, San Diego St. (I-A)	1971	10	18
Terry Glenn, Ohio St. (I-A)	1995	11	17
Chris Doering, Florida (I-A)	1995	12	17
Jeremy Loretz, St. John's (Minn.) (III)	1994	10	17
James Roe, Norfolk St. (II)	1994	10	17
Robert Williams, Valdosta St. (II)	1994	11	17
Bryan Reeves, Nevada (I-A)	1993	10	17
J. J. Stokes, UCLA (I-A)	1993	11	17
Sean Munroe, Mass.-Boston (III)	1992	9	17
Chris Bisaillon, Ill. Wesleyan (III)	1991	9	17
Mario Bailey, Washington (I-A)	1991	11	17
Clarkston Hines, Duke (I-A)	1989	11	17
Barry Wagner, Alabama A&M (II)	1989	11	17
Mark Carrier, Nicholls St. (I-AA)	1986	11	17
Dameon Reilly, Rhode Island (I-AA)	1985	11	17
Joe Thomas, Mississippi Val. (I-AA)	1985	11	17
Roy Banks, Eastern Ill. (I-AA)	1984	11	17
Alex Van Dyke, Nevada (I-A)	1995	11	16
Wayne Chrebet, Hofstra (I-AA)	1994	10	16
Brad Bailey, West Tex. A&M (II)	1994	11	16
Dave Cecchini, Lehigh (I-AA)	1993	11	16
Ryan Yarborough, Wyoming (I-A)	1993	11	16
Rodney Robinson, Gardner-Webb (II)	1992	11	16
Evan Elkington, Worcester Tech (III)	1989	10	16
Dan Bitson, Tulsa (I-A)	1989	11	16
Dan Fulton, Neb.-Omaha (II)	1976	10	16
Howard Twilley, Tulsa (I-A)	1965	10	16

**Record.*

SINGLE-GAME YARDS

Yds.	Div.	Player, Team (Opponent)	Date
370	I-AA	Michael Lerch, Princeton (Brown)	Oct. 12, 1991
370	II	Barry Wagner, Alabama A&M (Clark Atlanta)	Nov. 4, 1989
363	I-A	Randy Gatewood, UNLV (Idaho)	Sept. 17, 1994
363	II	Tom Nettles, San Diego St. (Southern Miss.)	Nov. 9, 1968
354	II	Robert Clark, N.C. Central (Jackson St.)	Aug. 30, 1986
349	I-A	Chuck Hughes, UTEP (North Texas)	Sept. 18, 1965
332	III	Sean Munroe, Mass.-Boston (Mass. Maritime)	Oct. 10, 1992
330	I-AA	Nate Singleton, Grambling (Virginia Union)	Sept. 14, 1991
327@	I-AA	Brian Forster, Rhode Island (Brown)	Sept. 28, 1985
325	II	Paul Zaeske, North Park (North Central)	Oct. 12, 1968
322	I-A	Rick Eber, Tulsa (Idaho St.)	Oct. 7, 1967
319	I-AA	Jason Cristino, Lehigh (Lafayette)	Nov. 21, 1992
318	I-A	Harry Wood, Tulsa (Idaho St.)	Oct. 7, 1967
317	II	Dan Fulton, Neb.-Omaha (South Dak.)	Sept. 4, 1976
316	I-AA	Marcus Hinton, Alcorn St. (Tenn.-Chatt.)	Sept. 10, 1994
316	I-A	Jeff Evans, New Mexico St. (Southern Ill.)	Sept. 30, 1978
314	I-A	Alex Van Dyke, Nevada (San Jose St.)	Nov. 18, 1995
310	II	Mike Collodi, Colorado Mines (Westminster, Utah)	Oct. 3, 1970
309	III	Dale Amos, Frank. & Marsh. (Western Md.)	Oct. 24, 1987

@Record for a tight end.

Interceptions

CAREER INTERCEPTIONS

Player, Team (Division[s])	Years	No.	Yards	Avg.
Tom Collins, Indianapolis (II)	1982-85	*37	390	10.5
Ralph Gebhardt, Rochester (II; III)	1972; 73-75	34	406	11.9
Dean Diaz, Humboldt St. (II)	1980-83	31	328	10.6
Bill Grantham, Mo.-Rolla (II)	1977-80	29	263	9.1
Eugene Hunter, Fort Valley St. (II; III)	1972; 73-74	29	479	16.5
Al Brosky, Illinois (I-A)	1950-52	29	356	12.3
Jason Johnson, Shepherd (II)	1991-94	28	321	11.5
Rick Bealer, Lycoming (III)	1987-90	28	279	10.0
Brian Fetterolf, Aurora (III)	1986-89	28	390	13.9
Dave Murphy, Holy Cross (I-AA)	1986-89	28	309	11.0
Tim Lennon, Curry (III)	1986-89	27	190	7.0
Scott Stanitous, Moravian (III)	1985-88	27	178	6.6
Mike Hintz, Wis.-Platteville (III)	1983-86	27	183	6.8
Martin Bayless, Bowling Green (I-A)	1980-83	27	266	9.9
John Provost, Holy Cross (I-A)	1972-74	27	470	17.4
Cory Mabry, Susquehanna (III)	1988-91	26	400	15.4
Tony Woods, Bloomsburg (II)	1982-85	26	105	4.0
Jeff Hughes, Ripon (III)	1975-78	26	333	12.8
Buster West, Gust. Adolphus (II)	1967-70	26	192	7.4

**Record.*

SEASON INTERCEPTIONS

Player, Team (Division)	Year	No.	Yards
Mark Dorner, Juniata (III)	†1987	*15	202
Eugene Hunter, Fort Valley St. (II)	†1972	14	211
Luther Howard, Delaware St. (II)	†1972	14	99
Tom Rezzuti, Northeastern (II)	†1971	14	153
Jim Blackwell, Southern-B.R. (II)	†1970	14	196
Carl Ray Harris, Fresno St. (II)	†1970	14	98
Al Worley, Washington (I-A)	†1968	14	130

**Record. †National champion.*

Punt Returns

CAREER AVERAGE

(Minimum 1.2 Returns Per Game; Minimum 30 Returns)

Player, Team (Division[s])	Years	No.	Yards	Avg.
Billy Johnson, Widener (II; III)	1971-72; 73	40	989	*24.7
Jack Mitchell, Oklahoma (I-A)	1946-48	39	922	23.6
Keith Winston, Knoxville (III)	1986-87	30	686	22.9
Kevin Doherty, Mass. Maritime (III)	1976-78, 80	45	939	20.9
Chuck Downey, Stony Brook (III)	1984-87	59	1,198	**20.3
Chuck Goehl, Monmouth (Ill.) (II)	1970-72	48	911	19.0
Eddie Macon, Pacific (Cal.) (I-A)	1949-51	48	907	18.9
Willie Canady, Fort Valley St. (III)	1979-82	41	772	18.8
Jackie Robinson, UCLA (I-A)	1939-40	37	694	18.8

**Record. **Record for minimum 50 returns.*

SEASON AVERAGE

(Minimum 1.2 Returns Per Game and Qualifiers for Championship)

Player, Team (Division)	Year	No.	Yards	Avg.
Billy Johnson, Widener (II)	†1972	15	511	*34.1
Chuck Downey, Stony Brook (III)	†1986	17	530	31.2
Kevin Doherty, Mass. Maritime (III)	†1976	11	332	30.2
Dennis Robinson, Wesleyan (Conn.) (III)	†1978	9	263	29.2
Robert Middlebrook, Knoxville (III)	†1984	9	260	28.9
Joe Troise, Kean (III)	†1974	12	342	28.5
William Williams, Livingstone (II)	†1976	16	453	28.3
Terry Egerdahl, Minn.-Duluth (II)	†1975	13	360	27.7
Melvin Dillard, Ferrum (III)	†1990	25	688	27.5
Eric Green, Ill. Benedictine (III)	†1993	13	346	26.6
Bill Blackstock, Tennessee (I-A)	1951	12	311	25.9
Ennis Thomas, Bishop (II)	†1971	18	450	25.0
George Sims, Baylor (I-A)	1948	15	375	25.0

**Record. †National champion.*

Kickoff Returns

CAREER AVERAGE

(Minimum 1.2 Returns Per Game; Minimum 30 Returns)

Player, Team (Division[s])	Years	No.	Yards	Avg.
Anthony Davis, Southern Cal (I-A)	1972-74	37	1,299	*35.1
Overton Curtis, Utah St. (I-A)	1957-58	32	991	31.0
Fred Montgomery, New Mexico St. (I-A)	1991-92	39	1,191	30.5
Karl Evans, Mo. Southern St. (II)	1991-92	32	959	30.0
Kevin Cannon, Millersville (II)	1992-95	67	1,999	29.8
Troy Brown, Marshall (I-AA)	1991-92	32	950	29.7
Dave Ludy, Winona St. (II)	1991-94	89	2,630	29.6
Charles Swann, Indiana St. (I-AA)	1989-91	45	1,319	29.3
Altie Taylor, Utah St. (I-A)	1966-68	40	1,170	29.3
Daryl Brown, Tufts (III)	1974-76	38	1,111	29.2
Stan Brown, Purdue (I-A)	1968-70	49	1,412	28.8
Henry White, Colgate (I-A)	1974-77	41	1,180	28.8
Doug Parrish, San Fran. St. (II)	1990	35	1,002	28.6
Craig Richardson, Eastern Wash. (I-AA)	1983-86	71	2,021	28.5

*Record.

SEASON AVERAGE

(Minimum 1.2 Returns Per Game and Qualifiers for Championship)

Player, Team (Division)	Year	No.	Yards	Avg.
Brandon Steinheim, Wesley (III)	†1994	10	422	*42.2
Paul Allen, Brigham Young (I-A)	1961	12	481	40.1
Jason Martin, Coe (III)	†1992	11	438	39.8
LaVon Reis, Western St. (II)	†1993	14	552	39.4
Danny Lee, Jacksonville St. (II)	†1992	12	473	39.4
Leeland McElroy, Texas A&M (I-A)	†1993	15	590	39.3
Fran DeFalco, Assumption (II)	1993	12	461	38.4
Forrest Hall, San Francisco (I-A)	1946	15	573	@38.2
David Fraterrigo, Canisius (I-AA)	†1993	13	485	37.3
Nate Kirtman, Pomona-Pitzer (III)	†1990	14	515	36.8
Kendall James, Carson-Newman (II)	1993	15	549	36.6
Kerry Hayes, Western Caro. (I-AA)	1993	16	584	36.5
Tom Myers, Coe (III)	†1983	11	401	36.5
Tony Ball, Tenn.-Chatt. (I-A)	†1977	13	473	36.4
Ron Scott, Occidental (III)	1983	10	363	36.3
Alan Hill, DePauw (III)	1980	12	434	36.2
Roscoe Word, Jackson St. (II)	†1973	18	650	36.1
Steve Levenseller, Puget Sound (II)	†1978	17	610	35.9
George Marinkov, North Caro. St. (I-A)	1954	13	465	35.8

*Record. †National champion. @ Record for minimum 1.5 returns per game.

Field Goals

(One-inch tees were permitted in 1949, two-inch tees were permitted in 1965, and use of tees was eliminated before the 1989 season. The goal posts were widened from 18 feet, 6 inches to 23 feet, 4 inches in 1959 and were narrowed back to 18 feet, 6 inches before the 1991 season. The hash marks were moved six feet, eight inches closer to the center of the field to 60 feet from each sideline in 1993.)

CAREER FIELD GOALS

Player, Team (Division[s])	Years	FGM	FGA	Pct.
Jeff Jaeger, Washington (S) (I-A)	1983-86	*80	99	.808
John Lee, UCLA (S) (I-A)	1982-85	79	92	*.859
Philip Doyle, Alabama (S) (I-A)	1987-90	78	*105	.743
Luis Zendejas, Arizona St. (S) (I-A)	1981-84	78	*105	.743
Max Zendejas, Arizona (S) (I-A)	1982-85	77	104	.740
Kevin Butler, Georgia (S) (I-A)	1981-84	77	98	.786
Carlos Huerta, Miami (Fla.) (S) (I-A)	1988-91	73	91	.802
Derek Schmidt, Florida St. (S) (I-A)	1984-87	73	104	.702
Marty Zendejas, Nevada (S) (I-AA)	1984-87	72	90	.800
Kirk Roach, Western Caro. (S) (I-AA)	1984-87	71	102	.696
Fuad Reveiz, Tennessee (S) (I-A)	1981-84	71	95	.747
Roman Anderson, Houston (S) (I-A)	1988-91	70	101	.693
Barry Belli, Fresno St. (S) (I-A)	1984-87	70	99	.707
Tony Zendejas, Nevada (S) (I-AA)	1981-83	70	86	.814
Collin Mackie, South Caro. (S) (I-A)	1987-90	69	95	.726
Gary Gussman, Miami (Ohio) (S) (I-A)	1984-87	68	94	.723
Larry Roach, Oklahoma St. (S) (I-A)	1981-84	68	101	.673
Michael Proctor, Alabama (S) (I-A)	1992-95	65	91	.714
Paul Woodside, West Va. (S) (I-A)	1981-84	65	81	.802

*Record. (S) Soccer-style kicker.

SEASON FIELD GOALS

Player, Team (Division)	Year	FGM	FGA	Pct.
John Lee, UCLA (S) (I-A)	1984	*29	33	.879
Luis Zendejas, Arizona St. (S) (I-A)	1983	28	37	.757
Paul Woodside, West Va. (S) (I-A)	1982	28	31	.903
Fuad Reveiz, Tennessee (S) (I-A)	1982	27	31	.871
Brian Mitchell, Northern Iowa (S) (I-AA)	1990	26	27	*.963
Tony Zendejas, Nevada (S) (I-AA)	1982	26	33	.788
Chris Jacke, UTEP (S) (I-A)	1988	25	27	.926
John Diettrich, Ball St. (S) (I-A)	1985	25	29	.862
Chuck Nelson, Washington (S) (I-A)	1982	25	26	.962
Remy Hamilton, Michigan (S) (I-A)	1994	24	29	.828
Philip Doyle, Alabama (S) (I-A)	1990	24	29	.828
Kendall Trainor, Arkansas (S) (I-A)	1988	24	27	.889
Kirk Roach, Western Caro. (S) (I-AA)	1986	24	28	.857
Carlos Reveiz, Tennessee (S) (I-A)	1985	24	28	.857
George Benyola, Louisiana Tech (S) (I-AA)	1985	24	31	.774
Chris White, Illinois (S) (I-A)	1984	24	28	.857
Mike Prindle, Western Mich. (S) (I-A)	1984	24	30	.800
Bruce Kallmeyer, Kansas (S) (I-A)	1983	24	29	.828

*Record. (S) Soccer-style kicker. (Record for attempts is 38)

LONGEST FIELD GOALS

Yds.	Div.	Player, Team (Opponent)	Year
67	II	Tom Odle, Fort Hays St. (Washburn)	1988
67	I-A	Joe Williams, Wichita St. (Southern Ill.)	1978
67	I-A	Russell Erxleben, Texas (Rice)	1977
67	I-A	Steve Little, Arkansas (Texas)	1977
65	I-A	Tony Franklin, Texas A&M (Baylor)	1976
64	I-A	Russell Erxleben, Texas (Oklahoma)	1977
64	I-A	Tony Franklin, Texas A&M (Baylor)	1976
63	I-AA	Tim Foley, Ga. Southern (James Madison)	1987
63	I-AA	Scott Roper, Arkansas St. (North Texas)	1987
63	I-A	Morten Andersen, Michigan St. (Ohio St.)	1981
63	I-A	Clark Kemble, Colorado St. (Arizona)	1975
63	II	Joe Duren, Arkansas St. (McNeese St.)	1974
62*	I-A	Jason Hanson, Washington St. (UNLV)	1991
62	I-A	John Diettrich, Ball St. (Ohio)	1986
62	I-AA	Paul Hickert, Murray St. (Eastern Ky.)	1986
62#	I-A	Chip Lohmiller, Minnesota (Iowa)	1986
62	I-A	Tom Whelihan, Missouri (Colorado)	1986
62	I-A	Dan Christopulos, Wyoming (Colorado St.)	1977
62	I-A	Iseed Khoury, North Texas (Richmond)	1977
62	III	Dom Antonini, Rowan (Salisbury St.)	1976
62	I-A	Dave Lawson, Air Force (Iowa St.)	1975
62	II	Mike Flater, Colorado Mines (Western St.)	1973

*Longest collegiate field goal without use of a tee and also longest collegiate field goal with narrower goal posts (18 feet, 6 inches). #Longest field goal made indoors.

Special Reference: Ove Johannson, Abilene Christian (not an NCAA-member college at the time), kicked a 69-yard field goal against East Texas State, Oct. 16, 1976.

Punting

CAREER PUNTING AVERAGE

(Minimum 150 Punts)

Player, Team (Division[s])	Years	No.	Yards	Avg.
Todd Sauerbrun, West Va. (I-A)	1991-94	167	7,733	*46.3
Reggie Roby, Iowa (I-A)	1979-82	172	7,849	45.6
Greg Montgomery, Michigan St. (I-A)	1985-87	170	7,721	45.4
Tom Tupa, Ohio St. (I-A)	1984-87	196	8,854	45.2
Barry Helton, Colorado (I-A)	1984-87	153	6,873	44.9
Ray Guy, Southern Miss. (I-A)	1970-72	200	8,934	44.7
Bucky Scribner, Kansas (I-A)	1980-82	217	9,670	44.6
Terry Daniel, Auburn (I-A)	1992-94	169	7,522	44.5
Greg Horne, Arkansas (I-A)	1983-86	180	8,002	44.5
Ray Criswell, Florida (I-A)	1982-85	161	7,153	44.4
Pumpy Tudors, Tenn.-Chatt. (I-AA)	1988-91	181	8,041	44.4
Bill Smith, Mississippi (I-A)	1983-86	254	11,260	44.3
Tim Baer, Colorado Mines (II)	1986-89	235	10,406	44.3
Russell Erxleben, Texas (I-A)	1975-78	214	9,467	44.2
Mark Simon, Air Force (I-A)	1984-86	156	6,898	44.2
Johnny Evans, North Caro. St. (I-A)	1974-77	185	8,143	44.0
Chuck Ramsey, Wake Forest (I-A)	1971-73	205	9,010	44.0

*Record.

SEASON PUNTING AVERAGE

(Qualifiers for Championship)

Player, Team (Division)	Year	No.	Yards	Avg.
Reggie Roby, Iowa (I-A)	†1981	44	2,193	*49.8
Kirk Wilson, UCLA (I-A)	†1956	30	1,479	49.3
Steve Ecker, Shippensburg (II)	†1965	32	1,570	49.1
Todd Sauerbrun, West Va. (I-A)	†1994	72	3,486	48.4
Zack Jordan, Colorado (I-A)	†1950	38	1,830	48.2
Ricky Anderson, Vanderbilt (I-A)	†1984	58	2,793	48.2
Reggie Roby, Iowa (I-A)	†1982	52	2,501	48.1

Player, Team (Division)	Year	No.	Yards	Avg.
Marv Bateman, Utah (I-A)	†1971	68	3,269	48.1
Don Cockroft, Adams St. (II)	†1966	36	1,728	48.0
Owen Price, UTEP (I-A)	†1940	30	1,440	48.0
Jack Jacobs, Oklahoma (I-A)	1940	31	1,483	47.8
Bill Smith, Mississippi (I-A)	1984	44	2,099	47.7

**Record. †National champion.*

LONGEST PUNTS

Yds.	Div.	Player, Team (Opponent)	Year
99	I-A	Pat Brady, Nevada (Loyola Marymount)	1950
97	II	Earl Hurst, Emporia St. (Central Mo. St.)	1964
96	II	Alex Campbell, Morris Brown (Clark Atlanta)	1994
96	II	Gary Frens, Hope (Olivet)	1966
96	II	Jim Jarrett, North Dak. (South Dak.)	1957
96	I-A	George O'Brien, Wisconsin (Iowa)	1952
94	I-A	John Hadl, Kansas (Oklahoma)	1959
94	I-A	Carl Knox, Texas Christian (Oklahoma St.)	1947
94	I-A	Preston Johnson, Southern Methodist (Pittsburgh)	1940
93	II	Elliot Mills, Carleton (Monmouth, Ill.)	1970
93	II	Kasper Fitins, Taylor (Georgetown, Ky.)	1966
93	II	Leeroy Sweeney, Pomona-Pitzer (UC Riverside)	1960
93	I-A	Bob Handke, Drake (Wichita St.)	1949

All-Purpose Yards

CAREER YARDS

Player, Team (Division[s])	Years	Rush	Rcv.	Int.	PR	KO	Yds.
Carey Bender, Coe (III)	1991-94	6,125	1,751	0	7	87	*7,970
Johnny Bailey, Tex. A&M-Kingsville (II)	1986-89	*6,320	452	0	20	1,011	7,803
Kenny Gamble, Colgate (I-AA)	1984-87	5,220	536	0	104	1,763	7,623
Howard Stevens, Randolph-Macon (II); Louisville (I-A)	1968-69; 71-72	5,297	738	0	781	748	7,564
Roger Graham, New Haven (II)	1991-94	5,953	393	0	0	870	7,216
Napoleon McCallum, Navy (I-A)	$1981-85	4,179	796	0	858	1,339	7,172
Dave Ludy, Winona St. (II)	1991-94	3,501	906	0	34	2,630	7,071
Albert Fann, Cal St. Northridge (II)	1987-90	4,090	803	0	0	2,141	7,032
Kirk Matthieu, Maine Maritime (III)	$1989-93	5,107	315	0	254	1,279	6,955
Curtis Delgardo, Portland St. (II)	$1986-90	4,178	1,258	0	318	1,188	6,942
Darrin Nelson, Stanford (I-A)	1977-78, 80-81	4,033	2,368	0	471	13	6,885
Eric Frees, Western Md. (III)	1988-91	5,281	392	0	47	1,158	6,878
Johnny Cox, Fort Lewis (II)	1990-93	112	3,611	0	495	2,476	6,694
Steve Roberts, Butler (II)	1986-89	4,623	1,201	0	272	578	6,674
Anthony Russo, St. John's (N.Y.) (III; I-AA)	1990-92; 93	5,834	405	0	25	379	6,643
Richard Huntley, Winston-Salem (II)	1992-95	6,286	333	0	0	0	6,619
Tony Dorsett, Pittsburgh (I-A)	1973-76	6,082	406	0	0	127	6,615
Paul Palmer, Temple (I-A)	1983-86	4,895	705	0	0	997	6,609
Charles White, Southern Cal (I-A)	1976-79	5,598	507	0	0	440	6,545
Trevor Cobb, Rice (I-A)	1989-92	4,948	892	0	21	651	6,512
Joe Dudek, Plymouth St. (III)	1982-85	5,570	348	0	0	243	6,509
Glyn Milburn, Oklahoma/Stanford (I-A)	1988, 90-92	2,302	1,495	0	1,145	1,246	6,188
Adam Henry, Carleton (III)	1990-93	3,482	601	0	186	1,839	6,108
Chris Cobb, Eastern Ill. (II)	1976-79	5,042	520	0	37	478	6,077
Don Aleksiewicz, Hobart (II)	1969-72	4,525	470	0	320	748	6,063
Gary Trettel, St. Thomas (Minn.) (III)	1988-90	3,724	853	0	0	1,467	6,044
Archie Griffin, Ohio St. (I-A)	1972-75	5,177	286	0	0	540	6,003
Ron "Po" James, New Mexico St. (I-A)	1968-71	3,884	217	0	8	1,870	5,979
Eric Wilkerson, Kent (I-A)	1985-88	3,830	506	0	0	1,638	5,974

**Record. $See page 6 for explanation.*

Stanford sports information photo by David K. Madison

When Stanford running back Darrin Nelson finished his collegiate career in 1981, he ranked second in collegiate history in all-purpose yards. Fourteen seasons later, his total of 6,885 yards is still good for 11th place.

CAREER YARDS PER GAME

(Minimum 3,500 Yards)

Player, Team (Division[s])	Years	G	Rush	Rcv.	Int.	PR	KO	Yds.	Yd.PG
Ryan Benjamin, Pacific (Cal.) (I-A)	1990-92	24	3,119	1,063	0	100	1,424	5,706	*237.8
Chris George, Glenville St. (II)	1993-94	20	23	3,215	0	391	1,050	4,679	234.0
Kirk Matthieu, Maine Maritime (III)	$1989-93	33	5,107	315	0	254	1,279	6,955	210.8
Sheldon Canley, San Jose St. (I-A)	1988-90	25	2,513	828	0	5	1,800	5,146	205.8
Carey Bender, Coe (III)	1991-94	39	6,125	1,751	0	7	87	*7,970	204.4
Johnny Bailey, Tex. A&M-Kingsville (II)	1986-89	39	*6,320	452	0	20	1,011	7,803	200.1
Howard Stevens, Randolph-Macon (II); Louisville (I-A)	1968-69; 71-72	38	5,297	738	0	781	748	7,564	199.1
Gary Trettel, St. Thomas (Minn.) (III)	1988-90	29	3,483	834	0	0	1,407	5,724	197.4
Arnold Mickens, Butler (I-AA)	1994-95	22	3,813	47	0	0	87	3,947	197.4
Tim Hall, Robert Morris (I-AA)	1994-95	19	2,908	793	0	0	0	3,701	194.8
Billy Johnson, Widener (II; III)	1971-72; 73	28	3,737	27	0	43	989	5,404	193.0
O. J. Simpson, Southern Cal (I-A)	1967-68	19	3,124	235	0	0	307	3,666	192.9
Steve Roberts, Butler (II)	1986-89	35	4,623	1,201	0	272	578	6,674	190.7

**Record. $See page 6 for explanation.*

SEASON YARDS

Player, Team (Division)	Year	Rush	Rcv.	Int.	PR	KO	Yds.
Barry Sanders, Oklahoma St. (I-A)	†1988	*2,628	106	0	95	421	*3,250
Ryan Benjamin, Pacific (Cal.) (I-A)	†1991	1,581	612	0	4	798	2,995
Mike Pringle, Cal St. Fullerton (I-A)	†1989	1,727	249	0	0	714	2,690
Steve Roberts, Butler (II)	†1989	1,450	532	0	272	415	2,669
Carey Bender, Coe (III)	†1994	2,243	319	0	7	87	2,656
Paul Palmer, Temple (I-A)	†1986	1,866	110	0	0	657	2,633
Chris George, Glenville St. (II)	†1993	23	*1,876	0	157	562	2,618

All-purpose yardage *is the combined net yards gained by rushing, receiving, interception (and fumble) returns, punt returns, kickoff returns and runbacks of field goal attempts. All-purpose yardage does not include forward passing yardage.*

Total offense *is the total of net gain rushing and net gain forward passing. Receiving and runback yards are not included in total offense.*

Player, Team (Division)	Year	Rush	Rcv.	Int.	PR	KO	Yds.
Ryan Benjamin, Pacific (Cal.) (I-A)	†1992	1,441	434	0	96	626	2,597
Marcus Allen, Southern Cal (I-A)	†1981	2,342	217	0	0	0	2,559
Sheldon Canley, San Jose St. (I-A)	1989	1,201	353	0	0	959	2,513
Mike Rozier, Nebraska (I-A)	1983	2,148	106	0	0	232	2,486
Troy Davis, Iowa St. (I-A)	†1995	2,010	159	0	0	297	2,466
Alex Van Dyke, Nevada (I-A)	1995	6	1,854	0	0	583	2,443
Johnny Bailey, Tex. A&M-Kingsville (II)	†1986	2,011	54	0	20	340	2,425
Kenny Gamble, Colgate (I-AA)	†1986	1,816	198	0	40	391	2,425
Theo Blanco, Wis.-Stevens Point (III)	1987	454	1,616	0	245	103	2,418
Rick Wegher, South Dak. St. (II)	1984	1,317	264	0	0	824	2,405
Steve Papin, Portland St. (II)	†1995	1,619	525	0	1	252	2,397
Ronald Moore, Pittsburg St. (II)	1992	1,864	141	0	0	388	2,393
Chuck Weatherspoon, Houston (I-A)	1989	1,146	735	0	415	95	2,391
Anthony Thompson, Indiana (I-A)	1989	1,793	201	0	0	394	2,388
Ricky Gales, Simpson (III)	†1989	2,035	102	0	0	248	2,385
Napoleon McCallum, Navy (I-A)	†1983	1,587	166	0	272	360	2,385
Rashaan Salaam, Colorado (I-A)	†1994	2,055	294	0	0	0	2,349
Gary Trettel, St. Thomas (Minn.) (III)	1989	1,502	337	0	0	496	2,335
Michael Clemons, William & Mary (I-AA)	1986	1,065	516	0	330	423	2,334
Napoleon McCallum, Navy (I-A)	†1985	1,327	358	0	157	488	2,330
Gary Trettel, St. Thomas (Minn.) (III)	1990	1,620	388	0	0	319	2,327
Roger Graham, New Haven (II)	1993	1,687	116	0	0	516	2,319
Brian Pruitt, Central Mich. (I-A)	1994	1,890	69	0	0	330	2,289

**Record. †National champion.*

SEASON YARDS PER GAME

Player, Team (Division)	Year	G	Rush	Rcv.	Int.	PR	KO	Yds.	Yd.PG
Barry Sanders, Oklahoma St. (I-A)	†1988	11	*2,628	106	0	0	95	*3,250	*295.5
Steve Roberts, Butler (II)	†1989	10	1,450	532	0	272	415	2,669	266.9
Carey Bender, Coe (III)	†1994	10	2,243	319	0	7	87	2,656	265.6
Bobby Felix, Western N.M. (II)	†1994	8	439	853	0	150	667	2,109	263.6
Chris George, Glenville St. (II)	†1993	10	23	*1,876	0	157	562	2,618	261.8
Billy Johnson, Widener (II)	1972	9	1,556	40	43	511	115	2,265	251.7
Ryan Benjamin, Pacific (Cal.) (I-A)	†1991	12	1,581	612	0	4	798	2,995	249.6
Byron "Whizzer" White, Colorado (I-A)	†1937	8	1,121	0	103	587	159	1,970	246.3
Mike Pringle, Cal St. Fullerton (I-A)	†1989	11	1,727	249	0	0	714	2,690	244.6
Kirk Matthieu, Maine Maritime (III)	†1992	9	1,733	91	0	56	308	2,188	243.1
Paul Palmer, Temple (I-A)	†1986	11	1,866	110	0	0	657	2,633	239.4
Ricky Gales, Simpson (III)	†1989	10	2,035	102	0	0	248	2,385	238.5
Ryan Benjamin, Pacific (Cal.) (I-A)	†1992	11	1,441	434	0	96	626	2,597	236.1
Gary Trettel, St. Thomas (Minn.) (III)	1989	10	1,502	337	0	0	496	2,335	233.5
Kirk Matthieu, Maine Maritime (III)	1990	9	1,428	77	0	99	495	2,099	233.2
Gary Trettel, St. Thomas (Minn.) (III)	1990	10	1,620	388	0	0	319	2,327	232.7

**Record. †National champion.*

Scoring

CAREER POINTS

Player, Team (Division[s])	Years	TD	XPt.	FG	Pts.
Carey Bender, Coe (III)	1991-94	*86	12	0	*528
Joe Dudek, Plymouth St. (III)	1982-85	79	0	0	474
Walter Payton, Jackson St. (II)	1971-74	66	53	5	464
Shawn Graves, Wofford (QB) (II)	1989-92	72	3	0	438
Johnny Bailey, Tex. A&M-Kingsville (II)	1986-89	70	3	0	426
Roger Graham, New Haven (II)	1991-94	70	2	0	424
Roman Anderson, Houston (I-A)	1988-91	0	213	70	423
Howard Stevens, Randolph-Macon (II); Louisville (I-A)	1968-69; 71-72	69	4	0	418
Dale Mills, Truman St. (II)	1957-60	64	23	0	407
Jeremy Monroe, Michigan Tech (II)	1990-93	67	0	0	402
Carlos Huerta, Miami (Fla.) (I-A)	1988-91	0	178	73	397
Jason Elam, Hawaii (I-A)	$1988-92	0	158	79	395
Anthony Thompson, Indiana (I-A)	1986-89	65	4	0	394
Garney Henley, Huron (II)	1956-59	63	16	0	394
Derek Schmidt, Florida St. (I-A)	1984-87	0	174	73	393
Steve Roberts, Butler (II)	1986-89	63	4	0	386
Jeff Bentrim, North Dak. St. (QB) (II)	1983-86	64	2	0	386
Marty Zendejas, Nevada (I-AA)	1984-87	0	169	72	385
Leo Lewis, Lincoln (Mo.) (II)	1951-54	64	0	0	384
Chris Bisaillon, Ill. Wesleyan (III)	1989-92	61	12	0	378
Heath Sherman, Tex. A&M-Kingsville (II)	1985-88	63	0	0	378
Marshall Faulk, San Diego St. (I-A)	1991-93	62	4	0	376
Chris Babirad, Wash. & Jeff. (III)	1989-92	62	2	0	374
Billy Johnson, Widener (II; III)	1971-72; 73	62	0	0	372
Tank Younger, Grambling (II)	1945-48	60	9	0	369
Richard Huntley, Winston-Salem (II)	1992-95	60	8	0	368
Luis Zendejas, Arizona St. (I-A)	1981-84	0	134	78	368
Sherriden May, Idaho (I-AA)	1991-94	61	0	0	366
Bill Cooper, Muskingum (II)	1957-60	54	37	1	364
Charvez Foger, Nevada (I-AA)	1985-88	60	2	0	362
Ole Gunderson, St. Olaf (II)	1969-71	60	2	0	362
Rob Marchitello, Maine Maritime (III)	1993-95	59	4	0	358
Jeff Jaeger, Washington (I-A)	1983-86	0	118	*80	358
Tony Dorsett, Pittsburgh (I-A)	1973-76	59	2	0	356
Glenn Davis, Army (I-A)	1943-46	59	0	0	354

**Record.* *$See page 6 for explanation.*

CAREER POINTS PER GAME

(Minimum 225 Points)

Player, Team (Division[s])	Years	G	TD	XPt.	FG	Pts.	Pt.PG
Rob Marchitello, Maine Maritime (III)	1993-95	26	59	4	0	358	*13.8
Carey Bender, Coe (III)	1991-94	39	*86	12	0	*528	13.5
Ole Gunderson, St. Olaf (II)	1969-71	27	60	2	0	362	13.4
Billy Johnson, Widener (II; III)	1971-72; 73	28	62	0	0	372	13.3
Leon Burns, Long Beach St. (II)	1969-70	22	47	2	0	284	12.9
Marshall Faulk, San Diego St. (I-A)	1991-93	31	62	4	0	376	12.1
Ed Marinaro, Cornell (I-A)	1969-71	27	52	6	0	318	11.8
Joe Dudek, Plymouth St. (III)	1982-85	41	79	0	0	474	11.6
Bill Burnett, Arkansas (I-A)	1968-70	26	49	0	0	294	11.3
Dale Mills, Truman St. (II)	1957-60	36	64	23	0	407	11.3
Steve Owens, Oklahoma (I-A)	1967-69	30	56	0	0	336	11.2
Walter Payton, Jackson St. (II)	1971-74	42	66	53	5	464	11.0
Steve Roberts, Butler (II)	1986-89	35	63	4	0	386	11.0
Jeff Bentrim, North Dak. St. (II)	1983-86	35	64	2	0	386	11.0
Shawn Graves, Wofford (II)	1989-92	40	72	3	0	438	11.0
Johnny Bailey, Tex. A&M-Kingsville (II)	1986-89	39	70	3	0	426	10.9
Eddie Talboom, Wyoming (I-A)	1948-50	28	34	99	0	303	10.8
Chris Babirad, Wash. & Jeff. (III)	1989-92	35	62	2	0	374	10.7
Keith Elias, Princeton (I-AA)	1991-93	30	52	8	0	320	10.7

**Record.*

SEASON POINTS

Player, Team (Division)	Year	TD	XPt.	FG	Pts.
Barry Sanders, Oklahoma St. (I-A)	†1988	*39	0	0	*234
Carey Bender, Coe (III)	†1994	32	2	0	194
Terry Metcalf, Long Beach St. (II)	1971	29	4	0	178
Mike Rozier, Nebraska (I-A)	†1983	29	0	0	174
Lydell Mitchell, Penn St. (I-A)	1971	29	0	0	174
Geoff Mitchell, Weber St. (I-AA)	†1991	28	2	0	170
Stanley Drayton, Allegheny (III)	†1991	28	0	0	168
Jim Switzer, Col. of Emporia (II)	†1963	28	0	0	168
Carl Herakovich, Rose-Hulman (II)	†1958	25	18	0	168
Ted Scown, Sul Ross St. (II)	†1948	28	0	0	168
Ronald Moore, Pittsburg St. (II)	1992	27	4	0	166
Ricky Gales, Simpson (III)	†1989	26	10	0	166
Art Luppino, Arizona (I-A)	†1954	24	22	0	166
Matt Malmberg, St. John's (Minn.) (III)	†1993	27	2	0	164
Leon Burns, Long Beach St. (II)	†1969	27	2	0	164
Jerry Rice, Mississippi Val. (I-AA)	†1984	27	0	0	162
Mike Deutsch, North Dak. (II)	1972	27	0	0	162
Billy Johnson, Widener (II)	†1972	27	0	0	162
Bobby Reynolds, Nebraska (I-A)	†1950	22	25	0	157

**Record. †National champion.*

SEASON POINTS PER GAME

Player, Team (Division)	Year	G	TD	XPt.	FG	Pts.	Pt.PG
Barry Sanders, Oklahoma St. (I-A)	†1988	11	*39	0	0	*234	*21.3
Carl Herakovich, Rose-Hulman (II)	†1958	8	25	18	0	168	21.0
Carey Bender, Coe (III)	†1994	10	32	2	0	194	19.4
Jim Switzer, Col. of Emporia (II)	†1963	9	28	0	0	168	18.7
Billy Johnson, Widener (II)	†1972	9	27	0	0	162	18.0
Carl Garrett, N.M. Highlands (II)	†1966	9	26	2	0	158	17.6
Bobby Reynolds, Nebraska (I-A)	†1950	9	22	25	0	157	17.4
Rob Marchitello, Maine Maritime (III)	1994	9	25	4	0	154	17.1
Stanley Drayton, Allegheny (III)	†1991	10	28	0	0	168	16.8
Ted Scown, Sul Ross St. (II)	†1948	10	28	0	0	168	16.8
Ricky Gales, Simpson (III)	†1989	10	26	10	0	166	16.6
Art Luppino, Arizona (I-A)	†1954	10	24	22	0	166	16.6
Ed Marinaro, Cornell (I-A)	†1971	9	24	4	0	148	16.4
Matt Malmberg, St. John's (Minn.) (III)	†1993	10	27	2	0	164	16.4
Jerry Rice, Mississippi Val. (I-AA)	†1984	10	27	0	0	162	16.2
Chris Babirad, Wash. & Jeff. (III)	†1992	9	24	0	0	144	16.0
Larry Ras, Michigan Tech (II)	†1971	9	24	0	0	144	16.0
Trent Nauholz, Simpson (III)	†1992	8	21	2	0	128	16.0
Lydell Mitchell, Penn St. (I-A)	1971	11	29	0	0	174	15.8
Marshall Faulk, San Diego St. (I-A)	†1991	9	23	2	0	140	15.6

**Record. †National champion.*

SINGLE-GAME POINTS

Pts.	Div.	Player, Team (Opponent)	Date
48	III	Carey Bender, Coe (Beloit)	Nov. 12, 1994
48	I-A	Howard Griffith, Illinois (Southern Ill.)	Sept. 22, 1990
48	II	Paul Zaeske, North Park (North Central)	Oct. 12, 1968
48	II	Junior Wolf, Okla. Panhandle St. (St. Mary, Kan.)	Nov. 8, 1958
44	I-A	Marshall Faulk, San Diego St. (Pacific, Cal.)	Sept. 14, 1991
43	I-A	Jim Brown, Syracuse (Colgate)	Nov. 17, 1956
42	I-A	Arnold "Showboat" Boykin, Mississippi (Mississippi St.)	Dec. 1, 1951
42	I-A	Fred Wendt, UTEP (New Mexico St.)	Nov. 25, 1948

Award Winners

Consensus All-America Selections, 1889-1995

In 1950, the National Collegiate Athletic Bureau (the NCAA's service bureau) compiled the first official comprehensive roster of all-time all-Americans. The compilation of the all-American roster was supervised by a panel of analysts working in large part with the historical records contained in the files of the Dr. Baker Football Information Service.

The roster consists of only those players who were first-team selections on one or more of the all-America teams that were selected for the national audience and received nationwide circulation. Not included are the thousands of players who received mention on all-America second or third teams, nor the numerous others who were selected by newspapers or agencies with circulations that were not primarily national and with viewpoints, therefore, that were not normally nationwide in scope.

The following chart indicates, by year (in left column), which national media and organizations selected all-America teams. The headings at the top of each column refer to the selector (see legend after chart).

All-America Selectors

	AA	AP	C	COL	CP	FBW	FC	FN	FW	INS	L	LIB	M	N	NA	NEA	SN	UP	UPI	W	WCF
1889	-	-	-	-	-	-	-	-	-	-	-	-	-	-	-	-	-	-	-	√	-
1890	-	-	-	-	-	-	-	-	-	-	-	-	-	-	-	-	-	-	-	√	-
1891	-	-	-	-	-	-	-	-	-	-	-	-	-	-	-	-	-	-	-	√	-
1892	-	-	-	-	-	-	-	-	-	-	-	-	-	-	-	-	-	-	-	√	-
1893	-	-	-	-	-	-	-	-	-	-	-	-	-	-	-	-	-	-	-	√	-
1894	-	-	-	-	-	-	-	-	-	-	-	-	-	-	-	-	-	-	-	√	-
1895	-	-	-	-	-	-	-	-	-	-	-	-	-	-	-	-	-	-	-	√	-
1896	-	-	-	-	-	-	-	-	-	-	-	-	-	-	-	-	-	-	-	√	-
1897	-	-	-	-	-	-	-	-	-	-	-	-	-	-	-	-	-	-	-	√	-
1898	-	-	√	-	-	-	-	-	-	-	-	-	-	-	-	-	-	-	-	√	-
1899	-	-	√	-	-	-	-	-	-	-	-	-	-	-	-	-	-	-	-	√	-
1900	-	-	√	-	-	-	-	-	-	-	-	-	-	-	-	-	-	-	-	√	-
1901	-	-	√	-	-	-	-	-	-	-	-	-	-	-	-	-	-	-	-	√	-
1902	-	-	√	-	-	-	-	-	-	-	-	-	-	-	-	-	-	-	-	√	-
1903	-	-	√	-	-	-	-	-	-	-	-	-	-	-	-	-	-	-	-	√	-
1904	-	-	√	-	-	-	-	-	-	-	-	-	-	-	-	-	-	-	-	√	-
1905	-	-	√	-	-	-	-	-	-	-	-	-	-	-	-	-	-	-	-	√	-
1906	-	-	√	-	-	-	-	-	-	-	-	-	-	-	-	-	-	-	-	√	-
1907	-	-	√	-	-	-	-	-	-	-	-	-	-	-	-	-	-	-	-	√	-
1908	-	-	√	-	-	-	-	-	-	-	-	-	-	-	-	-	-	-	-	√	-
1909	-	-	√	-	-	-	-	-	-	-	-	-	-	-	-	-	-	-	-	-	-
1910	-	-	√	-	-	-	-	-	-	-	-	-	-	-	-	-	-	-	-	-	-
1911	-	-	√	-	-	-	-	-	-	-	-	-	-	-	-	-	-	-	-	-	-
1912	-	-	√	-	-	-	-	-	-	-	-	-	-	-	-	-	-	-	-	-	-
1913	-	-	√	-	-	-	-	-	-	√	-	-	-	-	-	-	-	-	-	-	-
1914	-	-	√	-	-	-	-	-	-	√	-	-	-	-	-	-	-	-	-	-	-
1915	-	-	√	-	-	-	-	-	-	√	-	-	-	-	-	-	-	-	-	-	-
1916	-	-	√	-	-	-	-	-	-	√	-	-	√	-	-	-	-	-	-	-	-
1917	-	-	(*)	-	-	-	-	-	-	√	-	-	√	-	-	√	-	-	-	-	-
1918	-	-	√	-	-	-	-	-	-	-	-	-	√	-	-	-	-	-	-	-	-
1919	-	-	√	-	-	-	-	-	-	-	-	-	√	-	-	-	-	-	-	-	-
1920	-	-	√	-	-	√	-	-	-	√	-	-	√	-	-	-	-	-	-	-	-
1921	-	-	√	-	-	-	-	-	-	-	-	-	-	-	-	-	-	-	-	-	-
1922	-	-	√	-	-	-	-	-	-	-	-	-	-	-	-	-	-	-	-	-	-
1923	-	-	√	-	-	√	-	-	-	-	-	-	-	-	-	-	-	-	-	-	-
1924	√	-	√	-	-	√	-	-	-	√	-	√	-	-	-	√	-	-	-	-	-
1925	√	√	-	√	-	√	-	-	-	√	-	√	-	-	-	√	-	√	-	-	-
1926	√	√	-	√	-	-	-	-	-	√	-	-	-	-	-	√	-	√	-	-	-
1927	√	√	-	√	-	-	-	-	-	√	-	-	-	-	√	√	-	√	-	-	-
1928	√	√	-	√	-	-	-	-	-	√	-	-	-	-	√	√	-	√	-	-	-
1929	√	√	-	√	-	-	-	-	-	√	-	-	-	-	√	√	-	√	-	-	-
1930	√	√	-	√	-	-	-	-	-	√	-	-	-	-	√	√	-	√	-	-	-
1931	√	√	-	√	-	-	-	-	-	√	-	√	-	-	-	√	-	√	-	-	-
1932	√	√	-	√	-	-	-	-	-	√	-	√	-	-	√	√	-	√	-	-	-
1933	√	√	-	√	-	-	-	-	-	√	-	√	-	-	√	√	-	√	-	-	-
1934	√	√	-	√	-	-	-	-	-	√	-	√	-	-	√	√	√	√	-	-	-
1935	√	√	-	√	-	-	-	-	-	√	-	√	-	-	√	√	√	√	-	-	-
1936	√	√	-	√	-	-	-	-	-	√	-	√	-	-	√	√	√	√	-	-	-
1937	√	√	-	√	-	-	-	-	-	√	-	√	-	√	√	√	√	√	-	-	-
1938	√	√	-	√	-	-	-	-	-	√	-	√	-	√	-	√	√	√	-	-	-
1939	√	√	-	√	-	-	-	-	-	√	-	√	-	√	-	√	√	√	-	-	-
1940	√	√	-	√	-	-	-	-	-	√	-	√	-	√	-	√	√	√	-	-	-
1941	√	√	-	√	-	-	-	-	-	√	-	√	-	√	-	√	√	√	-	-	-
1942	√	√	-	√	-	-	-	-	-	√	√	-	-	√	-	√	√	√	-	-	-
1943	√	√	-	√	-	-	-	√	-	√	√	-	-	-	-	-	√	√	-	-	-
1944	√	√	-	√	-	-	-	√	√	√	√	-	-	-	-	√	√	√	-	-	-
1945	√	√	-	√	-	-	√	-	√	√	√	-	-	-	-	√	√	√	-	-	-
1946	√	√	-	√	-	-	√	-	√	√	(†)	-	-	-	-	√	√	√	-	-	-
1947	-	√	-	√	-	-	√	-	√	√	-	-	-	-	-	√	√	√	-	-	-
1948	-	√	-	(§)	-	-	√	-	√	(#)√	-	-	-	-	-	√	√	√	-	-	-
1949	√	√	-	-	-	-	√	-	√	√	-	-	-	-	-	√	√	√	-	-	-
1950	√	√	-	-	-	-	√	-	√	√	-	-	-	-	-	√	√	√	-	-	-
1951	√	√	-	-	-	-	√	-	√	√	-	-	-	-	-	√	√	√	-	-	-
1952	√	√	-	-	-	-	√	-	√	√	-	-	-	-	-	√	√	√	-	-	-
1953	√	√	-	-	-	-	√	-	√	√	-	-	-	-	-	√	√	√	-	-	-

	AA	AP	C	COL	CP	FBW	FC	FN	FW	INS	L	LIB	M	N	NA	NEA	SN	UP	UPI	W	WCF
1954	√	√	-	-	-	-	√	-	√	√	-	-	-	-	-	√	√	√	-	-	-
1955	√	√	-	-	-	-	√	-	√	√	-	-	-	-	-	√	√	√	-	-	-
1956	-	√	-	-	-	-	√	-	√	√	-	-	-	-	-	√	√	√	-	-	-
1957	-	√	-	-	-	-	√	-	√	√	-	-	-	-	-	√	√	√	-	-	-
1958	-	√	-	-	-	-	√	-	√	-	-	-	-	-	-	√	√	-	√	-	-
1959	-	√	-	-	-	-	√	-	√	-	-	-	-	-	-	√	√	-	√	-	-
1960	-	√	-	-	-	-	√	-	√	-	-	-	-	-	-	√	√	-	√	-	-
1961	-	√	-	-	-	-	√	-	√	-	-	-	-	-	-	√	√	-	√	-	-
1962	-	√	-	-	-	-	√	-	√	-	-	-	-	-	-	√	√	-	√	-	-
1963	-	√	-	-	√	-	√	-	√	-	-	-	-	-	-	√	√	-	√	-	-
1964	-	√	-	-	√	-	√	-	√	-	-	-	-	-	-	√	-	-	√	-	-
1965	-	√	-	-	√	-	√	-	√	-	-	-	-	-	-	√	-	-	√	-	-
1966	-	√	-	-	√	-	√	-	√	-	-	-	-	-	-	√	-	-	√	-	-
1967	-	√	-	-	√	-	√	-	√	-	-	-	-	-	-	√	-	-	√	-	-
1968	-	√	-	-	√	-	√	-	√	-	-	-	-	-	-	√	-	-	√	-	-
1969	-	√	-	-	√	-	√	-	√	-	-	-	-	-	-	√	-	-	√	-	-
1970	-	√	-	-	√	-	√	-	√	-	-	-	-	-	-	√	-	-	√	-	-
1971	-	√	-	-	-	-	√	-	√	-	-	-	-	-	-	√	-	-	√	-	-
1972	-	√	-	-	-	-	√	-	√	-	-	-	-	-	-	√	-	-	√	-	√
1973	-	√	-	-	-	-	√	-	√	-	-	-	-	-	-	√	-	-	√	-	√
1974	-	√	-	-	-	-	√	-	√	-	-	-	-	-	-	-	-	-	√	-	√
1975	-	√	-	-	-	-	√	-	√	-	-	-	-	-	-	-	-	-	√	-	-
1976	-	√	-	-	-	-	√	-	√	-	-	-	-	-	-	-	-	-	√	-	-
1977	-	√	-	-	-	-	√	-	√	-	-	-	-	-	-	-	-	-	√	-	-
1978	-	√	-	-	-	-	√	-	√	-	-	-	-	-	-	-	-	-	√	-	-
1979	-	√	-	-	-	-	√	-	√	-	-	-	-	-	-	-	-	-	√	-	-
1980	-	√	-	-	-	-	√	-	√	-	-	-	-	-	-	-	-	-	√	-	-
1981	-	√	-	-	-	-	√	-	√	-	-	-	-	-	-	-	-	-	√	-	-
1982	-	√	-	-	-	-	√	-	√	-	-	-	-	-	-	-	-	-	√	-	-
1983	-	√	-	-	-	-	√	-	√	-	-	-	-	-	-	-	-	-	√	-	√
1984	-	√	-	-	-	-	√	-	√	-	-	-	-	-	-	-	-	-	√	-	√
1985	-	√	-	-	-	-	√	-	√	-	-	-	-	-	-	-	-	-	√	-	√
1986	-	√	-	-	-	-	√	-	√	-	-	-	-	-	-	-	-	-	√	-	√
1987	-	√	-	-	-	-	√	-	√	-	-	-	-	-	-	-	-	-	√	-	√
1988	-	√	-	-	-	-	√	-	√	-	-	-	-	-	-	-	-	-	√	-	√
1989	-	√	-	-	-	-	√	-	√	-	-	-	-	-	-	-	-	-	√	-	√
1990	-	√	-	-	-	-	√	-	√	-	-	-	-	-	-	-	-	-	√	-	√
1991	-	√	-	-	-	-	√	-	√	-	-	-	-	-	-	-	-	-	√	-	√
1992	-	√	-	-	-	-	√	-	√	-	-	-	-	-	-	-	-	-	√	-	√
1993	-	√	-	-	-	-	√	√	√	-	-	-	-	-	-	-	√	-	√	-	√
1994	-	√	-	-	-	-	√	√	√	-	-	-	-	-	-	-	√	-	√	-	√
1995	-	√	-	-	-	-	√	√	√	-	-	-	-	-	-	-	√	-	√	-	√

**In 1917, Walter Camp selected an all-Service, all-America team composed of military personnel. †During 1946-70, Look Magazine published the Football Writers Association of America's selections, listed under FW. §During 1948-56, Collier's Magazine published the American Football Coaches Association's selections, listed under FC. #International News Service was the first to select offensive and defensive teams.*

LEGEND FOR SELECTORS

AA—All-America Board
AP—Associated Press
C—Walter Camp (published in Harper's Weekly, 1897; in Collier's Magazine, 1898-1924)
COL—Collier's Magazine (selections by Grantland Rice, 1925-47; published American Football Coaches Association teams, 1948-56, listed under FC)
CP—Central Press
FBW—Football World Magazine
FC—American Football Coaches Association (published in Saturday Evening Post Magazine, 1945-47; in Collier's Magazine, 1948-56; sponsored by General Mills in 1957-59 and by Eastman Kodak from 1960)
FN—Football News
FW—Football Writers Association of America (published in Look Magazine, 1946-70)
INS—International News Service (merged with United Press in 1958 to form UPI)
L—Look Magazine (published Football Writers Association of America teams, 1946-70, listed under FW)
LIB—Liberty Magazine
M—Frank Menke Syndicate
N—Newsweek
NA—North American Newspaper Alliance
NEA—Newspaper Enterprise Association
SN—Sporting News
UP—United Press (merged with International News Service in 1958 to form UPI)
UPI—United Press International
W—Caspar Whitney (published in The Week's Sport in association with Walter Camp, 1889-90; published in Harper's Weekly, 1891-96, and in Outing Magazine, which he owned, 1898-1908; Walter Camp substituted for Whitney, who was on a world sports tour, and selected Harper's Weekly's team for 1897)
WCF—Walter Camp Foundation

All-America Selections

Listed on the following pages are the consensus all-Americans (i.e., the players who were accorded a majority of votes at their positions by the selectors). Included are the selections of 1889-97, 1909-12 and 1921-22 when there was only one selector.

1889
E—Amos Alonzo Stagg, Yale; Arthur Cumnock, Harvard; T—Hector Cowan, Princeton; Charles Gill, Yale; G—Pudge Heffelfinger, Yale; John Cranston, Harvard; C—William George, Princeton; B—Edgar Allan Poe, Princeton; Roscoe Channing, Princeton; Knowlton Ames, Princeton; James Lee, Harvard.

1890
E—Frank Hallowell, Harvard; Ralph Warren, Princeton; T—Marshall Newell, Harvard; William Rhodes, Yale; G—Pudge Heffelfinger, Yale; Jesse Riggs, Princeton; C—John Cranston, Harvard; B—Thomas McClung, Yale; Sheppard Homans, Princeton; Dudley Dean, Harvard; John Corbett, Harvard.

1891
E—Frank Hinkey, Yale; John Hartwell, Yale; T—Wallace Winter, Yale; Marshall Newell, Harvard; G—Pudge Heffelfinger, Yale; Jesse Riggs, Princeton; C—John Adams, Pennsylvania; B—Philip King, Princeton; Everett Lake, Harvard; Thomas McClung, Yale; Sheppard Homans, Princeton.

1892
E—Frank Hinkey, Yale; Frank Hallowell, Harvard; T—Marshall Newell, Harvard; A. Hamilton Wallis, Yale; G—Arthur Wheeler, Princeton; Bertram Waters, Harvard; C—William Lewis, Harvard; B—Charles Brewer, Harvard; Vance McCormick, Yale; Philip King, Princeton; Harry Thayer, Pennsylvania.

1893
E—Frank Hinkey, Yale; Thomas Trenchard, Princeton; T—Langdon Lea, Princeton; Marshall Newell, Harvard; G—Arthur Wheeler, Princeton; William Hickok, Yale; C—William Lewis, Harvard; B—Philip King, Princeton; Charles Brewer, Harvard; Franklin Morse, Princeton; Frank Butterworth, Yale.

1894
E—Frank Hinkey, Yale; Charles Gelbert, Pennsylvania; T—Bertram Waters, Harvard; Langdon Lea, Princeton; G—Arthur Wheeler, Princeton; William Hickok, Yale; C—Philip Stillman, Yale; B—George Adee, Yale; Arthur Knipe, Pennsylvania; George Brooke, Pennsylvania; Frank Butterworth, Yale.

1895
E—Norman Cabot, Harvard; Charles Gelbert, Pennsylvania; T—Langdon Lea, Princeton; Fred Murphy, Yale; G—Charles Wharton, Pennsylvania; Dudley Riggs, Princeton; C—Alfred Bull, Pennsylvania; B—Clinton Wyckoff, Cornell; Samuel Thorne, Yale; Charles Brewer, Harvard; George Brooke, Pennsylvania.

1896
E—Norman Cabot, Harvard; Charles Gelbert, Pennsylvania; T—William Church, Princeton; Fred Murphy, Yale; G—Charles Wharton, Pennsylvania; Wylie Woodruff, Pennsylvania; C—Robert Gailey, Princeton; B—Clarence Fincke, Yale; Edgar Wrightington, Harvard; Addison Kelly, Princeton; John Baird, Princeton.

1897
E—Garrett Cochran, Princeton; John Hall, Yale; T—Burr Chamberlain, Yale; John Outland, Pennsylvania; G—T. Truxton Hare, Pennsylvania; Gordon Brown, Yale; C—Alan Doucette, Harvard; B—Charles DeSaulles, Yale; Benjamin Dibblee, Harvard; Addison Kelly, Princeton; John Minds, Pennsylvania.

1898
E—Lew Palmer, Princeton; John Hallowell, Harvard; T—Arthur Hillebrand, Princeton; Burr Chamberlain, Yale; G—T. Truxton Hare, Pennsylvania; Gordon Brown, Yale; Walter Boal, Harvard; C—Pete Overfield, Pennsylvania; William Cunningham, Michigan; B—Charles Daly, Harvard; Benjamin Dibblee, Harvard; John Outland, Pennsylvania; Clarence Herschberger, Chicago; Malcolm McBride, Yale; Charles Romeyn, Army.

1899
E—David Campbell, Harvard; Arthur Poe, Princeton; T—Arthur Hillebrand, Princeton; George Stillman, Yale; G—T. Truxton Hare, Pennsylvania; Gordon Brown, Yale; C—Pete Overfield, Pennsylvania; B—Charles Daly, Harvard; Josiah McCracken, Pennsylvania; Malcolm McBride, Yale; Isaac Seneca, Carlisle; Albert Sharpe, Yale; Howard Reiter, Princeton.

1900
E—John Hallowell, Harvard; David Campbell, Harvard; William Smith, Army; T—George Stillman, Yale; James Bloomer, Yale; G—Gordon Brown, Yale; T. Truxton Hare, Pennsylvania; C—Herman Olcott, Yale; Walter Bachman, Lafayette; B—Bill Morley, Columbia; George Chadwick, Yale; Perry Hale, Yale; William Fincke, Yale; Charles Daly, Harvard; Raymond Starbuck, Cornell.

1901
E—David Campbell, Harvard; Ralph Davis, Princeton; Edward Bowditch, Harvard; Neil Snow, Michigan; T—Oliver Cutts, Harvard; Paul Bunker, Army; Crawford Blagden, Harvard; G—William Warner, Cornell; William Lee, Harvard; Charles Barnard, Harvard; Sanford Hunt, Cornell; C—Henry Holt, Yale; Walter Bachman, Lafayette; B—Robert Kernan, Harvard; Charles Daly, Army; Thomas Graydon, Harvard; Harold Weekes, Columbia; Bill Morley, Columbia.

1902
E—Thomas Shevlin, Yale; Edward Bowditch, Harvard; T—Ralph Kinney, Yale; James Hogan, Yale; Paul Bunker, Army; G—Edgar Glass, Yale; John DeWitt, Princeton; William Warner, Cornell; C—Henry Holt, Yale; Robert Boyers, Army; B—Foster Rockwell, Yale; George Chadwick, Yale; Thomas Graydon, Harvard; Thomas Barry, Brown.

1903
E—Howard Henry, Princeton; Charles Rafferty, Yale; T—Daniel Knowlton, Harvard; James Hogan, Yale; Fred Schacht, Minnesota; G—John DeWitt, Princeton; Andrew Marshall, Harvard; James Bloomer, Yale; C—Henry Hooper, Dartmouth; B—Willie Heston, Michigan; J. Dana Kafer, Princeton; James Johnson, Carlisle; Richard Smith, Columbia; Myron Witham, Dartmouth; W. Ledyard Mitchell, Yale.

1904
E—Thomas Shevlin, Yale; Fred Speik, Chicago; T—James Hogan, Yale; James Cooney, Princeton; G—Frank Piekarski, Pennsylvania; Joseph Gilman, Dartmouth; Ralph Kinney, Yale; C—Arthur Tipton, Army; B—Daniel Hurley, Harvard; Walter Eckersall, Chicago; Vincent Stevenson, Pennsylvania; Willie Heston, Michigan; Andrew Smith, Pennsylvania; Foster Rockwell, Yale; Henry Torney, Army.

1905
E—Thomas Shevlin, Yale; Ralph Glaze, Dartmouth; Mark Catlin, Chicago; T—Otis Lamson, Pennsylvania; Beaton Squires, Harvard; Karl Brill, Harvard; G—Roswell Tripp, Yale; Francis Burr, Harvard; C—Robert Torrey, Pennsylvania; B—Walter Eckersall, Chicago; Howard Roome, Yale; John Hubbard, Amherst; James McCormick, Princeton; Guy Hutchinson, Yale; Daniel Hurley, Harvard; Henry Torney, Army.

1906
E—Robert Forbes, Yale; L. Casper Wister, Princeton; T—L. Horatio Biglow, Yale; James Cooney, Princeton; Charles Osborne, Harvard; G—Francis Burr, Harvard; Elmer Thompson, Cornell; August Ziegler, Pennsylvania; C—William Dunn, Penn St.; William Newman, Cornell; B—Walter Eckersall, Chicago; Hugh Knox, Yale; Edward Dillon, Princeton; John Mayhew, Brown; William Hollenback, Pennsylvania; Paul Veeder, Yale.

1907
E—Bill Dague, Navy; Clarence Alcott, Yale; Albert Exendine, Carlisle; L. Casper Wister, Princeton; T—Dexter Draper, Pennsylvania; L. Horatio Biglow, Yale; G—August Ziegler, Pennsylvania; William Erwin, Army; C—Adolph Schulz, Michigan; Patrick Grant, Harvard; B—John Wendell, Harvard; Thomas A. D. Jones, Yale; Edwin Harlan, Princeton; James McCormick, Princeton; Edward Coy, Yale; Peter Hauser, Carlisle.

1908
E—Hunter Scarlett, Pennsylvania; George Schildmiller, Dartmouth; T—Hamilton Fish, Harvard; Frank Horr, Syracuse; Percy Northcroft, Navy; G—Clark Tobin, Dartmouth; William Goebel, Yale; Hamlin Andrus, Yale; Bernard O'Rourke, Cornell; C—Charles Nourse, Harvard; B—Edward Coy, Yale; Frederick Tibbott, Princeton; William Hollenback, Pennsylvania; Walter Steffen, Chicago; Ed Lange, Navy; Hamilton Corbett, Harvard.

1909
E—Adrian Regnier, Brown; John Kilpatrick, Yale; T—Hamilton Fish, Harvard; Henry Hobbs, Yale; G—Albert Benbrook, Michigan; Hamlin Andrus, Yale; C—Carroll Cooney, Yale; B—Edward Coy, Yale; John McGovern, Minnesota; Stephen Philbin, Yale; Wayland Minot, Harvard.

1910
E—John Kilpatrick, Yale; Stanfield Wells, Michigan; T—Robert McKay, Harvard; James Walker, Minnesota; G—Robert Fisher, Harvard; Albert Benbrook, Michigan; C—Ernest Cozens, Pennsylvania; B—E. LeRoy Mercer, Pennsylvania; Percy Wendell, Harvard; Earl Sprackling, Brown; Talbot Pendleton, Princeton.

1911
E—Douglass Bomeisler, Yale; Sanford White, Princeton; T—Edward Hart, Princeton; Leland Devore, Army; G—Robert Fisher, Harvard; Joseph Duff, Princeton; C—Henry Ketcham, Yale; B—Jim Thorpe, Carlisle; Percy Wendell, Harvard; Arthur Howe, Yale; Jack Dalton, Navy.

1912
E—Samuel Felton, Harvard; Douglass Bomeisler, Yale; T—Wesley Englehorn, Dartmouth; Robert Butler, Wisconsin; G—Stanley Pennock, Harvard; John Logan, Princeton; C—Henry Ketcham, Yale; B—Charles Brickley, Harvard; Jim Thorpe, Carlisle; George Crowther, Brown; E. LeRoy Mercer, Pennsylvania.

1913
E—Robert Hogsett, Dartmouth; Louis Merrillat, Army; T—Harold Ballin, Princeton; Nelson Talbott, Yale; Miller Pontius, Michigan; Harvey Hitchcock, Harvard; G—John Brown, Navy; Stanley Pennock, Harvard; Ray Keeler, Wisconsin; C—Paul Des Jardien, Chicago; B—Charles Brickley, Harvard; Edward Mahan, Harvard; Jim Craig, Michigan; Ellery Huntington, Colgate; Gus Dorais, Notre Dame.

1914
E—Huntington Hardwick, Harvard; John O'Hearn, Cornell; Perry Graves, Illinois; T—Harold Ballin, Princeton; Walter Trumbull, Harvard; G—Stanley Pennock, Harvard; Ralph Chapman, Illinois; Clarence Spears, Dartmouth; C—John McEwan, Army; B—John Maulbetsch, Michigan; Edward Mahan, Harvard; Charles Barrett, Cornell; John Spiegel, Wash. & Jeff.; Harry LeGore, Yale.

1915
E—Murray Shelton, Cornell; Guy Chamberlin, Nebraska; T—Joseph Gilman, Harvard; Howard Buck, Wisconsin; G—Clarence Spears, Dartmouth; Harold White, Syracuse; C—Robert Peck, Pittsburgh; B—Charles Barrett, Cornell; Edward Mahan, Harvard; Richard King, Harvard; Bart Macomber, Illinois; Eugene Mayer, Virginia; Neno Jerry DaPrato, Michigan St.

1916
E—Bert Baston, Minnesota; James Herron, Pittsburgh; T—Clarence Horning, Colgate; D. Belford West, Colgate; G—Clinton Black, Yale; Harrie Dadmun, Harvard; Frank Hogg, Princeton; C—Robert Peck, Pittsburgh; B—Elmer Oliphant, Army; Oscar Anderson, Colgate; Fritz Pollard, Brown; Charles Harley, Ohio St.

1917
E—Charles Bolen, Ohio St.; Paul Robeson, Rutgers; Henry Miller, Pennsylvania; T—Alfred Cobb, Syracuse; George Hauser, Minnesota; G—Dale Seis, Pittsburgh; John Sutherland, Pittsburgh; Eugene Neely, Dartmouth; C—Frank Rydzewski, Notre Dame; B—Elmer Oliphant, Army; Ben Boynton, Williams; Everett Strupper, Georgia Tech; Charles Harley, Ohio St.

1918

E—Paul Robeson, Rutgers; Bill Fincher, Georgia Tech; T—Wilbur Henry, Wash. & Jeff.; Leonard Hilty, Pittsburgh; Lou Usher, Syracuse; Joe Guyon, Georgia Tech; G—Joe Alexander, Syracuse; Lyman Perry, Navy; C—Ashel Day, Georgia Tech; John Depler, Illinois; B—Frank Murrey, Princeton; Tom Davies, Pittsburgh; Wolcott Roberts, Navy; George McLaren, Pittsburgh.

1919

E—Bob Higgins, Penn St.; Henry Miller, Pennsylvania; Lester Belding, Iowa; T—Wilbur Henry, Wash. & Jeff.; D. Belford West, Colgate; G—Joe Alexander, Syracuse; Adolph Youngstrom, Dartmouth; C—James Weaver, Centre; Charles Carpenter, Wisconsin; B—Charles Harley, Ohio St.; Ira Rodgers, West Va.; Edward Casey, Harvard; Bo McMillin, Centre; Ben Boynton, Williams.

1920

E—Luke Urban, Boston College; Charles Carney, Illinois; Bill Fincher, Georgia Tech; T—Stan Keck, Princeton; Ralph Scott, Wisconsin; G—Tim Callahan, Yale; Tom Woods, Harvard; Iolas Huffman, Ohio St.; C—Herb Stein, Pittsburgh; B—George Gipp, Notre Dame; Donold Lourie, Princeton; Gaylord Stinchcomb, Ohio St.; Charles Way, Penn St.

1921

E—Brick Muller, California; Eddie Anderson, Notre Dame; T—Dan McMillan, California; Iolas Huffman, Ohio St.; G—Frank Schwab, Lafayette; John Brown, Harvard; Stan Keck, Princeton; C—Herb Stein, Pittsburgh; B—Aubrey Devine, Iowa; Glenn Killinger, Penn St.; Bo McMillin, Centre; Malcolm Aldrich, Yale; Edgar Kaw, Cornell.

1922

E—Brick Muller, California; Wendell Taylor, Navy; T—C. Herbert Treat, Princeton; John Thurman, Pennsylvania; G—Frank Schwab, Lafayette; Charles Hubbard, Harvard; C—Ed Garbisch, Army; B—Harry Kipke, Michigan; Gordon Locke, Iowa; John Thomas, Chicago; Edgar Kaw, Cornell.

1923

E—Pete McRae, Syracuse; Ray Ecklund, Minnesota; Lynn Bomar, Vanderbilt; T—Century Milstead, Yale; Marty Below, Wisconsin; G—Charles Hubbard, Harvard; James McMillen, Illinois; C—Jack Blott, Michigan; B—George Pfann, Cornell; Red Grange, Illinois; William Mallory, Yale; Harry Wilson, Penn St.

Beginning in 1924, unanimous selections are indicated by (*).

1924

E—Jim Lawson, Stanford, 5-11, 190, Long Beach, Calif.; (tie) E—Dick Luman, Yale, 6-1, 176, Pinedale, Wyo.; E—Henry Wakefield, Vanderbilt, 5-10, 160, Petersburg, Tenn.; T—Ed McGinley, Pennsylvania, 5-11, 185, Swarthmore, Pa.; T—Ed Weir, Nebraska, 6-1, 194, Superior, Neb.; G—Joe Pondelik, Chicago, 5-11, 215, Cicero, Ill.; G—Carl Diehl, Dartmouth, 6-1, 205, Chicago, Ill.; C—Edwin Horrell, California, 5-11, 185, Pasadena, Calif.; B—*Red Grange, Illinois, 5-10, 170, Wheaton, Ill.; B—Harry Stuhldreher, Notre Dame, 5-7, 151, Massillon, Ohio; B—Jimmy Crowley, Notre Dame, 5-11, 162, Green Bay, Wis.; B—Elmer Layden, Notre Dame, 6-0, 162, Davenport, Iowa.

1925

E—Bennie Oosterbaan, Michigan, 6-0, 180, Muskegon, Mich.; E—George Tully, Dartmouth, 5-10, 175, Orange, N.J.; T—*Ed Weir, Nebraska, 6-1, 194, Superior, Neb.; T—Ralph Chase, Pittsburgh, 6-3, 202, Easton, Pa.; G—Carl Diehl, Dartmouth, 6-1, 205, Chicago, Ill.; G—Ed Hess, Ohio St., 6-1, 190, Cincinnati, Ohio; C—Ed McMillan, Princeton, 6-0, 208, Pittsburgh, Pa.; B—*Andy Oberlander, Dartmouth, 6-0, 197, Everett, Mass.; B—Red Grange, Illinois, 5-10, 170, Wheaton, Ill.; B—Ernie Nevers, Stanford, 6-0, 200, Superior, Wis.; (tie) B—Benny Friedman, Michigan, 5-8, 170, Cleveland, Ohio; B—George Wilson, Washington, 5-11, 190, Everett, Wash.

1926

E—Bennie Oosterbaan, Michigan, 6-0, 186, Muskegon, Mich.; E—Vic Hanson, Syracuse, 5-10, 174, Syracuse, N.Y.; T—*Frank Wickhorst, Navy, 6-0, 218, Oak Park, Ill.; T—Bud Sprague, Army, 6-2, 210, Dallas, Texas; G—Harry Connaughton, Georgetown, 6-2, 275, Philadelphia, Pa.; G—Bernie Shively, Illinois, 6-4, 208, Oliver, Ill.; C—Bud Boeringer, Notre Dame, 6-1, 186, St. Paul, Minn.; B—Benny Friedman, Michigan, 5-8, 172, Cleveland, Ohio; B—Mort Kaer, Southern Cal, 5-11, 167, Red Bluff, Calif.; B—Ralph Baker, Northwestern, 5-10, 172, Rockford, Ill.; B—Herb Joesting, Minnesota, 6-1, 192, Owatonna, Minn.

1927

E—*Bennie Oosterbaan, Michigan, 6-0, 186, Muskegon, Mich.; E—Tom Nash, Georgia, 6-3, 200, Washington, Ga.; T—Jesse Hibbs, Southern Cal, 5-11, 185, Glendale, Calif.; T—Ed Hake, Pennsylvania, 6-0, 190, Philadelphia, Pa.; G—Bill Webster, Yale, 6-0, 200, Shelton, Conn.; G—John Smith, Notre Dame, 5-9, 164, Hartford, Conn.; (tie) C—Larry Bettencourt, St. Mary's (Cal.), 5-10, 187, Centerville, Calif.; C—John Charlesworth, Yale, 5-11, 198, North Adams, Mass.; B—*Gibby Welch, Pittsburgh, 5-11, 170, Parkersburg, W. Va.; B—Morley Drury, Southern Cal, 6-0, 185, Long Beach, Calif.; B—Red Cagle, Army, 5-9, 167, Merryville, La.; B—Herb Joesting, Minnesota, 6-1, 192, Owatonna, Minn.

1928

E—Irv Phillips, California, 6-1, 188, Salinas, Calif.; E—Wes Fesler, Ohio St., 6-0, 173, Youngstown, Ohio; T—Otto Pommerening, Michigan, 6-0, 178, Ann Arbor, Mich.; T—Mike Getto, Pittsburgh, 6-2, 198, Jeannette, Pa.; G—Seraphim Post, Stanford, 6-0, 190, Berkeley, Calif.; (tie) G—Don Robesky, Stanford, 5-11, 198, Bakersfield, Calif.; G—Edward Burke, Navy, 6-0, 180, Larksville, Pa.; C—Pete Pund, Georgia Tech, 6-0, 195, Augusta, Ga.; B—*Red Cagle, Army, 5-9, 167, Merryville, La.; B—Paul Scull, Pennsylvania, 5-8, 187, Bala, Pa.; B—(tie) Ken Strong, New York U., 6-0, 201, West Haven, Conn.; Howard Harpster, Carnegie Mellon, 6-1, 160, Akron, Ohio; B—Charles Carroll, Washington, 6-0, 190, Seattle, Wash.

1929

E—*Joe Donchess, Pittsburgh, 6-0, 175, Youngstown, Ohio; E—Wes Fesler, Ohio St., 6-0, 183, Youngstown, Ohio; T—Bronko Nagurski, Minnesota, 6-2, 217, International Falls, Minn.; T—Elmer Sleight, Purdue, 6-2, 193, Morris, Ill.; G—Jack Cannon, Notre Dame, 5-11, 193, Columbus, Ohio; G—Ray Montgomery, Pittsburgh, 6-1, 188, Wheeling, W.Va.; C—Ben Ticknor, Harvard, 6-2, 193, New York, N.Y.; B—*Frank Carideo, Notre Dame, 5-7, 175, Mount Vernon, N.Y.; B—Ralph Welch, Purdue, 6-1, 189, Whitesboro, Texas; B—Red Cagle, Army, 5-9, 167, Merryville, La.; B—Gene McEver, Tennessee, 5-10, 185, Bristol, Va.

1930

E—*Wes Fesler, Ohio St., 6-0, 185, Youngstown, Ohio; E—Frank Baker, Northwestern, 6-2, 175, Cedar Rapids, Iowa; T—*Fred Sington, Alabama, 6-2, 215, Birmingham, Ala.; T—Milo Lubratovich, Wisconsin, 6-2, 216, Duluth, Minn.; G—Ted Beckett, California, 6-1, 190, Oroville, Calif.; G—Barton Koch, Baylor, 5-10, 195, Temple, Texas; C—*Ben Ticknor, Harvard, 6-2, 193, New York, N.Y.; B—*Frank Carideo, Notre Dame, 5-7, 175, Mount Vernon, N.Y.; B—Marchy Schwartz, Notre Dame, 5-11, 172, Bay St. Louis, Miss.; B—Erny Pinckert, Southern Cal, 6-0, 189, San Bernardino, Calif.; B—Leonard Macaluso, Colgate, 6-2, 210, East Aurora, N.Y.

1931

E—*Jerry Dalrymple, Tulane, 5-10, 175, Arkadelphia, Ark.; E—Vernon Smith, Georgia, 6-2, 190, Macon, Ga.; T—Jesse Quatse, Pittsburgh, 5-8, 198, Greensburg, Pa.; (tie) T—Jack Riley, Northwestern, 6-2, 218, Wilmette, Ill.; T—Dallas Marvil, Northwestern, 6-3, 227, Laurel, Del.; G—Biggie Munn, Minnesota, 5-10, 217, Minneapolis, Minn.; G—John Baker, Southern Cal, 5-10, 185, Kingsburg, Calif.; C—Tommy Yarr, Notre Dame, 5-11, 197, Chimacum, Wash.; B—Gus Shaver, Southern Cal, 5-11, 185, Covina, Calif.; B—Marchy Schwartz, Notre Dame, 5-11, 178, Bay St. Louis, Miss.; B—Pug Rentner, Northwestern, 6-1, 185, Joliet, Ill.; B—Barry Wood, Harvard, 6-1, 173, Milton, Mass.

1932

E—*Paul Moss, Purdue, 6-2, 185, Terre Haute, Ind.; E—Joe Skladany, Pittsburgh, 5-10, 185, Larksville, Pa.; T—*Joe Kurth, Notre Dame, 6-2, 204, Madison, Wis.; T—*Ernie Smith, Southern Cal, 6-2, 215, Los Angeles, Calif.; G—Milt Summerfelt, Army, 6-0, 181, Benton Harbor, Mich.; G—Bill Corbus, Stanford, 5-11, 188, Vallejo, Calif.; C—Pete Gracey, Vanderbilt, 6-0, 188, Franklin, Tenn.; B—*Harry Newman, Michigan, 5-7, 175, Detroit, Mich.; B—*Warren Heller, Pittsburgh, 6-0, 170, Steelton, Pa.; B—Don Zimmerman, Tulane, 5-10, 190, Lake Charles, La.; B—Jimmy Hitchcock, Auburn, 5-11, 172, Union Springs, Ala.

1933

E—Joe Skladany, Pittsburgh, 5-10, 190, Larksville, Pa.; E—Paul Geisler, Centenary (La.), 6-2, 189, Berwick, La.; T—Fred Crawford, Duke, 6-2, 195, Waynesville, N.C.; T—Francis Wistert, Michigan, 6-3, 212, Chicago, Ill.; G—Bill Corbus, Stanford, 5-11, 195, Vallejo, Calif.; G—Aaron Rosenberg, Southern Cal, 6-0, 210, Los Angeles, Calif.; C—*Chuck Bernard, Michigan, 6-2, 215, Benton Harbor, Mich.; B—*Cotton Warburton, Southern Cal, 5-7, 147, San Diego, Calif.; B—George Sauer, Nebraska, 6-2, 195, Lincoln, Neb.; B—Beattie Feathers, Tennessee, 5-10, 180, Bristol, Va.; B—Duane Purvis, Purdue, 6-1, 190, Mattoon, Ill.

1934

E—Don Hutson, Alabama, 6-1, 185, Pine Bluff, Ark.; E—Frank Larson, Minnesota, 6-3, 190, Duluth, Minn.; T—Bill Lee, Alabama, 6-2, 225, Eutaw, Ala.; T—Bob Reynolds, Stanford, 6-4, 220, Okmulgee, Okla.; G—Chuck Hartwig, Pittsburgh, 6-0, 190, Benwood, W.Va.; G—Bill Bevan, Minnesota, 5-11, 194, St. Paul, Minn.; C—Jack Robinson, Notre Dame, 6-3, 195, Huntington, N.Y.; B—Bobby Grayson, Stanford, 5-11, 186, Portland, Ore.; B—Pug Lund, Minnesota, 5-11, 185, Rice Lake, Wis.; B—Dixie Howell, Alabama, 5-10, 164, Hartford, Ala.; B—Fred Borries, Navy, 6-0, 175, Louisville, Ky.

1935

E—Wayne Millner, Notre Dame, 6-0, 184, Salem, Mass.; (tie) E—James Moscrip, Stanford, 6-0, 186, Adena, Ohio; E—Gaynell Tinsley, LSU, 6-0, 188, Homer, La.; T—Ed Widseth, Minnesota, 6-2, 220, McIntosh, Minn.; T—Larry Lutz, California, 6-0, 201, Santa Ana, Calif.; G—John Weller, Princeton, 6-0, 195, Wynnewood, Pa.; (tie) G—Sidney Wagner, Michigan St., 5-11, 186, Lansing, Mich.; G—J. C. Wetsel, Southern Methodist, 5-10, 185, Dallas, Texas; (tie) C—Gomer Jones, Ohio St., 5-8, 210, Cleveland, Ohio; C—Darrell Lester, Texas Christian, 6-4, 218, Jacksboro, Texas; B—*Jay Berwanger, Chicago, 6-0, 195, Dubuque, Iowa; B—*Bobby Grayson, Stanford, 5-11, 190, Portland, Ore.; B—Bobby Wilson, Southern Methodist, 5-10, 147, Corsicana, Texas; B—Riley Smith, Alabama, 6-1, 195, Columbus, Miss.

1936

E—*Larry Kelley, Yale, 6-1, 190, Williamsport, Pa.; E—*Gaynell Tinsley, LSU, 6-0, 196, Homer, La.; T—*Ed Widseth, Minnesota, 6-2, 220, McIntosh, Minn.; T—Averell Daniell, Pittsburgh, 6-3, 200, Mt. Lebanon, Pa.; G—Steve Reid, Northwestern, 5-9, 192, Chicago, Ill.; G—Max Starcevich, Washington, 5-10, 198, Duluth, Minn.; (tie) C—Alex Wojciechowicz, Fordham, 6-0, 192, South River, N.J.; C—Mike Basrak, Duquesne, 6-1, 210, Bellaire, Ohio; B—Sammy Baugh, Texas Christian, 6-2, 180, Sweetwater, Texas; B—Ace Parker, Duke, 5-11, 175, Portsmouth, Va.; B—Ray Buivid, Marquette, 6-1, 193, Port Washington, Wis.; B—Sam Francis, Nebraska, 6-1, 207, Oberlin, Kan.

1937

E—Chuck Sweeney, Notre Dame, 6-0, 190, Bloomington, Ill.; E—Andy Bershak, North Caro., 6-0, 190, Clairton, Pa.; T—Ed Franco, Fordham, 5-8, 196, Jersey City, N.J.; T—Tony Matisi, Pittsburgh, 6-0, 224, Endicott, N.Y.; G—Joe Routt, Texas A&M, 6-0, 193, Chappel Hill, Texas; G—Leroy Monsky, Alabama, 6-0, 198, Montgomery, Ala.; C—Alex Wojciechowicz, Fordham, 6-0, 196, South River, N.J.; B—*Clint Frank, Yale, 5-10, 190, Evanston, Ill.; B—Marshall Goldberg, Pittsburgh, 5-11, 185, Elkins, W.Va.; B—Byron "Whizzer" White, Colorado, 6-1, 185, Wellington, Colo.; B—Sam Chapman, California, 6-0, 190, Tiburon, Calif.

1938

E—Waddy Young, Oklahoma, 6-2, 203, Ponca City, Okla.; (tie) E—Brud Holland, Cornell, 6-1, 205, Auburn, N.Y.; E—Bowden Wyatt, Tennessee, 6-1, 190, Kingston, Tenn.; T—*Ed Beinor, Notre Dame, 6-2, 207, Harvey, Ill.; T—Alvord Wolff, Santa Clara, 6-2, 220, San Francisco, Calif.; G—*Ralph Heikkinen, Michigan, 5-10, 185, Ramsey, Mich.; G—Ed Bock, Iowa St., 6-0, 202, Fort Dodge, Iowa; C—Ki Aldrich, Texas Christian, 5-11, 195, Temple, Texas; B—*Davey O'Brien, Texas Christian, 5-7, 150, Dallas, Texas; B—*Marshall

Goldberg, Pittsburgh, 6-0, 190, Elkins, W.Va.; B—Bob MacLeod, Dartmouth, 6-0, 190, Glen Ellyn, Ill.; B—Vic Bottari, California, 5-9, 182, Vallejo, Calif.

1939

E—Esco Sarkkinen, Ohio St., 6-0, 192, Fairport Harbor, Ohio; E—Ken Kavanaugh, LSU, 6-3, 203, Little Rock, Ark.; T—Nick Drahos, Cornell, 6-3, 200, Cedarhurst, N.Y.; T—Harley McCollum, Tulane, 6-4, 235, Wagoner, Okla.; G—*Harry Smith, Southern Cal, 5-11, 218, Ontario, Calif.; G—Ed Molinski, Tennessee, 5-10, 190, Massillon, Ohio; C—John Schiechl, Santa Clara, 6-2, 220, San Francisco, Calif.; B—Nile Kinnick, Iowa, 5-8, 167, Omaha, Neb.; B—Tom Harmon, Michigan, 6-0, 195, Gary, Ind.; B—John Kimbrough, Texas A&M, 6-2, 210, Haskell, Texas; B—George Cafego, Tennessee, 6-0, 174, Scarbro, W.Va.

1940

E—Gene Goodreault, Boston College, 5-10, 184, Haverhill, Mass.; E—Dave Rankin, Purdue, 6-1, 190, Warsaw, Ind.; T—Nick Drahos, Cornell, 6-3, 212, Cedarhurst, N.Y.; (tie) T—Alf Bauman, Northwestern, 6-1, 210, Chicago, Ill.; T—Urban Odson, Minnesota, 6-3, 247, Clark, S.D.; G—*Bob Suffridge, Tennessee, 6-0, 190, Knoxville, Tenn.; G—Marshall Robnett, Texas A&M, 6-1, 205, Klondike, Texas; C—Rudy Mucha, Washington, 6-2, 210, Chicago, Ill.; B—*Tom Harmon, Michigan, 6-0, 195, Gary, Ind.; B—*John Kimbrough, Texas A&M, 6-2, 221, Haskell, Texas; B—Frank Albert, Stanford, 5-9, 170, Glendale, Calif.; B—George Franck, Minnesota, 6-0, 175, Davenport, Iowa.

1941

E—Holt Rast, Alabama, 6-1, 185, Birmingham, Ala.; E—Bob Dove, Notre Dame, 6-2, 195, Youngstown, Ohio; T—Dick Wildung, Minnesota, 6-0, 210, Luverne, Minn.; T—Ernie Blandin, Tulane, 6-3, 245, Keighley, Kan.; G—*Endicott Peabody, Harvard, 6-0, 181, Syracuse, N.Y.; G—Ray Frankowski, Washington, 5-10, 210, Hammond, Ind.; C—Darold Jenkins, Missouri, 6-0, 195, Higginsville, Mo.; B—Bob Westfall, Michigan, 5-8, 190, Ann Arbor, Mich.; B—Bruce Smith, Minnesota, 6-0, 193, Faribault, Minn.; B—Frank Albert, Stanford, 5-9, 173, Glendale, Calif.; (tie) B—Bill Dudley, Virginia, 5-10, 175, Bluefield, Va.; B—Frank Sinkwich, Georgia, 5-8, 180, Youngstown, Ohio.

1942

E—*Dave Schreiner, Wisconsin, 6-2, 198, Lancaster, Wis.; E—Bob Dove, Notre Dame, 6-2, 195, Youngstown, Ohio; T—Dick Wildung, Minnesota, 6-0, 215, Luverne, Minn.; T—Albert Wistert, Michigan, 6-2, 205, Chicago, Ill.; G—Chuck Taylor, Stanford, 5-11, 200, San Jose, Calif.; (tie) G—Harvey Hardy, Georgia Tech, 5-10, 185, Thomaston, Ga.; G—Julie Franks, Michigan, 6-0, 187, Hamtramck, Mich.; C—Joe Domnanovich, Alabama, 6-1, 200, South Bend, Ind.; B—*Frank Sinkwich, Georgia, 5-8, 185, Youngstown, Ohio; B—Paul Governali, Columbia, 5-11, 186, New York, N.Y.; B—Mike Holovak, Boston College, 6-2, 214, Lansford, Pa.; B—Billy Hillenbrand, Indiana, 6-0, 195, Evansville, Ind.

1943

E—Ralph Heywood, Southern Cal, 6-2, 195, Huntington Park, Calif.; E—John Yonakor, Notre Dame, 6-4, 220, Dorchester, Mass.; T—Jim White, Notre Dame, 6-2, 210, Edgewater, N.J.; T—Don Whitmire, Navy, 5-11, 215, Decatur, Ala.; G—Alex Agase, Purdue, 5-10, 190, Evanston, Ill.; G—Pat Filley, Notre Dame, 5-8, 175, South Bend, Ind.; C—*Casimir Myslinski, Army, 5-11, 186, Steubenville, Ohio; B—*Bill Daley, Michigan, 6-2, 206, St. Cloud, Minn.; B—Angelo Bertelli, Notre Dame, 6-1, 173, West Springfield, Mass.; B—Creighton Miller, Notre Dame, 6-0, 185, Wilmington, Del.; B—Bob Odell, Pennsylvania, 5-11, 182, Sioux City, Iowa.

1944

E—Phil Tinsley, Georgia Tech, 6-1, 188, Bessemer, Ala.; (tie) E—Paul Walker, Yale, 6-3, 203, Oak Park, Ill.; E—Jack Dugger, Ohio St., 6-3, 210, Canton, Ohio; T—*Don Whitmire, Navy, 5-11, 215, Decatur, Ala.; T—John Ferraro, Southern Cal, 6-3, 235, Maywood, Calif.; G—Bill Hackett, Ohio St., 5-9, 191, London, Ohio; G—Ben Chase, Navy, 6-1, 195, San Diego, Calif.; C—John Tavener, Indiana, 6-0, 220, Granville, Ohio; B—*Les Horvath, Ohio St., 5-10, 167, Parma, Ohio; B—Glenn Davis, Army, 5-9, 170, Claremont, Calif.; B—Doc Blanchard, Army, 6-0, 205, Bishopville, S.C.; B—Bob Jenkins, Navy, 6-1, 195, Talladega, Ala.

1945

E—Dick Duden, Navy, 6-2, 203, New York, N.Y.; (tie) E—Hubert Bechtol, Texas, 6-2, 190, Lubbock, Texas; E—Bob Ravensberg, Indiana, 6-1, 180, Bellevue, Ky.; E—Max Morris, Northwestern, 6-2, 195, West Frankfort, Ill.; T—Tex Coulter, Army, 6-3, 220, Fort Worth, Texas; T—George Savitsky, Pennsylvania, 6-3, 250, Camden, N.J.; G—*Warren Amling, Ohio St., 6-0, 197, Pana, Ill.; G—John Green, Army, 5-11, 190, Shelbyville, Ky.; C—Vaughn Mancha, Alabama, 6-0, 235, Birmingham, Ala.; B—*Glenn Davis, Army, 5-9, 170, Claremont, Calif.; B—*Doc Blanchard, Army, 6-0, 205, Bishopville, S.C.; B—*Herman Wedemeyer, St. Mary's (Cal.), 5-10, 173, Honolulu, Hawaii; B—Bob Fenimore, Oklahoma St., 6-2, 188, Woodward, Okla.

1946

E—*Burr Baldwin, UCLA, 6-1, 196, Bakersfield, Calif.; E—(tie) Hubert Bechtol, Texas, 6-2, 201, Lubbock, Texas; Hank Foldberg, Army, 6-1, 200, Dallas, Texas; T—George Connor, Notre Dame, 6-3, 225, Chicago, Ill.; (tie) T—Warren Amling, Ohio St., 6-0, 197, Pana, Ill.; T—Dick Huffman, Tennessee, 6-2, 230, Charleston, W.Va.; G—Alex Agase, Illinois, 5-10, 191, Evanston, Ill.; G—Weldon Humble, Rice, 6-1, 214, San Antonio, Texas; C—Paul Duke, Georgia Tech, 6-1, 210, Atlanta, Ga.; B—*John Lujack, Notre Dame, 6-0, 180, Connellsville, Pa.; B—*Charley Trippi, Georgia, 5-11, 185, Pittston, Pa.; B—*Glenn Davis, Army, 5-9, 170, Claremont, Calif.; B—*Doc Blanchard, Army, 6-0, 205, Bishopville, S.C.

1947

E—Paul Cleary, Southern Cal, 6-1, 195, Santa Ana, Calif.; E—Bill Swiacki, Columbia, 6-2, 198, Southbridge, Mass.; T—Bob Davis, Georgia Tech, 6-4, 220, Columbus, Ga.; T—George Connor, Notre Dame, 6-3, 225, Chicago, Ill.; G—Joe Steffy, Army, 5-11, 190, Chattanooga, Tenn.; G—Bill Fischer, Notre Dame, 6-2, 230, Chicago, Ill.; C—Chuck Bednarik, Pennsylvania, 6-3, 220, Bethlehem, Pa.; B—*John Lujack, Notre Dame, 6-0, 180, Connellsville, Pa.; B—*Bob Chappuis, Michigan, 6-0, 180, Toledo, Ohio; B—Doak Walker, Southern Methodist, 5-11, 170, Dallas, Texas; (tie) B—Charley Conerly, Mississippi, 6-0, 184, Clarksdale, Miss.; B—Bobby Layne, Texas, 6-0, 191, Dallas, Texas.

1948

E—Dick Rifenburg, Michigan, 6-3, 197, Saginaw, Mich.; E—Leon Hart, Notre Dame, 6-4, 225, Turtle Creek, Pa.; T—Leo Nomellini, Minnesota, 6-2, 248, Chicago, Ill.; T—Alvin Wistert, Michigan, 6-3, 218, Chicago, Ill.; G—Buddy Burris, Oklahoma, 5-11, 214, Muskogee, Okla.; G—Bill Fischer, Notre Dame, 6-2, 233, Chicago, Ill.; C—Chuck Bednarik, Pennsylvania, 6-3, 220, Bethlehem, Pa.; B—*Doak Walker, Southern Methodist, 5-11, 168, Dallas, Texas; B—Charlie Justice, North Caro., 5-10, 165, Asheville, N.C.; B—Jackie Jensen, California, 5-11, 195, Oakland, Calif.; (tie) B—Emil Sitko, Notre Dame, 5-8, 180, Fort Wayne, Ind.; B—Clyde Scott, Arkansas, 6-0, 175, Smackover, Ark.

1949

E—*Leon Hart, Notre Dame, 6-5, 260, Turtle Creek, Pa.; E—James Williams, Rice, 6-0, 197, Waco, Texas; T—Leo Nomellini, Minnesota, 6-2, 255, Chicago, Ill.; T—Alvin Wistert, Michigan, 6-3, 223, Chicago, Ill.; G—*Rod Franz, California, 6-1, 198, San Francisco, Calif.; G—Ed Bagdon, Michigan St., 5-10, 200, Dearborn, Mich.; C—*Clayton Tonnemaker, Minnesota, 6-3, 240, Minneapolis, Minn.; B—*Emil Sitko, Notre Dame, 5-8, 180, Fort Wayne, Ind.; B—Doak Walker, Southern Methodist, 5-11, 170, Dallas, Texas; B—Arnold Galiffa, Army, 6-2, 190, Donora, Pa.; B—Bob Williams, Notre Dame, 6-1, 180, Baltimore, Md.

1950

E—*Dan Foldberg, Army, 6-1, 185, Dallas, Texas; E—Bill McColl, Stanford, 6-4, 225, San Diego, Calif.; T—Bob Gain, Kentucky, 6-3, 230, Weirton, W.Va.; T—Jim Weatherall, Oklahoma, 6-4, 220, White Deer, Texas; G—Bud McFadin, Texas, 6-3, 225, Iraan, Texas; G—Les Richter, California, 6-2, 220, Fresno, Calif.; C—Jerry Groom, Notre Dame, 6-3, 215, Des Moines, Iowa; B—*Vic Janowicz, Ohio St., 5-9, 189, Elyria, Ohio; B—Kyle Rote, Southern Methodist, 6-0, 190, San Antonio, Texas; B—Babe Parilli, Kentucky, 6-1, 183, Rochester, Pa.; B—Leon Heath, Oklahoma, 6-1, 195, Hollis, Okla.

1951

E—*Bill McColl, Stanford, 6-4, 225, San Diego, Calif.; E—Bob Carey, Michigan St., 6-5, 215, Charlevoix, Mich.; T—*Don Coleman, Michigan St., 5-10, 185, Flint, Mich.; T—*Jim Weatherall, Oklahoma, 6-4, 230, White Deer, Texas; G—*Bob Ward, Maryland, 5-10, 185, Elizabeth, N.J.; G—Les Richter, California, 6-2, 230, Fresno, Calif.; C—Dick Hightower, Southern Methodist, 6-1, 215, Tyler, Texas; B—*Dick Kazmaier, Princeton, 5-11, 171, Maumee, Ohio; B—*Hank Lauricella, Tennessee, 5-10, 169, New Orleans, La.; B—Babe Parilli, Kentucky, 6-1, 188, Rochester, Pa.; B—Johnny Karras, Illinois, 5-11, 171, Argo, Ill.

1952

E—Frank McPhee, Princeton, 6-3, 203, Youngstown, Ohio; E—Bernie Flowers, Purdue, 6-1, 189, Erie, Pa.; T—Dick Modzelewski, Maryland, 6-0, 235, West Natrona, Pa.; T—Hal Miller, Georgia Tech, 6-4, 235, Kingsport, Tenn.; G—John Michels, Tennessee, 5-10, 195, Philadelphia, Pa.; G—Elmer Wilhoite, Southern Cal, 6-2, 216, Winton, Calif.; C—Donn Moomaw, UCLA, 6-4, 220, Santa Ana, Calif.; B—*Jack Scarbath, Maryland, 6-1, 190, Baltimore, Md.; B—*Johnny Lattner, Notre Dame, 6-1, 190, Chicago, Ill.; B—Billy Vessels, Oklahoma, 6-0, 185, Cleveland, Okla.; B—Jim Sears, Southern Cal, 5-9, 167, Inglewood, Calif.

1953

E—Don Dohoney, Michigan St., 6-1, 193, Ann Arbor, Mich.; E—Carlton Massey, Texas, 6-4, 210, Rockwall, Texas; T—*Stan Jones, Maryland, 6-0, 235, Lemoyne, Pa.; T—Art Hunter, Notre Dame, 6-2, 226, Akron, Ohio; G—J. D. Roberts, Oklahoma, 5-10, 210, Dallas, Texas; G—Crawford Mims, Mississippi, 5-10, 200, Greenwood, Miss.; C—Larry Morris, Georgia Tech, 6-0, 205, Decatur, Ga.; B—*Johnny Lattner, Notre Dame, 6-1, 190, Chicago, Ill.; B—*Paul Giel, Minnesota, 5-11, 185, Winona, Minn.; B—Paul Cameron, UCLA, 6-0, 185, Burbank, Calif.; B—J. C. Caroline, Illinois, 6-0, 184, Columbia, S.C.

1954

E—Max Boydston, Oklahoma, 6-2, 207, Muskogee, Okla.; E—Ron Beagle, Navy, 6-0, 185, Covington, Ky.; T—Jack Ellena, UCLA, 6-3, 214, Susanville, Calif.; T—Sid Fournet, LSU, 5-11, 225, Baton Rouge, La.; G—*Bud Brooks, Arkansas, 5-11, 200, Wynne, Ark.; G—Calvin Jones, Iowa, 6-0, 200, Steubenville, Ohio; C—Kurt Burris, Oklahoma, 6-1, 209, Muskogee, Okla.; B—*Ralph Guglielmi, Notre Dame, 6-0, 185, Columbus, Ohio; B—*Howard Cassady, Ohio St., 5-10, 177, Columbus, Ohio; B—*Alan Ameche, Wisconsin, 6-0, 215, Kenosha, Wis.; B—Dicky Maegle, Rice, 6-0, 175, Taylor, Texas.

1955

E—*Ron Beagle, Navy, 6-0, 186, Covington, Ky.; E—Ron Kramer, Michigan, 6-3, 218, East Detroit, Mich.; T—Norman Masters, Michigan St., 6-2, 225, Detroit, Mich.; T—Bruce Bosley, West Va., 6-2, 225, Green Bank, W.Va.; G—Bo Bolinger, Oklahoma, 5-10, 206, Muskogee, Okla.; (tie) G—Calvin Jones, Iowa, 6-0, 220, Steubenville, Ohio; G—Hardiman Cureton, UCLA, 6-0, 213, Duarte, Calif.; C—*Bob Pellegrini, Maryland, 6-2, 225, Yatesboro, Pa.; B—*Howard Cassady, Ohio St., 5-10, 172, Columbus, Ohio; B—*Jim Swink, Texas Christian, 6-1, 180, Rusk, Texas; B—Earl Morrall, Michigan St., 6-1, 180, Muskegon, Mich.; B—Paul Hornung, Notre Dame, 6-2, 205, Louisville, Ky.

1956

E—*Joe Walton, Pittsburgh, 5-11, 205, Beaver Falls, Pa.; E—*Ron Kramer, Michigan, 6-3, 220, East Detroit, Mich.; T—John Witte, Oregon St., 6-2, 232, Klamath Falls, Ore.; T—Lou Michaels, Kentucky, 6-2, 229, Swoyersville, Pa.; G—*Jim Parker, Ohio St., 6-2, 251, Toledo, Ohio; G—*Bill Glass, Baylor, 6-4, 220, Corpus Christi, Texas; C—*Jerry Tubbs, Oklahoma, 6-2, 205, Breckenridge, Texas; B—*Jim Brown, Syracuse, 6-2, 212, Manhasset, N.Y.; B—*John Majors, Tennessee, 5-10, 162, Huntland, Tenn.; B—Tommy McDonald, Oklahoma, 5-9, 169, Albuquerque, N.M.; B—John Brodie, Stanford, 6-1, 190, Oakland, Calif.

1957

E—*Jimmy Phillips, Auburn, 6-2, 205, Alexander City, Ala.; E—Dick Wallen, UCLA, 6-0, 185, Alhambra, Calif.; T—Lou Michaels, Kentucky, 6-2, 235, Swoyersville, Pa.; T—Alex Karras, Iowa, 6-2, 233, Gary, Ind.; G—Bill Krisher, Oklahoma, 6-1, 213, Midwest City, Okla.; G—

Al Ecuyer, Notre Dame, 5-10, 190, New Orleans, La.; C—Dan Currie, Michigan St., 6-3, 225, Detroit, Mich.; B—*John David Crow, Texas A&M, 6-2, 214, Springhill, La.; B—Walt Kowalczyk, Michigan St., 6-0, 205, Westfield, Mass.; B—Bob Anderson, Army, 6-2, 200, Cocoa, Fla.; B—Clendon Thomas, Oklahoma, 6-2, 188, Oklahoma City, Okla.

1958

E—Buddy Dial, Rice, 6-1, 185, Magnolia, Texas; E—Sam Williams, Michigan St., 6-5, 225, Dansville, Mich.; T—Ted Bates, Oregon St., 6-2, 215, Los Angeles, Calif.; T—Brock Strom, Air Force, 6-0, 217, Ironwood, Mich.; G—John Guzik, Pittsburgh, 6-3, 223, Lawrence, Pa.; (tie) G—Zeke Smith, Auburn, 6-2, 210, Uniontown, Ala.; G—George Deiderich, Vanderbilt, 6-1, 198, Toronto, Ohio; C—Bob Harrison, Oklahoma, 6-2, 206, Stamford, Texas; B—*Randy Duncan, Iowa, 6-0, 180, Des Moines, Iowa; B—*Pete Dawkins, Army, 6-1, 197, Royal Oak, Mich.; B—*Billy Cannon, LSU, 6-1, 200, Baton Rouge, La.; B—Bob White, Ohio St., 6-2, 212, Covington, Ky.

1959

E—Bill Carpenter, Army, 6-2, 210, Springfield, Pa.; E—Monty Stickles, Notre Dame, 6-4, 225, Poughkeepsie, N.Y.; T—*Dan Lanphear, Wisconsin, 6-2, 214, Madison, Wis.; T—Don Floyd, Texas Christian, 6-3, 215, Midlothian, Texas; G—*Roger Davis, Syracuse, 6-2, 228, Solon, Ohio; G—Bill Burrell, Illinois, 6-0, 210, Chebanse, Ill.; C—Maxie Baughan, Georgia Tech, 6-1, 212, Bessemer, Ala.; B—Richie Lucas, Penn St., 6-1, 185, Glassport, Pa.; B—Billy Cannon, LSU, 6-1, 208, Baton Rouge, La.; B—Charlie Flowers, Mississippi, 6-0, 198, Marianna, Ark.; B—Ron Burton, Northwestern, 5-9, 185, Springfield, Ohio.

1960

E—*Mike Ditka, Pittsburgh, 6-3, 215, Aliquippa, Pa.; E—*Danny LaRose, Missouri, 6-4, 220, Crystal City, Mo.; T—*Bob Lilly, Texas Christian, 6-5, 250, Throckmorton, Texas; T—Ken Rice, Auburn, 6-3, 250, Bainbridge, Ga.; G—*Tom Brown, Minnesota, 6-0, 225, Minneapolis, Minn.; G—Joe Romig, Colorado, 5-10, 197, Lakewood, Colo.; C—E. J. Holub, Texas Tech, 6-4, 215, Lubbock, Texas; B—*Jake Gibbs, Mississippi, 6-0, 185, Grenada, Miss.; B—*Joe Bellino, Navy, 5-9, 181, Winchester, Mass.; B—*Bob Ferguson, Ohio St., 6-0, 217, Troy, Ohio; B—Ernie Davis, Syracuse, 6-2, 205, Elmira, N.Y.

1961

E—Gary Collins, Maryland, 6-3, 205, Williamstown, Pa.; E—Bill Miller, Miami (Fla.), 6-0, 188, McKeesport, Pa.; T—*Billy Neighbors, Alabama, 5-11, 229, Tuscaloosa, Ala.; T—Merlin Olsen, Utah St., 6-5, 265, Logan, Utah; G—*Roy Winston, LSU, 6-1, 225, Baton Rouge, La.; G—Joe Romig, Colorado, 5-10, 199, Lakewood, Colo.; C—Alex Kroll, Rutgers, 6-2, 228, Leechburg, Pa.; B—*Ernie Davis, Syracuse, 6-2, 210, Elmira, N.Y.; B—*Bob Ferguson, Ohio St., 6-0, 217, Troy, Ohio; B—*Jimmy Saxton, Texas, 5-11, 160, Palestine, Texas; B—Sandy Stephens, Minnesota, 6-0, 215, Uniontown, Pa.

1962

E—Hal Bedsole, Southern Cal, 6-5, 225, Northridge, Calif.; E—Pat Richter, Wisconsin, 6-5, 229, Madison, Wis.; T—*Bobby Bell, Minnesota, 6-4, 214, Shelby, N.C.; T—Jim Dunaway, Mississippi, 6-4, 260, Columbia, Miss.; G—*Johnny Treadwell, Texas, 6-1, 194, Austin, Texas; G—Jack Cvercko, Northwestern, 6-0, 230, Campbell, Ohio; C—*Lee Roy Jordan, Alabama, 6-2, 207, Monroeville, Ala.; B—*Terry Baker, Oregon St., 6-3, 191, Portland, Ore.; B—*Jerry Stovall, LSU, 6-2, 195, West Monroe, La.; B—Mel Renfro, Oregon, 5-11, 190, Portland, Ore.; B—George Saimes, Michigan St., 5-10, 186, Canton, Ohio.

1963

E—Vern Burke, Oregon St., 6-4, 195, Bakersfield, Calif.; E—Lawrence Elkins, Baylor, 6-1, 187, Brownwood, Texas; T—*Scott Appleton, Texas, 6-3, 235, Brady, Texas; T—Carl Eller, Minnesota, 6-6, 241, Winston-Salem, N.C.; G—*Bob Brown, Nebraska, 6-5, 259, Cleveland, Ohio; G—Rick Redman, Washington, 5-11, 210, Seattle, Wash.; C—*Dick Butkus, Illinois, 6-3, 234, Chicago, Ill.; B—*Roger Staubach, Navy, 6-2, 190, Cincinnati, Ohio; B—Sherman Lewis, Michigan St., 5-8, 154, Louisville, Ky.; B—Jim Grisham, Oklahoma, 6-2, 205, Olney, Texas; (tie) B—Gale Sayers, Kansas, 6-0, 196, Omaha, Neb.; B—Paul Martha, Pittsburgh, 6-1, 180, Wilkinsburg, Pa.

1964

E—Jack Snow, Notre Dame, 6-2, 210, Long Beach, Calif.; E—Fred Biletnikoff, Florida St., 6-1, 186, Erie, Pa.; T—*Larry Kramer, Nebraska, 6-2, 240, Austin, Minn.; T—Ralph Neely, Oklahoma, 6-5, 243, Farmington, N.M.; G—Rick Redman, Washington, 5-11, 215, Seattle, Wash.; G—Glenn Ressler, Penn St., 6-2, 230, Dornsife, Pa.; C—Dick Butkus, Illinois, 6-3, 237, Chicago, Ill.; B—John Huarte, Notre Dame, 6-0, 180, Anaheim, Calif.; B—Gale Sayers, Kansas, 6-0, 194, Omaha, Neb.; B—Lawrence Elkins, Baylor, 6-1, 187, Brownwood, Texas; B—Tucker Frederickson, Auburn, 6-2, 210, Hollywood, Fla.

Beginning in 1965, offense and defense selected.

1965

Offense E—*Howard Twilley, Tulsa, 5-10, 180, Galena Park, Texas; E—Freeman White, Nebraska, 6-5, 220, Detroit, Mich.; T—Sam Ball, Kentucky, 6-4, 241, Henderson, Ky.; T—Glen Ray Hines, Arkansas, 6-5, 235, El Dorado, Ark.; G—*Dick Arrington, Notre Dame, 5-11, 232, Erie, Pa.; G—Stas Maliszewski, Princeton, 6-1, 215, Davenport, Iowa; C—Paul Crane, Alabama, 6-2, 188, Prichard, Ala.; B—*Mike Garrett, Southern Cal, 5-9, 185, Los Angeles, Calif.; B—*Jim Grabowski, Illinois, 6-2, 211, Chicago, Ill.; B—Bob Griese, Purdue, 6-1, 185, Evansville, Ind.; B—Donny Anderson, Texas Tech, 6-3, 210, Stinnett, Texas.

Defense E—Aaron Brown, Minnesota, 6-4, 230, Port Arthur, Texas; E—Bubba Smith, Michigan St., 6-7, 268, Beaumont, Texas; T—Walt Barnes, Nebraska, 6-3, 235, Chicago, Ill.; T—Loyd Phillips, Arkansas, 6-3, 221, Longview, Texas; T—Bill Yearby, Michigan, 6-3, 222, Detroit, Mich.; LB—Carl McAdams, Oklahoma, 6-3, 215, White Deer, Texas; LB—Tommy Nobis, Texas, 6-2, 230, San Antonio, Texas; LB—Frank Emanuel, Tennessee, 6-3, 228, Newport News, Va.; B—George Webster, Michigan St., 6-4, 204, Anderson, S.C.; B—Johnny Roland, Missouri, 6-2, 198, Corpus Christi, Texas; B—Nick Rassas, Notre Dame, 6-0, 185, Winnetka, Ill.

1966

Offense E—*Jack Clancy, Michigan, 6-1, 192, Detroit, Mich.; E—Ray Perkins, Alabama, 6-0, 184, Petal, Miss.; T—*Cecil Dowdy, Alabama, 6-0, 206, Cherokee, Ala.; T—Ron Yary, Southern Cal, 6-6, 265, Bellflower, Calif.; G—Tom Regner, Notre Dame, 6-1, 245, Kenosha, Wis.; G—LaVerne Allers, Nebraska, 6-0, 209, Davenport, Iowa; C—Jim Breland, Georgia Tech, 6-2, 223, Blacksburg, Va.; B—*Steve Spurrier, Florida, 6-2, 203, Johnson City, Tenn.; B—*Nick Eddy, Notre Dame, 6-0, 195, Lafayette, Calif.; B—Mel Farr, UCLA, 6-2, 208, Beaumont, Texas; B—Clint Jones, Michigan St., 6-0, 206, Cleveland, Ohio.

Defense E—*Bubba Smith, Michigan St., 6-7, 283, Beaumont, Texas; E—Alan Page, Notre Dame, 6-5, 238, Canton, Ohio; T—*Loyd Phillips, Arkansas, 6-3, 230, Longview, Texas; T—Tom Greenlee, Washington, 6-0, 195, Seattle, Wash.; MG—Wayne Meylan, Nebraska, 6-0, 239, Bay City, Mich.; MG—John LaGrone, Southern Methodist, 5-10, 232, Borger, Texas; LB—*Jim Lynch, Notre Dame, 6-1, 225, Lima, Ohio; LB—Paul Naumoff, Tennessee, 6-1, 209, Columbus, Ohio; B—*George Webster, Michigan St., 6-4, 218, Anderson, S.C.; B—Tom Beier, Miami (Fla.), 5-11, 197, Fremont, Ohio; B—Nate Shaw, Southern Cal, 6-2, 205, San Diego, Calif.

1967

Offense E—Dennis Homan, Alabama, 6-0, 182, Muscle Shoals, Ala.; E—Ron Sellers, Florida St., 6-4, 187, Jacksonville, Fla.; T—*Ron Yary, Southern Cal, 6-6, 245, Bellflower, Calif.; T—Ed Chandler, Georgia, 6-2, 222, Cedartown, Ga.; G—Harry Olszewski, Clemson, 5-11, 237, Baltimore, Md.; G—Rich Stotter, Houston, 5-11, 225, Shaker Heights, Ohio; C—*Bob Johnson, Tennessee, 6-4, 232, Cleveland, Tenn.; B—Gary Beban, UCLA, 6-0, 191, Redwood City, Calif.; B—*Leroy Keyes, Purdue, 6-3, 199, Newport News, Va.; B—*O. J. Simpson, Southern Cal, 6-2, 205, San Francisco, Calif.; B—*Larry Csonka, Syracuse, 6-3, 230, Stow, Ohio.

Defense E—*Ted Hendricks, Miami (Fla.), 6-8, 222, Miami Springs, Fla.; E—Tim Rossovich, Southern Cal, 6-5, 235, Mountain View, Calif.; T—Dennis Byrd, North Caro. St., 6-4, 250, Lincolnton, N.C.; MG—*Granville Liggins, Oklahoma, 5-11, 216, Tulsa, Okla.; MG—Wayne Meylan, Nebraska, 6-0, 231, Bay City, Mich.; LB—Adrian Young, Southern Cal, 6-1, 210, La Puente, Calif.; LB—Don Manning, UCLA, 6-2, 204, Culver City, Calif.; B—Tom Schoen, Notre Dame, 5-11, 178, Euclid, Ohio; B—Frank Loria, Virginia Tech, 5-9, 174, Clarksburg, W.Va.; B—Bobby Johns, Alabama, 6-1, 180, Birmingham, Ala.; B—Dick Anderson, Colorado, 6-2, 204, Boulder, Colo.

1968

Offense E—*Ted Kwalick, Penn St., 6-4, 230, McKees Rocks, Pa.; E—Jerry LeVias, Southern Methodist, 5-10, 170, Beaumont, Texas; T—*Dave Foley, Ohio St., 6-5, 246, Cincinnati, Ohio; T—George Kunz, Notre Dame, 6-5, 240, Arcadia, Calif.; G—*Charles Rosenfelder, Tennessee, 6-1, 220, Humboldt, Tenn.; (tie) G—Jim Barnes, Arkansas, 6-4, 227, Pine Bluff, Ark.; G—Mike Montler, Colorado, 6-4, 235, Columbus, Ohio; C—*John Didion, Oregon St., 6-4, 242, Woodland, Calif.; B—*O. J. Simpson, Southern Cal, 6-2, 205, San Francisco, Calif.; B—*Leroy Keyes, Purdue, 6-3, 205, Newport News, Va.; B—Terry Hanratty, Notre Dame, 6-1, 200, Butler, Pa.; B—Chris Gilbert, Texas, 5-11, 176, Spring, Texas.

Defense E—*Ted Hendricks, Miami (Fla.), 6-8, 222, Miami Springs, Fla.; E—John Zook, Kansas, 6-4, 230, Larned, Kan.; T—Bill Stanfill, Georgia, 6-5, 245, Cairo, Ga.; T—Joe Greene, North Texas, 6-4, 274, Temple, Texas; MG—Ed White, California, 6-3, 245, Palm Desert, Calif.; MG—Chuck Kyle, Purdue, 6-1, 225, Fort Thomas, Ky.; LB—Steve Kiner, Tennessee, 6-1, 205, Tampa, Fla.; LB—Dennis Onkotz, Penn St., 6-2, 205, Northampton, Pa.; B—Jake Scott, Georgia, 6-1, 188, Arlington, Va.; B—Roger Wehrli, Missouri, 6-0, 184, King City, Mo.; B—Al Worley, Washington, 6-0, 175, Wenatchee, Wash.

1969

Offense E—Jim Mandich, Michigan, 6-3, 222, Solon, Ohio; (tie) E—Walker Gillette, Richmond, 6-5, 200, Capron, Va.; E—Carlos Alvarez, Florida, 5-11, 180, Miami, Fla.; T—Bob McKay, Texas, 6-6, 245, Crane, Texas; T—John Ward, Oklahoma St., 6-5, 248, Tulsa, Okla.; G—Chip Kell, Tennessee, 6-0, 255, Decatur, Ga.; G—Bill Bridges, Houston, 6-2, 230, Carrollton, Texas; C—Rodney Brand, Arkansas, 6-2, 218, Newport, Ark.; B—*Mike Phipps, Purdue, 6-3, 206, Columbus, Ind.; B—*Steve Owens, Oklahoma, 6-2, 215, Miami, Okla.; B—Jim Otis, Ohio St., 6-0, 214, Celina, Ohio; B—Bob Anderson, Colorado, 6-0, 208, Boulder, Colo.

Defense E—Jim Gunn, Southern Cal, 6-1, 210, San Diego, Calif.; E—Phil Olsen, Utah St., 6-5, 255, Logan, Utah; T—*Mike Reid, Penn St., 6-3, 240, Altoona, Pa.; T—*Mike McCoy, Notre Dame, 6-5, 274, Erie, Pa.; MG—Jim Stillwagon, Ohio St., 6-0, 216, Mount Vernon, Ohio; LB—*Steve Kiner, Tennessee, 6-1, 215, Tampa, Fla.; LB—Dennis Onkotz, Penn St., 6-2, 212, Northampton, Pa.; LB—Mike Ballou, UCLA, 6-3, 230, Los Angeles, Calif.; B—Jack Tatum, Ohio St., 6-0, 204, Passaic, N.J.; B—Buddy McClinton, Auburn, 5-11, 190, Montgomery, Ala.; B—Tom Curtis, Michigan, 6-1, 190, Aurora, Ohio.

1970

Offense E—Tom Gatewood, Notre Dame, 6-2, 208, Baltimore, Md.; E—Ernie Jennings, Air Force, 6-0, 172, Kansas City, Mo.; E—Elmo Wright, Houston, 6-0, 195, Brazoria, Texas; T—Dan Dierdorf, Michigan, 6-4, 250, Canton, Ohio; (tie) T—Bobby Wuensch, Texas, 6-3, 230, Houston, Texas; T—Bob Newton, Nebraska, 6-4, 248, LaMirada, Calif.; G—*Chip Kell, Tennessee, 6-0, 240, Decatur, Ga.; G—Larry DiNardo, Notre Dame, 6-1, 235, New York, N.Y.; C—Don Popplewell, Colorado, 6-2, 240, Raytown, Mo.; QB—Jim Plunkett, Stanford, 6-3, 204, San Jose, Calif.; RB—Steve Worster, Texas, 6-0, 210, Bridge City, Texas; RB—Don McCauley, North Caro., 6-0, 211, Garden City, N.Y.

Defense E—Bill Atessis, Texas, 6-3, 255, Houston, Texas; E—Charlie Weaver, Southern Cal, 6-2, 214, Richmond, Calif.; T—Rock Perdoni, Georgia Tech, 5-11, 236, Wellesley, Mass.; T—Dick Bumpas, Arkansas, 6-1, 225, Fort Smith, Ark.; MG—*Jim Stillwagon, Ohio St., 6-0, 220, Mount Vernon, Ohio; LB—Jack Ham, Penn St., 6-3, 212, Johnstown, Pa.; LB—Mike Anderson, LSU, 6-3, 225, Baton Rouge, La.; B—*Jack Tatum, Ohio St., 6-0, 208, Passaic, N.J.; B—Larry Willingham, Auburn, 6-1, 185, Birmingham, Ala.; B—Dave Elmendorf, Texas A&M, 6-1, 190, Houston, Texas; B—Tommy Casanova, LSU, 6-1, 191, Crowley, La.

1971

Offense E—*Terry Beasley, Auburn, 5-11, 184, Montgomery, Ala.; E—Johnny Rodgers, Nebraska, 5-10, 171, Omaha, Neb.; T—*Jerry Sisemore, Texas, 6-4, 255, Plainview, Texas; T—Dave Joyner, Penn St., 6-0, 235, State College, Pa.; G—*Royce Smith, Georgia, 6-3, 240, Savannah, Ga.; G—Reggie McKenzie, Michigan, 6-4, 232, Highland Park, Mich.; C—Tom Brahaney, Oklahoma, 6-2, 231, Midland, Texas; QB—*Pat Sullivan, Auburn, 6-0, 191, Birmingham, Ala.; RB—*Ed Marinaro, Cornell, 6-3, 210, New Milford, N.J.; RB—*Greg Pruitt, Oklahoma, 5-9, 176, Houston, Texas; RB—Johnny Musso, Alabama, 5-11, 194, Birmingham, Ala.

Defense E—*Walt Patulski, Notre Dame, 6-5, 235, Liverpool, N.Y.; E—Willie Harper, Nebraska, 6-3, 207, Toledo, Ohio; T—Larry Jacobson, Nebraska, 6-6, 250, Sioux Falls, S.D.; T—Mel Long, Toledo, 6-1, 230, Toledo, Ohio; T—Sherman White, California, 6-5, 250, Portsmouth, N.H.; LB—*Mike Taylor, Michigan, 6-2, 224, Detroit, Mich.; LB—Jeff Siemon, Stanford, 6-2, 225, Bakersfield, Calif.; B—*Bobby Majors, Tennessee, 6-1, 197, Sewanee, Tenn.; B—Clarence Ellis, Notre Dame, 6-0, 178, Grand Rapids, Mich.; B—Ernie Jackson, Duke, 5-10, 170, Hopkins, S.C.; B—Tommy Casanova, LSU, 6-2, 195, Crowley, La.

1972

Offense WR—*Johnny Rodgers, Nebraska, 5-9, 173, Omaha, Neb.; TE—*Charles Young, Southern Cal, 6-4, 228, Fresno, Calif.; T—*Jerry Sisemore, Texas, 6-4, 260, Plainview, Texas; T—Paul Seymour, Michigan, 6-5, 250, Berkley, Mich.; G—*John Hannah, Alabama, 6-3, 282, Albertville, Ala.; G—Ron Rusnak, North Caro., 6-1, 223, Prince George, Va.; C—Tom Brahaney, Oklahoma, 6-2, 227, Midland, Texas; QB—Bert Jones, LSU, 6-3, 205, Ruston, La.; RB—*Greg Pruitt, Oklahoma, 5-9, 177, Houston, Texas; RB—Otis Armstrong, Purdue, 5-11, 197, Chicago, Ill.; RB—Woody Green, Arizona St., 6-1, 190, Portland, Ore.

Defense E—Willie Harper, Nebraska, 6-2, 207, Toledo, Ohio; E—Bruce Bannon, Penn St., 6-3, 224, Rockaway, N.J.; T—*Greg Marx, Notre Dame, 6-5, 265, Redford, Mich.; T—Dave Butz, Purdue, 6-7, 279, Park Ridge, Ill.; MG—*Rich Glover, Nebraska, 6-1, 234, Jersey City, N.J.; LB—Randy Gradishar, Ohio St., 6-3, 232, Champion, Ohio; LB—John Skorupan, Penn St., 6-2, 208, Beaver, Pa.; B—*Brad VanPelt, Michigan St., 6-5, 221, Owosso, Mich.; B—Cullen Bryant, Colorado, 6-2, 215, Colorado Springs, Colo.; B—Robert Popelka, Southern Methodist, 6-1, 190, Temple, Texas; B—Randy Logan, Michigan, 6-2, 192, Detroit, Mich.

1973

Offense WR—Lynn Swann, Southern Cal, 6-0, 180, Foster City, Calif.; TE—Dave Casper, Notre Dame, 6-3, 252, Chilton, Wis.; T—*John Hicks, Ohio St., 6-3, 258, Cleveland, Ohio; T—Booker Brown, Southern Cal, 6-3, 270, Santa Barbara, Calif.; G—Buddy Brown, Alabama, 6-2, 242, Tallahassee, Fla.; G—Bill Yoest, North Caro. St., 6-0, 235, Pittsburgh, Pa.; C—Bill Wyman, Texas, 6-2, 235, Spring, Texas; QB—Dave Jaynes, Kansas, 6-2, 212, Bonner Springs, Kan.; RB—*John Cappelletti, Penn St., 6-1, 206, Upper Darby, Pa.; RB—Roosevelt Leaks, Texas, 5-11, 209, Brenham, Texas; RB—Woody Green, Arizona St., 6-1, 202, Portland, Ore.; RB—Kermit Johnson, UCLA, 6-0, 185, Los Angeles, Calif.

Defense L—*John Dutton, Nebraska, 6-7, 248, Rapid City, S.D.; L—Dave Gallagher, Michigan, 6-4, 245, Piqua, Ohio; L—*Lucious Selmon, Oklahoma, 5-11, 236, Eufaula, Okla.; L—Tony Cristiani, Miami (Fla.), 5-10, 215, Brandon, Fla.; LB—*Randy Gradishar, Ohio St., 6-3, 236, Champion, Ohio; LB—Rod Shoate, Oklahoma, 6-1, 214, Spiro, Okla.; LB—Richard Wood, Southern Cal, 6-2, 217, Elizabeth, N.J.; B—Mike Townsend, Notre Dame, 6-3, 183, Hamilton, Ohio; B—Artimus Parker, Southern Cal, 6-3, 215, Sacramento, Calif.; B—Dave Brown, Michigan, 6-1, 188, Akron, Ohio; B—Randy Rhino, Georgia Tech, 5-10, 179, Charlotte, N.C.

1974

Offense WR—Pete Demmerle, Notre Dame, 6-1, 190, New Canaan, Conn.; TE—Bennie Cunningham, Clemson, 6-5, 252, Seneca, S.C.; T—Kurt Schumacher, Ohio St., 6-4, 250, Lorain, Ohio; T—Marvin Crenshaw, Nebraska, 6-6, 240, Toledo, Ohio; G—Ken Huff, North Caro., 6-4, 261, Coronado, Calif.; G—John Roush, Oklahoma, 6-0, 252, Arvada, Colo.; G—Gerry DiNardo, Notre Dame, 6-1, 237, New York, N.Y.; C—Steve Myers, Ohio St., 6-2, 244, Kent, Ohio; QB—Steve Bartkowski, California, 6-4, 215, Santa Clara, Calif.; RB—*Archie Griffin, Ohio St., 5-9, 184, Columbus, Ohio; RB—*Joe Washington, Oklahoma, 5-10, 178, Port Arthur, Texas; RB—*Anthony Davis, Southern Cal, 5-9, 183, San Fernando, Calif.

Defense L—*Randy White, Maryland, 6-4, 238, Wilmington, Del.; L—Mike Hartenstine, Penn St., 6-4, 233, Bethlehem, Pa.; L—Pat Donovan, Stanford, 6-5, 240, Helena, Mont.; L—Jimmy Webb, Mississippi St., 6-5, 245, Florence, Miss.; L—Leroy Cook, Alabama, 6-4, 205, Abbeville, Ala.; MG—Louie Kelcher, Southern Methodist, 6-5, 275, Beaumont, Texas; MG—Rubin Carter, Miami (Fla.), 6-3, 260, Ft. Lauderdale, Fla.; LB—*Rod Shoate, Oklahoma, 6-1, 213, Spiro, Okla.; LB—Richard Wood, Southern Cal, 6-2, 213, Elizabeth, N.J.; LB—Ken Bernich, Auburn, 6-2, 240, Gretna, La.; LB—Woodrow Lowe, Alabama, 6-0, 211, Phenix City, Ala.; B—*Dave Brown, Michigan, 6-1, 188, Akron, Ohio; B—Pat Thomas, Texas A&M, 5-9, 180, Plano, Texas; B—John Provost, Holy Cross, 5-10, 180, Quincy, Mass.

1975

Offense E—Steve Rivera, California, 6-0, 185, Wilmington, Calif.; E—Larry Seivers, Tennessee, 6-4, 198, Clinton, Tenn.; T—Bob Simmons, Texas, 6-5, 245, Temple, Texas; T—Dennis Lick, Wisconsin, 6-3, 262, Chicago, Ill.; G—Randy Johnson, Georgia, 6-2, 250, Rome, Ga.; G—Ted Smith, Ohio St., 6-1, 242, Gibsonburg, Ohio; C—*Rik Bonness, Nebraska, 6-4, 223, Bellevue, Neb.; QB—John Sciarra, UCLA, 5-10, 178, Alhambra, Calif.; RB—*Archie Griffin, Ohio St., 5-9, 182, Columbus, Ohio; RB—*Ricky Bell, Southern Cal, 6-2, 215, Los Angeles, Calif.; RB—Chuck Muncie, California, 6-3, 220, Uniontown, Pa.

Defense E—*Leroy Cook, Alabama, 6-4, 205, Abbeville, Ala.; E—Jimbo Elrod, Oklahoma, 6-0, 210, Tulsa, Okla.; T—*Lee Roy Selmon, Oklahoma, 6-2, 256, Eufaula, Okla.; T—*Steve Niehaus, Notre Dame, 6-5, 260, Cincinnati, Ohio; MG—Dewey Selmon, Oklahoma, 6-1, 257, Eufaula, Okla.; LB—*Ed Simonini, Texas A&M, 6-0, 215, Las Vegas, Nev.; LB—Greg Buttle, Penn St., 6-3, 220, Linwood, N.J.; LB—Sammy Green, Florida, 6-2, 228, Ft. Meade, Fla.; B—*Chet Moeller, Navy, 6-0, 189, Kettering, Ohio; B—Tim Fox, Ohio St., 6-0, 186, Canton, Ohio; B—Pat Thomas, Texas A&M, 5-10, 180, Plano, Texas.

1976

Offense SE—Larry Seivers, Tennessee, 6-4, 200, Clinton, Tenn.; TE—Ken MacAfee, Notre Dame, 6-4, 251, Brockton, Mass.; T—Mike Vaughan, Oklahoma, 6-5, 275, Ada, Okla.; T—Chris Ward, Ohio St., 6-4, 274, Dayton, Ohio; G—Joel Parrish, Georgia, 6-3, 232, Douglas, Ga.; G—Mark Donahue, Michigan, 6-3, 245, Oak Lawn, Ill.; C—Derrel Gofourth, Oklahoma St., 6-2, 250, Parsons, Kan.; QB—Tommy Kramer, Rice, 6-2, 190, San Antonio, Texas; RB—*Tony Dorsett, Pittsburgh, 5-11, 192, Aliquippa, Pa.; RB—*Ricky Bell, Southern Cal, 6-2, 218, Los Angeles, Calif.; RB—Rob Lytle, Michigan, 6-1, 195, Fremont, Ohio; PK—Tony Franklin, Texas A&M, 5-10, 170, Fort Worth, Texas.

Defense E—*Ross Browner, Notre Dame, 6-3, 248, Warren, Ohio; E—Bob Brudzinski, Ohio St., 6-4, 228, Fremont, Ohio; T—Wilson Whitley, Houston, 6-3, 268, Brenham, Texas; T—Gary Jeter, Southern Cal, 6-5, 255, Cleveland, Ohio; T—Joe Campbell, Maryland, 6-6, 255, Wilmington, Del.; MG—Al Romano, Pittsburgh, 6-3, 230, Solvay, N.Y.; LB—*Robert Jackson, Texas A&M, 6-2, 228, Houston, Texas; LB—Jerry Robinson, UCLA, 6-3, 208, Santa Rosa, Calif.; B—*Bill Armstrong, Wake Forest, 6-4, 205, Randolph, N.J.; B—Gary Green, Baylor, 5-11, 182, San Antonio, Texas; B—Dennis Thurman, Southern Cal, 5-11, 170, Santa Monica, Calif.; B—Dave Butterfield, Nebraska, 5-10, 182, Kersey, Colo.

1977

Offense WR—John Jefferson, Arizona St., 6-1, 184, Dallas, Texas; WR—Ozzie Newsome, Alabama, 6-4, 210, Leighton, Ala.; TE—*Ken MacAfee, Notre Dame, 6-4, 250, Brockton, Mass.; T—*Chris Ward, Ohio St., 6-4, 272, Dayton, Ohio; T—Dan Irons, Texas Tech, 6-7, 260, Lubbock, Texas; G—*Mark Donahue, Michigan, 6-3, 245, Oak Lawn, Ill.; G—Leotis Harris, Arkansas, 6-1, 254, Little Rock, Ark.; C—Tom Brzoza, Pittsburgh, 6-3, 240, New Castle, Pa.; QB—Guy Benjamin, Stanford, 6-4, 202, Sepulveda, Calif.; RB—*Earl Campbell, Texas, 6-1, 220, Tyler, Texas; RB—*Terry Miller, Oklahoma St., 6-0, 196, Colorado Springs, Colo.; RB—Charles Alexander, LSU, 6-1, 215, Galveston, Texas; K—Steve Little, Arkansas, 6-0, 179, Overland Park, Kan.

Defense L—*Ross Browner, Notre Dame, 6-3, 247, Warren, Ohio; L—*Art Still, Kentucky, 6-8, 247, Camden, N.J.; L—*Brad Shearer, Texas, 6-4, 255, Austin, Texas; L—Randy Holloway, Pittsburgh, 6-6, 228, Sharon, Pa.; L—Dee Hardison, North Caro., 6-4, 252, Newton Grove, N.C.; LB—*Jerry Robinson, UCLA, 6-3, 208, Santa Rosa, Calif.; LB—Tom Cousineau, Ohio St., 6-3, 228, Fairview Park, Ohio; LB—Gary Spani, Kansas St., 6-2, 222, Manhattan, Kan.; B—*Dennis Thurman, Southern Cal, 5-11, 173, Santa Monica, Calif.; B—*Zac Henderson, Oklahoma, 6-1, 184, Burkburnett, Texas; B—Luther Bradley, Notre Dame, 6-2, 204, Muncie, Ind.; B—Bob Jury, Pittsburgh, 6-0, 190, Library, Pa.

1978

Offense WR—Emanuel Tolbert, Southern Methodist, 5-10, 180, Little Rock, Ark.; TE—Kellen Winslow, Missouri, 6-6, 235, East St. Louis, Ill.; T—*Keith Dorney, Penn St., 6-5, 257, Allentown, Pa.; T—Kelvin Clark, Nebraska, 6-4, 275, Odessa, Texas; G—*Pat Howell, Southern Cal, 6-6, 255, Fresno, Calif.; G—*Greg Roberts, Oklahoma, 6-3, 238, Nacogdoches, Texas; C—Dave Huffman, Notre Dame, 6-5, 245, Dallas, Texas; C—Jim Ritcher, North Caro. St., 6-3, 242, Hinckley, Ohio; QB—*Chuck Fusina, Penn St., 6-1, 195, McKees Rocks, Pa.; RB—*Billy Sims, Oklahoma, 6-0, 205, Hooks, Texas; RB—*Charles White, Southern Cal, 5-11, 183, San Fernando, Calif.; RB—Ted Brown, North Caro. St., 5-10, 195, High Point, N.C.; RB—Charles Alexander, LSU, 6-1, 214, Galveston, Texas.

Defense L—*Al Harris, Arizona St., 6-5, 240, Wheeler AFB, Hawaii; L—*Bruce Clark, Penn St., 6-3, 246, New Castle, Pa.; L—Hugh Green, Pittsburgh, 6-2, 215, Natchez, Miss.; L—Mike Bell, Colorado St., 6-5, 265, Wichita, Kan.; L—Marty Lyons, Alabama, 6-6, 250, St. Petersburg, Fla.; LB—*Bob Golic, Notre Dame, 6-3, 244, Willowick, Ohio; LB—*Jerry Robinson, UCLA, 6-3, 209, Santa Rosa, Calif.; LB—Tom Cousineau, Ohio St., 6-3, 227, Fairview Park, Ohio; B—*Johnnie Johnson, Texas, 6-2, 183, LaGrange, Texas; B—Kenny Easley, UCLA, 6-2, 202, Chesapeake, Va.; B—Jeff Nixon, Richmond, 6-4, 195, Glendale, Ariz.

1979

Offense WR—Ken Margerum, Stanford, 6-1, 175, Fountain Valley, Calif.; TE—*Junior Miller, Nebraska, 6-4, 222, Midland, Texas; T—*Greg Kolenda, Arkansas, 6-1, 258, Kansas City, Kan.; T—Jim Bunch, Alabama, 6-2, 240, Mechanicsville, Va.; G—*Brad Budde, Southern Cal, 6-5, 253, Kansas City, Mo.; G—Ken Fritz, Ohio St., 6-3, 238, Ironton, Ohio; C—*Jim Ritcher, North Caro. St., 6-3, 245, Hinckley, Ohio; QB—*Marc Wilson, Brigham Young, 6-5, 204, Seattle, Wash.; RB—*Charles White, Southern Cal, 6-0, 185, San Fernando, Calif.; RB—*Billy Sims, Oklahoma, 6-0, 205, Hooks, Texas; RB—Vagas Ferguson, Notre Dame, 6-1, 194, Richmond, Ind.; PK—Dale Castro, Maryland, 6-1, 170, Shady Side, Md.

Defense L—*Hugh Green, Pittsburgh, 6-2, 220, Natchez, Miss.; L—*Steve McMichael, Texas, 6-2, 250, Freer, Texas; L—Bruce Clark, Penn St., 6-3, 255, New Castle, Pa.; L—Jim Stuckey, Clemson, 6-5, 241, Cayce, S.C.; MG—Ron Simmons, Florida St., 6-1, 235, Warner Robins, Ga.; LB—*George Cumby, Oklahoma, 6-0, 205, Tyler, Texas; LB—Ron Simpkins, Michigan, 6-2, 220, Detroit, Mich.; LB—Mike Singletary, Baylor, 6-1, 224, Houston, Texas; B—*Kenny Easley, UCLA, 6-3, 204, Chesapeake, Va.; B—*Johnnie Johnson, Texas, 6-2, 190, LaGrange, Texas; B—Roland James, Tennessee, 6-2, 182, Jamestown, Ohio; P—Jim Miller, Mississippi, 5-11, 183, Ripley, Miss.

1980

Offense WR—*Ken Margerum, Stanford, 6-1, 175, Fountain Valley, Calif.; TE—*Dave Young, Purdue, 6-6, 242, Akron, Ohio; L—*Mark May, Pittsburgh, 6-6, 282, Oneonta, N.Y.; L—Keith Van Horne, Southern Cal, 6-7, 265, Fullerton, Calif.; L—Nick Eyre, Brigham Young, 6-5, 276, Las Vegas, Nev.; L—Louis Oubre, Oklahoma, 6-4, 262, New Orleans, La.; L—Randy Schleusener, Nebraska, 6-7, 242, Rapid City, S.D.; C—*John Scully, Notre Dame, 6-5, 255, Huntington, N.Y.; QB—*Mark Herrmann, Purdue, 6-4, 187, Carmel, Ind.; RB—*George Rogers, South Caro., 6-2, 220, Duluth, Ga.; RB—*Herschel Walker, Georgia, 6-2, 220, Wrightsville, Ga.; RB—Jarvis Redwine, Nebraska, 5-11, 204, Inglewood, Calif.

Defense L—*Hugh Green, Pittsburgh, 6-2, 222, Natchez, Miss.; L—*E. J. Junior, Alabama, 6-3, 227, Nashville, Tenn.; L—Kenneth Sims, Texas, 6-6, 265, Groesbeck, Texas; L—Leonard Mitchell, Houston, 6-7, 270, Houston,

Texas; MG—Ron Simmons, Florida St., 6-1, 230, Warner Robins, Ga.; LB—*Mike Singletary, Baylor, 6-1, 232, Houston, Texas; LB—*Lawrence Taylor, North Caro., 6-3, 237, Williamsburg, Va.; LB—David Little, Florida, 6-1, 228, Miami, Fla.; LB—Bob Crable, Notre Dame, 6-3, 222, Cincinnati, Ohio; B—*Kenny Easley, UCLA, 6-3, 206, Chesapeake, Va.; B—*Ronnie Lott, Southern Cal, 6-2, 200, Rialto, Calif.; B—John Simmons, Southern Methodist, 5-11, 188, Little Rock, Ark.

1981

Offense WR—*Anthony Carter, Michigan, 5-11, 161, Riviera Beach, Fla.; TE—*Tim Wrightman, UCLA, 6-3, 237, San Pedro, Calif.; L—*Sean Farrell, Penn St., 6-3, 266, Westhampton Beach, N.Y.; L—Roy Foster, Southern Cal, 6-4, 265, Overland Park, Kan.; L—Terry Crouch, Oklahoma, 6-1, 275, Dallas, Texas; L—Ed Muransky, Michigan, 6-7, 275, Youngstown, Ohio; L—Terry Tausch, Texas, 6-4, 265, New Braunfels, Texas; L—Kurt Becker, Michigan, 6-6, 260, Aurora, Ill.; C—*Dave Rimington, Nebraska, 6-3, 275, Omaha, Neb.; QB—*Jim McMahon, Brigham Young, 6-0, 185, Roy, Utah; RB—*Marcus Allen, Southern Cal, 6-2, 202, San Diego, Calif.; RB—*Herschel Walker, Georgia, 6-2, 222, Wrightsville, Ga.

Defense L—*Billy Ray Smith, Arkansas, 6-4, 228, Plano, Texas; L—*Kenneth Sims, Texas, 6-6, 265, Groesbeck, Texas; L—Andre Tippett, Iowa, 6-4, 235, Newark, N.J.; L—Tim Krumrie, Wisconsin, 6-3, 237, Mondovi, Wis.; LB—Bob Crable, Notre Dame, 6-3, 225, Cincinnati, Ohio; LB—Jeff Davis, Clemson, 6-0, 223, Greensboro, N.C.; LB—Sal Sunseri, Pittsburgh, 6-0, 220, Pittsburgh, Pa.; DB—Tommy Wilcox, Alabama, 5-11, 187, Harahan, La.; DB—Mike Richardson, Arizona St., 6-1, 192, Compton, Calif.; DB—Terry Kinard, Clemson, 6-1, 183, Sumter, S.C.; DB—Fred Marion, Miami (Fla.), 6-3, 194, Gainesville, Fla.; P—Reggie Roby, Iowa, 6-3, 215, Waterloo, Iowa.

1982

Offense WR—*Anthony Carter, Michigan, 5-11, 161, Riviera Beach, Fla.; TE—*Gordon Hudson, Brigham Young, 6-4, 224, Salt Lake City, Utah; L—*Don Mosebar, Southern Cal, 6-7, 270, Visalia, Calif.; L—*Steve Korte, Arkansas, 6-2, 270, Littleton, Colo.; L—Jimbo Covert, Pittsburgh, 6-5, 279, Conway, Pa.; L—Bruce Matthews, Southern Cal, 6-5, 265, Arcadia, Calif.; C—*Dave Rimington, Nebraska, 6-3, 290, Omaha, Neb.; QB—*John Elway, Stanford, 6-4, 202, Northridge, Calif.; RB—*Herschel Walker, Georgia, 6-2, 222, Wrightsville, Ga.; RB—*Eric Dickerson, Southern Methodist, 6-2, 215, Sealy, Texas; RB—Mike Rozier, Nebraska, 5-11, 210, Camden, N.J.; PK—*Chuck Nelson, Washington, 5-11, 178, Everett, Wash.

Defense L—*Billy Ray Smith, Arkansas, 6-3, 228, Plano, Texas; L—Vernon Maxwell, Arizona St., 6-2, 225, Carson, Calif.; L—Mike Pitts, Alabama, 6-5, 255, Baltimore, Md.; L—Wilber Marshall, Florida, 6-1, 230, Titusville, Fla.; L—Gabriel Rivera, Texas Tech, 6-3, 270, San Antonio, Texas; L—Rick Bryan, Oklahoma, 6-4, 260, Coweta, Okla.; MG—George Achica, Southern Cal, 6-5, 260, San Jose, Calif.; LB—*Darryl Talley, West Va., 6-4, 210, East Cleveland, Ohio; LB—Ricky Hunley, Arizona, 6-1, 230, Petersburg, Va.; LB—Marcus Marek, Ohio St., 6-2, 224, Masury, Ohio; DB—*Terry Kinard, Clemson, 6-1, 189, Sumter, S.C.; DB—Mike Richardson, Arizona St., 6-0, 190, Compton, Calif.; DB—Terry Hoage, Georgia, 6-3, 196, Huntsville, Texas; P—*Jim Arnold, Vanderbilt, 6-3, 205, Dalton, Ga.

1983

Offense WR—*Irving Fryar, Nebraska, 6-0, 200, Mount Holly, N.J.; TE—*Gordon Hudson, Brigham Young, 6-4, 231, Salt Lake City, Utah; L—*Bill Fralic, Pittsburgh, 6-5, 270, Penn Hills, Pa.; L—Terry Long, East Caro., 6-0, 280, Columbia, S.C.; L—Dean Steinkuhler, Nebraska, 6-3, 270, Burr, Neb.; L—Doug Dawson, Texas, 6-3, 263, Houston, Texas; C—Tony Slaton, Southern Cal, 6-4, 260, Merced, Calif.; QB—*Steve Young, Brigham Young, 6-1, 198, Greenwich, Conn.; RB—*Mike Rozier, Nebraska, 5-11, 210, Camden, N.J.; RB—Bo Jackson, Auburn, 6-1, 222, Bessemer, Ala.; RB—Greg Allen, Florida St., 6-0, 200, Milton, Fla.; RB—Napoleon McCallum, Navy, 6-2, 208, Milford, Ohio; PK—Luis Zendejas, Arizona St., 5-9, 186, Chino, Calif.

Defense L—*Rick Bryan, Oklahoma, 6-4, 260, Coweta, Okla.; L—*Reggie White, Tennessee, 6-5, 264, Chattanooga, Tenn.; L—William Perry, Clemson, 6-3, 320, Aiken, S.C.; L—William Fuller, North Caro., 6-4, 250, Chesapeake, Va.; LB—*Ricky Hunley, Arizona, 6-2, 230, Petersburg, Va.; LB—Wilber Marshall, Florida, 6-1, 230, Titusville, Fla.; LB—Ron Rivera, California, 6-3, 225, Monterey, Calif.; LB—Jeff Leiding, Texas, 6-4, 240, Tulsa, Okla.; DB—*Russell Carter, Southern Methodist, 6-3, 193, Ardmore, Pa.; DB—Jerry Gray, Texas, 6-1, 183, Lubbock, Texas; DB—Terry Hoage, Georgia, 6-3, 196, Huntsville, Texas; DB—Don Rogers, UCLA, 6-2, 208, Sacramento, Calif.; P—Jack Weil, Wyoming, 5-11, 171, Northglenn, Colo.

1984

Offense WR—*David Williams, Illinois, 6-3, 195, Los Angeles, Calif.; WR—Eddie Brown, Miami (Fla.), 6-0, 185, Miami, Fla.; TE—Jay Novacek, Wyoming, 6-4, 211, Gothenburg, Neb.; T—*Bill Fralic, Pittsburgh, 6-5, 285, Penn Hills, Pa.; T—Lomas Brown, Florida, 6-5, 277, Miami, Fla.; G—Del Wilkes, South Caro., 6-3, 255, Columbia, S.C.; G—Jim Lachey, Ohio St., 6-6, 274, St. Henry, Ohio; G—Bill Mayo, Tennessee, 6-3, 280, Dalton, Ga.; C—*Mark Traynowicz, Nebraska, 6-6, 265, Bellevue, Neb.; QB—*Doug Flutie, Boston College, 5-9, 177, Natick, Mass.; RB—*Keith Byars, Ohio St., 6-2, 233, Dayton, Ohio; RB—*Kenneth Davis, Texas Christian, 5-11, 205, Temple, Texas; RB—Rueben Mayes, Washington St., 6-0, 200, North Battleford, Saskatchewan, Canada; PK—Kevin Butler, Georgia, 6-1, 190, Stone Mountain, Ga.

Defense DL—Bruce Smith, Virginia Tech, 6-4, 275, Norfolk, Va.; DL—Tony Degrate, Texas, 6-4, 280, Snyder, Texas; DL—Ron Holmes, Washington, 6-4, 255, Lacey, Wash.; DL—Tony Casillas, Oklahoma, 6-3, 272, Tulsa, Okla.; LB—Gregg Carr, Auburn, 6-2, 215, Birmingham, Ala.; LB—Jack Del Rio, Southern Cal, 6-4, 235, Hayward, Calif.; LB—Larry Station, Iowa, 5-11, 233, Omaha, Neb.; DB—*Jerry Gray, Texas, 6-1, 183, Lubbock, Texas; DB—Tony Thurman, Boston College, 6-0, 179, Lynn, Mass.; DB—Jeff Sanchez, Georgia, 6-0, 183, Yorba Linda, Calif.; DB—David Fulcher, Arizona St., 6-3, 220, Los Angeles, Calif.; DB—Rod Brown, Oklahoma St., 6-3, 188, Gainesville, Texas; P—*Ricky Anderson, Vanderbilt, 6-2, 190, St. Petersburg, Fla.

1985

Offense WR—*David Williams, Illinois, 6-3, 195, Los Angeles, Calif.; WR—Tim McGee, Tennessee, 5-10, 181, Cleveland, Ohio; TE—Willie Smith, Miami (Fla.), 6-2, 230, Jacksonville, Fla.; L—*Jim Dombrowski, Virginia, 6-5, 290, Williamsville, N.Y.; L—Jeff Bregel, Southern Cal, 6-4, 280, Granada Hills, Calif.; L—Brian Jozwiak, West Va., 6-6, 290, Catonsville, Md.; L—John Rienstra, Temple, 6-4, 280, Colorado Springs, Colo.; L—J. D. Maarleveld, Maryland, 6-5, 300, Rutherford, N.J.; L—Jamie Dukes, Florida St., 6-0, 272, Orlando, Fla.; C—Pete Anderson, Georgia, 6-3, 264, Glen Ridge, N.J.; QB—*Chuck Long, Iowa, 6-4, 213, Wheaton, Ill.; RB—*Bo Jackson, Auburn, 6-1, 222, Bessemer, Ala.; RB—*Lorenzo White, Michigan St., 5-11, 205, Fort Lauderdale, Fla.; RB—Thurman Thomas, Oklahoma St., 5-11, 186, Missouri City, Texas; RB—Reggie Dupard, Southern Methodist, 6-0, 201, New Orleans, La.; RB—Napoleon McCallum, Navy, 6-2, 214, Milford, Ohio; PK—*John Lee, UCLA, 5-11, 187, Downey, Calif.

Defense L—*Tim Green, Syracuse, 6-2, 246, Liverpool, N.Y.; L—*Leslie O'Neal, Oklahoma St., 6-3, 245, Little Rock, Ark.; L—Tony Casillas, Oklahoma, 6-3, 280, Tulsa, Okla.; L—Mike Ruth, Boston College, 6-2, 250, Norristown, Pa.; L—Mike Hammerstein, Michigan, 6-4, 240, Wapakoneta, Ohio; LB—*Brian Bosworth, Oklahoma, 6-2, 234, Irving, Texas; LB—*Larry Station, Iowa, 5-11, 227, Omaha, Neb.; LB—Johnny Holland, Texas A&M, 6-2, 219, Hempstead, Texas; DB—David Fulcher, Arizona St., 6-3, 228, Los Angeles, Calif.; DB—Brad Cochran, Michigan, 6-3, 219, Royal Oak, Mich.; DB—Scott Thomas, Air Force, 6-0, 185, San Antonio, Texas; P—Barry Helton, Colorado, 6-3, 195, Simla, Colo.

1986

Offense WR—Cris Carter, Ohio St., 6-3, 194, Middletown, Ohio; TE—*Keith Jackson, Oklahoma, 6-3, 241, Little Rock, Ark.; L—Jeff Bregel, Southern Cal, 6-4, 280, Granada Hills, Calif.; L—Randy Dixon, Pittsburgh, 6-4, 286, Clewiston, Fla.; L—Danny Villa, Arizona St., 6-5, 284, Nogales, Ariz.; L—John Clay, Missouri, 6-5, 285, St. Louis, Mo.; C—*Ben Tamburello, Auburn, 6-3, 268, Birmingham, Ala.; QB—*Vinny Testaverde, Miami (Fla.), 6-5, 218, Elmont, N.Y.; RB—*Brent Fullwood, Auburn, 5-11, 209, St. Cloud, Fla.; RB—*Paul Palmer, Temple, 5-10, 180, Potomac, Md.; RB—Terrence Flagler, Clemson, 6-1, 200, Fernandina Beach, Fla.; RB—Brad Muster, Stanford, 6-3, 226, Novato, Calif.; RB—D. J. Dozier, Penn St., 6-1, 204, Virginia Beach, Va.; PK—Jeff Jaeger, Washington, 5-11, 191, Kent, Wash.

Defense L—*Jerome Brown, Miami (Fla.), 6-2, 285, Brooksville, Fla.; L—*Danny Noonan, Nebraska, 6-4, 280, Lincoln, Neb.; L—Tony Woods, Pittsburgh, 6-4, 240, Newark, N.J.; L—Jason Buck, Brigham Young, 6-6, 270, St. Anthony, Idaho; L—Reggie Rogers, Washington, 6-6, 260, Sacramento, Calif.; LB—*Cornelius Bennett, Alabama, 6-4, 235, Birmingham, Ala.; LB—Shane Conlan, Penn St., 6-3, 225, Frewsburg, N.Y.; LB—Brian Bosworth, Oklahoma, 6-2, 240, Irving, Texas; LB—Chris Spielman, Ohio St., 6-2, 227, Massillon, Ohio; DB—*Thomas Everett, Baylor, 5-9, 180, Daingerfield, Texas; DB—Tim McDonald, Southern Cal, 6-3, 205, Fresno, Calif.; DB—Bennie Blades, Miami (Fla.), 6-0, 207, Ft. Lauderdale, Fla.; DB—Rod Woodson, Purdue, 6-0, 195, Fort Wayne, Ind.; DB—Garland Rivers, Michigan, 6-1, 187, Canton, Ohio; P—Barry Helton, Colorado, 6-4, 200, Simla, Colo.

1987

Offense WR—*Tim Brown, Notre Dame, 6-0, 195, Dallas, Texas; WR—Wendell Davis, LSU, 6-0, 186, Shreveport, La.; TE—*Keith Jackson, Oklahoma, 6-3, 248, Little Rock, Ark.; L—*Mark Hutson, Oklahoma, 6-4, 282, Fort Smith, Ark.; L—Dave Cadigan, Southern Cal, 6-5, 280, Newport Beach, Calif.; L—John Elliott, Michigan, 6-7, 306, Lake Ronkonkoma, N.Y.; L—Randall McDaniel, Arizona St., 6-5, 261, Avondale, Ariz.; C—*Nacho Albergamo, LSU, 6-2, 257, Marrera, La.; QB—*Don McPherson, Syracuse, 6-0, 182, West Hempstead, N.Y.; RB—Lorenzo White, Michigan St., 5-11, 211, Fort Lauderdale, Fla.; RB—Craig Heyward, Pittsburgh, 6-0, 260, Passaic, N.J.; PK—David Treadwell, Clemson, 6-1, 165, Jacksonville, Fla.

Defense L—*Daniel Stubbs, Miami (Fla.), 6-4, 250, Red Bank, N.J.; L—*Chad Hennings, Air Force, 6-5, 260, Elboron, Iowa; L—Tracy Rocker, Auburn, 6-3, 258, Atlanta, Ga.; L—Ted Gregory, Syracuse, 6-1, 260, East Islip, N.Y.; L—John Roper, Texas A&M, 6-2, 215, Houston, Texas; LB—*Chris Spielman, Ohio St., 6-2, 236, Massillon, Ohio; LB—Aundray Bruce, Auburn, 6-6, 236, Montgomery, Ala.; LB—Dante Jones, Oklahoma, 6-2, 235, Dallas, Texas; DB—*Bennie Blades, Miami (Fla.), 6-0, 215, Fort Lauderdale, Fla.; DB—*Deion Sanders, Florida St., 6-0, 192, Fort Myers, Fla.; DB—Rickey Dixon, Oklahoma, 5-10, 184, Dallas, Texas; DB—Chuck Cecil, Arizona, 6-0, 185, Red Bluff, Calif.; P—*Tom Tupa, Ohio St., 6-5, 215, Brecksville, Ohio.

1988

Offense WR—Jason Phillips, Houston, 5-9, 175, Houston, Texas; WR—Hart Lee Dykes, Oklahoma St., 6-4, 220, Bay City, Texas; TE—Marv Cook, Iowa, 6-4, 243, West Branch, Iowa; L—*Tony Mandarich, Michigan St., 6-6, 315, Oakville, Ontario, Canada; L—*Anthony Phillips, Oklahoma, 6-3, 286, Tulsa, Okla.; L—Mike Utley, Washington St., 6-6, 302, Seattle, Wash.; L—Mark Stepnoski, Pittsburgh, 6-3, 265, Erie, Pa.; C—Jake Young, Nebraska, 6-5, 260, Midland, Texas; C—John Vitale, Michigan, 6-1, 273, Detroit, Mich.; QB—Steve Walsh, Miami (Fla.), 6-3, 195, St. Paul, Minn.; QB—Troy Aikman, UCLA, 6-4, 217, Henryetta, Okla.; RB—*Barry Sanders, Oklahoma St., 5-8, 197, Wichita, Kan.; RB—Anthony Thompson, Indiana, 6-0, 205, Terre Haute, Ind.; RB—Tim Worley, Georgia, 6-2, 216, Lumberton, N.C.; PK—Kendall Trainor, Arkansas, 6-2, 205, Fredonia, Kan.

Defense L—*Mark Messner, Michigan, 6-3, 244, Hartland, Mich.; L—*Tracy Rocker, Auburn, 6-3, 278, Atlanta, Ga.; L—Wayne Martin, Arkansas, 6-5, 263, Cherry Valley, Ark.; L—Frank Stams, Notre Dame, 6-4, 237, Akron, Ohio; L—Bill Hawkins, Miami (Fla.), 6-6, 260, Hollywood, Fla.; LB—*Derrick Thomas, Alabama, 6-4, 230, Miami, Fla.; LB—*Broderick Thomas, Nebraska, 6-3, 235, Houston, Texas; LB—Michael Stonebreaker, Notre Dame, 6-1, 228, River Ridge, La.; DB—*Deion Sanders, Florida St., 6-0, 195, Fort Myers, Fla.; DB—Donnell Woolford, Clemson, 5-10, 195, Fayetteville, N.C.; DB—Louis Oliver, Florida, 6-2, 222, Bell Glade, Fla.; DB—Darryl Henley, UCLA, 5-10, 165, Ontario, Calif.; P—Keith English, Colorado, 6-3, 215, Greeley, Colo.

1989

Offense WR—*Clarkston Hines, Duke, 6-1, 170, Chapel Hill, N.C.; WR—Terance Mathis, New Mexico, 5-9, 167, Stone Mountain, Ga.; TE—Mike Busch, Iowa

St., 6-5, 252, Donahue, Iowa; L—Jim Mabry, Arkansas, 6-4, 262, Memphis, Tenn.; L—Bob Kula, Michigan St., 6-4, 282, West Bloomfield, Mich.; L—Mohammed Elewonibi, Brigham Young, 6-5, 290, Kamloops, British Columbia, Canada; L—Joe Garten, Colorado, 6-3, 280, Placentia, Calif.; L—*Eric Still, Tennessee, 6-3, 283, Germantown, Tenn.; C—Jake Young, Nebraska, 6-4, 270, Midland, Texas; QB—Andre Ware, Houston, 6-2, 205, Dickinson, Texas; RB—*Anthony Thompson, Indiana, 6-0, 209, Terre Haute, Ind.; RB—*Emmitt Smith, Florida, 5-10, 201, Pensacola, Fla.; PK—*Jason Hanson, Washington St., 6-0, 164, Spokane, Wash.

Defense L—Chris Zorich, Notre Dame, 6-1, 268, Chicago, Ill.; L—Greg Mark, Miami (Fla.), 6-4, 255, Pennsauken, N.J.; L—Tim Ryan, Southern Cal, 6-5, 260, San Jose, Calif.; L—*Moe Gardner, Illinois, 6-2, 250, Indianapolis, Ind.; LB—*Percy Snow, Michigan St., 6-3, 240, Canton, Ohio; LB—*Keith McCants, Alabama, 6-5, 256, Mobile, Ala.; LB—Alfred Williams, Colorado, 6-6, 230, Houston, Texas; DB—*Todd Lyght, Notre Dame, 6-1, 181, Flint, Mich.; DB—*Mark Carrier, Southern Cal, 6-1, 185, Long Beach, Calif.; DB—*Tripp Welborne, Michigan, 6-1, 193, Greensboro, N.C.; DB—LeRoy Butler, Florida St., 6-0, 194, Jacksonville, Fla.; P—Tom Rouen, Colorado, 6-3, 220, Littleton, Colo.

1990

Offense WR—*Raghib Ismail, Notre Dame, 5-10, 175, Wilkes-Barre, Pa.; WR—Herman Moore, Virginia, 6-5, 197, Danville, Va.; TE—*Chris Smith, Brigham Young, 6-4, 230, La Canada, Calif.; OL—*Antone Davis, Tennessee, 6-4, 310, Fort Valley, Ga.; OL—*Joe Garten, Colorado, 6-3, 280, Placentia, Calif.; OL—*Ed King, Auburn, 6-4, 284, Phenix City, Ala.; OL—Stacy Long, Clemson, 6-2, 275, Griffin, Ga.; C—John Flannery, Syracuse, 6-4, 301, Pottsville, Pa.; QB—Ty Detmer, Brigham Young, 6-0, 175, San Antonio, Texas; RB—*Eric Bieniemy, Colorado, 5-7, 195, West Covina, Calif.; RB—Darren Lewis, Texas A&M, 6-0, 220, Dallas, Texas; PK—*Philip Doyle, Alabama, 6-1, 190, Birmingham, Ala.

Defense DL—*Russell Maryland, Miami (Fla.), 6-2, 273, Chicago, Ill.; DL—*Chris Zorich, Notre Dame, 6-1, 266, Chicago, Ill.; DL—Moe Gardner, Illinois, 6-2, 258, Indianapolis, Ind.; DL—David Rocker, Auburn, 6-4, 264, Atlanta, Ga.; LB—*Alfred Williams, Colorado, 6-6, 236, Houston, Texas; LB—*Michael Stonebreaker, Notre Dame, 6-1, 228, River Ridge, La.; LB—Maurice Crum, Miami (Fla.), 6-0, 222, Tampa, Fla.; DB—*Tripp Welborne, Michigan, 6-1, 201, Greensboro, N.C.; DB—*Darryll Lewis, Arizona, 5-9, 186, West Covina, Calif.; DB—*Ken Swilling, Georgia Tech, 6-3, 230, Toccoa, Ga.; DB—Todd Lyght, Notre Dame, 6-1, 184, Flint, Mich.; P—Brian Greenfield, Pittsburgh, 6-1, 210, Sherman Oaks, Calif.

1991

Offense WR—*Desmond Howard, Michigan, 5-9, 176, Cleveland, Ohio; WR—Mario Bailey, Washington, 5-9, 167, Seattle, Wash.; TE—Kelly Blackwell, Texas Christian, 6-2, 242, Fort Worth, Texas; OL—*Greg Skrepenak, Michigan, 6-8, 322, Wilkes-Barre, Pa.; OL—Bob Whitfield, Stanford, 6-7, 300, Carson, Calif.; OL—Jeb Flesch, Clemson, 6-3, 266, Morrow, Ga.; OL—(tie) Jerry Ostroski, Tulsa, 6-4, 305, Collegeville, Pa.; Mirko Jurkovic, Notre Dame, 6-4, 289, Calumet City, Ill.; C—*Jay Leeuwenburg, Colorado, 6-3, 265, Kirkwood, Mo.; QB—Ty Detmer, Brigham Young, 6-0, 175, San Antonio, Texas; RB—*Vaughn Dunbar, Indiana, 6-0, 207, Fort Wayne, Ind.; RB—(tie) Trevor Cobb, Rice, 5-9, 180, Houston, Texas; Russell White, California, 6-0, 210, Van Nuys, Calif.; PK—Carlos Huerta, Miami (Fla.), 5-9, 186, Miami, Fla.

Defense DL—*Steve Emtman, Washington, 6-4, 280, Cheney, Wash.; DL—*Santana Dotson, Baylor, 6-5, 264, Houston, Texas; DL—Brad Culpepper, Florida, 6-2, 263, Tallahassee, Fla.; DL—Leroy Smith, Iowa, 6-2, 214, Sicklerville, N. J.; LB—*Robert Jones, East Caro., 6-3, 234, Blackstone, Va.; LB—Marvin Jones, Florida St., 6-2, 220, Miami, Fla.; LB—Levon Kirkland, Clemson, 6-2, 245, Lamar, S.C.; DB—*Terrell Buckley, Florida St., 5-10, 175, Pascagoula, Miss.; DB—Dale Carter, Tennessee, 6-2, 182, Oxford, Ga.; DB—Kevin Smith, Texas A&M, 6-0, 180, Orange, Texas; DB—Darryl Williams, Miami (Fla.), 6-2, 190, Miami, Fla.; P—*Mark Bounds, Texas Tech, 5-11, 185, Stamford, Texas.

1992

Offense WR—O. J. McDuffie, Penn St., 5-11, 185, Warrensville Heights, Ohio; WR—Sean Dawkins, California, 6-4, 205, Sunnyvale, Calif.; TE—*Chris Gedney, Syracuse, 6-5, 256, Liverpool, N.Y.; OL—*Lincoln Kennedy, Washington, 6-7, 325, San Diego, Calif.; OL—*Will Shields, Nebraska, 6-1, 305, Lawton, Okla.; OL—Aaron Taylor, Notre Dame, 6-4, 294, Concord, Calif.; OL—(tie) Willie Roaf, Louisiana Tech, 6-5, 300, Pine Bluff, Ark.; Everett Lindsay, Mississippi, 6-5, 290, Raleigh, N.C.; C—Mike Compton, West Va., 6-7, 289, Richlands, Va.; QB—*Gino Torretta, Miami (Fla.), 6-3, 205, Pinole, Calif.; RB—*Marshall Faulk, San Diego St., 5-10, 200, New Orleans, La.; RB—*Garrison Hearst, Georgia, 5-11, 202, Lincolnton, Ga.; PK—Joe Allison, Memphis, 6-0, 184, Atlanta, Ga.

Defense DL—Eric Curry, Alabama, 6-6, 265, Thomasville, Ga.; DL—John Copeland, Alabama, 6-3, 261, Lanett, Ala.; DL—Chris Slade, Virginia, 6-5, 235, Tabb, Va.; DL—Rob Waldrop, Arizona, 6-2, 265, Phoenix, Ariz.; LB—*Marcus Buckley, Texas A&M, 6-4, 230, Fort Worth, Texas; LB—*Marvin Jones, Florida St., 6-2, 235, Miami, Fla.; LB—Micheal Barrow, Miami (Fla.), 6-2, 230, Homestead, Fla.; DB—*Carlton McDonald, Air Force, 6-0, 185, Jacksonville, Fla.; DB—Carlton Gray, UCLA, 6-0, 194, Cincinnati, Ohio; DB—Deon Figures, Colorado, 6-1, 195, Compton, Calif.; DB—Ryan McNeil, Miami (Fla.), 6-2, 185, Fort Pierce, Fla.; P—Sean Snyder, Kansas St., 6-1, 190, Greenville, Texas.

1993

Offense WR—*J. J. Stokes, UCLA, 6-5, 214, San Diego, Calif.; WR—Johnnie Morton, Southern Cal, 6-0, 190, Torrance, Calif.; OL—Mark Dixon, Virginia, 6-4, 283, Jamestown, N.C.; OL—Stacy Seegars, Clemson, 6-4, 320, Kershaw, S.C.; OL—*Aaron Taylor, Notre Dame, 6-4, 299, Concord, Calif.; OL—Wayne Gandy, Auburn, 6-5, 275, Haines City, Fla.; C—*Jim Pyne, Virginia Tech, 6-2, 280, Milford, Mass.; QB—*Charlie Ward, Florida St., 6-2, 190, Thomasville, Ga.; RB—*Marshall Faulk, San Diego St., 5-10, 200, New Orleans, La.; RB—*LeShon Johnson, Northern Ill., 6-0, 201, Haskell, Okla.; PK—Bjorn Merten, UCLA, 6-0, 203, Centreville, Va.; KR—David Palmer, Alabama, 5-9, 170, Birmingham, Ala.

Defense DL—*Rob Waldrop, Arizona, 6-2, 275, Phoenix, Ariz.; DL—Dan Wilkinson, Ohio St., 6-5, 300, Dayton, Ohio; DL—Sam Adams, Texas A&M, 6-4, 269, Cypress, Texas; LB—*Trev Alberts, Nebraska, 6-4, 240, Cedar Falls, Iowa; LB—*Derrick Brooks, Florida St., 6-1, 225, Pensacola, Fla.; LB—Jamir Miller, UCLA, 6-4, 233, El Cerrito, Calif.; DB—*Antonio Langham, Alabama, 6-1, 170, Town Creek, Ala.; DB—Aaron Glenn, Texas A&M, 5-10, 182, Aldine, Texas; DB—Jeff Burris, Notre Dame, 6-0, 204, Rock Hill, S.C.; DB—Corey Sawyer, Florida St., 5-11, 171, Key West, Fla.; P—Terry Daniel, Auburn, 6-1, 226, Valley, Ala.

1994

Offense WR—Jack Jackson, Florida, 5-9, 171, Moss Point, Miss.; WR—Michael Westbrook, Colorado, 6-4, 210, Detroit, Mich.; TE—Pete Mitchell, Boston College, 6-2, 238, Bloomfield Hills, Mich.; OL—*Zach Wiegert, Nebraska, 6-5, 300, Fremont, Neb.; OL—Tony Boselli, Southern Cal, 6-8, 305, Boulder, Colo.; OL—Korey Stringer, Ohio St., 6-5, 315, Warren, Ohio; OL—Brenden Stai, Nebraska, 6-4, 300, Yorba Linda, Calif.; C—Cory Raymer, Wisconsin, 6-4, 290, Fond du Lac, Wis.; QB—Kerry Collins, Penn St., 6-5, 235, West Lawn, Pa.; RB—*Rashaan Salaam, Colorado, 6-1, 210, San Diego, Calif.; RB—*Ki-Jana Carter, Penn St., 5-10, 212, Westerville, Ohio; PK—Steve McLaughlin, Arizona, 6-1, 175, Tucson, Ariz.; KR—Leeland McElroy, Texas A&M, 5-11, 200, Beaumont, Texas.

Defense DL—*Warren Sapp, Miami (Fla.), 6-3, 284, Plymouth, Fla.; DL—Tedy Bruschi, Arizona, 6-1, 255, Roseville, Calif.; DL—Luther Elliss, Utah, 6-6, 288, Mancos, Colo.; DL—Kevin Carter, Florida, 6-6, 265, Tallahassee, Fla.; LB—*Dana Howard, Illinois, 6-0, 235, East St. Louis, Ill.; LB—Ed Stewart, Nebraska, 6-1, 215, Chicago, Ill.; LB—Derrick Brooks, Florida St., 6-1, 226, Pensacola, Fla.; DB—Clifton Abraham, Florida St., 5-9, 185, Dallas, Texas; DB—Bobby Taylor, Notre Dame, 6-3, 201, Longview, Texas; DB—Chris Hudson, Colorado, 5-11, 195, Houston, Texas; DB—Brian Robinson, Auburn, 6-3, 194, Fort Lauderdale, Fla.; DB—Tony Bouie, Arizona, 5-10, 183, New Orleans, La.; P—*Todd Sauerbrun, West Va., 6-0, 205, Setauket, N.Y.

1995

Offense WR—Terry Glenn, Ohio St., 5-11, 185, Columbus, Ohio; WR—*Keyshawn Johnson, Southern Cal, 6-4, 210, Los Angeles, Calif.; TE—*Marco Battaglia, Rutgers, 6-3, 240, Queens, N.Y.; OL—*Jonathan Ogden, UCLA, 6-8, 310, Washington, D.C.; OL—*Jason Odom, Florida, 6-5, 291, Bartow, Fla.; OL—*Orlando Pace, Ohio St., 6-6, 320, Sandusky, Ohio; OL—Jeff Hartings, Penn St., 6-3, 278, St. Henry, Ohio; C—(tie) Clay Shiver, Florida St., 6-2, 285, Tifton, Ga.; Bryan Stoltenberg, Colorado, 6-2, 280, Sugarland, Texas; QB—Tommie Frazier, Nebraska, 6-2, 205, Bradenton, Fla.; RB—*Eddie George, Ohio St., 6-3, 230, Philadelphia, Pa.; RB—Troy Davis, Iowa St., 5-8, 182, Miami, Fla.; PK—Michael Reeder, Texas Christian, 6-0, 160, Sulphur, La.

Defense DL—*Tedy Bruschi, Arizona, 6-1, 253, Roseville, Calif.; DL—Cornell Brown, Virginia Tech, 6-2, 240, Lynchburg, Va.; DL—Marcus Jones, North Caro., 6-6, 270, Jacksonville, N.C.; DL—Tony Brackens, Texas, 6-4, 250, Fairfield, Texas; LB—*Zach Thomas, Texas Tech, 6-0, 232, Pampa, Texas; LB—Kevin Hardy, Illinois, 6-4, 243, Evansville, Ind.; LB—Pat Fitzgerald, Northwestern, 6-4, 228, Orland Park, Ill.; DB—Chris Canty, Kansas St., 5-10, 190, Voorhees, N.J.; DB—*Lawyer Milloy, Washington, 6-2, 200, Tacoma, Wash.; DB—Aaron Beasley, West Va., 6-0, 190, Pottstown, Pa.; DB—Greg Myers, Colorado St., 6-2, 191, Windsor, Colo.; P—Brad Maynard, Ball St., 6-1, 175, Atlanta, Ind.

1995 Selectors: Associated Press, United Press International, Football Writers Association of America, American Football Coaches Association (Kodak), Walter Camp Foundation, The Football News and The Sporting News.

**Indicates unanimous selection.*

Consensus All-Americans by College

Beginning in 1924, unanimous selections are indicated by (*).

AIR FORCE
58— Brock Strom, T
70— Ernie Jennings, E
85— Scott Thomas, DB
87—*Chad Hennings, DL
92—*Carlton McDonald, DB

ALABAMA
30—*Fred Sington, T
34— Don Hutson, E
Bill Lee, T
Dixie Howell, B
35— Riley Smith, B
37— Leroy Monsky, G
41— Holt Rast, E
42— Joe Domnanovich, C
45— Vaughn Mancha, C
61—*Billy Neighbors, T
62—*Lee Roy Jordan, C
65— Paul Crane, C
66— Ray Perkins, E
*Cecil Dowdy, T
67— Dennis Homan, E
Bobby Johns, DB
71— Johnny Musso, B
72—*John Hannah, G
73— Buddy Brown, G
74— Leroy Cook, DL
Woodrow Lowe, LB
75—*Leroy Cook, DE
77— Ozzie Newsome, WR
78— Marty Lyons, DL
79— Jim Bunch, T
80—*E. J. Junior, DL
81— Tommy Wilcox, DB
82— Mike Pitts, DL
86—*Cornelius Bennett, LB
88—*Derrick Thomas, LB
89—*Keith McCants, LB
90—*Philip Doyle, PK
92— John Copeland, DL
Eric Curry, DL
93— David Palmer, KR
*Antonio Langham, DB

AMHERST
05— John Hubbard, B

ARIZONA
82— Ricky Hunley, LB
83—*Ricky Hunley, LB
87— Chuck Cecil, DB
90—*Darryll Lewis, DB
92— Rob Waldrop, DL
93—*Rob Waldrop, DL
94— Steve McLaughlin, PK
Tedy Bruschi, DL
Tony Bouie, DB
95—*Tedy Bruschi, DL

ARIZONA ST.
72— Woody Green, B
73— Woody Green, B
77— John Jefferson, WR
78—*Al Harris, DL
81— Mike Richardson, DB
82— Mike Richardson, DB
Vernon Maxwell, DL
83— Luis Zendejas, PK
84— David Fulcher, DB
85— David Fulcher, DB
86— Danny Villa, OL
87— Randall McDaniel, OL

ARKANSAS
48— Clyde Scott, B
54—*Bud Brooks, G
65— Glen Ray Hines, T
Loyd Phillips, DT
66—*Loyd Phillips, DT
68— Jim Barnes, G
69— Rodney Brand, C
70— Dick Bumpas, DT
77— Leotis Harris, G
Steve Little, K
79—*Greg Kolenda, T
81—*Billy Ray Smith, DL
82—*Billy Ray Smith, DL
*Steve Korte, OL
88— Kendall Trainor, PK
Wayne Martin, DL
89— Jim Mabry, OL

ARMY
98— Charles Romeyn, B
00— William Smith, E
01— Paul Bunker, T
Charles Daly, B
02— Paul Bunker, T-B
Robert Boyers, C
04— Arthur Tipton, C
Henry Torney, B
05— Henry Torney, B
07— William Erwin, G
11— Leland Devore, T
13— Louis Merillat, E
14— John McEwan, C
16— Elmer Oliphant, B
17— Elmer Oliphant, B
22— Ed Garbisch, C
26— Bud Sprague, T
27— Red Cagle, B
28—*Red Cagle, B
29— Red Cagle, B
32— Milt Summerfelt, G
43—*Casimir Myslinski, C
44— Glenn Davis, B
Doc Blanchard, B
45— Tex Coulter, T
John Green, G
*Glenn Davis, B
*Doc Blanchard, B
46— Hank Foldberg, E
*Glenn Davis, B
*Doc Blanchard, B
47— Joe Steffy, G
49— Arnold Galiffa, B
50—*Dan Foldberg, E
57— Bob Anderson, B
58—*Pete Dawkins, B
59— Bill Carpenter, E

AUBURN
32— Jimmy Hitchcock, B
57—*Jimmy Phillips, E
58— Zeke Smith, G
60— Ken Rice, T
64— Tucker Frederickson, B
69— Buddy McClinton, DB
70— Larry Willingham, DB
71—*Pat Sullivan, QB
*Terry Beasley, E
74— Ken Bernich, LB
83— Bo Jackson, RB
84— Gregg Carr, LB
85—*Bo Jackson, RB
86—*Ben Tamburello, C
*Brent Fullwood, RB
87— Tracy Rocker, DL
Aundray Bruce, LB
88—*Tracy Rocker, DL
90—*Ed King, OL
David Rocker, DL
93— Wayne Gandy, OL
Terry Daniel, P
94— Brian Robinson, DB

BALL ST.
95— Brad Maynard, P

BAYLOR
30— Barton Koch, G
56—*Bill Glass, G
63— Lawrence Elkins, E
64— Lawrence Elkins, B
76— Gary Green, DB
79— Mike Singletary, LB
80—*Mike Singletary, LB
86—*Thomas Everett, DB
91—*Santana Dotson, DL

BOSTON COLLEGE
20— Luke Urban, E
40— Gene Goodreault, E
42— Mike Holovak, B
84—*Doug Flutie, QB
Tony Thurman, DB
85— Mike Ruth, DL
94— Pete Mitchell, TE

BRIGHAM YOUNG
79—*Marc Wilson, QB
80— Nick Eyre, OL
81—*Jim McMahon, QB
82—*Gordon Hudson, TE
83—*Gordon Hudson, TE
*Steve Young, QB
86— Jason Buck, DL
89— Mohammed Elewonibi, OL
90— Ty Detmer, QB
*Chris Smith, TE
91— Ty Detmer, QB

BROWN
02— Thomas Barry, B
06— John Mayhew, B
09— Adrian Regnier, E
10— Earl Sprackling, B
12— George Crowther, B
16— Fritz Pollard, B

CALIFORNIA
21— Brick Muller, E
Dan McMillan, T
22— Brick Muller, E
24— Edwin Horrell, C
28— Irv Phillips, E
30— Ted Beckett, G
35— Larry Lutz, T
37— Sam Chapman, B
38— Vic Bottari, B
48— Jackie Jensen, B
49—*Rod Franz, G
50— Les Richter, G
51— Les Richter, G
68— Ed White, MG
71— Sherman White, DT
74— Steve Bartkowski, QB
75— Chuck Muncie, RB
Steve Rivera, E
83— Ron Rivera, LB
91— Russell White, RB
92— Sean Dawkins, WR

CARLISLE
99— Isaac Seneca, B
03— James Johnson, B
07— Albert Exendine, E
Peter Hauser, B
11— Jim Thorpe, B
12— Jim Thorpe, B

CARNEGIE MELLON
28— Howard Harpster, B

CENTENARY (LA.)
33— Paul Geisler, E

CENTRE
19— James Weaver, C
Bo McMillin, B
21— Bo McMillin, B

CHICAGO
98— Clarence Herschberger, B
04— Fred Speik, E
Walter Eckersall, B
05— Mark Catlin, E
Walter Eckersall, B
06— Walter Eckersall, B
08— Walter Steffen, B
13— Paul Des Jardien, C
22— John Thomas, B
24— Joe Pondelik, G
35—*Jay Berwanger, B

CLEMSON
67— Harry Olszewski, G
74— Bennie Cunningham, TE
79— Jim Stuckey, DL
81— Jeff Davis, LB
Terry Kinard, DB
82—*Terry Kinard, DB
83— William Perry, DL
86— Terrence Flagler, RB
87— David Treadwell, PK
88— Donnell Woolford, DB
90— Stacy Long, OL
91— Jeb Flesch, OL
Levon Kirkland, LB
93— Stacy Seegars, OL

COLGATE
13— Ellery Huntington, B
16— Clarence Horning, T
D. Belford West, T
Oscar Anderson, B
19— D. Belford West, T
30— Leonard Macaluso, B

COLORADO
37— Byron White, B
60— Joe Romig, G
61— Joe Romig, G
67— Dick Anderson, DB
68— Mike Montler, G
69— Bob Anderson, B
70— Don Popplewell, C
72— Cullen Bryant, DB
85— Barry Helton, P
86— Barry Helton, P

AWARD WINNERS

Photo from Ball State sports information

Punter Brad Maynard was Ball State's first consensus Division I-A all-America selection in 1995.

88— Keith English, P
89— Joe Garten, OL
Alfred Williams, LB
Tom Rouen, P
90— *Eric Bieniemy, RB
*Joe Garten, OL
*Alfred Williams, LB
91— *Jay Leeuwenburg, OL
92— Deon Figures, DB
94— Michael Westbrook, WR
*Rashaan Salaam, RB
Chris Hudson, DB
95— Bryan Stoltenberg, C

COLORADO ST.
78— Mike Bell, DL
95— Greg Myers, DB

COLUMBIA
00— Bill Morley, B
01— Harold Weekes, B
Bill Morley, B
03— Richard Smith, B
42— Paul Governali, B
47— Bill Swiacki, E

CORNELL
95— Clinton Wyckoff, B
00— Raymond Starbuck, B
01— William Warner, G
Sanford Hunt, G
02— William Warner, G
06— Elmer Thompson, G
William Newman, C
08— Bernard O'Rourke, G
14— John O'Hearn, E
Charles Barrett, B
15— Murray Shelton, E
Charles Barrett, B
21— Edgar Kaw, B
22— Edgar Kaw, B
23— George Pfann, B
38— Brud Holland, E
39— Nick Drahos, T
40— Nick Drahos, T
71— *Ed Marinaro, B

DARTMOUTH
03— Henry Hooper, C
Myron Witham, B
04— Joseph Gilman, G
05— Ralph Glaze, E
08— George Schildmiller, E
Clark Tobin, G
12— Wesley Englehorn, T
13— Robert Hogsett, E
14— Clarence Spears, G
15— Clarence Spears, G
17— Eugene Neely, G
19— Adolph Youngstrom, G
24— Carl Diehl, G
25— Carl Diehl, G
George Tully, E
*Andy Oberlander, B
38— Bob MacLeod, B

DUKE
33— Fred Crawford, T
36— Ace Parker, B
71— Ernie Jackson, DB
89— *Clarkston Hines, WR

DUQUESNE
36— Mike Basrak, C

EAST CARO.
83— Terry Long, OL
91— *Robert Jones, LB

FLORIDA
66— *Steve Spurrier, B
69— Carlos Alvarez, E
75— Sammy Green, LB
80— David Little, LB
82— Wilber Marshall, DL
83— Wilber Marshall, LB
84— Lomas Brown, OT
88— Louis Oliver, DB
89— *Emmitt Smith, RB
91— Brad Culpepper, DL
94— Jack Jackson, WR
Kevin Carter, DL
95— *Jason Odom, OL

FLORIDA ST.
64— Fred Biletnikoff, E
67— Ron Sellers, E
79— Ron Simmons, MG
80— Ron Simmons, MG
83— Greg Allen, RB
85— Jamie Dukes, OL
87— *Deion Sanders, DB
88— *Deion Sanders, DB
89— LeRoy Butler, DB
91— *Terrell Buckley, DB
Marvin Jones, LB
92— *Marvin Jones, LB
93— *Charlie Ward, QB
*Derrick Brooks, LB
Corey Sawyer, DB
94— Derrick Brooks, LB
Clifton Abraham, DB
95— Clay Shiver, C

FORDHAM
36— Alex Wojciechowicz, C
37— Ed Franco, T
Alex Wojciechowicz, C

GEORGETOWN
26— Harry Connaughton, G

GEORGIA
27— Tom Nash, E
31— Vernon Smith, E
41— Frank Sinkwich, B
42— *Frank Sinkwich, B
46— *Charley Trippi, B
67— Ed Chandler, T
68— Bill Stanfill, DT
Jake Scott, DB
71— *Royce Smith, G
75— Randy Johnson, G
76— Joel Parrish, G
80— *Herschel Walker, RB
81— *Herschel Walker, RB
82— *Herschel Walker, RB
Terry Hoage, DB
83— Terry Hoage, DB
84— Kevin Butler, PK
Jeff Sanchez, DB
85— Pete Anderson, C
88— Tim Worley, RB
92— *Garrison Hearst, RB

GEORGIA TECH
17— Everett Strupper, B
18— Bill Fincher, E
Joe Guyon, T
Ashel Day, C
20— Bill Fincher, E
28— Pete Pund, C
42— Harvey Hardy, G
44— Phil Tinsley, E
46— Paul Duke, C
47— Bob Davis, T
52— Hal Miller, T
53— Larry Morris, C
59— Maxie Baughan, C
66— Jim Breland, C
70— Rock Perdoni, DT
73— Randy Rhino, DB
90— *Ken Swilling, DB

HARVARD
89— Arthur Cumnock, E
John Cranston, G
James Lee, B
90— Frank Hallowell, E
Marshall Newell, T
John Cranston, C
Dudley Dean, B
John Corbett, B
91— Marshall Newell, T
Everett Lake, B
92— Frank Hallowell, E
Marshall Newell, T
Bertram Waters, G
William Lewis, C
Charles Brewer, B
93— Marshall Newell, T
William Lewis, C
Charles Brewer, B
94— Bertram Waters, T
95— Norman Cabot, E
Charles Brewer, B
96— Norman Cabot, E
Edgar Wrightington, B
97— Alan Doucette, C
Benjamin Dibblee, B
98— John Hallowell, E
Walter Boal, G
Charles Daly, B
Benjamin Dibblee, B
99— David Campbell, E
Charles Daly, B
00— John Hallowell, E
David Campbell, E
Charles Daly, B
01— David Campbell, E
Edward Bowditch, E
Oliver Cutts, T
Crawford Blagden, T
William Lee, G
Charles Barnard, G
Robert Kernan, B
Thomas Graydon, B
02— Edward Bowditch, E
Thomas Graydon, B
03— Daniel Knowlton, T
Andrew Marshall, G
04— Daniel Hurley, B
05— Beaton Squires, T
Karl Brill, T
Francis Burr, G
Daniel Hurley, B
06— Charles Osborne, T
Francis Burr, G
07— Patrick Grant, C
John Wendell, B
08— Hamilton Fish, T
Charles Nourse, C
Hamilton Corbett, B
09— Hamilton Fish, T
Wayland Minot, B
10— Robert McKay, T
Robert Fisher, G
Percy Wendell, B
11— Robert Fisher, G
Percy Wendell, B
12— Samuel Felton, E
Stanley Pennock, G
Charles Brickley, B
13— Harvey Hitchcock, T
Stanley Pennock, G
Charles Brickley, B
Edward Mahan, B
14— Huntington Hardwick, E
Walter Trumbull, T
Stanley Pennock, G
Edward Mahan, B
15— Joseph Gilman, T
Edward Mahan, B
Richard King, B
16— Harrie Dadmun, G
19— Edward Casey, B
20— Tom Woods, G
21— John Brown, G
22— Charles Hubbard, G
23— Charles Hubbard, G
29— Ben Ticknor, C
30— *Ben Ticknor, C
31— Barry Wood, B
41— *Endicott Peabody, G

HOLY CROSS
74— John Provost, DB

HOUSTON
67— Rich Stotter, G
69— Bill Bridges, G
70— Elmo Wright, E
76— Wilson Whitley, DT
80— Leonard Mitchell, DL
88— Jason Phillips, WR
89— Andre Ware, QB

ILLINOIS
14— Perry Graves, E
Ralph Chapman, G
15— Bart Macomber, B
18— John Depler, C
20— Charles Carney, E
23— James McMillen, G
Red Grange, B
24— *Red Grange, B
25— Red Grange, B
26— Bernie Shively, G
46— Alex Agase, G
51— Johnny Karras, B
53— J. C. Caroline, B
59— Bill Burrell, G
63— *Dick Butkus, C
64— Dick Butkus, C
65— *Jim Grabowski, B
84— *David Williams, WR
85— *David Williams, WR
89— *Moe Gardner, DL
90— Moe Gardner, DL
94— *Dana Howard, LB
95— Kevin Hardy, LB

INDIANA
42— Billy Hillenbrand, B
44— John Tavener, C
45— Bob Ravensberg, E
88— Anthony Thompson, RB
89— *Anthony Thompson, RB
91— *Vaughn Dunbar, RB

IOWA
19— Lester Belding, E
21— Aubrey Devine, B
22— Gordon Locke, B
39— Nile Kinnick, B
54— Calvin Jones, G
55— Calvin Jones, G
57— Alex Karras, T
58— *Randy Duncan, B
81— Andre Tippett, DL
Reggie Roby, P
84— Larry Station, LB
85— *Chuck Long, QB
*Larry Station, LB
88— Marv Cook, TE
91— Leroy Smith, DL

IOWA ST.
38— Ed Bock, G
89— Mike Busch, TE
95— Troy Davis, RB

KANSAS
63— Gale Sayers, B
64— Gale Sayers, B
68— John Zook, DE
73— David Jaynes, QB

KANSAS ST.
77— Gary Spani, LB
92— Sean Snyder, P
95— Chris Canty, DB

KENTUCKY
50— Bob Gain, T
Babe Parilli, B
51— Babe Parilli, B
56— Lou Michaels, T
57— Lou Michaels, T
65— Sam Ball, T
77— *Art Still, DL

LAFAYETTE
00— Walter Bachman, C
01— Walter Bachman, C
21— Frank Schwab, G
22— Frank Schwab, G

LSU
35— Gaynell Tinsley, E
36— *Gaynell Tinsley, E
39— Ken Kavanaugh, E
54— Sid Fournet, T
58— *Billy Cannon, B
59— Billy Cannon, B
61— *Roy Winston, G
62— *Jerry Stovall, B
70— Mike Anderson, LB
Tommy Casanova, DB
71— Tommy Casanova, DB
72— Bert Jones, QB
77— Charles Alexander, RB
78— Charles Alexander, RB
87— Wendell Davis, WR
*Nacho Albergamo, C

LOUISIANA TECH
92— Willie Roaf, OL

MARQUETTE
36— Ray Buivid, B

MARYLAND
51— *Bob Ward, G
52— Dick Modzelewski, T
*Jack Scarbath, B
53— *Stan Jones, T
55— *Bob Pellegrini, C
61— Gary Collins, E
74— *Randy White, DL
76— Joe Campbell, DT

79— Dale Castro, PK
85— J. D. Maarleveld, OL

MEMPHIS
92— Joe Allison, PK

MIAMI (FLA.)
61— Bill Miller, E
66— Tom Beier, DB
67—*Ted Hendricks, DE
68—*Ted Hendricks, DE
73— Tony Cristiani, DL
74— Rubin Carter, MG
81— Fred Marion, DB
84— Eddie Brown, WR
85— Willie Smith, TE
86—*Vinny Testaverde, QB
*Jerome Brown, DL
Bennie Blades, DB
87—*Daniel Stubbs, DL
*Bennie Blades, DB
88— Steve Walsh, QB
Bill Hawkins, DL
89— Greg Mark, DL
90— Maurice Crum, LB
*Russell Maryland, DL
91— Carlos Huerta, PK
Darryl Williams, DB
92—*Gino Torretta, QB
Micheal Barrow, LB
Ryan McNeil, DB
94—*Warren Sapp, DL

MICHIGAN
98— William Cunningham, C
01— Neil Snow, E
03— Willie Heston, B
04— Willie Heston, B
07— Adolph Schulz, C
09— Albert Benbrook, G
10— Stanfield Wells, E
Albert Benbrook, G
13— Miller Pontius, T
Jim Craig, B
14— John Maulbetsch, B
22— Harry Kipke, B
23— Jack Blott, C
25— Bennie Oosterbaan, E
Benny Friedman, B
26— Bennie Oosterbaan, E
Benny Friedman, B
27—*Bennie Oosterbaan, E
28— Otto Pommerening, T
32—*Harry Newman, B
33— Francis Wistert, T
*Chuck Bernard, C
38—*Ralph Heikkinen, G
39— Tom Harmon, B
40—*Tom Harmon, B
41— Bob Westfall, B
42— Albert Wistert, T
Julie Franks, G
43—*Bill Daley, B
47—*Bob Chappuis, B
48— Dick Rifenburg, E
Alvin Wistert, T
49— Alvin Wistert, T
55— Ron Kramer, E
56—*Ron Kramer, E
65— Bill Yearby, DT
66—*Jack Clancy, E
69—*Jim Mandich, E
Tom Curtis, DB
70— Dan Dierdorf, T
71— Reggie McKenzie, G
*Mike Taylor, LB
72— Paul Seymour, T
Randy Logan, DB
73— Dave Gallagher, DL
Dave Brown, DB
74—*Dave Brown, DB
76— Rob Lytle, RB
Mark Donahue, G
77—*Mark Donahue, G
79— Ron Simpkins, LB
81—*Anthony Carter, WR
Ed Muransky, OL
Kurt Becker, OL
82—*Anthony Carter, WR
85— Mike Hammerstein, DL
Brad Cochran, DB
86— Garland Rivers, DB
87— John Elliott, OL
88— John Vitale, C
*Mark Messner, DL
89—*Tripp Welborne, DB
90—*Tripp Welborne, DB
91—*Desmond Howard, WR
*Greg Skrepenak, OL

MICHIGAN ST.
15— Neno Jerry DaPrato, B
35— Sidney Wagner, G
49— Ed Bagdon, G
51— Bob Carey, E
*Don Coleman, T
53— Don Dohoney, E
55— Norman Masters, T
Earl Morrall, B
57— Dan Currie, C
Walt Kowalczyk, B
58— Sam Williams, E
62— George Saimes, B
63— Sherman Lewis, B
65— Bubba Smith, DE
*George Webster, DB
66— Clint Jones, B
*Bubba Smith, DE
*George Webster, DB
72—*Brad VanPelt, DB
85—*Lorenzo White, RB
87— Lorenzo White, RB
88— Tony Mandarich, OL
89—*Percy Snow, LB
Bob Kula, OL

MINNESOTA
03— Fred Schacht, T
09— John McGovern, B
10— James Walker, T
16— Bert Baston, E
17— George Hauser, T
23— Ray Ecklund, E
26— Herb Joesting, B
27— Herb Joesting, B
29— Bronko Nagurski, T
31— Biggie Munn, G
34— Frank Larson, E
Bill Bevan, G
Pug Lund, B
35— Ed Widseth, T
36—*Ed Widseth, T
40— Urban Odson, T
George Franck, B
41— Dick Wildung, T
Bruce Smith, B
42— Dick Wildung, T
48— Leo Nomellini, T
49— Leo Nomellini, T
*Clayton Tonnemaker, C
53—*Paul Giel, B
60—*Tom Brown, G
61— Sandy Stephens, B
62—*Bobby Bell, T
63— Carl Eller, T
65— Aaron Brown, DE

MISSISSIPPI
47— Charley Conerly, B
53— Crawford Mims, G
59— Charlie Flowers, B
60—*Jake Gibbs, B
62— Jim Dunaway, T
79— Jim Miller, P
92— Everett Lindsay, OL

MISSISSIPPI ST.
74— Jimmy Webb, DL

MISSOURI
41— Darold Jenkins, C
60—*Danny LaRose, E
65— Johnny Roland, DB
68— Roger Wehrli, DB
78— Kellen Winslow, TE
86— John Clay, OL

NAVY
07— Bill Dague, E
08— Percy Northcroft, T
Ed Lange, B
11— Jack Dalton, B
13— John Brown, G
18— Lyman Perry, G
Wolcott Roberts, B
22— Wendell Taylor, T
26—*Frank Wickhorst, T
28— Edward Burke, G
34— Fred Borries, B
43— Don Whitmire, T
44—*Don Whitmire, T
Ben Chase, G
Bob Jenkins, B
45— Dick Duden, E
54— Ron Beagle, E
55—*Ron Beagle, E
60—*Joe Bellino, B
63—*Roger Staubach, B
75—*Chet Moeller, DB
83— Napoleon McCallum, RB
85— Napoleon McCallum, RB

NEBRASKA
15— Guy Chamberlin, E
24— Ed Weir, T
25—*Ed Weir, T
33— George Sauer, B
36— Sam Francis, B
63—*Bob Brown, G
64—*Larry Kramer, T
65— Freeman White, E
Walt Barnes, DT
66— LaVerne Allers, G
Wayne Meylan, MG
67— Wayne Meylan, MG
70— Bob Newton, T
71— Johnny Rodgers, FL
Willie Harper, DE
Larry Jacobson, DT
72—*Johnny Rodgers, FL
Willie Harper, DE
*Rich Glover, MG
73—*John Dutton, DL
74— Marvin Crenshaw, OT
75—*Rik Bonness, C
76— Dave Butterfield, DB
78— Kelvin Clark, OT
79—*Junior Miller, TE
80— Randy Schleusener, OL
Jarvis Redwine, RB
81—*Dave Rimington, C
82—*Dave Rimington, C
Mike Rozier, RB
83—*Irving Fryar, WR
Dean Steinkuhler, OL
*Mike Rozier, RB
84—*Mark Traynowicz, C
86—*Danny Noonan, DL
88— Jake Young, C
*Broderick Thomas, LB
89— Jake Young, C
92—*Will Shields, OL
93—*Trev Alberts, LB
94—*Zach Wiegert, OL
Brenden Stai, OL
Ed Stewart, LB
95— Tommie Frazier, QB

NEW MEXICO
89— Terance Mathis, WR

NEW YORK U.
28— Ken Strong, B

NORTH CARO.
37— Andy Bershak, E
48— Charlie Justice, B
70— Don McCauley, B
72— Ron Rusnak, G
74— Ken Huff, G
77— Dee Hardison, DL
80—*Lawrence Taylor, LB
83— William Fuller, DL
95— Marcus Jones, DL

NORTH CARO. ST.
67— Dennis Byrd, DT
73— Bill Yoest, G
78— Jim Ritcher, C
Ted Brown, RB
79—*Jim Ritcher, C

NORTH TEXAS
68— Joe Greene, DT

NORTHERN ILL.
93—*LeShon Johnson, RB

NORTHWESTERN
26— Ralph Baker, B
30— Frank Baker, E
31— Jack Riley, T
Dallas Marvil, T
Pug Rentner, B
36— Steve Reid, G
40— Alf Bauman, T
45— Max Morris, E
59— Ron Burton, B
62— Jack Cvercko, G
95— Pat Fitzgerald, LB

NOTRE DAME
13— Gus Dorais, B
17— Frank Rydzewski, C
20— George Gipp, B
21— Eddie Anderson, E
24— Harry Stuhldreher, B
Jimmy Crowley, B
Elmer Layden, B
26— Bud Boeringer, C
27— John Smith, G
29— Jack Cannon, G
*Frank Carideo, B
30—*Frank Carideo, B
Marchy Schwartz, B
31— Tommy Yarr, C
Marchy Schwartz, B
32—*Joe Kurth, T
34— Jack Robinson, C
35— Wayne Millner, E
37— Chuck Sweeney, E
38—*Ed Beinor, T
41— Bob Dove, E
42— Bob Dove, E
43— John Yonakor, E
Jim White, T
Pat Filley, G
Angelo Bertelli, B
Creighton Miller, B
46— George Connor, T
*John Lujack, B
47— George Connor, T
Bill Fischer, G
*John Lujack, B
48— Leon Hart, E
Bill Fischer, G
Emil Sitko, B
49—*Leon Hart, E
*Emil Sitko, B
Bob Williams, B
50— Jerry Groom, C
52—*Johnny Lattner, B
53— Art Hunter, T
*Johnny Lattner, B
54—*Ralph Guglielmi, B
55— Paul Hornung, B
57— Al Ecuyer, G
59— Monty Stickles, E
64— Jack Snow, E
John Huarte, B
65—*Dick Arrington, G
Nick Rassas, B
66— Tom Regner, G
*Nick Eddy, B
Alan Page, DE
*Jim Lynch, LB
67— Tom Schoen, DB
68— George Kunz, T
Terry Hanratty, QB
69—*Mike McCoy, DT
70— Tom Gatewood, E
Larry DiNardo, G
71—*Walt Patulski, DE
Clarence Ellis, DB
72—*Greg Marx, DT
73— Dave Casper, TE
Mike Townsend, DB
74— Pete Demmerle, WR
Gerry DiNardo, G
75—*Steve Niehaus, DT
76— Ken MacAfee, TE
*Ross Browner, DE
77—*Ken MacAfee, TE
*Ross Browner, DL
Luther Bradley, DB
78— Dave Huffman, C
*Bob Golic, LB
79— Vagas Ferguson, RB
80—*John Scully, C
Bob Crable, LB
81— Bob Crable, LB
87—*Tim Brown, WR
88— Frank Stams, DL
Michael Stonebreaker, LB
89—*Todd Lyght, DB
Chris Zorich, DL

AWARD WINNERS

90— *Raghib Ismail, WR
Todd Lyght, DB
*Michael Stonebreaker, LB
*Chris Zorich, DL
91— Mirko Jurkovic, OL
92— Aaron Taylor, OL
93— *Aaron Taylor, OL
Jeff Burris, DB
94— Bobby Taylor, DB

OHIO ST.
16— Charles Harley, B
17— Charles Bolen, E
Charles Harley, B
19— Charles Harley, B
20— Iolas Huffman, G
Gaylord Stinchcomb, B
21— Iolas Huffman, T
25— Ed Hess, G
28— Wes Fesler, E
29— Wes Fesler, E
30— *Wes Fesler, E
35— Gomer Jones, C
39— Esco Sarkkinen, E
44— Jack Dugger, E
Bill Hackett, G
*Les Horvath, B
45— *Warren Amling, G
46— Warren Amling, T
50— *Vic Janowicz, B
54— *Howard Cassady, B
55— *Howard Cassady, B
56— *Jim Parker, G
58— Bob White, B
60— *Bob Ferguson, B
61— *Bob Ferguson, B
68— *Dave Foley, T
69— Jim Otis, B
Jim Stillwagon, MG
Jack Tatum, DB
70— *Jim Stillwagon, MG
*Jack Tatum, DB
72— Randy Gradishar, LB
73— *John Hicks, OT
*Randy Gradishar, LB
74— Kurt Schumacher, OT
Steve Myers, C
*Archie Griffin, RB
75— *Archie Griffin, RB
Ted Smith, G
Tim Fox, DB
76— Chris Ward, T
Bob Brudzinski, DE
77— *Chris Ward, T
Tom Cousineau, LB
78— Tom Cousineau, LB
79— Ken Fritz, G
82— Marcus Marek, LB
84— Jim Lachey, OG
*Keith Byars, RB
86— Cris Carter, WR
Chris Spielman, LB
87— *Chris Spielman, LB
*Tom Tupa, P
93— Dan Wilkinson, DL
94— Korey Stringer, OL
95— Terry Glenn, WR
*Orlando Pace, OL
*Eddie George, RB

OKLAHOMA
38— Waddy Young, E
48— Buddy Burris, G
50— Jim Weatherall, T
Leon Heath, B
51— *Jim Weatherall, T
52— Billy Vessels, B
53— J. D. Roberts, G
54— Max Boydston, E
Kurt Burris, C
55— Bo Bolinger, G
56— *Jerry Tubbs, C
Tommy McDonald, B
57— Bill Krisher, G
Clendon Thomas, B
58— Bob Harrison, C
63— Jim Grisham, B
64— Ralph Neely, T
65— Carl McAdams, LB
67— *Granville Liggins, MG
69— *Steve Owens, B
71— *Greg Pruitt, B
Tom Brahaney, C
72— *Greg Pruitt, B
Tom Brahaney, C
73— *Lucious Selmon, DL
Rod Shoate, LB
74— John Roush, G
*Joe Washington, RB
*Rod Shoate, LB
75— *Lee Roy Selmon, DT
Dewey Selmon, MG
Jimbo Elrod, DE
76— *Mike Vaughan, OT
77— *Zac Henderson, DB
78— *Greg Roberts, G
*Billy Sims, RB
79— *Billy Sims, RB
*George Cumby, LB
80— Louis Oubre, OL
81— Terry Crouch, OL
82— Rick Bryan, DL
83— *Rick Bryan, DL
84— Tony Casillas, DL
85— Tony Casillas, DL
*Brian Bosworth, LB
86— *Keith Jackson, TE
*Brian Bosworth, LB
87— *Keith Jackson, TE
*Mark Hutson, OL
Dante Jones, LB
Rickey Dixon, DB
88— *Anthony Phillips, OL

OKLAHOMA ST.
45— Bob Fenimore, B
69— John Ward, T
76— Derrel Gofourth, C
77— *Terry Miller, RB
84— Rod Brown, DB
85— Thurman Thomas, RB
*Leslie O'Neal, DL
88— Hart Lee Dykes, WR
*Barry Sanders, RB

OREGON
62— Mel Renfro, B

OREGON ST.
56— John Witte, T
58— Ted Bates, T
62— *Terry Baker, B
63— Vern Burke, E
68— *John Didion, C

PENNSYLVANIA
91— John Adams, C
92— Harry Thayer, B
94— Charles Gelbert, E
Arthur Knipe, B
George Brooke, B
95— Charles Gelbert, E
Charles Wharton, G
Alfred Bull, C
George Brooke, B
96— Charles Gelbert, E
Charles Wharton, G
Wylie Woodruff, G
97— John Outland, T
T. Truxton Hare, G
John Minds, B
98— T. Truxton Hare, G
Pete Overfield, C
John Outland, B
99— T. Truxton Hare, G
Pete Overfield, C
Josiah McCracken, B
00— T. Truxton Hare, G
04— Frank Piekarski, G
Vincent Stevenson, B
Andrew Smith, B
05— Otis Lamson, T
Robert Torrey, C
06— August Ziegler, G
William Hollenback, B
07— Dexter Draper, T
August Ziegler, G
08— Hunter Scarlett, E
William Hollenback, B
10— Ernest Cozens, C
E. LeRoy Mercer, B
12— E. LeRoy Mercer, B
17— Henry Miller, E
19— Henry Miller, E
22— John Thurman, T
24— Ed McGinley, T
27— Ed Hake, T
28— Paul Scull, B
43— Bob Odell, B
45— George Savitsky, T
47— Chuck Bednarik, C
48— Chuck Bednarik, C

PENN ST.
06— William Dunn, C
19— Bob Higgins, E
20— Charles Way, B
21— Glenn Killinger, B
23— Harry Wilson, B
59— Richie Lucas, B
64— Glenn Ressler, G
68— *Ted Kwalick, E
Dennis Onkotz, LB
69— *Mike Reid, DT
Dennis Onkotz, LB
70— Jack Ham, LB
71— Dave Joyner, T
72— Bruce Bannon, DE
John Skorupan, LB
73— *John Cappelletti, B
74— Mike Hartenstine, DL
75— Greg Buttle, LB
78— *Keith Dorney, OT
*Chuck Fusina, QB
*Bruce Clark, DL
79— Bruce Clark, DL
81— *Sean Farrell, OL
86— D. J. Dozier, RB
Shane Conlan, LB
92— O. J. McDuffie, WR
94— Kerry Collins, QB
*Ki-Jana Carter, RB
95— Jeff Hartings, OL

PITTSBURGH
15— Robert Peck, C
16— James Herron, E
Robert Peck, C
17— Dale Seis, G
John Sutherland, G
18— Leonard Hilty, T
Tom Davies, B
George McLaren, B
20— Herb Stein, C
21— Herb Stein, C
25— Ralph Chase, T
27— *Gibby Welch, B
28— Mike Getto, T
29— *Joe Donchess, E
Ray Montgomery, G
31— Jesse Quatse, T
32— Joe Skladany, E
*Warren Heller, B
33— Joe Skladany, E
34— Chuck Hartwig, G
36— Averell Daniell, T
37— Tony Matisi, T
Marshall Goldberg, B
38— *Marshall Goldberg, B
56— *Joe Walton, E
58— John Guzik, G
60— *Mike Ditka, E
63— Paul Martha, B
76— *Tony Dorsett, RB
Al Romano, MG
77— Tom Brzoza, C
Randy Holloway, DL
Bob Jury, DB
78— Hugh Green, DL
79— *Hugh Green, DL
80— *Hugh Green, DL
*Mark May, OL
81— Sal Sunseri, LB
82— Jimbo Covert, OL
83— *Bill Fralic, OL
84— *Bill Fralic, OT
86— Randy Dixon, OL
Tony Woods, DL
87— Craig Heyward, RB
88— Mark Stepnoski, OL
90— Brian Greenfield, P

PRINCETON
89— Hector Cowan, T
William George, C
Edgar Allan Poe, B
Roscoe Channing, B
Knowlton Ames, B
90— Ralph Warren, E
Jesse Riggs, G
Sheppard Homans, B
91— Jesse Riggs, G
Philip King, B
Sheppard Homans, B
92— Arthur Wheeler, G
Philip King, B
93— Thomas Trenchard, E
Langdon Lea, T
Arthur Wheeler, G
Philip King, B
Franklin Morse, B
94— Langdon Lea, T
Arthur Wheeler, G
95— Langdon Lea, T
Dudley Riggs, G
96— William Church, T
Robert Gailey, C
Addison Kelly, B
John Baird, B
97— Garrett Cochran, E
Addison Kelly, B
98— Lew Palmer, E
Arthur Hillebrand, T
99— Arthur Hillebrand, T
Arthur Poe, E
Howard Reiter, B
01— Ralph Davis, E
02— John DeWitt, G
03— Howard Henry, E
John DeWitt, G
J. Dana Kafer, B
04— James Cooney, T
05— James McCormick, B
06— L. Casper Wister, E
James Cooney, T
Edward Dillon, B
07— L. Casper Wister, E
Edwin Harlan, B
James McCormick, B
08— Frederick Tibbott, B
10— Talbot Pendleton, B
11— Sanford White, E
Edward Hart, T
Joseph Duff, G
12— John Logan, G
13— Harold Ballin, T
14— Harold Ballin, T
16— Frank Hogg, G
18— Frank Murrey, B
20— Stan Keck, T
Donold Lourie, B
21— Stan Keck, G
22— C. Herbert Treat, T
25— Ed McMillan, C
35— John Weller, G
51— *Dick Kazmaier, B
52— Frank McPhee, E
65— Stas Maliszewski, G

PURDUE
29— Elmer Sleight, T
Ralph Welch, B
32— *Paul Moss, E
33— Duane Purvis, B
40— Dave Rankin, E
43— Alex Agase, G
52— Bernie Flowers, E
65— Bob Griese, QB
67— *Leroy Keyes, B
68— *Leroy Keyes, B
Chuck Kyle, MG
69— *Mike Phipps, QB
72— Otis Armstrong, B
Dave Butz, DT
80— *Dave Young, TE
*Mark Herrmann, QB
86— Rod Woodson, DB

RICE
46— Weldon Humble, G
49— James Williams, E
54— Dicky Maegle, B
58— Buddy Dial, E
76— Tommy Kramer, QB
91— Trevor Cobb, RB

RICHMOND
69— Walker Gillette, E
78— Jeff Nixon, DB

RUTGERS
17— Paul Robeson, E
18— Paul Robeson, E
61— Alex Kroll, C
95—*Marco Battaglia, TE

ST. MARY'S (CAL.)
27— Larry Bettencourt, C
45—*Herman Wedemeyer, B

SAN DIEGO ST.
92—*Marshall Faulk, RB
93—*Marshall Faulk, RB

SANTA CLARA
38— Alvord Wolff, T
39— John Schiechl, C

SOUTH CARO.
80—*George Rogers, RB
84— Del Wilkes, OG

SOUTHERN CAL
26— Mort Kaer, B
27— Jesse Hibbs, T
Morley Drury, B
30— Erny Pinckert, B
31— John Baker, G
Gus Shaver, B
32—*Ernie Smith, T
33— Aaron Rosenberg, G
*Cotton Warburton, B
39—*Harry Smith, G
43— Ralph Heywood, E
44— John Ferraro, T
47— Paul Cleary, E
52— Elmer Willhoite, G
Jim Sears, B
62— Hal Bedsole, E
65—*Mike Garrett, B
66— Ron Yary, T
Nate Shaw, DB
67—*Ron Yary, T
*O. J. Simpson, B
Tim Rossovich, DE
Adrian Young, LB
68—*O. J. Simpson, B
69— Jim Gunn, DE
70— Charlie Weaver, DE
72—*Charles Young, TE
73— Lynn Swann, WR
Booker Brown, OT
Richard Wood, LB
Artimus Parker, DB
74—*Anthony Davis, RB
Richard Wood, LB
75—*Ricky Bell, RB
76—*Ricky Bell, RB
Gary Jeter, DT
Dennis Thurman, DB
77—*Dennis Thurman, DB
78—*Pat Howell, G
*Charles White, RB
79—*Brad Budde, G
*Charles White, RB
80— Keith Van Horne, OL
*Ronnie Lott, DB
81— Roy Foster, OL
*Marcus Allen, RB
82—*Don Mosebar, OL
Bruce Matthews, OL
George Achica, MG
83— Tony Slaton, C
84— Jack Del Rio, LB
85— Jeff Bregel, OL
86— Jeff Bregel, OL
Tim McDonald, DB
87— Dave Cadigan, OL
89—*Mark Carrier, DB
Tim Ryan, DL
93— Johnnie Morton, WR
94— Tony Boselli, OL
95—*Keyshawn Johnson, WR

SOUTHERN METHODIST
35— J. C. Wetsel, G
Bobby Wilson, B
47— Doak Walker, B
48—*Doak Walker, B
49— Doak Walker, B
50— Kyle Rote, B
51— Dick Hightower, C
66— John LaGrone, MG
68— Jerry LeVias, E
72— Robert Popelka, DB
74— Louie Kelcher, G
78— Emanuel Tolbert, WR
80— John Simmons, DB
82—*Eric Dickerson, RB
83—*Russell Carter, DB
85— Reggie Dupard, RB

STANFORD
24— Jim Lawson, E
25— Ernie Nevers, B
28— Seraphim Post, G
Don Robesky, G
32— Bill Corbus, G
33— Bill Corbus, G
34— Bob Reynolds, T
Bobby Grayson, B
35— James Moscrip, E
*Bobby Grayson, B
40— Frank Albert, B
41— Frank Albert, B
42— Chuck Taylor, G
50— Bill McColl, E
51—*Bill McColl, E
56— John Brodie, QB
70— Jim Plunkett, QB
71— Jeff Siemon, LB
74— Pat Donovan, DL
77— Guy Benjamin, QB
79— Ken Margerum, WR
80—*Ken Margerum, WR
82—*John Elway, QB
86— Brad Muster, RB
91— Bob Whitfield, OL

SYRACUSE
08— Frank Horr, T
15— Harold White, G
17— Alfred Cobb, T
18— Lou Usher, T
Joe Alexander, G
19— Joe Alexander, G
23— Pete McRae, E
26— Vic Hanson, E
56—*Jim Brown, B
59—*Roger Davis, G
60— Ernie Davis, B
61—*Ernie Davis, B
67—*Larry Csonka, B
85—*Tim Green, DL
87—*Don McPherson, QB
Ted Gregory, DL
90— John Flannery, C
92—*Chris Gedney, TE

TEMPLE
85— John Rienstra, OL
86—*Paul Palmer, RB

TENNESSEE
29— Gene McEver, B
33— Beattie Feathers, B
38— Bowden Wyatt, E
39— Ed Molinski, G
George Cafego, B
40—*Bob Suffridge, G
46— Dick Huffman, T
51—*Hank Lauricella, B
52— John Michels, G
56—*John Majors, B
65— Frank Emanuel, LB
66— Paul Naumoff, LB
67—*Bob Johnson, C
68—*Charles Rosenfelder, G
Steve Kiner, LB
69— Chip Kell, G
*Steve Kiner, LB
70—*Chip Kell, G
71—*Bobby Majors, DB
75— Larry Seivers, E
76— Larry Seivers, SE
79— Roland James, DB
83—*Reggie White, DL
84— Bill Mayo, OG
85— Tim McGee, WR
89—*Eric Still, OL
90—*Antone Davis, OL
91— Dale Carter, DB

TEXAS
45— Hubert Bechtol, E
46— Hubert Bechtol, E
47— Bobby Layne, B
50—*Bud McFadin, G
53— Carlton Massey, E
61—*Jimmy Saxton, B
62—*Johnny Treadwell, G
63—*Scott Appleton, T
65— Tommy Nobis, LB
68— Chris Gilbert, B
69— Bob McKay, T
70— Bobby Wuensch, T
Steve Worster, B
Bill Atessis, DE
71—*Jerry Sisemore, T
72—*Jerry Sisemore, T
73—*Bill Wyman, C
Roosevelt Leaks, B
75— Bob Simmons, T
77—*Earl Campbell, RB
*Brad Shearer, DL
78—*Johnnie Johnson, DB
79—*Steve McMichael, DL
*Johnnie Johnson, DB
80— Kenneth Sims, DL
81— Terry Tausch, OL
*Kenneth Sims, DL
83— Doug Dawson, OL
Jeff Leiding, LB
Jerry Gray, DB
84— Tony Degrate, DL
*Jerry Gray, DB
95— Tony Brackens, DL

TEXAS A&M
37— Joe Routt, G
39— John Kimbrough, B
40— Marshall Robnett, G
*John Kimbrough, B
57—*John David Crow, B
70— Dave Elmendorf, DB
74— Pat Thomas, DB
75—*Ed Simonini, LB
Pat Thomas, DB
76— Tony Franklin, PK
*Robert Jackson, LB
85— Johnny Holland, LB
87— John Roper, DL
90— Darren Lewis, RB
91— Kevin Smith, DB
92—*Marcus Buckley, LB
93— Aaron Glenn, DB
Sam Adams, DL
94— Leeland McElroy, KR

TEXAS CHRISTIAN
35— Darrell Lester, C
36— Sammy Baugh, B
38— Ki Aldrich, C
*Davey O'Brien, B
55—*Jim Swink, B
59— Don Floyd, T
60—*Bob Lilly, T
84—*Kenneth Davis, RB
91— Kelly Blackwell, TE
95— Michael Reeder, PK

TEXAS TECH
60— E. J. Holub, C
65— Donny Anderson, B
77— Dan Irons, T
82— Gabriel Rivera, DL
91—*Mark Bounds, P
95—*Zach Thomas, LB

TOLEDO
71— Mel Long, DT

TULANE
31—*Jerry Dalrymple, E
32— Don Zimmerman, B
39— Harley McCollum, T
41— Ernie Blandin, T

TULSA
65—*Howard Twilley, E
91— Jerry Ostroski, OL

UCLA
46—*Burr Baldwin, E
52— Donn Moomaw, C
53— Paul Cameron, B
54— Jack Ellena, T
55— Hardiman Cureton, G
57— Dick Wallen, E
66— Mel Farr, B
67—*Gary Beban, B
Don Manning, LB
69— Mike Ballou, LB
73— Kermit Johnson, B
75— John Sciarra, QB
76— Jerry Robinson, LB
77—*Jerry Robinson, LB
78—*Jerry Robinson, LB
Kenny Easley, DB
79—*Kenny Easley, DB
80—*Kenny Easley, DB
81—*Tim Wrightman, TE
83— Don Rogers, DB
85—*John Lee, PK
88— Troy Aikman, QB
Darryl Henley, DB
92— Carlton Gray, DB
93—*J. J. Stokes, WR
Bjorn Merten, PK
Jamir Miller, LB
95—*Jonathan Ogden, OL

UTAH
94— Luther Elliss, DL

UTAH ST.
61— Merlin Olsen, T
69— Phil Olsen, DE

VANDERBILT
23— Lynn Bomar, E
24— Henry Wakefield, E
32— Pete Gracey, C
58— George Deiderich, G
82—*Jim Arnold, P
84—*Ricky Anderson, P

VIRGINIA
15— Eugene Mayer, B
41— Bill Dudley, B
85—*Jim Dombrowski, OL
90— Herman Moore, WR
92— Chris Slade, DL
93— Mark Dixon, OL

VIRGINIA TECH
67— Frank Loria, DB
84— Bruce Smith, DL
93—*Jim Pyne, C
95— Cornell Brown, DL

WAKE FOREST
76—*Bill Armstrong, DB

WASH. & JEFF.
14— John Spiegel, B
18— Wilbur Henry, T
19— Wilbur Henry, T

WASHINGTON
25— George Wilson, B
28— Charles Carroll, B
36— Max Starcevich, G
40— Rudy Mucha, C
41— Ray Frankowski, G
63— Rick Redman, G
64— Rick Redman, G
66— Tom Greenlee, DT
68— Al Worley, DB
82—*Chuck Nelson, PK
84— Ron Holmes, DL
86— Jeff Jaeger, PK
Reggie Rogers, DL
91—*Steve Emtman, DL
Mario Bailey, WR
92—*Lincoln Kennedy, OL
95—*Lawyer Milloy, DB

WASHINGTON ST.
84— Rueben Mayes, RB
88— Mike Utley, OL
89—*Jason Hanson, PK

WEST VA.
19— Ira Rodgers, B
55— Bruce Bosley, T
82—*Darryl Talley, LB
85— Brian Jozwiak, OL
92— Mike Compton, C
94—*Todd Sauerbrun, P
95— Aaron Beasley, DB

WILLIAMS
17— Ben Boynton, B
19— Ben Boynton, B

WISCONSIN
12— Robert Butler, T
13— Ray Keeler, G
15— Howard Buck, T
19— Charles Carpenter, C
20— Ralph Scott, T

23— Marty Below, T
30— Milo Lubratovich, T
42— *Dave Schreiner, E
54— *Alan Ameche, B
59— *Dan Lanphear, T
62— Pat Richter, E
75— Dennis Lick, T
81— Tim Krumrie, DL
94— Cory Raymer, C

WYOMING
83— Jack Weil, P
84— Jay Novacek, TE

YALE
89— Amos Alonzo Stagg, E
Charles Gill, T
Pudge Heffelfinger, G
90— William Rhodes, T
Pudge Heffelfinger, G
Thomas McClung, B
91— Frank Hinkey, E
John Hartwell, E
Wallace Winter, T
Pudge Heffelfinger, G
Thomas McClung, B
92— Frank Hinkey, E
A. Hamilton Wallis, T
Vance McCormick, B
93— Frank Hinkey, E
William Hickok, G
Frank Butterworth, B
94— Frank Hinkey, E
William Hickok, G
Philip Stillman, C
George Adee, B
Frank Butterworth, B
95— Fred Murphy, T
Samuel Thorne, B
96— Fred Murphy, T
Clarence Fincke, B
97— John Hall, E
Burr Chamberlin, T
Gordon Brown, G
Charles DeSaulles, B
98— Burr Chamberlin, T
Gordon Brown, G
Malcolm McBride, B
99— George Stillman, T
Gordon Brown, G
Malcolm McBride, B
Albert Sharpe, B
00— George Stillman, T
James Bloomer, T
Gordon Brown, G
Herman Olcott, C
George Chadwick, B
Perry Hale, B
William Fincke, B
01— Henry Holt, C
02— Thomas Shevlin, E
Ralph Kinney, T
James Hogan, T
Edgar Glass, G
Henry Holt, C
Foster Rockwell, B
George Chadwick, B
03— Charles Rafferty, E
James Hogan, T
James Bloomer, G
W. Ledyard Mitchell, B
04— Thomas Shevlin, E
James Hogan, T
Ralph Kinney, G
Foster Rockwell, B
05— Thomas Shevlin, E
Roswell Tripp, G
Howard Roome, B
Guy Hutchinson, B
06— Robert Forbes, E
L. Horatio Biglow, T
Hugh Knox, B
Paul Veeder, B
07— Clarence Alcott, E
L. Horatio Biglow, T
Thomas A. D. Jones, B
Edward Coy, B
08— William Goebel, G
Hamlin Andrus, G
Edward Coy, B
09— John Kilpatrick, E
Henry Hobbs, T
Hamlin Andrus, G
Carroll Cooney, C
Edward Coy, B
Stephen Philbin, B
10— John Kilpatrick, E
11— Douglass Bomeisler, E
Henry Ketcham, C
Arthur Howe, B
12— Douglass Bomeisler, E
Henry Ketcham, C
13— Nelson Talbott, T
14— Harry LeGore, B
16— Clinton Black, G
20— Tim Callahan, G
21— Malcolm Aldrich, B
23— Century Milstead, T
William Mallory, B
24— Dick Luman, E
27— Bill Webster, G
John Charlesworth, C
36— Larry Kelley, E
37— *Clint Frank, B
44— Paul Walker, E

Team Leaders in Consensus All-Americans

(Ranked on Total Number of Selections)

Team	No.	Players
Yale	100	69
Notre Dame	93	77
Harvard	89	59
Michigan	65	53
Princeton	65	49
Southern Cal	60	53
Ohio St.	58	43
Oklahoma	52	43
Pittsburgh	46	39
Pennsylvania	46	32
Nebraska	44	37
Army	37	28
Alabama	36	35
Texas	33	29
Penn St.	29	27
Minnesota	29	25
Tennessee	28	25
UCLA	28	24
Miami (Fla.)	25	23
Stanford	25	20
Michigan St.	24	21
Auburn	23	21
Navy	23	20
Colorado	23	19
Illinois	23	18
California	21	19
Georgia	21	17
Texas A&M	19	17
Cornell	19	15
Syracuse	18	16
Florida St.	18	14
Georgia Tech	17	16
Purdue	17	16
Washington	17	16
Arkansas	17	15
Dartmouth	17	15
Southern Methodist	16	14
LSU	16	12
Iowa	15	13
Wisconsin	14	14
Clemson	14	13
Florida	13	12
Arizona St.	12	9
Northwestern	11	11
Brigham Young	11	9
Chicago	11	9
Maryland	10	10
Texas Christian	10	10
Arizona	10	7
North Caro.	9	9
Oklahoma St.	9	9
Baylor	9	7
Boston College	7	7
Houston	7	7
Mississippi	7	7
West Va.	7	7
Kentucky	7	5
Brown	6	6
Missouri	6	6
Rice	6	6
Texas Tech	6	6
Vanderbilt	6	6
Virginia	6	6
Carlisle	6	5
Colgate	6	5
Columbia	6	5
Indiana	6	5
Air Force	5	5
Oregon St.	5	5
North Caro. St.	5	4

1995 First-Team All-America Teams

AMERICAN FOOTBALL COACHES ASSOCIATION

Offense QB—Tommie Frazier, Nebraska; RB—Eddie George, Ohio St.; RB—Troy Davis, Iowa St.; WR—Keyshawn Johnson, Southern Cal; WR—Marcus Harris, Wyoming; TE—Marco Battaglia, Rutgers; C—Clay Shiver, Florida St.; OL—Jeff Hartings, Penn St.; OL—Jason Odom, Florida; OL—Jonathan Ogden, UCLA; OL—Orlando Pace, Ohio St.; PK—Michael Reeder, Texas Christian.

Defense DL—Tedy Bruschi, Arizona; DL—Tim Colston, Kansas St.; DL—Marcus Jones, North Caro.; DL—Jason Horn, Michigan; DL—Tony Brackens, Texas; LB—Zach Thomas, Texas Tech; LB—Pat Fitzgerald, Northwestern; DB—Aaron Beasley, West Va.; DB—Lawyer Milloy, Washington; DB—Alex Molden, Oregon; DB—Adrian Robinson, Baylor; P—Brad Maynard, Ball St.

ASSOCIATED PRESS

Offense QB—Tommie Frazier, Nebraska; RB—Eddie George, Ohio St.; RB—Troy Davis, Iowa St.; WR—Terry Glenn, Ohio St.; WR—Keyshawn Johnson, Southern Cal; TE—Marco Battaglia, Rutgers; C—Aaron Graham, Nebraska; OL—Jonathan Ogden, UCLA; OL—Jason Odom, Florida; OL—Orlando Pace, Ohio St.; OL—Heath Irwin, Colorado; AP—Leeland McElroy, Texas A&M; PK—Michael Reeder, Texas Christian.

Defense DL—Tedy Bruschi, Arizona; DL—Cornell Brown, Virginia Tech; DL—Marcus Jones, North Caro.; DL—Jared Tomich, Nebraska; LB—Ray Lewis, Miami (Fla.); LB—Pat Fitzgerald, Northwestern; LB—Zach Thomas, Texas Tech; LB—Kevin Hardy, Illinois; DB—Chris Canty, Kansas St.; DB—Lawyer Milloy, Washington; DB—Greg Myers, Colorado St.; P—Brad Maynard, Ball St.

FOOTBALL NEWS

Offense QB—Danny Wuerffel, Florida; RB—Troy Davis, Iowa St.; RB—Eddie George, Ohio St.; WR—Keyshawn Johnson, Southern Cal; WR—Terry Glenn, Ohio St.; TE—Marco Battaglia, Rutgers; OL—Aaron Graham, Nebraska; OL—Bryan Stoltenberg, Colorado; OL—Orlando Pace, Ohio St.; OL—Jonathan Ogden, UCLA; OL—Jason Odom, Florida; PK—Michael Reeder, Texas Christian.

Defense DL—Cornell Brown, Virginia Tech; DL—Mike Vrabel, Ohio St.; DL—Tedy Bruschi, Arizona; LB—Simeon Rice, Illinois; LB—Duane Clemons, California; LB—Zach Thomas, Texas Tech; LB—Kevin Hardy, Illinois; DB—Aaron Beasley, West Va.; DB—Lawyer Milloy, Washington; DB—Percy Ellsworth, Virginia; DB—Chris Canty, Kansas St.; P—Brad Maynard, Ball St.

FOOTBALL WRITERS ASSOCIATION OF AMERICA

Offense QB—Tommie Frazier, Nebraska; RB—Eddie George, Ohio St.; RB—Karim Abdul-Jabbar, UCLA; WR—Keyshawn Johnson, Southern Cal; WR—Terry Glenn, Ohio St.; TE—Marco Battaglia, Rutgers; C—Clay Shiver, Florida St.; OL—Jonathan Ogden, UCLA; OL—Orlando Pace, Ohio St.; OL—Jason Odom, Florida; OL—Dan Neil, Texas; KR—Marvin Harrison, Syracuse; PK—Michael Reeder, Texas Christian.

Defense DL—Tony Brackens, Texas; DL—Cedric Jones, Oklahoma; DL—Tedy Bruschi, Arizona; DL—Cornell Brown, Virginia Tech; LB—Kevin Hardy, Illinois; LB—Zach Thomas, Texas Tech; LB—Pat Fitzgerald, Northwestern; DB—Lawyer Milloy, Washington; DB—Marcus Coleman, Texas Tech; DB—Chris Canty, Kansas St.; DB—Kevin Abrams, Syracuse; P—Will Brice, Virginia.

SPORTING NEWS

Offense QB—Tommie Frazier, Nebraska; RB—Eddie George, Ohio St.; RB—Troy Davis, Iowa St.; WR—Keyshawn Johnson, Southern Cal; WR—Terry Glenn, Ohio St.; TE—Marco Battaglia, Rutgers; OL—Jonathan Ogden, UCLA; OL—Orlando Pace, Ohio St.; OL—Jeff Hartings, Penn St.; OL—Jason Odom, Florida; OL—Clay Shiver, Florida St.; KR—Marvin Harrison, Syracuse; PK—Michael Reeder, Texas Christian.

Defense DL—Tedy Bruschi, Arizona; DL—Cedric Jones, Oklahoma; DL—Tony Brackens, Texas; DL—Cornell Brown, Virginia Tech; LB—Kevin Hardy, Illinois; LB—Zach Thomas, Texas Tech; LB—Pat Fitzgerald, Northwestern; DB—Chris Canty, Kansas St.; DB—Lawyer Milloy, Washington; DB—Kevin Abrams, Syracuse; DB—Greg Myers, Colorado St.; P—Brad Maynard, Ball St.

UNITED PRESS INTERNATIONAL

Offense QB—Tommie Frazier, Nebraska; RB—Troy Davis, Iowa St.; RB—Eddie George, Ohio St.; WR—Terry Glenn, Ohio St.; WR—Keyshawn Johnson, Southern Cal; TE—Marco Battaglia, Rutgers; OL—Jeff Hartings, Penn St.; OL—Jason Odom, Florida; OL—Jonathan Ogden, UCLA;

OL—Orlando Pace, Ohio St.; OL—Bryan Stoltenberg, Colorado; PK—Michael Reeder, Texas Christian.

Defense DL—Cornell Brown, Virginia Tech; DL—Tedy Bruschi, Arizona; DL—Marcus Jones, North Caro.; LB—Pat Fitzgerald, Northwestern; LB—Kevin Hardy, Illinois; LB—Ray Lewis, Miami (Fla.); LB—Zach Thomas, Texas Tech; DB—Aaron Beasley, West Va.; DB—Chris Canty, Kansas St.; DB—Lawyer Milloy, Washington; DB—Greg Myers, Colorado St.; P—Brad Maynard, Ball St.

WALTER CAMP FOOTBALL FOUNDATION

Offense QB—Tommie Frazier, Nebraska; RB—Troy Davis, Iowa St.; RB—Eddie George, Ohio St.; WR—Terry Glenn, Ohio St.; WR—Keyshawn Johnson, Southern Cal; TE—Marco Battaglia, Rutgers; C—Bryan Stoltenberg, Colorado; OL—Jeff Hartings, Penn St.; OL—Jason Odom, Florida; OL—Jonathan Ogden, UCLA; OL—Orlando Pace, Ohio St.; PK—Sam Valenzisi, Northwestern.

Defense DL—Tedy Bruschi, Arizona; DL—Tim Colston, Kansas St.; DL—Marcus Jones, North Caro.; DL—Brandon Mitchell, Texas A&M; LB—Kevin Hardy, Illinois; LB—Simeon Rice, Illinois; LB—Zach Thomas, Texas Tech; DB—Aaron Beasley, West Va.; DB—Ray Mickens, Texas A&M; DB—Lawyer Milloy, Washington; DB—Greg Myers, Colorado St.; P—Brad Maynard, Ball St.

Special Awards

HEISMAN MEMORIAL TROPHY

Originally presented in 1935 as the DAC Trophy by the Downtown Athletic Club of New York City to the best college player east of the Mississippi River. In 1936, players across the country were eligible and the award was renamed the Heisman Memorial Trophy to honor former college coach and DAC athletics director John W. Heisman. The award now goes to the outstanding college football player in the United States.

Year	Player (Winner Bold), School, Position	Points
1935	**Jay Berwanger,** Chicago, HB	84
	2nd—Monk Meyer, Army	29
	3rd—Bill Shakespeare, Notre Dame, HB	23
	4th—Pepper Constable, Princeton, FB	20
1936	**Larry Kelley,** Yale, E	219
	2nd—Sam Francis, Nebraska, FB	47
	3rd—Ray Buivid, Marquette, HB	43
	4th—Sammy Baugh, Texas Christian, HB	39
1937	**Clint Frank,** Yale, HB	524
	2nd—Byron White, Colorado, HB	264
	3rd—Marshall Goldberg, Pittsburgh, HB	211
	4th—Alex Wojciechowicz, Fordham, C	85
1938	**Davey O'Brien,** Texas Christian, QB	519
	2nd—Marshall Goldberg, Pittsburgh, HB	294
	3rd—Sid Luckman, Columbia, QB	154
	4th—Bob MacLeod, Dartmouth, HB	78
1939	**Nile Kinnick,** Iowa, HB	651
	2nd—Tom Harmon, Michigan, HB	405
	3rd—Paul Christman, Missouri, QB	391
	4th—George Cafego, Tennessee, QB	296
1940	**Tom Harmon,** Michigan, HB	1,303
	2nd—John Kimbrough, Texas A&M, FB	841
	3rd—George Franck, Minnesota, HB	102
	4th—Frankie Albert, Stanford, QB	90
1941	**Bruce Smith,** Minnesota, HB	554
	2nd—Angelo Bertelli, Notre Dame, QB	345
	3rd—Frankie Albert, Stanford, QB	336
	4th—Frank Sinkwich, Georgia, HB	249
1942	**Frank Sinkwich,** Georgia, HB	1,059
	2nd—Paul Governali, Columbia, QB	218
	3rd—Clint Castleberry, Georgia Tech, HB	99
	4th—Mike Holovak, Boston College, FB	95
1943	**Angelo Bertelli,** Notre Dame, QB	648
	2nd—Bob Odell, Pennsylvania, HB	177
	3rd—Otto Graham, Northwestern, QB	140
	4th—Creighton Miller, Notre Dame, HB	134
1944	**Les Horvath,** Ohio St., QB/HB	412
	2nd—Glenn Davis, Army, HB	287
	3rd—Doc Blanchard, Army, FB	237
	4th—Don Whitmire, Navy, T	115
1945 *	**Doc Blanchard,** Army, FB	860
	2nd—Glenn Davis, Army, HB	638
	3rd—Bob Fenimore, Oklahoma St., HB	187
	4th—Herman Wedermeyer, St. Mary's (Cal.), HB	152
1946	**Glenn Davis,** Army, HB	792
	2nd—Charlie Trippi, Georgia, HB	435
	3rd—Johnny Lujack, Notre Dame, QB	379
	4th—Doc Blanchard, Army, FB	267
1947	**Johnny Lujack,** Notre Dame, QB	742
	2nd—Bob Chappius, Michigan, HB	555
	3rd—Doak Walker, Southern Methodist, HB	196
	4th—Charlie Conerly, Mississippi, QB	186
1948 *	**Doak Walker,** Southern Methodist, HB	778
	2nd—Charlie Justice, North Caro., HB	443
	3rd—Chuck Bednarik, Pennsylvania, C	336
	4th—Jackie Jensen, California, HB	143
1949	**Leon Hart,** Notre Dame, E	995
	2nd—Charlie Justice, North Caro., HB	272
	3rd—Doak Walker, Southern Methodist, HB	229
	4th—Arnold Galiffa, Army, QB	196
1950 *	**Vic Janowicz,** Ohio St., HB	633
	2nd—Kyle Rote, Southern Methodist, HB	280
	3rd—Reds Bagnell, Pennsylvania, HB	231
	4th—Babe Parilli, Kentucky, QB	214
1951	**Dick Kazmaier,** Princeton, HB	1,777
	2nd—Hank Lauricella, Tennessee, HB	424
	3rd—Babe Pirilli, Kentucky, QB	344
	4th—Bill McColl, Stanford, E	313
1952	**Billy Vessels,** Oklahoma, HB	525
	2nd—Jack Scarbath, Maryland, QB	367
	3rd—Paul Giel, Minnesota, HB	329
	4th—Donn Moomaw, UCLA, C	257
1953	**Johnny Lattner,** Notre Dame, HB	1,850
	2nd—Paul Giel, Minnesota, HB	1,794
	3rd—Paul Cameron, UCLA, HB	444
	4th—Bernie Faloney, Maryland, QB	258
1954	**Alan Ameche,** Wisconsin, FB	1,068
	2nd—Kurt Burris, Oklahoma, C	838
	3rd—Howard Cassady, Ohio St., HB	810
	4th—Ralph Guglielmi, Notre Dame, QB	691
1955	**Howard Cassady,** Ohio St., HB	2,219
	2nd—Jim Swink, Texas Christian, HB	742
	3rd—George Welsh, Navy, QB	383
	4th—Earl Morrall, Michigan St., QB	323
1956	**Paul Hornung,** Notre Dame, QB	1,066
	2nd—Johnny Majors, Tennessee, HB	994
	3rd—Tommy McDonald, Oklahoma, HB	973
	4th—Jerry Tubbs, Oklahoma, C	724
1957	**John David Crow,** Texas A&M, HB	1,183
	2nd—Alex Karras, Iowa, T	693
	3rd—Walt Kowalczyk, Michigan St., HB	630
	4th—Lou Michaels, Kentucky, T	330
1958	**Pete Dawkins,** Army, HB	1,394
	2nd—Randy Duncan, Iowa, QB	1,021
	3rd—Billy Cannon, LSU, HB	975
	4th—Bob White, Ohio St., HB	365
1959	**Billy Cannon,** LSU, HB	1,929
	2nd—Richie Lucas, Penn St., QB	613
	3rd—Don Meredith, Southern Meth., QB	286
	4th—Bill Burrell, Illinois, G	196
1960	**Joe Bellino,** Navy, HB	1,793
	2nd—Tom Brown, Minnesota, G	731
	3rd—Jake Gibbs, Mississippi, QB	453
	4th—Ed Dyas, Auburn, HB	319
1961	**Ernie Davis,** Syracuse, HB	824
	2nd—Bob Ferguson, Ohio St., HB	771
	3rd—Jimmy Saxton, Texas, HB	551
	4th—Sandy Stephens, Minnesota, QB	543
1962	**Terry Baker,** Oregon St., QB	707
	2nd—Jerry Stovall, LSU, HB	618
	3rd—Bobby Bell, Minnesota, T	429
	4th—Lee Roy Jordan, Alabama, C	321
1963 *	**Roger Staubach,** Navy, QB	1,860
	2nd—Billy Lothridge, Georgia Tech, QB	504
	3rd—Sherman Lewis, Michigan St., HB	369
	4th—Don Trull, Baylor, QB	253
1964	**John Huarte,** Notre Dame, QB	1,026
	2nd—Jerry Rhome, Tulsa, QB	952
	3rd—Dick Butkus, Illinois, C	505
	4th—Bob Timberlake, Michigan, QB	361
1965	**Mike Garrett,** Southern Cal, HB	926
	2nd—Howard Twilley, Tulsa, E	528
	3rd—Jim Grabowski, Illinois, FB	481
	4th—Donny Anderson, Texas Tech, HB	408
1966	**Steve Spurrier,** Florida, QB	1,679
	2nd—Bob Griese, Purdue, QB	816
	3rd—Nick Eddy, Notre Dame, HB	456
	4th—Gary Beban, UCLA, QB	318
1967	**Gary Beban,** UCLA, QB	1,968
	2nd—O. J. Simpson, Southern Cal, HB	1,722
	3rd—Leroy Keyes, Purdue, HB	1,366
	4th—Larry Csonka, Syracuse, FB	136
1968	**O. J. Simpson,** Southern Cal, HB	2,853
	2nd—Leroy Keyes, Purdue, HB	1,103
	3rd—Terry Hanratty, Notre Dame, QB	387
	4th—Ted Kwalik, Penn St., TE	254
1969	**Steve Owens,** Oklahoma, HB	1,488
	2nd—Mike Phipps, Purdue, QB	1,344
	3rd—Rex Kern, Ohio St., QB	856
	4th—Archie Manning, Mississippi, QB	582
1970	**Jim Plunkett,** Stanford, QB	2,229
	2nd—Joe Theismann, Notre Dame, QB	1,410
	3rd—Archie Manning, Mississippi, QB	849
	4th—Steve Worster, Texas, RB	398
1971	**Pat Sullivan,** Auburn, QB	1,597
	2nd—Ed Marinaro, Cornell, RB	1,445
	3rd—Greg Pruitt, Oklahoma, RB	586
	4th—Johnny Musso, Alabama, RB	365
1972	**Johnny Rodgers,** Nebraska, WR	1,310
	2nd—Greg Pruitt, Oklahoma, RB	966
	3rd—Rich Glover, Nebraska, MG	652
	4th—Bert Jones, LSU, QB	351
1973	**John Cappelletti,** Penn St., RB	1,057
	2nd—John Hicks, Ohio St., OT	524
	3rd—Roosevelt Leaks, Texas, RB	482
	4th—David Jaynes, Kansas, QB	394
1974 *	**Archie Griffin,** Ohio St., RB	1,920
	2nd—Anthony Davis, Southern Cal, RB	819
	3rd—Joe Washington, Oklahoma, RB	661
	4th—Tom Clements, Notre Dame, QB	244
1975	**Archie Griffin,** Ohio St., RB	1,800
	2nd—Chuck Muncie, California, RB	730
	3rd—Ricky Bell, Southern Cal, RB	708
	4th—Tony Dorsett, Pittsburgh, RB	616
1976	**Tony Dorsett,** Pittsburgh, RB	2,357
	2nd—Ricky Bell, Southern Cal, RB	1,346
	3rd—Rob Lytle, Michigan, RB	413
	4th—Terry Miller, Oklahoma St., RB	197
1977	**Earl Campbell,** Texas, RB	1,547
	2nd—Terry Miller, Oklahoma St., RB	812
	3rd—Ken MacAfee, Notre Dame, TE	343
	4th—Doug Williams, Grambling, QB	266
1978 *	**Billy Sims,** Oklahoma, RB	827
	2nd—Chuck Fusina, Penn St., QB	750
	3rd—Rick Leach, Michigan, QB	435
	4th—Charles White, Southern Cal, RB	354
1979	**Charles White,** Southern Cal, RB	1,695
	2nd—Billy Sims, Oklahoma, RB	773
	3rd—Marc Wilson, Brigham Young, QB	589
	4th—Art Schlichter, Ohio St., QB	251
1980	**George Rogers,** South Caro., RB	1,128
	2nd—Hugh Green, Pittsburgh, DE	861
	3rd—Herschel Walker, Georgia, RB	683
	4th—Mark Hermann, Purdue, QB	405
1981	**Marcus Allen,** Southern Cal, RB	1,797
	2nd—Herschel Walker, Georgia, RB	1,199
	3rd—Jim McMahon, Brigham Young, QB	706
	4th—Dan Marino, Pittsburgh, QB	256
1982 *	**Herschel Walker,** Georgia, RB	1,926
	2nd—John Elway, Stanford, QB	1,231
	3rd—Eric Dickerson, Southern Meth., RB	465
	4th—Anthony Carter, Michigan, WR	142
1983	**Mike Rozier,** Nebraska, RB	1,801
	2nd—Steve Young, Brigham Young, QB	1,172
	3rd—Doug Flutie, Boston College, QB	253
	4th—Turner Gill, Nebraska, QB	190
1984	**Doug Flutie,** Boston College, QB	2,240
	2nd—Keith Byars, Ohio St., RB	1,251
	3rd—Robbie Bosco, Brigham Young, QB	443
	4th—Bernie Kosar, Miami (Fla.), QB	320
1985	**Bo Jackson,** Auburn, RB	1,509
	2nd—Chuck Long, Iowa, QB	1,464
	3rd—Robbie Bosco, Brigham Young, QB	459
	4th—Lorenzo White, Michigan St., RB	391

1986 **Vinny Testaverde,** Miami (Fla.), QB.....2,213
2nd—Paul Palmer, Temple, RB 672
3rd—Jim Harbaugh, Michigan, QB 458
4th—Brian Bosworth, Oklahoma, LB 395

1987 **Tim Brown,** Notre Dame, WR..............1,442
2nd—Don McPherson, Syracuse, QB...........831
3rd—Gordie Lockbaum, Holy Cross, WR/DB .657
4th—Lorenzo White, Michigan St., RB 632

1988 ***Barry Sanders,** Oklahoma St., RB 1,878
2nd—Rodney Peete, Southern Cal, QB 912
3rd—Troy Aikman, UCLA, QB 582
4th—Steve Walsh, Miami (Fla.), QB 341

1989 ***Andre Ware,** Houston, QB 1,073
2nd—Anthony Thompson, Indiana, RB......1,003
3rd—Major Harris, West Va., QB..............709
4th—Tony Rice, Notre Dame, QB................523

1990 ***Ty Detmer,** Brigham Young, QB 1,482
2nd—Raghib Ismail, Notre Dame, WR 1,177
3rd—Eric Bieniemy, Colorado, RB 798
4th—Shawn Moore, Virginia, QB................465

1991 #**Desmond Howard,** Michigan, WR......2,077
2nd—Casey Weldon, Florida St., QB..........503
3rd—Ty Detmer, Brigham Young, QB 445
4th—Steve Emtman, Washington, DT...........357

1992 **Gino Torretta,** Miami (Fla.), QB 1,400
2nd—Marshall Faulk, San Diego St., RB ...1,080
3rd—Garrison Hearst, Georgia, RB 982
4th—Marvin Jones, Florida St., LB................392

1993 **Charlie Ward,** Florida St., QB 2,310
2nd—Heath Shuler, Tennessee, QB 688
3rd—David Palmer, Alabama, RB 292
4th—Marshall Faulk, San Diego St., RB 250

1994 ***Rashaan Salaam,** Colorado, RB..........1,743
2nd—Ki-Jana Carter, Penn St., RB................901
3rd—Steve McNair, Alcorn St., QB.............655
4th—Kerry Collins, Penn St., QB..................639

**Winner as junior (all others seniors). #Had one year of eligibility remaining.*

1995 Heisman Voting

(Voting on a 3-2-1 basis)	1st	2nd	3rd	Total
1. Eddie George, RB, Ohio St.	268	248	160	1,460
2. Tommie Frazier, QB, Nebraska	218	192	158	1,196
3. *Danny Wuerffel, QB, Florida	185	152	128	987
4. *Darnell Autry, RB, Northwestern...........	87	78	118	535
5. #Troy Davis, RB, Iowa St.	41	80	119	402
6. #Peyton Manning, QB, Tennessee	10	21	37	109
7. Keyshawn Johnson, WR, Southern Cal	9	10	12	59
8. *Tim Biakabutuka, RB, Michigan.................	1	11	6	31
9. *Warrick Dunn, RB, Florida St.................	2	3	17	29
10. Bobby Hoying, QB, Ohio St.	0	9	10	28

**Junior. #Sophomore. All others seniors.*

OUTLAND TROPHY

Honoring the outstanding interior lineman in the nation, first presented in 1946 by the Football Writers Association of America. The award is named for its benefactor, Dr. John H. Outland.

Year	Player, College, Position
1946	George Connor, Notre Dame, T
1947	Joe Steffy, Army, G
1948	Bill Fischer, Notre Dame, G
1949	Ed Bagdon, Michigan St., G
1950	Bob Gain, Kentucky, T
1951	Jim Weatherall, Oklahoma, T
1952	Dick Modzelewski, Maryland, T
1953	J. D. Roberts, Oklahoma, G
1954	Bill Brooks, Arkansas, G
1955	Calvin Jones, Iowa, G
1956	Jim Parker, Ohio St., G
1957	Alex Karras, Iowa, T
1958	Zeke Smith, Auburn, G
1959	Mike McGee, Duke, T
1960	Tom Brown, Minnesota, G
1961	Merlin Olsen, Utah St., T
1962	Bobby Bell, Minnesota, T
1963	Scott Appleton, Texas, T
1964	Steve DeLong, Tennessee, T
1965	Tommy Nobis, Texas, G
1966	Loyd Phillips, Arkansas, T
1967	Ron Yary, Southern Cal, T
1968	Bill Stanfill, Georgia, T
1969	Mike Reid, Penn St., DT
1970	Jim Stillwagon, Ohio St., MG
1971	Larry Jacobson, Nebraska, DT
1972	Rich Glover, Nebraska, MG
1973	John Hicks, Ohio St., OT
1974	Randy White, Maryland, DE
1975	Lee Roy Selmon, Oklahoma, DT
1976	*Ross Browner, Notre Dame, DE
1977	Brad Shearer, Texas, DT
1978	Greg Roberts, Oklahoma, G
1979	Jim Ritcher, North Caro. St., C
1980	Mark May, Pittsburgh, OT
1981	*Dave Rimington, Nebraska, C
1982	Dave Rimington, Nebraska, C
1983	Dean Steinkuhler, Nebraska, G
1984	Bruce Smith, Virginia Tech, DT
1985	Mike Ruth, Boston College, NG
1986	Jason Buck, Brigham Young, DT
1987	Chad Hennings, Air Force, DT
1988	Tracy Rocker, Auburn, DT
1989	Mohammed Elewonibi, Brigham Young, G
1990	Russell Maryland, Miami (Fla.), DT
1991	*Steve Emtman, Washington, DT
1992	Will Shields, Nebraska, G
1993	Rob Waldrop, Arizona, NG
1994	Zach Wiegert, Nebraska, OT
1995	Jonathan Ogden, UCLA, OT

**Junior (all others seniors).*

VINCE LOMBARDI/ROTARY AWARD

Honoring the outstanding college lineman of the year, first presented in 1970 by the Rotary Club of Houston, Texas. The award is named after professional football coach Vince Lombardi, a member of the legendary "Seven Blocks of Granite" at Fordham in the 1930s.

Year	Player, College, Position
1970	Jim Stillwagon, Ohio St., MG
1971	Walt Patulski, Notre Dame, DE
1972	Rich Glover, Nebraska, MG
1973	John Hicks, Ohio St., OT
1974	Randy White, Maryland, DT
1975	Lee Roy Selmon, Oklahoma, DT
1976	Wilson Whitley, Houston, DT
1977	Ross Browner, Notre Dame, DE
1978	Bruce Clark, Penn St., DT
1979	Brad Budde, Southern Cal, G
1980	Hugh Green, Pittsburgh, DE
1981	Kenneth Sims, Texas, DT
1982	Dave Rimington, Nebraska, C
1983	Dean Steinkuhler, Nebraska, G
1984	Tony Degrate, Texas, DT
1985	Tony Casillas, Oklahoma, NG
1986	Cornelius Bennett, Alabama, LB
1987	Chris Spielman, Ohio St., LB
1988	Tracy Rocker, Auburn, DT
1989	Percy Snow, Michigan St., LB
1990	Chris Zorich, Notre Dame, NT
1991	Steve Emtman, Washington, DT
1992	Marvin Jones, Florida St., LB
1993	Aaron Taylor, Notre Dame, OT
1994	Warren Sapp, Miami (Fla.), DT
1995	Orlando Pace, Ohio St., OT

MAXWELL AWARD

Honoring the nation's outstanding college football player, first presented in 1937 by the Maxwell Memorial Football Club of Philadelphia. The award is named after Robert "Tiny" Maxwell, a Philadelphia native who played at the University of Chicago as a lineman near the turn of the century.

Year	Player, College, Position
1937	Clint Frank, Yale, HB
1938	Davey O'Brien, Texas Christian, QB
1939	Nile Kinnick, Iowa, HB
1940	Tom Harmon, Michigan, HB
1941	Bill Dudley, Virginia, HB
1942	Paul Governali, Columbia, QB
1943	Bob Odell, Pennsylvania, HB
1944	Glenn Davis, Army, HB
1945	Doc Blanchard, Army, FB
1946	Charley Trippi, Georgia, HB
1947	Doak Walker, Southern Methodist, HB
1948	Chuck Bednarik, Pennsylvania, C
1949	Leon Hart, Notre Dame, E
1950	Reds Bagnell, Pennsylvania, HB
1951	Dick Kazmaier, Princeton, HB
1952	Johnny Lattner, Notre Dame, HB
1953	Johnny Lattner, Notre Dame, HB
1954	Ron Beagle, Navy, E
1955	Howard Cassady, Ohio St., HB
1956	Tommy McDonald, Oklahoma, HB
1957	Bob Reifsnyder, Navy, T
1958	Pete Dawkins, Army, HB
1959	Rich Lucas, Penn St., QB
1960	Joe Bellino, Navy, HB
1961	Bob Ferguson, Ohio St., FB
1962	Terry Baker, Oregon St., QB
1963	Roger Staubach, Navy, QB
1964	Glenn Ressler, Penn St., C
1965	Tommy Nobis, Texas, LB
1966	Jim Lynch, Notre Dame, LB
1967	Gary Beban, UCLA, QB
1968	O. J. Simpson, Southern Cal, RB
1969	Mike Reid, Penn St., DT
1970	Jim Plunkett, Stanford, QB
1971	Ed Marinaro, Cornell, RB
1972	Brad VanPelt, Michigan St., DB
1973	John Cappelletti, Penn St., RB
1974	Steve Joachim, Temple, QB
1975	Archie Griffin, Ohio St., RB
1976	Tony Dorsett, Pittsburgh, RB
1977	Ross Browner, Notre Dame, DE
1978	Chuck Fusina, Penn St., QB
1979	Charles White, Southern Cal, RB
1980	Hugh Green, Pittsburgh, DE
1981	Marcus Allen, Southern Cal, RB
1982	Herschel Walker, Georgia, RB
1983	Mike Rozier, Nebraska, RB
1984	Doug Flutie, Boston College, QB
1985	Chuck Long, Iowa, QB
1986	Vinny Testaverde, Miami (Fla.), QB
1987	Don McPherson, Syracuse, QB
1988	Barry Sanders, Oklahoma St., RB
1989	Anthony Thompson, Indiana, RB
1990	Ty Detmer, Brigham Young, QB
1991	Desmond Howard, Michigan, WR
1992	Gino Torretta, Miami (Fla.), QB
1993	Charlie Ward, Florida St., QB
1994	Kerry Collins, Penn St., QB
1995	Eddie George, Ohio St., RB

WALTER CAMP AWARD

Honoring the nation's outstanding football player, first presented in 1937 by the Walter Camp Football Foundation in balloting by Division I-A coaches and sports information directors. The award is named after Walter Camp, one of the giants of football who introduced many of the innovations that led to the evolution of the American style of football.

Year	Player, College, Position
1937	Marshall Goldberg, Pittsburgh, HB
1938	Davey O'Brien, Texas Christian, QB
1939	Nile Kinnick, Iowa, HB
1940	Tom Harmon, Michigan, HB
1941	Bill Dudley, Virginia, HB
1942	Frank Sinkwich, Georgia, HB
1943	Angelo Bertelli, Notre Dame, QB
1944	Glenn Davis, Army, HB
1945	Doc Blanchard, Army, FB
1946	Charley Trippi, Georgia, HB
1947	Johnny Lujack, Notre Dame, QB
1948	Charlie Justice, North Caro., HB
1949	Emil Sitko, Notre Dame, HB
1950	Babe Parilli, Kentucky, QB
1951	Dick Kazmaier, Princeton, TB
1952	Don McAuliffe, Michigan St., HB

Year	Player, College, Position
1953	Alan Ameche, Wisconsin, FB
	Bernie Faloney, Maryland, QB
	Paul Giel, Minnesota, HB
	Johnny Lattner, Notre Dame, HB
1954	Ralph Guglielmi, Notre Dame, QB
1955	Howard Cassady, Ohio St., HB
1956	Paul Hornung, Notre Dame, QB
1957	John David Crow, Texas A&M, HB
1958	Randy Duncan, Iowa, QB
1959	Billy Cannon, LSU, HB
1960	Joe Bellino, Navy, HB
1961	Ernie Davis, Syracuse, HB
1962	Jerry Stovall, LSU, HB
1963	Roger Staubach, Navy, QB
1964	Jerry Rhome, Tulsa, QB
1965	Jim Grabowski, Illinois, FB
1966	Steve Spurrier, Florida, QB
1967	Gary Beban, UCLA, QB
1968	O. J. Simpson, Southern Cal, HB
1969	Archie Manning, Mississippi, QB
1970	Ed Marinaro, Cornell, RB
1971	Ed Marinaro, Cornell, RB
1972	Greg Pruitt, Oklahoma, RB
1973	John Cappelletti, Penn St., RB
1974	Anthony Davis, Southern Cal, HB
1975	Chuck Muncie, California, HB
1976	Tony Dorsett, Pittsburgh, RB
1977	Earl Campbell, Texas, HB
1978	Chuck Fusina, Penn St., QB
1979	Charles White, Southern Cal, RB
1980	Herschel Walker, Georgia, RB
1981	Art Schlichter, Ohio St., QB
1982	John Elway, Stanford, QB
1983	Mike Rozier, Nebraska, RB
1984	Keith Byars, Ohio St., RB
1985	Lorenzo White, Michigan St., RB
1986	Paul Palmer, Temple, RB
1987	Tim Brown, Notre Dame, WR
1988	Barry Sanders, Oklahoma St., RB
1989	Anthony Thompson, Indiana, RB
1990	Raghib Ismail, Notre Dame, RB/WR
1991	Desmond Howard, Michigan, WR
1992	Gino Torretta, Miami (Fla.), QB
1993	Charlie Ward, Florida St., QB
1994	Rashaan Salaam, Colorado, RB
1995	Eddie George, Ohio St., RB

BUTKUS AWARD

First presented in 1985 to honor the nation's best collegiate linebacker by the Downtown Athletic Club of Orlando, Fla. The award is named after Dick Butkus, two-time consensus all-American at Illinois and six-time all-pro linebacker with the Chicago Bears.

Year	Player, College
1985	Brian Bosworth, Oklahoma
1986	Brian Bosworth, Oklahoma
1987	Paul McGowan, Florida St.
1988	Derrick Thomas, Alabama
1989	Percy Snow, Michigan St.
1990	Alfred Williams, Colorado
1991	Erick Anderson, Michigan
1992	Marvin Jones, Florida St.
1993	Trev Alberts, Nebraska
1994	Dana Howard, Illinois
1995	Kevin Hardy, Illinois

JIM THORPE AWARD

First presented in 1986 to honor the nation's best defensive back by the Jim Thorpe Athletic Club of Oklahoma City. The award is named after Jim Thorpe, Olympic champion, two-time consensus all-American halfback at Carlisle and professional football player.

Year	Player, College
1986	Thomas Everett, Baylor
1987	(tie) Bennie Blades, Miami (Fla.)
	Rickey Dixon, Oklahoma
1988	Deion Sanders, Florida St.
1989	Mark Carrier, Southern Cal
1990	Darryll Lewis, Arizona
1991	Terrell Buckley, Florida St.
1992	Deon Figures, Colorado
1993	Antonio Langham, Alabama
1994	Chris Hudson, Colorado
1995	Greg Myers, Colorado St.

DAVEY O'BRIEN NATIONAL QUARTERBACK AWARD

First presented in 1977 as the O'Brien Memorial Trophy to the outstanding player in the Southwest. In 1981, the Davey O'Brien Educational and Charitable Trust of Fort Worth, Texas, renamed the award the Davey O'Brien National Quarterback Award, and it now honors the nation's best quarterback.

MEMORIAL TROPHY

Year	Player, College, Position
1977	Earl Campbell, Texas, RB
1978	Billy Sims, Oklahoma, RB
1979	Mike Singletary, Baylor, LB
1980	Mike Singletary, Baylor, LB

NATIONAL QB AWARD

Year	Player, College
1981	Jim McMahon, Brigham Young
1982	Todd Blackledge, Penn St.
1983	Steve Young, Brigham Young
1984	Doug Flutie, Boston College
1985	Chuck Long, Iowa
1986	Vinny Testaverde, Miami (Fla.)
1987	Don McPherson, Syracuse
1988	Troy Aikman, UCLA
1989	Andre Ware, Houston
1990	Ty Detmer, Brigham Young
1991	Ty Detmer, Brigham Young
1992	Gino Torretta, Miami (Fla.)
1993	Charlie Ward, Florida St.
1994	Kerry Collins, Penn St.
1995	Danny Wuerffel, Florida

DOAK WALKER NATIONAL RUNNING BACK AWARD

Presented for the first time in 1990 to honor the nation's best running back among Division I-A juniors or seniors who combine outstanding achievements on the field, in the classroom and in the community. Sponsored by the GTE/Southern Methodist Athletic Forum in Dallas, Texas, a $10,000 scholarship is donated to the recipient's university in his name. It is voted on by a 16-member panel of media and former college football standouts. The award is named after Doak Walker, Southern Methodist's three-time consensus all-American halfback and 1948 Heisman Trophy winner.

Year	Player, College
1990	Greg Lewis, Washington
1991	Trevor Cobb, Rice
1992	Garrison Hearst, Georgia
1993	Byron Morris, Texas Tech
1994	Rashaan Salaam, Colorado
1995	Eddie George, Ohio St.

LOU GROZA COLLEGIATE PLACE-KICKER AWARD

Presented for the first time in 1992 to honor the nation's top collegiate place-kicker. Sponsored by the Palm Beach County Sports Authority in conjunction with the Orange Bowl Committee. The award is named after NFL Hall of Fame kicker Lou Groza.

Year	Player, College
1992	Joe Allison, Memphis
1993	Judd Davis, Florida
1994	Steve McLaughlin, Arizona
1995	Michael Reeder, Texas Christian

FRED BILETNIKOFF RECEIVER AWARD

First presented in 1994 to honor the nation's top collegiate pass receiver. Sponsored by the Downtown Athletic Club of Orlando, Fla. The award is named after Fred Biletnikoff, former Florida State all-American and NFL Oakland Raider receiver, a member of both the College Football Hall of Fame and Pro Football Hall of Fame.

Year	Player, College
1994	Bobby Engram, Penn St.
1995	Terry Glenn, Ohio St.

Photo from St. John's (Minnesota) sports information

St. John's (Minnesota) wide receiver Chris Palmer won the 1995 Gagliardi Trophy, presented to the nation's outstanding Division III player. The award is named after John Gagliardi, who coached Palmer at St. John's.

AWARD WINNERS

WALTER PAYTON PLAYER OF THE YEAR AWARD

First presented in 1987 to honor the top Division I-AA football player by the Sports Network and voted on by Division I-AA sports information directors. The award is named after Walter Payton, former Jackson State player and the National Football League's all-time leading rusher.

Year	Player, College, Position
1987	Kenny Gamble, Colgate, RB
1988	Dave Meggett, Towson St., RB
1989	John Friesz, Idaho, QB
1990	Walter Dean, Grambling, RB
1991	Jamie Martin, Weber St., QB
1992	Michael Payton, Marshall, QB
1993	Doug Nussmeier, Idaho, QB
1994	Steve McNair, Alcorn St., QB
1995	Dave Dickenson, Montana, QB

ERNIE DAVIS AWARD

First presented in 1992 to honor a Division I-AA college football player who has overcome personal, athletic or academic adversity and performs in an exemplary manner. The annual award is presented by the American Sports Wire of Saugus, Calif., and is named after the late Ernie Davis, Syracuse halfback who won the Heisman Trophy in 1961.

Year	Player, College, Position
1992	Gilad Landau, Grambling, PK
1993	Jay Walker, Howard, QB
1994	Steve McNair, Alcorn St., QB
1995	Earl Holmes, Florida A&M, LB

HARLON HILL TROPHY

First presented in 1986 to honor the best Division II player by Division II sports information directors. The award is named after Harlon Hill, former receiver at North Alabama and the National Football League's most valuable player for the Chicago Bears in 1955.

Year	Player, College, Position
1986	Jeff Bentrim, North Dak. St., QB
1987	Johnny Bailey, Tex. A&M-Kingsville, RB
1988	Johnny Bailey, Tex. A&M-Kingsville, RB
1989	Johnny Bailey, Tex. A&M-Kingsville, RB
1990	Chris Simdorn, North Dak. St., QB
1991	Ronnie West, Pittsburg St., WR
1992	Ronald Moore, Pittsburg St., RB
1993	Roger Graham, New Haven, RB
1994	Chris Hatcher, Valdosta St., QB
1995	Ronald McKinnon, North Ala., LB

BRONKO NAGURSKI AWARD

First presented in 1993 to honor the nation's top collegiate defensive player. Presented by the Football Writers Association of America.

Year	Player, College, Position
1993	Rob Waldrop, Arizona, DL
1994	Warren Sapp, Miami (Fla.), DT
1995	Pat Fitzgerald, Northwestern, LB

EDDIE ROBINSON TROPHY

First presented in 1994 to the top college football player from a historically black college. Presented by a panel of sportswriters, sports information directors and coaches.

Year	Player, College, Position
1994	Steve McNair, Alcorn St., QB

GAGLIARDI TROPHY

First presented in 1993 to the nation's outstanding Division III player. Presented by the St. John's (Minn.) J-Club. The award is named after John Gagliardi, St. John's head coach for 43 seasons and one of only five coaches in college football history to win 300 games.

Year	Player, College, Position
1993	Jim Ballard, Mount Union, QB
1994	Carey Bender, Coe, RB
1995	Chris Palmer, St. John's (Minn.), WR

MELBERGER AWARD

First presented in 1995 to the nation's outstanding Division III player by the Wilkes-Barre (Pa.) Touchdown Club.

Year	Player, College, Position
1995	Craig Kusick, Wis.-La Crosse, QB

1995 COACHING AWARDS

Home Depot Coach of the Year—Gary Barnett, Northwestern

Bear Bryant Coach of the Year—Gary Barnett, Northwestern

American Football Coaches Association Coach of the Year (I-A)—Gary Barnett, Northwestern

American Football Coaches Association Coach of the Year (I-AA)—Don Read, Montana

American Football Coaches Association Coach of the Year (NCAA II & NAIA I)—Bobby Wallace, North Ala.

American Football Coaches Association Coach of the Year (NCAA III & NAIA II)—Roger Harring, Wis.-La Crosse

COLLEGE FOOTBALL HALL OF FAME

Established: In 1947, by the National Football Foundation and College Hall of Fame, Inc. The first class of enshrinees was inducted in 1951. **Eligibility:** A nominated player must be out of college at least 10 years and a first-team all-America selection by a major selector during his career. Coaches must be retired three years. The voting is done by a 12-member panel made up of athletics directors, conference and bowl officials, and media representatives.

Class of 1996 (to be inducted at the National Football Foundation and College Hall of Fame's 39th annual awards dinner December 10 in New York, N.Y.): Players—FB Bob Ferguson, Ohio St. (1959-61); DE Hugh Green, Pittsburgh (1977-80); T Frank Merritt, Army (1940-43); G John Michels, Tennessee (1950-52); C/LB Bob Pellegrini, Maryland (1953-55); E Pat Richter, Wisconsin (1960-62); LB Jerry Robinson, UCLA (1975-78); RB James Saxton, Texas (1959-61); C/LB Jerry Tubbs, Oklahoma (1954-56); RB Charles White, Southern Cal (1976-79); QB Marc Wilson, Brigham Young (1977-79). Coach—Henry "Red" Sanders, Vanderbilt (1940-42, 46-48) and UCLA 1949-57).

Member players are listed with the final year they played in college, and member coaches are listed with their year of induction. (†) Indicates deceased members. (#) Indicates dual member of Pro Football Hall of Fame.

Hall Facts: Only two individuals are enshrined in the College Football Hall of Fame as both a player and a coach. Amos Alonzo Stagg was an all-American at Yale (1889) and was inducted as a coach in 1951. The other two-way inductee is Bobby Dodd, who played at Tennessee (1930) and was inducted as a coach in 1993.

PLAYERS

Player, College	Year
†Earl Abell, Colgate	1915
Alex Agase, Purdue/Illinois	1946
†Harry Agganis, Boston U.	1952
Frank Albert, Stanford	1941
†Ki Aldrich, Texas Christian	1938
†Malcolm Aldrich, Yale	1921
†Joe Alexander, Syracuse	1920
Lance Alworth, Arkansas#	1961
†Alan Ameche, Wisconsin	1954
†Knowlton Ames, Princeton	1889
Warren Amling, Ohio St.	1946
Dick Anderson, Colorado	1967
Donny Anderson, Texas Tech	1966
†Hunk Anderson, Notre Dame	1921
Doug Atkins, Tennessee#	1952
Bob Babich, Miami (Ohio)	1968
†Everett Bacon, Wesleyan	1912
†Reds Bagnell, Pennsylvania	1950
†Hobey Baker, Princeton	1913
†John Baker, Southern Cal	1931
†Moon Baker, Northwestern	1926
Terry Baker, Oregon St.	1962
†Harold Ballin, Princeton	1914
†Bill Banker, Tulane	1929
Vince Banonis, Detroit	1941
†Stan Barnes, California	1921
†Charles Barrett, Cornell	1915
†Bert Baston, Minnesota	1916
†Cliff Battles, West Va. Wesleyan#	1931
Sammy Baugh, Texas Christian#	1936
Maxie Baughan, Georgia Tech	1959
†James Bausch, Kansas	1930
Ron Beagle, Navy	1955
Gary Beban, UCLA	1967
Hub Bechtol, Texas	1946
†John Beckett, Oregon	1916
Chuck Bednarik, Pennsylvania#	1948
Forrest Behm, Nebraska	1940
Bobby Bell, Minnesota#	1962
Joe Bellino, Navy	1960
†Marty Below, Wisconsin	1923
†Al Benbrook, Michigan	1910
†Charlie Berry, Lafayette	1924
Angelo Bertelli, Notre Dame	1943
Jay Berwanger, Chicago	1935
†Lawrence Bettencourt, St. Mary's (Cal.)	1927
Fred Biletnikoff, Florida St.#	1964
Doc Blanchard, Army	1946
†Al Blozis, Georgetown	1942
Ed Bock, Iowa St.	1938
†Lynn Bomar, Vanderbilt	1924
†Douglass Bomeisler, Yale	1913
†Albie Booth, Yale	1931
†Fred Borries, Navy	1934
Bruce Bosely, West Va.	1955
Don Bosseler, Miami (Fla.)	1956
Vic Bottari, California	1938
†Ben Boynton, Williams	1920
†Charles Brewer, Harvard	1895
†Johnny Bright, Drake	1951
John Brodie, Stanford	1956
†George Brooke, Pennsylvania	1895
Bob Brown, Nebraska	1963
George Brown, Navy/San Diego St.	1947
†Gordon Brown, Yale	1900
Jim Brown, Syracuse#	1956
†John Brown Jr., Navy	1913
†Johnny Mack Brown, Alabama	1925
†Tay Brown, Southern Cal	1932
†Paul Bunker, Army	1902
Chris Burford, Stanford	1959
Ron Burton, Northwestern	1959
Dick Butkus, Illinois#	1964
†Robert Butler, Wisconsin	1912
George Cafego, Tennessee	1939
†Red Cagle, Southwestern La./Army	1929
†John Cain, Alabama	1932
Ed Cameron, Wash. & Lee	1924
†David Campbell, Harvard	1901
Earl Campbell, Texas#	1977
†Jack Cannon, Notre Dame	1929
John Cappelletti, Penn St.	1973
†Frank Carideo, Notre Dame	1930
†Charles Carney, Illinois	1921
J. C. Caroline, Illinois	1954
Bill Carpenter, Army	1959
†Hunter Carpenter, Virginia Tech	1905
Charles Carroll, Washington	1928
Tommy Casanova, LSU	1971
†Edward Casey, Harvard	1919
Howard Cassady, Ohio St.	1955
†Guy Chamberlin, Nebraska#	1915
Sam Chapman, California	1938
Bob Chappuis, Michigan	1947
†Paul Christman, Missouri	1940
†Dutch Clark, Colorado Col.#	1929
Paul Cleary, Southern Cal	1947
†Zora Clevenger, Indiana	1903
Jack Cloud, William & Mary	1948
†Gary Cochran, Princeton	1897
†Josh Cody, Vanderbilt	1919
Don Coleman, Michigan St.	1951
†Charlie Conerly, Mississippi	1947
George Connor, Holy Cross/Notre Dame#	1947
†William Corbin, Yale	1888
William Corbus, Stanford	1933
†Hector Cowan, Princeton	1889
†Edward Coy, Yale	1909
†Fred Crawford, Duke	1933
John David Crow, Texas A&M	1957
†Jim Crowley, Notre Dame	1924
Larry Csonka, Syracuse#	1967
Slade Cutter, Navy	1934
†Ziggie Czarobski, Notre Dame	1947
Carroll Dale, Virginia Tech	1959
†Gerald Dalrymple, Tulane	1931
†John Dalton, Navy	1911
†Charles Daly, Harvard/Army	1902
Averell Daniell, Pittsburgh	1936
†James Daniell, Ohio St.	1941
†Tom Davies, Pittsburgh	1921
†Ernie Davis, Syracuse	1961
Glenn Davis, Army	1946
Robert Davis, Georgia Tech	1947
Pete Dawkins, Army	1958
Steve DeLong, Tennessee	1964
Al DeRogatis, Duke	1948
†Paul DesJardien, Chicago	1914
†Aubrey Devine, Iowa	1921
†John DeWitt, Princeton	1903
Buddy Dial, Rice	1958
Mike Ditka, Pittsburgh#	1960
Glenn Dobbs, Tulsa	1942
†Bobby Dodd, Tennessee	1930
Holland Donan, Princeton	1950
†Joseph Donchess, Pittsburgh	1929
Tony Dorsett, Pittsburgh#	1976
†Nathan Dougherty, Tennessee	1909
Nick Drahos, Cornell	1940
†Paddy Driscoll, Northwestern#	1917
†Morley Drury, Southern Cal	1927
Bill Dudley, Virginia#	1941
Kenny Easley, UCLA	1980
†Walter Eckersall, Chicago	1906
†Turk Edwards, Washington St.	1931
†William Edwards, Princeton	1899
†Ray Eichenlaub, Notre Dame	1914
Steve Eisenhauer, Navy	1953
Lawrence Elkins, Baylor	1964
Bump Elliott, Michigan/Purdue	1947
Pete Elliott, Michigan	1948
Ray Evans, Kansas	1947
†Albert Exendine, Carlisle	1907

Player, College	Year
†Nello Falaschi, Santa Clara	1936
Tom Fears, Santa Clara/UCLA#	1947
†Beattie Feathers, Tennessee	1933
Bob Fenimore, Oklahoma St.	1946
†Doc Fenton, LSU	1909
John Ferraro, Southern Cal	1944
†Wes Fesler, Ohio St.	1930
†Bill Fincher, Georgia Tech	1920
Bill Fischer, Notre Dame	1948
†Hamilton Fish, Harvard	1909
†Robert Fisher, Harvard	1911
†Allen Flowers, Georgia Tech	1920
†Danny Fortmann, Colgate#	1935
Sam Francis, Nebraska	1936
†Ed Franco, Fordham	1937
†Clint Frank, Yale	1937
Rodney Franz, California	1949
Tucker Frederickson, Auburn	1964
†Benny Friedman, Michigan	1926
Roman Gabriel, North Caro. St.	1961
Bob Gain, Kentucky	1950
†Arnold Galiffa, Army	1949
Hugh Gallarneau, Stanford	1940
†Edgar Garbisch, Wash. & Jeff./Army	1924
Mike Garrett, Southern Cal	1965
†Charles Gelbert, Pennsylvania	1896
†Forest Geyer, Oklahoma	1915
Jake Gibbs, Mississippi	1960
Paul Giel, Minnesota	1953
Frank Gifford, Southern Cal#	1951
†Walter Gilbert, Auburn	1936
Harry Gilmer, Alabama	1947
†George Gipp, Notre Dame	1920
†Chet Gladchuk, Boston College	1940
Bill Glass, Baylor	1956
Rich Glover, Nebraska	1972
Marshall Goldberg, Pittsburgh	1938
Gene Goodreault, Boston College	1940
†Walter Gordon, California	1918
†Paul Governali, Columbia	1942
Jim Grabowski, Illinois	1965
Otto Graham, Northwestern#	1943
†Red Grange, Illinois#	1925
†Bobby Grayson, Stanford	1935
†Jack Green, Tulane/Army	1945
Joe Greene, North Texas#	1968
Bob Griese, Purdue#	1966
Archie Griffin, Ohio St.	1975
Jerry Groom, Notre Dame	1950
†Merle Gulick, Toledo/Hobart	1929
†Joe Guyon, Georgia Tech#	1918
John Hadl, Kansas	1961
†Edwin Hale, Mississippi Col.	1921
L. Parker Hall, Mississippi	1938
Jack Ham, Penn St.#	1970
Bob Hamilton, Stanford	1935
†Tom Hamilton, Navy	1926
†Vic Hanson, Syracuse	1926
†Pat Harder, Wisconsin	1942
†Tack Hardwick, Harvard	1914
†T. Truxton Hare, Pennsylvania	1900
†Chick Harley, Ohio St.	1919
†Tom Harmon, Michigan	1940
†Howard Harpster, Carnegie Mellon	1928
†Edward Hart, Princeton	1911
Leon Hart, Notre Dame	1949
Bill Hartman, Georgia	1937
†Homer Hazel, Rutgers	1924
†Matt Hazeltine, California	1954
†Ed Healey, Dartmouth#	1916
†Pudge Heffelfinger, Yale	1891
†Mel Hein, Washington St.#	1930
†Don Heinrich, Washington	1952
Ted Hendricks, Miami (Fla.)#	1968
†Wilbur Henry, Wash. & Jeff.#	1919
†Clarence Herschberger, Chicago	1898
†Robert Herwig, California	1937
†Willie Heston, Michigan	1904
†Herman Hickman, Tennessee	1931
†William Hickok, Yale	1894
†Dan Hill, Duke	1938
†Art Hillebrand, Princeton	1899

Player, College	Year
†Frank Hinkey, Yale	1894
†Carl Hinkle, Vanderbilt	1937
†Clarke Hinkle, Bucknell#	1931
Elroy Hirsch, Wisconsin/Michigan#	1943
†James Hitchcock, Auburn	1932
Frank Hoffmann, Notre Dame	1931
†James J. Hogan, Yale	1904
†Brud Holland, Cornell	1938
†Don Holleder, Army	1955
†Bill Hollenback, Pennsylvania	1908
Mike Holovak, Boston College	1942
E. J. Holub, Texas Tech	1960
Paul Hornung, Notre Dame#	1956
†Edwin Horrell, California	1924
†Les Horvath, Ohio St.	1944
†Arthur Howe, Yale	1911
†Dixie Howell, Alabama	1934
†Cal Hubbard, Centenary (La.)#	1926
†John Hubbard, Amherst	1906
†Pooley Hubert, Alabama	1925
Sam Huff, West Va.#	1955
Weldon Humble, Rice	1946
†Joel Hunt, Texas A&M	1927
†Ellery Huntington, Colgate	1914
Don Hutson, Alabama#	1934
†Jonas Ingram, Navy	1906
†Cecil Isbell, Purdue	1937
†Harvey Jablonsky, Army/Washington	1933
†Vic Janowicz, Ohio St.	1951
†Darold Jenkins, Missouri	1941
†Jackie Jensen, California	1948
†Herbert Joesting, Minnesota	1927
Bob Johnson, Tennessee	1967
†Jimmie Johnson, Carlisle/Northwestern	1903
Ron Johnson, Michigan	1968
†Calvin Jones, Iowa	1955
†Gomer Jones, Ohio St.	1935
Lee Roy Jordan, Alabama	1962
†Frank Juhan, Sewanee	1910
Charlie Justice, North Caro.	1949
†Mort Kaer, Southern Cal	1926
Alex Karras, Iowa	1957
Ken Kavanaugh, LSU	1939
†Edgar Kaw, Cornell	1922
Dick Kazmaier, Princeton	1951
†Stan Keck, Princeton	1921
Larry Kelley, Yale	1936
†Wild Bill Kelly, Montana	1926
Doug Kenna, Army	1944
†George Kerr, Boston College	1941
†Henry Ketcham, Yale	1913
Leroy Keyes, Purdue	1968
†Glenn Killinger, Penn St.	1921
†John Kilpatrick, Yale	1910
John Kimbrough, Texas A&M	1940
†Frank Kinard, Mississippi#	1937
†Phillip King, Princeton	1893
†Nile Kinnick, Iowa	1939
†Harry Kipke, Michigan	1923
†John Kitzmiller, Oregon	1930
†Barton Koch, Baylor	1931
†Walt Koppisch, Columbia	1924
Ron Kramer, Michigan	1956
Charlie Krueger, Texas A&M	1957
Malcolm Kutner, Texas	1941
Ted Kwalick, Penn St.	1968
†Steve Lach, Duke	1941
†Myles Lane, Dartmouth	1927
Johnny Lattner, Notre Dame	1953
Hank Lauricella, Tennessee	1952
†Lester Lautenschlaeger, Tulane	1925
†Elmer Layden, Notre Dame	1924
†Bobby Layne, Texas#	1947
†Langdon Lea, Princeton	1895
Eddie LeBaron, Pacific (Cal.)	1949
†James Leech, Va. Military	1920
†Darrell Lester, Texas Christian	1935
Bob Lilly, Texas Christian#	1960
†Augie Lio, Georgetown	1940
Floyd Little, Syracuse	1966
†Gordon Locke, Iowa	1922
†Don Lourie, Princeton	1921
Richie Lucas, Penn St.	1959

Player, College	Year
Sid Luckman, Columbia#	1938
Johnny Lujack, Notre Dame	1947
†Pug Lund, Minnesota	1934
Jim Lynch, Notre Dame	1966
Robert MacLeod, Dartmouth	1938
†Bart Macomber, Illinois	1915
Dicky Maegle, Rice	1954
†Ned Mahon, Harvard	1915
Johnny Majors, Tennessee	1956
†William Mallory, Yale	1923
Vaughn Mancha, Alabama	1947
†Gerald Mann, Southern Methodist	1927
Archie Manning, Mississippi	1970
Edgar Manske, Northwestern	1933
Ed Marinaro, Cornell	1971
Vic Markov, Washington	1937
†Bobby Marshall, Minnesota	1906
Jim Martin, Notre Dame	1949
Ollie Matson, San Francisco#	1952
Ray Matthews, Texas Christian	1927
†John Maulbetsch, Michigan	1914
†Pete Mauthe, Penn St.	1912
†Robert Maxwell, Chicago/Swarthmore	1906
George McAfee, Duke#	1939
†Thomas McClung, Yale	1891
Bill McColl, Stanford	1951
†Jim McCormick, Princeton	1907
Tommy McDonald, Oklahoma	1956
†Jack McDowall, North Caro. St.	1927
Hugh McElhenny, Washington#	1951
†Gene McEver, Tennessee	1931
†John McEwan, Army	1916
Banks McFadden, Clemson	1939
Bud McFadin, Texas	1950
Mike McGee, Duke	1959
†Edward McGinley, Pennsylvania	1924
†John McGovern, Minnesota	1910
Thurman McGraw, Colorado St.	1949
†Mike McKeever, Southern Cal	1960
†George McLaren, Pittsburgh	1918
†Dan McMillan, Southern Cal/California	1922
†Bo McMillin, Centre	1921
†Bob McWhorter, Georgia	1913
†LeRoy Mercer, Pennsylvania	1912
Don Meredith, Southern Methodist	1959
†Bert Metzger, Notre Dame	1930
†Wayne Meylan, Nebraska	1967
Lou Michaels, Kentucky	1957
Abe Mickal, LSU	1935
Creighton Miller, Notre Dame	1943
†Don Miller, Notre Dame	1924
†Eugene Miller, Penn St.	1913
†Fred Miller, Notre Dame	1928
†Rip Miller, Notre Dame	1924
†Wayne Millner, Notre Dame#	1935
†Century Milstead, Wabash/Yale	1923
†John Minds, Pennsylvania	1897
Skip Minisi, Pennsylvania/Navy	1947
Dick Modzelewski, Maryland	1952
†Alex Moffat, Princeton	1883
†Ed Molinski, Tennessee	1940
Cliff Montgomery, Columbia	1933
Donn Moomaw, UCLA	1952
†William Morley, Columbia	1902
George Morris, Georgia Tech	1952
Larry Morris, Georgia Tech	1954
†Bill Morton, Dartmouth	1931
Craig Morton, California	1964
†Monk Moscrip, Stanford	1935
†Brick Muller, California	1922
†Bronko Nagurski, Minnesota#	1929
†Ernie Nevers, Stanford#	1925
†Marshall Newell, Harvard	1893
Harry Newman, Michigan	1932
Ozzie Newsome, Alabama	1977
Gifford Nielsen, Brigham Young	1977
Tommy Nobis, Texas	1965
Leo Nomellini, Minnesota#	1949
†Andrew Oberlander, Dartmouth	1925
†Davey O'Brien, Texas Christian	1938
†Pat O'Dea, Wisconsin	1899
Bob Odell, Pennsylvania	1943

Player, College	Year
†Jack O'Hearn, Cornell	1915
Robin Olds, Army	1942
†Elmer Oliphant, Army/Purdue	1917
Merlin Olsen, Utah St.#	1961
†Bennie Oosterbaan, Michigan	1927
Charles O'Rourke, Boston College	1940
†John Orsi, Colgate	1931
†Win Osgood, Cornell/Pennsylvania	1894
Bill Osmanski, Holy Cross	1938
†George Owen, Harvard	1922
Jim Owens, Oklahoma	1949
Steve Owens, Oklahoma	1969
Alan Page, Notre Dame#	1966
Jack Pardee, Texas A&M	1956
Babe Parilli, Kentucky	1951
Ace Parker, Duke#	1936
Jackie Parker, Mississippi St.	1953
Jim Parker, Ohio St.#	1956
†Vince Pazzetti, Lehigh	1912
Chub Peabody, Harvard	1941
†Robert Peck, Pittsburgh	1916
†Stan Pennock, Harvard	1914
George Pfann, Cornell	1923
†H. D. Phillips, Sewanee	1904
Loyd Phillips, Arkansas	1966
Pete Pihos, Indiana#	1946
†Erny Pinckert, Southern Cal	1931
John Pingel, Michigan St.	1938
Jim Plunkett, Stanford	1970
†Arthur Poe, Princeton	1899
†Fritz Pollard, Brown	1916
George Poole, Mississippi/North Caro./Army	1947
Marvin Powell, Southern Cal	1976
Merv Pregulman, Michigan	1943
†Eddie Price, Tulane	1949
†Peter Pund, Georgia Tech	1928
Garrard Ramsey, William & Mary	1942
Rick Redman, Washington	1964
†Claude Reeds, Oklahoma	1913
Mike Reid, Penn St.	1969
Steve Reid, Northwestern	1936
†William Reid, Harvard	1899
Mel Renfro, Oregon	1963
†Pug Rentner, Northwestern	1932
†Bob Reynolds, Stanford	1935
†Bobby Reynolds, Nebraska	1952
Les Richter, California	1951
†Jack Riley, Northwestern	1931
†Charles Rinehart, Lafayette	1897
J. D. Roberts, Oklahoma	1953
†Paul Robeson, Rutgers	1918
†Ira Rodgers, West Va.	1919
†Edward Rogers, Carlisle/Minnesota	1903
Joe Romig, Colorado	1961
†Aaron Rosenberg, Southern Cal	1933
Kyle Rote, Southern Methodist	1950
†Joe Routt, Texas A&M	1937
†Red Salmon, Notre Dame	1903
†George Sauer, Nebraska	1933
George Savitsky, Pennsylvania	1947
Gale Sayers, Kansas#	1964
Jack Scarbath, Maryland	1952
†Hunter Scarlett, Pennsylvania	1908
Bob Schloredt, Washington	1960
†Wear Schoonover, Arkansas	1929
†Dave Schreiner, Wisconsin	1942
†Germany Schultz, Michigan	1908
†Dutch Schwab, Lafayette	1922
†Marchy Schwartz, Notre Dame	1931
†Paul Schwegler, Washington	1931
Clyde Scott, Navy/Arkansas	1948
Richard Scott, Navy	1947
Tom Scott, Virginia	1953
†Henry Seibels, Sewanee	1899
Ron Sellers, Florida St.	1968
Lee Roy Selmon, Oklahoma#	1975
†Bill Shakespeare, Notre Dame	1935
†Murray Shelton, Cornell	1915
†Tom Shevlin, Yale	1905
†Bernie Shively, Illinois	1926
†Monk Simons, Tulane	1934
O. J. Simpson, Southern Cal#	1968
Billy Sims, Oklahoma	1979

Player, College	Year
Mike Singletary, Baylor	1980
Fred Sington, Alabama	1930
†Frank Sinkwich, Georgia	1942
†Emil Sitko, Notre Dame	1949
†Joe Skladany, Pittsburgh	1933
†Duke Slater, Iowa	1921
†Bruce Smith, Minnesota	1941
Bubba Smith, Michigan St.	1966
†Clipper Smith, Notre Dame	1927
†Ernie Smith, Southern Cal	1932
Harry Smith, Southern Cal	1939
Jim Ray Smith, Baylor	1954
Riley Smith, Alabama	1935
†Vernon Smith, Georgia	1931
†Neil Snow, Michigan	1901
Al Sparlis, UCLA	1945
†Clarence Spears, Dartmouth	1915
†W. D. Spears, Vanderbilt	1927
†William Sprackling, Brown	1911
†Bud Sprague, Army/Texas	1928
Steve Spurrier, Florida	1966
Harrison Stafford, Texas	1932
†Amos Alonzo Stagg, Yale	1889
†Max Starcevich, Washington	1936
Roger Staubach, Navy#	1964
†Walter Steffen, Chicago	1908
Joe Steffy, Tennessee/Army	1947
†Herbert Stein, Pittsburgh	1921
Bob Steuber, Missouri	1943
†Mal Stevens, Yale	1923
†Vincent Stevenson, Pennsylvania	1905
Jim Stillwagon, Ohio St.	1970
†Pete Stinchcomb, Ohio St.	1920
Brock Strom, Air Force	1959
†Ken Strong, New York U.#	1928
†George Strupper, Georgia Tech	1917
†Harry Stuhldreher, Notre Dame	1924
†Herb Sturhan, Yale	1926
†Joe Stydahar, West Va.#	1935
†Bob Suffridge, Tennessee	1940
†Steve Suhey, Penn St.	1947
Pat Sullivan, Auburn	1971
†Frank Sundstrom, Cornell	1923
Lynn Swann, Southern Cal	1973
†Clarence Swanson, Nebraska	1921
†Bill Swiacki, Columbia	1947
Jim Swink, Texas Christian	1956
George Taliaferro, Indiana	1948
Fran Tarkenton, Georgia#	1960
John Tavener, Indiana	1944
†Chuck Taylor, Stanford	1942
Aurelius Thomas, Ohio St.	1957
†Joe Thompson, Pittsburgh	1907
†Samuel Thorne, Yale	1895
†Jim Thorpe, Carlisle#	1912
†Ben Ticknor, Harvard	1930
†John Tigert, Vanderbilt	1904
Gaynell Tinsley, LSU	1936
Eric Tipton, Duke	1938
Clayton Tonnemaker, Minnesota	1949
†Bob Torrey, Pennsylvania	1905
†Brick Travis, Missouri	1920
Charley Trippi, Georgia#	1946
†Edward Tryon, Colgate	1925
Bulldog Turner, Hardin-Simmons#	1939
Howard Twilley, Tulsa	1965
†Joe Utay, Texas A&M	1907
†Norm Van Brocklin, Oregon#	1948
†Dale Van Sickel, Florida	1929
†H. Van Surdam, Wesleyan	1905
†Dexter Very, Penn St.	1912
Billy Vessels, Oklahoma	1952
†Ernie Vick, Michigan	1921
†Hube Wagner, Pittsburgh	1913
Doak Walker, Southern Methodist#	1949
†Bill Wallace, Rice	1935
†Adam Walsh, Notre Dame	1924
†Cotton Warburton, Southern Cal	1934
Bob Ward, Maryland	1951
†William Warner, Cornell	1904
†Kenny Washington, UCLA	1939
†Jim Weatherall, Oklahoma	1951

Player, College	Year
George Webster, Michigan St.	1966
Herman Wedemeyer, St. Mary's (Cal.)	1947
†Harold Weekes, Columbia	1902
Art Weiner, North Caro.	1949
†Ed Weir, Nebraska	1925
†Gus Welch, Carlisle	1914
†John Weller, Princeton	1935
†Percy Wendell, Harvard	1912
†Belford West, Colgate	1919
†Bob Westfall, Michigan	1941
†Babe Weyand, Army	1915
†Buck Wharton, Pennsylvania	1896
†Arthur Wheeler, Princeton	1894
Byron White, Colorado	1938
Randy White, Maryland#	1974
†Don Whitmire, Navy/Alabama	1944
†Frank Wickhorst, Navy	1926
Ed Widseth, Minnesota	1936
†Dick Wildung, Minnesota	1942
Bob Williams, Notre Dame	1950
Froggie Williams, Rice	1949
Bill Willis, Ohio St.	1944
Bobby Wilson, Southern Methodist	1935
†George Wilson, Washington	1925
†Harry Wilson, Army/Penn St.	1926
Mike Wilson, Lafayette	1928
Albert Wistert, Michigan	1942
Alvin Wistert, Michigan	1949
†Whitey Wistert, Michigan	1933
†Alex Wojciechowicz, Fordham#	1937
†Barry Wood, Harvard	1931
†Andy Wyant, Chicago	1894
†Bowden Wyatt, Tennessee	1938
†Clint Wyckoff, Cornell	1895
†Tommy Yarr, Notre Dame	1931
Ron Yary, Southern Cal	1967
†Lloyd Yoder, Carnegie Mellon	1926
†Buddy Young, Illinois	1946
†Harry Young, Wash. & Lee	1916
†Waddy Young, Oklahoma	1938
Jack Youngblood, Florida	1970
Gust Zarnas, Ohio St.	1937

COACHES

Coach	Year
†Joe Aillet	1989
†Bill Alexander	1951
†Ed Anderson	1971
†Ike Armstrong	1957
†Charlie Bachman	1978
Earl Banks	1992
†Harry Baujan	1990
†Matty Bell	1955
†Hugo Bezdek	1954
†Dana X. Bible	1951
†Bernie Bierman	1955
Bob Blackman	1987
†Earl (Red) Blaik	1965
Frank Broyles	1983
†Paul (Bear) Bryant	1986
†Charlie Caldwell	1961
†Walter Camp	1951
Len Casanova	1977
†Frank Cavanaugh	1954
†Dick Colman	1990
†Fritz Crisler	1954
†Duffy Daugherty	1984
Bob Devaney	1981
Dan Devine	1985
†Gil Dobie	1951
†Bobby Dodd	1993
†Michael Donohue	1951
Vince Dooley	1994
†Gus Dorais	1954
†Bill Edwards	1986
†Rip Engle	1973
†Don Faurot	1961
†Jake Gaither	1973
Sid Gillman#	1989
†Ernest Godfrey	1972
Ray Graves	1990
†Andy Gustafson	1985
†Edward Hall	1951

Coach	Year
†Jack Harding	1980
†Richard Harlow	1954
†Harvey Harman	1981
†Jesse Harper	1971
†Percy Haughton	1951
†Woody Hayes	1983
†John W. Heisman	1954
†Robert Higgins	1954
†Babe Hollingberry	1979
†Frank Howard	1989
†Bill Ingram	1973
†Morley Jennings	1973
†Biff Jones	1954
†Howard Jones	1951
†Tad Jones	1958
†Lloyd Jordan	1978
†Ralph (Shug) Jordan	1982
†Andy Kerr	1951
Frank Kush	1995
†Frank Leahy	1970
†George Little	1955
†Lou Little	1960
†Slip Madigan	1974
Dave Maurer	1991
Charlie McClendon	1986
Herb McCracken	1973
†Dan McGugin	1951
John McKay	1988
Allyn McKeen	1991
†Tuss McLaughry	1962
John Merritt	1994
†Dutch Meyer	1956
†Jack Mollenkopf	1988
†Bernie Moore	1954
†Scrappy Moore	1980
†Ray Morrison	1954
†George Munger	1976
†Clarence (Biggie) Munn	1959
†Bill Murray	1974
†Frank Murray	1983
†Ed (Hooks) Mylin	1974
†Earle (Greasy) Neale	1967
†Jess Neely	1971
†David Nelson	1987
†Robert Neyland	1956
†Homer Norton	1971
†Frank (Buck) O'Neill	1951
†Bennie Owen	1951
Ara Parseghian	1980
†Doyt Perry	1988
†Jimmy Phelan	1973
†Tommy Prothro	1991
John Ralston	1992
†E. N. Robinson	1955
†Knute Rockne	1951
†Dick Romney	1954
†Bill Roper	1951
Darrell Royal	1983
†George Sanford	1971
Glenn (Bo) Schembechler	1993
†Francis Schmidt	1971
†Ben Schwartzwalder	1982
†Clark Shaughnessy	1968
†Buck Shaw	1972
†Andy Smith	1951
†Carl Snavely	1965
†Amos Alonzo Stagg	1951
†Jock Sutherland	1951
†Jim Tatum	1984
†Frank Thomas	1951
†Thad Vann	1987
Johnny Vaught	1979
†Wallace Wade	1955
†Lynn (Pappy) Waldorf	1966
†Glenn (Pop) Warner	1951
†E. E. (Tad) Wieman	1956
†John Wilce	1954
†Bud Wilkinson	1969
†Henry Williams	1951
†George Woodruff	1963
Warren Woodson	1989
†Fielding (Hurry Up) Yost	1951
†Bob Zuppke	1951

First-Team All-Americans Below Division I-A

1995 Selectors (and division[s]): American Football Coaches Association (I-AA, II, III); Associated Press (I-AA, II, III); College Sports Information Directors of America (II); Football Gazette (I-AA, II, III); Hewlett-Packard (III); Sports Network (I-AA); Walter Camp (I-AA)

Selection of Associated Press Little All-America Teams began in 1934. Early AP selectors were not bound by NCAA membership classifications; therefore, several current Division I-A teams are included in this list.

The American Football Coaches Association began selecting all-America teams below Division I-A in 1967 for two College-Division classifications. Its College-Division I team includes NCAA Division II and National Association of Intercollegiate Athletics (NAIA) Division I players. The AFCA College-Division II team includes NCAA Division III and NAIA Division II players. The AFCA added a Division I-AA team in 1979; AP began selecting a Division I-AA team in 1982; the Sports Network added a Division I-AA team in 1994; and these players are included. In 1993, the College Sports Information Directors of America Division II team was added, selected by sports information directors from every NCAA Division II institution. In 1990, the Champion USA Division III team was added, selected by a panel of 25 sports information directors and replaced by the Hewlett-Packard Division III team in 1995. In 1993, Football Gazette's team was added for Divisions I-AA, II and III.

Nonmembers of the NCAA are included in this list, as are colleges that no longer play varsity football.

Players selected to a Division I-AA all-America team are indicated by (†). Current members of Division I-A are indicated by (*).

All-Americans are listed by college, year selected and position.

ABILENE CHRISTIAN (16)
48— V. T. Smith, B
51— Lester Wheeler, OT
52— Wallace Bullington, DB
65— Larry Cox, OT
69— Chip Bennett, LB
70— Jim Lindsey, QB
73— Wilbert Montgomery, RB
74— Chip Martin, DL
77— Chuck Sitton, DB
82— Grant Feasel, C
83— Mark Wilson, DB
84— Dan Remsberg, OT
87— Richard Van Druten, OT
89— John Layfield, OG
90— Dennis Brown, PK
91— Jay Jones, LB

ADAMS ST. (4)
79— Ronald Johnson, DB
84— Bill Stone, RB
87— Dave Humann, DB
95— Chris Perry, WR

AKRON* (9)
69— John Travis, OG
71— Michael Hatch, DB
76— Mark Van Horn, OG
Steve Cockerham, LB
77— Steve Cockerham, LB
80—†Brad Reece, LB
81—†Brad Reece, LB
85—†Wayne Grant, DL
86—†Mike Clark, RB

ALA.-BIRMINGHAM* (1)
94—†Derrick Ingram, WR

ALABAMA A&M (3)
87— Howard Ballard, OL
88— Fred Garner, DB
89— Barry Wagner, WR

ALABAMA ST. (3)
90—†Eddie Robinson, LB
91—†Patrick Johnson, OL
†Eddie Robinson, LB

ALBANY (N.Y.) (2)
92— Scott Turrin, OL
94— Scott Turrin, OL

ALBANY ST. (GA.) (1)
72— Harold Little, DE

ALBION (12)
40— Walter Ptak, G
58— Tom Taylor, E
76— Steve Spencer, DL
86— Joe Felton, OG
Mike Grant, DB
91— Hank Wineman, RB
93— Ron Dawson, OL
Jeff Brooks, OL
94— Jeff Robinson, RB
Martin Heyboer, C
David Lefere, DB
95— David Lefere, DB

ALBRIGHT (4)
36— Richard Riffle, B
37— Richard Riffle, B
75— Chris Simcic, OL
95— Dennis Unger, PK

ALCORN ST. (13)
69— David Hadley, DB
70— Fred Carter, DT
71— Harry Gooden, LB
72— Alex Price, DT
73— Leonard Fairley, DB
74— Jerry Dismuke, OG
75— Lawrence Pillers, DE
76— Augusta Lee, RB
Larry Warren, DT
79—†Leslie Frazier, DB
84—†Issiac Holt, DB
93—†Goree White, KR
94—†Steve McNair, QB

ALFRED (7)
51— Ralph DiMicco, B
52— Ralph DiMicco, B
55— Charles Schultz, E
56— Charles Schultz, E
75— Joseph Van Cura, DE
82— Brian O'Neil, DB
92— Mark Obuszewski, DB

ALLEGHENY (17)
75— Charles Slater, OL
87— Mike Mates, OL
88— Mike Parker, DL
90— Jeff Filkovski, QB
David LaCarte, DB
John Marzca, C
91— Ron Bendekovic, OT
Stanley Drayton, RB
Tony Bifulco, DB
92— Ron Bendekovic, OT
Stanley Drayton, RB
94— Matt Allison, OL
Paul Bell, QB
Marvin Farr, DB
95— Brian Adams, C
Nick Reiser, DE
Anson Park, OL

AMERICAN INT'L (10)
71— Bruce Laird, RB
80— Ed Cebula, C
82— Paul Thompson, DT
85— Keith Barry, OL
86— Jon Provost, OL
87— Jon Provost, OL
88— Greg Doherty, OL
89— Lamont Cato, DB
90— George Patterson, DL
91— Gabe Mokwuah, DL

AMHERST (3)
42— Adrian Hasse, E
72— Richard Murphy, QB
73— Fred Scott, FL

ANGELO ST. (13)
75— James Cross, DB
78— Jerry Aldridge, RB
Kelvin Smith, LB
81— Clay Weishuhn, LB
82— Mike Elarms, WR
83— Mike Thomas, K
85— Henry Jackson, LB
86— Pierce Holt, DL

AWARD WINNERS

87— Pierce Holt, DL
88— Henry Alsbrooks, LB
92— Jimmy Morris, P
93— Anthony Hooper, DB
95— Greg Stokes, LB

APPALACHIAN ST. (19)
48— John Caskey, E
63— Greg Van Orden, G
85— †Dino Hackett, LB
87— †Anthony Downs, DE
88— †Bjorn Nittmo, PK
89— †Derrick Graham, OL
†Keith Collins, DB
91— †Harold Alexander, P
92— †Avery Hall, DL
†Harold Alexander, P
94— †Chip Miller, DL
†William Peebles, DL
†Brad Ohrt, OL
†Dexter Coakley, LB
†Matt Stevens, DB
95— †Dexter Coakley, LB
†Matt Stevens, DB
†Chip Miller, DL
†Scott Kadlub, C

ARIZONA* (1)
41— Henry Stanton, E

ARKANSAS ST.* (17)
53— Richard Woit, B
64— Dan Summers, OG
65— Dan Summers, OG
68— Bill Bergey, LB
69— Dan Buckley, C
Clovis Swinney, DT
70— Bill Phillips, OG
Calvin Harrell, HB
71— Calvin Harrell, RB
Dennis Meyer, DB
Wayne Dorton, OG
73— Doug Lowrey, OG
84— †Carter Crawford, DL
85— †Carter Crawford, DL
86— †Randy Barnhill, OG
87— †Jim Wiseman, C
†Charlie Fredrick, DT

ARKANSAS TECH (3)
58— Edward Meador, B
61— Powell McClellan, E
95— Piotr Styczen, PK

ASHLAND (9)
70— Len Pettigrew, LB
78— Keith Dare, DL
85— Jeff Penko, OL
86— Vince Mazza, PK
89— Douglas Powell, DB
90— Morris Furman, LB
91— Ron Greer, LB
93— Bill Royce, DL
94— Sam Hohler, DE

AUGUSTANA (ILL.) (11)
72— Willie Van, DT
73— Robert Martin, OT
83— Kurt Kapischke, OL
84— Greg King, C
86— Lynn Thomsen, DL
87— Carlton Beasley, DL
88— John Bothe, OL
90— Barry Reade, PK
91— Mike Hesler, DB
92— George Annang, DL
95— Rusty Van Wetzinga, LB

AUGUSTANA (S.D.) (4)
60— John Simko, E
87— Tony Adkins, DL
88— Pete Jaros, DB
94— Bryan Schwartz, LB

AUSTIN (10)
37— Wallace Johnson, C
79— Price Clifford, LB
80— Chris Luper, DB
81— Larry Shillings, QB
83— Ed Holt, DL
84— Jeff Timmons, PK
87— Otis Amy, WR
88— Otis Amy, WR
90— Jeff Cordell, DB
94— Brent Badger, P

AUSTIN PEAY (8)
65— Tim Chilcutt, DB
66— John Ogles, FB
70— Harold Roberts, OE
77— Bob Bible, LB
78— Mike Betts, DB
80— Brett Williams, DE
82— Charlie Tucker, OL
92— †Richard Darden, DL

AZUSA PACIFIC (2)
86— Christian Okoye, RB
95— Jake Wiersma, OL

BAKER (3)
83— Chris Brown, LB
85— Kevin Alewine, RB
90— John Campbell, OL

BALDWIN-WALLACE (11)
50— Norbert Hecker, E
68— Bob Quackenbush, DT
78— Jeff Jenkins, OL
80— Dan Delfino, DE
82— Pete Primeau, DL
83— Steve Varga, K
89— Doug Halbert, DL
91— John Koz, QB
Jim Clardy, LB
94— Chris Kondik, PK
Phil Sahley, DL

BALL ST.* (4)
67— Oscar Lubke, OT
68— Amos Van Pelt, HB
72— Douglas Bell, C
73— Terry Schmidt, DB

BATES (1)
81— Larry DiGammarino, WR

BELOIT (1)
95— Maurice Redd, DB

BEMIDJI ST. (1)
83— Bruce Ecklund, TE

BENEDICTINE (1)
36— Leo Deutsch, E

BETHANY (W.VA.) (2)
77— Scott Lanz, P
93— Brian Darden, PK

BETHEL (KAN.) (1)
80— David Morford, C

BETHUNE-COOKMAN (2)
75— Willie Lee, DE
81— Booker Reese, DE

BIRMINGHAM-SOUTHERN (1)
37— Walter Riddle, T

BISHOP (1)
81— Carlton Nelson, DL

BLOOMSBURG (7)
79— Mike Morucci, RB
82— Mike Blake, TE
83— Frank Sheptock, LB
84— Frank Sheptock, LB
85— Frank Sheptock, LB
Tony Woods, DB
91— Eric Jonassen, OL

BOISE ST. (23)
72— Al Marshall, OE
73— Don Hutt, WR
74— Jim McMillan, QB
75— John Smith, FL
77— Chris Malmgren, DT
Terry Hutt, WR
Harold Cotton, OT
79— †Joe Aliotti, QB
†Doug Scott, DT
80— †Randy Trautman, DT
81— †Randy Trautman, DT
†Rick Woods, DB
82— †John Rade, DL
†Carl Keever, LB
84— †Carl Keever, LB
85— †Marcus Koch, DL
87— †Tom DeWitz, OG
†Pete Kwiatkowski, DT
90— †Erik Helgeson, DL
91— †Frank Robinson, DB
92— †Michael Dodd, PK
94— †Joe O'Brien, DL
†Rashid Gayle, DB

BOSTON U. (17)
67— Dick Farley, DB
68— Bruce Taylor, DB
69— Bruce Taylor, DB
79— †Mal Najarian, RB
†Tom Pierzga, DL
81— †Bob Speight, OT
†Gregg Drew, RB
82— †Mike Mastrogiacomo, OG
83— †Paul Lewis, RB
84— †Paul Lewis, RB
86— †Kevin Murphy, DT
87— †Mark Seals, DB
88— †Mark Seals, DB
89— †Daren Altieri, WR
93— †Chris Helon, DB
†Andre Maksimov, C
94— †Andre Maksimov, C

BOWDOIN (1)
77— Steve McCabe, OL

BOWIE ST. (2)
80— Victor Jackson, CB
81— Marco Tongue, DB

BOWLING GREEN* (2)
59— Bob Zimpfer, T
82— †Andre Young, DL

BRADLEY (1)
38— Ted Panish, B

BRANDEIS (2)
54— William McKenna, E
56— James Stehlin, B

BRIDGEPORT (1)
72— Dennis Paldin, DB

BRI'WATER (MASS.) (1)
92— Erik Arthur, DL

BRIDGEWATER (VA.) (1)
75— C. J. DeWitt, SE

BROCKPORT ST. (2)
90— Ed Smart, TE
93— Steve Milne, PK

BUCKNELL (8)
51— George Young, DT
60— Paul Terhes, B
64— Tom Mitchell, OE
65— Tom Mitchell, OE
74— Larry Schoenberger, LB
80— Mike McDonald, OT
90— †Mike Augsberger, DB
95— †Ed Burman, DL

BUENA VISTA (4)
72— Joe Kotval, OG
73— Joe Kotval, OG
76— Keith Kerkhoff, DL
87— Jim Higley, LB

BUFFALO (3)
84— Gerry Quinlivan, LB
87— Steve Wojciechowski, LB
95— †Pete Conley, LB

BUFFALO ST. (1)
93— John Mattey, OL

BUTLER (2)
88— Steve Roberts, RB
94— †Arnold Mickens, RB

UC DAVIS (11)
72— Bob Biggs, QB
David Roberts, OT
76— Andrew Gagnon, OL
77— Chuck Fomasi, DT
78— Casey Merrill, DL
79— Jeffrey Allen, DB
82— Ken O'Brien, QB
83— Bo Eason, DB
84— Scott Barry, QB
85— Mike Wise, DL
94— Aaron Bennetts, TE

UC RIVERSIDE (1)
75— Michael Johnson, SE

UC SANTA BARB. (3)
36— Douglas Oldershaw, G
37— Douglas Oldershaw, G
67— Paul Vallerga, DB

CALIF. (PA.) (1)
83— Perry Kemp, WR

CAL LUTHERAN (3)
72— Brian Kelley, LB
79— Mike Hagen, SE
95— Jeff Shea, P

CAL POLY SLO (13)
53— Stan Sheriff, C
58— Charles Gonzales, G
66— David Edmondson, C
72— Mike Amos, DB
73— Fred Stewart, OG
78— Louis Jackson, RB
80— Louis Jackson, RB
Robbie Martin, FL
81— Charles Daum, OL
84— Nick Frost, DB
89— Robert Morris, DL
90— Pat Moore, DL
91— Doug O'Neill, P

CAL ST. CHICO (1)
87— Chris Verhulst, TE

CAL ST. HAYWARD (4)
75— Greg Blankenship, LB
84— Ed Lively, DT
86— Fred Williams, OL
93— Jeff Williamson, TE

CAL ST. NORTHRIDGE (6)
75— Mel Wilson, DB
82— Pat Hauser, OT
83— Pat Hauser, OT
87— Kip Dukes, DB
91— Don Goodman, OL
94— †Joe Vaughn, DB

CAL ST. SACRAMENTO (4)
64— William Fuller, OT
91— Troy Mills, RB
Jim Crouch, PK
92— Jon Kirksey, DL

CANISIUS (3)
87— Tom Doctor, LB
88— Marty Hurley, DB
94— †Aaron Fix, PR

CAPITAL (3)
74— Greg Arnold, OG
80— John Phillips, DL
Steve Wigton, C

CARLETON (1)
90— Jim Bradford, WR

CARNEGIE MELLON (4)
81— Ken Murawski, LB
85— Robert Butts, OL
91— Chuck Jackson, OT
93— Chad Wilson, LB

CARROLL (MONT.) (5)
76— Richard Dale, DB
79— Don Diggins, DL
87— Jeff Beaudry, DB
88— Paul Petrino, QB
89— Suitoa Keleti, OL

CARROLL (WIS.) (3)
74— Robert Helf, TE
90— Bill Nolan, P
93— Andy Ostrand, DB

CARSON-NEWMAN (8)
78— Tank Black, FL
80— Brad Payne, S
83— Dwight Wilson, OL
90— Robert Hardy, RB
92— Darryl Gooden, LB
93— Kendall James, KR
95— Steve Mellon, DL
Anthony Davis, LB

CASE RESERVE (4)
41— Mike Yurcheshen, E
52— Al Feeny, DE
84— Fred Manley, DE
85— Mark Raiff, OL

CATAWBA (5)
34— Charles Garland, T
35— Charles Garland, T
45— Carroll Bowen, B
72— David Taylor, OT
74— Mike McDonald, LB

CATHOLIC (2)
84— Chris McMahon, DB
94— Steve Wilkerson, WR

CENTRAL (IOWA) (14)
70— Vernon Den Herder, DT
74— Al Dorenkamp, LB
77— Donald Taylor, RB
84— Scott Froehle, DB
85— Rich Thomas, DL
88— Mike Stumberg, DL
89— Mike Estes, DL
Kris Reis, LB
92— Bill Maulder, LB
93— Jeff Helle, OL
94— Jeff Helle, OL
Mark Kacmarynski, RB
Rick Sanger, LB
95— Rick Sanger, LB

CENTRAL ARK. (4)
80— Otis Chandler, MG
84— David Burnette, DT
91— David Henson, DL
95— Bart Reynolds, DL

CENTRAL CONN. ST. (4)
74— Mike Walton, C
84— Sal Cintorino, LB
88— Doug Magazu, DL
89— Doug Magazu, DL

CENTRAL FLA.* (4)
87— Bernard Ford, WR
Ed O'Brien, PK
93—†David Rhodes, WR
94—†Charlie Pierce, PK

CENTRAL MICH.* (4)
42— Warren Schmakel, G
59— Walter Beach, B
62— Ralph Soffredine, G
74— Rick Newsome, DL

CENTRAL MO. ST. (5)
68— Jim Urczyk, OT
85— Steve Huff, PK
88— Jeff Wright, DL
92— Bart Woods, DL
93— Bart Woods, DL

CENTRAL OKLA. (4)
65— Jerome Bell, OE
78— Gary Smith, TE
94— Elton Rhoades, DB
Joe Aska, RB

CENTRAL ST. (9)
83— Mark Corbin, RB
84— Dave Dunham, OT
85— Mark Corbin, RB
86— Terry Morrow, RB
89— Kenneth Vines, OG
90— Eric Williams, OL
92— Marvin Coleman, DB
93— Marvin Coleman, DB
94— Hugh Douglas, DL

CENTRAL WASH. (4)
48— Robert Osgood, G
50— Jack Hawkins, G
88— Mike Estes, DL
91— Eric Lamphere, OL

CENTRE (6)
55— Gene Scott, B
84— Teel Bruner, DB
85— Teel Bruner, DB
86— Jeff Leonard, OL
88— John Gohmann, DL
89— Jeff Bezold, LB

CHADRON ST. (4)
74— Dennis Fitzgerald, DB
78— Rick Mastey, OL
90— David Jones, RB
94— Scott Doyle, PK

CHICAGO (4)
91— Neal Cawi, DE
Jeff Stolte, P
93— Frank Baker, FB
95— Derrick Brooms, KR

CITADEL (10)
82— Jim Ettari, DL
84— Jim Gabrish, OL
85— Jim Gabrish, OL
86— Scott Thompson, DT
88—†Carlos Avalos, OL
90—†DeRhon Robinson, OL
92—†Corey Cash, OL
†Lester Smith, DB
94—†Levi Davis, OL
95—†Brad Keeney, DL

CLARION (9)
78— Jeff Langhans, OL
80— Steve Scillitani, MG
Gary McCauley, TE
81— Gary McCauley, TE
83— Elton Brown, RB
85— Chuck Duffy, OL
87— Lou Weiers, DL
93— Tim Brown, TE
95— Kim Neidbala, DB

CLARK ATLANTA (1)
79— Curtis Smith, OL

CLINCH VALLEY (1)
95— Shonn Bell, TE

COAST GUARD (2)
90— Ron Davies, DB
91— Ron Davies, DB

COE (7)
74— Dan Schmidt, OG
76— Paul Wagner, OT
85— Mike Matzen, P
90— Richard Matthews, DB
93— Carey Bender, RB
Craig Chmelicek, OL
94— Carey Bender, RB

COLGATE (7)
82—†Dave Wolf, LB
83—†Rich Erenberg, RB
84—†Tom Stenglein, WR
85—†Tom Stenglein, WR
86—†Kenny Gamble, RB
87—†Kenny Gamble, RB
†Greg Manusky, LB

COL. OF EMPORIA (1)
51— William Chai, OG

COL. OF IDAHO (2)
53— Norman Hayes, T
54— R. C. Owens, E

COLORADO COL. (4)
72— Ed Smith, DE
73— Darryl Crawford, DB
82— Ray Bridges, DL
93— Todd Mays, DL

COLORADO MINES (6)
39— Lloyd Madden, B
41— Dick Moe, T
59— Vince Tesone, B
72— Roger Cirimotich, DB
86— Tim Baer, P
94— Pat Hogelin, P

CONCORD (2)
86— Kevin Johnson, LB
92— Chris Hairston, RB

CONCORDIA-M'HEAD (4)
77— Barry Bennett, DT
90— Mike Gindorff, DT
Shayne Lindsay, NG
95— Tim Lowry, OL

CONNECTICUT (7)
45— Walter Trojanowski, B
73— Richard Foye, C
80—†Reggie Eccleston, WR
83—†John Dorsey, LB
88—†Glenn Antrum, WR
89—†Troy Ashley, LB
91—†Mark Didio, WR

CORNELL (3)
82—†Dan Suren, TE
86—†Tom McHale, DE
93—†Chris Zingo, LB

CORNELL COLLEGE (2)
82— John Ward, WR
92— Brent Sands, DB

CORTLAND ST. (5)
67— Rodney Verkey, DE
89— Jim Cook, OL
90— Chris Lafferty, OG
Vinny Swanda, LB
91— Vinny Swanda, LB

CUMBERLAND (KY.) (4)
87— David Carmichael, DB
89— Ralph McWilliams, OL
93— Doug Binkley, DB
94— Doug Binkley, LB

DAKOTA WESLEYAN (1)
45— Robert Kirkman, T

DARTMOUTH (2)
91—†Al Rosier, RB
92—†Dennis Durkin, PK

DAVIDSON (1)
34— John Mackorell, B

DAYTON (10)
36— Ralph Niehaus, T
78— Rick Chamberlin, LB
81— Chris Chaney, DB
84— David Kemp, LB
86— Gerry Meyer, OL
89— Mike Duvic, PK
90— Steve Harder, OL
91— Brian Olson, OG
92— Andy Pellegrino, OL
94—†Tim Duvic, PK

DEFIANCE (1)
93— Sammy Williams, WR

DELAWARE (31)
42— Hugh Bogovich, G
46— Tony Stalloni, T
54— Don Miller, B
63— Mike Brown, B
66— Herb Slattery, OT
69— John Favero, LB
70— Conway Hayman, OG
71— Gardy Kahoe, RB
72— Joe Carbone, DE
Dennis Johnson, DT
73— Jeff Cannon, DT
74— Ed Clark, LB
Ray Sweeney, OG
75— Sam Miller, DE
76— Robert Pietuszka, DB
78— Jeff Komlo, QB
79—†Herb Beck, OG
†Scott Brunner, QB
80—†Gary Kuhlman, OT
81—†Gary Kuhlman, OL
82—†George Schmitt, DB
85—†Jeff Rosen, OL
86—†Darrell Booker, LB
87—†James Anderson, WR
88—†Mike Renna, DL
89—†Mike Renna, DL
91—†Warren McIntire, DB
92—†Matt Morrill, DL
93—†Matt Morrill, DL
94—†Daryl Brown, RB
95—†Kenny Bailey, DB

DELAWARE ST. (4)
84— Gene Lake, RB
86— Joe Burton, DB
91—†Rod Milstead, OL
92—†LeRoy Thompson, DL

DELTA ST. (2)
67— Leland Hughes, OG
95— Jerome Williams, DB

DENISON (5)
47— William Hart, E
48— William Wehr, C
75— Dennis Thome, DL
79— Clay Sampson, RB
86— Dan Holland, DL

DePAUW (1)
63— Richard Dean, C

DETROIT TECH (1)
39— Mike Kostiuk, T

DICKINSON (3)
91— Shaughn White, DB
92— Brian Ridgway, DL
94— Jason Fox, LB

DICKINSON ST. (2)
81— Tony Moore, DL
92— Rory Farstveet, OL

DOANE (1)
66— Fred Davis, OT

DRAKE (4)
72— Mike Samples, DT
82— Pat Dunsmore, TE
Craig Wederquist, OT
95—†Matt Garvis, LB

DREXEL (2)
55— Vincent Vidas, T
56— Vincent Vidas, T

EAST CARO.* (1)
64— Bill Cline, HB

EAST CENTRAL (1)
84— Don Wilson, C

EAST STROUDSBURG (7)
65— Barry Roach, DB
75— William Stem, DB
79— Ronald Yakavonis, DL
83— Mike Reichenbach, LB
84— Andy Baranek, QB
91— Curtis Bunch, DB
94— Steve Hynes, OL

EAST TENN. ST. (6)
53— Hal Morrison, E
68— Ron Overbay, DB
70— William Casey, DB
85— George Cimadevilla, P
86— George Cimadevilla, P
94—†Jeff Johnson, WR

EAST TEX. ST. (18)
38— Darrell Tully, B
53— Bruno Ashley, G
58— Sam McCord, B
59— Sam McCord, B
68— Chad Brown, OT
70— William Lewis, C
72— Curtis Wester, OG
73— Autry Beamon, DB
84— Alan Veingrad, OG
88— Kim Morton, DL
90— Terry Bagsby, DL
91— Eric Turner, DB
Dwayne Phorne, OL
92— Eric Turner, DB
Pat Williams, DB
93— Fred Woods, LB
Billy Watkins, PK
95— Kevin Mathis, DB

EASTERN ILL. (18)
72— Nate Anderson, RB
76— Ted Petersen, C
78— James Warring, WR
79— Chris Cobb, RB
Pete Catan, DE
80— Pete Catan, DE
81—†Kevin Grey, DB
82—†Robert Williams, DB
†Bob Norris, OG
83—†Robert Williams, DB
†Chris Nicholson, DT
84—†Jerry Wright, WR
86—†Roy Banks, WR
88—†John Jurkovic, DL
89—†John Jurkovic, DL
90—†Tim Lance, DB
95—†Willie High, RB
†Tim Carver, LB

EASTERN KY. (26)
69— Teddy Taylor, MG
74— Everett Talbert, RB
75— Junior Hardin, MG
76— Roosevelt Kelly, OL
79—†Bob McIntyre, LB
80—†George Floyd, DB
81—†George Floyd, DB
†Kevin Greve, OG
82—†Steve Bird, WR
83—†Chris Sullivan, OL
84—†Chris Sullivan, C
85—†Joe Spadafino, OL
86—†Fred Harvey, LB
87—†Aaron Jones, DL
88—†Elroy Harris, RB
†Jessie Small, DL
89—†Al Jacevicius, OL
90—†Kelly Blount, LB
†Al Jacevicius, OL
91—†Carl Satterly, OL
†Ernest Thompson, DL
92—†Markus Thomas, RB
93—†Chad Bratzke, DL
94—†James Hand, OL

AWARD WINNERS

95—†James Hand, OL
†Marc Collins, P

EASTERN MICH.* (5)
68— John Schmidt, C
69— Robert Lints, MG
70— Dave Pureifory, DT
71— Dave Pureifory, DT
73— Jim Pietrzak, OT

EASTERN N.M. (7)
81— Brad Beck, RB
83— Kevin Kott, QB
87— Earl Jones, OL
89— Murray Garrett, DL
90— Anthony Pertile, DB
94— Conrad Hamilton, DB
95— Conrad Hamilton, DB

EASTERN WASH. (7)
57— Richard Huston, C
65— Mel Stanton, HB
73— Scott Garske, TE
81— John Tighe, OL
86— Ed Simmons, OT
87—†Eric Stein, P
91—†Kevin Sargent, OL

EDINBORO (5)
82— Rick Ruszkiewicz, K
89— Elbert Cole, RB
90— Ernest Priester, WR
93— Mike Kegarise, OL
95— Pat Schuster, DL

ELMHURST (1)
82— Lindsay Barich, OL

ELON (9)
50— Sal Gero, T
68— Richard McGeorge, OE
69— Richard McGeorge, OE
73— Glenn Ellis, DT
76— Ricky Locklear, DT
Dan Bass, OL
77— Dan Bass, OL
80— Bobby Hedrick, RB
86— Ricky Sigmon, OL

EMORY & HENRY (14)
50— Robert Miller, B
51— Robert Miller, B
56— William Earp, C
68— Sonny Wade, B
85— Keith Furr, DB
Rob McMillen, DL
86— Sandy Rogers, RB
87— Gary Collier, QB
88— Steve Bowman, DL
89— Doug Reavis, DB
90— Billy Salyers, OL
91— Jason Grooms, DL
92— Pat Buchanan, OL
Scott Pruner, DL

EMPORIA ST. (5)
35— James Fraley, B
37— Harry Klein, E
68— Bruce Cerone, OE
69— Bruce Cerone, OE
91— Quincy Tillmon, RB

EUREKA (1)
95— Kurt Barth, WR

EVANSVILLE (3)
46— Robert Hawkins, T
93—†Hanz Hoag, TE
94—†Hanz Hoag, TE

FDU-MADISON (4)
84— Ira Epstein, DL
86— Eric Brey, DB
87— Frank Illidge, DL
93— Vic Moncato, P

FAIRMONT ST. (3)
67— Dave Williams, DT
84— Ed Coleman, WR
88— Lou Mabin, DB

FAYETTEVILLE ST. (1)
90— Terrence Smith, LB

FERRIS ST. (5)
76— Charles Evans, RB
92— Monty Brown, LB
93— Ed Phillion, DL
94— Tyree Dye, RB
95— Bill Love, QB

FERRUM (5)
87— Dave Harper, LB
88— Dave Harper, LB
89— Chris Warren, RB
90— Melvin Dillard, DB/KR
91— John Sheets, OG

FINDLAY (4)
65— Allen Smith, HB
80— Nelson Bolden, FB
85— Dana Wright, RB
90— Tim Russ, OL

FLORIDA A&M (13)
61— Curtis Miranda, C
62— Robert Paremore, B
67— Major Hazelton, DB
John Eason, OE
73— Henry Lawrence, OT
75— Frank Poole, LB
77— Tyrone McGriff, OG
78— Tyrone McGriff, OG
79—†Tyrone McGriff, OG
†Kiser Lewis, C
80—†Gifford Ramsey, DB
83—†Ray Alexander, WR
95—†Earl Holmes, LB

FLORIDA ST.* (1)
51— William Dawkins, OG

FORT HAYS ST. (2)
95— Lance Schwindt, TE
Shawn Behr, QB

FORT LEWIS (3)
89— Eric Fadness, P
92— Johnny Cox, WR
93— Johnny Cox, AP

FORT VALLEY ST. (7)
74— Fred Harris, OT
80— Willie Canady, DB
81— Willie Canady, DB
83— Tugwan Taylor, DB
92— Joseph Best, DB
93— Joseph Best, DB
94— Tyrone Poole, DB

FRANKLIN (2)
82— Joe Chester, WR
95— Michael Brouwer, DB

FRANK. & MARSH. (9)
35— Woodrow Sponaugle, C
38— Sam Roeder, B
40— Alex Schibanoff, T
47— William Iannicelli, E
50— Charles Cope, C
81— Vin Carioscia, OL
82— Vin Carioscia, OL
89— Dale Amos, WR
95— Steve DeLuca, LB

FRESNO ST.* (5)
39— Jack Mulkey, E
40— Jack Mulkey, E
60— Douglas Brown, G
68— Tom McCall, LB
Erv Hunt, DB

FROSTBURG ST. (10)
80— Terry Beamer, LB
82— Steve Forsythe, WR
83— Kevin Walsh, DL
85— Bill Bagley, WR
86— Marcus Wooley, LB
88— Ken Boyd, DB
89— Ken Boyd, DB
93— Russell Williams, DB
94— Joe Holland, DL
Ariel Bell, KR

FURMAN (11)
82—†Ernest Gibson, DB
83—†Ernest Gibson, DB
84—†Rock Hurst, LB
85—†Gene Reeder, C
88—†Jeff Blankenship, LB
89—†Kelly Fletcher, DL
90—†Steve Duggan, C
†Kevin Kendrick, LB
91—†Eric Walter, OL
92—†Kota Suttle, LB
94—†Jim Richter, PK

GALLAUDET (1)
87— Shannon Simon, OL

GARDNER-WEBB (4)
73— Richard Grissom, LB
87— Jeff Parker, PK
92— Rodney Robinson, WR
93— Gabe Wilkins, DL

GEORGETOWN (3)
73— Robert Morris, DE
74— Robert Morris, DE
91— Chris Murphy, DE

GEORGETOWN (KY.) (8)
74— Charles Pierson, DL
78— John Martinelli, OL
85— Rob McCrary, RB
87— Chris Reed, C
88— Chris Reed, OL
89— Steve Blankenbaker, DL
91— Chris Hogan, DL
92— Chris Hogan, DL

GA. SOUTHERN (17)
85—†Vance Pike, OL
†Tim Foley, PK
86—†Fred Stokes, OT
†Tracy Ham, QB
87—†Flint Matthews, LB
†Dennis Franklin, C
†Tim Foley, PK
88—†Dennis Franklin, C
†Darren Alford, DL
89—†Joe Ross, RB
†Giff Smith, DL
90—†Giff Smith, DL
91—†Rodney Oglesby, DB
92—†Alex Mash, DL
93—†Alex Mash, DL
†Franklin Stephens, OL
94—†Franklin Stephens, OL

GA. SOUTHWESTERN (2)
85— Roger Glover, LB
86— Roger Glover, LB

GETTYSBURG (5)
66— Joseph Egresitz, DE
83— Ray Condren, RB
84— Ray Condren, RB
85— Brian Barr, DB
94— Dwayne Marcus, FB

GLENVILLE ST. (5)
73— Scotty Hamilton, DB
83— Byron Brooks, RB
84— Mike Payne, DB
93— Chris George, WR
94— Chris George, WR

GONZAGA (2)
34— Ike Peterson, B
39— Tony Canadeo, B

GRAMBLING (28)
62— Junious Buchanan, T
64— Alphonse Dotson, OT
65— Willie Young, OG
Frank Cornish, DT
69— Billy Manning, C
70— Richard Harris, DE
Charles Roundtree, DT
71— Solomon Freelon, OG
John Mendenhall, DE
72— Steve Dennis, DB
Gary Johnson, DT
73— Gary Johnson, DT
Willie Bryant, DB
74— Gary Johnson, DT
75— Sammie White, WR
James Hunter, DB
79—†Joe Gordon, DT
†Aldrich Allen, LB
†Robert Salters, DB
80—†Trumaine Johnson, WR
†Mike Barker, DT
81—†Andre Robinson, LB
82—†Trumaine Johnson, WR
83—†Robert Smith, DL
85—†James Harris, LB
90—†Walter Dean, RB
†Jake Reed, WR
94—†Curtis Ceaser, WR

GRAND VALLEY ST. (5)
79— Ronald Essink, OL
89— Todd Tracey, DL
91— Chris Tiede, C
94— Mike Sheldon, OL
95— Diriki Mose, WR

GROVE CITY (1)
87— Doug Hart, PK

GUILFORD (3)
75— Steve Musulin, OT
91— Rodney Alexander, DE
94— Bryan Garland, OL

GUST. ADOLPHUS (7)
37— Wendell Butcher, B
50— Calvin Roberts, T
51— Haldo Norman, OE
52— Calvin Roberts, DT
54— Gene Nei, G
67— Richard Jaeger, LB
84— Kurt Ploeger, DL

HAMILTON (2)
86— Joe Gilbert, OL
91— Eric Grey, RB

HAMLINE (4)
55— Dick Donlin, E
84— Kevin Graslewicz, WR
85— Ed Hitchcock, OL
89— Jon Voss, TE

HAMPDEN-SYDNEY (8)
48— Lynn Chewning, B
54— Stokeley Fulton, C
72— Michael Leidy, LB
74— Ed Kelley, DE
75— Ed Kelley, DE
77— Robert Wilson, OL
78— Tim Smith, DL
86— Jimmy Hondroulis, PK

HAMPTON (6)
84— Ike Readon, MG
85— Ike Readon, DL
93— Emerson Martin, OL
Christopher Williams, DL
94— John Meredith, LB
95—†Hugh Hunter, DL

HANOVER (4)
86— Jon Pinnick, QB
88— Mike Luker, WR
95— Ben Fox, WR
Terry Peebles, QB

HARDIN-SIMMONS (6)
37— Burns McKinney, B
39— Clyde Turner, C
40— Owen Goodnight, B
42— Rudy Mobley, B
46— Rudy Mobley, B
94— Colin McCormick, WR

HARDING (3)
74— Barney Crawford, DL
91— Pat Gill, LB
94— Paul Simmons, LB

HARVARD (2)
82—†Mike Corbat, OL
84—†Roger Caron, OL

HASTINGS (2)
84— Dennis Sullivan, OL
94— Jeff Drake, DL

HAWAII* (2)
41— Nolle Smith, B
68— Tim Buchanan, LB

HENDERSON ST. (2)
90— Todd Jones, OL
93— Chris Carter, P

HILLSDALE (9)
49— William Young, B
55— Nate Clark, B
56— Nate Clark, B
75— Mark Law, OG
81— Mike Broome, OG
82— Ron Gladnick, DE
86— Al Huge, DL
87— Al Huge, DL
88— Rodney Patterson, LB

HOBART (4)
72— Don Aleksiewicz, RB
75— Rich Kowalski, RB
86— Brian Verdon, DB
93— Bill Palmer, DB

HOFSTRA (8)
83— Chuck Choinski, DL
86— Tom Salamone, P
88— Tom Salamone, DB
90— George Tischler, LB
94—†Brian Clark, DB
95—†Dave Fiore, OL
†Dave Ettinger, PK
†Buck Buchanan, LB

HOLY CROSS (14)
83—†Bruce Kozerski, OT
†Steve Raquet, DL
84—†Bill McGovern, DB
†Kevin Garvey, OG
85—†Gill Fenerty, RB
86—†Gordie Lockbaum, RB-DB
87—†Jeff Wiley, QB
†Gordie Lockbaum, WR-SP
88—†Dennis Golden, OL
89—†Dave Murphy, DB
90—†Craig Callahan, LB
91—†Jerome Fuller, RB
93—†Rob Milanette, LB
95—†Tom Claro, OL

HOPE (2)
79— Craig Groendyk, OL
82— Kurt Brinks, C

HOWARD (2)
75— Ben Harris, DL
87—†Harvey Reed, RB

HOWARD PAYNE (6)
61— Ray Jacobs, T
72— Robert Woods, LB
73— Robert Woods, LB
92— Scott Lichner, QB
94— Steven Seale, OL
95— Sean Witherwax, DL

HUMBOLDT ST. (6)
61— Drew Roberts, E
62— Drew Roberts, E
76— Michael Gooing, OL
82— David Rush, MG
83— Dean Diaz, DB
95— Randy Matyshock, TE

HURON (1)
76— John Aldridge, OL

IDAHO (14)
83—†Ken Hobart, QB
85—†Eric Yarber, WR
88—†John Friesz, QB
89—†John Friesz, QB
†Lee Allen, WR
90—†Kasey Dunn, WR
91—†Kasey Dunn, WR
92—†Yo Murphy, WR
†Jeff Robinson, DL
93—†Doug Nussmeier, QB
†Mat Groshong, C
94—†Sherriden May, RB
†Jim Mills, OL
95—†Ryan Phillips, DL

IDAHO ST. (6)
69— Ed Bell, OE
77— Ray Allred, MG
81—†Case de Bruijn, P
†Mike Machurek, QB
83—†Jeff Kaiser, P
84—†Steve Anderson, DL

ILL. BENEDICTINE (3)
72— Mike Rogowski, LB
92— Bob McMillen, TE
93— Eric Green, KR

ILLINOIS COLL. (1)
81— Joe Aiello, DL

ILLINOIS ST. (5)
68— Denny Nelson, OT
85—†Jim Meyer, OL
86—†Brian Gant, LB
88—†Mike McCabe, P
93—†Todd Kurz, PK

ILL. WESLEYAN (4)
34— Tony Blazine, T
74— Caesar Douglas, OT
91— Chris Bisaillon, WR
92— Chris Bisaillon, WR

INDIANA (PA.) (18)
75— Lynn Hieber, QB
76— Jim Haslett, DE
77— Jim Haslett, DE
78— Jim Haslett, DE
79— Terrence Skelley, OE
80— Joe Cuigari, DT
84— Gregg Brenner, WR
86— Jim Angelo, OL
87— Troy Jackson, LB
88— Dean Cottrill, LB
90— Andrew Hill, WR
91— Tony Aliucci, QB
93— Matt Dalverny, OL
Mike Geary, PK
Michael Mann, RB
94— Jeff Turnage, DL
95— Jon Ruff, PK
Jeff Turnage, DL

INDIANA ST. (11)
69— Jeff Keller, DE
75— Chris Hicks, OL
Vince Allen, RB
83—†Ed Martin, DE
84—†Wayne Davis, DB
85—†Vencie Glenn, DB
86—†Mike Simmonds, OL
93—†Shawn Moore, OL
94—†Dan Brandenburg, DL
95—†Dan Bradenburg, DL
†Tom Allison, PK

INDIANAPOLIS (6)
83— Mark Bless, DL
84— Paul Loggan, DB
85— Tom Collins, DB
86— Dan Jester, TE
87— Thurman Montgomery, DL
91— Greg Matheis, DL

IOWA WESLEYAN (1)
87— Mike Wiggins, P

ITHACA (12)
72— Robert Wojnar, OT
74— David Remick, RB
75— Larry Czarnecki, DT
79— John Laper, LB
80— Bob Ferrigno, HB
84— Bill Sheerin, DL
85— Tim Torrey, LB
90— Jeff Wittman, FB
91— Jeff Wittman, FB
92— Jeff Wittman, FB
Dave Brumfield, OL
95— Scott Connolly, DL

JACKSON ST. (18)
62— Willie Richardson, E
69— Joe Stephens, OG
71— Jerome Barkum, OE
74— Walter Payton, RB
Robert Brazile, LB
78— Robert Hardy, DT
80—†Larry Werts, LB
81—†Mike Fields, OT
85—†Jackie Walker, LB
86—†Kevin Dent, DB
87—†Kevin Dent, DB
88—†Lewis Tillman, RB
†Kevin Dent, DB
89—†Darion Conner, LB
90—†Robert Turner, DB
91—†Deltrich Lockridge, OL
92—†Lester Holmes, OL
95—†Picasso Nelson, DB

JACKSONVILLE ST. (9)
52— Jodie Connell, OG
66— Ray Vinson, DB
70— Jimmy Champion, C
77— Jesse Baker, DT
78— Jesse Baker, DT
82— Ed Lett, QB
86— Joe Billingsley, OT
88— Joe Billingsley, OT
95—†Darron Edwards, DB

JAMES MADISON (11)
77— Woody Bergeria, DT
78— Rick Booth, OL
85—†Charles Haley, LB
86—†Carlo Bianchini, OG
89—†Steve Bates, DL
90—†Eupton Jackson, DB
93—†David McLeod, WR
94—†Dwight Robinson, DB
95—†John Coursey, PK
†David Bailey, C
†Ed Perry, TE

JAMESTOWN (2)
76— Brent Tischer, OL
81— Ron Hausauer, OL

JOHN CARROLL (5)
50— Carl Taseff, B
74— Tim Barrett, RB
94— Jason Goldberg, PK
Ryan Haley, P
95— Chris Anderson, LB

JOHNS HOPKINS (2)
80— Bill Stromberg, WR
81— Bill Stromberg, WR

JOHNSON SMITH (2)
82— Dan Beauford, DE
88— Ronald Capers, LB

JUNIATA (3)
54— Joe Veto, T
86— Steve Yerger, OL
87— Mark Dorner, DB

KANSAS WESLEYAN (2)
35— Virgil Baker, G
56— Larry Houdek, B

KEAN (1)
87— Kevin McGuirl, TE

KENTUCKY ST. (1)
72— Wiley Epps, LB

KENYON (1)
74— Jim Myers, WR

KNOX (2)
86— Rich Schiele, TE
87— Chris Vogel, WR

KNOXVILLE (1)
77— Dwight Treadwell, OL

KUTZTOWN (2)
77— Steve Head, OG
95— John Mobley, LB

LA SALLE (2)
38— George Somers, T
39— Frank Loughney, G

LA VERNE (3)
72— Dana Coleman, DT
91— Willie Reyna, QB
95— Anthony Jones, RB

LAFAYETTE (5)
79—†Rich Smith, TE
81—†Joe Skladany, LB
82—†Tony Green, DL
88—†Frank Baur, QB
92—†Edward Hudak, OL

LAKELAND (1)
89— Jeff Ogiego, P

LAMAR (5)
57— Dudley Meredith, T
61— Bobby Jancik, B
67— Spergon Wynn, OG
83—†Eugene Seale, LB
85—†Burton Murchison, RB

LAMBUTH (2)
93— Jo Jo Jones, RB
94— Jo Jo Jones, RB

LANE (1)
73— Edward Taylor, DT

LANGSTON (2)
73— Thomas Henderson, DE
94— Paul Reed, DB

LAWRENCE (10)
49— Claude Radtke, E
67— Charles McKee, QB
77— Frank Bouressa, C
78— Frank Bouressa, C
80— Scott Reppert, HB
81— Scott Reppert, HB
82— Scott Reppert, RB
83— Murray McDonough, DB
86— Dan Galante, DL
95— Brad Olson, RB

LEHIGH (19)
49— Robert Numbers, C
50— Dick Doyne, B
57— Dan Nolan, B
59— Walter Meincke, T
69— Thad Jamula, OT
71— John Hill, C
73— Kim McQuilken, QB
75— Joe Sterrett, QB
77— Steve Kreider, WR
Mike Reiker, QB
79—†Dave Melone, OT
†Jim McCormick, DL
80—†Bruce Rarig, LB
83—†John Shigo, LB
85—†Rennie Benn, WR
90—†Keith Petzold, OL
93—†Dave Cecchini, WR
95—†Brian Klingerman, WR
†Rabih Abdullah, RB

LENOIR-RHYNE (5)
52— Steve Trudnak, B
62— Richard Kemp, B
67— Eddie Joyner, OT
92— Jason Monday, PK
94— Leonard Davis, RB

LEWIS & CLARK (2)
68— Bill Bailey, DT
91— Dan Ruhl, RB

LIBERTY (4)
82— John Sanders, LB
86— Mark Mathis, DB
95—†Andrew McFadden, KR
†Tony Dews, TE

LINCOLN (MO.) (2)
53— Leo Lewis, B
54— Leo Lewis, B

LINFIELD (9)
57— Howard Morris, G
64— Norman Musser, C
72— Bernard Peterson, OE
75— Ken Cutcher, OL
78— Paul Dombroski, DB
80— Alan Schmidlin, QB
83— Steve Lopes, OL
84— Steve Boyea, OL
94— Darrin Causey, LB

LIVINGSTONE (1)
84— Jo Jo White, RB

LOCK HAVEN (1)
45— Robert Eyer, E

LONG BEACH ST. (4)
68— Bill Parks, OE
69— Leon Burns, FB
70— Leon Burns, RB
71— Terry Metcalf, RB

LIU-C. W. POST (5)
71— Gary Wichard, QB
77— John Mohring, DE
78— John Mohring, DE
81— Tom DeBona, WR
89— John Levelis, DL

LORAS (2)
47— Robert Hanlon, B
84— James Drew, P

LOS ANGELES ST. (1)
64— Walter Johnson, OG

LOUISIANA COLLEGE (1)
50— Bernard Calendar, E

LOUISIANA TECH* (15)
41— Garland Gregory, G
46— Mike Reed, G
68— Terry Bradshaw, QB
69— Terry Bradshaw, QB
72— Roger Carr, WR
73— Roger Carr, FL
74— Mike Barber, TE
Fred Dean, DT
82—†Matt Dunigan, QB
84—†Doug Landry, LB
†Walter Johnson, DE
85—†Doug Landry, LB
86—†Walter Johnson, LB-DE
87—†Glenell Sanders, LB
88—†Glenell Sanders, LB

LOUISVILLE* (1)
57— Leonard Lyles, B

LOYOLA (ILL.) (2)
35— Billy Roy, B
37— Clay Calhoun, B

LOYOLA MARYMOUNT (1)
42— Vince Pacewic, B

LUTHER (1)
57— Bruce Hartman, T

LYCOMING (7)
83— John Whalen, OL
85— Walt Zataveski, OL
89— Rick Bealer, DB
90— Rick Bealer, DB
91— Darrin Kenney, OT
Don Kinney, DL
Bill Small, LB

MAINE (6)
65— John Huard, LB
66— John Huard, LB
80—†Lorenzo Bouier, RB
89—†Carl Smith, RB
†Scott Hough, OL
90—†Claude Pettaway, DB

MAINE MARITIME (2)
92— Kirk Matthieu, RB
95— Rob Marchitello, RB

MANKATO ST. (6)
73— Marty Kranz, DB
87— Duane Goldammer, OG
91— John Kelling, DB
93— Jamie Pass, QB
94— Josh Nelsen, WR
95— Mark Erickson, AP

MARS HILL (3)
78— Alan Rice, OL
79— Steven Campbell, DB
87— Lee Marchman, LB

MARSHALL (22)
37— William Smith, E
40— Jackie Hunt, B
41— Jackie Hunt, B
87—†Mike Barber, WR
†Sean Doctor, TE
88—†Mike Barber, WR
†Sean Doctor, TE
90—†Eric Ihnat, TE
91—†Phil Ratliff, OL
92—†Michael Payton, QB
†Troy Brown, WR
†Phil Ratliff, OL
93—†Chris Deaton, OL
†William King, LB
†Roger Johnson, DB
94—†Roger Johnson, DB
†William Pannell, OL
†Travis Colquitt, P
95—†Chris Parker, RB
†William Pannell, OL
†Billy Lyon, DL
†Melvin Cunningham, DB

MD.-EAST. SHORE (2)
64— John Smith, DT
68— Bill Thompson, DB

MARYVILLE (TENN.) (5)
67— Steve Dockery, DB
73— Earl McMahon, OG
77— Wayne Dunn, LB
92— Tom Smith, OL
93— Tom Smith, OL

MASSACHUSETTS (22)
52— Tony Chambers, OE
63— Paul Graham, T
64— Milt Morin, DE
67— Greg Landry, QB
71— William DeFlavio, MG
72— Steve Schubert, OE
73— Tim Berra, OE
75— Ned Deane, OL
76— Ron Harris, DB
77— Kevin Cummings, TE
Bruce Kimball, OL
78— Bruce Kimball, OG
80—†Bob Manning, DB
81—†Garry Pearson, RB
82—†Garry Pearson, RB
85—†Mike Dwyer, DL
88—†John McKeown, LB
90—†Paul Mayberry, OL
92—†Don Caparotti, DB
93—†Bill Durkin, OL
94—†Breon Parker, DB
95—†Rene Ingoglia, RB

MASS.-BOSTON (1)
92— Sean Munroe, WR

MASS. MARITIME (1)
95— Paul Diamantopoulos, DE

McMURRY (6)
49— Brad Rowland, B
50— Brad Rowland, B
58— Charles Davis, G
68— Telly Windham, DE
74— Randy Roemisch, OT
80— Rick Nolly, OL

McNEESE ST. (13)
52— Charles Kuehn, DE
69— Glenn Kidder, OG
72— James Moore, TE
74— James Files, OT
82—†Leonard Smith, DB
92—†Terry Irving, LB
93—†Jose Larios, PK
†Terry Irving, LB
94—†Ronald Cherry, OL
95—†Kavika Pittman, DL
†Marsh Buice, DL
†Zack Bronson, DB
†Vincent Landrum, LB

MEMPHIS* (1)
54— Robert Patterson, G

MERCHANT MARINE (3)
52— Robert Wiechard, LB
69— Harvey Adams, DE
90— Harold Krebs, DB

MESA ST. (8)
82— Dean Haugum, DT
83— Dean Haugum, DL
84— Don Holmes, DB
85— Mike Berk, OL
86— Mike Berk, OL
88— Tracy Bennett, PK
89— Jeff Russell, OT
90— Brian Johnson, LB

MIAMI (FLA.)* (2)
45— Ed Cameron, G
William Levitt, C

MIAMI (OHIO)* (1)
82—†Brian Pillman, MG

MICHIGAN TECH (1)
76— Jim VanWagner, RB

MIDDLE TENN. ST. (12)
64— Jimbo Pearson, S
65— Keith Atchley, LB
83—†Robert Carroll, OL
84—†Kelly Potter, PK
85—†Don Griffin, DB
88—†Don Thomas, LB
90—†Joe Campbell, RB
91—†Steve McAdoo, OL
†Joe Campbell, RB
92—†Steve McAdoo, OL
93—†Pat Hicks, OL
95—†Nathaniel Claybrooks, DL

MIDDLEBURY (2)
36— George Anderson, G
83— Jonathan Good, DL

MIDLAND LUTHERAN (2)
76— Dave Marreel, DE
79— Scott Englehardt, OL

MILLERSVILLE (7)
76— Robert Parr, DB
80— Rob Riddick, RB
81— Mark Udovich, C
86— Jeff Hannis, DL
93— Scott Martin, DL
Greg Faulkner, OL
95— Kevin Cannon, AP

MILLIKIN (2)
42— Virgil Wagner, B
92— Mike Hall, KR

MILLSAPS (12)
72— Rowan Torrey, DB
73— Michael Reams, LB
76— Rickie Haygood, QB
78— David Culpepper, LB
79— David Culpepper, LB
83— Edmond Donald, RB
85— Tommy Powell, LB
90— Sean Brewer, DL
91— Sean Brewer, DL
92— Sean Brewer, DL
93— Mitch Holloway, P
94— Kelvin Gladney, RB

MINN.-DULUTH (4)
74— Mark Johnson, DB
75— Terry Egerdahl, RB
76— Ted McKnight, RB
82— Gary Birkholz, OG

MISSISSIPPI COL. (11)
72— Ricky Herzog, FL
79— Calvin Howard, RB
80— Bert Lyles, DE
82— Major Everett, RB
83— Wayne Frazier, OL
85— Earl Conway, DL
88— Terry Fleming, DL
89— Terry Fleming, DL
90— Fred McAfee, RB
92— Johnny Poole, OL
93— Kelly Ray, C

MISSISSIPPI VAL. (6)
79—†Carl White, OG
83—†Jerry Rice, WR
84—†Jerry Rice, WR
†Willie Totten, QB
87—†Vincent Brown, LB
91—†Ashley Ambrose, DB

MO.-ROLLA (5)
41— Ed Kromka, T
69— Frank Winfield, OG
74— Merle Dillow, TE
80— Bill Grantham, S
93— Elvind Listerud, PK

MO. SOUTHERN ST. (3)
93— Rod Smith, WR
Ron Burton, LB
95— Yancy McKnight, OL

MISSOURI VALLEY (3)
47— James Nelson, G
48— James Nelson, G
49— Herbert McKinney, T

MONMOUTH (ILL.) (1)
75— Ron Baker, RB

MONTANA (17)
67— Bob Beers, LB
70— Ron Stein, DB
76— Greg Anderson, DB
79—†Jim Hard, FL
83—†Brian Salonen, TE
85—†Mike Rice, P
87—†Larry Clarkson, OL
88—†Tim Hauck, DB
89—†Kirk Scafford, OL
†Tim Hauck, DB
93—†Dave Dickenson, QB
†Todd Ericson, DB
94—†Scott Gragg, OL
95—†Dave Dickenson, QB
†Matt Wells, WR
†Mike Agee, OL
†Eric Simonson, OL

MONTANA ST. (11)
66— Don Hass, HB
67— Don Hass, HB
70— Gary Gustafson, LB
73— Bill Kollar, DT
75— Steve Kracher, RB
76— Lester Leininger, DL
78— Jon Borchardt, OT
81—†Larry Rubens, OL
84—†Mark Fellows, LB
†Dirk Nelson, P
93—†Sean Hill, DB

MONTANA TECH (3)
73— James Persons, OT
80— Steve Hossler, HB
81— Craig Opatz, OL

MONTCLAIR ST. (13)
75— Barry Giblin, DB
77— Mario Benimeo, DT
79— Tom Morton, OL
80— Sam Mills, LB
81— Terrance Porter, WR
82— Mark Casale, QB
84— Jim Rennae, OL
85— Dan Zakashefski, DL
86— Dan Zakashefski, DL
89— Paul Cioffi, LB
90— Paul Cioffi, LB
93— Jeff Bargiel, DL
95— Jeff Bargiel, DL

MOORHEAD ST. (2)
76— Rocky Gullickson, OG
84— Randy Sullivan, DB

MOREHEAD ST. (5)
38— John Horton, C
42— Vincent Zachem, C
69— Dave Haverdick, DT
82—†John Christopher, P
86—†Randy Poe, OG

MORGAN ST. (8)
65— Willie Lanier, LB
67— Jeff Queen, DE
70— Willie Germany, DB
72— Stan Cherry, LB
73— Eugene Simms, LB
78— Joe Fowlkes, DB
80— Mike Holston, WR
93—†Matthew Steeple, DL

MORNINGSIDE (2)
49— Connie Callahan, B
91— Jorge Diaz, PK

MOUNT UNION (14)
84— Troy Starr, LB
87— Russ Kring, RB
90— Ken Edelman, PK
Dave Lasecki, LB
92— Mike Elder, OL
Jim Ballard, QB
Chris Dattilio, LB
93— Rob Atwood, TE
Jim Ballard, QB
Ed Bubonics, WR
Mike Hallet, DL
94— Rob Rodgers, LB
95— Mike Wonderfer, OG
Matt Liggett, DL

MUHLENBERG (3)
46— George Bibighaus, E
47— Harold Bell, B
93— Rob Lokerson, WR

MURRAY ST. (6)
37— Elmer Cochran, G
73— Don Clayton, RB
79—†Terry Love, DB
86—†Charley Wiles, OL
95—†Derrick Cullors, RB
†William Hampton, DB

MUSKINGUM (5)
40— Dave Evans, T
60— Bill Cooper, B
66— Mark DeVilling, DT
75— Jeff Heacock, DB
95— Connon Thompson, DB

NEB.-KEARNEY (3)
76— Dale Mitchell Johnson, DB
78— Doug Peterson, DL
95— Matt Bruggeman, DL

NEB.-OMAHA (9)
64— Gerald Allen, HB
68— Dan Klepper, OG
76— Dan Fulton, WR
77— Dan Fulton, OE
80— Tom Sutko, LB
82— John Walker, DT
83— Tim Carlson, LB
84— Ron Petersen, OT
86— Keith Coleman, LB

NEB. WESLEYAN (3)
90— Brad Bohn, DB
91— Darren Stohlmann, TE
92— Darren Stohlmann, TE

NEVADA* (23)
52— Neil Garrett, DB
74— Greg Grouwinkel, DB
78— James Curry, MG
Frank Hawkins, RB
79— †Frank Hawkins, RB
†Lee Fobbs, DB
80— †Frank Hawkins, RB
†Bubba Puha, DL
81— †John Ramatici, LB
†Tony Zendejas, K
82— †Tony Zendejas, K
†Charles Mann, DT
83— †Tony Zendejas, K
†Jim Werbeckes, OG
†Tony Shaw, DB
85— †Greg Rea, OL
†Marty Zendejas, PK
†Pat Hunter, DB
86— †Henry Rolling, DE-LB
88— †Bernard Ellison, DB
90— †Bernard Ellison, DB
†Treamelle Taylor, KR
91— †Matt Clafton, LB

UNLV* (3)
73— Mike Thomas, RB
74— Mike Thomas, RB
75— Joseph Ingersoll, DL

NEW HAMPSHIRE (11)
50— Ed Douglas, G
68— Al Whittman, DT
75— Kevin Martell, C
76— Bill Burnham, RB
77— Bill Burnham, RB
Grady Vigneau, OT
85— †Paul Dufault, OL
87— †John Driscoll, OL
91— †Barry Bourassa, RB
†Dwayne Sabb, LB
94— †Mike Foley, DL

NEW HAVEN (11)
85— David Haubner, OL
87— Erik Lesinski, LB
88— Rob Thompson, OL
90— Jay McLucas, QB
92— Scott Emmert, OL
Roger Graham, RB
93— Roger Graham, RB
George Byrd, DB
Tony Willis, WR
94— Roger Graham, RB
95— Scott Riggs, LB

N.M. HIGHLANDS (7)
66— Carl Garrett, HB
67— Carl Garrett, HB
68— Carl Garrett, HB
81— Jay Lewis, DL
85— Neil Windham, LB
86— Tim Salz, PK
93— Rus Bailey, WR

NEWBERRY (2)
40— Dominic Collangelo, B
81— Stan Stanton, DL

NICHOLLS ST. (7)
76— Gerald Butler, OE
77— Rusty Rebowe, LB
81— †Dwight Walker, WR
82— †Clint Conque, LB
84— †Dewayne Harrison, TE
86— †Mark Carrier, WR
94— †Darryl Pounds, DB

NICHOLS (1)
81— Ed Zywien, LB

NORFOLK ST. (5)
79— Mike Ellis, DB
89— Arthur Jimmerson, LB
94— James Roe, WR
95— James Roe, WR
Aaron Sparrow, QB

NORTH ALA. (17)
82— Don Smith, C
84— Daryl Smith, DB
85— Bruce Jones, DB
90— James Davis, LB
Mike Nord, OL
92— Harvey Summerhill, DB
93— Jeff Redcross, DL
Tyrone Rush, RB
Jeff Surbaugh, OL
Ronald McKinnon, LB
94— Jon Thompson, OL
Ronald McKinnon, LB
Marcus Keyes, DL
95— Jon Thompson, OL
Israel Raybon, DE
Ronald McKinnon, LB
Marcus Keyes, DL

NORTH CARO. A&T (7)
69— Merl Code, DB
70— Melvin Holmes, OT
81— †Mike West, OL
86— †Ernest Riddick, NG
88— †Demetrius Harrison, LB
93— †Ronald Edwards, OL
95— †Jamain Stephens, OL

N.C. CENTRAL (4)
68— Doug Wilkerson, MG
69— Doug Wilkerson, OT
74— Charles Smith, DE
88— Earl Harvey, QB

NORTH DAK. (18)
55— Steve Myhra, G
56— Steve Myhra, G
63— Neil Reuter, T
65— Dave Lince, DE
66— Roger Bonk, LB
71— Jim LeClair, LB
Dan Martinsen, DB
72— Mike Deutsch, RB
75— Bill Deutsch, RB
79— Paul Muckenhirn, TE
80— Todd Thomas, OT
81— Milson Jones, RB
89— Cory Solberg, PK
91— Shannon Burnell, RB
93— Shannon Burnell, RB
Kevin Robson, OL
94— Mike Mooney, LB
95— Dave Hillesheim, DE

NORTH DAK. ST. (28)
34— Melvin Hanson, B
46— Cliff Rothrock, C
66— Walt Odegaard, MG
67— Jim Ferge, LB
68— Jim Ferge, DT
Paul Hatchett, B
69— Paul Hatchett, HB
Joe Cichy, DB
70— Joe Cichy, DB
74— Jerry Dahl, DE
76— Rick Budde, LB
77— Lew Curry, OL
81— Wayne Schluchter, DB
82— Cliff Carmody, OG
Steve Garske, LB
83— Mike Whetstone, OG
84— Greg Hagfors, C
86— Jeff Bentrim, QB
Jim Dick, LB
87— Mike Favor, C
88— Matt Tracy, OL
Mike Favor, C
Yorrick Byers, LB
90— Phil Hansen, DL
Chris Simdorn, QB
93— Scott Fuchs, OL
T. R. McDonald, WR
95— Brad Servais, OL

NORTH PARK (2)
72— Greg Nugent, OE
90— John Love, QB

NORTH TEXAS* (6)
47— Frank Whitlow, T
51— Ray Renfro, DB
83— †Ronnie Hickman, DE
†Rayford Cooks, DL
88— †Rex Johnson, DL
90— †Mike Davis, DL

NORTHEAST LA.* (19)
67— Vic Bender, C
70— Joe Profit, RB
72— Jimmy Edwards, RB
73— Glenn Fleming, MG
74— Glenn Fleming, MG
82— †Arthur Christophe, C
†Bruce Daigle, DB
83— †Mike Grantham, OG
84— †Mike Grantham, OG
85— †Mike Turner, DB
87— †John Clement, OT
†Claude Brumfield, DT
88— †Cyril Crutchfield, DB
89— †Jackie Harris, E
92— †Jeff Blackshear, OL
†Vic Zordan, OL
†Roosevelt Potts, RB
93— †Raymond Batiste, OL
†James Folston, DL

NORTHEASTERN (2)
72— Tom Rezzuti, DB
78— Dan Ross, TE

NORTHEASTERN ST. (5)
69— Manuel Britto, HB
71— Roosevelt Manning, DT
74— Kevin Goodlet, DB
82— Cedric Mack, WR
94— Ricky Ceasar, DL

NORTHERN ARIZ. (16)
66— Rick Ries, LB
67— Bill Hanna, DE
68— Larry Small, OG
77— Larry Friedrichs, OL
Tom Jurich, K
78— Jerry Lumpkin, LB
79— †Ed Judie, LB
82— †Pete Mandley, WR
83— †Pete Mandley, WR
†James Gee, DT
86— †Goran Lingmerth, PK
89— †Darrell Jordan, LB
93— †Terry Belden, P
95— †Rayna Stewart, DB
†Kevin O'Leary, P
†Ben Petrucci, DL

NORTHERN COLO. (12)
68— Jack O'Brien, DB
80— Todd Volkart, DT
81— Brad Wimmer, OL
82— Mark Mostek, OG
Kevin Jelden, PK
89— Vance Lechman, DB
90— Frank Wainwright, TE
92— David Oliver, OL
93— Jeff Pease, LB
94— Jeff Pease, LB
95— Tony Ramirez, OL
Tim Bowie, DB

NORTHERN ILL.* (2)
62— George Bork, B
63— George Bork, B

NORTHERN IOWA (15)
52— Lou Bohnsack, C
60— George Asleson, G
61— Wendell Williams, G
64— Randy Schultz, FB
65— Randy Schultz, FB
67— Ray Pedersen, MG
75— Mike Timmermans, OT
85— Joe Fuller, DB
87— †Carl Boyd, RB
90— †Brian Mitchell, PK
91— †Brian Mitchell, PK
92— †Kenny Shedd, WR
†William Freeney, LB
94— †Andre Allen, LB
95— †Dedric Ward, WR

NORTHERN MICH. (6)
75— Daniel Stencil, OL
76— Maurice Mitchell, FL
77— Joseph Stemo, DB
82— George Works, RB
87— Jerry Woods, DB
88— Jerry Woods, DB

NORTHERN ST. (1)
76— Larry Kolbo, DL

NORTHWEST MO. ST. (3)
39— Marion Rogers, G
84— Steve Hansley, WR
89— Jason Agee, DB

N'WESTERN (IOWA) (1)
71— Kevin Korvor, DE

NORTHWESTERN ST. (12)
66— Al Dodd, DB
80— †Warren Griffith, C
†Joe Delaney, RB
81— †Gary Reasons, LB
82— †Gary Reasons, LB
83— †Gary Reasons, LB
84— †Arthur Berry, DT
87— †John Kulakowski, DE
91— †Andre Carron, LB
92— †Adrian Hardy, DB
†Marcus Spears, OL
93— †Marcus Spears, OL

NORTHWOOD (2)
73— Bill Chandler, DT
74— Bill Chandler, DT

NORWICH (3)
79— Milt Williams, RB
84— Beau Almodobar, WR
85— Mike Norman, OL

OBERLIN (1)
45— James Boswell, B

OCCIDENTAL (6)
76— Rick Fry, FL
77— Rick Fry, SE
82— Dan Osborn, P
83— Ron Scott, DB
89— David Hodges, LB
90— Peter Tucker, OL

OHIO* (2)
35— Art Lewis, T
60— Dick Grecni, C

OHIO NORTHERN (1)
95— LaVant King, WR

OHIO WESLEYAN (7)
34— John Turley, B
51— Dale Bruce, OE
71— Steve Dutton, DE
83— Eric DiMartino, LB
90— Jeff Court, OG
Neil Ringers, DL
91— Kevin Rucker, DL

OKLA PANHANDLE ST. (2)
82— Tom Rollison, DB
83— Tom Rollison, DB

OTTERBEIN (3)
82— Jim Hoyle, K
90— Ron Severance, WR
91— Ron Severance, WR

OUACHITA BAPTIST (1)
79— Ezekiel Vaughn, LB

PACIFIC (CAL.) (4)
34— Cris Kjeldsen, G
47— Eddie LeBaron, B
48— Eddie LeBaron, B
49— Eddie LeBaron, B

PACIFIC LUTHERAN (9)
40— Marv Tommervik, B
41— Marv Tommervik, B
47— Dan D'Andrea, C
52— Ron Billings, DB
65— Marvin Peterson, C
78— John Zamberlin, LB
85— Mark Foege, PK
Tim Shannon, DL
88— Jon Kral, DL

PENNSYLVANIA (7)
86— †Marty Peterson, OL
88— †John Zinser, OL
90— †Joe Valerio, OL
93— †Miles Macik, WR
94— †Pat Goodwillie, LB
95— †Miles Macik, WR
†Tom McGarrity, DL

PEPPERDINE (2)
47— Darwin Horn, B
55— Wixie Robinson, G

PERU ST. (4)
52— Robert Lade, OT
53— Robert Lade, T
81— Alvin Holder, RB
91— Tim Herman, DL

PILLSBURY (1)
85— Calvin Addison, RB

PITTSBURG ST. (14)
61— Gary Snadon, B
70— Mike Potchard, OT
78— Brian Byers, OL
88— Jesse Wall, OL
89— John Roderique, LB
90— Ron West, WR
91— Ron West, WR
92— Ronald Moore, RB
93— Doug Bullard, OL
94— Andy Sweet, LB
Chris Brown, DB
95— Phil Schepens, OT
B. J. McGivern, LB
Chris Brown, DB

PLYMOUTH ST. (8)
74— Robert Gibson, DB
82— Mark Barrows, LB
83— Joe Dudek, RB
84— Joe Dudek, RB
85— Joe Dudek, RB
91— Scott Allen, LB
94— Colby Compton, LB
95— Colby Compton, LB

POMONA-PITZER (1)
74— Larry Cenotto, QB

PORTLAND ST.* (15)
76— June Jones, QB
77— Dave Stief, OE
79—†Stuart Gaussoin, SE
†Kurt Ijanoff, OT
80—†Neil Lomax, QB
84— Doug Mikolas, DL
88— Bary Naone, TE
Chris Crawford, QB
89— Darren Del'Andrae, QB
91— James Fuller, DB
92— John Charles, QB
93— Rick Cruz, LB
94— Sam Peoples, DB
Jesus Moreno, OT
95— Steve Papin, RB

PRAIRIE VIEW (2)
64— Otis Taylor, OE
70— Bivian Lee, DB

PRESBYTERIAN (8)
45— Andy Kavounis, G
46— Hank Caver, B
52— Joe Kirven, OE
68— Dan Eckstein, DB
71— Robert Norris, LB
78— Roy Walker, OL
79— Roy Walker, OL
83— Jimmie Turner, LB

PRINCETON (4)
87—†Dean Cain, DB
89—†Judd Garrett, RB
92—†Keith Elias, RB
93—†Keith Elias, RB

PRINCIPIA (1)
93— Matt Newton, WR

PUGET SOUND (9)
56— Robert Mitchell, G
63— Ralph Bauman, G
66— Joseph Peyton, OE
75— Bill Linnenkohl, LB
76— Dan Kuehl, DL
81— Bob Jackson, MG
82— Mike Bos, WR
83— Larry Smith, DB
87— Mike Oliphant, RB

RANDOLPH-MACON (6)
47— Albert Oley, G
57— Dave Young, G
79— Rick Eades, DL
80— Rick Eades, DL
84— Cody Dearing, QB
88— Aaron Boston, OL

REDLANDS (2)
77— Randy Van Horn, OL
92— James Shields, DL

Plymouth State sports information photo from C.W. Pack Sports

Plymouth State linebacker Colby Compton was a Division III all-American in 1994 and 1995.

RHODE ISLAND (8)
55— Charles Gibbons, T
82—†Richard Pelzer, OL
83—†Tony DeLuca, DL
84—†Brian Forster, TE
85—†Brian Forster, TE
†Tom Ehrhardt, QB
90—†Kevin Smith, DB
92—†Darren Rizzi, TE

RHODES (5)
36— Henry Hammond, E
38— Gaylon Smith, B
76— Conrad Bradburn, DB
85— Jim Hever, PK
88— Larry Hayes, OL

RICHMOND (1)
84—†Eddie Martin, OL

RIPON (6)
57— Peter Kasson, E
75— Dick Rehbein, C
76— Dick Rehbein, OL
79— Art Peters, TE
82— Bob Wallner, OL
95— Jim Wallace, DB

ROANOKE (1)
38— Kenneth Moore, E

ROCHESTER (7)
51— Jack Wilson, DE
52— Donald Bardell, DG
67— Dave Ragusa, LB
75— Ralph Gebhardt, DB
90— Craig Chodak, P
92— Brian Laudadio, DL
93— Geoff Long, DL

ROCKHURST (1)
41— Joe Kiernan, T

ROLLINS (1)
40— Charles Lingerfelt, E

ROSE-HULMAN (2)
77— Gary Ellis, DB
92— Todd Holthaus, PK

ROWAN (3)
78— Dino Hall, RB
93— Bill Fisher, DL
95— LeRoi Jones, LB

SAGINAW VALLEY (4)
81— Eugene Marve, LB
84— Joe Rice, DL
90— David Cook, DB
92— Bill Schafer, TE

ST. AMBROSE (4)
40— Nick Kerasiotis, G
51— Robert Flanagan, B
58— Robert Webb, B
87— Jerry Klosterman, DL

ST. BONAVENTURE (2)
46— Phil Colella, B
48— Frank LoVuola, E

ST. CLOUD ST. (2)
85— Mike Lambrecht, DL
95— Randy Martin, RB

ST. JOHN'S (MINN.) (9)
65— Pat Whalin, DB
79— Ernie England, MG
82— Rick Bell, RB
83— Chris Biggins, TE
91— Pat Mayew, QB
93— Burt Chamberlin, OL
Jim Wagner, DL
94— Jim Wagner, DL
95— Chris Palmer, WR

ST. JOHN'S (N.Y.) (1)
83— Todd Jamison, QB

ST. LAWRENCE (2)
51— Ken Spencer, LB
77— Mitch Brown, DB

ST. MARY (KAN.) (1)
86— Joe Brinson, RB

ST. MARY'S (CAL.) (4)
79— Fran McDermott, DB
80— Fran McDermott, DB
88— Jon Braff, TE
92— Mike Estrella, PK

ST. MARY'S (TEX.) (1)
36— Douglas Locke, B

ST. NORBERT (2)
57— Norm Jarock, B
64— Dave Jauquet, DE

ST. OLAF (3)
53— John Gustafson, E
78— John Nahorniak, LB
80— Jon Anderson, DL

ST. THOMAS (MINN.) (8)
45— Theodore Molitor, E
48— Jack Salscheider, B
84— Neal Guggemos, DB
85— Neal Guggemos, DB
90— Gary Trettel, RB
91— Kevin DeVore, OL
94— Ryan Davis, TE
95— Ryan Davis, TE

SALISBURY ST. (5)
82— Mark Lagowski, LB
84— Joe Mammano, OL
85— Robb Disbennett, QB
86— Tom Kress, DL
95— Mark Hannah, LB

SAM HOUSTON ST. (3)
49— Charles Williams, E
52— Don Gottlob, B
91—†Michael Bankston, DL

SAMFORD (2)
36— Norman Cooper, C
94—†Anthony Jordan, AP

SAN DIEGO (3)
73— Bob Dulich, QB
81— Dan Herbert, DB
92— Robert Ray, P

SAN DIEGO ST.* (6)
35— John Butler, G
66— Don Horn, QB
67— Steve Duich, OT
Haven Moses, OE
68— Fred Dryer, DE
Lloyd Edwards, B

SAN FRANCISCO (1)
42— John Sanchez, T

SAN FRAN. ST. (7)
51— Robert Williamson, OT
60— Charles Fuller, B
67— Joe Koontz, OE
76— Forest Hancock, LB
78— Frank Duncan, DB
82— Poncho James, RB
84— Jim Jones, TE

SAN JOSE ST.* (2)
38— Lloyd Thomas, E
39— LeRoy Zimmerman, B

SANTA CLARA (8)
64— Lou Pastorini, LB
71— Ronald Sani, C
79— Jim Leonard, C
80— Brian Sullivan, K
82— Gary Hoffman, OT
83— Alex Vlahos, C
Mike Rosselli, LB
85— Brent Jones, TE

SAVANNAH ST. (2)
79— Timothy Walker, DL
89— Shannon Sharpe, TE

SEWANEE (8)
63— Martin Agnew, B
73— Mike Lumpkin, DE
77— Nino Austin, DB
79— John Hill, DB
80— Mallory Nimocs, TE
81— Greg Worsowicz, DB
86— Mark Kent, WR
90— Ray McGowan, DL

SHIPPENSBURG (3)
53— Robert Adams, G
91— Jeff Fickes, DB
94— Doug Seidenstricker, DB

SIENA (1)
95—†Reggie Greene, AP

SIMON FRASER (1)
90— Nick Mazzoli, WR

SIMPSON (1)
89— Ricky Gales, RB

SLIPPERY ROCK (6)
74— Ed O'Reilly, RB
75— Jerry Skocik, TE
76— Chris Thull, LB
77— Bob Schrantz, TE
78— Bob Schrantz, TE
85— Jeff Williams, P

SONOMA ST. (3)
86— Mike Henry, LB
92— Larry Allen, OL
93— Larry Allen, OL

SOUTH CARO. ST. (20)
67— Tyrone Caldwell, DE
71— James Evans, LB
72— Barney Chavous, DE
73— Donnie Shell, DB
75— Harry Carson, DE
76— Robert Sims, DL
77— Ricky Anderson, RB
79—†Phillip Murphy, DL
80—†Edwin Bailey, OG
81—†Anthony Reed, FB
†Dwayne Jackson, DL
82—†Dwayne Jackson, DE
†Anthony Reed, RB
†Ralph Green, OT
†John Courtney, DT
83—†Ralph Green, OT
89—†Eric Douglas, OL
91—†Robert Porcher, DL
93—†Anthony Cook, DE
94—†Anthony Cook, DL

SOUTH DAK. (10)
68— John Kohler, OT
69— John Kohler, OT
71— Gene Macken, OG
72— Gary Kipling, OG
78— Bill Moats, DB
79— Benjamin Long, LB
83— Kurt Seibel, K
86— Jerry Glinsky, C
Todd Salat, DB
88— Doug VanderEsch, LB

SOUTH DAK. ST. (14)
67— Darwin Gonnerman, HB
68— Darwin Gonnerman, FB
74— Lynn Boden, OT
77— Bill Matthews, DE
79— Charles Loewen, OL
84— Rick Wegher, RB
85— Jeff Tiefenthaler, WR
86— Jeff Tiefenthaler, WR
91— Kevin Tetzlaff, OL
92— Doug Miller, LB
93— Adam Timmerman, DL
94— Jake Hines, TE
Adam Vinatieri, P
Adam Timmerman, OL

SOUTH DAK. TECH (1)
73— Charles Waite, DB

SOUTHEAST MO. ST. (3)
37— Wayne Goddard, T
94—†Doug Berg, DL
95—†Frank Russell, DB

SOUTHEASTERN LA. (3)
70— Ronnie Hornsby, LB
83—†Bret Wright, P
85—†Willie Shepherd, DL

SOUTHERN-B.R. (7)
70— Isiah Robertson, LB
72— James Wright, OG
73— Godwin Turk, LB
79—†Ken Times, DL
87—†Gerald Perry, OT
93—†Sean Wallace, DB
95—†Kendell Shello, DL

SOUTHERN ARK. (2)
84— Greg Stuman, LB
85— Greg Stuman, LB

SOUTHERN CONN. ST. (8)
82— Mike Marshall, DB
83— Kevin Gray, OL
84— William Sixsmith, LB
86— Rick Atkinson, DB
91— Ron Lecointe, OL
92— Steve Lawrence, LB
94— Anthony Idone, DL
95—†Joe Andruzzi, OL

SOUTHERN ILL. (4)
70— Lionel Antoine, OE
71— Lionel Antoine, OE
83—†Donnell Daniel, DB
†Terry Taylor, DB

SOUTHERN MISS.* (4)
53— Hugh Pepper, B
56— Don Owens, T
58— Robert Yencho, E
59— Hugh McInnis, E

SOUTHERN ORE. ST. (1)
75— Dennis Webber, LB

SOUTHERN UTAH (5)
79— Lane Martino, DL
87— Jeff McComb, P
89— Randy Bostic, C
90— Randy Bostic, C
95—†Micah Deckert, TE

SOUTHWEST MO. ST. (7)
66— William Stringer, OG
87—†Matt Soraghan, LB
89—†Mark Christenson, OL
90—†DeAndre Smith, QB
91—†Bill Walter, DL
93—†Adrion Smith, DB
95—†DeLaun Fowler, LB

SOUTHWEST ST. (2)
87— James Ashley, WR
91— Wayne Hawkins, DE

SOUTHWEST TEX. ST. (11)
53— Pence Dacus, B
63— Jerry Cole, E
64— Jerry Cole, DB
72— Bob Daigle, C
75— Bobby Kotzur, DT
82— Tim Staskus, LB
83— Tim Staskus, LB
84—†Scott Forester, C
90—†Reggie Rivers, RB
91—†Ervin Thomas, C
94—†Don Wilkerson, RB

SOUTHWESTERN (KAN.) (2)
82— Tom Audley, DL
84— Jackie Jenson, RB

SOUTHWESTERN LA.* (1)
69— Glenn LaFleur, LB

SOUTHWESTERN OKLA. (2)
77— Louis Blanton, DB
82— Richard Lockman, LB

SPRINGFIELD (12)
68— Dick Dobbert, C
70— John Curtis, OE
76— Roy Samuelsen, MG
78— Jack Quinn, DB
79— Jack Quinn, DB
80— Steve Foster, OT
81— Jon Richardson, LB
83— Wally Case, DT
Ed Meachum, TE
85— Jim Anderson, LB
91— Fran Papasedero, DL
94— Matt Way, OL

STEPHEN F. AUSTIN (10)
51— James Terry, DE
79— Ronald Haynes, DL
85— James Noble, WR
86—†Darrell Harkless, DB
88—†Eric Lokey, LB
89—†David Whitmore, DB
93—†Cedric Walker, DB
95—†Joey Wylie, OL
†Lee Kirk, OL
†Damiyon Bell, DB

STONY BROOK (2)
87— Chuck Downey, DB
88— David Lewis, P

SUL ROSS ST. (2)
65— Tom Nelson, DE
88— Francis Jones, DB

SUSQUEHANNA (3)
51— James Hazlett, C
90— Keith Henry, DL
92— Andy Watkins, LB

SWARTHMORE (1)
89— Marshall Happer, OL

TAMPA (5)
65— John Perry, DB
68— Ron Brown, MG
70— Leon McQuay, RB
71— Ron Mikolajczyk, OT
Sammy Gellerstedt, MG

TENN.-CHATT. (22)
35— Robert Klein, E
38— Robert Sutton, G
39— Jack Gregory, T
45— Thomas Stewart, T
46— Gene Roberts, B
48— Ralph Hutchinson, T
49— Vincent Sarratore, G
51— Chester LaGod, DT
52— Chester LaGod, DT
54— Richard Young, B
57— Howard Clark, E
58— John Green, B
60— Charles Long, T
64— Jerry Harris, S
66— Harry Sorrell, OG
76— Tim Collins, LB
86—†Mike Makins, DL
89—†Pumpy Tudors, P
†Junior Jackson, LB
90—†Troy Boeck, DL
†Tony Hill, DL
†Pumpy Tudors, P

TENN.-MARTIN (3)
68— Julian Nunnamaker, OG
88— Emanuel McNeil, DL
91— Oscar Bunch, TE

TENNESSEE ST. (17)
67— Claude Humphrey, DT
68— Jim Marsalis, DB
69— Joe Jones, DE
70— Vernon Holland, OT
71— Cliff Brooks, DB
Joe Gilliam, QB
72— Robert Woods, OT
Waymond Bryant, LB
73— Waymond Bryant, LB
Ed Jones, DE
74— Cleveland Elam, DE
81—†Mike Jones, WR
†Malcolm Taylor, DT
82—†Walter Tate, OL
86—†Onzy Elam, LB
90—†Colin Godfrey, P
93—†Brent Alexander, DB

TENNESSEE TECH (10)
52— Tom Fann, OT
59— Tom Hackler, E
60— Tom Hackler, E
61— David Baxter, T
69— Larry Schreiber, HB
71— Jim Youngblood, LB
72— Jim Youngblood, LB
74— Elois Grooms, DE
76— Ed Burns, OT
89—†Ryan Weeks, PK

TENN. WESLEYAN (1)
92— Derrick Scott, PK

TEXAS-ARLINGTON (5)
66— Ken Ozee, DT
67— Robert Diem, OG
Robert Willbanks, S
83—†Mark Cannon, C
84—†Bruce Collie, OL

TEX. A&M-KINGSVILLE (48)
40— Stuart Clarkson, C
41— Stuart Clarkson, C
59— Gerald Lambert, G
60— William Crafts, T
62— Douglas Harvey, C
63— Sid Banks, B
65— Randy Johnson, QB
66— Dwayne Nix, OE
67— Dwayne Nix, OE
68— Dwayne Nix, OE
Ray Hickl, OG
70— Dwight Harrison, DB
Margarito Guerrero, MG
71— Eldridge Small, OE
Levi Johnson, DB
72— Ernest Price, DE
74— Don Hardeman, RB
75— David Hill, TE
76— Richard Ritchie, QB
Larry Grunewald, LB
77— Larry Collins, RB
John Barefield, DE
78— Billy John, OT
79— Andy Hawkins, LB
80— Don Washington, CB
81— Durwood Roquemore, DB
82— Darrell Green, DB
83— Loyd Lewis, OG
84— Neal Lattue, PK
85— Charles Smith, C
86— Johnny Bailey, RB
Moses Horn, OG
87— Johnny Bailey, RB
Moses Horn, OG
88— Rod Mounts, OL
Johnny Bailey, RB
John Randle, DL
89— Johnny Bailey, RB
90— Keithen DeGrate, OL
91— Brian Nielsen, OL
92— Earl Dotson, OL
93— Anthony Phillips, DB
Moke Simon, DL
94— Jeff Rodgers, DL
Kevin Dogins, C
95— Jermane Mayberry, OT
Jaime Martinez, OG
Kevin Dogins, C

TEXAS LUTHERAN (3)
73— David Wehmeyer, RB
74— D. W. Rutledge, LB
75— Jerry Ellis, OL

TEXAS SOUTHERN (3)
70— Nathaniel Allen, DB
76— Freddie Dean, OL
92—†Michael Strahan, DL

TEXAS TECH* (2)
35— Herschel Ramsey, E
45— Walter Schlinkman, B

THOMAS MORE (1)
93— Mike Flesch, OL

TIFFIN (1)
93— Brian Diliberto, RB

TOLEDO* (1)
38— Dan Buckwick, G

TOWSON ST. (11)
75— Dan Dullea, QB
76— Skip Chase, OE
77— Randy Bielski, DB
78— Ken Snoots, SE
82— Sean Landeta, P
83— Gary Rubeling, DB
84— Terry Brooks, OG
85— Stan Eisentooth, OL
86— David Haden, LB
93—†Tony Vinson, RB
94—†Mark Orlando, WR

TRENTON ST. (3)
74— Eric Hamilton, C
83— John Aromando, WR
91— Chris Shaw, C

TRINITY (CONN.) (8)
35— Mickey Kobrosky, B
36— Mickey Kobrosky, B
55— Charles Sticka, B
59— Roger LeClerc, C
70— David Kiarsis, HB
78— Pat McNamara, FL
93— Eric Mudry, DB
94— Greg Schramm, DB

TRINITY (TEX.) (5)
54— Alvin Beal, B
55— Hubert Cook, C
56— Milton Robichaux, E
67— Marvin Upshaw, DT
94— James Vallerie, LB

TROY ST. (12)
39— Sherrill Busby, E
73— Mark King, C

74— Mark King, C
76— Perry Griggs, OE
78— Tim Tucker, LB
80— Willie Tullis, QB
84— Mitch Geier, OG
86— Freddie Thomas, DB
87— Mike Turk, QB
Freddie Thomas, DB
94—†Bob Hall, OL
95—†Bob Hall, OL

TRUMAN ST. (4)
60— Dale Mills, B
65— Richard Rhodes, OT
85— Chris Hegg, QB
93— Mike Roos, DL

TUFTS (6)
34— William Grinnell, E
76— Tim Whelan, RB
78— Mark Buben, DL
79— Chris Connors, QB
80— Mike Brown, OL
86— Bob Patz, DL

TULSA* (1)
34— Rudy Prochaska, C

TUSCULUM (2)
94— Matt Schults, OL
95— Eric Claridy, RB

UNION (N.Y.) (9)
39— Sam Hammerstrom, B
82— Steve Bodmer, DL
83— Tim Howell, LB
84— Brian Cox, DE
85— Anthony Valente, DL
86— Rich Romer, DL
87— Rich Romer, DL
91— Greg Harrison, PK
93— Marco Lainez, LB

UNION (TENN.) (2)
41— James Jones, B
42— James Jones, B

U.S. INT'L (2)
72— Jerry Robinson, DB
75— Steve Matson, FL

UPSALA (1)
64— Dick Giessuebel, LB

VALDOSTA ST. (6)
82— Mark Catano, OL
86— Jessie Tuggle, LB
89— Randy Fisher, WR
90— Deon Searcy, DB
93— Chris Hatcher, QB
94— Chris Hatcher, QB

VALPARAISO (5)
51— Joe Pahr, B
71— Gary Puetz, OT
72— Gary Puetz, OT
76— John Belskis, DB
85— Mike Healey, WR

VILLANOVA (5)
88—†Paul Berardelli, OL
89—†Bryan Russo, OL
91—†Curtis Eller, LB
92—†Curtis Eller, LB
94—†Tyrone Frazier, LB

VA. MILITARY (2)
88—†Mark Stock, WR
95—†Thomas Haskins, RB

VIRGINIA ST. (3)
71— Larry Brooks, DT
84— John Greene, LB
85— James Ward, DL

VIRGINIA UNION (12)
73— Herb Scott, OG
74— Herb Scott, OG
75— Anthony Leonard, DB
77— Frank Dark, DB
79— Plummer Bullock, DE
80— William Dillon, DB
81— William Dillon, DB
82— William Dillon, DB
83— Larry Curtis, DT
88— Leroy Gause, LB
91— Paul DeBerry, DB
Kevin Williams, LB

WABASH (5)
76— Jimmy Parker, DB
77— David Harvey, QB
81— Pete Metzelaars, TE
88— Tim Pliske, PK
89— Mike Funk, WR

WAGNER (9)
67— John Gloistein, OT
80— Phil Theis, OL
81— Alonzo Patterson, RB
82— Alonzo Patterson, RB
83— Selwyn Davis, OT
86— Charles Stinson, DL
87— Rich Negrin, OT
88— Terry Underwood, RB
91— Walter Lopez, PK

WARTBURG (3)
94— Jamey Parker, OL
Vince Penningroth, DL
95— Vince Penningroth, DL

WASHBURN (2)
64— Robert Hardy, DB
88— Troy Slusser, WR

WASHINGTON (MO.) (6)
72— Shelby Jordan, LB
73— Stu Watkins, OE
74— Marion Stallings, DB
88— Paul Matthews, TE
94— Matt Gomric, LB
95— Chris Nalley, DB

WASH. & JEFF. (13)
84— Ed Kusko, OL
87— A. J. Pagano, RB
91— Chris Babirad, RB
Gilbert Floyd, DB
92— Chris Babirad, RB
Todd Pivnick, OL
Kevin Pintar, OL
93— Jason Moore, OL
Shawn Prendergast, LB
94— Matt Szczypinski, DL
Mike Jones, OL
Mike Brooder, DL
95— Mike Jones, OL

WASH. & LEE (5)
76— Tony Perry, OE
81— Mike Pressler, DL
83— Glenn Kirschner, OL
86— John Packett, OL
95— Robert Hall, DL

WAYNE ST. (NEB.) (3)
84— Herve Roussel, PK
85— Ruben Mendoza, OL
95— Brad Ottis, DL

WAYNESBURG (1)
41— Nick George, G

WEBER ST. (15)
66— Ronald McCall, DE
67— Lee White, FB
Jim Schmedding, OG
69— Carter Campbell, DE
70— Henry Reed, DE
71— David Taylor, OT
77— Dennis Duncanson, DB
78— Dennis Duncanson, DB
Randy Jordan, WR
80—†Mike Humiston, LB
89—†Peter Macon, WR
91—†Jamie Martin, QB
†Alfred Pupunu, WR
93—†Pat McNarney, TE
95—†Pokey Eckford, WR

WESLEY (2)
91— Fran Naselli, KR
95— Brandon Steinheim, RB

WESLEYAN (CONN.) (6)
46— Bert VanderClute, G
48— Jack Geary, T
72— Robert Heller, C
73— Robert Heller, C
76— John McVicar, DL
77— John McVicar, DL

WEST ALA. (4)
82— Charles Martin, DT
84— Andrew Fields, WR
87— Ronnie Glanton, DL
93— Matt Carman, WR

WEST CHESTER (9)
52— Charles Weber, DG
58— Richard Emerich, T
61— Joe Iacone, B
62— Joe Iacone, B
72— Tim Pierantozzi, QB
76— William Blystone, RB
87— Ralph Tamm, OL
88— Bill Hess, WR
92— Lee Woodall, DL

WEST TEX. A&M (5)
86— Stan Carraway, WR
90— Mark Bounds, P
94— Brad Bailey, WR
Brian Hurley, OL
95— Jon Mason, P

WEST VA.* (1)
34— Tod Goodwin, E

WEST VA. TECH (3)
82— Elliott Washington, DB
86— Calvin Wallace, DL
89— Phil Hudson, WR

WEST VA. WESLEYAN (2)
36— George Mike, T
82— Jerry Free, T

WESTERN CARO. (13)
49— Arthur Byrd, G
71— Steve Williams, DT
73— Mark Ferguson, OT
74— Jerry Gaines, SE
Steve Yates, LB
84—†Louis Cooper, DL
†Kirk Roach, PK
†Steve Kornegay, P
85—†Clyde Simmons, DL
86—†Alonzo Carmichael, TE
†Kirk Roach, PK
87—†Kirk Roach, PK
93—†Kerry Hayes, KR/WR

WESTERN ILL. (16)
59— Bill Larson, B
61— Leroy Jackson, B
74— John Passananti, OT
76— Scott Levenhagen, TE
Greg Lee, DB
77— Craig Phalen, DT
78— Bill Huskisson, DL
80— Mike Maher, TE
Don Greco, OG
83—†Chris Gunderson, MG
84—†Chris Gunderson, T
86—†Frank Winters, C
†Todd Auer, DL
88—†Marlin Williams, DL
93—†Rodney Harrison, DB
94—†Ross Schulte, P

WESTERN KY. (16)
64— Dale Lindsey, LB
70— Lawrence Brame, DE
73— Mike McKoy, DB
74— John Bushong, DL
Virgil Livers, DB
75— Rick Green, LB
77— Chip Carpenter, OL
80—†Pete Walters, OG
†Tim Ford, DL
81—†Donnie Evans, DE
82—†Paul Gray, LB
83—†Paul Gray, LB
87—†James Edwards, DB
88—†Dean Tiebout, OL
†Joe Arnold, RB
95—†Brian Bixler, C

WESTERN MD. (3)
51— Victor Makovitch, DG
78— Ricci Bonaccorsy, DL
79— Ricci Bonaccorsy, DL

WESTERN MICH.* (1)
82—†Matt Meares, OL

WESTERN N.M. (2)
83— Jay Ogle, WR
88— Pat Maxwell, P

WESTERN ST. (6)
56— Bill Rhodes, B
78— Bill Campbell, DB
80— Justin Cross, OT
84— Jeff Guy, P
92— Reggie Alexander, WR
94— Derren Bryan, OL

WESTERN WASH. (3)
51— Norman Hash, DB
79— Patrick Locker, RB
95— Orlando Steinauer, DB

WESTMINSTER (PA.) (10)
73— Robert Pontius, DB
77— Rex Macey, FL
82— Gary DeGruttola, LB
83— Scott Higgins, DB
86— Joe Keaney, LB
88— Kevin Myers, LB
89— Joe Micchia, QB
90— Brad Tokar, RB
91— Brian DeLorenzo, DL
92— Matt Raich, LB

WHEATON (ILL.) (7)
55— Dave Burnham, B
58— Robert Bakke, T
77— Larry Wagner, LB
78— Scott Hall, QB
83— Keith Bishop, QB
95— Doug Johnston, OL
Chip Parrish, LB

WHITTIER (3)
38— Myron Claxton, T
62— Richard Peter, T
77— Michael Ciacci, DB

WHITWORTH (4)
52— Pete Swanson, OG
54— Larry Paradis, T
85— Wayne Ralph, WR
86— Wayne Ralph, WR

WIDENER (13)
72— Billy Johnson, RB
73— Billy Johnson, RB
75— John Warrington, DB
76— Al Senni, OL
77— Chip Zawoiski, RB
79— Tom Deery, DB
80— Tom Deery, DB
81— Tom Deery, DB
82— Tony Stefanoni, DL
88— Dave Duffy, DL
94— O. J. McElroy, DL
Antoine Moore, DB
95— Blaise Coleman, LB

WILKES (2)
73— Jeff Grandinetti, DT
93— Jason Feese, DL

WILLAMETTE (11)
34— Loren Grannis, G
35— John Oravec, B
36— Richard Weisgerber, B
46— Marvin Goodman, E
58— William Long, C
59— Marvin Cisneros, G
64— Robert Burles, DT
65— Robert Burles, DT
69— Calvin Lee, LB
75— Gary Johnson, DL
82— Richard Milroy, DB

WILLIAM & MARY (6)
83—†Mario Shaffer, OL
86—†Michael Clemons, RB
89—†Steve Christie, P
90—†Pat Crowley, DL
93—†Craig Staub, DL
95—†Darren Sharper, DB

WILLIAM JEWELL (4)
52— Al Conway, B
73— John Strada, OE
81— Guy Weber, DL
83— Mark Mundel, OL

WM. PATERSON (2)
92— Craig Paskas, DB
93— Craig Paskas, DB

WILLIAM PENN (1)
72— Bruce Polen, DB

WILLIAMS (7)
51— Charles Salmon, DG
69— Jack Maitland, HB

74— John Chandler, LB
78— Greg McAleenan, DB
90— George Rogers, DL
94— Bobby Walker, LB
95— Ethan Brooks, DL

WILMINGTON (OHIO) (2)
72— William Roll, OG
94— Jason Tincher, WR

WINGATE (1)
89— Jimmy Sutton, OT

WINONA ST. (2)
92— Dave Ludy, AP
94— Dave Ludy, AP

WINSTON-SALEM (5)
77— Cornelius Washington, DB
78— Tim Newsome, RB
84— Danny Moore, OG
87— Barry Turner, G
95— Richard Huntley, RB

WIS.-EAU CLAIRE (1)
81— Roger Vann, RB

WIS.-LA CROSSE (13)
52— Ted Levanhagen, LB
72— Bryon Buelow, DB
78— Joel Williams, LB
83— Jim Byrne, DL
85— Tom Newberry, OL
88— Ted Pretasky, RB
89— Terry Strouf, OL
91— Jon Lauscher, LB
92— Norris Thomas, DB
Mike Breit, LB
93— Rick Schaaf, DL
95— Craig Kusick, QB
Erik Halverson, OL

WIS.-MILWAUKEE (1)
70— Pete Papara, LB

WIS.-PLATTEVILLE (2)
73— William Vander Velden, DE
86— Mike Hintz, DB

WIS.-RIVER FALLS (4)
80— Gerald Sonsalla, OG
82— Roland Hall, LB
87— Greg Corning, RB
95— Brian Izdepski, OT

WIS.-STEVENS POINT (5)
77— Reed Giordana, QB
81— Chuck Braun, WR
92— Randy Simpson, DB
93— Jimmy Henderson, RB
94— Randy Simpson, LB

WIS.-STOUT (1)
79— Joseph Bullis, DL

WIS.-SUPERIOR (3)
66— Mel Thake, DB
83— Larry Banks, MG
85— Phil Eiting, LB

WIS.-WHITEWATER (4)
75— William Barwick, OL
79— Jerry Young, WR
82— Daryl Schleim, DE
90— Reggie White, OL

WITTENBERG (22)
62— Donald Hunt, G
63— Bob Cherry, E
64— Chuck Green, QB
68— Jim Felts, DE
73— Steve Drongowski, OT
74— Arthur Thomas, LB
75— Robert Foster, LB
76— Dean Caven, DL
78— Dave Merritt, RB
79— Joe Govern, DL
80— Mike Dowds, DE
81— Bill Beach, DB
83— Bryant Lemon, DL
87— Eric Horstman, OL
88— Ken Bonner, OT
Eric Horstman, OL
90— Jon Warga, RB
92— Taver Johnson, LB
93— Taver Johnson, LB
Greg Brame, PK
95— Ron Cunningham, OT
Jimmy Watts, PK

WOFFORD (11)
42— Aubrey Faust, E
47— Ken Dubard, T
49— Elbert Hammett, T
51— Jack Beeler, DB
57— Charles Bradshaw, B
61— Dan Lewis, G
70— Sterling Allen, OG
79— Keith Kinard, OL
90— David Wiley, OL
91— Tom Colter, OL
94— Brian Porzio, PK

WOOSTER (1)
79— Blake Moore, C

WORCESTER ST. (3)
92— Chris Butts, DB
93— Chris Butts, DB
94— Brian Fitzpatrick, DB

XAVIER (OHIO) (1)
51— Tito Carinci, LB

YALE (1)
84— †John Zanieski, DL

YOUNGSTOWN ST. (22)
74— Don Calloway, DB
75— Don Calloway, DB
78— Ed McGlasson, OL
79— James Ferranti, OE
Jeff Lear, OT
80— Jeff Gergel, LB
81— †Paris Wicks, RB
82— †Paris Wicks, RB
88— †Jim Zdelar, OL
89— †Paul Soltis, LB
90— †Tony Bowens, DL
91— †Pat Danko, DL
92— †Dave Roberts, DB
93— †Drew Garber, OL
†Tamron Smith, RB
†Jeff Wilkins, PK
94— †Randy Smith, KR
†Leon Jones, LB
†Lester Weaver, DB
†Chris Sammarone, OL
95— †Leon Jones, LB
†Jermaine Hopkins, DL

NCAA Postgraduate Scholarship Winners

Following are football players who are NCAA postgraduate scholarship winners, whether or not they were able to accept the grant, plus all alternates (indicated by *) who accepted grants. The program began with the 1964 season. (Those who played in 1964 are listed as 1965 winners, those who played in 1965 as 1966 winners, etc.) To qualify, student-athletes must maintain a 3.000 grade-point average (on a 4.000 scale) during their collegiate careers and perform with distinction in varsity football.

ABILENE CHRISTIAN
71— James Lindsey
83— *Grant Feasel
85— Daniel Remsberg
86— *James Embry
Craig Huff
90— William Clayton

ADRIAN
94— Jeffrey Toner

AIR FORCE
65— Edward Fausti
67— James Hogarty
68— Kenneth Zagzebski
69— *Richard Rivers Jr.
70— Charles Longnecker
*Alfred Wurglitz
71— Ernest Jennings
Robert Parker Jr.
72— Darryl Haas
73— Mark Prill
75— *Joseph Debes
84— Jeffrey Kubiak
86— Derek Brown
88— Chad Hennings
89— David Hlatky
90— Steven Wilson
91— Christopher Howard
92— Ronald James
93— Scott Hufford
95— Preston McConnell
96— Bret Cillessen

ALABAMA
69— Donald Sutton
72— John Musso Jr.
75— Randy Hall
80— Steadman Shealy

ALABAMA ST.
92— Edward Robinson Jr.

ALBANY (N.Y.)
88— *Thomas Higgins

ALBION
81— Joel Manby
94— Michael Montico
95— Jeffrey Shooks
96— Timothy Schafer

ALBRIGHT
67— *Paul Chaiet

ALLEGHENY
65— David Wion
92— Darren Hadlock

ALMA
67— Keith Bird Jr.
79— Todd Friesner

AMHERST
66— David Greenblatt
76— Geoffrey Miller
85— Raymond Nurme
96— Gregory Schneider

APPALACHIAN ST.
78— Gill Beck
93— D. J. Campbell

ARIZONA
69— William Michael Moody
78— Jon Abbott
80— Jeffrey Whitton
88— Charles Cecil

ARIZONA ST.
78— John Harris
90— Mark Tingstad

ARKANSAS
70— Terry Stewart
71— William Burnett
79— William Bradford Shoup
85— *Mark Lee

ARKANSAS ST.
72— John Meyer
77— Thomas Humphreys

ARMY
66— Samuel Champi Jr.
68— Bohdan Neswiacheny
69— James McCall Jr.
Thomas Wheelock
70— Theodore Shadid Jr.
78— Curtis Downs
81— *Stanley March
86— Donald Smith
Douglas Black
88— William Conner
90— Michael Thorson
93— Michael McElrath
95— Eric Oliver

ASHLAND
78— Daniel Bogden
88— David Biondo
90— Douglas Powell

AUBURN
66— John Cochran
69— *Roger Giffin
85— Gregg Carr
90— James Lyle IV

AUGSBURG
90— Terry Mackenthun

AUGUSTANA (ILL.)
69— *Jeffrey Maurus
71— Kenneth Anderson
77— Joe Thompson
86— Steven Sanders
96— Thomas King

AUGUSTANA (S.D.)
72— Michael Olson
75— David Zelinsky
77— James Clemens
78— Dee Donlin
Roger Goebel
90— *David Gubbrud
91— Scott Boyens

BALL ST.
67— *John Hostrawser
73— Gregory Mack
77— Arthur Yaroch
84— Richard Chitwood
88— Ronald Duncan
90— Theodore Ashburn
93— Troy Hoffer

BATES
79— Christopher Howard

BAYLOR
65— Michael Kennedy
66— Edward Whiddon
94— John Eric Joe

BOISE ST.
72— Brent McIver
76— *Glenn Sparks
79— Samuel Miller
82— Kip Bedard
92— Larry Stayner
93— David Tingstad

BOSTON COLLEGE
66— *Lawrence Marzetti
67— Michael O'Neill
69— Gary Andrachik
70— Robert Bouley
78— Richard Scudellari
87— Michael Degnan

BOSTON U.
69— Suren Donabedian Jr.
81— David Bengtson

BOWDOIN
65— Steven Ingram
67— Thomas Allen

BOWIE ST.
92— Mark Fitzgerald

BOWLING GREEN
77— Richard Preston
78— Mark Miller
91— Patrick Jackson

BRIDGEPORT
70— Terry Sparker

BRIGHAM YOUNG
67— Virgil Carter
76— Orrin Olsen
77— *Stephen Miller
78— Gifford Nielsen
80— Marc Wilson
82— Daniel Plater
83— Bart Oates
84— Steve Young
85— Marvin Allen
89— Charles Cutler
94— Eric Drage

BROWN
65— John Kelly Jr.
70— James Lukens
74— Douglas Jost
75— William Taylor
77— Scott Nelson
78— Louis Cole
79— Robert Forster
82— Travis Holcombe
95— Rene Abdalah

BUCKNELL
71— *Kenneth Donahue
74— John Dailey
75— Steve Leskinen
77— Lawrence Brunt
85— David Kucera
93— David Berardinelli

BUENA VISTA
77— Steven Trost
87— Michael Habben
94— Cary Murphy

BUFFALO ST.
87— James Dunbar

BUTLER
72— George Yearsich
78— William Ginn
85— Stephen Kollias

CALIFORNIA
66— William Krum
67— John Schmidt
68— Robert Crittenden
70— James Calkins
71— Robert Richards
83— Harvey Salem
94— Douglas Brien

UC DAVIS
76— Daniel Carmazzi
David Gellerman
77— Rolf Benirschke
79— Mark Markel
86— Robert Hagenau
90— *James Tomasin
92— Robert Kincade
Michael Shepard
93— Brian Andersen

UC RIVERSIDE
72— Tyrone Hooks
74— Gary Van Jandegian

CAL LUTHERAN
90— *Gregory Maw

CAL POLY SLO
69— William Creighton

CAL TECH
67— William Mitchell
68— John Frazzini
74— Frank Hobbs Jr.

CANISIUS
84— Thomas Schott

CAPITAL
84— *Michael Linton

CARLETON
67— Robert Paarlberg
73— Mark Williams
83— Paul Vaaler
93— Arthur Gilliland

CARNEGIE MELLON
80— Gusty Sunseri
91— Robert O'Toole

CARROLL (WIS.)
77— Stephen Thompson
95— Christopher Klippel

CARTHAGE
70— William Radakovitz

CASE RESERVE
89— Christopher Nutter
91— James Meek

CENTRAL (IOWA)
71— Vernon Den Herder
87— Scott Lindell
89— Eric Perry
92— Richard Kacmarynski
96— Rick Sanger

CENTRAL ARK.
96— Brian Barnett

CENTRAL MICH.
77— John Wunderlich
80— *Michael Ball
85— Kevin Egnatuk
88— Robert Stebbins
92— Jeffrey Bender

CENTRAL WASH.
70— Danny Collins

CENTRE
69— Glenn Shearer
86— Casteel "Teel" Bruner II
88— *Robert Clark
90— James Ellington

CHADRON ST.
96— Corey Campbell

CHEYNEY
76— Steven Anderson

CHICAGO
86— *Bruce Montella
89— Paul Haar
94— Frank Baker

CINCINNATI
71— *Earl Willson

CITADEL
74— Thomas Leitner
79— Kenneth Caldwell
84— *William West IV

CLAREMONT-M-S
68— Craig Dodel
70— *Gregory Long
71— Stephen Endemano
73— Christopher Stecher
74— Samuel Reece

CLEMSON
65— James Bell Jr.
68— James Addison
73— Benjamin Anderson
79— Stephen Fuller

COAST GUARD
73— Rodney Leis
74— Leonard Kelly
81— Bruce Hensel
89— *Ty Rinoski
*Jeffery Peters
90— Richard Schachner
91— John Freda

COE
67— Lynn Harris

COLBY
71— Ronald Lupton
Frank Apantaku

COLGATE
73— Kenneth Nelson
80— Angelo Colosimo
89— Donald Charney

COLORADO
93— James Hansen

COLORADO COL.
69— Steven Ehrhart
72— Randy Bobier
75— Bruce Kolbezen
84— Herman Motz III

COLORADO MINES
66— Stuart Bennett
67— Michael Greensburg
Charles Kirby
75— David Chambers

COLORADO ST.
65— Russel Mowrer
76— Mark Driscoll

87— Stephan Bartalo
88— Joseph Brookhart
93— Gregory Primus
96— Gregory Myers

COLUMBIA
72— John Sefcik
80— Mario Biaggi Jr.

CONNECTICUT
77— *Bernard Palmer

CORNELL
68— Ronald Kipicki
72— Thomas Albright
84— Derrick Harmon

CORNELL COLLEGE
65— Steven Miller
72— David Hilmers
73— Robert Ash
79— Brian Farrell
Thomas Zinkula
81— *Timothy Garry
83— John Ward
93— Brent Sands
94— Matthew Miller
95— Mark McDermott

DARTMOUTH
66— Anthony Yezer
68— Henry Paulson Jr.
69— Randolph Wallick
71— Willie Bogan
73— Frederick Radke
74— Thomas Csatari
*Robert Funk
77— Patrick Sullivan
89— Paul Sorensen
95— O. Josh Bloom

DAVIDSON
66— Stephen Smith
71— Rick Lyon
72— Robert Norris
86— *Louis Krempel

DAYTON
73— Timothy Quinn
76— Roy Gordon III
83— *Michael Pignatiello
91— Daniel Sharley

DELAWARE
86— Brian Farrell

DELAWARE VALLEY
85— Daniel Glowatski

DELTA ST.
76— William Hood

DENISON
70— Richard Trumball
73— Steven Smiljanich
76— *Dennis Thome
78— David Holcombe
86— Brian Gearinger
88— Grant Jones
92— Jonathan Fortkamp

DePAUW
68— Bruce Montgomerie
78— Mark Frazer
81— Jay True
85— Richard Bonaccorsi
86— Anthony deNicola
92— Thomas Beaulieu

DICKINSON
66— Robert Averback
71— *John West
75— *Gerald Urich

DOANE
68— John Lothrop
70— Richard Held

DRAKE
73— Joseph Worobec

DREXEL
72— Blake Lynn Ferguson

DUBUQUE
82— Timothy Finn

DUKE
68— Robert Lasky
71— *Curt Rawley

EAST CARO.
92— Keith Arnold

EAST TENN. ST.
82— Jay Patterson

EASTERN KY.
78— Steven Frommeyer

EASTERN N.M.
66— Richard James

ELIZABETH CITY ST.
73— Darnell Johnson
80— David Nickelson

ELMHURST
80— Richard Green

EMORY & HENRY
82— Thomas Browder Jr.

EVANSVILLE
75— David Mattingly
76— Charles Uhde Jr.
79— *Neil Saunders

FERRIS ST.
79— Robert Williams
93— Monty Brown

FLORIDA
72— Carlos Alvarez
77— Darrell Carpenter
85— Garrison Rolle
87— Bret Wiechmann
90— *Cedric Smith
91— Huey Richardson
95— Michael Gilmore

FLORIDA ST.
88— David Palmer
91— David Roberts
94— Kenneth Alexander
95— Derrick Brooks

FORDHAM
91— Eric Schweiker

FORT HAYS ST.
94— David Foster

FRANK. & MARSH.
69— Frank deGenova
83— *Robert Shepardson

FRESNO ST.
70— *Henry Corda
74— Dwayne Westphal
83— William Griever Jr.

FURMAN
77— Thomas Holcomb III
82— Charles Anderson
84— Ernest Gibson
86— *David Jager
87— Stephen Squire
90— Christopher Roper
92— Paul Siffri
Eric Von Walter
96— William Phillip Jones

GEORGETOWN
75— James Chesley Jr.

GEORGIA
68— Thomas Lawhorne Jr.
69— William Payne
71— Thomas Lyons
72— Thomas Nash Jr.
Raleigh Mixon Robinson
78— Jeffrey Lewis
80— Jeffrey Pyburn
81— Christopher Welton
84— Terrell Hoage
88— Kim Stephens
89— Richard Tardits

GEORGIA TECH
68— William Eastman
75— James Robinson
81— Sheldon Fox
83— Ellis Gardner
86— John Ivemeyer

GETTYSBURG
70— *Herbert Ruby III
80— Richard Swartz

GRAMBLING
73— Stephen Dennis

GRINNELL
72— Edward Hirsch
80— *Derek Muehrcke

GROVE CITY
95— Stephen Sems

GUST. ADOLPHUS
74— James Goodwin
81—*David Najarian

HAMLINE
85— Kyle Aug
91— Robert Hackney

HAMPDEN-SYDNEY
78—*Wilson Newell
80— Timothy Maxa

HARVARD
68— Alan Bersin
71—*Richard Frisbie
75— Patrick McInally
76— William Emper
81— Charles Durst
85— Brian Bergstrom
87— Scott Collins

HAWAII
68— James Roberts
73—*Don Satterlee

HIRAM
68— Sherman Riemenschneider
74— Donald Brunetti

HOLY CROSS
84—*Bruce Kozerski
89— Jeffrey Wiley
91— John Lavalette

HOPE
74— Ronald Posthuma
80— Craig Groendyk
83— Kurt Brinks
85—*Scott Jecmen

HOUSTON
86— Gary Schoppe
87— Robert Brezina

IDAHO
67— Michael Lavens
Joseph McCollum Jr.
84— Boyce Bailey

IDAHO ST.
76— Richard Rodgers
92— Steven Boyenger

ILLINOIS
72— Robert Bucklin
73— Laurence McCarren Jr.
91— Curtis Lovelace
92— Michael Hopkins
93— John Wright

ILL. BENEDICTINE
70— David Cyr
71— Thomas Danaher

ILL. WESLEYAN
93— Christopher Bisaillon

INDIANA
73— Glenn Scolnik
79— David Abrams
81— Kevin Speer

INDIANA (PA.)
78—*John Mihota
84— Kenneth Moore

INDIANA ST.
86— Jeffrey Miller

INDIANAPOLIS
76— Rodney Pawlik

IONA
81— Neal Kurtti
82—*Paul Rupp

IOWA
69— Michael Miller
76— Robert Elliott
78— Rodney Sears
86— Larry Station Jr.
88— Michael Flagg
89— Charles Hartlieb

IOWA ST.
70— William Bliss

JACKSON ST.
80—*Lester Walls

JACKSONVILLE ST.
79— Dewey Barker

JAMES MADISON
79— Warren Coleman
90— Mark Kiefer

JOHNS HOPKINS
73— Joseph Ouslander
74— Gunter Glocker
94— Steuart Markley
95— Michael House

JUNIATA
72— Maurice Taylor
87— Robert Crossey

KANSAS
65— Ronald Oelschlager
69— David Morgan
72— Michael McCoy
73— John Schroll
78— Tom Fitch
87— Mark Henderson

KANSAS ST.
66—*Larry Anderson
83— James Gale
88— Matthew Garver

KENTUCKY
76— Thomas Ranieri
79— James Kovach
84—*Keith Martin

KENTUCKY ST.
68— James Jackson

KENYON
75— Patrick Clements

KNOX
88— Robert Monroe

LAFAYETTE
71— William Sprecher
76— Michael Kline
78— Victor Angeline III

LAMAR
73—*Richard Kubiak

LAWRENCE
68— Charles McKee
83— Christopher Matheus

LEBANON VALLEY
74—*Alan Shortell

LEHIGH
66— Robert Adelaar
68— Richard Miller
73—*Thomas Benfield
75— James Addonizio
76—*Robert Liptak
77—*Michael Yaszemski
80— David Melone

LONG BEACH ST.
84— Joseph Donohue

LIU-C.W. POST
79— John Luchsinger

LSU
79— Robert Dugas
83— James Britt
88— Ignazio Albergamo
91— Solomon Graves
94— Chad Loup
95— Michael Blanchard

LUTHER
67— Thomas Altemeier
78—*Mark Larson
85— Larry Bonney

MANKATO ST.
70— Bernard Maczuga

MARYLAND
78— Jonathan Claiborne

MARYVILLE (TENN.)
67— Frank Eggers II

MIT
91— Darcy Prather
92— Rodrigo Rubiano
93— Roderick Tranum
95— Corey Foster

McNEESE ST.
81— Daryl Burckel
86— Ross Leger

MEMPHIS
77—*James Mincey Jr.

MERCHANT MARINE
70— Robert Lavinia
76—*John Castagna

MIAMI (FLA.)
90— Robert Chudzinski
91— Michael Sullivan

MICHIGAN
67— David Fisher
74— David Gallagher
81—*John Wangler
82— Norm Betts
84— Stefan Humphries
Thomas Dixon
86— Clayton Miller
87— Kenneth Higgins
93— Christopher Hutchinson
94— Marc Milia

MICHIGAN ST.
69— Allen Brenner
70— Donald Baird
94— Steven Wasylk

MICHIGAN TECH
72— Larry Ras
74— Bruce Trusock
75— Daniel Rhude

MIDDLE TENN. ST.
73—*Edwin Zaunbrecher

MIDDLEBURY
79— Franklin Kettle

MIDLAND LUTHERAN
76— Thomas Hale

MILLERSVILLE
92— Thomas Burns III

Photo from Illinois Wesleyan sports information

In addition to holding the Division III record with 55 career touchdown catches, Illinois Wesleyan wide receiver Chris Bisaillon (99) was an NCAA Postgraduate Scholarship winner in 1993.

MILLIKIN
90—*Charles Martin

MILLSAPS
67— Edward Weller
73—*Russell Gill
92— David Harrison Jr.

MINNESOTA
69— Robert Stein
71— Barry Mayer
73— Douglas Kingsriter
78— Robert Weber

MISSISSIPPI
66— Stanley Hindman
69— Steve Hindman
81— Kenneth Toler Jr.
86— Richard Austin
87— Jeffrey Noblin
88— Daniel Hoskins
89— Charles Walls
91— Todd Sandroni

MISSISSIPPI COL.
80— Stephen Johnson

MISSISSIPPI ST.
69— William Nelson
73— Frank Dowsing Jr.
75— James Webb
77— William Coltharp
93— Daniel Boyd

MISSOURI
66— Thomas Lynn
67— James Whitaker
69—*Charles Weber
71— John Weisenfels
79— Christopher Garlich
82— Van Darkow

MO.-ROLLA
69— Robert Nicodemus
73— Kim Colter
81— Paul Janke

MONMOUTH (ILL.)
72— Dale Brooks
90— Brent Thurness

MONTANA
75— Rock Svennungsen
79— Steven Fisher
84— Brian Salonen
91— Michael McGowan
96— David Dickenson

MONTANA ST.
65— Gene Carlson
68— Russell Dodge
71— Jay Groepper
77— Bert Markovich
79— Jon Borchardt
James Mickelson
90— Derrick Isackson
92— Travis Annette

MORAVIAN
73— Daniel Joseph
94— Judson Frank

MOREHEAD ST.
92— James Appel

MORNINGSIDE
65— Larry White

MORRIS BROWN
83— Arthur Knight Jr.

MOUNT UNION
89— Paul Hrics

MUHLENBERG
73— Edward Salo
76— Eric Butler
78— Mark Stull
81— Arthur Scavone
91— Michael Hoffman

MURRAY ST.
71— Matthew Haug
78— Edward McFarland
81—*Kris Robbins
90— Eric Crigler

NAVY
65— William Donnelly
69— William Newton
70— Daniel Pike
75—*Timothy Harden
76— Chester Moeller II
81— Theodore Dumbauld

NEBRASKA
70— Randall Reeves
71—*John Decker
72— Larry Jacobson
73— David Mason
74— Daniel Anderson
76— Thomas Heiser
77— Vince Ferragamo
78— Ted Harvey
79— James Pillen
80— Timothy Smith
81— Randy Schleusener
Jeffrey Finn
82— Eric Lindquist
85— Scott Strasburger
88— Jeffrey Jamrog
89— Mark Blazek
90— Gerald Gdowski
Jacob Young III
91— David Edeal
Patrick Tyrance Jr.
92— Patrick Engelbert
93— Michael Stigge
94— Trev Alberts
95— Robert Zatechka
96— Aaron Graham

NEB.-OMAHA
84— Kirk Hutton
Clark Toner

UNLV
95— Howard McGowan

NEW HAMPSHIRE
85— Richard Leclerc

NEW MEXICO
72— Roderick Long
76— Robert Berg
79— Robert Rumbaugh
83— George Parks

NEW MEXICO ST.
76— Ralph Jackson
77—*Joseph Fox

NORTH ALA.
82—*Warren Moore

NORTH CARO.
75— Christopher Kupec
81— William Donnalley
83— David Drechsler
91— Kevin Donnalley

N.C. CENTRAL
91— Anthony Cooley

NORTH CARO. ST.
75— Justus Everett
82—*Calvin Warren Jr.

NORTH DAK.
79— Dale Lian
81— Douglas Moen
82— Paul Franzmeier
85— Glen Kucera
88— Kurt Otto
89— Matthew Gulseth
93— Timothy Gelinske

NORTH DAK. ST.
66— James Schindler
69—*Stephen Stephens
71— Joseph Cichy
75— Paul Cichy
84— Doug Hushka
89— Charles Stock
94— Arden Beachy

NORTH TEXAS
68— Ruben Draper
77— Peter Morris

NORTHEAST LA.
93— Darren Rimmer
94— Robert Cobb
Michael Young

NORTHERN ARIZ.
78— Larry Friedrichs

NORTHERN COLO.
76— Robert Bliss
91— Thomas Langer

NORTHERN IOWA
81— Owen Dockter

NORTHERN MICH.
73— Guy Falkenhagen
81— Phil Kessel
86— Keith Nelsen

NORTHWEST MO. ST.
82— Robert Gregory

NORTHWESTERN
70—*Bruce Hubbard
74— Steven Craig
77— Randolph Dean
81— Charles Kern
96— Salvatore Valenzisi
Ryan Padgett

NORTHWESTERN ST.
95— John Dippel

NORWICH
68— Richard Starbuck
74— Matthew Hincks

NOTRE DAME
67— Frederick Schnurr
68— James Smithberger
69— George Kunz
70— Michael Oriard
71— Lawrence DiNardo
72— Thomas Gatewood
73— Gregory Marx
74— David Casper
75— Peter Demmerle
Reggie Barnett
79— Joseph Restic
81— Thomas Gibbons
82— John Krimm Jr.
86— Gregory Dingens
89— Reginald Ho
94— Timothy Ruddy

OCCIDENTAL
66— James Wanless
67— Richard Verry
69— John St. John
78— Richard Fry
80—*Timothy Bond
89—*Curtis Page
95— Davin Lundquist

OHIO
78—*Robert Weidaw
80— Mark Geisler

OHIO NORTHERN
79— Mark Palmer
82— Larry Egbert

OHIO ST.
65— Arnold Chonko
66— Donald Unverferth
67— Ray Pryor
69— David Foley
71— Rex Kern
74— Randolph Gradishar
76— Brian Baschnagel
77— William Lukens
80— James Laughlin
84— John Frank
85— David Crecelius
86— Michael Lanese

OKLAHOMA
72— Larry Jack Mildren Jr.
73— Joe Wylie
81— Jay Jimerson
89— Anthony Phillips
91— Michael Sawatzky

OKLAHOMA ST.
83—*Doug Freeman

OLIVET
75— William Ziem

OREGON
79—*Willie Blasher Jr.
91— William Musgrave

OREGON ST.
69— William Enyart
69—*Jerry Belcher

PACIFIC (CAL.)
72—*Byron Cosgrove
78— Brian Peets
80— Bruce Filarsky

PENNSYLVANIA
68— Ben Mortensen
95— Michael Turner

PENN ST.
66— Joseph Bellas
67— John Runnells III
71— Robert Holuba
72— David Joyner
73— Bruce Bannon
74— Mark Markovich
75— John Baiorunos
79—*Charles Correal
80—*Michael Guman
81— John Walsh
84— Harry Hamilton
85— Douglas Strange
87— Brian Silverling
90— Roger Thomas Duffy
94— Craig Fayak
95— Charles Pittman

PITTSBURGH
79— Jeff Delaney
86— Robert Schilken
89— Mark Stepnoski

POMONA-PITZER
69—*Lee Piatek
77— Scott Borg
83—*Calvin Oishi
85—*Derek Watanabe
88— Edward Irick
93— Torin Cunningham

PORTLAND ST.
79— John Urness

PRINCETON
67— Charles Peters
69— Richard Sandler
70— Keith Mauney
76— Ronald Beible
81— Mark Bailey
83— Brent Woods
86— James Petrucci
87— John Hammond

PUGET SOUND
68— Stephen Doolittle
79—*Patrick O'Loughlin
83—*Anthony Threlkeld

PURDUE
70— Michael Phipps
74— Robert Hoftiezer
75— Lawrence Burton

REDLANDS
65— Robert Jones

RENSSELAER
67— Robert Darnall
69— John Contento

RHODES
71— John Churchill
79—*Philip Mischke
81— Jeffrey Lane
83—*Russell Ashford
85—*John Foropoulos
89— James Augustine

RICE
81—*Lamont Jefferson
91— Donald Hollas
96— James Lamy

RICHMOND
86— Leland Melvin

RIPON
65— Phillip Steans
69— Steven Thompson
80— Thomas Klofta

RUTGERS
90— Steven Tardy

ST. CLOUD ST.
90— Richard Rodgers

ST. FRANCIS (PA.)
87— Christopher Tantlinger

ST. JOHN'S (MINN.)
92— Denis McDonough
96— Christopher Palmer

ST. JOSEPH'S (IND.)
80— Michael Bettinger

ST. NORBERT
66— Michael Ryan
88— Matthew Lang

ST. PAUL'S
80— Gerald Hicks

ST. THOMAS (MINN.)
75— Mark Dienhart

SAN DIEGO
96— Douglas Popovich

SANTA CLARA
72— Ronald Sani
77— Mark Tiernan
81— *David Alfaro
85— Alexis Vlahos
87— Patrick Sende

SEWANEE
65— Frank Stubblefield
66— Douglas Paschall
69— James Beene
71— John Popham IV
77— Dudley West
82— Gregory Worsowicz
Domenick Reina
83— Michael York
84— Michael Jordan
93— Jason Forrester
94— Frederick Cravens
96— Stephen Tudor

SHIPPENSBURG
77— Anthony Winter

SIMPSON
71— Richard Clogg
74— Hugh Lickiss
90— Roger Grover
94— Chad Earwood

SOUTH CARO.
67— Steven Stanley Juk Jr.

SOUTH DAK.
79— Michael Schurrer
87— Todd Salat
93— Jason Seurer

SOUTH DAK. ST.
80— Charles Loewen
81— Paul Kippley
88— Daniel Sonnek
95— Jacob Hines

SOUTHEASTERN LA.
74— William Percy Jr.

SOUTHERN-B.R.
70— Alden Roche

SOUTHERN CAL
66— Charles Arrobio
69— Steven Sogge
70— Harry Khasigian
Steve Lehmer
74— Monte Doris
75— Patrick Haden
76— Kevin Bruce
78— Gary Bethel
80— Brad Budde
Paul McDonald
81— Gordon Adams
*Jeffrey Fisher
85— Duane Bickett
86— Anthony Colorito
*Matthew Koart
87— Jeffrey Bregel
90— John Jackson
96— Jeremy Hogue

SOUTHERN COLO.
70— Gregory Smith
73— Collon Kennedy III

SOUTHERN METHODIST
83— *Brian O'Meara
85— *Monte Goen
87— David Adamson
93— Cary Brabham

SOUTHERN MISS.
83— Richard Thompson
84— Stephen Carmody

SOUTHERN UTAH
92— Stephen McDowell

SOUTHWEST MO. ST.
80— Richard Suchenski
Mitchel Ware
85— Michael Armentrout

SOUTHWEST TEX. ST.
82— Michael Miller

SOUTHWESTERN LA.
71— *George Coussa

STANFORD
65— *Joe Neal
66— *Terry DeSylvia
68— John Root
71— John Sande III
72— Jackie Brown
74— Randall Poltl
75— *Keith Rowen
76— Gerald Wilson
77— Duncan McColl
81— Milton McColl
84— John Bergren
85— Scott Carpenter
86— Matthew Soderlund
87— Brian Morris
88— Douglas Robison
95— Stephen Stenstrom
96— Eric Abrams
David Walker

STONEHILL
93— Kevin Broderick

SUSQUEHANNA
77— Gerald Huesken
82— Daniel Distasio

SWARTHMORE
72— Christopher Leinberger
83— *John Walsh

SYRACUSE
78— *Robert Avery
86— Timothy Green
94— Patrick O'Neill
95— Eric Chenoweth

TEMPLE
74— Dwight Fulton

TENNESSEE
71— Donald Denbo
Timothy Priest
77— Michael Mauck
81— Timothy Irwin

TENN.-CHATT.
67— Harvey Ouzts
72— *Frank Webb
74— John McBrayer
76— Russell Gardner

TEXAS
69— Corbin Robertson Jr.
71— Willie Zapalac Jr.
73— *Michael Bayer
74— Patrick Kelly
75— Wade Johnston
76— Robert Simmons
77— William Hamilton

TEXAS-ARLINGTON
69— Michael Baylor

UTEP
80— Eddie Forkerway
89— Patrick Hegarty
92— Robert Sesich

TEXAS A&M
69— Edward Hargett
71— David Elmendorf
72— Stephen Luebbehusen
88— Kip Corrington

TEXAS CHRISTIAN
67— John Richards
68— Eldon Gresham Jr.
73— Scott Walker
75— Terry Drennan
88— J. Clinton Hailey

TEXAS SOUTHERN
65— Leon Hardy

TEXAS TECH
65— James Ellis Jr.
68— John Scovell
75— Jeffrey Jobe
78— *Richard Arledge
85— *Bradford White
90— Thomas Mathiasmeier

TOLEDO
82— Tad Wampfler
89— Kenneth Moyer
95— Chadd Dehn

TRINITY (CONN.)
67— *Howard Wrzosek
68— Keith Miles

TRINITY (TEX.)
84— *Peter Broderick
95— Martin Thompson

TROY ST.
75— Mark King

TRUMAN ST.
83— Roy Pettibone

TUFTS
65— Peter Smith
70— Robert Bass
79— *Don Leach
80— *James Ford
82— *Brian Gallagher
87— Robert Patz
92— Paulo Oliveira

TULSA
67— *Larry Williams
75— James Mack Lancaster II

TUSKEGEE
68— James Greene

UCLA
67— *Raymond Armstrong
Dallas Grider
70— Gregory Jones
74— Steven Klosterman
76— John Sciarra
77— Jeffrey Dankworth
78— John Fowler Jr.
83— Cormac Carney
84— Richard Neuheisel
86— Michael Hartmeier
90— Richard Meyer
93— Carlton Gray
96— George Kase

UNION (N.Y.)
88— Richard Romer

UTAH
81— James Baldwin
93— Steven Young
95— Jason Jones

UTAH ST.
67— Ronnie Edwards
68— Garth Hall
70— Gary Anderson
76— Randall Stockham

VALDOSTA ST.
95— Christopher Hatcher

VALPARAISO
75— *Richard Seall

VANDERBILT
73— Barrett Sutton Jr.
75— Douglas Martin

VILLANOVA
77— David Graziano
89— Richard Spugnardi

VIRGINIA
67— Frederick Jones
83— Patrick Chester
94— Thomas Burns Jr.
96— Patrick Jeffers

VA. MILITARY
79— Robert Bookmiller
80— Richard Craig Jones

VIRGINIA TECH
73— Thomas Carpenito

WABASH
74— *Mark Nicolini
81— *Melvin Gore
83— David Broecker
87— James Herrmann
92— William Padgett

WAKE FOREST
70— Joseph Dobner
74— *Daniel Stroup
76— Thomas Fehring
78— *Michael McGlamry
83— Philip Denfeld
87— Toby Cole Jr.

WARTBURG
75— Conrad Mandsager
76— James Charles Peterson
82— *Rod Feddersen
94— Koby Kreinbring
96— Vincent Penningroth

WASHINGTON
65— William Douglas
67— Michael Ryan
72— *James Krieg
73— John Brady
77— Scott Phillips
78— Blair Bush
80— Bruce Harrell
82— Mark Jerue
83— Charles Nelson
Mark Stewart
88— David Rill
92— Edward Cunningham

WASHINGTON (MO.)
94— Aaron Keen

WASH. & JEFF.
70— Edward Guna
82— Max Regula
91— David Conn
93— Raymond Cross Jr.
95— Michael Jones

WASH. & LEE
70— Michael Thornton
74— William Wallace Jr.
78— Jeffrey Slatcoff
79— Richard Wiles
80— *Scott Smith
81— Lonnie Nunley III
89— Michael Magoline

WASHINGTON ST.
67— Richard Sheron
68— A. Douglas Flansburg
83— Gregory Porter
84— Patrick Lynch Jr.
85— Daniel Lynch

WAYNE ST. (MICH.)
76— Edward Skowneski Jr.
81— Phillip Emery

WEBER ST.
68— Phillip Tuckett
74— *Douglas Smith
92— David Hall
94— Deric Gurley

WESLEYAN (CONN.)
67— John Dwyer
69— Stuart Blackburn
71— James Lynch
78— John McVicar

WEST TEX. A&M
75— *Ben Bentley
82— Kevin Dennis

WEST VA.
74— Ade Dillion
*Daniel Larcamp
82— Oliver Luck

WESTERN CARO.
94— Thomas Jackson III

WESTERN ILL.
89— Paul Singer

WESTERN KY.
72— Jimmy Barber
80— Charles DeLacey

WESTERN MICH.
68— Martin Barski
71— Jonathan Bull

WESTERN N.M.
68— Richard Mahoney

WHEATON (ILL.)
89— David Lauber
93— Bart Moseman
96— Pedro Arruza

WHITTIER
76— John Getz
79— Mark Deven
87— *Timothy Younger

WILLAMETTE
87—*Gerry Preston

WILLIAM & MARY
78— G. Kenneth Smith
80— Clarence Gaines
85— Mark Kelso

WILLIAM JEWELL
66— Charles Scrogin
70— Thomas Dunn
John Johnston

WILLIAMS
65— Jerry Jones
72— John Murray
95— Nathan Sleeper
96— Medley Gatewood

WINONA ST.
95— Nathan Gruber

WINSTON-SALEM
84— Eddie Sauls

WISCONSIN
66— David Fronek
80— Thomas Stauss
82—*David Mohapp
83— Mathew Vanden Boom

WIS.-PLATTEVILLE
87— Michael Hintz

WIS.-WHITEWATER
96— Scott Hawig

WITTENBERG
82— William Beach

WOOSTER
80— Edward Blake Moore

WYOMING
74— Steven Cockreham
85— Bob Gustafson
89— Randall Welniak
96— Joseph Cummings

XAVIER (OHIO)
65— William Eastlake

YALE
66—*James Groninger
67— Howard Hilgendorf Jr.
69— Frederick Morris
71— Thomas Neville
72— David Bliss
75— John Burkus
77—*Stone Phillips
79— William Crowley
82— Richard Diana
91— Vincent Mooney
96— Matthew Siskosky

YOUNGSTOWN ST.
96— Mark Brungard

Academic All-America Hall of Fame

Since its inception in 1988, 28 former NCAA football players have been inducted into the GTE Academic All-America Hall of Fame. They were selected from among nominees by the College Sports Information Directors of America from past academic all-Americans of the 1950s, '60s and '70s. Following are the football selections by the year selected and each player's team, position and last year played:

1988
Pete Dawkins, Army, HB, 1958
Pat Haden, Southern Cal, QB, 1974
Rev. Donn Moomaw, UCLA, LB, 1953
Merlin Olsen, Utah St., T, 1961

1989
Carlos Alvarez, Florida, WR, 1971
Willie Bogan, Dartmouth, DB, 1970
Steve Bramwell, Washington, DB, 1965
Joe Romig, Colorado, G, 1961
Jim Swink, Texas Christian, B, 1956
John Wilson, Michigan St., DB, 1952

1990
Joe Theismann, Notre Dame, QB, 1970
Howard Twilley, Tulsa, TE, 1965

1991
Terry Baker, Oregon St., QB, 1962
Joe Holland, Cornell, RB, 1978
David Joyner, Penn St., OT, 1971
Brock Strom, Air Force, T, 1958

1992
Alan Ameche, Wisconsin, RB, 1954
Stephen Eisenhauer, Navy, G, 1953
Randy Gradishar, Ohio St., LB, 1973

1993
Raymond Berry, Southern Methodist, E, 1954
Dave Casper, Notre Dame, E, 1973
Jim Grabowski, Illinois, FB, 1965

1994
Richard Mayo, Air Force, QB, 1961
Lee Roy Selmon, Oklahoma, DT, 1975

1995
Pat Richter, Wisconsin, E, 1962

1996
Wade Mitchell, Georgia Tech, QB, 1956
Bob Thomas, Notre Dame, K, 1973
Byron "Whizzer" White, Colorado, HB, 1937 (honorary selection)

Academic All-Americans by School

Since 1952, academic all-America teams have been selected by the College Sports Information Directors of America. To be eligible, student-athletes must be regular performers and have at least a 3.200 grade-point average (on a 4.000 scale) during their college careers. University division teams (I-A and I-AA) are complete in this list, but college division teams (II, III, NAIA) before 1970 are missing from CoSIDA archives, with few exceptions. Following are all known first-team selections:

ABILENE CHRISTIAN
63—Jack Griggs, LB
70—Jim Lindsey, QB
74—Greg Stirman, E
76—Bill Curbo, T
77—Bill Curbo, T
87—Bill Clayton, DL
88—Bill Clayton, DL
89—Bill Clayton, DL
90—Sean Grady, WR

ADRIAN
84—Steve Dembowski, QB
94—Jay Overmyer, DB

AIR FORCE
58—Brock Strom, T
59—Rich Mayo, B
60—Rich Mayo, B
70—Ernie Jennings, E
71—Darryl Haas, LB/K
72—Bob Homburg, DE
Mark Prill, LB
73—Joe Debes, OT
74—Joe Debes, OT
78—Steve Hoog, WR
81—Mike France, LB
83—Jeff Kubiak, P
86—Chad Hennings, DL
87—Chad Hennings, DL
88—David Hlatky, OL
90—Chris Howard, RB
92—Grant Johnson, LB

AKRON
80—Andy Graham, PK

ALABAMA
61—Tommy Brooker, E
Pat Trammell, B
64—Gaylon McCollough, C
65—Steve Sloan, QB
Dennis Homan, HB
67—Steve Davis, K
Bob Childs, LB
70—Johnny Musso, HB
71—Johnny Musso, HB
73—Randy Hall, DT
74—Randy Hall, DT
75—Danny Ridgeway, KS
79—Major Ogilvie, RB

ALABAMA A&M
89—Tracy Kendall, QB
90—Tracy Kendall, QB

ALBANY (N.Y.)
86—Thomas Higgins, OT
87—Thomas Higgins, OT
94—Andy Shein, WR
95—Rich Tallarico, OL

ALBION
82—Bruce Drogosch, LB
86—Michael Grant, DB
90—Scott Bissell, DB
93—Eric Baxmann, LB
Jeffrey Shooks, P
94—Jeffrey Shooks, P
95—David Lefere, DB

ALFRED
89—Mark Szynkowski, OL

ALLEGHENY
81—Kevin Baird, P
91—Adam Lechman, OL
Darren Hadlock, LB

ALMA
86—Greg Luczak, TE

AMERICAN INT'L
81—Todd Scyocurka, LB

APPALACHIAN ST.
77—Gill Beck, C
92—D. J. Campbell, QB

ARIZONA
68—Mike Moody, OG
75—Jon Abbott, LB
76—Jon Abbott, T/LB
77—Jon Abbott, T/LB
79—Jeffrey Whitton, DL
87—Charles Cecil, DB

ARIZONA ST.
66—Ken Dyer, OE
88—Mark Tingstad, LB

ARKANSAS
57—Gerald Nesbitt, FB
61—Lance Alworth, B
64—Ken Hatfield, B
65—Randy Stewart, C
Jim Lindsey, HB
Jack Brasuell, DB
68—Bob White, K
69—Bill Burnett, HB
Terry Stewart, DB
78—Brad Shoup, DB

ARK.-MONTICELLO
85—Ray Howard, OG
88—Sean Rochelle, QB

ARKANSAS ST.
59—Larry Zabrowski, OT
61—Jim McMurray, QB

ARKANSAS TECH
90—Karl Kuhn, TE
91—Karl Kuhn, TE

ARMY
55—Ralph Chesnauskas, E
57—James Kernan, C
Pete Dawkins, HB
58—Pete Dawkins, HB
59—Don Usry, E
65—Sam Champi, DE
67—Bud Neswiacheny, DE
69—Theodore Shadid, C
89—Michael Thorson, DB
92—Mike McElrath, DB
94—Eric Oliver, LB

ASHLAND
73—Mark Gulling, DB
74—Ron Brown, LB
76—Dan Bogden, E
77—Bruce Niehm, LB
81—Mark Braun, C
91—Thomas Shiban, RB
93—Jerry Spatny, DL

AUBURN
57—Jimmy Phillips, E
59—Jackie Burkett, C
60—Ed Dyas, B
65—Bill Cody, LB
69—Buddy McClinton, DB
74—Bobby Davis, LB
75—Chuck Fletcher, DT
76—Chris Vacarella, RB
84—Gregg Carr, LB
94—Matt Hawkins, PK

AUGSBURG
81—Paul Elliott, DL

AUGUSTANA (ILL.)
75—George Wesbey, T
80—Bill Dannehl, WR
84—Steve Sanders, OT
85—Steve Sanders, OT
95—Ryan Carpenter, OL

AUGUSTANA (S.D.)
72—Pat McNerney, T
73—Pat McNerney, T

74—Jim Clemens, G
75—Jim Clemens, C
77—Stan Biondi, K
86—David Gubbrud, DL
87—David Gubbrud, DL
88—David Gubbrud, LB
89—David Gubbrud, LB

AUSTIN
81—Gene Branum, PK

AUSTIN PEAY
74—Gregory Johnson, G

BAKER
61—John Jacobs, B

BALDWIN-WALLACE
70—Earl Stolberg, DB
72—John Yezerski, G
78—Roger Andrachik, RB
Greg Monda, LB
81—Chuck Krajacic, OG
88—Shawn Gorman, P
91—Tom Serdinak, P
93—Adrian Allison, DL
David Coverdale, DL
94—David Coverdale, DL

BALL ST.
83—Rich Chitwood, C
85—Ron Duncan, TE
86—Ron Duncan, TE
87—Ron Duncan, TE
88—Ted Ashburn, OL
Greg Shackelford, DL
89—Ted Ashburn, OL
David Haugh, DB
91—Troy Hoffer, DB
92—Troy Hoffer, DB

BATES
82—Neal Davidson, DB

BAYLOR
61—Ronnie Bull, RB
62—Don Trull, QB
63—Don Trull, QB
76—Cris Quinn, DE
89—Mike Welch, DB
90—Mike Welch, DB

BELOIT
90—Shane Stadler, RB

BETHANY (KAN.)
86—Wade Gaeddert, DB

BLOOMSBURG
83—Dave Pepper, DL

BOISE ST.
71—Brent McIver, IL
73—Glenn Sparks, G
78—Sam Miller, DB

BOSTON COLLEGE
77—Richard Scudellari, LB
86—Michael Degnan, DL

BOSTON U.
83—Steve Shapiro, K
85—Brad Hokin, DB
93—Andre Maksimov, OL
94—Andre Maksimov, OL

BOWDOIN
84—Mike Siegel, P
93—Michael Turmelle, DB

BOWLING GREEN
75—John Boles, DE
89—Pat Jackson, LB
90—Pat Jackson, TE

BRIGHAM YOUNG
73—Steve Stratton, RB
80—Scott Phillips, RB
81—Dan Plater, WR
87—Chuck Cutler, WR
88—Chuck Cutler, WR
Tim Clark, DL
89—Fred Whittingham, RB
90—Andy Boyce, WR
93—Eric Drage, WR

BROWN
81—Travis Holcombe, OG
82—Dave Folsom, DB
86—Marty Edwards, C
87—John Cuozzo, C

BUCKNELL
72—Douglas Nauman, T
John Ondrasik, DB
73—John Dailey, LB
74—Steve Leskinen, T
75—Larry Brunt, E
76—Larry Brunt, E
84—Rob Masonis, RB
Jim Reilly, TE
86—Mike Morrow, WR
91—David Berardinelli, WR
92—David Berardinelli, WR

BUFFALO
63—Gerry Philbin, T
84—Gerry Quinlivan, LB
85—James Dunbar, C
86—James Dunbar, C

BUFFALO ST.
87—Clint Morano, OT

BUTLER
84—Steve Kollias, L

CALIFORNIA
67—Bob Crittenden, DG
70—Robert Richards, OT
82—Harvey Salem, OT

UC DAVIS
72—Steve Algeo, LB
75—Dave Gellerman, LB
90—Mike Shepard, DL

UC RIVERSIDE
71—Tyrone Hooks, HB

CAL LUTHERAN
81—John Walsh, OT

CANISIUS
82—Tom Schott, WR
83—Tom Schott, TE
86—Mike Panepinto, RB

CAPITAL
70—Ed Coy, E
83—Mike Linton, G
85—Kevin Sheets, WR

CARLETON
92—Scott Hanks, TE

CARNEGIE MELLON
76—Rick Lackner, LB
Dave Nackoul, E
84—Roger Roble, WR
87—Bryan Roessler, DL
Chris Haupt, LB
89—Robert O'Toole, LB
90—Frank Bellante, RB
Robert O'Toole, LB
94—Aaron Neal, TE
Merle Atkinson, DL

CARROLL (WIS.)
76—Stephen Thompson, QB

CARSON-NEWMAN
61—David Dale, E
93—Chris Horton, OL
94—Chris Horton, OL

CARTHAGE
61—Bob Halsey, B
77—Mark Phelps, QB

CASE RESERVE
75—John Kosko, T
82—Jim Donnelly, RB
83—Jim Donnelly, RB
84—Jim Donnelly, RB
88—Chris Hutter, TE
90—Michael Bissler, DB
95—Doug Finefrock, LB

CENTRAL (IOWA)
79—Chris Adkins, LB
85—Scott Lindrell, LB
86—Scott Lindrell, LB
91—Rich Kacmarynski, RB

CENTRAL MICH.
70—Ralph Burde, DL
74—Mike Franckowiak, QB
John Wunderlich, T
79—Mike Ball, WR
84—John DeBoer, WR
91—Jeff Bender, QB

CENTRE
84—Teel Bruner, DB
85—Teel Bruner, DB
89—Bryan Ellington, DB
91—Eric Horstmeyer, WR

CHADRON ST.
73—Jerry Sutton, LB
75—Bob Lacey, KS
79—Jerry Carder, TE
95—Corey Campbell, RB

CHEYNEY
75—Steve Anderson, G

CHICAGO
87—Paul Haar, OG
88—Paul Haar, OL
93—Frank Baker, RB

CINCINNATI
81—Kari Yli-Renko, OT
90—Kyle Stroh, DL
91—Kris Bjorson, TE

CITADEL
63—Vince Petno, E
76—Kenny Caldwell, LB
77—Kenny Caldwell, LB
78—Kenny Caldwell, LB
87—Thomas Frooman, RB
89—Thomas Frooman, RB

CLEMSON
59—Lou Cordileone, T
78—Steve Fuller, QB

COAST GUARD
70—Charles Pike, LB
71—Bruce Melnick, DB
81—Mark Butt, DB

COE
93—Marcus Adkins, DL

COLGATE
78—Angelo Colosimo, RB
79—Angelo Colosimo, RB
85—Tom Stenglein, WR
89—Jeremy Garvey, TE

COLORADO
60—Joe Romig, G
61—Joe Romig, G
67—Kirk Tracy, OG
70—Jim Cooch, DB
73—Rick Stearns, LB
74—Rick Stearns, LB
75—Steve Young, DT
87—Eric McCarty, LB
90—Jim Hansen, OL
91—Jim Hansen, OL
92—Jim Hansen, OL

COLORADO MINES
72—Dave Chambers, RB
83—Charles Lane, T

COLORADO ST.
55—Gary Glick, B
69—Tom French, OT
86—Steve Bartalo, RB
95—Greg Myers, DB

COLUMBIA
52—Mitch Price, B
53—John Gasella, T
56—Claude Benham, B
71—John Sefcik, HB

CORNELL
77—Joseph Holland, RB
78—Joseph Holland, RB
82—Derrick Harmon, RB
83—Derrick Harmon, RB
85—Dave Van Metre, DL

CORNELL COLLEGE
72—Rob Ash, QB
Dewey Birkhofer, S
76—Joe Lauterbach, G
Tom Zinkula, DT
77—Tom Zinkula, DT
78—Tom Zinkula, DL
82—John Ward, WR
91—Bruce Feldmann, QB
92—Brent Sands, DB
93—Mark McDermott, DB
94—Mark McDermott, DB
95—Mike Tressel, DB

CULVER-STOCKTON
95—Mason Kaiser, DB

DARTMOUTH
70—Willie Bogan, DB
83—Michael Patsis, DB
87—Paul Sorensen, LB
88—Paul Sorensen, LB
90—Brad Preble, DB
91—Mike Bobo, WR
Tom Morrow, LB
92—Russ Torres, RB
94—David Shearer, WR
Zach Lehman, DL

DAYTON
71—Tim Quinn, LB
72—Tim Quinn, DT
79—Scott Terry, QB
84—Greg French, K
David Kemp, LB
Jeff Slayback, L
85—Greg French, K
86—Gerry Meyer, OT
91—Brett Cuthbert, DB
Dan Rosenbaum, DB
92—Steve Lochow, DL
Dan Rosenbaum, DB
93—Steve Lochow, DL
Brad Mager, DB
94—David Overhoiser, RB

DEFIANCE
80—Jill Bailey, OT
Mark Bockelman, TE

DELAWARE
70—Yancey Phillips, T
71—Robert Depew, DE
72—Robert Depew, DE

DELAWARE VALLEY
84—Dan Glowatski, WR

DELTA ST.
70—Hal Posey, RB
74—Billy Hood, E
Ricky Lewis, LB
Larry Miller, RB
75—Billy Hood, E
78—Terry Moody, DB
79—Charles Stavley, G

DENISON
75—Dennis Thome, LB
87—Grant Jones, DB

DePAUW
70—Jim Ceaser, LB
71—Jim Ceaser, LB
73—Neil Oslos, RB
80—Jay True, WR
85—Tony deNicola, QB
87—Michael Sherman, DB
90—Tom Beaulieu, DL
91—Tom Beaulieu, DL
Matt Nelson, LB
94—Mike Callahan, LB

DICKINSON
74—Gerald Urich, RB
79—Scott Mumma, RB

DRAKE
74—Todd Gaffney, KS
83—Tom Holt, RB

DREXEL
70—Lynn Ferguson, S

DUBUQUE
80—Tim Finn, RB

DUKE
66—Roger Hayes, DE
67—Bob Lasky, DT
70—Curt Rawley, DT
86—Mike Diminick, DB
87—Mike Diminick, DB
88—Mike Diminick, DB
89—Doug Key, DL
93—Travis Pearson, DL

EAST STROUDSBURG
84—Ernie Siegrist, TE

EAST TENN. ST.
71—Ken Oster, DB

EAST TEX. ST.
77—Mike Hall, OT

EASTERN ILL.
95—Tim Carver, LB

EASTERN KY.
77—Steve Frommeyer, S

EASTERN N.M.
80—Tom Sager, DL
81—Tom Sager, DL

ELON
73—John Rascoe, E
79—Bryan Burney, DB

EMORY & HENRY
71—Tom Wilson, LB

EMPORIA ST.
79—Tom Lingg, DL

EVANSVILLE
74—David Mattingly, S
76—Michael Pociask, C
87—Jeffery Willman, TE

FERRIS ST.
81—Vic Trecha, OT
92—Monty Brown, LB

FLORIDA
65—Charles Casey, E
69—Carlos Alvarez, WR
71—Carlos Alvarez, WR
76—David Posey, KS
77—Wes Chandler, RB
80—Cris Collinsworth, WR
91—Brad Culpepper, DL
93—Michael Gilmore, DB
94—Terry Dean, QB
Michael Gilmore, DB
95—Danny Wuerffel, QB

FLORIDA A&M
90—Irvin Clark, DL

FLORIDA ST.
72—Gary Huff, QB
79—William Jones, DB
Phil Williams, WR
80—William Jones, DB
81—Rohn Stark, P
94—Derrick Brooks, LB

FORDHAM
90—Eric Schweiker, OL

FORT HAYS ST.
75—Greg Custer, RB
82—Ron Johnson, P
85—Paul Nelson, DL
86—Paul Nelson, DL
89—Dean Gengler, OL

FORT LEWIS
72—Dee Tennison, E

FRANK. & MARSH.
77—Joe Fry, DB
78—Joe Fry, DB

FURMAN
76—Jeff Holcomb, T
85—Brian Jager, RB
88—Kelly Fletcher, DL
89—Kelly Fletcher, DL
Chris Roper, LB
91—Eric Walter, OL

GEORGETOWN
71—Gerry O'Dowd, HB
86—Andrew Phelan, OG

GEORGETOWN (KY.)
89—Eric Chumbley, OL
92—Bobby Wasson, PK

GEORGIA
60—Francis Tarkenton, QB
65—Bob Etter, K
66—Bob Etter, K
Lynn Hughes, DB
68—Bill Stanfill, DT
71—Tom Nash, OT
Mixon Robinson, DE
77—Jeff Lewis, LB
82—Terry Hoage, DB
83—Terry Hoage, DB
92—Todd Peterson, PK

GA. SOUTHERN
95—Rob Stockton, DB

GA. SOUTHWESTERN
87—Gregory Slappery, RB

GEORGIA TECH
52—Ed Gossage, T
Cecil Trainer, DE
Larry Morris, LB
55—Wade Mitchell, B
56—Allen Ecker, G
66—Jim Breland, C
W. J. Blaine, LB
Bill Eastman, DB
67—Bill Eastman, DB
80—Sheldon Fox, LB
90—Stefen Scotton, RB

GETTYSBURG
79—Richard Swartz, LB

GRAMBLING
72—Floyd Harvey, RB
93—Gilad Landau, PK

GRAND VALLEY ST.
91—Mark Smith, OL
Todd Wood, DB

GRINNELL
71—Edward Hirsch, E
81—David Smiley, TE

GROVE CITY
74—Pat McCoy, LB
89—Travis Croll, P

GUST. ADOLPHUS
80—Dave Najarian, DL
81—Dave Najarian, LB

HAMLINE
73—Thomas Dufresne, E
89—Jon Voss, TE

HAMPDEN-SYDNEY
82—John Dickinson, OG
90—W. R. Jones, OL
91—David Brickhill, PK

HAMPTON
93—Tim Benson, WR

HARVARD
84—Brian Bergstrom, DB

HEIDELBERG
82—Jeff Kurtzman, DL

HILLSDALE
61—James Richendollar, T
72—John Cervini, G
81—Mark Kellogg, LB
93—Jason Ahee, DB

HOLY CROSS
83—Bruce Kozerski, T
85—Kevin Reilly, OT
87—Jeff Wiley, QB
91—Pete Dankert, DL

HOPE
73—Ronald Posthuma, T
79—Craig Groendyk, T
80—Greg Bekius, PK
82—Kurt Brinks, C
84—Scott Jecmen, DB
86—Timothy Chase, OG

HOUSTON
64—Horst Paul, E
76—Mark Mohr, DB
Kevin Rollwage, OT
77—Kevin Rollwage, OT

IDAHO
70—Bruce Langmeade, T

IDAHO ST.
84—Brent Koetter, DB
91—Steve Boyenger, DB

ILLINOIS
52—Bob Lenzini, DT
64—Jim Grabowski, FB
65—Jim Grabowski, FB
66—John Wright, E
70—Jim Rucks, DE
71—Bob Bucklin, DE
80—Dan Gregus, DL
81—Dan Gregus, DL
82—Dan Gregus, DL
91—Mike Hopkins, DB
92—John Wright Jr., WR
94—Brett Larsen, P

ILLINOIS COL.
80—Jay Wessler, RB
94—Warren Dodson, OL

ILLINOIS ST.
76—Tony Barnes, C
80—Jeff Hembrough, DL
89—Dan Hackman, OL
95—Keith Goodnight, RB

ILL. WESLEYAN
71—Keith Ihlanfeldt, DE
80—Jim Eaton, DL
Rick Hanna, DL
Mike Watson, DB
81—Mike Watson, DB
91—Chris Bisaillon, WR
92—Chris Udovich, DL
95—Jason Richards, TE

INDIANA
67—Harry Gonso, HB
72—Glenn Scolnik, RB
80—Kevin Speer, C
94—John Hammerstein, DL

INDIANA (PA.)
82—Kenny Moore, DB
83—Kenny Moore, DB

INDIANA ST.
71—Gary Brown, E
72—Michael Eads, E

INDIANAPOLIS
76—William Willan, E
95—Ted Munson, DL

IONA
80—Neal Kurtti, DL

IOWA
52—Bill Fenton, DE
53—Bill Fenton, DE
75—Bob Elliott, DB
85—Larry Station, LB

IOWA ST.
52—Max Burkett, DB
82—Mark Carlson, LB

ITHACA
72—Dana Hallenbeck, LB
85—Brian Dougherty, DB
89—Peter Burns, OL

JACKSONVILLE ST.
77—Dewey Barker, E
78—Dewey Barker, TE

JAMES MADISON
78—Warren Coleman, OT

JOHN CARROLL
83—Nick D'Angelo, LB
Jim Sferra, DL
85—Joe Burrello, LB
86—Joe Burrello, LB

JOHNS HOPKINS
77—Charles Hauck, DT
93—Michael House, DL
94—Michael House, DL

JUNIATA
70—Ray Grabiak, DL
71—Ray Grabiak, DE
Maurice Taylor, IL

KALAMAZOO
92—Sean Mullendore, LB

KANSAS
64—Fred Elder, T
67—Mike Sweatman, LB
68—Dave Morgan, LB
71—Mike McCoy, C
76—Tom Fitch, S
95—Darrin Simmons, P

KANSAS ST.
74—Don Lareau, LB
77—Floyd Dorsey, OG
81—Darren Gale, DB
82—Darren Gale, DB
Mark Hundley, RB
85—Troy Faunce, P
95—Kevin Lockett, WR

KENT
72—Mark Reiheld, DB
91—Brad Smith, RB

KENTUCKY
74—Tom Ranieri, LB
78—Mark Keene, C
Jim Kovach, LB
85—Ken Pietrowiak, C

KENYON
77—Robert Jennings, RB
85—Dan Waldeck, TE

LA VERNE
82—Scott Shier, OT

LAFAYETTE
70—William Sprecher, T
74—Mike Kline, DB
79—Ed Rogusky, RB
80—Ed Rogusky, RB

LAWRENCE
81—Chris Matheus, DL
Scott Reppert, RB
82—Chris Matheus, DL

LEHIGH
90—Shon Harker, DB

LEWIS & CLARK
61—Pat Clock, G
81—Dan Jones, WR

LONG BEACH ST.
83—Joe Donohue, LB

LIU-C.W. POST
70—Art Canario, T
75—Frank Prochilo, RB
84—Bob Jahelka, DB
93—Jim Byrne, WR

LORAS
84—John Coyle, DL
Pete Kovatisis, DB
85—John Coyle, DL
91—Mark Goedken, DL
93—Travis Michaels, LB

LSU
59—Mickey Mangham, E
60—Charles Strange, C
61—Billy Booth, T
71—Jay Michaelson, KS
73—Tyler Lafauci, OG
Joe Winkler, DB
74—Brad Davis, RB
77—Robert Dugas, OT
84—Juan Carlos Betanzos, PK
94—Michael Blanchard, OL

LUTHER
83—Larry Bonney, DL
84—Larry Bonney, DL
89—Larry Anderson, RB
90—Joel Nerem, DL
91—Joel Nerem, DL
95—Karl Borge, DL

LYCOMING
74—Thomas Vanaskie, DB
85—Mike Kern, DL

MACALESTER
82—Lee Schaefer, OG

MANKATO ST.
74—Dan Miller, C

MANSFIELD
83—John Delate, DB

MARIETTA
83—Matt Wurtzbacher, DL

MARS HILL
92—Brent Taylor, DL

MARYLAND
53—Bernie Faloney, B
75—Kim Hoover, DE
78—Joe Muffler, DL

MASS.-LOWELL
85—Don Williams, RB

MIT
89—Anthony Lapes, WR
90—Darcy Prather, LB
91—Rodrigo Rubiano, DL
92—Roderick Tranum, WR
93—Corey Foster, OL

94—Corey Foster, OL
95—Scott Vollrath, P

McGILL
87—Bruno Pietrobon, WR

McNEESE ST.
78—Jim Downing, OT
79—Jim Downing, OT
90—David Easterling, DB

MEMPHIS
92—Pat Jansen, DL

MIAMI (FLA.)
59—Fran Curci, B
84—Bernie Kosar, QB

MIAMI (OHIO)
73—Andy Pederzolli, DB

MICHIGAN
52—Dick Balzhiser, B
55—Jim Orwig, T
57—Jim Orwig, T
64—Bob Timberlake, QB
66—Dave Fisher, FB
Dick Vidmer, FB
69—Jim Mandich, OE
70—Phil Seymour, DE
71—Bruce Elliott, DB
72—Bill Hart, OG
74—Kirk Lewis, OG
75—Dan Jilek, DE
81—Norm Betts, TE
82—Stefan Humphries, OG
Robert Thompson, LB
83—Stefan Humphries, OG
85—Clay Miller, OT
86—Kenneth Higgins, WR

MICHIGAN ST.
52—John Wilson, DB
53—Don Dohoney, E
55—Buck Nystrom, G
57—Blanche Martin, HB
65—Don Bierowicz, DT
Don Japinga, DB
66—Pat Gallinagh, DT
68—Al Brenner, E/DB
69—Ron Saul, OG
Rich Saul, DE
73—John Shinsky, DT
79—Alan Davis, DB
85—Dean Altobelli, DB
86—Dean Altobelli, DB
86—Shane Bullough, LB
92—Steve Wasylk, DB
93—Steve Wasylk, DB

MICHIGAN TECH
71—Larry Ras, HB
73—Bruce Trusock, C
76—Jim Van Wagner, RB
92—Kurt Coduti, QB

MIDWESTERN ST.
95—Corby Walker, LB

MILLERSVILLE
91—Tom Burns, OL

MILLIKIN
61—Gerald Domesick, B
75—Frank Stone, G
78—Charlie Sammis, K
79—Eric Stevens, WR
83—Marc Knowles, WR
84—Tom Kreller, RB
85—Cary Bottorff, LB
Tom Kreller, RB
90—Tim Eimermann, PK

MINNESOTA
56—Bob Hobert, T
60—Frank Brixius, T
68—Bob Stein, DE
70—Barry Mayer, RB
89—Brent Herbel, P
94—Justin Conzemius, DB

MISSISSIPPI
54—Harold Easterwood, C
59—Robert Khayat, T
Charlie Flowers, B
61—Doug Elmore, B
65—Stan Hindman, G
68—Steve Hindman, HB
69—Julius Fagan, K
74—Greg Markow, DE
77—Robert Fabris, OE
George Plasketes, DE
80—Ken Toler, WR
86—Danny Hoskins, OG
87—Danny Hoskins, OG
88—Wesley Walls, TE
89—Todd Sandroni, DB

MISSISSIPPI COL.
75—Anthony Saway, S
78—Steve Johnson, OT
79—Steve Johnson, OT
83—Wayne Frazier, C

MISSISSIPPI ST.
53—Jackie Parker, B
56—Ron Bennett, E
72—Frank Dowsing, DB
73—Jimmy Webb, DE
76—Will Coltharp, DE
89—Stacy Russell, DB

MISSOURI
62—Tom Hertz, G
66—Dan Schuppan, DE
Bill Powell, DT
68—Carl Garber, MG
70—John Weisenfels, LB
72—Greg Hill, KS
81—Van Darkow, LB
93—Matt Burgess, OL

MO.-ROLLA
72—Kim Colter, DB
80—Paul Janke, OG
86—Tom Reed, RB
87—Jim Pfeiffer, OT
88—Jim Pfeiffer, OL
91—Don Huff, DB
92—Don Huff, DB
94—Brian Gilmore, LB
95—Brian Gilmore, LB

MO. SOUTHERN ST.
85—Mike Testman, DB
93—Chris Tedford, OL
94—Chris Tedford, OL

MONMOUTH (ILL.)
83—Robb Long, QB

MONTANA
77—Steve Fisher, DE
79—Ed Cerkovnik, DB
88—Michael McGowan, LB
89—Michael McGowan, LB
90—Michael McGowan, LB
93—Dave Dickenson, QB
95—Matt Wells, WR

MONTANA ST.
84—Dirk Nelson, P
88—Anders Larsson, PK

MONTCLAIR ST.
70—Bill Trimmer, DL
82—Daniel Deneher, KS

MOORHEAD ST.
88—Brad Shamla, DL

MORAVIAN
87—Jeff Pollock, WR

MOREHEAD ST.
74—Don Russell, KS
90—James Appel, OL
91—James Appel, OL

MOUNT UNION
71—Dennis Montgomery, QB
84—Rick Marabito, L
86—Scott Gindlesberger, QB
87—Paul Hrics, C

MUHLENBERG
70—Edward Salo, G
71—Edward Salo, IL
72—Edward Salo, C
75—Keith Ordemann, LB
80—Arthur Scavone, OT
89—Joe Zeszotarski, DL
90—Mike Hoffman, DB

MURRAY ST.
76—Eddie McFarland, DB

MUSKINGUM
78—Dan Radalia, DL
79—Dan Radalia, DL

NAVY
53—Steve Eisenhauer, G
57—Tom Forrestal, QB
58—Joe Tranchini, B
69—Dan Pike, RB
80—Ted Dumbauld, LB

NEBRASKA
62—James Huge, E
63—Dennis Calridge, B
66—Marv Mueller, DB
69—Randy Reeves, DB
71—Larry Jacobson, DT
Jeff Kinney, HB
73—Frosty Anderson, E
75—Rik Bonness, C
Tom Heiser, RB
76—Vince Ferragamo, QB
Ted Harvey, DB
77—Ted Harvey, DB
78—George Andrews, DL
James Pillen, DB
79—Rod Horn, DL
Kelly Saalfeld, C
Randy Schleusener, OG
80—Jeff Finn, TE
Randy Schleusener, OG
81—Eric Lindquist, DB
David Rimington, C
Randy Theiss, OT
82—David Rimington, C
83—Scott Strasburger, DL
Rob Stuckey, DL
84—Scott Strasburger, DL
Rob Stuckey, DL
Mark Traynowicz, C
86—Dale Klein, K
Thomas Welter, OT
87—Jeffrey Jamrog, DL
Mark Blazek, DB
88—Mark Blazek, DB
John Kroeker, P
89—Gerry Gdowski, QB
Jake Young, OL
90—David Edeal, OL
Pat Tyrance, LB
Jim Wanek, OL
91—Pat Engelbert, DL
Mike Stigge, P
92—Mike Stigge, P
93—Rob Zatechka, OL
Terry Connealy, DL
Trev Alberts, LB
94—Matt Shaw, TE
Rob Zatechka, OL
Terry Connealy, DL
95—Aaron Graham, OL

NEB.-KEARNEY
70—John Makovicka, RB
75—Tim Brodahl, E

NEB.-OMAHA
82—Kirk Hutton, DB
Clark Toner, LB
83—Kirk Hutton, DB
84—Jerry Kripal, QB

NEB. WESLEYAN
87—Pat Sweeney, DB
88—Pat Sweeney, DB
Mike Surls, LB
89—Scott Shaffer, RB
Scott Shipman, DB
95—Justin Rice, DL

NEVADA
82—David Heppe, P

NEW HAMPSHIRE
52—John Driscoll, T
84—Dave Morton, OL

NEW MEXICO
75—Bob Johnson, S
77—Robert Rumbaugh, DT
78—Robert Rumbaugh, DL
93—Justin Hall, OL

NEW MEXICO ST.
66—Jim Bohl, B
74—Ralph Jackson, OG
75—Ralph Jackson, OG
85—Andy Weiler, KS
92—Todd Cutler, TE
Shane Hackney, OL

Tim Mauck, LB
93—Tim Mauck, LB

NICHOLS
89—David Kane, DB

NORTH CARO.
64—Ken Willard, QB
85—Kevin Anthony, QB

NORTH CARO. ST.
60—Roman Gabriel, QB
63—Joe Scarpati, B
67—Steve Warren, OT
71—Craig John, OG
73—Justus Everett, C
Stan Fritts, RB
74—Justus Everett, C
80—Calvin Warren, P

NORTH DAK.
87—Kurt Otto, QB
88—Chuck Clairmont, OL
Matt Gulseth, DB
92—Tim Gelinske, WR
Mark Ewen, LB

NORTH DAK. ST.
71—Tomm Smail, DT
93—T. R. McDonald, WR

NORTH PARK
83—Mike Lilgegren, DB
85—Scott Love, WR
86—Todd Love, WR
87—Todd Love, WR

NORTH TEXAS
75—Pete Morris, LB
76—Pete Morris, LB

NORTHEAST LA.
70—Tom Miller, KS
74—Mike Bialas, T

NORTHEASTERN
85—Shawn O'Malley, LB

NORTHERN ARIZ.
89—Chris Baniszewski, WR

NORTHERN COLO.
71—Charles Putnik, OG
81—Duane Hirsch, DL
Ray Sperger, DB
82—Jim Bright, RB
89—Mike Yonkovich, DL
Tom Langer, LB
90—Tom Langer, LB

NORTHERN MICH.
83—Bob Stefanski, WR

NORTHWEST MO. ST.
81—Robert "Chip" Gregory, LB

NORTHWESTERN
56—Al Viola, G
58—Andy Cvercko, T
61—Larry Onesti, C
62—Paul Flatley, B
63—George Burman, E
70—Joe Zigulich, OG
76—Randolph Dean, E
80—Jim Ford, OT
86—Michael Baum, OT
Bob Dirkes, DL
Todd Krehbiel, DB
87—Mike Baum, OL
88—Mike Baum, OL
90—Ira Adler, PK
95—Sam Valenzisi, PK

N'WESTERN (IOWA)
83—Mark Muilenberg, RB
92—Joel Bundt, OL

N'WESTERN (OKLA.)
61—Stewart Arthurs, B

NORTHWESTERN ST.
92—Guy Hedrick, RB
94—John Dippel, OL

NORWICH
70—Gary Fry, RB

NOTRE DAME
52—Joe Heap, B
53—Joe Heap, B
54—Joe Heap, B
55—Don Schaefer, B

58—Bob Wetoska, E
63—Bob Lehmann, G
66—Tom Regner, OG
Jim Lynch, LB
67—Jim Smithberger, DB
68—George Kunz, OT
69—Jim Reilly, OT
70—Tom Gatewood, E
Larry DiNardo, OG
Joe Theismann, QB
71—Greg Marx, DT
Tom Gatewood, E
72—Michael Creaney, E
Greg Marx, DT
73—David Casper, E
Gary Potempa, LB
Bob Thomas, K
74—Reggie Barnett, DB
Pete Demmerle, E
77—Ken MacAfee, E
Joe Restic, S
Dave Vinson, OG
78—Joe Restic, DB
80—Bob Burger, OG
Tom Gibbons, DB
81—John Krimm, DB
85—Greg Dingens, DL
87—Ted Gradel, PK
Vince Phelan, P
92—Tim Ruddy, OL
93—Tim Ruddy, OL

OCCIDENTAL
88—Curtis Page, DL

OHIO
71—John Rousch, HB

OHIO NORTHERN
76—Jeff McFarlin, S
79—Robert Coll, WR
86—David Myers, DL
90—Chad Hummell, OL

OHIO ST.
52—John Borton, B
54—Dick Hilinski, T
58—Bob White, B
61—Tom Perdue, E
65—Bill Ridder, MG
66—Dave Foley, OT
68—Dave Foley, OT
Mark Stier, LB
69—Bill Urbanik, DT
71—Rick Simon, OG
73—Randy Gradishar, LB
74—Brian Baschnagel, RB
75—Brian Baschnagel, RB
76—Pete Johnson, RB
Bill Lukens, OG
77—Jeff Logan, RB
80—Marcus Marek, LB
82—John Frank, TE
Joseph Smith, OT
83—John Frank, TE
84—David Crecelius, DL
Michael Lanese, WR
85—Michael Lanese, WR
89—Joseph Staysniak, OL
92—Leonard Hartman, OL
Gregory Smith, DL
95—Greg Bellisari, LB

OHIO WESLEYAN
70—Tony Heald, LB
Tom Liller, E
81—Ric Kinnan, WR
85—Kevin Connell, OG
94—Craig Anderson, LB
95—Craig Anderson, LB

OKLAHOMA
52—Tom Catlin, C
54—Carl Allison, E
56—Jerry Tubbs, C
57—Doyle Jenning, T
58—Ross Coyle, E
62—Wayne Lee, C
63—Newt Burton, G
64—Newt Burton, G
66—Ron Shotts, HB
67—Ron Shotts, HB
68—Eddie Hinton, DB
70—Joe Wylie, RB
71—Jack Mildren, QB
72—Joe Wylie, RB
74—Randy Hughes, S
75—Dewey Selmon, LB
Lee Roy Selmon, DT
80—Jay Jimerson, DB
86—Brian Bosworth, LB

OKLA. PANHANDLE ST.
76—Larry Johnson, G

OKLAHOMA ST.
54—Dale Meinert, G
72—Tom Wolf, OT
73—Doug Tarrant, LB
74—Tom Wolf, OT
77—Joe Avanzini, DE

OREGON
62—Steve Barnett, T
65—Tim Casey, LB
86—Mike Preacher, P
90—Bill Musgrave, QB

OREGON ST.
62—Terry Baker, B
67—Bill Enyart, FB
68—Bill Enyart, FB
93—Chad Paulson, RB

OUACHITA BAPTIST
78—David Cowling, OG

PACIFIC (CAL.)
78—Bruce Filarsky, OG
79—Bruce Filarsky, DL

PACIFIC LUTHERAN
82—Curt Rodin, TE

PENNSYLVANIA
86—Rich Comizio, RB

PENN ST.
65—Joe Bellas, T
John Runnells, LB
66—John Runnells, LB
67—Rich Buzin, OT
69—Charlie Pittman, HB
Dennis Onkotz, LB
71—Dave Joyner, OT
72—Bruce Bannon, DE
73—Mark Markovich, OG
76—Chuck Benjamin, OT
78—Keith Dorney, OT
82—Todd Blackledge, QB
Harry Hamilton, DB
Scott Radicec, LB
83—Harry Hamilton, LB
84—Lance Hamilton, DB
Carmen Masciantonio, LB
85—Lance Hamilton, DB
86—John Shaffer, QB
94—Jeff Hartings, OL
Tony Pittman, DB
95—Jeff Hartings, OL

PITTSBURG ST.
72—Jay Sperry, RB
89—Brett Potts, DL
91—Mike Brockel, OL
92—Mike Brockel, OL

PITTSBURGH
52—Dick Deitrick, DT
54—Lou Palatella, T
56—Joe Walton, E
58—John Guzik, G
76—Jeff Delaney, LB
80—Greg Meisner, DL
81—Rob Fada, OG
82—Rob Fada, OG
J. C. Pelusi, DL
88—Mark Stepnoski, OL

PORTLAND ST.
72—Bill Dials, T
77—John Urness, WR
78—John Urness, WR

PRINCETON
68—Dick Sandler, DT
76—Kevin Fox, OG
82—Kevin Guthrie, WR
83—Kevin Guthrie, WR

PUGET SOUND
82—Buster Crook, DB

PURDUE
56—Len Dawson, QB
60—Jerry Beabout, T
65—Sal Ciampi, G
67—Jim Beirne, E
Lance Olssen, DT
68—Tim Foley, DB
69—Tim Foley, DB
Mike Phipps, QB
Bill Yanchar, DT
73—Bob Hoftiezer, DE
79—Ken Loushin, DL
80—Tim Seneff, DB
81—Tim Seneff, DB
89—Bruce Brineman, OL

RENSSELAER
95—Alic Scott, OL

RHODE ISLAND
76—Richard Moser, RB
77—Richard Moser, RB

RHODES
90—Robert Heck, DL

RICE
52—Richard Chapman, DG
53—Richard Chapman, DG
54—Dicky Maegle, B
69—Steve Bradshaw, DG
79—LaMont Jefferson, LB
83—Brian Patterson, DB
95—Jay Lamy, DB

ROCHESTER
82—Bob Cordaro, LB
92—Jeremy Hurd, RB
93—Jeremy Hurd, RB

ROSE-HULMAN
78—Rick Matovich, DL
79—Scott Lindner, DL
80—Scott Lindner, DL
Jim Novacek, P
83—Jack Grote, LB
84—Jack Grote, LB
88—Greg Kremer, LB
Shawn Ferron, PK
89—Shawn Ferron, PK
90—Ed Huonden, WR
92—Greg Hubbard, OL
93—Greg Hubbard, OL

SAGINAW VALLEY
93—Troy Hendrickson, PK

ST. CLOUD ST.
88—Rick Rodgers, DB
89—Rick Rodgers, DB

ST. FRANCIS (PA.)
93—Todd Eckenroad, WR

ST. JOHN'S (MINN.)
72—Jim Kruzich, E
79—Terry Geraghty, DB
94—Chris Palmer, WR
Matthew Malmberg, RB
95—Chris Palmer, WR

ST. JOHN'S (N.Y.)
93—Anthony Russo, RB

ST. JOSEPH'S (IND.)
77—Mike Bettinger, DB
78—Mike Bettinger, DB
79—Mike Bettinger, DB
85—Ralph Laura, OT
88—Keith Woodason, OL
89—Jeff Fairchild, P

ST. NORBERT
86—Matthew Lang, LB
Karl Zacharias, P
87—Karl Zacharias, PK
Matthew Lang, LB
88—Mike Whitehouse, WR
89—Mike Whitehouse, WR

ST. OLAF
61—Dave Hindermann, T

ST. THOMAS (MINN.)
73—Mark Dienhart, T
74—Mark Dienhart, T
77—Tom Kelly, OG
80—Doug Groebner, C
94—Curt Behrns, DB

SAM HOUSTON ST.
72—Walter Anderson, KS
73—Walter Anderson, KS
93—Kevin Riley, DB

SAN DIEGO
87—Bryan Day, DB
88—Bryan Day, DB
94—Doug Popovich, DB
95—Doug Popovich, DB

SAN JOSE ST.
75—Tim Toews, OG

SANTA CLARA
71—Ron Sani, IL
73—Alex Damascus, RB
74—Steve Lagorio, LB
75—Mark Tiernan, LB
76—Lou Marengo, KS
Mark Tiernan, LB
80—Dave Alfaro, QB

SHIPPENSBURG
76—Tony Winter, LB
82—Dave Butler, DL
94—Joel Yohn, PK
95—Joel Yohn, PK

SOUTH CARO.
87—Mark Fryer, OL
88—Mark Fryer, OL
91—Joe Reeves, LB

SOUTH DAK.
78—Scott Pollock, QB
82—Jerus Campbell, DL
83—Jeff Sime, T
87—Dan Sonnek, RB

SOUTH DAK. ST.
74—Bob Gissler, E
75—Bill Matthews, T
77—Bill Matthews, DE
79—Tony Harris, PK
Paul Kippley, DB

SOUTHERN CAL
52—Dick Nunis, DB
59—Mike McKeever, G
60—Mike McKeever, G
Marlin McKeever, E
65—Charles Arrobio, T
67—Steve Sogge, QB
68—Steve Sogge, QB
69—Harry Khasigian, OG
73—Pat Haden, QB
74—Pat Haden, QB
78—Rich Dimler, DL
79—Brad Budde, OG
Paul McDonald, QB
Keith Van Horne, T
84—Duane Bickett, LB
85—Matt Koart, DL
86—Jeffrey Bregel, OG
88—John Jackson, WR
89—John Jackson, WR
95—Jeremy Hogue, OL
Matt Keneley, DL

SOUTHERN COLO.
83—Dan DeRose, LB

SOUTHERN CONN. ST.
84—Gerald Carbonaro, OL

SOUTHERN ILL.
70—Sam Finocchio, G
88—Charles Harmke, RB
91—Dwayne Summers, DL
Jon Manley, LB

SOUTHERN METHODIST
52—Dave Powell, E
53—Darrell Lafitte, G
54—Raymond Berry, E
55—David Hawk, G
57—Tom Koenig, G
58—Tom Koenig, G
62—Raymond Schoenke, T
66—John LaGrone, MG
Lynn Thornhill, OG
68—Jerry LeVias, OE
72—Cleve Whitener, LB
83—Brian O'Meara, T

SOUTHERN MISS.
92—James Singleton, DL

SOUTHERN UTAH
88—Jim Andrus, RB
90—Steve McDowell, P

SOUTHWEST MO. ST.
73—Kent Stringer, QB
75—Kent Stringer, QB
78—Steve Newbold, WR

SOUTHWEST ST.
88—Bruce Saugstad, DB

SOUTHWEST TEX. ST.
72—Jimmy Jowers, LB
73—Jimmy Jowers, LB
78—Mike Ferris, OG
79—Mike Ferris, G
Allen Kiesling, DL
81—Mike Miller, QB

SPRINGFIELD
71—Bruce Rupert, LB
84—Sean Flanders, DL
85—Sean Flanders, DL

STANFORD
70—John Sande, C
Terry Ewing, DB
75—Don Stevenson, RB
76—Don Stevenson, RB
77—Guy Benjamin, QB
78—Vince Mulroy, WR
Jim Stephens, OG
79—Pat Bowe, TE
Milt McColl, LB
Joe St. Geme, DB
81—John Bergren, DL
Darrin Nelson, RB
82—John Bergren, DL
83—John Bergren, DL
85—Matt Soderlund, LB
87—Brad Muster, RB
90—Ed McCaffrey, WR
91—Tommy Vardell, RB
94—Justin Armour, WR

SUL ROSS ST.
73—Archie Nexon, RB

SUSQUEHANNA
75—Gerry Huesken, T
76—Gerry Huesken, T
80—Dan Distasio, LB

SYRACUSE
60—Fred Mautino, E
71—Howard Goodman, LB
83—Tony Romano, LB
84—Tim Green, DL
85—Tim Green, DL

TARLETON ST.
81—Ricky Bush, RB
90—Mike Loveless, OL

TENNESSEE
56—Charles Rader, T
57—Bill Johnson, G
65—Mack Gentry, DT
67—Bob Johnson, C
70—Tim Priest, DB
80—Timothy Irwin, OT
82—Mike Terry, DL

TENN.-MARTIN
74—Randy West, E

TENNESSEE TECH
87—Andy Rittenhouse, DL

TEXAS
59—Maurice Doke, G
61—Johnny Treadwell, G
62—Johnny Treadwell, G
Pat Culpepper, B
63—Duke Carlisle, B
66—Gene Bledsoe, OT
67—Mike Perrin, DE
Corby Robertson, LB
68—Corby Robertson, LB
Scott Henderson, LB
69—Scott Henderson, LB
Bill Zapalac, DE
70—Scott Henderson, LB
Bill Zapalac, LB
72—Mike Bayer, DB
Tommy Keel, S
Steve Oxley, T
73—Tommy Keel, S
83—Doug Dawson, G
88—Lee Brockman, DL
95—Pat Fitzgerald, TE

UTEP
88—Pat Hegarty, QB

TEXAS A&M
56—Jack Pardee, B
71—Steve Luebbehusen, LB
76—Kevin Monk, LB
77—Kevin Monk, LB
85—Kip Corrington, DB
86—Kip Corrington, DB
87—Kip Corrington, DB

TEX. A&M-KINGSVILLE
72—Floyd Goodwin, T
73—Johnny Jackson, E
76—Wade Whitmer, DL
77—Joe Henke, LB
Wade Whitmer, DL
78—Wade Whitmer, DL

TEXAS CHRISTIAN
52—Marshall Harris, T
55—Hugh Pitts, C
Jim Swink, B
56—Jim Swink, B
57—John Nikkel, E
68—Jim Ray, G
72—Scott Walker, C
74—Terry Drennan, DB
80—John McClean, DL

TEXAS TECH
72—Jeff Jobe, E
79—Maury Buford, P
83—Chuck Alexander, DB
93—Robert King, P

TOLEDO
83—Michael Matz, DL
95—Craig Dues, LB

TRINITY (TEX.)
92—Jeff Bryan, OL

TRUMAN ST.
73—Tom Roberts, T
78—Keith Driscoll, LB
79—Keith Driscoll, LB
92—K. C. Conaway, P

TUFTS
70—Bruce Zinsmeister, DL
81—Brian Gallagher, OG
83—Richard Guiunta, G

TULANE
71—David Hebert, DB

TULSA
64—Howard Twilley, E
65—Howard Twilley, E
74—Mack Lancaster, T
95—David Millwee, OL

UCLA
52—Ed Flynn, G
Donn Moomaw, LB
53—Ira Pauly, C
54—Sam Boghosian, G
66—Ray Armstrong, E
75—John Sciarra, QB
77—John Fowler, LB
81—Cormac Carney, WR
Tim Wrightman, TE
82—Cormac Carney, WR
85—Mike Hartmeier, OG
92—Carlton Gray, DB
95—George Kase, DL

UNION (N.Y.)
71—Tom Anacher, LB
73—Dave Ricks, DB
87—Richard Romer, DL
93—Greg Oswitt, OL

URSINUS
86—Chuck Odgers, DB
87—Chuck Odgers, LB

UTAH
64—Mel Carpenter, T
71—Scott Robbins, DB
73—Steve Odom, RB
76—Dick Graham, E

UTAH ST.
61—Merlin Olsen, T
69—Gary Anderson, LB
74—Randy Stockham, DE
75—Randy Stockham, DE

VALDOSTA ST.
93—Chris Hatcher, QB
94—Chris Hatcher, QB

VANDERBILT
58—Don Donnell, C
68—Jim Burns, DB
74—Doug Martin, E
75—Damon Regen, LB
77—Greg Martin, K
83—Phil Roach, WR

VILLANOVA
86—Ron Sency, RB
88—Peter Lombardi, RB
92—Tim Matas, DL

VIRGINIA
72—Tom Kennedy, OG
75—Bob Meade, DT
92—Tom Burns, LB
93—Tom Burns, LB
95—Tiki Barber, RB

VA. MILITARY
78—Craig Jones, PK
79—Craig Jones, PK
84—David Twillie, OL
86—Dan Young, DL
88—Anthony McIntosh, DB

VIRGINIA TECH
67—Frank Loria, DB
72—Tommy Carpenito, LB

WABASH
70—Roscoe Fouts, DB
71—Kendrick Shelburne, DT
82—Dave Broecker, QB

WARTBURG
75—James Charles Peterson, DB
76—Randy Groth, DB
77—Neil Mandsager, LB
90—Jerrod Staack, OL
93—Koby Kreinbring, LB
94—Vince Penningroth, DL
95—Vince Penningroth, DL

WASHINGTON
55—Jim Houston, E
63—Mike Briggs, T
64—Rick Redman, G
65—Steve Bramwell, DB
79—Bruce Harrell, LB
81—Mark Jerue, LB
Chuck Nelson, PK
82—Chuck Nelson, PK
86—David Rill, LB
87—David Rill, LB
91—Ed Cunningham, OL

WASH. & JEFF.
92—Raymond Cross, DL
93—Michael Jones, OL
94—Michael Jones, OL

WASH. & LEE
75—John Cocklereece, DB
78—George Ballantyne, LB
92—Evans Edwards, OL

WASHINGTON ST.
89—Jason Hanson, PK
90—Lee Tilleman, DL
Jason Hanson, PK
91—Jason Hanson, PK

WAYNE ST. (MICH.)
71—Gary Schultz, DB
72—Walt Stasinski, DB

WAYNESBURG
77—John Culp, RB
78—John Culp, RB
89—Andrew Barrish, OL
90—Andrew Barrish, OL
91—Karl Petrof, OL

WEST CHESTER
83—Eric Wentling, K
86—Gerald Desmond, K

WEST VA.
52—Paul Bischoff, E
54—Fred Wyant, B
55—Sam Huff, T
70—Kim West, K
80—Oliver Luck, QB
81—Oliver Luck, QB
83—Jeff Hostetler, QB
92—Mike Compton, OL
94—Matt Taffoni, LB

WESTERN CARO.
75—Mike Wade, E
76—Mike Wade, LB
84—Eddie Maddox, RB

WESTERN ILL.
61—Jerry Blew, G
85—Jeff McKinney, RB
91—David Fierke, OL

WESTERN KY.
71—James Barber, LB
81—Tim Ford, DL
84—Mark Fatkin, OL
85—Mark Fatkin, OG
95—Brian Bixler, OL

WESTERN MD.
73—Chip Chaney, S

WESTERN MICH.
70—Jon Bull, OT
94—Rich Kaiser, DL
95—Rich Kaiser, DL

WESTERN OREGON
61—Francis Tresler, C

WESTERN ST.
78—Bill Campbell, DB
88—Damon Lockhart, RB

WESTMINSTER (PA.)
73—Bob Clark, G
77—Scott McLuckey, LB
93—Brian Wilson, OL

WHEATON (ILL.)
73—Bill Hyer, E
75—Eugene Campbell, RB
76—Eugene Campbell, RB
88—Paul Sternenberg, DL
92—Bart Moseman, DB
94—Pedro Arruza, RB
95—Jeff Brown, QB
Pedro Arruzo, RB

WHITTIER
86—Brent Kane, DL

WILKES
70—Al Kenney, C

WILLAMETTE
61—Stuart Hall

WILLIAM & MARY
74—John Gerdelman, RB
75—Ken Smith, DB
77—Ken Smith, DB
78—Robert Muscalus, TE
84—Mark Kelso, DB
88—Chris Gessner, DB
90—Jeff Nielsen, LB
93—Craig Staub, DL

WM. PATERSON
92—John Trust, RB

WINONA ST.
93—Nathan Gruber, DB
94—Nathan Gruber, DB

WISCONSIN
52—Bob Kennedy, DG
53—Alan Ameche, B
54—Alan Ameche, B
58—Jon Hobbs, B
59—Dale Hackbart, B
62—Pat Richter, E
63—Ken Bowman, C
72—Rufus Ferguson, RB
82—Kyle Borland, LB
87—Don Davey, DL
88—Don Davey, DL
89—Don Davey, DL
90—Don Davey, DL

WIS.-EAU CLAIRE
74—Mark Anderson, RB
80—Mike Zeihen, DB

WIS.-LA CROSSE
95—Troy Harcey, WR

WIS.-PLATTEVILLE
85—Mark Hintz, DB
Mark Rae, P

86—Mike Hintz, QB
87—Mark Rae, P

WIS.-RIVER FALLS
91—Mike Olson, LB
95—Brian Izdepski, OT

WIS.-WHITEWATER
95—Scott Hawig, OL

WITTENBERG
80—Bill Beach, DB
81—Bill Beach, DB
82—Tom Jones, OT
88—Paul Kungl, WR
90—Victor Terebuh, DB

WOOSTER
73—Dave Foy, LB
77—Blake Moore, C
78—Blake Moore, C
79—Blake Moore, C
80—Dale Fortner, DB
John Weisensell, OG

WYOMING
65—Bob Dinges, DE
67—George Mills, OG
73—Mike Lopiccolo, OT
84—Bob Gustafson, OT
87—Patrick Arndt, OG
94—Ryan Christopherson, RB
95—Joe Cummings, DL

YALE
68—Fred Morris, C
70—Tom Neville, DT
78—William Crowley, LB
81—Rich Diana, RB
Frederick Leone, DL
89—Glover Lawrence, DL
91—Scott Wagner, DB

YOUNGSTOWN ST.
93—John Quintana, TE

Bowl/All-Star Game Records

1996-97 Bowl Schedule

(All Starting Times Eastern; Conference Affiliations as of June 15, 1996)

BUILDERS SQUARE ALAMO BOWL
December 29, 1996, 8 p.m.
Alamodome
San Antonio, Texas
Televising Network: ESPN
Conference Affiliation: Big 12 No. 4 vs. Big Ten No. 4

CARQUEST BOWL
December 27, 1996, 7:30 p.m.
Joe Robbie Stadium
Miami, Florida
Televising Network: TBS/Raycom
Conference Affiliation: Big East No. 3 vs. Atlantic Coast No. 4

CompUSA FLORIDA CITRUS BOWL
January 1, 1997, 1 p.m.
Florida Citrus Bowl
Orlando, Florida
Televising Network: ABC
Conference Affiliation: Southeastern No. 2 vs. Big Ten No. 2

COPPER BOWL
December 27, 1996, 8 p.m.
Arizona Stadium
Tucson, Arizona
Televising Network: ESPN
Conference Affiliation: Big 12 No. 5 vs. Western Athletic No. 2

COTTON BOWL CLASSIC
January 1, 1997, 1:30 p.m.
Cotton Bowl
Dallas, Texas
Televising Network: CBS
Conference Affiliation: Big 12 No. 2 vs. Pacific-10 No. 2 or Western Athletic Champion

FEDEX ORANGE BOWL
December 31, 1996, 7 p.m.
Joe Robbie Stadium
Miami, Florida
Televising Network: CBS
Conference Affiliation: Alliance (Selections 4 and 6)

HAKA BOWL
December 26, 1996, 8 p.m.
Eden Park
Auckland, New Zealand
Televising Network: ESPN
Conference Affiliation: Pacific-10 No. 3 vs. At-Large

JEEP EAGLE ALOHA BOWL
December 25, 1996, 3:30 p.m.
Aloha Stadium
Honolulu, Hawaii
Televising Network: ABC
Conference Affiliation: Big 12 No. 6 vs. Pacific-10 No. 4

LAS VEGAS BOWL
December 19, 1996, 9:30 p.m.
Sam Boyd Stadium
Las Vegas, Nevada
Televising Network: ESPN
Conference Affiliation: Big West Champion vs. Mid-American Champion

NOKIA SUGAR BOWL
January 2, 1997, 8 p.m.
Louisiana Superdome
New Orleans, Louisiana
Televising Network: ABC
Conference Affiliation: Alliance (Selections 1 and 2)

NORWEST BANK SUN BOWL
December 31, 1996, 2:30 p.m.
Sun Bowl
El Paso, Texas
Televising Network: CBS
Conference Affiliation: Pacific-10 No. 5 vs. Big Ten No. 5

OUTBACK BOWL
January 1, 1997, 11 a.m.
Tampa Stadium
Tampa, Florida
Televising Network: ESPN
Conference Affiliation: Big Ten No. 3 vs. Southeastern No. 3

PEACH BOWL
December 28, 1996, 8 p.m.
Georgia Dome
Atlanta, Georgia
Televising Network: ESPN
Conference Affiliation: Atlantic Coast No. 3 vs. Southeastern No. 4

PLYMOUTH HOLIDAY BOWL
December 30, 1996, 8 p.m.
San Diego Jack Murphy Stadium
San Diego, California
Televising Network: ESPN
Conference Affiliation: Western Athletic Champion or Pacific-10 No. 2 vs. Big 12 No. 3

POULAN/WEED EATER INDEPENDENCE BOWL
December 31, 1996, 4 p.m.
Independence Stadium
Shreveport, Louisiana
Televising Network: ESPN
Conference Affiliation: Southeastern No. 5 vs. At-Large

ROSE BOWL
January 1, 1997, 5 p.m.
Rose Bowl
Pasadena, California
Televising Network: ABC
Conference Affiliation: Pacific-10 Champion vs. Big Ten Champion

ST. JUDE LIBERTY BOWL
December 27 or 28, 1996, noon or 1:30 p.m.
Liberty Bowl Memorial Stadium
Memphis, Tennessee
Televising Network: ESPN
Conference Affiliation: Conference USA No. 1 vs. Big East No. 4

TOSTITOS FIESTA BOWL
January 1, 1997, 8:30 p.m.
Sun Devil Stadium
Tempe, Arizona
Televising Network: CBS
Conference Affiliation: Alliance (Selections 3 and 5)

TOYOTA GATOR BOWL
January 1, 1997, 12:30 p.m.
Jacksonville Municipal Stadium
Jacksonville, Florida
Televising Network: NBC
Conference Affiliation: Big East No. 2 vs. Atlantic Coast No. 2

1995-96 Bowl Results

Game-by-Game Summaries

LAS VEGAS BOWL
December 14, 1995
Sam Boyd Stadium
Las Vegas, Nevada

Synopsis: Wasean Tait rushed for a Las Vegas Bowl record 185 yards and scored four touchdowns to lead Toledo to a 40-37 victory over Nevada in the first overtime bowl game.

Toledo	7	14	6	7	6	— 40
Nevada	7	7	10	10	3	— 37

TOL—Huzjak 31 run (Spring kick)
NEV—Minor 2 run (Shea kick)
TOL—Tait 18 run (Spring kick)
TOL—Tait 31 run (Spring kick)
NEV—Minor 1 run (Shea kick)
NEV—Shea 34 field goal
TOL—Harris 16 run (kick failed)
NEV—Bennett 4 run (Shea kick)
TOL—Tait 26 run (Spring kick)
NEV—Minor 1 run (Shea kick)
NEV—Shea 26 field goal
NEV—Shea 22 field goal
TOL—Tait 3 rush

Game Statistics	TOL	NEV
First Downs	33	23
Rushes-Yards	54-307	29-83
Passing Yards	254	330
Comp.-Att.-Int.	23-41-1	27-51-0
Punts-Avg.	3-37	5-50
Fumbles-Lost	0-0	3-3
Penalties-Yards	9-84	3-15
Time of Possession	34:29	25:31

Weather: Cool, 52 degrees
Attendance: 11,127

JEEP EAGLE ALOHA BOWL
December 25, 1995
Aloha Stadium
Honolulu, Hawaii

Synopsis: Led by quarterback Mark Williams, Kansas piled up 548 yards in total offense and dominated UCLA, 50-31, to win the Aloha Bowl.

UCLA	0	0	7	23	— 30
Kansas	7	10	20	14	— 51

KAN—Moore pass from Williams (McCord kick)
KAN—Henley 49 run (McCord kick)
KAN—McCord 27 field goal
KAN—Henley 2 run (kick failed)
UCLA—Melsby 8 pass from McNown (Merten kick)
KAN—Byrd 77 pass from Williams (McCord kick)
KAN—Carter 27 pass from Williams (McCord kick)
UCLA—Jordan 8 pass from McNown (Merten kick)
UCLA—Abdul-Jabbar 5 run (Melsby pass from McNown)
KAN—Williams 6 run (McCord kick)
UCLA—Melsby 7 pass from McNown (Abdul-Jabbar run)
KAN—Vann 67 run (McCord kick)

Game Statistics	UCLA	KAN
First Downs	21	21
Rushes-Yards	45-259	43-256
Passing Yards	136	292
Comp.-Att.-Int.	15-38-0	19-28-1
Punts-Avg.	4-45	2-48
Fumbles-Lost	1-1	1-0
Penalties-Yards	6-37	4-32
Time of Possession	29:42	30:18

Weather: Mostly sunny, 84 degrees
Attendance: 41,112

WEISER LOCK COPPER BOWL
December 27, 1995
Arizona Stadium
Tucson, Arizona

Synopsis: Texas Tech got a Copper Bowl record 260 yards rushing and four touchdowns from Byron Hanspard as the Red Raiders rolled over Air Force, 55-41.

Air Force	7	6	15	13	— 41
Texas Tech	21	10	7	17	— 55

TT—Mitchell 38 pass from Lethridge (Rogers kick)
AF—Addison 2 run (Thompson kick)
TT—Hanspard 2 run (Rogers kick)
TT—Hanspard 11 run (Rogers kick)
TT—Lethridge 1 run (Rogers kick)
AF—Johnson 71 run (kick failed)
TT—Rogers 24 field goal
AF—Campbell 7 run (Addison run)
AF—Johnson 60 run (Roberts kick)
TT—Hanspard 2 run (Rogers kick)
TT—Lethridge 3 run (Rogers kick)
TT—Rogers 31 field goal
AF—Morgan 1 run (Roberts kick)
TT—Hanspard 29 run (Rogers kick)
AF—Addison 7 run (run failed)

Game Statistics	AF	TT
First Downs	25	28
Rushes-Yards	67-431	39-361

Passing Yards	83	245
Comp.-Att.-Int.	7-13-0	22-41-1
Punts-Avg.	3-39.3	3-43.3
Fumbles-Lost	3-1	1-0
Penalties-Yards	6-51	11-90
Time of Possession	35:08	24:52

Weather: Clear, 58 degrees
Attendance: 41,004

BUILDERS SQUARE ALAMO BOWL

December 28, 1995
Alamodome
San Antonio, Texas

Synopsis: Kyle Bryant kicked five field goals to lead Texas A&M to a 22-20 victory over Michigan in the Builders Square Alamo Bowl.

Michigan	7	3	3	7	— 20
Texas A&M	10	3	3	6	— 22

TAM—Bernard 9 run (Bryant kick)
MIC—Toomer 41 pass from Griese (Hamilton kick)
TAM—Bryant 27 field goal
MIC—Hamilton 28 field goal
TAM—Bryant 49 field goal
TAM—Bryant 47 field goal
MIC—Hamilton 26 field goal
TAM—Bryant 31 field goal
TAM—Bryant 37 field goal
MIC—Toomer 44 pass from Griese (Hamilton kick)

Game Statistics	**MIC**	**TAM**
First Downs	19	17
Rushes-Yards	38-129	45-140
Passing Yards	182	136
Comp.-Att.-Int.	9-23-1	12-22-0
Punts-Avg.	7-36.0	5-43.0
Fumbles-Lost	2-1	2-1
Penalties-Yards	6-60	11-110
Time of Possession	31:54	28:01

Weather: Indoors, perfect
Attendance: 64,597

SUN BOWL

December 29, 1995
Sun Bowl
El Paso, Texas

Synopsis: Iowa's Sedrick Shaw rushed for 135 yards as the Hawkeyes rolled off 24 straight points and raced to a 38-18 win over Washington in the Sun Bowl.

Iowa	10	11	10	7	— 38
Washington	0	0	6	12	— 18

IOWA—Shaw 58 run (Bromert kick)
IOWA—Hurley 49 field goal
IOWA—Safety, punt snap rolls out of end zone
IOWA—Bromert 33 field goal
IOWA—Bromert 34 field goal
IOWA—Hurley 47 field goal
IOWA—Hurley 50 field goal
WASH—Pathon 30 pass from Fortney (pass failed)
IOWA—Burger 8 run (Bromert kick)
IOWA—Burger 1 run (Bromert kick)
WASH—Coleman 3 pass from Huard (pass failed)
WASH—Conwell 20 pass from Huard (run failed)

Game Statistics	**IOWA**	**WASH**
First Downs	18	14
Rushes-Yards	50-286	29-96
Passing Yards	135	250
Comp.-Att.-Int.	11-26-2	19-37-0
Punts-Avg.	5-39.4	7-27.1
Fumbles-Lost	1-0	3-3
Penalties-Yards	12-106	8-58
Time of Possession	35:32	24:28

Weather: Sunny, 56 degrees
Attendance: 49,116

POULAN/WEED EATER INDEPENDENCE BOWL

December 29, 1995
Independence Stadium
Shreveport, Louisiana

Synopsis: LSU's Kevin Faulk rushed for 234 yards and two touchdowns and Eddie Kennison caught five passes for 124 yards as the Tigers drilled Michigan State, 45-26, in the Poulan/Weed Eater Independence Bowl.

LSU	7	14	21	3	— 45
MSU	7	17	0	2	— 26

MSU—Muhammed 78 pass from Banks (Gardner kick)
LSU—Cleveland 6 run (Lafleur kick)
MSU—Greene 3 run (kick blocked)
LSU—Kennison 92 kickoff return (Lafleur kick)
MSU—Mason 100 kickoff return (Greene run)
LSU—Faulk 51 run (Lafleur kick)
MSU—Gardner 37 field goal
LSU—Faulk 5 run (Lafleur kick)
LSU—Northern 37 fumble return (Lafleur kick)
LSU—Kennison 27 pass from Tyler (Lafleur kick)
LSU—Richey 48 field goal
MSU—Safety

Game Statistics	**LSU**	**MSU**
First Downs	17	23
Rushes-Yards	48-272	35-100
Passing Yards	164	348
Comp.-Att.-Int.	10-20-1	22-44-3
Punts-Avg.	4-44.5	6-37.5
Fumbles-Lost	2-1	4-3
Penalties-Yards	5-42	9-80
Time of Possession	29:50	30:10

Weather: Fair, 46 degrees
Attendance: 48,835

PLYMOUTH HOLIDAY BOWL

December 29, 1995
San Diego Jack Murphy Stadium
San Diego, California

Synopsis: Kansas State rolled up 536 yards in total offense and raced to a 54-21 victory over Colorado State in the Plymouth Holiday Bowl.

Colorado St.	7	0	14	0	— 21
Kansas St.	7	19	21	7	— 54

KSU—Hickson 4 run (Gramatica kick)
CSU—Blake 2 run (McDougal kick)
KSU—Lawrence 5 run (kick failed)
KSU—Kelly 18 run (pass failed)
KSU—Lojka 12 pass from Kavanagh (Gramatica kick)
KSU—Schwieger 18 pass from Kavanagh (Gramatica kick)
CSU—Watson 3 run (McDougal kick)
KSU—Lawrence 5 run (Gramatica kick)
CSU—Washington 12 run (McDougal kick)
KSU—Lockett 4 pass from Kavanagh (Gramatica kick)
KSU—Running 33 pass from Kavanagh (Gramatica kick)

Game Statistics	**CSU**	**KSU**
First Downs	14	30
Rushes-Yards	30-169	48-212
Passing Yards	132	324
Comp.-Att.-Int.	6-30-3	24-32-1
Punts-Avg.	8-28.4	3-45.0
Fumbles-Lost	2-1	0-0
Penalties-Yards	11-95	12-124
Time of Possession	23:43	36:17

Weather: Clear, 61 degrees
Attendance: 51,051

ST. JUDE LIBERTY BOWL CLASSIC

December 30, 1995
Liberty Bowl Memorial Stadium
Memphis, Tennessee

Synopsis: Chad Holcomb kicked four field goals to lead East Carolina to a 19-13 victory over Stanford in the St. Jude Liberty Bowl Classic.

Stanford	0	7	6	0	— 13
East Caro.	7	9	0	3	— 19

ECU—Hart 39 interception return (Holcomb kick)
ECU—Holcomb 46 field goal
ECU—Holcomb 26 field goal
STA—Salina 1 run (Abrams kick)
ECU—Holcomb 41 field goal
STA—Ellis 2 blocked punt return (kick failed)
ECU—Holcomb 34 field goal

Game Statistics	**STA**	**ECU**
First Downs	11	18
Rushes-Yards	37-72	40-129
Passing Yards	139	218
Comp.-Att.-Int.	15-27-2	19-46-1
Punts-Avg.	7-36.9	6-28.5
Fumbles-Lost	2-2	0-0
Penalties-Yards	3-18	4-25
Time of Possession	27:43	32:17

Weather: Sunny, 43 degrees
Attendance: 47,398

CARQUEST BOWL

December 30, 1995
Joe Robbie Stadium
Miami, Florida

Synopsis: North Carolina's Leon Johnson rushed for a Carquest Bowl record 195 yards and Mike Thomas threw two scoring passes as the Tar Heels posted a 20-10 victory over Arkansas.

North Caro.	7	0	13	0	— 20
Arkansas	7	0	3	0	— 10

ARK—Lucas 25 pass from Lunney (Latourette kick)
UNC—Ashford 18 pass from Thomas (Welch kick)
ARK—Latourette 26 field goal
UNC—Johnson 28 run (Welch kick)
UNC—Stevens 87 pass from Thomas (kick failed)

Game Statistics	**UNC**	**ARK**
First Downs	20	26
Rushes-Yards	49-242	44-162
Passing Yards	177	227
Comp.-Att.-Int.	10-23-0	16-35-2
Punts-Avg.	4-32.5	4-38.8
Fumbles-Lost	0-0	1-1
Penalties-Yards	4-31	3-36
Time of Possession	29:57	30:03

Weather: Cloudy, 74 degrees
Attendance: 34,428

PEACH BOWL

December 30, 1995
Georgia Dome
Atlanta, Georgia

Synopsis: Demetrius Allen returned a kickoff 83 yards for a touchdown with 57 seconds left and Virginia beat Georgia, 34-27, in the Peach Bowl.

Georgia	3	11	3	10	— 27
Virginia	14	10	3	7	— 34

VA—Barber 1 run (Garcia kick)
VA—Brooks 5 run (Garcia kick)
GA—Parkman 36 field goal
GA—Parkman 37 field goal
VA—Garcia 36 field goal
VA—Allen 83 pass from Groh (Garcia kick)
GA—Ward 1 run (Hunter pass from Ward)
GA—Parkman 20 field goal
VA—Garcia 36 field goal
GA—Parkman 42 field goal
GA—Ferguson 10 fumble return (Parkman kick)
VA—Allen 83 kickoff return (Garcia kick)

Game Statistics	**GA**	**VA**
First Downs	20	10
Rushes-Yards	36-112	34-100
Passing Yards	413	156
Comp.-Att.-Int.	31-59-2	10-20-1
Punts-Avg.	5-33.0	8-42.0
Fumbles-Lost	1-1	4-2
Penalties-Yards	6-40	3-30
Time of Possession	34:25	25:35

Weather: Indoors, perfect
Attendance: 70,825

NOKIA SUGAR BOWL

December 31, 1995
Louisiana Superdome
New Orleans, Louisiana

Synopsis: Virginia Tech blitzed Texas into submission and rode two long touchdowns by Bryan Still to a 28-10 victory in the Nokia Sugar Bowl.

Virginia Tech	0	7	7	14	— 28
Texas	7	3	0	0	— 10

TEX—Fitzgerald 4 pass from Brown (Dawson kick)
TEX—Dawson 52 field goal
VT—Still 60 punt return (Larsen kick)
VT—Parker 2 run (Larsen kick)
VT—Still 54 pass from Druckenmiller (Larsen kick)
VT—Baron 20 fumble return (Larsen kick)

Game Statistics	**VT**	**TEX**
First Downs	20	15
Rushes-Yards	32-96	33-78
Passing Yards	266	148
Comp.-Att.-Int.	18-34-1	14-37-3
Punts-Avg.	8-37.0	9-40.0
Fumbles-Lost	5-2	2-1
Penalties-Yards	11-99	9-91
Time of Possession	30:25	29:35

Weather: Indoors, perfect
Attendance: 70,283

OUTBACK BOWL

January 1, 1996
Tampa Stadium
Tampa, Florida

Synopsis: Despite a steady downpour of rain, Penn State finally adjusted to the conditions and blitzed Auburn, 43-14, behind the play of receiver Bobby Engram in the Outback Bowl.

Auburn	0	7	0	7	— 14
Penn St.	3	13	27	0	— 43

PSU—Conway 19 field goal
AUB—Baker 25 pass from Nix (Hawkins kick)
PSU—Conway 22 field goal
PSU—Conway 38 field goal
PSU—Archie 8 pass from Richardson (Conway kick)
PSU—Engram 9 pass from Richardson (Conway kick)
PSU—Pitts 4 pass from Richardson (pass failed)
PSU—Enis 1 run (Conway kick)
PSU—Engram 20 pass from Richardson (Conway kick)
AUB—McLeod 12 run (Hawkins kick)

Game Statistics	**AUB**	**PSU**
First Downs	19	22
Rushes-Yards	40-220	49-266
Passing Yards	94	221
Comp.-Att.-Int.	8-33-2	14-29-2
Punts-Avg.	8-39.1	4-35.7
Fumbles-Lost	5-2	2-1
Penalties-Yards	5-59	6-35
Time of Possession	27:49	32:11

Weather: Rain, muddy, 70 degrees
Attendance: 65,313

CompUSA FLORIDA CITRUS BOWL

January 1, 1996
Florida Citrus Bowl
Orlando, Florida

Synopsis: Tennessee's Jay Graham rushed 26 times for 154 yards to lead the Volunteers to a 20-14 victory over Ohio State in the CompUSA Florida Citrus Bowl.

Ohio St.	7	0	0	7	— 14
Tennessee	0	7	7	6	— 20

OSU—George 2 run (Jackson kick)
TENN—Graham 69 run (Hall kick)
TENN—Kent 47 pass from Manning (Hall kick)
OSU—Dudley 32 pass from Hoying (Jackson kick)
TENN—Hall 29 field goal
TENN—Hall 25 field goal

Game Statistics	**OSU**	**TENN**
First Downs	17	15
Rushes-Yards	36-89	32-145
Passing Yards	246	182
Comp.-Att.-Int.	19-38-1	20-35-0
Punts-Avg.	7-48.1	9-34.2
Fumbles-Lost	5-3	1-1
Penalties-Yards	6-57	8-43
Time of Possession	29:21	30:39

Weather: Rain, cloudy, 70 degrees
Attendance: 70,797

TOYOTA GATOR BOWL

January 1, 1996
Jacksonville Municipal Stadium
Jacksonville, Florida

Synopsis: Freshman Donovan McNabb threw for 309 yards and three touchdowns as Syracuse totally dominated Clemson, 41-0, in the Toyota Gator Bowl.

Syracuse	20	0	14	7	— 41
Clemson	0	0	0	0	— 0

SYR—Thomas 1 run (Mare kick)
SYR—McNabb 5 run (kick blocked)
SYR—Harrison 38 pass from McNabb (Mare kick)
SYR—Thomas 2 run (Mare kick)
SYR—Harrison 56 pass from McNabb (Mare kick)
SYR—Sincero 15 pass from McNabb (Mare kick)

Game Statistics	**SYR**	**CLE**
First Downs	21	12
Rushes-Yards	50-158	34-90
Passing Yards	309	69
Comp.-Att.-Int.	13-23-1	11-24-2
Punts-Avg.	4-43.5	6-49.3
Fumbles-Lost	1-0	1-0
Penalties-Yards	7-65	1-16
Time of Possession	35:02	24:58

Weather: Cloudy, 67 degrees
Attendance: 45,202

COTTON BOWL CLASSIC

January 1, 1996
Cotton Bowl
Dallas, Texas

Synopsis: Marcus Washington stunned Oregon with a 95-yard interception return for a score and John Hessler threw for two touchdowns as Colorado beat the Ducks, 38-6, in a chilly Cotton Bowl.

Oregon	6	0	0	0	— 6
Colorado	0	13	19	6	— 38

ORE—Smith 25 field goal
ORE—Smith 33 field goal
COL—Hessler 1 run (Voskeritchian kick)
COL—Washington 95 interception return (kick failed)
COL—Lepsis 2 pass from Hessler (Voskeritchian kick)
COL—Troutman 6 run (kick failed)
COL—Savoy 12 pass from Hessler (kick failed)
COL—Abdul-Rahmaan 5 run (kick failed)

Game Statistics	**ORE**	**COL**
First Downs	16	16
Rushes-Yards	29-105	41-170
Passing Yards	162	143
Comp.-Att.-Int.	21-44-2	12-27-2
Punts-Avg.	5-38.0	4-29.0
Fumbles-Lost	4-3	2-1
Penalties-Yards	8-67	6-41
Time of Possession	30:01	29:59

Weather: Rain, cold, 26-degree wind chill
Attendance: 58,214

ROSE BOWL

January 1, 1996
Rose Bowl
Pasadena, California

Synopsis: Brad Otton threw for 391 yards and two touchdowns and Keyshawn Johnson caught 12 passes for 216 yards and one score to pace Southern Cal to a 41-32 victory over Northwestern in the Rose Bowl.

Southern Cal	7	17	7	10	— 41
Northwestern	7	3	16	6	— 32

USC—Woods 1 run (Abrams kick)
NW—Autry 3 run (Gowins kick)
USC—Barnum 21 pass from Otton (Abrams kick)
USC—Abrams 30 field goal
USC—McCutcheon 53 fumble return (Abrams kick)
NW—Gowins 29 field goal
NW—Gowins 28 field goal
NW—Autry 9 run (pass failed)
USC—Johnson 56 pass from Otton (Abrams kick)
NW—Schnur 1 run (Gowins kick)
NW—Autry 2 run (pass failed)
USC—Abrams 46 field goal
USC—Washington 2 run (Abrams kick)

Game Statistics	**USC**	**NW**
First Downs	22	23
Rushes-Yards	27-29	39-139
Passing Yards	391	336
Comp.-Att.-Int.	29-44-0	23-39-1
Punts-Avg.	2-44.5	2-38.5
Fumbles-Lost	1-1	1-1
Penalties-Yards	11-86	7-72
Time of Possession	29:47	30:13

Weather: Partly cloudy, 75 degrees
Attendance: 100,102

FEDEX ORANGE BOWL

January 1, 1996
Orange Bowl Stadium
Miami, Florida

Synopsis: Danny Kanell, Warrick Dunn and Andre Cooper all had a big hand in leading Florida State to a dramatic come-from-behind 31-26 victory over Notre Dame in the FedEx Orange Bowl.

Florida St.	7	7	0	17	— 31
Notre Dame	10	0	7	9	— 26

ND—Mayes 39 pass from Krug (Cengia kick)
FS—Cooper 15 pass from Kanell (Bentley kick)
ND—Cengia 20 field goal
FS—Cooper 10 pass from Kanell (Bentley kick)
ND—Mayes 33 pass from Krug (Cengia kick)
ND—Safety
ND—Chryplewicz 5 pass from Krug (Cengia kick)
FS—Green 11 pass from Kanell (Bentley kick)
FS—Cooper 3 pass from Kanell (Cooper pass from Kanell)
FS—Safety

Game Statistics	**FS**	**ND**
First Downs	26	17
Rushes-Yards	37-188	45-256
Passing Yards	290	169
Comp.-Att.-Int.	20-33-2	15-26-1
Punts-Avg.	3-44.0	5-42.4
Fumbles-Lost	1-0	2-1
Penalties-Yards	7-59	7-55
Time of Possession	28:13	31:47

Weather: Cloudy, humid, 79 degrees
Attendance: 72,198

TOSTITOS FIESTA BOWL

January 2, 1996
Sun Devil Stadium
Tempe, Arizona

Synopsis: Nebraska's Tommie Frazier rushed for 199 yards and two touchdowns and the Cornhusker defense sacked Danny Wuerffel seven times as Nebraska slammed Florida, 62-24, for a second straight national championship in the Tostitos Fiesta Bowl.

Nebraska	6	29	14	13	— 62
Florida	10	0	8	6	— 24

FLA—Edmiston 23 field goal
NEB—Phillips 16 pass from Frazier (kick blocked)
FLA—Wuerffel 1 run (Edmiston kick)
NEB—Phillips 42 run (Brown kick)
NEB—Safety
NEB—Green 1 run (Brown kick)
NEB—Brown 26 field goal
NEB—Booker 42 interception return (Brown kick)
NEB—Brown 24 field goal
NEB—Frazier 35 run (Brown kick)
FLA—Hilliard 35 pass from Wuerffel (Anthony pass from Wuerffel)
NEB—Frazier 75 run (Brown kick)
NEB—Phillips 15 run (kick blocked)
NEB—Berringer 1 run (Retzlaff kick)
FLA—Anthony 93 kickoff return (run failed)

Game Statistics	**NEB**	**FLA**
First Downs	27	15
Rushes-Yards	68-524	21-(-28)
Passing Yards	105	297
Comp.-Att.-Int.	6-15-2	20-38-3
Punts-Avg.	1-36.0	4-41.3
Fumbles-Lost	1-0	1-1
Penalties-Yards	4-30	9-78
Time of Possession	35:17	24:43

Weather: Clear, 58 degrees
Attendance: 79,864

All-Time Bowl-Game Results

Major Bowl Games

ROSE BOWL

Present Site: Pasadena, Calif.
Stadium (Capacity): Rose Bowl (98,252)
Playing Surface: Grass
Playing Sites: Tournament Park, Pasadena (1902, 1916-22); Rose Bowl, Pasadena (1923-41); Duke Stadium, Durham, N.C. (1942); Rose Bowl (since 1943)

1-1-02—Michigan 49, Stanford 0
1-1-16—Washington St. 14, Brown 0
1-1-17—Oregon 14, Pennsylvania 0
1-1-18—Mare Island 19, Camp Lewis 7
1-1-19—Great Lakes 17, Mare Island 0

1-1-20—Harvard 7, Oregon 6
1-1-21—California 28, Ohio St. 0
1-2-22—California 0, Wash. & Jeff. 0
1-1-23—Southern Cal 14, Penn St. 3
1-1-24—Navy 14, Washington 14

1-1-25—Notre Dame 27, Stanford 10
1-1-26—Alabama 20, Washington 19
1-1-27—Alabama 7, Stanford 7
1-2-28—Stanford 7, Pittsburgh 6
1-1-29—Georgia Tech 8, California 7

1-1-30—Southern Cal 47, Pittsburgh 14
1-1-31—Alabama 24, Washington St. 0
1-1-32—Southern Cal 21, Tulane 12
1-2-33—Southern Cal 35, Pittsburgh 0
1-1-34—Columbia 7, Stanford 0

1-1-35—Alabama 29, Stanford 13
1-1-36—Stanford 7, Southern Methodist 0
1-1-37—Pittsburgh 21, Washington 0
1-1-38—California 13, Alabama 0
1-2-39—Southern Cal 7, Duke 3

1-1-40—Southern Cal 14, Tennessee 0
1-1-41—Stanford 21, Nebraska 13
1-1-42—Oregon St. 20, Duke 16 (at Durham)
1-1-43—Georgia 9, UCLA 0
1-1-44—Southern Cal 29, Washington 0

1-1-45—Southern Cal 25, Tennessee 0
1-1-46—Alabama 34, Southern Cal 14
1-1-47—Illinois 45, UCLA 14
1-1-48—Michigan 49, Southern Cal 0
1-1-49—Northwestern 20, California 14

1-2-50—Ohio St. 17, California 14
1-1-51—Michigan 14, California 6
1-1-52—Illinois 40, Stanford 7
1-1-53—Southern Cal 7, Wisconsin 0
1-1-54—Michigan St. 28, UCLA 20

1-1-55—Ohio St. 20, Southern Cal 7
1-2-56—Michigan St. 17, UCLA 14
1-1-57—Iowa 35, Oregon St. 19
1-1-58—Ohio St. 10, Oregon 7
1-1-59—Iowa 38, California 12

1-1-60—Washington 44, Wisconsin 8
1-2-61—Washington 17, Minnesota 7
1-1-62—Minnesota 21, UCLA 3
1-1-63—Southern Cal 42, Wisconsin 37
1-1-64—Illinois 17, Washington 7

1-1-65—Michigan 34, Oregon St. 7
1-1-66—UCLA 14, Michigan St. 12
1-2-67—Purdue 14, Southern Cal 13
1-1-68—Southern Cal 14, Indiana 3
1-1-69—Ohio St. 27, Southern Cal 16

1-1-70—Southern Cal 10, Michigan 3
1-1-71—Stanford 27, Ohio St. 17
1-1-72—Stanford 13, Michigan 12
1-1-73—Southern Cal 42, Ohio St. 17
1-1-74—Ohio St. 42, Southern Cal 21

1-1-75—Southern Cal 18, Ohio St. 17
1-1-76—UCLA 23, Ohio St. 10
1-1-77—Southern Cal 14, Michigan 6
1-2-78—Washington 27, Michigan 20
1-1-79—Southern Cal 17, Michigan 10

1-1-80—Southern Cal 17, Ohio St. 16
1-1-81—Michigan 23, Washington 6
1-1-82—Washington 28, Iowa 0
1-1-83—UCLA 24, Michigan 14
1-2-84—UCLA 45, Illinois 9

1-1-85—Southern Cal 20, Ohio St. 17
1-1-86—UCLA 45, Iowa 28
1-1-87—Arizona St. 22, Michigan 15
1-1-88—Michigan St. 20, Southern Cal 17
1-2-89—Michigan 22, Southern Cal 14

1-1-90—Southern Cal 17, Michigan 10
1-1-91—Washington 46, Iowa 34
1-1-92—Washington 34, Michigan 14
1-1-93—Michigan 38, Washington 31
1-1-94—Wisconsin 21, UCLA 16

1-2-95—Penn St. 38, Oregon 20
1-1-96—Southern Cal 41, Northwestern 32

ORANGE BOWL

Present Site: Miami, Fla.
Stadium (Capacity): Joe Robbie Stadium (74,913)
Playing Surface: Prescription Athletic Turf
Name Changes: Orange Bowl (1935-88); Federal Express Orange Bowl (since 1989)
Playing Sites: Miami Field Stadium (1935-37); Orange Bowl (1938-96); Joe Robbie Stadium (since 1997)

1-1-35—Bucknell 26, Miami (Fla.) 0
1-1-36—Catholic 20, Mississippi 19
1-1-37—Duquesne 13, Mississippi St. 12
1-1-38—Auburn 6, Michigan St. 0
1-2-39—Tennessee 17, Oklahoma 0

1-1-40—Georgia Tech 21, Missouri 7
1-1-41—Mississippi St. 14, Georgetown 7
1-1-42—Georgia 40, Texas Christian 26

1-1-43—Alabama 37, Boston College 21
1-1-44—LSU 19, Texas A&M 14

1-1-45—Tulsa 26, Georgia Tech 12
1-1-46—Miami (Fla.) 13, Holy Cross 6
1-1-47—Rice 8, Tennessee 0
1-1-48—Georgia Tech 20, Kansas 14
1-1-49—Texas 41, Georgia 28

1-2-50—Santa Clara 21, Kentucky 13
1-1-51—Clemson 15, Miami (Fla.) 14
1-1-52—Georgia Tech 17, Baylor 14
1-1-53—Alabama 61, Syracuse 6
1-1-54—Oklahoma 7, Maryland 0

1-1-55—Duke 34, Nebraska 7
1-2-56—Oklahoma 20, Maryland 6
1-1-57—Colorado 27, Clemson 21
1-1-58—Oklahoma 48, Duke 21
1-1-59—Oklahoma 21, Syracuse 6

1-1-60—Georgia 14, Missouri 0
1-2-61—Missouri 21, Navy 14
1-1-62—LSU 25, Colorado 7
1-1-63—Alabama 17, Oklahoma 0
1-1-64—Nebraska 13, Auburn 7

1-1-65—Texas 21, Alabama 17
1-1-66—Alabama 39, Nebraska 28
1-2-67—Florida 27, Georgia Tech 12
1-1-68—Oklahoma 26, Tennessee 24
1-1-69—Penn St. 15, Kansas 14

1-1-70—Penn St. 10, Missouri 3
1-1-71—Nebraska 17, LSU 12
1-1-72—Nebraska 38, Alabama 6
1-1-73—Nebraska 40, Notre Dame 6
1-1-74—Penn St. 16, LSU 9

1-1-75—Notre Dame 13, Alabama 11
1-1-76—Oklahoma 14, Michigan 6
1-1-77—Ohio St. 27, Colorado 10
1-2-78—Arkansas 31, Oklahoma 6
1-1-79—Oklahoma 31, Nebraska 24

1-1-80—Oklahoma 24, Florida St. 7
1-1-81—Oklahoma 18, Florida St. 17
1-1-82—Clemson 22, Nebraska 15
1-1-83—Nebraska 21, LSU 20
1-2-84—Miami (Fla.) 31, Nebraska 30

1-1-85—Washington 28, Oklahoma 17
1-1-86—Oklahoma 25, Penn St. 10
1-1-87—Oklahoma 42, Arkansas 8
1-1-88—Miami (Fla.) 20, Oklahoma 14
1-2-89—Miami (Fla.) 23, Nebraska 3

1-1-90—Notre Dame 21, Colorado 6
1-1-91—Colorado 10, Notre Dame 9
1-1-92—Miami (Fla.) 22, Nebraska 0
1-1-93—Florida St. 27, Nebraska 14
1-1-94—Florida St. 18, Nebraska 16

1-1-95—Nebraska 24, Miami (Fla.) 17
1-1-96—Florida St. 31, Notre Dame 26

SUGAR BOWL

Present Site: New Orleans, La.
Stadium (Capacity): Louisiana Superdome (72,704)
Playing Surface: AstroTurf
Name Changes: Sugar Bowl (1935-87); USF&G Sugar Bowl (1988-95); Nokia Sugar Bowl (since 1996)
Playing Sites: Tulane Stadium, New Orleans (1935-74); Louisiana Superdome (since 1975)

1-1-35—Tulane 20, Temple 14
1-1-36—Texas Christian 3, LSU 2
1-1-37—Santa Clara 21, LSU 14
1-1-38—Santa Clara 6, LSU 0
1-2-39—Texas Christian 15, Carnegie Mellon 7

1-1-40—Texas A&M 14, Tulane 13
1-1-41—Boston College 19, Tennessee 13
1-1-42—Fordham 2, Missouri 0
1-1-43—Tennessee 14, Tulsa 7
1-1-44—Georgia Tech 20, Tulsa 18

1-1-45—Duke 29, Alabama 26
1-1-46—Oklahoma St. 33, St. Mary's (Cal.) 13
1-1-47—Georgia 20, North Caro. 10
1-1-48—Texas 27, Alabama 7
1-1-49—Oklahoma 14, North Caro. 6

1-2-50—Oklahoma 35, LSU 0
1-1-51—Kentucky 13, Oklahoma 7
1-1-52—Maryland 28, Tennessee 13
1-1-53—Georgia Tech 24, Mississippi 7
1-1-54—Georgia Tech 42, West Va. 19

1-1-55—Navy 21, Mississippi 0
1-2-56—Georgia Tech 7, Pittsburgh 0
1-1-57—Baylor 13, Tennessee 7
1-1-58—Mississippi 39, Texas 7
1-1-59—LSU 7, Clemson 0

1-1-60—Mississippi 21, LSU 0
1-2-61—Mississippi 14, Rice 6
1-1-62—Alabama 10, Arkansas 3
1-1-63—Mississippi 17, Arkansas 13
1-1-64—Alabama 12, Mississippi 7

1-1-65—LSU 13, Syracuse 10
1-1-66—Missouri 20, Florida 18
1-2-67—Alabama 34, Nebraska 7
1-1-68—LSU 20, Wyoming 13
1-1-69—Arkansas 16, Georgia 2

1-1-70—Mississippi 27, Arkansas 22
1-1-71—Tennessee 34, Air Force 13
1-1-72—Oklahoma 40, Auburn 22
12-31-72—Oklahoma 14, Penn St. 0
12-31-73—Notre Dame 24, Alabama 23

12-31-74—Nebraska 13, Florida 10
12-31-75—Alabama 13, Penn St. 6
1-1-77—Pittsburgh 27, Georgia 3
1-2-78—Alabama 35, Ohio St. 6
1-1-79—Alabama 14, Penn St. 7

1-1-80—Alabama 24, Arkansas 9
1-1-81—Georgia 17, Notre Dame 10
1-1-82—Pittsburgh 24, Georgia 20
1-1-83—Penn St. 27, Georgia 23
1-2-84—Auburn 9, Michigan 7

1-1-85—Nebraska 28, LSU 10
1-1-86—Tennessee 35, Miami (Fla.) 7
1-1-87—Nebraska 30, LSU 15
1-1-88—Auburn 16, Syracuse 16
1-2-89—Florida St. 13, Auburn 7

1-1-90—Miami (Fla.) 33, Alabama 25
1-1-91—Tennessee 23, Virginia 22
1-1-92—Notre Dame 39, Florida 28
1-1-93—Alabama 34, Miami (Fla.) 13
1-1-94—Florida 41, West Va. 7

1-2-95—Florida St. 23, Florida 17
12-31-95—Virginia Tech 28, Texas 10

COTTON BOWL

Present Site: Dallas, Texas
Stadium (Capacity): Cotton Bowl (68,245)
Playing Surface: Grass
Name Changes: Cotton Bowl (1937-88, since 1996); Mobil Cotton Bowl (1989-95)
Playing Sites: Fair Park Stadium, Dallas (1937); Cotton Bowl (since 1938)

1-1-37—Texas Christian 16, Marquette 6
1-1-38—Rice 28, Colorado 14
1-2-39—St. Mary's (Cal.) 20, Texas Tech 13
1-1-40—Clemson 6, Boston College 3
1-1-41—Texas A&M 13, Fordham 12

1-1-42—Alabama 29, Texas A&M 21
1-1-43—Texas 14, Georgia Tech 7
1-1-44—Randolph Field 7, Texas 7
1-1-45—Oklahoma St. 34, Texas Christian 0
1-1-46—Texas 40, Missouri 27

1-1-47—Arkansas 0, LSU 0
1-1-48—Penn St. 13, Southern Methodist 13
1-1-49—Southern Methodist 21, Oregon 13
1-2-50—Rice 27, North Caro. 13
1-1-51—Tennessee 20, Texas 14

1-1-52—Kentucky 20, Texas Christian 7
1-1-53—Texas 16, Tennessee 0
1-1-54—Rice 28, Alabama 6
1-1-55—Georgia Tech 14, Arkansas 6
1-2-56—Mississippi 14, Texas Christian 13

1-1-57—Texas Christian 28, Syracuse 27
1-1-58—Navy 20, Rice 7
1-1-59—Air Force 0, Texas Christian 0
1-1-60—Syracuse 23, Texas 14
1-2-61—Duke 7, Arkansas 6

1-1-62—Texas 12, Mississippi 7
1-1-63—LSU 13, Texas 0
1-1-64—Texas 28, Navy 6
1-1-65—Arkansas 10, Nebraska 7
1-1-66—LSU 14, Arkansas 7

12-31-66—Georgia 24, Southern Methodist 9
1-1-68—Texas A&M 20, Alabama 16
1-1-69—Texas 36, Tennessee 13

1-1-70—Texas 21, Notre Dame 17
1-1-71—Notre Dame 24, Texas 11

1-1-72—Penn St. 30, Texas 6
1-1-73—Texas 17, Alabama 13
1-1-74—Nebraska 19, Texas 3
1-1-75—Penn St. 41, Baylor 20
1-1-76—Arkansas 31, Georgia 10

1-1-77—Houston 30, Maryland 21
1-2-78—Notre Dame 38, Texas 10
1-1-79—Notre Dame 35, Houston 34
1-1-80—Houston 17, Nebraska 14
1-1-81—Alabama 30, Baylor 2

1-1-82—Texas 14, Alabama 12
1-1-83—Southern Methodist 7, Pittsburgh 3
1-2-84—Georgia 10, Texas 9
1-1-85—Boston College 45, Houston 28
1-1-86—Texas A&M 36, Auburn 16

1-1-87—Ohio St. 28, Texas A&M 12
1-1-88—Texas A&M 35, Notre Dame 10
1-2-89—UCLA 17, Arkansas 3
1-1-90—Tennessee 31, Arkansas 27
1-1-91—Miami (Fla.) 46, Texas 3

1-1-92—Florida St. 10, Texas A&M 2
1-1-93—Notre Dame 28, Texas A&M 3
1-1-94—Notre Dame 24, Texas A&M 21
1-2-95—Southern Cal 55, Texas Tech 14
1-1-96—Colorado 38, Oregon 6

NORWEST BANK SUN BOWL

Present Site: El Paso, Texas
Stadium (Capacity): Sun Bowl (51,270)
Playing Surface: AstroTurf
Name Changes: Sun Bowl (1936-86, 1994-95); John Hancock Sun Bowl (1987-88); John Hancock Bowl (1989-93); Norwest Bank Sun Bowl (since 1996)
Playing Sites: Kidd Field, UTEP, El Paso (1936-62); Sun Bowl (since 1963)

1-1-36—Hardin-Simmons 14, New Mexico St. 14
1-1-37—Hardin-Simmons 34, UTEP 6
1-1-38—West Va. 7, Texas Tech 6
1-2-39—Utah 26, New Mexico 0
1-1-40—Arizona St. 0, Catholic 0

1-1-41—Case Reserve 26, Arizona St. 13
1-1-42—Tulsa 6, Texas Tech 0
1-1-43—Second Air Force 13, Hardin-Simmons 7
1-1-44—Southwestern (Tex.) 7, New Mexico 0
1-1-45—Southwestern (Tex.) 35, U. of Mexico 0

1-1-46—New Mexico 34, Denver 24
1-1-47—Cincinnati 18, Virginia Tech 6
1-1-48—Miami (Ohio) 13, Texas Tech 12
1-1-49—West Va. 21, UTEP 12
1-2-50—UTEP 33, Georgetown 20

1-1-51—West Tex. A&M 14, Cincinnati 13
1-1-52—Texas Tech 25, Pacific (Cal.) 14
1-1-53—Pacific (Cal.) 26, Southern Miss. 7
1-1-54—UTEP 37, Southern Miss. 14
1-1-55—UTEP 47, Florida St. 20

1-2-56—Wyoming 21, Texas Tech 14
1-1-57—Geo. Washington 13, UTEP 0
1-1-58—Louisville 34, Drake 20
12-31-58—Wyoming 14, Hardin-Simmons 6
12-31-59—New Mexico St. 28, North Texas 8

12-31-60—New Mexico St. 20, Utah St. 13
12-30-61—Villanova 17, Wichita St. 9
12-31-62—West Tex. A&M 15, Ohio 14
12-31-63—Oregon 21, Southern Methodist 14
12-26-64—Georgia 7, Texas Tech 0

12-31-65—UTEP 13, Texas Christian 12
12-24-66—Wyoming 28, Florida St. 20
12-30-67—UTEP 14, Mississippi 7
12-28-68—Auburn 34, Arizona 10
12-20-69—Nebraska 45, Georgia 6

12-19-70—Georgia Tech 17, Texas Tech 9
12-18-71—LSU 33, Iowa St. 15
12-30-72—North Caro. 32, Texas Tech 28
12-29-73—Missouri 34, Auburn 17
12-28-74—Mississippi St. 26, North Caro. 24

12-26-75—Pittsburgh 33, Kansas 19
1-2-77—Texas A&M 37, Florida 14
12-31-77—Stanford 24, LSU 14
12-23-78—Texas 42, Maryland 0
12-22-79—Washington 14, Texas 7

12-27-80—Nebraska 31, Mississippi St. 17
12-26-81—Oklahoma 40, Houston 14
12-25-82—North Caro. 26, Texas 10
12-24-83—Alabama 28, Southern Methodist 7
12-22-84—Maryland 28, Tennessee 27

12-28-85—Arizona 13, Georgia 13
12-25-86—Alabama 28, Washington 6
12-25-87—Oklahoma St. 35, West Va. 33
12-24-88—Alabama 29, Army 28
12-30-89—Pittsburgh 31, Texas A&M 28

12-31-90—Michigan St. 17, Southern Cal 16
12-31-91—UCLA 6, Illinois 3
12-31-92—Baylor 20, Arizona 15
12-24-93—Oklahoma 41, Texas Tech 10
12-30-94—Texas 35, North Caro. 31

12-29-95—Iowa 38, Washington 18

GATOR BOWL

Present Site: Jacksonville, Fla.
Stadium (Capacity): Jacksonville Municipal Stadium (73,000)
Playing Surface: Grass
Name Changes: Gator Bowl (1946-85, 1991); Mazda Gator Bowl (1986-90); Outback Steakhouse Gator Bowl (1992-94); Toyota Gator Bowl (since 1995)
Playing Sites: Gator Bowl (1946-93, 1996); Ben Hill Griffin Stadium, Gainesville, Fla. (1994); Jacksonville Municipal Stadium (since 1996)

1-1-46—Wake Forest 26, South Caro. 14
1-1-47—Oklahoma 34, North Caro. St. 13
1-1-48—Georgia 20, Maryland 20
1-1-49—Clemson 24, Missouri 23
1-2-50—Maryland 20, Missouri 7

1-1-51—Wyoming 20, Wash. & Lee 7
1-1-52—Miami (Fla.) 14, Clemson 0
1-1-53—Florida 14, Tulsa 13
1-1-54—Texas Tech 35, Auburn 13
12-31-54—Auburn 33, Baylor 13

12-31-55—Vanderbilt 25, Auburn 13
12-29-56—Georgia Tech 21, Pittsburgh 14
12-28-57—Tennessee 3, Texas A&M 0
12-27-58—Mississippi 7, Florida 3
1-2-60—Arkansas 14, Georgia Tech 7

12-31-60—Florida 13, Baylor 12
12-30-61—Penn St. 30, Georgia Tech 15
12-29-62—Florida 17, Penn St. 7
12-28-63—North Caro. 35, Air Force 0
1-2-65—Florida St. 36, Oklahoma 19

12-31-65—Georgia Tech 31, Texas Tech 21
12-31-66—Tennessee 18, Syracuse 12
12-30-67—Florida St. 17, Penn St. 17
12-28-68—Missouri 35, Alabama 10
12-27-69—Florida 14, Tennessee 13

1-2-71—Auburn 35, Mississippi 28
12-31-71—Georgia 7, North Caro. 3
12-30-72—Auburn 24, Colorado 3
12-29-73—Texas Tech 28, Tennessee 19
12-30-74—Auburn 27, Texas 3

12-29-75—Maryland 13, Florida 0
12-27-76—Notre Dame 20, Penn St. 9
12-30-77—Pittsburgh 34, Clemson 3
12-29-78—Clemson 17, Ohio St. 15
12-28-79—North Caro. 17, Michigan 15

12-29-80—Pittsburgh 37, South Caro. 9
12-28-81—North Caro. 31, Arkansas 27
12-30-82—Florida St. 31, West Va. 12
12-30-83—Florida 14, Iowa 6
12-28-84—Oklahoma St. 21, South Caro. 14

12-30-85—Florida St. 34, Oklahoma St. 23
12-27-86—Clemson 27, Stanford 21
12-31-87—LSU 30, South Caro. 13
1-1-89—Georgia 34, Michigan St. 27
12-30-89—Clemson 27, West Va. 7

1-1-91—Michigan 35, Mississippi 3
12-29-91—Oklahoma 48, Virginia 14
12-31-92—Florida 27, North Caro. St. 10
12-31-93—Alabama 24, North Caro. 10
12-30-94—Tennessee 45, Virginia Tech 23 (at Gainesville)

1-1-96—Syracuse 41, Clemson 0

FLORIDA CITRUS BOWL

Present Site: Orlando, Fla.
Stadium (Capacity): Florida Citrus Bowl (70,349)
Playing Surface: Grass
Name Changes: Tangerine Bowl (1947-82); Florida Citrus Bowl (1983-93); CompUSA Florida Citrus Bowl (since 1994)
Playing Sites: Tangerine Bowl, Orlando (1947-72); Florida Field, Gainesville (1973); Tangerine Bowl (now Florida Citrus Bowl) (1974-82); Orlando Stadium (now Florida Citrus Bowl) (1983-85); Florida Citrus Bowl (since 1986)

1-1-47—Catawba 31, Maryville (Tenn.) 6
1-1-48—Catawba 7, Marshall 0
1-1-49—Murray St. 21, Sul Ross St. 21
1-2-50—St. Vincent 7, Emory & Henry 6
1-1-51—Morris Harvey 35, Emory & Henry 14

1-1-52—Stetson 35, Arkansas St. 20
1-1-53—East Tex. St. 33, Tennessee Tech 0
1-1-54—Arkansas St. 7, East Tex. St. 7
1-1-55—Neb.-Omaha 7, Eastern Ky. 6
1-2-56—Juniata 6, Missouri Valley 6

1-1-57—West Tex. A&M 20, Southern Miss. 13
1-1-58—East Tex. St. 10, Southern Miss. 9
12-27-58—East Tex. St. 26, Missouri Valley 7
1-1-60—Middle Tenn. St. 21, Presbyterian 12
12-30-60—Citadel 27, Tennessee Tech 0

12-29-61—Lamar 21, Middle Tenn. St. 14
12-22-62—Houston 49, Miami (Ohio) 21
12-28-63—Western Ky. 27, Coast Guard 0
12-12-64—East Caro. 14, Massachusetts 13
12-11-65—East Caro. 31, Maine 0

12-10-66—Morgan St. 14, West Chester 6
12-16-67—Tenn.-Martin 25, West Chester 8
12-27-68—Richmond 49, Ohio 42
12-26-69—Toledo 56, Davidson 33
12-28-70—Toledo 40, William & Mary 12

12-28-71—Toledo 28, Richmond 3
12-29-72—Tampa 21, Kent 18
12-22-73—Miami (Ohio) 16, Florida 7
12-21-74—Miami (Ohio) 21, Georgia 10
12-20-75—Miami (Ohio) 20, South Caro. 7

12-18-76—Oklahoma St. 49, Brigham Young 21
12-23-77—Florida St. 40, Texas Tech 17
12-23-78—North Caro. St. 30, Pittsburgh 17
12-22-79—LSU 34, Wake Forest 10
12-20-80—Florida 35, Maryland 20

12-19-81—Missouri 19, Southern Miss. 17
12-18-82—Auburn 33, Boston College 26
12-17-83—Tennessee 30, Maryland 23
12-22-84—Florida St. 17, Georgia 17
12-28-85—Ohio St. 10, Brigham Young 7

1-1-87—Auburn 16, Southern Cal 7
1-1-88—Clemson 35, Penn St. 10
1-2-89—Clemson 13, Oklahoma 6
1-1-90—Illinois 31, Virginia 21
1-1-91—Georgia Tech 45, Nebraska 21

1-1-92—California 37, Clemson 13
1-1-93—Georgia 21, Ohio St. 14
1-1-94—Penn St. 31, Tennessee 13
1-2-95—Alabama 24, Ohio St. 17
1-1-96—Tennessee 20, Ohio St. 14

Note: No classified major teams participated in games from January 1, 1947, through January 1, 1960, or in 1961 and 1963 through 1967.

LIBERTY BOWL

Present Site: Memphis, Tenn.
Stadium (Capacity): Liberty Bowl Memorial Stadium (62,380)
Playing Surface: Prescription Athletic Turf
Name Changes: Liberty Bowl (1959-92); St. Jude Liberty Bowl (since 1993)
Playing Sites: Municipal Stadium, Philadelphia (1959-63); Convention Hall, Atlantic City, N.J. (1964); Liberty Bowl Memorial Stadium (since 1965)

12-19-59—Penn St. 7, Alabama 0
12-17-60—Penn St. 41, Oregon 12
12-16-61—Syracuse 15, Miami (Fla.) 14
12-15-62—Oregon St. 6, Villanova 0
12-21-63—Mississippi St. 16, North Caro. St. 12

12-19-64—Utah 32, West Va. 6
12-18-65—Mississippi 13, Auburn 7
12-10-66—Miami (Fla.) 14, Virginia Tech 7
12-16-67—North Caro. St. 14, Georgia 7
12-14-68—Mississippi 34, Virginia Tech 17

12-13-69—Colorado 47, Alabama 33
12-12-70—Tulane 17, Colorado 3

12-20-71—Tennessee 14, Arkansas 13
12-18-72—Georgia Tech 31, Iowa St. 30
12-17-73—North Caro. St. 31, Kansas 18

12-16-74—Tennessee 7, Maryland 3
12-22-75—Southern Cal 20, Texas A&M 0
12-20-76—Alabama 36, UCLA 6
12-19-77—Nebraska 21, North Caro. 17
12-23-78—Missouri 20, LSU 15

12-22-79—Penn St. 9, Tulane 6
12-27-80—Purdue 28, Missouri 25
12-30-81—Ohio St. 31, Navy 28
12-29-82—Alabama 21, Illinois 15
12-29-83—Notre Dame 19, Boston College 18

12-27-84—Auburn 21, Arkansas 15
12-27-85—Baylor 21, LSU 7
12-29-86—Tennessee 21, Minnesota 14
12-29-87—Georgia 20, Arkansas 17
12-28-88—Indiana 34, South Caro. 10

12-28-89—Mississippi 42, Air Force 29
12-27-90—Air Force 23, Ohio St. 11
12-29-91—Air Force 38, Mississippi St. 15
12-31-92—Mississippi 13, Air Force 0
12-28-93—Louisville 18, Michigan St. 7

12-31-94—Illinois 30, East Caro. 0
12-30-95—East Caro. 19, Stanford 13

PEACH BOWL

Present Site: Atlanta, Ga.
Stadium (Capacity): Georgia Dome (71,548)
Playing Surface: AstroTurf
Playing Sites: Grant Field, Atlanta (1968-70); Atlanta/Fulton County (1971-92); Georgia Dome (since 1993)

12-30-68—LSU 31, Florida St. 27
12-30-69—West Va. 14, South Caro. 3
12-30-70—Arizona St. 48, North Caro. 26
12-30-71—Mississippi 41, Georgia Tech 18
12-29-72—North Caro. St. 49, West Va. 13

12-28-73—Georgia 17, Maryland 16
12-28-74—Texas Tech 6, Vanderbilt 6
12-31-75—West Va. 13, North Caro. St. 10
12-31-76—Kentucky 21, North Caro. 0
12-31-77—North Caro. St. 24, Iowa St. 14

12-25-78—Purdue 41, Georgia Tech 21
12-31-79—Baylor 24, Clemson 18
1-2-81—Miami (Fla.) 20, Virginia Tech 10
12-31-81—West Va. 26, Florida 6
12-31-82—Iowa 28, Tennessee 22

12-30-83—Florida St. 28, North Caro. 3
12-31-84—Virginia 27, Purdue 24
12-31-85—Army 31, Illinois 29
12-31-86—Virginia Tech 25, North Caro. St. 24
1-2-88—Tennessee 27, Indiana 22

12-31-88—North Caro. St. 28, Iowa 23
12-30-89—Syracuse 19, Georgia 18
12-29-90—Auburn 27, Indiana 23
1-1-92—East Caro. 37, North Caro. St. 34
1-2-93—North Caro. 21, Mississippi St. 17

12-31-93—Clemson 14, Kentucky 13
1-1-95—North Caro. St. 28, Mississippi St. 24
12-30-95—Virginia 34, Georgia 27

FIESTA BOWL

Present Site: Tempe, Ariz.
Stadium (Capacity): Sun Devil Stadium (73,471)
Playing Surface: Grass
Name Changes: Fiesta Bowl (1971-85, 1991-92); Sunkist Fiesta Bowl (1986-90); IBM OS/2 Fiesta Bowl (1993-95); Tostitos Fiesta Bowl (since 1996)
Playing Sites: Sun Devil Stadium (since 1971)

12-27-71—Arizona St. 45, Florida St. 38
12-23-72—Arizona St. 49, Missouri 35
12-21-73—Arizona St. 28, Pittsburgh 7
12-28-74—Oklahoma St. 16, Brigham Young 6
12-26-75—Arizona St. 17, Nebraska 14

12-25-76—Oklahoma 41, Wyoming 7
12-25-77—Penn St. 42, Arizona St. 30
12-25-78—Arkansas 10, UCLA 10
12-25-79—Pittsburgh 16, Arizona 10
12-26-80—Penn St. 31, Ohio St. 19

1-1-82—Penn St. 26, Southern Cal 10
1-1-83—Arizona St. 32, Oklahoma 21

1-2-84—Ohio St. 28, Pittsburgh 23
1-1-85—UCLA 39, Miami (Fla.) 37
1-1-86—Michigan 27, Nebraska 23

1-2-87—Penn St. 14, Miami (Fla.) 10
1-1-88—Florida St. 31, Nebraska 28
1-2-89—Notre Dame 34, West Va. 21
1-1-90—Florida St. 41, Nebraska 17
1-1-91—Louisville 34, Alabama 7

1-1-92—Penn St. 42, Tennessee 17
1-1-93—Syracuse 26, Colorado 22
1-1-94—Arizona 29, Miami (Fla.) 0
1-2-95—Colorado 41, Notre Dame 24
1-2-96—Nebraska 62, Florida 24

INDEPENDENCE BOWL

Present Site: Shreveport, La.
Stadium (Capacity): Independence Stadium (50,459)
Playing Surface: Grass
Name Changes: Independence Bowl (1976-89); Poulan Independence Bowl (1990); Poulan/Weed Eater Independence Bowl (since 1991)
Playing Sites: Independence Stadium (since 1976)

12-13-76—McNeese St. 20, Tulsa 16
12-17-77—Louisiana Tech 24, Louisville 14
12-16-78—East Caro. 35, Louisiana Tech 13
12-15-79—Syracuse 31, McNeese St. 7
12-13-80—Southern Miss. 16, McNeese St. 14

12-12-81—Texas A&M 33, Oklahoma St. 16
12-11-82—Wisconsin 14, Kansas St. 3
12-10-83—Air Force 9, Mississippi 3
12-15-84—Air Force 23, Virginia Tech 7
12-21-85—Minnesota 20, Clemson 13

12-20-86—Mississippi 20, Texas Tech 17
12-19-87—Washington 24, Tulane 12
12-23-88—Southern Miss. 38, UTEP 18
12-16-89—Oregon 27, Tulsa 24
12-15-90—Louisiana Tech 34, Maryland 34

12-29-91—Georgia 24, Arkansas 15
12-31-92—Wake Forest 39, Oregon 35
12-31-93—Virginia Tech 45, Indiana 20
12-28-94—Virginia 20, Texas Christian 10
12-29-95—LSU 45, Michigan St. 26

HOLIDAY BOWL

Present Site: San Diego, Calif.
Stadium (Capacity): San Diego Jack Murphy Stadium (63,039)
Playing Surface: Grass
Name Changes: Holiday Bowl (1978-85); Sea World Holiday Bowl (1986-90); Thrifty Car Rental Holiday Bowl (1991-94); Plymouth Holiday Bowl (since 1995)
Playing Sites: San Diego Jack Murphy Stadium (since 1978)

12-22-78—Navy 23, Brigham Young 16
12-21-79—Indiana 38, Brigham Young 37
12-19-80—Brigham Young 46, Southern Methodist 45
12-18-81—Brigham Young 38, Washington St. 36
12-17-82—Ohio St. 47, Brigham Young 17

12-23-83—Brigham Young 21, Missouri 17
12-21-84—Brigham Young 24, Michigan 17
12-22-85—Arkansas 18, Arizona St. 17
12-30-86—Iowa 39, San Diego St. 38
12-30-87—Iowa 20, Wyoming 19

12-30-88—Oklahoma St. 62, Wyoming 14
12-29-89—Penn St. 50, Brigham Young 39
12-29-90—Texas A&M 65, Brigham Young 14
12-30-91—Brigham Young 13, Iowa 13
12-30-92—Hawaii 27, Illinois 17

12-30-93—Ohio St. 28, Brigham Young 21
12-30-94—Michigan 24, Colorado St. 14
12-29-95—Kansas St. 54, Colorado St. 21

ALOHA BOWL

Present Site: Honolulu, Hawaii
Stadium (Capacity): Aloha Stadium (50,000)
Playing Surface: AstroTurf
Name Changes: Aloha Bowl (1982-84); Eagle Aloha Bowl (1985-88); Jeep Eagle Aloha Bowl (since 1989)
Playing Sites: Aloha Stadium (since 1982)

12-25-82—Washington 21, Maryland 20
12-26-83—Penn St. 13, Washington 10

12-29-84—Southern Methodist 27, Notre Dame 20
12-28-85—Alabama 24, Southern Cal 3
12-27-86—Arizona 30, North Caro. 21

12-25-87—UCLA 20, Florida 16
12-25-88—Washington St. 24, Houston 22
12-25-89—Michigan St. 33, Hawaii 13
12-25-90—Syracuse 28, Arizona 0
12-25-91—Georgia Tech 18, Stanford 17

12-25-92—Kansas 23, Brigham Young 20
12-25-93—Colorado 41, Fresno St. 30
12-25-94—Boston College 12, Kansas St. 7
12-25-95—Kansas 51, UCLA 30

OUTBACK BOWL (Formerly Hall of Fame)

Present Site: Tampa, Fla.
Stadium (Capacity): Tampa Stadium (74,350)
Playing Surface: Grass
Name Changes: Hall of Fame Bowl (1986-95); Outback Bowl (since 1996)
Playing Sites: Tampa Stadium (since 1986)

12-23-86—Boston College 27, Georgia 24
1-2-88—Michigan 28, Alabama 24
1-2-89—Syracuse 23, LSU 10
1-1-90—Auburn 31, Ohio St. 14
1-1-91—Clemson 30, Illinois 0

1-1-92—Syracuse 24, Ohio St. 17
1-1-93—Tennessee 38, Boston College 23
1-1-94—Michigan 42, North Caro. St. 7
1-2-95—Wisconsin 34, Duke 20
1-1-96—Penn St. 43, Auburn 14

COPPER BOWL

Present Site: Tucson, Ariz.
Stadium (Capacity): Arizona Stadium (56,167)
Playing Surface: Grass
Name Changes: Copper Bowl (1989); Domino's Pizza Copper Bowl (1990-91); Weiser Lock Copper Bowl (1992-95)
Playing Sites: Arizona Stadium (since 1989)

12-31-89—Arizona 17, North Caro. St. 10
12-31-90—California 17, Wyoming 15
12-31-91—Indiana 24, Baylor 0
12-29-92—Washington St. 31, Utah 28
12-29-93—Kansas St. 52, Wyoming 17

12-29-94—Brigham Young 31, Oklahoma 6
12-27-95—Texas Tech 55, Air Force 41

CARQUEST BOWL

Present Site: Miami, Fla.
Stadium (Capacity): Joe Robbie Stadium (74,913)
Playing Surface: Prescription Athletic Turf
Name Changes: Blockbuster Bowl (1990-93); Carquest Bowl (since 1994)
Playing Sites: Joe Robbie Stadium (since 1990)

12-28-90—Florida St. 24, Penn St. 17
12-28-91—Alabama 30, Colorado 25
1-1-93—Stanford 24, Penn St. 3
1-1-94—Boston College 31, Virginia 13
1-2-95—South Caro. 24, West Va. 21

12-30-95—North Caro. 20, Arkansas 10

LAS VEGAS BOWL

Present Site: Las Vegas, Nev.
Stadium (Capacity): Sam Boyd Stadium (32,000)
Playing Surface: Monsanto Turf (retractable)
Playing Sites: Sam Boyd Stadium (since 1992)

12-18-92—Bowling Green 35, Nevada 34
12-17-93—Utah St. 42, Ball St. 33
12-15-94—UNLV 52, Central Mich. 24
12-14-95—Toledo 40, Nevada 37 (OT)

ALAMO BOWL

Present Site: San Antonio, Texas
Stadium (Capacity): Alamodome (65,000)
Playing Surface: AstroTurf
Playing Sites: Alamodome (since 1993)

12-31-93—California 37, Iowa 3
12-31-94—Washington St. 10, Baylor 3
12-28-95—Texas A&M 22, Michigan 20

Bowl-Game Title Sponsors

Bowl	Title Sponsor (Year Began)	Bowl Name (Years)
Alamo	Builders Square (since 1993)	Builders Square Alamo (since 1993)
Aloha	Jeep Eagle (since 1985)	Aloha (1982-84) Eagle Aloha (1985-88) Jeep Eagle Aloha (since 1989)
Carquest	Blockbuster (1990-93) Carquest Auto Parts (since 1994)	Blockbuster (1990-93) Carquest (since 1994)
Copper	Domino's Pizza (1990-91) Weiser Lock (since 1992)	Copper (1989) Domino's Pizza Copper (1990-91) Weiser Lock Copper (since 1992)
Cotton	Mobil (1989-95)	Cotton (1937-88; since 1996) Mobil Cotton (1989-95)
Fiesta	Sunkist (1986-90) IBM (1993-95) Tostitos (since 1996)	Fiesta (1971-85; 1991-92) Sunkist Fiesta (1986-90) IBM OS/2 Fiesta (1993-95) Tostitos Fiesta (since 1996)
Florida Citrus	CompUSA (since 1994)	Tangerine (1947-82) Florida Citrus (1983-93) CompUSA Florida Citrus (since 1994)
Gator	Mazda (1986-91) Outback Steakhouse (1992-95) Toyota (since 1995)	Gator (1946-85) Mazda Gator (1986-91) Outback Steakhouse Gator (1992-94) Toyota Gator (since 1995)
Holiday	Sea World (1986-90) Thrifty Car Rental (1991-95) Plymouth (since 1995)	Holiday (1978-85) Sea World Holiday (1986-90) Thrifty Car Rental Holiday (1991-94) Plymouth Holiday (since 1995)
Independence	Poulan (since 1990)	Independence (1976-89) Poulan Independence (1990) Poulan/Weed Eater Independence (since 1991)
Las Vegas	None (since 1992)	Las Vegas (since 1992)
Liberty	St. Jude (since 1993)	Liberty (1959-92) St. Jude Liberty (since 1993)
Orange	Federal Express (since 1989)	Orange (1935-88) Federal Express Orange (since 1989)
Outback	None (1986-95)	Hall of Fame (1986-95) Outback (since 1996)
Peach	None (since 1968)	Peach (since 1968)
Rose	None (1902, since 1916)	Rose (since 1902)
Sugar	USF&G Sugar (1988-95) Nokia (since 1996)	Sugar (1935-87) USF&G Sugar (1988-95) Nokia Sugar (since 1996)
Sun	John Hancock (1987-93) Norwest Bank (since 1996)	John Hancock Sun (1987-88) John Hancock (1989-93) Sun (1936-86, 1994-95) Norwest Bank Sun (since 1996)

Rich Clarkson/NCAA photos

Brian Kavanagh, called into duty when Kansas State starting quarterback Matt Miller went out with an injury, passed for 242 yards and four touchdowns to lead the Wildcats to a 54-21 victory over Colorado State in the 1995 Holiday Bowl. For his efforts, Kavanagh was named the game's offensive MVP.

Bowl Financial Analysis, 1976-96

Year	No. Bowls	No. Teams	Total Payout	Per-Game Payout	Per-Team Payout
1976-77	11	22	$11,345,851	$515,714	$257,857
1977-78	12	24	13,323,638	1,110,303	555,152
1978-79	13	26	15,506,516	1,192,809	596,405
1979-80	13	26	17,219,624	1,324,586	662,293
1980-81	13	26	19,517,938	1,501,380	750,690
1981-82	14	28	21,791,222	1,556,516	778,258
1982-83	15	30	26,682,486	1,778,832	889,416
1983-84	15	30	32,535,788	2,169,052	1,084,526
1984-85	16	32	36,666,738	2,291,671	1,145,836
1985-86	16	32	36,995,864	2,312,242	1,156,121
1986-87	17	34	45,830,906	2,695,936	1,347,968
1987-88	17	34	48,251,516	2,838,324	1,419,162
1988-89	17	34	52,905,426	3,112,084	1,556,042
1989-90	18	36	58,208,058	3,233,781	1,616,891
1990-91	19	38	60,378,362	3,177,809	1,588,904
1991-92	18	36	63,494,554	3,527,475	1,763,738
1992-93	18	36	67,950,000	3,775,000	1,887,500
1993-94	19	38	71,006,000	3,737,158	1,868,579
1994-95	19	38	72,416,000	3,811,368	1,905,684
1995-96	18	36	101,390,000	5,632,778	2,816,389

27 Former Major Bowl Games

(Games in which at least one team was classified major that season)

ALAMO
(San Antonio, Texas)

1-4-47—Hardin-Simmons 20, Denver 0

ALL-AMERICAN
(Called Hall of Fame Classic, 1977-85)
(Birmingham, Ala.)

12-22-77—Maryland 17, Minnesota 7
12-20-78—Texas A&M 28, Iowa St. 12
12-29-79—Missouri 24, South Caro. 14
12-27-80—Arkansas 34, Tulane 15
12-31-81—Mississippi St. 10, Kansas 0

12-31-82—Air Force 36, Vanderbilt 28
12-22-83—West Va. 20, Kentucky 16
12-29-84—Kentucky 20, Wisconsin 19
12-31-85—Georgia Tech 17, Michigan St. 14
12-31-86—Florida St. 27, Indiana 13

12-22-87—Virginia 22, Brigham Young 16
12-29-88—Florida 14, Illinois 10
12-28-89—Texas Tech 49, Duke 21
12-28-90—North Caro. St. 31, Southern Miss. 27

AVIATION
(Dayton, Ohio)

12-9-61—New Mexico 28, Western Mich. 12

BACARDI
(Cuban National Sports Festival at Havana)

1-1-37—Auburn 7, Villanova 7

BLUEBONNET
(Houston, Texas)

12-19-59—Clemson 23, Texas Christian 7
12-17-60—Alabama 3, Texas 3
12-16-61—Kansas 33, Rice 7
12-22-62—Missouri 14, Georgia Tech 10
12-21-63—Baylor 14, LSU 7

12-19-64—Tulsa 14, Mississippi 7
12-18-65—Tennessee 27, Tulsa 6
12-17-66—Texas 19, Mississippi 0
12-23-67—Colorado 31, Miami (Fla.) 21
12-31-68—Southern Methodist 28, Oklahoma 27

12-31-69—Houston 36, Auburn 7
12-31-70—Alabama 24, Oklahoma 24
12-31-71—Colorado 29, Houston 17
12-30-72—Tennessee 24, LSU 17
12-29-73—Houston 47, Tulane 7

12-23-74—Houston 31, North Caro. St. 31
12-27-75—Texas 38, Colorado 21
12-31-76—Nebraska 27, Texas Tech 24
12-31-77—Southern Cal 47, Texas A&M 28
12-31-78—Stanford 25, Georgia 22

12-31-79—Purdue 27, Tennessee 22
12-31-80—North Caro. 16, Texas 7
12-31-81—Michigan 33, UCLA 14
12-31-82—Arkansas 28, Florida 24
12-31-83—Oklahoma St. 24, Baylor 14

12-31-84—West Va. 31, Texas Christian 14
12-31-85—Air Force 24, Texas 16
12-31-86—Baylor 21, Colorado 9
12-31-87—Texas 32, Pittsburgh 27

BLUEGRASS
(Louisville, Ky.)

12-13-58—Oklahoma St. 15, Florida St. 6

CALIFORNIA
(Fresno, Calif.)

12-19-81—Toledo 27, San Jose St. 25
12-18-82—Fresno St. 29, Bowling Green 28
12-17-83—Northern Ill. 20, Cal St. Fullerton 13
12-15-84—UNLV 30, *Toledo 13
12-14-85—Fresno St. 51, Bowling Green 7

12-13-86—San Jose St. 37, Miami (Ohio) 7
12-12-87—Eastern Mich. 30, San Jose St. 27
12-10-88—Fresno St. 35, Western Mich. 30
12-9-89—Fresno St. 27, Ball St. 6
12-8-90—San Jose St. 48, Central Mich. 24

12-14-91—Bowling Green 28, Fresno St. 21

** Won by forfeit.*

CAMELLIA
(Lafayette, La.)

12-30-48—Hardin-Simmons 49, Wichita St. 12

CHERRY
(Pontiac, Mich.)

12-22-84—Army 10, Michigan St. 6
12-21-85—Maryland 35, Syracuse 18

DELTA
(Memphis, Tenn.)

1-1-48—Mississippi 13, Texas Christian 9
1-1-49—William & Mary 20, Oklahoma St. 0

DIXIE BOWL
(Birmingham, Ala.)

1-1-48—Arkansas 21, William & Mary 19
1-1-49—Baylor 20, Wake Forest 7

DIXIE CLASSIC
(Dallas, Texas)

1-2-22—Texas A&M 22, Centre 14
1-1-25—West Va. Wesleyan 9, Southern Methodist 7
1-1-34—Arkansas 7, Centenary (La.) 7

FORT WORTH CLASSIC
(Fort Worth, Texas)

1-1-21—Centre 63, Texas Christian 7

FREEDOM BOWL
(Anaheim, Calif.)

12-26-84—Iowa 55, Texas 17
12-30-85—Washington 20, Colorado 17
12-30-86—UCLA 31, Brigham Young 10
12-30-87—Arizona St. 33, Air Force 28
12-29-88—Brigham Young 20, Colorado 17

12-30-89—Washington 34, Florida 7
12-29-90—Colorado St. 32, Oregon 31
12-30-91—Tulsa 28, San Diego St. 17
12-29-92—Fresno St. 24, Southern Cal 7
12-30-93—Southern Cal 28, Utah 21

12-27-94—Utah 16, Arizona 13

GARDEN STATE
(East Rutherford, N.J.)

12-16-78—Arizona St. 34, Rutgers 18
12-15-79—Temple 28, California 17
12-14-80—Houston 35, Navy 0
12-13-81—Tennessee 28, Wisconsin 21

GOTHAM
(New York, N.Y.)

12-9-61—Baylor 24, Utah St. 9
12-15-62—Nebraska 36, Miami (Fla.) 34

GREAT LAKES
(Cleveland, Ohio)

12-6-47—Kentucky 24, Villanova 14

HARBOR
(San Diego, Calif.)

1-1-47—Montana St. 13, New Mexico 13
1-1-48—Hardin-Simmons 53, San Diego St. 0
1-1-49—Villanova 27, Nevada 7

LOS ANGELES CHRISTMAS FESTIVAL
(Los Angeles, Calif.)

12-25-24—Southern Cal 20, Missouri 7

MERCY
(Los Angeles, Calif.)

11-23-61—Fresno St. 36, Bowling Green 6

OIL
(Houston, Texas)

1-1-46—Georgia 20, Tulsa 6
1-1-47—Georgia Tech 41, St. Mary's (Cal.) 19

PASADENA
(Called Junior Rose in 1967)
(Pasadena, Calif.)

12-2-67—West Tex. A&M 35, Cal St. Northridge 13
12-6-69—San Diego St. 28, Boston U. 7
12-19-70—Long Beach St. 24, Louisville 24
12-18-71—Memphis 28, San Jose St. 9

PRESIDENTIAL CUP
(College Park, Md.)

12-9-50—Texas A&M 40, Georgia 20

RAISIN
(Fresno, Calif.)

1-1-46—Drake 13, Fresno St. 12
1-1-47—San Jose St. 20, Utah St. 0
1-1-48—Pacific (Cal.) 26, Wichita St. 14
1-1-49—Occidental 21, Colorado St. 20
12-31-49—San Jose St. 20, Texas Tech 13

SALAD
(Phoenix, Ariz.)

1-1-48—Nevada 13, North Texas 6
1-1-49—Drake 14, Arizona 13
1-1-50—Xavier (Ohio) 33, Arizona St. 21
1-1-51—Miami (Ohio) 34, Arizona St. 21
1-1-52—Houston 26, Dayton 21

SAN DIEGO EAST-WEST CHRISTMAS CLASSIC
(San Diego, Calif.)

12-26-21—Centre 38, Arizona 0
12-25-22—West Va. 21, Gonzaga 13

SHRINE
(Little Rock, Ark.)

12-18-48—Hardin-Simmons 40, Ouachita Baptist 12

Other Major Postseason Games

There was a proliferation of postseason benefit games specially scheduled at the conclusion of the regular season during the Great Depression (principally in 1931) to raise money for relief of the unemployed in response to the President's Committee on Mobilization of Relief Resources and for other charitable causes.

The exact number of these games is unknown, but it is estimated that more than 100 college games were played nationwide during this period, often irrespective of the competing teams' records.

Most notable among these postseason games were the Tennessee-New York University game of 1931 and the Army-Navy contests of 1930 and 1931 (the two academies had severed athletics relations during 1928-31 and did not meet in regular-season play). All three games were played before huge crowds in New York City's Yankee Stadium.

Following is a list of the principal postseason benefit and charity games involving at least one major college. Not included (nor included in all-time team won-lost records) are several special feature, same-day double-header tournaments in 1931 in which four participating teams were paired to play halves or modified quarters.

Date	Site	Opposing Teams
12-6-30	New York	Colgate 7, New York U. 0
12-13-30	New York	Army 6, Navy 0
11-28-31	Kansas City	Temple 38, Missouri 6
11-28-31	Chicago	Purdue 7, Northwestern 0
11-28-31	Minneapolis	Minnesota 19, Ohio St. 7
11-28-31	Ann Arbor	Michigan 16, Wisconsin 0
11-28-31	Philadelphia	Penn St. 31, Lehigh 0
12-2-31	Chattanooga	Alabama 49, Tenn.-Chatt. 0
12-3-31	Brooklyn	Manhattan 7, Rutgers 6
12-5-31	Denver	Nebraska 20, Colorado St. 7
12-5-31	Pittsburgh	Carnegie Mellon 0, Duquesne 0
12-5-31	New York	Tennessee 13, New York U. 0
12-5-31	St. Louis	St. Louis 31, Missouri 6
12-5-31	Topeka	Kansas 6, Washburn 0
12-5-31	Wichita	Kansas St. 20, Wichita St. 6
12-5-31	Columbia	Centre 9, South Caro. 7
12-5-31	Norman	Oklahoma City 6, Oklahoma 0
12-12-31	New York	Army 17, Navy 7
12-12-31	Tulsa	Oklahoma 20, Tulsa 7
1-2-33	El Paso	Southern Methodist 26, UTEP 0
12-8-34	St. Louis	Southern Methodist 7, Washington (Mo.) 0

Team-by-Team Bowl Results

All-Time Bowl-Game Records

This list includes all bowls played by a current major team, providing its opponent was classified major that season or it was a major team then. The list excludes games in which a home team served as a predetermined, preseason host regardless of its record and/or games scheduled before the season, thus eliminating the old Pineapple, Glass and Palm Festival. Following is the alphabetical list showing the record of each current major team in all major bowls.

Team	W	L	T
Air Force	6	6	1
Alabama	27	17	3
Arizona	3	7	1
Arizona St.	9	5	1
Arkansas	9	16	3
Army	2	1	0
Auburn	12	10	2
Ball St.	0	2	0
Baylor	8	8	0
Boston College	5	5	0
Bowling Green	2	3	0
Brigham Young	6	12	1
California	5	6	1
Central Mich.	0	2	0
Cincinnati	1	1	0
Clemson	12	8	0
Colorado	8	12	0
Colorado St.	1	3	0
Duke	3	5	0
East Caro.	3	1	0
Eastern Mich.	1	0	0
Florida	10	13	0
Florida St.	15	7	2
Fresno St.	6	3	0
Georgia	15	14	3
Georgia Tech	17	8	0
Hawaii	1	1	0
Houston	7	5	1
Illinois	5	7	0
Indiana	3	5	0
Iowa	7	6	1
Iowa St.	0	4	0
Kansas	3	5	0
Kansas St.	2	2	0
Kent	0	1	0
Kentucky	5	3	0
LSU	12	16	1
Louisiana Tech	1	1	1
Louisville	3	1	1
Maryland	6	9	2
Memphis	1	0	0
Miami (Fla.)	10	11	0
Miami (Ohio)	5	2	0
Michigan	13	14	0
Michigan St.	5	7	0
Minnesota	2	3	0
Mississippi	14	11	0
Mississippi St.	4	5	0
Missouri	8	11	0
Navy	3	4	1
Nebraska	16	18	0
Nevada	1	3	0
UNLV	#2	0	0
New Mexico	2	2	1
New Mexico St.	2	0	1
North Caro.	8	12	0
North Caro. St.	8	8	1
North Texas	0	2	0
Northern Ill.	1	0	0
Northwestern	1	1	0
Notre Dame	13	8	0
Ohio	0	2	0
Ohio St.	12	16	0
Oklahoma	20	11	1
Oklahoma St.	9	3	0
Oregon	3	8	0
Oregon St.	2	2	0
Penn St.	20	10	2
Pittsburgh	8	10	0
Purdue	4	1	0
Rice	4	3	0
Rutgers	0	1	0
San Diego St.	1	3	0
San Jose St.	4	3	0
South Caro.	1	8	0
Southern Cal	25	13	0
Southern Methodist	4	6	1
Southern Miss.	2	4	0
Stanford	8	8	1
Syracuse	9	6	1
Temple	1	1	0
Tennessee	20	16	0
Texas	17	17	2
UTEP	5	4	0
Texas A&M	12	10	0
Texas Christian	4	10	1
Texas Tech	5	15	1
Toledo	5	1	0
Tulane	2	6	0
Tulsa	4	7	0
UCLA	10	9	1
Utah	3	2	0
Utah St.	1	3	0
Vanderbilt	1	1	1
Virginia	4	4	0
Virginia Tech	3	6	0
Wake Forest	2	2	0
Washington	12	9	1
Washington St.	4	2	0
West Va.	8	9	0
Western Mich.	0	2	0
Wisconsin	3	5	0
Wyoming	4	6	0
TOTALS	**626**	**628**	**42**

#Later lost game by forfeit.

The following current Division I-A teams have not played in a major bowl game: Akron, Ala.-Birmingham, Arkansas St., Central Fla., North Texas, Northeast La. and Southwestern La.

Major Bowl Records of Non-Division I-A Teams

Boston U. 0-1-0; Brown 0-1-0; Bucknell 1-0-0; Cal St. Fullerton 0-1-0; Cal St. Northridge 0-1-0; Carnegie Mellon 0-1-0; Case Reserve 1-0-0; Catholic 1-0-1; Centenary (La.) 0-0-1; Centre 2-1-0; Citadel 1-0-0; Columbia 1-0-0; Davidson 0-1-0; Dayton 0-1-0; Denver 0-2-0; Drake 2-1-0; Duquesne 1-0-0; Fordham 1-1-0; Geo. Washington 1-0-0; Georgetown 0-2-0; Gonzaga 0-1-0; Hardin-Simmons 5-2-1; Harvard 1-0-0; Holy Cross 0-1-0; Long Beach St. 0-0-1; Marquette 0-1-0; McNeese St. 1-2-0; Montana St. 0-0-1; Occidental 1-0-0; Ouachita Baptist 0-1-0; Pacific (Cal.) 2-1-0; Pennsylvania 0-1-0; Randolph Field 0-0-1; Richmond 1-1-0; St. Mary's (Cal.) 1-2-0; Santa Clara 3-0-0; Second Air Force 1-0-0; Southwestern (Tex.) 2-0-0; Tampa 1-0-0; Tennessee Tech 0-1-0; U. of Mexico 0-1-0; Villanova 2-2-1; Wash. & Jeff. 0-0-1; Wash. & Lee 0-1-0; West Tex. A&M 3-0-0; West Va. Wesleyan 1-0-0; Wichita St. 0-3-0; William & Mary 1-2-0; Xavier (Ohio) 1-0-0. **TOTALS: 39-37-8**

All-Time Bowl Appearances

(Must be classified as a major bowl game where one team was considered a major college at the time.)

Team	Appearances
Alabama	47
Southern Cal	38
Tennessee	36
Texas	36
Nebraska	34
Georgia	32
Oklahoma	32
Penn St.	32
LSU	29
Arkansas	28
Ohio St.	28
Michigan	27
Georgia Tech	25
Mississippi	25
Auburn	24
Florida St.	24
Florida	23
Texas A&M	22
Washington	22
Miami (Fla.)	21
Notre Dame	21
Texas Tech	21
Clemson	20
Colorado	20
North Caro.	20
UCLA	20
Brigham Young	19
Missouri	19
Pittsburgh	18
Maryland	17
North Caro. St.	17
Stanford	17
West Va.	17

All-Time Bowl Victories

(Includes bowls where at least one team was classified a major college at the time.)

Team	Victories	Team	Victories
Alabama	27	Texas A&M	12
Southern Cal	25	Washington	12
Oklahoma	20	Florida	10
Penn St.	20	Miami (Fla.)	10
Tennessee	20	UCLA	10
Georgia Tech	17	Arizona St.	9
Texas	17	Arkansas	9
Nebraska	16	Oklahoma St.	9
Florida St.	15	Syracuse	9
Georgia	15	Baylor	8
Mississippi	14	Colorado	8
Michigan	13	Missouri	8
Notre Dame	13	North Caro.	8
Auburn	12	North Caro. St.	8
Clemson	12	Pittsburgh	8
LSU	12	Stanford	8
Ohio St.	12	West Va.	8

Team-by-Team Major Bowl Scores With Coach of Each Bowl Team

Listed below are the 103 I-A teams that have participated in history's 690 major bowl games (the term "major bowl" is defined above the alphabetical list of team bowl records). The teams are listed alphabetically, with each coach listed along with the bowl participated in, date played, opponent, score and team's all-time bowl-game record. Following the I-A list is a group of 49 teams that played in a major bowl game or games but are no longer classified as I-A.

School/Coach	Bowl/Date	Opponent/Score
AIR FORCE		
Ben Martin	Cotton 1-1-59	Texas Christian 0-0
Ben Martin	Gator 12-28-63	North Caro. 0-35
Ben Martin	Sugar 1-1-71	Tennessee 13-34
Ken Hatfield	Hall of Fame 12-31-82	Vanderbilt 36-28
Ken Hatfield	Independence 12-10-83	Mississippi 9-3
Fisher DeBerry	Independence 12-15-84	Virginia Tech 23-7
Fisher DeBerry	Bluebonnet 12-31-85	Texas 24-16
Fisher DeBerry	Freedom 12-30-87	Arizona St. 28-33
Fisher DeBerry	Liberty 12-28-89	Mississippi 29-42
Fisher DeBerry	Liberty 12-27-90	Ohio St. 23-11
Fisher DeBerry	Liberty 12-29-91	Mississippi St. 38-15
Fisher DeBerry	Liberty 12-31-92	Mississippi 0-13
Fisher DeBerry	Copper 12-27-95	Texas Tech 41-55
All bowls 6-6-1		
ALABAMA		
Wallace Wade	Rose 1-1-26	Washington 20-19
Wallace Wade	Rose 1-1-27	Stanford 7-7
Wallace Wade	Rose 1-1-31	Washington St. 24-0
Frank Thomas	Rose 1-1-35	Stanford 29-13
Frank Thomas	Rose 1-1-38	California 0-13
Frank Thomas	Cotton 1-1-42	Texas A&M 29-21
Frank Thomas	Orange 1-1-43	Boston College 37-21
Frank Thomas	Sugar 1-1-45	Duke 26-29
Frank Thomas	Rose 1-1-46	Southern Cal 34-14
Harold "Red" Drew	Sugar 1-1-48	Texas 7-27
Harold "Red" Drew	Orange 1-1-53	Syracuse 61-6
Harold "Red" Drew	Cotton 1-1-54	Rice 6-28
Paul "Bear" Bryant	Liberty 12-19-59	Penn St. 0-7
Paul "Bear" Bryant	Bluebonnet 12-17-60	Texas 3-3
Paul "Bear" Bryant	Sugar 1-1-62	Arkansas 10-3
Paul "Bear" Bryant	Orange 1-1-63	Oklahoma 17-0
Paul "Bear" Bryant	Sugar 1-1-64	Mississippi 12-7
Paul "Bear" Bryant	Orange 1-1-65	Texas 17-21
Paul "Bear" Bryant	Orange 1-1-66	Nebraska 39-28
Paul "Bear" Bryant	Sugar 1-2-67	Nebraska 34-7
Paul "Bear" Bryant	Cotton 1-1-68	Texas A&M 16-20
Paul "Bear" Bryant	Gator 12-28-68	Missouri 10-35
Paul "Bear" Bryant	Liberty 12-13-69	Colorado 33-47
Paul "Bear" Bryant	Bluebonnet 12-31-70	Oklahoma 24-24
Paul "Bear" Bryant	Orange 1-1-72	Nebraska 6-38
Paul "Bear" Bryant	Cotton 1-1-73	Texas 13-17
Paul "Bear" Bryant	Sugar 12-31-73	Notre Dame 23-24
Paul "Bear" Bryant	Orange 1-1-75	Notre Dame 11-13
Paul "Bear" Bryant	Sugar 12-31-75	Penn St. 13-6
Paul "Bear" Bryant	Liberty 12-20-76	UCLA 36-6
Paul "Bear" Bryant	Sugar 1-2-78	Ohio St. 35-6
Paul "Bear" Bryant	Sugar 1-1-79	Penn St. 14-7
Paul "Bear" Bryant	Sugar 1-1-80	Arkansas 24-9
Paul "Bear" Bryant	Cotton 1-1-81	Baylor 30-2
Paul "Bear" Bryant	Cotton 1-1-82	Texas 12-14
Paul "Bear" Bryant	Liberty 12-29-82	Illinois 21-15
Ray Perkins	Sun 12-24-83	Southern Methodist 28-7
Ray Perkins	Aloha 12-28-85	Southern Cal 24-3
Ray Perkins	Sun 12-25-86	Washington 28-6
Bill Curry	Hall of Fame 1-2-88	Michigan 24-28
Bill Curry	Sun 12-24-88	Army 29-28
Bill Curry	Sugar 1-1-90	Miami (Fla.) 25-33
Gene Stallings	Fiesta 1-1-91	Louisville 7-34
Gene Stallings	Blockbuster 12-28-91	Colorado 30-25
Gene Stallings	Sugar 1-1-93	Miami (Fla.) 34-13
Gene Stallings	Gator 12-31-93	North Caro. 24-10
Gene Stallings	Florida Citrus 1-2-95	Ohio St. 24-17
All bowls 27-17-3		
ARIZONA		
J. F. "Pop" McKale	San Diego East-West Christmas Classic 12-26-21	Centre 0-38
Miles Casteel	Salad 1-1-49	Drake 13-14
Darrell Mudra	Sun 12-28-68	Auburn 10-34
Tony Mason	Fiesta 12-25-79	Pittsburgh 10-16
Larry Smith	Sun 12-28-85	Georgia 13-13
Larry Smith	Aloha 12-27-86	North Caro. 30-21
Dick Tomey	Copper 12-31-89	North Caro. St. 17-10
Dick Tomey	Aloha 12-25-90	Syracuse 0-28
Dick Tomey	John Hancock 12-31-92	Baylor 15-20
Dick Tomey	Fiesta 1-1-94	Miami (Fla.) 29-0
Dick Tomey	Freedom 12-27-94	Utah 13-16
All bowls 3-7-1		
ARIZONA ST.		
Millard "Dixie" Howell	Sun 1-1-40	Catholic 0-0
Millard "Dixie" Howell	Sun 1-1-41	Case Reserve 13-26
Ed Doherty	Salad 1-1-50	Xavier (Ohio) 21-33
Ed Doherty	Salad 1-1-51	Miami (Ohio) 21-34
Frank Kush	Peach 12-30-70	North Caro. 48-26
Frank Kush	Fiesta 12-27-71	Florida St. 45-38
Frank Kush	Fiesta 12-23-72	Missouri 49-35
Frank Kush	Fiesta 12-21-73	Pittsburgh 28-7
Frank Kush	Fiesta 12-26-75	Nebraska 17-14
Frank Kush	Fiesta 12-25-77	Penn St. 30-42
Frank Kush	Garden State 12-16-78	Rutgers 34-18
Darryl Rogers	Fiesta 1-1-83	Oklahoma 32-21
John Cooper	Holiday 12-22-85	Arkansas 17-18
John Cooper	Rose 1-1-87	Michigan 22-15
John Cooper	Freedom 12-30-87	Air Force 33-28
All bowls 9-5-1		
ARKANSAS		
Fred Thomsen	Dixie Classic 1-1-34	Centenary (La.) 7-7
John Barnhill	Cotton 1-1-47	LSU 0-0
John Barnhill	Dixie 1-1-48	William & Mary 21-19
Bowden Wyatt	Cotton 1-1-55	Georgia Tech 6-14
Frank Broyles	Gator 1-2-60	Georgia Tech 14-7
Frank Broyles	Cotton 1-2-61	Duke 6-7
Frank Broyles	Sugar 1-1-62	Alabama 3-10
Frank Broyles	Sugar 1-1-63	Mississippi 13-17
Frank Broyles	Cotton 1-1-65	Nebraska 10-7
Frank Broyles	Cotton 1-1-66	LSU 7-14
Frank Broyles	Sugar 1-1-69	Georgia 16-2
Frank Broyles	Sugar 1-1-70	Mississippi 22-27
Frank Broyles	Liberty 12-20-71	Tennessee 13-14
Frank Broyles	Cotton 1-1-76	Georgia 31-10
Lou Holtz	Orange 1-2-78	Oklahoma 31-6
Lou Holtz	Fiesta 12-25-78	UCLA 10-10
Lou Holtz	Sugar 1-1-80	Alabama 9-24
Lou Holtz	Hall of Fame 12-27-80	Tulane 34-15
Lou Holtz	Gator 12-28-81	North Caro. 27-31
Lou Holtz	Bluebonnet 12-31-82	Florida 28-24
Ken Hatfield	Liberty 12-27-84	Auburn 15-21
Ken Hatfield	Holiday 12-22-85	Arizona St. 18-17
Ken Hatfield	Orange 1-1-87	Oklahoma 8-42
Ken Hatfield	Liberty 12-29-87	Georgia 17-20
Ken Hatfield	Cotton 1-2-89	UCLA 3-17
Ken Hatfield	Cotton 1-1-90	Tennessee 27-31
Jack Crowe	Independence 12-29-91	Georgia 15-24
Danny Ford	Carquest 12-30-95	North Caro. 10-20
All bowls 9-16-3		
ARMY		
Jim Young	Cherry 12-22-84	Michigan St. 10-6
Jim Young	Peach 12-31-85	Illinois 31-29
Jim Young	Sun 12-24-88	Alabama 28-29
All bowls 2-1-0		

BOWL/ALL-STAR RECORDS

School/Coach	Bowl/Date	Opponent/Score
AUBURN		
Jack Meagher	Bacardi, Cuba 1-1-37	Villanova 7-7
Jack Meagher	Orange 1-1-38	Michigan St. 6-0
Ralph "Shug" Jordan	Gator 1-1-54	Texas Tech 13-35
Ralph "Shug" Jordan	Gator 12-31-54	Baylor 33-13
Ralph "Shug" Jordan	Gator 12-31-55	Vanderbilt 13-25
Ralph "Shug" Jordan	Orange 1-1-64	Nebraska 7-13
Ralph "Shug" Jordan	Liberty 12-18-65	Mississippi 7-13
Ralph "Shug" Jordan	Sun 12-28-68	Arizona 34-10
Ralph "Shug" Jordan	Bluebonnet 12-31-69	Houston 7-36
Ralph "Shug" Jordan	Gator 1-2-71	Mississippi 35-28
Ralph "Shug" Jordan	Sugar 1-1-72	Oklahoma 22-40
Ralph "Shug" Jordan	Gator 12-30-72	Colorado 24-3
Ralph "Shug" Jordan	Sun 12-29-73	Missouri 17-34
Ralph "Shug" Jordan	Gator 12-30-74	Texas 27-3
Pat Dye	Tangerine 12-18-82	Boston College 33-26
Pat Dye	Sugar 1-2-84	Michigan 9-7
Pat Dye	Liberty 12-27-84	Arkansas 21-15
Pat Dye	Cotton 1-1-86	Texas A&M 16-36
Pat Dye	Florida Citrus 1-1-87	Southern Cal 16-7
Pat Dye	Sugar 1-1-88	Syracuse 16-16
Pat Dye	Sugar 1-2-89	Florida St. 7-13
Pat Dye	Hall of Fame 1-1-90	Ohio St. 31-24
Pat Dye	Peach 12-29-90	Indiana 27-23
Terry Bowden	Outback 1-1-96	Penn St. 14-43
All bowls 12-10-2		
BALL ST.		
Paul Schudel	California 12-9-89	Fresno St. 6-27
Paul Schudel	Las Vegas 12-17-93	Utah St. 33-42
All bowls 0-2-0		
BAYLOR		
Bob Woodruff	Dixie 1-1-49	Wake Forest 20-7
George Sauer	Orange 1-1-52	Georgia Tech 14-17
George Sauer	Gator 12-31-54	Auburn 13-33
Sam Boyd	Sugar 1-1-57	Tennessee 13-7
John Bridgers	Gator 12-31-60	Florida 12-13
John Bridgers	Gotham 12-9-61	Utah St. 24-9
John Bridgers	Bluebonnet 12-21-63	LSU 14-7
Grant Teaff	Cotton 1-1-75	Penn St. 20-41
Grant Teaff	Peach 12-31-79	Clemson 24-18
Grant Teaff	Cotton 1-1-81	Alabama 2-30
Grant Teaff	Bluebonnet 12-31-83	Oklahoma St. 14-24
Grant Teaff	Liberty 12-27-85	LSU 21-7
Grant Teaff	Bluebonnet 12-31-86	Colorado 21-9
Grant Teaff	Copper 12-31-91	Indiana 0-24
Grant Teaff	John Hancock 12-31-92	Arizona 20-15
Chuck Reedy	Alamo 12-31-94	Washington St. 3-10
All bowls 8-8-0		
BOSTON COLLEGE		
Frank Leahy	Cotton 1-1-40	Clemson 3-6
Frank Leahy	Sugar 1-1-41	Tennessee 19-13
Denny Myers	Orange 1-1-43	Alabama 21-37
Jack Bicknell	Tangerine 12-18-82	Auburn 26-33
Jack Bicknell	Liberty 12-29-83	Notre Dame 18-19
Jack Bicknell	Cotton 1-1-85	Houston 45-28
Jack Bicknell	Hall of Fame 12-23-86	Georgia 27-24
Tom Coughlin	Hall of Fame 1-1-93	Tennessee 23-38
Tom Coughlin	Carquest 1-1-94	Virginia 31-13
Dan Henning	Aloha 12-25-94	Kansas St. 12-7
All bowls 5-5-0		
BOWLING GREEN		
Doyt Perry	Mercy 11-23-61	Fresno St. 6-36
Denny Stolz	California 12-18-82	Fresno St. 28-29
Denny Stolz	California 12-14-85	Fresno St. 7-51
Gary Blackney	California 12-14-91	Fresno St. 28-21
Gary Blackney	Las Vegas 12-18-92	Nevada 35-34
All bowls 2-3-0		
BRIGHAM YOUNG		
LaVell Edwards	Fiesta 12-28-74	Oklahoma St. 6-16
LaVell Edwards	Tangerine 12-18-76	Oklahoma St. 21-49
LaVell Edwards	Holiday 12-22-78	Navy 16-23
LaVell Edwards	Holiday 12-21-79	Indiana 37-38
LaVell Edwards	Holiday 12-19-80	Southern Methodist 46-45
LaVell Edwards	Holiday 12-18-81	Washington St. 38-36
LaVell Edwards	Holiday 12-17-82	Ohio St. 17-47
LaVell Edwards	Holiday 12-23-83	Missouri 21-17
LaVell Edwards	Holiday 12-21-84	Michigan 24-17
LaVell Edwards	Florida Citrus 12-28-85	Ohio St. 7-10
LaVell Edwards	Freedom 12-30-86	UCLA 10-31
LaVell Edwards	All-American 12-22-87	Virginia 16-22
LaVell Edwards	Freedom 12-29-88	Colorado 20-17

School/Coach	Bowl/Date	Opponent/Score
LaVell Edwards	Holiday 12-29-89	Penn St. 39-50
LaVell Edwards	Holiday 12-29-90	Texas A&M 14-65
LaVell Edwards	Holiday 12-30-91	Iowa 13-13
LaVell Edwards	Aloha 12-25-92	Kansas 20-23
LaVell Edwards	Holiday 12-30-93	Ohio St. 21-28
LaVell Edwards	Copper 12-29-94	Oklahoma 31-6
All bowls 6-12-1		
CALIFORNIA		
Andy Smith	Rose 1-1-21	Ohio St. 28-0
Andy Smith	Rose 1-2-22	Wash. & Jeff. 0-0
Clarence "Nibs" Price	Rose 1-1-29	Georgia Tech 7-8
Leonard "Stub" Allison	Rose 1-1-38	Alabama 13-0
Lynn "Pappy" Waldorf	Rose 1-1-49	Northwestern 14-20
Lynn "Pappy" Waldorf	Rose 1-2-50	Ohio St. 14-17
Lynn "Pappy" Waldorf	Rose 1-1-51	Michigan 6-14
Pete Elliott	Rose 1-1-59	Iowa 12-38
Roger Theder	Garden State 12-15-79	Temple 17-28
Bruce Snyder	Copper 12-31-90	Wyoming 17-15
Bruce Snyder	Florida Citrus 1-1-92	Clemson 37-13
Keith Gilbertson	Alamo 12-31-93	Iowa 37-3
All bowls 5-6-1		
CENTRAL MICH.		
Herb Deromedi	California 12-8-90	San Jose St. 24-48
Dick Flynn	Las Vegas 12-15-94	UNLV 24-52
All bowls 0-2-0		
CINCINNATI		
Ray Nolting	Sun 1-1-47	Virginia Tech 18-6
Sid Gillman	Sun 1-1-51	West Tex. A&M 13-14
All bowls 1-1-0		
CLEMSON		
Jess Neely	Cotton 1-1-40	Boston College 6-3
Frank Howard	Gator 1-1-49	Missouri 24-23
Frank Howard	Orange 1-1-51	Miami (Fla.) 15-14
Frank Howard	Gator 1-1-52	Miami (Fla.) 0-14
Frank Howard	Orange 1-1-57	Colorado 21-27
Frank Howard	Sugar 1-1-59	LSU 0-7
Frank Howard	Bluebonnet 12-19-59	Texas Christian 23-7
Charley Pell	Gator 12-30-77	Pittsburgh 3-34
Danny Ford	Gator 12-29-78	Ohio St. 17-15
Danny Ford	Peach 12-31-79	Baylor 18-24
Danny Ford	Orange 1-1-82	Nebraska 22-15
Danny Ford	Independence 12-21-85	Minnesota 13-20
Danny Ford	Gator 12-27-86	Stanford 27-21
Danny Ford	Florida Citrus 1-1-88	Penn St. 35-10
Danny Ford	Florida Citrus 1-2-89	Oklahoma 23-6
Danny Ford	Gator 12-30-89	West Va. 27-7
Ken Hatfield	Hall of Fame 1-1-91	Illinois 30-0
Ken Hatfield	Florida Citrus 1-1-92	California 13-37
Tommy West	Peach 12-31-93	Kentucky 14-13
Tommy West	Gator 1-1-96	Syracuse 0-41
All bowls 12-8-0		
COLORADO		
Bernard "Bunnie" Oaks	Cotton 1-1-38	Rice 14-28
Dallas Ward	Orange 1-1-57	Clemson 27-21
Sonny Grandelius	Orange 1-1-62	LSU 7-25
Eddie Crowder	Bluebonnet 12-23-67	Miami (Fla.) 31-21
Eddie Crowder	Liberty 12-13-69	Alabama 47-33
Eddie Crowder	Liberty 12-12-70	Tulane 3-17
Eddie Crowder	Bluebonnet 12-31-71	Houston 29-17
Eddie Crowder	Gator 12-30-72	Auburn 3-24
Bill Mallory	Bluebonnet 12-27-75	Texas 21-38
Bill Mallory	Orange 1-1-77	Ohio St. 10-27
Bill McCartney	Freedom 12-30-85	Washington 17-20
Bill McCartney	Bluebonnet 12-31-86	Baylor 9-21
Bill McCartney	Freedom 12-29-88	Brigham Young 17-20
Bill McCartney	Orange 1-1-90	Notre Dame 6-21
Bill McCartney	Orange 1-1-91	Notre Dame 10-9
Bill McCartney	Blockbuster 12-28-91	Alabama 25-30
Bill McCartney	Fiesta 1-1-93	Syracuse 22-26
Bill McCartney	Aloha 12-25-93	Fresno St. 41-30
Bill McCartney	Fiesta 1-2-95	Notre Dame 41-24
Rick Neuheisel	Cotton 1-1-96	Oregon 38-6
All bowls 8-12-0		
COLORADO ST.		
Bob Davis	Raisin 1-1-49	Occidental 20-21
Earle Bruce	Freedom 12-24-90	Oregon 32-31
Sonny Lubick	Holiday 12-30-94	Michigan 14-24
Sonny Lubick	Holiday 12-29-95	Kansas St. 21-54
All bowls 1-3-0		

School/Coach	Bowl/Date	Opponent/Score
DUKE		
Wallace Wade	Rose 1-2-39	Southern Cal 3-7
Wallace Wade	Rose 1-1-42	Oregon St. 16-20
Eddie Cameron	Sugar 1-1-45	Alabama 29-26
Bill Murray	Orange 1-1-55	Nebraska 34-7
Bill Murray	Orange 1-1-58	Oklahoma 21-48
Bill Murray	Cotton 1-2-61	Arkansas 7-6
Steve Spurrier	All-American 12-28-89	Texas Tech 21-49
Fred Goldsmith	Hall of Fame 1-2-95	Wisconsin 20-34
All bowls 3-5-0		
EAST CARO.		
Pat Dye	Independence 12-16-78	Louisiana Tech 35-13
Bill Lewis	Peach 1-1-92	North Caro. St. 37-34
Steve Logan	Liberty 12-31-94	Illinois 0-30
Steve Logan	Liberty 12-30-95	Stanford 19-13
All bowls 3-1-0		
EASTERN MICH.		
Jim Harkema	California 12-12-87	San Jose St. 30-27
All bowls 1-0-0		
FLORIDA		
Bob Woodruff	Gator 1-1-53	Tulsa 14-13
Bob Woodruff	Gator 12-27-58	Mississippi 3-7
Ray Graves	Gator 12-31-60	Baylor 13-12
Ray Graves	Gator 12-29-62	Penn St. 17-7
Ray Graves	Sugar 1-1-66	Missouri 18-20
Ray Graves	Orange 1-2-67	Georgia Tech 27-12
Ray Graves	Gator 12-27-69	Tennessee 14-13
Doug Dickey	Tangerine 12-22-73	Miami (Ohio) 7-16
Doug Dickey	Sugar 12-31-74	Nebraska 10-13
Doug Dickey	Gator 12-29-75	Maryland 0-13
Doug Dickey	Sun 1-2-77	Texas A&M 14-37
Charley Pell	Tangerine 12-20-80	Maryland 35-20
Charley Pell	Peach 12-31-81	West Va. 6-26
Charley Pell	Bluebonnet 12-31-82	Arkansas 24-28
Charley Pell	Gator 12-30-83	Iowa 14-6
Galen Hall	Aloha 12-25-87	UCLA 16-20
Galen Hall	All-American 12-29-88	Illinois 14-10
Gary Darnell	Freedom 12-30-89	Washington 7-34
Steve Spurrier	Sugar 1-1-92	Notre Dame 28-39
Steve Spurrier	Gator 12-31-92	North Caro. St. 27-10
Steve Spurrier	Sugar 1-1-94	West Va. 41-7
Steve Spurrier	Sugar 1-2-95	Florida St. 17-23
Steve Spurrier	Fiesta 1-2-96	Nebraska 24-62
All bowls 10-13-0		
FLORIDA ST.		
Tom Nugent	Sun 1-1-55	UTEP 20-47
Tom Nugent	Bluegrass 12-13-58	Oklahoma St. 6-15
Bill Peterson	Gator 1-2-65	Oklahoma 36-19
Bill Peterson	Sun 12-24-66	Wyoming 20-28
Bill Peterson	Gator 12-30-67	Penn St. 17-17
Bill Peterson	Peach 12-30-68	LSU 27-31
Larry Jones	Fiesta 12-27-71	Arizona St. 38-45
Bobby Bowden	Tangerine 12-23-77	Texas Tech 40-17
Bobby Bowden	Orange 1-1-80	Oklahoma 7-24
Bobby Bowden	Orange 1-1-81	Oklahoma 17-18
Bobby Bowden	Gator 12-30-82	West Va. 31-12
Bobby Bowden	Peach 12-30-83	North Caro. 28-3
Bobby Bowden	Florida Citrus 12-22-84	Georgia 17-17
Bobby Bowden	Gator 12-30-85	Oklahoma St. 34-23
Bobby Bowden	All-American 12-31-86	Indiana 27-13
Bobby Bowden	Fiesta 1-1-88	Nebraska 31-28
Bobby Bowden	Sugar 1-2-89	Auburn 13-7
Bobby Bowden	Fiesta 1-1-90	Nebraska 41-17
Bobby Bowden	Blockbuster 12-28-90	Penn St. 24-17
Bobby Bowden	Cotton 1-1-92	Texas A&M 10-2
Bobby Bowden	Orange 1-1-93	Nebraska 27-14
Bobby Bowden	Orange 1-1-94	Nebraska 18-16
Bobby Bowden	Sugar 1-2-95	Florida 23-17
Bobby Bowden	Orange 1-1-96	Notre Dame 31-26
All bowls 15-7-2		
FRESNO ST.		
Alvin "Pix" Pierson	Raisin 1-1-46	Drake 12-13
Cecil Coleman	Mercy 11-23-61	Bowling Green 36-6
Jim Sweeney	California 12-18-82	Bowling Green 29-28
Jim Sweeney	California 12-14-85	Bowling Green 51-7
Jim Sweeney	California 12-10-88	Western Mich. 35-30
Jim Sweeney	California 12-9-89	Ball St. 27-6
Jim Sweeney	California 12-14-91	Bowling Green 21-28
Jim Sweeney	Freedom 12-29-92	Southern Cal 24-7
Jim Sweeney	Aloha 12-25-93	Colorado 30-41
All bowls 6-3-0		

School/Coach	Bowl/Date	Opponent/Score
GEORGIA		
Wally Butts	Orange 1-1-42	Texas Christian 40-26
Wally Butts	Rose 1-1-43	UCLA 9-0
Wally Butts	Oil 1-1-46	Tulsa 20-6
Wally Butts	Sugar 1-1-47	North Caro. 20-10
Wally Butts	Gator 1-1-48	Maryland 20-20
Wally Butts	Orange 1-1-49	Texas 28-41
Wally Butts	Presidential 12-9-50	Texas A&M 20-40
Wally Butts	Orange 1-1-60	Missouri 14-0
Vince Dooley	Sun 12-26-64	Texas Tech 7-0
Vince Dooley	Cotton 12-31-66	Southern Methodist 24-9
Vince Dooley	Liberty 12-16-67	North Caro. St. 7-14
Vince Dooley	Sugar 1-1-69	Arkansas 2-16
Vince Dooley	Sun 12-20-69	Nebraska 6-45
Vince Dooley	Gator 12-31-71	North Caro. 7-3
Vince Dooley	Peach 12-28-73	Maryland 17-16
Vince Dooley	Tangerine 12-21-74	Miami (Ohio) 10-21
Vince Dooley	Cotton 1-1-76	Arkansas 10-31
Vince Dooley	Sugar 1-1-77	Pittsburgh 3-27
Vince Dooley	Bluebonnet 12-31-78	Stanford 22-25
Vince Dooley	Sugar 1-1-81	Notre Dame 17-10
Vince Dooley	Sugar 1-1-82	Pittsburgh 20-24
Vince Dooley	Sugar 1-1-83	Penn St. 23-27
Vince Dooley	Cotton 1-2-84	Texas 10-9
Vince Dooley	Florida Citrus 12-22-84	Florida St. 17-17
Vince Dooley	Sun 12-28-85	Arizona 13-13
Vince Dooley	Hall of Fame 12-23-86	Boston College 24-27
Vince Dooley	Liberty 12-29-87	Arkansas 20-17
Vince Dooley	Gator 1-1-89	Michigan St. 34-27
Ray Goff	Peach 12-30-89	Syracuse 18-19
Ray Goff	Independence 12-29-91	Arkansas 24-15
Ray Goff	Florida Citrus 1-1-93	Ohio St. 21-14
Ray Goff	Peach 12-30-95	Virginia 27-34
All bowls 15-14-3		
GEORGIA TECH		
Bill Alexander	Rose 1-1-29	California 8-7
Bill Alexander	Orange 1-1-40	Missouri 21-7
Bill Alexander	Cotton 1-1-43	Texas 7-14
Bill Alexander	Sugar 1-1-44	Tulsa 20-18
Bill Alexander	Orange 1-1-45	Tulsa 12-26
Bobby Dodd	Oil 1-1-47	St. Mary's (Cal.) 41-19
Bobby Dodd	Orange 1-1-48	Kansas 20-14
Bobby Dodd	Orange 1-1-52	Baylor 17-14
Bobby Dodd	Sugar 1-1-53	Mississippi 24-7
Bobby Dodd	Sugar 1-1-54	West Va. 42-19
Bobby Dodd	Cotton 1-1-55	Arkansas 14-6
Bobby Dodd	Sugar 1-2-56	Pittsburgh 7-0

Photo from East Carolina sports information

Chad Holcomb kicked four field goals to lead East Carolina to a 19-13 victory over Stanford in last year's Liberty Bowl.

School/Coach	Bowl/Date	Opponent/Score
Bobby Dodd	Gator 12-29-56	Pittsburgh 21-14
Bobby Dodd	Gator 1-2-60	Arkansas 7-14
Bobby Dodd	Gator 12-30-61	Penn St. 15-30
Bobby Dodd	Bluebonnet 12-22-62	Missouri 10-14
Bobby Dodd	Gator 12-31-65	Texas Tech 31-21
Bobby Dodd	Orange 1-2-67	Florida 12-27
Bud Carson	Sun 12-19-70	Texas Tech 17-9
Bud Carson	Peach 12-30-71	Mississippi 18-41
Bill Fulcher	Liberty 12-18-72	Iowa St. 31-30
Pepper Rodgers	Peach 12-25-78	Purdue 21-41
Bill Curry	Hall of Fame 12-31-85	Michigan St. 17-14
Bobby Ross	Florida Citrus 1-1-91	Nebraska 45-21
Bobby Ross	Aloha 12-25-91	Stanford 18-17
All bowls 17-8-0		
HAWAII		
Bob Wagner	Aloha 12-25-89	Michigan St. 13-33
Bob Wagner	Holiday 12-30-92	Illinois 27-17
All bowls 1-1-0		
HOUSTON		
Clyde Lee	Salad 1-1-52	Dayton 26-21
Bill Yeoman	Tangerine 12-22-62	Miami (Ohio) 49-21
Bill Yeoman	Bluebonnet 12-31-69	Auburn 36-7
Bill Yeoman	Bluebonnet 12-31-71	Colorado 17-29
Bill Yeoman	Bluebonnet 12-29-73	Tulane 47-7
Bill Yeoman	Bluebonnet 12-23-74	North Caro. St. 31-31
Bill Yeoman	Cotton 1-1-77	Maryland 30-21
Bill Yeoman	Cotton 1-1-79	Notre Dame 34-35
Bill Yeoman	Cotton 1-1-80	Nebraska 17-14
Bill Yeoman	Garden State 12-14-80	Navy 35-0
Bill Yeoman	Sun 12-26-81	Oklahoma 14-40
Bill Yeoman	Cotton 1-1-85	Boston College 28-45
Jack Pardee	Aloha 12-25-88	Washington St. 22-24
All bowls 7-5-1		
ILLINOIS		
Ray Eliot	Rose 1-1-47	UCLA 45-14
Ray Eliot	Rose 1-1-52	Stanford 40-7
Pete Elliott	Rose 1-1-64	Washington 17-7
Mike White	Liberty 12-29-82	Alabama 15-21
Mike White	Rose 1-2-84	UCLA 9-45
Mike White	Peach 12-31-85	Army 29-31
John Mackovic	All-American 12-29-88	Florida 10-14
John Mackovic	Florida Citrus 1-1-90	Virginia 31-21
John Mackovic	Hall of Fame 1-1-91	Clemson 0-30
Lou Tepper	John Hancock 12-31-91	UCLA 3-6
Lou Tepper	Holiday 12-30-92	Hawaii 17-27
Lou Tepper	Liberty 12-31-94	East Caro. 30-0
All bowls 5-7-0		
INDIANA		
John Pont	Rose 1-1-68	Southern Cal 3-14
Lee Corso	Holiday 12-21-79	Brigham Young 38-37
Bill Mallory	All-American 12-31-86	Florida St. 13-27
Bill Mallory	Peach 1-2-88	Tennessee 22-27
Bill Mallory	Liberty 12-28-88	South Caro. 34-10
Bill Mallory	Peach 12-29-90	Auburn 23-27
Bill Mallory	Copper 12-31-91	Baylor 24-0
Bill Mallory	Independence 12-31-93	Virginia Tech 20-45
All bowls 3-5-0		
IOWA		
Forest Evashevski	Rose 1-1-57	Oregon St. 35-19
Forest Evashevski	Rose 1-1-59	California 38-12
Hayden Fry	Rose 1-1-82	Washington 0-28
Hayden Fry	Peach 12-31-82	Tennessee 28-22
Hayden Fry	Gator 12-30-83	Florida 6-14
Hayden Fry	Freedom 12-26-84	Texas 55-17
Hayden Fry	Rose 1-1-86	UCLA 28-45
Hayden Fry	Holiday 12-30-86	San Diego St. 39-38
Hayden Fry	Holiday 12-30-87	Wyoming 20-19
Hayden Fry	Peach 12-31-88	North Caro. St. 23-28
Hayden Fry	Rose 1-1-91	Washington 34-46
Hayden Fry	Holiday 12-30-91	Brigham Young 13-13
Hayden Fry	Alamo 12-31-93	California 3-37
Hayden Fry	Sun 12-29-95	Washington 38-18
All bowls 7-6-1		
IOWA ST.		
Johnny Majors	Sun 12-18-71	LSU 15-33
Johnny Majors	Liberty 12-18-72	Georgia Tech 30-31
Earle Bruce	Peach 12-31-77	North Caro. St. 14-24
Earle Bruce	Hall of Fame 12-20-78	Texas A&M 12-28
All bowls 0-4-0		
KANSAS		
George Sauer	Orange 1-1-48	Georgia Tech 14-20
Jack Mitchell	Bluebonnet 12-16-61	Rice 33-7
Pepper Rodgers	Orange 1-1-69	Penn St. 14-15
Don Fambrough	Liberty 12-17-73	North Caro. St. 18-31
Bud Moore	Sun 12-26-75	Pittsburgh 19-33
Don Fambrough	Hall of Fame 12-31-81	Mississippi St. 0-10
Glen Mason	Aloha 12-25-92	Brigham Young 23-20
Glen Mason	Aloha 12-25-95	UCLA 51-30
All bowls 3-5-0		
KANSAS ST.		
Jim Dickey	Independence 12-11-82	Wisconsin 3-14
Bill Snyder	Copper 12-29-93	Wyoming 52-17
Bill Snyder	Aloha 12-25-94	Boston College 7-12
Bill Snyder	Holiday 12-29-95	Colorado St. 54-21
All bowls 2-2-0		
KENT		
Don James	Tangerine 12-29-72	Tampa 18-21
All bowls 0-1-0		
KENTUCKY		
Paul "Bear" Bryant	Great Lakes 12-6-47	Villanova 24-14
Paul "Bear" Bryant	Orange 1-2-50	Santa Clara 13-21
Paul "Bear" Bryant	Sugar 1-1-51	Oklahoma 13-7
Paul "Bear" Bryant	Cotton 1-1-52	Texas Christian 20-7
Fran Curci	Peach 12-31-76	North Caro. 21-0
Jerry Claiborne	Hall of Fame 12-22-83	West Va. 16-20
Jerry Claiborne	Hall of Fame 12-29-84	Wisconsin 20-19
Bill Curry	Peach 12-31-93	Clemson 13-14
All bowls 5-3-0		
LSU		
Bernie Moore	Sugar 1-1-36	Texas Christian 2-3
Bernie Moore	Sugar 1-1-37	Santa Clara 14-21
Bernie Moore	Sugar 1-1-38	Santa Clara 0-6
Bernie Moore	Orange 1-1-44	Texas A&M 19-14
Bernie Moore	Cotton 1-1-47	Arkansas 0-0
Gaynell Tinsley	Sugar 1-2-50	Oklahoma 0-35
Paul Dietzel	Sugar 1-1-59	Clemson 7-0
Paul Dietzel	Sugar 1-1-60	Mississippi 0-21
Paul Dietzel	Orange 1-1-62	Colorado 25-7
Charlie McClendon	Cotton 1-1-63	Texas 13-0
Charlie McClendon	Bluebonnet 12-21-63	Baylor 7-14
Charlie McClendon	Sugar 1-1-65	Syracuse 13-10
Charlie McClendon	Cotton 1-1-66	Arkansas 14-7
Charlie McClendon	Sugar 1-1-68	Wyoming 20-13
Charlie McClendon	Peach 12-30-68	Florida St. 31-27
Charlie McClendon	Orange 1-1-71	Nebraska 12-17
Charlie McClendon	Sun 12-18-71	Iowa St. 33-15
Charlie McClendon	Bluebonnet 12-30-72	Tennessee 17-24
Charlie McClendon	Orange 1-1-74	Penn St. 9-16
Charlie McClendon	Sun 12-31-77	Stanford 14-24
Charlie McClendon	Liberty 12-23-78	Missouri 15-20
Charlie McClendon	Tangerine 12-22-79	Wake Forest 34-10
Jerry Stovall	Orange 1-1-83	Nebraska 20-21
Bill Arnsparger	Sugar 1-1-85	Nebraska 10-28
Bill Arnsparger	Liberty 12-27-85	Baylor 7-21
Bill Arnsparger	Sugar 1-1-87	Nebraska 15-30
Mike Archer	Gator 12-31-87	South Caro. 30-13
Mike Archer	Hall of Fame 1-2-89	Syracuse 10-23
Gerry DiNardo	Independence 12-29-95	Michigan St. 45-26
All bowls 12-16-1		
LOUISIANA TECH		
Maxie Lambright	Independence 12-17-77	Louisville 24-14
Maxie Lambright	Independence 12-16-78	East Caro. 13-35
Joe Raymond Peace	Independence 12-15-90	Maryland 34-34
All bowls 1-1-1		
LOUISVILLE		
Frank Camp	Sun 1-1-58	Drake 34-20
Lee Corso	Pasadena 12-19-70	Long Beach St. 24-24
Vince Gibson	Independence 12-17-77	Louisiana Tech 14-24
Howard Schnellenberger	Fiesta 1-1-91	Alabama 34-7
Howard Schnellenberger	Liberty 12-28-93	Michigan St. 18-7
All bowls 3-1-1		
MARYLAND		
Jim Tatum	Gator 1-1-48	Georgia 20-20
Jim Tatum	Gator 1-2-50	Missouri 20-7
Jim Tatum	Sugar 1-1-52	Tennessee 28-13
Jim Tatum	Orange 1-1-54	Oklahoma 0-7
Jim Tatum	Orange 1-2-56	Oklahoma 6-20
Jerry Claiborne	Peach 12-28-73	Georgia 16-17
Jerry Claiborne	Liberty 12-16-74	Tennessee 3-7
Jerry Claiborne	Gator 12-29-75	Florida 13-0
Jerry Claiborne	Cotton 1-1-77	Houston 21-30
Jerry Claiborne	Hall of Fame 12-22-77	Minnesota 17-7

School/Coach	Bowl/Date	Opponent/Score
Jerry Claiborne	Sun 12-23-78	Texas 0-42
Jerry Claiborne	Tangerine 12-20-80	Florida 20-35
Bobby Ross	Aloha 12-25-82	Washington 20-21
Bobby Ross	Florida Citrus 12-17-83	Tennessee 23-30
Bobby Ross	Sun 12-22-84	Tennessee 27-26
Bobby Ross	Cherry 12-21-85	Syracuse 35-18
Joe Krivak	Independence 12-15-90	Louisiana Tech 34-34
All bowls 6-9-2		
MEMPHIS		
Billy Murphy	Pasadena 12-18-71	San Jose St. 28-9
All bowls 1-0-0		
MIAMI (FLA.)		
Tom McCann	Orange 1-1-35	Bucknell 0-26
Jack Harding	Orange 1-1-46	Holy Cross 13-6
Andy Gustafson	Orange 1-1-51	Clemson 14-15
Andy Gustafson	Gator 1-1-52	Clemson 14-0
Andy Gustafson	Liberty 12-16-61	Syracuse 14-15
Andy Gustafson	Gotham 12-15-62	Nebraska 34-36
Charlie Tate	Liberty 12-10-66	Virginia Tech 14-7
Charlie Tate	Bluebonnet 12-31-67	Colorado 21-31
Howard Schnellenberger	Peach 1-2-81	Virginia Tech 20-10
Howard Schnellenberger	Orange 1-2-84	Nebraska 31-30
Jimmy Johnson	Fiesta 1-1-85	UCLA 37-39
Jimmy Johnson	Sugar 1-1-86	Tennessee 7-35
Jimmy Johnson	Fiesta 1-2-87	Penn St. 10-14
Jimmy Johnson	Orange 1-1-88	Oklahoma 20-14
Jimmy Johnson	Orange 1-2-89	Nebraska 23-3
Dennis Erickson	Sugar 1-1-90	Alabama 33-25
Dennis Erickson	Cotton 1-1-91	Texas 46-3
Dennis Erickson	Orange 1-1-92	Nebraska 22-0
Dennis Erickson	Sugar 1-1-93	Alabama 13-34
Dennis Erickson	Fiesta 1-1-94	Arizona 0-29
Dennis Erickson	Orange 1-1-95	Nebraska 17-24
All bowls 10-11-0		
MIAMI (OHIO)		
Sid Gillman	Sun 1-1-48	Texas Tech 13-12
Woody Hayes	Salad 1-1-51	Arizona St. 34-21
John Pont	Tangerine 12-22-62	Houston 21-49
Bill Mallory	Tangerine 12-22-73	Florida 16-7
Dick Crum	Tangerine 12-21-74	Georgia 21-10
Dick Crum	Tangerine 12-20-75	South Caro. 20-7
Tim Rose	California 12-13-86	San Jose St. 7-37
All bowls 5-2-0		
MICHIGAN		
Fielding "Hurry Up" Yost	Rose 1-1-02	Stanford 49-0
H. O. "Fritz" Crisler	Rose 1-1-48	Southern Cal 49-0
Bennie Oosterbaan	Rose 1-1-51	California 14-6
Chalmers "Bump" Elliott	Rose 1-1-65	Oregon St. 34-7
Glenn "Bo" Schembechler	Rose 1-1-70	Southern Cal 3-10
Glenn "Bo" Schembechler	Rose 1-1-72	Stanford 12-13
Glenn "Bo" Schembechler	Orange 1-1-76	Oklahoma 6-14
Glenn "Bo" Schembechler	Rose 1-1-77	Southern Cal 6-14
Glenn "Bo" Schembechler	Rose 1-2-78	Washington 20-27
Glenn "Bo" Schembechler	Rose 1-1-79	Southern Cal 10-17
Glenn "Bo" Schembechler	Gator 12-28-79	North Caro. 15-17
Glenn "Bo" Schembechler	Rose 1-1-81	Washington 23-6
Glenn "Bo" Schembechler	Bluebonnet 12-31-81	UCLA 33-14
Glenn "Bo" Schembechler	Rose 1-1-83	UCLA 14-24
Glenn "Bo" Schembechler	Sugar 1-2-84	Auburn 7-9
Glenn "Bo" Schembechler	Holiday 12-21-84	Brigham Young 17-24
Glenn "Bo" Schembechler	Fiesta 1-1-86	Nebraska 27-23
Glenn "Bo" Schembechler	Rose 1-1-87	Arizona St. 15-22
Glenn "Bo" Schembechler	Hall of Fame 1-2-88	Alabama 28-24
Glenn "Bo" Schembechler	Rose 1-2-89	Southern Cal 22-14
Glenn "Bo" Schembechler	Rose 1-1-90	Southern Cal 10-17
Gary Moeller	Gator 1-1-91	Mississippi 35-3
Gary Moeller	Rose 1-1-92	Washington 14-34
Gary Moeller	Rose 1-1-93	Washington 38-31
Gary Moeller	Hall of Fame 1-1-94	North Caro. St. 42-7
Gary Moeller	Holiday 12-30-94	Colorado St. 24-14
Lloyd Carr	Alamo 12-28-95	Texas A&M 20-22
All bowls 13-14-0		
MICHIGAN ST.		
Charlie Bachman	Orange 1-1-38	Auburn 0-6
Clarence "Biggie" Munn	Rose 1-1-54	UCLA 28-20
Duffy Daugherty	Rose 1-2-56	UCLA 17-14
Duffy Daugherty	Rose 1-1-66	UCLA 12-14
George Perles	Cherry 12-22-84	Army 6-10
George Perles	Hall of Fame 12-31-85	Georgia Tech 14-17
George Perles	Rose 1-1-88	Southern Cal 20-17
George Perles	Gator 1-1-89	Georgia 27-34
George Perles	Aloha 12-25-89	Hawaii 33-13
George Perles	John Hancock 12-31-90	Southern Cal 17-6
George Perles	Liberty 12-28-93	Louisville 7-18
Nick Saban	Independence 12-29-95	LSU 26-45
All bowls 5-7-0		
MINNESOTA		
Murray Warmath	Rose 1-2-61	Washington 7-17
Murray Warmath	Rose 1-1-62	UCLA 21-3
Cal Stoll	Hall of Fame 12-22-77	Maryland 7-17
John Gutekunst	Independence 12-21-85	Clemson 20-13
John Gutekunst	Liberty 12-29-86	Tennessee 14-21
All bowls 2-3-0		
MISSISSIPPI		
Ed Walker	Orange 1-1-36	Catholic 19-20
John Vaught	Delta 1-1-48	Texas Christian 13-9
John Vaught	Sugar 1-1-53	Georgia Tech 7-24
John Vaught	Sugar 1-1-55	Navy 0-21
John Vaught	Cotton 1-2-56	Texas Christian 14-13
John Vaught	Sugar 1-1-58	Texas 39-7
John Vaught	Gator 12-27-58	Florida 7-3
John Vaught	Sugar 1-1-60	LSU 21-0
John Vaught	Sugar 1-2-61	Rice 14-6
John Vaught	Cotton 1-1-62	Texas 7-12
John Vaught	Sugar 1-1-63	Arkansas 17-13
John Vaught	Sugar 1-1-64	Alabama 7-12
John Vaught	Bluebonnet 12-19-64	Tulsa 7-14
John Vaught	Liberty 12-18-65	Auburn 13-7
John Vaught	Bluebonnet 12-17-66	Texas 0-19
John Vaught	Sun 12-30-67	UTEP 7-14
John Vaught	Liberty 12-14-68	Virginia Tech 34-17
John Vaught	Sugar 1-1-70	Arkansas 27-22
John Vaught	Gator 1-2-71	Auburn 28-35
Billy Kinard	Peach 12-30-71	Georgia Tech 41-18
Billy Brewer	Independence 12-10-83	Air Force 3-9
Billy Brewer	Independence 12-20-86	Texas Tech 20-17
Billy Brewer	Liberty 12-28-89	Air Force 42-29
Billy Brewer	Gator 1-1-91	Michigan 3-35
Billy Brewer	Liberty 12-31-92	Air Force 13-0
All bowls 14-11-0		
MISSISSIPPI ST.		
Ralph Sasse	Orange 1-1-37	Duquesne 12-13
Allyn McKeen	Orange 1-1-41	Georgetown 14-7
Paul Davis	Liberty 12-21-63	North Caro. St. 16-12
Bob Tyler	Sun 12-28-74	North Caro. 26-24
Emory Bellard	Sun 12-27-80	Nebraska 17-31
Emory Bellard	Hall of Fame 12-31-81	Kansas 10-0
Jackie Sherrill	Liberty 12-29-91	Air Force 15-38
Jackie Sherrill	Peach 1-2-93	North Caro. 17-21
Jackie Sherrill	Peach 1-1-95	North Caro. St. 24-28
All bowls 4-5-0		
MISSOURI		
Gwinn Henry	Los Angeles Christmas Festival 12-25-24	Southern Cal 7-20
Don Faurot	Orange 1-1-40	Georgia Tech 7-21
Don Faurot	Sugar 1-1-42	Fordham 0-2
Chauncey Simpson	Cotton 1-1-46	Texas 27-40
Don Faurot	Gator 1-1-49	Clemson 23-24
Don Faurot	Gator 1-2-50	Maryland 7-20
Dan Devine	Orange 1-1-60	Georgia 0-40
Dan Devine	Orange 1-2-61	Navy 21-14
Dan Devine	Bluebonnet 12-22-62	Georgia Tech 14-10
Dan Devine	Sugar 1-1-66	Florida 20-18
Dan Devine	Gator 12-28-68	Alabama 35-10
Dan Devine	Orange 1-1-70	Penn St. 3-10
Al Onofrio	Fiesta 12-23-72	Arizona St. 35-49
Al Onofrio	Sun 12-29-73	Auburn 34-17
Warren Powers	Liberty 12-23-78	LSU 20-15
Warren Powers	Hall of Fame 12-29-79	South Caro. 24-14
Warren Powers	Liberty 12-27-80	Purdue 25-28
Warren Powers	Tangerine 12-19-81	Southern Miss. 19-17
Warren Powers	Holiday 12-23-83	Brigham Young 17-21
All bowls 8-11-0		
NAVY		
Bob Folwell	Rose 1-1-24	Washington 14-14
Eddie Erdelatz	Sugar 1-1-55	Mississippi 21-0
Eddie Erdelatz	Cotton 1-1-58	Rice 20-7
Wayne Hardin	Orange 1-1-61	Missouri 14-21
Wayne Hardin	Cotton 1-1-64	Texas 6-28
George Welsh	Holiday 12-22-78	Brigham Young 23-16
George Welsh	Garden State 12-14-80	Houston 0-35
George Welsh	Liberty 12-30-81	Ohio St. 28-31
All bowls 3-4-1		

BOWL/ALL-STAR RECORDS

School/Coach	Bowl/Date	Opponent/Score
NEBRASKA		
Lawrence McC. "Biff" Jones	Rose 1-1-41	Stanford 13-21
Bill Glassford	Orange 1-1-55	Duke 7-34
Bob Devaney	Gotham 12-15-62	Miami (Fla.) 36-34
Bob Devaney	Orange 1-1-64	Auburn 13-7
Bob Devaney	Cotton 1-1-65	Arkansas 7-10
Bob Devaney	Orange 1-1-66	Alabama 28-39
Bob Devaney	Sugar 1-2-67	Alabama 7-34
Bob Devaney	Sun 12-20-69	Georgia 45-6
Bob Devaney	Orange 1-1-71	LSU 17-12
Bob Devaney	Orange 1-1-72	Alabama 38-6
Bob Devaney	Orange 1-1-73	Notre Dame 40-6
Tom Osborne	Cotton 1-1-74	Texas 19-3
Tom Osborne	Sugar 12-31-74	Florida 13-10
Tom Osborne	Fiesta 12-26-75	Arizona St. 14-17
Tom Osborne	Bluebonnet 12-31-76	Texas Tech 27-24
Tom Osborne	Liberty 12-19-77	North Caro. 21-17
Tom Osborne	Orange 1-1-79	Oklahoma 24-31
Tom Osborne	Cotton 1-1-80	Houston 14-17
Tom Osborne	Sun 12-27-80	Mississippi St. 31-17
Tom Osborne	Orange 1-1-82	Clemson 15-22
Tom Osborne	Orange 1-1-83	LSU 21-20
Tom Osborne	Orange 1-2-84	Miami (Fla.) 30-31
Tom Osborne	Sugar 1-1-85	LSU 28-10
Tom Osborne	Fiesta 1-1-86	Michigan 23-27
Tom Osborne	Sugar 1-1-87	LSU 30-15
Tom Osborne	Fiesta 1-1-88	Florida St. 28-31
Tom Osborne	Orange 1-2-89	Miami (Fla.) 3-23
Tom Osborne	Fiesta 1-1-90	Florida St. 17-41
Tom Osborne	Florida Citrus 1-1-91	Georgia Tech 21-45
Tom Osborne	Orange 1-1-92	Miami (Fla.) 0-22
Tom Osborne	Orange 1-1-93	Florida St. 14-27
Tom Osborne	Orange 1-1-94	Florida St. 16-18
Tom Osborne	Orange 1-1-95	Miami (Fla.) 24-17
Tom Osborne	Fiesta 1-2-96	Florida 62-24
All bowls 16-18-0		
NEVADA		
Joe Sheeketski	Salad 1-1-48	North Texas 13-6
Joe Sheeketski	Harbor 1-1-49	Villanova 7-27
Chris Ault	Las Vegas 12-18-92	Bowling Green 34-35
Chris Ault	Las Vegas 12-14-95	Toledo 37-40 (OT)
All bowls 1-3-0		
UNLV		
Harvey Hyde	California 12-15-84	Toledo 30-13
Jeff Horton	Las Vegas 12-15-94	Central Mich. 52-24
All bowls 2-0-0		
NEW MEXICO		
Ted Shipkey	Sun 1-2-39	Utah 0-26
Willis Barnes	Sun 1-1-44	Southwestern (Tex.) 0-7
Willis Barnes	Sun 1-1-46	Denver 34-24
Willis Barnes	Harbor 1-1-47	Montana St. 13-13
Bill Weeks	Aviation 12-9-61	Western Mich. 28-12
All bowls 2-2-1		
NEW MEXICO ST.		
Jerry Hines	Sun 1-1-36	Hardin-Simmons 14-14
Warren Woodson	Sun 12-31-59	North Texas 28-8
Warren Woodson	Sun 12-31-60	Utah St. 20-13
All bowls 2-0-1		
NORTH CARO.		
Carl Snavely	Sugar 1-1-47	Georgia 10-20
Carl Snavely	Sugar 1-1-49	Oklahoma 6-14
Carl Snavely	Cotton 1-2-50	Rice 13-27
Jim Hickey	Gator 12-28-63	Air Force 35-0
Bill Dooley	Peach 12-30-70	Arizona St. 26-48
Bill Dooley	Gator 12-31-71	Georgia 3-7
Bill Dooley	Sun 12-30-72	Texas Tech 32-28
Bill Dooley	Sun 12-28-74	Mississippi St. 24-26
Bill Dooley	Peach 12-31-76	Kentucky 0-21
Bill Dooley	Liberty 12-19-77	Nebraska 17-21
Dick Crum	Gator 12-28-79	Michigan 17-15
Dick Crum	Bluebonnet 12-31-80	Texas 16-7
Dick Crum	Gator 12-28-81	Arkansas 31-27
Dick Crum	Sun 12-25-82	Texas 26-10
Dick Crum	Peach 12-30-83	Florida St. 3-28
Dick Crum	Aloha 12-27-86	Arizona 21-30
Mack Brown	Peach 1-2-93	Mississippi St. 21-17
Mack Brown	Gator 12-31-93	Alabama 10-24
Mack Brown	Sun 12-30-94	Texas 31-35
Mack Brown	Carquest 12-30-95	Arkansas 20-10
All bowls 8-12-0		

School/Coach	Bowl/Date	Opponent/Score
NORTH CARO. ST.		
Beattie Feathers	Gator 1-1-47	Oklahoma 13-34
Earle Edwards	Liberty 12-21-63	Mississippi St. 12-16
Earle Edwards	Liberty 12-16-67	Georgia 14-7
Lou Holtz	Peach 12-29-72	West Va. 49-13
Lou Holtz	Liberty 12-17-73	Kansas 31-18
Lou Holtz	Bluebonnet 12-23-74	Houston 31-31
Lou Holtz	Peach 12-31-75	West Va. 10-13
Bo Rein	Peach 12-31-77	Iowa St. 24-14
Bo Rein	Tangerine 12-23-78	Pittsburgh 30-17
Dick Sheridan	Peach 12-31-86	Virginia Tech 24-25
Dick Sheridan	Peach 12-31-88	Iowa 28-23
Dick Sheridan	Copper 12-31-89	Arizona 10-17
Dick Sheridan	All-American 12-28-90	Southern Miss. 31-27
Dick Sheridan	Peach 1-1-92	East Caro. 34-37
Dick Sheridan	Gator 12-31-92	Florida 10-27
Mike O'Cain	Hall of Fame 1-1-94	Michigan 7-42
Mike O'Cain	Peach 1-1-95	Mississippi St. 28-24
All bowls 8-8-1		
NORTH TEXAS		
Odus Mitchell	Salad 1-1-48	Nevada 6-13
Odus Mitchell	Sun 12-31-59	New Mexico St. 8-28
All bowls 0-2-0		
NORTHERN ILL.		
Bill Mallory	California 12-17-83	Cal St. Fullerton 20-13
All bowls 1-0-0		
NORTHWESTERN		
Bob Voigts	Rose 1-1-49	California 20-14
Gary Barnett	Rose 1-1-96	Southern Cal 32-41
All bowls 1-1-0		
NOTRE DAME		
Knute Rockne	Rose 1-1-25	Stanford 27-10
Ara Parseghian	Cotton 1-1-70	Texas 17-21
Ara Parseghian	Cotton 1-1-71	Texas 24-11
Ara Parseghian	Orange 1-1-73	Nebraska 6-40
Ara Parseghian	Sugar 12-31-73	Alabama 24-23
Ara Parseghian	Orange 1-1-75	Alabama 13-11
Dan Devine	Gator 12-27-76	Penn St. 20-9
Dan Devine	Cotton 1-2-78	Texas 38-10
Dan Devine	Cotton 1-1-79	Houston 35-34
Dan Devine	Sugar 1-1-81	Georgia 10-17
Gerry Faust	Liberty 12-29-83	Boston College 19-18
Gerry Faust	Aloha 12-29-84	Southern Methodist 20-27
Lou Holtz	Cotton 1-1-88	Texas A&M 10-35
Lou Holtz	Fiesta 1-2-89	West Va. 34-21
Lou Holtz	Orange 1-1-90	Colorado 21-6
Lou Holtz	Orange 1-1-91	Colorado 9-10
Lou Holtz	Sugar 1-1-92	Florida 39-28
Lou Holtz	Cotton 1-1-93	Texas A&M 28-3
Lou Holtz	Cotton 1-1-94	Texas A&M 24-21
Lou Holtz	Fiesta 1-2-95	Colorado 24-41
Lou Holtz	Orange 1-1-96	Florida St. 26-31
All bowls 13-8-0		
OHIO		
Bill Hess	Sun 12-31-62	West Tex. A&M 14-15
Bill Hess	Tangerine 12-27-68	Richmond 42-49
All bowls 0-2-0		
OHIO ST.		
John Wilce	Rose 1-1-21	California 0-28
Wes Fesler	Rose 1-2-50	California 17-14
Woody Hayes	Rose 1-1-55	Southern Cal 20-7
Woody Hayes	Rose 1-1-58	Oregon 10-7
Woody Hayes	Rose 1-1-69	Southern Cal 27-16
Woody Hayes	Rose 1-1-71	Stanford 17-27
Woody Hayes	Rose 1-1-73	Southern Cal 17-42
Woody Hayes	Rose 1-1-74	Southern Cal 42-21
Woody Hayes	Rose 1-1-75	Southern Cal 17-18
Woody Hayes	Rose 1-1-76	UCLA 10-23
Woody Hayes	Orange 1-1-77	Colorado 27-10
Woody Hayes	Sugar 1-2-78	Alabama 6-35
Woody Hayes	Gator 12-29-78	Clemson 15-17
Earle Bruce	Rose 1-1-80	Southern Cal 16-17
Earle Bruce	Fiesta 12-26-80	Penn St. 19-31
Earle Bruce	Liberty 12-30-81	Navy 31-28
Earle Bruce	Holiday 12-17-82	Brigham Young 47-17
Earle Bruce	Fiesta 1-2-84	Pittsburgh 28-23
Earle Bruce	Rose 1-1-85	Southern Cal 17-20
Earle Bruce	Florida Citrus 12-28-85	Brigham Young 10-7
Earle Bruce	Cotton 1-1-87	Texas A&M 28-12
John Cooper	Hall of Fame 1-1-90	Auburn 14-31
John Cooper	Liberty 12-27-90	Air Force 11-23

School/Coach	Bowl/Date	Opponent/Score
John Cooper	Hall of Fame 1-1-92	Syracuse 17-24
John Cooper	Florida Citrus 1-1-93	Georgia 14-21
John Cooper	Holiday 12-30-93	Brigham Young 28-21
John Cooper	Florida Citrus 1-2-95	Alabama 17-24
John Cooper	Florida Citrus 1-1-96	Tennessee 14-20
All bowls 12-16-0		

OKLAHOMA

School/Coach	Bowl/Date	Opponent/Score
Tom Stidham	Orange 1-2-39	Tennessee 0-17
Jim Tatum	Gator 1-1-47	North Caro. St. 34-13
Bud Wilkinson	Sugar 1-1-49	North Caro. 14-6
Bud Wilkinson	Sugar 1-2-50	LSU 35-0
Bud Wilkinson	Sugar 1-1-51	Kentucky 7-13
Bud Wilkinson	Orange 1-1-54	Maryland 7-0
Bud Wilkinson	Orange 1-2-56	Maryland 20-6
Bud Wilkinson	Orange 1-1-58	Duke 48-21
Bud Wilkinson	Orange 1-1-59	Syracuse 21-6
Bud Wilkinson	Orange 1-1-63	Alabama 0-17
Gomer Jones	Gator 1-2-65	Florida St. 19-36
Chuck Fairbanks	Orange 1-1-68	Tennessee 26-24
Chuck Fairbanks	Bluebonnet 12-31-68	Southern Methodist 27-28
Chuck Fairbanks	Bluebonnet 12-31-70	Alabama 24-24
Chuck Fairbanks	Sugar 1-1-72	Auburn 40-22
Chuck Fairbanks	Sugar 12-31-72	Penn St. 14-0
Barry Switzer	Orange 1-1-76	Michigan 14-6
Barry Switzer	Fiesta 12-25-76	Wyoming 41-7
Barry Switzer	Orange 1-2-78	Arkansas 6-31
Barry Switzer	Orange 1-1-79	Nebraska 31-24
Barry Switzer	Orange 1-1-80	Florida St. 24-7
Barry Switzer	Orange 1-1-81	Florida St. 18-17
Barry Switzer	Sun 12-26-81	Houston 40-14
Barry Switzer	Fiesta 1-1-83	Arizona St. 21-32
Barry Switzer	Orange 1-1-85	Washington 17-28
Barry Switzer	Orange 1-1-86	Penn St. 25-10
Barry Switzer	Orange 1-1-87	Arkansas 42-8
Barry Switzer	Orange 1-1-88	Miami (Fla.) 14-20
Barry Switzer	Florida Citrus 1-2-89	Clemson 6-13
Gary Gibbs	Gator 12-29-91	Virginia 48-14
Gary Gibbs	John Hancock 12-24-93	Texas Tech 41-10
Gary Gibbs	Copper 12-29-94	Brigham Young 6-31
All bowls 20-11-1		

OKLAHOMA ST.

School/Coach	Bowl/Date	Opponent/Score
Jim Lookabaugh	Cotton 1-1-45	Texas Christian 34-0
Jim Lookabaugh	Sugar 1-1-46	St. Mary's (Cal.) 33-13
Jim Lookabaugh	Delta 1-1-49	William & Mary 0-20
Cliff Speegle	Bluegrass 12-13-58	Florida St. 15-6
Jim Stanley	Fiesta 12-28-74	Brigham Young 16-6
Jim Stanley	Tangerine 12-18-76	Brigham Young 49-12
Jimmy Johnson	Independence 12-12-81	Texas A&M 16-33
Jimmy Johnson	Bluebonnet 12-31-83	Baylor 24-14
Pat Jones	Gator 12-28-84	South Caro. 21-14
Pat Jones	Gator 12-30-85	Florida St. 23-34
Pat Jones	Sun 12-25-87	West Va. 35-33
Pat Jones	Holiday 12-30-88	Wyoming 62-14
All bowls 9-3-0		

OREGON

School/Coach	Bowl/Date	Opponent/Score
Hugo Bezdek	Rose 1-1-17	Pennsylvania 14-0
Charles "Shy" Huntington	Rose 1-1-20	Harvard 6-7
Jim Aiken	Cotton 1-1-49	Southern Methodist 13-21
Len Casanova	Rose 1-1-58	Ohio St. 7-10
Len Casanova	Liberty 12-17-60	Penn St. 12-41
Len Casanova	Sun 12-31-63	Southern Methodist 21-14
Rich Brooks	Independence 12-16-89	Tulsa 27-24
Rich Brooks	Freedom 12-29-90	Colorado St. 31-32
Rich Brooks	Independence 12-31-92	Wake Forest 35-39
Rich Brooks	Rose 1-2-95	Penn St. 20-38
Mike Bellotti	Cotton 1-1-96	Colorado 6-38
All bowls 3-8-0		

OREGON ST.

School/Coach	Bowl/Date	Opponent/Score
Lon Stiner	Rose 1-1-42	Duke 20-16
Tommy Prothro	Rose 1-1-57	Iowa 19-35
Tommy Prothro	Liberty 12-15-62	Villanova 6-0
Tommy Prothro	Rose 1-1-65	Michigan 7-34
All bowls 2-2-0		

PENN ST.

School/Coach	Bowl/Date	Opponent/Score
Hugo Bezdek	Rose 1-1-23	Southern Cal 3-14
Bob Higgins	Cotton 1-1-48	Southern Methodist 13-13
Charles "Rip" Engle	Liberty 12-19-59	Alabama 7-0
Charles "Rip" Engle	Liberty 12-17-60	Oregon 41-12
Charles "Rip" Engle	Gator 12-30-61	Georgia Tech 30-15
Charles "Rip" Engle	Gator 12-29-62	Florida 7-17
Joe Paterno	Gator 12-30-67	Florida St. 17-17
Joe Paterno	Orange 1-1-69	Kansas 15-14
Joe Paterno	Orange 1-1-70	Missouri 10-3
Joe Paterno	Cotton 1-1-72	Texas 30-6
Joe Paterno	Sugar 12-31-72	Oklahoma 0-14
Joe Paterno	Orange 1-1-74	LSU 16-9
Joe Paterno	Cotton 1-1-75	Baylor 41-20
Joe Paterno	Sugar 12-31-75	Alabama 6-13
Joe Paterno	Gator 12-27-76	Notre Dame 9-20
Joe Paterno	Fiesta 12-25-77	Arizona St. 42-30
Joe Paterno	Sugar 1-1-79	Alabama 7-14
Joe Paterno	Liberty 12-22-79	Tulane 9-6
Joe Paterno	Fiesta 12-26-80	Ohio St. 31-19
Joe Paterno	Fiesta 1-1-82	Southern Cal 26-10
Joe Paterno	Sugar 1-1-83	Georgia 27-23
Joe Paterno	Aloha 12-26-83	Washington 13-10
Joe Paterno	Orange 1-1-86	Oklahoma 10-25
Joe Paterno	Fiesta 1-2-87	Miami (Fla.) 14-10
Joe Paterno	Florida Citrus 1-1-88	Clemson 10-35
Joe Paterno	Holiday 12-29-89	Brigham Young 50-39
Joe Paterno	Blockbuster 12-28-90	Florida St. 17-24
Joe Paterno	Fiesta 1-1-92	Tennessee 42-17
Joe Paterno	Blockbuster 1-1-93	Stanford 3-24
Joe Paterno	Florida Citrus 1-1-94	Tennessee 31-13
Joe Paterno	Rose 1-2-95	Oregon 38-20
Joe Paterno	Outback 1-1-96	Auburn 43-14
All bowls 20-10-2		

PITTSBURGH

School/Coach	Bowl/Date	Opponent/Score
Jock Sutherland	Rose 1-2-28	Stanford 6-7
Jock Sutherland	Rose 1-1-30	Southern Cal 14-47
Jock Sutherland	Rose 1-2-33	Southern Cal 0-35
Jock Sutherland	Rose 1-1-37	Washington 21-0
John Michelosen	Sugar 1-2-56	Georgia Tech 0-7
John Michelosen	Gator 12-29-56	Georgia Tech 14-21
Johnny Majors	Fiesta 12-21-73	Arizona St. 7-28
Johnny Majors	Sun 12-26-75	Kansas 33-19
Johnny Majors	Sugar 1-1-77	Georgia 27-3
Jackie Sherrill	Gator 12-30-77	Clemson 34-3
Jackie Sherrill	Tangerine 12-23-78	North Caro. St. 17-30
Jackie Sherrill	Fiesta 12-25-79	Arizona 16-10
Jackie Sherrill	Gator 12-29-80	South Caro. 37-9
Jackie Sherrill	Sugar 1-1-82	Georgia 24-20
Foge Fazio	Cotton 1-1-83	Southern Methodist 3-7
Foge Fazio	Fiesta 1-2-84	Ohio St. 23-28
Mike Gottfried	Bluebonnet 12-31-87	Texas 27-32
Paul Hackett	John Hancock 12-30-89	Texas A&M 31-28
All bowls 8-10-0		

PURDUE

School/Coach	Bowl/Date	Opponent/Score
Jack Mollenkopf	Rose 1-2-67	Southern Cal 14-13
Jim Young	Peach 12-25-78	Georgia Tech 41-21
Jim Young	Bluebonnet 12-31-79	Tennessee 27-22
Jim Young	Liberty 12-27-80	Missouri 28-25
Leon Burtnett	Peach 12-31-84	Virginia 24-27
All bowls 4-1-0		

RICE

School/Coach	Bowl/Date	Opponent/Score
Jimmy Kitts	Cotton 1-1-38	Colorado 28-14
Jess Neely	Orange 1-1-47	Tennessee 8-0
Jess Neely	Cotton 1-2-50	North Caro. 27-13
Jess Neely	Cotton 1-1-54	Alabama 28-6
Jess Neely	Cotton 1-1-58	Navy 7-20
Jess Neely	Sugar 1-2-61	Mississippi 6-14
Jess Neely	Bluebonnet 12-16-61	Kansas 7-33
All bowls 4-3-0		

RUTGERS

School/Coach	Bowl/Date	Opponent/Score
Frank Burns	Garden State 12-16-78	Arizona St. 18-34
All bowls 0-1-0		

SAN DIEGO ST.

School/Coach	Bowl/Date	Opponent/Score
Bill Schutte	Harbor 1-1-48	Hardin-Simmons 0-53
Don Coryell	Pasadena 12-6-69	Boston U. 28-7
Denny Stolz	Holiday 12-30-86	Iowa 38-39
Al Luginbill	Freedom 12-30-91	Tulsa 17-28
All bowls 1-3-0		

SAN JOSE ST.

School/Coach	Bowl/Date	Opponent/Score
Bill Hubbard	Raisin 1-1-47	Utah St. 20-0
Bill Hubbard	Raisin 12-31-49	Texas Tech 20-13
Dewey King	Pasadena 12-18-71	Memphis 9-28
Jack Elway	California 12-19-81	Toledo 25-27
Claude Gilbert	California 12-31-86	Miami (Ohio) 37-7
Claude Gilbert	California 12-12-87	Eastern Mich. 27-30
Terry Shea	California 12-8-90	Central Mich. 48-24
All bowls 4-3-0		

School/Coach	Bowl/Date	Opponent/Score
SOUTH CARO.		
Johnny McMillan	Gator 1-1-46	Wake Forest 14-26
Paul Dietzel	Peach 12-30-69	West Va. 3-14
Jim Carlen	Tangerine 12-20-75	Miami (Ohio) 7-20
Jim Carlen	Hall of Fame 12-29-79	Missouri 14-24
Jim Carlen	Gator 12-29-80	Pittsburgh 9-37
Joe Morrison	Gator 12-28-84	Oklahoma St. 14-21
Joe Morrison	Gator 12-31-87	LSU 13-30
Joe Morrison	Liberty 12-28-88	Indiana 10-34
Brad Scott	Carquest 1-2-95	West Va. 24-21
All bowls 1-8-0		
SOUTHERN CAL		
Elmer "Gus" Henderson	Rose 1-1-23	Penn St. 14-3
Elmer "Gus" Henderson	Los Angeles Christmas Festival 12-25-24	Missouri 20-7
Howard Jones	Rose 1-1-30	Pittsburgh 47-14
Howard Jones	Rose 1-1-32	Tulane 21-12
Howard Jones	Rose 1-2-33	Pittsburgh 35-0
Howard Jones	Rose 1-2-39	Duke 7-3
Howard Jones	Rose 1-1-40	Tennessee 14-0
Jeff Cravath	Rose 1-1-44	Washington 29-0
Jeff Cravath	Rose 1-1-45	Tennessee 25-0
Jeff Cravath	Rose 1-1-46	Alabama 14-34
Jeff Cravath	Rose 1-1-48	Michigan 0-49
Jess Hill	Rose 1-1-53	Wisconsin 7-0
Jess Hill	Rose 1-1-55	Ohio St. 7-20
John McKay	Rose 1-1-63	Wisconsin 42-37
John McKay	Rose 1-2-67	Purdue 13-14
John McKay	Rose 1-1-68	Indiana 14-3
John McKay	Rose 1-1-69	Ohio St. 16-27
John McKay	Rose 1-1-70	Michigan 10-3
John McKay	Rose 1-1-73	Ohio St. 42-17
John McKay	Rose 1-1-74	Ohio St. 21-42
John McKay	Rose 1-1-75	Ohio St. 18-17
John McKay	Liberty 12-22-75	Texas A&M 20-0
John Robinson	Rose 1-1-77	Michigan 14-6
John Robinson	Bluebonnet 12-31-77	Texas A&M 47-28
John Robinson	Rose 1-1-79	Michigan 17-10
John Robinson	Rose 1-1-80	Ohio St. 17-16
John Robinson	Fiesta 1-1-82	Penn St. 10-26
Ted Tollner	Rose 1-1-85	Ohio St. 20-17
Ted Tollner	Aloha 12-28-85	Alabama 3-24
Ted Tollner	Florida Citrus 1-1-87	Auburn 7-16
Larry Smith	Rose 1-1-88	Michigan St. 17-20
Larry Smith	Rose 1-2-89	Michigan 14-22
Larry Smith	Rose 1-1-90	Michigan 17-10
Larry Smith	John Hancock 12-31-90	Michigan St. 16-17
Larry Smith	Freedom 12-29-92	Fresno St. 7-24
John Robinson	Freedom 12-30-93	Utah 28-21
John Robinson	Cotton 1-2-95	Texas Tech 55-14
John Robinson	Rose 1-1-96	Northwestern 41-32
All bowls 25-13-0		
SOUTHERN METHODIST		
Ray Morrison	Dixie Classic 1-1-25	West Va. Wesleyan 7-9
Matty Bell	Rose 1-1-36	Stanford 0-7
Matty Bell	Cotton 1-1-48	Penn St. 13-13
Matty Bell	Cotton 1-1-49	Oregon 21-13
Hayden Fry	Sun 12-31-63	Oregon 14-21
Hayden Fry	Cotton 12-31-66	Georgia 9-24
Hayden Fry	Bluebonnet 12-31-68	Oklahoma 28-27
Ron Meyer	Holiday 12-19-80	Brigham Young 45-46
Bobby Collins	Cotton 1-1-83	Pittsburgh 7-3
Bobby Collins	Sun 12-24-83	Alabama 7-28
Bobby Collins	Aloha 12-29-84	Notre Dame 27-20
All bowls 4-6-1		
SOUTHERN MISS.		
Thad "Pie" Vann	Sun 1-1-53	Pacific (Cal.) 7-26
Thad "Pie" Vann	Sun 1-1-54	UTEP 14-37
Bobby Collins	Independence 12-13-80	McNeese St. 16-14
Bobby Collins	Tangerine 12-19-81	Missouri 17-19
Curley Hallman	Independence 12-23-88	UTEP 38-18
Jeff Bower	All-American 12-28-90	North Caro. St. 27-31
All bowls 2-4-0		
STANFORD		
Charlie Fickert	Rose 1-1-02	Michigan 0-49
Glenn "Pop" Warner	Rose 1-1-25	Notre Dame 10-27
Glenn "Pop" Warner	Rose 1-1-27	Alabama 7-7
Glenn "Pop" Warner	Rose 1-2-28	Pittsburgh 7-6
Claude "Tiny" Thornhill	Rose 1-1-34	Columbia 0-7
Claude "Tiny" Thornhill	Rose 1-1-35	Alabama 13-29
Claude "Tiny" Thornhill	Rose 1-1-36	Southern Methodist 7-0
Clark Shaughnessy	Rose 1-1-41	Nebraska 21-13
Chuck Taylor	Rose 1-1-52	Illinois 7-40
John Ralston	Rose 1-1-71	Ohio St. 27-17
John Ralston	Rose 1-1-72	Michigan 13-12
Bill Walsh	Sun 12-31-77	LSU 24-14
Bill Walsh	Bluebonnet 12-31-78	Georgia 25-22
Jack Elway	Gator 12-27-86	Clemson 21-27
Dennis Green	Aloha 12-25-91	Georgia Tech 17-18
Bill Walsh	Blockbuster 1-1-93	Penn St. 24-3
Tyrone Willingham	Liberty 12-30-95	East Caro. 13-19
All bowls 8-8-1		
SYRACUSE		
Ben Schwartzwalder	Orange 1-1-53	Alabama 6-61
Ben Schwartzwalder	Cotton 1-1-57	Texas Christian 27-28
Ben Schwartzwalder	Orange 1-1-59	Oklahoma 6-21
Ben Schwartzwalder	Cotton 1-1-60	Texas 23-14
Ben Schwartzwalder	Liberty 12-16-61	Miami (Fla.) 15-14
Ben Schwartzwalder	Sugar 1-1-65	LSU 10-13
Ben Schwartzwalder	Gator 12-31-66	Tennessee 12-18
Frank Maloney	Independence 12-15-79	McNeese St. 31-7
Dick MacPherson	Cherry 12-21-85	Maryland 18-35
Dick MacPherson	Sugar 1-1-88	Auburn 16-16
Dick MacPherson	Hall of Fame 1-2-89	LSU 23-10
Dick MacPherson	Peach 12-30-89	Georgia 19-18
Dick MacPherson	Aloha 12-25-90	Arizona 28-0
Paul Pasqualoni	Hall of Fame 1-1-92	Ohio St. 24-17
Paul Pasqualoni	Fiesta 1-1-93	Colorado 26-22
Paul Pasqualoni	Gator 1-1-96	Clemson 41-0
All bowls 9-6-1		
TEMPLE		
Glenn "Pop" Warner	Sugar 1-1-35	Tulane 14-20
Wayne Hardin	Garden State 12-15-79	California 28-17
All bowls 1-1-0		
TENNESSEE		
Bob Neyland	Orange 1-2-39	Oklahoma 17-0
Bob Neyland	Rose 1-1-40	Southern Cal 0-14
Bob Neyland	Sugar 1-1-41	Boston College 13-19
John Barnhill	Sugar 1-1-43	Tulsa 14-7
John Barnhill	Rose 1-1-45	Southern Cal 0-25
Bob Neyland	Orange 1-1-47	Rice 0-8
Bob Neyland	Cotton 1-1-51	Texas 20-14
Bob Neyland	Sugar 1-1-52	Maryland 13-28
Bob Neyland	Cotton 1-1-53	Texas 0-16
Bowden Wyatt	Sugar 1-1-57	Baylor 7-13
Bowden Wyatt	Gator 12-28-57	Texas A&M 3-0
Doug Dickey	Bluebonnet 12-18-65	Tulsa 27-6
Doug Dickey	Gator 12-31-66	Syracuse 18-12
Doug Dickey	Orange 1-1-68	Oklahoma 24-26
Doug Dickey	Cotton 1-1-69	Texas 13-36
Doug Dickey	Gator 12-27-69	Florida 13-14
Bill Battle	Sugar 1-1-71	Air Force 34-13
Bill Battle	Liberty 12-20-71	Arkansas 14-13
Bill Battle	Bluebonnet 12-30-72	LSU 24-17
Bill Battle	Gator 12-29-73	Texas Tech 19-28
Bill Battle	Liberty 12-16-74	Maryland 7-3
Johnny Majors	Bluebonnet 12-31-79	Purdue 22-27
Johnny Majors	Garden State 12-13-81	Wisconsin 28-21
Johnny Majors	Peach 12-31-82	Iowa 22-28
Johnny Majors	Florida Citrus 12-17-83	Maryland 30-23
Johnny Majors	Sun 12-24-84	Maryland 26-27
Johnny Majors	Sugar 1-1-86	Miami (Fla.) 35-7
Johnny Majors	Liberty 12-29-86	Minnesota 21-14
Johnny Majors	Peach 1-2-88	Indiana 27-22
Johnny Majors	Cotton 1-1-90	Arkansas 31-27
Johnny Majors	Sugar 1-1-91	Virginia 23-22
Johnny Majors	Fiesta 1-1-92	Penn St. 17-42
Phillip Fulmer	Hall of Fame 1-1-93	Boston College 38-23
Phillip Fulmer	Florida Citrus 1-1-94	Penn St. 13-31
Phillip Fulmer	Gator 12-30-94	Virginia Tech 45-23
Phillip Fulmer	Florida Citrus 1-1-96	Ohio St. 20-14
All bowls 20-16-0		
TEXAS		
Dana Bible	Cotton 1-1-43	Georgia Tech 14-7
Dana Bible	Cotton 1-1-44	Randolph Field 7-7
Dana Bible	Cotton 1-1-46	Missouri 40-27
Blair Cherry	Sugar 1-1-48	Alabama 27-7
Blair Cherry	Orange 1-1-49	Georgia 41-28
Blair Cherry	Cotton 1-1-51	Tennessee 14-20
Ed Price	Cotton 1-1-53	Tennessee 16-0
Darrell Royal	Sugar 1-1-58	Mississippi 7-39
Darrell Royal	Cotton 1-1-60	Syracuse 14-23
Darrell Royal	Bluebonnet 12-17-60	Alabama 3-3

School/Coach	Bowl/Date	Opponent/Score
Darrell Royal	Cotton 1-1-62	Mississippi 12-7
Darrell Royal	Cotton 1-1-63	LSU 0-13
Darrell Royal	Cotton 1-1-64	Navy 28-6
Darrell Royal	Orange 1-1-65	Alabama 21-17
Darrell Royal	Bluebonnet 12-17-66	Mississippi 19-0
Darrell Royal	Cotton 1-1-69	Tennessee 36-13
Darrell Royal	Cotton 1-1-70	Notre Dame 21-17
Darrell Royal	Cotton 1-1-71	Notre Dame 11-24
Darrell Royal	Cotton 1-1-72	Penn St. 6-30
Darrell Royal	Cotton 1-1-73	Alabama 17-13
Darrell Royal	Cotton 1-1-74	Nebraska 3-19
Darrell Royal	Gator 12-30-74	Auburn 3-27
Darrell Royal	Bluebonnet 12-27-75	Colorado 38-21
Fred Akers	Cotton 1-2-78	Notre Dame 10-38
Fred Akers	Sun 12-23-78	Maryland 42-0
Fred Akers	Sun 12-22-79	Washington 7-14
Fred Akers	Bluebonnet 12-31-80	North Caro. 7-16
Fred Akers	Cotton 1-1-82	Alabama 14-12
Fred Akers	Sun 12-25-82	North Caro. 10-26
Fred Akers	Cotton 1-2-84	Georgia 9-10
Fred Akers	Freedom 12-26-84	Iowa 17-55
Fred Akers	Bluebonnet 12-31-85	Air Force 16-24
David McWilliams	Bluebonnet 12-31-87	Pittsburgh 32-27
David McWilliams	Cotton 1-1-91	Miami (Fla.) 3-46
John Mackovic	Sun 12-30-94	North Caro. 35-31
John Mackovic	Sugar 12-31-95	Virginia Tech 10-28

All bowls 17-17-2

UTEP

School/Coach	Bowl/Date	Opponent/Score
Mack Saxon	Sun 1-1-37	Hardin-Simmons 6-34
Jack "Cactus Jack" Curtice	Sun 1-1-49	West Va. 12-21
Jack "Cactus Jack" Curtice	Sun 1-2-50	Georgetown 33-20
Mike Brumbelow	Sun 1-1-54	Southern Miss. 37-14
Mike Brumbelow	Sun 1-1-55	Florida St. 47-20
Mike Brumbelow	Sun 1-1-57	Geo. Washington 0-13
Bobby Dobbs	Sun 12-31-65	Texas Christian 13-12
Bobby Dobbs	Sun 12-30-67	Mississippi 14-7
Bob Stull	Independence 12-23-88	Southern Miss. 18-38

All bowls 5-4-0

TEXAS A&M

School/Coach	Bowl/Date	Opponent/Score
Dana Bible	Dixie Classic 1-2-22	Centre 22-14
Homer Norton	Sugar 1-1-40	Tulane 14-13
Homer Norton	Cotton 1-1-41	Fordham 13-12
Homer Norton	Cotton 1-1-42	Alabama 21-29
Homer Norton	Orange 1-1-44	LSU 14-19
Harry Stiteler	Presidential 12-9-50	Georgia 40-20
Paul "Bear" Bryant	Gator 12-28-57	Tennessee 0-3
Gene Stallings	Cotton 1-1-68	Alabama 20-16
Emory Bellard	Liberty 12-22-75	Southern Cal 0-20
Emory Bellard	Sun 1-2-77	Florida 37-14
Emory Bellard	Bluebonnet 12-31-77	Southern Cal 28-47
Tom Wilson	Hall of Fame 12-20-78	Iowa St. 28-12
Tom Wilson	Independence 12-12-81	Oklahoma St. 33-16
Jackie Sherrill	Cotton 1-1-86	Auburn 36-16
Jackie Sherrill	Cotton 1-1-87	Ohio St. 12-28
Jackie Sherrill	Cotton 1-1-88	Notre Dame 35-10
R. C. Slocum	John Hancock 12-30-89	Pittsburgh 28-31
R. C. Slocum	Holiday 12-29-90	Brigham Young 65-14
R. C. Slocum	Cotton 1-1-92	Florida St. 2-10
R. C. Slocum	Cotton 1-1-93	Notre Dame 3-28
R. C. Slocum	Cotton 1-1-94	Notre Dame 21-24
R. C. Slocum	Alamo 12-28-95	Michigan 22-20

All bowls 12-10-0

TEXAS CHRISTIAN

School/Coach	Bowl/Date	Opponent/Score
Bill Driver	Fort Worth Classic 1-1-21	Centre 7-63
Leo "Dutch" Meyer	Sugar 1-1-36	LSU 3-2
Leo "Dutch" Meyer	Cotton 1-1-37	Marquette 16-6
Leo "Dutch" Meyer	Sugar 1-2-39	Carnegie Mellon 15-7
Leo "Dutch" Meyer	Orange 1-1-42	Georgia 26-40
Leo "Dutch" Meyer	Cotton 1-1-45	Oklahoma St. 0-34
Leo "Dutch" Meyer	Delta 1-1-48	Mississippi 9-13
Leo "Dutch" Meyer	Cotton 1-1-52	Kentucky 7-20
Abe Martin	Cotton 1-2-56	Mississippi 13-14
Abe Martin	Cotton 1-1-57	Syracuse 28-27
Abe Martin	Cotton 1-1-59	Air Force 0-0
Abe Martin	Bluebonnet 12-19-59	Clemson 7-23
Abe Martin	Sun 12-31-65	UTEP 12-13
Jim Wacker	Bluebonnet 12-31-84	West Va. 14-31
Pat Sullivan	Independence 12-28-94	Virginia 10-20

All bowls 4-10-1

TEXAS TECH

School/Coach	Bowl/Date	Opponent/Score
Pete Cawthon	Sun 1-1-38	West Va. 6-7
Pete Cawthon	Cotton 1-2-39	St. Mary's (Cal.) 13-20
Dell Morgan	Sun 1-1-42	Tulsa 0-6
Dell Morgan	Sun 1-1-48	Miami (Ohio) 12-13
Dell Morgan	Raisin 12-31-49	San Jose St. 13-20
DeWitt Weaver	Sun 1-1-52	Pacific (Cal.) 25-14
DeWitt Weaver	Gator 1-1-54	Auburn 35-13
DeWitt Weaver	Sun 1-2-56	Wyoming 14-21
J. T. King	Sun 12-26-64	Georgia 0-7
J. T. King	Gator 12-31-65	Georgia Tech 21-31
Jim Carlen	Sun 12-19-70	Georgia Tech 9-17
Jim Carlen	Sun 12-30-72	North Caro. 28-32
Jim Carlen	Gator 12-29-73	Tennessee 28-19
Jim Carlen	Peach 12-28-74	Vanderbilt 6-6
Steve Sloan	Bluebonnet 12-31-76	Nebraska 24-27
Steve Sloan	Tangerine 12-23-77	Florida St. 17-40
Spike Dykes	Independence 12-20-86	Mississippi 17-20
Spike Dykes	All-American 12-28-89	Duke 49-21
Spike Dykes	John Hancock 12-24-93	Oklahoma 10-41
Spike Dykes	Cotton 1-2-95	Southern Cal 14-55
Spike Dykes	Copper 12-27-95	Air Force 55-41

All bowls 5-15-1

TOLEDO

School/Coach	Bowl/Date	Opponent/Score
Frank Lauterbur	Tangerine 12-26-69	Davidson 56-33
Frank Lauterbur	Tangerine 12-28-70	William & Mary 40-12
Jack Murphy	Tangerine 12-28-71	Richmond 28-3
Chuck Stobart	California 12-19-81	San Jose St. 27-25
Dan Simrell	California 12-15-84	UNLV 13-30
Gary Pinkel	Las Vegas 12-14-95	Nevada 40-37 (OT)

All bowls 5-1-0

TULANE

School/Coach	Bowl/Date	Opponent/Score
Bernie Bierman	Rose 1-1-32	Southern Cal 12-21
Ted Cox	Sugar 1-1-35	Temple 20-14
Lowell "Red" Dawson	Sugar 1-1-40	Texas A&M 13-14
Jim Pittman	Liberty 12-12-70	Colorado 17-3
Bennie Ellender	Bluebonnet 12-29-73	Houston 7-47
Larry Smith	Liberty 12-22-79	Penn St. 6-9
Vince Gibson	Hall of Fame 12-27-80	Arkansas 15-34
Mack Brown	Independence 12-19-87	Washington 12-24

All bowls 2-6-0

TULSA

School/Coach	Bowl/Date	Opponent/Score
Henry Frnka	Sun 1-1-42	Texas Tech 6-0
Henry Frnka	Sugar 1-1-43	Tennessee 7-14
Henry Frnka	Sugar 1-1-44	Georgia Tech 18-20
Henry Frnka	Orange 1-1-45	Georgia Tech 26-12
Henry Frnka	Oil 1-1-46	Georgia 6-20
J. O. "Buddy" Brothers	Gator 1-1-53	Florida 13-14
Glenn Dobbs	Bluebonnet 12-19-64	Mississippi 14-7
Glenn Dobbs	Bluebonnet 12-18-65	Tennessee 6-27
F. A. Dry	Independence 12-13-76	McNeese St. 16-20
Dave Rader	Independence 12-16-89	Oregon 24-27
Dave Rader	Freedom 12-30-91	San Diego St. 28-17

All bowls 4-7-0

UCLA

School/Coach	Bowl/Date	Opponent/Score
Edwin "Babe" Horrell	Rose 1-1-43	Georgia 0-9
Bert LaBrucherie	Rose 1-1-47	Illinois 14-45
Henry "Red" Sanders	Rose 1-1-54	Michigan St. 20-28
Henry "Red" Sanders	Rose 1-2-56	Michigan St. 14-17
Bill Barnes	Rose 1-1-62	Minnesota 3-21
Tommy Prothro	Rose 1-1-66	Michigan St. 14-12
Dick Vermeil	Rose 1-1-76	Ohio St. 23-10
Terry Donahue	Liberty 12-20-76	Alabama 6-36
Terry Donahue	Fiesta 12-25-78	Arkansas 10-10
Terry Donahue	Bluebonnet 12-31-81	Michigan 14-33
Terry Donahue	Rose 1-1-83	Michigan 24-14
Terry Donahue	Rose 1-2-84	Illinois 45-9
Terry Donahue	Fiesta 1-1-85	Miami (Fla.) 39-37
Terry Donahue	Rose 1-1-86	Iowa 45-28
Terry Donahue	Freedom 12-30-86	Brigham Young 31-10
Terry Donahue	Aloha 12-25-87	Florida 20-16
Terry Donahue	Cotton 1-1-89	Arkansas 17-3
Terry Donahue	John Hancock 12-31-91	Illinois 6-3
Terry Donahue	Rose 1-1-94	Wisconsin 16-21
Terry Donahue	Aloha 12-25-95	Kansas 30-51

All bowls 10-9-1

UTAH

School/Coach	Bowl/Date	Opponent/Score
Ike Armstrong	Sun 1-2-39	New Mexico 26-0
Ray Nagel	Liberty 12-19-64	West Va. 32-6
Ron McBride	Copper 12-29-92	Washington St. 28-31
Ron McBride	Freedom 12-30-93	Southern Cal 21-28
Ron McBride	Freedom 12-27-94	Arizona 16-13

All bowls 3-2-0

UTAH ST.

School/Coach	Bowl/Date	Opponent/Score
E. L. "Dick" Romney	Raisin 1-1-47	San Jose St. 0-20
John Ralston	Sun 12-31-60	New Mexico St. 13-20
John Ralston	Gotham 12-9-61	Baylor 9-24

School/Coach	Bowl/Date	Opponent/Score
Charlie Weatherbie	Las Vegas 12-17-93	Ball St. 42-33
All bowls 1-3-0		
VANDERBILT		
Art Guepe	Gator 12-31-55	Auburn 25-13
Steve Sloan	Peach 12-28-74	Texas Tech 6-6
George MacIntyre	Hall of Fame 12-31-82	Air Force 28-36
All bowls 1-1-1		
VIRGINIA		
George Welsh	Peach 12-31-84	Purdue 27-24
George Welsh	All-American 12-22-87	Brigham Young 22-16
George Welsh	Florida Citrus 1-1-90	Illinois 21-31
George Welsh	Sugar 1-1-91	Tennessee 22-23
George Welsh	Gator 12-29-91	Oklahoma 14-48
George Welsh	Carquest 1-1-94	Boston College 13-31
George Welsh	Independence 12-28-94	Texas Christian 20-10
George Welsh	Peach 12-30-95	Georgia 34-27
All bowls 4-4-0		
VIRGINIA TECH		
Jimmy Kitts	Sun 1-1-47	Cincinnati 6-18
Jerry Claiborne	Liberty 12-10-66	Miami (Fla.) 7-14
Jerry Claiborne	Liberty 12-14-68	Mississippi 17-34
Bill Dooley	Peach 1-2-81	Miami (Fla.) 10-20
Bill Dooley	Independence 12-15-84	Air Force 7-23
Bill Dooley	Peach 12-31-86	North Caro. St. 25-24
Frank Beamer	Independence 12-31-93	Indiana 45-20
Frank Beamer	Gator 12-30-94	Tennessee 23-45
Frank Beamer	Sugar 12-31-95	Texas 28-10
All bowls 3-6-0		
WAKE FOREST		
D. C. "Peahead" Walker	Gator 1-1-46	South Caro. 26-14
D. C. "Peahead" Walker	Dixie 1-1-49	Baylor 7-20
John Mackovic	Tangerine 12-22-79	LSU 10-34
Bill Dooley	Independence 12-31-92	Oregon 39-35
All bowls 2-2-0		
WASHINGTON		
Enoch Bagshaw	Rose 1-1-24	Navy 14-14
Enoch Bagshaw	Rose 1-1-26	Alabama 19-20
Jimmy Phelan	Rose 1-1-37	Pittsburgh 0-21
Ralph "Pest" Welch	Rose 1-1-44	Southern Cal 0-29
Jim Owens	Rose 1-1-60	Wisconsin 44-8
Jim Owens	Rose 1-2-61	Minnesota 17-7
Jim Owens	Rose 1-1-64	Illinois 7-17
Don James	Rose 1-2-78	Michigan 27-20
Don James	Sun 12-22-79	Texas 14-7
Don James	Rose 1-1-81	Michigan 6-23
Don James	Rose 1-1-82	Iowa 28-0
Don James	Aloha 12-25-82	Maryland 21-20
Don James	Aloha 12-26-83	Penn St. 10-13
Don James	Orange 1-1-85	Oklahoma 28-17
Don James	Freedom 12-30-85	Colorado 20-17
Don James	Sun 12-25-86	Alabama 6-28
Don James	Independence 12-19-87	Tulane 24-12
Don James	Freedom 12-30-89	Florida 34-7
Don James	Rose 1-1-91	Iowa 46-34
Don James	Rose 1-1-92	Michigan 34-14
Don James	Rose 1-1-93	Michigan 31-38
Jim Lambright	Sun 12-29-95	Iowa 18-38
All bowls 12-9-1		
WASHINGTON ST.		
Bill "Lone Star" Dietz	Rose 1-1-16	Brown 14-0
Orin "Babe" Hollingbery	Rose 1-1-31	Alabama 0-24
Jim Walden	Holiday 12-18-81	Brigham Young 36-38
Dennis Erickson	Aloha 12-25-88	Houston 24-22
Mike Price	Copper 12-29-92	Utah 31-28
Mike Price	Alamo 12-31-94	Baylor 10-3
All bowls 4-2-0		
WEST VA.		
Clarence "Doc" Spears	San Diego East-West Christmas Classic 12-25-22	Gonzaga 21-13
Marshall "Little Sleepy" Glenn	Sun 1-1-38	Texas Tech 7-6
Dud DeGroot	Sun 1-1-49	UTEP 21-12
Art Lewis	Sugar 1-1-54	Georgia Tech 19-42
Gene Corum	Liberty 12-19-64	Utah 6-32
Jim Carlen	Peach 12-30-69	South Caro. 14-3
Bobby Bowden	Peach 12-29-72	North Caro. St. 13-49
Bobby Bowden	Peach 12-31-75	North Caro. St. 13-10
Don Nehlen	Peach 12-31-81	Florida 26-6
Don Nehlen	Gator 12-30-82	Florida St. 12-31
Don Nehlen	Hall of Fame 12-22-83	Kentucky 20-16
Don Nehlen	Bluebonnet 12-31-84	Texas Christian 31-14
Don Nehlen	Sun 12-25-87	Oklahoma St. 33-35
Don Nehlen	Fiesta 1-2-89	Notre Dame 21-34
Don Nehlen	Gator 12-30-89	Clemson 7-27
Don Nehlen	Sugar 1-1-94	Florida 7-41
Don Nehlen	Carquest 1-2-95	South Caro. 21-24
All bowls 8-9-0		
WESTERN MICH.		
Merle Schlosser	Aviation 12-9-61	New Mexico 12-28
Al Molde	California 12-10-88	Fresno St. 30-35
All bowls 0-2-0		
WISCONSIN		
Ivy Williamson	Rose 1-1-53	Southern Cal 0-7
Milt Bruhn	Rose 1-1-60	Washington 8-44
Milt Bruhn	Rose 1-2-63	Southern Cal 37-42
Dave McClain	Garden State 12-13-81	Tennessee 21-28
Dave McClain	Independence 12-11-82	Kansas St. 14-3
Dave McClain	Hall of Fame 12-29-84	Kentucky 19-20
Barry Alvarez	Rose 1-1-94	UCLA 21-16
Barry Alvarez	Hall of Fame 1-2-95	Duke 34-20
All bowls 3-5-0		
WYOMING		
Bowden Wyatt	Gator 1-1-51	Wash. & Lee 20-7
Phil Dickens	Sun 1-2-56	Texas Tech 21-14
Bob Devaney	Sun 12-31-58	Hardin-Simmons 14-6
Lloyd Eaton	Sun 12-24-66	Florida St. 28-20
Lloyd Eaton	Sugar 1-1-68	LSU 13-20
Fred Akers	Fiesta 12-25-76	Oklahoma 7-41
Paul Roach	Holiday 12-30-87	Iowa 19-20
Paul Roach	Holiday 12-30-88	Oklahoma St. 14-62
Paul Roach	Copper 12-31-90	California 15-17
Joe Tiller	Copper 12-29-93	Kansas St. 17-52
All bowls 4-6-0		

Played in Major Bowl—No Longer I-A

School/Coach	Bowl/Date	Opponent/Score
BOSTON U.		
Larry Naviaux	Pasadena 12-6-69	San Diego St. 7-28
All bowls 0-1-0		
BROWN		
Ed Robinson	Rose 1-1-16	Washington St. 0-14
All bowls 0-1-0		
BUCKNELL		
Edward "Hook" Mylin	Orange 1-1-35	Miami (Fla.) 26-0
All bowls 1-0-0		
CAL ST. FULLERTON		
Gene Murphy	California 12-17-83	Northern Ill. 13-20
All bowls 0-1-0		
CAL ST. NORTHRIDGE		
Sam Winningham	Pasadena 12-2-67	West Tex. A&M 13-35
All bowls 0-1-0		
CARNEGIE MELLON		
Bill Kern	Sugar 1-2-39	Texas Christian 7-15
All bowls 0-1-0		
CASE RESERVE		
Bill Edwards	Sun 1-1-41	Arizona St. 26-13
All bowls 1-0-0		
CATHOLIC		
Arthur "Dutch" Bergman	Orange 1-1-36	Mississippi 20-19
Arthur "Dutch" Bergman	Sun 1-1-40	Arizona St. 0-0
All bowls 1-0-1		
CENTENARY (LA.)		
Homer Norton	Dixie Classic 1-1-34	Arkansas 7-7
All bowls 0-0-1		
CENTRE		
Charley Moran	Fort Worth Classic 1-1-21	Texas Christian 63-7
Charley Moran	San Diego East-West Christmas Classic 12-26-21	Arizona 38-0
Charley Moran	Dixie Classic 1-2-22	Texas A&M 14-22
All bowls 2-1-0		
CITADEL		
Eddie Teague	Tangerine 12-30-60	Tennessee Tech 27-0
All bowls 1-0-0		

School/Coach	Bowl/Date	Opponent/Score
COLUMBIA		
Lou Little	Rose 1-1-34	Stanford 7-0
All bowls 1-0-0		
DAVIDSON		
Homer Smith	Tangerine 12-26-69	Toledo 33-56
All bowls 0-1-0		
DAYTON		
Joe Gavin	Salad 1-1-52	Houston 21-26
All bowls 0-1-0		
DENVER		
Clyde "Cac" Hubbard	Sun 1-1-46	New Mexico 24-34
Clyde "Cac" Hubbard	Alamo 1-4-47	Hardin-Simmons 0-20
All bowls 0-2-0		
DRAKE		
Vee Green	Raisin 1-1-46	Fresno St. 13-12
Al Kawal	Salad 1-1-49	Arizona 14-13
Warren Gaer	Sun 1-1-58	Louisville 20-34
All bowls 2-1-0		
DUQUESNE		
John "Little Clipper" Smith	Orange 1-1-37	Mississippi St. 13-12
All bowls 1-0-0		
FORDHAM		
Jim Crowley	Cotton 1-1-41	Texas A&M 12-13
Jim Crowley	Sugar 1-1-42	Missouri 2-0
All bowls 1-1-0		
GEO. WASHINGTON		
Eugene "Bo" Sherman	Sun 1-1-57	UTEP 13-0
All bowls 1-0-0		
GEORGETOWN		
Jack Hagerty	Orange 1-1-41	Mississippi St. 7-14
Bob Margarita	Sun 1-2-50	UTEP 20-33
All bowls 0-2-0		
GONZAGA		
Charles "Gus" Dorais	San Diego East-West Christmas Classic 12-15-22	West Va. 13-21
All bowls 0-1-0		
HARDIN-SIMMONS		
Frank Kimbrough	Sun 1-1-36	New Mexico St. 14-14
Frank Kimbrough	Sun 1-1-37	UTEP 34-6
Warren Woodson	Sun 1-1-43	Second Air Force 7-13
Warren Woodson	Alamo 1-4-47	Denver 20-6
Warren Woodson	Harbor 1-1-48	San Diego St. 53-0
Warren Woodson	Shrine 12-18-48	Ouachita Baptist 40-12
Warren Woodson	Camellia 12-30-48	Wichita St. 29-12
Sammy Baugh	Sun 12-31-58	Wyoming 6-14
All bowls 5-2-1		
HARVARD		
Robert Fisher	Rose 1-1-20	Oregon 7-6
All bowls 1-0-0		
HOLY CROSS		
John "Ox" Da Grosa	Orange 1-1-46	Miami (Fla.) 6-13
All bowls 0-1-0		
LONG BEACH ST.		
Jim Stangeland	Pasadena 12-19-70	Louisville 24-24
All bowls 0-0-1		
MARQUETTE		
Frank Murray	Cotton 1-1-37	Texas Christian 6-16
All bowls 0-1-0		
McNEESE ST.		
Jack Doland	Independence 12-13-76	Tulsa 20-16
Ernie Duplechin	Independence 12-15-79	Syracuse 7-31
Ernie Duplechin	Independence 12-13-80	Southern Miss. 14-16
All bowls 1-2-0		
MONTANA ST.		
Clyde Carpenter	Harbor 1-1-47	New Mexico 13-13
All bowls 0-0-1		
OCCIDENTAL		
Roy Dennis	Raisin 1-1-49	Colorado St. 21-20
All bowls 1-0-0		
OUACHITA BAPTIST		
Wesley Bradshaw	Shrine 12-18-48	Hardin-Simmons 12-40
All bowls 0-1-0		

School/Coach	Bowl/Date	Opponent/Score
PACIFIC (CAL.)		
Larry Siemering	Raisin 1-1-48	Wichita St. 26-14
Ernie Jorge	Sun 1-1-52	Texas Tech 14-25
Ernie Jorge	Sun 1-1-53	Southern Miss. 26-7
All bowls 2-1-0		
PENNSYLVANIA		
Bob Folwell	Rose 1-1-17	Oregon 0-14
All bowls 0-1-0		
RANDOLPH FIELD		
Frank Tritico	Cotton 1-1-44	Texas 7-7
All bowls 0-0-1		
RICHMOND		
Frank Jones	Tangerine 12-27-68	Ohio 49-42
Frank Jones	Tangerine 12-28-71	Toledo 3-28
All bowls 1-1-0		
ST. MARY'S (CAL.)		
Edward "Slip" Madigan	Cotton 1-2-39	Texas Tech 20-13
Jimmy Phelan	Sugar 1-1-46	Oklahoma St. 13-33
Jimmy Phelan	Oil 1-1-47	Georgia Tech 19-41
All bowls 1-2-0		
SANTA CLARA		
Lawrence "Buck" Shaw	Sugar 1-1-37	LSU 21-14
Lawrence "Buck" Shaw	Sugar 1-1-38	LSU 6-0
Len Casanova	Orange 1-2-50	Kentucky 21-13
All bowls 3-0-0		
SECOND AIR FORCE		
Red Reese	Sun 1-1-43	Hardin-Simmons 13-7
All bowls 1-0-0		
SOUTHWESTERN (TEX.)		
Randolph R. M. Medley	Sun 1-1-44	New Mexico 7-0
Randolph R. M. Medley	Sun 1-1-45	U. of Mexico 35-0
All bowls 2-0-0		
TAMPA		
Earle Bruce	Tangerine 12-29-72	Kent 21-18
All bowls 1-0-0		
TENNESSEE TECH		
Wilburn Tucker	Tangerine 12-30-60	Citadel 0-27
All bowls 0-1-0		
U. OF MEXICO		
Bernard A. Hoban	Sun 1-1-45	Southwestern (Tex.) 0-35
All bowls 0-1-0		
VILLANOVA		
Maurice "Clipper" Smith	Bacardi, Cuba 1-1-37	Auburn 7-7
Jordan Olivar	Great Lakes 12-6-47	Kentucky 14-24
Jordan Olivar	Harbor 1-1-49	Nevada 27-7
Alex Bell	Sun 12-30-61	Wichita St. 17-9
Alex Bell	Liberty 12-15-62	Oregon St. 0-6
All bowls 2-2-1		
WASH. & JEFF.		
Earle "Greasy" Neale	Rose 1-2-22	California 0-0
All bowls 0-0-1		
WASH. & LEE		
George Barclay	Gator 1-1-51	Wyoming 7-20
All bowls 0-1-0		
WEST TEX. A&M		
Frank Kimbrough	Sun 1-1-51	Cincinnati 14-13
Joe Kerbel	Sun 12-31-62	Ohio 15-14
Joe Kerbel	Pasadena 12-2-67	Cal St. Northridge 35-13
All bowls 3-0-0		
WEST VA. WESLEYAN		
Bob Higgins	Dixie Classic 1-1-25	Southern Methodist 9-7
All bowls 1-0-0		
WICHITA ST.		
Ralph Graham	Raisin 1-1-48	Pacific (Cal.) 14-26
Jim Trimble	Camellia 12-30-48	Hardin-Simmons 12-49
Hank Foldberg	Sun 12-30-61	Villanova 9-17
All bowls 0-3-0		
WILLIAM & MARY		
Rube McCray	Dixie 1-1-48	Arkansas 19-21
Rube McCray	Delta 1-1-49	Oklahoma St. 20-0
Lou Holtz	Tangerine 12-28-70	Toledo 12-40
All bowls 1-2-0		
XAVIER (OHIO)		
Ed Kluska	Salad 1-1-50	Arizona St. 33-21
All bowls 1-0-0		

Major Bowl-Game Attendance

Total Yearly Attendance

Year	No. Bowls	Total Attendance	Per/Game Average
1902	1	8,000	8,000
1916	1	7,000	7,000
1917	1	26,000	26,000
1920	1	30,000	30,000
1921	2	51,000	25,500
1922	3	57,000	19,000
1923	2	48,000	24,000
1924	1	40,000	40,000
1925	3	107,000	35,667
1926	1	50,000	50,000
1927	1	57,417	57,417
1928	1	65,000	65,000
1929	1	66,604	66,604
1930	1	72,000	72,000
1931	1	60,000	60,000
1932	1	75,562	75,562
1933	1	78,874	78,874
1934	2	47,000	23,500
1935	3	111,634	37,211
1936	4	137,042	34,261
1937	6	176,396	29,399
1938	5	202,972	40,594
1939	5	224,643	44,929
1940	5	226,478	45,296
1941	5	253,735	50,747
1942	5	215,786	43,157
1943	5	240,166	48,033
1944	5	195,203	39,041
1945	5	236,279	47,256
1946	8	308,071	38,509
1947	10	304,316	30,432
1948	12	404,772	33,731
1949	13	442,531	34,041
1950	8	384,505	48,063
1951	8	392,548	49,069
1952	7	388,588	55,513
1953	6	366,299	61,050
1954	6	359,285	59,881
1955	6	357,871	59,645
1956	6	379,723	63,287
1957	6	369,162	61,527
1958	6	385,427	64,238
1959	7	392,394	56,056
1960	8	481,814	60,227
1961	9	490,113	54,457
1962	11	509,654	46,332
1963	10	481,722	48,172
1964	8	460,720	57,590
1965	8	448,541	56,068
1966	8	482,106	60,263
1967	8	521,427	65,178
1968	9	532,113	59,124
1969	10	585,621	58,562
1970	11	649,915	59,083
1971	11	623,072	56,643
1972	12	668,031	55,669
1973	11	668,461	60,769
1974	11	631,229	57,384
1975	11	597,079	54,280
1976	11	650,881	59,171
1977	12	660,429	55,036
1978	13	730,078	56,160
1979	15	726,064	48,404
1980	15	865,236	57,682
1981	15	856,730	57,115
1982	16	871,594	54,475
1983	16	919,193	57,450
1984	16	867,319	54,207
1985	18	977,374	54,299
1986	18	975,756	54,209
1987	18	958,933	53,274
1988	18	995,830	55,324
1989	17	937,323	55,137
1990	18	1,047,772	58,210
1991	19	1,048,306	55,174
1992	18	1,049,694	58,316
1993	18	973,570	54,087
1994	19	1,036,950	54,576
1995	19	1,064,640	56,034
1996	18	1,021,466	56,748

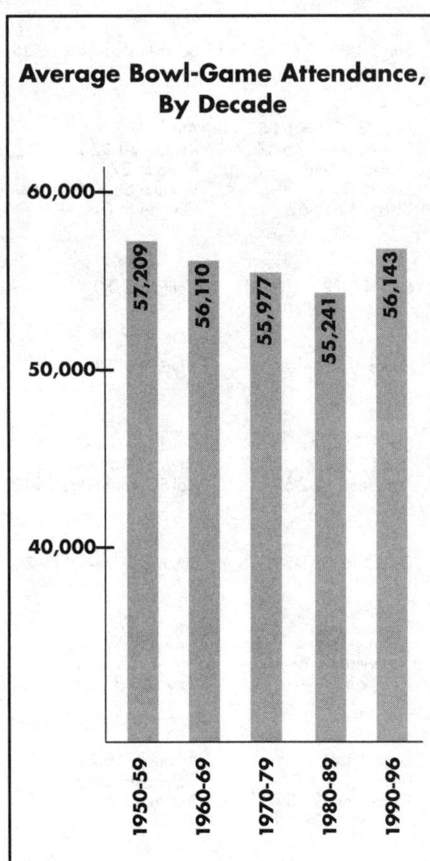

Bowl-by-Bowl Attendance

(Current site and stadium capacity in parentheses. For participating teams, refer to pages 250-255.)

ROSE BOWL

(Rose Bowl, Pasadena, Calif.; Capacity: 98,252)

Date	Attendance
1-1-02	8,000
1-1-16	7,000
1-1-17	26,000
1-1-20	30,000
1-1-21	42,000
1-2-22	40,000
1-1-23	43,000
1-1-24	40,000
1-1-25	53,000
1-1-26	50,000
1-1-27	57,417
1-2-28	65,000
1-1-29	66,604
1-1-30	72,000
1-1-31	60,000
1-1-32	75,562
1-2-33	78,874
1-1-34	35,000
1-1-35	84,474
1-1-36	84,474
1-1-37	87,196
1-1-38	90,000
1-2-39	89,452
1-1-40	92,200
1-1-41	91,500
1-1-42#	56,000
1-1-43	93,000
1-1-44	68,000
1-1-45	91,000
1-1-46	93,000
1-1-47	90,000
1-1-48	93,000
1-1-49	93,000
1-2-50	100,963
1-1-51	98,939
1-1-52	96,825
1-1-53	101,500
1-1-54	101,000
1-1-55	89,191
1-2-56	100,809
1-1-57	97,126
1-1-58	98,202
1-1-59	98,297
1-1-60	100,809
1-2-61	97,314
1-1-62	98,214
1-1-63	98,698
1-1-64	96,957
1-1-65	100,423
1-1-66	100,087
1-2-67	100,807
1-1-68	102,946
1-1-69	102,063
1-1-70	103,878
1-1-71	103,839
1-1-72	103,154
1-1-73	*106,869
1-1-74	105,267
1-1-75	106,721
1-1-76	105,464
1-1-77	106,182
1-2-78	105,312
1-1-79	105,629
1-1-80	105,526
1-1-81	104,863
1-1-82	105,611
1-1-83	104,991
1-2-84	103,217
1-1-85	102,594
1-1-86	103,292
1-1-87	103,168
1-1-88	103,847
1-2-89	101,688
1-1-90	103,450
1-1-91	101,273
1-1-92	103,566
1-1-93	94,236
1-1-94	101,237
1-2-95	102,247
1-1-96	100,102

**Record attendance. #Game held at Duke, Durham, N.C., due to war-time West Coast restrictions.*

ORANGE BOWL

(Joe Robbie Stadium, Miami, Fla.; Capacity: 74,913)

Date	Attendance
1-1-35	5,134
1-1-36	6,568
1-1-37	9,210
1-1-38	18,972
1-2-39	32,191
1-1-40	29,278
1-1-41	29,554
1-1-42	35,786
1-1-43	25,166
1-1-44	25,203
1-1-45	23,279
1-1-46	35,709
1-1-47	36,152
1-1-48	59,578
1-1-49	60,523
1-2-50	64,816
1-1-51	65,181
1-1-52	65,839
1-1-53	66,280
1-1-54	68,640
1-1-55	68,750
1-2-56	76,561
1-1-57	73,280

1-1-58	76,561
1-1-59	75,281
1-1-60	72,186
1-2-61	72,212
1-1-62	68,150
1-1-63	72,880
1-1-64	72,647
1-1-65	72,647
1-1-66	72,214
1-2-67	72,426
1-1-68	77,993
1-1-69	77,719
1-1-70	77,282
1-1-71	80,699
1-1-72	78,151
1-1-73	80,010
1-1-74	60,477
1-1-75	71,801
1-1-76	76,799
1-1-77	65,537
1-2-78	60,987
1-1-79	66,365
1-1-80	66,714
1-1-81	71,043
1-1-82	72,748
1-1-83	68,713
1-2-84	72,549
1-1-85	56,294
1-1-86	74,178
1-1-87	52,717
1-1-88	74,760
1-2-89	79,480
1-1-90	81,190
1-1-91	77,062
1-1-92	77,747
1-1-93	57,324
1-1-94	81,536
1-1-95	*81,753
1-1-96	72,198

**Record attendance.*

SUGAR BOWL

(Louisiana Superdome, New Orleans, La.; Capacity: 72,704)

Date	Attendance
1-1-35	22,026
1-1-36	35,000
1-1-37	41,000
1-1-38	45,000
1-2-39	50,000
1-1-40	73,000
1-1-41	73,181
1-1-42	72,000
1-1-43	70,000
1-1-44	69,000
1-1-45	72,000
1-1-46	75,000
1-1-47	73,300
1-1-48	72,000
1-1-49	82,000
1-2-50	82,470
1-1-51	82,000
1-1-52	82,000
1-1-53	82,000
1-1-54	76,000
1-1-55	82,000
1-2-56	80,175
1-1-57	81,000
1-1-58	82,000
1-1-59	82,000
1-1-60	83,000
1-2-61	82,851
1-1-62	82,910
1-1-63	82,900
1-1-64	80,785
1-1-65	65,000
1-1-66	67,421
1-2-67	82,000
1-1-68	78,963
1-1-69	82,113
1-1-70	82,500
1-1-71	78,655
1-1-72	84,031
12-31-72	80,123
12-31-73	*85,161
12-31-74	67,890
12-31-75	75,212
1-1-77	76,117
1-2-78	76,811
1-1-79	76,824
1-1-80	77,486
1-1-81	77,895
1-1-82	77,224
1-1-83	78,124
1-2-84	77,893
1-1-85	75,608
1-1-86	77,432
1-1-87	76,234
1-1-88	75,495
1-2-89	61,934
1-1-90	77,452
1-1-91	75,132
1-1-92	76,447
1-1-93	76,789
1-1-94	75,437
1-2-95	76,224
12-31-95	70,283

**Record attendance.*

COTTON BOWL

(Cotton Bowl, Dallas, Texas; Capacity: 68,245)

Date	Attendance
1-1-37	17,000
1-1-38	37,000
1-2-39	40,000
1-1-40	20,000
1-1-41	45,500
1-1-42	38,000
1-1-43	36,000
1-1-44	15,000
1-1-45	37,000
1-1-46	45,000
1-1-47	38,000
1-1-48	43,000
1-1-49	69,000
1-2-50	75,347
1-1-51	75,349
1-1-52	75,347
1-1-53	75,504
1-1-54	75,504
1-1-55	75,504
1-2-56	75,504
1-1-57	68,000
1-1-58	75,504
1-1-59	75,504
1-1-60	75,504
1-2-61	74,000
1-1-62	75,504
1-1-63	75,504
1-1-64	75,504
1-1-65	75,504
1-1-66	76,200
12-31-66	75,400
1-1-68	75,504
1-1-69	72,000
1-1-70	73,000
1-1-71	72,000
1-1-72	72,000
1-1-73	72,000
1-1-74	67,500
1-1-75	67,500
1-1-76	74,500
1-1-77	54,500
1-2-78	*76,601
1-1-79	32,500
1-1-80	72,032
1-1-81	74,281
1-1-82	73,243
1-1-83	60,359
1-2-84	67,891
1-1-85	56,522
1-1-86	73,137
1-1-87	74,188
1-1-88	73,006
1-2-89	74,304
1-1-90	74,358
1-1-91	73,521
1-1-92	73,728
1-1-93	71,615
1-1-94	69,855
1-2-95	70,218
1-1-96	58,214

**Record attendance.*

SUN BOWL#

(Sun Bowl, El Paso, Texas; Capacity: 51,270)

Date	Attendance
1-1-36	11,000
1-1-37	10,000
1-1-38	12,000
1-2-39	13,000
1-1-40	12,000
1-1-41	14,000
1-1-42	14,000
1-1-43	16,000
1-1-44	18,000
1-1-45	13,000
1-1-46	15,000
1-1-47	10,000
1-1-48	18,000
1-1-49	13,000
1-2-50	15,000
1-1-51	16,000
1-1-52	17,000
1-1-53	11,000
1-1-54	9,500
1-1-55	14,000
1-2-56	14,500
1-1-57	13,500
1-1-58	12,000
12-31-58	13,000
12-31-59	14,000
12-31-60	16,000
12-30-61	15,000
12-31-62	16,000
12-31-63	26,500
12-26-64	28,500
12-31-65	27,450
12-24-66	24,381
12-30-67	34,685
12-28-68	32,307
12-20-69	29,723
12-19-70	30,512
12-18-71	33,503
12-30-72	31,312
12-29-73	30,127
12-28-74	30,131
12-26-75	33,240
1-2-77	33,252
12-31-77	31,318
12-23-78	33,122
12-22-79	33,412
12-27-80	34,723
12-26-81	33,816
12-25-82	31,359
12-24-83	41,412
12-22-84	50,126
12-28-85	*52,203
12-25-86	48,722
12-25-87	43,240
12-24-88	48,719
12-30-89	44,887
12-31-90	50,562
12-31-91	42,821
12-31-92	41,622
12-24-93	43,848
12-30-94	50,612
12-29-95	49,116

**Record attendance. #Named John Hancock, 1989-93.*

GATOR BOWL

(Jacksonville Municipal Stadium, Jacksonville, Fla.; Capacity: 73,000)

Date	Attendance
1-2-46	7,362
1-1-47	10,134
1-1-48	16,666
1-1-49	32,939
1-2-50	18,409

1-1-51	19,834
1-1-52	34,577
1-1-53	30,015
1-1-54	28,641
12-31-54	28,426
12-31-55	32,174
12-29-56	36,256
12-28-57	41,160
12-27-58	41,312
1-2-60	45,104
12-31-60	50,112
12-30-61	50,202
12-29-62	50,026
12-28-63	50,018
1-2-65	50,408
12-31-65	60,127
12-31-66	60,312
12-30-67	68,019
12-28-68	68,011
12-27-69	72,248
1-2-71	71,136
12-31-71	71,208
12-30-72	71,114
12-29-73	62,109
12-30-74	63,811
12-29-75	64,012
12-27-76	67,827
12-30-77	72,289
12-29-78	72,011
12-28-79	70,407
12-29-80	72,297
12-28-81	71,009
12-30-82	80,913
12-30-83	81,293
12-28-84	82,138
12-30-85	79,417
12-27-86	80,104
12-31-87	82,119
1-1-89	76,236
12-30-89	*82,911
1-1-91	68,927
12-29-91	62,003
12-31-92	71,233
12-31-93	67,205
12-30-94†	62,200
1-1-96	45,202

Record attendance. †Played at Gainesville, Fla.

LIBERTY BOWL†

(Liberty Bowl Memorial Stadium, Memphis, Tenn.; Capacity: 62,380)

Date	Attendance
12-19-59	36,211
12-17-60	16,624
12-16-61	15,712
12-15-62	17,048
12-31-63	8,309
12-19-64	6,059
12-18-65	38,607
12-10-66	39,101
12-16-67	35,045
12-14-68	46,206
12-13-69	50,042
12-12-70	44,640
12-20-71	51,410
12-18-72	50,021
12-17-73	50,011
12-16-74	51,284
12-22-75	52,129
12-20-76	52,736
12-19-77	49,456
12-23-78	53,064
12-22-79	50,021
12-27-80	53,667
12-30-81	43,216
12-29-82	54,123
12-29-83	38,229
12-27-84	50,108
12-27-85	40,186
12-29-86	51,327
12-29-87	53,249
12-28-88	39,210
12-28-89	60,128
12-27-90	13,144
12-29-91	*61,497
12-31-92	32,107
12-28-93	21,097
12-31-94	33,280
12-30-95	47,398

Record attendance. †Played at Philadelphia, 1959-63; Atlantic City, 1964; Memphis, from 1965.

FLORIDA CITRUS BOWL#

(Florida Citrus Bowl, Orlando, Fla.; Capacity: 70,349)

Date	Attendance
12-30-60	13,000
12-22-62	7,500
12-27-68	16,114
12-26-69	16,311
12-28-70	15,164
12-28-71	16,750
12-29-72	20,062
12-22-73@	37,234
12-21-74	20,246
12-20-75	20,247
12-18-76	37,812
12-23-77	44,502
12-23-78	31,356
12-22-79	38,666
12-20-80	52,541
12-19-81	50,045
12-18-82	51,296
12-17-83	50,183
12-22-84	51,821
12-28-85	50,920
1-1-87	51,113
1-1-88	53,152
1-2-89	53,571
1-1-90	60,016
1-1-91	72,328
1-1-92	64,192
1-1-93	65,861
1-1-94	*72,456
1-2-95	71,195
1-1-96	70,797

Record attendance. #Named Tangerine Bowl before 1982. The first 14 games in the Tangerine Bowl, through 1-1-60, are not listed because no major teams were involved. The same is true for those games played in December 1961, 1963, 1964, 1965, 1966 and 1967. @ Played at Gainesville, Fla.

PEACH BOWL

(Georgia Dome, Atlanta, Ga.; Capacity: 71,548)

Date	Attendance
12-30-68	35,545
12-30-69	48,452
12-30-70	52,126
12-30-71	36,771
12-29-72	52,671
12-28-73	38,107
12-28-74	31,695
12-31-75	45,134
12-31-76	54,132
12-31-77	36,733
12-25-78	20,277
12-31-79	57,371
1-2-81	45,384
12-31-81	37,582
12-31-82	50,134
12-30-83	25,648
12-31-84	41,107
12-31-85	29,857
12-31-86	53,668
1-2-88	58,737
12-31-88	44,635
12-30-89	44,991
12-29-90	38,912
1-1-92	59,322
1-2-93	69,125
12-31-93	63,416
1-1-95	64,902
12-30-95	*70,825

Record attendance.

FIESTA BOWL

(Sun Devil Stadium, Tempe, Ariz.; Capacity: 73,471)

Date	Attendance
12-27-71	51,089
12-23-72	51,318
12-21-73	50,878
12-28-74	50,878
12-26-75	51,396
12-25-76	48,174
12-25-77	57,727
12-25-78	55,227
12-25-79	55,347
12-26-80	66,738
1-1-82	71,053
1-1-83	70,533
1-2-84	66,484
1-1-85	60,310
1-1-86	72,454
1-2-87	73,098
1-1-88	72,112
1-2-89	74,911
1-1-90	73,953
1-1-91	69,098
1-1-92	71,133
1-1-93	70,224
1-1-94	72,260
1-2-95	73,968
1-2-96	*79,864

Record attendance.

INDEPENDENCE BOWL

(Independence Stadium, Shreveport, La.; Capacity: 50,459)

Date	Attendance
12-13-76	15,542
12-17-77	18,500
12-16-78	18,200
12-15-79	27,234
12-13-80	45,000
12-12-81	47,300
12-11-82	*49,503
12-10-83	41,274
12-15-84	41,000
12-21-85	42,800
12-20-86	46,369
12-19-87	41,683
12-23-88	20,242
12-16-89	30,333
12-15-90	48,325
12-29-91	46,932
12-31-92	31,337
12-31-93	33,819
12-28-94	27,242
12-29-95	48,835

Record attendance.

HOLIDAY BOWL

(San Diego Jack Murphy Stadium, San Diego, Calif.; Capacity: 63,039)

Date	Attendance
12-28-78	52,500
12-21-79	52,200
12-19-80	50,214
12-18-81	52,419
12-17-82	52,533
12-23-83	51,480
12-21-84	61,243
12-22-85	42,324
12-30-86	59,473
12-30-87	*61,892
12-30-88	60,718
12-29-89	61,113
12-29-90	61,441
12-30-91	60,646
12-30-92	44,457
12-30-93	52,108
12-30-94	59,453
12-29-95	51,051

Record attendance.

ALOHA BOWL

(Aloha Stadium, Honolulu, Hawaii; Capacity: 50,000)

Date	Attendance
12-25-82	30,055
12-26-83	37,212
12-29-84	41,777
12-28-85	35,183
12-27-86	26,743

Date	Attendance
12-25-87	24,839
12-25-88	35,132
12-25-89	*50,000
12-25-90	14,185
12-25-91	34,433
12-25-92	42,933
12-25-93	44,009
12-25-94	44,862
12-25-95	41,112

Record attendance.

OUTBACK BOWL (Formerly Hall of Fame)

(Tampa Stadium, Tampa, Fla.; Capacity: 74,350)

Date	Attendance
12-23-86	25,368
1-2-88	60,156
1-2-89	51,112
1-1-90	52,535
1-1-91	63,154
1-1-92	57,789
1-1-93	52,056
1-1-94	52,649
1-2-95	61,384
1-1-96	*65,313

**Record attendance.*

COPPER BOWL

(Arizona Stadium, Tucson, Ariz.; Capacity: 56,167)

Date	Attendance
12-31-89	37,237
12-31-90	36,340
12-31-91	35,752
12-29-92	40,876
12-29-93	*49,075
12-29-94	45,122
12-27-95	41,004

**Record attendance.*

CARQUEST BOWL#

(Joe Robbie Stadium, Miami, Fla.; Capacity: 74,913)

Date	Attendance
12-28-90	*74,021
12-28-91	52,644
1-1-93	45,554
1-1-94	38,516
1-2-95	50,833
12-30-95	34,428

**Record attendance. #Named Blockbuster Bowl before 1993.*

LAS VEGAS BOWL

(Sam Boyd Stadium, Las Vegas, Nev.; Capacity: 32,000)

Date	Attendance
12-18-92	15,476
12-17-93	15,508
12-15-94	*17,562
12-14-95	11,127

**Record attendance.*

ALAMO BOWL

(Alamodome, San Antonio, Texas; Capacity: 65,000)

Date	Attendance
12-31-93	45,716
12-31-94	44,106
12-28-95	*64,597

Former Major Bowl Games

ALAMO

(San Antonio, Texas)

Date	Attendance
1-4-47	3,730

ALL-AMERICAN

(Birmingham, Ala.)

Date	Attendance
12-22-77	47,000
12-20-78	41,500
12-29-79	62,785
12-27-80	30,000
12-31-81	41,672
12-31-82	75,000
12-22-83	42,000
12-29-84	47,300
12-31-85	45,000
12-31-86	30,000
12-22-87	37,000
12-29-88	48,218
12-28-89	47,750
12-28-90	44,000

(Named Hall of Fame Classic until 1986 and then discontinued after 1990 game; played at Legion Field, capacity 75,952)

AVIATION

(Dayton, Ohio)

Date	Attendance
12-9-61	3,694

BACARDI

(Havana, Cuba)

Date	Attendance
1-1-37	12,000

BLUEBONNET

(Houston, Texas)

Date	Attendance
12-19-59	55,000
12-17-60	68,000
12-16-61	52,000
12-22-62	55,000
12-21-63	50,000
12-19-64	50,000
12-18-65	40,000
12-17-66	67,000
12-23-67	30,156
12-31-68	53,543
12-31-69	55,203
12-31-70	53,829
12-31-71	54,720
12-30-72	52,961
12-29-73	44,358
12-23-74	35,122
12-27-75	52,748
12-31-76	48,618
12-31-77	52,842
12-31-78	34,084
12-31-79	40,542
12-31-80	36,667
12-31-81	40,309
12-31-82	31,557
12-31-83	50,090
12-31-84	43,260
12-31-85	42,000
12-31-86	40,476
12-31-87	23,282

(Played at Rice Stadium 1959-67 and 1985, Astrodome 1968-84 and from 1986; Astrodome capacity 60,000)

BLUEGRASS

(Louisville, Ky.)

Date	Attendance
12-13-58	7,000

CALIFORNIA

(Fresno, Calif.)

Date	Attendance
12-19-81	15,565
12-18-82	30,000
12-17-83	20,464
12-15-84	21,741
12-14-85	32,554
12-13-86	10,743
12-12-87	24,000
12-10-88	31,272
12-9-89	31,610
12-8-90	25,431
12-14-91	34,825

CAMELLIA

(Lafayette, La.)

Date	Attendance
12-30-48	4,500

CHERRY

(Pontiac, Mich.)

Date	Attendance
12-22-84	70,332
12-21-85	51,858

DELTA

(Memphis, Tenn.)

Date	Attendance
1-1-48	28,120
1-1-49	15,069

DIXIE BOWL

(Birmingham, Ala.)

Date	Attendance
1-1-48	22,000
1-1-49	20,000

DIXIE CLASSIC

(Dallas, Texas)

Date	Attendance
1-2-22	12,000
1-1-25	7,000
1-1-34	12,000

FORT WORTH CLASSIC

(Fort Worth, Texas)

Date	Attendance
1-1-21	9,000

FREEDOM BOWL

(Anaheim, Calif.)

Date	Attendance
12-26-84	24,093
12-30-85	30,961
12-30-86	55,422
12-30-87	33,261
12-29-88	35,941
12-30-89	33,858
12-29-90	41,450
12-30-91	34,217
12-29-92	50,745
12-30-93	37,203
12-27-94	27,477

GARDEN STATE

(East Rutherford, N.J.)

Date	Attendance
12-16-78	33,402
12-15-79	55,493
12-14-80	41,417
12-13-81	38,782

GOTHAM

(New York, N.Y.)

Date	Attendance
12-9-61	15,123
12-15-62	6,166

GREAT LAKES

(Cleveland, Ohio)

Date	Attendance
12-6-47	14,908

HARBOR

(San Diego, Calif.)

Date	Attendance
1-1-47	7,000
1-1-48	12,000
1-1-49	20,000

LOS ANGELES CHRISTMAS FESTIVAL
(Los Angeles, Calif.)

Date	Attendance
12-25-24	47,000

MERCY
(Los Angeles, Calif.)

Date	Attendance
11-23-61	33,145

OIL
(Houston, Texas)

Date	Attendance
1-1-46	27,000
1-1-47	23,000

PASADENA
(Pasadena, Calif.)

Date	Attendance
12-2-67	28,802
12-6-69	41,276
12-19-70	20,472
12-18-71	15,244

PRESIDENTIAL CUP
(College Park, Md.)

Date	Attendance
12-9-50	12,245

RAISIN
(Fresno, Calif.)

Date	Attendance
1-1-46	10,000
1-1-47	13,000
1-1-48	13,000
1-1-49	10,000
12-31-49	9,000

SALAD
(Phoenix, Ariz.)

Date	Attendance
1-1-48	12,500
1-1-49	17,500
1-1-50	18,500
1-1-51	23,000
1-1-52	17,000

SAN DIEGO EAST-WEST CHRISTMAS CLASSIC
(San Diego, Calif.)

Date	Attendance
12-26-21	5,000
12-25-22	5,000

SHRINE
(Little Rock, Ark.)

Date	Attendance
12-18-48	5,000

Individual Records

Only official records after 1937 are included. Prior records are included if able to be substantiated. Each team's score is in parentheses after the team name. The year listed is the actual (calendar) year the game was played; the date is included if the bowl was played twice (i.e., January and December) during one calendar year. The list also includes discontinued bowls, marked with (D). Bowls are listed by the name of the bowl at the time it was played: The Florida Citrus Bowl was the Tangerine Bowl in 1947-82; the first Hall of Fame Bowl (1977-85) was called the All-American Bowl in 1986-90; the second Hall of Fame Bowl (1986-95) is now called the Outback Bowl and is played in Tampa, Fla.; the Sun Bowl was called the John Hancock Bowl in 1989-93, the John Hancock Sun Bowl in 1987-88, and reverted to Sun Bowl in 1994; and the Blockbuster Bowl changed its name to Carquest Bowl in 1993. The NCAA Statistics Service thanks former staff member Steve Boda for his valuable assistance in compiling these records.

Total Offense

MOST TOTAL PLAYS
74—(D) Tony Kimbrough, Western Mich. (30) vs. Fresno St. (35) (California, 1988) (431 yards)

MOST TOTAL YARDS
594—Ty Detmer, Brigham Young (39) vs. Penn St. (50) (Holiday, 1989) (576 passing yards, 67 plays)

HIGHEST AVERAGE PER PLAY
(Min. 10 Plays)
24.1—Dicky Maegle, Rice (28) vs. Alabama (6) (Cotton, 1954) (11 for 265)

MOST TOUCHDOWNS RESPONSIBLE FOR
(TDs Scored & Passed For)
6—(D) Chuck Long, Iowa (55) vs. Texas (17) (Freedom, 1984) (6 pass); Bobby Layne, Texas (40) vs. Missouri (27) (Cotton, 1946) (3 rush, 2 pass, 1 catch)

Rushing

MOST RUSHING ATTEMPTS
46—(D) Ron Jackson, Tulsa (28) vs. San Diego St. (17) (Freedom, 1991) (211 yards)

MOST NET RUSHING YARDS
280—(D) James Gray, Texas Tech (49) vs. Duke (21) (All-American, 1989) (33 carries)

MOST NET RUSHING YARDS BY A QUARTERBACK
199—Tommie Frazier, Nebraska (62) vs. Florida (24) (Fiesta, 1996) (16 carries)

HIGHEST AVERAGE PER RUSH
(Min. 9 Carries)
24.1—Dicky Maegle, Rice (28) vs. Alabama (6) (Cotton, 1954) (11 for 265)

MOST NET RUSHING YARDS BY TWO RUSHERS, SAME TEAM, OVER 100 YARDS RUSHING EACH
373—Woody Green (202) & Brent McClanahan (171), Arizona St. (49) vs. Missouri (35) (Fiesta, 1972)

MOST RUSHING TOUCHDOWNS
5—Barry Sanders, Oklahoma St. (62) vs. Wyoming (14) (Holiday, 1988) (runs of 33, 2, 67, 1, 10 yards); Neil Snow, Michigan (49) vs. Stanford (0) (Rose, 1902) (touchdowns counted as five-point scores)

Passing

MOST PASS ATTEMPTS
63—Trent Dilfer, Fresno St. (30) vs. Colorado (41) (Aloha, 1993) (completed 37)

MOST PASS COMPLETIONS
43—(D) Steve Clarkson, San Jose St. (25) vs. Toledo (27) (California, 1981) (attempted 62)

MOST CONSECUTIVE PASS COMPLETIONS
10—Danny Wuerffel, Florida (17) vs. Florida St. (23) (Sugar, Jan. 2, 1995); Rick Neuheisel, UCLA (45) vs. Illinois (9) (Rose, 1984)

MOST NET PASSING YARDS
576—Ty Detmer, Brigham Young (39) vs. Penn St. (50) (Holiday, 1989) (42 of 59 with 2 interceptions)

MOST NET PASSING YARDS, ONE QUARTER
223—Browning Nagle, Louisville (34) vs. Alabama (7) (Fiesta, 1991) (1st quarter, 9 of 16)

MOST TOUCHDOWN PASSES THROWN
6—(D) Chuck Long, Iowa (55) vs. Texas (17) (Freedom, 1984) (29 of 39 with no interceptions) (touchdown passes of 6, 11, 33, 49, 4, 15 yards)

MOST PASSES HAD INTERCEPTED
6—Bruce Lee, Arizona (10) vs. Auburn (34) (Sun, 1968) (6 of 24)

HIGHEST COMPLETION PERCENTAGE
(Min. 10 Attempts)
.917—Bobby Layne, Texas (40) vs. Missouri (27) (Cotton, 1946) (11 of 12 with no interceptions)

MOST YARDS PER PASS ATTEMPT
(Min. 10 Attempts)
19.4—Tony Rice, Notre Dame (34) vs. West Va. (21) (Fiesta, 1989) (11 for 213 yards)

MOST YARDS PER PASS COMPLETION
(Min. 7 Completions)
30.4—Tony Rice, Notre Dame (34) vs. West Va. (21) (Fiesta, 1989) (7 for 213 yards); Duke Carlisle, Texas (28) vs. Navy (6) (Cotton, 1964) (7 for 213 yards)

Receiving

MOST PASS RECEPTIONS
20—(D) Norman Jordan, Vanderbilt (28) vs. Air Force (36) (Hall of Fame, 1982) (173 yards); Walker Gillette, Richmond (49) vs. Ohio (42) (Tangerine, 1968) (242 yards)

MOST PASS RECEIVING YARDS
252—Andre Rison, Michigan St. (27) vs. Georgia (34) (Gator, Jan. 1, 1989) (9 catches)

HIGHEST AVERAGE PER CATCH
(Min. 3 Receptions)
52.3—Phil Harris, Texas (28) vs. Navy (6) (Cotton, 1964) (3 for 157 yards)

MOST TOUCHDOWNS RECEIVING
4—Fred Biletnikoff, Florida St. (36) vs. Oklahoma (19) (Gator, Jan. 2, 1965) (13 catches); (D) Bob McChesney, Hardin-Simmons (49) vs. Wichita St. (12) (Camellia, 1948) (8 catches)

Scoring

MOST POINTS SCORED
30—(D) Sheldon Canley, San Jose St. (48) vs. Central Mich. (24) (California, 1990) (5 touchdowns); Barry Sanders, Oklahoma St. (62) vs. Wyoming (14) (Holiday, 1988) (5 touchdowns)

MOST POINTS RESPONSIBLE FOR (TDs SCORED & PASSED FOR, EXTRA POINTS, AND FGs)
40—Bobby Layne, Texas (40) vs. Missouri (27) (Cotton, 1946) (18 rushing, 12 passing, 6 receiving and 4 PATs)

MOST TOUCHDOWNS SCORED
5—(D) Sheldon Canley, San Jose St. (48) vs. Central Mich. (24) (California, 1990) (4 rushing, 1 receiving); Barry Sanders, Oklahoma St. (62) vs. Wyoming (14) (Holiday, 1988) (5 rushing); Neil Snow, Michigan (49) vs. Stanford (0) (Rose, 1902) (5 rushing five-point TDs)

MOST TWO-POINT CONVERSIONS
2—Ernie Davis, Syracuse (23) vs. Texas (14) (Cotton, 1960) (2 receptions)

Kicking

MOST FIELD GOALS ATTEMPTED
6—Kyle Bryant, Texas A&M (22) vs. Michigan (20) (Alamo, 1995)

MOST FIELD GOALS MADE
5—Kyle Bryant, Texas A&M (22) vs. Michigan (20) (Alamo, 1995) (27, 49, 47, 31, 37 yards); Tim Rogers, Mississippi St. (24) vs. North Caro. St. (28) (Peach, Jan. 1, 1995) (37, 21, 29, 36, 30 yards); Arden Czyzewski, Florida (28) vs. Notre Dame (39) (Sugar, 1992) (26, 24, 36, 37, 24 yards); Jess

Atkinson, Maryland (23) vs. Tennessee (30) (Florida Citrus, 1983) (18, 48, 31, 22, 26 yards)

MOST EXTRA-POINT KICK ATTEMPTS
9—Layne Talbot, Texas A&M (65) vs. Brigham Young (14) (Holiday, 1990) (9 made); Bobby Luna, Alabama (61) vs. Syracuse (6) (Orange, 1953) (7 made); (D) James Weaver, Centre (63) vs. Texas Christian (7) (Fort Worth Classic, 1921) (9 made)

MOST EXTRA-POINT KICKS MADE
9—Layne Talbot, Texas A&M (65) vs. Brigham Young (14) (Holiday, 1990) (9 attempts); (D) James Weaver, Centre (63) vs. Texas Christian (7) (Fort Worth Classic, 1921) (9 attempts)

MOST POINTS BY A KICKER
16—Kyle Bryant, Texas A&M (22) vs. Michigan (20) (Alamo, 1995) (5 FGs, 1 PAT); Tim Rogers, Mississippi St. (24) vs. North Caro. St. (28) (Peach, Jan. 1, 1995) (5 FGs, 1 PAT); Arden Czyzewski, Florida (28) vs. Notre Dame (39) (Sugar, 1992) (5 FGs, 1 PAT)

Punting

MOST PUNTS
21—Everett Sweeney, Michigan (49) vs. Stanford (0) (Rose, 1902)

HIGHEST AVERAGE PER PUNT (Min. 5 Punts)
52.7—Des Koch, Southern Cal (7) vs. Wisconsin (0) (Rose, 1953) (7 for 369 yards)

Punt Returns

MOST PUNT RETURNS
9—Buzy Rosenberg, Georgia (7) vs. North Caro. (3) (Gator, Dec. 31, 1971) (54 yards); Paddy Driscoll, Great Lakes (17) vs. Mare Island (0) (Rose, 1919) (115 yards)

MOST PUNT RETURN YARDS
136—Johnny Rodgers, Nebraska (38) vs. Alabama (6) (Orange, 1972) (6 returns)

HIGHEST PUNT RETURN AVERAGE (Min. 3 Returns)
40.7—George Fleming, Washington (44) vs. Wisconsin (8) (Rose, 1960) (3 for 122 yards)

MOST TOUCHDOWNS ON PUNT RETURNS
2—James Henry, Southern Miss. (38) vs. UTEP (18) (Independence, 1988) (65 and 45 yards)

Kickoff Returns

MOST KICKOFF RETURNS
7—Dale Carter, Tennessee (17) vs. Penn St. (42) (Fiesta, 1992) (132 yards); Jeff Sydner, Hawaii (13) vs. Michigan St. (33) (Aloha, 1989) (174 yards); Homer Jones, Brigham Young (37) vs. Indiana (38) (Holiday, 1979) (126 yards)

MOST KICKOFF RETURN YARDS
203—Mike Fink, Missouri (35) vs. Arizona St. (49) (Fiesta, 1972) (6 returns)

HIGHEST KICKOFF RETURN AVERAGE (Min. 2 Returns)
60.5—(D) Bob Smith, Texas A&M (40) vs. Georgia (20) (Presidential Cup, 1950) (2 for 121 yards)

MOST TOUCHDOWNS ON KICKOFF RETURNS
1—Many players tied

Interceptions

MOST INTERCEPTIONS MADE
4—Jim Dooley, Miami (Fla.) (14) vs. Clemson (0) (Gator, 1952); (D) Manuel Aja, Arizona St. (21) vs. Xavier (Ohio) (33) (Salad, 1950)

MOST INTERCEPTION RETURN YARDAGE
148—Elmer Layden, Notre Dame (27) vs. Stanford (10) (Rose, 1925) (2 interceptions)

All-Purpose Yards

(Includes All Runs From Scrimmage, Pass Receptions and All Returns)

MOST ALL-PURPOSE PLAYS (Must Have at Least One Reception or Return)
47—(D) Ron Jackson, Tulsa (28) vs. San Diego St. (17) (Freedom, 1991) (46 rushes, 1 reception)

MOST ALL-PURPOSE YARDS GAINED (Must Have at Least One Reception or Return)
359—Sherman Williams, Alabama (24) vs. Ohio St. (17) (Florida Citrus, 1995) (166 rushing, 155 receiving, 38 kickoff returns)

Defensive Statistics

MOST TOTAL TACKLES MADE (Includes Assists)
31—Lee Roy Jordan, Alabama (17) vs. Oklahoma (0) (Orange, 1963)

MOST UNASSISTED TACKLES
18—Rod Smith, Notre Dame (39) vs. Florida (28) (Sugar, 1992)

MOST TACKLES MADE FOR LOSSES
5—(D) Michael Jones, Colorado (17) vs. Brigham Young (20) (Freedom, 1988) (20 yards in losses); Jimmy Walker, Arkansas (10) vs. UCLA (10) (Fiesta, 1978)

MOST QUARTERBACK SACKS
4—Rusty Medearis, Miami (Fla.) (22) vs. Nebraska (0) (Orange, 1992); Bobby Bell, Missouri (17) vs. Brigham Young (21) (Holiday, 1983)

MOST FUMBLE RECOVERIES
2—Randall Brown, Ohio St. (17) vs. Alabama (24) (Florida Citrus, 1995); (D) Michael Stewart, Fresno St. (51) vs. Bowling Green (7) (California, 1985); Rod Kirby, Pittsburgh (7) vs. Arizona St. (28) (Fiesta, 1973)

MOST BLOCKED KICKS
2—Carlton Williams, Pittsburgh (7) vs. Arizona St. (28) (Fiesta, 1973)

MOST PASSES BROKEN UP
3—Barron Miles, Nebraska (24) vs. Miami (Fla.) (17) (Orange, 1995); Perry Ellsworth, Virginia (20) vs. Texas Christian (10) (Independence, 1994); Sam McKiver, Virginia (20) vs. Texas Christian (10) (Independence, 1994); Tyrone Williams, Nebraska (16) vs. Florida St. (18) (Orange, 1994); (D) John Herpin, Southern Cal (28) vs. Utah (21) (Freedom, 1993); Demouy Williams, Washington (24) vs. Tulane (12) (Independence, 1987)

Team Records

Totals for each team in both-team records are in brackets after the team's score.

Total Offense

MOST TOTAL PLAYS
96—North Caro. St. (10) vs. Arizona (17) (Copper, 1989) (310 yards)

MOST TOTAL PLAYS, BOTH TEAMS
175—Toledo (40) [95] & Nevada (37) [80] (OT) (Las Vegas, 1995) (974 yards)

MOST YARDS GAINED
718—Arizona St. (49) vs. Missouri (35) (Fiesta, 1972) (452 rush, 266 pass)

MOST YARDS GAINED, BOTH TEAMS
1,143—(D) Southern Cal (47) [624] & Texas A&M (28) [519] (Bluebonnet, 1977) (148 plays)

HIGHEST AVERAGE GAINED PER PLAY
9.5—Louisville (34) vs. Alabama (7) (Fiesta, 1991) (60 plays for 571 yards)

FEWEST PLAYS
35—Tennessee (0) vs. Texas (16) (Cotton, 1953) (29 rush, 6 pass)

FEWEST PLAYS, BOTH TEAMS
107—Texas Christian (16) [54] & Marquette (6) [53] (Cotton, 1937)

FEWEST YARDS
Minus 21—U. of Mexico (0) vs. Southwestern (Tex.) (35) (Sun, 1945) (29 rush, -50 pass)

FEWEST YARDS, BOTH TEAMS
260—Randolph Field (7) [150] & Texas (7) [110] (Cotton, 1944)

LOWEST AVERAGE GAINED PER PLAY
0.9—Tennessee (0) vs. Texas (16) (Cotton, 1953) (35 plays for 32 yards)

Rushing

MOST RUSHING ATTEMPTS
87—Oklahoma (40) vs. Auburn (22) (Sugar, Jan. 1, 1972) (439 yards)

MOST RUSHING ATTEMPTS, BOTH TEAMS
122—(D) Southern Cal (47) [50] & Texas A&M (28) [72] (Bluebonnet, 1977) (864 yards); Mississippi St. (26) [68] & North Caro. (24) [54] (Sun, 1974) (732 yards)

MOST NET RUSHING YARDS
524—Nebraska (62) vs. Florida (24) (Fiesta, 1996) (68 attempts)

MOST NET RUSHING YARDS, BOTH TEAMS
864—(D) Southern Cal (47) [378] & Texas A&M (28) [486] (Bluebonnet, 1977) (122 attempts)

HIGHEST RUSHING AVERAGE (Min. 30 Attempts)
9.3—Texas Tech (55) vs. Air Force (41) (Copper, 1995) (39 for 361 yards)

FEWEST RUSHING ATTEMPTS
12—(D) Vanderbilt (28) vs. Air Force (36) (Hall of Fame, 1982) (35 yards)

FEWEST RUSHING ATTEMPTS, BOTH TEAMS
57—Iowa (20) [36] & Wyoming (19) [21] (Holiday, 1987)

FEWEST RUSHING YARDS
Minus 61—Kansas St. (7) vs. Boston College (12) (Aloha, 1994) (23 attempts)

FEWEST RUSHING YARDS, BOTH TEAMS
51—(D) Utah (16) [6] & Arizona (13) [45] (Freedom, 1994)

LOWEST RUSHING AVERAGE (Min. 20 Attempts)
Minus 2.7—Kansas St. (7) vs. Boston College (12) (Aloha, 1994) (23 for -61 yards)

RUSHING DEFENSE, FEWEST YARDS ALLOWED
Minus 61—Boston College (12) vs. Kansas St. (7) (Aloha, 1994) (23 attempts)

Passing

MOST PASS ATTEMPTS
63—(D) San Jose St. (25) vs. Toledo (27) (California, 1981) (43 completions, 5 interceptions, 467 yards)

MOST PASS ATTEMPTS, BOTH TEAMS
92—Toledo (40) [41] & Nevada (37) [51] (OT) (Las Vegas, 1995) (50 completions); Penn St. (38) [31] & Oregon (20) [61] (Rose, 1995) (61 completions); Air Force (13) [46] & Tennessee (34) [46] (Sugar, 1971) (47 completions)

MOST PASS COMPLETIONS
43—(D) San Jose St. (25) vs. Toledo (27) (California, 1981) (63 attempts, 5 interceptions, 467 yards)

MOST PASS COMPLETIONS, BOTH TEAMS
61—Penn St. (38) [20] & Oregon (20) [41] (Rose, 1995) (92 attempts)

MOST PASSING YARDS
576—Brigham Young (39) vs. Penn St. (50) (Holiday, 1989) (42 completions, 59 attempts, 2 interceptions)

MOST PASSING YARDS, BOTH TEAMS
808—Washington St. (31) [492] & Utah (28) [316] (Copper, 1992) (88 attempts)

MOST PASSES HAD INTERCEPTED
8—Arizona (10) vs. Auburn (34) (Sun, 1968)

MOST PASSES HAD INTERCEPTED, BOTH TEAMS
12—Auburn (34) [4] & Arizona (10) [8] (Sun, 1968)

MOST PASSES ATTEMPTED WITHOUT AN INTERCEPTION
57—(D) Western Mich. (30) vs. Fresno St. (35) (California, 1988) (24 completions)

MOST PASSES ATTEMPTED BY BOTH TEAMS WITHOUT AN INTERCEPTION
90—Bowling Green (35) [49] & Nevada (34) [41] (Las Vegas, 1992) (54 completions)

HIGHEST COMPLETION PERCENTAGE (Min. 10 Attempts)
.929—Texas (40) vs. Missouri (27) (Cotton, 1946) (13 of 14, no interceptions, 234 yards)

MOST YARDS PER ATTEMPT (Min. 10 Attempts)
21.7—Southern Cal (47) vs. Pittsburgh (14) (Rose, 1930) (13 for 282 yards)

MOST YARDS PER COMPLETION (Min. 8 Completions)
35.2—Southern Cal (47) vs. Pittsburgh (14) (Rose, 1930) (8 for 282 yards)

FEWEST PASS ATTEMPTS
2—Air Force (38) vs. Mississippi St. (15) (Liberty, 1991) (1 completion); (D) Army (10) vs. Michigan St. (6) (Cherry, 1984) (1 completion); West Va. (14) vs. South Caro. (3) (Peach, 1969) (1 completion)

FEWEST PASS ATTEMPTS, BOTH TEAMS
9—Fordham (2) [4] & Missouri (0) [5] (Sugar, 1942)

FEWEST PASS COMPLETIONS
0—13 teams tied (see Team Record Lists)

FEWEST PASS COMPLETIONS, BOTH TEAMS
3—Arizona St. (0) [0] & Catholic (0) [3] (Sun, 1940)

FEWEST PASSING YARDS
Minus 50—U. of Mexico (0) vs. Southwestern (Tex.) (35) (Sun, 1945) (2 completions, 9 attempts, 3 interceptions)

FEWEST PASSING YARDS, BOTH TEAMS
15—Rice (8) [-17] & Tennessee (0) [32] (Orange, 1947)

LOWEST COMPLETION PERCENTAGE
.000—13 teams tied (see Team Record Lists)

FEWEST YARDS PER PASS ATTEMPT
Minus 5.6—U. of Mexico (0) vs. Southwestern (Tex.) (35) (Sun, 1945) (9 for -50 yards)

FEWEST YARDS PER PASS COMPLETION (Min. 1 Completion)
Minus 25.0—U. of Mexico (0) vs. Southwestern (Tex.) (35) (Sun, 1945) (2 for -50 yards)

Scoring

MOST TOUCHDOWNS
9—Texas A&M (65) vs. Brigham Young (14) (Holiday, 1990) (5 rush, 4 pass); Alabama (61) vs. Syracuse (6) (Orange, 1953) (4 rush, 3 pass, 1 punt return, 1 interception return); (D) Centre (63) vs. Texas Christian (7) (Fort Worth Classic, 1921) (8 rush, 1 blocked punt recovery in end zone)

MOST TOUCHDOWNS, BOTH TEAMS
13—Texas Tech (55) [7] & Air Force (41) [6] (Copper, 1995); Richmond (49) [7] & Ohio (42) [6] (Tangerine, 1968)

MOST TOUCHDOWNS RUSHING
8—(D) Centre (63) vs. Texas Christian (7) (Fort Worth Classic, 1921)

MOST TOUCHDOWNS RUSHING, BOTH TEAMS
12—Texas Tech (55) [6] & Air Force (41) [6] (Copper, 1995)

MOST TOUCHDOWNS PASSING
6—(D) Iowa (55) vs. Texas (17) (Freedom, 1984)

MOST TOUCHDOWNS PASSING, BOTH TEAMS
8—(D) Iowa (55) [6] & Texas (17) [2] (Freedom, 1984); Richmond (49) [4] & Ohio (42) [4] (Tangerine, 1968)

MOST FIELD GOALS MADE
5—Texas A&M (22) vs. Michigan (20) (Alamo, 1995) (27, 49, 47, 31, 37 yards); Mississippi St. (24) vs. North Caro. St. (28) (Peach, Jan. 1, 1995) (37, 21, 29, 36, 30 yards); Florida (28) vs. Notre Dame (39) (Sugar, 1992) (26, 24, 36, 37, 24 yards); Maryland (23) vs. Tennessee (30) (Florida Citrus, 1983) (18, 48, 31, 22, 26 yards)

MOST FIELD GOALS MADE, BOTH TEAMS
7—Texas A&M (22) [5] & Michigan (20) [2] (Alamo, 1995); North Caro. St. (28) [2] & Mississippi St. (24) [5] (Peach, Jan. 1, 1995)

MOST POINTS, WINNING TEAM
65—Texas A&M vs. Brigham Young (14) (Holiday, 1990)

MOST POINTS, LOSING TEAM
45—Southern Methodist vs. Brigham Young (46) (Holiday, 1980)

MOST POINTS, BOTH TEAMS
96—Texas Tech (55) & Air Force (41) (Copper, 1995)

LARGEST MARGIN OF VICTORY
55—Alabama (61) vs. Syracuse (6) (Orange, 1953)

FEWEST POINTS, WINNING TEAM
2—Fordham vs. Missouri (0) (Sugar, 1942)

FEWEST POINTS, LOSING TEAM
0—By many teams

FEWEST POINTS, BOTH TEAMS
0—Air Force (0) & Texas Christian (0) (Cotton, 1959); Arkansas (0) & LSU (0) (Cotton, 1947); Arizona St. (0) & Catholic (0) (Sun, 1940); California (0) & Wash. & Jeff. (0) (Rose, 1922)

MOST POINTS SCORED IN FIRST HALF
42—Toledo (56) vs. Davidson (33) (Tangerine, 1969)

MOST POINTS SCORED IN SECOND HALF
45—Oklahoma St. (62) vs. Wyoming (14) (Holiday, 1988)

MOST POINTS SCORED IN FIRST HALF, BOTH TEAMS
49—Arizona St. (45) [21] & Florida St. (38) [28] (Fiesta, 1971); Toledo (56) [42] & Davidson (33) [7] (Tangerine, 1969)

MOST POINTS SCORED IN SECOND HALF, BOTH TEAMS
64—Kansas (51) [34] & UCLA (30) [30] (Aloha, 1995); Penn St. (50) [38] & Brigham Young (39) [26] (Holiday, 1989)

MOST POINTS SCORED EACH QUARTER
1st: 28—Southern Cal (55) vs. Texas Tech (14) (Cotton, 1995)
2nd: 29—Nebraska (62) vs. Florida (24) (Fiesta, 1996)
3rd: 31—(D) Iowa (55) vs. Texas (17) (Freedom, 1984)
4th: 30—Oklahoma (40) vs. Houston (14) (Sun, 1981)

MOST POINTS SCORED EACH QUARTER, BOTH TEAMS
1st: 28—Texas Tech (55) [21] & Air Force (41) [7] (Copper, 1995); Southern Cal (55) [28] & Texas Tech (14) [0] (Cotton, 1995); Indiana (38) [14] & Brigham Young (37) [14] (Holiday, 1979); Louisiana Tech (24) [21] & Louisville (14) [7] (Independence, 1977)
2nd: 40—Arizona St. (48) [14] & North Caro. (26) [26] (Peach, 1970)
3rd: 35—Kansas St. (54) [21] & Colorado St. (21) [14] (Holiday, 1995); Oklahoma St. (62) [28] & Wyoming (14) [7] (Holiday, 1988)
4th: 37—Kansas (51) [14] & UCLA (30) [23] (Aloha, 1995); Oklahoma (40) [30] & Houston (14) [7] (Sun, 1981)

First Downs

MOST FIRST DOWNS
36—Oklahoma (48) vs. Virginia (14) (Gator, Dec. 29, 1991) (16 rush, 18 pass, 2 penalty)

MOST FIRST DOWNS, BOTH TEAMS
61—Penn St. (50) [26] & Brigham Young (39) [35] (Holiday, 1989)

MOST FIRST DOWNS RUSHING
26—Oklahoma (40) vs. Auburn (22) (Sugar, Jan. 1, 1972)

MOST FIRST DOWNS RUSHING, BOTH TEAMS
36—Miami (Fla.) (46) [16] & Texas (3) [20] (Cotton, 1991); Colorado (47) [24] & Alabama (33) [12] (Liberty, 1969)

MOST FIRST DOWNS PASSING
27—Brigham Young (39) vs. Penn St. (50) (Holiday, 1989)

MOST FIRST DOWNS PASSING, BOTH TEAMS
32—Southern Cal (41) [21] & Northwestern (32) [11] (Rose, 1996)

MOST FIRST DOWNS BY PENALTY
6—Texas (3) vs. Miami (Fla.) (46) (Cotton, 1991)

MOST FIRST DOWNS BY PENALTY, BOTH TEAMS
8—Texas A&M (22) [4] & Michigan (20) [4] (Alamo, 1995); Miami (Fla.) (46) [2] & Texas (3) [6] (Cotton, 1991)

FEWEST FIRST DOWNS
1—Arkansas (0) vs. LSU (0) (Cotton, 1947) (1 rush); Alabama (29) vs. Texas A&M (21) (Cotton, 1942) (1 pass)

FEWEST FIRST DOWNS, BOTH TEAMS
10—Randolph Field (7) [7] & Texas (7) [3] (Cotton, 1944)

FEWEST FIRST DOWNS RUSHING
0—Florida (18) vs. Missouri (20) (Sugar, 1966); Navy (6) vs. Texas (28) (Cotton, 1964); Alabama (29) vs. Texas A&M (21) (Cotton, 1942)

FEWEST FIRST DOWNS RUSHING, BOTH TEAMS
3—Alabama (29) [0] & Texas A&M (21) [3] (Cotton, 1942)

FEWEST FIRST DOWNS PASSING
0—By 13 teams (see Team Record Lists)

FEWEST FIRST DOWNS PASSING, BOTH TEAMS
1—Alabama (10) [0] & Arkansas (3) [1] (Sugar, 1962)

Punting

MOST PUNTS
17—Duke (3) vs. Southern Cal (7) (Rose, 1939)

MOST PUNTS, BOTH TEAMS
28—Rice (8) [13] & Tennessee (0) [15] (Orange, 1947); Santa Clara (6) [14] & LSU (0) [14] (Sugar, 1938)

HIGHEST PUNTING AVERAGE (Min. 5 Punts)
53.9—Southern Cal (7) vs. Wisconsin (0) (Rose, 1953) (8 for 431)

FEWEST PUNTS
0—Oklahoma St. (62) vs. Wyoming (14) (Holiday, 1988); Oklahoma (41) vs. Wyoming (7) (Fiesta, 1976)

LOWEST PUNTING AVERAGE (Min. 3 Punts)
17.0—Nevada (34) vs. Bowling Green (35) (Las Vegas, 1992) (4 for 68 yards)

MOST PUNTS BLOCKED BY ONE TEAM
2—North Caro. St. (14) vs. Georgia (7) (Liberty, 1967)

Punt Returns

MOST PUNT RETURNS
9—Georgia (7) vs. North Caro. (3) (Gator, Dec. 31, 1971) (6.8 average)

MOST PUNT RETURN YARDS
136—Nebraska (38) vs. Alabama (6) (Orange, 1972) (6 returns)

HIGHEST PUNT RETURN AVERAGE (Min. 3 Returns)
33.0—Kent (18) vs. Tampa (21) (Tangerine, 1972) (3 for 99 yards)

Kickoff Returns

MOST KICKOFF RETURNS
10—Florida (24) vs. Nebraska (62) (Fiesta, 1996) (26.8 average); Wyoming (14) vs. Oklahoma St. (62) (Holiday, 1988) (20.5 average)

MOST KICKOFF RETURN YARDS
268—Florida (24) vs. Nebraska (62) (Fiesta, 1996) (10 returns)

HIGHEST KICKOFF RETURN AVERAGE (Min. 3 Returns)
42.5—Tennessee (27) vs. Maryland (28) (Sun, 1984) (4 for 170 yards)

Fumbles

MOST FUMBLES
11—Mississippi (7) vs. Alabama (12) (Sugar, 1964) (lost 6)

MOST FUMBLES, BOTH TEAMS
17—Alabama (12) [6] & Mississippi (7) [11] (Sugar, 1964) (lost 9)

MOST FUMBLES LOST
6—By five teams (see Team Record Lists)

MOST FUMBLES LOST, BOTH TEAMS
9—Alabama (12) [3] & Mississippi (7) [6] (Sugar, 1964) (17 fumbles)

Penalties

MOST PENALTIES
20—(D) Fresno St. (35) vs. Western Mich. (30) (California, 1988) (166 yards)

MOST PENALTIES, BOTH TEAMS
29—McNeese St. (20) [13] & Tulsa (16) [16] (Independence, 1976) (205 yards)

MOST YARDS PENALIZED
202—Miami (Fla.) (46) vs. Texas (3) (Cotton, 1991) (16 penalties)

MOST YARDS PENALIZED, BOTH TEAMS
270—Miami (Fla.) (46) [202] & Texas (3) [68] (Cotton, 1991)

FEWEST PENALTIES
0—By eight teams (see Team Record Lists)

FEWEST PENALTIES, BOTH TEAMS
3—In five games (see Team Record Lists)

FEWEST YARDS PENALIZED
0—By eight teams (see Team Record Lists)

FEWEST YARDS PENALIZED, BOTH TEAMS
10—Duquesne (13) [5] & Mississippi St. (12) [5] (Orange, 1937)

Individual Record Lists

Only official records after 1937 are included. Prior records are included if able to be substantiated. Each team's score is in parentheses after the team name. The year listed is the actual (calendar) year the game was played; the date is included if the bowl was played twice (i.e., January and December) during one calendar year. The list also includes discontinued bowls, marked with (D). Bowls are listed by the name of the bowl at the time it was played: The Florida Citrus Bowl was the Tangerine Bowl in 1947-82; the first Hall of Fame Bowl (1977-85) was called the All-American Bowl in 1986-90; the second Hall of Fame Bowl (1986-95) is now called the Outback Bowl and is played in Tampa, Fla.; the Sun Bowl was called the John Hancock Bowl in 1989-93, the John Hancock Sun Bowl in 1987-88, and reverted to the Sun Bowl in 1994; and the Blockbuster Bowl changed its name to Carquest Bowl in 1993.

Total Offense

MOST PLAYS
74—(D) Tony Kimbrough, Western Mich. (30) vs. Fresno St. (35) (California, 1988)
68—Hines Ward, Georgia (27) vs. Virginia (34) (Peach, Dec. 30, 1995)
67—Ty Detmer, Brigham Young (39) vs. Penn St. (50) (Holiday, 1989)
65—Shane Matthews, Florida (28) vs. Notre Dame (39) (Sugar, 1992)
65—Tony Eason, Illinois (15) vs. Alabama (21) (Liberty, 1982)
65—Buster O'Brien, Richmond (49) vs. Ohio (42) (Tangerine, 1968)
63—(D) Steve Clarkson, San Jose St. (25) vs. Toledo (27) (California, 1981)
62—Mark Young, Mississippi (20) vs. Texas Tech (17) (Independence, 1986)
62—Jack Trudeau, Illinois (29) vs. Army (31) (Peach, 1985)
62—Dennis Sproul, Arizona St. (30) vs. Penn St. (42) (Fiesta, 1977)
61—Jeff Blake, East Caro. (37) vs. North Caro. St. (34) (Peach, 1992)
61—Shawn Halloran, Boston College (27) vs. Georgia (24) (Hall of Fame, 1986)
61—Kim Hammond, Florida St. (17) vs. Penn St. (17) (Gator, 1967)
59—Vinny Testaverde, Miami (Fla.) (10) vs. Penn St. (14) (Fiesta, 1987)
59—Jim McMahon, Brigham Young (46) vs. Southern Methodist (45) (Holiday, 1980)
58—Terrence Jones, Tulane (12) vs. Washington (24) (Independence, 1987)
58—(D) Jerry Rhome, Tulsa (14) vs. Mississippi (7) (Bluebonnet, 1964)

MOST TOTAL YARDS
594—Ty Detmer, Brigham Young (39) vs. Penn St. (50) (Holiday, 1989) (576 pass)
486—Buster O'Brien, Richmond (49) vs. Ohio (42) (Tangerine, 1968) (447 pass)
481—(D) Chuck Long, Iowa (55) vs. Texas (17) (Freedom, 1984) (461 pass)
474—Trent Dilfer, Fresno St. (30) vs. Colorado (41) (Aloha, 1993) (523 pass)
469—Hines Ward, Georgia (27) vs. Virginia (34) (Peach, Dec. 30, 1995) (413 pass)
464—(D) Steve Clarkson, San Jose St. (25) vs. Toledo (27) (California, 1981) (467 pass)
454—John Walsh, Brigham Young (31) vs. Oklahoma (6) (Copper, 1994) (454 pass)
446—(D) Whit Taylor, Vanderbilt (28) vs. Air Force (36) (Hall of Fame, 1982) (452 pass)
446—Jim McMahon, Brigham Young (46) vs. Southern Methodist (45) (Holiday, 1980) (446 pass)
431—Browning Nagle, Louisville (34) vs. Alabama (7) (Fiesta, 1991) (451 pass)
431—(D) Tony Kimbrough, Western Mich. (30) vs. Fresno St. (35) (California, 1988) (366 pass)
420—(D) Ralph Martini, San Jose St. (48) vs. Central Mich. (24) (California, 1990) (404 pass)
414—Peter Tom Willis, Florida St. (41) vs. Nebraska (17) (Fiesta, 1990) (422 pass)
413—Tony Eason, Illinois (15) vs. Alabama (21) (Liberty, 1982) (423 pass)
412—David Smith, Alabama (29) vs. Army (28) (John Hancock Sun, 1988) (412 pass)
410—Chuck Hartlieb, Iowa (23) vs. North Caro. St. (28) (Peach, Dec. 31, 1988) (428 pass)
408—Marc Wilson, Brigham Young (37) vs. Indiana (38) (Holiday, 1979) (380 pass)
407—Jack Trudeau, Illinois (29) vs. Army (31) (Peach, 1985) (401 pass)

HIGHEST AVERAGE PER PLAY (Minimum 10 Plays)
24.1—Dicky Maegle, Rice (28) vs. Alabama (6) (Cotton, 1954) (11 for 265 yards)
14.1—Marcus Dupree, Oklahoma (21) vs. Arizona St. (32) (Fiesta, 1983) (17 for 239 yards)
14.0—Bucky Richardson, Texas A&M (65) vs. Brigham Young (14) (Holiday, 1990) (23 for 322 yards)
13.2—Kordell Stewart, Colorado (41) vs. Notre Dame (24) (Fiesta, 1995) (28 for 369)
12.2—Ger Schwedes, Syracuse (23) vs. Texas (14) (Cotton, 1960) (10 for 122 yards)
12.0—Tony Rice, Notre Dame (34) vs. West Va. (21) (Fiesta, 1989) (24 for 288 yards)
11.3—Rob Johnson, Southern Cal (55) vs. Texas Tech (14) (Cotton, 1995) (24 for 271 yards)
11.2—(D) Dwight Ford, Southern Cal (47) vs. Texas A&M (28) (Bluebonnet, 1977) (14 for 157 yards)
11.1—Browning Nagle, Louisville (34) vs. Alabama (7) (Fiesta, 1991) (39 for 431 yards)
10.8—Byron Hanspard, Texas Tech (55) vs. Air Force (41) (Copper, 1995) (24 for 260 yards)
10.8—Danny White, Arizona St. (49) vs. Missouri (35) (Fiesta, 1972) (27 for 291 yards)
10.8—(D) Ralph Martini, San Jose St. (48) vs. Central Mich. (24) (California, 1990) (39 for 420 yards)
10.5—(D) Chuck Long, Iowa (55) vs. Texas (17) (Freedom, 1984) (46 for 481 yards)
10.4—Frank Sinkwich, Georgia (40) vs. Texas Christian (26) (Orange, 1942) (35 for 365 yards)
10.3—Chuck Curtis, Texas Christian (28) vs. Syracuse (27) (Cotton, 1957) (18 for 185 yards)

MOST TOUCHDOWNS RESPONSIBLE FOR (TDS SCORED & PASSED FOR)
6—(D) Chuck Long, Iowa (55) vs. Texas (17) (Freedom, 1984) (6 pass)
6—Bobby Layne, Texas (40) vs. Missouri (27) (Cotton, 1946) (3 rush, 2 pass, 1 catch)
5—Jeff Blake, East Caro. (37) vs. North Caro. St. (34) (Peach, 1992) (4 pass, 1 rush)
5—Peter Tom Willis, Florida St. (41) vs. Nebraska (17) (Fiesta, 1990) (5 pass)
5—(D) Sheldon Canley, San Jose St. (48) vs. Central Mich. (24) (California, 1990) (4 rush, 1 pass)
5—Buster O'Brien, Richmond (49) vs. Ohio (42) (Tangerine, 1968) (4 pass, 1 rush)
5—Steve Tensi, Florida St. (36) vs. Oklahoma (19) (Gator, Jan. 2, 1965) (5 pass)
5—Neil Snow, Michigan (49) vs. Stanford (0) (Rose, 1902) (5 rush)

Rushing

MOST RUSHING ATTEMPTS
46—(D) Ron Jackson, Tulsa (28) vs. San Diego St. (17) (Freedom, 1991) (211 yards)
41—Blake Ezor, Michigan St. (33) vs. Hawaii (13) (Aloha, 1989) (179 yards)
39—Terrell Fletcher, Wisconsin (34) vs. Duke (20) (Hall of Fame, 1995) (241 yards)
39—Raymont Harris, Ohio St. (28) vs. Brigham Young (21) (Holiday, 1993) (235 yards)
39—Errict Rhett, Florida (27) vs. North Caro. St. (10) (Gator, 1992) (182 yards)
39—Charlie Wysocki, Maryland (20) vs. Florida (35) (Tangerine, 1980) (159 yards)
39—Charles White, Southern Cal (17) vs. Ohio St. (16) (Rose, 1980) (247 yards)
37—(D) Charles Davis, Colorado (29) vs. Houston (17) (Bluebonnet, 1971) (202 yards)

BOWL/ALL-STAR RECORDS

36—Brent Moss, Wisconsin (21) vs. UCLA (16) (Rose, 1994) (158 yards)
36—Herschel Walker, Georgia (17) vs. Notre Dame (10) (Sugar, 1981) (150 yards)
36—Don McCauley, North Caro. (26) vs. Arizona St. (48) (Peach, 1970) (143 yards)
35—Blair Thomas, Penn St. (50) vs. Brigham Young (39) (Holiday, 1989) (186 yards)
35—Lorenzo White, Michigan St. (20) vs. Southern Cal (17) (Rose, 1988) (113 yards)
35—(D) Robert Newhouse, Houston (17) vs. Colorado (29) (Bluebonnet, 1971) (168 yards)
35—Ed Williams, West Va. (14) vs. South Caro. (3) (Peach, 1969) (208 yards)
35—Bob Anderson, Colorado (47) vs. Alabama (33) (Liberty, 1969) (254 yards)
34—(D) Curtis Dickey, Texas A&M (28) vs. Iowa St. (12) (Hall of Fame, 1978) (276 yards)
34—Vic Bottari, California (13) vs. Alabama (0) (Rose, 1938) (137 yards)
34—Ernie Nevers, Stanford (10) vs. Notre Dame (27) (Rose, 1925) (114 yards)

MOST NET RUSHING YARDS

280—(D) James Gray, Texas Tech (49) vs. Duke (21) (All-American, 1989) (33 carries)
276—(D) Curtis Dickey, Texas A&M (28) vs. Iowa St. (12) (Hall of Fame, 1978) (34 carries)
266—(D) Gaston Green, UCLA (31) vs. Brigham Young (10) (Freedom, 1986) (33 carries)
265—Dicky Maegle, Rice (28) vs. Alabama (6) (Cotton, 1954) (11 carries)
260—Byron Hanspard, Texas Tech (55) vs. Air Force (41) (Copper, 1995) (24 carries)
254—Bob Anderson, Colorado (47) vs. Alabama (33) (Liberty, 1969) (35 carries)
250—Chuck Webb, Tennessee (31) vs. Arkansas (27) (Cotton, 1990) (26 carries)
247—Charles White, Southern Cal (17) vs. Ohio St. (16) (Rose, 1980) (39 carries)
241—Terrell Fletcher, Wisconsin (34) vs. Duke (20) (Hall of Fame, 1995) (39 carries)
239—Marcus Dupree, Oklahoma (21) vs. Arizona St. (32) (Fiesta, 1983) (17 carries)
235—Tyrone Wheatley, Michigan (38) vs. Washington (31) (Rose, 1993) (15 carries)
235—Raymont Harris, Ohio St. (28) vs. Brigham Young (21) (Holiday, 1993) (39 carries)
234—Kevin Faulk, LSU (45) vs. Michigan St. (26) (Independence, 1995) (25 carries)
234—Jamie Morris, Michigan (28) vs. Alabama (24) (Hall of Fame, 1988) (23 carries)
227—Eric Ball, UCLA (45) vs. Iowa (28) (Rose, 1986) (22 carries)
225—Craig James, Southern Methodist (45) vs. Brigham Young (46) (Holiday, 1980) (23 carries)
222—Barry Sanders, Oklahoma St. (62) vs. Wyoming (14) (Holiday, 1988) (29 carries)
216—Floyd Little, Syracuse (12) vs. Tennessee (18) (Gator, 1966) (29 carries)
211—(D) Ron Jackson, Tulsa (28) vs. San Diego St. (17) (Freedom, 1991) (46 carries)
208—Ed Williams, West Va. (14) vs. South Caro. (3) (Peach, 1969) (35 carries)
205—(D) Sammie Smith, Florida St. (27) vs. Indiana (13) (All-American, 1986) (25 carries)
205—Roland Sales, Arkansas (31) vs. Oklahoma (6) (Orange, 1978) (22 carries)
202—Tony Dorsett, Pittsburgh (27) vs. Georgia (3) (Sugar, 1977) (32 carries)
202—Woody Green, Arizona St. (49) vs. Missouri (35) (Fiesta, 1972) (25 carries)
202—(D) Charles Davis, Colorado (29) vs. Houston (17) (Bluebonnet, 1971) (37 carries)

MOST NET RUSHING YARDS BY A QUARTERBACK

199—Tommie Frazier, Nebraska (62) vs. Florida (24) (Fiesta, 1996) (16 carries)
180—(D) Mike Mosley, Texas A&M (28) vs. Southern Cal (47) (Bluebonnet, 1977) (20 carries)
164—Eddie Phillips, Texas (11) vs. Notre Dame (24) (Cotton, 1971) (23 carries)
143—Kordell Stewart, Colorado (41) vs. Notre Dame (24) (Fiesta, 1995) (7 carries)
136—(D) Nate Sassaman, Army (10) vs. Michigan St. (6) (Cherry, 1984) (28 carries)
133—(D) Eddie Wolgast, Arizona (13) vs. Drake (14) (Salad, 1949) (22 carries) (listed in newspaper accounts as halfback but also attempted 15 passes in game)
129—Beau Morgan, Air Force (41) vs. Texas Tech (55) (Copper, 1995) (22 carries)
129—Rex Kern, Ohio St. (17) vs. Stanford (27) (Rose, 1971) (20 carries)
127—J. C. Watts, Oklahoma (24) vs. Florida St. (7) (Orange, 1980) (12 carries)
119—Bucky Richardson, Texas A&M (65) vs. Brigham Young (14) (Holiday, 1990) (12 carries)
113—Harry Gilmer, Alabama (34) vs. Southern Cal (14) (Rose, 1946)
107—Darrell Shepard, Oklahoma (40) vs. Houston (14) (Sun, 1981) (12 carries)
103—Major Harris, West Va. (33) vs. Oklahoma St. (35) (John Hancock Sun, 1987)

HIGHEST AVERAGE PER RUSH
(Minimum 9 Carries)

24.1—Dicky Maegle, Rice (28) vs. Alabama (6) (Cotton, 1954) (11 for 265 yards)
21.6—Bob Jeter, Iowa (38) vs. California (12) (Rose, 1959) (9 for 194 yards)
15.7—Tyrone Wheatley, Michigan (38) vs. Washington (31) (Rose, 1993) (15 for 235 yards)
14.2—(D) Gary Anderson, Arkansas (34) vs. Tulane (15) (Hall of Fame, 1980) (11 for 156 yards)
14.1—Mike Holovak, Boston College (21) vs. Alabama (37) (Orange, 1943) (10 for 141 yards)
14.1—Marcus Dupree, Oklahoma (21) vs. Arizona St. (32) (Fiesta, 1983) (17 for 239 yards)
12.6—Randy Baldwin, Mississippi (42) vs. Air Force (29) (Liberty, 1989) (14 for 177 yards)
12.6—Ben Barnett, Army (28) vs. Alabama (29) (John Hancock Sun, 1988) (14 for 177 yards)
12.4—Tommie Frazier, Nebraska (62) vs. Florida (24) (Fiesta, 1996) (16 for 199 yards)
12.3—George Smith, Texas Tech (28) vs. North Caro. (32) (Sun, 1972) (14 for 172 yards)
11.2—(D) Dwight Ford, Southern Cal (47) vs. Texas A&M (28) (Bluebonnet, 1977) (14 for 157 yards)
11.2—Elliott Walker, Pittsburgh (33) vs. Kansas (19) (Sun, 1975) (11 for 123 yards)
10.9—Rodney Hampton, Georgia (34) vs. Michigan St. (27) (Gator, Jan. 1, 1989) (10 for 109 yards)
10.8—Bobby Cavazos, Texas Tech (35) vs. Auburn (13) (Gator, Jan. 1, 1954) (13 for 141 yards)
10.8—Byron Hanspard, Texas Tech (55) vs. Air Force (41) (Copper, 1995) (24 for 260 yards)
10.6—J. C. Watts, Oklahoma (24) vs. Florida St. (7) (Orange, 1980) (12 for 127 yards)
10.5—Ray Brown, Mississippi (39) vs. Texas (7) (Sugar, 1958) (15 for 157 yards)
10.3—Eric Ball, UCLA (45) vs. Iowa (28) (Rose, 1986) (22 for 227 yards)
10.2—(D) Bill Tobin, Missouri (14) vs. Georgia Tech (10) (Bluebonnet, 1962) (11 for 112 yards)
10.2—Jamie Morris, Michigan (28) vs. Alabama (24) (Hall of Fame, 1988) (23 for 234 yards)

THREE RUSHERS, SAME TEAM, GAINING MORE THAN 100 YARDS

366—Tony Dorsett (142), Elliott Walker (123) & Robert Haygood (QB) (101), Pittsburgh (33) vs. Kansas (19) (Sun, 1975)

TWO RUSHERS, SAME TEAM, GAINING MORE THAN 100 YARDS

373—Woody Green (202) & Brent McClanahan (171), Arizona St. (49) vs. Missouri (35) (Fiesta, 1972)
365—(D) George Woodard (185) & Mike Mosley (QB) (180), Texas A&M (28) vs. Southern Cal (47) (Bluebonnet, 1977)
365—Bob Anderson (254) & Jim Bratten (111), Colorado (47) vs. Alabama (33) (Liberty, 1969)
364—Tommie Frazier (QB) (199) & Lawrence Phillips (165), Nebraska (62) vs. Florida (24) (Fiesta, 1996)
347—Walter Packer (183) & Terry Vitrano (164), Mississippi St. (26) vs. North Caro. (24) (Sun, 1974)
343—(D) Charles White (186) & Dwight Ford (157), Southern Cal (47) vs. Texas A&M (28) (Bluebonnet, 1977)
330—Floyd Little (216) & Larry Csonka (114), Syracuse (12) vs. Tennessee (18) (Gator, 1966)
297—Monroe Eley (173) & Bob Thomas (124), Arizona St. (48) vs. North Caro. (26) (Peach, 1970)
292—Kelvin Bryant (148) & Ethan Horton (144), North Caro. (31) vs. Arkansas (27) (Gator, 1981)
291—Billy Sims (164) & J. C. Watts (QB) (127), Oklahoma (24) vs. Florida St. (7) (Orange, 1980)
288—Billy Sims (181) & Darrell Shepard (QB) (107), Oklahoma (40) vs. Houston (14) (Sun, 1981)
277—Danta Johnson (148) & Beau Morgan (QB) (129), Air Force (41) vs. Texas Tech (55) (Copper, 1995)
277—Willie Heston (170) & Neil Snow (107), Michigan (49) vs. Stanford (0) (Rose, 1902)
270—Anthony Brown (167) & Major Harris (QB) (103), West Va. (33) vs. Oklahoma St. (35) (John Hancock Sun, 1987)
257—Sedrick Shaw (135) & Tavian Banks (122), Iowa (38) vs. Washington (18) (Sun, 1995)
253—Alois Blackwell (149) & Dyral Thomas (104), Houston (30) vs. Maryland (21) (Cotton, 1977)
246—T. Robert Hopkins (125) & Leonard Brown (121), Missouri (27) vs. Texas (40) (Cotton, 1946)
240—Jon Vaughn (128) & Ricky Powers (112), Michigan (35) vs. Mississippi (3) (Gator, Jan. 1, 1991)
237—James Rouse (134) & Barry Foster (103), Arkansas (27) vs. Tennessee (31) (Cotton, 1990)
237—Raymond Bybee (127) & Thomas Reamon (110), Missouri (34) vs. Auburn (17) (Sun, 1973)
230—Rex Kern (QB) (129) & John Brockington (101), Ohio St. (17) vs. Stanford (27) (Rose, 1971)
223—Bucky Richardson (QB) (119) & Darren Lewis (104), Texas A&M (65) vs. Brigham Young (14) (Holiday, 1990)
222—(D) Marshall Johnson (114) & Donnie McGraw (108), Houston (47) vs. Tulane (7) (Bluebonnet, 1973)
218—Travis Sims (113) & Michael Carter (105), Hawaii (27) vs. Illinois (17) (Holiday, 1992)
218—Steve Giese (111) & Bob Torrey (107), Penn St. (42) vs. Arizona St. (30) (Fiesta, 1977)
215—Jeff Atkins (112) & Reggie Dupard (103), Southern Methodist (27) vs. Notre Dame (20) (Aloha, 1984)
215—Allen Pinkett (111) & Chris Smith (104), Notre Dame (19) vs. Boston College (18) (Liberty, 1983)
204—Johnny "Ham" Jones (104) & Johnny "Jam" Jones (100), Texas (42) vs. Maryland (0) (Sun, 1978)
201—Jerome Heavens (101) & Vagas Ferguson (100), Notre Dame (38) vs. Texas (10) (Cotton, 1978)

MOST RUSHING TOUCHDOWNS

5—Barry Sanders, Oklahoma St. (62) vs. Wyoming (14) (Holiday, 1988) (runs of 33, 2, 67, 1, 10)
5—Neil Snow, Michigan (49) vs. Stanford (0) (Rose, 1902) (five-point scores)
4—Byron Hanspard, Texas Tech (55) vs. Air Force (41) (Copper, 1995) (runs of 2, 11, 2, 29)
4—Wasean Tait, Toledo (40) vs. Nevada (37) (OT) (Las Vegas, 1995) (runs of 18, 31, 26, 3)
4—(D) Ron Jackson, Tulsa (28) vs. San Diego St. (17) (Freedom, 1991) (runs of 10, 6, 3, 4)
4—(D) Sheldon Canley, San Jose St. (48) vs. Central Mich. (24) (California, 1990) (runs of 5, 22, 59, 5)

4—(D) James Gray, Texas Tech (49) vs. Duke (21) (All-American, 1989) (runs of 2, 54, 18, 32)
4—Thurman Thomas, Oklahoma St. (35) vs. West Va. (33) (John Hancock Sun, 1987) (runs of 5, 9, 4, 4)
4—Eric Ball, UCLA (45) vs. Iowa (28) (Rose, 1986) (runs of 30, 40, 6, 32)
4—Terry Miller, Oklahoma St. (49) vs. Brigham Young (21) (Tangerine, 1976) (runs of 3, 78, 6, 1)
4—Sam Cunningham, Southern Cal (42) vs. Ohio St. (17) (Rose, 1973) (runs of 2, 1, 1, 1)
4—Woody Green, Arizona St. (49) vs. Missouri (35) (Fiesta, 1972) (runs of 2, 12, 17, 21)
4—Charles Cole, Toledo (56) vs. Davidson (33) (Tangerine, 1969) (runs of 1, 11, 16, 1)
4—(D) Gene Shannon, Houston (26) vs. Dayton (21) (Salad, 1952) (runs of 15, 19, 1, 10)

Passing

MOST PASS ATTEMPTS
63—Trent Dilfer, Fresno St. (30) vs. Colorado (41) (Aloha, 1993)
62—(D) Steve Clarkson, San Jose St. (25) vs. Toledo (27) (California, 1981)
61—Danny O'Neil, Oregon (20) vs. Penn St. (38) (Rose, 1995)
61—(D) Sean Covey, Brigham Young (16) vs. Virginia (22) (All-American, 1987)
59—Hines Ward, Georgia (27) vs. Virginia (34) (Peach, Dec. 30, 1995)
59—Ty Detmer, Brigham Young (39) vs. Penn St. (50) (Holiday, 1989)
58—Shane Matthews, Florida (28) vs. Notre Dame (39) (Sugar, 1992)
58—Buster O'Brien, Richmond (49) vs. Ohio (42) (Tangerine, 1968)
57—(D) Tony Kimbrough, Western Mich. (30) vs. Fresno St. (35) (California, 1988)
56—Gino Torretta, Miami (Fla.) (13) vs. Alabama (34) (Sugar, 1993)
55—Jack Trudeau, Illinois (29) vs. Army (31) (Peach, 1985)
55—Tony Eason, Illinois (15) vs. Alabama (21) (Liberty, 1982)
53—Tim Cowan, Washington (21) vs. Maryland (20) (Aloha, 1982)
53—Kim Hammond, Florida St. (17) vs. Penn St. (17) (Gator, 1967)
52—David Smith, Alabama (29) vs. Army (28) (John Hancock Sun, 1988)
52—Shawn Halloran, Boston College (27) vs. Georgia (24) (Hall of Fame, 1986)
51—Jeff Blake, East Caro. (37) vs. North Caro. St. (34) (Peach, 1992)
51—Danny McManus, Florida St. (31) vs. Nebraska (28) (Fiesta, 1988)
51—Chuck Hartlieb, Iowa (23) vs. North Caro. St. (28) (Peach, Dec. 31, 1988)
51—Craig Burnett, Wyoming (19) vs. Iowa (20) (Holiday, 1987)
51—(D) Whit Taylor, Vanderbilt (28) vs. Air Force (36) (Hall of Fame, 1982)

MOST PASS COMPLETIONS
43—(D) Steve Clarkson, San Jose St. (25) vs. Toledo (27) (California, 1981)
42—Ty Detmer, Brigham Young (39) vs. Penn St. (50) (Holiday, 1989)
41—Danny O'Neil, Oregon (20) vs. Penn St. (38) (Rose, 1995)
39—Buster O'Brien, Richmond (49) vs. Ohio (42) (Tangerine, 1968)
38—Jack Trudeau, Illinois (29) vs. Army (31) (Peach, 1985)
38—(D) Whit Taylor, Vanderbilt (28) vs. Air Force (36) (Hall of Fame, 1982)
37—Trent Dilfer, Fresno St. (30) vs. Colorado (41) (Aloha, 1993)
37—(D) Sean Covey, Brigham Young (16) vs. Virginia (22) (All-American, 1987)
37—Kim Hammond, Florida St. (17) vs. Penn St. (17) (Gator, 1967)
35—Tony Eason, Illinois (15) vs. Alabama (21) (Liberty, 1982)
33—David Smith, Alabama (29) vs. Army (28) (John Hancock Sun, 1988)
33—Tim Cowan, Washington (21) vs. Maryland (20) (Aloha, 1982)
33—Ron VanderKelen, Wisconsin (37) vs. Southern Cal (42) (Rose, 1963)
32—Jim McMahon, Brigham Young (46) vs. Southern Methodist (45) (Holiday, 1980)
31—Hines Ward, Georgia (27) vs. Virginia (34) (Peach, Dec. 30, 1995)
31—John Walsh, Brigham Young (31) vs. Oklahoma (6) (Copper, 1994)
31—Jeff Blake, East Caro. (37) vs. North Caro. St. (34) (Peach, 1992)
31—Stan White, Auburn (27) vs. Indiana (23) (Peach, 1990)
31—Shawn Halloran, Boston College (27) vs. Georgia (24) (Hall of Fame, 1986)
31—Mark Young, Mississippi (20) vs. Texas Tech (17) (Independence, 1986)
31—Bernie Kosar, Miami (Fla.) (37) vs. UCLA (39) (Fiesta, 1985)
31—John Congemi, Pittsburgh (23) vs. Ohio St. (28) (Fiesta, 1984)
31—(D) Jeff Tedford, Fresno St. (29) vs. Bowling Green (28) (California, 1982)

MOST CONSECUTIVE PASS COMPLETIONS
10—Danny Wuerffel, Florida (17) vs. Florida St. (23) (Sugar, Jan. 2, 1995)
10—Rick Neuheisel, UCLA (45) vs. Illinois (9) (Rose, 1984)
9—(D) Rob Johnson, Southern Cal (28) vs. Utah (21) (Freedom, 1993)
9—Bill Montgomery, Arkansas (16) vs. Georgia (2) (Sugar, 1969)
9—Glenn Dobbs, Tulsa (7) vs. Tennessee (14) (Sugar, 1943)
8—Billy Roland, Houston (49) vs. Miami (Ohio) (21) (Tangerine, 1962)
8—Bobby Layne, Texas (40) vs. Missouri (27) (Cotton, 1946)
8—Harry Gilmer, Alabama (26) vs. Duke (29) (Sugar, 1945)
7—(D) Daniel Ford, Arizona St. (33) vs. Air Force (28) (Freedom, 1987)

MOST NET PASSING YARDS
(Followed by Comp.-Att.-Int.)
576—Ty Detmer, Brigham Young (39) vs. Penn St. (50) (Holiday, 1989) (42-59-2)
523—Trent Dilfer, Fresno St. (30) vs. Colorado (41) (Aloha, 1993) (37-63-1)
476—Drew Bledsoe, Washington St. (31) vs. Utah (28) (Copper, 1992) (30-46-1)
467—(D) Steve Clarkson, San Jose St. (25) vs. Toledo (27) (California, 1981) (43-62-5)
461—(D) Chuck Long, Iowa (55) vs. Texas (17) (Freedom, 1984) (29-39-0)
456—Danny O'Neil, Oregon (20) vs. Penn St. (38) (Rose, 1995) (41-61-2)
454—John Walsh, Brigham Young (31) vs. Oklahoma (6) (Copper, 1994) (31-45-0)

Photo from Toledo sports information

Toledo's Wasean Tait rushed for four touchdowns, including the game winner in overtime, to lead the Rockets to a 40-37 victory over Nevada in the 1995 Las Vegas Bowl, the first bowl game decided with the NCAA tiebreaker. Only two players have rushed for more touchdowns in a single bowl game.

452—(D) Whit Taylor, Vanderbilt (28) vs. Air Force (36) (Hall of Fame, 1982) (38-51-3)
451—Browning Nagle, Louisville (34) vs. Alabama (7) (Fiesta, 1991) (20-33-1)
447—Buster O'Brien, Richmond (49) vs. Ohio (42) (Tangerine, 1968) (39-58-2)
446—Jim McMahon, Brigham Young (46) vs. Southern Methodist (45) (Holiday, 1980) (32-49-1)
428—Chuck Hartlieb, Iowa (23) vs. North Caro. St. (28) (Peach, Dec. 31, 1988) (30-51-4)
423—Tony Eason, Illinois (15) vs. Alabama (21) (Liberty, 1982) (35-55-4)
422—Peter Tom Willis, Florida St. (41) vs. Nebraska (17) (Fiesta, 1990) (25-40-0)
413—Hines Ward, Georgia (27) vs. Virginia (34) (Peach, Dec. 30, 1995) (31-59-2)
412—David Smith, Alabama (29) vs. Army (28) (John Hancock Sun, 1988) (33-52-1)
404—(D) Ralph Martini, San Jose St. (48) vs. Central Mich. (24) (California, 1990) (27-36-1)
401—Jack Trudeau, Illinois (29) vs. Army (31) (Peach, 1985) (38-55-2)
401—Ron VanderKelen, Wisconsin (37) vs. Southern Cal (42) (Rose, 1963) (33-48-3)

MOST NET PASSING YARDS, ONE QUARTER
223—Browning Nagle, Louisville (34) vs. Alabama (7) (Fiesta, 1991) (1st, 9 of 16)
202—(D) Bret Stafford, Texas (32) vs. Pittsburgh (27) (Bluebonnet, 1987) (1st)

MOST TOUCHDOWN PASSES THROWN
6—(D) Chuck Long, Iowa (55) vs. Texas (17) (Freedom, 1984) (29-39-0) (6, 11, 33, 49, 4, 15 yards)
5—Peter Tom Willis, Florida St. (41) vs. Nebraska (17) (Fiesta, 1990)
5—Steve Tensi, Florida St. (36) vs. Oklahoma (19) (Gator, Jan. 2, 1965)
4—Danny Kanell, Florida St. (31) vs. Notre Dame (26) (Orange, 1996)
4—Wally Richardson, Penn St. (43) vs. Auburn (14) (Outback, 1996)
4—Brian Kavanagh, Kansas St. (54) vs. Colorado St. (21) (Holiday, 1995)
4—Johnny Johnson, Illinois (30) vs. East Caro. (0) (Liberty, 1994)
4—John Walsh, Brigham Young (31) vs. Oklahoma (6) (Copper, 1994)
4—Tony Sacca, Penn St. (42) vs. Tennessee (17) (Fiesta, 1992)
4—Jeff Blake, East Caro. (37) vs. North Caro. St. (34) (Peach, 1992)
4—Elvis Grbac, Michigan (35) vs. Mississippi (3) (Gator, Jan. 1, 1991)
4—Rick Neuheisel, UCLA (45) vs. Illinois (9) (Rose, 1984)
4—Jim McMahon, Brigham Young (46) vs. Southern Methodist (45) (Holiday, 1980)
4—Mark Herrmann, Purdue (28) vs. Missouri (25) (Liberty, 1980)
4—(D) Rob Hertel, Southern Cal (47) vs. Texas A&M (28) (Bluebonnet, 1977)
4—Matt Cavanaugh, Pittsburgh (34) vs. Clemson (3) (Gator, 1977)
4—Gordon Slade, Davidson (33) vs. Toledo (55) (Tangerine, 1969)
4—Buster O'Brien, Richmond (49) vs. Ohio (42) (Tangerine, 1968)
4—Cleve Bryant, Ohio (42) vs. Richmond (49) (Tangerine, 1968)
4—Pete Beathard, Southern Cal (42) vs. Wisconsin (37) (Rose, 1963)

MOST PASSES HAD INTERCEPTED
(Followed by Comp.-Att.-Int.)

6—Bruce Lee, Arizona (10) vs. Auburn (34) (Sun, 1968) (6-24-6)
5—Wade Hill, Arkansas (15) vs. Georgia (24) (Independence, 1991) (12-31-5)
5—Kevin Murray, Texas A&M (12) vs. Ohio St. (28) (Cotton, 1987) (12-31-5)
5—Vinny Testaverde, Miami (Fla.) (10) vs. Penn St. (14) (Fiesta, 1987) (26-50-5)
5—Jeff Wickersham, LSU (10) vs. Nebraska (28) (Sugar, 1985) (20-38-5)
5—(D) Steve Clarkson, San Jose St. (25) vs. Toledo (27) (California, 1981) (43-62-5)
5—Terry McMillan, Missouri (3) vs. Penn St. (10) (Orange, 1970) (6-28-5)
5—Paul Gilbert, Georgia (6) vs. Nebraska (45) (Sun, 1969) (10-30-5)

HIGHEST COMPLETION PERCENTAGE
(Minimum 10 Attempts) (Followed by Comp.-Att.-Int.)

.917—Bobby Layne, Texas (40) vs. Missouri (27) (Cotton, 1946) (11-12-0)
.900—Ken Ploen, Iowa (35) vs. Oregon St. (19) (Rose, 1957) (9-10-0)
.846—Tom Sorley, Nebraska (21) vs. North Caro. (17) (Liberty, 1977) (11-13-0)
.833—Mike Gundy, Oklahoma St. (62) vs. Wyoming (14) (Holiday, 1988) (20-24-0)
.833—Richard Todd, Alabama (13) vs. Penn St. (6) (Sugar, 1975) (10-12-0)
.818—Bucky Richardson, Texas A&M (65) vs. Brigham Young (14) (Holiday, 1990) (9-11-0)
.806—Cale Gundy, Oklahoma (48) vs. Virginia (14) (Gator, Dec. 29, 1991) (25-31-0)
.800—Art Schlichter, Ohio St. (15) vs. Clemson (17) (Gator, 1978) (16-20-1)
.800—Jim Stevens, Georgia Tech (31) vs. Iowa St. (30) (Liberty, 1972) (12-15-0)
.800—Don Altman, Duke (7) vs. Arkansas (6) (Cotton, 1961) (12-15-0)
.800—Chuck Curtis, Texas Christian (28) vs. Syracuse (27) (Cotton, 1957) (12-15-0)
.789—Charles Ortmann, Michigan (14) vs. California (6) (Rose, 1951) (15-19-0)
.786—Mark Herrmann, Purdue (28) vs. Missouri (25) (Liberty, 1980) (22-28-0)

MOST YARDS PER PASS ATTEMPT
(Minimum 10 Attempts)

19.4—Tony Rice, Notre Dame (34) vs. West Va. (21) (Fiesta, 1989) (11 for 213)
18.7—Frank Sinkwich, Georgia (40) vs. Texas Christian (26) (Orange, 1942) (13 for 243)
18.5—Bucky Richardson, Texas A&M (65) vs. Brigham Young (14) (Holiday, 1990) (11 for 203)
17.3—Don Rumley, New Mexico (34) vs. Denver (24) (Sun, 1946) (12 for 207)
16.4—(D) Rob Hertel, Southern Cal (47) vs. Texas A&M (28) (Bluebonnet, 1977) (15 for 246)
15.4—James Street, Texas (36) vs. Tennessee (13) (Cotton, 1969) (13 for 200)
14.2—Danny White, Arizona St. (28) vs. Pittsburgh (7) (Fiesta, 1973) (19 for 269)
13.8—Rob Johnson, Southern Cal (55) vs. Texas Tech (14) (Cotton, 1995) (21 for 289)
13.7—Browning Nagle, Louisville (34) vs. Alabama (7) (Fiesta, 1991) (33 for 451)
13.6—Bob Churchich, Nebraska (28) vs. Alabama (39) (Orange, 1966) (17 for 232)
13.4—Donovan McNabb, Syracuse (41) vs. Clemson (0) (Gator, 1996) (23 for 309)
13.2—Bobby Layne, Texas (40) vs. Missouri (27) (Cotton, 1946) (12 for 158)

MOST YARDS PER PASS COMPLETION
(Minimum 7 Completions)

30.4—Tony Rice, Notre Dame (34) vs. West Va. (21) (Fiesta, 1989) (7 for 213)
30.4—Duke Carlisle, Texas (28) vs. Navy (6) (Cotton, 1964) (7 for 213)
28.6—James Street, Texas (36) vs. Tennessee (13) (Cotton, 1969) (7 for 200)
27.0—Frank Sinkwich, Georgia (40) vs. Texas Christian (26) (Orange, 1942) (9 for 243)

Receiving

MOST PASS RECEPTIONS

20—(D) Norman Jordan, Vanderbilt (28) vs. Air Force (36) (Hall of Fame, 1982) (173 yards)
20—Walker Gillette, Richmond (49) vs. Ohio (42) (Tangerine, 1968) (242 yards)
18—(D) Gerald Willhite, San Jose St. (25) vs. Toledo (27) (California, 1981) (124 yards)
15—(D) Stephone Paige, Fresno St. (29) vs. Bowling Green (28) (California, 1982) (246 yards)
14—Alex Van Dyke, Nevada (37) vs. Toledo (40) (OT) (Las Vegas, 1995) (176 yards)
14—J. J. Stokes, UCLA (16) vs. Wisconsin (21) (Rose, 1994) (176 yards)
14—Ron Sellers, Florida St. (17) vs. Penn St. (17) (Gator, 1967) (145 yards)
13—Fred Biletnikoff, Florida St. (36) vs. Oklahoma (19) (Gator, Jan. 2, 1965) (192 yards)
12—Keyshawn Johnson, Southern Cal (41) vs. Northwestern (32) (Rose, 1996) (216 yards)
12—Luke Fisher, East Caro. (37) vs. North Caro. St. (34) (Peach, 1992) (144 yards)
12—Chuck Dicus, Arkansas (16) vs. Georgia (2) (Sugar, 1969) (169 yards)
12—Bill Moremen, Florida St. (17) vs. Penn St. (17) (Gator, 1967) (106 yards)
11—Josh Wilcox, Oregon (20) vs. Penn St. (38) (Rose, 1995) (135 yards)
11—Bill Khayat, Duke (20) vs. Wisconsin (34) (Hall of Fame, 1995) (109 yards)
11—(D) Mark Szlachcic, Bowling Green (28) vs. Fresno St. (21) (California, 1991) (189 yards)
11—Ronnie Harmon, Iowa (28) vs. UCLA (45) (Rose, 1986) (102 yards)
11—David Mills, Brigham Young (24) vs. Michigan (17) (Holiday, 1984) (103 yards)
11—(D) Chip Otten, Bowling Green (28) vs. Fresno St. (29) (California, 1982) (76 yards)
11—(D) Anthony Hancock, Tennessee (28) vs. Wisconsin (21) (Garden State, 1981) (196 yards)
11—Pat Richter, Wisconsin (37) vs. Southern Cal (42) (Rose, 1963) (163 yards)
11—(D) James Ingram, Baylor (14) vs. LSU (7) (Bluebonnet, 1963) (163 yards)
10—Larry Bowie, Georgia (27) vs. Virginia (34) (Peach, Dec. 30, 1995) (156 yards)
10—Johnnie Morton, Southern Cal (28) vs. Utah (21) (Freedom, 1993) (147 yards)
10—Mike Blair, Ball St. (33) vs. Utah St. (42) (Las Vegas, 1993) (66 yards)
10—Matt Bellini, Brigham Young (39) vs. Penn St. (50) (Holiday, 1989) (124 yards)
10—Hart Lee Dykes, Oklahoma St. (62) vs. Wyoming (14) (Holiday, 1988) (163 yards)
10—(D) David Miles, Brigham Young (16) vs. Virginia (22) (All-American, 1987) (188 yards)
10—Lakei Heimuli, Brigham Young (7) vs. Ohio St. (10) (Florida Citrus, 1985)
10—Bobby Joe Edmonds, Arkansas (15) vs. Auburn (21) (Liberty, 1984)
10—David Williams, Illinois (9) vs. UCLA (45) (Rose, 1984)
10—Kelly Smith, Brigham Young (24) vs. Michigan (17) (Holiday, 1984) (88 yards)
10—Paul Skansi, Washington (21) vs. Maryland (20) (Aloha, 1982) (87 yards)
10—(D) Tim Kearse, San Jose St. (25) vs. Toledo (27) (California, 1981) (104 yards)
10—Scott Phillips, Brigham Young (46) vs. Southern Methodist (45) (Holiday, 1980) (81 yards)
10—Gordon Jones, Pittsburgh (34) vs. Clemson (3) (Gator, 1977) (163 yards)
10—Bobby Crockett, Arkansas (7) vs. LSU (14) (Cotton, Jan. 1, 1966)
10—Ron Stover, Oregon (7) vs. Ohio St. (10) (Rose, 1958) (144 yards)

MOST PASS RECEIVING YARDS

252—Andre Rison, Michigan St. (27) vs. Georgia (34) (Gator, Jan. 1, 1989) (9 catches)
246—(D) Stephone Paige, Fresno St. (29) vs. Bowling Green (28) (California, 1982) (15 catches)
242—(D) Tony Jones, Texas (32) vs. Pittsburgh (27) (Bluebonnet, 1987) (8 catches)
242—Walker Gillette, Richmond (49) vs. Ohio (42) (Tangerine, 1968) (20 catches)
222—Keyshawn Johnson, Southern Cal (55) vs. Texas Tech (14) (Cotton, 1995) (8 catches)
216—Keyshawn Johnson, Southern Cal (41) vs. Northwestern (32) (Rose, 1996) (12 catches)
212—Phillip Bobo, Washington St. (31) vs. Utah (28) (Copper, 1992) (7 catches)
201—(D) Bob McChesney, Hardin-Simmons (49) vs. Wichita St. (12) (Camellia, 1948) (8 catches)
196—(D) Anthony Hancock, Tennessee (28) vs. Wisconsin (21) (Garden State, 1981) (11 catches)
192—Fred Biletnikoff, Florida St. (36) vs. Oklahoma (19) (Gator, Jan. 2, 1965) (13 catches)
189—(D) Mark Szlachcic, Bowling Green (28) vs. Fresno St. (21) (California, 1991) (11 catches)
188—(D) David Miles, Brigham Young (16) vs. Virginia (22) (All-American, 1987) (10 catches)
186—Greg Hudson, Arizona St. (28) vs. Pittsburgh (7) (Fiesta, 1973) (8 catches)
182—Rob Turner, Indiana (34) vs. South Caro. (10) (Liberty, 1988) (5 catches)
178—Ray Perkins, Alabama (34) vs. Nebraska (7) (Sugar, 1967) (7 catches)
177—Thomas Lewis, Indiana (20) vs. Virginia Tech (45) (Independence, 1993) (6 catches)
176—Alex Van Dyke, Nevada (37) vs. Toledo (40) (OT) (Las Vegas, 1995) (14 catches)
176—J. J. Stokes, UCLA (16) vs. Wisconsin (21) (Rose, 1994) (14 catches)
173—Marvin Harrison, Syracuse (41) vs. Clemson (0) (Gator, 1996) (7 catches)
173—(D) Norman Jordan, Vanderbilt (28) vs. Air Force (36) (Hall of Fame, 1982) (20 catches)
172—Cris Carter, Ohio St. (17) vs. Southern Cal (20) (Rose, 1985) (9 catches)

HIGHEST AVERAGE PER RECEPTION
(Minimum 3 Receptions)

52.3—Phil Harris, Texas (28) vs. Navy (6) (Cotton, 1964) (3 for 157 yards)
39.7—Ike Hilliard, Florida (17) vs. Florida St. (23) (Sugar, Jan. 2, 1995) (3 for 119 yards)
36.4—Rob Turner, Indiana (34) vs. South Caro. (10) (Liberty, 1988) (5 for 182 yards)
36.3—Clarence Cannon, Boston College (31) vs. Virginia (13) (Carquest, 1994) (3 for 109 yards)
35.5—Rodney Harris, Kansas (23) vs. Brigham Young (20) (Aloha, 1992) (4 for 142 yards)
35.3—Anthony Carter, Michigan (15) vs. North Caro. (17) (Gator, 1979) (4 for 141 yards)
34.3—(D) Andre Alexander, Fresno St. (35) vs. Western Mich. (30) (California, 1988) (3 for 103 yards)
34.3—Ron Beverly, Arizona St. (49) vs. Missouri (35) (Fiesta, 1972) (3 for 103 yards)
34.0—Jimmy Cefalo, Penn St. (41) vs. Baylor (20) (Cotton, 1975) (3 for 102 yards)
33.7—Justin Shull, Colorado St. (14) vs. Michigan (24) (Holiday, 1994) (3 for 101 yards)
33.7—J. D. Hill, Arizona St. (48) vs. North Caro. (26) (Peach, 1970) (3 for 101 yards)
33.3—Tony Buford, Indiana (34) vs. South Caro. (10) (Liberty, 1988) (3 for 100 yards)
33.2—Melvin Bonner, Baylor (20) vs. Arizona (15) (John Hancock, 1992) (5 for 166 yards)
33.2—Todd Dixon, Wake Forest (39) vs. Oregon (35) (Independence, 1992) (5 for 166 yards)
33.0—Ed Hervey, Southern Cal (55) vs. Texas Tech (14) (Cotton, 1995) (3 for 99 yards)
32.2—Cotton Speyrer, Texas (36) vs. Tennessee (13) (Cotton, 1969) (5 for 161 yards)
31.0—Olanda Truitt, Pittsburgh (31) vs. Texas A&M (28) (John Hancock, 1989) (4 for 124 yards)
31.0—Clay Brown, Brigham Young (46) vs. Southern Methodist (45) (Holiday, 1980) (5 for 155 yards)

MOST TOUCHDOWNS RECEIVING

4—Fred Biletnikoff, Florida St. (36) vs. Oklahoma (19) (Gator, Jan. 2, 1965) (13 catches)
4—(D) Bob McChesney, Hardin-Simmons (49) vs. Wichita St. (12) (Camellia, 1948) (8 catches)
3—Keyshawn Johnson, Southern Cal (55) vs. Texas Tech (14) (Cotton, 1995) (8 catches)
3—(D) Ken Ealy, Central Mich. (24) vs. San Jose St. (48) (California, 1990) (7 catches)
3—Wendell Davis, LSU (30) vs. South Caro. (13) (Gator, 1987) (9 catches)
3—Anthony Allen, Washington (21) vs. Maryland (20) (Aloha, 1982) (8 catches)

3—(D) Norman Jordan, Vanderbilt (28) vs. Air Force (36) (Hall of Fame, 1982) (20 catches)
3—(D) Dwayne Dixon, Florida (24) vs. Arkansas (28) (Bluebonnet, 1982) (8 catches)
3—(D) Mervyn Fernandez, San Jose St. (25) vs. Toledo (27) (California, 1981) (9 catches)
3—Clay Brown, Brigham Young (46) vs. Southern Methodist (45) (Holiday, 1980) (5 catches)
3—Elliott Walker, Pittsburgh (34) vs. Clemson (3) (Gator, 1977) (6 catches)
3—Rhett Dawson, Florida St. (38) vs. Arizona St. (45) (Fiesta, 1971) (8 catches)
3—George Hannen, Davidson (33) vs. Toledo (56) (Tangerine, 1969)
3—Todd Snyder, Richmond (49) vs. Ohio (42) (Tangerine, 1968)

Scoring

MOST POINTS SCORED

30—(D) Sheldon Canley, San Jose St. (48) vs. Central Mich. (24) (California, 1990) (5 TDs)
30—Barry Sanders, Oklahoma St. (62) vs. Wyoming (14) (Holiday, 1988) (5 TDs)
28—Bobby Layne, Texas (40) vs. Missouri (27) (Cotton, 1946) (4 TDs, 4 PATs)
25—Neil Snow, Michigan (49) vs. Stanford (0) (Rose, 1902) (5 five-point TDs)
24—Byron Hanspard, Texas Tech (55) vs. Air Force (41) (Copper, 1995) (4 TDs)
24—Wasean Tait, Toledo (40) vs. Nevada (37) (OT) (Las Vegas, 1995) (4 TDs)
24—(D) Ron Jackson, Tulsa (28) vs. San Diego St. (17) (Freedom, 1991) (4 TDs)
24—(D) James Gray, Texas Tech (49) vs. Duke (21) (All-American, 1989) (4 TDs)
24—Thurman Thomas, Oklahoma St. (35) vs. West Va. (33) (John Hancock Sun, 1987) (4 TDs)
24—Eric Ball, UCLA (45) vs. Iowa (28) (Rose, 1986) (4 TDs)
24—Terry Miller, Oklahoma St. (49) vs. Brigham Young (21) (Tangerine, 1976) (4 TDs)
24—Sam Cunningham, Southern Cal (42) vs. Ohio St. (17) (Rose, 1973) (4 TDs)
24—Johnny Rodgers, Nebraska (40) vs. Notre Dame (6) (Orange, 1973) (4 TDs)
24—Woody Green, Arizona St. (49) vs. Missouri (35) (Fiesta, 1972) (4 TDs)
24—Charles Cole, Toledo (56) vs. Davidson (33) (Tangerine, 1969) (4 TDs)
24—Fred Biletnikoff, Florida St. (36) vs. Oklahoma (19) (Gator, Jan. 2, 1965) (4 TDs)
24—Joe Lopasky, Houston (49) vs. Miami (Ohio) (21) (Tangerine, 1962) (4 TDs)
24—(D) Gene Shannon, Houston (26) vs. Dayton (21) (Salad, 1952) (4 TDs)
24—(D) Bob McChesney, Hardin-Simmons (49) vs. Wichita St. (12) (Camellia, 1948) (4 TDs)

MOST POINTS RESPONSIBLE FOR
(TDs Scored & Passed For, Extra Points, and FGs)

40—Bobby Layne, Texas (40) vs. Missouri (27) (Cotton, 1946) (18 rush, 12 pass, 6 receiving and 4 PATs)
36—(D) Chuck Long, Iowa (55) vs. Texas (17) (Freedom, 1984) (36 pass)
30—Jeff Blake, East Caro. (37) vs. North Caro. St. (34) (Peach, 1992) (24 pass, 6 rush)
30—(D) Sheldon Canley, San Jose St. (48) vs. Central Mich. (24) (California, 1990) (24 rush, 6 receiving)
30—Peter Tom Willis, Florida St. (41) vs. Nebraska (17) (Fiesta, 1990) (30 pass)
30—Barry Sanders, Oklahoma St. (62) vs. Wyoming (14) (Holiday, 1988) (30 rush)
30—Johnny Rodgers, Nebraska (40) vs. Notre Dame (6) (Orange, 1973) (18 rush, 6 pass, 6 receiving)
30—Steve Tensi, Florida St. (36) vs. Oklahoma (19) (Gator, Jan. 2, 1965) (30 pass)

MOST TOUCHDOWNS

5—(D) Sheldon Canley, San Jose St. (48) vs. Central Mich. (24) (California, 1990) (4 rush, 1 catch)
5—Barry Sanders, Oklahoma St. (62) vs. Wyoming (14) (Holiday, 1988) (5 rush)
5—Neil Snow, Michigan (49) vs. Stanford (0) (Rose, 1902) (5 rush five-point TDs)
4—Byron Hanspard, Texas Tech (55) vs. Air Force (41) (Copper, 1995) (4 rush)
4—Wasean Tait, Toledo (40) vs. Nevada (37) (OT) (Las Vegas, 1995) (4 rush)
4—(D) Ron Jackson, Tulsa (28) vs. San Diego St. (17) (Freedom, 1991) (4 rush)
4—(D) James Gray, Texas Tech (49) vs. Duke (21) (All-American, 1989) (4 rush)
4—Thurman Thomas, Oklahoma St. (35) vs. West Va. (33) (John Hancock Sun, 1987) (4 rush)
4—Eric Ball, UCLA (45) vs. Iowa (28) (Rose, 1986) (4 rush)
4—Terry Miller, Oklahoma St. (49) vs. Brigham Young (21) (Tangerine, 1976) (4 rush)
4—Sam Cunningham, Southern Cal (42) vs. Ohio St. (17) (Rose, 1973) (4 rush)
4—Johnny Rodgers, Nebraska (40) vs. Notre Dame (6) (Orange, 1973) (3 rush, 1 catch)
4—Woody Green, Arizona St. (49) vs. Missouri (35) (Fiesta, 1972) (4 rush)
4—Charles Cole, Toledo (56) vs. Davidson (33) (Tangerine, 1969) (4 rush)
4—Fred Biletnikoff, Florida St. (36) vs. Oklahoma (19) (Gator, Jan. 2, 1965) (4 catch)
4—Joe Lopasky, Houston (49) vs. Miami (Ohio) (21) (Tangerine, 1962) (2 rush, 1 catch, 1 punt return)
4—(D) Gene Shannon, Houston (26) vs. Dayton (21) (Salad, 1952) (4 rush)
4—(D) Bob McChesney, Hardin-Simmons (49) vs. Wichita St. (12) (Camellia, 1948) (4 catch)
4—Bobby Layne, Texas (40) vs. Missouri (27) (Cotton, 1946) (3 rush, 1 catch)
4—(D) Alvin McMillin, Centre (63) vs. Texas Christian (7) (Fort Worth Classic, 1921) (4 rush)

MOST TWO-POINT CONVERSIONS

2—Ernie Davis, Syracuse (23) vs. Texas (14) (Cotton, 1960) (2 pass receptions)

Kicking

MOST FIELD GOALS ATTEMPTED

6—Kyle Bryant, Texas A&M (22) vs. Michigan (20) (Alamo, 1995) (5 made)
5—Chad Holcomb, East Caro. (19) vs. Stanford (13) (Liberty, 1995) (4 made)
5—Dan Mowrey, Florida St. (23) vs. Florida (17) (Sugar, Jan. 2, 1995) (3 made)
5—Tim Rogers, Mississippi St. (24) vs. North Caro. St. (28) (Peach, Jan. 1, 1995) (5 made)
5—Scott Bentley, Florida St. (18) vs. Nebraska (16) (Orange, 1994) (4 made)
5—Arden Czyzewski, Florida (28) vs. Notre Dame (39) (Sugar, 1992) (5 made)
5—Jess Atkinson, Maryland (23) vs. Tennessee (30) (Florida Citrus, 1983) (5 made)
5—Bob White, Arkansas (16) vs. Georgia (2) (Sugar, 1969) (3 made)
5—Tim Davis, Alabama (12) vs. Mississippi (7) (Sugar, 1964) (4 made)
4—Brett Conway, Penn St. (43) vs. Auburn (14) (Outback, 1996) (3 made)
4—Kanon Parkman, Georgia (27) vs. Virginia (34) (Peach, Dec. 30, 1995) (4 made)
4—Carlos Huerta, Miami (Fla.) (22) vs. Nebraska (0) (Orange, 1992) (3 made)
4—Greg Worker, Wyoming (19) vs. Iowa (20) (Holiday, 1987) (2 made)
4—Tim Lashar, Oklahoma (25) vs. Penn St. (10) (Orange, 1986) (4 made)
4—Kent Bostrom, Arizona St. (17) vs. Arkansas (18) (Holiday, 1985) (3 made)
4—(D) Todd Gregoire, Wisconsin (19) vs. Kentucky (20) (Hall of Fame, 1984) (4 made)
4—Bill Capece, Florida St. (17) vs. Oklahoma (18) (Orange, 1981) (1 made)
4—David Hardy, Texas A&M (33) vs. Oklahoma St. (16) (Independence, 1981) (4 made)
4—Bob Lucchesi, Missouri (19) vs. Southern Miss. (17) (Tangerine, 1981) (4 made)
4—Paul Woodside, West Va. (26) vs. Florida (6) (Peach, Dec. 31, 1981) (4 made)
4—(D) Fuad Reveiz, Tennessee (28) vs. Wisconsin (21) (Garden State, 1981) (2 made)
4—Dale Castro, Maryland (20) vs. Florida (35) (Tangerine, 1980) (4 made)
4—Brent Johnson, Brigham Young (37) vs. Indiana (38) (Holiday, 1979) (3 made)
4—Ricky Townsend, Tennessee (19) vs. Texas Tech (28) (Gator, 1973) (2 made)
4—Paul Rogers, Nebraska (45) vs. Georgia (6) (Sun, 1969) (4 made)

MOST FIELD GOALS MADE

5—Kyle Bryant, Texas A&M (22) vs. Michigan (20) (Alamo, 1995) (27, 49, 47, 31, 37 yards)
5—Tim Rogers, Mississippi St. (24) vs. North Caro. St. (28) (Peach, Jan. 1, 1995) (37, 21, 29, 36, 30 yards)
5—Arden Czyzewski, Florida (28) vs. Notre Dame (39) (Sugar, 1992) (26, 24, 36, 37, 24 yards)
5—Jess Atkinson, Maryland (23) vs. Tennessee (30) (Florida Citrus, 1983) (18, 48, 31, 22, 26 yards)
4—Chad Holcomb, East Caro. (19) vs. Stanford (13) (Liberty, 1995) (46, 26, 41, 34 yards)
4—Kanon Parkman, Georgia (27) vs. Virginia (34) (Peach, Dec. 30, 1995) (36, 37, 20, 42 yards)
4—Scott Bentley, Florida St. (18) vs. Nebraska (16) (Orange, 1994) (34, 25, 39, 22 yards)
4—Tim Lashar, Oklahoma (25) vs. Penn St. (10) (Orange, 1986) (26, 31, 21, 22 yards)
4—(D) Todd Gregoire, Wisconsin (19) vs. Kentucky (20) (Hall of Fame, 1984) (40, 27, 20, 40 yards)
4—David Hardy, Texas A&M (33) vs. Oklahoma St. (16) (Independence, 1981) (33, 32, 50, 18 yards)
4—Paul Woodside, West Va. (26) vs. Florida (6) (Peach, Dec. 31, 1981) (35, 42, 49, 24 yards)
4—Bob Lucchesi, Missouri (19) vs. Southern Miss. (17) (Tangerine, 1981) (45, 41, 30, 28 yards)
4—Dale Castro, Maryland (20) vs. Florida (35) (Tangerine, 1980) (35, 27, 27, 43 yards)
4—Paul Rogers, Nebraska (45) vs. Georgia (6) (Sun, 1969) (50, 32, 42, 37 yards, all in 1st quarter)
4—Tim Davis, Alabama (12) vs. Mississippi (7) (Sugar, 1964) (31, 46, 22, 48 yards)

MOST EXTRA-POINT KICK ATTEMPTS

9—Layne Talbot, Texas A&M (65) vs. Brigham Young (14) (Holiday, 1990) (9 made)
9—Bobby Luna, Alabama (61) vs. Syracuse (6) (Orange, 1953) (7 made)
9—(D) James Weaver, Centre (63) vs. Texas Christian (7) (Fort Worth Classic, 1921) (9 made)
8—Cary Blanchard, Oklahoma St. (62) vs. Wyoming (14) (Holiday, 1988) (8 made)
8—Ken Crots, Toledo (56) vs. Davidson (33) (Tangerine, 1969) (8 made)
7—Tony Rogers, Texas Tech (55) vs. Air Force (41) (Copper, 1995) (7 made)
7—Cole Ford, Southern Cal (55) vs. Texas Tech (14) (Cotton, 1995) (7 made)
7—Scott Blanton, Oklahoma (48) vs. Virginia (14) (Gator, Dec. 29, 1991) (6 made)
7—(D) Barry Belli, Fresno St. (51) vs. Bowling Green (7) (California, 1985) (7 made)
7—(D) Tom Nichol, Iowa (55) vs. Texas (17) (Freedom, 1984) (7 made)
7—Juan Cruz, Arizona St. (49) vs. Missouri (35) (Fiesta, 1972) (7 made)
7—Ron Sewell, North Caro. St. (49) vs. West Va. (13) (Peach, 1972) (7 made)
7—Don Ekstrand, Arizona St. (48) vs. North Caro. (26) (Peach, 1970) (6 made)
7—Bill McMillan, Houston (49) vs. Miami (Ohio) (21) (Tangerine, 1962) (7 made)
7—Jesse Whittenton, UTEP (47) vs. Florida St. (20) (Sun, 1955) (5 made)
7—Jim Brieske, Michigan (49) vs. UCLA (0) (Rose, 1948) (7 made)
7—(D) Pat Bailey, Hardin-Simmons (49) vs. Wichita St. (12) (Camellia, 1948) (7 made)

MOST EXTRA-POINT KICKS MADE

9—Layne Talbot, Texas A&M (65) vs. Brigham Young (14) (Holiday, 1990) (9 attempts)
9—(D) James Weaver, Centre (63) vs. Texas Christian (7) (Fort Worth Classic, 1921) (9 attempts)
8—Cary Blanchard, Oklahoma St. (62) vs. Wyoming (14) (Holiday, 1988) (8 attempts)
8—Ken Crots, Toledo (56) vs. Davidson (33) (Tangerine, 1969) (8 attempts)
7—Tony Rogers, Texas Tech (55) vs. Air Force (41) (Copper, 1995) (7 attempts)

7—Cole Ford, Southern Cal (55) vs. Texas Tech (14) (Cotton, 1995) (7 attempts)
7—(D) Barry Belli, Fresno St. (51) vs. Bowling Green (7) (California, 1985) (7 attempts)
7—(D) Tom Nichol, Iowa (55) vs. Texas (17) (Freedom, 1984) (7 attempts)
7—Juan Cruz, Arizona St. (49) vs. Missouri (35) (Fiesta, 1972) (7 attempts)
7—Ron Sewell, North Caro. St. (49) vs. West Va. (13) (Peach, 1972) (7 attempts)
7—Bill McMillan, Houston (49) vs. Miami (Ohio) (21) (Tangerine, 1962) (7 attempts)
7—Bobby Luna, Alabama (61) vs. Syracuse (6) (Orange, 1953) (9 attempts)
7—Jim Brieske, Michigan (49) vs. UCLA (0) (Rose, 1948) (7 attempts)
7—(D) Pat Bailey, Hardin-Simmons (49) vs. Wichita St. (12) (Camellia, 1948) (7 attempts)

MOST POINTS BY A KICKER

16—Kyle Bryant, Texas A&M (22) vs. Michigan (20) (Alamo, 1995) (5 FGs, 1 PAT)
16—Tim Rogers, Mississippi St. (24) vs. North Caro. St. (28) (Peach, Jan. 1, 1995) (5 FGs, 1 PAT)
16—Arden Czyzewski, Florida (28) vs. Notre Dame (39) (Sugar, 1992) (5 FGs, 1 PAT)
15—Jess Atkinson, Maryland (23) vs. Tennessee (30) (Florida Citrus, 1983) (5 FGs)
15—David Hardy, Texas A&M (33) vs. Oklahoma St. (16) (Independence, 1981) (4 FGs, 3 PATs)
15—Paul Rogers, Nebraska (45) vs. Georgia (6) (John Hancock, 1969) (4 FGs, 3 PATs)
14—Cary Blanchard, Oklahoma St. (62) vs. Wyoming (14) (Holiday, 1988) (2 FGs, 8 PATs)
14—Paul Woodside, West Va. (26) vs. Florida (6) (Peach, Dec. 31, 1981) (4 FGs, 2 PATs)
13—Chad Holcomb, East Caro. (19) vs. Stanford (13) (Liberty, 1995) (4 FGs, 1 PAT)
13—Kanon Parkman, Georgia (27) vs. Virginia (34) (Peach, Dec. 30, 1995) (4 FGs, 1 PAT)
13—Tony Rogers, Texas Tech (55) vs. Air Force (41) (Copper, 1995) (2 FGs, 7 PATs)
13—Damon Shea, Nevada (37) vs. Toledo (40) (OT) (Las Vegas, 1995) (3 FGs, 4 PATs)
13—Cole Ford, Southern Cal (55) vs. Texas Tech (14) (Cotton, 1995) (2 FGs, 7 PATs)
13—Tim Lashar, Oklahoma (25) vs. Penn. St. (10) (Orange, 1986) (4 FGs, 1 PAT)
13—John Lee, UCLA (39) vs. Miami (Fla.) (37) (Fiesta, 1985) (3 FGs, 4 PATs)
13—(D) Tom Nichol, Iowa (55) vs. Texas (17) (Freedom, 1984) (2 FGs, 7 PATs)
13—(D) Todd Gregoire, Wisconsin (19) vs. Kentucky (20) (Hall of Fame, 1984) (4 FGs, 1 PAT)
13—Bob Lucchesi, Missouri (19) vs. Southern Miss. (17) (Tangerine, 1981) (4 FGs, 1 PAT)
13—Dave Johnson, Brigham Young (37) vs. Indiana (38) (Holiday, 1979) (3 FGs, 4 PATs)
12—Scott Bentley, Florida St. (18) vs. Nebraska (16) (Orange, 1994) (4 FGs)
12—Chris Gardocki, Clemson (30) vs. Illinois (0) (Hall of Fame, 1991) (3 FGs, 3 PATs)
12—Ray Tarasi, Penn St. (50) vs. Brigham Young (39) (Holiday, 1989) (3 FGs, 3 PATs)
12—Luis Zendejas, Arizona St. (32) vs. Oklahoma (21) (Fiesta, 1983) (3 FGs, 3 PATs)
12—Dale Castro, Maryland (20) vs. Florida (35) (Tangerine, 1980) (4 FGs)
12—Nathan Ritter, North Caro. St. (30) vs. Pittsburgh (17) (Tangerine, 1978) (3 FGs, 3 PATs)
12—Buckey Berrey, Alabama (36) vs. UCLA (6) (Liberty, 1976) (3 FGs, 3 PATs)
12—Al Vitiello, Penn St. (30) vs. Texas (6) (Cotton, 1972) (3 FGs, 3 PATs)
12—Frank Fontes, Florida St. (38) vs. Arizona St. (45) (Fiesta, 1971) (3 FGs, 3 PATs)

Punting

MOST PUNTS

21—Everett Sweeney, Michigan (49) vs. Stanford (0) (Rose, 1902)
16—Lem Pratt, New Mexico St. (14) vs. Hardin-Simmons (14) (Sun, 1936) (38.4 average)
14—Sammy Baugh, Texas Christian (3) vs. LSU (2) (Sugar, 1936)
13—Hugh Keeney, Rice (8) vs. Tennessee (0) (Orange, 1947)
13—N. A. Keithley, Tulsa (6) vs. Texas Tech (0) (Sun, 1942) (37.0 average)
13—Hugh McCullough, Oklahoma (0) vs. Tennessee (17) (Orange, 1939) (40.6 average)
13—Tyler, Hardin-Simmons (14) vs. New Mexico St. (14) (Sun, 1936) (45.2 average)
13—(D) Tom Murphy, Arkansas (7) vs. Centenary (La.) (7) (Dixie Classic, 1934) (44.0 average)
12—Mitch Berger, Colorado (25) vs. Alabama (30) (Blockbuster, 1991) (41.0 average)
12—Bob Parsons, Penn St. (10) vs. Missouri (3) (Orange, 1970) (42.6 average)
12—Jim Callahan, Texas Tech (0) vs. Tulsa (6) (Sun, 1942) (43.0 average)
12—Mike Palm, Penn St. (3) vs. Southern Cal (14) (Rose, 1923)

HIGHEST AVERAGE PER PUNT
(Minimum 5 Punts)

52.7—Des Koch, Southern Cal (7) vs. Wisconsin (0) (Rose, 1953) (7 for 369 yards) (adjusted to current statistical rules)
52.4—Mike Sochko, Maryland (21) vs. Houston (30) (Cotton, 1977) (5 for 262 yards)
51.0—Chris Clauss, Penn St. (10) vs. Clemson (35) (Florida Citrus, 1988) (5 for 255 yards)
50.0—Dana Moore, Mississippi St. (17) vs. Nebraska (31) (Sun, 1980) (5 for 250 yards)
49.3—Chris McInally, Clemson (0) vs. Syracuse (41) (Gator, 1996) (6 for 296)
49.2—(D) Mark Simon, Air Force (24) vs. Texas (16) (Bluebonnet, 1985) (11 for 541 yards)
49.2—Allen Meacham, Arkansas (3) vs. UCLA (17) (Cotton, 1989) (6 for 295 yards)
49.0—Jim DiGuilio, Indiana (24) vs. Baylor (0) (Copper, 1991) (6 for 294 yards)
49.0—(D) Dana Moore, Mississippi St. (10) vs. Kansas (0) (Hall of Fame, 1981) (9 for 441 yards)
48.1—Brent Bartholomew, Ohio St. (14) vs. Tennessee (20) (Florida Citrus, 1996) (7 for 337)
48.0—Dan Eichloff, Kansas (23) vs. Brigham Young (20) (Aloha, 1992) (8 for 384 yards)
47.9—Doug Helkowski, Penn St. (42) vs. Tennessee (17) (Fiesta, 1992) (9 for 431 yards)
47.8—(D) Kevin Buenafe, UCLA (14) vs. Michigan (33) (Bluebonnet, 1981) (8 for 382 yards)
47.6—Todd Thomsen, Oklahoma (42) vs. Arkansas (8) (Orange, 1987) (5 for 238 yards)
47.5—Jerry Dowd, St. Mary's (Cal.) (20) vs. Texas Tech (13) (Cotton, 1939) (11 for 523 yards)
47.4—Jason Bender, Georgia Tech (18) vs. Stanford (17) (Aloha, 1991) (7 for 332 yards)
47.4—(D) Mike Mancini, Fresno St. (51) vs. Bowling Green (7) (California, 1985) (7 for 332 yards)
47.4—(D) Jimmy Colquitt, Tennessee (28) vs. Wisconsin (21) (Garden State, 1981) (5 for 237 yards)

Punt Returns

MOST PUNT RETURNS

9—Buzy Rosenberg, Georgia (7) vs. North Caro. (3) (Gator, Dec. 31, 1971) (54 yards)
9—Paddy Driscoll, Great Lakes (17) vs. Mare Island (0) (Rose, 1919) (115 yards)
8—Thomas Lewis, Indiana (20) vs. Virginia Tech (45) (Independence, 1993) (58 yards)
6—Dale Carter, Tennessee (17) vs. Penn St. (42) (Fiesta, 1992)
6—Joey Smith, Louisville (34) vs. Alabama (7) (Fiesta, 1991) (35 yards)
6—David Palmer, Alabama (30) vs. Colorado (25) (Blockbuster, 1991) (74 yards)
6—(D) Hesh Colar, San Jose St. (48) vs. Central Mich. (24) (California, 1990)
6—David Kintigh, Miami (Fla.) (10) vs. Penn St. (14) (Fiesta, 1987) (32 yards)
6—(D) Eric Metcalf, Texas (16) vs. Air Force (24) (Bluebonnet, 1985) (49 yards)
6—Vai Sikahema, Brigham Young (7) vs. Ohio St. (10) (Florida Citrus, 1985)
6—Ray Horton, Washington (21) vs. Maryland (20) (Aloha, 1982) (28 yards)
6—Bill Gribble, Washington St. (36) vs. Brigham Young (38) (Holiday, 1981) (39 yards)
6—Johnny Rodgers, Nebraska (38) vs. Alabama (6) (Orange, 1972) (136 yards)
6—Rick Sygar, Michigan (34) vs. Oregon St. (7) (Rose, 1965) (50 yards)
6—Billy Hair, Clemson (0) vs. Miami (Fla.) (14) (Gator, 1952) (73 yards)
6—Don Zimmerman, Tulane (12) vs. Southern Cal (21) (Rose, 1932)

MOST PUNT RETURN YARDS

136—Johnny Rodgers, Nebraska (38) vs. Alabama (6) (Orange, 1972) (6 returns)
122—George Fleming, Washington (44) vs. Wisconsin (8) (Rose, 1960) (3 returns)
122—Bobby Kellogg, Tulane (13) vs. Texas A&M (14) (Sugar, 1940) (5 returns)
115—Paddy Driscoll, Great Lakes (17) vs. Mare Island (0) (Rose, 1919) (9 returns)
110—James Henry, Southern Miss. (38) vs. UTEP (18) (Independence, 1988) (2 returns, touchdowns of 65 and 45 yards)
106—Kevin Baugh, Penn St. (27) vs. Georgia (23) (Sugar, 1983) (5 returns)
106—Steve Holden, Arizona St. (45) vs. Florida St. (38) (Fiesta, 1971) (3 returns)
104—Leo Daniels, Texas A&M (21) vs. Alabama (29) (Cotton, 1942) (5 returns)
103—Jon Staggers, Missouri (3) vs. Penn St. (10) (Orange, 1970)
89—Lawrence Williams, Texas Tech (28) vs. North Caro. (32) (Sun, 1972) (5 returns)
87—Vai Sikahema, Brigham Young (46) vs. Southern Methodist (45) (Holiday, 1980) (2 returns)
86—Bobby Majors, Tennessee (34) vs. Air Force (13) (Sugar, 1971) (4 returns)
86—Aramis Dandoy, Southern Cal (7) vs. Ohio St. (20) (Rose, 1955) (1 return)
82—Marcus Wall, North Caro. (31) vs. Texas (35) (Sun, 1994) (1 return)
82—Willie Drewrey, West Va. (12) vs. Florida St. (31) (Gator, 1982) (1 return)
80—(D) Gary Anderson, Arkansas (34) vs. Tulane (15) (Hall of Fame, 1980) (2 returns)
80—Cecil Ingram, Alabama (61) vs. Syracuse (6) (Orange, 1953) (1 return)

HIGHEST PUNT RETURN AVERAGE
(Minimum 3 Returns)

40.7—George Fleming, Washington (44) vs. Wisconsin (8) (Rose, 1960) (3 for 122 yards)
35.3—Steve Holden, Arizona St. (45) vs. Florida St. (38) (Fiesta, 1971) (3 for 106 yards)
24.4—Bobby Kellogg, Tulane (13) vs. Texas A&M (14) (Sugar, 1940) (5 for 122 yards)
24.0—Shayne Wasden, Auburn (31) vs. Ohio St. (14) (Hall of Fame, 1990) (3 for 72 yards)
22.7—Johnny Rodgers, Nebraska (38) vs. Alabama (6) (Orange, 1972) (6 for 136 yards)
21.5—Bobby Majors, Tennessee (34) vs. Air Force (13) (Sugar, 1971) (4 for 86 yards)
21.0—Tiki Barber, Virginia (34) vs. Georgia (27) (Peach, Dec. 30, 1995) (3 for 63 yards)
21.0—(D) Brian Williams, Kentucky (16) vs. West Va. (20) (Hall of Fame, 1983) (3 for 63 yards)
20.8—Leo Daniels, Texas A&M (21) vs. Alabama (29) (Cotton, 1942) (5 for 104 yards)
19.5—(D) Zippy Morocco, Georgia (20) vs. Texas A&M (40) (Presidential Cup, 1950) (4 for 78 yards)
19.3—Dave Liegi, Nebraska (14) vs. Houston (17) (Cotton, 1980) (3 for 58 yards)
19.0—Gary Moss, Georgia (10) vs. Texas (9) (Cotton, 1984) (3 for 57 yards)

Kickoff Returns

MOST KICKOFF RETURNS

7—Dale Carter, Tennessee (17) vs. Penn St. (42) (Fiesta, 1992) (132 yards)
7—Jeff Sydner, Hawaii (13) vs. Michigan St. (33) (Aloha, 1989) (174 yards)
7—Homer Jones, Brigham Young (37) vs. Indiana (38) (Holiday, 1979) (126 yards)
6—Eugene Napoleon, West Va. (21) vs. Notre Dame (34) (Fiesta, 1989) (107 yards)
6—Tim Brown, Notre Dame (10) vs. Texas A&M (35) (Cotton, 1988) (129 yards)
6—Leroy Thompson, Penn St. (10) vs. Clemson (35) (Florida Citrus, 1988)
6—(D) Anthony Roberson, Air Force (28) vs. Arizona St. (33) (Freedom, 1987) (109 yards)

6—Casey Tiumalu, Brigham Young (17) vs. Ohio St. (47) (Holiday, 1982) (116 yards)
6—Brian Nelson, Texas Tech (17) vs. Florida St. (40) (Tangerine, 1977) (143 yards)
6—Wally Henry, UCLA (6) vs. Alabama (36) (Liberty, 1976)
6—Steve Williams, Alabama (6) vs. Nebraska (38) (Orange, 1972)
6—Mike Fink, Missouri (35) vs. Arizona St. (49) (Fiesta, 1972) (203 yards)

MOST KICKOFF RETURN YARDS

203—Mike Fink, Missouri (35) vs. Arizona St. (49) (Fiesta, 1972) (6 returns)
178—Al Hoisch, UCLA (14) vs. Illinois (45) (Rose, 1947) (4 returns)
174—Jeff Sydner, Hawaii (13) vs. Michigan St. (33) (Aloha, 1989) (7 returns)
166—Willie Jones, Iowa St. (30) vs. Georgia Tech (31) (Liberty, 1972) (4 returns)
154—Dave Lowery, Brigham Young (21) vs. Oklahoma St. (49) (Tangerine, 1976) (4 returns)
154—(D) Martin Mitchell, Tulane (7) vs. Houston (47) (Bluebonnet, 1973) (5 returns)
148—Earl Allen, Houston (28) vs. Boston College (45) (Cotton, 1985) (4 returns)
147—Carlos Snow, Ohio St. (17) vs. Syracuse (24) (Hall of Fame, 1992) (4 returns)
144—Clint Johnson, Notre Dame (39) vs. Florida (28) (Sugar, 1992) (5 returns)
143—Brian Nelson, Texas Tech (17) vs. Florida St. (40) (Tangerine, 1977) (6 returns)
143—Barry Smith, Florida St. (38) vs. Arizona St. (45) (Fiesta, 1971) (5 returns)

HIGHEST KICKOFF RETURN AVERAGE
(Minimum 2 Returns)

60.5—(D) Bob Smith, Texas A&M (40) vs. Georgia (20) (Presidential Cup, 1950) (2 for 121 yards)
58.0—Eddie Kennison, LSU (45) vs. Michigan St. (26) (Independence, 1995) (2 for 116 yards)
57.5—Pete Panuska, Tennessee (27) vs. Maryland (28) (Sun, 1984) (2 for 115 yards)
55.5—Todd Snyder, Ohio (42) vs. Richmond (49) (Tangerine, 1968) (2 for 111 yards)
46.7—(D) Cal Beck, Utah (16) vs. Arizona (13) (Freedom, 1994) (3 for 140 yards)
44.5—Al Hoisch, UCLA (14) vs. Illinois (45) (Rose, 1947) (4 for 178 yards)
43.7—Larry Key, Florida St. (40) vs. Texas Tech (17) (Tangerine, 1977) (3 for 131 yards)
41.5—Willie Jones, Iowa St. (30) vs. Georgia Tech (31) (Liberty, 1972) (4 for 166 yards)
41.0—Kevin Williams, Miami (Fla.) (46) vs. Texas (3) (Cotton, 1991) (2 for 82 yards)
40.3—(D) Willie Gault, Tennessee (28) vs. Wisconsin (21) (Garden State, 1981) (3 for 121 yards)
39.0—Damon Dunn, Stanford (13) vs. East Caro. (19) (Liberty, 1995) (3 for 117 yards)
37.0—Earl Allen, Houston (28) vs. Boston College (45) (Cotton, 1985) (4 for 148 yards)
36.8—Carlos Snow, Ohio St. (17) vs. Syracuse (24) (Hall of Fame, 1992) (4 for 147 yards)
33.8—Mike Fink, Missouri (35) vs. Arizona St. (49) (Fiesta, 1972) (6 for 203 yards)
33.8—Demetrius Allen, Virginia (34) vs. Georgia (27) (Peach, Dec. 30, 1995) (4 for 135)
33.2—Hudhaifa Ismaeli, Northwestern (32) vs. Southern Cal (41) (Rose, 1996) (5 for 166)
33.0—Derrick Mason, Michigan St. (26) vs. LSU (45) (Independence, 1995) (4 for 132)
32.6—Jim McElroy, UCLA (30) vs. Kansas (51) (Aloha, 1995) (5 for 163)
32.5—Reidel Anthony, Florida (24) vs. Nebraska (62) (Fiesta, 1996) (6 for 195)
32.0—(D) Eric Alozie, Washington (34) vs. Florida (7) (Freedom, 1989) (2 for 64 yards)
32.0—Jim Brown, Syracuse (27) vs. Texas Christian (28) (Cotton, 1957) (3 for 96 yards)
32.0—Harry Jones, Kentucky (20) vs. Texas Christian (7) (Cotton, 1952) (2 for 64 yards)

Interceptions

MOST INTERCEPTIONS MADE

4—Jim Dooley, Miami (Fla.) (14) vs. Clemson (0) (Gator, 1952)
4—(D) Manuel Aja, Arizona St. (21) vs. Xavier (Ohio) (33) (Salad, 1950)
3—Michael Brooks, North Caro. St. (28) vs. Iowa (23) (Peach, Dec. 31, 1988)
3—Bud Hebert, Oklahoma (24) vs. Florida St. (7) (Orange, 1980)
3—Louis Campbell, Arkansas (13) vs. Tennessee (14) (Liberty, 1971)
3—Bud McClinton, Auburn (34) vs. Arizona (10) (Sun, 1968)
3—(D) Les Derrick, Texas (19) vs. Mississippi (0) (Bluebonnet, 1966)
3—(D) Tommy Luke, Mississippi (0) vs. Texas (19) (Bluebonnet, 1966)
3—Jerry Cook, Texas (12) vs. Mississippi (7) (Cotton, 1962)
3—Ray Brown, Mississippi (39) vs. Texas (7) (Sugar, 1958)
3—Bill Paulman, Stanford (7) vs. Southern Methodist (0) (Rose, 1936)
3—Shy Huntington, Oregon (14) vs. Pennsylvania (0) (Rose, 1917)

MOST INTERCEPTION RETURN YARDAGE

148—Elmer Layden, Notre Dame (27) vs. Stanford (10) (Rose, 1925) (2 interceptions)
94—David Baker, Oklahoma (48) vs. Duke (21) (Orange, 1958) (1 interception)
90—Norm Beal, Missouri (21) vs. Navy (14) (Orange, 1961) (1 interception)
90—Charlie Brembs, South Caro. (14) vs. Wake Forest (26) (Gator, 1946) (1 interception)
89—Al Hudson, Miami (Fla.) (13) vs. Holy Cross (6) (Orange, 1946) (1 interception)
81—Gary Moss, Georgia (24) vs. Boston College (27) (Hall of Fame, 1986) (1 interception)
80—(D) Russ Meredith, West Va. (21) vs. Gonzaga (13) (San Diego East-West Christmas Classic, 1922) (1 interception)
77—George Halas, Great Lakes (17) vs. Mare Island (0) (Rose, 1919) (1 interception)
75—Hugh Morrow, Alabama (26) vs. Duke (29) (Sugar, 1945) (1 interception)
72—Alton Montgomery, Houston (22) vs. Washington St. (24) (Aloha, 1988) (1 interception)
70—Robert Bailey, Mississippi (34) vs. Virginia Tech (17) (Liberty, 1968) (1 interception)
70—(D) Mel McGaha, Arkansas (21) vs. William & Mary (19) (Dixie, 1948) (1 interception)
69—Chris Carter, Texas (35) vs. North Caro. (31) (Sun, 1994) (1 interception)
69—Howard Ehler, Florida St. (36) vs. Oklahoma (19) (Gator, Jan. 2, 1965) (1 interception)
67—John Matsock, Michigan St. (28) vs. UCLA (20) (Rose, 1954) (2 interceptions)

All-Purpose Yards

(Includes All Runs From Scrimmage, Pass Receptions and All Returns)

MOST ALL-PURPOSE PLAYS
(Must Have at Least One Reception or Return)

47—(D) Ron Jackson, Tulsa (28) vs. San Diego St. (17) (Freedom, 1991) (46 rush, 1 reception)
46—Errict Rhett, Florida (27) vs. North Caro. St. (10) (Gator, 1992) (39 rush, 7 receptions)
42—Blake Ezor, Michigan St. (33) vs. Hawaii (13) (Aloha, 1989) (41 rush, 1 reception)
41—Terrell Fletcher, Wisconsin (34) vs. Duke (20) (Hall of Fame, 1995) (39 rush, 1 reception, 1 kickoff return)
39—(D) Marshall Faulk, San Diego St. (17) vs. Tulsa (28) (Freedom, 1991) (30 rush, 9 receptions)
37—Wasean Tait, Toledo (40) vs. Nevada (37) (OT) (Las Vegas, 1995) (31 rush, 6 receptions)
37—Sherman Williams, Alabama (24) vs. Ohio St. (17) (Florida Citrus, 1995) (27 rush, 8 receptions, 2 kickoff returns)
37—O. J. Simpson, Southern Cal (16) vs. Ohio St. (27) (Rose, 1969) (28 rush, 8 receptions, 1 kickoff return)
36—Thurman Thomas, Oklahoma St. (35) vs. West Va. (33) (John Hancock Sun, 1987) (33 rush, 6 receptions)
36—Bob Anderson, Colorado (47) vs. Alabama (33) (Liberty, 1969) (35 rush, 1 kickoff return)
35—Ricky Ervins, Southern Cal (17) vs. Michigan (10) (Rose, 1990) (30 rush, 5 receptions)
35—(D) Eric Bieniemy, Colorado (17) vs. Brigham Young (20) (Freedom, 1988) (33 rush, 2 receptions)
33—Shaumbe Wright-Fair, Washington St. (31) vs. Utah (28) (Copper, 1992) (27 rush, 6 receptions)
33—(D) Greg Lewis, Washington (34) vs. Florida (7) (Freedom, 1989) (27 rush, 6 receptions)
33—Bo Jackson, Auburn (16) vs. Texas A&M (36) (Cotton, 1986) (31 rush, 2 receptions)

MOST ALL-PURPOSE YARDS GAINED
(Must Have at Least One Reception or Return)

359—Sherman Williams, Alabama (24) vs. Ohio St. (17) (Florida Citrus, 1995) (166 rush, 155 receptions, 38 kickoff returns)
303—(D) Bob Smith, Texas A&M (40) vs. Georgia (20) (Presidential Cup, 1950) (160 rush, 22 receptions, 121 kickoff returns)
278—Byron Hanspard, Texas Tech (55) vs. Air Force (41) (Copper, 1995) (260 rush, 18 receptions)
277—Bob Anderson, Colorado (47) vs. Alabama (33) (Liberty, 1969) (254 rush, 23 kickoff returns)
276—O. J. Simpson, Southern Cal (16) vs. Ohio St. (27) (Rose, 1969) (171 rush, 85 receptions, 20 kickoff returns)
256—Terrell Fletcher, Wisconsin (34) vs. Duke (20) (Hall of Fame, 1995) (241 rush, 8 receptions, 7 kickoff returns)
247—(D) Wilford White, Arizona St. (21) vs. Miami (Ohio) (34) (Salad, 1951) (106 rush, 87 receptions, 54 kickoff returns)
246—Demetrius Allen, Virginia (34) vs. Georgia (27) (Peach, Dec. 30, 1995) (111 receiving, 135 kickoff returns)
246—Ernie Jones, Indiana (22) vs. Tennessee (27) (Peach, 1987) (15 rush, 150 receptions, 81 kickoff returns)
242—Errict Rhett, Florida (27) vs. North Caro. St. (10) (Gator, 1992) (182 rush, 60 receptions)
239—Tyrone Wheatley, Michigan (38) vs. Washington (31) (Rose, 1993) (235 rush, 4 receptions)
238—Wasean Tait, Toledo (40) vs. Nevada (37) (OT) (Las Vegas, 1995) (185 rush, 53 receptions)
236—(D) Gary Anderson, Arkansas (34) vs. Tulane (15) (Hall of Fame, 1980) (156 rush, 80 punt returns)
230—Jamie Morris, Michigan (28) vs. Alabama (24) (Hall of Fame, 1987) (234 rush, -4 receptions)
228—Phillip Bobo, Washington St. (31) vs. Utah (28) (Copper, 1992) (16 rush, 212 receptions)
225—(D) Ron Jackson, Tulsa (28) vs. San Diego St. (17) (Freedom, 1991) (211 rush, 14 receptions)
223—Donny Anderson, Texas Tech (21) vs. Georgia Tech (31) (Gator, 1966) (85 rush, 138 receptions)
212—Troy Stradford, Boston College (45) vs. Houston (28) (Cotton, 1985) (196 rush, 16 receptions)
211—(D) Charles White, Southern Cal (47) vs. Texas A&M (28) (Bluebonnet, 1977) (186 rush, 25 receptions)
208—(D) Sheldon Canley, San Jose St. (48) vs. Central Mich. (24) (California, 1990) (164 rush, 44 receptions)

Defensive Statistics

MOST TOTAL TACKLES MADE
(Includes Assists)

31—Lee Roy Jordan, Alabama (17) vs. Oklahoma (0) (Orange, 1963)
22—Bubba Brown, Clemson (17) vs. Ohio St. (15) (Gator, 1978)
22—Gordy Ceresino, Stanford (24) vs. LSU (14) (Sun, Dec. 31, 1977)
20—Vada Murray, Michigan (10) vs. Southern Cal (17) (Rose, 1990)
20—(D) Gordy Ceresino, Stanford (25) vs. Georgia (22) (Bluebonnet, 1978)
18—Allen Stansberry, LSU (45) vs. Michigan St. (26) (Independence, 1995)
18—Ted Johnson, Colorado (41) vs. Notre Dame (24) (Fiesta, 1995)
18—Rod Smith, Notre Dame (39) vs. Florida (28) (Sugar, 1992)
18—Erick Anderson, Michigan (10) vs. Southern Cal (17) (Rose, 1990)
18—(D) Yepi Pauu, San Jose St. (27) vs. Eastern Mich. (30) (California, 1987)
18—Garland Rivers, Michigan (17) vs. Brigham Young (24) (Holiday, 1984)
18—(D) Terry Hubbard, Cal St. Fullerton (13) vs. Northern Ill. (20) (California, 1983)
18—(D) Don Turner, Fresno St. (29) vs. Bowling Green (28) (California, 1982)
18—Matt Millen, Penn St. (42) vs. Arizona St. (30) (Fiesta, 1977)

MOST UNASSISTED TACKLES

18—Rod Smith, Notre Dame (39) vs. Florida (28) (Sugar, 1992)
17—Garland Rivers, Michigan (17) vs. Brigham Young (24) (Holiday, 1984)
15—Randy Neal, Virginia (13) vs. Boston College (31) (Carquest, 1994)
15—(D) Ken Norton Jr., UCLA (31) vs. Brigham Young (10) (Freedom, 1986)
15—Lynn Evans, Missouri (35) vs. Arizona St. (49) (Fiesta, 1972)

MOST TACKLES MADE FOR LOSSES

5—(D) Michael Jones, Colorado (17) vs. Brigham Young (20) (Freedom, 1988) (20 yards)
5—Jimmy Walker, Arkansas (10) vs. UCLA (10) (Fiesta, 1978)
4—Matt Finkes, Ohio St. (14) vs. Tennessee (20) (Florida Citrus, 1996)
4—(D) Ken Norton Jr., UCLA (31) vs. Brigham Young (10) (Freedom, 1986)
3—Mike Vrabel, Ohio St. (14) vs. Tennessee (20) (Florida Citrus, 1996)
3—Nate Hemsley, Syracuse (41) vs. Clemson (0) (Gator, 1996)
3—Marcus Jones, North Caro. (20) vs. Arkansas (10) (Carquest, Dec. 30, 1995)
3—(D) Guy Boliaux, Wisconsin (21) vs. Tennessee (28) (Garden State, 1981)

MOST QUARTERBACK SACKS

4—Rusty Medearis, Miami (Fla.) (22) vs. Nebraska (0) (Orange, 1992)
4—Bobby Bell, Missouri (17) vs. Brigham Young (21) (Holiday, 1983)
3—Gabe Northern, LSU (45) vs. Michigan St. (26) (Independence, 1995)
3—James Gillyard, LSU (45) vs. Michigan St. (26) (Independence, 1995)
3—Dewayne Harris, Nebraska (24) vs. Miami (Fla.) (17) (Orange, 1995)
3—Trev Alberts, Nebraska (16) vs. Florida St. (18) (Orange, 1994)
3—(D) Alfred Williams, Colorado (17) vs. Brigham Young (20) (Freedom, 1988)
3—(D) Jim Wahler, UCLA (31) vs. Brigham Young (10) (Freedom, 1986)
3—James Mosley, Texas Tech (17) vs. Mississippi (20) (Independence, 1986)
3—(D) Ernie Barnes, Mississippi St. (10) vs. Kansas (0) (Hall of Fame, 1981)

FUMBLE RECOVERIES

2—Randall Brown, Ohio St. (17) vs. Alabama (24) (Florida Citrus, 1995)
2—(D) Michael Stewart, Fresno St. (51) vs. Bowling Green (7) (California, 1985)
2—Rod Kirby, Pittsburgh (7) vs. Arizona St. (28) (Fiesta, 1973)

BLOCKED KICKS

2—Bracey Walker, North Caro. (21) vs. Mississippi St. (17) (Peach, Jan. 2, 1993)
2—Carlton Williams, Pittsburgh (7) vs. Arizona St. (28) (Fiesta, 1973)

PASSES BROKEN UP

3—Mark Tate, Penn St. (43) vs. Auburn (14) (Outback, 1996)
3—Kwame Ellis, Stanford (13) vs. East Caro. (19) (Liberty, 1995)
3—Mickey Dalton, Air Force (41) vs. Texas Tech (55) (Copper, 1995)
3—Barron Miles, Nebraska (24) vs. Miami (Fla.) (17) (Orange, 1995)
3—Sam McKiver, Virginia (20) vs. Texas Christian (10) (Independence, 1994)
3—Percy Ellsworth, Virginia (20) vs. Texas Christian (10) (Independence, 1994)
3—Tyrone Williams, Nebraska (16) vs. Florida St. (18) (Orange, 1994)
3—(D) John Herpin, Southern Cal (28) vs. Utah (21) (Freedom, 1993)
3—Demouy Williams, Washington (24) vs. Tulane (12) (Independence, 1987)

Team Record Lists

Only official records after 1937 are included. Prior records are included if able to be substantiated. Each team's score is in parentheses after the team name. Totals for each team in both-team records are in brackets after the team's score. The year listed is the actual (calendar) year the game was played; the date is included if the bowl was played twice (i.e., January and December) during one calendar year. The list also includes discontinued bowls, marked with (D). Bowls are listed by the name of the bowl at the time it was played: The Florida Citrus Bowl was the Tangerine Bowl in 1947-82; the first Hall of Fame Bowl (1977-85) was called the All-American Bowl in 1986-90; the second Hall of Fame Bowl (1986-95) is now called the Outback Bowl and is played in Tampa, Fla.; the Sun Bowl was called the John Hancock Bowl in 1989-93, the John Hancock Sun Bowl in 1987-88, and reverted to the Sun Bowl in 1994; and the Blockbuster Bowl changed its name to Carquest Bowl in 1993.

Total Offense

MOST TOTAL PLAYS

96—North Caro. St. (10) vs. Arizona (17) (Copper, 1989) (310 yards)
95—Georgia (27) vs. Virginia (34) (Peach, Dec. 30, 1995) (525 yards)
95—Toledo (40) vs. Nevada (37) (OT) (Las Vegas, 1995) (561 yards)
95—North Caro. St. (28) vs. Iowa (23) (Peach, Dec. 31, 1988) (431 yards)
94—Arkansas (27) vs. Tennessee (31) (Cotton, 1990) (568 yards)
93—Miami (Fla.) (10) vs. Penn St. (14) (Fiesta, 1987) (445 yards)
92—Oregon (20) vs. Penn St. (38) (Rose, 1995) (501 yards)
92—Washington St. (24) vs. Houston (22) (Aloha, 1988) (460 yards)
92—(D) Western Mich. (30) vs. Fresno St. (35) (California, 1988) (503 yards)
92—(D) Purdue (27) vs. Tennessee (22) (Bluebonnet, 1979) (483 yards)
92—Arizona St. (30) vs. Penn St. (42) (Fiesta, 1977) (426 yards)
91—Florida (28) vs. Notre Dame (39) (Sugar, 1992) (511 yards)
91—Baylor (21) vs. LSU (7) (Liberty, 1985) (489 yards)
90—Virginia Tech (25) vs. North Caro. St. (24) (Peach, 1986) (487 yards)
90—Maryland (0) vs. Texas (42) (Sun, 1978) (248 yards)
90—Nebraska (40) vs. Notre Dame (6) (Orange, 1973) (560 yards)
90—(D) Oklahoma (27) vs. Southern Methodist (28) (Bluebonnet, 1968)
90—Richmond (49) vs. Ohio (42) (Tangerine, 1968) (556 yards)

MOST TOTAL PLAYS, BOTH TEAMS

175—Toledo (40) [95] & Nevada (37) [80] (OT) (Las Vegas, 1995) (974 yards)
171—Auburn (34) [82] & Arizona (10) [89] (Sun, 1968) (537 yards)
167—(D) Fresno St. (35) [75] & Western Mich. (30) [92] (California, 1988) (943 yards)
167—Arizona St. (45) [86] & Florida St. (38) [81] (Fiesta, 1971) (863 yards)
166—Colorado (47) [86] & Alabama (33) [80] (Liberty, 1969) (930 yards)
165—North Caro. St. (28) [95] & Iowa (23) [70] (Peach, Dec. 31, 1988)
165—East Caro. (35) [80] & Louisiana Tech (13) [85] (Independence, 1978) (607 yards)
165—Penn St. (42) [73] & Arizona St. (30) [92] (Fiesta, 1977) (777 yards)
163—Nebraska (45) [88] & Georgia (6) [75] (Sun, 1969) (540 yards)
162—Penn St. (38) [70] & Oregon (20) [92] (Rose, 1995) (931 yards)
161—Ohio St. (28) [78] & Pittsburgh (23) [83] (Fiesta, 1984) (897 yards)
161—Auburn (35) [84] & Mississippi (28) [77] (Gator, Jan. 2, 1971) (1,024 yards)
160—Texas Tech (55) [80] & Air Force (41) [80] (Copper, 1995) (1,120 yards)
160—Mississippi (42) [78] & Air Force (29) [82] (Liberty, 1989) (1,047 yards)
159—Notre Dame (39) [68] & Florida (28) [91] (Sugar, 1992) (944 yards)
159—Notre Dame (38) [85] & Texas (10) [74] (Cotton, 1978) (690 yards)
159—Texas (42) [69] & Maryland (0) [90] (Sun, 1978) (517 yards)

MOST YARDS GAINED

718—Arizona St. (49) vs. Missouri (35) (Fiesta, 1972) (452 rush, 266 pass)
715—Michigan (35) vs. Mississippi (3) (Gator, Jan. 1, 1991) (324 rush, 391 pass)
698—Oklahoma St. (62) vs. Wyoming (14) (Holiday, 1988) (320 rush, 378 pass)
680—Texas A&M (65) vs. Brigham Young (14) (Holiday, 1989) (356 rush, 324 pass)
655—(D) Houston (47) vs. Tulane (7) (Bluebonnet, 1973) (402 rush, 253 pass)
651—Brigham Young (39) vs. Penn St. (50) (Holiday, 1989) (75 rush, 576 pass)
642—(D) San Jose St. (48) vs. Central Mich. (24) (California, 1990) (200 rush, 442 pass)
629—Nebraska (62) vs. Florida (24) (Fiesta, 1996) (524 rush, 105 pass)
624—(D) Southern Cal (47) vs. Texas A&M (28) (Bluebonnet, 1977) (378 rush, 246 pass)
618—Oklahoma (48) vs. Virginia (14) (Gator, Dec. 29, 1991) (261 rush, 357 pass)
606—Texas Tech (55) vs. Air Force (41) (Copper, 1995) (361 rush, 245 pass)
596—Alabama (61) vs. Syracuse (6) (Orange, 1953) (296 rush, 300 pass)
589—UNLV (52) vs. Central Mich. (24) (Las Vegas, 1994) (301 rush, 288 pass)
578—Southern Cal (55) vs. Texas Tech (14) (Cotton, 1995) (143 rush, 435 pass)
575—Indiana (34) vs. South Caro. (10) (Liberty, 1988) (185 rush, 390 pass)
571—Louisville (34) vs. Alabama (7) (Fiesta, 1991) (113 rush, 458 pass)
569—Florida St. (34) vs. Oklahoma St. (23) (Gator, 1985) (231 rush, 338 pass)
568—Arkansas (27) vs. Tennessee (31) (Cotton, 1990) (361 rush, 207 pass)
566—Pittsburgh (34) vs. Clemson (3) (Gator, 1977) (179 rush, 387 pass)

MOST YARDS GAINED, BOTH TEAMS

1,143—(D) Southern Cal (47) [624] & Texas A&M (28) [519] (Bluebonnet, 1977) (148 plays)
1,129—Arizona St. (49) [718] & Missouri (35) [411] (Fiesta, 1972) (134 plays)
1,120—Texas Tech (55) [606] & Air Force (41) [514] (Copper, 1995) (160 plays)
1,115—Penn St. (50) [464] & Brigham Young (39) [651] (Holiday, 1989) (157 plays)
1,048—Michigan (35) [715] & Mississippi (3) [333] (Gator, Jan. 1, 1991) (153 plays)
1,047—Mississippi (42) [533] & Air Force (29) [514] (Liberty, 1989) (160 plays)
1,038—Tennessee (31) [470] & Arkansas (27) [568] (Cotton, 1990) (155 plays)
1,024—Auburn (35) [559] & Mississippi (28) [465] (Gator, Jan. 2, 1971) (161 plays)
1,007—(D) Toledo (27) [486] & San Jose St. (25) [521] (California, 1981) (158 plays)
978—Pittsburgh (31) [530] & Texas A&M (28) [448] (John Hancock, 1989) (158 plays)
974—Toledo (40) [561] & Nevada (37) [413] (OT) (Las Vegas, 1995) (175 plays)
965—UNLV (52) [589] & Central Mich. (24) [376] (Las Vegas, 1994) (145 plays)
954—Mississippi (27) [427] & Arkansas (22) [527] (Sugar, 1970)
950—Texas (40) [436] & Missouri (27) [514] (Cotton, 1946)
944—Notre Dame (39) [433] & Florida (28) [511] (Sugar, 1992) (159 plays)

HIGHEST AVERAGE GAINED PER PLAY
9.5—Louisville (34) vs. Alabama (7) (Fiesta, 1991) (60 for 571 yards)
8.7—Oklahoma St. (62) vs. Wyoming (14) (Holiday, 1988) (80 for 698 yards)
8.4—Michigan (35) vs. Mississippi (3) (Gator, Jan. 1, 1991) (85 for 715 yards)
8.3—Texas A&M (65) vs. Brigham Young (14) (Holiday, 1990) (82 for 680 yards)
8.1—Arizona St. (49) vs. Missouri (35) (Fiesta, 1972) (89 for 718 yards)
7.9—Brigham Young (39) vs. Penn St. (50) (Holiday, 1989) (82 for 651 yards)
7.7—Alabama (61) vs. Syracuse (6) (Orange, 1953) (77 for 596 yards)
7.7—(D) Vanderbilt (28) vs. Air Force (36) (Hall of Fame, 1982) (63 for 487 yards)
7.7—Kansas (51) vs. UCLA (30) (Aloha, 1995) (71 for 548 yards)
7.7—Tennessee (31) vs. Arkansas (27) (Cotton, 1990) (61 for 470 yards)
7.6—Florida St. (41) vs. Nebraska (17) (Fiesta, 1990) (65 for 494 yards)
7.6—Nebraska (62) vs. Florida (24) (Fiesta, 1996) (83 for 629 yards)
7.6—Texas Tech (55) vs. Air Force (41) (Copper, 1995) (80 for 606 yards)
7.5—(D) Houston (47) vs. Tulane (7) (Bluebonnet, 1973) (87 for 655 yards)
7.5—Iowa (38) vs. California (12) (Rose, 1959) (69 for 516 yards)
7.4—(D) UCLA (31) vs. Brigham Young (10) (Freedom, 1986) (70 for 518 yards)
7.3—(D) UNLV (30) vs. Toledo (13) (California, 1984) (56 for 409 yards)
7.3—(D) San Jose St. (48) vs. Central Mich. (24) (California, 1990) (88 for 642 yards)

FEWEST PLAYS
35—Tennessee (0) vs. Texas (16) (Cotton, 1953) (29 rush, 6 pass)
36—Arkansas (3) vs. UCLA (17) (Cotton, 1989) (22 rush, 14 pass)
37—Texas Christian (0) vs. Oklahoma St. (34) (Cotton, 1945) (27 rush, 10 pass)
38—Iowa (3) vs. California (37) (Alamo, 1993) (21 rush, 17 pass)

FEWEST PLAYS, BOTH TEAMS
107—Texas Christian (16) [54] & Marquette (6) [53] (Cotton, 1937)

FEWEST YARDS
-21—U. of Mexico (0) vs. Southwestern (Tex.) (35) (Sun, 1945) (29 rush, -50 pass)
23—Alabama (10) vs. Missouri (35) (Gator, 1968) (-45 rush, 68 pass)
32—Tennessee (0) vs. Texas (16) (Cotton, 1953) (-14 rush, 46 pass)
38—Miami (Fla.) (0) vs. Bucknell (26) (Orange, 1935) (20 rush, 18 pass)
41—Southern Cal (14) vs. Alabama (34) (Rose, 1946) (6 rush, 35 pass)
42—Arkansas (3) vs. UCLA (17) (Cotton, 1989) (21 rush, 21 pass)
48—New Mexico (0) vs. Southwestern (Tex.) (7) (Sun, 1944) (38 rush, 10 pass)
54—Arkansas (0) vs. LSU (0) (Cotton, 1947) (54 rush, 0 pass)
57—Michigan St. (0) vs. Auburn (6) (Orange, 1938) (32 rush, 25 pass)

FEWEST YARDS, BOTH TEAMS
260—Randolph Field (7) [150] & Texas (7) [110] (Cotton, 1944)
263—LSU (19) [92] & Texas A&M (14) [171] (Orange, 1944)

Rushing

MOST RUSHING ATTEMPTS
87—Oklahoma (40) vs. Auburn (22) (Sugar, Jan. 1, 1972) (439 yards)
82—Missouri (35) vs. Alabama (10) (Gator, 1968) (402 yards)
79—West Va. (14) vs. South Caro. (3) (Peach, 1969) (356 yards)
79—Georgia Tech (31) vs. Texas Tech (21) (Gator, Dec. 31, 1965) (364 yards)
78—(D) Houston (35) vs. Navy (0) (Garden State, 1980) (405 yards)
78—Texas (16) vs. Tennessee (0) (Cotton, 1953) (296 yards)
76—Oklahoma (14) vs. Penn St. (0) (Sugar, Dec. 31, 1972) (278 yards)
74—Oklahoma (41) vs. Wyoming (7) (Fiesta, 1976) (415 yards)
74—Michigan (12) vs. Stanford (13) (Rose, 1972) (264 yards)
74—Ohio St. (20) vs. Southern Cal (7) (Rose, 1955) (305 yards)
73—Syracuse (31) vs. McNeese St. (7) (Independence, 1979) (276 yards)
73—Penn St. (41) vs. Oregon (12) (Liberty, 1960) (301 yards)
72—Arkansas (27) vs. Tennessee (31) (Cotton, 1990) (361 yards)
72—North Caro. St. (28) vs. Iowa (23) (Peach, Dec. 31, 1988) (236 yards)
72—(D) Texas A&M (28) vs. Southern Cal (47) (Bluebonnet, 1977) (486 yards)

MOST RUSHING ATTEMPTS, BOTH TEAMS
122—(D) Southern Cal (47) [50] & Texas A&M (28) [72] (Bluebonnet, 1977) (864 yards)
122—Mississippi St. (26) [68] & North Caro. (24) [54] (Sun, 1974) (732 yards)
120—Pittsburgh (33) [53] & Kansas (19) [67] (Sun, 1975) (714 yards)
117—Oklahoma (14) [65] & Michigan (6) [52] (Orange, 1976) (451 yards)
117—West Va. (14) [79] & South Caro. (3) [38] (Peach, 1969) (420 yards)
116—Oklahoma (41) [74] & Wyoming (7) [42] (Fiesta, 1976) (568 yards)
116—Colorado (47) [70] & Alabama (33) [46] (Liberty, 1969) (628 yards)
115—Southern Cal (7) [47] & Wisconsin (0) [68] (Rose, 1953) (259 yards)
113—Oklahoma (40) [54] & Houston (14) [59] (Sun, 1981) (566 yards)
113—(D) Houston (35) [78] & Navy (0) [35] (Garden State, 1980) (540 yards)
113—Missouri (34) [71] & Auburn (17) [42] (Sun, 1973) (408 yards)
112—Arkansas (31) [65] & Georgia (10) [47] (Cotton, 1976) (426 yards)
112—(D) Colorado (29) [62] & Houston (17) [50] (Bluebonnet, 1971) (552 yards)

MOST NET RUSHING YARDS
524—Nebraska (62) vs. Florida (24) (Fiesta, 1996) (68 attempts)
486—(D) Texas A&M (28) vs. Southern Cal (47) (Bluebonnet, 1977) (72 attempts)
473—Colorado (47) vs. Alabama (33) (Liberty, 1969) (70 attempts)
455—Mississippi St. (26) vs. North Caro. (24) (Sun, 1974) (68 attempts)
452—Arizona St. (49) vs. Missouri (35) (Fiesta, 1972) (65 attempts)
439—Oklahoma (40) vs. Auburn (22) (Sugar, Jan. 1, 1972) (87 attempts)
434—Oklahoma (41) vs. Wyoming (7) (Fiesta, 1976) (74 attempts)
431—Air Force (41) vs. Texas Tech (55) (Copper, 1995) (67 attempts)
429—Iowa (38) vs. California (12) (Rose, 1959) (55 attempts)
423—(D) UCLA (31) vs. Brigham Young (10) (Freedom, 1986) (49 attempts)
423—Auburn (33) vs. Baylor (13) (Gator, Dec. 31, 1954) (48 attempts)
417—Oklahoma (21) vs. Arizona St. (32) (Fiesta, 1983) (63 attempts)
411—Oklahoma (24) vs. Florida St. (7) (Orange, 1980) (62 attempts)
409—Oklahoma (40) vs. Houston (14) (Sun, 1981) (54 attempts)
408—Missouri (27) vs. Texas (40) (Cotton, 1946)
405—(D) Houston (35) vs. Navy (0) (Garden State, 1980) (78 attempts)
402—(D) Houston (47) vs. Tulane (7) (Bluebonnet, 1973) (58 attempts)

MOST NET RUSHING YARDS, BOTH TEAMS
864—(D) Southern Cal (47) [378] & Texas A&M (28) [486] (Bluebonnet, 1977) (122 attempts)
792—Texas Tech (55) [361] & Air Force (41) [431] (Copper, 1995) (107 attempts)
732—Mississippi St. (26) [455] & North Caro. (24) [277] (Sun, 1974) (122 attempts)
714—Pittsburgh (33) [372] & Kansas (19) [342] (Sun, 1975) (120 attempts)
701—Arizona St. (49) [453] & Missouri (35) [248] (Fiesta, 1972) (109 attempts)
681—Tennessee (31) [320] & Arkansas (27) [361] (Cotton, 1990) (110 attempts)
643—Iowa (38) [429] & California (12) [214] (Rose, 1959) (108 attempts)
628—Colorado (47) [473] & Alabama (33) [155] (Liberty, 1969) (116 attempts)
616—Oklahoma (41) [434] & Wyoming (7) [182] (Fiesta, 1976) (116 attempts)
610—Texas (40) [202] & Missouri (27) [408] (Cotton, 1946)

HIGHEST RUSHING AVERAGE
(Minimum 30 Attempts)
9.3—Texas Tech (55) vs. Air Force (41) (Copper, 1995) (39 for 361 yards)
8.6—(D) UCLA (31) vs. Brigham Young (10) (Freedom, 1986) (49 for 423 yards)
8.6—Michigan (38) vs. Washington (31) (Rose, 1993) (36 for 308 yards)
8.4—Tennessee (31) vs. Arkansas (27) (Cotton, 1990) (38 for 320 yards)
8.0—Toledo (56) vs. Davidson (33) (Tangerine, 1969) (42 for 334 yards)
7.8—Iowa (38) vs. California (12) (Rose, 1959) (55 for 429 yards)
7.7—Texas Tech (28) vs. North Caro. (32) (Sun, 1972) (38 for 293 yards)
7.7—Nebraska (62) vs. Florida (24) (Fiesta, 1996) (68 for 524 yards)
7.6—Oklahoma (42) vs. Arkansas (8) (Orange, 1987) (48 for 366 yards)
7.6—Oklahoma (40) vs. Houston (14) (Sun, 1981) (54 for 409 yards)
7.6—(D) Southern Cal (47) vs. Texas A&M (28) (Bluebonnet, 1977) (50 for 378 yards)
7.4—Michigan (35) vs. Mississippi (3) (Gator, Jan. 1, 1991) (53 for 391 yards)
7.1—Boston College (45) vs. Houston (28) (Cotton, 1985) (50 for 353 yards)
7.0—Pittsburgh (33) vs. Kansas (19) (Sun, 1975) (53 for 372 yards)
7.0—Arizona St. (49) vs. Missouri (35) (Fiesta, 1972) (65 for 453 yards)

FEWEST RUSHING ATTEMPTS
12—(D) Vanderbilt (28) vs. Air Force (36) (Hall of Fame, 1982) (35 yards)
16—Florida (18) vs. Missouri (20) (Sugar, 1966) (-2 yards)
16—Colorado (7) vs. LSU (25) (Orange, 1962) (24 yards)
17—(D) Duke (21) vs. Texas Tech (49) (All-American, 1989) (67 yards)
17—Illinois (9) vs. UCLA (45) (Rose, 1984) (0 yards)
18—Brigham Young (46) vs. Southern Methodist (45) (Holiday, 1980) (-2 yards)
19—Iowa (23) vs. North Caro. St. (28) (Peach, Dec. 31, 1988) (46 yards)
19—Baylor (13) vs. Auburn (33) (Gator, Dec. 31, 1954) (108 yards)
20—(D) San Jose St. (27) vs. Eastern Mich. (30) (California, 1987) (81 yards)
20—Tulane (6) vs. Penn St. (9) (Liberty, 1979) (-8 yards)
21—Florida (24) vs. Nebraska (62) (Fiesta, 1996) (-28 yards)
21—Iowa (3) vs. California (37) (Alamo, 1993) (20 yards)
21—Brigham Young (14) vs. Texas A&M (65) (Holiday, 1990) (-12 yards)
21—Houston (22) vs. Washington St. (24) (Aloha, 1988) (68 yards)
21—Wyoming (19) vs. Iowa (20) (Holiday, 1987) (43 yards)
21—(D) San Jose St. (25) vs. Toledo (27) (California, 1981) (54 yards)

FEWEST RUSHING ATTEMPTS, BOTH TEAMS
57—Iowa (20) [36] & Wyoming (19) [21] (Holiday, 1987)
63—(D) Southern Cal (28) [38] & Utah (21) [25] (Freedom, 1993)
66—Southern Cal (41) [27] & Northwestern (32) [39] (Rose, 1996)
66—Brigham Young (13) [33] & Iowa (13) [33] (Holiday, 1991)
66—Miami (Fla.) (23) [28] & Nebraska (3) [38] (Orange, 1989)
66—Texas Christian (16) [34] & Marquette (6) [32] (Cotton, 1937)
67—UCLA (6) [41] & Illinois (3) [26] (John Hancock, 1991)
67—Southern Cal (7) [39] & Duke (3) [28] (Rose, 1939)
68—Tennessee (20) [32] & Ohio St. (14) [36] (Florida Citrus, 1996)
68—(D) Fresno St. (29) [24] & Bowling Green (28) [44] (California, 1982)
69—(D) Utah (16) [32] & Arizona (13) [37] (Freedom, 1994)
70—Colorado (38) [41] & Oregon (6) [29] (Cotton, 1996)
70—Arizona (29) [50] & Miami (Fla.) (0) [20] (Fiesta, 1994)
70—Florida St. (41) [24] & Nebraska (17) [46] (Fiesta, 1990)
70—Florida St. (24) [39] & Penn St. (17) [31] (Blockbuster, 1990)

FEWEST RUSHING YARDS
-61—Kansas St. (7) vs. Boston College (12) (Aloha, 1994) (23 attempts)
-45—Alabama (10) vs. Missouri (35) (Gator, 1968) (29 attempts)
-30—Florida (6) vs. West Va. (26) (Peach, Dec. 31, 1981) (34 attempts)
-28—Florida (24) vs. Nebraska (62) (Fiesta, 1996) (21 attempts)
-21—Florida St. (20) vs. Wyoming (28) (Sun, 1966) (31 attempts)
-15—LSU (0) vs. Mississippi (20) (Sugar, 1960)
-14—Navy (6) vs. Texas (28) (Cotton, 1964) (29 attempts)
-14—Tennessee (0) vs. Texas (16) (Cotton, 1953) (29 attempts)
-12—Brigham Young (14) vs. Texas A&M (65) (Holiday, 1990) (21 attempts)
-12—Air Force (13) vs. Tennessee (34) (Sugar, 1971)
-11—Colorado (25) vs. Alabama (30) (Blockbuster, 1991) (30 attempts)

-8—Tulane (6) vs. Penn St. (9) (Liberty, 1979) (20 attempts)
-8—Navy (14) vs. Missouri (21) (Orange, 1961) (24 attempts)
-2—Brigham Young (46) vs. Southern Methodist (45) (Holiday, 1980) (24 attempts)
-2—Florida (18) vs. Missouri (20) (Sugar, 1966) (16 attempts)

FEWEST RUSHING YARDS, BOTH TEAMS
51—(D) Utah (16) [6] & Arizona (13) [45] (Freedom, 1994)
74—Tennessee (34) [86] & Air Force (13) [-12] (Sugar, 1971)
81—Florida St. (23) [76] & Florida (17) [5] (Sugar, Jan. 2, 1995)
81—Washington St. (10) [7] & Baylor (3) [74] (Alamo, 1994)
88—Boston College (12) [149] & Kansas St. (7) [-61] (Aloha, 1994)
137—Iowa (20) [94] & Wyoming (19) [43] (Holiday, 1987)
143—Brigham Young (31) [71] & Oklahoma (6) [72] (Copper, 1994)
145—Arkansas (10) [45] & Nebraska (7) [100] (Cotton, 1965)
147—(D) San Jose St. (37) [123] & Miami (Ohio) (7) [24] (California, 1986)

LOWEST RUSHING AVERAGE
(Minimum 20 Attempts)
-2.7—Kansas St. (7) vs. Boston College (12) (Aloha, 1994) (23 for -61 yards)
-1.6—Alabama (10) vs. Missouri (35) (Gator, 1968) (29 for -45 yards)
-1.3—Florida (24) vs. Nebraska (62) (Fiesta, 1996) (21 for -28 yards)
-0.9—Florida (6) vs. West Va. (26) (Peach, Dec. 31, 1981) (32 for -30 yards)
-0.7—Florida St. (20) vs. Wyoming (28) (Sun, 1966) (31 for -21 yards)
-0.6—Brigham Young (14) vs. Texas A&M (65) (Holiday, 1990) (21 for -12 yards)
-0.5—Navy (6) vs. Texas (28) (Cotton, 1964) (29 for -14 yards)
-0.5—Tennessee (0) vs. Texas (16) (Cotton, 1953) (29 for -14 yards)
-0.4—Colorado (25) vs. Alabama (30) (Blockbuster, 1991) (30 for -11 yards)
-0.3—Navy (14) vs. Missouri (21) (Orange, 1961) (24 for -8 yards)

RUSHING DEFENSE, FEWEST YARDS ALLOWED
-61—Boston College (12) vs. Kansas St. (7) (Aloha, 1994) (23 attempts)
-45—Missouri (35) vs. Alabama (10) (Gator, 1968) (29 attempts)
-30—West Va. (26) vs. Florida (6) (Peach, Dec. 31, 1981) (32 attempts)
-28—Nebraska (62) vs. Florida (24) (Fiesta, 1996) (21 attempts)
-21—Wyoming (28) vs. Florida St. (20) (Sun, 1966) (31 attempts)
-15—Mississippi (20) vs. LSU (0) (Sugar, 1960)
-14—Texas (28) vs. Navy (6) (Cotton, 1964) (29 attempts)
-14—Texas (16) vs. Tennessee (0) (Cotton, 1953) (29 attempts)
-12—Texas A&M (65) vs. Brigham Young (14) (Holiday, 1990) (21 attempts)
-12—Tennessee (34) vs. Air Force (13) (Sugar, 1971)
-11—Alabama (30) vs. Colorado (25) (Blockbuster, 1991) (30 attempts)
-8—Penn St. (9) vs. Tulane (6) (Liberty, 1979) (20 attempts)
-8—Missouri (21) vs. Navy (14) (Orange, 1961) (24 attempts)
-2—Southern Methodist (45) vs. Brigham Young (46) (Holiday, 1980) (24 attempts)
-2—Missouri (20) vs. Florida (18) (Sugar, 1966) (16 attempts)

Passing

MOST PASS ATTEMPTS
(Followed by Comp.-Att.-Int. and Yardage)
63—Fresno St. (30) vs. Colorado (41) (Aloha, 1993) (37-63-1, 523 yards)
63—(D) San Jose St. (25) vs. Toledo (27) (California, 1981) (43-63-5, 467 yards)
61—Oregon (20) vs. Penn St. (38) (Rose, 1995) (41-61-2, 456 yards)
61—(D) Brigham Young (16) vs. Virginia (22) (All-American, 1987) (37-61-1, 394 yards)
59—Georgia (27) vs. Virginia (34) (Peach, Dec. 30, 1995) (31-59-2, 413 yards)
59—Brigham Young (39) vs. Penn St. (50) (Holiday, 1989) (42-59-2, 576 yards)
58—Florida (28) vs. Notre Dame (39) (Sugar, 1992) (28-58-2, 370 yards)
58—Illinois (15) vs. Alabama (21) (Liberty, 1982) (35-58-7, 423 yards)
58—Richmond (49) vs. Ohio (42) (Tangerine, 1968) (39-58-2, 447 yards)
57—(D) Western Mich. (30) vs. Fresno St. (35) (California, 1988) (24-57-0, 366 yards)
56—Miami (Fla.) (13) vs. Alabama (34) (Sugar, 1993) (24-56-3, 278 yards)
56—Washington (21) vs. Maryland (20) (Aloha, 1982) (35-56-0, 369 yards)
55—Illinois (29) vs. Army (31) (Peach, 1985) (38-55-2, 401 yards)
55—Florida St. (17) vs. Penn St. (17) (Gator, 1967) (38-55-4, 363 yards)
52—Alabama (29) vs. Army (28) (John Hancock Sun, 1988) (33-52-1, 412 yards)
52—Louisiana Tech (13) vs. East Caro. (35) (Independence, 1978) (18-52-3, 263 yards)

MOST PASS ATTEMPTS, BOTH TEAMS
92—Toledo (40) [41] & Nevada (37) [51] (OT) (Las Vegas, 1995) (50 completed)
92—Penn St. (38) [31] & Oregon (20) [61] (Rose, 1995) (61 completed)
92—Tennessee (34) [46] & Air Force (13) [46] (Sugar, 1971) (47 completed)
91—Richmond (49) [58] & Ohio (42) [33] (Tangerine, 1968) (56 completed)
90—Bowling Green (35) [41] & Nevada (34) [49] (Las Vegas, 1992) (54 completed)
90—Mississippi (20) [50] & Texas Tech (17) [40] (Independence, 1986) (48 completed)
88—Washington St. (31) [48] & Utah (28) [40] (Copper, 1992) (53 completed)
88—Washington (21) [56] & Maryland (20) [32] (Aloha, 1982) (54 completed)
86—(D) Fresno St. (35) [29] & Western Mich. (30) [57] (California, 1988) (39 completed)
86—Iowa (20) [35] & Wyoming (19) [51] (Holiday, 1987) (49 completed)
85—Ohio St. (10) [35] & Brigham Young (7) [50] (Florida Citrus, 1985) (45 completed)
85—(D) Toledo (27) [22] & San Jose St. (25) [63] (California, 1981) (54 completed)
84—Florida St. (23) [41] & Florida (17) [43] (Sugar, Jan. 2, 1995) (54 completed)
84—(D) Southern Cal (28) [44] & Utah (21) [40] (Freedom, 1993) (53 completed)
83—Southern Cal (41) [44] & Northwestern (32) [39] (Rose, 1996) (52 completed)
83—Auburn (35) [44] & Mississippi (28) [39] (Gator, Jan. 2, 1971) (50 completed)
82—(D) Fresno St. (29) [50] & Bowling Green (28) [32] (California, 1982) (53 completed)
80—Penn St. (50) [21] & Brigham Young (39) [59] (Holiday, 1989) (53 completed)
80—(D) Virginia (22) [19] & Brigham Young (16) [61] (All-American, 1987) (47 completed)
80—(D) San Jose St. (37) [39] & Miami (Ohio) (7) [41] (California, 1986) (40 completed)

MOST PASS COMPLETIONS
(Followed by Comp.-Att.-Int. and Yardage)
43—(D) San Jose St. (25) vs. Toledo (27) (California, 1981) (43-63-5, 467 yards)
42—Brigham Young (39) vs. Penn St. (50) (Holiday, 1989) (42-59-2, 576 yards)
41—Oregon (20) vs. Penn St. (38) (Rose, 1995) (41-61-2, 456 yards)
39—Richmond (49) vs. Ohio (42) (Tangerine, 1968) (39-58-2, 447 yards)
38—Illinois (29) vs. Army (31) (Peach, 1985) (38-55-2, 401 yards)
38—(D) Vanderbilt (28) vs. Air Force (36) (Hall of Fame, 1982) (38-51-3, 452 yards)
38—Florida St. (17) vs. Penn St. (17) (Gator, 1967) (38-55-4, 363 yards)
37—Fresno St. (30) vs. Colorado (41) (Aloha, 1993) (37-63-1, 523 yards)
37—(D) Brigham Young (16) vs. Virginia (22) (All-American, 1987) (37-61-1, 394 yards)
35—Brigham Young (24) vs. Michigan (17) (Holiday, 1984) (35-49-3, 371 yards)
35—Illinois (15) vs. Alabama (21) (Liberty, 1982) (35-58-7, 423 yards)
35—Washington (21) vs. Maryland (20) (Aloha, 1982) (35-56-0, 369 yards)
34—Wisconsin (37) vs. Southern Cal (42) (Rose, 1963) (34-49-3, 419 yards)
33—Alabama (29) vs. Army (28) (John Hancock Sun, 1988) (33-52-1, 412 yards)

MOST PASS COMPLETIONS, BOTH TEAMS
61—Penn St. (38) [20] & Oregon (20) [41] (Rose, 1995) (92 attempted)
56—Richmond (49) [39] & Ohio (42) [17] (Tangerine, 1968) (91 attempted)
54—Florida St. (23) [24] & Florida (17) [30] (Sugar, Jan. 2, 1995) (84 attempted)
54—Bowling Green (35) [25] & Nevada (34) [29] (Las Vegas, 1992) (90 attempted)
54—Washington (21) [35] & Maryland (20) [19] (Aloha, 1982) (88 attempted)
54—(D) Toledo (27) [11] & San Jose St. (25) [43] (California, 1981) (85 attempted)
53—(D) Southern Cal (28) [30] & Utah (21) [23] (Freedom, 1993) (84 attempted)
53—Washington St. (31) [32] & Utah (28) [21] (Copper, 1992) (88 attempted)
53—Penn St. (50) [11] & Brigham Young (39) [42] (Holiday, 1989) (80 attempted)
53—(D) Fresno St. (29) [31] & Bowling Green (28) [22] (California, 1982) (82 attempted)
52—Southern Cal (41) [29] & Northwestern (32) [23] (Rose, 1996) (83 attempted)
50—Toledo (40) [23] & Nevada (37) [27] (OT) (Las Vegas, 1995) (92 attempted)
50—Auburn (35) [27] & Mississippi (28) [23] (Gator, Jan. 2, 1971) (83 attempted)
49—Iowa (20) [21] & Wyoming (19) [28] (Holiday, 1987) (86 attempted)
49—UCLA (39) [18] & Miami (Fla.) (37) [31] (Fiesta, 1985) (71 attempted)
49—(D) Air Force (36) [11] & Vanderbilt (28) [38] (Hall of Fame, 1982) (68 attempted)
48—Brigham Young (13) [29] & Iowa (13) [19] (Holiday, 1991) (72 attempted)
48—LSU (30) [20] & South Caro. (13) [28] (Gator, 1987) (79 attempted)
48—Mississippi (20) [31] & Texas Tech (17) [17] (Independence, 1986) (90 attempted)

MOST PASSING YARDS
(Followed by Comp.-Att.-Int.)
576—Brigham Young (39) vs. Penn St. (50) (Holiday, 1989) (42-59-2)
523—Fresno St. (30) vs. Colorado (41) (Aloha, 1993) (37-63-1)
492—Washington St. (31) vs. Utah (28) (Copper, 1992) (32-48-1)
485—Brigham Young (31) vs. Oklahoma (6) (Copper, 1994) (23-46-0)
469—(D) Iowa (55) vs. Texas (17) (Freedom, 1984) (30-40-0)
467—(D) San Jose St. (25) vs. Toledo (27) (California, 1981) (43-63-5)
458—Louisville (34) vs. Alabama (7) (Fiesta, 1991) (21-39-3)
456—Oregon (20) vs. Penn St. (38) (Rose, 1995) (41-61-2)
455—Florida St. (40) vs. Texas Tech (17) (Tangerine, 1977) (25-35-0)
452—(D) Vanderbilt (28) vs. Air Force (36) (Hall of Fame, 1982) (38-51-3)
449—Florida (17) vs. Florida St. (23) (Sugar, Jan. 2, 1995) (30-43-1)
447—Richmond (49) vs. Ohio (42) (Tangerine, 1968) (39-58-2)
446—Brigham Young (46) vs. Southern Methodist (45) (Holiday, 1980) (32-49-1)
442—(D) San Jose St. (48) vs. Central Mich. (24) (California, 1990) (32-43-1)
435—Southern Cal (55) vs. Texas Tech (14) (Cotton, 1995) (24-35-0)
428—Iowa (23) vs. North Caro. St. (28) (Peach, Dec. 31, 1988) (30-51-4)
423—Illinois (15) vs. Alabama (21) (Liberty, 1982) (35-58-7)
422—Florida St. (41) vs. Nebraska (17) (Fiesta, 1990) (25-41-0)
419—Wisconsin (37) vs. Southern Cal (42) (Rose, 1963) (34-49-3)
413—Georgia (27) vs. Virginia (34) (Peach, Dec. 30, 1995) (31-59-2)
412—Alabama (29) vs. Army (28) (John Hancock Sun, 1988) (33-52-1)

MOST PASSING YARDS, BOTH TEAMS
808—Washington St. (31) [492] & Utah (28) [316] (Copper, 1992) (88 attempted)
791—Penn St. (50) [215] & Brigham Young (39) [576] (Holiday, 1989) (80 attempted)
774—Florida St. (23) [325] & Florida (17) [449] (Sugar, Jan. 2, 1995) (84 attempted)
734—Florida St. (40) [455] & Texas Tech (17) [279] (Tangerine, 1977) (63 attempted)
732—(D) Toledo (27) [265] & San Jose St. (25) [467] (California, 1981) (85 attempted)
727—Southern Cal (41) [391] & Northwestern (32) [336] (Rose, 1996) (83 attempted)
672—Southern Cal (42) [253] & Wisconsin (37) [419] (Rose, 1963) (69 attempted)
662—(D) San Jose St. (48) [442] & Central Mich. (24) [220] (California, 1990) (68 attempted)
658—Penn St. (38) [202] & Oregon (20) [456] (Rose, 1995) (92 attempted)

654—(D) Iowa (55) [469] & Texas (17) [185] (Freedom, 1984) (74 attempted)
648—Brigham Young (31) [485] & Oklahoma (6) [163] (Copper, 1994) (76 attempted)
647—Colorado (41) [124] & Fresno St. (30) [523] (Aloha, 1993) (78 attempted)
640—Southern Cal (55) [435] & Texas Tech (14) [205] (Cotton, 1995) (72 attempted)
631—(D) Southern Cal (28) [345] & Utah (21) [286] (Freedom, 1993) (84 attempted)
629—Florida St. (41) [422] & Nebraska (17) [207] (Fiesta, 1990) (67 attempted)
623—North Caro. St. (28) [195] & Iowa (23) [428] (Peach, Dec. 31, 1988) (74 attempted)
620—Washington (21) [369] & Maryland (20) [251] (Aloha, 1982) (88 attempted)
619—(D) Fresno St. (29) [373] & Bowling Green (28) [246] (California, 1982) (82 attempted)
611—Arizona St. (45) [250] & Florida St. (38) [361] (Fiesta, 1971) (77 attempted)
611—Mississippi (27) [273] & Arkansas (22) [338] (Sugar, 1970) (70 attempted)
607—Auburn (35) [351] & Mississippi (28) [256] (Gator, Jan. 2, 1971) (83 attempted)
606—(D) Fresno St. (35) [240] & Western Mich. (30) [366] (California, 1988) (86 attempted)

MOST PASSES HAD INTERCEPTED
8—Arizona (10) vs. Auburn (34) (Sun, 1968)
7—Illinois (15) vs. Alabama (21) (Liberty, 1982)
7—Missouri (3) vs. Penn St. (10) (Orange, 1970)
7—Texas A&M (21) vs. Alabama (29) (Cotton, 1942)
6—Georgia (6) vs. Nebraska (45) (Sun, 1969)
6—Texas Christian (26) vs. Georgia (40) (Orange, 1942)
6—Southern Methodist (0) vs. Stanford (7) (Rose, 1936)

MOST PASSES HAD INTERCEPTED, BOTH TEAMS
12—Auburn (34) [4] & Arizona (10) [8] (Sun, 1968)
10—Georgia (40) [6] & Texas Christian (26) [4] (Orange, 1942)
9—Alabama (21) [2] & Illinois (15) [7] (Liberty, 1982)
8—Ohio St. (28) [3] & Texas A&M (12) [5] (Cotton, 1987)
8—Nebraska (28) [3] & LSU (10) [5] (Sugar, 1985)
8—Penn St. (10) [1] & Missouri (3) [7] (Orange, 1970)
8—Nebraska (45) [2] & Georgia (6) [6] (Sun, 1969)
8—Texas (12) [3] & Mississippi (7) [5] (Cotton, 1962)

MOST PASSES ATTEMPTED WITHOUT AN INTERCEPTION
(Followed by Comp.-Att.-Int. and Yardage)
57—(D) Western Mich. (30) vs. Fresno St. (35) (California, 1988) (24-57-0, 366 yards)
51—Nevada (37) vs. Toledo (40) (OT) (Las Vegas, 1995) (27-51-0, 330 yards)

MOST PASSES ATTEMPTED BY BOTH TEAMS WITHOUT AN INTERCEPTION
(Followed by Comp.-Att.-Int. and Yardage)
90—Bowling Green (35) [49] & Nevada (34) [41] (Las Vegas, 1992) (54-90-0, 597 yards)

HIGHEST COMPLETION PERCENTAGE
(Minimum 10 Attempts) (Followed by Comp.-Att.-Int. and Yardage)
.929—Texas (40) vs. Missouri (27) (Cotton, 1946) (13-14-0, 234 yards)
.900—Mississippi (13) vs. Air Force (0) (Liberty, 1992) (9-10-0, 163 yards)
.889—Texas A&M (65) vs. Brigham Young (14) (Holiday, 1990) (16-18-0, 324 yards)
.833—Alabama (13) vs. Penn St. (6) (Sugar, 1975) (10-12-0, 210 yards)
.828—Oklahoma St. (62) vs. Wyoming (14) (Holiday, 1988) (24-29-0, 378 yards)
.824—Nebraska (21) vs. North Caro. (17) (Liberty, 1977) (14-17-2, 161 yards)
.813—Texas Christian (28) vs. Syracuse (27) (Cotton, 1957) (13-16-0, 202 yards)
.800—Ohio St. (15) vs. Clemson (17) (Gator, 1978) (16-20-1, 205 yards)
.800—Georgia Tech (31) vs. Iowa St. (30) (Liberty, 1972) (12-15-1, 157 yards)
.778—Tennessee (27) vs. Indiana (22) (Peach, 1987) (21-27-0, 230 yards)
.771—Washington St. (10) vs. Baylor (3) (Alamo, 1994) (27-35-0, 286 yards)
.765—Illinois (17) vs. Hawaii (27) (Holiday, 1992) (26-34-1, 248 yards)
.765—Duke (7) vs. Arkansas (6) (Cotton, 1961) (13-17-1, 93 yards)
.763—Iowa (28) vs. UCLA (45) (Rose, 1986) (29-38-1, 319 yards)
.750—Kansas St. (54) vs. Colorado St. (21) (Holiday, 1995) (24-32-1, 324 yards)
.750—Oklahoma (48) vs. Virginia (14) (Gator, Dec. 29, 1991) (27-36-0, 357 yards)
.750—(D) Iowa (55) vs. Texas (17) (Freedom, 1984) (30-40-0, 469 yards)

MOST YARDS PER ATTEMPT
(Minimum 10 Attempts)
21.7—Southern Cal (47) vs. Pittsburgh (14) (Rose, 1930) (13 for 282 yards)
18.0—Texas A&M (65) vs. Brigham Young (14) (Holiday, 1990) (18 for 324 yards)
17.5—Alabama (13) vs. Penn St. (6) (Sugar, 1975) (12 for 210 yards)
16.7—Texas (36) vs. Tennessee (13) (Cotton, 1969) (14 for 234 yards)
16.7—Texas (40) vs. Missouri (27) (Cotton, 1946) (14 for 234 yards)

MOST YARDS PER COMPLETION
(Minimum 8 Completions)
35.2—Southern Cal (47) vs. Pittsburgh (14) (Rose, 1930) (8 for 282 yards)
29.3—Texas (36) vs. Tennessee (13) (Cotton, 1969) (8 for 234 yards)
29.3—Texas (28) vs. Navy (6) (Cotton, 1964) (8 for 234 yards)

FEWEST PASS ATTEMPTS
2—Air Force (38) vs. Mississippi St. (15) (Liberty, 1991) (completed 1)
2—(D) Army (10) vs. Michigan St. (6) (Cherry, 1984) (completed 1)
2—West Va. (14) vs. South Caro. (3) (Peach, 1969) (completed 1)
3—Air Force (23) vs. Ohio St. (11) (Liberty, 1990) (completed 1)
3—Oklahoma (31) vs. Nebraska (24) (Orange, 1979) (completed 2)
3—Georgia Tech (21) vs. Pittsburgh (14) (Gator, 1956) (completed 3)
3—Georgia Tech (7) vs. Pittsburgh (0) (Sugar, 1956) (completed 0)
3—Miami (Fla.) (14) vs. Clemson (0) (Gator, 1952) (completed 2)
3—Hardin-Simmons (7) vs. Second Air Force (13) (Sun, 1943) (completed 1)
3—Catholic (20) vs. Mississippi (19) (Orange, 1936) (completed 1)

FEWEST PASS ATTEMPTS, BOTH TEAMS
9—Fordham (2) [4] & Missouri (0) [5] (Sugar, 1942)
13—Colorado (27) [9] & Clemson (21) [4] (Orange, 1957)
14—Texas (16) [8] & Tennessee (0) [6] (Cotton, 1953)
15—LSU (7) [11] & Clemson (0) [4] (Sugar, 1959)
15—Utah (26) [4] & New Mexico (0) [11] (Sun, 1939)

FEWEST PASS COMPLETIONS
(Followed by Comp.-Att.-Int.)
0—Army (28) vs. Alabama (29) (John Hancock Sun, 1988) (0-6-1)
0—Missouri (35) vs. Alabama (10) (Gator, 1968) (0-6-2)
0—(D) Missouri (14) vs. Georgia Tech (10) (Bluebonnet, 1962) (0-7-2)
0—(D) New Mexico (28) vs. Western Mich. (12) (Aviation, 1961) (0-4-0)
0—Utah St. (13) vs. New Mexico St. (20) (Sun, 1960) (0-4-0)
0—Georgia Tech (7) vs. Pittsburgh (0) (Sugar, 1956) (0-3-1)
0—Arkansas (0) vs. LSU (0) (Cotton, 1947) (0-4-1)
0—Rice (8) vs. Tennessee (0) (Orange, 1947) (0-6-2)
0—Miami (Fla.) (13) vs. Holy Cross (6) (Orange, 1946) (0-10-3)
0—Fordham (2) vs. Missouri (0) (Sugar, 1942) (0-4-0)
0—Arizona St. (0) vs. Catholic (0) (Sun, 1940) (0-7-2)
0—Tulane (13) vs. Texas A&M (14) (Sugar, 1940) (0-4-0)
0—West Va. (7) vs. Texas Tech (6) (Sun, 1938) (0-7-0)

FEWEST PASS COMPLETIONS, BOTH TEAMS
3—Arizona St. (0) [0] & Catholic (0) [3] (Sun, 1940)
4—Penn St. (7) [2] & Alabama (0) [2] (Liberty, 1959)
5—Oklahoma (14) [3] & Michigan (6) [2] (Orange, 1976)
5—Kentucky (21) [2] & North Caro. (0) [3] (Peach, 1976)
5—Texas (16) [2] & Tennessee (0) [3] (Cotton, 1953)
5—Arkansas (0) [0] & LSU (0) [5] (Cotton, 1947)
5—Wake Forest (26) [1] & South Caro. (14) [4] (Gator, 1946)
5—Utah (26) [1] & New Mexico (0) [4] (Sun, 1939)

FEWEST PASSING YARDS
(Followed by Comp.-Att.-Int.)
-50—U. of Mexico (0) vs. Southwestern (Tex.) (35) (Sun, 1945) (2-9-3)
-17—Rice (8) vs. Tennessee (0) (Orange, 1947) (0-6-2)
-2—Oklahoma (40) vs. Houston (14) (Sun, 1981) (1-5-1)
0—Army (28) vs. Alabama (29) (John Hancock Sun, 1988) (0-6-1)
0—Missouri (35) vs. Alabama (10) (Gator, 1968) (0-6-2)
0—(D) Missouri (14) vs. Georgia Tech (10) (Bluebonnet, 1962) (0-7-2)
0—(D) New Mexico (28) vs. Western Mich. (12) (Aviation, 1961) (0-4-0)
0—Utah St. (13) vs. New Mexico St. (20) (Sun, 1960)
0—Georgia Tech (7) vs. Pittsburgh (0) (Sugar, 1956) (0-3-1)
0—Arkansas (0) vs. LSU (0) (Cotton, 1947) (0-4-1)
0—Miami (Fla.) (13) vs. Holy Cross (6) (Orange, 1946) (0-10-3)
0—Fordham (2) vs. Missouri (0) (Sugar, 1942) (0-4-0)
0—Tulane (13) vs. Texas A&M (14) (Sugar, 1940)
0—Arizona St. (0) vs. Catholic (0) (Sun, 1940) (0-7-2)
0—West Va. (7) vs. Texas Tech (6) (Sun, 1938) (0-7-0)
0—California (0) vs. Wash. & Jeff. (0) (Rose, 1922)
0—Oregon (6) vs. Harvard (7) (Rose, 1920)

FEWEST PASSING YARDS, BOTH TEAMS
15—Rice (8) [-17] & Tennessee (0) [32] (Orange, 1947)
16—Arkansas (0) [0] & LSU (0) [16] (Cotton, 1947)
16—Arizona St. (0) [0] & Catholic (0) [16] (Sun, 1940)
21—Fordham (2) [0] & Missouri (0) [21] (Sugar, 1942)
52—Colorado (27) [25] & Clemson (21) [27] (Orange, 1957)
59—Miami (Fla.) (13) [0] & Holy Cross (6) [59] (Orange, 1946)
68—Missouri (35) [0] & Alabama (10) [68] (Gator, 1968)
68—Penn St. (7) [41] & Alabama (0) [27] (Liberty, 1959)
74—Oklahoma (41) [23] & Wyoming (7) [51] (Fiesta, 1976)
75—Southwestern (Tex.) (7) [65] & New Mexico (0) [10] (Sun, 1944)
77—Utah (26) [18] & New Mexico (0) [59] (Sun, 1939)
78—Texas (16) [32] & Tennessee (0) [46] (Cotton, 1953)

LOWEST COMPLETION PERCENTAGE
(Followed by Comp.-Att.-Int.)
.000—Army (28) vs. Alabama (29) (John Hancock Sun, 1988) (0-6-1)
.000—Missouri (35) vs. Alabama (10) (Gator, 1968) (0-6-2)
.000—(D) Missouri (14) vs. Georgia Tech (10) (Bluebonnet, 1962) (0-7-2)
.000—(D) New Mexico (28) vs. Western Mich. (12) (Aviation, 1961) (0-4-0)
.000—Utah St. (13) vs. New Mexico St. (20) (Sun, 1960) (0-4-0)
.000—Georgia Tech (7) vs. Pittsburgh (0) (Sugar, 1956) (0-3-1)
.000—Arkansas (0) vs. LSU (0) (Cotton, 1947) (0-4-1)
.000—Rice (8) vs. Tennessee (0) (Orange, 1947) (0-6-2)
.000—Miami (Fla.) (13) vs. Holy Cross (6) (Orange, 1946) (0-10-3)
.000—Fordham (2) vs. Missouri (0) (Sugar, 1942) (0-4-0)
.000—Arizona St. (0) vs. Catholic (0) (Sun, 1940) (0-7-2)
.000—Tulane (13) vs. Texas A&M (14) (Sugar, 1940) (0-4-0)
.000—West Va. (7) vs. Texas Tech (6) (Sun, 1938) (0-7-0)

FEWEST YARDS PER PASS ATTEMPT
-5.6—U. of Mexico (0) vs. Southwestern (Tex.) (35) (Sun, 1945) (9 for -50 yards)
-2.8—Rice (8) vs. Tennessee (0) (Orange, 1947) (6 for -17 yards)
-0.4—Oklahoma (40) vs. Houston (14) (Sun, 1981) (5 for -2 yards)
0.0—Army (28) vs. Alabama (29) (John Hancock Sun, 1988) (6 for 0 yards)
0.0—Missouri (35) vs. Alabama (10) (Gator, 1968) (6 for 0 yards)
0.0—(D) Missouri (14) vs. Georgia Tech (10) (Bluebonnet, 1962) (7 for 0 yards)

0.0—(D) New Mexico (28) vs. Western Mich. (12) (Aviation, 1961) (4 for 0 yards)
0.0—Utah St. (13) vs. New Mexico St. (20) (Sun, 1960) (4 for 0 yards)
0.0—Georgia Tech (7) vs. Pittsburgh (0) (Sugar, 1956) (3 for 0 yards)
0.0—Arkansas (0) vs. LSU (0) (Cotton, 1947) (4 for 0 yards)
0.0—Miami (Fla.) (13) vs. Holy Cross (6) (Orange, 1946) (10 for 0 yards)
0.0—Fordham (2) vs. Missouri (0) (Sugar, 1942) (4 for 0 yards)
0.0—Arizona St. (0) vs. Catholic (0) (Sun, 1940) (7 for 0 yards)
0.0—Tulane (13) vs. Texas A&M (14) (Sugar, 1940) (4 for 0 yards)
0.0—West Va. (7) vs. Texas Tech (6) (Sun, 1938) (7 for 0 yards)

FEWEST YARDS PER PASS COMPLETION
(Minimum 1 completion)
-25.0—U. of Mexico (0) vs. Southwestern (Tex.) (35) (Sun, 1945) (2 for -50 yards)
-2.0—Oklahoma (40) vs. Houston (14) (Sun, 1981) (1 for -2 yards)
3.0—West Va. (14) vs. South Caro. (3) (Peach, 1969) (1 for 3 yards)
3.2—LSU (0) vs. Arkansas (0) (Cotton, 1947) (5 for 16 yards)
3.3—New Mexico (0) vs. Southwestern (Tex.) (7) (Sun, 1944) (3 for 10 yards)
4.5—Alabama (34) vs. Miami (Fla.) (13) (Sugar, 1993) (4 for 18 yards)
4.6—Texas (14) vs. Georgia Tech (7) (Cotton, 1943) (5 for 23 yards)
4.8—UTEP (33) vs. Georgetown (20) (Sun, 1950) (5 for 24 yards)
5.3—Case Reserve (26) vs. Arizona St. (13) (Sun, 1941) (3 for 16 yards)
5.3—Arkansas (3) vs. UCLA (17) (Cotton, 1989) (4 for 21 yards)

Scoring

MOST TOUCHDOWNS
9—Texas A&M (65) vs. Brigham Young (14) (Holiday, 1990) (5 rush, 4 pass)
9—Alabama (61) vs. Syracuse (6) (Orange, 1953) (4 rush, 3 pass, 1 punt return, 1 interception return)
9—(D) Centre (63) vs. Texas Christian (7) (Fort Worth Classic, 1921) (8 rush, 1 blocked punt recovery in end zone)
8—Nebraska (62) vs. Florida (24) (Fiesta, 1996) (6 rush, 1 pass, 1 interception return)
8—Kansas St. (54) vs. Colorado St. (21) (Holiday, 1995) (4 rush, 4 pass)
8—Oklahoma St. (62) vs. Wyoming (14) (Holiday, 1988) (6 rush, 2 pass)
8—Toledo (56) vs. Davidson (33) (Tangerine, 1969) (4 rush, 3 pass, 1 fumble return)
7—Texas Tech (55) vs. Air Force (41) (Copper, 1995) (6 rush, 1 pass)
7—Southern Cal (55) vs. Texas Tech (14) (Cotton, 1995) (1 rush, 5 pass, 1 interception retrun)
7—UNLV (52) vs. Central Mich. (24) (Las Vegas, 1994) (3 rush, 3 pass, 1 fumble return)
7—Kansas St. (52) vs. Wyoming (17) (Copper, 1993) (3 rush, 2 pass, 1 punt return, 1 interception return)
7—Oklahoma (48) vs. Virginia (14) (Gator, Dec. 29, 1991) (4 rush, 2 pass, 1 blocked punt return)
7—(D) Texas Tech (49) vs. Duke (21) (All-American, 1989) (6 rush, 1 pass)
7—(D) Fresno St. (51) vs. Bowling Green (7) (California, 1985) (4 rush, 3 pass)
7—(D) Iowa (55) vs. Texas (17) (Freedom, 1984) (1 rush, 6 pass)
7—(D) Houston (47) vs. Tulane (7) (Bluebonnet, 1973) (7 rush)
7—Arizona St. (49) vs. Missouri (35) (Fiesta, 1972) (5 rush, 2 pass)
7—North Caro. St. (49) vs. West Va. (13) (Peach, 1972) (4 rush, 3 pass)
7—Arizona St. (48) vs. North Caro. (26) (Peach, 1970) (6 rush, 1 pass)
7—Houston (49) vs. Miami (Ohio) (21) (Tangerine, 1962) (4 rush, 2 pass, 1 punt return)
7—Oklahoma (48) vs. Duke (21) (Orange, 1958) (3 rush, 2 pass, 1 pass interception return, 1 intercepted lateral return)
7—UTEP (47) vs. Florida St. (20) (Sun, 1955) (4 rush, 3 pass)
7—Michigan (49) vs. Southern Cal (0) (Rose, 1948) (3 rush, 4 pass)
7—Illinois (45) vs. UCLA (14) (Rose, 1947) (5 rush, 2 pass interception returns)

MOST TOUCHDOWNS, BOTH TEAMS
13—Texas Tech (55) [7] & Air Force (41) [6] (Copper, 1995)
13—Richmond (49) [7] & Ohio (42) [6] (Tangerine, 1968)
11—Nebraska (62) [8] & Florida (24) [3] (Fiesta, 1996)
11—Kansas St. (54) [8] & Colorado St. (21) [3] (Holiday, 1995)
11—Washington (46) [6] & Iowa (34) [5] (Rose, 1991)
11—Texas A&M (65) [9] & Brigham Young (14) [2] (Holiday, 1990)
11—Penn St. (50) [6] & Brigham Young (39) [5] (Holiday, 1989)
11—Arizona St. (49) [7] & Missouri (35) [4] (Fiesta, 1971)
11—Arizona St. (48) [7] & North Caro. (26) [4] (Peach, 1970)
11—Southern Cal (42) [6] & Wisconsin (37) [5] (Rose, 1963)
10—UNLV (52) [7] & Central Mich. (24) [3] (Las Vegas, 1994)
10—Utah St. (42) [6] & Ball St. (33) [4] (Las Vegas, 1993)
10—East Caro. (37) [5] & North Caro. St. (34) [5] (Peach, 1992)
10—(D) Texas Tech (49) [7] & Duke (21) [3] (All-American, 1989)
10—Mississippi (42) [6] & Air Force (29) [4] (Liberty, 1989)
10—Oklahoma St. (62) [8] & Wyoming (14) [2] (Holiday, 1988)
10—Boston College (45) [6] & Houston (28) [4] (Cotton, 1985)
10—Colorado (47) [6] & Alabama (33) [4] (Liberty, 1969)
10—(D) Nebraska (36) [5] & Miami (Fla.) (34) [5] (Gotham, 1962)
10—UTEP (47) [7] & Florida St. (20) [3] (Sun, 1955)
10—Alabama (61) [9] & Syracuse (6) [1] (Orange, 1953)

MOST TOUCHDOWNS RUSHING
8—(D) Centre (63) vs. Texas Christian (7) (Fort Worth Classic, 1921)
7—(D) Houston (47) vs. Tulane (7) (Bluebonnet, 1973)
6—Nebraska (62) vs. Florida (24) (Fiesta, 1996)
6—Texas Tech (55) vs. Air Force (41) (Copper, 1995)
6—Air Force (41) vs. Texas Tech (55) (Copper, 1995)
6—(D) Texas Tech (49) vs. Duke (21) (All-American, 1989)
6—Oklahoma St. (62) vs. Wyoming (14) (Holiday, 1988)
6—Oklahoma (42) vs. Arkansas (8) (Orange, 1987)
6—Ohio St. (47) vs. Brigham Young (17) (Holiday, 1982)
6—Oklahoma St. (49) vs. Brigham Young (21) (Tangerine, 1976)
6—Arizona St. (48) vs. North Caro. (26) (Peach, 1970)
6—Michigan (49) vs. Stanford (0) (Rose, 1902)

MOST TOUCHDOWNS RUSHING, BOTH TEAMS
12—Texas Tech (55) [6] & Air Force (41) [6] (Copper, 1995)
9—Arizona St. (48) [6] & North Caro. (26) [3] (Peach, 1970)
8—Oklahoma St. (62) [6] & Wyoming (14) [2] (Holiday, 1988)
8—Colorado (47) [5] & Alabama (33) [3] (Liberty, 1969)
7—Nebraska (62) [6] & Florida (24) [1] (Fiesta, 1996)
7—Kansas St. (54) [4] & Colorado St. (21) [3] (Holiday, 1995)
7—Oklahoma (42) [6] & Arkansas (8) [1] (Orange, 1987)
7—Oklahoma St. (35) [4] & West Va. (33) [3] (John Hancock Sun, 1987)
7—UCLA (45) [5] & Iowa (28) [2] (Rose, 1986)
7—Oklahoma St. (49) [6] & Brigham Young (21) [1] (Tangerine, 1976)
7—Arizona St. (49) [5] & Missouri (35) [2] (Fiesta, 1972)
7—Penn St. (41) [5] & Oregon (12) [2] (Liberty, 1960)

MOST TOUCHDOWNS PASSING
6—(D) Iowa (55) vs. Texas (17) (Freedom, 1984)
5—Southern Cal (55) vs. Texas Tech (14) (Cotton, 1995)
5—Florida St. (41) vs. Nebraska (17) (Fiesta, 1990)
5—Florida St. (36) vs. Oklahoma (19) (Gator, Jan. 2, 1965)
4—Florida St. (31) vs. Notre Dame (26) (Orange, 1996)
4—Penn St. (43) vs. Auburn (14) (Outback, 1996)
4—Kansas St. (54) vs. Colorado St. (21) (Holiday, 1995)
4—East Caro. (37) vs. North Caro. St. (34) (Peach, 1992)
4—Miami (Fla.) (46) vs. Texas (3) (Cotton, 1991)
4—Michigan (35) vs. Mississippi (3) (Gator, Jan. 1, 1991)
4—Texas A&M (65) vs. Brigham Young (14) (Holiday, 1990)
4—UCLA (45) vs. Illinois (9) (Rose, 1984)
4—Purdue (28) vs. Missouri (25) (Liberty, 1980)
4—Pittsburgh (34) vs. Clemson (3) (Gator, 1977)
4—Florida St. (40) vs. Texas Tech (17) (Tangerine, 1977)
4—Davidson (33) vs. Toledo (56) (Tangerine, 1969)
4—Richmond (49) vs. Ohio (42) (Tangerine, 1968)
4—Ohio (42) vs. Richmond (49) (Tangerine, 1968)
4—Southern Cal (42) vs. Wisconsin (37) (Rose, 1963)
4—Michigan (49) vs. Southern Cal (0) (Rose, 1948)
4—Georgia (40) vs. Texas Christian (26) (Orange, 1942)
4—Southern Cal (47) vs. Pittsburgh (14) (Rose, 1930)

MOST TOUCHDOWNS PASSING, BOTH TEAMS
8—(D) Iowa (55) [6] & Texas (17) [2] (Freedom, 1984)
8—Richmond (49) [4] & Ohio (42) [4] (Tangerine, 1968)
7—Florida St. (31) [4] & Notre Dame (26) [3] (Orange, 1996)
7—East Caro. (37) [4] & North Caro. St. (34) [3] (Peach, 1992)
7—Toledo (56) [3] & Davidson (33) [4] (Tangerine, 1969)
7—Georgia (40) [4] & Texas Christian (26) [3] (Orange, 1942)
6—Southern Cal (55) [5] & Texas Tech (14) [1] (Cotton, 1995)
6—Kansas (51) [3] & UCLA (30) [3] (Aloha, 1995)
6—Utah St. (42) [3] & Ball St. (33) [3] (Las Vegas, 1993)
6—Miami (Fla.) (33) [3] & Alabama (25) [3] (Sugar, 1990)
6—Florida St. (41) [5] & Nebraska (17) [1] (Fiesta, 1990)
6—Texas A&M (65) [4] & Brigham Young (14) [2] (Holiday, 1990)
6—Florida St. (36) [5] & Oklahoma (19) [1] (Gator, Jan. 2, 1965)
6—Southern Cal (42) [4] & Wisconsin (37) [2] (Rose, 1963)

MOST FIELD GOALS MADE
5—Texas A&M (22) vs. Michigan (20) (Alamo, 1995) (27, 49, 47, 31, 37 yards)
5—Mississippi St. (24) vs. North Caro. St. (28) (Peach, Jan. 1, 1995) (37, 21, 29, 36, 30 yards)
5—Florida (28) vs. Notre Dame (39) (Sugar, 1992) (26, 24, 36, 37, 24 yards)
5—Maryland (23) vs. Tennessee (30) (Florida Citrus, 1983) (18, 48, 31, 22, 26 yards)
4—East Caro. (19) vs. Stanford (13) (Liberty, 1995) (46, 26, 41, 34 yards)
4—Oklahoma (25) vs. Penn St. (10) (Orange, 1986) (26, 31, 21, 22 yards)
4—North Caro. (26) vs. Texas (10) (Sun, 1982) (53, 47, 24, 42 yards)
4—Texas A&M (33) vs. Oklahoma St. (16) (Independence, 1981) (33, 32, 50, 18 yards)
4—West Va. (26) vs. Florida (6) (Peach, Dec. 31, 1981) (35, 42, 49, 24 yards)
4—Missouri (19) vs. Southern Miss. (17) (Tangerine, 1981) (45, 41, 30, 28 yards)
4—Nebraska (45) vs. Georgia (6) (Sun, 1969) (50, 32, 42, 37 yards)
4—Alabama (12) vs. Mississippi (7) (Sugar, 1964) (46, 31, 34, 48 yards)

MOST FIELD GOALS MADE, BOTH TEAMS
7—Texas A&M (22) [5] & Michigan (20) [2] (Alamo, 1995)
7—North Caro. St. (28) [2] & Mississippi St. (24) [5] (Peach, Jan. 1, 1995)
6—Notre Dame (39) [1] & Florida (28) [5] (Sugar, 1992)
6—Syracuse (16) [3] & Auburn (16) [3] (Sugar, 1988)
6—Tennessee (30) [1] & Maryland (23) [5] (Florida Citrus, 1983)

5—Penn St. (50) [3] & Brigham Young (39) [2] (Holiday, 1989)
5—Oklahoma (25) [4] & Penn St. (10) [1] (Orange, 1986)
5—North Caro. (26) [4] & Texas (10) [1] (Sun, 1982)
5—Texas A&M (33) [4] & Oklahoma St. (16) [1] (Independence, 1981)
5—Missouri (19) [4] & Southern Miss. (17) [1] (Tangerine, 1981)
5—Penn St. (9) [3] & Tulane (6) [2] (Liberty, 1979)
5—Penn St. (30) [3] & Texas (6) [2] (Cotton, 1972)

MOST POINTS, WINNING TEAM

65—Texas A&M vs. Brigham Young (14) (Holiday, 1990)
62—Nebraska vs. Florida (24) (Fiesta, 1996)
62—Oklahoma St. vs. Wyoming (14) (Holiday, 1988)
61—Alabama vs. Syracuse (6) (Orange, 1953)
56—Toledo vs. Davidson (33) (Tangerine, 1969)
55—Texas Tech vs. Air Force (41) (Copper, 1995)
55—Southern Cal vs. Texas Tech (14) (Cotton, 1995)
55—(D) Iowa vs. Texas (17) (Freedom, 1984)
54—Kansas St. vs. Colorado St. (21) (Holiday, 1995)
52—UNLV vs. Central Mich. (24) (Las Vegas, 1994)
52—Kansas St. vs. Wyoming (17) (Copper, 1993)
51—Kansas vs. UCLA (30) (Aloha, 1995)
51—(D) Fresno St. vs. Bowling Green (7) (California, 1985)
50—Penn St. vs. Brigham Young (39) (Holiday, 1989)
49—(D) Texas Tech vs. Duke (21) (All-American, 1989)
49—Oklahoma St. vs. Brigham Young (21) (Tangerine, 1976)
49—North Caro. St. vs. West Va. (13) (Peach, 1972)
49—Arizona St. vs. Missouri (35) (Fiesta, 1972)
49—Richmond vs. Ohio (42) (Tangerine, 1968)
49—Michigan vs. Southern Cal (0) (Rose, 1948)

MOST POINTS, LOSING TEAM

45—Southern Methodist vs. Brigham Young (46) (Holiday, 1980)
42—Ohio vs. Richmond (49) (Tangerine, 1968)
41—Air Force vs. Texas Tech (55) (Copper, 1995)
39—Brigham Young vs. Penn St. (50) (Holiday, 1989)
38—San Diego St. vs. Iowa (39) (Holiday, 1986)
38—Florida St. vs. Arizona St. (45) (Fiesta, 1971)
37—Nevada vs. Toledo (40) (OT) (Las Vegas, 1995)
37—Miami (Fla.) vs. UCLA (39) (Fiesta, 1985)
37—Brigham Young vs. Indiana (38) (Holiday, 1979)
37—Wisconsin vs. Southern Cal (42) (Rose, 1963)
36—Washington St. vs. Brigham Young (38) (Holiday, 1981)
35—Oregon vs. Wake Forest (39) (Independence, 1992)
35—Missouri vs. Arizona St. (49) (Fiesta, 1972)
34—Nevada vs. Bowling Green (35) (Las Vegas, 1992)
34—North Caro. St. vs. East Caro. (37) (Peach, 1992)
34—Iowa vs. Washington (46) (Rose, 1991)
34—Houston vs. Notre Dame (35) (Cotton, 1979)
34—(D) Miami (Fla.) vs. Nebraska (36) (Gotham, 1962)

MOST POINTS, BOTH TEAMS

96—Texas Tech (55) & Air Force (41) (Copper, 1995)
91—Brigham Young (46) & Southern Methodist (45) (Holiday, 1980)
91—Richmond (49) & Ohio (42) (Tangerine, 1968)
89—Penn St. (50) & Brigham Young (39) (Holiday, 1989)
89—Toledo (56) & Davidson (33) (Tangerine, 1969)
86—Nebraska (62) & Florida (24) (Fiesta, 1996)
84—Arizona St. (49) & Missouri (35) (Fiesta, 1972)
83—Arizona St. (45) & Florida St. (38) (Fiesta, 1971)
81—Kansas (51) & UCLA (30) (Aloha, 1995)
80—Washington (46) & Iowa (34) (Rose, 1991)
80—Colorado (47) & Alabama (33) (Liberty, 1969)
79—Texas A&M (65) & Brigham Young (14) (Holiday, 1990)
79—Southern Cal (42) & Wisconsin (37) (Rose, 1963)
77—Toledo (40) & Nevada (37) (OT) (Las Vegas, 1995)
77—Iowa (39) & San Diego St. (38) (Holiday, 1986)
76—UNLV (52) & Central Mich. (24) (Las Vegas, 1994)
76—Oklahoma St. (62) & Wyoming (14) (Holiday, 1988)
76—UCLA (39) & Miami (Fla.) (37) (Fiesta, 1985)
75—Kansas St. (54) & Colorado St. (21) (Holiday, 1995)
75—Utah St. (42) & Ball St. (33) (Las Vegas, 1993)
75—Indiana (38) & Brigham Young (37) (Holiday, 1979)
75—Houston (47) & Miami (Ohio) (28) (Tangerine, 1962)

LARGEST MARGIN OF VICTORY

55—Alabama (61) vs. Syracuse (6) (Orange, 1953)
51—Texas A&M (65) vs. Brigham Young (14) (Holiday, 1990)
48—Oklahoma St. (62) vs. Wyoming (14) (Holiday, 1988)
44—(D) Fresno St. (51) vs. Bowling Green (7) (California, 1985)
43—Miami (Fla.) (46) vs. Texas (3) (Cotton, 1991)
42—Texas (42) vs. Maryland (0) (Sun, 1978)
41—Syracuse (41) vs. Clemson (0) (Gator, 1996)
41—Southern Cal (55) vs. Texas Tech (14) (Cotton, 1995)
40—(D) Houston (47) vs. Tulane (7) (Bluebonnet, 1973)
39—Nebraska (45) vs. Georgia (6) (Sun, 1969)
38—Nebraska (62) vs. Florida (24) (Fiesta, 1996)
38—(D) Iowa (55) vs. Texas (17) (Freedom, 1984)
36—North Caro. St. (49) vs. West Va. (13) (Peach, 1972)
35—Michigan (42) vs. North Caro. St. (7) (Hall of Fame, 1994)
35—Kansas St. (52) vs. Wyoming (17) (Copper, 1993)
35—(D) Houston (35) vs. Navy (0) (Garden State, 1980)
35—North Caro. (35) vs. Air Force (0) (Gator, 1963)
35—Oklahoma (35) vs. LSU (0) (Sugar, 1950)
35—Southwestern (Tex.) (35) vs. U. of Mexico (0) (Sun, 1945)

FEWEST POINTS, WINNING TEAM

2—Fordham vs. Missouri (0) (Sugar, 1942)
3—Tennessee vs. Texas A&M (0) (Gator, 1957)
3—Texas Christian vs. LSU (2) (Sugar, 1936)
6—UCLA vs. Illinois (3) (John Hancock, 1991)
6—Oregon St. vs. Villanova (0) (Liberty, 1962)
6—Tulsa vs. Texas Tech (0) (Sun, 1942)
6—Clemson vs. Boston College (3) (Cotton, 1940)
6—Auburn vs. Michigan St. (0) (Orange, 1938)
6—Santa Clara vs. LSU (0) (Sugar, 1938)

FEWEST POINTS, LOSING TEAM

0—By many teams

FEWEST POINTS, BOTH TEAMS

0—Air Force (0) & Texas Christian (0) (Cotton, 1959)
0—Arkansas (0) & LSU (0) (Cotton, 1947)
0—Arizona St. (0) & Catholic (0) (Sun, 1940)
0—California (0) & Wash. & Jeff. (0) (Rose, 1922)

MOST POINTS SCORED IN ONE HALF

45—Oklahoma St. (62) vs. Wyoming (14) (Holiday, 1988) (2nd half)
42—Toledo (56) vs. Davidson (33) (Tangerine, 1969) (1st half)
40—Alabama (61) vs. Syracuse (6) (Orange, 1953) (2nd half)
38—Penn St. (50) vs. Brigham Young (39) (Holiday, 1989) (2nd half)
38—Penn St. (41) vs. Baylor (20) (Cotton, 1975) (2nd half)
38—Mississippi (41) vs. Georgia Tech (18) (Peach, 1971) (1st half)
37—Texas A&M (65) vs. Brigham Young (14) (Holiday, 1990) (1st half)
35—Nebraska (62) vs. Florida (24) (Fiesta, 1996) (1st half)
35—Tennessee (45) vs. Virginia Tech (23) (Gator, 1994) (1st half)
35—Penn St. (42) vs. Tennessee (17) (Fiesta, 1992) (2nd half)
35—Southern Cal (42) vs. Ohio St. (17) (Rose, 1973) (2nd half)
35—North Caro. St. (49) vs. West Va. (13) (Peach, 1972) (2nd half)
35—Houston (49) vs. Miami (Ohio) (21) (Tangerine, 1962) (1st half)
34—Kansas (51) vs. UCLA (30) (Aloha, 1995) (2nd half)
34—Southern Cal (55) vs. Texas Tech (14) (Cotton, 1995) (1st half)
34—Oklahoma (48) vs. Virginia (14) (Gator, Dec. 29, 1991) (1st half)
34—Purdue (41) vs. Georgia Tech (21) (Peach, 1978) (1st half)
34—Oklahoma (48) vs. Duke (21) (Orange, 1958) (2nd half)
34—UTEP (47) vs. Florida St. (20) (Sun, 1955) (1st half)

Photo from Texas Tech sports information

Texas Tech running back Byron Hanspard sparked an offensive explosion in the 1995 Copper Bowl by rushing for 260 yards and four touchdowns. The Red Raiders' 55-41 victory over Air Force was the highest-scoring bowl game in history.

MOST POINTS SCORED IN ONE HALF, BOTH TEAMS
64—Kansas (51) [34] & UCLA (30) [30] (Aloha, 1995) (2nd half)
64—Penn St. (50) [38] & Brigham Young (39) [26] (Holiday, 1989) (2nd half)
54—Utah St. (42) [21] & Ball St. (33) [33] (Las Vegas, 1993) (2nd half)
52—Texas Tech (55) [24] & Air Force (41) [28] (Copper, 1995) (2nd half)
52—Oklahoma St. (62) [45] & Wyoming (14) [7] (Holiday, 1988) (2nd half)
51—Penn St. (41) [38] & Baylor (20) [13] (Cotton, 1975) (2nd half)
49—Brigham Young (46) [33] & Southern Methodist (45) [16] (Holiday, 1980) (2nd half)
49—(D) Houston (31) [28] & North Caro. St. (31) [21] (Bluebonnet, 1974) (2nd half)
49—Arizona St. (49) [21] & Missouri (35) [28] (Fiesta, 1972) (2nd half)
49—Arizona St. (45) [21] & Florida St. (38) [28] (Fiesta, 1971) (1st half)
49—Toledo (56) [42] & Davidson (33) [7] (Tangerine, 1969) (1st half)
49—Richmond (49) [28] & Ohio (42) [21] (Tangerine, 1968) (1st half)
48—Oklahoma (48) [34] & Duke (21) [14] (Orange, 1958) (2nd half)
47—Arizona St. (48) [21] & North Caro. (26) [26] (Peach, 1970) (1st half)
45—LSU (45) [21] & Michigan St. (26) [24] (Independence, 1995) (1st half)
45—Tennessee (45) [35] & Virginia Tech (23) [10] (Gator, 1994) (1st half)
45—Boston College (45) [31] & Houston (28) [14] (Cotton, 1985) (1st half)
45—Southern Cal (42) [35] & Ohio St. (17) [10] (Rose, 1973) (2nd half)

MOST POINTS SCORED IN ONE QUARTER
31—(D) Iowa (55) vs. Texas (17) (Freedom, 1984) (3rd quarter)
30—Oklahoma (40) vs. Houston (14) (Sun, 1981) (4th quarter)
29—Nebraska (62) vs. Florida (24) (Fiesta, 1996) (2nd quarter)
28—Southern Cal (55) vs. Texas Tech (14) (Cotton, 1995) (1st quarter)
28—Oklahoma St. (62) vs. Wyoming (14) (Holiday, 1988) (3rd quarter)
28—Missouri (34) vs. Auburn (17) (Sun, 1973) (2nd quarter)
28—Mississippi (41) vs. Georgia Tech (18) (Peach, 1971) (2nd quarter)
28—Toledo (56) vs. Davidson (33) (Tangerine, 1969) (2nd quarter)
28—Houston (49) vs. Miami (Ohio) (21) (Tangerine, 1962) (2nd quarter)
27—Penn St. (43) vs. Auburn (14) (Outback, 1996) (3rd quarter)
27—Oklahoma (48) vs. Virginia (14) (Gator, Dec. 29, 1991) (2nd quarter)
27—Brigham Young (46) vs. Southern Methodist (45) (Holiday, 1980) (4th quarter)
27—Oklahoma (48) vs. Duke (21) (Orange, 1958) (4th quarter)
27—UTEP (47) vs. Florida St. (20) (Sun, 1955) (2nd quarter)
27—Illinois (40) vs. Stanford (7) (Rose, 1952) (4th quarter)
26—North Caro. (26) vs. Arizona St. (48) (Peach, 1970) (2nd quarter)
25—Louisville (34) vs. Alabama (7) (Fiesta, 1991) (1st quarter)

MOST POINTS SCORED IN ONE QUARTER, BOTH TEAMS
40—Arizona St. (48) [14] & North Caro. (26) [26] (Peach, 1970) (2nd quarter)
38—Missouri (34) [28] & Auburn (17) [10] (Sun, 1973) (2nd quarter)
37—Kansas (51) [14] & UCLA (30) [23] (Aloha, 1995) (4th quarter)
37—Oklahoma (40) [30] & Houston (14) [7] (Sun, 1981) (4th quarter)
35—Kansas St. (54) [21] & Colorado St. (21) [14] (Holiday, 1995) (3rd quarter)
35—Oklahoma St. (62) [28] & Wyoming (14) [7] (Holiday, 1988) (3rd quarter)
35—Oklahoma St. (49) [21] & Brigham Young (21) [14] (Tangerine, 1976) (2nd quarter)
35—(D) Houston (31) [21] & North Caro. St. (31) [14] (Bluebonnet, 1974) (4th quarter)
35—Arizona St. (49) [21] & Missouri (35) [14] (Fiesta, 1972) (4th quarter)
35—Richmond (49) [21] & Ohio (42) [14] (Tangerine, 1968) (2nd quarter)
34—Oklahoma (48) [27] & Virginia (14) [7] (Gator, Dec. 29, 1991) (2nd quarter)
34—Penn St. (50) [21] & Brigham Young (39) [13] (Holiday, 1989) (4th quarter)
34—Brigham Young (46) [27] & Southern Methodist (45) [7] (Holiday, 1980) (4th quarter)
34—Penn St. (42) [18] & Arizona St. (30) [16] (Fiesta, 1977) (4th quarter)
34—Mississippi (41) [28] & Georgia Tech (18) [6] (Peach, 1971) (2nd quarter)
34—Oklahoma (48) [27] & Duke (21) [7] (Orange, 1958) (4th quarter)

First Downs

MOST FIRST DOWNS
36—Oklahoma (48) vs. Virginia (14) (Gator, Dec. 29, 1991) (16 rush, 18 pass, 2 penalty)
35—Michigan (35) vs. Mississippi (3) (Gator, Jan. 1, 1991) (20 rush, 14 pass, 1 penalty)
35—Brigham Young (39) vs. Penn St. (50) (Holiday, 1989) (8 rush, 27 pass, 0 penalty)
34—Fresno St. (30) vs. Colorado (41) (Aloha, 1993) (4 rush, 25 pass, 5 penalty)
34—Oklahoma St. (62) vs. Wyoming (14) (Holiday, 1988) (15 rush, 17 pass, 2 penalty)
34—(D) Miami (Fla.) (34) vs. Nebraska (36) (Gotham, 1962)
33—Toledo (40) vs. Nevada (37) (OT) (Las Vegas, 1995) (19 rush, 12 pass, 2 penalty)
33—Arizona St. (49) vs. Missouri (35) (Fiesta, 1972) (22 rush, 11 pass, 0 penalty)
32—Brigham Young (24) vs. Michigan (17) (Holiday, 1984)
32—Richmond (49) vs. Ohio (42) (Tangerine, 1968) (8 rush, 24 pass, 0 penalty)
32—Wisconsin (37) vs. Southern Cal (42) (Rose, 1963) (7 rush, 23 pass, 2 penalty)
31—UCLA (16) vs. Wisconsin (21) (Rose, 1994)
31—Arkansas (27) vs. Tennessee (31) (Cotton, 1990) (21 rush, 10 pass, 0 penalty)
31—Florida St. (34) vs. Oklahoma St. (23) (Gator, 1985) (10 rush, 21 pass, 0 penalty)
31—Brigham Young (37) vs. Indiana (38) (Holiday, 1979) (9 rush, 21 pass, 1 penalty)
31—(D) Purdue (27) vs. Tennessee (22) (Bluebonnet, 1979)
31—(D) Houston (26) vs. Dayton (21) (Salad, 1952) (25 rush, 6 pass, 0 penalty)

MOST FIRST DOWNS, BOTH TEAMS
61—Penn St. (50) [26] & Brigham Young (39) [35] (Holiday, 1989)
56—Toledo (40) [33] & Nevada (37) [23] (OT) (Las Vegas, 1995)
56—Mississippi (42) [30] & Air Force (29) [26] (Liberty, 1989)
55—Michigan (35) [35] & Mississippi (3) [20] (Gator, Jan. 1, 1991)
54—UCLA (45) [29] & Iowa (28) [25] (Rose, 1986)
54—Florida St. (34) [31] & Oklahoma St. (23) [23] (Gator, 1985)
53—Texas Tech (55) [28] & Air Force (41) [25] (Copper, 1995)
53—Colorado (41) [19] & Fresno St. (30) [34] (Aloha, 1993)
53—Tennessee (23) [28] & Virginia (22) [25] (Sugar, 1991)
53—Colorado (47) [29] & Alabama (33) [24] (Liberty, 1969)
52—Wisconsin (21) [21] & UCLA (16) [31] (Rose, 1994)
52—Notre Dame (39) [23] & Florida (28) [29] (Sugar, 1992)
52—Indiana (38) [21] & Brigham Young (37) [31] (Holiday, 1979)
51—Texas (35) & North Caro. (31) (Sun, 1994)
51—(D) Arkansas (28) [28] & Florida (24) [23] (Bluebonnet, 1982)
50—(D) Toledo (27) [21] & San Jose St. (25) [29] (California, 1981)
50—Texas (21) [25] & Notre Dame (17) [25] (Cotton, 1970)

MOST FIRST DOWNS RUSHING
26—Oklahoma (40) vs. Auburn (22) (Sugar, Jan. 1, 1972)
25—(D) Houston (26) vs. Dayton (21) (Salad, 1952)
24—Colorado (47) vs. Alabama (33) (Liberty, 1969)
23—Georgia Tech (31) vs. Texas Tech (21) (Gator, Dec. 31, 1965)
22—(D) Arkansas (28) vs. Florida (24) (Bluebonnet, 1982)
22—Oklahoma (41) vs. Wyoming (7) (Fiesta, 1976)
22—Arizona St. (49) vs. Missouri (35) (Fiesta, 1972)
21—Nebraska (62) vs. Florida (24) (Fiesta, 1996)
21—Arkansas (27) vs. Tennessee (31) (Cotton, 1990)
21—Florida St. (7) vs. Oklahoma (24) (Orange, 1980)
21—(D) Houston (35) vs. Navy (0) (Garden State, 1980)
21—Mississippi St. (26) vs. North Caro. (24) (Sun, 1974)
21—Missouri (35) vs. Alabama (10) (Gator, 1968)

MOST FIRST DOWNS RUSHING, BOTH TEAMS
36—Miami (Fla.) (46) [16] & Texas (3) [20] (Cotton, 1991)
36—Colorado (47) [24] & Alabama (33) [12] (Liberty, 1969)
32—Texas Tech (55) [15] & Air Force (41) [17] (Copper, 1995)
32—Tennessee (31) [11] & Arkansas (27) [21] (Cotton, 1990)
32—Oklahoma (41) [22] & Wyoming (7) [10] (Fiesta, 1976)
32—Arizona St. (49) [22] & Missouri (35) [10] (Fiesta, 1972)
32—Texas (21) [19] & Notre Dame (17) [13] (Cotton, 1970)
31—Air Force (38) [18] & Mississippi St. (15) [13] (Liberty, 1991)

MOST FIRST DOWNS PASSING
27—Brigham Young (39) vs. Penn St. (50) (Holiday, 1989)
25—Fresno St. (30) vs. Colorado (41) (Aloha, 1993)
24—Richmond (49) vs. Ohio (42) (Tangerine, 1968)
23—(D) San Jose St. (25) vs. Toledo (27) (California, 1981)
23—Wisconsin (37) vs. Southern Cal (42) (Rose, 1963)
21—Southern Cal (41) vs. Northwestern (32) (Rose, 1996)
21—(D) Fresno St. (29) vs. Bowling Green (28) (California, 1982)
21—Brigham Young (46) vs. Southern Methodist (45) (Holiday, 1980)
21—Brigham Young (37) vs. Indiana (38) (Holiday, 1979)
20—Mississippi (20) vs. Texas Tech (17) (Independence, 1986)
20—Brigham Young (24) vs. Michigan (17) (Holiday, 1984)
20—(D) Vanderbilt (28) vs. Air Force (36) (Hall of Fame, 1982)
19—Brigham Young (21) vs. Ohio St. (28) (Holiday, 1993)
19—(D) Oregon (31) vs. Colorado St. (32) (Freedom, 1990)
19—Florida St. (31) vs. Nebraska (28) (Fiesta, 1988)
19—Florida St. (34) vs. Oklahoma (23) (Gator, 1985)
19—Illinois (29) vs. Army (31) (Peach, 1985)

MOST FIRST DOWNS PASSING, BOTH TEAMS
32—Southern Cal (41) [21] & Northwestern (32) [11] (Rose, 1996)
30—Colorado (41) [5] & Fresno St. (30) [25] (Aloha, 1993)
30—(D) Fresno St. (29) [21] & Bowling Green (28) [9] (California, 1982)
30—Richmond (49) [24] & Ohio (42) [6] (Tangerine, 1968)
29—Mississippi (42) [17] & Air Force (29) [12] (Liberty, 1989)
29—Indiana (38) [8] & Brigham Young (37) [21] (Holiday, 1979)
28—Ohio St. (28) [12] & Pittsburgh (23) [16] (Fiesta, 1984)
27—Florida St. (23) [12] & Florida (17) [15] (Sugar, Jan. 2, 1995)
27—Brigham Young (31) [18] & Oklahoma (6) [9] (Copper, 1994)
27—Arizona St. (45) [13] & Florida St. (38) [14] (Fiesta, 1971)
26—Boston College (31) [16] & Virginia (13) [10] (Carquest, 1994)
26—(D) Southern Cal (28) [15] & Utah (21) [11] (Freedom, 1993)
26—Brigham Young (24) [20] & Michigan (17) [6] (Holiday, 1984)
26—Washington (21) [15] & Maryland (20) [11] (Aloha, 1982)
26—(D) Air Force (36) [6] & Vanderbilt (28) [20] (Hall of Fame, 1982)
25—Wisconsin (34) [8] & Duke (20) [17] (Hall of Fame, 1995)
25—Texas (35) [9] & North Caro. (31) [16] (Sun, 1994)
25—Oklahoma St. (62) [17] & Wyoming (14) [8] (Holiday, 1988)
25—Florida St. (31) [19] & Nebraska (28) [6] (Fiesta, 1988)
25—Miami (Fla.) (31) [15] & Nebraska (30) [10] (Orange, 1984)
25—Brigham Young (46) [21] & Southern Methodist (45) [4] (Holiday, 1980)

MOST FIRST DOWNS BY PENALTY
6—Texas (3) vs. Miami (Fla.) (46) (Cotton, 1991)
5—(D) Arizona (13) vs. Utah (16) (Freedom, 1994)
5—Fresno St. (30) vs. Colorado (41) (Aloha, 1993)
5—West Va. (21) vs. Notre Dame (34) (Fiesta, 1989)
5—(D) Washington (34) vs. Florida (7) (Freedom, 1989)

5—(D) Western Mich. (30) vs. Fresno St. (35) (California, 1988)
5—Miami (Fla.) (7) vs. Tennessee (35) (Sugar, 1986)
5—(D) Miami (Ohio) (7) vs. San Jose St. (37) (California, 1986)
4—Texas A&M (22) vs. Michigan (20) (Alamo, 1995)
4—Michigan (20) vs. Texas A&M (22) (Alamo, 1995)
4—Texas (35) vs. North Caro. (31) (Sun, 1994)
4—Alabama (25) vs. Miami (Fla.) (33) (Sugar, 1990)
4—Brigham Young (14) vs. Texas A&M (65) (Holiday, 1990)
4—Georgia (10) vs. Texas (9) (Cotton, 1984)
4—(D) Iowa (55) vs. Texas (17) (Freedom, 1984)
4—(D) Vanderbilt (28) vs. Air Force (36) (Hall of Fame, 1982)
4—Maryland (20) vs. Florida (35) (Tangerine, 1980)
4—Baylor (20) vs. Penn St. (41) (Cotton, 1975)
4—Arkansas (13) vs. Tennessee (14) (Liberty, 1971)
4—Arizona St. (45) vs. Florida St. (38) (Fiesta, 1971)
4—Alabama (33) vs. Colorado (47) (Liberty, 1969)
4—Texas A&M (21) vs. Alabama (29) (Cotton, 1942)

MOST FIRST DOWNS BY PENALTY, BOTH TEAMS
8—Texas A&M (22) [4] & Michigan (20) [4] (Alamo, 1995)
8—Miami (Fla.) (46) [2] & Texas (3) [6] (Cotton, 1991)
7—(D) Washington (34) [5] & Florida (7) [2] (Freedom, 1989)
7—Tennessee (35) [2] & Miami (Fla.) (7) [5] (Sugar, 1986)
6—Colorado (41) [1] & Fresno St. (30) [5] (Aloha, 1993)
6—Miami (Fla.) (33) [2] & Alabama (25) [4] (Sugar, 1990)
5—Texas (35) [4] & North Caro. (31) [1] (Sun, 1994)
5—(D) Utah (16) [0] & Arizona (13) [5] (Freedom, 1994)
5—Florida (41) [3] & West Va. (7) [2] (Sugar, 1994)
5—Texas A&M (65) [1] & Brigham Young (14) [4] (Holiday, 1990)
5—Notre Dame (34) [0] & West Va. (21) [5] (Fiesta, 1989)
5—Georgia (10) [4] & Texas (9) [1] (Cotton, 1984)
5—Southern Methodist (7) [3] & Pittsburgh (3) [2] (Cotton, 1983)
5—Pittsburgh (16) [3] & Arizona (10) [2] (Fiesta, 1979)
5—Penn St. (41) [1] & Baylor (20) [4] (Cotton, 1975)

FEWEST FIRST DOWNS
1—Arkansas (0) vs. LSU (0) (Cotton, 1947) (rushing)
1—Alabama (29) vs. Texas A&M (21) (Cotton, 1942) (passing)
2—Michigan St. (0) vs. Auburn (6) (Orange, 1938) (1 rushing, 1 passing)

FEWEST FIRST DOWNS, BOTH TEAMS
10—Texas (7) [3] & Randolph Field (7) [7] (Cotton, 1944)
12—LSU (19) [4] & Texas A&M (14) [8] (Orange, 1944)

FEWEST FIRST DOWNS RUSHING
0—Florida (18) vs. Missouri (20) (Sugar, 1966)
0—Navy (6) vs. Texas (28) (Cotton, 1964)
0—Alabama (29) vs. Texas A&M (21) (Cotton, 1942)

FEWEST FIRST DOWNS RUSHING, BOTH TEAMS
3—Alabama (29) [0] & Texas A&M (21) [3] (Cotton, 1942)
8—(D) Southern Cal (28) [4] & Utah (21) [4] (Freedom, 1993)
9—Florida St. (41) [2] & Nebraska (17) [7] (Fiesta, 1990)
9—Texas (28) [9] & Navy (6) [0] (Cotton, 1964)

FEWEST FIRST DOWNS PASSING
0—Army (28) vs. Alabama (29) (John Hancock Sun, 1988)
0—Oklahoma (40) vs. Houston (10) (Sun, 1981)
0—West Va. (14) vs. South Caro. (3) (Peach, 1969)
0—Missouri (35) vs. Alabama (10) (Gator, 1968)
0—Virginia Tech (7) vs. Miami (Fla.) (14) (Liberty, 1966)
0—Auburn (7) vs. Mississippi (13) (Liberty, 1965)
0—Alabama (10) vs. Arkansas (3) (Sugar, 1962)
0—(D) Missouri (14) vs. Georgia Tech (10) (Bluebonnet, 1962)
0—Utah St. (13) vs. New Mexico St. (20) (Sun, 1960)
0—Arkansas (0) vs. LSU (0) (Cotton, 1947)
0—Fordham (2) vs. Missouri (0) (Sugar, 1942)
0—Arizona St. (0) vs. Catholic (0) (Sun, 1940)
0—West Va. (7) vs. Texas Tech (6) (Sun, 1938)

FEWEST FIRST DOWNS PASSING, BOTH TEAMS
1—Alabama (10) [0] & Arkansas (3) [1] (Sugar, 1962)
4—Oklahoma (41) [1] & Wyoming (7) [3] (Fiesta, 1976)
4—Texas (16) [2] & Tennessee (0) [2] (Cotton, 1953)
4—Rice (28) [3] & Colorado (14) [1] (Cotton, 1938)

Punting

MOST PUNTS
17—Duke (3) vs. Southern Cal (7) (Rose, 1939)
16—Alabama (29) vs. Texas A&M (21) (Cotton, 1942)
16—New Mexico St. (14) vs. Hardin-Simmons (14) (Sun, 1936)
15—Tennessee (0) vs. Rice (8) (Orange, 1947)
14—Tulsa (7) vs. Tennessee (14) (Sugar, 1943)
14—Santa Clara (6) vs. LSU (0) (Sugar, 1938)
14—LSU (0) vs. Santa Clara (6) (Sugar, 1938)
14—Texas Christian (3) vs. LSU (2) (Sugar, 1936)
13—Rice (8) vs. Tennessee (0) (Orange, 1947)
13—Tennessee (0) vs. Southern Cal (25) (Rose, 1945)
13—Oklahoma (0) vs. Tennessee (17) (Orange, 1939)
13—Catholic (20) vs. Mississippi (19) (Orange, 1936)
13—LSU (2) vs. Texas Christian (3) (Sugar, 1936)
13—Miami (Fla.) (0) vs. Bucknell (26) (Orange, 1935)

MOST PUNTS, BOTH TEAMS
28—Rice (8) [13] & Tennessee (0) [15] (Orange, 1947)
28—Santa Clara (6) [14] & LSU (0) [14] (Sugar, 1938)
27—Texas Christian (3) [14] & LSU (2) [13] (Sugar, 1936)
25—Tennessee (17) [12] & Oklahoma (0) [13] (Orange, 1939)
24—Catholic (20) [13] & Mississippi (19) [11] (Orange, 1936)
23—UTEP (14) [12] & Mississippi (7) [11] (Sun, 1967)
22—Auburn (6) [10] & Michigan St. (0) [12] (Orange, 1938)

HIGHEST PUNTING AVERAGE
(Minimum 5 Punts)
53.9—Southern Cal (7) vs. Wisconsin (0) (Rose, 1953) (8 for 431 yards)
51.0—Penn St. (10) vs. Clemson (35) (Florida Citrus, 1988) (5 for 255 yards)
50.0—Nevada (37) vs. Toledo (40) (OT) (Las Vegas, 1995) (5 for 250 yards)
50.0—Mississippi St. (17) vs. Nebraska (31) (Sun, 1980) (5 for 250 yards)
49.3—Clemson (0) vs. Syracuse (41) (Gator, 1996) (6 for 296 yards)
49.2—(D) Air Force (24) vs. Texas (16) (Bluebonnet, 1985) (11 for 541 yards)
49.2—Arkansas (3) vs. UCLA (17) (Cotton, 1989) (6 for 295 yards)
49.0—Indiana (24) vs. Baylor (0) (Copper, 1991) (6 for 294 yards)
49.0—(D) Mississippi St. (10) vs. Kansas (0) (Hall of Fame, 1981) (9 for 441 yards)
48.1—Ohio St. (14) vs. Tennessee (20) (Florida Citrus, 1996) (7 for 337 yards)
48.0—Oklahoma (41) vs. Texas Tech (10) (John Hancock, 1993) (7 for 336 yards)
48.0—Kansas (23) vs. Brigham Young (20) (Aloha, 1992) (8 for 384 yards)
47.9—Penn St. (42) vs. Tennessee (17) (Fiesta, 1992) (9 for 431 yards)
47.9—Oregon St. (20) vs. Duke (16) (Rose, 1942) (7 for 335 yards)
47.6—Oklahoma (42) vs. Arkansas (8) (Orange, 1987) (5 for 238 yards)
47.5—St. Mary's (Cal.) (20) vs. Texas Tech (13) (Cotton, 1939) (11 for 523 yards)
47.4—Georgia Tech (18) vs. Stanford (17) (Aloha, 1991) (7 for 332 yards)
47.4—(D) Fresno St. (51) vs. Bowling Green (7) (California, 1985) (7 for 332 yards)
47.4—(D) Tennessee (28) vs. Wisconsin (21) (Garden State, 1981) (5 for 237 yards)

FEWEST PUNTS
0—Oklahoma St. (62) vs. Wyoming (14) (Holiday, 1988)
0—Oklahoma (41) vs. Wyoming (7) (Fiesta, 1976)
1—Nebraska (62) vs. Florida (24) (Fiesta, 1996)
1—Brigham Young (39) vs. Penn St. (50) (Holiday, 1989)
1—Nebraska (21) vs. LSU (20) (Orange, 1983)
1—North Caro. St. (31) vs. Kansas (18) (Liberty, 1973)
1—Utah (32) vs. West Va. (6) (Liberty, 1964)
1—(D) Miami (Fla.) (34) vs. Nebraska (36) (Gotham, 1962)
1—Georgia Tech (42) vs. West Va. (19) (Sugar, 1954)
1—West Va. (19) vs. Georgia Tech (42) (Sugar, 1954)
1—Missouri (23) vs. Clemson (24) (Gator, 1949)

LOWEST PUNTING AVERAGE
(Minimum 3 Punts)
17.0—Nevada (34) vs. Bowling Green (35) (Las Vegas, 1992) (4 for 68 yards)
19.0—Cincinnati (18) vs. Virginia Tech (6) (Sun, 1947) (6 for 114 yards)
22.0—Mississippi St. (16) vs. North Caro. St. (12) (Liberty, 1963) (3 for 66 yards)
23.0—Bowling Green (35) vs. Nevada (34) (Las Vegas, 1992) (5 for 115 yards)
25.5—Houston (34) vs. Notre Dame (35) (Cotton, 1979) (10 for 255 yards)
26.3—Oklahoma St. (34) vs. Texas Christian (0) (Cotton, 1945) (6 for 158 yards)
26.3—Notre Dame (35) vs. Houston (34) (Cotton, 1979) (7 for 184 yards)
26.3—Rice (28) vs. Alabama (6) (Cotton, 1954) (8 for 210 yards)

MOST PUNTS BLOCKED BY ONE TEAM
2—North Caro. (21) vs. Mississippi St. (17) (Peach, Jan. 2, 1993)
2—North Caro. St. (14) vs. Georgia (7) (Liberty, 1967)

Punt Returns

MOST PUNT RETURNS
9—Georgia (7) vs. North Caro. (3) (Gator, Dec. 31, 1971) (6.8 average)
8—Indiana (20) vs. Virginia Tech (45) (Independence, 1993) (7.3 average)
8—Tennessee (34) vs. Air Force (13) (Sugar, 1971) (10.8 average)
8—Mississippi (7) vs. UTEP (14) (Sun, 1967) (9.4 average)
8—Michigan (34) vs. Oregon St. (7) (Rose, 1965) (10.6 average)
7—Louisville (34) vs. Alabama (7) (Fiesta, 1991) (7.3 average)
6—Ohio St. (14) vs. Tennessee (20) (Florida Citrus, 1996) (5.0 average)
6—Tennessee (17) vs. Penn St. (42) (Fiesta, 1992) (8.2 average)
6—Clemson (30) vs. Illinois (0) (Hall of Fame, 1991)
6—(D) San Jose St. (48) vs. Central Mich. (24) (California, 1990)
6—Brigham Young (7) vs. Ohio St. (10) (Florida Citrus, 1985)
6—Texas (9) vs. Georgia (10) (Cotton, 1984) (2.5 average)
6—Washington (21) vs. Maryland (20) (Aloha, 1982) (4.7 average)
6—(D) Vanderbilt (28) vs. Air Force (36) (Hall of Fame, 1982)
6—Washington St. (36) vs. Brigham Young (38) (Holiday, 1981)
6—Nebraska (38) vs. Alabama (6) (Orange, 1972) (22.7 average)
6—Miami (Fla.) (14) vs. Syracuse (15) (Liberty, 1961) (13.0 average)
6—Air Force (0) vs. Texas Christian (0) (Cotton, 1959) (5.8 average)

6—Tulane (13) vs. Texas A&M (14) (Sugar, 1940) (21.0 average)
6—Tulane (20) vs. Temple (14) (Sugar, 1935)
6—Tulane (12) vs. Southern Cal (21) (Rose, 1932)

MOST PUNT RETURN YARDS

136—Nebraska (38) vs. Alabama (6) (Orange, 1972) (6 returns)
128—Oklahoma (48) vs. Duke (21) (Orange, 1958)
126—Tulane (13) vs. Texas A&M (14) (Sugar, 1940) (6 returns)
124—California (37) vs. Clemson (13) (Florida Citrus, 1992) (5 returns)
124—Washington (44) vs. Wisconsin (8) (Rose, 1960) (4 returns)
108—Southern Miss. (38) vs. UTEP (18) (Independence, 1988) (2 returns)
107—Arizona St. (45) vs. Florida St. (38) (Fiesta, 1971) (5 returns)
104—Texas A&M (21) vs. Alabama (29) (Cotton, 1942) (5 returns)
100—Virginia (34) vs. Georgia (27) (Peach, Dec. 30, 1995) (4 returns)
99—Kent (18) vs. Tampa (21) (Tangerine, 1972) (3 returns)
98—Brigham Young (46) vs. Southern Methodist (45) (Holiday, 1980) (3 returns)
94—Denver (24) vs. New Mexico (34) (Sun, 1946)
93—Auburn (35) vs. Mississippi (28) (Gator, Jan. 2, 1971) (4 returns)
92—Southern Cal (7) vs. Ohio St. (20) (Rose, 1955) (2 returns)
89—Nebraska (28) vs. Florida St. (31) (Fiesta, 1988) (3 returns)
88—Penn St. (42) vs. Arizona St. (30) (Fiesta, 1977) (2 returns)

HIGHEST PUNT RETURN AVERAGE
(Minimum 3 Returns)

33.0—Kent (18) vs. Tampa (21) (Tangerine, 1972) (3 for 99 yards)
32.7—Brigham Young (46) vs. Southern Methodist (45) (Holiday, 1980) (3 for 98 yards)
31.0—Washington (44) vs. Wisconsin (8) (Rose, 1960) (4 for 124 yards)
30.7—Michigan (42) vs. North Caro. St. (7) (Hall of Fame, 1994) (3 for 92 yards)
29.7—Nebraska (28) vs. Florida St. (31) (Fiesta, 1988) (3 for 89 yards)
27.6—Kansas St. (52) vs. Wyoming (17) (Copper, 1993) (3 for 83 yards)
25.0—Virginia (34) vs. Georgia (27) (Peach, Dec. 30, 1995) (4 for 100 yards)
24.8—California (37) vs. Clemson (13) (Florida Citrus, 1992) (5 for 124 yards)
24.0—Auburn (31) vs. Ohio St. (14) (Hall of Fame, 1990) (3 for 72 yards)
23.3—Auburn (35) vs. Mississippi (28) (Gator, Jan. 2, 1971) (4 for 93 yards)
22.7—Nebraska (38) vs. Alabama (6) (Orange, 1972) (6 for 136 yards)
21.4—Arizona St. (45) vs. Florida St. (38) (Fiesta, 1971) (5 for 107 yards)
21.0—Arkansas (6) vs. Duke (7) (Cotton, 1961) (3 for 63 yards)
21.0—Tulane (13) vs. Texas A&M (14) (Sugar, 1940) (6 for 126 yards)
20.8—Texas A&M (21) vs. Alabama (29) (Cotton, 1942) (5 for 104 yards)
19.5—(D) Georgia (20) vs. Texas A&M (40) (Presidential Cup, 1950) (4 for 78 yards)
19.3—Nebraska (14) vs. Houston (17) (Cotton, 1980) (3 for 58 yards)

Kickoff Returns

MOST KICKOFF RETURNS

10—Florida (24) vs. Nebraska (62) (Fiesta, 1996) (26.8 average)
10—Wyoming (14) vs. Oklahoma St. (62) (Holiday, 1988) (20.5 average)
9—Brigham Young (14) vs. Texas A&M (65) (Holiday, 1990) (18.2 average)
8—Northwestern (32) vs. Southern Cal (41) (Rose, 1996) (28.1 average)
8—Nebraska (21) vs. Georgia Tech (45) (Florida Citrus, 1991) (23.6 average)
8—Notre Dame (10) vs. Texas A&M (35) (Cotton, 1988) (18.9 average)
8—Texas Tech (17) vs. Florida St. (40) (Tangerine, 1977)
8—UCLA (6) vs. Alabama (36) (Liberty, 1976) (17.6 average)
8—Brigham Young (21) vs. Oklahoma St. (49) (Tangerine, 1976)
8—(D) Tulane (7) vs. Houston (47) (Bluebonnet, 1973) (28.1 average)
8—Missouri (35) vs. Arizona St. (49) (Fiesta, 1972) (32.3 average)
8—Arizona St. (45) vs. Florida St. (38) (Fiesta, 1971) (16.4 average)
8—Florida St. (38) vs. Arizona St. (45) (Fiesta, 1971) (23.0 average)
8—Colorado (47) vs. Alabama (33) (Liberty, 1969) (27.8 average)
8—Ohio (42) vs. Richmond (49) (Tangerine, 1968)
8—Florida St. (20) vs. UTEP (47) (Sun, 1955)
8—UCLA (14) vs. Illinois (45) (Rose, 1947) (32.4 average)

MOST KICKOFF RETURN YARDS

268—Florida (24) vs. Nebraska (62) (Fiesta, 1996) (10 returns)
259—UCLA (14) vs. Illinois (45) (Rose, 1947) (8 returns)
258—Missouri (35) vs. Arizona St. (49) (Fiesta, 1972) (8 returns)
225—Northwestern (32) vs. Southern Cal (41) (Rose, 1996) (8 returns)
225—(D) Tulane (7) vs. Houston (47) (Bluebonnet, 1973) (8 returns)
222—Colorado (47) vs. Alabama (33) (Liberty, 1969) (8 returns)
205—Wyoming (14) vs. Oklahoma (62) (Holiday, 1988) (10 returns)
204—Brigham Young (21) vs. Oklahoma St. (49) (Tangerine, 1976) (8 returns)
191—Houston (22) vs. Washington St. (24) (Aloha, 1988) (5 returns)
189—Nebraska (21) vs. Georgia Tech (45) (Florida Citrus, 1991) (8 returns)
188—Stanford (13) vs. East Caro. (19) (Liberty, 1995) (6 returns)
187—Houston (28) vs. Boston College (45) (Cotton, 1985) (7 returns)
184—Florida St. (38) vs. Arizona St. (45) (Fiesta, 1971) (8 returns)
174—Hawaii (13) vs. Michigan St. (33) (Aloha, 1989) (7 returns)
170—Tennessee (27) vs. Maryland (28) (John Hancock, 1984) (4 returns)
169—Oregon St. (19) vs. Iowa (35) (Rose, 1957) (5 returns)
164—Brigham Young (14) vs. Texas A&M (65) (Holiday, 1990) (9 returns)

HIGHEST KICKOFF RETURN AVERAGE
(Minimum 3 Returns)

42.5—Tennessee (27) vs. Maryland (28) (John Hancock, 1984) (4 for 170 yards)
38.3—Fresno St. (30) vs. Colorado (41) (Aloha, 1993) (3 for 115 yards)
38.3—Ohio St. (28) vs. Pittsburgh (23) (Fiesta, 1984) (4 for 153 yards)
38.2—Houston (22) vs. Washington St. (24) (Aloha, 1988) (5 for 191 yards)
37.5—LSU (45) vs. Michigan St. (26) (Independence, 1995) (4 for 150 yards)
37.5—Notre Dame (24) vs. Alabama (23) (Sugar, 1973) (4 for 150 yards)
36.8—Ohio St. (17) vs. Syracuse (24) (Hall of Fame, 1992) (4 for 147 yards)
36.7—Indiana (20) vs. Virginia Tech (45) (Independence, 1993) (3 for 110 yards)
33.8—Oregon St. (19) vs. Iowa (35) (Rose, 1957) (5 for 169 yards)
32.8—Florida St. (40) vs. Texas Tech (17) (Tangerine, 1977) (4 for 131 yards)
32.6—UCLA (30) vs. Kansas (51) (Aloha, 1995) (5 for 163 yards)
32.4—UCLA (14) vs. Illinois (45) (Rose, 1947) (8 for 259 yards)
32.3—Missouri (35) vs. Arizona St. (49) (Fiesta, 1972) (8 for 258 yards)
31.7—Penn St. (41) vs. Baylor (20) (Cotton, 1975) (3 for 95 yards)
31.3—Stanford (13) vs. East Caro. (19) (Liberty, 1995) (6 for 188 yards)
29.4—Virginia (34) vs. Georgia (27) (Peach, Dec. 30, 1995) (5 for 147 yards)
29.0—Mississippi St. (17) vs. Nebraska (31) (Sun, 1980) (4 for 116 yards)
28.1—Northwestern (32) vs. Southern Cal (41) (Rose, 1996) (8 for 225 yards)
27.8—Brigham Young (21) vs. Ohio St. (28) (Holiday, 1993) (5 for 139 yards)
27.0—Arizona St. (17) vs. Arkansas (18) (Holiday, 1985) (3 for 81 yards)
26.8—Florida (24) vs. Nebraska (62) (Fiesta, 1996) (10 for 268 yards)
26.7—Houston (28) vs. Boston College (45) (Cotton, 1985) (7 for 187 yards)

Fumbles

MOST FUMBLES

11—Mississippi (7) vs. Alabama (12) (Sugar, 1964) (lost 6)
9—Texas (11) vs. Notre Dame (24) (Cotton, 1971) (lost 5)
8—North Caro. St. (28) vs. Iowa (23) (Peach, Dec. 31, 1988) (lost 5)
8—(D) Houston (35) vs. Navy (0) (Garden State, 1980) (lost 3)
8—Louisville (14) vs. Louisiana Tech (24) (Independence, 1977) (lost 3)
8—North Texas (8) vs. New Mexico St. (28) (Sun, 1959) (lost 6)
8—Texas Christian (0) vs. Air Force (0) (Cotton, 1959) (lost 3)
8—Colorado (27) vs. Clemson (21) (Orange, 1957) (lost 3)
7—(D) Florida (7) vs. Washington (34) (Freedom, 1989) (lost 3)
7—Hawaii (13) vs. Michigan St. (33) (Aloha, 1989) (lost 4)
7—(D) Toledo (27) vs. San Jose St. (25) (California, 1981) (lost 2)
7—(D) Texas A&M (28) vs. Southern Cal (47) (Bluebonnet, 1977) (lost 5)
7—Auburn (27) vs. Texas (3) (Gator, 1974) (lost 5)
7—Tennessee (34) vs. Air Force (13) (Sugar, 1971) (lost 4)
7—Air Force (13) vs. Tennessee (34) (Sugar, 1971) (lost 3)
7—Georgia (2) vs. Arkansas (16) (Sugar, 1969) (lost 5)
7—Alabama (0) vs. Penn St. (7) (Liberty, 1959) (lost 4)
7—Southern Cal (7) vs. Ohio St. (20) (Rose, 1955) (lost 3)
7—Wash. & Lee (7) vs. Wyoming (20) (Gator, 1951) (lost 2)
7—Missouri (7) vs. Maryland (20) (Gator, 1950) (lost 5)
7—(D) Georgia (20) vs. Texas A&M (40) (Presidential Cup, 1950)
7—(D) Arizona St. (21) vs. Xavier (Ohio) (33) (Salad, 1950) (lost 6)

MOST FUMBLES, BOTH TEAMS

17—Alabama (12) [6] & Mississippi (7) [11] (Sugar, 1964) (lost 9)
14—Louisiana Tech (24) [6] & Louisville (14) [8] (Independence, 1977) (lost 6)
14—Tennessee (34) [7] & Air Force (13) [7] (Sugar, 1971) (lost 7)
13—Texas Christian (0) [8] & Air Force (0) [5] (Cotton, 1959) (lost 6)
12—North Caro. St. (28) [8] & Iowa (23) [4] (Peach, Dec. 31, 1988) (lost 8)
12—(D) Houston (35) [8] & Navy (0) [4] (Garden State, 1980) (lost 6)
12—New Mexico St. (28) [4] & North Texas (8) [8] (Sun, 1959) (lost 8)
11—(D) Toledo (27) [7] & San Jose St. (25) [4] (California, 1981) (lost 3)
11—Oklahoma (41) [6] & Wyoming (7) [5] (Fiesta, 1976)
10—Alabama (30) [5] & Baylor (2) [5] (Cotton, 1981) (lost 5)
10—(D) Houston (31) [5] & North Caro. St. (31) [5] (Bluebonnet, 1974) (lost 4)
10—Notre Dame (24) [1] & Texas (11) [9] (Cotton, 1971) (lost 6)
10—Illinois (17) [5] & Washington (7) [5] (Rose, 1964) (lost 6)
10—Navy (20) [5] & Rice (7) [5] (Cotton, 1958) (lost 8)
10—Mississippi (7) [5] & Florida (3) [5] (Gator, 1958) (lost 5)
10—Texas (16) [5] & Tennessee (0) [5] (Cotton, 1953) (lost 6)

MOST FUMBLES LOST

6—Texas A&M (2) vs. Florida St. (10) (Cotton, 1992) (6 fumbles)
6—East Caro. (31) vs. Maine (0) (Tangerine, 1965) (6 fumbles)
6—Mississippi (7) vs. Alabama (12) (Sugar, 1964) (11 fumbles)
6—North Texas (8) vs. New Mexico St. (28) (Sun, 1959) (8 fumbles)
6—(D) Arizona St. (21) vs. Xavier (Ohio) (33) (Salad, 1950) (7 fumbles)
5—UCLA (16) vs. Wisconsin (21) (Rose, 1994) (5 fumbles)
5—North Caro. St. (28) vs. Iowa (23) (Peach, Dec. 31, 1988) (8 fumbles)
5—North Caro. (21) vs. Arizona (30) (Aloha, 1986) (5 fumbles)
5—(D) Bowling Green (7) vs. Fresno St. (51) (California, 1985) (6 fumbles)
5—(D) Georgia (22) vs. Stanford (25) (Bluebonnet, 1978) (6 fumbles)
5—(D) Texas A&M (28) vs. Southern Cal (47) (Bluebonnet, 1977) (7 fumbles)
5—Auburn (27) vs. Texas (3) (Gator, 1974) (7 fumbles)
5—Texas (11) vs. Notre Dame (24) (Cotton, 1971) (9 fumbles)
5—Georgia (2) vs. Arkansas (16) (Sugar, 1969) (7 fumbles)
5—(D) Utah St. (9) vs. Baylor (24) (Gotham, 1961) (5 fumbles)
5—Rice (7) vs. Navy (20) (Cotton, 1958) (5 fumbles)
5—Auburn (13) vs. Vanderbilt (25) (Gator, 1955) (5 fumbles)
5—Oklahoma (7) vs. Kentucky (13) (Sugar, 1951)
5—Missouri (7) vs. Maryland (20) (Gator, 1950) (7 fumbles)
5—Texas A&M (21) vs. Alabama (29) (Cotton, 1942) (6 fumbles)

MOST FUMBLES LOST, BOTH TEAMS
9—Alabama (12) [3] & Mississippi (7) [6] (Sugar, 1964) (17 fumbles)
8—North Caro. St. (28) [5] & Iowa (23) [3] (Peach, Dec. 31, 1988) (12 fumbles)
8—New Mexico St. (28) [2] & North Texas (8) [6] (Sun, 1959) (12 fumbles)
8—Navy (20) [3] & Rice (7) [5] (Cotton, 1958) (10 fumbles)
7—Florida St. (10) [1] & Texas A&M (2) [6] (Cotton, 1992) (7 fumbles)
7—Texas A&M (37) [3] & Florida (14) [4] (Sun, Jan. 2, 1977) (8 fumbles)
7—Arizona St. (28) [3] & Pittsburgh (7) [4] (Fiesta, 1973) (9 fumbles)
7—Tennessee (34) [4] & Air Force (13) [3] (Sugar, 1971) (14 fumbles)
7—Michigan St. (28) [4] & UCLA (20) [3] (Rose, 1954) (8 fumbles)

Penalties

MOST PENALTIES
20—(D) Fresno St. (35) vs. Western Mich. (30) (California, 1988) (166 yards)
18—Washington St. (31) vs. Utah (28) (Copper, 1992) (136 yards)
17—Tennessee (17) vs. Oklahoma (0) (Orange, 1939) (157 yards)
16—Miami (Fla.) (46) vs. Texas (3) (Cotton, 1991) (202 yards)
16—Tulsa (16) vs. McNeese St. (20) (Independence, 1976) (100 yards)
15—Washington St. (10) vs. Baylor (3) (Alamo, 1994) (110 yards)
15—Illinois (30) vs. East Caro. (0) (Liberty, 1994) (164 yards)
15—Utah St. (42) vs. Ball St. (33) (Las Vegas, 1993) (150 yards)
15—Miami (Fla.) (7) vs. Tennessee (35) (Sugar, 1986) (120 yards)
15—(D) Michigan (33) vs. UCLA (14) (Bluebonnet, 1981) (148 yards)
14—(D) San Jose St. (37) vs. Miami (Ohio) (7) (California, 1986) (163 yards)
13—Florida St. (41) vs. Nebraska (17) (Fiesta, 1990) (135 yards)
13—(D) San Jose St. (27) vs. Eastern Mich. (30) (California, 1987) (103 yards)
13—(D) Washington (20) vs. Colorado (17) (Freedom, 1985) (88 yards)
13—Miami (Fla.) (31) vs. Nebraska (30) (Orange, 1984) (101 yards)
13—McNeese St. (20) vs. Tulsa (16) (Independence, 1976) (105 yards)
13—Lamar (21) vs. Middle Tenn. St. (14) (Tangerine, 1961) (140 yards)

MOST PENALTIES, BOTH TEAMS
29—McNeese St. (20) [13] & Tulsa (16) [16] (Independence, 1976) (205 yards)
28—(D) Fresno St. (35) [20] & Western Mich. (30) [8] (California, 1988) (231 yards)
26—Tennessee (35) [11] & Miami (Fla.) (7) [15] (Sugar, 1986) (245 yards)
26—Tennessee (17) [17] & Oklahoma (0) [9] (Orange, 1939) (221 yards)
25—Washington St. (31) [18] & Utah (28) [7] (Copper, 1992) (191 yards)
24—Miami (Fla.) (46) [16] & Texas (3) [8] (Cotton, 1991) (270 yards)
24—(D) San Jose St. (37) [14] & Miami (Ohio) (7) [10] (California, 1986) (264 yards)
24—(D) Michigan (33) [15] & UCLA (14) [9] (Bluebonnet, 1981) (242 yards)
23—Kansas St. (54) [12] & Colorado St. (21) [11] (Holiday, 1995) (219 yards)
23—(D) Fresno St. (51) [12] & Bowling Green (7) [11] (California, 1985) (183 yards)
22—(D) Eastern Mich. (30) [9] & San Jose St. (27) [13] (California, 1987) (162 yards)
21—Illinois (30) [15] & East Caro. (0) [6] (Liberty, 1994) (204 yards)
21—Florida St. (18) [10] & Nebraska (16) [11] (Orange, 1994) (184 yards)
21—Ohio St. (47) [12] & Brigham Young (17) [9] (Holiday, 1982) (184 yards)
21—Oklahoma St. (16) [12] & Brigham Young (6) [9] (Fiesta, 1974) (150 yards)
20—Virginia Tech (28) [11] & Texas (10) [9] (Sugar, Dec. 31, 1995) (190 yards)
20—Iowa (38) [12] & Washington (18) [8] (Sun, 1995) (164 yards)
20—Utah St. (42) [15] & Ball St. (33) [5] (Las Vegas, 1993) (180 yards)
20—Penn St. (50) [10] & Brigham Young (39) [10] (Holiday, 1989) (181 yards)
20—Washington St. (24) [11] & Houston (22) [9] (Aloha, 1988) (153 yards)
20—Brigham Young (24) [9] & Michigan (17) [11] (Holiday, 1984) (194 yards)

MOST YARDS PENALIZED
202—Miami (Fla.) (46) vs. Texas (3) (Cotton, 1991) (16 penalties)
166—(D) Fresno St. (35) vs. Western Mich. (30) (California, 1988) (20 penalties)
164—Illinois (30) vs. East Caro. (0) (Liberty, 1994) (15 penalties)
163—(D) San Jose St. (37) vs. Miami (Ohio) (7) (California, 1986) (14 penalties)
150—Utah St. (42) vs. Ball St. (33) (Las Vegas, 1993) (15 penalties)
150—Oklahoma (48) vs. Duke (21) (Orange, 1958) (12 penalties)
148—(D) Michigan (33) vs. UCLA (14) (Bluebonnet, 1981) (15 penalties)
143—Miami (Fla.) (22) vs. Nebraska (0) (Orange, 1992) (12 penalties)
140—Lamar (21) vs. Middle Tenn. St. (14) (Tangerine, 1961) (13 penalties)
136—Washington St. (31) vs. Utah (28) (Copper, 1992) (18 penalties)
135—Florida St. (41) vs. Nebraska (17) (Fiesta, 1990) (13 penalties)
130—LSU (15) vs. Nebraska (30) (Sugar, 1987) (12 penalties)
130—Tennessee (17) vs. Oklahoma (0) (Orange, 1939)
128—Oklahoma (48) vs. Virginia (14) (Gator, Dec. 29, 1991) (12 penalties)
126—Penn St. (42) vs. Arizona St. (30) (Fiesta, 1977) (12 penalties)
125—Tennessee (35) vs. Miami (Fla.) (7) (Sugar, 1986) (11 penalties)
124—Kansas St. (54) vs. Colorado St. (21) (Holiday, 1995) (12 penalties)
122—Mississippi St. (16) vs. North Caro. St. (12) (Liberty, 1963) (11 penalties)

MOST YARDS PENALIZED, BOTH TEAMS
270—Miami (Fla.) (46) [202] & Texas (3) [68] (Cotton, 1991)
264—(D) San Jose St. (37) [163] & Miami (Ohio) (7) [101] (California, 1986)
245—Tennessee (35) [125] & Miami (Fla.) (7) [120] (Sugar, 1986)
242—(D) Michigan (33) [148] & UCLA (14) [94] (Bluebonnet, 1981)
231—(D) Fresno St. (35) [166] & Western Mich. (30) [65] (California, 1988)
221—Tennessee (17) [130] & Oklahoma (0) [91] (Orange, 1939)
219—Kansas St. (54) [124] & Colorado St. (21) [95] (Holiday, 1995)
205—McNeese St. (20) [105] & Tulsa (16) [100] (Independence, 1976)
204—Illinois (30) [164] & East Caro. (0) [40] (Liberty, 1994)
194—Brigham Young (24) [82] & Michigan (17) [112] (Holiday, 1984)
191—Washington St. (31) [136] & Utah (28) [55] (Copper, 1992)
190—Virginia Tech (28) [99] & Texas (10) [91] (Sugar, Dec. 31, 1995)
184—Florida St. (18) [69] & Nebraska (16) [115] (Orange, 1994)
183—Florida St. (41) [135] & Nebraska (17) [48] (Fiesta, 1990)
183—(D) Fresno St. (51) [112] & Bowling Green (7) [71] (California, 1985)
181—Penn St. (50) [93] & Brigham Young (39) [88] (Holiday, 1989)
180—Utah St. (42) [150] & Ball St. (33) [30] (Las Vegas, 1993)
179—Miami (Fla.) (22) [143] & Nebraska (0) [36] (Orange, 1992)
176—Oklahoma (48) [128] & Virginia (14) [48] (Gator, Dec. 29, 1991)
175—Oklahoma (48) [150] & Duke (21) [25] (Orange, 1958)

FEWEST PENALTIES
0—Southern Methodist (7) vs. Alabama (28) (Sun, 1983)
0—Louisiana Tech (13) vs. East Caro. (35) (Independence, 1978)
0—Texas (17) vs. Alabama (13) (Cotton, 1973)
0—(D) Rice (7) vs. Kansas (33) (Bluebonnet, 1961)
0—Pittsburgh (14) vs. Georgia Tech (21) (Gator, 1956)
0—Clemson (0) vs. Miami (Fla.) (14) (Gator, 1952)
0—Texas (7) vs. Randolph Field (7) (Cotton, 1944)
0—Alabama (20) vs. Washington (19) (Rose, 1926)

FEWEST PENALTIES, BOTH TEAMS
3—Alabama (28) [3] & Southern Methodist (7) [0] (Sun, 1983)
3—Penn St. (30) [2] & Texas (6) [1] (Cotton, 1972)
3—Texas (21) [1] & Notre Dame (17) [2] (Cotton, 1970)
3—Penn St. (15) [1] & Kansas (14) [2] (Orange, 1969)
3—(D) Kansas (33) [3] & Rice (7) [0] (Bluebonnet, 1961)

FEWEST YARDS PENALIZED
0—Southern Methodist (7) vs. Alabama (28) (Sun, 1983)
0—Louisiana Tech (13) vs. East Caro. (35) (Independence, 1978)
0—Texas (17) vs. Alabama (13) (Cotton, 1973)
0—(D) Rice (7) vs. Kansas (33) (Bluebonnet, 1961)
0—Pittsburgh (14) vs. Georgia Tech (21) (Gator, 1956)
0—Clemson (0) vs. Miami (Fla.) (14) (Gator, 1952)
0—Texas (7) vs. Randolph Field (7) (Cotton, 1944)
0—Alabama (20) vs. Washington (19) (Rose, 1926)

FEWEST YARDS PENALIZED, BOTH TEAMS
10—Duquesne (13) [5] & Mississippi St. (12) [5] (Orange, 1937)
15—Texas (21) [5] & Notre Dame (17) [10] (Cotton, 1970)
15—(D) Kansas (33) [15] vs. Rice (7) [0] (Bluebonnet, 1961)

Miscellaneous Records

SCORELESS TIES#
1959—Air Force 0, Texas Christian 0 (Cotton)
1947—Arkansas 0, LSU 0 (Cotton)
1940—Arizona St. 0, Catholic 0 (Sun)
1922—California 0, Wash. & Jeff. 0 (Rose)

TIE GAMES#
(Not Scoreless)
1991—Brigham Young 13, Iowa 13 (Holiday)
1990—Louisiana Tech 34, Maryland 34 (Independence)
1988—Auburn 16, Syracuse 16 (Sugar)
1985—Arizona 13, Georgia 13 (Sun)
1984—Florida St. 17, Georgia 17 (Florida Citrus)
1978—Arkansas 10, UCLA 10 (Fiesta)
1977—(D) Maryland 17, Minnesota 17 (Hall of Fame)
1974—Texas Tech 6, Vanderbilt 6 (Peach)
1974—(D) Houston 31, North Caro. St. 31 (Bluebonnet)
1970—(D) Alabama 24, Oklahoma 24 (Bluebonnet)
1970—(D) Long Beach St. 24, Louisville 24 (Pasadena)
1967—Florida St. 17, Penn St. 17 (Gator)
1960—(D) Alabama 3, Texas 3 (Bluebonnet)
1948—Georgia 20, Maryland 20 (Gator)
1948—Penn St. 13, Southern Methodist 13 (Cotton)
1947—(D) Montana St. 13, New Mexico 13 (Harbor)
1944—Randolph Field 7, Texas 7 (Cotton)
1937—(D) Auburn 7, Villanova 7 (Bacardi)
1936—Hardin-Simmons 14, New Mexico St. 14 (Sun)
1934—(D) Arkansas 7, Centenary (La.) 7 (Dixie Classic)
1927—Alabama 7, Stanford 7 (Rose)
1924—Navy 14, Washington 14 (Rose)

LARGEST DEFICIT OVERCOME TO WIN
22—Brigham Young (46) vs. Southern Methodist (45) (Holiday, 1980) (trailed 35-13 in 3rd quarter and then trailed 45-25 with four minutes remaining in the game)
22—Notre Dame (35) vs. Houston (34) (Cotton, 1979) (trailed 34-12 in 4th quarter)
21—(D) Fresno St. (29) vs. Bowling Green (28) (California, 1982) (trailed 21-0 in 2nd quarter)
19—Wake Forest (39) vs. Oregon (35) (Independence, 1992) (trailed 29-10 in 3rd quarter)

14—Rice (28) vs. Colorado (14) (Cotton, 1938) (trailed 14-0 in 2nd quarter)
13—Mississippi (14) vs. Texas Christian (13) (Cotton, 1956) (trailed 13-0 in 2nd quarter)
11—Michigan (27) vs. Nebraska (23) (Fiesta, 1986) (trailed 14-3 in 3rd quarter)

OVERTIME GAMES#

1995—Toledo (40) vs. Nevada (37) (Las Vegas) (1 OT)

#Beginning in 1995-96, tied bowl games were allowed to use a tiebreaker system.

Longest Plays

(D) Denotes discontinued bowl. Year listed is actual year bowl was played.

LONGEST RUNS FROM SCRIMMAGE

Yds.	Player, Team (Score) vs. Opponent (Score)	Bowl, Year
99*	Terry Baker (QB), Oregon St. (6) vs. Villanova (0)	Liberty, 1962
95*#	Dicky Maegle, Rice (28) vs. Alabama (6)	Cotton, 1954
94*(D)	Dwight Ford, Southern Cal (47) vs. Texas A&M (28)	Bluebonnet, 1977
94*	Larry Smith, Florida (27) vs. Georgia Tech (12)	Orange, 1967
94*	Hascall Henshaw, Arizona St. (13) vs. Case Reserve (26)	Sun, 1941

*#Famous bench-tackle play; Maegle tackled on Alabama 40-yard line by Tommy Lewis, awarded touchdown. *Scored touchdown on play.*

LONGEST PASS PLAYS

Yds.	Player, Team (Score) vs. Opponent (Score)	Bowl, Year
95*	Ronnie Fletcher to Ben Hart, Oklahoma (19) vs. Florida St. (36)	Gator, Jan. 2, 1965
93*(D)	Stan Heath to Tommy Kalminir, Nevada (13) vs. North Texas (6)	Salad, 1948
91*(D)	Mark Barsotti to Stephen Shelley, Fresno St. (27) vs. Ball St. (6)	California, 1989
88*	Dave Schnell to Rob Turner, Indiana (34) vs. South Caro. (10)	Liberty, 1988
87*	Mike Thomas to L. C. Stevens, North Caro. (20) vs. Arkansas (10)	Carquest, Dec. 30, 1995
87*	Drew Bledsoe to Phillip Bobo, Washington St. (31) vs. Utah (28)	Copper, 1992
87*	Randy Wright to Tim Stracka, Wisconsin (14) vs. Kansas St. (3)	Independence, 1982
87*	Ger Schwedes to Ernie Davis, Syracuse (23) vs. Texas (14)	Cotton, 1960
86*	Brad Otton to Keyshawn Johnson, Southern Cal (55) vs. Texas Tech (14)	Cotton, 1995

**Scored touchdown on play.*

LONGEST FIELD GOALS

Yds.	Player, Team (Score) vs. Opponent (Score)	Bowl, Year
62	Tony Franklin, Texas A&M (37) vs. Florida (14)	Sun, Jan. 2, 1977
56	Greg Cox, Miami (Fla.) (20) vs. Oklahoma (14)	Orange, 1988
55(D)	Russell Erxleben, Texas (38) vs. Colorado (21)	Bluebonnet, 1975
54	Carlos Huerta, Miami (Fla.) (22) vs. Nebraska (0)	Orange, 1992
54	Quin Rodriguez, Southern Cal (16) vs. Michigan St. (17)	John Hancock, 1990
54	Luis Zendejas, Arizona St. (32) vs. Oklahoma (21)	Fiesta, 1983

LONGEST PUNTS

Yds.	Player, Team (Score) vs. Opponent (Score)	Bowl, Year
84$	Kyle Rote, Southern Methodist (21) vs. Oregon (13)	Cotton, 1949
82	Ike Pickle, Mississippi St. (12) vs. Duquesne (13)	Orange, 1937
80	Elmer Layden, Notre Dame (27) vs. Stanford (10)	Rose, 1925
79$	Doak Walker, Southern Methodist (21) vs. Oregon (13)	Cotton, 1949
77	Mike Sochko, Maryland (21) vs. Houston (30)	Cotton, 1977
73	Sean Reali, Syracuse (41) vs. Clemson (0)	Gator, 1996

$Quick kick.

LONGEST PUNT RETURNS

Yds.	Player, Team (Score) vs. Opponent (Score)	Bowl, Year
86*	Aramis Dandoy, Southern Cal (7) vs. Ohio St. (20)	Rose, 1955
83*	Vai Sikahema, Brigham Young (46) vs. Southern Methodist (45)	Holiday, 1980
82*	Marcus Wall, North Caro. (31) vs. Texas (35)	Sun, 1994
82	Willie Drewrey, West Va. (12) vs. Florida St. (31)	Gator, 1982
80*(D)	Gary Anderson, Arkansas (34) vs. Tulane (15)	Hall of Fame, 1980
80*	Cecil Ingram, Alabama (61) vs. Syracuse (6)	Orange, 1953

**Scored touchdown on play.*

LONGEST KICKOFF RETURNS

Yds.	Player, Team (Score) vs. Opponent (Score)	Bowl, Year
100*	Derrick Mason, Michigan St. (26) vs. LSU (45)	Independence, 1995
100*	Kirby Dar Dar, Syracuse (26) vs. Colorado (22)	Fiesta, 1993
100*	Pete Panuska, Tennessee (27) vs. Maryland (28)	Sun, 1984
100*	Dave Lowery, Brigham Young (21) vs. Oklahoma St. (49)	Tangerine, 1976
100*	Mike Fink, Missouri (35) vs. Arizona St. (49)	Fiesta, 1972
100*(D)	Bob Smith, Texas A&M (40) vs. Georgia (20)	Presidential Cup, 1950
100*!	Al Hoisch, UCLA (14) vs. Illinois (45)	Rose, 1947

**Scored touchdown on play. !Rose Bowl records carry as 103-yard return.*

LONGEST INTERCEPTION RETURNS

Yds.	Player, Team (Score) vs. Opponent (Score)	Bowl, Year
95*	Marcus Washington, Colorado (38) vs. Oregon (6)	Cotton, 1996
94*	David Baker, Oklahoma (48) vs. Duke (21)	Orange, 1958
91*	Don Hoover, Ohio (14) vs. West Tex. A&M (15)	Sun, 1962
90*	Norm Beal, Missouri (21) vs. Navy (14)	Orange, 1961
90*	Charlie Brembs, South Caro. (14) vs. Wake Forest (26)	Gator, 1946
90*(D)	G. P. Jackson, Texas Christian (7) vs. Centre (63)	Fort Worth Classic, 1921

**Scored touchdown on play.*

LONGEST MISCELLANEOUS RETURNS

Yds.	Player, Team (Score) vs. Opponent (Score)	Bowl, Year
98	Greg Mather, Navy (14) vs. Missouri (21) (Int. Lat.)	Orange, 1961
80	Antonio Banks, Virginia Tech (45) vs. Indiana (20) (Blocked field goal return)	Independence, 1993
73	Dick Carpenter, Oklahoma (48) vs. Duke (21) (Int. Lat.)	Orange, 1958
65	Steve Manstedt, Nebraska (19) vs. Texas (3) (Live Fum.)	Cotton, 1974

Bowl Coaching Records

All-Time Bowl Appearances

(Ranked by Most Bowl Games Coached)

Coach (Teams Taken to Bowl)	G	W-L-T	Pct.
Bear Bryant, Alabama, Texas A&M, Kentucky	29	15-12-2	.552
*Joe Paterno, Penn St.	26	17-8-1	.673
*Tom Osborne, Nebraska	23	10-13-0	.435
*Lou Holtz, William & Mary, North Caro. St., Arkansas, Notre Dame	20	10-8-2	.550
Vince Dooley, Georgia	20	8-10-2	.450
*Bobby Bowden, West Va., Florida St.	19	15-3-1	.816
*LaVell Edwards, Brigham Young	19	6-12-1	.342
John Vaught, Mississippi	18	10-8-0	.556
Bo Schembechler, Michigan	17	5-12-0	.294
*Johnny Majors, Iowa St., Pittsburgh, Tennessee	16	9-7-0	.563
Darrell Royal, Texas	16	8-7-1	.531
Don James, Kent, Washington	15	10-5-0	.667
*Hayden Fry, Southern Methodist, Iowa	15	6-8-1	.433
Bobby Dodd, Georgia Tech	13	9-4-0	.692
Terry Donahue, UCLA	13	8-4-1	.654
Barry Switzer, Oklahoma	13	8-5-0	.615
Charlie McClendon, LSU	13	7-6-0	.538
Earle Bruce, Ohio St., Colorado St.	12	7-5-0	.583
Woody Hayes, Miami (Ohio), Ohio St.	12	6-6-0	.500
Shug Jordan, Auburn	12	5-7-0	.417
Bill Yeoman, Houston	11	6-4-1	.591
*George Welsh, Navy, Virginia	11	5-6-0	.455
Jerry Claiborne, Virginia Tech, Maryland, Kentucky	11	3-8-0	.273

**Active coach.*

All-Time Bowl Victories

Coach	Wins	Record	Coach	Wins	Record
*Joe Paterno	17	17-8-1	Terry Donahue	8	8-4-1
*Bobby Bowden	15	15-3-1	Barry Switzer	8	8-5-0
Bear Bryant	15	15-12-2	Darrell Royal	8	8-7-1
Don James	10	10-5-0	Vince Dooley	8	8-10-2
John Vaught	10	10-8-0	*John Robinson	7	7-1-0
*Lou Holtz	10	10-8-2	Bob Devaney	7	7-3-0
*Tom Osborne	10	10-13-0	Dan Devine	7	7-3-0
Bobby Dodd	9	9-4-0	Earle Bruce	7	7-5-0
*Johnny Majors	9	9-7-0	Charlie McClendon	7	7-6-0

**Active coach.*

All-Time Bowl Winning Percentage

(Minimum 11 Games)

Coach, Last Team Coached	G	W-L-T	Pct.
*Bobby Bowden, Florida St.	19	15-3-1	.816
Bobby Dodd, Georgia Tech	13	9-4-0	.692
*Joe Paterno, Penn St.	26	17-8-1	.673
Don James, Washington	15	10-5-0	.667
Terry Donahue, UCLA	13	8-4-1	.654
Barry Switzer, Oklahoma	13	8-5-0	.615
Bill Yeoman, Houston	11	6-4-1	.591
Earle Bruce, Colorado St.	12	7-5-0	.583
*Johnny Majors, Pittsburgh	16	9-7-0	.563
John Vaught, Mississippi	18	10-8-0	.556
Bear Bryant, Alabama	29	15-12-2	.552
*Lou Holtz, Notre Dame	20	10-8-2	.550
Charlie McClendon, LSU	13	7-6-0	.538
Darrell Royal, Texas	16	8-7-1	.531
Woody Hayes, Ohio St.	12	6-6-0	.500
*George Welsh, Virginia	11	5-6-0	.455
Vince Dooley, Georgia	20	8-10-2	.450
*Tom Osborne, Nebraska	23	10-13-0	.435
*Hayden Fry, Iowa	15	6-8-1	.433
Shug Jordan, Auburn	12	5-7-0	.417
*LaVell Edwards, Brigham Young	19	6-12-1	.342
Bo Schembechler, Michigan	17	5-12-0	.294
Jerry Claiborne, Kentucky	11	3-8-0	.273

**Active coach.*

All-Time Bowl Coaching History

A total of 423 coaches have head-coached in history's 690 major bowl games (the term "major bowl" is defined above the alphabetical list of team bowl records). Below is an alphabetical list of all 423 bowl coaches, with their alma mater and year, their birth date, and their game-by-game bowl records, with name and date of each bowl, opponent, final score (own score first) and opposing coach (in parentheses). A handful coached service teams or colleges never in the major category but are included because they coached against a major team in a major bowl.

Coach/School	Bowl/Date	Opponent/Score (Coach)
JIM AIKEN, 0-1-0 (Wash. & Jeff. '22) Born 5-26-99		
Oregon	Cotton 1-1-49	Southern Methodist 12-21 (Matty Bell)
FRED AKERS, 2-8-0 (Arkansas '60) Born 3-17-38		
Wyoming	Fiesta 12-19-76	Oklahoma 7-41 (Barry Switzer)
Texas	Cotton 1-2-78	Notre Dame 10-38 (Dan Devine)
Texas	Sun 12-23-78	Maryland 42-0 (Jerry Claiborne)
Texas	Sun 12-22-79	Washington 7-14 (Don James)
Texas	Bluebonnet 12-31-80	North Caro. 7-16 (Dick Crum)
Texas	Cotton 1-1-82	Alabama 14-12 (Paul "Bear" Bryant)
Texas	Sun 12-25-82	North Caro. 10-26 (Dick Crum)
Texas	Cotton 1-2-84	Georgia 9-10 (Vince Dooley)
Texas	Freedom 12-26-84	Iowa 17-55 (Hayden Fry)
Texas	Bluebonnet 12-31-85	Air Force 16-24 (Fisher DeBerry)
BILL ALEXANDER, 3-2-0 (Georgia Tech '12) Born 6-6-89		
Georgia Tech	Rose 1-1-29	California 8-7 (Clarence "Nibs" Price)
Georgia Tech	Orange 1-1-40	Missouri 21-7 (Don Faurot)
Georgia Tech	Cotton 1-1-43	Texas 7-14 (Dana Bible)
Georgia Tech	Sugar 1-1-44	Tulsa 20-18 (Henry Frnka)
Georgia Tech	Orange 1-1-45	Tulsa 12-26 (Henry Frnka)
LEONARD "STUB" ALLISON, 1-0-0 (Carleton '17) Born 1892		
California	Rose 1-1-38	Alabama 13-0 (Frank Thomas)
BARRY ALVAREZ, 2-0-0 (Nebraska '69) Born 12-30-46		
Wisconsin	Rose 1-1-94	UCLA 21-16 (Terry Donahue)
Wisconsin	Hall of Fame 1-2-95	Duke 34-20 (Fred Goldsmith)
MIKE ARCHER, 1-1-0 (Miami, Fla. '75) Born 7-26-53		
LSU	Gator 12-31-87	South Caro. 30-13 (Joe Morrison)
LSU	Hall of Fame 1-2-89	Syracuse 10-23 (Dick MacPherson)
IKE ARMSTRONG, 1-0-0 (Drake '23) Born 6-8-95		
Utah	Sun 1-2-39	New Mexico 16-0 (Ted Shipkey)
BILL ARNSPARGER, 0-3-0 (Miami, Ohio '50) Born 12-16-26		
LSU	Sugar 1-1-85	Nebraska 10-28 (Tom Osborne)
LSU	Liberty 12-27-85	Baylor 7-21 (Grant Teaff)
LSU	Sugar 1-1-87	Nebraska 15-30 (Tom Osborne)
CHRIS AULT, 0-2-0 (Nevada '68) Born 11-8-47		
Nevada	Las Vegas 12-18-92	Bowling Green 34-35 (Gary Blackney)
Nevada	Las Vegas 12-14-95	Toledo 37-40 OT (Gary Pinkel)
CHARLEY BACHMAN, 0-1-0 (Notre Dame '17) Born 12-1-92		
Michigan St.	Orange 1-1-38	Auburn 0-6 (Jack Meagher)
ENOCH BAGSHAW, 0-1-1 (Washington '08) Born 1884		
Washington	Rose 1-1-24	Navy 14-14 (Bob Folwell)
Washington	Rose 1-1-26	Alabama 19-20 (Wallace Wade)

Coach/School	Bowl/Date	Opponent/Score (Coach)
GEORGE BARCLAY, 0-1-0 (North Caro. '35) Born 5-14-11		
Wash. & Lee	Gator 1-1-51	Wyoming 7-20 (Bowden Wyatt)
BILL BARNES, 0-1-0 (Tennessee '41) Born 10-20-17		
UCLA	Rose 1-1-62	Minnesota 3-21 (Murray Warmath)
WILLIS BARNES, 1-1-1 (Nebraska) Born 10-22-00		
New Mexico	Sun 1-1-44	Southwestern (Tex.) 0-7 (R. M. Medley)
New Mexico	Sun 1-1-46	Denver 34-24 (Clyde "Cac" Hubbard)
New Mexico	Harbor 1-1-47	Montana St. 13-13 (Clyde Carpenter)
GARY BARNETT, 0-1-0 (Missouri '69) Born 5-23-46		
Northwestern	Rose 1-1-96	Southern Cal 32-41 (John Robinson)
JOHN BARNHILL, 2-1-1 (Tennessee '28) Born 2-21-03		
Tennessee	Sugar 1-1-43	Tulsa 14-7 (Henry Frnka)
Tennessee	Rose 1-1-45	Southern Cal 0-25 (Jeff Cravath)
Arkansas	Cotton 1-1-47	LSU 0-0 (Bernie Moore)
Arkansas	Dixie 1-1-48	William & Mary 21-19 (Rube McCray)
BILL BATTLE, 4-1-0 (Alabama '63) Born 12-8-41		
Tennessee	Sugar 1-1-71	Air Force 34-13 (Ben Martin)
Tennessee	Liberty 12-20-71	Arkansas 14-13 (Frank Broyles)
Tennessee	Bluebonnet 12-30-72	LSU 24-17 (Charlie McClendon)
Tennessee	Gator 12-29-73	Texas Tech 19-28 (Jim Carlen)
Tennessee	Liberty 12-16-74	Maryland 7-3 (Jerry Claiborne)
SAMMY BAUGH, 0-1-0 (Texas Christian '37) Born 3-17-14		
Hardin-Simmons	Sun 12-31-58	Wyoming 6-14 (Bob Devaney)
FRANK BEAMER, 2-1-0 (Virginia Tech '69) Born 10-18-46		
Virginia Tech	Independence 12-31-93	Indiana 45-20 (Bill Mallory)
Virginia Tech	Gator 12-30-94	Tennessee 23-45 (Phillip Fulmer)
Virginia Tech	Sugar 12-31-95	Texas 28-10 (John Mackovic)
ALEX BELL, 1-1-0 (Villanova '38) Born 8-12-15		
Villanova	Sun 12-20-61	Wichita St. 17-9 (Hank Foldberg)
Villanova	Liberty 12-15-62	Oregon St. 0-6 (Tommy Prothro)
MATTY BELL, 1-1-1 (Centre '20) Born 2-22-99		
Southern Methodist	Rose 1-1-36	Stanford 0-7 (Claude "Tiny" Thornhill)
Southern Methodist	Cotton 1-1-48	Penn St. 13-13 (Bob Higgins)
Southern Methodist	Cotton 1-1-49	Oregon 21-13 (Jim Aiken)
EMORY BELLARD, 2-3-0 (Southwest Tex. St. '49) Born 12-17-27		
Texas A&M	Liberty 12-22-75	Southern Cal 0-20 (John McKay)
Texas A&M	Sun 1-2-77	Florida 37-14 (Doug Dickey)
Texas A&M	Bluebonnet 12-31-77	Southern Cal 28-47 (John Robinson)
Mississippi St.	Sun 12-27-80	Nebraska 17-31 (Tom Osborne)
Mississippi St.	Hall of Fame 12-31-81	Kansas 10-0 (Don Fambrough)
MIKE BELLOTTI, 0-1-0 (UC Davis '73) Born 12-21-50		
Oregon	Cotton 1-1-96	Colorado 6-38 (Rick Neuheisel)
ARTHUR "DUTCH" BERGMAN, 1-0-1 (Notre Dame '20) Born 2-23-95		
Catholic	Orange 1-1-36	Mississippi 20-19 (Ed Walker)
Catholic	Sun 1-1-40	Arizona St. 0-0 (Millard "Dixie" Howell)
HUGO BEZDEK, 1-1-0 (Chicago '06) Born 4-1-84		
Oregon	Rose 1-1-17	Pennsylvania 14-0 (Bob Folwell)
Penn St.	Rose 1-1-23	Southern Cal 3-14 (Elmer "Gus" Henderson)
DANA BIBLE, 3-0-1 (Carson-Newman '12) Born 10-8-91		
Texas A&M	Dixie Classic 1-2-22	Centre 22-14 (Charley Moran)
Texas	Cotton 1-1-43	Georgia Tech 14-7 (Bill Alexander)
Texas	Cotton 1-1-44	Randolph Field 7-7 (Frank Tritico)
Texas	Cotton 1-1-46	Missouri 40-27 (Chauncey Simpson)
JACK BICKNELL, 2-2-0 (Montclair St. '60) Born 2-20-38		
Boston College	Tangerine 12-18-82	Auburn 26-33 (Pat Dye)
Boston College	Liberty 12-29-83	Notre Dame 18-19 (Gerry Faust)
Boston College	Cotton 1-1-85	Houston 45-28 (Bill Yeoman)
Boston College	Hall of Fame 12-23-86	Georgia 27-24 (Vince Dooley)
BERNIE BIERMAN, 0-1-0 (Minnesota '16) Born 3-11-94		
Tulane	Rose 1-1-32	Southern Cal 12-21 (Howard Jones)
GARY BLACKNEY, 2-0-0 (Connecticut '67) Born 12-10-55		
Bowling Green	California 12-14-91	Fresno St. 28-21 (Jim Sweeney)
Bowling Green	Las Vegas 12-18-92	Nevada 35-34 (Chris Ault)
BOBBY BOWDEN, 15-3-1 (Samford '53) Born 11-8-29		
West Va.	Peach 12-29-72	North Caro. St. 13-49 (Lou Holtz)
West Va.	Peach 12-31-75	North Caro. St. 13-10 (Lou Holtz)
Florida St.	Tangerine 12-23-77	Texas Tech 40-17 (Steve Sloan)
Florida St.	Orange 1-1-80	Oklahoma 7-24 (Barry Switzer)
Florida St.	Orange 1-1-81	Oklahoma 17-18 (Barry Switzer)
Florida St.	Gator 12-30-82	West Va. 31-12 (Don Nehlen)
Florida St.	Peach 12-30-83	North Caro. 28-3 (Dick Crum)
Florida St.	Fla. Citrus 12-22-84	Georgia 17-17 (Vince Dooley)
Florida St.	Gator 12-30-85	Oklahoma St. 34-23 (Pat Jones)
Florida St.	All-American 12-31-86	Indiana 27-13 (Bill Mallory)
Florida St.	Fiesta 1-1-88	Nebraska 31-28 (Tom Osborne)
Florida St.	Sugar 1-2-89	Auburn 13-7 (Pat Dye)
Florida St.	Fiesta 1-1-90	Nebraska 41-17 (Tom Osborne)
Florida St.	Blockbuster 12-28-90	Penn St. 24-17 (Joe Paterno)
Florida St.	Cotton 1-1-92	Texas A&M 10-2 (R. C. Slocum)
Florida St.	Orange 1-1-93	Nebraska 27-14 (Tom Osborne)

Coach/School	Bowl/Date	Opponent/Score (Coach)
Florida St.	Orange 1-1-94	Nebraska 18-16 (Tom Osborne)
Florida St.	Sugar 1-2-95	Florida 23-17 (Steve Spurrier)
Florida St.	Orange 1-1-96	Notre Dame 31-26 (Lou Holtz)
TERRY BOWDEN, 0-1-0 (West Va. '78) Born 2-24-56		
Auburn	Outback 1-1-96	Penn St. 14-43 (Joe Paterno)
JEFF BOWER, 0-1-0 (Southern Miss. '76) Born 5-28-53		
Southern Miss.	All-American 12-28-90	North Caro. St. 27-31 (Dick Sheridan)
SAM BOYD, 1-0-0 (Baylor '38) Born 8-12-15		
Baylor	Sugar 1-1-57	Tennessee 13-7 (Bowden Wyatt)
WESLEY BRADSHAW, 0-1-0 (Baylor '23) Born 11-26-98		
Ouachita Baptist	Shrine 12-18-48	Hardin-Simmons 12-40 (Warren Woodson)
BILLY BREWER, 3-2-0 (Mississippi '61) Born 10-8-35		
Mississippi	Independence 12-10-83	Air Force 3-9 (Ken Hatfield)
Mississippi	Independence 12-20-86	Texas Tech 20-17 (Spike Dykes)
Mississippi	All-American 12-29-89	Air Force 42-29 (Fisher DeBerry)
Mississippi	Gator 1-1-91	Michigan 3-35 (Gary Moeller)
Mississippi	Liberty 12-31-92	Air Force 13-0 (Fisher DeBerry)
JOHN BRIDGERS, 2-1-0 (Auburn '47) Born 1-13-22		
Baylor	Gator 12-31-60	Florida 12-13 (Ray Graves)
Baylor	Gotham 12-9-61	Utah St. 24-9 (John Ralston)
Baylor	Bluebonnet 12-21-63	LSU 14-7 (Charlie McClendon)
RICH BROOKS, 1-3-0 (Oregon St. '63) Born 8-20-41		
Oregon	Independence 12-16-89	Tulsa 27-24 (Dave Rader)
Oregon	Freedom 12-29-90	Colorado St. 31-32 (Earle Bruce)
Oregon	Independence 12-31-92	Wake Forest 35-39 (Bill Dooley)
Oregon	Rose 1-2-95	Penn St. 20-38 (Joe Paterno)
J. O. "BUDDY" BROTHERS, 0-1-0 (Texas Tech '31) Born 5-29-09		
Tulsa	Gator 1-1-53	Florida 13-14 (Bob Woodruff)
MACK BROWN, 2-3-0 (Florida St. '74) Born 8-27-51		
Tulane	Independence 12-19-87	Washington 12-24 (Don James)
North Caro.	Peach 1-2-93	Mississippi St. 21-17 (Jackie Sherrill)
North Caro.	Gator 12-31-93	Alabama 10-24 (Gene Stallings)
North Caro.	Sun 12-30-94	Texas 31-35 (John Mackovic)
North Caro.	Carquest 12-30-95	Arkansas 20-10 (Danny Ford)
FRANK BROYLES, 4-6-0 (Georgia Tech '47) Born 12-26-24		
Arkansas	Gator 1-2-60	Georgia Tech 14-7 (Bobby Dodd)
Arkansas	Cotton 1-2-61	Duke 6-7 (Bill Murray)
Arkansas	Sugar 1-1-62	Alabama 3-10 (Paul "Bear" Bryant)
Arkansas	Sugar 1-1-63	Mississippi 13-17 (John Vaught)
Arkansas	Cotton 1-1-65	Nebraska 10-7 (Bob Devaney)
Arkansas	Cotton 1-1-66	LSU 7-14 (Charlie McClendon)
Arkansas	Sugar 1-1-69	Georgia 16-2 (Vince Dooley)
Arkansas	Sugar 1-1-70	Mississippi 22-27 (John Vaught)
Arkansas	Liberty 12-20-71	Tennessee 13-14 (Bill Battle)
Arkansas	Cotton 1-1-76	Georgia 31-10 (Vince Dooley)
EARLE BRUCE, 7-5-0 (Ohio St. '53) Born 3-8-31		
Tampa	Tangerine 12-29-72	Kent 21-18 (Don James)
Iowa St.	Peach 12-31-77	North Caro. St. 14-24 (Bo Rein)
Iowa St.	Hall of Fame 12-20-78	Texas A&M 12-28 (Tom Wilson)
Ohio St.	Rose 1-1-80	Southern Cal 16-17 (John Robinson)
Ohio St.	Fiesta 12-26-80	Penn St. 19-31 (Joe Paterno)
Ohio St.	Liberty 12-30-81	Navy 31-28 (George Welsh)
Ohio St.	Holiday 12-17-82	Brigham Young 47-17 (LaVell Edwards)
Ohio St.	Fiesta 1-2-84	Pittsburgh 28-23 (Foge Fazio)
Ohio St.	Rose 1-1-85	Southern Cal 17-20 (Ted Tollner)
Ohio St.	Fla. Citrus 12-28-85	Brigham Young 10-7 (LaVell Edwards)
Ohio St.	Cotton 1-1-87	Texas A&M 28-12 (Jackie Sherrill)
Colorado St.	Freedom 12-29-90	Oregon 32-31 (Rich Brooks)
MILT BRUHN, 0-2-0 (Minnesota '35) Born 7-28-12		
Wisconsin	Rose 1-1-60	Washington 8-44 (Jim Owens)
Wisconsin	Rose 1-2-63	Southern Cal 37-42 (John McKay)
MIKE BRUMBELOW, 2-1-0 (Texas Christian '30) Born 7-13-06		
UTEP	Sun 1-1-54	Southern Miss. 37-14 (Thad "Pie" Vann)
UTEP	Sun 1-1-55	Florida St. 47-20 (Tom Nugent)
UTEP	Sun 1-1-57	Geo. Washington 0-13 (Eugene "Bo" Sherman)
PAUL "BEAR" BRYANT, 15-12-2 (Alabama '36) Born 9-11-13		
Kentucky	Great Lakes 12-6-47	Villanova 24-14 (Jordan Oliver)
Kentucky	Orange 1-2-50	Santa Clara 13-21 (Len Casanova)
Kentucky	Sugar 1-1-51	Oklahoma 13-7 (Bud Wilkinson)
Kentucky	Cotton 1-1-52	Texas Christian 20-7 (Leo "Dutch" Meyer)
Texas A&M	Gator 12-28-57	Tennessee 0-3 (Bowden Wyatt)
Alabama	Liberty 12-19-59	Penn St. 0-7 (Charles "Rip" Engle)
Alabama	Bluebonnet 12-17-60	Texas 3-3 (Darrell Royal)
Alabama	Sugar 1-1-62	Arkansas 10-3 (Frank Broyles)
Alabama	Orange 1-1-63	Oklahoma 17-0 (Bud Wilkinson)
Alabama	Sugar 1-1-64	Mississippi 12-7 (John Vaught)
Alabama	Orange 1-1-65	Texas 17-21 (Darrell Royal)
Alabama	Orange 1-1-66	Nebraska 39-28 (Bob Devaney)
Alabama	Sugar 1-2-67	Nebraska 34-7 (Bob Devaney)
Alabama	Cotton 1-1-68	Texas A&M 16-20 (Gene Stallings)
Alabama	Gator 12-28-68	Missouri 10-35 (Dan Devine)
Alabama	Liberty 12-13-69	Colorado 33-47 (Eddie Crowder)
Alabama	Bluebonnet 12-31-70	Oklahoma 24-24 (Chuck Fairbanks)
Alabama	Orange 1-1-72	Nebraska 6-38 (Bob Devaney)
Alabama	Cotton 1-1-73	Texas 13-17 (Darrell Royal)
Alabama	Sugar 12-31-73	Notre Dame 23-24 (Ara Parseghian)
Alabama	Orange 1-1-75	Notre Dame 11-13 (Ara Parseghian)
Alabama	Sugar 12-31-75	Penn St. 13-6 (Joe Paterno)
Alabama	Liberty 12-20-76	UCLA 36-6 (Terry Donahue)
Alabama	Sugar 1-2-78	Ohio St. 35-6 (Woody Hayes)
Alabama	Sugar 1-1-79	Penn St. 14-7 (Joe Paterno)
Alabama	Sugar 1-1-80	Arkansas 24-9 (Lou Holtz)
Alabama	Cotton 1-1-81	Baylor 30-2 (Grant Teaff)
Alabama	Cotton 1-1-82	Texas 12-14 (Fred Akers)
Alabama	Liberty 12-29-82	Illinois 21-15 (Mike White)
FRANK BURNS, 0-1-0 (Rutgers '49) Born 3-16-28		
Rutgers	Garden State 12-16-78	Arizona St. 18-34 (Frank Kush)
LEON BURTNETT, 0-1-0 (Southwestern, Kan. '65) Born 5-30-43		
Purdue	Peach 12-31-84	Virginia 24-27 (George Welsh)
WALLY BUTTS, 5-2-1 (Mercer '28) Born 2-7-05		
Georgia	Orange 1-1-42	Texas Christian 40-26 (Leo "Dutch" Meyer)
Georgia	Rose 1-1-43	UCLA 9-0 (Edwin "Babe" Horrell)
Georgia	Oil 1-1-46	Tulsa 20-6 (Henry Frnka)
Georgia	Sugar 1-1-47	North Caro. 20-10 (Carl Snavely)
Georgia	Gator 1-1-48	Maryland 20-20 (Jim Tatum)
Georgia	Orange 1-1-49	Texas 28-41 (Blair Cherry)
Georgia	Presidential Cup 12-9-50	Texas A&M 20-40 (Harry Stiteler)
Georgia	Orange 1-1-60	Missouri 14-0 (Dan Devine)
EDDIE CAMERON, 1-0-0 (Wash. & Lee '24) Born 4-22-02		
Duke	Sugar 1-1-45	Alabama 29-26 (Frank Thomas)
FRANK CAMP, 1-0-0 (Transylvania '30) Born 12-23-05		
Louisville	Sun 1-1-58	Drake 34-20 (Warren Gaer)
JIM CARLEN, 2-5-1 (Georgia Tech '55) Born 7-11-33		
West Va.	Peach 12-30-69	South Caro. 14-3 (Paul Dietzel)
Texas Tech	Sun 12-19-70	Georgia Tech 9-17 (Bud Carson)
Texas Tech	Sun 12-30-72	North Caro. 28-32 (Bill Dooley)
Texas Tech	Gator 12-29-73	Tennessee 28-19 (Bill Battle)
Texas Tech	Peach 12-28-74	Vanderbilt 6-6 (Steve Sloan)
South Caro.	Tangerine 12-20-75	Miami (Ohio) 7-20 (Dick Crum)
South Caro.	Hall of Fame 12-29-79	Missouri 14-24 (Warren Powers)
South Caro.	Gator 12-29-80	Pittsburgh 8-37 (Jackie Sherrill)
CLYDE CARPENTER, 0-0-1 (Montana '32) Born 4-17-08		
Montana St.	Harbor 1-1-47	New Mexico 13-13 (Willis Barnes)
LLOYD CARR, 0-1-0 (Northern Mich. '68) Born 7-30-45		
Michigan	Alamo 12-28-95	Texas A&M 20-22 (R. C. Slocum)
BUD CARSON, 1-1-0 (North Caro. '52) Born 4-28-30		
Georgia Tech	Sun 12-19-70	Texas Tech 17-9 (Jim Carlen)
Georgia Tech	Peach 12-30-71	Mississippi 18-41 (Billy Kinard)
LEN CASANOVA, 2-2-0 (Santa Clara '27) Born 6-12-05		
Santa Clara	Orange 1-2-50	Kentucky 21-13 (Paul "Bear" Bryant)
Oregon	Rose 1-1-58	Ohio St. 7-10 (Woody Hayes)
Oregon	Liberty 12-17-60	Penn St. 12-41 (Charles "Rip" Engle)
Oregon	Sun 12-31-63	Southern Methodist 21-14 (Hayden Fry)
MILES CASTEEL, 0-1-0 (Kalamazoo '25) Born 12-30-96		
Arizona	Salad 1-1-49	Drake 13-14 (Al Kawal)
PETE CAWTHON, 0-2-0 (Southwestern, Tex. '20) Born 8-24-98		
Texas Tech	Sun 1-1-38	West Va. 6-7 (Marshall "Little Sleepy" Glenn)
Texas Tech	Cotton 1-2-39	St. Mary's (Cal.) 13-20 (Edward "Slip" Madigan)
BLAIR CHERRY, 2-1-0 (Texas Christian '24) Born 9-7-01		
Texas	Sugar 1-1-48	Alabama 27-7 (Harold "Red" Drew)
Texas	Orange 1-1-49	Georgia 41-28 (Wally Butts)
Texas	Cotton 1-1-51	Tennessee 14-20 (Bob Neyland)
JERRY CLAIBORNE, 3-8-0 (Kentucky '50) Born 8-26-28		
Virginia Tech	Liberty 12-10-66	Miami (Fla.) 7-14 (Charlie Tate)
Virginia Tech	Liberty 12-14-68	Mississippi 17-34 (John Vaught)
Maryland	Peach 12-28-73	Georgia 16-17 (Vince Dooley)
Maryland	Liberty 12-16-74	Tennessee 3-7 (Bill Battle)
Maryland	Gator 12-29-75	Florida 13-0 (Doug Dickey)
Maryland	Cotton 1-1-77	Houston 21-30 (Bill Yeoman)
Maryland	Hall of Fame 12-22-77	Minnesota 17-7 (Cal Stoll)
Maryland	Sun 12-23-78	Texas 0-42 (Fred Akers)
Maryland	Tangerine 12-20-80	Florida 20-35 (Charley Pell)
Kentucky	Hall of Fame 12-22-83	West Va. 16-20 (Don Nehlen)
Kentucky	Hall of Fame 12-29-84	Wisconsin 20-19 (Dave McClain)
CECIL COLEMAN, 1-0-0 (Arizona St. '50) Born 4-12-26		
Fresno St.	Mercy 11-23-61	Bowling Green 36-6 (Doyt Perry)
BOBBY COLLINS, 3-2-0 (Mississippi St. '55) Born 10-25-33		
Southern Miss.	Independence 12-13-70	McNeese St. 16-14 (Ernie Duplechin)
Southern Miss.	Tangerine 12-19-81	Missouri 17-19 (Warren Powers)
Southern Methodist	Cotton 1-1-83	Pittsburgh 7-3 (Foge Fazio)

Coach/School	Bowl/Date	Opponent/Score (Coach)
Southern Methodist	Sun 12-24-83	Alabama 7-28 (Ray Perkins)
Southern Methodist	Aloha 12-29-84	Notre Dame 27-20 (Gerry Faust)
JOHN COOPER, 3-7-0 (Iowa St. '62) Born 7-2-37		
Arizona St.	Holiday 12-22-85	Arkansas 17-18 (Ken Hatfield)
Arizona St.	Rose 1-1-87	Michigan 22-15 (Glenn "Bo" Schembechler)
Arizona St.	Freedom 12-30-87	Air Force 33-28 (Fisher DeBerry)
Ohio St.	Hall of Fame 1-1-90	Auburn 14-31 (Pat Dye)
Ohio St.	Liberty 12-27-90	Air Force 11-23 (Fisher DeBerry)
Ohio St.	Hall of Fame 1-1-92	Syracuse 17-24 (Paul Pasqualoni)
Ohio St.	Fla. Citrus 1-1-93	Georgia 14-21 (Ray Goff)
Ohio St.	Holiday 12-30-93	Brigham Young 28-21 (LaVell Edwards)
Ohio St.	Fla. Citrus 1-2-95	Alabama 17-24 (Gene Stallings)
Ohio St.	Fla. Citrus 1-1-96	Tennessee 14-20 (Phillip Fulmer)
LEE CORSO, 1-0-1 (Florida St. '57) Born 8-7-35		
Louisville	Pasadena 12-19-70	Long Beach St. 24-24 (Jim Stangeland)
Indiana	Holiday 12-21-79	Brigham Young 38-37 (LaVell Edwards)
GENE CORUM, 0-1-0 (West Va. '48) Born 5-29-21		
West Va.	Liberty 12-19-64	Utah 6-32 (Ray Nagel)
DON CORYELL, 1-0-0 (Washington '50) Born 10-17-24		
San Diego St.	Pasadena 12-6-69	Boston U. 28-7 (Larry Naviaux)
TOM COUGHLIN, 1-1-0 (Syracuse '68) Born 8-31-46		
Boston College	Hall of Fame 1-1-93	Tennessee 23-38 (Phillip Fulmer)
Boston College	Carquest 1-1-94	Virginia 31-13 (George Welsh)
TED COX, 1-0-0 (Minnesota '26) Born 6-30-03		
Tulane	Sugar 1-1-35	Temple 20-14 (Glenn "Pop" Warner)
JEFF CRAVATH, 2-2-0 (Southern Cal '27) Born 2-5-05		
Southern Cal	Rose 1-1-44	Washington 29-0 (Ralph "Pest" Welch)
Southern Cal	Rose 1-1-45	Tennessee 25-0 (John Barnhill)
Southern Cal	Rose 1-1-46	Alabama 14-34 (Frank Thomas)
Southern Cal	Rose 1-1-48	Michigan 0-49 (H. O. "Fritz" Crisler)
H. O. "FRITZ" CRISLER, 1-0-0 (Chicago '22) Born 1-2-99		
Michigan	Rose 1-1-48	Southern Cal 49-0 (Jeff Cravath)
EDDIE CROWDER, 3-2-0 (Oklahoma '55) Born 8-26-31		
Colorado	Bluebonnet 12-23-67	Miami (Fla.) 31-21 (Charlie Tate)
Colorado	Liberty 12-13-69	Alabama 47-33 (Paul "Bear" Bryant)
Colorado	Liberty 12-12-70	Tulane 3-17 (Jim Pittman)
Colorado	Bluebonnet 12-31-71	Houston 29-17 (Bill Yeoman)
Colorado	Gator 12-20-72	Auburn 3-24 (Ralph "Shug" Jordan)
JACK CROWE, 0-1-0 (Ala.-Birmingham '70) Born 4-6-48		
Arkansas	Independence 12-29-91	Georgia 15-24 (Ray Goff)
JIM CROWLEY, 1-1-0 (Notre Dame '25) Born 9-10-02		
Fordham	Cotton 1-1-41	Texas A&M 12-13 (Homer Norton)
Fordham	Sugar 1-1-42	Missouri 2-0 (Don Faurot)
DICK CRUM, 6-2-0 (Mount Union '57) Born 4-29-34		
Miami (Ohio)	Tangerine 12-21-74	Georgia 21-10 (Vince Dooley)
Miami (Ohio)	Tangerine 12-20-75	South Caro. 20-7 (Jim Carlen)
North Caro.	Gator 12-28-79	Michigan 17-15 (Glenn "Bo" Schembechler)
North Caro.	Bluebonnet 12-31-80	Texas 16-7 (Fred Akers)
North Caro.	Gator 12-28-81	Arkansas 31-27 (Lou Holtz)
North Caro.	Sun 12-25-82	Texas 26-10 (Fred Akers)
North Caro.	Peach 12-30-83	Florida St. 3-28 (Bobby Bowden)
North Caro.	Aloha 12-27-86	Arizona 21-30 (Larry Smith)
FRAN CURCI, 1-0-0 (Miami, Fla. '60) Born 6-11-38		
Kentucky	Peach 12-31-76	North Caro. 21-0 (Bill Dooley)
BILL CURRY, 2-3-0 (Georgia Tech '65) Born 10-21-42		
Georgia Tech	Hall of Fame 12-31-85	Michigan St. 17-14 (George Perles)
Alabama	Hall of Fame 1-2-88	Michigan 24-28 (Glenn "Bo" Schembechler)
Alabama	Sun 12-24-88	Army 29-28 (Jim Young)
Alabama	Sugar 1-1-90	Miami (Fla.) 25-33 (Dennis Erickson)
Kentucky	Peach 12-31-93	Clemson 13-14 (Tommy West)
JACK "CACTUS JACK" CURTICE, 1-1-0 (Transylvania '30) Born 5-24-07		
UTEP	Sun 1-1-49	West Va. 12-21 (Dud DeGroot)
UTEP	Sun 1-2-50	Georgetown 33-20 (Bob Margarita)
JOHN "OX" Da GROSA, 0-1-0 (Colgate '26) Born 2-17-02		
Holy Cross	Orange 1-1-46	Miami (Fla.) 6-13 (Jack Harding)
GARY DARNELL, 0-1-0 (Oklahoma St. '71) Born 10-15-48		
Florida	Freedom 12-29-89	Washington 7-34 (Don James)
DUFFY DAUGHERTY, 1-1-0 (Syracuse '40) Born 9-8-15		
Michigan St.	Rose 1-2-56	UCLA 17-14 (Henry "Red" Sanders)
Michigan St.	Rose 1-1-66	UCLA 12-14 (Tommy Prothro)
BOB DAVIS, 0-1-0 (Utah '30) Born 2-13-08		
Colorado St.	Raisin 1-1-49	Occidental 20-21 (Roy Dennis)
PAUL DAVIS, 1-0-0 (Mississippi '47) Born 2-3-22		
Mississippi St.	Liberty 12-21-63	North Caro. St. 16-12 (Earle Edwards)
LOWELL "RED" DAWSON, 0-1-0 (Tulane '30) Born 12-26-06		
Tulane	Sugar 1-1-40	Texas A&M 13-14 (Homer Norton)

Coach/School	Bowl/Date	Opponent/Score (Coach)
FISHER DeBERRY, 4-4-0 (Wofford '60) Born 9-9-38		
Air Force	Independence 12-15-84	Virginia Tech 23-7 (Bill Dooley)
Air Force	Bluebonnet 12-31-85	Texas 24-16 (Fred Akers)
Air Force	Freedom 12-30-87	Arizona St. 28-33 (John Cooper)
Air Force	Liberty 12-29-89	Mississippi 29-42 (Billy Brewer)
Air Force	Liberty 12-27-90	Ohio St. 23-11 (John Cooper)
Air Force	Liberty 12-29-91	Mississippi St. 38-15 (Jackie Sherrill)
Air Force	Liberty 12-31-92	Mississippi 0-13 (Billy Brewer)
Air Force	Copper 12-27-95	Texas Tech 41-55 (Spike Dykes)
DUD DeGROOT, 1-0-0 (Stanford '24) Born 11-20-95		
West Va.	Sun 1-1-49	UTEP 21-12 (Jack "Cactus Jack" Curtice)
ROY DENNIS, 1-0-0 (Occidental '33) Born 5-13-05		
Occidental	Raisin 1-1-49	Colorado St. 21-20 (Bob Davis)
HERB DEROMEDI, 0-1-0 (Michigan '60) Born 5-26-39		
Central Mich.	California 12-8-90	San Jose St. 24-48 (Terry Shea)
BOB DEVANEY, 7-3-0 (Alma '39) Born 4-2-15		
Wyoming	Sun 12-31-58	Hardin-Simmons 14-6 (Sammy Baugh)
Nebraska	Gotham 12-15-62	Miami (Fla.) 36-34 (Andy Gustafson)
Nebraska	Orange 1-1-64	Auburn 13-7 (Ralph "Shug" Jordan)
Nebraska	Cotton 1-1-65	Arkansas 7-10 (Frank Broyles)
Nebraska	Orange 1-1-66	Alabama 28-39 (Paul "Bear" Bryant)
Nebraska	Sugar 1-2-67	Alabama 7-34 (Paul "Bear" Bryant)
Nebraska	Sun 12-20-69	Georgia 45-6 (Vince Dooley)
Nebraska	Orange 1-1-71	LSU 17-12 (Charlie McClendon)
Nebraska	Orange 1-1-72	Alabama 38-6 (Paul "Bear" Bryant)
Nebraska	Orange 1-1-73	Notre Dame 40-6 (Ara Parseghian)
DAN DEVINE, 7-3-0 (Minn.-Duluth '48) Born 12-23-24		
Missouri	Orange 1-1-60	Georgia 0-14 (Wally Butts)
Missouri	Orange 1-2-61	Navy 21-14 (Wayne Hardin)
Missouri	Bluebonnet 12-22-62	Georgia Tech 14-10 (Bobby Dodd)
Missouri	Sugar 1-1-66	Florida 20-18 (Ray Graves)
Missouri	Gator 12-28-68	Alabama 35-10 (Paul "Bear" Bryant)
Missouri	Orange 1-1-70	Penn St. 3-10 (Joe Paterno)
Notre Dame	Gator 12-27-76	Penn St. 20-9 (Joe Paterno)
Notre Dame	Cotton 1-2-78	Texas 38-10 (Fred Akers)
Notre Dame	Cotton 1-1-79	Houston 35-34 (Bill Yeoman)
Notre Dame	Sugar 1-1-81	Georgia 10-17 (Vince Dooley)
PHIL DICKENS, 1-0-0 (Tennessee '37) Born 6-29-14		
Wyoming	Sun 1-2-56	Texas Tech 21-14 (DeWitt Weaver)
DOUG DICKEY, 2-7-0 (Florida '54) Born 6-24-32		
Tennessee	Bluebonnet 12-18-65	Tulsa 27-6 (Glenn Dobbs)
Tennessee	Gator 12-31-66	Syracuse 18-12 (Ben Schwartzwalder)
Tennessee	Orange 1-1-68	Oklahoma 24-26 (Chuck Fairbanks)
Tennessee	Cotton 1-1-69	Texas 13-35 (Darrell Royal)
Tennessee	Gator 12-27-69	Florida 13-14 (Ray Graves)
Florida	Tangerine 12-22-73	Miami (Ohio) 7-16 (Bill Mallory)
Florida	Sugar 12-31-74	Nebraska 10-13 (Tom Osborne)
Florida	Gator 12-29-75	Maryland 0-13 (Jerry Claiborne)
Florida	Sun 1-2-77	Texas A&M 14-37 (Emory Bellard)
JIM DICKEY, 0-1-0 (Houston '56) Born 3-22-34		
Kansas St.	Independence 12-11-82	Wisconsin 3-14 (Dave McClain)
BILL "LONE STAR" DIETZ, 1-0-0 (Carlisle '12) Born 8-15-85		
Washington St.	Rose 1-1-16	Brown 14-0 (Ed Robinson)
PAUL DIETZEL, 2-2-0 (Miami, Ohio '48) Born 9-5-24		
LSU	Sugar 1-1-59	Clemson 7-0 (Frank Howard)
LSU	Sugar 1-1-60	Mississippi 0-21 (John Vaught)
LSU	Orange 1-1-62	Colorado 25-7 (Sonny Grandelius)
South Caro.	Peach 12-20-69	West Va. 3-14 (Jim Carlen)
GERRY DiNARDO, 1-0-0 (Notre Dame '75) Born 11-10-52		
LSU	Independence 12-29-95	Michigan St. 45-26 (Nick Saban)
BOBBY DOBBS, 2-0-0 (Army '46) Born 10-13-22		
UTEP	Sun 12-31-65	Texas Christian 13-12 (Abe Martin)
UTEP	Sun 12-30-67	Mississippi 14-7 (John Vaught)
GLENN DOBBS, 1-1-0 (Tulsa '43) Born 7-12-20		
Tulsa	Bluebonnet 12-19-64	Mississippi 14-7 (John Vaught)
Tulsa	Bluebonnet 12-18-65	Tennessee 6-27 (Doug Dickey)
BOBBY DODD, 9-4-0 (Tennessee '31) Born 11-11-08		
Georgia Tech	Oil 1-1-47	St. Mary's (Cal.) 41-19 (Jimmy Phelan)
Georgia Tech	Orange 1-1-48	Kansas 20-14 (George Sauer)
Georgia Tech	Orange 1-1-52	Baylor 17-14 (George Sauer)
Georgia Tech	Sugar 1-1-53	Mississippi 24-7 (John Vaught)
Georgia Tech	Sugar 1-1-54	West Va. 42-19 (Art Lewis)
Georgia Tech	Cotton 1-1-55	Arkansas 14-6 (Bowden Wyatt)
Georgia Tech	Sugar 1-2-56	Pittsburgh 7-0 (John Michelosen)
Georgia Tech	Gator 12-29-56	Pittsburgh 21-14 (John Michelosen)
Georgia Tech	Gator 1-2-60	Arkansas 7-14 (Frank Broyles)
Georgia Tech	Gator 12-30-61	Penn St. 15-30 (Charles "Rip" Engle)
Georgia Tech	Bluebonnet 12-22-62	Missouri 10-14 (Dan Devine)
Georgia Tech	Gator 12-31-65	Texas Tech 31-21 (J. T. King)
Georgia Tech	Orange 1-2-67	Florida 12-27 (Ray Graves)

BOWL/ALL-STAR RECORDS

Coach/School	Bowl/Date	Opponent/Score (Coach)
ED DOHERTY, 0-2-0 (Boston College '44) Born 7-25-18		
Arizona St.	Salad 1-1-50	Xavier (Ohio) 21-33 (Ed Kluska)
Arizona St.	Salad 1-1-51	Miami (Ohio) 21-34 (Woody Hayes)
JACK DOLAND, 1-0-0 (Tulane '50) Born 3-3-28		
McNeese St.	Independence 12-13-76	Tulsa 20-16 (F. A. Dry)
TERRY DONAHUE, 8-4-1 (UCLA '67) Born 6-24-44		
UCLA	Liberty 12-30-76	Alabama 6-36 (Paul "Bear" Bryant)
UCLA	Fiesta 12-25-78	Arkansas 10-10 (Lou Holtz)
UCLA	Bluebonnet 12-31-81	Michigan 14-33 (Glenn "Bo" Schembechler)
UCLA	Rose 1-1-83	Michigan 24-14 (Glenn "Bo" Schembechler)
UCLA	Rose 1-2-84	Illinois 45-9 (Mike White)
UCLA	Fiesta 1-1-85	Miami (Fla.) 39-37 (Jimmy Johnson)
UCLA	Rose 1-1-86	Iowa 45-28 (Hayden Fry)
UCLA	Freedom 12-30-86	Brigham Young 31-10 (LaVell Edwards)
UCLA	Aloha 12-25-87	Florida 20-16 (Galen Hall)
UCLA	Cotton 1-2-89	Arkansas 17-3 (Ken Hatfield)
UCLA	John Hancock 12-31-91	Illinois 6-3 (Lou Tepper)
UCLA	Rose 1-1-94	Wisconsin 16-21 (Barry Alvarez)
UCLA	Aloha 12-25-95	Kansas 30-51 (Glen Mason)
BILL DOOLEY, 3-7-0 (Mississippi St. '56) Born 5-19-34		
North Caro.	Peach 12-30-70	Arizona St. 26-48 (Frank Kush)
North Caro.	Gator 12-31-71	Georgia 3-7 (Vince Dooley)
North Caro.	Sun 12-30-72	Texas Tech 32-28 (Jim Carlen)
North Caro.	Sun 12-28-74	Mississippi St. 24-26 (Bob Tyler)
North Caro.	Peach 12-31-76	Kentucky 0-21 (Fran Curci)
North Caro.	Liberty 12-19-77	Nebraska 17-21 (Tom Osborne)
Virginia Tech	Peach 1-2-81	Miami (Fla.) 10-20 (Howard Schnellenberger)
Virginia Tech	Independence 12-15-84	Air Force 7-23 (Fisher DeBerry)
Virginia Tech	Peach 12-31-86	North Caro. St. 25-24 (Dick Sheridan)
Wake Forest	Independence 12-31-92	Oregon 39-35 (Rich Brooks)
VINCE DOOLEY, 8-10-2 (Auburn '54) Born 9-4-32		
Georgia	Sun 12-26-64	Texas Tech 7-0 (J. T. King)
Georgia	Cotton 12-31-66	Southern Methodist 24-9 (Hayden Fry)
Georgia	Liberty 12-16-67	North Caro. St. 7-14 (Earle Edwards)
Georgia	Sugar 1-1-69	Arkansas 2-16 (Frank Broyles)
Georgia	Sun 12-20-69	Nebraska 6-45 (Bob Devaney)
Georgia	Gator 12-31-71	North Caro. 7-3 (Bill Dooley)
Georgia	Peach 12-28-73	Maryland 17-16 (Jerry Claiborne)
Georgia	Tangerine 12-21-74	Miami (Ohio) 10-21 (Dick Crum)
Georgia	Cotton 1-1-76	Arkansas 10-31 (Frank Broyles)
Georgia	Sugar 1-1-77	Pittsburgh 3-27 (Johnny Majors)
Georgia	Bluebonnet 12-31-78	Stanford 22-25 (Bill Walsh)
Georgia	Sugar 1-1-81	Notre Dame 17-10 (Dan Devine)
Georgia	Sugar 1-1-82	Pittsburgh 20-24 (Jackie Sherrill)
Georgia	Sugar 1-1-83	Penn St. 23-27 (Joe Paterno)
Georgia	Cotton 1-2-84	Texas 10-9 (Fred Akers)
Georgia	Fla. Citrus 12-22-84	Florida St. 17-17 (Bobby Bowden)
Georgia	Sun 12-28-85	Arizona 13-13 (Larry Smith)
Georgia	Hall of Fame 12-23-86	Boston College 24-27 (Jack Bicknell)
Georgia	Liberty 12-29-87	Arkansas 20-17 (Ken Hatfield)
Georgia	Gator 1-1-89	Michigan St. 34-27 (George Perles)
CHARLES "GUS" DORAIS, 0-1-0 (Notre Dame '14) Born 7-21-91		
Gonzaga	San Diego East-West Christmas Classic 12-25-22	West Va. 13-21 (Clarence "Doc" Spears)
HAROLD "RED" DREW, 1-2-0 (Bates '16) Born 11-9-94		
Alabama	Sugar 1-1-48	Texas 7-27 (Blair Cherry)
Alabama	Orange 1-1-53	Syracuse 61-6 (Ben Schwartzwalder)
Alabama	Cotton 1-1-54	Rice 6-28 (Jess Neely)
BILL DRIVER, 0-1-0 (Missouri '09) Born 11-7-83		
Texas Christian	Fort Worth Classic 1-1-21	Centre 7-63 (Charley Moran)
F. A. DRY, 0-1-0 (Oklahoma St. '53) Born 9-2-31		
Tulsa	Independence 12-13-76	McNeese St. 16-20 (Jack Doland)
ERNIE DUPLECHIN, 0-2-0 (Louisiana Col. '55) Born 7-19-32		
McNeese St.	Independence 12-15-79	Syracuse 7-31 (Frank Maloney)
McNeese St.	Independence 12-13-80	Southern Miss. 14-16 (Bobby Collins)
PAT DYE, 7-2-1 (Georgia '62) Born 11-6-39		
East Caro.	Independence 12-16-78	Louisiana Tech 35-13 (Maxie Lambright)
Auburn	Tangerine 12-18-82	Boston College 33-26 (Jack Bicknell)
Auburn	Sugar 1-2-84	Michigan 9-7 (Glenn "Bo" Schembechler)
Auburn	Liberty 12-27-84	Arkansas 21-15 (Ken Hatfield)
Auburn	Cotton 1-1-86	Texas A&M 16-36 (Jackie Sherrill)
Auburn	Fla. Citrus 1-1-87	Southern Cal 16-7 (Ted Tollner)
Auburn	Sugar 1-1-88	Syracuse 16-16 (Dick MacPherson)
Auburn	Sugar 1-2-89	Florida St. 7-13 (Bobby Bowden)
Auburn	Hall of Fame 1-1-90	Ohio St. 31-14 (John Cooper)
Auburn	Peach 12-29-90	Indiana 27-23 (Bill Mallory)
SPIKE DYKES, 2-3-0 (Stephen F. Austin '59) Born 4-15-38		
Texas Tech	Independence 12-20-86	Mississippi 17-20 (Billy Brewer)

Coach/School	Bowl/Date	Opponent/Score (Coach)
Texas Tech	All-American 12-28-89	Duke 49-21 (Steve Spurrier)
Texas Tech	John Hancock 12-24-93	Oklahoma 10-41 (Gary Gibbs)
Texas Tech	Cotton 1-2-95	Southern Cal 14-55 (John Robinson)
Texas Tech	Copper 12-27-95	Air Force 55-41 (Fisher DeBerry)
LLOYD EATON, 1-1-0 (Black Hills St. '40) Born 3-23-18		
Wyoming	Sun 12-24-66	Florida St. 28-20 (Bill Peterson)
Wyoming	Sugar 1-1-68	LSU 13-20 (Charlie McClendon)
BILL EDWARDS, 1-0-0 (Wittenberg '31) Born 6-21-05		
Case Reserve	Sun 1-1-41	Arizona St. 26-13 (Millard "Dixie" Howell)
EARLE EDWARDS, 1-1-0 (Penn St. '31) Born 11-10-08		
North Caro. St.	Liberty 12-21-63	Mississippi St. 12-16 (Paul Davis)
North Caro. St.	Liberty 12-16-67	Georgia 14-7 (Vince Dooley)
LaVELL EDWARDS, 6-12-1 (Utah St. '52) Born 10-11-30		
Brigham Young	Fiesta 12-28-74	Oklahoma St. 6-16 (Jim Stanley)
Brigham Young	Tangerine 12-18-76	Oklahoma St. 21-49 (Jim Stanley)
Brigham Young	Holiday 12-22-78	Navy 16-23 (George Welsh)
Brigham Young	Holiday 12-21-79	Indiana 37-38 (Lee Corso)
Brigham Young	Holiday 12-19-80	Southern Methodist 46-45 (Ron Meyer)
Brigham Young	Holiday 12-18-81	Washington St. 38-36 (Jim Walden)
Brigham Young	Holiday 12-17-82	Ohio St. 17-47 (Earle Bruce)
Brigham Young	Holiday 12-23-83	Missouri 21-17 (Warren Powers)
Brigham Young	Holiday 12-21-84	Michigan 24-17 (Glenn "Bo" Schembechler)
Brigham Young	Fla. Citrus 12-28-85	Ohio St. 7-10 (Earle Bruce)
Brigham Young	Freedom 12-30-86	UCLA 10-31 (Terry Donahue)
Brigham Young	All-American 12-22-87	Virginia 16-22 (George Welsh)
Brigham Young	Freedom 12-29-88	Colorado 20-17 (Bill McCartney)
Brigham Young	Holiday 12-29-89	Penn St. 39-50 (Joe Paterno)
Brigham Young	Holiday 12-29-90	Texas A&M 14-65 (R. C. Slocum)
Brigham Young	Holiday 12-30-91	Iowa 13-13 (Hayden Fry)
Brigham Young	Aloha 12-25-92	Kansas 20-23 (Glen Mason)
Brigham Young	Holiday 12-30-93	Ohio St. 21-28 (John Cooper)
Brigham Young	Copper 12-29-94	Oklahoma 31-6 (Gary Gibbs)
RAY ELIOT, 2-0-0 (Illinois '32) Born 6-13-05		
Illinois	Rose 1-1-47	UCLA 45-14 (Bert LaBrucherie)
Illinois	Rose 1-1-52	Stanford 40-7 (Chuck Taylor)
BENNIE ELLENDER, 0-1-0 (Tulane '48) Born 3-2-25		
Tulane	Bluebonnet 12-29-73	Houston 7-47 (Bill Yeoman)
CHALMERS "BUMP" ELLIOTT, 1-0-0 (Michigan '48) Born 1-30-25		
Michigan	Rose 1-1-65	Oregon St. 34-7 (Tommy Prothro)
PETE ELLIOTT, 1-1-0 (Michigan '49) Born 9-29-26		
California	Rose 1-1-59	Iowa 12-38 (Forest Evashevski)
Illinois	Rose 1-1-64	Washington 17-7 (Jim Owens)
JACK ELWAY, 0-2-0 (Washington St. '53) Born 5-30-31		
San Jose St.	California 12-19-81	Toledo 25-27 (Chuck Stobart)
Stanford	Gator 12-27-86	Clemson 21-27 (Danny Ford)
CHARLES "RIP" ENGLE, 3-1-0 (Western Md. '30) Born 3-26-06		
Penn St.	Liberty 12-19-53	Alabama 7-0 (Paul "Bear" Bryant)
Penn St.	Liberty 12-17-60	Oregon 41-12 (Len Casanova)
Penn St.	Gator 12-30-61	Georgia Tech 30-15 (Bobby Dodd)
Penn St.	Gator 12-29-62	Florida 7-17 (Ray Graves)
EDDIE ERDELATZ, 2-0-0 (St. Mary's, Cal. '36) Born 4-21-13		
Navy	Sugar 1-1-55	Mississippi 21-0 (John Vaught)
Navy	Cotton 1-1-58	Rice 20-7 (Jess Neely)
DENNIS ERICKSON, 4-3-0 (Montana St. '70) Born 3-24-47		
Washington St.	Aloha 12-25-88	Houston 24-22 (Jack Pardee)
Miami (Fla.)	Sugar 1-1-90	Alabama 33-25 (Bill Curry)
Miami (Fla.)	Cotton 1-1-91	Texas 46-3 (David McWilliams)
Miami (Fla.)	Orange 1-1-92	Nebraska 22-0 (Tom Osborne)
Miami (Fla.)	Sugar 1-1-93	Alabama 13-34 (Gene Stallings)
Miami (Fla.)	Fiesta 1-1-94	Arizona 0-24 (Dick Tomey)
Miami (Fla.)	Orange 1-1-95	Nebraska 17-24 (Tom Osborne)
FOREST EVASHEVSKI, 2-0-0 (Michigan '41) Born 2-19-18		
Iowa	Rose 1-1-57	Oregon St. 35-19 (Tommy Prothro)
Iowa	Rose 1-1-59	California 38-12 (Pete Elliott)
CHUCK FAIRBANKS, 3-1-1 (Michigan St. '55) Born 6-10-33		
Oklahoma	Orange 1-1-68	Tennessee 26-24 (Doug Dickey)
Oklahoma	Bluebonnet 12-31-68	Southern Methodist 27-28 (Hayden Fry)
Oklahoma	Bluebonnet 12-31-70	Alabama 24-24 (Paul "Bear" Bryant)
Oklahoma	Sugar 1-1-72	Auburn 40-22 (Ralph "Shug" Jordan)
Oklahoma	Sugar 12-31-72	Penn St. 14-0 (Joe Paterno)
DON FAMBROUGH, 0-2-0 (Kansas '48) Born 10-19-22		
Kansas	Liberty 12-17-73	North Caro. St. 18-31 (Lou Holtz)
Kansas	Hall of Fame 12-31-81	Mississippi St. 0-10 (Emory Bellard)
DON FAUROT, 0-4-0 (Missouri '25) Born 6-23-02		
Missouri	Orange 1-1-40	Georgia Tech 7-21 (Bill Alexander)
Missouri	Sugar 1-1-42	Fordham 0-2 (Jim Crowley)
Missouri	Gator 1-1-49	Clemson 23-24 (Frank Howard)
Missouri	Gator 1-2-50	Maryland 7-21 (Jim Tatum)

Coach/School	Bowl/Date	Opponent/Score (Coach)
GERRY FAUST, 1-1-0 (Dayton '58) Born 5-21-35		
Notre Dame	Liberty 12-29-83	Boston College 19-18 (Jack Bicknell)
Notre Dame	Aloha 12-29-84	Southern Methodist 20-27 (Bobby Collins)
FOGE FAZIO, 0-2-0 (Pittsburgh '60) Born 2-28-39		
Pittsburgh	Cotton 1-1-83	Southern Methodist 3-7 (Bobby Collins)
Pittsburgh	Fiesta 1-2-84	Ohio St. 23-28 (Earle Bruce)
BEATTIE FEATHERS, 0-1-0 (Tennessee '34) Born 6-1-12		
North Caro. St.	Gator 1-1-47	Oklahoma 13-34 (Jim Tatum)
WES FESLER, 1-0-0 (Ohio St. '32) Born 6-29-08		
Ohio St.	Rose 1-2-50	California 17-14 (Lynn "Pappy" Waldorf)
CHARLIE FICKERT, 0-1-0 (Stanford '98) Born 2-23-73		
Stanford	Rose 1-1-02	Michigan 0-49 (Fielding "Hurry Up" Yost)
ROBERT FISHER, 1-0-0 (Harvard '12) Born 12-3-88		
Harvard	Rose 1-1-20	Oregon 7-6 (Charles "Shy" Huntington)
DICK FLYNN, 0-1-0 (Michigan St. '65) Born 7-17-43		
Central Mich.	Las Vegas 12-15-94	UNLV 24-52 (Jeff Horton)
HANK FOLDBERG, 0-1-0 (Army '48) Born 3-12-23		
Wichita St.	Sun 12-30-61	Villanova 9-17 (Alex Bell)
BOB FOLWELL, 0-1-1 (Pennsylvania '08) Born 1885		
Pennsylvania	Rose 1-1-17	Oregon 0-14 (Hugo Bezdek)
Navy	Rose 1-1-24	Washington 14-14 (Enoch Bagshaw)
DANNY FORD, 6-3-0 (Alabama '70) Born 4-2-48		
Clemson	Gator 12-29-78	Ohio St. 17-15 (Woody Hayes)
Clemson	Peach 12-31-79	Baylor 18-24 (Grant Teaff)
Clemson	Orange 1-1-82	Nebraska 22-15 (Tom Osborne)
Clemson	Independence 12-21-85	Minnesota 13-20 (John Gutekunst)
Clemson	Gator 12-27-86	Stanford 27-21 (Jack Elway)
Clemson	Fla. Citrus 1-1-88	Penn St. 35-10 (Joe Paterno)
Clemson	Fla. Citrus 1-2-89	Oklahoma 23-6 (Barry Switzer)
Clemson	Gator 12-30-89	West Va. 27-7 (Don Nehlen)
Arkansas	Carquest 12-30-95	North Caro. 10-20 (Mack Brown)
HENRY FRNKA, 2-3-0 (Austin '26) Born 3-16-03		
Tulsa	Sun 1-1-42	Texas Tech 6-0 (Dell Morgan)
Tulsa	Sugar 1-1-43	Tennessee 7-14 (John Barnhill)
Tulsa	Sugar 1-1-44	Georgia Tech 18-20 (Bill Alexander)
Tulsa	Orange 1-1-45	Georgia Tech 26-12 (Bill Alexander)
Tulsa	Oil 1-1-46	Georgia 6-20 (Wally Butts)
HAYDEN FRY, 6-8-1 (Baylor '51) Born 2-28-29		
Southern Methodist	Sun 12-31-63	Oregon 13-21 (Len Casanova)
Southern Methodist	Cotton 12-31-66	Georgia 9-24 (Vince Dooley)
Southern Methodist	Bluebonnet 12-31-68	Oklahoma 28-27 (Chuck Fairbanks)
Iowa	Rose 1-1-82	Washington 0-28 (Don James)
Iowa	Peach 12-31-82	Tennessee 28-22 (Johnny Majors)
Iowa	Gator 12-30-83	Florida 6-14 (Charley Pell)
Iowa	Freedom 12-26-84	Texas 55-17 (Fred Akers)
Iowa	Rose 1-1-86	UCLA 28-45 (Terry Donahue)
Iowa	Holiday 12-30-86	San Diego St. 39-38 (Denny Stolz)
Iowa	Holiday 12-30-87	Wyoming 20-19 (Paul Roach)
Iowa	Peach 12-31-88	North Caro. St. 23-29 (Dick Sheridan)
Iowa	Rose 1-1-91	Washington 34-46 (Don James)
Iowa	Holiday 12-30-91	Brigham Young 13-13 (LaVell Edwards)
Iowa	Alamo 12-31-93	California 3-37 (Keith Gilbertson)
Iowa	Sun 12-29-95	Washington 38-18 (Jim Lambright)
BILL FULCHER, 1-0-0 (Georgia Tech '57) Born 2-9-34		
Georgia Tech	Liberty 12-18-72	Iowa St. 31-30 (Johnny Majors)
PHILLIP FULMER, 3-1-0 (Tennessee '72) Born 9-1-50		
Tennessee	Hall of Fame 1-1-93	Boston College 38-23 (Tom Coughlin)
Tennessee	Fla. Citrus 1-1-94	Penn St. 13-31 (Joe Paterno)
Tennessee	Gator 12-30-94	Virginia Tech 45-23 (Frank Beamer)
Tennessee	Fla. Citrus 1-1-96	Ohio St. 20-14 (John Cooper)
WARREN GAER, 0-1-0 (Drake '35) Born 2-7-12		
Drake	Sun 1-1-58	Louisville 20-34 (Frank Camp)
JOE GAVIN, 0-1-0 (Notre Dame '31) Born 3-20-08		
Dayton	Salad 1-1-52	Houston 21-26 (Clyde Lee)
GARY GIBBS, 2-1-0 (Oklahoma '75) Born 8-13-52		
Oklahoma	Gator 12-29-91	Virginia 48-14 (George Welsh)
Oklahoma	John Hancock 12-24-93	Texas Tech 41-10 (Spike Dykes)
Oklahoma	Copper 12-29-94	Brigham Young 6-31 (LaVell Edwards)
VINCE GIBSON, 0-2-0 (Florida St. '55) Born 3-27-33		
Louisville	Independence 12-17-77	Louisiana Tech 14-24 (Maxie Lambright)
Tulane	Hall of Fame 12-27-80	Arkansas 15-34 (Lou Holtz)
CLAUDE GILBERT, 1-1-0 (San Jose St. '59) Born 7-10-32		
San Jose St.	California 12-13-86	Miami (Ohio) 37-7 (Tim Rose)
San Jose St.	California 12-12-87	Eastern Mich. 27-30 (Jim Harkema)
KEITH GILBERTSON, 1-0-0 (Central Wash. '71) Born 5-15-48		
California	Alamo 12-31-93	Iowa 37-3 (Hayden Fry)

Coach/School	Bowl/Date	Opponent/Score (Coach)
SID GILLMAN, 1-1-0 (Ohio St. '34) Born 10-26-11		
Miami (Ohio)	Sun 1-1-48	Texas Tech 13-12 (Dell Morgan)
Cincinnati	Sun 1-1-51	West Tex. A&M 13-14 (Frank Kimbrough)
BILL GLASSFORD, 0-1-0 (Pittsburgh '37) Born 3-8-14		
Nebraska	Orange 1-1-55	Duke 7-34 (Bill Murray)
MARSHALL "LITTLE SLEEPY" GLENN, 1-0-0 (West Va. '31) Born 4-22-08		
West Va.	Sun 1-1-38	Texas Tech 7-6 (Pete Cawthon)
RAY GOFF, 2-2-0 (Georgia '78) Born 7-10-55		
Georgia	Peach 12-30-89	Syracuse 18-19 (Dick MacPherson)
Georgia	Independence 12-29-91	Arkansas 24-15 (Jack Crowe)
Georgia	Fla. Citrus 1-1-93	Ohio St. 21-14 (John Cooper)
Georgia	Peach 12-30-95	Virginia 27-34 (George Welsh)
FRED GOLDSMITH, 0-1-0 (Florida '67) Born 3-3-44		
Duke	Hall of Fame 1-2-95	Wisconsin 20-34 (Barry Alvarez)
MIKE GOTTFRIED, 0-1-0 (Morehead St. '66) Born 12-17-44		
Pittsburgh	Bluebonnet 12-31-87	Texas 27-32 (David McWilliams)
RALPH GRAHAM, 0-1-0 (Kansas St. '34) Born 8-16-10		
Wichita St.	Raisin 1-1-48	Pacific (Cal.) 14-26 (Larry Siemering)
SONNY GRANDELIUS, 0-1-0 (Michigan St. '51) Born 4-16-29		
Colorado	Orange 1-1-62	LSU 7-25 (Paul Dietzel)
RAY GRAVES, 4-1-0 (Tennessee '43) Born 12-31-18		
Florida	Gator 12-31-60	Baylor 13-12 (John Bridgers)
Florida	Gator 12-29-62	Penn St. 17-7 (Charles "Rip" Engle)
Florida	Sugar 1-1-66	Missouri 18-20 (Dan Devine)
Florida	Orange 1-2-67	Georgia Tech 27-12 (Bobby Dodd)
Florida	Gator 12-27-69	Tennessee 14-13 (Doug Dickey)
DENNIS GREEN, 0-1-0 (Iowa '71) Born 2-17-49		
Stanford	Aloha 12-25-91	Georgia Tech 17-18 (Bobby Ross)
VEE GREEN, 1-0-0 (Illinois '24) Born 10-9-00		
Drake	Raisin 1-1-46	Fresno St. 13-12 (Alvin "Pix" Pierson)
ART GUEPE, 1-0-0 (Marquette '37) Born 1-28-15		
Vanderbilt	Gator 12-31-55	Auburn 25-13 (Ralph "Shug" Jordan)
ANDY GUSTAFSON, 1-3-0 (Pittsburgh '26) Born 4-3-03		
Miami (Fla.)	Orange 1-1-51	Clemson 14-15 (Frank Howard)
Miami (Fla.)	Gator 1-1-52	Clemson 14-0 (Frank Howard)
Miami (Fla.)	Liberty 12-16-61	Syracuse 14-15 (Ben Schwartzwalder)
Miami (Fla.)	Gotham 12-15-62	Nebraska 34-36 (Bob Devaney)
JOHN GUTEKUNST, 1-1-0 (Duke '66) Born 4-13-44		
Minnesota	Independence 12-21-85	Clemson 20-13 (Danny Ford)
Minnesota	Liberty 12-29-86	Tennessee 14-21 (Johnny Majors)
PAUL HACKETT, 1-0-0 (UC Davis '69) Born 6-5-47		
Pittsburgh	John Hancock 12-30-89	Texas A&M 31-28 (R. C. Slocum)
JACK HAGERTY, 0-1-0 (Georgetown '26) Born 7-3-03		
Georgetown	Orange 1-1-41	Mississippi St. 7-14 (Alvin McKeen)

File photo

Quarterback Jack Mildren, playing in the final game of his brilliant collegiate career, scored three rushing touchdowns and earned game MVP honors in Oklahoma's 40-22 victory over Auburn in the January 1, 1972, Sugar Bowl. The win was the second of three bowl victories that Sooners coach Chuck Fairbanks would earn.

Coach/School	Bowl/Date	Opponent/Score (Coach)
GALEN HALL, 1-1-0 (Penn St. '62) Born 8-14-40		
Florida	Aloha 12-25-87	UCLA 16-20 (Terry Donahue)
Florida	All-American 12-29-88	Illinois 14-10 (John Mackovic)
CURLEY HALLMAN, 1-0-0 (Texas A&M '70) Born 9-3-47		
Southern Miss.	Independence 12-23-88	UTEP 38-18 (Bob Stull)
WAYNE HARDIN, 1-2-0 (Pacific, Cal. '50) Born 3-23-27		
Navy	Orange 1-2-61	Missouri 14-21 (Dan Devine)
Navy	Cotton 1-1-64	Texas 6-28 (Darrell Royal)
Temple	Garden State 12-15-79	California 28-17 (Roger Theder)
JACK HARDING, 1-0-0 (Pittsburgh '26) Born 1-5-98		
Miami (Fla.)	Orange 1-1-48	Holy Cross 13-6 (John "Ox" Da Grosa)
JIM HARKEMA, 1-0-0 (Kalamazoo '64) Born 6-25-42		
Eastern Mich.	California 12-12-87	San Jose St. 30-27 (Claude Gilbert)
KEN HATFIELD, 4-6-0 (Arkansas '65) Born 6-8-43		
Air Force	Hall of Fame 12-31-82	Vanderbilt 36-28 (George MacIntyre)
Air Force	Independence 12-10-83	Mississippi 9-3 (Billy Brewer)
Arkansas	Liberty 12-27-84	Auburn 15-21 (Pat Dye)
Arkansas	Holiday 12-22-85	Arizona St. 18-17 (John Cooper)
Arkansas	Orange 1-1-87	Oklahoma 8-42 (Barry Switzer)
Arkansas	Liberty 12-29-87	Georgia 17-20 (Vince Dooley)
Arkansas	Cotton 1-2-89	UCLA 3-17 (Terry Donahue)
Arkansas	Cotton 1-1-90	Tennessee 27-31 (Johnny Majors)
Clemson	Hall of Fame 1-1-91	Illinois 30-0 (John Mackovic)
Clemson	Fla. Citrus 1-1-92	California 13-37 (Bruce Snyder)
WOODY HAYES, 6-6-0 (Denison '35) Born 2-14-13		
Miami (Ohio)	Salad 1-1-51	Arizona St. 34-21 (Ed Doherty)
Ohio St.	Rose 1-1-55	Southern Cal 20-7 (Jess Hill)
Ohio St.	Rose 1-1-58	Oregon 10-7 (Len Casanova)
Ohio St.	Rose 1-1-69	Southern Cal 27-16 (John McKay)
Ohio St.	Rose 1-1-71	Stanford 17-27 (John Ralston)
Ohio St.	Rose 1-1-73	Southern Cal 17-42 (John McKay)
Ohio St.	Rose 1-1-74	Southern Cal 42-21 (John McKay)
Ohio St.	Rose 1-1-75	Southern Cal 17-18 (John McKay)
Ohio St.	Rose 1-1-76	UCLA 10-23 (Dick Vermeil)
Ohio St.	Orange 1-1-77	Colorado 27-10 (Bill Mallory)
Ohio St.	Sugar 1-2-78	Alabama 6-35 (Paul "Bear" Bryant)
Ohio St.	Gator 12-29-78	Clemson 15-17 (Danny Ford)
ELMER "GUS" HENDERSON, 2-0-0 (Oberlin '12) Born 3-10-89		
Southern Cal	Rose 1-1-23	Penn St. 14-3 (Hugo Bezdek)
Southern Cal	L.A. Christmas Festival 12-25-24	Missouri 20-7 (Gwinn Henry)
DAN HENNING, 1-0-0 (William & Mary '64) Born 7-21-42		
Boston College	Aloha 12-25-94	Kansas St. 12-7 (Bill Snyder)
GWINN HENRY, 0-1-0 (Howard Payne '17) Born 8-5-87		
Missouri	L.A. Christmas Festival 12-25-24	Southern Cal 7-20 (Elmer "Gus" Henderson)
BILL HESS, 0-2-0 (Ohio '47) Born 2-5-23		
Ohio	Sun 12-31-62	West Tex. A&M 14-15 (Joe Kerbel)
Ohio	Tangerine 12-27-68	Richmond 42-49 (Frank Jones)
JIM HICKEY, 1-0-0 (William & Mary '42) Born 1-22-20		
North Caro.	Gator 12-28-63	Air Force 35-0 (Ben Martin)
BOB HIGGINS, 1-0-1 (Penn St. '20) Born 12-24-93		
West Va. Wesleyan	Dixie Classic 1-1-25	Southern Methodist 9-7 (Ray Morrison)
Penn St.	Cotton 1-1-48	Southern Methodist 13-13 (Matty Bell)
JESS HILL, 1-1-0 (Southern Cal '30) Born 1-20-07		
Southern Cal	Rose 1-1-53	Wisconsin 7-0 (Ivy Williamson)
Southern Cal	Rose 1-1-55	Ohio St. 7-20 (Woody Hayes)
JERRY HINES, 0-0-1 (New Mexico St. '26) Born 10-11-03		
New Mexico St.	Sun 1-1-36	Hardin-Simmons 14-14 (Frank Kimbrough)
BERNARD A. HOBAN, 0-1-0 (Dartmouth '12) Born 4-21-90		
U. of Mexico	Sun 1-1-45	Southwestern (Tex.) 0-35 (Randolph R. M. Medley)
ORIN "BABE" HOLLINGBERY, 0-1-0 (No college) Born 7-15-93		
Washington St.	Rose 1-1-31	Alabama 0-24 (Wallace Wade)
LOU HOLTZ, 10-8-2 (Kent '59) Born 1-6-37		
William & Mary	Tangerine 12-28-70	Toledo 12-40 (Frank Lauterbur)
North Caro. St.	Peach 12-29-72	West Va. 49-13 (Bobby Bowden)
North Caro. St.	Liberty 12-17-73	Kansas 31-18 (Don Fambrough)
North Caro. St.	Bluebonnet 12-23-74	Houston 31-31 (Bill Yeoman)
North Caro. St.	Peach 12-31-75	West Va. 10-13 (Bobby Bowden)
Arkansas	Orange 1-2-78	Oklahoma 31-6 (Barry Switzer)
Arkansas	Fiesta 12-25-78	UCLA 10-10 (Terry Donahue)
Arkansas	Sugar 1-1-80	Alabama 9-24 (Paul "Bear" Bryant)
Arkansas	Hall of Fame 12-27-80	Tulane 34-15 (Vince Gibson)
Arkansas	Gator 12-28-81	North Caro. 27-31 (Dick Crum)
Arkansas	Bluebonnet 12-31-82	Florida 28-24 (Charley Pell)
Notre Dame	Cotton 1-1-88	Texas A&M 10-35 (Jackie Sherrill)
Notre Dame	Fiesta 1-2-89	West Va. 34-21 (Don Nehlen)
Notre Dame	Orange 1-1-90	Colorado 21-6 (Bill McCartney)

Coach/School	Bowl/Date	Opponent/Score (Coach)
Notre Dame	Orange 1-1-91	Colorado 9-10 (Bill McCartney)
Notre Dame	Sugar 1-1-92	Florida 39-28 (Steve Spurrier)
Notre Dame	Cotton 1-1-93	Texas A&M 28-3 (R. C. Slocum)
Notre Dame	Cotton 1-1-94	Texas A&M 24-21 (R. C. Slocum)
Notre Dame	Fiesta 1-2-95	Colorado 24-41 (Bill McCartney)
Notre Dame	Orange 1-1-96	Florida St. 26-31 (Bobby Bowden)
EDWIN "BABE" HORRELL, 0-1-0 (California '26) Born 9-29-02		
UCLA	Rose 1-1-43	Georgia 0-9 (Wally Butts)
JEFF HORTON, 1-0-0 (Nevada '81) Born 7-13-57		
UNLV	Las Vegas 12-15-94	Central Mich. 52-24 (Dick Flynn)
FRANK HOWARD, 3-3-0 (Alabama '31) Born 3-25-09		
Clemson	Gator 1-1-49	Missouri 24-23 (Don Faurot)
Clemson	Orange 1-1-51	Miami (Fla.) 15-14 (Andy Gustafson)
Clemson	Gator 1-1-52	Miami (Fla.) 0-14 (Andy Gustafson)
Clemson	Orange 1-1-57	Colorado 21-27 (Dallas Ward)
Clemson	Sugar 1-1-59	LSU 0-7 (Paul Dietzel)
Clemson	Bluebonnet 12-19-59	Texas Christian 23-7 (Abe Martin)
MILLARD "DIXIE" HOWELL, 0-1-1 (Alabama '35) Born 11-24-12		
Arizona St.	Sun 1-1-40	Catholic 0-0 (Arthur "Dutch" Bergman)
Arizona St.	Sun 1-1-41	Case Reserve 13-26 (Bill Edwards)
BILL HUBBARD, 2-0-0 (Stanford '30) Born 2-5-07		
San Jose St.	Raisin 1-1-47	Utah St. 20-0 (E. L. "Dick" Romney)
San Jose St.	Raisin 12-31-49	Texas Tech 20-13 (Dell Morgan)
CLYDE "CAC" HUBBARD, 0-2-0 (Oregon St. '21) Born 9-13-97		
Denver	Sun 1-1-46	New Mexico 24-34 (Willis Barnes)
Denver	Alamo 1-4-47	Hardin-Simmons 0-20 (Warren Woodson)
CHARLES "SHY" HUNTINGTON, 0-1-0 (Oregon) Born 7-7-91		
Oregon	Rose 1-1-20	Harvard 6-7 (Robert Fisher)
HARVEY HYDE, 1-0-0 (Redlands '62) Born 7-13-39		
UNLV	California 12-15-84	Toledo 30-13 (Dan Simrell)
DON JAMES, 10-5-0 (Miami, Fla. '54) Born 12-31-32		
Kent	Tangerine 12-29-72	Tampa 18-21 (Earle Bruce)
Washington	Rose 1-2-78	Michigan 27-20 (Glenn "Bo" Schembechler)
Washington	Sun 12-22-79	Texas 14-7 (Fred Akers)
Washington	Rose 1-1-81	Michigan 6-23 (Glenn "Bo" Schembechler)
Washington	Rose 1-1-82	Iowa 28-0 (Hayden Fry)
Washington	Aloha 12-25-82	Maryland 21-20 (Bobby Ross)
Washington	Aloha 12-26-83	Penn St. 10-13 (Joe Paterno)
Washington	Orange 1-1-85	Oklahoma 28-17 (Barry Switzer)
Washington	Freedom 12-30-85	Colorado 20-17 (Bill McCartney)
Washington	Sun 12-25-86	Alabama 6-28 (Ray Perkins)
Washington	Independence 12-18-87	Tulane 24-12 (Mack Brown)
Washington	Freedom 12-29-89	Florida 34-7 (Gary Darnell)
Washington	Rose 1-1-91	Iowa 46-34 (Hayden Fry)
Washington	Rose 1-1-92	Michigan 34-14 (Gary Moeller)
Washington	Rose 1-1-93	Michigan 31-38 (Gary Moeller)
JIMMY JOHNSON, 3-4-0 (Arkansas '65) Born 7-16-43		
Oklahoma St.	Independence 12-12-81	Texas A&M 16-33 (Tom Wilson)
Oklahoma St.	Bluebonnet 12-31-83	Baylor 24-14 (Grant Teaff)
Miami (Fla.)	Fiesta 1-1-85	UCLA 37-39 (Terry Donahue)
Miami (Fla.)	Sugar 1-1-86	Tennessee 7-35 (Johnny Majors)
Miami (Fla.)	Fiesta 1-2-87	Penn St. 10-14 (Joe Paterno)
Miami (Fla.)	Orange 1-1-88	Oklahoma 20-14 (Barry Switzer)
Miami (Fla.)	Orange 1-2-89	Nebraska 23-3 (Tom Osborne)
FRANK JONES, 1-1-0 (North Caro. '48) Born 8-30-21		
Richmond	Tangerine 12-27-68	Ohio 49-42 (Bill Hess)
Richmond	Tangerine 12-28-71	Toledo 3-28 (John Murphy)
GOMER JONES, 0-1-0 (Ohio St. '36) Born 2-26-14		
Oklahoma	Gator 1-2-65	Florida St. 19-36 (Bill Peterson)
HOWARD JONES, 5-0-0 (Yale '08) Born 8-23-85		
Southern Cal	Rose 1-1-30	Pittsburgh 47-14 (Jock Sutherland)
Southern Cal	Rose 1-1-32	Tulane 21-12 (Bernie Bierman)
Southern Cal	Rose 1-2-33	Pittsburgh 35-0 (Jock Sutherland)
Southern Cal	Rose 1-2-39	Duke 7-3 (Wallace Wade)
Southern Cal	Rose 1-1-40	Tennessee 14-0 (Bob Neyland)
LARRY JONES, 0-1-0 (LSU '54) Born 12-18-33		
Florida St.	Fiesta 12-27-71	Arizona St. 38-45 (Frank Kush)
LAWRENCE McC. "BIFF" JONES, 0-1-0 (Army '17) Born 10-8-95		
Nebraska	Rose 1-1-41	Stanford 13-21 (Clark Shaughnessy)
PAT JONES, 3-1-0 (Arkansas '69) Born 11-4-47		
Oklahoma St.	Gator 12-28-84	South Caro. 21-14 (Joe Morrison)
Oklahoma St.	Gator 12-30-85	Florida St. 23-34 (Bobby Bowden)
Oklahoma St.	Sun 12-25-87	West Va. 35-33 (Don Nehlen)
Oklahoma St.	Holiday 12-30-88	Wyoming 62-14 (Paul Roach)
RALPH "SHUG" JORDAN, 5-7-0 (Auburn '32) Born 9-25-10		
Auburn	Gator 1-1-54	Texas Tech 13-35 (DeWitt Weaver)
Auburn	Gator 12-31-54	Baylor 33-13 (George Sauer)
Auburn	Gator 12-31-55	Vanderbilt 13-25 (Art Gueppe)

Coach/School	Bowl/Date	Opponent/Score (Coach)
Auburn	Orange 1-1-64	Nebraska 7-13 (Bob Devaney)
Auburn	Liberty 12-18-65	Mississippi 7-13 (John Vaught)
Auburn	Sun 12-28-68	Arizona 34-10 (Darrell Mudra)
Auburn	Bluebonnet 12-31-69	Houston 7-36 (Bill Yeoman)
Auburn	Gator 1-2-71	Mississippi 35-28 (John Vaught)
Auburn	Sugar 1-1-72	Oklahoma 22-40 (Chuck Fairbanks)
Auburn	Gator 12-30-72	Colorado 24-3 (Eddie Crowder)
Auburn	Sun 12-29-73	Missouri 17-34 (Al Onofrio)
Auburn	Gator 12-30-74	Texas 27-3 (Darrell Royal)
ERNIE JORGE, 1-1-0 (St. Mary's, Cal. '36) Born 10-7-14		
Pacific (Cal.)	Sun 1-1-52	Texas Tech 14-25 (DeWitt Weaver)
Pacific (Cal.)	Sun 1-1-53	Southern Miss. 26-7 (Thad "Pie" Vann)
AL KAWAL, 1-0-0 (Northwestern '35) Born 7-4-12		
Drake	Salad 1-1-49	Arizona 14-13 (Miles Casteel)
JOE KERBEL, 2-0-0 (Oklahoma '47) Born 5-3-21		
West Tex. A&M	Sun 12-21-62	Ohio 15-14 (Bill Hess)
West Tex. A&M	Pasadena 12-2-67	Cal St. Northridge 35-13 (Sam Winningham)
BILL KERN, 0-1-0 (Pittsburgh '28) Born 9-2-06		
Carnegie Mellon	Sugar 1-2-39	Texas Christian 7-15 (Leo "Dutch" Meyer)
FRANK KIMBROUGH, 2-0-1 (Hardin-Simmons '26) Born 6-24-04		
Hardin-Simmons	Sun 1-1-36	New Mexico St. 14-14 (Jerry Hines)
Hardin-Simmons	Sun 1-1-37	UTEP 34-6 (Max Saxon)
West Tex. A&M	Sun 1-1-51	Cincinnati 14-13 (Sid Gillman)
BILLY KINARD, 1-0-0 (Mississippi '56) Born 12-16-33		
Mississippi	Peach 12-30-71	Georgia Tech 41-18 (Bud Carson)
DEWEY KING, 0-1-0 (North Dak. '50) Born 10-1-25		
San Jose St.	Pasadena 12-18-71	Memphis 9-28 (Billy Murphy)
J. T. KING, 0-2-0 (Texas '38) Born 10-22-12		
Texas Tech	Sun 12-26-64	Georgia 0-7 (Vince Dooley)
Texas Tech	Gator 12-31-65	Georgia Tech 21-31 (Bobby Dodd)
JIMMY KITTS, 1-1-0 (Southern Methodist) Born 6-14-00		
Rice	Cotton 1-1-38	Colorado 28-14 (Bernard "Bunnie" Oakes)
Virginia Tech	Sun 1-1-47	Cincinnati 6-18 (Ray Nolting)
ED KLUSKA, 1-0-0 (Xavier, Ohio '40) Born 5-21-18		
Xavier (Ohio)	Salad 1-1-50	Arizona St. 33-21 (Ed Doherty)
JOE KRIVAK, 0-0-1 (Syracuse '57) Born 3-20-35		
Maryland	Independence 12-15-90	Louisiana Tech 34-34 (Joe Raymond Peace)
FRANK KUSH, 6-1-0 (Michigan St. '53) Born 1-20-29		
Arizona St.	Peach 12-30-70	North Caro. 48-26 (Bill Dooley)
Arizona St.	Fiesta 12-27-71	Florida St. 45-38 (Larry Jones)
Arizona St.	Fiesta 12-23-72	Missouri 49-35 (Al Onofrio)
Arizona St.	Fiesta 12-21-73	Pittsburgh 28-7 (Johnny Majors)
Arizona St.	Fiesta 12-26-75	Nebraska 17-14 (Tom Osborne)
Arizona St.	Fiesta 12-25-77	Penn St. 30-42 (Joe Paterno)
Arizona St.	Garden State 12-16-78	Rutgers 34-18 (Frank Burns)
BERT LaBRUCHERIE, 0-1-0 (UCLA '29) Born 1-19-05		
UCLA	Rose 1-1-47	Illinois 14-45 (Ray Eliot)
JIM LAMBRIGHT, 0-1-0 (Washington '65) Born 4-26-42		
Washington	Sun 12-29-95	Iowa 18-38 (Hayden Fry)
MAXIE LAMBRIGHT, 1-1-0 (Southern Miss. '49) Born 6-3-24		
Louisiana Tech	Independence 12-17-77	Louisville 24-14 (Vince Gibson)
Louisiana Tech	Independence 12-16-78	East Caro. 13-35 (Pat Dye)
FRANK LAUTERBUR, 2-0-0 (Mount Union '49) Born 8-8-25		
Toledo	Tangerine 12-26-69	Davidson 56-33 (Homer Smith)
Toledo	Tangerine 12-28-70	William & Mary 40-12 (Lou Holtz)
FRANK LEAHY, 1-1-0 (Notre Dame '31) Born 8-27-08		
Boston College	Cotton 1-1-40	Clemson 3-6 (Jess Neely)
Boston College	Sugar 1-1-41	Tennessee 19-13 (Bob Neyland)
CLYDE LEE, 1-0-0 (Centenary, La. '32) Born 2-11-08		
Houston	Salad 1-1-52	Dayton 26-21 (Joe Gavin)
ART LEWIS, 0-1-0 (Ohio '36) Born 2-18-11		
West Va.	Sugar 1-1-54	Georgia Tech 19-42 (Bobby Dodd)
BILL LEWIS, 1-0-0 (East Stroudsburg '63) Born 8-5-41		
East Caro.	Peach 1-1-92	North Caro. St. 37-34 (Dick Sheridan)
LOU LITTLE, 1-0-0 (Pennsylvania '20) Born 12-6-93		
Columbia	Rose 1-1-34	Stanford 7-0 (Claude "Tiny" Thornhill)
STEVE LOGAN, 1-1-0 (Tulsa '75) Born 2-3-53		
East Caro.	Liberty 12-31-94	Illinois 0-30 (Lou Tepper)
East Caro.	Liberty 12-30-95	Stanford 19-13 (Tyrone Willingham)
JIM LOOKABAUGH, 2-1-0 (Oklahoma St. '25) Born 6-15-02		
Oklahoma St.	Cotton 1-1-45	Texas Christian 34-0 (Leo "Dutch" Meyer)
Oklahoma St.	Sugar 1-1-46	St. Mary's (Cal.) 33-13 (Jimmy Phelan)
Oklahoma St.	Delta 1-1-49	William & Mary 0-20 (Rube McCray)
SONNY LUBICK, 0-2-0 (Western Mont. '60) Born 3-12-37		
Colorado St.	Holiday 12-30-94	Michigan 14-24 (Gary Moeller)
Colorado St.	Holiday 12-29-95	Kansas St. 21-54 (Bill Snyder)
AL LUGINBILL, 0-1-0 (Cal Poly Pomona '67) Born 11-3-46		
San Diego St.	Freedom 12-30-91	Tulsa 17-28 (Dave Rader)
GEORGE MacINTYRE, 0-1-0 (Miami, Fla. '61) Born 4-30-39		
Vanderbilt	Hall of Fame 12-31-82	Air Force 28-36 (Ken Hatfield)
JOHN MACKOVIC, 2-4-0 (Wake Forest '65) Born 10-1-43		
Wake Forest	Tangerine 12-22-79	LSU 10-34 (Charlie McClendon)
Illinois	All-American 12-29-88	Florida 10-14 (Galen Hall)
Illinois	Fla. Citrus 1-1-90	Virginia 31-21 (George Welsh)
Illinois	Hall of Fame 1-1-91	Clemson 0-30 (Ken Hatfield)
Texas	Sun 12-30-94	North Caro. 35-31 (Mack Brown)
Texas	Sugar 12-31-95	Virginia Tech 10-28 (Frank Beamer)
DICK MacPHERSON, 3-1-1 (Springfield '58) Born 11-4-30		
Syracuse	Cherry 12-21-85	Maryland 18-35 (Bobby Ross)
Syracuse	Sugar 1-1-88	Auburn 16-16 (Pat Dye)
Syracuse	Hall of Fame 1-2-89	LSU 23-10 (Mike Archer)
Syracuse	Peach 12-30-89	Georgia 19-18 (Ray Goff)
Syracuse	Aloha 12-25-90	Arizona 28-0 (Dick Tomey)
EDWARD "SLIP" MADIGAN, 1-0-0 (Notre Dame '20) Born 11-18-95		
St. Mary's (Cal.)	Cotton 1-2-39	Texas Tech 20-13 (Pete Cawthon)
JOHNNY MAJORS, 9-7-0 (Tennessee '57) Born 5-21-35		
Iowa St.	Sun 12-18-71	LSU 15-33 (Charlie McClendon)
Iowa St.	Liberty 12-18-72	Georgia Tech 30-31 (Bill Fulcher)
Pittsburgh	Fiesta 12-21-73	Arizona St. 7-28 (Frank Kush)
Pittsburgh	Sun 12-26-75	Kansas 33-19 (Bud Moore)
Pittsburgh	Sugar 1-1-77	Georgia 27-3 (Vince Dooley)
Tennessee	Bluebonnet 12-31-79	Purdue 22-27 (Jim Young)
Tennessee	Garden State 12-13-81	Wisconsin 28-21 (Dave McClain)
Tennessee	Peach 12-31-82	Iowa 22-28 (Hayden Fry)
Tennessee	Fla. Citrus 12-17-83	Maryland 30-23 (Bobby Ross)
Tennessee	Sun 12-24-84	Maryland 26-27 (Bobby Ross)
Tennessee	Sugar 1-1-86	Miami (Fla.) 35-7 (Jimmy Johnson)
Tennessee	Liberty 12-29-86	Minnesota 21-14 (John Gutekunst)
Tennessee	Peach 1-2-88	Indiana 27-22 (Bill Mallory)
Tennessee	Cotton 1-1-90	Arkansas 31-27 (Ken Hatfield)
Tennessee	Sugar 1-1-91	Virginia 23-22 (George Welsh)
Tennessee	Fiesta 1-1-92	Penn St. 17-42 (Joe Paterno)
BILL MALLORY, 4-6-0 (Miami, Ohio '57) Born 5-30-35		
Miami (Ohio)	Tangerine 12-22-73	Florida 16-7 (Doug Dickey)
Colorado	Bluebonnet 12-27-75	Texas 21-38 (Darrell Royal)
Colorado	Orange 1-1-77	Ohio St. 10-27 (Woody Hayes)
Northern Ill.	California 12-17-83	Cal St. Fullerton 20-13 (Gene Murphy)
Indiana	All-American 12-31-86	Florida St. 13-27 (Bobby Bowden)
Indiana	Peach 1-2-88	Tennessee 22-27 (Johnny Majors)
Indiana	Liberty 12-28-88	South Caro. 34-10 (Joe Morrison)
Indiana	Peach 12-29-90	Auburn 23-27 (Pat Dye)
Indiana	Copper 12-31-91	Baylor 24-0 (Grant Teaff)
Indiana	Independence 12-31-93	Virginia Tech 20-45 (Frank Beamer)
FRANK MALONEY, 1-0-0 (Michigan '62) Born 9-26-40		
Syracuse	Independence 12-15-79	McNeese St. 31-7 (Ernie Duplechin)
BOB MARGARITA, 0-1-0 (Brown '44) Born 11-3-20		
Georgetown	Sun 1-2-50	UTEP 20-33 (Jack "Cactus Jack" Curtice)
ABE MARTIN, 1-3-1 (Texas Christian '32) Born 10-8-08		
Texas Christian	Cotton 1-2-56	Mississippi 13-14 (John Vaught)
Texas Christian	Cotton 1-1-57	Syracuse 28-27 (Ben Schwartzwalder)
Texas Christian	Cotton 1-1-59	Air Force 0-0 (Ben Martin)
Texas Christian	Bluebonnet 12-19-59	Clemson 7-23 (Frank Howard)
Texas Christian	Sun 12-31-65	UTEP 12-13 (Bobby Dobbs)
BEN MARTIN, 0-2-1 (Navy '46) Born 6-28-21		
Air Force	Cotton 1-1-59	Texas Christian 0-0 (Abe Martin)
Air Force	Gator 12-28-63	North Caro. 0-35 (Jim Hickey)
Air Force	Sugar 1-1-71	Tennessee 13-34 (Bill Battle)
GLEN MASON, 2-0-0 (Ohio St. '72) Born 4-9-50		
Kansas	Aloha 12-25-92	Brigham Young 23-20 (LaVell Edwards)
Kansas	Aloha 12-25-95	UCLA 51-30 (Terry Donahue)
TONY MASON, 0-1-0 (Clarion '50) Born 3-2-30		
Arizona	Fiesta 12-25-79	Pittsburgh 10-16 (Jackie Sherrill)
RON McBRIDE, 1-2-0 (San Jose St. '63) Born 10-14-39		
Utah	Copper 12-29-92	Washington St. 28-31 (Mike Price)
Utah	Freedom 12-30-93	Southern Cal 21-28 (John Robinson)
Utah	Freedom 12-27-94	Arizona 16-13 (Dick Tomey)
TOM McCANN, 0-1-0 (Illinois '24) Born 11-7-98		
Miami (Fla.)	Orange 1-1-35	Bucknell 0-26 (Edward "Hook" Mylin)
BILL McCARTNEY, 3-6-0 (Missouri '62) Born 8-22-40		
Colorado	Freedom 12-30-85	Washington 17-20 (Don James)
Colorado	Bluebonnet 12-31-86	Baylor 9-21 (Grant Teaff)
Colorado	Freedom 12-29-88	Brigham Young 17-20 (LaVell Edwards)
Colorado	Orange 1-1-90	Notre Dame 6-21 (Lou Holtz)
Colorado	Orange 1-1-91	Notre Dame 10-9 (Lou Holtz)

Coach/School	Bowl/Date	Opponent/Score (Coach)
Colorado	Blockbuster 12-28-91	Alabama 25-30 (Gene Stallings)
Colorado	Fiesta 1-1-93	Syracuse 22-26 (Paul Pasqualoni)
Colorado	Aloha 12-25-93	Fresno St. 41-30 (Jim Sweeney)
Colorado	Fiesta 1-2-95	Notre Dame 41-24 (Lou Holtz)
DAVE McCLAIN, 1-2-0 (Bowling Green '60) Born 1-28-38		
Wisconsin	Garden State 12-13-81	Tennessee 21-28 (Johnny Majors)
Wisconsin	Independence 12-11-82	Kansas St. 14-3 (Jim Dickey)
Wisconsin	Hall of Fame 12-29-84	Kentucky 19-20 (Jerry Claiborne)
CHARLIE McCLENDON, 7-6-0 (Kentucky '50) Born 10-17-22		
LSU	Cotton 1-1-63	Texas 13-0 (Darrell Royal)
LSU	Bluebonnet 12-21-63	Baylor 7-14 (John Bridgers)
LSU	Sugar 1-1-65	Syracuse 13-10 (Ben Schwartzwalder)
LSU	Cotton 1-1-66	Arkansas 14-7 (Frank Broyles)
LSU	Sugar 1-1-68	Wyoming 20-13 (Lloyd Eaton)
LSU	Peach 12-30-68	Florida St. 31-27 (Bill Peterson)
LSU	Orange 1-1-71	Nebraska 12-17 (Bob Devaney)
LSU	Sun 12-18-71	Iowa St. 33-15 (Johnny Majors)
LSU	Bluebonnet 12-30-72	Tennessee 17-24 (Bill Battle)
LSU	Orange 1-1-74	Penn St. 9-16 (Joe Paterno)
LSU	Sun 12-31-77	Stanford 14-24 (Bill Walsh)
LSU	Liberty 12-23-78	Missouri 15-20 (Warren Powers)
LSU	Tangerine 12-22-79	Wake Forest 34-10 (John Mackovic)
RUBE McCRAY, 1-1-0 (Ky. Wesleyan '30) Born 6-13-05		
William & Mary	Dixie 1-1-48	Arkansas 19-21 (John Barnhill)
William & Mary	Delta 1-1-49	Oklahoma St. 20-0 (Jim Lookabaugh)
J. F. "POP" McKALE, 0-1-0 (Albion '10) Born 6-12-87		
Arizona	San Diego East-West Christmas Classic 12-26-21	Centre 0-38 (Charley Moran)
JOHN McKAY, 6-3-0 (Oregon St. '50) Born 7-5-23		
Southern Cal	Rose 1-2-63	Wisconsin 42-37 (Milt Bruhn)
Southern Cal	Rose 1-2-67	Purdue 13-14 (Jack Mollenkopf)
Southern Cal	Rose 1-1-68	Indiana 14-3 (John Pont)
Southern Cal	Rose 1-1-69	Ohio St. 16-27 (Woody Hayes)
Southern Cal	Rose 1-1-70	Michigan 10-3 (Glenn "Bo" Schembechler)
Southern Cal	Rose 1-1-73	Ohio St. 42-17 (Woody Hayes)
Southern Cal	Rose 1-1-74	Ohio St. 21-42 (Woody Hayes)
Southern Cal	Rose 1-1-75	Ohio St. 18-17 (Woody Hayes)
Southern Cal	Liberty 12-22-75	Texas A&M 20-0 (Emory Bellard)
ALLYN McKEEN, 1-0-0 (Tennessee '29) Born 1-26-05		
Mississippi St.	Orange 1-1-41	Georgetown 14-7 (Jack Hagerty)
JOHNNIE McMILLAN, 0-1-0 (South Caro. '41) Born 1-27-19		
South Caro.	Gator 1-1-46	Wake Forest 14-26 (D. C. "Peahead" Walker)
DAVID McWILLIAMS, 1-1-0 (Texas '64) Born 4-18-42		
Texas	Bluebonnet 12-31-87	Pittsburgh 32-27 (Mike Gottfried)
Texas	Cotton 1-1-91	Miami (Fla.) 3-46 (Dennis Erickson)
JACK MEAGHER, 1-0-1 (Notre Dame '17) Born 7-4-94		
Auburn	Bacardi, Cuba 1-1-37	Villanova 7-7 (Maurice "Clipper" Smith)
Auburn	Orange 1-1-38	Michigan St. 6-0 (Charlie Bachman)
RANDOLPH R. M. MEDLEY, 2-0-0 (Mo. Wesleyan '21) Born 9-22-98		
Southwestern (Tex.)	Sun 1-1-44	New Mexico 7-0 (Willis Barnes)
Southwestern (Tex.)	Sun 1-1-45	U. of Mexico 35-0 (Bernard A. Hoban)
LEO "DUTCH" MEYER, 3-4-0 (Texas Christian '22) Born 1-15-98		
Texas Christian	Sugar 1-1-36	LSU 3-2 (Bernie Moore)
Texas Christian	Cotton 1-1-37	Marquette 16-6 (Frank Murray)
Texas Christian	Sugar 1-2-39	Carnegie Mellon 15-7 (Bill Kern)
Texas Christian	Orange 1-1-42	Georgia 26-40 (Wally Butts)
Texas Christian	Cotton 1-1-45	Oklahoma St. 0-34 (Jim Lookabaugh)
Texas Christian	Delta 1-1-48	Mississippi 9-13 (John Vaught)
Texas Christian	Cotton 1-1-52	Kentucky 7-20 (Paul "Bear" Bryant)
RON MEYER, 0-1-0 (Purdue '63) Born 2-17-41		
Southern Methodist	Holiday 12-19-80	Brigham Young 45-46 (LaVell Edwards)
JOHN MICHELOSEN, 0-2-0 (Pittsburgh '38) Born 2-13-16		
Pittsburgh	Sugar 1-2-56	Georgia Tech 0-7 (Bobby Dodd)
Pittsburgh	Gator 12-29-56	Georgia Tech 14-21 (Bobby Dodd)
JACK MITCHELL, 1-0-0 (Oklahoma '49) Born 12-3-24		
Kansas	Bluebonnet 12-16-61	Rice 33-7 (Jess Neely)
ODUS MITCHELL, 0-2-0 (West Tex. A&M '25) Born 6-29-99		
North Texas	Salad 1-1-48	Nevada 6-13 (Joe Sheeketski)
North Texas	Sun 12-31-59	New Mexico St. 8-28 (Warren Woodson)
GARY MOELLER, 4-1-0 (Ohio St. '63) Born 1-26-41		
Michigan	Gator 1-1-91	Mississippi 35-3 (Billy Brewer)
Michigan	Rose 1-1-92	Washington 14-34 (Don James)
Michigan	Rose 1-1-93	Washington 38-31 (Don James)
Michigan	Hall of Fame 1-1-94	North Caro. St. 42-7 (Mike O'Cain)
Michigan	Holiday 12-30-94	Colorado St. 24-14 (Sonny Lubick)
AL MOLDE, 0-1-0 (Gust. Adolphus '66) Born 11-15-43		
Western Mich.	California 12-10-88	Fresno St. 30-35 (Jim Sweeney)

Coach/School	Bowl/Date	Opponent/Score (Coach)
JACK MOLLENKOPF, 1-0-0 (Bowling Green '31) Born 11-24-05		
Purdue	Rose 1-2-67	Southern Cal 14-13 (John McKay)
BERNIE MOORE, 1-3-1 (Carson-Newman '17) Born 4-30-95		
LSU	Sugar 1-1-36	Texas Christian 2-3 (Leo "Dutch" Meyer)
LSU	Sugar 1-1-37	Santa Clara 14-21 (Lawrence "Buck" Shaw)
LSU	Sugar 1-1-38	Santa Clara 0-6 (Lawrence "Buck" Shaw)
LSU	Orange 1-1-44	Texas A&M 19-14 (Homer Norton)
LSU	Cotton 1-1-47	Arkansas 0-0 (John Barnhill)
BUD MOORE, 0-1-0 (Alabama '61) Born 10-16-39		
Kansas	Sun 12-26-75	Pittsburgh 19-33 (Johnny Majors)
CHARLEY MORAN, 2-1-0 (Tennessee '98) Born 2-22-78		
Centre	Fort Worth Classic 1-1-21	Texas Christian 63-7 (Bill Driver)
Centre	San Diego East-West Christmas Classic 12-26-21	Arizona 38-0 (J. F. "Pop" McKale)
Centre	Dixie Classic 1-2-22	Texas A&M 14-22 (Dana Bible)
DELL MORGAN, 0-3-0 (Austin '25) Born 2-14-02		
Texas Tech	Sun 1-1-42	Tulsa 0-6 (Henry Frnka)
Texas Tech	Sun 1-1-48	Miami (Ohio) 12-13 (Sid Gillman)
Texas Tech	Raisin 12-31-49	San Jose St. 13-20 (Bill Hubbard)
JOE MORRISON, 0-3-0 (Cincinnati '59) Born 8-21-37		
South Caro.	Gator 12-28-84	Oklahoma St. 14-21 (Pat Jones)
South Caro.	Gator 12-31-87	LSU 13-30 (Mike Archer)
South Caro.	Liberty 12-28-88	Indiana 10-34 (Bill Mallory)
RAY MORRISON, 0-1-0 (Vanderbilt '12) Born 2-28-85		
Southern Methodist	Dixie Classic 1-1-25	West Va. Wesleyan 7-9 (Bob Higgins)
DARRELL MUDRA, 0-1-0 (Peru St. '51) Born 1-4-29		
Arizona	Sun 12-28-68	Auburn 10-34 (Ralph "Shug" Jordan)
CLARENCE "BIGGIE" MUNN, 1-0-0 (Minnesota '32) Born 9-11-08		
Michigan St.	Rose 1-1-54	UCLA 28-20 (Henry "Red" Sanders)
BILLY MURPHY, 1-0-0 (Mississippi St. '47) Born 1-13-21		
Memphis	Pasadena 12-18-71	San Jose St. 28-9 (Dewey King)
GENE MURPHY, 0-1-0 (North Dak. '62) Born 8-6-39		
Cal St. Fullerton	California 12-17-83	Northern Ill. 13-20 (Bill Mallory)
JACK MURPHY, 1-0-0 (Heidelberg '54) Born 8-6-32		
Toledo	Tangerine 12-28-71	Richmond 28-3 (Frank Jones)
BILL MURRAY, 2-1-0 (Duke '31) Born 9-9-08		
Duke	Orange 1-1-55	Nebraska 34-7 (Bill Glassford)
Duke	Orange 1-1-58	Oklahoma 21-48 (Bud Wilkinson)
Duke	Cotton 1-2-61	Arkansas 7-6 (Frank Broyles)
FRANK MURRAY, 0-1-0 (Tufts '08) Born 2-12-85		
Marquette	Cotton 1-1-37	Texas Christian 6-16 (Leo "Dutch" Meyer)
DENNY MYERS, 0-1-0 (Iowa '30) Born 11-10-05		
Boston College	Orange 1-1-43	Alabama 21-37 (Frank Thomas)
EDWARD "HOOK" MYLIN, 1-0-0 (Frank. & Marsh.) Born 10-23-97		
Bucknell	Orange 1-1-35	Miami (Fla.) 26-0 (Tom McCann)
RAY NAGEL, 1-0-0 (UCLA '50) Born 5-18-27		
Utah	Liberty 12-19-64	West Va. 32-6 (Gene Corum)
LARRY NAVIAUX, 0-1-0 (Nebraska '59) Born 12-17-36		
Boston U.	Pasadena 12-6-69	San Diego St. 7-28 (Don Coryell)
EARLE "GREASY" NEALE, 0-0-1 (West Va. Wesleyan '14) Born 11-5-91		
Wash. & Jeff.	Rose 1-2-22	California 0-0 (Andy Smith)
JESS NEELY, 4-3-0 (Vanderbilt '23) Born 1-4-98		
Clemson	Cotton 1-1-40	Boston College 6-3 (Frank Leahy)
Rice	Orange 1-1-47	Tennessee 8-0 (Bob Neyland)
Rice	Cotton 1-2-50	North Caro. 27-13 (Carl Snavely)
Rice	Cotton 1-1-54	Alabama 28-6 (Harold "Red" Drew)
Rice	Cotton 1-1-58	Navy 7-20 (Eddie Erdelatz)
Rice	Sugar 1-2-61	Mississippi 6-14 (John Vaught)
Rice	Bluebonnet 12-16-61	Kansas 7-33 (Jack Mitchell)
DON NEHLEN, 3-6-0 (Bowling Green '58) Born 1-1-36		
West Va.	Peach 12-31-81	Florida 26-6 (Charley Pell)
West Va.	Gator 12-30-82	Florida St. 12-31 (Bobby Bowden)
West Va.	Hall of Fame 12-22-83	Kentucky 20-16 (Jerry Claiborne)
West Va.	Bluebonnet 12-31-84	Texas Christian 31-14 (Jim Wacker)
West Va.	Sun 12-25-87	Oklahoma St. 33-35 (Pat Jones)
West Va.	Fiesta 1-2-89	Notre Dame 21-34 (Lou Holtz)
West Va.	Gator 12-30-89	Clemson 7-27 (Danny Ford)
West Va.	Sugar 1-1-94	Florida 7-41 (Steve Spurrier)
West Va.	Carquest 1-2-95	South Caro. 21-24 (Brad Scott)
RICK NEUHEISEL, 1-0-0 (UCLA '84) Born 2-7-61		
Colorado	Cotton 1-1-96	Oregon 38-6 (Mike Bellotti)
BOB NEYLAND, 2-5-0 (Army '16) Born 2-17-92		
Tennessee	Orange 1-2-39	Oklahoma 17-0 (Tom Stidham)

Coach/School	Bowl/Date	Opponent/Score (Coach)
Tennessee	Rose 1-1-40	Southern Cal 0-14 (Howard Jones)
Tennessee	Sugar 1-1-41	Boston College 13-19 (Frank Leahy)
Tennessee	Orange 1-1-47	Rice 0-8 (Jess Neely)
Tennessee	Cotton 1-1-51	Texas 20-14 (Blair Cherry)
Tennessee	Sugar 1-1-52	Maryland 13-28 (Jim Tatum)
Tennessee	Cotton 1-1-53	Texas 0-16 (Ed Price)

RAY NOLTING, 1-0-0 (Cincinnati '36) Born 11-8-13

Cincinnati	Sun 1-1-47	Virginia Tech 18-6 (Jimmy Kitts)

HOMER NORTON, 2-2-1 (Birmingham Southern '16) Born 12-30-96

Centenary (La.)	Dixie Classic 1-1-34	Arkansas 7-7 (Fred Thomsen)
Texas A&M	Sugar 1-1-40	Tulane 14-13 (Lowell "Red" Dawson)
Texas A&M	Cotton 1-1-41	Fordham 13-12 (Jim Crowley)
Texas A&M	Cotton 1-1-42	Alabama 21-29 (Frank Thomas)
Texas A&M	Orange 1-1-44	LSU 14-19 (Bernie Moore)

TOM NUGENT, 0-2-0 (Ithaca '36) Born 2-24-16

Florida St.	Sun 1-1-55	UTEP 20-47 (Mike Brumbelow)
Florida St.	Bluegrass 12-13-58	Oklahoma St. 6-15 (Cliff Speegle)

MIKE O'CAIN, 1-1-0 (Clemson '77) Born 7-20-54

North Caro. St.	Hall of Fame 1-1-94	Michigan 7-42 (Gary Moeller)
North Caro. St.	Peach 1-1-95	Mississippi St. 28-24 (Jackie Sherrill)

BERNARD "BUNNIE" OAKES, 0-1-0 (Illinois '24) Born 9-15-98

Colorado	Cotton 1-1-38	Rice 14-28 (Jimmy Kitts)

JORDAN OLIVAR, 1-1-0 (Villanova '38) Born 1-30-15

Villanova	Great Lakes 12-6-47	Kentucky 14-24 (Paul "Bear" Bryant)
Villanova	Harbor 1-1-49	Nevada 27-7 (Joe Sheeketski)

AL ONOFRIO, 1-1-0 (Arizona St. '43) Born 3-15-21

Missouri	Fiesta 12-23-72	Arizona St. 35-49 (Frank Kush)
Missouri	Sun 12-29-73	Auburn 34-17 (Ralph "Shug" Jordan)

BENNIE OOSTERBAAN, 1-0-0 (Michigan '28) Born 2-24-06

Michigan	Rose 1-1-51	California 14-6 (Lynn "Pappy" Waldorf)

TOM OSBORNE, 10-13-0 (Hastings '59) Born 2-23-37

Nebraska	Cotton 1-1-74	Texas 19-3 (Darrell Royal)
Nebraska	Sugar 12-31-74	Florida 13-10 (Doug Dickey)
Nebraska	Fiesta 12-26-75	Arizona St. 14-17 (Frank Kush)
Nebraska	Bluebonnet 12-31-76	Texas Tech 27-24 (Steve Sloan)
Nebraska	Liberty 12-19-77	North Caro. 21-17 (Bill Dooley)
Nebraska	Orange 1-1-79	Oklahoma 24-31 (Barry Switzer)
Nebraska	Cotton 1-1-80	Houston 14-17 (Bill Yeoman)
Nebraska	Sun 12-27-80	Mississippi St. 31-17 (Emory Bellard)
Nebraska	Orange 1-1-82	Clemson 15-22 (Danny Ford)
Nebraska	Orange 1-1-83	LSU 21-20 (Jerry Stovall)
Nebraska	Orange 1-2-84	Miami (Fla.) 30-31 (Howard Schnellenberger)
Nebraska	Sugar 1-1-85	LSU 28-10 (Bill Arnsparger)
Nebraska	Fiesta 1-1-86	Michigan 23-27 (Glenn "Bo" Schembechler)
Nebraska	Sugar 1-1-87	LSU 30-15 (Bill Arnsparger)
Nebraska	Fiesta 1-1-88	Florida St. 28-31 (Bobby Bowden)
Nebraska	Orange 1-2-89	Miami (Fla.) 3-23 (Jimmy Johnson)
Nebraska	Fiesta 1-1-90	Florida St. 17-41 (Bobby Bowden)
Nebraska	Fla. Citrus 1-1-91	Georgia Tech 21-45 (Bobby Ross)
Nebraska	Orange 1-1-92	Miami (Fla.) 0-22 (Dennis Erickson)
Nebraska	Orange 1-1-93	Florida St. 14-27 (Bobby Bowden)
Nebraska	Orange 1-1-94	Florida St. 16-18 (Bobby Bowden)
Nebraska	Orange 1-1-95	Miami (Fla.) 24-17 (Dennis Erickson)
Nebraska	Fiesta 1-2-96	Florida 62-24 (Steve Spurrier)

JIM OWENS, 2-1-0 (Oklahoma '50) Born 3-6-27

Washington	Rose 1-1-60	Wisconsin 44-8 (Milt Bruhn)
Washington	Rose 1-2-61	Minnesota 17-7 (Murray Warmath)
Washington	Rose 1-1-64	Illinois 7-17 (Pete Elliott)

JACK PARDEE, 0-1-0 (Texas A&M '57) Born 4-9-36

Houston	Aloha 12-25-88	Washington St. 22-24 (Dennis Erickson)

ARA PARSEGHIAN, 3-2-0 (Miami, Ohio '49) Born 5-21-23

Notre Dame	Cotton 1-1-70	Texas 17-21 (Darrell Royal)
Notre Dame	Cotton 1-1-71	Texas 24-11 (Darrell Royal)
Notre Dame	Orange 1-1-73	Nebraska 6-40 (Bob Devaney)
Notre Dame	Sugar 12-31-73	Alabama 24-23 (Paul "Bear" Bryant)
Notre Dame	Orange 1-1-75	Alabama 13-11 (Paul "Bear" Bryant)

PAUL PASQUALONI, 3-0-0 (Penn St. '72) Born 8-16-49

Syracuse	Hall of Fame 1-1-92	Ohio St. 24-17 (John Cooper)
Syracuse	Fiesta 1-1-93	Colorado 26-22 (Bill McCartney)
Syracuse	Gator 1-1-96	Clemson 41-0 (Tommy West)

JOE PATERNO, 17-8-1 (Brown '50) Born 12-21-26

Penn St.	Gator 12-30-67	Florida St. 17-17 (Bill Peterson)
Penn St.	Orange 1-1-69	Kansas 15-14 (Pepper Rodgers)
Penn St.	Orange 1-1-70	Missouri 10-3 (Dan Devine)
Penn St.	Cotton 1-1-72	Texas 30-6 (Darrell Royal)
Penn St.	Sugar 12-31-72	Oklahoma 0-14 (Chuck Fairbanks)
Penn St.	Orange 1-1-74	LSU 16-9 (Charlie McClendon)
Penn St.	Cotton 1-1-75	Baylor 41-20 (Grant Teaff)
Penn St.	Sugar 12-31-75	Alabama 6-13 (Paul "Bear" Bryant)
Penn St.	Gator 12-27-76	Notre Dame 9-20 (Dan Devine)

Coach/School	Bowl/Date	Opponent/Score (Coach)
Penn St.	Fiesta 12-25-77	Arizona St. 42-30 (Frank Kush)
Penn St.	Sugar 1-1-79	Alabama 7-14 (Paul "Bear" Bryant)
Penn St.	Liberty 12-22-79	Tulane 9-6 (Larry Smith)
Penn St.	Fiesta 12-26-80	Ohio St. 31-19 (Earle Bruce)
Penn St.	Fiesta 1-1-82	Southern Cal 26-10 (John Robinson)
Penn St.	Sugar 1-1-83	Georgia 27-23 (Vince Dooley)
Penn St.	Aloha 12-26-83	Washington 13-10 (Don James)
Penn St.	Orange 1-1-86	Oklahoma 10-25 (Barry Switzer)
Penn St.	Fiesta 1-1-87	Miami (Fla.) 14-10 (Jimmy Johnson)
Penn St.	Fla. Citrus 1-1-88	Clemson 10-35 (Danny Ford)
Penn St.	Holiday 12-29-89	Brigham Young 50-39 (LaVell Edwards)
Penn St.	Blockbuster 12-28-90	Florida St. 17-24 (Bobby Bowden)
Penn St.	Fiesta 1-1-92	Tennessee 42-17 (Johnny Majors)
Penn St.	Blockbuster 1-1-93	Stanford 3-24 (Bill Walsh)
Penn St.	Fla. Citrus 1-1-94	Tennessee 31-13 (Phillip Fulmer)
Penn St.	Rose 1-2-95	Oregon 38-20 (Rich Brooks)
Penn St.	Outback 1-1-96	Auburn 43-14 (Terry Bowden)

JOE RAYMOND PEACE, 0-0-1 (Louisiana Tech '68) Born 6-5-45

Louisiana Tech	Independence 12-15-90	Maryland 34-34 (Joe Krivak)

CHARLEY PELL, 2-3-0 (Alabama '64) Born 2-27-41

Clemson	Gator 12-30-77	Pittsburgh 3-34 (Jackie Sherrill)
Florida	Tangerine 12-20-80	Maryland 35-20 (Jerry Claiborne)
Florida	Peach 12-31-81	West Va. 6-26 (Don Nehlen)
Florida	Bluebonnet 12-31-82	Arkansas 24-28 (Lou Holtz)
Florida	Gator 12-30-83	Iowa 14-6 (Hayden Fry)

RAY PERKINS, 3-0-0 (Alabama '67) Born 11-6-41

Alabama	Sun 12-24-83	Southern Methodist 28-7 (Bobby Collins)
Alabama	Aloha 12-28-85	Southern Cal 24-3 (Ted Tollner)
Alabama	Sun 12-26-86	Washington 28-6 (Don James)

GEORGE PERLES, 3-4-0 (Michigan St. '60) Born 7-16-34

Michigan St.	Cherry 12-22-84	Army 6-10 (Jim Young)
Michigan St.	Hall of Fame 12-31-85	Georgia Tech 14-17 (Bill Curry)
Michigan St.	Rose 1-1-88	Southern Cal 20-17 (Larry Smith)
Michigan St.	Gator 1-1-89	Georgia 27-34 (Vince Dooley)
Michigan St.	Aloha 12-25-89	Hawaii 33-13 (Bob Wagner)
Michigan St.	John Hancock 12-31-90	Southern Cal 17-16 (Larry Smith)
Michigan St.	Liberty 12-28-93	Louisville 7-18 (Howard Schnellenberger)

DOYT PERRY, 0-1-0 (Bowling Green '32) Born 1-6-10

Bowling Green	Mercy 11-23-61	Fresno St. 6-36 (Cecil Coleman)

BILL PETERSON, 1-2-1 (Ohio Northern '46) Born 5-14-20

Florida St.	Gator 1-2-65	Oklahoma 36-19 (Gomer Jones)
Florida St.	Sun 12-24-66	Wyoming 20-28 (Lloyd Eaton)
Florida St.	Gator 12-30-67	Penn St. 17-17 (Joe Paterno)
Florida St.	Peach 12-30-68	LSU 27-31 (Charlie McClendon)

JIMMY PHELAN, 0-3-0 (Notre Dame '19) Born 12-5-92

Washington	Rose 1-1-37	Pittsburgh 0-21 (Jock Sutherland)
St. Mary's (Cal.)	Sugar 1-1-46	Oklahoma St. 12-33 (Jim Lookabaugh)
St. Mary's (Cal.)	Oil 1-1-47	Georgia Tech 19-41 (Bobby Dodd)

ALVIN "PIX" PIERSON, 0-1-0 (Nevada '22) Born 7-25-98

Fresno St.	Raisin 1-1-46	Drake 12-13 (Vee Green)

GARY PINKEL, 1-0-0 (Kent '75) Born 4-27-52

Toledo	Las Vegas 12-14-95	Nevada 40-37 OT (Chris Ault)

JIM PITTMAN, 1-0-0 (Mississippi St. '50) Born 8-28-25

Tulane	Liberty 12-12-70	Colorado 17-3 (Eddie Crowder)

JOHN PONT, 0-2-0 (Miami, Ohio '52) Born 11-13-27

Miami (Ohio)	Tangerine 12-22-52	Houston 21-49 (Bill Yeoman)
Indiana	Rose 1-1-68	Southern Cal 3-14 (John McKay)

WARREN POWERS, 3-2-0 (Nebraska '63) Born 2-19-41

Missouri	Liberty 12-23-78	LSU 20-15 (Charlie McClendon)
Missouri	Hall of Fame 12-29-79	South Caro. 24-14 (Jim Carlen)
Missouri	Liberty 12-27-80	Purdue 25-28 (Jim Young)
Missouri	Tangerine 12-19-81	Southern Miss. 19-17 (Bobby Collins)
Missouri	Holiday 12-23-83	Brigham Young 17-21 (LaVell Edwards)

CLARENCE "NIBS" PRICE, 0-1-0 (California '14) Born 1889

California	Rose 1-1-29	Georgia Tech 7-8 (Bill Alexander)

ED PRICE, 1-0-0 (Texas '33) Born 1-12-09

Texas	Cotton 1-1-53	Tennessee 16-0 (Bob Neyland)

MIKE PRICE, 2-0-0 (Puget Sound '69) Born 4-6-46

Washington St.	Copper 12-29-92	Utah 31-28 (Ron McBride)
Washington St.	Alamo 12-31-94	Baylor 10-3 (Chuck Reedy)

TOMMY PROTHRO, 2-2-0 (Duke '42) Born 7-20-20

Oregon St.	Rose 1-1-57	Iowa 19-35 (Forest Evashevski)
Oregon St.	Liberty 12-15-62	Villanova 6-0 (Alex Bell)
Oregon St.	Rose 1-1-65	Michigan 7-34 (Chalmers "Bump" Elliott)
UCLA	Rose 1-1-66	Michigan St. 14-12 (Duffy Daugherty)

DAVE RADER, 1-1-0 (Tulsa '80) Born 3-9-57

Tulsa	Independence 12-16-89	Oregon 24-27 (Rich Brooks)
Tulsa	Freedom 12-30-91	San Diego St. 28-17 (Al Luginbill)

Coach/School	Bowl/Date	Opponent/Score (Coach)
JOHN RALSTON, 2-2-0 (California '54) Born 4-25-27		
Utah St.	Sun 12-31-60	New Mexico St. 13-20 (Warren Woodson)
Utah St.	Gotham 12-9-61	Baylor 9-24 (John Bridgers)
Stanford	Rose 1-1-71	Ohio St. 27-17 (Woody Hayes)
Stanford	Rose 1-1-72	Michigan 13-12 (Glenn "Bo" Schembechler)
CHUCK REEDY, 0-1-0 (Appalachian St. '71) Born 5-31-49		
Baylor	Alamo 12-31-94	Washington St. 3-10 (Mike Price)
RED REESE, 1-0-0 (Washington St. '25) Born 3-2-99		
Second Air Force	Sun 1-1-43	Hardin-Simmons 13-7 (Warren Woodson)
BO REIN, 2-0-0 (Ohio St. '68) Born 7-20-45		
North Caro. St.	Peach 12-31-77	Iowa St. 24-14 (Earle Bruce)
North Caro. St.	Tangerine 12-23-78	Pittsburgh 30-17 (Jackie Sherrill)
PAUL ROACH, 0-3-0 (Black Hills St. '52) Born 10-24-27		
Wyoming	Holiday 12-30-87	Iowa 19-20 (Hayden Fry)
Wyoming	Holiday 12-30-88	Oklahoma St. 14-62 (Pat Jones)
Wyoming	Copper 12-31-90	California 15-17 (Bruce Snyder)
ED ROBINSON, 0-1-0 (Brown '96) Born 10-15-73		
Brown	Rose 1-1-16	Washington St. 0-14 (Bill "Lone Star" Dietz)
JOHN ROBINSON, 7-1-0 (Oregon '58) Born 7-25-35		
Southern Cal	Rose 1-1-77	Michigan 14-6 (Glenn "Bo" Schembechler)
Southern Cal	Bluebonnet 12-31-77	Texas A&M 47-28 (Emory Bellard)
Southern Cal	Rose 1-1-79	Michigan 17-10 (Glenn "Bo" Schembechler)
Southern Cal	Rose 1-1-80	Ohio St. 17-16 (Earle Bruce)
Southern Cal	Fiesta 1-1-82	Penn St. 10-26 (Joe Paterno)
Southern Cal	Freedom 12-30-93	Utah 28-21 (Ron McBride)
Southern Cal	Cotton 1-2-95	Texas Tech 55-14 (Spike Dykes)
Southern Cal	Rose 1-1-96	Northwestern 41-32 (Gary Barnett)
KNUTE ROCKNE, 1-0-0 (Notre Dame '14) Born 3-4-88		
Notre Dame	Rose 1-1-25	Stanford 27-10 (Glenn "Pop" Warner)
PEPPER RODGERS, 0-2-0 (Georgia Tech '55) Born 10-8-31		
Kansas	Orange 1-1-69	Penn St. 14-15 (Joe Paterno)
Georgia Tech	Peach 12-25-78	Purdue 21-41 (Jim Young)
DARRYL ROGERS, 1-0-0 (Fresno St. '57) Born 5-28-34		
Arizona St.	Fiesta 1-1-83	Oklahoma 32-21 (Barry Switzer)
E. L. "DICK" ROMNEY, 0-1-0 (Utah '17) Born 2-12-95		
Utah St.	Raisin 1-1-47	San Jose St. 0-20 (Bill Hubbard)
TIM ROSE, 0-1-0 (Xavier, Ohio '62) Born 10-14-41		
Miami (Ohio)	California 12-13-86	San Jose St. 7-37 (Claude Gilbert)
BOBBY ROSS, 4-2-0 (Va. Military '59) Born 12-23-36		
Maryland	Aloha 12-25-82	Washington 20-21 (Don James)
Maryland	Fla. Citrus 12-17-83	Tennessee 23-30 (Johnny Majors)
Maryland	Sun 12-22-84	Tennessee 27-26 (Johnny Majors)
Maryland	Cherry 12-21-85	Syracuse 35-18 (Dick MacPherson)
Georgia Tech	Fla. Citrus 1-1-91	Nebraska 45-21 (Tom Osborne)
Georgia Tech	Aloha 12-25-91	Stanford 18-17 (Dennis Green)
DARRELL ROYAL, 8-7-1 (Oklahoma '50) Born 7-6-24		
Texas	Sugar 1-1-58	Mississippi 7-39 (John Vaught)
Texas	Cotton 1-1-60	Syracuse 14-23 (Ben Schwartzwalder)
Texas	Bluebonnet 12-17-60	Alabama 3-3 (Paul "Bear" Bryant)
Texas	Cotton 1-1-62	Mississippi 12-7 (John Vaught)
Texas	Cotton 1-1-63	LSU 0-13 (Charlie McClendon)
Texas	Cotton 1-1-64	Navy 28-6 (Wayne Hardin)
Texas	Orange 1-1-65	Alabama 21-17 (Paul "Bear" Bryant)
Texas	Bluebonnet 12-17-66	Mississippi 19-0 (John Vaught)
Texas	Cotton 1-1-69	Tennessee 36-13 (Doug Dickey)
Texas	Cotton 1-1-70	Notre Dame 21-17 (Ara Parseghian)
Texas	Cotton 1-1-71	Notre Dame 11-24 (Ara Parseghian)
Texas	Cotton 1-1-72	Penn St. 6-30 (Joe Paterno)
Texas	Cotton 1-1-73	Alabama 17-13 (Paul "Bear" Bryant)
Texas	Cotton 1-1-74	Nebraska 3-19 (Tom Osborne)
Texas	Gator 12-30-74	Auburn 3-27 (Ralph "Shug" Jordan)
Texas	Bluebonnet 12-27-75	Colorado 38-21 (Bill Mallory)
NICK SABAN, 0-1-0 (Kent '73) Born 10-31-51		
Michigan St.	Independence 12-29-95	LSU 26-45 (Gerry DiNardo)
HENRY "RED" SANDERS, 0-2-0 (Vanderbilt '27) Born 3-7-05		
UCLA	Rose 1-1-54	Michigan St. 20-28 (Clarence "Biggie" Munn)
UCLA	Rose 1-2-56	Michigan St. 14-17 (Duffy Daugherty)
RALPH SASSE, 0-1-0 (Army '10) Born 7-19-89		
Mississippi St.	Orange 1-1-37	Duquesne 12-13 (John Smith)
GEORGE SAUER, 0-3-0 (Nebraska '34) Born 12-11-10		
Kansas	Orange 1-1-48	Georgia Tech 14-20 (Bobby Dodd)
Baylor	Orange 1-1-52	Georgia Tech 14-17 (Bobby Dodd)
Baylor	Gator 12-31-54	Auburn 13-33 (Ralph "Shug" Jordan)
MACK SAXON, 0-1-0 (Texas) Born 1901		
UTEP	Sun 1-1-37	Hardin-Simmons 6-34 (Frank Kimbrough)
GLENN "BO" SCHEMBECHLER, 5-12-0 (Miami, Ohio '51) Born 4-1-29		
Michigan	Rose 1-1-70	Southern Cal 3-10 (John McKay)
Michigan	Rose 1-1-72	Stanford 12-13 (John Ralston)
Michigan	Orange 1-1-76	Oklahoma 6-14 (Barry Switzer)
Michigan	Rose 1-1-77	Southern Cal 6-14 (John Robinson)
Michigan	Rose 1-2-78	Washington 20-27 (Don James)
Michigan	Rose 1-1-79	Southern Cal 10-17 (John Robinson)
Michigan	Gator 12-28-79	North Caro. 15-17 (Dick Crum)
Michigan	Rose 1-1-81	Washington 23-6 (Don James)
Michigan	Bluebonnet 12-31-81	UCLA 33-14 (Terry Donahue)
Michigan	Rose 1-1-83	UCLA 14-24 (Terry Donahue)
Michigan	Sugar 1-2-84	Auburn 7-9 (Pat Dye)
Michigan	Holiday 12-21-84	Brigham Young 17-24 (LaVell Edwards)
Michigan	Fiesta 1-1-86	Nebraska 27-23 (Tom Osborne)
Michigan	Rose 1-1-87	Arizona St. 15-22 (John Cooper)
Michigan	Hall of Fame 1-2-88	Alabama 28-24 (Bill Curry)
Michigan	Rose 1-2-89	Southern Cal 22-14 (Larry Smith)
Michigan	Rose 1-1-90	Southern Cal 10-17 (Larry Smith)
MERLE SCHLOSSER, 0-1-0 (Illinois '50) Born 10-14-27		
Western Mich.	Aviation 12-9-61	New Mexico 12-28 (Bill Weeks)
HOWARD SCHNELLENBERGER, 4-0-0 (Kentucky '56) Born 3-16-34		
Miami (Fla.)	Peach 1-2-81	Virginia Tech 20-10 (Bill Dooley)
Miami (Fla.)	Orange 1-2-84	Nebraska 31-30 (Tom Osborne)
Louisville	Fiesta 1-1-91	Alabama 34-7 (Gene Stallings)
Louisville	Liberty 12-28-93	Michigan St. 18-7 (George Perles)
PAUL SCHUDEL, 0-2-0 (Miami, Ohio '66) Born 7-2-44		
Ball St.	California 12-9-89	Fresno St. 6-27 (Jim Sweeney)
Ball St.	Las Vegas 12-17-93	Utah St. 33-42 (Charlie Weatherbie)
BILL SCHUTTE, 0-1-0 (Idaho '33) Born 5-7-10		
San Diego St.	Harbor 1-1-48	Hardin-Simmons 0-53 (Warren Woodson)
BEN SCHWARTZWALDER, 2-5-0 (West Va. '35) Born 6-2-09		
Syracuse	Orange 1-1-53	Alabama 6-61 (Harold "Red" Drew)
Syracuse	Cotton 1-1-57	Texas Christian 27-28 (Abe Martin)
Syracuse	Orange 1-1-59	Oklahoma 6-21 (Bud Wilkinson)
Syracuse	Cotton 1-1-60	Texas 23-14 (Darrell Royal)
Syracuse	Liberty 12-16-61	Miami (Fla.) 15-14 (Andy Gustafson)
Syracuse	Sugar 1-1-65	LSU 10-13 (Charlie McClendon)
Syracuse	Gator 12-31-66	Tennessee 12-18 (Doug Dickey)
BRAD SCOTT, 1-0-0 (Mo.-Rolla '76) Born 9-30-54		
South Caro.	Carquest 1-2-95	West Va. 24-21 (Don Nehlen)
CLARK SHAUGHNESSY, 1-0-0 (Minnesota '14) Born 3-6-92		
Stanford	Rose 1-1-41	Nebraska 21-13 (Lawrence McC. "Biff" Jones)
LAWRENCE "BUCK" SHAW, 2-0-0 (Notre Dame '22) Born 3-28-99		
Santa Clara	Sugar 1-1-37	LSU 21-14 (Bernie Moore)
Santa Clara	Sugar 1-1-38	LSU 6-0 (Bernie Moore)
TERRY SHEA, 1-0-0 (Oregon '68) Born 6-12-46		
San Jose St.	California 12-8-90	Central Mich. 48-24 (Herb Deromedi)
JOE SHEEKETSKI, 1-1-0 (Notre Dame '33) Born 4-15-09		
Nevada	Salad 1-1-48	North Texas 13-6 (Odus Mitchell)
Nevada	Harbor 1-1-49	Villanova 7-27 (Jordan Olivar)
DICK SHERIDAN, 2-4-0 (South Caro. '64) Born 8-9-41		
North Caro. St.	Peach 12-31-86	Virginia Tech 24-25 (Bill Dooley)
North Caro. St.	Peach 12-31-88	Iowa 28-23 (Hayden Fry)
North Caro. St.	Copper 12-31-89	Arizona 10-17 (Dick Tomey)
North Caro. St.	All-American 12-28-90	Southern Miss. 31-27 (Jeff Bower)
North Caro. St.	Peach 1-1-92	East Caro. 34-37 (Bill Lewis)
North Caro. St.	Gator 12-31-92	Florida 10-27 (Steve Spurrier)
EUGENE "BO" SHERMAN, 1-0-0 (Henderson St. '30) Born 7-5-08		
Geo. Washington	Sun 1-1-57	UTEP 13-0 (Mike Brumbelow)
JACKIE SHERRILL, 6-5-0 (Alabama '66) Born 11-28-43		
Pittsburgh	Gator 12-30-77	Clemson 34-3 (Charley Pell)
Pittsburgh	Tangerine 12-23-78	North Caro. St. 17-30 (Bo Rein)
Pittsburgh	Fiesta 12-25-79	Arizona 16-10 (Tony Mason)
Pittsburgh	Gator 12-29-80	South Caro. 37-9 (Jim Carlen)
Pittsburgh	Sugar 1-1-82	Georgia 24-20 (Vince Dooley)
Texas A&M	Cotton 1-1-86	Auburn 36-16 (Pat Dye)
Texas A&M	Cotton 1-1-87	Ohio St. 12-28 (Earle Bruce)
Texas A&M	Cotton 1-1-88	Notre Dame 35-10 (Lou Holtz)
Mississippi St.	Liberty 12-29-91	Air Force 15-38 (Fisher DeBerry)
Mississippi St.	Peach 1-2-93	North Caro. 17-21 (Mack Brown)
Mississippi St.	Peach 1-1-95	North Caro. St. 24-28 (Mike O'Cain)
TED SHIPKEY, 0-1-0 (Stanford '27) Born 9-28-04		
New Mexico	Sun 1-2-39	Utah 0-28 (Ike Armstrong)
LARRY SIEMERING, 1-0-0 (San Francisco '35) Born 11-24-10		
Pacific (Cal.)	Raisin 1-1-48	Wichita St. 26-14 (Ralph Graham)
CHAUNCEY SIMPSON, 0-1-0 (Missouri '25) Born 12-21-02		
Missouri	Cotton 1-1-46	Texas 27-40 (Dana Bible)

Coach/School	Bowl/Date	Opponent/Score (Coach)
DAN SIMRELL, 0-1-0 (Toledo '65) Born 4-9-43		
Toledo	California 12-15-84	UNLV 13-30 (Harvey Hyde)
STEVE SLOAN, 0-2-1 (Alabama '66) Born 8-19-44		
Vanderbilt	Peach 12-28-74	Texas Tech 6-6 (Jim Carlen)
Texas Tech	Bluebonnet 12-31-76	Nebraska 24-27 (Tom Osborne)
Texas Tech	Tangerine 12-23-77	Florida St. 17-40 (Bobby Bowden)
R. C. SLOCUM, 2-4-0 (McNeese St. '67) Born 11-7-44		
Texas A&M	John Hancock 12-30-89	Pittsburgh 28-31 (Paul Hackett)
Texas A&M	Holiday 12-29-90	Brigham Young 65-14 (LaVell Edwards)
Texas A&M	Cotton 1-1-92	Florida St. 2-10 (Bobby Bowden)
Texas A&M	Cotton 1-1-93	Notre Dame 3-28 (Lou Holtz)
Texas A&M	Cotton 1-1-94	Notre Dame 21-24 (Lou Holtz)
Texas A&M	Alamo 12-28-95	Michigan 22-20 (Lloyd Carr)
ANDY SMITH, 1-0-1 (Pennsylvania '06) Born 9-10-83		
California	Rose 1-1-21	Ohio St. 28-0 (John Wilce)
California	Rose 1-2-22	Wash. & Jeff. 0-0 (Earle "Greasy" Neale)
HOMER SMITH, 0-1-0 (Princeton '54) Born 10-9-31		
Davidson	Tangerine 12-26-69	Toledo 33-56 (Frank Lauterbur)
JOHN "LITTLE CLIPPER" SMITH, 1-0-0 (Notre Dame '29) Born 12-12-04		
Duquesne	Orange 1-1-37	Mississippi St. 13-12 (Ralph Sasse)
LARRY SMITH, 2-5-1 (Bowling Green '62) Born 9-12-39		
Tulane	Liberty 12-22-79	Penn St. 6-9 (Joe Paterno)
Arizona	Sun 12-28-85	Georgia 13-13 (Vince Dooley)
Arizona	Aloha 12-27-86	North Caro. 30-21 (Dick Crum)
Southern Cal	Rose 1-1-88	Michigan St. 17-20 (George Perles)
Southern Cal	Rose 1-2-89	Michigan 14-22 (Glenn "Bo" Schembechler)
Southern Cal	Rose 1-1-90	Michigan 17-10 (Glenn "Bo" Schembechler)
Southern Cal	John Hancock 12-31-90	Michigan St. 16-17 (George Perles)
Southern Cal	Freedom 12-29-92	Fresno St. 7-24 (Jim Sweeney)
MAURICE "CLIPPER" SMITH, 0-0-1 (Notre Dame '21) Born 10-15-98		
Villanova	Bacardi, Cuba 1-1-37	Auburn 7-7 (Jack Meagher)
CARL SNAVELY, 0-3-0 (Lebanon Valley '15) Born 7-30-94		
North Caro.	Sugar 1-1-47	Georgia 10-20 (Wally Butts)
North Caro.	Sugar 1-1-49	Oklahoma 6-14 (Bud Wilkinson)
North Caro.	Cotton 1-2-50	Rice 13-27 (Jess Neely)
BILL SNYDER, 2-1-0 (William Jewell '63) Born 10-7-41		
Kansas St.	Copper 12-29-93	Wyoming 52-17 (Joe Tiller)
Kansas St.	Aloha 12-25-94	Boston College 7-12 (Dan Henning)
Kansas St.	Holiday 12-29-95	Colorado St. 54-21 (Sonny Lubick)
BRUCE SNYDER, 2-0-0 (Oregon '62) Born 3-14-40		
California	Copper 12-31-90	Wyoming 17-15 (Paul Roach)
California	Fla. Citrus 1-1-92	Clemson 37-13 (Ken Hatfield)
CLARENCE "DOC" SPEARS, 1-0-0 (Dartmouth '16) Born 7-24-94		
West Va.	San Diego East-West Christmas Classic 12-25-22	Gonzaga 21-13 (Charles "Gus" Dorais)
CLIFF SPEEGLE, 1-0-0 (Oklahoma '41) Born 11-4-17		
Oklahoma St.	Bluegrass 12-13-58	Florida St. 15-6 (Tom Nugent)
STEVE SPURRIER, 2-4-0 (Florida '67) Born 4-20-45		
Duke	All-American 12-28-89	Texas Tech 21-49 (Spike Dykes)
Florida	Sugar 1-1-92	Notre Dame 28-39 (Lou Holtz)
Florida	Gator 12-31-92	North Caro. St. 27-10 (Dick Sheridan)
Florida	Sugar 1-1-94	West Va. 41-7 (Don Nehlen)
Florida	Sugar 1-2-95	Florida St. 17-23 (Bobby Bowden)
Florida	Fiesta 1-2-96	Nebraska 24-62 (Tom Osborne)
GENE STALLINGS, 5-1-0 (Texas A&M '57) Born 3-2-35		
Texas A&M	Cotton 1-1-68	Alabama 20-16 (Paul "Bear" Bryant)
Alabama	Fiesta 1-1-91	Louisville 7-34 (Howard Schnellenberger)
Alabama	Blockbuster 12-28-91	Colorado 30-25 (Bill McCartney)
Alabama	Sugar 1-1-93	Miami (Fla.) 34-13 (Dennis Erickson)
Alabama	Gator 12-31-93	North Caro. 24-10 (Mack Brown)
Alabama	Fla. Citrus 1-2-95	Ohio St. 24-17 (John Cooper)
JIM STANGELAND, 0-0-1 (Arizona St. '48) Born 12-21-21		
Long Beach St.	Pasadena 12-19-70	Louisville 24-24 (Lee Corso)
JIM STANLEY, 2-0-0 (Texas A&M '59) Born 5-22-35		
Oklahoma St.	Fiesta 12-28-74	Brigham Young 16-6 (LaVell Edwards)
Oklahoma St.	Tangerine 12-18-76	Brigham Young 49-12 (LaVell Edwards)
TOM STIDHAM, 0-1-0 (Haskell '27) Born 3-27-04		
Oklahoma	Orange 1-2-39	Tennessee 0-17 (Bob Neyland)
LON STINER, 1-0-0 (Nebraska '27) Born 6-20-03		
Oregon St.	Rose 1-1-42	Duke 20-16 (Wallace Wade)
HARRY STITELER, 1-0-0 (Texas A&M '31) Born 9-17-09		
Texas A&M	Presidential Cup 12-9-50	Georgia 40-20 (Wally Butts)
CHUCK STOBART, 1-0-0 (Ohio '59) Born 10-27-34		
Toledo	California 12-19-81	San Jose St. 27-25 (Jack Elway)

Coach/School	Bowl/Date	Opponent/Score (Coach)
CAL STOLL, 0-1-0 (Minnesota '50) Born 12-12-23		
Minnesota	Hall of Fame 12-22-77	Maryland 7-17 (Jerry Claiborne)
DENNY STOLZ, 0-3-0 (Alma '55) Born 9-12-34		
Bowling Green	California 12-18-82	Fresno St. 28-29 (Jim Sweeney)
Bowling Green	California 12-14-85	Fresno St. 7-51 (Jim Sweeney)
San Diego St.	Holiday 12-30-86	Iowa 38-39 (Hayden Fry)
JERRY STOVALL, 0-1-0 (LSU '63) Born 4-30-41		
LSU	Orange 1-1-83	Nebraska 20-21 (Tom Osborne)
BOB STULL, 0-1-0 (Kansas St. '68) Born 11-21-45		
UTEP	Independence 12-23-88	Southern Miss. 18-38 (Curley Hallman)
PAT SULLIVAN, 0-1-0 (Auburn '72) Born 1-18-50		
Texas Christian	Independence 12-28-94	Virginia 10-20 (George Welsh)
JOCK SUTHERLAND, 1-3-0 (Pittsburgh '18) Born 3-21-89		
Pittsburgh	Rose 1-1-28	Stanford 6-7 (Glenn "Pop" Warner)
Pittsburgh	Rose 1-1-30	Southern Cal 14-47 (Howard Jones)
Pittsburgh	Rose 1-2-33	Southern Cal 0-35 (Howard Jones)
Pittsburgh	Rose 1-1-37	Washington 21-0 (Jimmy Phelan)
JIM SWEENEY, 5-2-0 (Portland '51) Born 9-1-29		
Fresno St.	California 12-18-82	Bowling Green 29-28 (Denny Stolz)
Fresno St.	California 12-14-85	Bowling Green 51-7 (Denny Stolz)
Fresno St.	California 12-10-88	Western Mich. 35-30 (Al Molde)
Fresno St.	California 12-9-89	Ball St. 27-8 (Paul Schudel)
Fresno St.	California 12-13-91	Bowling Green 21-28 (Gary Blackney)
Fresno St.	Freedom 12-29-92	Southern Cal 24-7 (Larry Smith)
Fresno St.	Aloha 12-25-93	Colorado 30-41 (Bill McCartney)
BARRY SWITZER, 8-5-0 (Arkansas '60) Born 10-5-37		
Oklahoma	Orange 1-1-76	Michigan 14-6 (Glenn "Bo" Schembechler)
Oklahoma	Fiesta 12-25-76	Wyoming 41-7 (Fred Akers)
Oklahoma	Orange 1-2-78	Arkansas 6-31 (Lou Holtz)
Oklahoma	Orange 1-1-79	Nebraska 31-24 (Tom Osborne)
Oklahoma	Orange 1-1-80	Florida St. 24-7 (Bobby Bowden)
Oklahoma	Orange 1-1-81	Florida St. 18-17 (Bobby Bowden)
Oklahoma	Sun 12-26-81	Houston 40-14 (Bill Yeoman)
Oklahoma	Fiesta 1-1-83	Arizona St. 21-32 (Darryl Rogers)
Oklahoma	Orange 1-1-85	Washington 17-28 (Don James)
Oklahoma	Orange 1-1-86	Penn St. 25-10 (Joe Paterno)
Oklahoma	Orange 1-1-87	Arkansas 42-8 (Ken Hatfield)
Oklahoma	Orange 1-1-88	Miami (Fla.) 14-20 (Jimmy Johnson)
Oklahoma	Fla. Citrus 1-2-89	Clemson 6-13 (Danny Ford)
CHARLIE TATE, 1-1-0 (Florida '42) Born 2-20-21		
Miami (Fla.)	Liberty 12-10-66	Virginia Tech 14-7 (Jerry Claiborne)
Miami (Fla.)	Bluebonnet 12-23-67	Colorado 21-31 (Eddie Crowder)
JIM TATUM, 3-2-1 (North Caro. '35) Born 7-22-13		
Oklahoma	Gator 1-1-47	North Caro. St. 34-13 (Beattie Feathers)
Maryland	Gator 1-1-48	Georgia 20-20 (Wally Butts)
Maryland	Gator 1-2-50	Missouri 20-7 (Don Faurot)
Maryland	Sugar 1-1-52	Tennessee 28-13 (Bob Neyland)
Maryland	Orange 1-1-54	Oklahoma 0-7 (Bud Wilkinson)
Maryland	Orange 1-2-56	Oklahoma 6-20 (Bud Wilkinson)
CHUCK TAYLOR, 0-1-0 (Stanford '43) Born 1-24-20		
Stanford	Rose 1-1-52	Illinois 7-40 (Ray Eliot)
GRANT TEAFF, 4-4-0 (McMurry '56) Born 11-12-33		
Baylor	Cotton 1-1-75	Penn St. 20-41 (Joe Paterno)
Baylor	Peach 12-31-79	Clemson 24-18 (Danny Ford)
Baylor	Cotton 1-1-81	Alabama 2-30 (Paul "Bear" Bryant)
Baylor	Bluebonnet 12-31-83	Oklahoma St. 14-24 (Jimmy Johnson)
Baylor	Liberty 12-27-85	LSU 21-7 (Bill Arnsparger)
Baylor	Bluebonnet 12-31-86	Colorado 21-9 (Bill McCartney)
Baylor	Copper 12-31-91	Indiana 0-24 (Bill Mallory)
Baylor	John Hancock 12-31-92	Arizona 20-15 (Dick Tomey)
EDDIE TEAGUE, 1-0-0 (North Caro. '44) Born 12-14-21		
Citadel	Tangerine 12-30-60	Tennessee Tech 27-0 (Wilburn Tucker)
LOU TEPPER, 1-2-0 (Rutgers '67) Born 7-21-45		
Illinois	John Hancock 12-31-91	UCLA 3-6 (Terry Donahue)
Illinois	Holiday 12-30-92	Hawaii 17-27 (Bob Wagner)
Illinois	Liberty 12-31-94	East Caro. 30-0 (Steve Logan)
ROBERT THEDER, 0-1-0 (Western Mich. '63) Born 9-22-39		
California	Garden State 12-15-79	Temple 17-28 (Wayne Hardin)
FRANK THOMAS, 4-2-0 (Notre Dame '23) Born 11-14-98		
Alabama	Rose 1-1-35	Stanford 29-13 (Claude "Tiny" Thornhill)
Alabama	Rose 1-1-38	California 0-13 (Leonard "Stub" Allison)
Alabama	Cotton 1-1-42	Texas A&M 29-21 (Homer Norton)
Alabama	Orange 1-1-43	Boston College 37-21 (Denny Myers)
Alabama	Sugar 1-1-45	Duke 26-29 (Eddie Cameron)
Alabama	Rose 1-1-46	Southern Cal 34-14 (Jeff Cravath)
FRED THOMSEN, 0-0-1 (Nebraska '25) Born 4-25-97		
Arkansas	Dixie Classic 1-1-34	Centenary (La.) 7-7 (Homer Norton)
CLAUDE "TINY" THORNHILL, 1-2-0 (Pittsburgh '17) Born 4-14-93		
Stanford	Rose 1-1-34	Columbia 0-7 (Lou Little)

BOWL/ALL-STAR RECORDS

Coach/School **Bowl/Date** **Opponent/Score (Coach)**
Stanford .... Rose 1-1-35 Alabama 13-29 (Frank Thomas)
Stanford .... Rose 1-1-36 Southern Methodist 7-0 (Matty Bell)

JOE TILLER, 0-1-0 (Montana St. '64) Born 12-7-42
Wyoming .... Copper 12-29-93 Kansas St. 17-52 (Bill Snyder)

GAYNELL TINSLEY, 0-1-0 (LSU '37) Born 2-1-15
LSU .... Sugar 1-2-50 Oklahoma 0-35 (Bud Wilkinson)

TED TOLLNER, 1-2-0 (Cal Poly SLO '62) Born 5-29-40
Southern Cal .... Rose 1-1-85 Ohio St. 20-17 (Earle Bruce)
Southern Cal .... Aloha 12-28-85 Alabama 3-24 (Ray Perkins)
Southern Cal .... Fla. Citrus 1-1-87 Auburn 7-16 (Pat Dye)

DICK TOMEY, 2-3-0 (DePauw '61) Born 6-20-38
Arizona .... Copper 12-30-89 North Caro. St. 17-10 (Dick Sheridan)
Arizona .... Aloha 12-28-90 Syracuse 0-28 (Dick MacPherson)
Arizona .... John Hancock 12-31-92 Baylor 15-20 (Grant Teaff)
Arizona .... Fiesta 1-1-94 Miami (Fla.) 29-0 (Dennis Erickson)
Arizona .... Freedom 12-27-94 Utah 13-16 (Ron McBride)

JIM TRIMBLE, 0-1-0 (Indiana '42) Born 5-29-18
Wichita St. .... Camellia 12-30-48 Hardin-Simmons 12-49 (Warren Woodson)

FRANK TRITICO, 0-0-1 (Southwestern La. '34) Born 3-25-09
Randolph Field .... Cotton 1-1-44 Texas 7-7 (Dana Bible)

WILBURN TUCKER, 0-1-0 (Tennessee Tech '43) Born 8-11-20
Tennessee Tech .... Tangerine 12-30-60 Citadel 0-27 (Eddie Teague)

BOB TYLER, 1-0-0 (Mississippi '58) Born 7-4-32
Mississippi St. .... Sun 12-28-74 North Caro. 26-24 (Bill Dooley)

THAD "PIE" VANN, 0-2-0 (Mississippi '28) Born 9-22-07
Southern Miss. .... Sun 1-1-53 Pacific (Cal.) 7-26 (Ernie Jorge)
Southern Miss. .... Sun 1-1-54 UTEP 14-37 (Mike Brumbelow)

JOHN VAUGHT, 10-8-0 (Texas Christian '33) Born 5-6-08
Mississippi .... Delta 1-1-48 Texas Christian 13-9 (Leo "Dutch" Meyer)
Mississippi .... Sugar 1-1-53 Georgia Tech 7-24 (Bobby Dodd)
Mississippi .... Sugar 1-1-55 Navy 0-21 (Eddie Erdelatz)
Mississippi .... Cotton 1-2-56 Texas Christian 14-13 (Abe Martin)
Mississippi .... Sugar 1-1-58 Texas 39-7 (Darrell Royal)
Mississippi .... Gator 12-27-58 Florida 7-3 (Bob Woodruff)
Mississippi .... Sugar 1-1-60 LSU 21-0 (Paul Dietzel)
Mississippi .... Sugar 1-2-61 Rice 14-6 (Jess Neely)
Mississippi .... Cotton 1-1-62 Texas 7-12 (Darrell Royal)
Mississippi .... Sugar 1-1-63 Arkansas 17-13 (Frank Broyles)
Mississippi .... Sugar 1-1-64 Alabama 7-12 (Paul "Bear" Bryant)
Mississippi .... Bluebonnet 12-19-64 Tulsa 7-14 (Glenn Dobbs)
Mississippi .... Liberty 12-18-65 Auburn 13-7 (Ralph "Shug" Jordan)
Mississippi .... Bluebonnet 12-17-66 Texas 0-19 (Darrell Royal)
Mississippi .... Sun 12-30-67 UTEP 7-14 (Bobby Dobbs)
Mississippi .... Liberty 12-14-68 Virginia Tech 34-17 (Jerry Claiborne)
Mississippi .... Sugar 1-1-70 Arkansas 27-22 (Frank Broyles)
Mississippi .... Gator 1-2-71 Auburn 28-35 (Ralph "Shug" Jordan)

DICK VERMEIL, 1-0-0 (San Jose St. '58) Born 10-30-36
UCLA .... Rose 1-1-76 Ohio St. 23-10 (Woody Hayes)

BOB VOIGTS, 1-0-0 (Northwestern '39) Born 3-29-16
Northwestern .... Rose 1-1-49 California 20-14 (Lynn "Pappy" Waldorf)

JIM WACKER, 0-1-0 (Valparaiso '60) Born 4-28-37
Texas Christian .... Bluebonnet 12-31-84 West Va. 14-31 (Don Nehlen)

WALLACE WADE, 2-2-1 (Brown '17) Born 6-15-92
Alabama .... Rose 1-1-26 Washington 20-19 (Enoch Bagshaw)
Alabama .... Rose 1-1-27 Stanford 7-7 (Glenn "Pop" Warner)
Alabama .... Rose 1-1-31 Washington St. 24-0 (Orin "Babe" Hollingbery)
Duke .... Rose 1-2-39 Southern Cal 3-7 (Howard Jones)
Duke .... Rose 1-1-42 Oregon St. 16-20 (Lon Stiner)

BOB WAGNER, 1-1-0 (Wittenberg '69) Born 5-16-47
Hawaii .... Aloha 12-25-89 Michigan St. 13-33 (George Perles)
Hawaii .... Holiday 12-30-92 Illinois 27-17 (Lou Tepper)

JIM WALDEN, 0-1-0 (Wyoming '60) Born 4-10-38
Washington St. .... Holiday 12-18-81 Brigham Young 36-38 (LaVell Edwards)

LYNN "PAPPY" WALDORF, 0-3-0 (Syracuse '25) Born 10-3-02
California .... Rose 1-1-49 Northwestern 14-20 (Bob Voigts)
California .... Rose 1-2-50 Ohio St. 14-17 (Wes Fesler)
California .... Rose 1-1-51 Michigan 6-14 (Bennie Oosterbaan)

D. C. "PEAHEAD" WALKER, 1-1-0 (Samford '22) Born 2-17-00
Wake Forest .... Gator 1-1-46 South Caro. 26-14 (Johnnie McMillan)
Wake Forest .... Dixie 1-1-49 Baylor 7-20 (Bob Woodruff)

ED WALKER, 0-1-0 (Stanford '27) Born 3-25-01
Mississippi .... Orange 1-1-36 Catholic 19-20 (Arthur "Dutch" Bergman)

BILL WALSH, 3-0-0 (San Jose St. '54) Born 11-30-31
Stanford .... Sun 12-31-77 LSU 24-14 (Charlie McClendon)

Coach/School **Bowl/Date** **Opponent/Score (Coach)**
Stanford .... Bluebonnet 12-31-78 Georgia 25-22 (Vince Dooley)
Stanford .... Blockbuster 1-1-93 Penn St. 24-3 (Joe Paterno)

DALLAS WARD, 1-0-0 (Oregon St. '27) Born 8-11-06
Colorado .... Orange 1-1-57 Clemson 27-21 (Frank Howard)

MURRAY WARMATH, 1-1-0 (Tennessee '35) Born 12-26-13
Minnesota .... Rose 1-2-61 Washington 7-17 (Jim Owens)
Minnesota .... Rose 1-1-62 UCLA 21-3 (Bill Barnes)

GLENN "POP" WARNER, 1-2-1 (Cornell '95) Born 4-5-71
Stanford .... Rose 1-1-25 Notre Dame 10-27 (Knute Rockne)
Stanford .... Rose 1-1-27 Alabama 7-7 (Wallace Wade)
Stanford .... Rose 1-2-28 Pittsburgh 7-6 (Jock Sutherland)
Temple .... Sugar 1-1-35 Tulane 14-20 (Ted Cox)

CHARLIE WEATHERBIE, 1-0-0 (Oklahoma St. '77) Born 1-17-55
Utah St. .... Las Vegas 12-17-93 Ball St. 42-33 (Paul Schudel)

DeWITT WEAVER, 2-1-0 (Tennessee '37) Born 5-11-12
Texas Tech .... Sun 1-1-52 Pacific (Cal.) 25-14 (Ernie Jorge)
Texas Tech .... Gator 1-1-54 Auburn 35-13 (Ralph "Shug" Jordan)
Texas Tech .... Sun 1-2-56 Wyoming 14-21 (Phil Dickens)

BILL WEEKS, 1-0-0 (Iowa St. '51) Born 10-20-29
New Mexico .... Aviation 12-9-61 Western Mich. 28-12 (Merle Schlosser)

RALPH "PEST" WELCH, 0-1-0 (Purdue '30) Born 8-11-07
Washington .... Rose 1-1-44 Southern Cal 0-29 (Jeff Cravath)

GEORGE WELSH, 5-6-0 (Navy '56) Born 8-26-33
Navy .... Holiday 12-22-78 Brigham Young 23-16 (LaVell Edwards)
Navy .... Garden State 12-14-80 Houston 0-35 (Bill Yeoman)
Navy .... Liberty 12-30-81 Ohio St. 28-31 (Earle Bruce)
Virginia .... Peach 12-31-84 Purdue 27-24 (Leon Burtnett)
Virginia .... All-American 12-22-87 Brigham Young 22-16 (LaVell Edwards)
Virginia .... Fla. Citrus 1-1-90 Illinois 21-31 (John Mackovic)
Virginia .... Sugar 1-1-91 Tennessee 22-23 (Johnny Majors)
Virginia .... Gator 12-29-91 Oklahoma 14-48 (Gary Gibbs)
Virginia .... Carquest 1-1-94 Boston College 13-31 (Tom Coughlin)
Virginia .... Independence 12-28-94 Texas Christian 20-10 (Pat Sullivan)
Virginia .... Peach 12-30-95 Georgia 34-27 (Ray Goff)

TOMMY WEST, 1-1-0 (Tennessee '75) Born 7-31-54
Clemson .... Peach 12-31-93 Kentucky 14-13 (Bill Curry)
Clemson .... Gator 1-1-96 Syracuse 0-41 (Paul Pasqualoni)

MIKE WHITE, 0-3-0 (California '58) Born 1-3-36
Illinois .... Liberty 12-29-82 Alabama 15-21 (Paul "Bear" Bryant)
Illinois .... Rose 1-2-84 UCLA 9-45 (Terry Donahue)
Illinois .... Peach 12-31-85 Army 29-31 (Jim Young)

JOHN WILCE, 0-1-0 (Wisconsin '10) Born 5-12-88
Ohio St. .... Rose 1-1-21 California 0-28 (Andy Smith)

BUD WILKINSON, 6-2-0 (Minnesota '37) Born 4-12-16
Oklahoma .... Sugar 1-1-49 North Caro. 14-6 (Carl Snavely)
Oklahoma .... Sugar 1-2-50 LSU 35-0 (Gaynell Tinsley)
Oklahoma .... Sugar 1-1-51 Kentucky 7-13 (Paul "Bear" Bryant)
Oklahoma .... Orange 1-1-54 Maryland 7-0 (Jim Tatum)
Oklahoma .... Orange 1-2-56 Maryland 20-6 (Jim Tatum)
Oklahoma .... Orange 1-1-58 Duke 48-21 (Bill Murray)
Oklahoma .... Orange 1-1-59 Syracuse 21-6 (Ben Schwartzwalder)
Oklahoma .... Orange 1-1-63 Alabama 0-17 (Paul "Bear" Bryant)

IVY WILLIAMSON, 0-1-0 (Michigan '33) Born 2-4-11
Wisconsin .... Rose 1-1-53 Southern Cal 0-7 (Jess Hill)

TYRONE WILLINGHAM, 0-1-0 (Michigan St. '77) Born 12-30-53
Stanford .... Liberty 12-30-95 East Caro. 13-19 (Steve Logan)

TOM WILSON, 2-0-0 (Texas Tech '66) Born 2-24-44
Texas A&M .... Hall of Fame 12-20-78 Iowa St. 28-12 (Earle Bruce)
Texas A&M .... Independence 12-12-81 Oklahoma St. 33-16 (Jimmy Johnson)

SAM WINNINGHAM, 0-1-0 (Colorado '50) Born 10-11-26
Cal St. Northridge .... Pasadena 12-2-67 West Tex. A&M 13-35 (Joe Kerbel)

BOB WOODRUFF, 2-1-0 (Tennessee '39) Born 3-14-16
Baylor .... Dixie 1-1-49 Wake Forest 20-7 (D. C. "Peahead" Walker)
Florida .... Gator 1-1-53 Tulsa 14-13 (J. O. "Buddy" Brothers)
Florida .... Gator 12-27-58 Mississippi 3-7 (John Vaught)

WARREN WOODSON, 6-1-0 (Baylor '24) Born 2-24-03
Hardin-Simmons .... Sun 1-1-43 Second Air Force 7-13 (Red Reese)
Hardin-Simmons .... Alamo 1-4-47 Denver 20-6 (Clyde "Cac" Hubbard)
Hardin-Simmons .... Harbor 1-1-48 San Diego St. 53-0 (Bill Schutte)
Hardin-Simmons .... Shrine 12-18-48 Ouachita Baptist 40-12 (Wesley Bradshaw)
Hardin-Simmons .... Camellia 12-30-48 Wichita St. 49-12 (Jim Trimble)
New Mexico St. .... Sun 12-31-59 North Texas 28-8 (Odus Mitchell)
New Mexico St. .... Sun 12-31-60 Utah St. 20-13 (John Ralston)

BOWDEN WYATT, 2-2-0 (Tennessee '39) Born 11-3-17
Wyoming .... Gator 1-1-51 Wash. & Lee 20-7 (George Barclay)
Arkansas .... Cotton 1-1-55 Georgia Tech 6-14 (Bobby Dodd)
Tennessee .... Sugar 1-1-57 Baylor 7-13 (Sam Boyd)
Tennessee .... Gator 12-26-57 Texas A&M 3-0 (Paul "Bear" Bryant)

Coach/School	Bowl/Date	Opponent/Score (Coach)
BILL YEOMAN, 6-4-1 (Army '50) Born 12-26-27		
Houston	Tangerine 12-22-62	Miami (Ohio) 49-21 (John Pont)
Houston	Bluebonnet 12-31-69	Auburn 36-7 (Ralph "Shug" Jordan)
Houston	Bluebonnet 12-31-71	Colorado 17-29 (Eddie Crowder)
Houston	Bluebonnet 12-29-73	Tulane 47-7 (Bennie Ellender)
Houston	Bluebonnet 12-23-74	North Caro. St. 31-31 (Lou Holtz)
Houston	Cotton 1-1-77	Maryland 30-21 (Jerry Claiborne)
Houston	Cotton 1-1-79	Notre Dame 34-35 (Dan Devine)
Houston	Cotton 1-1-80	Nebraska 17-14 (Tom Osborne)
Houston	Garden State 12-14-80	Navy 35-0 (George Welsh)
Houston	Sun 12-26-81	Oklahoma 14-40 (Barry Switzer)
Houston	Cotton 1-1-85	Boston College 28-45 (Jack Bicknell)
FIELDING "HURRY UP" YOST, 1-0-0 (Lafayette '97) Born 4-30-71		
Michigan	Rose 1-1-02	Stanford 49-0 (Charlie Fickert)
JIM YOUNG, 5-1-0 (Bowling Green '57) Born 4-21-35		
Purdue	Peach 12-25-78	Georgia Tech 41-21 (Pepper Rodgers)
Purdue	Bluebonnet 12-31-79	Tennessee 27-22 (Johnny Majors)
Purdue	Liberty 12-27-80	Missouri 28-25 (Warren Powers)
Army	Cherry 12-22-84	Michigan St. 10-6 (George Perles)
Army	Peach 12-31-85	Illinois 31-29 (Mike White)
Army	Sun 12-24-88	Alabama 28-29 (Bill Curry)

Coaches Who Have Taken More Than One Team to a Bowl Game

FOUR TEAMS (3)

Earle Bruce: Tampa, Iowa St., Ohio St. & Colorado St.
*Lou Holtz: William & Mary, North Caro. St., Arkansas & Notre Dame
*Bill Mallory: Miami (Ohio), Colorado, Northern Ill. & Indiana

THREE TEAMS (11)

Bear Bryant: Kentucky, Texas A&M & Alabama
Jim Carlen: West Va., Texas Tech & South Caro.
Jerry Claiborne: Virginia Tech, Maryland & Kentucky
*Bill Curry: Georgia Tech, Alabama & Kentucky
Bill Dooley: North Caro., Virginia Tech & Wake Forest

*Ken Hatfield: Air Force, Arkansas & Clemson
*John Mackovic: Wake Forest, Illinois & Texas
*Johnny Majors: Iowa St., Pittsburgh & Tennessee
*Jackie Sherrill: Pittsburgh, Texas A&M & Mississippi St.
*Larry Smith: Tulane, Arizona & Southern Cal

Bowden Wyatt: Wyoming, Arkansas & Tennessee

TWO TEAMS (54)

Fred Akers: Wyoming & Texas
John Barnhill: Tennessee & Arkansas
Emory Bellard: Texas A&M & Mississippi St.
Hugo Bezdek: Oregon & Penn St.
Dana X. Bible: Texas A&M & Texas

*Bobby Bowden: West Va. & Florida St.
*Mack Brown: Tulane & North Caro.
Len Casanova: Santa Clara & Oregon
Bobby Collins: Southern Miss. & Southern Methodist
*John Cooper: Arizona St. & Ohio St.

Lee Corso: Louisville & Indiana
Dick Crum: Miami (Ohio) & North Caro.
Bob Devaney: Wyoming & Nebraska
Dan Devine: Missouri & Notre Dame
Doug Dickey: Tennessee & Florida

Paul Dietzel: LSU & South Caro.
Pat Dye: East Caro. & Auburn
Pete Elliott: California & Illinois
Jack Elway: San Jose St. & Stanford
Dennis Erickson: Washington St. & Miami (Fla.)

Bob Folwell: Pennsylvania & Navy
*Danny Ford: Clemson & Arkansas
*Hayden Fry: Southern Methodist & Iowa
Vince Gibson: Louisville & Tulane
Sid Gillman: Miami (Ohio) & Cincinnati

Wayne Hardin: Navy & Temple
Woody Hayes: Miami (Ohio) & Ohio St.
Bob Higgins: West Va. Wesleyan & Penn St.
Don James: Kent & Washington
Jimmy Johnson: Oklahoma St. & Miami (Fla.)

Frank Kimbrough: Hardin-Simmons & West Tex. A&M
Jimmy Kitts: Rice & Virginia Tech
Jess Neely: Clemson & Rice
Homer Norton: Centenary (La.) & Texas A&M
Charley Pell: Clemson & Florida

Jimmy Phelan: Washington & St. Mary's (Cal.)
John Pont: Miami (Ohio) & Indiana

Tommy Prothro: Oregon St. & UCLA
*John Ralston: Utah St. & Stanford
Pepper Rodgers: Kansas & Georgia Tech

Bobby Ross: Maryland & Georgia Tech
George Sauer: Kansas & Baylor
Howard Schnellenberger: Miami (Fla.) & Louisville
Steve Sloan: Vanderbilt & Texas Tech
*Steve Spurrier: Duke & Florida

*Gene Stallings: Texas A&M & Alabama
Denny Stolz: Bowling Green & San Diego St.
Jim Tatum: Oklahoma & Maryland
Wallace Wade: Alabama & Duke
Pop Warner: Stanford & Temple

*George Welsh: Navy & Virginia
Bob Woodruff: Baylor & Florida
Warren Woodson: Hardin-Simmons & New Mexico St.
Jim Young: Purdue & Army

Active coach.

Coaches With the Most Years Taking One College to a Bowl Game

Coach, Team Taken	Bowls	Consecutive Years
*Joe Paterno, Penn St.	26	13 (1971-83)
Bear Bryant, Alabama	24	24 (1959-82)
*Tom Osborne, Nebraska	23	23 (1973-95)
Vince Dooley, Georgia	20	9 (1980-88)
*LaVell Edwards, Brigham Young	19	17 (1978-94)
John Vaught, Mississippi	18	14 (1957-70)
Bo Schembechler, Michigan	17	15 (1975-89)
*Bobby Bowden, Florida St.	16	14 (1982-95)
Darrell Royal, Texas	16	8 (1968-75)
Don James, Washington	14	9 (1979-87)
Bobby Dodd, Georgia Tech	13	6 (1951-56)
Terry Donahue, UCLA	13	8 (1981-88)
Charlie McClendon, LSU	13	4 (1970-73)
Barry Switzer, Oklahoma	13	8 (1975-82)
*Hayden Fry, Iowa	12	8 (1981-88)
Ralph Jordan, Auburn	12	7 (1968-74)
Woody Hayes, Ohio St.	11	7 (1972-78)
*Johnny Majors, Tennessee	11	7 (1981-87)
Bill Yeoman, Houston	11	4 (1978-81)
Frank Broyles, Arkansas	10	4 (1959-62)
Fred Akers, Texas	9	9 (1977-85)
Bob Devaney, Nebraska	9	5 (1962-66)
Pat Dye, Auburn	9	9 (1982-90)
*Lou Holtz, Notre Dame	9	9 (1987-95)
John McKay, Southern Cal	9	4 (1966-69; 1972-75)
Earle Bruce, Ohio St.	8	8 (1979-86)
Wally Butts, Georgia	8	4 (1945-48)
*Fisher DeBerry, Air Force	8	4 (1989-92)
*Danny Ford, Clemson	8	5 (1985-89)
*Don Nehlen, West Va.	8	4 (1981-84)
*John Robinson, Southern Cal	8	4 (1976-79)
Grant Teaff, Baylor	8	2 (1979-80; 1985-86; 1991-92)
*George Welsh, Virginia	8	3 (1989-91; 1993-95)
Bud Wilkinson, Oklahoma	8	3 (1948-50)

Active coach.

Conference Bowl Records

1995-96 Bowl Records by Conference

Conference (Teams in Bowls)	W-L-T	Pct.
Big Eight Conference (4)	4-0-0	1.000
Big East Conference (2)	2-0-0	1.000
Mid-American Conference (1)	1-0-0	1.000
Atlantic Coast Conference (4)	3-1-0	.750
Southwest Conference (3)	2-1-0	.667
Independents (2)	1-1-0	.500
Big Ten Conference (6)	2-4-0	.333
Southeastern Conference (6)	2-4-0	.333
Pacific-10 Conference (5)	1-4-0	.200
Big West Conference (1)	0-1-0	.000
Western Athletic Conference (2)	0-2-0	.000

All-Time Conference Bowl Records

(Through 1995-96 Bowls, Using Present Conference Alignments)

ATLANTIC COAST CONFERENCE

School	Bowls	W-L-T	Pct.	Last Appearance
Clemson	20	12-8-0	.600	1996 Gator
Duke	8	3-5-0	.375	1995 Hall of Fame
Florida St.	24	15-7-2	.667	1996 Orange
Georgia Tech	25	17-8-0	.680	1991 Aloha
Maryland	17	6-9-2	.412	1990 Independence
North Caro.	20	8-12-0	.400	1995 Carquest (Dec. 30)
North Caro. St.	17	8-8-1	.500	1995 Peach (Jan. 1)
Virginia	8	4-4-0	.500	1995 Peach (Dec. 30)
Wake Forest	4	2-2-0	.500	1992 Independence
Current Members	**143**	**75-63-5**	**.542**	

BIG EAST CONFERENCE

School	Bowls	W-L-T	Pct.	Last Appearance
Boston College	10	5-5-0	.500	1994 Aloha
Miami (Fla.)	21	10-11-0	.476	1995 Orange
Pittsburgh	18	8-10-0	.444	1989 John Hancock
Rutgers	1	0-1-0	.000	1978 Garden State
Syracuse	16	9-6-1	.594	1996 Gator
Temple	2	1-1-0	.500	1979 Garden State
Virginia Tech	9	3-6-0	.333	1995 Sugar (Dec. 31)
West Va.	17	8-9-0	.471	1995 Carquest (Jan. 2)
Current Members	**94**	**44-49-1**	**.473**	

BIG TEN CONFERENCE

School	Bowls	W-L-T	Pct.	Last Appearance
Illinois	12	5-7-0	.417	1994 Liberty
Indiana	8	3-5-0	.375	1993 Independence
Iowa	14	7-6-1	.536	1995 Sun
Michigan	27	13-14-0	.481	1995 Alamo
Michigan St.	12	5-7-0	.417	1995 Independence
Minnesota	5	2-3-0	.400	1986 Liberty
Northwestern	2	1-1-0	.500	1996 Rose
Ohio St.	28	12-16-0	.429	1996 Florida Citrus
Penn St.	32	20-10-2	.656	1996 Outback
Purdue	5	4-1-0	.800	1984 Peach
Wisconsin	8	3-5-0	.375	1995 Hall of Fame
Current Members	**153**	**75-75-3**	**.500**	

BIG 12 CONFERENCE

School	Bowls	W-L-T	Pct.	Last Appearance
Baylor	16	8-8-0	.500	1994 Alamo
Colorado	20	8-12-0	.400	1996 Cotton
Iowa St.	4	0-4-0	.000	1978 Hall of Fame
Kansas	8	3-5-0	.375	1995 Aloha
Kansas St.	4	2-2-0	.500	1995 Holiday
Missouri	18	8-10-0	.444	1983 Holiday
Nebraska	34	16-18-0	.471	1996 Fiesta
Oklahoma	32	20-11-1	.641	1994 Copper
Oklahoma St.	12	9-3-0	.750	1988 Holiday
Texas	36	17-17-2	.500	1995 Sugar (Dec. 31)
Texas A&M	22	12-10-0	.545	1995 Alamo
Texas Tech	21	5-15-1	.262	1995 Copper
Current Members	**227**	**108-115-4**	**.485**	

BIG WEST CONFERENCE

School	Bowls	W-L-T	Pct.	Last Appearance
*Boise St.	0	0-0-0	.000	Has never appeared
*Idaho	0	0-0-0	.000	Has never appeared
Nevada	4	1-3-0	.250	1995 Las Vegas
New Mexico St.	3	2-0-1	.833	1960 Sun
North Texas	2	0-2-0	.000	1959 Sun
Utah St.	4	1-3-0	.250	1993 Las Vegas
Current Members	**13**	**4-8-1**	**.346**	

**Both Boise St. and Idaho are Division I-AA members.*

CONFERENCE USA

School	Bowls	W-L-T	Pct.	Last Appearance
Cincinnati	2	1-1-0	.500	1951 Sun
Houston	13	7-5-1	.577	1988 Aloha
Louisville	5	3-1-1	.700	1993 Liberty
Memphis	1	1-0-0	1.000	1971 Pasadena
Southern Miss.	6	2-4-0	.333	1990 All-American
Tulane	8	2-6-0	.250	1987 Independence
Current Members	**35**	**16-17-2**	**.486**	

MID-AMERICAN CONFERENCE

School	Bowls	W-L-T	Pct.	Last Appearance
Akron	0	0-0-0	.000	Has never appeared
Ball St.	2	0-2-0	.000	1993 Las Vegas
Bowling Green	5	2-3-0	.400	1992 Las Vegas
Central Mich.	2	0-2-0	.000	1994 Las Vegas
Eastern Mich.	1	1-0-0	1.000	1987 California
Kent	1	0-1-0	.000	1972 Tangerine
Miami (Ohio)	7	5-2-0	.714	1986 California
Ohio	2	0-2-0	.000	1968 Tangerine
Toledo	6	5-1-0	.833	1995 Las Vegas
Western Mich.	2	0-2-0	.000	1988 California
Current Members	**28**	**13-15-0**	**.464**	

PACIFIC-10 CONFERENCE

School	Bowls	W-L-T	Pct.	Last Appearance
Arizona	11	3-7-1	.318	1994 Freedom
Arizona St.	15	9-5-1	.633	1987 Freedom
California	12	5-6-1	.458	1993 Alamo
Oregon	11	3-8-0	.273	1996 Cotton
Oregon St.	4	2-2-0	.500	1965 Rose
Southern Cal	38	25-13-0	.658	1996 Rose
Stanford	17	8-8-1	.500	1995 Liberty
UCLA	20	10-9-1	.525	1995 Aloha
Washington	22	12-9-1	.568	1995 Sun
Washington St.	6	4-2-0	.667	1994 Alamo
Current Members	**156**	**81-69-6**	**.538**	

SOUTHEASTERN CONFERENCE

School	Bowls	W-L-T	Pct.	Last Appearance
Alabama	47	27-17-3	.606	1995 Florida Citrus
Arkansas	28	9-16-3	.375	1995 Carquest (Dec. 30)
Auburn	24	12-10-2	.542	1996 Outback
Florida	23	10-13-0	.435	1996 Fiesta
Georgia	32	15-14-3	.517	1995 Peach (Dec. 30)
Kentucky	8	5-3-0	.625	1993 Peach (Dec. 31)
LSU	29	12-16-1	.431	1995 Independence
Mississippi	25	14-11-0	.560	1992 Liberty
Mississippi St.	9	4-5-0	.444	1995 Peach (Jan. 1)
South Caro.	9	1-8-0	.111	1995 Carquest (Jan. 2)
Tennessee	36	20-16-0	.556	1996 Florida Citrus
Vanderbilt	3	1-1-1	.500	1982 Hall of Fame
Current Members	**273**	**130-130-13**	**.500**	

WESTERN ATHLETIC CONFERENCE

School	Bowls	W-L-T	Pct.	Last Appearance
Air Force	13	6-6-1	.500	1995 Copper
Brigham Young	19	6-12-1	.342	1994 Copper
Colorado St.	4	1-3-0	.250	1995 Holiday
Fresno St.	9	6-3-0	.667	1993 Aloha
Hawaii	2	1-1-0	.500	1992 Holiday
UNLV	2	2-0-0	1.000	1994 Las Vegas
New Mexico	5	2-2-1	.500	1961 Aviation
Rice	7	4-3-0	.571	1961 Bluebonnet
San Diego St.	4	1-3-0	.250	1991 Freedom
San Jose St.	7	4-3-0	.571	1990 California
Southern Methodist	11	4-6-1	.409	1984 Aloha
UTEP	9	5-4-0	.556	1988 Independence
Texas Christian	15	4-10-1	.300	1994 Independence
Tulsa	11	4-7-0	.364	1991 Freedom
Utah	5	3-2-0	.600	1994 Freedom
Wyoming	10	4-6-0	.400	1993 Copper
Current Members	**133**	**57-71-5**	**.447**	

INDEPENDENTS

School	Bowls	W-L-T	Pct.	Last Appearance
Ala.-Birmingham	0	0-0-0	.000	Has never appeared
Arkansas St.	0	0-0-0	.000	Has never appeared
Army	3	2-1-0	.667	1988 Sun
Central Fla.	0	0-0-0	.000	Has never appeared
East Caro.	4	3-1-0	.750	1995 Liberty
Louisiana Tech	3	1-1-1	.500	1990 Independence
Navy	8	3-4-1	.438	1981 Liberty
Northeast La.	0	0-0-0	.000	Has never appeared
Northern Ill.	1	1-0-0	1.000	1983 California
Notre Dame	21	13-8-0	.619	1996 Orange
Southwestern La.	0	0-0-0	.000	Has never appeared
Current Members	**40**	**23-15-2**	**.600**	

Award Winners in Bowl Games

Most Valuable Players in Major Bowls

Bowls that are played twice in the same calendar year (i.e., January and December) are listed in chronological order.

ALAMO BOWL

Year Player, Team, Position
1993 Dave Barr, California, quarterback (offense)
Jerrott Willard, California, linebacker (defense)
Larry Blue, Iowa, defensive tackle (sportsmanship award)
1994 Chad Davis, Washington St., quarterback (offense)
Ron Childs, Washington St., linebacker (defense)
Adrian Robinson, Baylor, defensive back (sportsmanship award)
1995 Kyle Bryant, Texas A&M, kicker (offense)
Keith Mitchell, Texas A&M, linebacker (defense)
Jarrett Irons, Michigan, linebacker (sportsmanship award)

ALOHA BOWL

Year Player, Team, Position
1982 Offense—Tim Cowan, Washington, quarterback
Defense—Tony Caldwell, Washington, linebacker
1983 Offense—Danny Greene, Washington, wide receiver
Defense—George Reynolds, Penn St., punter
1984 Offense—Jeff Atkins, Southern Methodist, running back
Defense—Jerry Ball, Southern Methodist, nose guard
1985 Offense—Gene Jelks, Alabama, running back
Defense—Cornelius Bennett, Alabama, linebacker
1986 Offense—Alfred Jenkins, Arizona, quarterback
Defense—Chuck Cecil, Arizona, safety
1987* Troy Aikman, UCLA, quarterback
Emmitt Smith, Florida, running back
1988 David Dacus, Houston, quarterback
Victor Wood, Washington St., wide receiver
1989 Blake Ezor, Michigan St., tailback
Chris Roscoe, Hawaii, wide receiver
1990 Todd Burden, Arizona, cornerback
Marvin Graves, Syracuse, quarterback
1991 Tommy Vardell, Stanford, running back
Shawn Jones, Georgia Tech, quarterback
1992 Tom Young, Brigham Young, quarterback
Dana Stubblefield, Kansas, defensive tackle
1993 Rashaan Salaam, Colorado, tailback
Trent Dilfer, Fresno St., quarterback
1994 David Green, Boston College, running back (offense)
Mike Mamula, Boston College, defensive end (defense)
Joe Gordon, Kansas St., cornerback
1995 Mark Williams, Kansas, quarterback
Karim Abdul-Jabbar, UCLA, running back

**Began selecting one MVP for each team.*

CARQUEST BOWL

(Named Blockbuster Bowl, 1990-92)

Brian Piccolo Most Valuable Player Award
Year Player, Team, Position
1990 Amp Lee, Florida St., running back
1991 David Palmer, Alabama, wide receiver
1992 Darrien Gordon, Stanford, cornerback
1993 Glenn Foley, Boston College, quarterback
1995 Steve Taneyhill, South Caro., quarterback
1995 Leon Johnson, North Caro., running back

COPPER BOWL

Year Player, Team, Position
1989 Shane Montgomery, North Caro. St., quarterback
Scott Geyer, Arizona, defensive back
1990 Mike Pawlawski, California, quarterback
Robert Midgett, Wyoming, linebacker
1991 Vaughn Dunbar, Indiana, tailback
Mark Hagen, Indiana, linebacker
1992 Drew Bledsoe, Washington St., quarterback (overall)
Phillip Bobo, Washington St., wide receiver (offense)
Kareem Leary, Utah, defensive back (defense)
1993 Andre Coleman, Kansas St., wide receiver (offense)
Kenny McEntyre, Kansas St., cornerback (defense)
1994 John Walsh, Brigham Young, quarterback (overall)
Jamal Willis, Brigham Young, running back (offense)
Broderick Simpson, Oklahoma, linebacker (defense)
1995 Byron Hanspard, Texas Tech, running back (overall)
Zebbie Lethridge, Texas Tech, quarterback (offense)
Mickey Dalton, Air Force, cornerback (defense)

COTTON BOWL

Year Player, Team, Position
1937 Ki Aldrich, Texas Christian, center
Sammy Baugh, Texas Christian, quarterback
L. D. Meyer, Texas Christian, end
1938 Ernie Lain, Rice, back
Byron "Whizzer" White, Colorado, quarterback
1939 Jerry Dowd, St. Mary's (Tex.), center
Elmer Tarbox, Texas Tech, back
1940 Banks McFadden, Clemson, back
1941 Charles Henke, Texas A&M, guard
John Kimbrough, Texas A&M, fullback
Chip Routt, Texas A&M, tackle
Lou De Filippo, Fordham, center
Joe Ungerer, Fordham, tackle
1942 Martin Ruby, Texas A&M, tackle
Jimmy Nelson, Alabama, halfback
Holt Rast, Alabama, end
Don Whitmire, Alabama, tackle
1943 Jack Freeman, Texas, guard
Roy McKay, Texas, fullback
Stanley Mauldin, Texas, tackle
Harvey Hardy, Georgia Tech, guard
Jack Marshall, Georgia Tech, end
1944 Joe Parker, Texas, end
Martin Ruby, Randolph Field, tackle
Glenn Dobbs, Randolph Field, quarterback
1945 Neil Armstrong, Oklahoma St., end
Bob Fenimore, Oklahoma St., back
Ralph Foster, Oklahoma St., tackle
1946 Hub Bechtol, Texas, end
Bobby Layne, Texas, back
Jim Kekeris, Missouri, tackle
1947 Alton Baldwin, Arkansas, end
Y. A. Tittle, LSU, quarterback
1948 Doak Walker, Southern Methodist, back
Steve Suhey, Penn St., guard
1949 Kyle Rote, Southern Methodist, back
Doak Walker, Southern Methodist, back
Brad Ecklund, Oregon, center
Norm Van Brocklin, Oregon, quarterback
1950 Billy Burkhalter, Rice, halfback
Joe Watson, Rice, center
James "Froggie" Williams, Rice, end
1951 Bud McFadin, Texas, guard
Andy Kozar, Tennessee, fullback
Hank Lauricella, Tennessee, halfback
Horace "Bud" Sherrod, Tennessee, defensive end
1952 Keith Flowers, Texas Christian, fullback
Emery Clark, Kentucky, halfback
Ray Correll, Kentucky, guard
Vito "Babe" Parilli, Kentucky, quarterback
1953 Richard Ochoa, Texas, fullback
Harley Sewell, Texas, guard
Bob Griesbach, Tennessee, linebacker
1954 Richard Chapman, Rice, tackle
Dan Hart, Rice, end
Dicky Maegle, Rice, halfback
1955 Bud Brooks, Arkansas, guard
George Humphreys, Georgia Tech, fullback
1956 Buddy Alliston, Mississippi, guard
Eagle Day, Mississippi, quarterback
1957 Norman Hamilton, Texas Christian, tackle
Jim Brown, Syracuse, halfback
1958 Tom Forrestal, Navy, quarterback
Tony Stremic, Navy, guard
1959 Jack Spikes, Texas Christian, fullback
Dave Phillips, Air Force, tackle
1960 Maurice Doke, Texas, guard
Ernie Davis, Syracuse, halfback
1961 Lance Alworth, Arkansas, halfback
Dwight Bumgarner, Duke, tackle
1962 Mike Cotten, Texas, quarterback
Bob Moser, Texas, end

Photo from Virginia sports information

Tiki Barber rushed 20 times for 103 yards and a touchdown to lead Virginia to a 34-27 victory over Georgia in last year's Peach Bowl. He was named the Cavaliers' offensive player of the game.

1963 Johnny Treadwell, Texas, guard
Lynn Amedee, LSU, quarterback
1964 Scott Appleton, Texas, tackle
Duke Carlisle, Texas, quarterback
1965 Ronnie Caveness, Arkansas, linebacker
Fred Marshall, Arkansas, quarterback
1966 Joe Labruzzo, LSU, tailback
David McCormick, LSU, tackle
1966 Kent Lawrence, Georgia, tailback
George Patton, Georgia, tackle
1968 Grady Allen, Texas A&M, defensive end
Edd Hargett, Texas A&M, quarterback
Bill Hobbs, Texas A&M, linebacker
1969 Tom Campbell, Texas, linebacker
Charles "Cotton" Speyrer, Texas, wide receiver
James Street, Texas, quarterback
1970 Steve Worster, Texas, fullback
Bob Olson, Notre Dame, linebacker
1971 Eddie Phillips, Texas, quarterback
Clarence Ellis, Notre Dame, cornerback
1972 Bruce Bannon, Penn St., defensive end
Lydell Mitchell, Penn St., running back
1973 Randy Braband, Texas, linebacker
Alan Lowry, Texas, quarterback
1974 Wade Johnston, Texas, linebacker
Tony Davis, Nebraska, tailback
1975 Ken Quesenberry, Baylor, safety
Tom Shuman, Penn St., quarterback
1976 Ike Forte, Arkansas, running back
Hal McAfee, Arkansas, linebacker
1977 Alois Blackwell, Houston, running back
Mark Mohr, Houston, cornerback
1978 Vagas Ferguson, Notre Dame, running back
Bob Golic, Notre Dame, linebacker
1979 David Hodge, Houston, linebacker
Joe Montana, Notre Dame, quarterback
1980 Terry Elston, Houston, quarterback
David Hodge, Houston, linebacker
1981 Warren Lyles, Alabama, nose guard
Major Ogilvie, Alabama, running back
1982 Robert Brewer, Texas, quarterback
Robbie Jones, Alabama, linebacker
1983 Wes Hopkins, Southern Methodist, strong safety
Lance McIlhenny, Southern Methodist, quarterback
1984 Jeff Leiding, Texas, linebacker
John Lastinger, Georgia, quarterback
1985 Bill Romanowski, Boston College, linebacker
Steve Strachan, Boston College, fullback

1986 Domingo Bryant, Texas A&M, strong safety
Bo Jackson, Auburn, tailback
1987 Chris Spielman, Ohio St., linebacker
Roger Vick, Texas A&M, fullback
1988 Adam Bob, Texas A&M, linebacker
Bucky Richardson, Texas A&M, quarterback
1989 LaSalle Harper, Arkansas, linebacker
Troy Aikman, UCLA, quarterback
1990 Carl Pickens, Tennessee, free safety
Chuck Webb, Tennessee, tailback
1991 Craig Erickson, Miami (Fla.), quarterback
Russell Maryland, Miami (Fla.), defensive lineman
1992 Sean Jackson, Florida St., running back
Chris Crooms, Texas A&M, safety
1993 Rick Mirer, Notre Dame, quarterback
Devon McDonald, Notre Dame, defensive end
1994 Lee Becton, Notre Dame, running back
Antonio Shorter, Texas A&M, linebacker
1995 Keyshawn Johnson, Southern Cal, wide receiver
John Herpin, Southern Cal, cornerback
1996 Herchell Troutman, Colorado, running back
Marcus Washington, Colorado, defensive back

FIESTA BOWL

Year Player, Team, Position
1971 Gary Huff, Florida St., quarterback
Junior Ah You, Arizona St., defensive end
1972 Woody Green, Arizona St., halfback
Mike Fink, Missouri, defensive back
1973 Greg Hudson, Arizona St., split end
Mike Haynes, Arizona St., cornerback
1974 Kenny Walker, Oklahoma St., running back
Phillip Dokes, Oklahoma St., defensive tackle
1975 John Jefferson, Arizona St., split end
Larry Gordon, Arizona St., linebacker
1976 Thomas Lott, Oklahoma, quarterback
Terry Peters, Oklahoma, cornerback
1977 Matt Millen, Penn St., linebacker
Dennis Sproul, Arizona St., quarterback (sportsmanship award)
1978 James Owens, UCLA, running back
Jimmy Walker, Arkansas, defensive tackle
Kenny Easley, UCLA, safety (sportsmanship award)
1979 Mark Schubert, Pittsburgh, kicker
Dave Liggins, Arizona, safety
Dan Fidler, Pittsburgh, offensive guard (sportsmanship award)
1980 Curt Warner, Penn St., running back
Frank Case, Penn St., defensive end (sportsmanship award)
1982 Curt Warner, Penn St., running back
Leo Wisniewski, Penn St., nose tackle
George Achica, Southern Cal, nose guard (sportsmanship award)
1983 Marcus Dupree, Oklahoma, running back
Jim Jeffcoat, Arizona St., defensive lineman
Paul Ferrer, Oklahoma, center (sportsmanship award)
1984 John Congemi, Pittsburgh, quarterback
Rowland Tatum, Ohio St., linebacker (sportsmanship award)
1985 Gaston Green, UCLA, tailback
James Washington, UCLA, defensive back
Bruce Fleming, Miami (Fla.), linebacker (sportsmanship award)
1986 Jamie Morris, Michigan, running back
Mark Messner, Michigan, defensive tackle
Mike Mallory, Michigan, linebacker (sportsmanship award)
1987 D. J. Dozier, Penn St., running back
Shane Conlan, Penn St., linebacker
Paul O'Connor, Miami (Fla.), offensive guard (sportsmanship award)
1988 Danny McManus, Florida St., quarterback
Neil Smith, Nebraska, defensive lineman
Steve Forch, Nebraska, linebacker (sportsmanship award)
1989 Tony Rice, Notre Dame, quarterback
Frank Stams, Notre Dame, defensive end
Chris Parker, West Va., defensive lineman (sportsmanship award)
1990 Peter Tom Willis, Florida St., quarterback
Odell Haggins, Florida St., nose guard
Jake Young, Nebraska, center (sportsmanship award)
1991 Browning Nagle, Louisville, quarterback
Ray Buchanan, Louisville, free safety
1992 O. J. McDuffie, Penn St., wide receiver
Reggie Givens, Penn St., outside linebacker
1993 Marvin Graves, Syracuse, quarterback
Kevin Mitchell, Syracuse, nose guard
1994 Chuck Levy, Arizona, running back
Tedy Bruschi, Arizona, defensive end
Paul White, Miami (Fla.), cornerback (sportsmanship award)
1995 Kordell Stewart, Colorado, quarterback
Shannon Clavelle, Colorado, defensive tackle
Oliver Gibson, Notre Dame, nose guard (sportsmanship award)
1996 Tommie Frazier, Nebraska, quarterback
Michael Booker, Nebraska, cornerback
Danny Wuerffel, Florida, quarterback (sportsmanship award)

FLORIDA CITRUS BOWL

(Named Tangerine Bowl, 1947-82)

Players of the Game (Pre-1977)

Year Player, Team, Position
1949 Dale McDaniels, Murray St.
Ted Scown, Sul Ross St.
1950 Don Henigan, St. Vincent
Chick Davis, Emory & Henry
1951 Pete Anania, Morris Harvey
Charles Hubbard, Morris Harvey
1952 Bill Johnson, Stetson
Dave Laude, Stetson
1953 Marvin Brown, East Tex. St.
1954 Billy Ray Norris, East Tex. St.
Bobby Spann, Arkansas St.
1955 Bill Englehardt, Nebraska-Omaha
1956 Pat Tarquinio, Juniata
1957 Ron Mills, West Tex. A&M
1958 Garry Berry, East Tex. St.
Neal Hinson, East Tex. St.
1958 Sam McCord, East Tex. St.
1960 Bucky Pitts, Middle Tenn. St.
Bob Waters, Presbyterian
1960 Jerry Nettles, Citadel
1961 Win Herbert, Lamar
1962 Joe Lopasky, Houston
Billy Roland, Houston
1963 Sharon Miller, Western Ky.
1964 Bill Cline, East Caro.
Jerry Whelchel, Massachusetts
1965 Dave Alexander, East Caro.
1966 Willie Lanier, Morgan St.
1967 Errol Hook, Tenn.-Martin
Gordon Lambert, Tenn.-Martin
1968 Buster O'Brien, Richmond, back
Walker Gillette, Richmond, lineman
1969 Chuck Ealy, Toledo, back
Dan Crockett, Toledo, lineman
1970 Chuck Ealy, Toledo, back
Vince Hubler, William & Mary, lineman
1971 Chuck Ealy, Toledo, back
Mel Long, Toledo, lineman
1972 Freddie Solomon, Tampa, back
Jack Lambert, Kent, lineman
1973 Chuck Varner, Miami (Ohio), back
Brad Cousino, Miami (Ohio), lineman
1974 Sherman Smith, Miami (Ohio), back
Brad Cousino, Miami (Ohio), lineman (tie)
John Roudebush, Miami (Ohio), lineman (tie)
1975 Rob Carpenter, Miami (Ohio), back
Jeff Kelly, Miami (Ohio), lineman
1976 Terry Miller, Oklahoma St., back
Phillip Dokes, Oklahoma St., lineman

Most Valuable Player (1977-Present)

Year Player, Team, Position
1977 Jimmy Jordan, Florida St., quarterback
1978 Ted Brown, North Caro. St., running back
1979 David Woodley, LSU, quarterback
1980 Cris Collinsworth, Florida, wide receiver
1981 Jeff Gaylord, Missouri, linebacker
1982 Randy Campbell, Auburn, quarterback
1983 Johnnie Jones, Tennessee, running back
1984 James Jackson, Georgia, quarterback
1985 Larry Kolic, Ohio St., middle guard
1987 Aundray Bruce, Auburn, linebacker
1988 Rodney Williams, Clemson, quarterback
1989 Terry Allen, Clemson, tailback
1990 Jeff George, Illinois, quarterback
1991 Shawn Jones, Georgia Tech, quarterback
1992 Mike Pawlawski, California, quarterback
1993 Garrison Hearst, Georgia, running back
1994 Bobby Engram, Penn St., wide receiver (overall)
Charlie Garner, Tennessee, tailback (offense)
Lee Rubin, Penn St., free safety (defense)
Raymond Austin, Tennessee, strong safety (defense)
1995 Sherman Williams, Alabama, running back (overall)
Joey Galloway, Ohio St., wide receiver (offense)
Dameian Jeffries, Alabama, defensive end (defense)
Matt Finkes, Ohio St., defensive end (defense)
1996 Jay Graham, Tennessee, running back (overall)
Rickey Dudley, Ohio St., tight end (offense)
Leonard Little, Tennessee, defensive end (defense)
Matt Finkes, Ohio St., defensive end (defense)

GATOR BOWL

Year Player, Team
1946 Nick Sacrinty, Wake Forest
1947 Joe Golding, Oklahoma
1948 Lu Gambino, Maryland
1949 Bobby Gage, Clemson
1950 Bob Ward, Maryland
1951 Eddie Talboom, Wyoming
1952 Jim Dooley, Miami (Fla.)
1953 Marv Matuszak, Tulsa
John Hall, Florida
1954 Vince Dooley, Auburn
Bobby Cavazos, Texas Tech
1954 Billy Hooper, Baylor
Joe Childress, Auburn
1955 Joe Childress, Auburn
Don Orr, Vanderbilt
1956 Corny Salvaterra, Pittsburgh
Wade Mitchell, Georgia Tech
1957 John David Crow, Texas A&M
Bobby Gordon, Tennessee
1958 Dave Hudson, Florida
Bobby Franklin, Mississippi
1960 Maxie Baughan, Georgia Tech
Jim Mooty, Arkansas
1960 Bobby Ply, Baylor
Larry Libertore, Florida
1961 Joe Auer, Georgia Tech
Galen Hall, Penn St.
1962 Dave Robinson, Penn St.
Tom Shannon, Florida
1963 David Sicks, Air Force
Ken Willard, North Caro.
1965 Carl McAdams, Oklahoma
Fred Biletnikoff, Florida St.
Steve Tensi, Florida
1965 Donny Anderson, Texas Tech
Lenny Snow, Georgia Tech
1966 Floyd Little, Syracuse
Dewey Warren, Tennessee
1967 Tom Sherman, Penn St.
Kim Hammond, Florida St.
1968 Mike Hall, Alabama
Terry McMillan, Missouri
1969 Curt Watson, Tennessee
Mike Kelley, Florida
1971 Archie Manning, Mississippi
Pat Sullivan, Auburn
1971 James Webster, North Caro.
Jimmy Poulos, Georgia
1972 Mark Cooney, Colorado
Wade Whatley, Auburn
1973 Haskell Stanback, Tennessee
Joe Barnes, Texas Tech
1974 Earl Campbell, Texas
Phil Gargis, Auburn
1975 Sammy Green, Florida
Steve Atkins, Maryland
1976 Jim Cefalo, Penn St.
Al Hunter, Notre Dame
1977 Jerry Butler, Clemson
Matt Cavanaugh, Pittsburgh
1978 Art Schlichter, Ohio St.
Steve Fuller, Clemson
1979 John Wangler, Michigan
Anthony Carter, Michigan
Matt Kupec, North Caro.
Amos Lawrence, North Caro.
1980 George Rogers, South Caro.
Rick Trocano, Pittsburgh
1981 Gary Anderson, Arkansas
Kelvin Bryant, North Caro.
Ethan Horton, North Caro.
1982 Paul Woodside, West Va.
Greg Allen, Florida St.
1983 Owen Gill, Iowa
Tony Lilly, Florida
1984 Mike Hold, South Caro.
Thurman Thomas, Oklahoma St.

1985 Thurman Thomas, Oklahoma St.
Chip Ferguson, Florida St.
1986 Brad Muster, Stanford
Rodney Williams, Clemson
1987 Harold Green, South Caro.
Wendell Davis, LSU
1989 Andre Rison, Michigan St.
Wayne Johnson, Georgia
1989 Mike Fox, West Va.
Levon Kirkland, Clemson
1991 Tyrone Ashley, Mississippi
Michigan offensive line: Tom Dohring, Matt Elliott, Steve Everitt, Dean Dingman, Greg Skrepenak
1991 Cale Gundy, Oklahoma
Tyrone Lewis, Virginia
1992 Errict Rhett, Florida
Reggie Lawrence, North Caro. St.
1993 Brian Burgdorf, Alabama
Corey Holliday, North Caro.
1994 James Stewart, Tennessee
Dwayne Thomas, Virginia Tech
1996 Donovan McNabb, Syracuse, quarterback
Peter Ford, Clemson, cornerback

HOLIDAY BOWL

Year Player, Team, Position
1978 Phil McConkey, Navy, wide receiver
1979 Marc Wilson, Brigham Young, quarterback
Tim Wilbur, Indiana, cornerback
1980 Jim McMahon, Brigham Young, quarterback
Craig James, Southern Methodist, running back
1981 Jim McMahon, Brigham Young, quarterback
Kyle Whittingham, Brigham Young, linebacker
1982 Tim Spencer, Ohio St., running back
Garcia Lane, Ohio St., cornerback
1983 Steve Young, Brigham Young, quarterback
Bobby Bell, Missouri, defensive end
1984 Robbie Bosco, Brigham Young, quarterback
Leon White, Brigham Young, linebacker
1985 Bobby Joe Edmonds, Arkansas, running back
Greg Battle, Arizona St., linebacker
1986 Todd Santos, San Diego St., quarterback (co-offensive)
Mark Vlasic, Iowa, quarterback (co-offensive)
Richard Brown, San Diego St., linebacker
1987 Craig Burnett, Wyoming, quarterback
Anthony Wright, Iowa, cornerback
1988 Barry Sanders, Oklahoma St., running back
Sim Drain, Oklahoma St., linebacker
1989 Blair Thomas, Penn St., running back
Ty Detmer, Brigham Young, quarterback
1990 Bucky Richardson, Texas A&M, quarterback
William Thomas, Texas A&M, linebacker
1991 Ty Detmer, Brigham Young, quarterback
Josh Arnold, Brigham Young, defensive back (co-defensive)
Carlos James, Iowa, defensive back (co-defensive)
1992 Michael Carter, Hawaii, quarterback
Junior Tagoai, Hawaii, defensive tackle
1993 John Walsh, Brigham Young, quarterback (co-offensive)
Raymont Harris, Ohio St., running back (co-offensive)
Lorenzo Styles, Ohio St., linebacker
1994 Todd Collins, Michigan, quarterback (co-offensive)
Anthoney Hill, Colorado St., quarterback (co-offensive)
Matt Dyson, Michigan, linebacker
1995 Brian Kavanagh, Kansas St., quarterback (offense)
Mario Smith, Kansas St., defensive back (defense)

INDEPENDENCE BOWL

Year Player, Team, Position
1976 Terry McFarland, McNeese St., quarterback
Terry Clark, Tulsa, cornerback
1977 Keith Thibodeaux, Louisiana Tech, quarterback
Otis Wilson, Louisville, linebacker
1978 Theodore Sutton, East Caro., fullback
Zack Valentine, East Caro., defensive end
1979 Joe Morris, Syracuse, running back
Clay Carroll, McNeese St., defensive tackle
1980 Stephan Starring, McNeese St., quarterback
Jerald Baylis, Southern Miss., nose guard
1981 Gary Kubiak, Texas A&M, quarterback
Mike Green, Oklahoma St., linebacker
1982 Randy Wright, Wisconsin, quarterback
Tim Krumrie, Wisconsin, nose guard
1983 Marty Louthan, Air Force, quarterback
Andre Townsend, Mississippi, defensive tackle
1984 Bart Weiss, Air Force, quarterback
Scott Thomas, Air Force, safety
1985 Rickey Foggie, Minnesota, quarterback
Bruce Holmes, Minnesota, linebacker
1986 Mark Young, Mississippi, quarterback
James Mosley, Texas Tech, defensive end
1987 Chris Chandler, Washington, quarterback
David Rill, Washington, linebacker
1988 James Henry, Southern Miss., punt returner/cornerback
1989 Bill Musgrave, Oregon, quarterback
Chris Oldham, Oregon, defensive back
1990 Mike Richardson, Louisiana Tech, running back
Lorenzo Baker, Louisiana Tech, linebacker
1991 Andre Hastings, Georgia, flanker
Torrey Evans, Georgia, linebacker
1992 Todd Dixon, Wake Forest, split end
1993 Maurice DeShazo, Virginia Tech, quarterback
Antonio Banks, Virginia Tech, safety
1994 Mike Groh, Virginia, quarterback
Mike Frederick, Virginia, defensive end
1995 Kevin Faulk, LSU, running back
Gabe Northern, LSU, defensive end

LAS VEGAS BOWL

Year Player, Team, Position
1992 Chris Vargas, Nevada, quarterback
1993 Anthony Calvillo, Utah St., quarterback
Mike Neu, Ball St., quarterback
1994 Henry Bailey, UNLV, running back
1995 Wasean Tait, Toledo, running back
Alex Van Dyke, Nevada, wide receiver

LIBERTY BOWL

Year Player, Team
1959 Jay Huffman, Penn St.
1960 Dick Hoak, Penn St.
1961 Ernie Davis, Syracuse
1962 Terry Baker, Oregon St.
1963 Ode Burrell, Mississippi St.
1964 Ernest Adler, Utah
1965 Tom Bryan, Auburn
1966 Jimmy Cox, Miami (Fla.)
1967 Jim Donnan, North Caro. St.
1968 Steve Hindman, Mississippi
1969 Bob Anderson, Colorado
1970 Dave Abercrombie, Tulane
1971 Joe Ferguson, Arkansas
1972 Jim Stevens, Georgia Tech
1973 Stan Fritts, North Caro. St.
1974 Randy White, Maryland
1975 Ricky Bell, Southern Cal
1976 Barry Krauss, Alabama
1977 Matt Kupec, North Caro.
1978 James Wilder, Missouri
1979 Roch Hontas, Tulane
1980 Mark Herrmann, Purdue
1981 Eddie Meyers, Navy
1982 Jeremiah Castille, Alabama
1983 Doug Flutie, Boston College
1984 Bo Jackson, Auburn
1985 Cody Carlson, Baylor
1986 Jeff Francis, Tennessee
1987 Greg Thomas, Arkansas
1988 Dave Schnell, Indiana
1989 Randy Baldwin, Mississippi
1990 Rob Perez, Air Force
1991 Rob Perez, Air Force
1992 Cassius Ware, Mississippi
1993 Jeff Brohm, Louisville
1994 Johnny Johnson, Illinois
1995 Kwame Ellis, Stanford, cornerback

ORANGE BOWL

Year Player, Team, Position
1965 Joe Namath, Alabama, quarterback
1966 Steve Sloan, Alabama, quarterback
1967 Larry Smith, Florida, tailback
1968 Bob Warmack, Oklahoma, quarterback
1969 Donnie Shanklin, Kansas, halfback
1970 Chuck Burkhart, Penn St., quarterback
Mike Reid, Penn St., defensive tackle
1971 Jerry Tagge, Nebraska, quarterback
Willie Harper, Nebraska, defensive end
1972 Jerry Tagge, Nebraska, quarterback
Rich Glover, Nebraska, defensive guard
1973 Johnny Rodgers, Nebraska, wingback
Rich Glover, Nebraska, defensive guard
1974 Tom Shuman, Penn St., quarterback
Randy Crowder, Penn St., defensive tackle
1975 Wayne Bullock, Notre Dame, fullback
Leroy Cook, Alabama, defensive end
1976 Steve Davis, Oklahoma, quarterback
Lee Roy Selmon, Oklahoma, defensive tackle
1977 Rod Gerald, Ohio St., quarterback
Tom Cousineau, Ohio St., linebacker
1978 Roland Sales, Arkansas, running back
Reggie Freeman, Arkansas, nose guard
1979 Billy Sims, Oklahoma, running back
Reggie Kinlaw, Oklahoma, nose guard
1980 J. C. Watts, Oklahoma, quarterback
Bud Hebert, Oklahoma, free safety
1981 J. C. Watts, Oklahoma, quarterback
Jarvis Coursey, Florida St., defensive end
1982 Homer Jordan, Clemson, quarterback
Jeff Davis, Clemson, linebacker
1983 Turner Gill, Nebraska, quarterback
Dave Rimington, Nebraska, center
1984 Bernie Kosar, Miami (Fla.), quarterback
Jack Fernandez, Miami (Fla.), linebacker
1985 Jacque Robinson, Washington, tailback
Ron Holmes, Washington, defensive tackle
1986 Sonny Brown, Oklahoma, defensive back
Tim Lashar, Oklahoma, kicker
1987 Dante Jones, Oklahoma, linebacker
Spencer Tillman, Oklahoma, halfback
1988 Bernard Clark, Miami (Fla.), linebacker
Darrell Reed, Oklahoma, defensive end
1989 Steve Walsh, Miami (Fla.), quarterback
Charles Fryar, Nebraska, cornerback
1990 Raghib Ismail, Notre Dame, tailback/wide receiver
Darian Hagan, Colorado, quarterback
1991 Charles Johnson, Colorado, quarterback
Chris Zorich, Notre Dame, nose guard
1992 Larry Jones, Miami (Fla.), running back
Tyrone Leggett, Nebraska, cornerback
1993 Charlie Ward, Florida St., quarterback
Corey Dixon, Nebraska, split end
1994 Tommie Frazier, Nebraska, quarterback
Charlie Ward, Florida St., quarterback
1995 Tommie Frazier, Nebraska, quarterback
Chris T. Jones, Miami (Fla.), cornerback
1996 Andre Cooper, Florida St., wide receiver
Derrick Mayes, Notre Dame, wide receiver

OUTBACK BOWL (Formerly Hall of Fame, 1986-95)

Year Player, Team, Position
1986 Shawn Halloran, Boston College, quarterback
James Jackson, Georgia, quarterback
1988 Jamie Morris, Michigan, tailback
Bobby Humphrey, Alabama, tailback
1989 Robert Drummond, Syracuse, running back
1990 Reggie Slack, Alabama, quarterback
Derek Isaman, Ohio St., linebacker
1991 DeChane Cameron, Clemson, quarterback
1992 Marvin Graves, Syracuse, quarterback
1993 Heath Shuler, Tennessee, quarterback
1994 Tyrone Wheatley, Michigan, running back
1995 Terrell Fletcher, Wisconsin, running back
1996 Bobby Engram, Penn St., wide receiver

PEACH BOWL

Year Player, Team, Position
1968 Mike Hillman, LSU (offense)
Buddy Millican, Florida St. (defense)
1969 Ed Williams, West Va. (offense)
Carl Crennel, West Va. (defense)
1970 Monroe Eley, Arizona St. (offense)
Junior Ah You, Arizona St. (defense)
1971 Norris Weese, Mississippi (offense)
Crowell Armstrong, Mississippi (defense)
1972 Dave Buckey, North Caro. St. (offense)
George Bell, North Caro. St. (defense)
1973 Louis Carter, Maryland (offense)
Sylvester Boler, Georgia (defense)
1974 Larry Isaac, Texas Tech (offense)
Dennis Harrison, Vanderbilt (defense)
1975 Dan Kendra, West Va. (offense)
Ray Marshall, West Va. (defense)
1976 Rod Stewart, Kentucky (offense)
Mike Martin, Kentucky (defense)
1977 Johnny Evans, North Caro. St. (offense)
Richard Carter, North Caro. St. (defense)

1978 Mark Herrmann, Purdue (offense)
Calvin Clark, Purdue (defense)
1979 Mike Brannan, Baylor (offense)
Andrew Melontree, Baylor (defense)
1980 Jim Kelly, Miami (Fla.) (offense)
Jim Burt, Miami (Fla.) (defense)
1981 Mickey Walczak, West Va. (offense)
Don Stemple, West Va. (defense)
1982 Chuck Long, Iowa (offense)
Clay Uhlenhake, Iowa (defense)
1983 Eric Thomas, Florida St. (offense)
Alphonso Carreker, Florida St. (defense)
1984 Howard Petty, Virginia (offense)
Ray Daly, Virginia (defense)
1985 Rob Healy, Army (offense)
Peel Chronister, Army (defense)
1986 Erik Kramer, North Caro. St. (offense)
Derrick Taylor, North Caro. St. (defense)
1987 Reggie Cobb, Tennessee (offense)
Van Waiters, Indiana (defense)
1988 Shane Montgomery, North Caro. St. (offense)
Michael Brooks, North Caro. St. (defense)
1989 Michael Owens, Syracuse (offense)
Rodney Hampton, Georgia (offense)
Terry Wooden, Syracuse (defense)
Morris Lewis, Georgia (defense)
1990 Stan White, Auburn (offense)
Vaughn Dunbar, Indiana (offense)
Darrel Crawford, Auburn (defense)
Mike Dumas, Indiana (defense)
1991 Jeff Blake, East Caro. (offense)
Terry Jordan, North Caro. St. (offense)
Robert Jones, East Caro. (defense)
Billy Ray Haynes, North Caro. St. (defense)
1993 Natrone Means, North Caro., running back (offense)
Greg Plump, Mississippi St., quarterback (offense)
Bracey Walker, North Caro., strong safety (defense)
Marc Woodard, Mississippi St., linebacker (defense)
1993 Emory Smith, Clemson, fullback (offense)
Pookie Jones, Kentucky, quarterback (offense)
Brentson Buckner, Clemson, tackle (defense)
Zane Beehn, Kentucky, end (defense)
1995 Treymayne Stephens, North Caro. St., running back
1995 Tiki Barber, Virginia, running back (offense)
Hines Ward, Georgia, quarterback (offense)
Skeet Jones, Virginia, linebacker (defense)
Whit Marshall, Georgia, linebacker (defense)

ROSE BOWL

Year Player, Team, Position
1902 Neil Snow, Michigan, fullback
1916 Carl Dietz, Washington St., fullback
1917 John Beckett, Oregon, tackle
1918 Hollis Huntington, Mare Island, fullback
1919 George Halas, Great Lakes, end
1920 Edward Casey, Harvard, halfback
1921 Harold "Brick" Muller, California, end
1922 Russell Stein, Wash. & Jeff., tackle
1923 Leo Calland, Southern Cal, guard
1924 Ira McKee, Navy, quarterback
1925 Elmer Layden, Notre Dame, fullback
Ernie Nevers, Stanford, fullback
1926 Johnny Mack Brown, Alabama, halfback
George Wilson, Washington, halfback
1927 Fred Pickhard, Alabama, tackle
1928 Clifford Hoffman, Stanford, fullback
1929 Benjamin Lom, California, halfback
1930 Russell Saunders, Southern Cal, quarterback
1931 John "Monk" Campbell, Alabama, quarterback
1932 Ernie Pinckert, Southern Cal, halfback
1933 Homer Griffith, Southern Cal, quarterback
1934 Cliff Montgomery, Columbia, quarterback
1935 Millard "Dixie" Howell, Alabama, halfback
1936 James "Monk" Moscrip, Stanford, end
Keith Topping, Stanford, end
1937 William Daddio, Pittsburgh, end
1938 Victor Bottari, California, halfback
1939 Doyle Nave, Southern Cal, quarterback
Alvin Krueger, Southern Cal, end
1940 Ambrose Schindler, Southern Cal, quarterback
1941 Peter Kmetovic, Stanford, halfback
1942 Donald Durdan, Oregon St., halfback
1943 Charles Trippi, Georgia, halfback
1944 Norman Verry, Southern Cal, guard
1945 James Hardy, Southern Cal, quarterback
1946 Harry Gilmer, Alabama, halfback
1947 Claude "Buddy" Young, Illinois, halfback
Julius Rykovich, Illinois, halfback
1948 Robert Chappius, Michigan, halfback
1949 Frank Aschenbrenner, Northwestern, halfback
1950 Fred Morrison, Ohio St., fullback
1951 Donald Dufek, Michigan, fullback
1952 William Tate, Illinois, halfback
1953 Rudy Bukich, Southern Cal, quarterback
1954 Billy Wells, Michigan St., halfback
1955 Dave Leggett, Ohio St., quarterback
1956 Walter Kowalczyk, Michigan St., halfback
1957 Kenneth Ploen, Iowa, quarterback
1958 Jack Crabtree, Oregon, quarterback
1959 Bob Jeter, Iowa, halfback
1960 Bob Schloredt, Washington, quarterback
George Fleming, Washington, halfback
1961 Bob Schloredt, Washington, quarterback
1962 Sandy Stephens, Minnesota, quarterback
1963 Pete Beathard, Southern Cal, quarterback
Ron VanderKelen, Wisconsin, quarterback
1964 Jim Grabowski, Illinois, fullback
1965 Mel Anthony, Michigan, fullback
1966 Bob Stiles, UCLA, defensive back
1967 John Charles, Purdue, halfback
1968 O. J. Simpson, Southern Cal, tailback
1969 Rex Kern, Ohio St., quarterback
1970 Bob Chandler, Southern Cal, flanker
1971 Jim Plunkett, Stanford, quarterback
1972 Don Bunce, Stanford, quarterback
1973 Sam Cunningham, Southern Cal, fullback
1974 Cornelius Greene, Ohio St., quarterback
1975 Pat Haden, Southern Cal, quarterback
John McKay Jr., Southern Cal, split end
1976 John Sciarra, UCLA, quarterback
1977 Vince Evans, Southern Cal, quarterback
1978 Warren Moon, Washington, quarterback
1979 Charles White, Southern Cal, tailback
Rick Leach, Michigan, quarterback
1980 Charles White, Southern Cal, tailback
1981 Butch Woolfolk, Michigan, running back
1982 Jacque Robinson, Washington, running back
1983 Don Rogers, UCLA, free safety
Tom Ramsey, UCLA, quarterback
1984 Rick Neuheisel, UCLA, quarterback
1985 Tim Green, Southern Cal, quarterback
Jack Del Rio, Southern Cal, linebacker
1986 Eric Ball, UCLA, tailback
1987 Jeff Van Raaphorst, Arizona St., quarterback
1988 Percy Snow, Michigan St., linebacker
1989 Leroy Hoard, Michigan, fullback
1990 Ricky Ervins, Southern Cal, tailback
1991 Mark Brunell, Washington, quarterback
1992 Steve Emtman, Washington, defensive tackle
Billy Joe Hobert, Washington, quarterback
1993 Tyrone Wheatley, Michigan, running back
1994 Brent Moss, Wisconsin, tailback
1995 Danny O'Neil, Oregon, quarterback
Ki-Jana Carter, Penn St., running back
1996 Keyshawn Johnson, Southern Cal, wide receiver

SUGAR BOWL

Miller-Digby Memorial Trophy
Year Player, Team, Position
1948 Bobby Layne, Texas, quarterback
1949 Jack Mitchell, Oklahoma, quarterback
1950 Leon Heath, Oklahoma, fullback
1951 Walt Yowarsky, Kentucky, tackle
1952 Ed Modzelewski, Maryland, fullback
1953 Leon Hardemann, Georgia Tech, halfback
1954 "Pepper" Rodgers, Georgia Tech, quarterback
1955 Joe Gattuso, Navy, fullback
1956 Franklin Brooks, Georgia Tech, guard
1957 Del Shofner, Baylor, halfback
1958 Raymond Brown, Mississippi, quarterback
1959 Billy Cannon, LSU, halfback
1960 Bobby Franklin, Mississippi, quarterback
1961 Jake Gibbs, Mississippi, quarterback
1962 Mike Fracchia, Alabama, fullback
1963 Glynn Griffing, Mississippi, quarterback
1964 Tim Davis, Alabama, kicker
1965 Doug Moreau, LSU, flanker
1966 Steve Spurrier, Florida, quarterback
1967 Kenny Stabler, Alabama, quarterback
1968 Glenn Smith, LSU, halfback
1969 Chuck Dicus, Arkansas, flanker
1970 Archie Manning, Mississippi, quarterback
1971 Bobby Scott, Tennessee, quarterback
1972 Jack Mildren, Oklahoma, quarterback
1972 Tinker Owens, Oklahoma, flanker
1973 Tom Clements, Notre Dame, quarterback
1974 Tony Davis, Nebraska, fullback
1975 Richard Todd, Alabama, quarterback
1977 Matt Cavanaugh, Pittsburgh, quarterback
1978 Jeff Rutledge, Alabama, quarterback
1979 Barry Krauss, Alabama, linebacker
1980 Major Ogilvie, Alabama, running back
1981 Herschel Walker, Georgia, running back
1982 Dan Marino, Pittsburgh, quarterback
1983 Todd Blackledge, Penn St., quarterback
1984 Bo Jackson, Auburn, running back
1985 Craig Sundberg, Nebraska, quarterback
1986 Daryl Dickey, Tennessee, quarterback
1987 Steve Taylor, Nebraska, quarterback
1988 Don McPherson, Syracuse, quarterback
1989 Sammie Smith, Florida St., running back
1990 Craig Erickson, Miami (Fla.), quarterback
1991 Andy Kelly, Tennessee, quarterback
1992 Jerome Bettis, Notre Dame, fullback
1993 Derrick Lassic, Alabama, running back
1994 Errict Rhett, Florida, running back
1995 Warrick Dunn, Florida St., running back
1995 Bryan Still, Virginia Tech, wide receiver

SUN BOWL

(Named Sun Bowl, 1936-86, 1994-95; John Hancock Sun Bowl, 1987-88; John Hancock Bowl, 1989-93); Norwest Bank Sun Bowl (since 1996)

C. M. Hendricks Most Valuable Player Trophy (1954-Present)
Jimmy Rogers Jr. Most Valuable Lineman Trophy (1961-Present)
John Folmer Most Valuable Special Teams Trophy (1994)

Year Player, Team, Position
1950 Harvey Gabriel, UTEP, halfback
1951 Bill Cross, West Tex. A&M, end
1952 Junior Arteburn, Texas Tech, quarterback
1953 Tom McCormick, Pacific (Cal.), halfback
1954 Dick Shinaut, UTEP, quarterback
1955 Jesse Whittenton, UTEP, quarterback
1956 Jim Crawford, Wyoming, halfback
1957 Claude Austin, Geo. Washington
1958 Leonard Kucewski, Wyoming, guard
1959 Charley Johnson, New Mexico St., quarterback
1960 Charley Johnson, New Mexico St., quarterback
1961 Billy Joe, Villanova, fullback
Richie Ross, Villanova, guard
1962 Jerry Logan, West Tex. A&M, halfback
Don Hoovler, Ohio, guard
1963 Bob Berry, Oregon, quarterback
John Hughes, Southern Methodist, guard
1964 Preston Ridlehuber, Georgia, quarterback
Jim Wilson, Georgia, tackle
1965 Billy Stevens, UTEP, quarterback
Ronny Nixon, Texas Christian, tackle
1966 Jim Kiick, Wyoming, tailback
Jerry Durling, Wyoming, middle guard
1967 Billy Stevens, UTEP, quarterback
Fred Carr, UTEP, linebacker
1968 Buddy McClintock, Auburn, defensive back
David Campbell, Auburn, tackle
1969 Paul Rogers, Nebraska, halfback
Jerry Murtaugh, Nebraska, linebacker
1970 Rock Perdoni, Georgia Tech, defensive tackle
Bill Flowers, Georgia Tech, linebacker
1971 Bert Jones, LSU, quarterback
Matt Blair, Iowa St., linebacker
1972 George Smith, Texas Tech, halfback
Ecomet Burley, Texas Tech, defensive tackle
1973 Ray Bybee, Missouri, fullback
John Kelsey, Missouri, tight end
1974 Terry Vitrano, Mississippi St., fullback
Jimmy Webb, Mississippi St., defensive tackle
1975 Robert Haygood, Pittsburgh, quarterback
Al Romano, Pittsburgh, middle guard
1977 Tony Franklin, Texas A&M, kicker
Edgar Fields, Texas A&M, defensive tackle
1977 Charles Alexander, LSU, tailback
Gordy Ceresino, Stanford, linebacker
1978 Johnny "Ham" Jones, Texas, running back
Dwight Jefferson, Texas, defensive end
1979 Paul Skansi, Washington, flanker
Doug Martin, Washington, defensive tackle
1980 Jeff Quinn, Nebraska, quarterback
Jimmy Williams, Nebraska, defensive end
1981 Darrell Shepard, Oklahoma, quarterback
Rick Bryan, Oklahoma, defensive tackle
1982 Ethan Horton, North Caro., tailback
Ronnie Mullins, Texas, defensive end

1983 Walter Lewis, Alabama, quarterback
Wes Neighbors, Alabama, center
1984 Rick Badanjek, Maryland, fullback
Carl Zander, Tennessee, linebacker
1985 Max Zendejas, Arizona, kicker
Peter Anderson, Georgia, center
1986 Cornelius Bennett, Alabama, defensive end
Steve Alvord, Washington, middle guard
1987 Thurman Thomas, Oklahoma St., running back
Darnell Warren, West Va., linebacker
1988 David Smith, Alabama, quarterback
Derrick Thomas, Alabama, linebacker
1989 Alex Van Pelt, Pittsburgh, quarterback
Anthony Williams, Texas A&M, linebacker
1990 Courtney Hawkins, Michigan St., wide receiver
Craig Hartsuyker, Southern Cal, linebacker
1991 Arnold Ale, UCLA, inside linebacker
Jimmy Rogers Jr., Illinois, lineman
1992 Melvin Bonner, Baylor, flanker
1993 Jerald Moore, Oklahoma, running back
1994 Priest Holmes, Texas, running back
Blake Brockermeyer, Texas, offensive lineman
Marcus Wall, North Caro., wide receiver
1995 Sedrick Shaw, Iowa, running back
Jared DeVries, Iowa, defensive tackle
Brion Hurley, Iowa, kicker

Most Valuable Players in Former Major Bowls

ALL-AMERICAN BOWL

(Birmingham, Ala.; Known as Hall of Fame Classic, 1977-85)

Year Player, Team, Position
1977 Chuck White, Maryland, split end
Charles Johnson, Maryland, defensive tackle
1978 Curtis Dickey, Texas A&M, running back
1979 Phil Bradley, Missouri, quarterback
1980 Gary Anderson, Arkansas, running back
Billy Ray Smith, Arkansas, linebacker
1981 John Bond, Mississippi St., quarterback
Johnie Cooks, Mississippi St., linebacker
1982 Whit Taylor, Vanderbilt, quarterback
Carl Dieudonne, Air Force, defensive end
1983 Jeff Hostetler, West Va., quarterback
1984 Mark Logan, Kentucky, running back
Todd Gregoire, Wisconsin, placekicker
1985 Mark Ingram, Michigan St., wide receiver
1986 Sammie Smith, Florida St., running back
1987 Scott Secules, Virginia, quarterback
1988 Emmitt Smith, Florida, running back
1989 Jerry Gray, Texas Tech, running back
1990 Brett Favre, Southern Miss., quarterback

AVIATION BOWL

(Dayton, Ohio)

Year Player, Team, Position
1961 Bobby Santiago, New Mexico, running back
Chuck Cummings, New Mexico, guard

BLUEBONNET BOWL

(Houston, Texas)

Year Player, Team
1959 Lowndes Shingles, Clemson
Bob Lilly, Texas Christian
1960 James Saxton, Texas
Lee Roy Jordan, Alabama
1961 Ken Coleman, Kansas
Elvin Basham, Kansas
1962 Bill Tobin, Missouri
Conrad Hitchler, Missouri
1963 Don Trull, Baylor
James Ingram, Baylor
1964 Jerry Rhome, Tulsa
Willy Townes, Tulsa
1965 Dewey Warren, Tennessee
Frank Emanuel, Tennessee
1966 Chris Gilbert, Texas
Fred Edwards, Texas
1967 Bob Anderson, Colorado
Ted Hendricks, Miami (Fla.)
1968 Joe Pearce, Oklahoma
Rufus Cormier, Southern Methodist
1969 Jim Strong, Houston
Jerry Drones, Houston
1970 Greg Pruitt, Oklahoma
Jeff Rouzie, Alabama
1971 Charlie Davis, Colorado
Butch Brezina, Houston
1972 Condredge Holloway, Tennessee
Carl Johnson, Tennessee
1973 D. C. Nobles, Houston
Deryl McGallion, Houston
1974 John Housmann, Houston
Mack Mitchell, Houston
1975 Earl Campbell, Texas
Tim Campbell, Texas
1976 Chuck Malito, Nebraska
Rodney Allison, Texas Tech
1977 Rob Hertel, Southern Cal
Walt Underwood, Southern Cal
1978 Steve Dils, Stanford
Gordy Ceresino, Stanford
1979 Mark Herrmann, Purdue
Roland James, Tennessee
1980 Amos Lawrence, North Caro.
Steve Streater, North Caro.
1981 Butch Woolfolk, Michigan
Ben Needham, Michigan
1982 Gary Anderson, Arkansas
Dwayne Dixon, Florida
1983 Rusty Hilger, Oklahoma St.
Alfred Anderson, Baylor
1984 Willie Drewrey, West Va.
1985 Pat Evans, Air Force
James McKinney, Texas
1986 Ray Berry, Baylor
Mark Hatcher, Colorado
1987 Tony Jones, Texas
Zeke Gadson, Pittsburgh

BLUEGRASS BOWL

(Louisville, Ky.)

Year Player, Team
1958 Forrest Campbell, Oklahoma St.

CALIFORNIA RAISIN BOWL

(Beginning in 1992, Mid-American Conference and Big West Conference winners met in Las Vegas Bowl)

Year Player, Team, Position
1981 Arnold Smiley, Toledo, running back
Marlin Russell, Toledo, linebacker
1982 Chip Otten, Bowling Green, tailback
Jac Tomasello, Bowling Green, defensive back
1983 Lou Wicks, Northern Ill., fullback
James Pruitt, Cal St. Fullerton, wide receiver
1984 Randall Cunningham, UNLV, quarterback
Steve Morgan, Toledo, tailback
1985 Mike Mancini, Fresno St., punter
Greg Meehan, Bowling Green, flanker
1986 Mike Perez, San Jose St., quarterback
Andrew Marlatt, Miami (Ohio), defensive tackle
1987 Gary Patton, Eastern Mich., tailback
Mike Perez, San Jose St., quarterback
1988 Darrell Rosette, Fresno St., running back
Tony Kimbrough, Western Mich., quarterback
1989 Ron Cox, Fresno St., linebacker
Sean Jones, Ball St., wide receiver
1990 Sheldon Canley, San Jose St., tailback
Ken Ealy, Central Mich., wide receiver
1991 Mark Szlachcic, Bowling Green, wide receiver
Mark Barsotti, Fresno St., quarterback

CHERRY BOWL

(Pontiac, Mich.)

Year Player, Team
1984 Nate Sassaman, Army
1985 Stan Gelbaugh, Maryland
Scott Shankweiler, Maryland

DELTA BOWL

(Memphis, Tenn.)

Year Player, Team
1948 Charlie Conerly, Mississippi

FREEDOM BOWL

(Anaheim, Calif.)

Year Player, Team, Position
1984 Chuck Long, Iowa, quarterback
William Harris, Texas, tight end
1985 Chris Chandler, Washington, quarterback
Barry Helton, Colorado, punter
1986 Gaston Green, UCLA, tailback
Shane Shumway, Brigham Young, defensive back
1987 Daniel Ford, Arizona St., quarterback
Chad Hennings, Air Force, defensive tackle
1988 Ty Detmer, Brigham Young, quarterback
Eric Bieniemy, Colorado, halfback
1989 Cary Conklin, Washington, quarterback
Huey Richardson, Florida, linebacker
1990 Todd Yert, Colorado St., running back
Bill Musgrave, Oregon, quarterback
1991 Marshall Faulk, San Diego St., running back
Ron Jackson, Tulsa, running back
1992 Lorenzo Neal, Fresno St., fullback
Estrus Crayton, Southern Cal, tailback
1993 Johnnie Morton, Southern Cal, wide receiver
Henry Lusk, Utah, wide receiver
1994 Tedy Bruschi, Arizona, defensive end
Cal Beck, Utah, kick returner

GARDEN STATE BOWL

(East Rutherford, N.J.)

Year Player, Team
1978 John Mistler, Arizona St.
1979 Mark Bright, Temple
1980 Terald Clark, Houston
1981 Steve Alatorre, Tennessee
Anthony Hancock, Tennessee
Randy Wright, Wisconsin

GOTHAM BOWL

(New York, N.Y.)

Year Player, Team
1961 Don Trull, Baylor
1962 Willie Ross, Nebraska
George Mira, Miami (Fla.)

HARBOR BOWL

(San Diego, Calif.)

Year Player, Team
1947 Bryan Brock, New Mexico
Bill Nelson, Montana St.

MERCY BOWL

(Los Angeles, Calif.)

Year Player, Team
1961 Beau Carter, Fresno St.

PASADENA BOWL

(Pasadena, Calif.; called Junior Rose Bowl in 1967)

Year Player, Team
1967 Eugene "Mercury" Morris, West Tex. A&M
Albie Owens, West Tex. A&M
1969 John Featherstone, San Diego St.
1970 Leon Burns, Long Beach St.
Paul Mattingly, Louisville
1971 Tom Carlsen, Memphis
Dornell Harris, Memphis

PRESIDENTIAL CUP

(College Park, Md.)

Year Player, Team
1950 Bob Smith, Texas A&M
Zippy Morocco, Georgia

SALAD BOWL

(Phoenix, Ariz.)

Year Player, Team
1950 Bob McQuade, Xavier (Ohio)
Wilford White, Arizona St.
1951 Jim Bailey, Miami (Ohio)
1952 Gene Shannon, Houston

Heisman Trophy Winners in Bowl Games

YEAR-BY-YEAR BOWL RESULTS FOR HEISMAN WINNERS

(Includes bowl games immediately after award of Heisman Trophy)

Of the 60 winners of the 61 Heisman Trophies (Archie Griffin won twice), 36 played in bowl games after they received their prize. Of those 36 players, only 16 were on the winning team in the bowl.

Houston's Andre Ware is the only Heisman recipient to miss a bowl date since 1969. The Cougars were on probation during the 1989 season and were ineligible for selection to a bowl. Before that lapse, Oklahoma's Steve Owens in 1969 was the last Heisman awardee not to participate in a bowl game.

Only three of the first 22 Heisman Trophy winners played in bowl games after receiving the award—Texas Christian's Davey O'Brien in 1938, Georgia's Frank Sinkwich in 1942 and Southern Methodist's Doak Walker in 1948.

Year	Heisman Winner, Team, Position	Bowl (Opponent, Result)
1935	Jay Berwanger, Chicago, HB	Did not play in bowl
1936	Larry Kelley, Yale, E	Did not play in bowl
1937	Clint Frank, Yale, HB	Did not play in bowl
1938	Davey O'Brien, Texas Christian, QB	Sugar (Carnegie Mellon, W 15-7)
1939	Nile Kinnick, Iowa, HB	Did not play in bowl
1940	Tom Harmon, Michigan, HB	Did not play in bowl
1941	Bruce Smith, Minnesota, HB	Did not play in bowl
1942	Frank Sinkwich, Georgia, HB	Rose (UCLA, W 9-0)
1943	Angelo Bertelli, Notre Dame, QB	Did not play in bowl
1944	Les Horvath, Ohio St., QB	Did not play in bowl
1945	Doc Blanchard, Army, FB	Did not play in bowl
1946	Glenn Davis, Army, HB	Did not play in bowl
1947	Johnny Lujack, Notre Dame, QB	Did not play in bowl
1948	Doak Walker, Southern Methodist, HB	Cotton (Oregon, W 21-13)
1949	Leon Hart, Notre Dame, E	Did not play in bowl
1950	Vic Janowicz, Ohio St., HB	Did not play in bowl
1951	Dick Kazmeier, Princeton, HB	Did not play in bowl
1952	Billy Vessels, Oklahoma, HB	Did not play in bowl
1953	John Lattner, Notre Dame, HB	Did not play in bowl
1954	Alan Ameche, Wisconsin, FB	Did not play in bowl
1955	Howard Cassady, Ohio St., HB	Did not play in bowl
1956	Paul Hornung, Notre Dame, QB	Did not play in bowl
1957	John David Crow, Texas A&M, HB	Gator (Tennessee, L 3-0)
1958	Pete Dawkins, Army, HB	Did not play in bowl
1959	Billy Cannon, LSU, HB	Sugar (Mississippi, L 21-0)
1960	Joe Bellino, Navy, HB	Orange (Missouri, L 21-14)
1961	Ernie Davis, Syracuse, HB	Liberty (Miami, Fla., W 15-14)
1962	Terry Baker, Oregon St., QB	Liberty (Villanova, W 6-0)
1963	Roger Staubach, Navy, QB	Cotton (Texas, L 28-6)
1964	John Huarte, Notre Dame, QB	Did not play in bowl
1965	Mike Garrett, Southern Cal, HB	Did not play in bowl
1966	Steve Spurrier, Florida, QB	Orange (Georgia Tech, W 27-12)
1967	Gary Beban, UCLA, QB	Did not play in bowl
1968	O. J. Simpson, Southern Cal, HB	Rose (Ohio St., L 27-16)
1969	Steve Owens, Oklahoma, HB	Did not play in bowl
1970	Jim Plunkett, Stanford, QB	Rose (Ohio St., W 27-17)
1971	Pat Sullivan, Auburn, QB	Sugar (Oklahoma, L 40-22)
1972	Johnny Rodgers, Nebraska, FL	Orange (Notre Dame, W 40-6)
1973	John Cappelletti, Penn St., HB	Orange (LSU, W 16-9)
1974	Archie Griffin, Ohio St., HB	Rose (Southern Cal, L 18-17)
1975	Archie Griffin, Ohio St., HB	Rose (UCLA, L 23-10)
1976	Tony Dorsett, Pittsburgh, HB	Sugar (Georgia, W 27-3)
1977	Earl Campbell, Texas, HB	Cotton (Notre Dame, L 38-10)
1978	Billy Sims, Oklahoma, HB	Orange (Nebraska, W 31-24)
1979	Charles White, Southern Cal, HB	Rose (Ohio St., W 17-16)
1980	George Rogers, South Caro., HB	Gator (Pittsburgh, L 37-9)
1981	Marcus Allen, Southern Cal, HB	Fiesta (Penn St., L 26-10)
1982	Herschel Walker, Georgia, HB	Sugar (Penn St., L 27-23)
1983	Mike Rozier, Nebraska, HB	Orange (Miami, Fla., L 31-30)
1984	Doug Flutie, Boston College, QB	Cotton (Houston, W 45-28)
1985	Bo Jackson, Auburn, HB	Cotton (Texas A&M, L 36-16)
1986	Vinny Testaverde, Miami (Fla.), QB	Fiesta (Penn St., L 14-10)
1987	Tim Brown, Notre Dame, WR	Cotton (Texas A&M, L 35-10)
1988	Barry Sanders, Oklahoma St., RB	Holiday (Wyoming, W 62-14)
1989	Andre Ware, Houston, QB	Did not play in bowl
1990	Ty Detmer, Brigham Young, QB	Holiday (Texas A&M, L 65-14)
1991	Desmond Howard, Michigan, WR	Rose (Washington, L 34-14)
1992	Gino Torretta, Miami (Fla.), QB	Sugar (Alabama, L 34-13)
1993	Charlie Ward, Florida St., QB	Orange (Nebraska, W 18-16)
1994	Rashaan Salaam, Colorado, RB	Fiesta (Notre Dame, W 41-24)
1995	Eddie George, Ohio St., RB	Fla. Citrus (Tennessee, L 20-14)

TOP BOWLS FOR HEISMAN WINNERS

Bowl	Heisman Winner Year	Heisman Winners
Orange	1960, 1966, 1972, 1973, 1978, 1983, 1993	7
Rose	1942, 1968, 1970, 1974, 1975, 1979, 1991	7
Cotton	1948, 1963, 1977, 1984, 1985, 1987	6
Sugar	1938, 1959, 1971, 1976, 1982, 1992	6
Fiesta	1981, 1986, 1995	3
Gator	1957, 1980	2
Holiday	1988, 1990	2
Liberty	1961, 1962	2

HEISMAN TROPHY WINNERS WHO WERE BOWL-GAME MVPs

Heisman Winner, Team (Year Won)	Bowl, Year Played
Doak Walker, Southern Methodist (1948)	Cotton, 1948
Doak Walker, Southern Methodist (1948)	Cotton, 1949
John David Crow, Texas A&M (1957)	Gator, 1957
Billy Cannon, LSU (1959)	Sugar, 1959
Ernie Davis, Syracuse (1961)	Cotton, 1960
Ernie Davis, Syracuse (1961)	Liberty, 1961
Terry Baker, Oregon St. (1962)	Liberty, 1962
Steve Spurrier, Florida (1966)	Sugar, 1966
O. J. Simpson, Southern Cal (1968)	Rose, 1968
Jim Plunkett, Stanford (1970)	Rose, 1971
Pat Sullivan, Auburn (1971)	Gator, 1971
Johnny Rodgers, Nebraska (1972)	Orange, 1973
Earl Campbell, Texas (1977)	Gator, 1974
Earl Campbell, Texas (1977)	Bluebonnet, 1975*
Billy Sims, Oklahoma (1978)	Orange, 1979
Charles White, Southern Cal (1979)	Rose, 1979
Charles White, Southern Cal (1979)	Rose, 1980
George Rogers, South Caro. (1980)	Gator, 1980
Herschel Walker, Georgia (1982)	Sugar, 1981
Doug Flutie, Boston College (1984)	Liberty, 1983
Bo Jackson, Auburn (1985)	Sugar, 1984
Bo Jackson, Auburn (1985)	Liberty, 1984
Bo Jackson, Auburn (1985)	Cotton, 1986
Barry Sanders, Oklahoma St. (1988)	Holiday, 1988
Ty Detmer, Brigham Young (1990)	Freedom, 1988*
Ty Detmer, Brigham Young (1990)	Holiday, 1989
Ty Detmer, Brigham Young (1990)	Holiday, 1991
Charlie Ward, Florida St. (1993)	Orange, 1994

**Discontinued bowl.*

Bowls and Polls

Associated Press No. 1 Teams Defeated in Bowl Games

Date	Bowl	Teams Involved	Score	New No. 1
1-1-51	Sugar	No. 7 Kentucky beat No. 1 Oklahoma	13-7	Same
1-1-52	Sugar	No. 3 Maryland beat No. 1 Tennessee	28-13	Same
1-1-54	Orange	No. 4 Oklahoma beat No. 1 Maryland	7-0	Same
1-1-61	Rose	No. 6 Washington beat No. 1 Minnesota	17-7	Same
1-1-65	Orange	No. 5 Texas beat No. 1 Alabama	21-17	Same
1-1-71	Cotton	No. 6 Notre Dame beat No. 1 Texas	24-11	Nebraska
12-31-73	Sugar	No. 3 Notre Dame beat No. 1 Alabama	24-23	Notre Dame
1-1-76	Rose	No. 11 UCLA beat No. 1 Ohio St.	23-10	Oklahoma
1-2-78	Cotton	No. 5 Notre Dame beat No. 1 Texas	38-10	Notre Dame
1-1-79	Sugar	No. 2 Alabama beat No. 1 Penn St.	14-7	Alabama
1-1-83	Sugar	No. 2 Penn St. beat No. 1 Georgia	27-23	Penn St.
1-2-84	Orange	No. 5 Miami (Fla.) beat No. 1 Nebraska	31-30	Miami (Fla.)
1-1-86	Orange	No. 3 Oklahoma beat No. 1 Penn St.	25-10	Oklahoma
1-2-87	Fiesta	No. 2 Penn St. beat No. 1 Miami (Fla.)	14-10	Penn St.
1-1-88	Orange	No. 2 Miami (Fla.) beat No. 1 Oklahoma	20-14	Miami (Fla.)
1-1-90	Orange	No. 4 Notre Dame beat No. 1 Colorado	21-6	Miami (Fla.)
1-1-93	Sugar	No. 2 Alabama beat No. 1 Miami (Fla.)	34-13	Alabama

Associated Press No. 1 Vs. No. 2 in Bowl Games

Date	Bowl	Teams, Score
1-1-63	Rose	No. 1 Southern Cal 42, No. 2 Wisconsin 37
1-1-64	Cotton	No. 1 Texas 28, No. 2 Navy 6
1-1-69	Rose	No. 1 Ohio St. 27, No. 2 Southern Cal 16
1-1-72	Orange	No. 1 Nebraska 28, No. 2 Alabama 6
1-1-79	Sugar	No. 2 Alabama 14, No. 1 Penn St. 7
1-1-83	Sugar	No. 2 Penn St. 27, No. 1 Georgia 23
1-2-87	Fiesta	No. 2 Penn St. 14, No. 1 Miami (Fla.) 10

Date	Bowl	Teams, Score
1-1-88	Orange	No. 2 Miami (Fla.) 20, No. 1 Oklahoma 14
1-1-93	Sugar*	No. 2 Alabama 34, No. 1 Miami (Fla.) 13
1-1-94	Orange*	No. 1 Florida St. 18, No. 2 Nebraska 16
1-2-96	Fiesta*	No. 1 Nebraska 62, No. 2 Florida 24

**Bowl alliance matched the No. 1 and No. 2 teams.*

Bowl Games and the National Championship

(How the bowl games determined the national champion from 1965 to present. Year listed is the football season before the bowl games.)

Note: The national champion was selected before the bowl games as follows: Associated Press (1936-64 and 1966-67); United Press International (1950-73); Football Writers Association of America (1954), and National Football Foundation and Hall of Fame (1959-70).

1965 The Associated Press (AP) selected Alabama as national champion after it defeated Nebraska, 39-28, in the Orange Bowl on January 1, 1966.

1968 AP selected Ohio State as national champion after it defeated Southern California, 27-16, in the Rose Bowl on January 1, 1969.

1969 AP selected Texas as national champion after it defeated Notre Dame, 21-17, in the Cotton Bowl on January 1, 1970.

1970 AP selected Nebraska as national champion after it defeated LSU, 17-12, in the Orange Bowl on January 1, 1971.

1971 AP selected Nebraska as national champion after it defeated Alabama, 38-6, in the Orange Bowl on January 1, 1972.

1972 AP selected Southern California as national champion after it defeated Ohio State, 42-17, in the Rose Bowl on January 1, 1973.

1973 AP selected Notre Dame as national champion after it defeated Alabama, 24-23, in the Sugar Bowl on December 31, 1973.

Beginning in 1974, all four of the national polls waited until after the bowl-game results before selecting a national champion. The following list shows how the bowl games figured in the final national championship polls for AP and UPI:

1974 First year of the agreement between the American Football Coaches Association (AFCA) and the UPI Board of Coaches to declare any teams on NCAA probation ineligible for the poll. AP—Oklahoma (11-0-0) did not participate in a bowl game because of NCAA probation. UPI—Southern California (10-1-1) defeated Ohio State, 18-17, in the Rose Bowl on January 1, 1975.

1975 AP and UPI both selected Oklahoma (11-1-0). Coach Barry Switzer's Sooners defeated Michigan, 14-6, in the Orange Bowl on January 1, 1976. Ohio State had led the AP poll for nine consecutive weeks until a 23-10 loss to UCLA in the Rose Bowl on January 1, 1976. Oklahoma had led the AP poll for the first four weeks of the year.

1976 AP and UPI both selected Tony Dorsett-led Pittsburgh (12-0-0). Pittsburgh whipped Georgia, 27-3, in the Sugar Bowl on January 1, 1977. Pittsburgh took over the No. 1 position from Michigan in the ninth week of the season en route to an undefeated year.

1977 AP and UPI were in agreement again, picking Notre Dame as national titlist. The Irish crushed previously undefeated and top-ranked Texas, 38-10, in the Cotton Bowl on January 2, 1978. Notre Dame was the sixth team to be ranked No. 1 during the 1977 season in the AP poll.

1978 This was the last time until the 1991 season that the two polls split on a national champion, with AP selecting Alabama (11-1-0) and UPI going for Southern California (12-1-0). Alabama, ranked No. 2 in the AP poll, upset No. 1 Penn State, 14-7, in the Sugar Bowl on January 1, 1979. Alabama had been ranked No. 1 in the first two weeks of the season until a 24-14 loss to Southern California.

1979 Unbeaten Alabama (12-0-0) was the unanimous choice of both polls. Bear Bryant's Tide whipped Arkansas easily, 24-9, in the Sugar Bowl on January 1, 1980, to claim the title.

1980 Georgia made it three No. 1's in a row for the Southeastern Conference with an undefeated season (12-0-0) to take the top spot in both polls. Vince Dooley's Bulldogs downed Notre Dame, 17-10, behind freshman phenom Herschel Walker in the Sugar Bowl on January 1, 1981.

1981 Both polls selected unbeaten Clemson (12-0-0). The Tigers gave coach Danny Ford the first Clemson national football championship with a 22-15 victory over Nebraska in the Orange Bowl on January 1, 1982. Clemson did not take over the AP No. 1 slot until the next-to-last poll of the year.

1982 AP and UPI both selected Penn State (11-1-0). The Nittany Lions were No. 2 in the AP poll but knocked off No. 1 Georgia, 27-23, in the Sugar Bowl on January 1, 1983. Georgia had led the AP poll for the final five weeks of the season.

1983 AP and UPI had no choice but to select Miami (Florida) as the unanimous champion after the No. 2 Hurricanes downed No. 1 Nebraska, 31-30, in the Orange Bowl on January 2, 1984. Many observers felt this may have been the most exciting Orange Bowl ever played as the Cornhuskers failed on a two-point conversion attempt with 48 seconds remaining. Nebraska had led the AP poll since the first week of the season.

1984 Unknown and a victim of the Mountain time zone, Brigham Young (13-0-0) overcame many obstacles to ascend to No. 1 in both polls. Coach LaVell Edwards' Cougars downed Michigan, 24-17, in the Holiday Bowl on December 21, 1984. BYU took over the top spot in the AP poll with three weeks left in the season after four other teams came and went as the top-rated team.

1985 Oklahoma (11-1-0) returned as the unanimous choice of both polls. Barry Switzer's Sooners knocked off top-rated Penn State, 25-10, in the Orange Bowl on January 1, 1986, to claim the national title.

1986 Penn State (12-0-0) had to battle top-rated Miami (Florida) in the Fiesta Bowl to take the top slot in both polls. Joe Paterno's No. 2 Nittany Lions upset the Hurricanes, 14-10, on January 2, 1987, to claim the championship. Miami (Florida) had been ranked No. 1 for the final 10 weeks of the season.

1987 Miami (Florida) (12-0-0) bounced back to a similar scenario as Jimmy Johnson's Hurricanes played underdog and finished ranked first in both polls. The No. 2 Hurricanes beat No. 1-ranked Oklahoma, 20-14, in the Orange Bowl on January 1, 1988. The Sooners had been the top-rated AP team for 13 of the season's 15 polls.

1988 Notre Dame (12-0-0) finished as the top team in both polls and gave the Fiesta Bowl its second national title game in three seasons. Lou Holtz's Irish whipped West Virginia, 34-21, on January 2, 1989, to claim their eighth AP title. Notre Dame took over the top spot in the poll from UCLA in the ninth week of the season.

1989 Miami (Florida) (11-1-0) claimed its second national title in three years in both polls. The Hurricanes downed Alabama, 33-25, in the Sugar Bowl on January 1, 1990, while No. 1-ranked Colorado lost to Notre Dame, 21-6, in the Orange Bowl to clear the way. Notre Dame led the AP poll for 12 of the 15 weeks.

1990 Colorado (11-1-0) and Georgia Tech (11-0-1) split the polls for the first time since 1978 with the Buffs taking the AP vote and the Jackets the UPI. Colorado bounced back from a disappointing 1989 title march to edge Notre Dame, 10-9, in the Orange Bowl on January 1, 1991. Georgia Tech had little trouble with Nebraska, 45-21, in the Florida Citrus Bowl on January 1, 1991, to finish as Division I-A's only undefeated team.

1991 Miami (Florida) (12-0-0) and Washington (12-0-0) kept Division I-A playoff talk alive with a split in the national polls for the second consecutive year. The Hurricanes took the AP vote, while the Huskies took both the USA Today/CNN and UPI polls. If either had stumbled in a bowl, then the other would have been a unanimous selection. However, Washington drubbed Michigan, 34-14, in the Rose Bowl, and Miami (Florida) had little trouble shutting out Nebraska, 22-0, in the Orange Bowl later that evening.

1992 No. 2 Alabama (13-0-0) turned in a magnificent performance in the Sugar Bowl by upsetting No. 1 Miami (Florida), 34-13, in a game dominated by the Crimson Tide. It marked the first year of the bowl coalition, and the bowlmeisters managed to match the top two teams for the national championship. It also marked the 17th time that a No. 1 team in the AP poll was knocked off in a bowl game since 1951. Alabama was named No. 1 in all polls after the January 1, 1993, matchup.

1993 No. 1 Florida State downed No. 2 Nebraska, 18-16, in the Orange Bowl to become a unanimous national champion. Notre Dame, winner over Texas A&M (24-21) in the Cotton Bowl, wanted to claim the title after beating the Seminoles in the regular season. But a late-season loss to Boston College cost the Irish in the polls. Florida State was No. 1 in all polls after the bowls.

1994 No. 1 Nebraska halted a seven-game bowl losing streak by posting a come-from-behind victory, 24-17, over Miami (Florida) in the Orange Bowl to cap a perfect 13-0 season with the national title. No. 2 Penn State, also undefeated at 12-0, downed Oregon, 38-20, in the Rose Bowl but had to settle for second place in the polls. Nebraska was No. 1 in all polls after the bowls.

1995 Another unanimous year for undefeated and No. 1 Nebraska. The Cornhuskers posted back-to-back national titles with a convincing 62-24 victory over No. 2 Florida in the bowl alliance's Fiesta Bowl matchup.

Bowl Results of Teams Ranked in The Associated Press Poll

The bowls and national polls have been perpetually linked since 1936, when The Associated Press introduced its weekly college football poll. The final AP poll was released at the end of the regular season until 1965, when bowl results were included for one year, dropped for two more and then added again in 1968 until the present. This is a list of the key bowl games as they related to the AP poll since 1936 (with pertinent references made to other polls where applicable).

(Key to polls: AP, Associated Press; UPI, United Press International; FW, Football Writers; NFF, National Football Foundation and Hall of Fame; USA/CNN, USA Today/Cable News Network; USA/NFF, USA Today/National Football Foundation and Hall of Fame; UPI/NFF, United Press International/National Football Foundation and Hall of Fame.)

1936 SUGAR—No. 6 Santa Clara beat No. 2 LSU, 21-14; ROSE—No. 3 Pittsburgh beat No. 5 Washington, 21-0; ORANGE—No. 14 Duquesne beat unranked Mississippi St., 13-12; COTTON—No. 16 Texas Christian beat No. 20 Marquette, 16-6. (Minnesota selected No. 1 but did not play in a bowl)

1937 ROSE—No. 2 California beat No. 4 Alabama, 13-0; SUGAR—No. 9 Santa Clara beat No. 8 LSU, 6-0; COTTON—No. 18 Rice beat No. 17 Colorado, 28-14. (Pittsburgh selected No. 1 but did not play in a bowl)

1938 SUGAR—No. 1 Texas Christian beat No. 6 Carnegie Mellon, 15-7; ORANGE—No. 2 Tennessee beat No. 4 Oklahoma, 17-0; ROSE—No. 7 Southern Cal beat No. 3 Duke, 7-3; COTTON—Unranked St. Mary's (Cal.) beat No. 11 Texas Tech, 20-13. (Texas Christian selected No. 1)

1939 SUGAR—No. 1 Texas A&M beat No. 5 Tulane, 14-13; ROSE—No. 3 Southern Cal beat No. 2 Tennessee, 14-0; ORANGE—No. 16 Georgia Tech beat No. 6 Missouri, 21-7; COTTON—No. 12 Clemson beat No. 11 Boston College, 6-3. (Texas A&M selected No. 1)

1940 ROSE—No. 2 Stanford beat No. 7 Nebraska, 21-13; SUGAR—No. 5 Boston College beat No. 4 Tennessee, 19-13; COTTON—No. 6 Texas A&M beat No. 12 Fordham, 13-12; ORANGE—No. 9 Mississippi St. beat No. 13 Georgetown, 14-7. (Minnesota selected No. 1 but did not play in a bowl)

1941 ROSE—No. 12 Oregon St. beat No. 2 Duke, 20-16 (played at Durham, N.C., because of World War II); SUGAR—No. 6 Fordham beat No. 7 Missouri, 2-0; COTTON—No. 20 Alabama beat No. 9 Texas A&M, 29-21; ORANGE—No. 14 Georgia beat unranked Texas Christian, 40-26. (Minnesota selected No. 1 but did not play in a bowl)

1942 ROSE—No. 2 Georgia beat No. 13 UCLA, 9-0; SUGAR—No. 7 Tennessee beat No. 4 Tulsa, 14-7; COTTON—No. 11 Texas beat No. 5 Georgia Tech, 14-7; ORANGE—No. 10 Alabama beat No. 8 Boston College, 37-21. (Ohio St. selected No. 1 but did not play in a bowl)

1943 ROSE—Unranked Southern Cal beat No. 12 Washington, 29-0; COTTON—No. 14 Texas tied unranked Randolph Field, 7-7; SUGAR—No. 13 Georgia Tech beat No. 15 Tulsa, 20-18. (Notre Dame selected No. 1 but did not play in a bowl)

1944 ROSE—No. 7 Southern Cal beat No. 12 Tennessee, 25-0; ORANGE—Unranked Tulsa beat No. 13 Georgia Tech, 26-12; No. 3 Randolph Field beat No. 20 Second Air Force, 13-6, in a battle of military powers. (Army selected No. 1 but did not play in a bowl)

1945 ROSE—No. 2 Alabama beat No. 11 Southern Cal, 34-14; COTTON—No. 10 Texas beat unranked Missouri, 40-27; ORANGE—Unranked Miami (Fla.) beat No. 16 Holy Cross, 13-6; SUGAR—No. 5 Oklahoma St. beat No. 7 St. Mary's (Cal.), 33-13. (Army selected No. 1 but did not play in a bowl)

1946 COTTON—No. 8 LSU tied No. 16 Arkansas, 0-0; ROSE—No. 5 Illinois beat No. 4 UCLA, 45-14; SUGAR—No. 3 Georgia beat No. 9 North Caro., 20-10; ORANGE—No. 10 Rice beat No. 7 Tennessee, 8-0. (Notre Dame selected No. 1 but did not play in a bowl)

1947 ORANGE—No. 10 Georgia Tech beat No. 12 Kansas, 20-14; ROSE—No. 2 Michigan beat No. 8 Southern Cal, 49-0; SUGAR—No. 5 Texas beat No. 6 Alabama, 27-7; COTTON—No. 3 Southern Methodist tied No. 4 Penn St., 13-13. (Notre Dame selected No. 1 but did not play in a bowl; Michigan also declared champion in vote after Rose Bowl victory but AP kept Notre Dame as vote of record)

1948 ROSE—No. 7 Northwestern beat No. 4 California, 20-14; COTTON—No. 10 Southern Methodist beat No. 9 Oregon, 21-13; SUGAR—No. 5 Oklahoma beat No. 3 North Caro., 14-6; ORANGE—Unranked Texas beat No. 8 Georgia, 41-28. (Michigan selected No. 1 but did not play in a bowl)

1949 ORANGE—No. 15 Santa Clara beat No. 11 Kentucky, 21-13; COTTON—No. 5 Rice beat No. 16 North Caro., 27-13; ROSE—No. 6 Ohio St. beat No. 3 California, 17-14; SUGAR—No. 2 Oklahoma beat No. 9 LSU, 35-0. (Notre Dame selected No. 1 but did not play in a bowl)

1950 ROSE—No. 9 Michigan beat No. 5 California, 14-6; SUGAR—No. 7 Kentucky beat No. 1 Oklahoma, 13-7; ORANGE—No. 10 Clemson beat No. 15 Miami (Fla.), 15-14; COTTON—No. 4 Tennessee beat No. 3 Texas, 20-14. (Oklahoma selected No. 1 in vote before losing in Sugar Bowl)

1951 COTTON—No. 15 Kentucky beat No. 11 Texas Christian, 20-7; ORANGE—No. 5 Georgia Tech beat No. 9 Baylor, 17-14; ROSE—No. 4 Illinois beat No. 7 Stanford, 40-7; SUGAR—No. 3 Maryland beat No. 1 Tennessee, 28-13. (Tennessee selected No. 1 in vote before losing in Sugar Bowl)

1952 ROSE—No. 5 Southern Cal beat No. 11 Wisconsin, 7-0; SUGAR—No. 2 Georgia Tech beat No. 7 Mississippi, 24-7; ORANGE—No. 9 Alabama beat No. 14 Syracuse, 61-6; COTTON—No. 10 Texas beat No. 8 Tennessee, 16-0. (Michigan St. selected No. 1 but did not play in a bowl)

1953 SUGAR—No. 8 Georgia Tech beat No. 10 West Va., 42-19; ORANGE—No. 4 Oklahoma beat No. 1 Maryland, 7-0; COTTON—No. 5 Rice beat No. 13 Alabama, 28-6; ROSE—No. 3 Michigan St. beat No. 5 UCLA, 28-20. (Maryland selected No. 1 before losing in Orange Bowl)

1954 ROSE—No. 1 Ohio St. beat No. 17 Southern Cal, 20-7; ORANGE—No. 14 Duke beat unranked Nebraska, 34-7; SUGAR—No. 5 Navy beat No. 6 Mississippi, 21-0; COTTON—Unranked Georgia Tech beat No. 10 Arkansas, 14-6. (Ohio St. remained No. 1 but UCLA named in UPI and FW polls)

1955 GATOR—Unranked Vanderbilt beat No. 8 Auburn, 25-13; ROSE—No. 2 Michigan St. beat No. 4 UCLA, 17-14; ORANGE—No. 1 Oklahoma beat No. 3 Maryland, 20-6; COTTON—No. 10 Mississippi beat No. 6 Texas Christian, 14-13; SUGAR—No. 7 Georgia Tech beat No. 11 Pittsburgh, 7-0. (Oklahoma remained No. 1)

1956 SUGAR—No. 11 Baylor beat No. 2 Tennessee, 13-7; ORANGE—No. 20 Colorado beat No. 19 Clemson, 27-21; GATOR—No. 4 Georgia Tech beat No. 13 Pittsburgh, 21-14; ROSE—No. 3 Iowa beat No. 10 Oregon St., 35-19; COTTON—No. 14 Texas Christian beat No. 8 Syracuse, 28-27. (Oklahoma selected No. 1 but did not play in a bowl)

1957 GATOR—No. 13 Tennessee beat No. 9 Texas A&M, 3-0; ROSE—No. 2 Ohio St. beat unranked Oregon, 10-7; COTTON—No. 5 Navy beat No. 8 Rice, 20-7; ORANGE—No. 4 Oklahoma beat No. 16 Duke, 48-21; SUGAR—No. 7 Mississippi beat No. 11 Texas, 39-7. (Auburn selected No. 1 but did not play in a bowl; Ohio St. selected No. 1 in both UPI and FW polls)

1958 SUGAR—No. 1 LSU beat No. 12 Clemson, 7-0; COTTON—No. 6 Air Force tied No. 10 Texas Christian, 0-0; ROSE—No. 2 Iowa beat No. 16 California, 38-12; ORANGE—No. 5 Oklahoma beat No. 9 Syracuse, 21-6. (LSU remained No. 1 in AP and UPI but Iowa selected in FW poll)

1959 COTTON—No. 1 Syracuse beat No. 4 Texas, 23-14; ROSE—No. 8 Washington beat No. 6 Wisconsin, 44-8; ORANGE—No. 5 Georgia beat No. 18 Missouri, 14-0; SUGAR—No. 2 Mississippi beat No. 3 LSU, 21-0; BLUEBONNET—No. 11 Clemson beat No. 7 Texas Christian, 23-7; LIBERTY—No. 12 Penn St. beat No. 10 Alabama, 7-0; GATOR—No. 9 Arkansas beat unranked Georgia Tech, 14-7. (Syracuse selected No. 1 by all four polls)

1960 ROSE—No. 6 Washington beat No. 1 Minnesota, 17-7; COTTON—No. 10 Duke beat No. 7 Arkansas, 7-6; SUGAR—No. 2 Mississippi beat unranked Rice, 14-6; ORANGE—No. 5 Missouri beat No. 4 Navy, 21-14; BLUEBONNET—No. 9 Alabama tied unranked Texas, 3-3. (Minnesota selected No. 1 by AP, UPI and NFF before losing in Rose Bowl; Mississippi named No. 1 in FW poll)

1961 COTTON—No. 3 Texas beat No. 5 Mississippi, 12-7; SUGAR—No. 1 Alabama beat No. 9 Arkansas, 10-3; ORANGE—No. 4 LSU beat No. 7 Colorado, 25-7; GOTHAM—Unranked Baylor beat No. 10 Utah St., 24-9; ROSE—No. 6 Minnesota beat No. 16 UCLA, 21-3. (Alabama selected No. 1 in AP, UPI and NFF, but Ohio St. picked by FW poll)

1962 ROSE—No. 1 Southern Cal beat No. 2 Wisconsin, 42-37; SUGAR—No. 3 Mississippi beat No. 6 Arkansas, 17-13; COTTON—No. 7 LSU beat No. 4 Texas, 13-0; GATOR—Unranked Florida beat No. 9 Penn St., 17-7; ORANGE—No. 5 Alabama beat No. 8 Oklahoma, 17-0. (Southern Cal selected No. 1 by all four polls)

1963 COTTON—No. 1 Texas beat No. 2 Navy, 28-6; ORANGE—No. 6 Nebraska beat No. 5 Auburn, 13-7; ROSE—No. 3 Illinois beat unranked Washington, 17-7; SUGAR—No. 8 Alabama beat No. 7 Mississippi, 12-7. (Texas selected No. 1 by all four polls)

1964 ORANGE—No. 5 Texas beat No. 1 Alabama, 21-17; ROSE—No. 4 Michigan beat No. 8 Oregon St., 34-7; COTTON—No. 2 Arkansas beat No. 6 Nebraska, 10-7; SUGAR—No. 7 LSU beat unranked Syracuse, 13-10. (Alabama selected No. 1 by AP and UPI before losing in the Orange Bowl, while Arkansas No. 1 in FW poll and Notre Dame No. 1 in NFF poll)

1965 ***(First year final poll taken after bowl games)*** ROSE—No. 5 UCLA beat No. 1 Michigan St., 14-12; COTTON—Unranked LSU beat No. 2 Arkansas, 14-7; SUGAR—No. 6 Missouri beat unranked Florida, 20-18; ORANGE—No. 4 Alabama beat No. 3 Nebraska, 39-28; BLUEBONNET—No. 7 Tennessee beat unranked Tulsa, 27-6; GATOR—Unranked Georgia Tech beat No. 10 Texas Tech, 31-21. (Alabama selected No. 1 in final poll but Michigan St. named by UPI and NFF polls and they tied in FW poll)

1966 ***(Returned to final poll taken before bowls)*** SUGAR—No. 3 Alabama beat No. 6 Nebraska, 34-7; ROSE—No. 7 Purdue beat unranked Southern Cal, 14-13; COTTON—No. 4 Georgia beat No. 10 Southern Methodist, 24-9; ORANGE—Unranked Florida beat No. 8 Georgia Tech, 27-12; LIBERTY—No. 9 Miami (Fla.) beat unranked Virginia Tech, 14-7. (Notre Dame selected No. 1 by AP, UPI and FW polls and tied with Michigan St. in NFF poll; neither team played in a bowl game and they tied in a regular-season game)

1967 ROSE—No. 1 Southern Cal beat No. 4 Indiana, 14-3; SUGAR—Unranked LSU beat No. 6 Wyoming, 20-13; ORANGE—No. 3 Oklahoma beat No. 2 Tennessee, 26-24; COTTON—Unranked Texas A&M beat No. 8 Alabama, 20-16; GATOR—No. 10 Penn St. tied unranked Florida St., 17-17. (Southern Cal selected No. 1 in all four polls)

1968 ***(Returned to final poll taken after bowl games)*** ROSE—No. 1 Ohio St. beat No. 2 Southern Cal, 27-16; SUGAR—No. 9 Arkansas beat No. 4 Georgia, 16-2; ORANGE—No. 3 Penn St. beat No. 6 Kansas, 15-14; COTTON—No. 5 Texas beat No. 8 Tennessee, 36-13; BLUEBONNET—No. 20 Southern Methodist beat No. 10 Oklahoma, 28-27; GATOR—No. 16 Missouri beat No. 12 Alabama, 35-10. (Ohio St. remained No. 1)

1969 COTTON—No. 1 Texas beat No. 9 Notre Dame, 21-17; SUGAR—No. 13 Mississippi beat No. 3 Arkansas, 27-22; ORANGE—No. 2 Penn St. beat No. 6 Missouri, 10-3; ROSE—No. 5 Southern Cal beat No. 7 Michigan, 10-3. (Texas remained No. 1)

1970 ROSE—No. 12 Stanford beat No. 2 Ohio St., 27-17; COTTON—No. 6 Notre Dame beat No. 1 Texas, 24-11; ROSE—No. 12 Stanford beat No. 2 Ohio St., 27-17; SUGAR—No. 5 Tennessee beat No. 11 Air Force, 34-13; ORANGE—No. 3 Nebraska beat No. 8 LSU, 17-12; PEACH—No. 9 Arizona St. beat unranked North Caro., 48-26. (Nebraska selected No. 1 in AP and FW polls while Texas was No. 1 in UPI and tied with Ohio St. in NFF poll)

1971 ORANGE—No. 1 Nebraska beat No. 2 Alabama, 38-6; SUGAR—No. 3 Oklahoma beat No. 5 Auburn, 40-22; ROSE—No. 16 Stanford beat No. 4 Michigan, 13-12; GATOR—No. 6 Georgia beat unranked North Caro., 7-3; COTTON—No. 10 Penn St. beat No. 12 Texas, 30-6; FIESTA—No. 8 Arizona St. beat unranked Florida St., 45-38; BLUEBONNET—No. 7 Colorado beat No. 15 Houston, 29-17. (Nebraska remained No. 1 in all four polls)

1972 ROSE—No. 1 Southern Cal beat No. 3 Ohio St., 42-17; COTTON—No. 7 Texas beat No. 4 Alabama, 17-13; SUGAR—No. 2 Oklahoma beat No. 5 Penn St., 14-0; ORANGE—No. 9 Nebraska beat No. 12 Notre Dame, 40-6; GATOR—No. 6 Auburn beat No. 13 Colorado, 24-3; BLUEBONNET—No. 11 Tennessee beat No. 10 LSU, 24-17. (Southern Cal remained No. 1 in all four polls)

1973 SUGAR—No. 3 Notre Dame beat No. 1 Alabama, 24-23; ROSE—No. 4 Ohio St. beat No. 7 Southern Cal, 42-21; ORANGE—No. 6 Penn St. beat No. 13 LSU, 16-9; COTTON—No. 12 Nebraska beat No. 8 Texas, 19-3; FIESTA—No. 10 Arizona St. beat unranked Pittsburgh, 28-7; BLUEBONNET—No. 14 Houston beat No. 17 Tulane, 47-7. (Notre Dame selected No. 1 in AP, FW and NFF polls, Alabama named No. 1 by UPI but No. 2 Oklahoma was on probation and could not go to a bowl game)

1974 ROSE—No. 5 Southern Cal beat No. 3 Ohio St., 18-17; ORANGE—No. 9 Notre Dame beat No. 2 Alabama, 13-11; GATOR—No. 6 Auburn beat No. 11 Texas, 27-3; COTTON—No. 7 Penn St. beat No. 12 Baylor, 41-20; SUGAR—No. 8 Nebraska beat No. 18 Florida, 13-10; LIBERTY—Unranked Tennessee beat No. 10 Maryland, 7-3. (Oklahoma selected No. 1 in AP poll despite being on probation and not able to participate in bowl game; Southern Cal named No. 1 by UPI, FW and NFF polls)

1975 ROSE—No. 11 UCLA beat No. 1 Ohio St., 23-10; ORANGE—No. 3 Oklahoma beat No. 5 Michigan, 14-6; LIBERTY—No. 17 Southern Cal beat No. 2 Texas A&M, 20-0; SUGAR—No. 4 Alabama beat No. 8 Penn St., 13-6; FIESTA—No. 7 Arizona St. beat No. 6 Nebraska, 17-14; COTTON—No. 18 Arkansas beat No. 12 Georgia, 31-10; BLUEBONNET—No. 9 Texas beat No. 10 Colorado, 38-21. (Oklahoma selected No. 1 in all four polls)

1976 SUGAR—No. 1 Pittsburgh beat No. 5 Georgia, 27-3; ROSE—No. 3 Southern Cal beat No. 2 Michigan, 14-6; COTTON—No. 6 Houston beat No. 4 Maryland, 30-21; LIBERTY—No. 16 Alabama beat No. 7 UCLA, 36-6; ORANGE—No. 11 Ohio St. beat No. 12 Colorado, 27-10; FIESTA—No. 8 Oklahoma beat unranked Wyoming, 41-7; SUN—No. 10 Texas A&M beat unranked Florida, 37-14; BLUEBONNET—No. 13 Nebraska beat No. 9 Texas Tech, 27-24. (Pittsburgh remained No. 1 in all four polls)

1977 COTTON—No. 5 Notre Dame beat No. 1 Texas, 38-10; ORANGE—No. 6 Arkansas beat No. 2 Oklahoma, 31-6; SUGAR—No. 3 Alabama beat No. 9 Ohio St.,

35-6; ROSE—No. 13 Washington beat No. 4 Michigan, 27-20; FIESTA—No. 8 Penn St. beat No. 15 Arizona St., 42-30; GATOR—No. 10 Pittsburgh beat No. 11 Clemson, 34-3. (Notre Dame selected No. 1 in all four polls)

1978 SUGAR—No. 2 Alabama beat No. 1 Penn St., 14-7; ROSE—No. 3 Southern Cal beat No. 5 Michigan, 17-10; ORANGE—No. 4 Oklahoma beat No. 6 Nebraska, 31-24; COTTON—No. 10 Notre Dame beat No. 9 Houston, 35-34; GATOR—No. 7 Clemson beat No. 20 Ohio St., 17-15; FIESTA—No. 8 Arkansas tied No. 15 UCLA, 10-10. (Alabama selected No. 1 in AP, FW and NFF polls, while Southern Cal named in UPI)

1979 ROSE—No. 3 Southern Cal beat No. 1 Ohio St., 17-16; SUGAR—No. 2 Alabama beat No. 6 Arkansas, 24-9; ORANGE—No. 5 Oklahoma beat No. 4 Florida St., 24-7; COTTON—No. 8 Houston beat No. 7 Nebraska, 17-14; SUN—No. 13 Washington beat No. 11 Texas, 14-7; FIESTA—No. 10 Pittsburgh beat unranked Arizona, 16-10. (Alabama selected No. 1 in all four polls)

1980 SUGAR—No. 1 Georgia beat No. 7 Notre Dame, 17-10; ORANGE—No. 4 Oklahoma beat No. 2 Florida St., 18-17; ROSE—No. 5 Michigan beat No. 16 Washington, 23-6; COTTON—No. 9 Alabama beat No. 6 Baylor, 30-2; GATOR—No. 3 Pittsburgh beat No. 18 South Caro., 37-9; SUN—No. 8 Nebraska beat No. 17 Mississippi St., 31-17; FIESTA—No. 10 Penn St. beat No. 11 Ohio St., 31-19; BLUEBONNET—No. 13 North Caro. beat unranked Texas, 16-7. (Georgia remained No. 1 in all four polls)

1981 ORANGE—No. 1 Clemson beat No. 4 Nebraska, 22-15; SUGAR—No. 10 Pittsburgh beat No. 2 Georgia, 24-20; COTTON—No. 6 Texas beat No. 3 Alabama, 14-12; GATOR—No. 11 North Caro. beat unranked Arkansas, 31-27; ROSE—No. 12 Washington beat No. 13 Iowa, 28-0; FIESTA—No. 7 Penn St. beat No. 8 Southern Cal, 26-10. (Clemson remained No. 1 in all four polls)

1982 SUGAR—No. 2 Penn St. beat No. 1 Georgia, 27-23; ORANGE—No. 3 Nebraska beat No. 13 LSU, 21-20; COTTON—No. 4 Southern Methodist beat No. 6 Pittsburgh, 7-3; ROSE—No. 5 UCLA beat No. 19 Michigan, 24-14; ALOHA—No. 9 Washington beat No. 16 Maryland, 21-20; FIESTA—No. 11 Arizona St. beat No. 12 Oklahoma, 32-21; BLUEBONNET—No. 14 Arkansas beat unranked Florida, 28-24. (Penn St. selected No. 1 in all four polls)

1983 ORANGE—No. 5 Miami (Fla.) beat No. 1 Nebraska, 31-30; COTTON—No. 7 Georgia beat No. 2 Texas, 10-9; SUGAR—No. 3 Auburn beat No. 8 Michigan, 9-7; ROSE—Unranked UCLA beat No. 4 Illinois, 45-9; HOLIDAY—No. 9 Brigham Young beat unranked Missouri, 21-17; GATOR—No. 11 Florida beat No. 10 Iowa, 14-6; FIESTA—No. 14 Ohio St. beat No. 15 Pittsburgh, 28-23. (Miami, Fla., selected No. 1 in all four polls)

1984 HOLIDAY—No. 1 Brigham Young beat unranked Michigan, 24-17; ORANGE—No. 4 Washington beat No. 2 Oklahoma, 28-17; SUGAR—No. 5 Nebraska beat No. 11 LSU, 28-10; ROSE—No. 18 Southern Cal beat No. 6 Ohio St., 20-17; COTTON—No. 8 Boston College beat unranked Houston, 45-28; GATOR—No. 9 Oklahoma St. beat No. 7 South Caro., 21-14; ALOHA—No. 10 Southern Methodist beat No. 17 Notre Dame, 27-20. (Brigham Young remained No. 1 in all four polls)

1985 ORANGE—No. 3 Oklahoma beat No. 1 Penn St., 25-10; SUGAR—No. 8 Tennessee beat No. 2 Miami (Fla.), 35-7; ROSE—No. 13 UCLA beat No. 4 Iowa, 45-28; COTTON—No. 11 Texas A&M beat No. 16 Auburn, 36-16; FIESTA—No. 5 Michigan beat No. 7 Nebraska, 27-23; BLUEBONNET—No. 10 Air Force beat unranked Texas, 24-16. (Oklahoma selected No. 1 in all four polls)

1986 FIESTA—No. 2 Penn St. beat No. 1 Miami (Fla.), 14-10; ORANGE—No. 3 Oklahoma beat No. 9 Arkansas, 42-8; ROSE—No. 7 Arizona St. beat No. 4 Michigan, 22-15; SUGAR—No. 6 Nebraska beat No. 5 LSU, 30-15; COTTON—No. 11 Ohio St. beat No. 8 Texas A&M, 28-12; CITRUS—No. 10 Auburn beat unranked Southern Cal, 16-7; SUN—No. 13 Alabama beat No. 12 Washington, 28-6. (Penn St. selected No. 1 in all four polls)

1987 ORANGE—No. 2 Miami (Fla.) beat No. 1 Oklahoma, 20-14; FIESTA—No. 3 Florida St. beat No. 5 Nebraska, 31-28; SUGAR—No. 4 Syracuse tied No. 6 Auburn, 16-16; ROSE—No. 8 Michigan St. beat No. 16 Southern Cal, 20-17; COTTON—No. 13 Texas A&M beat No. 12 Notre Dame, 35-10; GATOR—No. 7 LSU beat No. 9 South Caro., 30-13; ALOHA—No. 10 UCLA beat unranked Florida, 20-16. (Miami, Fla., selected No. 1 in all four polls)

1988 FIESTA—No. 1 Notre Dame beat No. 3 West Va., 34-21; ORANGE—No. 2 Miami (Fla.) beat No. 6 Nebraska, 23-3; SUGAR—No. 4 Florida St. beat No. 7 Auburn, 13-7; ROSE—No. 11 Michigan beat No. 5 Southern Cal, 22-14; COTTON—No. 9 UCLA beat No. 8 Arkansas, 17-3; CITRUS—No. 13 Clemson beat No. 10 Oklahoma, 13-6. (Notre Dame selected No. 1 in all four polls)

1989 ORANGE—No. 4 Notre Dame beat No. 1 Colorado, 21-6; SUGAR—No. 2 Miami (Fla.) beat No. 7 Alabama, 33-25; ROSE—No. 12 Southern Cal beat No. 3 Michigan, 17-10; COTTON—No. 8 Tennessee beat No. 10 Arkansas, 31-27; FIESTA—No. 5 Florida St. beat No. 6 Nebraska, 41-17; HALL OF FAME—No. 9 Auburn beat No. 21 Ohio St., 31-14; CITRUS—No. 11 Illinois beat No. 15 Virginia, 31-21. (Miami, Fla., selected No. 1 in all four polls)

1990 ORANGE—No. 1 Colorado beat No. 5 Notre Dame, 10-9; CITRUS—No. 2 Georgia Tech beat No. 19 Nebraska, 45-21; COTTON—No. 4 Miami (Fla.) beat No. 3 Texas, 46-3; BLOCKBUSTER—No. 6 Florida St. beat No. 7 Penn St., 24-17; ROSE—No. 8 Washington beat No. 17 Iowa, 46-34; GATOR—No. 12 Michigan beat No. 15 Mississippi, 35-3; SUGAR—No. 10 Tennessee beat unranked Virginia, 23-22. (Colorado selected No. 1 in AP, FW and NFF polls, but Georgia Tech picked in UPI poll)

1991 ORANGE—No. 1 Miami (Fla.) beat No. 11 Nebraska, 22-0; ROSE—No. 2 Washington beat No. 4 Michigan, 34-14; COTTON—No. 5 Florida St. beat No. 9 Texas A&M, 10-3; BLOCKBUSTER—No. 8 Alabama beat No. 15 Colorado, 30-25; SUGAR—No. 18 Notre Dame beat No. 3 Florida, 39-28; FIESTA—No. 6 Penn St. beat No. 10 Tennessee, 42-17; CITRUS—No. 14 California beat No. 13 Clemson, 37-13; PEACH—No. 12 East Caro. beat No. 21 North Caro. St., 37-34; HOLIDAY—No. 7 Iowa tied unranked Brigham Young, 13-13. (Miami, Fla., selected No. 1 in AP poll, while Washington named in USA/CNN, NFF and FW polls)

1992 SUGAR—No. 2 Alabama beat No. 1 Miami (Fla.), 34-13; GATOR—No. 14 Florida beat No. 12 North Caro. St., 27-10; COTTON—No. 5 Notre Dame beat No. 4 Texas A&M, 28-3; HALL OF FAME—No. 17 Tennessee beat No. 16 Boston College, 38-23; CITRUS—No. 8 Georgia beat No. 15 Ohio St., 21-14; ROSE—No. 7 Michigan beat No. 9 Washington, 38-31; ORANGE—No. 3 Florida St. beat No. 11 Nebraska, 27-14; FIESTA—No. 6 Syracuse beat No. 10 Colorado, 26-22; BLOCKBUSTER—No. 13 Stanford beat No. 21 Penn St., 24-3; PEACH—No. 19 North Caro. beat No. 24 Mississippi St., 21-17; COPPER—No. 18 Washington St. beat unranked Utah, 31-28. (Alabama selected No. 1 in all four polls)

1993 ORANGE—No. 1 Florida St. beat No. 2 Nebraska, 18-16; SUGAR—No. 8 Florida beat No. 3 West Va., 41-7; ROSE—No. 9 Wisconsin beat No. 14 UCLA, 21-16; COTTON—No. 4 Notre Dame beat No. 7 Texas A&M, 24-21; CARQUEST—No. 15 Boston College beat unranked Virginia, 31-13; FIESTA—No. 16 Arizona beat No. 10 Miami (Fla.), 29-0; FLORIDA CITRUS—No. 13 Penn St. beat No. 6 Tennessee, 31-13; HALL OF FAME—No. 23 Michigan beat unranked North Caro. St., 42-7; GATOR—No. 18 Alabama beat No. 12 North Caro., 24-10; PEACH—No. 24 Clemson beat unranked Kentucky, 14-13; INDEPENDENCE—No. 22 Virginia Tech beat unranked Indiana, 45-20; HOLIDAY—No. 11 Ohio St. beat unranked Brigham Young, 28-21; COPPER—No. 20 Kansas St. beat unranked Wyoming, 52-17; LIBERTY—No. 25 Louisville beat unranked Michigan St., 18-7; ALOHA—No. 17 Colorado beat No. 25 Fresno St., 41-30; JOHN HANCOCK—No. 19 Oklahoma beat unranked Texas Tech, 41-10. (Florida St. selected in all four major polls—AP, FW, USA/CNN and USA/NFF)

1994 ORANGE—No. 1 Nebraska beat No. 3 Miami (Fla.), 24-17; ROSE—No. 2 Penn St. beat No. 12 Oregon, 38-20; FIESTA—No. 4 Colorado beat unranked Notre Dame, 41-24; SUGAR—No. 7 Florida St. beat No. 5 Florida, 23-17; FLORIDA CITRUS—No. 6 Alabama beat No. 13 Ohio St., 24-17; FREEDOM—No. 14 Utah beat No. 15 Arizona, 16-13; ALOHA—Unranked Boston College beat No. 11 Kansas St., 12-7; HOLIDAY—No. 20 Michigan beat No. 10 Colorado St., 24-14; PEACH—No. 23 North Caro. St. beat No. 16 Mississippi St., 28-24; INDEPENDENCE—No. 18 Virginia beat unranked Texas Christian, 20-10; SUN—Unranked Texas beat No. 19 North Caro., 35-31; GATOR—Unranked Tennessee beat No. 17 Virginia Tech, 45-23. (Nebraska selected in all four major polls—AP, UPI, USA/CNN and FW)

1995 FIESTA—No. 1 Nebraska beat No. 2 Florida, 62-24; ROSE—No. 17 Southern Cal beat No. 3 Northwestern, 41-32; FLORIDA CITRUS—No. 4 Tennessee beat No. 4 Ohio St., 20-14; ORANGE—No. 8 Florida St. beat No. 6 Notre Dame, 31-26; COTTON—No. 7 Colorado beat No. 12 Oregon, 38-6; SUGAR—No. 13 Virginia Tech beat No. 9 Texas, 28-10; HOLIDAY—No. 10 Kansas St. beat unranked Colorado St., 54-21; ALOHA—No. 11 Kansas beat unranked UCLA, 51-30; ALAMO—No. 19 Texas A&M beat No. 14 Michigan, 22-20; OUTBACK—No. 15 Penn St. beat No. 16 Auburn, 43-14; PEACH—No. 18 Virginia beat unranked Georgia, 34-27. (Nebraska selected in all four major polls—AP, UPI, USA/CNN and FW)

Most Consecutive Bowl-Game Victories

(Bowls do not have to be in consecutive years; year listed is calendar year in which bowl was played)

College	Victories (Years)
Florida St.	11 (1985-86-88-89-90-90-92-93-94-95-96)
Southern Cal	9 (1923-24-30-32-33-39-40-44-45)
UCLA	8 (1983-84-85-86-86-87-89-91)
Georgia Tech	8 (1947-48-52-53-54-55-56-56)
Syracuse	6 (1989-89-90-92-93-96)
Alabama	6 (1975-76-78-79-80-81)
Nebraska	6 (1969-71-72-73-74-74)
Notre Dame	5 (1973-75-76-78-79)
Arizona St.	5 (1970-71-72-73-75)
Alabama	4 (1991-93-93-95)
Alabama	4 (1982-83-85-86)
Air Force	4 (1982-83-84-85)
North Caro.	4 (1979-80-81-82)
Michigan	4 (1902-48-51-65)
Colorado	3 (1993-95-96)
Penn St.	3 (1994-95-96)
Southern Cal	3 (1993-95-96)
Notre Dame	3 (1992-93-94)
California	3 (1990-92-93)

Most Consecutive Seasons With Bowl-Game Victories

*11 Florida St.—85 Gator, Oklahoma St. 34-23; 86 All-American, Indiana 27-13; 87 Fiesta, Nebraska 31-28; 88 Sugar, Auburn 13-7; 89 Fiesta, Nebraska 41-17; 90 Blockbuster, Penn St. 24-17; 92 Cotton, Texas A&M 10-2; 93 Orange, Nebraska 27-14; 94 Orange, Nebraska 18-16; 95 Sugar, Florida 23-17; 96 Orange, Notre Dame 31-26. Coach: Bobby Bowden.

7 UCLA—83 Rose, Michigan 24-14; 84 Rose, Illinois 45-9; 85 Fiesta, Miami (Fla.) 39-37; 86 Rose, Iowa 45-28; 86 Freedom, Brigham Young 31-10; 87 Aloha, Florida 20-16; 89 Cotton, Arkansas, 17-3. Coach: Terry Donahue.

6 Alabama—75 Sugar, Penn St. 13-6; 76 Liberty, UCLA 36-6; 78 Sugar, Ohio St. 35-6; 79 Sugar, Penn St. 14-7; 80 Sugar, Arkansas 24-9; 81 Cotton, Baylor 30-2. Coach: Paul "Bear" Bryant.

6 Nebraska—69 Sun, Georgia 45-6; 71 Orange, LSU 17-12; 72 Orange, Alabama 38-6; 73 Orange, Notre Dame 40-6; 74 Cotton, Texas 19-3; 74 Sugar, Florida 13-10. Coaches: Bob Devaney first 4 games, Tom Osborne last 2.

BOWL/ALL-STAR RECORDS

6 Georgia Tech—52 Orange, Baylor 17-14; 53 Sugar, Mississippi 24-7; 54 Sugar, West Va. 42-19; 55 Cotton, Arkansas 14-6; 56 Sugar, Pittsburgh 7-0; 56 Gator, Pittsburgh 21-14. Coach: Bobby Dodd.

*Active streak.

Active Consecutive Appearances in Bowl Games

(Must have appeared in 1995-96 bowls)

Team	Appearances	Team	Appearances
Nebraska	27	Colorado	7
Michigan	21	Penn St.	7
Florida St.	14	Tennessee	7
Notre Dame	9	Ohio St.	6

Most Bowl Teams Faced in 1995

(Teams that faced the most 1995-96 bowl teams during their 1995 regular-season schedule)

Team	No. Faced	Team	No. Faced
Illinois	7	Alabama	5
Wisconsin	7	Cincinnati	5
Arizona St.	6	Colorado	5
Boston College	6	Georgia Tech	5
Florida	6	Iowa St.	5
Houston	6	Kentucky	5
Indiana	6	Michigan	5
Minnesota	6	Mississippi	5
Notre Dame	6	Missouri	5
Penn St.	6	Northwestern	5
Purdue	6	Ohio St.	5
South Caro.	6	Oklahoma	5
Virginia	6	Oklahoma St.	5
Washington	6	Temple	5
Washington St.	6	Vanderbilt	5

Undefeated, Untied Team Matchups in Bowl Games

Bowl	Date	Winner (Record Going In, Coach)	Loser (Record Going In, Coach)
Rose	1-1-21	California 28 (8-0, Andy Smith)	Ohio St. 0 (7-0, John Wilce)
Rose	1-2-22	0-0 tie: California (9-0, Andy Smith) Wash. & Jeff. (10-0, Earle "Greasy" Neale)	
Rose	1-1-27	7-7 tie: Alabama (9-0, Wallace Wade) Stanford (10-0, Glenn "Pop" Warner)	
Rose	1-1-31	Alabama 24 (9-0, Wallace Wade)	Washington St. 0 (9-0, Orin "Babe" Hollingbery)
Orange	1-2-39	Tennessee 17 (10-0, Bob Neyland)	Oklahoma 0 (10-0, Tom Stidham)
Sugar	1-1-41	Boston College 19 (10-0, Frank Leahy)	Tennessee 13 (10-0, Bob Neyland)
Sugar	1-1-52	Maryland 28 (9-0, Jim Tatum)	Tennessee 13 (10-0, Bob Neyland)
Orange	1-2-56	Oklahoma 20 (10-0, Bud Wilkinson)	Maryland 6 (10-0, Jim Tatum)
Orange	1-1-72	Nebraska 38 (12-0, Bob Devaney)	Alabama 6 (11-0, Paul "Bear" Bryant)
Sugar	12-31-73	Notre Dame 24 (10-0, Ara Parseghian)	Alabama 23 (11-0, Paul "Bear" Bryant)
Fiesta	1-2-87	Penn St. 14 (11-0, Joe Paterno)	Miami (Fla.) 10 (11-0, Jimmy Johnson)
Orange	1-1-88	Miami (Fla.) 20 (11-0, Jimmy Johnson)	Oklahoma 14 (11-0, Barry Switzer)
Fiesta	1-2-89	Notre Dame 34 (11-0, Lou Holtz)	West Va. 21 (11-0, Don Nehlen)
Sugar	1-1-93	Alabama 34 (12-0, Gene Stallings)	Miami (Fla.) 13 (11-0, Dennis Erickson)
Fiesta	1-2-96	Nebraska 62 (11-0, Tom Osborne)	Florida 24 (12-0, Steve Spurrier)

Undefeated Team Matchups in Bowl Games

(Both teams were undefeated but one or both was tied one or more times)

Bowl	Date	Winner (Record Going In, Coach)	Loser (Record Going In, Coach)
Rose	1-1-25	Notre Dame 27 (9-0, Knute Rockne)	Stanford 10 (7-0-1, Glenn "Pop" Warner)
Rose	1-1-26	Alabama 20 (9-0, Wallace Wade)	Washington 19 (10-0-1, Enoch Bagshaw)
Rose	1-2-33	Southern Cal 35 (9-0, Howard Jones)	Pittsburgh 0 (8-0-2, Jock Sutherland)
Rose	1-1-35	Alabama 29 (9-0, Frank Thomas)	Stanford 13 (9-0-1, Claude "Tiny" Thornhill)
Rose	1-1-38	California 13 (9-0-1, Leonard "Stub" Allison)	Alabama 0 (9-0, Frank Thomas)
Rose	1-1-40	Southern Cal 14 (7-0-2, Howard Jones)	Tennessee 0 (10-0, Bob Neyland)
Sugar	1-1-40	Texas A&M 14 (10-0, Homer Norton)	Tulane 13 (8-0-1, Lowell "Red" Dawson)
Rose	1-1-45	Southern Cal 25 (7-0-2, Jeff Cravath)	Tennessee 0 (7-0-1, John Barnhill)
Cotton	1-1-48	13-13 tie: Penn St. (9-0, Bob Higgins) Southern Methodist (9-0-1, Matty Bell)	
Orange	1-1-51	Clemson 15 (8-0-1, Frank Howard)	Miami (Fla.) 14 (9-0-1, Andy Gustafson)
Sugar	1-1-53	Georgia Tech 24 (11-0, Bobby Dodd)	Mississippi 7 (8-0-2, John Vaught)
Rose	1-1-69	Ohio St. 27 (9-0, Woody Hayes)	Southern Cal 16 (9-0-1, John McKay)
Rose	1-1-80	Southern Cal 17 (10-0-1, John Robinson)	Ohio St. 16 (11-0, Earle Bruce)
California	12-14-85	Fresno St. 51 (10-0-1, Jim Sweeney)	Bowling Green 7 (11-0, Denny Stolz)

Bowl Rematches of Regular-Season Opponents

Date	Regular Season	Date	Bowl-Game Rematch
10-9-43	Texas A&M 28, LSU 13	1-1-44	(Orange) LSU 19, Texas A&M 14
10-6-56	Iowa 14, Oregon St. 13	1-1-57	(Rose) Iowa 35, Oregon St. 19
10-31-59	LSU 7, Mississippi 3	1-1-60	(Sugar) Mississippi 21, LSU 0
9-18-65	Michigan St. 13, UCLA 3	1-1-66	(Rose) UCLA 14, Michigan St. 12
10-4-75	Ohio St. 41, UCLA 20	1-1-76	(Rose) UCLA 23, Ohio St. 10
11-11-78	Nebraska 17, Oklahoma 14	1-1-79	(Orange) Oklahoma 31, Nebraska 24
9-25-82	UCLA 31, Michigan 27	1-1-83	(Rose) UCLA 24, Michigan 14
9-7-87	Michigan St. 27, Southern Cal 13	1-1-88	(Rose) Michigan St. 20, Southern Cal 17
11-26-94	Florida 31, Florida St. 31	1-2-95	(Sugar) Florida St. 23, Florida 17
9-23-95	Toledo 49, Nevada 35	12-14-95	(Las Vegas) Toledo 40, Nevada 37 (OT)

Bowl-Game Facts

The Bowl/Basketball Connection

Nine times in history, a football bowl winner also won the NCAA men's basketball championship during the same academic year. They are as follows:

Year	School	Bowl	Date of Bowl
1992-93	North Caro.	Peach	1-2-93
1988-89	Michigan	Rose	1-2-89
1981-82	North Caro.	Gator	12-28-81
1973-74	North Caro. St.	Liberty	12-17-73
1965-66	UTEP	Sun	12-31-65
1950-51	Kentucky	Sugar	1-1-51
1947-48	Kentucky	Great Lakes	12-6-47
1945-46	Oklahoma St.	Sugar	1-1-46
1944-45	Oklahoma St.	Cotton	1-1-45

One-Time Wonders

Six major-college teams have played in only one bowl game in their football history, and three of those have posted victories. The winners were Eastern Michigan, Memphis and Northern Illinois. The one-time bowlers are as follows:

School	Date	Bowl	Opponent (Score)
Eastern Mich.	12-12-87	California	San Jose St. (30-27)
Kent	12-29-72	Tangerine	Tampa (18-21)
Long Beach St.	12-19-70	Pasadena	Louisville (24-24)
Memphis	12-18-71	Pasadena	San Jose St. (28-9)
Northern Ill.	12-17-83	California	Cal St. Fullerton (20-13)
Rutgers	12-16-78	Garden State	Arizona St. (18-34)

Year-by-Year Bowl Facts

(A note about bowl-game dates: Traditionally, bowl games have been played on January 1, but as more bowl games joined the holiday lineup, schedule adjustments were made whereby some bowl games are now played as early as mid-December. In the interest of avoiding confusion, all years referred to in bowl records are the actual calendar year in which the bowl game was played.)

1917 Coach Hugo Bezdek led the first of three teams to the Rose Bowl from 1917 to 1923. His Oregon team beat Pennsylvania, 14-0, in 1917; his Mare Island squad defeated Camp Lewis, 19-7, in 1918; and his Penn State team lost to Southern California, 14-3, in 1923. In his 1923 trip with the Nittany Lions, Bezdek almost came to blows with Southern California coach Elmer "Gloomy Gus" Henderson because Penn State did not arrive for the game until an hour after the scheduled kickoff time. Henderson accused Bezdek of not taking the field until the hot California sun had gone down to give his winterized Easterners an advantage.

1919 George Halas (yes, "Papa Bear") was the player of the game for Great Lakes Naval Training Station in Chicago as the Sailors shut out Mare Island, 17-0, in another of the wartime Rose Bowls.

1923 The first Rose Bowl game actually played in the stadium in Pasadena saw Southern California defeat Penn State, 14-3.

1926 Johnny Mack Brown, one of Hollywood's most famous movie cowboys, also was one of college football's most exciting players at Alabama. He was selected player of the game for the Rose Bowl in the Crimson Tide's 20-19 victory over Washington.

1927 The Rose Bowl becomes the first coast-to-coast radio broadcast of a sporting event.

1929 The Rose Bowl game became one of the most famous in bowl history because of California player Roy Riegels' now-legendary wrong-way run. Early in the second quarter, with each team just changing possessions, Georgia Tech was on its own 20. Tech halfback Stumpy Thompson broke for a seven-yard run, fumbled, and Riegels picked up the ball, momentarily headed for the Tech goal, then reversed his field and started running the wrong way. Teammate Benny Lom tried to stop him and finally did on the California one-yard line, where the dazed Riegels was pounced on by a group of Tech tacklers. Lom went back to punt on the next play and the kick was blocked out of the end zone for a safety, which decided the contest, eventually won by Tech, 8-7.

1938 The first Orange Bowl played in Miami's new stadium, which seated 22,000 at the time, saw Auburn edge Michigan State, 6-0. Also, in the second annual Cotton Bowl, Colorado's do-it-all standout Byron "Whizzer" White, the Rhodes Scholar and future U.S. Supreme Court justice, passed for one score and returned a pass interception for another, but the Buffs lost to Rice, 28-14.

1941 On December 6, 1941, Hawaii defeated Willamette, 20-6, but a second post-season game, scheduled with San Jose State for the next week, was cancelled after the attack on Pearl Harbor.

1942 You would think a team making only one first down and gaining only 75 yards to its opponent's 309 yards could not come out of a game a 29-21 victor, but it happened in the Cotton Bowl as Alabama downed Texas A&M. The Tide intercepted seven of A&M's 42 passes and recovered five Aggie fumbles. Also, the Rose Bowl was moved for one year to Durham, N.C., because of wartime considerations that precluded large gatherings on the West Coast, and Oregon State downed Duke, 20-16.

1946 The first and only bowl game decided after time expired was the Orange Bowl when Miami (Florida) downed Holy Cross, 13-6. Time expired as Miami halfback Al Hudson returned an 89-yard intercepted pass for the deciding score.

1949 A Pacific Coast team had never been allowed to play in a major bowl other than the Rose Bowl, but the conference leadership let Oregon play in the Cotton Bowl against Southern Methodist. Doak Walker and Kyle Rote led Southern Methodist to a 20-13 victory over the Ducks and quarterback Norm Van Brocklin. John McKay, later the head coach at Southern California, also was on the Oregon roster.

1953 The Rose, Cotton, Sugar and Orange Bowls were televised nationally for the first time.

1954 Dicky Maegle of Rice may be the best-remembered bowl player, not because of his 265 yards rushing and three touchdowns vs. Alabama in 1954, but because of what happened on a 95-yard scoring run. Alabama's Tommy Lewis became infamous by coming off the bench to tackle Maegle in the Cotton Bowl, won by Rice, 28-6.

1960 In one of those pupil-vs.-teacher battles, former Georgia Tech player and assistant coach Frank Broyles led his Arkansas Razorbacks to a 14-7 Gator Bowl victory over his former coach, Bobby Dodd, and the Yellow Jackets.

1962 Oregon State quarterback Terry Baker turned in the longest run in bowl history with a 99-yard scamper to down Villanova, 6-0, in the Liberty Bowl. Baker, an outstanding athlete, became the only Heisman Trophy winner to play in an NCAA Final Four basketball game later that academic year (1963).

1964 Utah and West Virginia became the first teams to play a major bowl game indoors when they met in the Atlantic City Convention Hall. Utah won, 32-6, beneath the bright indoor lights.

1965 The first Orange Bowl played under the lights in Miami saw Texas stun national champion Alabama and quarterback Joe Namath, 21-17.

1968 It was the student beating the teacher in the Cotton Bowl as Texas A&M head coach Gene Stallings saw his Aggies hold on for a 20-16 victory over Alabama and legendary head coach Paul "Bear" Bryant. Stallings had played (at Texas A&M) and coached (at Alabama) under Bryant. The "Bear" met Stallings at midfield after the contest and lifted the 6-foot-3 Aggie coach up in admiration. Also, the Astro-Bluebonnet Bowl (also known as the Bluebonnet Bowl) became the first bowl game to be played in a domed stadium as the Astrodome served as the site of the December 31, 1968, game between Southern Methodist (28) and Oklahoma (27).

1970 Three of the four legendary Four Horsemen of Notre Dame came to Dallas to watch the Fighting Irish drop a 21-17 Cotton Bowl game to Texas. The only other time Notre Dame had played in a bowl game was the 1925 Rose Bowl, when the Four Horsemen led the Irish to a 27-10 victory over Stanford.

1971 Notre Dame snapped the second-longest winning streak going into a bowl game by halting Texas' 30-game string, 24-11, in the Cotton Bowl. In 1951, Kentucky had stopped Oklahoma's 31-game streak in the Sugar Bowl, 13-7.

1976 Archie Griffin started his fourth straight Rose Bowl for Ohio State (1973-76), totaling 412 yards on 79 carries in the four games. The Buckeyes, under legendary head coach Woody Hayes, won only the 1974 contest, but Griffin is the only player to win two Heisman Trophies (1974-75).

1989 Texas Tech's James Gray set a college bowl record with 280 yards rushing in the All-American Bowl against Duke. Brigham Young's Ty Detmer set the bowl passing mark with 576 yards versus Penn State in the Holiday Bowl.

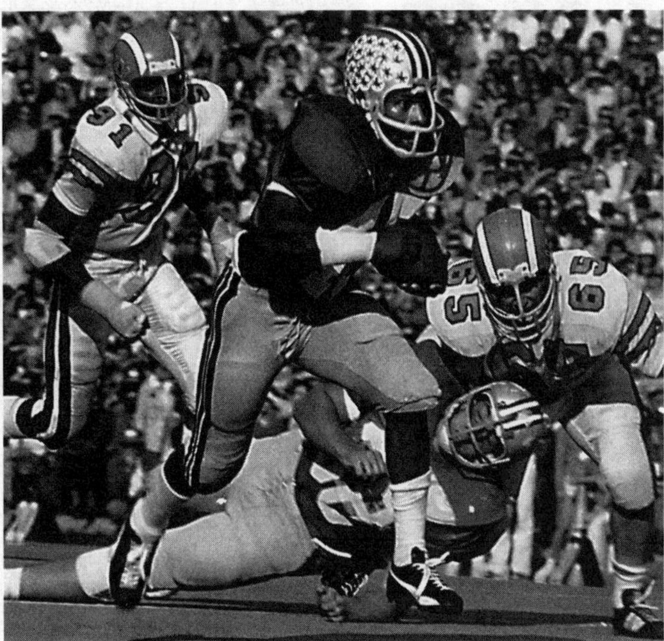

File photo

Two-time Heisman Trophy winner Archie Griffin started four straight Rose Bowls for Ohio State (1973-76).

Special Regular- and Postseason Games

Postseason Games

UNSANCTIONED OR OTHER BOWLS

The following bowl games were unsanctioned by the NCAA or otherwise had no team classified as major college at the time of the bowl. Most are postseason games; in many cases, complete dates and/or statistics are not available and the scores are listed only to provide a historical reference. Attendance of the game, if known, is listed in parentheses after the score.

ALL-SPORTS BOWL
(Oklahoma City, Okla.)
12-9-61—Okla. Panhandle St. 28, Langston 14 (8,000)
12-8-62—Neb.-Omaha 34, East Central 21 (2,500)
12-7-63—Northeastern St. 59, Slippery Rock 12
12-5-64—Sul Ross St. 21, East Central 13

ALUMINUM BOWL (NAIA Title Game)
(Little Rock, Ark.)
12-22-56—Montana St. 0, St. Joseph's (Ind.) 0

ANGEL BOWL
(Los Angeles, Calif.)
12-28-46—Florida A&M 6, Wiley 6 (12,000)

AZALEA BOWL
(Orlando, Fla.)
1-1-46—Knoxville 18, Florida Normal 0 (4,000)

AZALEA CLASSIC
(Mobile, Ala.)
12-4-71—Jackson St. 40, Alabama A&M 21
12-7-74—Bethune-Cookman 19, Langston 3 (1,000)

AZTEC BOWL
(Mexico City, Mexico)
12-50—Whittier 27, Mexico All-Stars 14
12-53—Mexico City 45, Eastern N.M. 26

BEAN BOWL
(Scottsbluff, Neb.)
11-24-49—Idaho St. 20, Chadron St. 2
11-23-50—Doane 14, Northern Colo. 6

BEAVER BOWL
(Corry, Pa.)
11-15-58—Slippery Rock 6, Edinboro 0 (3,000)

BICENTENNIAL BOWL
(Little Rock, Ark.)
11-29-75—Henderson St. 27, East Central 14 (2,000)

BICENTENNIAL BOWL
(Richmond, Va.)
12-11-76—South Caro. St. 26, Norfolk St. 10 (7,500)

BOOT HILL BOWL
(Dodge City, Kan.)
12-70—Cameron 13, N.M. Highlands 12
12-4-71—Dakota St. 23, Northwestern Okla. 20 (2,000)
12-2-72—William Penn 17, Emporia St. 14 (2,000)
12-1-73—Millikin 51, Bethany (Kan.) 7 (1,600)
11-30-74—Washburn 21, Millikin 7 (2,500)
11-22-75—Buena Vista 24, St. Mary's (Kan.) 21 (2,700)
11-20-76—Benedictine 29, Washburn 14 (3,000)
11-19-77—Mo. Western St. 35, Benedictine 30 (1,000)
11-18-78—Chadron St. 30, Baker (Kan.) 19 (3,000)
11-17-79—Pittsburg St. 43, Peru St. 14 (2,800)
11-21-80—Cameron 34, Adams St. 16

BOTANY BOWL
11-24-55—Neb.-Kearney 34, Northern St. 13

BOY'S RANCH BOWL
(Abilene, Texas)
12-13-47—Missouri Valley 20, McMurry (Tex.) 13 (2,500)

BURLEY BOWL
(Johnson City, Tenn.)
1-1-46—High Point 7, Milligan 7 (3,500)
11-28-46—Southeastern La. 21, Milligan 13 (7,500)
11-27-47—West Chester 20, Carson-Newman 6 (10,000)
11-25-48—West Chester 7, Appalachian St. 2 (12,000)
11-24-49—Emory & Henry 32, Hanover 0 (12,000)
11-23-50—Emory & Henry 26, Appalachian St. 6 (12,000)
11-22-51—Morris Harvey (now Charleston) 27, Lebanon Valley 20 (9,000)
11-27-52—East Tenn. St. 34, Emory & Henry 16
11-26-53—East Tenn. St. 48, Emory & Henry 12
11-25-54—Appalachian St. 28, East Tenn. St. 13
11-24-55—East Tenn. St. 7, Appalachian St. 0
11-22-56—Memphis 32, East Tenn. St. 12

CAJUN BOWL
12-47—McNeese St. 0, Southern Ark. 0

CATTLE BOWL
(Fort Worth, Texas)
1-1-47—Ark.-Pine Bluff 7, Lane 0 (1,000)
1-1-48—Samuel Huston 7, Philander Smith 0 (800)

CEMENT BOWL
(Allentown, Pa.)
12-8-62—West Chester 46, Hofstra 12

CHARITY BOWL
(Los Angeles, Calif.)
12-25-37—Fresno St. 27, Central Ark. 26 (5,000)

CHRISTMAS BOWL
(Natchitoches, La.)
12-6-58—Northwestern St. 18, Sam Houston St. 11
12-5-59—Delta St. 19, East Central 0

CIGAR BOWL
(Tampa, Fla.)
1-1-47—Delaware 21, Rollins 7 (9,500)
1-1-48—Missouri Valley 26, West Chester 7 (10,000)
1-1-49—Missouri Valley 13, St. Thomas (Minn.) 13 (11,000)
1-2-50—Florida St. 19, Wofford 6 (14,000)
1-1-51—Wis.-La Crosse 47, Valparaiso 14 (12,000)
12-29-51—Brooke Army Medical 20, Camp Lejeune Marines 0 (7,500) (see Cigar Bowl in Service Games)
12-13-52—Tampa 21, Lenoir-Rhyne 12 (7,500)
1-1-54—Missouri Valley 12, Wis.-La Crosse 12 (5,000)
12-17-54—Tampa 21, Morris Harvey (now Charleston) 0

CITRACADO BOWL
(see Citracado Bowl in Service Games)

COCONUT BOWL
(Miami, Fla.)
1-1-42—Florida Normal 0, Miami All-Stars 0 (9,000)
1-1-46—Bethune-Cookman 32, Albany St. (Ga.) 0 (5,000)
1-1-47—Bethune-Cookman 13, Columbia (S.C.) Sporting Club 0 (5,000)

CORN BOWL
(Bloomington, Ill.)
11-27-47—Southern Ill. 21, North Central 0 (5,500)
11-25-48—Ill. Wesleyan 6, Eastern Ill. 0 (8,500)
11-24-49—Western Ill. 13, Wheaton (Ill.) 0 (4,567)
11-23-50—Mo.-Rolla 7, Illinois St. 6 (2,500)
11-22-51—Lewis 21, William Jewell 12 (2,000)
11-26-53—Western Ill. 32, Iowa Wesleyan 0
11-24-55—Luther 24, Western Ill. 20 (3,100)

COSMOPOLITAN BOWL
(Alexandria, La.)
12-51—McNeese St. 13, Louisiana Col. 6

COTTON-TOBACCO BOWL
(Greensboro, N.C.)
1-1-46—Johnson Smith 18, Allen 6
1-1-47—Norfolk St. 0, Richmond 0 (10,000)

COWBOY BOWL
(Lawton, Okla.)
12-11-71—Howard Payne 16, Cameron 13
12-9-72—Harding 30, Langston 27

DOLL AND TOY CHARITY GAME
(Gulfport, Miss.)
12-3-37—Southern Miss. 7, Appalachian St. 0 (2,000)

EASTERN BOWL
(Allentown, Pa.)
12-14-63—East Caro. 27, Northeastern 6 (2,700)

ELKS BOWL
1-2-54—Morris Harvey (now Charleston) 12, East Caro. 0 (4,500) (at Greenville, N.C.)
12-11-54—Newberry 20, Appalachian St. 13 (at Raleigh, N.C.)

FISH BOWL
(Corpus Christi, Texas)
11-48—Southwestern (Tex.) 7, Corpus Christi 0

FISH BOWL
(Norfolk, Va.)
12-4-48—Hampton 20, Central St. 19

FLOWER BOWL
(Jacksonville, Fla.)
1-1-42—Johnson Smith 13, Lane 0 (4,500)
1-1-43—North Caro. A&T 14, Southern-B.R. 6 (2,000)
1-1-44—Allen 33, Winston-Salem 0 (2,000)
1-1-45—Texas College 18, North Caro. A&T 0 (5,000)
1-1-46—Grambling 19, Lane 6 (6,000)
1-1-47—Delaware St. 7, Florida Normal 6 (3,000)
1-1-48—Bethune-Cookman 6, Lane 0 (3,000)

FRUIT BOWL
(San Francisco, Calif.)
12-14-47—Central St. 26, Prairie View 0 (9,000)
12-5-48—Southern-B.R. 30, San Fran. St. 0 (5,000)

GATE CITY BOWL
(Atlanta, Ga.)
12-21-74—Tuskegee 15, Norfolk St. 14 (6,252)

GLASS BOWL
(Toledo, Ohio)
12-7-46—Toledo 21, Bates 12 (12,000)
12-6-47—Toledo 20, New Hampshire 14 (13,500)
12-4-48—Toledo 27, Oklahoma City 14 (8,500)
12-3-49—Cincinnati 33, Toledo 13

GOLD BOWL
(Richmond, Va.)
12-3-77—South Caro. St. 10, Winston-Salem 7 (14,000)
12-2-78—Virginia Union 21, North Caro. A&T 6 (7,500)
12-1-79—South Caro. St. 39, Norfolk St. 7 (8,000)
12-6-80—North Caro. A&T 37, N.C. Central 0 (3,374)

GOLDEN ISLES BOWL
(Brunswick, Ga.)
12-1-62—McNeese St. 21, Samford 14

GRAPE BOWL
(Lodi, Calif.)
12-13-47—Pacific (Cal.) 35, Utah St. 21 (12,000)
12-11-48—Hardin-Simmons 35, Pacific (Cal.) 35 (10,000)

GREAT LAKES BOWL
(Cleveland, Ohio)
12-5-48—John Carroll 14, Canisius 13 (18,000)

GREAT SOUTHWEST BOWL
(Grand Prairie, Texas)
12-31-60—Tex. A&M-Kingsville 45, Arkansas Tech 14 (3,900)

HOLIDAY BOWL
(St. Petersburg, Fla.)
12-21-57—Pittsburg St. 27, Hillsdale 26
12-20-58—Northeastern St. 19, Northern Ariz. 13
12-19-59—Tex. A&M-Kingsville 20, Lenoir-Rhyne 7 (9,500)
12-10-60—Lenoir-Rhyne 15, Humboldt St. 14 (also served as NAIA national title game)

HOOSIER BOWL
(See Turkey Bowl)

INTERNATIONAL BOWL
12-52—Tex. A&M-Kingsville 49, Hereico Colegio Military 0

IODINE BOWL
(Charleston, S.C.)
12-3-49—Johnson Smith 20, Allen 12
12-9-50—Allen 20, Bethune-Cookman 0 (1,000)
12-1-51—Allen 33, Morris College 14 (3,000)
12-5-53—Allen 33, Paul Quinn 6

KICKAPOO BOWL
(Wichita Falls, Texas)
12-5-47—Midwestern St. 39, Central Ark. 20 (5,000)

LIONS BOWL
(Ruston, La.)
12-46—Grambling 69, Miss. Industrial 12
12-5-47—Grambling 47, Bethune-Cookman 6
12-49—Grambling 21, Texas College 18
12-2-50—Bishop 35, Grambling 0
12-1-51—Grambling 52, Bishop 0 (at Shreveport, La.)
12-6-52—Grambling 27, Alcorn St. 13 (at Monroe, La.)

LIONS BOWL
(Salisbury, N.C.)
12-13-52—Clarion 13, East Caro. 6 (3,000)

MERCY BOWL II
(Anaheim, Calif.)
12-11-71—Cal St. Fullerton 17, Fresno St. 14 (16,854)

MINERAL WATER BOWL
(Excelsior Springs, Mo.)
11-25-54—Hastings 20, Col. of Emporia 14 (4,000)
11-24-55—Missouri Valley 31, Hastings 7

11-22-56—St. Benedict's 14, Northeastern St. 13 (2,000)
11-30-57—William Jewell 33, Hastings 14 (2,000)
11-22-58—Lincoln (Mo.) 21, Emporia St. 0 (2,500)
11-28-59—Col. of Emporia 21, Austin (Tex.) 20 (3,000)
11-26-60—Hillsdale 17, Northern Iowa 6 (6,000)
11-25-61—Truman St. 22, Parsons 8 (8,000)
11-24-62—Adams St. 23, Northern Ill. 20
11-30-63—Northern Ill. 21, Southwest Mo. St. 14
11-28-64—North Dak. St. 14, Western St. 13 (4,500)
11-27-65—North Dak. 37, Northern Ill. 20
11-26-66—Adams St. 14, Southwest Mo. St. 8 (5,500)
11-25-67—Doane 14, William Jewell 14 (6,500)
11-30-68—Doane 10, Central Mo. St. 0 (6,000)
11-29-69—St. John's (Minn.) 21, Simpson 0 (5,000)
11-28-70—Franklin 40, Wayne St. (Neb.) 12 (2,500)
12-4-71—Bethany (Kan.) 17, Missouri Valley 14 (2,500)
11-18-72—Ottawa 27, Friends 20 (4,500)
11-73—William Jewell 20, St. Mary's (Kan.) 9
11-23-74—Midland 32, Friends 6 (1,500)
11-22-75—Mo. Western St. 44, Graceland (Ia.) 0 (3,300)

MIRZA SHRINE BOWL
(Pittsburg, Kan.)
12-1-50—Central Mo. St. 32, Pittsburg St. 21

MISSOURI-KANSAS BOWL
(Kansas City, Mo.)
12-4-48—Emporia St. 34, Southwest Mo. St. 20

MOILA SHRINE CLASSIC
(St. Joseph, Mo.)
11-24-79—Mo. Western St. 72, William Jewell 44 (1,600)
11-22-80—Truman St. 17, Pittsburg St. 14 (500)

NATIONAL CLASSIC
(Greensboro, N.C.)
12-4-54—N.C. Central 19, Tennessee St. 6

NEW YEAR'S CLASSIC
(Honolulu, Hawaii)
1-1-34—Santa Clara 26, Hawaii 7
1-1-35—Hawaii 14, California 0 (later called Poi Bowl)

OIL BOWL
(Houston, Texas)
1-1-44—Southwestern La. 24, Ark.-Monticello 7 (12,000)

OLEANDER BOWL
(Galveston, Texas)
1-2-50—McMurry 19, Missouri Valley 13 (7,500)

OLYMPIAN BOWL
(see Pythian Bowl)

OPTIMIST BOWL
(Houston, Texas)
12-21-46—North Texas 14, Pacific (Cal.) 13 (5,000)

ORANGE BLOSSOM CLASSIC
(Miami, Fla.)
12-2-33—Florida A&M 9, Howard 6
12-13-34—Florida A&M 13, Virginia St. 12
12-12-35—Kentucky St. 19, Florida A&M 10
12-5-36—Prairie View 25, Florida A&M 0
12-9-37—Florida A&M 25, Hampton 20
12-8-38—Florida A&M 9, Kentucky St. 7
12-9-39—Florida A&M 42, Wiley 0
12-7-40—Central St. 0, Florida A&M 0
12-6-41—Florida A&M 15, Tuskegee 7
12-12-42—Florida A&M 12, Texas College 6
12-4-43—Hampton 39, Florida A&M 0
12-9-44—Virginia St. 19, Florida A&M 6
12-8-45—Wiley 32, Florida A&M 6
12-7-46—Lincoln (Pa.) 20, Florida A&M 0 (at Tampa)
12-6-47—Florida A&M 7, Hampton 0
12-4-48—Virginia Union 10, Florida A&M 6 (16,000)
12-10-49—North Caro. A&T 20, Florida A&M 14
12-2-50—Central St. 13, Florida A&M 6
12-1-51—Florida A&M 67, N.C. Central 6
12-6-52—Florida A&M 29, Virginia St. 7
12-5-53—Prairie View 33, Florida A&M 27
12-4-54—Florida A&M 67, Md.-East. Shore 19
12-3-55—Grambling 28, Florida A&M 21
12-1-56—Tennessee St. 41, Florida A&M 39
12-14-57—Florida A&M 27, Md.-East. Shore 21
12-13-58—Prairie View 26, Florida A&M 8
12-5-59—Florida A&M 28, Prairie View 7
12-10-60—Florida A&M 40, Langston 26
12-9-61—Florida A&M 14, Jackson St. 8 (47,791)
12-8-62—Jackson St. 22, Florida A&M 6
12-14-63—Morgan St. 30, Florida A&M 7
12-5-64—Florida A&M 42, Grambling 15
12-4-65—Morgan St. 36, Florida A&M 7
12-3-66—Florida A&M 43, Alabama A&M 26
12-2-67—Grambling 28, Florida A&M 25
12-7-68—Alcorn St. 36, Florida A&M 9 (37,398)
12-6-69—Florida A&M 23, Grambling 19 (36,784) (at Tallahassee, Fla.)
12-12-70—Jacksonville St. 21, Florida A&M 7 (31,184)
12-11-71—Florida A&M 27, Kentucky St. 9 (26,161)
12-2-72—Florida A&M 41, Md.-East. Shore 21 (21,606)
12-8-73—Florida A&M 23, South Caro. St. 12 (18,996)
12-7-74—Florida A&M 17, Howard 13 (20,166)
12-6-75—Florida A&M 40, Kentucky St. 13 (27,875)
12-4-76—Florida A&M 26, Central St. 21 (18,000)
12-3-77—Florida A&M 37, Delaware St. 15 (29,493)
12-2-78—Florida A&M 31, Grambling 7

ORCHID BOWL
(Mexico City, Mexico)
1-1-42—Louisiana Col. 10, U. of Mexico 0 (8,000)
12-28-46—Mississippi Col. 43, U. of Mexico 7 (7,500)

PALM FESTIVAL
(Miami, Fla.)
1-2-33—Miami (Fla.) 7, Manhattan 0 (6,000)
1-1-34—Duquesne 33, Miami (Fla.) 7 (3,500) (forerunner to Orange Bowl)

PALMETTO SHRINE
(Columbia, S.C.)
12-10-55—Lenoir-Rhyne 14, Newberry 13 (6,000)

PAPER BOWL
(Pensacola, Fla.)
12-18-48—Jacksonville St. 19, Troy St. 0
12-16-49—Jacksonville St. 12, West Ala. 7 (3,000)
12-2-50—Pensacola Alumni Cardinals 7, Jacksonville St. 6 (3,600)

PEACH BLOSSOM CLASSIC
(Atlanta, Ga.)
12-9-39—Morris Brown 13, Virginia St. 7
12-6-40—Morris Brown 28, Kentucky St. 6 (1,500)
12-6-41—Morris Brown 7, N.C. Central 6 (6,000) (at Columbus, Ga.)
12-4-42—Morris Brown 20, Lane 0 (3,000) (at Columbus, Ga.)

PEACH BOWL
(Macon, Ga.)
12-13-46—Tenn. Wesleyan 14, Ga. Military 13 (5,000)
12-6-47—Virginia St. 48, Morris Brown 0
12-3-49—Morris Brown 33, Texas College 28 (at Atlanta, Ga.)

PEANUT BOWL
(Dothan, Ala.)
12-21-68—Ouachita Baptist 39, West Ala. 6

PEAR BOWL
(Medford, Ore.)
11-28-46—Southern Ore. St. 13, Central Wash. 8 (3,000) (at Ashland, Ore.)
11-27-47—Pacific Lutheran 27, Southern Ore. St. 21
11-25-48—Col. of Idaho 27, Southern Ore. St. 20 (2,500)
11-24-49—Pacific (Ore.) 33, UC Davis 15 (4,000)
11-23-50—Lewis & Clark 61, San Fran. St. 7 (4,000)
11-24-51—Pacific (Ore.) 25, UC Davis 7 (4,000)

PECAN BOWL
(Orangeburg, S.C.)
12-7-46—South Caro. St. 13, Johnson Smith 6
12-13-47—South Caro. St. 7, Allen 0 (3,000)

PELICAN BOWL
(New Orleans, La.)
12-2-72—Grambling 56, N.C. Central 6 (22,500) (at Durham, N.C.)
12-7-74—Grambling 28, South Caro. St. 7 (30,120)
12-27-75—Southern-B.R. 15, South Caro. St. 12 (6,748)

PENINSULA BOWL
(Charleston, S.C.)
12-2-50—Allen 47, South Caro. St. 13 (7,500)

PHILLIPS FIELD BOWL
(Tampa, Fla.)
12-8-51—Tampa 7, Brandeis 0

PIEDMONT TOBACCO BOWL
(Fayetteville, N.C.)
12-7-46—Allen 40, Fayetteville St. 6 (900)

PINEAPPLE BOWL
(Honolulu, Hawaii)
1-1-40—Oregon St. 39, Hawaii 6 (formerly called Poi Bowl)
1-1-41—Fresno St. 3, Hawaii 0
1-1-47—Hawaii 19, Utah 16 (25,000)
1-1-48—Hawaii 33, Redlands 32 (12,000)
1-1-49—Oregon St. 47, Hawaii 27 (15,000)
1-2-50—Stanford 74, Hawaii 20
1-1-51—Hawaii 28, Denver 27
1-1-52—San Diego St. 34, Hawaii 13

PITTSBURGH CHARITY GAME
(Pittsburgh, Pa.)
12-5-31—Carnegie Mellon 0, Duquesne 0 (42,539) (see Other Postseason Games)

POI BOWL
(Honolulu, Hawaii)
1-1-36—Southern Cal 38, Hawaii 6
1-2-37—Hawaii 18, Honolulu All-Stars 12
1-1-38—Washington 53, Hawaii 13 (13,500)
1-2-39—UCLA 32, Hawaii 7 (later called Pineapple Bowl)

POULTRY BOWL
(Gainesville, Ga.)
12-8-73—Stephen F. Austin 31, Gardner-Webb 10 (2,500)
12-7-74—Guilford 7, William Penn 7 (1,000) (at Greensboro, N.C.) (Guilford awarded win on 10-8 edge in first downs)

PRAIRIE VIEW BOWL
(Also called Bayou City Bowl)
(Houston, Texas)
1-1-29—Atlanta 7, Prairie View 0
1-1-30—Fisk 20, Prairie View 0
1-1-31—Tuskegee 19, Prairie View 7
1-1-32—Prairie View 27, Alabama St. 2
1-1-33—Prairie View 14, Tuskegee 0
1-1-34—Prairie View 20, Langston 7
1-1-35—Tuskegee 15, Prairie View 6
1-1-36—Wiley 7, Prairie View 6
1-1-37—Tuskegee 6, Prairie View 0 (3,000)
1-1-38—Prairie View 27, Florida A&M 14
1-2-39—Prairie View 34, Tuskegee 0
1-1-40—Prairie View 7, Xavier (La.) 6
1-1-41—Prairie View 7, Alabama St. 6
1-1-42—Kentucky St. 19, Prairie View 13
1-1-43—Langston 18, Prairie View 13
1-1-44—Prairie View 6, Wiley 0 (5,000)
1-1-45—Wiley 26, Prairie View 0 (4,000)
1-1-46—Prairie View 12, Tuskegee 0 (10,000)
1-1-47—Prairie View 14, Lincoln (Mo.) 0 (1,500) (called Houston Bowl)
1-1-48—Texas Southern 13, Prairie View 0
1-1-49—Central St. 6, Prairie View 0 (9,000)
1-2-50—Prairie View 27, Fisk 6 (4,718)
1-1-51—Prairie View 6, Bishop 0
1-1-52—Prairie View 27, Ark.-Pine Bluff 26
1-1-53—Texas Southern 13, Prairie View 12 (13,000)
1-1-54—Prairie View 33, Texas Southern 8
1-1-55—Prairie View 14, Texas Southern 12 (10,000)
1-2-56—Prairie View 59, Fisk 0 (7,500)
1-1-57—Prairie View 27, Texas Southern 6
1-1-58—Prairie View 6, Texas Southern 6 (3,500)
1-1-59—Prairie View 34, Langston 8
1-1-60—Prairie View 47, Wiley 10 (1,200)
12-31-60—Prairie View 19, Ark.-Pine Bluff 8 (1,400)
12-1-62—Prairie View 37, Central St. 16

PRETZEL BOWL
(Reading, Pa.)
11-24-51—West Chester 32, Albright 9 (7,500)

PYTHIAN BOWL
(Salisbury, N.C.)
11-26-49—Appalachian St. 21, Catawba 7
12-9-50—West Liberty St. 28, Appalachian St. 26
12-8-51—Lenoir-Rhyne 13, Calif. (Pa.) 7 (4,500)

REFRIGERATOR BOWL
(Evansville Ind.)
12-4-48—Evansville 13, Missouri Valley 7 (7,500)
12-3-49—Evansville 22, Hillsdale 7
12-2-50—Abilene Christian 13, Gust. Adolphus 7 (8,000)
12-2-51—Arkansas St. 46, Camp Breckinridge 12 (10,000)
12-7-52—Western Ky. 34, Arkansas St. 19 (9,500)
12-6-53—Sam Houston St. 14, Col. of Idaho 12 (7,500)
12-5-54—Delaware 19, Kent 7 (4,500)
12-4-55—Jacksonville St. 12, Rhode Island 10 (7,000)
12-1-56—Sam Houston St. 27, Middle Tenn. St. 13 (3,000)

RICE BOWL
(Stuggart, Ark.)
12-57—Arkansas Tech 19, Ark.-Monticello 7
12-58—Louisiana Col. 39, Arkansas Tech 12
12-2-60—East Central 25, Henderson St. 7

ROCKET BOWL
(Huntsville, Ala.)
11-19-60—Maryville (Tenn.) 19, Millsaps 0

SAN JACINTO SHRINE BOWL
(Pasadena, Texas)
12-4-76—Abilene Christian 22, Harding 12 (8,000)

SHARE BOWL
(Knoxville, Tenn.)
12-11-71—Carson-Newman 54, Fairmont St. 3 (1,200)

SHRIMP BOWL
(Galveston, Texas)
12-27-52—Sam Houston St. 41, Northeastern St. 20 (3,500)

SHRINE BOWL
(Ardmore, Okla.)
12-9-72—Southwestern Okla. 28, Angelo St. 6

SILVER BOWL
(Mexico City, Mexico)
12-20-47—Mexico All-Stars 24, Randolph Field 19
12-11-48—Pacific Fleet 33, Mexico All-Stars 26
12-17-49—Trinity (Tex.) 52, Mexico 6

SMOKY MOUNTAIN BOWL
(Bristol, Tenn.)
11-24-49—West Liberty St. 20, Western Caro. 0 (1,000)

SPACE CITY BOWL
(Huntsville, Ala.)
11-24-66—Jacksonville St. 41, Ark.-Monticello 30
12-9-67—Samford 20, Ark.-Monticello 7

STEEL BOWL
(Birmingham, Ala.)
1-1-41—Morris Brown 19, Central St. 3 (8,000)
1-1-42—Southern College All-Stars 26, Nashville Pros 13
1-1-52—Bethune-Cookman 27, Texas College 13 (1,500) (see Vulcan Bowl)

SUGAR CUP CLASSIC
(New Orleans, La.)
11-28-64—Grambling 42, Bishop 6

TANGERINE BOWL#
(Orlando, Fla.)
1-1-47—Catawba 31, Maryville (Tenn.) 6
1-1-48—Catawba 7, Marshall 0
1-1-49—Murray St. 21, Sul Ross St. 21
1-2-50—St. Vincent (Pa.) 7, Emory & Henry 6
1-1-51—Morris Harvey (now Charleston) 35, Emory & Henry 14
1-1-52—Stetson 35, Arkansas St. 20 (12,500)
1-1-53—East Tex. St. 33, Tennessee Tech 0 (12,340)
1-1-54—Arkansas St. 7, East Tex. St. 7
1-1-55—Neb.-Omaha 7, Eastern Ky. 6
1-2-56—Juniata 6, Missouri Valley 6 (10,000)
1-1-57—West Tex. A&M 20, Southern Miss. 13 (11,000)
1-1-58—East Tex. St. 10, Southern Miss. 9
12-27-58—East Tex. St. 26, Missouri Valley 7 (4,000)
1-1-60—Middle Tenn. St. 21, Presbyterian 12 (12,500)
12-29-61—Lamar 21, Middle Tenn. St. 14
12-28-63—Western Ky. 27, Coast Guard 0 (7,500)
12-12-64—East Caro. 14, Massachusetts 13
12-11-65—East Caro. 31, Maine 0 (8,350)
12-10-66—Morgan St. 14, West Chester 6
12-16-67—Tenn.-Martin 25, West Chester 8

TEXHOMA BOWL
(Denison, Texas)
12-10-48—Ouachita Baptist 7, Southeastern Okla. 0
11-25-49—Austin (Tex.) 27, East Central 6

TEXTILE BOWL
(Spartanburg, S.C.)
11-30-74—Wofford 20, South Caro. St. 0 (3,000)

TOBACCO BOWL
(Lexington, Ky.)
12-14-46—Muhlenberg 26, St. Bonaventure 25 (3,000)

TROPICAL BOWL
12-18-51—Morris Brown 21, Alcorn St. 0
12-13-52—Bethune-Cookman 54, Albany St. (Ga.) 0
12-12-53—Virginia Union 13, Bethune-Cookman 0

TURKEY BOWL
11-28-46—Evansville 19, Northern Ill. 7 (12,000) (also called Hoosier Bowl)

VULCAN BOWL
(Birmingham, Ala.)
1-1-42—Langston 13, Morris Brown 0 (7,000)
1-1-43—Texas College 13, Tuskegee 10 (6,000)
1-1-44—Tuskegee 12, Clark (Ga.) 7 (6,000)
1-1-45—Tennessee St. 13, Tuskegee 0 (5,000)
1-1-46—Tennessee St. 33, Texas College 6 (9,000)
1-1-47—Tennessee St. 32, Louisville Municipal 0 (4,000)
1-2-48—Central St. 27, Grambling 21 (8,000)
1-1-49—Kentucky St. 23, North Caro. A&T 13 (5,000)
1-1-52—Bethune-Cookman 27, Texas College 13 (1,500) (see Steel Bowl)

WILL ROGERS BOWL
(Oklahoma City, Okla.)
1-1-47—Pepperdine 38, Neb. Wesleyan 13 (800)

YAM BOWL
(Dallas, Texas)
12-25-46—Texas Southern 64, Tuskegee 7 (5,000)
12-25-47—Southern-B.R. 46, Fort Valley St. 0 (1,200)

#Became Florida Citrus Bowl (no classified major teams participated in games from January 1, 1947, through January 1, 1960, or in 1961 and 1963 through 1967.

SERVICE GAMES

AIRBORNE BOWL
12-15-57—101st Airborne 20, 82nd Airborne 14
12-5-59—Fort Campbell 26, Fort Bragg 7

ARAB BOWL
(Oran, Africa)
1-1-44—Army 10, Navy 7 (15,000)

ARMY ALL-STAR GAMES
8-30-42—Washington Redskins 26, Western Army All-Stars 7 (at Los Angeles, Calif.)
9-6-42—Western Army All-Stars 16, Chicago Cardinals 10 (at Denver, Colo.)
9-9-42—Western Army All-Stars 12, Detroit Lions 0 (at Detroit, Mich.)
9-12-42—Eastern Army All-Stars 16, New York Giants 0 (at New York, N.Y.)
9-13-42—Green Bay Packers 36, Western Army All-Stars 21 (at Milwaukee, Wis.)
9-16-42—Eastern Army All-Stars 13, Brooklyn Dodgers 7 (at Baltimore, Md.)
9-19-42—New York Giants 10, Western Army All-Stars 7 (at New York, N.Y.)
9-20-42—Chicago Bears 14, Eastern Army All-Stars 7 (at Boston, Mass.)

ARMY PACIFIC OLYMPICS
(Osaka, Japan)
1-13-46—11th Airborne Angels 27, Clark Field 6
1-27-46—11th Airborne Angels 18, Honolulu All-Stars 0

ARMY-NAVY BENEFIT BOWL
(Tallahassee, Fla.)
12-20-52—Parris Island 49, Fort Benning 0

ATOM BOWL
(Nagasaki, Japan)
12-45—Nishahaya Tigers 14, Bertelli's Bears 13 (2,000)

BAMBINO BOWL
(Bari, Italy)
11-23-44—Technical School 13, Playboys 0 (5,000)

BAMBOO BOWL
(Manila, Philippines)
1-1-46—Clark Field Acpacs 14, Leyte Base 12 (40,000)
1-1-47—Manila Raiders 13, Scofield Barracks 6 (12,000)
12-47—Ryukgus Command Sea Horses 21, Hawaiian Mid-Pacific Commandos 0
1-1-50—All-Navy Guam 19, Clark Air Force Base 7

BLUEBONNET BOWL
(Houston, Texas)
12-25-46—Texas Southern 49, Camp Hood 0

CHERRY BOWL
(Yokohama, Japan)
1-1-52—Camp Drake 26, Yoksuka Naval Base 12

CHIGGER BOWL
(Dutch Guiana)
1-1-45—Army Air Base Bonecrushers 6, Army Airway Rams 0 (1,200)

CHINA BOWL
(Shanghai)
1-27-46—Navy All-Stars 12, Army All-Stars 0
1-1-47—11th Airborne 12, Army-Navy All-Stars 6
1-1-48—Marines (Guam) 45, China All-Stars 0

CIGAR BOWL
12-29-51—Brooke Army Medical 20, Camp LeJeune 0 (7,500)

CITRICADO BOWL
12-56—San Diego Marines 25, UC Santa Barb. 14

COCONUT BOWL
(New Guinea)
1-6-45—Bulldogs 18, Crimson Tide 7 (3,000)

COFFEE BOWL
(London, England)
3-19-44—United States 18, Canada 0

CONCH BOWL
(Key West, Fla.)
11-24-57—Keesler Air Force Base 27, Maxwell Air Force Base 7
11-28-58—Keesler Air Force Base 14, Maxwell Air Force Base 8

COSMOPOLITAN BOWL
(Alexandria, La.)
12-50—Camp Polk 26, Louisiana Col. 7
12-52—Louisiana Col. 14, Alexander Air Base 0

ELECTRONICS BOWL
(Biloxi, Miss.)
12-9-51—Keesler Air Force Base 13, Camp LeJeune 0
12-53—Eglin Air Force Base 19, Keesler Air Force Base 8
12-54—Shaw Air Force Base 20, Keesler Air Force Base 19

EUROPEAN "ORANGE BOWL"
(Heidelberg, Germany)
12-7-46—1st Division Artillery 27, 60th Infantry 13

EUROPEAN "ROSE BOWL"
(Augsburg, Germany)
12-7-46—9th Division 20, 16th Infantry 7 (3,000)

EUROPEAN "SUGAR BOWL"
(Nuremberg, Germany)
12-7-46—Grafenwohr Military 0, 39th Infantry 0

G. I. BOWL
(London, England)
11-12-44—Army G.I.'s 20, Navy Bluejackets 0 (60,000)

ICE BOWL
(Fairbanks, Alaska)
1-1-49—Ladd Air Force Base 0, University of Alaska 0 (500)
1-2-50—University of Alaska 3, Ladd Air Force Base 0
1-1-51—University of Alaska 0, Ladd Air Force Base 0
12-30-52—Ladd Air Force Base 47, University of Alaska 0

IRANIAN BOWL
(Teheran, Iran)
12-12-44—Camp Amirabad 20, Camp Khorramsahr 0 (9,000)

JUNGLE BOWL
(Southwest Pacific)
1-1-45—American All-Stars 49, Marines 0 (6,400)

LILY BOWL
(Hamilton, Bermuda)
1-3-43—Army 19, Navy 18
1-1-44—Navy 19, Army 0
1-7-45—Navy 39, Army 6 (11,000)
1-5-47—Army 7, Navy 7 (9,000)
1-1-48—Air Force 12, Navy 12
1-1-49—Navy All-Stars 25, Kindley Fliers 6

MARINE BOWL
(Pritchard Field, Southwest Pacific)
12-24-44—4th Marines 0, 29th Marines 0 (7,000)

MISSILE BOWL
(Orlando, Fla.)
12-3-60—Quantico Marines 36, Pensacola Air Force Base 6
12-9-61—Fort Eustis 25, Quantico Marines 24
12-15-62—Fort Campbell 14, Lackland Air Force Base 10
12-14-63—Quantico Marines 13, San Diego Marines 10
12-5-64—Fort Benning 9, Fort Eustis 3

PALMETTO SHRINE
(Charleston, S.C.)
1-1-55—Fort Jackson 26, Shaw Air Force Base 21

PARC DES PRINCES BOWL
(Paris, France)
12-19-44—9th Air Force 6, 1st General Hospital 0 (20,000)

POI BOWL
(Honolulu, Hawaii)
(Pacific Ocean Areas Service Championship)
1-8-45—Navy 14, Army Air Force 0 (29,000)

POINSETTIA BOWL
(San Diego, Calif.)
12-20-52—Bolling Air Force Base 35, San Diego NTC 14

12-19-53—Fort Ord 55, Quantico Marines 19
12-19-54—Fort Sill 27, Bolling Air Force Base 6
12-17-55—Fort Ord 35, Pensacola NAS 13

POTATO BOWL
(Belfast, Ireland)
1-1-44—Galloping Gaels 0, Wolverines 0

RICE BOWL
(Tokyo, Japan)
1-1-46—11th Airborne Angels 25, 41st Division 12 (15,000)
12-46—Yokota Air Base 13, 1st AD 8 (7,000)
1-1-48—Korea All-Stars 19, Japan All-Stars 13
1-1-49—Army Ground Forces 13, Air Force 7 (20,000)
1-1-50—Air Force All-Stars 18, Army All-Stars 14
1-1-53—Camp Drake 25, Yokosuka Naval Base 6
1-1-54—Camp Fisher 19, Nagoya Air Base 13
1-1-55—Air Force 21, Marines 14
12-31-55—Air Force 33, Army 14 (40,000)
12-30-56—Army 21, Air Force 6
12-7-57—Johnson Air Base Vanguards 6, Marine Corps Sukiran Streaks 0
12-20-58—Air Force 20, Army 0

RIVIERA BOWL
(Marseille, France)
1-1-45—Railway Shop Battalion Unit 37, Army All-Stars 0 (18,000)

SALAD BOWL
(Phoenix, Ariz.)
1-1-53—San Diego Navy 81, 101st Airborne 20
1-1-54—Fort Ord 67, Great Lakes 12

SATELLITE BOWL
(Cocoa, Fla.)
12-29-57—Fort Carson 12, Fort Dix 6

SHRIMP BOWL
(Galveston, Texas)
1-1-55—Fort Ord 36, Fort Hood 0
12-18-55—Fort Hood 33, Little Creek 13
12-8-56—Bolling Air Force Base 29, Fort Hood 14
12-15-57—Bolling Air Force Base 28, San Diego Marines 7
12-14-58—Eglin Air Force Base 15, Brooke Medics 7
12-13-59—Quantico Marines 90, McClellan Air Force Base 0

SHURI BOWL
12-58—Air Force 60, Marine Corps 0

SPAGHETTI BOWL
(Florence, Italy)
1-1-45—5th Army 20, 12th Air Force 0 (20,000)
1-1-53—Salzburg Army 12, Wiesbaden AFC 7 (at Leghorn, Italy)

SUKIYAKI BOWL
12-56—Air Force 29, Marines 7

TEA BOWL
(London, England)
2-13-44—Canada 16, United States 6 (30,000)
12-31-44—Air Service Command Warriors 13, 8th Air Force Shuttle Raiders 0 (12,000)

TREASURY BOWL
(New York, N.Y.)
12-16-44—Randolph Field 13, 2nd Air Force 6 (8,356)

TYPHOON BOWL
12-56—Army 13, Marines 0

VALOR BOWL
(Chattanooga, Tenn.)
12-7-57—Hamilton Air Force Base 12, Quantico Marines 6

POSTSEASON BOWL INVOLVING NON-I-A TEAMS

HERITAGE BOWL
Site: Atlanta, Ga.
Stadium (Capacity): Georgia Dome (71,596)
Name Changes: Alamo Heritage Bowl (1991); Heritage Bowl (1993-94); Jim Walters Heritage Bowl (1995)
Playing Surface: AstroTurf
Playing Sites: Joe Robbie Stadium, Miami (1991); Bragg Memorial Stadium, Tallahassee (1993); Georgia Dome, Atlanta (since 1994)

Date	Score (Attendance)
12-21-91	Alabama St. 36, North Caro. A&T 13 (7,724)
1-2-93	Grambling 45, Florida A&M 15 (11,273)
1-1-94	Southern-B.R. 11, South Caro. St. 0 (36,128)
12-30-94	South Caro. St. 31, Grambling 27 (22,179)
12-29-95	Southern-B.R. 30, Florida A&M 25 (25,164)

NCAA-CERTIFIED ALL-STAR GAMES

EAST-WEST SHRINE CLASSIC
Present Site: Palo Alto, Calif.
Stadium (Capacity): Stanford (85,500)
Playing Surface: Grass
Playing Sites: Ewing Field, San Francisco (1925); Kezar Stadium, San Francisco (1927-41); Sugar Bowl, New Orleans (1942); Kezar Stadium, San Francisco (1943-66); Candlestick Park, San Francisco (1967-68); Stanford Stadium, Palo Alto (1969); Oakland Coliseum (1971); Candlestick Park, San Francisco (1971-73); Stanford Stadium, Palo Alto (since 1974)

Date	Score (Attendance)
12-26-25	West 7-0 (20,000)
1-1-27	West 7-3 (15,000)
12-26-27	West 16-6 (27,500)
12-29-28	East 20-0 (55,000)
1-1-30	East 19-7 (58,000)
12-27-30	West 3-0 (40,000)
1-1-32	East 6-0 (45,000)
1-2-33	West 21-13 (45,000)
1-1-34	West 12-0 (35,000)
1-1-35	West 19-13 (52,000)
1-1-36	East 19-3 (55,000)
1-1-37	East 3-0 (38,000)
1-1-38	Tie 0-0 (55,000)
1-2-39	West 14-0 (60,000)
1-1-40	West 28-11 (50,000)
1-1-41	West 20-14 (60,000)
1-3-42	Tie 6-6 (35,000)
1-1-43	East 13-12 (57,000)
1-1-44	Tie 13-13 (55,000)
1-1-45	West 13-7 (60,000)
1-1-46	Tie 7-7 (60,000)
1-1-47	West 13-9 (60,000)
1-1-48	East 40-9 (60,000)
1-1-49	East 14-12 (59,000)
12-31-49	East 28-6 (60,000)
12-30-50	West 16-7 (60,000)
12-29-51	East 15-14 (60,000)
12-27-52	East 21-20 (60,000)
1-2-54	West 31-7 (60,000)
1-1-55	East 13-12 (60,000)
12-31-55	East 29-6 (60,000)
12-29-56	West 7-6 (60,000)
12-28-57	West 27-13 (60,000)
12-27-58	East 26-14 (60,000)
1-2-60	West 21-14 (60,000)
12-31-60	East 7-0 (60,000)
12-30-61	West 21-8 (60,000)
12-29-62	East 25-19 (60,000)
12-28-63	Tie 6-6 (60,000)
1-2-65	West 11-7 (60,000)
12-31-65	West 22-7 (47,000)
12-31-66	East 45-22 (46,000)
12-30-67	East 16-14 (29,000)
12-28-68	West 18-7 (29,000)
12-27-69	West 15-0 (70,000)
1-2-71	West 17-13 (50,000)
12-31-71	West 17-13 (35,000)
12-30-72	East 9-3 (37,000)
12-29-73	East 35-7 (30,000)
12-28-74	East 16-14 (35,000)
1-3-76	West 21-14 (75,000)
1-2-77	West 30-14 (45,000)
12-31-77	West 23-3 (65,000)
1-6-79	East 56-17 (72,000)
1-5-80	West 20-10 (75,000)
1-10-81	East 21-3 (76,000)
1-9-82	West 20-13 (75,000)
1-15-83	East 26-25 (72,999)
1-7-84	East 27-19 (77,000)
1-5-85	West 21-10 (72,000)
1-11-86	East 18-7 (77,000)
1-10-87	West 24-21 (74,000)
1-16-88	West 16-13 (62,000)
1-15-89	East 24-6 (76,000)
1-21-90	West 22-21 (78,000)
1-26-91	West 24-21 (70,000)
1-19-92	West 14-6 (83,000)
1-24-93	East 31-17 (84,000)
1-15-94	West 29-28 (60,000)
1-14-95	West 30-28 (35,079)
1-13-96	West 34-18 (68,500)

Series record: West won 38, East 28, 5 ties.

BLUE-GRAY ALL-STAR CLASSIC
Present Site: Montgomery, Ala.
Stadium (Capacity): Cramton Bowl (24,600)
Playing Surface: Grass
Playing Sites: Cramton Bowl, Montgomery (since 1939)

Date	Score (Attendance)
1-2-39	Blue 7-0 (8,000)
12-30-39	Gray 33-20 (10,000)
12-28-40	Blue 14-12 (14,000)
12-27-41	Gray 16-0 (15,571)
12-26-42	Gray 24-0 (16,000)
1943	No Game
12-30-44	Gray 24-7 (16,000)
12-29-45	Blue 26-0 (20,000)
12-28-46	Gray 20-13 (22,500)
12-27-47	Gray 33-6 (22,500)
12-25-48	Blue 19-13 (15,000)
12-31-49	Gray 27-13 (21,500)
12-30-50	Gray 31-6 (21,000)
12-29-51	Gray 20-14 (22,000)
12-27-52	Gray 28-7 (22,000)
12-26-53	Gray 40-20 (18,500)
12-25-54	Blue 14-7 (18,000)
12-31-55	Gray 20-19 (19,000)
12-29-56	Blue 14-0 (21,000)
12-28-57	Gray 21-20 (16,000)
12-27-58	Blue 16-0 (16,000)
12-26-59	Blue 20-8 (20,000)
12-31-60	Blue 35-7 (18,000)
12-30-61	Gray 9-7 (18,000)
12-29-62	Blue 10-6 (20,000)
12-28-63	Gray 21-14 (20,000)
12-26-64	Blue 10-6 (16,000)
12-25-65	Gray 23-19 (18,000)
12-24-66	Blue 14-9 (18,000)
12-30-67	Blue 22-16 (23,350)
12-28-68	Gray 28-7 (18,000)
12-27-69	Tie 6-6 (21,500)
12-28-70	Gray 38-7 (23,000)
12-28-71	Gray 9-0 (24,000)
12-27-72	Gray 27-15 (20,000)
12-18-73	Blue 20-14 (21,000)
12-17-74	Blue 29-24 (12,000)
12-19-75	Blue 14-13 (10,000)
12-24-76	Gray 31-10 (16,000)
12-30-77	Blue 20-16 (5,000)
12-29-78	Gray 28-24 (18,380)
12-25-79	Blue 22-13 (18,312)
12-25-80	Blue 24-23 (25,000)
12-25-81	Blue 21-9 (19,000)
12-25-82	Gray 20-10 (21,000)
12-25-83	Gray 17-13 (2,000)
12-25-84	Gray 33-6 (24,080)
12-25-85	Blue 27-20 (18,500)
12-25-86	Blue 31-7 (18,500)
12-25-87	Gray 12-10 (20,300)
12-25-88	Blue 22-21 (20,000)
12-25-89	Gray 28-10 (16,000)
12-25-90	Blue 17-14 (17,500)
12-25-91	Gray 20-12 (21,000)
12-25-92	Gray 27-17 (20,500)
12-25-93	Gray 17-10 (18,500)
12-25-94	Blue 38-27 (23,500)
12-25-95	Blue 26, Gray 7 (18,500)

Series record: Gray won 30, Blue 26, 1 tie.

HULA BOWL
Present Site: Honolulu, Hawaii
Stadium (Capacity): Aloha (50,000)
Playing Surface: AstroTurf
Format: From 1947 through 1950, the College All-Stars played the Hawaii All-Stars. Beginning in 1951, the Hawaiian team was augmented by players from the National Football League. This format, however, was changed to an all-collegiate contest—first between the East and West, then between North and South (in 1963), and then back to East and West in 1974. In 1994, the format went to a collection of collegiate all-stars versus a collection of Hawaiian former collegiate players. In 1995, it reverted back to East-West.

Playing Sites: Honolulu Stadium (1960-74); Aloha Stadium (since 1975)

Date	Score (Attendance)
1-10-60	East 34-8 (23,000)
1-8-61	East 14-7 (17,017)
1-7-62	Tie 7-7 (20,598)
1-6-63	North 20-13 (20,000)
1-4-64	North 20-13 (18,177)
1-9-65	South 16-14 (22,100)
1-8-66	North 27-26 (25,000)
1-7-67	North 28-27 (23,500)
1-6-68	North 50-6 (21,000)
1-4-69	North 13-7 (23,000)
1-10-70	South 35-13 (25,000)
1-9-71	North 42-32 (23,500)
1-8-72	North 24-7 (23,000)
1-6-73	South 17-3 (23,000)
1-5-74	East 24-14 (23,000)
1-4-75	East 34-25 (22,000)
1-10-76	East 16-0 (45,458)
1-8-77	West 20-17 (45,579)
1-7-78	West 42-22 (48,197)
1-6-79	East 29-24 (49,132)
1-5-80	East 17-10 (47,096)
1-10-81	West 24-17 (39,010)
1-9-82	West 26-23 (43,002)
1-15-83	East 30-14 (39,456)
1-7-84	West 21-16 (34,216)
1-5-85	East 34-14 (30,767)
1-11-86	West 23-10 (29,564)
1-10-87	West 16-14 (17,775)
1-16-88	West 20-18 (26,737)
1-7-89	East 21-10 (25,000)
1-13-90	West 21-13 (28,742)
1-19-91	East 23-10 (21,926)
1-11-92	West 27-20 (23,112)
1-16-93	West 13-10 (25,479)
1-22-94	College All-Stars 28-15 (33,947)
1-22-95	East 20-9 (19,074)
1-21-96	East 17-10 (25,112)

Series records: North-South (1963-73)—North won 8, South 3; East-West (1960-62, 1974-93 and 1995 to present)—East won 13, West 11, 1 tie; College All-Stars vs. Hawaiian All-Stars (1994)—College All-Stars won 1, Hawaiian All-Stars 0.

SENIOR BOWL

Played at Ladd Memorial Stadium in Mobile, Ala., since 1951 under the auspices of the National Football League. North and South teams are composed of senior players who have used all of their collegiate eligibility. In 1991, the teams switched from North and South to AFC and NFC; in 1994, the teams switched back to North and South.

Date	Score (Attendance)
1-7-50	South 22, North 13 (at Jacksonville, Fla.)
1-6-51	South 19, North 18
1-5-52	North 20, South 6
1-3-53	North 28, South 13
1-9-54	North 20, South 14
1-8-55	South 12, North 6
1-7-56	South 12, North 2
1-5-57	South 21, North 7
1-11-58	North 15, South 13
1-3-59	South 21, North 12
1-9-60	North 26, South 7 (40,119)
1-7-61	South 33, North 26
1-6-62	South 42, North 7
1-5-63	South 33, North 27
1-4-64	South 28, North 21 (37,094)
1-9-65	Tie 7-7 (40,605)
1-8-66	South 27, North 18
1-7-67	North 35, South 13
1-6-68	South 34, North 21
1-11-69	North 27, South 16
1-10-70	Tie 37-37
1-9-71	North 31, South 13 (40,646)
1-8-72	North 26, South 21 (40,646)
1-6-73	South 33, North 30 (40,646)
1-12-74	North 16, South 13 (40,646)
1-11-75	Tie 17-17 (40,646)
1-10-76	North 42, South 35 (40,646)
1-9-77	North 27, South 24 (40,646)
1-7-78	Tie 17-17 (40,646)
1-13-79	South 41, North 21 (40,100)
1-12-80	North 57, South 3 (40,646)
1-17-81	North 23, South 10 (40,102)
1-16-82	South 27, North 10 (39,410)
1-22-83	North 14, South 6 (37,511)
1-14-84	South 21, North 20 (38,254)
1-12-85	South 23, North 7 (33,500)
1-18-86	North 31, South 17 (40,646)
1-17-87	South 42, North 38
1-23-88	North 21, South 7
1-21-89	South 13, North 12 (39,742)
1-20-90	North 41, South 0 (42,400)
1-19-91	AFC 38, NFC 28 (37,500)
1-18-92	AFC 13, NFC 10 (37,100)
1-16-93	NFC 21, AFC 6 (37,124)
1-22-94	South 35, North 32 (39,200)
1-21-95	South 14, North 7 (40,007)
1-20-96	North 25, South 10 (40,700)

Series records: North-South (1950-90 and 1994 to present)—South won 21, North 19, 4 ties; AFC-NFC (1991-93)—AFC won 2, NFC 1.

DISCONTINUED ALL-STAR FOOTBALL GAMES

Many of these games were identified without complete information such as scores, teams, sites or dates. Please send any updates or additional information to: NCAA Statistics Service, 6201 College Boulevard, Overland Park, Kansas 66211-2422.

ALL-AMERICAN BOWL (1969-77) (Tampa, Fla.)

Date	Score (Attendance)
1-4-69	North 21, South 15 (16,380)
1-3-70	South 24, North 23 (17,642)
1-10-71	North 39, South 2 (12,000)
1-9-72	North 27, South 8 (20,137)
1-7-73	North 10, South 6 (23,416)
1-6-74	North 28, South 7 (24,536)
1-5-75	South 28, North 22 (19,246)
1-10-76	North 21, South 14 (15,321)
1-2-77	North 21, South 20 (14,207)

AMERICAN COLLEGE ALL-STAR GAME (1948) (Los Angeles, Calif.)

Date	Score
12-18-48	American All-Stars 43, Canadian All-Stars 0
12-26-48	American All-Stars 14, Hawaiian All-Stars 0

BLACK COLLEGE ALL-STAR BOWL (1979-82)

Date	Score (Location, Attendance)
1-7-79	East 25, West 20 (at New Orleans, La.)
1-5-80	West 27, East 21 (OT) (at New Orleans, La.)
1-17-81	West 19, East 10 (at Jackson, Miss., 7,500)
1-16-82	West 7, East 0 (at Jackson, Miss.)

CAMP FOOTBALL FOUNDATION BOWL (1974)

CANADIAN-AMERICAN BOWL (1978-79) (Tampa, Fla.)

Date	Score (Attendance)
1-8-78	U.S. All-Stars 22, Canadian All-Stars 7 (11,328)
1-6-79	U.S. All-Stars 34, Canadian All-Stars 14 (11,033)

CHALLENGE BOWL (1978-79) (Seattle, Wash.)

Date	Score (Attendance)
1-14-78	Pacific-8 27, Big Ten 20 (20,578)
1-13-79	Pacific-10 36, Big Eight 23 (23,961)

CHICAGO COLLEGE ALL-STAR FOOTBALL GAME (1934-76)

An all-star team composed of the top senior collegiate players met the National Football League champions (1933-66) or the Super Bowl champions (1967-75) from the previous season, beginning in 1934. The only time the all-stars did not play the league champions was in 1935. All games were played at Soldier Field, Chicago, Ill.

Date	Score (Attendance)
8-31-34	(Tie) Chicago Bears 0-0 (79,432)
8-29-35	Chicago Bears 5, All-Stars 0 (77,450)
9-2-36	(Tie) Detroit 7-7 (76,000)
9-1-37	All-Stars 6, Green Bay 0 (84,560)
8-31-38	All-Stars 28, Washington 16 (74,250)
8-30-39	New York Giants 9, All-Stars 0 (81,456)
8-29-40	Green Bay 45, All-Stars 28 (84,567)
8-28-41	Chicago Bears 37, All-Stars 13 (98,203)
8-28-42	Chicago Bears 21, All-Stars 0 (101,100)
8-25-43	All-Stars 27, Washington 7 (48,471)
8-30-44	Chicago Bears 24, All-Stars 21 (48,769)
8-30-45	Green Bay 19, All-Stars 7 (92,753)
8-23-46	All-Stars 16, Los Angeles 0 (97,380)
8-22-47	All-Stars 16, Chicago Bears 0 (105,840)
8-20-48	Chicago Cardinals 28, All-Stars 0 (101,220)
8-12-49	Philadelphia 38, All-Stars 0 (93,780)
8-11-50	All-Stars 17, Philadelphia 7 (88,885)
8-17-51	Cleveland 33, All-Stars 0 (92,180)
8-15-52	Los Angeles 10, All-Stars 7 (88,316)
8-14-53	Detroit 24, All-Stars 10 (93,818)
8-13-54	Detroit 31, All-Stars 6 (93,470)
8-12-55	All-Stars 30, Cleveland 27 (75,000)
8-10-56	Cleveland 26, All-Stars 0 (75,000)
8-9-57	New York Giants 22, All-Stars 12 (75,000)
8-15-58	All-Stars 35, Detroit 19 (70,000)
8-14-59	Baltimore 29, All-Stars 0 (70,000)
8-12-60	Baltimore 32, All-Stars 7 (70,000)
8-4-61	Philadelphia 28, All-Stars 14 (66,000)
8-3-62	Green Bay 42, All-Stars 20 (65,000)
8-2-63	All-Stars 20, Green Bay 17 (65,000)
8-7-64	Chicago Bears 28, All-Stars 17 (65,000)
8-6-65	Cleveland 24, All-Stars 16 (68,000)
8-5-66	Green Bay 38, All-Stars 0 (72,000)
8-4-67	Green Bay 27, All-Stars 0 (70,934)
8-2-68	Green Bay 34, All-Stars 17 (69,917)
8-1-69	New York Jets 26, All-Stars 24 (74,208)
7-31-70	Kansas City 24, All-Stars 3 (69,940)
7-30-71	Baltimore 24, All-Stars 17 (52,289)
7-28-72	Dallas 20, All-Stars 7 (54,162)
7-27-73	Miami 14, All-Stars 3 (54,103)
1974	No game played
8-1-75	Pittsburgh 21, All-Stars 14 (54,103)
7-23-76	*Pittsburgh 24, All-Stars 0 (52,895)

**Game was not completed due to thunderstorms.*

CHRISTIAN BOWL (1955) (Murfreesboro, Tenn.)

Date	Score (Attendance)
12-26-55	East 21, West 10 (4,000)

COACHES ALL-AMERICAN GAME (1961-76)

Date	Score (Attendance)
at Buffalo, N.Y.	
6-23-61	West 30, East 20 (12,913)
6-29-62	East 13, West 8 (22,759)
6-29-63	West 22, East 21 (20,840)
6-27-64	East 18, West 15 (21,112)
6-26-65	East 34, West 14 (25,501)
at Atlanta, Ga.	
7-9-66	West 24, East 7 (38,236)
7-9-67	East 12, West 9 (29,145)
6-28-68	West 34, East 20 (21,120)
6-28-69	West 14, East 10 (17,008)
at Lubbock, Texas	
6-28-70	East 34, West 27 (42,150)
6-26-71	West 33, East 28 (43,320)
6-24-72	East 42, West 20 (42,314)
6-23-73	West 20, East 6 (43,272)
6-22-74	West 36, East 6 (42,368)
6-21-75	East 23, West 21 (36,108)
6-19-76	West 35, East 17 (36,504)

COPPER BOWL (1958-60) (Tempe, Ariz.)

Date	Score (Attendance)
12-20-58	Southwest All-Stars 22, National All-Stars 13 (12,000)
12-26-59	National All-Stars 21, Southwest All-Stars 6 (16,000)
12-31-60	National All-Stars 27, Southwest All-Stars 8 (8,000)

CRUSADE BOWL (1963) (Baltimore, Md.)

Date	Score (Attendance)
1-6-63	East 38, West 10 (2,400)

DALLAS ALL-STAR GAME (1936-39) (Dallas, Texas)

Date	Score
9-7-36	Southwest All-Stars 7, Chicago Bears 6
9-6-37	Southwest All-Stars 6, Chicago Bears 0

9-5-38 Southwest All-Stars 13, Washington Redskins 7
9-4-39 Green Bay Packers 31, Southwest All-Stars 20

DIXIE CLASSIC (1928-31)
(Dallas, Texas)

Date	Score (Attendance)
12-29-28	Southwest Conference 14, Small Texas Schools 6
1-1-29	Big Six Conference 14, Southwest Conference 6 (10,000)
1-1-30	Midwest 25, Southwest Conference 12 (15,000)
1-1-31	Southwest Conference 18, Midwest 0 (14,000)

EAST-WEST BLACK ALL-STAR GAME (1971)
(Houston, Texas)

Date	Score (Attendance)
12-11-71	East 19, West 10 (5,156)

EAST-WEST COLLEGE ALL-STAR GAME (1932)
(Demonstrated at Tenth Olympiad, Los Angeles, Calif.; East team composed of players from Harvard, Princeton and Yale, West team composed of players from California, Southern Cal and Stanford)

Date	Score (Attendance)
8-8-32	West 7, East 6 (50,000)

FREEDOM BOWL ALL-STAR CLASSIC (1984-86)
(Atlanta, Ga.)
Southwestern Athletic Conference vs. Mid-Eastern Athletic Conference.

Date	Score (Attendance)
1-14-84	SWAC 36, MEAC 22 (16,097)
1-12-85	SWAC 14, MEAC 0 (18,352)
1-11-86	SWAC 16, MEAC 14 (10,200)

FREEDOM BOWL ALL-STAR CLASSIC (1990)
(Houston, Texas)

Date	Score
1-13-90	North 14, South 13

FREEDOM CLASSIC (1976)

Year	Score (Attendance)
1976	West 12, East 9 (6,654)

JAPAN BOWL
(Yokohama, Japan)

Date	Score (Attendance)
1-18-76	West 27-18 (68,000)
1-16-77	West 21-10 (58,000)
1-15-78	East 26-10 (32,500)
1-14-79	East 33-14 (55,000)
1-13-80	West 28-17 (27,000)
1-17-81	West 25-13 (30,000)
1-16-82	West 28-17 (28,000)
1-23-83	West 30-21 (30,000)
1-15-84	West 26-21 (26,000)
1-13-85	West 28-14 (30,000)
1-11-86	East 31-14 (30,000)
1-11-87	West 24-17 (30,000)
1-10-88	West 17-3 (30,000)
1-15-89	East 30-7 (29,000)
1-13-90	East 24-10 (27,000)
1-12-91	West 20-14 (30,000)
1-11-92	East 14-13 (50,000)
1-9-93	East 27-13 (46,000)

LOS ANGELES ALL-STAR GAME (1948)
(Los Angeles, Calif.)

Date	Score
1-18-48	West 34, East 20

MARTIN LUTHER KING ALL-AMERICA CLASSIC (1990-91)
(Division I-A vs. all other divisions)

Date	Score (Attendance)
1-15-90	All Div. All-Stars 35, I-A All-Stars 24 (350) (at San Jose, Calif.)
1-14-91	I-A All-Stars 21, All Div. All-Stars 14 (6,272) (at St. Petersburg, Fla.)

NORTH-SOUTH ALL-STAR SHRINE GAME
(1930-34, 1948-73, 1976)

Date	Score (Attendance)
1-1-30	North 21, South 12 (20,000) (at Atlanta, Ga.) (Southern Conference All-Star Game)
12-28-30	South 7, North 0 (2,000) (at New York, N.Y.)
12-10-32	South 7, North 6 (500) (at Baltimore, Md.)
12-24-33	North 3, South 0 (5,000) (at New York, N.Y.)
1-1-34	North 7, South 0 (12,000) (at Knoxville, Tenn.) (Southeastern Conference All-Star Game)

at Miami, Fla.

Date	Score (Attendance)
12-25-48	South 24, North 14 (33,056)
12-25-49	North 20, South 14 (37,378)
12-25-50	South 14, North 9 (39,132)
12-25-51	South 35, North 7 (39,995)
12-25-52	North 21, South 21 (42,866)
12-25-53	South 20, North 0 (44,715)
12-25-54	South 20, North 17 (37,847)
12-26-55	South 20, North 7 (42,179)
12-26-56	North 17, South 7 (39,181)
12-25-57	North 23, South 20 (28,303)
12-27-58	South 49, North 20 (35,519)
12-26-59	North 27, South 17 (35,185)
12-26-60	North 41, South 14 (26,146)
12-25-61	South 35, North 16 (18,892)
12-22-62	South 15, North 14 (16,952)
12-21-63	South 23, North 14 (19,120)
12-25-64	North 37, South 30 (29,124)
12-25-65	South 21, North 14 (25,640)
12-26-66	North 27, South 14 (28,569)
12-25-67	North 24, South 0 (17,400)
12-25-68	North 3, South 0 (18,063)
12-25-69	North 31, South 10 (23,527)
12-25-70	North 28, South 7 (15,402)
12-27-71	South 7, North 6 (18,640)
12-25-72	North 17, South 10 (18,013)
12-25-73	South 27, North 6 (10,672)

at Pontiac, Mich.

Date	Score (Attendance)
12-17-76	South 24, North 0 (41,627)

OHIO SHRINE BOWL (1972-76)
(Columbus, Ohio)

Date	Score
12-9-72	East 20, West 7
12-1-73	East 8, West 6
12-7-74	East 27, West 6
1975	West 17, East 7
12-4-76	East 24, West 8 (played elsewhere)

OLYMPIA GOLD BOWL (1982)
(San Diego, Calif.)

Date	Score (Attendance)
1-16-82	National All-Stars 30, American All-Stars 21 (22,316)

OLYMPIC GAME (1933)
(Chicago, Ill.)

Date	Score (Attendance)
8-24-33	East 13, West 7 (50,000)

OPTIMIST ALL-AMERICA BOWL (1958-62)
(Tucson, Ariz.)

Date	Score (Attendance)
1-4-58	College All-Stars 56, Tucson Cowboys 28
1-3-59	Major-College 14, Small-College 12 (10,000)
1-2-60	Major College 53, Small-College 0 (14,500)
12-26-60	Major-College 25, Small-College 12
12-30-61	Major-College 31, Small-College 0 (14,000)
12-29-62	Small-College 14, Major-College 13

POTATO BOWL (1967)
(Bakersfield, Calif.)

Date	Score (Attendance)
12-23-67	North 23, South 7 (5,600)

ROCKY MOUNTAIN CONFERENCE-NORTH CENTRAL CONFERENCE GAME (1930)
(Elks Charity Bowl)
(Denver, Colo.)

Date	Score
1-1-30	North Central 13, Rocky Mountain 6

SALAD BOWL ALL-STAR GAME (1955)
(Phoenix, Ariz.)

Date	Score (Attendance)
1-1-55	Skyline Conference 20, Border Conference 13 (8,000)
12-31-55	Border Conference 13, Skyline Conference 10

SHERIDAN BLACK ALL-STAR GAME (1979-82)
(See Black College All-Star Bowl)

SMOKE BOWL (1941)
(Richmond, Va.)

Date	Score (Attendance)
1-1-41	Norfolk All-Stars 16, Richmond All-Stars 2 (5,000)

SOUTHWEST CHALLENGE BOWL (1963-64)
(Corpus Christi, Texas)

Date	Score (Attendance)
1-5-63	National 33, Southwest 13
1-4-64	National 66, Southwest 14 (10,200)

U.S. BOWL (1962)
(Washington, D. C.)
(Teams were composed of players selected in the recent NFL draft)

Date	Score
1-7-62	West 33, East 19

Special Regular-Season Games

REGULAR-SEASON GAMES PLAYED IN USA

KICKOFF CLASSIC
Present Site: East Rutherford, N.J.
Stadium (Capacity): Giants Stadium (76,000)
Playing Surface: AstroTurf
Sponsor: National Association of Collegiate Directors of Athletics (NACDA). It is a permitted 12th regular-season game.
Playing Sites: Giants Stadium (since 1983)

Date	Teams, Score (Attendance)
8-29-83	Nebraska 44, Penn St. 6 (71,123)
8-27-84	Miami (Fla.) 20, Auburn 18 (51,131)
8-29-85	Brigham Young 28, Boston College 14 (51,227)
8-27-86	Alabama 16, Ohio St. 10 (68,296)
8-30-87	Tennessee 23, Iowa 22 (54,681)
8-27-88	Nebraska 23, Texas A&M 14 (58,172)
8-31-89	Notre Dame 36, Virginia 13 (77,323)
8-31-90	Southern Cal 34, Syracuse 16 (57,293)
8-28-91	Penn St. 34, Georgia Tech 22 (77,409)
8-29-92	North Caro. St. 24, Iowa 14 (46,251)
8-28-93	Florida St. 42, Kansas 0 (51,734)
8-28-94	Nebraska 31, West Va. 0 (58,233)
8-27-95	Ohio St. 38, Boston College 6 (62,711)
8-26-96	Penn St. vs. Southern Cal

PIGSKIN CLASSIC
Present Site: Provo, Utah
Stadium (Capacity): Cougar Stadium (65,000)
Playing Surface: Grass
Sponsor: None. It is a permitted 12th regular-season game.
Playing Sites: Anaheim Stadium (1990-94); Michigan Stadium (1995)

Date	Teams, Score (Attendance)
8-26-90	Colorado 31, Tennessee 31 (33,458)
8-29-91	Florida St. 44, Brigham Young 28 (38,363)
8-26-92	Texas A&M 10, Stanford 7 (35,240)
8-29-93	North Caro. 31, Southern Cal 9 (49,309)
8-29-94	Ohio St. 34, Fresno St. 10 (28,513)
8-26-95	Michigan 18, Virginia 17 (101,444)
8-24-96	Brigham Young vs. Texas A&M

SOUTHEASTERN CONFERENCE CHAMPIONSHIP
Present Site: Atlanta, Ga.
Stadium (Capacity): Georgia Dome (71,548)
Playing Surface: AstroTurf
Playing Sites: Legion Field (1992-93); Georgia Dome (since 1994)

Date	Teams, Score (Attendance)
12-5-92	Alabama (Western Div.) 28, Florida (Eastern Div.) 21 (83,091) (at Birmingham, Ala.)
12-4-93	Florida (Eastern Div.) 28, Alabama (Western Div.) 13 (76,345) (at Birmingham, Ala.)
12-3-94	Florida (Eastern Div.) 24, Alabama (Western Div.) 23 (74,751)
12-2-95	Florida (Eastern Div.) 34, Arkansas (Western Div.) 3 (71,325)

REGULAR-SEASON GAMES PLAYED IN FOREIGN COUNTRIES

TOKYO, JAPAN
(Called Mirage Bowl 1976-85, Coca-Cola Classic from 1986. Played at Tokyo Olympic Memorial Stadium 1976-87, Tokyo Dome from 1988.)

Date	Teams, Score (Attendance)
9-4-76	Grambling 42, Morgan St. 16 (50,000)

Date	Teams, Score (Attendance)
12-11-77	Grambling 35, Temple 32 (50,000)
12-10-78	Temple 28, Boston College 24 (55,000)
11-24-79	Notre Dame 40, Miami (Fla.) 15 (62,574)
11-30-80	UCLA 34, Oregon St. 3 (86,000)
11-28-81	Air Force 21, San Diego St. 16 (80,000)
11-27-82	Clemson 21, Wake Forest 17 (64,700)
11-26-83	Southern Methodist 34, Houston 12 (70,000)
11-17-84	Army 45, Montana 31 (60,000)
11-30-85	Southern Cal 20, Oregon 6 (65,000)
11-30-86	Stanford 29, Arizona 24 (55,000)
11-28-87	California 17, Washington St. 17 (45,000)
12-3-88	Oklahoma St. 45, Texas Tech 42 (56,000)
12-4-89	Syracuse 24, Louisville 13 (50,000)
12-2-90	Houston 62, Arizona St. 45 (50,000)
11-30-91	Clemson 33, Duke 21 (50,000)
12-6-92	Nebraska 38, Kansas St. 24 (50,000)
12-5-93	Wisconsin 41, Michigan St. 20 (51,500)

MELBOURNE, AUSTRALIA

Date	Teams, Score (Attendance)
12-6-85*	Wyoming 24, UTEP 21 (22,000)
12-4-87†	Brigham Young 30, Colorado St. 26 (76,652)

**Played at V.F.L. Park. †Played at Princes Park.*

YOKOHAMA, JAPAN

Date	Teams, Score (Attendance)
12-2-78	Brigham Young 28, UNLV 24 (27,500)

OSAKA, JAPAN

Date	Teams, Score (Attendance)
9-3-78	Utah St. 10, Idaho St. 0 (15,000)

DUBLIN, IRELAND

(Called Emerald Isle Classic. Played at Lansdowne Road Stadium.)

Date	Teams, Score (Attendance)
11-19-88	Boston College 38, Army 24 (45,525)
12-2-89	Pittsburgh 46, Rutgers 29 (19,800)
11-2-96	Navy vs. Notre Dame

LONDON, ENGLAND

Date	Teams, Score (Attendance)
10-16-88	Richmond 20, Boston U. 17 (6,000)

MILAN, ITALY

(Played at The Arena.)

Date	Teams, Score (Attendance)
10-28-89	Villanova 28, Rhode Island 25 (5,000)

LIMERICK, IRELAND

(Wild Geese Classic. Played at Limerick Gaelic Grounds.)

Date	Teams, Score (Attendance)
11-16-91	Holy Cross 24, Fordham 19 (17,411)

FRANKFURT, GERMANY

(Played at Wald Stadium.)

Date	Teams, Score (Attendance)
9-19-92	Heidelberg 7, Otterbein 7 (4,351)

GALWAY, IRELAND

(Called Christopher Columbus Classic.)

Date	Teams, Score (Attendance)
11-29-92	Bowdoin 7, Tufts 6 (2,500)

HAMILTON, BERMUDA

(Played at Bermuda National Soccer Stadium.)

Date	Teams, Score (Attendance)
11-20-93	Georgetown 17, Wash. & Lee 14 (3,218)
11-19-94	Davidson 28, Sewanee 14 (2,000)
10-28-95	Fordham17, Holy Cross 10 (2,436)

COLLEGE FOOTBALL TROPHY GAMES

Following is a list of the current college football trophy games. The games are listed alphabetically by the trophy-object name. The date refers to the season the trophy was first exchanged and is not necessarily the start of competition between the participants. A game involving interdivision teams is listed in the higher-division classification.

DIVISION I-A

Trophy	Date	Colleges
Anniversary Award	1985	Bowling Green-Kent
Apple Cup	1962	Washington-Washington St.
Axe	1933	California-Stanford
Bayou Bucket	1974	Houston-Rice
Beehive Boot	1971	Brigham Young, Utah, Weber St.
Beer Barrel	1925	Kentucky-Tennessee
Bell	1927	Missouri-Nebraska
Bell Clapper	1931	Oklahoma-Oklahoma St.
Big Game	1979	Arizona-Arizona St.
Blue Key Victory Bell	1940	Ball St.-Indiana St.
Bourbon Barrel	1967	Indiana-Kentucky
Brass Spittoon	1950	Indiana-Michigan St.
Brass Spittoon	1981	New Mexico St.-UTEP
Bronze Boot	1968	Colorado St.-Wyoming
Cannon	1943	Illinois-Purdue
Commander in Chief's	1972	Air Force, Army, Navy
Cy-Hawk	1977	Iowa-Iowa St.
Floyd of Rosedale	1935	Iowa-Minnesota
Foy-O.D.K.	1948	Alabama-Auburn
Fremont Cannon	1970	Nevada-UNLV
Golden Egg	1927	Mississippi-Mississippi St.
Golden Hat	1941	Oklahoma-Texas
Governor's	1969	Kansas-Kansas St.
Governor's Cup	1958	Florida-Florida St.
Governor's Cup	1983	Colorado-Colorado St.
Governor's Flag*	1953	Arizona-Arizona St.
Governor's Victory Bell	1993	Minnesota-Penn St.
Illibuck	1925	Illinois-Ohio St.
Indian War Drum	1935	Kansas-Missouri
Iron Bowl	1983	Alabama-Auburn
Keg of Nails	1950	Cincinnati-Louisville
Kit Carson Rifle	1938	Arizona-New Mexico
Land Grant Trophy	1993	Michigan St.-Penn St.
Little Brown Jug	1909	Michigan-Minnesota
Mayor's Cup	1981	Bethune-Cookman—Central Fla.
Megaphone	1949	Michigan St.-Notre Dame
Old Oaken Bucket	1925	Indiana-Purdue
Old Wagon Wheel	1948	Brigham Young-Utah St.
Paniolo Trophy	1979	Hawaii-Wyoming
Paul Bunyan Axe	1948	Minnesota-Wisconsin
Paul Bunyan-Governor of Michigan	1953	Michigan-Michigan St.
Peace Pipe	1929	Missouri-Oklahoma
Peace Pipe	1955	Miami (Ohio)-Western Mich.
Peace Pipe	1980	Bowling Green-Toledo
Ram-Falcon	1980	Air Force-Colorado St.
Sabine Shoe	1937	Lamar-Southwestern La.
Shillelagh	1952	Notre Dame-Southern Cal
Shillelagh	1958	Notre Dame-Purdue
Silver Spade	1955	New Mexico St.-UTEP
Steel Tire	1976	Akron-Youngstown St.
Telephone	1960	Iowa St.-Missouri
Textile Bowl	1981	Clemson-North Caro. St.
Tomahawk	1945	Illinois-Northwestern
Victory Bell	1942	Southern Cal-UCLA
Victory Bell	1948	Cincinnati-Miami (Ohio)
Victory Bell	1948	Duke-North Caro.
Wagon Wheel	1946	Akron-Kent

DIVISION I-AA

Trophy	Date	Colleges
Bill Knight	1986	Massachusetts-New Hampshire
Brice-Colwell Musket	1946	Maine-New Hampshire
Chief Caddo	1962	Northwestern St.-Stephen F. Austin
Field Cup	1983	Evansville-Ky. Wesleyan
Gem State	1978	Boise St., Idaho, Idaho St.
Golden Circle	1988	Drake-Simpson
Governor's	1979	Central Conn. St.-Southern Conn. St.
Governor's Cup	1972	Brown-Rhode Island
Governor's Cup	1975	Dartmouth-Princeton
Governor's Cup	1984	Eastern Wash.-Idaho
Grizzly-Bobcat Painting	1984	Montana-Montana St.
Harvey—Shin-A-Ninny Totem Pole	1961	Middle Tenn. St.-Tennessee Tech
Little Brown Stein	1938	Idaho-Montana
Mare's	1987	Murray St.—Tenn.-Martin
Ol' Mountain Jug	1937	Appalachian St.-Western Caro.
Ol' School Bell	1988	Jacksonville St.-Troy St.
Red Belt	1978	Murray St.-Western Ky.
Ron Rogerson Memorial	1988	Maine-Rhode Island
Silver Shako	1976	Citadel-Va. Military
Team of Game's MVP	1960	Lafayette-Lehigh
Top Dog	1971	Butler-Indianapolis
Victory Carriage	1960	UC Davis-Cal St. Sacramento

DIVISION II

Trophy	Date	Colleges
Axe	1946	Cal St. Chico-Humboldt St.
Axe Bowl	1975	Northwood-Saginaw Valley
Backyard Bowl	1987	Cheyney-West Chester
Battle Axe	1948	Bemidji St.-Moorhead St.
Battle of the Ravine	1976	Henderson St.-Ouachita Baptist
Bishop's	1970	Lenoir-Rhyne—Newberry
Bronze Derby	1946	Newberry-Presbyterian
Eagle-Rock	1980	Black Hills St.-Chadron St.
East Meets West	1987	Chadron St.-Peru St.
Elm City	1983	New Haven-Southern Conn. St.
Heritage Bell	1979	Delta St.-Mississippi Col.
Miner's Bowl	1986	Mo. Southern St.-Pittsburg St.
Nickel	1938	North Dak.-North Dak. St.
Old Hickory Stick	1931	Northwest Mo. St.-Truman St.
Old Settler's Musket	1975	Adams St.-Fort Lewis
Sitting Bull	1953	North Dak.-South Dak.
Springfield Mayor's	1941	American Int'l-Springfield
Textile	1960	Clark Atlanta-Fort Valley St.

Trophy	Date	Colleges
Traveling	1976	Ashland-Hillsdale
Wagon Wheel	1986	Eastern N.M.-West Tex. A&M
Wooden Shoes	1977	Grand Valley St.-Wayne St. (Mich.)

DIVISION III

Trophy	Date	Colleges
Academic Bowl	1986	Carnegie Mellon-Case Reserve
Admiral's Cup	1980	Maine Maritime-Mass. Maritime
Baird Bros. Golden Stringer	1984	Case Reserve-Wooster
Bell	†1931	Franklin-Hanover
Bill Edwards Trophy	1989	Case Reserve-Wittenberg
Bridge Bowl	1990	Mt. St. Joseph-Thomas More
Bronze Turkey	1929	Knox-Monmouth (Ill.)
CBB	1966	Bates, Bowdoin, Colby
Conestoga Wagon	1963	Dickinson-Frank. & Marsh.
Cortaca Jug	1959	Cortland St.-Ithaca
Cranberry Bowl	1979	Bri'water (Mass.)-Mass. Maritime
Doehling-Heselton Helmet	1988	Lawrence-Ripon
Drum	1940	Occidental—Pomona-Pitzer
Dutchman's Shoes	1950	Rensselaer-Union (N.Y.)
Edmund Orgill	1954	Rhodes-Sewanee
Founder's	1987	Chicago-Washington (Mo.)
Goal Post	1953	Juniata-Susquehanna
Goat	1931	Carleton-St. Olaf
John Wesley	1984	Ky. Wesleyan-Union (Ky.)
Keystone Cup	1981	Delaware Valley-Widener
Little Brass Bell	1947	North Central-Wheaton (Ill.)
Little Brown Bucket	1938	Dickinson-Gettysburg
Little Three	1971	Amherst, Wesleyan (Conn.), Williams
Mercer County Cup	1984	Grove City-Thiel
Monon Bell	1932	DePauw-Wabash
Mug	1931	Coast Guard-Norwich
Old Goal Post	1953	Juniata-Susquehanna
Old Musket	1964	Carroll (Wis.)-Carthage
Old Rocking Chair	1980	Hamilton-Middlebury
Old Tin Cup	1954	Gettysburg-Muhlenberg
Old Water Bucket	1989	Maranatha Baptist-Martin Luther
Paint Bucket	1965	Hamline-Macalester
Pella Corporation Classic	1988	Central (Iowa)-William Penn
President's Cup	1971	Case Reserve-John Carroll
Secretary's Cup	1981	Coast Guard-Merchant Marine
Shoes	1946	Occidental-Whittier
Shot Glass	1938	Coast Guard-Rensselaer
Steve Dean Memorial	1976	Catholic-Georgetown
Transit	1980	Rensselaer-Worcester Tech
Victory Bell	1946	Loras-St. Thomas (Minn.)
Victory Bell	1949	Upper Iowa-Wartburg
Wadsworth	1977	Middlebury-Norwich
Wilson Brothers Cup	1986	Hamline-St. Thomas (Minn.)
Wooden Shoes	1946	Hope-Kalamazoo

NON-NCAA MEMBERS

Trophy	Date	Colleges
Baptist Bible Bowl	1982	Maranatha Baptist-Pillsbury
Home Stake-Gold Mine	1950	Black Hills St.-South Dak. Tech
KTEN Savage-Tiger	1979	East Central-Southeastern Okla.
Paint Bucket	1961	Jamestown-Valley City St.
Wagon Wheel	1957	Lewis & Clark-Willamette

**Changed to Big Game Trophy. †Was reinstated in 1988 after a 17-year lapse.*

BOWL/ALL-STAR RECORDS

Coaching Records

All-Division Coaching Records

Coaches With Career Winning Percentage of .800 or Better

This list includes all coaches in history with a winning percentage of at least .800 over a career of at least 10 seasons at four-year colleges (regardless of division or association). Bowl and playoff games included.

Coach (Alma Mater) (Colleges Coached, Tenure)	Years	Won	Lost	Tied	Pct.
Knute Rockne (Notre Dame '14) (Notre Dame 1918-30)	13	105	12	5	.881
Frank Leahy (Notre Dame '31) (Boston College 1939-40; Notre Dame 1941-43, 1946-53)	13	107	13	9	.864
Bob Reade (Cornell College '54) (Augustana, Ill. 1979-94)	†16	146	23	1	.862
Doyt Perry (Bowling Green '32) (Bowling Green 1955-64)	†10	77	11	5	.855
#Larry Kehres (Mount Union '71) (Mount Union 1986—)	†10	96	16	3	.848
George Woodruff (Yale '89) (Pennsylvania 1892-1901; Illinois 1903; Carlisle 1905)	12	142	25	2	.846
Jake Gaither (Knoxville '27) (Florida A&M 1945-69)	†25	203	36	4	.844
Dave Maurer (Denison '54) (Wittenberg 1969-83)	†15	129	23	3	.842
#Mike Kelly (Manchester '70) (Dayton 1981—)	†15	145	27	1	.841
Paul Hoereman (Heidelberg '38) (Heidelberg 1946-59)	†14	102	18	4	.839
Barry Switzer (Arkansas '60) (Oklahoma 1973-88)	16	157	29	4	.837
Don Coryell (Washington '50) (Whittier 1957-59; San Diego St. 1961-72)	†15	127	24	3	.834
Percy Haughton (Harvard '99) (Cornell 1899-1900; Harvard 1908-16; Columbia 1923-24)	13	96	17	6	.832
Bob Neyland (Army '16) (Tennessee 1926-34, 1936-40, 1946-52)	21	173	31	12	.829
Fielding Yost (Lafayette '97) (Ohio Wesleyan 1897; Nebraska 1898; Kansas 1899; Stanford 1900; Michigan 1901-23, 1925-26)	29	196	36	12	.828
#Tom Osborne (Hastings '59) (Nebraska 1973—)	23	231	47	3	.827
#Al Bagnoli (Central Conn. St. '74) (Union, N.Y. 1982-91; Pennsylvania 1992—)	†14	119	25	0	.826
Bud Wilkinson (Minnesota '37) (Oklahoma 1947-63)	17	145	29	4	.826
Chuck Klausing (Slippery Rock '48) (Indiana, Pa. 1964-69; Carnegie Mellon 1976-85)	†16	123	26	2	.821
Vernon McCain (Langston '31) (Md.-East. Shore 1948-63)	†16	102	21	5	.816
Jock Sutherland (Pittsburgh '18) (Lafayette 1919-23; Pittsburgh 1924-38)	20	144	28	14	.812
#Ron Schipper (Hope '52) (Central, Iowa 1961—)	†35	280	64	3	.811
Bob Devaney (Alma '39) (Wyoming 1957-61; Nebraska 1962-72)	16	136	30	7	.806
Biggie Munn (Minnesota '32) (Albright 1935-36; Syracuse 1946; Michigan St. 1947-53)	10	71	16	3	.805
#John Luckhardt (Purdue '67) (Wash. & Jeff. 1982—)	†14	118	28	2	.804
Sid Gillman (Ohio St. '34) (Miami, Ohio 1944-47; Cincinnati 1949-54)	†10	81	19	2	.804

†Zero to nine years in Division I-A. #Active coach.

Coaches With 200 or More Career Victories

This list includes all coaches who have won at least 200 games at four-year colleges (regardless of classification or association). Bowl and playoff games included.

Coach (Alma Mater) (Colleges Coached, Tenure)	Years	Won	Lost	Tied	Pct.
#Eddie Robinson (Leland '41) (Grambling 1941-42, 1945—)	†53	402	149	15	.724
Bear Bryant (Alabama '36) (Maryland 1945; Kentucky 1946-53; Texas A&M 1954-57; Alabama 1958-82)	38	323	85	17	.780
Pop Warner (Cornell '95) (Georgia 1895-96; Cornell 1897-98; Carlisle 1899-1903; Cornell 1904-06; Carlisle 1907-14; Pittsburgh 1915-23; Stanford 1924-32; Temple 1933-38)	44	319	106	32	.733
#John Gagliardi (Colorado Col. '49) (Carroll, Mont. 1949-52; St. John's, Minn. 1953—)	†47	325	99	11	.760
Amos Alonzo Stagg (Yale '88) (Springfield 1890-91; Chicago 1892-1932; Pacific, Cal. 1933-46)	57	314	199	35	.605
#Ron Schipper (Hope '52) (Central, Iowa 1961—)	†35	280	64	3	.811
#Joe Paterno (Brown '50) (Penn St. 1966—)	30	278	72	3	.792
#Roy Kidd (Eastern Ky. '54) (Eastern Ky. 1964—)	†32	266	94	8	.734
#Bobby Bowden (Samford '53) (Samford 1959-62; West Va. 1970-75; Florida St. 1976—)	30	259	81	4	.759
#Tubby Raymond (Michigan '50) (Delaware 1966—)	†30	250	97	3	.719
#Jim Malosky (Minnesota '51) (Minn.-Duluth 1958—)	†38	243	116	13	.671
Woody Hayes (Denison '35) (Denison 1946-48; Miami, Ohio 1949-50; Ohio St. 1951-78)	33	238	72	10	.759
Bo Schembechler (Miami, Ohio '51) (Miami, Ohio 1963-68; Michigan 1969-89)	27	234	65	8	.775
Arnett Mumford (Wilberforce '24) (Jarvis 1924-26; Bishop 1927-29; Texas College 1931-35; Southern-B.R. 1936-42, 1944-61)	†36	233	85	23	.717
#Roger Harring (Wis.-La Crosse '58) (Wis.-La Crosse 1969—)	†27	232	62	7	.782
††John Merritt (Kentucky St. '50) (Jackson St. 1953-62; Tennessee St. 1963-83)	†31	232	65	11	.771
#Tom Osborne (Hastings '59) (Nebraska 1973—)	23	231	47	3	.827
Fred Long (Millikin '18) (Paul Quinn 1921-22; Wiley 1923-47; Prairie View 1948; Texas College 1949-55; Wiley 1956-65)	†45	227	151	31	.593
Fred Martinelli (Otterbein '51) (Ashland 1959-93)	†35	217	119	12	.641
#LaVell Edwards (Utah St. '52) (Brigham Young 1972—)	24	214	80	3	.726
#Hayden Fry (Baylor '51) (Southern Methodist 1962-72; North Texas 1973-78; Iowa 1979—)	34	213	162	10	.566
#Lou Holtz (Kent '59) (William & Mary 1969-71); North Caro. St. 1972-75; Arkansas 1977-83; Minnesota 1984-85; Notre Dame 1986—)	26	208	92	7	.689
Jess Neely (Vanderbilt '24) (Southwestern, Tenn. 1924-27; Clemson 1931-39; Rice 1940-66)	40	207	176	19	.539
Jim Butterfield (Maine '53) (Ithaca 1967-93)	†27	206	71	1	.743
Jake Gaither (Knoxville '27) (Florida A&M 1945-69)	†25	203	36	4	.844
Warren Woodson (Baylor '24) (Conway St. 1935-40; Hardin-Simmons 1941-42, 1946-51; Arizona 1952-56; New Mexico St. 1958-67; Trinity, Tex. 1972-73)	31	203	95	14	.673
Vince Dooley (Auburn '54) (Georgia 1964-88)	25	201	77	10	.715
Eddie Anderson (Notre Dame '22) (Loras 1922-24; DePaul 1925-31; Holy Cross 1933-38; Iowa 1939-42, 1946-49; Holy Cross 1950-64)	39	201	128	15	.606
Darrell Mudra (Peru St. '51) (Adams St. 1959-62; North Dak. St. 1963-65; Arizona 1967-68; Western Ill. 1969-73; Florida St. 1974-75; Eastern Ill. 1978-82; Northern Iowa 1983-87)	†26	200	81	4	.709

†Zero to nine years in Division I-A. ††Tennessee State's participation in 1981 and 1982 Division I-AA championships (1-2 record) vacated by action of the NCAA Committee on Infractions. #Active coach.

Matchups of Coaches Each With 200 Victories

Date	Coaches, Teams (Victories Going In)	Winner (Score)
11-11-61	Arnett Mumford, Southern-B.R. (232)	
	Fred Long, Wiley (215)	Wiley (21-19)
1-1-78	Bear Bryant, Alabama (272)	Alabama (35-6)
Sugar Bowl	Woody Hayes, Ohio St. (231)	
10-11-80	Eddie Robinson, Grambling (284)	Grambling (52-27)
	John Merritt, Tennessee St. (200)	
10-10-81	Eddie Robinson, Grambling (294)	
	John Merritt, Tennessee St. (209)	Tennessee St. (14-10)
10-9-82	Eddie Robinson, Grambling (301)	
	John Merritt, Tennessee St. (218)	Tennessee St. (22-8)
10-8-83	Eddie Robinson, Grambling (308)	Tie (7-7)
	John Merritt, Tennessee St. (228)	
11-28-87	John Gagliardi, St. John's (Minn.) (251)	
	...wa) (202)	Central (Iowa) (13-3)
	...s (Minn.) (268)	St. John's (Minn.) (27-24)
	...wa) (224)	
	...9)	
	...t. (204)	Florida St. (24-17)
	... (Minn.) (305)	St. John's (Minn.) (47-25)
	...rosse (210)	
	...t. (238)	Florida St. (18-16)
	...(206)	
	...3)	Penn St. (61-21)
	...3)	Penn St. (41-27)
	... (258)	Florida St. (31-26)
	...08)	

...or ...One College

	Years	Won	Lost	Tied	Pct.
...45—)	†53	402	149	15	.724
...	†43	300	93	10	.757
...	†35	280	64	3	.811
...	30	278	72	3	.792
...	†32	266	94	8	.734
...	†30	250	97	3	.719
...	41	244	111	27	.674
...	†38	243	116	13	.671
...	25	232	46	9	.824
...	†27	232	62	7	.782
...	23	231	47	3	.827
...	†35	217	119	12	.641
...	24	214	80	3	.726
...	†27	206	71	1	.743
...	28	205	61	10	.761
...	†25	203	36	4	.844
...	25	201	77	10	.715

...oach.

x-did not coach in Independence Bowl; y-won national championship

From Knute to Lou

Notre Dame coaches since 1918:

Years	Coach	W-L-T
1918-30	Knute Rockne	105-12-5
1931-33	Hunk Anderson	16-9-2
1934-40	Elmer Layden	47-13-3
1941-43, 1946-53	Frank Leahy	87-11-9
1944	Ed McKeever	8-2-0
1945, '63	Hugh Devore	9-9-1
1954-58	Terry Brennan	32-18-0
1959-62	Joe Kuharich	17-23-0
1964-74	Ara Parseghian	95-17-4
1975-80	Dan Devine	53-16-1
1981-85	Gerry Faust	30-26-1
1986-96	Lou Holtz	99-29-2

Coaching Records

Winningest Active Division I-A Coaches

(Minimum Five Years as Division I-A Head Coach; Record at Four-Year Colleges Only)

BY PERCENTAGE

Coach, College	Years	Won	Lost	Tied	†Pct.	Bowls W-L-T
Tom Osborne, Nebraska	23	231	47	3	.827	10-13-0
R. C. Slocum, Texas A&M	7	68	15	2	.812	2-4-0
Joe Paterno, Penn St.	30	278	72	3	.792	17-8-1
John Robinson, Southern Cal	10	92	24	4	.783	7-1-0
Bobby Bowden, Florida St.!	30	259	81	4	.759	15-3-1
Steve Spurrier, Florida	9	81	26	2	.752	2-4-0
Gary Blackney, Bowling Green	5	41	14	2	.737	2-0-0
LaVell Edwards, Brigham Young	24	214	80	3	.726	6-12-1
Danny Ford, Arkansas@$	15	114	45	5	.710	6-3-0
Paul Pasqualoni, Syracuse	10	76	32	1	.702	*3-1-0
Lou Holtz, Notre Dame	26	208	92	7	.689	10-8-2
John Cooper, Ohio St.	19	146	69	6	.674	3-7-0
Jackie Sherrill, Mississippi St.$	18	134	72	4	.648	6-5-0
Gary Pinkel, Toledo	5	34	19	3	.634	1-0-0
Al Molde, Western Mich.	25	166	95	8	.632	*3-6-0
Fisher DeBerry, Air Force	12	92	55	1	.625	4-4-0
Don Nehlen, West Va.	25	168	103	8	.616	3-6-0
Ken Hatfield, Rice	17	120	76	4	.610	4-6-0
Dick Tomey, Arizona	19	123	86	7	.586	2-3-0
George Welsh, Virginia	23	153	109	4	.583	5-6-0
John Mackovic, Texas	11	73	52	3	.582	2-4-0
Bill Snyder, Kansas St.	7	46	33	1	.581	2-1-0
Johnny Majors, Pittsburgh	28	181	130	10	.579	9-7-0
Ron McBride, Utah	6	41	30	0	.577	1-2-0
Jim Hess, New Mexico St.	21	133	98	5	.574	*5-3-0
Bill Mallory, Indiana	26	164	122	4	.572	4-6-0
Jim Sweeney, Fresno St.	31	196	147	4	.571	*6-3-0
Hayden Fry, Iowa	34	213	162	10	.566	6-8-1
John Ralston, San Jose St.	16	94	72	4	.565	2-2-0
Frank Beamer, Virginia Tech	15	93	72	4	.562	*2-2-0
Jim Wacker, Minnesota	25	156	123	3	.559	*13-2-0
Randy Walker, Miami (Ohio)	6	34	27	5	.553	0-0-0
Ted Tollner, San Diego St.	6	38	31	1	.550	1-2-0
Larry Smith, Missouri	19	116	96	7	.546	2-5-1
Spike Dykes, Texas Tech#	10	56	47	1	.543	2-3-0
Gene Stallings, Alabama!	13	79	67	1	.541	5-1-0
Lou Tepper, Illinois	5	23	22	2	.511	1-2-0
Joe Tiller, Wyoming	5	29	28	1	.509	0-1-0
Bruce Snyder, Arizona St.	16	87	85	6	.506	2-0-0
Barry Alvarez, Wisconsin	6	32	32	4	.500	2-0-0
Mike Price, Washington St.	15	84	85	0	.497	*3-1-0
Nelson Stokley, Southwestern La.	10	54	55	1	.495	0-0-0
Glen Mason, Kansas	10	55	57	1	.491	2-0-0
Mack Brown, North Caro.	12	66	71	1	.482	2-3-0
Gerry DiNardo, LSU$	5	26	29	1	.473	1-0-0
Jeff Bower, Southern Miss.$	6	26	29	1	.473	0-1-0
Bill Curry, Kentucky	16	79	98	4	.448	2-3-0
Bob Sutton, Army	5	24	30	1	.445	0-0-0
Dave Rader, Tulsa	8	38	51	1	.428	1-1-0
Fred Goldsmith, Duke	8	36	50	1	.420	0-1-0
Jerry Pettibone, Oregon St.	11	44	75	2	.372	0-0-0
Jim Colletto, Purdue	10	34	73	4	.324	0-0-0
Charlie Bailey, UTEP	6	17	42	2	.295	0-0-0
Tom Rossley, Southern Methodist	5	10	42	3	.209	0-0-0
Less Than 5 Years in Division I-A (school followed by years in I-A, includes record at all four-year colleges):						
Jim Donnan, Georgia (0)	6	64	21	0	.753	*15-4-0
Bill Lynch, Ball St. (1)	6	43	16	3	.718	*0-1-0
Terry Bowden, Auburn (3)	12	92	41	2	.689	*2-5-0
Mark Duffner, Maryland (4)	10	75	34	1	.686	0-0-0
Dennis Franchione, New Mexico (4)	13	98	46	2	.678	*6-5-0
John L. Smith, Utah St. (1)	7	57	28	0	.671	*3-5-0
Sonny Lubick, Colorado St. (3)	7	44	31	0	.587	0-2-0
Rip Scherer, Memphis (1)	5	32	27	0	.542	*2-2-0
Mike Bellotti, Oregon (1)	6	30	28	2	.517	0-1-0
Bob Toledo, UCLA (4)	6	29	36	0	.446	0-0-0
Buddy Teevens, Tulane (4)$	11	48	67	2	.419	0-0-0
Gary Barnett, Northwestern (4)	6	26	37	2	.415	1-0-0

*†Ties computed as half won and half lost. Overall record includes bowl and playoff games. *Includes record in NCAA and/or NAIA championships. @Win in Gator Bowl in first game. #Loss in Independence Bowl in first game. !Includes games forfeited by action of NCAA Committee on Infractions. $Includes forfeit victory over Alabama in 1993 by action of NCAA Committee on Infractions.*

BY VICTORIES

(Minimum 100 Victories)

Coach, College, Winning Percentage	Won
Joe Paterno, Penn St. .792	278
Bobby Bowden, Florida St. .759	259
Tom Osborne, Nebraska .827	231
LaVell Edwards, Brigham Young .726	214
Hayden Fry, Iowa .566	213
Lou Holtz, Notre Dame .689	208
Jim Sweeney, Fresno St. .571	196
Johnny Majors, Pittsburgh .579	181
Don Nehlen, West Va. .616	168
Al Molde, Western Mich. .632	166
Bill Mallory, Indiana .572	164
Jim Wacker, Minnesota .559	156
George Welsh, Virginia .583	153
John Cooper, Ohio St. .674	146
Jackie Sherrill, Mississippi St. .648	134
Jim Hess, New Mexico St. .574	133
Dick Tomey, Arizona .586	123
Ken Hatfield, Rice .610	120
Larry Smith, Missouri .546	116
Danny Ford, Arkansas .710	114

COACHING RECORDS

Winningest All-Time Division I-A Coaches

Minimum 10 years as head coach at Division I institutions; record at four-year colleges only; bowl games included; ties computed as half won, half lost. Active coaches indicated by (*). College Football Hall of Fame members indicated by (†).

BY PERCENTAGE

Coach (Alma Mater) (Colleges Coached, Tenure)	Years	Won	Lost	Tied	Pct.
Knute Rockne (Notre Dame '14)† (Notre Dame 1918-30)	13	105	12	5	.881
Frank Leahy (Notre Dame '31)† (Boston College 1939-40; Notre Dame 1941-43, 1946-53)	13	107	13	9	.864
George Woodruff (Yale '89)† (Pennsylvania 1892-01; Illinois 1903; Carlisle 1905)	12	142	25	2	.846
Barry Switzer (Arkansas '60) (Oklahoma 1973-88)	16	157	29	4	.837
Percy Haughton (Harvard '99)† (Cornell 1899-00; Harvard 1908-16; Columbia 1923-24)	13	96	17	6	.832
Bob Neyland (Army '16)† (Tennessee 1926-34, 1936-40, 1946-52)	21	173	31	12	.829
Fielding Yost (West Va. '95)† (Ohio Wesleyan 1897; Nebraska 1898; Kansas 1899; Stanford 1900; Michigan 1901-23, 1925-26)	29	196	36	12	.828
*Tom Osborne (Hastings '59) (Nebraska 1973—)	23	231	47	3	.827
Bud Wilkinson (Minnesota '37)† (Oklahoma 1947-63)	17	145	29	4	.826
Jock Sutherland (Pittsburgh '18)† (Lafayette 1919-23; Pittsburgh 1924-38)	20	144	28	14	.812
Bob Devaney (Alma '39)† (Wyoming 1957-61; Nebraska 1962-72)	16	136	30	7	.806
Frank Thomas (Notre Dame '23)† (Tenn.-Chatt. 1925-28; Alabama 1931-42, 1944-46)	19	141	33	9	.795
*Joe Paterno (Brown '50) (Penn St. 1966—)	30	278	72	3	.792
Henry Williams (Yale '91)† (Army 1891; Minnesota 1900-21)	23	141	34	12	.786
*John Robinson (Oregon '58) (Southern Cal 1976-82, 1993—)	10	92	24	4	.783
Gil Dobie (Minnesota '02)† (North Dak. St. 1906-07; Washington 1908-16; Navy 1917-19; Cornell 1920-35; Boston College 1936-38)	33	180	45	15	.781
Bear Bryant (Alabama '36)† (Maryland 1945; Kentucky 1946-53; Texas A&M 1954-57; Alabama 1958-82)	38	323	85	17	.780
Fred Folsom (Dartmouth '95) (Colorado 1895-99, 1901-02; Dartmouth 1903-06; Colorado 1908-15)	19	106	28	6	.779
Bo Schembechler (Miami, Ohio '51)† (Miami, Ohio 1963-68; Michigan 1969-89)	27	234	65	8	.775
Fritz Crisler (Chicago '22)† (Minnesota 1930-31; Princeton 1932-37; Michigan 1938-47)	18	116	32	9	.768
Charley Moran (Tennessee '98) (Texas A&M 1909-14; Centre 1919-23; Bucknell 1924-26; Catawba 1930-33)	18	122	33	12	.766
Wallace Wade (Brown '17)† (Alabama 1923-30; Duke 1931-41, 1946-50)	24	171	49	10	.765
Frank Kush (Michigan St. '53)† (Arizona St. 1958-79)	22	176	54	1	.764
Dan McGugin (Michigan '04)† (Vanderbilt 1904-17, 1919-34)	30	197	55	19	.762
Jimmy Crowley (Notre Dame '25)# (Michigan St. 1929-32; Fordham 1933-41)	13	78	21	10	.761
Andy Smith (Penn St., Pennsylvania '05)† (Pennsylvania 1909-12; Purdue 1913-15; California 1916-25)	17	116	32	13	.761
Woody Hayes (Denison '35)† (Denison 1946-48; Miami, Ohio 1949-50; Ohio St. 1951-78)	33	238	72	10	.759
Red Blaik (Miami, Ohio '18; Army '20)† (Dartmouth 1934-40; Army 1941-58)	25	166	48	14	.759
*Bobby Bowden (Samford '53)√ (Samford 1959-62; West Va. 1970-75; Florida St. 1976—)	30	259	81	4	.759
Darrell Royal (Oklahoma '50)† (Mississippi St. 1954-55; Washington 1956; Texas 1957-76)	23	184	60	5	.749
John McKay (Oregon '50)† (Southern Cal 1960-75)	16	127	40	8	.749
John Vaught (Texas Christian '33)† (Mississippi 1947-70, 1973)	25	190	61	12	.745
Dan Devine (Minn.-Duluth '48)† (Arizona St. 1955-57; Missouri 1958-70; Notre Dame 1975-80)	22	172	57	9	.742
Gus Henderson (Oberlin '12) (Southern Cal 1919-24; Tulsa 1925-35; Occidental 1940-42)	20	126	42	7	.740
Ara Parseghian (Miami, Ohio '49)† (Miami, Ohio 1951-55; Northwestern 1956-63; Notre Dame 1964-74)	24	170	58	6	.739
Elmer Layden (Notre Dame '25)# (Loras 1925-26; Duquesne 1927-33; Notre Dame 1934-40)	16	103	34	11	.733
Pop Warner (Cornell '95)† (Georgia 1895-96; Cornell 1897-98; Carlisle 1899-1903; Cornell 1904-06; Carlisle 1907-14; Pittsburgh 1915-23; Stanford 1924-32; Temple 1933-38)	44	319	106	32	.733
Howard Jones (Yale '08)† (Syracuse 1908; Yale 1909; Ohio St. 1910; Yale 1913; Iowa 1916-23; Duke 1924; Southern Cal 1925-40)	29	194	64	21	.733
Frank Cavanaugh (Dartmouth '97)† (Cincinnati 1898; Holy Cross 1903-05; Dartmouth 1911-16; Boston College 1919-26; Fordham 1927-32)	24	145	48	17	.731
Jim Tatum (North Caro. '35)† (North Caro. 1942; Oklahoma 1946; Maryland 1947-55; North Caro. 1956-58)	14	100	35	7	.729
*LaVell Edwards (Utah St. '52) (Brigham Young 1972—)	24	214	80	3	.726
Francis Schmidt (Nebraska '14)† (Tulsa 1919-21; Arkansas 1922-28; Texas Christian 1929-33; Ohio St. 1934-40; Idaho 1941-42)	24	158	57	11	.723
Bill Roper (Princeton '03)† (Va. Military 1903-04; Princeton 1906-08; Missouri 1909; Princeton 1910-11; Swarthmore 1915-16; Princeton 1919-30)	22	112	37	19	.723
Doc Kennedy (Kansas & Pennsylvania '03) (Kansas 1904-10; Haskell 1911-16)	13	85	31	7	.720
Tad Jones (Yale '08)† (Syracuse 1909-10; Yale 1916, 1920-27)	11	66	24	6	.719
Vince Dooley (Auburn '54)† (Georgia 1964-88)	25	201	77	10	.715
Dana Bible (Carson-Newman '12)† (Mississippi Col. 1913-15; LSU 1916; Texas A&M 1917, 1919-28; Nebraska 1929-36; Texas 1937-46)	33	198	72	23	.715
Bobby Dodd (Tennessee '31)†# (Georgia Tech 1945-66)	22	165	64	8	.713
John Heisman (Brown '90, Pennsylvania '92)† (Oberlin 1892; Akron 1893; Oberlin 1894; Auburn 1895-99; Clemson 1900-03; Georgia Tech 1904-19; Pennsylvania 1920-22; Wash. & Jeff. 1923; Rice 1924-27)	36	185	70	17	.711
*Danny Ford (Alabama '70) (Clemson 1978-89; Arkansas 1993—)	‡15	114	45	5	.710
Jumbo Stiehm (Wisconsin '09) (Ripon 1910; Nebraska 1911-15; Indiana 1916-21)	12	59	23	4	.709
Red Sanders (Vanderbilt '27)† (Vanderbilt 1940-42, 1946-48; UCLA 1949-57)	15	102	41	3	.709
Pat Dye (Georgia '62) (East Caro. 1974-79; Wyoming 1980; Auburn 1981-92)	19	153	62	5	.707
Chick Meehan (Syracuse '18) (Syracuse 1920-24; New York U. 1925-31; Manhattan 1932-37)	18	115	44	14	.705
John McEwan (Army '17) (Army 1923-25; Oregon 1926-29; Holy Cross 1930-32)	10	59	23	6	.705
Bennie Owen (Kansas '00)† (Washburn 1900; Bethany, Kan. 1901-04; Oklahoma 1905-26)	27	155	60	19	.703
Ike Armstrong (Drake '23)† (Utah 1925-49)	25	140	55	15	.702
Frank Broyles (Georgia Tech '47)† (Missouri 1957; Arkansas 1958-76)	20	149	62	6	.700
Biff Jones (Army '17)† (Army 1926-29; LSU 1932-34; Oklahoma 1935-36; Nebraska 1937-41)	14	87	33	15	.700

#Member of College Football Hall of Fame as a player. ‡Last game of 1978 season counted as full season. √Includes games forfeited, team and/or individual statistics abrogated, and coaching records changed by action of the NCAA Committee on Infractions.

All-Time Division I-A Coaching Victories

Minimum 10 years as head coach at Division I institutions; record at four-year colleges only; bowl games included. After each coach's name is his alma mater, year graduated, total years coached, won-lost record and percentage, tenure at each college coached, and won-lost record there. Active coaches are denoted by an asterisk (*).

(Minimum 150 Victories)

323 Bear Bryant (Born 9-11-13 Moro Bottoms, Ark.; Died 1-26-83)
Alabama 1936 (38: 323-85-17 .780)
Maryland 1945 (6-2-1); Kentucky 1946-53 (60-23-5); Texas A&M 1954-57 (25-14-2); Alabama 1958-82 (232-46-9)

319 Pop Warner (Born 4-5-1871 Springville, N.Y.; Died 9-7-54)
Cornell 1895 (44: 319-106-32 .733)
Georgia 1895-96 (7-4-0); Cornell 1897-98, 1904-06 (36-13-3); Carlisle 1899-1903, 1907-14 (114-42-8); Pittsburgh 1915-23 (60-12-4); Stanford 1924-32 (71-17-8); Temple 1933-38 (31-18-9)

314 Amos Alonzo Stagg (Born 8-16-1862 West Orange, N.J.; Died 3-17-65)
Yale 1888 (57: 314-199-35 .605)
Springfield 1890-91 (10-11-1); Chicago 1892-1932 (244-111-27); Pacific (Cal.) 1933-46 (60-77-7)

278 *Joe Paterno (Born 12-21-26 Brooklyn, N.Y.)
Brown 1951 (30: 278-72-3 .792)
Penn St. 1966-95 (278-72-3)

259 *Bobby Bowden (Born 11-8-29 Birmingham, Ala.)
Samford 1953 (√30: 259-81-4 .759)
Samford 1959-62 (31-6-0); West Va. 1970-75 (√42-26-0); Florida St. 1976-95 (186-49-4)

238 Woody Hayes (Born 2-13-14 Clifton, Ohio; Died 3-12-87)
Denison 1935 (33: 238-72-10 .759)
Denison 1946-48 (19-6-0); Miami (Ohio) 1949-50 (14-5-0); Ohio St. 1951-78 (205-61-10)

234 Bo Schembechler (Born 9-1-29 Barberton, Ohio)
Miami (Ohio) 1951 (27: 234-65-8 .775)
Miami (Ohio) 1963-68 (40-17-3); Michigan 1969-89 (194-48-5)

231 *Tom Osborne (Born 2-23-37 Hastings, Neb.)
Hastings 1959 (23: 231-47-3 .827)
Nebraska 1973-95 (231-47-3)

214 *LaVell Edwards (Born 10-11-30 Provo, Utah)
Utah St. 1952 (24: 214-80-3 .726)
Brigham Young 1972-95 (214-80-3)

213 *Hayden Fry (Born 2-28-29 Odessa, Texas)
Baylor 1951 (√34: 213-162-10 .566)
Southern Methodist 1962-72 (49-66-1); North Texas 1973-78 (√40-23-3); Iowa 1979-95 (124-73-6)

208 *Lou Holtz (Born 1-6-37 Follansbee, W.Va.)
Kent 1959 (26: 208-92-7 .689)
William & Mary 1969-71 (13-20-0); North Caro. St. 1972-75 (33-12-3); Arkansas 1977-83 (60-21-2); Minnesota 1984-85 (10-12-0); Notre Dame 1986-95 (92-27-2)

207 Jess Neely (Born 1-4-1898 Smyrna, Tenn.; Died 4-9-83)
Vanderbilt 1924 (40: 207-176-19 .539)
Rhodes 1924-27 (20-17-2); Clemson 1931-39 (43-35-7); Rice 1940-66 (144-124-10)

203 Warren Woodson (Born 2-24-03 Fort Worth, Texas)
Baylor 1924 (31: 203-95-14 .673)
Central Ark. 1935-39 (40-8-3); Hardin-Simmons 1941-42, 1946-51 (58-24-6); Arizona 1952-56 (26-22-2); New Mexico St. 1958-67 (63-36-3); Trinity (Tex.) 1972-73 (16-5-0)

201 Vince Dooley (Born 9-4-32 Mobile, Ala.)
Auburn 1954 (25: 201-77-10 .715)
Georgia 1964-88 (201-77-10)

201 Eddie Anderson (Born 11-13-1900 Mason City, Iowa; Died 4-26-74)
Notre Dame 1922 (39: 201-128-15 .606)
Loras 1922-24 (16-6-2); DePaul 1925-31 (21-22-3); Holy Cross 1933-38, 1950-64 (129-67-8); Iowa 1939-42, 1946-49 (35-33-2)

198 Dana X. Bible (Born 10-8-1891 Jefferson City, Tenn.; Died 1-19-80)
Carson-Newman 1912 (33: 198-72-23 .715)
Mississippi Col. 1913-15 (12-7-2); LSU 1916 (1-0-2); Texas A&M 1917, 1919-28 (72-19-9); Nebraska 1929-36 (50-15-7); Texas 1937-46 (63-31-3)

197 Dan McGugin (Born 7-29-1879 Tingley, Iowa; Died 1-19-36)
Michigan 1904 (30: 197-55-19 .762)
Vanderbilt 1904-17, 1919-34 (197-55-19)

196 Fielding Yost (Born 4-30-1871 Fairview, W.Va.; Died 8-20-46)
West Va. '95 (29: 196-36-12 .828)
Ohio Wesleyan 1897 (7-1-1); Nebraska 1898 (7-4-0); Kansas 1899 (10-0-0); Stanford 1900 (7-2-1); Michigan 1901-23, 1925-26 (165-29-10)

196 *Jim Sweeney (Born 9-1-29 Butte, Mont.)
Portland 1951 (31: 196-147-4 .571)
Montana St. 1963-67 (31-20-0); Washington St. 1968-75 (26-59-1); Fresno St. 1976-77, 1980-95 (139-68-3)

194 Howard Jones (Born 8-23-1885 Excello, Ohio; Died 7-27-41)
Yale 1908 (29: 194-64-21 .733)
Syracuse 1908 (6-3-1); Yale 1909, 1913 (15-2-3); Ohio St. 1910 (6-1-3); Iowa 1916-23 (42-17-1); Duke 1924 (4-5-0); Southern Cal 1925-40 (121-36-13)

190 John Vaught (Born 5-6-08 Olney, Texas)
Texas Christian 1933 (25: 190-61-12 .745)
Mississippi 1947-70, 1973 (190-61-12)

185 John Heisman (Born 10-23-1869 Cleveland, Ohio; Died 10-3-36)
Brown 1890 (36: 185-70-17 .711)
Oberlin 1892, 1894 (11-3-1); Akron 1893 (5-2-0); Auburn 1895-99 (12-4-2); Clemson 1900-03 (19-3-2); Georgia Tech 1904-19 (102-29-6); Pennsylvania 1920-22 (16-10-2); Wash. & Jeff. 1923 (6-1-1); Rice 1924-27 (14-18-3)

184 Darrell Royal (Born 7-6-24 Hollis, Okla.)
Oklahoma 1950 (23: 184-60-5 .749)
Mississippi St. 1954-55 (12-8-0); Washington 1956 (5-5-0); Texas 1957-76 (167-47-5)

181 *Johnny Majors (Born 5-21-35 Lynchburg, Tenn.)
Tennessee 1957 (28: 181-130-10 .579)
Iowa St. 1968-72 (24-30-1); Pittsburgh 1973-76, 1993-95 (41-38-1); Tennessee 1977-92 (116-62-8)

180 Gil Dobie (Born 1-31-1879 Hastings, Minn.; Died 12-24-48)
Minnesota 1902 (33: 180-45-15 .781)
North Dak. St. 1906-07 (7-0-0); Washington 1908-16 (58-0-3); Navy 1917-19 (17-3-0); Cornell 1920-35 (82-36-7); Boston College 1936-38 (16-6-5)

180 Carl Snavely (Born 7-30-1894 Omaha, Neb.; Died 7-12-75)
Lebanon Valley 1915 (32: 180-96-16 .644)
Bucknell 1927-33 (42-16-8); North Caro. 1934-35, 1945-52 (59-35-5); Cornell 1936-44 (46-26-3); Washington (Mo.) 1953-58 (33-19-0)

179 Jerry Claiborne (Born 8-26-28 Hopkinsville, Ky.)
Kentucky 1950 (28: 179-122-8 .592)
Virginia Tech 1961-70 (61-39-2); Maryland 1972-81 (77-37-3); Kentucky 1982-89 (41-46-3)

178 Ben Schwartzwalder (Born 6-2-09 Point Pleasant, W.Va.; Died 4-28-93)
West Va. 1933 (28: 178-96-3 .648)
Muhlenberg 1946-48 (25-5-0); Syracuse 1949-73 (153-91-3)

176 Frank Kush (Born 1-20-29 Windber, Pa.)
Michigan St. 1953 (22: 176-54-1 .764)
Arizona St. 1958-79 (176-54-1)

176 Don James (Born 12-31-32 Massillon, Ohio)
Miami (Fla.) 1954 (22: 176-78-3 .691)
Kent 1971-74 (25-19-1); Washington 1975-92 (151-59-2)

176 Ralph Jordan (Born 9-25-10 Selma, Ala.; Died 7-17-80)
Auburn 1932 (√25: 176-83-6 .675)
Auburn 1951-75 (√176-83-6)

174 Pappy Waldorf (Born 10-3-02 Clifton Springs, N.Y.; Died 8-15-81)
Syracuse 1925 (31: 174-100-22 .625)
Oklahoma City 1925-27 (17-11-3); Oklahoma St. 1929-33 (34-10-7); Kansas St. 1934 (7-2-1); Northwestern 1935-46 (49-45-7); California 1947-56 (67-32-4)

173 Bob Neyland (Born 2-17-92 Greenville, Texas; Died 3-28-62)
Army 1916 (21: 173-31-12 .829)
Tennessee 1926-34, 1936-40, 1946-52 (173-31-12)

172 Dan Devine (Born 12-23-24 Augusta, Wis.)
Minn.-Duluth 1948 (22: 172-57-9 .742)
Arizona St. 1955-57 (27-3-1); Missouri 1958-70 (92-38-7); Notre Dame 1975-80 (53-16-1)

171 Wallace Wade (Born 6-15-1892 Trenton, Tenn.; Died 10-7-86)
Brown 1917 (24: 171-49-10 .765)
Alabama 1923-30 (61-13-3); Duke 1931-41, 1946-50 (110-36-7)

170 Ara Parseghian (Born 5-21-23 Akron, Ohio)
Miami (Ohio) 1949 (24: 170-58-6 .739)
Miami (Ohio) 1951-55 (39-6-1); Northwestern 1956-63 (36-35-1); Notre Dame 1964-74 (95-17-4)

170 Grant Teaff (Born 11-12-33 Hermleigh, Texas)
McMurry 1956 (30: 170-151-8 .529)
McMurry 1960-65 (23-35-2); Angelo St. 1969-71 (19-11-0); Baylor 1972-92 (128-105-6)

168 *Don Nehlen (Born 1-1-36 Canton, Ohio)
Bowling Green 1958 (25: 168-103-8 .616)
Bowling Green 1968-76 (53-35-4); West Va. 1980-95 (115-68-4)

168 Bob Blackman (Born 7-7-18 De Soto, Iowa)
Southern Cal 1941 (30: 168-112-7 .598)
Denver 1953-54 (12-6-2); Dartmouth 1955-70 (104-37-3); Illinois 1971-76 (29-36-1); Cornell 1977-82 (23-33-1)

166 Red Blaik (Born 2-17-1897 Detroit, Mich.; Died 5-6-89)
Miami (Ohio) 1918; Army 1920 (25: 166-48-14 .759)
Dartmouth 1934-40 (45-15-4); Army 1941-58 (121-33-10)

165 Bobby Dodd (Born 11-11-08 Galax, Va.; Died 6-21-88)
Tennessee 1931 (22: 165-64-8 .713)
Georgia Tech 1945-66 (165-64-8)

165 Frank Howard (Born 3-25-09 Barlow Bend, Ala.; Died 1-25-96)
Alabama 1931 (30: 165-118-12 .580)
Clemson 1940-69 (165-118-12)

164 *Bill Mallory (Born 5-30-35 Sandusky, Ohio)
Miami (Ohio) 1957 (26: 164-122-4 .572)
Miami (Ohio) 1969-73 (39-12-0); Colorado 1974-78 (35-21-1); Northern Ill. 1980-83 (25-19-0); Indiana 1984-95 (65-70-3)

163 Don Faurot (Born 6-23-02 Mountain Grove, Mo.; Died 10-18-95)
Missouri 1925 (28: 163-93-13 .630)
Truman St. 1926-34 (63-13-3); Missouri 1935-42, 1946-56 (100-80-10)

162 Ossie Solem (Born 12-13-1891 Minneapolis, Minn.; Died 10-26-70)
Minnesota 1915 (37: 162-117-20 .575)
Luther 1920 (5-1-1); Drake 1921-31 (54-35-2); Iowa 1932-36 (15-21-4); Syracuse 1937-45 (30-27-6); Springfield 1946-57 (58-33-7)

161 Bill Dooley (Born 5-19-34 Mobile, Ala.)
Mississippi St. 1956 (26: 161-127-5 .558)
North Caro. 1967-77 (69-53-2); Virginia Tech 1978-86 (64-37-1); Wake Forest 1987-92 (29-36-2)

160 Bill Yeoman (Born 12-26-27 Elnora, Ind.)
Army 1949 (25: 160-108-8 .595)
Houston 1962-86 (160-108-8)

158 Francis Schmidt (Born 12-3-1885 Downs, Kan.; Died 9-19-44)
Nebraska 1914 (24: 158-57-11 .723)
Tulsa 1919-21 (24-3-2); Arkansas 1922-28 (42-20-3); Texas Christian 1929-33 (46-6-5); Ohio St. 1934-40 (39-16-1); Idaho 1941-42 (7-12-0)

157 Barry Switzer (Born 10-5-37 Crossett, Ark.)
Arkansas 1960 (16: 157-29-4 .837)
Oklahoma 1973-88 (157-29-4)

157 Edward Robinson (Born 10-15-1873 Lynn, Miss.; Died 3-10-45)
Brown 1896 (27: 157-88-13 .632)
Nebraska 1896-97 (11-4-1); Brown 1898-1901, 1904-07, 1910-1925 (140-82-12); Maine 1902 (6-2-0)

156 *Jim Wacker (Born 4-28-37 Detroit, Mich.)
Valparaiso 1960 (25: 156-123-3 .559)
Texas Lutheran 1971-75 (38-16-0); North Dak. St. 1976-78 (24-9-1); Southwest Tex. St. 1979-82 (42-8-0); Texas Christian 1983-91 (40-58-2); Minnesota 1992-95 (12-32-0)

155 Bennie Owen (Born 7-24-1875 Chicago, Ill.; Died 2-9-70)
Kansas 1900 (27: 155-60-19 .703)
Washburn 1900 (6-2-0); Bethany (Kan.) 1901-04 (27-4-3); Oklahoma 1905-26 (122-54-16)

155 Ray Morrison (Born 2-28-1885 Switzerland Co., Ind.; Died 11-19-82)
Vanderbilt 1912 (34: 155-130-33 .539)
Southern Methodist 1915-16, 1922-34 (84-44-22); Vanderbilt 1918, 1935-39 (29-22-2); Temple 1940-48 (31-38-9); Austin 1949-52 (11-26-0)

154 Earle Bruce (Born 3-8-31 Massillon, Ohio)
Ohio St. 1953 (21: 154-90-2 .630)
Tampa 1972 (10-2-0); Iowa St. 1973-78 (36-32-0); Ohio St. 1979-87 (81-26-1); Northern Iowa 1988 (5-6-0); Colorado St. 1989-92 (22-24-1)

153 Pat Dye (Born 11-6-39 Augusta, Ga.)
Georgia 1962 (19: 153-62-5 .707)
East Caro. 1974-79 (48-18-1); Wyoming 1980 (6-5-0); Auburn 1981-92 (99-39-4)

153 Morley Jennings (Born 1-23-1885 Holland, Mich.; Died 5-13-85)
Mississippi St. 1912 (29: 153-75-18 .658)
Ouachita Baptist 1912-25 (70-15-12); Baylor 1926-40 (83-60-6)

153 Matty Bell (Born 2-22-1899 Baylor Co., Texas; Died 6-30-83)
Centre 1920 (26: 153-87-16 .630)
Haskell 1920-21 (13-6-0); Carroll (Wis.) 1922 (4-3-0); Texas Christian 1923-28 (33-17-5); Texas A&M 1929-33 (24-21-3); Southern Methodist 1935-41, 1945-49 (79-40-8)

153 *George Welsh (Born 8-26-33 Coaldale, Pa.)
Navy 1960 (23: 153-109-4 .583)
Navy 1973-81 (55-46-1); Virginia 1982-95 (98-63-3)

151 Lou Little (Born 12-6-1893 Leominster, Mass.; Died 5-28-79)
Pennsylvania 1920 (33: 151-128-13 .539)
Georgetown 1924-29 (41-12-3); Columbia 1930-56 (110-116-10)

√Includes games forfeited, team and/or individual statistics abrogated, and coaching records changed by action of the NCAA Committee on Infractions.

Division I-A Best Career Starts by Wins

(Head coaches with at least half their seasons at major college at the time and minimum five years coached)

1 SEASON

Coach, Team	Season	W	L	T	Pct.
George Woodruff, Pennsylvania	1892	15	1	0	.938
Walter Camp, Yale	1888	13	0	0	1.000
Bill Battle, Tennessee	1970	11	1	0	.917
*Gary Blackney, Bowling Green	1991	11	1	0	.917
*John Robinson, Southern Cal	1976	11	1	0	.917
Dick Crum, Miami (Ohio)	1974	10	0	1	.955
Barry Switzer, Oklahoma	1973	10	0	1	.955
Chuck Fairbanks, Oklahoma	1967	10	1	0	.909
Larry Siemering, Pacific (Cal.)	1947	10	1	0	.909
Dwight Wallace, Ball St.	1978	10	1	0	.909
Mike Archer, LSU	1987	10	1	1	.875

2 SEASONS

Coach, Team	Seasons	W	L	T	Pct.
Walter Camp, Yale	1888-89	28	1	0	.966
George Woodruff, Pennsylvania	1892-93	27	4	0	.871
Barry Switzer, Oklahoma	1973-74	21	0	1	.977
Dick Crum, Miami (Ohio)	1974-75	21	1	1	.935
Bill Battle, Tennessee	1970-71	21	3	0	.875
*Gary Blackney, Bowling Green	1991-92	21	3	0	.875
Frank Leahy, Boston College	1939-40	20	2	0	.909
Ron Meyer, UNLV	1973-74	20	4	0	.833
*Fisher DeBerry, Air Force	1984-85	20	5	0	.800
Dutch Meyer, Texas Christian	1934-35	20	5	0	.800
Herb Deromedi, Central Mich.	1978-79	19	2	1	.886
*John Robinson, Southern Cal	1976-77	19	5	0	.792

3 SEASONS

Coach, Team(s)	Seasons	W	L	T	Pct.
Walter Camp, Yale	1888-90	41	2	0	.953
George Woodruff, Pennsylvania	1892-94	39	4	0	.907
Barry Switzer, Oklahoma	1973-75	32	1	1	.956
Bill Battle, Tennessee	1970-72	31	5	0	.861
*John Robinson, Southern Cal	1976-78	31	6	0	.838
Dutch Meyer, Texas Christian	1934-36	29	7	2	.789
Frank Leahy, Boston College, Notre Dame	1939-41	28	2	1	.919
Larry Siemering, Pacific (Cal.)	1947-49	28	2	2	.906
Bud Wilkinson, Oklahoma	1947-49	28	3	1	.891
Herb Deromedi, Central Mich.	1978-80	28	4	1	.864
*Tom Osborne, Nebraska	1973-75	28	7	1	.792

4 SEASONS

Coach, Team(s)	Seasons	W	L	T	Pct.
Walter Camp, Yale	1888-91	54	2	0	.964
George Woodruff, Pennsylvania	1892-95	53	4	0	.930
*John Robinson, Southern Cal	1976-79	42	6	1	.867
Barry Switzer, Oklahoma	1973-76	41	3	2	.935
Bill Battle, Tennessee	1970-73	39	9	0	.813
*R. C. Slocum, Texas A&M	1989-92	39	10	1	.790
Bud Wilkinson, Oklahoma	1947-50	38	4	1	.895
*Tom Osborne, Nebraska	1973-76	37	10	2	.776
*Gary Blackney, Bowling Green	1991-94	36	8	2	.804
Frank Leahy, Boston College, Notre Dame	1939-42	35	4	3	.869
Larry Siemering, Pacific (Cal.)	1947-50	35	5	3	.849
*Joe Paterno, Penn St.	1966-69	35	7	1	.826
Claude Gilbert, San Diego St.	1973-76	35	7	2	.818
Herb Deromedi, Central Mich.	1978-81	35	8	1	.807
*Fisher DeBerry, Air Force	1984-87	35	14	0	.714

5 SEASONS

Coach, Team(s)	Seasons	W	L	T	Pct.
Walter Camp, Yale, Stanford	1888-92	69	2	2	.959
George Woodruff, Pennsylvania	1892-96	67	5	0	.931
Barry Switzer, Oklahoma	1973-77	51	5	2	.896
*John Robinson, Southern Cal	1976-80	50	8	2	.850
*R. C. Slocum, Texas A&M	1989-93	49	12	1	.798
Henry Williams, Army, Minnesota	1891, 1900-03	47	4	6	.877
Bud Wilkinson, Oklahoma	1947-51	46	6	1	.877
Bill Battle, Tennessee	1970-74	46	12	2	.783
*Tom Osborne, Nebraska	1973-77	46	13	2	.770
Claude Gilbert, San Diego St.	1973-77	45	8	2	.836

6 SEASONS

Coach, Team(s)	Seasons	W	L	T	Pct.
George Woodruff, Pennsylvania	1892-97	82	5	0	.943
Walter Camp, Yale, Stanford	1888-92, 94	75	5	2	.927
Barry Switzer, Oklahoma	1973-78	62	6	2	.900
Henry Williams, Army, Minnesota	1891, 1900-04	60	4	6	.900
*John Robinson, Southern Cal	1976-81	59	11	2	.833
*R. C. Slocum, Texas A&M	1989-94	59	12	2	.822
*Tom Osborne, Nebraska	1973-78	55	16	2	.767
Bud Wilkinson, Oklahoma	1947-52	54	7	2	.873
Fielding Yost, Ohio Wesleyan, Nebraska, Kansas, Stanford, Michigan	1897-1902	53	7	2	.871
*Joe Paterno, Penn St.	1966-71	53	11	1	.823
*Jackie Sherrill, Washington St., Pittsburgh	1976-81	53	17	1	.754
Bill Battle, Tennessee	1970-75	53	17	2	.750

7 SEASONS

Coach, Team(s)	Seasons	W	L	T	Pct.
George Woodruff, Pennsylvania	1892-98	94	6	0	.940
Walter Camp, Yale, Stanford	1888-92, 94-95	79	5	3	.925
Barry Switzer, Oklahoma	1973-79	73	7	2	.902
Henry Williams, Army, Minnesota	1891, 1900-05	70	5	6	.901
*R. C. Slocum, Texas A&M	1989-95	68	15	2	.812
*John Robinson, Southern Cal	1976-82	67	14	2	.819
*Tom Osborne, Nebraska	1973-79	65	18	2	.776
Fielding Yost, Ohio Wesleyan, Nebraska, Kansas, Stanford, Michigan	1897-1903	64	7	3	.897
Bud Wilkinson, Oklahoma	1947-53	63	8	3	.872
*Joe Paterno, Penn St.	1966-72	63	13	1	.825
Amos Alonzo Stagg, Springfield, Chicago	1890-96	63	31	7	.658

8 SEASONS

Coach, Team(s)	Seasons	W	L	T	Pct.
George Woodruff, Pennsylvania	1892-99	102	9	2	.912
Barry Switzer, Oklahoma	1973-80	83	9	2	.894
*Joe Paterno, Penn St.	1966-73	75	13	1	.848
*John Robinson, Southern Cal	1976-82, 93	75	19	2	.792
*Tom Osborne, Nebraska	1973-80	75	20	2	.784
Fielding Yost, Ohio Wesleyan, Nebraska, Kansas, Stanford, Michigan	1897-1904	74	7	3	.898
Henry Williams, Army, Minnesota	1891, 1900-06	74	6	6	.895
Amos Alonzo Stagg, Springfield, Chicago	1890-97	74	32	7	.686
Bud Wilkinson, Oklahoma	1947-54	73	8	3	.887
Frank Leahy, Boston College, Notre Dame	1939-43, 46-48	70	5	5	.882

9 SEASONS

Coach, Team(s)	Seasons	W	L	T	Pct.
George Woodruff, Pennsylvania	1892-1900	114	10	2	.913
Barry Switzer, Oklahoma	1973-81	90	13	3	.863
Fielding Yost, Ohio Wesleyan, Nebraska, Kansas, Stanford, Michigan	1897-1905	86	8	3	.902
*Joe Paterno, Penn St.	1966-74	85	15	1	.847
Bud Wilkinson, Oklahoma	1947-55	84	8	3	.900
*Tom Osborne, Nebraska	1973-81	84	23	2	.780
*John Robinson, Southern Cal	1976-82, 93-94	83	22	3	.782
Amos Alonzo Stagg, Springfield, Chicago	1890-98	83	34	7	.698
*Steve Spurrier, Duke, Florida	1987-95	81	26	2	.752
Frank Leahy, Boston College, Notre Dame	1939-43, 46-49	80	5	5	.917
Bob Neyland, Tennessee	1926-34	76	7	5	.892
Henry Williams, Army, Minnesota	1891, 1900-07	76	8	7	.874
Dick Crum, Miami (Ohio), North Caro.	1974-82	76	26	2	.740
Fred Akers, Wyoming, Texas	1975-83	76	30	1	.715

10 SEASONS

Coach, Team(s)	Seasons	W	L	T	Pct.
George Woodruff, Pennsylvania	1892-1901	124	15	2	.887
Barry Switzer, Oklahoma	1973-82	98	17	3	.843
*Tom Osborne, Nebraska	1973-82	96	24	2	.795
Amos Alonzo Stagg, Springfield, Chicago	1890-99	95	34	9	.721
Bud Wilkinson, Oklahoma	1947-56	94	8	3	.910
*Joe Paterno, Penn St.	1966-75	94	18	1	.836
*John Robinson, Southern Cal	1976-82, 93-95	92	24	4	.783
Fielding Yost, Ohio Wesleyan, Nebraska, Kansas, Stanford, Michigan	1897-1906	90	9	3	.897
Frank Leahy, Boston College, Notre Dame	1939-43, 46-50	84	9	6	.879
Dick Crum, Miami (Ohio), North Caro.	1974-83	84	30	2	.733
Dennis Erickson, Idaho, Wyoming, Washington St., Miami (Fla.)	1982-91	83	34	1	.708
Fred Akers, Wyoming, Texas	1975-84	83	34	2	.706

11 SEASONS

Coach, Team(s)	Seasons	W	L	T	Pct.
George Woodruff, Pennsylvania, Illinois	1892-1901, 03	132	21	2	.858
*Tom Osborne, Nebraska	1973-83	108	25	2	.807
Barry Switzer, Oklahoma	1973-83	106	21	3	.827
Bud Wilkinson, Oklahoma	1947-57	104	9	3	.909
Amos Alonzo Stagg, Springfield, Chicago	1890-1900	102	39	10	.709
*Joe Paterno, Penn St.	1966-76	101	23	1	.812
Fielding Yost, Ohio Wesleyan, Nebraska, Kansas, Stanford, Michigan	1897-1907	95	10	3	.894
Dennis Erickson, Idaho, Wyoming, Washington St., Miami (Fla.)	1982-92	94	35	1	.727
Frank Leahy, Boston College, Notre Dame	1939-43, 46-51	91	11	7	.867
Bobby Dodd, Georgia Tech	1945-55	91	27	3	.764
Fred Akers, Wyoming, Texas	1975-85	91	38	2	.702

12 SEASONS

Coach, Team(s)	Seasons	W	L	T	Pct.
George Woodruff, Pennsylvania, Illinois, Carlisle	1892-1901, 03, 05	142	25	2	.846
*Tom Osborne, Nebraska	1973-84	118	27	2	.810
Barry Switzer, Oklahoma	1973-84	115	23	4	.824
Bud Wilkinson, Oklahoma	1947-58	114	10	3	.909
*Joe Paterno, Penn St.	1966-77	112	24	1	.821
Amos Alonzo Stagg, Springfield, Chicago	1890-1901	107	44	12	.693
Dennis Erickson, Idaho, Wyoming, Washington St., Miami (Fla.)	1982-93	103	38	1	.729
Bobby Dodd, Georgia Tech	1945-56	101	28	3	.777
Fielding Yost, Ohio Wesleyan, Nebraska, Kansas, Stanford, Michigan	1897-1908	100	12	4	.879
Bob Neyland, Tennessee	1926-34, 36-38	99	12	8	.866

13 SEASONS

Coach, Team(s)	Seasons	W	L	T	Pct.
*Tom Osborne, Nebraska	1973-85	127	30	2	.805
Barry Switzer, Oklahoma	1973-85	126	24	4	.831
*Joe Paterno, Penn St.	1966-78	123	25	1	.829
Bud Wilkinson, Oklahoma	1947-59	121	13	3	.894
*LaVell Edwards, Brigham Young	1972-84	118	37	1	.760
Amos Alonzo Stagg, Springfield, Chicago	1890-1902	118	45	12	.709
Dennis Erickson, Idaho, Wyoming, Washington St., Miami (Fla.)	1982-94	113	40	1	.737
Bob Neyland, Tennessee	1926-34, 36-39	109	13	8	.869
Terry Donahue, UCLA	1976-88	108	38	7	.729
Frank Leahy, Boston College, Notre Dame	1939-43, 46-53	107	13	9	.864

14 SEASONS

Coach, Team(s)	Seasons	W	L	T	Pct.
Barry Switzer, Oklahoma	1973-86	137	25	4	.837
*Tom Osborne, Nebraska	1973-86	137	32	2	.807
*Joe Paterno, Penn St.	1966-79	131	29	1	.817
*LaVell Edwards, Brigham Young	1972-85	129	40	1	.762
Amos Alonzo Stagg, Springfield, Chicago.	1890-1903	128	47	13	.715
Bud Wilkinson, Oklahoma	1947-60	124	19	4	.857
Bob Neyland, Tennessee	1926-34, 36-40	119	14	8	.872
Bo Schembechler, Miami (Ohio), Michigan	1963-76	116	28	6	.793
Pat Dye, East Caro., Wyoming, Auburn	1974-87	115	44	3	.719
Bob Devaney, Wyoming, Nebraska	1957-70	114	28	6	.791

15 SEASONS

Coach, Team(s)	Seasons	W	L	T	Pct.
Barry Switzer, Oklahoma	1973-87	148	26	4	.843
*Tom Osborne, Nebraska	1973-87	147	34	2	.809
*Joe Paterno, Penn St.	1966-80	141	31	1	.818
*LaVell Edwards, Brigham Young	1972-86	137	45	1	.751
Amos Alonzo Stagg, Springfield, Chicago	1890-1904	136	48	14	.722
Bud Wilkinson, Oklahoma	1947-61	129	24	4	.834
Bob Neyland, Tennessee	1926-34, 36-40, 46	128	16	8	.868
Bob Devaney, Wyoming, Nebraska	1957-71	127	28	6	.807
Bo Schembechler, Miami (Ohio), Michigan	1963-77	126	30	6	.796
Pat Dye, East Caro., Wyoming, Auburn	1974-88	125	46	3	.727

16 SEASONS

Coach, Team(s)	Seasons	W	L	T	Pct.
*Tom Osborne, Nebraska	1973-88	158	36	2	.811
Barry Switzer, Oklahoma	1973-88	157	29	4	.837
*Joe Paterno, Penn St.	1966-81	151	33	1	.819
*LaVell Edwards, Brigham Young	1972-87	146	49	1	.747
Amos Alonzo Stagg, Springfield, Chicago	1890-1905	146	48	14	.736
Bud Wilkinson, Oklahoma	1947-62	137	27	4	.827
Bob Devaney, Wyoming, Nebraska	1957-72	136	30	7	.806
Bo Schembechler, Miami (Ohio), Michigan	1963-78	136	32	6	.799
Pat Dye, East Caro., Wyoming, Auburn	1974-89	135	48	3	.734
Bob Neyland, Tennessee	1926-34, 36-40, 46-47	133	21	8	.846

17 SEASONS

Coach, Team(s)	Seasons	W	L	T	Pct.
*Tom Osborne, Nebraska	1973-89	168	38	2	.813
*Joe Paterno, Penn St.	1966-82	162	34	1	.825
*LaVell Edwards, Brigham Young	1972-88	155	53	1	.744
Amos Alonzo Stagg, Springfield, Chicago	1890-1906	150	49	15	.736
Bud Wilkinson, Oklahoma	1947-63	145	29	4	.826
Bo Schembechler, Miami (Ohio), Michigan	1963-79	144	36	6	.790
Pat Dye, East Caro., Wyoming, Auburn	1974-90	143	51	4	.732
Frank Kush, Arizona St.	1958-74	139	39	1	.779
Bob Neyland, Tennessee	1926-34, 36-40, 46-48	137	25	10	.826
Johnny Vaught, Mississippi	1947-63	137	32	9	.795
Tony Knap, Utah St., Boise St., UNLV	1963-66, 68-80	137	47	4	.739

18 SEASONS

Coach, Team(s)	Seasons	W	L	T	Pct.
*Tom Osborne, Nebraska	1973-90	177	41	2	.809
*Joe Paterno, Penn St.	1966-83	170	38	2	.814
*LaVell Edwards, Brigham Young	1972-89	165	56	1	.745
Bo Schembechler, Miami (Ohio), Michigan	1963-80	154	38	6	.793
Amos Alonzo Stagg, Springfield, Chicago	1890-1907	154	50	15	.737
Frank Kush, Arizona St.	1958-75	151	39	1	.793
Pat Dye, East Caro., Wyoming, Auburn	1974-91	148	57	4	.718
Bob Neyland, Tennessee	1926-34, 36-40, 46-49	144	27	11	.821
Darrell Royal, Mississippi St., Washington, Texas	1954-71	143	45	4	.755
Tony Knap, Utah St., Boise St., UNLV	1963-66, 68-81	143	53	4	.725

19 SEASONS

Coach, Team(s)	Seasons	W	L	T	Pct.
*Tom Osborne, Nebraska	1973-91	186	43	3	.808
*Joe Paterno, Penn St.	1966-84	176	43	2	.801
*LaVell Edwards, Brigham Young	1972-90	175	59	1	.747
Bo Schembechler, Miami (Ohio), Michigan	1963-81	163	41	6	.790
Amos Alonzo Stagg, Springfield, Chicago	1890-1908	159	50	16	.742
Bob Neyland, Tennessee	1926-34, 36-40, 46-50	155	28	11	.827
Frank Kush, Arizona St.	1958-76	155	46	1	.770
Darrell Royal, Mississippi St., Washington, Texas	1954-72	153	46	4	.764
Pat Dye, East Caro., Wyoming, Auburn	1974-92	153	62	5	.707
Pop Warner, Georgia, Cornell, Carlisle	1895-1913	152	50	10	.741

20 SEASONS

Coach, Team(s)	Seasons	W	L	T	Pct.
*Tom Osborne, Nebraska	1973-92	195	46	3	.805
*Joe Paterno, Penn St.	1966-85	187	44	2	.807
*LaVell Edwards, Brigham Young	1972-91	183	62	3	.744
Bo Schembechler, Miami (Ohio), Michigan	1963-82	171	45	6	.784
Bob Neyland, Tennessee	1926-34, 36-40, 46-51	165	29	11	.832
Frank Kush, Arizona St.	1958-77	164	49	1	.769
Amos Alonzo Stagg, Springfield, Chicago	1890-1909	163	51	18	.741
Darrell Royal, Mississippi St., Washington, Texas	1954-73	161	49	4	.762
Vince Dooley, Georgia	1964-83	161	60	7	.721
Johnny Vaught, Mississippi	1947-66	157	44	10	.768
Pop Warner, Georgia, Cornell, Carlisle	1895-1914	157	59	11	.716

21 SEASONS

Coach, Team(s)	Seasons	W	L	T	Pct.
*Tom Osborne, Nebraska	1973-93	206	47	3	.811
*Joe Paterno, Penn St.	1966-86	199	44	2	.816
*LaVell Edwards, Brigham Young	1972-92	191	67	3	.738
Bo Schembechler, Miami (Ohio), Michigan	1963-83	180	48	6	.782
Bob Neyland, Tennessee	1926-34, 36-40, 46-52	173	31	12	.829
Frank Kush, Arizona St.	1958-78	173	52	1	.768
Darrell Royal, Mississippi St., Washington, Texas	1954-74	169	53	4	.757
Vince Dooley, Georgia	1964-84	168	64	8	.717
Don James, Kent, Washington	1971-91	167	75	3	.688
Amos Alonzo Stagg, Springfield, Chicago	1890-1910	165	56	18	.728
Pop Warner, Georgia, Cornell, Carlisle, Pittsburgh	1895-1915	165	59	11	.726

22 SEASONS

Coach, Team(s)	Seasons	W	L	T	Pct.
*Tom Osborne, Nebraska	1973-94	219	47	3	.820
*Joe Paterno, Penn St.	1966-87	207	48	2	.809
*LaVell Edwards, Brigham Young	1972-93	197	73	3	.727
Bo Schembechler, Miami (Ohio), Michigan	1963-84	186	54	6	.768
Darrell Royal, Mississippi St., Washington, Texas	1954-75	179	55	4	.761
Frank Kush, Arizona St.	1958-79	176	54	1	.764
Don James, Kent, Washington	1971-92	176	78	3	.691
Vince Dooley, Georgia	1964-85	175	67	10	.714
*Bobby Bowden, Samford, West Va., Florida St.	1959-62, 70-87	174	69	3	.713
Pop Warner, Georgia, Cornell, Carlisle, Pittsburgh	1895-1916	173	59	11	.735

23 SEASONS

Coach, Team(s)	Seasons	W	L	T	Pct.
*Tom Osborne, Nebraska	1973-95	231	47	3	.827
*Joe Paterno, Penn St.	1966-88	212	54	2	.795
*LaVell Edwards, Brigham Young	1972-94	207	76	3	.729
Bo Schembechler, Miami (Ohio), Michigan	1963-85	196	55	7	.773
*Bobby Bowden, Samford, West Va., Florida St.	1959-62, 70-88	185	70	3	.723
Darrell Royal, Mississippi St., Washington, Texas	1954-76	184	60	5	.749
Pop Warner, Georgia, Cornell, Carlisle, Pittsburgh	1895-1917	183	59	11	.745
Vince Dooley, Georgia	1964-86	183	71	10	.712
*Lou Holtz, William & Mary, North Caro. St., Arkansas, Minnesota, Notre Dame	1969-92	182	83	6	.683
Bear Bryant, Maryland, Kentucky, Texas A&M, Alabama	1945-67	179	53	15	.755
Johnny Vaught, Mississippi	1947-69	178	54	12	.754

24 SEASONS

Coach, Team(s)	Seasons	W	L	T	Pct.
*Joe Paterno, Penn St.	1966-89	220	57	3	.791
*LaVell Edwards, Brigham Young	1972-95	214	80	3	.726
Bo Schembechler, Miami (Ohio), Michigan	1963-86	207	57	7	.777
*Bobby Bowden, Samford, West Va., Florida St.	1959-62, 70-89	195	72	3	.728
*Lou Holtz, William & Mary, North Caro. St., Arkansas, Minnesota, Notre Dame	1969-93	193	84	6	.693
Vince Dooley, Georgia	1964-87	192	74	10	.714
Bear Bryant, Maryland, Kentucky, Texas A&M, Alabama	1945-68	187	56	15	.754
Pop Warner, Georgia, Cornell, Carlisle, Pittsburgh	1895-1918	187	60	11	.746
Johnny Vaught, Mississippi	1947-70	185	58	12	.749
Amos Alonzo Stagg, Springfield, Chicago	1890-1913	184	58	18	.742

25 SEASONS

Coach, Team(s)	Seasons	W	L	T	Pct.
*Joe Paterno, Penn St.	1966-90	229	60	3	.789
Bo Schembechler, Miami (Ohio), Michigan	1963-87	215	61	7	.772
*Bobby Bowden, Samford, West Va., Florida St.	1959-62, 70-90	205	74	3	.732
Vince Dooley, Georgia	1964-88	201	77	10	.715
*Lou Holtz, William & Mary, North Caro. St., Arkansas, Minnesota, Notre Dame	1969-94	199	89	7	.686
Bear Bryant, Maryland, Kentucky, Texas A&M, Alabama	1945-69	193	61	15	.745
Pop Warner, Georgia, Cornell, Carlisle, Pittsburgh	1895-1919	193	62	12	.745
Johnny Vaught, Mississippi	1947-70, 73	190	61	12	.745
Amos Alonzo Stagg, Springfield, Chicago	1890-1914	188	60	19	.740

26 SEASONS

Coach, Team(s)	Seasons	W	L	T	Pct.
*Joe Paterno, Penn St.	1966-91	240	62	3	.792
Bo Schembechler, Miami (Ohio), Michigan	1963-88	224	63	8	.773
*Bobby Bowden, Samford, West Va., Florida St.	1959-62, 70-91	216	76	3	.737
*Lou Holtz, William & Mary, North Caro. St., Arkansas, Minnesota, Notre Dame	1969-95	208	92	7	.689
Pop Warner, Georgia, Cornell, Carlisle, Pittsburgh	1895-1920	199	62	14	.749
Bear Bryant, Maryland, Kentucky, Texas A&M, Alabama	1945-70	199	66	16	.737
Amos Alonzo Stagg, Springfield, Chicago	1890-1915	193	62	19	.739

27 SEASONS

Coach, Team(s)	Seasons	W	L	T	Pct.
*Joe Paterno, Penn St.	1966-92	247	67	3	.784
Bo Schembechler, Miami (Ohio), Michigan	1963-89	234	65	8	.775
*Bobby Bowden, Samford, West Va., Florida St.	1959-62, 70-92	227	77	3	.744
Bear Bryant, Maryland, Kentucky, Texas A&M, Alabama	1945-71	210	67	16	.744
Pop Warner, Georgia, Cornell, Carlisle, Pittsburgh	1895-1921	204	65	15	.745
Amos Alonzo Stagg, Springfield, Chicago	1890-1916	196	66	19	.731

28 SEASONS

Coach, Team(s)	Seasons	W	L	T	Pct.
*Joe Paterno, Penn St.	1966-93	257	69	3	.786
*Bobby Bowden, Samford, West Va., Florida St.	1959-62, 70-93	239	78	3	.752
Bear Bryant, Maryland, Kentucky, Texas A&M, Alabama	1945-72	220	69	16	.748
Pop Warner, Georgia, Cornell, Carlisle, Pittsburgh	1895-1922	212	67	15	.747
Amos Alonzo Stagg, Springfield, Chicago	1890-1917	199	68	20	.728
Woody Hayes, Denison, Miami (Ohio), Ohio St.	1946-73	192	60	8	.754
Howard Jones, Syracuse, Yale, Ohio St., Iowa, Duke, Southern Cal	1908-10, 13, 16-39	191	60	19	.743

29 SEASONS

Coach, Team(s)	Seasons	W	L	T	Pct.
*Joe Paterno, Penn St.	1966-94	269	69	3	.793
*Bobby Bowden, Samford, West Va., Florida St.	1959-62, 70-94	249	79	4	.756
Bear Bryant, Maryland, Kentucky, Texas A&M, Alabama	1945-73	231	70	16	.754
Pop Warner, Georgia, Cornell, Carlisle, Pittsburgh	1895-1923	217	71	15	.741
Woody Hayes, Denison, Miami (Ohio), Ohio St.	1946-74	202	62	8	.757

Coach, Team(s)	Seasons	W	L	T	Pct.
Amos Alonzo Stagg, Springfield, Chicago	1890-1918	199	74	20	.713
Fielding Yost, Ohio Wesleyan, Nebraska, Kansas, Stanford, Michigan	1897-1923, 25-26	196	36	12	.828
Howard Jones, Syracuse, Yale, Ohio St., Iowa, Duke, Southern Cal	1908-10, 13, 16-40	194	64	21	.733
Dan McGugin, Vanderbilt	1904-17, 19-33	191	52	19	.765

30 SEASONS

Coach, Team(s)	Seasons	W	L	T	Pct.
*Joe Paterno, Penn St.	1966-95	278	72	3	.792
*Bobby Bowden, Samford, West Va., Florida St.	1959-62, 70-95	259	81	4	.759
Bear Bryant, Maryland, Kentucky, Texas A&M, Alabama	1945-74	242	71	16	.760
Pop Warner, Georgia, Cornell, Carlisle, Pittsburgh, Stanford	1895-1924	224	72	16	.744
Woody Hayes, Denison, Miami (Ohio), Ohio St.	1946-75	213	63	8	.764
Amos Alonzo Stagg, Springfield, Chicago	1890-1919	204	76	20	.713

31 SEASONS

Coach, Team(s)	Seasons	W	L	T	Pct.
Bear Bryant, Maryland, Kentucky, Texas A&M, Alabama	1945-75	253	72	16	.765
Pop Warner, Georgia, Cornell, Carlisle, Pittsburgh, Stanford	1895-1925	231	74	16	.745
Woody Hayes, Denison, Miami (Ohio), Ohio St.	1946-76	222	65	9	.765
Amos Alonzo Stagg, Springfield, Chicago	1890-1920	207	80	20	.707
Warren Woodson, Central Ark., Hardin-Simmons, Arizona, New Mexico St., Trinity (Tex.)	1935-42, 46-56, 58-67, 72-73	203	95	14	.673
Dana X. Bible, Mississippi Col., LSU, Texas A&M, Nebraska, Texas	1913-17, 19-44	180	69	23	.704

32 SEASONS

Coach, Team(s)	Seasons	W	L	T	Pct.
Bear Bryant, Maryland, Kentucky, Texas A&M, Alabama	1945-76	262	75	16	.765
Pop Warner, Georgia, Cornell, Carlisle, Pittsburgh, Stanford	1895-1926	241	74	17	.752
Woody Hayes, Denison, Miami (Ohio), Ohio St.	1946-77	231	68	9	.765
Amos Alonzo Stagg, Springfield, Chicago	1890-1921	213	81	20	.710
*Hayden Fry, Southern Methodist, North Texas, Iowa	1962-93	200	153	9	.565
Dana X. Bible, Mississippi Col., LSU, Texas A&M, Nebraska, Texas	1913-17, 19-45	190	70	23	.712

33 SEASONS

Coach, Team(s)	Seasons	W	L	T	Pct.
Bear Bryant, Maryland, Kentucky, Texas A&M, Alabama	1945-77	273	76	16	.770
Pop Warner, Georgia, Cornell, Carlisle, Pittsburgh, Stanford	1895-1927	249	76	18	.752
Woody Hayes, Denison, Miami (Ohio), Ohio St.	1946-78	238	72	10	.759
Amos Alonzo Stagg, Springfield, Chicago	1890-1922	219	82	20	.713
*Hayden Fry, Southern Methodist, North Texas, Iowa	1962-94	205	158	10	.563
Dana X. Bible, Mississippi Col., LSU, Texas A&M, Nebraska, Texas	1913-17, 19-46	198	72	23	.715

34 SEASONS

Coach, Team(s)	Seasons	W	L	T	Pct.
Bear Bryant, Maryland, Kentucky, Texas A&M, Alabama	1945-78	284	77	16	.775
Pop Warner, Georgia, Cornell, Carlisle, Pittsburgh, Stanford	1895-1928	257	79	19	.751
Amos Alonzo Stagg, Springfield, Chicago	1890-1923	226	83	20	.717
*Hayden Fry, Southern Methodist, North Texas, Iowa	1962-95	213	162	10	.566

35 SEASONS

Coach, Team(s)	Seasons	W	L	T	Pct.
Bear Bryant, Maryland, Kentucky, Texas A&M, Alabama	1945-79	296	77	16	.781
Pop Warner, Georgia, Cornell, Carlisle, Pittsburgh, Stanford	1895-1929	266	81	19	.753
Amos Alonzo Stagg, Springfield, Chicago	1890-1924	230	84	23	.717

36 SEASONS

Coach, Team(s)	Seasons	W	L	T	Pct.
Bear Bryant, Maryland, Kentucky, Texas A&M, Alabama	1945-80	306	79	16	.783
Pop Warner, Georgia, Cornell, Carlisle, Pittsburgh, Stanford	1895-1930	275	82	20	.756
Amos Alonzo Stagg, Springfield, Chicago	1890-1925	233	88	24	.710

37 SEASONS

Coach, Team(s)	Seasons	W	L	T	Pct.
Bear Bryant, Maryland, Kentucky, Texas A&M, Alabama	1945-81	315	81	17	.783
Pop Warner, Georgia, Cornell, Carlisle, Pittsburgh, Stanford	1895-1931	282	84	22	.755
Amos Alonzo Stagg, Springfield, Chicago	1890-1926	235	94	24	.700

38 SEASONS

Coach, Team(s)	Seasons	W	L	T	Pct.
Bear Bryant, Maryland, Kentucky, Texas A&M, Alabama	1945-82	323	85	17	.780
Pop Warner, Georgia, Cornell, Carlisle, Pittsburgh, Stanford	1895-1932	288	88	23	.751
Amos Alonzo Stagg, Springfield, Chicago	1890-1927	239	98	24	.695
Jess Neely, Rhodes, Clemson, Rice	1924-27, 31-64	203	160	19	.556

39 SEASONS

Coach, Team(s)	Seasons	W	L	T	Pct.
Pop Warner, Georgia, Cornell, Carlisle, Pittsburgh, Stanford, Temple	1895-1933	293	91	23	.748
Amos Alonzo Stagg, Springfield, Chicago	1890-1928	241	105	24	.684
Jess Neely, Rhodes, Clemson, Rice	1924-27, 31-65	205	168	19	.539
Eddie Anderson, Loras, DePaul, Holy Cross, Iowa	1922-42, 46-64	201	128	15	.606

40 SEASONS

Coach, Team(s)	Seasons	W	L	T	Pct.
Pop Warner, Georgia, Cornell, Carlisle, Pittsburgh, Stanford, Temple	1895-1934	300	92	25	.749
Amos Alonzo Stagg, Springfield, Chicago	1890-1929	248	108	24	.684
Jess Neely, Rhodes, Clemson, Rice	1924-27, 31-66	207	176	19	.539

41 SEASONS

Coach, Team(s)	Seasons	W	L	T	Pct.
Pop Warner, Georgia, Cornell, Carlisle, Pittsburgh, Stanford, Temple	1895-1935	307	95	25	.748
Amos Alonzo Stagg, Springfield, Chicago	1890-1930	249	113	26	.675

42 SEASONS

Coach, Team(s)	Seasons	W	L	T	Pct.
Pop Warner, Georgia, Cornell, Carlisle, Pittsburgh, Stanford, Temple	1895-1936	313	98	27	.745
Amos Alonzo Stagg, Springfield, Chicago	1890-1931	251	118	27	.668

43 SEASONS

Coach, Team(s)	Seasons	W	L	T	Pct.
Pop Warner, Georgia, Cornell, Carlisle, Pittsburgh, Stanford, Temple	1895-1937	316	100	31	.742
Amos Alonzo Stagg, Springfield, Chicago	1890-1932	254	122	28	.663

44 SEASONS

Coach, Team(s)	Seasons	W	L	T	Pct.
Pop Warner, Georgia, Cornell, Carlisle, Pittsburgh, Stanford, Temple	1895-1938	319	106	32	.733
Amos Alonzo Stagg, Springfield, Chicago, Pacific (Cal.)	1890-1933	259	127	28	.659

*Active coach.

Division I-A Best Career Starts by Percentage

(Head coaches with at least half their seasons at major college at the time and minimum five years coached)

1 SEASON

Coach, Team	Season	W	L	T	Pct.
Walter Camp, Yale	1888	13	0	0	1.000
Dan McGugin, Vanderbilt	1904	9	0	0	1.000
Bennie Oosterbaan, Michigan	1948	9	0	0	1.000
Carroll Widdoes, Ohio St.	1944	9	0	0	1.000
Galen Hall, Florida	1984	8	0	0	1.000
William Dietz, Washington St.	1915	7	0	0	1.000
John Heisman, Oberlin	1892	7	0	0	1.000

Coach, Team	Season	W	L	T	Pct.
Dick Crum, Miami (Ohio)	1974	10	0	1	.955
Barry Switzer, Oklahoma	1973	10	0	1	.955
Aldo Donelli, Duquesne	1939	8	0	1	.944
Francis Schmidt, Tulsa	1919	8	0	1	.944

2 SEASONS

Coach, Team	Seasons	W	L	T	Pct.
Barry Switzer, Oklahoma	1973-74	21	0	1	.977
Walter Camp, Yale	1888-89	28	1	0	.966
Francis Schmidt, Tulsa	1919-20	18	0	2	.950
John Bateman, Rutgers	1960-61	17	1	0	.944
Dan McGugin, Vanderbilt	1904-05	16	1	0	.941
Dick Crum, Miami (Ohio)	1974-75	21	1	1	.935
Galen Hall, Florida	1984-85	17	1	1	.921
Bob Neyland, Tennessee	1926-27	16	1	1	.917
Aldo Donelli, Duquesne	1939-40	15	1	1	.912
Charley Moran, Texas A&M	1909-10	15	1	1	.912

3 SEASONS

Coach, Team(s)	Seasons	W	L	T	Pct.
Barry Switzer, Oklahoma	1973-75	32	1	1	.956
Walter Camp, Yale	1888-90	41	2	0	.953
Aldo Donelli, Duquesne	1939-41	23	1	1	.940
Bob Neyland, Tennessee	1926-28	25	1	2	.929
Dan McGugin, Vanderbilt	1904-06	24	2	0	.923
Frank Leahy, Boston College, Notre Dame	1939-41	28	2	1	.919
Knute Rockne, Notre Dame	1918-20	21	1	2	.917
Elmer Henderson, Southern Cal	1919-21	20	2	0	.909
George Woodruff, Pennsylvania	1892-94	39	4	0	.907
Larry Siemering, Pacific (Cal.)	1947-49	28	2	2	.906

4 SEASONS

Coach, Team(s)	Seasons	W	L	T	Pct.
Gil Dobie, North Dak. St., Washington	1906-09	20	0	1	.976
Walter Camp, Yale	1888-91	54	2	0	.964
Barry Switzer, Oklahoma	1973-76	41	3	2	.935
Bob Neyland, Tennessee	1926-29	34	1	3	.934
George Woodruff, Pennsylvania	1892-95	53	4	0	.930
Knute Rockne, Notre Dame	1918-21	31	2	2	.914
Elmer Henderson, Southern Cal	1919-22	30	3	0	.909
Wallace Wade, Alabama	1923-26	34	3	2	.897
William Murray, Delaware	1940-42, 46	30	3	1	.897
Bud Wilkinson, Oklahoma	1947-50	38	4	1	.895

5 SEASONS

Coach, Team(s)	Seasons	W	L	T	Pct.
Gil Dobie, North Dak. St., Washington	1906-10	26	0	1	.981
Walter Camp, Yale, Stanford	1888-92	69	2	2	.959
George Woodruff, Pennsylvania	1892-96	67	5	0	.931
Bob Neyland, Tennessee	1926-30	43	2	3	.927
Knute Rockne, Notre Dame	1918-22	39	3	3	.900
Barry Switzer, Oklahoma	1973-77	51	5	2	.896
Elmer Henderson, Southern Cal	1919-23	36	5	0	.878
Bud Wilkinson, Oklahoma	1947-51	46	6	1	.877
Henry Williams, Army, Minnesota	1891, 1900-03	47	4	6	.877
Frank Leahy, Boston College, Notre Dame	1939-43	44	5	3	.875

6 SEASONS

Coach, Team(s)	Seasons	W	L	T	Pct.
Gil Dobie, North Dak. St., Washington	1906-11	33	0	1	.985
George Woodruff, Pennsylvania	1892-97	82	5	0	.943
Bob Neyland, Tennessee	1926-31	52	2	4	.931
Walter Camp, Yale, Stanford	1888-92, 94	75	5	2	.927
Knute Rockne, Notre Dame	1918-23	48	4	3	.900
Barry Switzer, Oklahoma	1973-78	62	6	2	.900
Henry Williams, Army, Minnesota	1891, 1900-04	60	4	6	.900
Frank Leahy, Boston College, Notre Dame	1939-43, 46	52	5	4	.885
Bud Wilkinson, Oklahoma	1947-52	54	7	2	.873
Fielding Yost, Ohio Wesleyan, Nebraska, Kansas, Stanford, Michigan	1897-1902	53	7	2	.871

7 SEASONS

Coach, Team(s)	Seasons	W	L	T	Pct.
Gil Dobie, North Dak. St., Washington	1906-12	39	0	1	.988
George Woodruff, Pennsylvania	1892-98	94	6	0	.940
Bob Neyland, Tennessee	1926-32	61	2	5	.934
Walter Camp, Yale, Stanford	1888-92, 94-95	79	5	3	.925
Knute Rockne, Notre Dame	1918-24	58	4	3	.915
Barry Switzer, Oklahoma	1973-79	73	7	2	.902
Henry Williams, Army, Minnesota	1891, 1900-05	70	5	6	.901
Frank Leahy, Boston College, Notre Dame	1939-43, 46-47	61	5	4	.900
Fielding Yost, Ohio Wesleyan, Nebraska, Kansas, Stanford, Michigan	1897-1903	64	7	3	.897
Bud Wilkinson, Oklahoma	1947-53	63	8	3	.872

8 SEASONS

Coach, Team(s)	Seasons	W	L	T	Pct.
Gil Dobie, North Dak. St., Washington	1906-13	46	0	1	.989
George Woodruff, Pennsylvania	1892-99	102	9	2	.912
Bob Neyland, Tennessee	1926-33	68	5	5	.904
Fielding Yost, Ohio Wesleyan, Nebraska, Kansas, Stanford, Michigan	1897-1904	74	7	3	.898
Henry Williams, Army, Minnesota	1891, 1900-06	74	6	6	.895
Barry Switzer, Oklahoma	1973-80	83	9	2	.894
Knute Rockne, Notre Dame	1918-25	65	6	4	.893
Bud Wilkinson, Oklahoma	1947-54	73	8	3	.887
Frank Leahy, Boston College, Notre Dame	1939-43, 46-48	70	5	5	.882
Percy Haughton, Cornell, Harvard	1899-1900, 08-13	66	8	3	.877

9 SEASONS

Coach, Team(s)	Seasons	W	L	T	Pct.
Gil Dobie, North Dak. St., Washington	1906-14	52	0	2	.981
Frank Leahy, Boston College, Notre Dame	1939-43, 46-49	80	5	5	.917
George Woodruff, Pennsylvania	1892-1900	114	10	2	.913
Fielding Yost, Ohio Wesleyan, Nebraska, Kansas, Stanford, Michigan	1897-1905	86	8	3	.902
Bud Wilkinson, Oklahoma	1947-55	84	8	3	.900
Knute Rockne, Notre Dame	1918-26	74	7	4	.894
Bob Neyland, Tennessee	1926-34	76	7	5	.892
Percy Haughton, Cornell, Harvard	1899-1900, 08-14	73	8	5	.878
Henry Williams, Army, Minnesota	1891, 1900-07	76	8	7	.874
Barry Switzer, Oklahoma	1973-81	90	13	3	.863

10 SEASONS

Coach, Team(s)	Seasons	W	L	T	Pct.
Gil Dobie, North Dak. St., Washington	1906-15	59	0	2	.984
Bud Wilkinson, Oklahoma	1947-56	94	8	3	.910
Fielding Yost, Ohio Wesleyan, Nebraska, Kansas, Stanford, Michigan	1897-1906	90	9	3	.897
Knute Rockne, Notre Dame	1918-27	81	8	5	.888
George Woodruff, Pennsylvania	1892-1901	124	15	2	.887
Percy Haughton, Cornell, Harvard	1899-1900, 08-15	81	9	5	.879
Frank Leahy, Boston College, Notre Dame	1939-43, 46-50	84	9	6	.879
Bob Neyland, Tennessee	1926-34, 36	82	9	7	.872
Henry Williams, Army, Minnesota	1891, 1900-08	79	10	8	.856
Barry Switzer, Oklahoma	1973-82	98	17	3	.843

11 SEASONS

Coach, Team(s)	Seasons	W	L	T	Pct.
Gil Dobie, North Dak. St., Washington	1906-16	65	0	3	.978
Bud Wilkinson, Oklahoma	1947-57	104	9	3	.909
Fielding Yost, Ohio Wesleyan, Nebraska, Kansas, Stanford, Michigan	1897-1907	95	10	3	.894
Frank Leahy, Boston College, Notre Dame	1939-43, 46-51	91	11	7	.867
Percy Haughton, Cornell, Harvard	1899-1900, 08-16	88	12	5	.862
Knute Rockne, Notre Dame	1918-28	86	12	5	.859
George Woodruff, Pennsylvania, Illinois	1892-1901, 03	132	21	2	.858
Henry Williams, Army, Minnesota	1891, 1900-09	85	11	8	.856
Bob Neyland, Tennessee	1926-34, 36-37	88	12	8	.852
Charley Moran, Texas A&M, Centre	1909-14, 19-23	80	14	5	.833

12 SEASONS

Coach, Team(s)	Seasons	W	L	T	Pct.
Gil Dobie, North Dak. St., Washington, Navy	1906-17	72	1	3	.967
Bud Wilkinson, Oklahoma	1947-58	114	10	3	.909
Fielding Yost, Ohio Wesleyan, Nebraska, Kansas, Stanford, Michigan	1897-1908	100	12	4	.879
Knute Rockne, Notre Dame	1918-29	95	12	5	.871
Bob Neyland, Tennessee	1926-34, 36-38	99	12	8	.866
Frank Leahy, Boston College, Notre Dame	1939-43, 46-52	98	13	8	.857
Henry Williams, Army, Minnesota	1891, 1900-10	91	12	8	.856
George Woodruff, Pennsylvania, Illinois, Carlisle	1892-1901, 03, 05	142	25	2	.846
Percy Haughton, Cornell, Harvard, Columbia	1899-1900, 08-16, 23	92	16	6	.833
Charley Moran, Texas A&M, Centre, Bucknell	1909-14, 19-24	88	16	5	.830

13 SEASONS

Coach, Team(s)	Seasons	W	L	T	Pct.
Gil Dobie, North Dak. St., Washington, Navy	1906-18	76	2	3	.957
Bud Wilkinson, Oklahoma	1947-59	121	13	3	.894

Coach, Team(s)	Seasons	W	L	T	Pct.
Knute Rockne, Notre Dame	1918-30	105	12	5	.881
Fielding Yost, Ohio Wesleyan, Nebraska, Kansas, Stanford, Michigan	1897-1909	106	13	4	.878
Bob Neyland, Tennessee	1926-34, 36-39	109	13	8	.869
Frank Leahy, Boston College, Notre Dame	1939-43, 46-53	107	13	9	.864
Henry Williams, Army, Minnesota	1891, 1900-11	97	12	9	.860
Percy Haughton, Cornell, Harvard, Columbia	1899-1900, 08-16, 23-24	96	17	6	.832
Barry Switzer, Oklahoma	1973-85	126	24	4	.831
*Joe Paterno, Penn St.	1966-78	123	25	1	.829

14 SEASONS

Coach, Team(s)	Seasons	W	L	T	Pct.
Gil Dobie, North Dak. St., Washington, Navy	1906-19	82	3	3	.949
Bob Neyland, Tennessee	1926-34, 36-40	119	14	8	.872
Fielding Yost, Ohio Wesleyan, Nebraska, Kansas, Stanford, Michigan	1897-1910	109	13	7	.872
Bud Wilkinson, Oklahoma	1947-60	124	19	4	.857
Henry Williams, Army, Minnesota	1891, 1900-12	101	15	9	.844
Barry Switzer, Oklahoma	1973-86	137	25	4	.837
*Joe Paterno, Penn St.	1966-79	131	29	1	.817
Fred Folsom, Colorado, Dartmouth	1895-99, 1901-06, 08-10	83	17	5	.814
Elmer Henderson, Southern Cal, Tulsa	1919-32	101	23	3	.807
*Tom Osborne, Nebraska	1973-86	137	32	2	.807

15 SEASONS

Coach, Team(s)	Seasons	W	L	T	Pct.
Gil Dobie, North Dak. St., Washington, Navy, Cornell	1906-20	88	5	3	.932
Bob Neyland, Tennessee	1926-34, 36-40, 46	128	16	8	.868
Fielding Yost, Ohio Wesleyan, Nebraska, Kansas, Stanford, Michigan	1897-1911	114	14	9	.858
Barry Switzer, Oklahoma	1973-87	148	26	4	.843
Henry Williams, Army, Minnesota	1891, 1900-13	106	17	9	.837
Bud Wilkinson, Oklahoma	1947-61	129	24	4	.834
Fred Folsom, Colorado, Dartmouth	1895-99, 1901-06, 08-11	89	17	5	.824
*Joe Paterno, Penn St.	1966-80	141	31	1	.818
Elmer Henderson, Southern Cal, Tulsa	1919-33	107	24	3	.810
*Tom Osborne, Nebraska	1973-87	147	34	2	.809

16 SEASONS

Coach, Team(s)	Seasons	W	L	T	Pct.
Gil Dobie, North Dak. St., Washington, Navy, Cornell	1906-21	96	5	3	.938
Fielding Yost, Ohio Wesleyan, Nebraska, Kansas, Stanford, Michigan	1897-1912	119	16	9	.858
Bob Neyland, Tennessee	1926-34, 36-40, 46-47	133	21	8	.846
Henry Williams, Army, Minnesota	1891, 1900-14	112	18	9	.838
Barry Switzer, Oklahoma	1973-88	157	29	4	.837
Bud Wilkinson, Oklahoma	1947-62	137	27	4	.827
*Joe Paterno, Penn St.	1966-81	151	33	1	.819
Fred Folsom, Colorado, Dartmouth	1895-99, 1901-06, 08-12	95	20	5	.813
*Tom Osborne, Nebraska	1973-88	158	36	2	.811
Bob Devaney, Wyoming, Nebraska	1957-72	136	30	7	.806

17 SEASONS

Coach, Team(s)	Seasons	W	L	T	Pct.
Gil Dobie, North Dak. St., Washington, Navy, Cornell	1906-22	104	5	3	.942
Fielding Yost, Ohio Wesleyan, Nebraska, Kansas, Stanford, Michigan	1897-1913	125	17	9	.858
Henry Williams, Army, Minnesota	1891, 1900-15	118	18	10	.842
Bud Wilkinson, Oklahoma	1947-63	145	29	4	.826
Bob Neyland, Tennessee	1926-34, 36-40, 46-48	137	25	10	.826
*Joe Paterno, Penn St.	1966-82	162	34	1	.825
*Tom Osborne, Nebraska	1973-89	168	38	2	.813
Fred Folsom, Colorado, Dartmouth	1895-99, 1901-06, 08-13	100	21	6	.811
Wallace Wade, Alabama, Duke	1923-39	130	29	6	.806
Red Blaik, Dartmouth, Army	1934-50	120	26	10	.801
Jock Sutherland, Lafayette, Pittsburgh	1919-35	119	25	12	.801

18 SEASONS

Coach, Team(s)	Seasons	W	L	T	Pct.
Gil Dobie, North Dak. St., Washington, Navy, Cornell	1906-23	112	5	3	.946
Fielding Yost, Ohio Wesleyan, Nebraska Kansas, Stanford, Michigan	1897-1914	131	20	9	.847

UPI/Bettmann photo

Gil Dobie, who coached at five different schools, holds the best career record (based on winning percentage) of all coaches after four to 28 years of coaching.

Coach, Team(s)	Seasons	W	L	T	Pct.
Henry Williams, Army, Minnesota	1891, 1900-16	124	19	10	.843
Bob Neyland, Tennessee	1926-34, 36-40, 46-49	144	27	11	.821
*Joe Paterno, Penn St.	1966-83	170	38	2	.814
Fred Folsom, Colorado, Dartmouth	1895-99, 1901-06, 08-14	105	22	6	.812
*Tom Osborne, Nebraska	1973-90	177	41	2	.809
Frank Thomas, Tenn.-Chatt., Alabama	1925-28, 31-42, 44-45	134	29	9	.805
Wallace Wade, Alabama, Duke	1923-40	137	31	6	.805
Jock Sutherland, Lafayette, Pittsburgh	1919-36	127	26	13	.804

19 SEASONS

Coach, Team(s)	Seasons	W	L	T	Pct.
Gil Dobie, North Dak. St., Washington, Navy, Cornell	1906-24	116	9	3	.918
Henry Williams, Army, Minnesota	1891, 1900-17	128	20	10	.842
Fielding Yost, Ohio Wesleyan, Nebraska, Kansas, Stanford, Michigan	1897-1915	135	23	10	.833
Bob Neyland, Tennessee	1926-34, 36-40, 46-50	155	28	11	.827
Jock Sutherland, Lafayette, Pittsburgh	1919-37	136	26	14	.813
Wallace Wade, Alabama, Duke	1923-41	146	32	6	.810
*Tom Osborne, Nebraska	1973-91	186	43	3	.808
*Joe Paterno, Penn St.	1966-84	176	43	2	.801
Frank Thomas, Tenn.-Chatt., Alabama	1925-28, 31-42, 44-46	141	33	9	.795
Bo Schembechler, Miami (Ohio), Michigan	1963-81	163	41	6	.790

20 SEASONS

Coach, Team(s)	Seasons	W	L	T	Pct.
Gil Dobie, North Dak. St., Washington, Navy, Cornell	1906-25	122	11	3	.908
Henry Williams, Army, Minnesota	1891, 1900-18	133	22	11	.834
Bob Neyland, Tennessee	1926-34, 36-40, 46-51	165	29	11	.832
Fielding Yost, Ohio Wesleyan, Nebraska, Kansas, Stanford, Michigan	1897-1916	142	25	10	.831
Jock Sutherland, Lafayette, Pittsburgh	1919-38	144	28	14	.812
*Joe Paterno, Penn St.	1966-85	187	44	2	.807
*Tom Osborne, Nebraska	1973-92	195	46	3	.805
Wallace Wade, Alabama, Duke	1923-41, 46	150	37	6	.793
Bo Schembechler, Miami (Ohio), Michigan	1963-82	171	45	6	.784
Dan McGugin, Vanderbilt	1904-17, 19-24	131	33	12	.778

21 SEASONS

Coach, Team(s)	Seasons	W	L	T	Pct.
Gil Dobie, North Dak. St., Washington, Navy, Cornell	1906-26	128	12	4	.903
Fielding Yost, Ohio Wesleyan, Nebraska, Kansas, Stanford, Michigan	1897-1917	150	27	10	.829
Bob Neyland, Tennessee	1926-34, 36-40, 46-52	173	31	12	.829
Henry Williams, Army, Minnesota	1891, 1900-19	137	24	12	.827
*Joe Paterno, Penn St.	1966-86	199	44	2	.816
*Tom Osborne, Nebraska	1973-93	206	47	3	.811
Wallace Wade, Alabama, Duke	1923-41, 46-47	154	40	8	.782
Bo Schembechler, Miami (Ohio), Michigan	1963-83	180	48	6	.782
Howard Jones, Syracuse, Yale, Ohio St., Iowa, Duke, Southern Cal	1908-10, 13, 16-32	147	38	10	.779
Dan McGugin, Vanderbilt	1904-17, 19-25	137	36	12	.773

22 SEASONS

Coach, Team(s)	Seasons	W	L	T	Pct.
Gil Dobie, North Dak. St., Washington, Navy, Cornell	1906-27	131	15	6	.882
Fielding Yost, Ohio Wesleyan, Nebraska, Kansas, Stanford, Michigan	1897-1918	155	27	10	.833
*Tom Osborne, Nebraska	1973-94	219	47	3	.820
*Joe Paterno, Penn St.	1966-87	207	48	2	.809
Henry Williams, Army, Minnesota	1891, 1900-20	138	30	12	.800
Howard Jones, Syracuse, Yale, Ohio St., Iowa, Duke, Southern Cal	1908-10, 13, 16-33	157	39	11	.785
Dan McGugin, Vanderbilt	1904-17, 19-26	145	37	12	.778
Wallace Wade, Alabama, Duke	1923-41, 46-48	158	43	10	.773
Bo Schembechler, Miami (Ohio), Michigan	1963-84	186	54	6	.768
Bear Bryant, Maryland, Kentucky, Texas A&M, Alabama	1945-66	171	51	14	.767

23 SEASONS

Coach, Team(s)	Seasons	W	L	T	Pct.
Gil Dobie, North Dak. St., Washington, Navy, Cornell	1906-28	134	18	8	.863
*Tom Osborne, Nebraska	1973-95	231	47	3	.827
Fielding Yost, Ohio Wesleyan, Nebraska, Kansas, Stanford, Michigan	1897-1919	158	31	10	.819
*Joe Paterno, Penn St.	1966-88	212	54	2	.795
Henry Williams, Army, Minnesota	1891, 1900-21	141	34	12	.786
Dan McGugin, Vanderbilt	1904-17, 19-27	153	38	14	.780
Bo Schembechler, Miami (Ohio), Michigan	1963-85	196	55	7	.773
Wallace Wade, Alabama, Duke	1923-41, 46-49	164	46	10	.768
Howard Jones, Syracuse, Yale, Ohio St., Iowa, Duke, Southern Cal	1908-10, 13, 16-34	161	45	12	.766
Bear Bryant, Maryland, Kentucky, Texas A&M, Alabama	1945-67	179	53	15	.755
Johnny Vaught, Mississippi	1947-69	178	54	12	.754

24 SEASONS

Coach, Team(s)	Seasons	W	L	T	Pct.
Gil Dobie, North Dak. St., Washington, Navy, Cornell	1906-29	140	20	8	.857
Fielding Yost, Ohio Wesleyan, Nebraska, Kansas, Stanford, Michigan	1897-1920	163	33	10	.816
*Joe Paterno, Penn St.	1966-89	220	57	3	.791
Dan McGugin, Vanderbilt	1904-17, 19-28	161	40	14	.781
Bo Schembechler, Miami (Ohio), Michigan	1963-86	207	57	7	.777
Wallace Wade, Alabama, Duke	1923-41, 46-50	171	49	10	.765
Bear Bryant, Maryland, Kentucky, Texas A&M, Alabama	1945-68	187	56	15	.754
Red Blaik, Dartmouth, Army	1934-57	158	48	13	.751
Johnny Vaught, Mississippi	1947-70	185	58	12	.749
Howard Jones, Syracuse, Yale, Ohio St., Iowa, Duke, Southern Cal	1908-10, 13, 16-35	166	52	12	.748

25 SEASONS

Coach, Team(s)	Seasons	W	L	T	Pct.
Gil Dobie, North Dak. St., Washington, Navy, Cornell	1906-30	146	22	8	.852
Fielding Yost, Ohio Wesleyan, Nebraska, Kansas, Stanford, Michigan	1897-1921	168	34	11	.815
*Joe Paterno, Penn St.	1966-90	229	60	3	.789
Dan McGugin, Vanderbilt	1904-17, 19-29	168	42	14	.781
Bo Schembechler, Miami (Ohio), Michigan	1963-87	215	61	7	.772
Red Blaik, Dartmouth, Army	1934-58	166	48	14	.759
John Heisman, Oberlin, Akron, Auburn, Clemson, Georgia Tech	1892-1916	127	37	11	.757
Howard Jones, Syracuse, Yale, Ohio St., Iowa, Duke, Southern Cal	1908-10, 13, 16-36	170	54	15	.755
Woody Hayes, Denison, Miami (Ohio), Ohio St.	1946-70	167	54	7	.748
Bear Bryant, Maryland, Kentucky, Texas A&M, Alabama	1945-69	193	61	15	.745

26 SEASONS

Coach, Team(s)	Seasons	W	L	T	Pct.
Gil Dobie, North Dak. St., Washington, Navy, Cornell	1906-31	153	23	8	.853
Fielding Yost, Ohio Wesleyan, Nebraska, Kansas, Stanford, Michigan	1897-1922	174	34	12	.818
*Joe Paterno, Penn St.	1966-91	240	62	3	.792
Dan McGugin, Vanderbilt	1904-17, 19-30	176	44	14	.782
Bo Schembechler, Miami (Ohio), Michigan	1963-88	224	63	8	.773
John Heisman, Oberlin, Akron, Auburn, Clemson, Georgia Tech	1892-1917	136	37	11	.769
Pop Warner, Georgia, Cornell, Carlisle, Pittsburgh	1895-1920	199	62	14	.749
Woody Hayes, Denison, Miami (Ohio), Ohio St.	1946-71	173	58	7	.742
Amos Alonzo Stagg, Springfield, Chicago	1890-1915	193	62	19	.739
*Bobby Bowden, Samford, West Va., Florida St.	1959-62, 70-91	216	76	3	.737

27 SEASONS

Coach, Team(s)	Seasons	W	L	T	Pct.
Gil Dobie, North Dak. St., Washington, Navy, Cornell	1906-32	158	25	9	.846
Fielding Yost, Ohio Wesleyan, Nebraska, Kansas, Stanford, Michigan	1897-1923	182	34	12	.825
*Joe Paterno, Penn St.	1966-92	247	67	3	.784
Bo Schembechler, Miami (Ohio), Michigan	1963-89	234	65	8	.775
Dan McGugin, Vanderbilt	1904-17, 19-31	181	48	14	.774
John Heisman, Oberlin, Akron, Auburn, Clemson, Georgia Tech	1892-1918	142	38	11	.772
Woody Hayes, Denison, Miami (Ohio), Ohio St.	1946-72	182	60	7	.745
Pop Warner, Georgia, Cornell, Carlisle, Pittsburgh	1895-1921	204	65	15	.745
*Bobby Bowden, Samford, West Va., Florida St.	1959-62, 70-92	227	77	3	.744
Bear Bryant, Maryland, Kentucky, Texas A&M, Alabama	1945-71	210	67	16	.744

28 SEASONS

Coach, Team(s)	Seasons	W	L	T	Pct.
Gil Dobie, North Dak. St., Washington, Navy, Cornell	1906-33	162	28	9	.837
Fielding Yost, Ohio Wesleyan, Nebraska, Kansas, Stanford, Michigan	1897-1923, 25	189	35	12	.826
*Joe Paterno, Penn St.	1966-93	257	69	3	.786
Dan McGugin, Vanderbilt	1904-17, 19-32	187	49	16	.774
John Heisman, Oberlin, Akron, Auburn, Clemson, Georgia Tech	1892-1919	149	41	11	.769
Woody Hayes, Denison, Miami (Ohio), Ohio St.	1946-73	192	60	8	.754
*Bobby Bowden, Samford, West Va., Florida St.	1959-62, 70-93	239	78	3	.752
Bear Bryant, Maryland, Kentucky, Texas A&M, Alabama	1945-72	220	69	16	.748
Pop Warner, Georgia, Cornell, Carlisle, Pittsburgh	1895-1922	212	67	15	.747
Howard Jones, Syracuse, Yale, Ohio St., Iowa, Duke, Southern Cal	1908-10, 13, 16-39	191	60	19	.743

29 SEASONS

Coach, Team(s)	Seasons	W	L	T	Pct.
Fielding Yost, Ohio Wesleyan, Nebraska, Kansas, Stanford, Michigan	1897-1923, 25-26	196	36	12	.828
Gil Dobie, North Dak. St., Washington, Navy, Cornell	1906-34	164	33	9	.818
*Joe Paterno, Penn St.	1966-94	269	69	3	.793
Dan McGugin, Vanderbilt	1904-17, 19-33	191	52	19	.765
John Heisman, Oberlin, Akron, Auburn, Clemson, Georgia Tech, Pennsylvania	1892-1920	155	45	11	.761
Woody Hayes, Denison, Miami (Ohio), Ohio St.	1946-74	202	62	8	.757
*Bobby Bowden, Samford, West Va., Florida St.	1959-62, 70-94	249	79	4	.756
Bear Bryant, Maryland, Kentucky, Texas A&M, Alabama	1945-73	231	70	16	.754
Pop Warner, Georgia, Cornell, Carlisle, Pittsburgh	1895-1923	217	71	15	.741
Howard Jones, Syracuse, Yale, Ohio St., Iowa, Duke, Southern Cal	1908-10, 13, 16-40	194	64	21	.733

30 SEASONS

Coach, Team(s)	Seasons	W	L	T	Pct.
Gil Dobie, North Dak. St., Washington, Navy, Cornell	1906-35	164	39	10	.793
*Joe Paterno, Penn St.	1966-95	278	72	3	.792
Woody Hayes, Denison, Miami (Ohio), Ohio St.	1946-75	213	63	8	.764
Dan McGugin, Vanderbilt	1904-17, 19-34	197	55	19	.762
Bear Bryant, Maryland, Kentucky, Texas A&M, Alabama	1945-74	242	71	16	.760
*Bobby Bowden, Samford, West Va., Florida St.	1959-62, 70-95	259	81	4	.759
John Heisman, Oberlin, Akron, Auburn, Clemson, Georgia Tech, Pennsylvania	1892-1921	159	48	13	.752
Pop Warner, Georgia, Cornell, Carlisle, Pittsburgh, Stanford	1895-1924	224	72	16	.744
Amos Alonzo Stagg, Springfield, Chicago	1890-1919	204	76	20	.713
Dana X. Bible, Mississippi Col., LSU, Texas A&M, Nebraska, Texas	1913-17, 19-43	175	67	23	.704

31 SEASONS

Coach, Team(s)	Seasons	W	L	T	Pct.
Gil Dobie, North Dak. St., Washington, Navy, Cornell, Boston College	1906-36	170	40	12	.793
Bear Bryant, Maryland, Kentucky, Texas A&M, Alabama	1945-75	253	72	16	.765
Woody Hayes, Denison, Miami (Ohio), Ohio St.	1946-76	222	65	9	.765
John Heisman, Oberlin, Akron, Auburn, Clemson, Georgia Tech, Pennsylvania	1892-1922	165	51	13	.749
Pop Warner, Georgia, Cornell, Carlisle, Pittsburgh, Stanford	1895-1925	231	74	16	.745
Amos Alonzo Stagg, Springfield, Chicago	1890-1920	207	80	20	.707
Dana X. Bible, Mississippi Col., LSU, Texas A&M, Nebraska, Texas	1913-17, 19-44	180	69	23	.704

32 SEASONS

Coach, Team(s)	Seasons	W	L	T	Pct.
Gil Dobie, North Dak. St., Washington, Navy, Cornell, Boston College	1906-37	174	44	13	.781
Bear Bryant, Maryland, Kentucky, Texas A&M, Alabama	1945-76	262	75	16	.765
Woody Hayes, Denison, Miami (Ohio), Ohio St.	1946-77	231	68	9	.765
Pop Warner, Georgia, Cornell, Carlisle, Pittsburgh, Stanford	1895-1926	241	74	17	.752
John Heisman, Oberlin, Akron, Auburn, Clemson, Georgia Tech, Pennsylvania, Wash. & Jeff.	1892-1923	171	52	14	.751
Dana X. Bible, Mississippi Col., LSU, Texas A&M, Nebraska, Texas	1913-17, 19-45	190	70	23	.712
Amos Alonzo Stagg, Springfield, Chicago	1890-1921	213	81	20	.710

33 SEASONS

Coach, Team(s)	Seasons	W	L	T	Pct.
Gil Dobie, North Dak. St., Washington, Navy, Cornell, Boston College	1906-38	180	45	15	.781
Bear Bryant, Maryland, Kentucky, Texas A&M, Alabama	1945-77	273	76	16	.770
Woody Hayes, Denison, Miami (Ohio), Ohio St.	1946-78	238	72	10	.759
Pop Warner, Georgia, Cornell, Carlisle, Pittsburgh, Stanford	1895-1927	249	76	18	.752
John Heisman, Oberlin, Akron, Auburn, Clemson, Georgia Tech, Pennsylvania, Wash. & Jeff., Rice	1892-1924	175	56	14	.743
Dana X. Bible, Mississippi Col., LSU, Texas A&M, Nebraska, Texas	1913-17, 19-46	198	72	23	.715
Amos Alonzo Stagg, Springfield, Chicago	1890-1922	219	82	20	.713

34 SEASONS

Coach, Team(s)	Seasons	W	L	T	Pct.
Bear Bryant, Maryland, Kentucky, Texas A&M, Alabama	1945-78	284	77	16	.775
Pop Warner, Georgia, Cornell, Carlisle, Pittsburgh, Stanford	1895-1928	257	79	19	.751
John Heisman, Oberlin, Akron, Auburn, Clemson, Georgia Tech, Pennsylvania, Wash. & Jeff., Rice	1892-1925	179	60	15	.734
Amos Alonzo Stagg, Springfield, Chicago.	1890-1923	226	83	20	.717

35 SEASONS

Coach, Team(s)	Seasons	W	L	T	Pct.
Bear Bryant, Maryland, Kentucky, Texas A&M, Alabama	1945-79	296	77	16	.781
Pop Warner, Georgia, Cornell, Carlisle, Pittsburgh, Stanford	1895-1929	266	81	19	.753
John Heisman, Oberlin, Akron, Auburn, Clemson, Georgia Tech, Pennsylvania, Wash. & Jeff., Rice	1892-1926	183	64	16	.726
Amos Alonzo Stagg, Springfield, Chicago.	1890-1924	230	84	23	.717

36 SEASONS

Coach, Team(s)	Seasons	W	L	T	Pct.
Bear Bryant, Maryland, Kentucky, Texas A&M, Alabama	1945-80	306	79	16	.783
Pop Warner, Georgia, Cornell, Carlisle, Pittsburgh, Stanford	1895-1930	275	82	20	.756
John Heisman, Oberlin, Akron, Auburn, Clemson, Georgia Tech, Pennsylvania, Wash. & Jeff., Rice	1892-1927	185	70	17	.711
Amos Alonzo Stagg, Springfield, Chicago.	1890-1925	233	88	24	.710

37 SEASONS

Coach, Team(s)	Seasons	W	L	T	Pct.
Bear Bryant, Maryland, Kentucky, Texas A&M, Alabama	1945-81	315	81	17	.783
Pop Warner, Georgia, Cornell, Carlisle, Pittsburgh, Stanford	1895-1931	282	84	22	.755
Amos Alonzo Stagg, Springfield, Chicago.	1890-1926	235	94	24	.700
Eddie Anderson, Loras, DePaul, Holy Cross, Iowa	1922-31, 33-42, 46-62	194	117	14	.618

38 SEASONS

Coach, Team(s)	Seasons	W	L	T	Pct.
Bear Bryant, Maryland, Kentucky, Texas A&M, Alabama	1945-82	323	85	17	.780
Pop Warner, Georgia, Cornell, Carlisle, Pittsburgh, Stanford	1895-1932	288	88	23	.751
Amos Alonzo Stagg, Springfield, Chicago	1890-1927	239	98	24	.695
Eddie Anderson, Loras, DePaul, Holy Cross, Iowa	1922-31, 33-42, 46-63	196	123	15	.609

39 SEASONS

Coach, Team(s)	Seasons	W	L	T	Pct.
Pop Warner, Georgia, Cornell, Carlisle, Pittsburgh, Stanford, Temple	1895-1933	293	91	23	.748
Amos Alonzo Stagg, Springfield, Chicago	1890-1928	241	105	24	.684
Eddie Anderson, Loras, DePaul, Holy Cross, Iowa	1922-31, 33-42, 46-64	201	128	15	.606

40 SEASONS

Coach, Team(s)	Seasons	W	L	T	Pct.
Pop Warner, Georgia, Cornell, Carlisle, Pittsburgh, Stanford, Temple	1895-1934	300	92	25	.749
Amos Alonzo Stagg, Springfield, Chicago	1890-1929	248	108	24	.684

41 SEASONS

Coach, Team(s)	Seasons	W	L	T	Pct.
Pop Warner, Georgia, Cornell, Carlisle, Pittsburgh, Stanford, Temple	1895-1935	307	95	25	.748
Amos Alonzo Stagg, Springfield, Chicago	1890-1930	249	113	26	.675

42 SEASONS

Coach, Team(s)	Seasons	W	L	T	Pct.
Pop Warner, Georgia, Cornell, Carlisle, Pittsburgh, Stanford, Temple	1895-1936	313	98	27	.745
Amos Alonzo Stagg, Springfield, Chicago	1890-1931	251	118	27	.668

43 SEASONS

Coach, Team(s)	Seasons	W	L	T	Pct.
Pop Warner, Georgia, Cornell, Carlisle, Pittsburgh, Stanford, Temple	1895-1937	316	100	31	.742
Amos Alonzo Stagg, Springfield, Chicago	1890-1932	254	122	28	.663

44 SEASONS

Coach, Team(s)	Seasons	W	L	T	Pct.
Pop Warner, Georgia, Cornell, Carlisle, Pittsburgh, Stanford, Temple	1895-1938	319	106	32	.733
Amos Alonzo Stagg, Springfield, Chicago, Pacific (Cal.)	1890-1933	259	127	28	.659

**Active coach.*

Photo from Ohio State sports information

Ohio State's John Cooper coached his 100th career victory in 1990 in his 14th season as a head coach.

Coaches to Reach 100, 200 and 300 Victories

(Must have five years or 50 victories at a school that was classified as a major college at the time)

100 VICTORIES

Coach (Date Reached Milestone) (Schools Coached and Years)	WHEN MILESTONE REACHED Age in Yrs.-Days	Career Game (Record)	Career Yr.-Game
FRED AKERS (9-17-88) (Wyoming 1975-76, Texas 1977-86, Purdue 1987-90)	50-184	155th (100-52-3)	14-2
WILLIAM ALEXANDER (11-18-39) (Georgia Tech 1920-44)	49-233	189th (100-74-15)	20-7
EDDIE ANDERSON (10-12-46) (Loras 1922-24, DePaul 1925-31, Holy Cross 1933-38, Iowa 1939-42, 1946-49, Holy Cross 1950-64)	45-333	160th (100-50-10)	21-4
IKE ARMSTRONG (10-17-42) (Utah 1925-49)	47-131	141st (100-30-11)	18-4
MATTY BELL (11-5-38) (Haskell 1920-21, Carroll, Wis. 1922, Texas Christian 1923-28, Texas A&M 1929-33, Southern Methodist 1935-41, 1945-49)	39-256	169th (100-60-9)	18-6
HUGO BEZDEK (11-22-24) (Oregon 1906, Arkansas 1908-12, Oregon 1913-17, Penn St. 1918-29, Delaware Valley 1949)	40-120	147th (100-34-13)	18-9
DANA X. BIBLE (11-21-31) (Mississippi Col. 1913-15, LSU 1916, Texas A&M 1917, 1919-28, Nebraska 1929-36, Texas 1937-46)	40-44	149th (100-31-18)	18-8
BERNIE BIERMAN (11-11-39) (Montana St. 1919-21, Mississippi St. 1925-26, Tulane 1927-31, Minnesota 1932-41, 1945-50)	45-245	149th (100-38-11)	18-6
BOB BLACKMAN (9-27-69) (Denver 1953-54, Dartmouth 1955-70, Illinois 1971-76, Cornell 1977-82)	51-82	147th (100-42-5)	17-1
RED BLAIK (10-23-48) (Dartmouth 1934-40, Army 1941-58)	51-249	134th (100-25-9)	15-5
#BOBBY BOWDEN (10-7-78) (Samford 1959-62, West Va. 1970-75, Florida St. 1976-95)	48-333	144th (100-44-0)	14-5
BILLY BREWER (10-6-90) (Southeast La. 1974-79, Louisiana Tech 1980-82, Mississippi 1983-93)	54-363	184th (100-78-6)	17-5
FRANK BROYLES (11-27-69) (Missouri 1957, Arkansas 1958-76)	44-336	138th (100-36-2)	13-9
EARLE BRUCE (11-3-84) (Tampa 1972, Iowa St. 1973-78, Ohio St. 1979-87, Northern Iowa 1988, Colorado St. 1989-92)	53-240	149th (100-49-0)	13-9
BEAR BRYANT (11-7-59) (Maryland 1945, Kentucky 1946-53, Texas A&M 1954-57, Alabama 1958-82)	46-57	154th (100-44-10)	15-7
WALLY BUTTS (11-15-52) (Georgia 1939-60)	47-281	151st (100-44-7)	14-9
CHARLIE CALDWELL (10-21-50) (Williams 1928-42, Princeton 1945-56)	48-80	163rd (100-55-8)	21-4
FRANK CAMP (10-23-65) (Louisville 1946-68)	60-39	182nd (100-80-2)	20-6
JIM CARLEN (11-8-80) (West Va. 1966-69, Texas Tech 1970-74, South Caro. 1975-81)	47-120	167th (100-61-6)	15-9
LEN CASANOVA (10-2-65) (Santa Clara 1946-49, Pittsburgh 1950, Oregon 1951-66)	59-263	192nd (100-82-10)	20-3
FRANK CAVANAUGH (10-3-25) (Cincinnati 1898, Holy Cross 1903-05, Dartmouth 1911-16, Boston College 1919-26, Fordham 1927-32)	49-158	143rd (100-32-11)	17-1
JERRY CLAIBORNE (11-6-76) (Virginia Tech 1961-70, Maryland 1972-81, Kentucky 1982-89)	48-72	158th (100-54-4)	15-9
#JOHN COOPER (11-17-90) (Tulsa 1977-84, Arizona St. 1985-87, Ohio St. 1988-95)	53-137	162nd (100-57-5)	14-10
FRITZ CRISLER (11-24-45) (Minnesota 1930-31, Princeton 1932-37, Michigan 1938-47)	46-316	138th (100-30-8)	16-10
DICK CRUM (11-15-86) (Miami, Ohio 1974-77, North Caro. 1978-87, Kent 1988-90)	52-200	148th (100-44-4)	13-10
JACK CURTICE (10-3-64) (West Tex. A&M 1940-41, UTEP 1946-49, Utah 1950-57, Stanford 1958-61, UC Santa Barb. 1962-69)	56-118	202nd (100-95-7)	21-1
DUFFY DAUGHERTY (9-25-71) (Michigan St. 1954-72)	56-17	164th (100-60-4)	18-3
DUDLEY DeGROOT (9-17-49) (UC Santa Barb. 1926-28, 1931, San Jose St. 1932-39, Rochester 1940-43, West Va. 1948-49, New Mexico 1950-52)	49-302	152nd (100-44-8)	17-1
HERB DEROMEDI (11-16-91) (Central Mich. 1978-93)	52-171	153rd (100-43-10)	14-11
BOB DEVANEY (11-8-69) (Wyoming 1957-61, Nebraska 1962-72)	54-209	133rd (100-28-5)	13-8
DAN DEVINE (10-12-68) (Arizona St. 1955-57, Missouri 1958-70, Notre Dame 1975-80)	43-293	139th (100-31-8)	14-4
DOUG DICKEY (11-27-77) (Tennessee 1964-69, Florida 1970-78)	45-202	156th (100-50-6)	14-10
PAUL DIETZEL (10-6-73) (LSU 1955-61, Army 1962-65, South Caro. 1966-74)	47-188	191st (100-86-5)	19-4

Coach (Date Reached Milestone) (Schools Coached and Years)	WHEN MILESTONE REACHED Age in Yrs.-Days	Career Game (Record)	Career Yr.-Game
GIL DOBIE (10-20-22) (North Dak. St. 1906-07, Washington 1908-16, Navy 1917-19, Cornell 1920-35, Boston College 1936-38)	43-262	108th (100-5-3)	17-4
BOBBY DODD (12-1-56) (Georgia Tech 1945-66)	48-20	131st (100-28-3)	12-10
MIKE DONAHUE (9-29-23) (Auburn 1904-06, 1908-22, LSU 1923-27)	42-111	140th (100-35-5)	19-1
TERRY DONAHUE (9-10-88) (UCLA 1976-95)	44-78	143rd (100-36-7)	13-2
ALDO DONELLI (10-16-65) (Duquesne 1939-42, Boston U. 1947-56, Columbia 1957-67)	58-86	197th (100-89-8)	23-4
BILL DOOLEY (11-27-82) (North Caro. 1967-77, Virginia Tech 1978-86, Wake Forest 1987-92)	48-192	180th (100-78-2)	16-11
VINCE DOOLEY (9-24-77) (Georgia 1964-88)	45-20	149th (100-44-5)	14-3
FRED DUNLAP (10-29-83) (Lehigh 1965-75, Colgate 1976-87)	55-194	195th (100-91-4)	19-8
PAT DYE (10-4-86) (East Caro. 1974-79, Wyoming 1980, Auburn 1981-92)	46-332	142nd (100-41-1)	13-4
LLOYD EATON (10-4-69) (Alma 1949-55, Northern Mich. 1956, Wyoming 1962-70)	51-101	145th (100-40-5)	16-3
#LaVELL EDWARDS (10-22-83) (Brigham Young 1972-95)	53-11	138th (100-37-1)	12-7
RAY ELIOT (10-10-59) (Illinois Col. 1933-36, Illinois 1942-59)	54-119	191st (100-79-12)	22-3
RIP ENGLE (10-21-61) (Brown 1944-49, Penn St. 1950-65)	55-209	161st (100-53-8)	18-5
DENNIS ERICKSON (10-30-93) (Idaho 1982-85, Wyoming 1986, Washington St. 1987-88, Miami, Fla. 1989-94)	46-334	137th (100-36-1)	12-7
DON FAUROT (11-1-41) (Northeast Mo. St. 1926-34, Missouri 1935-42, 1946-56)	39-131	171st (100-63-8)	16-6
FRED FOLSOM (11-1-13) (Colorado 1895-1902, Dartmouth 1903-06, Colorado 1908-15)	41-357	126th (100-20-6)	17-6
#DANNY FORD (11-13-93) (Clemson 1978-89, Arkansas 1993-95)	45-225	139th (100-34-5)	13-9
#HAYDEN FRY (9-26-81) (Southern Methodist 1962-72, North Texas 1973-78, Iowa 1979-95)	52-185	207th (100-103-4)	20-3
ANDY GUSTAFSON (9-29-61) (Virginia Tech 1926-29, Miami, Fla. 1948-63)	58-179	168th (100-64-4)	18-3
WAYNE HARDIN (10-13-79) (Navy 1959-64, Temple 1970-82)	52-204	159th (100-54-5)	16-6
JIM HARKEMA (9-16-89) (Grand Valley St. 1973-82, Eastern Mich. 1983-92)	47-83	167th (100-63-4)	17-3
DICK HARLOW (11-3-34) (Penn St. 1915-17, Colgate 1922-25, Western Md. 1926-34, Harvard 1935-42, 1945-47)	44-67	142nd (100-31-11)	16-5
HARVEY HARMAN (10-4-47) (Haverford 1922-29, Sewanee 1930, Pennsylvania 1931-37, Rutgers 1938-55)	46-334	177th (100-70-7)	22-2
#KEN HATFIELD (11-20-91) (Air Force 1979-83, Arkansas 1984-89, Clemson 1990-93, Rice 1994-95)	48-174	155th (100-52-3)	13-11
WOODY HAYES (10-21-61) (Denison 1946-48, Miami, Ohio 1949-50, Ohio St. 1951-78)	48-249	140th (100-34-6)	16-4
JOHN HEISMAN (9-27-13) (Oberlin 1892, Akron 1893, Oberlin 1894, Auburn 1895-99, Clemson 1900-03, Georgia Tech 1904-19, Pennsylvania 1920-22, Wash. & Jeff. 1923, Rice 1924-27)	43-339	142nd (100-33-9)	22-1
GUS HENDERSON (11-24-32) (Southern Cal 1919-24, Tulsa 1925-35, Occidental 1940-42)	43-259	126th (100-23-3)	14-8
BILL HESS (9-4-76) (Ohio 1958-77)	51-106	182nd (100-78-4)	19-1
#JIM HESS (9-5-87) (Angelo St. 1974-81, Stephen F. Austin 1982-88, New Mexico St. 1990-95)	50-278	147th (100-43-4)	14-1
#LOU HOLTZ (12-31-82) (William & Mary 1969-71, North Caro. St. 1972-75, Arkansas 1977-83, Minnesota 1984-85, Notre Dame 1986-95)	45-359	153rd (100-48-5)	13-12
FRANK HOWARD (9-27-58) (Clemson 1940-69)	49-186	175th (100-65-10)	19-2
DON JAMES (9-15-84) (Kent 1971-74, Washington 1975-92)	51-258	153rd (100-52-1)	14-2
MORLEY JENNINGS (10-3-31) (Ouachita Baptist 1912-25, Baylor 1926-40)	46-253	136th (100-33-3)	20-1
HOWARD JONES (12-3-27) (Syracuse 1908, Yale 1909, Ohio St. 1910, Yale 1913, Iowa 1916-23, Duke 1924, Southern Cal 1925-40)	42-102	142nd (100-33-9)	16-10
LLOYD JORDAN (10-27-56) (Amherst 1932-49, Harvard 1950-56)	55-317	172nd (100-65-7)	22-4
SHUG JORDAN (10-9-65) (Auburn 1951-75)	55-14	148th (100-43-5)	15-4
FRANK KIMBROUGH (9-29-56) (Hardin-Simmons 1935-40, Baylor 1941-42, 1945-46, West Tex. A&M 1947-57)	52-97	181st (100-73-8)	20-3

Photo from New Mexico State sports information

Jim Hess, currently head coach at New Mexico State, earned his 100th career coaching victory in 1987 when he was at the helm of Stephen F. Austin.

Photo from West Virginia sports information

Don Nehlen, head coach at West Virginia since 1980, earned his 100th career victory in 1985. Coming into this season, he had coached 68 more wins in the ensuing 10 seasons.

	WHEN MILESTONE REACHED		
Coach (Date Reached Milestone) (Schools Coached and Years)	**Age in Yrs.-Days**	**Career Game (Record)**	**Career Yr.-Game**
TONY KNAP (10-2-76) (Utah St. 1963-66, Boise St. 1968-75, UNLV 1976-81)	61-298	135th (100-33-2)	13-4
FRANK KUSH (12-30-70) (Arizona St. 1958-79)	41-344	131st (100-30-1)	13-11
ELMER LAYDEN (10-26-40) (Loras 1925-26, Duquesne 1927-33, Notre Dame 1934-40)	37-175	143rd (100-32-11)	16-4
FRANK LEAHY (10-3-53) (Boston College 1939-40, Notre Dame 1941-53)	45-37	121st (100-13-8)	13-2
LOU LITTLE (9-26-42) (Georgetown 1924-29, Columbia 1930-56)	48-294	161st (100-49-12)	19-1
DICK MacPHERSON (10-28-89) (Massachusetts 1971-77, Syracuse 1981-90)	58-358	171st (100-68-3)	16-7
#JOHNNY MAJORS (11-19-83) (Iowa St. 1968-72, Pittsburgh 1973-76, Tennessee 1977-92, Pittsburgh 1993-95)	48-181	185th (100-81-4)	16-10
#BILL MALLORY (9-14-85) (Miami, Ohio 1969-73, Colorado 1974-78, Northern Ill. 1980-83, Indiana 1984-95)	50-107	164th (100-63-1)	16-1
BEN MARTIN (11-20-76) (Virginia 1956-57, Air Force 1958-77)	55-145	217th (100-108-9)	21-11
CHARLIE McCLENDON (11-2-74) (LSU 1962-79)	46-222	141st (100-35-6)	13-7
DAN McGUGIN (11-15-19) (Vanderbilt 1904-34)	40-78	132nd (100-25-7)	15-7
JOHN McKAY (1-1-73) (Southern Cal 1960-75)	49-209	139th (100-33-6)	13-12
TUSS McLAUGHRY (10-25-41) (Westminster 1916-18, 1921, Amherst 1922-25, Brown 1926-40, Dartmouth 1941-42, 1945-54)	48-109	196th (100-86-10)	23-5
CHICK MEEHAN (9-28-35) (Syracuse 1920-24, New York U. 1925-31, Manhattan 1932-37)	42-23	146th (100-34-12)	16-2
DUTCH MEYER (9-29-51) (Texas Christian 1934-52)	53-204	182nd (100-71-11)	18-2
CHUCK MILLS (9-15-84) (Pomona-Pitzer 1959-61, Indiana, Pa. 1962-63, Merchant Marine 1964, Utah St. 1967-72, Wake Forest 1973-77, Southern Ore. St. 1980-88)	55-287	213th (100-109-4)	22-2
ODUS MITCHELL (11-25-61) (North Texas 1946-66)	59-116	167th (100-59-8)	16-10
#AL MOLDE (10-11-86) (Sioux Falls 1971-72, Minn.-Morris 1973-79, Central Mo. St. 1980-82, Eastern Ill. 1983-86, Western Mich. 1987-95)	42-330	162nd (100-56-6)	16-6
CHARLEY MORAN (9-27-30) (Texas A&M 1909-14, Centre 1919-23, Bucknell 1924-26, Catawba 1930-33)	52-217	131st (100-24-7)	15-1
JOE MORRISON (10-29-88) (Tenn.-Chatt. 1973-79, New Mexico 1980-82, South Caro. 1983-88)	51-69	176th (100-69-7)	16-8
RAY MORRISON (10-2-37) (Southern Methodist 1915-16, Vanderbilt 1918, Southern Methodist 1922-34, Vanderbilt 1935-39, Temple 1940-48, Austin College 1949-52)	52-216	177th (100-54-23)	19-2
BILL MURRAY (11-22-58) (Delaware 1940-42, 1946-50, Duke 1951-65)	50-74	149th (100-40-9)	16-10
JESS NEELY (10-19-46) (Rhodes 1924-27, Clemson 1931-39, Rice 1940-66)	48-288	190th (100-79-11)	20-4
#DON NEHLEN (11-16-85) (Bowling Green 1968-76, West Va. 1980-95)	48-319	162nd (100-57-5)	15-10
BOB NEYLAND (9-29-39) (Tennessee 1926-34, 1936-40, 1946-52)	47-224	120th (100-12-8)	13-1
BOB ODELL (9-24-77) (Bucknell 1958-64, Pennsylvania 1965-70, Williams 1971-86)	55-203	166th (100-64-2)	20-1
JORDAN OLIVAR (10-15-60) (Villanova 1943-48, Loyola Marymount 1949-51, Yale 1952-60)	45-258	159th (100-53-6)	18-4
#TOM OSBORNE (9-24-83) (Nebraska 1973-95)	46-211	126th (100-24-2)	11-4
BENNIE OWEN (10-4-15) (Washburn 1900, Bethany, Kan. 1901-04, Oklahoma 1905-26)	40-72	136th (100-28-8)	16-5
ARA PARSEGHIAN (11-26-66) (Miami, Ohio 1951-55, Northwestern 1956-63, Notre Dame 1964-74)	43-189	147th (100-43-4)	16-10
#JOE PATERNO (11-6-76) (Penn St. 1966-95)	49-320	122nd (100-21-1)	11-9
TOMMY PROTHRO (9-19-70) (Oregon St. 1955-64, UCLA 1965-70)	50-38	155th (100-50-5)	16-2
EDWARD ROBINSON (11-6-15) (Nebraska 1896-97, Brown 1898-1901, Maine 1902, Brown 1904-07, 1910-25)	41-344	165th (100-56-9)	17-7
KNUTE ROCKNE (11-1-30) (Notre Dame 1918-30)	42-242	117th (100-12-5)	13-5
DARRYL ROGERS (9-12-81) (Cal St. Hayward 1965, Fresno St. 1966-72, San Jose St. 1973-75, Michigan St. 1976-79, Arizona St. 1980-84)	47-106	176th (100-70-6)	17-1

Coach (Date Reached Milestone) (Schools Coached and Years)	WHEN MILESTONE REACHED Age in Yrs.-Days	Career Game (Record)	Career Yr.-Game
BILL ROPER (10-8-27) (Va. Military 1903-04, Princeton 1906-08, Missouri 1909, Princeton 1910-11, Swarthmore 1915-16, Princeton 1919-30)	47-47	141st (100-26-15)	19-2
DARRELL ROYAL (10-7-67) (Mississippi St. 1954-55, Washington 1956, Texas 1957-76)	43-93	141st (100-38-3)	14-3
RED SANDERS (11-9-57) (Vanderbilt 1940-48, UCLA 1949-57)	52-216	144th (100-41-3)	15-8
PHILIP SARBOE (12-1-60) (Central Wash. 1941-42, Washington St. 1945-49, Humboldt St. 1951-65, Hawaii 1966)	48-233	160th (100-53-7)	17-11
BO SCHEMBECHLER (10-4-75) (Miami, Ohio 1963-68, Michigan 1969-89)	46-33	130th (100-24-6)	13-4
FRANCIS SCHMIDT (11-5-32) (Tulsa 1919-21, Arkansas 1922-28, Texas Christian 1929-33, Ohio St. 1934-40, Idaho 1941-42)	46-336	136th (100-27-9)	14-8
HOWARD SCHNELLENBERGER (10-28-95) (Miami, Fla. 1979-83, Louisville 1985-94, Oklahoma 1995)	61-226	177th (100-74-3)	16-8
BEN SCHWARTZWALDER (9-30-65) (Muhlenberg 1946-48, Syracuse 1949-73)	52-120	143rd (100-41-2)	16-2
CLARK SHAUGHNESSY (10-20-34) (Tulane 1915-20, 1922-26, Loyola, Ill. 1927-32, Chicago 1933-39, Stanford 1940-41, Maryland 1942, Pittsburgh 1943-45, Maryland 1946, Hawaii 1965)	42-228	164th (100-50-14)	19-3
DICK SHERIDAN (10-6-90) (Furman 1978-85, North Caro. St. 1986-92)	49-58	147th (100-43-4)	13-6
#JACKIE SHERRILL (10-8-88) (Washington St. 1976, Pittsburgh 1977-81, Texas A&M 1982-88, Mississippi St. 1991-95)	44-314	145th (100-43-2)	13-5
ANDY SMITH (11-10-23) (Pennsylvania 1909-12, Purdue 1913-15, California 1916-25)	40-71	140th (100-29-11)	15-8
CLIPPER SMITH (11-6-42) (Gonzaga 1925-28, Santa Clara 1929-35, Villanova 1936-42, San Francisco 1946, Lafayette 1949-51)	44-81	159th (100-47-12)	18-5
#LARRY SMITH (11-10-90) (Tulane 1976-79, Arizona 1980-86, Southern Cal 1987-92, Missouri 1994-95)	51-59	170th (100-65-5)	15-10
CARL SNAVELY (9-30-44) (Bucknell 1927-33, North Caro. 1934-35, Cornell 1936-44, North Caro. 1945-52, Washington, Mo. 1953-58)	50-60	152nd (100-40-12)	18-2
OSSIE SOLEM (10-24-42) (Luther 1920, Drake 1921-31, Iowa 1932-36, Syracuse 1937-45, Springfield 1946-57)	50-315	183rd (100-71-12)	23-5
AMOS ALONZO STAGG (10-6-1900) (Springfield 1890-91, Chicago 1892-1932, Pacific, Cal. 1933-46)	38-51	143rd (100-34-9)	11-6
DENNY STOLZ (9-14-85) (Alma 1965-70, Michigan St. 1973-75, Bowling Green 1977-85, San Diego St. 1986-88)	51-2	175th (100-73-2)	18-2
ABE STUBER (10-16-48) (Westminster, Mo. 1929-31, Southeast Mo. St. 1932-44, 1946, Iowa St. 1947-52)	43-338	162nd (100-54-8)	19-5
JOCK SUTHERLAND (10-14-33) (Lafayette 1919-23, Pittsburgh 1924-38)	44-207	132nd (100-22-10)	15-4
#JIM SWEENEY (9-8-84) (Montana St. 1963-67, Washington St. 1968-75, Fresno St. 1976-77, 1980-95)	55-7	206th (100-105-1)	20-2
BARRY SWITZER (9-24-83) (Oklahoma 1973-88)	45-353	122nd (100-18-4)	11-3
JIM TATUM (11-8-58) (North Caro. 1942, Oklahoma 1946, Maryland 1947-55, North Caro. 1956-58)	45-78	140th (100-33-7)	14-8
GRANT TEAFF (9-25-82) (McMurry 1960-65, Angelo St. 1969-71, Baylor 1972-92)	48-317	206th (100-101-5)	20-3
FRANK THOMAS (11-9-40) (Tenn.-Chatt. 1925-28, Alabama 1931-42, 1944-46)	41-359	128th (100-21-7)	14-6
#DICK TOMEY (9-4-93) (Hawaii 1977-86, Arizona 1987-95)	55-76	182nd (100-75-7)	17-1
PIE VANN (10-6-62) (Southern Miss. 1949-68)	55-14	137th (100-36-1)	14-4
JOHNNY VAUGHT (11-28-59) (Mississippi 1947-73)	51-206	135th (100-29-6)	13-10
#JIM WACKER (11-14-81) (Texas Lutheran 1971-75, North Dak. St. 1976-78, Southwest Tex. St. 1979-82, Texas Christian 1983-91, Minnesota 1992-95)	44-200	134th (100-33-1)	12-10
WALLACE WADE (10-3-36) (Alabama 1923-30, Duke 1931-41, 1946-50)	44-110	129th (100-24-5)	14-3
PAPPY WALDORF (10-27-45) (Oklahoma City 1925-27, Oklahoma St. 1929-33, Kansas St. 1934, Northwestern 1935-46, California 1947-56)	43-24	173rd (100-56-17)	20-5
POP WARNER (11-26-08) (Georgia 1895-96, Cornell 1897-98, Carlisle 1899-1903, Cornell 1904-06, Carlisle 1907-14, Pittsburgh 1915-23, Stanford 1924-32, Temple 1933-38)	37-235	145th (100-38-7)	14-11
#GEORGE WELSH (10-14-89) (Navy 1973-81, Virginia 1982-95)	56-49	188th (100-85-3)	17-7

Photo from Arizona sports information

Arizona coach Dick Tomey kicked off his 17th season as a head coach by chalking up his 100th career victory, a 24-6 win over UTEP on September 4, 1993.

COACHING RECORDS

Photo from Notre Dame sports information

When his Fighting Irish beat Purdue, 35-28, on September 9, 1995, Lou Holtz became just the 15th coach to reach the coveted 200-win plateau (among coaches with 10 years at a major college).

Coach (Date Reached Milestone) (Schools Coached and Years)	WHEN MILESTONE REACHED Age in Yrs.-Days	Career Game (Record)	Career Yr.-Game
BUD WILKINSON (11-2-57) (Oklahoma 1947-63)	41-193	111th (100-8-3)	11-6
HENRY WILLIAMS (10-2-12) (Army 1891, Minnesota 1900-21)	43-98	122nd (100-13-9)	14-4
GEORGE WOODRUFF (11-11-1898) (Pennsylvania 1892-1901, Illinois 1903, Carlisle 1905)	35-261	109th (100-9-0)	8-11
WARREN WOODSON (9-27-52) (Conway 1935-40, Hardin-Simmons 1941-51, Arizona St. 1952-56, New Mexico St. 1958-67, Trinity, Tex. 1972-73)	49-215	141st (100-32-9)	15-2
BILL YEOMAN (9-12-77) (Houston 1962-86)	49-260	161st (100-56-5)	16-1
FIELDING YOST (11-7-08) (Ohio Wesleyan 1897, Nebraska 1898, Kansas 1899, Stanford 1900, Michigan 1901-23, 1925-26)	37-191	114th (100-10-4)	12-6
JIM YOUNG (9-10-88) (Arizona 1973-76, Purdue 1977-81, Army 1983-90)	53-142	160th (100-58-2)	15-1
JOHN YOVICSIN (11-16-68) (Gettysburg 1952-56, Harvard 1957-70)	50-131	150th (100-45-5)	17-8
JOSEPH YUKICA (11-20-82) (New Hampshire 1966-67, Boston College 1968-77, Dartmouth 1978-86)	51-177	169th (100-68-1)	17-10
ROBERT ZUPPKE (11-12-32) (Illinois 1913-41)	53-102	152nd (100-44-8)	20-9

#Active coach.

200 VICTORIES

Coach (Date Reached Milestone)	WHEN MILESTONE REACHED Age in Yrs.-Days	Career Game (Record)	Career Yr.-Game
Eddie Anderson (11-14-64)	64-1	342nd (200-127-15)	39-8
#Bobby Bowden (10-27-90)	60-353	279th (200-76-3)	25-7
Bear Bryant (9-10-71)	57-364	282nd (200-66-16)	27-1
Vince Dooley (11-26-88)	56-84	286th (200-76-10)	25-11
#LaVell Edwards (9-24-94)	64-348	277th (200-74-3)	23-4
#Hayden Fry (11-20-93)	64-265	361st (200-152-9)	32-11
Woody Hayes (11-2-74)	61-261	268th (200-60-8)	29-8
#Lou Holtz (9-9-95)	58-243	297th (200-90-7)	26-2
Jess Neely (9-26-64)	66-265	373rd (200-155-18)	38-1
#Tom Osborne (10-7-93)	56-224	249th (200-46-3)	21-5
#Joe Paterno (9-5-87)	60-258	246th (200-44-2)	22-1
Bo Schembechler (10-4-86)	57-33	262nd (200-55-7)	24-4
Amos Alonzo Stagg (10-11-19)	57-56	294th (200-74-20)	30-1
Pop Warner (9-24-21)	50-172	276th (200-62-14)	28-1
Warren Woodson (10-13-73)	70-231	307th (200-93-14)	31-6

#Active coach.

300 VICTORIES

Coach (Date Reached Milestone)	WHEN MILESTONE REACHED Age in Yrs.-Days	Career Game (Record)	Career Yr.-Game
Bear Bryant (10-3-80)	67-22	393rd (300-77-16)	36-4
Amos Alonzo Stagg (11-6-43)	81-82	507th (300-173-34)	54-7
Pop Warner (11-24-34)	63-233	415th (300-91-24)	41-8

Other Coaching Milestones

(Must have five years or 50 victories at a school that was classified as a major college at the time)

YOUNGEST COACHES TO REACH 100 VICTORIES

Coach	Age in Yrs.-Days
George Woodruff	35-261
Elmer Layden	37-175
Fielding Yost	37-191
Pop Warner	37-235
Amos Alonzo Stagg	38-51
Don Faurot	39-131
Matty Bell	39-256
Dana Bible	40-44
Andy Smith	40-71
Bennie Owen	40-72
Dan McGugin	40-78
Hugo Bezdek	40-120

YOUNGEST COACHES TO REACH 200 VICTORIES

Coach	Age in Yrs.-Days
Pop Warner	50-172
Vince Dooley	56-84
*Tom Osborne	56-224
Bo Schembechler	57-33
Amos Alonzo Stagg	57-56
Bear Bryant	57-364
Lou Holtz	58-243

*Active coach.

YOUNGEST COACHES TO REACH 300 VICTORIES

Coach	Age in Yrs.-Days
Pop Warner	63-233
Bear Bryant	67-22
Amos Alonzo Stagg	81-82

FEWEST GAMES TO REACH 100 VICTORIES

Coach	Career Game (Record at Time)
Gil Dobie	108 (100-5-3)
George Woodruff	109 (100-9-0)
Bud Wilkinson	111 (100-8-3)
Fielding Yost	114 (100-10-4)
Knute Rockne	117 (100-12-5)
Bob Neyland	120 (100-12-8)
Frank Leahy	121 (100-13-8)
*Joe Paterno	122 (100-21-1)
Barry Switzer	122 (100-18-4)
Henry Williams	122 (100-13-9)
Fred Folsom	126 (100-20-6)
Gus Henderson	126 (100-23-3)
*Tom Osborne	126 (100-24-2)
Frank Thomas	128 (100-21-7)
Wallace Wade	129 (100-24-5)
Bo Schembechler	130 (100-24-6)
Bobby Dodd	131 (100-28-3)
Frank Kush	131 (100-30-1)
Charley Moran	131 (100-24-7)
Dan McGugin	132 (100-25-7)
Jock Sutherland	132 (100-22-10)
Bob Devaney	133 (100-28-5)
Red Blaik	134 (100-25-9)
*Jim Wacker	134 (100-33-1)
Tony Knap	135 (100-33-2)
Johnny Vaught	135 (100-29-6)
Morley Jennings	136 (100-33-3)
Bennie Owen	136 (100-28-8)
Francis Schmidt	136 (100-27-9)
Dennis Erickson	137 (100-36-1)
Pie Vann	137 (100-36-1)
Frank Broyles	138 (100-36-2)
Fritz Crisler	138 (100-30-8)
*LaVell Edwards	138 (100-37-1)
Dan Devine	139 (100-31-8)
*Danny Ford	139 (100-34-5)
John McKay	139 (100-33-6)

*Active coach.

FEWEST GAMES TO REACH 200 VICTORIES

Coach	Career Game (Record at Time)
*Joe Paterno	246 (200-44-2)
*Tom Osborne	249 (200-46-3)
Bo Schembechler	262 (200-55-7)
Woody Hayes	268 (200-60-8)
Pop Warner	276 (200-62-14)
*LaVell Edwards	277 (200-74-3)
*Bobby Bowden	279 (200-76-3)
Bear Bryant	282 (200-66-16)
Vince Dooley	286 (200-76-10)
Amos Alonzo Stagg	294 (200-74-20)

*Active coach.

FEWEST GAMES TO REACH 300 VICTORIES

Coach	Career Game (Record at Time)
Bear Bryant	393 (300-77-16)
Pop Warner	415 (300-91-24)
Amos Alonzo Stagg	507 (300-173-34)

All-Time Division I Coaching Longevity Records

(Minimum 10 Head-Coaching Seasons in Division I; Bowl Games Included)

MOST GAMES

Games	Coach, School(s) and Years
548	Amos Alonzo Stagg, Springfield 1890-91, Chicago 1892-1932, Pacific (Cal.) 1933-46
457	Pop Warner, Georgia 1895-96, Cornell 1897-98 and 1904-06, Carlisle 1899-1903 and 1907-14, Pittsburgh 1915-23, Stanford 1924-32, Temple 1933-38
425	Bear Bryant, Maryland 1945, Kentucky 1946-53, Texas A&M 1954-57, Alabama 1958-82
402	Jess Neely, Rhodes 1924-27, Clemson 1931-39, Rice 1940-66
385	*Hayden Fry, Southern Methodist 1962-72, North Texas 1973-78, Iowa 1979-95
353	*Joe Paterno, Penn St. 1966-95
347	*Jim Sweeney, Montana St. 1963-67, Washington St. 1968-75, Fresno St. 1976-77 and 1980-95
344	Eddie Anderson, Loras 1922-24, DePaul 1925-31, Holy Cross 1933-38 and 1950-64, Iowa 1939-42 and 1946-49
344	*Bobby Bowden, Samford 1959-62, West Va. 1970-75, Florida St. 1976-95
329	Grant Teaff, McMurry 1960-65, Angelo St. 1969-71, Baylor 1972-92
321	*Johnny Majors, Iowa St. 1968-72, Pittsburgh 1973-76 and 1993-95, Tennessee 1977-92
320	Woody Hayes, Denison 1946-48, Miami (Ohio) 1949-50, Ohio St. 1951-78
318	Ray Morrison, Southern Methodist 1915-16 and 1922-34, Vanderbilt 1918 and 1935-39, Temple 1940-48, Austin 1949-52
312	Warren Woodson, Central Ark. 1935-39, Hardin-Simmons 1941-42 and 1946-51, Arizona 1952-56, New Mexico St. 1958-67, Trinity (Tex.) 1972-73
309	Jerry Claiborne, Virginia Tech 1961-70, Maryland 1972-81, Kentucky 1982-89
307	*Lou Holtz, William & Mary 1969-71, North Caro. St. 1972-75, Arkansas 1977-83, Minnesota 1984-85, Notre Dame 1986-95
307	Bo Schembechler, Miami (Ohio) 1963-68, Michigan 1969-89
299	Ossie Solem, Luther 1920, Drake 1921-31, Iowa 1932-36, Syracuse 1937-42 and 1944-45, Springfield 1946-57
297	*LaVell Edwards, Brigham Young 1972-95
296	Tuss McLaughry, Westminster 1916, 1918 and 1921, Amherst 1922-25, Brown 1926-40, Dartmouth 1941-54
296	Pappy Waldorf, Oklahoma City 1925-27, Oklahoma St. 1929-33, Kansas St. 1934, Northwestern 1935-46, California 1947-56
295	Frank Howard, Clemson 1940-69
293	Dana X. Bible, Mississippi Col. 1913-15, LSU 1916, Texas A&M 1917 and 1919-28, Nebraska 1929-36, Texas 1937-46
293	Bill Dooley, North Caro. 1967-77, Virginia Tech 1978-86, Wake Forest 1987-92
292	Lou Little, Georgetown 1924-29, Columbia 1930-56
292	Carl Snavely, Bucknell 1927-33, North Caro. 1934-35 and 1945-52, Cornell 1936-44, Washington (Mo.) 1953-58
290	*Bill Mallory, Miami (Ohio) 1969-73, Colorado 1974-78, Northern Ill. 1980-83, Indiana 1984-95
288	Vince Dooley, Georgia 1964-88
287	Bob Blackman, Denver 1953-54, Dartmouth 1955-70, Illinois 1971-76, Cornell 1977-82
282	Clark Shaughnessy, Tulane 1915-20 and 1922-26, Loyola (Ill.) 1927-32, Chicago 1933-39, Stanford 1940-41, Maryland 1942 and 1946, Pittsburgh 1943-45, Hawaii 1965
282	*Jim Wacker, Texas Lutheran 1971-75, North Dak. St. 1976-78, Southwest Tex. St. 1979-82, Texas Christian 1983-91, Minnesota 1992-95
281	*Tom Osborne, Nebraska 1973-95
279	Howard Jones, Syracuse 1908, Yale 1909 and 1913, Ohio St. 1910, Iowa 1916-23, Duke 1924, Southern Cal 1925-40

Games	Coach, School(s) and Years
279	*Don Nehlen, Bowling Green 1968-76, West Va. 1980-95
277	Ben Schwartzwalder, Muhlenberg 1946-48, Syracuse 1949-73
276	Bill Yeoman, Houston 1962-86
272	John Heisman, Oberlin 1892 and 1894, Akron 1893, Auburn 1895-99, Clemson 1900-03, Georgia Tech 1904-19, Pennsylvania 1920-22, Wash. & Jeff. 1923, Rice 1924-27
271	Dan McGugin, Vanderbilt 1904-17 and 1919-34
269	Don Faurot, Truman St. 1926-34, Missouri 1935-42 and 1946-56
266	*George Welsh, Navy 1973-81, Virginia 1982-95
265	Shug Jordan, Auburn 1951-75
263	John Vaught, Mississippi 1947-70 and 1973
260	Jack Curtice, West Tex. A&M 1940-41, UTEP 1946-49, Utah 1950-57, Stanford 1958-61, UC Santa Barb. 1962-69
260	Frank Dobson, Georgia 1909, Clemson 1910-12, Richmond 1913-17 and 1919-33, South Caro. 1918, Maryland 1935-39
260	Chuck Mills, Pomona-Pitzer 1959-61, Indiana (Pa.) 1962-63, Merchant Marine 1964, Utah St. 1967-72, Wake Forest 1973-77, Southern Ore. St. 1980-88
258	Edward Robinson, Nebraska 1896-97, Brown 1898-1901, 1904-07 and 1910-25
257	Don James, Kent 1971-74, Washington 1975-92
256	Matty Bell, Haskell 1920-21, Carroll (Wis.) 1922, Texas Christian 1923-28, Texas A&M 1929-33, Southern Methodist 1935-41 and 1945-49
252	Harvey Harman, Haverford 1922-29, Sewanee 1930, Pennsylvania 1931-37, Rutgers 1938-55

**Active.*

MOST YEARS

Years	Coach, School(s) and Years
57	Amos Alonzo Stagg, Springfield 1890-91, Chicago 1892-1932, Pacific (Cal.) 1933-46
44	Pop Warner, Georgia 1895-96, Cornell 1897-98 and 1904-06, Carlisle 1899-1903 and 1907-14, Pittsburgh 1915-23, Stanford 1924-32, Temple 1933-38
40	Jess Neely, Rhodes 1924-27, Clemson 1931-39, Rice 1940-66
39	Eddie Anderson, Loras 1922-24, DePaul 1925-31, Holy Cross 1933-38 and 1950-54, Iowa 1939-42 and 1946-49
38	Bear Bryant, Maryland 1945, Kentucky 1946-53, Texas A&M 1954-57, Alabama 1958-82
37	Ossie Solem, Luther 1920, Drake 1921-31, Iowa 1932-36, Syracuse 1937-45, Springfield 1946-57
36	John Heisman, Oberlin 1892 and 1894, Akron 1893, Auburn 1895-99, Clemson 1900-03, Georgia Tech 1904-19, Pennsylvania 1920-22, Wash. & Jeff. 1923, Rice 1924-27
34	*Hayden Fry, Southern Methodist 1962-72, North Texas 1973-78, Iowa 1979-95
34	Tuss McLaughry, Westminster 1916, 1918 and 1921, Amherst 1922-25, Brown 1926-40, Dartmouth 1941-54
34	Ray Morrison, Southern Methodist 1915-16 and 1922-34, Vanderbilt 1918 and 1935-39, Temple 1940-48, Austin 1949-52
33	Dana X. Bible, Mississippi Col. 1913-15, LSU 1916, Texas A&M 1917 and 1919-28, Nebraska 1929-36, Texas 1937-46
33	Gil Dobie, North Dak. St. 1906-07, Washington 1908-16, Navy 1917-19, Cornell 1920-35, Boston College 1936-38
33	Woody Hayes, Denison 1946-48, Miami (Ohio) 1949-50, Ohio St. 1951-78
33	Lou Little, Georgetown 1924-29, Columbia 1930-56
32	Clark Shaughnessy, Tulane 1915-20 and 1922-26, Loyola (Ill.) 1927-32, Chicago 1933-39, Stanford 1940-41, Maryland 1942 and 1946, Pittsburgh 1943-45, Hawaii 1965
32	Carl Snavely, Bucknell 1927-33, North Caro. 1934-35 and 1945-52, Cornell 1936-44, Washington (Mo.) 1953-58
32	William Spaulding, Western Mich. 1907-21, Minnesota 1922-24, UCLA 1925-38
31	*Jim Sweeney, Montana St. 1963-67, Washington St. 1968-75, Fresno St. 1976-77 and 1980-95
31	Pappy Waldorf, Oklahoma City 1925-27, Oklahoma St. 1929-33, Kansas St. 1934, Northwestern 1935-46, California 1947-56
31	Warren Woodson, Central Ark. 1935-39, Hardin-Simmons 1941-42 and 1946-51, Arizona 1952-56, New Mexico St. 1958-67, Trinity (Tex.) 1972-73
30	Bob Blackman, Denver 1953-54, Dartmouth 1955-70, Illinois 1971-76, Cornell 1977-82
30	*Bobby Bowden, Samford 1959-62, West Va. 1970-75, Florida St. 1976-95
30	Frank Dobson, Georgia 1909, Clemson 1910-12, Richmond 1913-17 and 1919-33, South Caro. 1918, Maryland 1935-39
30	Harvey Harman, Haverford 1922-29, Sewanee 1930, Pennsylvania 1931-37, Rutgers 1938-55
30	Frank Howard, Clemson 1940-69
30	Dan McGugin, Vanderbilt 1904-17 and 1919-34
30	*Joe Paterno, Penn St. 1966-95
30	Grant Teaff, McMurry 1960-65, Angelo St. 1969-71, Baylor 1972-92

**Active.*

MOST SCHOOLS

(Must Have Coached at Least One Division I or Major-College Team)

Schools	Coach, Schools and Years
8	John Heisman, Oberlin 1892 and 1894, Akron 1893, Auburn 1895-99, Clemson 1900-03, Georgia Tech 1904-19, Pennsylvania 1920-22, Wash. & Jeff. 1923, Rice 1924-27
7	Darrell Mudra, Adams St. 1959-62, North Dak. St. 1963-65, Arizona 1967-68, Western Ill. 1969-73, Florida St. 1974-75, Eastern Ill. 1978-82, Northern Iowa 1983-87
7	Lou Saban, Case Reserve 1950-52, Northwestern 1955, Western Ill. 1957-59, Maryland 1966, Miami (Fla.) 1977-78, Army 1979, Central Fla. 1983-84
7	Clark Shaughnessy, Tulane 1915-20 and 1922-26, Loyola (Ill.) 1927-32, Chicago 1933-39, Stanford 1940-41, Maryland 1942 and 1946, Pittsburgh 1943-45, Hawaii 1965
7	Clarence Spears, Dartmouth 1917-20, West Va. 1921-24, Minnesota 1925-29, Oregon 1930-31, Wisconsin 1932-35, Toledo 1936-42, Maryland 1943-44
6	Howard Jones, Syracuse 1908, Yale 1909 and 1913, Ohio St. 1910, Iowa 1916-23, Duke 1924, Southern Cal 1925-40
6	Chuck Mills, Pomona-Pitzer 1959-61, Indiana (Pa.) 1962-63, Merchant Marine 1964, Utah St. 1967-72, Wake Forest 1973-77, Southern Ore. St. 1980-88
6	Pop Warner, Georgia 1895-96, Cornell 1897-98 and 1904-06, Carlisle 1899-1903 and 1907-14, Pittsburgh 1915-23, Stanford 1924-32, Temple 1933-38
5	Matty Bell, Haskell 1920-21, Carroll (Wis.) 1922, Texas Christian 1923-28, Texas A&M 1929-33, Southern Methodist 1935-41 and 1945-49
5	Dana X. Bible, Mississippi Col. 1913-15, LSU 1916, Texas A&M 1917 and 1919-28, Nebraska 1929-36, Texas 1937-46
5	*Watson Brown, Austin Peay 1979-80, Cincinnati 1983, Rice 1984-85, Vanderbilt 1986-90, Ala.-Birmingham 1995
5	Earle Bruce, Tampa 1972, Iowa St. 1973-78, Ohio St. 1979-87, Northern Iowa 1988, Colorado St. 1989-92
5	Frank Cavanaugh, Cincinnati 1898, Holy Cross 1903-05, Dartmouth 1911-16, Boston College 1919-26, Fordham 1927-32
5	Jack Curtice, West Tex. A&M 1940-41, UTEP 1946-49, Utah 1950-57, Stanford 1958-61, UC Santa Barb. 1962-69
5	Gil Dobie, North Dak. St. 1906-07, Washington 1908-16, Navy 1917-19, Cornell 1920-35, Boston College 1936-38
5	Frank Dobson, Georgia 1909, Clemson 1910-12, Richmond 1913-17 and 1919-33, South Caro. 1918, Maryland 1935-39
5	Ed Doherty, Arizona St. 1947-50, Rhode Island 1951, Arizona 1957-58, Xavier (Ohio) 1959-61, Holy Cross 1971-75
5	Red Drew, Trinity (Conn.) 1921-23, Birmingham So. 1924-27, Tenn.-Chatt. 1929-30, Mississippi 1946, Alabama 1947-54
5	Stuart Holcomb, Findlay 1932-35, Muskingum 1936-40, Wash. & Jeff. 1941, Miami (Ohio) 1942-43, Purdue 1947-55
5	*Lou Holtz, William & Mary 1969-71, North Caro. St. 1972-75, Arkansas 1977-83, Minnesota 1984-85, Notre Dame 1986-95
5	*Al Molde, Sioux Falls 1971-72, Minn.-Morris 1973-79, Central Mo. St. 1980-82, Eastern Ill. 1983-86, Western Mich. 1987-95
5	Darryl Rogers, Cal St. Hayward 1965, Fresno St. 1966-72, San Jose St. 1973-75, Michigan St. 1976-79, Arizona St. 1980-84
5	John Rowland, Henderson St. 1925-30, Ouachita Baptist 1931, Citadel 1940-42, Oklahoma City 1946-47, Geo. Washington 1948-51
5	Francis Schmidt, Tulsa 1919-21, Arkansas 1922-28, Texas Christian 1929-33, Ohio St. 1934-40, Idaho 1941-42
5	Clipper Smith, Gonzaga 1925-28, Santa Clara 1929-35, Villanova 1936-42, San Francisco 1946, Lafayette 1949-51
5	Ossie Solem, Luther 1920, Drake 1921-31, Iowa 1932-36, Syracuse 1937-45, Springfield 1946-57
5	Skip Stahley, Delaware 1934, Brown 1941-43, Geo. Washington 1946-47, Toledo 1948-49, Idaho 1954-60
5	*Jim Wacker, Texas Lutheran 1971-75, North Dak. St. 1976-78, Southwest Tex. St. 1979-82, Texas Christian 1983-91, Minnesota 1992-95
5	Pappy Waldorf, Oklahoma City 1925-27, Oklahoma St. 1929-33, Kansas St. 1934, Northwestern 1935-46, California 1947-56
5	Warren Woodson, Central Ark. 1935-39, Hardin-Simmons 1941-42, Arizona 1952-56, New Mexico St. 1958-67, Trinity (Tex.) 1972-73
5	Fielding Yost, Ohio Wesleyan 1897, Nebraska 1898, Kansas 1899, Stanford 1900, Michigan 1901-23 and 1925-26
4	Eddie Anderson, Loras 1922-24, DePaul 1925-31, Holy Cross 1933-38 and 1950-64, Iowa 1939-42 and 1946-49
4	Charles Bachman, Northwestern 1919, Kansas St. 1920-27, Florida 1928-32, Michigan St. 1933-42 and 1944-46
4	Jerry Berndt, DePauw 1979-80, Pennsylvania 1981-85, Rice 1986-88, Temple 1989-92
4	Bob Blackman, Denver 1953-54, Dartmouth 1955-70, Illinois 1971-76, Cornell 1977-82
4	Bear Bryant, Maryland 1945, Kentucky 1946-53, Texas A&M 1954-57, Alabama 1958-82
4	Dudley DeGroot, UC Santa Barb. 1926-31, San Jose St. 1932-43, West Va. 1948-49, New Mexico 1950-52
4	Pete Elliott, Nebraska 1956, California 1957-59, Illinois 1960-66, Miami (Fla.) 1973-74
4	Dennis Erickson, Idaho 1982-85, Wyoming 1986, Washington St. 1987-88, Miami (Fla.) 1989-94
4	Wesley Fesler, Wesleyan (Conn.) 1941-42, Pittsburgh 1946, Ohio St. 1947-50, Minnesota 1951-53

Schools	Coach, Schools and Years
4	*Dennis Franchione, S'western (Kan.) 1981-82, Pittsburg St. 1985-89, Southwest Tex. St. 1990-91, New Mexico 1992-95
4	Mike Gottfried, Murray St. 1978-80, Cincinnati 1981-82, Kansas 1983-85, Pittsburgh 1986-89
4	Harvey Harman, Haverford 1922-29, Sewanee 1930, Pennsylvania 1931-37, Rutgers 1938-55
4	*Ken Hatfield, Air Force 1979-83, Arkansas 1984-89, Clemson 1990-93, Rice 1994-95
4	*Bill Mallory, Miami (Ohio) 1969-73, Colorado 1974-78, Northern Ill. 1980-83, Indiana 1984-95
4	Tuss McLaughry, Westminster 1916, 1918 and 1921, Amherst 1922-25, Brown 1926-40, Dartmouth 1941-54
4	Joe McMullen, Stetson 1950-51, Wash. & Jeff. 1952-53, Akron 1954-60, San Jose St. 1969-70
4	Bill Meek, Kansas St. 1951-54, Houston 1955-56, Southern Methodist 1957-61, Utah 1968-73
4	Charley Moran, Texas A&M 1909-14, Centre 1919-23, Bucknell 1924-26, Catawba 1930-31
4	Ray Morrison, Southern Methodist 1915-16 and 1922-34, Vanderbilt 1918 and 1935-39, Temple 1940-48, Austin 1949-52
4	Frank Navarro, Williams 1963-67, Columbia 1968-73, Wabash 1974-77, Princeton 1978-84
4	John Pont, Miami (Ohio) 1956-62, Yale 1963-64, Indiana 1965-72, Northwestern 1973-77
4	Bill Roper, Va. Military 1903-04, Princeton 1906-08, 1910-11 and 1919-30, Missouri 1909, Swarthmore 1915-16
4	Philip Sarboe, Central Wash. 1941-42, Washington St. 1945-49, Humboldt St. 1951-65, Hawaii 1966
4	George Sauer, New Hampshire 1937-41, Kansas 1946-47, Navy 1948-49, Baylor 1950-55
4	*Jackie Sherrill, Washington St. 1976, Pittsburgh 1977-81, Texas A&M 1982-88, Mississippi St. 1991-95
4	Steve Sloan, Vanderbilt 1973-74, Texas Tech 1975-77, Mississippi 1978-82, Duke 1983-86
4	*Larry Smith, Tulane 1976-79, Arizona 1980-86, Southern Cal 1987-92, Missouri 1994-95
4	Carl Snavely, Bucknell 1927-33, North Caro. 1934-35 and 1945-52, Cornell 1936-44, Washington (Mo.) 1953-58
4	Denny Stolz, Alma 1965-70, Michigan St. 1973-75, Bowling Green 1977-85, San Diego St. 1986-88

**Active.*

MOST YEARS COACHED AT ONE COLLEGE

(Minimum 15 Years)

Coach, College (Years)	Years	School W-L-T	Overall W-L-T
Amos Alonzo Stagg, Chicago (1892-1932)	41	244-111-27	314-199-35
Frank Howard, Clemson (1940-69)	30 #	165-118-12	165-118-12
Dan McGugin, Vanderbilt (1904-17, 1919-34)	30 #	197-55-19	197-55-19
*Joe Paterno, Penn St. (1966-95)	30 #	278-72-3	278-72-3
Robert Zuppke, Illinois (1913-41)	29 #	131-81-13	131-81-13
Woody Hayes, Ohio St. (1951-78)	28	205-61-10	238-72-10
Lou Little, Columbia (1930-56)	27	110-116-10	151-128-13
Jess Neely, Rice (1940-66)	27	144-124-10	207-176-19
William Alexander, Georgia Tech (1920-44)	25 #	134-95-15	134-95-15
Ike Armstrong, Utah (1925-49)	25 #	140-55-15	140-55-15
Bear Bryant, Alabama (1958-82)	25	232-46-9	323-85-17
Vince Dooley, Georgia (1964-88)	25 #	201-77-10	201-77-10
Ralph Jordan, Auburn (1951-75)	25 #	176-83-6	176-83-6
Ben Schwartzwalder, Syracuse (1949-73)	25	153-91-3	178-96-3
John Vaught, Mississippi (1947-70, 1973)	25 #	190-61-12	190-61-12
Bill Yeoman, Houston (1962-86)	25 #	160-108-8	160-108-8
Fielding Yost, Michigan (1901-23, 1925-26)	25	165-29-10	196-36-12
*LaVell Edwards, Brigham Young (1972-95)	24 #	214-80-3	214-80-3
Edward Robinson, Brown (1898-1901, 1904-07, 1910-25)	24	140-82-12	157-88-13
Frank Camp, Louisville (1946-68)	23 #	118-96-2	118-96-2
*Tom Osborne, Nebraska (1973-95)	23 #	231-47-3	231-47-3
Wally Butts, Georgia (1939-60)	22 #	140-86-9	140-86-9
Bobby Dodd, Georgia Tech (1945-66)	22 #	165-64-8	165-64-8
Frank Kush, Arizona St. (1958-79)	22 #	176-54-1	176-54-1
Bennie Owen, Oklahoma (1905-26)	22	122-54-16	155-60-19
Henry Williams, Minnesota (1900-21)	22	140-33-11	141-34-12
Eddie Anderson, Holy Cross (1933-38, 1950-64)	21	129-67-8	201-128-15
Bob Neyland, Tennessee (1926-34, 1936-40, 1946-52)	21 #	173-31-12	173-31-12
Bo Schembechler, Michigan (1969-89)	21	194-48-5	234-65-8
Grant Teaff, Baylor (1972-92)	21	128-105-6	170-151-8
*Bobby Bowden, Florida St. (1976-95)	20	186-49-4	259-81-4
Terry Donahue, UCLA (1976-95)	20 #	151-74-8	151-74-8
Bill Hess, Ohio (1958-77)	20 #	107-92-4	107-92-4
Ben Martin, Air Force (1958-77)	20	96-103-9	102-116-10
Darrell Royal, Texas (1957-76)	20	167-47-5	184-60-5
Pie Vann, Southern Miss. (1949-68)	20 #	139-59-2	139-59-2
Chris Ault, Nevada (1976-92, 1994-95)	19 #	163-63-1	163-63-1
Frank Broyles, Arkansas (1958-76)	19	144-58-5	149-62-6
Robert Higgins, Penn St. (1930-48)	19	91-57-10	123-79-18
Red Blaik, Army (1941-58)	18	121-33-10	166-48-14
Rich Brooks, Oregon (1977-94)	18 #	91-109-4	91-109-4
Ray Eliot, Illinois (1942-59)	18	83-73-11	102-82-13
Don James, Washington (1975-92)	18	151-59-2	176-78-3
Charlie McClendon, LSU (1962-79)	18 #	137-59-7	137-59-7
Jim Owens, Washington (1957-74)	18 #	99-82-6	99-82-6
*Jim Sweeney, Fresno St. (1976-77, 1980-95)	18	139-68-3	196-147-4
Murray Warmath, Minnesota (1954-71)	18	87-78-7	97-84-10
Earle Edwards, North Caro. St. (1954-70)	17 #	77-88-8	77-88-8
*Hayden Fry, Iowa (1979-95)	17	124-73-6	213-162-10
Bud Wilkinson, Oklahoma (1947-63)	17 #	145-29-4	145-29-4
Bob Blackman, Dartmouth (1955-70)	16	104-37-3	168-112-7
Len Casanova, Oregon (1951-66)	16	82-73-8	104-94-11
Herb Deromedi, Central Mich. (1978-93)	16 #	110-55-10	110-55-10
Gil Dobie, Cornell (1920-35)	16	82-36-7	180-45-15
Rip Engle, Penn St. (1950-65)	16	104-48-4	132-68-8
Andy Gustafson, Miami (Fla.) (1948-63)	16	93-65-3	115-78-4
John Heisman, Georgia Tech (1904-19)	16	102-29-6	185-70-17
Howard Jones, Southern Cal (1925-40)	16	121-36-13	194-64-21
*Johnny Majors, Tennessee (1977-92)	16	116-62-8	181-130-10
John McKay, Southern Cal (1960-75)	16 #	127-40-8	127-40-8
*Don Nehlen, West Va. (1980-95)	16	115-68-4	168-103-8
Barry Switzer, Oklahoma (1973-88)	16 #	157-29-4	157-29-4
Wallace Wade, Duke (1931-41, 1946-50)	16	110-36-7	171-49-10
Rex Enright, South Caro. (1938-42, 1946-55)	15 #	64-69-7	64-69-7
Morley Jennings, Baylor (1926-40)	15	83-60-6	153-75-18
Ray Morrison, Southern Methodist (1915-16, 1922-34)	15	84-44-22	155-130-33
Bill Murray, Duke (1951-65)	15	83-51-9	142-67-11
Jock Sutherland, Pittsburgh (1924-38)	15	111-20-12	144-28-14
Frank Thomas, Alabama (1931-42, 1944-46)	15	115-24-7	141-33-9

**Active coach. #Never coached at any other college.*

UPI/Bettmann photo

In addition to holding a host of major-college records for the quality of his coaching, Amos Alonzo Stagg possesses several records for quantity. He coached the most games (548), most years (57) and most years at one school (41 at Chicago).

Active Coaching Longevity Records

(Minimum Five Years as a Division I-A Head Coach; Includes Bowl Games)

MOST GAMES

Games	Coach, School(s) and Years
385	Hayden Fry, Southern Methodist 1962-72, North Texas 1973-78, Iowa 1979-95
353	Joe Paterno, Penn St., 1966-95
347	Jim Sweeney, Montana St. 1963-67, Washington St. 1968-75, Fresno St. 1976-77 and 1980-95
344	Bobby Bowden, Samford 1959-62, West Va. 1970-75, Florida St. 1976-95
321	Johnny Majors, Iowa St. 1968-72, Pittsburgh 1973-76 and 1993-95, Tennessee 1977-92
307	Lou Holtz, William & Mary 1969-71, North Caro. St. 1972-75, Arkansas 1977-83, Minnesota 1984-85, Notre Dame 1986-95
297	LaVell Edwards, Brigham Young 1972-95
290	Bill Mallory, Miami (Ohio) 1969-73, Colorado 1974-78, Northern Ill. 1980-83, Indiana 1984-95
282	Jim Wacker, Texas Lutheran 1971-75, North Dak. St. 1976-78, Southwest Tex. St. 1979-82, Texas Christian 1983-91, Minnesota 1992-95
281	Tom Osborne, Nebraska 1973-95
279	Don Nehlen, Bowling Green 1968-76, West Va. 1980-95
269	Al Molde, Sioux Falls 1971-72, Minn.-Morris 1973-79, Central Mo. St. 1980-82, Eastern Ill. 1983-86, Western Mich. 1987-95
266	George Welsh, Navy 1973-81, Virginia 1982-95

MOST YEARS

Years	Coach, School(s) and Years
34	Hayden Fry, Southern Methodist 1962-72, North Texas 1973-78, Iowa 1979-95
31	Jim Sweeney, Montana St. 1963-67, Washington St. 1968-75, Fresno St. 1976-77 and 1980-95
30	Bobby Bowden, Samford 1959-62, West Va. 1970-75, Florida St. 1976-95
30	Joe Paterno, Penn St. 1966-95
28	Johnny Majors, Iowa St. 1968-72, Pittsburgh 1973-76 and 1993-95, Tennessee 1977-92
26	Lou Holtz, William & Mary 1969-71, North Caro. St. 1972-75, Arkansas 1977-83, Minnesota 1984-85, Notre Dame 1986-95
26	Bill Mallory, Miami (Ohio) 1969-73, Colorado 1974-78, Northern Ill. 1980-83, Indiana 1984-95
25	Al Molde, Sioux Falls 1971-72, Minn.-Morris 1973-79, Central Mo. St. 1980-82, Eastern Ill. 1983-86, Western Mich. 1987-95
25	Don Nehlen, Bowling Green 1968-76, West Va. 1980-95
25	Jim Wacker, Texas Lutheran 1971-75, North Dak. St. 1976-78, Southwest Tex. St. 1979-82, Texas Christian 1983-91, Minnesota 1992-95
24	LaVell Edwards, Brigham Young 1972-95
23	Tom Osborne, Nebraska 1973-95
23	George Welsh, Navy 1973-81, Virginia 1982-95
21	Jim Hess, Angelo St. 1974-81, Stephen F. Austin 1982-88, New Mexico St. 1990-95
19	John Cooper, Tulsa 1977-84, Arizona 1985-87, Ohio St. 1988-95
19	Larry Smith, Tulane 1976-79, Arizona 1980-86, Southern Cal 1987-92, Missouri 1994-95
19	Dick Tomey, Hawaii 1977-86, Arizona 1987-95
18	Jackie Sherrill, Washington St. 1976, Pittsburgh 1977-81, Texas A&M 1982-88, Mississippi St. 1991-95
17	Ken Hatfield, Air Force 1979-83, Arkansas 1984-89, Clemson 1990-93, Rice 1994-95
16	Bill Curry, Georgia Tech 1980-86, Alabama 1987-89, Kentucky 1990-95
16	John Ralston, Utah St. 1959-62, Stanford 1963-71, San Jose St. 1993-95
16	Bruce Snyder, Utah St. 1976-82, California 1987-91, Arizona St. 1992-95

MOST YEARS AT CURRENT SCHOOL

Years	Coach, School and Years
30	Joe Paterno, Penn St. 1966-95
24	LaVell Edwards, Brigham Young 1972-95
23	Tom Osborne, Nebraska 1973-95
20	Bobby Bowden, Florida St. 1976-95
18	Jim Sweeney, Fresno St. 1976-77, 1980-95
17	Hayden Fry, Iowa 1979-95
16	Don Nehlen, West Va. 1980-95
14	George Welsh, Virginia 1982-95
12	Fisher DeBerry, Air Force 1984-95
12	Bill Mallory, Indiana 1984-95
10	Spike Dykes, Texas Tech 1986-95
10	Lou Holtz, Notre Dame 1986-95
10	John Robinson, Southern Cal 1976-82, 1993-95
10	Nelson Stokley, Southwestern La. 1986-95
Less Than 5 Years as Division I-A Head Coach:	
11	Gene McDowell, Central Fla. 1985-95

MOST SCHOOLS

Schools	Coach, Schools and Years
5	Watson Brown, Austin Peay 1979-80, Cincinnati 1983, Rice 1984-85, Vanderbilt 1986-90, Ala.-Birmingham 1995
5	Lou Holtz, William & Mary 1969-71, North Caro. St. 1972-75, Arkansas 1977-83, Minnesota 1984-85, Notre Dame 1986-95
5	Al Molde, Sioux Falls 1971-72, Minn.-Morris 1973-79, Central Mo. St. 1980-82, Eastern Ill. 1983-86, Western Mich. 1987-95
5	Jim Wacker, Texas Lutheran 1971-75, North Dak. St. 1976-78, Southwest Tex. St. 1979-82, Texas Christian 1983-91, Minnesota 1992-95
4	Ken Hatfield, Air Force 1979-83, Arkansas 1984-89, Clemson 1990-93, Rice 1994-95
4	Bill Mallory, Miami (Ohio) 1969-73, Colorado 1974-78, Northern Ill. 1980-83, Indiana 1984-95
4	Jackie Sherrill, Washington St. 1976, Pittsburgh 1977-81, Texas A&M 1982-88, Mississippi St. 1991-95
4	Larry Smith, Tulane 1976-79, Arizona 1980-86, Southern Cal 1987-92, Missouri 1994-95
3	Bobby Bowden, Samford 1959-62, West Va. 1970-75, Florida St. 1976-95
3	Mack Brown, Appalachian St. 1983, Tulane 1985-87, North Caro. 1988-95
3	John Cooper, Tulsa 1977-84, Arizona St. 1985-87, Ohio St. 1988-95
3	Bill Curry, Georgia Tech 1980-86, Alabama 1987-89, Kentucky 1990-95
3	Hayden Fry, Southern Methodist 1962-72, North Texas 1973-78, Iowa 1979-95
3	Fred Goldsmith, Slippery Rock 1981, Rice 1989-93, Duke 1994-95
3	Jim Hess, Angelo St. 1974-81, Stephen F. Austin 1982-88, New Mexico St. 1990-95
3	John Mackovic, Wake Forest 1978-80, Illinois 1988-91, Texas 1992-95
3	Johnny Majors, Iowa St. 1968-72, Pittsburgh 1973-76 and 1993-95, Tennessee 1977-92
3	John Ralston, Utah St. 1959-62, Stanford 1963-71, San Jose St. 1993-95
3	Bruce Snyder, Utah St. 1976-82, California 1987-91, Arizona St. 1992-95
3	Jim Sweeney, Montana St. 1963-67, Washington St. 1968-75, Fresno St. 1976-77 and 1980-95
Less Than 5 Years as Division I-A Head Coach:	
4	Dennis Franchione, S'western (Kan.) 1981-82, Pittsburg St. 1985-89, Southwest Tex. St. 1990-91, New Mexico 1992-95
3	Terry Bowden, Salem Teikyo 1984-86, Samford 1987-92, Auburn 1993-95
3	Buddy Teevens, Maine 1985-86, Dartmouth 1987-91, Tulane 1992-95
3	Bob Toledo, UC Riverside 1974-75, Pacific (Cal.) 1979-82, UCLA 1996

Major-College Brother vs. Brother Coaching Matchups

(Each brother's victories in parentheses)

Mack Brown, Tulane (2), vs. Watson, Vanderbilt (0), 1986-87

Vince Dooley, Georgia (1), vs. Bill, North Caro. (0), 1971 Gator Bowl

Bump Elliott, Michigan (6), vs. Pete, Illinois (1), 1960-66

Howard Jones, Yale 1909 and Iowa 1922 (2), vs. Tad, Syracuse 1909 and Yale 1922 (0)

Annual Division I-A Head-Coaching Changes

Year	Changes	Teams	Pct.
1947	27	125	.216
1948	24	121	.198
1949	22	114	.193
1950	23	119	.193
1951	23	115	.200
1952	15	113	.133
1953	18	111	.162
1954	14	103	.136
1955	23	103	.223
1956	19	105	.181
1957	22	108	.204
1958	18	109	.165
1959	18	110	.164
1960	18	114	.158
1961	11	112	.098
1962	20	119	.168
1963	12	118	.102
1964	14	116	.121
1965	16	114	.140
1966	16	116	.138
1967	21	114	.184
1968	14	114	.123
1969	22	118	.186
1970	13	118	.110
1971	27	119	.227
1972	17	121	.140
1973	36	126	†.286
1974	28	128	.219
1975	18	134	.134
1976	23	137	.168

Year	Changes	Teams	Pct.	Year	Changes	Teams	Pct.	Year	Changes	Teams	Pct.
1977	27	144	.188	1984	16	105	.152	1991	16	106	.151
1978	27	139	.194	1985	15	105	.143	1992	16	107	.150
1979	26	139	.187	1986	22	105	.210	1993	15	106	.142
1980	27	139	.194	1987	24	104	.231	1994	15	107	.140
1981	17	137	.123	1988	9	104	.087	1995	21	108	.194
1982	17	97	.175	1989	19	106	.179	1996	9	111	*.081
1983	22	105	.210	1990	20	106	.189				

**Record low. †Record high.*

Records of Division I-A First-Year Head Coaches

(Coaches with no previous head-coaching experience at a four-year college.)

							Team's Previous Season Record				
Year	No.	Won	Lost	Tied	Pct.	Bowl Record	Won	Lost	Tied	Pct.	Bowl Record
1948	14	56	68	7	.454	0-1	76	52	8	.588	2-1
1949	8	26	49	3	.353	0-1	35	41	4	.463	0-0
1950	10	37	56	4	.402	0-0	49	42	6	.536	2-0
1951	13	60	67	4	.473	1-2	39	88	7	.317	1-1
1952	8	31	42	3	.428	0-0	38	40	0	.487	0-0
1953	8	29	45	5	.399	0-0	48	28	7	.620	1-2
1954	8	31	43	4	.423	0-0	40	33	7	.543	1-0
1955	9	36	50	4	.422	0-1	36	52	1	.410	0-0
1956	14	47	80	11	.380	1-0	61	68	6	.474	0-1
1957	9	32	50	6	.398	0-0	44	42	2	.511	0-0
1958	7	26	44	0	.371	0-0	37	31	2	.543	0-0
1959	8	34	43	2	.443	0-0	41	35	2	.538	0-1
1960	14	54	80	5	.406	1-0	57	78	2	.423	0-0
1961	8	26	50	0	.342	0-0	38	38	2	.500	0-0
1962	12	40	74	4	.356	2-0	52	66	2	.442	1-1
1963	8	23	49	6	.333	0-0	32	46	1	.411	0-1
1964	12	45	67	7	.408	1-1	42	71	4	.376	0-0
1965	8	28	47	2	.377	0-0	36	42	1	.462	0-0
1966	10	46	50	3	.480	0-0	38	56	5	.409	0-0
1967	18	58	114	5	.342	1-0	60	116	4	.344	0-1
1968	6	19	40	1	.325	0-0	20	38	2	.350	0-0
1969	15	49	90	1	.353	0-0	62	85	3	.423	0-1
1970	10	45	61	1	.425	1-0	46	54	0	.460	0-2
1971	12	57	72	0	.442	1-1	64	61	0	.512	0-1
1972	11	57	64	1	.471	1-0	53	64	2	.454	1-0
1973	14	84	63	8	.568	1-0	83	71	2	.538	3-0
1974	17	63	116	5	.356	1-0	78	105	1	.427	1-0
1975	10	38	72	0	.345	0-1	43	67	0	.391	0-0
1976	15	57	109	2	.345	3-1	72	91	5	.443	3-1
1977	14	55	94	5	.373	1-0	66	88	3	.430	0-2
1978	16	68	104	3	.397	0-0	77	96	3	.446	0-1
1979	11	53	66	3	.447	0-0	66	57	1	.536	2-2
1980	12	54	75	2	.420	0-0	60	68	3	.469	1-0
1981	6	25	40	0	.385	0-0	31	35	1	.470	0-1
1982	10	51	59	1	.464	0-1	58	57	2	.504	2-2
1983	12	51	82	2	.385	1-0	60	73	1	.451	1-1
1984	7	47	28	1	*.625	2-1	45	35	1	.562	3-0
1985	5	19	37	0	.339	0-0	20	32	4	.393	0-0
1986	12	53	81	0	.396	0-1	56	76	3	.426	1-1
1987	9	51	49	3	.510	1-1	52	50	1	.510	0-2
1988	4	25	20	0	.556	1-0	22	23	1	.489	1-1
1989	7	32	49	1	.396	0-2	39	43	0	.476	1-2
1990	9	46	42	2	.522	1-1	41	48	1	.461	0-1
1991	10	38	72	1	.347	1-0	46	64	2	.420	0-2
1992	4	15	20	1	.431	0-0	32	14	0	.696	1-1
1993	8	29	58	2	.337	0-1	41	51	1	.446	2-2
1994	7	30	40	2	.431	2-1	40	39	0	.506	1-0
1995	10	57	56	2	.504	1-2	45	65	3	.412	2-1

**Record percentage for first-year coaches. 1984 coaches and their records, with bowl game indicated by an asterisk (*): Pat Jones, Oklahoma St. (*10-2-0); Galen Hall, Florida (8-0-0, took over from Charley Pell after three games); Bill Arnsparger, LSU (8-*3-1); Fisher DeBerry, Air Force (*8-4-0); Dick Anderson, Rutgers (7-3-0); Mike Sheppard, Long Beach St. (4-7-0); Ron Chismar, Wichita St. (2-9-0).*

Most Victories by First-Year Head Coaches

Coach, College, Year	W	L	T
Rick Neuheisel, Colorado, 1995	*11	1	0
Gary Blackney, Bowling Green, 1991	*11	1	0
John Robinson, Southern Cal, 1976	*11	1	0
Bill Battle, Tennessee, 1970	*11	1	0
Dick Crum, Miami (Ohio), 1974	*10	0	1
Barry Switzer, Oklahoma, 1973	10	0	1
John Jenkins, Houston, 1990	10	1	0
Dwight Wallace, Ball St., 1978	10	1	0
Chuck Fairbanks, Oklahoma, 1967	*10	1	0
Mike Archer, LSU, 1987	*10	1	1
Curley Hallman, Southern Miss., 1988	*10	2	0
Pat Jones, Oklahoma St., 1984	*10	2	0
Earle Bruce, Tampa, 1972	*10	2	0
Billy Kinard, Mississippi, 1971	*10	2	0

**Bowl game victory included.*

Only first-year coach to win a national championship: Bennie Oosterbaan, Michigan, 1948 (9-0-0).

Division I-AA Coaching Records

Winningest Active Division I-AA Coaches

(Minimum Five Years as a Division I-A and/or Division I-AA Head Coach; Record at Four-Year Colleges Only)

BY PERCENTAGE

Coach, College	Years	Won	Lost	Tied	*Pct.	Playoffs# W-L-T
Roy Kidd, Eastern Ky.	32	266	94	8	.734	17-15-0
Terry Allen, Northern Iowa	7	63	24	0	.724	4-6-0
Eddie Robinson, Grambling	53	402	149	15	.724	10-8-0
Tubby Raymond, Delaware	30	250	97	3	.719	18-12-0
Bobby Keasler, McNeese St.	6	53	21	2	.711	5-5-0
Steve Tosches, Princeton	9	61	27	2	.689	0-0-0
Jim Tressel, Youngstown St.	10	87	41	2	.677	16-4-0
Houston Markham, Alabama St.	9	62	31	5	.658	1-0-0
Cardell Jones, Alcorn St.	5	34	18	3	.645	0-2-0
Bill Hayes, North Caro. A&T	20	141	78	2	.643	1-5-0
Boots Donnelly, Middle Tenn. St.	19	139	78	1	.640	6-7-0
Bill Collick, Delaware St.	11	75	43	0	.636	0-0-0
Bill Bowes, New Hampshire	24	158	90	5	.634	1-4-0
Carmen Cozza, Yale	31	177	111	5	.613	0-0-0
Willie Jeffries, South Caro. St.	23	148	98	6	.599	3-3-0
Andy Talley, Villanova	16	95	64	2	.596	1-4-0
Ron Randleman, Sam Houston St.	27	166	115	6	.589	3-5-1
Jimmye Laycock, William & Mary	16	105	74	2	.586	1-4-0
Jim Hofher, Cornell	6	35	25	0	.583	0-0-0
Sam Rutigliano, Liberty	7	44	32	0	.579	0-0-0
Jack McClarien, Bethune-Cookman	14	69	51	3	.573	0-0-0
Jim Reid, Richmond	7	43	32	3	.571	0-2-0
Steve Wilson, Howard	7	44	34	0	.564	0-1-0
Bill Russo, Lafayette	18	103	85	4	.547	0-1-0
Charlie Taaffe, Citadel	9	55	47	1	.539	1-3-0
Bill Thomas, Texas Southern	7	40	35	3	.532	1-1-0
Dan Allen, Holy Cross	6	36	33	0	.522	1-2-0
Jerry Moore, Appalachian St.	14	82	77	2	.516	2-5-0
Bob Spoo, Eastern Ill.	9	52	49	1	.515	1-2-0
Dave Arslanian, Weber St.	7	40	38	0	.513	0-1-0
Sam Goodwin, Northwestern St.	15	82	80	4	.506	1-1-0
Stephen Axman, Northern Ariz.	6	33	33	0	.500	0-0-0
Randy Ball, Western Ill.	6	33	33	1	.500	0-1-0

Coach, College	Years	Won	Lost	Tied	*Pct.	Playoffs# W-L-T
Floyd Keith, Rhode Island	7	35	38	2	.480	0-0-0
Dennis Raetz, Indiana St.	16	84	93	1	.475	1-2-0
Jack Harbaugh, Western Ky.	12	55	71	3	.438	0-0-0
Larry Dorsey, Mississippi Val.	6	25	34	3	.427	0-0-0
Steve Hodgin, Western Caro.	6	27	38	0	.415	0-0-0
John Mumford, Southeast Mo. St.	6	27	39	0	.409	0-0-0
Tim Murphy, Harvard	9	38	59	1	.393	0-1-0
Ray Tellier, Columbia	12	37	78	3	.326	0-1-0
Barry Gallup, Northeastern	5	17	37	1	.318	0-0-0
Roy Gregory, Austin Peay	5	16	39	0	.291	0-0-0
Less Than 5 Years as Division I-A and/or Division I-AA Head Coach (school followed by years in I-A or I-AA, includes record at all four-year colleges):						
Mike Kelly, Dayton (3)	15	145	27	1	.841	13-8-0
Al Bagnoli, Pennsylvania (4)	14	119	25	0	.826	7-6-0
Larry Blakeney, Troy St. (3)	5	46	13	1	.775	2-3-0
Pete Richardson, Southern-B.R. (3)	8	69	21	1	.764	1-3-0
Joe Gardi, Hofstra (3)	6	48	15	2	.754	2-2-0
Walt Hameline, Wagner (3)	15	117	39	2	.747	6-2-0
Billy Joe, Florida A&M (2)	22	184	67	4	.729	12-6-0
Joe Taylor, Hampton (1)	13	100	36	4	.729	1-5-0
Mark Whipple, Brown (2)	8	60	25	0	.706	3-2-0
Pokey Allen, Boise St. (3)	10	85	40	2	.677	13-6-0
Bill Burgess, Jacksonville St. (1)	11	83	40	4	.669	12-4-0
Mike Rasmussen, St. Mary's (Cal.) (3)	6	39	20	1	.658	0-0-0
Rob Ash, Drake (3)	16	98	57	5	.628	0-0-0
Bob Ricca, St. John's (N.Y.) (3)	18	113	69	1	.620	1-0-0
Robin Cooper, Evansville (3)	8	46	29	0	.613	0-0-0
Mike Cavan, East Tenn. St. (4)	10	57	46	2	.552	0-0-0
Mike Ayers, Wofford (4)	11	62	58	2	.516	0-2-0
Matt Ballard, Morehead St. (2)	8	37	44	1	.457	0-0-0
Don McLeary, Tenn.-Martin (4)	12	59	71	0	.454	1-1-0
Harold Crocker, Iona (3)	11	48	60	1	.445	0-1-0
Tom Horne, Valparaiso (3)	10	39	61	2	.392	0-0-0
David Dowd, Charleston So. (3)	5	9	42	0	.176	0-0-0

**Ties computed as half won and half lost. Overall record includes bowl and playoff games. #Playoffs include all divisional championships as well as bowl games, conference playoff games and NAIA playoffs.*

BY VICTORIES

(Minimum 100 Victories)

Coach, College, Winning Percentage	Won
Eddie Robinson, Grambling .724	402
Roy Kidd, Eastern Ky. .734	266
Tubby Raymond, Delaware .719	250
Carmen Cozza, Yale .613	177
Ron Randleman, Sam Houston St. .589	166
Bill Bowes, New Hampshire .634	158
Willie Jeffries, South Caro. St. .599	148
Bill Hayes, North Caro. A&T .643	141
Boots Donnelly, Middle Tenn. St. .640	139
Jimmye Laycock, William & Mary .586	105
Bill Russo, Lafayette .547	103
Less Than 5 Yrs. as a I-A/I-AA Head Coach:	
Billy Joe, Florida A&M .729	184
Mike Kelly, Dayton .841	145
Al Bagnoli, Pennsylvania .826	119
Walt Hameline, Wagner .747	117
Bob Ricca, St. John's (N.Y.) .620	113
Joe Taylor, Hampton .729	100

Annual Division I-AA Head-Coaching Changes

(From the 1982 reorganization of the division for parallel comparisons)

Year	Changes	Teams	Pct.
1982	7	92	.076
1983	17	84	.202
1984	14	87	.161
1985	11	87	.126
1986	18	86	.209
1987	13	87	.149
1988	12	88	.136
1989	21	89	†.236
1990	16	89	.180
1991	6	87	*.069
1992	14	89	.157
1993	13	#115	.113
1994	17	116	.147
1995	11	119	.092
1996	11	118	.093

**Record low. †Record high. #Twenty-seven teams switched from Divisions II & III to I-AA.*

Division I-AA Championship Coaches

All coaches who have coached teams in the Division I-AA championship playoffs since 1978 are listed here with their playoff record, alma mater and year graduated, team, year coached, opponent, and score.

Dan Allen (1-2) (Hanover '78)
Boston U. 93 Northern Iowa 27-21 (2 OT)
Boston U. 93 Idaho 14-21
Boston U. 94 Eastern Ky. 23-30

Pokey Allen (3-1) (Utah '65)
Boise St. 94 North Texas 42-20
Boise St. 94 Appalachian St. 17-14
Boise St. 94 Marshall 28-24
Boise St. 94 Youngstown St. 14-28

Terry Allen (4-6) (Northern Iowa '79)
Northern Iowa 90 Boise St. 3-20
Northern Iowa 91 Weber St. 38-21
Northern Iowa 91 Marshall 13-41
Northern Iowa 92 Eastern Wash. 17-14
Northern Iowa 92 McNeese St. 29-7
Northern Iowa 92 Youngstown St. 7-19
Northern Iowa 93 Boston U. 21-27 (2 OT)
Northern Iowa 94 Montana 20-23
Northern Iowa 95 Murray St. 35-34
Northern Iowa 95 Marshall 24-41

Dave Arnold (3-0) (Drake '67)
Montana St. 84 Arkansas St. 31-24
Montana St. 84 Rhode Island 32-20
Montana St. 84* Louisiana Tech 19-6

Dave Arslanian (0-1) (Weber St. '72)
Weber St. 91 Northern Iowa 21-38

Chris Ault (9-7) (Nevada '68)
Nevada 78 Massachusetts 21-44
Nevada 79 Eastern Ky. 30-33
Nevada 83 Idaho St. 27-20
Nevada 83 North Texas 20-17 (OT)
Nevada 83 Southern Ill. 7-23
Nevada 85 Arkansas St. 24-23
Nevada 85 Furman 12-35
Nevada 86 Idaho 27-7
Nevada 86 Tennessee St. 33-6
Nevada 86 Ga. Southern 38-48
Nevada 90 Northeast La. 27-14
Nevada 90 Furman 42-35 (3 OT)
Nevada 90 Boise St. 59-52 (3 OT)
Nevada 90 Ga. Southern 13-36
Nevada 91 McNeese St. 22-16
Nevada 91 Youngstown St. 28-30

Randy Ball (0-1) (Truman St. '73)
Western Ill. 91 Marshall 17-20 (OT)

Frank Beamer (0-1) (Virginia Tech '69)
Murray St. 86 Eastern Ill. 21-28

Larry Blakeney (2-3) (Auburn '70)
Troy St. 93 Stephen F. Austin 42-20
Troy St. 93 McNeese St. 35-28
Troy St. 93 Marshall 21-24
Troy St. 94 James Madison 26-45
Troy St. 95 Ga. Southern 21-24

Terry Bowden (2-2) (West Va. '78)
Samford 91 New Hampshire 29-13
Samford 91 James Madison 24-21
Samford 91 Youngstown St. 0-10
Samford 92 Delaware 21-56

Bill Bowes (0-2) (Penn St. '65)
New Hampshire 91 Samford 13-29
New Hampshire 94 Appalachian St. 10-17 (OT)

Jesse Branch (1-2) (Arkansas '64)
Southwest Mo. St. 89 Maine 38-35
Southwest Mo. St. 89 Stephen F. Austin 25-55
Southwest Mo. St. 90 Idaho 35-41

Billy Brewer (1-1) (Mississippi '61)
Louisiana Tech 82 South Caro. St. 38-3
Louisiana Tech 82 Delaware 0-17

James Carson (0-1) (Jackson St. '63)
Jackson St. 95 Marshall 8-38

Rick Carter (0-1) (Earlham '65)
Holy Cross 83 Western Caro. 21-28

Marino Casem (0-1) (Xavier, La. '56)
Alcorn St. 84 Louisiana Tech 21-44

George Chaump (4-2) (Bloomsburg '58)
Marshall 87 James Madison 41-12
Marshall 87 Weber St. 51-23
Marshall 87 Appalachian St. 24-10
Marshall 87 Northeast La. 42-43
Marshall 88 North Texas 7-0
Marshall 88 Furman 9-13

Pat Collins (4-0) (Louisiana Tech '63)
Northeast La. 87 North Texas 30-9
Northeast La. 87 Eastern Ky. 33-32
Northeast La. 87 Northern Iowa 44-41 (OT)
Northeast La. 87* Marshall 43-42

Archie Cooley Jr. (0-1) (Jackson St. '62)
Mississippi Val. 84 Louisiana Tech 19-66

Bruce Craddock (0-1) (Truman St. '66)
Western Ill. 88 Western Ky. 32-35

Jim Criner (3-1) (Cal Poly Pomona '61)
Boise St. 80 Grambling 14-9
Boise St. 80* Eastern Ky. 31-29
Boise St. 81 Jackson St. 19-7
Boise St. 81 Eastern Ky. 17-23

Bill Davis (2-2) (Johnson Smith '65)
South Caro. St. 81 Tennessee St. 26-25
South Caro. St. 81 Idaho St. 12-41
South Caro. St. 82 Furman 17-0
South Caro. St. 82 Louisiana Tech 3-38

Rey Dempsey (3-0) (Geneva '58)
Southern Ill. 83 Indiana St. 23-7
Southern Ill. 83 Nevada 23-7
Southern Ill. 83* Western Caro. 43-7

Jim Dennison (0-1) (Wooster '60)
Akron 85 Rhode Island 27-35

Jim Donnan (15-4) (North Caro. St. '67)
Marshall 91 Western Ill. 20-17 (OT)
Marshall 91 Northern Iowa 41-13
Marshall 91 Eastern Ky. 14-7

Marshall................. 91 Youngstown St. 17-25
Marshall................. 92 Eastern Ky. 44-0
Marshall................. 92 Middle Tenn. St. 35-21
Marshall................. 92 Delaware 28-7
Marshall................. 92* Youngstown St. 31-28
Marshall................. 93 Howard 28-14
Marshall................. 93 Delaware 34-31
Marshall................. 93 Troy St. 24-21
Marshall................. 93 Youngstown St. 5-17
Marshall................. 94 Middle Tenn. St. 49-14
Marshall................. 94 James Madison 28-21 (OT)
Marshall................. 94 Boise St. 24-28
Marshall................. 95 Jackson St. 38-8
Marshall................. 95 Northern Iowa 41-24
Marshall................. 95 McNeese St. 25-13
Marshall................. 95 Montana 20-22

Boots Donnelly (6-7) (Middle Tenn. St. '65)
Middle Tenn. St. ..... 84 Eastern Ky. 27-10
Middle Tenn. St. ..... 84 Indiana St. 42-41 (3 OT)
Middle Tenn. St. ..... 84 Louisiana Tech 13-21
Middle Tenn. St. ..... 85 Ga. Southern 21-28
Middle Tenn. St. ..... 89 Appalachian St. 24-21
Middle Tenn. St. ..... 89 Ga. Southern 3-45
Middle Tenn. St. ..... 90 Jackson St. 28-7
Middle Tenn. St. ..... 90 Boise St. 13-20
Middle Tenn. St. ..... 91 Sam Houston St. 20-19 (OT)
Middle Tenn. St. ..... 91 Eastern Ky. 13-23
Middle Tenn. St. ..... 92 Appalachian St. 35-10
Middle Tenn. St. ..... 92 Marshall 21-35
Middle Tenn. St. ..... 94 Marshall 14-49

Larry Donovan (0-1) (Nebraska '64)
Montana .... 82 Idaho 7-21

Fred Dunlap (1-2) (Colgate '50)
Colgate.................. 82 Boston U. 21-7
Colgate.................. 82 Delaware 13-20
Colgate.................. 83 Western Caro. 23-24

Dennis Erickson (1-2) (Montana St. '70)
Idaho..................... 82 Montana 21-7
Idaho..................... 82 Eastern Ky. 30-38
Idaho..................... 85 Eastern Wash. 38-42

Mo Forte (0-1) (Minnesota '71)
North Caro. A&T .... 86 Ga. Southern 21-52

Joe Gardi (0-1) (Maryland '60)
Hofstra.................. 95 Delaware 17-38

Keith Gilbertson (2-3) (Central Wash. '71)
Idaho..................... 86 Nevada 7-27
Idaho..................... 87 Weber St. 30-59
Idaho..................... 88 Montana 38-19
Idaho..................... 88 Northwestern St. 38-30
Idaho..................... 88 Furman 7-38

Sam Goodwin (1-1) (Henderson St. '66)
Northwestern St. ..... 88 Boise St. 22-13
Northwestern St. ..... 88 Idaho 30-38

W. C. Gorden (0-9) (Tennessee St. '52)
Jackson St. .... 78 Florida A&M 10-15
Jackson St. .... 81 Boise St. 7-19
Jackson St. .... 82 Eastern Ill. 13-16 (OT)
Jackson St. .... 85 Ga. Southern 0-27
Jackson St. .... 86 Tennessee St. 23-32
Jackson St. .... 87 Arkansas St. 32-35
Jackson St. .... 88 Stephen F. Austin 0-24
Jackson St. .... 89 Montana 7-48
Jackson St. .... 90 Middle Tenn. St. 7-28

Mike Gottfried (0-1) (Morehead St. '66)
Murray St............... 79 Lehigh 9-28

Lynn Graves (%3-1) (Stephen F. Austin '65)
Stephen F. Austin .... 89% Grambling 59-56
Stephen F. Austin .... 89% Southwest Mo. St. 55-25
Stephen F. Austin .... 89% Furman 21-19
Stephen F. Austin .... 89% Ga. Southern 34-37

Bob Griffin (2-3) (Southern Conn. St. '63)
Rhode Island .... 81 Idaho St. 0-51
Rhode Island .... 84 Richmond 23-17
Rhode Island .... 84 Montana St. 20-32
Rhode Island .... 85 Akron 35-27
Rhode Island .... 85 Furman 15-59

Skip Hall (2-2) (Concordia-M'head '66)
Boise St.................. 88 Northwestern St. 13-22
Boise St.................. 90 Northern Iowa 20-3
Boise St.................. 90 Middle Tenn. St. 20-13
Boise St.................. 90 Nevada 52-59 (3 OT)

Bill Hayes (0-1) (N.C. Central '64)
North Caro. A&T .... 92 Citadel 0-44

Jim Hess (1-1) (Southeastern Okla. '59)
Stephen F. Austin .... 88 Jackson St. 24-0
Stephen F. Austin .... 88 Ga. Southern 6-27

Rudy Hubbard (2-0) (Ohio St. '68)
Florida A&M .... 78 Jackson St. 15-10
Florida A&M .... 78* Massachusetts 35-28

Sonny Jackson (1-1) (Nicholls St. '63)
Nicholls St............. 86 Appalachian St. 28-26
Nicholls St............. 86 Ga. Southern 31-55

Cardell Jones (0-2) (Alcorn St. '65)
Alcorn St................ 92 Northeast La. 27-78
Alcorn St................ 94 Youngstown St. 20-63

Bobby Keasler (5-5) (Northeast La. '70)
McNeese St. .... 91 Nevada 16-22
McNeese St. .... 92 Idaho 23-20
McNeese St. .... 92 Northern Iowa 7-29
McNeese St. .... 93 William & Mary 34-28
McNeese St. .... 93 Troy St. 28-35
McNeese St. .... 94 Idaho 38-21
McNeese St. .... 94 Montana 28-30
McNeese St. .... 95 Idaho 33-3
McNeese St. .... 95 Delaware 52-18
McNeese St. .... 95 Marshall 13-25

Roy Kidd (16-14) (Eastern Ky. '54)
Eastern Ky............. 79 Nevada 33-30
Eastern Ky............. 79* Lehigh 30-7
Eastern Ky............. 80 Lehigh 23-20
Eastern Ky............. 80 Boise St. 29-31
Eastern Ky............. 81 Delaware 35-28
Eastern Ky............. 81 Boise St. 23-17
Eastern Ky............. 81 Idaho St. 23-34
Eastern Ky............. 82 Idaho St. 38-30
Eastern Ky............. 82 Tennessee St. 13-7
Eastern Ky............. 82* Delaware 17-14
Eastern Ky............. 83 Boston U. 20-24
Eastern Ky............. 84 Middle Tenn. St. 10-27
Eastern Ky............. 86 Furman 23-10
Eastern Ky............. 86 Eastern Ill. 24-22
Eastern Ky............. 86 Arkansas St. 10-24
Eastern Ky............. 87 Western Ky. 40-17
Eastern Ky............. 87 Northeast La. 32-33
Eastern Ky............. 88 Massachusetts 28-17
Eastern Ky............. 88 Western Ky. 41-24
Eastern Ky............. 88 Ga. Southern 17-21
Eastern Ky............. 89 Youngstown St. 24-28
Eastern Ky............. 90 Furman 17-45
Eastern Ky............. 91 Appalachian St. 14-3
Eastern Ky............. 91 Middle Tenn. St. 23-13
Eastern Ky............. 91 Marshall 7-14
Eastern Ky............. 92 Marshall 0-44
Eastern Ky............. 93 Ga. Southern 12-14
Eastern Ky............. 94 Boston U. 30-23
Eastern Ky............. 94 Youngstown St. 15-18
Eastern Ky............. 95 Montana 0-48

Jim Koetter (0-1) (Idaho St. '61)
Idaho St................. 83 Nevada 20-27

Dave Kragthorpe (3-0) (Utah St. '55)
Idaho St................. 81 Rhode Island 51-0
Idaho St................. 81 South Caro. St. 41-12
Idaho St................. 81* Eastern Ky. 34-23

Larry Lacewell (6-4) (Ark.-Monticello '59)
Arkansas St. .... 84 Tenn.-Chatt. 37-10
Arkansas St. .... 84 Montana St. 14-31
Arkansas St. .... 85 Grambling 10-7
Arkansas St. .... 85 Nevada 23-24
Arkansas St. .... 86 Sam Houston St. 48-7
Arkansas St. .... 86 Delaware 55-14
Arkansas St. .... 86 Eastern Ky. 24-10
Arkansas St. .... 86 Ga. Southern 21-48
Arkansas St. .... 87 Jackson St. 35-32
Arkansas St. .... 87 Northern Iowa 28-49

Jimmye Laycock (1-4) (William & Mary '70)
William & Mary...... 86 Delaware 17-51
William & Mary...... 89 Furman 10-24
William & Mary...... 90 Massachusetts 38-0
William & Mary...... 90 Central Fla. 38-52
William & Mary...... 93 McNeese St. 28-34

Tom Lichtenberg (0-1) (Louisville '62)
Maine.................... 89 Southwest Mo. St. 35-38

Gene McDowell (2-2) (Florida St. '63)
Central Fla. .... 90 Youngstown St. 20-17
Central Fla. .... 90 William & Mary 52-38
Central Fla. .... 90 Ga. Southern 7-44
Central Fla. .... 93 Youngstown St. 30-56

John Merritt (†1-2) (Kentucky St. '50)
Tennessee St........... 81† South Caro. St. 25-26 (OT)
Tennessee St........... 82† Eastern Ill. 20-19
Tennessee St........... 82† Eastern Ky. 7-13

Al Molde (1-2) (Gust. Adolphus '66)
Eastern Ill. .... 83 Indiana St. 13-16 (2 OT)
Eastern Ill. .... 86 Murray St. 28-21
Eastern Ill. .... 86 Eastern Ky. 22-24

Jerry Moore (2-5) (Baylor '61)
Appalachian St....... 89 Middle Tenn. St. 21-24
Appalachian St....... 91 Eastern Ky. 3-14
Appalachian St....... 92 Middle Tenn. St. 10-35
Appalachian St....... 94 New Hampshire 17-10 (OT)
Appalachian St....... 94 Boise St. 14-17
Appalachian St....... 95 James Madison 31-24
Appalachian St....... 95 Stephen F. Austin 17-27

Darrell Mudra (4-3) (Peru St. '51)
Eastern Ill. .... 82 Jackson St. 16-13 (OT)
Eastern Ill. .... 82 Tennessee St. 19-20
Northern Iowa .... 85 Eastern Wash. 17-14
Northern Iowa .... 85 Ga. Southern 33-40
Northern Iowa .... 87 Youngstown St. 31-28
Northern Iowa .... 87 Arkansas St. 49-28
Northern Iowa .... 87 Northeast La. 41-44 (OT)

Tim Murphy (0-1) (Springfield '78)
Maine.................... 87 Ga. Southern 28-31 (OT)

Corky Nelson (0-3) (Southwest Tex. St. '64)
North Texas............ 83 Nevada 17-20 (OT)
North Texas............ 87 Northeast La. 9-30
North Texas............ 88 Marshall 0-7

Buddy Nix (0-1) (West Ala. '61)
Tenn.-Chatt. .... 84 Arkansas St. 10-37

Houston Nutt (0-1) (Oklahoma St. '81)
Murray St............... 95 Northern Iowa 34-35

John Pearce (2-2) (East Tex. St. '70)
Stephen F. Austin .... 93 Troy St. 20-42
Stephen F. Austin .... 95 Eastern Ill. 34-29
Stephen F. Austin .... 95 Appalachian St. 27-17
Stephen F. Austin .... 95 Montana 14-70

Bob Pickett (1-1) (Maine '59)
Massachusetts......... 78 Nevada 44-21
Massachusetts......... 78 Florida A&M 28-35

Mike Price (1-1) (Puget Sound '69)
Weber St. .... 87 Idaho 59-30
Weber St. .... 87 Marshall 23-51

Joe Purzycki (0-1) (Delaware '71)
James Madison....... 87 Marshall 12-41

Dennis Raetz (1-2) (Nebraska '68)
Indiana St. .... 83 Eastern Ill. 16-13 (2 OT)
Indiana St. .... 83 Southern Ill. 7-23
Indiana St. .... 84 Middle Tenn. St. 41-42 (3 OT)

Ron Randleman (0-2) (William Penn '64)
Sam Houston St. ..... 86 Arkansas St. 7-48
Sam Houston St. ..... 91 Middle Tenn. St. 19-20 (OT)

Tubby Raymond (7-8) (Michigan '50)
Delaware .... 81 Eastern Ky. 28-35
Delaware .... 82 Colgate 20-13
Delaware .... 82 Louisiana Tech 17-0
Delaware .... 82 Eastern Ky. 14-17
Delaware .... 86 William & Mary 51-17
Delaware .... 86 Arkansas St. 14-55
Delaware .... 88 Furman 7-21
Delaware .... 91 James Madison 35-42 (2 OT)
Delaware .... 92 Samford 56-21
Delaware .... 92 Northeast La. 41-18
Delaware .... 92 Marshall 7-28
Delaware .... 93 Montana 49-48
Delaware .... 93 Marshall 31-34
Delaware .... 95 Hofstra 38-17
Delaware .... 95 McNeese St. 18-52

Don Read (8-4) (Cal St. Sacramento '59)
Montana .... 88 Idaho 19-38
Montana .... 89 Jackson St. 48-7
Montana .... 89 Eastern Ill. 25-19
Montana .... 89 Ga. Southern 15-45
Montana .... 93 Delaware 48-49
Montana .... 94 Northern Iowa 23-20
Montana .... 94 McNeese St. 30-28
Montana .... 94 Youngstown St. 9-28
Montana .... 95 Eastern Ky. 48-0
Montana .... 95 Ga. Southern 45-0
Montana .... 95 Stephen F. Austin 70-14
Montana .... 95* Marshall 22-20

Jim Reid (0-2) (Maine '73)
Massachusetts......... 88 Eastern Ky. 17-28
Massachusetts......... 90 William & Mary 0-38

Dave Roberts (2-5) (Western Caro. '68)
Western Ky. .... 87 Eastern Ky. 17-40
Western Ky. .... 88 Western Ill. 35-32
Western Ky. .... 88 Eastern Ky. 24-41
Northeast La.......... 90 Nevada 14-27
Northeast La.......... 92 Alcorn St. 78-27
Northeast La.......... 92 Delaware 18-41
Northeast La.......... 93 Idaho 31-34

Eddie Robinson (0-3) (Leland '41)
Grambling............. 80 Boise St. 9-14
Grambling............. 85 Arkansas St. 7-10
Grambling............. 89 Stephen F. Austin 56-59

Erk Russell (16-2) (Auburn '49)
Ga. Southern.......... 85 Jackson St. 27-0
Ga. Southern.......... 85 Middle Tenn. St. 28-21
Ga. Southern.......... 85 Northern Iowa 40-33
Ga. Southern.......... 85* Furman 44-42
Ga. Southern.......... 86 North Caro. A&T 52-21
Ga. Southern.......... 86 Nicholls St. 55-31
Ga. Southern.......... 86 Nevada 48-38
Ga. Southern.......... 86* Arkansas St. 48-21
Ga. Southern.......... 87 Maine 31-28 (OT)
Ga. Southern.......... 87 Appalachian St. 0-19
Ga. Southern.......... 88 Citadel 38-20
Ga. Southern.......... 88 Stephen F. Austin 27-6
Ga. Southern.......... 88 Eastern Ky. 21-17
Ga. Southern.......... 88 Furman 12-17
Ga. Southern.......... 89 Villanova 52-36
Ga. Southern.......... 89 Middle Tenn. St. 45-3
Ga. Southern.......... 89 Montana 45-15
Ga. Southern.......... 89* Stephen F. Austin 37-34

Jimmy Satterfield (7-3) (South Caro. '62)
Furman .... 86 Eastern Ky. 10-23
Furman .... 88 Delaware 21-7
Furman .... 88 Marshall 13-9
Furman .... 88 Idaho 38-7
Furman .... 88* Ga. Southern 17-12
Furman .... 89 William & Mary 24-10
Furman .... 89 Youngstown St. 42-23
Furman .... 89 Stephen F. Austin 19-21
Furman .... 90 Eastern Ky. 45-17
Furman .... 90 Nevada 35-42 (3 OT)

Rip Scherer (2-2) (William & Mary '74)
James Madison....... 91 Delaware 42-35 (2 OT)
James Madison....... 91 Samford 21-24
James Madison....... 94 Troy St. 45-26
James Madison....... 94 Marshall 21-28 (OT)

Dal Shealy (1-2) (Carson-Newman '60)
Richmond.............. 84 Boston U. 35-33
Richmond.............. 84 Rhode Island 17-23
Richmond.............. 87 Appalachian St. 3-20

Dick Sheridan (3-3) (South Caro. '64)
Furman .... 82 South Caro. St. 0-17
Furman .... 83 Boston U. 35-16
Furman .... 83 Western Caro. 7-14
Furman .... 85 Rhode Island 59-15
Furman .... 85 Nevada 35-12
Furman .... 85 Ga. Southern 42-44

Matt Simon (0-1) (Eastern N.M. '76)
North Texas........... 94 Boise St. 20-24

John L. Smith (3-5) (Weber St. '71)
Idaho.................... 89 Eastern Ill. 21-38
Idaho.................... 90 Southwest Mo. St. 41-35
Idaho.................... 90 Ga. Southern 27-28
Idaho.................... 92 McNeese St. 20-23
Idaho.................... 93 Northeast La. 34-31
Idaho.................... 93 Boston U. 21-14
Idaho.................... 93 Youngstown St. 16-35
Idaho.................... 94 McNeese St. 21-38

Bob Spoo (1-2) (Purdue '60)
Eastern Ill. .... 89 Idaho 38-21
Eastern Ill. .... 89 Montana 19-25
Eastern Ill. .... 95 Stephen F. Austin 29-34

Tim Stowers (6-2) (Auburn '79)
Ga. Southern.......... 90 Citadel 31-0
Ga. Southern.......... 90 Idaho 28-27
Ga. Southern.......... 90 Central Fla. 44-7
Ga. Southern.......... 90* Nevada 36-13
Ga. Southern.......... 93 Eastern Ky. 14-12
Ga. Southern.......... 93 Youngstown St. 14-34
Ga. Southern.......... 95 Troy St. 24-21
Ga. Southern.......... 95 Montana 0-45

Charlie Taaffe (1-3) (Siena '73)
Citadel.................. 88 Ga. Southern 20-38
Citadel.................. 90 Ga. Southern 0-31
Citadel.................. 92 North Caro. A&T 44-0
Citadel.................. 92 Youngstown St. 17-42

Andy Talley (0-3) (Southern Conn. St. '67)
Villanova............... 89 Ga. Southern 36-52
Villanova............... 91 Youngstown St. 16-17
Villanova............... 92 Youngstown St. 20-23

Rick Taylor (1-3) (Gettysburg '64)
Boston U. .... 82 Colgate 7-21
Boston U. .... 83 Eastern Ky. 24-20
Boston U. .... 83 Furman 16-35
Boston U. .... 84 Richmond 33-35

Bill Thomas (1-1) (Tennessee St. '71)
Tennessee St.......... 86 Jackson St. 32-23
Tennessee St.......... 86 Nevada 6-33

Chris Tormey (0-1) (Idaho '78)
Idaho.................... 95 McNeese St. 3-33

Jim Tressel (16-4) (Baldwin-Wallace '75)
Youngstown St........ 87 Northern Iowa 28-31
Youngstown St........ 89 Eastern Ky. 28-24
Youngstown St........ 89 Furman 23-42
Youngstown St........ 90 Central Fla. 17-20
Youngstown St........ 91 Villanova 17-16
Youngstown St........ 91 Nevada 30-28
Youngstown St........ 91 Samford 10-0
Youngstown St........ 91* Marshall 25-17
Youngstown St........ 92 Villanova 23-20
Youngstown St........ 92 Citadel 42-17
Youngstown St........ 92 Northern Iowa 19-7
Youngstown St........ 92 Marshall 28-31
Youngstown St........ 93 Central Fla. 56-30
Youngstown St........ 93 Ga. Southern 34-14
Youngstown St........ 93 Idaho 35-16
Youngstown St........ 93* Marshall 17-5
Youngstown St........ 94 Alcorn St. 63-20
Youngstown St........ 94 Eastern Ky. 18-15
Youngstown St........ 94 Montana 28-9
Youngstown St........ 94* Boise St. 28-14

Bob Waters (3-1) (Presbyterian '60)
Western Caro......... 83 Colgate 24-23
Western Caro......... 83 Holy Cross 28-21
Western Caro......... 83 Furman 14-7
Western Caro......... 83 Southern Ill. 7-43

John Whitehead (1-2) (East Stroudsburg '50)
Lehigh.................... 79 Murray St. 28-9
Lehigh.................... 79 Eastern Ky. 7-30
Lehigh.................... 80 Eastern Ky. 20-23

A. L. Williams (3-1) (Louisiana Tech '57)
Louisiana Tech........ 84 Mississippi Val. 66-19
Louisiana Tech........ 84 Alcorn St. 44-21
Louisiana Tech........ 84 Middle Tenn. St. 21-13
Louisiana Tech........ 84 Montana St. 6-19

Steve Wilson (0-1) (Howard '79)
Howard .... 93 Marshall 14-28

Alex Wood (0-1) (Iowa '79)
James Madison....... 95 Appalachian St. 24-31

Sparky Woods (2-2) (Carson-Newman '76)
Appalachian St....... 86 Nicholls St. 26-28
Appalachian St....... 87 Richmond 20-3
Appalachian St....... 87 Ga. Southern 19-0
Appalachian St....... 87 Marshall 10-24

Dick Zornes (1-2) (Eastern Wash. '68)
Eastern Wash......... 85 Idaho 42-38
Eastern Wash......... 85 Northern Iowa 14-17
Eastern Wash......... 92 Northern Iowa 14-17

**National championship. †Tennessee State's participation vacated by action of the NCAA Committee on Infractions. %Stephen F. Austin's participation vacated by action of the NCAA Committee on Infractions.*

Division II Coaching Records

Winningest Active Division II Coaches

(Minimum Five Years as a College Head Coach; Record at Four-Year Colleges Only)

BY PERCENTAGE

Coach, College	Years	Won	Lost	Tied	*Pct.
Chuck Broyles, Pittsburg St.	6	69	8	2	.886
Peter Yetten, Bentley	8	59	14	1	.804
Rocky Hager, North Dak. St.	9	85	21	1	.799
Ken Sparks, Carson-Newman	16	149	40	2	.785
Ron Taylor, Quincy	6	43	15	2	.733
Bob Cortese, Fort Hays St.	16	127	45	6	.730
Danny Hale, Bloomsburg	8	62	23	1	.727
Mike Isom, Central Ark.	6	47	18	4	.710
Gene Carpenter, Millersville	27	184	74	6	.708
Frank Cignetti, Indiana (Pa.)	14	117	48	1	.708
Tom Hollman, Edinboro	12	85	35	3	.703
Bobby Wallace, North Ala.	8	67	28	1	.703
Brian Kelly, Grand Valley St.	5	39	16	2	.702
Dick Lowry, Hillsdale	22	166	70	3	.701
Hal Mumme, Valdosta St.	7	54	25	1	.681
Tim Walsh, Portland St.	7	52	25	0	.675
Jim Malosky, Minn.-Duluth	38	243	116	13	.671
Eric Holm, Northern Mich.	6	44	22	0	.667
Carl Iverson, Western St.	13	85	42	3	.665
Willard Bailey, Virginia Union	23	158	80	7	.659
Ron Harms, Tex. A&M-Kingsville	27	186	98	4	.653
Jerry Vandergriff, Angelo St.	14	96	53	2	.642
Fred Whitmire, Humboldt St.	5	32	18	2	.635
Claire Boroff, Neb.-Kearney	24	146	87	5	.632
Jon Lantz, Mo. Southern St.	10	63	37	3	.626
Mike Daly, South Dak. St.	5	33	20	0	.623
Stan McGarvey, Mo. Western St.	11	72	43	4	.622
Joe Glenn, Northern Colo.	11	72	44	1	.620
Brad Smith, Chadron St.	9	57	35	1	.618
Rick Daniels, West Chester	7	47	29	1	.617
Lou Anderson, Virginia St.	5	31	20	0	.608
Dennis Douds, East Stroudsburg	22	133	87	3	.603
Malen Luke, Clarion	8	47	31	0	.603
Tony DeMeo, Washburn	13	69	45	4	.602
Dennis Miller, Northern St.	10	66	44	0	.600
Hampton Smith, Albany St. (Ga.)	20	122	81	4	.599
Kevin Donley, Calif. (Pa.)	18	111	77	1	.590
Doug Porter, Fort Valley St.	26	149	106	5	.583
George Mihalik, Slippery Rock	8	46	33	4	.578
Gary Howard, Central Okla.	19	109	79	6	.577
Dennis Wagner, Wayne St. (Neb.)	7	41	30	1	.576
Rocky Rees, Shippensburg	11	68	50	2	.575
Denny Creehan, South Dak.	11	64	50	1	.561
Noel Martin, St. Cloud St.	13	77	62	0	.554

Coach, College	Years	Won	Lost	Tied	*Pct.
Rich Rodriquez, Glenville St.	7	39	32	2	.548
Terry Noland, Central Mo. St.	13	74	61	2	.547
Monte Cater, Shepherd	15	80	66	2	.547
Tom Marshall, LIU-C.W. Post	13	69	57	2	.547
Robert Ford, Albany (N.Y.)	27	139	117	1	.543
Mel Tjeerdsma, Northwest Mo. St.	12	65	55	4	.540
Roger Thomas, North Dak.	12	67	58	2	.535
Eddie Vowell, East Tex. St.	10	60	52	1	.535
Jeff Geiser, Adams St.	12	64	56	2	.532
Tom Herman, Gannon	7	34	30	2	.530
Woody Fish, Gardner-Webb	12	70	62	1	.530
Bob Mullett, Concord (W.Va.)	7	36	33	2	.521
Bud Elliott, Eastern N.M.	28	149	138	9	.519
Bob Eaton, West Liberty St.	6	30	29	1	.508
Charles Forbes, Lenoir-Rhyne	20	97	95	3	.505
Joe Kimble, Mercyhurst	11	52	51	2	.505
Sam Kornhauser, Stony Brook	12	57	56	2	.504
Bernie Anderson, Michigan Tech	9	44	44	0	.500
Dan Runkle, Mankato St.	15	83	83	2	.500
Terry McMillan, Mississippi Col.	5	23	24	5	.490
George Moody, Elizabeth City St.	13	63	68	3	.481
Bill Struble, West Va. Wesleyan	13	62	67	0	.481
Pat Behrns, Neb.-Omaha	8	40	44	0	.476
Larry Little, N.C. Central	12	59	66	1	.472
Dominic Livedoti, Wayne St. (Mich.)	6	24	29	3	.455
John Perry, Presbyterian	12	59	73	0	.447
Richard Cavanaugh, Southern Conn. St.	11	48	61	1	.441
Jim Heinitz, Augustana (S.D.)	8	37	49	1	.431
Willie Hunter, Clark Atlanta	6	25	34	1	.425
Doug Sams, Fairmont St.	5	21	29	0	.420
Maurice Hunt, Morehouse	17	69	101	4	.402
Ralph Micheli, Moorhead St.	13	48	73	2	.398
Gary Houser, Cal St. Chico	7	24	40	3	.381
Gary Reho, Sacred Heart	5	14	32	0	.304
Bob Gobel, West Va. Tech	7	18	52	1	.261

**Ties computed as half won and half lost; bowl and postseason games included.*

BY VICTORIES

(Minimum 80 Victories)

Coach, College, Winning Percentage	Won
Jim Malosky, Minn.-Duluth .671	243
Ron Harms, Tex. A&M-Kingsville .653	186
Gene Carpenter, Millersville .708	184
Dick Lowry, Hillsdale .701	166
Willard Bailey, Virginia Union .659	158
Ken Sparks, Carson-Newman .785	149
Doug Porter, Fort Valley St. .583	149
Bud Elliott, Eastern N.M. .519	149
Claire Boroff, Neb.-Kearney .632	146
Robert Ford, Albany (N.Y.) .543	139
Dennis Douds, East Stroudsburg .603	133
Bob Cortese, Fort Hays St. .730	127
Hampton Smith, Albany St. (Ga.) .599	122
Frank Cignetti, Indiana (Pa.) .708	117
Kevin Donley, Calif. (Pa.) .590	111
Gary Howard, Central Okla. .577	109
Charles Forbes, Lenoir-Rhyne .505	97
Jerry Vandergriff, Angelo St. .642	96
Rocky Hager, North Dak. St. .799	85
Tom Hollman, Edinboro .703	85
Carl Iverson, Western St. .665	85
Dan Runkle, Mankato St. .500	83
Monte Cater, Shepherd .547	80

Division II Championship Coaches

All coaches who have coached teams in the Division II championship playoffs since 1973 are listed here with their playoff record, alma mater and year graduated, team, year coached, opponent, and score.

Phil Albert (1-3) (Arizona '66)
Towson St. .... 83 North Dak. St. 17-24
Towson St. .... 84 Norfolk St. 31-21
Towson St. .... 84 Troy St. 3-45
Towson St. .... 86 Central St. 0-31

Pokey Allen (10-5) (Utah '65)
Portland St............. 87 Mankato St. 27-21
Portland St............. 87 Northern Mich. 13-7
Portland St............. 87 Troy St. 17-31
Portland St............. 88 Bowie St. 34-17
Portland St............. 88 Jacksonville St. 20-13
Portland St............. 88 Tex. A&M-Kingsville 35-27
Portland St............. 88 North Dak. St. 21-35
Portland St............. 89 West Chester 56-50 (3 OT)
Portland St............. 89 Indiana (Pa.) 0-17
Portland St............. 91 Northern Colo. 28-24
Portland St............. 91 Mankato St. 37-27
Portland St............. 91 Pittsburg St. 21-53
Portland St............. 92 UC Davis 42-28
Portland St............. 92 Tex. A&M-Kingsville 35-30
Portland St............. 92 Pittsburg St. 38-41

Mike Ayers (0-2) (Georgetown, Ky. '74)
Wofford................ 90 Mississippi Col. 19-70
Wofford................ 91 Mississippi Col. 15-28

Willard Bailey (0-6) (Norfolk St. '62)
Virginia Union .... 79 Delaware 28-58
Virginia Union .... 80 North Ala. 8-17
Virginia Union .... 81 Shippensburg 27-40
Virginia Union .... 82 North Dak. St. 20-21
Virginia Union .... 83 North Ala. 14-16
Norfolk St.............. 84 Towson St. 21-31

Bob Bartolomeo (0-1) (Butler '77)
Butler .... 91 Pittsburg St. 16-26

Tom Beck (0-2) (Northern Ill. '61)
Grand Valley St...... 89 Indiana (Pa.) 24-34
Grand Valley St...... 90 East Tex. St. 14-20

Bob Biggs (1-1) (UC Davis '73)
UC Davis............... 93 Fort Hays St. 37-34
UC Davis............... 93 Tex. A&M-Kingsville 28-51

Bob Blasi (0-1) (Colorado St. '53)
Northern Colo. .... 80 Eastern Ill. 14-21

Bill Bowes (1-2) (Penn St. '65)
New Hampshire ..... 75 Lehigh 35-21
New Hampshire ..... 75 Western Ky. 3-14
New Hampshire ..... 76 Montana St. 16-17

Chuck Broyles (12-5) (Pittsburg St. '70)
Pittsburg St. .... 90 Truman St. 59-3
Pittsburg St. .... 90 East Tex. St. 60-28
Pittsburg St. .... 90 North Dak. St. 29-39
Pittsburg St. .... 91 Butler 26-16
Pittsburg St. .... 91 East Tex. St. 38-28
Pittsburg St. .... 91 Portland St. 53-21
Pittsburg St. .... 91* Jacksonville St. 23-6
Pittsburg St. .... 92 North Dak. 26-21
Pittsburg St. .... 92 North Dak. St. 38-37 (OT)
Pittsburg St. .... 92 Portland St. 41-38
Pittsburg St. .... 92 Jacksonville St. 13-17
Pittsburg St. .... 93 North Dak. 14-17
Pittsburg St. .... 94 North Dak. St. 12-18 (3 OT)
Pittsburg St. .... 95 Northern Colo. 36-17
Pittsburg St. .... 95 North Dak. St. 9-7
Pittsburg St. .... 95 Tex. A&M-Kingsville 28-25 (OT)
Pittsburg St. .... 95 North Ala. 7-27

Sandy Buda (1-2) (Kansas '67)
Neb.-Omaha.......... 78 Youngstown St. 14-21
Neb.-Omaha.......... 84 Northwest Mo. St. 28-15
Neb.-Omaha.......... 84 North Dak. St. 14-25

Bill Burgess (12-4) (Auburn '63)
Jacksonville St........ 88 West Chester 63-24
Jacksonville St........ 88 Portland St. 13-20
Jacksonville St........ 89 Alabama A&M 33-9
Jacksonville St........ 89 North Dak. St. 21-17
Jacksonville St........ 89 Angelo St. 34-16
Jacksonville St........ 89 Mississippi Col. 0-3
Jacksonville St........ 90 North Ala. 38-14
Jacksonville St........ 90 Mississippi Col. 7-14
Jacksonville St........ 91 Winston-Salem 49-24
Jacksonville St........ 91 Mississippi Col. 35-7
Jacksonville St........ 91 Indiana (Pa.) 27-20
Jacksonville St........ 91 Pittsburg St. 6-23
Jacksonville St........ 92 Savannah St. 41-16
Jacksonville St........ 92 North Ala. 14-12
Jacksonville St......... 92 New Haven 46-35
Jacksonville St......... 92* Pittsburg St. 17-13

Bob Burt (0-1) (Cal St. Los Angeles '62)
Cal St. Northridge .. 90 Cal Poly SLO 7-14

Gene Carpenter (1-2) (Huron '63)
Millersville .... 88 Indiana (Pa.) 27-24
Millersville .... 88 North Dak. St. 26-36
Millersville .... 95 Ferris St. 26-36

Marino Casem (0-1) (Xavier, La. '56)
Alcorn St. .... 74 UNLV 22-35

Frank Cignetti (12-7) (Indiana, Pa. '60)
Indiana (Pa.)........... 87 Central Fla. 10-12
Indiana (Pa.)........... 88 Millersville 24-27
Indiana (Pa.)........... 89 Grand Valley St. 34-24
Indiana (Pa.)........... 89 Portland St. 17-0
Indiana (Pa.)........... 89 Mississippi Col. 14-26
Indiana (Pa.)........... 90 Winston-Salem 48-0
Indiana (Pa.)........... 90 Edinboro 14-7
Indiana (Pa.)........... 90 Mississippi Col. 27-8
Indiana (Pa.)........... 90 North Dak. St. 11-51
Indiana (Pa.)........... 91 Virginia Union 56-7
Indiana (Pa.)........... 91 Shippensburg 52-7
Indiana (Pa.)........... 91 Jacksonville St. 20-27
Indiana (Pa.)........... 93 Ferris St. 28-21
Indiana (Pa.)........... 93 New Haven 38-35
Indiana (Pa.)........... 93 North Dak. 21-6
Indiana (Pa.)........... 93 North Ala. 34-41
Indiana (Pa.)........... 94 Grand Valley St. 35-27
Indiana (Pa.)........... 94 Ferris St. 21-17
Indiana (Pa.)........... 94 Tex. A&M-Kingsville 20-46

Bob Cortese (0-2) (Colorado '67)
Fort Hays St............ 93 UC Davis 34-37
Fort Hays St............ 95 Tex. A&M-Kingsville 28-59

Bruce Craddock (0-1) (Truman St. '66)
Truman St. .... 82 Jacksonville St. 21-34

Rick Daniels (0-3) (West Chester '75)
West Chester.......... 89 Portland St. 50-56 (3 OT)
West Chester.......... 92 New Haven 26-38
West Chester.......... 94 Ferris St. 40-43

Bill Davis (0-1) (Johnson Smith '65)
Savannah St. .... 92 Jacksonville St. 16-41

Rey Dempsey (0-1) (Geneva '58)
Youngstown St........ 74 Delaware 14-35

Jim Dennison (2-1) (Wooster '60)
Akron .... 76 UNLV 26-6
Akron .... 76 Northern Mich. 29-26
Akron .... 76 Montana St. 13-24

Dennis Douds (0-1) (Slippery Rock '63)
East Stroudsburg ..... 91 Shippensburg 33-34

Fred Dunlap (0-2) (Colgate '50)
Lehigh.................... 73 Western Ky. 16-25
Lehigh.................... 75 New Hampshire 21-35

Bud Elliott (0-1) (Baker '53)
Northwest Mo. St.... 89 Pittsburg St. 7-28

Jimmy Feix (4-2) (Western Ky. '53)
Western Ky. .... 73 Lehigh 25-16
Western Ky. .... 73 Grambling 28-20
Western Ky. .... 73 Louisiana Tech 0-34

Western Ky. .... 75 Northern Iowa 14-12
Western Ky. .... 75 New Hampshire 14-3
Western Ky. .... 75 Northern Mich. 14-16

Charlie Fisher (0-1) (Springfield '81)
West Ga. .... 95 Carson-Newman 26-37

Bob Foster (0-2) (UC Davis '62)
UC Davis .... 89 Angelo St. 23-28
UC Davis .... 92 Portland St. 28-42

Dennis Franchione (1-1) (Pittsburg St. '73)
Pittsburg St. .... 89 Northwest Mo. St. 28-7
Pittsburg St. .... 89 Angelo St. 21-24

Fred Freeman (0-1) (Mississippi Val. '66)
Hampton .... 85 Bloomsburg 28-38

Jim Fuller (3-5) (Alabama '67)
Jacksonville St. .... 77 Northern Ariz. 35-0
Jacksonville St. .... 77 North Dak. St. 31-7
Jacksonville St. .... 77 Lehigh 0-33
Jacksonville St. .... 78 Delaware 27-42
Jacksonville St. .... 80 Cal Poly SLO 0-15
Jacksonville St. .... 81 Southwest Tex. St. 22-38
Jacksonville St. .... 82 Truman St. 34-21
Jacksonville St. .... 82 Southwest Tex. St. 14-19

Chan Gailey (3-0) (Florida '74)
Troy St. .... 84 Central St. 31-21
Troy St. .... 84 Towson St. 45-3
Troy St. .... 84* North Dak. St. 18-17

Joe Glenn (0-3) (South Dak. '71)
Northern Colo. .... 90 North Dak. St. 7-17
Northern Colo. .... 91 Portland St. 24-28
Northern Colo. .... 95 Pittsburg St. 17-36

Ray Greene (1-1) (Akron '63)
Alabama A&M .... 79 Morgan St. 27-7
Alabama A&M .... 79 Youngstown St. 0-52

John Gregory (0-1) (Northern Iowa '61)
South Dak. St. .... 79 Youngstown St. 7-50

Herb Grenke (1-1) (Wis.-Milwaukee '63)
Northern Mich. .... 87 Angelo St. 23-20 (OT)
Northern Mich. .... 87 Portland St. 7-13

Wayne Grubb (4-3) (Tennessee '61)
North Ala. .... 80 Virginia Union 17-8
North Ala. .... 80 Eastern Ill. 31-56
North Ala. .... 83 Virginia Union 16-14
North Ala. .... 83 Central St. 24-27
North Ala. .... 85 Fort Valley St. 14-7
North Ala. .... 85 Bloomsburg 34-0
North Ala. .... 85 North Dak. St. 7-35

Photo from Bloomsburg sports information

Entering his fourth season at Bloomsburg, Danny Hale has a .727 winning percentage in eight years as a head coach, a mark that ranks seventh among active Division II coaches.

Rocky Hager (12-5) (Minot St. '74)
North Dak. St. .... 88 Augustana (S.D.) 49-7
North Dak. St. .... 88 Millersville 36-26
North Dak. St. .... 88 Cal St. Sacramento 42-20
North Dak. St. .... 88* Portland St. 35-21
North Dak. St. .... 89 Edinboro 45-32
North Dak. St. .... 89 Jacksonville St. 17-21
North Dak. St. .... 90 Northern Colo. 17-7
North Dak. St. .... 90 Cal Poly SLO 47-0
North Dak. St. .... 90 Pittsburg St. 39-29
North Dak. St. .... 90* Indiana (Pa.) 51-11
North Dak. St. .... 91 Mankato St. 7-27
North Dak. St. .... 92 Truman St. 42-7
North Dak. St. .... 92 Pittsburg St. 37-38 (OT)
North Dak. St. .... 94 Pittsburg St. 18-12 (3 OT)
North Dak. St. .... 94 North Dak. 7-14
North Dak. St. .... 95 North Dak. 41-10
North Dak. St. .... 95 Pittsburg St. 7-9

Danny Hale (0-1) (West Chester '68)
West Chester .... 88 Jacksonville St. 24-63

Ron Harms (10-6) (Valparaiso '59)
Tex. A&M-Kingsville .. 88 Mississippi Col. 39-15
Tex. A&M-Kingsville .. 88 Tenn.-Martin 34-0
Tex. A&M-Kingsville .. 88 Portland St. 27-35
Tex. A&M-Kingsville .. 89 Mississippi Col. 19-34
Tex. A&M-Kingsville .. 92 Western St. 22-13
Tex. A&M-Kingsville .. 92 Portland St. 30-35
Tex. A&M-Kingsville .. 93 Portland St. 50-15
Tex. A&M-Kingsville .. 93 UC Davis 51-28
Tex. A&M-Kingsville .. 93 North Ala. 25-27
Tex. A&M-Kingsville .. 94 Western St. 43-7
Tex. A&M-Kingsville .. 94 Portland St. 21-16
Tex. A&M-Kingsville .. 94 Indiana (Pa.) 46-20
Tex. A&M-Kingsville .. 94 North Ala. 10-16
Tex. A&M-Kingsville .. 95 Fort Hays St. 59-28
Tex. A&M-Kingsville .. 95 Portland St. 30-3
Tex. A&M-Kingsville .. 95 Pittsburg St. 25-28 (OT)

Joe Harper (3-1) (UCLA '59)
Cal Poly SLO .... 78 Winston-Salem 0-17
Cal Poly SLO .... 80 Jacksonville St. 15-0
Cal Poly SLO .... 80 Santa Clara 38-14
Cal Poly SLO .... 80* Eastern Ill. 21-13

Bill Hayes (1-2) (N.C. Central '64)
Winston-Salem .... 78 Cal Poly SLO 17-0
Winston-Salem .... 78 Delaware 0-41
Winston-Salem .... 87 Troy St. 14-45

Jim Heinitz (0-2) (South Dak. St. '72)
Augustana (S.D.) ..... 88 North Dak. St. 7-49
Augustana (S.D.) ..... 89 St. Cloud St. 20-27

Andy Hinson (0-1) (Bethune-Cookman '53)
Bethune-Cookman ... 77 UC Davis 16-34

Sonny Holland (3-0) (Montana St. '60)
Montana St. .... 76 New Hampshire 17-16
Montana St. .... 76 North Dak. St. 10-3
Montana St. .... 76* Akron 24-13

Tom Hollman (1-5) (Ohio Northern '68)
Edinboro .... 89 North Dak. St. 32-45
Edinboro .... 90 Virginia Union 38-14
Edinboro .... 90 Indiana (Pa.) 7-14
Edinboro .... 92 Ferris St. 15-19
Edinboro .... 93 New Haven 28-48
Edinboro .... 95 New Haven 12-27

Eric Holm (0-3) (Truman St. '81)
Truman St. .... 90 Pittsburg St. 3-59
Truman St. .... 92 North Dak. St. 7-42
Truman St. .... 94 North Dak. 6-18

Carl Iverson (0-2) (Whitman '62)
Western St. .... 92 Tex. A&M-Kingsville 13-22
Western St. .... 94 Tex. A&M-Kingsville 7-43

Billy Joe (3-4) (Villanova '63)
Central St. .... 83 Southwest Tex. St. 24-16
Central St. .... 83 North Ala. 27-24
Central St. .... 83 North Dak. St. 21-41
Central St. .... 84 Troy St. 21-31
Central St. .... 85 South Dak. 10-13 (2 OT)
Central St. .... 86 Towson St. 31-0
Central St. .... 86 North Dak. St. 12-35

Brian Kelly (0-2) (Assumption '83)
Grand Valley St. ..... 91 East Tex. St. 15-36
Grand Valley St. ..... 94 Indiana (Pa.) 27-35

Roy Kidd (0-1) (Eastern Ky. '54)
Eastern Ky. .... 76 North Dak. St. 7-10

Jim King (1-1)
West Ala. .... 75 North Dak. 34-14
West Ala. .... 75 Northern Mich. 26-28

Tony Knap (1-4) (Idaho '39)
Boise St. .... 73 South Dak. 53-10
Boise St. .... 73 Louisiana Tech 34-38
Boise St. .... 74 Central Mich. 6-20
Boise St. .... 75 Northern Mich. 21-24
UNLV .... 76 Akron 6-26

Roy Kramer (3-0) (Maryville, Tenn. '53)
Central Mich. .... 74 Boise St. 20-6
Central Mich. .... 74 Louisiana Tech 35-14
Central Mich. .... 74* Delaware 54-14

Gil Krueger (4-2) (Marquette '52)
Northern Mich. .... 75 Boise St. 24-21
Northern Mich. .... 75 West Ala. 28-26
Northern Mich. .... 75* Western Ky. 16-14
Northern Mich. .... 76 Delaware 28-17
Northern Mich. .... 76 Akron 26-29
Northern Mich. .... 77 North Dak. St. 6-20

Maxie Lambright (4-1) (Southern Miss. '49)
Louisiana Tech .... 73 Western Ill. 18-13
Louisiana Tech .... 73 Boise St. 38-34
Louisiana Tech .... 73* Western Ky. 34-0
Louisiana Tech .... 74 Western Caro. 10-7
Louisiana Tech .... 74 Central Mich. 14-35

George Landis (1-1) (Penn St. '71)
Bloomsburg .... 85 Hampton 38-28
Bloomsburg .... 85 North Ala. 0-34

Jon Lantz (0-1) (Okla. Panhandle St. '74)
Mo. Southern St. ..... 93 Mankato St. 13-34

Henry Lattimore (1-1) (Jackson St. '57)
N.C. Central .... 88 Winston-Salem 31-16
N.C. Central .... 88 Cal St. Sacramento 7-56

Bill Lynch (0-1) (Butler '77)
Butler .... 88 Tenn.-Martin 6-23

Dick MacPherson (0-1) (Springfield '58)
Massachusetts .... 77 Lehigh 23-30

Pat Malley (1-1) (Santa Clara '53)
Santa Clara .... 80 Northern Mich. 27-26
Santa Clara .... 80 Cal Poly SLO 14-38

Noel Martin (1-1) (Nebraska '63)
St. Cloud St. .... 89 Augustana (S.D.) 27-20
St. Cloud St. .... 89 Mississippi Col. 24-55

Fred Martinelli (0-1) (Otterbein '51)
Ashland .... 86 North Dak. St. 0-50

Bob Mattos (2-1) (Cal St. Sacramento '64)
Cal St. Sacramento .. 88 UC Davis 35-14
Cal St. Sacramento .. 88 N.C. Central 56-7
Cal St. Sacramento .. 88 North Dak. St. 20-42

Gene McDowell (1-1) (Florida St. '65)
Central Fla. .... 87 Indiana (Pa.) 12-10
Central Fla. .... 87 Troy St. 10-31

Don McLeary (1-1) (Tennessee '70)
Tenn.-Martin .... 88 Butler 23-6
Tenn.-Martin .... 88 Tex. A&M-Kingsville 0-34

Terry McMillan (1-1) (Southern Miss. '69)
Mississippi Col. ...... 91 Wofford 28-15
Mississippi Col. ...... 91 Jacksonville St. 7-35

Ron Meyer (1-1) (Purdue '63)
UNLV .... 74 Alcorn St. 35-22
UNLV .... 74 Delaware 11-49

Don Morton (8-3) (Augustana, Ill. '69)
North Dak. St. .... 81 Puget Sound 24-10
North Dak. St. .... 81 Shippensburg 18-6
North Dak. St. .... 81 Southwest Tex. St. 13-42
North Dak. St. .... 82 Virginia Union 21-20
North Dak. St. .... 82 UC Davis 14-19
North Dak. St. .... 83 Towson St. 24-17
North Dak. St. .... 83 UC Davis 26-17
North Dak. St. .... 83* Central St. 41-21
North Dak. St. .... 84 UC Davis 31-23
North Dak. St. .... 84 Neb.-Omaha 25-14
North Dak. St. .... 84 Troy St. 17-18

Darrell Mudra (5-2) (Peru St. '51)
Western Ill. .... 73 Louisiana Tech 13-18
Eastern Ill. .... 78 UC Davis 35-31
Eastern Ill. .... 78 Youngstown St. 26-22
Eastern Ill. .... 78* Delaware 10-9
Eastern Ill. .... 80 Northern Colo. 21-14

Team	Year	Opponent, Score
Eastern Ill.	80	North Ala. 56-31
Eastern Ill.	80	Cal Poly SLO 13-21

Hal Mumme (1-1) (Tarleton St. '75)

Team	Year	Opponent, Score
Valdosta St.	94	Albany St. (Ga.) 14-7
Valdosta St.	94	North Ala. 24-27 (2 OT)

Gene Murphy (0-1) (North Dak. '62)

Team	Year	Opponent, Score
North Dak.	79	Mississippi Col. 15-35

Bill Narduzzi (3-2) (Miami, Ohio '59)

Team	Year	Opponent, Score
Youngstown St.	78	Neb.-Omaha 21-14
Youngstown St.	78	Eastern Ill. 22-26
Youngstown St.	79	South Dak. St. 50-7
Youngstown St.	79	Alabama A&M 52-0
Youngstown St.	79	Delaware 21-38

John O'Hara (0-1) (Okla. Panhandle St. '67)

Team	Year	Opponent, Score
Southwest Tex. St.	83	Central St. 16-24

Jerry Olson (0-1) (Valley City St. '55)

Team	Year	Opponent, Score
North Dak.	75	West Ala. 14-34

Keith Otterbein (2-3) (Ferris St. '79)

Team	Year	Opponent, Score
Ferris St.	92	Edinboro 19-15
Ferris St.	92	New Haven 13-35
Ferris St.	93	Indiana (Pa.) 21-28
Ferris St.	94	West Chester 43-40
Ferris St.	94	Indiana (Pa.) 17-21

Jeff Pierce (2-1) (Ferris St. '79)

Team	Year	Opponent, Score
Ferris St.	95	Millersville 36-26
Ferris St.	95	New Haven 17-9
Ferris St.	95	North Ala. 7-45

Doug Porter (0-1) (Xavier, La. '52)

Team	Year	Opponent, Score
Fort Valley St.	82	Southwest Tex. St. 6-27

George Pugh (0-1) (Alabama '76)

Team	Year	Opponent, Score
Alabama A&M	89	Jacksonville St. 9-33

Bill Rademacher (1-3) (Northern Mich. '63)

Team	Year	Opponent, Score
Northern Mich.	80	Santa Clara 6-27
Northern Mich.	81	Elizabeth City St. 55-6
Northern Mich.	81	Southwest Tex. St. 0-62
Northern Mich.	82	UC Davis 21-42

Vito Ragazzo (1-1) (William & Mary '51)

Team	Year	Opponent, Score
Shippensburg	81	Virginia Union 40-27
Shippensburg	81	North Dak. St. 6-18

Tubby Raymond (7-4) (Michigan '50)

Team	Year	Opponent, Score
Delaware	73	Grambling 8-17
Delaware	74	Youngstown St. 35-14
Delaware	74	UNLV 49-11
Delaware	74	Central Mich. 14-54
Delaware	76	Northern Mich. 17-28
Delaware	78	Jacksonville St. 42-27
Delaware	78	Winston-Salem 41-0
Delaware	78	Eastern Ill. 9-10
Delaware	79	Virginia Union 58-28
Delaware	79	Mississippi Col. 60-10
Delaware	79*	Youngstown St. 38-21

Rocky Rees (1-1) (West Chester '71)

Team	Year	Opponent, Score
Shippensburg	91	East Stroudsburg 34-33
Shippensburg	91	Indiana (Pa.) 7-52

Rick Rhodes (4-1)

Team	Year	Opponent, Score
Troy St.	86	Virginia Union 31-7
Troy St.	86	South Dak. 28-42
Troy St.	87	Winston-Salem 45-14
Troy St.	87	Central Fla. 31-10
Troy St.	87*	Portland St. 31-17

Pete Richardson (0-3) (Dayton '68)

Team	Year	Opponent, Score
Winston-Salem	88	N.C. Central 16-31
Winston-Salem	90	Indiana (Pa.) 0-48
Winston-Salem	91	Jacksonville St. 24-49

Eddie Robinson (1-1) (Leland '41)

Team	Year	Opponent, Score
Grambling	73	Delaware 17-8
Grambling	73	Western Ky. 20-28

Dan Runkle (2-3) (Illinois Col. '68)

Team	Year	Opponent, Score
Mankato St.	87	Portland St. 21-27
Mankato St.	91	North Dak. St. 27-7
Mankato St.	91	Portland St. 27-37
Mankato St.	93	Mo. Southern St. 34-13
Mankato St.	93	North Dak. 21-54

Joe Salem (0-2) (Minnesota '61)

Team	Year	Opponent, Score
South Dak.	73	Boise St. 10-53
Northern Ariz.	77	Jacksonville St. 0-35

Lyle Setencich (1-1) (Fresno St. '68)

Team	Year	Opponent, Score
Cal Poly SLO	90	Cal St. Northridge 14-7
Cal Poly SLO	90	North Dak. St. 0-47

Stan Sheriff (0-1) (Cal Poly SLO '54)

Team	Year	Opponent, Score
Northern Iowa	75	Western Ky. 12-14

Sanders Shiver (0-1) (Carson-Newman '76)

Team	Year	Opponent, Score
Bowie St.	88	Portland St. 17-34

Ron Simonson (0-1) (Portland St. '65)

Team	Year	Opponent, Score
Puget Sound	81	North Dak. St. 10-24

Hampton Smith (0-3) (Mississippi Val. '57)

Team	Year	Opponent, Score
Albany St. (Ga.)	93	Hampton 7-33
Albany St. (Ga.)	94	Valdosta St. 7-14
Albany St. (Ga.)	95	North Ala. 28-38

Jim Sochor (4-8) (San Fran. St. '60)

Team	Year	Opponent, Score
UC Davis	77	Bethune-Cookman 34-16
UC Davis	77	Lehigh 30-39
UC Davis	78	Eastern Ill. 31-35
UC Davis	82	Northern Mich. 42-21
UC Davis	82	North Dak. St. 19-14
UC Davis	82	Southwest Tex. St. 9-34
UC Davis	83	Butler 25-6
UC Davis	83	North Dak. St. 17-26
UC Davis	84	North Dak. St. 23-31
UC Davis	85	North Dak. St. 12-31
UC Davis	86	South Dak. 23-26
UC Davis	88	Cal St. Sacramento 14-35

Earle Solomonson (6-0) (Augsburg '69)

Team	Year	Opponent, Score
North Dak. St.	85	UC Davis 31-12
North Dak. St.	85	South Dak. 16-7
North Dak. St.	85*	North Ala. 35-7
North Dak. St.	86	Ashland 50-0
North Dak. St.	86	Central St. 35-12
North Dak. St.	86*	South Dak. 27-7

Tony Sparano (1-1) (New Haven '82)

Team	Year	Opponent, Score
New Haven	95	Edinboro 27-12
New Haven	95	Ferris St. 9-17

Ken Sparks (1-3) (Carson-Newman '68)

Team	Year	Opponent, Score
Carson-Newman	93	North Ala. 28-38
Carson-Newman	94	North Ala. 13-17
Carson-Newman	95	West Ga. 37-26
Carson-Newman	95	North Ala. 7-28

Bill Sylvester (0-1) (Butler '50)

Team	Year	Opponent, Score
Butler	83	UC Davis 6-25

Joe Taylor (1-5) (Western Ill. '72)

Team	Year	Opponent, Score
Virginia Union	86	Troy St. 7-31
Virginia Union	90	Edinboro 14-38
Virginia Union	91	Indiana (Pa.) 7-56
Hampton	92	North Ala. 21-33
Hampton	93	Albany St. (Ga.) 33-7
Hampton	93	North Ala. 20-45

Clarence Thomas (0-1)

Team	Year	Opponent, Score
Morgan St.	79	Alabama A&M 7-27

Roger Thomas (4-4) (Augustana, Ill. '69)

Team	Year	Opponent, Score
North Dak.	92	Pittsburg St. 21-26
North Dak.	93	Pittsburg St. 17-14
North Dak.	93	Mankato St. 54-21
North Dak.	93	Indiana (Pa.) 6-21
North Dak.	94	Truman St. 18-6
North Dak.	94	North Dak. St. 14-7
North Dak.	94	North Ala. 7-35
North Dak.	95	North Dak. St. 10-41

Vern Thomsen (0-1) (Peru St. '61)

Team	Year	Opponent, Score
Northwest Mo. St.	84	Neb.-Omaha 15-28

Dave Triplett (3-2) (Iowa '72)

Team	Year	Opponent, Score
South Dak.	85	Central St. 13-10 (2 OT)
South Dak.	85	North Dak. St. 7-16
South Dak.	86	UC Davis 26-23
South Dak.	86	Troy St. 42-28
South Dak.	86	North Dak. St. 7-27

Jerry Vandergriff (2-3) (Corpus Christi '65)

Team	Year	Opponent, Score
Angelo St.	87	Northern Mich. 20-23 (OT)
Angelo St.	89	UC Davis 28-23
Angelo St.	89	Pittsburg St. 24-21
Angelo St.	89	Jacksonville St. 16-34
Angelo St.	94	Portland St. 0-29

Eddie Vowell (2-3) (Southwestern Okla. '69)

Team	Year	Opponent, Score
East Tex. St.	90	Grand Valley St. 20-14
East Tex. St.	90	Pittsburg St. 28-60
East Tex. St.	91	Grand Valley St. 36-15
East Tex. St.	91	Pittsburg St. 28-38
East Tex. St.	95	Portland St. 35-56

Jim Wacker (8-2) (Valparaiso '60)

Team	Year	Opponent, Score
North Dak. St.	76	Eastern Ky. 10-7
North Dak. St.	76	Montana St. 3-10
North Dak. St.	77	Northern Mich. 20-6
North Dak. St.	77	Jacksonville St. 7-31
Southwest Tex. St.	81	Jacksonville St. 38-22
Southwest Tex. St.	81	Northern Mich. 62-0
Southwest Tex. St.	81*	North Dak. St. 42-13
Southwest Tex. St.	82	Fort Valley St. 27-6
Southwest Tex. St.	82	Jacksonville St. 19-14
Southwest Tex. St.	82*	UC Davis 34-9

Gerald Walker (0-1) (Lincoln, Mo. '62)

Team	Year	Opponent, Score
Fort Valley St.	85	North Ala. 7-14

Bobby Wallace (13-2) (Mississippi St. '76)

Team	Year	Opponent, Score
North Ala.	90	Jacksonville St. 14-38
North Ala.	92	Hampton 33-21
North Ala.	92	Jacksonville St. 12-14
North Ala.	93	Carson-Newman 38-28
North Ala.	93	Hampton 45-20
North Ala.	93	Tex. A&M-Kingsville 27-25
North Ala.	93*	Indiana (Pa.) 41-34
North Ala.	94	Carson-Newman 17-13
North Ala.	94	Valdosta St. 27-24 (2 OT)
North Ala.	94	North Dak. 35-7
North Ala.	94*	Tex. A&M-Kingsville 16-10
North Ala.	95	Albany St. (Ga.) 38-28
North Ala.	95	Carson-Newman 28-7
North Ala.	95	Ferris St. 45-7
North Ala.	95*	Pittsburg St. 27-7

Tim Walsh (2-3) (UC Riverside '77)

Team	Year	Opponent, Score
Portland St.	93	Tex. A&M-Kingsville 15-50
Portland St.	94	Angelo St. 29-0
Portland St.	94	Tex. A&M-Kingsville 16-21
Portland St.	95	East Tex. St. 56-35
Portland St.	95	Tex. A&M-Kingsville 3-30

Johnnie Walton (0-1) (Elizabeth City St. '69)

Team	Year	Opponent, Score
Elizabeth City St.	81	Northern Mich. 6-55

Bob Waters (0-1) (Presbyterian '60)

Team	Year	Opponent, Score
Western Caro.	74	Louisiana Tech 7-10

Mark Whipple (3-2) (Brown '79)

Team	Year	Opponent, Score
New Haven	92	West Chester 38-26
New Haven	92	Ferris St. 35-13
New Haven	92	Jacksonville St. 35-46
New Haven	93	Edinboro 48-28
New Haven	93	Indiana (Pa.) 35-38

John Whitehead (3-0) (East Stroudsburg '50)

Team	Year	Opponent, Score
Lehigh	77	Massachusetts 30-23
Lehigh	77	UC Davis 39-30
Lehigh	77*	Jacksonville St. 33-0

John Williams (†7-3) (Mississippi Col. '57)

Team	Year	Opponent, Score
Mississippi Col.	79	North Dak. 35-15
Mississippi Col.	79	Delaware 10-60
Mississippi Col.	88	Tex. A&M-Kingsville 15-39
Mississippi Col.	89†	Tex. A&M-Kingsville 34-19
Mississippi Col.	89†	St. Cloud St. 55-24
Mississippi Col.	89†	Indiana (Pa.) 26-14
Mississippi Col.	89†*	Jacksonville St. 3-0
Mississippi Col.	90†	Wofford 70-19
Mississippi Col.	90†	Jacksonville St. 14-7
Mississippi Col.	90†	Indiana (Pa.) 8-27

**National championship. †Mississippi College's participation vacated by action of the NCAA Committee on Infractions.*

Division III Coaching Records

Winningest Active Division III Coaches

(Minimum Five Years as a College Head Coach; Record at Four-Year Colleges Only)

BY PERCENTAGE

Coach, College	Years	Won	Lost	Tied	*Pct.
Ken O'Keefe, Allegheny	6	60	7	1	.890
Dick Farley, Williams	9	60	9	3	.854
Larry Kehres, Mount Union	10	96	16	3	.848
Ron Schipper, Central (Iowa)	35	280	64	3	.811
John Luckhardt, Wash. & Jeff.	14	118	28	2	.804
Vic Clark, Thomas More	6	47	13	0	.783
Roger Harring, Wis.-La Crosse	27	232	62	7	.782
Bob Packard, Baldwin-Wallace	15	117	33	2	.776
Pete Schmidt, Albion	13	95	26	4	.776
John Gagliardi, St. John's (Minn.)	47	325	99	11	.760
Rich Lackner, Carnegie Mellon	10	73	24	2	.747
Doug Neibuhr, Millikin	7	50	18	1	.732
Tony DeCarlo, John Carroll	9	63	22	4	.730
Frank Girardi, Lycoming	24	169	62	5	.727
D. J. LeRoy, Coe	13	98	38	2	.717
Lou Wacker, Emory & Henry	14	106	43	0	.711
Jack Siedlecki, Amherst	8	49	20	2	.704
Don Miller, Trinity (Conn.)	29	160	67	5	.700
Jim Christopherson, Concordia-M'head	27	189	79	7	.700
Steve Briggs, Susquehanna	6	44	19	0	.698
Scot Dapp, Moravian	9	64	28	1	.694
John Miech, Wis.-Stevens Point	8	55	24	2	.691
Rick Giancola, Montclair St.	13	91	41	2	.687
Bob Nielson, Wis.-Eau Claire	7	48	22	1	.683
Jimmie Keeling, Hardin-Simmons	6	45	21	0	.682
Joe King, Rensselaer	7	44	20	2	.682
Dale Widolff, Occidental	14	88	41	2	.679
Jim Williams, Simpson	9	61	29	1	.676
Tom Gilburg, Frank. & Marsh.	21	136	65	2	.675
C. Wayne Perry, Hanover	14	92	45	2	.669
John Audino, Union (N.Y.)	6	41	21	0	.661
Greg Carlson, Wabash	13	79	40	2	.661
Mike Maynard, Redlands	8	48	25	1	.655
Bob Berezowitz, Wis.-Whitewater	11	74	38	4	.655
Norm Eash, Ill. Wesleyan	9	53	29	1	.645
John O'Grady, Wis.-River Falls	7	44	24	3	.641
Mike Clary, Rhodes	12	66	40	6	.616
Eric Hamilton, Trenton St.	19	114	70	6	.616
Dick Tressel, Hamline	18	107	68	2	.610
Bob Bierie, Loras	16	98	62	5	.609
Scott Duncan, Rose-Hulman	10	60	39	1	.605
Charlie Pravata, Merchant Marine	5	27	18	2	.596
Dave Murray, Cortland St.	6	38	26	1	.592
Nick Mourouzis, DePauw	15	86	59	4	.591
Barry Streeter, Gettysburg	18	105	73	5	.587
Ron Ernst, Ripon	5	27	19	0	.587
Jim Morretti, Alfred	11	63	44	3	.586
Steve Miller, Cornell College	17	90	64	3	.583
Mike Hollway, Ohio Wesleyan	13	74	53	2	.581
Brien Cullen, Worcester St.	11	58	43	0	.574
Craig Rundle, Colorado Col.	10	54	40	1	.574
Rich Parrinello, Rochester	8	43	32	0	.573
Joe McDaniel, Centre	30	155	115	5	.573
Jim Scott, Aurora	10	48	36	3	.569
Kelly Kane, Monmouth (Ill.)	12	63	48	0	.568
Don Ruggeri, Mass. Maritime	23	116	89	1	.566
Larry Kindbom, Washington (Mo.)	13	71	56	1	.559
Ed Sweeney, Frostburg St.	11	62	49	4	.557
Mickey Heinecken, Middlebury	23	101	81	2	.554
Steve Frank, Hamilton	11	48	39	1	.551
Don Canfield, St. Olaf	23	119	98	1	.548
Joe Bush, Hampden-Sydney	11	59	49	1	.546
Ken Visser, Chapman	5	24	20	1	.544
Ed DeGeorge, Beloit	19	94	79	1	.543
Peter Mazzaferro, Bri'water (Mass.)	32	151	127	11	.542
Bob Sullivan, Carleton	17	89	76	0	.539
Rich Johanningmeier, Illinois Col.	11	60	51	5	.539
A. Wallace Hood, Otterbein	19	93	81	8	.533
Joe Riccio, Randolph-Macon	5	25	22	2	.531
Steve Johnson, Bethel (Minn.)	7	36	32	1	.529
Tim Keating, Western Md.	8	39	35	3	.526
Bill Samko, Tufts	9	41	37	1	.525
Jim Margraff, Johns Hopkins	6	30	27	3	.525
Tom Bell, Macalester	20	93	86	6	.519
Jeff Heacock, Muskingum	15	74	69	4	.517
Jim Cole, Alma	5	23	22	0	.511
Mike DeLong, Springfield	14	68	65	2	.511
Bill Kavanaugh, Mass.-Dartmouth	6	29	28	0	.509
Tommy Ranager, Millsaps	7	32	31	2	.508
Phil Wilks, Maryville (Tenn.)	8	40	39	0	.506
Jerry Boyes, Buffalo St.	10	49	48	0	.505
Merle Masonholder, Carroll (Wis.)	14	63	62	0	.504
Dennis Gorsline, Martin Luther	25	91	92	1	.497
Tom Austin, Colby	10	39	40	1	.494
Steve Marino, Westfield St.	6	28	29	1	.491
Dave Warmack, Kalamazoo	6	26	27	1	.491
Dick West, Heidelberg	12	56	62	2	.475
Mike Ketchum, Guilford	5	23	26	0	.469
Karl Miran, Swarthmore	6	25	31	1	.447
Paul Vosburgh, St. John Fisher	5	21	26	0	.447
Howard Vandersea, Bowdoin	20	75	95	3	.442
Dennis Riccio, St. Lawrence	9	38	48	0	.442
Mike Manley, Anderson (Ind.)	14	59	75	3	.442
Paul Rudolph, Upper Iowa	5	22	28	0	.440
Steven Mohr, Trinity (Tex.)	6	26	34	0	.433
Carlin Carpenter, Bluffton	17	67	89	1	.430
Jack Osberg, Augsburg	5	21	28	0	.429
Gerry Gallagher, Wm. Paterson	10	41	55	1	.428
Mike McClure, Franklin	7	29	39	1	.428
Jim Monos, Lebanon Valley	10	41	56	2	.424
Roger Welsh, Capital	10	40	56	4	.420
Randy Oberembt, Knox	11	41	57	1	.419
Gene Epley, Marietta	9	36	52	3	.412
Steve Gilbert, Ursinus	8	32	46	0	.410
Dale Sprague, Blackburn	10	35	52	2	.404
Jim Lyall, Adrian	6	21	32	1	.398
Roy Miller, Jersey City St.	11	42	64	0	.396
Tom Kaczkowski, Ohio Northern	10	38	59	2	.394
Chris Smith, Grove City	12	41	66	2	.385
Ron Crado, Wis.-Oshkosh	12	44	72	4	.383
Jim Braun, Concordia (Ill.)	17	57	93	4	.383
Dwight Smith, MIT	8	23	38	1	.379
Steve Stetson, Hartwick	10	33	56	2	.374
Randy Awrey, Lakeland	6	20	38	1	.347
Bill Klika, FDU-Madison	22	62	129	1	.326
John Welty, Ill. Benedictine	6	18	38	1	.325
Rick Pardy, Bates	7	18	42	2	.306
Mike Wallace, Wilmington (Ohio)	5	14	33	1	.302
Greg Quick, St. Norbert	7	18	49	0	.269
Joe Rotellini, Salisbury St.	6	15	41	0	.268
Frank Carr, Earlham	11	28	77	0	.267
Gerry Martin, Western New Eng.	5	11	32	1	.261
Tim Rucks, Carthage	6	12	38	4	.259
Steve Hackett, Norwich	5	11	35	0	.239
Greg Wallace, Grinnell	8	15	55	1	.218

**Ties computed as half won and half lost; bowl and postseason games included.*

BY VICTORIES

(Minimum 100 Victories)

Coach, College, Winning Percentage	Won
John Gagliardi, St. John's (Minn.) .760	325
Ron Schipper, Central (Iowa) .811	280
Roger Harring, Wis.-La Crosse .782	232
Jim Christopherson, Concordia-M'head .700	189
Frank Girardi, Lycoming .727	169
Don Miller, Trinity (Conn.) .700	160
Joe McDaniel, Centre .573	155
Peter Mazzaferro, Bri'water (Mass.) .542	151
Tom Gilburg, Frank. & Marsh. .675	136
Don Canfield, St. Olaf .548	119
John Luckhardt, Wash. & Jeff. .804	118
Bob Packard, Baldwin-Wallace .776	117
Don Ruggeri, Mass. Maritime .566	116
Eric Hamilton, Trenton St. .616	114
Dick Tressel, Hamline .610	107
Lou Wacker, Emory & Henry .711	106
Barry Streeter, Gettysburg .587	105
Mickey Heinecken, Middlebury .554	101

Division III Championship Coaches

All coaches who have coached teams in the Division III championship playoffs since 1973 are listed here with their playoff record, alma mater and year graduated, team, year coached, opponent, and score.

Phil Albert (2-1) (Arizona '66)
Towson St. .... 76 LIU-C.W. Post 14-10
Towson St. .... 76 St. Lawrence 38-36
Towson St. .... 76 St. John's (Minn.) 28-31

Dom Anile (0-1) (LIU-C.W. Post '59)
LIU-C.W. Post .... 76 Towson St. 10-14

John Audino (1-2) (Notre Dame '75)
Union (N.Y.).......... 93 Wm. Paterson 7-17
Union (N.Y.).......... 95 Plymouth St. 24-7
Union (N.Y.).......... 95 Rowan 7-38

Don Ault (0-1) (West Liberty St. '52)
Bethany (W.Va.)..... 80 Widener 12-43

Al Bagnoli (7-6) (Central Conn. St. '74)
Union (N.Y.).......... 83 Hofstra 51-19
Union (N.Y.).......... 83 Salisbury St. 23-21
Union (N.Y.).......... 83 Augustana (Ill.) 17-21
Union (N.Y.).......... 84 Plymouth St. 26-14
Union (N.Y.).......... 84 Augustana (Ill.) 6-23
Union (N.Y.).......... 85 Ithaca 12-13
Union (N.Y.).......... 86 Ithaca 17-24 (OT)
Union (N.Y.).......... 89 Cortland St. 42-14
Union (N.Y.).......... 89 Montclair St. 45-6
Union (N.Y.).......... 89 Ferrum 37-21
Union (N.Y.).......... 89 Dayton 7-17
Union (N.Y.).......... 91 Mass.-Lowell 55-16
Union (N.Y.).......... 91 Ithaca 23-35

Bob Berezowitz (1-2) (Wis.-Whitewater '67)
Wis.-Whitewater..... 88 Simpson 29-27
Wis.-Whitewater..... 88 Central (Iowa) 13-16
Wis.-Whitewater..... 90 St. Thomas (Minn.) 23-24

Don Birmingham (0-2) (Westmar '62)
Dubuque .... 79 Ithaca 7-27
Dubuque .... 80 Minn.-Morris 35-41

J. R. Bishop (1-1) (Franklin '61)
Wheaton (Ill.) .... 95 Wittenberg 63-41
Wheaton (Ill.) .... 95 Mount Union 14-40

Jim Blackburn (0-1) (Virginia '71)
Randolph-Macon..... 84 Wash. & Jeff. 21-22

Bill Bless (0-1) (Indianapolis '63)
Indianapolis........... 75 Wittenberg 13-17

Jerry Boyes (1-4) (Ithaca '76)
Buffalo St. .... 92 Ithaca 28-26
Buffalo St. .... 92 Rowan 19-28
Buffalo St. .... 93 Rowan 6-29
Buffalo St. .... 94 Ithaca 7-10 (2 OT)
Buffalo St. .... 95 Rowan 7-46

Darwin Breaux (0-1) (West Chester '77)
Dickinson .... 94 Widener 0-14

Steve Briggs (2-1) (Springfield '84)
Susquehanna.......... 91 Dickinson 21-20
Susquehanna.......... 91 Lycoming 31-24
Susquehanna.......... 91 Ithaca 13-49

Don Brown (1-2) (Norwich '77)
Plymouth St............ 94 Merchant Marine 19-18
Plymouth St............ 94 Ithaca 7-22
Plymouth St............ 95 Union (N.Y.) 7-24

John Bunting (2-2) (North Caro. '72)
Rowan .... 91 Ithaca 10-31
Rowan .... 92 Worcester Tech 41-14
Rowan .... 92 Buffalo St. 28-19
Rowan .... 92 Wash. & Jeff. 13-18

Jim Butterfield (21-8) (Maine '53)
Ithaca .... 74 Slippery Rock 27-14
Ithaca .... 74 Central (Iowa) 8-10
Ithaca .... 75 Fort Valley St. 41-12
Ithaca .... 75 Widener 23-14
Ithaca .... 75 Wittenberg 0-28
Ithaca .... 78 Wittenberg 3-6
Ithaca .... 79 Dubuque 27-7
Ithaca .... 79 Carnegie Mellon 15-6
Ithaca .... 79* Wittenberg 14-10
Ithaca .... 80 Wagner 41-13
Ithaca .... 80 Minn.-Morris 36-0
Ithaca .... 80 Dayton 0-63
Ithaca .... 85 Union (N.Y.) 13-12
Ithaca .... 85 Montclair St. 50-28
Ithaca .... 85 Gettysburg 34-0
Ithaca .... 85 Augustana (Ill.) 7-20
Ithaca .... 86 Union (N.Y.) 24-17 (OT)
Ithaca .... 86 Montclair St. 29-15
Ithaca .... 86 Salisbury St. 40-44
Ithaca .... 88 Wagner 34-31 (OT)
Ithaca .... 88 Cortland St. 24-17
Ithaca .... 88 Ferrum 62-28
Ithaca .... 88* Central (Iowa) 39-24
Ithaca .... 90 Trenton St. 14-24
Ithaca .... 91 Rowan 31-10
Ithaca .... 91 Union (N.Y.) 35-23
Ithaca .... 91 Susquehanna 49-13
Ithaca .... 91* Dayton 34-20
Ithaca .... 92 Buffalo St. 26-28

Jim Byers (0-1) (Michigan '59)
Evansville .... 74 Central (Iowa) 16-17

Don Canfield (0-1)
Wartburg .... 82 Bishop 7-32

Jerry Carle (0-1) (Northwestern '48)
Colorado Col. .... 75 Millsaps 21-28

Gene Carpenter (0-1) (Huron '63)
Millersville .... 79 Wittenberg 14-21

Rick Carter (3-1) (Earlham '65)
Dayton.................. 78 Carnegie Mellon 21-24
Dayton.................. 80 Baldwin-Wallace 34-0
Dayton.................. 80 Widener 28-24
Dayton.................. 80* Ithaca 63-0

Don Charlton (0-1) (Lock Haven '65)
Hiram .... 87 Augustana (Ill.) 0-53

Jim Christopherson (2-3) (Concordia-M'head '60)
Concordia-M'head .. 86 Wis.-Stevens Point 24-15
Concordia-M'head .. 86 Central (Iowa) 17-14
Concordia-M'head .. 86 Augustana (Ill.) 7-41
Concordia-M'head .. 88 Central (Iowa) 0-7
Concordia-M'head .. 95 Wis.-La Crosse 7-45

Vic Clark (0-1) (Indiana St. '71)
Thomas More .... 92 Emory & Henry 0-17

Mike Clary (0-1) (Rhodes '77)
Rhodes.................. 88 Ferrum 10-35

Jay Cottone (0-1) (Norwich '71)
Plymouth St............ 84 Union (N.Y.) 14-26

Bill Cubit (1-2) (Delaware '75)
Widener .... 94 Dickinson 14-0
Widener .... 94 Wash. & Jeff. 21-37
Widener .... 95 Lycoming 27-31

Scot Dapp (1-2) (West Chester '73)
Moravian .... 88 Widener 17-7
Moravian .... 88 Ferrum 28-49
Moravian .... 93 Wash. & Jeff. 7-27

Harper Davis (1-1) (Mississippi St. '49)
Millsaps .... 75 Colorado Col. 28-21
Millsaps .... 75 Wittenberg 22-55

Tony DeCarlo (0-1) (Kent '62)
John Carroll............ 89 Dayton 10-35

Joe DeMelfi (0-1) (Delta St. '66)
Wilkes .... 93 Frostburg St. 25-26

Bob Di Spirito (0-1) (Rhode Island '53)
Slippery Rock .... 74 Ithaca 14-27

Norm Eash (1-1) (Ill. Wesleyan '75)
Ill. Wesleyan .... 92 Aurora 21-12
Ill. Wesleyan .... 92 Mount Union 27-49

Ed Farrell (0-1) (Rutgers '56)
Bridgeport .... 73 Juniata 14-35

Bob Ford (1-1) (Springfield '59)
Albany (N.Y.) .... 77 Hampden-Sydney 51-45
Albany (N.Y.) .... 77 Widener 15-33

Stokeley Fulton (0-1) (Hampden-Sydney '55)
Hampden-Sydney .... 77 Albany (N.Y.) 45-51

John Gagliardi (12-7) (Colorado Col. '49)
St. John's (Minn.) .... 76 Augustana (Ill.) 46-7
St. John's (Minn.) .... 76 Buena Vista 61-0
St. John's (Minn.) .... 76* Towson St. 31-28
St. John's (Minn.) .... 77 Wabash 9-20
St. John's (Minn.) .... 85 Occidental 10-28
St. John's (Minn.) .... 87 Gust. Adolphus 7-3
St. John's (Minn.) .... 87 Central (Iowa) 3-13
St. John's (Minn.) .... 89 Simpson 42-35
St. John's (Minn.) .... 89 Central (Iowa) 27-24
St. John's (Minn.) .... 89 Dayton 0-28
St. John's (Minn.) .... 91 Coe 75-2
St. John's (Minn.) .... 91 Wis.-La Crosse 29-10
St. John's (Minn.) .... 91 Dayton 7-19
St. John's (Minn.) .... 93 Coe 32-14
St. John's (Minn.) .... 93 Wis.-La Crosse 47-25
St. John's (Minn.) .... 93 Mount Union 8-56
St. John's (Minn.) .... 94 La Verne 51-12
St. John's (Minn.) .... 94 Wartburg 42-14
St. John's (Minn.) .... 94 Albion 16-19

Gerry Gallagher (1-1) (Wm. Paterson '74)
Wm. Paterson......... 93 Union (N.Y.) 17-7
Wm. Paterson......... 93 Rowan 0-37

Joe Gardi (2-1) (Maryland '60)
Hofstra.................. 90 Cortland St. 35-9
Hofstra.................. 90 Trenton St. 38-3
Hofstra.................. 90 Lycoming 10-20

Rick Giancola (3-3) (Rowan '68)
Montclair St........... 85 Western Conn. St. 28-0
Montclair St........... 85 Ithaca 28-50
Montclair St........... 86 Hofstra 24-21
Montclair St........... 86 Ithaca 15-29
Montclair St........... 89 Hofstra 23-6
Montclair St........... 89 Union (N.Y.) 6-45

Frank Girardi (6-6) (West Chester '61)
Lycoming............... 85 Gettysburg 10-14
Lycoming............... 89 Dickinson 21-0
Lycoming............... 89 Ferrum 24-49
Lycoming............... 90 Carnegie Mellon 17-7
Lycoming............... 90 Wash. & Jeff. 24-0
Lycoming............... 90 Hofstra 20-10
Lycoming............... 90 Allegheny 14-21 (OT)
Lycoming............... 91 Wash. & Jeff. 18-16
Lycoming............... 91 Susquehanna 24-31
Lycoming............... 92 Wash. & Jeff. 0-33
Lycoming............... 95 Widener 31-27
Lycoming............... 95 Wash. & Jeff. 0-48

Larry Glueck (1-1) (Villanova '63)
Fordham .... 87 Hofstra 41-6
Fordham .... 87 Wagner 0-21

Walt Hameline (4-2) (Brockport St. '75)
Wagner................. 82 St. Lawrence 34-43
Wagner................. 87 Rochester 38-14
Wagner................. 87 Fordham 21-0
Wagner................. 87 Emory & Henry 20-15
Wagner................. 87* Dayton 19-3
Wagner................. 88 Ithaca 31-34 (OT)

Eric Hamilton (1-1) (Trenton St. '75)
Trenton St............. 90 Ithaca 24-14
Trenton St............. 90 Hofstra 3-38

Roger Harring (11-3) (Wis.-La Crosse '58)
Wis.-La Crosse........ 83 Occidental 43-42
Wis.-La Crosse........ 83 Augustana (Ill.) 15-21
Wis.-La Crosse........ 91 Simpson 28-13
Wis.-La Crosse........ 91 St. John's (Minn.) 10-29
Wis.-La Crosse........ 92 Redlands 47-26
Wis.-La Crosse........ 92 Central (Iowa) 34-9
Wis.-La Crosse........ 92 Mount Union 29-24
Wis.-La Crosse........ 92* Wash. & Jeff. 16-12
Wis.-La Crosse........ 93 Wartburg 55-26
Wis.-La Crosse........ 93 St. John's (Minn.) 25-47
Wis.-La Crosse........ 95 Concordia-M'head 45-7
Wis.-La Crosse........ 95 Wis.-River Falls 28-14
Wis.-La Crosse........ 95 Mount Union 20-17
Wis.-La Crosse........ 95* Rowan 36-7

Jim Hershberger (1-2) (Northern Iowa '57)
Buena Vista .... 76 Carroll (Wis.) 20-14 (OT)
Buena Vista .... 76 St. John's (Minn.) 0-61
Buena Vista .... 86 Central (Iowa) 0-37

Fred Hill (1-1) (Upsala '57)
Montclair St........... 81 Alfred 13-12
Montclair St........... 81 Widener 12-23

Rex Huigens (0-1) (La Verne '70)
La Verne .... 94 St. John's (Minn.) 12-51

James Jones (1-1) (Bishop '49)
Bishop .... 82 Wartburg 32-7
Bishop .... 82 West Ga. 6-27

Frank Joranko (0-1) (Albion '52)
Albion................... 77 Minn.-Morris 10-13

Dennis Kayser (1-2) (Ithaca '74)
Cortland St............. 88 Hofstra 32-27

COACHING RECORDS

Cortland St. .... 88 Ithaca 17-24
Cortland St. .... 89 Union (N.Y.) 14-42

K. C. Keeler (6-2) (Delaware '81)
Rowan .... 93 Buffalo St. 29-6
Rowan .... 93 Wm. Paterson 37-0
Rowan .... 93 Wash. & Jeff. 23-16
Rowan .... 93 Mount Union 24-34
Rowan .... 95 Buffalo St. 46-7
Rowan .... 95 Union (N.Y.) 38-7
Rowan .... 95 Wash. & Jeff. 28-15
Rowan .... 95 Wis.-La Crosse 7-36

Larry Kehres (10-5) (Mount Union '71)
Mount Union .... 86 Dayton 42-36
Mount Union .... 86 Augustana (Ill.) 7-16
Mount Union .... 90 Allegheny 15-26
Mount Union .... 92 Dayton 27-10
Mount Union .... 92 Ill. Wesleyan 49-27
Mount Union .... 92 Wis.-La Crosse 24-29
Mount Union .... 93 Allegheny 40-7
Mount Union .... 93 Albion 30-16
Mount Union .... 93 St. John's (Minn.) 56-8
Mount Union .... 93* Rowan 34-24
Mount Union .... 94 Allegheny 28-19
Mount Union .... 94 Albion 33-34
Mount Union .... 95 Hanover 52-18
Mount Union .... 95 Wheaton (Ill.) 40-14
Mount Union .... 95 Wis.-La Crosse 17-20

Mike Kelly (13-8) (Manchester '70)
Dayton .... 81 Augustana (Ill.) 19-7
Dayton .... 81 Lawrence 38-0
Dayton .... 81 Widener 10-17
Dayton .... 84 Augustana (Ill.) 13-14
Dayton .... 86 Mount Union 36-42
Dayton .... 87 Capital 52-28
Dayton .... 87 Augustana (Ill.) 38-36
Dayton .... 87 Central (Iowa) 34-0
Dayton .... 87 Wagner 3-19
Dayton .... 88 Wittenberg 28-35 (2 OT)
Dayton .... 89 John Carroll 35-10
Dayton .... 89 Millikin 28-16
Dayton .... 89 St. John's (Minn.) 28-0
Dayton .... 89* Union (N.Y.) 17-7
Dayton .... 90 Augustana (Ill.) 24-14
Dayton .... 90 Allegheny 23-31
Dayton .... 91 Baldwin-Wallace 27-10
Dayton .... 91 Allegheny 28-25 (OT)
Dayton .... 91 St. John's (Minn.) 19-7
Dayton .... 91 Ithaca 20-34
Dayton .... 92 Mount Union 10-27

Chuck Klausing (2-4) (Slippery Rock '48)
Carnegie Mellon ..... 78 Dayton 24-21
Carnegie Mellon ..... 78 Baldwin-Wallace 6-31
Carnegie Mellon ..... 79 Minn.-Morris 31-25
Carnegie Mellon ..... 79 Ithaca 6-15
Carnegie Mellon ..... 83 Salisbury St. 14-16
Carnegie Mellon ..... 85 Salisbury St. 22-35

Mickey Kwiatkowski (0-5) (Delaware '70)
Hofstra .... 83 Union (N.Y.) 19-51
Hofstra .... 86 Montclair St. 21-24
Hofstra .... 87 Fordham 6-41
Hofstra .... 88 Cortland St. 27-32
Hofstra .... 89 Montclair St. 6-23

Ron Labadie (0-2) (Adrian '71)
Adrian .... 83 Augustana (Ill.) 21-22
Adrian .... 88 Augustana (Ill.) 7-25

Rich Lackner (0-1) (Carnegie Mellon '79)
Carnegie Mellon ..... 90 Lycoming 7-17

Don LaViolette (0-1) (St. Norbert '54)
St. Norbert .... 89 Central (Iowa) 7-55

D. J. LeRoy (0-3) (Wis.-Eau Claire '79)
Wis.-Stevens Point ... 86 Concordia-M'head 15-24
Coe .... 91 St. John's (Minn.) 2-75
Coe .... 93 St. John's (Minn.) 14-32

Leon Lomax (0-1) (Fort Valley St. '43)
Fort Valley St. .... 75 Ithaca 12-41

John Luckhardt (13-10) (Purdue '67)
Wash. & Jeff. .... 84 Randolph-Macon 22-21
Wash. & Jeff. .... 84 Central (Iowa) 0-20
Wash. & Jeff. .... 86 Susquehanna 20-28
Wash. & Jeff. .... 87 Allegheny 23-17 (OT)
Wash. & Jeff. .... 87 Emory & Henry 16-23
Wash. & Jeff. .... 89 Ferrum 7-41
Wash. & Jeff. .... 90 Ferrum 10-7
Wash. & Jeff. .... 90 Lycoming 0-24
Wash. & Jeff. .... 91 Lycoming 16-18
Wash. & Jeff. .... 92 Lycoming 33-0
Wash. & Jeff. .... 92 Emory & Henry 51-15
Wash. & Jeff. .... 92 Rowan 18-13
Wash. & Jeff. .... 92 Wis.-La Crosse 12-16
Wash. & Jeff. .... 93 Moravian 27-7
Wash. & Jeff. .... 93 Frostburg St. 28-7
Wash. & Jeff. .... 93 Rowan 16-23
Wash. & Jeff. .... 94 Trinity (Tex.) 28-0
Wash. & Jeff. .... 94 Widener 37-21
Wash. & Jeff. .... 94 Ithaca 23-19
Wash. & Jeff. .... 94 Albion 15-38
Wash. & Jeff. .... 95 Emory & Henry 35-16
Wash. & Jeff. .... 95 Lycoming 48-0
Wash. & Jeff. .... 95 Rowan 15-28

Mike Manley (0-1) (Anderson, Ind. '73)
Anderson (Ind.) .... 93 Albion 21-41

Bill Manlove (9-5) (Temple '58)
Widener .... 75 Albright 14-6
Widener .... 75 Ithaca 14-23
Widener .... 77 Central (Iowa) 19-0
Widener .... 77 Albany (N.Y.) 33-15
Widener .... 77* Wabash 39-36
Widener .... 79 Baldwin-Wallace 29-8
Widener .... 79 Wittenberg 14-17
Widener .... 80 Bethany (W.Va.) 43-12
Widener .... 80 Dayton 24-28
Widener .... 81 West Ga. 10-3
Widener .... 81 Montclair St. 23-12
Widener .... 81* Dayton 17-10
Widener .... 82 West Ga. 24-31 (3 OT)
Widener .... 88 Moravian 7-17

Dave Maurer (9-2) (Denison '54)
Wittenberg .... 73 San Diego 21-14
Wittenberg .... 73* Juniata 41-0
Wittenberg .... 75 Indianapolis 17-13
Wittenberg .... 75 Millsaps 55-22
Wittenberg .... 75* Ithaca 28-0
Wittenberg .... 78 Ithaca 6-3
Wittenberg .... 78 Minn.-Morris 35-14
Wittenberg .... 78 Baldwin-Wallace 10-24
Wittenberg .... 79 Millersville 21-14
Wittenberg .... 79 Widener 17-14
Wittenberg .... 79 Ithaca 10-14

Mike Maynard (0-2) (Ill. Wesleyan '80)
Redlands .... 90 Central (Iowa) 14-24
Redlands .... 92 Wis.-La Crosse 26-47

Mike McGlinchey (6-4) (Delaware '67)
Salisbury St. .... 83 Carnegie Mellon 16-14
Salisbury St. .... 83 Union (N.Y.) 21-23
Salisbury St. .... 85 Carnegie Mellon 35-22
Salisbury St. .... 85 Gettysburg 6-22
Salisbury St. .... 86 Emory & Henry 34-20
Salisbury St. .... 86 Susquehanna 31-17
Salisbury St. .... 86 Ithaca 44-40
Salisbury St. .... 86 Augustana (Ill.) 3-31
Frostburg St. .... 93 Wilkes 26-25
Frostburg St. .... 93 Wash. & Jeff. 7-28

Steve Miller (0-1) (Cornell College '65)
Carroll (Wis.) .... 76 Buena Vista 14-20 (OT)

Steve Mohr (0-1) (Denison '76)
Trinity (Tex.) .... 94 Wash. & Jeff. 0-28

Al Molde (2-3) (Gust. Adolphus '66)
Minn.-Morris .... 77 Albion 13-10
Minn.-Morris .... 77 Wabash 21-37
Minn.-Morris .... 78 St. Olaf 23-10
Minn.-Morris .... 78 Wittenberg 14-35
Minn.-Morris .... 79 Carnegie Mellon 25-31

Ron Murphy (1-1) (Wittenberg '60)
Wittenberg .... 88 Dayton 35-28 (2 OT)
Wittenberg .... 88 Augustana (Ill.) 14-28

Dave Murray (0-1) (Springfield '81)
Cortland St. .... 90 Hofstra 9-35

Walt Nadzak (1-1) (Denison '57)
Juniata .... 73 Bridgeport 35-14
Juniata .... 73 Wittenberg 0-41

Frank Navarro (2-1) (Maryland '53)
Wabash .... 77 St. John's (Minn.) 20-9
Wabash .... 77 Minn.-Morris 37-21
Wabash .... 77 Widener 36-39

Doug Neibuhr (0-1) (Millikin '75)
Wittenberg .... 95 Wheaton (Ill.) 41-63

Ben Newcomb (0-1) (Augustana, S.D. '57)
Augustana (Ill.) .... 76 St. John's (Minn.) 7-46

Bob Nielson (1-2) (Wartburg '81)
Wartburg .... 93 Wis.-La Crosse 26-55
Wartburg .... 94 Central (Iowa) 22-21
Wartburg .... 94 St. John's (Minn.) 14-42

Hank Norton (4-4) (Lynchburg '51)
Ferrum .... 87 Emory & Henry 7-49
Ferrum .... 88 Rhodes 35-10
Ferrum .... 88 Moravian 49-28
Ferrum .... 88 Ithaca 28-62
Ferrum .... 89 Wash. & Jeff. 41-7
Ferrum .... 89 Lycoming 49-24
Ferrum .... 89 Union (N.Y.) 21-37
Ferrum .... 90 Wash. & Jeff. 7-10

John O'Grady (1-1) (Wis.-River Falls '79)
Wis.-River Falls .... 95 Central (Iowa) 10-7
Wis.-River Falls .... 95 Wis.-La Crosse 14-28

Ken O'Keefe (5-3) (John Carroll '75)
Allegheny .... 90 Mount Union 26-15
Allegheny .... 90 Dayton 31-23
Allegheny .... 90 Central (Iowa) 24-7
Allegheny .... 90* Lycoming 21-14 (OT)
Allegheny .... 91 Albion 24-21 (OT)
Allegheny .... 91 Dayton 25-28 (OT)
Allegheny .... 93 Mount Union 7-40
Allegheny .... 94 Mount Union 19-28

Bob Packard (0-2) (Baldwin-Wallace '65)
Baldwin-Wallace ..... 82 Augustana (Ill.) 22-28
Baldwin-Wallace ..... 91 Dayton 10-27

Paul Pasqualoni (0-1) (Penn St. '72)
Western Conn. St. .. 85 Montclair St. 0-28

Bobby Pate (3-1) (Georgia '63)
West Ga. .... 81 Widener 3-10
West Ga. .... 82 Widener 31-24 (3 OT)
West Ga. .... 82 Bishop 27-6
West Ga. .... 82* Augustana (Ill.) 14-0

C. Wayne Perry (0-1) (DePauw '72)
Hanover .... 95 Mount Union 18-52

Keith Piper (0-1) (Baldwin-Wallace '48)
Denison .... 85 Mount Union 3-35

Carl Poelker (1-1) (Millikin '68)
Millikin .... 89 Augustana (Ill.) 21-12
Millikin .... 89 Dayton 16-28

Tom Porter (0-1) (St. Olaf '51)
St. Olaf .... 78 Minn.-Morris 10-23

John Potsklan (0-2) (Penn St. '49)
Albright .... 75 Widener 6-14
Albright .... 76 St. Lawrence 7-26

Charlie Pravata (0-1) (Adelphi '72)
Merchant Marine .... 94 Plymouth St. 18-19

Steve Raarup (0-1) (Gust. Adolphus '53)
Gust. Adolphus .... 87 St. John's (Minn.) 3-7

Bob Reade (19-7) (Cornell College '54)
Augustana (Ill.) .... 81 Dayton 7-19
Augustana (Ill.) .... 82 Baldwin-Wallace 28-22
Augustana (Ill.) .... 82 St. Lawrence 14-0
Augustana (Ill.) .... 82 West Ga. 0-14
Augustana (Ill.) .... 83 Adrian 22-21
Augustana (Ill.) .... 83 Wis.-La Crosse 21-15
Augustana (Ill.) .... 83* Union (N.Y.) 21-17
Augustana (Ill.) .... 84 Dayton 14-13
Augustana (Ill.) .... 84 Union (N.Y.) 23-6
Augustana (Ill.) .... 84* Central (Iowa) 21-12
Augustana (Ill.) .... 85 Albion 26-10
Augustana (Ill.) .... 85 Mount Union 21-14
Augustana (Ill.) .... 85 Central (Iowa) 14-7
Augustana (Ill.) .... 85* Ithaca 20-7
Augustana (Ill.) .... 86 Hope 34-10
Augustana (Ill.) .... 86 Mount Union 16-7
Augustana (Ill.) .... 86 Concordia-M'head 41-7
Augustana (Ill.) .... 86* Salisbury St. 31-3
Augustana (Ill.) .... 87 Hiram 53-0
Augustana (Ill.) .... 87 Dayton 36-38
Augustana (Ill.) .... 88 Adrian 25-7
Augustana (Ill.) .... 88 Wittenberg 28-14
Augustana (Ill.) .... 88 Central (Iowa) 17-23 (2 OT)
Augustana (Ill.) .... 89 Millikin 12-21
Augustana (Ill.) .... 90 Dayton 14-24
Augustana (Ill.) .... 94 Albion 21-28

Rocky Rees (1-1) (West Chester '71)
Susquehanna .... 86 Wash. & Jeff. 28-20
Susquehanna .... 86 Salisbury St. 17-31

Ron Roberts (1-1) (Wisconsin '54)
Lawrence............... 81 Minn.-Morris 21-14 (OT)
Lawrence............... 81 Dayton 0-38

Bill Russo (0-1)
Wagner................. 80 Ithaca 13-41

Sam Sanders (0-1) (Buffalo '60)
Alfred .... 81 Montclair St. 12-13

Dennis Scannell (0-1) (Villanova '74)
Mass.-Lowell........... 91 Union (N.Y.) 16-55

Ron Schipper (16-11) (Hope '52)
Central (Iowa)......... 74 Evansville 17-16
Central (Iowa)......... 74* Ithaca 10-8
Central (Iowa)......... 77 Widener 0-19
Central (Iowa)......... 84 Occidental 23-22
Central (Iowa)......... 84 Wash. & Jeff. 20-0
Central (Iowa)......... 84 Augustana (Ill.) 12-21
Central (Iowa)......... 85 Coe 27-7
Central (Iowa)......... 85 Occidental 71-0
Central (Iowa)......... 85 Augustana (Ill.) 7-14
Central (Iowa)......... 86 Buena Vista 37-0
Central (Iowa)......... 86 Concordia-M'head 14-17
Central (Iowa)......... 87 Menlo 17-0
Central (Iowa)......... 87 St. John's (Minn.) 13-3
Central (Iowa)......... 87 Dayton 0-34
Central (Iowa)......... 88 Concordia-M'head 7-0
Central (Iowa)......... 88 Wis.-Whitewater 16-13
Central (Iowa)......... 88 Augustana (Ill.) 23-17 (2 OT)
Central (Iowa)......... 88 Ithaca 24-39
Central (Iowa)......... 89 St. Norbert 55-7
Central (Iowa)......... 89 St. John's (Minn.) 24-27
Central (Iowa)......... 90 Redlands 24-14
Central (Iowa)......... 90 St. Thomas (Minn.) 33-32
Central (Iowa)......... 90 Allegheny 7-24
Central (Iowa)......... 92 Carleton 20-8
Central (Iowa)......... 92 Wis.-La Crosse 9-34
Central (Iowa)......... 94 Wartburg 21-22
Central (Iowa)......... 95 Wis.-River Falls 7-10

Pete Schmidt (5-3) (Alma '70)
Albion.................... 85 Augustana (Ill.) 10-26
Albion.................... 91 Allegheny 21-24 (OT)
Albion.................... 93 Anderson (Ind.) 41-21
Albion.................... 93 Mount Union 16-30
Albion.................... 94 Augustana (Ill.) 28-21
Albion.................... 94 Mount Union 34-33
Albion.................... 94 St. John's (Minn.) 19-16
Albion.................... 94* Wash. & Jeff. 38-15

Jim Scott (0-1) (Luther '61)
Aurora.................. 92 Ill. Wesleyan 12-21

Jack Siedlecki (0-1) (Union, N.Y. '73)
Worcester Tech ...... 92 Rowan 14-41

Dick Smith (1-2) (Coe '68)
Minn.-Morris........... 80 Dubuque 41-35
Minn.-Morris........... 80 Ithaca 0-36
Minn.-Morris........... 81 Lawrence 14-21 (OT)

Ray Smith (0-1) (UCLA '61)
Hope .... 86 Augustana (Ill.) 10-34

Ray Solari (0-1) (California '51)
Menlo .... 87 Central (Iowa) 0-17

Ted Stratford (1-2) (St. Lawrence '57)
St. Lawrence........... 76 Albright 26-7
St. Lawrence........... 76 Towson St. 36-38
St. Lawrence........... 78 Baldwin-Wallace 7-71

Barry Streeter (2-1) (Lebanon Valley '71)
Gettysburg .... 85 Lycoming 14-10
Gettysburg .... 85 Salisbury St. 22-6
Gettysburg .... 85 Ithaca 0-34

Bob Sullivan (0-1) (St. John's, Minn. '59)
Carleton................ 92 Central (Iowa) 8-20

Ed Sweeney (0-2) (LIU-C.W. Post '71)
Dickinson .... 89 Lycoming 0-21
Dickinson .... 91 Susquehanna 20-21

Andy Talley (1-1) (Southern Conn. St. '67)
St. Lawrence........... 82 Wagner 43-34
St. Lawrence........... 82 Augustana (Ill.) 0-14

Ray Tellier (0-1) (Connecticut '73)
Rochester .... 87 Wagner 14-38

Bob Thurness (0-1) (Coe '62)
Coe .... 85 Central (Iowa) 7-27

Lee Tressel (3-2) (Baldwin-Wallace '48)
Baldwin-Wallace..... 78 St. Lawrence 71-7
Baldwin-Wallace..... 78 Carnegie Mellon 31-6
Baldwin-Wallace..... 78* Wittenberg 24-10
Baldwin-Wallace..... 79 Widener 8-29
Baldwin-Wallace..... 80 Dayton 0-34

Peter Vaas (0-1) (Holy Cross '74)
Allegheny.............. 87 Wash. & Jeff. 17-23 (OT)

Andy Vinci (0-1) (Cal St. Los Angeles '63)
San Diego.............. 73 Wittenberg 14-21

Ken Wable (1-1) (Muskingum '52)
Mount Union .... 85 Denison 35-3
Mount Union .... 85 Augustana (Ill.) 14-21

Lou Wacker (3-4) (Richmond '56)
Emory & Henry....... 86 Salisbury St. 20-34
Emory & Henry....... 87 Ferrum 49-7
Emory & Henry....... 87 Wash. & Jeff. 23-16
Emory & Henry....... 87 Wagner 15-20
Emory & Henry....... 92 Thomas More 17-0
Emory & Henry....... 92 Wash. & Jeff. 15-51
Emory & Henry....... 95 Wash. & Jeff. 16-35

Vic Wallace (1-1) (Cornell College '65)
St. Thomas (Minn.).. 90 Wis.-Whitewater 24-23
St. Thomas (Minn.).. 90 Central (Iowa) 32-33

Michael Welch (2-1) (Ithaca '73)
Ithaca .... 94 Buffalo St. 10-7 (2 OT)
Ithaca .... 94 Plymouth St. 22-7
Ithaca .... 94 Wash. & Jeff. 19-23

Roger Welsh (0-1) (Muskingum '64)
Capital.................. 87 Dayton 28-52

Dale Widolff (1-3) (Indiana Central '75)
Occidental .... 83 Wis.-La Crosse 42-43
Occidental .... 84 Central (Iowa) 22-23
Occidental .... 85 St. John's (Minn.) 28-10
Occidental .... 85 Central (Iowa) 0-71

Jim Williams (0-3) (Northern Iowa '60)
Simpson................ 88 Wis.-Whitewater 27-29
Simpson................ 89 St. John's (Minn.) 35-42
Simpson................ 91 Wis.-La Crosse 13-28

**National championship.*

Coaching Honors

Division I-A Coach-of-the-Year Award

(Selected by the American Football Coaches Association and the Football Writers Association of America)

AFCA

1935 Lynn Waldorf, Northwestern
1936 Dick Harlow, Harvard
1937 Edward Mylin, Lafayette
1938 Bill Kern, Carnegie Mellon
1939 Eddie Anderson, Iowa
1940 Clark Shaughnessy, Stanford
1941 Frank Leahy, Notre Dame
1942 Bill Alexander, Georgia Tech
1943 Amos Alonzo Stagg, Pacific (Cal.)
1944 Carroll Widdoes, Ohio St.
1945 Bo McMillin, Indiana
1946 Red Blaik, Army
1947 Fritz Crisler, Michigan
1948 Bennie Oosterbaan, Michigan
1949 Bud Wilkinson, Oklahoma
1950 Charlie Caldwell, Princeton
1951 Chuck Taylor, Stanford
1952 Biggie Munn, Michigan St.
1953 Jim Tatum, Maryland
1954 Red Sanders, UCLA
1955 Duffy Daugherty, Michigan St.
1956 Bowden Wyatt, Tennessee
1957 Woody Hayes, Ohio St.
1958 Paul Dietzel, LSU
1959 Ben Schwartzwalder, Syracuse
1960 Murray Warmath, Minnesota
1961 Bear Bryant, Alabama
1962 John McKay, Southern Cal
1963 Darrell Royal, Texas
1964 Frank Broyles, Arkansas, and Ara Parseghian, Notre Dame
1965 Tommy Prothro, UCLA
1966 Tom Cahill, Army
1967 John Pont, Indiana
1968 Joe Paterno, Penn St.
1969 Bo Schembechler, Michigan
1970 Charlie McClendon, LSU, and Darrell Royal, Texas
1971 Bear Bryant, Alabama
1972 John McKay, Southern Cal
1973 Bear Bryant, Alabama
1974 Grant Teaff, Baylor
1975 Frank Kush, Arizona St.
1976 Johnny Majors, Pittsburgh
1977 Don James, Washington
1978 Joe Paterno, Penn St.
1979 Earle Bruce, Ohio St.
1980 Vince Dooley, Georgia
1981 Danny Ford, Clemson
1982 Joe Paterno, Penn St.
1983 Ken Hatfield, Air Force
1984 LaVell Edwards, Brigham Young
1985 Fisher DeBerry, Air Force
1986 Joe Paterno, Penn St.
1987 Dick MacPherson, Syracuse
1988 Don Nehlen, West Va.
1989 Bill McCartney, Colorado
1990 Bobby Ross, Georgia Tech
1991 Bill Lewis, East Caro.
1992 Gene Stallings, Alabama
1993 Barry Alvarez, Wisconsin
1994 Tom Osborne, Nebraska
1995 Gary Barnett, Northwestern

FWAA

1957 Woody Hayes, Ohio St.
1958 Paul Dietzel, LSU
1959 Ben Schwartzwalder, Syracuse
1960 Murray Warmath, Minnesota
1961 Darrell Royal, Texas
1962 John McKay, Southern Cal
1963 Darrell Royal, Texas
1964 Ara Parseghian, Notre Dame
1965 Duffy Daugherty, Michigan St.
1966 Tom Cahill, Army
1967 John Pont, Indiana
1968 Woody Hayes, Ohio St.
1969 Bo Schembechler, Michigan
1970 Alex Agase, Northwestern
1971 Bob Devaney, Nebraska
1972 John McKay, Southern Cal
1973 Johnny Majors, Pittsburgh
1974 Grant Teaff, Baylor
1975 Woody Hayes, Ohio St.
1976 Johnny Majors, Pittsburgh
1977 Lou Holtz, Arkansas
1978 Joe Paterno, Penn St.
1979 Earle Bruce, Ohio St.
1980 Vince Dooley, Georgia
1981 Danny Ford, Clemson
1982 Joe Paterno, Penn St.
1983 Howard Schnellenberger, Miami (Fla.)
1984 LaVell Edwards, Brigham Young
1985 Fisher DeBerry, Air Force
1986 Joe Paterno, Penn St.
1987 Dick MacPherson, Syracuse
1988 Lou Holtz, Notre Dame
1989 Bill McCartney, Colorado
1990 Bobby Ross, Georgia Tech
1991 Don James, Washington
1992 Gene Stallings, Alabama
1993 Terry Bowden, Auburn
1994 Rich Brooks, Oregon
1995 Gary Barnett, Northwestern

Division I-AA Coach-of-the-Year Award

(Selected by the American Football Coaches Association)

1983 Rey Dempsey, Southern Ill.
1984 Dave Arnold, Montana St.
1985 Dick Sheridan, Furman

1986 Erk Russell, Ga. Southern
1987 Mark Duffner, Holy Cross

1988 Jimmy Satterfield, Furman
1989 Erk Russell, Ga. Southern
1990 Tim Stowers, Ga. Southern
1991 Mark Duffner, Holy Cross
1992 Charlie Taafe, Citadel

1993 Dan Allen, Boston U.
1994 Jim Tressel, Youngstown St.
1995 Don Read, Montana

Small College Coach-of-the-Year Awards

(Selected by the American Football Coaches Association)

COLLEGE DIVISION

1960 Warren Woodson, New Mexico St.
1961 Jake Gaither, Florida A&M
1962 Bill Edwards, Wittenberg
1963 Bill Edwards, Wittenberg
1964 Clarence Stasavich, East Caro.

1965 Jack Curtice, UC Santa Barb.
1966 Dan Jessee, Trinity (Conn.)
1967 Scrappy Moore, Tenn.-Chatt.
1968 Jim Root, New Hampshire
1969 Larry Naviaux, Boston U.

1970 Bennie Ellender, Arkansas St.
1971 Tubby Raymond, Delaware
1972 Tubby Raymond, Delaware
1973 Dave Maurer, Wittenberg
1974 Roy Kramer, Central Mich.

1975 Dave Maurer, Wittenberg
1976 Jim Dennison, Akron
1977 Bill Manlove, Widener
1978 Lee Tressel, Baldwin-Wallace
1979 Bill Narduzzi, Youngstown St.

1980 Rick Carter, Dayton
1981 Vito Ragazzo, Shippensburg
1982 Jim Wacker, Southwest Tex. St.

COLLEGE DIVISION I

(NCAA Division II and NAIA Division I)

1983 Don Morton, North Dak. St.
1984 Chan Gailey, Troy St.
1985 George Landis, Bloomsburg
1986 Earle Solomonson, North Dak. St.
1987 Rick Rhoades, Troy St.

1988 Rocky Hager, North Dak. St.
1989 John Williams, Mississippi Col.
1990 Rocky Hager, North Dak. St.
1991 Frank Cignetti, Indiana (Pa.)
1992 Bill Burgess, Jacksonville St.

1993 Bobby Wallace, North Ala.
1994 Bobby Wallace, North Ala.
1995 Bobby Wallace, North Ala.

COLLEGE DIVISION II

(NCAA Division III and NAIA Division II)

1983 Bob Reade, Augustana (Ill.)
1984 Bob Reade, Augustana (Ill.)
1985 Bob Reade, Augustana (Ill.)
1986 Bob Reade, Augustana (Ill.)
1987 Walt Hameline, Wagner

1988 Jim Butterfield, Ithaca
1989 Mike Kelly, Dayton
1990 Ken O'Keefe, Allegheny
1991 Mike Kelly, Dayton
1992 John Luckhardt, Wash. & Jeff.

1993 Larry Kehres, Mount Union
1994 Pete Schmidt, Albion
1995 Roger Harring, Wis.-La Crosse

Added and Discontinued Programs

Nationally Prominent Teams That Permanently Dropped Football

Listed alphabetically at right are the all-time records of teams formerly classified as major college that permanently discontinued football. Also included are those teams that, retroactively, are considered to have been major college (before the advent of official classification in 1937) by virtue of their schedules (i.e., at least half of their games versus other major-college opponents). All schools listed were considered to have been major college or classified in either Division I-A or I-AA for a minimum of 10 consecutive seasons.

Team	Inclusive Seasons	Years	Won	Lost	Tied	Pct.†
Cal St. Fullerton	1970-1992	23	107	150	3	.417
Carlisle Indian School	1893-1917	25	167	88	13	.647
Centenary (La.)	1894-1947	36	148	100	21	.589
Creighton	1900-1942	43	183	139	27	.563
Denver	1885-1960	73	273	262	40	.510
Detroit	1896-1964	64	305	200	25	.599
Geo. Washington	1890-1966	58	209	240	34	.468
Gonzaga	1892-1941	39	130	99	20	.562
Haskell Institute	1896-1938	43	199	166	18	.543
Lamar	1951-1989	39	171	225	9	.433
Long Beach St.	1955-1991	37	199	183	4	.521
Manhattan	1923-1942	20	77	75	11	.506
Marquette	1892-1960	68	273	220	38	.550
New York U.	1873-1952	66	201	231	32	.468
Pacific (Cal.)	1919-1995	77	346	397	23	.467
Saint Louis	1899-1949	49	235	179	33	.563
San Francisco	*1924-1951; 1959-1971	38	133	169	20	.444
Texas-Arlington	1959-1985	27	129	150	2	.463
Wichita St.	1897-1986	89	375	402	47	.484
Xavier (Ohio)	1900-1973	61	302	223	21	.572

*†Ties computed as half won and half lost. *Discontinued football during 1952 after having been classified major college. Resumed at the Division II level during 1959-71, when it was discontinued again.*

Added or Resumed Programs Since 1968

NCAA Member Colleges

1968 (4)
Boise St.; *Chicago; Jersey City St.; UNLV.

1969 (2)
*Adelphi (dropped 1972); Towson St.

1970 (6)
Cal St. Fullerton (dropped 1993); *Fordham; *Georgetown; Plattsburgh St. (dropped 1979); Plymouth St.; *St. Mary's (Cal.).

1971 (6)
Boston St. (dropped 1982); D.C. Teachers (dropped 1974); Federal City (dropped 1975); *New England Col. (dropped 1973); Rochester Tech (dropped 1978); St. Peter's (suspended after one game 1984, resumed 1985, dropped 1988, resumed 1989).

1972 (6)
Kean; *Lake Forest; Nicholls St.; Salisbury St.; *San Diego; Wm. Paterson.

1973 (7)
Albany St. (N.Y.); *Benedictine; Bowie St.; James Madison; New Haven; New York Tech (dropped 1984); Seton Hall (dropped 1982).

1974 (2)
FDU-Madison; Framingham St.

1975 (2)
*Brooklyn (dropped 1991); *Canisius.

1976 (1)
Oswego St. (dropped 1977).

1977 (2)
*Catholic; *Mankato St.

1978 (7)
*Buffalo; Dist. Columbia; Iona; Marist; Pace; *St. Francis (Pa.); *St. John's (N.Y.).

1979 (2)
Central Fla.; *Duquesne.

1980 (5)
*Loras; Mass.-Lowell; *Miles (dropped 1989, resumed 1990); Ramapo (dropped 1993); *Sonoma St.

1981 (4)
Buffalo St.; Mercyhurst; *West Ga.; Western New Eng.

1982 (2)
Valdosta St.; Westfield St.

1983 (2)
*Ky. Wesleyan; Stony Brook.

1984 (3)
Fitchburg St.; *Ga. Southern; *Samford.

1985 (6)
Ferrum; MacMurray; N.Y. Maritime (dropped 1986, resumed 1987, dropped 1989); *St. Peter's (dropped 1988, resumed 1989); *Villanova; Worcester St.

1986 (4)
*UC Santa Barb.; Menlo; *Quincy; Wesley.

1987 (5)
*Aurora; *Drake; Gallaudet; *N.Y. Maritime (dropped 1989); St. John Fisher.

1988 (7)
Assumption; Bentley; Mass.-Boston; Mass.-Dartmouth; *MIT (last team was in 1901); Siena; Stonehill.

1989 (4)
*Gannon; Methodist; *St. Peter's; *Southern Methodist.

1990 (3)
*Hardin-Simmons; *Miles; Thomas More.

1991 (3)
Ala.-Birmingham; Charleston So.; Sacred Heart.

1992 (1)
*West Tex. A&M.

1993 (3)
*King's (Pa.); Monmouth (N.J.); Salve Regina.

1994 (2)
Chapman; Robert Morris.

1996 (2)
Fairfield; Merrimack.

**Previously dropped football.*

Non-NCAA Senior Colleges

1968 (2)
#Mo. Southern St.; #Southwest St.

1970 (1)
#Mo. Western St.

1971 (3)
Concordia (St. Paul); #Gardner-Webb; #Grand Valley St.

1972 (5)
Dr. Martin Luther; #Mars Hill; N'western (Minn.); Pillsbury; #Western Conn. St.

1973 (2)
#Liberty; #Mass. Maritime.

1974 (3)
#*N.M. Highlands; #Northeastern Ill. (dropped 1988); #Saginaw Valley.

1976 (2)
Maranatha Baptist; #Mesa St.

1977 (2)
Evangel; Olivet Nazarene.

1978 (3)
*Baptist Christian (dropped 1983); *St. Ambrose; *Yankton (dropped 1984).

1979 (2)
Fort Lauderdale (dropped 1982); Lubbock Christian (dropped 1983).

1980 (1)
Mid-America Nazarene.

1983 (2)
Ga. Southwestern (dropped 1989); #Loras.

1984 (3)
St. Paul Bible; #Southwest Baptist; *Union (Ky.).

1985 (4)
*Cumberland (Ky.); *Lambuth; *Tenn. Wesleyan; Tiffin.

1986 (4)
*St. Francis (Ill.); Trinity Bible (N.D.); Urbana; #Wingate.

1987 (1)
Greenville.

1988 (5)
Campbellsville; Mary; Midwestern St.; Trinity (Ill.); *Western Mont.

1990 (3)
*Cumberland; Lindenwood; Mt. St. Joseph (Ohio).

1991 (3)
Clinch Valley; Lees-McRae (dropped 1994); *Tusculum.

1993 (6)
Ark.-Pine Bluff; *Bethel (Tenn.); Chowan; Malone; St. Xavier (Ill.); Sue Bennett.

**Previously dropped football. #Now NCAA member.*

Discontinued Programs Since 1950

(Includes NCAA member colleges and non-member colleges; also colleges that closed or merged with other institutions.)

1950 (9)
Alliance; Canisius (resumed 1975); Huntington; Oklahoma City; *Portland; Rio Grande; Rollins; *Saint Louis; Steubenville.

1951 (38)
Arkansas Col.; Atlantic Christian; Canterbury; Catholic (resumed 1977); CCNY; Corpus Christi (resumed 1954, dropped 1967); Daniel Baker; Detroit Tech; *Duquesne (resumed 1979); East Tex. Baptist; Gannon (resumed 1989); *Georgetown (resumed 1970); Glassboro St. (resumed 1964—name changed to Rowan in 1992); Hartwick; High Point; LeMoyne-Owen; Lowell Textile; Lycoming (resumed 1954); McKendree; Milligan; Mt. St. Mary's (Md.); Nevada (resumed 1952); New Bedford Textile; New England Col. (resumed 1971, dropped 1973); Niagara; Northern Idaho; Panzer; St. Mary's (Cal.) (resumed 1970); St. Michael's (N.M.); Shurtleff (resumed 1953, dropped 1954); Southern Idaho; Southwestern (Tenn.) (resumed 1952—name changed to Rhodes in 1986); Southwestern (Tex.); Tillotson; Tusculum (resumed 1991); Washington (Md.); West Va. Wesleyan (resumed 1953); William Penn (resumed 1953).

1952 (13)
Aquinas; Clarkson; Erskine; Louisville Municipal; *Loyola Marymount; Nebraska Central; Rider; Samuel Huston; *San Francisco (resumed 1959, dropped 1972); Shaw (resumed 1953, dropped 1979); St. Bonaventure; St. Martin's; Teikyo Westmar (resumed 1953).

1953 (10)
Arnold; Aurora; Bethel (Tenn.) (resumed 1993); Cedarville; Champlain; Davis & Elkins (resumed 1955, dropped 1962); Georgetown (Ky.) (resumed 1955); *New York U.; *Santa Clara (resumed 1959, dropped 1993); Union (Tenn.).

1954 (8)
Adelphi (resumed 1969, dropped 1972); Case Tech (resumed 1955); Quincy (resumed 1986); St. Francis (Pa.) (resumed 1978); St. Michael's (Vt.); Shurtleff; *Wash. & Lee (resumed 1955); York (Neb.).

1955 (2)
*Fordham (resumed 1970); St. Mary's (Minn.).

1956 (4)
Brooklyn (resumed 1975, dropped 1991); Hendrix (resumed 1957, dropped 1961); William Carey; Wisconsin Extension.

1957 (4)
Lewis; Midwestern (Iowa) (resumed 1966); Morris Harvey; Stetson.

1959 (2)
Florida N&I; West Ga. (resumed 1981).

1960 (5)
Brandeis; Leland; Loras (resumed 1980); St. Ambrose (resumed 1978); Xavier (La.).

1961 (9)
*Denver; Hawaii (resumed 1962); Hendrix; Lincoln (Pa.); *Marquette; Paul Quinn; Scranton; Texas College; Tougaloo.

1962 (5)
Azusa Pacific (resumed 1965); Davis & Elkins; San Diego (resumed 1972); Southern Cal Col.; Westminster (Utah) (resumed 1965, dropped 1979).

1963 (3)
Benedictine (resumed 1973); *Hardin-Simmons (resumed 1990); St. Vincent (Pa.).

1964 (2)
King's (Pa.) (resumed 1993); Paine.

1965 (7)
Claflin; *Detroit; Dillard; Miss. Industrial; Morris; Philander Smith; Rust.

1966 (1)
St. Augustine's.

1967 (6)
Benedict; Corpus Christi; *Geo. Washington; Jarvis Christian; Ozarks; South Caro. Trade.

1968 (2)
Edward Waters; Frederick.

1969 (6)
Allen; Case Tech and Western Reserve merged to form Case Western Reserve; George Fox; Louisiana Col.; UC San Diego; Wiley.

1971 (5)
Bradley; *Buffalo (resumed 1978); Hiram Scott; Lake Forest (resumed 1972); Parsons.

1972 (8)
Adelphi; UC Santa Barb. (resumed 1986); Haverford; North Dak.-Ellendale; Northern Mont.; Northwood (Tex.); San Francisco; Sonoma St. (resumed 1980).

1973 (2)
New England Col.; N.M. Highlands (resumed 1974).

1974 (6)
Col. of Emporia; D.C. Teachers; Drexel; Ill.-Chicago; Samford (resumed 1984); *Xavier (Ohio).

1975 (6)
Baptist Christian (resumed 1978, dropped 1983); Bridgeport; Federal City; *Tampa; Vermont; Wis.-Milwaukee.

1976 (3)
UC Riverside; Mankato St. (resumed 1977); Northland.

1977 (4)
Cal Tech; Oswego St.; Whitman; Yankton (resumed 1978, dropped 1984).

1978 (3)
Cal St. Los Angeles; Col. of Idaho; Rochester Tech.

1979 (5)
Miles (resumed 1980, dropped 1989, resumed 1990); Mont. St.-Billings; Plattsburgh St.; Shaw; Westminster (Utah).

1980 (3)
†Gallaudet; Md.-East. Shore; U.S. Int'l.

1981 (2)
Bluefield St.; *Villanova (resumed 1985).

1982 (4)
Boston St.; Fort Lauderdale; Milton; Seton Hall.

1983 (3)
Baptist Christian; Cal Poly Pomona; Lubbock Christian.

1984 (5)
Fisk; New York Tech; St. Peter's (suspended after one game, resumed 1985, dropped 1988, resumed 1989); So. Dak.-Springfield; Yankton.

1985 (1)
Southern Colo.

1986 (4)
Drake (resumed 1987); N.Y. Maritime (resumed 1987, dropped 1989); Southeastern La.; *Texas-Arlington.

1987 (4)
Bishop; *Southern Methodist (resumed 1989); Western Mont. (resumed 1988); *Wichita St.

1988 (4)
Northeastern Ill.; St. Paul's; St. Peter's (resumed 1989); Texas Lutheran.

1989 (3)
Ga. Southwestern; Miles (resumed 1990); N.Y. Maritime.

1990 (2)
*Lamar; Lincoln (Mo.).

1991 (3)
Brooklyn; Tarkio; West Tex. A&M (resumed 1992).

1992 (3)
*Long Beach St.; Pacific (Ore.); St. Mary of the Plains.

1993 (5)
*Cal St. Fullerton; Cameron; Ramapo; Santa Clara; Wis.-Superior.

1994 (4)
Cal St. Hayward; Lees-McRae; Oregon Tech; Upsala.

1995 (1)
San Fran St.

1996 (1)
*Pacific (Cal.).

**Classified major college previous year. †Did not play a 7-game varsity schedule, 1980-86, and returned to club status in 1995.*

Championship Results

Jason Burfield/NCAA photos

Montana's Matt Wells (left), Jeff Zellick (center) and Marc Bebout (right) begin celebrating the Grizzlies' 22-20 victory over Marshall in the 1995 Division I-AA Football Championship title game.

Division I-AA Championship

1995 Title Game Summary

MARSHALL UNIVERSITY STADIUM, HUNTINGTON, W.VA.; DECEMBER 16, 1995

	Montana			Marshall
First Downs	21			17
Rushes-Net Yardage	29-49			32-112
Passing Yardage	281			246
Return Yardage (Punts, Int. & Fum.)	23			0
Passes (Comp.-Att.-Int.)	29-48-1			23-41-1
Punts (Number-Average)	8-28.1			5-37.0
Fumbles (Number-Lost)	0-0			4-1
Penalties (Number-Yards)	4-18			12-109
Montana	3	7	2	10—22
Marshall	0	3	7	10—20

Game Conditions: Temperature, 51 degrees; wind, 5 mph from northeast; weather, sunny. Attendance: 32,106.

FIRST QUARTER

Montana—Andy Larson 48 field goal (13 yards in 6 plays, 6:09 left)

SECOND QUARTER

Marshall—Tim Openlander 39 field goal (51 yards in 11 plays, 12:54 left)
Montana—Matt Wells 24 pass from Dave Dickenson (Larson kick) (77 yards in 5 plays, 0:59 left)

THIRD QUARTER

Marshall—Chris Parker 10 run (Openlander kick) (48 yards in 11 plays, 9:46 left)
Montana—Safety, Chad Pennington intentional grounding in end zone (6:54 left)

FOURTH QUARTER

Montana—Wells 1 pass from Dickenson (Larson kick) (20 yards in 4 plays, 12:30 left)
Marshall—Openlander 21 field goal (51 yards in 7 plays, 10:05 left)
Marshall—Parker 26 run (Openlander kick) (76 yards in 8 plays, 4:45 left)
Montana—Larson 25 field goal (72 yards in 12 plays, 0:39 left)

INDIVIDUAL LEADERS

Rushing—Montana: Josh Branen, 33 yards on 6 carries; Marshall: Parker, 94 yards on 23 carries.
Passing—Montana: Dickenson, 29 of 48 for 281 yards; Marshall: Pennington, 23 of 40 for 246 yards.
Receiving—Montana: Joe Douglass, 8 catches for 102 yards; Marshall: Jermaine Wiggins, 5 catches for 81 yards.

NCAA I-AA Football Championship History

1978 At the 72nd NCAA Convention (January 1978) in Atlanta, Ga., the membership voted to establish the Division I-AA Football Championship and a statistics program for the division. The format for the first I-AA championship, held in Wichita Falls, Texas, was a single-elimination, four-team tournament. Florida A&M defeated Massachusetts, 35-28, in the title game. The game was televised by ABC.

1981 The championship expanded to include eight teams in a single-elimination tournament.

1982 The championship expanded to include 12 teams. Eight teams played first-round games at campus sites, and the top four teams, seeded by the Division I-AA Football Committee, received byes.

1986 The championship field expanded to its current format of 16 teams with each team playing a first-round game.

1987 Northeast Louisiana defeated Marshall, 43-42, in the closest game in championship history.

1989 A then-record 25,725 fans watched Georgia Southern down Stephen F. Austin, 37-34, in the championship game at Allen E. Paulson Stadium in Statesboro, Ga.

1990 Georgia Southern won its fourth I-AA championship, adding to its titles in 1985, 1986 and 1989.

1991 Youngstown State won its first national championship with a 25-17 victory over Marshall. Penguin head coach Jim Tressel joined his father, Lee, as the only father-son combination to win NCAA football titles. Lee Tressel won the 1978 Division III championship at Baldwin-Wallace.

1992 A then-record crowd of 31,304 in Huntington, W.Va., saw Marshall return the favor with a 31-28 win over Youngstown State for its first I-AA title.

1993 The I-AA championship provided for a maximum field of 16 teams. Six member conferences (Big Sky, Gateway, Ohio Valley, Southern, Southland and Yankee) were granted automatic qualification for their respective winners. Youngstown State won its second I-AA title with a 17-5 victory over Marshall before a crowd of 29,218 in Huntington.

1994 Youngstown State won its third national title in four years with a 28-14 victory over Boise State.

1995 Montana won its first Division I-AA championship before a championship record crowd of 32,106 in Huntington, W.Va.

Division I-AA All-Time Championship Results

Year	Champion	Coach	Score	Runner-Up	Site
1978	Florida A&M	Rudy Hubbard	35-28	Massachusetts	Wichita Falls, Texas
1979	Eastern Ky.	Roy Kidd	30-7	Lehigh	Orlando, Fla.
1980	Boise St.	Jim Criner	31-29	Eastern Ky.	Sacramento, Calif.
1981	Idaho St.	Dave Kragthorpe	34-23	Eastern Ky.	Wichita Falls, Texas
1982	Eastern Ky.	Roy Kidd	17-14	Delaware	Wichita Falls, Texas
1983	Southern Ill.	Rey Dempsey	43-7	Western Caro.	Charleston, S.C.
1984	Montana St.	Dave Arnold	19-6	Louisiana Tech	Charleston, S.C.
1985	Ga. Southern	Erk Russell	44-42	Furman	Tacoma, Wash.
1986	Ga. Southern	Erk Russell	48-21	Arkansas St.	Tacoma, Wash.
1987	Northeast La.	Pat Collins	43-42	Marshall	Pocatello, Idaho
1988	Furman	Jimmy Satterfield	17-12	Ga. Southern	Pocatello, Idaho
1989	Ga. Southern	Erk Russell	37-34	*Stephen F. Austin	Statesboro, Ga.
1990	Ga. Southern	Tim Stowers	36-13	Nevada	Statesboro, Ga.
1991	Youngstown St.	Jim Tressel	25-17	Marshall	Statesboro, Ga.
1992	Marshall	Jim Donnan	31-28	Youngstown St.	Huntington, W.Va.
1993	Youngstown St.	Jim Tressel	17-5	Marshall	Huntington, W.Va.
1994	Youngstown St.	Jim Tressel	28-14	Boise St.	Huntington, W.Va.
1995	Montana	Don Read	22-20	Marshall	Huntington, W.Va.

**Stephen F. Austin's participation in 1989 Division I-AA championship vacated.*

Jason Burfield/NCAA photos

Marshall's Chad Pennington passes under intense pressure from the Montana defense during the 1995 Division I-AA title game, won by Montana, 22-20.

1995 Division I-AA Championship Results

FIRST ROUND
McNeese St. 33, Idaho 3
Delaware 38, Hofstra 17
Northern Iowa 35, Murray St. 34
Marshall 38, Jackson St. 8
Appalachian St. 31, James Madison 24
Stephen F. Austin 34, Eastern Ill. 29
Ga. Southern 24, Troy St. 21
Montana 48, Eastern Ky. 0

QUARTERFINALS
McNeese St. 52, Delaware 18
Marshall 41, Northern Iowa 24
Stephen F. Austin 27, Appalachian St. 17
Montana 45, Ga. Southern 0

SEMIFINALS
Marshall 25, McNeese St. 13
Montana 70, Stephen F. Austin 14

CHAMPIONSHIP
Montana 22, Marshall 20

Championship Records

INDIVIDUAL: SINGLE GAME

NET YARDS RUSHING
250—Greg Robinson, Northeast La. (78) vs. Alcorn St. (27), 11-28-92.

RUSHES ATTEMPTED
46—Tamron Smith, Youngstown St. (10) vs. Samford (0), 12-14-91.

TOUCHDOWNS BY RUSHING
6—Sean Sanders, Weber St. (59) vs. Idaho (30), 11-28-87.

NET YARDS PASSING
517—Todd Hammel, Stephen F. Austin (59) vs. Grambling (56), 11-25-89.

PASSES ATTEMPTED
82—Steve McNair, Alcorn St. (20) vs. Youngstown St. (63), 11-25-94.

PASSES COMPLETED
52—Steve McNair, Alcorn St. (20) vs. Youngstown St. (63), 11-25-94.

PASSES HAD INTERCEPTED
7—Jeff Gilbert, Western Caro. (7) vs. Southern Ill. (43), 12-17-83.

TOUCHDOWN PASSES COMPLETED
6—Mike Smith, Northern Iowa (41) vs. Northeast La. (44), 12-12-87; Clemente Gordon, Grambling (56) vs. Stephen F. Austin (59), 11-25-89.

COMPLETION PERCENTAGE (Min. 15 Attempts)
.841—Dave Dickenson, Montana (48) vs. Delaware (49), 11-27-93 (37 of 44).

NET YARDS RUSHING AND PASSING
539—Todd Hammel, Stephen F. Austin (59) vs. Grambling (56), 11-25-89 (517 passing, 22 rushing).

NUMBER OF RUSHING AND PASSING PLAYS
91—Steve McNair, Alcorn St. (20) vs. Youngstown St. (63), 11-25-94.

PUNTING AVERAGE (Min. 3 Punts)
50.3—Steve Rowe, Eastern Ky. (38) vs. Idaho (30), 12-4-82.

NUMBER OF PUNTS
14—Fred McRae, Jackson St. (0) vs. Stephen F. Austin (24), 11-26-88.

PASSES CAUGHT
18—Brian Forster, Rhode Island (23) vs. Richmond (17), 12-1-84.

NET YARDS RECEIVING
264—Winky White, Boise St. (52) vs. Nevada (59), 3 OT, 12-8-90 (11 catches).

TOUCHDOWN PASSES CAUGHT
4—Tony DiMaggio, Rhode Island (35) vs. Akron (27), 11-30-85.

PASSES INTERCEPTED
4—Greg Shipp, Southern Ill. (43) vs. Western Caro. (7), 12-17-83.

YARDS GAINED ON INTERCEPTION RETURNS
117—Kevin Sullivan, Massachusetts (44) vs. Nevada (21), 12-9-78.

YARDS GAINED ON PUNT RETURNS
95—Troy Brown, Marshall (44) vs. Eastern Ky. (0), 11-28-92.

YARDS GAINED ON KICKOFF RETURNS
232—Mike Cadore, Eastern Ky. (32) vs. Northeast La. (33), 12-5-87, 6 returns, 1 for 99-yard TD.

YARDS GAINED ON FUMBLE RETURNS
95—Randy Smith, Youngstown St. (63) vs. Alcorn St. (20), 11-25-94.

POINTS
36—Sean Sanders, Weber St. (59) vs. Idaho (30), 11-28-87.

TOUCHDOWNS
6—Sean Sanders, Weber St. (59) vs. Idaho (30), 11-28-87.

EXTRA POINTS
10—Andy Larson, Montana (70) vs. Stephen F. Austin (14), 12-9-95.

FIELD GOALS
4—Jeff Wilkins, Youngstown St. (19) vs. Northern Iowa (7), 12-12-92; Jose Larios, McNeese St. (33) vs. Idaho (3), 11-25-95.

INDIVIDUAL: TOURNAMENT

NET YARDS RUSHING
661—Tracy Ham, Ga. Southern, 1986 (128 vs. North Caro. A&T, 191 vs. Nicholls St., 162 vs. Nevada, 180 vs. Arkansas St.).

RUSHES ATTEMPTED
123—Ray Whalen, Nevada, 1990 (21 vs. Northeast La., 34 vs. Furman, 44 vs. Boise St., 24 vs. Ga. Southern).

NET YARDS PASSING
1,500—Dave Dickenson, Montana, 1995 (441 vs. Eastern Ky., 408 vs. Ga. Southern, 370 vs. Stephen F. Austin, 281 vs. Marshall).

PASSES ATTEMPTED
177—Jeff Gilbert, Western Caro., 1983 (47 vs. Colgate, 52 vs. Holy Cross, 45 vs. Furman, 33 vs. Southern Ill.).

PASSES COMPLETED
122—Dave Dickenson, Montana, 1995 (31 vs. Eastern Ky., 37 vs. Ga. Southern, 25 vs. Stephen F. Austin, 29 vs. Marshall).

TOUCHDOWN PASSES COMPLETED
14—Todd Hammel, Stephen F. Austin, 1989 (5 vs. Grambling, 4 vs. Southwest Mo. St., 2 vs. Furman, 3 vs. Ga. Southern).

COMPLETION PERCENTAGE (Min. 50 Completions)
.722—Dave Dickenson, Montana, 1995, 122 of 169 (31-39 vs. Eastern Ky., 37-46 vs. Ga. Southern, 25-36 vs. Stephen F. Austin, 29-48 vs. Marshall).

PASSES HAD INTERCEPTED
11—Todd Hammel, Stephen F. Austin, 1989 (0 vs. Grambling, 4 vs. Southwest Mo. St., 2 vs. Furman, 5 vs. Ga. Southern).

PASSES CAUGHT
36—Ross Ortega, Nevada, 1990 (1 vs. Northeast La., 15 vs. Furman, 10 vs. Boise St., 10 vs. Ga. Southern).

NET YARDS RECEIVING
545—Troy Brown, Marshall, 1992 (188 vs. Eastern Ky., 189 vs. Middle Tenn. St., 53 vs. Delaware, 115 vs. Youngstown St.).

TOUCHDOWN PASSES CAUGHT
6—Keith Baxter, Marshall, 1987 (1 vs. James Madison, 3 vs. Weber St., 0 vs. Appalachian St., 2 vs. Northeast La.).

POINTS
66—Gerald Harris, Ga. Southern, 1986 (30 vs. North Caro. A&T, 18 vs. Nicholls St., 12 vs. Nevada, 6 vs. Arkansas St.).

TOUCHDOWNS
11—Gerald Harris, Ga. Southern, 1986 (5 vs. North Caro. A&T, 3 vs. Nicholls St., 2 vs. Nevada, 1 vs. Arkansas St.).

INDIVIDUAL: LONGEST PLAYS

LONGEST RUSH
90—Henry Fields, McNeese St. (38) vs. Idaho (21), 11-26-94.

LONGEST PASS (INCLUDING RUN)
90—Paul Singer 22 pass to Derek Swanson and 68 fumble recovery advancement by Steve Williams, Western Ill. (32) vs. Western Ky. (35), 11-26-88.

LONGEST FIELD GOAL
56—Tony Zendejas, Nevada (27) vs. Idaho St. (20), 11-26-83.

LONGEST PUNT
88—Mike Cassidy, Rhode Island (20) vs. Montana St. (32), 12-8-84.

LONGEST PUNT RETURN
84—Rob Friese, Eastern Wash. (14) vs. Northern Iowa (17), 12-7-85, TD.

LONGEST KICKOFF RETURN
100—Chris Fontenette, McNeese St. (7) vs. Northern Iowa (29), 12-5-92, TD.

LONGEST FUMBLE RETURN
95—Randy Smith, Youngstown St. (63) vs. Alcorn St. (20), 11-25-94.

LONGEST INTERCEPTION RETURN
100—Melvin Cunningham, Marshall (28) vs. James Madison (21), OT, 12-3-94, TD; Paul Williams, Delaware (38) vs. Hofstra (17), 11-25-95, TD.

TEAM: SINGLE GAME

FIRST DOWNS
41—Montana (45) vs. Ga. Southern (0), 12-2-95.

FIRST DOWNS BY RUSHING
29—Alcorn St. (20) vs. Youngstown St. (63), 11-25-94.

FIRST DOWNS BY PASSING
28—Rhode Island (35) vs. Akron (27), 11-30-85.

RUSHES ATTEMPTED
81—Youngstown St. (10) vs. Samford (0), 12-14-91.

NET YARDS RUSHING
518—Arkansas St. (55) vs. Delaware (14), 12-6-86.

NET YARDS PASSING
537—Montana (30) vs. McNeese St. (28), 12-3-94.

PASSES ATTEMPTED
90—Rhode Island (15) vs. Furman (59), 12-7-85.

PASSES COMPLETED
52—Alcorn St. (20) vs. Youngstown St. (63), 11-25-94.

COMPLETION PERCENTAGE
(Min. 10 Attempts)
.841—Montana (48) vs. Delaware (49), 11-27-93 (37 of 44).

PASSES HAD INTERCEPTED
7—Western Caro. (7) vs. Southern Ill. (43), 12-17-83; Rhode Island (15) vs. Furman (59), 12-7-85; Weber St. (23) vs. Marshall (51), 12-5-87.

NET YARDS RUSHING AND PASSING
742—Northeast La. (78) vs. Alcorn St. (27), 11-28-92.

RUSHING AND PASSING PLAYS
114—Nevada (42) vs. Furman (35), 3 OT, 12-1-90 (47 rushing, 67 passing).

PUNTING AVERAGE
(Min. 4 Punts)
50.2—Montana St. (32) vs. Rhode Island (20), 12-8-84.

NUMBER OF PUNTS
14—Jackson St. (0) vs. Stephen F. Austin (24), 11-26-88.

PUNTS HAD BLOCKED
2—Florida A&M (35) vs. Massachusetts (28), 12-16-78; Boise St. (14) vs. Grambling (9), 12-13-80.

YARDS GAINED ON PUNT RETURNS
115—Youngstown St. (19) vs. Northern Iowa (7), 12-12-92.

YARDS GAINED ON KICKOFF RETURNS
232—Eastern Ky. (32) vs. Northeast La. (33), 12-5-87.

YARDS GAINED ON INTERCEPTION RETURNS
164—Marshall (51) vs. Weber St. (23), 12-5-87.

YARDS PENALIZED
172—Tennessee St. (32) vs. Jackson St. (23), 11-29-86.

FUMBLES LOST
6—South Caro. St. (12) vs. Idaho St. (41), 12-12-81; Idaho (38) vs. Eastern Wash. (42), 11-30-85.

POINTS
78—Northeast La. vs. Alcorn St. (27), 11-28-92.

TEAM: TOURNAMENT

FIRST DOWNS
125—Montana, 1995 (25 vs. Eastern Ky., 41 vs. Ga. Southern, 38 vs. Stephen F. Austin, 21 vs. Marshall).

NET YARDS RUSHING
1,522—Ga. Southern, 1986 (442 vs. North Caro. A&T, 317 vs. Nicholls St., 466 vs. Nevada, 297 vs. Arkansas St.).

NET YARDS PASSING
1,607—Montana, 1995 (407 vs. Eastern Ky., 446 vs. Ga. Southern, 473 vs. Stephen F. Austin, 281 vs. Marshall).

NET YARDS RUSHING AND PASSING
2,241—Ga. Southern, 1986 (541 vs. North Caro. A&T, 484 vs. Nicholls St., 613 vs. Nevada, 603 vs. Arkansas St.).

PASSES ATTEMPTED
196—Montana, 1995 (46 vs. Eastern Ky., 54 vs. Ga. Southern, 48 vs. Stephen F. Austin, 48 vs. Marshall).

PASSES COMPLETED
137—Montana, 1995 (35 vs. Eastern Ky., 42 vs. Ga. Southern, 31 vs. Stephen F. Austin, 29 vs. Marshall).

PASSES HAD INTERCEPTED
11—Stephen F. Austin, 1989 (0 vs. Grambling, 4 vs. Southwest Mo. St., 2 vs. Furman, 5 vs. Ga. Southern).

NUMBER OF PUNTS
29—Northern Iowa, 1992 (11 vs. Eastern Wash., 10 vs. McNeese St., 8 vs. Youngstown St.).

YARDS PENALIZED
350—Ga. Southern, 1986 (106 vs. North Caro. A&T, 104 vs. Nicholls St., 75 vs. Nevada, 65 vs. Arkansas St.).

FUMBLES LOST
9—Nevada, 1983 (3 vs. Idaho St., 4 vs. North Texas, 2 vs. Southern Ill.); Youngstown St., 1991 (3 vs. Villanova, 1 vs. Nevada, 4 vs. Samford, 1 vs. Marshall).

POINTS
203—Ga. Southern, 1986 (52 vs. North Caro. A&T, 55 vs. Nicholls St., 48 vs. Nevada, 48 vs. Arkansas St.).

INDIVIDUAL: CHAMPIONSHIP GAME

NET YARDS RUSHING
207—Mike Solomon, Florida A&M (35) vs. Massachusetts (28), 1978 (27 carries).

RUSHES ATTEMPTED
31—Joe Ross, Ga. Southern (37) vs. Stephen F. Austin (34), 1989 (152 yards); Raymond Gross, Ga. Southern (36) vs. Nevada (13), 1990 (145 yards).

TOUCHDOWNS BY RUSHING
4—John Bagwell, Furman (42) vs. Ga. Southern (44), 1985.

NET YARDS PASSING
474—Tony Peterson, Marshall (42) vs. Northeast La. (43), 1987 (28 of 54).

PASSES ATTEMPTED
57—Kelly Bradley, Montana St. (19) vs. Louisiana Tech (6), 1984 (32 completions).

PASSES COMPLETED
32—Kelly Bradley, Montana St. (19) vs. Louisiana Tech (6), 1984 (57 attempts).

PASSES HAD INTERCEPTED
7—Jeff Gilbert, Western Caro. (7) vs. Southern Ill. (43), 1983.

TOUCHDOWN PASSES COMPLETED
4—Tracy Ham, Ga. Southern (44) vs. Furman (42), 1985; Tony Peterson, Marshall (42) vs. Northeast La. (43), 1987.

COMPLETION PERCENTAGE
(Min. 8 Attempts)
.875—Mark Brungard, Youngstown St. (17) vs. Marshall (5), 1993 (7 of 8).

NET YARDS RUSHING AND PASSING
509—Tracy Ham, Ga. Southern (44) vs. Furman (42), 1985 (56 plays).

NUMBER OF RUSHING AND PASSING PLAYS
66—Dave Dickenson, Montana (22) vs. Marshall (20), 1995 (18 rush, 48 pass, 346 yards).

PUNTING AVERAGE
(Min. 3 Punts)
48.3—Todd Fugate, Marshall (42) vs. Northeast La. (43), 1987 (3 punts).

NUMBER OF PUNTS
10—Rick Titus, Delaware (14) vs. Eastern Ky. (17), 1982 (41.6 average).

PASSES CAUGHT
11—Kipp Bedard, Boise St. (31) vs. Eastern Ky. (29), 1980 (212 yards).

NET YARDS RECEIVING
212—Kipp Bedard, Boise St. (31) vs. Eastern Ky. (29), 1980 (11 catches).

TOUCHDOWN PASSES CAUGHT
2—Steve Bird, Eastern Ky. (23) vs. Idaho St. (34), 1981; Joseph Bignell, Montana St. (19) vs. Louisiana Tech (6), 1984; Frank Johnson, Ga. Southern (44) vs. Furman (42), 1985; Keith Baxter, Marshall (42) vs. Northeast La. (43), 1987; Larry Centers, Stephen F. Austin (34) vs. Ga. Southern (37), 1989; Randy Matyschock, Boise St. (14) vs. Youngstown St. (28), 1994; Matt Wells, Montana (22) vs. Marshall (20), 1995.

PASSES INTERCEPTED
4—Greg Shipp, Southern Ill. (43) vs. Western Caro. (7), 1983.

YARDS GAINED ON INTERCEPTION RETURNS
58—Chris Cook, Boise St. (14) vs. Youngstown St. (28), 1994 (1 interception).

YARDS GAINED ON PUNT RETURNS
67—Rodney Oglesby, Ga. Southern (36) vs. Nevada (13), 1990 (6 returns).

YARDS GAINED ON KICKOFF RETURNS
207—Eric Rasheed, Western Caro. (7) vs. Southern Ill. (43), 1983 (6 returns).

POINTS
24—John Bagwell, Furman (42) vs. Ga. Southern (44), 1985.

TOUCHDOWNS
4—John Bagwell, Furman (42) vs. Ga. Southern (44), 1985.

EXTRA POINTS
6—Keven Esval, Furman (42) vs. Ga. Southern (44), 1985.

FIELD GOALS
4—Tim Foley, Ga. Southern (48) vs. Arkansas St. (21), 1986.

LONGEST RUSH
58—Dale Patton, Eastern Ky. (30) vs. Lehigh (7), 1979.

LONGEST PASS COMPLETION
79—Tracy Ham to Ricky Harris, Ga. Southern (48) vs. Arkansas St. (21), 1986.

LONGEST FIELD GOAL
55—David Cool, Ga. Southern (12) vs. Furman (17), 1988.

LONGEST PUNT
72—Rick Titus, Delaware (14) vs. Eastern Ky. (17), 1982.

TEAM: CHAMPIONSHIP GAME

FIRST DOWNS
28—Furman (42) vs. Ga. Southern (44), 1985; Ga. Southern (48) vs. Arkansas St. (21), 1986; Northeast La. (43) vs. Marshall (42), 1987.

FIRST DOWNS BY RUSHING
19—Florida A&M (35) vs. Massachusetts (28), 1978.

FIRST DOWNS BY PASSING
19—Marshall (42) vs. Northeast La. (43), 1987.

FIRST DOWNS BY PENALTY
3—Eastern Ky. (23) vs. Idaho St. (34), 1981; Furman (42) vs. Ga. Southern (44), 1985; Northeast La. (43) vs. Marshall (42), 1987.

NET YARDS RUSHING
470—Florida A&M (35) vs. Massachusetts (28), 1978 (76 attempts).

RUSHES ATTEMPTED
76—Florida A&M (35) vs. Massachusetts (28), 1978 (470 yards).

NET YARDS PASSING
474—Marshall (42) vs. Northeast La. (43), 1987 (28 of 54).

PASSES ATTEMPTED
57—Montana St. (19) vs. Louisiana Tech (6), 1984 (32 completions).

PASSES COMPLETED
32—Montana St. (19) vs. Louisiana Tech (6), 1984 (57 attempts).

COMPLETION PERCENTAGE (Min. 10 Attempts)
.760—Southern Ill. (43) vs. Western Caro. (7), 1983 (19 of 25).

PASSES HAD INTERCEPTED
7—Western Caro. (7) vs. Southern Ill. (43), 1983.

NET YARDS RUSHING AND PASSING
640—Ga. Southern (44) vs. Furman (42), 1985 (77 plays).

RUSHING AND PASSING PLAYS
86—Boise St. (31) vs. Eastern Ky. (29), 1980 (510 yards); Nevada (13) vs. Ga. Southern (36), 1990 (321 yards).

PUNTING AVERAGE (Min. 3 Punts)
48.3—Marshall (42) vs. Northeast La. (43), 1987 (3 punts).

NUMBER OF PUNTS
10—Delaware (14) vs. Eastern Ky. (17), 1982 (41.6 average).

YARDS GAINED ON PUNT RETURNS
67—Ga. Southern (36) vs. Nevada (13), 1990 (6 returns).

YARDS GAINED ON KICKOFF RETURNS
229—Western Caro. (7) vs. Southern Ill. (43), 1983 (8 returns).

YARDS GAINED ON INTERCEPTION RETURNS
70—Marshall (31) vs. Youngstown St. (28), 1992 (2 interceptions).

YARDS PENALIZED
162—Idaho St. (34) vs. Eastern Ky. (23), 1981 (12 penalties).

FUMBLES
5—Eastern Ky. (17) vs. Delaware (14), 1982; Western Caro. (7) vs. Southern Ill. (43), 1983; Louisiana Tech (6) vs. Montana St. (19), 1984; Northeast La. (43) vs. Marshall (42), 1987; Ga. Southern (12) vs. Furman (17), 1988; Ga. Southern (36) vs. Nevada (13), 1990.

FUMBLES LOST
4—Northeast La. (43) vs. Marshall (42), 1987; Ga. Southern (36) vs. Nevada (13), 1990.

POINTS
48—Ga. Southern vs. Arkansas St. (21), 1986.

ATTENDANCE
32,106—Marshall University Stadium, Huntington, W.Va., 1995.

Year-by-Year Division I-AA Championship Results

Year (Number of Teams)	Coach	Record	Result
1978 (4)			
Florida A&M	Rudy Hubbard	2-0	Champion
Massachusetts	Bob Pickett	1-1	Second
Jackson St.	W. C. Gorden	0-1	Lost 1st Round
Nevada	Chris Ault	0-1	Lost 1st Round
1979 (4)			
Eastern Ky.	Roy Kidd	2-0	Champion
Lehigh	John Whitehead	1-1	Second
Murray St.	Mike Gottfried	0-1	Lost 1st Round
Nevada	Chris Ault	0-1	Lost 1st Round
1980 (4)			
Boise St.	Jim Criner	2-0	Champion
Eastern Ky.	Roy Kidd	1-1	Second
Grambling	Eddie Robinson	0-1	Lost 1st Round
Lehigh	John Whitehead	0-1	Lost 1st Round
1981 (8)			
Idaho St.	Dave Kragthorpe	3-0	Champion
Eastern Ky.	Roy Kidd	2-1	Second
Boise St.	Jim Criner	1-1	Semifinalist
South Caro. St.	Bill Davis	1-1	Semifinalist
Delaware	Tubby Raymond	0-1	Lost 1st Round
Jackson St.	W. C. Gorden	0-1	Lost 1st Round
Rhode Island	Bob Griffin	0-1	Lost 1st Round
*Tennessee St.	John Merritt	0-1	Vacated
1982 (12)			
Eastern Ky.	Roy Kidd	3-0	Champion
Delaware	Tubby Raymond	2-1	Second
Louisiana Tech	Billy Brewer	1-1	Semifinalist
*Tennessee St.	John Merritt	1-1	Vacated
Colgate	Fred Dunlap	1-1	Quarterfinalist
Eastern Ill.	Darrell Mudra	1-1	Quarterfinalist
Idaho	Dennis Erickson	1-1	Quarterfinalist
South Caro. St.	Bill Davis	1-1	Quarterfinalist
Boston U.	Rick Taylor	0-1	Lost 1st Round
Furman	Dick Sheridan	0-1	Lost 1st Round
Jackson St.	W. C. Gorden	0-1	Lost 1st Round
Montana	Larry Donovan	0-1	Lost 1st Round
1983 (12)			
Southern Ill.	Rey Dempsey	3-0	Champion
Western Caro.	Bob Waters	3-1	Second
Furman	Dick Sheridan	1-1	Semifinalist
Nevada	Chris Ault	2-1	Semifinalist
Boston U.	Rick Taylor	1-1	Quarterfinalist
Holy Cross	Rick Carter	0-1	Quarterfinalist
Indiana St.	Dennis Raetz	1-1	Quarterfinalist
North Texas	Corky Nelson	0-1	Quarterfinalist
Colgate	Fred Dunlap	0-1	Lost 1st Round
Eastern Ill.	Al Molde	0-1	Lost 1st Round
Eastern Ky.	Roy Kidd	0-1	Lost 1st Round
Idaho St.	Jim Koetter	0-1	Lost 1st Round
1984 (12)			
Montana St.	Dave Arnold	3-0	Champion
Louisiana Tech	A. L. Williams	3-1	Second
Middle Tenn. St.	James Donnelly	2-1	Semifinalist
Rhode Island	Bob Griffin	1-1	Semifinalist
Alcorn St.	Marino Casem	0-1	Quarterfinalist
Arkansas St.	Larry Lacewell	1-1	Quarterfinalist
Indiana St.	Dennis Raetz	0-1	Quarterfinalist
Richmond	Dal Shealy	1-1	Quarterfinalist
Boston U.	Rick Taylor	0-1	Lost 1st Round
Eastern Ky.	Roy Kidd	0-1	Lost 1st Round
Mississippi Val.	Archie Cooley Jr.	0-1	Lost 1st Round
Tenn.-Chatt.	Buddy Nix	0-1	Lost 1st Round
1985 (12)			
Ga. Southern	Erk Russell	4-0	Champion
Furman	Dick Sheridan	2-1	Second
Nevada	Chris Ault	1-1	Semifinalist
Northern Iowa	Darrell Mudra	1-1	Semifinalist
Arkansas St.	Larry Lacewell	1-1	Quarterfinalist
Eastern Wash.	Dick Zornes	1-1	Quarterfinalist
Middle Tenn. St.	James Donnelly	0-1	Quarterfinalist
Rhode Island	Bob Griffin	1-1	Quarterfinalist
Akron	Jim Dennison	0-1	Lost 1st Round
Grambling	Eddie Robinson	0-1	Lost 1st Round
Idaho	Dennis Erickson	0-1	Lost 1st Round
Jackson St.	W. C. Gorden	0-1	Lost 1st Round
1986 (16)			
Ga. Southern	Erk Russell	4-0	Champion
Arkansas St.	Larry Lacewell	3-1	Second
Eastern Ky.	Roy Kidd	2-1	Semifinalist
Nevada	Chris Ault	2-1	Semifinalist
Delaware	Tubby Raymond	1-1	Quarterfinalist
Eastern Ill.	Al Molde	1-1	Quarterfinalist
Nicholls St.	Sonny Jackson	1-1	Quarterfinalist
Tennessee St.	William Thomas	1-1	Quarterfinalist
Appalachian St.	Sparky Woods	0-1	Lost 1st Round
Furman	Jimmy Satterfield	0-1	Lost 1st Round
Idaho	Keith Gilbertson	0-1	Lost 1st Round
Jackson St.	W. C. Gorden	0-1	Lost 1st Round
Murray St.	Frank Beamer	0-1	Lost 1st Round

Year (Number of Teams)	Coach	Record	Result
North Caro. A&T	Maurice Forte	0-1	Lost 1st Round
Sam Houston St.	Ron Randleman	0-1	Lost 1st Round
William & Mary	Jimmye Laycock	0-1	Lost 1st Round
1987 (16)			
Northeast La.	Pat Collins	4-0	Champion
Marshall	George Chaump	3-1	Second
Appalachian St.	Sparky Woods	2-1	Semifinalist
Northern Iowa	Darrell Mudra	2-1	Semifinalist
Arkansas St.	Larry Lacewell	1-1	Quarterfinalist
Eastern Ky.	Roy Kidd	1-1	Quarterfinalist
Ga. Southern	Erk Russell	1-1	Quarterfinalist
Weber St.	Mike Price	1-1	Quarterfinalist
Idaho	Keith Gilbertson	0-1	Lost 1st Round
Jackson St.	W. C. Gorden	0-1	Lost 1st Round
James Madison	Joe Purzycki	0-1	Lost 1st Round
Maine	Tim Murphy	0-1	Lost 1st Round
North Texas	Corky Nelson	0-1	Lost 1st Round
Richmond	Dal Shealy	0-1	Lost 1st Round
Western Ky.	Dave Roberts	0-1	Lost 1st Round
Youngstown St.	Jim Tressel	0-1	Lost 1st Round
1988 (16)			
Furman	Jimmy Satterfield	4-0	Champion
Ga. Southern	Erk Russell	3-1	Second
Eastern Ky.	Roy Kidd	2-1	Semifinalist
Idaho	Keith Gilbertson	2-1	Semifinalist
Marshall	George Chaump	1-1	Quarterfinalist
Northwestern St.	Sam Goodwin	1-1	Quarterfinalist
Stephen F. Austin	Jim Hess	1-1	Quarterfinalist
Western Ky.	Dave Roberts	1-1	Quarterfinalist
Boise St.	Skip Hall	0-1	Lost 1st Round
Citadel	Charlie Taaffe	0-1	Lost 1st Round
Delaware	Tubby Raymond	0-1	Lost 1st Round
Jackson St.	W. C. Gorden	0-1	Lost 1st Round
Massachusetts	Jim Reid	0-1	Lost 1st Round
Montana	Don Read	0-1	Lost 1st Round
North Texas	Corky Nelson	0-1	Lost 1st Round
Western Ill.	Bruce Craddock	0-1	Lost 1st Round
1989 (16)			
Ga. Southern	Erk Russell	4-0	Champion
*Stephen F. Austin	Lynn Graves	3-1	Vacated
Furman	Jimmy Satterfield	2-1	Semifinalist
Montana	Don Read	2-1	Semifinalist
Eastern Ill.	Bob Spoo	1-1	Quarterfinalist
Middle Tenn. St.	James Donnelly	1-1	Quarterfinalist
Southwest Mo. St.	Jesse Branch	1-1	Quarterfinalist
Youngstown St.	Jim Tressel	1-1	Quarterfinalist
Appalachian St.	Jerry Moore	0-1	Lost 1st Round
Eastern Ky.	Roy Kidd	0-1	Lost 1st Round
Grambling	Eddie Robinson	0-1	Lost 1st Round
Idaho	John L. Smith	0-1	Lost 1st Round
Jackson St.	W. C. Gorden	0-1	Lost 1st Round
Maine	Tom Lichtenberg	0-1	Lost 1st Round
Villanova	Andy Talley	0-1	Lost 1st Round
William & Mary	Jimmye Laycock	0-1	Lost 1st Round
1990 (16)			
Ga. Southern	Tim Stowers	4-0	Champion
Nevada	Chris Ault	3-1	Second
Boise St.	Skip Hall	2-1	Semifinalist
Central Fla.	Gene McDowell	2-1	Semifinalist
Furman	Jimmy Satterfield	1-1	Quarterfinalist
Idaho	John L. Smith	1-1	Quarterfinalist
Middle Tenn. St.	James Donnelly	1-1	Quarterfinalist
William & Mary	Jimmye Laycock	1-1	Quarterfinalist
Citadel	Charlie Taaffe	0-1	Lost 1st Round
Eastern Ky.	Roy Kidd	0-1	Lost 1st Round
Jackson St.	W. C. Gorden	0-1	Lost 1st Round
Massachusetts	Jim Reid	0-1	Lost 1st Round
Northeast La.	Dave Roberts	0-1	Lost 1st Round
Northern Iowa	Terry Allen	0-1	Lost 1st Round
Southwest Mo. St.	Jesse Branch	0-1	Lost 1st Round
Youngstown St.	Jim Tressel	0-1	Lost 1st Round
1991 (16)			
Youngstown St.	Jim Tressel	4-0	Champion
Marshall	Jim Donnan	3-1	Second
Eastern Ky.	Roy Kidd	2-1	Semifinalist
Samford	Terry Bowden	2-1	Semifinalist
James Madison	Rip Scherer	1-1	Quarterfinalist
Middle Tenn. St.	James Donnelly	1-1	Quarterfinalist
Nevada	Chris Ault	1-1	Quarterfinalist
Northern Iowa	Terry Allen	1-1	Quarterfinalist
Appalachian St.	Jerry Moore	0-1	Lost 1st Round
Delaware	Tubby Raymond	0-1	Lost 1st Round
McNeese St.	Bobby Keasler	0-1	Lost 1st Round
New Hampshire	Bill Bowes	0-1	Lost 1st Round
Sam Houston St.	Ron Randleman	0-1	Lost 1st Round
Villanova	Andy Talley	0-1	Lost 1st Round
Weber St.	Dave Arslanian	0-1	Lost 1st Round
Western Ill.	Randy Ball	0-1	Lost 1st Round
1992 (16)			
Marshall	Jim Donnan	4-0	Champion
Youngstown St.	Jim Tressel	3-1	Second
Delaware	Tubby Raymond	2-1	Semifinalist
Northern Iowa	Terry Allen	2-1	Semifinalist
Citadel	Charlie Taaffe	1-1	Quarterfinalist
McNeese St.	Bobby Keasler	1-1	Quarterfinalist
Middle Tenn. St.	James Donnelly	1-1	Quarterfinalist
Northeast La.	Dave Roberts	1-1	Quarterfinalist
Alcorn St.	Cardell Jones	0-1	Lost 1st Round
Appalachian St.	Jerry Moore	0-1	Lost 1st Round
Eastern Ky.	Roy Kidd	0-1	Lost 1st Round
Eastern Wash.	Dick Zornes	0-1	Lost 1st Round
Idaho	John L. Smith	0-1	Lost 1st Round
North Caro. A&T	Bill Hayes	0-1	Lost 1st Round
Samford	Terry Bowden	0-1	Lost 1st Round
Villanova	Andy Talley	0-1	Lost 1st Round
1993 (16)			
Youngstown St.	Jim Tressel	4-0	Champion
Marshall	Jim Donnan	3-1	Second
Idaho	John L. Smith	2-1	Semifinalist
Troy St.	Larry Blakeney	2-1	Semifinalist
Boston U.	Dan Allen	1-1	Quarterfinalist
Delaware	Tubby Raymond	1-1	Quarterfinalist
Ga. Southern	Tim Stowers	1-1	Quarterfinalist
McNeese St.	Bobby Keasler	1-1	Quarterfinalist
Central Fla.	Gene McDowell	0-1	Lost 1st Round
Eastern Ky.	Roy Kidd	0-1	Lost 1st Round
Howard	Steve Wilson	0-1	Lost 1st Round
Montana	Don Read	0-1	Lost 1st Round
Northeast La.	Dave Roberts	0-1	Lost 1st Round
Northern Iowa	Terry Allen	0-1	Lost 1st Round
Stephen F. Austin	John Pearce	0-1	Lost 1st Round
William & Mary	Jimmye Laycock	0-1	Lost 1st Round
1994 (16)			
Youngstown St.	Jim Tressel	4-0	Champion
Boise St.	Pokey Allen	3-1	Second
Marshall	Jim Donnan	2-1	Semifinalist
Montana	Don Read	2-1	Semifinalist
Appalachian St.	Jerry Moore	1-1	Quarterfinalist
Eastern Ky.	Roy Kidd	1-1	Quarterfinalist
James Madison	Rip Scherer	1-1	Quarterfinalist
McNeese St.	Bobby Keasler	1-1	Quarterfinalist
Alcorn St.	Cardell Jones	0-1	Lost 1st Round
Boston U.	Dan Allen	0-1	Lost 1st Round
Idaho	John L. Smith	0-1	Lost 1st Round
Middle Tenn. St.	James Donnelly	0-1	Lost 1st Round
New Hampshire	Bill Bowes	0-1	Lost 1st Round
North Texas	Matt Simon	0-1	Lost 1st Round
Northern Iowa	Terry Allen	0-1	Lost 1st Round
Troy St.	Larry Blakeney	0-1	Lost 1st Round
1995 (16)			
Montana	Don Read	4-0	Champion
Marshall	Jim Donnan	3-1	Second
McNeese St.	Bobby Keasler	2-1	Semifinalist
Stephen F. Austin	John Pearce	2-1	Semifinalist
Appalachian St.	Jerry Moore	1-1	Quarterfinalist
Delaware	Tubby Raymond	1-1	Quarterfinalist
Ga. Southern	Tim Stowers	1-1	Quarterfinalist
Northern Iowa	Terry Allen	1-1	Quarterfinalist
Eastern Ill.	Bob Spoo	0-1	Lost 1st Round
Eastern Ky.	Roy Kidd	0-1	Lost 1st Round
Hofstra	Joe Gardi	0-1	Lost 1st Round
Idaho	Chris Tormey	0-1	Lost 1st Round
Jackson St.	James Carson	0-1	Lost 1st Round
James Madison	Alex Wood	0-1	Lost 1st Round
Murray St.	Houston Nutt	0-1	Lost 1st Round
Troy St.	Larry Blakeney	0-1	Lost 1st Round

**Competition in championship vacated by action of the NCAA Committee on Infractions.*

Division I-AA Championship Record of Each College by Coach

(62 Colleges; 1978-95)

	Yrs	Won	Lost	CH	2D
AKRON					
Jim Dennison (Wooster '60) 85	1	0	1	0	0
ALCORN ST.					
Marino Casem (Xavier, La. '56) 84	1	0	1	0	0
Cardell Jones (Alcorn St. '65) 92, 94	2	0	2	0	0
TOTAL	3	0	3	0	0
APPALACHIAN ST.					
Sparky Woods (Carson-Newman '76) 86, 87	2	2	2	0	0
Jerry Moore (Baylor '61) 89, 91, 92, 94, 95	5	2	5	0	0
TOTAL	7	4	7	0	0
ARKANSAS ST.					
Larry Lacewell (Ark.-Monticello '59) 84, 85, 86-2D, 87	4	6	4	0	1
BOISE ST.					
Jim Criner (Cal Poly Pomona '61) 80-CH, 81	2	3	1	1	0
Skip Hall (Concordia-M'head '66) 88, 90	2	2	2	0	0
Pokey Allen (Utah '65) 94-2D	1	3	1	0	1
TOTAL	5	8	4	1	1
BOSTON U.					
Rick Taylor (Gettysburg '64) 82, 83, 84	3	1	3	0	0
Dan Allen (Hanover '78) 93, 94	2	1	2	0	0
TOTAL	5	2	5	0	0
CENTRAL FLA.					
Gene McDowell (Florida St. '63) 90, 93	2	2	2	0	0
CITADEL					
Charlie Taaffe (Siena '73) 88, 90, 92	3	1	3	0	0
COLGATE					
Fred Dunlap (Colgate '50) 82, 83	2	1	2	0	0
DELAWARE					
Harold "Tubby" Raymond (Michigan '50) 81, 82-2D, 86, 88, 91, 92, 93, 95	8	7	8	0	1
EASTERN ILL.					
Darrell Mudra (Peru St. '51) 82	1	1	1	0	0
Al Molde (Gust. Adolphus '66) 83, 86	2	1	2	0	0
Bob Spoo (Purdue '60) 89, 95	2	1	2	0	0
TOTAL	5	3	5	0	0
EASTERN KY.					
Roy Kidd (Eastern Ky. '54) 79-CH, 80-2D, 81-2D, 82-CH, 83, 84, 86, 87, 88, 89, 90, 91, 92, 93, 94, 95	16	16	14	2	2
EASTERN WASH.					
Dick Zornes (Eastern Wash. '68) 85, 92	2	1	2	0	0
FLORIDA A&M					
Rudy Hubbard (Ohio St. '68) 78-CH	1	2	0	1	0
FURMAN					
Dick Sheridan (South Caro. '64) 82, 83, 85-2D	3	3	3	0	1
Jimmy Satterfield (South Caro. '62) 86, 88-CH, 89, 90	4	7	3	1	0
TOTAL	7	10	6	1	1
GA. SOUTHERN					
Erk Russell (Auburn '49) 85-CH, 86-CH, 87, 88-2D, 89-CH	5	16	2	3	1
Tim Stowers (Auburn '79) 90-CH, 93, 95	3	6	2	1	0
TOTAL	8	22	4	4	1
GRAMBLING					
Eddie Robinson (Leland '41) 80, 85, 89	3	0	3	0	0
HOFSTRA					
Joe Gardi (Maryland '60) 95	1	0	1	0	0
HOLY CROSS					
Rick Carter (Earlham '65) 83	1	0	1	0	0
HOWARD					
Steve Wilson (Howard '79) 93	1	0	1	0	0
IDAHO					
Dennis Erickson (Montana St. '70) 82, 85	2	1	2	0	0
Keith Gilbertson (Central Wash. '71) 86, 87, 88	3	2	3	0	0
John L. Smith (Weber St. '71) 89, 90, 92, 93, 94	5	3	5	0	0
Chris Tormey (Idaho '78) 95	1	0	1	0	0
TOTAL	11	6	11	0	0
IDAHO ST.					
Dave Kragthorpe (Utah St. '55) 81-CH	1	3	0	1	0
Jim Koetter (Idaho St. '61) 83	1	0	1	0	0
TOTAL	2	3	1	1	0
INDIANA ST.					
Dennis Raetz (Nebraska '68) 83, 84	2	1	2	0	0
JACKSON ST.					
W. C. Gorden (Tennessee St. '52) 78, 81, 82, 85, 86, 87, 88, 89, 90	9	0	9	0	0
James Carson (Jackson St. '63) 95	1	0	1	0	0
TOTAL	10	0	10	0	0
JAMES MADISON					
Joe Purzycki (Delaware '71) 87	1	0	1	0	0
Rip Scherer (William & Mary '74) 91, 94	2	2	2	0	0
Alex Wood (Iowa '79) 95	1	0	1	0	0
TOTAL	4	2	4	0	0
LEHIGH					
John Whitehead (East Stroudsburg '50) 79-2D, 80	2	1	2	0	1
LOUISIANA TECH					
Billy Brewer (Mississippi '61) 82	1	1	1	0	0
A. L. Williams (Louisiana Tech '57) 84-2D	1	3	1	0	1
TOTAL	2	4	2	0	1
MAINE					
Tim Murphy (Springfield '78) 87	1	0	1	0	0
Tom Lichtenberg (Louisville '62) 89	1	0	1	0	0
TOTAL	2	0	2	0	0
MARSHALL					
George Chaump (Bloomsburg '58) 87-2D, 88	2	4	2	0	1
Jim Donnan (North Caro. St. '67) 91-2D, 92-CH, 93-2D, 94, 95-2D	5	15	4	1	3
TOTAL	7	19	6	1	4
MASSACHUSETTS					
Bob Pickett (Maine '59) 78-2D	1	1	1	0	1
Jim Reid (Maine '73) 88, 90	2	0	2	0	0
TOTAL	3	1	3	0	1
McNEESE ST.					
Bobby Keasler (Northeast La. '70) 91, 92, 93, 94, 95	5	5	5	0	0
MIDDLE TENN. ST.					
James "Boots" Donnelly (Middle Tenn. St. '65) 84, 85, 89, 90, 91, 92, 94	7	6	7	0	0
MISSISSIPPI VAL.					
Archie Cooley Jr. (Jackson St. '62) 84	1	0	1	0	0
MONTANA					
Larry Donovan (Nebraska '64) 82	1	0	1	0	0
Don Read (Cal St. Sacramento '59) 88, 89, 93, 94, 95-CH	5	8	4	1	0
TOTAL	6	8	5	1	0
MONTANA ST.					
Dave Arnold (Drake '67) 84-CH	1	3	0	1	0
MURRAY ST.					
Mike Gottfried (Morehead St. '66) 79	1	0	1	0	0
Frank Beamer (Virginia Tech '69) 86	1	0	1	0	0
Houston Nutt (Oklahoma St. '81) 95	1	0	1	0	0
TOTAL	3	0	3	0	0
NEVADA					
Chris Ault (Nevada '68) 78, 79, 83, 85, 86, 90-2D, 91	7	9	7	0	1
NEW HAMPSHIRE					
Bill Bowes (Penn St. '65) 91, 94	2	0	2	0	0
NICHOLLS ST.					
Sonny Jackson (Nicholls St. '63) 86	1	1	1	0	0
NORTH CARO. A&T					
Maurice "Mo" Forte (Minnesota '71) 86	1	0	1	0	0
Bill Hayes (N.C. Central '64) 92	1	0	1	0	0
TOTAL	2	0	2	0	0
NORTH TEXAS					
Corky Nelson (Southwest Tex. St. '64) 83, 87, 88	3	0	3	0	0
Matt Simon (Eastern N.M. '76) 94	1	0	1	0	0
TOTAL	4	0	4	0	0
NORTHEAST LA.					
Pat Collins (Louisiana Tech '63) 87-CH	1	4	0	1	0
Dave Roberts (Western Caro. '68) 90, 92, 93	3	1	3	0	0
TOTAL	4	5	3	1	0

	Yrs	Won	Lost	CH	2D
NORTHERN IOWA					
Darrell Mudra (Peru St. '51) 85, 87	2	3	2	0	0
Terry Allen (Northern Iowa '79) 90, 91, 92, 93, 94, 95	6	4	6	0	0
TOTAL	8	7	8	0	0
NORTHWESTERN ST.					
Sam Goodwin (Henderson St. '66) 88	1	1	1	0	0
RHODE ISLAND					
Bob Griffin (Southern Conn. St. '63) 81, 84, 85	3	2	3	0	0
RICHMOND					
Dal Shealy (Carson-Newman '60) 84, 87	2	1	2	0	0
SAM HOUSTON ST.					
Ron Randleman (William Penn '64) 86, 91	2	0	2	0	0
SAMFORD					
Terry Bowden (West Va. '78) 91, 92	2	2	2	0	0
SOUTH CARO. ST.					
Bill Davis (Johnson Smith '65) 81, 82	2	2	2	0	0
SOUTHERN ILL.					
Rey Dempsey (Geneva '58) 83-CH	1	3	0	1	0
SOUTHWEST MO. ST.					
Jesse Branch (Arkansas '64) 89, 90	2	1	2	0	0
STEPHEN F. AUSTIN¢					
Jim Hess (Southeastern Okla. '59) 88	1	1	1	0	0
Lynn Graves (Stephen F. Austin '65) 89-2D	1	3	1	0	1
John Pearce (East Tex. St. '70) 93, 95	2	2	2	0	0
TOTAL	4	6	4	0	1
TENN.-CHATT.					
Buddy Nix (West Ala. '61) 84	1	0	1	0	0

	Yrs	Won	Lost	CH	2D
TENNESSEE ST.*					
John Merritt (Kentucky St. '50) 81, 82	2	1	2	0	0
Bill Thomas (Tennessee St. '71) 86	1	1	1	0	0
TOTAL	3	2	3	0	0
TROY ST.					
Larry Blakeney (Auburn '70) 93, 94, 95	3	2	3	0	0
VILLANOVA					
Andy Talley (Southern Conn. St. '67) 89, 91, 92	3	0	3	0	0
WEBER ST.					
Mike Price (Puget Sound '69) 87	1	1	1	0	0
Dave Arslanian (Weber St. '72) 91	1	0	1	0	0
TOTAL	2	1	2	0	0
WESTERN CARO.					
Bob Waters (Presbyterian '60) 83-2D	1	3	1	0	1
WESTERN ILL.					
Bruce Craddock (Truman St. '66) 88	1	0	1	0	0
Randy Ball (Truman St. '73) 91	1	0	1	0	0
TOTAL	2	0	2	0	0
WESTERN KY.					
Dave Roberts (Western Caro. '68) 87, 88	2	1	2	0	0
WILLIAM & MARY					
Jimmye Laycock (William & Mary '70) 86, 89, 90, 93	4	1	4	0	0
YOUNGSTOWN ST.					
Jim Tressel (Baldwin-Wallace '75) 87, 89, 90, 91-CH, 92-2D, 93-CH, 94-CH	7	16	4	3	1

**Tennessee State's competition in the 1981 and 1982 Division I-AA championships was vacated by action of the NCAA Committee on Infractions (official record is 1-1). ¢Stephen F. Austin's competition in the 1989 Division I-AA championship was vacated by action of the NCAA Committee on Infractions (official record is 1-2).*

All-Time Results

1978 First Round: Florida A&M 15, Jackson St. 10; Massachusetts 44, Nevada 21. **Championship:** Florida A&M 35, Massachusetts 28.

1979 First Round: Lehigh 28, Murray St. 9; Eastern Ky. 33, Nevada 30 (2 OT). **Championship:** Eastern Ky. 30, Lehigh 7.

1980 First Round: Eastern Ky. 23, Lehigh 20; Boise St. 14, Grambling 9. **Championship:** Boise St. 31, Eastern Ky. 29.

1981 First Round: Eastern Ky. 35, Delaware 28; Boise St. 19, Jackson St. 7; Idaho St. 51, Rhode Island 0; South Caro. St. 26, *Tennessee St. 25 (OT). **Semifinals:** Eastern Ky. 23, Boise St. 17; Idaho St. 41, South Caro. St. 12. **Championship:** Idaho St. 34, Eastern Ky. 23.

**Tennessee State's participation in 1981 playoff vacated.*

1982 First Round: Idaho 21, Montana 7; Eastern Ill. 16, Jackson St. 13 (OT); South Caro. St. 17, Furman 0; Colgate 21, Boston U. 7. **Quarterfinals:** Eastern Ky. 38, Idaho 30; *Tennessee St. 20, Eastern Ill. 19; Louisiana Tech 38, South Caro. St. 3; Delaware 20, Colgate 13. **Semifinals:** Eastern Ky. 13, *Tennessee St. 7; Delaware 17, Louisiana Tech 0. **Championship:** Eastern Ky. 17, Delaware 14.

**Tennessee State's participation in 1982 playoff vacated.*

1983 First Round: Indiana St. 16, Eastern Ill. 13 (2 OT); Nevada 27, Idaho St. 20; Western Caro. 24, Colgate 23; Boston U. 24, Eastern Ky. 20. **Quarterfinals:** Southern Ill. 23, Indiana St. 7; Nevada 20, North Texas 17 (OT); Western Caro. 28, Holy Cross 21; Furman 35, Boston U. 16. **Semifinals:** Southern Ill. 23, Nevada 7; Western Caro. 14, Furman 7. **Championship:** Southern Ill. 43, Western Caro. 7.

1984 First Round: Louisiana Tech 66, Mississippi Val. 19; Middle Tenn. St. 27, Eastern Ky. 10; Richmond 35, Boston U. 33; Arkansas St. 37, Tenn.-Chatt. 10. **Quarterfinals:** Louisiana Tech 44, Alcorn St. 21; Middle Tenn. St. 42, Indiana St. 41 (3 OT); Rhode Island 23, Richmond 17; Montana St. 31, Arkansas St. 14. **Semifinals:** Louisiana Tech 21, Middle Tenn. St. 13; Montana St. 32, Rhode Island 20. **Championship:** Montana St. 19, Louisiana Tech 6.

1985 First Round: Ga. Southern 27, Jackson St. 0; Eastern Wash. 42, Idaho 38; Rhode Island 35, Akron 27; Arkansas St. 10, Grambling 7. **Quarterfinals:** Ga. Southern 28, Middle Tenn. St. 21; Northern Iowa 17, Eastern Wash. 14; Furman 59, Rhode Island 15; Nevada 24, Arkansas St. 23. **Semifinals:** Ga. Southern 40, Northern Iowa 33; Furman 35, Nevada 12. **Championship:** Ga. Southern 44, Furman 42.

1986 First Round: Nevada 27, Idaho 7; Tennessee St. 32, Jackson St. 23; Ga. Southern 52, North Caro. A&T 21; Nicholls St. 28, Appalachian St. 26; Arkansas St. 48, Sam Houston St. 7; Delaware 51, William & Mary 17; Eastern Ill. 28, Murray St. 21; Eastern Ky. 23, Furman 10. **Quarterfinals:** Nevada 33, Tennessee St. 6; Ga. Southern 55, Nicholls St. 31; Arkansas St. 55, Delaware 14; Eastern Ky. 24, Eastern Ill. 22. **Semifinals:** Ga. Southern 48, Nevada 38; Arkansas St. 24, Eastern Ky. 10. **Championship:** Ga. Southern 48, Arkansas St. 21.

1987 First Round: Appalachian St. 20, Richmond 3; Ga. Southern 31, Maine 28 (OT); Weber St. 59, Idaho 30; Marshall 41, James Madison 12; Northeast La. 30, North Texas 9; Eastern Ky. 40, Western Ky. 17; Northern Iowa 31, Youngstown St. 28; Arkansas St. 35, Jackson St. 32. **Quarterfinals:** Appalachian St. 19, Ga. Southern 0; Marshall 51, Weber St. 23; Northeast La. 33, Eastern Ky. 32; Northern Iowa 49, Arkansas St. 28. **Semifinals:** Marshall 24, Appalachian St. 10; Northeast La. 44, Northern Iowa 41 (2 OT). **Championship:** Northeast La. 43, Marshall 42.

1988 First Round: Idaho 38, Montana 19; Northwestern St. 22, Boise St. 13; Furman 21, Delaware 7; Marshall 7, North Texas 0; Ga. Southern 38, Citadel 20; Stephen F. Austin 24, Jackson St. 0; Western Ky. 35, Western Ill. 32; Eastern Ky. 28, Massachusetts 17. **Quarterfinals:** Idaho 38, Northwestern St. 30; Furman 13, Marshall 9; Ga. Southern 27, Stephen F. Austin 6; Eastern Ky. 41, Western Ky. 24. **Semifinals:** Furman 38, Idaho 7; Ga. Southern 21, Eastern Ky. 17. **Championship:** Furman 17, Ga. Southern 12.

1989 First Round: Ga. Southern 52, Villanova 36; Middle Tenn. St. 24, Appalachian St. 21; Eastern Ill. 38, Idaho 21; Montana 48, Jackson St. 7; Furman 24, William & Mary 10; Youngstown St. 28, Eastern Ky. 24; ¢Stephen F. Austin 59, Grambling 56; Southwest Mo. St. 38, Maine 35. **Quarterfinals:** Ga. Southern 45, Middle Tenn. St. 3; Montana 25, Eastern Ill. 19; Furman 42, Youngstown St. 23; ¢Stephen F. Austin 55, Southwest Mo. St. 25. **Semifinals:** Ga. Southern 45, Montana 15; ¢Stephen F. Austin 21, Furman 19. **Championship:** Ga. Southern 37, ¢Stephen F. Austin 34.

¢Stephen F. Austin's participation in 1989 playoff vacated.

1990 First Round: Middle Tenn. St. 28, Jackson St. 7; Boise St. 20, Northern Iowa 3; Nevada 27, Northeast La. 14; Furman 45, Eastern Ky. 17; Central Fla. 20, Youngstown St. 17; William & Mary 38, Massachusetts 0; Ga. Southern 31, Citadel 0; Idaho 41, Southwest Mo. St. 35. **Quarterfinals:** Boise St. 20, Middle Tenn. St. 13; Nevada 42, Furman 35 (3 OT); Central Fla. 52, William & Mary 38; Ga. Southern 28, Idaho 27. **Semifinals:** Nevada 59, Boise St. 52 (3 OT); Ga. Southern 44, Central Fla. 7. **Championship:** Ga. Southern 36, Nevada 13.

1991 First Round: Nevada 22, McNeese St. 16; Youngstown St. 17, Villanova 16; James Madison 42, Delaware 35 (2 OT); Samford 29, New Hampshire 13; Eastern Ky. 14, Appalachian St. 3; Middle Tenn. St. 20, Sam Houston St. 19 (OT); Northern Iowa 38, Weber St. 21; Marshall 20, Western Ill. 17 (OT). **Quarterfinals:** Youngstown St. 30, Nevada 28; Samford 24, James Madison 21; Eastern Ky. 23, Middle Tenn. St. 13; Marshall 41, Northern Iowa 13. **Semifinals:** Youngstown St. 10, Samford 0; Marshall 14, Eastern Ky. 7. **Championship:** Youngstown St. 25, Marshall 17.

1992 First Round: Northeast La. 78, Alcorn St. 27; Delaware 56, Samford 21; Middle Tenn. St. 35, Appalachian St. 10; Marshall 44, Eastern Ky. 0; Citadel 44, North Caro. A&T 0; Youngstown St. 23, Villanova 20; Northern Iowa 17, Eastern Wash. 14; McNeese St. 23, Idaho 20. **Quarterfinals:** Delaware 41, Northeast La. 18; Marshall 35, Middle Tenn. St. 21; Youngstown St. 42, Citadel 17; Northern Iowa 29, McNeese St. 7. **Semifinals:** Marshall 28, Delaware 7; Youngstown St. 19, Northern Iowa 7. **Championship:** Marshall 31, Youngstown St. 28.

1993 First Round: Ga. Southern 14, Eastern Ky. 12; Youngstown St. 56, Central Fla. 30; Boston U. 27, Northern Iowa 21 (2 OT); Idaho 34, Northeast La. 31; Delaware 49, Montana 48; Marshall 28, Howard 14; McNeese St. 34, William & Mary 28; Troy St. 42, Stephen F. Austin 20. **Quarterfinals:** Youngstown St. 34, Ga. Southern 14; Idaho 21, Boston U. 14; Marshall 34, Delaware 31; Troy St. 35, McNeese St. 28. **Semifinals:** Youngstown St. 35, Idaho 16; Marshall 24,

Troy St. 21. **Championship:** Youngstown St. 17, Marshall 5.

1994 First Round: Youngstown St. 63, Alcorn St. 20; Eastern Ky. 30, Boston U. 23; McNeese St. 38, Idaho 21; Montana 23, Northern Iowa 20; Marshall 49, Middle Tenn. St. 14; James Madison 45, Troy St. 26; Boise St. 24, North Texas 20; Appalachian St. 17, New Hampshire 10 (OT). **Quarterfinals:** Youngstown St. 18, Eastern Ky. 15; Montana 30, McNeese St. 28; Marshall 28, James Madison 21 (OT); Boise St. 17, Appalachian St. 14. **Semifinals:** Youngstown St. 28, Montana 9; Boise St. 28, Marshall 24. **Championship:** Youngstown St. 28, Boise St. 14.

1995 First Round: McNeese St. 33, Idaho 3; Delaware 38, Hofstra 17; Northern Iowa 35, Murray St. 34; Marshall 38, Jackson St. 8; Appalachian St. 31, James Madison 24; Stephen F. Austin 34, Eastern Ill. 29; Ga. Southern 24, Troy St. 21; Montana 48, Eastern Ky. 0. **Quarterfinals:** McNeese St. 52, Delaware 18; Marshall 41, Northern Iowa 24; Stephen F. Austin 27, Appalachian St. 17; Montana 45, Ga. Southern 0. **Semifinals:** Marshall 25, McNeese St. 13; Montana 70, Stephen F. Austin 14. **Championship:** Montana 22, Marshall 20.

Division II Championship

1995 Title Game Summary

BRALY MUNICIPAL STADIUM, FLORENCE, ALA.; DECEMBER 9, 1995

	Pittsburg St.	North Ala.
First Downs	10	21
Rushes-Net Yardage	27-99	58-249
Passing Yardage	77	131
Return Yardage (Punts, Int. & Fum.)	10	3
Passes (Comp.-Att.-Int.)	6-19-4	10-24-1
Punts (Number-Average)	7-38.3	7-32.8
Fumbles (Number-Lost)	2-1	3-1
Penalties (Number-Yards)	6-61	7-75

Pittsburg St.	0	0	0	7	— 7
North Ala.	7	14	0	6	—27

Game Conditions: Temperature, 31 degrees; wind, 13 mph from north; weather, sunny. Attendance: 15,241.

FIRST QUARTER
North Ala.—Jermaine Roberts 28 run (Jamie Stoddard kick) (76 yards in 12 plays, 8:04 left)

SECOND QUARTER
North Ala.—Roberts 5 run (Stoddard kick) (29 yards in 5 plays, 11:16 left)
North Ala.—Michael Edwards 13 pass from Cody Gross (Stoddard kick) (69 yards in 11 plays, 0:05 left)

FOURTH QUARTER
Pittsburg St.—Chris Hudson 15 pass from Jeff Moreland (Josh Barcus kick) (15 yards in 1 play, 9:30 left)
North Ala.—Nate George 1 run (kick failed) (44 yards in 9 plays, 0:34 left)

INDIVIDUAL LEADERS
Rushing—Pittsburg St.: Michael Mayfield, 43 yards on 4 carries; North Ala.: Roberts, 107 yards on 20 carries.
Passing—Pittsburg St.: Moreland, 6 of 19 for 77 yards; North Ala.: Gross, 8 of 13 for 102 yards.
Receiving—Pittsburg St.: Hudson, 3 catches for 34 yards; North Ala.: Demetrea Shelton, 5 catches for 59 yards.

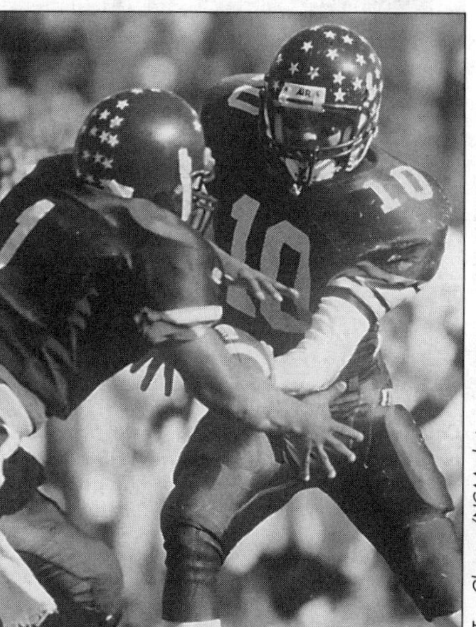

Troy Glasgow/NCAA photos

North Alabama quarterback Cale Manley hands off to Jermaine Roberts during the 1995 Division II Football Championship title game. Roberts rushed for 107 yards and two touchdowns to lead the Lions to a 27-7 victory over Pittsburg State.

Division II All-Time Championship Results

Year	Champion	Coach	Score	Runner-Up	Site
1973	Louisiana Tech	Maxie Lambright	34-0	Western Ky.	Sacramento, Calif.
1974	Central Mich.	Roy Kramer	54-14	Delaware	Sacramento, Calif.
1975	Northern Mich.	Gil Krueger	16-14	Western Ky.	Sacramento, Calif.
1976	Montana St.	Sonny Holland	24-13	Akron	Wichita Falls, Texas
1977	Lehigh	John Whitehead	33-0	Jacksonville St.	Wichita Falls, Texas
1978	Eastern Ill.	Darrell Mudra	10-9	Delaware	Longview, Texas
1979	Delaware	Tubby Raymond	38-21	Youngstown St.	Albuquerque, N.M.
1980	Cal Poly SLO	Joe Harper	21-13	Eastern Ill.	Albuquerque, N.M.
1981	Southwest Tex. St.	Jim Wacker	42-13	North Dak. St.	McAllen, Texas
1982	Southwest Tex. St.	Jim Wacker	34-9	UC Davis	McAllen, Texas
1983	North Dak. St.	Don Morton	41-21	Central St.	McAllen, Texas
1984	Troy St.	Chan Gailey	18-17	North Dak. St.	McAllen, Texas
1985	North Dak. St.	Earle Solomonson	35-7	North Ala.	McAllen, Texas
1986	North Dak. St.	Earle Solomonson	27-7	South Dak.	Florence, Ala.
1987	Troy St.	Rick Rhoades	31-17	Portland St.	Florence, Ala.
1988	North Dak. St.	Rocky Hager	35-21	Portland St.	Florence, Ala.
1989	*Mississippi Col.	John Williams	3-0	Jacksonville St.	Florence, Ala.
1990	North Dak. St.	Rocky Hager	51-11	Indiana (Pa.)	Florence, Ala.
1991	Pittsburg St.	Chuck Broyles	23-6	Jacksonville St.	Florence, Ala.
1992	Jacksonville St.	Bill Burgess	17-13	Pittsburg St.	Florence, Ala.
1993	North Ala.	Bobby Wallace	41-34	Indiana (Pa.)	Florence, Ala.
1994	North Ala.	Bobby Wallace	16-10	Tex. A&M-Kingsville	Florence, Ala.
1995	North Ala.	Bobby Wallace	27-7	Pittsburg St.	Florence, Ala.

**Mississippi College's participation in 1989 Division II championship vacated.*

Troy Glasgow/NCAA photos

Chuckey Aiken of Pittsburg State finds little running room against a tough North Alabama defense in the 1995 Division II title game. The Lion defense held the potent Pittsburg State attack to just 176 yards of total offense in North Alabama's 27-7 win.

Regional Championship Results

Before 1973, there was no Division II Football Championship. Instead, four regional bowl games were played in order to provide postseason action for what then were called NCAA College Division member institutions. Following are the results of those bowl games:

Year	Champion	Coach	Score	Runner-Up	Site
EAST (TANGERINE BOWL)					
1964	East Caro.	Clarence Stasavich	14-13	Massachusetts	Orlando, Fla.
1965	East Caro.	Clarence Stasavich	31-0	Maine	Orlando, Fla.
1966	Morgan St.	Earl Banks	14-6	West Chester	Orlando, Fla.
1967	Tenn.-Martin	Robert Carroll	25-8	West Chester	Orlando, Fla.
EAST (BOARDWALK BOWL)					
1968	Delaware	Tubby Raymond	31-24	Indiana (Pa.)	Atlantic City, N.J.
1969	Delaware	Tubby Raymond	31-13	N.C. Central	Atlantic City, N.J.
1970	Delaware	Tubby Raymond	38-23	Morgan St.	Atlantic City, N.J.
1971	Delaware	Tubby Raymond	72-22	LIU-C.W. Post	Atlantic City, N.J.
1972	Massachusetts	Dick MacPherson	35-14	UC Davis	Atlantic City, N.J.
MIDEAST (GRANTLAND RICE BOWL)					
1964	Middle Tenn. St.	Charles Murphy	20-0	Muskingum	Murfreesboro, Tenn.
1965	Ball St. Tennessee St.	Ray Louthen John Merritt	14-14	—	Murfreesboro, Tenn.
1966	Tennessee St.	John Merritt	34-7	Muskingum	Murfreesboro, Tenn.
1967	Eastern Ky.	Roy Kidd	27-13	Ball St.	Murfreesboro, Tenn.
1968	Louisiana Tech	Maxie Lambright	33-13	Akron	Murfreesboro, Tenn.
1969	East Tenn. St.	John Bell	34-14	Louisiana Tech	Baton Rouge, La.
1970	Tennessee St.	John Merritt	26-25	Southwestern La.	Baton Rouge, La.
1971	Tennessee St.	John Merritt	26-23	McNeese St.	Baton Rouge, La.
1972	Louisiana Tech	Maxie Lambright	35-0	Tennessee Tech	Baton Rouge, La.
MIDWEST (PECAN BOWL)					
1964	Northern Iowa	Stan Sheriff	19-17	Lamar	Abilene, Texas
1965	North Dak. St.	Darrell Mudra	20-7	Grambling	Abilene, Texas
1966	North Dak.	Marv Helling	42-24	Parsons	Abilene, Texas
1967	Texas-Arlington	Burley Bearden	13-0	North Dak. St.	Abilene, Texas
1968	North Dak. St.	Ron Erhardt	23-14	Arkansas St.	Arlington, Texas
1969	Arkansas St.	Bennie Ellender	29-21	Drake	Arlington, Texas
1970	Arkansas St.	Bennie Ellender	38-21	Central Mo. St.	Arlington, Texas
MIDWEST (PIONEER BOWL)					
1971	Louisiana Tech	Maxie Lambright	14-3	Eastern Mich.	Wichita Falls, Texas
1972	Tennessee St.	John Merritt	29-7	Drake	Wichita Falls, Texas
WEST (CAMELLIA BOWL)					
1964	Montana St.	Jim Sweeney	28-7	Cal St. Sacramento	Sacramento, Calif.
1965	Cal St. Los Angeles	Homer Beatty	18-10	UC Santa Barb.	Sacramento, Calif.
1966	San Diego St.	Don Coryell	28-7	Montana St.	Sacramento, Calif.
1967	San Diego St.	Don Coryell	27-6	San Fran. St.	Sacramento, Calif.
1968	Humboldt St.	Frank VanDeren	29-14	Fresno St.	Sacramento, Calif.
1969	North Dak. St.	Ron Erhardt	30-3	Montana	Sacramento, Calif.
1970	North Dak. St.	Ron Erhardt	31-16	Montana	Sacramento, Calif.
1971	Boise St.	Tony Knap	32-28	Cal St. Chico	Sacramento, Calif.
1972	North Dak.	Jerry Olson	38-21	Cal Poly SLO	Sacramento, Calif.

1995 Division II Championship Results

FIRST ROUND
Ferris St. 36, Millersville 26
New Haven 27, Edinboro 12
North Ala. 38, Albany St. (Ga.) 28
Carson-Newman 37, West Ga. 26
Pittsburg St. 36, Northern Colo. 17
North Dak. St. 41, North Dak. 10
Tex. A&M-Kingsville 59, Fort Hays St. 28
Portland St. 56, East Tex. St. 35

QUARTERFINALS
Ferris St. 17, New Haven 9
North Ala. 28, Carson-Newman 7
Pittsburg St. 9, North Dak. St. 7
Tex. A&M-Kingsville 30, Portland St. 3

SEMIFINALS
North Ala. 45, Ferris St. 7
Pittsburg St. 28, Tex. A&M-Kingsville 25 (OT)

CHAMPIONSHIP
North Ala. 27, Pittsburg St. 7

Championship Records

INDIVIDUAL: SINGLE GAME

NET YARDS RUSHING
379—Ronald Moore, Pittsburg St. (41) vs. Portland St. (38), 12-5-92.

RUSHES ATTEMPTED
51—Terry Morrow, Central St. (31) vs. Towson St. (0), 11-28-86.

TOUCHDOWNS BY RUSHING
5—Ronald Moore, Pittsburg St. (38) vs. North Dak. St. (37), OT, 11-28-92; Ronald Moore, Pittsburg St. (41) vs. Portland St. (38), 12-5-92.

NET YARDS PASSING
443—Tom Bertoldi, Northern Mich. (55) vs. Elizabeth City St. (6), 11-28-81.

PASSES ATTEMPTED
59—Bob Biggs, UC Davis (14) vs. Massachusetts (35), 12-9-72.

PASSES COMPLETED
32—Darren Del'Andrae, Portland St. (56) vs. West Chester (50), 3 OT, 11-18-89.

PASSES HAD INTERCEPTED
7—George Coussan, Southwestern La. (25) vs. Tennessee St. (26), 12-12-70.

TOUCHDOWN PASSES COMPLETED
6—Darren Del'Andrae, Portland St. (56) vs. West Chester (50), 3 OT, 11-18-89.

COMPLETION PERCENTAGE
(Min. 8 Attempts)
.833—Tony Aliucci, Indiana (Pa.) (56) vs. Virginia Union (7), 11-23-91 (10 of 12).

NET YARDS RUSHING AND PASSING
444—Tom Bertoldi, Northern Mich. (55) vs. Elizabeth City St. (6), 11-28-81.

NUMBER OF RUSHING AND PASSING PLAYS
66—Jamie Pass, Mankato St. (21) vs. North Dak. (54), 11-27-93.

PUNTING AVERAGE
(Min. 3 Punts)
53.7—Chris Humes, UC Davis (23) vs. Angelo St. (28), 11-18-89.

NUMBER OF PUNTS
12—Dan Gentry, Tennessee Tech (0) vs. Louisiana Tech (35), 12-9-72.

PASSES CAUGHT
14—Don Hutt, Boise St. (34) vs. Louisiana Tech (38), 12-8-73.

NET YARDS RECEIVING
220—Steve Hansley, Northwest Mo. St. (15) vs. Neb.-Omaha (28), 11-24-84.

TOUCHDOWN PASSES CAUGHT
4—Steve Kreider, Lehigh (30) vs. Massachusetts (23), 11-26-77; Scott Asman, West Chester (50) vs. Portland St. (56), 3 OT, 11-18-89; Brian Penecale, West Chester (40) vs. Ferris St. (43), 11-19-94.

PASSES INTERCEPTED
5—Don Pinson, Tennessee St. (26) vs. Southwestern La. (25), 12-12-70.

YARDS GAINED ON INTERCEPTION RETURNS
113—Darren Ryals, Millersville (27) vs. Indiana (Pa.) (24), 2 returns for 53- and 60-yard TDs, 11-19-88.

YARDS GAINED ON PUNT RETURNS
138—Rick Caswell, Western Ky. (14) vs. New Hampshire (3), 12-6-75.

YARDS GAINED ON KICKOFF RETURNS
182—Larry Anderson, LIU-C.W. Post (22) vs. Delaware (72), 12-11-71.

POINTS
32—Ronald Moore, Pittsburg St. (38) vs. North Dak. St. (37), OT, 11-28-92; Ronald Moore, Pittsburg St. (41) vs. Portland St. (38), 12-5-92.

TOUCHDOWNS
5—Ronald Moore, Pittsburg St. (38) vs. North Dak. St. (37), OT, 11-28-92; Ronald Moore, Pittsburg St. (41) vs. Portland St. (38), 12-5-92; Dexter Deese, Tex. A&M-Kingsville (43) vs. Western St. (7), 11-19-94.

EXTRA POINTS
10—Larry Washington, Delaware (72) vs. LIU-C.W. Post (22), 12-11-71.

FIELD GOALS
4—Mario Ferretti, Northern Mich. (55) vs. Elizabeth City St. (6), 11-28-81; Ken Kubisz, North Dak. St. (26) vs. UC Davis (17), 12-3-83.

INDIVIDUAL: TOURNAMENT

NET YARDS RUSHING
721—Ronald Moore, Pittsburg St., 1992 (108 vs. North Dak., 151 vs. North Dak. St., 379 vs. Portland St., 83 vs. Jacksonville St.).

RUSHES ATTEMPTED
117—Ronald Moore, Pittsburg St., 1992 (29 vs. North Dak., 31 vs. North Dak. St., 37 vs. Portland St., 20 vs. Jacksonville St.).

NET YARDS PASSING
1,226—Chris Crawford, Portland St., 1988 (248 vs. Bowie St., 375 vs. Jacksonville St., 270 vs. Tex. A&M-Kingsville, 333 vs. North Dak. St.).

PASSES ATTEMPTED
139—Chris Crawford, Portland St., 1988 (31 vs. Bowie St., 41 vs. Jacksonville St., 32 vs. Tex. A&M-Kingsville, 35 vs. North Dak. St.).

PASSES COMPLETED
94—Chris Crawford, Portland St., 1988 (20 vs. Bowie St., 27 vs. Jacksonville St., 25 vs. Tex. A&M-Kingsville, 22 vs. North Dak. St.).

TOUCHDOWN PASSES COMPLETED
10—Chris Crawford, Portland St., 1988 (2 vs. Bowie St., 2 vs. Jacksonville St., 3 vs. Tex. A&M-Kingsville, 3 vs. North Dak. St.).

COMPLETION PERCENTAGE
(Min. 2 Games)
.824—Mike Turk, Troy St., 1984, 14 of 17 (4-5 vs. Central St., 5-5 vs. Towson St., 5-7 vs. North Dak. St.).

PASSES HAD INTERCEPTED
9—Dennis Tomek, Western Ky., 1973 (0 vs. Lehigh, 6 vs. Grambling, 3 vs. Louisiana Tech).

PASSES CAUGHT
27—Don Hutt, Boise St., 1973 (13 vs. South Dak., 14 vs. Louisiana Tech).

NET YARDS RECEIVING
452—Henry Newson, Portland St., 1991 (94 vs. Northern Colo., 209 vs. Mankato St., 149 vs. Pittsburg St.).

TOUCHDOWN PASSES CAUGHT
7—Steve Kreider, Lehigh, 1977 (4 vs. Massachusetts, 1 vs. UC Davis, 2 vs. Jacksonville St.).

POINTS
88—Ronald Moore, Pittsburg St., 1992 (18 vs. North Dak., 32 vs. North Dak. St., 32 vs. Portland St., 6 vs. Jacksonville St.).

TOUCHDOWNS
14—Ronald Moore, Pittsburg St., 1992 (3 vs. North Dak., 5 vs. North Dak. St., 5 vs. Portland St., 1 vs. Jacksonville St.).

INDIVIDUAL: LONGEST PLAYS

LONGEST RUSH
98—Wesley Whiten, Tex. A&M-Kingsville (59) vs. Fort Hays St. (28), 11-18-95.

LONGEST PASS COMPLETION
99—Ken Suhl to Tony Willis, New Haven (35) vs. Ferris St. (13), 11-28-92, TD.

LONGEST FIELD GOAL
50—Ted Clem, Troy St. (18) vs. North Dak. St. (17), 12-8-84.

LONGEST PUNT
76—Chris Humes, UC Davis (23) vs. Angelo St. (28), 11-18-89.

LONGEST PUNT RETURN
91—Winford Wilborn, Louisiana Tech (14) vs. Eastern Mich. (3), 12-11-71, TD.

LONGEST KICKOFF RETURN
100—Ken Bowles, UNLV (6) vs. Akron (26), 11-26-76, TD.

LONGEST INTERCEPTION RETURN
100—Charles Harris, Jacksonville St. (34) vs. Truman St. (21), 11-27-82, TD.

LONGEST FUMBLE RETURN
93—Ray Neal, Middle Tenn. St. (20) vs. Muskingum (0), 12-12-64, TD.

TEAM: SINGLE GAME

FIRST DOWNS
34—Delaware (60) vs. Mississippi Col. (10), 12-1-79; Cal St. Sacramento (56) vs. N.C. Central (7), 11-26-88.

FIRST DOWNS BY RUSHING
27—Delaware (72) vs. LIU-C.W. Post (22), 12-11-71.

FIRST DOWNS BY PASSING
23—Central Fla. (10) vs. Troy St. (31), 12-5-87; Portland St. (56) vs. West Chester (50), 3 OT, 11-18-89.

NET YARDS RUSHING
566—Jacksonville St. (63) vs. West Chester (24), 11-19-88.

RUSHES ATTEMPTED
84—Southwest Tex. St. (34) vs. UC Davis (9), 12-11-82.

NET YARDS PASSING
464—Northern Mich. (55) vs. Elizabeth City St. (6), 11-28-81.

PASSES ATTEMPTED
60—Central Fla. (10) vs. Troy St. (31), 12-5-87.

PASSES COMPLETED
36—Central Fla. (10) vs. Troy St. (31), 12-5-87.

COMPLETION PERCENTAGE
(Min. 10 Attempts)
.813—Delaware (60) vs. Mississippi Col. (10), 12-1-79 (13 of 16); Tex. A&M-Kingsville (51) vs. UC Davis (28), 11-27-93 (13 of 16).

PASSES HAD INTERCEPTED
8—Southwestern La. (25) vs. Tennessee St. (26), 12-12-70.

NET YARDS RUSHING AND PASSING
695—Northern Mich. (55) vs. Elizabeth City St. (6), 11-28-81.

RUSHING AND PASSING PLAYS
98—Northern Mich. (55) vs. Elizabeth City St. (6), 11-28-81.

PUNTING AVERAGE
53.7—UC Davis (23) vs. Angelo St. (28), 11-18-89.

NUMBER OF PUNTS
12—Delaware (8) vs. Grambling (17), 12-1-73; Western Ky. (0) vs. Louisiana Tech (34), 12-15-73.

PUNTS HAD BLOCKED
2—Truman St. (21) vs. Jacksonville St. (34), 11-27-82.

YARDS GAINED ON PUNT RETURNS
140—Southwest Tex. St. (62) vs. Northern Mich. (0), 12-5-81.

YARDS GAINED ON KICKOFF RETURNS
251—LIU-C.W. Post (22) vs. Delaware (72), 12-11-71.

YARDS GAINED ON INTERCEPTION RETURNS
131—Millersville (27) vs. Indiana (Pa.) (24), 11-19-88.

YARDS PENALIZED
185—Tex. A&M-Kingsville (30) vs. Portland St. (3), 11-25-95.

NUMBER OF PENALTIES
21—San Diego St. (27) vs. San Fran. St. (6), 12-9-67.

FUMBLES
10—Winston-Salem (0) vs. Delaware (41), 12-2-78.

FUMBLES LOST
7—Louisiana Tech (10) vs. Western Caro. (7), 11-30-74.

POINTS
*63—Jacksonville St. vs. West Chester (24), 11-19-88.
**Mississippi Col. defeated Wofford, 70-19, on 11-17-90, but its participation was vacated.*

TEAM: TOURNAMENT

FIRST DOWNS
99—North Ala., 1993 (25 vs. Carson-Newman, 30 vs. Hampton, 23 vs. Tex. A&M-Kingsville, 21 vs. Indiana, Pa.).

NET YARDS RUSHING
1,660—North Dak. St., 1988 (474 vs. Augustana, S.D., 434 vs. Millersville, 413 vs. Cal St. Sacramento, 339 vs. Portland St.).

NET YARDS PASSING
1,226—Portland St., 1988 (248 vs. Bowie St., 375 vs. Jacksonville St., 270 vs. Tex. A&M-Kingsville, 333 vs. North Dak. St.).

NET YARDS RUSHING AND PASSING
2,032—North Ala., 1993 (455 vs. Carson-Newman, 570 vs. Hampton, 470 vs. Tex. A&M-Kingsville, 537 vs. Indiana, Pa.).

PASSES ATTEMPTED
139—Portland St., 1988 (31 vs. Bowie St., 41 vs. Jacksonville St., 32 vs. Tex. A&M-Kingsville, 35 vs. North Dak. St.).

PASSES COMPLETED
94—Portland St., 1988 (20 vs. Bowie St., 27 vs. Jacksonville St., 25 vs. Tex. A&M-Kingsville, 22 vs. North Dak. St.).

PASSES HAD INTERCEPTED
10—Western Ky., 1973 (0 vs. Lehigh, 6 vs. Grambling, 4 vs. Louisiana Tech).

NUMBER OF PUNTS
29—Western Ky., 1973 (6 vs. Lehigh, 11 vs. Grambling, 12 vs. Louisiana Tech).

YARDS PENALIZED
355—New Haven, 1992 (114 vs. West Chester, 146 vs. Ferris St., 95 vs. Jacksonville St.).

FUMBLES
16—Delaware, 1978 (8 vs. Jacksonville St., 2 vs. Winston-Salem, 6 vs. Eastern Ill.).

FUMBLES LOST
12—Delaware, 1978 (6 vs. Jacksonville St., 2 vs. Winston-Salem, 4 vs. Eastern Ill.).

POINTS
162—North Dak. St., 1988 (49 vs. Augustana, S.D., 36 vs. Millersville, 42 vs. Cal St. Sacramento, 35 vs. Portland St.).

Year-by-Year Division II Championship Results

Year (Number of Teams)	Coach	Record	Result
1973 (8)			
Louisiana Tech	Maxie Lambright	3-0	Champion
Western Ky.	Jimmy Feix	2-1	Second
Boise St.	Tony Knap	1-1	Semifinalist
Grambling	Eddie Robinson	1-1	Semifinalist
Delaware	Tubby Raymond	0-1	Lost 1st Round
Lehigh	Fred Dunlap	0-1	Lost 1st Round
South Dak.	Joe Salem	0-1	Lost 1st Round
Western Ill.	Darrell Mudra	0-1	Lost 1st Round
1974 (8)			
Central Mich.	Roy Kramer	3-0	Champion
Delaware	Tubby Raymond	2-1	Second
Louisiana Tech	Maxie Lambright	1-1	Semifinalist
UNLV	Ron Meyer	1-1	Semifinalist
Alcorn St.	Marino Casem	0-1	Lost 1st Round
Boise St.	Tony Knap	0-1	Lost 1st Round
Western Caro.	Bob Waters	0-1	Lost 1st Round
Youngstown St.	Rey Dempsey	0-1	Lost 1st Round
1975 (8)			
Northern Mich.	Gil Krueger	3-0	Champion
Western Ky.	Jimmy Feix	2-1	Second
New Hampshire	Bill Bowes	1-1	Semifinalist
West Ala.	Jim King	1-1	Semifinalist
Boise St.	Tony Knap	0-1	Lost 1st Round
Lehigh	Fred Dunlap	0-1	Lost 1st Round
North Dak.	Jerry Olson	0-1	Lost 1st Round
Northern Iowa	Stan Sheriff	0-1	Lost 1st Round
1976 (8)			
Montana St.	Sonny Holland	3-0	Champion
Akron	Jim Dennison	2-1	Second
North Dak. St.	Jim Wacker	1-1	Semifinalist
Northern Mich.	Gil Krueger	1-1	Semifinalist
Delaware	Tubby Raymond	0-1	Lost 1st Round
Eastern Ky.	Roy Kidd	0-1	Lost 1st Round
UNLV	Tony Knap	0-1	Lost 1st Round
New Hampshire	Bill Bowes	0-1	Lost 1st Round
1977 (8)			
Lehigh	John Whitehead	3-0	Champion
Jacksonville St.	Jim Fuller	2-1	Second
UC Davis	Jim Sochor	1-1	Semifinalist
North Dak. St.	Jim Wacker	1-1	Semifinalist
Bethune-Cookman	Andy Hinson	0-1	Lost 1st Round
Massachusetts	Dick MacPherson	0-1	Lost 1st Round
Northern Ariz.	Joe Salem	0-1	Lost 1st Round
Northern Mich.	Gil Krueger	0-1	Lost 1st Round
1978 (8)			
Eastern Ill.	Darrell Mudra	3-0	Champion
Delaware	Tubby Raymond	2-1	Second
Winston-Salem	Bill Hayes	1-1	Semifinalist
Youngstown St.	Bill Narduzzi	1-1	Semifinalist
UC Davis	Jim Sochor	0-1	Lost 1st Round
Cal Poly SLO	Joe Harper	0-1	Lost 1st Round
Jacksonville St.	Jim Fuller	0-1	Lost 1st Round
Neb.-Omaha	Sandy Buda	0-1	Lost 1st Round
1979 (8)			
Delaware	Tubby Raymond	3-0	Champion
Youngstown St.	Bill Narduzzi	2-1	Second
Alabama A&M	Ray Greene	1-1	Semifinalist
Mississippi Col.	John Williams	1-1	Semifinalist
Morgan St.	Clarence Thomas	0-1	Lost 1st Round
North Dak.	Gene Murphy	0-1	Lost 1st Round
South Dak. St.	John Gregory	0-1	Lost 1st Round
Virginia Union	Willard Bailey	0-1	Lost 1st Round
1980 (8)			
Cal Poly SLO	Joe Harper	3-0	Champion
Eastern Ill.	Darrell Mudra	2-1	Second
North Ala.	Wayne Grubb	1-1	Semifinalist
Santa Clara	Pat Malley	1-1	Semifinalist
Jacksonville St.	Jim Fuller	0-1	Lost 1st Round
Northern Colo.	Bob Blasi	0-1	Lost 1st Round
Northern Mich.	Bill Rademacher	0-1	Lost 1st Round
Virginia Union	Willard Bailey	0-1	Lost 1st Round
1981 (8)			
Southwest Tex. St.	Jim Wacker	3-0	Champion
North Dak. St.	Don Morton	2-1	Second
Northern Mich.	Bill Rademacher	1-1	Semifinalist
Shippensburg	Vito Ragazzo	1-1	Semifinalist
Elizabeth City St.	Johnnie Walton	0-1	Lost 1st Round
Jacksonville St.	Jim Fuller	0-1	Lost 1st Round
Puget Sound	Ron Simonson	0-1	Lost 1st Round
Virginia Union	Willard Bailey	0-1	Lost 1st Round
1982 (8)			
Southwest Tex. St.	Jim Wacker	3-0	Champion
UC Davis	Jim Sochor	2-1	Second
Jacksonville St.	Jim Fuller	1-1	Semifinalist
North Dak. St.	Don Morton	1-1	Semifinalist
Fort Valley St.	Doug Porter	0-1	Lost 1st Round
Northern Mich.	Bill Rademacher	0-1	Lost 1st Round
Truman St.	Bruce Craddock	0-1	Lost 1st Round
Virginia Union	Willard Bailey	0-1	Lost 1st Round
1983 (8)			
North Dak. St.	Don Morton	3-0	Champion
Central St.	Billy Joe	2-1	Second
UC Davis	Jim Sochor	1-1	Semifinalist
North Ala.	Wayne Grubb	1-1	Semifinalist
Butler	Bill Sylvester	0-1	Lost 1st Round
Southwest Tex. St.	John O'Hara	0-1	Lost 1st Round
Towson St.	Phil Albert	0-1	Lost 1st Round
Virginia Union	Willard Bailey	0-1	Lost 1st Round
1984 (8)			
Troy St.	Chan Gailey	3-0	Champion
North Dak. St.	Don Morton	2-1	Second
Neb.-Omaha	Sandy Buda	1-1	Semifinalist
Towson St.	Phil Albert	1-1	Semifinalist
UC Davis	Jim Sochor	0-1	Lost 1st Round
Central St.	Billy Joe	0-1	Lost 1st Round
Norfolk St.	Willard Bailey	0-1	Lost 1st Round
Northwest Mo. St.	Vern Thomsen	0-1	Lost 1st Round
1985 (8)			
North Dak. St.	Earle Solomonson	3-0	Champion
North Ala.	Wayne Grubb	2-1	Second
Bloomsburg	George Landis	1-1	Semifinalist
South Dak.	Dave Triplett	1-1	Semifinalist
UC Davis	Jim Sochor	0-1	Lost 1st Round
Central St.	Billy Joe	0-1	Lost 1st Round
Fort Valley St.	Gerald Walker	0-1	Lost 1st Round
Hampton	Fred Freeman	0-1	Lost 1st Round
1986 (8)			
North Dak. St.	Earle Solomonson	3-0	Champion
South Dak.	Dave Triplett	2-1	Second
Central St.	Billy Joe	1-1	Semifinalist
Troy St.	Rick Rhodes	1-1	Semifinalist
Ashland	Fred Martinelli	0-1	Lost 1st Round
UC Davis	Jim Sochor	0-1	Lost 1st Round
Towson St.	Phil Albert	0-1	Lost 1st Round
Virginia Union	Joe Taylor	0-1	Lost 1st Round
1987 (8)			
Troy St.	Rick Rhodes	3-0	Champion
Portland St.	Pokey Allen	2-1	Second
Central Fla.	Gene McDowell	1-1	Semifinalist
Northern Mich.	Herb Grenke	1-1	Semifinalist
Angelo St.	Jerry Vandergriff	0-1	Lost 1st Round
Indiana (Pa.)	Frank Cignetti	0-1	Lost 1st Round
Mankato St.	Dan Runkle	0-1	Lost 1st Round
Winston-Salem	Bill Hayes	0-1	Lost 1st Round
1988 (16)			
North Dak. St.	Rocky Hager	4-0	Champion
Portland St.	Pokey Allen	3-1	Second
Cal St. Sacramento	Bob Mattos	2-1	Semifinalist
Tex. A&M-Kingsville	Ron Harms	2-1	Semifinalist
Jacksonville St.	Bill Burgess	1-1	Quarterfinalist
Millersville	Gene Carpenter	1-1	Quarterfinalist
N.C. Central	Henry Lattimore	1-1	Quarterfinalist
Tenn.-Martin	Don McLeary	1-1	Quarterfinalist
Augustana (S.D.)	Jim Heinitz	0-1	Lost 1st Round
Bowie St.	Sanders Shiver	0-1	Lost 1st Round
Butler	Bill Lynch	0-1	Lost 1st Round
UC Davis	Jim Sochor	0-1	Lost 1st Round
Indiana (Pa.)	Frank Cignetti	0-1	Lost 1st Round
Mississippi Col.	John Williams	0-1	Lost 1st Round
West Chester	Danny Hale	0-1	Lost 1st Round
Winston-Salem	Pete Richardson	0-1	Lost 1st Round
1989 (16)			
*Mississippi Col.	John Williams	4-0	Champion
Jacksonville St.	Bill Burgess	3-1	Second
Angelo St.	Jerry Vandergriff	2-1	Semifinalist
Indiana (Pa.)	Frank Cignetti	2-1	Semifinalist
North Dak. St.	Rocky Hager	1-1	Quarterfinalist

Year (Number of Teams)	Coach	Record	Result
Pittsburg St.	Dennis Franchione	1-1	Quarterfinalist
Portland St.	Pokey Allen	1-1	Quarterfinalist
St. Cloud St.	Noel Martin	1-1	Quarterfinalist
Alabama A&M	George Pugh	0-1	Lost 1st Round
Augustana (S.D.)	Jim Heinitz	0-1	Lost 1st Round
UC Davis	Bob Foster	0-1	Lost 1st Round
Edinboro	Tom Hollman	0-1	Lost 1st Round
Grand Valley St.	Tom Beck	0-1	Lost 1st Round
Northwest Mo. St.	Bud Elliott	0-1	Lost 1st Round
Tex. A&M-Kingsville	Ron Harms	0-1	Lost 1st Round
West Chester	Rick Daniels	0-1	Lost 1st Round
1990 (16)			
North Dak. St.	Rocky Hager	4-0	Champion
Indiana (Pa.)	Frank Cignetti	3-1	Second
*Mississippi Col.	John Williams	2-1	Semifinalist
Pittsburg St.	Chuck Broyles	2-1	Semifinalist
Cal Poly SLO	Lyle Setencich	1-1	Quarterfinalist
East Tex. St.	Eddie Vowell	1-1	Quarterfinalist
Edinboro	Tom Hollman	1-1	Quarterfinalist
Jacksonville St.	Bill Burgess	1-1	Quarterfinalist
Cal St. Northridge	Bob Burt	0-1	Lost 1st Round
Grand Valley St.	Tom Beck	0-1	Lost 1st Round
North Ala.	Bobby Wallace	0-1	Lost 1st Round
Northern Colo.	Joe Glenn	0-1	Lost 1st Round
Truman St.	Eric Holm	0-1	Lost 1st Round
Virginia Union	Joe Taylor	0-1	Lost 1st Round
Winston-Salem	Pete Richardson	0-1	Lost 1st Round
Wofford	Mike Ayers	0-1	Lost 1st Round
1991 (16)			
Pittsburg St.	Chuck Broyles	4-0	Champion
Jacksonville St.	Bill Burgess	3-1	Second
Indiana (Pa.)	Frank Cignetti	2-1	Semifinalist
Portland St.	Pokey Allen	2-1	Semifinalist
East Tex. St.	Eddie Vowell	1-1	Quarterfinalist
Mankato St.	Dan Runkle	1-1	Quarterfinalist
Mississippi Col.	Terry McMillan	1-1	Quarterfinalist
Shippensburg	Rocky Rees	1-1	Quarterfinalist
Butler	Bob Bartolomeo	0-1	Lost 1st Round
East Stroudsburg	Dennis Douds	0-1	Lost 1st Round
Grand Valley St.	Brian Kelly	0-1	Lost 1st Round
North Dak. St.	Rocky Hager	0-1	Lost 1st Round
Northern Colo.	Joe Glenn	0-1	Lost 1st Round
Virginia Union	Joe Taylor	0-1	Lost 1st Round
Winston-Salem	Pete Richardson	0-1	Lost 1st Round
Wofford	Mike Ayers	0-1	Lost 1st Round
1992 (16)			
Jacksonville St.	Bill Burgess	4-0	Champion
Pittsburg St.	Chuck Broyles	3-1	Second
New Haven	Mark Whipple	2-1	Semifinalist
Portland St.	Pokey Allen	2-1	Semifinalist
Ferris St.	Keith Otterbein	1-1	Quarterfinalist
North Ala.	Bobby Wallace	1-1	Quarterfinalist
North Dak. St.	Rocky Hager	1-1	Quarterfinalist
Tex. A&M-Kingsville	Ron Harms	1-1	Quarterfinalist
UC Davis	Bob Foster	0-1	Lost 1st Round
Edinboro	Tom Hollman	0-1	Lost 1st Round
Hampton	Joe Taylor	0-1	Lost 1st Round
North Dak.	Roger Thomas	0-1	Lost 1st Round
Savannah St.	Bill Davis	0-1	Lost 1st Round
Truman St.	Eric Holm	0-1	Lost 1st Round
West Chester	Rick Daniels	0-1	Lost 1st Round
Western St.	Carl Iverson	0-1	Lost 1st Round
1993 (16)			
North Ala.	Bobby Wallace	4-0	Champion
Indiana (Pa.)	Frank Cignetti	3-1	Second
North Dak.	Roger Thomas	2-1	Semifinalist
Tex. A&M-Kingsville	Ron Harms	2-1	Semifinalist
UC Davis	Bob Biggs	1-1	Quarterfinalist
Hampton	Joe Taylor	1-1	Quarterfinalist
Mankato St.	Dan Runkle	1-1	Quarterfinalist
New Haven	Mark Whipple	1-1	Quarterfinalist
Albany St. (Ga.)	Hampton Smith	0-1	Lost 1st Round
Carson-Newman	Ken Sparks	0-1	Lost 1st Round
Edinboro	Tom Hollman	0-1	Lost 1st Round
Ferris St.	Keith Otterbein	0-1	Lost 1st Round
Fort Hays St.	Bob Cortese	0-1	Lost 1st Round
Mo. Southern St.	Jon Lantz	0-1	Lost 1st Round
Pittsburg St.	Chuck Broyles	0-1	Lost 1st Round
Portland St.	Tim Walsh	0-1	Lost 1st Round
1994 (16)			
North Ala.	Bobby Wallace	4-0	Champion
Tex. A&M-Kingsville	Ron Harms	3-1	Second

Year (Number of Teams)	Coach	Record	Result
Indiana (Pa.)	Frank Cignetti	2-1	Semifinalist
North Dak.	Roger Thomas	2-1	Semifinalist
Ferris St.	Keith Otterbein	1-1	Quarterfinalist
North Dak. St.	Rocky Hager	1-1	Quarterfinalist
Portland St.	Tim Walsh	1-1	Quarterfinalist
Valdosta St.	Hal Mumme	1-1	Quarterfinalist
Albany St. (Ga.)	Hampton Smith	0-1	Lost 1st Round
Angelo St.	Jerry Vandergriff	0-1	Lost 1st Round
Carson-Newman	Ken Sparks	0-1	Lost 1st Round
Grand Valley St.	Brian Kelly	0-1	Lost 1st Round
Pittsburg St.	Chuck Broyles	0-1	Lost 1st Round
Truman St.	Eric Holm	0-1	Lost 1st Round
West Chester	Rick Daniels	0-1	Lost 1st Round
Western St.	Carl Iverson	0-1	Lost 1st Round
1995 (16)			
North Ala.	Bobby Wallace	4-0	Champion
Pittsburg St.	Chuck Broyles	3-1	Second
Ferris St.	Jeff Pierce	2-1	Semifinalist
Tex. A&M-Kingsville	Ron Harms	2-1	Semifinalist
Carson-Newman	Ken Sparks	1-1	Quarterfinalist
New Haven	Tony Sparano	1-1	Quarterfinalist
North Dak. St.	Rocky Hager	1-1	Quarterfinalist
Portland St.	Tim Walsh	1-1	Quarterfinalist
Albany St. (Ga.)	Hampton Smith	0-1	Lost 1st Round
East Tex. St.	Eddie Vowell	0-1	Lost 1st Round
Edinboro	Tom Hollman	0-1	Lost 1st Round
Fort Hays St.	Bob Cortese	0-1	Lost 1st Round
Millersville	Gene Carpenter	0-1	Lost 1st Round
North Dak.	Roger Thomas	0-1	Lost 1st Round
Northern Colo.	Joe Glenn	0-1	Lost 1st Round
West Ga.	Charlie Fisher	0-1	Lost 1st Round

**Competition in championship vacated by action of the NCAA Committee on Infractions.*

Division II Championship Record of Each College by Coach

(85 Colleges; 1973-95)	Yrs	Won	Lost	CH	2D
AKRON					
Jim Dennison (Wooster '60) 76-2D	1	2	1	0	1
ALABAMA A&M					
Ray Green (Akron '63) 79	1	1	1	0	0
George Pugh (Alabama '76) 89	1	0	1	0	0
TOTAL	2	1	2	0	0
ALBANY ST. (GA.)					
Hampton Smith (Mississippi Val. '57) 93, 94, 95	3	0	3	0	0
ALCORN ST.					
Marino Casem (Xavier, La. '56) 74	1	0	1	0	0
ANGELO ST.					
Jerry Vandergriff (Corpus Christi '65) 87, 89, 94	3	2	3	0	0
ASHLAND					
Fred Martinelli (Otterbein '51) 86	1	0	1	0	0
AUGUSTANA (S.D.)					
Jim Heinitz (South Dak. St. '72) 88, 89	2	0	2	0	0
BETHUNE-COOKMAN					
Andy Hinson (Bethune-Cookman '53) 77	1	0	1	0	0
BLOOMSBURG					
George Landis (Penn St. '71) 85	1	1	1	0	0
BOISE ST.					
Tony Knap (Idaho '39) 73, 74, 75	3	1	3	0	0
BOWIE ST.					
Sanders Shiver (Carson-Newman '76) 88	1	0	1	0	0
BUTLER					
Bill Sylvester (Butler '50) 83	1	0	1	0	0
Bill Lynch (Butler '77) 88	1	0	1	0	0
Bob Bartolomeo (Butler '77) 91	1	0	1	0	0
TOTAL	3	0	3	0	0
UC DAVIS					
Jim Sochor (San Fran. St. '60) 77, 78, 82-2D, 83, 84, 85, 86, 88	8	4	8	0	1
Bob Foster (UC Davis '62) 89, 92	2	0	2	0	0
Bob Biggs (UC Davis '73) 93	1	1	1	0	0
TOTAL	11	5	11	0	1
CAL POLY SLO					
Joe Harper (UCLA '59) 78, 80-CH	2	3	1	1	0
Lyle Setencich (Fresno St. '68) 90	1	1	1	0	0
TOTAL	3	4	2	1	0

	Yrs	Won	Lost	CH	2D
CAL ST. NORTHRIDGE					
Bob Burt (Cal St. Los Angeles '62) 90	1	0	1	0	0
CAL ST. SACRAMENTO					
Bob Mattos (Cal St. Sacramento '64) 88	1	2	1	0	0
CARSON-NEWMAN					
Ken Sparks (Carson-Newman '68) 93, 94, 95	3	1	3	0	0
CENTRAL FLA.					
Gene McDowell (Florida St. '65) 87	1	1	1	0	0
CENTRAL MICH.					
Roy Kramer (Maryville, Tenn. '53) 74-CH	1	3	0	1	0
CENTRAL ST.					
Billy Joe (Villanova '63) 83-2D, 84, 85, 86	4	3	4	0	1
DELAWARE					
Harold "Tubby" Raymond (Michigan '50) 73, 74-2D, 76, 78-2D, 79-CH	5	7	4	1	2
EAST STROUDSBURG					
Dennis Douds (Slippery Rock '63) 91	1	0	1	0	0
EAST TEX. ST.					
Eddie Vowell (Southwestern Okla. '69) 90, 91, 95	3	2	3	0	0
EASTERN ILL.					
Darrell Mudra (Peru St. '51) 78-CH, 80-2D	2	5	1	1	1
EASTERN KY.					
Roy Kidd (Eastern Ky. '54) 76	1	0	1	0	0
EDINBORO					
Tom Hollman (Ohio Northern '68) 89, 90, 92, 93, 95	5	1	5	0	0
ELIZABETH CITY ST.					
Johnnie Walton (Elizabeth City St. '69) 81	1	0	1	0	0
FERRIS ST.					
Keith Otterbein (Ferris St. '79) 92, 93, 94	3	2	3	0	0
Jeff Pierce (Ferris St. '79) 95	1	2	1	0	0
TOTAL	4	4	4	0	0
FORT HAYS ST.					
Bob Cortese (Colorado '67) 93, 95	2	0	2	0	0
FORT VALLEY ST.					
Doug Porter (Xavier, La. '52) 82	1	0	1	0	0
Gerald Walker (Lincoln, Mo. '62) 85	1	0	1	0	0
TOTAL	2	0	2	0	0
GRAMBLING					
Eddie Robinson (Leland '41) 73	1	1	1	0	0
GRAND VALLEY ST.					
Tom Beck (Northern Ill. '61) 89, 90	2	0	2	0	0
Brian Kelly (Assumption '83) 91, 94	2	0	2	0	0
TOTAL	4	0	4	0	0
HAMPTON					
Fred Freeman (Mississippi Val. '66) 85	1	0	1	0	0
Joe Taylor (Western Ill. '72) 92, 93	2	1	2	0	0
TOTAL	3	1	3	0	0
INDIANA (PA.)					
Frank Cignetti (Indiana, Pa. '60) 87, 88, 89, 90-2D, 91, 93-2D, 94	7	12	7	0	2
JACKSONVILLE ST.					
Jim Fuller (Alabama '67) 77-2D, 78, 80, 81, 82	5	3	5	0	1
Bill Burgess (Auburn '63) 88, 89-2D, 90, 91-2D, 92-CH	5	12	4	1	2
TOTAL	10	15	9	1	3
LEHIGH					
Fred Dunlap (Colgate '50) 73, 75	2	0	2	0	0
John Whitehead (East Stroudsburg '50) 77-CH	1	3	0	1	0
TOTAL	3	3	2	1	0
LOUISIANA TECH					
Maxie Lambright (Southern Miss. '49) 73-CH, 74	2	4	1	1	0
MANKATO ST.					
Dan Runkle (Illinois Col. '68) 87, 91, 93	3	2	3	0	0
MASSACHUSETTS					
Dick MacPherson (Springfield '58) 77	1	0	1	0	0
MILLERSVILLE					
Gene Carpenter (Huron '63) 88, 95	2	1	2	0	0
MISSISSIPPI COL.*					
John Williams (Mississippi Col. '57) 79, 88, 89-CH, 90	4	7	3	1	0
Terry McMillan (Southern Miss. '69) 91	1	1	1	0	0
TOTAL	5	8	4	1	0

	Yrs	Won	Lost	CH	2D
MO. SOUTHERN ST.					
Jon Lantz (Okla. Panhandle St. '74) 93	1	0	1	0	0
MONTANA ST.					
Sonny Holland (Montana St. '60) 76-CH	1	3	0	1	0
MORGAN ST.					
Clarence Thomas 79	1	0	1	0	0
NEB.-OMAHA					
Sandy Buda (Kansas '67) 78, 84	2	1	2	0	0
UNLV					
Ron Meyer (Purdue '63) 74	1	1	1	0	0
Tony Knap (Idaho '39) 76	1	0	1	0	0
TOTAL	2	1	2	0	0
NEW HAMPSHIRE					
Bill Bowes (Penn St. '65) 75, 76	2	1	2	0	0
NEW HAVEN					
Mark Whipple (Brown '79) 92, 93	2	3	2	0	0
Tony Sparano (New Haven '82) 95	1	1	1	0	0
TOTAL	3	4	3	0	0
NORFOLK ST.					
Willard Bailey (Norfolk St. '62) 84	1	0	1	0	0
NORTH ALA.					
Wayne Grubb (Tennessee '61) 80, 83, 85-2D	3	4	3	0	1
Bobby Wallace (Mississippi St. '76) 90, 92, 93-CH, 94-CH, 95-CH	5	13	2	3	0
TOTAL	8	17	5	3	1
N.C. CENTRAL					
Henry Lattimore (Jackson St. '57) 88	1	1	1	0	0
NORTH DAK.					
Jerry Olson (Valley City St. '55) 75	1	0	1	0	0
Gene Murphy (North Dak. '62) 79	1	0	1	0	0
Roger Thomas (Augustana, Ill. '69) 92, 93, 94, 95	4	4	4	0	0
TOTAL	6	4	6	0	0
NORTH DAK. ST.					
Jim Wacker (Valparaiso '60) 76, 77	2	2	2	0	0
Don Morton (Augustana, Ill. '69) 81-2D, 82, 83-CH, 84-2D	4	8	3	1	2
Earle Solomonson (Augsburg '69) 85-CH, 86-CH	2	6	0	2	0
Rocky Hager (Minot St. '74) 88-CH, 89, 90-CH, 91, 92, 94, 95	7	12	5	2	0
TOTAL	15	28	10	5	2
NORTHERN ARIZ.					
Joe Salem (Minnesota '61) 77	1	0	1	0	0
NORTHERN COLO.					
Bob Blasi (Colorado St. '53) 80	1	0	1	0	0
Joe Glenn (South Dak. '71) 90, 91, 95	3	0	3	0	0
TOTAL	4	0	4	0	0
NORTHERN IOWA					
Stan Sheriff (Cal Poly SLO '54) 75	1	0	1	0	0
NORTHERN MICH.					
Gil Krueger (Marquette '52) 75-CH, 76, 77	3	4	2	1	0
Bill Rademacher (Northern Mich. '63) 80, 81, 82	3	1	3	0	0
Herb Grenke (Wis.-Milwaukee '63) 87	1	1	1	0	0
TOTAL	7	6	6	1	0
NORTHWEST MO. ST.					
Vern Thomsen (Peru St. '61) 84	1	0	1	0	0
Bud Elliott (Baker '53) 89	1	0	1	0	0
TOTAL	2	0	2	0	0
PITTSBURG ST.					
Dennis Franchione (Pittsburg St. '73) 89	1	1	1	0	0
Chuck Broyles (Pittsburg St. '70) 90, 91-CH, 92-2D, 93, 94, 95-2D	6	12	5	1	2
TOTAL	7	13	6	1	2
PORTLAND ST.					
Pokey Allen (Utah '65) 87-2D, 88-2D, 89, 91, 92	5	10	5	0	2
Tim Walsh (UC Riverside '77) 93, 94, 95	3	2	3	0	0
TOTAL	8	12	8	0	2
PUGET SOUND					
Ron Simonson (Portland St. '65) 81	1	0	1	0	0
ST. CLOUD ST.					
Noel Martin (Nebraska '63) 89	1	1	1	0	0
SANTA CLARA					
Pat Malley (Santa Clara '53) 80	1	1	1	0	0

	Yrs	Won	Lost	CH	2D
SAVANNAH ST.					
Bill Davis (Johnson Smith '65) 92	1	0	1	0	0
SHIPPENSBURG					
Vito Ragazzo (William & Mary '51) 81	1	1	1	0	0
Rocky Rees (West Chester '71) 91	1	1	1	0	0
TOTAL	2	2	2	0	0
SOUTH DAK.					
Joe Salem (Minnesota '61) 73	1	0	1	0	0
Dave Triplett (Iowa '72) 85, 86-2D	2	3	2	0	1
TOTAL	3	3	3	0	1
SOUTH DAK. ST.					
John Gregory (Northern Iowa '61) 79	1	0	1	0	0
SOUTHWEST TEX. ST.					
Jim Wacker (Valparaiso '60) 81-CH, 82-CH	2	6	0	2	0
John O'Hara (Okla. Panhandle St. '67) 83	1	0	1	0	0
TOTAL	3	6	1	2	0
TENN.-MARTIN					
Don McLeary (Tennessee '70) 88	1	1	1	0	0
TEX. A&M-KINGSVILLE					
Ron Harms (Valparaiso '59) 88, 89, 92, 93, 94-2D, 95	6	10	6	0	1
TOWSON ST.					
Phil Albert (Arizona '66) 83, 84, 86	3	1	3	0	0
TROY ST.					
Chan Gailey (Florida '74) 84-CH	1	3	0	1	0
Rick Rhodes 86, 87-CH	2	4	1	1	0
TOTAL	3	7	1	2	0
TRUMAN ST.					
Bruce Craddock (Truman St. '66) 82	1	0	1	0	0
Eric Holm (Truman St. '81) 90, 92, 94	3	0	3	0	0
TOTAL	4	0	4	0	0
VALDOSTA ST.					
Hal Mumme (Tarleton St. '75) 94	1	1	1	0	0
VIRGINIA UNION					
Willard Bailey (Norfolk St. '62) 79, 80, 81, 82, 83	5	0	5	0	0
Joe Taylor (Western Ill. '72) 86, 90, 91	3	0	3	0	0
TOTAL	8	0	8	0	0
WEST ALA.					
Jim King 75	1	1	1	0	0
WEST CHESTER					
Danny Hale (West Chester '68) 88	1	0	1	0	0
Rick Daniels (West Chester '75) 89, 92, 94	3	0	3	0	0
TOTAL	4	0	4	0	0
WEST GA.					
Charlie Fisher (Springfield '81) 95	1	0	1	0	0
WESTERN CARO.					
Bob Waters (Presbyterian '60) 74	1	0	1	0	0
WESTERN ILL.					
Darrell Mudra (Peru St. '51) 73	1	0	1	0	0
WESTERN KY.					
Jimmy Feix (Western Ky. '53) 73-2D, 75-2D	2	4	2	0	2
WESTERN ST.					
Carl Iverson (Whitman '62) 92, 94	2	0	2	0	0
WINSTON-SALEM					
Bill Hayes (N.C. Central '64) 78, 87	2	1	2	0	0
Pete Richardson (Dayton '68) 88, 90, 91	3	0	3	0	0
TOTAL	5	1	5	0	0
WOFFORD					
Mike Ayers (Georgetown, Ky. '74) 90, 91	2	0	2	0	0
YOUNGSTOWN ST.					
Rey Dempsey (Geneva '58) 74	1	0	1	0	0
Bill Narduzzi (Miami, Ohio '59) 78, 79-2D	2	3	2	0	1
TOTAL	3	3	3	0	1

**Mississippi College's competition in the 1989 and 1990 Division II championships was vacated by action of the NCAA Committee on Infractions (official record is 2-3).*

CHAMPIONSHIP RESULTS

All-Time Results

1973 First Round: Grambling 17, Delaware 8; Western Ky. 25, Lehigh 16; Louisiana Tech 18, Western Ill. 13; Boise St. 53, South Dak. 10. **Semifinals:** Western Ky. 28, Grambling 20; Louisiana Tech 38, Boise St. 34. **Championship:** Louisiana Tech 34, Western Ky. 0.

1974 First Round: Central Mich. 20, Boise St. 6; Louisiana Tech 10, Western Caro. 7; UNLV 35, Alcorn St. 22; Delaware 35, Youngstown St. 14. **Semifinals:** Central Mich. 35, Louisiana Tech 14; Delaware 49, UNLV 11. **Championship:** Central Mich. 54, Delaware 14.

1975 First Round: Northern Mich. 24, Boise St. 21; West Ala. 34, North Dak. 14; Western Ky. 14, Northern Iowa 12; New Hampshire 35, Lehigh 21. **Semifinals:** Northern Mich. 28, West Ala. 26; Western Ky. 14, New Hampshire 3. **Championship:** Northern Mich. 16, Western Ky. 14.

1976 First Round: Akron 26, UNLV 6; Northern Mich. 28, Delaware 17; North Dak. St. 10, Eastern Ky. 7; Montana St. 17, New Hampshire 16. **Semifinals:** Akron 29, Northern Mich. 26; Montana St. 10, North Dak. St. 3. **Championship:** Montana St. 24, Akron 13.

1977 First Round: UC Davis 34, Bethune-Cookman 16; Lehigh 30, Massachusetts 23; North Dak. St. 20, Northern Mich. 6; Jacksonville St. 35, Northern Ariz. 0. **Semifinals:** Lehigh 39, UC Davis 30; Jacksonville St. 31, North Dak. St. 7. **Championship:** Lehigh 33, Jacksonville St. 0.

1978 First Round: Winston-Salem 17, Cal Poly SLO 0; Delaware 42, Jacksonville St. 27; Youngstown St. 21, Neb.-Omaha 14; Eastern Ill. 35, UC Davis 31. **Semifinals:** Delaware 41, Winston-Salem 0; Eastern Ill. 26, Youngstown St. 22. **Championship:** Eastern Ill. 10, Delaware 9.

1979 First Round: Delaware 58, Virginia Union 28; Mississippi Col. 35, North Dak. 15; Youngstown St. 50, South Dak. St. 7; Alabama A&M 27, Morgan St. 7. **Semifinals:** Delaware 60, Mississippi Col. 10; Youngstown St. 52, Alabama A&M 0. **Championship:** Delaware 38, Youngstown St. 21.

1980 First Round: Eastern Ill. 21, Northern Colo. 14; North Ala. 17, Virginia Union 8; Santa Clara 27, Northern Mich. 26; Cal Poly SLO 15, Jacksonville St. 0. **Semifinals:** Eastern Ill. 56, North Ala. 31; Cal Poly SLO 38, Santa Clara 14. **Championship:** Cal Poly SLO 21, Eastern Ill. 13.

1981 First Round: Northern Mich. 55, Elizabeth City St. 6; Southwest Tex. St. 38, Jacksonville St. 22; North Dak. St. 24, Puget Sound 10; Shippensburg 40, Virginia Union 27. **Semifinals:** Southwest Tex. St. 62, Northern Mich. 0; North Dak. St. 18, Shippensburg 6. **Championship:** Southwest Tex. St. 42, North Dak. St. 13.

1982 First Round: Southwest Tex. St. 27, Fort Valley St. 6; Jacksonville St. 34, Truman St. 21; North Dak. St. 21, Virginia Union 20; UC Davis 42, Northern Mich. 21. **Semifinals:** Southwest Tex. St. 19, Jacksonville St. 14; UC Davis 19, North Dak. St. 14. **Championship:** Southwest Tex. St. 34, UC Davis 9.

1983 First Round: UC Davis 25, Butler 6; North Dak. St. 24, Towson St. 17; North Ala. 16, Virginia Union 14; Central St. 24, Southwest Tex. St. 16. **Semifinals:** North Dak. St. 26, UC Davis 17; Central St. 27, North Ala. 24. **Championship:** North Dak. St. 41, Central St. 21.

1984 First Round: North Dak. St. 31, UC Davis 23; Neb.-Omaha 28, Northwest Mo. St. 15; Troy St. 31, Central St. 21; Towson St. 31, Norfolk St. 21. **Semifinals:** North Dak. St. 25, Neb.-Omaha 14; Troy St. 45, Towson St. 3. **Championship:** Troy St. 18, North Dak. St. 17.

1985 First Round: North Dak. St. 31, UC Davis 12; South Dak. 13, Central St. 10 (2 OT); Bloomsburg 38, Hampton 28; North Ala. 14, Fort Valley St. 7. **Semifinals:** North Dak. St. 16, South Dak. 7; North Ala. 34, Bloomsburg 0. **Championship:** North Dak. St. 35, North Ala. 7.

1986 First Round: North Dak. St. 50, Ashland 0; Central St. 31, Towson St. 0; Troy St. 31, Virginia Union 7; South Dak. 26, UC Davis 23. **Semifinals:** North Dak. St. 35, Central St. 12; South Dak. 42, Troy St. 28. **Championship:** North Dak. St. 27, South Dak. 7.

1987 First Round: Portland St. 27, Mankato St. 21; Northern Mich. 23, Angelo St. 20 (OT); Central Fla. 12, Indiana (Pa.) 10; Troy St. 45, Winston-Salem 14. **Semifinals:** Portland St. 13, Northern Mich. 7; Troy St. 31, Central Fla. 10. **Championship:** Troy St. 31, Portland St. 17.

1988 First Round: North Dak. St. 49, Augustana (S.D.) 7; Millersville 27, Indiana (Pa.) 24; Cal St. Sacramento 35, UC Davis 14; N.C. Central 31, Winston-Salem 16; Tex. A&M-Kingsville 39, Mississippi Col. 15; Tenn.-Martin 23, Butler 6; Portland St. 34, Bowie St. 17; Jacksonville St. 63, West Chester 24. **Quarterfinals:** North Dak. St. 36, Millersville 26; Cal St. Sacramento 56, N.C. Central 7; Tex. A&M-Kingsville 34, Tenn.-Martin 0; Portland St. 20, Jacksonville St. 13. **Semifinals:** North Dak. St. 42, Cal St. Sacramento 20; Portland St. 35, Tex. A&M-Kingsville 27. **Championship:** North Dak. St. 35, Portland St. 21.

1989 First Round: *Mississippi Col. 34, Tex. A&M-Kingsville 19; St. Cloud St. 27, Augustana (S.D.) 20; Portland St. 56, West Chester 50 (3 OT); Indiana (Pa.) 34, Grand Valley St. 24; Pittsburg St. 28, Northwest Mo. St. 7; Angelo St. 28, UC Davis 23; North Dak. St. 45, Edinboro 32; Jacksonville St. 33, Alabama A&M 9. **Quarterfinals:** *Mississippi Col. 55, St. Cloud St. 24; Indiana (Pa.) 17, Portland St. 0; Angelo St. 24, Pittsburg St. 21; Jacksonville St. 21, North Dak. St. 17. **Semifinals:** *Mississippi Col. 26, Indiana (Pa.) 14; Jacksonville St. 34, Angelo St. 16. **Championship:** *Mississippi Col. 3, Jacksonville St. 0.

**Mississippi College's participation in 1989 playoff vacated.*

1990 First Round: *Mississippi Col. 70, Wofford 19; Jacksonville St. 38, North Ala. 14; Indiana (Pa.) 48, Winston-Salem 0; Edinboro 38, Virginia Union 14; North Dak. St. 17, Northern Colo. 7; Cal Poly SLO 14, Cal St. Northridge 7; Pittsburg St. 59, Truman St. 3; East Tex. St. 20, Grand Valley St. 14. **Quarterfinals:** *Mississippi Col. 14, Jacksonville St. 7; Indiana (Pa.) 14, Edinboro 7; North Dak. St. 47, Cal Poly SLO 0; Pittsburg St. 60, East Tex. St. 28. **Semifinals:** Indiana (Pa.) 27, *Mississippi Col. 8; North Dak. St. 39, Pittsburg St. 29. **Championship:** North Dak. St. 51, Indiana (Pa.) 11.

**Mississippi College's participation in 1990 playoff vacated.*

1991 First Round: Pittsburg St. 26, Butler 16; East Tex. St. 36, Grand Valley St. 15; Portland St. 28, Northern Colo. 24; Mankato St. 27, North Dak. St. 7; Jacksonville

St. 49, Winston-Salem 24; Mississippi Col. 28, Wofford 15; Indiana (Pa.) 56, Virginia Union 7; Shippensburg 34, East Stroudsburg 33 (OT). **Quarterfinals:** Pittsburg St. 38, East Tex. St. 28; Portland St. 37, Mankato St. 27; Jacksonville St. 35, Mississippi Col. 7; Indiana (Pa.) 52, Shippensburg 7. **Semifinals:** Pittsburg St. 53, Portland St. 21; Jacksonville St. 27, Indiana (Pa.) 20. **Championship:** Pittsburg St. 23, Jacksonville St. 6.

1992 First Round: Ferris St. 19, Edinboro 15; New Haven 38, West Chester 26; Jacksonville St. 41, Savannah St. 16; North Ala. 33, Hampton 21; Tex. A&M-Kingsville 22, Western St. 13; Portland St. 42, UC Davis 28; Pittsburg St. 26, North Dak. 21; North Dak. St. 42, Truman St. 7. **Quarterfinals:** New Haven 35, Ferris St. 13; Jacksonville St. 14, North Ala. 12; Portland St. 35, Tex. A&M-Kingsville 30; Pittsburg St. 38, North Dak. St. 37 (OT). **Semifinals:** Jacksonville St. 46, New Haven 35; Pittsburg St. 41, Portland St. 38. **Championship:** Jacksonville St. 17, Pittsburg St. 13.

1993 First Round: North Ala. 38, Carson-Newman 28; Hampton 33, Albany St. (Ga.) 7; Tex. A&M-Kingsville 50, Portland St. 15; UC Davis 37, Fort Hays St. 34; Mankato St. 34, Mo. Southern St. 13; North Dak. 17, Pittsburg St. 14; New Haven 48, Edinboro 28; Indiana (Pa.) 28, Ferris St. 21. **Quarterfinals:** North Ala. 45, Hampton 20; Tex. A&M-Kingsville 51, UC Davis 28; North Dak. 54, Mankato St. 21; Indiana (Pa.) 38, New Haven 35. **Semifinals:** North Ala. 27, Tex. A&M-Kingsville 25; Indiana (Pa.) 21, North Dak. 6. **Championship:** North Ala. 41, Indiana (Pa.) 34.

1994 First Round: Ferris St. 43, West Chester 40; Indiana (Pa.) 35, Grand Valley St. 27; Tex. A&M-Kingsville 43, Western St. 7; Portland St. 29, Angelo St. 0; North Dak. St. 18, Pittsburg St. 12 (3 OT); North Dak. 18, Truman St. 6; North Ala. 17, Carson-Newman 13; Valdosta St. 14, Albany St. (Ga.) 7. **Quarterfinals:** Indiana (Pa.) 21, Ferris St. 17; Tex. A&M-Kingsville 21, Portland St. 16; North Dak. 14, North Dak. St. 7; North Ala. 27, Valdosta St. 24 (2 OT). **Semifinals:** Tex. A&M-Kingsville 46, Indiana (Pa.) 20; North Ala. 35, North Dak. 7. **Championship:** North Ala. 16, Tex. A&M-Kingsville 10.

1995 First Round: Ferris St. 36, Millersville 26; New Haven 27, Edinboro 12; North Ala. 38, Albany St. (Ga.) 28; Carson-Newman 37, West Ga. 26; Pittsburg St. 36, Northern Colo. 17; North Dak. St. 41, North Dak. 10; Tex. A&M-Kingsville 59, Fort Hays St. 28; Portland St. 56, East Tex. St. 35. **Quarterfinals:** Ferris St. 17, New Haven 9; North Ala. 28, Carson-Newman 7; Pittsburg St. 9, North Dak. St. 7; Tex. A&M-Kingsville 30, Portland St. 3. **Semifinals:** North Ala. 45, Ferris St. 7; Pittsburg St. 28, Tex. A&M-Kingsville 25 (OT). **Championship:** North Ala. 27, Pittsburg St. 7.

Andres Alonso/NCAA photos

Craig Kusick passed for 281 yards and four touchdowns to lead Wisconsin-La Crosse to a convincing 36-7 victory over Rowan in the 1995 Division III Football Championship title game. It was the Eagles' second title in four years.

Division III Championship

1995 Title Game Summary

AMOS ALONZO STAGG BOWL, SALEM STADIUM, SALEM, VA.; DECEMBER 9, 1995

	Rowan	Wis.-La Crosse
First Downs	9	25
Rushes-Net Yardage	27-61	54-155
Passing Yardage	92	296
Return Yardage (Punts, Int. & Fum.)	49	90
Passes (Comp.-Att.-Int.)	8-30-4	21-35-1
Punts (Number-Average)	9-34.6	7-31.4
Fumbles (Number-Lost)	3-2	2-2
Penalties (Number-Yards)	4-26	7-102

Rowan	7	0	0	0— 7
Wis.-La Crosse	0	16	7	13—36

Game Conditions: Temperature, 45 degrees; wind, 17-35 mph from the south; weather, sunny. Attendance: 4,905.

FIRST QUARTER
Rowan—Aaron Bosco 1 run (Tim Huckel kick) (7 yards in 2 plays, 7:28 left)

SECOND QUARTER
Wis.-La Crosse—Dave Nagel 4 pass from Craig Kusick (Thad Dugan kick) (79 yards in 12 plays, 9:15 left)
Wis.-La Crosse—Safety, Mike Ivey tackled Eugene Foster in end zone (9:02 left)
Wis.-La Crosse—Jeremy Earp 85 pass from Kusick (Dugan kick) (85 yards in 1 play, 0:04 left)

THIRD QUARTER
Wis.-La Crosse—Erick Jenkins 35 pass from Kusick (Dugan kick) (51 yards in 4 plays, 1:44 left)

FOURTH QUARTER
Wis.-La Crosse—John Barrett 3 pass from Kusick (Dugan kick) (27 yards in 5 plays, 14:56 left)
Wis.-La Crosse—Jason Tarkowski 6 run (kick failed) (10 yards in 2 plays, 13:34 left)

INDIVIDUAL LEADERS
Rushing—Rowan: Foster, 46 yards on 14 carries; Wis.-La Crosse: Tarkowski, 74 yards on 17 carries.
Passing—Rowan: Greg Lister, 7 of 27 for 60 yards; Wis.-La Crosse: Kusick, 19 of 31 for 281 yards.
Receiving—Rowan: Gantry Fox, 6 catches for 80 yards; Wis.-La Crosse: Troy Harcey, 7 catches for 61 yards.

Division III All-Time Championship Results

Year	Champion	Coach	Score	Runner-Up	Site
1973	Wittenberg	Dave Maurer	41-0	Juniata	Phenix City, Ala.
1974	Central (Iowa)	Ron Schipper	10-8	Ithaca	Phenix City, Ala.
1975	Wittenberg	Dave Maurer	28-0	Ithaca	Phenix City, Ala.
1976	St. John's (Minn.)	John Gagliardi	31-28	Towson St.	Phenix City, Ala.
1977	Widener	Bill Manlove	39-36	Wabash	Phenix City, Ala.
1978	Baldwin-Wallace	Lee Tressel	24-10	Wittenberg	Phenix City, Ala.
1979	Ithaca	Jim Butterfield	14-10	Wittenberg	Phenix City, Ala.
1980	Dayton	Rick Carter	63-0	Ithaca	Phenix City, Ala.
1981	Widener	Bill Manlove	17-10	Dayton	Phenix City, Ala.
1982	West Ga.	Bobby Pate	14-0	Augustana (Ill.)	Phenix City, Ala.
1983	Augustana (Ill.)	Bob Reade	21-17	Union (N.Y.)	Kings Island, Ohio
1984	Augustana (Ill.)	Bob Reade	21-12	Central (Iowa)	Kings Island, Ohio
1985	Augustana (Ill.)	Bob Reade	20-7	Ithaca	Phenix City, Ala.
1986	Augustana (Ill.)	Bob Reade	31-3	Salisbury St.	Phenix City, Ala.
1987	Wagner	Walt Hameline	19-3	Dayton	Phenix City, Ala.
1988	Ithaca	Jim Butterfield	39-24	Central (Iowa)	Phenix City, Ala.
1989	Dayton	Mike Kelly	17-7	Union (N.Y.)	Phenix City, Ala.

Year	Champion	Coach	Score	Runner-Up	Site
1990	Allegheny	Ken O'Keefe	21-14 (OT)	Lycoming	Bradenton, Fla.
1991	Ithaca	Jim Butterfield	34-20	Dayton	Bradenton, Fla.
1992	Wis.-La Crosse	Roger Harring	16-12	Wash. & Jeff.	Bradenton, Fla.
1993	Mount Union	Larry Kehres	34-24	Rowan	Salem, Va.
1994	Albion	Pete Schmidt	38-15	Wash. & Jeff.	Salem, Va.
1995	Wis.-La Crosse	Roger Harring	36-7	Rowan	Salem, Va.

Wheaton (Illinois) sports information photo by Michael Hudson

Wheaton (Illinois) running back Dane Shaw gains some of his 79 rushing yards in Wheaton's 63-41 victory over Wittenberg in the first round of the 1995 Division III Football Championship.

Regional Championship Results

(Before Division III Championship)

Year	Champion	Coach	Score	Runner-Up	Site
EAST (KNUTE ROCKNE BOWL)					
1969	Randolph-Macon	Ted Keller	47-28	Bridgeport	Bridgeport, Conn.
1970	Montclair St.	Clary Anderson	7-6	Hampden-Sydney	Atlantic City, N.J.
1971	Bridgeport	Ed Farrell	17-12	Hampden-Sydney	Atlantic City, N.J.
1972	Bridgeport	Ed Farrell	27-22	Slippery Rock	Atlantic City, N.J.
WEST (AMOS ALONZO STAGG BOWL)					
1969	Wittenberg	Dave Maurer	27-21	William Jewell	Springfield, Ohio
1970	Capital	Gene Slaughter	34-21	Luther	Columbus, Ohio
1971	Vacated		20-10	Ohio Wesleyan	Phenix City, Ala.
1972	Heidelberg	Pete Riesen	28-16	Fort Valley St.	Phenix City, Ala.

CHAMPIONSHIP RESULTS

1995 Division III Championship Results

REGIONALS

Mount Union 52, Hanover 18
Wheaton (Ill.) 63, Wittenberg 41
Wis.-La Crosse 45, Concordia-M'head 7
Wis.-River Falls 10, Central (Iowa) 7
Wash. & Jeff. 35, Emory & Henry 16
Lycoming 31, Widener 27
Rowan 46, Buffalo St. 7
Union (N.Y.) 24, Plymouth St. 7

QUARTERFINALS

Mount Union 40, Wheaton (Ill.) 14
Wis.-La Crosse 28, Wis.-River Falls 14
Wash. & Jeff. 48, Lycoming 0
Rowan 38, Union (N.Y.) 7

SEMIFINALS

Wis.-La Crosse 20, Mount Union 17
Rowan 28, Wash. & Jeff. 15

CHAMPIONSHIP

Wis.-La Crosse 36, Rowan 7

Championship Records

INDIVIDUAL: SINGLE GAME

NET YARDS RUSHING
389—Ricky Gales, Simpson (35) vs. St. John's (Minn.) (42), 11-18-89.

RUSHES ATTEMPTED
51—Ricky Gales, Simpson (35) vs. St. John's (Minn.) (42), 11-18-89.

TOUCHDOWNS BY RUSHING
5—Jeff Norman, St. John's (Minn.) (46) vs. Augustana (Ill.) (7), 11-20-76; Mike Coppa, Salisbury St. (44) vs. Ithaca (40), 12-6-86; Paul Parker, Ithaca (62) vs. Ferrum (28), 12-3-88; Kevin Hofacre, Dayton (35) vs. John Carroll (10), 11-18-89.

NET YARDS PASSING
584—Bill Borchert, Mount Union (52) vs. Hanover (18), 11-18-95.

PASSES ATTEMPTED
67—Terry Peebles, Hanover (18) vs. Mount Union (52), 11-18-95; Vic Ameye, Widener (27) vs. Lycoming (31), 11-18-95.

PASSES COMPLETED
37—Bill Borchert, Mount Union (52) vs. Hanover (18), 11-18-95.

PASSES HAD INTERCEPTED
7—Rick Steil, Dubuque (7) vs. Ithaca (27), 11-17-79.

TOUCHDOWN PASSES COMPLETED
8—Jim Ballard, Mount Union (56) vs. St. John's (Minn.) (8), 12-4-93.

COMPLETION PERCENTAGE (Min. 8 Attempts)
.900—Robb Disbennett, Salisbury St. (16) vs. Carnegie Mellon (14), 11-19-83 (18 of 20).

NET YARDS RUSHING AND PASSING
595—Bill Borchert, Mount Union (52) vs. Hanover (18) 11-18-95.

NUMBER OF RUSHING AND PASSING PLAYS
77—Terry Peebles, Hanover (18) vs. Mount Union (52), 11-18-95.

PUNTING AVERAGE (Min. 3 Punts)
48.5—Phil Macken, Minn.-Morris (25) vs. Carnegie Mellon (31), 11-17-79.

NUMBER OF PUNTS
14—Tim Flynn, Gettysburg (14) vs. Lycoming (10), 11-23-85.

PASSES CAUGHT
16—Todd Zufra, Mount Union (52) vs. Hanover (18), 11-18-95; Mark Loeffler, Wheaton (Ill.) (14) vs. Mount Union (40), 11-25-95.

NET YARDS RECEIVING
265—Todd Zufra, Mount Union (52) vs. Hanover (18), 11-18-95.

TOUCHDOWN PASSES CAUGHT
4—Kirk Liesimer, Ill. Wesleyan (27) vs. Mount Union (49), 11-28-92; Rob Atwood, Mount Union (56) vs. St. John's (Minn.) (8), 12-4-93.

PASSES INTERCEPTED
3—By nine players. Most recent: Arnell Palmer, Rowan (28) vs. Wash. & Jeff. (15), 12-2-95.

YARDS GAINED ON INTERCEPTION RETURNS
100—Jay Zunic, Ithaca (31) vs. Rowan (10), 11-23-91 (2 interceptions, 1 for 100-yard TD).

YARDS GAINED ON PUNT RETURNS
98—Leroy Horn, Montclair St. (28) vs. Western Conn. St. (0), 11-23-85.

YARDS GAINED ON KICKOFF RETURNS
190—George Day, Susquehanna (31) vs. Lycoming (24), 11-30-91.

POINTS
36—Mike Coppa, Salisbury St. (44) vs. Ithaca (40), 12-6-86.

TOUCHDOWNS
6—Mike Coppa, Salisbury St. (44) vs. Ithaca (40), 12-6-86.

EXTRA POINTS
9—Tim Robinson, Baldwin-Wallace (71) vs. St. Lawrence (7), 11-18-78.

INDIVIDUAL: TOURNAMENT

NET YARDS RUSHING
882—Chris Babirad, Wash. & Jeff., 1992 (285 vs. Lycoming, 286 vs. Emory & Henry, 207 vs. Rowan, 104 vs. Wis.-La Crosse).

RUSHES ATTEMPTED
129—Chris Babirad, Wash. & Jeff., 1992 (37 vs. Lycoming, 31 vs. Emory & Henry, 36 vs. Rowan, 25 vs. Wis.-La Crosse).

NET YARDS PASSING
1,251—Jim Ballard, Mount Union, 1993 (347 vs. Allegheny, 192 vs. Albion, 325 vs. St. John's, Minn., 387 vs. Rowan).

PASSES ATTEMPTED
141—Brett Russ, Union (N.Y.), 1989 (23 vs. Cortland St., 37 vs. Montclair St., 38 vs. Ferrum, 43 vs. Dayton); Jim Ballard, Mount Union, 1993 (40 vs. Allegheny, 28 vs. Albion, 28 vs. St. John's, Minn., 45 vs. Rowan).

PASSES COMPLETED
90—Jim Ballard, Mount Union, 1993 (26 vs. Allegheny, 16 vs. Albion, 20 vs. St. John's, Minn., 28 vs. Rowan).

TOUCHDOWN PASSES COMPLETED
17—Jim Ballard, Mount Union, 1993 (5 vs. Allegheny, 1 vs. Albion, 8 vs. St. John's, Minn., 3 vs. Rowan).

COMPLETION PERCENTAGE (Min. 2 Games)
.676—Bill Borchert, Mount Union, 1994, 46 of 68 (23-34 vs. Allegheny, 23-34 vs. Albion).

PASSES HAD INTERCEPTED
9—Rollie Wiebers, Buena Vista, 1976 (4 vs. Carroll, Wis., 5 vs. St. John's, Minn.).

PASSES CAUGHT
39—Nick Ismailoff, Ithaca, 1991 (12 vs. Rowan, 6 vs. Union, N.Y., 11 vs. Susquehanna, 10 vs. Dayton).

NET YARDS RECEIVING
599—Nick Ismailoff, Ithaca, 1991 (179 vs. Rowan, 122 vs. Union, N.Y., 105 vs. Susquehanna, 193 vs. Dayton).

TOUCHDOWN PASSES CAUGHT
6—Rob Atwood, Mount Union, 1993 (0 vs. Allegheny, 0 vs. Albion, 4 vs. St. John's, Minn., 2 vs. Rowan).

POINTS
60—By four players. Most recent: Chris Babirad, Wash. & Jeff., 1992 (18 vs. Lycoming, 24 vs. Emory & Henry, 12 vs. Rowan, 6 vs. Wis.-La Crosse).

TOUCHDOWNS
10—Brad Price, Augustana (Ill.), 1986 (4 vs. Hope, 1 vs. Mount Union, 2 vs. Concordia-M'head, 3 vs. Salisbury St.); Mike Coppa, Salisbury St., 1986 (1 vs. Emory & Henry, 3 vs. Susquehanna, 6 vs. Ithaca, 0 vs. Augustana, Ill.); Chris Babirad, Wash. & Jeff., 1992 (3 vs. Lycoming, 4 vs. Emory & Henry, 2 vs. Rowan, 1 vs. Wis.-La Crosse).

INDIVIDUAL: LONGEST PLAYS

LONGEST RUSH
93—Rick Papke, Augustana (Ill.) (17) vs. Central (Iowa) (23), 12-3-88, TD.

LONGEST PASS COMPLETION
96—Mark Blom to Tom McDonald, Central (Iowa) (37) vs. Buena Vista (0), 11-22-86, TD.

LONGEST FIELD GOAL
52—Rod Vesling, St. Lawrence (43) vs. Wagner (34), 11-20-82.

LONGEST PUNT
79—Tom Hansen, Ithaca (3) vs. Wittenberg (6), 11-18-78.

LONGEST PUNT RETURN
78—Pete Minturn, Ithaca (34) vs. Gettysburg (0), 12-7-85, TD.

LONGEST KICKOFF RETURN
100—Tom Deery, Widener (23) vs. Montclair St. (12), 11-30-81, TD.

LONGEST INTERCEPTION RETURN
100—Jay Zunic, Ithaca (31) vs. Rowan (10), 11-23-91, TD.

TEAM: SINGLE GAME

FIRST DOWNS
40—Mount Union (52) vs. Hanover (18), 11-18-95.

FIRST DOWNS BY RUSHING
30—Central (Iowa) (71) vs. Occidental (0), 12-7-85.

FIRST DOWNS BY PASSING
34—Mount Union (52) vs. Hanover (18), 11-18-95.

NET YARDS RUSHING
530—St. John's (Minn.) (46) vs. Augustana (Ill.) (7), 11-20-76.

RUSHES ATTEMPTED
83—Capital (34) vs. Luther (21), 11-28-70; Baldwin-Wallace (31) vs. Carnegie Mellon (6), 11-25-78.

NET YARDS PASSING
614—Mount Union (52) vs. Hanover (18), 11-18-95.

PASSES ATTEMPTED
67—Hanover (18) vs. Mount Union (52), 11-18-95; Widener (27) vs. Lycoming (31), 11-18-95.

PASSES COMPLETED
39—Mount Union (52) vs. Hanover (18), 11-18-95.

COMPLETION PERCENTAGE (Min. 10 Attempts)
.857—Salisbury St. (16) vs. Carnegie Mellon (14), 11-19-83 (18 of 21).

PASSES HAD INTERCEPTED
9—Dubuque (7) vs. Ithaca (27), 11-17-79.

NET YARDS RUSHING AND PASSING
773—Mount Union (52) vs. Hanover (18), 11-18-95.

RUSHING AND PASSING PLAYS
101—Union (N.Y.) (45) vs. Montclair St. (6), 11-25-89.

PUNTING AVERAGE
48.5—Minn.-Morris (25) vs. Carnegie Mellon (31), 11-17-79.

NUMBER OF PUNTS
14—Gettysburg (14) vs. Lycoming (10), 11-23-85.

YARDS GAINED ON PUNT RETURNS
109—Plymouth St. (7) vs. Union (N.Y.) (24), 11-18-95.

YARDS GAINED ON KICKOFF RETURNS
234—Ithaca (40) vs. Salisbury St. (44), 12-6-86.

YARDS GAINED ON INTERCEPTION RETURNS
176—Augustana (Ill.) (14) vs. St. Lawrence (0), 11-27-82.

YARDS PENALIZED
166—Ferrum (49) vs. Moravian (28), 11-26-88.

FUMBLES LOST
6—Albright (7) vs. St. Lawrence (26), 11-20-76; St. John's (Minn.) (7) vs. Dayton (19), 12-7-91.

POINTS
75—St. John's (Minn.) vs. Coe (2), 11-23-91.

TEAM: TOURNAMENT

FIRST DOWNS
94—Ithaca, 1991 (22 vs. Rowan, 15 vs. Union, N.Y., 28 vs. Susquehanna, 29 vs. Dayton).

NET YARDS RUSHING
1,377—Ithaca, 1988 (251 vs. Wagner, 293 vs. Cortland St., 425 vs. Ferrum, 408 vs. Central, Iowa).

NET YARDS PASSING
1,268—Mount Union, 1993 (347 vs. Allegheny, 192 vs. Albion, 342 vs. St. John's, Minn., 387 vs. Rowan).

NET YARDS RUSHING AND PASSING
1,867—Ithaca, 1991 (486 vs. Rowan, 350 vs. Union, N.Y., 473 vs. Susquehanna, 558 vs. Dayton).

PASSES ATTEMPTED
150—Hofstra, 1990 (51 vs. Cortland St., 50 vs. Trenton St., 49 vs. Lycoming).

PASSES COMPLETED
92—Mount Union, 1993 (26 vs. Allegheny, 16 vs. Albion, 22 vs. St. John's, Minn., 28 vs. Rowan).

PASSES HAD INTERCEPTED
11—Hofstra, 1990 (5 vs. Cortland St., 3 vs. Trenton St., 3 vs. Lycoming).

NUMBER OF PUNTS
30—Central (Iowa), 1988 (12 vs. Concordia-M'head, 8 vs. Wis.-Whitewater, 5 vs. Augustana, Ill., 5 vs. Ithaca).

YARDS PENALIZED
331—Wagner, 1987 (61 vs. Rochester, 80 vs. Fordham, 87 vs. Emory & Henry, 103 vs. Dayton).

FUMBLES LOST
10—Wittenberg, 1978 (4 vs. Ithaca, 2 vs. Minn.-Morris, 4 vs. Baldwin-Wallace).

POINTS
160—Mount Union, 1993 (40 vs. Allegheny, 30 vs. Albion, 56 vs. St. John's, Minn., 34 vs. Rowan).

Year-by-Year Division III Championship Results

Year (Number of Teams)	Coach	Record	Result
1973 (4)			
Wittenberg	Dave Maurer	2-0	Champion
Juniata	Walt Nadzak	1-1	Second
Bridgeport	Ed Farrell	0-1	Semifinalist
San Diego	Andy Vinci	0-1	Semifinalist
1974 (4)			
Central (Iowa)	Ron Schipper	2-0	Champion
Ithaca	Jim Butterfield	1-1	Second
Evansville	Jim Byers	0-1	Semifinalist
Slippery Rock	Bob Di Spirito	0-1	Semifinalist
1975 (8)			
Wittenberg	Dave Maurer	3-0	Champion
Ithaca	Jim Butterfield	2-1	Second
Millsaps	Harper Davis	1-1	Semifinalist
Widener	Bill Manlove	1-1	Semifinalist
Albright	John Potsklan	0-1	Lost 1st Round
Colorado Col.	Jerry Carle	0-1	Lost 1st Round
Fort Valley St.	Leon Lomax	0-1	Lost 1st Round
Indianapolis	Bill Bless	0-1	Lost 1st Round
1976 (8)			
St. John's (Minn.)	John Gagliardi	3-0	Champion
Towson St.	Phil Albert	2-1	Second
Buena Vista	Jim Hershberger	1-1	Semifinalist
St. Lawrence	Ted Stratford	1-1	Semifinalist
Albright	John Potsklan	0-1	Lost 1st Round
Augustana (Ill.)	Ben Newcomb	0-1	Lost 1st Round
Carroll (Wis.)	Steve Miller	0-1	Lost 1st Round
LIU-C.W. Post	Dom Anile	0-1	Lost 1st Round
1977 (8)			
Widener	Bill Manlove	3-0	Champion
Wabash	Frank Navarro	2-1	Second
Albany (N.Y.)	Bob Ford	1-1	Semifinalist

Year (Number of Teams)	Coach	Record	Result
Minn.-Morris	Al Molde	1-1	Semifinalist
Albion	Frank Joranko	0-1	Lost 1st Round
Central (Iowa)	Ron Schipper	0-1	Lost 1st Round
Hampden-Sydney	Stokeley Fulton	0-1	Lost 1st Round
St. John's (Minn.)	John Gagliardi	0-1	Lost 1st Round

1978 (8)

Year (Number of Teams)	Coach	Record	Result
Baldwin-Wallace	Lee Tressel	3-0	Champion
Wittenberg	Dave Maurer	2-1	Second
Carnegie Mellon	Chuck Klausing	1-1	Semifinalist
Minn.-Morris	Al Molde	1-1	Semifinalist
Dayton	Rick Carter	0-1	Lost 1st Round
Ithaca	Jim Butterfield	0-1	Lost 1st Round
St. Lawrence	Ted Stratford	0-1	Lost 1st Round
St. Olaf	Tom Porter	0-1	Lost 1st Round

1979 (8)

Year (Number of Teams)	Coach	Record	Result
Ithaca	Jim Butterfield	3-0	Champion
Wittenberg	Dave Maurer	2-1	Second
Carnegie Mellon	Chuck Klausing	1-1	Semifinalist
Widener	Bill Manlove	1-1	Semifinalist
Baldwin-Wallace	Lee Tressel	0-1	Lost 1st Round
Dubuque	Don Birmingham	0-1	Lost 1st Round
Millersville	Gene Carpenter	0-1	Lost 1st Round
Minn.-Morris	Al Molde	0-1	Lost 1st Round

1980 (8)

Year (Number of Teams)	Coach	Record	Result
Dayton	Rick Carter	3-0	Champion
Ithaca	Jim Butterfield	2-1	Second
Minn.-Morris	Dick Smith	1-1	Semifinalist
Widener	Bill Manlove	1-1	Semifinalist
Baldwin-Wallace	Lee Tressel	0-1	Lost 1st Round
Bethany (W.Va.)	Don Ault	0-1	Lost 1st Round
Dubuque	Don Birmingham	0-1	Lost 1st Round
Wagner	Bill Russo	0-1	Lost 1st Round

1981 (8)

Year (Number of Teams)	Coach	Record	Result
Widener	Bill Manlove	3-0	Champion
Dayton	Mike Kelly	2-1	Second
Lawrence	Ron Roberts	1-1	Semifinalist
Montclair St.	Fred Hill	1-1	Semifinalist
Alfred	Sam Sanders	0-1	Lost 1st Round
Augustana (Ill.)	Bob Reade	0-1	Lost 1st Round
Minn.-Morris	Dick Smith	0-1	Lost 1st Round
West Ga.	Bobby Pate	0-1	Lost 1st Round

1982 (8)

Year (Number of Teams)	Coach	Record	Result
West Ga.	Bobby Pate	3-0	Champion
Augustana (Ill.)	Bob Reade	2-1	Second
Bishop	James Jones	1-1	Semifinalist
St. Lawrence	Andy Talley	1-1	Semifinalist
Baldwin-Wallace	Bob Packard	0-1	Lost 1st Round
Wagner	Walt Hameline	0-1	Lost 1st Round
Wartburg	Don Canfield	0-1	Lost 1st Round
Widener	Bill Manlove	0-1	Lost 1st Round

1983 (8)

Year (Number of Teams)	Coach	Record	Result
Augustana (Ill.)	Bob Reade	3-0	Champion
Union (N.Y.)	Al Bagnoli	2-1	Second
Salisbury St.	Mike McGlinchey	1-1	Semifinalist
Wis.-La Crosse	Roger Harring	1-1	Semifinalist
Adrian	Ron Labadie	0-1	Lost 1st Round
Carnegie Mellon	Chuck Klausing	0-1	Lost 1st Round
Hofstra	Mickey Kwiatkowski	0-1	Lost 1st Round
Occidental	Dale Widolff	0-1	Lost 1st Round

1984 (8)

Year (Number of Teams)	Coach	Record	Result
Augustana (Ill.)	Bob Reade	3-0	Champion
Central (Iowa)	Ron Schipper	2-1	Second
Union (N.Y.)	Al Bagnoli	1-1	Semifinalist
Wash. & Jeff.	John Luckhardt	1-1	Semifinalist
Dayton	Mike Kelly	0-1	Lost 1st Round
Occidental	Dale Widolff	0-1	Lost 1st Round
Plymouth St.	Jay Cottone	0-1	Lost 1st Round
Randolph-Macon	Jim Blackburn	0-1	Lost 1st Round

1985 (16)

Year (Number of Teams)	Coach	Record	Result
Augustana (Ill.)	Bob Reade	4-0	Champion
Ithaca	Jim Butterfield	3-1	Second
Central (Iowa)	Ron Schipper	2-1	Semifinalist
Gettysburg	Barry Streeter	2-1	Semifinalist
Montclair St.	Rick Giancola	1-1	Quarterfinalist
Mount Union	Ken Wable	1-1	Quarterfinalist
Occidental	Dale Widolff	1-1	Quarterfinalist
Salisbury St.	Mike McGlinchey	1-1	Quarterfinalist
Albion	Pete Schmidt	0-1	Lost 1st Round
Carnegie Mellon	Chuck Klausing	0-1	Lost 1st Round
Coe	Bob Thurness	0-1	Lost 1st Round
Denison	Keith Piper	0-1	Lost 1st Round
Lycoming	Frank Girardi	0-1	Lost 1st Round
St. John's (Minn.)	John Gagliardi	0-1	Lost 1st Round
Union (N.Y.)	Al Bagnoli	0-1	Lost 1st Round
Western Conn. St.	Paul Pasqualoni	0-1	Lost 1st Round

1986 (16)

Year (Number of Teams)	Coach	Record	Result
Augustana (Ill.)	Bob Reade	4-0	Champion
Salisbury St.	Mike McGlinchey	3-1	Second
Concordia-M'head	Jim Christopherson	2-1	Semifinalist
Ithaca	Jim Butterfield	2-1	Semifinalist
Central (Iowa)	Ron Schipper	1-1	Quarterfinalist
Montclair St.	Rick Giancola	1-1	Quarterfinalist
Mount Union	Larry Kehres	1-1	Quarterfinalist
Susquehanna	Rocky Rees	1-1	Quarterfinalist
Buena Vista	Jim Hershberger	0-1	Lost 1st Round
Dayton	Mike Kelly	0-1	Lost 1st Round
Emory & Henry	Lou Wacker	0-1	Lost 1st Round
Hofstra	Mickey Kwiatkowski	0-1	Lost 1st Round
Hope	Ray Smith	0-1	Lost 1st Round
Union (N.Y.)	Al Bagnoli	0-1	Lost 1st Round
Wash. & Jeff.	John Luckhardt	0-1	Lost 1st Round
Wis.-Stevens Point	D. J. LeRoy	0-1	Lost 1st Round

1987 (16)

Year (Number of Teams)	Coach	Record	Result
Wagner	Walt Hameline	4-0	Champion
Dayton	Mike Kelly	3-1	Second
Central (Iowa)	Ron Schipper	2-1	Semifinalist
Emory & Henry	Lou Wacker	2-1	Semifinalist
Augustana (Ill.)	Bob Reade	1-1	Quarterfinalist
Fordham	Larry Glueck	1-1	Quarterfinalist
St. John's (Minn.)	John Gagliardi	1-1	Quarterfinalist
Wash. & Jeff.	John Luckhardt	1-1	Quarterfinalist
Allegheny	Peter Vaas	0-1	Lost 1st Round
Capital	Roger Welsh	0-1	Lost 1st Round
Ferrum	Hank Norton	0-1	Lost 1st Round
Gust. Adolphus	Steve Raarup	0-1	Lost 1st Round
Hiram	Don Charlton	0-1	Lost 1st Round
Hofstra	Mickey Kwiatkowski	0-1	Lost 1st Round
Menlo	Ray Solari	0-1	Lost 1st Round
Rochester	Ray Tellier	0-1	Lost 1st Round

1988 (16)

Year (Number of Teams)	Coach	Record	Result
Ithaca	Jim Butterfield	4-0	Champion
Central (Iowa)	Ron Schipper	3-1	Second
Augustana (Ill.)	Bob Reade	2-1	Semifinalist
Ferrum	Hank Norton	2-1	Semifinalist
Cortland St.	Dennis Kayser	1-1	Quarterfinalist
Moravian	Scot Dapp	1-1	Quarterfinalist
Wis.-Whitewater	Bob Berezowitz	1-1	Quarterfinalist
Wittenberg	Ron Murphy	1-1	Quarterfinalist
Adrian	Ron Labadie	0-1	Lost Regionals
Concordia-M'head	Jim Christopherson	0-1	Lost Regionals
Dayton	Mike Kelly	0-1	Lost Regionals
Hofstra	Mickey Kwiatkowski	0-1	Lost Regionals
Rhodes	Mike Clary	0-1	Lost Regionals
Simpson	Jim Williams	0-1	Lost Regionals
Wagner	Walt Hameline	0-1	Lost Regionals
Widener	Bill Manlove	0-1	Lost Regionals

1989 (16)

Year (Number of Teams)	Coach	Record	Result
Dayton	Mike Kelly	4-0	Champion
Union (N.Y.)	Al Bagnoli	3-1	Second
Ferrum	Hank Norton	2-1	Semifinalist
St. John's (Minn.)	John Gagliardi	2-1	Semifinalist
Central (Iowa)	Ron Schipper	1-1	Quarterfinalist
Lycoming	Frank Girardi	1-1	Quarterfinalist
Millikin	Carl Poelker	1-1	Quarterfinalist
Montclair St.	Rick Giancola	1-1	Quarterfinalist
Augustana (Ill.)	Bob Reade	0-1	Lost Regionals
Cortland St.	Dennis Kayser	0-1	Lost Regionals
Dickinson	Ed Sweeney	0-1	Lost Regionals
Hofstra	Mickey Kwiatkowski	0-1	Lost Regionals
John Carroll	Tony DeCarlo	0-1	Lost Regionals
St. Norbert	Don LaViolette	0-1	Lost Regionals
Simpson	Jim Williams	0-1	Lost Regionals
Wash. & Jeff.	John Luckhardt	0-1	Lost Regionals

1990 (16)

Year (Number of Teams)	Coach	Record	Result
Allegheny	Ken O'Keefe	4-0	Champion
Lycoming	Frank Girardi	3-1	Second
Central (Iowa)	Ron Schipper	2-1	Semifinalist
Hofstra	Joe Gardi	2-1	Semifinalist
Dayton	Mike Kelly	1-1	Quarterfinalist
St. Thomas (Minn.)	Vic Wallace	1-1	Quarterfinalist
Trenton St.	Eric Hamilton	1-1	Quarterfinalist
Wash. & Jeff.	John Luckhardt	1-1	Quarterfinalist

Year (Number of Teams)	Coach	Record	Result
Augustana (Ill.)	Bob Reade	0-1	Lost Regionals
Carnegie Mellon	Rich Lackner	0-1	Lost Regionals
Cortland St.	Dave Murray	0-1	Lost Regionals
Ferrum	Hank Norton	0-1	Lost Regionals
Ithaca	Jim Butterfield	0-1	Lost Regionals
Mount Union	Larry Kehres	0-1	Lost Regionals
Redlands	Mike Maynard	0-1	Lost Regionals
Wis.-Whitewater	Bob Berezowitz	0-1	Lost Regionals
1991 (16)			
Ithaca	Jim Butterfield	4-0	Champion
Dayton	Mike Kelly	3-1	Second
St. John's (Minn.)	John Gagliardi	2-1	Semifinalist
Susquehanna	Steve Briggs	2-1	Semifinalist
Allegheny	Ken O'Keefe	1-1	Quarterfinalist
Lycoming	Frank Girardi	1-1	Quarterfinalist
Union (N.Y.)	Al Bagnoli	1-1	Quarterfinalist
Wis.-La Crosse	Roger Harring	1-1	Quarterfinalist
Albion	Pete Schmidt	0-1	Lost Regionals
Baldwin-Wallace	Bob Packard	0-1	Lost Regionals
Coe	D. J. LeRoy	0-1	Lost Regionals
Dickinson	Ed Sweeney	0-1	Lost Regionals
Mass.-Lowell	Dennis Scannell	0-1	Lost Regionals
Rowan	John Bunting	0-1	Lost Regionals
Simpson	Jim Williams	0-1	Lost Regionals
Wash. & Jeff.	John Luckhardt	0-1	Lost Regionals
1992 (16)			
Wis.-La Crosse	Roger Harring	4-0	Champion
Wash. & Jeff.	John Luckhardt	3-1	Second
Mount Union	Larry Kehres	2-1	Semifinalist
Rowan	John Bunting	2-1	Semifinalist
Buffalo St.	Jerry Boyes	1-1	Quarterfinalist
Central (Iowa)	Ron Schipper	1-1	Quarterfinalist
Emory & Henry	Lou Wacker	1-1	Quarterfinalist
Ill. Wesleyan	Norm Eash	1-1	Quarterfinalist
Aurora	Jim Scott	0-1	Lost Regionals
Carleton	Bob Sullivan	0-1	Lost Regionals
Dayton	Mike Kelly	0-1	Lost Regionals
Ithaca	Jim Butterfield	0-1	Lost Regionals
Lycoming	Frank Girardi	0-1	Lost Regionals
Redlands	Mike Maynard	0-1	Lost Regionals
Thomas More	Vic Clark	0-1	Lost Regionals
Worcester Tech	Jack Siedlecki	0-1	Lost Regionals
1993 (16)			
Mount Union	Larry Kehres	4-0	Champion
Rowan	K. C. Keeler	3-1	Second
St. John's (Minn.)	John Gagliardi	2-1	Semifinalist
Wash. & Jeff.	John Luckhardt	2-1	Semifinalist
Albion	Pete Schmidt	1-1	Quarterfinalist
Frostburg St.	Mike McGlinchey	1-1	Quarterfinalist
Wm. Paterson	Gerry Gallagher	1-1	Quarterfinalist
Wis.-La Crosse	Roger Harring	1-1	Quarterfinalist
Allegheny	Ken O'Keefe	0-1	Lost Regionals
Anderson (Ind.)	Mike Manley	0-1	Lost Regionals
Buffalo St.	Jerry Boyes	0-1	Lost Regionals
Coe	D. J. LeRoy	0-1	Lost Regionals
Moravian	Scot Dapp	0-1	Lost Regionals
Union (N.Y.)	John Audino	0-1	Lost Regionals
Wartburg	Bob Nielson	0-1	Lost Regionals
Wilkes	Joe DeMelfi	0-1	Lost Regionals
1994 (16)			
Albion	Pete Schmidt	4-0	Champion
Wash. & Jeff.	John Luckhardt	3-1	Second
Ithaca	Michael Welch	2-1	Semifinalist
St. John's (Minn.)	John Gagliardi	2-1	Semifinalist
Mount Union	Larry Kehres	1-1	Quarterfinalist
Plymouth St.	Don Brown	1-1	Quarterfinalist
Wartburg	Bob Nielson	1-1	Quarterfinalist
Widener	Bill Cubit	1-1	Quarterfinalist
Allegheny	Ken O'Keefe	0-1	Lost Regionals
Augustana (Ill.)	Bob Reade	0-1	Lost Regionals
Buffalo St.	Jerry Boyes	0-1	Lost Regionals
Central (Iowa)	Ron Schipper	0-1	Lost Regionals
Dickinson	Darwin Breaux	0-1	Lost Regionals
La Verne	Rex Huigens	0-1	Lost Regionals
Merchant Marine	Charlie Pravata	0-1	Lost Regionals
Trinity (Tex.)	Steven Mohr	0-1	Lost Regionals
1995 (16)			
Wis.-La Crosse	Roger Harring	4-0	Champion
Rowan	K. C. Keeler	3-1	Second
Mount Union	Larry Kehres	2-1	Semifinalist
Wash. & Jeff.	John Luckhardt	2-1	Semifinalist
Lycoming	Frank Girardi	1-1	Quarterfinalist
Union (N.Y.)	John Audino	1-1	Quarterfinalist
Wheaton (Ill.)	J. R. Bishop	1-1	Quarterfinalist
Wis.-River Falls	John O'Grady	1-1	Quarterfinalist
Buffalo St.	Jerry Boyes	0-1	Lost Regionals
Central (Iowa)	Ron Schipper	0-1	Lost Regionals
Concordia-M'head	Jim Christopherson	0-1	Lost Regionals
Emory & Henry	Lou Wacker	0-1	Lost Regionals
Hanover	C. Wayne Perry	0-1	Lost Regionals
Plymouth St.	Don Brown	0-1	Lost Regionals
Widener	Bill Cubit	0-1	Lost Regionals
Wittenberg	Doug Neibuhr	0-1	Lost Regionals

Division III Championship Record of Each College by Coach

(98 Colleges; 1973-95)

	Yrs	Won	Lost	CH	2D
ADRIAN					
Ron Labadie (Adrian '71) 83, 88	2	0	2	0	0
ALBANY (N.Y.)					
Bob Ford (Springfield '59) 77	1	1	1	0	0
ALBION					
Frank Joranko (Albion '52) 77	1	0	1	0	0
Pete Schmidt (Alma '70) 85, 91, 93, 94-CH	4	5	3	1	0
TOTAL	5	5	4	1	0
ALBRIGHT					
John Potsklan (Penn St. '49) 75, 76	2	0	2	0	0
ALFRED					
Sam Sanders (Buffalo '60) 81	1	0	1	0	0
ALLEGHENY					
Peter Vaas (Holy Cross '74) 87	1	0	1	0	0
Ken O'Keefe (John Carroll '75) 90-CH, 91, 93, 94	4	5	3	1	0
TOTAL	5	5	4	1	0
ANDERSON (IND.)					
Mike Manley (Anderson, Ind. '73) 93	1	0	1	0	0
AUGUSTANA (ILL.)					
Ben Newcomb 76	1	0	1	0	0
Bob Reade (Cornell College '54) 81, 82-2D, 83-CH, 84-CH, 85-CH, 86-CH, 87, 88, 89, 90, 94	11	19	7	4	1
TOTAL	12	19	8	4	1
AURORA					
Jim Scott (Luther '61) 92	1	0	1	0	0
BALDWIN-WALLACE					
Lee Tressel (Baldwin-Wallace '48) 78-CH, 79, 80	3	3	2	1	0
Bob Packard (Baldwin-Wallace '65) 82, 91	2	0	2	0	0
TOTAL	5	3	4	1	0
BETHANY (W.VA.)					
Don Ault (West Liberty St. '52) 80	1	0	1	0	0
BISHOP					
James Jones (Bishop '49) 82	1	1	1	0	0
BRIDGEPORT					
Ed Farrell (Rutgers '56) 73	1	0	1	0	0
BUENA VISTA					
Jim Hershberger (Northern Iowa '57) 76, 86	2	1	2	0	0
BUFFALO ST.					
Jerry Boyes (Ithaca '76) 92, 93, 94, 95	4	1	4	0	0
CAPITAL					
Roger Welsh (Muskingum '64) 87	1	0	1	0	0
CARLETON					
Bob Sullivan (St. John's, Minn. '59) 92	1	0	1	0	0
CARNEGIE MELLON					
Chuck Klausing (Slippery Rock '48) 78, 79, 83, 85	4	2	4	0	0
Rich Lackner (Carnegie Mellon '79) 90	1	0	1	0	0
TOTAL	5	2	5	0	0
CARROLL (WIS.)					
Steve Miller (Cornell College '65) 76	1	0	1	0	0
CENTRAL (IOWA)					
Ron Schipper (Hope '52) 74-CH, 77, 84-2D, 85, 86, 87, 88-2D, 89, 90, 92, 94, 95	12	16	11	1	2

	Yrs	Won	Lost	CH	2D
COE					
Bob Thurness (Coe '62) 85	1	0	1	0	0
D. J. LeRoy (Wis.-Eau Claire '79) 91, 93	2	0	2	0	0
TOTAL	3	0	3	0	0
COLORADO COL.					
Jerry Carle (Northwestern '48) 75	1	0	1	0	0
CONCORDIA-M'HEAD					
Jim Christopherson (Concordia-M'head '60) 86, 88, 95	3	2	3	0	0
CORTLAND ST.					
Dennis Kayser (Ithaca '74) 88, 89	2	1	2	0	0
Dave Murray (Springfield '81) 90	1	0	1	0	0
TOTAL	3	1	3	0	0
DAYTON					
Rick Carter (Earlham '65) 78, 80-CH	2	3	1	1	0
Mike Kelly (Manchester '70) 81-2D, 84, 86, 87-2D, 88, 89-CH, 90, 91-2D, 92	9	13	8	1	3
TOTAL	11	16	9	2	3
DENISON					
Keith Piper (Baldwin-Wallace '48) 85	1	0	1	0	0
DICKINSON					
Ed Sweeney (LIU-C.W. Post '71) 89, 91	2	0	2	0	0
Darwin Breaux (West Chester '77) 94	1	0	1	0	0
TOTAL	3	0	3	0	0
DUBUQUE					
Don Birmingham (Westmar '62) 79, 80	2	0	2	0	0
EMORY & HENRY					
Lou Wacker (Richmond '56) 86, 87, 92, 95	4	3	4	0	0
EVANSVILLE					
Jim Byers (Michigan '59) 74	1	0	1	0	0
FERRUM					
Hank Norton (Lynchburg '51) 87, 88, 89, 90	4	4	4	0	0
FORDHAM					
Larry Glueck (Villanova '63) 87	1	1	1	0	0
FORT VALLEY ST.					
Leon Lomax (Fort Valley St. '43) 75	1	0	1	0	0
FROSTBURG ST.					
Mike McGlinchey (Delaware '67) 93	1	1	1	0	0
GETTYSBURG					
Barry Streeter (Lebanon Valley '71) 85	1	2	1	0	0
GUST. ADOLPHUS					
Steve Raarup (Gust. Adolphus '53) 87	1	0	1	0	0
HAMPDEN-SYDNEY					
Stokeley Fulton (Hampden-Sydney '55) 77	1	0	1	0	0
HANOVER					
C. Wayne Perry (DePauw '72) 95	1	0	1	0	0
HIRAM					
Don Charlton (Lock Haven '65) 87	1	0	1	0	0
HOFSTRA					
Mickey Kwiatkowski (Delaware '70) 83, 86, 87, 88, 89	5	0	5	0	0
Joe Gardi (Maryland '60) 90	1	2	1	0	0
TOTAL	6	2	6	0	0
HOPE					
Ray Smith (UCLA '61) 86	1	0	1	0	0
ILL. WESLEYAN					
Norm Eash (Ill. Wesleyan '75) 92	1	1	1	0	0
INDIANAPOLIS					
Bill Bless (Indianapolis '63) 75	1	0	1	0	0
ITHACA					
Jim Butterfield (Maine '53) 74-2D, 75-2D, 78, 79-CH, 80-2D, 85-2D, 86, 88-CH, 90, 91-CH, 92	11	21	8	3	4
Michael Welch (Ithaca '73) 94	1	2	1	0	0
TOTAL	12	23	9	3	4
JOHN CARROLL					
Tony DeCarlo (Kent '62) 89	1	0	1	0	0
JUNIATA					
Walt Nadzak (Denison '57) 73-2D	1	1	1	0	1
LA VERNE					
Rex Huigens (La Verne '70) 94	1	0	1	0	0
LAWRENCE					
Ron Roberts (Wisconsin '54) 81	1	1	1	0	0
LIU-C.W. POST					
Dom Anile (LIU-C.W. Post '59) 76	1	0	1	0	0

	Yrs	Won	Lost	CH	2D
LYCOMING					
Frank Girardi (West Chester '61) 85, 89, 90-2D, 91, 92, 95	6	6	6	0	1
MASS.-LOWELL					
Dennis Scannell (Villanova '74) 91	1	0	1	0	0
MENLO					
Ray Solari (California '51) 87	1	0	1	0	0
MERCHANT MARINE					
Charlie Pravata (Adelphi '72) 94	1	0	1	0	0
MILLERSVILLE					
Gene Carpenter (Huron '63) 79	1	0	1	0	0
MILLIKIN					
Carl Poelker (Millikin '68) 89	1	1	1	0	0
MILLSAPS					
Harper Davis (Mississippi St. '49) 75	1	1	1	0	0
MINN.-MORRIS					
Al Molde (Gust. Adolphus '66) 77, 78, 79	3	2	3	0	0
Dick Smith (Coe '68) 80, 81	2	1	2	0	0
TOTAL	5	3	5	0	0
MONTCLAIR AT.					
Fred Hill (Upsala '57) 81	1	1	1	0	0
Rick Giancola (Rowan '68) 85, 86, 89	3	3	3	0	0
TOTAL	4	4	4	0	0
MORAVIAN					
Scot Dapp (West Chester '73) 88, 93	2	1	2	0	0
MOUNT UNION					
Ken Wable (Muskingum '52) 85	1	1	1	0	0
Larry Kehres (Mount Union '71) 86, 90, 92, 93-CH, 94, 95	6	10	5	1	0
TOTAL	7	11	6	1	0
OCCIDENTAL					
Dale Widolff (Indiana Central '75) 83, 84, 85	3	1	3	0	0
PLYMOUTH ST.					
Jay Cottone (Norwich '71) 84	1	0	1	0	0
Don Brown (Norwich '77) 94, 95	2	1	2	0	0
TOTAL	3	1	3	0	0
RANDOLPH-MACON					
Jim Blackburn (Virginia '71) 84	1	0	1	0	0
REDLANDS					
Mike Maynard (Ill. Wesleyan '80) 90, 92	2	0	2	0	0
RHODES					
Mike Clary (Rhodes '77) 88	1	0	1	0	0
ROCHESTER					
Ray Tellier (Connecticut '73) 87	1	0	1	0	0
ROWAN					
John Bunting (North Caro. '72) 91, 92	2	2	2	0	0
K. C. Keeler (Delaware '81) 93-2D, 95-2D	2	6	2	0	2
TOTAL	4	8	4	0	2
ST. JOHN'S (MINN.)					
John Gagliardi (Colorado Col. '49) 76-CH, 77, 85, 87, 89, 91, 93, 94	8	12	7	1	0
ST. LAWRENCE					
Ted Stratford (St. Lawrence '57) 76, 78	2	1	2	0	0
Andy Talley (Southern Conn. St. '67) 82	1	1	1	0	0
TOTAL	3	2	3	0	0
ST. NORBERT					
Don LaViolette (St. Norbert '54) 89	1	0	1	0	0
ST. OLAF					
Tom Porter (St. Olaf '51) 78	1	0	1	0	0
ST. THOMAS (MINN.)					
Vic Wallace (Cornell College '65) 90	1	1	1	0	0
SALISBURY ST.					
Mike McGlinchey (Delaware '67) 83, 85, 86-2D	3	5	3	0	1
SAN DIEGO					
Andy Vinci (Cal St. Los Angeles '63) 73	1	0	1	0	0
SIMPSON					
Jim Williams (Northern Iowa '60) 88, 89, 91	3	0	3	0	0
SLIPPERY ROCK					
Bob Di Spirito (Rhode Island '53) 74	1	0	1	0	0
SUSQUEHANNA					
Rocky Rees (West Chester '71) 86	1	1	1	0	0
Steve Briggs (Springfield '84) 91	1	2	1	0	0
TOTAL	2	3	2	0	0

	Yrs	Won	Lost	CH	2D
THOMAS MORE					
Vic Clark (Indiana St. '71) 92	1	0	1	0	0
TOWSON ST.					
Phil Albert (Arizona '66) 76-2D	1	2	1	0	1
TRENTON ST.					
Eric Hamilton (Trenton St. '75) 90	1	1	1	0	0
TRINITY (TEX.)					
Steven Mohr (Denison '76) 94	1	0	1	0	0
UNION (N.Y.)					
Al Bagnoli (Central Conn. St. '74) 83-2D, 84, 85, 86, 89-2D, 91	6	7	6	0	2
John Audino (Notre Dame '75) 93, 95	2	1	2	0	0
TOTAL	8	8	8	0	2
WABASH					
Frank Navarro (Maryland '53) 77-2D	1	2	1	0	1
WAGNER					
Bill Russo 80	1	0	1	0	0
Walt Hameline (Brockport St. '75) 82, 87-CH, 88	3	4	2	1	0
TOTAL	4	4	3	1	0
WARTBURG					
Don Canfield 82	1	0	1	0	0
Bob Nielson (Wartburg '81) 93, 94	2	1	2	0	0
TOTAL	3	1	3	0	0
WASH. & JEFF.					
John Luckhardt (Purdue '67) 84, 86, 87, 89, 90, 91 92-2D, 93, 94-2D, 95	10	13	10	0	2
WEST GA.					
Bobby Pate (Georgia '63) 81, 82-CH	2	3	1	1	0
WESTERN CONN. ST.					
Paul Pasqualoni (Penn St. '72) 85	1	0	1	0	0
WHEATON (ILL.)					
J. R. Bishop (Franklin '61) 95	1	1	1	0	0
WIDENER					
Bill Manlove (Temple '58) 75, 77-CH, 79, 80, 81-CH, 82, 88	7	9	5	2	0
Bill Cubit (Delaware '75) 94, 95	2	1	2	0	0
TOTAL	9	10	7	2	0
WILKES					
Joe DeMelfi (Delta St. '66) 93	1	0	1	0	0
WM. PATERSON					
Gerry Gallagher (Wm. Paterson '74) 93	1	1	1	0	0
WIS.-LA CROSSE					
Roger Harring (Wis.-La Crosse '58) 83, 91, 92-CH, 93, 95-CH	5	11	3	2	0
WIS.-RIVER FALLS					
John O'Grady (Wis.-River Falls '79) 95	1	1	1	0	0
WIS.-STEVENS POINT					
D. J. LeRoy (Wis.-Eau Claire '79) 86	1	0	1	0	0
WIS.-WHITEWATER					
Bob Berezowitz (Wis.-Whitewater '67) 88, 90	2	1	2	0	0
WITTENBERG					
Dave Maurer (Denison '54) 73-CH, 75-CH, 78-2D, 79-2D	4	9	2	2	2
Ron Murphy 88	1	1	1	0	0
Doug Neibuhr (Millikin '75) 95	1	0	1	0	0
TOTAL	6	10	4	2	2
WORCESTER TECH					
Jack Siedlecki (Union, N.Y. '73) 92	1	0	1	0	0

All-Time Results

1973 Semifinals: Juniata 35, Bridgeport 14; Wittenberg 21, San Diego 14. **Championship:** Wittenberg 41, Juniata 0.

1974 Semifinals: Central (Iowa) 17, Evansville 16; Ithaca 27, Slippery Rock 14. **Championship:** Central (Iowa) 10, Ithaca 8.

1975 First Round: Widener 14, Albright 6; Ithaca 41, Fort Valley St. 12; Wittenberg 17, Indianapolis 13; Millsaps 28, Colorado Col. 21. **Semifinals:** Ithaca 23, Widener 14; Wittenberg 55, Millsaps 22. **Championship:** Wittenberg 28, Ithaca 0.

1976 First Round: St. John's (Minn.) 46, Augustana (Ill.) 7; Buena Vista 20, Carroll (Wis.) 14 (OT); St. Lawrence 26, Albright 7; Towson St. 14, LIU-C.W. Post 10. **Semifinals:** St. John's (Minn.) 61, Buena Vista 0; Towson St. 38, St. Lawrence 36. **Championship:** St. John's (Minn.) 31, Towson St. 28.

1977 First Round: Minn.-Morris 13, Albion 10; Wabash 20, St. John's (Minn.) 9; Widener 19, Central (Iowa) 0; Albany (N.Y.) 51, Hampden-Sydney 45. **Semifinals:** Wabash 37, Minn.-Morris 21; Widener 33, Albany (N.Y.) 15. **Championship:** Widener 39, Wabash 36.

1978 First Round: Minn.-Morris 23, St. Olaf 10; Wittenberg 6, Ithaca 3; Carnegie Mellon 24, Dayton 21; Baldwin-Wallace 71, St. Lawrence 7. **Semifinals:** Wittenberg 35, Minn.-Morris 14; Baldwin-Wallace 31, Carnegie Mellon 6. **Championship:** Baldwin-Wallace 24, Wittenberg 10.

1979 First Round: Wittenberg 21, Millersville 14; Widener 29, Baldwin-Wallace 8; Carnegie Mellon 31, Minn.-Morris 25; Ithaca 27, Dubuque 7. **Semifinals:** Wittenberg 17, Widener 14; Ithaca 15, Carnegie Mellon 6. **Championship:** Ithaca 14, Wittenberg 10.

1980 First Round: Ithaca 41, Wagner 13; Minn.-Morris 41, Dubuque 35; Dayton 34, Baldwin-Wallace 0; Widener 43, Bethany (W.Va.) 12. **Semifinals:** Ithaca 36, Minn.-Morris 0; Dayton 28, Widener 24. **Championship:** Dayton 63, Ithaca 0.

1981 First Round: Dayton 19, Augustana (Ill.) 7; Lawrence 21, Minn.-Morris 14 (OT); Montclair St. 13, Alfred 12; Widener 10, West Ga. 3. **Semifinals:** Dayton 38, Lawrence 0; Widener 23, Montclair St. 12. **Championship:** Widener 17, Dayton 10.

1982 First Round: Augustana (Ill.) 28, Baldwin-Wallace 22; St. Lawrence 43, Wagner 34; Bishop 32, Wartburg 7; West Ga. 31, Widener 24 (3 OT). **Semifinals:** Augustana (Ill.) 14, St. Lawrence 0; West Ga. 27, Bishop 6. **Championship:** West Ga. 14, Augustana (Ill.) 0.

1983 First Round: Union (N.Y.) 51, Hofstra 19; Salisbury St. 16, Carnegie Mellon 14; Augustana (Ill.) 22, Adrian 21; Wis.-La Crosse 43, Occidental 42. **Semifinals:** Union (N.Y.) 23, Salisbury St. 21; Augustana (Ill.) 21, Wis.-La Crosse 15. **Championship:** Augustana (Ill.) 21, Union (N.Y.) 17.

1984 First Round: Union (N.Y.) 26, Plymouth St. 14; Augustana (Ill.) 14, Dayton 13; Wash. & Jeff. 22, Randolph-Macon 21; Central (Iowa) 23, Occidental 22. **Semifinals:** Augustana (Ill.) 23, Union (N.Y.) 6; Central (Iowa) 20, Wash. & Jeff. 0. **Championship:** Augustana (Ill.) 21, Central (Iowa) 12.

1985 First Round: Ithaca 13, Union (N.Y.) 12; Montclair St. 28, Western Conn. St. 0; Salisbury St. 35, Carnegie Mellon 22; Gettysburg 14, Lycoming 10; Augustana (Ill.) 26, Albion 10; Mount Union 35, Denison 3; Central (Iowa) 27, Coe 7; Occidental 28, St. John's (Minn.) 10. **Quarterfinals:** Ithaca 50, Montclair St. 28; Gettysburg 22, Salisbury St. 6; Augustana (Ill.) 21, Mount Union 14; Central (Iowa) 71, Occidental 0. **Semifinals:** Ithaca 34, Gettysburg 0; Augustana (Ill.) 14, Central (Iowa) 7. **Championship:** Augustana (Ill.) 20, Ithaca 7.

1986 First Round: Ithaca 24, Union (N.Y.) 17 (OT); Montclair St. 24, Hofstra 21; Susquehanna 28, Wash. & Jeff. 20; Salisbury St. 34, Emory & Henry 20; Mount Union 42, Dayton 36; Augustana (Ill.) 34, Hope 10; Central (Iowa) 37, Buena Vista 0; Concordia-M'head 24, Wis.-Stevens Point 15. **Quarterfinals:** Ithaca 29, Montclair St. 15; Salisbury St. 31, Susquehanna 17; Augustana (Ill.) 16, Mount Union 7; Concordia-M'head 17, Central (Iowa) 14. **Semifinals:** Salisbury St. 44, Ithaca 40; Augustana (Ill.) 41, Concordia-M'head 7. **Championship:** Augustana (Ill.) 31, Salisbury St. 3.

1987 First Round: Wagner 38, Rochester 14; Fordham 41, Hofstra 6; Wash. & Jeff. 23, Allegheny 17 (OT); Emory & Henry 49, Ferrum 7; Dayton 52, Capital 28; Augustana (Ill.) 53, Hiram 0; St. John's (Minn.) 7, Gust. Adolphus 3; Central (Iowa) 17, Menlo 0. **Quarterfinals:** Wagner 21, Fordham 0; Emory & Henry 23, Wash. & Jeff. 16; Dayton 38, Augustana (Ill.) 36; Central (Iowa) 13, St. John's (Minn.) 3. **Semifinals:** Wagner 20, Emory & Henry 15; Dayton 34, Central (Iowa) 0. **Championship:** Wagner 19, Dayton 3.

1988 Regionals: Cortland St. 32, Hofstra 27; Ithaca 34, Wagner 31 (OT); Ferrum 35, Rhodes 10; Moravian 17, Widener 7; Wittenberg 35, Dayton 28 (OT); Augustana (Ill.) 25, Adrian 7; Central (Iowa) 7, Concordia-M'head 0; Wis.-Whitewater 29, Simpson 27. **Quarterfinals:** Ithaca 24, Cortland St. 17; Ferrum 49, Moravian 28; Augustana (Ill.) 28, Wittenberg 14; Central (Iowa) 16, Wis.-Whitewater 13. **Semifinals:** Ithaca 62, Ferrum 28; Central (Iowa) 23, Augustana (Ill.) 17 (2 OT). **Championship:** Ithaca 39, Central (Iowa) 24.

1989 Regionals: Union (N.Y.) 42, Cortland St. 14; Montclair St. 23, Hofstra 6; Lycoming 21, Dickinson 0; Ferrum 41, Wash. & Jeff. 7; Dayton 35, John Carroll 10; Millikin 21, Augustana (Ill.) 12; Central (Iowa) 55, St. Norbert 7; St. John's (Minn.) 42, Simpson 35. **Quarterfinals:** Union (N.Y.) 45, Montclair St. 6; Ferrum 49, Lycoming 24; Dayton 28, Millikin 16; St. John's (Minn.) 27, Central (Iowa) 24. **Semifinals:** Union (N.Y.) 37, Ferrum 21; Dayton 28, St. John's (Minn.) 0. **Championship:** Dayton 17, Union (N.Y.) 7.

1990 Regionals: Hofstra 35, Cortland St. 9; Trenton St. 24, Ithaca 14; Wash. & Jeff. 10, Ferrum 7; Lycoming 17, Carnegie Mellon 7; Dayton 24, Augustana (Ill.) 14; Allegheny 26, Mount Union 15; St. Thomas (Minn.) 24, Wis.-Whitewater 23; Central (Iowa) 24, Redlands 14. **Quarterfinals:** Hofstra 38, Trenton St. 3; Lycoming 24, Wash. & Jeff. 0; Allegheny 31, Dayton 23; Central (Iowa) 33, St. Thomas (Minn.) 32. **Semifinals:** Lycoming 20, Hofstra 10; Allegheny 24, Central (Iowa) 7. **Championship:** Allegheny 21, Lycoming 14 (OT).

1991 Regionals: St. John's (Minn.) 75, Coe 2; Wis.-La Crosse 28, Simpson 13; Allegheny 24, Albion 21 (OT); Dayton 27, Baldwin-Wallace 10; Ithaca 31, Rowan 10; Union (N.Y.) 55, Mass.-Lowell 16; Lycoming 18, Wash. & Jeff. 16; Susquehanna 21, Dickinson 20. **Quarterfinals:** St. John's (Minn.) 29, Wis.-La Crosse 10; Dayton 28, Allegheny 25 (OT); Ithaca 35, Union (N.Y.) 23; Susquehanna 31, Lycoming 24. **Semifinals:** Dayton 19, St. John's (Minn.) 7; Ithaca 49, Susquehanna 13. **Championship:** Ithaca 34, Dayton 20.

1992 Regionals: Mount Union 27, Dayton 10; Ill. Wesleyan 21, Aurora 12; Central (Iowa) 20, Carleton 8; Wis.-La Crosse 47, Redlands 26; Emory & Henry 17, Thomas More 0; Wash. & Jeff. 33, Lycoming 0; Rowan 41, Worcester Tech 14; Buffalo St. 28, Ithaca 26.

Quarterfinals: Mount Union 49, Ill. Wesleyan 27; Wis.-La Crosse 34, Central (Iowa) 9; Wash. & Jeff. 51, Emory & Henry 15; Rowan 28, Buffalo St. 19. **Semifinals:** Wis.-La Crosse 29, Mount Union 24; Wash. & Jeff. 18, Rowan 13. **Championship:** Wis.-La Crosse 16, Wash. & Jeff. 12.

1993 Regionals: Mount Union 40, Allegheny 7; Albion 41, Anderson (Ind.) 21; Wis.-La Crosse 55, Wartburg 26; St. John's (Minn.) 32, Coe 14; Wash. & Jeff. 27, Moravian 7; Frostburg St. 26, Wilkes 25; Rowan 29, Buffalo St. 6; Wm. Paterson 17, Union (N.Y.) 7. **Quarterfinals:** Mount Union 30, Albion 16; St. John's (Minn.) 47, Wis.-La Crosse 25; Wash. & Jeff. 28, Frostburg St. 7; Rowan 37, Wm. Paterson 0. **Semifinals:** Mount Union 56, St. John's (Minn.) 8; Rowan 23, Wash. & Jeff. 16. **Championship:** Mount Union 34, Rowan 24.

1994 Regionals: Mount Union 28, Allegheny 19; Albion 28, Augustana (Ill.) 21; Wartburg 22, Central (Iowa) 21; St. John's (Minn.) 51, La Verne 12; Widener 14, Dickinson 0; Wash. & Jeff. 28, Trinity (Tex.) 0; Plymouth St. 19, Merchant Marine 18; Ithaca 10, Buffalo St. 7 (2 OT). **Quarterfinals:** Albion 34, Mount Union 33; St. John's (Minn.) 42, Wartburg 14; Wash. & Jeff. 37, Widener 21; Ithaca 22, Plymouth St. 7. **Semifinals:** Albion 19, St. John's (Minn.) 16; Wash. & Jeff. 23, Ithaca 19. **Championship:** Albion 38, Wash. & Jeff. 15.

1995 Regionals: Mount Union 52, Hanover 18; Wheaton (Ill.) 63, Wittenberg 41; Wis.-La Crosse 45, Concordia-M'head 7; Wis.-River Falls 10, Central (Iowa) 7; Wash. & Jeff. 35, Emory & Henry 16; Lycoming 31, Widener 27; Rowan 46, Buffalo St. 7; Union (N.Y.) 24, Plymouth St. 7. **Quarterfinals:** Mount Union 40, Wheaton (Ill.) 14; Wis.-La Crosse 28, Wis.-River Falls 14; Wash. & Jeff. 48, Lycoming 0; Rowan 38, Union (N.Y.) 7. **Semifinals:** Wis.-La Crosse 20, Mount Union 17; Rowan 28, Wash. & Jeff. 15. **Championship:** Wis.-La Crosse 36, Rowan 7.

Attendance Records

All-Time College Football Attendance

(Includes all divisions and non-NCAA teams)

Year	No. Teams	G	Total Attendance	P/G Avg.	Yearly Change Total	Percent
1948	685	—	19,134,159	—	—	—
1949	682	—	19,651,995	—	Up 517,836	+2.71
1950	674	—	18,961,688	—	Dn 690,307	-3.51
1951	635	—	17,480,533	—	Dn 1,481,155	-7.81
1952	625	—	17,288,062	—	Dn 192,471	-1.10
1953	618	—	16,681,731	—	Dn 606,331	-3.51
1954	614	—	17,048,603	—	Up 366,872	+2.20
1955	621	—	17,266,556	—	Up 217,953	+1.28
1956	618	—	18,031,805	—	Up 765,249	+4.43
1957	618	2,586	18,290,724	7,073	Up 258,919	+1.44
1958	618	2,673	19,280,709	7,213	Up 989,985	+5.41
1959	623	2,695	19,615,344	7,278	Up 334,635	+1.74
1960	620	2,711	20,403,409	7,526	Up 788,065	+4.02
1961	616	2,697	20,677,604	7,667	Up 274,195	+1.34
1962	610	2,679	21,227,162	7,924	Up 549,558	+2.66
1963	616	2,686	22,237,094	8,279	Up 1,009,932	+4.76
1964	622	2,745	23,354,477	8,508	Up 1,117,383	+5.02
1965	616	2,749	24,682,572	8,979	Up 1,328,095	+5.69
1966	616	2,768	25,275,899	9,131	Up 593,327	+2.40
1967	610	2,764	26,430,639	9,562	Up 1,154,740	+4.57
1968	612	2,786	27,025,846	9,701	Up 595,207	+2.25
1969	615	2,820	27,626,160	9,797	Up 600,314	+2.22
1970	617	2,895	29,465,604	10,178	Up 1,839,444	+6.66
1971	618	2,955	30,455,442	10,306	Up 989,838	+3.36
1972	620	2,997	30,828,802	10,287	Up 373,360	+1.23
1973	630	3,062	31,282,540	10,216	Up 453,738	+1.47
1974	634	3,101	31,234,855	10,073	Dn 47,685	-0.15
1975	634	3,089	31,687,847	10,258	Up 452,992	+1.45
1976	637	3,108	32,012,008	10,299	Up 324,161	+1.02
1977	638	3,145	32,905,178	10,463	Up 893,170	+2.79

Beginning in 1978, attendance includes NCAA teams only.

All-Time NCAA Attendance

Annual Total NCAA Attendance

(Includes Only NCAA Teams, All Divisions)

Year	No. Teams	G	Total Attendance	P/G Avg.	Yearly Change Total	Percent
1978	484	2,422	32,369,730	13,365	—	—
1979	478	2,381	32,874,755	13,807	Up 505,025	+1.56
1980	485	2,451	33,707,772	13,753	Up 833,017	+2.53
1981	497	2,505	34,230,471	13,665	Up 522,699	+1.55
1982	510	2,569	35,176,195	13,693	Up 945,724	+2.76
1983	505	2,557	34,817,264	13,616	Dn 358,931	-1.02
1984	501	2,542	35,211,076	*13,852	Up 393,812	+1.13
1985	509	2,599	34,951,548	13,448	Dn 259,528	-0.74
1986	510	2,605	35,030,902	13,448	Up 79,354	+2.27
1987	507	2,589	35,007,541	13,522	Dn 23,361	-0.07
1988	524	2,644	34,323,842	12,982	Dn 683,699	-1.95
1989	524	2,630	35,116,188	13,352	Up 792,346	-2.31
1990	533	2,704	35,329,946	13,066	Up 213,758	+0.61
1991	548	2,776	35,528,220	12,798	Up 198,274	+0.56
1992	552	2,824	35,225,431	12,474	Dn 302,789	-0.65
1993	560	2,888	34,870,634	12,074	Dn 354,797	-1.01
1994	*568	2,907	*36,459,896	12,542	*Up 1,591,352	*+4.56
1995	565	*2,923	35,637,784	12,192	Dn 822,112	-2.25

**Record.*

Annual Division I-A Attendance

Year	Teams	G	Attendance	Avg.
1976	137	796	23,917,522	30,047
1977	144	799	24,613,285	30,805
1978	139	772	25,017,915	32,407
1979	139	774	25,862,801	33,414
1980	139	776	26,499,022	34,148
1981	137	768	*26,588,688	34,621
1982	97	567	24,771,855	*43,689
1983	105	602	25,381,761	42,162
1984	105	606	25,783,807	42,548
1985	105	605	25,434,412	42,040
1986	105	611	25,692,095	42,049
1987	104	607	25,471,744	41,963
1988	104	605	25,079,490	41,454
1989	106	603	25,307,915	41,970
1990	106	615	25,513,098	41,485
1991	106	610	25,646,067	42,043
1992	107	617	25,402,046	41,170
1993	106	613	25,305,438	41,281
1994	107	614	25,590,190	41,678
1995	108	623	25,836,469	41,471

**Record.*

Annual Division I-AA Attendance

Year	Teams	G	Attendance	Avg.
1978	38	201	2,032,766	10,113
1979	39	211	2,073,890	9,829
1980	46	251	2,617,932	10,430
1981	50	270	2,950,156	10,927
1982	92	483	5,655,519	*11,709
1983	84	450	4,879,709	10,844
1984	87	465	5,061,480	10,885
1985	87	471	5,143,077	10,919
1986	86	456	5,044,992	11,064
1987	87	460	5,129,250	11,151
1988	88	465	4,801,637	10,326
1989	89	471	5,278,520	11,020
1990	87	473	5,328,477	11,265
1991	89	490	5,386,425	10,993
1992	88	485	5,057,955	10,429
1993	115	623	5,356,873	8,599
1994	117	643	*6,193,989	9,633
1995	119	647	5,660,329	8,749

**Record.*

Annual Division II Attendance

Year	Teams	G	Attendance	Avg.
1978	103	518	*2,871,683	*5,544
1979	105	526	2,775,569	5,277
1980	111	546	2,584,765	4,734
1981	121	589	2,726,537	4,629
1982	126	618	2,745,964	4,443
1983	122	611	2,705,892	4,429
1984	114	568	2,413,947	4,250
1985	114	569	2,475,325	4,350
1986	111	551	2,404,852	4,365
1987	107	541	2,424,041	4,481
1988	117	580	2,570,964	4,493
1989	116	579	2,572,496	4,428
1990	120	580	2,472,811	4,263
1991	128	622	2,490,929	4,005
1992	129	643	2,733,094	4,251
1993	142	718	2,572,053	3,582
1994	142	704	2,791,074	3,965
1995	138	705	2,459,792	3,489

**Record.*

Annual Division III Attendance

Year	Teams	G	Attendance	Avg.
1978	204	931	*2,447,366	*2,629
1979	195	870	2,162,495	2,486
1980	189	878	2,006,053	2,285
1981	189	878	1,965,090	2,238
1982	195	901	2,002,857	2,223
1983	194	894	1,849,902	2,069
1984	195	903	1,951,842	2,162
1985	203	954	1,898,734	1,990
1986	208	987	1,888,963	1,914
1987	209	981	1,982,506	2,021
1988	215	994	1,871,751	1,883
1989	213	977	1,957,257	1,948
1990	220	1,036	2,015,560	1,946
1991	225	1,054	2,004,799	1,902
1992	228	1,079	2,032,336	1,884
1993	197	934	1,636,270	1,752
1994	202	946	1,884,643	1,992
1995	200	948	1,681,194	1,773

**Record.*

Annual Conference Attendance Leaders

(Based on per-game average; minimum 20 games)

Division I-A

Year	Conference	Teams	Attendance	P/G Avg.
1978	Big Ten	10	3,668,926	61,149
1979	Big Ten	10	3,865,170	63,363
1980	Big Ten	10	3,781,232	64,089
1981	Big Ten	10	3,818,728	63,645
1982	Big Ten	10	3,935,722	66,707
1983	Big Ten	10	3,710,931	67,471
1984	Big Ten	10	3,943,802	*67,997
1985	Big Ten	10	4,015,693	66,928
1986	Big Ten	10	4,006,845	65,686
1987	Big Ten	10	3,990,524	65,418
1988	Southeastern	10	3,912,241	63,101
1989	Southeastern	10	4,123,005	65,445
1990	Southeastern	10	4,215,400	63,870
1991	Southeastern	10	4,063,190	66,610
1992	Southeastern	12	4,844,014	63,737
1993	Big Ten	11	4,320,397	63,535
1994	Big Ten	11	4,452,839	66,460
1995	Big Ten	11	4,592,499	67,537

**Record. Note: The total attendance record is 4,897,564 by the Southeastern Conference in 1993.*

Division I-AA

Year	Conference	Teams	Attendance	P/G Avg.
1978	Southwestern Athletic	5	483,159	17,895
1979	Southwestern Athletic	6	513,768	16,055
1980	Southwestern Athletic	7	611,234	16,085
1981	Southwestern Athletic	7	662,221	18,921
1982	Southwestern Athletic	7	634,505	18,129
1983	Southwestern Athletic	8	709,160	16,117
1984	Southwestern Athletic	8	702,186	17,555
1985	Southwestern Athletic	8	790,296	17,961
1986	Southwestern Athletic	8	621,584	16,357
1987	Southwestern Athletic	8	697,534	16,608
1988	Southwestern Athletic	8	541,127	14,240
1989	Southwestern Athletic	8	796,844	18,110
1990	Southwestern Athletic	7	828,169	20,704
1991	Southwestern Athletic	8	856,491	18,223
1992	Southwestern Athletic	8	873,772	20,804
1993	Southwestern Athletic	8	772,714	18,398
1994	Southwestern Athletic	8	*958,508	*23,378
1995	Southwestern Athletic	8	628,702	16,545

**Record.*

Division II

Year	Conference	Teams	Attendance	P/G Avg.
1978	Mid-Continent	6	237,458	9,133
1979	Mid-Continent	6	313,790	9,509
1980	Southern Intercollegiate	12	356,744	7,280
1981	Lone Star	8	340,876	7,575
1982	Lone Star	8	348,780	8,507
1983	Lone Star	8	296,350	7,228
1984	Central Intercollegiate	12	418,075	6,743
1985	Central Intercollegiate	12	378,160	6,099
1986	Central Intercollegiate	12	380,172	6,670
1987	Lone Star	6	208,709	6,325
1988	Central Intercollegiate	12	343,070	6,473
1989	Lone Star	8	249,570	5,942
1990	Southern Intercollegiate	9	264,741	6,967
1991	Central Intercollegiate	11	349,962	6,603
1992	Southern Intercollegiate	9	344,504	7,489
1993	Southern Intercollegiate	9	342,446	8,352
1994	Southern Intercollegiate	9	*456,289	*10,140
1995	Southern Intercollegiate	10	321,751	6,846

**Record.*

Division III

Year	Conference	Teams	Attendance	P/G Avg.
1979	Great Lakes	6	90,531	3,482
1980	Great Lakes	7	113,307	3,333
1981	Ohio Athletic	14	*196,640	2,979
1982	New Jersey State	7	98,502	2,985
1983	Heartland	7	121,825	3,384
1984	Heartland	7	107,500	2,986
1985	Ohio Athletic	9	125,074	2,719
1986	Heartland	7	91,793	2,550
1987	Heartland	6	84,815	3,029
1988	Heartland	5	82,966	2,963
1989	Old Dominion	5	70,676	2,945
1990	Old Dominion	6	86,238	2,974
1991	Old Dominion	6	101,774	3,283
1992	Old Dominion	6	100,132	3,338
1993	Old Dominion	6	96,526	3,218
1994	Old Dominion	6	111,334	*3,976
1995	Old Dominion	6	105,819	3,527

**Record. Note: 1978 figures not available.*

Large Regular-Season Crowds

Largest Regular-Season Crowds*

Crowd	Date	Home	Visitor
106,867	11-20-93	Michigan 28,	Ohio St. 0
106,851	9-11-93	Michigan 23,	Notre Dame 27
106,832	10-15-94	Michigan 24,	Penn St. 31
106,788	10-10-92	Michigan 35,	Michigan St. 10
106,579	10-24-92	Michigan 63,	Minnesota 13
106,481	11-14-92	Michigan 22,	Illinois 22
106,427	9-24-94	Michigan 26,	Colorado 27
106,385	10-23-93	Michigan 21,	Illinois 24
106,288	11-25-95	Michigan 31,	Ohio St. 23
106,272	10-8-94	Michigan 40,	Michigan St. 20
106,255	11-17-79	Michigan 15,	Ohio St. 18
106,209	10-29-94	Michigan 19,	Wisconsin 31
106,208	10-8-88	Michigan 17,	Michigan St. 3
106,188	10-13-90	Michigan 27,	Michigan St. 28
106,156	11-23-91	Michigan 31,	Ohio St. 3
106,145	9-28-91	Michigan 31,	Florida St. 51
106,141	10-11-86	Michigan 27,	Michigan St. 6
106,138	9-14-91	Michigan 24,	Notre Dame 14
106,137	11-25-89	Michigan 28,	Ohio St. 18
106,132	10-3-92	Michigan 52,	Iowa 28
106,115	11-19-83	Michigan 24,	Ohio St. 21
106,113	10-9-82	Michigan 31,	Michigan St. 17

**In the 48 seasons official national attendance records have been maintained.*

WEEKS WITH LARGEST TOTAL ATTENDANCE FOR THE TOP-10 ATTENDED GAMES

Total	Date
862,941	9-4-93
857,115	10-10-92
854,835	9-30-95
834,370	10-8-94
833,285	10-22-83
828,869	10-28-95
828,253	10-2-93
828,034	9-24-94
827,232	9-16-89
825,455	9-22-84
825,260	9-9-95
820,668	11-18-89
820,545	11-19-94
819,980	10-18-86
819,501	9-25-93
816,954	9-14-91
816,618	9-28-91
816,458	10-13-84
815,853	11-10-90
815,423	11-5-88

Largest Regular-Season Crowds for Games Not Played at Michigan

Attendance	Date	Score (Home Team in Boldface)	Site
101,799	11-30-68	Army 21, Navy 14	Philadelphia, Pa.*
100,428	12-2-67	Navy 19, Army 14	Philadelphia, Pa.*
97,731	9-28-91	**Tennessee** 30, Auburn 21	Knoxville, Tenn.
97,388	10-17-92	Alabama 17, **Tennessee** 10	Knoxville, Tenn.
97,372	11-30-85	**Tennessee** 30, Vanderbilt 0	Knoxville, Tenn.
97,137	9-19-92	**Tennessee** 31, Florida 14	Knoxville, Tenn.
97,123	11-11-90	Notre Dame 34, **Tennessee** 29	Knoxville, Tenn.
97,117	9-14-91	**Tennessee** 30, UCLA 16	Knoxville, Tenn.
97,079	10-29-94	**Penn St.** 63, Ohio St. 14	University Park, Pa.
96,874	10-13-90	**Tennessee** 45, Florida 3	Knoxville, Tenn.
96,856	10-15-94	Alabama 17, **Tennessee** 13	Knoxville, Tenn.
96,748	10-18-80	Alabama 27, **Tennessee** 0	Knoxville, Tenn.
96,732	10-20-90	Alabama 9, **Tennessee** 6	Knoxville, Tenn.
96,719	10-16-93	Michigan 21, **Penn St.** 13	University Park, Pa.
96,704	10-10-92	Miami (Fla.) 17, **Penn St.** 14	University Park, Pa.
96,672	11-16-91	**Penn St.** 35, Notre Dame 13	University Park, Pa.
96,664	11-2-91	**Tennessee** 52, Memphis 24	Knoxville, Tenn.
96,656	9-17-94	Florida 31, **Tennessee** 0	Knoxville, Tenn.
96,655	10-7-95	Ohio St. 28, **Penn St.** 25	University Park, Pa.
96,597	9-26-92	**Tennessee** 40, Cincinnati 0	Knoxville, Tenn.
96,540	9-30-95	Wisconsin 17, **Penn St.** 9	University Park, Pa.
96,493	11-26-94	**Penn St.** 59, Michigan St. 31	University Park, Pa.
96,445	10-26-91	**Penn St.** 51, West Va. 6	University Park, Pa.
96,391	10-28-95	**Penn St.** 45, Indiana 21	University Park, Pa.
96,383	11-19-94	**Penn St.** 45, Northwestern 17	University Park, Pa.
96,304	9-21-91	**Penn St.** 33, Brigham Young 7	University Park, Pa.
96,173	10-2-93	**Tennessee** 52, Duke 19	Knoxville, Tenn.
96,130	10-17-92	Boston College 35, **Penn St.** 32	University Park, Pa.
96,058	10-7-89	**Tennessee** 17, Georgia 14	Knoxville, Tenn.
96,034	9-9-95	**Penn St.** 24, Texas Tech 23	University Park, Pa.

**Neutral site.*

Pre-1948 Regular-Season Crowds in Excess of 100,000†

Crowd	Date	Site	Opponents, Score
120,000*	11-26-27	Soldier Field, Chicago	Notre Dame 7, Southern Cal 6
120,000*	10-13-28	Soldier Field, Chicago	Notre Dame 7, Navy 0
112,912	11-16-29	Soldier Field, Chicago	Notre Dame 13, Southern Cal 12
110,000*	11-27-26	Soldier Field, Chicago	Army 21, Navy 21
110,000*	11-29-30	Soldier Field, Chicago	Notre Dame 7, Army 6
104,953	12-6-47	Los Angeles	Notre Dame 38, Southern Cal 7

**Estimated attendance; others are audited figures. †Since 1956, when Michigan Stadium's capacity was increased to 101,000, there have been 147 100,000-plus crowds at Michigan. The 22 largest crowds are listed on the previous page. Therefore, there has been a total of 155 regular-season crowds in excess of 100,000.*

Additional Records

Highest Average Attendance Per Home Game: 106,217, Michigan, 1994 (637,300 in 6)

Highest Total Home Attendance: 739,620, Michigan, 1993 (7 games)

Highest Total Attendance, Home and Away: 1,040,351, Michigan, 1995 (12 games); 1,035,998, Michigan, 1993 (11 games)

Highest Bowl Game Attendance: 106,869, 1973 Rose Bowl (Southern Cal 42, Ohio St. 17)

Most Consecutive Home Sellout Crowds: 207, Nebraska (current, from Nov. 3, 1962)

Most Consecutive 100,000-Plus Crowds: 129, Michigan (current, from Nov. 8, 1975)

1995 Attendance

Division I-A

	G	Attendance	Average	Change
1. Michigan	7	726,368	103,767	Down 2,450
2. Tennessee	7	662,857	94,694	Down 943
3. Penn St.	6	561,546	93,591	Down 2,698
4. Ohio St.	6	561,057	93,510	Up 407
5. Florida	6	510,832	85,139	Down 145
6. Georgia	6	503,687	83,948	Up 2,509
7. Auburn	7	568,266	81,181	Down 107
8. Wisconsin	6	469,330	78,222	Up 894
9. Nebraska	7	529,616	75,659	Up 89
10. Florida St.	6	448,150	74,692	Down 1,843
11. LSU	6	446,148	74,358	Up 10,118
12. Washington	6	445,608	74,268	Up 4,196
13. Alabama	7	516,797	73,828	Down 1,474
14. Michigan St.	6	431,583	71,931	Up 4,904
15. Clemson	6	427,774	71,296	Up 1,574
16. Oklahoma	6	425,812	70,969	Up 8,321
17. South Caro.	7	485,988	69,427	Down 1,043
18. Iowa	6	410,198	68,366	Up 113
19. Texas	6	399,134	66,522	Down 1,620
20. Texas A&M	6	374,744	62,457	Down 420
21. Brigham Young	6	371,780	61,963	Up 1,307
22. Illinois	6	364,471	60,745	Up 451
23. Southern Cal	6	358,333	59,722	Up 1,184
24. Notre Dame	6	354,450	59,075	0
25. Arizona	6	310,494	51,749	Down 4,863
26. Colorado	6	302,757	50,460	Down 356
27. Purdue	6	301,895	50,316	Up 7,831
28. West Va.	6	301,780	50,297	Down 1,423
29. Kentucky	6	299,772	49,962	Down 325
30. Minnesota	6	296,597	49,433	Up 7,247
31. UCLA	6	294,643	49,107	Down 2,289
32. Arizona St.	6	282,940	47,157	Down 1,289
33. North Caro.	6	280,800	46,800	Down 1,867
34. Stanford	5	231,123	46,225	Up 2,297
35. Arkansas	6	275,876	45,979	Down 2,217
36. North Caro. St.	6	271,753	45,292	Up 289
37. Boston College	5	222,500	44,500	0
38. Air Force	6	266,768	44,461	Up 6,034
39. Oregon	6	265,169	44,195	Up 10,136
40. Syracuse	6	259,654	43,276	Down 4,438
41. Maryland	5	206,822	41,364	Up 12,402
42. Georgia Tech	6	247,420	41,237	Up 485
43. Virginia Tech	5	205,962	41,192	Down 1,624
44. Baylor	5	202,707	40,541	Up 4,493
45. Virginia	6	240,400	40,067	Up 607
46. Kansas	6	237,600	39,600	Down 467
47. Miami (Fla.)	6	234,223	39,037	Down 21,294
48. Kansas St.	7	271,400	38,771	Up 1,046
49. Northwestern	6	229,380	38,230	Down 1,579
50. Texas Tech	5	190,819	38,184	Up 8,200
51. Rutgers	6	225,657	37,610	Up 4,765
52. Iowa St.	7	262,187	37,455	Up 1,862
53. Oklahoma St.	5	184,100	36,820	Down 2,079
54. Pittsburgh	6	211,645	35,274	Up 3,702
55. Indiana	7	240,074	34,296	Down 4,804
56. California	6	202,455	33,743	Down 9,662
57. Mississippi St.	6	201,517	33,586	Down 2,929
58. Missouri	6	201,332	33,555	Down 7,809
59. Fresno St.	6	200,991	33,499	Down 1,808
60. Army	6	196,789	32,798	Down 387
61. Louisville	6	193,177	32,196	Down 5,077
62. Mississippi	6	191,531	31,922	Down 2,567
63. Washington St.	5	153,395	30,679	Down 4,040
64. Texas Christian	5	152,864	30,573	Down 6,561
65. East Caro.	5	151,889	30,378	Down 1,583
66. Utah	7	210,027	30,004	Down 2,306
67. San Diego St.	7	204,986	29,284	Down 5,739
68. Hawaii	7	197,620	28,231	Down 10,143
69. Navy	6	168,544	28,091	Up 3,892
70. Vanderbilt	6	164,563	27,427	Down 3,544
71. Oregon St.	5	136,350	27,270	Down 3,216
72. Colorado St.	5	134,860	26,972	Down 4,297
73. Southern Miss.	4	102,605	25,651	Up 11,591
74. Rice	5	126,800	25,360	Up 2,780
75. Duke	5	122,940	24,588	Down 6,257

	G	Attendance	Average	Change
76. Nevada	6	144,378	24,063	Up 3,532
77. Eastern Mich.	4	94,644	23,661	Up 16,090
78. New Mexico	7	164,359	23,480	Down 3,734
79. Toledo	5	115,249	23,050	Down 2,517
80. UTEP	6	126,862	21,144	Down 788
81. New Mexico St.	5	99,678	19,936	Up 1,262
82. Memphis	5	99,629	19,926	Down 5,065
83. Central Mich.	5	97,285	19,457	Down 2,006
84. Western Mich.	5	96,883	19,377	Up 1,065
85. Southern Methodist	6	115,533	19,256	Down 1,032
86. Wyoming	6	109,607	18,268	Down 702
87. Tulane	5	91,320	18,264	Down 7,068
88. Houston	5	91,287	18,257	Down 3,349
89. Northeast La.	4	72,497	18,124	Up 3,241
90. Southwestern La.	5	88,640	17,728	Down 1,787
91. Tulsa	5	87,598	17,520	Down 209
92. Cincinnati	5	87,204	17,441	Down 328
93. UNLV	5	86,728	17,346	Up 4,773
94. Wake Forest	5	83,809	16,762	Down 2,236
95. Louisiana Tech	4	66,530	16,633	Up 2,559
96. North Texas	3	49,291	16,430	Down 4,310
97. Bowling Green	5	76,635	15,327	Down 4,808
98. Utah St.	6	90,595	15,099	Down 3,228
99. Ball St.	5	73,985	14,797	Up 8,058
100. San Jose St.	5	67,900	13,580	Up 3,151
101. Miami (Ohio)	5	66,854	13,371	Down 1,543
102. Northern Ill.	5	55,140	11,028	Up 338
103. Pacific (Cal.)	4	43,012	10,753	Up 2,209
104. Ohio	5	45,717	9,143	Down 2,564
105. Akron	5	42,557	8,511	Down 2,176
106. Arkansas St.	6	50,851	8,475	Down 216
107. Kent	6	38,329	6,388	Down 2,264
108. Temple	4	17,622	4,406	Down 11,116

Division I-AA

	G	Attendance	Average	Change
1. Jackson St.	5	174,245	34,849	Up 11,448
2. Boise St.	7	150,551	21,507	Down 180
3. Marshall	6	126,239	21,040	Down 2,213
4. Grambling	5	103,044	20,609	Up 268
5. Southern-B.R.	5	102,012	20,402	Down 1,260
6. Yale	5	101,717	20,343	Up 6,966
7. Delaware	6	108,015	18,003	Up 2,036
8. Florida A&M	4	68,642	17,161	Down 3,843
9. McNeese St.	6	100,061	16,677	Up 677
10. Pennsylvania	5	80,493	16,099	Up 1,224
11. Tennessee St.	5	79,157	15,831	Up 2,492
12. South Caro. St.	4	59,636	14,909	Up 1,547
13. Idaho	4	59,550	14,888	Up 4,562
14. Montana	6	84,689	14,115	Up 593
15. Appalachian St.	5	69,801	13,960	Down 961
16. Citadel	6	83,209	13,868	Down 1,158
17. Ga. Southern	5	67,523	13,505	Down 38
18. Texas Southern	7	93,782	13,397	Up 1,235
19. Youngstown St.	7	91,944	13,135	Down 1,938
20. Central Fla.	7	89,811	12,830	Down 10,006
21. Alabama St.	5	62,102	12,420	Down 4,740
22. North Caro. A&T	5	61,615	12,323	Down 5,988
23. James Madison	6	73,000	12,167	Up 2,021
24. Richmond	5	60,659	12,132	Up 1,939
25. Troy St.	5	57,821	11,564	Down 1,189
26. Northern Iowa	6	69,057	11,510	Down 3,226
27. Murray St.	5	57,336	11,467	Up 5,271
28. William & Mary	5	56,360	11,272	Down 319
29. Stephen F. Austin	6	67,113	11,186	Up 1,090
30. Middle Tenn. St.	5	55,500	11,100	Up 1,249
31. Southwest Mo. St.	6	65,467	10,911	Up 1,981
32. Howard	3	32,679	10,893	Down 2,483
33. Sam Houston St.	5	54,305	10,861	Up 3,949
34. Connecticut	6	64,778	10,796	Down 1,200
35. Jacksonville St. #	4	42,814	10,704	Up 934
36. Ala.-Birmingham	6	64,010	10,668	Down 9,683
37. Alcorn St.	4	41,705	10,426	Down 15,777
38. Princeton	5	52,091	10,418	Down 1,321
39. Lehigh	5	51,750	10,350	Down 93
40. Furman	5	51,281	10,256	Down 2,208
41. Northern Ariz.	6	60,450	10,075	Up 1,968
42. Northwestern St.	5	48,578	9,716	Up 726
43. Western Ky.	4	38,700	9,675	Up 425
44. Mississippi Val.	4	36,774	9,194	Down 7,804
45. Weber St.	6	54,455	9,076	Down 3,777
46. Harvard	6	52,717	8,786	Down 4,496
47. Idaho St.	6	51,852	8,642	Up 1,668
48. Eastern Ky.	6	49,400	8,233	Down 5,587
49. Southern Ill.	6	49,000	8,167	Down 253
50. Montana St.	6	48,032	8,005	Down 812
51. Cornell	5	39,273	7,855	Down 1,663
52. Western Caro.	5	39,257	7,851	Down 2,451
53. Massachusetts	5	38,906	7,781	Down 2,357
54. Bucknell	4	28,266	7,067	Up 2,015
55. Va. Military	5	34,973	6,995	Down 1,507
56. Bethune-Cookman	5	33,590	6,718	Up 374
57. Illinois St.	6	39,125	6,521	Down 177
58. Western Ill.	5	32,443	6,489	Up 1,277
59. Rhode Island	6	38,137	6,356	Up 2,149
60. Tenn.-Chatt.	6	37,176	6,196	Up 1,095
61. Holy Cross	5	30,541	6,108	Down 3,663
62. Villanova	6	36,309	6,052	Down 3,011
63. Liberty	7	42,001	6,000	Down 782
64. Eastern Ill.	6	35,763	5,961	Up 1,806
65. Lafayette	4	23,830	5,958	Down 2,458
66. Southwest Tex. St.	6	35,508	5,918	Down 1,488
67. Southeast Mo. St.	6	35,357	5,893	Down 1,783
68. Dayton	7	40,883	5,840	Down 1,679
69. Dartmouth	5	28,987	5,797	Down 2,587
70. East Tenn. St.	4	23,071	5,768	Down 1,365
71. Boston U.	5	28,062	5,612	Down 3,439
72. Southern Utah	5	27,677	5,535	Up 697
73. Hampton#	4	21,878	5,470	Down 1,761
74. New Hampshire	6	31,355	5,226	Down 3,855
75. Cal Poly SLO	6	30,452	5,075	Up 87
76. Samford	6	30,264	5,044	Down 407
77. Prairie View	3	15,038	5,013	Down 12,315
78. Columbia	5	24,340	4,868	Down 2,589
79. Austin Peay	6	27,625	4,604	Up 207
80. Tennessee Tech	5	22,850	4,570	Down 20
81. Indiana St.	6	26,677	4,446	Down 417
82. Maine	5	22,061	4,412	Down 1,001
83. Hofstra	5	21,898	4,380	Down 281
84. Tenn.-Martin	6	25,680	4,280	Up 1,026
85. Drake	5	21,228	4,246	Up 411
86. Northeastern	5	21,100	4,220	Down 520
87. Buffalo	7	28,886	4,127	Up 166
88. Eastern Wash.	5	20,443	4,089	Down 477
89. Cal St. Sacramento	7	28,467	4,067	Up 1,290
90. Delaware St.	6	23,534	3,922	Down 4,640
91. Butler	5	18,688	3,738	Down 1,316
92. Morehead St.	6	21,062	3,510	Down 90
93. San Diego	5	16,983	3,397	Down 382
94. Monmouth (N.J.)	5	16,470	3,294	Down 875
95. Wofford#	4	12,718	3,180	Down 2,088
96. Morgan St.	4	12,501	3,125	Down 8,822
97. Brown	6	16,921	2,820	Down 2,705
98. Duquesne	5	13,520	2,704	Down 616
99. St. Mary's (Cal.)	5	13,263	2,653	Up 389
100. Robert Morris	5	12,113	2,423	Down 523
101. Fordham	6	14,215	2,369	Up 257
102. Cal St. Northridge	5	11,202	2,240	Down 1,029
103. Nicholls St.	5	10,861	2,172	Down 2,830
104. Valparaiso	5	10,360	2,072	Down 202
105. Marist	5	9,772	1,954	Up 381
106. Towson St.	5	9,708	1,942	Down 935
107. Colgate	5	9,023	1,805	Down 1,567
108. Charleston So.	5	7,864	1,573	Down 240
109. Davidson	5	7,864	1,573	Up 168
110. Georgetown	4	6,196	1,549	Down 260
111. Evansville	5	7,006	1,401	Down 116
112. Central Conn. St.	5	6,745	1,349	Down 467
113. St. John's (N.Y.)	5	5,783	1,157	Down 23
114. St. Peter's	4	4,623	1,156	Up 420
115. Iona	5	5,364	1,073	Up 204
116. Wagner	5	4,951	990	Down 1,077
117. Siena	4	3,001	750	Down 529
118. Canisius	5	3,290	658	Down 169
119. St. Francis (Pa.)	6	3,720	620	Down 303

Note: Minimum three home games.
#First year in Division I-AA.

Division II

	G	Attendance	Average	Change
1. Norfolk St.	6	99,555	16,593	Up 3,965
2. Clark Atlanta	2	28,700	14,350	Down 5,873
3. North Dak. St.	6	71,128	11,855	Down 2,251
4. Tex. A&M-Kingsville	4	45,500	11,375	Up 935
5. Tuskegee	4	42,026	10,507	Down 2,813
6. Morris Brown	4	38,250	9,536	Down 3,087
7. Portland St.	6	55,775	9,296	Down 3,501
8. North Dak.	5	43,099	8,620	Up 2,641
9. North Ala.	5	37,935	7,587	Down 2,759
10. Albany St. (Ga.)	5	37,137	7,427	Up 1,251
11. Morehouse	6	42,168	7,028	0
12. Angelo St.	5	34,602	6,920	Down 1,280
13. Winston-Salem	6	39,426	6,571	0
14. Alabama A&M	5	32,785	6,557	Up 850
15. Central Ark.	5	30,450	6,090	Up 797
16. South Dak. St.	6	36,206	6,034	Down 351
17. West Tex. A&M	7	41,737	5,962	Down 904
18. Fort Valley St.	5	28,361	5,672	Down 684
19. Pittsburg St.	7	39,300	5,614	Down 453
20. Northwest Mo. St.	5	28,000	5,600	Up 1,483
21. UC Davis	5	27,798	5,560	Down 1,169
22. Savannah St.	6	32,624	5,437	Down 1,205
23. N.C. Central	5	27,158	5,432	Down 2,491
24. Mo. Southern St.	5	25,900	5,180	Up 1,920
25. Valdosta St.	5	24,602	4,920	Down 2,025

Division III

	G	Attendance	Average	Change
1. St. John's (Minn.)	5	32,871	6,574	Up 1,410
2. Emory & Henry	5	27,816	5,563	Down 165
3. Ithaca	4	21,706	5,427	Up 3,337
4. Hampden-Sydney	5	22,700	4,540	Down 2,074
5. Randolph-Macon	5	19,900	3,980	Up 2,097
6. Williams	4	15,157	3,789	Up 685
7. Montclair St.	3	10,857	3,619	Up 937
8. Amherst	4	14,334	3,584	Up 23
9. Alma	4	14,303	3,576	Down 602
10. Concordia-M'head	6	21,200	3,533	Down 436
11. Redlands	5	17,250	3,450	Down 372
12. Chapman	5	16,970	3,394	Up 85
13. Gust. Adolphus	5	16,919	3,384	Up 691
14. Wash. & Jeff.	5	16,820	3,364	Down 96
15. Anderson (Ind.)	4	13,050	3,263	Up 1,603
16. Trinity (Conn.)	4	12,775	3,194	Down 1,509
17. Wesley	7	21,966	3,138	0
18. Baldwin-Wallace	5	14,900	2,980	Down 1,291
Cortland St.	5	14,900	2,980	Down 800
20. Alfred	4	11,900	2,975	Up 338
21. Hardin-Simmons	5	14,819	2,964	Up 1,346
22. Wartburg	6	17,600	2,933	Down 767
23. Albion	5	14,515	2,903	Down 332
24. Union (N.Y.)	5	14,400	2,880	Down 420
25. Wesleyan (Conn.)	4	11,500	2,875	Down 525
Wheaton (Ill.)	4	11,500	2,875	Down 125

File photo

With all of its stadiums filled to more than 90 percent of capacity year after year, the Southeastern Conference does not experience much change in its average annual attendance. But the change from 1994 to 1995 was minute by any standard: Only three fewer fans attended the average SEC game in 1995.

Divisions I-A and I-AA Conferences and Independent Groups

	Teams	G	Attendance	Avg. P/G	Change† in Avg.	Change† in Total
1. Big Ten (I-A)	11	68	*4,592,499	67,537	Up 1,077	Up 139,660
2. Southeastern (I-A)	12	76	4,827,834	63,524	Dn 3	Dn 63,781
3. Big Eight (I-A)	8	50	2,414,804	48,296	Up 588	Up 220,259
4. Pacific-10 (I-A)	10	57	2,680,510	47,026	Dn 184	Dn 104,863
5. Atlantic Coast (I-A)	9	51	2,329,868	*45,684	Up 1,592	Up 81,168
6. Southwest (I-A)	8	43	1,653,888	38,463	Up 1,511	Up 64,933
7. Big East (I-A)	8	44	1,679,043	38,160	Dn 3,190	Dn 223,053
8. Western Athletic (I-A)	10	63	1,987,860	31,553	Dn 2,719	Dn 103,260
9. I-A Independents#	12	60	1,654,993	27,583	Dn 323	Dn 103,070
10. Southwestern (I-AA)	8	38	628,702	16,545	Dn 6,833	Dn 329,806
11. Big West (I-A)	10	51	*793,452	15,558	Up 1,159	Up 87,913
12. Mid-American (I-A)	10	50	748,138	14,963	Up 173	Dn 6,158
13. Big Sky (I-AA)	8	46	530,022	11,522	Up 244	Dn 67
14. Southern (I-AA)	9	47	532,530	11,330	Dn 1,260	Dn 134,753
15. Southland (I-AA)#	6	33	316,426	9,589	Up 560	Dn 35,692
16. Mid-Eastern (I-AA)#	8	37	350,770	9,480	Dn 2,922	Dn 182,535
17. Ivy (I-AA)	8	42	396,539	9,441	Dn 1,176	Dn 49,361
18. Yankee (I-AA)	12	66	578,742	8,769	Dn 647	Dn 52,105
19. Gateway (I-AA)	7	41	317,344	7,740	Up 404	Up 23,907
20. Ohio Valley (I-AA)	9	50	373,967	7,479	Up 236	Up 19,064
21. I-AA Independents#	20	108	603,565	5,589	Dn 1,610	Dn 130,712
22. Patriot (I-AA)	6	29	157,625	5,435	Dn 761	Dn 40,649
23. American West (I-AA)	4	23	*97,798	*4,252	Up 103	Up 14,812
24. Pioneer (I-AA)	6	32	115,148	3,598	Dn 454	Dn 14,530
25. Metro Atlantic (I-AA)#	8	37	*51,549	*1,393	Dn 56	Dn 6,413
I-A Neutral Sites		9	473,580	52,620	— —	— —
I-AA Neutral Sites		18	609,602	33,867	— —	— —
DIVISION I-A#	108	623	25,836,469	41,471	Dn 209	Up 246,279
DIVISION I-AA#	119	647	5,660,329	8,749	Dn 908	Dn 533,660
I-A & I-AA Combined	227	1,270	31,496,798	24,801	Dn 580	Dn 287,381
DIVISION II#	138	705	2,459,792	3,489	Dn 335	Dn 331,282
DIVISION III#	200	948	1,681,194	1,773	Dn 209	Dn 203,449
ALL NCAA TEAMS	**565**	**2,923**	**35,637,784**	**12,192**	**Dn 350**	**Dn 822,112**

By Percentage of Capacity

Div. I-A: 75.31 percent—Southeastern 93.61, Big Ten 91.43, Atlantic Coast 87.69, Big Eight 86.52, Western Athletic 70.52, Pacific-10 68.98, Big East 68.38, Div. I-A Independents 63.21, Southwest 61.60, Mid-American 56.59, Big West 49.87.

Div. I-AA: 47.53 percent—Big Sky 75.24, Southland 63.88, Southern 63.05, Yankee 62.40, Ohio Valley 56.11, Southwestern 51.73, Gateway 49.00, Metro Atlantic 48.93, Mid-Eastern 45.93, Patriot 38.26, American West 37.13, Pioneer 35.75, I-AA Independents 34.11, Ivy 25.55.

*# Did not have same lineup in 1995 as in 1994. * Record high for this conference. † The 1995 figures used for comparison reflect changes in conference and division lineups to provide parallel, valid comparisons.*

Conferences and Independent Groups Below Division I-AA

	Teams	G	Attendance	Avg. P/G	Change† in Avg.	Change† in Total
1. Southern Intercollegiate (II)#	10	47	321,751	6,846	Dn 2,750	Dn 148,438
2. Central Intercollegiate (II)#	10	49	295,384	6,028	Dn 335	Dn 22,746
3. North Central (II)	10	55	283,779	5,160	Up 200	Up 15,932
4. Lone Star (II)#	8	41	201,845	4,923	Dn 374	Dn 15,315
5. Gulf South (II)	8	41	175,666	4,285	Dn 803	Dn 22,756
6. Mid-America Intercoll. (II)	10	53	194,449	3,669	Up 165	Up 15,732
7. Old Dominion (III)	6	30	105,819	3,527	Dn 449	Dn 5,515
8. Pennsylvania (II)	14	70	203,851	2,912	Dn 763	Dn 53,430
9. South Atlantic (II)	8	42	117,302	2,793	Dn 508	Dn 8,137
10. Michigan Intercollegiate (III)	6	29	72,248	2,491	Dn 219	Up 4,486
11. New England Small Coll. (III)	10	40	97,552	2,439	Dn 224	Dn 8,954
12. Minnesota Intercollegiate (III)	10	48	116,390	2,425	Up 137	Up 6,584
13. Indiana Collegiate (III)	7	34	76,448	2,248	Dn 175	Dn 10,795
14. Midwest Intercollegiate (II)	12	62	135,690	2,189	Dn 62	Dn 6,137
15. Division II Independents#	18	87	185,223	2,129	Dn 473	Dn 41,142
16. Rocky Mountain (II)	9	46	95,822	2,083	Dn 100	Dn 4,598
17. Middle Atlantic (III)#	11	54	105,504	1,954	Dn 310	Dn 9,953
18. Mideast (III)	4	18	35,008	1,945	Up 38	Up 2,594
19. Ohio Athletic (III)	10	49	95,059	1,940	Dn 989	Dn 54,341
20. Northern California (II)#	3	12	22,565	1,880	Dn 332	Dn 1,765
21. Wisconsin State University (III)	8	37	69,476	1,878	Dn 297	Dn 13,179
22. Iowa Intercollegiate (III)	9	43	80,558	1,873	Dn 73	Dn 1,156
23. West Va. Intercollegiate (II)	7	34	61,027	1,795	Dn 473	Dn 41,142
24. Centennial (III)	8	41	70,530	1,720	Dn 132	Dn 3,558
25. Presidents Athletic (III)	5	26	43,581	1,676	Dn 207	Up 2,161
26. University Athletic (III)	5	27	45,176	1,673	Dn 113	Up 4,088
27. New Jersey (III)	6	26	42,735	1,644	Dn 474	Dn 25,027
28. Northern Sun (II)	7	31	50,703	1,636	Dn 237	Dn 11,120
29. Freedom Football (III)#	6	28	45,297	1,618	Dn 1,266	Dn 26,805
30. Division III Independents#	34	159	257,166	1,617	Up 54	Up 7,085
31. North Coast (III)	9	44	67,681	1,538	Dn 394	Dn 21,205
32. Southern California (III)	7	32	48,356	1,511	Dn 185	Dn 4,233
33. Illinois & Wisconsin (III)	8	34	50,975	1,499	Dn 222	Dn 14,433
34. Southern Collegiate (III)	5	24	33,105	1,379	Dn 201	Dn 6,397
35. Eastern Collegiate (II & III)	9	43	52,866	1,229	Up 46	Up 6,729
II Teams	4	20	34,546	1,727	Up 272	Up 6,905
III Teams	5	23	18,320	797	Dn 128	Dn 176
36. Midwest Intercollegiate (III)	12	54	64,858	1,201	Dn 1,050	Dn 76,969
37. New England Football (III)	9	42	29,859	710	Dn 304	Dn 12,718

 # Did not have the same lineup in 1995 as in 1994. † The figures used for comparison reflect changes in conference and division lineups to provide parallel, valid comparison.

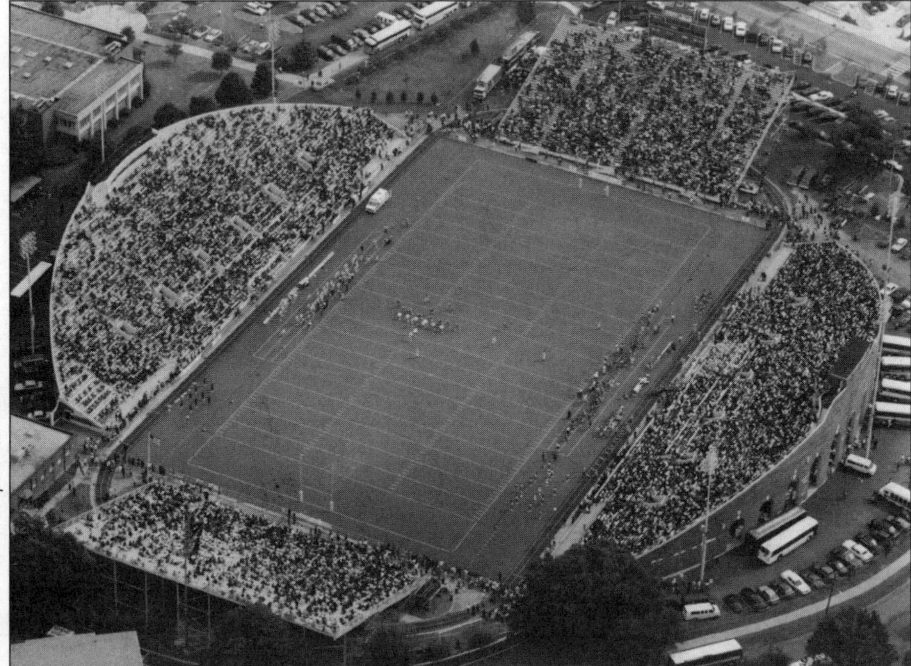

Photo from Norfolk State sports information

Norfolk State averaged 16,593 fans in six games at Foreman Field in 1995 to lead Division II in per-game attendance and help the Central Intercollegiate Athletic Association rank second in the division.

Annual Team Attendance Leaders

Annual Leading Division I-A Teams in Per-Game Home Attendance

Year/Teams	G	Attendance	Avg.
1949			
Michigan	6	563,363	93,894
Ohio St.	5	382,146	76,429
Southern Methodist	8	484,000	60,500
1950			
Michigan	6	493,924	82,321
Ohio St.	5	368,021	73,604
Southern Methodist	5	309,000	61,800
1951			
Ohio St.	6	455,737	75,956
Michigan	6	445,635	74,273
Illinois	4	237,035	59,259
1952			
Ohio St.	6	453,911	75,652
Michigan	6	395,907	65,985
Texas	#5	311,160	62,232
1953			
Ohio St.	5	397,998	79,600
Southern Cal	6	413,617	68,936
Michigan	6	353,860	58,977
1954			
Ohio St.	6	479,840	79,973
Michigan	6	409,454	68,242
UCLA	5	318,371	63,674
1955			
Michigan	7	544,838	77,834
Ohio St.	7	493,178	70,454
Southern Cal	7	467,085	66,726
1956			
Ohio St.	6	494,575	82,429
Michigan	7	566,145	80,878
Minnesota	6	375,407	62,568
1957			
Michigan	6	504,954	84,159
Ohio St.	6	484,118	80,686
Minnesota	5	319,942	63,988
1958			
Ohio St.	6	499,352	82,225
Michigan	6	405,115	67,519
LSU	5	296,576	59,315
1959			
Ohio St.	6	495,536	82,589
Michigan	6	456,385	76,064
LSU	7	408,727	58,390
1960			
Ohio St.	5	413,583	82,717
Michigan St.	4	274,367	68,592
Michigan	6	374,682	62,447
1961			
Ohio St.	5	414,712	82,942
Michigan	7	514,924	73,561
LSU	6	381,409	63,651
1962			
Ohio St.	6	497,644	82,941
Michigan St.	4	272,568	68,142
LSU	6	397,701	66,284
1963			
Ohio St.	5	416,023	83,205
LSU	6	396,846	66,141
Michigan St.	5	326,597	65,319
1964			
Ohio St.	7	583,740	83,391
Michigan St.	4	284,933	71,233
Michigan	6	388,829	64,805

Year/Teams	G	Attendance	Avg.
1965			
Ohio St.	5	416,282	83,256
Michigan	6	480,487	80,081
Michigan St.	5	346,296	69,259
1966			
Ohio St.	6	488,399	81,400
Michigan St.	6	426,750	71,125
Michigan	6	413,599	68,933
1967			
Ohio St.	5	383,502	76,700
Michigan	6	447,289	74,548
Michigan St.	6	411,916	68,653
1968			
Ohio St.	6	482,564	80,427
Southern Cal	5	354,945	70,989
Michigan St.	6	414,177	69,030
1969			
Ohio St.	5	431,175	86,235
Michigan	6	428,780	71,463
Michigan St.	5	352,123	70,425
1970			
Ohio St.	5	432,451	86,490
Michigan	6	476,164	79,361
Purdue	5	340,090	68,018
1971			
Ohio St.	6	506,699	84,450
Michigan	7	564,376	80,625
Wisconsin	6	408,885	68,148
1972			
Michigan	6	513,398	85,566
Ohio St.	6	509,420	84,903
Nebraska	6	456,859	76,143
1973			
Ohio St.	6	523,369	87,228
Michigan	7	595,171	85,024
Nebraska	6	456,726	76,121
1974			
Michigan	6	562,105	93,684
Ohio St.	6	525,314	87,552
Nebraska	7	534,388	76,341
1975			
Michigan	7	689,146	98,449
Ohio St.	6	527,141	87,856
Nebraska	7	533,368	76,195
1976			
Michigan	7	722,113	103,159
Ohio St.	6	526,216	87,702
Tennessee	7	564,922	80,703
1977			
Michigan	7	729,418	104,203
Ohio St.	6	525,535	87,589
Tennessee	7	582,979	83,283
1978			
Michigan	6	629,690	104,948
Ohio St.	7	614,881	87,840
Tennessee	†8	627,381	78,422
1979			
Michigan	7	730,315	104,331
Ohio St.	7	611,794	87,399
Tennessee	6	512,139	85,357
1980			
Michigan	6	625,750	104,292
Tennessee	†8	709,193	88,649
Ohio St.	7	615,476	87,925
1981			
Michigan	6	632,990	105,498
Tennessee	6	558,996	93,166
Ohio St.	6	521,760	86,960
1982			
Michigan	6	631,743	105,291
Tennessee	6	561,102	93,517
Ohio St.	7	623,152	89,022
1983			
Michigan	6	626,916	104,486
Ohio St.	6	534,110	89,018
Tennessee	†8	679,420	84,928
1984			
Michigan	7	726,734	103,819
Tennessee	7	654,602	93,515
Ohio St.	6	536,691	89,449
1985			
Michigan	6	633,530	105,588
Tennessee	7	658,690	94,099
Ohio St.	6	535,284	89,214
1986			
Michigan	6	631,261	105,210
Tennessee	7	643,317	91,902
Ohio St.	6	536,210	89,368
1987			
Michigan	7	731,281	104,469
Tennessee	‡8	705,434	88,179
Ohio St.	6	511,772	85,295
1988			
Michigan	6	628,807	104,801
Tennessee	6	551,677	91,946
Ohio St.	6	516,972	86,162
1989			
Michigan	6	632,136	105,356
Tennessee	6	563,502	93,917
Ohio St.	6	511,812	85,302
1990			
Michigan	6	627,046	104,508
Tennessee	7	666,540	95,220
Ohio St.	6	536,297	89,383
1991			
Michigan	6	632,024	105,337
Tennessee	6	578,389	96,398
Penn St.	6	575,077	95,846
1992			
Michigan	6	635,201	105,867
Tennessee	6	575,544	95,924
Penn St.	6	569,195	94,866
1993			
Michigan	7	*739,620	105,660
Tennessee	7	667,280	95,326
Penn St.	6	564,190	94,032
1994			
Michigan	6	637,300	*106,217
Penn St.	6	577,731	96,289
Tennessee	6	573,821	95,637
1995			
Michigan	7	726,368	103,767
Tennessee	7	662,857	94,694
Penn St.	6	561,546	93,591

**Record. #Includes neutral-site game (Oklahoma) at Dallas counted as a home game (75,500). †Includes neutral-site game at Memphis counted as a home game. Attendance: 1978 (40,879), 1980 (50,003), 1983 (20,135). ‡Includes neutral-site game at East Rutherford (54,681).*

Annual Leading Division I-AA Teams in Per-Game Home Attendance

Year	Team	Avg.
1978	Southern-B.R.	28,333
1979	Grambling	29,900
1980	Southern-B.R.	29,708
1981	Grambling	30,835
1982	Southern-B.R.	32,265
1983	Jackson St.	29,117
1984	Jackson St.	29,215
1985	Yale	29,347
1986	Jackson St.	25,177
1987	Jackson St.	32,734
1988	Jackson St.	26,500
1989	Jackson St.	32,269
1990	Grambling	30,152
1991	Grambling	27,181
1992	Southern-B.R.	28,906
1993	Jackson St.	28,917
1994	Alcorn St.	26,203
1995	Jackson St.	*34,849

**Record.*

Annual Leading Division II Teams in Per-Game Home Attendance

Year	Team	Avg.
1958	Southern Miss.	11,998
1959	Southern Miss.	13,964
1960	Florida A&M	12,083
1961	Akron	12,988
1962	Mississippi Col.	13,125
1963	San Diego St.	14,200
1964	Southern-B.R.	12,633
1965	San Diego St.	15,227
1966	San Diego St.	15,972
1967	San Diego St.	*41,030
1968	San Diego St.	36,969
1969	Grambling	27,680
1970	Tampa	24,204
1971	Grambling	29,341
1972	Grambling	22,663
1973	Morgan St.	22,371
1974	Southern-B.R.	33,563
1975	Texas Southern	22,800
1976	Southern-B.R.	25,864
1977	Florida A&M	21,376
1978	Delaware	18,981
1979	Delaware	19,644
1980	Alabama A&M	15,820
1981	Norfolk St.	19,750
1982	Norfolk St.	16,183
1983	Norfolk St.	15,417
1984	Norfolk St.	18,500
1985	Norfolk St.	18,430
1986	Norfolk St.	13,836
1987	North Dak. St.	14,120
1988	Central Fla.	21,905
1989	North Dak. St.	16,833
1990	Norfolk St.	14,904
1991	Norfolk St.	16,779
1992	Norfolk St.	14,196
1993	Norfolk St.	15,346
1994	Clark Atlanta	20,223
1995	Norfolk St.	16,593

**Record.*

Annual Leading Division III Teams in Per-Game Home Attendance

Year	Team	Avg.
1974	Albany St. (Ga.)	9,380
1975	Wittenberg	7,000
1976	Morehouse	11,600
1977	Dayton	10,315
1978	Dayton	9,827
1979	Central Fla.	11,240
1980	Central Fla.	10,450
1981	Dayton	10,025
1982	Dayton	7,906
1983	Dayton	6,542
1984	Dayton	8,332
1985	Villanova	11,740
1986	Villanova	*11,883
1987	Trinity (Conn.)	6,254
1988	St. John's (Minn.)	5,788
1989	Dayton	5,962
1990	Dayton	6,185
1991	Dayton	7,657
1992	Dayton	6,098
1993	St. John's (Minn.)	6,655
1994	Hampden-Sydney	6,614
1995	St. John's (Minn.)	6,574

**Record.*

1995 Statistical Leaders

Northwestern media services photo by Stephen Serio

Running back Darnell Autry led Northwestern to its first bowl appearance in 47 years by rushing for 152.3 yards per game, fourth best in Division I-A last season.

1995 Division I-A Individual Leaders

Rushing

	1995 Class	G	Car.	Yards	Avg.	TD	Yds.PG
Troy Davis, Iowa St.	So.	11	345	2,010	5.8	15	182.73
Wasean Tait, Toledo	Jr.	11	357	1,905	5.3	20	173.18
George Jones, San Diego St.	Jr.	12	305	1,842	6.0	23	153.50
Darnell Autry, Northwestern	So.	11	355	1,675	4.7	14	152.27
Eddie George, Ohio St.	Sr.	12	303	1,826	6.0	23	152.17
Deland McCullough, Miami (Ohio)	Sr.	11	321	1,627	5.1	14	147.91
Moe Williams, Kentucky	Jr.	11	294	1,600	5.4	17	145.45
Tim Biakabutuka, Michigan	Jr.	12	279	1,724	6.2	12	143.67
Karim Abdul-Jabbar, UCLA	Jr.	10	270	1,419	5.3	11	141.90
Charles Talley, Northern Ill.	Jr.	11	285	1,540	5.4	7	140.00
Abu Wilson, Utah St.	Sr.	11	275	1,476	5.4	15	134.18
Jay Graham, Tennessee	Jr.	11	272	1,438	5.3	12	130.73
Mike Alstott, Purdue	Sr.	11	243	1,436	5.9	11	130.55
David Thompson, Oklahoma St.	Jr.	12	256	1,509	5.9	8	125.75
Byron Hanspard, Texas Tech	So.	11	248	1,374	5.5	11	124.91
Sedrick Shaw, Iowa	Jr.	11	295	1,342	4.5	14	122.00
Joe Abdullah, Pacific (Cal.)	Sr.	11	263	1,334	5.1	11	121.27
Raymond Priester, Clemson	So.	11	223	1,286	5.8	6	116.91
Kin Minor, Nevada	Sr.	9	218	1,052	4.8	9	116.89
Tiki Barber, Virginia	Jr.	12	265	1,397	5.3	14	116.42
Madre Hill, Arkansas	So.	12	307	1,387	4.5	15	115.58
Toraino Singleton, UTEP	Sr.	12	268	1,358	5.1	8	113.17
Warrick Dunn, Florida St.	Jr.	11	166	1,242	7.5	13	112.91
Leeland McElroy, Texas A&M	Jr.	10	246	1,122	4.6	13	112.20
Beau Morgan, Air Force	Jr.	12	229	1,285	5.6	19	107.08
Carl McCullough, Wisconsin	So.	10	236	1,038	4.4	3	103.80
C. J. Williams, Georgia Tech	So.	11	245	1,138	4.6	12	103.45
Denvis Manns, New Mexico St.	Fr.	11	157	1,120	7.1	7	101.82
Jerod Douglas, Baylor	So.	11	211	1,114	5.3	8	101.27
Jerald Moore, Oklahoma	Jr.	10	165	1,001	6.1	9	100.10

Passing Efficiency

(Min. 15 att. per game)	1995 Class	G	Att.	Cmp.	Cmp. Pct.	Int.	Int. Pct.	Yards	Yds./ Att.	TD	TD Pct.	Rating Points
Danny Wuerffel, Florida	Jr.	11	325	210	64.62	10	3.08	3,266	10.05	35	10.77	178.4
Bobby Hoying, Ohio St.	Sr.	12	303	192	63.37	11	3.63	3,023	9.98	28	9.24	170.4
Donovan McNabb, Syracuse	Fr.	11	207	128	61.84	6	2.90	1,991	9.62	16	7.73	162.3
Mike Maxwell, Nevada	Sr.	9	409	277	67.73	17	4.16	3,611	8.83	33	8.07	160.2
Matt Miller, Kansas St.	Sr.	11	240	154	64.17	11	4.58	2,059	8.58	22	9.17	157.3
Steve Taneyhill, South Caro.	Sr.	11	389	261	67.10	9	2.31	3,094	7.95	29	7.46	153.9
Jim Arellanes, Fresno St.	Jr.	9	172	102	59.30	6	3.49	1,539	8.95	13	7.56	152.4
Donald Sellers, New Mexico	Jr.	10	195	121	62.05	3	1.54	1,693	8.68	11	5.64	150.5
Steve Sarkisian, Brigham Young	Jr.	11	385	250	64.94	14	3.64	3,437	8.93	20	5.19	149.8
Josh Wallwork, Wyoming	Jr.	10	271	163	60.15	13	4.80	2,363	8.72	21	7.75	149.4
Peyton Manning, Tennessee	So.	11	380	244	64.21	4	1.05	2,954	7.77	22	5.79	146.5
Billy Blanton, San Diego St.	Jr.	12	389	243	62.47	14	3.60	3,300	8.48	23	5.91	146.0
Danny Kanell, Florida St.	Sr.	11	402	257	63.93	13	3.23	2,957	7.36	32	7.96	145.5
John Hessler, Colorado	So.	11	266	154	57.89	9	3.38	2,136	8.03	20	7.52	143.4
Damon Huard, Washington	Sr.	11	287	184	64.11	6	2.09	2,415	8.41	11	3.83	143.3
Ron Powlus, Notre Dame	Jr.	10	217	124	57.14	7	3.23	1,853	8.54	12	5.53	140.7
Matt Sherman, Iowa	So.	11	271	159	58.67	14	5.17	2,406	8.88	14	5.17	140.0
Kyle Wachholtz, Southern Cal	Sr.	11	171	105	61.40	3	1.75	1,231	7.20	11	6.43	139.6
Moses Moreno, Colorado St.	So.	10	175	99	56.57	6	3.43	1,439	8.22	11	6.29	139.5
Raymond Philyaw, Northeast La.	Jr.	10	320	167	52.19	7	2.19	2,627	8.21	22	6.88	139.5
Darrell Bevell, Wisconsin	Sr.	11	300	195	65.00	11	3.67	2,273	7.58	15	5.00	137.8
Nealon Greene, Clemson	So.	11	183	107	58.47	6	3.28	1,474	8.05	10	5.46	137.6
Brad Otton, Southern Cal	Jr.	11	212	130	61.32	4	1.89	1,532	7.23	12	5.66	136.9
Mark Butterfield, Stanford	Sr.	11	333	194	58.26	9	2.70	2,533	7.61	19	5.71	135.6
Patrick Nix, Auburn	Sr.	11	331	201	60.73	9	2.72	2,574	7.78	15	4.53	135.6
Cody Ledbetter, New Mexico St.	Sr.	11	453	259	57.17	20	4.42	3,501	7.73	30	6.62	135.1
Cory Sauter, Minnesota	So.	11	338	204	60.36	13	3.85	2,600	7.69	18	5.33	134.9
Mike Fouts, Utah	Jr.	11	323	179	55.42	12	3.72	2,581	7.99	18	5.57	133.5
Jake Delhomme, Southwestern La.	Jr.	11	351	190	54.13	10	2.85	2,761	7.87	20	5.70	133.3
Jake Plummer, Arizona St.	Jr.	11	301	173	57.48	9	2.99	2,222	7.38	17	5.65	132.1

Total Offense

	RUSHING				PASSING		TOTAL OFFENSE				
	Car.	Gain	Loss	Net	Att.	Yards	Plays	Yards	Avg.	TDR*	Yds.PG
Mike Maxwell, Nevada	34	91	79	12	409	3,611	443	3,623	8.18	34	402.56
Cody Ledbetter, New Mexico St.	90	405	182	223	453	3,501	543	3,724	6.86	32	338.55
Steve Sarkisian, Brigham Young	82	136	303	-167	385	3,437	467	3,270	7.00	22	297.27
Charlie Batch, Eastern Mich.	61	157	105	52	421	3,177	482	3,229	6.70	24	293.55
Danny Wuerffel, Florida	46	65	206	-141	325	3,266	371	3,125	8.42	37	284.09
Steve Taneyhill, South Caro.	66	203	241	-38	389	3,094	455	3,056	6.72	29	277.82
Billy Blanton, San Diego St.	69	225	201	24	389	3,300	458	3,324	7.26	23	277.00
Tony Graziani, Oregon	70	333	95	238	389	2,491	459	2,729	5.95	17	272.90
Peyton Manning, Tennessee	41	90	84	6	380	2,954	421	2,960	7.03	27	269.09
Marcus Crandell, East Caro.	94	327	126	201	447	2,751	541	2,952	5.46	24	268.36
Danny Kanell, Florida St.	19	30	71	-41	402	2,957	421	2,916	6.93	32	265.09
Raymond Philyaw, Northeast La.	49	112	155	-43	320	2,627	369	2,584	7.00	22	258.40
Bobby Hoying, Ohio St.	52	193	160	33	303	3,023	355	3,056	8.61	30	254.67
Rusty LaRue, Wake Forest	84	269	243	26	421	2,775	505	2,801	5.55	17	254.64
Josh Wallwork, Wyoming	49	249	68	181	271	2,363	320	2,544	7.95	25	254.40
Spence Fischer, Duke	64	215	111	104	438	2,668	502	2,772	5.52	15	252.00
Jake Delhomme, S'western La.	51	205	197	8	351	2,761	402	2,769	6.89	21	251.73
Patrick Mullins, Utah St.	38	76	172	-96	383	2,774	421	2,678	6.36	15	243.45
Patrick Nix, Auburn	48	177	113	64	331	2,574	379	2,638	6.96	18	239.82
Jason Martin, Louisiana Tech	36	85	83	2	370	2,606	406	2,608	6.42	25	237.09

**Touchdowns responsible for are players' TDs scored and passed for.*

Photo from Eastern Michigan sports information

Eastern Michigan quarterback Charlie Batch ranked fourth in Division I-A total offense last season with an average of 293.5 yards per game.

Receptions Per Game

	1995 Class	G	Rec.	Yards	TD	Rec.PG
Alex Van Dyke, Nevada	Sr.	11	129	1,854	16	11.73
Kevin Alexander, Utah St.	Sr.	11	92	1,400	6	8.36
Chad Mackey, Louisiana Tech	Jr.	11	90	1,255	9	8.18
Keyshawn Johnson, Southern Cal	Sr.	11	90	1,218	6	8.18
Will Blackwell, San Diego St.	So.	11	86	1,207	8	7.82
Marcus Harris, Wyoming	Jr.	11	78	1,423	14	7.09
Brandon Stokley, Southwestern La.	Fr.	11	75	1,121	9	6.82
Jermaine Lewis, Maryland	Sr.	10	66	937	3	6.60
Andre Cooper, Florida St.	Jr.	11	71	1,002	15	6.45
Joey Kent, Tennessee	Jr.	11	69	1,055	9	6.27
Marco Battaglia, Rutgers	Sr.	11	69	894	10	6.27
Eric Moulds, Mississippi St.	Sr.	10	62	779	6	6.20
Marlon Estes, Wake Forest	Sr.	11	68	833	9	6.18
Stepfret Williams, Northeast La.	Sr.	11	66	1,056	12	6.00
Brian Roche, San Jose St.	Sr.	11	66	729	5	6.00
Charlie Jones, Fresno St.	Sr.	12	71	1,171	9	5.92
Chris Doering, Florida	Sr.	12	70	1,045	17	5.83
Bobby Engram, Penn St.	Sr.	11	63	1,084	11	5.73
Steve Clay, Eastern Mich.	Sr.	11	63	999	7	5.73
Stanley Pritchett, South Caro.	Sr.	11	62	664	4	5.64

Receiving Yards Per Game

	1995 Class	G	Rec.	Yards	TD	Yds.PG
Alex Van Dyke, Nevada	Sr.	11	129	1,854	16	168.55
Marcus Harris, Wyoming	Jr.	11	78	1,423	14	129.36
Kevin Alexander, Utah St.	Sr.	11	92	1,400	6	127.27
Terry Glenn, Ohio St.	Jr.	11	57	1,316	17	119.64
Chad Mackey, Louisiana Tech	Jr.	11	90	1,255	9	114.09
Keyshawn Johnson, Southern Cal	Sr.	11	90	1,218	6	110.73
Will Blackwell, San Diego St.	So.	11	86	1,207	8	109.73
Marvin Harrison, Syracuse	Sr.	11	56	1,131	8	102.82
Brandon Stokley, Southwestern La.	Fr.	11	75	1,121	9	101.91
Bobby Engram, Penn St.	Sr.	11	63	1,084	11	98.55
Charlie Jones, Fresno St.	Sr.	12	71	1,171	9	97.58
Stepfret Williams, Northeast La.	Sr.	11	66	1,056	12	96.00
Joey Kent, Tennessee	Jr.	11	69	1,055	9	95.91
Keith Poole, Arizona St.	Jr.	11	55	1,036	7	94.18
Jermaine Lewis, Maryland	Sr.	10	66	937	3	93.70
Lucious Davis, New Mexico St.	Sr.	11	57	1,018	12	92.55
Cristin McLemore, Oregon	Sr.	11	61	1,010	4	91.82
Ike Hilliard, Florida	So.	11	57	1,008	15	91.64
Rae Carruth, Colorado	Jr.	11	53	1,008	9	91.64
E. G. Green, Florida St.	So.	11	60	1,007	10	91.55

Interceptions

	1995 Class	G	Int.	Yards	TD	Int.PG
Willie Smith, Louisiana Tech	Jr.	10	8	65	0	.80
Chris Canty, Kansas St.	So.	11	8	117	2	.73
Sean Andrews, Navy	So.	11	8	30	0	.73
Sam Madison, Louisville	Jr.	11	7	136	0	.64
Plez Atkins, Iowa	So.	10	6	97	2	.60
Harold Lusk, Utah	Jr.	10	6	40	0	.60
Kevin Abrams, Syracuse	Jr.	10	6	13	0	.60
Emmanuel McDaniel, East Caro.	Sr.	11	6	111	1	.55
Sam Garnes, Cincinnati	Jr.	11	6	101	0	.55
Jeremy Bunch, Tulsa	Jr.	11	6	76	1	.55
James Crockett, Louisiana Tech	Jr.	11	6	61	0	.55
Brian Dawkins, Clemson	Sr.	11	6	55	1	.55
Andreal Johnson, Maryland	Jr.	11	6	46	0	.55
Craig Dues, Toledo	Jr.	11	6	39	1	.55
Corey Sampson, Northeast La.	Jr.	11	6	22	0	.55
Jamal Belt, Toledo	Sr.	11	6	12	0	.55
Ricky Parker, San Diego St.	Jr.	12	6	203	1	.50
Chris Carter, Texas	Jr.	12	6	146	0	.50
Rob Clifford, Boston College	Sr.	12	6	28	0	.50
Percy Ellsworth, Virginia	Sr.	12	6	21	0	.50
Paul London, Virginia	Sr.	12	6	20	0	.50

Scoring

	1995 Class	G	TD	XP	FG	Pts.	Pts.PG
Eddie George, Ohio St.	Sr.	12	24	0	0	144	12.00
George Jones, San Diego St.	Jr.	12	23	0	0	138	11.50
Wasean Tait, Toledo	Jr.	11	20	0	0	120	10.91
Scott Greene, Michigan St.	Sr.	10	17	2	0	104	10.40
Byron Hanspard, Texas Tech	So.	11	18	0	0	108	9.82
Leeland McElroy, Texas A&M	Jr.	10	16	0	0	96	9.60
Beau Morgan, Air Force	Jr.	12	19	0	0	114	9.50
Terry Glenn, Ohio St.	Jr.	11	17	2	0	104	9.45
Stephen Davis, Auburn	Sr.	11	17	0	0	102	9.27
Moe Williams, Kentucky	Jr.	11	17	0	0	102	9.27
Kris Brown, Nebraska	Fr.	11	0	58	13	97	8.82
Troy Davis, Iowa St.	So.	11	16	0	0	96	8.73
Warrick Dunn, Florida St.	Jr.	11	16	0	0	96	8.73
Ahman Green, Nebraska	Fr.	11	16	0	0	96	8.73
Alex Van Dyke, Nevada	Sr.	11	16	0	0	96	8.73
Jeff Hall, Tennessee	Fr.	11	0	47	16	95	8.64
Scott Bentley, Florida St.	Jr.	11	0	67	9	94	8.55
Chris Doering, Florida	Sr.	12	17	0	0	102	8.50
Keffer McGee, Mississippi St.	So.	11	15	2	0	92	8.36

Photo from Ohio State sports information

On his way to the 1995 Heisman Trophy, Ohio State running back Eddie George averaged 185.4 all-purpose yards per game, which ranked fourth in Division I-A.

All-Purpose Yards

	1995 Class	G	Rush	Rec.	PR	KOR	Total Yards	Yds.PG
Troy Davis, Iowa St.	So.	11	2,010	159	0	297	2,466	224.18
Alex Van Dyke, Nevada	Sr.	11	6	1854	0	583	2,443	222.09
Wasean Tait, Toledo	Jr.	11	1,905	183	0	0	2,088	189.82
Eddie George, Ohio St.	Sr.	12	1,826	399	0	0	2,225	185.42
Abu Wilson, Utah St.	Sr.	11	1,476	375	0	153	2,004	182.18
Winslow Oliver, New Mexico	Sr.	11	915	228	101	666	1,910	173.64
Corey Walker, Arkansas St.	Jr.	11	1,013	411	0	459	1,883	171.18
Leeland McElroy, Texas A&M	Jr.	10	1,122	379	0	208	1,709	170.90
Darnell Autry, Northwestern	So.	11	1,675	130	0	45	1,850	168.18
Byron Hanspard, Texas Tech	So.	11	1,374	474	0	0	1,848	168.00
Moe Williams, Kentucky	Jr.	11	1,600	153	0	73	1,826	166.00
Ricky Whittle, Oregon	Sr.	11	971	419	0	414	1,804	164.00
George Jones, San Diego St.	Jr.	12	1,842	119	0	0	1,961	163.42
Joe Abdullah, Pacific (Cal.)	Sr.	11	1,334	460	0	0	1,794	163.09
Derrick Mason, Michigan St.	Jr.	11	0	713	234	815	1,762	160.18
Tiki Barber, Virginia	Jr.	12	1,397	216	272	21	1,906	158.83
Karim Abdul-Jabbar, UCLA	Jr.	10	1,419	154	0	0	1,573	157.30
Deland McCullough, Miami (Ohio)	Sr.	11	1,627	97	0	0	1,724	156.73
Robert Tate, Cincinnati	Jr.	11	35	895	240	515	1,685	153.18
Denvis Manns, New Mexico St.	Fr.	11	1,120	267	0	296	1,683	153.00

Punt Returns

(Min. 1.2 per game)	1995 Class	No.	Yds.	TD	Avg.
James Dye, Brigham Young	Jr.	20	438	2	21.90
Brian Roberson, Fresno St.	Jr.	19	346	1	18.21
Marvin Harrison, Syracuse	Sr.	22	369	2	16.77
Greg Myers, Colorado St.	Sr.	35	555	3	15.86
Paul Guidry, UCLA	Jr.	24	370	1	15.42
Ray Peterson, San Diego St.	Sr.	22	320	0	14.55
Kenyatta Watson, Boston College	Jr.	17	245	2	14.41
Dane Johnson, Texas Tech	So.	15	214	0	14.27
Brian Musso, Northwestern	Jr.	28	393	1	14.04
Mike Fullman, Nebraska	Jr.	21	285	1	13.57
Eddie Kennison, LSU	Jr.	19	253	0	13.32
Jermaine Lewis, Maryland	Sr.	12	152	1	12.67
Dee Feaster, Florida St.	Fr.	25	314	0	12.56
Nathan Perryman, Georgia Tech	Jr.	29	362	0	12.48
Antwuan Wyatt, Clemson	Jr.	20	245	0	12.25
John Washington, Texas Christian	Jr.	21	257	1	12.24
Ray Mickens, Texas A&M	Sr.	24	281	0	11.71
Dean Jackson, Louisiana Tech	Jr.	18	203	0	11.28
Tremayne Banks, Miami (Ohio)	Jr.	16	180	0	11.25
Reidel Anthony, Florida	So.	11	122	0	11.09

Kickoff Returns

(Min. 1.2 per game)	1995 Class	No.	Yds.	TD	Avg.
Robert Tate, Cincinnati	Jr.	15	515	1	34.33
Winslow Oliver, New Mexico	Sr.	21	666	1	31.71
Damon Dunn, Stanford	So.	19	539	1	28.37
Steve Clay, Eastern Mich.	Sr.	14	395	1	28.21
Emmett Mosley, Notre Dame	Jr.	15	419	0	27.93
Marlon Evans, Stanford	Sr.	16	446	1	27.88
Silas Massey, Central Mich.	Fr.	16	434	0	27.13
Chris Buckhalter, Southern Miss.	Sr.	14	377	0	26.93
Vertis McKinney, North Texas	Sr.	14	373	0	26.64
Derrick Mason, Michigan St.	Jr.	31	815	1	26.29
Corey Walker, Arkansas St.	Jr.	18	459	1	25.50
Jake Campbell, Air Force	Sr.	19	475	0	25.00
Antwuan Wyatt, Clemson	Jr.	17	425	0	25.00
Kenny Gunn, Tulsa	Sr.	16	399	0	24.94
Reidel Anthony, Florida	So.	19	472	1	24.84
Brian Smith, North Texas	Sr.	15	371	1	24.73
Marcus Wall, North Caro.	Sr.	20	492	1	24.60
Mike Adams, Texas	Jr.	17	417	0	24.53
Dwayne Harris, Toledo	So.	18	438	0	24.33
Ron Thomas, Army	Jr.	14	340	0	24.29

Punting

(Min. 3.6 per game)	1995 Class	No.	Avg.
Brad Maynard, Ball St.	Jr.	66	46.53
Brian Gragert, Wyoming	Sr.	40	45.20
Greg Ivy, Oklahoma St.	Sr.	66	44.65
Chad Kessler, LSU	So.	47	44.09
Sean Liss, Florida St.	Jr.	49	43.94
Darrin Simmons, Kansas	Sr.	51	43.78
Tucker Phillips, Rice	Jr.	57	43.63
John Stonehouse, Southern Cal	Sr.	44	43.59
Sean Terry, Texas A&M	Sr.	60	43.30
Steve Carr, Air Force	Sr.	45	43.24
George Martin, Washington St.	Sr.	67	43.16
Sean Reali, Syracuse	Jr.	40	43.13
Noel Prefontaine, San Diego St	Jr.	52	42.98
Nate Cochran, Pittsburgh	Jr.	71	42.92
Ty Grude, Toledo	Jr.	46	42.80
Bill Marinangel, Vanderbilt	Jr.	70	42.66
Chris Sailer, UCLA	Fr.	55	42.16
Alan Sutkowski, Indiana	So.	67	42.07
Toby Gowin, North Texas	Jr.	78	42.05
Beau Stephens, Texas Christian	Sr.	56	42.04

Field Goals

	1995 Class	G	FGA	FG	Pct.	FGPG
Michael Reeder, Texas Christian	So.	11	25	23	.920	2.09
Rafael Garcia, Virginia	Jr.	12	27	20	.741	1.67
Dan Pulsipher, Utah	Jr.	11	22	17	.773	1.55
Eric Abrams, Stanford	Sr.	11	18	16	.889	1.45
Brett Conway, Penn St.	Jr.	11	24	16	.667	1.45
Eric Richards, Cincinnati	So.	11	24	16	.667	1.45
Jeff Hall, Tennessee	Fr.	11	25	16	.640	1.45
Remy Hamilton, Michigan	Jr.	12	25	17	.680	1.42
Josh Smith, Oregon	Fr.	10	21	14	.667	1.40
Jeff Sauve, Clemson	Sr.	11	20	15	.750	1.36
Jeremy Alexander, Oklahoma	So.	11	16	14	.875	1.27
Chris Pierce, Southern Miss.	Sr.	11	17	14	.824	1.27
Tom Cochran, Duke	Sr.	11	18	14	.778	1.27
Cory Wedel, Wyoming	So.	11	18	14	.778	1.27
Brad Blasy, Central Mich.	Sr.	11	20	14	.700	1.27
Chris Ferencik, Pittsburgh	Fr.	10	13	12	.923	1.20
Matt Hawkins, Auburn	Sr.	11	15	13	.867	1.18
Kris Brown, Nebraska	Fr.	11	16	13	.813	1.18
Andre Lafleur, LSU	Sr.	11	19	13	.684	1.18
Tim Montz, Mississippi	Jr.	11	19	13	.684	1.18
Kanon Parkman, Georgia	Sr.	11	19	13	.684	1.18
Jarvis Van Dyke, Baylor	Sr.	11	23	13	.565	1.18

1995 Division I-A Team Leaders

Total Offense

	G	Plays	Yds.	Avg.	TD*	Yds.PG
Nevada	11	917	6,263	6.8	63	569.36
Nebraska	11	855	6,119	7.2	69	556.27
Florida St.	11	885	6,067	6.9	71	551.55
Florida	12	867	6,413	7.4	72	534.42
Ohio St.	12	865	5,887	6.8	60	490.58
Colorado	11	809	5,353	6.6	48	486.64
San Diego St.	12	883	5,785	6.6	51	482.08
New Mexico St.	11	811	5,248	6.5	46	477.09
Auburn	11	788	5,049	6.4	54	459.00
Fresno St.	12	899	5,479	6.1	47	456.58
Tennessee	11	833	5,003	6.0	48	454.82
Wyoming	11	784	4,961	6.3	37	451.00
Eastern Mich.	11	820	4,940	6.0	44	449.09
Louisiana Tech	11	815	4,934	6.1	41	448.55
Southwestern La.	11	856	4,780	5.6	45	434.55
Utah St.	11	811	4,776	5.9	34	434.18
Texas	12	848	5,199	6.1	46	433.25
Air Force	12	850	5,180	6.1	48	431.67
South Caro.	11	783	4,717	6.0	50	428.82
Rutgers	11	900	4,701	5.2	36	427.36

**Touchdowns scored by rushing/passing only.*

Total Defense

	G	Plays	Yds.	Avg.	TD*	Yds.PG
Kansas St.	11	673	2,759	4.1	16	250.8
Miami (Ohio)	11	738	2,764	3.7	15	251.3
Texas A&M	11	773	2,835	3.7	16	257.7
Ball St.	11	712	2,850	4.0	22	259.1
Baylor	11	709	2,903	4.1	19	263.9
North Caro.	11	729	2,940	4.0	25	267.3
Arizona	11	739	2,976	4.0	19	270.5
Western Mich.	11	686	3,092	4.5	23	281.1
Alabama	11	727	3,125	4.3	21	284.1
Virginia Tech	11	782	3,145	4.0	18	285.9
Michigan	12	813	3,436	4.2	21	286.3
Oregon	11	735	3,222	4.4	26	292.9
Nebraska	11	726	3,235	4.5	20	294.1
West Va.	11	738	3,294	4.5	26	299.5
Oklahoma	11	735	3,307	4.5	27	300.6
Oregon St.	11	796	3,342	4.2	28	303.8
LSU	11	789	3,398	4.3	19	308.9
Navy	11	754	3,448	4.6	24	313.5
Southwestern La.	11	744	3,471	4.7	30	315.5
Florida	12	815	3,787	4.6	22	315.6

**Touchdowns scored by rushing or passing only.*

Rushing Offense

	G	Car.	Yds.	Avg.	TD	Yds.PG
Nebraska	11	627	4,398	7.0	51	399.8
Air Force	12	672	3,989	5.9	36	332.4
Army	11	699	3,632	5.2	36	330.2
Clemson	11	611	2,855	4.7	24	259.5
Toledo	11	564	2,690	4.8	32	244.5
Notre Dame	11	562	2,572	4.6	29	233.8
Navy	11	574	2,570	4.5	21	233.6
Purdue	11	522	2,567	4.9	25	233.4
Iowa St.	11	506	2,513	5.0	23	228.5
Northern Ill.	11	546	2,497	4.6	18	227.0
Hawaii	12	559	2,688	4.8	27	224.0
Florida St.	11	420	2,451	5.8	35	222.8
Rice	11	559	2,447	4.4	19	222.5
Ohio St.	12	530	2,643	5.0	28	220.3
New Mexico	11	516	2,380	4.6	19	216.4
Baylor	11	539	2,325	4.3	25	211.4
Georgia Tech	11	523	2,321	4.4	22	211.0
Oregon St.	11	586	2,302	3.9	15	209.3
Penn St.	11	484	2,294	4.7	21	208.5
UCLA	11	501	2,291	4.6	25	208.3

Rushing Defense

	G	Car.	Yds.	Avg.	TD	Yds.PG
Virginia Tech	11	429	851	2.0	7	77.4
Nebraska	11	341	862	2.5	6	78.4
Michigan	12	419	1,081	2.6	12	90.1
Georgia Tech	11	372	1,003	2.7	17	91.2
Arkansas	12	424	1,251	3.0	15	104.3
Alabama	11	380	1,158	3.0	9	105.3
Oregon	11	416	1,163	2.8	15	105.7
Texas A&M	11	444	1,164	2.6	8	105.8
Oklahoma	11	424	1,200	2.8	11	109.1
Virginia	12	424	1,310	3.1	15	109.2
Miami (Ohio)	11	435	1,220	2.8	4	110.9
Baylor	11	399	1,242	3.1	12	112.9
Tennessee	11	392	1,243	3.2	12	113.0
Western Mich.	11	387	1,246	3.2	13	113.3
Kansas St.	11	404	1,254	3.1	4	114.0
North Caro.	11	450	1,304	2.9	15	118.5
Penn St.	11	418	1,318	3.2	13	119.8
Clemson	11	365	1,342	3.7	9	122.0
Oregon St.	11	442	1,346	3.0	15	122.4
Southwestern La.	11	396	1,372	3.5	17	124.7

Scoring Offense

	G	Pts.	Avg.
Nebraska	11	576	52.4
Florida St.	11	532	48.4
Florida	12	534	44.5
Nevada	11	484	44.0
Auburn	11	424	38.5
Ohio St.	12	461	38.4
Tennessee	11	411	37.4
Colorado	11	406	36.9
Kansas St.	11	402	36.5
South Caro.	11	401	36.5
Toledo	11	371	33.7
San Diego St.	12	401	33.4
Notre Dame	11	366	33.3
Eastern Mich.	11	363	33.0
Penn St.	11	356	32.4
Southwestern La.	11	351	31.9
New Mexico St.	11	349	31.7
Texas	12	380	31.7
Fresno St.	12	371	30.9
Syracuse	11	334	30.4

Scoring Defense

	G	Pts.	Avg.
Northwestern	11	140	12.7
Kansas St.	11	145	13.2
Texas A&M	11	148	13.5
Nebraska	11	150	13.6
Virginia Tech	11	155	14.1
LSU	11	160	14.5
Louisville	11	165	15.0
Miami (Ohio)	11	165	15.0
Baylor	11	166	15.1
Clemson	11	178	16.2
Southern Cal	11	180	16.4
Ohio St.	12	200	16.7
Florida	12	201	16.8
Michigan	12	201	16.8
Ball St.	11	187	17.0
Alabama	11	188	17.1
Navy	11	189	17.2
Western Mich.	11	190	17.3
Cincinnati	11	197	17.9
Illinois	11	198	18.0

Passing Offense

	G	Att.	Cmp.	Int.	Pct.	Yards	Yds./ Att.	TD	Yds.PG
Nevada	11	509	337	22	66.2	4,579	9.0	39	416.3
Florida	12	457	287	12	62.8	4,330	9.5	48	360.8
Florida St.	11	465	297	14	63.9	3,616	7.8	36	328.7
New Mexico St.	11	454	260	20	57.3	3,540	7.8	30	321.8
Brigham Young	11	388	252	14	64.9	3,469	8.9	20	315.4
South Caro.	11	420	282	10	67.1	3,373	8.0	32	306.6
Eastern Mich.	11	441	254	19	57.6	3,323	7.5	23	302.1
Colorado	11	366	222	11	60.7	3,269	8.9	28	297.2
Fresno St.	12	432	247	17	57.2	3,483	8.1	25	290.3
Wake Forest	11	483	289	18	59.8	3,073	6.4	19	279.4
San Diego St.	12	396	246	14	62.1	3,352	8.5	24	279.3
Tennessee	11	391	250	4	63.9	3,031	7.8	22	275.5
Wyoming	11	358	204	21	57.0	3,005	8.4	23	273.2
Utah St.	11	421	228	17	54.2	2,975	7.1	12	270.5
Ohio St.	12	335	210	12	62.7	3,244	9.7	32	270.3
Oregon	11	443	239	10	54.0	2,902	6.6	14	263.8
Auburn	11	375	233	10	62.1	2,891	7.7	19	262.8
Minnesota	11	384	222	16	57.8	2,863	7.5	20	260.3
Northeast La.	11	365	186	8	51.0	2,861	7.8	22	260.1
Louisiana Tech	11	420	227	14	54.0	2,848	6.8	24	258.9

Photo from Louisville sports information

Paced by defensive back Sam Madison's seven interceptions, Louisville finished ninth in Division I-A in pass efficiency defense in 1995.

Pass Efficiency Defense

	G	Att.	Cmp.	Cmp. Pct.	Int.	Int. Pct.	Yards	Yds./ Att.	TD	TD Pct.	Rating Points
Miami (Ohio)	11	303	137	45.21	22	7.26	1,544	5.10	11	3.63	85.48
Texas A&M	11	329	150	45.59	13	3.95	1,671	5.08	8	2.43	88.38
Texas Tech	11	372	153	41.13	15	4.03	2,020	5.43	14	3.76	91.10
Ball St.	11	303	128	42.24	10	3.30	1,469	4.85	14	4.62	91.62
Baylor	11	310	148	47.74	13	4.19	1,661	5.36	7	2.26	91.81
LSU	11	343	158	46.06	13	3.79	1,907	5.56	8	2.33	92.88
East Caro.	11	332	157	47.29	19	5.72	1,988	5.99	7	2.11	93.10
Cincinnati	11	347	162	46.69	20	5.76	2,011	5.80	11	3.17	94.30
Louisville	11	350	175	50.00	24	6.86	2,130	6.09	8	2.29	94.95
Miami (Fla.)	11	302	145	48.01	12	3.97	1,631	5.40	10	3.31	96.36
Northwestern	11	365	204	55.89	16	4.38	2,029	5.56	5	1.37	98.34
Alabama	11	347	173	49.86	18	5.19	1,967	5.67	12	3.46	98.51
Kansas St.	11	269	125	46.47	13	4.83	1,505	5.59	12	4.46	98.52
Arizona	11	291	138	47.42	6	2.06	1,577	5.42	10	3.44	100.16
Florida	12	378	187	49.47	14	3.70	2,225	5.89	11	2.91	101.11
Clemson	11	376	190	50.53	21	5.59	2,255	6.00	13	3.46	101.15
Illinois	11	325	171	52.62	18	5.54	1,976	6.08	9	2.77	101.75
Southwestern La.	11	348	160	45.98	11	3.16	2,099	6.03	13	3.74	102.65
Ohio St.	12	327	169	51.68	24	7.34	2,203	6.74	9	2.75	102.68
Western Mich.	11	299	151	50.50	16	5.35	1,846	6.17	10	3.34	102.70

Net Punting

	Punts	Avg.	No. Ret.	Yds. Ret.	Net Avg.
Ball St.	66	46.5	29	346	41.3
Wyoming	40	45.2	13	184	40.6
Rice	57	43.6	23	181	40.5
Oklahoma St.	67	44.0	31	260	40.1
Texas A&M	60	43.3	23	196	40.0
Syracuse	40	43.1	13	131	39.8
North Texas	78	42.1	29	190	39.6
Kansas	53	42.4	20	159	39.4
Texas Christian	56	42.0	25	150	39.4
Vanderbilt	74	41.0	29	140	39.1
Arizona	80	40.9	29	171	38.8
New Mexico St.	42	40.6	14	87	38.5
Mississippi St.	50	40.6	13	109	38.4
Southern Cal	45	42.6	19	190	38.4
Southern Miss.	71	41.3	31	220	38.2
Pittsburgh	74	41.3	37	229	38.2
Nebraska	29	38.6	5	12	38.1
Iowa	49	41.7	18	177	38.1
Iowa St.	53	40.6	24	135	38.1
Texas Tech	69	40.7	26	180	38.1

Punt Returns

	G	No.	Yds.	TD	Avg.
Eastern Mich.	11	8	166	1	20.8
Brigham Young	11	26	492	2	18.9
Fresno St.	12	22	398	2	18.1
Syracuse	11	23	390	2	17.0
Colorado St.	11	36	562	3	15.6
San Diego St.	12	23	338	0	14.7
Boston College	12	20	284	2	14.2
UCLA	11	31	433	2	14.0
Northwestern	11	30	418	1	13.9
Michigan St.	11	25	337	2	13.5
Kansas	11	13	172	1	13.2
Pacific (Cal.)	11	11	138	0	12.5
Texas	12	24	299	1	12.5
Kansas St.	11	40	492	3	12.3
Iowa St.	11	7	86	0	12.3
Texas Christian	11	21	257	1	12.2
Notre Dame	11	22	269	1	12.2
Texas A&M	11	27	328	0	12.1
Maryland	11	16	194	1	12.1
Georgia Tech	11	34	404	0	11.9

Kickoff Returns

	G	No.	Yds.	TD	Avg.
New Mexico	11	35	947	1	27.1
Stanford	11	39	1,024	2	26.3
Cincinnati	11	37	930	1	25.1
Tennessee	11	30	752	0	25.1
Air Force	12	38	922	0	24.3
Baylor	11	25	604	0	24.2
South Caro.	11	46	1,084	1	23.6
Florida	12	38	886	1	23.3
Southern Miss.	11	42	965	1	23.0
Michigan St.	11	42	961	1	22.9
Tulsa	11	50	1,138	1	22.8
Clemson	11	33	749	0	22.7
Arizona St.	11	45	1,011	1	22.5
Memphis	11	39	874	0	22.4
Arkansas St.	11	38	850	1	22.4

	G	No.	Yds.	TD	Avg.
North Caro.	11	25	559	1	22.4
Notre Dame	11	36	793	0	22.0
Oregon	11	31	679	1	21.9
Duke	11	55	1,201	0	21.8
Mississippi	11	26	564	0	21.7

Turnover Margin

	TURNOVERS GAINED			TURNOVERS LOST			Margin/
	Fum.	Int.	Total	Fum.	Int.	Total	Game
Toledo	16	18	34	6	6	12	2.00
Louisville	17	24	41	12	8	20	1.91
Northwestern	16	16	32	6	6	12	1.82
Florida St.	18	16	34	6	14	20	1.27
Nebraska	8	20	28	9	6	15	1.18
Washington	12	16	28	9	6	15	1.18
Miami (Ohio)	9	22	31	8	11	19	1.09
Virginia	8	25	33	9	11	20	1.08
Louisiana Tech	19	20	39	14	14	28	1.00
Missouri	13	16	29	9	9	18	1.00
Tennessee	7	16	23	8	4	12	1.00
Ohio St.	7	24	31	8	12	20	.92
Notre Dame	14	16	30	12	8	20	.91
Syracuse	10	19	29	13	6	19	.91
Tulsa	18	14	32	15	7	22	.91
San Diego St.	11	26	37	13	14	27	.83
Kentucky	13	12	25	8	8	16	.82
Arkansas	12	16	28	8	11	19	.75

Longest Division I-A Plays of 1995

Rushing

Player, Team (Opponent)	Yards
Eddie George, Ohio St. (Minnesota)	87
Winslow Oliver, New Mexico (Northern Ariz.)	82
Lawrence Phillips, Nebraska (Oklahoma St.)	80
James Sims, Nebraska (Michigan St.)	80
David Thompson, Oklahoma St. (Nebraska)	*79
Eric Hines-Tucker, Auburn (Tenn.-Chatt.)	77
Lee Ragsdale, Louisiana Tech (South Caro.)	76
Moe Williams, Kentucky (South Caro.)	76
Yoncy Edmonds, Rice (UNLV)	75
George Jones, San Diego St. (Fresno St.)	*75
Jay Graham, Tennessee (Alabama)	75

**Did not score.*

Passing

Passer-Receiver, Team (Opponent)	Yards
Donovan McNabb-Marvin Harrison, Syracuse (West Va.)	96
Eric Kressler-Jacquez Green, Florida (Northern Ill.)	96
Steve Taneyhill-Monty Means, South Caro. (Louisiana Tech)	93
Steve Taneyhill-Stanley Pritchett, South Caro. (Kentucky)	92
Dan White-Richard Dice, Arizona (Pacific, Cal.)	89
Koy Detmer-Herchell Troutman, Colorado (Colorado St.)	*89
Eric Bennett-Alex Van Dyke, Nevada (San Jose St.)	89
Mike Maxwell-Alex Van Dyke, Nevada (Louisiana Tech)	87
Chris McCoy-Matt Scornavacchi, Navy (Tulane)	87

**Did not score.*

Interception Returns

Player, Team (Opponent)	Yards
Cedric Anderson, Tulane (Louisville)	96
Darrell Baker, Arkansas St. (UNLV)	95
Isaac Walker, Oregon (Washington St.)	82
Aaron Collins, Penn St. (Indiana)	80
James Reddish, Houston (Southern Methodist)	78
Chris Martin, Northwestern (Purdue)	76
Rod Thomas, Southern Miss. (Tulane)	75
Cyrill Weems, Wisconsin (Purdue)	75
Gary Ellison, Hawaii (UNLV)	73
Chris Hewitt, Cincinnati (Memphis)	73

Punt Returns

Player, Team (Opponent)	Yards
Marvin Harrison, Syracuse (Minnesota)	94
James Dye, Brigham Young (Wyoming)	90
Brian Musso, Northwestern (Indiana)	86
Brian Roberson, Fresno St. (Hawaii)	86
James Dye, Brigham Young (San Diego St.)	84
Greg Myers, Colorado St. (San Diego St.)	84
Steve Clay, Eastern Mich. (Ball St.)	78
Mark Butler, Pittsburgh (Temple)	76
James Dye, Brigham Young (Tulsa)	75
Kendrick Lee, Southern Miss. (Tulane)	74

Kickoff Returns

Player, Team (Opponent)	Yards
Jason Jacoby, Tulsa (Brigham Young)	100
Aaron Stecker, Wisconsin (Minnesota)	100
Lee Johnson, Purdue (Ball St.)	99
Cedric Johnson, UTEP (Tulsa)	98
Winslow Oliver, New Mexico (UTEP)	98
Shaun Springs, Ohio St. (Boston College)	97
Marlon Evans, Stanford (Oregon)	96
Fred Brock, Southern Miss. (Northern Ill.)	95
Steve Clay, Eastern Mich. (Pittsburgh)	93
Lew Lawhorn, Akron (Eastern Mich.)	93

Field Goals

Player, Team (Opponent)	Yards
Derek Schorejs, Bowling Green (Toledo)	60
John Hall, Wisconsin (Minnesota)	60
Jon Prasuhn, Arizona (Pacific, Cal.)	57
Brett Conway, Penn St. (Michigan)	57
Micah Knorr, Utah St. (Northern Ill.)	56
Rafael Garcia, Virginia (Texas)	56
Steve Yenner, Vanderbilt (Louisiana Tech)	55
Chad Seitz, Miami, Ohio (Michigan)	54
Jeff Hall, Tennessee (Oklahoma St.)	53
Mike Shafer, Southwestern La. (New Mexico St.)	53

Punts

Player, Team (Opponent)	Yards
Paul Burton, Northwestern (Indiana)	90
Ian Hughes, Army (Air Force)	88
Brett Larson, Illinois (Arizona)	80
Lonny Calicchio, Mississippi (Auburn)	79
Sean Terry, Texas A&M (Colorado)	76
Nick Gallery, Iowa (Indiana)	75
Andy Mitchell, Colorado (Kansas)	73
Ty Atteberry, Baylor (Texas Tech)	72

Fumble Returns

Player, Team (Opponent)	Yards
Paul Rivers, Rutgers (Pittsburgh)	100
Ben Hanks, Florida (Arkansas)	95
Marcus Coleman, Texas Tech (New Mexico)	92
Clark Watkins, Arkansas St. (Northern Ill.)	76
Steve Rosga, Colorado (Wisconsin)	75
Donnell Leomiti, Colorado (Iowa St.)	75
Hassan Saamsid-Deen, North Caro. St. (Duke)	68
Damani Shakoor, Iowa (Iowa St.)	67
Maylon Wesley, Oklahoma (San Diego St.)	65

Cornell sports information photo by Tim McKinney

Cornell running back Chad Levitt averaged 142.8 rushing yards per game last season, good for a sixth-place ranking in Division I-AA.

1995 Division I-AA Individual Leaders

Rushing

	1995 Class	G	Car.	Yards	Avg.	TD	Yds.PG
Reggie Greene, Siena	So.	9	273	1,461	5.4	11	162.33
Derrick Cullors, Murray St.	Sr.	11	269	1,765	6.6	16	160.45
Tim Hall, Robert Morris	Sr.	10	239	1,572	6.6	16	157.20
Arnold Mickens, Butler	Sr.	10	354	1,558	4.4	11	155.80
Kito Lockwood, Wagner	Sr.	7	212	1,018	4.8	10	145.43
Chad Levitt, Cornell	Jr.	10	292	1,428	4.9	13	142.80
Bill Green, Duquesne	Sr.	10	284	1,427	5.0	9	142.70
Thomas Haskins, Va. Military	Jr.	11	248	1,548	6.2	17	140.73
Rabih Abdullah, Lehigh	Jr.	11	257	1,536	6.0	11	139.64
Marquette Smith, Central Fla.	Sr.	11	274	1,511	5.5	14	137.36
Willie High, Eastern Ill.	Sr.	11	314	1,458	4.6	12	132.55
Michael Hicks, South Caro. St.	Sr.	10	228	1,299	5.7	13	129.90
Chris Parker, Marshall	Sr.	11	254	1,390	5.5	12	126.36
Clarence Matthews, Northwestern St.	Jr.	11	230	1,384	6.0	13	125.82
Larry Washington, Towson St.	Sr.	9	205	1,101	5.4	12	122.33
Rich Lemon, Bucknell	Jr.	11	293	1,297	4.4	9	117.91
Fabian Thorne, Delaware St.	Sr.	11	240	1,296	5.4	7	117.82
Claude Mathis, Southwest Tex. St.	So.	11	244	1,286	5.3	11	116.91
Frank Alessio, Massachusetts	Jr.	11	161	1,276	7.9	9	116.00
Tory Taylor, Connecticut	Fr.	11	208	1,262	6.1	6	114.73
Damon Scott, Appalachian St.	Jr.	11	243	1,256	5.2	13	114.18
Andre Pam, Maine	Jr.	11	191	1,250	6.5	8	113.64
Derek Fitzgerald, William & Mary	Sr.	11	255	1,223	4.8	7	111.18
Eion Hu, Harvard	Jr.	10	230	1,101	4.8	8	110.10
Michael Penix, Tennessee Tech	Sr.	11	249	1,208	4.9	14	109.82
Tyrone Mayer, Hampton	So.	11	204	1,193	5.8	8	108.45
Alfredo Anderson, Idaho St.	Jr.	11	208	1,192	5.7	11	108.36
Kwame Vidal, Florida A&M	Sr.	11	263	1,189	4.5	14	108.09
Rene Ingoglia, Massachusetts	Sr.	11	262	1,178	4.5	19	107.09
Matt Engelking, Montana St.	Jr.	11	258	1,176	4.6	4	106.91

Passing Efficiency

(Min. 15 att. per game)	1995 Class	G	Att.	Cmp.	Cmp. Pct.	Int.	Int. Pct.	Yards	Yds./ Att.	TD	TD Pct.	Rating Points
Brian Kadel, Dayton	Sr.	11	183	115	62.84	6	3.28	1,880	10.27	18	9.84	175.0
Dave Dickenson, Montana	Sr.	11	455	309	67.91	9	1.98	4,176	9.18	38	8.35	168.6
Leo Hamlett, Delaware	Jr.	11	174	95	54.60	6	3.45	1,849	10.63	15	8.62	165.4
Chris Berg, Northern Iowa	Sr.	10	206	113	54.85	6	2.91	2,144	10.41	15	7.28	160.5
Jeff Lewis, Northern Ariz.	Sr.	10	313	209	66.77	3	.96	2,426	7.75	22	7.03	153.2
Mike Cherry, Murray St.	Jr.	11	225	135	60.00	10	4.44	2,084	9.26	16	7.11	152.4
James Ritchey, Stephen F. Austin	Sr.	10	203	113	55.67	6	2.96	1,667	8.21	17	8.37	146.4
David Loya, Duquesne	So.	10	188	108	57.45	5	2.66	1,667	8.87	11	5.85	145.9
Tony Hilde, Boise St.	Jr.	11	279	154	55.20	5	1.79	2,386	8.55	18	6.45	144.7
Sean Laird, St. Mary's (Cal.)	So.	10	244	141	57.79	6	2.46	1,909	7.82	18	7.38	142.9
Brad Laird, Northwestern St.	Sr.	11	213	130	61.03	6	2.82	1,895	8.90	5	2.35	137.9
Bob Aylsworth, Lehigh	Sr.	11	400	240	60.00	11	2.75	2,899	7.25	27	6.75	137.7
Tommy Luginbill, Eastern Ky.	Sr.	11	196	112	57.14	7	3.57	1,608	8.20	11	5.61	137.4
Eric Randall, Southern-B.R.	Sr.	11	255	159	62.35	6	2.35	1,877	7.36	13	5.10	136.3
Kerry Joseph, McNeese St.	Sr.	11	253	134	52.96	12	4.74	1,952	7.72	21	8.30	135.7
Steve Joyce, Cornell	Sr.	10	274	156	56.93	9	3.28	2,255	8.23	13	4.74	135.2
Shane Stafford, Connecticut	Fr.	10	182	99	54.40	8	4.40	1,492	8.20	11	6.04	134.4
Mike Fisher, Cal Poly SLO	Sr.	11	338	188	55.62	15	4.44	2,660	7.87	22	6.51	134.3
Maseo Bolin, North Caro. A&T	Sr.	11	299	162	54.18	5	1.67	2,276	7.61	17	5.69	133.5
Dan Sabella, Monmouth (N.J.)	So.	10	303	175	57.76	5	1.65	2,149	7.09	17	5.61	132.5
Jason McCullough, Brown	Jr.	10	351	190	54.13	12	3.42	2,406	6.85	22	6.27	125.6
Jason Miletic, Wagner	Jr.	9	201	112	55.72	6	2.99	1,321	6.57	12	5.97	124.7
Grailyn Pratt, Jackson St.	So.	11	345	191	55.36	15	4.35	2,372	6.88	21	6.09	124.5
Chad Pennington, Marshall	Fr.	11	236	140	59.32	9	3.81	1,650	6.99	10	4.24	124.4
Jeff Hecklinski, Western Ill.	So.	11	281	162	57.65	13	4.63	2,149	7.65	10	3.56	124.4
Antwan Chiles, Liberty	Sr.	11	285	157	55.09	8	2.81	2,026	7.11	12	4.21	123.1
Daunte Culpepper, Central Fla.	Fr.	11	294	168	57.14	10	3.40	2,071	7.04	12	4.08	123.0
Scott Satterfield, Appalachian St.	Sr.	10	168	94	55.95	5	2.98	1,160	6.90	7	4.17	121.8
Chris Hixson, Rhode Island	Jr.	11	330	190	57.58	14	4.24	2,250	6.82	15	4.55	121.4
Mike Cawley, James Madison	Sr.	11	361	196	54.29	11	3.05	2,459	6.81	17	4.71	121.0

Total Offense

	RUSHING				PASSING		TOTAL OFFENSE				
	Car.	Gain	Loss	Net	Att.	Yards	Plays	Yards	Avg.	TDR*	Yds.PG
Dave Dickenson, Montana	89	322	289	33	455	4,176	544	4,209	7.74	41	382.64
Kevin Foley, Boston U.	53	46	226	-180	476	3,192	529	3,012	5.69	17	273.82
Kharon Brown, Hofstra	151	1,133	156	977	320	1,860	471	2,837	6.02	24	257.91
Jason McCullough, Brown	82	328	177	151	351	2,406	433	2,557	5.91	25	255.70
Bob Aylsworth, Lehigh	54	93	182	-89	400	2,899	454	2,810	6.19	27	255.45
Tom Proudian, Iona	50	89	191	-102	367	2,396	417	2,294	5.50	14	254.89
Jeff Lewis, Northern Ariz.	51	225	105	120	313	2,426	364	2,546	6.99	24	254.60
Tony Hilde, Boise St.	114	606	231	375	279	2,386	393	2,761	7.03	27	251.00
David Williams, SW Tex. St.	41	102	111	-9	349	2,395	390	2,386	6.12	20	238.60
Michael Moore, Morgan St.	118	402	275	127	369	2,469	487	2,596	5.33	14	236.00
Grailyn Pratt, Jackson St.	140	476	277	199	345	2,372	485	2,571	5.30	24	233.73
Mike Fisher, Cal Poly SLO	39	95	194	-99	338	2,660	377	2,561	6.79	22	232.82
Joe Moorhead, Fordham	35	25	160	-135	426	2,687	461	2,552	5.54	15	232.00
Leo Hamlett, Delaware	158	919	217	702	174	1,849	332	2,551	7.68	24	231.91
Greg Ryan, East Tenn. St.	83	254	176	78	387	2,473	470	2,551	5.43	17	231.91
Nick Browder, Valparaiso	138	712	174	538	279	1,780	417	2,318	5.56	21	231.80
Tony Corbin, Cal St. S'mento	53	202	189	13	368	2,532	421	2,545	6.05	18	231.36
Todd Walker, Bethune-Cookman	28	57	55	2	423	2,535	451	2,537	5.63	19	230.64
Mike Cawley, James Madison	99	320	250	70	361	2,459	460	2,529	5.50	21	229.91
Jeff McCrone, Tenn.-Martin	34	49	91	-42	395	2,516	429	2,474	5.77	19	224.91

**Touchdowns responsible for are players' TDs scored and passed for.*

Photo from Boston University sports information

Boston University quarterback Kevin Foley ranked second in Division I-AA in total offense last season with an average of 273.8 yards per game.

Receptions Per Game

	1995 Class	G	Rec.	Yards	TD	Rec.PG
Ed Mantie, Boston U.	Sr.	11	81	943	1	7.36
Pokey Eckford, Weber St.	Sr.	11	77	1,074	6	7.00
Brian Klingerman, Lehigh	Sr.	11	77	1,040	10	7.00
Miles Macik, Pennsylvania	Sr.	10	68	816	5	6.80
Lenny Harris, Tenn.-Martin	Jr.	8	53	790	5	6.63
Tim Hilton, Cal St. Northridge	Jr.	10	64	565	1	6.40
Kobie Jenkins, Alcorn St.	Jr.	11	70	875	4	6.36
David Patten, Western Caro.	Sr.	10	59	887	7	5.90
Rod Marshall, Northern Ariz.	Sr.	11	64	732	9	5.82
Morris Nobles, Bethune-Cookman	Sr.	11	63	853	6	5.73
Joe Douglass, Montana	Jr.	11	63	832	7	5.73
Nikki Jackson, Tenn.-Martin	Jr.	11	63	425	0	5.73
Jon Peck, Cal Poly SLO	Jr.	11	62	1,009	8	5.64
Matt Wells, Montana	Sr.	11	61	1,008	10	5.55
Cy Butler, Rhode Island	Jr.	11	60	700	2	5.45
Ralph Dupont, Iona	So.	8	43	457	2	5.38
Kamil Loud, Cal Poly SLO	So.	11	57	1,098	9	5.18
Nick Johnson, Hofstra	Sr.	10	51	596	6	5.10
James Adderly, Bethune-Cookman	Fr.	11	56	861	7	5.09

Receiving Yards Per Game

	1995 Class	G	Rec.	Yards	TD	Yds.PG
Dedric Ward, Northern Iowa	Jr.	10	44	1,164	12	116.40
Mick Oliver, Cal St. Sacramento	Sr.	9	45	907	11	100.78
Kamil Loud, Cal Poly SLO	So.	11	57	1,098	9	99.82
Lenny Harris, Tenn.-Martin	Jr.	8	53	790	5	98.75
Pokey Eckford, Weber St.	Sr.	11	77	1,074	6	97.64
Brian Klingerman, Lehigh	Sr.	11	77	1,040	10	94.55
Jon Peck, Cal Poly SLO	Jr.	11	62	1,009	8	91.73
Matt Wells, Montana	Sr.	11	61	1,008	10	91.64
Scott Hinrichs, Valparaiso	Sr.	10	50	911	6	91.10
David Patten, Western Caro.	Sr.	10	59	887	7	88.70
Joey Stockton, Western Ky.	So.	10	33	863	6	86.30
Ed Mantie, Boston U.	Sr.	11	81	943	1	85.73
Dwight McKinzie, Idaho	Sr.	10	50	850	9	85.00
Demetric Mostiller, Middle Tenn. St.	Jr.	11	37	934	6	84.91
Miles Macik, Pennsylvania	Sr.	10	68	816	5	81.60
Terence Davis, McNeese St.	Sr.	11	46	890	13	80.91
Kobie Jenkins, Alcorn St.	Jr.	11	70	875	4	79.55
Mike Erhardt, Montana	Jr.	10	47	792	10	79.20
James Adderly, Bethune-Cookman	Fr.	11	56	861	7	78.27
Chris Love, Cal St. Northridge	Sr.	10	49	779	4	77.90

Interceptions

	1995 Class	G	Int.	Yards	TD	Int.PG
Picasso Nelson, Jackson St.	Sr.	9	8	101	0	.89
Damani Leech, Princeton	So.	10	8	17	0	.80
William Hampton, Murray St.	Jr.	11	8	280	4	.73
Mark Wallrapp, Yale	Sr.	10	7	65	0	.70
Adam Hunt, Marist	Fr.	9	6	107	1	.67
Chris Johnston, Georgetown	Sr.	9	6	68	1	.67
Darren Sharper, William & Mary	Jr.	11	7	144	1	.64
Helshma Northern, Southern-B.R.	Sr.	11	7	126	0	.64
Kalvin Robinson, Alcorn St.	Sr.	11	7	95	1	.64
Chris Carlson, Canisius	Jr.	10	6	43	0	.60
Doug Knopp, Cornell	Sr.	10	6	18	0	.60
Paul Serie, Siena	Fr.	9	5	27	0	.56
Robert Taylor, Tennessee Tech	Jr.	11	6	197	2	.55
Buck Phillips, Western Ill.	Sr.	11	6	121	1	.55
Quincy Waller, James Madison	Sr.	11	6	107	2	.55
Richard White, Alcorn St.	So.	11	6	84	0	.55
Darnell Hendricks, Southern Ill.	Sr.	11	6	70	1	.55
Tyree Talton, Northern Iowa	Fr.	11	6	57	0	.55
Derek Carter, Maine	So.	11	6	51	0	.55
Willie Oglesby, Bethune-Cookman	Jr.	11	6	41	0	.55
Mark Hopkins, Northeastern	Sr.	11	6	36	0	.55
Willie Parks, Southwest Mo. St.	Sr.	11	6	36	0	.55
Marvin Brown, Cal St. Sacramento	Sr.	11	6	28	1	.55

Scoring

	1995 Class	G	TD	XP	FG	Pts.	Pts.PG
Alcede Surtain, Alabama St.	Sr.	11	21	6	0	132	12.00
Tim Hall, Robert Morris	Sr.	10	20	0	0	120	12.00
Derrick Cullors, Murray St.	Sr.	11	20	0	0	120	10.91
William Murrell, Eastern Ky.	Jr.	10	18	0	0	108	10.80
Kito Lockwood, Wagner	Sr.	7	12	2	0	74	10.57
Rene Ingoglia, Massachusetts	Sr.	11	19	0	0	114	10.36
Thomas Haskins, Va. Military	Jr.	11	17	4	0	106	9.64
Melvin Williams, Southern-B.R.	So.	11	17	0	0	102	9.27
Chad Levitt, Cornell	Jr.	10	15	2	0	92	9.20
David Ettinger, Hofstra	Jr.	11	0	35	22	101	9.18
Michael Hicks, South Caro. St.	Sr.	10	14	4	0	88	8.80
Lawrence Worthington, Liberty	So.	11	16	0	0	96	8.73
Reggie Greene, Siena	So.	9	13	0	0	78	8.67
Carlos Leach, Southern-B.R.	Jr.	11	0	54	13	93	8.45
Chris Dill, Murray St.	Sr.	11	1	56	9	89	8.09
Kevin O'Leary, Northern Ariz.	Sr.	11	0	41	16	89	8.09
Tim Openlander, Marshall	Jr.	11	0	44	15	89	8.09
Larry Washington, Towson St.	Sr.	9	12	0	0	72	8.00
Jay Sutton, Appalachian St.	Jr.	11	0	39	16	87	7.91
Rabih Abdullah, Lehigh	Jr.	11	14	2	0	86	7.82

Photo from Southwest Texas State sports information

Southwest Texas State running back Claude Mathis averaged 205.5 all-purpose yards per game last season, good for fourth place on the list of division leaders.

All-Purpose Yards

	1995 Class	G	Rush	Rec.	PR	KOR	Total Yards	Yds.PG
Reggie Greene, Siena	So.	9	1,461	77	53	363	1,954	217.11
Derrick Cullors, Murray St.	Sr.	11	1,765	312	0	201	2,278	207.09
Clarence Matthews, Northwestern St.	Jr.	11	1,384	194	145	554	2,277	207.00
Claude Mathis, Southwest Tex. St.	So.	11	1,286	315	352	308	2,261	205.55
Joey Stockton, Western Ky.	So.	10	46	863	147	934	1,990	199.00
Thomas Haskins, Va. Military	Jr.	11	1,548	33	0	553	2,134	194.00
Tim Hall, Robert Morris	Sr.	10	1,572	333	0	0	1,905	190.50
Kito Lockwood, Wagner	Sr.	7	1,018	187	0	127	1,332	190.29
Rabih Abdullah, Lehigh	Jr.	11	1,536	382	0	0	1,918	174.36
Arnold Mickens, Butler	Sr.	10	1,558	40	0	87	1,685	168.50
Alfredo Anderson, Idaho St.	Jr.	11	1,192	393	10	218	1,813	164.82
Ozzie Young, Valparaiso	Sr.	10	524	255	160	690	1,629	162.90
Andre Pam, Maine	Jr.	11	1,250	89	0	416	1,755	159.55
Dione Tyler, Southeast Mo. St.	Sr.	11	1,005	353	178	204	1,740	158.18
Michael Stewart, Cal St. Sacramento	Jr.	11	1,161	121	0	425	1,707	155.18
Chad Levitt, Cornell	Jr.	10	1,428	122	0	0	1,550	155.00
William Murrell, Eastern Ky.	Jr.	10	982	76	73	403	1,534	153.40
Brigham Lyons, Middle Tenn. St.	Sr.	11	876	213	57	541	1,687	153.36
Bill Green, Duquesne	Sr.	10	1,427	95	0	0	1,522	152.20
Archie Amerson, Northern Ariz.	Jr.	11	1,117	222	0	294	1,633	148.45

Punt Returns

(Min. 1.2 per game)	1995 Class	No.	Yds.	TD	Avg.
Reggie Barlow, Alabama St.	Sr.	12	249	1	20.75
Claude Mathis, Southwest Tex. St.	So.	20	352	0	17.60
Roy Hanks, Columbia	So.	20	320	2	16.00
Dexter Dawson, Ga. Southern	Sr.	17	271	1	15.94
William Hampton, Murray St.	Jr.	24	344	1	14.33
Cedrick Buchannon, Ala.-Birmingham	Sr.	23	312	2	13.57
Cy Butler, Rhode Island	Jr.	31	404	3	13.03
Jason Gaines, Texas Southern	Sr.	23	288	0	12.52
Keith James, Grambling	Sr.	17	205	0	12.06
Buck Phillips, Western Ill.	Sr.	16	192	1	12.00
Patrick Plott, Jacksonville St.	Fr.	14	168	1	12.00
Reggie Fowler, Southern Ill.	So.	27	322	0	11.93
Tim Martin, Marshall	Jr.	33	393	1	11.91
Ricky Ellis, St. Mary's (Cal.)	Jr.	17	201	1	11.82
Cedric Redden, Howard	So.	32	377	1	11.78
Andrew McFadden, Liberty	Jr.	26	306	2	11.77
Marvin Brown, Cal St. Sacramento	Sr.	15	172	0	11.47
Maurice Stringer, Troy St.	Jr.	32	362	0	11.31
Dione Tyler, Southeast Mo. St.	Sr.	16	178	1	11.13
Darren Sharper, William & Mary	Jr.	30	333	0	11.10

Punting

(Min. 3.6 per game)	1995 Class	No.	Avg.
Kevin O'Leary, Northern Ariz.	Sr.	44	42.75
Marc Collins, Eastern Ky.	Sr.	43	42.72
Josh Siefken, Tenn.-Chatt.	Sr.	60	41.40
Craig VanWoerkom, Southern Utah	Sr.	62	41.13
Chris Hurst, Southwest Mo. St.	Sr.	68	41.12
Brandon Thomas, Middle Tenn. St.	So.	64	41.08
Todd Kurz, Illinois St.	Jr.	70	41.01
Cory Collins, East Tenn. St.	Sr.	50	40.86
Eric Colvard, Liberty	Sr.	41	40.73
James Ferrell, Idaho St.	So.	59	40.66
Tom Antongiovanni, St. Mary's (Cal.)	So.	42	40.55
Justin Spiva, Idaho	Fr.	51	40.27
Scott Holmes, Samford	Sr.	52	40.25
Mark Gagliano, Southern Ill.	Jr.	74	40.15
Steve Fill, William & Mary	Fr.	40	39.88
Andre Seoldo, Northeastern	Sr.	74	39.86
Ken Hinsley, Western Caro.	Fr.	60	39.83
Joe Lafirenza, Cal St. Northridge	Jr.	43	39.77
James Tuthill, Cal Poly SLO	So.	47	39.77
Nelson Garner, James Madison	So.	62	39.76

Kickoff Returns

(Min. 1.2 per game)	1995 Class	No.	Yds.	TD	Avg.
Josh Cole, Furman	Jr.	17	546	1	32.12
Jermine Sharp, Southern-B.R.	So.	16	504	2	31.50
Kenny Bynum, South Caro. St.	Jr.	13	389	0	29.92
Karlton Carpenter, Southern Ill.	Fr.	14	401	1	28.64
Ricky Ellis, St. Mary's (Cal.)	Jr.	14	399	2	28.50
Kenyatta Sparks, Southern-B.R.	Sr.	15	424	1	28.27
James Griffith, Samford	Fr.	18	479	1	26.61
Buck Phillips, Western Ill.	Sr.	23	610	0	26.52
Maurice Sydnor, Towson St.	Jr.	14	371	1	26.50
Garrick Haltiwanger, Citadel	Jr.	14	370	1	26.43
Dexter Dawson, Ga. Southern	Sr.	15	389	0	25.93
Tom Bernardo, Canisius	Jr.	16	407	0	25.44
Clarence Matthews, Northwestern St.	Jr.	22	554	0	25.18
D'athony Cameron, Morgan St.	Sr.	19	467	1	24.58
Anthony Taylor, Northern Iowa	Sr.	14	343	0	24.50
Joe Rosato, Duquesne	So.	13	318	1	24.46
Reggie Greene, Siena	So.	15	363	2	24.20
Eric Anderson, Sam Houston St.	Sr.	15	362	0	24.13
Dwight McKinzie, Idaho	Sr.	12	289	0	24.08
Mark McCain, William & Mary	Sr.	17	409	1	24.06

Field Goals

	1995 Class	G	FGA	FG	Pct.	FGPG
David Ettinger, Hofstra	Jr.	11	33	22	.667	2.00
Todd Kurz, Illinois St.	Jr.	11	25	19	.760	1.73
Tom Allison, Indiana St.	Sr.	11	23	18	.783	1.64
Gerald Carlson, Buffalo	Jr.	11	22	17	.773	1.55
David Dearmas, Connecticut	Sr.	11	23	17	.739	1.55
Scott Shields, Weber St.	Fr.	11	18	16	.889	1.45
Kevin O'Leary, Northern Ariz.	Sr.	11	22	16	.727	1.45
Jay Sutton, Appalachian St.	Jr.	11	23	16	.696	1.45
Steve Largent, Eastern Ill.	Sr.	11	26	16	.615	1.45
Greg Erickson, Boise St.	Sr.	11	20	15	.750	1.36
Tim Openlander, Marshall	Jr.	11	20	15	.750	1.36
Brandon Hanes, Northeastern	So.	11	23	15	.652	1.36
Jeremiah Greathouse, Pennsylvania	So.	10	20	13	.650	1.30
John Coursey, James Madison	Jr.	11	14	14	1.000	1.27
Brian Shallcross, William & Mary	So.	11	19	14	.737	1.27
Wayne Boyer, Southwest Mo. St.	Jr.	11	24	14	.583	1.27
James Tuthill, Cal Poly SLO	So.	11	25	14	.560	1.27
Ryan Woolverton, Idaho	Sr.	10	18	12	.667	1.20
Carlos Leach, Southern-B.R.	Jr.	11	21	13	.619	1.18
Dave Regula, Dartmouth	So.	10	15	11	.733	1.10

1995 Division I-AA Team Leaders

Total Offense

	G	Plays	Yds.	Avg.	TD*	Yds.PG
Montana	11	820	5,637	6.9	60	512.45
Cal Poly SLO	11	812	5,455	6.7	50	495.91
Murray St.	11	782	4,959	6.3	49	450.82
Delaware	11	747	4,939	6.6	45	449.00
Hofstra	11	806	4,924	6.1	39	447.64
Weber St.	11	846	4,922	5.8	37	447.45
Northern Ariz.	11	793	4,891	6.2	49	444.64
Southern-B.R.	11	878	4,725	5.4	53	429.55
Lehigh	11	795	4,700	5.9	41	427.27
Dayton	11	755	4,667	6.2	57	424.27
Marshall	11	812	4,642	5.7	43	422.00
Cornell	10	746	4,199	5.6	34	419.90
Brown	10	791	4,169	5.3	36	416.90
Eastern Ky.	11	741	4,544	6.1	48	413.09
Troy St.	11	712	4,510	6.3	54	410.00
Boise St.	11	772	4,487	5.8	41	407.91
Stephen F. Austin	10	658	4,045	6.1	39	404.50
Monmouth (N.J.)	10	712	4,039	5.7	38	403.90
Connecticut	11	799	4,371	5.5	33	397.36
Hampton	11	779	4,363	5.6	44	396.64

**Touchdowns scored by rushing or passing only.*

Total Defense

	G	Plays	Yds.	Avg.	TD*	Yds.PG
Georgetown	9	580	1,948	3.4	12	216.4
Marshall	11	673	2,710	4.0	18	246.4
Monmouth (N.J.)	10	604	2,488	4.1	16	248.8
Wagner	9	533	2,262	4.2	25	251.3
Jackson St.	11	711	2,779	3.9	23	252.6
Murray St.	11	690	2,786	4.0	16	253.3
Towson St.	10	671	2,546	3.8	16	254.6
New Hampshire	11	727	2,813	3.9	20	255.7
Canisius	10	650	2,690	4.1	21	269.0
Duquesne	10	603	2,691	4.5	19	269.1
Drake	10	631	2,717	4.3	13	271.7
McNeese St.	11	736	2,993	4.1	10	272.1
Troy St.	11	699	2,996	4.3	18	272.4
Robert Morris	10	657	2,761	4.2	20	276.1
Dartmouth	10	689	2,799	4.1	17	279.9
Bucknell	11	768	3,100	4.0	21	281.8
Northern Iowa	11	729	3,100	4.3	15	281.8
Dayton	11	709	3,100	4.4	23	281.8
Hampton	11	749	3,104	4.1	30	282.2
Indiana St.	11	751	3,109	4.1	20	282.6

**Touchdowns scored by rushing or passing only.*

Rushing Offense

	G	Car.	Yds.	Avg.	TD	Yds.PG
Massachusetts	11	626	3,328	5.3	36	302.5
Western Ky.	10	610	2,752	4.5	24	275.2
Delaware	11	556	3,010	5.4	30	273.6
Troy St.	11	519	2,985	5.8	37	271.4
Hofstra	11	470	2,879	6.1	22	261.7
Appalachian St.	11	590	2,874	4.9	31	261.3
Murray St.	11	537	2,804	5.2	33	254.9
Morehead St.	10	536	2,452	4.6	19	245.2
Jacksonville St.	11	601	2,653	4.4	22	241.2
Citadel	11	537	2,651	4.9	19	241.0
Eastern Ky.	11	508	2,639	5.2	35	239.9
South Caro. St.	10	444	2,377	5.4	23	237.7
Hampton	11	539	2,609	4.8	29	237.2
Wagner	9	468	2,134	4.6	23	237.1
Maine	11	505	2,596	5.1	16	236.0
Alabama St.	11	461	2,586	5.6	35	235.1
Wofford	11	620	2,582	4.2	20	234.7
Ga. Southern	11	589	2,572	4.4	24	233.8
Dayton	11	540	2,554	4.7	38	232.2
Eastern Ill.	11	581	2,539	4.4	21	230.8

Rushing Defense

	G	Car.	Yds.	Avg.	TD	Yds.PG
McNeese St.	11	317	670	2.1	4	60.9
Georgetown	9	336	614	1.8	7	68.2
Wagner	9	288	642	2.2	9	71.3
Idaho	10	342	812	2.4	7	81.2
Florida A&M	11	371	924	2.5	13	84.0
Towson St.	10	374	963	2.6	10	96.3
Hofstra	11	424	1,072	2.5	6	97.5
Dartmouth	10	368	985	2.7	5	98.5
Drake	10	353	987	2.8	6	98.7
Eastern Ill.	11	378	1,125	3.0	8	102.3
Northern Ariz.	11	372	1,128	3.0	13	102.5
Delaware	11	420	1,161	2.8	10	105.5
New Hampshire	11	443	1,183	2.7	12	107.5
Princeton	10	378	1,089	2.9	8	108.9
Murray St.	11	368	1,214	3.3	10	110.4
Marshall	11	417	1,226	2.9	9	111.5
Jackson St.	11	419	1,250	3.0	9	113.6
St. Mary's (Cal.)	10	342	1,147	3.4	15	114.7
Marist	10	451	1,165	2.6	13	116.5
Stephen F. Austin	10	377	1,167	3.1	5	116.7

Scoring Offense

	G	Pts.	Avg.
Montana	11	467	42.5
Southern-B.R.	11	445	40.5
Troy St.	11	425	38.6
Dayton	11	422	38.4
Murray St.	11	421	38.3
Cal Poly SLO	11	411	37.4
Northern Ariz.	11	403	36.6
Hofstra	11	376	34.2
Marshall	11	368	33.5
St. Mary's (Cal.)	10	334	33.4
Delaware	11	367	33.4
Eastern Ky.	11	363	33.0
Boise St.	11	361	32.8
Liberty	11	352	32.0
Stephen F. Austin	10	317	31.7
Alabama St.	11	348	31.6
McNeese St.	11	346	31.5
Hampton	11	342	31.1
Grambling	11	340	30.9
James Madison	11	337	30.6

Scoring Defense

	G	Pts.	Avg.
McNeese St.	11	98	8.9
Hofstra	11	112	10.2
Murray St.	11	114	10.4
Drake	10	104	10.4
Georgetown	9	99	11.0
Monmouth (N.J.)	10	118	11.8
Princeton	10	124	12.4
Stephen F. Austin	10	126	12.6
Troy St.	11	144	13.1
Dartmouth	10	137	13.7
Evansville	10	139	13.9
Duquesne	10	143	14.3
Northern Iowa	11	161	14.6
Northern Ariz.	11	163	14.8
Eastern Ky.	11	164	14.9
Towson St.	10	150	15.0
Eastern Ill.	11	167	15.2
Jackson St.	11	168	15.3
Delaware	11	169	15.4
Ga. Southern	11	171	15.5
New Hampshire	11	171	15.5

Passing Offense

	G	Att.	Cmp.	Int.	Pct.	Yards	Yds./ Att.	TD	Yds.PG
Montana	11	500	336	12	67.2	4,490	9.0	38	408.2
Cal Poly SLO	11	441	253	16	57.4	3,794	8.6	33	344.9
Weber St.	11	468	284	12	60.7	3,640	7.8	26	330.9
Boston U.	11	497	298	18	60.0	3,299	6.6	16	299.9
Tenn.-Martin	11	471	287	23	60.9	3,061	6.5	20	278.3
Lehigh	11	413	248	11	60.0	3,022	7.3	28	274.7
Iona	9	389	205	25	52.7	2,423	6.2	14	269.2
Fordham	11	457	245	14	53.6	2,854	6.2	16	259.5
Alcorn St.	11	422	216	18	51.2	2,764	6.5	12	251.3
Cal St. Sacramento	11	393	188	17	47.8	2,762	7.0	22	251.1
Brown	10	379	201	14	53.0	2,510	6.6	24	251.0
Bethune-Cookman	11	462	226	17	48.9	2,745	5.9	21	249.5
Southwest Tex. St.	11	419	209	16	49.9	2,729	6.5	19	248.1
Northern Ariz.	11	348	231	5	66.4	2,638	7.6	23	239.8
Northern Iowa	11	250	139	7	55.6	2,616	10.5	18	237.8
Boise St.	11	322	178	7	55.3	2,614	8.1	19	237.6
Idaho St.	11	409	219	13	53.5	2,593	6.3	21	235.7
Southern Utah	11	354	189	16	53.4	2,586	7.3	12	235.1
Idaho	10	312	162	11	51.9	2,347	7.5	20	234.7
Southwest Mo. St.	11	382	198	16	51.8	2,581	6.8	9	234.6

Photo from Jackson State sports information

Safety Picasso Nelson's eight interceptions helped Jackson State post the sixth best pass efficiency defense rating (86.9) in Division I-AA last season.

Pass Efficiency Defense

	G	Att.	Cmp.	Cmp. Pct.	Int.	Int. Pct.	Yards	Yds./ Att.	TD	TD Pct.	Rating Points
Canisius	10	203	81	39.90	21	10.34	1,010	4.98	5	2.46	69.13
Murray St.	11	322	139	43.17	19	5.90	1,572	4.88	6	1.86	78.52
Georgetown	9	244	104	42.62	17	6.97	1,334	5.47	5	2.05	81.38
Dayton	11	261	109	41.76	14	5.36	1,396	5.35	7	2.68	84.81
Liberty	11	246	98	39.84	16	6.50	1,355	5.51	9	3.66	85.17
Jackson St.	11	292	133	45.55	27	9.25	1,529	5.24	14	4.79	86.86
Hofstra	11	381	175	45.93	20	5.25	2,141	5.62	7	1.84	88.70
Robert Morris	10	252	111	44.05	18	7.14	1,403	5.57	10	3.97	89.62
William & Mary	11	281	141	50.18	21	7.47	1,603	5.70	7	2.49	91.37
McNeese St.	11	419	206	49.16	17	4.06	2,323	5.54	6	1.43	92.35
Duquesne	10	240	116	48.33	13	5.42	1,332	5.55	6	2.50	92.37
Northern Iowa	11	300	145	48.33	12	4.00	1,703	5.68	5	1.67	93.52
Bucknell	11	289	144	49.83	16	5.54	1,536	5.31	9	3.11	93.68
Towson St.	10	297	148	49.83	11	3.70	1,583	5.33	6	2.02	93.86
James Madison	11	337	169	50.15	16	4.75	1,878	5.57	7	2.08	94.32
Grambling	11	316	157	49.68	19	6.01	1,817	5.75	9	2.85	95.36
Princeton	10	310	158	50.97	22	7.10	1,939	6.25	6	1.94	95.70
Troy St.	11	246	117	47.56	16	6.50	1,557	6.33	6	2.44	95.77
Northeastern	11	238	110	46.22	14	5.88	1,503	6.32	6	2.52	95.82
San Diego	10	300	146	48.67	14	4.67	1,718	5.73	8	2.67	96.24

Net Punting

	Punts	Avg.	No. Ret.	Yds. Ret.	Net Avg.
Eastern Ky.	43	42.7	21	100	40.4
Northern Ariz.	44	42.8	19	124	39.9
Troy St.	38	40.5	16	89	38.2
Sam Houston St.	65	39.6	24	156	37.2
Howard	67	39.1	27	147	36.9
Southwest Mo. St.	69	40.5	21	255	36.8
Montana	43	38.9	14	94	36.7
McNeese St.	56	38.8	26	124	36.6
Stephen F. Austin	39	37.1	13	20	36.6
Illinois St.	70	41.0	26	319	36.5
Idaho	63	38.8	26	156	36.4
Appalachian St.	47	38.5	16	101	36.3
Ga. Southern	49	37.2	12	43	36.3
Samford	52	40.3	27	216	36.1
Northwestern St.	46	38.3	18	108	36.0
San Diego	74	38.0	22	153	35.9
Boise St.	57	38.0	22	120	35.9
Cal Poly SLO	48	39.7	22	183	35.9
Murray St.	46	38.1	19	108	35.7
James Madison	66	37.8	23	137	35.7

Punt Returns

	G	No.	Yds.	TD	Avg.
Southwest Tex. St.	11	23	443	0	19.3
Alabama St.	11	27	432	1	16.0
Columbia	10	24	377	2	15.7
Samford	11	12	184	1	15.3
Ga. Southern	11	25	347	1	13.9
Charleston So.	11	14	185	2	13.2
Ala.-Birmingham	11	24	312	2	13.0
Murray St.	11	32	402	1	12.6
Southern Ill.	11	30	372	1	12.4
Western Ill.	11	22	272	1	12.4
Morgan St.	11	16	195	0	12.2
James Madison	11	23	278	2	12.1
Howard	11	39	471	4	12.1
Rhode Island	11	36	430	4	11.9
Troy St.	11	33	391	0	11.8
St. Mary's (Cal.)	10	20	233	1	11.6
Marshall	11	34	393	1	11.6
Villanova	11	29	334	1	11.5
Grambling	11	21	239	0	11.4
Jacksonville St.	11	28	313	2	11.2

Kickoff Returns

	G	No.	Yds.	TD	Avg.
Southern-B.R.	11	39	1,054	3	27.0
Idaho	10	29	740	1	25.5
Liberty	11	30	745	2	24.8
Furman	11	37	904	1	24.4
San Diego	10	32	767	1	24.0
Sam Houston St.	10	34	790	0	23.2
St. Mary's (Cal.)	10	36	826	2	22.9
Citadel	11	45	1,028	1	22.8
Northern Iowa	11	32	726	0	22.7
Canisius	10	35	793	0	22.7
Marshall	11	27	609	0	22.6
Western Ill.	11	41	921	0	22.5
Murray St.	11	24	535	0	22.3
Cal Poly SLO	11	37	818	0	22.1
Troy St.	11	28	610	0	21.8

	G	No.	Yds.	TD	Avg.
Howard	11	44	958	1	21.8
Dayton	11	37	803	0	21.7
Tennessee Tech	11	49	1,044	0	21.3
Stephen F. Austin	10	29	616	0	21.2
Appalachian St.	11	30	637	0	21.2
Northern Ariz.	11	30	637	0	21.2

Turnover Margin

	TURNOVERS GAINED			TURNOVERS LOST			Margin/
	Fum.	Int.	Total	Fum.	Int.	Total	Game
Princeton	15	22	37	10	5	15	2.20
Eastern Ill.	15	19	34	6	4	10	2.18
Hofstra	12	20	32	6	3	9	2.09
Southern-B.R.	15	21	36	10	6	16	1.82
Middle Tenn. St.	21	17	38	6	13	19	1.73
Jackson St.	20	27	47	14	15	29	1.64
Troy St.	17	16	33	11	5	16	1.55
Monmouth (N.J.)	14	13	27	7	5	12	1.50
Jacksonville St.	16	17	33	11	6	17	1.45
St. Mary's (Cal.)	16	13	29	8	7	15	1.40
Northern Ariz.	23	9	32	13	5	18	1.27
Robert Morris	13	18	31	10	9	19	1.20
Northeastern	14	14	28	11	5	16	1.09
Ga. Southern	11	18	29	11	7	18	1.00
San Diego	16	14	30	17	3	20	1.00
Florida A&M	14	18	32	12	10	22	.91
Howard	22	14	36	13	13	26	.91
McNeese St.	23	17	40	18	12	30	.91
Dartmouth	17	10	27	9	9	18	.90
Liberty	13	16	29	11	9	20	.82

Longest Division I-AA Plays of 1995

Rushing

Player, Team (Opponent)	Yards
Pat Williams, Delaware (West Chester)	97
Brett Chappell, Western Caro. (Elon)	95
Kevin Francis, Monmouth, N.J. (St. John's, N.Y.)	92
Nakia Lumar, Nicholls St. (Samford)	91
Kenny Bynum, South Caro. St. (Morgan St.)	89
Alfredo Anderson, Idaho St. (Southern Utah)	85
Dione Tyler, Southeast Mo. St. (Eastern Ky.)	85
Alcede Surtain, Alabama St. (Alabama A&M)	84
Frank Alessio, Massachusetts (Boston U.)	84
Tim Hall, Robert Morris (Monmouth, N.J.)	82
Michael Hicks, South Caro. St. (Charleston So.)	82

Passing

Passer-Receiver, Team (Opponent)	Yards
Derek Jensen-Jason Cannon, Southwest Mo. St. (Eastern Ill.)	98
Jonathan Quinn-Dee Mostiller, Middle Tenn. St. (Tennessee Tech)	98
Chris Berg-Dedric Ward, Northern Iowa (Western Ill.)	96
Dave Dickenson-Matt Wells, Montana (Boise St.)	90
Keith Poindexter-Dewayne Barnett, Mississippi Val. (Texas Southern)	89
Steve Joyce-Steve Busch, Cornell (Brown)	88
Bryan Martin-Pokey Eckford, Weber St. (St. Mary's, Cal.)	88
Bryan Martin–Joel Pelagio-Williams, Weber St. (Cal Poly SLO)	87
Jonathan Quinn-Dee Mostiller, Middle Tenn. St. (Tenn.-Martin)	*87

*Did not score.

Interception Returns

Player, Team (Opponent)	Yards
Robert Taylor, Tennessee Tech (Southeast Mo. St.)	96
Dana Lyons, Pennsylvania (Lafayette)	94
Joe Wright, Hofstra (Fordham)	90
Jimmy Clark, Boise St. (Portland St.)	81
Bill Randles, Illinois St. (Northern Iowa)	*81

Player, Team (Opponent)	Yards
Ed Burman, Bucknell (Fordham)	79
Raasan Haralson, Southern-B.R. (Texas Southern)	79
Jason Ozolins, Canisius (Siena)	77
Mark Pryce, Wagner (Robert Morris)	*77
Gabe Garcia, Fordham (Lafayette)	77

*Did not score.

Punt Returns

Player, Team (Opponent)	Yards
Andrew McFadden, Liberty (Delaware St.)	93
Patrick Plott, Jacksonville St. (Southwest Mo. St.)	93
Kirk Pointer, Austin Peay (Tennessee Tech)	86
Reggie Barlow, Alabama St. (Alabama A&M)	86
Dexter Dawson, Ga. Southern (Citadel)	85
Cy Butler, Rhode Island (Delaware St.)	83
Cedrick Buchannon, Ala.-Birmingham (Wofford)	77
Winston October, Richmond (Citadel)	74
Dione Tyler, Southeast Mo. St. (Tennessee St.)	73
Tony McDonald, Southeast Mo. St. (Tenn.-Martin)	70

Kickoff Returns

Player, Team (Opponent)	Yards
Joe Rosato, Duquesne (Robert Morris)	100
Chris Watson, Eastern Ill. (Northern Iowa)	100
Shaun Marshall, James Madison (Boston U.)	98
Bert Rich, Maine (Central Fla.)	97
Karlton Carpenter, Southern Ill. (Southeast Mo. St.)	96
Evan Hlavacek, San Diego (Cal Lutheran)	95
Andre Pam, Maine (Lock Haven)	94
Josh Cole, Furman (Va. Military)	93
Larry Leith, Fordham (Bucknell)	90
Ryan Ikebe, Boise St. (Eastern Wash.)	90

Field Goals

Player, Team (Opponent)	Yards
Kevin O'Leary, Northern Ariz. (Montana)	55
David Ettinger, Hofstra (Lafayette)	54
Frank Venezia, Villanova (Connecticut)	53
Gerald Carlson, Buffalo (Villanova)	52
Matt Waller, Northern Iowa (Indiana St.)	52
Ryan Woolverton, Idaho (Weber St.)	52
Jason Haslam, Southern Utah (Idaho St.)	51
Gerald Carlson, Buffalo (Massachusetts)	51
Tim Openlander, Marshall (East Tenn. St.)	51
David Ettinger, Hofstra (Rhode Island)	51
Todd Kurz, Illinois St. (Youngstown St.)	51
David Ettinger, Hofstra (Marshall)	51

Punts

Player, Team (Opponent)	Yards
Josh Siefken, Tenn.-Chatt. (Furman)	77
Barry Cantrell, Fordham (Dartmouth)	73
Nelson Garner, James Madison (Boston U.)	73
Todd Kurz, Illinois St. (Ohio)	71
Marc Collins, Eastern Ky. (Tennessee Tech)	70
Kevin O'Leary, Northern Ariz. (Weber St.)	69
Charlie Pierce, Central Fla. (Maine)	69
Cory Collins, East Tenn. St. (Appalachian St.)	67
Josh Siefken, Tenn.-Chatt. (Appalachian St.)	67
Clifford Green, Tennessee St. (Austin Peay)	66

Fumble Returns

Player, Team (Opponent)	Yards
Marcus LeBlanc, McNeese St. (Youngstown St.)	100
Tim Denton, Sam Houston St. (Southwest Tex. St.)	98
Clifford Green, Tennessee St. (Florida A&M)	94
Richard Freeman, Tennessee St. (Tenn.-Martin)	85
Maurice Gerald, Charleston So. (Wofford)	*85
Greg Klund, Southeast Mo. St. (Southern Ill.)	80
Brian Regan/Terrance Browning, Holy Cross (Brown)	77
Eric Austin, Jackson St. (Alabama A&M)	75
Arthur Griffin, Mississippi Val. (Alcorn St.)	70

*Did not score.

Photo from Lane sports information

Running back Fred Lane (6) was much more than just a namesake for Lane College last year. He finished second in Division II rushing with an average of 183.3 yards per game.

1995 Division II Individual Leaders

Rushing

	1995 Class	G	Car.	Yards	TD	Yds.PG
Richard Huntley, Winston-Salem	Sr.	10	273	1,889	16	188.9
Fred Lane, Lane	Jr.	10	273	1,833	19	183.3
Randy Martin, St. Cloud St.	Jr.	9	265	1,426	10	158.4
Chris Pulliams, Ferris St.	Jr.	10	262	1,489	19	148.9
Steve Papin, Portland St.	Sr.	11	257	1,619	18	147.2
Mesiah Porter, Fort Valley St.	Jr.	11	274	1,537	5	139.7
Jarrett Anderson, Truman St.	Jr.	11	232	1,502	16	136.5
Antonio Leroy, Albany St. (Ga.)	Jr.	11	219	1,430	21	130.0
Murray Dillon, Western St.	Sr.	10	222	1,291	10	129.1
John Fisher, Mo. Western St.	Sr.	10	240	1,274	11	127.4
Steve Gorrie, Presbyterian	Sr.	11	247	1,312	16	119.3
Gerald Thompson, Edinboro	Fr.	10	205	1,191	9	119.1
Keath Porterfield, Newberry	Jr.	11	244	1,307	14	118.8
Chris Ryan, Clark Atlanta	Sr.	10	169	1,185	8	118.5
Derrick Johnson, Eastern N.M.	Jr.	11	238	1,265	12	115.0
Tim McGlynn, Moorhead St.	So.	10	163	1,143	6	114.3
Mike Lodice, Neb.-Kearney	Fr.	8	159	912	11	114.0
Rashid Thomas, American Int'l	Sr.	10	224	1,127	6	112.7
Corey Campbell, Chadron St.	Sr.	10	233	1,123	7	112.3
Joel Rogers, Morningside	So.	11	263	1,229	5	111.7
Chris Chachere, Savannah St.	Sr.	11	247	1,221	14	111.0
Michael McSharry, Stonehill	Jr.	10	223	1,106	6	110.6
Brian Ihlefeld, Sacred Heart	Jr.	10	207	1,057	7	105.7
Marcus Bishop, Wayne St. (Neb.)	Jr.	10	163	1,031	14	103.1
Marvin Melton, Lenoir-Rhyne	Sr.	10	240	1,028	11	102.8
Albert Bland, Mo. Southern St.	Sr.	10	216	1,018	16	101.8
Sheldon Cooper, West Va. Wesleyan	Jr.	10	209	1,000	9	100.0
Ed Christian, West Liberty St.	Sr.	9	155	898	8	99.8
Darrien Peoples, Kutztown	Jr.	10	226	988	7	98.8
Billy Smith, Pace	Jr.	10	225	976	7	97.6

Passing Efficiency

(Min. 15 att. per game)	1995 Class	G	Att.	Cmp.	Pct.	Int.	Yards	TD	Rating Points
Shawn Behr, Fort Hays St.	Sr.	11	318	191	60.0	6	3,158	31	171.9
Bill Love, Ferris St.	Sr.	10	271	170	62.7	4	2,469	19	159.4
Jarrod Furgason, Fairmont St.	So.	10	349	222	63.6	8	2,696	35	157.0
Greg Moylan, Millersville	Jr.	10	275	175	63.6	6	2,310	22	156.2
Chris Shipe, Humboldt St.	Jr.	9	224	149	66.5	5	2,025	9	151.3
Kevin Klancher, North Dak.	So.	10	206	125	60.6	8	1,693	18	150.8
Paul Kaiser, Central Mo. St.	Jr.	10	277	163	58.8	10	2,306	24	150.1
Mike Rymsha, Bentley	Sr.	10	202	120	59.4	7	1,718	16	150.0
Aaron Sparrow, Norfolk St.	Sr.	10	409	238	58.1	14	3,434	32	147.7
Scott Otis, Glenville St.	Sr.	10	344	205	59.5	8	2,784	22	144.0
Dan Field, Stonehill	Sr.	10	204	104	50.9	12	1,589	24	143.5
Glen McNamee, Bloomsburg	Jr.	11	222	127	57.2	10	1,884	15	141.8
Casey Bradshaw, Adams St.	So.	10	293	167	57.0	15	2,370	24	141.8
Jarrod DeGeorgia, Wayne St. (Neb.)	Jr.	8	225	142	63.1	6	1,773	12	141.6
Sultan Cooper, Albany St. (Ga.)	Sr.	11	209	104	49.7	8	1,718	19	141.2
Jason Richards, West Liberty St.	Sr.	10	221	116	52.4	12	1,896	18	140.6
Jason Davis, Western St.	Jr.	10	291	153	52.5	5	2,237	23	139.8
Chad Vogt, Slippery Rock	Jr.	11	282	167	59.2	10	2,188	19	139.5
Grady Benton, West Tex. A&M	Sr.	9	277	163	58.8	9	2,077	19	138.0
Mark Grieb, UC Davis	Jr.	10	286	163	56.9	6	2,226	17	137.7
Scott Kieser, Michigan Tech	Sr.	10	209	123	58.8	7	1,605	13	137.2
Kwame McKinnon, Grand Valley St.	Sr.	11	275	146	53.0	5	2,124	19	137.1
Tom Beck, Northern Colo.	Jr.	11	275	151	54.9	12	2,239	18	136.2
Nate Minnis, Truman St.	So.	11	210	119	56.6	9	1,750	11	135.4
Oktay Basci, Tex. A&M-Kingsville	So.	10	172	89	51.7	8	1,424	12	135.0
Lance Funderburk, Valdosta St.	Jr.	11	544	356	65.4	12	3,706	26	134.0
Chris Weibel, Clarion	Jr.	9	268	159	59.3	9	2,017	14	133.1
Eric Stockton, Ky. Wesleyan	Sr.	10	336	177	52.6	10	2,505	24	132.9
Timm Schroeder, Stony Brook	Sr.	10	296	168	56.7	14	2,029	25	132.7
Greg Teale, Northwest Mo. St.	Jr.	11	363	198	54.5	9	2,434	27	130.5

Total Offense

	1995 Class	G	Plays	Yards	Yds.PG
Aaron Sparrow, Norfolk St.	Sr.	10	464	3,300	330.0
Lance Funderburk, Valdosta St.	Jr.	11	581	3,549	322.6
Scott Otis, Glenville St.	Sr.	10	438	2,943	294.3
Pat Graham, Augustana (S.D.)	Jr.	10	477	2,830	283.0
Bob McLaughlin, Lock Haven	Sr.	11	576	3,092	281.1
Shawn Behr, Fort Hays St.	Sr.	11	398	3,070	279.1
John Hebgen, Mankato St.	Jr.	11	516	2,917	265.2
Jarrod Furgason, Fairmont St.	So.	10	383	2,615	261.5
Chad Roanhaus, N.M. Highlands	Fr.	11	466	2,800	254.5
Casey Bradshaw, Adams St.	So.	10	366	2,506	250.6
Kwame McKinnon, Grand Valley St.	Sr.	11	404	2,676	243.3
Eric Stockton, Ky. Wesleyan	Sr.	10	399	2,422	242.2
Alfred Montez, Western N.M.	Sr.	9	355	2,158	239.8
Bill Love, Ferris St.	Sr.	10	299	2,389	238.9
Greg Teale, Northwest Mo. St.	Jr.	11	451	2,612	237.5
Chris Weibel, Clarion	So.	9	351	2,133	237.0
Grady Benton, West Tex. A&M	Sr.	9	339	2,132	236.9
Greg Moylan, Millersville	Jr.	10	319	2,362	236.2
Rodney Granger, Virginia St.	Jr.	10	372	2,353	235.3
Paul Kaiser, Central Mo. St.	Jr.	10	317	2,310	231.0

Receptions Per Game

	1995 Class	G	Rec.	Yards	TD	Rec.PG
Sean Pender, Valdosta St.	Jr.	11	111	983	2	10.1
Jarett Vito, Emporia St.	Fr.	10	94	932	7	9.4
Chris Perry, Adams St.	Sr.	10	88	1,719	21	8.8
Carlos Ferralls, Glenville St.	So.	10	80	1,252	17	8.0
Jon Spinosa, Lock Haven	Sr.	10	80	613	0	8.0
Kevin Cannon, Millersville	Sr.	9	71	918	11	7.9
Kevin Swayne, Wayne St. (Neb.)	Jr.	9	65	818	4	7.2
Glenn Saenz, Stony Brook	Jr.	10	69	947	13	6.9
Matt McPhie, Augustana (S.D.)	Jr.	9	62	779	6	6.9
Preston Cunningham, Southwest St.	Sr.	8	53	514	4	6.6
James Roe, Norfolk St.	Sr.	10	64	1,248	15	6.4
Sedrick Robinson, Ky. Wesleyan	Jr.	10	64	1,105	17	6.4
Derek Woods, Emporia St	Sr.	10	63	966	8	6.3
John Davis, Mankato St.	Jr.	11	68	865	8	6.2
Brian Penecale, West Chester	Sr.	10	61	901	14	6.1
Anthony Simpson, Central Mo. St.	Sr.	9	54	673	7	6.0
Bobby Barnette, New Haven	Sr.	10	59	582	4	5.9
Jeff McElroy, North Dak.	Sr.	10	58	867	11	5.8
Ted Murphy, Fairmont St.	Jr.	10	58	620	9	5.8
Robert Ferrera, Colorado Mines	Jr.	10	57	661	5	5.7

Receiving Yards Per Game

	1995 Class	G	Rec.	Yards	TD	Yds.PG
Chris Perry, Adams St.	Sr.	10	88	1,719	21	171.9
Carlos Ferralls, Glenville St.	So.	10	80	1,252	17	125.2
James Roe, Norfolk St.	Sr.	10	64	1,248	15	124.8
Michael Dritlein, Washburn	Sr.	10	48	1,112	8	111.2
Sedrick Robinson, Ky. Wesleyan	Jr.	10	64	1,105	17	110.5
Lance Schwindt, Fort Hays St.	Sr.	11	53	1,148	14	104.4
Kevin Cannon, Millersville	Sr.	9	71	918	11	102.0
Bryan McGinty, Lock Haven	Jr.	11	62	1,081	5	98.3
Derek Woods, Emporia St	Sr.	10	63	966	8	96.6
Ryan Gentry, Western St.	Sr.	10	53	959	10	95.9
Cory Brooks, Chadron St.	Sr.	10	56	958	4	95.8
Chad Walker, West Ga.	Sr.	10	56	955	7	95.5
Glenn Saenz, Stony Brook	Jr.	10	69	947	13	94.7
Brian Dugan, West Va. Wesleyan	Sr.	10	51	944	9	94.4
Jarett Vito, Emporia St.	Fr.	10	94	932	7	93.2
Buck Eardley, Bloomsburg	Sr.	11	58	1,006	10	91.5
Floyd Lanier, Virginia St.	Jr.	10	56	914	9	91.4
Kevin Swayne, Wayne St. (Neb.)	Jr.	9	65	818	4	90.9
Kahn Powell, Fort Hays St.	Sr.	11	59	993	6	90.3
Brian Penecale, West Chester	Sr.	10	61	901	14	90.1

All-Purpose Yards

	1995 Class	G	Rush	Rec.	PR	KOR	Total Yards	Yds.PG
Steve Papin, Portland St.	Sr.	11	1,619	525	1	252	2,397	217.91
Fred Lane, Lane	Jr.	10	1,833	209	0	0	2,042	204.20
Richard Huntley, Winston-Salem	Sr.	10	1,889	89	0	0	1,978	197.80
Mike Smith, Neb.-Kearney	So.	10	251	766	384	568	1,969	196.90
Rashid Thomas, American Int'l	Sr.	10	1,127	193	0	620	1,940	194.00
Kevin Cannon, Millersville	Sr.	9	-17	918	277	463	1,641	182.33
Jermaine Rucker, UC Davis	Jr.	10	916	162	0	744	1,822	182.20
Chris Pulliams, Ferris St.	Jr.	10	1,489	296	0	0	1,785	178.50
Jermaine Hill, Neb.-Omaha	Sr.	11	805	86	324	721	1,936	176.00
Chris Perry, Adams St.	Sr.	10	8	1,719	17	0	1,744	174.40
Mark Erickson, Mankato St.	Sr.	11	1,019	482	14	347	1,862	169.27
Kahn Powell, Fort Hays St.	Sr.	11	0	993	237	610	1,840	167.27
Diriki Mose, Grand Valley St.	Sr.	11	-10	931	380	511	1,812	164.73
Randy Martin, St. Cloud St.	Jr.	9	1,426	18	0	37	1,481	164.56
Sedrick Robinson, Ky. Wesleyan	Jr.	10	-2	1,105	64	403	1,570	157.00
Chris Ryan, Clark Atlanta	Sr.	10	1,185	73	76	212	1,546	154.60
Michael McSharry, Stonehill	Jr.	10	1,106	82	151	198	1,537	153.70
Antonio Leroy, Albany St. (Ga.)	Jr.	11	1,430	240	0	0	1,670	151.82
John Fisher, Mo. Western St.	Sr.	10	1,274	163	19	12	*1,493	149.30
Jarrett Anderson, Truman St.	Jr.	11	1,502	126	0	6	1,634	148.55

**Includes 25 yards in interception returns.*

Photo from Portland State sports information

Portland State running back Steve Papin led Division II with an average of 217.9 all-purpose yards per game last year.

Interceptions

	1995 Class	G	No.	Yards	Int.PG
Chenelle Jones, Western N.M.	Sr.	8	7	61	.9
Telley Priester, Virginia St.	So.	10	8	104	.8
Mitch Mason, Mo. Western St.	Sr.	11	8	126	.7
Pat Davis, Neb.-Omaha	Jr.	11	8	18	.7
Dale Reed, Millersville	Jr.	10	7	80	.7
Roderick Johnson, Morehouse	Sr.	10	7	95	.7
Pete Iten, Minn.-Morris	Jr.	9	6	111	.7
Deon Hampton, Cal St. Chico	Jr.	9	6	80	.7
Jerome Williams, Delta St.	Sr.	11	7	133	.6
Jeff Rickert, Fort Lewis	Sr.	10	6	66	.6
George O'Connor, Bentley	Sr.	10	6	65	.6
Rodrick Dunlap, Livingstone	So.	10	6	49	.6
Gilbert Diaz, Chadron St.	Sr.	10	6	33	.6
Fred Hager, Ky. Wesleyan	Jr.	10	6	29	.6
Aaron Dunlap, Fort Lewis	Jr.	10	6	0	.6
Steve Carter, Elizabeth City St.	Fr.	9	5	68	.6
Chris Watson, Virginia St.	Jr.	9	5	34	.6

Scoring

	1995 Class	G	TD	XP	FG	Pts.	Pts.PG
Antonio Leroy, Albany St. (Ga.)	Jr.	11	24	0	0	144	13.1
Chris Perry, Adams St.	Sr.	10	21	4	0	130	13.0
Fred Lane, Lane	Jr.	10	20	6	0	126	12.6
Chris Pulliams, Ferris St.	Jr.	10	21	0	0	126	12.6
Sedrick Robinson, Ky. Wesleyan	Jr.	10	17	14	0	116	11.6
Steve Papin, Portland St.	Sr.	11	21	0	0	126	11.5
Robert Morgan, Virginia St.	Jr.	10	18	6	0	114	11.4
Steve Gorrie, Presbyterian	Sr.	11	20	2	0	122	11.1
Albert Bland, Mo. Southern St.	Sr.	10	18	2	0	110	11.0
Jermaine Rucker, UC Davis	Jr.	10	18	0	0	108	10.8
Jason Gibson, Fairmont St.	Sr.	10	17	4	0	106	10.6
Carlos Ferralls, Glenville St.	So.	10	17	2	0	104	10.4
Richard Huntley, Winston-Salem	Sr.	10	17	0	0	102	10.2
James Roe, Norfolk St.	Sr.	10	15	10	0	100	10.0
Robert Reeves, Saginaw Valley	Sr.	9	15	0	0	90	10.0
Mike Lodice, Neb.-Kearney	Fr.	8	13	0	0	78	9.8
Kevin Cannon, Millersville	Sr.	9	14	0	0	84	9.3
Kevin Feeney, North Dak. St.	Fr.	10	15	2	0	92	9.2
Clint Bedore, Fort Hays St.	Sr.	11	16	4	0	100	9.1
Percy McGee, Humboldt St.	Jr.	10	15	0	0	90	9.0
Steve Witte, Clarion	Jr.	10	15	0	0	90	9.0

Punt Returns

(Min. 1.2 per game)	1995 Class	No.	Yds.	Avg.
Kevin Cannon, Millersville	Sr.	16	277	17.3
Charles Davis, Saginaw Valley	Jr.	25	406	16.2
Diriki Mose, Grand Valley St.	Sr.	27	380	14.1
Valery Jackson, Angelo St.	Jr.	25	351	14.0
Troy Myers, East Stroudsburg	Jr.	17	236	13.9
Greg Smith, Western St.	Sr.	25	343	13.7
John Mobley, Kutztown	Sr.	15	202	13.5
Sean Smith, Bloomsburg	Jr.	24	309	12.9
Brian Claunch, Adams St.	So.	12	152	12.7
Mike Smith, Neb.-Kearney	So.	32	384	12.0
Shawn Brown, Shippensburg	Sr.	16	186	11.6
Darren Thornton, Virginia St.	Sr.	14	156	11.1
Chris Ortiz, Southern Conn. St.	Jr.	14	153	10.9
Michael McSharry, Stonehill	Jr.	14	151	10.8
James Cheatham, North Dak.	Jr.	16	172	10.8
Gilbert Grantlin, Edinboro	Sr.	27	290	10.7
Brian Pinks, Northern Mich.	So.	19	203	10.7
Travis Schafer, Northern St.	So.	18	192	10.7
Chad Moran, Central Ark.	Fr.	21	222	10.6
Jermaine Hill, Neb.-Omaha	Sr.	31	324	10.5

Kickoff Returns

(Min. 1.2 per game)	1995 Class	No.	Yds.	Avg.
Melvin German, Southwest St.	Sr.	9	413	45.9
Norman Miller, Tex. A&M-Kingsville	Jr.	12	405	33.8
Kevin Cannon, Millersville	Sr.	14	463	33.1
Jermaine Hill, Neb.-Omaha	Sr.	22	721	32.8
Jurome Lee, Angelo St.	Jr.	13	390	30.0
Kahn Powell, Fort Hays St.	Sr.	21	610	29.0
Jeff Gipson, Chadron St.	Fr.	17	476	28.0
Charles Davis, Saginaw Valley	Jr.	14	385	27.5
Justin Taylor, Mo. Southern St.	So.	12	326	27.2
Paul Hudson, Albany (N.Y.)	Fr.	13	353	27.2
Jerry Reitan, St. Cloud St.	Fr.	13	352	27.1
Jeremy Frisch, Assumption	Fr.	18	487	27.1
Mike Smith, Neb.-Kearney	So.	21	568	27.0
Chris Hamilton, Presbyterian	So.	19	513	27.0
Sean Smith, Bloomsburg	Jr.	25	674	27.0
Raphael McCuien, Central Ark.	So.	20	534	26.7
Peter Yu, Fort Lewis	Sr.	14	370	26.4
Monte Southerland, N.C. Central	Jr.	35	920	26.3
James Cheatham, North Dak.	Jr.	15	393	26.2
Albert Bland, Mo. Southern St.	Sr.	13	339	26.1

Punting

(Min. 3.6 per game)	1995 Class	No.	Avg.
Jon Mason, West Tex. A&M	Sr.	54	45.5
Jason Van Dyke, Adams St.	Fr.	54	42.9
John McGhee, Indiana (Pa.)	Sr.	41	42.0
Brian Moorman, Pittsburg St.	Fr.	45	41.5
Jack Hankins, West Ala.	Sr.	63	41.3
Kevin Thornewell, Tex. A&M-Kingsville	So.	41	41.3
Chris Dolan, East Tex. St.	Sr.	49	41.1
Sean Hegarty, N.M. Highlands	Jr.	56	41.1
Lynn Wendelin, Chadron St.	Sr.	52	40.7
Bryan Standfest, Carson-Newman	Sr.	42	40.6
Gene Adair, New Haven	Sr.	59	40.5
Michael Kramer, East Stroudsburg	Jr.	57	40.4
Chad Kraemer, Western N.M.	Sr.	51	40.3
John Torrance, North Dak. St.	So.	45	40.2
Tony Bilic, Portland St.	So.	35	40.1
Wayne DeVane, Valdosta St.	So.	41	40.0
Tony Faggioni, North Ala.	Fr.	39	39.7
David McCormack, Mo.-Rolla	Fr.	63	39.7
Alex Campbell, Morris Brown	Sr.	67	39.5
Stan Whitlock, Wingate	Sr.	57	39.4

Field Goals

	1995 Class	G	FGA	FG	Pct.	FGPG
Jon Ruff, Indiana (Pa.)	Sr.	11	23	18	78.3	1.64
David Dell, East Tex. St.	Fr.	11	26	17	65.4	1.55
Eric Myers, West Va. Wesleyan	Jr.	10	22	15	68.2	1.50
Mike Foster, Mesa St.	So.	10	20	14	70.0	1.40
Jason Lipke, Ferris St.	Sr.	10	20	14	70.0	1.40
Scott Doyle, Chadron St.	Sr.	10	22	14	63.6	1.40
Ryan Anderson, Northern Colo.	Sr.	11	18	15	83.3	1.36
Sean Hegarty, N.M. Highlands	Jr.	11	16	13	81.3	1.18
Josh Barcus, Pittsburg St.	Fr.	10	15	11	73.3	1.10
Brandon Lynch, Millersville	Jr.	10	20	11	55.0	1.10
Brett Gorden, South Dak. St.	Fr.	11	13	12	92.3	1.09
Steve Opstad, South Dak.	Sr.	11	15	12	80.0	1.09
Shane Meyer, Central Mo. St.	Fr.	10	15	10	66.7	1.00
Kurt Buterbaugh, Northern Mich.	Jr.	10	16	10	62.5	1.00
Mike Rowen, Neb.-Kearney	Sr.	10	17	10	58.8	1.00
Stan Whitlock, Wingate	Sr.	11	25	11	44.0	1.00
Craig Moses, Henderson St.	Jr.	11	14	10	71.4	.91
Michael Sierra, Mo. Western St.	Jr.	11	16	10	62.5	.91
Paul Kosel, Neb.-Omaha	Fr.	11	18	10	55.6	.91
Brian McManus, American Int'l	Sr.	10	17	9	52.9	.90

1995 Division II Team Leaders

Total Offense

	G	Plays	Yds.	Yds.PG
Portland St.	11	826	5,192	472.0
Wayne St. (Neb.)	10	754	4,701	470.1
Norfolk St.	10	751	4,678	467.8
Millersville	10	740	4,605	460.5
Ferris St.	10	705	4,591	459.1
Fort Hays St.	11	774	5,003	454.8
Tex. A&M-Kingsville	10	697	4,502	450.2
Emporia St.	11	922	4,935	448.6
Glenville St.	10	766	4,480	448.0
Grand Valley St.	11	761	4,861	441.9
UC Davis	10	756	4,362	436.2
Truman St.	11	759	4,764	433.1
Humboldt St.	10	683	4,298	429.8
Indiana (Pa.)	11	770	4,721	429.2
Valdosta St.	11	812	4,675	425.0
Pittsburg St.	10	737	4,234	423.4
Adams St.	10	736	4,227	422.7
Chadron St.	10	774	4,219	421.9
Western St.	10	767	4,216	421.6
Bloomsburg	11	785	4,614	419.5

Total Defense

	G	Plays	Yds.	Yds.PG
Kentucky St.	11	621	2,256	205.1
North Ala.	10	596	2,090	209.0
Lane	10	640	2,191	219.1
Bentley	10	573	2,207	220.7
Virginia St.	10	631	2,227	222.7
LIU-C.W. Post	10	659	2,294	229.4
Millersville	10	631	2,342	234.2
Pittsburg St.	10	632	2,396	239.6
Albany St. (Ga.)	11	571	2,637	239.7
Glenville St.	10	557	2,402	240.2
Edinboro	10	643	2,469	246.9
Alabama A&M	11	705	2,750	250.0
West Ga.	10	659	2,574	257.4
Angelo St.	10	674	2,585	258.5
Minn.-Duluth	11	687	2,848	258.9
South Dak.	11	649	2,850	259.1
Tex. A&M-Kingsville	10	662	2,596	259.6
Central Okla.	11	710	2,860	260.0
Pace	10	592	2,602	260.2
Kutztown	10	696	2,612	261.2

Rushing Offense

	G	Car.	Yds.	Yds.PG
Pittsburg St.	10	609	3,188	318.8
Moorhead St.	10	564	3,121	312.1
North Ala.	10	535	3,070	307.0
Saginaw Valley	10	507	2,897	289.7
Tex. A&M-Kingsville	10	499	2,860	286.0
Winston-Salem	10	528	2,644	264.4
Carson-Newman	10	499	2,589	258.9
North Dak. St.	11	594	2,819	256.3
South Dak.	11	573	2,785	253.2
Northwood	10	617	2,521	252.1
Indiana (Pa.)	11	505	2,725	247.7
Bloomsburg	11	562	2,720	247.3
Grand Valley St.	11	480	2,691	244.6
Lane	10	454	2,389	238.9
Mars Hill	10	467	2,379	237.9
Edinboro	10	466	2,366	236.6
Catawba	10	503	2,304	230.4
Truman St.	11	462	2,529	229.9
Henderson St.	11	547	2,524	229.5
Michigan Tech	10	497	2,286	228.6

Rushing Defense

	G	Car.	Yds.	Yds.PG
North Ala.	10	309	568	56.8
Lane	10	356	606	60.6
Livingstone	10	301	630	63.0
Millersville	10	316	635	63.5
Pittsburg St.	10	331	675	67.5
Western St.	10	352	708	70.8
Virginia St.	10	379	801	80.1
South Dak.	11	332	902	82.0
New Haven	10	351	834	83.4
Tex. A&M-Kingsville	10	349	864	86.4
West Va. Wesleyan	10	357	892	89.2
Glenville St.	10	312	931	93.1
Chadron St.	10	348	960	96.0
Kutztown	10	383	972	97.2
Edinboro	10	356	987	98.7
Central Okla.	11	416	1,088	98.9
Eastern N.M.	11	379	1,093	99.4
Humboldt St.	10	332	1,013	101.3
North Dak.	10	371	1,016	101.6
West Liberty St.	10	366	1,047	104.7

Scoring Offense

	G	TD	XP	2XP	DXP	FG	SAF	Pts.	Avg.
Tex. A&M-Kingsville	10	55	42	2	0	7	2	401	40.1
Virginia St.	10	55	30	11	0	0	0	382	38.2
Albany St. (Ga.)	11	59	41	0	0	7	1	418	38.0
Ferris St.	10	49	40	1	0	14	1	380	38.0
Fort Hays St.	11	59	39	5	0	5	0	418	38.0
North Ala.	10	53	37	3	0	5	0	376	37.6
Pittsburg St.	10	49	35	3	0	12	1	373	37.3
Grand Valley St.	11	57	40	5	0	5	0	407	37.0
Norfolk St.	10	53	22	7	0	0	3	360	36.0
Saginaw Valley	10	50	42	1	0	5	0	359	35.9
Bloomsburg	11	53	39	4	0	8	1	391	35.5
Indiana (Pa.)	11	48	43	2	0	18	0	389	35.4
Millersville	10	46	38	1	0	11	2	353	35.3
Bentley	10	49	23	8	0	6	0	351	35.1
Humboldt St.	10	47	36	3	0	8	0	348	34.8
Glenville St.	10	47	32	8	0	5	0	345	34.5
Northern Colo.	11	48	40	2	0	15	1	379	34.5
Wayne St. (Neb.)	10	48	35	1	0	4	0	337	33.7
Western St.	10	46	39	2	0	6	0	337	33.7
Truman St.	11	49	40	4	0	8	0	366	33.3

Scoring Defense

	G	TD	XP	2XP	DXP	FG	SAF	Pts.	Avg.
North Ala.	10	14	10	0	0	4	0	106	10.6
Pittsburg St.	10	14	10	0	0	5	0	109	10.9
Kutztown	10	14	12	0	0	6	0	114	11.4
Central Okla.	11	18	12	0	0	2	0	126	11.5
Bentley	10	18	7	1	0	0	1	119	11.9
Glenville St.	10	16	13	1	0	4	0	123	12.3
Edinboro	10	17	12	1	0	4	0	128	12.8
New Haven	10	15	10	0	0	9	1	129	12.9
West Ga.	10	18	12	0	0	4	0	132	13.2
Hillsdale	11	21	15	0	0	2	0	147	13.4
Angelo St.	10	18	17	0	0	4	0	137	13.7
Lane	10	20	8	2	0	1	2	139	13.9
Millersville	10	19	11	1	0	4	0	139	13.9
Tex. A&M-Kingsville	10	17	14	0	0	8	0	140	14.0
Virginia St.	10	19	6	1	0	4	3	140	14.0
LIU-C.W. Post	10	19	14	1	1	5	0	147	14.7
Indiana (Pa.)	11	22	16	2	0	4	0	164	14.9
Kentucky St.	11	25	13	2	0	0	0	167	15.2
Clark Atlanta	10	22	16	1	0	1	0	153	15.3
St. Cloud St.	10	18	10	4	0	9	0	153	15.3

Passing Offense

	G	Att.	Cmp.	Pct.	Int.	Yards	Yds.PG
Norfolk St.	10	447	256	57.3	16	3,674	367.4
Emporia St.	11	623	322	51.7	25	3,862	351.1
Valdosta St.	11	570	373	65.4	14	3,842	349.3
Augustana (S.D.)	10	454	259	57.0	13	3,141	314.1
Glenville St.	10	387	234	60.5	11	3,129	312.9
Fort Hays St.	11	342	202	59.1	7	3,338	303.5
West Tex. A&M	11	451	255	56.5	21	3,225	293.2
Fairmont St.	10	378	234	61.9	9	2,902	290.2
Adams St.	10	352	202	57.4	18	2,882	288.2
Wayne St. (Neb.)	10	366	219	59.8	13	2,788	278.8
N.M. Highlands	11	457	240	52.5	19	3,047	277.0
Portland St.	11	395	200	50.6	15	3,023	274.8
Western N.M.	9	382	204	53.4	8	2,448	272.0
Lock Haven	11	512	254	49.6	27	2,984	271.3
Central Mo. St.	10	322	191	59.3	12	2,658	265.8
Ky. Wesleyan	10	350	183	52.3	11	2,627	262.7
UC Davis	10	340	194	57.1	9	2,590	259.0
Ferris St.	10	290	179	61.7	4	2,566	256.6
Mankato St.	11	431	243	56.4	13	2,822	256.5
Humboldt St.	10	297	181	60.9	10	2,549	254.9

Pass Efficiency Defense

	G	Att.	Cmp.	Pct.	Int.	Yards	TD	Rating Points
Savannah St.	11	272	108	39.7	21	1,243	8	72.4
Kentucky St.	11	234	86	36.7	17	1,017	10	72.8
Clark Atlanta	10	245	103	42.0	16	1,162	4	74.2
Virginia St.	10	252	95	37.7	23	1,426	9	78.8
Bentley	10	196	70	35.7	17	1,123	8	80.0
Albany St. (Ga.)	11	238	97	40.7	16	1,183	8	80.2
Edinboro	10	287	115	40.0	16	1,482	8	81.5
Stonehill	10	282	120	42.5	20	1,552	8	84.0
Gardner-Webb	10	261	108	41.3	13	1,403	6	84.2
Kutztown	10	313	142	45.3	17	1,640	6	84.8
Newberry	11	249	102	40.9	14	1,446	5	85.1
North Ala.	10	287	132	45.9	17	1,522	8	87.9
Tex. A&M-Kingsville	10	313	134	42.8	14	1,732	8	88.8

	G	Att.	Cmp.	Pct.	Int.	Yards	TD	Rating Points
Morris Brown	10	232	92	39.6	15	1,223	13	89.5
West Ga.	10	303	140	46.2	7	1,493	6	89.5
Lane	10	284	113	39.7	14	1,585	12	90.8
Emporia St.	11	278	104	37.4	20	1,658	15	90.9
Portland St.	11	333	152	45.6	13	1,634	12	90.9
LIU-C.W. Post	10	251	113	45.0	10	1,237	10	91.6
Glenville St.	10	245	112	45.7	17	1,471	7	91.7

Net Punting

	Punts	Yds.	Avg.	No. Ret.	Yds. Ret.	Net Avg.
New Haven	59	2,390	40.50	17	104	38.74
Chadron St.	55	2,253	40.96	20	150	38.23
Indiana (Pa.)	42	1,724	41.04	24	120	38.19
Carson-Newman	45	1,791	39.80	17	96	37.66
Morris Brown	67	2,646	39.49	26	126	37.61
Adams St.	54	2,317	42.90	19	289	37.55
East Tex. St.	51	2,014	39.49	19	106	37.41
Western N.M.	51	2,056	40.31	22	153	37.31
West Tex. A&M	63	2,766	43.90	28	423	37.19
Western St.	41	1,629	39.73	19	105	37.17
Wingate	58	2,259	38.94	21	113	37.00
Valdosta St.	42	1,639	39.02	16	87	36.95
Northern Colo.	48	1,902	39.62	26	145	36.60
East Stroudsburg	58	2,319	39.98	20	204	36.46
North Ala.	41	1,578	38.48	14	84	36.43
Pittsburg St.	47	1,873	39.85	30	180	36.02
West Liberty St.	47	1,747	37.17	18	87	35.31
UC Davis	49	1,894	38.65	21	175	35.08
Gardner-Webb	59	2,224	37.69	18	164	34.91
Neb.-Kearney	74	2,880	38.91	29	300	34.86

Punt Returns

	G	No.	Yds.	TD	Avg.
Elizabeth City St.	11	16	370	0	23.12
Alabama A&M	11	22	406	0	18.45
Saginaw Valley	10	27	446	0	16.51
Millersville	10	25	362	1	14.48
Grand Valley St.	11	27	380	2	14.07
Adams St.	10	16	215	2	13.43
North Dak.	10	18	236	3	13.11
Angelo St.	10	31	406	2	13.09
Neb.-Kearney	10	36	471	0	13.08
Northern Colo.	11	41	522	5	12.73
Bloomsburg	11	33	405	1	12.27
Western St.	10	30	363	1	12.10
West Ala.	11	13	155	0	11.92
Savannah St.	11	28	328	0	11.71
East Stroudsburg	10	23	266	0	11.56
Virginia St.	10	19	213	1	11.21
Norfolk St.	10	19	210	0	11.05
Neb.-Omaha	11	33	362	2	10.96
Tarleton St.	11	25	273	1	10.92
Mansfield	10	15	162	1	10.80

Kickoff Returns

	G	No.	Yds.	TD	Avg.
Millersville	10	23	599	2	26.04
Tex. A&M-Kingsville	10	27	695	3	25.74
Fort Hays St.	11	31	781	0	25.19
New Haven	10	32	781	1	24.40
Bloomsburg	11	31	744	1	24.00
Neb.-Omaha	11	49	1,165	1	23.77
Neb.-Kearney	10	29	686	2	23.65
Lane	10	19	449	0	23.63
Chadron St.	10	30	701	0	23.36
St. Cloud St.	10	21	489	1	23.28
Angelo St.	10	26	604	1	23.23
Northwood	10	43	989	0	23.00
Presbyterian	11	29	663	0	22.86
Mo. Southern St.	10	33	737	1	22.33
North Dak.	10	26	579	0	22.26
UC Davis	10	42	935	0	22.26
North Dak. St.	11	35	778	0	22.22
East Stroudsburg	10	38	842	1	22.15
Slippery Rock	11	33	728	0	22.06
N.C. Central	11	49	1,079	2	22.02

Turnover Margin

		TURNOVERS GAINED			TURNOVERS LOST			Margin/
	G	Fum.	Int.	Total	Fum.	Int.	Total	Game
Central Okla.	11	28	17	45	12	4	16	2.63
Lane	10	33	14	47	13	13	26	2.10
St. Cloud St.	10	17	15	32	7	7	14	1.80
Northwest Mo. St.	11	22	15	37	9	10	19	1.63
Bentley	10	12	17	29	6	7	13	1.60
Virginia St.	10	14	23	37	8	13	21	1.60
Western St.	10	14	21	35	14	5	19	1.60
Fort Hays St.	11	18	21	39	15	7	22	1.54
Glenville St.	10	19	17	36	10	11	21	1.50
Northern Mich.	10	17	14	31	10	7	17	1.40
Bloomsburg	11	12	22	34	10	10	20	1.27
Kutztown	10	13	17	30	12	6	18	1.20
Norfolk St.	10	19	17	36	8	16	24	1.20
East Tex. St.	11	19	18	37	14	10	24	1.18
Indiana (Pa.)	11	21	17	38	13	12	25	1.18
Fort Valley St.	11	19	14	33	8	13	21	1.09
Mo. Western St.	11	17	18	35	12	11	23	1.09
Grand Valley St.	11	12	13	25	9	5	14	1.00
Mars Hill	10	11	12	23	8	5	13	1.00
Slippery Rock	11	18	17	35	12	12	24	1.00

Longest Division II Plays of 1995

Rushing

Player, Team (Opponent)	Yards
Chris Pulliams, Ferris St. (Saginaw Valley)	97
Leon Williams, Mars Hill (Newberry)	92
Alex Colbert, Central Ark. (Mississippi Col.)	88
Rodney Harrell, Central Mo. St. (Emporia St.)	88
Fred Lane, Lane (West Ala.)	87
Chris Ryan, Clark Atlanta (Morehouse)	86
Fred Bradley, Sonoma St. (Cal St. Chico)	83
Troy Jackson, Henderson St. (West Ala.)	83
Steve Wilson, Concord (West Va. Wesleyan)	83
Tyrone Baker, Central Okla. (West Tex. A&M)	82
Karega Scott, Truman St. (Central Mo. St.)	82
Ronel Saintvil, Carson-Newman (Elon)	81
Gerald Wright, Mars Hill (Catawba)	81

Passing

Passer-Receiver, Team (Opponent)	Yards
Bob McLaughlin-Bryan McGinty, Lock Haven (Shippensburg)	96
Sean Ponder-Chet Pobolish, Emporia St. (Mo.-Rolla)	96
Oktay Basci-Karl Williams, Tex. A&M-Kingsville (East Tex. St.)	95
Pete Jelovic-Erik Guberman, Emporia St. (Mo.-Rolla)	95
Ian Page-Anthony Campbell, Mo. Western St. (Mo. Southern St.)	95
Joe Knapp-Elliott Jackson, Mo.-Rolla (Mo. Western St.)	93
Josh Racanelli-Jachon Ramseur, Portland St. (Western N.M.)	90
Joel Staehr-Mike Smith, Neb.-Kearney (Northwestern Okla.)	90
Pete Jelovic-Derek Woods, Emporia St. (Truman St.)	89
Brian Cavanaugh-Ron Simpson, Calif., Pa. (West Chester)	88
Kevin Feeney-Kelly Artz, North Dak. St. (Northern Colo.)	88
Mike Mullen-Jamie Merloni, Assumption (MIT)	88
Aaron Sparrow-James Roe, Norfolk St. (Livingstone)	87
Mike Rymsha-John Ferguson, Bentley (Curry)	86

Interception Returns

Player, Team (Opponent)	Yards
Brian Oliver, New Haven (Bloomsburg)	100
Troy Myers, East Stroudsburg (Slippery Rock)	95
Mike Lankas, Fort Hays St. (Mesa St.)	92
Quincy Morgan, Livingstone (Johnson Smith)	91
Brad Vesperman, Mankato St. (Augustana, S.D.)	91
Jason Ney, Western N.M. (Adams St.)	85
Reade Sands, Pace (Stonehill)	85
Darryl Stewart, Clark Atlanta (Savannah St.)	83

Punt Returns

Player, Team (Opponent)	Yards
Colin Yocom, Tarleton St. (Midwestern St.)	89
Valery Jackson, Angelo St. (Central Okla.)	88
Brian Claunch, Adams St. (Colorado Mines)	82
Valery Jackson, Angelo St. (West Tex. A&M)	81
Ben Steinbacher, Lock Haven (Mansfield)	76
James Bell, Alabama A&M (Alabama St.)	75
Chad Moran, Central Ark. (West Ala.)	74
Kevin Cannon, Millersville (Shippensburg)	70

Kickoff Returns

Player, Team (Opponent)	Yards
Kevin Cannon, Millersville (Shepherd)	100
Jurome Lee, Angelo St. (West Tex. A&M)	100
Norman Miller, Tex. A&M-Kingsville (Portland St.)	100
Raphael McCuien, Central Ark. (Arkansas Tech)	97
Mike Smith, Neb.-Kearney (Southern Utah)	97
Rodney Brown, Valdosta St. (UTEP)	96
Jerry Reitan, St. Cloud St. (Minn.-Duluth)	96
Lamart Cooper, Wayne St., Neb. (Neb.-Omaha)	95
Monk Culbreth, West Chester (East Stroudsburg)	95
Edwin Franklin, Southwest Baptist (Pittsburg St.)	95
Jeremy Frisch, Assumption (Pace)	95
Rashid Thomas, American Int'l (East Stroudsburg)	95
Peter Yu, Fort Lewis (Adams St.)	95
Jason Smith, East Tex. St. (Tarleton St.)	94
Monte Southerland, N.C. Central (Howard)	94

Field Goals

Player, Team (Opponent)	Yards
Lance Privett, Mo.-Rolla (Truman St.)	54
Stan Whitlock, Wingate (Shepherd)	53
Sean Hegarty, N.M. Highlands (Colorado Mines)	52
Jon Ruff, Indiana, Pa. (Edinboro)	52
Ryan Anderson, Northern Colo. (Western St.)	51
Shane Meyer, Central Mo. St. (Northwest Mo. St.)	51
Jason Crowson, Eastern N.M. (West Tex. A&M)	49
Craig Bost, Mars Hill (Concord)	48
James Roberts, Albany St., Ga. (Morehouse)	48
Bryan Standfest, Carson-Newman (Newberry)	48
Steve Walter, Adams St. (Mesa St.)	48

Punts

Player, Team (Opponent)	Yards
Mike Bean, West Chester (Calif., Pa.)	80
George Moeke, Michigan Tech (Ashland)	79
John Torrance, North Dak. St. (North Dak.)	78
Jerry Willoughby, Concord (West Va. Wesleyan)	76
Jason Van Dyke, Adams St. (West Tex. A&M)	75
Jason Young, Winona St. (Minn.-Morris)	72
Tom Dusseau, Hillsdale (St. Joseph's, Ind.)	71
Kelly Hughes, Shepherd (West Va. Tech)	71
Dirk Johnson, Northern Colo. (Western St.)	70
Michael Kramer, East Stroudsburg (Millersville)	70
Jon Mason, West Tex. A&M (Angelo St.)	70
Billy Mentekidis, Pace (Stonehill)	70
Sean Hegarty, N.M. Highlands (Fort Hays St.)	68
Jerry Willoughby, Concord (West Va. St.)	67
David McCormack, Mo.-Rolla (Washburn)	66

1995 Division III Individual Leaders

Rushing

	1995 Class	G	Car.	Yards	TD	Yds.PG
Brad Olson, Lawrence	So.	9	242	1,760	16	195.6
Anthony Jones, La Verne	Sr.	8	200	1,453	19	181.6
Rob Marchitello, Maine Maritime	Sr.	8	292	1,413	19	176.6
Jamall Pollock, Williams	Sr.	8	216	1,319	7	164.9
Fredrick Nanhed, Cal Lutheran	Fr.	9	242	1,380	10	153.3
Dan McGovern, Rensselaer	So.	9	231	1,378	14	153.1
Mike Lee, Rhodes	Sr.	9	263	1,374	14	152.7
Ray Neosh, Coe	Fr.	9	209	1,354	14	150.4
Adam Kowles, Wis.-River Falls	Sr.	8	145	1,195	13	149.4
Rick Etienne, Franklin	Jr.	10	246	1,433	14	143.3
Darnell Morgan, Chapman	Sr.	9	119	1,289	18	143.2
Trenell Smith, Kean	Jr.	8	222	1,109	4	138.6
Brandon Steinheim, Wesley	Jr.	10	211	1,343	17	134.3
Brandon Graham, Hope	So.	9	221	1,139	8	126.6
Darnell Avery, Upper Iowa	Jr.	10	240	1,221	5	122.1
Doug Eastes, Wilmington (Ohio)	Sr.	9	229	1,093	13	121.4
Jim Callahan, Salve Regina	Jr.	9	209	1,092	14	121.3
Brad Madden, Millsaps	Jr.	8	202	950	7	118.8
Kris Garrett, Centre	Sr.	10	261	1,187	7	118.7
Mark Logan, Hobart	Fr.	10	273	1,175	10	117.5
Jose DeLeon, MIT	Jr.	8	167	929	8	116.1
Jeremy Tvedt, Bethel (Minn.)	Jr.	10	220	1,159	10	115.9
Scott Tumilty, Augustana (Ill.)	Sr.	9	180	1,040	17	115.6
John Wells, Western New Eng.	Sr.	8	176	918	6	114.8
Matt Figueroa, Redlands	Sr.	9	187	1,029	12	114.3
Ray Jones, Trinity (Conn.)	Jr.	8	175	907	9	113.4
Pat Rusch, St. Norbert	Sr.	9	222	1,017	5	113.0
Mark Pawelek, Hardin-Simmons	Jr.	9	208	1,009	10	112.1
Perez Dinkins, Buffalo St.	Jr.	10	235	1,117	15	111.7
John Klasen, Lake Forest	Sr.	9	207	1,003	6	111.4

Photo from Lawrence sports information

Lawrence running back Brad Olson led Division III in rushing (195.6 yards per game) last season as a sophomore.

Photo from Washington and Jefferson sports information

Washington and Jefferson quarterback Jason Baer finished second in Division III passing efficiency last season with a rating of 192.3.

Passing Efficiency

(Min. 15 att. per game)	1995 Class	G	Att.	Cmp.	Pct.	Int.	Yards	TD	Rating Points
Bill Borchert, Mount Union	So.	10	225	160	71.1	4	2,270	30	196.3
Jason Baer, Wash. & Jeff.	Jr.	8	146	95	65.0	3	1,536	19	192.3
Mike Donnelly, Wittenberg	Jr.	10	153	92	60.1	2	1,480	15	171.1
Kyle Adamson, Allegheny	So.	10	209	142	67.9	8	2,039	17	169.1
Brian Nelson, Wartburg	Jr.	10	171	95	55.5	3	1,600	19	167.3
John Furmaniak, Eureka	Sr.	10	361	210	58.1	11	3,372	34	161.6
Craig Kusick, Wis.-La Crosse	Sr.	10	252	155	61.5	8	2,275	21	158.5
Jeff Brown, Wheaton (Ill.)	Sr.	9	279	168	60.2	5	2,376	23	155.4
Marc Harris, Wesley	So.	8	183	107	58.4	8	1,633	13	148.1
Tracy Bacon, Buffalo St.	Jr.	10	182	96	52.7	5	1,630	14	147.9
Todd Baumann, Hardin-Simmons	Jr.	8	210	131	62.3	10	1,628	19	147.8
Chris Esterley, St. Thomas (Minn.)	Jr.	10	289	191	66.0	12	2,305	20	147.7
Kurt Ramler, St. John's (Minn.)	Jr.	10	307	177	57.6	7	2,462	25	147.3
Thor Larsen, Washington (Mo.)	So.	10	261	135	51.7	9	2,101	27	146.6
Tom Fitzgerald, Wis.-Stevens Point	Jr.	8	191	115	60.2	5	1,519	14	145.9
Vic Ameye, Widener	Sr.	10	333	195	58.5	9	2,669	21	141.4
Larry Hutson, Thomas More	Sr.	10	241	135	56.0	3	1,885	16	141.1
Terry Peebles, Hanover	Sr.	10	488	283	57.9	10	3,521	39	140.9
Peter Supino, Williams	So.	6	90	50	55.5	3	703	7	140.2
Jon Nielsen, Claremont-M-S	Sr.	9	338	189	55.9	9	2,690	23	139.9
Jack Ramirez, Pomona-Pitzer	So.	9	271	165	60.8	11	1,847	21	135.6
Kyle Klein, Albion	Jr.	8	148	74	50.0	3	1,181	10	135.3
Dan Runaas, Wis.-Whitewater	Sr.	10	196	115	58.6	3	1,379	11	133.3
Danny Green, Redlands	Jr.	9	291	185	63.5	7	2,044	13	132.5
Mark Barnes, Rensselaer	Sr.	9	184	106	57.6	6	1,307	11	130.5
Ross Panko, Hamline	Jr.	8	133	78	58.6	7	975	8	129.6
Mike Magistrelli, Coe	Jr.	9	179	93	51.9	4	1,194	14	129.3
Neal Weidman, Ithaca	Jr.	9	295	176	59.6	10	2,125	13	127.9
Nick Caserio, John Carroll	Fr.	10	299	180	60.2	14	2,135	14	126.3
Brad Jorgensen, Simpson	So.	10	244	148	60.6	11	1,852	8	126.2

Total Offense

	1995 Class	G	Plays	Yards	Yds.PG
Terry Peebles, Hanover	Sr.	10	572	3,981	398.1
John Furmaniak, Eureka	Sr.	10	414	3,503	350.3
Jon Nielsen, Claremont-M-S	Sr.	9	405	2,848	316.4
Eric Noble, Wilmington (Ohio)	Sr.	9	438	2,642	293.6
Jason Falk, Alma	Sr.	9	467	2,638	293.1
Greg McDonald, Kalamazoo	Jr.	9	420	2,538	282.0
Vic Ameye, Widener	Sr.	10	380	2,644	264.4
Chris Ings, Wabash	Sr.	10	447	2,629	262.9
Kurt Ramler, St. John's (Minn.)	Jr.	10	386	2,612	261.2
Brian Van Deusen, Western Md.	Sr.	10	522	2,546	254.6
Lon Erickson, Ill. Wesleyan	Jr.	9	380	2,281	253.4
Jeff Brown, Wheaton (Ill.)	Sr.	9	306	2,272	252.4
Bryan Snyder, Albright	So.	10	471	2,461	246.1
Steve Panning, Manchester	Jr.	10	407	2,454	245.4
Jack Ramirez, Pomona-Pitzer	So.	9	356	2,158	239.8
Jason Schneider, FDU-Madison	Sr.	9	405	2,121	235.7
Brad Ruderman, Hartwick	Sr.	9	328	2,106	234.0
Aaron Conte, Marietta	Jr.	10	385	2,318	231.8
Bill Borchert, Mount Union	So.	10	309	2,315	231.5
Jeff Kinziger, Lawrence	Sr.	9	387	2,079	231.0

Receptions Per Game

	1995 Class	G	Rec.	Yards	TD	Rec.PG
Ben Fox, Hanover	Sr.	9	95	1,087	15	10.6
Mike Cook, Claremont-M-S	Jr.	9	83	993	7	9.2
Todd Bloom, Hardin-Simmons	So.	9	72	744	4	8.0
Mike Gundersdorf, Wilkes	Jr.	10	79	1,269	8	7.9
Jake Doran, FDU-Madison	Sr.	9	70	1,201	11	7.8
Jeff Clay, Catholic	So.	9	66	881	7	7.3
Ryan Tusek, Ill. Wesleyan	Jr.	9	65	863	11	7.2
Nick Roudebush, Hanover	Sr.	8	57	692	11	7.1
Burnell Roques, Claremont-M-S	Sr.	9	64	1,169	14	7.1
Chris Palmer, St. John's (Minn.)	Sr.	10	71	1,197	13	7.1
Eric Nemec, Albright	Fr.	10	71	834	6	7.1
Michael LeFlore, Rochester	Sr.	9	62	868	8	6.9
Kurt Barth, Eureka	So.	10	68	1,337	18	6.8
Matt Ports, Heidelberg	Jr.	10	68	866	5	6.8
Russ Jacques, Wis.-Platteville	Sr.	10	68	556	2	6.8
David Sherwood, Kalamazoo	Sr.	9	60	743	3	6.7
Gary Furner, Hartwick	Sr.	9	60	698	6	6.7
Manny Pina, St. John Fisher	Jr.	10	66	603	8	6.6
Seth Haight, Hartwick	Sr.	8	52	923	10	6.5
Nathan Hutchings, Eureka	Sr.	9	58	814	6	6.4

Receiving Yards Per Game

	1995 Class	G	Rec.	Yards	TD	Yds.PG
Kurt Barth, Eureka	So.	10	68	1,337	18	133.7
Jake Doran, FDU-Madison	Sr.	9	70	1,201	11	133.4
Burnell Roques, Claremont-M-S	Sr.	9	64	1,169	14	129.9
Mike Gundersdorf, Wilkes	Jr.	10	79	1,269	8	126.9
Ben Fox, Hanover	Sr.	9	95	1,087	15	120.8
Chris Palmer, St. John's (Minn.)	Sr.	10	71	1,197	13	119.7
Seth Haight, Hartwick	Sr.	8	52	923	10	115.4
Mike Cook, Claremont-M-S	Jr.	9	83	993	7	110.3
R. J. Hoppe, Carroll (Wis.)	Jr.	9	49	905	13	100.6
Derrick Brooms, Chicago	Sr.	9	42	896	13	99.6
Steve Verton, Lycoming	Jr.	9	54	892	9	99.1
Jeff Clay, Catholic	So.	9	66	881	7	97.9
Bill Schultz, Ripon	Jr.	10	59	976	11	97.6
Josh Haza, Washington (Mo.)	Jr.	10	50	967	10	96.7
Chris Barnett, Albion	Sr.	9	57	870	7	96.7
LaVant King, Ohio Northern	Sr.	9	41	869	9	96.6
Michael LeFlore, Rochester	Sr.	9	62	868	8	96.4
Ramon Fulcher, Menlo	So.	9	52	863	7	95.9
Ryan Tusek, Ill. Wesleyan	Jr.	9	65	863	11	95.9
Ryan Smith, Olivet	Fr.	7	36	645	8	92.1

Interceptions

	1995 Class	G	No.	Yards	Int.PG
Mike Susi, Lebanon Valley	Sr.	8	8	153	1.0
LeMonde Zachary, St. Lawrence	Fr.	7	7	109	1.0
Jim Wallace, Ripon	Jr.	10	9	149	.9
Chris Nalley, Washington (Mo.)	Jr.	10	9	50	.9
Mike Brouwer, Franklin	Sr.	10	9	17	.9
Keith Murphy, Western New Eng.	Jr.	7	6	79	.9
Evan Jones, Randolph-Macon	Sr.	10	8	135	.8
Ken Pope, Wittenberg	Fr.	10	8	104	.8
Matt Bixler, Dickinson	Jr.	9	7	195	.8
Will Wagner, Hardin-Simmons	Sr.	9	7	100	.8
David Lefere, Albion	Jr.	9	7	70	.8
Rob Taylor, Rensselaer	Sr.	8	6	120	.8
Tony Aguilar, Hobart	Jr.	8	6	43	.8

Scoring

	1995 Class	G	TD	XP	FG	Pts.	Pts.PG
Anthony Jones, La Verne	Sr.	8	19	4	0	118	14.8
Rob Marchitello, Maine Maritime	Sr.	8	19	0	0	114	14.3
Darnell Morgan, Chapman	Sr.	9	21	0	0	126	14.0
Scott Tumilty, Augustana (Ill.)	Sr.	9	19	0	0	114	12.7
Kurt Barth, Eureka	So.	10	18	15	0	123	12.3
Ben Fox, Hanover	Sr.	9	18	0	0	108	12.0
Ray Neosh, Coe	Fr.	9	18	0	0	108	12.0
Mark Kossick, Williams	Jr.	7	13	2	0	80	11.4
Brandon Steinheim, Wesley	Jr.	10	18	0	0	108	10.8
Curt Weikart, Marietta	Sr.	10	18	0	0	108	10.8
Derrick Brooms, Chicago	Sr.	9	16	0	0	96	10.7
Brad Olson, Lawrence	So.	9	16	0	0	96	10.7
Anthony Rice, La Verne	Jr.	9	16	0	0	96	10.7
LaVant King, Ohio Northern	Sr.	9	15	2	0	92	10.2
Jason Regan, Simpson	Sr.	10	17	0	0	102	10.2
Jim Callahan, Salve Regina	Jr.	9	14	6	0	90	10.0
Adam Kowles, Wis.-River Falls	Sr.	8	13	2	0	80	10.0
Mike Lee, Rhodes	Sr.	9	15	0	0	90	10.0
Rick Etienne, Franklin	Jr.	10	16	2	0	98	9.8
Aaron Powers, Wittenberg	Jr.	10	16	2	0	98	9.8
R. J. Hoppe, Carroll (Wis.)	Jr.	9	14	4	0	88	9.8
Keith Miller, Wash. & Jeff.	Jr.	8	13	0	0	78	9.8

All-Purpose Yards

	1995 Class	G	Rush	Rec.	PR	KOR	Total Yards	Yds.PG
Brad Olson, Lawrence	So.	9	1,760	279	0	0	2,039	226.56
Ray Neosh, Coe	Fr.	9	1,354	218	0	254	1,826	202.89
Fredrick Nanhed, Cal Lutheran	Fr.	9	1,380	26	0	349	1,755	195.00
Anthony Jones, La Verne	Sr.	8	1,453	64	0	17	1,534	191.75
LaVant King, Ohio Northern	Sr.	9	153	869	296	378	1,696	188.44
Rob Marchitello, Maine Maritime	Sr.	8	1,413	93	0	0	1,506	188.25
John Wells, Western New Eng.	Sr.	8	918	75	11	490	1,494	186.75
Rick Etienne, Franklin	Jr.	10	1,433	352	0	0	1,785	178.50
Darnell Morgan, Chapman	Sr.	9	1,289	235	0	78	1,602	178.00
Dan McGovern, Rensselaer	So.	9	1,378	39	0	184	1,601	177.89
Mike Lee, Rhodes	Sr.	9	1,374	185	0	0	1,559	173.22
Matt Figueroa, Redlands	Sr.	9	1,029	275	0	249	1,553	172.56
Brandon Steinheim, Wesley	Jr.	10	1,343	101	0	249	1,693	169.30
Scott Tumilty, Augustana (Ill.)	Sr.	9	1,040	126	205	143	1,514	168.22
Derrick Brooms, Chicago	Sr.	9	3	896	175	422	1,496	166.22
A. J. Pittarino, Hartwick	Jr.	9	768	66	0	658	1,492	165.78
Mark Logan, Hobart	Fr.	10	1,175	87	0	394	1,656	165.60
Jamall Pollock, Williams	Sr.	8	1,319	0	0	0	1,319	164.88
Oscar Ford, Chapman	Jr.	8	164	423	345	373	1,305	163.13
Anthony Rice, La Verne	Jr.	9	899	374	0	190	1,463	162.56

Photo from New England Football Conference

Maine Maritime running back Rob Marchitello was among the Division III leaders in rushing, scoring and all-purpose yards last season.

Punt Returns

(Min. 1.2 per game)	1995 Class	No.	Yds.	Avg.
Jim Wallace, Ripon	Jr.	17	305	17.9
LaVant King, Ohio Northern	Sr.	18	296	16.4
David Sherwood, Kalamazoo	Sr.	11	179	16.3
Scott Tumilty, Augustana (Ill.)	Sr.	13	205	15.8
Josh Morris, Hartwick	So.	15	226	15.1
Oscar Ford, Chapman	Jr.	23	345	15.0
Eric Wolfe, Monmouth (Ill.)	So.	11	162	14.7
Alex Doran, Trinity (Tex.)	So.	11	160	14.5
Brett Bardellini, Plymouth St.	Fr.	38	538	14.2
Shannon Green, Rowan	Fr.	19	265	13.9
Andy Ehresman, Cornell College	Sr.	21	291	13.9
Jeff Harrison, Otterbein	Jr.	11	149	13.5
Matt Newland, Central (Iowa)	Sr.	41	546	13.3
Aaron Settles, Hampden-Sydney	Fr.	12	159	13.3
Joe Madigan, Gettysburg	So.	12	156	13.0
Richard Wemer, Grinnell	Fr.	13	167	12.8
Ron Contreras, Salve Regina	Sr.	22	278	12.6
Al Thompson, Coast Guard	So.	16	197	12.3
Jon Holloway, DePauw	Jr.	24	294	12.3
Keith Miller, Wash. & Jeff.	Jr.	13	158	12.2

Kickoff Returns

(Min. 1.2 per game)	1995 Class	No.	Yds.	Avg.
Derrick Brooms, Chicago	Sr.	12	422	35.2
Jeff Higgins, Ithaca	Jr.	12	407	33.9
Oscar Ford, Chapman	Jr.	11	373	33.9
Matt Gudorf, Adrian	So.	20	658	32.9
Freddy Grant, Salisbury St.	Jr.	11	347	31.5
Chris Turner, Emory & Henry	Sr.	13	408	31.4
R. J. Hoppe, Carroll (Wis.)	Jr.	17	496	29.2
Andy Ehresman, Cornell College	Sr.	15	428	28.5
Craig Roscoe, Knox	So.	11	312	28.4
George Lino, Wabash	Sr.	19	524	27.6
Richard Wemer, Grinnell	Fr.	20	546	27.3
Shane Abrams, Norwich	Sr.	15	407	27.1
Omar Darling, Cortland St.	So.	17	461	27.1
Mike Oursler, Albion	Jr.	16	433	27.1
Dante Brown, Marietta	So.	13	351	27.0
Andy Baribeau, Gettysburg	Sr.	21	559	26.6
Mike Bechtel, Wis.-Stout	Jr.	23	602	26.2
Damon Adams, Tufts	Sr.	10	261	26.1
Lelan Kawa, Menlo	Jr.	11	286	26.0
LaVant King, Ohio Northern	Sr.	15	378	25.2

Punting

(Min. 3.6 per game)	1995 Class	No.	Avg.
Jeff Shea, Cal Lutheran	So.	43	45.0
Mario Acosta, Chapman	So.	38	40.2
Tyler Laughery, Claremont-M-S	Jr.	39	39.6
David Heggie, Guilford	So.	39	39.3
Drew Thomas, Wash. & Lee	Sr.	33	38.7
Rusty Oglesby, Hardin-Simmons	Jr.	38	38.6
Augie Mitschke, Wilkes	So.	66	38.5
Von Lewis, Bridgewater (Va.)	Jr.	59	38.3
Tim Huckel, Rowan	So.	47	38.3
Sean Sahlberg, Lake Forest	Sr.	38	38.1
Dave Johnson, Lakeland	So.	39	38.1
Marc Widmer, Buffalo St.	Sr.	40	37.9
Erik Berendsen, Wis.-Stevens Point	So.	56	37.8
Erik Ward, Thomas More	Jr.	42	37.6
Jon Bushey, Frank. & Marsh.	Jr.	65	37.6
Andre Clements, Trenton St.	Fr.	61	37.5
John Beckwith, Trinity (Tex.)	Jr.	35	37.5
Chris Murray, Sewanee	Jr.	63	37.4
Chris Boglev, Rochester	Jr.	62	37.4
Bruce Lanning, Muskingum	Jr.	60	37.1

Field Goals

	1995 Class	G	FGA	FG	Pct.	FGPG
Dennis Unger, Albright	So.	10	20	16	80.0	1.60
Roger Egbert, Union (N.Y.)	Jr.	9	21	12	57.1	1.33
Eddie Rhodes, Blackburn	Jr.	8	13	10	76.9	1.25
Dave McQuilkin, Maine Maritime	So.	9	16	11	68.8	1.22
David Johnston, Trenton St.	Sr.	10	17	11	64.7	1.10
Mike Zahn, Alma	Sr.	9	10	9	90.0	1.00
Fred Galecke, Wis.-Stevens Point	So.	10	14	10	71.4	1.00
Jimmy Watts, Wittenberg	Jr.	10	14	10	71.4	1.00
David Waddell, Ferrum	Sr.	10	20	10	50.0	1.00
Erik Ward, Thomas More	Jr.	10	19	9	47.4	.90
Tony Labrador, Randolph-Macon	Sr.	9	12	8	66.7	.89
Juan Contreras, La Verne	Sr.	9	13	8	61.5	.89
George Mayer, Salisbury St.	Jr.	9	13	8	61.5	.89
Bret Roberts, Colorado Col.	Sr.	9	13	8	61.5	.89
Brian Beddow, Hardin-Simmons	So.	9	17	8	47.1	.89
Rick Kavan, Simpson	Jr.	10	10	8	80.0	.80
Michael Roberts, Anderson (Ind.)	Jr.	10	10	8	80.0	.80
Art Kirk, Hobart	So.	10	11	8	72.7	.80
Bryan Mader, Wis.-Whitewater	So.	10	15	8	53.3	.80

1995 Division III Team Leaders

Total Offense

	G	Plays	Yds.	Yds.PG
Mount Union	10	761	4,958	495.8
Hanover	10	771	4,850	485.0
Wittenberg	10	735	4,841	484.1
Lawrence	9	739	4,315	479.4
Wheaton (Ill.)	9	706	4,231	470.1
Allegheny	10	672	4,646	464.6
La Verne	9	630	4,139	459.9
Wilmington (Ohio)	9	756	4,120	457.8
Eureka	10	675	4,562	456.2
Widener	10	757	4,560	456.0
Wesley	10	723	4,464	446.4
Williams	8	588	3,556	444.5
Chapman	9	503	3,978	442.0
Simpson	10	790	4,325	432.5
Buffalo St.	10	670	4,279	427.9
St. John's (Minn.)	10	742	4,234	423.4
Central (Iowa)	10	702	4,229	422.9
Albion	9	677	3,750	416.7
Thomas More	10	734	4,131	413.1
Wartburg	10	732	4,126	412.6

Total Defense

	G	Plays	Yds.	Yds.PG
Mass. Maritime	9	513	1,451	161.2
Salve Regina	9	536	1,499	166.6
Worcester St.	10	633	1,679	167.9
Wesley	10	609	1,693	169.3
Mount Union	10	540	1,702	170.2
Union (N.Y.)	9	618	1,566	174.0
Wash. & Jeff.	8	444	1,435	179.4
Augustana (Ill.)	9	544	1,671	185.7
Williams	8	472	1,573	196.6
Central (Iowa)	10	679	2,019	201.9
Wittenberg	10	577	2,037	203.7
Plymouth St.	9	534	1,840	204.4
Wis.-La Crosse	10	649	2,061	206.1
Wartburg	10	633	2,093	209.3
Emory & Henry	10	649	2,094	209.4
Maine Maritime	9	538	1,934	214.9
Trinity (Tex.)	9	578	1,960	217.8
Marietta	10	638	2,321	232.1
La Verne	9	536	2,097	233.0
Thomas More	10	646	2,346	234.6

Rushing Offense

	G	Car.	Yds.	Yds.PG
Lawrence	9	574	3,096	344.0
La Verne	9	478	3,070	341.1
Wis.-River Falls	10	574	3,345	334.5
Wittenberg	10	551	3,040	304.0
Springfield	9	545	2,659	295.4
Cornell College	10	557	2,949	294.9
Chapman	9	381	2,639	293.2
Augustana (Ill.)	9	492	2,629	292.1
Rose-Hulman	10	537	2,897	289.7
Salve Regina	9	461	2,474	274.9
Maine Maritime	9	482	2,413	268.1
Coe	9	410	2,379	264.3
Central (Iowa)	10	492	2,597	259.7
Concordia-M'head	10	587	2,544	254.4
Buffalo St.	10	475	2,527	252.7
Wesley	10	481	2,510	251.0
Williams	8	408	1,993	249.1
Frostburg St.	10	554	2,482	248.2
Rensselaer	9	450	2,224	247.1
Simpson	10	530	2,436	243.6

Rushing Defense

	G	Car.	Yds.	Yds.PG
Marietta	10	318	462	46.2
Worcester St.	10	384	500	50.0
Mass. Maritime	9	301	464	51.6
Wash. & Jeff.	8	242	420	52.5
Wesley	10	369	525	52.5
Mount Union	10	306	567	56.7
Emory & Henry	10	367	572	57.2
Augustana (Ill.)	9	340	533	59.2
Wittenberg	10	331	658	65.8
Union (N.Y.)	9	360	602	66.9
Maine Maritime	9	325	604	67.1
Concordia-M'head	10	337	740	74.0
Trinity (Tex.)	9	304	700	77.8
Chapman	9	330	714	79.3
Salve Regina	9	356	767	85.2
Wartburg	10	380	855	85.5
Thomas More	10	364	869	86.9
Albion	9	320	795	88.3
John Carroll	10	379	886	88.6
La Verne	9	291	805	89.4

Scoring Offense

	G	TD	XP	2XP	DXP	FG	SAF	Pts.	Avg.
Chapman	9	59	54	0	0	5	1	425	47.2
Wittenberg	10	61	56	1	0	10	1	456	45.6
La Verne	9	56	46	2	0	8	0	410	45.6
Mount Union	10	62	43	4	0	5	0	438	43.8
Allegheny	10	59	49	2	0	6	0	425	42.5
Central (Iowa)	10	57	42	2	0	7	3	415	41.5
Widener	10	55	43	4	0	7	1	404	40.4
Wheaton (Ill.)	9	52	37	4	0	1	1	362	40.2
Wash. & Jeff.	8	44	35	2	0	5	0	318	39.8
Wartburg	10	56	42	3	0	2	3	396	39.6
Hanover	10	56	40	1	0	3	0	387	38.7
St. John's (Minn.)	10	55	40	6	0	1	0	385	38.5
Wesley	10	55	41	1	0	2	0	379	37.9
Marietta	10	51	33	2	1	5	2	364	36.4
Coe	9	43	38	1	0	7	1	321	35.7
Simpson	10	47	40	1	0	8	0	348	34.8
Lakeland	10	49	31	5	0	2	2	345	34.5
Thomas More	10	47	36	0	0	9	0	345	34.5
Lawrence	9	45	29	4	0	1	0	310	34.4
Salve Regina	9	46	12	11	0	0	0	310	34.4

Scoring Defense

	G	TD	XP	2XP	DXP	FG	SAF	Pts.	Avg.
Wash. & Jeff.	8	6	4	1	0	1	0	45	5.6
Williams	8	6	3	0	0	2	0	45	5.6
Central (Iowa)	10	8	7	0	0	2	0	61	6.1
Plymouth St.	9	10	5	0	0	1	1	70	7.8
Union (N.Y.)	9	10	5	0	0	2	0	71	7.9
Wis.-La Crosse	10	12	8	1	0	1	0	85	8.5
Rowan	10	11	8	0	0	3	2	87	8.7
Emory & Henry	10	11	7	1	1	5	0	92	9.2
Trinity (Tex.)	9	11	9	1	0	2	0	83	9.2
Allegheny	10	13	10	0	0	2	0	94	9.4
Salve Regina	9	12	5	1	0	3	1	90	10.0
Mount Union	10	14	9	1	0	2	0	101	10.1
Howard Payne	10	13	8	2	0	4	0	102	10.2
Wartburg	10	13	5	4	0	3	1	102	10.2
Moravian	10	13	9	1	0	5	0	104	10.4
Concordia-M'head	10	14	8	1	0	7	0	115	11.5
Wittenberg	10	16	10	3	0	2	0	118	11.8
Thomas More	10	16	12	1	0	3	0	119	11.9
Wesley	10	16	11	0	0	4	0	119	11.9
Muskingum	10	15	5	2	0	7	0	120	12.0

Passing Offense

	G	Att.	Cmp.	Pct.	Int.	Yards	Yds.PG
Hanover	10	507	291	57.4	11	3,628	362.8
Eureka	10	376	215	57.2	11	3,401	340.1
Claremont-M-S	9	395	213	53.9	13	2,984	331.6
Widener	10	378	218	57.7	10	2,934	293.4
Kalamazoo	9	390	211	54.1	16	2,579	286.6
Wilmington (Ohio)	9	404	192	47.5	23	2,553	283.7
Mount Union	10	278	196	70.5	4	2,815	281.5
Alma	9	383	197	51.4	8	2,510	278.9
Wheaton (Ill.)	9	295	176	59.7	5	2,455	272.8
Hartwick	9	351	167	47.6	22	2,412	268.0
St. John's (Minn.)	10	337	191	56.7	7	2,621	262.1
Albright	10	418	216	51.7	19	2,613	261.3
Hardin-Simmons	9	277	180	65.0	12	2,260	251.1
Ill. Wesleyan	9	326	177	54.3	11	2,256	250.7
St. Thomas (Minn.)	10	306	200	65.4	12	2,460	246.0
Western Md.	10	432	234	54.2	9	2,450	245.0
Ithaca	9	306	176	57.5	10	2,183	242.6
Wis.-La Crosse	10	269	167	62.1	8	2,421	242.1
Wabash	10	338	186	55.0	13	2,411	241.1
Lakeland	10	331	164	49.5	19	2,370	237.0

Pass Efficiency Defense

	G	Att.	Cmp.	Pct.	Int.	Yards	TD	Rating Points
Union (N.Y.)	9	258	94	36.4	22	964	3	54.6
Williams	8	173	65	37.5	11	638	1	57.7
Salve Regina	9	180	67	37.2	17	732	5	61.7
Frostburg St.	10	270	96	35.5	16	1,040	6	63.4
Central (Iowa)	10	259	108	41.7	16	951	3	64.0
Framingham St.	9	166	54	32.5	10	719	4	64.8
Hardin-Simmons	9	254	107	42.1	15	994	3	67.1
Worcester St.	10	249	78	31.3	19	1,179	9	67.8
Ursinus	10	254	107	42.1	20	1,113	4	68.4
Mass. Maritime	9	209	83	39.7	14	987	3	70.7
Plymouth St.	9	207	87	42.0	17	978	5	73.3
Simpson	10	313	131	41.8	17	1,364	6	73.9
Wheaton (Ill.)	9	244	106	43.4	14	1,159	3	75.9
Beloit	9	205	91	44.3	12	838	6	76.7
Amherst	8	161	66	40.9	13	800	5	76.8
Thomas More	10	282	117	41.4	26	1,477	9	77.6
Wash. & Jeff.	8	202	85	42.0	10	1,015	2	77.7
Moravian	10	268	122	45.5	26	1,454	6	79.1
Wis.-La Crosse	10	263	122	46.3	13	1,106	6	79.4
Wesley	10	240	106	44.1	16	1,168	6	80.0

Net Punting

	Punts	Yds.	Avg.	No. Ret.	Yds. Ret.	Net Avg.
Hardin-Simmons	42	1,616	38.47	15	26	37.85
Rowan	48	1,799	37.47	15	37	36.70
Trinity (Tex.)	47	1,807	38.44	21	109	36.12
Guilford	48	1,894	39.45	23	161	36.10
Wis.-Stevens Point	56	2,118	37.82	24	116	35.75
Cal Lutheran	44	1,933	43.93	30	362	35.70
Chapman	38	1,528	40.21	22	173	35.65
Thomas More	50	1,861	37.22	12	91	35.40
Albright	47	1,729	36.78	19	73	35.23
Lakeland	42	1,620	38.57	24	141	35.21
Washington (Mo.)	45	1,630	36.22	15	50	35.11
Sewanee	63	2,358	37.42	25	154	34.98
Bridgewater (Va.)	64	2,395	37.42	24	164	34.85
Wesleyan (Conn.)	59	2,108	35.72	14	70	34.54
Wis.-La Crosse	43	1,547	35.97	13	67	34.41
Wittenberg	33	1,182	35.81	10	49	34.33
Claremont-M-S	44	1,680	38.18	20	173	34.25
Redlands	44	1,577	35.84	16	73	34.18
Millsaps	55	1,950	35.45	16	76	34.07
Wilkes	70	2,659	37.98	35	280	33.98

Punt Returns

	G	No.	Yds.	TD	Avg.
Ohio Northern	10	19	314	2	16.52
Hartwick	9	17	245	0	14.41
Dickinson	10	36	506	2	14.05
Plymouth St.	9	40	557	3	13.92
Cornell College	10	25	336	1	13.44
Central (Iowa)	10	57	766	2	13.43
Ripon	10	28	373	1	13.32
Augustana (Ill.)	9	19	253	1	13.31
Claremont-M-S	9	17	222	3	13.05
Chapman	9	36	463	2	12.86
Salve Regina	9	28	357	4	12.75
Upper Iowa	10	21	264	0	12.57

	G	No.	Yds.	TD	Avg.
Monmouth (Ill.)	9	13	162	0	12.46
Otterbein	10	15	186	0	12.40
DePauw	10	25	309	1	12.36
Kean	9	23	282	0	12.26
Trenton St.	10	38	464	1	12.21
Marietta	10	44	522	1	11.86
Howard Payne	10	19	223	0	11.73
Curry	10	11	129	1	11.72

Kickoff Returns

	G	No.	Yds.	TD	Avg.
Howard Payne	10	15	442	0	29.46
Adrian	9	32	845	0	26.40
Hardin-Simmons	9	19	492	1	25.89
Buffalo St.	10	27	690	2	25.55
Trinity (Tex.)	9	18	459	0	25.50
Chicago	10	32	802	4	25.06
Salisbury St.	9	30	751	1	25.03
Emory & Henry	10	24	599	0	24.95
Salve Regina	9	17	416	2	24.47
Chapman	9	28	678	1	24.21
Ithaca	9	24	580	2	24.16
Norwich	9	30	712	0	23.73
Gettysburg	10	29	684	1	23.58
Cortland St.	10	33	776	1	23.51
Trinity (Conn.)	8	15	345	0	23.00
Plymouth St.	9	17	388	0	22.82
La Verne	9	21	477	0	22.71
Albion	9	24	545	0	22.70
Brockport St.	10	33	747	1	22.63
Cornell College	10	32	721	1	22.53

Turnover Margin

		TURNOVERS GAINED			TURNOVERS LOST			Margin/
	G	Fum.	Int.	Total	Fum.	Int.	Total	Game
Thomas More	10	21	26	47	15	4	19	2.80
Chapman	9	17	22	39	9	8	17	2.44
Wis.-River Falls	10	15	16	31	6	2	8	2.30
Wash. & Jeff.	8	17	10	27	8	3	11	2.00
Albion	9	17	15	32	5	10	15	1.88
Lycoming	9	13	24	37	10	10	20	1.88
Otterbein	10	17	18	35	7	10	17	1.80
Allegheny	10	22	13	35	9	9	18	1.70
Moravian	10	14	26	40	14	9	23	1.70
La Verne	9	16	13	29	10	4	14	1.66
Maine Maritime	9	17	20	37	17	5	22	1.66
Salve Regina	9	14	17	31	12	4	16	1.66
Anderson (Ind.)	10	21	18	39	14	9	23	1.60
Wartburg	10	16	13	29	8	5	13	1.60
Widener	10	20	18	38	12	10	22	1.60
Beloit	9	14	12	26	6	7	13	1.44
Rensselaer	9	10	19	29	10	6	16	1.44
Trinity (Tex.)	9	15	19	34	12	9	21	1.44
Union (N.Y.)	9	14	22	36	7	16	23	1.44
Eureka	10	11	21	32	7	11	18	1.40
Mount Union	10	4	16	20	2	4	6	1.40
Ursinus	10	13	20	33	6	13	19	1.40
Wis.-Whitewater	10	16	13	29	12	3	15	1.40

Longest Division III Plays of 1995

Rushing

Player, Team (Opponent)	Yards
Bill Casey, Mass.-Dartmouth (Norwich)	99
Chris Hohlbein, Albion (Wilmington, Ohio)	97
Ray Neosh, Coe (Lake Forest)	95
Jim Hart, Grinnell (Monmouth, Ill.)	92
Shawn Tarpey, Springfield (Merchant Marine)	91
Adam Kowles, Wis.-River Falls (Wis.-Stevens Point)	90
Trevor Shannon, Wartburg (Luther)	90
Josh Purdy, Baldwin-Wallace (Heidelberg)	90
Jeff Elser, Wooster (Denison)	89
Derek Walker, Elmhurst (Millikin)	88

Passing

Passer-Receiver, Team (Opponent)	Yards
Mike Schultz-R. J. Hoppe, Carroll, Wis. (Ripon)	99
Tracy Bacon-Lamont Rhim, Buffalo St. (Wash. & Jeff.)	98
Matt Lundeen-Mike Lundeen, Bethel, Minn. (Macalester)	96
Neil Rine-Mike Gundersdorf, Wilkes (FDU-Madison)	95
Jason Dyer-Jason Lobik, Fitchburg St. (Bri'water, Mass.)	95
Terry Peebles-Josh Habegger, Hanover (Centre)	92
Bill Poe-Todd Bloom, Hardin-Simmons (Sul Ross St.)	89
Marc Harris-Duane Martin, Wesley (Salisbury St.)	88
Larry Hutson-Jason Stiens, Thomas More (Mount Senario)	88
Scott Tekancic-LaVant King, Ohio Northern (Otterbein)	88

Interception Returns

Player, Team (Opponent)	Yards
Dan Gilson, Curry (Stonehill)	100
Tony Hinkle, Rose-Hulman (Millsaps)	100
Matt Bixler, Dickinson (Western Md.)	95

Punt Returns

Player, Team (Opponent)	Yards
Jim Wallace, Ripon (Illinois Col.)	86
Richard Wemer, Grinnell (Principia)	81
Vaughn Blythe, Upper Iowa (Ripon)	80
Brent Bardellini, Plymouth St. (Worcester Tech)	80

Kickoff Returns

Player, Team (Opponent)	Yards
Denarius Robinson, Hardin-Simmons (Sul Ross St.)	99
Mike Bechtel, Wis.-Stout (Wis.-Whitewater)	98
Scott Pietrzyk, Salve Regina (Bentley)	98
Derrick Brooms, Chicago (Rochester)	97
Oscar Ford, Chapman (Menlo)	97
Derrick Brooms, Chicago (Case Reserve)	96
George Lino, Wabash (Manchester)	96
Mike Smith, Franklin (Alma)	95
Derrick Brooms, Chicago (Washington, Mo.)	94
Ryan Glor, St. Norbert (Concordia, Wis.)	94
Al Thompson, Coast Guard (Worcester St.)	94

Field Goals

Player, Team (Opponent)	Yards
Joe Metzka, Knox (Beloit)	53
Brian Beddow, Hardin-Simmons (McMurry)	52
Eddie Rhodes, Blackburn (Tri-State)	50
Joel Buseman, Central, Iowa (Luther)	49
Ken Marzec, St. Norbert (Knox)	48
Scott Ernst, Ithaca (Mansfield)	48
Mike Grant, Ripon (Lakeland)	47
Bill Hamlin, Chapman (Occidental)	47
Jake Merski, Allegheny (Wooster)	47
Chad House, Rhodes (Sewanee)	46

Punts

Player, Team (Opponent)	Yards
Rob Sarvis, Norwich (Western Conn. St.)	84
Scott Ernst, Ithaca (Springfield)	79
Mike Sloan, Brockport St. (Western Conn. St.)	76
Doug Grigar, Trinity, Tex. (Centre)	75
Nate Holtey, Tufts (Bates)	73
Mike Moreno, Mass.-Boston (Framingham St.)	72
Bryan Weber, Wis.-Platteville (Wis.-Stout)	71
Ed Lizak, Chicago (Lawrence)	71
Chris Boglev, Rochester (Case Reserve)	70
Chris Ploucha, Olivet (Alma)	70
Jeff Timmons, Monmouth, Ill. (Beloit)	70
Brandon O'Connell, Albion (Adrian)	70

Conference Standings and Champions

1995 Conference Standings

(Full-Season Records Do Not Include Postseason Play; Ties in Standings Broken by Full-Season Records Unless Otherwise Noted)

Division I-A

ATLANTIC COAST CONFERENCE

	Conference				Full Season			
Team	W	L	T	Pct.	W	L	T	Pct.
Virginia*	7	1	0	.875	8	4	0	.667
Florida St.*	7	1	0	.875	9	2	0	.818
Clemson	6	2	0	.750	8	3	0	.727
Georgia Tech	5	3	0	.625	6	5	0	.545
Maryland#	4	4	0	.500	6	5	0	.545
North Caro.#	4	4	0	.500	6	5	0	.545
North Caro. St.	2	6	0	.250	3	8	0	.273
Duke	1	7	0	.125	3	8	0	.273
Wake Forest	0	8	0	.000	1	10	0	.091

**Virginia defeated Florida St., 33-28, on November 2. #Maryland defeated North Caro., 32-18, on September 9.*

Bowl Games (3-1): Florida St. (defeated Notre Dame, 31-26, in Orange Bowl); Clemson (lost to Syracuse, 41-0, in Gator Bowl); Virginia (defeated Georgia, 34-27, in Peach Bowl); North Caro. (defeated Arkansas, 20-10, in Carquest Bowl)

BIG EAST CONFERENCE

	Conference				Full Season			
Team	W	L	T	Pct.	W	L	T	Pct.
Virginia Tech	6	1	0	.857	9	2	0	.818
Miami (Fla.)	6	1	0	.857	8	3	0	.727
Syracuse	5	2	0	.714	8	3	0	.727
West Va.	4	3	0	.571	5	6	0	.455
Boston College	4	3	0	.571	4	8	0	.333
Rutgers	2	5	0	.286	4	7	0	.364
Temple	1	6	0	.143	1	10	0	.091
Pittsburgh	0	7	0	.000	2	9	0	.182

Bowl Games (2-0): Virginia Tech (defeated Texas, 28-10, in Sugar Bowl); Syracuse (defeated Clemson, 41-0, in Gator Bowl)

BIG EIGHT CONFERENCE

	Conference				Full Season			
Team	W	L	T	Pct.	W	L	T	Pct.
Nebraska	7	0	0	1.000	11	0	0	1.000
Colorado	5	2	0	.714	9	2	0	.818
Kansas	5	2	0	.714	9	2	0	.818
Kansas St.	5	2	0	.714	9	2	0	.818
Oklahoma	2	5	0	.286	5	5	1	.500
Oklahoma St.	2	5	0	.286	4	8	0	.333
Missouri*	1	6	0	.143	3	8	0	.273
Iowa St.*	1	6	0	.143	3	8	0	.273

**Missouri defeated Iowa St., 45-31, on November 18.*

Bowl Games (4-0): Nebraska (defeated Florida, 62-24, in Fiesta Bowl); Colorado (defeated Oregon, 38-6, in Cotton Bowl); Kansas (defeated UCLA, 51-30, in Aloha Bowl); Kansas St. (defeated Colorado St., 54-21, in Holiday Bowl)

BIG TEN CONFERENCE

	Conference				Full Season			
Team	W	L	T	Pct.	W	L	T	Pct.
Northwestern	8	0	0	1.000	10	1	0	.909
Ohio St.	7	1	0	.875	11	1	0	.917
Michigan	5	3	0	.625	9	3	0	.750
Penn St.	5	3	0	.625	8	3	0	.727
Michigan St.	4	3	1	.563	6	4	1	.591
Iowa	4	4	0	.500	7	4	0	.636
Illinois	3	4	1	.438	5	5	1	.500
Wisconsin	3	4	1	.438	4	5	2	.455
Purdue	2	5	1	.313	4	6	1	.409
Minnesota	1	7	0	.125	3	8	0	.273
Indiana	0	8	0	.000	2	9	0	.182

Bowl Games (2-4): Northwestern (lost to Southern Cal, 41-32, in Rose Bowl); Ohio St. (lost to Tennessee, 20-14, in Florida Citrus Bowl); Michigan (lost to Texas A&M, 22-20, in Alamo Bowl); Penn St. (defeated Auburn, 43-14, in Outback Bowl); Michigan St. (lost to LSU, 45-26, in Independence Bowl); Iowa (defeated Washington, 38-18, in Sun Bowl)

BIG WEST CONFERENCE

	Conference				Full Season			
Team	W	L	T	Pct.	W	L	T	Pct.
Nevada	6	0	0	1.000	9	2	0	.818
Southwestern La.	4	2	0	.667	6	5	0	.545
Utah St.	4	2	0	.667	4	7	0	.364
Arkansas St.	3	3	0	.500	6	5	0	.545
New Mexico St.	3	3	0	.500	4	7	0	.364
Northern Ill.	3	3	0	.500	3	8	0	.273
Louisiana Tech	2	4	0	.333	5	6	0	.455
Pacific (Cal.)*	2	4	0	.333	3	8	0	.273
San Jose St.*	2	4	0	.333	3	8	0	.273
UNLV	1	5	0	.167	2	9	0	.182

**Pacific (Cal.) defeated San Jose St., 32-30, on October 28.*

Bowl Games (0-1): Nevada (lost to Toledo, 40-37 in overtime, in Las Vegas Bowl)

MID-AMERICAN ATHLETIC CONFERENCE

	Conference				Full Season			
Team	W	L	T	Pct.	W	L	T	Pct.
Toledo	7	0	1	.938	10	0	1	.955
Miami (Ohio)	6	1	1	.813	8	2	1	.773
Ball St.*	6	2	0	.750	7	4	0	.636
Western Mich.*	6	2	0	.750	7	4	0	.636
Eastern Mich.	5	3	0	.625	6	5	0	.545
Bowling Green	3	5	0	.375	5	6	0	.455
Central Mich.	2	6	0	.250	4	7	0	.364
Akron	2	6	0	.250	2	9	0	.182
Ohio	1	6	1	.188	2	8	1	.227
Kent	0	7	1	.063	1	9	1	.136

**Ball St. defeated Western Mich., 10-0, on September 23.*

Bowl Games (1-0): Toledo (defeated Nevada, 40-37 in overtime, in Las Vegas Bowl)

PACIFIC-10 CONFERENCE

	Conference				Full Season			
Team	W	L	T	Pct.	W	L	T	Pct.
Southern Cal	6	1	1	.813	8	2	1	.773
Washington	6	1	1	.813	7	3	1	.682
Oregon	6	2	0	.750	9	2	0	.818
Stanford	5	3	0	.625	7	3	1	.682
UCLA	4	4	0	.500	7	4	0	.636
Arizona*	4	4	0	.500	6	5	0	.545
Arizona St.*	4	4	0	.500	6	5	0	.545
California#	2	6	0	.250	3	8	0	.273
Washington St.#	2	6	0	.250	3	8	0	.273
Oregon St.	0	8	0	.000	1	10	0	.091

**Arizona defeated Arizona St., 31-28, on November 24. #California defeated Washington St., 27-11, on November 4.*

Bowl Games (1-4): Southern Cal (defeated Northwestern, 41-32, in Rose Bowl); Washington (lost to Iowa, 38-18, in Sun Bowl); Oregon (lost to Colorado, 38-6, in Cotton Bowl); Stanford (lost to East Caro., 19-13, in Liberty Bowl); UCLA (lost to Kansas, 51-30, in Aloha Bowl)

SOUTHEASTERN CONFERENCE

	Conference				Full Season			
Team	W	L	T	Pct.	W	L	T	Pct.
Eastern Division								
Florida*#	8	0	0	1.000	12	0	0	1.000
Tennessee	7	1	0	.875	10	1	0	.909
Georgia	3	5	0	.375	6	5	0	.545
South Caro.	2	5	1	.313	4	6	1	.409
Kentucky	2	6	0	.250	4	7	0	.364
Vanderbilt	1	7	0	.125	2	9	0	.182
Western Division								
Arkansas*#	6	2	0	.750	8	4	0	.667
Auburn†	5	3	0	.625	8	3	0	.727
Alabama†	5	3	0	.625	8	3	0	.727
LSU	4	3	1	.563	6	4	1	.591
Mississippi	3	5	0	.375	6	5	0	.545
Mississippi St.	1	7	0	.125	3	8	0	.273

**Division champions. #Overall record includes SEC championship game in which Florida defeated Arkansas, 34-3, on December 2. †Auburn defeated Alabama, 31-27, on November 18.*

Bowl Games (2-4): Florida (lost to Nebraska, 62-24, in Fiesta Bowl); Tennessee (defeated Ohio St., 20-14, in Florida Citrus Bowl); Georgia (lost to Virginia, 34-27, in Peach Bowl); Arkansas (lost to North Caro., 20-10, in Carquest Bowl); Auburn (lost to Penn St., 43-14, in Outback Bowl); LSU (defeated Michigan St., 45-26, in Independence Bowl)

SOUTHWEST CONFERENCE

	Conference				Full Season			
Team	W	L	T	Pct.	W	L	T	Pct.
Texas	7	0	0	1.000	10	1	1	.875
Texas Tech*	5	2	0	.714	8	3	0	.727
Texas A&M*	5	2	0	.714	8	3	0	.727
Baylor	5	2	0	.714	7	4	0	.636
Texas Christian	3	4	0	.429	6	5	0	.545
Rice	1	6	0	.143	2	8	1	.227
Houston	2	5	0	.286	2	9	0	.182
Southern Methodist	0	7	0	.000	1	10	0	.091

**Texas Tech defeated Texas A&M, 14-7, on October 7.*

Bowl Games (2-1): Texas (lost to Virginia Tech, 28-10, in Sugar Bowl); Texas A&M (defeated Michigan, 22-20, in Alamo Bowl); Texas Tech (defeated Air Force, 55-41, in Copper Bowl)

WESTERN ATHLETIC CONFERENCE

	Conference				Full Season			
Team	W	L	T	Pct.	W	L	T	Pct.
Colorado St.	6	2	0	.750	8	3	0	.727
Air Force	6	2	0	.750	8	4	0	.667
Utah*	6	2	0	.750	7	4	0	.636
Brigham Young*	6	2	0	.750	7	4	0	.636
San Diego St.	5	3	0	.625	8	4	0	.667
Wyoming	4	4	0	.500	6	5	0	.545
Fresno St.	2	6	0	.250	5	7	0	.417
New Mexico	2	6	0	.250	4	7	0	.364
Hawaii	2	6	0	.250	4	8	0	.333
UTEP	1	7	0	.125	2	10	0	.167

**Utah defeated Brigham Young, 34-17, on November 18.*

Bowl Games (0-2): Colorado St. (lost to Kansas St., 54-21, in Holiday Bowl); Air Force (lost to Texas Tech, 55-41, in Copper Bowl)

DIVISION I-A INDEPENDENTS

	Full Season			
Team	W	L	T	Pct.
Notre Dame	9	2	0	.818
East Caro.	8	3	0	.727
Louisville	7	4	0	.636
Cincinnati	6	5	0	.545
Southern Miss.	6	5	0	.545
Army	5	5	1	.500
Navy	5	6	0	.455
Tulsa	4	7	0	.364
Memphis	3	8	0	.273
North Texas	2	9	0	.182
Northeast La.	2	9	0	.182
Tulane	2	9	0	.182

Bowl Games (1-1): Notre Dame (lost to Florida St., 31-26, in Orange Bowl); East Caro. (defeated Stanford, 19-13, in Liberty Bowl)

Division I-AA

AMERICAN WEST CONFERENCE

	Conference				Full Season			
Team	W	L	T	Pct.	W	L	T	Pct.
Cal St. Sacramento	3	0	0	1.000	4	6	1	.409
Cal Poly SLO	2	1	0	.667	5	6	0	.455
Cal St. Northridge	1	2	0	.333	2	8	0	.200
Southern Utah	0	3	0	.000	2	9	0	.182

BIG SKY CONFERENCE

	Conference				Full Season			
Team	W	L	T	Pct.	W	L	T	Pct.
Montana	6	1	0	.857	9	2	0	.818
Northern Ariz.*	4	3	0	.571	7	4	0	.636
Boise St.*	4	3	0	.571	7	4	0	.636
Idaho	4	3	0	.571	6	4	0	.600
Weber St.	4	3	0	.571	6	5	0	.545
Idaho St.	3	4	0	.429	6	5	0	.545
Montana St.	2	5	0	.286	5	6	0	.455
Eastern Wash.	1	6	0	.143	3	8	0	.273

**Northern Ariz. defeated Boise St., 32-13, on October 7.*

NCAA Division I-AA Playoffs (4-1): Montana (4-0: defeated Eastern Ky., 48-0, in first round; defeated Ga. Southern, 45-0, in quarterfinals; defeated Stephen F. Austin, 70-14, in semifinals; defeated Marshall, 22-20, in championship game); Idaho (0-1: lost to McNeese St., 33-3, in first round)

GATEWAY FOOTBALL CONFERENCE

	Conference				Full Season			
Team	**W**	**L**	**T**	**Pct.**	**W**	**L**	**T**	**Pct.**
Eastern Ill.*	5	1	0	.833	10	1	0	.909
Northern Iowa*	5	1	0	.833	7	4	0	.636
Indiana St.	3	3	0	.500	7	4	0	.636
Illinois St.	3	3	0	.500	5	6	0	.455
Southern Ill.	2	4	0	.333	5	6	0	.455
Western Ill.	2	4	0	.333	4	7	0	.364
Southwest Mo. St.	1	5	0	.167	4	7	0	.364

**Northern Iowa secured automatic Division I-AA playoff berth with 17-7 victory over Eastern Ill. on October 7.*

NCAA Division I-AA Playoffs (1-2): Northern Iowa (1-1: defeated Murray St., 35-34, in first round; lost to Marshall, 41-24, in quarterfinals); Eastern Ill. (0-1: lost to Stephen F. Austin, 34-29, in first round)

IVY GROUP

	Conference				Full Season			
Team	**W**	**L**	**T**	**Pct.**	**W**	**L**	**T**	**Pct.**
Princeton	5	1	1	.786	8	1	1	.850
Pennsylvania	5	2	0	.714	7	3	0	.700
Cornell	5	2	0	.714	6	4	0	.600
Dartmouth	4	2	1	.643	7	2	1	.750
Columbia	3	4	0	.429	3	6	1	.350
Brown	2	5	0	.286	5	5	0	.500
Yale	2	5	0	.286	3	7	0	.300
Harvard	1	6	0	.143	2	8	0	.200

Ivy Group teams do not participate in postseason play.

METRO ATLANTIC ATHLETIC CONFERENCE

	Conference				Full Season			
Team	**W**	**L**	**T**	**Pct.**	**W**	**L**	**T**	**Pct.**
Duquesne*	7	0	0	1.000	9	1	0	.900
Georgetown	5	2	0	.714	6	3	0	.667
Marist	4	3	0	.571	6	4	0	.600
Canisius	4	3	0	.571	4	6	0	.400
St. John's (N.Y.)	3	4	0	.429	4	6	0	.400
Iona	3	4	0	.429	3	6	0	.333
St. Peter's	2	5	0	.286	2	7	0	.222
Siena	0	7	0	.000	0	9	0	.000

**Does not include ECAC playoff victory, 44-20, over Wagner, November 18.*

MID-EASTERN ATHLETIC CONFERENCE

	Conference				Full Season			
Team	**W**	**L**	**T**	**Pct.**	**W**	**L**	**T**	**Pct.**
Florida A&M	6	0	0	1.000	9	2	0	.818
Delaware St.	5	1	0	.833	6	5	0	.545
South Caro. St.	4	2	0	.667	6	4	0	.600
Howard	2	4	0	.333	6	5	0	.545
North Caro. A&T	2	4	0	.333	4	7	0	.364
Bethune-Cookman	2	4	0	.333	3	8	0	.273
Morgan St.*	0	6	0	.000	1	10	0	.091
Hampton#	—	—	—	—	8	3	0	.727

**Morgan St. was not eligible for postseason competition. #Hampton was not eligible for the MEAC title.*

Postseason Game: Florida A&M (MEAC) lost to Southern-B.R. (SWAC), 30-25, on December 29 in the Jim Walter Homes Heritage Bowl V.

OHIO VALLEY CONFERENCE

	Conference				Full Season			
Team	**W**	**L**	**T**	**Pct.**	**W**	**L**	**T**	**Pct.**
Murray St.	8	0	0	1.000	11	0	0	1.000
Eastern Ky.	7	1	0	.875	9	2	0	.818
Middle Tenn. St.	6	2	0	.750	7	4	0	.636
Southeast Mo. St.	5	3	0	.625	5	6	0	.455
Tenn.-Martin	4	4	0	.500	5	6	0	.455
Austin Peay*	2	6	0	.250	3	8	0	.273
Tennessee Tech*	2	6	0	.250	3	8	0	.273
Morehead St.	1	7	0	.125	2	8	0	.200
Tennessee St.	1	7	0	.125	2	9	0	.182

**Austin Peay defeated Tennessee Tech, 20-17, on October 14.*

NCAA Division I-AA Playoffs (0-2): Murray St. (0-1: lost to Northern Iowa, 35-34, in first round); Eastern Ky. (0-1: lost to Montana, 48-0, in first round)

PATRIOT LEAGUE

	Conference				Full Season			
Team	**W**	**L**	**T**	**Pct.**	**W**	**L**	**T**	**Pct.**
Lehigh	5	0	0	1.000	8	3	0	.727
Bucknell	4	1	0	.800	7	4	0	.636
Lafayette	3	2	0	.600	4	6	1	.409
Fordham	2	3	0	.400	4	6	1	.409
Holy Cross	1	4	0	.200	2	9	0	.182
Colgate	0	5	0	.000	0	11	0	.000

Patriot League teams do not participate in postseason play.

PIONEER FOOTBALL LEAGUE

	Conference				Full Season			
Team	**W**	**L**	**T**	**Pct.**	**W**	**L**	**T**	**Pct.**
Drake	5	0	0	1.000	8	1	1	.850
Dayton	4	1	0	.800	9	2	0	.818
San Diego	3	2	0	.600	5	5	0	.500
Evansville*	1	4	0	.200	5	5	0	.500
Valparaiso*	1	4	0	.200	5	5	0	.500
Butler	1	4	0	.200	2	8	0	.200

**Evansville defeated Valparaiso, 7-6, on October 21.*

SOUTHERN CONFERENCE

	Conference				Full Season			
Team	**W**	**L**	**T**	**Pct.**	**W**	**L**	**T**	**Pct.**
Appalachian St.	8	0	0	1.000	11	0	0	1.000
Marshall	7	1	0	.875	9	2	0	.818
Ga. Southern	5	3	0	.625	8	3	0	.727
Furman	5	3	0	.625	6	5	0	.545
East Tenn. St.	4	4	0	.500	4	7	0	.364
Va. Military	3	5	0	.375	4	7	0	.364
Tenn.-Chatt.	2	6	0	.250	4	7	0	.364
Western Caro.	2	6	0	.250	3	7	0	.300
Citadel	0	8	0	.000	2	9	0	.182

NCAA Division I-AA Playoffs (5-3): Appalachian St. (1-1: defeated James Madison, 31-24, in first round; lost to Stephen F. Austin, 27-17, in quarterfinals); Marshall (3-1: defeated Jackson St., 38-8, in first round; defeated Northern Iowa, 41-24, in quarterfinals; defeated McNeese St., 25-13, in semifinals; lost to Montana, 22-20, in championship game); Ga. Southern (1-1: defeated Troy St., 24-21, in first round; lost to Montana, 45-0, in quarterfinals)

SOUTHLAND CONFERENCE

	Conference				Full Season			
Team	**W**	**L**	**T**	**Pct.**	**W**	**L**	**T**	**Pct.**
McNeese St.	5	0	0	1.000	11	0	0	1.000
Stephen F. Austin	4	1	0	.800	9	1	0	.900
Northwestern St.	2	3	0	.400	6	5	0	.545
Sam Houston St.	2	3	0	.400	5	5	0	.500
Southwest Tex. St.	2	3	0	.400	4	7	0	.364
Nicholls St.	0	5	0	.000	0	11	0	.000

NCAA Division I-AA Playoffs (4-2): McNeese St. (2-1: defeated Idaho, 33-3, in first round; defeated Delaware, 52-18, in quarterfinals; lost to Marshall, 25-13, in semifinals); Stephen F. Austin (2-1: defeated Eastern Ill., 34-29, in first round; defeated Appalachian St., 27-17, in quarterfinals; lost to Montana, 70-14, in semifinals)

SOUTHWESTERN ATHLETIC CONFERENCE

	Conference				Full Season			
Team	**W**	**L**	**T**	**Pct.**	**W**	**L**	**T**	**Pct.**
Jackson St.	7	0	0	1.000	9	2	0	.818
Southern-B.R.	6	1	0	.857	10	1	0	.909
Alabama St.	5	2	0	.714	8	3	0	.727
Grambling	4	3	0	.571	5	6	0	.455
Alcorn St.	3	4	0	.429	4	7	0	.364
Mississippi Val.	2	5	0	.286	2	9	0	.182
Texas Southern	1	6	0	.143	2	8	0	.200
Prairie View	0	7	0	.000	0	11	0	.000

NCAA Division I-AA Playoffs (0-1): Jackson St. (0-1: lost to Marshall, 38-8, in first round)

Postseason Game: Southern-B.R. (SWAC) defeated Florida A&M (MEAC), 30-25, on December 29 in the Jim Walter Homes Heritage Bowl V.

YANKEE CONFERENCE

	Conference				Full Season			
Team	**W**	**L**	**T**	**Pct.**	**W**	**L**	**T**	**Pct.**
New England Division								
Rhode Island*	6	2	0	.750	7	4	0	.636
Connecticut	5	3	0	.625	8	3	0	.727
New Hampshire	4	4	0	.500	6	5	0	.545
Massachusetts	3	5	0	.375	6	5	0	.545
Boston U.#	1	7	0	.125	3	8	0	.273
Maine#	1	7	0	.125	3	8	0	.273
Mid-Atlantic Division								
Delaware†	8	0	0	1.000	10	1	0	.909
James Madison	6	2	0	.750	8	3	0	.727
Richmond	5	3	0	.625	7	3	1	.682
William & Mary	5	3	0	.625	7	4	0	.636
Northeastern	2	6	0	.250	4	7	0	.364
Villanova	2	6	0	.250	3	8	0	.273

**New England Division champion. #Boston U. defeated Maine, 40-21, on September 16. †Yankee Conference and Mid-Atlantic Division champion.*

NCAA Division I-AA Playoffs (1-2): Delaware (1-1: defeated Hofstra, 38-17, in first round; lost to McNeese St., 52-18, in quarterfinals); James Madison (0-1: lost to Appalachian St., 31-24, in first round)

DIVISION I-AA INDEPENDENTS

	Full Season			
Team	**W**	**L**	**T**	**Pct.**
Troy St.	11	0	0	1.000
Hofstra	10	1	0	.909
Wagner*	8	1	0	.889
St. Mary's (Cal.)	8	2	0	.800
Liberty	8	3	0	.727
Monmouth (N.J.)	7	3	0	.700
Jacksonville St.	7	4	0	.636
Samford	7	4	0	.636
Robert Morris	6	4	0	.600
Towson St.	6	4	0	.600
Central Fla.	6	5	0	.545
Ala.-Birmingham	5	6	0	.455
Wofford	4	7	0	.364
Buffalo	3	8	0	.273
Youngstown St.	3	8	0	.273
Central Conn. St.	2	8	0	.200
Western Ky.	2	8	0	.200
Davidson	1	8	1	.150
Charleston So.	1	10	0	.091
St. Francis (Pa.)	0	10	0	.000

**Does not include ECAC playoff loss, 44-20, to Duquesne on November 18.*

NCAA Division I-AA Playoffs (0-2): Troy St. (0-1: lost to Ga. Southern, 24-21, in first round); Hofstra (0-1: lost to Delaware, 38-17, in first round)

Division II

CENTRAL INTERCOLLEGIATE ATHLETIC ASSOCIATION

	Conference				Full Season			
Team	**W**	**L**	**T**	**Pct.**	**W**	**L**	**T**	**Pct.**
Virginia St.	7	1	0	.875	8	2	0	.800
Norfolk St.	6	2	0	.750	7	3	0	.700
Elizabeth City St.	6	2	0	.750	7	4	0	.636
Livingstone	4	3	1	.563	5	4	1	.550
Winston-Salem	3	3	2	.500	4	4	2	.500
N.C. Central	4	4	0	.500	5	6	0	.455
Bowie St.	2	6	0	.250	3	8	0	.273
Johnson Smith	2	6	0	.250	2	8	0	.200
Fayetteville St.	1	5	2	.250	1	7	2	.200
Virginia Union	0	6	2	.125	0	8	2	.100

In designated conference games, Virginia Union tied Cheyney, 21-21, on September 9; Lane defeated Johnson Smith, 46-20, on September 30; and Delaware St. defeated Norfolk St., 20-14, on September 30.

EASTERN COLLEGIATE FOOTBALL CONFERENCE*

	Conference				Full Season			
Team	**W**	**L**	**T**	**Pct.**	**W**	**L**	**T**	**Pct.**
Stonehill#	8	0	0	1.000	9	1	0	.900
Bentley#	7	1	0	.875	9	1	0	.900

Team	W	L	T	Pct.	W	L	T	Pct.
Salve Regina	6	2	0	.750	7	2	0	.778
Assumption	5	3	0	.625	6	4	0	.600
MIT	3	4	0	.429	3	5	0	.375
Sacred Heart	2	4	0	.333	3	7	0	.300
Western New Eng.	2	6	0	.250	2	6	0	.250
Curry	1	7	0	.125	2	8	0	.200
Nichols	0	7	0	.000	0	9	0	.000

**Assumption, Bentley, Sacred Heart and Stonehill are Division II members, others are Division III. #Does not include Bentley's 46-3 ECAC playoff victory over Stonehill on November 18.*

GULF SOUTH CONFERENCE

	Conference				Full Season			
Team	**W**	**L**	**T**	**Pct.**	**W**	**L**	**T**	**Pct.**
North Ala.	8	0	0	1.000	10	0	0	1.000
West Ga.	7	1	0	.875	8	2	0	.800
Central Ark.	6	3	0	.667	7	4	0	.636
Henderson St.	6	3	0	.667	6	5	0	.545
Valdosta St.	4	3	0	.571	6	5	0	.545
Delta St.	5	4	0	.556	5	6	0	.455
Ark.-Monticello	3	3	0	.500	6	5	0	.545
Arkansas Tech	2	6	1	.278	3	6	1	.350
Mississippi Col.	2	7	1	.250	2	7	1	.250
Southern Ark.	1	6	0	.143	4	6	0	.400
West Ala.	0	8	0	.000	2	9	0	.182

NCAA Division II Playoffs (4-1): North Ala. (4-0: defeated Albany St., Ga., 38-28, in first round; defeated Carson-Newman, 28-7, in quarterfinals; defeated Ferris St., 45-7, in semifinals; defeated Pittsburg St., 27-7, in championship game); West Ga. (0-1: lost to Carson-Newman, 37-26, in first round)

LONE STAR CONFERENCE

	Conference				Full Season			
Team	**W**	**L**	**T**	**Pct.**	**W**	**L**	**T**	**Pct.**
Tex. A&M-Kingsville	7	0	0	.1000	9	1	0	.900
East Tex. St.	6	1	0	.857	8	3	0	.727
Angelo St.	4	2	1	.643	6	3	1	.650
Central Okla.	4	3	0	.571	8	3	0	.727
Eastern N.M.	3	3	1	.500	6	4	1	.591
Abilene Christian	2	5	0	.286	4	7	0	.364
West Tex. A&M	1	6	0	.143	5	6	0	.455
Tarleton St.	0	7	0	.000	1	10	0	.091

NCAA Division II Playoffs (2-2): Tex. A&M-Kingsville (2-1: defeated Fort Hays St., 59-28, in first round; defeated Portland St., 30-3, in quarterfinals; lost to Pittsburg St., 28-25 in overtime, in semifinals); East Tex. St. (0-1: lost to Portland St., 56-35, in first round)

MID-AMERICAN INTERCOLLEGIATE ATHLETICS ASSOCIATION

	Conference				Full Season			
Team	**W**	**L**	**T**	**Pct.**	**W**	**L**	**T**	**Pct.**
Pittsburg St.	9	0	0	1.000	9	0	1	.950
Mo. Western St.	6	3	0	.667	7	3	1	.682
Truman St.*	6	3	0	.667	6	5	0	.545
Northwest Mo. St.*	6	3	0	.667	6	5	0	.545
Mo. Southern St.	5	4	0	.556	6	4	0	.600
Emporia St.	4	5	0	.444	5	6	0	.455
Washburn#	3	6	0	.333	4	6	0	.400
Central Mo. St.#	3	6	0	.333	4	6	0	.400
Southwest Baptist	2	7	0	.222	2	8	0	.200
Mo.-Rolla	1	8	0	.111	1	9	0	.100

**Truman St. defeated Northwest Mo. St., 44-10, on October 7. #Washburn defeated Central Mo. St., 37-21, on October 7.*

NCAA Division II Playoffs (3-1): Pittsburg St. (3-1: defeated Northern Colo., 36-17, in first round; defeated North Dak. St., 9-7, in quarterfinals; defeated Tex. A&M-Kingsville, 28-25 in overtime, in semifinals; lost to North Ala., 27-7, in championship game)

MIDWEST INTERCOLLEGIATE FOOTBALL CONFERENCE

	Conference				Full Season			
Team	**W**	**L**	**T**	**Pct.**	**W**	**L**	**T**	**Pct.**
Ferris St.	10	0	0	1.000	10	0	0	1.000
Grand Valley St.	8	2	0	.800	8	3	0	.727
Northern Mich.*	7	3	0	.700	7	3	0	.700
Saginaw Valley*	7	3	0	.700	7	3	0	.700
Hillsdale	7	3	0	.700	7	4	0	.636
Michigan Tech	5	5	0	.500	5	5	0	.500
St. Francis (Ill.)	5	5	0	.500	5	6	0	.455
Indianapolis#	3	7	0	.300	3	8	0	.273
Wayne St. (Mich.)#	3	7	0	.300	3	8	0	.273
Northwood†	2	8	0	.200	2	8	0	.200
Ashland†	2	8	0	.200	2	8	0	.200
St. Joseph's (Ind.)	1	9	0	.100	1	9	0	.100

**Northern Mich. defeated Saginaw Valley, 13-12, on September 9. #Indianapolis defeated Wayne St. (Mich.), 21-7, on September 23. †Northwood defeated Ashland, 15-9, on September 30.*

NCAA Division II Playoffs (2-1): Ferris St. (2-1: defeated Millersville, 36-26, in first round; defeated New Haven, 17-9, in quarterfinals; lost to North Ala., 45-7, in semifinals)

NORTH CENTRAL INTERCOLLEGIATE ATHLETIC CONFERENCE

	Conference				Full Season			
Team	**W**	**L**	**T**	**Pct.**	**W**	**L**	**T**	**Pct.**
North Dak.	8	1	0	.889	9	1	0	.900
North Dak. St.*	7	2	0	.778	9	2	0	.818
Northern Colo.*	7	2	0	.778	9	2	0	.818
South Dak.	6	3	0	.667	8	3	0	.727
St. Cloud St.	5	4	0	.556	6	4	0	.600
South Dak. St.	4	5	0	.444	6	5	0	.545
Mankato St.	3	6	0	.333	4	7	0	.364
Augustana (S.D.)	2	6	1	.278	3	6	1	.350
Neb.-Omaha	2	7	0	.222	3	8	0	.273
Morningside	0	8	1	.056	0	9	2	.091

**North Dak. St. defeated Northern Colo., 42-38, on October 7.*

NCAA Division II Playoffs (1-3): North Dak. (0-1: lost to North Dak. St., 41-10, in first round); North Dak. St. (1-1: defeated North Dak., 41-10, in first round; lost to Pittsburg St., 9-7, in quarterfinals); Northern Colo. (0-1: lost to Pittsburg St., 36-17, in first round)

NORTHERN CALIFORNIA ATHLETIC CONFERENCE

	Conference				Full Season			
Team	**W**	**L**	**T**	**Pct.**	**W**	**L**	**T**	**Pct.**
Humboldt St.	4	0	0	1.000	8	1	1	.850
Cal St. Chico	1	2	1	.375	2	5	2	.333
Sonoma St.	0	3	1	.125	0	8	1	.056

NORTHERN SUN INTERCOLLEGIATE ATHLETIC CONFERENCE

	Conference				Full Season			
Team	**W**	**L**	**T**	**Pct.**	**W**	**L**	**T**	**Pct.**
Minn.-Duluth	5	0	1	.917	8	2	1	.773
Moorhead St.	5	0	1	.917	6	3	1	.650
Winona St.	3	3	0	.500	6	5	0	.545
Bemidji St.	3	3	0	.500	3	7	0	.300
Northern St.	2	4	0	.333	4	7	0	.364
Southwest St.	2	4	0	.333	2	8	0	.200
Minn.-Morris	0	6	0	.000	0	10	0	.000

PENNSYLVANIA STATE ATHLETIC CONFERENCE

	Conference				Full Season			
Team	**W**	**L**	**T**	**Pct.**	**W**	**L**	**T**	**Pct.**
Western Division								
Edinboro	6	0	0	1.000	9	1	0	.900
Indiana (Pa.)	5	1	0	.833	8	3	0	.727
Slippery Rock	4	2	0	.667	7	4	0	.636
Clarion	3	3	0	.500	6	4	0	.600
Shippensburg	2	4	0	.333	3	8	0	.273
Calif. (Pa.)	1	5	0	.167	2	9	0	.182
Lock Haven	0	6	0	.000	2	9	0	.182
Eastern Division								
Millersville*	5	0	1	.917	9	0	1	.950
Bloomsburg*	5	0	1	.917	9	1	1	.864
Kutztown	4	2	0	.667	6	4	0	.600
East Stroudsburg	3	3	0	.500	4	6	0	.400
West Chester	2	4	0	.333	4	6	1	.409
Mansfield	1	5	0	.167	1	9	0	.100
Cheyney	0	6	0	.000	0	10	1	.045

**PSAC Eastern Division cochampions.*

NCAA Division II Playoffs (0-2): Edinboro (0-1: lost to New Haven, 27-12, in first round); Millersville (0-1: lost to Ferris St., 36-26, in first round)

ROCKY MOUNTAIN ATHLETIC CONFERENCE

	Conference				Full Season			
Team	**W**	**L**	**T**	**Pct.**	**W**	**L**	**T**	**Pct.**
Fort Hays St.*	6	0	1	.929	8	1	2	.818
Western St.*	6	0	1	.929	7	2	1	.750
Chadron St.	5	2	0	.714	8	2	0	.800
Fort Lewis#	3	4	0	.429	4	6	0	.400
Adams St.#	3	4	0	.429	4	6	0	.400
N.M. Highlands	2	5	0	.286	4	7	0	.364
Mesa St.	2	5	0	.286	3	7	0	.300
Colorado Mines	0	7	0	.000	1	9	0	.100
Neb.-Kearney†	—	—	—	—	6	3	1	.650

**RMAC cochampions. #Fort Lewis defeated Adams St., 41-16, on October 28. †Neb.-Kearney not eligible for RMAC championship.*

NCAA Division II Playoffs (0-1): Fort Hays St. (0-1: lost to Tex. A&M-Kingsville, 59-28, in first round)

SOUTH ATLANTIC CONFERENCE

	Conference				Full Season			
Team	**W**	**L**	**T**	**Pct.**	**W**	**L**	**T**	**Pct.**
Carson-Newman	6	1	0	.857	8	2	0	.800
Catawba	5	2	0	.714	7	3	0	.700
Gardner-Webb*	4	3	0	.571	6	4	0	.600
Mars Hill*	4	3	0	.571	6	4	0	.600
Presbyterian	4	3	0	.571	6	5	0	.545
Elon	2	5	0	.286	4	7	0	.364
Lenior-Rhyne	2	5	0	.286	3	7	0	.300
Wingate	1	6	0	.143	4	7	0	.364

**Gardner-Webb defeated Mars Hill, 14-6, on November 11.*

NCAA Division II Playoffs (1-1): Carson-Newman (1-1: defeated West Ga., 37-26, in first round; lost to North Ala., 28-7, in quarterfinals)

SOUTHERN INTERCOLLEGIATE ATHLETIC CONFERENCE

	Conference				Full Season			
Team	**W**	**L**	**T**	**Pct.**	**W**	**L**	**T**	**Pct.**
Albany St. (Ga.)	7	1	0	.875	8	3	0	.727
Alabama A&M	5	3	0	.625	6	5	0	.545
Clark Atlanta	5	3	0	.625	5	5	0	.500
Morehouse	5	3	0	.625	5	6	0	.455
Savannah St.	4	4	0	.500	7	4	0	.636
Miles	4	4	0	.500	4	6	0	.400
Fort Valley St.	3	5	0	.375	3	8	0	.273
Tuskegee	2	6	0	.250	2	9	0	.182
Morris Brown	1	7	0	.125	1	9	0	.100
Kentucky St.*	—	—	—	—	7	4	0	.636

**Kentucky St. not eligible for conference championship.*

NCAA Division II Championship (0-1): Albany St. (Ga.) (0-1: lost to North Ala., 38-28, in first round)

WEST VIRGINIA INTERCOLLEGIATE ATHLETIC CONFERENCE

	Conference				Full Season			
Team	**W**	**L**	**T**	**Pct.**	**W**	**L**	**T**	**Pct.**
W. Va. Wesleyan*#	6	1	0	.857	8	2	0	.800
Glenville St.*#	6	1	0	.857	8	2	0	.800
West Liberty St.	5	2	0	.714	7	3	0	.700
Fairmont St.	5	2	0	.714	6	4	0	.600
Shepherd	3	4	0	.429	3	7	0	.300
Concord	2	5	0	.286	3	7	0	.300
West Va. St.	1	6	0	.143	1	9	0	.100
West Va. Tech	0	7	0	.000	0	10	0	.000

**WVIAC cochampions. #West Va. Wesleyan defeated Glenville St., 17-14, on October 7.*

DIVISION II INDEPENDENTS

	Full Season			
Team	**W**	**L**	**T**	**Pct.**
New Haven	9	0	1	.950
Lane	9	1	0	.900
Southern Conn. St.	8	3	0	.727
Gannon	7	3	0	.700
Mercyhurst	7	3	0	.700
Stony Brook*	7	3	0	.700
UC Davis	6	3	1	.650
Portland St.	7	4	0	.636
LIU-C.W. Post	6	4	0	.600

Team	W	L	T	Pct.
Pace	6	4	0	.600
Wayne St. (Neb.)	6	4	0	.600
Ky. Wesleyan	5	5	0	.500
Newberry	5	6	0	.455
Western N.M.	4	5	0	.444
Albany (N.Y.)	3	7	0	.300
American Int'l	2	8	0	.200
Mass.-Lowell*	0	10	0	.000
Quincy#	—	—	—	—

**Member of the Freedom Football Conference listed in Division III. #Did not play a varsity schedule in 1995.*

NCAA Division II Playoffs (2-2): New Haven (1-1: defeated Edinboro, 27-12, in first round; lost to Ferris St., 17-9, in quarterfinals); Portland St. (1-1: defeated East Tex. St., 56-35, in first round; lost to Tex. A&M-Kingsville, 30-3, in quarterfinals)

Division III

ASSOCIATION OF MID-EAST COLLEGES

Team	Conference W	L	T	Pct.	Full Season W	L	T	Pct.
Thomas More	3	0	0	1.000	10	0	0	1.000
Mt. St. Joseph	1	2	0	.333	5	4	0	.556
Bluffton	1	2	0	.333	5	5	0	.500
Wilmington (Ohio)	1	2	0	.333	2	6	1	.278

CENTENNIAL FOOTBALL CONFERENCE

Team	Conference W	L	T	Pct.	Full Season W	L	T	Pct.
Frank. & Marsh.	6	1	0	.857	7	3	0	.700
Dickinson	5	1	1	.786	7	2	1	.750
Johns Hopkins	4	2	1	.643	6	3	1	.650
Western Md.	3	2	2	.571	5	3	2	.600
Gettysburg	3	3	1	.500	5	4	1	.550
Swarthmore	3	4	0	.429	5	5	0	.500
Ursinus	1	6	0	.143	3	7	0	.300
Muhlenberg	0	6	1	.071	0	9	1	.050

COLLEGE CONFERENCE OF ILLINOIS AND WISCONSIN

Team	Conference W	L	T	Pct.	Full Season W	L	T	Pct.
Wheaton (Ill.)	7	0	0	1.000	9	0	0	1.000
Ill. Wesleyan	6	1	0	.857	6	3	0	.667
Augustana (Ill.)	5	2	0	.714	6	3	0	.667
Millikin	3	4	0	.429	5	4	0	.556
Carthage	2	4	1	.357	3	5	1	.389
Elmhurst	2	5	0	.286	2	7	0	.222
North Central	1	5	1	.214	3	5	1	.389
North Park	1	6	0	.143	2	7	0	.222

NCAA Division III Playoffs (1-1): Wheaton (Ill.) (1-1: defeated Wittenberg, 63-41, in first round; lost to Mount Union, 40-14, in quarterfinals)

EASTERN COLLEGIATE FOOTBALL CONFERENCE*

Team	Conference W	L	T	Pct.	Full Season W	L	T	Pct.
Stonehill#	8	0	0	1.000	9	1	0	.900
Bentley#	7	1	0	.875	9	1	0	.900
Salve Regina	6	2	0	.750	7	2	0	.778
Assumption	5	3	0	.625	6	4	0	.600
MIT	3	4	0	.429	3	5	0	.375
Sacred Heart	2	4	0	.333	3	7	0	.300
Western New Eng.	2	6	0	.250	2	6	0	.250
Curry	1	7	0	.125	2	8	0	.200
Nichols	0	7	0	.000	0	9	0	.000

**Curry, MIT, Nichols, Salve Regina and Western New Eng. are Division III members, others are Division II. #Does not include Stonehill's 46-3 loss to Bentley in ECAC playoff game on November 18.*

FREEDOM FOOTBALL CONFERENCE*

Team	Conference W	L	T	Pct.	Full Season W	L	T	Pct.
Plymouth St.	7	0	0	1.000	9	1	0	.900
Western Conn. St.	4	2	0	.667	6	3	1	.650
Springfield	3	2	0	.600	8	2	0	.800
Stony Brook	3	2	0	.600	7	3	0	.700
Worcester Tech	3	3	0	.500	4	5	0	.444
Merchant Marine	2	3	0	.400	5	4	0	.556
Coast Guard	2	4	0	.333	4	6	0	.400
Norwich	2	5	0	.286	3	6	0	.333
Mass.-Lowell	0	5	0	.000	0	10	0	.000

**Mass.-Lowell and Stony Brook are Division II members.*

NCAA Division III Playoffs (0-1): Plymouth St. (0-1: lost to Union, N.Y., 24-7, in first round)

INDIANA COLLEGIATE ATHLETIC CONFERENCE

Team	Conference W	L	T	Pct.	Full Season W	L	T	Pct.
Hanover	6	0	0	1.000	10	0	0	1.000
Rose-Hulman	4	2	0	.667	6	4	0	.600
Franklin	3	3	0	.500	6	4	0	.600
Manchester	3	3	0	.500	4	6	0	.400
Anderson (Ind.)	2	4	0	.333	6	4	0	.600
Wabash	2	4	0	.333	5	5	0	.500
DePauw	1	5	0	.167	3	7	0	.300

NCAA Division III Playoffs (0-1): Hanover (0-1: lost to Mount Union, 52-18, in first round)

IOWA INTERCOLLEGIATE ATHLETIC CONFERENCE

Team	Conference W	L	T	Pct.	Full Season W	L	T	Pct.
Central (Iowa)	8	0	0	1.000	10	0	0	1.000
Wartburg	7	1	0	.875	9	1	0	.900
Simpson	6	2	0	.750	7	3	0	.700
Loras	5	3	0	.625	6	4	0	.600
Upper Iowa	4	4	0	.500	4	6	0	.400
Buena Vista	2	6	0	.250	2	7	0	.222
Dubuque*	2	6	0	.250	2	8	0	.200
Luther*	2	6	0	.250	2	8	0	.200
William Penn	0	8	0	.000	0	10	0	.000

**Dubuque defeated Luther, 13-12, on October 28.*

NCAA Division III Playoffs (0-1): Central (Iowa) (0-1: lost to Wis.-River Falls, 10-7, in first round)

MICHIGAN INTERCOLLEGIATE ATHLETIC CONFERENCE

Team	Conference W	L	T	Pct.	Full Season W	L	T	Pct.
Albion	5	0	0	1.000	8	1	0	.889
Alma*	3	2	0	.600	6	3	0	.667
Adrian*	3	2	0	.600	6	3	0	.667
Kalamazoo	3	2	0	.600	4	5	0	.444
Hope	1	4	0	.200	2	7	0	.222
Olivet	0	5	0	.000	3	6	0	.333

**Alma defeated Adrian, 24-21, on October 28.*

MIDDLE ATLANTIC STATES COLLEGIATE ATHLETIC CONFERENCE

Team	Conference W	L	T	Pct.	Full Season W	L	T	Pct.
Commonwealth League								
Widener*	5	0	0	1.000	8	2	0	.800
Albright#	4	1	0	.800	7	3	0	.700
Moravian	2	2	1	.500	7	2	1	.750
Juniata	1	3	1	.300	2	7	1	.250
Susquehanna	1	4	0	.200	5	5	0	.500
Lebanon Valley	1	4	0	.200	3	7	0	.300
Freedom League								
Lycoming†	3	1	0	.750	7	2	0	.778
Wilkes†	3	1	0	.750	5	5	0	.500
FDU-Madison	2	2	0	.500	4	5	0	.444
Delaware Valley	1	3	0	.250	3	7	0	.300
King's (Pa.)	1	3	0	.250	1	9	0	.100

**MAC and Commonwealth League champion. #Does not include 20-10 victory over Salisbury St. in ECAC playoff game on November 18. †Freedom League cochampions.*

NCAA Division III Playoffs (1-2): Widener (0-1: lost to Lycoming, 31-27, in first round); Lycoming (1-1: defeated Widener, 31-27, in first round; lost to Wash. & Jeff., 48-0, in quarterfinals)

MIDWEST COLLEGIATE ATHLETIC CONFERENCE

Team	Conference* W	L	T	Pct.	Full Season W	L	T	Pct.
North Division								
Ripon#†	4	1	0	.800	8	2	0	.800
Beloit†	4	1	0	.800	8	1	0	.889
Carroll (Wis.)	4	1	0	.800	6	3	0	.667
Lawrence	2	3	0	.400	4	5	0	.444
St. Norbert	1	4	0	.200	1	8	0	.111
Lake Forest	0	5	0	.000	0	9	0	.000
South Division								
Cornell College#	5	0	0	1.000	9	1	0	.900
Coe	4	1	0	.800	7	2	0	.778
Knox	3	2	0	.600	6	3	0	.667
Grinnell	2	3	0	.400	4	5	0	.444
Illinois Col.	1	4	0	.200	2	7	0	.222
Monmouth (Ill.)	0	5	0	.000	0	9	0	.000

**Interdivision games count in conference statistics and also are used for tiebreaking criteria. #Cornell College defeated Ripon, 38-17, on November 12 for MCAC title. †Ripon defeated Beloit, 13-7, on October 7.*

MINNESOTA INTERCOLLEGIATE ATHLETIC CONFERENCE

Team	Conference W	L	T	Pct.	Full Season W	L	T	Pct.
Concordia-M'head*	7	1	1	.833	8	1	1	.850
St. John's (Minn.)*	7	1	1	.833	8	1	1	.850
Hamline	6	3	0	.667	7	3	0	.700
St. Thomas (Minn.)	6	3	0	.667	6	4	0	.600
Bethel (Minn.)#	5	4	0	.556	6	4	0	.600
Augsburg#	5	4	0	.556	6	4	0	.600
St. Olaf	4	5	0	.444	5	5	0	.500
Carleton	3	6	0	.333	3	7	0	.300
Gust. Adolphus	1	8	0	.111	1	9	0	.100
Macalester	0	9	0	.000	1	9	0	.100

**MIAC cochampions; the two teams tied, 14-14, on November 4. #Bethel (Minn.) defeated Augsburg, 20-7, on September 30.*

NCAA Division III Playoffs (0-1): Concordia-M'head (0-1: lost to Wis.-La Crosse, 45-7, in first round)

NEW ENGLAND FOOTBALL CONFERENCE

Team	Conference W	L	T	Pct.	Full Season W	L	T	Pct.
Worcester St.*	8	0	0	1.000	9	1	0	.900
Mass. Maritime#	6	2	0	.750	7	2	0	.778
Maine Maritime#	6	2	0	.750	7	2	0	.778
Bri'water (Mass.)	6	2	0	.750	6	4	0	.600
Mass.-Dartmouth	3	5	0	.375	4	6	0	.400
Westfield St.	3	5	0	.375	3	6	0	.333
Framingham St.	2	6	0	.250	2	7	0	.222
Mass.-Boston	1	7	0	.125	2	7	0	.222
Fitchburg St.	1	7	0	.125	1	8	0	.111

**Does not include 69-12 loss to Rensselaer in ECAC playoff game on November 18. #Mass. Maritime defeated Maine Maritime, 17-10, on September 30.*

NEW JERSEY ATHLETIC CONFERENCE

Team	Conference W	L	T	Pct.	Full Season W	L	T	Pct.
Rowan	5	0	0	1.000	7	2	1	.750
Trenton St.*	4	1	0	.800	7	3	0	.700
Kean	3	2	0	.600	3	4	2	.444
Montclair St.	2	3	0	.400	3	6	0	.333
Jersey City St.	1	4	0	.200	1	9	0	.100
Wm. Paterson	0	5	0	.000	0	10	0	.000

**Does not include 10-7 victory over Wesley in ECAC playoff game on November 18.*

NCAA Division III Playoffs (3-1): Rowan (3-1: defeated Buffalo St., 46-7, in first round; defeated Union, N.Y., 38-7, in quarterfinals; defeated Wash. & Jeff., 28-15, in semifinals; lost to Wis.-La Crosse, 36-7, in championship game)

NORTH COAST ATHLETIC CONFERENCE

Team	Conference W	L	T	Pct.	Full Season W	L	T	Pct.
Wittenberg	7	0	0	1.000	10	0	0	1.000
Allegheny	7	1	0	.875	9	1	0	.900
Ohio Wesleyan	6	2	0	.750	6	4	0	.600
Wooster	5	3	0	.625	5	5	0	.500
Kenyon	3	4	1	.438	3	6	1	.350
Denison	2	5	1	.313	2	7	1	.250
Earlham	2	6	0	.250	3	7	0	.300
Case Reserve*	1	5	0	.167	2	8	0	.200
Oberlin	0	7	0	.000	0	10	0	.000

**Also member of University Athletic Association.*

NCAA Division III Playoffs (3-1): Rowan (3-1: defeated Buffalo St., 46-7, in first round; defeated Union, N.Y., 38-7, in quarterfinals; defeated Wash. & Jeff., 28-15, in semifinals; lost to Wis.-La Crosse, 36-7 in championship game)

OHIO ATHLETIC CONFERENCE

Team	Conference W	L	T	Pct.	Full Season W	L	T	Pct.
Mount Union	9	0	0	1.000	10	0	0	1.000
Marietta	7	1	1	.833	8	1	1	.850
John Carroll	5	2	2	.667	6	2	2	.700
Baldwin-Wallace	6	3	0	.667	6	4	0	.600
Muskingum	5	3	1	.611	6	3	1	.650
Ohio Northern	4	5	0	.444	5	5	0	.500
Hiram	3	6	0	.333	4	6	0	.400
Otterbein	3	6	0	.333	3	7	0	.300
Capital	1	8	0	.111	1	9	0	.100
Heidelberg	0	9	0	.000	0	10	0	.000

NCAA Division III Playoffs (2-1): Mount Union (2-1: defeated Hanover, 52-18, in first round; defeated Wheaton, Ill., 40-14, in quarterfinals; lost to Wis.-La Crosse, 20-17, in semifinals)

OLD DOMINION ATHLETIC CONFERENCE

Team	Conference W	L	T	Pct.	Full Season W	L	T	Pct.
Emory & Henry	5	0	0	1.000	9	1	0	.900
Randolph-Macon	4	1	0	.800	6	3	1	.650
Wash. & Lee	3	2	0	.600	5	3	1	.611
Hampden-Sydney	2	3	0	.400	4	6	0	.400
Guilford	1	4	0	.200	3	6	0	.333
Bridgewater (Va.)	0	5	0	.000	0	9	1	.050

NCAA Division III Playoffs (0-1): Emory & Henry (0-1: lost to Wash. & Jeff., 35-16, in first round)

PRESIDENTS' ATHLETIC CONFERENCE

Team	Conference W	L	T	Pct.	Full Season W	L	T	Pct.
Wash. & Jeff.	4	0	0	1.000	8	0	0	1.000
Bethany (W.Va.)	3	1	0	.750	6	3	0	.667
Waynesburg	2	2	0	.500	5	4	0	.556
Grove City	1	3	0	.250	2	8	0	.200
Thiel	0	4	0	.000	0	10	0	.000

NCAA Division III Playoffs (2-1): Wash. & Jeff. (2-1: defeated Emory & Henry, 35-16, in first round; defeated Lycoming, 48-0, in quarterfinals; lost to Rowan, 28-15, in semifinals)

SOUTHERN CALIFORNIA INTERCOLLEGIATE ATHLETIC CONFERENCE

Team	Conference W	L	T	Pct.	Full Season W	L	T	Pct.
La Verne	6	0	0	1.000	9	0	0	1.000
Pomona-Pitzer	4	2	0	.667	6	3	0	.667
Cal Lutheran	4	2	0	.677	4	4	1	.500
Redlands	3	3	0	.500	4	5	0	.444
Claremont-M-S*	2	4	0	.333	3	6	0	.333
Occidental*	2	4	0	.333	3	6	0	.333
Whittier	0	6	0	.000	1	8	0	.111

**Claremont-M-S defeated Occidental, 51-13, on October 21.*

SOUTHERN COLLEGIATE ATHLETIC CONFERENCE

Team	Conference W	L	T	Pct.	Full Season W	L	T	Pct.
Trinity (Tex.)*	3	1	0	.750	6	3	0	.667
Centre*	3	1	0	.750	5	4	1	.550
Rhodes*	3	1	0	.750	4	5	0	.444
Sewanee	1	3	0	.250	3	6	0	.333
Millsaps	0	4	0	.000	2	7	0	.222

**SCAC trichampions.*

UNIVERSITY ATHLETIC ASSOCIATION

Team	Conference W	L	T	Pct.	Full Season W	L	T	Pct.
Carnegie Mellon*#	3	1	0	.750	7	3	0	.700
Washington (Mo.)*#	3	1	0	.750	9	1	0	.900
Chicago	2	2	0	.500	8	2	0	.800
Rochester	1	3	0	.250	4	5	0	.444
Case Reserve†	1	3	0	.250	2	8	0	.200

**Cochampions of UAA. #Carnegie Mellon defeated Washington (Mo.), 12-8, on October 14. †Also member of North Coast Athletic Conference.*

WISCONSIN STATE UNIVERSITY CONFERENCE

Team	Conference W	L	T	Pct.	Full Season W	L	T	Pct.
Wis.-La Crosse	7	0	0	1.000	10	0	0	1.000
Wis.-River Falls	6	1	0	.857	8	2	0	.800
Wis.-Stevens Point	5	2	0	.714	8	2	0	.800
Wis.-Whitewater	4	3	0	.571	7	3	0	.700
Wis.-Platteville	3	4	0	.429	5	5	0	.500
Wis.-Oshkosh	2	5	0	.286	5	5	0	.500
Wis.-Stout	1	6	0	.143	3	7	0	.300
Wis.-Eau Claire	0	7	0	.000	1	9	0	.100

NCAA Division III Playoffs (5-1): Wis.-La Crosse (4-0: defeated Concordia-M'head, 45-7, in first round; defeated Wis.-River Falls, 28-14, in quarterfinals; defeated Mount Union, 20-17, in semifinals; defeated Rowan, 36-7, in championship game); Wis.-River Falls (1-1: defeated Central, Iowa, 10-7, in first round; lost to Wis.-La Crosse, 28-14, in quarterfinals)

DIVISION III INDEPENDENTS

Team	Full Season W	L	T	Pct.
Williams*	7	0	1	.938
Buffalo St.	9	1	0	.900
Eureka	9	1	0	.900
Chapman	8	1	0	.889
Hardin-Simmons#	8	1	0	.889
Union (N.Y.)	8	1	0	.889
Wesley†	8	2	0	.800
Rensselaer^	7	2	0	.778
Salisbury St.%	7	2	0	.778
Springfield!	7	2	0	.778
Martin Luther	6	2	0	.750
Trinity (Conn.)*	6	2	0	.750
Howard Payne#	7	3	0	.700
St. John Fisher	7	3	0	.700
Amherst*	5	2	1	.688
Cortland St.!	6	3	1	.650
Lakeland	6	3	1	.650
Colby*@	5	3	0	.625
Hamilton*@	5	3	0	.625
Catholic	5	3	1	.611
Ferrum	6	4	0	.600
Frostburg St.	6	4	0	.600
Ithaca	5	4	0	.556
Blackburn	4	4	0	.500
Maryville (Tenn.)	5	5	0	.500
Methodist	5	5	0	.500
Tufts*	4	4	0	.500
Brockport St.	4	5	1	.450
Wesleyan (Conn.)*	3	5	0	.375
Alfred	3	6	0	.333
Aurora	3	6	0	.333
Colorado Col.	3	6	0	.333
Hartwick	3	6	0	.333
Hobart	3	7	0	.300
MacMurray	3	7	0	.300
Neb. Wesleyan¢	3	7	0	.300
Middlebury*	2	6	0	.250
St. Lawrence	2	6	0	.250
Defiance	2	7	0	.222
Bates*$	1	7	0	.125
Bowdoin*$	1	7	0	.125
Principia	1	7	0	.125
Concordia (Ill.)	1	8	0	.111
Ill. Benedictine	1	8	0	.111
Menlo	0	9	0	.000

**Member of New England Small College Athletic Conference but league does not keep standings. #Member of Texas Intercollegiate Athletic Conference. †Does not include 10-7 loss to Trenton St. in ECAC playoff game on November 18. ^Does not include 69-12 victory over Worcester St. in ECAC playoff game on November 18. %Does not include 20-10 loss to Albright in ECAC playoff game on November 18. !Does not include Cortland St. loss to Springfield, 49-26, in ECAC playoff game on November 18. @Hamilton defeated Colby, 16-10, on October 21. ¢Member of Nebraska-Iowa Athletic Conference. $Bates defeated Bowdoin, 33-29, on November 4.*

NCAA Division III Playoffs (1-2): Buffalo St. (0-1: lost to Rowan, 46-7, in first round); Union (N.Y.) (1-1: defeated Plymouth St., 24-7, in first round; lost to Rowan, 38-7, in quarterfinals)

NAIA Division II playoffs (1-2): Hardin-Simmons (1-1: defeated Howard Payne, 17-6, in first round; lost to Central Wash., 40-20, in quarterfinals); Howard Payne (0-1: lost to Hardin-Simmons, 17-6, in first round)

All-Time Conference Champions

Division I-A

ATLANTIC COAST CONFERENCE

Founded: In 1953 when charter members all left the Southern Conference to form the ACC. **Charter members** (7): Clemson, Duke, Maryland, North Caro., North Caro. St., South Caro. and Wake Forest. **Admitted later** (3): Virginia (1953), Georgia Tech (1978) and Florida St. (1992). **Withdrew later** (1): South Caro. (1971). **Current members** (9): Clemson, Duke, Florida St., Georgia Tech, Maryland, North Caro., North Caro. St., Virginia and Wake Forest.

Year	Champion (Record)
1953	Duke (4-0) & Maryland (3-0)
1954	Duke (4-0)
1955	Maryland (4-0) & Duke (4-0)
1956	Clemson (4-0-1)
1957	North Caro. St. (5-0-1)
1958	Clemson (5-1)
1959	Clemson (6-1)
1960	Duke (5-1)
1961	Duke (5-1)
1962	Duke (6-0)
1963	North Caro. (6-1) & North Caro. St. (6-1)
1964	North Caro. St. (5-2)
1965	Clemson (5-2) & North Caro. St. (5-2)
1966	Clemson (6-1)
1967	Clemson (6-0)
1968	North Caro. St. (6-1)
1969	South Caro. (6-0)
1970	Wake Forest (5-1)
1971	North Caro. (6-0)
1972	North Caro. (6-0)
1973	North Caro. St. (6-0)
1974	Maryland (6-0)
1975	Maryland (5-0)
1976	Maryland (5-0)
1977	North Caro. (5-0-1)
1978	Clemson (6-0)
1979	North Caro. St. (5-1)
1980	North Caro. (6-0)
1981	Clemson (6-0)
1982	Clemson (6-0)
1983	Maryland (5-0)
1984	Maryland (5-0)
1985	Maryland (6-0)
1986	Clemson (5-1-1)
1987	Clemson (6-1)
1988	Clemson (6-1)
1989	Virginia (6-1) & Duke (6-1)
1990	Georgia Tech (6-0-1)
1991	Clemson (6-0-1)
1992	Florida St. (8-0)
1993	Florida St. (8-0)
1994	Florida St. (8-0)
1995	Virginia (7-1) & Florida St. (7-1)*

**Virginia defeated Florida St., 33-28, on November 2.*

BIG EAST CONFERENCE

Founded: In 1991 when eight charter members all went from independent status to form the Big East. **Charter members** (8): Boston College, Miami (Fla.), Pittsburgh, Rutgers (football only), Syracuse, Temple (football only), Virginia Tech (football only) and West Va. (football only). **Current members** (8): Boston College, Miami (Fla.), Pittsburgh, Rutgers, Syracuse, Temple, Virginia Tech and West Va. **Note:** In 1991 and 1992, the team ranked highest in the USA Today/CNN coaches poll was declared champion. Beginning in 1993, the champion was decided by a seven-game round-robin schedule.

Year	Champion (Record)
1991	Miami (Fla.) (2-0, No. 1) & Syracuse (5-0, No. 16)
1992	Miami (Fla.) (4-0, No. 1)
1993	West Va. (7-0)
1994	Miami (Fla.) (7-0)
1995	Virginia Tech (6-1) & Miami (Fla.) (6-1)*

**Virginia Tech defeated Miami (Fla.), 13-7, on September 23.*

BIG TEN CONFERENCE

Founded: In 1895 as the Intercollegiate Conference of Faculty Representatives, better known as the Western Conference. **Charter members** (7): Chicago, Illinois, Michigan, Minnesota, Northwestern, Purdue and Wisconsin. **Admitted later** (5): Indiana (1899), Iowa (1899), Ohio St. (1912), Michigan St. (1950) and Penn St. (1993). **Withdrew later** (2): Michigan (1907, rejoined in 1917) and Chicago (1940). **Note:** Iowa belonged to both the Missouri Valley and Western Conferences from 1907 to 1910. Unofficially called the Big Ten from 1912 until after 1939, then Big Nine from 1940 until Michigan St. began conference play in 1953. Formally renamed **Big Ten** in 1984. **Current members** (11): Illinois, Indiana, Iowa, Michigan, Michigan St., Minnesota, Northwestern, Ohio St., Penn St., Purdue and Wisconsin.

Year	Champion (Record)
1896	Wisconsin (2-0-1)
1897	Wisconsin (3-0)
1898	Michigan (3-0)
1899	Chicago (4-0)
1900	Iowa (3-0-1) & Minnesota (3-0-1)
1901	Michigan (4-0) & Wisconsin (2-0)
1902	Michigan (5-0)
1903	Michigan (3-0-1), Minnesota (3-0-1) & Northwestern (1-0-2)
1904	Minnesota (3-0) & Michigan (2-0)
1905	Chicago (7-0)
1906	Wisconsin (3-0), Minnesota (2-0) & Michigan (1-0)
1907	Chicago (4-0)
1908	Chicago (5-0)
1909	Minnesota (3-0)
1910	Illinois (4-0) & Minnesota (2-0)
1911	Minnesota (3-0-1)
1912	Wisconsin (6-0)
1913	Chicago (7-0)
1914	Illinois (6-0)
1915	Minnesota (3-0-1) & Illinois (3-0-2)
1916	Ohio St. (4-0)
1917	Ohio St. (4-0)
1918	Illinois (4-0), Michigan (2-0) & Purdue (1-0)
1919	Illinois (6-1)
1920	Ohio St. (5-0)
1921	Iowa (5-0)
1922	Iowa (5-0) & Michigan (4-0)
1923	Illinois (5-0) & Michigan (4-0)
1924	Chicago (3-0-3)
1925	Michigan (5-1)
1926	Michigan (5-0) & Northwestern (5-0)
1927	Illinois (5-0)
1928	Illinois (4-1)
1929	Purdue (5-0)
1930	Michigan (5-0) & Northwestern (5-0)
1931	Purdue (5-1), Michigan (5-1) & Northwestern (5-1)
1932	Michigan (6-0)
1933	Michigan (5-0-1)
1934	Minnesota (5-0)
1935	Minnesota (5-0) & Ohio St. (5-0)
1936	Northwestern (6-0)
1937	Minnesota (5-0)
1938	Minnesota (4-1)
1939	Ohio St. (5-1)
1940	Minnesota (6-0)
1941	Minnesota (5-0)
1942	Ohio St. (5-1)
1943	Purdue (6-0) & Michigan (6-0)
1944	Ohio St. (6-0)
1945	Indiana (5-0-1)
1946	Illinois (6-1)
1947	Michigan (6-0)
1948	Michigan (6-0)
1949	Ohio St. (4-1-1) & Michigan (4-1-1)
1950	Michigan (4-1-1)
1951	Illinois (5-0-1)
1952	Wisconsin (4-1-1) & Purdue (4-1-1)
1953	Michigan St. (5-1) & Illinois (5-1)
1954	Ohio St. (7-0)
1955	Ohio St. (6-0)
1956	Iowa (5-1)
1957	Ohio St. (7-0)
1958	Iowa (5-1)
1959	Wisconsin (5-2)
1960	Minnesota (5-1) & Iowa (5-1)
1961	Ohio St. (6-0)
1962	Wisconsin (6-1)
1963	Illinois (5-1-1)
1964	Michigan (6-1)
1965	Michigan St. (7-0)
1966	Michigan St. (7-0)
1967	Indiana (6-1), Purdue (6-1) & Minnesota (6-1)
1968	Ohio St. (7-0)
1969	Ohio St. (6-1) & Michigan (6-1)
1970	Ohio St. (7-0)
1971	Michigan (8-0)
1972	Ohio St. (8-0) & Michigan (7-1)
1973	Ohio St. (7-0-1) & Michigan (7-0-1)
1974	Ohio St. (7-1) & Michigan (7-1)
1975	Ohio St. (8-0)
1976	Michigan (7-1) & Ohio St. (7-1)
1977	Michigan (7-1) & Ohio St. (7-1)
1978	Michigan (7-1) & Michigan St. (7-1)
1979	Ohio St. (8-0)
1980	Michigan (8-0)
1981	Iowa (6-2) & Ohio St. (6-2)
1982	Michigan (8-1)
1983	Illinois (9-0)
1984	Ohio St. (7-2)
1985	Iowa (7-1)
1986	Michigan (7-1) & Ohio St. (7-1)
1987	Michigan St. (7-0-1)
1988	Michigan (7-0-1)
1989	Michigan (8-0)
1990	Iowa (6-2), Michigan (6-2), Michigan St. (6-2) & Illinois (6-2)
1991	Michigan (8-0)
1992	Michigan (6-0-2)
1993	Ohio St. (6-1-1) & Wisconsin (6-1-1)
1994	Penn St. (8-0)
1995	Northwestern (8-0)

BIG WEST CONFERENCE

Founded: In 1969 as the Pacific Coast Athletic Association (PCAA). **Charter members** (7): UC Santa Barb., Cal St. Los Angeles, Fresno St., Long Beach St., Pacific (Cal.), San Diego St. and San Jose St. **Admitted later** (12): Cal St. Fullerton (1974), Utah St. (1977), UNLV (1982), New Mexico St. (1983), Nevada (1992), Arkansas St. (1993), Louisiana Tech (1993), Northern Ill. (1993), Southwestern La. (1993), Boise St. (1996), Idaho (1996) and North Texas (1996). **Withdrew later** (13): UC Santa Barb. (1972), Cal St. Los Angeles (1974), San Diego St. (1976), Fresno St. (1991), Long Beach St. (1991, dropped football), Cal St. Fullerton (1992, dropped football), Arkansas St. (1996), Louisiana Tech (1996), UNLV (1996), Northern Ill. (1996), Pacific (Cal.) (1996, dropped football), San Jose St. (1996) and Southwestern La. (1996). Renamed **Big West** in 1988. **Current members** (6): Boise St. (Div. II member), Idaho (Div. II member), Nevada, New Mexico St., North Texas and Utah St.

Year	Champion (Record)
1969	San Diego St. (6-0)
1970	Long Beach St. (5-1) & San Diego St. (5-1)
1971	Long Beach St. (5-1)
1972	San Diego St. (4-0)
1973	San Diego St. (3-0-1)
1974	San Diego St. (4-0)
1975	San Jose St. (5-0)
1976	San Jose St. (4-0)
1977	Fresno St. (4-0)
1978	San Jose St. (4-1) & Utah St. (4-1)
1979	Utah St. (5-0)
1980	Long Beach St. (5-0)
1981	San Jose St. (5-0)
1982	Fresno St. (6-0)
1983	Cal St. Fullerton (5-1)
1984	Cal St. Fullerton (6-1)#
1985	Fresno St. (7-0)
1986	San Jose St. (7-0)
1987	San Jose St. (7-0)
1988	Fresno St. (7-0)
1989	Fresno St. (7-0)
1990	San Jose St. (7-0)
1991	Fresno St. (6-1) & San Jose St. (6-1)
1992	Nevada (5-1)
1993	Southwestern La. (5-1) & Utah St. (5-1)
1994	Nevada (5-1), Southwestern La. (5-1) & UNLV (5-1)
1995	Nevada (6-0)

#UNLV forfeited title.

BIG 12 CONFERENCE

Founded: In 1996 when 12 charter members combined eight members of Big Eight Conference with four former Southwest Conference members. **Charter members** (12): Baylor, Colorado, Iowa St., Kansas, Kansas St., Missouri, Nebraska, Oklahoma, Oklahoma St., Texas, Texas A&M and Texas Tech. **Current members** (12): Baylor, Colorado, Iowa St., Kansas, Kansas St., Missouri, Nebraska, Oklahoma, Oklahoma St., Texas, Texas A&M and Texas Tech.

CONFERENCE USA

Founded: In 1996 when five charter members went from independent status and one former Southwest Conference member combined to form Conference USA. **Charter members** (6): Cincinnati, Houston, Louisville, Memphis, Southern Miss. and Tulane. **Current members** (6): Cincinnati, Houston, Louisville, Memphis, Southern Miss. and Tulane.

MID-AMERICAN ATHLETIC CONFERENCE

Founded: In 1946. **Charter members** (6): Butler, Cincinnati, Miami (Ohio), Ohio, Western Mich. and Western Reserve (now Case Reserve). **Admitted later** (9): Kent St. (now Kent) (1951), Toledo (1951), Bowling Green (1952), Marshall (1954), Central Mich. (1972), Eastern Mich. (1972), Ball St. (1973), Northern Ill. (1973) and Akron (1992). **Withdrew later** (5): Butler (1950), Cincinnati (1953), Case Reserve (1955), Marshall (1969) and Northern Ill. (1986). **Current members** (10): Akron, Ball St., Bowling Green, Central Mich., Eastern Mich., Kent, Miami (Ohio), Ohio, Toledo and Western Mich.

Year	Champion (Record)
1947	Cincinnati (3-1)
1948	Miami (Ohio) (4-0)
1949	Cincinnati (4-0)
1950	Miami (Ohio) (4-0)
1951	Cincinnati (3-0)
1952	Cincinnati (3-0)
1953	Ohio (5-0-1)
1954	Miami (Ohio) (4-0)
1955	Miami (Ohio) (5-0)
1956	Bowling Green (5-0-1)
1957	Miami (Ohio) (5-0)
1958	Miami (Ohio) (5-0)
1959	Bowling Green (6-0)
1960	Ohio (6-0)
1961	Bowling Green (5-1)
1962	Bowling Green (5-0-1)
1963	Ohio (5-1)
1964	Bowling Green (5-1)
1965	Bowling Green (5-1) & Miami (Ohio) (5-1)
1966	Miami (Ohio) (5-1) & Western Mich. (5-1)
1967	Toledo (5-1) & Ohio (5-1)
1968	Ohio (6-0)
1969	Toledo (5-0)
1970	Toledo (5-0)
1971	Toledo (5-0)
1972	Kent (4-1)
1973	Miami (Ohio) (5-0)
1974	Miami (Ohio) (5-0)
1975	Miami (Ohio) (6-0)
1976	Ball St. (4-1)
1977	Miami (Ohio) (5-0)
1978	Ball St. (8-0)
1979	Central Mich. (8-0-1)
1980	Central Mich. (7-2)
1981	Toledo (8-1)
1982	Bowling Green (7-2)
1983	Northern Ill. (8-1)
1984	Toledo (7-1-1)
1985	Bowling Green (9-0)
1986	Miami (Ohio) (6-2)
1987	Eastern Mich. (7-1)
1988	Western Mich. (7-1)
1989	Ball St. (6-1-1)
1990	Central Mich. (7-1)
1991	Bowling Green (8-0)
1992	Bowling Green (8-0)
1993	Ball St. (7-0-1)
1994	Central Mich. (8-1)
1995	Toledo (7-0-1)

PACIFIC-10 CONFERENCE

Founded: In 1915 as the **Pacific Coast Conference** by group of four charter members. **Charter members** (4): California, Oregon, Oregon St. and Washington. **Admitted later** (6): Washington St. (1917), Stanford (1918), Idaho (1922), Southern Cal (1922), Montana (1924) and UCLA (1928). **Withdrew later** (2): Montana (1950) and Idaho (1958).

The Pacific Coast Conference dissolved in 1959 and the Athletic Association of Western Universities was founded with five charter members. **Charter members** (5): California, Southern Cal, Stanford, UCLA and Washington. **Admitted later** (5): Washington St. (1962), Oregon (1964), Oregon St. (1964), Arizona (1978) and Arizona St. (1978). Conference renamed **Pacific-8** in 1968 and **Pacific-10** in 1978. **Current members** (10): Arizona, Arizona St., California, Oregon, Oregon St., Southern Cal, Stanford, UCLA, Washington and Washington St.

Year	Champion (Record)
1916	Washington (3-0-1)
1917	Washington (3-0)
1918	California (3-0)
1919	Oregon (2-1) & Washington (2-1)
1920	California (3-0)
1921	California (5-0)
1922	California (3-0)
1923	California (5-0)
1924	Stanford (3-0-1)
1925	Washington (5-0)
1926	Stanford (4-0)
1927	Southern Cal (4-0-1) & Stanford (4-0-1)
1928	Southern Cal (4-0-1)
1929	Southern Cal (6-1)
1930	Washington St. (6-0)
1931	Southern Cal (7-0)
1932	Southern Cal (6-0)
1933	Oregon (4-1) & Stanford (4-1)
1934	Stanford (5-0)
1935	California (4-1), Stanford (4-1) & UCLA (4-1)
1936	Washington (6-0-1)
1937	California (6-0-1)
1938	Southern Cal (6-1) & California (6-1)
1939	Southern Cal (5-0-2) & UCLA (5-0-3)
1940	Stanford (7-0)
1941	Oregon St. (7-2)
1942	UCLA (6-1)
1943	Southern Cal (4-0)
1944	Southern Cal (3-0-2)
1945	Southern Cal (6-0)
1946	UCLA (7-0)
1947	Southern Cal (6-0)
1948	California (6-0) & Oregon (6-0)
1949	California (7-0)
1950	California (5-0-1)
1951	Stanford (6-1)
1952	Southern Cal (6-0)
1953	UCLA (6-1)
1954	UCLA (6-0)
1955	UCLA (6-0)
1956	Oregon St. (6-1-1)
1957	Oregon (6-2) & Oregon St. (6-2)
1958	California (6-1)
1959	Washington (3-1), Southern Cal (3-1) & UCLA (3-1)
1960	Washington (4-0)
1961	UCLA (3-1)
1962	Southern Cal (4-0)
1963	Washington (4-1)
1964	Oregon St. (3-1) & Southern Cal (3-1)
1965	UCLA (4-0)
1966	Southern Cal (4-1)
1967	Southern Cal (6-1)
1968	Southern Cal (6-0)
1969	Southern Cal (6-0)
1970	Stanford (6-1)
1971	Stanford (6-1)
1972	Southern Cal (7-0)
1973	Southern Cal (7-0)
1974	Southern Cal (6-0-1)
1975	UCLA (6-1) & California (6-1)
1976	Southern Cal (7-0)
1977	Washington (6-1)
1978	Southern Cal (6-1)
1979	Southern Cal (6-0-1)
1980	Washington (6-1)
1981	Washington (6-2)
1982	UCLA (5-1-1)
1983	UCLA (6-1-1)
1984	Southern Cal (7-1)
1985	UCLA (6-2)
1986	Arizona St. (5-1-1)
1987	Southern Cal (7-1) & UCLA (7-1)
1988	Southern Cal (8-0)
1989	Southern Cal (6-0-1)
1990	Washington (7-1)
1991	Washington (8-0)
1992	Stanford (6-2) & Washington (6-2)
1993	UCLA (6-2), Arizona (6-2) & Southern Cal (6-2)
1994	Oregon (7-1)
1995	Southern Cal (6-1-1) & Washington (6-1-1)*

**Southern Cal tied Washington, 21-21, on October 28.*

SOUTHEASTERN CONFERENCE

Founded: In 1933 when charter members all left the **Southern Conference** to become the SEC. **Charter members** (13): Alabama, Auburn, Florida, Georgia, Georgia Tech, Kentucky, LSU, Mississippi, Mississippi St., Sewanee, Tennessee, Tulane and Vanderbilt. **Admitted later** (2): Arkansas (1992) and South Caro. (1992). **Withdrew later** (3): Sewanee (1940), Georgia Tech (1964) and Tulane (1966). **Current members** (12): Alabama, Arkansas, Auburn, Florida, Georgia, Kentucky, LSU, Mississippi, Mississippi St., South Caro., Tennessee and Vanderbilt.

Year	Champion (Record)
1933	Alabama (5-0-1)
1934	Tulane (8-0) & Alabama (7-0)
1935	LSU (5-0)
1936	LSU (6-0)
1937	Alabama (6-0)
1938	Tennessee (7-0)
1939	Tennessee (6-0), Georgia Tech (6-0) & Tulane (5-0)
1940	Tennessee (5-0)
1941	Mississippi St. (4-0-1)
1942	Georgia (6-1)
1943	Georgia Tech (4-0)
1944	Georgia Tech (4-0)
1945	Alabama (6-0)
1946	Georgia (5-0) & Tennessee (5-0)
1947	Mississippi (6-1)
1948	Georgia (6-0)
1949	Tulane (5-1)
1950	Kentucky (5-1)
1951	Georgia Tech (7-0) & Tennessee (5-0)
1952	Georgia (6-0)
1953	Alabama (4-0-3)
1954	Mississippi (5-1)
1955	Mississippi (5-1)
1956	Tennessee (6-0)
1957	Auburn (7-0)
1958	LSU (6-0)
1959	Georgia (7-0)
1960	Mississippi (5-0-1)
1961	Alabama (7-0) & LSU (6-0)
1962	Mississippi (6-0)
1963	Mississippi (5-0-1)
1964	Alabama (8-0)
1965	Alabama (6-1-1)
1966	Alabama (6-0) & Georgia (6-0)
1967	Tennessee (6-0)
1968	Georgia (5-0-1)
1969	Tennessee (5-1)
1970	LSU (5-0)
1971	Alabama (7-0)
1972	Alabama (7-1)
1973	Alabama (8-0)
1974	Alabama (6-0)
1975	Alabama (6-0)
1976	Georgia (5-1) & Kentucky (5-1)
1977	Alabama (7-0) & Kentucky (6-0)
1978	Alabama (6-0)
1979	Alabama (6-0)
1980	Georgia (6-0)
1981	Georgia (6-0) & Alabama (6-0)
1982	Georgia (6-0)
1983	Auburn (6-0)
1984	Florida (5-0-1)#
1985	Tennessee (5-1)*
1986	LSU (5-1)
1987	Auburn (5-0-1)
1988	Auburn (6-1) & LSU (6-1)
1989	Alabama (6-1), Tennessee (6-1) & Auburn (6-1)
1990	Tennessee (5-1-1)*
1991	Florida (7-0)
1992	Alabama (8-0)
1993	Florida (7-1)*
1994	Florida (7-1)
1995	Florida (8-0)

*#Title vacated. *Ineligible for title (probation): Florida (5-1) in 1985, Florida (6-1) in 1990 and Auburn (8-0) in 1993.*

Since 1992, the SEC has conducted a championship game to determine the league's representative in the alliance bowls. Following are the results year-by-year of the Western Division champion (W) vs. the Eastern Division champion (E):

1992	Alabama (W) 28, Florida (E) 21
1993	Florida (E) 28, Alabama (W) 13
1994	Florida (E) 24, Alabama (W) 23
1995	Florida (E) 34, Arkansas (W) 3

WESTERN ATHLETIC CONFERENCE

Founded: In 1962 when charter members left the Skyline and Border Conferences to form the WAC. In 1996, three former Southwest Conference members joined two former Big West members and one former independent team to form a 16-team league, the largest conference alignment ever in Division I-A. The league will be divided into Mountain and Pacific divisions. **Charter members** (6): Arizona (from Border), Arizona St. (from Border), Brigham Young (from Skyline), New Mexico (from Skyline), Utah (from Skyline) and Wyoming (from Skyline). **Admitted later** (12): Colorado St. (1968), UTEP (1968), San Diego St. (1978), Hawaii (1979), Air Force (1980), Fresno St. (1992), UNLV (1996), Rice (1996), San Jose St. (1996), Southern Methodist (1996), Texas Christian (1996) and Tulsa (1996). **Withdrew later** (2): Arizona (1978) and Arizona St. (1978). **Current members** (16): Air Force, Brigham Young, Colorado St., Fresno St., Hawaii, UNLV, New Mexico, Rice, San Diego St., San Jose St., Southern Methodist, UTEP, Texas Christian, Tulsa, Utah and Wyoming.

Year	Champion (Record)
1962	New Mexico (2-1-1)
1963	New Mexico (3-1)
1964	Arizona (3-1), Utah (3-1) & New Mexico (3-1)
1965	Brigham Young (4-1)
1966	Wyoming (5-0)
1967	Wyoming (5-0)
1968	Wyoming (6-1)
1969	Arizona St. (6-1)
1970	Arizona St. (7-0)
1971	Arizona St. (7-0)
1972	Arizona St. (5-1)
1973	Arizona (6-1) & Arizona St. (6-1)
1974	Brigham Young (6-0-1)
1975	Arizona St. (7-0)
1976	Brigham Young (6-1) & Wyoming (6-1)
1977	Arizona St. (6-1) & Brigham Young (6-1)
1978	Brigham Young (5-1)
1979	Brigham Young (7-0)
1980	Brigham Young (6-1)
1981	Brigham Young (7-1)
1982	Brigham Young (7-1)
1983	Brigham Young (7-0)
1984	Brigham Young (8-0)
1985	Air Force (7-1) & Brigham Young (7-1)
1986	San Diego St. (7-1)
1987	Wyoming (8-0)
1988	Wyoming (8-0)
1989	Brigham Young (7-1)
1990	Brigham Young (7-1)
1991	Brigham Young (7-0-1)
1992	Hawaii (6-2), Fresno St. (6-2) & Brigham Young (6-2)
1993	Wyoming (6-2), Fresno St. (6-2) & Brigham Young (6-2)
1994	Colorado St. (7-1)
1995	Colorado St. (6-2), Air Force (6-2), Utah (6-2) & Brigham Young (6-2)*

**Utah defeated Brigham Young, 34-17, on November 18.*

Division I-AA

BIG SKY CONFERENCE

Founded: In 1963 when six charter members—Gonzaga, Idaho, Idaho St., Montana, Montana St. and Weber St.—banded together to form the Big Sky. **Admitted later** (7): Boise St. (1970), Northern Ariz. (1970), Nevada (1979, replacing charter member

Gonzaga), Eastern Wash. (1987), Cal St. Northridge (1996), Cal St. Sacramento (1996) and Portland St. (1996). **Withdrew later** (4): Gonzaga (1979), Nevada (1992), Boise St. (1996) and Idaho (1996). **Current members** (9): Cal St. Northridge, Cal St. Sacramento, Eastern Wash., Idaho St., Montana, Montana St., Northern Ariz., Portland St. (Div. II member) and Weber St.

Year	Champion (Record)
1963	Idaho St. (3-1)
1964	Montana St. (3-0)
1965	Weber St. (3-1) & Idaho (3-1)
1966	Montana St. (4-0)
1967	Montana St. (4-0)
1968	Weber St. (3-1), Montana St. (3-1) & Idaho (3-1)
1969	Montana (4-0)#
1970	Montana (5-0)
1971	Idaho (4-1)
1972	Montana St. (5-1)
1973	Boise St. (6-0)#
1974	Boise St. (6-0)#
1975	Boise St. (5-0-1)#
1976	Montana St. (6-0)#
1977	Boise St. (6-0)
1978	Northern Ariz. (6-0)
1979	Montana St. (6-1)
1980	Boise St. (6-1)
1981	Idaho St. (6-1)*
1982	Montana (5-2)*
1983	Nevada (6-1)*
1984	Montana St. (6-1)*
1985	Idaho (6-1)*
1986	Nevada (7-0)*
1987	Idaho (7-1)*
1988	Idaho (7-1)*
1989	Idaho (8-0)*
1990	Nevada (7-1)*
1991	Nevada (8-0)*
1992	Idaho (6-1)* & Eastern Wash. (6-1)*
1993	Montana (7-0)*
1994	Boise St. (6-1)*
1995	Montana (6-1)*

#Participated in NCAA Division II Championship.
**Participated in NCAA Division I-AA Championship.*

GATEWAY FOOTBALL CONFERENCE

Founded: In 1982 as a women's athletics organization by 10 Midwestern universities. Six members started as a football conference in 1985. **Charter members** (6): (Football) Eastern Ill., Illinois St., Northern Iowa, Southern Ill., Southwest Mo. St. and Western Ill. Four members—Eastern Ill., Northern Iowa, Southwest Mo. St. and Western Ill.—were members of the Mid-Continent Conference for football. **Admitted later** (1): Indiana St. (1986). **Withdrew later** (1): Eastern Ill. (1996). **Current members** (6): Illinois St., Indiana St., Northern Iowa, Southern Ill., Southwest Mo. St. and Western Ill.

Year	Champion (Record)
1985	Northern Iowa (5-0)*
1986	Eastern Ill. (5-1)*
1987	Northern Iowa (6-0)*
1988	Western Ill. (6-0)*
1989	Southwest Mo. St. (5-1)*
1990	Northern Iowa (5-1)*
1991	Northern Iowa (5-1)*
1992	Northern Iowa (5-1)*
1993	Northern Iowa (5-1)*
1994	Northern Iowa (6-0)*
1995	Northern Iowa (5-1)* & Eastern Ill. (5-1)*#

**Participated in NCAA Division I-AA Championship.*
#Northern Iowa defeated Eastern Ill., 17-7, on October 7.

IVY GROUP

Founded: In 1956 by a group of eight charter members. **Charter members** (8): Brown, Columbia, Cornell, Dartmouth, Harvard, Pennsylvania, Princeton and Yale. **Current members** (8): Brown, Columbia, Cornell, Dartmouth, Harvard, Pennsylvania, Princeton and Yale.

Year	Champion (Record)
1956	Yale (7-2)
1957	Princeton (6-1)
1958	Dartmouth (6-1)
1959	Pennsylvania (6-1)
1960	Yale (7-0)
1961	Columbia (6-1) & Harvard (6-1)
1962	Dartmouth (7-0)
1963	Dartmouth (5-2) & Princeton (5-2)
1964	Princeton (7-0)
1965	Dartmouth (7-0)
1966	Dartmouth (6-1), Harvard (6-1) & Princeton (6-1)
1967	Yale (7-0)
1968	Harvard (6-0-1) & Yale (6-0-1)
1969	Dartmouth (6-1), Yale (6-1) & Princeton (6-1)
1970	Dartmouth (7-0)
1971	Cornell (6-1) & Dartmouth (6-1)
1972	Dartmouth (5-1-1)
1973	Dartmouth (6-1)
1974	Harvard (6-1) & Yale (6-1)
1975	Harvard (6-1)
1976	Brown (6-1) & Yale (6-1)
1977	Yale (6-1)
1978	Dartmouth (6-1)
1979	Yale (6-1)
1980	Yale (6-1)
1981	Yale (6-1) & Dartmouth (6-1)
1982	Harvard (5-2), Pennsylvania (5-2) & Dartmouth (5-2)
1983	Harvard (5-1-1) & Pennsylvania (5-1-1)
1984	Pennsylvania (7-0)
1985	Pennsylvania (6-1)
1986	Pennsylvania (7-0)
1987	Harvard (6-1)
1988	Pennsylvania (6-1) & Cornell (6-1)
1989	Princeton (6-1) & Yale (6-1)
1990	Cornell (6-1) & Dartmouth (6-1)
1991	Dartmouth (6-0-1)
1992	Dartmouth (6-1) & Princeton (6-1)
1993	Pennsylvania (7-0)
1994	Pennsylvania (7-0)
1995	Princeton (5-1-1)

METRO ATLANTIC ATHLETIC CONFERENCE

Founded: Began in Division I-AA in 1993 with Canisius, Georgetown, Iona, St. John's (N.Y.), St. Peter's and Siena as charter members. **Admitted later** (3): Duquesne (1994), Marist (1994) and Fairfield (1996). **Withdrew later** (0): None. **Current members** (9): Canisius, Duquesne, Fairfield, Georgetown, Iona, Marist, St. John's (N.Y.), St. Peter's and Siena.

Year	Champion (Record)
1993	Iona (5-0)
1994	Marist (6-1) & St. John's (N.Y.) (6-1)
1995	Duquesne (7-0)

MID-EASTERN ATHLETIC CONFERENCE

Founded: In 1970 with first playing season in 1971 by six charter members. **Charter members** (6): Delaware St., Howard, Morgan St., North Caro. A&T, N.C. Central and South Caro. St. **Admitted later** (3): Bethune-Cookman (1979), Florida A&M (1979) and Hampton (1996). **Withdrew later** (3): Morgan St. (1979), N.C. Central (1979) and Florida A&M (1984). **Readmitted** (2): Morgan St. (1984) and Florida A&M (1986). **Current members** (8): Bethune-Cookman, Delaware St., Florida A&M, Hampton, Howard, Morgan St., North Caro. A&T and South Caro. St.

Year	Champion (Record)
1971	Morgan St. (5-0-1)
1972	N.C. Central (5-1)
1973	N.C. Central (5-1)
1974	South Caro. St. (5-1)
1975	South Caro. St. (5-1)
1976	South Caro. St. (5-1)
1977	South Caro. St. (6-0)
1978	South Caro. St. (5-0-1)
1979	Morgan St. (5-0)#
1980	South Caro. St. (5-0)
1981	South Caro. St. (5-0)*
1982	South Caro. St. (4-1)*
1983	South Caro. St. (4-0)
1984	Bethune-Cookman (4-0)
1985	Delaware St. (4-0)
1986	North Caro. A&T (4-1)*
1987	Howard (5-0)
1988	Bethune-Cookman (4-2), Florida A&M (4-2) & Delaware St. (4-2)
1989	Delaware St. (5-1)
1990	Florida A&M (6-0)
1991	North Caro. A&T (5-1)√
1992	North Caro. A&T (5-1)*
1993	Howard (6-0)*
1994	South Caro. St. (6-0)√
1995	Florida A&M (6-0)√

#Participated in NCAA Division II Championship.
**Participated in NCAA Division I-AA Championship.*
√Participated in Division I-AA Heritage Bowl.

NORTHEAST CONFERENCE

Founded: In 1996 when five charter members all went from independent status to form the Northeast Conference. **Charter members** (5): Central Conn. St., Monmouth (N.J.), Robert Morris, St. Francis (Pa.) and Wagner. **Current members** (5): Central Conn. St., Monmouth (N.J.), Robert Morris, St. Francis (Pa.) and Wagner.

OHIO VALLEY CONFERENCE

Founded: In 1948 by six charter members, five of which withdrew from the Kentucky Intercollegiate Athletic Conference (Eastern Ky., Louisville, Morehead St., Murray St. and Western Ky.), plus Evansville. **Charter members** (6): Eastern Ky., Evansville, Louisville, Morehead St., Murray St. and Western Ky. **Admitted later** (11): Marshall (1949), Tennessee Tech (1949), Middle Tenn. St. (1952), East Tenn. St. (1957), Austin Peay (1962), Akron (1979), Youngstown St. (1980), Tennessee St. (1988), Southeast Mo. St. (1991), Tenn.-Martin (1992) and Eastern Ill. (1996). **Withdrew later** (8): Louisville (1949), Evansville (1952), Marshall (1952), East Tenn. St. (1979), Western Ky. (1982), Akron (1987), Youngstown St. (1988) and Morehead St. (1996). **Current members** (9): Austin Peay, Eastern Ill., Eastern Ky., Middle Tenn. St., Murray St., Southeast Mo. St., Tenn.-Martin, Tennessee St. and Tennessee Tech.

Team	Champion (Record)
1948	Murray St. (3-1)
1949	Evansville (3-1)
1950	Murray St. (5-0-1)
1951	Murray St. (5-1)
1952	Tennessee St. (4-1) & Western Ky. (4-1)
1953	Tennessee Tech (5-0)
1954	Eastern Ky. (5-0)
1955	Tennessee Tech (5-0)
1956	Middle Tenn. St. (5-0)
1957	Middle Tenn. St. (5-0)
1958	Middle Tenn. St. (5-1) & Tennessee Tech (5-1)
1959	Middle Tenn. St. (5-0-1) & Tennessee Tech (5-0-1)
1960	Tennessee Tech (6-0)
1961	Tennessee Tech (6-0)
1962	East Tenn. St. (4-2)
1963	Western Ky. (7-0)
1964	Middle Tenn. St. (6-1)#
1965	Middle Tenn. St. (7-0)
1966	Morehead St. (6-1)
1967	Eastern Ky. (5-0-2)#
1968	Eastern Ky. (7-0)
1969	East Tenn. St. (6-0-1)#
1970	Western Ky. (5-1-1)
1971	Western Ky. (5-2)
1972	Tennessee Tech (7-0)#
1973	Western Ky. (7-0)#
1974	Eastern Ky. (6-1)
1975	Tennessee Tech (6-1) & Western Ky. (6-1)#
1976	Eastern Ky. (6-1)#
1977	Austin Peay (6-1)
1978	Western Ky. (6-0)
1979	Murray St. (6-0)*
1980	Western Ky. (6-1)
1981	Eastern Ky. (8-0)*
1982	Eastern Ky. (7-0)*
1983	Eastern Ky. (6-1)*
1984	Eastern Ky. (6-1)*
1985	Middle Tenn. St. (7-0)*
1986	Murray St. (5-2)
1987	Eastern Ky. (5-1)* & Youngstown St. (5-1)
1988	Eastern Ky. (6-0)*
1989	Middle Tenn. St. (6-0)*
1990	Middle Tenn. St. (5-1)* & Eastern Ky. (5-1)*
1991	Eastern Ky. (7-0)*
1992	Middle Tenn. St. (8-0)*
1993	Eastern Ky. (8-0)*
1994	Eastern Ky. (8-0)*
1995	Murray St. (8-0)*

#Participated in NCAA Division II Championship.
**Participated in NCAA Division I-AA Championship.*

PATRIOT LEAGUE

Founded: In 1984 originally as the Colonial League with six charter members. **Charter members** (6): Bucknell, Colgate, Davidson, Holy Cross, Lafayette and Lehigh. **Admitted later** (1): Fordham (1990). **Withdrew later**

(1): Davidson (1989). **Current members** (6): Bucknell, Colgate, Fordham, Holy Cross, Lafayette and Lehigh.

Year	Champion (Record)
1986	Holy Cross (4-0)
1987	Holy Cross (4-0)
1988	Lafayette (5-0)
1989	Holy Cross (4-0)
1990	Holy Cross (5-0)
1991	Holy Cross (5-0)
1992	Lafayette (5-0)
1993	Lehigh (4-1)
1994	Lafayette (5-0)
1995	Lehigh (5-0)

PIONEER FOOTBALL LEAGUE

Founded: Started in 1993 with Division I-AA charter members Butler, Dayton, Drake, Evansville, San Diego and Valparaiso. **Admitted later** (0): None. **Withdrew later** (0): None. **Current members** (6): Butler, Dayton, Drake, Evansville, San Diego and Valparaiso.

Year	Champion (Record)
1993	Dayton (5-0)
1994	Dayton (4-1) & Butler (4-1)
1995	Drake (5-0)

SOUTHERN CONFERENCE

Founded: In 1921 by 14 institutions to form the Southern Intercollegiate Conference. Roots for the conference can actually be traced back to 1894 when several football-playing schools formed a confederation known as the Southeastern Intercollegiate Athletic Association. **Charter members** (14): Alabama, Auburn, Clemson, Georgia, Georgia Tech, Kentucky, Maryland, Mississippi St., North Caro., North Caro. St., Tennessee, Virginia, Virginia Tech and Wash. & Lee. **Admitted later** (16): Florida (1922), LSU (1922), Mississippi (1922), South Caro. (1922), Tulane (1922), Vanderbilt (1922), Va. Military (1924), Citadel (1936), Furman (1936), West Va. (1951), Appalachian St. (1971), Marshall (1976), Tenn.-Chatt. (1976), Western Caro. (1976), East Tenn. St. (1978) and Ga. Southern (1992). **Withdrew later:** Since 1922, membership has changed drastically, with a total of 38 schools having been affiliated with the league, including 11 of the 12 schools currently comprising the Southeastern Conference and eight of the nine schools currently comprising the Atlantic Coast Conference. **Current members** (9): Appalachian St., Citadel, East Tenn. St., Furman, Ga. Southern, Marshall, Tenn.-Chatt., Va. Military and Western Caro.

Year	Champion (Record√)
1922	Georgia Tech
1923	Vanderbilt
1924	Alabama
1925	Alabama
1926	Alabama
1927	Georgia Tech
1928	Georgia Tech
1929	Tulane
1930	Alabama & Tulane
1931	Tulane
1932	Tennessee & Auburn
1933	Duke (4-0)
1934	Wash. & Lee (4-0)
1935	Duke (5-0)
1936	Duke (7-0)
1937	Maryland (2-0)
1938	Duke (5-0)
1939	Clemson (4-0)
1940	Clemson (4-0)
1941	Duke (5-0)
1942	William & Mary (4-0)
1943	Duke (4-0)
1944	Duke (4-0)
1945	Duke (4-0)
1946	North Caro. (4-0-1)
1947	William & Mary (7-1)
1948	Clemson (5-0)
1949	North Caro. (5-0)
1950	Wash. & Lee (6-0)
1951	Maryland (5-0) & Va. Military (5-0)
1952	Duke (5-0)
1953	West Va. (4-0)
1954	West Va. (3-0)
1955	West Va. (4-0)
1956	West Va. (5-0)
1957	Va. Military (6-0)
1958	West Va. (4-0)
1959	Va. Military (6-0-1)
1960	Va. Military (4-1)
1961	Citadel (5-1)
1962	Va. Military (6-0)
1963	Virginia Tech (5-0)
1964	West Va. (5-0)
1965	West Va. (4-0)
1966	East Caro. (4-1-1) & William & Mary (4-1-1)
1967	West Va. (4-0-1)
1968	Richmond (6-0)
1969	Davidson (5-1) & Richmond (5-1)
1970	William & Mary (3-1)
1971	Richmond (5-1)
1972	East Caro. (7-0)
1973	East Caro. (7-0)
1974	Va. Military (5-1)
1975	Richmond (5-1)
1976	East Caro. (4-1)
1977	Tenn.-Chatt. (4-1) & Va. Military (4-1)
1978	Furman (4-1) & Tenn.-Chatt. (4-1)
1979	Tenn.-Chatt. (5-1)
1980	Furman (7-0)
1981	Furman (5-2)
1982	Furman (6-1)*
1983	Furman (6-0-1)*
1984	Tenn.-Chatt. (5-1)*
1985	Furman (6-0)*
1986	Appalachian St. (6-0-1)*
1987	Appalachian St. (7-0)*
1988	Furman (6-1)* & Marshall (6-1)*
1989	Furman (7-0)*
1990	Furman (6-1)*
1991	Appalachian St. (6-1)*
1992	Citadel (6-1)*
1993	Ga. Southern (7-1)*
1994	Marshall (7-1)*
1995	Appalachian St. (8-0)*

**Participated in NCAA Division I-AA Championship. √No records available until 1933.*

SOUTHLAND FOOTBALL LEAGUE

Founded: In 1963 by a group of five institutions. **Charter members** (5): Abilene Christian, Arkansas St., Lamar, Texas-Arlington and Trinity (Tex.). **Admitted later** (12): Louisiana Tech (1971), Southwestern La. (1971), McNeese St. (1972), North Texas (1982), Northeast La. (1982), Northwestern St. (1987), Sam Houston St. (1987), Southwest Tex. St. (1987), Stephen F. Austin (1987), Nicholls St. (1992), Jacksonville St. (1996) and Troy St. (1996). **Withdrew later** (9): Trinity (Tex.) (1972), Abilene Christian (1973), Southwestern La. (1982), Texas-Arlington (1986, dropped football), Arkansas St. (1987), Lamar (1987), Louisiana Tech (1987), North Texas (1995) and Northeast La. (1996). **Current members** (8): Jacksonville St., McNeese St., Nicholls St., Northwestern St., Sam Houston St., Southwest Tex. St., Stephen F. Austin and Troy St.

Year	Champion (Record)
1964	Lamar (3-0-1)
1965	Lamar (3-1)
1966	Texas-Arlington (3-1)
1967	Texas-Arlington (4-0)
1968	Arkansas St. (3-0-1)
1969	Arkansas St. (4-0)
1970	Arkansas St. (4-0)
1971	Louisiana Tech (4-1)
1972	Louisiana Tech (5-0)
1973	Louisiana Tech (5-0)
1974	Louisiana Tech (5-0)
1975	Arkansas St. (5-0)
1976	McNeese St. (4-1) & Southwestern La. (4-1)
1977	Louisiana Tech (4-0-1)
1978	Louisiana Tech (4-1)
1979	McNeese St. (5-0)
1980	McNeese St. (5-0)
1981	Texas-Arlington (4-1)
1982	Louisiana Tech (5-0)*
1983	North Texas (5-1)* & Northeast La. (5-1)
1984	Louisiana Tech (5-1)*
1985	Arkansas St. (5-1)*
1986	Arkansas St. (5-0)*
1987	Northeast La. (6-0)*
1988	Northwestern St. (6-0)*
1989	Stephen F. Austin (5-0-1)*
1990	Northeast La. (5-1)*
1991	McNeese St. (4-1-2)*
1992	Northeast La. (7-0)*
1993	McNeese St. (7-0)*
1994	North Texas (5-0-1)*
1995	McNeese St. (5-0)*

**Participated in NCAA Division I-AA Championship.*

SOUTHWESTERN ATHLETIC CONFERENCE

Founded: In 1920 by a group of six institutions. **Charter members** (6): Bishop, Paul Quinn, Prairie View, Sam Houston College, Texas College and Wiley. **Admitted later** (9): Langston (1931), Southern-B.R. (1934), Arkansas AM&N (1936), Texas Southern (1954), Grambling (1958), Jackson St. (1958), Alcorn St. (1962), Mississippi Val. (1968) and Alabama St. (1982). **Withdrew later** (8): Paul Quinn (1929), Bishop (1956), Langston (1957), Sam Houston College (1959), Texas College (1961), Wiley (1968), Arkansas AM&N (1970) and Prairie View (1990, dropped program, readmitted 1991). **Current members** (8): Alabama St., Alcorn St., Grambling, Jackson St., Mississippi Val., Prairie View, Southern-B.R. and Texas Southern.

Year	Champion (Record√)
1921	Wiley
1922	Paul Quinn
1923	Wiley
1924	Paul Quinn
1925	Bishop
1926	Sam Houston College
1927	Wiley
1928	Wiley
1929	Wiley
1930	Wiley
1931	Prairie View
1932	Wiley
1933	Langston & Prairie View
1934	Texas College
1935	Texas College
1936	Texas College & Langston
1937	Southern-B.R. & Langston
1938	Southern-B.R. & Langston
1939	Langston
1940	Southern-B.R. & Langston
1941	No champion
1942	Texas College
1943	No champion
1944	Wiley (5-1), Texas College (5-1) & Langston (5-1)
1945	Wiley (6-0)
1946	Southern-B.R. (5-1)
1947	Southern-B.R. (7-0)
1948	Southern-B.R. (7-0)
1949	Southern-B.R. (6-0-1) & Langston (6-0-1)
1950	Southern-B.R. (7-0)
1951	Prairie View (6-1)
1952	Prairie View (6-0)
1953	Prairie View (6-0)
1954	Prairie View (6-0)
1955	Southern-B.R. (6-1)
1956	Texas Southern (5-1) & Langston (5-1)
1957	Wiley (6-0)
1958	Prairie View (5-0)
1959	Southern-B.R. (7-0)
1960	Southern-B.R. (6-1), Prairie View (6-1) & Grambling (6-1)
1961	Jackson St. (6-1)
1962	Jackson St. (6-1)
1963	Prairie View (7-0)
1964	Prairie View (7-0)
1965	Grambling (6-1)
1966	Southern-B.R. (4-2-1), Grambling (4-2-1), Texas Southern (4-2-1) & Arkansas AM&N (4-2-1)
1967	Grambling (6-1)
1968	Alcorn St. (6-1), Grambling (6-1) & Texas Southern (6-1)
1969	Alcorn St. (6-0-1)
1970	Alcorn St. (6-0)
1971	Grambling (5-1)
1972	Grambling (5-1) & Jackson St. (5-1)
1973	Grambling (5-1) & Jackson St. (5-1)
1974	Alcorn St. (5-1) & Grambling (5-1)
1975	Grambling (4-2) & Southern-B.R. (4-2)
1976	Alcorn St. (5-1)
1977	Grambling (6-0)
1978	Grambling (5-0-1)
1979	Grambling (5-1) & Alcorn St. (5-1)
1980	Grambling (5-1)* & Jackson St. (5-1)
1981	Jackson St. (5-1)*
1982	Jackson St. (6-0)*
1983	Grambling (6-0-1)
1984	Alcorn St. (7-0)*
1985	Jackson St. (6-1)* & Grambling (6-1)*
1986	Jackson St. (7-0)*
1987	Jackson St. (7-0)*
1988	Jackson St. (7-0)*

Year	Champion (Record√)
1989	Jackson St. (7-0)*
1990	Jackson St. (5-1)*
1991	Alabama St. (6-0-1)#
1992	Alcorn St. (7-0)*
1993	Southern-B.R. (7-0)#
1994	Grambling (6-1)# & Alcorn St. (6-1)*
1995	Jackson St. (7-0)*

*√No records available until 1944. *Participated in NCAA Division I-AA Championship. #Participated in Division I-AA Heritage Bowl.*

YANKEE CONFERENCE

Founded: In 1947 by six institutions from the old New England College Conference. **Charter members** (6): Connecticut, Maine, Massachusetts, New Hampshire, Rhode Island and Vermont. **Admitted later** (8): Boston U. (1971), Holy Cross (1971), Delaware (1983), Richmond (1984), Villanova (1985), James Madison (1993), Northeastern (1993) and William & Mary (1993). **Withdrew later** (2): Holy Cross (1972) and Vermont (1974, dropped football). **Current members** (12): Boston U., Connecticut, Delaware, James Madison, Maine, Massachusetts, New Hampshire, Northeastern, Rhode Island, Richmond, Villanova and William & Mary. **Note:** The league is divided into the New England and Mid-Atlantic Divisions.

Year	Champion (Record)
1947	New Hampshire (4-0)
1948	New Hampshire (3-1)
1949	Connecticut (2-0-1) & Maine (2-0-1)
1950	New Hampshire (4-0)
1951	Maine (3-0-1)
1952	Connecticut (3-1), Maine (3-1) & Rhode Island (3-1)
1953	New Hampshire (3-1) & Rhode Island (3-1)
1954	New Hampshire (4-0)
1955	Rhode Island (4-0-1)
1956	Connecticut (3-0-1)
1957	Connecticut (3-0-1) & Rhode Island (3-0-1)
1958	Connecticut (4-0)
1959	Connecticut (4-0)
1960	Connecticut (3-1)
1961	Maine (5-0)
1962	New Hampshire (4-0-1)
1963	Massachusetts (5-0)
1964	Massachusetts (5-0)
1965	Maine (5-0)
1966	Massachusetts (5-0)
1967	Massachusetts (5-0)
1968	Connecticut (4-1) & New Hampshire (4-1)
1969	Massachusetts (5-0)
1970	Connecticut (4-0-1)
1971	Connecticut (3-1-1) & Massachusetts (3-1-1)
1972	Massachusetts (5-0)
1973	Connecticut (5-0-1)
1974	Maine (4-2) & Massachusetts (4-2)
1975	New Hampshire (5-0)
1976	New Hampshire (4-1)
1977	Massachusetts (5-0)
1978	Massachusetts (5-0)*
1979	Massachusetts (4-1)
1980	Boston U. (5-0)
1981	Rhode Island (4-1) & Massachusetts (4-1)
1982	Boston U. (3-2)*, Connecticut (3-2), Maine (3-2) and Massachusetts (3-2)
1983	Boston U. (4-1)* & Connecticut (4-1)
1984	Boston U. (4-1)* & Rhode Island (4-1)*
1985	Rhode Island (5-0)*
1986	Connecticut (5-2), Delaware (5-2)* & Massachusetts (5-2)
1987	Maine (6-1)* & Richmond (6-1)*
1988	Delaware (6-2)* & Massachusetts (6-2)*
1989	Connecticut (6-2), Maine (6-2)* & Villanova (6-2)*
1990	Massachusetts (7-1)*
1991	Delaware (7-1)* & Villanova (7-1)*
1992	Delaware (7-1)*
1993	Boston U. (9-0)*
1994	New Hampshire (8-0)*
1995	Delaware (8-0)*

**Participated in NCAA Division I-AA Championship.*

Discontinued Conferences

Division I-A

BIG EIGHT CONFERENCE

Founded: Originally founded in 1907 as the Missouri Valley Intercollegiate Athletic Association. Charter members were Iowa, Kansas, Missouri, Nebraska and Washington (Mo.). Six schools were admitted later: Drake (1908), Iowa St. (1908), Kansas St. (1913), Grinnell (1919), Oklahoma (1920) and Oklahoma St. (1925). Iowa withdrew in 1911. The Big Six Conference was founded in 1928 when charter members left the MVIAA. Iowa St., Kansas, Kansas St., Missouri, Nebraska and Oklahoma were joined by Colorado (1948) (known as Big Seven) and Oklahoma St. (1958) (known as Big Eight until 1996). All eight members of Big Eight joined four former Southwest Conference members (Baylor, Texas, Texas A&M and Texas Tech) to form Big 12 Conference in 1996.

Year	Champion (Record)
1907	Iowa (1-0) & Nebraska (1-0)
1908	Kansas (4-0)
1909	Missouri (4-0-1)
1910	Nebraska (2-0)
1911	Iowa St. (2-0-1) & Nebraska (2-0-1)
1912	Iowa St. (2-0) & Nebraska (2-0)
1913	Missouri (4-0) & Nebraska (3-0)
1914	Nebraska (3-0)
1915	Nebraska (4-0)
1916	Nebraska (3-1)
1917	Nebraska (2-0)
1918	No Champion—War
1919	Missouri (4-0-1)
1920	Oklahoma (4-0-1)
1921	Nebraska (3-0)
1922	Nebraska (5-0)
1923	Nebraska (3-0-2)
1924	Missouri (5-1)
1925	Missouri (5-1)
1926	Oklahoma St. (3-0-1)
1927	Missouri (5-1)
1928	Nebraska (4-0)
1929	Nebraska (3-0-2)
1930	Kansas (4-1)
1931	Nebraska (5-0)
1932	Nebraska (5-0)
1933	Nebraska (5-0)
1934	Kansas St. (5-0)
1935	Nebraska (4-0-1)
1936	Nebraska (5-0)
1937	Nebraska (3-0-2)
1938	Oklahoma (5-0)
1939	Missouri (5-0)
1940	Nebraska (5-0)
1941	Missouri (5-0)
1942	Missouri (4-0-1)
1943	Oklahoma (5-0)
1944	Oklahoma (4-0-1)
1945	Missouri (5-0)
1946	Oklahoma (4-1) & Kansas (4-1)
1947	Kansas (4-0-1) & Oklahoma (4-0-1)
1948	Oklahoma (5-0)
1949	Oklahoma (5-0)
1950	Oklahoma (6-0)
1951	Oklahoma (6-0)
1952	Oklahoma (5-0-1)
1953	Oklahoma (6-0)
1954	Oklahoma (6-0)
1955	Oklahoma (6-0)
1956	Oklahoma (6-0)
1957	Oklahoma (6-0)
1958	Oklahoma (6-0)
1959	Oklahoma (5-1)
1960	Missouri (7-0)
1961	Colorado (7-0)
1962	Oklahoma (7-0)
1963	Nebraska (7-0)
1964	Nebraska (6-1)
1965	Nebraska (7-0)
1966	Nebraska (6-1)
1967	Oklahoma (7-0)
1968	Kansas (6-1) & Oklahoma (6-1)
1969	Missouri (6-1) & Nebraska (6-1)
1970	Nebraska (7-0)
1971	Nebraska (7-0)
1972	Nebraska (5-1-1)*
1973	Oklahoma (7-0)
1974	Oklahoma (7-0)
1975	Nebraska (6-1) & Oklahoma (6-1)
1976	Colorado (5-2), Oklahoma (5-2) & Oklahoma St. (5-2)
1977	Oklahoma (7-0)
1978	Nebraska (6-1) & Oklahoma (6-1)
1979	Oklahoma (7-0)
1980	Oklahoma (7-0)
1981	Nebraska (7-0)
1982	Nebraska (7-0)
1983	Nebraska (7-0)
1984	Oklahoma (6-1) & Nebraska (6-1)
1985	Oklahoma (7-0)
1986	Oklahoma (7-0)
1987	Oklahoma (7-0)
1988	Nebraska (7-0)
1989	Colorado (7-0)
1990	Colorado (7-0)
1991	Colorado (6-0-1) & Nebraska (6-0-1)
1992	Nebraska (6-1)
1993	Nebraska (7-0)
1994	Nebraska (7-0)
1995	Nebraska (7-0)

**Oklahoma (5-1-1) forfeited title.*

BORDER INTERCOLLEGIATE ATHLETIC ASSOCIATION

Founded: In 1931 as Border Intercollegiate Athletic Association. Charters members were Arizona, Arizona St. Teachers' (Flagstaff) (now Northern Ariz.), Arizona St. Teachers' (Tempe) (now Arizona St.), New Mexico and New Mexico A&M (now New Mexico St.). Texas Tech admitted in 1932, Texas Mines (now UTEP) admitted in 1935, and Hardin-Simmons and West Texas St. Teachers' (now West Tex. A&M) in 1941.

Year	Champion (Record)
1931	Arizona St. (3-1)
1932	Texas Tech (2-0)*
1933	Texas Tech (1-0)*
1934	Texas Tech (1-0)*
1935	Arizona (4-0)
1936	Arizona (3-0-1)
1937	Texas Tech (3-0)
1938	New Mexico St. (4-1)** New Mexico (4-2)**
1939	Arizona St. (4-0)
1940	Arizona St. (3-0-1)
1941	Arizona (5-0)
1942	Hardin-Simmons (3-0-1) Texas Tech (3-0-1)
1943	No full conference program

**Texas Tech has been listed by some as conference champion for the years 1932, 1933 and 1934, but conference rules forbade an official conference championship. This was due to the fact that the conference covered such a large area that games between all members were not practical.*

***Texas Tech won its two conference games in 1938 but did not win the official championship since it did not meet the conference three-game requirement. Its victory over New Mexico did not count toward the championship, permitting New Mexico to share championship honors with New Mexico St.*

MISSOURI VALLEY CONFERENCE

Founded: Originally founded as the Missouri Valley Intercollegiate Athletic Association. Several charter members left in 1928 to form the Big Six Conference, which became the Big Eight later. But Drake, Grinnell, Iowa St., Kansas St., Oklahoma, Oklahoma A&M (now Oklahoma St.) and Washington (Mo.) continued the MVIAA. Creighton joined in 1928, Butler in 1932, Tulsa and Washburn in 1935, St. Louis in 1937, Wichita St. in 1947, Bradley and Detroit in 1949, and Houston in 1951.

Year	Champion
1928	Drake
1929	Drake
1930	Drake & Oklahoma St.
1931	Drake
1932	Oklahoma St.
1933	Drake & Oklahoma St.
1934	Washington (Mo.)
1935	Washington (Mo.) & Tulsa
1936	Tulsa & Creighton

Year	Champion
1937	Tulsa
1938	Tulsa
1939	Washington (Mo.)
1940	Tulsa
1941	Tulsa
1942	Tulsa
1943	Tulsa
1944	Oklahoma St.
1945	Oklahoma St.
1946	Tulsa
1947	Tulsa
1948	Oklahoma St.
1949	Detroit
1950	Tulsa
1951	Tulsa
1952	Houston
1953	Oklahoma St. & Detroit
1954	Wichita St.
1955	Wichita St. & Detroit
1956	Houston
1957	Houston
1958	North Texas
1959	North Texas & Houston
1960	Wichita St.
1961	Wichita St.
1962	Tulsa
1963	Cincinnati & Wichita St.
1964	Cincinnati
1965	Tulsa
1966	North Texas & Tulsa
1967	North Texas
1968	Memphis
1969	Memphis
1970	Louisville
1971	Memphis
1972	Louisville, West Tex. A&M & Drake
1973	North Texas
1974	Tulsa
1975	Tulsa
1976	Tulsa & New Mexico St.
1977	West Tex. A&M
1978	New Mexico St.
1979	West Tex. A&M
1980	Tulsa
1981	Drake & Tulsa
1982	Tulsa
1983	Tulsa
1984	Tulsa
1985	Tulsa

OLD ROCKY MOUNTAIN CONFERENCE

(Mountain States Athletic Conference and Big Seven Conference)

Founded: This conference predates every conference except the Big Ten and consisted of Brigham Young (1922), Colorado (1900), Colorado Agricultural College (now Colorado St.) (1900), Colorado St. College (1900), Denver (1900), Utah (1902), Utah St. (1902) and Wyoming (1905). Before 1938, these schools were part of the Rocky Mountain Conference, other members of which, at that time, were Colorado College, Colorado Mines, Greeley St. Teachers' (now Northern Colo.), Montana St. (1917) and Western St. Teachers' (now Western St.) (1925). A split took place in 1938, when the Mountain States Athletic Conference or "Big Seven" was formed. The name Rocky Mountain Conference was retained by the last six schools after 1938. Some members went into the Western Athletic Conference when the RMC was dissolved in 1962.

Year	Champion
1900	Colorado College
1901	Colorado
1902	Colorado
1903	Colorado
1904	Colorado Mines
1905	Colorado Mines
1906	Colorado Mines
1907	Colorado Mines
1908	Denver
1909	Denver
1910	Colorado
1911	Colorado
1912	Colorado Mines
1913	Colorado
1914	Colorado Mines
1915	Colorado Aggies
1916	Colorado Aggies
1917	Denver
1918	Colorado Mines
1919	Colorado Aggies
1920	Colorado Aggies
1921	Utah St.
1922	Utah
1923	Colorado
1924	Colorado
1925	Colorado Aggies
1926	Utah
1927	Colorado Aggies
1928	Utah
1929	Utah
1930	Utah
1931	Utah
1932	Utah
1933	Utah, Denver* & Colorado St.*
1934	Colorado, Northern Colo. & Colorado St.*
1935	Colorado & Utah St.*
1936	Utah St.
1937	Colorado
1938	Utah
1939	Colorado
1940	Utah
1941	Utah
1942	Colorado & Utah
1943	Colorado
1944	Colorado
1945	Denver
1946	Utah St. & Denver
1947	Utah
1948	Utah
1949	Wyoming
1950	Wyoming
1951	Utah
1952	Utah
1953	Utah
1954	Denver
1955	Colorado St.
1956	Wyoming
1957	Utah
1958	Wyoming
1959	Wyoming
1960	Wyoming & Utah St.
1961	Wyoming & Utah St.

**In final ratings, according to conference rules, tie games were not counted in awarding championships. Thus, teams marked with * shared the championship because one or more ties were not counted in their conference records.*

SOUTHLAND CONFERENCE

(I-A only 1975-79, now I-AA conference)

SOUTHWEST CONFERENCE

Founded: In 1914 as the Southwest Athletic Conference with charter members Arkansas, Baylor, Oklahoma, Oklahoma St., Rice, Southwestern (Tex.), Texas and Texas A&M. Five teams were added: Southern Methodist (1918), Phillips (1920), Texas Christian (1923), Texas Tech (1960) and Houston (1976). Five withdrew: Southwestern (Texas) (1917), Oklahoma (1920), Phillips (1921), Oklahoma St. (1925) and Arkansas (1992). Of the eight members in the final (1995) season, four (Baylor, Texas, Texas A&M and Texas Tech) joined with eight members of the Big Eight Conference to form the Big 12 Conference in 1996. The other members in 1996: Houston (to Conference USA), Rice (to Western Athletic Conference), Southern Methodist (to Western Athletic Conference) and Texas Christian (to Western Athletic Conference).

Year	Champion (Record)
1914	No champion
1915	Oklahoma (3-0)
1916	No champion
1917	Texas A&M (2-0)
1918	Texas (4-0)
1919	Texas A&M (4-0)
1920	Texas (5-0)
1921	Texas A&M (3-0-2)
1922	Baylor (5-0)
1923	Southern Methodist (5-0)
1924	Baylor (4-0-1)
1925	Texas A&M (4-1)
1926	Southern Methodist (5-0)
1927	Texas A&M (4-0-1)
1928	Texas (5-1)
1929	Texas Christian (4-0-1)
1930	Texas (4-1)
1931	Southern Methodist (5-0-1)
1932	Texas Christian (6-0)
1933	No champion*
1934	Rice (5-1)
1935	Southern Methodist (6-0)
1936	Arkansas (5-1)
1937	Rice (4-1-1)
1938	Texas Christian (6-0)
1939	Texas A&M (6-0)
1940	Texas A&M (5-1)
1941	Texas A&M (5-1)
1942	Texas (5-1)
1943	Texas (5-0)
1944	Texas Christian (3-1-1)
1945	Texas (5-1)
1946	Rice (5-1) & Arkansas (5-1)
1947	Southern Methodist (5-0-1)
1948	Southern Methodist (5-0-1)
1949	Rice (6-0)
1950	Texas (6-0)
1951	Texas Christian (5-1)
1952	Texas (6-0)
1953	Rice (5-1) & Texas (5-1)
1954	Arkansas (5-1)
1955	Texas Christian (5-1)
1956	Texas A&M (6-0)
1957	Rice (5-1)
1958	Texas Christian (5-1)
1959	Texas (5-1), Texas Christian (5-1) & Arkansas (5-1)
1960	Arkansas (6-1)
1961	Texas (6-1) & Arkansas (6-1)
1962	Texas (6-0-1)
1963	Texas (7-0)
1964	Arkansas (7-0)
1965	Arkansas (7-0)
1966	Southern Methodist (6-1)
1967	Texas A&M (6-1)
1968	Texas (6-1) & Arkansas (6-1)
1969	Texas (7-0)
1970	Texas (7-0)
1971	Texas (6-1)
1972	Texas (7-0)
1973	Texas (7-0)
1974	Baylor (6-1)
1975	Arkansas (6-1), Texas A&M (6-1) & Texas (6-1)
1976	Houston (7-1) & Texas Tech (7-1)
1977	Texas (8-0)
1978	Houston (7-1)
1979	Houston (7-1) & Arkansas (7-1)
1980	Baylor (8-0)
1981	Texas (6-1-1)*
1982	Southern Methodist (7-0-1)
1983	Texas (8-0)
1984	Southern Methodist (6-2) & Houston (6-2)
1985	Texas A&M (7-1)
1986	Texas A&M (7-1)
1987	Texas A&M (6-1)
1988	Arkansas (7-0)
1989	Arkansas (7-1)
1990	Texas (8-0)
1991	Texas A&M (8-0)
1992	Texas A&M (7-0)
1993	Texas A&M (7-0)
1994	Baylor (4-3), Rice (4-3), Texas (4-3), Texas Christian (4-3) & Texas Tech (4-3)*
1995	Texas (7-0)

**Forfeited title: Arkansas (4-1) in 1933, Southern Methodist (7-1) in 1981 on probation and Texas A&M (6-0-1) in 1994 on probation.*

Division I-AA

AMERICAN WEST CONFERENCE

Founded: Started Division I-AA play in 1993 with charter members Cal St. Northridge, Cal St. Sacramento and Southern Utah. Other members were UC Davis and Cal Poly SLO (both Division II members at the time). Cal Poly SLO became a Division I-AA member in 1994, and UC Davis withdrew in 1994. Last-year members were Cal Poly SLO (became independent), Cal St. Northridge (to Big Sky Conference), Cal St. Sacramento (to Big Sky Conference) and Southern Utah (became independent).

Year	Champion (Record)
1993	Southern Utah (3-1) & UC Davis (3-1)#
1994	Cal Poly SLO (3-0)
1995	Cal St. Sacramento (3-0)

#Participated in NCAA Division II Championship.

1996 Conference Alignment Changes

Division I-A

In Division I-A, the biggest shakeup in divisional changes is the addition of Alabama-Birmingham and Central Florida from Division I-AA. Pacific (California) dropped its football program after the 1995 season, thus bringing the Division I-A membership total to 109 teams in 1996.

In conference movement, the Big Eight Conference and the Southwest Conference will begin a merger of sorts in 1996 to form the Big 12 Conference. All Big Eight members (Colorado, Iowa State, Kansas, Kansas State, Missouri, Nebraska, Oklahoma and Oklahoma State) plus four of the Southwest members (Baylor, Texas, Texas A&M and Texas Tech) will comprise the new league.

The Big West Conference also has undergone dramatic realignment, adding Division II members Boise State and Idaho plus Division I-A independent North Texas. The league loses Arkansas State, Louisiana Tech, Northern Illinois and Southwestern Louisiana to independent status and San Jose State and UNLV to the Western Athletic Conference in 1996. The three new teams joining the Big West: Nevada, New Mexico State and Utah State.

Six teams will form brand-new Conference USA in 1996. Former Division I-A independents Cincinnati, Louisville, Memphis, Southern Mississippi and Tulane join former Southwest Conference member Houston in the new league.

The Western Athletic Conference becomes the largest Division I-A league at 16 teams by adding six new schools to its double-division fold. Former Southwest Conference members Rice, Southern Methodist and Texas Christian and independent Tulsa join Brigham Young, New Mexico, UTEP and Utah in the Mountain Division. Former Big West members UNLV and San Jose State join Air Force, Colorado State, Fresno State, Hawaii, San Diego State and Wyoming in the Pacific Division.

New Division I-A independents Alabama-Birmingham, Arkansas State, Central Florida, Louisiana Tech, Northern Illinois and Southwestern Louisiana join Army, East Carolina, Navy, Northeast Louisiana and Notre Dame to total 11 Division I-A teams without conference affiliation in 1996.

Division I-AA

Fairfield (starting a new football program) is the new member of Division I-AA in 1996. Alabama-Birmingham and Central Florida moved up to Division I-A. That makes 118 teams competing in Division I-AA in 1996.

In conference alignments, there is one new league and one that folded plus much movement for 1996. The new league will be the Northeast Conference, consisting of former Division I-AA independents Central Connecticut State, Monmouth (New Jersey), Robert Morris, St. Francis (Pennsylvania) and Wagner.

The Big Sky adds former American West Conference members Cal State Northridge and Cal State Sacramento as well as Portland State (Division II) and loses Boise State and Idaho to the Big West Conference (Division I-A). The new teams join Eastern Washington, Idaho State, Montana, Montana State, Northern Arizona and Weber State for a nine-team league.

The Gateway Conference loses Eastern Illinois to the Ohio Valley Conference, while newly outfitted Fairfield joins the Metro Atlantic Athletic Conference. Hampton goes from independent status to the Mid-Eastern Athletic Conference, and the Ohio Valley Conference adds Eastern Illinois and loses Morehead State to the ranks of independents.

The Southland Conference changes its name to Southland Football League and adds both Jacksonville State and Troy State from the independent ranks. The 14 independent teams in 1996 are newcomer Morehead State and old-timers Buffalo, Cal Poly San Luis Obispo, Charleston Southern, Davidson, Hofstra, Liberty, St. Mary's (California), Samford, Southern Utah, Towson State, Western Kentucky, Wofford and Youngstown State.

Division II

Only one new team has joined Division II for 1996: Merrimack (beginning a new football program). That brings the division total to 140 teams.

Merrimack will join the new Eastern Football Conference. Former Midwest Intercollegiate Football Conference member St. Joseph's (Indiana) moves to independent status. Northeast Missouri State, a Mid-America Intercollegiate Athletic Association member, has changed its name to Truman State.

Division III

With no new teams joining the division, the Division III membership totals 199 for 1996.

There are several conference alignment changes. Bluffton, Defiance, Thomas More and Wilmington (Ohio), all former Association of Mid-East Conference members, have changed to independent status. Two former independents have joined conferences: Springfield joins the Freedom Football Conference, and Alfred joins the Presidents' Athletic Conference.

1996 Schedules/ 1995 Results

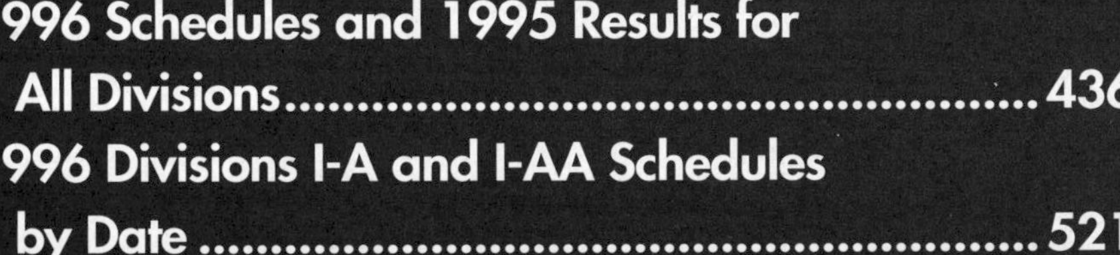

1996 Schedules and 1995 Results for All Divisions

Listed alphabetically in this section are 1996 schedules and 1995 results for all football-playing NCAA member institutions. The division designation for each school is indicated to the right of the school location.

Coaching records (below head coaches' names) are for all seasons as the head coach at any four-year collegiate institution.

Game dates and starting times are subject to change.
■ Designates home games.
*** Designates night games. Neutral sites are listed in brackets.**

ABILENE CHRISTIAN

Abilene, TX 79699 II

Coach: Jack Kiser, Abilene Christian '71
(First year as head coach)

1996 SCHEDULE

N.M. Highlands ■ .... *Aug. 31
Prairie View .... Sept. 7
Midwestern St. ■ .... *Sept. 21
Eastern N.M. ■ .... *Oct. 5
Central Okla. .... Oct. 12
Angelo St. ■ .... Oct. 19
Tarleton St. .... Oct. 26
East Tex. St. ■ .... Nov. 2
Tex. A&M-Kingsville .... *Nov. 9
West Tex. A&M ■ .... Nov. 16

1995 RESULTS (4-7-0)

31 N.M. Highlands 6
35 Prairie View 0
0 Northern Ariz. 62
7 New Haven 33
7 Eastern N.M. 17
7 Central Okla. 13
0 Angelo St. 24
38 Tarleton St. 18
24 East Tex. St. 31
7 Tex. A&M-Kingsville 54
21 West Tex. A&M 14
177 **272**

Nickname: Wildcats.
Stadium: Shotwell (1959), 15,000 capacity. Natural turf.
Colors: Purple & White.
Conference: Lone Star.
SID: Garner Roberts, 915-674-2693.
AD: Stan Lambert.

ADAMS ST.

Alamosa, CO 81102 II

Coach: Jeff Geiser, Colorado '76
Record: 12 Years, 64-56-2

1996 SCHEDULE

West Tex. A&M .... *Sept. 7
Western N.M. ■ .... Sept. 14
N.M. Highlands .... Sept. 21
Mesa St. .... Sept. 28
Northwestern Okla. ■ .... Oct. 5
Western St. ■ .... Oct. 12
Colorado Mines ■ .... Oct. 19
Chadron St. .... Oct. 26
Fort Lewis .... Nov. 2
Fort Hays St. ■ .... Nov. 9
Neb.-Kearney ■ .... Nov. 16

1995 RESULTS (4-6-0)

26 West Tex. A&M 44
27 Western N.M. 48
23 Northwestern Okla. 6
21 Western St. 42
27 Chadron St. 31
38 Colorado Mines 26
47 Fort Hays St. 50
16 Fort Lewis 41
52 Mesa St. 21
36 N.M. Highlands 26
313 **335**

Nickname: Grizzlies.
Stadium: Rex Field (1949), 2,800 capacity. Natural turf.
Colors: Green & White.
Conference: Rocky Mountain Athletic.
SID: Lloyd Engen, 719-589-7825.
AD: Rodger Jehlicka.

ADRIAN

Adrian, MI 49221 III

Coach: Jim Lyall, Michigan '74
Record: 6 Years, 21-32-1

1996 SCHEDULE

Heidelberg .... *Sept. 14
Defiance ■ .... *Sept. 21
Wilmington (Ohio) .... Sept. 28
Ill. Benedictine ■ .... Oct. 5
Hope .... Oct. 12
Olivet ■ .... Oct. 19
Albion ■ .... Oct. 26
Alma .... Nov. 2
Kalamazoo ■ .... Nov. 9

1995 RESULTS (6-3-0)

28 Heidelberg 14
24 Defiance 14
14 Augustana (Ill.) 35
41 Wilmington (Ohio) 37
24 Hope 9
27 Olivet 14
0 Albion 37
21 Alma 24
10 Kalamazoo 7
189 **191**

Nickname: Bulldogs.
Stadium: Maple (1960), 5,000 capacity. Natural turf.
Colors: Gold & Black.
Conference: Michigan Intercollegiate Athletic Association.
SID: Darcy Gifford, 517-264-3176.
AD: Henry Mensing.

AIR FORCE

Air Force Academy, CO 80840 .... I-A

Coach: Fisher DeBerry, Wofford '60
Record: 12 Years, 92-55-1

1996 SCHEDULE

San Jose St. ■ .... Aug. 31
UNLV .... *Sept. 7
Wyoming .... Sept. 21
Rice ■ .... Sept. 28
San Diego St. .... *Oct. 5
Navy ■ .... Oct. 12
Notre Dame .... Oct. 19
Hawaii ■ .... Oct. 26
Colorado St. ■ .... Nov. 2
Army .... Nov. 9
Fresno St. .... Nov. 16

1995 RESULTS (8-4-0)

38 Brigham Young 12
34 Wyoming 10
20 Colorado St. 27
6 Northwestern 30
27 New Mexico 24
56 UTEP 46
30 Navy 20
21 Utah 22
31 Fresno St. 20
38 Army 20
14 Notre Dame 44
45 Hawaii 28
360 **303**

Copper Bowl

41 Texas Tech 55

Nickname: Falcons.
Stadium: Falcon (1962), 52,480 capacity. Natural turf.
Colors: Blue & Silver.
Conference: Western Athletic.
SID: Dave Kellogg, 719-472-2313.
AD: Col. Randall Spetman.

AKRON

Akron, OH 44325 .... I-A

Coach: Lee Owens, Bluffton '77
Record: 1 Year, 2-9-0

1996 SCHEDULE

Ohio .... *Aug. 29
Virginia Tech ■ .... *Sept. 7
Toledo ■ .... *Sept. 14
Illinois .... Sept. 21
Western Mich. .... *Sept. 28
Kent .... Oct. 5
Central Mich. .... Oct. 12
Miami (Ohio) ■ .... Oct. 19
Northern Ill. .... Oct. 26
Bowling Green ■ .... Nov. 2
Eastern Mich. .... Nov. 9

1995 RESULTS (2-9-0)

29 Eastern Mich. 49
12 Bowling Green 50
0 Kansas St. 67
16 Central Mich. 13
3 Western Mich. 7
27 Virginia Tech 77
23 Ohio 29
14 Kent 6
10 Youngstown St. 24
7 Toledo 41
0 Miami (Ohio) 65
141 **428**

Nickname: Zips.
Stadium: Rubber Bowl (1940), 35,202 capacity. Artificial turf.
Colors: Blue & Gold.
Conference: Mid-American.
SID: Tom Liggett, 330-972-7968.
AD: Michael Bobinski.

ALABAMA

University, AL 35486 .... I-A

Coach: Gene Stallings, Texas A&M '57
Record: 13 Years, 79-67-1

1996 SCHEDULE

Bowling Green ■ .... Aug. 31
Southern Miss. ■ .... Sept. 7
Vanderbilt ■ .... Sept. 14
Arkansas [Little Rock, Ark.] .... *Sept. 21
Kentucky ■ .... Oct. 5
North Caro. St. .... Oct. 12
Mississippi ■ .... Oct. 19
Tennessee .... Oct. 26
LSU .... *Nov. 9
Mississippi St. .... Nov. 16
Auburn ■ .... Nov. 23

1995 RESULTS (8-3-0)

33 Vanderbilt 25
24 Southern Miss. 20
19 Arkansas 20
31 Georgia 0
27 North Caro. St. 11
14 Tennessee 41
23 Mississippi 9
38 North Texas 19
10 LSU 3
14 Mississippi St. 9
27 Auburn 31
260 **188**

Nickname: Crimson Tide.
Stadium: Bryant-Denny (1929), 70,123 capacity. Natural turf.

Colors: Crimson & White.
Conference: Southeastern.
SID: Larry White, 205-348-6084.
AD: Bob Bockrath.

ALA.-BIRMINGHAM

Birmingham, AL 35294 ....I-A

Coach: Watson Brown, Vanderbilt '73
Record: 11 Years, 37-83-1

1996 SCHEDULE

Auburn ....*Aug. 31
Maryland ....*Sept. 7
Arkansas St. ■..*Sept. 14
Jacksonville St. ■ ....*Sept. 21
Western Ky. ■..*Oct. 5
Southwestern La. ■..Oct. 19
Louisiana Tech ....*Oct. 26
Vanderbilt..Nov. 2
Central Fla. ■..Nov. 9
Cincinnati ■..Nov. 16
Charleston So. ■..*Nov. 21

1995 RESULTS (5-6-0)

3 Alabama St. 13
21 Southwestern La. 56
26 Jacksonville St. 28
18 Western Ky. 32
13 Middle Tenn. St. 28
28 Wofford..0
19 North Texas 14
7 Troy St. 60
40 Charleston So. 14
61 Knoxville..8
37 Miles 8
273 **261**

Nickname: Blazers.
Stadium: Legion Field (1927), 83,091 capacity. Natural turf.
Colors: Green, Gold & White.
Conference: I-A Independents.
SID: Grant Shingleton, 205-934-0722.
AD: Gene Bartow.

ALABAMA A&M

Normal, AL 35762....................................II

Coach: Kenneth Pettiford, Tennessee St. '75
Record: 4 Years, 11-32-0

1996 SCHEDULE

North Ala. ....*Sept. 7
Clark Atlanta ■..*Sept. 14
Savannah St. ■ ....Sept. 21
Morris Brown..Sept. 28
Morehouse ....Oct. 5
Albany St. (Ga.) ■..Oct. 12
Fort Valley St. ....Oct. 19
Alabama St. [Birmingham, Ala.]..Oct. 26
Miles ■..Nov. 2
Tuskegee..Nov. 9
Kentucky St. ■..Nov. 16

1995 RESULTS (6-5-0)

21 Jackson St. 20
0 North Ala. 49
7 Clark Atlanta..0
11 Savannah St. 8
26 Morris Brown 6
48 Morehouse..14
9 Albany St. (Ga.)..45
24 Fort Valley St. 20
20 Alabama St. 37
20 Miles 26
6 Tuskegee..19
192 **244**

Nickname: Bulldogs.
Stadium: Bulldog, 20,000 capacity. Natural turf.
Colors: Maroon & White.
Conference: Southern Intercollegiate Athletic.
SID: Antoine Bell, 205-851-5368.
AD: Jerome Fitch (Interim).

ALABAMA ST.

Montgomery, AL 36195..........................I-AA

Coach: Houston Markham, Alcorn St. '65
Record: 9 Years, 62-31-5

1996 SCHEDULE

Jackson St. [Birmingham, Ala.] ....*Sept. 1
Texas Southern ■..*Sept. 7
Southern-B.R. ....*Sept. 14
Alcorn St. ....*Sept. 21
Troy St. [Mobile, Ala.] ....*Oct. 5
Clark Atlanta [Mobile, Ala.] ....*Oct. 12
Prairie View..Oct. 19
Alabama A&M [Birmingham, Ala.]..Oct. 26
Grambling..Nov. 9
Mississippi Val. ■ ....Nov. 16
Tuskegee ■..Nov. 28

1995 RESULTS (7-3-1)

13 Ala.-Birmingham 3
19 Southern-B.R. 29
20 Alcorn St. 20
10 Troy St. 28
22 Jackson St. 24
27 Texas Southern 19
49 Prairie View 16
37 Alabama A&M..20
37 Grambling 16
56 Mississippi Val. 28
58 Tuskegee..20
348 **223**

Nickname: Hornets.
Stadium: Cramton (1922), 24,600 capacity. Natural turf.
Colors: Black & Old Gold.
Conference: Southwestern Athletic.
SID: Peter Forest, 205-293-4511.
AD: W. Curtis Williams.

ALBANY (N. Y.)

Albany, NY 12222 II

Coach: Robert Ford, Springfield '59
Record: 27 Years, 139-117-1

1996 SCHEDULE

Central Conn. St. ■ ....*Sept. 7
Mercyhurst ■..*Sept. 14
St. Lawrence ....Sept. 21
Rensselaer ....Sept. 28
Union (N.Y.) ■ ....Oct. 12
Stony Brook ....Oct. 19
Gannon ■ ....*Oct. 26
Pace..Nov. 2
Trenton St. ■..Nov. 9
King's (Pa.) ....Nov. 16

1995 RESULTS (3-7-0)

14 Dayton..40
17 Central Conn. St. 10
21 LIU-C.W. Post 27
7 Rensselaer..41
6 Union (N.Y.)..20
14 Southern Conn. St. 35
38 Pace..20
30 Trenton St. 43
50 King's (Pa.)..0
21 Stony Brook..40
218 **276**

Nickname: Great Danes.
Stadium: University Field (1967), 10,000 capacity. Natural turf.
Colors: Purple & Gold.
Conference: Division II Independents.
SID: Brian DePasquale, 518-442-3072.
AD: Milton Richards.

ALBANY ST. (GA.)

Albany, GA 31705 II

Coach: Hampton Smith, Mississippi Val. '57
Record: 20 Years, 122-81-4

1996 SCHEDULE

North Ala. ■..*Aug. 31
Miles ■ ....Sept. 7
Kentucky St. ....*Sept. 14
Morehouse ....Sept. 21
Tuskegee ■ ....Sept. 28
Savannah St. ■..Oct. 5
Alabama A&M ....Oct. 12
Clark Atlanta ■..Oct. 26
Morris Brown..Nov. 2
Fort Valley St. [Columbus, Ga.] ....Nov. 9

1995 RESULTS (8-3-0)

13 North Ala. 41
58 Miles 12
35 Kentucky St. 0
44 Morehouse..13
69 Tuskegee..0
48 Savannah St. 10
45 Alabama A&M..9
28 Bethune-Cookman..40
31 Clark Atlanta..23
53 Morris Brown 11
12 Fort Valley St. 16
436 **175**

II Championship

28 North Ala. 38

Nickname: Golden Rams.
Stadium: Mills Memorial (1957), 11,000 capacity. Natural turf.
Colors: Blue & Gold.
Conference: Southern Intercollegiate Athletic.
SID: Calvin Miles (Interim), 912-430-4672.
AD: Shirley Reese.

ALBION

Albion, MI 49224 III

Coach: Pete Schmidt, Alma '70
Record: 13 Years, 95-26-4

1996 SCHEDULE

Tiffin..Sept. 14
Wabash..Sept. 21
DePauw ■..Sept. 28
Kalamazoo..Oct. 12
Hope ■..Oct. 19
Adrian ....Oct. 26
Olivet ■ ....Nov. 2
Alma..Nov. 9
Thomas More ■..Nov. 16

1995 RESULTS (8-1-0)

43 Wilmington (Ohio)..3
21 Aurora..14
31 Wabash 21
3 DePauw 14
19 Kalamazoo 14
34 Hope..24
37 Adrian 0
48 Olivet 0
38 Alma 28
274 **118**

Nickname: Britons.
Stadium: Sprankle-Sprandel (1976), 5,010 capacity. Natural turf.
Colors: Purple & Gold.
Conference: Michigan Intercollegiate Athletic Association.
SID: Robin Hartman, 517-629-0434.
AD: Pete Schmidt.

ALBRIGHT

Reading, PA 19612....................................III

Coach: Ron Maier, Bentley '86
(First year as head coach)

1996 SCHEDULE

Lycoming..Sept. 14
Lebanon Valley ■..*Sept. 21
Moravian ....Sept. 28
Wilkes ■..Oct. 5
King's (Pa.) ■ ....Oct. 12
Widener..Oct. 19

FDU-Madison ■ ..... Oct. 26
Juniata ..... Nov. 2
Susquehanna ..... Nov. 9
Catholic ■ ..... Nov. 16

1995 RESULTS (7-3-0)

26	Lycoming	29
38	Lebanon Valley	3
26	Moravian	0
10	Wilkes	7
42	King's (Pa.)	24
17	Widener	31
19	FDU-Madison	10
10	Juniata	0
47	Susquehanna	14
16	Catholic	17
251		**135**

ECAC III Playoff

20 Salisbury St. 10

Nickname: Lions.
Stadium: Eugene L. Shirk (1925), 7,000 capacity. Natural turf.
Colors: Cardinal & White.
Conference: Middle Atlantic.
SID: Stan Hyman, 610-921-7833.
AD: Sally Miller.

ALCORN ST.

Lorman, MS 39096 ..... I-AA

Coach: Cardell Jones, Alcorn St. '65
Record: 5 Years, 34-18-3

1996 SCHEDULE

Troy St. ■ ..... Aug. 31
Grambling ..... *Sept. 7
Western Ill. ..... Sept. 14
Alabama St. ■ ..... *Sept. 21
Samford ..... *Sept. 28
Ark.-Pine Bluff ■ ..... *Oct. 5
Prairie View ..... Oct. 12
Texas Southern ■ ..... *Oct. 19
Southern-B.R. ■ ..... Oct. 26
Mississippi Val. ..... Nov. 9
Jackson St. ■ ..... Nov. 23

1995 RESULTS (4-6-1)

17	Grambling	39
7	Sam Houston St.	44
20	Alabama St.	20
21	Texas Southern	10
44	Ark.-Pine Bluff	28
17	Howard	21
13	Prairie View	2
51	Southern-B.R.	61
9	Samford	20
38	Mississippi Val.	27
7	Jackson St.	28
244		**300**

Nickname: Braves.
Stadium: Jack Spinks (1992), 25,000 capacity. Natural turf.
Colors: Purple & Gold.
Conference: Southwestern Athletic.
SID: Derick Hackett, 601-877-6466.
AD: Lloyd Hill.

ALFRED

Alfred, NY 14802 III

Coach: Jim Moretti, Alfred '72
Record: 11 Years, 63-44-3

1996 SCHEDULE

Ursinus ..... Sept. 7
Waynesburg ■ ..... Sept. 14
Hartwick ■ ..... Sept. 21
Ithaca ..... Sept. 28
Bethany (W.Va.) ■ ..... Oct. 5
Thiel ..... Oct. 12
Hobart ..... Oct. 26
Union (N.Y.) ■ ..... Nov. 2
Wash. & Jeff. ■ ..... Nov. 9
Grove City ..... Nov. 16

1995 RESULTS (3-6-0)

14	Thomas More	17
21	Hartwick	28
13	Ithaca	12
35	St. John Fisher	52
42	St. Lawrence	0
17	Trenton St.	38
35	Hobart	14
14	Buffalo St.	37
28	Wesley	52
219		**250**

Nickname: Saxons.
Stadium: Merrill Field (1926), 5,000 capacity. Artificial turf.
Colors: Purple & Gold.
Conference: Presidents' Athletic.
SID: R. J. Hydorn, 607-871-2103.
AD: Hank Ford.

ALLEGHENY

Meadville, PA 16335 III

Coach: Ken O'Keefe, John Carroll '75
Record: 6 Years, 60-7-1

1996 SCHEDULE

Thiel ■ ..... Sept. 14
Wittenberg ..... Sept. 21
Ohio Wesleyan ■ ..... Sept. 28
Denison ..... Oct. 5
Case Reserve ■ ..... Oct. 12
Wooster ..... Oct. 19
Earlham ■ ..... Oct. 26
Brockport St. ..... Nov. 2
Kenyon ..... Nov. 9
Oberlin ■ ..... Nov. 16

1995 RESULTS (9-1-0)

34	Carnegie Mellon	7
31	Denison	7
17	Wittenberg	31
50	Case Reserve	0
34	Earlham	14
17	Westminster (Pa.)	10
69	Kenyon	13
57	Wooster	12
61	Ohio Wesleyan	0
55	Oberlin	0
425		**94**

Nickname: Gators.
Stadium: Robertson Field (1948), 5,000 capacity. Natural turf.
Colors: Blue & Gold.
Conference: North Coast Athletic.
SID: Steven Mest, 814-332-6755.
AD: Richard Creehan.

ALMA

Alma, MI 48801 III

Coach: Jim Cole, Alma '74
Record: 5 Years, 23-22-0

1996 SCHEDULE

Valparaiso ..... Sept. 14
Olivet Nazarene ..... Sept. 21
Elmhurst ■ ..... Sept. 28
Defiance ■ ..... Oct. 5
Olivet ..... Oct. 12
Kalamazoo ■ ..... Oct. 19
Hope ..... Oct. 26
Adrian ■ ..... Nov. 2
Albion ■ ..... Nov. 9

1995 RESULTS (6-3-0)

36	Olivet Nazarene	17
29	Elmhurst	6
25	Franklin	29
35	Ill. Benedictine	0
27	Olivet	17
23	Kalamazoo	30
31	Hope	17
24	Adrian	21
28	Albion	38
258		**175**

Nickname: Scots.
Stadium: Bahlke Field (1986), 4,000 capacity. Artificial turf.
Colors: Maroon & Cream.
Conference: Michigan Intercollegiate Athletic Association.
SID: Greg Baadte, 517-463-7323.
AD: Denny Griffin.

AMERICAN INT'L

Springfield, MA 01109 II

Coach: Art Wilkins, Bucknell '72
Record: 2 Years, 5-15-0

1996 SCHEDULE

Rhode Island ..... Aug. 31
Kutztown ■ ..... Sept. 7
Springfield ■ ..... Sept. 14
Bloomsburg ■ ..... Sept. 28
Southern Conn. St. ..... *Oct. 4
Bentley ..... *Oct. 11
Cheyney ..... Oct. 19
Ithaca ■ ..... Oct. 26
LIU-C.W. Post ■ ..... Nov. 9
New Haven ..... Nov. 16

1995 RESULTS (2-8-0)

19	East Stroudsburg	49
0	Millersville	39
7	Bloomsburg	40
22	LIU-C.W. Post	31
24	Ithaca	23
22	Stony Brook	23
17	Springfield	27
19	Towson St.	17
13	New Haven	23
45	Southern Conn. St.	48
188		**320**

Nickname: Yellow Jackets.
Stadium: J. H. Miller Field (1964), 5,000 capacity. Natural turf.
Colors: Gold & White.
Conference: Division II Independents.
SID: Chris Herman, 413-747-6544.
AD: Robert E. Burke.

AMHERST

Amherst, MA 01002 III

Coach: Jack Siedlecki, Union (N.Y.) '74
Record: 8 Years, 49-20-1

1996 SCHEDULE

Hamilton ■ ..... Sept. 21
Bowdoin ..... Sept. 28
Middlebury ..... Oct. 5
Colby ■ ..... Oct. 12
Wesleyan (Conn.) ..... Oct. 19
Tufts ■ ..... Oct. 26
Trinity (Conn.) ..... Nov. 2
Williams ■ ..... Nov. 9

1995 RESULTS (5-2-1)

34	Bates	12
27	Bowdoin	20
28	Middlebury	13
15	Colby	27
13	Wesleyan (Conn.)	0
28	Tufts	0
10	Trinity (Conn.)	33
0	Williams	0
155		**105**

Nickname: Lord Jeffs.
Stadium: Pratt Field (1891), 8,000 capacity. Natural turf.
Colors: Purple & White.
Conference: NESCAC.
SID: Rotating, 413-542-2390.
AD: Peter Gooding.

ANDERSON (IND.)

Anderson, IN 46012 III

Coach: Mike Manley, Anderson '73
Record: 14 Years, 59-75-3

1996 SCHEDULE

Walsh .... Sept. 7
Taylor ■ .... Sept. 14
Olivet .... Sept. 21
DePauw .... Oct. 5
Rose-Hulman .... Oct. 12
Franklin ■ .... Oct. 19
Hanover .... Oct. 26
Ill. Benedictine ■ .... Nov. 2
Wabash ■ .... Nov. 9
Manchester ■ .... Nov. 16

1995 RESULTS (6-4-0)

24 Mt. Senario 10
27 Olivet 26
27 Taylor 17
42 Rose-Hulman 14
28 Franklin 32
35 Hanover 41
36 Campbellsville 27
29 Wabash 21
13 DePauw 45
7 Manchester 10
268 **243**

Nickname: Ravens.
Stadium: Macholtz, 4,200 capacity. Natural turf.
Colors: Orange & Black.
Conference: Indiana Collegiate Athletic.
SID: Jim Hazen, 317-641-4479.
AD: A. Barrett Bates.

ANGELO ST.

San Angelo, TX 76909 II

Coach: Jerry Vandergriff, Corpus Christi '64
Record: 14 Years, 96-53-2

1996 SCHEDULE

Northeastern St. ■ .... *Aug. 31
Western N.M. ■ .... *Sept. 7
McNeese St. .... *Sept. 21
West Tex. A&M .... *Oct. 5
Eastern N.M. ■ .... *Oct. 12
Abilene Christian .... Oct. 19
Central Okla. ■ .... *Oct. 26
Tarleton St. .... Nov. 2
East Tex. St. .... Nov. 9
Tex. A&M-Kingsville ■ .... Nov. 16

1995 RESULTS (6-3-1)

14 Southern Utah 7
30 East Central 10
3 Stephen F. Austin 17
54 West Tex. A&M 14
10 Eastern N.M. 10
24 Abilene Christian 0
14 Central Okla. 7
35 Tarleton St. 7
21 East Tex. St. 24
20 Tex. A&M-Kingsville 41
225 **137**

Nickname: Rams.
Stadium: San Angelo (1962), 17,500 capacity. Natural turf.
Colors: Blue & Gold.
Conference: Lone Star.
SID: M. L. Stark Hinkle, 915-942-2248.
AD: Jerry Vandergriff.

APPALACHIAN ST.

Boone, NC 28608 .... I-AA

Coach: Jerry Moore, Baylor '61
Record: 14 Years, 82-77-2

1996 SCHEDULE

Wake Forest .... *Aug. 29
Tennessee Tech ■ .... *Sept. 7
Eastern Ky. .... *Sept. 21
Citadel ■ .... Sept. 28
East Tenn. St. .... *Oct. 5
Furman ■ .... Oct. 12
Ga. Southern .... Oct. 19
Marshall ■ .... Oct. 26
Tenn.-Chatt. .... Nov. 2
Western Caro. .... Nov. 16
Va. Military ■ .... Nov. 23

1995 RESULTS (11-0-0)

24 Wake Forest 22
44 Edinboro 7
38 North Caro. A&T 31
30 East Tenn. St. 23
41 Furman 28
27 Ga. Southern 17
10 Marshall 3
31 Tenn.-Chatt. 18
26 Va. Military 24
28 Western Caro. 3
28 Citadel 24
327 **200**

I-AA Championship

31 James Madison 24
17 Stephen F. Austin 27

Nickname: Mountaineers.
Stadium: Kidd Brewer (1962), 16,650 capacity. Artificial turf.
Colors: Black & Gold.
Conference: Southern.
SID: Rick Covington, 704-262-3080.
AD: Roachel Laney.

ARIZONA

Tucson, AZ 85721 .... I-A

Coach: Dick Tomey, DePauw '61
Record: 19 Years, 123-86-7

1996 SCHEDULE

UTEP ■ .... *Aug. 31
Iowa .... Sept. 7
Illinois ■ .... *Sept. 14
Washington .... Sept. 21
Washington St. ■ .... *Oct. 5
Southern Cal .... Oct. 12
Oregon St. ■ .... *Oct. 26
California .... Nov. 2
Oregon .... Nov. 9
UCLA ■ .... Nov. 16
Arizona St. ■ .... *Nov. 23

1995 RESULTS (6-5-0)

41 Pacific (Cal.) 9
20 Georgia Tech 19
7 Illinois 9
10 Southern Cal 31
20 California 15
10 UCLA 17
17 Washington 31
24 Washington St. 14
14 Oregon St. 9
13 Oregon 17
31 Arizona St. 28
207 **199**

Nickname: Wildcats.
Stadium: Arizona (1928), 57,803 capacity. Natural turf.
Colors: Cardinal & Navy.
Conference: Pacific-10.
SID: Tom Duddleston Jr., 602-621-4163.
AD: Jim Livengood.

ARIZONA ST.

Tempe, AZ 85287 .... I-A

Coach: Bruce Snyder, Oregon '63
Record: 16 Years, 87-85-6

1996 SCHEDULE

Washington ■ .... *Sept. 7
North Texas ■ .... *Sept. 14
Nebraska ■ .... *Sept. 21
Oregon ■ .... *Sept. 28
Boise St. ■ .... *Oct. 5
UCLA .... Oct. 12
Southern Cal ■ .... *Oct. 19
Stanford .... Oct. 26
Oregon St. .... Nov. 2
California ■ .... *Nov. 9
Arizona .... *Nov. 23

1995 RESULTS (6-5-0)

20 Washington 23
45 UTEP 20
28 Nebraska 77
20 Oregon St. 11
0 Southern Cal 31
28 Stanford 30
29 Brigham Young 21
35 Oregon 24
37 UCLA 33
38 California 29
28 Arizona 31
308 **330**

Nickname: Sun Devils.
Stadium: Sun Devil (1959), 73,656 capacity. Natural turf.
Colors: Maroon & Gold.
Conference: Pacific-10.
SID: Mark Brand, 602-965-6592.
AD: Kevin White.

ARKANSAS

Fayetteville, AR 72701 .... I-A

Coach: Danny Ford, Alabama '70
Record: 15 Years, 114-45-5

1996 SCHEDULE

Southern Methodist ■ .... Sept. 7
Alabama [Little Rock, Ark.] .... *Sept. 21
Northeast La. [Little Rock, Ark.] .... *Sept. 28
Florida ■ .... Oct. 5
Louisiana Tech [Little Rock, Ark.] .... *Oct. 12
South Caro. .... Oct. 19
Auburn .... Nov. 2
Mississippi ■ .... Nov. 9
Tennessee .... Nov. 16
Mississippi St. .... Nov. 23
LSU [Little Rock, Ark.] .... Nov. 29

1995 RESULTS (8-4-0)

14 Southern Methodist 17
51 South Caro. 21
20 Alabama 19
27 Memphis 20
35 Vanderbilt 7
31 Tennessee 49
13 Mississippi 6
30 Auburn 28
26 Mississippi St. 21
24 Southwestern La. 13
0 LSU 28
3 Florida 34
274 **263**

Carquest Bowl

10 North Caro. 20

Nickname: Razorbacks.
Stadium: Razorback (1938), 50,018 capacity. Natural turf.
Colors: Cardinal & White.
Conference: Southeastern.
SID: Rick Schaeffer, 501-575-2751.
AD: Frank Broyles.

ARKANSAS ST.

State University, AR 72467 .... I-A

Coach: John Bobo, Maryville (Tenn.) '80
Record: 3 Years, 9-23-1

1996 SCHEDULE

Brigham Young .... *Aug. 31
Austin Peay ■ .... *Sept. 7
Ala.-Birmingham .... *Sept. 14
Northern Ill. ■ .... *Sept. 21
Central Ark. ■ .... *Oct. 5
Southwestern La. .... Oct. 12
Southeast Mo. St. ■ .... Oct. 19
Mississippi .... *Oct. 26
East Caro. .... Nov. 2
Louisiana Tech ■ .... Nov. 9
Nevada .... Nov. 16

1995 RESULTS (6-5-0)

21 Utah St. 17
23 UNLV 28

14 Southern Ill. 9
25 Louisiana Tech 28
7 Minnesota 55
9 Southwestern La. 33
25 Texas Tech 63
37 Jacksonville St. 6
21 San Jose St. 7
28 Northern Ill. 21
55 Mississippi Val. 3
265 **270**

Nickname: Indians.
Stadium: Indian (1974), 33,410 capacity. Natural turf.
Colors: Scarlet & Black.
Conference: I-A Independents.
SID: Gina Bowman, 501-972-2541.
AD: Barry Dowd.

ARMY

West Point, NY 10996 .... I-A

Coach: Bob Sutton, Eastern Mich. '74
Record: 5 Years, 24-30-1

1996 SCHEDULE

Ohio ■ ....Sept. 14
Duke ■ ....Sept. 21
North Texas [Irving, Texas] ....Sept. 28
Yale ■ ....Oct. 5
Rutgers ....Oct. 12
Tulane ■ ....Oct. 19
Miami (Ohio) ....Oct. 26
Lafayette ■ ....Nov. 2
Air Force ■ ....Nov. 9
Syracuse ....Nov. 16
Navy [Philadelphia, Pa.] ....Dec. 7

1995 RESULTS (5-5-1)

42 Lehigh 9
21 Duke 23
13 Washington 21
21 Rice 21
27 Notre Dame 28
49 Boston College 7
56 Colgate 14
25 East Caro. 31
20 Air Force 38
37 Bucknell 6
14 Navy 13
325 **211**

Nickname: Cadets, Black Knights.
Stadium: Michie (1924), 39,929 capacity. Artificial turf.
Colors: Black, Gold & Gray.
Conference: I-A Independents.
SID: Bob Beretta, 914-938-3303.
AD: Al Vanderbush.

ASHLAND

Ashland, OH 44805 II

Coach: Gary Keller, Bluffton '73
Record: 2 Years, 8-12-0

1996 SCHEDULE

Ferris St. ■ ....*Aug. 29
Michigan Tech ....Sept. 7
Grand Valley St. ■ ....Sept. 14
Northwood ....Sept. 21
Hillsdale ■ ....Sept. 28
Saginaw Valley ....Oct. 5
Wayne St. (Mich.) ■ ....Oct. 12
Youngstown St. ....*Oct. 19
Northern Mich. ■ ....Oct. 26
St. Francis (Ill.) ....Nov. 2
Indianapolis ....Nov. 9

1995 RESULTS (2-8-0)

13 Ferris St. 20
32 Michigan Tech 28
17 Grand Valley St. 52
9 Northwood 15
7 Hillsdale 28
20 Saginaw Valley 32
24 Wayne St. (Mich.) 17
13 St. Joseph's (Ind.) 21
8 Northern Mich. 20
7 St. Francis (Ill.) 28
150 **261**

Nickname: Eagles.
Stadium: Community (1963), 5,700 capacity. Natural turf.
Colors: Purple & Gold.
Conference: Midwest Intercollegiate.
SID: Al King, 419-289-5442.
AD: William J. Weidner.

ASSUMPTION

Worcester, MA 01615 II

Coach: Mark Garrett, Westfield St. '91
(First year as head coach)

1996 SCHEDULE

Stonehill ....Sept. 14
MIT ■ ....Sept. 21
Curry ■ ....Sept. 28
Pace ....Oct. 5
Sacred Heart ....Oct. 12
Merrimack ■ ....Oct. 19
Mass.-Lowell ....Oct. 26
Bentley ....Nov. 2
Salve Regina ■ ....Nov. 9
Nichols ■ ....Nov. 16

1995 RESULTS (6-4-0)

14 Stonehill 35
20 MIT 6
20 Western New Eng. 14
20 Pace 28
8 Nichols 6
26 Sacred Heart 23
36 Curry 29
18 Bentley 48
26 Mass.-Lowell 13
0 Salve Regina 54
188 **256**

Nickname: Greyhounds.
Stadium: Rocheleau Field (1961), 1,200 capacity. Natural turf.
Colors: Royal Blue & White.
Conference: Division II Independents.
SID: Steve Morris, 508-767-7240.
AD: Rita Castagna.

AUBURN

Auburn, AL 36830 .... I-A

Coach: Terry Bowden, West Va. '78
Record: 12 Years, 92-41-2

1996 SCHEDULE

Ala.-Birmingham ■ ....*Aug. 31
Fresno St. ■ ....*Sept. 7
Mississippi ....*Sept. 14
LSU ■ ....Sept. 21
South Caro. ■ ....Oct. 5
Mississippi St. ....*Oct. 12
Florida ....Oct. 19
Arkansas ■ ....Nov. 2
Northeast La. ■ ....Nov. 9
Georgia ■ ....Nov. 16
Alabama ....Nov. 23

1995 RESULTS (8-3-0)

46 Mississippi 13
76 Tenn.-Chatt. 10
6 LSU 12
42 Kentucky 21
48 Mississippi St. 20
38 Florida 49
34 Western Mich. 13
28 Arkansas 30
38 Northeast La. 14
37 Georgia 31
31 Alabama 27
424 **240**

Outback Bowl

14 Penn St. 43

Nickname: Tigers.
Stadium: Jordan-Hare (1939), 85,214 capacity. Natural turf.
Colors: Burnt Orange & Navy Blue.
Conference: Southeastern.
SID: Kent Partridge, 334-844-9800.
AD: David Housel.

AUGSBURG

Minneapolis, MN 55454 III

Coach: Jack Osberg, Augsburg '62
Record: 5 Years, 21-28-0

1996 SCHEDULE

Mayville St. ■ ....*Sept. 7
St. Thomas (Minn.) ■ ....*Sept. 14
St. John's (Minn.) ....Sept. 21
St. Olaf ....Sept. 28
Hamline ■ ....Oct. 5
Carleton ....Oct. 12
Gust. Adolphus ■ ....Oct. 19
Concordia-M'head ....Oct. 26
Macalester ■ ....Nov. 2
Bethel (Minn.) [Minneapolis, Minn.] ....*Nov. 8

1995 RESULTS (6-4-0)

34 Mayville St. 24
6 Concordia-M'head 38
14 St. John's (Minn.) 41
7 Bethel (Minn.) 27
17 Macalester 7
7 Hamline 35
28 St. Thomas (Minn.) 7
23 Gust. Adolphus 20
20 Carleton 7
20 St. Olaf 12
176 **218**

Nickname: Auggies.
Stadium: Anderson-Nelson Field (1984), 2,000 capacity. Artificial turf.
Colors: Maroon & Gray.
Conference: Minnesota Intercollegiate Athletic.
SID: Chris Brown, 612-330-1677.
AD: Paul Grauer.

AUGUSTANA (ILL.)

Rock Island, IL 61201 III

Coach: Tom Schmulbach, Western Ill. '69
Record: 1 Year, 6-3-0

1996 SCHEDULE

Wartburg ....Sept. 14
Ill. Benedictine ....Sept. 28
Wheaton (Ill.) ■ ....Oct. 5
Carthage ....Oct. 12
North Park ■ ....Oct. 19
North Central ....Oct. 26
Ill. Wesleyan ....Nov. 2
Elmhurst ■ ....Nov. 9
Millikin ....Nov. 16

1995 RESULTS (6-3-0)

21 Wis.-Platteville 24
35 Adrian 14
12 Ill. Wesleyan 28
47 North Central 7
53 North Park 14
35 Elmhurst 7
36 Millikin 0
27 Wheaton (Ill.) 35
24 Carthage 0
290 **129**

Nickname: Vikings.
Stadium: Ericson Field (1938), 3,200 capacity. Natural turf.
Colors: Gold & Blue.
Conference: College Conf. of Illinois & Wisconsin.
SID: Dave Wrath, 309-794-7265.
AD: John Farwell.

AUGUSTANA (S.D.)

Sioux Falls, SD 57197 II

Coach: Jim Heinitz, South Dak. St. '72
Record: 8 Years, 37-49-1

1996 SCHEDULE

Central Mo. St. ....*Sept. 7
Southwest St. ....Sept. 14
South Dak. St. ■ ....Sept. 21
North Dak. ....Sept. 28
North Dak. St. ■ ....Oct. 5
Morningside ....Oct. 12
South Dak. ....Oct. 19
Neb.-Omaha ■ ....Oct. 26
Mankato St. ■ ....Nov. 2
St. Cloud St. ....Nov. 9
Northern Colo. ■ ....Nov. 16

1995 RESULTS (3-6-1)

40 Southwest St. 6
15 South Dak. St. 37
29 North Dak. 39
14 North Dak. St. 53
17 Morningside 17
7 South Dak. 24
28 Neb.-Omaha 14
38 Mankato St. 55
24 St. Cloud St. 14
21 Northern Colo. 55
233 **314**

Nickname: Vikings.
Stadium: Howard Wood (1957), 10,000 capacity. Natural turf.
Colors: Blue & Yellow.
Conference: North Central.
SID: Karen Madsen, 605-336-4335.
AD: Bill Gross.

AURORA

Aurora, IL 60506 III

Coach: Jim Scott, Luther '61
Record: 10 Years, 48-36-3

1996 SCHEDULE

Coe ■ ....Sept. 7
Wheaton (Ill.) ....Sept. 21
Kalamazoo ■ ....Sept. 28
Concordia (Wis.) ....Oct. 5
Ill. Benedictine ■ ....Oct. 12
Upper Iowa ....Oct. 19
Simpson ....Oct. 26
Drake ■ ....Nov. 2
Valparaiso ....Nov. 9

1995 RESULTS (3-6-0)

14 Albion 21
21 Wheaton (Ill.) 28
7 Drake 37
6 Hope 40
34 Olivet Nazarene 23
34 Ill. Benedictine 0
15 Trinity (Ill.) 12
15 Valparaiso 20
6 Evansville 18
152 **199**

Nickname: Spartans.
Stadium: Aurora Field, 1,500 capacity. Natural turf.
Colors: Royal Blue & White.
Conference: Division III Independents.
SID: Dave Beyer, 708-844-5479.
AD: Rita Yerkes.

AUSTIN PEAY

Clarksville, TN 37044 ....I-AA

Coach: Roy Gregory, Tenn.-Chatt. '68
Record: 5 Years, 16-39-0

1996 SCHEDULE

Arkansas St. ....*Sept. 7
Samford ....*Sept. 14
Western Ky. ■ ....*Sept. 21
Southeast Mo. St. ....Sept. 28
Murray St. ....Oct. 5
Middle Tenn. St. ....Oct. 12
Tennessee Tech ■ ....Oct. 19
Tennessee St. ....Oct. 26
Eastern Ill. ■ ....Nov. 2
Eastern Ky. ■ ....Nov. 16
Tenn.-Martin ■ ....Nov. 23

1995 RESULTS (3-8-0)

13 Eastern Ill. 31
32 Samford 42
38 Western Ky. 34
23 Southeast Mo. St. 38
17 Murray St. 45
0 Middle Tenn. St. 43
20 Tennessee Tech 17
28 Tennessee St. 6
13 Morehead St. 26
0 Eastern Ky. 28
28 Tenn.-Martin 31
212 **341**

Nickname: Governors.
Stadium: Governors (1946), 10,000 capacity. Artificial turf.
Colors: Red & White.
Conference: Ohio Valley.
SID: Brad Kirtley, 615-648-7561.
AD: Kaye Hart.

BALDWIN-WALLACE

Berea, OH 44017 III

Coach: Bob Packard, Baldwin-Wallace '65
Record: 15 Years, 117-33-2

1996 SCHEDULE

Wis.-Whitewater ....Sept. 14
Mount Union ....Sept. 21
Heidelberg ■ ....*Sept. 28
Marietta ....*Oct. 5
Capital ■ ....Oct. 12
Otterbein ■ ....Oct. 19
Hiram ....Oct. 26
Muskingum ■ ....Nov. 2
Ohio Northern ....Nov. 9
John Carroll ■ ....Nov. 16

1995 RESULTS (6-4-0)

3 Wis.-Whitewater 6
36 Heidelberg 13
10 Marietta 27
32 Otterbein 7
0 Muskingum 17
16 Mount Union 35
42 Hiram 21
43 Capital 13
40 Ohio Northern 22
31 John Carroll 3
253 **164**

Nickname: Yellow Jackets.
Stadium: George Finnie (1971), 8,100 capacity. Artificial turf.
Colors: Brown & Gold.
Conference: Ohio Athletic.
SID: Kevin Ruple, 216-826-2327.
AD: Steve Bankson.

BALL ST.

Muncie, IN 47306 ....I-A

Coach: Bill Lynch, Butler '77
Record: 6 Years, 43-16-3

1996 SCHEDULE

Kansas ....*Aug. 29
Miami (Ohio) ■ ....Sept. 7
Minnesota ....*Sept. 14
Central Fla. ■ ....Sept. 21
Western Mich. ....Oct. 5
Ohio ■ ....Oct. 12
Bowling Green ....Oct. 19
Central Mich. ....Oct. 26
Eastern Mich. ....Nov. 2
Kent ■ ....Nov. 9
Toledo ■ ....Nov. 16

1995 RESULTS (7-4-0)

17 Miami (Ohio) 15
20 Western Ill. 7
7 Minnesota 31
10 Western Mich. 0
13 Purdue 35
14 Toledo 17
30 Bowling Green 10
35 Eastern Mich. 40
6 Ohio 3
28 Kent 13
24 Central Mich. 16
204 **187**

Nickname: Cardinals.
Stadium: Ball St. (1967), 21,581 capacity. Natural turf.
Colors: Cardinal & White.
Conference: Mid-American.
SID: Joe Hernandez, 317-285-8242.
AD: Andrea Seger.

BATES

Lewiston, ME 04240 III

Coach: Rick Pardy, Ithaca '83
Record: 7 Years, 18-42-2

1996 SCHEDULE

Trinity (Conn.) ....Sept. 21
Tufts ....Sept. 28
Williams ■ ....Oct. 5
Wesleyan (Conn.) ■ ....Oct. 12
Middlebury ....Oct. 19
Colby ■ ....Oct. 26
Bowdoin ....Nov. 2
Hamilton ■ ....Nov. 9

1995 RESULTS (1-7-0)

12 Amherst 34
21 Tufts 40
0 Williams 35
16 Wesleyan (Conn.) 23
23 Middlebury 28
6 Colby 26
33 Bowdoin 29
14 Hamilton 34
125 **249**

Nickname: Bobcats.
Stadium: Garcelon Field (1900), 3,000 capacity. Natural turf.
Colors: Garnet.
Conference: NESCAC.
SID: Adam Levin, 207-786-6411.
AD: Suzanne Coffey.

BAYLOR

Waco, TX 76706 ....I-A

Coach: Chuck Reedy, Appalachian St. '71
Record: 3 Years, 19-15-0

1996 SCHEDULE

Louisiana Tech [Shreveport, La.] ....*Sept. 7
Louisville ....Sept. 14
Oregon St. ■ ....*Sept. 21
Texas Tech ....*Oct. 5
Nebraska ....Oct. 12
Oklahoma ■ ....Oct. 19
Iowa St. ■ ....Oct. 26
Texas ....Nov. 2
Texas A&M ■ ....Nov. 9
Missouri ■ ....Nov. 16
Oklahoma St. ....Nov. 23

1995 RESULTS (7-4-0)

37 Tulsa 5
21 Mississippi St. 30
14 North Caro. St. 0
9 Texas Tech 7
47 Houston 7
9 Texas A&M 24
27 Texas Christian 24
14 Miami (Fla.) 35
48 Southern Methodist 7
34 Rice 6
13 Texas 21
273 **166**

Nickname: Bears.
Stadium: Floyd Casey (1950), 50,000 capacity. Artificial turf.

SCHEDULES/RESULTS

Colors: Green & Gold.
Conference: Big 12.
SID: Maxey Parrish, 817-755-2743.
AD: Tom Stanton.

BELOIT

Beloit, WI 53511 III

Coach: Ed DeGeorge, Colorado Col. '64
Record: 19 Years, 94-79-1

1996 SCHEDULE

Knox ■ ....Sept. 7
Concordia (Wis.) ....Sept. 14
Grinnell ■ ....Sept. 21
Cornell College ....Sept. 28
Ripon ■ ....Oct. 5
Carroll (Wis.) ■ ....Oct. 12
Lawrence ....Oct. 19
St. Norbert ....Oct. 26
Lake Forest ■ ....Nov. 2

1995 RESULTS (8-1-0)

47 Knox....................24
17 Cornell College 8
23 Illinois Col. 0
40 Monmouth (Ill.) 0
7 Ripon....................13
20 Carroll (Wis.) 14
20 Lawrence 17
22 St. Norbert....................16
31 Lake Forest....................20
227 **112**

Nickname: Buccaneers.
Stadium: Strong (1934), 3,500 capacity. Natural turf.
Colors: Gold & Blue.
Conference: Midwest.
SID: Paul Erickson, 608-363-2229.
AD: Ed DeGeorge.

BEMIDJI ST.

Bemidji, MN 56601 II

Coach: Jeff Tesch, Moorhead St. '78
(First year as head coach)

1996 SCHEDULE

St. John's (Minn.)....................Sept. 7
Wis.-Stout ■ ....*Sept. 14
Wis.-Stevens Point ■ ....*Sept. 21
Southwest St. ....Sept. 28
Moorhead St. ■....................Oct. 5
Winona St.....................Oct. 12
Minn.-Morris ■ ....Oct. 19
Northern St.....................Oct. 26
Minn.-Duluth ■....................Nov. 9

1995 RESULTS (3-7-0)

0 North Dak....................63
17 Wis.-Stout 49
9 Minn.-Duluth....................40
6 Southwest St. 8
20 Moorhead St. 32
25 Winona St. 14
16 Minn.-Morris....................12
25 Northern St. 24
14 Wayne St. (Neb.)....................55
15 Winona St. 29
147 **326**

Nickname: Beavers.
Stadium: BSU (1937), 4,000 capacity. Natural turf.
Colors: Kelly Green & White.
Conference: Northern Sun Intercollegiate.
SID: Jim Grimm, 218-755-2763.
AD: Bob Peters.

BENTLEY

Waltham, MA 02154 II

Coach: Peter Yetten, Boston U. '71
Record: 8 Years, 59-14-1

1996 SCHEDULE

Mass.-Lowell ....Sept. 14
Merrimack ■ ....*Sept. 20
Stony Brook ■ ....Sept. 28
Salve Regina....................*Oct. 4
American Int'l ■....................*Oct. 11
LIU-C.W. Post....................Oct. 19
Sacred Heart ■....................Oct. 26
Assumption ■ ....Nov. 2
MIT ....Nov. 9
Stonehill ....Nov. 16

1995 RESULTS (9-1-0)

44 Mass.-Lowell....................7
44 Curry....................7
50 Nichols 0
26 Salve Regina 19
16 Sacred Heart....................7
24 LIU-C.W. Post 16
24 Western New Eng. 0
48 Assumption 18
39 MIT....................6
36 Stonehill....................39
351 **119**

ECAC II Playoff

46 Stonehill....................3

Nickname: Falcons.
Stadium: Bentley College (1990), 1,500 capacity. Natural turf.
Colors: Blue & Gold.
Conference: Division II Independents.
SID: Dick Lipe, 617-891-2334.
AD: Bob DeFelice.

BETHANY (W. VA.)

Bethany, WV 26032 III

Coach: Steve Campos, Indiana (Pa.) '82
Record: 3 Years, 13-13-1

1996 SCHEDULE

Capital....................Sept. 7
Bridgewater (Va.) ■ ....Sept. 14
Waynesburg....................Sept. 28
Alfred....................Oct. 5
Wash. & Jeff. ■....................Oct. 12
Thiel ■....................Oct. 19
Grove City ■....................Oct. 26
Salisbury St.....................Nov. 2
Wilmington (Ohio) ■....................Nov. 9
St. Francis (Pa.)....................Nov. 16

1995 RESULTS (6-3-0)

28 Bridgewater (Va.) 14
30 St. Francis (Pa.) 12
0 Wash. & Jeff. 51
40 Thiel 19
13 Grove City 6
17 Waynesburg 16
23 Salisbury St. 21
7 Robert Morris 32
14 Gannon 16
172 **187**

Nickname: Bison.
Stadium: Bethany Field (1938), 1,000 capacity. Natural turf.
Colors: Green & White.
Conference: Presidents' Athletic.
SID: John Stroh, 304-829-7292.
AD: Wally Neel.

BETHEL (MINN.)

St. Paul, MN 55112....................................III

Coach: Steve Johnson, Bethel (Minn.) '80
Record: 7 Years, 36-32-1

1996 SCHEDULE

Trinity (Ill.)....................Sept. 7
Hamline ....Sept. 14
Carleton ■ ....Sept. 21
Gust. Adolphus....................Sept. 28
Concordia-M'head ■....................Oct. 5
Macalester....................Oct. 12
St. Olaf ■....................Oct. 19
St. Thomas (Minn.) ■....................Oct. 26
St. John's (Minn.)....................Nov. 2
Augsburg [Minneapolis, Minn.] ....*Nov. 8

1995 RESULTS (6-4-0)

38 Lake Forest....................27
14 St. John's (Minn.) 49
34 Macalester 7
27 Augsburg 7
9 Hamline....................31
7 St. Thomas (Minn.)....................21
7 Gust. Adolphus....................0
21 Carleton....................7
42 St. Olaf....................7
14 Concordia-M'head....................32
213 **188**

Nickname: Royals.
Stadium: Bremer Field (1972), 3,000 capacity. Natural turf.
Colors: Royal Blue & Gold.
Conference: Minnesota Intercollegiate Athletic.
SID: Leland Christenson, 612-638-6394.
AD: Dave Klostreich.

BETHUNE-COOKMAN

Daytona Beach, FL 32015....................I-AA

Coach: Jack McClairen, Bethune-Cookman '53
Record: 14 Years, 69-51-3

1996 SCHEDULE

Morehouse ■....................Aug. 31
Morris Brown ■ ....Sept. 7
Morgan St. ....Sept. 14
Norfolk St. ■ ....Sept. 21
Delaware St. ■ ....Oct. 5
Howard....................Oct. 12
South Caro. St. ....Oct. 19
North Caro. A&T ....Nov. 2
Hampton ....Nov. 9
Valparaiso ■ ....Nov. 16
Florida A&M [Tampa, Fla.] ....Nov. 23

1995 RESULTS (3-8-0)

25 Howard....................15
33 Morgan St.....................10
6 Tenn.-Chatt.....................35
14 Hampton....................34
33 Norfolk St. 35
20 South Caro. St. 42
40 Albany St. (Ga.) 28
21 North Caro. A&T....................24
7 Central Fla. 38
20 Delaware St. 30
0 Florida A&M 43
219 **334**

Nickname: Wildcats.
Stadium: Municipal, 10,000 capacity. Natural turf.
Colors: Maroon & Gold.
Conference: Mid-Eastern Athletic.
SID: W. Earl Kitchings, 904-255-1401.
AD: Lynn Thompson.

BLACKBURN

Carlinville, IL 62626 III

Coach: Dale Sprague, American Int'l '76
Record: 10 Years, 35-52-2

1996 SCHEDULE

Tri-State ....Sept. 7
Greenville ■ ....Sept. 14
Eureka ■....................Sept. 21
North Central ■....................Sept. 28
Westminster (Mo.) ....Oct. 5
Principia....................Oct. 12
McKendree....................Oct. 19
Wartburg ■....................Nov. 2
MacMurray ■ ....Nov. 9

1995 RESULTS (4-4-0)

12 Eureka 31
15 Illinois Col. 6
17 Ky. Wesleyan....................51
33 MacMurray 12
15 Tri-State....................21
31 Principia 6
20 Sue Bennett....................0
23 Maranatha Baptist 29
166 **156**

Nickname: Beavers.
Stadium: Blackburn College (1989), 1,500 capacity. Natural turf.
Colors: Scarlet & Black.
Conference: St. Louis Intercollegiate Athletic.
SID: Brad Turner, 217-854-3231.
AD: Ira Zeff.

BLOOMSBURG

Bloomsburg, PA 17815 II

Coach: Danny Hale, West Chester '68
Record: 8 Years, 62-23-1

1996 SCHEDULE

Wayne St. (Mich.) ■ ....Aug. 31
Indiana (Pa.) ....*Sept. 14
Lock Haven ■ ....Sept. 21
American Int'l ....Sept. 28
Cheyney ....Oct. 5
Mansfield ■ ....Oct. 12
Millersville ....Oct. 19
Shippensburg ■ ....Oct. 26
Kutztown ■ ....Nov. 2
West Chester ....Nov. 9
East Stroudsburg ■ ....Nov. 16

1995 RESULTS (9-1-1)

20 New Haven 27
41 Shippensburg 34
24 Calif. (Pa.) 20
40 American Int'l 7
56 Mansfield 13
28 Millersville 28
53 Lock Haven 20
17 Kutztown 8
23 West Chester 18
34 East Stroudsburg 27
55 Cheyney 0
391 **202**

Nickname: Huskies.
Stadium: Redman (1974), 5,000 capacity. Natural turf.
Colors: Maroon & Gold.
Conference: Pennsylvania State Athletic.
SID: Scott Leightman, 717-389-4413.
AD: Mary Gardner.

BLUFFTON

Bluffton, OH 45817 III

Coach: Carlin Carpenter, Defiance '64
Record: 17 Years, 67-89-1

1996 SCHEDULE

Wittenberg ■ ....Sept. 7
Ohio Northern ....*Sept. 14
Thiel ....Sept. 21
Manchester ■ ....Sept. 28
Sue Bennett ■ ....Oct. 5
Thomas More ....Oct. 12
Grove City ■ ....Oct. 19
Mt. St. Joseph ....Oct. 26
Wilmington (Ohio) ■ ....Nov. 2
Defiance ■ ....Nov. 9

1995 RESULTS (5-5-0)

14 Ohio Northern 35
40 Grove City 27
18 Manchester 28
28 Thiel 0
35 Oberlin 26
17 Urbana 14
25 Mt. St. Joseph 35
34 Wilmington (Ohio) 33
13 Defiance 17
0 Thomas More 19
224 **234**

Nickname: Beavers.
Stadium: Salzman (1993), 3,000 capacity. Natural turf.
Colors: Purple & White.
Conference: Division III Independents.
SID: Ron Geiser, 419-358-3241.
AD: Carlin Carpenter.

BOISE ST.

Boise, ID 83725 ....I-AA

Coach: Pokey Allen, Utah '65
Record: 10 Years, 85-40-2

1996 SCHEDULE

Central Mich. ■ ....*Aug. 31
Portland St. ■ ....*Sept. 7
Eastern Wash. ■ ....*Sept. 14
Hawaii ....*Sept. 21
Northwestern St. ■ ....*Sept. 28
Arizona St. ....*Oct. 5
Nevada ....Oct. 12
Utah St. ■ ....*Oct. 19
Fresno St. ....*Nov. 2
North Texas ■ ....Nov. 9
New Mexico St. ....Nov. 16
Idaho ■ ....Nov. 23

1995 RESULTS (7-4-0)

38 Utah St. 14
38 Sam Houston St. 14
28 Montana 54
17 Northwestern St. 22
13 Northern Ariz. 32
40 Weber St. 14
27 Idaho St. 17
49 Portland St. 14
63 Eastern Wash. 44
35 Montana St. 7
13 Idaho 33
361 **265**

Nickname: Broncos.
Stadium: Bronco (1970), 22,600 capacity. Artificial turf.
Colors: Orange & Blue.
Conference: Big West.
SID: Max Corbet, 208-385-1515.
AD: Gene Bleymaier.

BOSTON COLLEGE

Chestnut Hill, MA 02167 ....I-A

Coach: Dan Henning, William & Mary '64
Record: 2 Years, 11-12-1

1996 SCHEDULE

Hawaii ....*Aug. 31
Virginia Tech ■ ....Sept. 14
Michigan ....Sept. 21
Navy ■ ....Sept. 28
West Va. ....Oct. 5
Cincinnati ....*Oct. 12
Rutgers ■ ....Oct. 19
Syracuse ■ ....Oct. 26
Pittsburgh ....*Oct. 31
Notre Dame ■ ....Nov. 9
Temple ■ ....Nov. 16
Miami (Fla.) ....Nov. 23

1995 RESULTS (4-8-0)

6 Ohio St. 38
20 Virginia Tech 14
13 Michigan 23
21 Michigan St. 25
17 Pittsburgh 0
19 West Va. 31
7 Army 49
10 Notre Dame 20
10 Temple 9
14 Miami (Fla.) 17
29 Syracuse 58
41 Rutgers 38
207 **322**

Nickname: Eagles.
Stadium: Alumni (1957), 44,500 capacity. Artificial turf.
Colors: Maroon & Gold.
Conference: Big East.
SID: Reid Oslin, 617-552-3004.
AD: Chet Gladchuk.

BOSTON U.

Boston, MA 02215 ....I-AA

Coach: Tom Masella, Wagner '81
(First year as head coach)

1996 SCHEDULE

St. Mary's (Cal.) ....Sept. 7
Maine ....Sept. 14
James Madison ■ ....Sept. 21
Richmond ■ ....Sept. 28
Delaware ....Oct. 5
Massachusetts ....Oct. 12
Hofstra ■ ....Oct. 19
Rhode Island ....Oct. 26
Connecticut ■ ....Nov. 2
Northeastern ....Nov. 9
New Hampshire ■ ....Nov. 16

1995 RESULTS (3-8-0)

21 Villanova 16
40 Maine 21
29 Delaware 41
6 Richmond 21
31 James Madison 38
19 Rhode Island 22
3 Northeastern 14
7 New Hampshire 35
17 Connecticut 28
23 Massachusetts 28
54 Buffalo 40
250 **304**

Nickname: Terriers.
Stadium: Nickerson Field (1930), 17,369 capacity. Artificial turf.
Colors: Scarlet & White.
Conference: Yankee.
SID: Ed Carpenter, 617-353-2872.
AD: Gary Strickler.

BOWDOIN

Brunswick, ME 04011 III

Coach: Howard Vandersea, Bates '63
Record: 20 Years, 75-95-3

1996 SCHEDULE

Middlebury ....Sept. 21
Amherst ■ ....Sept. 28
Tufts ■ ....Oct. 5
Hamilton ....Oct. 12
Trinity (Conn.) ■ ....Oct. 19
Wesleyan (Conn.) ....Oct. 26
Bates ■ ....Nov. 2
Colby ....Nov. 9

1995 RESULTS (1-7-0)

6 Williams 24
20 Amherst 27
26 Tufts 29
13 Hamilton 35
12 Trinity (Conn.) 14
22 Wesleyan (Conn.) 30
29 Bates 33
24 Colby 3
152 **195**

Nickname: Polar Bears.
Stadium: Whittier Field (1896), 6,000 capacity. Natural turf.
Colors: White.
Conference: NESCAC.
SID: Craig C. Cheslog, 207-725-3254.
AD: Sidney J. Watson.

BOWIE ST.

Bowie, MD 20715 II

Coach: Sherman Wood, Salisbury St. '84
Record: 3 Years, 8-22-1

1996 SCHEDULE

West Va. St. ....*Aug. 31
Norfolk St. ■ ....Sept. 7

Johnson Smith ■ ....Sept. 14
Cheyney [Atlantic City, N.J.] ....Sept. 21
Virginia Union ■ ....Sept. 28
Elizabeth City St. ■ ....Oct. 12
Livingstone ....Oct. 19
Fayetteville St. ....Oct. 26
Virginia St. ■ ....Nov. 2
N.C. Central ....Nov. 9

1995 RESULTS (3-8-0)

0 West Liberty St. 35
12 Norfolk St. 27
35 Knoxville 26
0 Virginia St. 7
23 Virginia Union 12
15 Livingstone 22
7 Elizabeth City St. 43
20 Winston-Salem 7
3 Fayetteville St. 6
0 New Haven 34
18 N.C. Central 27
133 **246**

Nickname: Bulldogs.
Stadium: Bulldog (1992), 6,000 capacity. Natural turf.
Colors: Black & Gold.
Conference: Central Intercollegiate Athletic Association.
SID: Scott Rouch, 301-464-7710.
AD: Charles Guilford.

BOWLING GREEN

Bowling Green, OH 43403 ....I-A

Coach: Gary Blackney, Connecticut '67
Record: 5 Years, 41-14-2

1996 SCHEDULE

Alabama ....Aug. 31
Temple ■ ....Sept. 14
Miami (Ohio) ....Sept. 21
Central Mich. ■ ....Sept. 28
Toledo ....*Oct. 5
Kent ■ ....Oct. 12
Ball St. ■ ....Oct. 19
Ohio ....Oct. 26
Akron ....Nov. 2
Western Mich. ■ ....Nov. 9
Central Fla. ....Nov. 16

1995 RESULTS (5-6-0)

21 Louisiana Tech 28
17 Missouri 10
50 Akron 12
16 Central Mich. 22
37 Temple 31
0 Miami (Ohio) 21
10 Ball St. 30
16 Toledo 35
0 Western Mich. 17
33 Ohio 7
26 Kent 15
226 **228**

Nickname: Falcons.
Stadium: Doyt Perry (1966), 30,599 capacity. Natural turf.
Colors: Orange & Brown.
Conference: Mid-American.
SID: Steve Barr, 419-372-7075.
AD: Ron Zwierlein.

BRI'WATER (MASS.)

Bridgewater, MA 02324 III

Coach: Peter Mazzaferro, Centre '54
Record: 32 Years, 151-127-11

1996 SCHEDULE

Western Conn. St. ■ ....Sept. 14
Maine Maritime ....Sept. 21
Mass.-Boston ■ ....Sept. 28
Fitchburg St. ....Oct. 5
Framingham St. ■ ....Oct. 12
Westfield St. ....Oct. 19
Plymouth St. ....Oct. 26
Worcester St. ■ ....Nov. 2
Mass. Maritime ....Nov. 9
Mass.-Dartmouth ■ ....Nov. 16

1995 RESULTS (6-4-0)

12 Frostburg St. 30
0 Maine Maritime 20
34 Mass.-Boston 0
56 Fitchburg St. 18
35 Framingham St. 13
20 Westfield St. 3
13 Plymouth St. 20
0 Worcester St. 13
25 Mass. Maritime 21
28 Mass.-Dartmouth 20
223 **158**

Nickname: Bears.
Stadium: College (1974), 3,000 capacity. Natural turf.
Colors: Crimson & White.
Conference: New England.
SID: Michael Storey, 617-697-1352.
AD: John C. Harper.

BRIDGEWATER (VA.)

Bridgewater, VA 22812 III

Coach: Michael Clark, Cincinnati '79
Record: 1 Year, 0-9-1

1996 SCHEDULE

Western Md. ....Sept. 7
Bethany (W.Va.) ....Sept. 14
Emory & Henry ....Sept. 21
Hampden-Sydney ■ ....Oct. 5
Methodist ■ ....Oct. 12
Guilford ....Oct. 19
Johns Hopkins ■ ....Oct. 26
Wash. & Lee ■ ....Nov. 2
Randolph-Macon ....Nov. 9
Davidson ■ ....Nov. 16

1995 RESULTS (0-9-1)

14 Bethany (W.Va.) 28
0 Emory & Henry 21
14 Clinch Valley 28
14 Hampden-Sydney 35
3 Methodist 27
3 Guilford 33
10 Frostburg St. 14
13 Wash. & Lee 24
20 Randolph-Macon 28
7 Davidson 7
98 **245**

Nickname: Eagles.
Stadium: Jopson Field (1971), 3,000 capacity. Natural turf.
Colors: Crimson & Gold.
Conference: Old Dominion Athletic.
SID: Douglas Barton, 703-828-5360.
AD: Tom Kinder.

BRIGHAM YOUNG

Provo, UT 84602 ....I-A

Coach: LaVell Edwards, Utah St. '52
Record: 24 Years, 214-80-3

1996 SCHEDULE

Texas A&M ■ ....Aug. 24
Arkansas St. ■ ....*Aug. 31
Washington ....Sept. 14
New Mexico ■ ....Sept. 21
Southern Methodist ■ ....Sept. 28
Utah St. ....*Oct. 4
UNLV ■ ....Oct. 12
Tulsa ....Oct. 19
Texas Christian ....Oct. 26
UTEP ■ ....Nov. 2
Rice ■ ....Nov. 9
Hawaii ....*Nov. 16
Utah ....Nov. 23

1995 RESULTS (7-4-0)

12 Air Force 38
9 UCLA 23
31 San Diego St. 19
28 Colorado St. 21
21 Arizona St. 29
23 Wyoming 20
45 Hawaii 7
45 Tulsa 35
31 New Mexico 14
17 Utah 34
45 Fresno St. 28
307 **268**

Nickname: Cougars.
Stadium: Cougar (1964), 65,000 capacity. Natural turf.
Colors: Royal Blue & White.
Conference: Western Athletic.
SID: Ralph Zobell, 801-378-4911.
AD: Rondo Fehlberg.

BROCKPORT ST.

Brockport, NY 14420 III

Coach: Rocco Salomone, Brockport St. '88
Record: 1 Year, 4-5-1

1996 SCHEDULE

Jersey City St. ....Sept. 14
Mercyhurst ■ ....Sept. 21
Montclair St. ....*Sept. 28
Buffalo St. ■ ....Oct. 5
Ithaca ■ ....Oct. 12
Frostburg St. ....Oct. 19
St. John Fisher ■ ....Oct. 26
Allegheny ■ ....Nov. 2
Kean ■ ....Nov. 9
Cortland St. ....Nov. 16

1995 RESULTS (4-5-1)

6 Montclair St. 19
24 Jersey City St. 6
6 Western Conn. St. 7
15 Mercyhurst 23
17 Buffalo St. 58
13 Cortland St. 21
14 Frostburg St. 7
28 St. John Fisher 23
3 Kean 3
8 Grove City 7
134 **174**

Nickname: Golden Eagles.
Stadium: Special Olympics (1979), 10,000 capacity. Natural turf.
Colors: Green & Gold.
Conference: Division III Independents.
SID: Mike Andriatch, 716-395-2218.
AD: Linda J. Case.

BROWN

Providence, RI 02912 ....I-AA

Coach: Mark Whipple, Brown '79
Record: 8 Years, 60-25-0

1996 SCHEDULE

Yale ■ ....Sept. 21
Rhode Island ....Sept. 28
Colgate ....Oct. 5
Princeton ....Oct. 12
Fordham ■ ....Oct. 19
Pennsylvania ■ ....Oct. 26
Cornell ....Nov. 2
Harvard ....Nov. 9
Dartmouth ■ ....Nov. 16
Columbia ....Nov. 23

1995 RESULTS (5-5-0)

38 Yale 42
31 Rhode Island 28
37 Holy Cross 14
19 Princeton 21
21 Colgate 6
21 Pennsylvania 58
28 Cornell 38
47 Harvard 8
7 Dartmouth 10
33 Columbia 14
282 **239**

Nickname: Bears.
Stadium: Brown (1925), 20,000 capacity. Natural turf.
Colors: Seal Brown, Cardinal & White.
Conference: Ivy League.

SID: Christopher Humm, 401-863-2219.
AD: David Roach.

BUCKNELL

Lewisburg, PA 17837 ....I-AA

Coach: Tom Gadd, UC Riverside '70
Record: 1 Year, 7-4-0

1996 SCHEDULE

Towson St. ■ ....Sept. 14
William & Mary ■ ....Sept. 21
Harvard ■ ....Sept. 28
Pennsylvania ■ ....Oct. 5
Yale ....Oct. 12
Princeton ■ ....Oct. 19
Holy Cross ....Oct. 26
Lehigh ....Nov. 2
Lafayette ....Nov. 9
Fordham ■ ....Nov. 16
Colgate ■ ....Nov. 23

1995 RESULTS (7-4-0)

20 Southern Conn. St. 0
28 Fordham 21
3 Princeton 20
19 Pennsylvania 20
23 Lehigh 30
10 Cornell 7
14 Towson St. 7
30 Lafayette 11
21 Holy Cross 7
21 Colgate 14
6 Army 37
195 **174**

Nickname: Bison.
Stadium: Christy Mathewson (1924), 13,100 capacity. Natural turf.
Colors: Orange & Blue.
Conference: Patriot League.
SID: Bo Smolka, 717-524-1227.
AD: Rick Hartzell.

BUENA VISTA

Storm Lake, IA 50588...............................III

Coach: Joe Hadachek, Northern Iowa '85
(First year as head coach)

1996 SCHEDULE

Northwestern Ia. ■ ....Sept. 14
William Penn ....Sept. 21
Luther ■ ....Sept. 28
Dana ....Oct. 5
Dubuque ....Oct. 12
Wartburg ■ ....Oct. 19
Upper Iowa ....Oct. 26
Loras ■ ....Nov. 2
Simpson ....Nov. 9
Central (Iowa) ■ ....Nov. 16

1995 RESULTS (2-7-0)

13 Colorado Col. 22
28 Loras 47
49 William Penn 0
20 Dubuque 7
18 Luther 20
7 Wartburg 33
12 Upper Iowa 28
0 Central (Iowa) 28
21 Simpson 29
168 **214**

Nickname: Beavers.
Stadium: J. Leslie Rollins (1980), 3,500 capacity. Natural turf.
Colors: Navy Blue & Gold.
Conference: Iowa Intercollegiate Athletic.
SID: Paul Misner, 712-749-2633.
AD: Roger Egland.

BUFFALO

Buffalo, NY 14260................................I-AA

Coach: Craig Cirbus, Buffalo '80
Record: 1 Year, 3-8-0

1996 SCHEDULE

Illinois St. ■ ....*Aug. 29
Connecticut ■ ....*Sept. 7
Colgate ....Sept. 14
Lehigh ....Sept. 21
Edinboro ■ ....*Sept. 28
Cornell ■ ....Oct. 5
Youngstown St. ■ ....Oct. 12
Massachusetts ....Oct. 19
Hofstra ....Nov. 2
New Haven ■ ....Nov. 9
Maine ....Nov. 16

1995 RESULTS (3-8-0)

49 Fordham 13
17 Lafayette 24
19 Illinois St. 6
25 Connecticut 26
3 Villanova 28
6 Maine 19
9 Massachusetts 33
14 Hofstra 17
7 Central St. 33
9 Youngstown St. 6
40 Boston U. 54
198 **259**

Nickname: Bulls.
Stadium: UB Stadium (1993), 16,500 capacity. Natural turf.
Colors: Royal Blue & White.
Conference: I-AA Independents.
SID: Paul Vecchio, 716-645-6311.
AD: Nelson E. Townsend.

BUFFALO ST.

Buffalo, NY 14222..................................III

Coach: Jerry Boyes, Ithaca '76
Record: 10 Years, 49-48-0

1996 SCHEDULE

St. John Fisher ....Sept. 14
Wash. & Jeff. ■ ....Sept. 21
Cortland St. ■ ....Sept. 28
Brockport St. ....Oct. 5
Southern Conn. St. ....Oct. 19
Kean ....Oct. 26
Mercyhurst ■ ....Nov. 2
Rochester ■ ....Nov. 9
Ithaca ....Nov. 16

1995 RESULTS (9-1-0)

46 Thiel 0
14 Wash. & Jeff. 31
36 Cortland St. 33
58 Brockport St. 17
31 Canisius 0
44 Mercyhurst 18
31 Kean 7
37 Alfred 14
22 St. John Fisher 8
24 Ithaca 6
343 **134**

III Championship

7 Rowan 46

Nickname: Bengals.
Stadium: Coyer Field (1964), 3,000 capacity. Natural turf.
Colors: Orange & Black.
Conference: Division III Independents.
SID: Keith Bullion, 716-878-6030.
AD: To be named.

BUTLER

Indianapolis, IN 46208 ....I-AA

Coach: Ken LaRose, Butler '80
Record: 4 Years, 21-19-0

1996 SCHEDULE

Towson St. ■ ....Sept. 7
Robert Morris ....Sept. 14
Millikin ■ ....Sept. 21
Clinch Valley ....Sept. 28
Drake ....Oct. 5
Valparaiso ....Oct. 12
Dayton ■ ....Oct. 19
San Diego ■ ....Oct. 26
Evansville ■ ....Nov. 2
St. Joseph's (Ind.) ....Nov. 9

1995 RESULTS (2-8-0)

17 Howard Payne 7
3 Towson St. 34
15 Millikin 27
0 Wis.-Stevens Point 37
8 Drake 29
42 Valparaiso 44
13 Dayton 49
29 Thomas More 37
14 Evansville 13
16 San Diego 37
157 **314**

Nickname: Bulldogs.
Stadium: Butler Bowl (1927), 19,000 capacity. Natural turf.
Colors: Blue & White.
Conference: Pioneer Football League.
SID: Jim McGrath, 317-940-9671.
AD: John Parry.

CALIFORNIA

Berkeley, CA 94720 ....I-A

Coach: Steve Mariucci, Northern Mich. '77
(First year as head coach)

1996 SCHEDULE

San Jose St. ....Sept. 7
San Diego St. ■ ....Sept. 14
Nevada ■ ....Sept. 21
Oregon St. ■ ....Sept. 28
Southern Cal ....Oct. 5
Washington St. ....Oct. 19
UCLA ■ ....Oct. 26
Arizona ■ ....Nov. 2
Arizona St. ....*Nov. 9
Oregon ....Nov. 16
Stanford ■ ....Nov. 23

1995 RESULTS (3-8-0)

9 San Diego St. 33
24 Fresno St. 25
40 San Jose St. 7
15 Arizona 20
16 Southern Cal 26
30 Oregon 52
13 Oregon St. 12
16 UCLA 33
27 Washington St. 11
29 Arizona St. 38
24 Stanford 29
243 **286**

Nickname: Golden Bears.
Stadium: Memorial (1923), 75,662 capacity. Natural turf.
Colors: Blue & Gold.
Conference: Pacific-10.
SID: Kevin Reneau, 510-642-5363.
AD: John Kasser.

UC DAVIS

Davis, CA 95616......................................II

Coach: Bob Biggs, UC Davis '73
Record: 3 Years, 22-9-1

1996 SCHEDULE

Cal St. Northridge ....*Sept. 14
Cal St. Sacramento ■ ....*Sept. 21
Cal St. Chico ....*Sept. 28
Humboldt St. ....Oct. 5
Portland St. ....*Oct. 12
Western N.M. ■ ....*Oct. 19
St. Mary's (Cal.) ■ ....*Oct. 26
Cal Poly SLO ....Nov. 2
Sonoma St. ....Nov. 9
Southern Utah ■ ....*Nov. 16

1995 RESULTS (6-3-1)

48 Western St. 3
31 Humboldt St. 31
35 Sonoma St. 0

20 Montana....41
13 Portland St. 40
24 St. Mary's (Cal.) 33
38 Cal St. Northridge 8
52 Cal St. Sacramento....42
37 Southern Utah 21
34 Cal Poly SLO....31
332 **250**

Nickname: Aggies.
Stadium: Toomey Field (1949), 10,111 capacity. Natural turf.
Colors: Blue & Gold.
Conference: Division II Independents.
SID: Doug Dull, 916-752-3505.
AD: Greg Warzecka.

CALIF. (PA.)

California, PA 15419 II

Coach: Kevin Donley, Anderson (Ind.) '73
Record: 18 Years, 111-77-1

1996 SCHEDULE

Tusculum ■ ....*Sept. 5
Fairmont St. ....Sept. 14
West Va. Wesleyan ■ ....*Sept. 21
St. Joseph's (Ind.) ....Sept. 28
Indiana (Pa.) ....Oct. 5
Edinboro ■....*Oct. 12
Clarion....Oct. 19
Lock Haven ■....Oct. 26
Shippensburg....Nov. 2
Kutztown ■....*Nov. 9
Slippery Rock ■....Nov. 16

1995 RESULTS (2-9-0)

28 Fairmont St....26
29 Glenville St....31
20 Bloomsburg....24
0 Kutztown....34
14 Slippery Rock 42
20 Indiana (Pa.) 44
7 Edinboro....31
10 Clarion 20
19 Lock Haven 14
15 Shippensburg 26
24 West Chester 25
186 **317**

Nickname: Vulcans.
Stadium: Adamson (1970), 5,000 capacity. Natural turf.
Colors: Red & Black.
Conference: Pennsylvania State Athletic.
SID: Bruce Wald, 412-938-4552.
AD: Tom Pucci.

CAL LUTHERAN

Thousand Oaks, CA 91360 III

Coach: Scott Squires, Pacific Lutheran '88
(First year as head coach)

1996 SCHEDULE

San Diego....*Sept. 14
La Verne ■....Sept. 21
Azusa Pacific....*Oct. 5
Chapman ■ ....Oct. 12
Occidental ■....Oct. 19
Claremont-M-S ....Oct. 26
Redlands ....*Nov. 2
Whittier....*Nov. 9
Menlo ■....Nov. 16

1995 RESULTS (4-4-1)

7 Chapman....38
21 San Diego....28
14 Azusa Pacific 14
21 Occidental 14
38 Claremont-M-S....24
42 Whittier 0
0 Pomona-Pitzer....9
21 Redlands....19
21 La Verne 31
185 **177**

Nickname: Kingsmen.
Stadium: Mt. Clef (1962), 2,000 capacity. Natural turf.
Colors: Purple & Gold.
Conference: Southern California Intercollegiate Athletic.
SID: John Czimbal, 805-493-3153.
AD: Bruce Bryde.

CAL POLY SLO

San Luis Obispo, CA 93407 ....I-AA

Coach: Andre Patterson, Montana '83
Record: 2 Years, 12-10-0

1996 SCHEDULE

Idaho St. ....*Sept. 7
Montana ....Sept. 14
Weber St. ■....*Sept. 21
Central Wash. ■ ....Sept. 28
Idaho ....Oct. 5
St. Mary's (Cal.) ■....Oct. 12
Southern Utah ■ ....Oct. 19
Western Ill. ....Oct. 26
UC Davis ■....Nov. 2
Montana St....Nov. 9
Cal St. Sacramento ....Nov. 23

1995 RESULTS (5-6-0)

57 Western Mont. 3
22 Idaho St. 28
10 Montana St. 13
43 Weber St....53
35 Southern Utah 20
56 Sonoma St. 10
36 Cal St. Sacramento....37
20 St. Mary's (Cal.) 31
49 Cal St. Northridge 7
31 UC Davis 34
52 Eastern Wash....35
411 **271**

Nickname: Mustangs.
Stadium: Mustang (1935), 8,500 capacity. Natural turf.
Colors: Green & Gold.
Conference: I-AA Independents.
SID: Eric McDowell, 805-756-6531.
AD: John McCutcheon.

CAL ST. CHICO

Chico, CA 95929 II

Coach: Gary Houser, Oregon St. '68
Record: 7 Years, 24-40-3

1996 SCHEDULE

San Diego ■ ....Sept. 7
Western Ore. ■....Sept. 14
Montana Tech....Sept. 21
UC Davis ■ ....*Sept. 28
Chapman ....*Oct. 5
Humboldt St. ■ ....Oct. 19
Azusa Pacific ■ ....Oct. 26
Sonoma St....Nov. 2
Humboldt St....Nov. 9
Sonoma St. ■ ....Nov. 16

1995 RESULTS (2-5-2)

20 San Diego....13
20 St. Mary's (Cal.) 44
22 Mesa St. 23
21 Cal St. Sacramento....21
21 Sonoma St. 21
7 Chapman....10
7 Humboldt St....47
26 Sonoma St. 14
13 Humboldt St. 31
157 **224**

Nickname: Wildcats.
Stadium: University (1952), 8,000 capacity. Natural turf.
Colors: Cardinal & White.
Conference: Northern California Athletic.
SID: Teresa Clements, 916-898-4658.
AD: Don W. Batie.

CAL ST. NORTHRIDGE

Northridge, CA 91330 ....I-AA

Coach: David Baldwin, Cal St. Northridge '78
Record: 1 Year, 2-8-0

1996 SCHEDULE

Utah St. ....*Sept. 7
UC Davis ■....*Sept. 14
New Mexico St....*Sept. 21
Northern Ariz. ....*Sept. 28
Portland St. ■ ....*Oct. 5
Weber St. ....Oct. 12
Montana St. ■....*Oct. 19
Cal St. Sacramento ....*Oct. 26
Montana ■....*Nov. 2
Idaho St. ....*Nov. 9
Eastern Wash. ■....Nov. 16

1995 RESULTS (2-8-0)

45 Menlo....2
0 Idaho St. 52
7 Northern Ariz....68
14 Southwest Tex. St....43
8 Western N.M. 27
8 UC Davis....38
34 Southern Utah 28
7 Cal Poly SLO....49
20 St. Mary's (Cal.) 28
16 Cal St. Sacramento....20
159 **355**

Nickname: Matadors.
Stadium: North Campus (1971), 6,000 capacity. Natural turf.
Colors: Red, White & Black.
Conference: Big Sky.
SID: Ryan Finney, 818-677-3243.
AD: Paul A. Bubb.

CAL ST. SACRAMENTO

Sacramento, CA 95819 ....I-AA

Coach: John Volek, UC Riverside '68
Record: 1 Year, 4-6-1

1996 SCHEDULE

Hofstra ....Sept. 7
UC Davis....*Sept. 21
Montana ■....*Sept. 28
Idaho St. ....*Oct. 5
Eastern Wash. ■....*Oct. 12
Northern Ariz. ....Oct. 19
Cal St. Northridge ■ ....*Oct. 26
Portland St. ....*Nov. 2
Weber St. ■....*Nov. 9
Montana St....Nov. 16
Cal Poly SLO ■....Nov. 23

1995 RESULTS (4-6-1)

7 Northern Ariz. 62
18 Eastern Wash....21
21 Cal St. Chico 21
16 Portland St. 54
15 Hofstra....55
12 Southwest Tex. St. 3
37 Cal Poly SLO....36
42 UC Davis 52
14 St. Mary's (Cal.) 28
53 Southern Utah 29
20 Cal St. Northridge 16
255 **377**

Nickname: Hornets.
Stadium: Hornet Field (1964), 21,418 capacity. Natural turf.
Colors: Green & Gold.
Conference: Big Sky.
SID: Jeff Minahan, 916-278-6896.
AD: To be named.

CANISIUS

Buffalo, NY 14208 ....I-AA

Coach: Chuck Williams, Brockport St. '55
Record: 1 Year, 4-6-0

1996 SCHEDULE

Gannon ....Sept. 14
St. Peter's ■....Sept. 28
Iona ....Oct. 5
Siena ■....Oct. 12
Fairfield....Oct. 19

St. John's (N.Y.) ■	Oct. 26
Georgetown	Nov. 2
Marist	Nov. 9
Duquesne ■	Nov. 16

1995 RESULTS (4-6-0)

	Opponent	
3	Mercyhurst	13
33	Siena	13
12	Gannon	20
13	Georgetown	7
0	Buffalo St.	31
13	St. John's (N.Y.)	30
13	Marist	34
22	St. Peter's	0
21	Iona	14
0	Duquesne	14
130		**176**

Nickname: Golden Griffins.
Stadium: Demske Sports Complex (1989), 1,000 capacity. Artificial turf.
Colors: Blue & Gold.
Conference: Metro Atlantic.
SID: John Maddock, 716-888-2977.
AD: Daniel P. Starr.

CAPITAL

Columbus, OH 43209 III

Coach: Roger Welsh, Muskingum '64
Record: 10 Years, 40-56-4

1996 SCHEDULE

Bethany (W.Va.) ■	Sept. 7
Marietta	*Sept. 21
Ohio Northern ■	Sept. 28
Muskingum	Oct. 5
Baldwin-Wallace	Oct. 12
Heidelberg ■	Oct. 19
John Carroll ■	Oct. 26
Hiram	Nov. 2
Mount Union	Nov. 9
Otterbein ■	Nov. 16

1995 RESULTS (1-9-0)

	Opponent	
9	Gannon	42
0	Ohio Northern	41
11	Muskingum	31
51	Heidelberg	50
19	Hiram	42
7	Marietta	69
6	John Carroll	39
13	Baldwin-Wallace	43
7	Mount Union	62
20	Otterbein	33
143		**452**

Nickname: Crusaders.
Stadium: Bernlohr (1928), 2,000 capacity. Natural turf.
Colors: Purple & White.
Conference: Ohio Athletic.
SID: Barry Katz, 614-236-6174.
AD: Roger Welsh.

CARLETON

Northfield, MN 55057 III

Coach: Bob Sullivan, St. John's (Minn.) '59
Record: 17 Years, 89-76-0

1996 SCHEDULE

Lawrence ■	Sept. 7
Macalester ■	Sept. 14
Bethel (Minn.)	Sept. 21
St. Thomas (Minn.) ■	Sept. 28
St. John's (Minn.)	Oct. 5
Augsburg ■	Oct. 12
Hamline	Oct. 19
St. Olaf	Oct. 26
Gust. Adolphus ■	Nov. 2
Concordia-M'head [Minneapolis, Minn.]	*Nov. 9

1995 RESULTS (3-7-0)

	Opponent	
13	Cornell College	15
14	St. Thomas (Minn.)	25
29	Gust. Adolphus	21
36	Macalester	13
21	St. Olaf	15
9	Concordia-M'head	41
14	St. John's (Minn.)	35
7	Bethel (Minn.)	21
7	Augsburg	20
6	Hamline	24
156		**230**

Nickname: Knights.
Stadium: Laird (1926), 7,500 capacity. Natural turf.
Colors: Maize & Blue.
Conference: Minnesota Intercollegiate Athletic.
SID: Ryan Beckers, 507-663-4045.
AD: Leon Lunder.

CARNEGIE MELLON

Pittsburgh, PA 15213 III

Coach: Rich Lackner, Carnegie Mellon '79
Record: 10 Years, 73-24-2

1996 SCHEDULE

Frank. & Marsh.	Sept. 7
Case Reserve	Sept. 14
Grove City ■	*Sept. 21
Rhodes ■	Sept. 28
Dickinson	Oct. 5
Washington (Mo.)	*Oct. 19
Chicago ■	Oct. 26
Rochester ■	Nov. 2
Muhlenberg	Nov. 9
Union (N.Y.) ■	Nov. 16

1995 RESULTS (7-3-0)

	Opponent	
27	Frank. & Marsh.	8
7	Allegheny	34
35	Rhodes	7
19	Merchant Marine	20
30	Grove City	25
12	Washington (Mo.)	8
35	Chicago	21
20	Rochester	10
39	Juniata	7
0	Case Reserve	3
224		**143**

Nickname: Tartans.
Stadium: Gesling (1990), 3,500 capacity. Artificial turf.
Colors: Cardinal, White & Gray.
Conference: University Athletic Association.
SID: E. J. Borghetti, 412-268-3087.
AD: John Harvey.

CARROLL (WIS.)

Waukesha, WI 53186 III

Coach: Merle Masonholder, Northern Iowa '66
Record: 14 Years, 63-62-0

1996 SCHEDULE

Wis.-Whitewater ■	Sept. 7
Carthage	Sept. 14
Knox ■	Sept. 21
Coe	Sept. 28
Lawrence ■	Oct. 5
Beloit	Oct. 12
Lake Forest ■	Oct. 19
Ripon	Oct. 26
St. Norbert ■	Nov. 2

1995 RESULTS (6-3-0)

	Opponent	
37	Carthage	20
13	North Central	29
42	Grinnell	19
18	Cornell College	36
37	Lawrence	28
14	Beloit	20
27	Lake Forest	24
25	Ripon	23
33	St. Norbert	19
246		**218**

Nickname: Pioneers.
Stadium: Van Male Field (1976), 4,200 capacity. Natural turf.
Colors: Orange & White.
Conference: Midwest.
SID: Shawn Ama, 414-524-7376.
AD: Merle Masonholder.

CARSON-NEWMAN

Jefferson City, TN 37760 II

Coach: Ken Sparks, Carson-Newman '68
Record: 16 Years, 149-40-2

1996 SCHEDULE

Lane ■	*Sept. 5
Edinboro ■	*Sept. 14
Presbyterian ■	*Sept. 21
Elon	Sept. 28
Catawba	Oct. 5
Wingate ■	Oct. 12
Mars Hill	Oct. 19
Gardner-Webb ■	Oct. 26
Lenoir-Rhyne	Nov. 2
Newberry ■	Nov. 9

1995 RESULTS (8-2-0)

	Opponent	
21	Wayne St. (Mich.)	0
21	Central Fla.	35
24	Presbyterian	21
29	Elon	6
41	Catawba	21
24	Wingate	25
42	Mars Hill	0
38	Gardner-Webb	10
40	Lenoir-Rhyne	21
39	Newberry	30
319		**169**

II Championship

	Opponent	
37	West Ga.	26
7	North Ala.	38

Nickname: Eagles.
Stadium: Burke-Tarr (1966), 5,000 capacity. Natural turf.
Colors: Orange & Blue.
Conference: South Atlantic.
SID: Eric Trainer, 423-471-3477.
AD: David Barger.

CARTHAGE

Kenosha, WI 53140 III

Coach: Tim Rucks, Carthage '83
Record: 6 Years, 12-38-4

1996 SCHEDULE

Carroll (Wis.) ■	Sept. 14
Lakeland	Sept. 21
North Central	*Oct. 5
Augustana (Ill.) ■	Oct. 12
Elmhurst	Oct. 19
Millikin ■	Oct. 26
Wheaton (Ill.) ■	Nov. 2
Ill. Wesleyan	Nov. 9
North Park ■	Nov. 16

1995 RESULTS (3-5-1)

	Opponent	
20	Carroll (Wis.)	37
20	Ill. Benedictine	12
7	Wheaton (Ill.)	47
6	Millikin	49
31	Elmhurst	19
7	Ill. Wesleyan	35
20	North Park	7
7	North Central	7
0	Augustana (Ill.)	24
118		**237**

Nickname: Redmen.
Stadium: Art Keller Field (1965), 3,100 capacity. Natural turf.
Colors: Red, White & Black.
Conference: College Conf. of Illinois & Wisconsin.
SID: Steve Marovich, 414-551-5740.
AD: Robert R. Bonn.

CASE RESERVE

Cleveland, OH 44106 III

Coach: Regis Scafe, Case Reserve '71
Record: 2 Years, 3-17-0

1996 SCHEDULE

Carnegie Mellon ■ .... Sept. 14
Washington (Mo.) .... Sept. 21
Wooster .... Sept. 28
Earlham ■ .... Oct. 5
Allegheny .... Oct. 12
Kenyon ■ .... Oct. 19
Oberlin .... Oct. 26
Wittenberg ■ .... Nov. 2
Chicago ■ .... Nov. 9
Rochester .... Nov. 16

1995 RESULTS (2-8-0)

5 Rochester 9
21 Chicago 24
3 Earlham 7
0 Allegheny 50
7 Kenyon 33
13 Wooster 14
7 Ohio Wesleyan 27
22 Washington (Mo.) 49
21 Denison 6
3 Carnegie Mellon 0
102 **219**

Nickname: Spartans.
Stadium: E.L. Finnigan Field (1968), 3,000 capacity. Natural turf.
Colors: Blue, Gray & White.
Conference: North Coast Athletic.
SID: Sue Herdle Penicka, 216-368-6517.
AD: David Hutter.

CATAWBA

Salisbury, NC 28144 II

Coach: David Bennett, Presbyterian '84
Record: 1 Year, 7-3-0

1996 SCHEDULE

Concord (W.Va.) ■ .... Sept. 7
West Va. Tech .... Sept. 14
Mars Hill .... Sept. 21
Tusculum ■ .... Sept. 28
Carson-Newman ■ .... Oct. 5
Presbyterian .... Oct. 12
Gardner-Webb .... Oct. 19
Elon ■ .... Oct. 26
Newberry .... *Nov. 2
Wingate .... Nov. 9
Lenoir-Rhyne ■ .... Nov. 16

1995 RESULTS (7-3-0)

52 Concord (W.Va.) 14
16 Mars Hill 35
21 Wofford 20
21 Carson-Newman 41
31 Presbyterian 28
21 Gardner-Webb 19
23 Elon 6
8 Newberry 17
42 Wingate 32
22 Lenoir-Rhyne 0
257 **212**

Nickname: Indians.
Stadium: Shuford Field (1926), 4,000 capacity. Natural turf.
Colors: Blue & White.
Conference: South Atlantic.
SID: Jim Lewis, 704-637-4720.
AD: Dennis Davidson.

CATHOLIC

Washington, DC 20064 III

Coach: Tom Clark, Maryland '86
Record: 2 Years, 13-5-1

1996 SCHEDULE

Muhlenberg .... Sept. 14
Randolph-Macon ■ .... Sept. 21
Merchant Marine .... Sept. 28
Salisbury St. ■ .... Oct. 5
FDU-Madison ■ .... Oct. 19
Hampden-Sydney .... Oct. 26
Newport News App. ■ .... Nov. 2
Thiel .... Nov. 9
Albright .... Nov. 16

1995 RESULTS (5-3-1)

45 Muhlenberg 0
50 Randolph-Macon 50
7 Merchant Marine 21
21 Trinity (Tex.) 18
21 St. John Fisher 29
34 Hampden-Sydney 0
21 Ursinus 20
2 Salisbury St. 12
17 Albright 16
218 **166**

Nickname: Cardinals.
Stadium: Cardinal Field (1985), 3,500 capacity. Natural turf.
Colors: Cardinal & Black.
Conference: Division III Independents.
SID: Michael Graber, 202-319-5610.
AD: Robert J. Talbot.

CENTRAL (IOWA)

Pella, IA 50219 III

Coach: Ron Schipper, Hope '52
Record: 35 Years, 280-64-3

1996 SCHEDULE

Marietta ■ .... Sept. 7
Wartburg ■ .... Sept. 21
Dubuque .... Sept. 28
William Penn ■ .... Oct. 5
Loras ■ .... Oct. 12
Simpson .... Oct. 19
Luther .... Oct. 26
Upper Iowa ■ .... Nov. 2
Washington (Mo.) .... Nov. 9
Buena Vista .... Nov. 16

1995 RESULTS (10-0-0)

44 Gust. Adolphus 17
64 Dubuque 7
27 Wartburg 0
50 Luther 7
31 Colorado Col. 9
24 Loras 14
37 Simpson 7
28 Buena Vista 0
68 William Penn 0
42 Upper Iowa 0
415 **61**

III Championship

7 Wis.-River Falls 10

Nickname: Flying Dutchmen.
Stadium: Kuyper (1977), 5,000 capacity. Natural turf.
Colors: Red & White.
Conference: Iowa Intercollegiate Athletic.
SID: Larry Happel, 515-628-5278.
AD: Sam Bedrosian.

CENTRAL ARK.

Conway, AR 72032 II

Coach: Mike Isom, Central Ark. '70
Record: 6 Years, 47-18-4

1996 SCHEDULE

Southern Ill. .... Aug. 31
Northeastern St. .... *Sept. 7
Southern Ark. .... *Sept. 21
Delta St. ■ .... *Sept. 28
Arkansas St. .... *Oct. 5
West Ga. ■ .... Oct. 12
Henderson St. .... *Oct. 19
Ark.-Monticello ■ .... Oct. 26
North Ala. .... Nov. 2
Valdosta St. .... Nov. 9
Arkansas Tech ■ .... Nov. 16

1995 RESULTS (7-4-0)

27 East Tex. St. 20
7 Mo. Southern St. 13
35 Arkansas Tech 19
44 Ark.-Monticello 24
30 Valdosta St. 24
0 Delta St. 19
7 North Ala. 28
34 West Ala. 10
26 Mississippi Col. 11
24 Southern Ark. 22
21 Henderson St. 31
255 **221**

Nickname: Bears.
Stadium: Estes (1939), 7,000 capacity. Natural turf.
Colors: Purple & Gray.
Conference: Gulf South.
SID: Steve East, 501-450-5743.
AD: Bill Stephens.

CENTRAL CONN. ST.

New Britain, CT 06050 .... I-AA

Coach: Sal Cintorio, Central Conn. St. '86
Record: 4 Years, 12-27-0

1996 SCHEDULE

Albany (N.Y.) .... *Sept. 7
Fairfield .... *Sept. 14
Frostburg St. .... Sept. 21
Robert Morris ■ .... Sept. 28
Towson St. .... *Oct. 5
Stony Brook ■ .... Oct. 12
Wagner ■ .... Oct. 26
St. Francis (Pa.) ■ .... Nov. 2
Southern Conn. St. .... Nov. 9
Monmouth (N.J.) .... Nov. 16

1995 RESULTS (2-8-0)

10 Albany (N.Y.) 17
9 Connecticut 54
0 LIU-C.W. Post 40
3 Robert Morris 45
10 Towson St. 24
24 Siena 7
15 St. Francis (Pa.) 13
35 Wagner 40
3 Southern Conn. St. 14
13 Monmouth (N.J.) 30
122 **284**

Nickname: Blue Devils.
Stadium: Arute Field (1969), 5,000 capacity. Natural turf.
Colors: Blue & White.
Conference: Northeast.
SID: Brent Rutkowski, 203-832-3089.
AD: Charles "C. J." Jones.

CENTRAL FLA.

Orlando, FL 32816 .... I-A

Coach: Gene McDowell, Florida St. '63
Record: 11 Years, 76-49-0

1996 SCHEDULE

William & Mary ■ .... *Aug. 29
South Caro. .... *Sept. 7
New Mexico .... *Sept. 14
Ball St. .... Sept. 21
East Caro. .... Sept. 28
Samford ■ .... Oct. 12
Northeast La. ■ .... Oct. 19
Georgia Tech .... Oct. 26
Illinois St. ■ .... Nov. 2
Ala.-Birmingham .... Nov. 9
Bowling Green ■ .... Nov. 16

1995 RESULTS (6-5-0)

40 Eastern Ky. 32
35 Carson-Newman 21
14 Florida St. 46
7 McNeese St. 49
41 Samford 14
6 Liberty 7
14 Hawaii 45
34 Northeast La. 14
38 Bethune-Cookman 7
17 Troy St. 28
37 Maine 17
283 **280**

Nickname: Golden Knights.
Stadium: Florida Citrus Bowl (1936), 70,188 capacity. Natural turf.
Colors: Black & Gold.
Conference: I-A Independents.
SID: John Marini, 407-823-2729.
AD: Steve Sloan.

CENTRAL MICH.

Mt. Pleasant, MI 48859.............................I-A

Coach: Dick Flynn, Michigan St. '65
Record: 2 Years, 13-10-0

1996 SCHEDULE

Boise St. ....*Aug. 31
Virginia ....*Sept. 7
Louisiana Tech ■....................Sept. 14
Western Mich. ■....................Sept. 21
Bowling Green....................Sept. 28
Miami (Ohio)....................Oct. 5
Akron ■....................Oct. 12
Eastern Mich. ■....................Oct. 19
Ball St. ■....................Oct. 26
Kent....................Nov. 2
Toledo....................Nov. 9

1995 RESULTS (4-7-0)

39	Weber St.	31
17	East Caro.	30
22	Bowling Green	16
13	Akron	16
24	Eastern Mich.	34
46	Youngstown St.	25
27	Kent	16
13	Miami (Ohio)	17
7	Toledo	19
16	Ball St.	24
31	Western Mich.	48
255		**276**

Nickname: Chippewas.
Stadium: Kelly-Shorts (1972), 20,086 capacity. Artificial turf.
Colors: Maroon & Gold.
Conference: Mid-American.
SID: Fred Stabley Jr., 517-774-3277.
AD: Herb Deromedi.

CENTRAL MO. ST.

Warrensburg, MO 64093...........................II

Coach: Terry Noland, Southwest Mo. St. '71
Record: 13 Years, 74-61-2

1996 SCHEDULE

Augustana (S.D.) ■....................*Sept. 7
Southwestern (Kan.) ■....................*Sept. 12
Pittsburg St. ■....................*Sept. 21
Mo. Southern St. ....*Sept. 28
Northwest Mo. St. ■....................Oct. 5
Washburn....................Oct. 12
Truman St. ....Oct. 19
Mo.-Rolla ■....................Oct. 26
Mo. Western St. ■....................Nov. 2
Southwest Baptist....................Nov. 9
Emporia St. ■....................Nov. 16

1995 RESULTS (4-6-0)

43	Upper Iowa	20
16	Pittsburg St.	37
32	Mo. Southern St.	37
23	Northwest Mo. St.	33
21	Washburn	37
34	Truman St.	45
50	Mo.-Rolla	19
20	Mo. Western St.	30
28	Southwest Baptist	7
52	Emporia St.	22
319		**287**

Nickname: Mules.
Stadium: Audrey J. Walton (1995), 10,000 capacity. Natural turf.
Colors: Cardinal & Black.
Conference: Mid-America Intercollegiate Athletic Assoc.
SID: Bill Turnage, 816-543-4312.
AD: Jerry Hughes.

CENTRAL OKLA.

Edmond, OK 73034 II

Coach: Gary Howard, Arkansas '64
Record: 19 Years, 109-79-6

1996 SCHEDULE

Mesa St. ■....................*Sept. 7
Southwestern Okla. ....*Sept. 14
Langston ■....................Sept. 28
East Tex. St. ■....................Oct. 5
Abilene Christian ■....................Oct. 12
Tex. A&M-Kingsville....................*Oct. 19
Angelo St. ....*Oct. 26
West Tex. A&M ■....................Nov. 2
Tarleton St. ■....................Nov. 9
Eastern N.M. ....Nov. 16

1995 RESULTS (8-3-0)

27	Mesa St.	0
20	Southwestern Okla.	6
28	Fort Hays St.	0
30	Langston	26
9	East Tex. St.	17
13	Abilene Christian	7
21	Tex. A&M-Kingsville	27
7	Angelo St.	14
43	West Tex. A&M	6
47	Tarleton St.	0
33	Eastern N.M.	23
278		**126**

Nickname: Bronchos.
Stadium: Wantland (1965), 10,000 capacity. Natural turf.
Colors: Bronze & Blue.
Conference: Lone Star.
SID: Mike Kirk, 405-341-2980.
AD: John "Skip" Wagnon.

CENTRE

Danville, KY 40422...................................III

Coach: Joe McDaniel, Muskingum '56
Record: 30 Years, 155-115-5

1996 SCHEDULE

Wooster....................Sept. 7
Denison....................Sept. 14
Hanover ■....................Sept. 21
Wash. & Lee ■....................Sept. 28
Sewanee ■....................Oct. 5
Millsaps....................Oct. 12
Maryville (Tenn.)....................Oct. 19
Trinity (Tex.) ■....................Oct. 26
Davidson....................Nov. 9
Rhodes....................Nov. 16

1995 RESULTS (5-4-1)

31	Denison	22
3	Hanover	14
7	Wash. & Lee	7
41	Sewanee	7
30	Millsaps	19
7	Maryville (Tenn.)	26
17	Trinity (Tex.)	7
21	Ky. Wesleyan	33
21	Davidson	6
10	Rhodes	14
188		**155**

Nickname: Colonels.
Stadium: Farris (1925), 2,500 capacity. Natural turf.
Colors: Gold & White.
Conference: Southern Collegiate Athletic.
SID: Kelly Kiernan, 606-238-8746.
AD: Ray Hammond.

CHADRON ST.

Chadron, NE 69337 II

Coach: Brad Smith, Western Ill. '72
Record: 9 Years, 57-35-1

1996 SCHEDULE

Fort Lewis [Aurora, Colo.]....................Sept. 7
Eastern N.M. ....*Sept. 14
Mesa St. ....Sept. 21
Neb.-Kearney ■....................Sept. 28
Western St. ■....................Oct. 5
N.M. Highlands....................Oct. 12
Peru St. ■....................Oct. 19
Adams St. ■....................Oct. 26
Fort Hays St. ....Nov. 2
Colorado Mines....................Nov. 9
Fort Lewis ■....................Nov. 16

1995 RESULTS (8-2-0)

46	South Dak. Tech	0
44	Black Hills St.	26
20	Peru St.	0
22	Mesa St.	19
31	Adams St.	27
24	N.M. Highlands	17
24	Colorado Mines	10
21	Western St.	28
5	Fort Hays St.	47
31	Fort Lewis	3
268		**177**

Nickname: Eagles.
Stadium: Elliott Field (1930), 2,500 capacity. Natural turf.
Colors: Cardinal & White.
Conference: Rocky Mountain Athletic.
SID: Con Marshall, 308-432-6212.
AD: Brad Smith.

CHAPMAN

Orange, CA 92666 III

Coach: Ken Visser, Occidental '68
Record: 5 Years, 24-20-1

1996 SCHEDULE

Eastern Ore. ■....................*Sept. 14
Redlands....................*Sept. 21
Cal St. Chico ■....................*Oct. 5
Cal Lutheran....................Oct. 12
Sonoma St. ■....................*Oct. 19
La Verne ■....................*Oct. 26
Occidental....................*Nov. 2
St. Mary's (Cal.)....................Nov. 9
Azusa Pacific....................Nov. 16

1995 RESULTS (8-1-0)

34	La Verne	35
38	Cal Lutheran	7
55	Claremont-M-S	25
47	Occidental	6
10	Cal St. Chico	7
79	Menlo	13
54	Redlands	24
45	Azusa Pacific	9
63	Whittier	7
425		**133**

Nickname: Panthers.
Stadium: Chapman, 3,000 capacity. Natural turf.
Colors: Cardinal & Gray.
Conference: Division III Independents.
SID: Jim Moore, 714-997-6900.
AD: David Currey.

CHARLESTON SO.

Charleston, SC 29423 ....I-AA

Coach: David Dowd, Guilford '76
Record: 5 Years, 9-42-0

1996 SCHEDULE

South Caro. St. ■....................Sept. 7
Presbyterian....................Sept. 14
West Va. St. ■....................Sept. 21
Hofstra ■....................Sept. 28
Morehead St. ■....................Oct. 5
Newberry ■....................Oct. 12
Liberty....................Oct. 26
New Haven ■....................Nov. 2
Tusculum ■....................Nov. 9
Wofford....................Nov. 16
Ala.-Birmingham....................*Nov. 21

1995 RESULTS (1-10-0)

0 Tenn.-Chatt. 41
6 Presbyterian 44
8 South Caro. St. 36
6 Ferrum 15
34 Morehead St. 22
10 Newberry 38
7 Troy St. 66
6 Hofstra 56
15 Liberty 19
14 Ala.-Birmingham 40
23 Wofford 31
129 408

Nickname: Buccaneers.
Stadium: CSU (1970), 3,000 capacity. Natural turf.
Colors: Blue & Gold.
Conference: I-AA Independents.
SID: Mike Hoffman, 803-863-7688.
AD: Howard Bagwell.

CHEYNEY

Cheyney, PA 19319 II

Coach: Vincent Williams, Cheyney '86
Record: 2 Years, 3-17-1

1996 SCHEDULE

West Chester ■ ....Aug. 31
Virginia Union ....*Sept. 14
Bowie St. [Atlantic City, N.J.] ....Sept. 21
Morgan St. ■ ....Sept. 28
Bloomsburg ■ ....Oct. 5
Kutztown ....Oct. 12
American Int'l ■ ....Oct. 19
East Stroudsburg ....Oct. 26
Edinboro ....Nov. 2
Mansfield ■ ....Nov. 9
Millersville ....Nov. 16

1995 RESULTS (0-10-1)

7 West Chester 56
21 Virginia Union 21
3 Southern Conn. St. 55
7 Morgan St. 38
7 Kutztown 17
9 Virginia St. 81
13 East Stroudsburg 40
0 Indiana (Pa.) 58
20 Mansfield 28
0 Millersville 54
0 Bloomsburg 55
87 503

Nickname: Wolves.
Stadium: O'Shield-Stevenson, 3,500 capacity. Natural turf.
Colors: Blue & White.
Conference: Pennsylvania State Athletic.
SID: To be named, 610-399-2287.
AD: Andrew Hinson.

CHICAGO

Chicago, IL 60637 III

Coach: Dick Maloney, Mass.-Boston '74
Record: 2 Years, 13-7-0

1996 SCHEDULE

DePauw ....Sept. 14
Concordia (Ill.) ....Sept. 21
Rose-Hulman ■ ....Sept. 28
Kalamazoo ....Oct. 5
Rochester ■ ....Oct. 19
Carnegie Mellon ....Oct. 26
Washington (Mo.) ■ ....Nov. 2
Case Reserve ....Nov. 9
Kenyon ■ ....Nov. 16

1995 RESULTS (8-2-0)

39 Lawrence 28
24 Case Reserve 21
46 Concordia (Ill.) 0
29 Kalamazoo 25
14 Washington (Mo.) 28
29 Rochester 18
21 Carnegie Mellon 35
47 Oberlin 0
40 Ky. Wesleyan 24
26 Rose-Hulman 7
315 186

Nickname: Maroons.
Stadium: Stagg Field (1969), 1,500 capacity. Natural turf.
Colors: White & Maroon.
Conference: University Athletic Association.
SID: Dave Hilbert, 312-702-4638.
AD: Tom Weingartner.

CINCINNATI

Cincinnati, OH 45221 ....I-A

Coach: Rick Minter, Henderson St. '77
Record: 2 Years, 8-13-1

1996 SCHEDULE

Tulane ■ ....*Aug. 30
Kentucky ■ ....Sept. 7
Kansas St. ....*Sept. 14
Miami (Ohio) ■ ....*Sept. 28
Memphis ....*Oct. 5
Boston College ■ ....*Oct. 12
Houston ■ ....Oct. 19
Louisville ....Oct. 26
Southern Miss. ....Nov. 2
Ala.-Birmingham ....Nov. 16
Northeast La. ■ ....Nov. 23

1995 RESULTS (6-5-0)

18 Kansas 23
21 Kansas St. 23
16 Virginia Tech 0
16 Miami (Ohio) 23
31 Toledo 45
13 East Caro. 10
16 Southern Miss. 13
28 Memphis 3
55 Northern Ill. 19
14 Kentucky 33
24 Tulsa 5
252 197

Nickname: Bearcats.
Stadium: Nippert (1916), 35,000 capacity. Artificial turf.
Colors: Red & Black.
Conference: Conference USA.
SID: Tom Hathaway, 513-556-5191.
AD: Gerald K. O'Dell.

CITADEL

Charleston, SC 29409 ....I-AA

Coach: Charlie Taaffe, Siena '73
Record: 9 Years, 55-47-1

1996 SCHEDULE

Miami (Fla.) ....Sept. 7
Richmond ■ ....*Sept. 14
Western Caro. ■ ....*Sept. 21
Appalachian St. ....Sept. 28
East Tenn. St. ■ ....Oct. 12
Furman ....Oct. 19
Ga. Southern ■ ....Oct. 26
Marshall ....Nov. 2
Tenn.-Chatt. ■ ....Nov. 9
Va. Military ....Nov. 16
Wofford ■ ....Nov. 23

1995 RESULTS (2-9-0)

21 Newberry 20
27 Wofford 10
13 Richmond 17
14 Western Caro. 31
13 East Tenn. St. 21
3 Furman 24
0 Ga. Southern 27
19 Marshall 21
24 Tenn.-Chatt. 29
7 Va. Military 34
24 Appalachian St. 28
165 262

Nickname: Bulldogs.
Stadium: Johnson Hagood (1948), 22,500 capacity. Natural turf.
Colors: Blue & White.
Conference: Southern.
SID: Clark Haptonstall, 803-953-5120.
AD: Walt Nadzak.

CLAREMONT-M-S

Claremont, CA 91711 III

Coach: Rick Candaele, Col. of Idaho '69
Record: 4 Years, 22-15-0

1996 SCHEDULE

Menlo ....Sept. 14
Trinity (Tex.) ■ ....Sept. 21
Occidental ....*Sept. 28
Menlo ■ ....Oct. 5
Redlands ....*Oct. 12
Whittier ■ ....Oct. 19
Cal Lutheran ■ ....Oct. 26
La Verne ■ ....Nov. 2
Pomona-Pitzer ....*Nov. 9

1995 RESULTS (3-6-0)

3 Trinity (Tex.) 28
25 Chapman 55
27 Redlands 47
41 Menlo 24
24 Cal Lutheran 38
51 Occidental 13
35 Whittier 31
17 La Verne 38
34 Pomona-Pitzer 38
257 312

Nickname: Stags.
Stadium: Zinda Field (1955), 3,000 capacity. Natural turf.
Colors: Maroon, Gold & White.
Conference: Southern California Intercollegiate Athletic.
SID: Kelly Beck, 909-607-3138.
AD: David Wells.

CLARION

Clarion, PA 16214 II

Coach: Malen Luke, Westminster (Pa.) '76
Record: 8 Years, 47-31-0

1996 SCHEDULE

West Va. Wesleyan ....Sept. 7
Westminster (Pa.) ■ ....Sept. 14
Glenville St. ■ ....Sept. 21
Youngstown St. ....*Sept. 28
Lock Haven ■ ....Oct. 5
Shippensburg ....Oct. 12
Calif. (Pa.) ■ ....Oct. 19
Slippery Rock ....Oct. 26
Indiana (Pa.) ■ ....Nov. 2
Edinboro ....Nov. 9
Mansfield ....Nov. 16

1995 RESULTS (6-4-0)

24 West Va. Wesleyan 23
42 Westminster (Pa.) 0
48 Fairmont St. 13
35 Millersville 41
49 Lock Haven 32
31 Shippensburg 9
20 Calif. (Pa.) 10
17 Slippery Rock 41
9 Indiana (Pa.) 14
6 Edinboro 28
281 211

Nickname: Golden Eagles.
Stadium: Memorial Field (1965), 5,000 capacity. Natural turf.
Colors: Blue & Gold.
Conference: Pennsylvania State Athletic.
SID: Rich Herman, 814-226-2334.
AD: Robert Carlson.

CLARK ATLANTA

Atlanta, GA 30314 II

Coach: Willie Hunter, Fort Valley St. '57
Record: 6 Years, 25-34-1

1996 SCHEDULE

Hampton ■ .... Sept. 1
Alabama A&M .... *Sept. 14
Kentucky St. ■ .... Sept. 21
Miles ■ .... *Sept. 28
Fort Valley St. ■ .... *Oct. 5
Alabama St. [Mobile, Ala.] .... *Oct. 12
Savannah St. .... Oct. 19
Albany St. (Ga.) .... Oct. 26
Tuskegee ■ .... Nov. 2
Morehouse ■ .... Nov. 9
Morris Brown ■ .... Nov. 16

1995 RESULTS (5-5-0)

15 Morris Brown 14
0 Texas Southern 28
0 Alabama A&M 7
0 Kentucky St. 7
30 Miles 26
12 Fort Valley St. 21
21 Savannah St. 7
23 Albany St. (Ga.) 31
7 Tuskegee 6
21 Morehouse 6
129 **153**

Nickname: Panthers.
Stadium: Georgia Dome (1992), 71,000 capacity. Artificial turf.
Colors: Red, Black & Gray.
Conference: Southern Intercollegiate Athletic.
SID: Roger Caruth, 404-880-8029.
AD: Richard Cosby.

CLEMSON

Clemson, SC 29633 .... I-A

Coach: Tommy West, Tennessee '76
Record: 4 Years, 18-17-0

1996 SCHEDULE

North Caro. .... Aug. 31
Furman ■ .... Sept. 7
Missouri .... *Sept. 21
Wake Forest ■ .... Sept. 28
Florida St. .... *Oct. 5
Duke .... Oct. 12
Georgia Tech ■ .... Oct. 19
Maryland ■ .... Nov. 2
Virginia .... Nov. 9
North Caro. St. ■ .... Nov. 16
South Caro. ■ .... Nov. 23

1995 RESULTS (8-3-0)

55 Western Caro. 9
26 Florida St. 45
29 Wake Forest 14
3 Virginia 22
43 North Caro. St. 22
17 Georgia 19
17 Maryland 0
24 Georgia Tech 3
17 North Caro. 10
34 Duke 17
38 South Caro. 17
303 **178**

Gator Bowl

0 Syracuse 41

Nickname: Tigers.
Stadium: Memorial (1942), 81,473 capacity. Natural turf.
Colors: Purple & Orange.
Conference: Atlantic Coast.
SID: Tim Bourret, 803-656-2114.
AD: Bobby Robinson.

COAST GUARD

New London, CT 06320 III

Coach: Bill Schmitz, Coast Guard '76
Record: 3 Years, 12-16-0

1996 SCHEDULE

Rensselaer ■ .... Sept. 14
Mass. Maritime ■ .... *Sept. 21
Springfield .... Sept. 28
Norwich .... Oct. 5
Westfield St. ■ .... Oct. 12
Western Conn. St. ■ .... Oct. 19
Union (N.Y.) .... Oct. 26
Plymouth St. ■ .... Nov. 2
Worcester Tech .... Nov. 9
Merchant Marine .... Nov. 16

1995 RESULTS (4-6-0)

35 Worcester St. 0
20 Rensselaer 21
20 Springfield 26
27 Norwich 6
12 Westfield St. 0
7 Western Conn. St. 28
0 Union (N.Y.) 23
2 Plymouth St. 9
13 Worcester Tech 34
27 Merchant Marine 9
163 **156**

Nickname: Cadets, Bears.
Stadium: Cadet Memorial Field (1932), 4,500 capacity. Natural turf.
Colors: Blue, White & Orange.
Conference: Freedom Football.
SID: Jason Southard, 860-437-6800.
AD: Chuck Mills.

COE

Cedar Rapids, IA 52402 III

Coach: D. J. LeRoy, Wis.-Eau Claire '79
Record: 13 Years, 98-38-2

1996 SCHEDULE

Aurora .... Sept. 7
Eureka .... Sept. 14
Lawrence .... Sept. 21
Carroll (Wis.) ■ .... Sept. 28
Grinnell ■ .... Oct. 5
Illinois Col. .... Oct. 12
Monmouth (Ill.) ■ .... Oct. 19
Knox .... Oct. 26
Cornell College ■ .... Nov. 2

1995 RESULTS (7-2-0)

31 Quincy 7
7 Wartburg 28
22 St. Norbert 0
52 Lake Forest 20
37 Grinnell 7
55 Illinois Col. 0
41 Monmouth (Ill.) 13
48 Knox 23
28 Cornell College 40
321 **138**

Nickname: Kohawks.
Stadium: Clark (1989), 1,100 capacity. Natural turf.
Colors: Crimson & Gold.
Conference: Midwest.
SID: Alice Davidson, 319-399-8570.
AD: Barron Bremner.

COLBY

Waterville, ME 04901 III

Coach: Tom Austin, Maine '63
Record: 10 Years, 39-40-1

1996 SCHEDULE

Williams .... Sept. 21
Middlebury ■ .... Sept. 28
Wesleyan (Conn.) ■ .... Oct. 5
Amherst .... Oct. 12
Hamilton ■ .... Oct. 19
Bates .... Oct. 26
Tufts .... Nov. 2
Bowdoin ■ .... Nov. 9

1995 RESULTS (5-3-0)

14 Trinity (Conn.) 11
24 Middlebury 41
24 Wesleyan (Conn.) 3
27 Amherst 15
10 Hamilton 16
26 Bates 6
33 Tufts 6
3 Bowdoin 24
161 **122**

Nickname: Mules.
Stadium: Seaverns (1948), 5,000 capacity. Natural turf.
Colors: Blue & Gray.
Conference: NESCAC.
SID: To be named, 207-872-3227.
AD: Richard Whitmore.

COLGATE

Hamilton, NY 13346 .... I-AA

Coach: Dick Biddle, Duke '71
(First year as head coach)

1996 SCHEDULE

Richmond .... Sept. 7
Buffalo ■ .... Sept. 14
Holy Cross ■ .... Sept. 21
Pennsylvania .... Sept. 28
Brown ■ .... Oct. 5
Towson St. .... Oct. 12
Cornell .... Oct. 19
Lafayette ■ .... Oct. 26
Fordham .... Nov. 9
Lehigh .... Nov. 16
Bucknell .... Nov. 23

1995 RESULTS (0-11-0)

3 Northeastern 44
9 Lehigh 20
8 Harvard 28
23 Princeton 34
14 Fordham 34
6 Brown 21
14 Dartmouth 35
14 Army 56
9 Lafayette 35
14 Bucknell 21
20 Holy Cross 39
134 **367**

Nickname: Red Raiders.
Stadium: Andy Kerr (1937), 10,221 capacity. Natural turf.
Color: Maroon.
Conference: Patriot League.
SID: Bob Cornell, 315-824-7616.
AD: Mark Murphy.

COLORADO

Boulder, CO 80309 .... I-A

Coach: Rick Neuheisel, UCLA '84
Record: 1 Year, 10-2-0

1996 SCHEDULE

Washington St. ■ .... Aug. 31
Colorado St. .... *Sept. 7
Michigan ■ .... Sept. 14
Texas A&M .... Sept. 28
Oklahoma St. ■ .... *Oct. 12
Kansas .... Oct. 19
Texas ■ .... Oct. 26
Missouri .... Nov. 2
Iowa St. ■ .... Nov. 9
Kansas St. ■ .... Nov. 16
Nebraska .... Nov. 29

1995 RESULTS (9-2-0)

43 Wisconsin 7
42 Colorado St. 14
66 Northeast La. 14
29 Texas A&M 21
38 Oklahoma 17
24 Kansas 40
50 Iowa St. 28
21 Nebraska 44
45 Oklahoma St. 32
21 Missouri 0
27 Kansas St. 17
406 **234**

Cotton Bowl

38 Oregon 6

Nickname: Buffaloes.
Stadium: Folsom (1924), 51,808 capacity. Artificial turf.

Colors: Silver, Gold & Black.
Conference: Big 12.
SID: David Plati, 303-492-5626.
AD: Bill Marolt.

COLORADO COL.

Colorado Springs, CO 80903 ... III

Coach: Craig Rundle, Albion '74
Record: 10 Years, 54-40-1

1996 SCHEDULE

Gust. Adolphus ■ ... Sept. 7
Pomona-Pitzer ■ ... Sept. 14
Neb. Wesleyan ... Sept. 21
Austin ■ ... Sept. 28
Trinity (Tex.) ... *Oct. 5
Kan. Wesleyan ■ ... Oct. 19
Rhodes ... Oct. 26
McPherson ■ ... Nov. 9

1995 RESULTS (3-6-0)

22 Buena Vista ... 13
10 Pomona-Pitzer ... 37
17 Millsaps ... 21
3 Kan. Wesleyan ... 41
9 Central (Iowa) ... 31
20 McPherson ... 6
34 Rhodes ... 26
3 Austin ... 6
0 Washington (Mo.) ... 42
118 **223**

Nickname: Tigers.
Stadium: Washburn Field (1898), 2,000 capacity. Natural turf.
Colors: Black & Gold.
Conference: Division III Independents.
SID: Dave Moross, 719-389-6755.
AD: Marty Scarano.

COLORADO MINES

Golden, CO 80401 ... II

Coach: Versie Wallace, Northwestern Okla. '81
Record: 1 Year, 1-9-0

1996 SCHEDULE

South Dak. Tech ... Sept. 7
Hastings ■ ... Sept. 14
Neb.-Kearney ... Sept. 21
Fort Lewis ... Sept. 28
N.M. Highlands ■ ... Oct. 5
Mesa St. ■ ... Oct. 12
Adams St. ... Oct. 19
Western St. ... Oct. 26
Humboldt St. ... Nov. 2
Chadron St. ■ ... Nov. 9
Fort Hays St. ■ ... Nov. 16

1995 RESULTS (1-9-0)

10 Doane ... 7
7 Hastings ... 16
15 Mesa St. ... 38
22 N.M. Highlands ... 41
0 Western St. ... 55
26 Adams St. ... 38
10 Chadron St. ... 24
17 Fort Hays St. ... 56
34 Fort Lewis ... 39
0 Neb.-Kearney ... 56
141 **370**

Nickname: Orediggers.
Stadium: Brooks Field (1922), 5,000 capacity. Natural turf.
Colors: Silver & Blue.
Conference: Rocky Mountain Athletic.
SID: Steve Smith, 303-273-3300.
AD: Marv Kay.

COLORADO ST.

Fort Collins, CO 80523 ... I-A

Coach: Sonny Lubick, Western Mont. '60
Record: 7 Years, 44-31-0

1996 SCHEDULE

Tenn.-Chatt. ■ ... Aug. 31
Colorado ■ ... *Sept. 7
Oregon ... Sept. 14
UNLV ■ ... Sept. 21
Nebraska ... Sept. 28
Hawaii ... Oct. 5
Tulsa ... Oct. 12
San Jose St. ■ ... Oct. 19
San Diego St. ■ ... Oct. 26
Air Force ... Nov. 2
Fresno St. ... *Nov. 9
Wyoming ■ ... Nov. 16

1995 RESULTS (8-3-0)

31 Montana St. ... 10
14 Colorado ... 42
27 Air Force ... 20
21 Brigham Young ... 28
59 Utah St. ... 17
19 Utah ... 14
14 New Mexico ... 22
31 Wyoming ... 24
56 UTEP ... 10
22 Hawaii ... 0
24 San Diego St. ... 13
318 **200**

Holiday Bowl

21 Kansas St. ... 54

Nickname: Rams.
Stadium: Hughes (1968), 30,000 capacity. Natural turf.
Colors: Green & Gold.
Conference: Western Athletic.
SID: Gary Ozzello, 303-491-5067.
AD: Tom Jurich.

COLUMBIA

New York, NY 10027 ... I-AA

Coach: Ray Tellier, Connecticut '73
Record: 12 Years, 37-78-3

1996 SCHEDULE

Harvard ■ ... Sept. 21
Fordham ... Sept. 28
Holy Cross ... Oct. 5
Pennsylvania ... Oct. 12
Lafayette ■ ... Oct. 19
Yale ... Oct. 26
Princeton ■ ... Nov. 2
Dartmouth ... Nov. 9
Cornell ■ ... Nov. 16
Brown ■ ... Nov. 23

1995 RESULTS (3-6-1)

28 Harvard ... 24
14 St. Mary's (Cal.) ... 34
10 Lafayette ... 10
24 Pennsylvania ... 14
35 Lehigh ... 37
21 Yale ... 7
14 Princeton ... 44
27 Dartmouth ... 43
14 Cornell ... 35
14 Brown ... 33
201 **281**

Nickname: Lions.
Stadium: Lawrence A. Wien (1984), 17,000 capacity. Artificial turf.
Colors: Columbia Blue & White.
Conference: Ivy League.
SID: Brian Bodine, 212-854-2534.
AD: John Reeves.

CONCORD

Athens, WV 24712 ... II

Coach: Bob Mullett, Concord '73
Record: 7 Years, 36-33-2

1996 SCHEDULE

Tusculum ... *Aug. 31
Catawba ... Sept. 7
Mars Hill ■ ... Sept. 14
Newport News App. ■ ... Sept. 21
Fairmont St. ■ ... Sept. 28
West Va. Tech ... Oct. 5
Shepherd ... Oct. 12
West Liberty St. ■ ... Oct. 19
Glenville St. ■ ... Oct. 26
West Va. Wesleyan ... Nov. 2
West Va. St. ... Nov. 9

1995 RESULTS (3-7-0)

14 Catawba ... 52
21 Mars Hill ... 38
17 Newport News App. ... 12
6 Fairmont St. ... 55
42 West Va. Tech ... 12
10 Shepherd ... 31
0 West Liberty St. ... 27
0 Glenville St. ... 54
14 West Va. Wesleyan ... 36
25 West Va. St. ... 18
149 **335**

Nickname: Mountain Lions.
Stadium: Callahan, 5,000 capacity. Natural turf.
Colors: Maroon & Gray.
Conference: West Virginia Intercollegiate Athletic.
SID: Don Christie, 304-384-5347.
AD: Don Christie.

CONCORDIA (ILL.)

River Forest, IL 60305 ... III

Coach: Jim Braun, Concordia (Ill.) '71
Record: 17 Years, 57-93-4

1996 SCHEDULE

Maranatha Baptist ... Sept. 7
Lawrence ... Sept. 14
Chicago ■ ... Sept. 21
Principia ■ ... Oct. 5
Eureka ■ ... Oct. 12
Greenville ... Oct. 19
Lakeland ■ ... Oct. 26
MacMurray ■ ... Nov. 2
Concordia (Wis.) ... Nov. 9

1995 RESULTS (1-8-0)

14 Maranatha Baptist ... 12
6 Northwestern Minn. ... 37
0 Chicago ... 46
0 MacMurray ... 15
13 Eureka ... 60
7 Quincy ... 9
0 Lakeland ... 42
7 Greenville ... 51
7 Concordia (Wis.) ... 28
54 **300**

Nickname: Cougars.
Stadium: Concordia, 1,500 capacity. Natural turf.
Colors: Maroon & Gold.
Conference: Division III Independents.
SID: Jim Egan, 708-209-3116.
AD: Janet Fisher.

CONCORDIA-M'HEAD

Moorhead, MN 56560 ... III

Coach: Jim Christopherson, Concordia-M'head '60
Record: 27 Years, 189-79-7

1996 SCHEDULE

Moorhead St. ... Sept. 7
Gust. Adolphus ... Sept. 14
St. Olaf ■ ... Sept. 21
Macalester ■ ... Sept. 28
Bethel (Minn.) ... Oct. 5
St. Thomas (Minn.) ■ ... Oct. 12
St. John's (Minn.) ... Oct. 19
Augsburg ■ ... Oct. 26
Hamline ... Nov. 2
Carleton [Minneapolis, Minn.] ... *Nov. 9

1995 RESULTS (8-1-1)

10 Moorhead St. ... 7
38 Augsburg ... 6
27 Hamline ... 3

28 St. Thomas (Minn.) 34
48 Gust. Adolphus 6
41 Carleton 9
48 St. Olaf 16
49 Macalester 6
14 St. John's (Minn.) 14
32 Bethel (Minn.) 14
335 **115**

III Championship

7 Wis.-La Crosse 45

Nickname: Cobbers.
Stadium: Jake Christiansen, 7,500 capacity. Natural turf.
Colors: Maroon & Gold.
Conference: Minnesota Intercollegiate Athletic.
SID: Jerry Pyle, 218-299-3194.
AD: Armin Pipho.

CONNECTICUT

Storrs, CT 06269 I-AA

Coach: Skip Holtz, Notre Dame '86
Record: 3 Years, 12-10-0

1996 SCHEDULE

Buffalo *Sept. 7
Northeastern ■ Sept. 14
New Hampshire Sept. 21
Yale Sept. 28
Villanova ■ Oct. 5
Maine ■ Oct. 12
Rhode Island ■ Oct. 19
Hofstra ■ Oct. 26
Boston U. Nov. 2
James Madison ■ Nov. 9
Massachusetts Nov. 16

1995 RESULTS (8-3-0)

23 New Hampshire 21
54 Central Conn. St. 9
26 Buffalo 25
39 Yale 20
14 Villanova 13
31 Maine 30
19 Rhode Island 24
9 Northeastern 10
28 Boston U. 17
16 James Madison 24
20 Massachusetts 7
279 **200**

Nickname: Huskies.
Stadium: Memorial (1953), 16,200 capacity. Natural turf.
Colors: National Flag Blue & White.
Conference: Yankee.
SID: Kyle Muncy, 203-486-3531.
AD: Lew Perkins.

CORNELL

Ithaca, NY 14853 I-AA

Coach: Jim Hofher, Cornell '79
Record: 6 Years, 35-25-0

1996 SCHEDULE

Princeton ■ Sept. 21
Lafayette Sept. 28
Buffalo Oct. 5
Harvard Oct. 12
Colgate ■ Oct. 19
Dartmouth ■ Oct. 26
Brown ■ Nov. 2
Yale Nov. 9
Columbia Nov. 16
Pennsylvania ■ Nov. 23

1995 RESULTS (6-4-0)

22 Princeton 24
28 Holy Cross 19
24 Dartmouth 19
28 Harvard 27
7 Bucknell 10
23 Lehigh 34
38 Brown 28
38 Yale 10
35 Columbia 14
18 Pennsylvania 37
261 **222**

Nickname: Big Red.
Stadium: Schoellkopf (1915), 27,000 capacity. Artificial turf.
Colors: Carnelian & White.
Conference: Ivy League.
SID: Dave Wohlhueter, 607-255-3753.
AD: Charles H. Moore.

CORNELL COLLEGE

Mt. Vernon, IA 52314 III

Coach: Steve Miller, Cornell College '65
Record: 17 Years, 90-64-3

1996 SCHEDULE

Simpson ■ Sept. 7
Dubuque ■ Sept. 14
Ripon Sept. 21
Beloit ■ Sept. 28
Knox ■ Oct. 5
Monmouth (Ill.) Oct. 12
Grinnell Oct. 19
Illinois Col. ■ Oct. 26
Coe Nov. 2

1995 RESULTS (9-1-0)

15 Carleton 13
8 Beloit 17
34 Lawrence 26
36 Carroll (Wis.) 18
23 Knox 16
43 Monmouth (Ill.) 0
32 Grinnell 17
52 Illinois Col. 7
40 Coe 28
38 Ripon 17
321 **159**

Nickname: Rams.
Stadium: Ash Park Field (1922), 2,500 capacity. Natural turf.
Colors: Purple & White.
Conference: Midwest.
SID: Greg Suckow, 319-895-4483.
AD: Ellen Whale.

CORTLAND ST.

Cortland, NY 13045 III

Coach: Dave Murray, Springfield '81
Record: 6 Years, 38-26-1

1996 SCHEDULE

Mansfield Sept. 7
Montclair St. Sept. 14
Kean ■ Sept. 21
Buffalo St. Sept. 28
St. Lawrence ■ Oct. 12
Rowan Oct. 19
Wm. Paterson ■ Oct. 26
Springfield Nov. 2
Ithaca ■ Nov. 9
Brockport St. ■ Nov. 16

1995 RESULTS (6-3-1)

21 Mansfield 20
24 Montclair St. 17
13 Ferrum 0
33 Buffalo St. 36
21 Brockport St. 13
14 Rowan 14
28 Newport News App. 0
7 Wash. & Jeff. 14
19 Ithaca 35
28 Jersey City St. 14
208 **163**

ECAC III Playoff

26 Springfield 49

Nickname: Red Dragons.
Stadium: Davis Field (1959), 5,000 capacity. Natural turf.
Colors: Red & White.
Conference: Division III Independents.
SID: Fran Elia, 607-753-5673.
AD: Lee Roberts.

CURRY

Milton, MA 02186 III

Coach: Chris House, Curry '88
Record: 1 Year, 2-8-0

1996 SCHEDULE

Framingham St. ■ Sept. 7
Fitchburg St. ■ Sept. 14
Stonehill ■ Sept. 21
Assumption Sept. 28
Merrimack Oct. 5
Nichols ■ Oct. 12
MIT Oct. 19
Salve Regina Nov. 1
Western New Eng. ■ Nov. 9
Mass.-Lowell ■ Nov. 16

1995 RESULTS (2-8-0)

38 Fitchburg St. 28
7 Bentley 44
6 MIT 33
33 Nichols 14
7 Salve Regina 47
0 Wesley 62
29 Assumption 36
19 Stonehill 40
14 Sacred Heart 62
30 Western New Eng. 36
183 **402**

Nickname: Colonels.
Stadium: D. Forbes Will Field, 1,500 capacity. Natural turf.
Colors: Purple, White & Silver.
Conference: Eastern Football.
SID: Adam Polgreen, 617-333-2324.
AD: Pam Samuelson.

DARTMOUTH

Hanover, NH 03755 I-AA

Coach: John Lyons, Pennsylvania '74
Record: 4 Years, 26-13-1

1996 SCHEDULE

Pennsylvania ■ Sept. 21
Lehigh Sept. 28
Fordham ■ Oct. 5
Holy Cross ■ Oct. 12
Yale ■ Oct. 19
Cornell Oct. 26
Harvard Nov. 2
Columbia ■ Nov. 9
Brown Nov. 16
Princeton Nov. 23

1995 RESULTS (7-2-1)

12 Pennsylvania 20
34 Fordham 14
19 Cornell 24
14 Lafayette 7
22 Yale 7
35 Colgate 14
23 Harvard 7
43 Columbia 27
10 Brown 7
10 Princeton 10
222 **137**

Nickname: Big Green.
Stadium: Memorial Field (1923), 20,416 capacity. Natural turf.
Colors: Dartmouth Green & White.
Conference: Ivy League.
SID: Kathy Slattery, 603-646-2468.
AD: Dick Jaeger.

DAVIDSON

Davidson, NC 28036 I-AA

Coach: Tim Landis, Randolph-Macon '86
Record: 3 Years, 10-19-1

1996 SCHEDULE

Maryville (Tenn.) ....Sept. 14
Sewanee ....Sept. 21
Emory & Henry ■ ....Sept. 28
Guilford ■ ....*Oct. 5
Wash. & Lee ■ ....Oct. 12
Methodist ....Oct. 19
Randolph-Macon ■ ....Oct. 26
Hampden-Sydney ....Nov. 2
Centre ■ ....Nov. 9
Bridgewater (Va.) ....Nov. 16

1995 RESULTS (1-8-1)

21 Sewanee 14
21 Maryville (Tenn.) 28
0 Emory & Henry 32
28 Guilford 31
13 Wash. & Lee 19
14 Methodist 16
0 Randolph-Macon 36
19 Hampden-Sydney 22
6 Centre 21
7 Bridgewater (Va.) 7
129 **226**

Nickname: Wildcats.
Stadium: Richardson Field (1924), 5,200 capacity. Natural turf.
Colors: Red & Black.
Conference: I-AA Independents.
SID: Emil Parker, 704-892-2374.
AD: Jim Murphy.

DAYTON

Dayton, OH 45469 ....I-AA

Coach: Mike Kelly, Manchester '70
Record: 15 Years, 145-27-1

1996 SCHEDULE

Morehead St. ■ ....*Sept. 7
Georgetown (Ky.) ■ ....*Sept. 14
Wis.-Platteville ■ ....Sept. 21
Towson St. ....Sept. 28
Evansville ....Oct. 5
Robert Morris ■ ....Oct. 12
Butler ....Oct. 19
Drake ■ ....Oct. 26
Valparaiso ....Nov. 2
Wofford ■ ....Nov. 9
San Diego ....*Nov. 16

1995 RESULTS (9-2-0)

40 Albany (N.Y.) 14
30 San Diego 3
38 Towson St. 0
28 Wis.-Platteville 7
55 Georgetown (Ky.) 30
49 Butler 13
23 Drake 34
44 Valparaiso 14
36 Evansville 10
55 West Va. St. 0
24 Wofford 55
422 **180**

Nickname: Flyers.
Stadium: Welcome (1949), 11,000 capacity. Artificial turf.
Colors: Red & Blue.
Conference: Pioneer Football League.
SID: Doug Hauschild, 513-229-4460.
AD: Ted Kissell.

DEFIANCE

Defiance, OH 43512 III

Coach: Greg Pscodna, Adrian '86
(First year as head coach)

1996 SCHEDULE

Mount Union ■ ....Sept. 14
Adrian ....*Sept. 21
Olivet ■ ....Sept. 28
Alma ....Oct. 5
Mt. St. Joseph ■ ....Oct. 12
Thomas More ....Oct. 19
Manchester ■ ....Oct. 26
Bluffton ....Nov. 9
Wash. & Jeff. ■ ....Nov. 16

1995 RESULTS (2-7-0)

31 Manchester 22
7 Mount Union 57
14 Adrian 24
20 Hanover 38
10 Olivet 23
14 Mt. St. Joseph 20
0 Wash. & Jeff. 42
0 Thomas More 33
17 Bluffton 13
113 **272**

Nickname: Yellow Jackets.
Stadium: Justin F. Coressel (1994), 4,176 capacity. Natural turf.
Colors: Purple & Gold.
Conference: Division III Independents.
SID: Tom Palombo, 419-783-2346.
AD: Marv Hohenberger.

DELAWARE

Newark, DE 19716 ....I-AA

Coach: Tubby Raymond, Michigan '50
Record: 30 Years, 250-97-3

1996 SCHEDULE

Lehigh ■ ....Sept. 7
Villanova ....Sept. 14
West Chester ■ ....Sept. 21
Maine ....Sept. 28
Boston U. ■ ....Oct. 5
Richmond ....Oct. 12
Northeastern ■ ....Oct. 19
James Madison ■ ....Oct. 26
William & Mary ....Nov. 2
Navy ....Nov. 9
Rhode Island ■ ....Nov. 16

1995 RESULTS (10-1-0)

49 West Chester 21
28 Villanova 7
41 Boston U. 29
37 Northeastern 10
34 Youngstown St. 13
15 Richmond 0
48 James Madison 19
61 Maine 0
23 William & Mary 20
7 Navy 31
24 Rhode Island 19
367 **169**

I-AA Championship

38 Hofstra 17
18 McNeese St. 52

Nickname: Fightin' Blue Hens.
Stadium: Delaware (1952), 23,000 capacity. Natural turf.
Colors: Blue & Gold.
Conference: Yankee.
SID: Scott Selheimer, 302-831-2186.
AD: Edgar Johnson.

DELAWARE ST.

Dover, DE 19901 ....I-AA

Coach: Bill Collick, Delaware '74
Record: 11 Years, 75-43-0

1996 SCHEDULE

Lock Haven ■ ....Sept. 7
Liberty ....Sept. 14
N.C. Central ■ ....Sept. 21
Norfolk St. ....Sept. 28
Bethune-Cookman ....Oct. 5
Hampton ■ ....Oct. 12
Florida A&M ■ ....Oct. 19
Morgan St. ....Oct. 26
South Caro. St. ■ ....Nov. 2
North Caro. A&T ■ ....Nov. 9
Howard ....Nov. 23

1995 RESULTS (6-5-0)

14 Rhode Island 17
14 Western Ill. 41
14 Liberty 41
20 Norfolk St. 14
21 Hampton 51
21 Florida A&M 24
41 Morgan St. 17
20 South Caro. St. 7
17 North Caro. A&T 10
30 Bethune-Cookman 20
20 Howard 13
232 **255**

Nickname: Hornets.
Stadium: Alumni Field (1957), 5,000 capacity. Natural turf.
Colors: Red & Blue.
Conference: Mid-Eastern Athletic.
SID: Craig Cotton, 302-739-4926.
AD: Bill Collick.

DELAWARE VALLEY

Doylestown, PA 18901 III

Coach: Chris Bockrath, Delaware Valley '70
(First year as head coach)

1996 SCHEDULE

Salisbury St. ....Sept. 7
Susquehanna ■ ....Sept. 14
Juniata ....Sept. 28
Moravian ■ ....Oct. 5
FDU-Madison ....Oct. 12
Lycoming ■ ....Oct. 19
King's (Pa.) ■ ....Oct. 26
Wilkes ....Nov. 2
Widener ■ ....Nov. 9
Lebanon Valley ....Nov. 16

1995 RESULTS (3-7-0)

14 Susquehanna 28
13 Jersey City St. 10
28 Juniata 26
0 Moravian 32
24 FDU-Madison 27
0 Lycoming 29
13 King's (Pa.) 0
9 Wilkes 10
14 Widener 49
7 Lebanon Valley 19
122 **230**

Nickname: Aggies.
Stadium: James Work (1978), 4,500 capacity. Natural turf.
Colors: Green & Gold.
Conference: Middle Atlantic.
SID: Matthew Levy, 215-345-1500.
AD: Frank Wolfgang.

DELTA ST.

Cleveland, MS 38733 II

Coach: Todd Knight, Ouachita Baptist '86
Record: 3 Years, 11-18-2

1996 SCHEDULE

Stephen F. Austin ....*Sept. 7
Arkansas Tech ....*Sept. 14
Ark.-Monticello ■ ....*Sept. 21
Central Ark. ....*Sept. 28
Southern Ark. ....*Oct. 5
Henderson St. ■ ....Oct. 12
North Ala. ....Oct. 19
West Ga. ....Oct. 26
Valdosta St. ■ ....Nov. 2
West Ala. ■ ....Nov. 9

1995 RESULTS (5-6-0)

13 North Dak. St. 16
14 Arkansas Tech 7
0 Northwestern St. 34
0 North Ala. 30
14 West Ga. 20
19 Central Ark. 0
17 Henderson St. 24
19 Valdosta St. 37
20 Southern Ark. 7

41 West Ala. 3
14 Mississippi Col. 0
171 **178**

Nickname: Statesmen.
Stadium: Travis E. Parker Field (1970), 8,000 capacity. Natural turf.
Colors: Green & White.
Conference: Gulf South.
SID: Rick Kindhart, 601-846-4677.
AD: Jim Jordan.

DENISON

Granville, OH 43023 III

Coach: Bill Wentworth, Purdue '80
Record: 3 Years, 8-21-1

1996 SCHEDULE

Muskingum ....Sept. 7
Centre ■ ....Sept. 14
Wooster ■ ....Sept. 21
Earlham....Sept. 28
Allegheny ■ ....Oct. 5
Kenyon....Oct. 12
Oberlin ■....Oct. 19
Wittenberg ....Oct. 26
Ohio Wesleyan ■....Nov. 2
Grove City....Nov. 9

1995 RESULTS (2-7-1)

0 Muskingum 34
22 Centre 31
7 Allegheny....31
7 Kenyon 7
7 Wooster....10
0 Ohio Wesleyan....20
30 Oberlin....10
0 Wittenberg....51
6 Case Reserve 21
13 Earlham....11
92 **226**

Nickname: Big Red.
Stadium: Deeds Field (1922), 5,000 capacity. Natural turf.
Colors: Red & White.
Conference: North Coast Athletic.
SID: Jack Hire, 614-587-6546.
AD: Larry Scheiderer.

DePAUW

Greencastle, IN 46135....III

Coach: Nick Mourouzis, Miami (Ohio) '59
Record: 15 Years, 86-59-4

1996 SCHEDULE

Chicago ■ ....Sept. 14
Hope ■....Sept. 21
Albion ....Sept. 28
Anderson (Ind.) ■....Oct. 5
Franklin ....Oct. 12
Hanover ■ ....Oct. 19
Rose-Hulman....Oct. 26
Manchester ■ ....Nov. 2
Ill. Benedictine....Nov. 9
Wabash....Nov. 16

1995 RESULTS (3-7-0)

35 Wittenberg....45
13 Hope....7
14 Albion 3
15 Franklin....23
25 Hanover....45
20 Rose-Hulman 21
8 Manchester 10
7 Mt. St. Joseph....14
45 Anderson (Ind.)....13
2 Wabash 7
184 **188**

Nickname: Tigers.
Stadium: Blackstock (1941), 4,000 capacity. Natural turf.
Colors: Old Gold & Black.
Conference: Indiana Collegiate Athletic.
SID: Bill Wagner, 317-658-4630.
AD: Ted Katula.

DICKINSON

Carlisle, PA 17013....III

Coach: Darwin Breaux, West Chester '77
Record: 3 Years, 24-7-1

1996 SCHEDULE

Hobart ....Sept. 14
Muhlenberg ■ ....Sept. 21
Susquehanna ....Sept. 28
Carnegie Mellon ■ ....Oct. 5
Frank. & Marsh. ■ ....Oct. 12
Western Md. ....Oct. 19
Swarthmore ■ ....Oct. 26
Johns Hopkins....Nov. 2
Gettysburg ■ ....Nov. 9
Ursinus ....Nov. 16

1995 RESULTS (7-2-1)

31 Hobart....14
35 Muhlenberg....0
30 Susquehanna....6
7 Union (N.Y.)....20
28 Frank. & Marsh. 21
38 Western Md.....24
18 Swarthmore....19
17 Johns Hopkins 14
7 Gettysburg 7
27 Ursinus....12
238 **137**

Nickname: Red Devils.
Stadium: Biddle Field (1909), 2,577 capacity. Natural turf.
Colors: Red & White.
Conference: Centennial.
SID: Matt Howell, 717-245-1652.
AD: Les Poolman.

DRAKE

Des Moines, IA 50311....I-AA

Coach: Rob Ash, Cornell College '73
Record: 16 Years, 98-57-5

1996 SCHEDULE

Morningside ■....Sept. 7
St. Norbert ....Sept. 14
San Diego ■ ....Sept. 21
St. Mary's (Cal.)....Sept. 28
Butler ■....Oct. 5
Evansville....Oct. 12
Valparaiso ■ ....Oct. 19
Dayton ....Oct. 26
Aurora ....Nov. 2
Wayne St. (Neb.) ■....Nov. 9
Northwestern Ia. ....Nov. 16

1995 RESULTS (8-1-1)

19 Mo. Western St.....19
23 St. Ambrose 0
7 Wis.-La Crosse 14
37 Aurora....7
29 Butler....8
23 Evansville....6
28 Valparaiso 21
34 Dayton....23
9 San Diego....0
28 Northwestern Ia.....6
237 **104**

Nickname: Bulldogs.
Stadium: Drake (1925), 18,000 capacity. Natural turf.
Colors: Blue & White.
Conference: Pioneer Football League.
SID: Mike Mahon, 515-271-3012.
AD: Lynn King.

DUBUQUE

Dubuque, IA 52001 III

Coach: Jim Collins, Wittenberg '88
Record: 2 Years, 3-17-0

1996 SCHEDULE

Cornell College....Sept. 14
Concordia (St. Paul) ....Sept. 21
Central (Iowa) ■ ....Sept. 28
Luther ....Oct. 5
Buena Vista ■....Oct. 12
William Penn ....Oct. 19
Wartburg ....Oct. 26
Simpson ■....Nov. 2
Loras ....Nov. 9
Upper Iowa ■....Nov. 16

1995 RESULTS (2-8-0)

3 Dana 7
7 Central (Iowa) 64
6 Loras 14
7 Buena Vista....20
0 Wartburg....54
0 Upper Iowa....30
22 Eureka....24
13 Luther....12
6 Simpson....41
39 William Penn....0
103 **266**

Nickname: Spartans.
Stadium: Chalmers Field (1942), 2,800 capacity. Natural turf.
Colors: Blue & White.
Conference: Iowa Intercollegiate Athletic.
SID: Greg Yoko, 319-589-3225.
AD: Connie Bandy-Hodge.

DUKE

Durham, NC 27706 ....I-A

Coach: Fred Goldsmith, Florida '67
Record: 8 Years, 36-50-1

1996 SCHEDULE

Florida St.....Sept. 7
Northwestern ■ ....Sept. 14
Army....Sept. 21
Georgia Tech ....*Sept. 26
Navy....Oct. 5
Clemson ■ ....Oct. 12
Maryland ■....Oct. 26
Virginia ■ ....Nov. 2
North Caro. St. ....Nov. 9
Wake Forest....Nov. 16
North Caro. ■ ....Nov. 23

1995 RESULTS (3-8-0)

26 Florida St. 70
24 Rutgers....14
23 Army 21
28 Maryland....41
9 Navy....30
21 Georgia Tech....37
30 Virginia....44
38 North Caro. St. 41
42 Wake Forest 26
17 Clemson 34
24 North Caro. 28
282 **386**

Nickname: Blue Devils.
Stadium: Wallace Wade (1929), 33,941 capacity. Natural turf.
Colors: Royal Blue & White.
Conference: Atlantic Coast.
SID: Mike Cragg, 919-684-2633.
AD: Tom Butters.

DUQUESNE

Pittsburgh, PA 15282....I-AA

Coach: Greg Gattuso, Penn St. '83
Record: 3 Years, 20-11-0

1996 SCHEDULE

Marist ■....Sept. 14
St. John's (N.Y.) ....Sept. 21
Gannon ■....Sept. 28
Siena ....Oct. 5
St. Francis (Pa.)....Oct. 12
Georgetown ■....Oct. 19
Iona ■ ....Oct. 26
Fairfield ■ ....Nov. 2
St. Peter's ....Nov. 9
Canisius ....Nov. 16

1995 RESULTS (9-1-0)

21 St. Francis (Pa.) 14
20 Robert Morris 38
13 Georgetown 7
44 Gannon 15
42 St. Peter's 13
16 Marist 14
21 Siena 7
30 Iona 13
48 St. John's (N.Y.) 22
14 Canisius 0
269 **143**

ECAC I-AA Playoff

44 Wagner 20

Nickname: Dukes.
Stadium: Arthur J. Rooney Field (1993), 2,500 capacity. Artificial turf.
Colors: Red & Blue.
Conference: Metro Atlantic.
SID: Sue Ryan, 412-396-5861.
AD: Brian Colleary.

EARLHAM

Richmond, IN 47374 III

Coach: Frank Carr, Albion '78
Record: 11 Years, 28-77-0

1996 SCHEDULE

Manchester ....Sept. 14
Ohio Wesleyan ....Sept. 21
Denison ■ ....Sept. 28
Case Reserve ....Oct. 5
Wooster ■ ....Oct. 12
Wilmington (Ohio) ■ ....Oct. 19
Allegheny ....Oct. 26
Kenyon ■ ....Nov. 2
Oberlin ....Nov. 9
Wittenberg ■ ....Nov. 16

1995 RESULTS (3-7-0)

21 Swarthmore 28
30 Wittenberg 45
7 Case Reserve 3
73 Principia 6
14 Allegheny 34
8 Kenyon 14
15 Wooster 17
14 Ohio Wesleyan 33
49 Oberlin 14
11 Denison 13
242 **207**

Nickname: Hustlin' Quakers.
Stadium: M. O. Ross Field (1975), 1,500 capacity. Natural turf.
Colors: Maroon & White.
Conference: North Coast Athletic.
SID: David Knight, 317-983-1416.
AD: Porter Miller.

EAST CARO.

Greenville, NC 27834 ....I-A

Coach: Steve Logan, Tulsa '75
Record: 4 Years, 23-23-0

1996 SCHEDULE

East Tenn. St. ■ ....Sept. 7
West Va. ....Sept. 14
South Caro. ....*Sept. 21
Central Fla. ■ ....Sept. 28
Southern Miss. ■ ....*Oct. 10
Miami (Fla.) ....Oct. 19
Arkansas St. ■ ....Nov. 2
Virginia Tech ....Nov. 9
Ohio ■ ....Nov. 16
Memphis ....Nov. 23
North Caro. St. [Charlotte, N.C.] ....Nov. 30

1995 RESULTS (8-3-0)

7 Tennessee 27
27 Syracuse 24
30 Central Mich. 17
0 Illinois 7
23 West Va. 20
10 Cincinnati 13
32 Temple 22
36 Southern Miss. 34
31 Army 25
28 Tulsa 7
31 Memphis 17
255 **213**

Liberty Bowl

19 Stanford 13

Nickname: Pirates.
Stadium: Dowdy-Ficklen (1963), 35,000 capacity. Natural turf.
Colors: Purple & Gold.
Conference: I-A Independents.
SID: Norm Reilly, 919-328-4522.
AD: Mike Hamrick.

EAST STROUDSBURG

East Stroudsburg, PA 18301 II

Coach: Dennis Douds, Slippery Rock '63
Record: 22 Years, 133-87-3

1996 SCHEDULE

New Haven ....Sept. 14
Southern Conn. St. ■ ....Sept. 21
Slippery Rock ....Sept. 28
Kutztown ■ ....Oct. 5
West Chester ....Oct. 12
Indiana (Pa.) ■ ....Oct. 19
Cheyney ■ ....Oct. 26
Mansfield ....Nov. 2
Millersville ■ ....Nov. 9
Bloomsburg ....Nov. 16

1995 RESULTS (4-6-0)

49 American Int'l 19
0 Eastern Ky. 26
10 Southern Conn. St. 19
34 West Chester 26
12 Slippery Rock 23
40 Cheyney 13
36 Mansfield 13
14 Millersville 19
27 Bloomsburg 34
7 Kutztown 28
229 **220**

Nickname: Warriors.
Stadium: Eiler-Martin (1969), 6,000 capacity. Natural turf.
Colors: Red & Black.
Conference: Pennsylvania State Athletic.
SID: Peter Nevins, 717-422-3312.
AD: Earl W. Edwards.

EAST TENN. ST.

Johnson City, TN 37614 ....I-AA

Coach: Mike Cavan, Georgia '72
Record: 10 Years, 57-46-2

1996 SCHEDULE

Liberty ■ ....*Aug. 29
East Caro. ....Sept. 7
Glenville St. ■ ....*Sept. 14
Va. Military ■ ....Sept. 21
Western Caro. ....*Sept. 28
Appalachian St. ■ ....*Oct. 5
Citadel ....Oct. 12
Furman ■ ....Oct. 26
Ga. Southern ....Nov. 2
Marshall ■ ....Nov. 9
Tenn.-Chatt. ....Nov. 16

1995 RESULTS (4-7-0)

7 Troy St. 31
20 Toledo 41
23 Va. Military 37
20 Tulsa 45
23 Appalachian St. 30
21 Citadel 13
15 Furman 21
21 Ga. Southern 16
0 Marshall 52
38 Tenn.-Chatt. 9
36 Western Caro. 10
224 **305**

Nickname: Buccaneers.
Stadium: Memorial (1977), 12,000 capacity. Artificial turf.
Colors: Blue & Gold.
Conference: Southern.
SID: Annabelle Vaughan, 615-929-4220.
AD: H. Keener Fry.

EAST TEX. ST.

Commerce, TX 75428 II

Coach: Eddie Vowell, Southwestern Okla. '69
Record: 10 Years, 60-52-1

1996 SCHEDULE

Harding ■ ....*Sept. 7
Henderson St. ■ ....*Sept. 14
Northwestern St. ....*Sept. 21
Ark.-Pine Bluff ....*Sept. 28
Central Okla. ....Oct. 5
Tex. A&M-Kingsville ■ ....*Oct. 12
West Tex. A&M ....*Oct. 19
Eastern N.M. ■ ....Oct. 26
Abilene Christian ....Nov. 2
Angelo St. ■ ....Nov. 9
Tarleton St. ....Nov. 16

1995 RESULTS (8-3-0)

20 Central Ark. 27
40 Harding 0
6 Henderson St. 3
17 Northwestern St. 45
17 Central Okla. 9
18 Tex. A&M-Kingsville 37
51 West Tex. A&M 7
28 Eastern N.M. 14
31 Abilene Christian 24
24 Angelo St. 21
48 Tarleton St. 3
300 **190**

II Championship

35 Portland St. 56

Nickname: Lions.
Stadium: Memorial (1950), 10,000 capacity. Natural turf.
Colors: Blue & Gold.
Conference: Lone Star.
SID: Kevin Carson, 903-886-5131.
AD: Margo Harbison.

EASTERN ILL.

Charleston, IL 61920 ....I-AA

Coach: Bob Spoo, Purdue '60
Record: 9 Years, 52-49-1

1996 SCHEDULE

Western Mich. ....*Aug. 29
Pittsburg St. ■ ....*Sept. 7
Indiana St. ■ ....*Sept. 14
Tenn.-Martin ....Sept. 28
Western Ill. ■ ....Oct. 12
Murray St. ■ ....Oct. 19
Tennessee Tech ....Oct. 26
Austin Peay ....Nov. 2
Southeast Mo. St. ....Nov. 9
Middle Tenn. St. ....Nov. 16
Eastern Ky. ■ ....Nov. 23

1995 RESULTS (10-1-0)

31 Austin Peay 13
34 Southeast Mo. St. 18
30 Tenn.-Martin 22
9 Southwest Mo. St. 7
33 Central St. 27
7 Northern Iowa 17
35 Western Ky. 9
31 Illinois St. 10
20 Western Ill. 17
42 Southern Ill. 21
27 Indiana St. 6
299 **167**

I-AA Championship

29 Stephen F. Austin 34

Nickname: Panthers.
Stadium: O'Brien (1970), 10,000 capacity. Natural turf.
Colors: Blue & Gray.
Conference: Ohio Valley.
SID: Dave Kidwell, 217-581-6408.
AD: Bob McBee.

EASTERN KY.

Richmond, KY 40475 ....I-AA

Coach: Roy Kidd, Eastern Ky. '54
Record: 32 Years, 266-94-8

1996 SCHEDULE

Troy St. ■ ....*Sept. 7
Western Ky. ....*Sept. 14
Appalachian St. ■ ....*Sept. 21
Tennessee Tech ■ ....*Sept. 28
Southeast Mo. St. ■ ....Oct. 5
Middle Tenn. St. ....Oct. 19
Tenn.-Martin ....Oct. 26
Tennessee St. ■ ....Nov. 2
Murray St. ■ ....Nov. 9
Austin Peay ....Nov. 16
Eastern Ill. ....Nov. 23

1995 RESULTS (9-2-0)

32 Central Fla. 40
38 Western Ky. 14
26 East Stroudsburg 0
21 Tennessee Tech 3
42 Southeast Mo. St. 24
34 Middle Tenn. St. 21
38 Tenn.-Martin 15
56 Tennessee St. 20
7 Murray St. 17
28 Austin Peay 0
41 Morehead St. 10
363 **164**

I-AA Championship

0 Montana 48

Nickname: Colonels.
Stadium: Roy Kidd (1969), 20,000 capacity. Natural turf.
Colors: Maroon & White.
Conference: Ohio Valley.
SID: Karl Park, 606-622-1253.
AD: Robert Baugh.

EASTERN MICH.

Ypsilanti, MI 48197 ....I-A

Coach: Rick Rasnick, San Jose St. '81
Record: 1 Year, 6-5-0

1996 SCHEDULE

Temple ■ ....*Aug. 31
Wisconsin ....Sept. 7
Western Mich. ....*Sept. 14
Toledo ■ ....*Sept. 21
Michigan St. ....Sept. 28
Ohio ....Oct. 5
Miami (Ohio) ■ ....*Oct. 12
Central Mich. ....Oct. 19
Kent ■ ....Oct. 26
Ball St. ■ ....Nov. 2
Akron ■ ....Nov. 9

1995 RESULTS (6-5-0)

49 Akron 29
30 Pittsburgh 66
51 UNLV 6
31 Ohio 20
34 Central Mich. 24
24 Syracuse 52
40 Ball St. 35
28 Toledo 34
23 Miami (Ohio) 39
13 Western Mich. 23
40 Kent 7
363 **335**

Nickname: Eagles.
Stadium: Rynearson (1969), 30,200 capacity. Artificial turf.
Colors: Dark Green & White.
Conference: Mid-American.
SID: Jim Streeter, 313-487-0317.
AD: Tim Weiser.

EASTERN N.M.

Portales, NM 88130 II

Coach: Bud Elliott, Baker (Kan.) '53
Record: 28 Years, 149-138-9

1996 SCHEDULE

Stephen F. Austin ....*Aug. 29
N.M. Highlands ....*Sept. 7
Chadron St. ■ ....*Sept. 14
Western N.M. ■ ....*Sept. 21
Abilene Christian ....*Oct. 5
Angelo St. ....*Oct. 12
Tarleton St. ■ ....*Oct. 19
East Tex. St. ....Oct. 26
Tex. A&M-Kingsville ■ ....Nov. 2
West Tex. A&M ....Nov. 9
Central Okla. ■ ....Nov. 16

1995 RESULTS (6-4-1)

14 Montana 41
27 Fort Lewis 17
22 N.M. Highlands 9
9 Western N.M. 3
17 Abilene Christian 7
10 Angelo St. 10
28 Tarleton St. 7
14 East Tex. St. 28
14 Tex. A&M-Kingsville 33
10 West Tex. A&M 7
23 Central Okla. 33
188 **195**

Nickname: Greyhounds.
Stadium: Greyhound (1969), 6,500 capacity. Natural turf.
Colors: Silver & Green.
Conference: Lone Star.
SID: Judy Willson, 505-562-4309.
AD: B. B. Lees (Interim).

EASTERN WASH.

Cheney, WA 99004 ....I-AA

Coach: Mike Kramer, Idaho '77
Record: 2 Years, 7-15-0

1996 SCHEDULE

Weber St. ....*Sept. 7
Boise St. ....*Sept. 14
Southwest Tex. St. ■ ....*Sept. 21
Portland St. ■ ....*Sept. 28
Montana St. ■ ....Oct. 5
Cal St. Sacramento ....*Oct. 12
Montana ■ ....Oct. 19
Idaho St. ....Oct. 26
Idaho ....Nov. 2
Northern Ariz. ■ ....Nov. 9
Cal St. Northridge ....Nov. 16

1995 RESULTS (3-8-0)

34 Southwest Tex. St. 16
21 Cal St. Sacramento 18
6 Portland St. 14
30 Weber St. 40
7 Idaho St. 14
10 Idaho 37
16 Northern Ariz. 30
28 Montana St. 10
44 Boise St. 63
7 Montana 63
35 Cal Poly SLO 52
238 **357**

Nickname: Eagles.
Stadium: Woodward (1967), 6,000 capacity. Natural turf.
Colors: Red & White.
Conference: Big Sky.
SID: Dave Cook, 509-359-6334.
AD: John Johnson.

EDINBORO

Edinboro, PA 16444 II

Coach: Tom Hollman, Ohio Northern '68
Record: 12 Years, 85-35-3

1996 SCHEDULE

Hillsdale ....*Sept. 7
Carson-Newman ....*Sept. 14
Buffalo ....*Sept. 28
Shippensburg ■ ....Oct. 5
Calif. (Pa.) ....*Oct. 12
Slippery Rock ■ ....Oct. 19
Indiana (Pa.) ....Oct. 26
Cheyney ■ ....Nov. 2
Clarion ■ ....Nov. 9
Lock Haven ....Nov. 16

1995 RESULTS (9-1-0)

21 Hillsdale 14
7 Appalachian St. 44
26 Portland St. 7
52 Lock Haven 12
40 Shippensburg 7
31 Calif. (Pa.) 7
22 Slippery Rock 13
35 Indiana (Pa.) 18
42 Mansfield 0
28 Clarion 6
304 **128**

II Championship

12 New Haven 27

Nickname: Fighting Scots.
Stadium: Sox Harrison (1965), 5,000 capacity. Natural turf.
Colors: Red & White.
Conference: Pennsylvania State Athletic.
SID: Todd Jay, 814-732-2811.
AD: Jody Mooradian.

ELIZABETH CITY ST.

Elizabeth City, NC 27909 II

Coach: George Moody, Virginia St. '60
Record: 13 Years, 63-68-3

1996 SCHEDULE

Livingstone ....*Aug. 31
Fayetteville St. ■ ....Sept. 7
Winston-Salem ■ ....Sept. 14
Johnson Smith ....*Sept. 21
N.C. Central ....Sept. 28
Virginia Union ■ ....Oct. 5
Bowie St. ....Oct. 12
New Haven ■ ....Oct. 19
Norfolk St. ■ ....Oct. 26
Virginia St. ■ ....Nov. 9

1995 RESULTS (7-4-0)

16 Livingstone 6
22 Fayetteville St. 7
22 Winston-Salem 19
50 Norfolk St. 62
28 N.C. Central 27
48 Virginia Union 20
43 Bowie St. 7
3 Virginia St. 44
13 Hampton 36
43 Knoxville 34
8 Grambling 48
296 **310**

Nickname: Vikings.
Stadium: Roebuck, 6,500 capacity. Natural turf.
Colors: Royal Blue & White.
Conference: Central Intercollegiate Athletic Association.
SID: Kirt Campbell, 919-335-3278.
AD: Ed McLean.

ELMHURST

Elmhurst, IL 60126 III

Coach: Paul Krohn, Mankato St. '76
Record: 3 Years, 6-20-1

1996 SCHEDULE

Ill. Benedictine ■	Sept. 21
Alma	Sept. 28
Millikin	Oct. 5
Wheaton (Ill.)	Oct. 12
Carthage ■	Oct. 19
North Park	Oct. 26
North Central ■	Nov. 2
Augustana (Ill.)	Nov. 9
Ill. Wesleyan ■	Nov. 16

1995 RESULTS (2-7-0)

	Opponent	
6	Alma	29
7	Ill. Benedictine	8
3	North Central	21
38	North Park	6
19	Carthage	31
7	Augustana (Ill.)	35
7	Ill. Wesleyan	41
28	Millikin	21
0	Wheaton (Ill.)	42
115		**234**

Nickname: Bluejays.
Stadium: Langhorst (1920), 2,500 capacity. Natural turf.
Colors: Navy & White.
Conference: College Conf. of Illinois & Wisconsin.
SID: John Quigley, 708-617-3380.
AD: Chris Ragsdale.

ELON

Elon College, NC 27244 II

Coach: Al Seagraves, Shippensburg '75
(First year as head coach)

1996 SCHEDULE

Newberry ■	*Sept. 7
N.C. Central ■	*Sept. 14
West Ga.	*Sept. 21
Carson-Newman ■	Sept. 28
Lenoir-Rhyne	*Oct. 5
Mars Hill	Oct. 12
Presbyterian ■	Oct. 19
Catawba	Oct. 26
Gardner-Webb ■	Nov. 2
Western Caro.	Nov. 9
Wingate [Rockingham, N.C.]	Nov. 16

1995 RESULTS (4-7-0)

	Opponent	
16	West Ga.	35
12	N.C. Central	5
14	Western Caro.	36
6	Carson-Newman	29
31	Lenoir-Rhyne	0
31	Mars Hill	51
7	Presbyterian	13
6	Catawba	23
20	Gardner-Webb	38
20	Wofford	16
28	Wingate	22
191		**268**

Nickname: Fightin' Christians.
Stadium: Burlington Memorial (1949), 10,000 capacity. Natural turf.
Colors: Maroon & Gold.
Conference: South Atlantic.
SID: David Hibbard, 910-584-2316.
AD: Alan White.

EMORY & HENRY

Emory, VA 24327 III

Coach: Lou Wacker, Richmond '56
Record: 14 Years, 106-43-0

1996 SCHEDULE

Wash. & Jeff.	Sept. 14
Bridgewater (Va.) ■	Sept. 21
Davidson	Sept. 28
Millsaps ■	Oct. 5
Hampden-Sydney	Oct. 12
Randolph-Macon ■	Oct. 19
Guilford	Oct. 26
Ferrum ■	Nov. 2
Wash. & Lee	Nov. 9
Maryville (Tenn.) ■	Nov. 16

1995 RESULTS (9-1-0)

	Opponent	
35	Wash. & Lee	22
21	Bridgewater (Va.)	0
32	Davidson	0
34	Millsaps	17
17	Hampden-Sydney	0
17	Randolph-Macon	14
38	Guilford	6
29	Clinch Valley	20
14	Ferrum	7
3	Maryville (Tenn.)	6
240		**92**

III Championship

	Opponent	
16	Wash. & Jeff.	35

Nickname: Wasps.
Stadium: Fullerton Field, 5,500 capacity. Natural turf.
Colors: Blue & Gold.
Conference: Old Dominion Athletic.
SID: Nathan Graybeal, 540-944-6830.
AD: Lou Wacker.

EMPORIA ST.

Emporia, KS 66801 II

Coach: Manny Matsakis, Capital '84
Record: 1 Year, 5-6-0

1996 SCHEDULE

Wayne St. (Neb.) ■	*Aug. 31
Fort Hays St. ■	*Sept. 7
Mo. Southern St. ■	Sept. 21
Mo. Western St.	*Sept. 28
Washburn	*Oct. 5
Mo.-Rolla ■	Oct. 12
Southwest Baptist	Oct. 19
Pittsburg St. ■	Oct. 26
Northwest Mo. St.	Nov. 2
Truman St. ■	Nov. 9
Central Mo. St.	Nov. 16

1995 RESULTS (5-6-0)

	Opponent	
16	Fort Hays St.	43
66	Friends	0
26	Mo. Southern St.	21
28	Mo. Western St.	35
25	Washburn	24
45	Mo.-Rolla	14
30	Southwest Baptist	35
12	Pittsburg St.	48
13	Northwest Mo. St.	23
36	Truman St.	19
22	Central Mo. St.	52
319		**314**

Nickname: Hornets.
Stadium: Welch (1937), 7,000 capacity. Natural turf.
Colors: Black & Old Gold.
Conference: Mid-America Intercollegiate Athletic Assoc.
SID: J. D. Campbell, 316-341-5454.
AD: Bill Quayle.

EUREKA

Eureka, IL 61530 III

Coach: Nicholas Fletcher, Johns Hopkins '76
Record: 1 Year, 9-1-0

1996 SCHEDULE

Monmouth (Ill.) ■	Sept. 7
Coe ■	Sept. 14
Blackburn	Sept. 21
Concordia (Wis.) ■	Sept. 28
MacMurray ■	Oct. 5
Concordia (Ill.)	Oct. 12
McKendree	Oct. 26
Lakeland	Nov. 2
Greenville ■	Nov. 9

1995 RESULTS (9-1-0)

	Opponent	
31	Blackburn	12
40	Monmouth (Ill.)	33
50	Lawrence	53
21	Greenville	14
19	Concordia (Wis.)	17
60	Concordia (Ill.)	13
24	Dubuque	22
33	Quincy	13
47	Lakeland	45
18	MacMurray	6
343		**228**

Nickname: Red Devils.
Stadium: McKinzie (1913), 3,000 capacity. Natural turf.
Colors: Maroon & Gold.
Conference: Division III Independents.
SID: Shellie Schwanke, 309-467-6370.
AD: Warner McCollum.

EVANSVILLE

Evansville, IN 47722 .... I-AA

Coach: Robin Cooper, Ill. Wesleyan '75
Record: 8 Years, 46-29-0

1996 SCHEDULE

Cumberland (Tenn.)	Sept. 14
Quincy	Sept. 21
Dayton ■	Oct. 5
Drake ■	Oct. 12
San Diego	*Oct. 19
Valparaiso ■	Oct. 26
Butler	Nov. 2
Ky. Wesleyan	Nov. 9
Morehead St. ■	Nov. 16

1995 RESULTS (5-5-0)

	Opponent	
42	Ky. Wesleyan	12
27	Cumberland (Tenn.)	7
28	Greenville	0
14	Thomas More	16
6	Drake	23
17	San Diego	19
7	Valparaiso	6
13	Butler	14
10	Dayton	36
18	Aurora	6
182		**139**

Nickname: Purple Aces.
Stadium: Arad McCutchan (1984), 3,000 capacity. Natural turf.
Colors: Purple & White.
Conference: Pioneer Football League.
SID: Bob Boxell, 812-479-2350.
AD: Jim Byers.

FAIRFIELD

Fairfield, CT 06430 .... I-AA

Coach: Kevin Kiesel, Gettysburg '81
Record: 3 Years, 15-15-1

1996 SCHEDULE

Central Conn. St. ■	*Sept. 14
Georgetown ■	Sept. 21
St. John's (N.Y.)	*Sept. 27
St. Peter's ■	*Oct. 5
Marist	Oct. 12
Canisius ■	Oct. 19
Siena	Oct. 26
Duquesne	Nov. 2
Iona ■	*Nov. 9

1995 RESULTS

None—1996 is first year of football

Nickname: Stags.
Stadium: Alumni, 3,000 capacity. Natural turf.
Color: Cardinal Red.
Conference: Metro Atlantic.
SID: Victor D'Ascenzo, 203-254-4000.
AD: Eugene P. Doris.

FDU-MADISON

Madison, NJ 07940 III

Coach: Bill Klika, Colgate '67
Record: 22 Years, 62-129-1

1996 SCHEDULE

Johns Hopkins ■ ....*Sept. 13
Widener....Sept. 21
Wilkes ■....*Sept. 27
Lycoming....Oct. 5
Delaware Valley ■....Oct. 12
Catholic....Oct. 19
Albright....Oct. 26
Moravian....Nov. 2
King's (Pa.) ■....*Nov. 8
Juniata ■....Nov. 16

1995 RESULTS (4-5-0)

20 Johns Hopkins....17
38 Widener....36
15 Wilkes....30
20 Lycoming....17
27 Delaware Valley....24
10 Albright....19
6 Moravian....17
40 King's (Pa.)....45
7 Juniata....14
183 219

Nickname: Devils.
Stadium: Devils (1973), 4,000 capacity. Natural turf.
Colors: Black, Blue & White.
Conference: Middle Atlantic.
SID: Alan Wickstrom, 201-443-8965.
AD: Bill Klika.

FAIRMONT ST.

Fairmont, WV 26554....II

Coach: Doug Sams, Oregon St. '78
Record: 5 Years, 21-29-0

1996 SCHEDULE

Indiana (Pa.) ■....Sept. 7
Calif. (Pa.) ■....Sept. 14
Slippery Rock....Sept. 21
Concord (W.Va.)....Sept. 28
West Va. St. ■....Oct. 5
West Va. Tech ■....Oct. 12
Glenville St....Oct. 19
Shepherd....Oct. 26
West Liberty St. ■....Nov. 2
West Va. Wesleyan....Nov. 9

1995 RESULTS (6-4-0)

26 Calif. (Pa.)....28
13 Clarion....48
55 Concord (W.Va.)....6
46 West Va. St....32
43 West Va. Tech....27
6 Glenville St....28
36 Shepherd....29
28 West Liberty St....35
48 West Va. Wesleyan....24
9 Tiffin....6
310 263

Nickname: Falcons.
Stadium: Rosier Field (1929), 6,000 capacity. Natural turf.
Colors: Maroon & White.
Conference: West Virginia Intercollegiate Athletic.
SID: Jim Brinkman, 304-367-4264.
AD: Colin Cameron.

FAYETTEVILLE ST.

Fayetteville, NC 28301....II

Coach: Jerome Harper, Alabama St. '74
Record: 3 Years, 16-21-4

1996 SCHEDULE

Knoxville ■....*Aug. 31
Elizabeth City St....Sept. 7
North Caro. A&T....Sept. 14
Virginia Union....Sept. 21
Winston-Salem....*Sept. 28
N.C. Central ■....*Oct. 5
Virginia St. ■....*Oct. 12
Johnson Smith....Oct. 19
Bowie St. ■....Oct. 26
Livingstone ■....Nov. 2

1995 RESULTS (1-7-2)

8 Knoxville....13
7 Elizabeth City St....22
21 Virginia Union....21
17 Winston-Salem....17
0 N.C. Central....45
0 Virginia St....48
9 Johnson Smith....14
6 Bowie St....3
21 Livingstone....39
7 Hampton....28
96 250

Nickname: Broncos.
Stadium: Jeralds Athletic Complex (1993), 6,100 capacity. Natural turf.
Colors: White & Royal Blue.
Conference: Central Intercollegiate Athletic Association.
SID: Marion Crowe Jr., 910-486-1349.
AD: Ralph Burns.

FERRIS ST.

Big Rapids, MI 49307....II

Coach: Jeff Pierce, Ferris St. '79
Record: 1 Year, 12-1-0

1996 SCHEDULE

Ashland....*Aug. 29
Indianapolis ■....Sept. 7
Hillsdale ■....*Sept. 14
Grand Valley St....Sept. 21
Northern Mich. ■....Sept. 28
Wayne St. (Mich.)....Oct. 5
Northwood ■....Oct. 12
Michigan Tech....Oct. 19
Saginaw Valley....Nov. 2
St. Francis (Ill.)....Nov. 9

1995 RESULTS (10-0-0)

20 Ashland....13
50 Indianapolis....0
17 Hillsdale....10
30 Grand Valley St....21
41 Northern Mich....27
39 Wayne St. (Mich.)....30
56 Northwood....14
38 Michigan Tech....17
43 St. Joseph's (Ind.)....26
46 Saginaw Valley....42
380 200

II Championship

36 Millersville....26
17 New Haven....9
7 North Ala....45

Nickname: Bulldogs.
Stadium: Top Taggart Field (1957), 9,100 capacity. Natural turf.
Colors: Crimson & Gold.
Conference: Midwest Intercollegiate.
SID: Joe Gorby, 616-592-2336.
AD: Larry Marfise.

FERRUM

Ferrum, VA 24088....III

Coach: Dave Davis, Elon '71
Record: 2 Years, 10-9-0

1996 SCHEDULE

Wesley....Sept. 6
Clinch Valley ■....Sept. 14
Rowan ■....Sept. 21
Newport News App....Oct. 5
Guilford....Oct. 12
Chowan ■....Oct. 19
Methodist....Oct. 26
Emory & Henry....Nov. 2
Frostburg St. ■....Nov. 9

1995 RESULTS (6-4-0)

0 Rowan....31
17 West Va. Tech....13
0 Cortland St....13
15 Charleston So....6
36 Newport News App....0
30 Guilford....24
29 Chowan....9
20 Methodist....13
6 Frostburg St....21
7 Emory & Henry....14
160 144

Nickname: Panthers.
Stadium: Adams (1970), 5,500 capacity. Natural turf.
Colors: Black & Gold.
Conference: Division III Independents.
SID: Gary Holden, 540-365-4306.
AD: Ted Kinder.

FITCHBURG ST.

Fitchburg, MA 01420....III

Coach: Chris Nugal, Worcester St. '91
(First year as head coach)

1996 SCHEDULE

Curry....Sept. 14
Framingham St. ■....Sept. 21
Westfield St....*Sept. 27
Bri'water (Mass.) ■....Oct. 5
Worcester St....Oct. 12
Mass. Maritime ■....Oct. 19
Mass.-Dartmouth....Oct. 26
Maine Maritime ■....Nov. 2
Mass.-Boston....Nov. 9

1995 RESULTS (1-8-0)

28 Curry....38
0 Framingham St....20
17 Westfield St....41
18 Bri'water (Mass.)....56
15 Worcester St....37
7 Mass. Maritime....50
0 Mass.-Dartmouth....23
6 Maine Maritime....51
14 Mass.-Boston....7
105 323

Nickname: Falcons.
Stadium: Robert Elliot (1984), 1,200 capacity. Natural turf.
Colors: Green, Gold & White.
Conference: New England.
SID: David Marsh, 508-665-3343.
AD: Sue Lauder.

FLORIDA

Gainesville, FL 32604....I-A

Coach: Steve Spurrier, Florida '67
Record: 9 Years, 81-26-2

1996 SCHEDULE

Southwestern La. ■....*Aug. 31
Ga. Southern ■....*Sept. 7
Tennessee....Sept. 21
Kentucky ■....Sept. 28
Arkansas....Oct. 5
LSU ■....Oct. 12
Auburn ■....Oct. 19
Georgia [Jacksonville, Fla.]....Nov. 2
Vanderbilt....Nov. 9
South Caro. ■....Nov. 16
Florida St....Nov. 30

1995 RESULTS (12-0-0)

45 Houston....21
42 Kentucky....7
62 Tennessee....37
28 Mississippi....10
28 LSU....10
49 Auburn....38
52 Georgia....17
58 Northern Ill....20
63 South Caro....7
38 Vanderbilt....7
35 Florida St....24
34 Arkansas....3
534 201

SCHEDULES/RESULTS

Fiesta Bowl

24 Nebraska..62

Nickname: Gators.
Stadium: Florida Field (1929), 83,000 capacity. Natural turf.
Colors: Blue & Orange.
Conference: Southeastern.
SID: John Humenik, 352-375-4683.
AD: Jeremy Foley.

FLORIDA A&M

Tallahassee, FL 32307 ....I-AA

Coach: Billy Joe, Villanova '63
Record: 22 Years, 184-67-4

1996 SCHEDULE

Tennessee St. ....*Aug. 31
Tuskegee ■...*Sept. 7
Jackson St..*Sept. 21
Howard ■...*Sept. 28
Hampton [Indianapolis, Ind.] ....Oct. 5
North Caro. A&T ■...Oct. 12
Delaware St...Oct. 19
Morgan St. ■..Nov. 2
Southern-B.R..*Nov. 9
South Caro. St. [Atlanta, Ga.] ....Nov. 16
Bethune-Cookman [Tampa, Fla.] ....Nov. 23

1995 RESULTS (9-2-0)

28 Tuskegee...16
3 Miami (Fla.) 49
15 Jackson St. 12
24 Tennessee St...7
29 Howard 18
20 North Caro. A&T...3
24 Delaware St. 21
47 Morgan St..9
38 Southern-B.R. 52
28 South Caro. St. 21
43 Bethune-Cookman 0
299 **208**

Heritage Bowl

25 Southern-B.R. 30

Nickname: Rattlers.
Stadium: Bragg Memorial (1957), 25,500 capacity. Natural turf.
Colors: Orange & Green.
Conference: Mid-Eastern Athletic.
SID: Alvin Hollins, 904-599-3200.
AD: Ken Riley.

FLORIDA ST.

Tallahassee, FL 32306...............................I-A

Coach: Bobby Bowden, Samford '53
Record: 30 Years, 259-81-4

1996 SCHEDULE

Duke ■...Sept. 7
North Caro. St. ....*Sept. 19
North Caro. ■ ....Sept. 28
Clemson ■ ....*Oct. 5
Miami (Fla.) ....Oct. 12
Virginia ■ ....Oct. 26
Georgia Tech..*Nov. 2
Wake Forest [Orlando, Fla.] ....Nov. 9
Southern Miss. ■..Nov. 16
Maryland [Fort Lauderdale, Fla.]......................Nov. 23
Florida ■..Nov. 30

1995 RESULTS (9-2-0)

70 Duke...26
45 Clemson 26
77 North Caro. St. 17
46 Central Fla. 14
41 Miami (Fla.) 17
72 Wake Forest 13
42 Georgia Tech 10
28 Virginia..33
28 North Caro. 12
59 Maryland 17
24 Florida 35
532 **220**

Orange Bowl

31 Notre Dame 26

Nickname: Seminoles.
Stadium: Doak S. Campbell (1950), 77,500 capacity. Natural turf.
Colors: Garnet & Gold.
Conference: Atlantic Coast.
SID: Rob Wilson, 904-644-1403.
AD: Dave Hart Jr.

FORDHAM

Bronx, NY 10458..................................I-AA

Coach: Nick Quartaro, Iowa '77
Record: 4 Years, 16-25-1

1996 SCHEDULE

Maine ■ ....Sept. 7
Lehigh ....Sept. 14
Villanova ....Sept. 21
Columbia ■..Sept. 28
Dartmouth..Oct. 5
Lafayette ■ ....Oct. 12
Brown ....Oct. 19
Georgetown ■...Oct. 26
Holy Cross ■ ....Nov. 2
Colgate ■ ....Nov. 9
Bucknell...Nov. 16

1995 RESULTS (4-6-1)

13 Buffalo 49
46 Marist..0
21 Bucknell 28
14 Dartmouth 34
24 Harvard..21
34 Colgate...14
15 Hofstra...36
3 Richmond 3
17 Holy Cross 10
0 Lehigh...17
21 Lafayette 24
208 **236**

Nickname: Rams.
Stadium: Jack Coffey Field (1930), 7,000 capacity. Natural turf.
Colors: Maroon & White.
Conference: Patriot League.
SID: Bill Holtz, 718-817-4240.
AD: Frank McLaughlin.

FORT HAYS ST.

Hays, KS 67601 II

Coach: Bob Cortese, Colorado '67
Record: 16 Years, 127-45-6

1996 SCHEDULE

Emporia St...*Sept. 7
Washburn ■..*Sept. 14
Fort Lewis ■...Sept. 21
Mesa St. ■ ....*Oct. 5
Neb.-Kearney ....Oct. 12
Western St..Oct. 19
N.M. Highlands ■ ....Oct. 26
Chadron St. ■ ....Nov. 2
Adams St...Nov. 9
Colorado Mines...Nov. 16

1995 RESULTS (8-1-2)

43 Emporia St. 16
16 Pittsburg St. 16
0 Central Okla. 28
31 Neb.-Kearney 6
35 Fort Lewis 27
51 N.M. Highlands 7
62 Mesa St. 13
50 Adams St. 47
56 Colorado Mines 17
47 Chadron St. 5
27 Western St. 27
418 **209**

II Championship

28 Tex. A&M-Kingsville 59

Nickname: Tigers.
Stadium: Lewis Field (1936), 7,000 capacity. Artificial turf.
Colors: Black & Gold.
Conference: Rocky Mountain Athletic.
SID: Jack Kuestermeyer, 913-628-5903.
AD: Tom Spicer.

FORT LEWIS

Durango, CO 81301 II

Coach: Todd Wash, North Dak. St. '94
(First year as head coach)

1996 SCHEDULE

Chadron St. [Aurora, Colo.]..............................Sept. 7
Montana Tech ■..Sept. 14
Fort Hays St..Sept. 21
Colorado Mines ■ ....Sept. 28
Neb.-Kearney ■...Oct. 5
N.M. Highlands ....Oct. 19
Mesa St. ....*Oct. 26
Adams St. ■...Nov. 2
Western St. ■ ....Nov. 9
Chadron St. ....Nov. 16

1995 RESULTS (4-6-0)

17 Eastern N.M..27
7 West Tex. A&M 44
31 Montana Tech 12
27 Fort Hays St. 35
20 Mesa St. 17
8 Western St. 26
16 N.M. Highlands 39
41 Adams St. 16
39 Colorado Mines 34
3 Chadron St. 31
209 **281**

Nickname: Skyhawks.
Stadium: Ray Dennison Memorial (1958), 4,000 capacity. Natural turf.
Colors: Blue & Gold.
Conference: Rocky Mountain Athletic.
SID: Chris Aaland, 970-247-7441.
AD: Daryl Leonard.

FORT VALLEY ST.

Fort Valley, GA 31030 II

Coach: Douglas Porter, Xavier (La.) '52
Record: 26 Years, 149-106-5

1996 SCHEDULE

Winston-Salem ■...*Aug. 31
Morehouse ■...*Sept. 7
Gardner-Webb ....*Sept. 14
Morris Brown ....*Sept. 21
Kentucky St. ■ ....*Sept. 28
Clark Atlanta ....*Oct. 5
Miles..Oct. 12
Alabama A&M ■..Oct. 19
Tuskegee ■ ....Oct. 26
Savannah St. ....Nov. 2
Albany St. (Ga.) [Columbus, Ga.]......................Nov. 9

1995 RESULTS (3-8-0)

6 Winston-Salem 33
12 Morehouse...18
0 Gardner-Webb..42
13 Morris Brown 0
12 Kentucky St. 17
21 Clark Atlanta 12
8 Miles 19
20 Alabama A&M...24
27 Tuskegee...28
7 Savannah St...28
16 Albany St. (Ga.) 12
142 **233**

Nickname: Wildcats.
Stadium: Wildcat (1957), 7,500 capacity. Natural turf.
Colors: Royal Blue & Old Gold.
Conference: Southern Intercollegiate Athletic.
SID: Russell Boone Jr., 912-825-6437.
AD: Douglas Porter.

FRAMINGHAM ST.

Framingham, MA 01701 III

Coach: Michael Strachan, Swedish Sports '90
Record: 1 Year, 2-7-0

1996 SCHEDULE

Curry ....Sept. 7
Fitchburg St. ....Sept. 21
Westfield St. ■ ....Oct. 5
Bri'water (Mass.) ....Oct. 12
Worcester St. ■ ....Oct. 19
Mass. Maritime ....Oct. 26
Mass.-Dartmouth ■ ....Nov. 2
Maine Maritime ....Nov. 9
Mass.-Boston ■ ....Nov. 16

1995 RESULTS (2-7-0)

0 Wesley 55
20 Fitchburg St. 0
10 Westfield St. 7
13 Bri'water (Mass.) 35
8 Worcester St. 31
6 Mass. Maritime 30
6 Mass.-Dartmouth 24
8 Maine Maritime 33
7 Mass.-Boston 8
78 **223**

Nickname: Rams.
Stadium: Maple Street Field, 1,500 capacity. Natural turf.
Colors: Black & Gold.
Conference: New England.
SID: John White, 508-626-4612.
AD: Lawrence Boyd.

FRANKLIN

Franklin, IN 46131 III

Coach: Mike McClure, Franklin '75
Record: 7 Years, 29-39-1

1996 SCHEDULE

Mt. St. Joseph ■ ....Sept. 7
Kalamazoo ....Sept. 21
Lakeland ■ ....Sept. 28
Olivet ■ ....Oct. 5
DePauw ■ ....Oct. 12
Anderson (Ind.) ....Oct. 19
Wabash ■ ....Oct. 26
Rose-Hulman ■ ....Nov. 2
Manchester ....Nov. 9
Hanover ....Nov. 16

1995 RESULTS (6-4-0)

28 Millikin 31
16 Kalamazoo 15
29 Alma 25
23 DePauw 15
32 Anderson (Ind.) 28
0 Wabash 48
27 Rose-Hulman 29
28 Manchester 27
50 MacMurray 18
22 Hanover 26
255 **262**

Nickname: Grizzlies.
Stadium: Goodell Field (1889), 2,000 capacity. Natural turf.
Colors: Old Gold & Navy Blue.
Conference: Indiana Collegiate Athletic.
SID: Kevin Elixman, 317-738-8184.
AD: Kerry Prather.

FRANK. & MARSH.

Lancaster, PA 17604 III

Coach: Tom Gilburg, Syracuse '61
Record: 21 Years, 136-65-2

1996 SCHEDULE

Carnegie Mellon ■ ....Sept. 7
Randolph-Macon ....Sept. 14
Ursinus ■ ....Sept. 21
Muhlenberg ....Sept. 28
Dickinson ....Oct. 12
Hobart ■ ....Oct. 19
Western Md. ■ ....Oct. 26
Swarthmore ....Nov. 2
Johns Hopkins ■ ....Nov. 9
Gettysburg ....Nov. 16

1995 RESULTS (7-3-0)

8 Carnegie Mellon 27
28 Randolph-Macon 27
14 Ursinus 0
38 Muhlenberg 10
21 Dickinson 28
7 Georgetown 31
24 Western Md. 7
42 Swarthmore 22
27 Johns Hopkins 22
14 Gettysburg 10
223 **184**

Nickname: Diplomats.
Stadium: Sponaugle-Williamson (1920), 4,000 capacity. Natural turf.
Colors: Blue & White.
Conference: Centennial.
SID: Tom Byrnes, 717-291-3838.
AD: William A. Marshall.

FRESNO ST.

Fresno, CA 93740 ....I-A

Coach: Jim Sweeney, Portland '51
Record: 31 Years, 196-147-4

1996 SCHEDULE

Oregon ■ ....*Aug. 31
Auburn ....*Sept. 7
Utah ....*Sept. 21
Hawaii ■ ....*Sept. 28
San Jose St. ■ ....*Oct. 12
Wyoming ....Oct. 19
UNLV ....Oct. 26
Boise St. ■ ....*Nov. 2
Colorado St. ■ ....*Nov. 9
Air Force ■ ....Nov. 16
San Diego St. ....*Nov. 23

1995 RESULTS (5-7-0)

31 Northeast La. 17
25 California 24
56 Pacific (Cal.) 24
21 Utah 25
21 UCLA 45
51 New Mexico 34
24 San Diego St. 48
20 Air Force 31
37 Hawaii 42
47 UTEP 14
10 Wyoming 38
28 Brigham Young 45
371 **387**

Nickname: Bulldogs.
Stadium: Bulldog (1980), 41,031 capacity. Natural turf.
Colors: Cardinal & Blue.
Conference: Western Athletic.
SID: Dave Haglund, 209-278-2509.
AD: Al Bohl.

FROSTBURG ST.

Frostburg, MD 21532 III

Coach: Ed Sweeney, LIU-C.W. Post '71
Record: 11 Years, 62-49-4

1996 SCHEDULE

North Greenville ■ ....Sept. 14
Central Conn. St. ■ ....Sept. 21
Salisbury St. ■ ....Sept. 28
Chowan ....Oct. 5
Wesley ....Oct. 12
Brockport St. ■ ....Oct. 19
Waynesburg ....Oct. 26
Sue Bennett ■ ....Nov. 2
Ferrum ....Nov. 9
Methodist ■ ....Nov. 16

1995 RESULTS (6-4-0)

30 Bri'water (Mass.) 12
21 Mercyhurst 7
28 Salisbury St. 35
20 Chowan 9
24 Newport News App. 33
7 Brockport St. 14
14 Bridgewater (Va.) 10
21 Ferrum 6
14 Waynesburg 20
7 Methodist 0
186 **146**

Nickname: Bobcats.
Stadium: Bobcat (1974), 4,000 capacity. Natural turf.
Colors: Red, White & Black.
Conference: Division III Independents.
SID: Jeffrey P. Krone, 301-687-4371.
AD: Loyal Park.

FURMAN

Greenville, SC 29613 ....I-AA

Coach: Bobby Johnson, Clemson '73
Record: 2 Years, 9-13-0

1996 SCHEDULE

Clemson ....Sept. 7
South Caro. St. ■ ....Sept. 14
Wofford ■ ....Sept. 21
Va. Military ....Sept. 28
Western Caro. ■ ....Oct. 5
Appalachian St. ....Oct. 12
Citadel ■ ....Oct. 19
East Tenn. St. ....Oct. 26
Ga. Southern ■ ....Nov. 9
Marshall ....Nov. 16
Tenn.-Chatt. ■ ....Nov. 23

1995 RESULTS (6-5-0)

7 Georgia Tech 51
21 South Caro. St. 27
38 Wofford 0
55 Va. Military 24
31 Western Caro. 21
28 Appalachian St. 41
24 Citadel 3
21 East Tenn. St. 15
20 Ga. Southern 27
6 Marshall 31
23 Tenn.-Chatt. 21
274 **261**

Nickname: Paladins.
Stadium: Paladin (1981), 16,000 capacity. Natural turf.
Colors: Purple & White.
Conference: Southern.
SID: Hunter Reid, 864-294-2061.
AD: John Block.

GANNON

Erie, PA 16541 II

Coach: Tom Herman, Edinboro '72
Record: 7 Years, 34-30-2

1996 SCHEDULE

John Carroll ■ ....*Sept. 6
Canisius ■ ....Sept. 14
St. Francis (Pa.) ■ ....Sept. 21
Duquesne ....Sept. 28
Robert Morris ....Oct. 5
Mercyhurst ....Oct. 12
Pace ■ ....Oct. 19
Albany (N.Y.) ....*Oct. 26
Thiel ■ ....*Nov. 2
St. John Fisher ....Nov. 9

1995 RESULTS (7-3-0)

29 St. Francis (Pa.) 14
42 Capital 9
23 Rochester 35
20 Canisius 12
15 Duquesne 44
30 Robert Morris 29
14 Waynesburg 10
21 Thiel 0

6 Mercyhurst 9
16 Bethany (W.Va.) 14
216 **176**

Nickname: Golden Knights.
Stadium: Erie Veterans Memorial (1958), 10,500 capacity. Artificial turf.
Colors: Maroon & Gold.
Conference: Eastern Football.
SID: Bob Shreve, 814-871-7418.
AD: Richard Dunford.

GARDNER-WEBB

Boiling Springs, NC 28017 II

Coach: Woody Fish, Gardner-Webb '73
Record: 12 Years, 70-62-1

1996 SCHEDULE

Valdosta St. ■ ....*Aug. 31
N.C. Central ■ ....*Sept. 7
Fort Valley St. ■ ....*Sept. 14
Newberry ....*Sept. 28
Wingate ■ ....Oct. 5
Lenoir-Rhyne ....*Oct. 12
Catawba ■ ....Oct. 19
Carson-Newman ....Oct. 26
Elon ....Nov. 2
Presbyterian ....Nov. 9
Mars Hill ■ ....Nov. 16

1995 RESULTS (6-4-0)

21 Valdosta St. 34
42 Fort Valley St. 0
21 Newberry 16
14 Wingate 10
30 Lenoir-Rhyne 13
19 Catawba 21
10 Carson-Newman 38
38 Elon 20
20 Presbyterian 34
14 Mars Hill 6
229 **192**

Nickname: Bulldogs.
Stadium: Spangler (1969), 5,000 capacity. Natural turf.
Colors: Scarlet, White & Black.
Conference: South Atlantic.
SID: Mark Wilson, 704-434-4355.
AD: Ozzie McFarland.

GEORGETOWN

Washington, DC 20057 ....I-AA

Coach: Bob Benson, Vermont '86
Record: 3 Years, 15-12-0

1996 SCHEDULE

Fairfield ....Sept. 21
Siena ....Sept. 28
Marist ■ ....Oct. 5
Iona ■ ....Oct. 12
Duquesne ....Oct. 19
Fordham ....Oct. 26
Canisius ■ ....Nov. 2
St. John's (N.Y.) ....*Nov. 8
St. Peter's ■ ....Nov. 16
Holy Cross ■ ....Nov. 23

1995 RESULTS (6-3-0)

27 Iona 14
7 Duquesne 13
7 Canisius 13
41 St. John's (N.Y.) 13
31 Frank. & Marsh. 7
3 Johns Hopkins 7
14 Marist 13
33 Siena 19
29 St. Peter's 0
192 **99**

Nickname: Hoyas.
Stadium: Kehoe Field (1979), 2,400 capacity. Artificial turf.
Colors: Blue & Gray.
Conference: Metro Atlantic.
SID: Bill Hurd, 202-687-2492.
AD: Joseph C. Lang.

GEORGIA

Athens, GA 30602 ....I-A

Coach: Jim Donnan, North Caro. St. '69
Record: 6 Years, 64-21-0

1996 SCHEDULE

Southern Miss. ■ ....Aug. 31
South Caro. ....*Sept. 14
Texas Tech ■ ....Sept. 21
Mississippi St. ....*Oct. 5
Tennessee ■ ....Oct. 12
Vanderbilt ■ ....Oct. 19
Kentucky ....*Oct. 26
Florida [Jacksonville, Fla.] ....Nov. 2
Auburn ....Nov. 16
Mississippi ■ ....Nov. 23
Georgia Tech ■ ....Nov. 30

1995 RESULTS (6-5-0)

42 South Caro. 23
27 Tennessee 30
40 New Mexico St. 13
10 Mississippi 18
0 Alabama 31
19 Clemson 17
17 Vanderbilt 6
12 Kentucky 3
17 Florida 52
31 Auburn 37
18 Georgia Tech 17
233 **247**

Peach Bowl

27 Virginia 34

Nickname: Bulldogs.
Stadium: Sanford (1929), 86,117 capacity. Natural turf.
Colors: Red & Black.
Conference: Southeastern.
SID: Claude Felton, 706-542-1621.
AD: Vince Dooley.

GA. SOUTHERN

Statesboro, GA 30460 ....I-AA

Coach: Frank Ellwood, Ohio St. '57
Record: 4 Years, 9-35-0

1996 SCHEDULE

South Caro. St. ....*Aug. 31
Florida ....*Sept. 7
Marshall ■ ....Sept. 21
Tenn.-Chatt. ....Sept. 28
Va. Military ■ ....Oct. 5
Western Caro. ....Oct. 12
Appalachian St. ■ ....Oct. 19
Citadel ....Oct. 26
East Tenn. St. ■ ....Nov. 2
Furman ....Nov. 9
Liberty ■ ....Nov. 16

1995 RESULTS (8-3-0)

27 South Caro. St. 12
34 Middle Tenn. St. 26
7 Marshall 37
35 Tenn.-Chatt. 9
42 Western Caro. 0
17 Appalachian St. 27
27 Citadel 0
16 East Tenn. St. 21
27 Furman 20
7 Liberty 6
31 Va. Military 13
270 **171**

I-AA Championship

24 Troy St. 21
0 Montana 45

Nickname: Eagles.
Stadium: Paulson (1984), 18,000 capacity. Natural turf.
Colors: Blue & White.
Conference: Southern.
SID: Matt Rogers, 912-681-5239.
AD: Sam Baker.

GEORGIA TECH

Atlanta, GA 30332 ....I-A

Coach: George O'Leary, New Hampshire '68
Record: 2 Years, 6-8-0

1996 SCHEDULE

North Caro. St. ....Sept. 7
Wake Forest ■ ....Sept. 14
North Caro. ....Sept. 21
Duke ■ ....*Sept. 26
Virginia ■ ....Oct. 5
Clemson ....Oct. 19
Central Fla. ■ ....Oct. 26
Florida St. ■ ....*Nov. 2
Maryland ....*Nov. 14
Navy ■ ....Nov. 23
Georgia ....Nov. 30

1995 RESULTS (6-5-0)

51 Furman 7
19 Arizona 20
14 Virginia 41
31 Maryland 3
37 Duke 21
27 North Caro. 25
10 Florida St. 42
3 Clemson 24
24 Wake Forest 23
27 North Caro. St. 19
17 Georgia 18
260 **243**

Nickname: Yellow Jackets.
Stadium: Bobby Dodd/Grant Field (1913), 46,000 capacity. Natural turf.
Colors: Old Gold & White.
Conference: Atlantic Coast.
SID: Mike Finn, 404-894-5445.
AD: Homer Rice.

GETTYSBURG

Gettysburg, PA 17325 III

Coach: Barry Streeter, Lebanon Valley '71
Record: 18 Years, 105-73-5

1996 SCHEDULE

Hampden-Sydney ■ ....Sept. 14
Western Md. ....Sept. 21
Swarthmore ■ ....Sept. 28
Johns Hopkins ....*Oct. 4
Randolph-Macon ....Oct. 12
Ursinus ■ ....Oct. 19
Muhlenberg ....Oct. 26
Merchant Marine ....Nov. 2
Dickinson ....Nov. 9
Frank. & Marsh. ■ ....Nov. 16

1995 RESULTS (5-4-1)

25 Hampden-Sydney 7
17 Western Md. 21
19 Swarthmore 15
16 Johns Hopkins 35
27 Randolph-Macon 23
7 Ursinus 3
28 Muhlenberg 16
0 Merchant Marine 25
7 Dickinson 7
10 Frank. & Marsh. 14
156 **166**

Nickname: Bullets.
Stadium: Musselman (1965), 6,176 capacity. Natural turf.
Colors: Orange & Blue.
Conference: Centennial.
SID: Robert Kenworthy, 717-337-6527.
AD: Chuck Winters.

GLENVILLE ST.

Glenville, WV 26351 II

Coach: Rich Rodriquez, West Va. '85
Record: 7 Years, 39-32-2

1996 SCHEDULE

Livingstone....Sept. 7
East Tenn. St....*Sept. 14
Clarion....Sept. 21
West Va. St. ■....*Sept. 28
West Liberty St....*Oct. 5
West Va. Wesleyan....Oct. 12
Fairmont St. ■....Oct. 19
Concord (W.Va.)....Oct. 26
West Va. Tech ■....Nov. 2
Shepherd ■....Nov. 9

1995 RESULTS (8-2-0)

31 Calif. (Pa.)....29
14 Indiana St....41
31 West Va. St....13
37 West Liberty St....7
14 West Va. Wesleyan....17
28 Fairmont St....6
54 Concord (W.Va.)....0
56 West Va. Tech....0
40 Shepherd....10
40 Livingstone....0
345 **123**

Nickname: Pioneers.
Stadium: Pioneer (1977), 5,000 capacity. Natural turf.
Colors: Blue & White.
Conference: West Virginia Intercollegiate Athletic.
SID: Rick Conklin, 304-462-4102.
AD: Rich Rodriquez.

GRAMBLING

Grambling, LA 71245....I-AA

Coach: Eddie Robinson, Leland '41
Record: 53 Years, 402-149-15

1996 SCHEDULE

Alcorn St. ■....*Sept. 7
Central St. [Pontiac, Mich.]....Sept. 14
Langston ■....*Sept. 21
Prairie View....Sept. 28
Mississippi Val....Oct. 12
Ark.-Pine Bluff [Shreveport, La.]....*Oct. 19
Jackson St. ■....Oct. 26
Texas Southern....Nov. 2
Alabama St. ■....Nov. 9
North Caro. A&T....Nov. 16
Southern-B.R. [New Orleans, La.]....Nov. 30

1995 RESULTS (5-6-0)

39 Alcorn St....17
7 Hampton....16
14 Central St....16
64 Prairie View....0
42 Mississippi Val....6
14 Ark.-Pine Bluff....17
28 Jackson St....29
54 Texas Southern....15
16 Alabama St....37
48 Elizabeth City St....8
14 Southern-B.R....30
340 **191**

Nickname: Tigers.
Stadium: Robinson (1983), 19,600 capacity. Natural turf.
Colors: Black & Gold.
Conference: Southwestern Athletic.
SID: Vernon Cheek, 318-274-2479.
AD: Fred Hobdy.

GRAND VALLEY ST.

Allendale, MI 49401....II

Coach: Brian Kelly, Assumption '83
Record: 5 Years, 39-16-2

1996 SCHEDULE

Southwest Tex. St....*Aug. 31
St. Francis (Ill.) ■....Sept. 7
Ashland....Sept. 14
Ferris St. ■....Sept. 21
Wayne St. (Mich.) ■....Sept. 28
Hillsdale....Oct. 5
Michigan Tech ■....Oct. 12
Northern Mich....Oct. 19
Saginaw Valley ■....Oct. 26
Northwood....Nov. 2
Indianapolis....Nov. 16

1995 RESULTS (8-3-0)

25 Indiana (Pa.)....28
56 Indianapolis....0
42 St. Francis (Ill.)....0
52 Ashland....17
21 Ferris St....30
42 Wayne St. (Mich.)....10
25 Hillsdale....20
54 Michigan Tech....52
26 Northern Mich....23
21 Saginaw Valley....24
43 Northwood....7
407 **211**

Nickname: Lakers.
Stadium: Arend D. Lubbers (1979), 4,146 capacity. Natural turf.
Colors: Blue, Black & White.
Conference: Midwest Intercollegiate.
SID: Don Thomas, 616-895-3275.
AD: Tim Selgo.

GRINNELL

Grinnell, IA 50112....III

Coach: Greg Wallace, Missouri Valley '70
Record: 8 Years, 15-55-1

1996 SCHEDULE

Pomona-Pitzer....*Sept. 7
Principia ■....Sept. 14
Beloit....Sept. 21
Ripon ■....Sept. 28
Coe....Oct. 5
Knox....Oct. 12
Cornell College ■....Oct. 19
Monmouth (Ill.) ■....Oct. 26
Illinois Col....Nov. 2

1995 RESULTS (4-5-0)

32 Trinity Bible (N.D.)....12
42 Principia....14
19 Carroll (Wis.)....42
8 Lawrence....29
7 Coe....37
0 Knox....23
17 Cornell College....32
27 Monmouth (Ill.)....13
26 Illinois Col....15
178 **217**

Nickname: Pioneers.
Stadium: Rosenbloom (1911), 1,750 capacity. Natural turf.
Colors: Scarlet & Black.
Conference: Midwest.
SID: Andy Hamilton, 515-269-3832.
AD: Dee Fairchild.

GROVE CITY

Grove City, PA 16127....III

Coach: Chris Smith, Grove City '72
Record: 12 Years, 41-66-2

1996 SCHEDULE

Kenyon ■....Sept. 7
Wooster ■....Sept. 14
Carnegie Mellon....*Sept. 21
Thiel ■....Sept. 28
Wash. & Jeff....Oct. 5
Waynesburg....Oct. 12
Bluffton....Oct. 19
Bethany (W.Va.)....Oct. 26
Denison ■....Nov. 9
Alfred ■....Nov. 16

1995 RESULTS (2-8-0)

31 Kenyon....16
27 Bluffton....40
0 Wash. & Jeff....48
7 Waynesburg....36
25 Carnegie Mellon....30
6 Bethany (W.Va.)....13
16 Thiel....14
27 Mercyhurst....38
16 Walsh....21
7 Brockport St....8
162 **264**

Nickname: Wolverines.
Stadium: Thorn Field (1981), 3,500 capacity. Natural turf.
Colors: Crimson & White.
Conference: Presidents' Athletic.
SID: Joe Klimchak, 412-458-3365.
AD: Chris Smith.

GUILFORD

Greensboro, NC 27410....III

Coach: Mike Ketchum, Guilford '78
Record: 5 Years, 23-26-0

1996 SCHEDULE

Methodist....Sept. 14
Wash. & Lee ■....Sept. 21
Hampden-Sydney....Sept. 28
Davidson....*Oct. 5
Ferrum ■....Oct. 12
Bridgewater (Va.) ■....Oct. 19
Emory & Henry ■....Oct. 26
Randolph-Macon....Nov. 2
Chowan....Nov. 23

1995 RESULTS (3-6-0)

16 Methodist....10
0 Hampden-Sydney....16
31 Davidson....28
24 Ferrum....30
33 Bridgewater (Va.)....3
6 Emory & Henry....38
10 Randolph-Macon....27
9 Wash. & Lee....13
13 Sewanee....20
142 **185**

Nickname: Quakers.
Stadium: Armfield Athletic (1960), 3,500 capacity. Natural turf.
Colors: Crimson & Gray.
Conference: Old Dominion Athletic.
SID: Brett Ayers, 910-316-2107.
AD: Gayle Currie.

GUST. ADOLPHUS

St. Peter, MN 56082....III

Coach: Jay Schoenebeck, Gust. Adolphus '80
Record: 2 Years, 6-14-0

1996 SCHEDULE

Colorado Col....Sept. 7
Concordia-M'head ■....Sept. 14
Macalester....Sept. 21
Bethel (Minn.) ■....Sept. 28
St. Thomas (Minn.)....Oct. 5
St. John's (Minn.) ■....Oct. 12
Augsburg....Oct. 19
Hamline ■....Oct. 26
Carleton....Nov. 2
St. Olaf [Minneapolis, Minn.]....*Nov. 9

1995 RESULTS (1-9-0)

17 Central (Iowa)....44
42 Macalester....18
21 Carleton....29
22 St. Olaf....28
6 Concordia-M'head....48
24 St. John's (Minn.)....35
0 Bethel (Minn.)....7
20 Augsburg....23
14 Hamline....21
14 St. Thomas (Minn.)....28
180 **281**

Nickname: Golden Gusties.
Stadium: Hollingsworth Field (1929), 5,500 capacity. Natural turf.
Colors: Black & Gold.
Conference: Minnesota Intercollegiate Athletic.
SID: Tim Kennedy, 507-933-7647.
AD: Jim Malmquist.

HAMILTON

Clinton, NY 13323....................................III

Coach: Steve Frank, Bridgeport '72
Record: 11 Years, 48-39-1

1996 SCHEDULE

Amherst..Sept. 21
Wesleyan (Conn.) ....Sept. 28
Trinity (Conn.) ■...Oct. 5
Bowdoin ■..Oct. 12
Colby..Oct. 19
Williams ■..Oct. 26
Middlebury ■ ....Nov. 2
Bates..Nov. 9

1995 RESULTS (5-3-0)

21 Tufts..35
34 Wesleyan (Conn.)...3
0 Trinity (Conn.)...26
35 Bowdoin 13
16 Colby 10
9 Williams 29
23 Middlebury 20
34 Bates 14
172 **150**

Nickname: Continentals.
Stadium: Steuben Field, 2,500 capacity. Natural turf.
Colors: Buff & Blue.
Conference: NESCAC.
SID: Marc Simon, 315-859-4685.
AD: Thomas Murphy.

HAMLINE

St. Paul, MN 55104..................................III

Coach: Dick Tressel, Baldwin-Wallace '70
Record: 18 Years, 107-68-2

1996 SCHEDULE

Lake Forest ....Sept. 7
Bethel (Minn.) ■...Sept. 14
St. Thomas (Minn.) ....Sept. 21
St. John's (Minn.) ■.......................................Sept. 28
Augsburg ....Oct. 5
St. Olaf..Oct. 12
Carleton ■..Oct. 19
Gust. Adolphus...Oct. 26
Concordia-M'head ■...Nov. 2
Macalester [Minneapolis, Minn.] ....Nov. 9

1995 RESULTS (7-3-0)

31 Minn.-Morris..14
20 St. Olaf...21
3 Concordia-M'head...27
20 St. John's (Minn.) 35
31 Bethel (Minn.) 9
35 Augsburg 7
21 Macalester 6
10 St. Thomas (Minn.)..7
21 Gust. Adolphus...14
24 Carleton...6
216 **146**

Nickname: Pipers.
Stadium: Norton (1921), 2,000 capacity. Natural turf.
Colors: Red & Gray.
Conference: Minnesota Intercollegiate Athletic.
SID: Tom Giller, 612-641-2242.
AD: Dick Tressel.

HAMPDEN-SYDNEY

Hampden-Sydney, VA 23943.....................III

Coach: Joe Bush, Va. Military '65
Record: 11 Years, 59-49-1

1996 SCHEDULE

Gettysburg...Sept. 14
Wesley ....Sept. 21
Guilford ■...Sept. 28
Bridgewater (Va.) ....Oct. 5
Emory & Henry ■...Oct. 12
Wash. & Lee ....Oct. 19
Catholic ■...Oct. 26
Davidson ■ ....Nov. 2
Methodist ....Nov. 9
Randolph-Macon ■ ....Nov. 16

1995 RESULTS (4-6-0)

7 Gettysburg 25
12 Wesley 47
16 Guilford 0
35 Bridgewater (Va.) 14
0 Emory & Henry...17
7 Wash. & Lee 21
0 Catholic..34
22 Davidson 19
29 Methodist...13
14 Randolph-Macon 35
142 **225**

Nickname: Tigers.
Stadium: Hundley (1964), 2,400 capacity. Natural turf.
Colors: Garnet & Gray.
Conference: Old Dominion Athletic.
SID: Dean E. Hybl, 804-223-6156.
AD: Joe Bush.

HAMPTON

Hampton, VA 23668 ....I-AA

Coach: Joe Taylor, Western Ill. '72
Record: 13 Years, 100-36-4

1996 SCHEDULE

Clark Atlanta ....Sept. 1
Howard...*Sept. 13
North Caro. A&T ■...Sept. 21
Central St. [East Rutherford, N.J.]...................*Sept. 28
Florida A&M [Indianapolis, Ind.] ....Oct. 5
Delaware St...Oct. 12
South Caro. St. ....Oct. 26
Liberty ■...Nov. 2
Bethune-Cookman ■...Nov. 9
Norfolk St. ■ ....Nov. 16
Morgan St. ....Nov. 23

1995 RESULTS (8-3-0)

42 Morehouse...14
22 Howard 34
16 Grambling 7
22 Southern-B.R. 45
34 Bethune-Cookman 14
51 Delaware St. 21
23 Norfolk St. 18
36 Elizabeth City St. 13
14 Liberty...28
28 Fayetteville St. 7
54 Morgan St. 20
342 **221**

Nickname: Pirates.
Stadium: Armstrong Field (1928), 11,000 capacity. Natural turf.
Colors: Royal Blue & White.
Conference: Mid-Eastern Athletic.
SID: LeCounte Conaway, 804-727-5757.
AD: Dennis Thomas.

HANOVER

Hanover, IN 47243...................................III

Coach: C. Wayne Perry, DePauw '72
Record: 14 Years, 92-45-2

1996 SCHEDULE

Otterbein ■ ....Sept. 7
North Central..*Sept. 14
Centre...Sept. 21
Mt. St. Joseph ■ ....Sept. 28
Manchester..Oct. 5
DePauw...Oct. 19
Anderson (Ind.) ■...Oct. 26
Wabash ....Nov. 2
Rose-Hulman ■ ....Nov. 9
Franklin ■...Nov. 16

1995 RESULTS (10-0-0)

24 Otterbein 7
14 Centre 3
38 Defiance 20
44 Mt. St. Joseph..33
45 DePauw 25
41 Anderson (Ind.)..35
41 Wabash 21
73 Rose-Hulman 23
41 Manchester 19
26 Franklin...22
387 **208**

III Championship

18 Mount Union 52

Nickname: Panthers.
Stadium: L. S. Ayers Field (1973), 4,000 capacity. Natural turf.
Colors: Red & Blue.
Conference: Indiana Collegiate Athletic.
SID: Carter Cloyd, 812-866-7010.
AD: Dick Naylor.

HARDIN-SIMMONS

Abilene, TX 79698 III

Coach: Jimmie Keeling, Howard Payne '58
Record: 6 Years, 45-21-0

1996 SCHEDULE

Prairie View ■ ....Sept. 14
Howard Payne..Sept. 21
McMurry...*Sept. 28
Sul Ross St. ■ ....Oct. 5
Mississippi Col. ■ ....Oct. 12
Midwestern St. ....*Oct. 19
Howard Payne ■ ....Oct. 26
McMurry ■..Nov. 2
Sul Ross St. ....Nov. 9
Austin ■..Nov. 16

1995 RESULTS (8-1-0)

9 Howard Payne 22
31 McMurry..14
38 Sul Ross St. 23
43 Austin 0
20 Midwestern St. 14
28 Howard Payne 27
27 McMurry..17
55 Sul Ross St. 7
31 Austin 0
282 **124**

NAIA II Championship

17 Howard Payne 6
20 Central Wash..40

Nickname: Cowboys.
Stadium: Shelton (1993), 4,000 capacity. Natural turf.
Colors: Purple & Gold.
Conference: Division III Independents.
SID: John Neese, 915-670-1273.
AD: Jimmie Keeling.

HARTWICK

Oneonta, NY 13820 III

Coach: Steve Stetson, Dartmouth '73
Record: 10 Years, 33-56-2

1996 SCHEDULE

Pace...Sept. 7
Lebanon Valley ■...Sept. 14
Alfred..Sept. 21
Jersey City St. ■ ....*Oct. 5
Lycoming ....Oct. 12
Norwich ■ ....Oct. 19
Rensselaer ....Oct. 26
Waynesburg...Nov. 2
Hobart ■...Nov. 9
St. Lawrence ■ ....Nov. 16

1995 RESULTS (3-6-0)

37 Lebanon Valley...6
28 Alfred 21
18 St. John Fisher 19
54 Rochester 20
26 Lycoming 38
19 Maine Maritime..22
19 Rensselaer...20

23	Hobart	27
14	St. Lawrence	21
238		**194**

Nickname: Hawks.
Stadium: AstroTurf Field (1985), 1,200 capacity. Artificial turf.
Colors: Royal Blue & White.
Conference: Division III Independents.
SID: Dave Caspole, 607-431-4703.
AD: Kenneth Kutler.

HARVARD

Cambridge, MA 02138 .... I-AA

Coach: Tim Murphy, Springfield '78
Record: 9 Years, 38-59-1

1996 SCHEDULE

Columbia	Sept. 21
Bucknell	Sept. 28
Lafayette ■	Oct. 5
Cornell ■	Oct. 12
Holy Cross	Oct. 19
Princeton	Oct. 26
Dartmouth ■	Nov. 2
Brown ■	Nov. 9
Pennsylvania	Nov. 16
Yale ■	Nov. 23

1995 RESULTS (2-8-0)

24	Columbia	28
28	Colgate	8
21	Fordham	24
27	Cornell	28
22	Holy Cross	27
3	Princeton	14
7	Dartmouth	23
8	Brown	47
21	Pennsylvania	38
22	Yale	21
183		**258**

Nickname: Crimson.
Stadium: Harvard (1903), 37,289 capacity. Natural turf.
Colors: Crimson, Black & White.
Conference: Ivy League.
SID: John Veneziano, 617-495-2206.
AD: William Cleary Jr.

HAWAII

Honolulu, HI 96822 .... I-A

Coach: Fred vonAppen, Linfield '64
(First year as head coach)

1996 SCHEDULE

Boston College ■	*Aug. 31
Ohio ■	*Sept. 7
Wyoming	Sept. 14
Boise St. ■	*Sept. 21
Fresno St.	*Sept. 28
Colorado St. ■	Oct. 5
San Diego St.	*Oct. 12
UNLV ■	*Oct. 19
Air Force	Oct. 26
San Jose St. ■	*Nov. 9
Brigham Young ■	*Nov. 16
Wisconsin ■	*Nov. 30

1995 RESULTS (4-8-0)

17	Texas	38
6	Wyoming	52
42	UTEP	21
58	UNLV	30
10	New Mexico	24
45	Central Fla.	14
7	Brigham Young	45
42	Fresno St.	37
0	Colorado St.	22
10	San Diego St.	49
28	Air Force	45
20	Oklahoma St.	24
285		**401**

Nickname: Rainbow Warriors.
Stadium: Aloha (1975), 50,000 capacity. Artificial turf.
Colors: Green & White.
Conference: Western Athletic.
SID: Lois Manin (interim), 808-956-7523.
AD: Hugh Yoshida.

HEIDELBERG

Tiffin, OH 44883 III

Coach: Dick West, Xavier (Ohio) '73
Record: 12 Years, 56-62-2

1996 SCHEDULE

Adrian ■	*Sept. 14
Muskingum ■	Sept. 21
Baldwin-Wallace	*Sept. 28
Hiram ■	Oct. 5
Mount Union	Oct. 12
Capital	Oct. 19
Otterbein ■	Oct. 26
John Carroll	Nov. 2
Marietta	Nov. 9
Ohio Northern ■	Nov. 16

1995 RESULTS (0-10-0)

14	Adrian	28
13	Baldwin-Wallace	36
0	Hiram	24
50	Capital	51
21	John Carroll	44
10	Muskingum	11
12	Otterbein	22
14	Mount Union	52
34	Marietta	50
7	Ohio Northern	57
175		**375**

Nickname: Student Princes.
Stadium: Columbian (1941), 7,500 capacity. Natural turf.
Colors: Red, Orange & Black.
Conference: Ohio Athletic.
SID: Dick Edmond, 419-448-2140.
AD: John Hill.

HENDERSON ST.

Arkadelphia, AR 71923 II

Coach: Ronnie Kerr, Henderson St. '66
Record: 2 Years, 8-13-1

1996 SCHEDULE

Ouachita Baptist ■	*Sept. 7
East Tex. St.	*Sept. 14
Mississippi Col.	*Sept. 21
West Ga.	*Sept. 28
West Ala. ■	Oct. 5
Delta St.	Oct. 12
Central Ark. ■	*Oct. 19
North Ala. ■	Oct. 26
Arkansas Tech	Nov. 2
Ark.-Monticello	Nov. 9
Southern Ark. ■	Nov. 16

1995 RESULTS (6-5-0)

24	Southern Ark.	10
18	Ark.-Monticello	23
3	East Tex. St.	6
6	Stephen F. Austin	31
48	West Ala.	43
45	Mississippi Col.	12
24	Delta St.	17
28	North Ala.	33
38	Arkansas Tech	14
10	West Ga.	16
31	Central Ark.	21
275		**226**

Nickname: Reddies.
Stadium: Carpenter-Haygood (1968), 9,600 capacity. Natural turf.
Colors: Red & Gray.
Conference: Gulf South.
SID: David Worlock, 501-230-5197.
AD: Ken Turner.

HILLSDALE

Hillsdale, MI 49242 II

Coach: Dick Lowry, Baldwin-Wallace '57
Record: 22 Years, 166-70-3

1996 SCHEDULE

St. Francis (Ill.) ■	*Aug. 29
Edinboro ■	*Sept. 7
Ferris St.	*Sept. 14
Indianapolis ■	Sept. 21
Ashland	Sept. 28
Grand Valley St. ■	Oct. 5
Northern Mich. ■	Oct. 12
Wayne St. (Mich.)	Oct. 19
Northwood ■	Oct. 26
Michigan Tech	Nov. 2
Saginaw Valley	Nov. 9

1995 RESULTS (7-4-0)

14	Edinboro	21
28	St. Francis (Ill.)	0
49	St. Joseph's (Ind.)	0
10	Ferris St.	17
10	Indianapolis	0
28	Ashland	7
20	Grand Valley St.	25
14	Northern Mich.	28
45	Wayne St. (Mich.)	13
44	Northwood	30
21	Michigan Tech	6
283		**147**

Nickname: Chargers.
Stadium: Frank Waters (1982), 8,500 capacity. Natural turf.
Colors: Royal Blue & White.
Conference: Midwest Intercollegiate.
SID: Greg Younger, 517-437-7364.
AD: Mike Kovalchik.

HIRAM

Hiram, OH 44234 III

Coach: Bobby Thomas, Hiram '79
Record: 4 Years, 9-31-0

1996 SCHEDULE

Oberlin	Sept. 14
Otterbein	*Sept. 21
Muskingum ■	Sept. 28
Heidelberg	Oct. 5
Ohio Northern ■	Oct. 12
Marietta	Oct. 19
Baldwin-Wallace ■	Oct. 26
Capital ■	Nov. 2
John Carroll	Nov. 9
Mount Union ■	Nov. 16

1995 RESULTS (4-6-0)

57	Oberlin	7
0	Muskingum	14
24	Heidelberg	0
7	Marietta	26
42	Capital	19
9	Otterbein	2
21	Baldwin-Wallace	42
7	Ohio Northern	22
7	John Carroll	33
0	Mount Union	21
174		**186**

Nickname: Terriers.
Stadium: Charles Henry Field (1963), 3,500 capacity. Natural turf.
Colors: Red & Columbia Blue.
Conference: Ohio Athletic.
SID: Tom Cammett, 216-569-5495.
AD: Bobby Thomas.

HOBART

Geneva, NY 14456 III

Coach: Mike Cragg, Slippery Rock '81
Record: 1 Year, 3-7-0

1996 SCHEDULE

Dickinson ■	Sept. 14
St. John Fisher	Sept. 21
Union (N.Y.)	Sept. 28
St. Lawrence ■	Oct. 5
Rochester	Oct. 12
Frank. & Marsh.	Oct. 19
Alfred ■	Oct. 26
Ithaca ■	Nov. 2
Hartwick	Nov. 9
Rensselaer ■	Nov. 16

1995 RESULTS (3-7-0)

14	Dickinson	31
20	St. John Fisher	35
15	Union (N.Y.)	39
20	St. Lawrence	16
17	Rochester	26
51	Swarthmore	0
14	Alfred	35
22	Ithaca	43
27	Hartwick	23
28	Rensselaer	40
228		**288**

Nickname: Statesmen.
Stadium: Boswell (1975), 4,500 capacity. Natural turf.
Colors: Orange & Purple.
Conference: Upstate Collegiate Athletic Association.
SID: Eric T. Reuscher, 315-781-3538.
AD: Michael J. Hanna.

HOFSTRA

Hempstead, NY 11550 .... I-AA

Coach: Joe Gardi, Maryland '60
Record: 6 Years, 48-15-2

1996 SCHEDULE

Cal St. Sacramento ■	Sept. 7
Southwest Tex. St.	*Sept. 14
Western Ill. ■	Sept. 21
Charleston So.	Sept. 28
Liberty	Oct. 12
Boston U.	Oct. 19
Connecticut	Oct. 26
Buffalo ■	Nov. 2
Maine ■	Nov. 9
Youngstown St. ■	Nov. 16
Rhode Island ■	Nov. 23

1995 RESULTS (10-1-0)

34	Nicholls St.	10
24	Holy Cross	9
26	Lafayette	0
27	Illinois St.	0
36	Liberty	10
55	Cal St. Sacramento	15
36	Fordham	15
56	Charleston So.	6
17	Buffalo	14
37	Rhode Island	3
28	Marshall	30
376		**112**

I-AA Championship

17	Delaware	38

Nickname: Flying Dutchmen.
Stadium: Hofstra (1963), 15,000 capacity. Artificial turf.
Colors: Blue, Gold & White.
Conference: I-AA Independents.
SID: Jim Sheehan, 516-463-6764.
AD: James Garvey.

HOLY CROSS

Worcester, MA 01610 .... I-AA

Coach: Dan Allen, Hanover '78
Record: 6 Years, 36-33-0

1996 SCHEDULE

Massachusetts ■	Sept. 14
Colgate	Sept. 21
Princeton	Sept. 28
Columbia ■	Oct. 5
Dartmouth	Oct. 12
Harvard ■	Oct. 19
Bucknell ■	Oct. 26
Fordham	Nov. 2
Lehigh ■	Nov. 9
Lafayette	Nov. 16
Georgetown	Nov. 23

1995 RESULTS (2-9-0)

9	Hofstra	24
0	Massachusetts	51
19	Cornell	28
14	Brown	37
17	Yale	28
27	Harvard	22
17	Lafayette	27
10	Fordham	17
7	Bucknell	21
21	Lehigh	51
39	Colgate	20
180		**326**

Nickname: Crusaders.
Stadium: Fitton Field (1924), 23,500 capacity. Natural turf.
Color: Royal Purple.
Conference: Patriot League.
SID: Frank Mastrandrea, 203-870-4750.
AD: Ron Perry.

HOPE

Holland, MI 49423 III

Coach: Dean Kreps, Monmouth (N.J.) '83
Record: 1 Year, 2-7-0

1996 SCHEDULE

Valparaiso ■	Sept. 7
Ill. Benedictine	Sept. 14
DePauw	Sept. 21
Wabash ■	Sept. 28
Adrian ■	Oct. 12
Albion	Oct. 19
Alma ■	Oct. 26
Kalamazoo	Nov. 2
Olivet	Nov. 9

1995 RESULTS (2-7-0)

7	Wheaton (Ill.)	48
7	DePauw	13
10	Wabash	35
40	Aurora	6
9	Adrian	24
24	Albion	34
17	Alma	31
16	Kalamazoo	28
33	Olivet	28
163		**247**

Nickname: Flying Dutchmen.
Stadium: Holland Municipal (1979), 5,322 capacity. Natural turf.
Colors: Orange & Blue.
Conference: Michigan Intercollegiate Athletic Association.
SID: Tom Renner, 616-395-7860.
AD: Ray Smith.

HOUSTON

Houston, TX 77204 .... I-A

Coach: Kim Helton, Florida '70
Record: 3 Years, 4-28-1

1996 SCHEDULE

Sam Houston St. ■	*Aug. 31
LSU	*Sept. 7
Pittsburgh	*Sept. 14
Southern Cal ■	Sept. 21
Southwestern La.	*Oct. 5
Memphis ■	*Oct. 12
Cincinnati	Oct. 19
North Caro. ■	*Oct. 26
Tulane	*Nov. 2
Southern Miss. ■	*Nov. 9
Louisville ■	*Nov. 16

1995 RESULTS (2-9-0)

21	Florida	45
7	Louisiana Tech	19
10	Southern Cal	45
13	Kansas	20
21	Texas Christian	31
7	Baylor	47
38	Southern Methodist	15
7	Texas A&M	31
20	Texas	52
26	Texas Tech	38
18	Rice	17
188		**360**

Nickname: Cougars.
Stadium: Astrodome (1965), 60,000 capacity. Artificial turf.
Colors: Scarlet & White.
Conference: Conference USA.
SID: Donna Turner, 713-743-9404.
AD: Bill Carr.

HOWARD

Washington, DC 20059 .... I-AA

Coach: Steve Wilson, Howard '79
Record: 7 Years, 44-34-0

1996 SCHEDULE

Marshall	*Sept. 7
Hampton ■	*Sept. 13
Virginia St. ■	Sept. 21
Florida A&M	*Sept. 28
Bethune-Cookman ■	Oct. 12
Morehouse	Oct. 19
North Caro. A&T ■	Oct. 26
Norfolk St. ■	Nov. 2
South Caro. St.	Nov. 9
Morgan St. ■	Nov. 16
Delaware St. ■	Nov. 23

1995 RESULTS (6-5-0)

15	Bethune-Cookman	25
34	Hampton	22
32	N.C. Central	37
23	Ark.-Pine Bluff	7
18	Florida A&M	29
21	Alcorn St.	17
20	North Caro. A&T	14
27	Morehouse	19
14	South Caro. St.	18
29	Morgan St.	17
13	Delaware St.	20
246		**225**

Nickname: Bison.
Stadium: Greene (1986), 7,500 capacity. Artificial turf.
Colors: Blue, White & Red.
Conference: Mid-Eastern Athletic.
SID: Edward Hill, 202-806-7188.
AD: To be named.

HOWARD PAYNE

Brownwood, TX 76801 III

Coach: Vance Gibson, Austin '75
Record: 4 Years, 24-15-0

1996 SCHEDULE

Thomas More	Sept. 7
McMurry	*Sept. 14
Hardin-Simmons ■	Sept. 21
Sul Ross St.	Sept. 28
Austin ■	Oct. 5
McMurry ■	Oct. 19
Hardin-Simmons	Oct. 26
Sul Ross St. ■	Nov. 2
Austin	Nov. 9
Mississippi Col. ■	Nov. 16

1995 RESULTS (7-2-0)

7	Butler	17
13	McMurry	0
22	Hardin-Simmons	9
21	Sul Ross St.	6
13	Austin	7
49	McMurry	18
27	Hardin-Simmons	28
21	Sul Ross St.	0
33	Austin	0
206		**85**

NAIA II Championship

6 Hardin-Simmons 17

Nickname: Yellow Jackets.
Stadium: Gordon Wood, 7,600 capacity. Natural turf.
Colors: Old Gold & Navy Blue.
Conference: Division III Independents.
SID: Mike Blackwell, 915-649-8034.
AD: Larry Nickell.

HUMBOLDT ST.

Arcata, CA 95521 II

Coach: Fred Whitmire, Humboldt St. '64
Record: 5 Years, 32-18-2

1996 SCHEDULE

Montana Tech .... Sept. 7
Western Mont. ■ .... *Sept. 14
Azusa Pacific .... Sept. 21
UC Davis ■ .... Oct. 5
Sonoma St. ■ .... *Oct. 12
Cal St. Chico .... Oct. 19
Sonoma St. .... Oct. 26
Colorado Mines ■ .... Nov. 2
Cal St. Chico ■ .... Nov. 9
St. Mary's (Cal.) .... Nov. 16

1995 RESULTS (8-1-1)

31 Montana Tech 10
21 Western Mont. 38
31 UC Davis 31
37 Azusa Pacific 13
38 St. Mary's (Cal.) 37
24 Sonoma St. 13
47 Cal St. Chico 7
35 Sonoma St. 7
53 Menlo 12
31 Cal St. Chico 13
348 **181**

Nickname: Lumberjacks.
Stadium: Redwood Bowl (1946), 7,000 capacity. Natural turf.
Colors: Green & Gold.
Conference: Northern California Athletic.
SID: Dan Pambianco, 707-826-3631.
AD: To be named.

IDAHO

Moscow, ID 83843 .... I-AA

Coach: Chris Tormey, Idaho '78
Record: 1 Year, 6-5-0

1996 SCHEDULE

Wyoming .... Aug. 31
San Diego St. .... *Sept. 7
St. Mary's (Cal.) ■ .... Sept. 14
Southwest Tex. St. .... *Sept. 28
Cal Poly SLO ■ .... Oct. 5
Nevada ■ .... Oct. 19
Utah St. .... Oct. 26
Eastern Wash. ■ .... Nov. 2
New Mexico St. ■ .... Nov. 9
North Texas .... Nov. 16
Boise St. .... Nov. 23

1995 RESULTS (6-4-0)

7 Oregon St. 14
66 Sonoma St. 3
21 Idaho St. 26
13 Montana St. 16
37 Eastern Wash. 10
55 Montana 43
19 Weber St. 25
17 Northern Ariz. 14
16 Northern Iowa 12
33 Boise St. 13
284 **176**

I-AA Championship

3 McNeese St. 33

Nickname: Vandals.
Stadium: Kibbie (1975), 16,000 capacity. Artificial turf.
Colors: Silver & Gold.
Conference: Big West.
SID: Sean Johnson, 208-885-0211.
AD: Pete Liske.

IDAHO ST.

Pocatello, ID 83209 .... I-AA

Coach: Brian McNeely, Wichita St. '79
Record: 4 Years, 17-27-0

1996 SCHEDULE

Mississippi .... *Aug. 31
Cal Poly SLO ■ .... *Sept. 7
Western Mont. ■ .... *Sept. 21
Montana St. .... Sept. 28
Cal St. Sacramento ■ .... *Oct. 5
Montana .... Oct. 12
Eastern Wash. ■ .... Oct. 26
Northern Ariz. .... *Nov. 2
Cal St. Northridge ■ .... *Nov. 9
Portland St. .... *Nov. 16
Weber St. ■ .... Nov. 23

1995 RESULTS (6-5-0)

28 Cal Poly SLO 22
52 Cal St. Northridge 0
48 Southern Utah 14
26 Idaho 21
14 Eastern Wash. 7
14 Montana St. 18
17 Boise St. 27
14 Northern Ariz. 42
21 Montana 35
38 North Texas 41
35 Weber St. 25
307 **252**

Nickname: Bengals.
Stadium: Holt Arena (1970), 12,000 capacity. Artificial turf.
Colors: Orange & Black.
Conference: Big Sky.
SID: Glenn Alford, 208-236-3651.
AD: Irv Cross.

ILLINOIS

Champaign, IL 61820 .... I-A

Coach: Lou Tepper, Rutgers '67
Record: 5 Years, 23-22-2

1996 SCHEDULE

Michigan .... Aug. 31
Southern Cal ■ .... Sept. 7
Arizona .... *Sept. 14
Akron ■ .... Sept. 21
Indiana ■ .... Oct. 5
Michigan St. .... Oct. 12
Northwestern .... Oct. 26
Iowa ■ .... Nov. 2
Ohio St. ■ .... Nov. 9
Minnesota .... *Nov. 16
Wisconsin ■ .... Nov. 23

1995 RESULTS (5-5-1)

14 Michigan 38
31 Oregon 34
9 Arizona 7
7 East Caro. 0
17 Indiana 10
21 Michigan St. 27
14 Northwestern 17
26 Iowa 7
3 Ohio St. 41
48 Minnesota 14
3 Wisconsin 3
193 **198**

Nickname: Fighting Illini.
Stadium: Memorial (1923), 70,904 capacity. Artificial turf.
Colors: Orange & Blue.
Conference: Big Ten.
SID: Dave Johnson, 217-333-1391.
AD: Ron Guenther.

ILL. BENEDICTINE

Lisle, IL 60532 III

Coach: John Welty, Ill. Benedictine '77
Record: 6 Years, 18-38-1

1996 SCHEDULE

Loras .... Sept. 7
Hope ■ .... Sept. 14
Elmhurst .... Sept. 21
Augustana (Ill.) ■ .... Sept. 28
Adrian .... Oct. 5
Aurora .... Oct. 12
Wabash ■ .... Oct. 19
Anderson (Ind.) .... Nov. 2
DePauw ■ .... Nov. 9

1995 RESULTS (1-8-0)

7 Loras 42
12 Carthage 20
8 Elmhurst 7
0 Alma 35
3 Wabash 40
0 Olivet Nazarene 33
0 Aurora 34
14 Trinity (Ill.) 56
0 Wittenberg 53
44 **320**

Nickname: Eagles.
Stadium: Alumni Memorial (1910), 2,500 capacity. Natural turf.
Colors: Cardinal & White.
Conference: Division III Independents.
SID: John Welty, 708-960-1500.
AD: John Welty.

ILLINOIS COL.

Jacksonville, IL 62650 III

Coach: Rich Johanningmeier, Southwest Mo. St. '64
Record: 11 Years, 60-51-5

1996 SCHEDULE

Principia .... Sept. 7
Washington (Mo.) ■ .... Sept. 14
Lake Forest ■ .... Sept. 21
St. Norbert .... Sept. 28
Monmouth (Ill.) .... Oct. 5
Coe ■ .... Oct. 12
Knox ■ .... Oct. 19
Cornell College .... Oct. 26
Grinnell ■ .... Nov. 2

1995 RESULTS (2-7-0)

29 Principia 24
6 Blackburn 15
0 Beloit 23
13 Ripon 53
42 Monmouth (Ill.) 26
0 Coe 55
7 Knox 28
7 Cornell College 52
15 Grinnell 26
119 **302**

Nickname: Blueboys.
Stadium: England Field (1960), 2,500 capacity. Natural turf.
Colors: Royal Blue & White.
Conference: Midwest.
SID: James T. Murphy, 217-245-3048.
AD: Rich Johanningmeier.

ILLINOIS ST.

Normal, IL 61761 .... I-AA

Coach: Todd Berry, Tulsa '83
(First year as head coach)

1996 SCHEDULE

Buffalo .... *Aug. 29
North Texas .... *Sept. 7
Southeast Mo. St. ■ .... *Sept. 14
Youngstown St. ■ .... *Sept. 21
Southern Ill. ■ .... Sept. 28

Northern Iowa ....Oct. 12
Indiana St. ....Oct. 19
Southwest Mo. St. ■ ....Oct. 26
Central Fla. ....Nov. 2
Western Ill. ....Nov. 9
Tennessee Tech ■ ....Nov. 16

1995 RESULTS (5-6-0)

45 St. Francis (Ill.) 3
6 Ohio 14
6 Buffalo 19
0 Hofstra 27
20 Southwest Mo. St. 17
11 Southern Ill. 14
22 Western Ill. 25
10 Eastern Ill. 31
31 Northern Iowa 29
25 Indiana St. 0
30 Youngstown St. 13
206 **192**

Nickname: Redbirds.
Stadium: Hancock (1967), 15,000 capacity. Artificial turf.
Colors: Red & White.
Conference: Gateway.
SID: Kenny Mossman, 309-438-3825.
AD: Rick Greenspan.

ILL. WESLEYAN

Bloomington, IL 61701 III

Coach: Norm Eash, Ill. Wesleyan '75
Record: 9 Years, 53-29-1

1996 SCHEDULE

Thomas More ■ ....Sept. 14
Washington (Mo.) ....Sept. 28
North Park ....Oct. 5
Millikin ■ ....Oct. 12
North Central ■ ....Oct. 19
Wheaton (Ill.) ....Oct. 26
Augustana (Ill.) ■ ....Nov. 2
Carthage ■ ....Nov. 9
Elmhurst ....Nov. 16

1995 RESULTS (6-3-0)

23 Washington (Mo.) 28
21 Simpson 24
28 Augustana (Ill.) 12
28 Wheaton (Ill.) 42
25 North Central 0
35 Carthage 7
41 Elmhurst 7
61 North Park 10
3 Millikin 0
265 **130**

Nickname: Titans.
Stadium: Wesleyan (1893), 3,500 capacity. Natural turf.
Colors: Green & White.
Conference: College Conf. of Illinois & Wisconsin.
SID: Stew Salowitz, 309-556-3206.
AD: Dennie Bridges.

INDIANA

Bloomington, IN 47405 ....I-A

Coach: Bill Mallory, Miami (Ohio) '57
Record: 26 Years, 164-122-4

1996 SCHEDULE

Toledo ....*Sept. 7
Miami (Ohio) ■ ....Sept. 14
Kentucky ....*Sept. 21
Northwestern ■ ....Sept. 28
Illinois ....Oct. 5
Iowa ■ ....Oct. 12
Michigan ....Oct. 19
Penn St. ■ ....Oct. 26
Michigan St. ....Nov. 9
Ohio St. ■ ....Nov. 16
Purdue ....Nov. 23

1995 RESULTS (2-9-0)

24 Western Mich. 10
10 Kentucky 17
27 Southern Miss. 26
7 Northwestern 31
10 Illinois 17
13 Iowa 22
17 Michigan 34
21 Penn St. 45
13 Michigan St. 31
3 Ohio St. 42
14 Purdue 51
159 **326**

Nickname: Fightin' Hoosiers.
Stadium: Memorial (1960), 52,354 capacity. Artificial turf.
Colors: Cream & Crimson.
Conference: Big Ten.
SID: Kit Klingelhoffer, 812-855-9610.
AD: Clarence Doninger.

INDIANA (PA.)

Indiana, PA 15705 II

Coach: Frank Cignetti, Indiana (Pa.) '60
Record: 14 Years, 117-48-1

1996 SCHEDULE

Fairmont St. ....Sept. 7
Bloomsburg ■ ....*Sept. 14
New Haven ■ ....*Sept. 28
Calif. (Pa.) ■ ....Oct. 5
Slippery Rock ....Oct. 12
East Stroudsburg ....Oct. 19
Edinboro ■ ....Oct. 26
Clarion ....Nov. 2
Lock Haven ■ ....Nov. 9
Shippensburg ....Nov. 16

1995 RESULTS (8-3-0)

28 Grand Valley St. 25
17 Central St. 20
19 New Haven 20
50 West Chester 7
62 Shippensburg 21
44 Calif. (Pa.) 20
41 Slippery Rock 7
58 Cheyney 0
18 Edinboro 35
14 Clarion 9
38 Lock Haven 0
389 **164**

Nickname: Indians.
Stadium: Miller (1962), 6,500 capacity. Artificial turf.
Colors: Crimson & Gray.
Conference: Pennsylvania State Athletic.
SID: Larry Judge, 412-357-2747.
AD: Frank Cignetti.

INDIANA ST.

Terre Haute, IN 47809 ....I-AA

Coach: Dennis Raetz, Nebraska '68
Record: 16 Years, 84-93-1

1996 SCHEDULE

Mars Hill ■ ....*Aug. 31
Kansas St. ....*Sept. 7
Eastern Ill. ....*Sept. 14
St. Joseph's (Ind.) ■ ....*Sept. 21
Liberty ....Sept. 28
Western Ill. ....Oct. 5
Southern Ill. ....Oct. 12
Illinois St. ■ ....Oct. 19
Western Ky. ....Oct. 26
Northern Iowa ■ ....Nov. 9
Southwest Mo. St. ■ ....Nov. 16

1995 RESULTS (7-4-0)

31 Mars Hill 0
10 Mississippi 56
41 Glenville St. 14
30 Western Ill. 13
52 Southern Ill. 3
16 Southwest Mo. St. 9
10 Northern Iowa 27
27 Western Ky. 6
13 Youngstown St. 6
0 Illinois St. 25
6 Eastern Ill. 27
236 **186**

Nickname: Sycamores.
Stadium: Memorial (1970), 20,500 capacity. Artificial turf.
Colors: Blue & White.
Conference: Gateway.
SID: Eric Ruden, 812-237-4160.
AD: Larry Gallo.

INDIANAPOLIS

Indianapolis, IN 46227 II

Coach: Joe Polizzi, Hillsdale '76
Record: 2 Years, 5-15-1

1996 SCHEDULE

St. Joseph's (Ind.) ....Aug. 31
Ferris St. ....Sept. 7
Wayne St. (Mich.) ■ ....Sept. 14
Hillsdale ....Sept. 21
Michigan Tech ■ ....Sept. 28
Northern Mich. ....Oct. 5
Saginaw Valley ■ ....Oct. 12
Northwood ....Oct. 19
St. Francis (Ill.) ■ ....Oct. 26
Ashland ■ ....Nov. 9
Grand Valley St. ■ ....Nov. 16

1995 RESULTS (3-8-0)

10 Slippery Rock 38
0 Grand Valley St. 56
0 Ferris St. 50
21 Wayne St. (Mich.) 7
0 Hillsdale 10
14 Michigan Tech 21
14 Northern Mich. 28
6 Saginaw Valley 42
30 Northwood 25
0 St. Francis (Ill.) 27
14 St. Joseph's (Ind.) 0
109 **304**

Nickname: Greyhounds.
Stadium: Key (1971), 5,500 capacity. Natural turf.
Colors: Crimson & Gray.
Conference: Midwest Intercollegiate.
SID: Joe Gentry, 317-788-3494.
AD: Dave Huffman.

IONA

New Rochelle, NY 10801 ....I-AA

Coach: Harold Crocker, Central Conn. St. '74
Record: 11 Years, 48-60-1

1996 SCHEDULE

Wagner ■ ....Sept. 14
Marist ....Sept. 21
Pace ....Sept. 28
Canisius ■ ....Oct. 5
Georgetown ....Oct. 12
Siena ■ ....Oct. 19
Duquesne ....Oct. 26
St. Peter's ■ ....Nov. 2
Fairfield ....*Nov. 9
St. John's (N.Y.) ■ ....Nov. 16

1995 RESULTS (3-6-0)

14 Georgetown 27
22 Pace 29
18 Siena 6
18 Marist 14
29 St. Peter's 0
0 Wagner 42
13 Duquesne 30
14 Canisius 21
13 St. John's (N.Y.) 17
141 **186**

Nickname: Gaels.
Stadium: Mazzella Field (1989), 1,200 capacity. Artificial turf.
Colors: Maroon & Gold.
Conference: Metro Atlantic.
SID: Shawn Brennan, 914-633-2334.
AD: Rich Petriccione.

IOWA

Iowa City, IA 52242 ....I-A

Coach: Hayden Fry, Baylor '51
Record: 34 Years, 213-162-10

1996 SCHEDULE

Arizona ■ ....Sept. 7
Iowa St. ■ ....Sept. 14
Tulsa ....*Sept. 21
Michigan St. ■ ....Oct. 5
Indiana ....Oct. 12
Penn St. ....Oct. 19
Ohio St. ■ ....Oct. 26
Illinois ....Nov. 2
Northwestern ■ ....Nov. 9
Wisconsin ■ ....Nov. 16
Minnesota ....*Nov. 23

1995 RESULTS (7-4-0)

34 Northern Iowa 13
27 Iowa St. 10
59 New Mexico St. 21
21 Michigan St. 7
22 Indiana 13
27 Penn St. 41
35 Ohio St. 56
7 Illinois 26
20 Northwestern 31
33 Wisconsin 20
45 Minnesota 3
330 **241**

Sun Bowl

38 Washington 18

Nickname: Hawkeyes.
Stadium: Kinnick (1929), 70,397 capacity. Natural turf.
Colors: Old Gold & Black.
Conference: Big Ten.
SID: Phil Haddy, 319-335-9411.
AD: Bob Bowlsby.

IOWA ST.

Ames, IA 50011 ....I-A

Coach: Dan McCarney, Iowa '75
Record: 1 Year, 3-8-0

1996 SCHEDULE

Wyoming ■ ....Sept. 7
Iowa ....Sept. 14
Northern Iowa ■ ....Sept. 21
Missouri ■ ....Sept. 28
Texas A&M ■ ....Oct. 12
Oklahoma St. ....Oct. 19
Baylor ....Oct. 26
Kansas ■ ....Nov. 2
Colorado ....Nov. 9
Nebraska ■ ....Nov. 16
Kansas St. ....Nov. 23

1995 RESULTS (3-8-0)

36 Ohio 21
10 Texas Christian 27
10 Iowa 27
57 UNLV 30
26 Oklahoma 39
7 Kansas 34
28 Colorado 50
38 Oklahoma St. 14
14 Nebraska 73
7 Kansas St. 49
31 Missouri 45
264 **409**

Nickname: Cyclones.
Stadium: Cyclone-Jack Trice (1975), 43,000 capacity. Natural turf.
Colors: Cardinal & Gold.
Conference: Big 12.
SID: Tom Kroeschell, 515-294-3372.
AD: Eugene Smith.

ITHACA

Ithaca, NY 14850 III

Coach: Michael Welch, Ithaca '73
Record: 2 Years, 15-7-0

1996 SCHEDULE

Mansfield ■ ....Sept. 21
Alfred ■ ....Sept. 28
Springfield ■ ....Oct. 5
Brockport St. ....Oct. 12
St. Lawrence ■ ....Oct. 19
American Int'l ....Oct. 26
Hobart ....Nov. 2
Cortland St. ....Nov. 9
Buffalo St. ■ ....Nov. 16

1995 RESULTS (5-4-0)

30 Mansfield 12
12 Alfred 13
24 Springfield 27
23 American Int'l 24
34 St. Lawrence 7
33 Montclair St. 7
43 Hobart 22
35 Cortland St. 19
6 Buffalo St. 24
240 **155**

Nickname: Bombers.
Stadium: Butterfield (1958), 5,000 capacity. Natural turf.
Colors: Blue & Gold.
Conference: Division III Independents.
SID: Pete Moore, 607-274-3825.
AD: Robert Deming.

JACKSON ST.

Jackson, MS 39217 ....I-AA

Coach: James Carson, Jackson St. '63
Record: 4 Years, 28-16-1

1996 SCHEDULE

Alabama St. [Birmingham, Ala.] ....*Sept. 1
Tennessee St. [Memphis, Tenn.] ....*Sept. 14
Florida A&M ■ ....*Sept. 21
Mississippi Val. ■ ....*Sept. 28
Texas Southern ■ ....Oct. 5
Southern-B.R. ....*Oct. 19
Grambling ....Oct. 26
Ark.-Pine Bluff [Little Rock, Ark.] ....Nov. 2
Central St. ■ ....*Nov. 9
Prairie View ■ ....Nov. 16
Alcorn St. ....Nov. 23

1995 RESULTS (9-2-0)

20 Alabama A&M 21
24 Tennessee St. 19
12 Florida A&M 15
47 Mississippi Val. 7
24 Alabama St. 22
16 Southern-B.R. 14
29 Grambling 28
29 Ark.-Pine Bluff 26
13 Texas Southern 9
68 Prairie View 0
28 Alcorn St. 7
310 **168**

I-AA Championship

8 Marshall 38

Nickname: Tigers.
Stadium: Mississippi Memorial (1949), 62,512 capacity. Natural turf.
Colors: Blue & White.
Conference: Southwestern Athletic.
SID: Samuel Jefferson, 601-968-2273.
AD: Paul Covington.

JACKSONVILLE ST.

Jacksonville, AL 36265 ....I-AA

Coach: Bill Burgess, Auburn '63
Record: 11 Years, 83-40-4

1996 SCHEDULE

West Ga. ■ ....*Sept. 7
Nicholls St. ....*Sept. 14
Ala.-Birmingham ....*Sept. 21
Southwest Mo. St. ....*Sept. 28
Middle Tenn. St. ■ ....Oct. 5
Western Ky. ■ ....Oct. 12
Samford ■ ....Oct. 19
Troy St. ■ ....*Oct. 26
Stephen F. Austin ....Nov. 9
Northeast La. ....*Nov. 16

1995 RESULTS (7-4-0)

16 Sam Houston St. 13
25 West Ga. 22
28 Ala.-Birmingham 26
21 North Caro. A&T 10
56 Knoxville 6
15 Western Ky. 17
35 Samford 14
7 Troy St. 35
6 Arkansas St. 37
32 Western Ill. 27
14 Southwest Mo. St. 49
255 **256**

Nickname: Gamecocks.
Stadium: Paul Snow (1947), 15,000 capacity. Natural turf.
Colors: Red & White.
Conference: Southland Football League.
SID: Mike Galloway, 205-782-5377.
AD: Jerry Cole.

JAMES MADISON

Harrisonburg, VA 22807 ....I-AA

Coach: Alex Wood, Iowa '79
Record: 1 Year, 8-4-0

1996 SCHEDULE

Shippensburg ■ ....*Sept. 7
McNeese St. ....*Sept. 14
Boston U. ....Sept. 21
New Hampshire ■ ....Sept. 28
Maine ■ ....Oct. 5
William & Mary ■ ....Oct. 12
Richmond ....Oct. 19
Delaware ....Oct. 26
Northeastern ■ ....Nov. 2
Connecticut ....Nov. 9
Villanova ■ ....Nov. 16

1995 RESULTS (8-3-0)

76 Morgan St. 7
24 William & Mary 17
24 McNeese St. 30
28 Villanova 27
21 Maine 17
38 Boston U. 31
23 New Hampshire 19
19 Delaware 48
33 Richmond 34
27 Northeastern 13
24 Connecticut 16
337 **259**

I-AA Championship

24 Appalachian St. 31

Nickname: Dukes.
Stadium: Bridgeforth (1974), 12,500 capacity. Artificial turf.
Colors: Purple & Gold.
Conference: Yankee.
SID: Gary Michael, 540-568-6154.
AD: Donald Lemish.

JERSEY CITY ST.

Jersey City, NJ 07305 III

Coach: Roy Miller, Jersey City St. '69
Record: 11 Years, 42-64-0

1996 SCHEDULE

Brockport St. ■ ....Sept. 14
Western Conn. St. ....*Sept. 21

Rowan ....*Sept. 27
Hartwick....*Oct. 5
St. John Fisher ■ ....Oct. 12
Kean ■ ....Oct. 19
Trenton St. ....Oct. 26
Wm. Paterson ....*Nov. 1
Montclair St. ■ ....Nov. 9
Wesley ■ ....Nov. 16

1995 RESULTS (1-9-0)

6 Brockport St. 24
10 Delaware Valley 13
0 Rowan 28
14 Wesley 28
6 St. John Fisher 7
7 Kean 14
0 Trenton St. 14
20 Wm. Paterson 7
14 Montclair St. 28
14 Cortland St. 28
91 **191**

Nickname: Gothic Knights.
Stadium: Thomas Gerrity Athletic Complex (1986), 3,000 capacity. Natural turf.
Colors: Green & Gold.
Conference: New Jersey Athletic.
SID: John Stallings, 201-200-3301.
AD: Larry Schiner.

JOHN CARROLL

Cleveland, OH 44118 III

Coach: Tony DeCarlo, Kent '62
Record: 9 Years, 63-22-4

1996 SCHEDULE

Gannon ....*Sept. 6
Ohio Northern ....Sept. 21
Marietta ■ ....Sept. 28
Otterbein ....*Oct. 5
Muskingum ■ ....Oct. 12
Mount Union ■ ....Oct. 19
Capital ....Oct. 26
Heidelberg ■ ....Nov. 2
Hiram ■ ....Nov. 9
Baldwin-Wallace ....Nov. 16

1995 RESULTS (6-2-2)

28 Ohio Wesleyan 13
21 Marietta 21
55 Otterbein 14
7 Mount Union 33
44 Heidelberg 21
38 Ohio Northern 6
39 Capital 6
7 Muskingum 7
33 Hiram 7
3 Baldwin-Wallace 31
275 **159**

Nickname: Blue Streaks.
Stadium: Wasmer Field (1968), 3,500 capacity. Artificial turf.
Colors: Blue & Gold.
Conference: Ohio Athletic.
SID: Chris Wenzler, 216-397-4676.
AD: Tony DeCarlo.

JOHNS HOPKINS

Baltimore, MD 21218 III

Coach: Jim Margraff, Johns Hopkins '82
Record: 6 Years, 30-27-3

1996 SCHEDULE

FDU-Madison ....*Sept. 13
Swarthmore ....Sept. 21
King's (Pa.) ■ ....*Sept. 27
Gettysburg ■ ....*Oct. 4
Ursinus ....Oct. 12
Muhlenberg ■ ....*Oct. 18
Bridgewater (Va.) ....Oct. 26
Dickinson ■ ....Nov. 2
Frank. & Marsh. ....Nov. 9
Western Md. ■ ....Nov. 16

1995 RESULTS (6-3-1)

17 FDU-Madison 20
25 Swarthmore 3
35 King's (Pa.) 6
35 Gettysburg 16
14 Ursinus 9
14 Muhlenberg 11
7 Georgetown 3
14 Dickinson 17
22 Frank. & Marsh. 27
14 Western Md. 14
197 **126**

Nickname: Blue Jays.
Stadium: Homewood Field (1906), 4,000 capacity. Artificial turf.
Colors: Blue & Black.
Conference: Centennial.
SID: Jennifer Hoover, 410-889-4636.
AD: Tom Calder.

JOHNSON SMITH

Charlotte, NC 28216 II

Coach: Daryl McNeill, South Caro. St. '82
Record: 1 Year, 2-8-0

1996 SCHEDULE

Benedict ■ ....*Aug. 31
Virginia St. ■ ....*Sept. 7
Bowie St. ....Sept. 14
Elizabeth City St. ■ ....*Sept. 21
South Caro. St. ....Sept. 28
Livingstone ....Oct. 12
Fayetteville St. ■ ....Oct. 19
Winston-Salem ■ ....Oct. 26
N.C. Central ....Nov. 2
Virginia Union ....Nov. 9
Lane ....Nov. 16

1995 RESULTS (2-8-0)

12 Wingate 33
18 Virginia St. 47
6 Lenoir-Rhyne 26
6 N.C. Central 45
20 Lane 46
12 Winston-Salem 28
25 Livingstone 49
14 Fayetteville St. 9
14 Norfolk St. 55
12 Virginia Union 0
139 **338**

Nickname: Golden Bulls.
Stadium: Bullpit (1990), 7,500 capacity. Natural turf.
Colors: Blue & Gold.
Conference: Central Intercollegiate Athletic Association.
SID: To be named, 704-378-1205.
AD: Stephen Wayne Joyner.

JUNIATA

Huntingdon, PA 16652 III

Coach: Tom Gibboney, Juniata '78
Record: 1 Year, 2-7-1

1996 SCHEDULE

Western Md. ■ ....Sept. 14
Moravian ....Sept. 21
Delaware Valley ■ ....Sept. 28
Widener ■ ....Oct. 5
Wilkes ....Oct. 12
Lebanon Valley ■ ....Oct. 19
Susquehanna ....Oct. 26
Albright ■ ....Nov. 2
Waynesburg ....Nov. 9
FDU-Madison ....Nov. 16

1995 RESULTS (2-7-1)

10 Western Md. 36
15 Moravian 15
26 Delaware Valley 28
21 Widener 56
28 Wilkes 29
0 Lebanon Valley 17
35 Susquehanna 28
0 Albright 10
7 Carnegie Mellon 39
14 FDU-Madison 7
156 **265**

Nickname: Eagles.
Stadium: Chuck Knox (1988), 3,000 capacity. Natural turf.
Colors: Yale Blue & Old Gold.
Conference: Middle Atlantic.
SID: Joseph Scialabba, 814-643-4310.
AD: Larry Bock.

KALAMAZOO

Kalamazoo, MI 49006 III

Coach: Dave Warmack, Western Mich. '71
Record: 6 Years, 26-27-1

1996 SCHEDULE

Wheaton (Ill.) ....Sept. 14
Franklin ■ ....Sept. 21
Aurora ....Sept. 28
Chicago ■ ....Oct. 5
Albion ■ ....Oct. 12
Alma ....Oct. 19
Olivet ....Oct. 26
Hope ■ ....Nov. 2
Adrian ....Nov. 9

1995 RESULTS (4-5-0)

32 Wooster 0
15 Franklin 16
39 Valparaiso 47
25 Chicago 29
14 Albion 19
30 Alma 23
41 Olivet 22
28 Hope 16
7 Adrian 10
231 **182**

Nickname: Hornets.
Stadium: Angell Field (1946), 3,000 capacity. Natural turf.
Colors: Orange & Black.
Conference: Michigan Intercollegiate Athletic Association.
SID: Michael Molde, 616-337-7287.
AD: Bob Kent.

KANSAS

Lawrence, KS 66045 ....I-A

Coach: Glen Mason, Ohio St. '72
Record: 10 Years, 55-57-1

1996 SCHEDULE

Ball St. ■ ....*Aug. 29
Texas Christian ....*Sept. 14
Utah ....*Sept. 28
Oklahoma ....Oct. 5
Texas Tech ■ ....Oct. 12
Colorado ■ ....Oct. 19
Nebraska ....Oct. 26
Iowa St. ....Nov. 2
Kansas St. ■ ....Nov. 9
Texas ■ ....Nov. 16
Missouri ....Nov. 23

1995 RESULTS (9-2-0)

23 Cincinnati 18
27 North Texas 10
38 Texas Christian 20
20 Houston 13
40 Colorado 24
34 Iowa St. 7
38 Oklahoma 17
7 Kansas St. 41
42 Missouri 23
3 Nebraska 41
22 Oklahoma St. 17
294 **231**

Aloha Bowl

51 UCLA 30

Nickname: Jayhawks.
Stadium: Memorial (1921), 50,250 capacity. Artificial turf.
Colors: Crimson & Blue.

Conference: Big 12.
SID: Doug Vance, 913-864-3417.
AD: Bob Frederick.

KANSAS ST.

Manhattan, KS 66506 ....I-A

Coach: Bill Snyder, William Jewell '63
Record: 7 Years, 46-33-1

1996 SCHEDULE

Texas Tech ■ ....Aug. 31
Indiana St. ■ ....*Sept. 7
Cincinnati ■ ....*Sept. 14
Rice ....*Sept. 21
Nebraska ■ ....Oct. 5
Missouri ....Oct. 12
Texas A&M ....Oct. 19
Oklahoma ■ ....Oct. 26
Kansas ....Nov. 9
Colorado ....Nov. 16
Iowa St. ■ ....Nov. 23

1995 RESULTS (9-2-0)

34 Temple 7
23 Cincinnati 21
67 Akron 0
44 Northern Ill. 0
30 Missouri 0
23 Oklahoma St. 17
25 Nebraska 49
41 Kansas 7
49 Oklahoma 10
49 Iowa St. 7
17 Colorado 27
402 **145**

Holiday Bowl

54 Colorado St. 21

Nickname: Wildcats.
Stadium: K S U (1968), 42,000 capacity. Artificial turf.
Colors: Purple & White.
Conference: Big 12.
SID: Ben Boyle, 913-532-6735.
AD: Max Urick.

KEAN

Union, NJ 07083 III

Coach: Brian Carlson, Montclair St. '82
Record: 4 Years, 21-13-4

1996 SCHEDULE

Lock Haven ■ ....Sept. 14
Cortland St. ....Sept. 21
Wm. Paterson ....*Oct. 5
Montclair St. ■ ....Oct. 12
Jersey City St. ....Oct. 19
Buffalo St. ■ ....Oct. 26
Rowan ■ ....Nov. 2
Brockport St. ....Nov. 9
Trenton St. ....Nov. 16

1995 RESULTS (3-4-2)

13 Western Conn. St. 13
13 Lock Haven 21
24 Wm. Paterson 6
6 Montclair St. 0
14 Jersey City St. 7
7 Buffalo St. 31
13 Rowan 42
3 Brockport St. 3
10 Trenton St. 20
103 **143**

Nickname: Cougars.
Stadium: Zweidinger Field, 2,200 capacity. Natural turf.
Colors: Royal Blue & Silver.
Conference: New Jersey Athletic.
SID: Adam Fenton, 908-527-2939.
AD: Glenn Hedden.

KENT

Kent, OH 44242 ....I-A

Coach: Jim Corrigall, Kent '70
Record: 2 Years, 3-18-1

1996 SCHEDULE

Miami (Ohio) ....Aug. 31
Pittsburgh ....*Sept. 7
Youngstown St. ■ ....*Sept. 14
Nevada ....Sept. 28
Akron ■ ....Oct. 5
Bowling Green ....Oct. 12
Ohio ■ ....Oct. 19
Eastern Mich. ....Oct. 26
Central Mich. ■ ....Nov. 2
Ball St. ....Nov. 9
Western Mich. ....Nov. 16

1995 RESULTS (1-9-1)

17 Youngstown St. 14
0 Miami (Ohio) 39
28 Ohio 28
6 West Va. 45
6 Western Mich. 52
14 South Caro. 77
16 Central Mich. 27
6 Akron 14
13 Ball St. 28
15 Bowling Green 26
7 Eastern Mich. 40
128 **390**

Nickname: Golden Flashes.
Stadium: Dix (1969), 30,520 capacity. Natural turf.
Colors: Navy Blue & Gold.
Conference: Mid-American.
SID: Dale Gallagher, 330-672-2110.
AD: Laing Kennedy.

KENTUCKY

Lexington, KY 40506 ....I-A

Coach: Bill Curry, Georgia Tech '65
Record: 16 Years, 79-98-4

1996 SCHEDULE

Louisville ■ ....*Aug. 31
Cincinnati ....Sept. 7
Indiana ■ ....*Sept. 21
Florida ....Sept. 28
Alabama ....Oct. 5
South Caro. ■ ....*Oct. 12
LSU ....*Oct. 19
Georgia ■ ....*Oct. 26
Mississippi St. ■ ....Nov. 9
Vanderbilt ■ ....Nov. 16
Tennessee ....Nov. 23

1995 RESULTS (4-7-0)

10 Louisville 13
7 Florida 42
17 Indiana 10
35 South Caro. 30
21 Auburn 42
24 LSU 16
3 Georgia 12
32 Mississippi St. 42
10 Vanderbilt 14
33 Cincinnati 14
31 Tennessee 34
223 **269**

Nickname: Wildcats.
Stadium: Commonwealth (1973), 57,800 capacity. Natural turf.
Colors: Blue & White.
Conference: Southeastern.
SID: Tony Neely, 606-257-3838.
AD: C. M. Newton.

KENTUCKY ST.

Frankfort, KY 40601 II

Coach: George Small, North Caro. A&T '79
Record: 1 Year, 7-4-0

1996 SCHEDULE

Miles ....Aug. 31
Georgetown (Ky.) ....Sept. 7
Albany St. (Ga.) ■ ....*Sept. 14
Clark Atlanta ....Sept. 21
Fort Valley St. ....*Sept. 28
Tuskegee ....Oct. 5
Lane ■ ....Oct. 12
Savannah St. ....Oct. 26
Morehouse ■ ....Nov. 2
Morris Brown ■ ....Nov. 9
Alabama A&M ....Nov. 16

1995 RESULTS (7-4-0)

14 Georgetown (Ky.) 7
19 West Va. St. 7
0 Albany St. (Ga.) 35
7 Clark Atlanta 0
17 Fort Valley St. 12
40 Ky. Wesleyan 0
12 Lane 28
18 Tuskegee 12
13 Savannah St. 20
13 Morehouse 6
6 Central St. 42
159 **169**

Nickname: Thorobreds.
Stadium: Alumni Field (1978), 6,000 capacity. Natural turf.
Colors: Green & Gold.
Conference: Southern Intercollegiate Athletic.
SID: Ron Braden, 502-227-6011.
AD: Don Lyons.

KY. WESLEYAN

Owensboro, KY 42301 II

Coach: John Johnson, Northern Mich. '84
Record: 2 Years, 10-10-0

1996 SCHEDULE

Western Ky. ....*Aug. 29
Bethel (Tenn.) ■ ....Sept. 14
Maryville (Tenn.) ....Sept. 21
Morehead St. ....*Sept. 28
Campbellsville ■ ....Oct. 5
Sue Bennett ....Oct. 12
Quincy ■ ....Oct. 19
Millsaps ....Oct. 26
St. Joseph's (Ind.) ....Nov. 2
Evansville ■ ....Nov. 9
Mt. St. Joseph ....Nov. 23

1995 RESULTS (5-5-0)

12 Evansville 42
11 Morehead St. 36
50 Quincy 29
57 Sue Bennett 24
51 Blackburn 17
0 Kentucky St. 40
28 Millsaps 21
33 Centre 21
24 Chicago 40
27 Valparaiso 36
293 **306**

Nickname: Panthers.
Stadium: Apollo (1989), 3,000 capacity. Natural turf.
Colors: Purple & White.
Conference: Division II Independents.
SID: Roy Pickerill, 502-926-3111.
AD: William Meadors.

KENYON

Gambier, OH 43022 III

Coach: Vince Arduini, Norwich '77
Record: 1 Year, 3-6-1

1996 SCHEDULE

Grove City ....Sept. 7
Oberlin ....Sept. 21
Wittenberg ■ ....Sept. 28
Ohio Wesleyan ....Oct. 5
Denison ■ ....Oct. 12
Case Reserve ....Oct. 19
Wooster ■ ....Oct. 26
Earlham ....Nov. 2
Allegheny ■ ....Nov. 9
Chicago ....Nov. 16

1995 RESULTS (3-6-1)

16 Grove City 31
30 Oberlin 6
7 Denison 7

14 Wittenberg....42
33 Case Reserve....7
14 Earlham....8
13 Allegheny....69
3 Waynesburg....32
14 Wooster....23
13 Ohio Wesleyan....33
157 **258**

Nickname: Lords.
Stadium: McBride Field (1962), 2,500 capacity. Natural turf.
Colors: Purple & White.
Conference: North Coast Athletic.
SID: Joe Wasiluk, 614-427-5471.
AD: Robert D. Bunnell.

KING'S (PA.)

Wilkes-Barre, PA 18711....III

Coach: Richard Mannello, Springfield '83
Record: 3 Years, 4-24-1

1996 SCHEDULE

Moravian ■....Sept. 14
Lycoming ■....Sept. 21
Johns Hopkins....*Sept. 27
Lebanon Valley....Oct. 5
Albright....Oct. 12
Wilkes ■....Oct. 19
Delaware Valley....Oct. 26
Widener ■....Nov. 2
FDU-Madison....*Nov. 8
Albany (N.Y.) ■....Nov. 16

1995 RESULTS (1-9-0)

0 Moravian....31
0 Lycoming....48
6 Johns Hopkins....35
11 Lebanon Valley....18
24 Albright....42
15 Wilkes....29
0 Delaware Valley....13
14 Widener....50
45 FDU-Madison....40
0 Albany (N.Y.)....50
115 **356**

Nickname: Monarchs.
Stadium: Monarch Fields, 3,000 capacity. Natural turf.
Colors: Red & Gold.
Conference: Middle Atlantic.
SID: Bob Ziadie, 717-826-5934.
AD: John Dorish.

KNOX

Galesburg, IL 61401....III

Coach: Andy Gibbons, Culver-Stockton '90
(First year as head coach)

1996 SCHEDULE

Beloit....Sept. 7
Lake Forest ■....Sept. 14
Carroll (Wis.)....Sept. 21
Lawrence ■....Sept. 28
Cornell College....Oct. 5
Grinnell ■....Oct. 12
Illinois Col.....Oct. 19
Coe ■....Oct. 26
Monmouth (Ill.)....Nov. 2

1995 RESULTS (6-3-0)

24 Principia....6
24 Beloit....47
24 Lake Forest....21
34 St. Norbert....30
16 Cornell College....23
23 Grinnell....0
28 Illinois Col.....7
23 Coe....48
28 Monmouth (Ill.)....14
224 **196**

Nickname: Prairie Fire.
Stadium: Knox Bowl (1968), 6,000 capacity. Natural turf.
Colors: Purple & Gold.
Conference: Midwest.
SID: Marc Wong, 309-341-7379.
AD: Harlan Knosher.

KUTZTOWN

Kutztown, PA 19530....II

Coach: Al Leonzi, Penn St. '64
Record: 4 Years, 15-25-1

1996 SCHEDULE

American Int'l....Sept. 7
Shippensburg ■....Sept. 21
Southern Conn. St. ■....Sept. 28
East Stroudsburg....Oct. 5
Cheyney ■....Oct. 12
Mansfield....Oct. 19
Millersville ■....Oct. 26
Bloomsburg....Nov. 2
Calif. (Pa.)....*Nov. 9
West Chester ■....Nov. 16

1995 RESULTS (6-4-0)

19 New Haven....28
14 West Va. Wesleyan....16
34 Calif. (Pa.)....0
17 Cheyney....7
23 Mansfield....0
20 Millersville....21
8 Bloomsburg....17
35 Shippensburg....6
21 West Chester....12
28 East Stroudsburg....7
219 **114**

Nickname: Golden Bears.
Stadium: University Field (1987), 5,600 capacity. Natural turf.
Colors: Maroon & Gold.
Conference: Pennsylvania State Athletic.
SID: Matt Santos, 610-683-4182.
AD: Clark Yeager.

LA VERNE

La Verne, CA 91750....III

Coach: Don Morel, La Verne '87
Record: 1 Year, 9-0-0

1996 SCHEDULE

Azusa Pacific....*Sept. 14
Cal Lutheran....Sept. 21
Sonoma St.....Sept. 28
Occidental ■....Oct. 5
Whittier....*Oct. 12
Chapman....*Oct. 26
Claremont-M-S....Nov. 2
Menlo ■....Nov. 9
Redlands ■....Nov. 16

1995 RESULTS (9-0-0)

35 Chapman....34
42 Redlands....17
51 Menlo....7
69 Pomona-Pitzer....14
59 Whittier....7
51 Azusa Pacific....17
34 Occidental....7
38 Claremont-M-S....17
31 Cal Lutheran....21
410 **141**

Nickname: Leopards.
Stadium: Ortmayer (1991), 1,500 capacity. Natural turf.
Colors: Orange & Green.
Conference: Southern California Intercollegiate Athletic.
SID: Mark Bagley, 909-593-3511.
AD: Jim Paschal.

LAFAYETTE

Easton, PA 18042....I-AA

Coach: Bill Russo, Brown '69
Record: 18 Years, 103-85-4

1996 SCHEDULE

Millersville ■....Sept. 14
Northeastern ■....Sept. 21
Cornell ■....Sept. 28
Harvard....Oct. 5
Fordham....Oct. 12
Columbia....Oct. 19
Colgate....Oct. 26
Army....Nov. 2
Bucknell ■....Nov. 9
Holy Cross ■....Nov. 16
Lehigh ■....Nov. 23

1995 RESULTS (4-6-1)

24 Buffalo....17
0 Hofstra....26
8 Pennsylvania....28
10 Columbia....10
7 Dartmouth....14
0 Princeton....41
27 Holy Cross....17
11 Bucknell....30
35 Colgate....9
24 Fordham....21
30 Lehigh....37
176 **250**

Nickname: Leopards.
Stadium: Fisher Field (1926), 13,750 capacity. Natural turf.
Colors: Maroon & White.
Conference: Patriot League.
SID: Scott D. Morse, 610-250-5122.
AD: Eve Atkinson.

LAKE FOREST

Lake Forest, IL 60045....III

Coach: Randy Moore, Iowa '84
Record: 1 Year, 0-9-0

1996 SCHEDULE

Hamline ■....Sept. 7
Knox....Sept. 14
Illinois Col.....Sept. 21
Monmouth (Ill.) ■....Sept. 28
St. Norbert ■....Oct. 5
Ripon....Oct. 12
Carroll (Wis.)....Oct. 19
Lawrence ■....Oct. 26
Beloit....Nov. 2

1995 RESULTS (0-9-0)

27 Bethel (Minn.)....38
14 North Park....34
21 Knox....24
20 Coe....52
17 St. Norbert....21
7 Ripon....42
24 Carroll (Wis.)....27
41 Lawrence....47
20 Beloit....31
191 **316**

Nickname: Foresters.
Stadium: Farwell Field, 2,000 capacity. Natural turf.
Colors: Red & Black.
Conference: Midwest.
SID: Mark Perlman, 708-735-6011.
AD: Jackie Slaats.

LAKELAND (WIS.)

Sheboygan, WI 53082....III

Coach: Randy Awrey, Northern Mich. '78
Record: 6 Years, 20-38-1

1996 SCHEDULE

Ripon ■....Sept. 7
Maranatha Baptist....Sept. 14
Carthage ■....Sept. 21
Franklin....Sept. 28
Greenville....Oct. 5
Concordia (Wis.) ■....Oct. 12
MacMurray ■....Oct. 19
Concordia (Ill.)....Oct. 26
Eureka ■....Nov. 2
Crown ■....Nov. 9

1995 RESULTS (6-3-1)

26 Ripon....30
33 Concordia (St. Paul)....33

42 Quincy 6
26 Crown 14
28 Greenville 27
14 Concordia (Wis.) 45
42 Concordia (Ill.) 0
67 MacMurray 14
45 Eureka 47
22 Mt. Senario 15
345 **231**

Nickname: Muskies.
Stadium: Taylor Field (1958), 1,500 capacity. Natural turf.
Colors: Navy & Gold.
Conference: Division III Independents.
SID: Dave Moyer, 414-565-1411.
AD: Jane Bouche.

LANE

Jackson, TN 38301 II

Coach: John P. Gore Jr., Tennessee St. '90
Record: 1 Year, 9-1-0

1996 SCHEDULE

Ark.-Pine Bluff [Little Rock, Ark.] ....*Aug. 31
Carson-Newman ....*Sept. 5
West Ala. ....Sept. 14
Texas Southern ....Sept. 21
Tennessee St. ....Oct. 5
Kentucky St. ....Oct. 12
Mississippi Val. ....Oct. 19
Knoxville ■ ....Oct. 26
Benedict ....Nov. 2
Johnson Smith ■ ....Nov. 16

1995 RESULTS (9-1-0)

25 Mississippi Val. 14
20 West Ala. 12
35 Knoxville 20
46 Johnson Smith 20
28 Kentucky St. 12
28 Miles 6
20 Morris Brown 10
7 Ark.-Pine Bluff 35
12 North Caro. A&T 4
49 Benedict 6
270 **139**

Nickname: Dragons.
Stadium: Rothrock (1930), 3,500 capacity. Natural turf.
Colors: Blue & Red.
Conference: Division II Independents.
SID: Donald D. Wilkes, 901-426-7651.
AD: J. L. Perry.

LAWRENCE

Appleton, WI 54911 III

Coach: Rick Coles, Coe '79
Record: 3 Years, 8-19-0

1996 SCHEDULE

Carleton ....Sept. 7
Concordia (Ill.) ■ ....Sept. 14
Coe ■ ....Sept. 21
Knox ....Sept. 28
Carroll (Wis.) ....Oct. 5
St. Norbert ■ ....Oct. 12
Beloit ■ ....Oct. 19
Lake Forest ....Oct. 26
Ripon ■ ....Nov. 2

1995 RESULTS (4-5-0)

28 Chicago 39
53 Eureka 50
26 Cornell College 34
29 Grinnell 8
28 Carroll (Wis.) 37
47 St. Norbert 31
17 Beloit 20
47 Lake Forest 41
35 Ripon 49
310 **309**

Nickname: Vikings.
Stadium: Banta Bowl (1965), 5,255 capacity. Natural turf.
Colors: Navy & White.
Conference: Midwest.
SID: Jeff School, 414-832-7346.
AD: Amy Proctor.

LEBANON VALLEY

Annville, PA 17003 III

Coach: James Monos, Shippensburg '72
Record: 9 Years, 41-56-2

1996 SCHEDULE

Hartwick ....Sept. 14
Albright ....*Sept. 21
Widener ....Sept. 28
King's (Pa.) ■ ....Oct. 5
Susquehanna ■ ....Oct. 12
Juniata ....Oct. 19
Moravian ■ ....Oct. 26
Western Md. ....Nov. 2
Lycoming ■ ....Nov. 9
Delaware Valley ■ ....Nov. 16

1995 RESULTS (3-7-0)

6 Hartwick 37
3 Albright 38
8 Widener 66
18 King's (Pa.) 11
26 Susquehanna 39
17 Juniata 0
7 Moravian 19
13 Western Md. 27
9 Lycoming 13
19 Delaware Valley 7
126 **257**

Nickname: Flying Dutchmen.
Stadium: Arnold Field (1969), 2,500 capacity. Natural turf.
Colors: Royal Blue & White.
Conference: Middle Atlantic.
SID: John Deamer, 717-867-6033.
AD: Louis Sorrentino.

LEHIGH

Bethlehem, PA 18015 ....I-AA

Coach: Kevin Higgins, West Chester '77
Record: 2 Years, 13-8-1

1996 SCHEDULE

Delaware ....Sept. 7
Fordham ■ ....Sept. 14
Buffalo ■ ....Sept. 21
Dartmouth ■ ....Sept. 28
Princeton ....Oct. 5
New Hampshire ....Oct. 12
Pennsylvania ....Oct. 19
Bucknell ■ ....Nov. 2
Holy Cross ....Nov. 9
Colgate ■ ....Nov. 16
Lafayette ....Nov. 23

1995 RESULTS (8-3-0)

9 Army 42
20 Colgate 9
21 Yale 10
14 New Hampshire 35
30 Bucknell 23
37 Columbia 35
34 Cornell 23
36 Massachusetts 44
17 Fordham 0
51 Holy Cross 21
37 Lafayette 30
306 **272**

Nickname: Mountain Hawks.
Stadium: Goodman (1988), 16,000 capacity. Natural turf.
Colors: Brown & White.
Conference: Patriot League.
SID: Glenn Hofmann, 610-758-3174.
AD: Joseph Sterrett.

LENOIR-RHYNE

Hickory, NC 28603 II

Coach: Charles Forbes, East Caro. '68
Record: 20 Years, 97-95-3

1996 SCHEDULE

Wofford ....*Sept. 7
Shepherd ....Sept. 21
Presbyterian ....Sept. 28
Elon ■ ....*Oct. 5
Gardner-Webb ■ ....*Oct. 12
Wingate ....Oct. 19
Newberry ■ ....Oct. 26
Carson-Newman ■ ....Nov. 2
Mars Hill ■ ....Nov. 9
Catawba ....Nov. 16

1995 RESULTS (3-7-0)

19 Wofford 23
26 Johnson Smith 6
35 Presbyterian 28
0 Elon 31
13 Gardner-Webb 30
13 Wingate 12
15 Newberry 36
21 Carson-Newman 40
14 Mars Hill 42
0 Catawba 22
156 **270**

Nickname: Bears.
Stadium: Moretz (1923), 8,500 capacity. Natural turf.
Colors: Red & Black.
Conference: South Atlantic.
SID: Dom Donnelly, 704-328-7174.
AD: Keith Ochs.

LIBERTY

Lynchburg, VA 24506 ....I-AA

Coach: Sam Rutigliano, Tulsa '56
Record: 7 Years, 44-32-0

1996 SCHEDULE

East Tenn. St. ....*Aug. 29
Western Caro. ■ ....*Sept. 7
Delaware St. ■ ....Sept. 14
Morgan St. ....Sept. 21
Indiana St. ■ ....Sept. 28
Hofstra ■ ....Oct. 12
Western Ky. ....*Oct. 19
Charleston So. ■ ....Oct. 26
Hampton ....Nov. 2
Livingstone ■ ....Nov. 9
Ga. Southern ....Nov. 16

1995 RESULTS (8-3-0)

76 West Va. Tech 6
31 Va. Military 50
48 Morgan St. 19
41 Delaware St. 14
10 Hofstra 36
7 Central Fla. 6
37 Wofford 0
19 Charleston So. 15
28 Hampton 14
6 Ga. Southern 7
49 Western Ky. 36
352 **203**

Nickname: Flames.
Stadium: Williams (1989), 12,000 capacity. Artificial turf.
Colors: Red, White & Blue.
Conference: I-AA Independents.
SID: Mike Montoro, 804-582-2292.
AD: Chuck Burch.

LIVINGSTONE

Salisbury, NC 28144 II

Coach: Rudy Abrams, Livingstone '64
Record: 2 Years, 10-9-1

1996 SCHEDULE

Elizabeth City St. ■ ....*Aug. 31
Glenville St. ■ ....Sept. 7
Norfolk St. ....*Sept. 14
Virginia St. ....Sept. 28
Winston-Salem ....Oct. 5
Johnson Smith ■ ....Oct. 12
Bowie St. ■ ....Oct. 19
N.C. Central ■ ....Oct. 26

Fayetteville St. ....Nov. 2
Liberty ....Nov. 9

1995 RESULTS (5-4-1)

6 Elizabeth City St. 16
28 Norfolk St. 42
17 Winston-Salem 17
24 Virginia St. 28
22 Bowie St. 15
49 Johnson Smith 25
49 Knoxville 14
60 N.C. Central 25
39 Fayetteville St. 21
0 Glenville St. 40
294 **243**

Nickname: Fighting Blue Bears.
Stadium: Alumni, 4,000 capacity. Natural turf.
Colors: Blue & Black.
Conference: Central Intercollegiate Athletic Association.
SID: Adrian Ferguson, 704-638-5586.
AD: Clifton Huff.

LOCK HAVEN

Lock Haven, PA 17745 II

Coach: Nick Polk, Lock Haven '86
(First year as head coach)

1996 SCHEDULE

Delaware St. ....Sept. 7
Kean ....Sept. 14
Bloomsburg ....Sept. 21
Mansfield ■ ....*Sept. 28
Clarion ....Oct. 5
Millersville ....*Oct. 12
Shippensburg ■ ....Oct. 19
Calif. (Pa.) ....Oct. 26
Slippery Rock ■ ....*Nov. 2
Indiana (Pa.) ....Nov. 9
Edinboro ■ ....Nov. 16

1995 RESULTS (2-9-0)

15 Maine 41
21 Kean 13
10 Northern Iowa 55
37 Mansfield 6
12 Edinboro 52
32 Clarion 49
20 Bloomsburg 53
29 Shippensburg 73
14 Calif. (Pa.) 19
6 Slippery Rock 34
0 Indiana (Pa.) 38
196 **433**

Nickname: Bald Eagles.
Stadium: Hubert Jack, 3,000 capacity. Artificial turf.
Colors: Crimson & White.
Conference: Pennsylvania State Athletic.
SID: Patrick Donghia, 717-893-2350.
AD: Sharon E. Taylor.

LIU-C.W. POST

Brookville, NY 11548 II

Coach: Tom Marshall, Detroit '62
Record: 13 Years, 69-57-2

1996 SCHEDULE

Wm. Paterson ....*Sept. 13
Wagner ....Sept. 21
Monmouth (N.J.) ■ ....Sept. 28
Trenton St. ■ ....Oct. 12
Bentley ■ ....Oct. 19
Stony Brook ....Oct. 26
Southern Conn. St. ■ ....Nov. 2
American Int'l ....Nov. 9
Robert Morris ....Nov. 16

1995 RESULTS (6-4-0)

23 Wm. Paterson 6
27 Albany (N.Y.) 21
40 Central Conn. St. 0
31 American Int'l 22
34 Trenton St. 23
16 Bentley 24
20 Rowan 0
23 Southern Conn. St. 24
6 Springfield 10
13 Mercyhurst 17
233 **147**

Nickname: Pioneers.
Stadium: Hickox Field (1966), 5,000 capacity. Natural turf.
Colors: Green & Gold.
Conference: Eastern Football.
SID: Jeremy Kniffin, 516-299-4156.
AD: Vin Salamone.

LORAS

Dubuque, IA 52001 III

Coach: Bob Bierie, Loras '65
Record: 16 Years, 98-62-5

1996 SCHEDULE

Ill. Benedictine ■ ....Sept. 7
Wis.-Platteville ....Sept. 14
Upper Iowa ....Sept. 21
Wartburg ■ ....Oct. 5
Central (Iowa) ....Oct. 12
Luther ■ ....Oct. 19
William Penn ■ ....Oct. 26
Buena Vista ....Nov. 2
Dubuque ■ ....Nov. 9
Simpson ....Nov. 16

1995 RESULTS (6-4-0)

0 Wis.-La Crosse 34
42 Ill. Benedictine 7
47 Buena Vista 28
14 Dubuque 6
12 Simpson 34
61 William Penn 0
14 Central (Iowa) 24
48 Luther 20
38 Upper Iowa 14
8 Wartburg 30
284 **197**

Nickname: Duhawks.
Stadium: Rock Bowl (1945), 3,000 capacity. Natural turf.
Colors: Purple & Gold.
Conference: Iowa Intercollegiate Athletic.
SID: Howard Thomas, 319-588-7407.
AD: Bob Bierie.

LSU

Baton Rouge, LA 70894 ....I-A

Coach: Gerry DiNardo, Notre Dame '75
Record: 5 Years, 26-29-1

1996 SCHEDULE

Houston ■ ....*Sept. 7
Auburn ....Sept. 21
New Mexico St. ■ ....*Sept. 28
Vanderbilt ■ ....*Oct. 5
Florida ....Oct. 12
Kentucky ■ ....*Oct. 19
Mississippi St. ■ ....*Oct. 26
Alabama ■ ....*Nov. 9
Mississippi ....Nov. 16
Tulane ■ ....*Nov. 23
Arkansas [Little Rock, Ark.] ....Nov. 29

1995 RESULTS (6-4-1)

17 Texas A&M 33
34 Mississippi St. 16
12 Auburn 6
52 Rice 7
20 South Caro. 20
10 Florida 28
16 Kentucky 24
49 North Texas 7
3 Alabama 10
38 Mississippi 9
28 Arkansas 0
279 **160**

Independence Bowl

45 Michigan St. 26

Nickname: Fighting Tigers.
Stadium: Tiger (1924), 79,940 capacity. Natural turf.
Colors: Purple & Gold.
Conference: Southeastern.
SID: Herb Vincent, 504-388-8226.
AD: Joe Dean.

LOUISIANA TECH

Ruston, LA 71272 ....I-A

Coach: Gary Crowton, Brigham Young '83
(First year as head coach)

1996 SCHEDULE

Middle Tenn. St. ■ ....*Aug. 31
Baylor [Shreveport, La.] ....*Sept. 7
Central Mich. ....Sept. 14
Mississippi St. ....*Sept. 21
Southwestern La. ■ ....*Sept. 28
Texas A&M ....Oct. 5
Arkansas [Little Rock, Ark.] ....*Oct. 12
Toledo ■ ....Oct. 19
Ala.-Birmingham ■ ....*Oct. 26
Northern Ill. ....Nov. 2
Arkansas St. ....Nov. 9

1995 RESULTS (5-6-0)

28 Bowling Green 21
19 Houston 7
21 South Caro. 68
28 Arkansas St. 25
27 Tulsa 23
13 New Mexico St. 48
41 Pacific (Cal.) 47
45 Nevada 49
33 Southwestern La. 40
6 Vanderbilt 29
59 Northern Ill. 14
320 **371**

Nickname: Bulldogs.
Stadium: Joe Aillet (1968), 30,600 capacity. Natural turf.
Colors: Red & Blue.
Conference: I-A Independents.
SID: To be named, 318-257-3144.
AD: Jim Oakes.

LOUISVILLE

Louisville, KY 40292 ....I-A

Coach: Ron Cooper, Jacksonville St. '83
Record: 3 Years, 16-17-0

1996 SCHEDULE

Kentucky ....*Aug. 31
Penn St. ....Sept. 7
Baylor ■ ....Sept. 14
Michigan St. ....Sept. 21
Southern Miss. ■ ....Sept. 28
Tulane ....*Oct. 12
Northern Ill. ■ ....Oct. 19
Cincinnati ■ ....Oct. 26
Memphis ■ ....Nov. 2
North Caro. ....Nov. 9
Houston ....*Nov. 16

1995 RESULTS (7-4-0)

13 Kentucky 10
34 Northern Ill. 21
7 Michigan St. 30
10 North Caro. 17
17 Memphis 7
21 Southern Miss. 25
20 Wyoming 27
31 Maryland 0
34 Tulane 14
39 Northeast La. 0
57 North Texas 14
283 **165**

Nickname: Cardinals.
Stadium: Cardinal (1956), 35,500 capacity. Artificial turf.
Colors: Red, Black & White.
Conference: Conference USA.
SID: Kenny Klein, 502-852-6581.
AD: William Olsen.

LUTHER

Decorah, IA 52101 III

Coach: Brad Pole, Rocky Mountain '79
(First year as head coach)

1996 SCHEDULE

St. Olaf ■ ....Sept. 7
Martin Luther ....Sept. 14
Simpson ■ ....Sept. 21
Buena Vista ....Sept. 28
Dubuque ■ ....Oct. 5
Loras ....Oct. 19
Central (Iowa) ■ ....Oct. 26
William Penn ■ ....Nov. 2
Upper Iowa ....Nov. 9
Wartburg ....Nov. 16

1995 RESULTS (2-8-0)

0 St. Olaf 23
28 William Penn 7
6 Upper Iowa 14
7 Central (Iowa) 50
20 Buena Vista 18
3 Simpson 49
20 Loras 48
12 Dubuque 13
28 Wartburg 50
17 Northern St. 41
141 **313**

Nickname: Norse.
Stadium: Carlson (1966), 5,000 capacity. Natural turf.
Colors: Blue & White.
Conference: Iowa Intercollegiate Athletic.
SID: Dave Blanchard, 319-387-1586.
AD: Joe Thompson.

LYCOMING

Williamsport, PA 17701 III

Coach: Frank Girardi, West Chester '61
Record: 24 Years, 169-62-5

1996 SCHEDULE

Albright ■ ....Sept. 14
King's (Pa.) ....Sept. 21
FDU-Madison ■ ....Oct. 5
Hartwick ■ ....Oct. 12
Delaware Valley ....Oct. 19
Widener ....Oct. 26
Susquehanna ■ ....Nov. 2
Lebanon Valley ....Nov. 9
Wilkes ■ ....Nov. 16

1995 RESULTS (7-2-0)

29 Albright 26
48 King's (Pa.) 0
17 FDU-Madison 20
38 Hartwick 26
29 Delaware Valley 0
16 Widener 15
14 Susquehanna 21
13 Lebanon Valley 9
28 Wilkes 9
232 **126**

III Championship

31 Widener 27
0 Wash. & Jeff. 48

Nickname: Warriors.
Stadium: Person Field (1962), 2,500 capacity. Natural turf.
Colors: Blue & Gold.
Conference: Middle Atlantic.
SID: Jeff Michaels, 717-321-4028.
AD: Frank Girardi.

MACALESTER

St. Paul, MN 55105 III

Coach: Tom Bell, Bri'water (Mass.) '66
Record: 19 Years, 93-86-6

1996 SCHEDULE

Crown ....Sept. 7
Carleton ....Sept. 14
Gust. Adolphus ■ ....Sept. 21
Concordia-M'head ....Sept. 28
St. Olaf ■ ....Oct. 5
Bethel (Minn.) ■ ....Oct. 12
St. Thomas (Minn.) ....Oct. 19
St. John's (Minn.) ■ ....Oct. 26
Augsburg ....Nov. 2
Hamline [Minneapolis, Minn.] ....Nov. 9

1995 RESULTS (1-9-0)

28 Crown 14
18 Gust. Adolphus 42
7 Bethel (Minn.) 34
13 Carleton 36
7 Augsburg 17
18 St. Olaf 35
6 Hamline 21
6 Concordia-M'head 49
0 St. Thomas (Minn.) 48
18 St. John's (Minn.) 45
121 **341**

Nickname: Scots.
Stadium: Macalester (1965), 4,000 capacity. Natural turf.
Colors: Orange & Blue.
Conference: Minnesota Intercollegiate Athletic.
SID: Andy Johnson, 612-696-6533.
AD: Ken Andrews.

MacMURRAY

Jacksonville, IL 62650 III

Coach: Bob Frey, Mount Union '85
Record: 1 Year, 3-7-0

1996 SCHEDULE

William Penn ■ ....Sept. 7
Monmouth (Ill.) ....Sept. 14
Principia ....Sept. 28
Eureka ....Oct. 5
Greenville ■ ....Oct. 12
Lakeland ....Oct. 19
Concordia (Wis.) ■ ....Oct. 26
Concordia (Ill.) ....Nov. 2
Blackburn ....Nov. 9
Westminster (Mo.) ■ ....Nov. 16

1995 RESULTS (3-7-0)

16 William Penn 9
19 Monmouth (Ill.) 10
13 Concordia (Wis.) 42
15 Concordia (Ill.) 0
12 Blackburn 33
21 Greenville 33
7 Quincy 31
14 Lakeland 67
18 Franklin 50
6 Eureka 18
141 **293**

Nickname: Fighting Highlanders.
Stadium: Highlander (1984), 5,000 capacity. Natural turf.
Colors: Navy & Scarlet.
Conference: St. Louis Intercollegiate Athletic.
SID: Tom Lenz, 217-479-7143.
AD: Bob Gay.

MAINE

Orono, ME 04469 ....I-AA

Coach: Jack Cosgrove, Maine '78
Record: 3 Years, 9-24-0

1996 SCHEDULE

Northeastern [Portland, Maine] ....*Aug. 29
Fordham ....Sept. 7
Boston U. ■ ....Sept. 14
Rhode Island ■ ....Sept. 21
Delaware ■ ....Sept. 28
James Madison ....Oct. 5
Connecticut ....Oct. 12
New Hampshire ■ ....Oct. 19
Massachusetts ....Nov. 2
Hofstra ....Nov. 9
Buffalo ■ ....Nov. 16

1995 RESULTS (3-8-0)

41 Lock Haven 15
13 Rhode Island 17
21 Boston U. 40
17 James Madison 21
19 Buffalo 6
30 Connecticut 31
0 New Hampshire 21
0 Delaware 61
24 Massachusetts 21
28 Northeastern 31
17 Central Fla. 37
210 **301**

Nickname: Black Bears.
Stadium: Alumni (1942), 10,000 capacity. Natural turf.
Colors: Blue & White.
Conference: Yankee.
SID: Matt Bourque, 207-581-1086.
AD: Suzanne Tyler.

MAINE MARITIME

Castine, ME 04420 III

Coach: Mike Hodgson, Maine '79
Record: 2 Years, 14-5-0

1996 SCHEDULE

Plymouth St. ■ ....Sept. 14
Bri'water (Mass.) ■ ....Sept. 21
Worcester St. ....Sept. 28
Mass. Maritime ■ ....Oct. 5
Mass.-Dartmouth ....Oct. 12
Salve Regina ....Oct. 19
Mass.-Boston ■ ....Oct. 26
Fitchburg St. ....Nov. 2
Framingham St. ■ ....Nov. 9
Westfield St. ....Nov. 16

1995 RESULTS (7-2-0)

20 Bri'water (Mass.) 0
22 Worcester St. 29
10 Mass. Maritime 17
27 Mass.-Dartmouth 24
22 Hartwick 19
48 Mass.-Boston 6
51 Fitchburg St. 6
33 Framingham St. 8
14 Westfield St. 7
247 **116**

Nickname: Mariners.
Stadium: Ritchie (1965), 3,500 capacity. Artificial turf.
Colors: Royal Blue & Gold.
Conference: New England.
SID: To be named, 207-326-2259.
AD: Bill Mottola.

MANCHESTER

North Manchester, IN 46962 III

Coach: Dave Harms, Drake '80
Record: 1 Year, 4-6-0

1996 SCHEDULE

Earlham ■ ....Sept. 14
Mt. St. Joseph ....Sept. 21
Bluffton ....Sept. 28
Hanover ■ ....Oct. 5
Wabash ....Oct. 12
Rose-Hulman ■ ....Oct. 19
Defiance ....Oct. 26
DePauw ....Nov. 2
Franklin ■ ....Nov. 9
Anderson (Ind.) ....Nov. 16

1995 RESULTS (4-6-0)

22 Defiance 31
27 Olivet 28
28 Bluffton 18
31 Wabash 29
44 Rose-Hulman 61
13 Walsh 21
10 DePauw 8
27 Franklin 28
19 Hanover 41
10 Anderson (Ind.) 7
231 **272**

Nickname: Spartans.
Stadium: Burt Memorial, 4,500 capacity. Natural turf.

Colors: Black & Old Gold.
Conference: Indiana Collegiate Athletic.
SID: Rob Nichols, 219-982-5035.
AD: Tom Jarman.

MANKATO ST.

Mankato, MN 56001 II

Coach: Dan Runkle, Illinois Col. '68
Record: 15 Years, 83-83-2

1996 SCHEDULE

Minn.-Duluth ■ ....*Sept. 7
Northwest Mo. St. ....Sept. 14
Neb.-Omaha ....*Sept. 21
Morningside ■ ....Sept. 28
Northern Colo. ....Oct. 5
St. Cloud St. ■ ....Oct. 12
North Dak. [Minneapolis, Minn.] ....Oct. 19
North Dak. St. ....*Oct. 26
Augustana (S.D.) ....Nov. 2
South Dak. ■ ....Nov. 9
South Dak. St. ....Nov. 16

1995 RESULTS (4-7-0)

10 Portland St. 42
59 Northwest Mo. St. 34
49 Neb.-Omaha 10
19 Morningside 17
7 Northern Colo. 31
6 St. Cloud St. 14
21 North Dak. 27
25 North Dak. St. 26
55 Augustana (S.D.) 38
7 South Dak. 28
32 South Dak. St. 39
290 **306**

Nickname: Mavericks.
Stadium: Blakeslee Field (1962), 7,500 capacity. Natural turf.
Colors: Purple & Gold.
Conference: North Central.
SID: Paul Allan, 507-389-2625.
AD: Don Amiot.

MANSFIELD

Mansfield, PA 16933 II

Coach: Joe Viadella, Rhode Island '83
Record: 1 Year, 1-9-0

1996 SCHEDULE

Cortland St. ■ ....Sept. 7
Southern Conn. St. ....Sept. 14
Ithaca ....Sept. 21
Lock Haven ....*Sept. 28
Millersville ■ ....Oct. 5
Bloomsburg ....Oct. 12
Kutztown ■ ....Oct. 19
West Chester ....Oct. 26
East Stroudsburg ■ ....Nov. 2
Cheyney ....Nov. 9
Clarion ■ ....Nov. 16

1995 RESULTS (1-9-0)

20 Cortland St. 21
12 Ithaca 30
6 Lock Haven 37
13 Bloomsburg 56
0 Kutztown 23
8 West Chester 24
13 East Stroudsburg 36
28 Cheyney 20
0 Edinboro 42
20 Millersville 41
120 **330**

Nickname: Mountaineers.
Stadium: Van Norman Field, 4,000 capacity. Natural turf.
Colors: Red & Black.
Conference: Pennsylvania State Athletic.
SID: Steve McCloskey, 717-662-4845.
AD: Roger Maisner.

MARIETTA

Marietta, OH 45750 III

Coach: Gene Epley, Indiana (Pa.) '65
Record: 9 Years, 36-52-3

1996 SCHEDULE

Central (Iowa) ....Sept. 7
Capital ■ ....*Sept. 21
John Carroll ....Sept. 28
Baldwin-Wallace ■ ....*Oct. 5
Otterbein ....Oct. 12
Hiram ■ ....Oct. 19
Ohio Northern ....Oct. 26
Mount Union ....Nov. 2
Heidelberg ■ ....Nov. 9
Muskingum ....Nov. 16

1995 RESULTS (8-1-1)

36 Thiel 0
21 John Carroll 21
27 Baldwin-Wallace 10
26 Hiram 7
37 Mount Union 41
69 Capital 7
29 Ohio Northern 27
45 Otterbein 14
50 Heidelberg 34
24 Muskingum 0
364 **161**

Nickname: Pioneers.
Stadium: Don Drumm Field (1935), 7,000 capacity. Natural turf.
Colors: Navy Blue & White.
Conference: Ohio Athletic.
SID: Jeff Schaly, 614-376-4891.
AD: Debora Lazorik.

MARIST

Poughkeepsie, NY 12601 ....I-AA

Coach: Jim Parady, Maine '84
Record: 4 Years, 22-17-1

1996 SCHEDULE

Duquesne ....Sept. 14
Iona ■ ....Sept. 21
Wagner ....Sept. 28
Georgetown ....Oct. 5
Fairfield ■ ....Oct. 12
St. John's (N.Y.) ■ ....Oct. 19
St. Peter's ....Oct. 26
Towson St. ■ ....Nov. 2
Canisius ■ ....Nov. 9
Siena ....Nov. 16

1995 RESULTS (6-4-0)

16 Monmouth (N.J.) 15
0 Fordham 46
20 St. Francis (Pa.) 17
36 St. John's (N.Y.) 29
14 Iona 18
14 Duquesne 16
34 Canisius 13
13 Georgetown 14
38 St. Peter's 0
49 Siena 6
234 **174**

Nickname: Red Foxes.
Stadium: Leonidoff Field (1972), 2,500 capacity. Natural turf.
Colors: Black, Red & White.
Conference: Metro Atlantic.
SID: Sean Morrison, 914-575-3000.
AD: Tim Murray.

MARS HILL

Mars Hill, NC 28754 II

Coach: Tim Clifton, Mercer '76
Record: 3 Years, 17-14-0

1996 SCHEDULE

Indiana St. ....*Aug. 29
Concord (W.Va.) ....Sept. 14
Catawba ■ ....Sept. 21
Wingate ....Sept. 28
Newberry ....*Oct. 5
Elon ■ ....Oct. 12
Carson-Newman ■ ....Oct. 19
Presbyterian ■ ....Oct. 26
Lenoir-Rhyne ....Nov. 9
Gardner-Webb ....Nov. 16

1995 RESULTS (6-4-0)

0 Indiana St. 31
38 Concord (W.Va.) 21
35 Catawba 16
28 Wingate 20
34 Newberry 14
51 Elon 31
0 Carson-Newman 42
7 Presbyterian 35
42 Lenoir-Rhyne 14
6 Gardner-Webb 14
241 **238**

Nickname: Lions.
Stadium: Meares (1965), 5,000 capacity. Natural turf.
Colors: Blue & Gold.
Conference: South Atlantic.
SID: Rick Baker, 704-689-1373.
AD: Ed Hoffmeyer.

MARSHALL

Huntington, WV 25715 ....I-AA

Coach: Bob Pruett, Marshall '65
(First year as head coach)

1996 SCHEDULE

Howard ■ ....*Sept. 7
West Va. St. ■ ....*Sept. 14
Ga. Southern ....Sept. 21
Western Ky. ■ ....*Sept. 28
Tenn.-Chatt. ■ ....*Oct. 5
Va. Military ....Oct. 12
Western Caro. ■ ....*Oct. 19
Appalachian St. ....Oct. 26
Citadel ■ ....Nov. 2
East Tenn. St. ....Nov. 9
Furman ■ ....Nov. 16

1995 RESULTS (9-2-0)

16 North Caro. St. 33
45 Tennessee Tech 14
37 Ga. Southern 7
35 Tenn.-Chatt. 32
56 Va. Military 21
42 Western Caro. 3
3 Appalachian St. 10
21 Citadel 19
52 East Tenn. St. 0
31 Furman 6
30 Hofstra 28
368 **173**

I-AA Championship

38 Jackson St. 8
41 Northern Iowa 24
25 McNeese St. 13
20 Montana 22

Nickname: Thundering Herd.
Stadium: Marshall University (1991), 30,000 capacity. Artificial turf.
Colors: Green & White.
Conference: Southern.
SID: Gary Richter, 304-696-5275.
AD: To be named.

MARTIN LUTHER

New Ulm, MN 56073 III

Coach: Dennis Gorsline, Northern Mich. '65
Record: 25 Years, 91-92-1

1996 SCHEDULE

Trinity Bible (N.D.) ....Sept. 7
Luther ■ ....Sept. 14
Minn.-Crookston ....Sept. 21
Concordia (St. Paul) ■ ....Sept. 28
Northwestern Minn. ....Oct. 5

Mt. Senario ■ .... Oct. 12
Crown ■ .... Oct. 19
Maranatha Baptist ■ .... Oct. 26

1995 RESULTS (5-2-0)

13 Maranatha Baptist 21
20 Mt. Senario 30
28 Northwestern Minn. 14
14 Crown 0
32 Minn.-Crookston 27
35 Concordia (St. Paul) 25
48 Trinity Bible (N.D.) 27
190 **144**

Nickname: Knights.
Stadium: Martin Luther, 2,000 capacity. Natural turf.
Colors: Black, Red & White.
Conference: Upper Midwest Athletic.
SID: Dave Wietzke, 507-354-8221.
AD: To be named.

MARYLAND

College Park, MD 20740 .... I-A

Coach: Mark Duffner, William & Mary '75
Record: 10 Years, 75-34-1

1996 SCHEDULE

Northern Ill. ■ .... *Aug. 31
Ala.-Birmingham ■ .... *Sept. 7
Virginia .... Sept. 14
West Va. .... Sept. 28
North Caro. St. ■ .... Oct. 5
North Caro. .... Oct. 12
Wake Forest ■ .... Oct. 19
Duke .... Oct. 26
Clemson .... Nov. 2
Georgia Tech ■ .... *Nov. 14
Florida St. [Fort Lauderdale, Fla.] .... Nov. 23

1995 RESULTS (6-5-0)

29 Tulane 10
32 North Caro. 18
31 West Va. 17
41 Duke 28
3 Georgia Tech 31
9 Wake Forest 6
0 Clemson 17
0 Louisville 31
30 North Caro. St. 13
18 Virginia 21
17 Florida St. 59
210 **251**

Nickname: Terrapins.
Stadium: Byrd (1950), 48,000 capacity. Natural turf.
Colors: Red, White, Black & Gold.
Conference: Atlantic Coast.
SID: Herb Hartnett, 301-314-7064.
AD: Debbie Yow.

MARYVILLE (TENN.)

Maryville, TN 37801 III

Coach: Phil Wilks, Marshall '70
Record: 8 Years, 40-39-0

1996 SCHEDULE

Davidson ■ .... Sept. 14
Ky. Wesleyan ■ .... Sept. 21
Sewanee ■ .... Sept. 28
Rhodes .... Oct. 5
Wittenberg .... Oct. 12
Centre ■ .... Oct. 19
Clinch Valley .... Oct. 26
Methodist ■ .... Nov. 2
Emory & Henry .... Nov. 16

1995 RESULTS (4-3-0)

28 Davidson 21
19 Sewanee 20
17 Rhodes 14
26 Centre 7
13 Methodist 23
7 Wittenberg 41
6 Emory & Henry 3
116 **129**

Nickname: Scots.
Stadium: Lloyd Thorton (1951), 2,500 capacity. Natural turf.
Colors: Orange & Garnet.
Conference: Division III Independents.
SID: Eric Etchison, 615-981-8283.
AD: Randy Lambert.

MASSACHUSETTS

Amherst, MA 01003 .... I-AA

Coach: Mike Hodges, Maine '67
Record: 4 Years, 26-17-0

1996 SCHEDULE

Villanova .... Sept. 7
Holy Cross .... Sept. 14
Richmond .... Sept. 21
Northeastern ■ .... Sept. 28
Rhode Island .... Oct. 5
Boston U. ■ .... Oct. 12
Buffalo ■ .... Oct. 19
New Hampshire .... Oct. 26
Maine ■ .... Nov. 2
William & Mary .... Nov. 9
Connecticut ■ .... Nov. 16

1995 RESULTS (6-5-0)

7 Richmond 21
51 Holy Cross 0
21 Northeastern 19
0 Rhode Island 34
29 New Hampshire 32
33 Buffalo 9
20 William & Mary 9
44 Lehigh 36
21 Maine 24
28 Boston U. 23
7 Connecticut 20
261 **227**

Nickname: Minutemen.
Stadium: Warren McGuirk (1965), 17,000 capacity. Natural turf.
Colors: Maroon & White.
Conference: Yankee.
SID: Bill Strickland, 413-545-2439.
AD: Bob Marcum.

MASS.-BOSTON

Boston, MA 02125 III

Coach: Gus Giardi, Syracuse '64
Record: 2 Years, 2-16-0

1996 SCHEDULE

Westfield St. ■ .... Sept. 21
Bri'water (Mass.) .... Sept. 28
Worcester St. ■ .... Oct. 5
Mass. Maritime .... Oct. 12
Mass.-Dartmouth ■ .... Oct. 19
Maine Maritime .... Oct. 26
MIT .... Nov. 2
Fitchburg St. ■ .... Nov. 9
Framingham St. .... Nov. 16

1995 RESULTS (2-7-0)

0 Westfield St. 35
0 Bri'water (Mass.) 34
22 Worcester St. 40
19 Mass. Maritime 33
12 Mass.-Dartmouth 36
6 Maine Maritime 48
18 MIT 14
7 Fitchburg St. 14
8 Framingham St. 7
92 **261**

Nickname: Beacons.
Stadium: Clark Field (1981), 750 capacity. Natural turf.
Colors: Blue & White.
Conference: New England.
SID: Chuck Sullivan, 617-287-7815.
AD: Charlie Titus.

MASS.-DARTMOUTH

North Dartmouth, MA 02747 III

Coach: William Kavanaugh, Stonehill '72
Record: 6 Years, 29-28-0

1996 SCHEDULE

Norwich .... Sept. 7
Worcester St. ■ .... Sept. 21
Mass. Maritime .... Sept. 28
Nichols .... Oct. 5
Maine Maritime ■ .... Oct. 12
Mass.-Boston .... Oct. 19
Fitchburg St. ■ .... Oct. 26
Framingham St. .... Nov. 2
Westfield St. ■ .... Nov. 9
Bri'water (Mass.) .... Nov. 16

1995 RESULTS (4-6-0)

13 Norwich 0
0 Plymouth St. 33
2 Worcester St. 16
7 Mass. Maritime 23
24 Maine Maritime 27
36 Mass.-Boston 12
23 Fitchburg St. 0
24 Framingham St. 6
0 Westfield St. 12
20 Bri'water (Mass.) 28
149 **157**

Nickname: Corsairs.
Stadium: University, 1,850 capacity. Natural turf.
Colors: Blue, Gold & White.
Conference: New England.
SID: William Gathright, 508-999-8727.
AD: Robert Dowd.

MASS.-LOWELL

Lowell, MA 01854 II

Coach: Sandy Ruggles, Northeastern '73
(First year as head coach)

1996 SCHEDULE

Bentley ■ .... Sept. 14
Norwich ■ .... Sept. 21
Sacred Heart .... Sept. 28
Western New Eng. .... Oct. 5
Salve Regina ■ .... Oct. 12
Stonehill .... Oct. 19
Assumption ■ .... Oct. 26
Merrimack ■ .... Nov. 2
Plymouth St. .... Nov. 9
Curry .... Nov. 16

1995 RESULTS (0-10-0)

7 Bentley 44
7 Norwich 35
13 Sacred Heart 41
3 Plymouth St. 52
7 Pace 42
6 Stonehill 35
0 Western Conn. St. 62
0 Worcester Tech 28
13 Assumption 26
0 Stony Brook 26
56 **391**

Nickname: River Hawks.
Stadium: Cawley Memorial, 7,000 capacity. Natural turf.
Colors: Red, White & Blue.
Conference: Division II Independents.
SID: Jim Seavy, 508-934-2306.
AD: Dana K. Skinner.

MIT

Cambridge, MA 02139 III

Coach: Dwight Smith, Bates '75
Record: 8 Years, 23-38-1

1996 SCHEDULE

Salve Regina .... Sept. 14
Assumption .... Sept. 21

SCHEDULES/RESULTS

Western New Eng. ■ ... Sept. 28
Stonehill ■ ... Oct. 5
Merrimack ... Oct. 12
Curry ■ ... Oct. 19
Nichols ... Oct. 26
Mass.-Boston ■ ... Nov. 2
Bentley ■ ... Nov. 9

1995 RESULTS (3-5-0)

13 Salve Regina ... 40
6 Assumption ... 20
33 Curry ... 6
14 Stonehill ... 21
42 Western New Eng. ... 24
35 Nichols ... 2
14 Mass.-Boston ... 18
6 Bentley ... 39
163 **170**

Nickname: Beavers.
Stadium: Steinbrenner (1980), 1,600 capacity. Natural turf.
Colors: Cardinal & Gray.
Conference: Eastern Football.
SID: Roger F. Crosley, 617-253-7946.
AD: Richard Hill.

MASS. MARITIME

Buzzards Bay, MA 02532 ... III

Coach: Don Ruggeri, Springfield '62
Record: 23 Years, 116-89-1

1996 SCHEDULE

Nichols ■ ... Sept. 14
Coast Guard ... *Sept. 21
Mass.-Dartmouth ■ ... Sept. 28
Maine Maritime ... Oct. 5
Mass.-Boston ■ ... Oct. 12
Fitchburg St. ... Oct. 19
Framingham St. ■ ... Oct. 26
Westfield St. ... *Nov. 1
Bri'water (Mass.) ■ ... Nov. 9
Worcester St. ... Nov. 16

1995 RESULTS (7-2-0)

16 Nichols ... 13
23 Mass.-Dartmouth ... 7
17 Maine Maritime ... 10
33 Mass.-Boston ... 19
50 Fitchburg St. ... 7
30 Framingham St. ... 6
37 Westfield St. ... 6
21 Bri'water (Mass.) ... 25
17 Worcester St. ... 22
244 **115**

Nickname: Buccaneers.
Stadium: Commander Ellis (1972), 3,000 capacity. Natural turf.
Colors: Blue & Gold.
Conference: New England.
SID: Leroy Thompson, 508-830-5054.
AD: Robert Corradi.

McNEESE ST.

Lake Charles, LA 70601 ... I-AA

Coach: Bobby Keasler, Northeast La. '70
Record: 6 Years, 53-21-2

1996 SCHEDULE

Southwest Mo. St. ■ ... *Sept. 7
James Madison ■ ... *Sept. 14
Angelo St. ■ ... *Sept. 21
Northern Iowa ... *Sept. 28
Ark.-Monticello ■ ... *Oct. 5
Troy St. ... *Oct. 12
Sam Houston St. ... Oct. 26
Stephen F. Austin ■ ... *Nov. 2
Southwest Tex. St. ■ ... *Nov. 9
Northwestern St. ... *Nov. 16
Nicholls St. ■ ... *Nov. 23

1995 RESULTS (11-0-0)

31 Southwest Mo. St. ... 2
45 Southeastern Okla. ... 10
30 James Madison ... 24
31 Youngstown St. ... 3
49 Central Fla. ... 7
27 Portland St. ... 13
20 Sam Houston St. ... 0
34 Stephen F. Austin ... 16
28 Southwest Tex. St. ... 7
20 Northwestern St. ... 10
31 Nicholls St. ... 6
346 **98**

I-AA Championship

33 Idaho ... 3
52 Delaware ... 18
13 Marshall ... 25

Nickname: Cowboys.
Stadium: Cowboy (1965), 17,500 capacity. Natural turf.
Colors: Blue & Gold.
Conference: Southland Football League.
SID: Louis Bonnette, 318-475-5207.
AD: Bobby Keasler.

MEMPHIS

Memphis, TN 38152 ... I-A

Coach: Rip Scherer, William & Mary '74
Record: 5 Years, 32-27-0

1996 SCHEDULE

Miami (Fla.) ■ ... *Aug. 31
Mississippi St. ■ ... *Sept. 7
Missouri ... *Sept. 14
Tulane ■ ... *Sept. 21
Cincinnati ■ ... *Oct. 5
Houston ... *Oct. 12
Southern Miss. ... Oct. 19
Southwestern La. ... *Oct. 26
Louisville ... Nov. 2
Tennessee ■ ... Nov. 9
East Caro. ■ ... Nov. 23

1995 RESULTS (3-8-0)

18 Mississippi St. ... 28
7 Michigan ... 24
33 Southwestern La. ... 19
20 Arkansas ... 27
7 Louisville ... 17
23 Tulane ... 8
3 Cincinnati ... 28
10 Tulsa ... 7
3 Mississippi ... 34
9 Southern Miss. ... 17
17 East Caro. ... 31
150 **240**

Nickname: Tigers.
Stadium: Liberty Bowl (1965), 62,380 capacity. Natural turf.
Colors: Blue & Gray.
Conference: Conference USA.
SID: Bob Winn, 901-678-2337.
AD: R. C. Johnson.

MENLO

Menlo Park, CA 94025 ... III

Coach: Doug Cosbie, Santa Clara '78
(First year as head coach)

1996 SCHEDULE

Claremont-M-S ■ ... Sept. 14
Occidental ■ ... Sept. 21
Redlands ... *Sept. 28
Claremont-M-S ... Oct. 5
Pomona-Pitzer ■ ... Oct. 12
Whittier ■ ... Oct. 26
Azusa Pacific ■ ... Nov. 2
La Verne ... Nov. 9
Cal Lutheran ... Nov. 16

1995 RESULTS (0-9-0)

2 Cal St. Northridge ... 45
16 Occidental ... 53
7 La Verne ... 51
7 Whittier ... 35
24 Claremont-M-S ... 41
13 Chapman ... 79
15 Pomona-Pitzer ... 56
21 Azusa Pacific ... 41
12 Humboldt St. ... 53
117 **454**

Nickname: Oaks.
Stadium: Connor Field (1972), 1,000 capacity. Natural turf.
Colors: Navy Blue & White.
Conference: Division III Independents.
SID: Matt Monroe, 415-688-3780.
AD: Doug Cosbie.

MERCHANT MARINE

Kings Point, NY 11024 ... III

Coach: Charlie Pravata, Adelphi '72
Record: 5 Years, 27-18-2

1996 SCHEDULE

Norwich ... Sept. 14
Springfield ■ ... Sept. 21
Catholic ■ ... Sept. 28
Plymouth St. ■ ... Oct. 12
Worcester Tech ... *Oct. 19
Ursinus ■ ... Oct. 26
Gettysburg ■ ... Nov. 2
Western Conn. St. ... Nov. 9
Coast Guard ■ ... Nov. 16

1995 RESULTS (5-4-0)

23 Norwich ... 0
0 Springfield ... 35
21 Catholic ... 7
20 Carnegie Mellon ... 19
10 Worcester Tech ... 0
7 Ursinus ... 14
25 Gettysburg ... 0
17 Western Conn. St. ... 27
9 Coast Guard ... 27
132 **129**

Nickname: Mariners.
Stadium: Capt. Tomb Field (1945), 5,840 capacity. Natural turf.
Colors: Blue & Gray.
Conference: Freedom Football.
SID: Craig Fink, 516-773-5455.
AD: Susan Petersen Lubow.

MERCYHURST

Erie, PA 16546 ... II

Coach: Joe Kimball, Syracuse '75
Record: 11 Years, 52-51-2

1996 SCHEDULE

Robert Morris ■ ... Sept. 7
Albany (N.Y.) ... *Sept. 14
Brockport St. ... Sept. 21
St. John Fisher ■ ... Sept. 28
Monmouth (N.J.) ■ ... Oct. 5
Gannon ■ ... Oct. 12
St. Francis (Pa.) ... Oct. 19
Buffalo St. ... Nov. 2
Ohio Wesleyan ... Nov. 9

1995 RESULTS (7-3-0)

13 Canisius ... 3
7 Frostburg St. ... 21
23 Brockport St. ... 15
57 St. Francis (Pa.) ... 21
14 Monmouth (N.J.) ... 35
18 Buffalo St. ... 44
21 Robert Morris ... 19
38 Grove City ... 27
9 Gannon ... 6
17 LIU-C.W. Post ... 13
217 **204**

Nickname: Lakers.
Stadium: Erie Veteran Memorial (1958), 10,500 capacity. Artificial turf.
Colors: Blue & Green.
Conference: Eastern Football.

SID: Ed Hess, 814-824-2525.
AD: Pete Russo.

MERRIMACK

North Andover, MA 01845 II

Coach: Thomas Caito, Boston U. '60
(First year as head coach)

1996 SCHEDULE

Western New Eng. ■ ....Sept. 14
Bentley ....*Sept. 20
Nichols ....Sept. 28
Curry ■ ....Oct. 5
MIT ■ ....Oct. 12
Assumption ....Oct. 19
Stonehill ■ ....Oct. 26
Mass.-Lowell ....Nov. 2
Sacred Heart ....Nov. 9

1995 RESULTS

None—1996 is first year of varsity football

Nickname: Warriors.
Stadium: Merrimack, 2,000 capacity. Natural turf.
Colors: Navy Blue & Gold.
Conference: Division II Independents.
SID: Tom Caraccioli, 508-837-5341.
AD: Bob DeGregorio.

MESA ST.

Grand Junction, CO 81501 II

Coach: Jay Hood, Ohio Wesleyan '86
Record: 2 Years, 7-14-0

1996 SCHEDULE

Central Okla. ....*Sept. 7
Northern Colo. ■ ....Sept. 14
Chadron St. ■ ....Sept. 21
Adams St. ■ ....Sept. 28
Fort Hays St. ....*Oct. 5
Colorado Mines ....Oct. 12
Neb.-Kearney ■ ....Oct. 19
Fort Lewis ■ ....*Oct. 26
N.M. Highlands ....Nov. 2
Western St. ....Nov. 16

1995 RESULTS (3-7-0)

0 Central Okla. 27
7 Northern Colo. 58
23 Cal St. Chico 22
38 Colorado Mines 15
19 Chadron St. 22
17 Fort Lewis 20
13 Fort Hays St. 62
9 Western St. 56
27 N.M. Highlands 14
21 Adams St. 52
174 **348**

Nickname: Mavericks.
Stadium: Stocker (1949), 8,000 capacity. Natural turf.
Colors: Maroon, White & Gold.
Conference: Rocky Mountain Athletic.
SID: Tish Elliott, 970-248-1143.
AD: Jim Paronto.

METHODIST

Fayetteville, NC 28311 III

Coach: Jim Sypult, West Va. '67
Record: 4 Years, 14-26-0

1996 SCHEDULE

Chowan ....Sept. 7
Guilford ■ ....Sept. 14
Salisbury St. ■ ....Sept. 21
Newport News App. ....Sept. 28
Bridgewater (Va.) ....Oct. 12
Davidson ■ ....Oct. 19
Ferrum ■ ....Oct. 26
Maryville (Tenn.) ....Nov. 2
Hampden-Sydney ■ ....Nov. 9
Frostburg St. ....Nov. 16

1995 RESULTS (5-5-0)

31 Chowan 13
10 Guilford 16
19 Salisbury St. 34
35 Newport News App. 30
27 Bridgewater (Va.) 3
16 Davidson 14
13 Ferrum 20
23 Maryville (Tenn.) 13
13 Hampden-Sydney 29
0 Frostburg St. 7
187 **179**

Nickname: Monarchs.
Stadium: Monarch Field (1989), 1,500 capacity. Natural turf.
Colors: Green & Gold.
Conference: Division III Independents.
SID: To be named, 910-630-7172.
AD: Rita S. Wiggs.

MIAMI (FLA.)

Coral Gables, FL 33124 ....I-A

Coach: Butch Davis, Arkansas '74
Record: 1 Year, 8-3-0

1996 SCHEDULE

Memphis ....*Aug. 31
Citadel ■ ....Sept. 7
Rutgers ....*Sept. 12
Pittsburgh ■ ....Sept. 28
Florida St. ■ ....Oct. 12
East Caro. ■ ....Oct. 19
West Va. ....Oct. 26
Temple ....Nov. 2
Virginia Tech ■ ....Nov. 16
Boston College ■ ....Nov. 23
Syracuse ....Nov. 30

1995 RESULTS (8-3-0)

8 UCLA 31
49 Florida A&M 3
7 Virginia Tech 13
17 Florida St. 41
56 Rutgers 21
17 Pittsburgh 16
36 Temple 12
35 Baylor 14
17 Boston College 14
17 West Va. 12
35 Syracuse 24
294 **201**

Nickname: Hurricanes.
Stadium: Orange Bowl (1935), 74,476 capacity. Natural turf.
Colors: Orange, Green & White.
Conference: Big East.
SID: Bob Burda, 305-284-3244.
AD: Paul Dee.

MIAMI (OHIO)

Oxford, OH 45056 ....I-A

Coach: Randy Walker, Miami (Ohio) '76
Record: 6 Years, 34-27-5

1996 SCHEDULE

Kent ■ ....Aug. 31
Ball St. ....Sept. 7
Indiana ....Sept. 14
Bowling Green ■ ....Sept. 21
Cincinnati ....*Sept. 28
Central Mich. ■ ....Oct. 5
Eastern Mich. ....*Oct. 12
Akron ....Oct. 19
Army ■ ....Oct. 26
Toledo ....Nov. 2
Ohio ■ ....Nov. 9

1995 RESULTS (8-2-1)

15 Ball St. 17
39 Kent 0
30 Northwestern 28
23 Cincinnati 16
19 Michigan 38
21 Bowling Green 0
28 Toledo 28
17 Central Mich. 13
39 Eastern Mich. 23
30 Ohio 2
65 Akron 0
326 **165**

Nickname: Redskins.
Stadium: Fred C. Yager (1983), 30,000 capacity. Natural turf.
Colors: Red & White.
Conference: Mid-American.
SID: John Estes, 513-529-4327.
AD: Eric Hyman.

MICHIGAN

Ann Arbor, MI 48109 ....I-A

Coach: Lloyd Carr, Northern Mich. '68
Record: 1 Year, 9-4-0

1996 SCHEDULE

Illinois ■ ....Aug. 31
Colorado ....Sept. 14
Boston College ■ ....Sept. 21
UCLA ■ ....Sept. 28
Northwestern ....Oct. 5
Indiana ■ ....Oct. 19
Minnesota ....*Oct. 26
Michigan St. ■ ....Nov. 2
Purdue ....Nov. 9
Penn St. ■ ....Nov. 16
Ohio St. ....Nov. 23

1995 RESULTS (9-3-0)

18 Virginia 17
38 Illinois 14
24 Memphis 7
23 Boston College 13
38 Miami (Ohio) 19
13 Northwestern 19
34 Indiana 17
52 Minnesota 17
25 Michigan St. 28
5 Purdue 0
17 Penn St. 27
31 Ohio St. 23
318 **201**

Alamo Bowl

20 Texas A&M 22

Nickname: Wolverines.
Stadium: Michigan (1927), 102,501 capacity. Natural turf.
Colors: Maize & Blue.
Conference: Big Ten.
SID: Bruce Madej, 313-763-4423.
AD: Joe Roberson.

MICHIGAN ST.

East Lansing, MI 48824 ....I-A

Coach: Nick Saban, Kent '73
Record: 2 Years, 15-7-1

1996 SCHEDULE

Purdue ■ ....Aug. 31
Nebraska ....Sept. 7
Louisville ■ ....Sept. 21
Eastern Mich. ■ ....Sept. 28
Iowa ....Oct. 5
Illinois ■ ....Oct. 12
Minnesota ....Oct. 19
Wisconsin ■ ....Oct. 26
Michigan ....Nov. 2
Indiana ■ ....Nov. 9
Penn St. ....Nov. 23

1995 RESULTS (6-4-1)

10 Nebraska 50
30 Louisville 7
35 Purdue 35
25 Boston College 21
7 Iowa 21
27 Illinois 21

34 Minnesota....31
14 Wisconsin....45
28 Michigan....25
31 Indiana....13
20 Penn St....24
261 **293**

Independence Bowl

26 LSU....45

Nickname: Spartans.
Stadium: Spartan (1957), 72,027 capacity. Artificial turf.
Colors: Green & White.
Conference: Big Ten.
SID: Ken Hoffman, 517-355-2271.
AD: Merritt J. Norvell Jr.

MICHIGAN TECH

Houghton, MI 49931 II

Coach: Bernie Anderson, Northern Mich. '78
Record: 9 Years, 44-44-0

1996 SCHEDULE

Northwood....*Aug. 29
Ashland ■....Sept. 7
Saginaw Valley ■....Sept. 21
Indianapolis....Sept. 28
St. Francis (Ill.) ■....Oct. 5
Grand Valley St....Oct. 12
Ferris St. ■....Oct. 19
Wayne St. (Mich.)....Oct. 26
Hillsdale ■....Nov. 2
Northern Mich. ■....Nov. 9

1995 RESULTS (5-5-0)

39 Northwood....25
28 Ashland....32
44 St. Joseph's (Ind.)....23
37 Saginaw Valley....35
21 Indianapolis....14
21 St. Francis (Ill.)....23
52 Grand Valley St....54
17 Ferris St....38
43 Wayne St. (Mich.)....3
6 Hillsdale....21
308 **268**

Nickname: Huskies.
Stadium: Sherman Field (1954), 3,000 capacity. Natural turf.
Colors: Silver & Gold.
Conference: Midwest Intercollegiate.
SID: Dave Fischer, 906-487-2350.
AD: Rick Yeo.

MIDDLE TENN. ST.

Murfreesboro, TN 37132....I-AA

Coach: Boots Donnelly, Middle Tenn. St. '65
Record: 19 Years, 139-78-1

1996 SCHEDULE

Louisiana Tech....*Aug. 31
Tennessee St....*Sept. 7
Tenn.-Chatt. ■....*Sept. 14
Murray St....*Sept. 28
Jacksonville St....Oct. 5
Austin Peay ■....Oct. 12
Eastern Ky. ■....Oct. 19
Southeast Mo. St....Oct. 26
Tenn.-Martin....Nov. 9
Eastern Ill. ■....Nov. 16
Tennessee Tech ■....Nov. 23

1995 RESULTS (7-4-0)

11 Tennessee St....7
26 Ga. Southern....34
42 Morehead St....0
0 Murray St....34
28 Ala.-Birmingham....13
43 Austin Peay....0
21 Eastern Ky....34
42 Southeast Mo. St....0
45 Tenn.-Martin....17
31 Tennessee Tech....6
14 Texas A&M....56
303 **201**

Nickname: Blue Raiders.
Stadium: Johnny Floyd (1969), 15,000 capacity. Artificial turf.
Colors: Blue & White.
Conference: Ohio Valley.
SID: Ed Given, 615-898-2450.
AD: Lee Fowler.

MIDDLEBURY

Middlebury, VT 05753 III

Coach: Mickey Heinecken, Delaware '61
Record: 23 Years, 101-81-2

1996 SCHEDULE

Bowdoin ■....Sept. 21
Colby....Sept. 28
Amherst ■....Oct. 5
Williams....Oct. 12
Bates ■....Oct. 19
Trinity (Conn.)....Oct. 26
Hamilton....Nov. 2
Tufts ■....Nov. 9

1995 RESULTS (2-6-0)

20 Wesleyan (Conn.)....28
41 Colby....24
13 Amherst....28
3 Williams....35
28 Bates....23
7 Trinity (Conn.)....19
20 Hamilton....23
12 Tufts....14
144 **194**

Nickname: Panthers.
Stadium: Alumni (1991), 3,500 capacity. Natural turf.
Colors: Blue & White.
Conference: NESCAC.
SID: Brad Nadeau, 802-443-5193.
AD: G. Thomas Lawson.

MILES

Birmingham, AL 35208 II

Coach: Cecil Leonard, Tuskegee '69
Record: 2 Years, 6-12-1

1996 SCHEDULE

Kentucky St. ■....Aug. 31
Albany St. (Ga.)....Sept. 7
Morehouse ■....Sept. 14
Tuskegee....Sept. 21
Clark Atlanta....*Sept. 28
Morris Brown ■....Oct. 5
Fort Valley St. ■....Oct. 12
Knoxville....Oct. 19
Alabama A&M....Nov. 2
Savannah St. ■....Nov. 9

1995 RESULTS (4-6-0)

12 Albany St. (Ga.)....58
6 Morehouse....19
37 Tuskegee....36
26 Clark Atlanta....30
42 Morris Brown....10
19 Fort Valley St....8
6 Lane....28
26 Alabama A&M....20
18 Savannah St....28
8 Ala.-Birmingham....37
200 **274**

Nickname: Golden Bears.
Stadium: Alumni, 3,400 capacity. Natural turf.
Colors: Purple & Gold.
Conference: Southern Intercollegiate Athletic.
SID: Willie K. Patterson Jr., 205-923-8323.
AD: Augustus James.

MILLERSVILLE

Millersville, PA 17551 II

Coach: Gene Carpenter, Huron '63
Record: 27 Years, 184-74-6

1996 SCHEDULE

Lafayette....Sept. 14
New Haven ■....Sept. 21
Shippensburg....Sept. 28
Mansfield....Oct. 5
Lock Haven ■....*Oct. 12
Bloomsburg ■....Oct. 19
Kutztown....Oct. 26
West Chester ■....*Nov. 2
East Stroudsburg....Nov. 9
Cheyney ■....Nov. 16

1995 RESULTS (9-0-1)

59 Shepherd....7
39 American Int'l....0
20 Shippensburg....3
41 Clarion....35
28 Bloomsburg....28
21 Kutztown....20
31 West Chester....12
19 East Stroudsburg....14
54 Cheyney....0
41 Mansfield....20
353 **139**

II Championship

26 Ferris St....36

Nickname: Marauders.
Stadium: Biemesderfer (1970), 6,500 capacity. Natural turf.
Colors: Black & Gold.
Conference: Pennsylvania State Athletic.
SID: Greg Wright, 717-872-3100.
AD: Gene Carpenter.

MILLIKIN

Decatur, IL 62522 III

Coach: Doug Neibuhr, Millikin '75
Record: 7 Years, 50-18-1

1996 SCHEDULE

Iowa Wesleyan ■....Sept. 7
Butler....Sept. 21
Elmhurst ■....Oct. 5
Ill. Wesleyan....Oct. 12
Wheaton (Ill.) ■....Oct. 19
Carthage....Oct. 26
North Park ■....Nov. 2
North Central....Nov. 9
Augustana (Ill.) ■....Nov. 16

1995 RESULTS (5-4-0)

31 Franklin....28
27 Butler....15
34 North Park....7
49 Carthage....6
21 Wheaton (Ill.)....42
21 North Central....19
0 Augustana (Ill.)....36
21 Elmhurst....28
0 Ill. Wesleyan....3
204 **184**

Nickname: Big Blue.
Stadium: Frank M. Lindsay Field (1987), 4,000 capacity. Natural turf.
Colors: Royal Blue & White.
Conference: College Conf. of Illinois & Wisconsin.
SID: Brett Clark, 217-424-6350.
AD: Merle Chapman.

MILLSAPS

Jackson, MS 39210....III

Coach: Ron Jurney, Millsaps '77
Record: 3 Years, 12-21-0

1996 SCHEDULE

Rose-Hulman....Sept. 7
Rhodes ■....Sept. 14
McMurry ■....Sept. 21
Greenville ■....Sept. 28
Emory & Henry....Oct. 5
Centre ■....Oct. 12
Ky. Wesleyan ■....Oct. 26
Sewanee....Nov. 2

Rhodes ....Nov. 9
Trinity (Tex.) ■ ....Nov. 16

1995 RESULTS (2-7-0)

15 Rose-Hulman 35
28 McMurry....18
21 Colorado Col. 17
17 Emory & Henry....34
19 Centre 30
7 Trinity (Tex.) 35
21 Ky. Wesleyan....28
6 Sewanee....7
26 Rhodes 34
160 **238**

Nickname: Majors.
Stadium: Alumni Field (1920), 4,000 capacity. Natural turf.
Colors: Purple & White.
Conference: Southern Collegiate Athletic.
SID: Trey Porter, 601-974-1195.
AD: Ron Jurney.

MINNESOTA

Minneapolis, MN 55455 ....I-A

Coach: Jim Wacker, Valparaiso '60
Record: 25 Years, 156-123-3

1996 SCHEDULE

Northeast La. ....*Sept. 7
Ball St. ■....*Sept. 14
Syracuse ■....*Sept. 21
Purdue....Oct. 5
Northwestern ....Oct. 12
Michigan St. ■ ....Oct. 19
Michigan ■....*Oct. 26
Ohio St. ....Nov. 2
Wisconsin ....Nov. 9
Illinois ■....*Nov. 16
Iowa ■....*Nov. 23

1995 RESULTS (3-8-0)

31 Ball St. 7
17 Syracuse 27
55 Arkansas St. 7
39 Purdue 38
17 Northwestern....27
31 Michigan St. 34
17 Michigan 52
21 Ohio St....49
27 Wisconsin....34
14 Illinois 48
3 Iowa....45
272 **368**

Nickname: Golden Gophers.
Stadium: Metrodome (1982), 63,669 capacity. Artificial turf.
Colors: Maroon & Gold.
Conference: Big Ten.
SID: Marc Ryan, 612-625-4090.
AD: Mark Dienhart.

MINN.-DULUTH

Duluth, MN 55812 II

Coach: James Malosky, Minnesota '51
Record: 38 Years, 243-116-13

1996 SCHEDULE

Mankato St. ....*Sept. 7
St. Cloud St. ■....Sept. 14
Montana St....Sept. 21
Wayne St. (Neb.) ■....Sept. 28
Southwest St. ■....Oct. 5
Moorhead St. ....Oct. 12
Winona St. ■ ....Oct. 19
Minn.-Morris ....Oct. 26
Northern St. ■ ....Nov. 2
Bemidji St. ....Nov. 9
Wis.-La Crosse [Minneapolis, Minn.]....*Nov. 17

1995 RESULTS (8-2-1)

21 Wis.-Stout 20
23 St. Cloud St. 29
6 Montana....54
40 Bemidji St....9
22 Wayne St. (Neb.) 15
28 Southwest St. 21
14 Moorhead St. 14
24 Winona St. 20
35 Minn.-Morris....0
28 Northern St. 7
13 Southwest St. 6
254 **195**

Nickname: Bulldogs.
Stadium: Griggs Field (1966), 4,000 capacity. Artificial turf.
Colors: Maroon & Gold.
Conference: Northern Sun Intercollegiate.
SID: Bob Nygaard, 218-726-8191.
AD: Bruce McLeod.

MINN.-MORRIS

Morris, MN 56267 II

Coach: John Parker, Missouri Valley '87
(First year as head coach)

1996 SCHEDULE

Minn.-Crookston ■ ....Sept. 14
Northwestern Ia. ....*Sept. 21
Winona St....Sept. 28
Minot St. ■....Oct. 5
Northern St. ■ ....Oct. 12
Bemidji St. ....Oct. 19
Minn.-Duluth ■....Oct. 26
Southwest St. ....Nov. 2
Moorhead St. ■....Nov. 9

1995 RESULTS (0-10-0)

14 Hamline....31
7 Northwestern Minn. 35
7 Moorhead St. 51
6 Winona St. 14
6 Minn.-Crookston 31
7 Northern St. 35
12 Bemidji St. 16
0 Minn.-Duluth....35
6 Southwest St....13
26 St. Ambrose 34
91 **295**

Nickname: Cougars.
Stadium: UMM Field, 5,000 capacity. Natural turf.
Colors: Maroon & Gold.
Conference: Northern Sun Intercollegiate.
SID: Broderick Powell, 612-589-6423.
AD: Mark Fohl.

MISSISSIPPI

University, MS 38677 ....I-A

Coach: Tommy Tuberville, Southern Ark. '76
Record: 1 Year, 6-5-0

1996 SCHEDULE

Idaho St. ■....*Aug. 31
Va. Military [Jackson, Miss.]....*Sept. 7
Auburn ■....*Sept. 14
Vanderbilt....*Sept. 21
Tennessee [Memphis, Tenn.]....*Oct. 3
Alabama....Oct. 19
Arkansas St. ■....*Oct. 26
Arkansas ....Nov. 9
LSU ■ ....Nov. 16
Georgia ....Nov. 23
Mississippi St. ■....*Nov. 30

1995 RESULTS (6-5-0)

13 Auburn 46
56 Indiana St. 10
18 Georgia....10
10 Florida....28
20 Tulane 17
6 Arkansas....13
9 Alabama 23
21 Vanderbilt....10
34 Memphis....3
9 LSU 38
13 Mississippi St....10
209 **208**

Nickname: Rebels.
Stadium: Vaught-Hemingway (1941), 42,577 capacity. Natural turf.
Colors: Cardinal Red & Navy Blue.
Conference: Southeastern.
SID: Langston Rogers, 601-232-7522.
AD: Pete Boone.

MISSISSIPPI COL.

Clinton, MS 39058 II

Coach: Terry McMillan, Southern Miss. '69
Record: 5 Years, 23-24-5

1996 SCHEDULE

Ark.-Monticello ■ ....*Sept. 7
Sul Ross St. ....Sept. 14
Henderson St. ■ ....*Sept. 21
Arkansas Tech ....*Oct. 5
Hardin-Simmons....Oct. 12
Tusculum....Oct. 19
West Ala. ■ ....Oct. 26
Austin ■ ....*Nov. 2
Southern Ark. ....Nov. 9
Howard Payne....Nov. 16

1995 RESULTS (2-7-1)

23 Southern Ark. 14
0 Ark.-Monticello 17
30 West Ala. 7
3 North Ala. 41
12 Henderson St. 45
15 West Ga....30
15 Arkansas Tech 15
11 Central Ark. 26
16 Valdosta St. 42
0 Delta St. 14
125 **251**

Nickname: Choctaws.
Stadium: Robinson-Hale (1985), 8,500 capacity. Natural turf.
Colors: Blue & Gold.
Conference: Division II Independents.
SID: Pete Smith, 601-925-3255.
AD: Terry McMillan.

MISSISSIPPI ST.

Mississippi State, MS 39762 ....I-A

Coach: Jackie Sherrill, Alabama '66
Record: 18 Years, 134-72-4

1996 SCHEDULE

Memphis ....*Sept. 7
Louisiana Tech ■....*Sept. 21
South Caro. ....Sept. 28
Georgia ■....*Oct. 5
Auburn ■ ....*Oct. 12
LSU....*Oct. 26
Northeast La. ■ ....Nov. 2
Kentucky....Nov. 9
Alabama ■ ....Nov. 16
Arkansas ■....Nov. 23
Mississippi....*Nov. 30

1995 RESULTS (3-8-0)

28 Memphis....18
16 LSU 34
30 Baylor....21
14 Tennessee 52
32 Northeast La....34
20 Auburn 48
39 South Caro. 65
42 Kentucky....32
21 Arkansas....26
9 Alabama 14
10 Mississippi 13
261 **357**

Nickname: Bulldogs.
Stadium: Scott Field (1935), 40,656 capacity. Natural turf.
Colors: Maroon & White.
Conference: Southeastern.
SID: Mike Nemeth, 601-325-2703.
AD: Larry Templeton.

MISSISSIPPI VAL.

Itta Bena, MS 38941 ....I-AA

Coach: Larry Dorsey, Tennessee St. '76
Record: 6 Years, 25-34-3

1996 SCHEDULE

Morris Brown ....Sept. 1
Ark.-Pine Bluff ■ ....*Sept. 7
Tenn.-Chatt. ....Sept. 21
Jackson St. ....*Sept. 28
Southern-B.R. ....*Oct. 5
Grambling ■ ....Oct. 12
Lane ■ ....Oct. 19
Texas Southern......................................Oct. 26
Prairie View ■ ....Nov. 2
Alcorn St. ■ ....Nov. 9
Alabama St. ....Nov. 16

1995 RESULTS (2-9-0)

16 Ark.-Pine Bluff 41
14 Lane 25
7 Jackson St. 47
6 Southern-B.R. 44
6 Grambling 42
12 Central St. 59
28 Texas Southern 21
35 Prairie View 14
27 Alcorn St. 38
28 Alabama St. 56
3 Arkansas St. 55
182 **442**

Nickname: Delta Devils.
Stadium: Magnolia (1958), 10,500 capacity. Natural turf.
Colors: Green & White.
Conference: Southwestern Athletic.
SID: Chuck Prophet, 601-254-3551.
AD: Chuck Prophet.

MISSOURI

Columbia, MO 65201 ....I-A

Coach: Larry Smith, Bowling Green '62
Record: 19 Years, 116-96-7

1996 SCHEDULE

Texas ....*Aug. 31
Memphis ■ ....*Sept. 14
Clemson ■ ....*Sept. 21
Iowa St. ....Sept. 28
Southern Methodist ....*Oct. 5
Kansas St. ■ ....Oct. 12
Oklahoma St. ■ ....Oct. 26
Colorado ■ ....Nov. 2
Nebraska ....Nov. 9
Baylor ....Nov. 16
Kansas ■ ....Nov. 23

1995 RESULTS (3-8-0)

28 North Texas 7
10 Bowling Green 17
14 Texas Tech 41
31 Northeast La. 22
0 Kansas St. 30
0 Nebraska 57
26 Oklahoma St. 30
9 Oklahoma 13
23 Kansas 42
0 Colorado 21
45 Iowa St. 31
186 **311**

Nickname: Tigers.
Stadium: Memorial/Faurot Field (1926), 62,000 capacity. Natural turf.
Colors: Old Gold & Black.
Conference: Big 12.
SID: Bob Brendel, 573-882-0712.
AD: Joe Castiglione.

MO.-ROLLA

Rolla, MO 65401 II

Coach: Jim Anderson, Missouri '69
Record: 4 Years, 11-30-1

1996 SCHEDULE

Quincy ■ ....Sept. 7
Missouri Valley ■ ....Sept. 14
Truman St. ■ ....Sept. 21
Northwest Mo. St. ....Sept. 28
Mo. Southern St. ■ ....Oct. 5
Emporia St. ....Oct. 12
Washburn ■ ....Oct. 19
Central Mo. St. ....Oct. 26
Southwest Baptist ....Nov. 2
Pittsburg St. ■ ....Nov. 9
Mo. Western St. ....Nov. 16

1995 RESULTS (1-9-0)

0 Missouri Valley 3
3 Truman St. 63
14 Northwest Mo. St. 48
17 Mo. Southern St. 56
14 Emporia St. 45
10 Washburn 21
19 Central Mo. St. 50
7 Southwest Baptist 12
10 Pittsburg St. 60
25 Mo. Western St. 21
119 **379**

Nickname: Miners.
Stadium: Jackling Field (1967), 8,000 capacity. Natural turf.
Colors: Silver & Gold.
Conference: Mid-America Intercollegiate Athletic Assoc.
SID: John Kean, 314-341-4140.
AD: Mark Mullin.

MO. SOUTHERN ST.

Joplin, MO 64801 II

Coach: Jon Lantz, Okla. Panhandle St. '74
Record: 10 Years, 63-37-3

1996 SCHEDULE

Northeastern St. ....*Sept. 14
Emporia St. ....Sept. 21
Central Mo. St. ■ ....*Sept. 28
Mo.-Rolla ....Oct. 5
Southwest Baptist ■ ....Oct. 12
Pittsburg St. ....*Oct. 19
Northwest Mo. St. ■ ....*Oct. 26
Truman St. ....Nov. 2
Mo. Western St. ■ ....Nov. 9
Washburn ■ ....Nov. 16

1995 RESULTS (6-4-0)

13 Central Ark. 7
21 Emporia St. 26
37 Central Mo. St. 32
56 Mo.-Rolla 17
44 Southwest Baptist 7
14 Pittsburg St. 15
33 Northwest Mo. St. 41
24 Truman St. 22
7 Mo. Western St. 43
25 Washburn 0
274 **210**

Nickname: Lions.
Stadium: Fred G. Hughes (1975), 7,000 capacity. Artificial turf.
Colors: Green & Gold.
Conference: Mid-America Intercollegiate Athletic Assoc.
SID: Dennis Slusher, 417-625-9359.
AD: Jim Frazier.

MO. WESTERN ST.

St. Joseph, MO 64507 II

Coach: Stan McGarvey, William Jewell '73
Record: 11 Years, 72-43-4

1996 SCHEDULE

Neb.-Kearney ....Sept. 7
Quincy ■ ....Sept. 14
Washburn ....*Sept. 21
Emporia St. ■ ....*Sept. 28
Southwest Baptist ....Oct. 5
Pittsburg St. ■ ....Oct. 12
Northwest Mo. St. ....Oct. 19
Truman St. ■ ....Oct. 26
Central Mo. St. ....Nov. 2
Mo. Southern St. ....Nov. 9
Mo.-Rolla ■ ....Nov. 16

1995 RESULTS (7-3-1)

19 Drake 19
44 Northeastern St. 7
17 Washburn 6
35 Emporia St. 28
45 Southwest Baptist 0
0 Pittsburg St. 31
24 Northwest Mo. St. 20
21 Truman St. 42
30 Central Mo. St. 20
43 Mo. Southern St. 7
21 Mo.-Rolla 25
299 **205**

Nickname: Griffons.
Stadium: Spratt (1979), 6,000 capacity. Natural turf.
Colors: Black & Gold.
Conference: Mid-America Intercollegiate Athletic Assoc.
SID: Paul Sweetgall, 816-271-4257.
AD: Don Kaverman.

MONMOUTH (ILL.)

Monmouth, IL 61462 III

Coach: Kelly Kane, Ill. Wesleyan '70
Record: 12 Years, 63-48-0

1996 SCHEDULE

Eureka ....Sept. 7
MacMurray ■ ....Sept. 14
St. Norbert ■ ....Sept. 21
Lake Forest ....Sept. 28
Illinois Col. ■ ....Oct. 5
Cornell College ■ ....Oct. 12
Coe ....Oct. 19
Grinnell ....Oct. 26
Knox ■ ....Nov. 2

1995 RESULTS (0-9-0)

33 Eureka 40
10 MacMurray 19
23 Ripon 31
0 Beloit 40
26 Illinois Col. 42
0 Cornell College 43
13 Coe 41
13 Grinnell 27
14 Knox 28
132 **311**

Nickname: Fighting Scots.
Stadium: Bobby Woll Field (1981), 3,000 capacity. Natural turf.
Colors: Crimson & White.
Conference: Midwest.
SID: Chris Pio, 309-457-2173.
AD: Terry Glasgow.

MONMOUTH (N.J.)

West Long Branch, NJ 07764 ....I-AA

Coach: Kevin Callahan, Rochester '77
Record: 2 Years, 14-5-0

1996 SCHEDULE

Southern Conn. St. ■ ....Sept. 7
St. Francis (Pa.) ■ ....Sept. 14
Pace ■ ....Sept. 21
LIU-C.W. Post ....Sept. 28
Mercyhurst ....Oct. 5
Wagner ....*Oct. 12
Towson St. ■ ....Oct. 19
Robert Morris ....Oct. 26
Siena ■ ....Nov. 9
Central Conn. St. ■ ....Nov. 16

1995 RESULTS (7-3-0)

15 Marist 16
16 Robert Morris 13
34 St. Peter's 10
47 St. John's (N.Y.) 0
15 Towson St. 31

35 Mercyhurst....14
41 Pace....0
35 St. Francis (Pa.)....0
20 Wagner....21
30 Central Conn. St....13
288 **118**

Nickname: Hawks.
Stadium: Kessler Field (1993), 4,600 capacity. Natural turf.
Colors: Royal Blue & White.
Conference: Northeast.
SID: Brian Ierardi, 908-728-7103.
AD: Marilyn McNeil.

MONTANA

Missoula, MT 59812 ....I-AA

Coach: Mick Dennehy, Montana '73
Record: 3 Years, 10-13-0

1996 SCHEDULE

Oregon St. ....Sept. 7
Cal Poly SLO ■ ....Sept. 14
Cal St. Sacramento ....*Sept. 28
Southern Utah ■ ....Oct. 5
Idaho St. ■....Oct. 12
Eastern Wash. ....Oct. 19
Northern Ariz. ■....Oct. 26
Cal St. Northridge....*Nov. 2
Portland St. ■ ....Nov. 9
Weber St. ....Nov. 16
Montana St. ■....Nov. 23

1995 RESULTS (9-2-0)

41 Eastern N.M....14
21 Washington St. 38
54 Minn.-Duluth....6
54 Boise St. 28
41 UC Davis....20
49 Weber St. 22
24 Northern Ariz....21
43 Idaho....55
35 Idaho St....21
63 Eastern Wash....7
42 Montana St. 33
467 **265**

I-AA Championship

48 Eastern Ky....0
45 Ga. Southern....0
70 Stephen F. Austin....14
22 Marshall 20

Nickname: Grizzlies.
Stadium: Washington-Grizzly (1986), 18,845 capacity. Natural turf.
Colors: Copper, Silver & Gold.
Conference: Big Sky.
SID: Dave Guffey, 406-243-6899.
AD: Wayne Hogan.

MONTANA ST.

Bozeman, MT 59717....I-AA

Coach: Cliff Hysell, Montana St. '66
Record: 4 Years, 19-25-0

1996 SCHEDULE

Nevada ....Sept. 14
Minn.-Duluth ■....Sept. 21
Idaho St. ■....Sept. 28
Eastern Wash. ....Oct. 5
Northern Ariz. ■....Oct. 12
Cal St. Northridge....*Oct. 19
Portland St. ■ ....Oct. 26
Weber St....Nov. 2
Cal Poly SLO ■....Nov. 9
Cal St. Sacramento ■....Nov. 16
Montana ....Nov. 23

1995 RESULTS (5-6-0)

10 Colorado St. 31
34 Central Wash....14
13 Cal Poly SLO....10
45 Southwest Tex. St....24
0 Northern Ariz....37
16 Idaho....13
18 Idaho St. 14
7 Weber St. 14
10 Eastern Wash....28
7 Boise St. 35
33 Montana....42
193 **262**

Nickname: Bobcats.
Stadium: Reno H. Sales (1973), 15,197 capacity. Natural turf.
Colors: Blue & Gold.
Conference: Big Sky.
SID: Bill Lamberty, 406-994-5133.
AD: Chuck Lindemenn.

MONTCLAIR ST.

Upper Montclair, NJ 07043 III

Coach: Rick Giancola, Glassboro St. '68
Record: 13 Years, 91-41-2

1996 SCHEDULE

Cortland St. ■ ....Sept. 14
Stony Brook ....Sept. 21
Brockport St. ■ ....*Sept. 28
St. John Fisher....Oct. 5
Kean....Oct. 12
Wm. Paterson ■ ....*Oct. 19
Wilkes....Oct. 26
Trenton St. ■....*Nov. 2
Jersey City St. ....Nov. 9
Rowan ■....*Nov. 16

1995 RESULTS (3-6-0)

19 Brockport St....6
17 Cortland St....24
14 Southern Conn. St....15
0 Kean 6
21 Wm. Paterson 15
7 Ithaca....33
44 Trenton St....50
28 Jersey City St....14
0 Rowan....30
150 **193**

Nickname: Red Hawks.
Stadium: Sprague (1934), 6,000 capacity. Artificial turf.
Colors: Scarlet & White.
Conference: New Jersey Athletic.
SID: Al Langer, 201-655-5249.
AD: Greg Lockard.

MOORHEAD ST.

Moorhead, MN 56563 II

Coach: Ralph Micheli, Macalester '70
Record: 13 Years, 48-73-2

1996 SCHEDULE

Concordia-M'head ■....Sept. 7
North Dak....Sept. 14
Wayne St. (Neb.) ....Sept. 21
Northern St. ■....Sept. 28
Bemidji St. ....Oct. 5
Minn.-Duluth ■....Oct. 12
Southwest St. ....Oct. 19
Winona St. ■ ....Nov. 2
Minn.-Morris ....Nov. 9
Wis.-River Falls [Minneapolis, Minn.] ....Nov. 17

1995 RESULTS (6-3-1)

7 Concordia-M'head....10
14 Neb.-Kearney....46
51 Minn.-Morris....7
35 Northern St. 13
32 Bemidji St. 20
14 Minn.-Duluth....14
27 Southwest St. 9
51 Wayne St. (Neb.)....28
46 Winona St. 25
16 Valley City 26
293 **198**

Nickname: Dragons.
Stadium: Alex Nemzek (1960), 5,000 capacity. Natural turf.
Colors: Scarlet & White.
Conference: Northern Sun Intercollegiate.
SID: Larry Scott, 218-236-2113.
AD: Katy Wilson.

MORAVIAN

Bethlehem, PA 18018....III

Coach: Scot Dapp, West Chester '73
Record: 9 Years, 64-28-1

1996 SCHEDULE

King's (Pa.) ....Sept. 14
Juniata ■....Sept. 21
Albright ■ ....Sept. 28
Delaware Valley....Oct. 5
Widener ■....Oct. 12
Susquehanna ....Oct. 19
Lebanon Valley ....Oct. 26
FDU-Madison ■ ....Nov. 2
Wilkes....Nov. 9
Muhlenberg ■ ....Nov. 16

1995 RESULTS (7-2-1)

31 King's (Pa.)....0
15 Juniata....15
0 Albright 26
32 Delaware Valley 0
10 Widener 31
19 Susquehanna....3
19 Lebanon Valley....7
17 FDU-Madison 6
34 Wilkes....9
38 Muhlenberg....7
215 **104**

Nickname: Greyhounds.
Stadium: Steel Field (1932), 2,200 capacity. Natural turf.
Colors: Blue & Gray.
Conference: Middle Atlantic.
SID: Mike Warwick, 610-861-1472.
AD: To be named.

MOREHEAD ST.

Morehead, KY 40351....I-AA

Coach: Matt Ballard, Gardner-Webb '79
Record: 8 Years, 37-44-1

1996 SCHEDULE

Dayton ....*Sept. 7
Valparaiso....Sept. 21
Ky. Wesleyan ■ ....*Sept. 28
Charleston So. ....Oct. 5
Wofford ....Oct. 12
St. Joseph's (Ind.) ■....Oct. 26
Quincy ■ ....Nov. 2
Western Ky. ■ ....Nov. 9
Evansville....Nov. 16

1995 RESULTS (2-8-0)

36 Ky. Wesleyan....11
0 Middle Tenn. St. 42
24 Tenn.-Martin 49
22 Charleston So....34
14 Tennessee St....45
13 Murray St....63
29 Tennessee Tech....36
26 Austin Peay 13
12 Southeast Mo. St. 21
10 Eastern Ky....41
186 **355**

Nickname: Eagles.
Stadium: Jayne (1964), 10,000 capacity. Artificial turf.
Colors: Blue & Gold.
Conference: Ohio Valley.
SID: Randy Stacy, 606-783-2500.
AD: Steve Hamilton.

MOREHOUSE

Atlanta, GA 30314 II

Coach: Maurice Hunt, Kentucky St. '67
Record: 17 Years, 69-101-4

1996 SCHEDULE

Bethune-Cookman....Aug. 31
Fort Valley St. ....*Sept. 7
Miles....Sept. 14
Albany St. (Ga.) ■....Sept. 21
Savannah St. ....Sept. 28
Alabama A&M ■....Oct. 5
Tuskegee [Columbus, Ga.]....*Oct. 12
Howard ■....Oct. 19
Morris Brown ■....Oct. 26
Kentucky St....Nov. 2
Clark Atlanta ....Nov. 9

1995 RESULTS (5-6-0)

14 Hampton....42
18 Fort Valley St....12
19 Miles 6
13 Albany St. (Ga.) 44
14 Savannah St....9
14 Alabama A&M....48
19 Tuskegee....6
28 Morris Brown 22
19 Howard 27
6 Kentucky St....13
6 Clark Atlanta....21
170 **250**

Nickname: Maroon Tigers/Tigers.
Stadium: B. T. Harvey (1983), 9,850 capacity. Natural turf.
Colors: Maroon & White.
Conference: Southern Intercollegiate Athletic.
SID: James E. Nix, 404-681-2800.
AD: Arthur J. McAfee Jr.

MORGAN ST.

Baltimore, MD 21239....I-AA

Coach: Stump Mitchell, Citadel '81
(First year as head coach)

1996 SCHEDULE

Central St. [Columbus, Ohio]....*Aug. 31
Bethune-Cookman ■....Sept. 14
Liberty ■....Sept. 21
Cheyney....Sept. 28
South Caro. St. ....Oct. 5
North Caro. A&T ....Oct. 19
Delaware St. ■....Oct. 26
Florida A&M....Nov. 2
Texas Southern....Nov. 9
Howard....Nov. 16
Hampton ■....Nov. 23

1995 RESULTS (1-10-0)

7 James Madison 76
10 Bethune-Cookman....33
19 Liberty....48
38 Cheyney 7
19 South Caro. St....31
32 North Caro. A&T....38
17 Delaware St....41
9 Florida A&M....47
24 Samford....35
17 Howard 29
20 Hampton....54
212 **439**

Nickname: Bears.
Stadium: Hughes (1934), 10,000 capacity. Natural turf.
Colors: Blue & Orange.
Conference: Mid-Eastern Athletic.
SID: Joe McIver, 410-319-3831.
AD: Garnett Purnell.

MORNINGSIDE

Sioux City, IA 51106 II

Coach: Dave Elliott, Michigan '75
(First year as head coach)

1996 SCHEDULE

Drake....Sept. 7
Wayne St. (Neb.) ■....*Sept. 14
South Dak. ■....*Sept. 21
Mankato St....Sept. 28
Neb.-Omaha ....*Oct. 5
Augustana (S.D.) ■....Oct. 12
St. Cloud St. ■....Oct. 19
South Dak. St....Oct. 26
North Dak....Nov. 2
Northern Colo. ■....Nov. 9
North Dak. St. ■....Nov. 16

1995 RESULTS (0-9-2)

10 Neb.-Kearney....10
27 Wayne St. (Neb.)....31
17 South Dak. 35
17 Mankato St....19
14 Neb.-Omaha....31
17 Augustana (S.D.) 17
6 St. Cloud St....39
17 South Dak. St. 39
21 North Dak....44
14 Northern Colo. 51
7 North Dak. St. 30
167 **346**

Nickname: Chiefs.
Stadium: Roberts (1939), 9,000 capacity. Natural turf.
Colors: Maroon & White.
Conference: North Central.
SID: Ron Christian, 712-274-5127.
AD: Bill Goldring.

MORRIS BROWN

Atlanta, GA 30314....II

Coach: Joseph C. Crosby Jr., North Caro. A&T '77
Record: 2 Years, 13-6-2

1996 SCHEDULE

Mississippi Val. ■....Sept. 1
Bethune-Cookman ....Sept. 7
Tuskegee....Sept. 14
Fort Valley St. ■....*Sept. 21
Alabama A&M ■....Sept. 28
Miles....Oct. 5
Savannah St. ■....Oct. 12
Morehouse....Oct. 26
Albany St. (Ga.) ■....Nov. 2
Kentucky St....Nov. 9
Clark Atlanta ....Nov. 16

1995 RESULTS (1-9-0)

14 Clark Atlanta....15
21 Tuskegee....19
0 Fort Valley St....13
6 Alabama A&M....26
10 Miles 42
16 Savannah St....19
22 Morehouse....28
10 Lane 20
11 Albany St. (Ga.)....53
12 Ark.-Pine Bluff....51
122 **286**

Nickname: Wolverines.
Stadium: A.F. Herndon, 20,000 capacity. Natural turf.
Colors: Purple & Black.
Conference: Southern Intercollegiate Athletic.
SID: Cecil McKay, 404-220-3628.
AD: Gene Bright.

MOUNT UNION

Alliance, OH 44601....III

Coach: Larry Kehres, Mount Union '71
Record: 10 Years, 96-16-3

1996 SCHEDULE

Defiance....Sept. 14
Baldwin-Wallace ■....Sept. 21
Otterbein ■....Sept. 28
Ohio Northern....Oct. 5
Heidelberg ■....Oct. 12
John Carroll....Oct. 19
Muskingum....Oct. 26
Marietta ■....Nov. 2
Capital ■....Nov. 9
Hiram....Nov. 16

1995 RESULTS (10-0-0)

57 Defiance 7
51 Otterbein 6
45 Ohio Northern....0
33 John Carroll....7
41 Marietta....37
35 Baldwin-Wallace 16
41 Muskingum 7
52 Heidelberg....14
62 Capital 7
21 Hiram 0
438 **101**

III Championship

52 Hanover....18
40 Wheaton (Ill.) 14
17 Wis.-La Crosse 20

Nickname: Purple Raiders.
Stadium: Mount Union (1915), 5,800 capacity. Natural turf.
Colors: Purple & White.
Conference: Ohio Athletic.
SID: Michael De Matteis, 216-823-6093.
AD: Larry Kehres.

MUHLENBERG

Allentown, PA 18104....III

Coach: Greg Olejack, Louisville '77
Record: 2 Years, 2-17-1

1996 SCHEDULE

Catholic ■....Sept. 14
Dickinson....Sept. 21
Frank. & Marsh. ■....Sept. 28
Western Md. ....Oct. 5
Swarthmore ■....Oct. 12
Johns Hopkins....*Oct. 18
Gettysburg ■....Oct. 26
Ursinus....Nov. 2
Carnegie Mellon ■ ....Nov. 9
Moravian ....Nov. 16

1995 RESULTS (0-9-1)

0 Catholic....45
0 Dickinson....35
10 Frank. & Marsh. 38
13 Western Md....13
7 Swarthmore....11
11 Johns Hopkins 14
16 Gettysburg....28
14 Union (N.Y.)....33
10 Ursinus....17
7 Moravian....38
88 **272**

Nickname: Mules.
Stadium: Muhlenberg Field (1928), 4,000 capacity. Natural turf.
Colors: Cardinal & Gray.
Conference: Centennial.
SID: Mike Falk, 610-821-3232.
AD: Connie Kunda (interim).

MURRAY ST.

Murray, KY 42071 ....I-AA

Coach: Houston Nutt, Oklahoma St. '81
Record: 3 Years, 20-14-0

1996 SCHEDULE

Western Ky. ■....*Sept. 7
Southern Ill. ■....*Sept. 14
Southeast Mo. St....Sept. 21
Middle Tenn. St. ■....*Sept. 28
Austin Peay ■....Oct. 5
Tenn.-Martin....*Oct. 12
Eastern Ill....Oct. 19
Tennessee Tech ■....Nov. 2
Eastern Ky....Nov. 9
Tennessee St. ■ ....Nov. 16

1995 RESULTS (11-0-0)

35 Western Ky. 14
35 Southern Ill....3
34 Southeast Mo. St. 0
34 Middle Tenn. St. 0
45 Austin Peay 17
33 Tenn.-Martin 9
63 Morehead St. 13

45 Tennessee Tech......14
17 Eastern Ky......7
24 Tennessee St......19
56 Western Ill. 18
421 **114**

I-AA Championship

34 Northern Iowa......35

Nickname: Racers.
Stadium: Stewart (1973), 16,800 capacity. Artificial turf.
Colors: Blue & Gold.
Conference: Ohio Valley.
SID: Brian Horgan, 502-762-4271.
AD: Mike Strickland.

MUSKINGUM

New Concord, OH 43762 III

Coach: Jeff Heacock, Muskingum '76
Record: 15 Years, 74-69-4

1996 SCHEDULE

Denison ■ ......Sept. 7
Heidelberg ......Sept. 21
Hiram ......Sept. 28
Capital ■ ......Oct. 5
John Carroll ......Oct. 12
Ohio Northern ■ ......Oct. 19
Mount Union ■ ......Oct. 26
Baldwin-Wallace ......Nov. 2
Otterbein ......Nov. 9
Marietta ■ ......Nov. 16

1995 RESULTS (6-3-1)

34 Denison 0
14 Hiram 0
31 Capital 11
20 Ohio Northern 18
17 Baldwin-Wallace 0
11 Heidelberg 10
7 Mount Union 41
7 John Carroll 7
6 Otterbein 9
0 Marietta 24
147 **120**

Nickname: Fighting Muskies.
Stadium: McConagha (1925), 5,000 capacity. Natural turf.
Colors: Black & Magenta.
Conference: Ohio Athletic.
SID: Craig McKendry, 614-826-8022.
AD: Jeff Heacock.

NAVY

Annapolis, MD 21402 ......I-A

Coach: Charlie Weatherbie, Oklahoma St. '77
Record: 4 Years, 20-25-0

1996 SCHEDULE

Rutgers ......*Sept. 7
Southern Methodist ■ ......*Sept. 21
Boston College ......Sept. 28
Duke ■ ......Oct. 5
Air Force ......Oct. 12
Wake Forest ......Oct. 26
Notre Dame [Dublin, Ireland] ......Nov. 2
Delaware ■ ......Nov. 9
Tulane ■ ......Nov. 16
Georgia Tech ......Nov. 23
Army [Philadelphia, Pa.] ......Dec. 7

1995 RESULTS (5-6-0)

33 Southern Methodist 2
17 Rutgers 27
7 Wake Forest 30
30 Duke 9
0 Virginia Tech 14
20 Air Force 30
20 Villanova 14
17 Notre Dame 35
31 Delaware 7
35 Tulane 7
13 Army 14
223 **189**

Nickname: Midshipmen.
Stadium: Navy-Marine Corps Memorial (1959), 30,000 capacity. Natural turf.
Colors: Navy Blue & Gold.
Conference: I-A Independents.
SID: Scott Strasemeier, 410-268-6226.
AD: Jack Lengyel.

NEBRASKA

Lincoln, NE 68588 ......I-A

Coach: Tom Osborne, Hastings '59
Record: 23 Years, 231-47-3

1996 SCHEDULE

Michigan St. ■ ......Sept. 7
Arizona St. ......*Sept. 21
Colorado St. ■ ......Sept. 28
Kansas St. ......Oct. 5
Baylor ■ ......Oct. 12
Texas Tech ......Oct. 19
Kansas ■ ......Oct. 26
Oklahoma ......Nov. 2
Missouri ■ ......Nov. 9
Iowa St. ......Nov. 16
Colorado ■ ......Nov. 29

1995 RESULTS (11-0-0)

64 Oklahoma St. 21
50 Michigan St. 10
77 Arizona St. 28
49 Pacific (Cal.) 7
35 Washington St. 21
57 Missouri 0
49 Kansas St. 25
44 Colorado 21
73 Iowa St. 14
41 Kansas 3
37 Oklahoma 0
576 **150**

Fiesta Bowl

62 Florida 24

Nickname: Cornhuskers.
Stadium: Memorial (1923), 72,700 capacity. Artificial turf.
Colors: Scarlet & Cream.
Conference: Big 12.
SID: Chris Anderson, 402-472-2263.
AD: Bill Byrne.

NEB.-KEARNEY

Kearney, NE 68849 II

Coach: Claire Boroff, Neb.-Kearney '59
Record: 24 Years, 146-87-5

1996 SCHEDULE

Mo. Western St. ■ ......Sept. 7
Neb.-Omaha ......Sept. 14
Colorado Mines ■ ......Sept. 21
Chadron St. ......Sept. 28
Fort Lewis ......Oct. 5
Fort Hays St. ■ ......Oct. 12
Mesa St. ......Oct. 19
Wayne St. (Neb.) ......Oct. 26
Western St. ■ ......Nov. 2
N.M. Highlands ■ ......Nov. 9
Adams St. ......Nov. 16

1995 RESULTS (6-3-1)

10 Morningside 10
14 Neb.-Omaha 19
46 Moorhead St. 14
6 Fort Hays St. 31
28 Northwestern Okla. 6
24 Wayne St. (Neb.) 14
21 Southern Utah 28
36 Northern St. 23
44 Western N.M. 28
56 Colorado Mines 0
285 **173**

Nickname: Antelopes.
Stadium: Foster Field (1929), 6,500 capacity. Natural turf.
Colors: Royal Blue & Old Gold.
Conference: Rocky Mountain Athletic.
SID: Aaron Babcock, 308-865-8334.
AD: Dick Dull.

NEB.-OMAHA

Omaha, NE 68182 II

Coach: Pat Behrns, Dakota St. '72
Record: 8 Years, 40-44-0

1996 SCHEDULE

Hastings ■ ......*Sept. 7
Neb.-Kearney ■ ......Sept. 14
Mankato St. ■ ......*Sept. 21
North Dak. St. ......*Sept. 28
Morningside ■ ......*Oct. 5
North Dak. ......Oct. 12
Northern Colo. ■ ......*Oct. 19
Augustana (S.D.) ......Oct. 26
St. Cloud St. ■ ......*Nov. 2
South Dak. St. ■ ......Nov. 9
South Dak. ......Nov. 16

1995 RESULTS (3-8-0)

30 Wayne St. (Neb.) 37
19 Neb.-Kearney 14
10 Mankato St. 49
23 North Dak. St. 34
31 Morningside 14
16 North Dak. 31
6 Northern Colo. 23
14 Augustana (S.D.) 28
7 St. Cloud St. 34
44 South Dak. St. 28
37 South Dak. 55
237 **347**

Nickname: Mavericks.
Stadium: Al F. Caniglia Field (1949), 9,500 capacity. Artificial turf.
Colors: Black & Crimson.
Conference: North Central.
SID: Gary Anderson, 402-554-2305.
AD: Dave Cox.

NEB. WESLEYAN

Lincoln, NE 68504 III

Coach: Brian Keller, Neb. Wesleyan '83
(First year as head coach)

1996 SCHEDULE

Austin ......Sept. 14
Colorado Col. ■ ......Sept. 21
Midland Lutheran ■ ......Sept. 28
Concordia (Neb.) ■ ......Oct. 5
Northwestern Ia. ......Oct. 12
Hastings ■ ......Oct. 19
Dana ......Oct. 26
Sioux Falls ■ ......Nov. 2
Doane ......Nov. 9
Peru St. ......Nov. 16

1995 RESULTS (3-7-0)

9 Mary 39
25 Carroll (Mont.) 52
33 Concordia (Neb.) 23
25 Northwestern Ia. 26
10 Hastings 20
7 Dana 27
10 St. Ambrose 47
13 Doane 6
6 Midland Lutheran 14
47 Peru St. 7
185 **261**

Nickname: Plainsmen.
Stadium: Abel (1986), 2,000 capacity. Natural turf.
Colors: Yellow & Brown.
Conference: Division III Independents.
SID: Jim Angele, 402-465-2151.
AD: Mary Beth Kennedy.

NEVADA

Reno, NV 89557 ......I-A

Coach: Jeff Tisdel, Nevada '77
(First year as head coach)

SCHEDULES/RESULTS

1996 SCHEDULE

Oregon .... Sept. 7
Montana St. ■ .... Sept. 14
California .... Sept. 21
Kent ■ .... Sept. 28
UNLV .... Oct. 5
Boise St. ■ .... Oct. 12
Idaho .... Oct. 19
North Texas .... Oct. 26
New Mexico St. ■ .... Nov. 2
Utah St. .... Nov. 9
Arkansas St. ■ .... Nov. 16

1995 RESULTS (9-2-0)

38 Southwestern La. 14
45 New Mexico St. 24
35 Toledo 49
27 San Diego St. 30
56 North Texas 24
59 Northeast La. 35
49 Louisiana Tech 45
55 UNLV 32
30 Utah St. 25
45 Pacific (Cal.) 29
45 San Jose St. 28
484 **335**

Las Vegas Bowl

37 Toledo 40

Nickname: Wolf Pack.
Stadium: Mackay (1967), 31,545 capacity. Natural turf.
Colors: Silver & Blue.
Conference: Big West.
SID: Paul Stuart, 702-784-4600.
AD: Chris Ault.

UNLV

Las Vegas, NV 89154 .... I-A

Coach: Jeff Horton, Nevada '81
Record: 3 Years, 16-18-0

1996 SCHEDULE

Tennessee .... *Aug. 31
Air Force ■ .... *Sept. 7
Wisconsin ■ .... *Sept. 14
Colorado St. .... Sept. 21
Wyoming ■ .... Sept. 28
Nevada ■ .... Oct. 5
Brigham Young .... Oct. 12
Hawaii .... *Oct. 19
Fresno St. ■ .... Oct. 26
Texas Christian .... Nov. 2
San Diego St. ■ .... Nov. 16
San Jose St. .... Nov. 23

1995 RESULTS (2-9-0)

0 Rice 38
28 Arkansas St. 23
6 Eastern Mich. 51
30 Iowa St. 57
30 Hawaii 58
14 Northern Ill. 62
14 San Jose St. 52
32 Nevada 55
34 North Texas 24
0 Utah St. 42
34 New Mexico St. 58
222 **520**

Nickname: Rebels.
Stadium: Sam Boyd (1971), 32,000 capacity. Artificial turf.
Colors: Scarlet & Gray.
Conference: Western Athletic.
SID: Mark Wallington, 702-895-4472.
AD: Charles Cavagnaro.

NEW HAMPSHIRE

Durham, NH 03824 .... I-AA

Coach: Bill Bowes, Penn St. '65
Record: 24 Years, 158-90-5

1996 SCHEDULE

Rhode Island .... Sept. 14
Connecticut ■ .... Sept. 21
James Madison .... Sept. 28
William & Mary .... Oct. 5
Lehigh ■ .... Oct. 12
Maine .... Oct. 19
Massachusetts ■ .... Oct. 26
Richmond ■ .... Nov. 2
Villanova ■ .... Nov. 9
Boston U. .... Nov. 16
Northeastern .... Nov. 23

1995 RESULTS (6-5-0)

21 Connecticut 23
7 Rhode Island 10
0 William & Mary 39
35 Lehigh 14
32 Massachusetts 29
19 James Madison 23
21 Maine 0
35 Boston U. 7
3 Richmond 7
12 Villanova 9
21 Northeastern 10
206 **171**

Nickname: Wildcats.
Stadium: Cowell (1936), 9,571 capacity. Natural turf.
Colors: Blue & White.
Conference: Yankee.
SID: John Sudsbury, 603-862-2585.
AD: Gilbert Chapman.

NEW HAVEN

West Haven, CT 06516 II

Coach: Tony Sparano, New Haven '82
Record: 2 Years, 17-4-1

1996 SCHEDULE

West Chester ■ .... Sept. 7
East Stroudsburg ■ .... Sept. 14
Millersville .... Sept. 21
Indiana (Pa.) .... *Sept. 28
Virginia Union ■ .... Oct. 12
Elizabeth City St. .... Oct. 19
Southern Conn. St. ■ .... Oct. 26
Charleston So. .... Nov. 2
Buffalo .... Nov. 9
American Int'l ■ .... Nov. 16

1995 RESULTS (9-0-1)

27 Bloomsburg 20
28 Kutztown 19
20 Indiana (Pa.) 19
33 Abilene Christian 7
36 West Chester 36
36 Virginia Union 9
24 Southern Conn. St. 6
50 Knoxville 0
34 Bowie St. 0
23 American Int'l 13
311 **129**

II Championship

27 Edinboro 12
9 Ferris St. 17

Nickname: Chargers.
Stadium: Robert B. Dodds, 3,500 capacity. Natural turf.
Colors: Blue & Gold.
Conference: Division II Independents.
SID: Jack Jones, 203-932-7025.
AD: Deborah Chin.

NEW MEXICO

Albuquerque, NM 87131 .... I-A

Coach: Dennis Franchione, Pittsburg St. '73
Record: 13 Years, 98-46-2

1996 SCHEDULE

New Mexico St. .... *Aug. 29
Northern Ariz. ■ .... *Sept. 7
Central Fla. ■ .... *Sept. 14
Brigham Young .... Sept. 21
Texas Christian ■ .... *Sept. 28
Rice .... *Oct. 5
San Diego St. ■ .... *Oct. 19
Southern Methodist .... *Oct. 26
Tulsa .... Nov. 2
Utah ■ .... Nov. 9
UTEP ■ .... Nov. 23

1995 RESULTS (4-7-0)

45 Northern Ariz. 21
9 Utah 36
36 New Mexico St. 24
24 Air Force 27
34 Fresno St. 51
24 Hawaii 10
22 Colorado St. 14
7 Texas Tech 34
29 San Diego St. 38
14 Brigham Young 31
12 UTEP 17
256 **303**

Nickname: Lobos.
Stadium: University (1960), 31,218 capacity. Natural turf.
Colors: Cherry & Silver.
Conference: Western Athletic.
SID: Greg Remington, 505-277-2026.
AD: Rudy Davalos.

N.M. HIGHLANDS

Las Vegas, NM 87701 II

Coach: Carl Ferrill, N.M. Highlands '69
(First year as head coach)

1996 SCHEDULE

Abilene Christian .... *Aug. 31
Eastern N.M. ■ .... *Sept. 7
Adams St. ■ .... Sept. 21
Western St. .... Sept. 28
Colorado Mines .... Oct. 5
Chadron St. ■ .... Oct. 12
Fort Lewis ■ .... Oct. 19
Fort Hays St. .... Oct. 26
Mesa St. ■ .... Nov. 2
Neb.-Kearney .... Nov. 9
Western N.M. .... Nov. 16

1995 RESULTS (4-7-0)

6 Abilene Christian 31
38 Western N.M. 22
9 Eastern N.M. 22
40 Midwestern St. 23
41 Colorado Mines 22
7 Fort Hays St. 51
17 Chadron St. 24
39 Fort Lewis 16
14 Mesa St. 27
20 Western St. 45
26 Adams St. 36
257 **319**

Nickname: Cowboys.
Stadium: Perkins, 5,000 capacity. Natural turf.
Colors: Purple & White.
Conference: Rocky Mountain Athletic.
SID: Jesse Gallegos, 505-454-3387.
AD: Rob Evers.

NEW MEXICO ST.

Las Cruces, NM 88003 .... I-A

Coach: Jim Hess, Southeastern Okla. '59
Record: 21 Years, 133-98-5

1996 SCHEDULE

New Mexico ■ .... *Aug. 29
Texas .... *Sept. 7
UTEP .... *Sept. 14
Cal St. Northridge ■ .... *Sept. 21
LSU .... *Sept. 28
Utah St. ■ .... *Oct. 12
North Texas .... Oct. 19
Southern Utah ■ .... *Oct. 26
Nevada .... Nov. 2
Idaho .... Nov. 9
Boise St. ■ .... Nov. 16

1995 RESULTS (4-7-0)

45 UTEP 17
24 Nevada 45
13 Georgia 40

24 New Mexico....36
21 Iowa....59
48 Louisiana Tech....13
26 Southwestern La....43
14 Utah St....27
39 Pacific (Cal.)....37
37 San Jose St....38
58 UNLV....34
349 **389**

Nickname: Aggies.
Stadium: Aggie Memorial (1978), 30,343 capacity. Natural turf.
Colors: Crimson & White.
Conference: Big West.
SID: Steve Shutt, 505-646-3929.
AD: Al Gonzales.

NEWBERRY

Newberry, SC 29108 II

Coach: Mike Taylor, Newberry '76
Record: 4 Years, 16-27-0

1996 SCHEDULE

West Ga. ■....*Aug. 31
Elon....*Sept. 7
Wingate....*Sept. 21
Gardner-Webb ■....*Sept. 28
Mars Hill ■....*Oct. 5
Charleston So....Oct. 12
Wofford ■....*Oct. 19
Lenoir-Rhyne....Oct. 26
Catawba ■....*Nov. 2
Carson-Newman....Nov. 9
Presbyterian....Nov. 16

1995 RESULTS (5-6-0)

20 Citadel....21
21 Wingate....27
7 West Liberty St....10
16 Gardner-Webb....21
14 Mars Hill....34
38 Charleston So....10
17 Wofford....15
36 Lenoir-Rhyne....15
17 Catawba....8
30 Carson-Newman....39
9 Presbyterian....8
225 **208**

Nickname: Indians.
Stadium: Setzler Field (1930), 4,000 capacity. Natural turf.
Colors: Scarlet & Gray.
Conference: Division II Independents.
SID: Marcie L. Cole, 803-321-5667.
AD: William Grafton Young.

NICHOLLS ST.

Thibodaux, LA 70301 ....I-AA

Coach: Darren Barbier, Nicholls St. '82
Record: 1 Year, 0-11-0

1996 SCHEDULE

Northeast La....*Aug. 29
Jacksonville St. ■....*Sept. 14
Troy St....*Sept. 21
Samford....Oct. 5
Northwestern St. ■....*Oct. 12
Stephen F. Austin ■....Oct. 19
Southwest Tex. St....Oct. 26
Southern-B.R. ■....*Nov. 2
Sam Houston St. ■....*Nov. 9
Harding ■....Nov. 16
McNeese St....*Nov. 23

1995 RESULTS (0-11-0)

10 Hofstra....34
21 Northeast La....34
3 Troy St....17
20 Southern Ill....48
20 Samford....36
14 Northwestern St....34
3 Stephen F. Austin....56
25 Southwest Tex. St....35
3 Southern-B.R....41
17 Sam Houston St....24
6 McNeese St....31
142 **390**

Nickname: Colonels.
Stadium: John L. Guidry (1972), 12,800 capacity. Natural turf.
Colors: Red & Gray.
Conference: Southland Football League.
SID: Ron Mears, 504-448-4282.
AD: Mike Knight.

NICHOLS

Dudley, MA 01570 III

Coach: Jim Foster, Oklahoma '69
(First year as head coach)

1996 SCHEDULE

Mass. Maritime....Sept. 14
Salve Regina ■....Sept. 21
Merrimack ■....Sept. 28
Mass.-Dartmouth ■....Oct. 5
Curry....Oct. 12
Sacred Heart ■....Oct. 19
MIT ■....Oct. 26
Western New Eng....Nov. 2
Worcester St....Nov. 9
Assumption....Nov. 16

1995 RESULTS (0-9-0)

13 Mass. Maritime....16
14 Stonehill....38
0 Bentley....50
14 Curry....33
6 Assumption....8
10 Salve Regina....60
2 MIT....35
0 Western New Eng....6
6 Worcester St....42
65 **288**

Nickname: Bison.
Stadium: Bison Bowl (1961), 3,000 capacity. Natural turf.
Colors: Black & Green.
Conference: Eastern Football.
SID: Scott Gibbons, 508-943-1560.
AD: Thomas R. Cafaro.

NORFOLK ST.

Norfolk, VA 23504 II

Coach: Darnell Moore, Elizabeth City St. '70
Record: 2 Years, 14-6-0

1996 SCHEDULE

Virginia St....*Aug. 31
Bowie St....Sept. 7
Livingstone ■....*Sept. 14
Bethune-Cookman....Sept. 21
Delaware St. ■....Sept. 28
Central St. ■....*Oct. 5
Virginia Union ■....Oct. 19
Elizabeth City St....Oct. 26
Howard....Nov. 2
Winston-Salem....*Nov. 9
Hampton....Nov. 16

1995 RESULTS (7-3-0)

22 Virginia St....41
27 Bowie St....12
42 Livingstone....28
62 Elizabeth City St....50
14 Delaware St....20
35 Bethune-Cookman....33
18 Hampton....23
58 Virginia Union....32
55 Johnson Smith....14
27 N.C. Central....6
360 **259**

Nickname: Spartans.
Stadium: Foreman Field (1935), 26,000 capacity. Artificial turf.
Colors: Green & Gold.
Conference: Central Intercollegiate Athletic Association.
SID: John Holley, 804-683-8444.
AD: William (Dick) Price.

NORTH ALA.

Florence, AL 35630....II

Coach: Bobby Wallace, Mississippi St. '76
Record: 8 Years, 67-28-1

1996 SCHEDULE

Albany St. (Ga.)....*Aug. 31
Alabama A&M ■....*Sept. 7
Southern Ark. ■....*Sept. 14
Tex. A&M-Kingsville....*Sept. 21
Arkansas Tech ■....Sept. 28
Valdosta St....Oct. 5
Delta St. ■....Oct. 19
Henderson St....Oct. 26
Central Ark. ■....Nov. 2
West Ga....*Nov. 7
West Ala....Nov. 16

1995 RESULTS (10-0-0)

41 Albany St. (Ga.)....13
49 Alabama A&M....0
30 Delta St....0
41 Mississippi Col....3
34 West Ga....19
28 Central Ark....7
33 Henderson St....28
26 Valdosta St....9
52 Arkansas Tech....17
42 West Ala....10
376 **106**

II Championship

38 Albany St. (Ga.)....28
38 Carson-Newman....7
45 Ferris St....7
27 Pittsburg St....7

Nickname: Lions.
Stadium: Braly (1940), 13,000 capacity. Natural turf.
Colors: Purple & Gold.
Conference: Gulf South.
SID: Jeff Hodges, 205-760-4595.
AD: Dan Summy.

NORTH CARO.

Chapel Hill, NC 27514....I-A

Coach: Mack Brown, Florida St. '74
Record: 12 Years, 66-71-1

1996 SCHEDULE

Clemson ■....Aug. 31
Syracuse....*Sept. 7
Georgia Tech ■....Sept. 21
Florida St....Sept. 28
Wake Forest....Oct. 5
Maryland ■....Oct. 12
Houston....*Oct. 26
North Caro. St. ■....Nov. 2
Louisville ■....Nov. 9
Virginia....Nov. 16
Duke....Nov. 23

1995 RESULTS (6-5-0)

9 Syracuse....20
18 Maryland....32
17 Louisville....10
62 Ohio....0
22 Virginia....17
25 Georgia Tech....27
31 Wake Forest....7
10 Clemson....17
12 Florida St....28
28 Duke....24
30 North Caro. St....28
264 **210**

Carquest Bowl

20 Arkansas....10

Nickname: Tar Heels.
Stadium: Kenan (1927), 52,000 capacity. Natural turf.
Colors: Carolina Blue & White.
Conference: Atlantic Coast.

SCHEDULES/RESULTS

SID: Rick Brewer, 919-962-2123.
AD: John Swofford.

NORTH CARO. A&T

Greensboro, NC 27411 ....I-AA

Coach: Bill Hayes, N.C. Central '65
Record: 20 Years, 141-78-2

1996 SCHEDULE

N.C. Central [Raleigh, N.C.]........................Aug. 31
Winston-Salem ■ ....Sept. 7
Fayetteville St. ■ ....Sept. 14
Hampton ....Sept. 21
Florida A&M........................Oct. 12
Morgan St. ■ ....Oct. 19
Howard........................Oct. 26
Bethune-Cookman ■........................Nov. 2
Delaware St........................Nov. 9
Grambling ■ ....Nov. 16
South Caro. St. [Charlotte, N.C.]........................Nov. 23

1995 RESULTS (4-7-0)

18 N.C. Central 17
45 Winston-Salem 21
31 Appalachian St. 38
10 Jacksonville St........................21
3 Florida A&M........................20
38 Morgan St........................32
14 Howard 20
24 Bethune-Cookman 21
10 Delaware St. 17
4 Lane 12
27 South Caro. St........................28
224 **247**

Nickname: Aggies.
Stadium: Aggie (1981), 21,000 capacity. Natural turf.
Colors: Blue & Gold.
Conference: Mid-Eastern Athletic.
SID: Bradford Evans Jr., 919-334-7141.
AD: Willie Burden.

N.C. CENTRAL

Durham, NC 27707........................II

Coach: Larry Little, Bethune-Cookman '66
Record: 12 Years, 59-66-1

1996 SCHEDULE

North Caro. A&T [Raleigh, N.C.] ....Aug. 31
Gardner-Webb ....*Sept. 7
Elon ....*Sept. 14
Delaware St........................Sept. 21
Elizabeth City St. ■........................Sept. 28
Fayetteville St. ....*Oct. 5
Winston-Salem ■ ....Oct. 12
Central St. ....Oct. 19
Livingstone........................Oct. 26
Johnson Smith ■........................Nov. 2
Bowie St. ■ ....Nov. 9

1995 RESULTS (5-6-0)

17 North Caro. A&T........................18
5 Elon........................12
37 Howard 32
45 Johnson Smith........................6
27 Elizabeth City St. 28
45 Fayetteville St. 0
42 Winston-Salem 19
30 Central St........................50
25 Livingstone 60
6 Norfolk St. 27
27 Bowie St. 18
306 **270**

Nickname: Eagles.
Stadium: O'Kelly-Riddick (1975), 11,500 capacity. Natural turf.
Colors: Maroon & Gray.
Conference: Central Intercollegiate Athletic Association.
SID: Kyle Serba, 919-560-5427.
AD: William E. Lide.

NORTH CARO. ST.

Raleigh, NC 27695 ....I-A

Coach: Mike O'Cain, Clemson '77
Record: 3 Years, 19-16-0

1996 SCHEDULE

Georgia Tech ■ ....Sept. 7
Florida St. ■ ....*Sept. 19
Purdue........................Sept. 28
Maryland ....Oct. 5
Alabama ■ ....Oct. 12
Virginia ....Oct. 19
North Caro. ....Nov. 2
Duke ■........................Nov. 9
Clemson ....Nov. 16
Wake Forest ■ ....Nov. 23
East Caro. [Charlotte, N. C.]........................Nov. 30

1995 RESULTS (3-8-0)

33 Marshall 16
24 Virginia........................29
17 Florida St. 77
0 Baylor........................14
22 Clemson 43
11 Alabama 27
41 Duke........................38
13 Maryland 30
19 Georgia Tech 27
52 Wake Forest 23
28 North Caro. 30
260 **354**

Nickname: Wolfpack.
Stadium: Carter-Finley (1966), 50,000 capacity. Natural turf.
Colors: Red & White.
Conference: Atlantic Coast.
SID: Mark Bockelman, 919-515-2102.
AD: Todd Turner.

NORTH CENTRAL

Naperville, IL 60540 III

Coach: Bill Mack, Beloit '58
Record: 3 Years, 9-17-1

1996 SCHEDULE

Hanover ■ ....*Sept. 14
Blackburn ....Sept. 28
Carthage ■ ....*Oct. 5
North Park........................Oct. 12
Ill. Wesleyan........................Oct. 19
Augustana (Ill.) ■........................Oct. 26
Elmhurst........................Nov. 2
Millikin ■........................Nov. 9
Wheaton (Ill.)........................Nov. 16

1995 RESULTS (3-5-1)

23 Quincy 21
29 Carroll (Wis.) 13
21 Elmhurst 3
7 Augustana (Ill.) 47
0 Ill. Wesleyan 25
19 Millikin........................21
16 Wheaton (Ill.) 34
7 Carthage 7
14 North Park 29
136 **200**

Nickname: Cardinals.
Stadium: Kroehler Field, 3,000 capacity. Natural turf.
Colors: Cardinal & White.
Conference: College Conf. of Illinois & Wisconsin.
SID: Mike Koon, 708-637-5302.
AD: Walter Johnson.

NORTH DAK.

Grand Forks, ND 58202 II

Coach: Roger Thomas, Augustana (Ill.) '69
Record: 12 Years, 67-58-2

1996 SCHEDULE

Moorhead St. ■ ....Sept. 14
Northern Colo. ....Sept. 21
Augustana (S.D.) ■ ....Sept. 28
South Dak. St. ....Oct. 5
Neb.-Omaha ■ ....Oct. 12
Mankato St. [Minneapolis, Minn.] ....Oct. 19
South Dak. ■........................Oct. 26
Morningside ■........................Nov. 2
North Dak. St........................*Nov. 9
St. Cloud St. ....Nov. 16

1995 RESULTS (9-1-0)

63 Bemidji St........................0
34 Northern Colo. 13
39 Augustana (S.D.) 29
14 South Dak. St. 3
31 Neb.-Omaha........................16
27 Mankato St. 21
0 South Dak. 35
44 Morningside........................21
21 North Dak. St. 7
35 St. Cloud St........................21
308 **166**

II Championship

10 North Dak. St. 41

Nickname: Sioux.
Stadium: Memorial (1927), 10,000 capacity. Artificial turf.
Colors: Kelly Green & White.
Conference: North Central.
SID: To be named, 701-777-2985.
AD: Terry Wanless.

NORTH DAK. ST.

Fargo, ND 58105........................II

Coach: Rocky Hager, Minot St. '74
Record: 9 Years, 85-21-1

1996 SCHEDULE

Tex. A&M-Kingsville ■........................*Sept. 7
St. Cloud St. ■........................Sept. 21
Neb.-Omaha ■ ....*Sept. 28
Augustana (S.D.) ....Oct. 5
Northern Colo. ....Oct. 12
South Dak. St. ■ ....*Oct. 19
Mankato St. ■ ....*Oct. 26
South Dak........................*Nov. 2
North Dak. ■........................*Nov. 9
Morningside ....Nov. 16

1995 RESULTS (9-2-0)

16 Delta St........................13
19 Valdosta St........................14
0 St. Cloud St........................34
34 Neb.-Omaha........................23
53 Augustana (S.D.) 14
42 Northern Colo. 38
26 South Dak. St. 17
26 Mankato St. 25
14 South Dak. 7
7 North Dak........................21
30 Morningside........................7
267 **213**

II Championship

41 North Dak........................10
7 Pittsburg St. 9

Nickname: Bison.
Stadium: FargoDome (1992), 18,700 capacity. Artificial turf.
Colors: Yellow & Green.
Conference: North Central.
SID: George Ellis, 701-231-8331.
AD: Robert Entzion.

NORTH PARK

Chicago, IL 60625 III

Coach: Mike Liljegren, North Park '85
Record: 1 Year, 2-7-0

1996 SCHEDULE

Ripon ....Sept. 14
Mt. Senario ■........................Sept. 21
Ill. Wesleyan ■........................Oct. 5
North Central ■........................Oct. 12
Augustana (Ill.)........................Oct. 19

Elmhurst ■ .... Oct. 26
Millikin .... Nov. 2
Wheaton (Ill.) ■ .... Nov. 9
Carthage .... Nov. 16

1995 RESULTS (2-7-0)

0 Concordia (Wis.) 17
34 Lake Forest 14
7 Millikin 34
6 Elmhurst 38
14 Augustana (Ill.) 53
10 Wheaton (Ill.) 44
7 Carthage 20
10 Ill. Wesleyan 61
29 North Central 14
117 **295**

Nickname: Vikings.
Stadium: Hedstrand Field (1955), 2,500 capacity. Natural turf.
Colors: Blue & Gold.
Conference: College Conf. of Illinois & Wisconsin.
SID: Steve VandenBranden, 312-244-5675.
AD: Jerry Chaplin.

NORTH TEXAS

Denton, TX 76203 .... I-A

Coach: Matt Simon, Eastern N.M. '76
Record: 2 Years, 9-13-1

1996 SCHEDULE

Illinois St. ■ .... *Sept. 7
Arizona St. .... *Sept. 14
Texas A&M .... Sept. 21
Army [Irving, Texas] .... Sept. 28
Northern Ill. .... Oct. 5
Vanderbilt ■ .... Oct. 12
New Mexico St. ■ .... Oct. 19
Nevada ■ .... Oct. 26
Utah St. .... Nov. 2
Boise St. .... Nov. 9
Idaho ■ .... Nov. 16

1995 RESULTS (2-9-0)

7 Missouri 28
10 Kansas 27
30 Oregon St. 27
10 Oklahoma 51
24 Nevada 56
14 Ala.-Birmingham 19
7 LSU 49
19 Alabama 38
24 UNLV 34
41 Idaho St. 38
14 Louisville 57
200 **424**

Nickname: Eagles.
Stadium: Fouts Field (1952), 30,500 capacity. Artificial turf.
Colors: Green & White.
Conference: Big West.
SID: Ann Wheelwright, 817-565-2476.
AD: Craig Helwig.

NORTHEAST LA.

Monroe, LA 71209 .... I-A

Coach: Ed Zaunbrecher, Middle Tenn. St. '71
Record: 2 Years, 5-17-0

1996 SCHEDULE

Nicholls St. ■ .... *Aug. 29
Minnesota ■ .... *Sept. 7
UCLA .... *Sept. 14
Sam Houston St. ■ .... *Sept. 21
Arkansas [Little Rock, Ark.] .... *Sept. 28
Northwestern St. ■ .... *Oct. 5
Central Fla. .... Oct. 19
Mississippi St. .... Nov. 2
Auburn .... Nov. 9
Jacksonville St. ■ .... *Nov. 16
Cincinnati .... Nov. 23

1995 RESULTS (2-9-0)

17 Fresno St. 31
34 Nicholls St. 21
14 Colorado 66
22 Missouri 31
34 Mississippi St. 32
10 Troy St. 20
35 Nevada 59
39 Northwestern St. 42
14 Central Fla. 34
14 Auburn 38
0 Louisville 39
233 **413**

Nickname: Indians.
Stadium: Malone (1978), 30,427 capacity. Natural turf.
Colors: Maroon & Gold.
Conference: I-A Independents.
SID: Robby Edwards, 318-342-5460.
AD: Richard Giannini.

NORTHEASTERN

Boston, MA 02115 .... I-AA

Coach: Barry Gallup, Boston College '69
Record: 5 Years, 17-37-1

1996 SCHEDULE

Maine [Portland, Maine] .... *Aug. 29
Connecticut .... Sept. 14
Lafayette .... Sept. 21
Massachusetts .... Sept. 28
Richmond ■ .... Oct. 5
Villanova ■ .... Oct. 12
Delaware .... Oct. 19
William & Mary .... Oct. 26
James Madison .... Nov. 2
Boston U. ■ .... Nov. 9
New Hampshire ■ .... Nov. 23

1995 RESULTS (4-7-0)

44 Colgate 3
0 William & Mary 32
19 Massachusetts 21
10 Delaware 37
23 Richmond 26
24 Villanova 27
14 Boston U. 3
10 Connecticut 9
13 James Madison 27
31 Maine 28
10 New Hampshire 21
198 **234**

Nickname: Huskies.
Stadium: E.S. Parsons (1933), 7,000 capacity. Artificial turf.
Colors: Red & Black.
Conference: Yankee.
SID: Jack Grinold, 617-373-2691.
AD: Barry Gallup.

NORTHERN ARIZ.

Flagstaff, AZ 86011 .... I-AA

Coach: Steve Axman, LIU-C.W. Post '69
Record: 6 Years, 33-33-0

1996 SCHEDULE

Western N.M. ■ .... *Aug. 29
New Mexico .... *Sept. 7
Southern Utah ■ .... *Sept. 14
Portland St. .... Sept. 21
Cal St. Northridge ■ .... *Sept. 28
Weber St. ■ .... Oct. 5
Montana St. .... Oct. 12
Cal St. Sacramento ■ .... Oct. 19
Montana .... Oct. 26
Idaho St. ■ .... *Nov. 2
Eastern Wash. .... Nov. 9

1995 RESULTS (7-4-0)

21 New Mexico 45
62 Cal St. Sacramento 7
62 Abilene Christian 0
68 Cal St. Northridge 7
37 Montana St. 0
32 Boise St. 13
21 Montana 24
30 Eastern Wash. 16
42 Idaho St. 14
14 Idaho 17
14 Weber St. 20
403 **163**

Nickname: Lumberjacks.
Stadium: Walkup Skydome (1977), 15,300 capacity. Artificial turf.
Colors: Blue & Gold.
Conference: Big Sky.
SID: To be named, 520-523-6792.
AD: Steve Holton.

NORTHERN COLO.

Greeley, CO 80639 II

Coach: Joe Glenn, South Dak. '71
Record: 11 Years, 72-44-1

1996 SCHEDULE

Western St. ■ .... Sept. 7
Mesa St. .... Sept. 14
North Dak. ■ .... Sept. 21
South Dak. .... Sept. 28
Mankato St. ■ .... Oct. 5
North Dak. St. ■ .... Oct. 12
Neb.-Omaha .... *Oct. 19
St. Cloud St. .... Oct. 26
South Dak. St. ■ .... Nov. 2
Morningside .... Nov. 9
Augustana (S.D.) .... Nov. 16

1995 RESULTS (9-2-0)

29 Western St. 19
58 Mesa St. 7
13 North Dak. 34
28 South Dak. 21
31 Mankato St. 7
38 North Dak. St. 42
23 Neb.-Omaha 6
30 St. Cloud St. 27
23 South Dak. St. 14
51 Morningside 14
55 Augustana (S.D.) 21
379 **212**

II Championship

17 Pittsburg St. 36

Nickname: Bears.
Stadium: Nottingham Field (1995), 7,000 capacity. Natural turf.
Colors: Navy & Gold.
Conference: North Central.
SID: Scott Leisinger, 303-351-2150.
AD: Jim Fallis.

NORTHERN ILL.

De Kalb, IL 60115 .... I-A

Coach: Joe Novak, Miami (Ohio) '67
(First year as head coach)

1996 SCHEDULE

Maryland .... *Aug. 31
Western Ill. ■ .... *Sept. 7
Penn St. .... Sept. 14
Arkansas St. .... *Sept. 21
UTEP ■ .... Sept. 28
North Texas ■ .... Oct. 5
Louisville .... Oct. 19
Akron ■ .... Oct. 26
Louisiana Tech ■ .... Nov. 2
Southwestern La. .... *Nov. 9
Oregon St. .... Nov. 16

1995 RESULTS (3-8-0)

13 Southern Miss. 45
21 Louisville 34
18 San Jose St. 17
25 Southwestern La. 24
0 Kansas St. 44
62 UNLV 14
7 Utah St. 42
19 Cincinnati 55
20 Florida 58

21 Arkansas St. 28
14 Louisiana Tech 59
220 **420**

Nickname: Huskies.
Stadium: Huskie (1965), 31,000 capacity. Artificial turf.
Colors: Cardinal & Black.
Conference: I-A Independents.
SID: Mike Korcek, 815-753-1706.
AD: Cary Groth.

NORTHERN IOWA

Cedar Falls, IA 50613 I-AA

Coach: Terry Allen, Northern Iowa '79
Record: 7 Years, 63-24-0

1996 SCHEDULE

Southern Utah *Aug. 31
St. Cloud St. ■ *Sept. 7
Stephen F. Austin ■ *Sept. 14
Iowa St. Sept. 21
McNeese St. ■ *Sept. 28
Illinois St. ■ Oct. 12
Southwest Mo. St. ■ *Oct. 19
Southern Ill. Oct. 26
Youngstown St. Nov. 2
Indiana St. Nov. 9
Western Ill. ■ *Nov. 16

1995 RESULTS (7-4-0)

7 Stephen F. Austin 26
13 Iowa 34
55 Lock Haven 10
38 Western Ill. 7
17 Eastern Ill. 7
27 Indiana St. 10
13 Southern Ill. 0
19 Southwest Mo. St. 17
29 Illinois St. 31
12 Idaho 16
48 Winona St. 3
278 **161**

I-AA Championship

35 Murray St. 34
24 Marshall 41

Nickname: Panthers.
Stadium: UNI-Dome (1976), 16,324 capacity. Artificial turf.
Colors: Purple & Old Gold.
Conference: Gateway.
SID: Nancy Justis, 319-273-6354.
AD: Christopher Ritrievi.

NORTHERN MICH.

Marquette, MI 49855 II

Coach: Eric Holm, Truman St. '81
Record: 6 Years, 44-22-0

1996 SCHEDULE

Northwood ■ Sept. 7
St. Francis (Ill.) *Sept. 14
Ferris St. Sept. 28
Indianapolis ■ Oct. 5
Hillsdale Oct. 12
Grand Valley St. ■ Oct. 19
Ashland Oct. 26
Wayne St. (Mich.) ■ Nov. 2
Michigan Tech Nov. 9
Saginaw Valley ■ Nov. 16

1995 RESULTS (7-3-0)

13 Saginaw Valley 12
21 Northwood 16
27 St. Francis (Ill.) 6
28 St. Joseph's (Ind.) 14
27 Ferris St. 41
28 Indianapolis 14
28 Hillsdale 14
23 Grand Valley St. 26
20 Ashland 8
15 Wayne St. (Mich.) 28
230 **179**

Nickname: Wildcats.
Stadium: Superior Dome (1991), 8,000 capacity. Artificial turf.
Colors: Old Gold & Olive Green.
Conference: Midwest Intercollegiate.
SID: Jim Pinar, 906-227-2720.
AD: Rick Comley.

NORTHERN ST.

Aberdeen, SD 57401 II

Coach: Dennis Miller, St. Cloud St. '81
Record: 10 Years, 66-44-0

1996 SCHEDULE

Wis.-Eau Claire ■ *Sept. 7
South Dak. ■ *Sept. 14
Wis.-Stout Sept. 21
Moorhead St. Sept. 28
Winona St. ■ Oct. 5
Minn.-Morris Oct. 12
Wayne St. (Neb.) Oct. 19
Bemidji St. ■ Oct. 26
Minn.-Duluth Nov. 2
Southwest St. ■ Nov. 9

1995 RESULTS (4-7-0)

21 Wis.-Eau Claire 13
13 South Dak. 56
14 Wayne St. (Neb.) 35
11 Southwest St. 0
13 Moorhead St. 35
23 Winona St. 26
35 Minn.-Morris 7
23 Neb.-Kearney 36
24 Bemidji St. 25
7 Minn.-Duluth 28
41 Luther 17
225 **278**

Nickname: Wolves.
Stadium: Swisher (1975), 6,000 capacity. Natural turf.
Colors: Maroon & Gold.
Conference: Northern Sun Intercollegiate.
SID: Deb Smith, 605-626-7748.
AD: Jim Kretchman.

NORTHWEST MO. ST.

Maryville, MO 64468 II

Coach: Mel Tjeerdsma, Southern St. '67
Record: 12 Years, 65-55-4

1996 SCHEDULE

South Dak. St. ■ Sept. 7
Mankato St. ■ Sept. 14
Southwest Baptist Sept. 21
Mo.-Rolla ■ Sept. 28
Central Mo. St. Oct. 5
Truman St. Oct. 12
Mo. Western St. ■ Oct. 19
Mo. Southern St. *Oct. 26
Emporia St. ■ Nov. 2
Washburn Nov. 9
Pittsburg St. ■ Nov. 16

1995 RESULTS (6-5-0)

6 South Dak. St. 10
34 Mankato St. 59
45 Southwest Baptist 13
48 Mo.-Rolla 14
33 Central Mo. St. 23
10 Truman St. 44
20 Mo. Western St. 24
41 Mo. Southern St. 33
23 Emporia St. 13
42 Washburn 21
14 Pittsburg St. 22
316 **276**

Nickname: Bearcats.
Stadium: Rickenbrode (1917), 7,500 capacity. Natural turf.
Colors: Green & White.
Conference: Mid-America Intercollegiate Athletic Assoc.
SID: Rocco Gasparro, 816-562-1118.
AD: Jim Redd.

NORTHWESTERN

Evanston, IL 60208 I-A

Coach: Gary Barnett, Missouri '69
Record: 6 Years, 26-37-2

1996 SCHEDULE

Wake Forest Sept. 7
Duke Sept. 14
Ohio ■ Sept. 21
Indiana Sept. 28
Michigan ■ Oct. 5
Minnesota ■ Oct. 12
Wisconsin Oct. 19
Illinois ■ Oct. 26
Penn St. Nov. 2
Iowa Nov. 9
Purdue ■ Nov. 16

1995 RESULTS (10-1-0)

17 Notre Dame 15
28 Miami (Ohio) 30
30 Air Force 6
31 Indiana 7
19 Michigan 13
27 Minnesota 17
35 Wisconsin 0
17 Illinois 14
21 Penn St. 10
31 Iowa 20
23 Purdue 8
279 **140**

Rose Bowl

32 Southern Cal 41

Nickname: Wildcats.
Stadium: Dyche (1926), 49,256 capacity. Artificial turf.
Colors: Purple & White.
Conference: Big Ten.
SID: Brad Hurlbut, 847-491-7503.
AD: Rick Taylor.

NORTHWESTERN ST.

Natchitoches, LA 71497 I-AA

Coach: Sam Goodwin, Henderson St. '66
Record: 15 Years, 82-80-4

1996 SCHEDULE

Southern-B.R. ■ *Sept. 7
East Tex. St. ■ *Sept. 21
Boise St. *Sept. 28
Northeast La. *Oct. 5
Nicholls St. *Oct. 12
Sam Houston St. ■ Oct. 19
Youngstown St. Oct. 26
Southwest Tex. St. Nov. 2
Troy St. ■ *Nov. 9
McNeese St. ■ *Nov. 16
Stephen F. Austin Nov. 23

1995 RESULTS (6-5-0)

7 Southern-B.R. 13
17 Troy St. 34
34 Delta St. 0
45 East Tex. St. 17
22 Boise St. 17
34 Nicholls St. 14
24 Sam Houston St. 2
42 Northeast La. 39
14 Southwest Tex. St. 28
10 McNeese St. 20
20 Stephen F. Austin 25
269 **209**

Nickname: Demons.
Stadium: Turpin (1976), 15,971 capacity. Artificial turf.
Colors: Purple & White.
Conference: Southland Football League.
SID: Doug Ireland, 318-357-6467.
AD: Tynes Hildebrand.

NORTHWOOD

Midland, MI 48640 II

Coach: Pat Riepma, Hillsdale '83
Record: 3 Years, 7-22-2

1996 SCHEDULE

Michigan Tech ■ .....*Aug. 29
Northern Mich. .....Sept. 7
Saginaw Valley .....Sept. 14
Ashland ■ .....Sept. 21
St. Francis (Ill.) .....Sept. 28
Thomas More ■ .....Oct. 5
Ferris St. .....Oct. 12
Indianapolis ■ .....Oct. 19
Hillsdale .....Oct. 26
Grand Valley St. ■ .....Nov. 2
Wayne St. (Mich.) ■ .....Nov. 9

1995 RESULTS (2-8-0)

25 Michigan Tech 39
16 Northern Mich. 21
21 Saginaw Valley 24
15 Ashland 9
3 St. Francis (Ill.) 13
19 St. Joseph's (Ind.) 18
14 Ferris St. 56
25 Indianapolis 30
30 Hillsdale 44
7 Grand Valley St. 43
175 **297**

Nickname: Northmen.
Stadium: Louis Juillerat (1964), 2,500 capacity. Natural turf.
Colors: Columbia Blue & White.
Conference: Midwest Intercollegiate.
SID: Fritz Reznor, 517-837-4239.
AD: Dave Coffey.

NORWICH

Northfield, VT 05663 III

Coach: Steve Hackett, Canisius '76
Record: 5 Years, 11-35-0

1996 SCHEDULE

Mass.-Dartmouth ■ .....Sept. 7
Merchant Marine ■ .....Sept. 14
Mass.-Lowell .....Sept. 21
Plymouth St. .....Sept. 28
Coast Guard ■ .....Oct. 5
Worcester Tech ■ .....Oct. 12
Hartwick .....Oct. 19
St. Lawrence .....Oct. 26
Springfield ■ .....Nov. 9
Western Conn. St. .....Nov. 16

1995 RESULTS (3-6-0)

0 Mass.-Dartmouth 13
0 Merchant Marine 23
35 Mass.-Lowell 7
21 Plymouth St. 24
6 Coast Guard 27
8 Worcester Tech 17
12 Stony Brook 27
24 St. Lawrence 0
14 Western Conn. St. 13
120 **151**

Nickname: Cadets.
Stadium: Sabine Field (1921), 5,000 capacity. Natural turf.
Colors: Maroon & Gold.
Conference: Freedom Football.
SID: Todd Bamford, 802-485-2160.
AD: Tony Mariano.

NOTRE DAME

Notre Dame, IN 46556...........................I-A

Coach: Lou Holtz, Kent '59
Record: 26 Years, 208-92-7

1996 SCHEDULE

Vanderbilt .....*Sept. 5
Purdue ■ .....Sept. 14
Texas .....Sept. 21
Ohio St. ■ .....Sept. 28
Washington ■ .....Oct. 12
Air Force ■ .....Oct. 19
Navy [Dublin, Ireland] .....Nov. 2
Boston College .....Nov. 9
Pittsburgh ■ .....Nov. 16
Rutgers ■ .....Nov. 23
Southern Cal .....Nov. 30

1995 RESULTS (9-2-0)

15 Northwestern 17
35 Purdue 28
41 Vanderbilt 0
55 Texas 27
26 Ohio St. 45
29 Washington 21
28 Army 27
38 Southern Cal 10
20 Boston College 10
35 Navy 17
44 Air Force 14
366 **216**

Orange Bowl

26 Florida St. 31

Nickname: Fighting Irish.
Stadium: Notre Dame (1930), 59,075 capacity. Natural turf.
Colors: Gold & Blue.
Conference: I-A Independents.
SID: John Heisler, 219-631-7516.
AD: Mike Wadsworth.

OBERLIN

Oberlin, OH 44074.................................III

Coach: Pete Peterson, Kalamazoo '74
Record: 2 Years, 0-19-0

1996 SCHEDULE

Thiel .....Sept. 7
Hiram ■ .....Sept. 14
Kenyon ■ .....Sept. 21
Wittenberg .....*Oct. 5
Ohio Wesleyan ■ .....Oct. 12
Denison .....Oct. 19
Case Reserve ■ .....Oct. 26
Wooster .....Nov. 2
Earlham ■ .....Nov. 9
Allegheny .....Nov. 16

1995 RESULTS (0-10-0)

7 Hiram 57
6 Kenyon 30
0 Wooster 27
6 Ohio Wesleyan 62
26 Bluffton 35
10 Denison 30
3 Wittenberg 77
0 Chicago 47
14 Earlham 49
0 Allegheny 55
72 **469**

Nickname: Yeomen.
Stadium: Dill Field (1925), 3,500 capacity. Natural turf.
Colors: Crimson & Gold.
Conference: North Coast Athletic.
SID: Scott Wargo, 216-775-8503.
AD: Donald Hunsinger.

OCCIDENTAL

Los Angeles, CA 90041 III

Coach: Dale Widolff, Indiana Central '75
Record: 14 Years, 88-41-1

1996 SCHEDULE

Menlo .....Sept. 21
Claremont-M-S ■ .....*Sept. 28
La Verne .....Oct. 5
Azusa Pacific ■ .....*Oct. 12
Cal Lutheran .....Oct. 19
Pomona-Pitzer ■ .....*Oct. 26
Chapman ■ .....*Nov. 2
Redlands .....*Nov. 9
Whittier ■ .....*Nov. 16

1995 RESULTS (3-6-0)

53 Menlo 16
21 Pomona-Pitzer 37
6 Chapman 47
14 Cal Lutheran 21
7 Azusa Pacific 28
13 Claremont-M-S 51
7 La Verne 34
10 Whittier 0
20 Redlands 15
151 **249**

Nickname: Tigers.
Stadium: Patterson Field (1900), 3,000 capacity. Natural turf.
Colors: Orange & Black.
Conference: Southern California Intercollegiate Athletic.
SID: James Kerman, 213-259-2699.
AD: Dale Widolff.

OHIO

Athens, OH 45701 ....I-A

Coach: Jim Grobe, Virginia '75
Record: 1 Year, 2-8-1

1996 SCHEDULE

Akron ■ .....*Aug. 29
Hawaii .....*Sept. 7
Army .....Sept. 14
Northwestern .....Sept. 21
Eastern Mich. ■ .....Oct. 5
Ball St. .....Oct. 12
Kent .....Oct. 19
Bowling Green ■ .....Oct. 26
Western Mich. .....Nov. 2
Miami (Ohio) .....Nov. 9
East Caro. .....Nov. 16
Toledo ■ .....Nov. 23

1995 RESULTS (2-8-1)

21 Iowa St. 36
14 Illinois St. 6
28 Kent 28
20 Eastern Mich. 31
0 North Caro. 62
17 Western Mich. 34
29 Akron 23
3 Ball St. 6
7 Bowling Green 33
2 Miami (Ohio) 30
20 Toledo 31
161 **320**

Nickname: Bobcats.
Stadium: Peden (1929), 20,000 capacity. Natural turf.
Colors: Ohio Green & White.
Conference: Mid-American.
SID: George Mauzy, 614-593-1299.
AD: Thomas Boeh.

OHIO NORTHERN

Ada, OH 45810.......................................III

Coach: Tom Kaczkowski, Illinois '78
Record: 10 Years, 38-59-2

1996 SCHEDULE

Bluffton ■ .....*Sept. 14
John Carroll ■ .....Sept. 21
Capital .....Sept. 28
Mount Union ■ .....Oct. 5
Hiram .....Oct. 12
Muskingum .....Oct. 19
Marietta ■ .....Oct. 26
Otterbein .....Nov. 2
Baldwin-Wallace ■ .....Nov. 9
Heidelberg .....Nov. 16

1995 RESULTS (5-5-0)

35 Bluffton 14
41 Capital 0
0 Mount Union 45
18 Muskingum 20
42 Otterbein 13

SCHEDULES/RESULTS

6 John Carroll....38
27 Marietta....29
22 Hiram....7
22 Baldwin-Wallace....40
57 Heidelberg....7
270 **213**

Nickname: Polar Bears.
Stadium: Ada Memorial (1948), 4,000 capacity. Natural turf.
Colors: Orange & Black.
Conference: Ohio Athletic.
SID: Tim Glon, 419-772-2046.
AD: Gale Daugherty.

OHIO ST.

Columbus, OH 43210 ....I-A

Coach: John Cooper, Iowa St. '62
Record: 19 Years, 146-69-6

1996 SCHEDULE

Rice ■....Sept. 7
Pittsburgh ■....Sept. 21
Notre Dame....Sept. 28
Penn St. ■....Oct. 5
Wisconsin ■....Oct. 12
Purdue....Oct. 19
Iowa....Oct. 26
Minnesota ■....Nov. 2
Illinois....Nov. 9
Indiana....Nov. 16
Michigan ■....Nov. 23

1995 RESULTS (11-1-0)

38 Boston College....6
30 Washington....20
54 Pittsburgh....14
45 Notre Dame....26
28 Penn St.....25
27 Wisconsin....16
28 Purdue....0
56 Iowa....35
49 Minnesota....21
41 Illinois....3
42 Indiana....3
23 Michigan....31
461 **200**

Citrus Bowl

14 Tennessee....20

Nickname: Buckeyes.
Stadium: Ohio (1922), 91,470 capacity. Natural turf.
Colors: Scarlet & Gray.
Conference: Big Ten.
SID: Steve Snapp, 614-292-6861.
AD: Andy Geiger.

OHIO WESLEYAN

Delaware, OH 43015 III

Coach: Mike Hollway, Michigan '74
Record: 13 Years, 74-53-2

1996 SCHEDULE

Olivet....Sept. 14
Earlham ■....Sept. 21
Allegheny....Sept. 28
Kenyon ■....Oct. 5
Oberlin....Oct. 12
Wittenberg ■....Oct. 19
Thomas More ■....Oct. 26
Denison....Nov. 2
Mercyhurst ■....Nov. 9
Wooster....Nov. 16

1995 RESULTS (6-4-0)

13 John Carroll....28
34 Wooster....7
17 Olivet....21
62 Oberlin....6
20 Denison....0
13 Wittenberg....15
27 Case Reserve....7
33 Earlham....14
0 Allegheny....61
33 Kenyon....13
252 **172**

Nickname: Battling Bishops.
Stadium: Selby (1929), 9,600 capacity. Natural turf.
Colors: Red & Black.
Conference: North Coast Athletic.
SID: Mark Beckenbach, 614-368-3340.
AD: John Martin.

OKLAHOMA

Norman, OK 73019 ....I-A

Coach: John Blake, Oklahoma '83
(First year as head coach)

1996 SCHEDULE

Texas Christian ■....Sept. 7
San Diego St.....Sept. 21
Tulsa ■....Sept. 28
Kansas ■....Oct. 5
Texas [Dallas, Texas]....Oct. 12
Baylor....Oct. 19
Kansas St.....Oct. 26
Nebraska ■....Nov. 2
Oklahoma St.....Nov. 9
Texas A&M....Nov. 16
Texas Tech ■....Nov. 23

1995 RESULTS (5-5-1)

38 San Diego St.....22
24 Southern Methodist....10
51 North Texas....10
17 Colorado....38
39 Iowa St.....26
24 Texas....24
17 Kansas....38
13 Missouri....9
10 Kansas St.....49
0 Oklahoma St.....12
0 Nebraska....37
233 **275**

Nickname: Sooners.
Stadium: Owen Field (1923), 75,004 capacity. Natural turf.
Colors: Crimson & Cream.
Conference: Big 12.
SID: Mike Prusinski, 405-325-8228.
AD: Larry Naifeh (Interim).

OKLAHOMA ST.

Stillwater, OK 74078 ....I-A

Coach: Bob Simmons, Bowling Green '71
Record: 1 Year, 4-8-0

1996 SCHEDULE

Southwest Mo. St. ■....*Aug. 31
Texas Tech [Dallas, Texas]....Sept. 7
Tulsa ■....*Sept. 14
Utah St. ■....*Sept. 21
Texas....Oct. 5
Colorado....*Oct. 12
Iowa St. ■....Oct. 19
Missouri....Oct. 26
Texas A&M ■....Nov. 2
Oklahoma ■....Nov. 9
Baylor ■....Nov. 23

1995 RESULTS (4-8-0)

21 Nebraska....64
23 Tulsa....24
35 Southwest Mo. St.....7
25 Wyoming....45
0 Tennessee....31
17 Kansas St.....23
30 Missouri....26
14 Iowa St.....38
32 Colorado....45
12 Oklahoma....0
17 Kansas....22
24 Hawaii....20
250 **345**

Nickname: Cowboys.
Stadium: Lewis (1920), 50,614 capacity. Artificial turf.
Colors: Orange & Black.
Conference: Big 12.
SID: Steve Buzzard, 405-744-5749.
AD: Terry Don Phillips.

OLIVET

Olivet, MI 49076 III

Coach: Dallas Hilliar, Central Mich. '68
Record: 3 Years, 5-22-0

1996 SCHEDULE

Ohio Wesleyan ■....Sept. 14
Anderson (Ind.) ■....Sept. 21
Defiance....Sept. 28
Franklin....Oct. 5
Alma ■....Oct. 12
Adrian....Oct. 19
Kalamazoo ■....Oct. 26
Albion....Nov. 2
Hope ■....Nov. 9

1995 RESULTS (3-6-0)

28 Manchester....27
26 Anderson (Ind.)....27
21 Ohio Wesleyan....17
23 Defiance....10
17 Alma....27
14 Adrian....27
22 Kalamazoo....41
0 Albion....48
28 Hope....33
179 **257**

Nickname: Comets.
Stadium: Griswold Field (1972), 3,500 capacity. Natural turf.
Colors: Red & White.
Conference: Michigan Intercollegiate Athletic Association.
SID: To be named, 616-749-7156.
AD: Dick Kaiser.

OREGON

Eugene, OR 97401 ....I-A

Coach: Mike Bellotti, UC Davis '73
Record: 6 Years, 30-28-2

1996 SCHEDULE

Fresno St.....*Aug. 31
Nevada ■....Sept. 7
Colorado St. ■....Sept. 14
Washington St.....Sept. 21
Arizona St.....*Sept. 28
UCLA ■....Oct. 5
Stanford....Oct. 12
Washington ■....Oct. 26
Arizona ■....Nov. 9
California ■....Nov. 16
Oregon St.....Nov. 23

1995 RESULTS (9-2-0)

27 Utah....20
34 Illinois....31
38 UCLA....31
21 Stanford....28
45 Pacific (Cal.)....7
52 California....30
26 Washington St.....7
24 Arizona St.....35
24 Washington....22
17 Arizona....13
12 Oregon St.....10
320 **234**

Cotton Bowl

6 Colorado....38

Nickname: Ducks.
Stadium: Autzen (1967), 41,678 capacity. Artificial turf.
Colors: Green & Yellow.
Conference: Pacific-10.
SID: David Williford, 503-346-5488.
AD: Bill Moos.

OREGON ST.

Corvallis, OR 97331 ....I-A

Coach: Jerry Pettibone, Oklahoma '63
Record: 11 Years, 44-75-2

1996 SCHEDULE

Montana ■ .... Sept. 7
Southern Cal .... Sept. 14
Baylor .... *Sept. 21
California .... Sept. 28
Washington St. ■ .... Oct. 12
Stanford ■ .... Oct. 19
Arizona .... *Oct. 26
Arizona St. ■ .... Nov. 2
Washington .... Nov. 9
Northern Ill. ■ .... Nov. 16
Oregon ■ .... Nov. 23

1995 RESULTS (1-10-0)

14 Idaho 7
10 Pacific (Cal.) 23
27 North Texas 30
11 Arizona St. 20
16 Washington 26
14 Washington St. 40
12 California 13
3 Stanford 24
9 Arizona 14
10 Southern Cal 28
10 Oregon 12
136 237

Nickname: Beavers.
Stadium: Parker (1953), 35,362 capacity. Artificial turf.
Colors: Orange & Black.
Conference: Pacific-10.
SID: Hal Cowan, 503-737-3720.
AD: Dutch Baughman.

OTTERBEIN

Westerville, OH 43081 III

Coach: A. Wallace Hood, Ohio Wesleyan '57
Record: 19 Years, 93-81-8

1996 SCHEDULE

Hanover .... Sept. 7
Hiram ■ .... *Sept. 21
Mount Union .... Sept. 28
John Carroll ■ .... *Oct. 5
Marietta ■ .... Oct. 12
Baldwin-Wallace .... Oct. 19
Heidelberg .... Oct. 26
Ohio Northern ■ .... Nov. 2
Muskingum ■ .... Nov. 9
Capital .... Nov. 16

1995 RESULTS (3-7-0)

7 Hanover 24
6 Mount Union 51
14 John Carroll 55
7 Baldwin-Wallace 32
13 Ohio Northern 42
2 Hiram 9
22 Heidelberg 12
14 Marietta 45
9 Muskingum 6
33 Capital 20
127 296

Nickname: Cardinals.
Stadium: Memorial (1946), 4,000 capacity. Natural turf.
Colors: Tan & Cardinal.
Conference: Ohio Athletic.
SID: Ed Syguda, 614-823-1600.
AD: Dick Reynolds.

PACE

Pleasantville, NY 10570 II

Coach: Gregory Lusardi, Slippery Rock '75
Record: 2 Years, 8-12-0

1996 SCHEDULE

Hartwick ■ .... Sept. 7
Stony Brook .... Sept. 14
Monmouth (N.J.) .... Sept. 21
Iona ■ .... Sept. 28
Assumption ■ .... Oct. 5
Gannon .... Oct. 19
Western Conn. St. ■ .... Oct. 26
Albany (N.Y.) ■ .... Nov. 2
Stonehill .... Nov. 9
Sacred Heart ■ .... Nov. 16

1995 RESULTS (6-4-0)

19 Stony Brook 21
17 St. John's (N.Y.) 7
29 Iona 22
28 Assumption 20
42 Mass.-Lowell 7
0 Monmouth (N.J.) 41
12 Salve Regina 34
20 Albany (N.Y.) 38
26 Stonehill 10
12 Sacred Heart 7
205 207

Nickname: Setters.
Stadium: Finnerty Field, 1,500 capacity. Natural turf.
Colors: Blue & Gold.
Conference: Division II Independents.
SID: Nick Renda, 914-773-3411.
AD: Christopher Bledsoe.

PENNSYLVANIA

Philadelphia, PA 19104 ....I-AA

Coach: Al Bagnoli, Central Conn. St. '74
Record: 14 Years, 119-25-0

1996 SCHEDULE

Dartmouth .... Sept. 21
Colgate ■ .... Sept. 28
Bucknell .... Oct. 5
Columbia ■ .... Oct. 12
Lehigh ■ .... Oct. 19
Brown .... Oct. 26
Yale ■ .... Nov. 2
Princeton .... Nov. 9
Harvard ■ .... Nov. 16
Cornell .... Nov. 23

1995 RESULTS (7-3-0)

20 Dartmouth 12
28 Lafayette 8
20 Bucknell 19
14 Columbia 24
34 William & Mary 48
58 Brown 21
16 Yale 6
9 Princeton 22
38 Harvard 21
37 Cornell 18
274 199

Nickname: Red & Blue, Quakers.
Stadium: Franklin Field (1895), 53,000 capacity. Artificial turf.
Colors: Red & Blue.
Conference: Ivy League.
SID: Shaun May, 215-898-6128.
AD: Steve Bilsky.

PENN ST.

University Park, PA 16802 ....I-A

Coach: Joe Paterno, Brown '50
Record: 30 Years, 278-72-3

1996 SCHEDULE

Southern Cal [East Rutherford, N.J.] .... Aug. 25
Louisville ■ .... Sept. 7
Northern Ill. ■ .... Sept. 14
Temple [East Rutherford, N.J.] .... Sept. 21
Wisconsin .... Sept. 28
Ohio St. .... Oct. 5
Purdue ■ .... Oct. 12
Iowa ■ .... Oct. 19
Indiana .... Oct. 26
Northwestern ■ .... Nov. 2
Michigan .... Nov. 16
Michigan St. ■ .... Nov. 23

1995 RESULTS (8-3-0)

24 Texas Tech 23
66 Temple 14
59 Rutgers 34
9 Wisconsin 17
25 Ohio St. 28
26 Purdue 23
41 Iowa 27
45 Indiana 21
10 Northwestern 21
27 Michigan 17
24 Michigan St. 20
356 245

Outback Bowl

43 Auburn 14

Nickname: Nittany Lions.
Stadium: Beaver (1960), 93,967 capacity. Natural turf.
Colors: Blue & White.
Conference: Big Ten.
SID: Jeff Nelson, 814-865-1757.
AD: Tim Curley.

PITTSBURG ST.

Pittsburg, KS 66762 II

Coach: Chuck Broyles, Pittsburg St. '70
Record: 6 Years, 69-8-2

1996 SCHEDULE

Eastern Ill. .... *Sept. 7
Central Mo. St. .... *Sept. 21
Southwest Baptist ■ .... *Sept. 28
Truman St. ■ .... Oct. 5
Mo. Western St. .... Oct. 12
Mo. Southern St. ■ .... *Oct. 19
Emporia St. .... Oct. 26
Washburn ■ .... Nov. 2
Mo.-Rolla .... Nov. 9
Northwest Mo. St. .... Nov. 16

1995 RESULTS (9-0-1)

16 Fort Hays St. 16
37 Central Mo. St. 16
64 Southwest Baptist 13
49 Truman St. 7
31 Mo. Western St. 0
15 Mo. Southern St. 14
48 Emporia St. 12
31 Washburn 7
60 Mo.-Rolla 10
22 Northwest Mo. St. 14
373 109

II Championship

36 Northern Colo. 17
9 North Dak. St. 7
28 Tex. A&M-Kingsville 25
7 North Ala. 27

Nickname: Gorillas.
Stadium: Carnie Smith (1924), 5,600 capacity. Natural turf.
Colors: Crimson & Gold.
Conference: Mid-America Intercollegiate Athletic Assoc.
SID: Dan Wilkes, 316-235-4147.
AD: Bill Samuels.

PITTSBURGH

Pittsburgh, PA 15213 ....I-A

Coach: Johnny Majors, Tennessee '57
Record: 28 Years, 181-130-10

1996 SCHEDULE

West Va. ■ .... *Aug. 31
Kent ■ .... *Sept. 7
Houston ■ .... *Sept. 14
Ohio St. .... Sept. 21
Miami (Fla.) .... Sept. 28
Temple ■ .... Oct. 5
Syracuse .... Oct. 12
Virginia Tech .... Oct. 26
Boston College ■ .... *Oct. 31
Notre Dame .... Nov. 16
Rutgers ■ .... Nov. 30

1995 RESULTS (2-9-0)

17 Washington St. 13
66 Eastern Mich. 30
27 Texas 38
14 Ohio St. 54
16 Virginia Tech 26
0 Boston College 17
27 Temple 29
16 Miami (Fla.) 17
24 Rutgers 42
10 Syracuse 42
0 West Va. 21
217 **329**

Nickname: Panthers.
Stadium: Pitt (1925), 56,500 capacity. Artificial turf.
Colors: Blue & Gold.
Conference: Big East.
SID: Ron Wahl, 412-648-8240.
AD: L. Oval Jaynes.

PLYMOUTH ST.

Plymouth, NH 03264 III

Coach: Mike Kemp, Notre Dame '75
(First year as head coach)

1996 SCHEDULE

Maine Maritime ....Sept. 14
Norwich ■ ....Sept. 28
Western Conn. St. ....Oct. 5
Merchant Marine ....Oct. 12
Springfield ....Oct. 19
Bri'water (Mass.) ■ ....Oct. 26
Coast Guard ....Nov. 2
Mass.-Lowell ■ ....Nov. 9
Worcester Tech ■ ....Nov. 16

1995 RESULTS (9-0-0)

33 Mass.-Dartmouth 0
24 Norwich 21
52 Mass.-Lowell 3
36 Western Conn. St. 6
31 Springfield 6
20 Bri'water (Mass.) 13
9 Coast Guard 2
20 Stony Brook 12
31 Worcester Tech 7
256 **70**

III Championship

7 Union (N.Y.) 24

Nickname: Panthers.
Stadium: Currier Memorial Field (1970), 1,000 capacity. Natural turf.
Colors: Green & White.
Conference: Freedom Football.
SID: Kent Cherrington, 603-535-2477.
AD: Steve Bamford.

POMONA-PITZER

Claremont, CA 91711 III

Coach: Roger Caron, Harvard '85
Record: 2 Years, 7-11-0

1996 SCHEDULE

Grinnell ■ ....*Sept. 7
Colorado Col. ....Sept. 14
Whittier ■ ....*Sept. 21
Trinity (Tex.) ■ ....Sept. 28
Menlo ....Oct. 12
Swarthmore ....Oct. 19
Occidental ....*Oct. 26
Claremont-M-S ■ ....*Nov. 9

1995 RESULTS (6-3-0)

0 Trinity (Tex.) 26
37 Colorado Col. 10
37 Occidental 21
14 La Verne 69
21 Whittier 10
28 Redlands 42
56 Menlo 15
9 Cal Lutheran 0
38 Claremont-M-S 34
240 **227**

Nickname: Sagehens.
Stadium: Merritt Field (1991), 2,000 capacity. Natural turf.
Colors: Blue, White & Orange.
Conference: Southern California Intercollegiate Athletic.
SID: Kirk Reynolds, 909-621-8429.
AD: Curt Tong.

PORTLAND ST.

Portland, OR 97201 II

Coach: Tim Walsh, UC Riverside '77
Record: 7 Years, 52-25-0

1996 SCHEDULE

Boise St. ....*Sept. 7
Sonoma St. ■ ....*Sept. 14
Northern Ariz. ■ ....Sept. 21
Eastern Wash. ....*Sept. 28
Cal St. Northridge ....*Oct. 5
UC Davis ■ ....*Oct. 12
Weber St. ■ ....*Oct. 19
Montana St. ....Oct. 26
Cal St. Sacramento ■ ....*Nov. 2
Montana ....Nov. 9
Idaho St. ■ ....*Nov. 16

1995 RESULTS (7-4-0)

42 Mankato St. 10
7 Tex. A&M-Kingsville 40
7 Edinboro 26
14 Eastern Wash. 6
54 Cal St. Sacramento 16
40 UC Davis 13
13 McNeese St. 27
55 Western N.M. 21
14 Boise St. 49
56 Ark.-Monticello 20
52 Sonoma St. 0
354 **228**

II Championship

56 East Tex. St. 35
3 Tex. A&M-Kingsville 30

Nickname: Vikings.
Stadium: Civic (1928), 23,150 capacity. Artificial turf.
Colors: Green & White.
Conference: Big Sky.
SID: Larry Sellers, 503-725-2525.
AD: Jim Sterk.

PRAIRIE VIEW

Prairie View, TX 77445 ....I-AA

Coach: Hensley W. Sapenter Jr., Prairie View '60
Record: 1 Year, 0-11-0

1996 SCHEDULE

Texas Southern [Houston, Texas] ....*Aug. 31
Abilene Christian ■ ....Sept. 7
Hardin-Simmons ....Sept. 14
Southern-B.R. [Houston, Texas] ....*Sept. 21
Grambling ■ ....Sept. 28
Langston ....Oct. 5
Alcorn St. ■ ....Oct. 12
Alabama St. ■ ....Oct. 19
Mississippi Val. ....Nov. 2
Midwestern St. ■ ....Nov. 9
Jackson St. ....Nov. 16

1995 RESULTS (0-11-0)

8 Texas Southern 50
0 Abilene Christian 35
6 Southern-B.R. 68
6 Tarleton St. 44
0 Grambling 64
12 Langston 48
2 Alcorn St. 13
16 Alabama St. 49
14 Mississippi Val. 35
15 Midwestern St. 37
0 Jackson St. 68
79 **511**

Nickname: Panthers.
Stadium: Blackshear (1960), 6,000 capacity. Natural turf.
Colors: Purple & Gold.
Conference: Southwestern Athletic.
SID: Harlan S. Robinson, 409-857-2114.
AD: Hensley W. Sapenter Jr.

PRESBYTERIAN

Clinton, SC 29325 II

Coach: John Perry, Presbyterian '72
Record: 12 Years, 59-73-0

1996 SCHEDULE

Shepherd ....Sept. 7
Charleston So. ■ ....Sept. 14
Carson-Newman ....*Sept. 21
Lenoir-Rhyne ■ ....Sept. 28
Wofford ....*Oct. 5
Catawba ■ ....Oct. 12
Elon ....Oct. 19
Mars Hill ....Oct. 26
Wingate ■ ....Nov. 2
Gardner-Webb ■ ....Nov. 9
Newberry ■ ....Nov. 16

1995 RESULTS (6-5-0)

20 Newport News App. 0
44 Charleston So. 6
21 Carson-Newman 24
28 Lenoir-Rhyne 35
20 Wofford 21
28 Catawba 31
13 Elon 7
35 Mars Hill 7
27 Wingate 16
34 Gardner-Webb 20
8 Newberry 9
278 **176**

Nickname: Blue Hose.
Stadium: Bailey Memorial, 5,000 capacity. Natural turf.
Colors: Garnet & Blue.
Conference: South Atlantic.
SID: Art Chase, 803-833-8252.
AD: Allen Morris.

PRINCETON

Princeton, NJ 08544 ....I-AA

Coach: Steve Tosches, Rhode Island '79
Record: 9 Years, 61-27-2

1996 SCHEDULE

Cornell ....Sept. 21
Holy Cross ■ ....Sept. 28
Lehigh ■ ....Oct. 5
Brown ■ ....Oct. 12
Bucknell ....Oct. 19
Harvard ■ ....Oct. 26
Columbia ....Nov. 2
Pennsylvania ■ ....Nov. 9
Yale ....Nov. 16
Dartmouth ■ ....Nov. 23

1995 RESULTS (8-1-1)

24 Cornell 22
20 Bucknell 3
34 Colgate 23
21 Brown 19
41 Lafayette 0
14 Harvard 3
44 Columbia 14
22 Pennsylvania 9
13 Yale 21
10 Dartmouth 10
243 **124**

Nickname: Tigers.
Stadium: Palmer (1914), 45,725 capacity. Natural turf.
Colors: Orange & Black.
Conference: Ivy League.
SID: Jerry Price, 609-258-3568.
AD: Gary D. Walters.

PRINCIPIA

Elsah, IL 62028 III

Coach: Todd Small, Principia '68
Record: 4 Years, 7-35-0

1996 SCHEDULE

Illinois Col. ■ ... Sept. 7
Grinnell ... Sept. 14
Maranatha Baptist ■ ... Sept. 21
MacMurray ■ ... Sept. 28
Concordia (Ill.) ... Oct. 5
Blackburn ■ ... Oct. 12
Greenville ... Oct. 26
Westminster (Mo.) ... Nov. 2

1995 RESULTS (1-7-0)

6 Knox ... 24
24 Illinois Col. ... 29
14 Grinnell ... 42
6 Maranatha Baptist ... 43
6 Earlham ... 73
24 Bapt. Christian ... 6
6 Blackburn ... 31
20 Crown ... 26
106 **274**

Nickname: Panthers.
Stadium: Clark Field (1937), 1,000 capacity. Natural turf.
Colors: Navy Blue & Gold.
Conference: St. Louis Intercollegiate Athletic.
SID: Phil Webster, 618-374-5372.
AD: Seth Johnson.

PURDUE

West Lafayette, IN 47907 ... I-A

Coach: Jim Colletto, UCLA '67
Record: 10 Years, 34-73-4

1996 SCHEDULE

Michigan St. ... Aug. 31
Notre Dame ... Sept. 14
West Va. ■ ... *Sept. 21
North Caro. St. ■ ... Sept. 28
Minnesota ■ ... Oct. 5
Penn St. ... Oct. 12
Ohio St. ■ ... Oct. 19
Wisconsin ... Nov. 2
Michigan ■ ... Nov. 9
Northwestern ... Nov. 16
Indiana ■ ... Nov. 23

1995 RESULTS (4-6-1)

26 West Va. ... 24
28 Notre Dame ... 35
35 Michigan St. ... 35
35 Ball St. ... 13
38 Minnesota ... 39
23 Penn St. ... 26
0 Ohio St. ... 28
38 Wisconsin ... 27
0 Michigan ... 5
8 Northwestern ... 23
51 Indiana ... 14
282 **269**

Nickname: Boilermakers.
Stadium: Ross-Ade (1924), 67,861 capacity. Natural turf.
Colors: Old Gold & Black.
Conference: Big Ten.
SID: Mark Adams, 317-494-3202.
AD: Morgan Burke.

QUINCY

Quincy, IL 62301 ... II

Coach: Ron Taylor, Missouri '61
Record: 6 Years, 43-15-2

1996 SCHEDULE

Mo.-Rolla ... Sept. 7
Mo. Western St. ... Sept. 14
Evansville ■ ... Sept. 21
St. Joseph's (Ind.) ... Oct. 5
St. Francis (Ill.) ■ ... Oct. 12
Ky. Wesleyan ... Oct. 19
Morehead St. ... Nov. 2
Winona St. ■ ... Nov. 9
Culver-Stockton ■ ... Nov. 16

1995 RESULTS (4-6-0)

7 Coe ... 31
21 North Central ... 23
29 Ky. Wesleyan ... 50
6 Lakeland ... 42
27 Greenville ... 19
42 Concordia (Wis.) ... 28
9 Concordia (Ill.) ... 7
31 MacMurray ... 7
13 Eureka ... 33
6 Culver-Stockton ... 9
191 **249**

Nickname: Hawks.
Stadium: QU (1938), 2,500 capacity. Natural turf.
Colors: Brown, White & Gold.
Conference: Eastern Football.
SID: Damian Becker, 217-228-5277.
AD: Jim Naumovich.

RANDOLPH-MACON

Ashland, VA 23005 ... III

Coach: Joe Riccio, Miami (Fla.) '76
Record: 5 Years, 25-22-2

1996 SCHEDULE

Frank. & Marsh. ■ ... Sept. 14
Catholic ... Sept. 21
Chowan ■ ... Sept. 28
Wash. & Lee ... Oct. 5
Gettysburg ■ ... Oct. 12
Emory & Henry ... Oct. 19
Davidson ... Oct. 26
Guilford ■ ... Nov. 2
Bridgewater (Va.) ■ ... Nov. 9
Hampden-Sydney ... Nov. 16

1995 RESULTS (6-3-1)

27 Frank. & Marsh. ... 28
50 Catholic ... 50
30 Chowan ... 7
24 Wash. & Lee ... 21
23 Gettysburg ... 27
14 Emory & Henry ... 17
36 Davidson ... 0
27 Guilford ... 10
28 Bridgewater (Va.) ... 20
35 Hampden-Sydney ... 14
294 **194**

Nickname: Yellow Jackets.
Stadium: Day Field (1953), 5,000 capacity. Natural turf.
Colors: Lemon & Black.
Conference: Old Dominion Athletic.
SID: Todd Hilder, 804-798-8372.
AD: Helmut Werner.

REDLANDS

Redlands, CA 92373 ... III

Coach: Mike Maynard, Ill. Wesleyan '80
Record: 8 Years, 48-25-1

1996 SCHEDULE

Lewis & Clark ... Sept. 7
Whittier ... *Sept. 14
Chapman ■ ... *Sept. 21
Menlo ■ ... *Sept. 28
Claremont-M-S ■ ... *Oct. 12
Azusa Pacific ... *Oct. 19
Cal Lutheran ■ ... *Nov. 2
Occidental ■ ... *Nov. 9
La Verne ... Nov. 16

1995 RESULTS (4-5-0)

17 Azusa Pacific ... 23
17 La Verne ... 42
31 Whittier ... 10
47 Claremont-M-S ... 27
42 Pomona-Pitzer ... 28
16 San Diego ... 3
24 Chapman ... 54
19 Cal Lutheran ... 21
15 Occidental ... 20
228 **228**

Nickname: Bulldogs.
Stadium: Ted Runner (1968), 7,000 capacity. Natural turf.
Colors: Maroon & Gray.
Conference: Southern California Intercollegiate Athletic.
SID: Chuck Sadowski, 909-335-4031.
AD: Carl Clapp.

RENSSELAER

Troy, NY 12180 ... III

Coach: Joe King, Siena '70
Record: 7 Years, 44-20-2

1996 SCHEDULE

Coast Guard ... Sept. 14
Rochester ... Sept. 21
Albany (N.Y.) ■ ... Sept. 28
Worcester Tech ■ ... Oct. 5
Union (N.Y.) ... Oct. 19
Hartwick ■ ... Oct. 26
St. John Fisher ■ ... Nov. 2
St. Lawrence ■ ... Nov. 9
Hobart ... Nov. 16

1995 RESULTS (7-2-0)

21 Coast Guard ... 20
41 Albany (N.Y.) ... 7
20 Worcester Tech ... 21
59 Siena ... 0
13 Union (N.Y.) ... 16
20 Hartwick ... 19
22 St. John Fisher ... 13
41 St. Lawrence ... 16
40 Hobart ... 28
277 **140**

ECAC III Playoff

69 Worcester St. ... 12

Nickname: Engineers.
Stadium: '86 Field (1912), 3,000 capacity. Natural turf.
Colors: Cherry & White.
Conference: Division III Independents.
SID: Leigh Jackman, 518-276-2187.
AD: Bob Ducatte.

RHODE ISLAND

Kingston, RI 02881 ... I-AA

Coach: Floyd Keith, Ohio Northern '70
Record: 7 Years, 35-38-2

1996 SCHEDULE

American Int'l ■ ... Aug. 31
William & Mary ■ ... Sept. 7
New Hampshire ■ ... Sept. 14
Maine ... Sept. 21
Brown ■ ... Sept. 28
Massachusetts ■ ... Oct. 5
Connecticut ... Oct. 19
Boston U. ■ ... Oct. 26
Villanova ... Nov. 2
Delaware ... Nov. 16
Hofstra ... Nov. 23

1995 RESULTS (7-4-0)

17 Delaware St. ... 14
17 Maine ... 13
10 New Hampshire ... 7
28 Brown ... 31
34 Massachusetts ... 0
14 William & Mary ... 23
22 Boston U. ... 19
24 Connecticut ... 19
27 Villanova ... 10
3 Hofstra ... 37
19 Delaware ... 24
215 **197**

Nickname: Rams.
Stadium: Meade Stadium (1928), 8,000 capacity. Natural turf.
Colors: Light Blue, Dark Blue & White.
Conference: Yankee.
SID: Mike Ballweg, 401-874-2401.
AD: Ron Petro.

RHODES

Memphis, TN 38112 III

Coach: Mike Clary, Rhodes '77
Record: 12 Years, 66-40-6

1996 SCHEDULE

Washington (Mo.) ■ ....Sept. 7
Millsaps...Sept. 14
Austin..Sept. 21
Carnegie Mellon ....Sept. 28
Maryville (Tenn.) ■.......................................Oct. 5
Sewanee..Oct. 19
Colorado Col. ■..Oct. 26
Trinity (Tex.) ....Nov. 2
Millsaps ■ ....Nov. 9
Centre ■ ....Nov. 16

1995 RESULTS (4-5-0)

7 Carnegie Mellon 35
19 Austin 12
7 Washington (Mo.) 28
14 Maryville (Tenn.)...17
17 Sewanee...13
26 Colorado Col. 34
7 Trinity (Tex.) 13
34 Millsaps..26
14 Centre 10
145 **188**

Nickname: Lynx.
Stadium: Fargason Field, 3,300 capacity. Natural turf.
Colors: Cardinal & Black.
Conference: Southern Collegiate Athletic.
SID: John Langdon, 901-726-3940.
AD: Mike Clary.

RICE

Houston, TX 77005 ....I-A

Coach: Ken Hatfield, Arkansas '65
Record: 17 Years, 120-76-4

1996 SCHEDULE

Ohio St. ....Sept. 7
Tulane ....*Sept. 14
Kansas St. ■...*Sept. 21
Air Force ....Sept. 28
New Mexico ■ ....*Oct. 5
Southern Methodist ■ ....Oct. 19
UTEP ....*Oct. 26
Utah ■ ....Nov. 2
Brigham Young ....Nov. 9
Texas Christian ....Nov. 16
Tulsa ■...Nov. 23

1995 RESULTS (2-8-1)

38 UNLV 0
15 Tulane 17
7 LSU 52
21 Army 21
13 Texas...37
28 Texas Christian 33
26 Texas Tech 31
34 Southern Methodist 24
10 Texas A&M..17
6 Baylor..34
17 Houston 18
215 **284**

Nickname: Owls.
Stadium: Rice (1950), 70,000 capacity. Artificial turf.
Colors: Blue & Gray.
Conference: Western Athletic.
SID: Bill Cousins, 713-527-4034.
AD: J. R. "Bobby" May.

RICHMOND

Richmond, VA 23173 ....I-AA

Coach: Jim Reid, Maine '73
Record: 7 Years, 43-32-3

1996 SCHEDULE

Colgate ■ ....Sept. 7
Citadel ....*Sept. 14
Massachusetts ■ ....Sept. 21
Boston U. ....Sept. 28
Northeastern...Oct. 5
Delaware ■...Oct. 12
James Madison ■ ....Oct. 19
Villanova ■ ....Oct. 26
New Hampshire...Nov. 2
Va. Military ....Nov. 9
William & Mary ■ ....Nov. 16

1995 RESULTS (7-3-1)

51 Va. Military...28
21 Massachusetts 7
17 Citadel..13
21 Boston U. 6
26 Northeastern 23
0 Delaware 15
3 Fordham 3
34 James Madison 33
7 New Hampshire 3
7 William & Mary 27
0 Villanova 28
187 **186**

Nickname: Spiders.
Stadium: Richmond (1929), 21,319 capacity. Natural turf.
Colors: Red & Blue.
Conference: Yankee.
SID: Phil Stanton, 804-289-8320.
AD: Chuck Boone.

RIPON

Ripon, WI 54971 III

Coach: Ron Ernst, Neb. Wesleyan '80
Record: 5 Years, 27-19-0

1996 SCHEDULE

Lakeland...Sept. 7
North Park ■ ....Sept. 14
Cornell College ■ ....Sept. 21
Grinnell..Sept. 28
Beloit...Oct. 5
Lake Forest ■..Oct. 12
St. Norbert ....Oct. 19
Carroll (Wis.) ■ ....Oct. 26
Lawrence..Nov. 2

1995 RESULTS (8-2-0)

30 Lakeland 26
21 Upper Iowa..20
31 Monmouth (Ill.) 23
53 Illinois Col. 13
13 Beloit 7
42 Lake Forest 7
21 St. Norbert...20
23 Carroll (Wis.) 25
49 Lawrence 35
17 Cornell College 38
300 **214**

Nickname: Red Hawks.
Stadium: Ingalls Field (1888), 2,500 capacity. Natural turf.
Colors: Crimson & White.
Conference: Midwest.
SID: Bret Atkins, 414-748-8133.
AD: Bob Gillespie.

ROBERT MORRIS

Coraopolis, PA 15108 ....I-AA

Coach: Joe Walton, Pittsburgh '57
Record: 2 Years, 13-5-1

1996 SCHEDULE

Mercyhurst...Sept. 7
Butler ■ ....Sept. 14
Towson St. ■..Sept. 21
Central Conn. St. ....Sept. 28
Gannon ■ ....Oct. 5
Dayton ....Oct. 12
Monmouth (N.J.) ■...Oct. 26
Wagner ....Nov. 2
St. Francis (Pa.) ....Nov. 9
LIU-C.W. Post ■...Nov. 16

1995 RESULTS (6-4-0)

41 Waynesburg 6
13 Monmouth (N.J.)...16
38 Duquesne..20
45 Central Conn. St. 3
29 Gannon 30
18 Wagner...16
19 Mercyhurst 21
14 Towson St. 34
32 Bethany (W.Va.) 7
21 St. Francis (Pa.)..6
270 **159**

Nickname: Colonials.
Stadium: Moon (1950), 7,000 capacity. Natural turf.
Colors: Blue & White.
Conference: Northeast.
SID: Marty Galosi, 412-262-8314.
AD: Bruce Corrie.

ROCHESTER

Rochester, NY 14627 III

Coach: Rich Parrinello, Rochester '72
Record: 8 Years, 43-32-0

1996 SCHEDULE

Rensselaer ■...Sept. 21
St. Lawrence...Sept. 28
Union (N.Y.) ■ ....Oct. 5
Hobart ■...Oct. 12
Chicago ....Oct. 19
Washington (Mo.) ■ ....Oct. 26
Carnegie Mellon ....Nov. 2
Buffalo St. ....Nov. 9
Case Reserve ■ ....Nov. 16

1995 RESULTS (4-5-0)

9 Case Reserve..5
35 Gannon 23
20 St. Lawrence...14
20 Hartwick 54
26 Hobart...17
18 Chicago...29
7 Washington (Mo.) 40
10 Carnegie Mellon 20
7 Union (N.Y.)..44
152 **246**

Nickname: Yellowjackets.
Stadium: Fauver (1930), 5,000 capacity. Artificial turf.
Colors: Yellow & Blue.
Conference: University Athletic Association.
SID: Dennis O'Donnell, 716-275-5955.
AD: Jeff Vennell.

ROSE-HULMAN

Terre Haute, IN 47803 III

Coach: Scott Duncan, Northwestern '80
Record: 10 Years, 60-39-1

1996 SCHEDULE

Millsaps ■ ....Sept. 7
Sewanee ....Sept. 14
Chicago..Sept. 28
Wabash ■ ....Oct. 5
Anderson (Ind.) ■..Oct. 12
Manchester...Oct. 19
DePauw ■...Oct. 26
Franklin ....Nov. 2
Hanover ....Nov. 9
Washington (Mo.) ■ ....Nov. 16

1995 RESULTS (6-4-0)

32 Washington (Mo.) 43
35 Millsaps 15
17 Sewanee..6
14 Anderson (Ind.)...42
61 Manchester 44
21 DePauw...20
29 Franklin...27
23 Hanover...73
41 Wabash 29
7 Chicago...26
280 **325**

Nickname: Fightin' Engineers.
Stadium: Phil Brown Field, 2,500 capacity. Natural turf.
Colors: Red & White.
Conference: Indiana Collegiate Athletic.
SID: Darin Bryan, 812-877-8180.
AD: Scott Duncan.

ROWAN

Glassboro, NJ 08028 III

Coach: K. C. Keeler, Delaware '81
Record: 3 Years, 27-8-1

1996 SCHEDULE

Newport News App. ■ ....Sept. 14
Ferrum ....Sept. 21
Jersey City St. ■ ....*Sept. 27
Trenton St. ....Oct. 5
Southern Conn. St. ....Oct. 12
Cortland St. ■ ....Oct. 19
Kean ....Nov. 2
Wm. Paterson ■ ....Nov. 9
Montclair St. ....*Nov. 16

1995 RESULTS (7-2-1)

31 Ferrum 0
35 Newport News App. 3
28 Jersey City St. 0
38 Trenton St. 10
20 Southern Conn. St. 21
14 Cortland St. 14
0 LIU-C.W. Post 20
42 Kean 13
41 Wm. Paterson 6
30 Montclair St. 0
279 **87**

III Championship

46 Buffalo St. 7
38 Union (N.Y.) 7
28 Wash. & Jeff. 15
7 Wis.-La Crosse 36

Nickname: Profs.
Stadium: John Page (1969), 5,000 capacity. Natural turf.
Colors: Brown & Gold.
Conference: New Jersey Athletic.
SID: Sheila Stevenson, 609-256-4252.
AD: Joy Reighn.

RUTGERS

New Brunswick, NJ 08903 ....I-A

Coach: Terry Shea, Oregon '68
Record: 2 Years, 15-6-2

1996 SCHEDULE

Villanova ■ ....*Aug. 31
Navy ■ ....*Sept. 7
Miami (Fla.) ■ ....*Sept. 12
Virginia Tech ....Sept. 21
Syracuse ....Oct. 5
Army ■ ....Oct. 12
Boston College ....Oct. 19
Temple ■ ....Oct. 26
West Va. ■ ....Nov. 9
Notre Dame ....Nov. 23
Pittsburgh ....Nov. 30

1995 RESULTS (4-7-0)

14 Duke 24
27 Navy 17
34 Penn St. 59
17 Syracuse 27
21 Miami (Fla.) 56
17 Virginia Tech 45
42 Pittsburgh 24
26 West Va. 59
45 Tulane 40
23 Temple 20
38 Boston College 41
304 **412**

Nickname: Scarlet Knights.
Stadium: Rutgers (1994), 41,500 capacity. Natural turf.
Colors: Scarlet.
Conference: Big East.
SID: Peter Kowalski, 908-445-4200.
AD: Frederick E. Gruninger.

SACRED HEART

Fairfield, CT 06432 II

Coach: Gary Reho, Springfield '76
Record: 5 Years, 14-32-0

1996 SCHEDULE

St. John's (N.Y.) ■ ....Sept. 14
Western New Eng. ....Sept. 21
Mass.-Lowell ■ ....Sept. 28
Stony Brook ....Oct. 5
Assumption ■ ....Oct. 12
Nichols ....Oct. 19
Bentley ....Oct. 26
Stonehill ■ ....Nov. 2
Merrimack ■ ....Nov. 9
Pace ....Nov. 16

1995 RESULTS (3-7-0)

42 Western New Eng. 3
41 Mass.-Lowell 13
17 Stony Brook 44
7 Bentley 16
23 Assumption 26
7 Stonehill 19
3 Salve Regina 28
62 Curry 14
7 Pace 12
20 St. John's (N.Y.) 35
229 **210**

Nickname: Pioneers.
Stadium: Campus Field (1993), 2,000 capacity. Artificial turf.
Colors: Scarlet & White.
Conference: Division II Independents.
SID: Mike Guastelle, 203-371-7885.
AD: Don Cook.

SAGINAW VALLEY ST.

University Center, MI 48710 II

Coach: Jerry Kill, Southwestern (Kan.) '83
Record: 2 Years, 13-7-0

1996 SCHEDULE

Wayne St. (Mich.) ....Sept. 7
Northwood ■ ....Sept. 14
Michigan Tech ....Sept. 21
Ashland ■ ....Oct. 5
Indianapolis ....Oct. 12
St. Francis (Ill.) ■ ....Oct. 19
Grand Valley St. ....Oct. 26
Ferris St. ■ ....Nov. 2
Hillsdale ■ ....Nov. 9
Northern Mich. ....Nov. 16

1995 RESULTS (7-3-0)

12 Northern Mich. 13
44 Wayne St. (Mich.) 14
24 Northwood 21
35 Michigan Tech 37
49 St. Joseph's (Ind.) 26
32 Ashland 20
42 Indianapolis 6
55 St. Francis (Ill.) 30
24 Grand Valley St. 21
42 Ferris St. 46
359 **234**

Nickname: Cardinals.
Stadium: Harvey R. Wickes (1975), 4,028 capacity. Natural turf.
Colors: Red, White & Blue.
Conference: Midwest Intercollegiate.
SID: Tom Waske, 517-790-4053.
AD: Bob Becker.

ST. CLOUD ST.

St.Cloud, MN 56301 II

Coach: Noel Martin, Nebraska '63
Record: 13 Years, 77-62-0

1996 SCHEDULE

Northern Iowa ....*Sept. 7
Minn.-Duluth ....Sept. 14
North Dak. St. ....Sept. 21
South Dak. St. ■ ....Sept. 28
South Dak. ■ ....Oct. 5
Mankato St. ....Oct. 12
Morningside ....Oct. 19
Northern Colo. ■ ....Oct. 26
Neb.-Omaha ....*Nov. 2
Augustana (S.D.) ■ ....Nov. 9
North Dak. ■ ....Nov. 16

1995 RESULTS (6-4-0)

29 Minn.-Duluth 23
34 North Dak. St. 0
34 South Dak. St. 10
7 South Dak. 12
14 Mankato St. 6
39 Morningside 6
27 Northern Colo. 30
34 Neb.-Omaha 7
14 Augustana (S.D.) 24
21 North Dak. 35
253 **153**

Nickname: Huskies.
Stadium: Selke Field (1937), 4,000 capacity. Natural turf.
Colors: Cardinal & Black.
Conference: North Central.
SID: Anne Abicht, 320-255-2141.
AD: Morris Kurtz.

ST. FRANCIS (ILL.)

Joliet, IL 60435 II

Coach: Mike Slovick, Lewis '71
Record: 2 Years, 6-16-0

1996 SCHEDULE

Hillsdale ....*Aug. 29
Grand Valley St. ....Sept. 7
Northern Mich. ■ ....*Sept. 14
Wayne St. (Mich.) ....Sept. 21
Northwood ■ ....Sept. 28
Michigan Tech ....Oct. 5
Quincy ....Oct. 12
Saginaw Valley ....Oct. 19
Indianapolis ....Oct. 26
Ashland ■ ....Nov. 2
Ferris St. ■ ....Nov. 9

1995 RESULTS (5-6-0)

3 Illinois St. 45
0 Hillsdale 28
0 Grand Valley St. 42
6 Northern Mich. 27
8 Wayne St. (Mich.) 9
13 Northwood 3
23 Michigan Tech 21
24 St. Joseph's (Ind.) 14
30 Saginaw Valley 55
27 Indianapolis 0
28 Ashland 7
162 **251**

Nickname: Fighting Saints.
Stadium: Joliet Memorial (1951), 10,000 capacity. Natural turf.
Colors: Brown & Gold.
Conference: Midwest Intercollegiate.
SID: Dave Laketa, 815-740-3842.
AD: Pat Sullivan.

ST. FRANCIS (PA.)

Loretto, PA 15940 ....I-AA

Coach: Pete Mayock, Dickinson '87
Record: 1 Year, 0-10-0

1996 SCHEDULE

Waynesburg ■ ....Sept. 7
Monmouth (N.J.) ....Sept. 14
Gannon ....Sept. 21
Wagner ■ ....Oct. 5
Duquesne ■ ....Oct. 12
Mercyhurst ■ ....Oct. 19

Towson St. ....Oct. 26
Central Conn. St. ....Nov. 2
Robert Morris ■ ....Nov. 9
Bethany (W.Va.) ■ ....Nov. 16

1995 RESULTS (0-10-0)

14 Gannon 29
14 Duquesne 21
17 Marist 20
12 Bethany (W.Va.) 30
21 Mercyhurst 57
21 Wagner 38
7 Towson St. 34
13 Central Conn. St. 15
0 Monmouth (N.J.) 35
6 Robert Morris 21
125 **300**

Nickname: Red Flash.
Stadium: Pine Bowl (1979), 1,500 capacity. Natural turf.
Colors: Red & White.
Conference: Northeast.
SID: Kevin Southard, 814-472-3128.
AD: Frank Pergolizzi.

ST. JOHN FISHER

Rochester, NY 14618 III

Coach: Paul Vosburgh, William Penn '75
Record: 5 Years, 21-26-0

1996 SCHEDULE

Buffalo St. ■ ....Sept. 14
Hobart ■ ....Sept. 21
Mercyhurst ....Sept. 28
Montclair St. ■ ....Oct. 5
Jersey City St. ....Oct. 12
Western New Eng. ....Oct. 19
Brockport St. ....Oct. 26
Rensselaer ....Nov. 2
Gannon ■ ....Nov. 9

1995 RESULTS (7-3-0)

31 Western Conn. St. 0
35 Hobart 20
19 Hartwick 18
52 Alfred 35
7 Jersey City St. 6
29 Catholic 21
23 Brockport St. 28
13 Rensselaer 22
8 Buffalo St. 22
48 Thiel 7
265 **179**

Nickname: Cardinals.
Stadium: Cardinal Field, 1,000 capacity. Natural turf.
Colors: Cardinal & Gold.
Conference: Division III Independents.
SID: Chuck Mitrano, 716-385-8309.
AD: Bob Ward.

ST. JOHN'S (MINN.)

Collegeville, MN 56321 III

Coach: John Gagliardi, Colorado Col. '49
Record: 47 Years, 325-99-11

1996 SCHEDULE

Bemidji St. ■ ....Sept. 7
St. Olaf ....Sept. 14
Augsburg ■ ....Sept. 21
Hamline ....Sept. 28
Carleton ■ ....Oct. 5
Gust. Adolphus ....Oct. 12
Concordia-M'head ■ ....Oct. 19
Macalester ....Oct. 26
Bethel (Minn.) ■ ....Nov. 2
St. Thomas (Minn.) [Minneapolis, Minn.] ....Nov. 9

1995 RESULTS (8-1-1)

61 Concordia (St. Paul) 14
49 Bethel (Minn.) 14
41 Augsburg 14
35 Hamline 20
49 St. Thomas (Minn.) 18
35 Gust. Adolphus 24
35 Carleton 14
21 St. Olaf 24
14 Concordia-M'head 14
45 Macalester 18
385 **174**

Nickname: Johnnies.
Stadium: St. John's (1908), 5,000 capacity. Natural turf.
Colors: Red & White.
Conference: Minnesota Intercollegiate Athletic.
SID: Tom Nelson, 320-363-2595.
AD: Jim Smith.

ST. JOHN'S (N. Y.)

Jamaica, NY 11439 ....I-AA

Coach: Bob Ricca, LIU-C.W. Post '69
Record: 18 Years, 113-69-1

1996 SCHEDULE

Sacred Heart ....Sept. 14
Duquesne ■ ....Sept. 21
Fairfield ■ ....*Sept. 27
St. Peter's ....*Oct. 11
Marist ....Oct. 19
Canisius ....Oct. 26
Siena ■ ....Nov. 2
Georgetown ■ ....*Nov. 8
Iona ....Nov. 16
Stony Brook ■ ....Nov. 28

1995 RESULTS (4-6-0)

7 Pace 17
0 Monmouth (N.J.) 47
29 Marist 36
13 Georgetown 41
30 Canisius 13
6 St. Peter's 9
22 Siena 21
22 Duquesne 48
17 Iona 13
35 Sacred Heart 20
181 **265**

Nickname: Red Storm.
Stadium: Da Silva (1961), 3,000 capacity. Artificial turf.
Colors: Red & White.
Conference: Metro Atlantic.
SID: To be named, 718-990-6367.
AD: Edward J. Manetta Jr.

ST. JOSEPH'S (IND.)

Rensselaer, IN 47978 II

Coach: Joe Palka, Eastern Mich. '87
Record: 1 Year, 1-9-0

1996 SCHEDULE

Indianapolis ■ ....Aug. 31
West Va. Tech ■ ....Sept. 7
Indiana St. ....*Sept. 21
Calif. (Pa.) ■ ....Sept. 28
Quincy ■ ....Oct. 5
Wilmington (Ohio) ....Oct. 12
Union (Ky.) ■ ....Oct. 19
Morehead St. ....Oct. 26
Ky. Wesleyan ■ ....Nov. 2
Butler ■ ....Nov. 9
West Liberty St. ....Nov. 16

1995 RESULTS (1-9-0)

9 Wayne St. (Mich.) 35
0 Hillsdale 49
23 Michigan Tech 44
14 Northern Mich. 28
26 Saginaw Valley 49
18 Northwood 19
14 St. Francis (Ill.) 24
21 Ashland 13
26 Ferris St. 43
0 Indianapolis 14
151 **318**

Nickname: Pumas.
Stadium: Alumni Field (1947), 4,000 capacity. Natural turf.
Colors: Cardinal & Purple.
Conference: Division II Independents.
SID: Joe Danahey, 219-866-6141.
AD: Lynn Plett.

ST. LAWRENCE

Canton, NY 13617 III

Coach: Dennis Riccio, Illinois St. '68
Record: 9 Years, 38-48-0

1996 SCHEDULE

Union (N.Y.) ....Sept. 14
Albany (N.Y.) ■ ....Sept. 21
Rochester ■ ....Sept. 28
Hobart ....Oct. 5
Cortland St. ....Oct. 12
Ithaca ....Oct. 19
Norwich ■ ....Oct. 26
Rensselaer ....Nov. 9
Hartwick ....Nov. 16

1995 RESULTS (2-6-0)

9 Union (N.Y.) 8
14 Rochester 20
16 Hobart 20
0 Alfred 42
7 Ithaca 34
0 Norwich 24
16 Rensselaer 41
21 Hartwick 14
83 **203**

Nickname: Saints.
Stadium: Weeks Field (1906), 3,000 capacity. Natural turf.
Colors: Scarlet & Brown.
Conference: Upstate Collegiate Athletic Association.
SID: Wally Johnson, 315-379-5588.
AD: John Clark.

ST. MARY'S (CAL.)

Moraga, CA 94575 ....I-AA

Coach: Mike Rasmussen, Michigan St. '72
Record: 6 Years, 39-20-1

1996 SCHEDULE

Boston U. ■ ....Sept. 7
Idaho ....Sept. 14
Sonoma St. ....Sept. 21
Drake ■ ....Sept. 28
San Diego ■ ....Oct. 5
Cal Poly SLO ....Oct. 12
UC Davis ....*Oct. 26
Southern Utah ....Nov. 2
Chapman ■ ....Nov. 9
Humboldt St. ■ ....Nov. 16

1995 RESULTS (8-2-0)

59 Sonoma St. 7
44 Cal St. Chico 20
14 Weber St. 49
34 Columbia 14
37 Humboldt St. 38
33 UC Davis 24
26 Southern Utah 24
31 Cal Poly SLO 20
28 Cal St. Sacramento 14
28 Cal St. Northridge 20
334 **230**

Nickname: Gaels.
Stadium: St. Mary's (1973), 5,000 capacity. Natural turf.
Colors: Red & Blue.
Conference: I-AA Independents.
SID: Steve Janisch, 510-631-4402.
AD: Rick Mazzuto.

ST. NORBERT

DePere, WI 54115 III

Coach: Greg Quick, Baldwin-Wallace '79
Record: 8 Years, 18-49-0

1996 SCHEDULE

Wis.-Oshkosh ....*Sept. 7
Drake ■ ....Sept. 14
Monmouth (Ill.) ....Sept. 21

Illinois Col. ■ .... Sept. 28
Lake Forest .... Oct. 5
Lawrence .... Oct. 12
Ripon ■ .... Oct. 19
Beloit ■ .... Oct. 26
Carroll (Wis.) .... Nov. 2

1995 RESULTS (1-8-0)

12 Wis.-Oshkosh 45
13 Concordia (Wis.) 36
0 Coe 22
30 Knox 34
21 Lake Forest 17
31 Lawrence 47
20 Ripon 21
16 Beloit 22
19 Carroll (Wis.) 33
162 **277**

Nickname: Green Knights.
Stadium: Minahan (1937), 3,100 capacity. Natural turf.
Colors: Green & Gold.
Conference: Midwest.
SID: Len Wagner, 414-337-4077.
AD: Larry Van Alstine.

ST. OLAF

Northfield, MN 55057 III

Coach: To be named

1996 SCHEDULE

Luther .... Sept. 7
St. John's (Minn.) ■ .... Sept. 14
Concordia-M'head .... Sept. 21
Augsburg ■ .... Sept. 28
Macalester .... Oct. 5
Hamline ■ .... Oct. 12
Bethel (Minn.) .... Oct. 19
Carleton ■ .... Oct. 26
St. Thomas (Minn.) .... Nov. 2
Gust. Adolphus [Minneapolis, Minn.] .... *Nov. 9

1995 RESULTS (5-5-0)

23 Luther 0
21 Hamline 20
14 St. Thomas (Minn.) 35
28 Gust. Adolphus 22
15 Carleton 21
35 Macalester 18
16 Concordia-M'head 48
24 St. John's (Minn.) 21
7 Bethel (Minn.) 42
12 Augsburg 20
195 **247**

Nickname: Oles.
Stadium: Manitou Field (1930), 5,000 capacity. Natural turf.
Colors: Black & Old Gold.
Conference: Minnesota Intercollegiate Athletic.
SID: Nancy Moe, 507-646-3834.
AD: Lee Swan.

ST. PETER'S

Jersey City, NJ 07306 .... I-AA

Coach: Mark Collins, Central Conn. St. '80
Record: 2 Years, 3-15-0

1996 SCHEDULE

Siena ■ .... Sept. 21
Canisius .... Sept. 28
Fairfield .... *Oct. 5
St. John's (N.Y.) ■ .... *Oct. 11
Wagner .... Oct. 19
Marist ■ .... Oct. 26
Iona .... Nov. 2
Duquesne ■ .... Nov. 9
Georgetown .... Nov. 16

1995 RESULTS (2-7-0)

10 Monmouth (N.J.) 34
25 Siena 19
24 Wagner 28
13 Duquesne 42
0 Iona 29
9 St. John's (N.Y.) 6
0 Canisius 22
0 Marist 38
0 Georgetown 29
81 **247**

Nickname: Peacocks.
Stadium: Cochrane (1990), 4,000 capacity. Natural turf.
Colors: Blue & White.
Conference: Metro Atlantic.
SID: Tim Camp, 201-915-9101.
AD: William Stein.

ST. THOMAS (MINN.)

St. Paul, MN 55105 III

Coach: Mal Scanlan, St. Thomas (Minn.) '65
Record: 3 Years, 18-12-0

1996 SCHEDULE

Concordia (St. Paul) ■ .... Sept. 7
Augsburg .... *Sept. 14
Hamline ■ .... Sept. 21
Carleton .... Sept. 28
Gust. Adolphus ■ .... Oct. 5
Concordia-M'head .... Oct. 12
Macalester ■ .... Oct. 19
Bethel (Minn.) .... Oct. 26
St. Olaf ■ .... Nov. 2
St. John's (Minn.) [Minneapolis, Minn.] .... Nov. 9

1995 RESULTS (6-4-0)

28 Wis.-River Falls 54
25 Carleton 14
35 St. Olaf 14
34 Concordia-M'head 28
18 St. John's (Minn.) 49
21 Bethel (Minn.) 7
7 Augsburg 28
7 Hamline 10
48 Macalester 0
28 Gust. Adolphus 14
251 **218**

Nickname: Tommies.
Stadium: O'Shaughnessy (1948), 5,025 capacity. Natural turf.
Colors: Purple & Gray.
Conference: Minnesota Intercollegiate Athletic.
SID: Gene McGivern, 612-962-5903.
AD: Steve Fritz.

SALISBURY ST.

Salisbury, MD 21801 III

Coach: Joe Rotellini, Bethany (W.Va.) '77
Record: 6 Years, 15-41-0

1996 SCHEDULE

Delaware Valley ■ .... Sept. 7
Trenton St. ■ .... Sept. 14
Methodist .... Sept. 21
Frostburg St. .... Sept. 28
Catholic .... Oct. 5
Chowan ■ .... Oct. 12
Wesley ■ .... Oct. 26
Bethany (W.Va.) ■ .... Nov. 2
Sue Bennett .... Nov. 16

1995 RESULTS (7-2-0)

3 Trenton St. 22
34 Methodist 19
35 Frostburg St. 28
21 Chowan 6
22 Newport News App. 10
24 Wesley 21
21 Bethany (W.Va.) 23
12 Catholic 2
49 Sue Bennett 15
221 **146**

ECAC III Playoff

10 Albright 20

Nickname: Sea Gulls.
Stadium: Sea Gull (1980), 2,500 capacity. Natural turf.
Colors: Maroon & Gold.
Conference: Division III Independents.
SID: G. Paul Ohanian, 410-543-6016.
AD: Michael Vienna.

SALVE REGINA

Newport, RI 02840 III

Coach: Tim Coen, Salve Regina '76
Record: 3 Years, 20-6-0

1996 SCHEDULE

MIT ■ .... Sept. 14
Nichols .... Sept. 21
Stonehill .... Sept. 28
Bentley ■ .... *Oct. 4
Mass.-Lowell .... Oct. 12
Maine Maritime ■ .... Oct. 19
Curry ■ .... Nov. 1
Assumption .... Nov. 9
Western New Eng. ■ .... Nov. 16

1995 RESULTS (7-2-0)

40 MIT 13
0 Stonehill 13
19 Bentley 26
47 Curry 7
60 Nichols 10
34 Pace 12
28 Sacred Heart 3
28 Western New Eng. 6
54 Assumption 0
310 **90**

Nickname: Newporters.
Stadium: Toppa Field, 1,500 capacity. Natural turf.
Colors: Blue, White & Green.
Conference: Eastern Football.
SID: Ed Habershaw, 401-847-6650.
AD: Lynn Sheedy.

SAM HOUSTON ST.

Huntsville, TX 77341 .... I-AA

Coach: Ron Randleman, William Penn '64
Record: 27 Years, 166-115-6

1996 SCHEDULE

Houston .... *Aug. 31
Central St. ■ .... *Sept. 7
Tex. A&M-Kingsville .... *Sept. 14
Northeast La. .... *Sept. 21
Texas Southern ■ .... Sept. 28
Stephen F. Austin .... Oct. 12
Northwestern St. .... Oct. 19
McNeese St. ■ .... Oct. 26
Nicholls St. .... *Nov. 9
Troy St. ■ .... Nov. 16
Southwest Tex. St. ■ .... Nov. 23

1995 RESULTS (5-5-0)

13 Jacksonville St. 16
44 Alcorn St. 7
14 Boise St. 38
24 Tex. A&M-Kingsville 23
24 Texas Southern 13
22 Stephen F. Austin 38
2 Northwestern St. 24
0 McNeese St. 20
24 Nicholls St. 17
26 Southwest Tex. St. 20
193 **216**

Nickname: Bearkats.
Stadium: Elliott T. Bowers (1986), 14,885 capacity. Artificial turf.
Colors: Orange & White.
Conference: Southland Football League.
SID: Paul Ridings Jr., 409-294-1764.
AD: Ronnie Choate.

SAMFORD

Birmingham, AL 35229 .... I-AA

Coach: Pete Hurt, Mississippi Col. '78
Record: 2 Years, 11-10-1

1996 SCHEDULE

Knoxville ■ .... *Sept. 7
Austin Peay ■ .... *Sept. 14
Tennessee Tech .... *Sept. 21
Alcorn St. ■ .... *Sept. 28
Nicholls St. ■ .... Oct. 5
Central Fla. .... Oct. 12
Jacksonville St. .... Oct. 19
Stephen F. Austin .... Oct. 26
Wofford ■ .... Nov. 2
Tenn.-Martin ■ .... Nov. 16
Troy St. .... *Nov. 21

1995 RESULTS (7-4-0)

24 Ark.-Monticello 7
42 Austin Peay 32
27 Tennessee Tech 24
36 Nicholls St. 20
14 Central Fla. 41
14 Jacksonville St. 35
10 Stephen F. Austin 31
20 Alcorn St. 9
35 Morgan St. 24
21 Tenn.-Martin 14
20 Troy St. 50
263 **287**

Nickname: Bulldogs.
Stadium: Seibert (1960), 6,700 capacity. Natural turf.
Colors: Crimson & Blue.
Conference: I-AA Independents.
SID: Riley Adair, 205-870-2799.
AD: Steve Allgood.

SAN DIEGO

San Diego, CA 92110 .... I-AA

Coach: Kevin McGarry, San Diego '79
(First year as head coach)

1996 SCHEDULE

Cal St. Chico .... Sept. 7
Cal Lutheran ■ .... *Sept. 14
Drake .... Sept. 21
Valparaiso ■ .... *Sept. 28
St. Mary's (Cal.) .... Oct. 5
Evansville ■ .... *Oct. 19
Butler .... Oct. 26
Whittier ■ .... Nov. 2
Azusa Pacific .... Nov. 9
Dayton ■ .... *Nov. 16

1995 RESULTS (5-5-0)

13 Cal St. Chico 20
3 Dayton 30
28 Cal Lutheran 21
35 Valparaiso 18
21 Azusa Pacific 0
19 Evansville 17
3 Redlands 16
0 Drake 9
37 Butler 16
17 Wagner 20
176 **167**

Nickname: Toreros.
Stadium: USD Torero (1955), 4,000 capacity. Natural turf.
Colors: Columbia Blue, Navy & White.
Conference: Pioneer Football League.
SID: Ted Gosen, 619-260-4745.
AD: Tom Iannacone.

SAN DIEGO ST.

San Diego, CA 92182 .... I-A

Coach: Ted Tollner, Cal Poly SLO '62
Record: 6 Years, 38-31-1

1996 SCHEDULE

Idaho ■ .... *Sept. 7
California .... Sept. 14
Oklahoma ■ .... Sept. 21
Air Force ■ .... *Oct. 5
Hawaii ■ .... *Oct. 12
New Mexico .... *Oct. 19
Colorado St. .... Oct. 26
San Jose St. .... Nov. 2
Wyoming ■ .... *Nov. 7
UNLV .... Nov. 16
Fresno St. ■ .... *Nov. 23

1995 RESULTS (8-4-0)

33 California 9
22 Oklahoma 38
19 Brigham Young 31
30 Nevada 27
24 Utah 21
48 Fresno St. 24
49 San Jose St. 20
45 UTEP 16
38 New Mexico 29
31 Wyoming 34
49 Hawaii 10
13 Colorado St. 24
401 **283**

Nickname: Aztecs.
Stadium: Jack Murphy (1967), 61,121 capacity. Natural turf.
Colors: Scarlet & Black.
Conference: Western Athletic.
SID: John Rosenthal, 619-594-5547.
AD: Rick Bay.

SAN JOSE ST.

San Jose, CA 95192 .... I-A

Coach: John Ralston, California '51
Record: 16 Years, 94-72-4

1996 SCHEDULE

Air Force .... Aug. 31
California ■ .... Sept. 7
Stanford .... Sept. 14
UTEP ■ .... Sept. 21
Washington St. .... Sept. 28
Wyoming ■ .... Oct. 5
Fresno St. .... *Oct. 12
Colorado St. .... Oct. 19
San Diego St. ■ .... Nov. 2
Hawaii .... *Nov. 9
Washington .... Nov. 16
UNLV ■ .... Nov. 23

1995 RESULTS (3-8-0)

33 Stanford 47
7 Southern Cal 45
17 Northern Ill. 18
7 California 40
32 Utah St. 30
52 UNLV 14
20 San Diego St. 49
30 Pacific (Cal.) 32
7 Arkansas St. 21
38 New Mexico St. 37
28 Nevada 45
271 **378**

Nickname: Spartans.
Stadium: Spartan (1933), 31,218 capacity. Natural turf.
Colors: Gold, White & Blue.
Conference: Western Athletic.
SID: Lawrence Fan, 408-924-1217.
AD: Thomas Brennan.

SAVANNAH ST.

Savannah, GA 31404 II

Coach: Wendell Avery, Minnesota '80
Record: 1 Year, 7-4-0

1996 SCHEDULE

Tuskegee ■ .... Aug. 31
Virginia Union ■ .... Sept. 7
Valdosta St. .... Sept. 14
Alabama A&M .... Sept. 21
Morehouse ■ .... Sept. 28
Albany St. (Ga.) .... Oct. 5
Morris Brown .... Oct. 12
Clark Atlanta ■ .... Oct. 19
Kentucky St. ■ .... Oct. 26
Fort Valley St. ■ .... Nov. 2
Miles .... Nov. 9

1995 RESULTS (7-4-0)

45 Virginia Union 6
10 Tuskegee 6
30 Virginia St. 14
8 Alabama A&M 11
9 Morehouse 14
10 Albany St. (Ga.) 48
19 Morris Brown 16
7 Clark Atlanta 21
20 Kentucky St. 13
28 Fort Valley St. 7
28 Miles 18
214 **174**

Nickname: Tigers.
Stadium: Ted Wright (1967), 7,500 capacity. Natural turf.
Colors: Blue & Orange.
Conference: Southern Intercollegiate Athletic.
SID: Lee Grant Pearson, 912-356-2446.
AD: Hornsby Howell (Interim).

SEWANEE

Sewanee, TN 37383 III

Coach: John Windham, Vanderbilt '86
(First year as head coach)

1996 SCHEDULE

Rose-Hulman ■ .... Sept. 14
Davidson ■ .... Sept. 21
Maryville (Tenn.) .... Sept. 28
Centre .... Oct. 5
Rhodes ■ .... Oct. 19
Wash. & Lee .... Oct. 26
Millsaps ■ .... Nov. 2
Trinity (Tex.) .... *Nov. 9

1995 RESULTS (3-6-0)

14 Davidson 21
6 Rose-Hulman 17
20 Maryville (Tenn.) 19
7 Centre 41
13 Rhodes 17
21 Wash. & Lee 36
7 Millsaps 6
7 Trinity (Tex.) 34
20 Guilford 13
115 **204**

Nickname: Tigers.
Stadium: McGee Field (1935), 1,500 capacity. Natural turf.
Colors: Purple & White.
Conference: Southern Collegiate Athletic.
SID: Larry Dagenhart, 615-598-1136.
AD: Mark Webb.

SHEPHERD

Shepherdstown, WV 25443 II

Coach: Monte Cater, Millikin '71
Record: 15 Years, 80-66-2

1996 SCHEDULE

Presbyterian ■ .... Sept. 7
Shippensburg .... Sept. 14
Lenoir-Rhyne ■ .... Sept. 21
West Liberty St. .... Sept. 28
West Va. Wesleyan ■ .... Oct. 5
Concord (W.Va.) ■ .... Oct. 12
West Va. Tech .... Oct. 19
Fairmont St. ■ .... Oct. 26
West Va. St. .... Nov. 2
Glenville St. .... Nov. 9

1995 RESULTS (3-7-0)

21 Shippensburg 24
7 Millersville 59
21 Wingate 35
19 West Liberty St. 24
7 West Va. Wesleyan 33
31 Concord (W.Va.) 10
45 West Va. Tech 6
29 Fairmont St. 36
38 West Va. St. 0
10 Glenville St. 40
228 **267**

Nickname: Rams.
Stadium: Ram (1959), 3,000 capacity. Natural turf.

Colors: Blue & Gold.
Conference: West Virginia Intercollegiate Athletic.
SID: Ernie Larossa, 304-876-5228.
AD: Monte Cater.

SHIPPENSBURG

Shippensburg, PA 17257 II

Coach: Rocky Rees, West Chester '71
Record: 11 Years, 68-50-2

1996 SCHEDULE

James Madison ....*Sept. 7
Shepherd ■ ....Sept. 14
Kutztown ....Sept. 21
Millersville ■ ....Sept. 28
Edinboro ....Oct. 5
Clarion ■ ....Oct. 12
Lock Haven ....Oct. 19
Bloomsburg ....Oct. 26
Calif. (Pa.) ■ ....Nov. 2
Slippery Rock ....Nov. 9
Indiana (Pa.) ■ ....Nov. 16

1995 RESULTS (3-8-0)

24 Shepherd 21
34 Bloomsburg 41
14 West Chester 25
3 Millersville 20
21 Indiana (Pa.) 62
7 Edinboro 40
9 Clarion 31
73 Lock Haven 29
6 Kutztown 35
26 Calif. (Pa.) 15
16 Slippery Rock 34
233 **353**

Nickname: Red Raiders.
Stadium: Grove (1972), 7,700 capacity. Natural turf.
Colors: Red & Blue.
Conference: Pennsylvania State Athletic.
SID: John R. Alosi, 717-532-9121.
AD: James Pribula.

SIENA

Loudonville, NY 12211 ....I-AA

Coach: Ed Zaloom, Cortland St. '75
(First year as head coach)

1996 SCHEDULE

St. Peter's ....Sept. 21
Georgetown ■ ....Sept. 28
Duquesne ■ ....Oct. 5
Canisius ....Oct. 12
Iona ....Oct. 19
Fairfield ■ ....Oct. 26
St. John's (N.Y.) ....Nov. 2
Monmouth (N.J.) ....Nov. 9
Marist ■ ....Nov. 16

1995 RESULTS (0-9-0)

13 Canisius 33
19 St. Peter's 25
6 Iona 18
0 Rensselaer 59
7 Central Conn. St. 24
7 Duquesne 21
21 St. John's (N.Y.) 22
19 Georgetown 33
6 Marist 49
98 **284**

Nickname: Saints.
Stadium: Heritage Park, 5,500 capacity. Natural turf.
Colors: Green & Gold.
Conference: Metro Atlantic.
SID: Chris Caporale, 518-783-2411.
AD: John D'Argenio.

SIMPSON

Indianola, IA 50125 III

Coach: Jim Williams, Northern Iowa '56
Record: 9 Years, 61-29-1

1996 SCHEDULE

Cornell College ....Sept. 7
Luther ....Sept. 21
William Penn ■ ....Sept. 28
Upper Iowa ....Oct. 5
Wartburg ....Oct. 12
Central (Iowa) ■ ....Oct. 19
Aurora ■ ....Oct. 26
Dubuque ....Nov. 2
Buena Vista ■ ....Nov. 9
Loras ■ ....Nov. 16

1995 RESULTS (7-3-0)

27 Wabash 30
10 Wartburg 23
24 Ill. Wesleyan 21
34 Loras 12
58 Upper Iowa 6
49 Luther 3
7 Central (Iowa) 37
69 William Penn 0
41 Dubuque 6
29 Buena Vista 21
348 **159**

Nickname: Storm.
Stadium: Simpson/Indianola Field (1990), 5,000 capacity. Natural turf.
Colors: Red & Gold.
Conference: Iowa Intercollegiate Athletic.
SID: Vicki Klinge, 515-961-1577.
AD: John Sirianni.

SLIPPERY ROCK

Slippery Rock, PA 16057..........................II

Coach: George Mihalik, Slippery Rock '74
Record: 8 Years, 46-33-4

1996 SCHEDULE

Youngstown St. ....*Sept. 7
West Va. Wesleyan ....Sept. 14
Fairmont St. ■ ....Sept. 21
East Stroudsburg ■ ....Sept. 28
West Chester ....Oct. 5
Indiana (Pa.) ■ ....Oct. 12
Edinboro ....Oct. 19
Clarion ■ ....Oct. 26
Lock Haven ....*Nov. 2
Shippensburg ■ ....Nov. 9
Calif. (Pa.) ....Nov. 16

1995 RESULTS (7-4-0)

38 Indianapolis 10
16 West Va. Wesleyan 20
12 Youngstown St. 28
21 Wis.-River Falls 17
42 Calif. (Pa.) 14
23 East Stroudsburg 12
7 Indiana (Pa.) 41
13 Edinboro 22
41 Clarion 17
34 Lock Haven 6
34 Shippensburg 16
281 **203**

Nickname: Rockets, The Rock.
Stadium: N. Kerr Thompson (1974), 10,000 capacity. Natural turf.
Colors: Green & White.
Conference: Pennsylvania State Athletic.
SID: John Carpenter, 412-738-2777.
AD: Paul Lueken.

SONOMA ST.

Rohnert Park, CA 94928 II

Coach: Frank Scalercio, UC Davis '83
Record: 3 Years, 5-22-1

1996 SCHEDULE

Western Mont. ■ ....Sept. 7
Portland St. ....*Sept. 14
St. Mary's (Cal.) ■ ....Sept. 21
La Verne ■ ....Sept. 28
Humboldt St. ....*Oct. 12
Chapman ....*Oct. 19
Humboldt St. ■ ....Oct. 26
Cal St. Chico ■ ....Nov. 2
UC Davis ■ ....Nov. 9
Cal St. Chico ....Nov. 16

1995 RESULTS (0-8-1)

7 St. Mary's (Cal.) 59
3 Idaho 66
0 UC Davis 35
21 Cal St. Chico 21
13 Humboldt St. 24
10 Cal Poly SLO 56
7 Humboldt St. 35
14 Cal St. Chico 26
0 Portland St. 52
75 **374**

Nickname: Cossacks.
Stadium: Cossack (1961), 3,000 capacity. Natural turf.
Colors: Navy Blue & White.
Conference: Northern California Athletic.
SID: Mitch Cox, 707-664-2701.
AD: Ralph Barkey.

SOUTH CARO.

Columbia, SC 29208 ....I-A

Coach: Brad Scott, South Fla. '79
Record: 2 Years, 11-11-1

1996 SCHEDULE

Central Fla. ■ ....*Sept. 7
Georgia ■ ....*Sept. 14
East Caro. ■ ....*Sept. 21
Mississippi St. ■ ....Sept. 28
Auburn ....Oct. 5
Kentucky ....*Oct. 12
Arkansas ■ ....Oct. 19
Vanderbilt ....Oct. 26
Tennessee ■ ....Nov. 2
Florida ....Nov. 16
Clemson ....Nov. 23

1995 RESULTS (4-6-1)

23 Georgia 42
21 Arkansas 51
68 Louisiana Tech 21
30 Kentucky 35
20 LSU 20
77 Kent 14
65 Mississippi St. 39
52 Vanderbilt 14
21 Tennessee 56
7 Florida 63
17 Clemson 38
401 **393**

Nickname: Fighting Gamecocks.
Stadium: Williams-Brice (1934), 80,250 capacity. Natural turf.
Colors: Garnet & Black.
Conference: Southeastern.
SID: Kerry Tharp, 803-777-5204.
AD: Mike McGee.

SOUTH CARO. ST.

Orangeburg, SC 29117 ....I-AA

Coach: Willie Jeffries, South Caro. St. '60
Record: 23 Years, 148-98-6

1996 SCHEDULE

Ga. Southern ■ ....*Aug. 31
Charleston So. ....Sept. 7
Furman ....Sept. 14
Johnson Smith ■ ....Sept. 28
Morgan St. ■ ....Oct. 5
Bethune-Cookman ■ ....Oct. 19
Hampton ■ ....Oct. 26
Delaware St. ....Nov. 2
Howard ■ ....Nov. 9
Florida A&M [Atlanta, Ga.] ....Nov. 16
North Caro. A&T [Charlotte, N.C.] ....Nov. 23

1995 RESULTS (6-4-0)

12 Ga. Southern 27
27 Furman 21

36	Charleston So.	8
14	Tennessee St.	15
31	Morgan St.	19
42	Bethune-Cookman	20
7	Delaware St.	20
18	Howard	14
21	Florida A&M	28
28	North Caro. A&T	27
236		**199**

Nickname: Bulldogs.
Stadium: Dawson Bulldog (1955), 22,000 capacity. Natural turf.
Colors: Garnet & Blue.
Conference: Mid-Eastern Athletic.
SID: Bill Hamilton, 803-536-7060.
AD: Tim Autry.

SOUTH DAK.

Vermillion, SD 57069 II

Coach: Dennis Creehan, Edinboro '71
Record: 11 Years, 65-50-1

1996 SCHEDULE

Wayne St. (Neb.) ■	Sept. 7
Northern St.	*Sept. 14
Morningside	*Sept. 21
Northern Colo. ■	Sept. 28
St. Cloud St.	Oct. 5
South Dak. St.	Oct. 12
Augustana (S.D.) ■	Oct. 19
North Dak.	Oct. 26
North Dak. St. ■	*Nov. 2
Mankato St.	Nov. 9
Neb.-Omaha ■	Nov. 16

1995 RESULTS (8-3-0)

27	Truman St.	10
56	Northern St.	13
35	Morningside	17
21	Northern Colo.	28
12	St. Cloud St.	7
3	South Dak. St.	31
24	Augustana (S.D.)	7
35	North Dak.	0
7	North Dak. St.	14
28	Mankato St.	7
55	Neb.-Omaha	37
303		**171**

Nickname: Coyotes.
Stadium: DakotaDome (1979), 10,000 capacity. Artificial turf.
Colors: Red & White.
Conference: North Central.
SID: Kyle Johnson, 605-677-5927.
AD: Jack Doyle.

SOUTH DAK. ST.

Brookings, SD 57007 II

Coach: Mike Daly, Augustana (S.D.) '71
Record: 5 Years, 33-20-0

1996 SCHEDULE

Northwest Mo. St.	Sept. 7
South Dak. Tech ■	Sept. 14
Augustana (S.D.)	Sept. 21
St. Cloud St.	Sept. 28
North Dak. ■	Oct. 5
South Dak. ■	Oct. 12
North Dak. St.	*Oct. 19
Morningside ■	Oct. 26
Northern Colo.	Nov. 2
Neb.-Omaha	Nov. 9
Mankato St. ■	Nov. 16

1995 RESULTS (6-5-0)

10	Northwest Mo. St.	6
48	South Dak. Tech	14
37	Augustana (S.D.)	15
10	St. Cloud St.	34
31	South Dak.	3
17	North Dak. St.	26
39	Morningside	17
14	Northern Colo.	23
28	Neb.-Omaha	44
39	Mankato St.	32
3	North Dak.	14
276		**228**

Nickname: Jackrabbits.
Stadium: Coughlin-Alumni (1962), 16,000 capacity. Natural turf.
Colors: Yellow & Blue.
Conference: North Central.
SID: Ron Lenz, 605-688-4623.
AD: Fred Oien.

SOUTHEAST MO. ST.

Cape Girardeau, MO 63701 .... I-AA

Coach: John Mumford, Pittsburg St. '79
Record: 6 Years, 27-39-0

1996 SCHEDULE

Illinois St.	*Sept. 14
Murray St. ■	Sept. 21
Austin Peay ■	Sept. 28
Eastern Ky.	Oct. 5
Tennessee Tech	Oct. 12
Arkansas St.	Oct. 19
Middle Tenn. St. ■	Oct. 26
Tenn.-Martin ■	Nov. 2
Eastern Ill. ■	Nov. 9
Southern Ill.	Nov. 16
Tennessee St.	Nov. 23

1995 RESULTS (5-6-0)

27	Southern Ill.	30
18	Eastern Ill.	34
0	Murray St.	34
38	Austin Peay	23
24	Eastern Ky.	42
33	Tennessee Tech	12
0	Middle Tenn. St.	42
38	Tenn.-Martin	17
21	Morehead St.	12
3	Southwest Mo. St.	39
41	Tennessee St.	24
243		**309**

Nickname: Indians.
Stadium: Houck (1930), 10,000 capacity. Natural turf.
Colors: Red & Black.
Conference: Ohio Valley.
SID: Ron Hines, 573-651-2294.
AD: Richard McDuffie.

SOUTHERN-B.R.

Baton Rouge, LA 70813 .... I-AA

Coach: Pete Richardson, Dayton '68
Record: 8 Years, 69-21-1

1996 SCHEDULE

Northwestern St.	*Sept. 7
Alabama St. ■	*Sept. 14
Prairie View [Houston, Texas]	*Sept. 21
Tennessee St. [Atlanta, Ga.]	Sept. 28
Mississippi Val. ■	*Oct. 5
Jackson St. ■	*Oct. 19
Alcorn St.	Oct. 26
Nicholls St.	*Nov. 2
Florida A&M ■	*Nov. 9
Texas Southern ■	Nov. 16
Grambling [New Orleans, La.]	Nov. 30

1995 RESULTS (10-1-0)

13	Northwestern St.	7
29	Alabama St.	19
68	Prairie View	6
45	Hampton	22
44	Mississippi Val.	6
14	Jackson St.	16
61	Alcorn St.	51
41	Nicholls St.	3
52	Florida A&M	38
48	Texas Southern	13
30	Grambling	14
445		**195**

Heritage Bowl

30	Florida A&M	25

Nickname: Jaguars.
Stadium: A.W. Mumford (1928), 24,000 capacity. Natural turf.
Colors: Blue & Gold.
Conference: Southwestern Athletic.
SID: Errol Domingue, 504-771-4142.
AD: Marino Casem.

SOUTHERN CAL

Los Angeles, CA 90089 .... I-A

Coach: John Robinson, Oregon '58
Record: 10 Years, 92-24-4

1996 SCHEDULE

Penn St. [East Rutherford, N.J.]	Aug. 25
Illinois	Sept. 7
Oregon St. ■	Sept. 14
Houston	Sept. 21
California ■	Oct. 5
Arizona ■	Oct. 12
Arizona St.	*Oct. 19
Washington St.	Oct. 26
Washington ■	Nov. 2
Stanford	Nov. 9
UCLA	Nov. 23
Notre Dame ■	Nov. 30

1995 RESULTS (8-2-1)

45	San Jose St.	7
45	Houston	10
31	Arizona	10
31	Arizona St.	0
26	California	16
26	Washington St.	14
10	Notre Dame	38
21	Washington	21
31	Stanford	30
28	Oregon St.	10
20	UCLA	24
314		**180**

Rose Bowl

41	Northwestern	32

Nickname: Trojans.
Stadium: L.A. Coliseum (1923), 92,000 capacity. Natural turf.
Colors: Cardinal & Gold.
Conference: Pacific-10.
SID: Tim Tessalone, 213-740-8480.
AD: Mike Garrett.

SOUTHERN CONN. ST.

New Haven, CT 06515 II

Coach: Richard Cavanaugh, American Int'l '76
Record: 11 Years, 48-61-1

1996 SCHEDULE

Monmouth (N.J.)	Sept. 7
Mansfield ■	Sept. 14
East Stroudsburg	Sept. 21
Kutztown	Sept. 28
American Int'l ■	*Oct. 4
Rowan ■	Oct. 12
Buffalo St. ■	Oct. 19
New Haven	Oct. 26
LIU-C.W. Post	Nov. 2
Central Conn. St. ■	Nov. 9
Stony Brook ■	Nov. 16

1995 RESULTS (8-3-0)

0	Bucknell	20
55	Cheyney	3
19	East Stroudsburg	10
15	Montclair St.	14
21	Rowan	20
35	Albany (N.Y.)	14
6	New Haven	24
24	LIU-C.W. Post	23
14	Central Conn. St.	3
7	Towson St.	38
48	American Int'l	45
244		**214**

Nickname: Owls.
Stadium: Jess Dow Field (1988), 6,000 capacity. Artificial turf.
Colors: Blue & White.
Conference: Eastern Football.
SID: Richard Leddy, 203-392-6005.
AD: Darryl Rogers.

SOUTHERN ILL.

Carbondale, IL 62901 ....I-AA

Coach: Shawn Watson, Southern Ill. '82
Record: 2 Years, 6-16-0

1996 SCHEDULE

Central Ark. ■ ....Aug. 31
Tenn.-Martin ■ ....Sept. 7
Murray St. ....*Sept. 14
Winston-Salem ■ ....Sept. 21
Illinois St. ....Sept. 28
Southwest Mo. St. ....Oct. 5
Indiana St. ■ ....Oct. 12
Western Ill. ■ ....Oct. 19
Northern Iowa ■ ....Oct. 26
Western Ky. ....Nov. 2
Southeast Mo. St. ■ ....Nov. 16

1995 RESULTS (5-6-0)

30 Southeast Mo. St. 27
3 Murray St. 35
9 Arkansas St. 14
48 Nicholls St. 20
3 Indiana St. 52
14 Illinois St. 11
33 Southwest Mo. St. 30
0 Northern Iowa 13
7 Western Ill. 19
30 Western Ky. 28
21 Eastern Ill. 42
198 **291**

Nickname: Salukis.
Stadium: McAndrew (1975), 17,324 capacity. Artificial turf.
Colors: Maroon & White.
Conference: Gateway.
SID: Fred Huff, 618-453-7235.
AD: Jim Hart.

SOUTHERN METHODIST

Dallas, TX 75275 ....I-A

Coach: Tom Rossley, Cincinnati '69
Record: 5 Years, 10-42-3

1996 SCHEDULE

Tulsa ■ ....*Aug. 31
Arkansas ....Sept. 7
Utah ■ ....*Sept. 14
Navy ....*Sept. 21
Brigham Young ....Sept. 28
Missouri ■ ....*Oct. 5
Rice ....Oct. 19
New Mexico ■ ....*Oct. 26
Wyoming ....Nov. 2
UTEP ....*Nov. 9
Texas Christian ■ ....*Nov. 21

1995 RESULTS (1-10-0)

17 Arkansas 14
2 Navy 33
10 Oklahoma 24
0 Wisconsin 42
10 Texas 35
17 Texas A&M 20
15 Houston 38
24 Rice 34
16 Texas Christian 19
7 Baylor 48
14 Texas Tech 45
132 **352**

Nickname: Mustangs.
Stadium: Cotton Bowl (1930), 68,252 capacity. Natural turf.
Colors: Red & Blue.
Conference: Western Athletic.
SID: Jon Jackson, 214-768-2883.
AD: Jim Copeland.

SOUTHERN MISS.

Hattiesburg, MS 39406 ....I-A

Coach: Jeff Bower, Southern Miss. '76
Record: 6 Years, 26-29-1

1996 SCHEDULE

Georgia ....Aug. 31
Alabama ....Sept. 7
Utah St. ■ ....Sept. 14
Southwestern La. ■ ....Sept. 21
Louisville ....Sept. 28
East Caro. ....*Oct. 10
Memphis ■ ....Oct. 19
Tulane ....*Oct. 26
Cincinnati ■ ....Nov. 2
Houston ....*Nov. 9
Florida St. ....Nov. 16

1995 RESULTS (6-5-0)

45 Northern Ill. 13
20 Alabama 24
24 Utah St. 21
26 Indiana 27
45 Tulane 0
25 Louisville 21
13 Cincinnati 16
34 East Caro. 36
0 Tennessee 42
17 Memphis 9
35 Southwestern La. 32
284 **241**

Nickname: Golden Eagles.
Stadium: Roberts (1976), 33,000 capacity. Natural turf.
Colors: Black & Gold.
Conference: Conference USA.
SID: M.R. Napier, 601-266-4503.
AD: Bill McLellan.

SOUTHERN UTAH

Cedar City, UT 84720 ....I-AA

Coach: Rich Ellerson, Hawaii '77
(First year as head coach)

1996 SCHEDULE

Northern Iowa ■ ....*Aug. 31
Northern Ariz. ....*Sept. 14
Western St. ■ ....*Sept. 21
Montana Tech ■ ....*Sept. 28
Montana ....Oct. 5
Southwest Tex. St. ■ ....Oct. 12
Cal Poly SLO ....Oct. 19
New Mexico St. ....*Oct. 26
St. Mary's (Cal.) ■ ....Nov. 2
UC Davis ....*Nov. 16

1995 RESULTS (2-9-0)

7 Angelo St. 14
26 Montana Tech 25
8 Western St. 36
14 Idaho St. 48
15 Southwest Tex. St. 65
20 Cal Poly SLO 35
28 Neb.-Kearney 21
24 St. Mary's (Cal.) 26
28 Cal St. Northridge 34
21 UC Davis 37
29 Cal St. Sacramento 53
220 **394**

Nickname: Thunderbirds.
Stadium: Coliseum of Southern Utah (1967), 6,500 capacity. Natural turf.
Colors: Scarlet & White.
Conference: I-AA Independents.
SID: Neil Gardner, 801-586-7753.
AD: Jack Bishop.

SOUTHWEST BAPTIST

Bolivar, MO 65613 II

Coach: Wayne Haynes, Pittsburg St. '76
Record: 3 Years, 5-25-1

1996 SCHEDULE

Ouachita Baptist ....*Sept. 14
Northwest Mo. St. ■ ....Sept. 21
Pittsburg St. ....*Sept. 28
Mo. Western St. ■ ....Oct. 5
Mo. Southern St. ....Oct. 12
Emporia St. ■ ....Oct. 19
Washburn ....Oct. 26
Mo.-Rolla ■ ....Nov. 2
Central Mo. St. ■ ....Nov. 9
Truman St. ....Nov. 16

1995 RESULTS (2-8-0)

10 Ouachita Baptist 24
13 Northwest Mo. St. 45
13 Pittsburg St. 64
0 Mo. Western St. 45
7 Mo. Southern St. 44
35 Emporia St. 30
20 Washburn 37
12 Mo.-Rolla 7
7 Central Mo. St. 28
21 Truman St. 56
138 **380**

Nickname: Bearcats.
Stadium: Plaster (1986), 2,500 capacity. Natural turf.
Colors: Purple & White.
Conference: Mid-America Intercollegiate Athletic Assoc.
SID: Christopher Johnson, 417-326-1799.
AD: Rex Brown.

SOUTHWEST MO. ST.

Springfield, MO 65804 ....I-AA

Coach: Del Miller, Central (Iowa) '72
Record: 1 Year, 4-7-0

1996 SCHEDULE

Oklahoma St. ....*Aug. 31
McNeese St. ....*Sept. 7
Truman St. ■ ....*Sept. 14
Tenn.-Martin ....*Sept. 21
Jacksonville St. ■ ....*Sept. 28
Southern Ill. ■ ....Oct. 5
Northern Iowa ....*Oct. 19
Illinois St. ....Oct. 26
Western Ill. ■ ....Nov. 2
Youngstown St. ■ ....Nov. 9
Indiana St. ....Nov. 16

1995 RESULTS (4-7-0)

2 McNeese St. 31
30 Truman St. 17
7 Oklahoma St. 35
7 Eastern Ill. 9
17 Illinois St. 20
9 Indiana St. 16
30 Southern Ill. 33
13 Western Ill. 7
17 Northern Iowa 19
39 Southeast Mo. St. 3
49 Jacksonville St. 14
220 **204**

Nickname: Bears.
Stadium: Plaster Field (1941), 16,300 capacity. Artificial turf.
Colors: Maroon & White.
Conference: Gateway.
SID: Mark Stillwell, 417-836-5402.
AD: Bill Rowe.

SOUTHWEST ST.

Marshall, MN 56258 II

Coach: Brent Jeffers, Bemidji St. '85
Record: 3 Years, 10-20-0

1996 SCHEDULE

Minot St. ■ ....Sept. 7
Augustana (S.D.) ■ ....Sept. 14
Wis.-River Falls ....Sept. 21
Bemidji St. ■ ....Sept. 28
Minn.-Duluth ....Oct. 5
Wayne St. (Neb.) ....Oct. 12
Moorhead St. ■ ....Oct. 19
Winona St. ....Oct. 26

Minn.-Morris ■ ...Nov. 2
Northern St. ...Nov. 9

1995 RESULTS (2-8-0)

6 Augustana (S.D.) ...40
8 Wis.-River Falls ...15
0 Northern St. ...11
8 Bemidji St. ...6
21 Minn.-Duluth ...28
28 Wayne St. (Neb.) ...33
9 Moorhead St. ...27
13 Winona St. ...22
13 Minn.-Morris ...6
6 Minn.-Duluth ...13
112 **201**

Nickname: Golden Mustangs.
Stadium: Mattke Field (1971), 5,000 capacity. Natural turf.
Colors: Brown & Gold.
Conference: Northern Sun Intercollegiate.
SID: Doug Terfehr, 507-537-7177.
AD: Gary Carney.

SOUTHWEST TEX. ST.

San Marcos, TX 78666 ...I-AA

Coach: Jim Bob Helduser, Texas Lutheran '79
Record: 4 Years, 15-28-1

1996 SCHEDULE

Grand Valley St. ■ ...*Aug. 31
Hofstra ■ ...*Sept. 14
Eastern Wash. ...*Sept. 21
Idaho ■ ...*Sept. 28
Southern Utah ...Oct. 12
Troy St. ...Oct. 19
Nicholls St. ■ ...Oct. 26
Northwestern St. ■ ...Nov. 2
McNeese St. ...*Nov. 9
Stephen F. Austin ■ ...Nov. 16
Sam Houston St. ...Nov. 23

1995 RESULTS (4-7-0)

16 Eastern Wash. ...34
12 Tex. A&M-Kingsville ...40
24 Montana St. ...45
65 Southern Utah ...15
43 Cal St. Northridge ...14
3 Cal St. Sacramento ...12
35 Nicholls St. ...25
28 Northwestern St. ...14
7 McNeese St. ...28
21 Stephen F. Austin ...50
20 Sam Houston St. ...26
274 **303**

Nickname: Bobcats.
Stadium: Bobcat (1981), 14,104 capacity. Natural turf.
Colors: Maroon & Gold.
Conference: Southland Football League.
SID: Tony Brubaker, 512-245-2966.
AD: Mike Alden.

SOUTHWESTERN LA.

Lafayette, LA 70506 ...I-A

Coach: Nelson Stokley, LSU '68
Record: 10 Years, 54-55-1

1996 SCHEDULE

Florida ...*Aug. 31
Texas A&M ■ ...*Sept. 14
Southern Miss. ...Sept. 21
Louisiana Tech ...*Sept. 28
Houston ■ ...*Oct. 5
Arkansas St. ■ ...Oct. 12
Ala.-Birmingham ...Oct. 19
Memphis ■ ...*Oct. 26
Virginia Tech ...Nov. 2
Northern Ill. ■ ...*Nov. 9
Texas Tech ...Nov. 16

1995 RESULTS (6-5-0)

14 Nevada ...38
56 Ala.-Birmingham ...21
19 Memphis ...33
24 Northern Ill. ...25
33 Arkansas St. ...9
43 New Mexico St. ...26
45 Pacific (Cal.) ...3
32 Tulane ...28
40 Louisiana Tech ...33
13 Arkansas ...24
32 Southern Miss. ...35
351 **275**

Nickname: Ragin' Cajuns.
Stadium: Cajun Field (1971), 31,000 capacity. Natural turf.
Colors: Vermilion & White.
Conference: I-A Independents.
SID: Dan McDonald, 318-482-6331.
AD: Nelson Schexnayder.

SPRINGFIELD

Springfield, MA 01109 ...III

Coach: Mike DeLong, Springfield '74
Record: 14 Years, 68-65-2

1996 SCHEDULE

Western Conn. St. ■ ...*Sept. 6
American Int'l ...Sept. 14
Merchant Marine ...Sept. 21
Coast Guard ■ ...Sept. 28
Ithaca ...Oct. 5
Plymouth St. ■ ...Oct. 19
Worcester Tech ...*Oct. 26
Cortland St. ■ ...Nov. 2
Norwich ...Nov. 9
Wm. Paterson ■ ...Nov. 16

1995 RESULTS (7-2-0)

35 Merchant Marine ...0
26 Coast Guard ...20
27 Ithaca ...24
22 Stony Brook ...33
6 Plymouth St. ...31
30 Worcester Tech ...7
27 American Int'l ...17
10 LIU-C.W. Post ...6
42 Wm. Paterson ...14
225 **152**

ECAC III Playoff

49 Cortland St. ...26

Nickname: Pride.
Stadium: Benedum Field (1971), 2,500 capacity. Artificial turf.
Colors: Maroon & White.
Conference: Freedom Football.
SID: Ken Cerino, 413-748-3341.
AD: Edward Bilik.

STANFORD

Stanford, CA 94305 ...I-A

Coach: Tyrone Willingham, Michigan St. '77
Record: 1 Year, 7-4-1

1996 SCHEDULE

Utah ■ ...Sept. 7
San Jose St. ■ ...Sept. 14
Wisconsin ...Sept. 21
Washington ...Oct. 5
Oregon ■ ...Oct. 12
Oregon St. ...Oct. 19
Arizona St. ■ ...Oct. 26
UCLA ...Nov. 2
Southern Cal ■ ...Nov. 9
Washington St. ■ ...Nov. 16
California ...Nov. 23

1995 RESULTS (7-3-1)

47 San Jose St. ...33
27 Utah ...20
24 Wisconsin ...24
28 Oregon ...21
30 Arizona St. ...28
28 Washington ...38
28 UCLA ...42
24 Oregon St. ...3
30 Southern Cal ...31
36 Washington St. ...24
29 California ...24
331 **288**

Liberty Bowl

13 East Caro. ...19

Nickname: Cardinal.
Stadium: Stanford (1921), 85,500 capacity. Natural turf.
Colors: Cardinal & White.
Conference: Pacific-10.
SID: Gary Migdol, 415-723-4418.
AD: Ted Leland.

STEPHEN F. AUSTIN

Nacogdoches, TX 75962 ...I-AA

Coach: John Pearce, East Tex. St. '70
Record: 4 Years, 28-17-2

1996 SCHEDULE

Eastern N.M. ■ ...*Aug. 29
Delta St. ■ ...*Sept. 7
Northern Iowa ...*Sept. 14
Troy St. ■ ...*Sept. 28
Sam Houston St. ■ ...Oct. 12
Nicholls St. ...Oct. 19
Samford ■ ...Oct. 26
McNeese St. ...*Nov. 2
Jacksonville St. ■ ...Nov. 9
Southwest Tex. St. ...Nov. 16
Northwestern St. ■ ...Nov. 23

1995 RESULTS (9-1-0)

26 Northern Iowa ...7
27 Youngstown St. ...0
17 Angelo St. ...3
31 Henderson St. ...6
38 Sam Houston St. ...22
56 Nicholls St. ...3
31 Samford ...10
16 McNeese St. ...34
50 Southwest Tex. St. ...21
25 Northwestern St. ...20
317 **126**

I-AA Championship

34 Eastern Ill. ...29
27 Appalachian St. ...17
14 Montana ...70

Nickname: Lumberjacks.
Stadium: Homer Bryce (1973), 14,575 capacity. Artificial turf.
Colors: Purple & White.
Conference: Southland Football League.
SID: Bill Powers, 409-468-2606.
AD: Steve McCarty.

STONEHILL

North Easton, MA 02356 ...II

Coach: Connie Driscoll, Mass.-Dartmouth '76
Record: 3 Years, 23-7-0

1996 SCHEDULE

Assumption ■ ...Sept. 14
Curry ...Sept. 21
Salve Regina ■ ...Sept. 28
MIT ...Oct. 5
Western New Eng. ...Oct. 12
Mass.-Lowell ■ ...Oct. 19
Merrimack ...Oct. 26
Sacred Heart ...Nov. 2
Pace ■ ...Nov. 9
Bentley ■ ...Nov. 16

1995 RESULTS (9-1-0)

35 Assumption ...14
38 Nichols ...14
13 Salve Regina ...0
21 MIT ...14
54 Western New Eng. ...19
35 Mass.-Lowell ...6
19 Sacred Heart ...7
40 Curry ...19

10 Pace 26
39 Bentley 36
304 **155**

ECAC II Playoff

3 Bentley 46

Nickname: Chieftains.
Stadium: Chieftain (1980), 2,000 capacity. Natural turf.
Colors: Purple & White.
Conference: Division II Independents.
SID: Bob Richards, 508-230-1352.
AD: Paula J. Sullivan.

STONY BROOK

Stony Brook, NY 11794 II

Coach: Sam Kornhauser, Missouri Valley '71
Record: 12 Years, 57-56-2

1996 SCHEDULE

Pace ■ .....Sept. 14
Montclair St. ■ .....Sept. 21
Bentley .....Sept. 28
Sacred Heart ■ .....Oct. 5
Central Conn. St. .....Oct. 12
Albany (N.Y.) ■ .....Oct. 19
LIU-C.W. Post ■ .....Oct. 26
Wagner ■ .....Nov. 9
Southern Conn. St. .....Nov. 16
St. John's (N.Y.) .....Nov. 28

1995 RESULTS (7-3-0)

21 Pace 19
27 Wagner 28
44 Sacred Heart 17
33 Springfield 22
27 Norwich 12
23 American Int'l 22
13 Western Conn. St. 21
12 Plymouth St. 20
26 Mass.-Lowell 0
40 Albany (N.Y.) 21
266 **182**

Nickname: Seawolves.
Stadium: Seawolves (1978), 2,000 capacity. Natural turf.
Colors: Scarlet & Gray.
Conference: Division II Independents.
SID: Ken Alber, 516-632-6312.
AD: Sandy Weeden.

SUSQUEHANNA

Selinsgrove, PA 17870 III

Coach: Steve Briggs, Springfield '84
Record: 6 Years, 44-19-0

1996 SCHEDULE

Delaware Valley .....Sept. 14
Wilkes .....Sept. 21
Dickinson ■ .....Sept. 28
Wilmington (Ohio) ■ .....Oct. 5
Lebanon Valley .....Oct. 12
Moravian ■ .....Oct. 19
Juniata ■ .....Oct. 26
Lycoming .....Nov. 2
Albright ■ .....Nov. 9
Widener .....Nov. 16

1995 RESULTS (5-5-0)

21 Western Md. 14
28 Delaware Valley 14
24 Wilkes 3
6 Dickinson 30
39 Lebanon Valley 26
3 Moravian 19
28 Juniata 35
21 Lycoming 14
14 Albright 47
26 Widener 28
210 **230**

Nickname: Crusaders.
Stadium: Amos Alonzo Stagg (1892), 4,600 capacity. Natural turf.
Colors: Orange & Maroon.
Conference: Middle Atlantic.
SID: Mike Ferlazzo, 717-372-4119.
AD: Don Harnum.

SWARTHMORE

Swarthmore, PA 19081 III

Coach: Karl Miran, Middlebury '77
Record: 6 Years, 25-31-1

1996 SCHEDULE

Newport News App. .....Sept. 7
Johns Hopkins ■ .....Sept. 21
Gettysburg .....Sept. 28
Ursinus ■ .....Oct. 5
Muhlenberg .....Oct. 12
Pomona-Pitzer ■ .....Oct. 19
Dickinson .....Oct. 26
Frank. & Marsh. ■ .....Nov. 2
Western Md. .....Nov. 9
Wash. & Lee ■ .....Nov. 16

1995 RESULTS (5-5-0)

28 Earlham 21
3 Johns Hopkins 25
15 Gettysburg 19
25 Ursinus 23
11 Muhlenberg 7
0 Hobart 51
19 Dickinson 18
22 Frank. & Marsh. 42
6 Western Md. 39
2 Wash. & Lee 0
131 **245**

Nickname: Garnet Tide.
Stadium: Clothier (1950), 2,000 capacity. Natural turf.
Colors: Garnet & White.
Conference: Centennial.
SID: Mark Duzenski, 610-328-8206.
AD: Robert Williams.

SYRACUSE

Syracuse, NY 13244 .....I-A

Coach: Paul Pasqualoni, Penn St. '72
Record: 10 Years, 76-32-1

1996 SCHEDULE

North Caro. ■ .....*Sept. 7
Minnesota .....*Sept. 21
Virginia Tech ■ .....Sept. 28
Rutgers ■ .....Oct. 5
Pittsburgh ■ .....Oct. 12
Boston College .....Oct. 26
West Va. .....Nov. 2
Tulane .....Nov. 9
Army ■ .....Nov. 16
Temple .....Nov. 23
Miami (Fla.) ■ .....Nov. 30

1995 RESULTS (8-3-0)

20 North Caro. 9
24 East Caro. 27
27 Minnesota 17
27 Rutgers 17
31 Temple 14
52 Eastern Mich. 24
22 West Va. 0
7 Virginia Tech 31
42 Pittsburgh 10
58 Boston College 29
24 Miami (Fla.) 35
334 **213**

Gator Bowl

41 Clemson 0

Nickname: Orangemen.
Stadium: Carrier Dome (1980), 50,000 capacity. Artificial turf.
Colors: Orange.
Conference: Big East.
SID: Larry Kimball, 315-443-2608.
AD: Jake Crouthamel.

TARLETON ST.

Stephenville, TX 76402 II

Coach: Todd Whitten, Stephen F. Austin '87
(First year as head coach)

1996 SCHEDULE

Midwestern St. ■ .....*Sept. 5
Southeastern Okla. ■ .....*Sept. 14
East Central .....*Sept. 21
Tex. A&M-Kingsville .....*Oct. 5
West Tex. A&M ■ .....*Oct. 12
Eastern N.M. .....*Oct. 19
Abilene Christian ■ .....Oct. 26
Angelo St. ■ .....Nov. 2
Central Okla. .....Nov. 9
East Tex. St. ■ .....Nov. 16

1995 RESULTS (1-10-0)

12 East Central 35
35 Midwestern St. 44
0 Southeastern Okla. 47
44 Prairie View 6
0 Tex. A&M-Kingsville 51
23 West Tex. A&M 46
7 Eastern N.M. 28
18 Abilene Christian 38
7 Angelo St. 35
0 Central Okla. 47
3 East Tex. St. 48
149 **425**

Nickname: Texans.
Stadium: Memorial (1976), 5,284 capacity. Natural turf.
Colors: Purple & White.
Conference: Lone Star.
SID: Reed Richmond, 817-968-9077.
AD: Lonn Reisman.

TEMPLE

Philadelphia, PA 19122 .....I-A

Coach: Ron Dickerson, Kansas St. '71
Record: 3 Years, 4-29-0

1996 SCHEDULE

Eastern Mich. .....*Aug. 31
Washington St. ■ .....Sept. 7
Bowling Green .....Sept. 14
Penn St. [East Rutherford, N.J.] .....Sept. 21
Pittsburgh .....Oct. 5
Virginia Tech .....Oct. 12
West Va. ■ .....Oct. 19
Rutgers .....Oct. 26
Miami (Fla.) ■ .....Nov. 2
Boston College .....Nov. 16
Syracuse ■ .....Nov. 23

1995 RESULTS (1-10-0)

7 Kansas St. 34
13 West Va. 24
14 Penn St. 66
31 Bowling Green 37
14 Syracuse 31
29 Pittsburgh 27
22 East Caro. 32
12 Miami (Fla.) 36
9 Boston College 10
16 Virginia Tech 38
20 Rutgers 23
187 **358**

Nickname: Owls.
Stadium: Veterans (1971), 66,592 capacity. Artificial turf.
Colors: Cherry & White.
Conference: Big East.
SID: Scott Cathcart, 215-204-7445.
AD: Dave O'Brien.

TENNESSEE

Knoxville, TN 37996 .....I-A

Coach: Phillip Fulmer, Tennessee '72
Record: 4 Years, 33-7-0

1996 SCHEDULE

UNLV ■ .... *Aug. 31
UCLA ■ .... *Sept. 7
Florida ■ .... Sept. 21
Mississippi [Memphis, Tenn.] .... *Oct. 3
Georgia .... Oct. 12
Alabama ■ .... Oct. 26
South Caro. .... Nov. 2
Memphis .... Nov. 9
Arkansas ■ .... Nov. 16
Kentucky ■ .... Nov. 23
Vanderbilt .... Nov. 30

1995 RESULTS (10-1-0)

27 East Caro. 7
30 Georgia 27
37 Florida 62
52 Mississippi St. 14
31 Oklahoma St. 0
49 Arkansas 31
41 Alabama 14
56 South Caro. 21
42 Southern Miss. 0
34 Kentucky 31
12 Vanderbilt 7
411 **214**

Citrus Bowl

20 Ohio St. 14

Nickname: Volunteers.
Stadium: Neyland (1921), 102,485 capacity. Natural turf.
Colors: Orange & White.
Conference: Southeastern.
SID: Bud Ford, 423-974-1212.
AD: Doug Dickey.

TENN.-CHATT.

Chattanooga, TN 37402 .... I-AA

Coach: Buddy Green, North Caro. St. '76
Record: 2 Years, 7-15-0

1996 SCHEDULE

Colorado St. .... Aug. 31
Middle Tenn. St. .... *Sept. 14
Mississippi Val. ■ .... Sept. 21
Ga. Southern ■ .... Sept. 28
Marshall .... *Oct. 5
Va. Military ■ .... Oct. 19
Western Caro. .... Oct. 26
Appalachian St. ■ .... Nov. 2
Citadel .... Nov. 9
East Tenn. St. ■ .... Nov. 16
Furman .... Nov. 23

1995 RESULTS (4-7-0)

41 Charleston So. 0
10 Auburn 76
35 Bethune-Cookman 6
9 Ga. Southern 35
32 Marshall 35
12 Va. Military 17
35 Western Caro. 14
18 Appalachian St. 31
29 Citadel 24
9 East Tenn. St. 38
21 Furman 23
251 **299**

Nickname: Moccasins.
Stadium: Chamberlain Field (1908), 10,501 capacity. Natural turf.
Colors: Navy Blue & Gold.
Conference: Southern.
SID: Scott McKinney, 423-755-4618.
AD: Ed Farrell.

TENN.-MARTIN

Martin, TN 38238 .... I-AA

Coach: Don McLeary, Tennessee '70
Record: 12 Years, 59-71-0

1996 SCHEDULE

Southern Ill. .... Sept. 7
Southwest Mo. St. ■ .... *Sept. 21
Eastern Ill. ■ .... Sept. 28
Tennessee Tech .... Oct. 5
Murray St. ■ .... *Oct. 12
Tennessee St. .... *Oct. 19
Eastern Ky. ■ .... Oct. 26
Southeast Mo. St. .... Nov. 2
Middle Tenn. St. ■ .... Nov. 9
Samford .... Nov. 16
Austin Peay .... Nov. 23

1995 RESULTS (5-6-0)

97 Bethel (Tenn.) 7
22 Eastern Ill. 30
49 Morehead St. 24
36 Tennessee Tech 31
9 Murray St. 33
28 Tennessee St. 7
15 Eastern Ky. 38
17 Southeast Mo. St. 38
17 Middle Tenn. St. 45
14 Samford 21
31 Austin Peay 28
335 **302**

Nickname: Skyhawks.
Stadium: UT Martin (1964), 7,500 capacity. Natural turf.
Colors: Orange, White & Royal Blue.
Conference: Ohio Valley.
SID: Lee Wilmot, 901-587-7630.
AD: Benny Hollis.

TENNESSEE ST.

Nashville, TN 37209 .... I-AA

Coach: L. C. Cole, Nebraska '80
(First year as head coach)

1996 SCHEDULE

Florida A&M ■ .... *Aug. 31
Middle Tenn. St. ■ .... *Sept. 7
Jackson St. [Memphis, Tenn.] .... *Sept. 14
Southern-B.R. [Atlanta, Ga.] .... Sept. 28
Lane ■ .... Oct. 5
Tenn.-Martin ■ .... *Oct. 19
Austin Peay ■ .... Oct. 26
Eastern Ky. .... Nov. 2
Tennessee Tech .... Nov. 9
Murray St. .... Nov. 16
Southeast Mo. St. ■ .... Nov. 23

1995 RESULTS (2-9-0)

7 Middle Tenn. St. 11
19 Jackson St. 24
7 Florida A&M 24
15 South Caro. St. 14
45 Morehead St. 14
7 Tenn.-Martin 28
6 Austin Peay 28
20 Eastern Ky. 56
24 Tennessee Tech 28
19 Murray St. 24
24 Southeast Mo. St. 41
193 **292**

Nickname: Tigers.
Stadium: W.J. Hale (1953), 16,000 capacity. Natural turf.
Colors: Royal Blue & White.
Conference: Ohio Valley.
SID: Johnny M. Franks, 615-963-5851.
AD: Howard Gentry Jr.

TENNESSEE TECH

Cookeville, TN 38505 .... I-AA

Coach: Mike Hennigan, Tennessee Tech '73
(First year as head coach)

1996 SCHEDULE

Appalachian St. .... *Sept. 7
Samford ■ .... *Sept. 21
Eastern Ky. .... *Sept. 28
Tenn.-Martin ■ .... Oct. 5
Southeast Mo. St. ■ .... Oct. 12
Austin Peay .... Oct. 19
Eastern Ill. ■ .... Oct. 26
Murray St. .... Nov. 2
Tennessee St. ■ .... Nov. 9
Illinois St. .... Nov. 16
Middle Tenn. St. .... Nov. 23

1995 RESULTS (3-8-0)

49 Campbellsville 0
14 Marshall 45
24 Samford 27
3 Eastern Ky. 21
31 Tenn.-Martin 36
12 Southeast Mo. St. 33
17 Austin Peay 20
36 Morehead St. 29
14 Murray St. 45
28 Tennessee St. 24
6 Middle Tenn. St. 31
234 **311**

Nickname: Golden Eagles.
Stadium: Tucker (1966), 16,500 capacity. Artificial turf.
Colors: Purple & Gold.
Conference: Ohio Valley.
SID: Rob Schabert, 615-372-3088.
AD: David Larimore.

TEXAS

Austin, TX 78712 .... I-A

Coach: John Mackovic, Wake Forest '65
Record: 11 Years, 73-52-3

1996 SCHEDULE

Missouri ■ .... *Aug. 31
New Mexico St. ■ .... *Sept. 7
Notre Dame ■ .... Sept. 21
Virginia .... *Sept. 28
Oklahoma St. ■ .... Oct. 5
Oklahoma [Dallas, Texas] .... Oct. 12
Colorado .... Oct. 26
Baylor ■ .... Nov. 2
Texas Tech .... Nov. 9
Kansas .... Nov. 16
Texas A&M ■ .... Nov. 29

1995 RESULTS (10-1-1)

38 Hawaii 17
38 Pittsburgh 27
27 Notre Dame 55
35 Southern Methodist 10
37 Rice 13
24 Oklahoma 24
17 Virginia 16
48 Texas Tech 7
52 Houston 20
27 Texas Christian 19
21 Baylor 13
16 Texas A&M 6
380 **227**

Sugar Bowl

10 Virginia Tech 28

Nickname: Longhorns.
Stadium: Memorial (1924), 75,512 capacity. Natural turf.
Colors: Burnt Orange & White.
Conference: Big 12.
SID: Bill Little, 512-471-7437.
AD: DeLoss Dodds.

UTEP

El Paso, TX 79968 .... I-A

Coach: Charlie Bailey, Tampa '62
Record: 6 Years, 17-42-2

1996 SCHEDULE

Arizona .... *Aug. 31
New Mexico St. ■ .... *Sept. 14
San Jose St. .... Sept. 21
Northern Ill. .... Sept. 28
Utah ■ .... *Oct. 5
Texas Christian .... *Oct. 12
Rice ■ .... *Oct. 26
Brigham Young .... Nov. 2
Southern Methodist ■ .... *Nov. 9
Tulsa ■ .... *Nov. 16
New Mexico .... Nov. 23

1995 RESULTS (2-10-0)
17 New Mexico St. 45
20 Arizona St. 45
34 Valdosta St. 24
21 Hawaii 42
21 Utah 34
46 Air Force 56
28 Tulsa 38
16 San Diego St. 45
10 Colorado St. 56
14 Fresno St. 47
17 New Mexico 12
19 Wyoming 42
263 **486**

Nickname: Miners.
Stadium: Sun Bowl (1963), 51,270 capacity. Artificial turf.
Colors: Orange, White & Blue.
Conference: Western Athletic.
SID: To be named, 915-747-5330.
AD: John Thompson.

TEXAS A&M

College Station, TX 77843 ....I-A

Coach: R. C. Slocum, McNeese St. '67
Record: 7 Years, 68-15-2

1996 SCHEDULE
Brigham Young ....Aug. 24
Southwestern La. ....*Sept. 14
North Texas ■ ....Sept. 21
Colorado ■ ....Sept. 28
Louisiana Tech ■ ....Oct. 5
Iowa St. ....Oct. 12
Kansas St. ■ ....Oct. 19
Texas Tech ■ ....Oct. 26
Oklahoma St. ....Nov. 2
Baylor ....Nov. 9
Oklahoma ■ ....Nov. 16
Texas ....Nov. 29

1995 RESULTS (8-3-0)
33 LSU 17
52 Tulsa 9
21 Colorado 29
7 Texas Tech 14
20 Southern Methodist 17
24 Baylor 9
31 Houston 7
17 Rice 10
56 Middle Tenn. St. 14
38 Texas Christian 6
6 Texas 16
305 **148**

Alamo Bowl
22 Michigan 20

Nickname: Aggies.
Stadium: Kyle Field (1925), 70,210 capacity. Natural turf.
Colors: Maroon & White.
Conference: Big 12.
SID: Alan Cannon, 409-845-5725.
AD: Wally Groff.

TEX. A&M-KINGSVILLE

Kingsville, TX 78363 II

Coach: Ron Harms, Valparaiso '59
Record: 27 Years, 186-98-4

1996 SCHEDULE
North Dak. St. ....*Sept. 7
Sam Houston St. ■ ....*Sept. 14
North Ala. ■ ....*Sept. 21
Tarleton St. ■ ....*Oct. 5
East Tex. St. ....*Oct. 12
Central Okla. ■ ....*Oct. 19
West Tex. A&M ■ ....*Oct. 26
Eastern N.M. ....Nov. 2
Abilene Christian ■ ....*Nov. 9
Angelo St. ....Nov. 16

1995 RESULTS (9-1-0)
40 Portland St. 7
40 Southwest Tex. St. 12
23 Sam Houston St. 24
51 Tarleton St. 0
37 East Tex. St. 18
27 Central Okla. 21
55 West Tex. A&M 17
33 Eastern N.M. 14
54 Abilene Christian 7
41 Angelo St. 20
401 **140**

II Championship
59 Fort Hays St. 28
30 Portland St. 3
25 Pittsburg St. 28

Nickname: Javelinas.
Stadium: Javelina (1950), 15,000 capacity. Natural turf.
Colors: Blue & Gold.
Conference: Lone Star.
SID: Fred Nuesch, 512-593-3908.
AD: Ron Harms.

TEXAS CHRISTIAN

Fort Worth, TX 76129 ....I-A

Coach: Pat Sullivan, Auburn '72
Record: 4 Years, 19-25-1

1996 SCHEDULE
Oklahoma ....Sept. 7
Kansas ■ ....*Sept. 14
New Mexico ....*Sept. 28
Tulane ....*Oct. 5
UTEP ■ ....*Oct. 12
Utah ....Oct. 19
Brigham Young ■ ....Oct. 26
UNLV ■ ....Nov. 2
Tulsa ....Nov. 9
Rice ■ ....Nov. 16
Southern Methodist ....*Nov. 21

1995 RESULTS (6-5-0)
27 Iowa St. 10
20 Kansas 38
16 Vanderbilt 3
31 Houston 21
33 Rice 28
16 Tulane 11
24 Baylor 27
19 Southern Methodist 16
6 Texas Tech 27
19 Texas 27
6 Texas A&M 38
217 **246**

Nickname: Horned Frogs.
Stadium: Amon G. Carter (1929), 46,000 capacity. Natural turf.
Colors: Purple & White.
Conference: Western Athletic.
SID: Glen Stone, 817-921-7969.
AD: Frank Windegger.

TEXAS SOUTHERN

Houston, TX 77004 ....I-AA

Coach: Bill Thomas, Tennessee St. '70
Record: 7 Years, 40-35-3

1996 SCHEDULE
Prairie View [Houston, Texas] ....*Aug. 31
Alabama St. ....*Sept. 7
Lane ■ ....Sept. 21
Sam Houston St. ....Sept. 28
Jackson St. ....Oct. 5
Ark.-Pine Bluff ■ ....*Oct. 12
Alcorn St. ....*Oct. 19
Mississippi Val. ■ ....Oct. 26
Grambling ■ ....Nov. 2
Morgan St. ■ ....Nov. 9
Southern-B.R. ....Nov. 16

1995 RESULTS (2-8-0)
50 Prairie View 8
28 Clark Atlanta 0
10 Alcorn St. 21
13 Sam Houston St. 24
22 Ark.-Pine Bluff 36
19 Alabama St. 27
21 Mississippi Val. 28
15 Grambling 54
9 Jackson St. 13
13 Southern-B.R. 48
200 **259**

Nickname: Tigers.
Stadium: Robertson (1965), 25,000 capacity. Natural turf.
Colors: Maroon & Gray.
Conference: Southwestern Athletic.
SID: Ellis Johnson, 713-527-7270.
AD: Bill Thomas.

TEXAS TECH

Lubbock, TX 79409 ....I-A

Coach: Spike Dykes, Stephen F. Austin '59
Record: 9 Years, 56-47-1

1996 SCHEDULE
Kansas St. ....Aug. 31
Oklahoma St. [Dallas, Texas] ....Sept. 7
Georgia ....Sept. 21
Utah St. ■ ....*Sept. 28
Baylor ■ ....*Oct. 5
Kansas ....Oct. 12
Nebraska ■ ....Oct. 19
Texas A&M ....Oct. 26
Texas ■ ....Nov. 9
Southwestern La. ■ ....Nov. 16
Oklahoma ....Nov. 23

1995 RESULTS (8-3-0)
23 Penn St. 24
41 Missouri 14
7 Baylor 9
14 Texas A&M 7
63 Arkansas St. 25
31 Rice 26
34 New Mexico 7
7 Texas 48
27 Texas Christian 6
45 Southern Methodist 14
38 Houston 26
330 **206**

Copper Bowl
55 Air Force 41

Nickname: Red Raiders.
Stadium: Jones (1947), 50,500 capacity. Artificial turf.
Colors: Scarlet & Black.
Conference: Big 12.
SID: Richard Kilwien, 806-742-2770.
AD: Gerald Myers (Interim).

THIEL

Greenville, PA 16125 III

Coach: David Armstrong, Mercyhurst '86
(First year as head coach)

1996 SCHEDULE
Oberlin ■ ....Sept. 7
Allegheny ....Sept. 14
Bluffton ■ ....Sept. 21
Grove City ....Sept. 28
Waynesburg ■ ....Oct. 5
Alfred ■ ....Oct. 12
Bethany (W.Va.) ....Oct. 19
Wash. & Jeff. ■ ....Oct. 26
Gannon ....*Nov. 2
Catholic ■ ....Nov. 9

1995 RESULTS (0-10-0)
0 Marietta 36
0 Buffalo St. 46
26 Waynesburg 31
0 Bluffton 28
19 Bethany (W.Va.) 40
8 Wash. & Jeff. 49
14 Grove City 16
0 Gannon 21
10 Malone 31
7 St. John Fisher 48
84 **346**

Nickname: Tomcats.
Stadium: Stewart Field (1954), 5,000 capacity. Natural turf.
Colors: Blue & Gold.
Conference: Presidents' Athletic.
SID: Matt Weaver, 412-589-2187.
AD: John A. Dickason.

THOMAS MORE

Crestview Hills, KY 41017 III

Coach: Vic Clark, Indiana St. '71
Record: 6 Years, 47-13-0

1996 SCHEDULE

Howard Payne ■ ....Sept. 7
Ill. Wesleyan ....Sept. 14
Wilmington (Ohio) ....Sept. 21
Northwood ....Oct. 5
Bluffton ■ ....Oct. 12
Defiance ■ ....Oct. 19
Ohio Wesleyan ....Oct. 26
Mt. Senario ■ ....Nov. 2
Knoxville ■ ....Nov. 9
Albion ....Nov. 16

1995 RESULTS (10-0-0)

30 Mt. Senario 6
17 Alfred 14
48 Wilmington (Ohio) 23
16 Evansville 14
48 Sue Bennett 0
37 Knoxville 6
37 Butler 29
33 Defiance 0
60 Mt. St. Joseph 27
19 Bluffton 0
345 **119**

Nickname: Saints.
Stadium: Gilligan (1945), 2,500 capacity. Natural turf.
Colors: Royal Blue, White & Silver.
Conference: Division III Independents.
SID: Ted Kiep, 606-344-3673.
AD: Vic Clark.

TOLEDO

Toledo, OH 43606 ....I-A

Coach: Gary Pinkel, Kent '75
Record: 5 Years, 34-19-3

1996 SCHEDULE

Indiana ■ ....*Sept. 7
Akron ....*Sept. 14
Eastern Mich. ....*Sept. 21
Weber St. ■ ....*Sept. 28
Bowling Green ■ ....*Oct. 5
Louisiana Tech ....Oct. 19
Western Mich. ■ ....Oct. 26
Miami (Ohio) ■ ....Nov. 2
Central Mich. ■ ....Nov. 9
Ball St. ....Nov. 16
Ohio ....Nov. 23

1995 RESULTS (10-0-1)

41 East Tenn. St. 20
31 Western Mich. 21
49 Nevada 35
45 Cincinnati 31
17 Ball St. 14
28 Miami (Ohio) 28
35 Bowling Green 16
34 Eastern Mich. 28
19 Central Mich. 7
41 Akron 7
31 Ohio 20
371 **227**

Las Vegas Bowl

40 Nevada 37

Nickname: Rockets.
Stadium: Glass Bowl (1937), 26,248 capacity. Artificial turf.
Colors: Blue & Gold.
Conference: Mid-American.
SID: Rod Brandt, 419-530-3790.
AD: To be named.

TOWSON ST.

Towson, MD 21204 ....I-AA

Coach: Gordy Combs, Towson St. '72
Record: 4 Years, 27-13-0

1996 SCHEDULE

Butler ....Sept. 7
Bucknell ....Sept. 14
Robert Morris ....Sept. 21
Dayton ■ ....Sept. 28
Central Conn. St. ■ ....*Oct. 5
Colgate ■ ....Oct. 12
Monmouth (N.J.) ....Oct. 19
St. Francis (Pa.) ■ ....Oct. 26
Marist ....Nov. 2
Wagner ■ ....Nov. 16

1995 RESULTS (6-4-0)

34 Butler 3
0 Dayton 38
15 Wagner 23
31 Monmouth (N.J.) 15
24 Central Conn. St. 10
34 St. Francis (Pa.) 7
7 Bucknell 14
34 Robert Morris 14
17 American Int'l 19
38 Southern Conn. St. 7
234 **150**

Nickname: Tigers.
Stadium: Minnegan Stadium (1978), 5,000 capacity. Natural turf.
Colors: Gold & White.
Conference: Eastern Football.
SID: Peter Schlehr, 410-830-2232.
AD: R. Wayne Edwards.

TRENTON ST.

Trenton, NJ 08650 III

Coach: Eric Hamilton, Trenton St. '75
Record: 19 Years, 114-70-6

1996 SCHEDULE

Salisbury St. ....Sept. 14
Wm. Paterson ■ ....*Sept. 20
Wesley ....Sept. 28
Rowan ■ ....Oct. 5
LIU-C.W. Post ....Oct. 12
Jersey City St. ■ ....Oct. 26
Montclair St. ....*Nov. 2
Albany (N.Y.) ....Nov. 9
Kean ■ ....Nov. 16

1995 RESULTS (7-3-0)

22 Salisbury St. 3
17 Wm. Paterson 14
3 Wesley 16
10 Rowan 38
23 LIU-C.W. Post 34
38 Alfred 17
14 Jersey City St. 0
50 Montclair St. 44
43 Albany (N.Y.) 30
20 Kean 10
240 **206**

ECAC III Playoff

10 Wesley 7

Nickname: Lions.
Stadium: Lions (1984), 5,000 capacity. Artificial turf.
Colors: Blue & Gold.
Conference: New Jersey Athletic.
SID: Ann Bready, 609-771-2517.
AD: Kevin McHugh.

TRINITY (CONN.)

Hartford, CT 06106 III

Coach: Don Miller, Delaware '55
Record: 29 Years, 160-67-5

1996 SCHEDULE

Bates ■ ....Sept. 21
Williams ....Sept. 28
Hamilton ....Oct. 5
Tufts ■ ....Oct. 12
Bowdoin ....Oct. 19
Middlebury ■ ....Oct. 26
Amherst ■ ....Nov. 2
Wesleyan (Conn.) ....Nov. 9

1995 RESULTS (6-2-0)

11 Colby 14
21 Williams 50
26 Hamilton 0
27 Tufts 7
14 Bowdoin 12
19 Middlebury 7
33 Amherst 10
22 Wesleyan (Conn.) 0
173 **100**

Nickname: Bantams.
Stadium: Jessee Field (1900), 6,500 capacity. Natural turf.
Colors: Blue & Gold.
Conference: NESCAC.
SID: Albert Carbone Jr., 203-297-2137.
AD: Rick Hazelton.

TRINITY (TEX.)

San Antonio, TX 78212 III

Coach: Steven Mohr, Denison '76
Record: 6 Years, 26-34-0

1996 SCHEDULE

Austin ■ ....*Sept. 7
McPherson ■ ....*Sept. 14
Claremont-M-S ....Sept. 21
Pomona-Pitzer ....Sept. 28
Colorado Col. ■ ....*Oct. 5
Washington (Mo.) ....*Oct. 12
Centre ....Oct. 26
Rhodes ■ ....Nov. 2
Sewanee ■ ....*Nov. 9
Millsaps ....Nov. 16

1995 RESULTS (6-3-0)

26 Pomona-Pitzer 0
28 Claremont-M-S 3
19 Washington (Mo.) 21
18 Catholic 21
35 Millsaps 7
7 Centre 17
13 Rhodes 7
34 Sewanee 7
33 Wooster 0
213 **83**

Nickname: Tigers.
Stadium: E. M. Stevens (1972), 3,500 capacity. Natural turf.
Colors: Maroon & White.
Conference: Southern Collegiate Athletic.
SID: Tony Ziner, 210-736-8447.
AD: Bob King.

TROY ST.

Troy, AL 36081 ....I-AA

Coach: Larry Blakeney, Auburn '70
Record: 5 Years, 46-13-1

1996 SCHEDULE

Alcorn St. ....Aug. 31
Eastern Ky. ....*Sept. 7
Nicholls St. ■ ....*Sept. 21
Stephen F. Austin ....*Sept. 28
Alabama St. ■ [Mobile, Ala.] ....*Oct. 5
McNeese St. ■ ....*Oct. 12
Southwest Tex. St. ■ ....Oct. 19
Jacksonville St. ....*Oct. 26
Northwestern St. ....*Nov. 9
Sam Houston St. ....Nov. 16
Samford ■ ....*Nov. 21

1995 RESULTS (11-0-0)

31 East Tenn. St. 7
34 Northwestern St. 17

17 Nicholls St. ... 3
28 Alabama St. ... 10
56 Western Ky. ... 39
20 Northeast La. ... 10
66 Charleston So. ... 7
35 Jacksonville St. ... 7
60 Ala.-Birmingham ... 7
28 Central Fla. ... 17
50 Samford ... 20
425 **144**

I-AA Championship

21 Ga. Southern ... 24

Nickname: Trojans.
Stadium: Memorial (1950), 12,000 capacity. Natural turf.
Colors: Cardinal, Gray & Black.
Conference: Southland Football League.
SID: Tom Ensey, 205-670-3480.
AD: John D. Williams.

TRUMAN ST. (formerly Northeast Mo. St.)

Kirksville, MO 63501 ... II

Coach: John Ware, Drake '81
Record: 1 Year, 6-5-0

1996 SCHEDULE

Valdosta St. ... Sept. 7
Southwest Mo. St. ... *Sept. 14
Mo.-Rolla ... Sept. 21
Washburn ■ ... Sept. 28
Pittsburg St. ... Oct. 5
Northwest Mo. St. ■ ... Oct. 12
Central Mo. St. ■ ... Oct. 19
Mo. Western St. ... Oct. 26
Mo. Southern St. ■ ... Nov. 2
Emporia St. ... Nov. 9
Southwest Baptist ■ ... Nov. 16

1995 RESULTS (6-5-0)

10 South Dak. ... 27
17 Southwest Mo. St. ... 30
63 Mo.-Rolla ... 3
41 Washburn ... 17
7 Pittsburg St. ... 49
44 Northwest Mo. St. ... 10
45 Central Mo. St. ... 34
42 Mo. Western St. ... 21
22 Mo. Southern St. ... 24
19 Emporia St. ... 36
56 Southwest Baptist ... 21
366 **272**

Nickname: Bulldogs.
Stadium: Stokes (1962), 4,000 capacity. Natural turf.
Colors: Purple & White.
Conference: Mid-America Intercollegiate Athletic Assoc.
SID: Melissa Ware, 816-785-4127.
AD: Walter H. Ryle.

TUFTS

Medford, MA 02155 ... III

Coach: Bill Samko, Connecticut '73
Record: 9 Years, 41-37-1

1996 SCHEDULE

Wesleyan (Conn.) ■ ... Sept. 21
Bates ■ ... Sept. 28
Bowdoin ... Oct. 5
Trinity (Conn.) ... Oct. 12
Williams ■ ... Oct. 19
Amherst ... Oct. 26
Colby ■ ... Nov. 2
Middlebury ... Nov. 9

1995 RESULTS (4-4-0)

35 Hamilton ... 21
40 Bates ... 21
29 Bowdoin ... 26
7 Trinity (Conn.) ... 27
6 Williams ... 34
0 Amherst ... 28
6 Colby ... 33
14 Middlebury ... 12
137 **202**

Nickname: Jumbos.
Stadium: Ellis Oval (1923), 6,000 capacity. Natural turf.
Colors: Brown & Blue.
Conference: NESCAC.
SID: Paul Sweeney, 617-627-3586.
AD: Rocco Carzo.

TULANE

New Orleans, LA 70118 ... I-A

Coach: Buddy Teevens, Dartmouth '79
Record: 10 Years, 48-67-2

1996 SCHEDULE

Cincinnati ... *Aug. 30
Rice ■ ... *Sept. 14
Memphis ... *Sept. 21
Texas Christian ■ ... *Oct. 5
Louisville ■ ... *Oct. 12
Army ... Oct. 19
Southern Miss. ■ ... *Oct. 26
Houston ■ ... *Nov. 2
Syracuse ■ ... Nov. 9
Navy ... Nov. 16
LSU ... *Nov. 23

1995 RESULTS (2-9-0)

10 Maryland ... 29
35 Wake Forest ... 9
17 Rice ... 15
0 Southern Miss. ... 45
17 Mississippi ... 20
8 Memphis ... 23
11 Texas Christian ... 16
28 Southwestern La. ... 32
14 Louisville ... 34
40 Rutgers ... 45
7 Navy ... 35
187 **303**

Nickname: Green Wave.
Stadium: Superdome (1975), 70,892 capacity. Artificial turf.
Colors: Olive Green & Sky Blue.
Conference: Conference USA.
SID: Lenny Vangilder, 504-865-5506.
AD: To be named.

TULSA

Tulsa, OK 74104 ... I-A

Coach: David Rader, Tulsa '80
Record: 8 Years, 38-51-1

1996 SCHEDULE

Southern Methodist ... *Aug. 31
Oklahoma St. ... *Sept. 14
Iowa ■ ... *Sept. 21
Oklahoma ... Sept. 28
Colorado St. ■ ... Oct. 12
Brigham Young ■ ... Oct. 19
Utah ... Oct. 26
New Mexico ■ ... Nov. 2
Texas Christian ■ ... Nov. 9
UTEP ... *Nov. 16
Rice ... Nov. 23

1995 RESULTS (4-7-0)

5 Baylor ... 37
24 Oklahoma St. ... 23
9 Texas A&M ... 52
45 East Tenn. St. ... 20
23 Louisiana Tech ... 27
35 Wyoming ... 6
38 UTEP ... 28
7 Memphis ... 10
35 Brigham Young ... 45
7 East Caro. ... 28
5 Cincinnati ... 24
233 **300**

Nickname: Golden Hurricane.
Stadium: Skelly (1930), 40,385 capacity. Artificial turf.
Colors: Blue & Gold.
Conference: Western Athletic.
SID: Don Tomkalski, 918-631-2395.
AD: Judy MacLeod.

TUSKEGEE

Tuskegee, AL 36088 ... II

Coach: Rick Comegy, Millersville '76
Record: 2 Years, 0-22-0

1996 SCHEDULE

Savannah St. ... Aug. 31
Florida A&M ... *Sept. 7
Morris Brown ■ ... Sept. 14
Miles ■ ... Sept. 21
Albany St. (Ga.) ... Sept. 28
Kentucky St. ■ ... Oct. 5
Morehouse [Columbus, Ga.] ... *Oct. 12
Fort Valley St. ... Oct. 26
Clark Atlanta ... Nov. 2
Alabama A&M ■ ... Nov. 9
Alabama St. ... Nov. 28

1995 RESULTS (2-9-0)

16 Florida A&M ... 28
6 Savannah St. ... 10
19 Morris Brown ... 21
36 Miles ... 37
0 Albany St. (Ga.) ... 69
6 Morehouse ... 19
12 Kentucky St. ... 18
28 Fort Valley St. ... 27
6 Clark Atlanta ... 7
19 Alabama A&M ... 6
20 Alabama St. ... 58
168 **300**

Nickname: Golden Tigers.
Stadium: Alumni Bowl (1925), 10,000 capacity. Natural turf.
Colors: Old Gold & Crimson.
Conference: Southern Intercollegiate Athletic.
SID: Arnold Houston, 334-727-8150.
AD: Rick Comegy.

UCLA

Los Angeles, CA 90024 ... I-A

Coach: Bob Toledo, San Fran. St. '68
Record: 6 Years, 27-36-0

1996 SCHEDULE

Tennessee ... *Sept. 7
Northeast La. ■ ... *Sept. 14
Michigan ... Sept. 28
Oregon ... Oct. 5
Arizona St. ■ ... Oct. 12
Washington ... Oct. 19
California ... Oct. 26
Stanford ■ ... Nov. 2
Washington St. ■ ... Nov. 9
Arizona ... Nov. 16
Southern Cal ■ ... Nov. 23

1995 RESULTS (7-4-0)

31 Miami (Fla.) ... 8
23 Brigham Young ... 9
31 Oregon ... 38
15 Washington St. ... 24
45 Fresno St. ... 21
17 Arizona ... 10
42 Stanford ... 28
33 California ... 16
33 Arizona St. ... 37
14 Washington ... 38
24 Southern Cal ... 20
308 **249**

Aloha Bowl

30 Kansas ... 51

Nickname: Bruins.
Stadium: Rose Bowl (1922), 100,089 capacity. Natural turf.
Colors: Blue & Gold.
Conference: Pacific-10.
SID: Marc Dellins, 310-206-6831.
AD: Peter Dalis.

UNION (N.Y.)

Schenectady, NY 12308 III

Coach: John Audino, Notre Dame '75
Record: 6 Years, 41-21-0

1996 SCHEDULE

St. Lawrence ■ ....Sept. 14
Worcester Tech ....Sept. 21
Hobart ■ ....Sept. 28
Rochester ....Oct. 5
Albany (N.Y.) ....Oct. 12
Rensselaer ■ ....Oct. 19
Coast Guard ■ ....Oct. 26
Alfred ....Nov. 2
Carnegie Mellon ....Nov. 16

1995 RESULTS (8-1-0)

8 St. Lawrence 9
44 Worcester Tech 0
39 Hobart 15
20 Dickinson 7
20 Albany (N.Y.) 6
16 Rensselaer 13
23 Coast Guard 0
33 Muhlenberg 14
44 Rochester 7
247 **71**

III Championship

24 Plymouth St. 7
7 Rowan 38

Nickname: Dutchmen.
Stadium: Frank Bailey Field (1981), 2,000 capacity. Artificial turf.
Color: Garnet.
Conference: Upstate Collegiate Athletic Association.
SID: George Cuttita, 518-388-6170.
AD: Richard Sakala.

UPPER IOWA

Fayette, IA 52142 III

Coach: Paul Rudolph, Minot St. '88
Record: 5 Years, 22-28-0

1996 SCHEDULE

Huron ....Sept. 14
Loras ■ ....Sept. 21
Wartburg ....Sept. 28
Simpson ■ ....Oct. 5
William Penn ....Oct. 12
Aurora ■ ....Oct. 19
Buena Vista ■ ....Oct. 26
Central (Iowa) ....Nov. 2
Luther ■ ....Nov. 9
Dubuque ....Nov. 16

1995 RESULTS (4-6-0)

20 Central Mo. St. 43
20 Ripon 21
14 Luther 6
26 William Penn 6
6 Simpson 58
30 Dubuque 0
28 Buena Vista 12
8 Wartburg 42
14 Loras 38
0 Central (Iowa) 42
166 **268**

Nickname: Peacocks.
Stadium: Eischeid (1993), 3,500 capacity. Natural turf.
Colors: Blue & White.
Conference: Iowa Intercollegiate Athletic.
SID: Julie Lentz, 319-425-5307.
AD: Paul Rudolph.

URSINUS

Collegeville, PA 19426 III

Coach: Steve Gilbert, West Chester '79
Record: 8 Years, 32-46-0

1996 SCHEDULE

Alfred ■ ....Sept. 7
Wash. & Lee ....Sept. 14
Frank. & Marsh. ....Sept. 21
Western Md. ■ ....Sept. 28
Swarthmore ....Oct. 5
Johns Hopkins ■ ....Oct. 12
Gettysburg ....Oct. 19
Merchant Marine ....Oct. 26
Muhlenberg ■ ....Nov. 2
Dickinson ■ ....Nov. 16

1995 RESULTS (3-7-0)

16 Worcester Tech 6
0 Frank. & Marsh. 14
7 Western Md. 27
23 Swarthmore 25
9 Johns Hopkins 14
3 Gettysburg 7
14 Merchant Marine 7
20 Catholic 21
17 Muhlenberg 10
12 Dickinson 27
121 **158**

Nickname: Bears.
Stadium: Patterson Field (1923), 2,500 capacity. Natural turf.
Colors: Old Gold, Red & Black.
Conference: Centennial.
SID: David M. Sherman, 610-409-3612.
AD: William E. Akin.

UTAH

Salt Lake City, UT 84112 ....I-A

Coach: Ron McBride, San Jose St. '63
Record: 6 Years, 41-30-0

1996 SCHEDULE

Utah St. ....*Aug. 31
Stanford ....Sept. 7
Southern Methodist ....*Sept. 14
Fresno St. ■ ....*Sept. 21
Kansas ■ ....*Sept. 28
UTEP ....*Oct. 5
Texas Christian ■ ....Oct. 19
Tulsa ■ ....Oct. 26
Rice ....Nov. 2
New Mexico ....Nov. 9
Brigham Young ■ ....Nov. 23

1995 RESULTS (7-4-0)

20 Oregon 27
20 Stanford 27
36 New Mexico 9
25 Fresno St. 21
34 UTEP 21
21 San Diego St. 24
14 Colorado St. 19
22 Air Force 21
40 Utah St. 20
30 Wyoming 24
34 Brigham Young 17
296 **230**

Nickname: Utes.
Stadium: Robert Rice (1927), 32,500 capacity. Natural turf.
Colors: Crimson & White.
Conference: Western Athletic.
SID: Liz Abel, 801-581-3511.
AD: Chris Hill.

UTAH ST.

Logan, UT 84322 ....I-A

Coach: John L. Smith, Weber St. '71
Record: 7 Years, 57-28-0

1996 SCHEDULE

Utah ■ ....*Aug. 31
Cal St. Northridge ■ ....*Sept. 7
Southern Miss. ....Sept. 14
Oklahoma St. ....*Sept. 21
Texas Tech ....*Sept. 28
Brigham Young ■ ....*Oct. 4
New Mexico St. ....*Oct. 12
Boise St. ....*Oct. 19
Idaho ■ ....Oct. 26
North Texas ■ ....Nov. 2
Nevada ■ ....Nov. 9

1995 RESULTS (4-7-0)

17 Arkansas St. 21
14 Boise St. 38
21 Southern Miss. 24
30 San Jose St. 32
17 Colorado St. 59
42 Northern Ill. 7
27 New Mexico St. 14
20 Utah 40
25 Nevada 30
42 UNLV 0
38 Pacific (Cal.) 22
293 **287**

Nickname: Aggies.
Stadium: E.L. Romney (1968), 30,257 capacity. Natural turf.
Colors: Navy Blue & White.
Conference: Big West.
SID: John Lewandowski, 801-797-1361.
AD: Chuck Bell.

VALDOSTA ST.

Valdosta, GA 31698 II

Coach: Hal Mumme, Tarleton St. '75
Record: 7 Years, 54-25-1

1996 SCHEDULE

Gardner-Webb ....*Aug. 31
Truman St. ■ ....Sept. 7
Savannah St. ■ ....Sept. 14
Arkansas Tech ....*Sept. 21
North Ala. ■ ....Oct. 5
Ark.-Monticello ....*Oct. 12
West Ala. ....Oct. 19
Southern Ark. ■ ....Oct. 26
Delta St. ....Nov. 2
Central Ark. ■ ....Nov. 9
West Ga. ■ ....Nov. 16

1995 RESULTS (6-5-0)

34 Gardner-Webb 21
14 North Dak. St. 19
24 UTEP 34
28 Arkansas Tech 0
24 Central Ark. 30
27 West Ala. 20
41 St. Ambrose 0
37 Delta St. 19
9 North Ala. 26
42 Mississippi Col. 16
6 West Ga. 44
286 **229**

Nickname: Blazers.
Stadium: Cleveland Field (1922), 11,500 capacity. Natural turf.
Colors: Red & Black.
Conference: Gulf South.
SID: Steve Roberts, 912-333-5890.
AD: Herb Reinhard.

VALPARAISO

Valparaiso, IN 46383 ....I-AA

Coach: Tom Horne, Wis.-La Crosse '76
Record: 10 Years, 39-61-2

1996 SCHEDULE

Hope ....Sept. 7
Alma ■ ....Sept. 14
Morehead St. ■ ....Sept. 21
San Diego ....*Sept. 28
Butler ■ ....Oct. 12
Drake ....Oct. 19
Evansville ....Oct. 26
Dayton ■ ....Nov. 2
Aurora ■ ....Nov. 9
Bethune-Cookman ....Nov. 16

1995 RESULTS (5-5-0)

41 St. Xavier (Ill.) 30
0 Wis.-Whitewater 47
47 Kalamazoo 39

18 San Diego....35
44 Butler....42
21 Drake....28
6 Evansville....7
14 Dayton....44
20 Aurora....15
36 Ky. Wesleyan....27
247 **314**

Nickname: Crusaders.
Stadium: Brown Field (1947), 5,000 capacity. Natural turf.
Colors: Brown & Gold.
Conference: Pioneer Football League.
SID: Bill Rogers, 219-464-5232.
AD: William Steinbrecher.

VANDERBILT

Nashville, TN 37212....I-A

Coach: Rod Dowhower, San Diego St. '68
Record: 2 Years, 7-14-1

1996 SCHEDULE

Notre Dame ■....*Sept. 5
Alabama....Sept. 14
Mississippi ■....*Sept. 21
LSU....*Oct. 5
North Texas....Oct. 12
Georgia....Oct. 19
South Caro. ■....Oct. 26
Ala.-Birmingham ■....Nov. 2
Florida ■....Nov. 9
Kentucky....Nov. 16
Tennessee ■....Nov. 30

1995 RESULTS (2-9-0)

25 Alabama....33
0 Notre Dame....41
3 Texas Christian....16
7 Arkansas....35
6 Georgia....17
14 South Caro....52
10 Mississippi....21
14 Kentucky....10
29 Louisiana Tech....6
7 Florida....38
7 Tennessee....12
122 **281**

Nickname: Commodores.
Stadium: Vanderbilt Stadium (1981), 41,000 capacity. Artificial turf.
Colors: Black & Gold.
Conference: Southeastern.
SID: Rod Williamson, 615-322-4121.
AD: To be named.

VILLANOVA

Villanova, PA 19085....I-AA

Coach: Andy Talley, Southern Conn. St. '67
Record: 16 Years, 95-64-2

1996 SCHEDULE

Rutgers....*Aug. 31
Massachusetts ■....Sept. 7
Delaware ■....Sept. 14
Fordham ■....Sept. 21
Connecticut....Oct. 5
Northeastern....Oct. 12
William & Mary ■....Oct. 19
Richmond....Oct. 26
Rhode Island ■....Nov. 2
New Hampshire....Nov. 9
James Madison....Nov. 16

1995 RESULTS (3-8-0)

16 Boston U....21
7 Delaware....28
27 James Madison....28
28 Buffalo....3
13 Connecticut....14
27 Northeastern....24
14 Navy....20
15 William & Mary....18
10 Rhode Island....27
9 New Hampshire....12
28 Richmond....0
194 **195**

Nickname: Wildcats.
Stadium: Villanova (1927), 12,000 capacity. Artificial turf.
Colors: Blue & White.
Conference: Yankee.
SID: Karen Frascona, 610-519-4120.
AD: Gene DeFilippo.

VIRGINIA

Charlottesville, VA 22903....I-A

Coach: George Welsh, Navy '56
Record: 23 Years, 153-109-4

1996 SCHEDULE

Central Mich. ■....*Sept. 7
Maryland ■....Sept. 14
Wake Forest....Sept. 21
Texas ■....*Sept. 28
Georgia Tech....Oct. 5
North Caro. St. ■....Oct. 19
Florida St....Oct. 26
Duke....Nov. 2
Clemson ■....Nov. 9
North Caro. ■....Nov. 16
Virginia Tech....Nov. 29

1995 RESULTS (8-4-0)

17 Michigan....18
40 William & Mary....16
29 North Caro. St....24
41 Georgia Tech....14
22 Clemson....3
35 Wake Forest....17
17 North Caro....22
44 Duke....30
16 Texas....17
33 Florida St....28
21 Maryland....18
29 Virginia Tech....36
344 **243**

Peach Bowl

34 Georgia....27

Nickname: Cavaliers.
Stadium: Harrison Field/Scott Stadium (1931), 40,000 capacity. Natural turf.
Colors: Orange & Blue.
Conference: Atlantic Coast.
SID: Rich Murray, 804-982-5500.
AD: Terry Holland.

VA. MILITARY

Lexington, VA 24450....I-AA

Coach: Bill Stewart, Fairmont St. '75
Record: 2 Years, 5-17-0

1996 SCHEDULE

Mississippi [Jackson, Miss.]....*Sept. 7
William & Mary....Sept. 14
East Tenn. St....Sept. 21
Furman ■....Sept. 28
Ga. Southern....Oct. 5
Marshall ■....Oct. 12
Tenn.-Chatt....Oct. 19
Western Caro. ■....Nov. 2
Richmond ■....Nov. 9
Citadel ■....Nov. 16
Appalachian St....Nov. 23

1995 RESULTS (4-7-0)

28 Richmond....51
50 Liberty....31
37 East Tenn. St....23
24 Furman....55
7 William & Mary....27
21 Marshall....56
17 Tenn.-Chatt....12
14 Western Caro....31
24 Appalachian St....26
34 Citadel....7
13 Ga. Southern....31
269 **350**

Nickname: Keydets.
Stadium: Alumni Field (1962), 10,000 capacity. Natural turf.
Colors: Red, White & Yellow.
Conference: Southern.
SID: Wade Branner, 703-464-7253.
AD: Davis Babb.

VIRGINIA ST.

Petersburg, VA 23806....II

Coach: Louis Anderson, Claflin '61
Record: 5 Years, 31-20-0

1996 SCHEDULE

Norfolk St. ■....*Aug. 31
Johnson Smith....*Sept. 7
West Chester ■....Sept. 14
Howard....Sept. 21
Livingstone ■....Sept. 28
Knoxville ■....Oct. 5
Fayetteville St....*Oct. 12
Winston-Salem ■....Oct. 19
Virginia Union....Oct. 26
Bowie St....Nov. 2
Elizabeth City St....Nov. 9

1995 RESULTS (8-2-0)

41 Norfolk St....22
47 Johnson Smith....18
14 Savannah St....30
7 Bowie St....0
28 Livingstone....24
81 Cheyney....9
48 Fayetteville St....0
44 Elizabeth City St....3
58 Virginia Union....14
14 Winston-Salem....20
382 **140**

Nickname: Trojans.
Stadium: Rogers (1950), 13,500 capacity. Natural turf.
Colors: Orange & Blue.
Conference: Central Intercollegiate Athletic Association.
SID: Gregory C. Goings, 804-524-5028.
AD: Alfreeda Goff.

VIRGINIA TECH

Blacksburg, VA 24061....I-A

Coach: Frank Beamer, Virginia Tech '69
Record: 15 Years, 93-72-4

1996 SCHEDULE

Akron....*Sept. 7
Boston College....Sept. 14
Rutgers ■....Sept. 21
Syracuse....Sept. 28
Temple ■....Oct. 12
Pittsburgh ■....Oct. 26
Southwestern La. ■....Nov. 2
East Caro. ■....Nov. 9
Miami (Fla.)....Nov. 16
West Va. ■....Nov. 23
Virginia ■....Nov. 29

1995 RESULTS (9-2-0)

14 Boston College....20
0 Cincinnati....16
13 Miami (Fla.)....7
26 Pittsburgh....16
14 Navy....0
77 Akron....27
45 Rutgers....17
27 West Va....0
31 Syracuse....7
38 Temple....16
36 Virginia....29
321 **155**

Sugar Bowl

28 Texas....10

Nickname: Gobblers, Hokies.
Stadium: Lane (1965), 50,000 capacity. Natural turf.
Colors: Orange & Maroon.
Conference: Big East.

SID: Dave Smith, 540-231-6726.
AD: Dave Braine.

VIRGINIA UNION

Richmond, VA 23220.................................II

Coach: Willard Bailey, Norfolk St. '62
Record: 23 Years, 158-80-7

1996 SCHEDULE

Savannah St. ....Sept. 7
Cheyney ■.......................................*Sept. 14
Fayetteville St. ■...............................Sept. 21
Bowie St. ....Sept. 28
Elizabeth City St. ....Oct. 5
New Haven ....Oct. 12
Norfolk St. ....Oct. 19
Virginia St. ■....................................Oct. 26
Winston-Salem ....*Nov. 2
Johnson Smith ■.................................Nov. 9

1995 RESULTS (0-8-2)

6 Savannah St. 45
21 Cheyney 21
21 Fayetteville St. 21
12 Bowie St. 23
20 Elizabeth City St. 48
9 New Haven 36
32 Norfolk St. 58
14 Virginia St. 58
0 Winston-Salem 43
0 Johnson Smith..............................12
135 **365**

Nickname: Panthers.
Stadium: Hovey Field, 10,000 capacity. Natural turf.
Colors: Steel Gray & Maroon.
Conference: Central Intercollegiate Athletic Association.
SID: Paul Williams, 804-342-1233.
AD: James Battle.

WABASH

Crawfordsville, IN 47933 III

Coach: Greg Carlson, Wis.-Oshkosh '70
Record: 13 Years, 79-40-2

1996 SCHEDULE

Wilmington (Ohio) ■............................Sept. 14
Albion ■..Sept. 21
Hope ....Sept. 28
Rose-Hulman ....Oct. 5
Manchester ■....................................Oct. 12
Ill. Benedictine...................................Oct. 19
Franklin ....Oct. 26
Hanover ■..Nov. 2
Anderson (Ind.) ....Nov. 9
DePauw ■...Nov. 16

1995 RESULTS (5-5-0)

30 Simpson.......................................27
21 Albion 31
35 Hope 10
29 Manchester 31
40 Ill. Benedictine 3
48 Franklin...0
21 Hanover.......................................41
21 Anderson (Ind.)............................29
29 Rose-Hulman 41
7 DePauw 2
281 **215**

Nickname: Little Giants.
Stadium: Little Giant (1967), 4,200 capacity. Natural turf.
Colors: Scarlet.
Conference: Indiana Collegiate Athletic.
SID: Jim Amidon, 317-361-6364.
AD: Max Servies.

WAGNER

Staten Island, NY 10301.........................I-AA

Coach: Walt Hameline, Brockport St. '75
Record: 15 Years, 117-39-2

1996 SCHEDULE

Iona ....Sept. 14
LIU-C.W. Post ■.................................Sept. 21
Marist ■...Sept. 28
St. Francis (Pa.) ....Oct. 5
Monmouth (N.J.) ■............................*Oct. 12
St. Peter's ■.....................................Oct. 19
Central Conn. St. ....Oct. 26
Robert Morris ■.................................Nov. 2
Stony Brook ....Nov. 9
Towson St. ....Nov. 16

1995 RESULTS (8-1-0)

28 Stony Brook..................................27
23 Towson St. 15
28 St. Peter's....................................24
38 St. Francis (Pa.) 21
16 Robert Morris 18
42 Iona..0
40 Central Conn. St. 35
21 Monmouth (N.J.)...........................20
20 San Diego.....................................17
256 **177**

ECAC I-AA Playoff

20 Duquesne.....................................44

Nickname: Seahawks.
Stadium: Fischer Memorial Field (1967), 5,000 capacity. Natural turf.
Colors: Green & White.
Conference: Northeast.
SID: Tom Dowd, 718-390-3227.
AD: Walt Hameline.

WAKE FOREST

Winston-Salem, NC 27109 ....I-A

Coach: Jim Caldwell, Iowa '77
Record: 3 Years, 6-27-0

1996 SCHEDULE

Appalachian St. ■..............................*Aug. 29
Northwestern ■..................................Sept. 7
Georgia Tech ....Sept. 14
Virginia ■..Sept. 21
Clemson ....Sept. 28
North Caro. ■.....................................Oct. 5
Maryland ....Oct. 19
Navy ■..Oct. 26
Florida St. [Orlando, Fla.] ....Nov. 9
Duke ■..Nov. 16
North Caro. St. ....Nov. 23

1995 RESULTS (1-10-0)

22 Appalachian St. 24
9 Tulane 35
14 Clemson 29
30 Navy 7
17 Virginia.......................................35
6 Maryland.......................................9
13 Florida St. 72
7 North Caro. 31
26 Duke 42
23 Georgia Tech 24
23 North Caro. St. 52
190 **360**

Nickname: Demon Deacons.
Stadium: Groves (1968), 31,500 capacity. Natural turf.
Colors: Old Gold & Black.
Conference: Atlantic Coast.
SID: John Justus, 910-759-5640.
AD: Ron Wellman.

WARTBURG

Waverly, IA 50677 III

Coach: Steve Hagen, Cal Lutheran '83
(First year as head coach)

1996 SCHEDULE

Augustana (Ill.) ■...............................Sept. 14
Central (Iowa)....................................Sept. 21
Upper Iowa ■.....................................Sept. 28
Loras ....Oct. 5
Simpson ■...Oct. 12
Buena Vista ....Oct. 19
Dubuque ■..Oct. 26
Blackburn ....Nov. 2
William Penn ....Nov. 9
Luther ■..Nov. 16

1995 RESULTS (9-1-0)

28 Coe..7
23 Simpson.......................................10
0 Central (Iowa) 27
69 Concordia (St. Paul) 7
54 Dubuque..0
33 Buena Vista 7
67 William Penn..................................0
42 Upper Iowa 8
50 Luther..28
30 Loras 8
396 **102**

Nickname: Knights.
Stadium: Schield (1956), 2,500 capacity. Natural turf.
Colors: Orange & Black.
Conference: Iowa Intercollegiate Athletic.
SID: Duane Schroeder, 319-352-8277.
AD: Gary Grace.

WASHBURN

Topeka, KS 66621 II

Coach: Tony DeMeo, Iona '71
Record: 13 Years, 69-45-4

1996 SCHEDULE

Fort Hays St. ....:..............................*Sept. 14
Mo. Western St. ■..............................*Sept. 21
Truman St. ....Sept. 28
Emporia St. ■....................................*Oct. 5
Central Mo. St. ■................................Oct. 12
Mo.-Rolla ....Oct. 19
Southwest Baptist ■............................Oct. 26
Pittsburg St. ....Nov. 2
Northwest Mo. St. ■............................Nov. 9
Mo. Southern St. ....Nov. 16

1995 RESULTS (4-6-0)

61 McPherson 0
6 Mo. Western St. 17
17 Truman St. 41
24 Emporia St. 25
37 Central Mo. St. 21
21 Mo.-Rolla 10
37 Southwest Baptist..........................20
7 Pittsburg St. 31
21 Northwest Mo. St. 42
0 Mo. Southern St.............................25
231 **232**

Nickname: Ichabods.
Stadium: Moore Bowl (1928), 7,200 capacity. Natural turf.
Colors: Yale Blue & White.
Conference: Mid-America Intercollegiate Athletic Assoc.
SID: To be named, 913-231-1010.
AD: Loren Ferre'.

WASHINGTON

Seattle, WA 98195 ....I-A

Coach: Jim Lambright, Washington '65
Record: 3 Years, 21-12-1

1996 SCHEDULE

Arizona St. ....*Sept. 7
Brigham Young ■................................Sept. 14
Arizona ■..Sept. 21
Stanford ■...Oct. 5
Notre Dame ....Oct. 12
UCLA ■...Oct. 19
Oregon ....Oct. 26
Southern Cal......................................Nov. 2
Oregon St. ■......................................Nov. 9
San Jose St. ■....................................Nov. 16
Washington St. ....Nov. 23

1995 RESULTS (7-3-1)

23 Arizona St.....................................20
20 Ohio St. 30
21 Army 13

26 Oregon St. 16
21 Notre Dame 29
38 Stanford 28
31 Arizona 17
21 Southern Cal 21
22 Oregon 24
38 UCLA 14
33 Washington St. 30
294 **242**

Sun Bowl

18 Iowa 38

Nickname: Huskies.
Stadium: Husky (1920), 72,500 capacity. Artificial turf.
Colors: Purple & Gold.
Conference: Pacific-10.
SID: Jim Daves, 206-543-2230.
AD: Barbara Hedges.

WASHINGTON (MO.)

St. Louis, MO 63130 III

Coach: Larry Kindbom, Kalamazoo '74
Record: 13 Years, 71-56-1

1996 SCHEDULE

Rhodes ....Sept. 7
Illinois Col. ....Sept. 14
Case Reserve ■ ....Sept. 21
Ill. Wesleyan ■ ....Sept. 28
Trinity (Tex.) ■ ....*Oct. 12
Carnegie Mellon ■ ....*Oct. 19
Rochester ....Oct. 26
Chicago ....Nov. 2
Central (Iowa) ■ ....Nov. 9
Rose-Hulman ....Nov. 16

1995 RESULTS (9-1-0)

43 Rose-Hulman 32
33 Central Methodist 0
28 Ill. Wesleyan 23
21 Trinity (Tex.) 19
28 Rhodes 7
28 Chicago 14
8 Carnegie Mellon 12
40 Rochester 7
49 Case Reserve 22
42 Colorado Col. 0
320 **136**

Nickname: Bears.
Stadium: Francis Field (1904), 4,000 capacity. Natural turf.
Colors: Red & Green.
Conference: University Athletic Association.
SID: Mike Wolf, 314-935-5077.
AD: John Schael.

WASH. & JEFF.

Washington, PA 15301 III

Coach: John Luckhardt, Purdue '67
Record: 14 Years, 118-28-2

1996 SCHEDULE

Emory & Henry ■ ....Sept. 14
Buffalo St. ....Sept. 21
Grove City ■ ....Oct. 5
Bethany (W.Va.) ....Oct. 12
Waynesburg ■ ....Oct. 19
Thiel ....Oct. 26
Mt. St. Joseph ■ ....Nov. 2
Alfred ....Nov. 9
Defiance ....Nov. 16

1995 RESULTS (8-0-0)

31 Buffalo St. 14
48 Grove City 0
51 Bethany (W.Va.) 0
58 Waynesburg 6
49 Thiel 8
42 Defiance 0
14 Cortland St. 7
25 Wesley 10
318 **45**

III Championship

35 Emory & Henry 16
48 Lycoming 0
15 Rowan 28

Nickname: Presidents.
Stadium: College Field (1958), 5,000 capacity. Natural turf.
Colors: Red & Black.
Conference: Presidents' Athletic.
SID: Susan Isola, 412-223-6074.
AD: John Luckhardt.

WASH. & LEE

Lexington, VA 24450 III

Coach: Frank Miriello, East Stroudsburg '67
Record: 1 Year, 5-3-1

1996 SCHEDULE

Ursinus ■ ....Sept. 14
Guilford ....Sept. 21
Centre ....Sept. 28
Randolph-Macon ■ ....Oct. 5
Davidson ....Oct. 12
Hampden-Sydney ■ ....Oct. 19
Sewanee ■ ....Oct. 26
Bridgewater (Va.) ....Nov. 2
Emory & Henry ■ ....Nov. 9
Swarthmore ....Nov. 16

1995 RESULTS (5-3-1)

22 Emory & Henry 35
7 Centre 7
21 Randolph-Macon 24
19 Davidson 13
21 Hampden-Sydney 7
36 Sewanee 21
24 Bridgewater (Va.) 13
13 Guilford 9
0 Swarthmore 2
163 **131**

Nickname: Generals.
Stadium: Wilson Field (1930), 7,000 capacity. Natural turf.
Colors: Royal Blue & White.
Conference: Old Dominion Athletic.
SID: Brian Logue, 540-463-8676.
AD: Mike Walsh.

WASHINGTON ST.

Pullman, WA 99164 ....I-A

Coach: Mike Price, Puget Sound '69
Record: 15 Years, 84-85-0

1996 SCHEDULE

Colorado ....Aug. 31
Temple ....Sept. 7
Oregon ■ ....Sept. 21
San Jose St. ■ ....Sept. 28
Arizona ....*Oct. 5
Oregon St. ....Oct. 12
California ■ ....Oct. 19
Southern Cal ■ ....Oct. 26
UCLA ....Nov. 9
Stanford ....Nov. 16
Washington ■ ....Nov. 23

1995 RESULTS (3-8-0)

13 Pittsburgh 17
38 Montana 21
24 UCLA 15
21 Nebraska 35
40 Oregon St. 14
14 Southern Cal 26
7 Oregon 26
14 Arizona 24
11 California 27
24 Stanford 36
30 Washington 33
236 **274**

Nickname: Cougars.
Stadium: Clarence D. Martin (1972), 37,600 capacity. Artificial turf.
Colors: Crimson & Gray.
Conference: Pacific-10.
SID: Rod Commons, 509-335-2684.
AD: Rick Dickson.

WAYNE ST. (MICH.)

Detroit, MI 48202 II

Coach: Dominic Livedoti, Olivet '65
Record: 6 Years, 24-29-3

1996 SCHEDULE

Bloomsburg ....Aug. 31
Saginaw Valley ■ ....Sept. 7
Indianapolis ....Sept. 14
St. Francis (Ill.) ■ ....Sept. 21
Grand Valley St. ....Sept. 28
Ferris St. ■ ....Oct. 5
Ashland ....Oct. 12
Hillsdale ■ ....Oct. 19
Michigan Tech ■ ....Oct. 26
Northern Mich. ....Nov. 2
Northwood ....Nov. 9

1995 RESULTS (3-8-0)

0 Carson-Newman 21
35 St. Joseph's (Ind.) 9
14 Saginaw Valley 44
7 Indianapolis 21
9 St. Francis (Ill.) 8
10 Grand Valley St. 42
30 Ferris St. 39
17 Ashland 24
13 Hillsdale 45
3 Michigan Tech 43
28 Northern Mich. 15
166 **311**

Nickname: Tartars.
Stadium: Wayne State (1968), 6,000 capacity. Natural turf.
Colors: Green & Gold.
Conference: Midwest Intercollegiate.
SID: Richard Thompson Jr., 313-577-7542.
AD: Bob Brennan.

WAYNE ST. (NEB.)

Wayne, NE 68787 II

Coach: Dennis Wagner, Utah '80
Record: 7 Years, 41-30-1

1996 SCHEDULE

Emporia St. ....*Aug. 31
South Dak. ....Sept. 7
Morningside ....*Sept. 14
Moorhead St. ■ ....Sept. 21
Minn.-Duluth ....Sept. 28
Southwest St. ■ ....Oct. 12
Northern St. ■ ....Oct. 19
Neb.-Kearney ■ ....Oct. 26
Western N.M. ....Nov. 2
Drake ....Nov. 9

1995 RESULTS (6-4-0)

37 Neb.-Omaha 30
31 Morningside 27
35 Northern St. 14
21 Winona St. 36
15 Minn.-Duluth 22
14 Neb.-Kearney 24
33 Southwest St. 28
28 Moorhead St. 51
55 Bemidji St. 14
68 Iowa Wesleyan 0
337 **246**

Nickname: Wildcats.
Stadium: Memorial (1931), 3,500 capacity. Natural turf.
Colors: Black & Gold.
Conference: Division II Independents.
SID: Jerry Rashid, 403-375-7326.
AD: Pete Chapman.

WAYNESBURG

Waynesburg, PA 15370 III

Coach: Dan Baranik, Shippensburg '84
Record: 2 Years, 9-9-0

1996 SCHEDULE

St. Francis (Pa.) .... Sept. 7
Alfred .... Sept. 14
Bethany (W.Va.) ■ .... Sept. 28
Thiel .... Oct. 5
Grove City ■ .... Oct. 12
Wash. & Jeff. .... Oct. 19
Frostburg St. ■ .... Oct. 26
Hartwick ■ .... Nov. 2
Juniata ■ .... Nov. 9

1995 RESULTS (5-4-0)

6 Robert Morris 41
37 Walsh 15
31 Thiel 26
36 Grove City 7
6 Wash. & Jeff. 58
10 Gannon 14
16 Bethany (W.Va.) 17
32 Kenyon 3
20 Frostburg St. 14
194 **195**

Nickname: Yellow Jackets.
Stadium: College Field (1904), 1,300 capacity. Natural turf.
Colors: Orange & Black.
Conference: Presidents' Athletic.
SID: David Walkosky, 412-852-3334.
AD: Rudy Marisa.

WEBER ST.

Ogden, UT 84408 .... I-AA

Coach: Dave Arslanian, Weber St. '72
Record: 7 Years, 40-38-0

1996 SCHEDULE

Eastern Wash. ■ .... *Sept. 7
Western St. ■ .... *Sept. 14
Cal Poly SLO .... *Sept. 21
Toledo .... *Sept. 28
Northern Ariz. .... Oct. 5
Cal St. Northridge ■ .... Oct. 12
Portland St. .... *Oct. 19
Montana St. ■ .... Nov. 2
Cal St. Sacramento .... *Nov. 9
Montana ■ .... Nov. 16
Idaho St. .... Nov. 23

1995 RESULTS (6-5-0)

21 Western Mich. 28
31 Central Mich. 39
49 St. Mary's (Cal.) 14
53 Cal Poly SLO 43
40 Eastern Wash. 30
22 Montana 49
14 Boise St. 40
14 Montana St. 7
25 Idaho 19
20 Northern Ariz. 14
25 Idaho St. 35
314 **318**

Nickname: Wildcats.
Stadium: Wildcat (1966), 17,500 capacity. Natural turf.
Colors: Royal Purple & White.
Conference: Big Sky.
SID: Brad Larsen, 801-626-6010.
AD: Dutch Belnap.

WESLEY

Dover, DE 19901 III

Coach: Mike Drass, Mansfield '83
Record: 3 Years, 23-8-1

1996 SCHEDULE

Ferrum ■ .... Sept. 6
Hampden-Sydney ■ .... Sept. 21
Trenton St. ■ .... Sept. 28
Clinch Valley .... Oct. 5
Frostburg St. ■ .... Oct. 12
Newport News App. ■ .... Oct. 19
Salisbury St. .... Oct. 26
Chowan .... Nov. 2
Jersey City St. .... Nov. 16

1995 RESULTS (8-2-0)

55 Framingham St. 0
47 Hampden-Sydney 12
16 Trenton St. 3
28 Jersey City St. 14
35 Wm. Paterson 7
62 Curry 0
21 Salisbury St. 24
47 Chowan 6
52 Alfred 28
10 Wash. & Jeff. 25
373 **119**

ECAC III Playoff

7 Trenton St. 10

Nickname: Wolverines.
Stadium: Wolverine (1989), 2,000 capacity. Natural turf.
Colors: Blue & White.
Conference: Division III Independents.
SID: Jason Bowen, 302-736-2557.
AD: Steve Clark.

WESLEYAN (CONN.)

Middletown, CT 06459 III

Coach: Frank Hauser, Wesleyan (Conn.) '79
Record: 4 Years, 15-17-0

1996 SCHEDULE

Tufts .... Sept. 21
Hamilton ■ .... Sept. 28
Colby .... Oct. 5
Bates .... Oct. 12
Amherst ■ .... Oct. 19
Bowdoin ■ .... Oct. 26
Williams .... Nov. 2
Trinity (Conn.) ■ .... Nov. 9

1995 RESULTS (3-5-0)

28 Middlebury 20
3 Hamilton 34
3 Colby 24
23 Bates 16
0 Amherst 13
30 Bowdoin 22
0 Williams 42
0 Trinity (Conn.) 22
87 **193**

Nickname: Cardinals.
Stadium: Andrus Field (1881), 8,000 capacity. Natural turf.
Colors: Red & Black.
Conference: NESCAC.
SID: Brian Katten, 203-685-2887.
AD: John Biddiscombe.

WEST ALA.

Livingston, AL 35470 II

Coach: Todd Stroud, Florida St. '85
Record: 2 Years, 3-18-0

1996 SCHEDULE

Arkansas Tech ■ .... *Sept. 7
Lane ■ .... Sept. 14
Harding .... Sept. 21
Ark.-Monticello .... Sept. 28
Henderson St. .... Oct. 5
Valdosta St. ■ .... Oct. 19
Mississippi Col. .... Oct. 26
West Ga. ■ .... Nov. 2
Delta St. .... Nov. 9
North Ala. ■ .... Nov. 16

1995 RESULTS (2-9-0)

15 Harding 14
28 Union (Ky.) 7
12 Lane 20
7 Mississippi Col. 30
43 Henderson St. 48
20 Valdosta St. 27
15 Arkansas Tech 53
10 Central Ark. 34
7 West Ga. 31
3 Delta St. 41
10 North Ala. 42
170 **347**

Nickname: Tigers.
Stadium: Tiger (1952), 8,500 capacity. Natural turf.
Colors: Red & White.
Conference: Gulf South.
SID: Fred Sington, 205-652-3596.
AD: Dee Outlaw.

WEST CHESTER

West Chester, PA 19383 II

Coach: Rick Daniels, West Chester '75
Record: 7 Years, 47-29-1

1996 SCHEDULE

Cheyney .... Aug. 31
New Haven .... Sept. 7
Virginia St. .... Sept. 14
Delaware .... Sept. 21
Slippery Rock ■ .... Oct. 5
East Stroudsburg ■ .... Oct. 12
Mansfield ■ .... Oct. 26
Millersville .... *Nov. 2
Bloomsburg ■ .... Nov. 9
Kutztown .... Nov. 16

1995 RESULTS (4-6-1)

56 Cheyney 7
21 Delaware 49
25 Shippensburg 14
7 Indiana (Pa.) 50
26 East Stroudsburg 34
36 New Haven 36
24 Mansfield 8
12 Millersville 31
18 Bloomsburg 23
12 Kutztown 21
25 Calif. (Pa.) 24
262 **297**

Nickname: Golden Rams.
Stadium: Farrell (1970), 7,500 capacity. Natural turf.
Colors: Purple & Gold.
Conference: Pennsylvania State Athletic.
SID: Tom Di Camillo, 610-436-3316.
AD: Edward M. Matejkovic.

WEST GA.

Carrollton, GA 30118 II

Coach: Charlie Fisher, Springfield '81
Record: 3 Years, 19-12-0

1996 SCHEDULE

Newberry .... *Aug. 31
Jacksonville St. .... *Sept. 7
Ark.-Monticello ■ .... *Sept. 14
Elon ■ .... *Sept. 21
Henderson St. ■ .... *Sept. 28
Tusculum ■ .... Oct. 5
Central Ark. .... Oct. 12
Delta St. ■ .... Oct. 26
West Ala. .... Nov. 2
North Ala. ■ .... *Nov. 7
Valdosta St. .... Nov. 16

1995 RESULTS (8-2-0)

35 Elon 16
22 Jacksonville St. 25
28 Southern Ark. 0
20 Delta St. 14
19 North Ala. 34
30 Mississippi Col. 15
40 Ark.-Monticello 7
31 West Ala. 7
16 Henderson St. 10
44 Valdosta St. 6
285 **134**

II Championship
26 Carson-Newman 37

Nickname: Braves.
Stadium: Grisham (1966), 6,500 capacity. Natural turf.
Colors: Red & Blue.
Conference: Gulf South.
SID: Mitch Gray, 770-836-6542.
AD: Ed Murphy.

WEST LIBERTY ST.

West Liberty, WV 26074 II

Coach: Bob Eaton, Glenville St. '78
Record: 6 Years, 30-29-1

1996 SCHEDULE

Westminster (Pa.) ....Sept. 7
Geneva ■ ....Sept. 14
Shepherd ■ ....Sept. 28
Glenville St. ■ ....*Oct. 5
West Va. St. ....Oct. 12
Concord (W.Va.) ....Oct. 19
West Va. Wesleyan ■ ....Oct. 26
Fairmont St. ....Nov. 2
West Va. Tech ....Nov. 9
St. Joseph's (Ind.) ■ ....Nov. 16

1995 RESULTS (7-3-0)

35 Bowie St. 0
13 Geneva 30
10 Newberry 7
24 Shepherd 19
7 Glenville St. 37
53 West Va. St. 14
27 Concord (W.Va.) 0
31 West Va. Wesleyan 33
35 Fairmont St. 28
35 West Va. Tech 0
270 **168**

Nickname: Hilltoppers.
Stadium: Russek Field (1960), 4,000 capacity. Natural turf.
Colors: Gold & Black.
Conference: West Virginia Intercollegiate Athletic.
SID: Lynn Ullom, 304-336-8320.
AD: James Watson.

WEST TEX. A&M

Canyon, TX 79016 II

Coach: Morris Stone, Midwestern St. '87
Record: 2 Years, 14-8-0

1996 SCHEDULE

Adams St. ■ ....*Sept. 7
Midwestern St. ....*Sept. 14
Southwestern Okla. ■ ....*Sept. 21
Angelo St. ■ ....*Oct. 5
Tarleton St. ....*Oct. 12
East Tex. St. ■ ....*Oct. 19
Tex. A&M-Kingsville ....*Oct. 26
Central Okla. ....Nov. 2
Eastern N.M. ■ ....Nov. 9
Abilene Christian ....Nov. 16

1995 RESULTS (5-6-0)

35 Western N.M. 23
44 Adams St. 26
44 Fort Lewis 7
38 Southwestern Okla. 21
14 Angelo St. 54
46 Tarleton St. 23
7 East Tex. St. 51
17 Tex. A&M-Kingsville 55
6 Central Okla. 43
7 Eastern N.M. 10
14 Abilene Christian 21
272 **334**

Nickname: Buffaloes.
Stadium: Kimbrough (1959), 20,000 capacity. Natural turf.
Colors: Maroon & White.
Conference: Division II Independents.
SID: Bill Kauffman, 806-656-2687.
AD: Ed Harris.

WEST VA.

Morgantown, WV 26505 ....I-A

Coach: Don Nehlen, Bowling Green '58
Record: 25 Years, 168-103-8

1996 SCHEDULE

Pittsburgh ....*Aug. 31
Western Mich. ■ ....Sept. 7
East Caro. ■ ....Sept. 14
Purdue ....*Sept. 21
Maryland ■ ....Sept. 28
Boston College ■ ....Oct. 5
Temple ....Oct. 19
Miami (Fla.) ■ ....Oct. 26
Syracuse ■ ....Nov. 2
Rutgers ....Nov. 9
Virginia Tech ....Nov. 23

1995 RESULTS (5-6-0)

24 Purdue 26
24 Temple 13
17 Maryland 31
45 Kent 6
20 East Caro. 23
31 Boston College 19
0 Syracuse 22
0 Virginia Tech 27
59 Rutgers 26
12 Miami (Fla.) 17
21 Pittsburgh 0
253 **210**

Nickname: Mountaineers.
Stadium: Mountaineer Field (1980), 63,500 capacity. Artificial turf.
Colors: Old Gold & Blue.
Conference: Big East.
SID: Shelly Poe, 304-293-2821.
AD: Ed Pastilong.

WEST VA. TECH

Montgomery, WV 25136 II

Coach: Paul Price, West Va. Wesleyan '83
(First year as head coach)

1996 SCHEDULE

St. Joseph's (Ind.) ....Sept. 7
Catawba ■ ....Sept. 14
Tusculum ....Sept. 21
West Va. Wesleyan ....Sept. 28
Concord (W.Va.) ■ ....Oct. 5
Fairmont St. ....Oct. 12
Shepherd ■ ....Oct. 19
West Va. St. ■ ....*Oct. 24
Glenville St. ....Nov. 2
West Liberty St. ■ ....Nov. 9

1995 RESULTS (0-10-0)

6 Liberty 76
13 Ferrum 17
7 West Va. Wesleyan 35
12 Concord (W.Va.) 42
27 Fairmont St. 43
6 Shepherd 45
20 West Va. St. 23
0 Glenville St. 56
0 West Liberty St. 35
9 Geneva 13
100 **385**

Nickname: Golden Bears.
Stadium: Martin, 3,000 capacity. Artificial turf.
Colors: Gold & Blue.
Conference: West Virginia Intercollegiate Athletic.
SID: Frank Costa, 304-442-3085.
AD: To be named.

WEST VA. WESLEYAN

Buckhannon, WV 26201 II

Coach: Bill Struble, West Va. Wesleyan '76
Record: 13 Years, 62-67-0

1996 SCHEDULE

Clarion ■ ....Sept. 7
Slippery Rock ■ ....Sept. 14
Calif. (Pa.) ....*Sept. 21
West Va. Tech ■ ....Sept. 28
Shepherd ....Oct. 5
Glenville St. ■ ....Oct. 12
West Va. St. ....Oct. 19
West Liberty St. ....Oct. 26
Concord (W.Va.) ■ ....Nov. 2
Fairmont St. ■ ....Nov. 9

1995 RESULTS (8-2-0)

23 Clarion 24
20 Slippery Rock 16
16 Kutztown 14
35 West Va. Tech 7
33 Shepherd 7
17 Glenville St. 14
42 West Va. St. 6
33 West Liberty St. 31
36 Concord (W.Va.) 14
24 Fairmont St. 48
279 **181**

Nickname: Bobcats.
Stadium: Cebe Ross Field (1957), 4,000 capacity. Natural turf.
Colors: Orange & Black.
Conference: West Virginia Intercollegiate Athletic.
SID: Peter Galarneau Jr., 304-473-8102.
AD: George Klebez.

WESTERN CARO.

Cullowhee, NC 28723 ....I-AA

Coach: Steve Hodgin, North Caro. '72
Record: 6 Years, 27-38-0

1996 SCHEDULE

Liberty ....*Sept. 7
Wofford ■ ....Sept. 14
Citadel ....*Sept. 21
East Tenn. St. ■ ....*Sept. 28
Furman ....Oct. 5
Ga. Southern ■ ....Oct. 12
Marshall ....*Oct. 19
Tenn.-Chatt. ■ ....Oct. 26
Va. Military ....Nov. 2
Elon ■ ....Nov. 9
Appalachian St. ■ ....Nov. 16

1995 RESULTS (3-7-0)

9 Clemson 55
36 Elon 14
31 Citadel 14
21 Furman 31
0 Ga. Southern 42
3 Marshall 42
14 Tenn.-Chatt. 35
31 Va. Military 14
3 Appalachian St. 28
10 East Tenn. St. 36
158 **311**

Nickname: Catamounts.
Stadium: E. J. Whitmire (1974), 12,000 capacity. Artificial turf.
Colors: Purple & Gold.
Conference: Southern.
SID: Steve White, 704-227-7171.
AD: Larry L. Travis.

WESTERN CONN. ST.

Danbury, CT 06810 III

Coach: John Cervino, West Va. Wesleyan '82
Record: 4 Years, 13-26-1

1996 SCHEDULE

Springfield ....*Sept. 6
Bri'water (Mass.) ....Sept. 14
Jersey City St. ■ ....*Sept. 21
Wm. Paterson ....*Sept. 27
Plymouth St. ■ ....Oct. 5
Coast Guard ....Oct. 19
Pace ....Oct. 26

Worcester Tech ■ ....Nov. 2
Merchant Marine ■ ....Nov. 9
Norwich ■ ....Nov. 16

1995 RESULTS (6-3-1)

13 Kean 13
0 St. John Fisher 31
7 Brockport St. 6
26 Wm. Paterson 13
6 Plymouth St. 36
28 Coast Guard 7
62 Mass.-Lowell 0
21 Stony Brook 13
27 Merchant Marine 17
13 Norwich 14
203 **150**

Nickname: Colonials.
Stadium: Midtown Campus Field, 3,500 capacity. Artificial turf.
Colors: Blue & White.
Conference: Freedom Football.
SID: Scott Ames, 203-837-9014.
AD: Ed Farrington.

WESTERN ILL.

Macomb, IL 61455 ....I-AA

Coach: Randy Ball, Truman St. '73
Record: 6 Years, 33-33-1

1996 SCHEDULE

Northwestern Okla. ■ ....*Aug. 29
Northern Ill. ....*Sept. 7
Alcorn St. ■ ....Sept. 14
Hofstra ....Sept. 21
Indiana St. ■ ....Oct. 5
Eastern Ill. ....Oct. 12
Southern Ill. ....Oct. 19
Cal Poly SLO ■ ....Oct. 26
Southwest Mo. St. ....Nov. 2
Illinois St. ■ ....Nov. 9
Northern Iowa ....*Nov. 16

1995 RESULTS (4-7-0)

86 Iowa Wesleyan 0
7 Ball St. 20
41 Delaware St. 14
13 Indiana St. 30
7 Northern Iowa 38
25 Illinois St. 22
7 Southwest Mo. St. 13
19 Southern Ill. 7
17 Eastern Ill. 20
27 Jacksonville St. 32
18 Murray St. 56
267 **252**

Nickname: Leathernecks.
Stadium: Hanson Field (1948), 15,000 capacity. Natural turf.
Colors: Purple & Gold.
Conference: Gateway.
SID: Greg Seiler, 309-298-1133.
AD: Helen Smiley.

WESTERN KY.

Bowling Green, KY 42101 ....I-AA

Coach: Jack Harbaugh, Bowling Green '61
Record: 12 Years, 55-71-3

1996 SCHEDULE

Ky. Wesleyan ■ ....*Aug. 29
Murray St. ....*Sept. 7
Eastern Ky. ■ ....*Sept. 14
Austin Peay ....*Sept. 21
Marshall ....*Sept. 28
Ala.-Birmingham ....*Oct. 5
Jacksonville St. ....Oct. 12
Liberty ■ ....*Oct. 19
Indiana St. ■ ....Oct. 26
Southern Ill. ■ ....Nov. 2
Morehead St. ....Nov. 9

1995 RESULTS (2-8-0)

14 Murray St. 35
14 Eastern Ky. 38
34 Austin Peay 38
32 Ala.-Birmingham 18
39 Troy St. 56
17 Jacksonville St. 15
9 Eastern Ill. 35
6 Indiana St. 27
28 Southern Ill. 30
36 Liberty 49
229 **341**

Nickname: Hilltoppers.
Stadium: L.T. Smith (1968), 17,500 capacity. Natural turf.
Colors: Red & White.
Conference: I-AA Independents.
SID: Paul Just, 502-745-4298.
AD: Lewis Mills.

WESTERN MD.

Westminster, MD 21157 III

Coach: Tim Keating, Bethany (W.Va.) '75
Record: 8 Years, 39-35-3

1996 SCHEDULE

Bridgewater (Va.) ■ ....Sept. 7
Juniata ....Sept. 14
Gettysburg ■ ....Sept. 21
Ursinus ....Sept. 28
Muhlenberg ■ ....Oct. 5
Dickinson ■ ....Oct. 19
Frank. & Marsh. ....Oct. 26
Lebanon Valley ■ ....Nov. 2
Swarthmore ■ ....Nov. 9
Johns Hopkins ....Nov. 16

1995 RESULTS (5-3-2)

14 Susquehanna 21
36 Juniata 10
21 Gettysburg 17
27 Ursinus 7
13 Muhlenberg 13
24 Dickinson 38
7 Frank. & Marsh. 24
27 Lebanon Valley 13
39 Swarthmore 6
14 Johns Hopkins 14
222 **163**

Nickname: Green Terror.
Stadium: Scott S. Bair (1981), 4,000 capacity. Natural turf.
Colors: Green & Gold.
Conference: Centennial.
SID: Scott E. Deitch, 410-857-2291.
AD: J. Richard Carpenter.

WESTERN MICH.

Kalamazoo, MI 49008 ....I-A

Coach: Al Molde, Gust. Adolphus '66
Record: 25 Years, 166-95-8

1996 SCHEDULE

Eastern Ill. ■ ....*Aug. 29
West Va. ....Sept. 7
Eastern Mich. ■ ....*Sept. 14
Central Mich. ....Sept. 21
Akron ■ ....*Sept. 28
Ball St. ■ ....Oct. 5
Wyoming ....Oct. 12
Toledo ....Oct. 26
Ohio ■ ....Nov. 2
Bowling Green ....Nov. 9
Kent ■ ....Nov. 16

1995 RESULTS (7-4-0)

28 Weber St. 21
10 Indiana 24
21 Toledo 31
0 Ball St. 10
52 Kent 6
7 Akron 3
34 Ohio 17
13 Auburn 34
17 Bowling Green 0
23 Eastern Mich. 13
48 Central Mich. 31
253 **190**

Nickname: Broncos.
Stadium: Waldo (1939), 30,200 capacity. Natural turf.
Colors: Brown & Gold.
Conference: Mid-American.
SID: John Beatty, 616-387-4138.
AD: Jim Weaver.

WESTERN NEW ENG.

Springfield, MA 01119 III

Coach: Gerry Martin, Connecticut '80
Record: 5 Years, 11-32-1

1996 SCHEDULE

Merrimack ....Sept. 14
Sacred Heart ■ ....Sept. 21
MIT ....Sept. 28
Mass.-Lowell ■ ....Oct. 5
Stonehill ■ ....Oct. 12
St. John Fisher ■ ....Oct. 19
Nichols ■ ....Nov. 2
Curry ....Nov. 9
Salve Regina ....Nov. 16

1995 RESULTS (2-6-0)

3 Sacred Heart 42
14 Assumption 20
19 Stonehill 54
24 MIT 42
0 Bentley 24
6 Nichols 0
6 Salve Regina 28
36 Curry 30
108 **240**

Nickname: Golden Bears.
Stadium: WNEC, 1,500 capacity. Natural turf.
Colors: Blue & Gold.
Conference: Eastern Football.
SID: Gene Gumbs, 413-782-1227.
AD: Eric Geldart.

WESTERN N.M.

Silver City, NM 88061 II

Coach: Land Jacobsen, Central Okla. '76
(First year as head coach)

1996 SCHEDULE

Northern Ariz. ....*Aug. 29
Angelo St. ....*Sept. 7
Adams St. ....Sept. 14
Eastern N.M. ....*Sept. 21
Midwestern St. ....Oct. 12
UC Davis ....*Oct. 19
Okla. Panhandle St. ■ ....Oct. 26
Wayne St. (Neb.) ■ ....Nov. 2
N.M. Highlands ■ ....Nov. 16

1995 RESULTS (4-5-0)

23 West Tex. A&M 35
22 N.M. Highlands 38
48 Adams St. 27
3 Eastern N.M. 9
54 Midwestern St. 24
27 Cal St. Northridge 8
21 Portland St. 55
28 Neb.-Kearney 44
34 Okla. Panhandle St. 23
260 **263**

Nickname: Mustangs.
Stadium: Silver Sports Complex (1969), 2,000 capacity. Natural turf.
Colors: Old Gold & Purple.
Conference: Division II Independents.
SID: Jason Reid, 505-538-6220.
AD: Dick Drangmeister.

WESTERN ST.

Gunnison, CO 81231 II

Coach: Carl Iverson, Whitman '62
Record: 13 Years, 85-42-3

1996 SCHEDULE

Northern Colo. ....Sept. 7
Weber St. ....*Sept. 14

Southern Utah ....*Sept. 21
N.M. Highlands ■ ....Sept. 28
Chadron St. ....Oct. 5
Adams St. ....Oct. 12
Fort Hays St. ■ ....Oct. 19
Colorado Mines ■ ....Oct. 26
Neb.-Kearney ....Nov. 2
Fort Lewis ....Nov. 9
Mesa St. ■ ....Nov. 16

1995 RESULTS (7-2-1)

19 Northern Colo. 29
3 UC Davis 48
36 Southern Utah 8
42 Adams St. 21
26 Fort Lewis 8
55 Colorado Mines 0
56 Mesa St. 9
28 Chadron St. 21
45 N.M. Highlands 20
27 Fort Hays St. 27
337 **191**

Nickname: Mountaineers.
Stadium: Mountaineer Bowl (1950), 2,400 capacity. Natural turf.
Colors: Crimson & Slate.
Conference: Rocky Mountain Athletic.
SID: J.W. Campbell, 303-943-2831.
AD: Greg Waggoner.

WESTFIELD ST.

Westfield, MA 01085 III

Coach: Steve Marino, Westfield St. '71
Record: 6 Years, 28-29-1

1996 SCHEDULE

Worcester Tech ....*Sept. 7
Mass.-Boston ....Sept. 21
Fitchburg St. ■ ....*Sept. 27
Framingham St. ....Oct. 5
Coast Guard ....Oct. 12
Bri'water (Mass.) ■ ....Oct. 19
Worcester St. ....Oct. 26
Mass. Maritime ■ ....*Nov. 1
Mass.-Dartmouth ....Nov. 9
Maine Maritime ■ ....Nov. 16

1995 RESULTS (3-6-0)

35 Mass.-Boston 0
41 Fitchburg St. 17
7 Framingham St. 10
0 Coast Guard 12
3 Bri'water (Mass.) 20
6 Worcester St. 17
6 Mass. Maritime 37
12 Mass.-Dartmouth 0
7 Maine Maritime 14
117 **127**

Nickname: Owls.
Stadium: Alumni Field (1982), 4,800 capacity. Artificial turf.
Colors: Royal Blue & White.
Conference: New England.
SID: Mickey Curtis, 413-572-5433.
AD: Ken Magarian.

WHEATON (ILL.)

Wheaton, IL 60187 III

Coach: Mike Swider, Wheaton (Ill.) '77
(First year as head coach)

1996 SCHEDULE

Kalamazoo ■ ....Sept. 14
Aurora ■ ....Sept. 21
Augustana (Ill.) ....Oct. 5
Elmhurst ■ ....Oct. 12
Millikin ....Oct. 19
Ill. Wesleyan ■ ....Oct. 26
Carthage ....Nov. 2
North Park ....Nov. 9
North Central ■ ....Nov. 16

1995 RESULTS (9-0-0)

48 Hope 7
28 Aurora 21
47 Carthage 7
42 Ill. Wesleyan 28
42 Millikin 21
44 North Park 10
34 North Central 16
35 Augustana (Ill.) 27
42 Elmhurst 0
362 **137**

III Championship

63 Wittenberg 14
14 Mount Union 40

Nickname: Crusaders.
Stadium: McCully Field (1956), 7,000 capacity. Natural turf.
Colors: Orange & Blue.
Conference: College Conf. of Illinois & Wisconsin.
SID: Steve Schwepker, 708-752-5747.
AD: Tony Ladd.

WHITTIER

Whittier, CA 90608 III

Coach: To be named

1996 SCHEDULE

Redlands ■ ....*Sept. 14
Pomona-Pitzer ....*Sept. 21
Azusa Pacific ■ ....*Sept. 28
La Verne ■ ....*Oct. 12
Claremont-M-S ....Oct. 19
Menlo ....Oct. 26
San Diego ....Nov. 2
Cal Lutheran ■ ....*Nov. 9
Occidental ....*Nov. 16

1995 RESULTS (1-8-0)

14 Azusa Pacific 42
10 Redlands 31
35 Menlo 7
10 Pomona-Pitzer 21
7 La Verne 59
0 Cal Lutheran 42
31 Claremont-M-S 35
0 Occidental 10
7 Chapman 63
114 **310**

Nickname: Poets.
Stadium: Memorial, 7,000 capacity. Natural turf.
Colors: Purple & Gold.
Conference: Southern California Intercollegiate Athletic.
SID: Rock Carter, 310-907-4271.
AD: Dave Jacobs.

WIDENER

Chester, PA 19013 III

Coach: Bill Cubit, Delaware '75
Record: 4 Years, 27-15-1

1996 SCHEDULE

Wilkes ....Sept. 14
FDU-Madison ■ ....Sept. 21
Lebanon Valley ■ ....Sept. 28
Juniata ....Oct. 5
Moravian ....Oct. 12
Albright ■ ....Oct. 19
Lycoming ■ ....Oct. 26
King's (Pa.) ....Nov. 2
Delaware Valley ....Nov. 9
Susquehanna ■ ....Nov. 16

1995 RESULTS (8-2-0)

42 Wilkes 35
36 FDU-Madison 38
66 Lebanon Valley 8
56 Juniata 21
31 Moravian 10
31 Albright 17
15 Lycoming 16
50 King's (Pa.) 14
49 Delaware Valley 14
28 Susquehanna 26
404 **199**

III Championship

27 Lycoming 31

Nickname: Pioneers.
Stadium: Leslie Quick Jr. (1994), 4,000 capacity. Natural turf.
Colors: Widener Blue & Gold.
Conference: Middle Atlantic.
SID: Susan Fumagalli, 610-499-4436.
AD: Bill Cubit.

WILKES

Wilkes-Barre, PA 18766 III

Coach: Frank Sheptock, Bloomsburg '86
(First year as head coach)

1996 SCHEDULE

Widener ■ ....Sept. 14
Susquehanna ■ ....Sept. 21
FDU-Madison ....*Sept. 27
Albright ....Oct. 5
Juniata ■ ....Oct. 12
King's (Pa.) ....Oct. 19
Montclair St. ■ ....Oct. 26
Delaware Valley ■ ....Nov. 2
Moravian ■ ....Nov. 9
Lycoming ....Nov. 16

1995 RESULTS (5-5-0)

35 Widener 42
3 Susquehanna 24
30 FDU-Madison 15
7 Albright 10
29 Juniata 28
29 King's (Pa.) 15
17 Wm. Paterson 0
10 Delaware Valley 9
9 Moravian 34
9 Lycoming 28
178 **205**

Nickname: Colonels.
Stadium: Ralston Field (1965), 4,000 capacity. Natural turf.
Colors: Navy & Gold.
Conference: Middle Atlantic.
SID: Thomas McGuire, 717-831-4777.
AD: Phil Wingert.

WILLIAM & MARY

Williamsburg, VA 23185 ....I-AA

Coach: Jimmye Laycock, William & Mary '70
Record: 16 Years, 105-74-2

1996 SCHEDULE

Central Fla. ....*Aug. 29
Rhode Island ....Sept. 7
Va. Military ■ ....Sept. 14
Bucknell ....Sept. 21
New Hampshire ■ ....Oct. 5
James Madison ....Oct. 12
Villanova ....Oct. 19
Northeastern ■ ....Oct. 26
Delaware ■ ....Nov. 2
Massachusetts ■ ....Nov. 9
Richmond ....Nov. 16

1995 RESULTS (7-4-0)

16 Virginia 40
17 James Madison 24
32 Northeastern 0
39 New Hampshire 0
27 Va. Military 7
23 Rhode Island 14
48 Pennsylvania 34
9 Massachusetts 20
18 Villanova 15
20 Delaware 23
27 Richmond 7
276 **184**

SCHEDULES/RESULTS

Nickname: Tribe.
Stadium: Walter Zable (1935), 15,000 capacity. Natural turf.
Colors: Green, Gold & Silver.
Conference: Yankee.
SID: Jean Elliott, 804-221-3344.
AD: Terry Driscoll.

WM. PATERSON

Wayne, NJ 07470 III

Coach: Gerry Gallagher, Wm. Paterson '74
Record: 10 Years, 41-55-1

1996 SCHEDULE

LIU-C.W. Post ■ .... *Sept. 13
Trenton St. .... *Sept. 20
Western Conn. St. ■ .... *Sept. 27
Kean ■ .... *Oct. 5
Newport News App. ■ .... *Oct. 11
Montclair St. .... *Oct. 19
Cortland St. .... Oct. 26
Jersey City St. ■ .... *Nov. 1
Rowan .... Nov. 9
Springfield .... Nov. 16

1995 RESULTS (0-10-0)

6 LIU-C.W. Post 23
14 Trenton St. 17
13 Western Conn. St. 26
6 Kean 24
7 Wesley 35
15 Montclair St. 21
0 Wilkes 17
7 Jersey City St. 20
6 Rowan 41
14 Springfield 42
88 **266**

Nickname: Pioneers.
Stadium: Wightman Field, 2,000 capacity. Natural turf.
Colors: Orange & Black.
Conference: New Jersey Athletic.
SID: Joe Martinelli, 201-595-2705.
AD: Arthur Eason.

WILLIAM PENN

Oskaloosa, IA 52577 III

Coach: Bob Borkenhagen, William Penn '77
Record: 2 Years, 1-19-0

1996 SCHEDULE

MacMurray .... Sept. 7
Central Methodist ■ .... Sept. 14
Buena Vista ■ .... Sept. 21
Simpson .... Sept. 28
Central (Iowa) .... Oct. 5
Upper Iowa ■ .... Oct. 12
Dubuque ■ .... Oct. 19
Loras .... Oct. 26
Luther .... Nov. 2
Wartburg ■ .... Nov. 9

1995 RESULTS (0-10-0)

9 MacMurray 16
7 Luther 28
0 Buena Vista 49
6 Upper Iowa 26
0 Loras 61
0 Central Methodist 21
0 Wartburg 67
0 Simpson 69
0 Central (Iowa) 68
0 Dubuque 39
22 **444**

Nickname: The Statesmen.
Stadium: Community, 5,000 capacity. Natural turf.
Colors: Navy Blue & Gold.
Conference: Iowa Intercollegiate Athletic.
SID: John Eberline, 515-673-1046.
AD: Mike Laird.

WILLIAMS

Williamstown, MA 01267 III

Coach: Dick Farley, Boston U. '68
Record: 9 Years, 60-9-3

1996 SCHEDULE

Colby ■ .... Sept. 21
Trinity (Conn.) ■ .... Sept. 28
Bates .... Oct. 5
Middlebury ■ .... Oct. 12
Tufts .... Oct. 19
Hamilton .... Oct. 26
Wesleyan (Conn.) ■ .... Nov. 2
Amherst .... Nov. 9

1995 RESULTS (7-0-1)

24 Bowdoin 6
50 Trinity (Conn.) 21
35 Bates 0
35 Middlebury 3
34 Tufts 6
29 Hamilton 9
42 Wesleyan (Conn.) 0
0 Amherst 0
249 **45**

Nickname: Ephs.
Stadium: Weston Field (1875), 7,500 capacity. Natural turf.
Color: Purple.
Conference: NESCAC.
SID: Dick Quinn, 413-597-4982.
AD: Robert R. Peck.

WILMINGTON (OHIO)

Wilmington, OH 45177 III

Coach: Mike Wallace, Bowling Green '68
Record: 5 Years, 14-33-1

1996 SCHEDULE

Urbana .... Sept. 7
Wabash .... Sept. 14
Thomas More ■ .... Sept. 21
Adrian ■ .... Sept. 28
Susquehanna .... Oct. 5
St. Joseph's (Ind.) ■ .... Oct. 12
Earlham .... Oct. 19
Bluffton .... Nov. 2
Bethany (W.Va.) .... Nov. 9
Mt. St. Joseph ■ .... Nov. 16

1995 RESULTS (2-6-1)

3 Albion 43
14 Malone 34
23 Thomas More 48
34 Tiffin 34
37 Adrian 41
14 Geneva 49
33 Bluffton 34
21 Urbana 10
32 Mt. St. Joseph 14
211 **307**

Nickname: Quakers.
Stadium: Williams (1983), 3,250 capacity. Natural turf.
Colors: Green & White.
Conference: Division III Independents.
SID: Brian Neal, 513-382-6661.
AD: Terry Rupert.

WINGATE

Wingate, NC 28174 II

Coach: Doug Malone, Carson-Newman '82
Record: 2 Years, 7-14-0

1996 SCHEDULE

Union (Ky.) ■ .... *Sept. 5
Tusculum .... Sept. 14
Newberry ■ .... *Sept. 21
Mars Hill ■ .... Sept. 28
Gardner-Webb .... Oct. 5
Carson-Newman .... Oct. 12
Lenoir-Rhyne ■ .... Oct. 19
Presbyterian .... Nov. 2
Catawba ■ .... Nov. 9
Elon [Rockingham, N.C.] .... Nov. 16

1995 RESULTS (4-7-0)

33 Johnson Smith 12
27 Newberry 21
35 Shepherd 21
20 Mars Hill 28
10 Gardner-Webb 14
25 Carson-Newman 24
12 Lenoir-Rhyne 13
7 Youngstown St. 56
16 Presbyterian 27
32 Catawba 42
22 Elon 28
239 **286**

Nickname: Bulldogs.
Stadium: Walter Bickett, 5,000 capacity. Natural turf.
Colors: Navy Blue & Old Gold.
Conference: South Atlantic.
SID: David Sherwood, 704-233-8186.
AD: Beth Lawrence.

WINONA ST.

Winona, MN 55987 II

Coach: Tom Sawyer, Winona St. '83
(First year as head coach)

1996 SCHEDULE

Wis.-River Falls ■ .... *Sept. 7
Wis.-La Crosse .... Sept. 14
Wis.-Eau Claire .... *Sept. 21
Minn.-Morris ■ .... Sept. 28
Northern St. .... Oct. 5
Bemidji St. ■ .... Oct. 12
Minn.-Duluth .... Oct. 19
Southwest St. ■ .... Oct. 26
Moorhead St. .... Nov. 2
Quincy .... Nov. 9
Wis.-Stout [Minneapolis, Minn.] .... *Nov. 17

1995 RESULTS (6-5-0)

23 Wis.-La Crosse 31
35 Wis.-Eau Claire 21
36 Wayne St. (Neb.) 21
14 Minn.-Morris 6
26 Northern St. 23
14 Bemidji St. 25
20 Minn.-Duluth 24
22 Southwest St. 13
25 Moorhead St. 46
29 Bemidji St. 15
3 Northern Iowa 48
247 **273**

Nickname: Warriors.
Stadium: Maxwell, 3,500 capacity. Natural turf.
Colors: Purple & White.
Conference: Northern Sun Intercollegiate.
SID: Michael R. Herzberg, 507-457-5576.
AD: To be named.

WINSTON-SALEM

Winston-Salem, NC 27102 II

Coach: Kermit Blount, Winston-Salem '80
Record: 3 Years, 16-13-3

1996 SCHEDULE

Fort Valley St. .... *Aug. 31
North Caro. A&T .... Sept. 7
Elizabeth City St. .... Sept. 14
Southern Ill. .... Sept. 21
Fayetteville St. ■ .... *Sept. 28
Livingstone ■ .... Oct. 5
N.C. Central .... Oct. 12
Virginia St. .... Oct. 19
Johnson Smith .... Oct. 26
Virginia Union ■ .... *Nov. 2
Norfolk St. ■ .... *Nov. 9

1995 RESULTS (4-4-2)

33 Fort Valley St. 6
21 North Caro. A&T 45

19	Elizabeth City St.	22
17	Livingstone	17
17	Fayetteville St.	17
28	Johnson Smith	12
19	N.C. Central	42
7	Bowie St.	20
43	Virginia Union	0
20	Virginia St.	14
224		**195**

Nickname: Rams.
Stadium: Bowman-Gray (1940), 18,000 capacity. Natural turf.
Colors: Scarlet & White.
Conference: Central Intercollegiate Athletic Association.
SID: Kevin Manns, 919-750-2143.
AD: Albert L. Roseboro.

WISCONSIN

Madison, WI 53711 .... I-A

Coach: Barry Alvarez, Nebraska '69
Record: 6 Years, 32-32-4

1996 SCHEDULE

Eastern Mich. ■	Sept. 7
UNLV	*Sept. 14
Stanford ■	Sept. 21
Penn St. ■	Sept. 28
Ohio St.	Oct. 12
Northwestern ■	Oct. 19
Michigan St.	Oct. 26
Purdue ■	Nov. 2
Minnesota ■	Nov. 9
Iowa	Nov. 16
Illinois	Nov. 23
Hawaii	*Nov. 30

1995 RESULTS (4-5-2)

7	Colorado	43
24	Stanford	24
42	Southern Methodist	0
17	Penn St.	9
16	Ohio St.	27
0	Northwestern	35
45	Michigan St.	14
27	Purdue	38
34	Minnesota	27
20	Iowa	33
3	Illinois	3
235		**253**

Nickname: Badgers.
Stadium: Camp Randall (1917), 76,129 capacity. Artificial turf.
Colors: Cardinal & White.
Conference: Big Ten.
SID: Steve Malchow, 608-262-1811.
AD: Pat Richter.

WIS.-EAU CLAIRE

Eau Claire, WI 54702 III

Coach: Bob Nielson, Wartburg '82
Record: 7 Years, 48-22-1

1996 SCHEDULE

Northern St.	*Sept. 7
Mayville St.	Sept. 14
Winona St. ■	*Sept. 21
Wis.-Stevens Point ■	Sept. 28
Wis.-Whitewater ■	Oct. 5
Wis.-Platteville	Oct. 12
Wis.-Stout	Oct. 19
Wis.-Oshkosh ■	Oct. 26
Wis.-La Crosse	Nov. 2
Wis.-River Falls ■	Nov. 9

1995 RESULTS (1-9-0)

13	Northern St.	21
21	Winona St.	35
67	Concordia (St. Paul)	7
0	Wis.-Stevens Point	17
14	Wis.-Whitewater	35
7	Wis.-Platteville	12
15	Wis.-Stout	20
28	Wis.-Oshkosh	29
13	Wis.-La Crosse	30
7	Wis.-River Falls	55
185		**261**

Nickname: Blugolds.
Stadium: Carson Park, 6,500 capacity. Natural turf.
Colors: Navy Blue & Old Gold.
Conference: Wisconsin State University.
SID: Tim Petermann, 715-836-4184.
AD: Mel Lewis.

WIS.-LA CROSSE

La Crosse, WI 54601 III

Coach: Roger Harring, Wis.-La Crosse '58
Record: 27 Years, 232-62-7

1996 SCHEDULE

Winona St. ■	Sept. 14
Huron ■	Sept. 21
Wis.-Oshkosh	Sept. 28
Wis.-Platteville ■	Oct. 5
Wis.-River Falls ■	Oct. 12
Wis.-Stevens Point	Oct. 19
Wis.-Stout	Oct. 26
Wis.-Eau Claire ■	Nov. 2
Wis.-Whitewater	Nov. 9
Minn.-Duluth [Minneapolis, Minn.]	*Nov. 17

1995 RESULTS (10-0-0)

34	Loras	0
31	Winona St.	23
14	Drake	7
44	Wis.-Oshkosh	0
33	Wis.-Platteville	0
14	Wis.-River Falls	13
25	Wis.-Stevens Point	15
56	Wis.-Stout	0
30	Wis.-Eau Claire	13
45	Wis.-Whitewater	14
326		**85**

III Championship

45	Concordia-M'head	7
28	Wis.-River Falls	14
20	Mount Union	17
36	Rowan	7

Nickname: Eagles.
Stadium: Memorial (1924), 4,349 capacity. Natural turf.
Colors: Maroon & Gray.
Conference: Wisconsin State University.
SID: Todd Clark, 608-785-8493.
AD: Bridget Belgiovine.

WIS.-OSHKOSH

Oshkosh, WI 54901 III

Coach: Ron Cardo, Wis.-Oshkosh '71
Record: 12 Years, 44-72-4

1996 SCHEDULE

St. Norbert ■	*Sept. 7
St. Xavier (Ill.) ■	Sept. 14
St. Ambrose	Sept. 21
Wis.-La Crosse ■	Sept. 28
Wis.-River Falls	Oct. 5
Wis.-Stevens Point	Oct. 12
Wis.-Platteville ■	Oct. 19
Wis.-Eau Claire	Oct. 26
Wis.-Whitewater ■	Nov. 2
Wis.-Stout	Nov. 9

1995 RESULTS (5-5-0)

45	St. Norbert	12
38	St. Xavier (Ill.)	20
33	St. Ambrose	23
0	Wis.-La Crosse	44
19	Wis.-River Falls	47
0	Wis.-Stevens Point	41
16	Wis.-Platteville	19
29	Wis.-Eau Claire	28
14	Wis.-Whitewater	48
28	Wis.-Stout	7
222		**289**

Nickname: Titans.
Stadium: Titan (1970), 9,680 capacity. Natural turf.
Colors: Gold, Black & White.
Conference: Wisconsin State University.
SID: Kennan Timm, 414-424-0365.
AD: Allen Ackerman.

WIS.-PLATTEVILLE

Platteville, WI 53818 III

Coach: Jim Kinder, Wisconsin '73
Record: 3 Years, 13-17-0

1996 SCHEDULE

Concordia (Wis.)	Sept. 7
Loras ■	Sept. 14
Dayton	Sept. 21
Wis.-Whitewater ■	Sept. 28
Wis.-La Crosse	Oct. 5
Wis.-Eau Claire ■	Oct. 12
Wis.-Oshkosh	Oct. 19
Wis.-River Falls ■	Oct. 26
Wis.-Stout ■	Nov. 2
Wis.-Stevens Point	Nov. 9

1995 RESULTS (5-5-0)

24	Augustana (Ill.)	21
27	St. Ambrose	10
7	Dayton	28
12	Wis.-Whitewater	17
0	Wis.-La Crosse	33
12	Wis.-Eau Claire	7
19	Wis.-Oshkosh	16
7	Wis.-River Falls	28
16	Wis.-Stout	9
10	Wis.-Stevens Point	32
134		**201**

Nickname: Pioneers.
Stadium: Ralph E. Davis Pioneer (1972), 10,000 capacity. Natural turf.
Colors: Orange & Blue.
Conference: Wisconsin State University.
SID: Becky Bohm, 608-342-1574.
AD: To be named.

WIS.-RIVER FALLS

River Falls, WI 54022 III

Coach: John O'Grady, Wis.-River Falls '79
Record: 7 Years, 44-24-3

1996 SCHEDULE

Winona St.	*Sept. 7
Southwest St. ■	Sept. 21
Wis.-Stout ■	Sept. 28
Wis.-Oshkosh ■	Oct. 5
Wis.-La Crosse	Oct. 12
Wis.-Whitewater ■	Oct. 19
Wis.-Platteville	Oct. 26
Wis.-Stevens Point ■	Nov. 2
Wis.-Eau Claire	Nov. 9
Moorhead St. [Minneapolis, Minn.]	Nov. 17

1995 RESULTS (8-2-0)

54	St. Thomas (Minn.)	28
15	Southwest St.	8
17	Slippery Rock	21
24	Wis.-Stout	7
47	Wis.-Oshkosh	19
13	Wis.-La Crosse	14
17	Wis.-Whitewater	7
28	Wis.-Platteville	7
28	Wis.-Stevens Point	18
55	Wis.-Eau Claire	7
298		**136**

III Championship

10	Central (Iowa)	7
14	Wis.-La Crosse	28

Nickname: Falcons.
Stadium: Ramer Field (1966), 4,800 capacity. Natural turf.
Colors: Red & White.
Conference: Wisconsin State University.
SID: Jim Thies, 715-425-3846.
AD: Rick Bowen.

WIS.-STEVENS POINT

Stevens Point, WI 54481 III

Coach: John Miech, Wis.-Stevens Point '75
Record: 8 Years, 55-24-2

1996 SCHEDULE

Wis.-Stout ....*Sept. 7
Bemidji St. ....*Sept. 21
Wis.-Eau Claire ....Sept. 28
Wis.-Oshkosh ■ ....Oct. 12
Wis.-La Crosse ■ ....Oct. 19
Wis.-Whitewater ....Oct. 26
Wis.-River Falls ....Nov. 2
Wis.-Platteville ■ ....Nov. 9

1995 RESULTS (8-2-0)

9 Minot St. 7
41 Iowa Wesleyan 13
37 Butler 0
17 Wis.-Eau Claire 0
52 Wis.-Stout 20
41 Wis.-Oshkosh 0
15 Wis.-La Crosse 25
31 Wis.-Whitewater 24
18 Wis.-River Falls 28
32 Wis.-Platteville 10
293 **127**

Nickname: Pointers.
Stadium: Goerke Field (1932), 4,000 capacity. Natural turf.
Colors: Purple & Gold.
Conference: Wisconsin State University.
SID: Terry Owens, 715-346-2840.
AD: Frank O'Brien.

WIS.-STOUT

Menomonie, WI 54751 III

Coach: Ed Meierkort, Dakota Wesleyan '81
Record: 3 Years, 9-21-0

1996 SCHEDULE

Wis.-Stevens Point ■ ....*Sept. 7
Bemidji St. ....*Sept. 14
Northern St. ■ ....Sept. 21
Wis.-River Falls ....Sept. 28
Wis.-Whitewater ....Oct. 12
Wis.-Eau Claire ■ ....Oct. 19
Wis.-La Crosse ■ ....Oct. 26
Wis.-Platteville ....Nov. 2
Wis.-Oshkosh ■ ....Nov. 9
Winona St. [Minneapolis, Minn.] ....*Nov. 17

1995 RESULTS (3-7-0)

20 Minn.-Duluth 21
50 Valley City 20
49 Bemidji St. 17
7 Wis.-River Falls 24
20 Wis.-Stevens Point 52
35 Wis.-Whitewater 48
20 Wis.-Eau Claire 15
0 Wis.-La Crosse 56
9 Wis.-Platteville 16
7 Wis.-Oshkosh 28
217 **297**

Nickname: Blue Devils.
Stadium: Nelson Field (1936), 5,000 capacity. Natural turf.
Colors: Navy Blue & White.
Conference: Wisconsin State University.
SID: Layne Pitt, 715-232-2275.
AD: Steve Terry.

WIS.-WHITEWATER

Whitewater, WI 53190 III

Coach: Bob Berezowitz, Wis.-Whitewater '67
Record: 10 Years, 74-38-4

1996 SCHEDULE

Carroll (Wis.) ....Sept. 7
Baldwin-Wallace ■ ....Sept. 14
Iowa Wesleyan ....Sept. 21
Wis.-Platteville ....Sept. 28
Wis.-Eau Claire ....Oct. 5
Wis.-Stout ■ ....Oct. 12
Wis.-River Falls ....Oct. 19
Wis.-Stevens Point ■ ....Oct. 26
Wis.-Oshkosh ....Nov. 2
Wis.-La Crosse ■ ....Nov. 9

1995 RESULTS (7-3-0)

6 Baldwin-Wallace 3
47 Valparaiso 0
28 Iowa Wesleyan 7
17 Wis.-Platteville 12
35 Wis.-Eau Claire 14
48 Wis.-Stout 35
7 Wis.-River Falls 17
24 Wis.-Stevens Point 31
48 Wis.-Oshkosh 14
14 Wis.-La Crosse 45
274 **178**

Nickname: Warhawks.
Stadium: Warhawk (1970), 11,000 capacity. Natural turf.
Colors: Purple & White.
Conference: Wisconsin State University.
SID: Tom Fick, 414-472-1147.
AD: Willie Myers.

WITTENBERG

Springfield, OH 45501 III

Coach: Joe Fincham, Ohio '88
(First year as head coach)

1996 SCHEDULE

Bluffton ....Sept. 7
Allegheny ■ ....Sept. 21
Kenyon ....Sept. 28
Oberlin ■ ....*Oct. 5
Maryville (Tenn.) ■ ....Oct. 12
Ohio Wesleyan ....Oct. 19
Denison ■ ....Oct. 26
Case Reserve ....Nov. 2
Wooster ■ ....Nov. 9
Earlham ....Nov. 16

1995 RESULTS (10-0-0)

45 DePauw 35
45 Earlham 30
31 Allegheny 17
42 Kenyon 14
56 Wooster 0
15 Ohio Wesleyan 13
77 Oberlin 3
51 Denison 0
41 Maryville (Tenn.) 7
53 Ill. Benedictine 0
456 **119**

III Championship

41 Wheaton (Ill.) 63

Nickname: Tigers.
Stadium: Edwards-Maurer (1994), 2,400 capacity. Artificial turf.
Colors: Red & White.
Conference: North Coast Athletic.
SID: Alan Aldinger, 513-327-6115.
AD: Carl Schraibman.

WOFFORD

Spartanburg, SC 29303 ....I-AA

Coach: Mike Ayers, Georgetown (Ky.) '74
Record: 11 Years, 62-58-2

1996 SCHEDULE

Youngstown St. ....*Aug. 29
Lenoir-Rhyne ■ ....*Sept. 7
Western Caro. ....Sept. 14
Furman ....Sept. 21
Presbyterian ■ ....*Oct. 5
Morehead St. ■ ....Oct. 12
Newberry ....*Oct. 19
Samford ....Nov. 2
Dayton ....Nov. 9
Charleston So. ■ ....Nov. 16
Citadel ....Nov. 23

1995 RESULTS (4-7-0)

23 Lenoir-Rhyne 19
10 Citadel 27
0 Furman 38
20 Catawba 21
21 Presbyterian 20
0 Ala.-Birmingham 28
15 Newberry 17
0 Liberty 37
16 Elon 20
31 Charleston So. 23
55 Dayton 24
191 **274**

Nickname: Terriers.
Stadium: Gibbs (1996), 8,500 capacity. Natural turf.
Colors: Old Gold & Black.
Conference: I-AA Independents.
SID: Mark Cohen, 864-597-4093.
AD: Danny Morrison.

WOOSTER

Wooster, OH 44691 III

Coach: Jim Barnes, Augustana (Ill.) '81
Record: 1 Year, 5-5-0

1996 SCHEDULE

Centre ■ ....Sept. 7
Grove City ....Sept. 14
Denison ....Sept. 21
Case Reserve ■ ....Sept. 28
Earlham ....Oct. 12
Allegheny ■ ....Oct. 19
Kenyon ....Oct. 26
Oberlin ■ ....Nov. 2
Wittenberg ....Nov. 9
Ohio Wesleyan ■ ....Nov. 16

1995 RESULTS (5-5-0)

0 Kalamazoo 32
7 Ohio Wesleyan 34
27 Oberlin 0
10 Denison 7
0 Wittenberg 56
14 Case Reserve 13
17 Earlham 15
12 Allegheny 57
23 Kenyon 14
0 Trinity (Tex.) 33
110 **261**

Nickname: Fighting Scots.
Stadium: John P. Papp (1991), 4,500 capacity. Natural turf.
Colors: Black & Old Gold.
Conference: North Coast Athletic.
SID: John Finn, 330-263-2374.
AD: To be named.

WORCESTER ST.

Worcester, MA 01602 III

Coach: Brien Cullen, Worcester St. '77
Record: 11 Years, 58-43-0

1996 SCHEDULE

Worcester Tech ■ ....Sept. 14
Mass.-Dartmouth ....Sept. 21
Maine Maritime ■ ....Sept. 28
Mass.-Boston ....Oct. 5
Fitchburg St. ■ ....Oct. 12
Framingham St. ....Oct. 19
Westfield St. ■ ....Oct. 26
Bri'water (Mass.) ....Nov. 2
Nichols ■ ....Nov. 9
Mass. Maritime ■ ....Nov. 16

1995 RESULTS (9-1-0)

0 Coast Guard 35
16 Mass.-Dartmouth 2
29 Maine Maritime 22
40 Mass.-Boston 22
37 Fitchburg St. 15

31 Framingham St. 8
17 Westfield St. 6
13 Bri'water (Mass.) 0
42 Nichols 6
22 Mass. Maritime 17
247 **133**

ECAC III Playoff

12 Rensselaer 69

Nickname: Lancers.
Stadium: John Coughlin Memorial (1976), 2,500 capacity. Natural turf.
Colors: Royal Blue & Gold.
Conference: New England.
SID: Bruce Baker, 508-793-8128.
AD: Susan E. Chapman.

WORCESTER TECH

Worcester, MA 01609 III

Coach: Kevin Morris, Williams '86
Record: 3 Years, 14-13-0

1996 SCHEDULE

Westfield St. ■ ....*Sept. 7
Worcester St. ....Sept. 14
Union (N.Y.) ■ ....Sept. 21
Rensselaer ....Oct. 5
Norwich ....Oct. 12
Merchant Marine ■ ....*Oct. 19
Springfield ■ ....*Oct. 26
Western Conn. St. ....Nov. 2
Coast Guard ■ ....Nov. 9
Plymouth St. ....Nov. 16

1995 RESULTS (4-5-0)

6 Ursinus 16
0 Union (N.Y.) 44
21 Rensselaer 20
17 Norwich 8
0 Merchant Marine 10
7 Springfield 30
28 Mass.-Lowell 0
34 Coast Guard 13
7 Plymouth St. 31
120 **172**

Nickname: Engineers.
Stadium: Alumni Field (1916), 2,800 capacity. Artificial turf.
Colors: Crimson & Gray.
Conference: Freedom Football.
SID: Geoff Hassard, 508-831-5328.
AD: Raymond Gilbert.

WYOMING

Laramie, WY 82071 ....I-A

Coach: Joe Tiller, Montana St. '65
Record: 5 Years, 29-28-1

1996 SCHEDULE

Idaho ■ ....Aug. 31
Iowa St. ....Sept. 7
Hawaii ■ ....Sept. 14
Air Force ■ ....Sept. 21
UNLV ....Sept. 28
San Jose St. ....Oct. 5
Western Mich. ■ ....Oct. 12
Fresno St. ■ ....Oct. 19
Southern Methodist ■ ....Nov. 2
San Diego St. ....*Nov. 7
Colorado St. ....Nov. 16

1995 RESULTS (6-5-0)

10 Air Force 34
52 Hawaii 6
45 Oklahoma St. 25
6 Tulsa 35
27 Louisville 20
20 Brigham Young 23
24 Colorado St. 31
24 Utah 30
34 San Diego St. 31
38 Fresno St. 10
42 UTEP 19
322 **264**

Nickname: Cowboys.
Stadium: War Memorial (1950), 33,500 capacity. Natural turf.
Colors: Brown & Yellow.
Conference: Western Athletic.
SID: Kevin McKinney, 307-766-2256.
AD: Lee Moon.

YALE

New Haven, CT 06520 ....I-AA

Coach: Carmen Cozza, Miami (Ohio) '52
Record: 31 Years, 177-111-5

1996 SCHEDULE

Brown ....Sept. 21
Connecticut ■ ....Sept. 28
Army ....Oct. 5
Bucknell ■ ....Oct. 12
Dartmouth ....Oct. 19
Columbia ■ ....Oct. 26
Pennsylvania ....Nov. 2
Cornell ■ ....Nov. 9
Princeton ■ ....Nov. 16
Harvard ....Nov. 23

1995 RESULTS (3-7-0)

42 Brown 38
10 Lehigh 21
20 Connecticut 39
28 Holy Cross 17
7 Dartmouth 22
7 Columbia 21
6 Pennsylvania 16
10 Cornell 38
21 Princeton 13
21 Harvard 22
172 **247**

Nickname: Elis, Bulldogs.
Stadium: Yale Bowl (1914), 60,000 capacity. Natural turf.
Colors: Yale Blue & White.
Conference: Ivy League.
SID: Steve Conn, 203-432-1456.
AD: Tom Beckett.

YOUNGSTOWN ST.

Youngstown, OH 44555 ....I-AA

Coach: Jim Tressel, Baldwin-Wallace '75
Record: 10 Years, 87-41-2

1996 SCHEDULE

Wofford ■ ....*Aug. 29
Slippery Rock ■ ....*Sept. 7
Kent ....*Sept. 14
Illinois St. ....*Sept. 21
Clarion ■ ....*Sept. 28
Buffalo ....Oct. 12
Ashland ■ ....*Oct. 19
Northwestern St. ■ ....Oct. 26
Northern Iowa ■ ....Nov. 2
Southwest Mo. St. ....Nov. 9
Hofstra ....Nov. 16

1995 RESULTS (3-8-0)

14 Kent 17
0 Stephen F. Austin 27
28 Slippery Rock 12
3 McNeese St. 31
13 Delaware 34
25 Central Mich. 46
56 Wingate 7
6 Indiana St. 13
24 Akron 10
6 Buffalo 9
13 Illinois St. 30
188 **236**

Nickname: Penguins.
Stadium: Arnold D. Stambaugh (1982), 16,000 capacity. Artificial turf.
Colors: Red & White.
Conference: I-AA Independents.
SID: Greg Gulas, 216-742-3192.
AD: Jim Tressel.

1996 Divisions I-A and I-AA Schedules by Date

This listing by dates includes all 1996 season games involving Divisions I-A and I-AA teams, as of printing deadline.

Neutral sites, indicated by footnote numbers, are listed at the end of each date. Asterisks (*) before the visiting team indicate night games.

Game dates and starting times are subject to change.

SATURDAY, AUGUST 24

HOME **OPPONENT**
Brigham Young ....Texas A&M

SUNDAY, AUGUST 25

HOME **OPPONENT**
Penn St. [1] ....Southern Cal
[1] East Rutherford, N.J.

THURSDAY, AUGUST 29

HOME **OPPONENT**
Buffalo ....*Illinois St.
Central Fla. ....*William & Mary
East Tenn. St. ....*Liberty
Kansas ....*Ball St.
Maine [1] ....*Northeastern
New Mexico St. ....*New Mexico
Northeast La. ....*Nicholls St.
Northern Ariz. ....*Western N.M.
Ohio ....*Akron
Stephen F. Austin ....*Eastern N.M.
Wake Forest ....*Appalachian St.
Western Ill. ....*Northwestern Okla.
Western Ky. ....*Ky. Wesleyan
Western Mich. ....*Eastern Ill.
Youngstown St. ....*Wofford
[1] Portland, Maine

FRIDAY, AUGUST 30

HOME **OPPONENT**
Cincinnati ....*Tulane

SATURDAY, AUGUST 31

HOME **OPPONENT**
Air Force ....San Jose St.
Alabama ....Bowling Green
Alcorn St. ....Troy St.
Arizona ....*UTEP
Auburn ....*Ala.-Birmingham
Bethune-Cookman ....Morehouse
Boise St. ....*Central Mich.
Brigham Young ....*Arkansas St.
Central St. [1] ....*Morgan St.
Colorado ....Washington St.
Colorado St. ....Tenn.-Chatt.
Eastern Mich. ....*Temple
Florida ....*Southwestern La.
Fresno St. ....*Oregon
Georgia ....Southern Miss.
Hawaii ....*Boston College
Houston ....*Sam Houston St.
Indiana St. ....*Mars Hill
Kansas St. ....Texas Tech
Kentucky ....*Louisville
Louisiana Tech ....*Middle Tenn. St.

SCHEDULES/RESULTS

Maryland	*Northern Ill.
Memphis	*Miami (Fla.)
Miami (Ohio)	Kent
Michigan	Illinois
Michigan St.	Purdue
Mississippi	*Idaho St.
North Caro.	Clemson
North Caro. A&T [2]	N.C. Central
Oklahoma St.	*Southwest Mo. St.
Pittsburgh	*West Va.
Prairie View [3]	*Texas Southern
Rhode Island	American Int'l
Rutgers	*Villanova
South Caro. St.	*Ga. Southern
Southern Ill.	Central Ark.
Southern Methodist	*Tulsa
Southern Utah	*Northern Iowa
Southwest Tex. St.	*Grand Valley St.
Tennessee	*UNLV
Tennessee St.	*Florida A&M
Texas	*Missouri
Utah St.	*Utah
Wyoming	Idaho

[1] Columbus, Ohio
[2] Raleigh, N.C.
[3] Houston, Texas

SUNDAY, SEPTEMBER 1

HOME	OPPONENT
Alabama St. [1]	*Jackson St.
Clark Atlanta	Hampton
Morris Brown	Mississippi Val.

[1] Birmingham, Ala.

THURSDAY, SEPTEMBER 5

HOME	OPPONENT
Vanderbilt	*Notre Dame

SATURDAY, SEPTEMBER 7

HOME	OPPONENT
Akron	*Virginia Tech
Alabama	Southern Miss.
Alabama St.	*Texas Southern
Albany (N.Y.)	*Central Conn. St.
Appalachian St.	*Tennessee Tech
Arizona St.	*Washington
Arkansas	Southern Methodist
Arkansas St.	*Austin Peay
Auburn	*Fresno St.
Ball St.	Miami (Ohio)
Bethune-Cookman	Morris Brown
Boise St.	*Portland St.
Buffalo	*Connecticut
Butler	Towson St.
Cal St. Chico	San Diego
Charleston So.	South Caro. St.
Cincinnati	Kentucky
Clemson	Furman
Colorado St.	*Colorado
Dayton	*Morehead St.
Delaware	Lehigh
Delaware St.	Lock Haven
Drake	Morningside
East Caro.	East Tenn. St.
Eastern Ill.	*Pittsburg St.
Eastern Ky.	*Troy St.
Florida	*Ga. Southern
Florida A&M	*Tuskegee
Florida St.	Duke
Fordham	Maine
Grambling	*Alcorn St.
Hawaii	*Ohio
Hofstra	Cal St. Sacramento
Hope	Valparaiso
Idaho St.	*Cal Poly SLO
Illinois	Southern Cal
Iowa	Arizona
Iowa St.	Wyoming
Jacksonville St.	*West Ga.
James Madison	*Shippensburg
Kansas St.	*Indiana St.
Liberty	*Western Caro.
LSU	*Houston
Louisiana Tech [1]	*Baylor
Marshall	*Howard
Maryland	*Ala.-Birmingham
McNeese St.	*Southwest Mo. St.
Memphis	*Mississippi St.
Mercyhurst	Robert Morris
Miami (Fla.)	Citadel
Mississippi [2]	*Va. Military
Mississippi Val.	*Ark.-Pine Bluff
Monmouth (N.J.)	Southern Conn. St.
Murray St.	*Western Ky.
Nebraska	Michigan St.
UNLV	*Air Force
New Mexico	*Northern Ariz.
North Caro. A&T	Winston-Salem
North Caro. St.	Georgia Tech
North Texas	*Illinois St.
Northeast La.	*Minnesota
Northern Ill.	*Western Ill.
Northern Iowa	*St. Cloud St.
Northwestern St.	*Southern-B.R.
Ohio St.	Rice
Oklahoma	Texas Christian
Oregon	Nevada
Oregon St.	Montana
Penn St.	Louisville
Pittsburgh	*Kent
Prairie View	Abilene Christian
Rhode Island	William & Mary
Richmond	Colgate
Rutgers	*Navy
St. Francis (Pa.)	Waynesburg
St. Mary's (Cal.)	Boston U.
Sam Houston St.	*Central St.
Samford	*Knoxville
San Diego St.	*Idaho
San Jose St.	California
South Caro.	*Central Fla.
Southern Ill.	Tenn.-Martin
Stanford	Utah
Stephen F. Austin	*Delta St.
Syracuse	*North Caro.
Temple	Washington St.
Tennessee	*UCLA
Tennessee St.	*Middle Tenn. St.
Texas	*New Mexico St.
Texas Tech [3]	Oklahoma St.
Toledo	*Indiana
Utah St.	*Cal St. Northridge
Villanova	Massachusetts
Virginia	*Central Mich.
Wake Forest	Northwestern
Weber St.	*Eastern Wash.
West Va.	Western Mich.
Wisconsin	Eastern Mich.
Wofford	*Lenoir-Rhyne
Youngstown St.	*Slippery Rock

[1] Shreveport, La.
[2] Jackson, Miss.
[3] Dallas, Texas

THURSDAY, SEPTEMBER 12

HOME	OPPONENT
Rutgers	*Miami (Fla.)

FRIDAY, SEPTEMBER 13

HOME	OPPONENT
Howard	*Hampton

SATURDAY, SEPTEMBER 14

HOME	OPPONENT
Akron	*Toledo
Alabama	Vanderbilt
Ala.-Birmingham	*Arkansas St.
Arizona	*Illinois
Arizona St.	*North Texas
Army	Ohio
Boise St.	*Eastern Wash.
Boston College	Virginia Tech
Bowling Green	Temple
Bucknell	Towson St.
California	San Diego St.
Cal St. Northridge	*UC Davis
Central Mich.	Louisiana Tech
Citadel	*Richmond
Colgate	Buffalo
Colorado	Michigan
Connecticut	Northeastern
Cumberland (Tenn.)	Evansville
Dayton	*Georgetown (Ky.)
Duke	Northwestern
Duquesne	Marist
East Tenn. St.	*Glenville St.
Eastern Ill.	*Indiana St.
Fairfield	*Central Conn. St.
Furman	South Caro. St.
Gannon	Canisius
Georgia Tech	Wake Forest
Grambling [1]	Central St
Hardin-Simmons	Prairie View
Holy Cross	Massachusetts
Idaho	St. Mary's (Cal.)
Illinois St.	*Southeast Mo. St.
Indiana	Miami (Ohio)
Iona	Wagner
Iowa	Iowa St.
Kansas St.	*Cincinnati
Kent	*Youngstown St.
Lafayette	Millersville
Lehigh	Fordham
Liberty	Delaware St.
Louisville	Baylor
Maine	Boston U.
Marshall	*West Va. St.
Maryville (Tenn.)	Davidson
McNeese St.	*James Madison
Middle Tenn. St.	*Tenn.-Chatt.
Minnesota	*Ball St.
Mississippi	*Auburn
Missouri	*Memphis
Monmouth (N.J.)	St. Francis (Pa.)
Montana	Cal Poly SLO
Morgan St.	Bethune-Cookman
Murray St.	*Southern Ill.
Nevada	Montana St.
UNLV	*Wisconsin
New Mexico	*Central Fla.
Nicholls St.	*Jacksonville St.
North Caro. A&T	Fayetteville St.
Northern Ariz.	*Southern Utah
Northern Iowa	*Stephen F. Austin
Notre Dame	Purdue
Oklahoma St.	*Tulsa
Oregon	Colorado St.
Penn St.	Northern Ill.
Pittsburgh	*Houston
Presbyterian	Charleston So.
Rhode Island	New Hampshire
Robert Morris	Butler
Sacred Heart	St. John's (N.Y.)
St. Norbert	Drake
Samford	*Austin Peay
San Diego	*Cal Lutheran
South Caro.	*Georgia
Southern-B.R.	*Alabama St.
Southern Cal	Oregon St.
Southern Methodist	*Utah
Southern Miss.	Utah St.
Southwest Mo. St.	*Truman St.
Southwest Tex. St.	*Hofstra
Southwestern La.	*Texas A&M
Stanford	San Jose St.
Tennessee St. [2]	*Jackson St.
UTEP	*New Mexico St.
Tex. A&M-Kingsville	*Sam Houston St.
Texas Christian	*Kansas
Tulane	*Rice
UCLA	*Northeast La.
Valparaiso	Alma

HOME	OPPONENT
Villanova	Delaware
Virginia	Maryland
Washington	Brigham Young
Weber St.	*Western St.
West Va.	East Caro.
Western Caro.	Wofford
Western Ill.	Alcorn St.
Western Ky.	*Eastern Ky.
Western Mich.	*Eastern Mich.
William & Mary	Va. Military
Wyoming	Hawaii

[1] Pontiac, Mich.
[2] Memphis, Tenn.

THURSDAY, SEPTEMBER 19

HOME	OPPONENT
North Caro. St.	*Florida St.

SATURDAY, SEPTEMBER 21

HOME	OPPONENT
Ala.-Birmingham	*Jacksonville St.
Alcorn St.	*Alabama St.
Arizona St.	*Nebraska
Arkansas [1]	*Alabama
Arkansas St.	*Northern Ill.
Army	Duke
Auburn	LSU
Austin Peay	*Western Ky.
Ball St.	Central Fla.
Baylor	*Oregon St.
Bethune-Cookman	Norfolk St.
Boston U.	James Madison
Brigham Young	New Mexico
Brown	Yale
Bucknell	William & Mary
Butler	Millikin
California	Nevada
UC Davis	*Cal St. Sacramento
Cal Poly SLO	*Weber St.
Central Mich.	Western Mich.
Charleston So.	West Va. St.
Citadel	*Western Caro.
Colgate	Holy Cross
Colorado St.	UNLV
Columbia	Harvard
Cornell	Princeton
Dartmouth	Pennsylvania
Dayton	Wis.-Platteville
Delaware	West Chester
Delaware St.	N.C. Central
Drake	San Diego
East Tenn. St.	Va. Military
Eastern Ky.	*Appalachian St.
Eastern Mich.	*Toledo
Eastern Wash.	*Southwest Tex. St.
Fairfield	Georgetown
Frostburg St.	Central Conn. St.
Furman	Wofford
Gannon	St. Francis (Pa.)
Georgia	Texas Tech
Ga. Southern	Marshall
Grambling	*Langston
Hampton	North Caro. A&T
Hawaii	*Boise St.
Hofstra	Western Ill.
Houston	Southern Cal
Howard	Virginia St.
Idaho St.	*Western Mont.
Illinois	Akron
Illinois St.	*Youngstown St.
Indiana St.	*St. Joseph's (Ind.)
Iowa St.	Northern Iowa
Jackson St.	*Florida A&M
Kentucky	*Indiana
Lafayette	Northeastern
Lehigh	Buffalo
Maine	Rhode Island
Marist	Iona
McNeese St.	*Angelo St.
Memphis	*Tulane
Miami (Ohio)	Bowling Green
Michigan	Boston College
Michigan St.	Louisville
Minnesota	*Syracuse
Mississippi St.	*Louisiana Tech
Missouri	*Clemson
Monmouth (N.J.)	Pace
Montana St.	Minn.-Duluth
Morgan St.	Liberty
Navy	*Southern Methodist
New Hampshire	Connecticut
New Mexico St.	*Cal St. Northridge
North Caro.	Georgia Tech
Northeast La.	*Sam Houston St.
Northwestern	Ohio
Northwestern St.	*East Tex. St.
Ohio St.	Pittsburgh
Oklahoma St.	*Utah St.
Portland St.	Northern Ariz.
Prairie View [2]	*Southern-B.R.
Purdue	*West Va.
Quincy	Evansville
Rice	*Kansas St.
Richmond	Massachusetts
Robert Morris	Towson St.
St. John's (N.Y.)	Duquesne
St. Peter's	Siena
San Diego St.	Oklahoma
San Jose St.	UTEP
Sewanee	Davidson
Sonoma St.	St. Mary's (Cal.)
South Caro.	*East Caro.
Southeast Mo. St.	Murray St.
Southern Ill.	Winston-Salem
Southern Miss.	Southwestern La.
Southern Utah	*Western St.
Temple [3]	Penn St.
Tennessee	Florida
Tenn.-Chatt.	Mississippi Val.
Tenn.-Martin	*Southwest Mo. St.
Tennessee Tech	*Samford
Texas	Notre Dame
Texas A&M	North Texas
Texas Southern	Lane
Troy St.	*Nicholls St.
Tulsa	*Iowa
Utah	*Fresno St.
Valparaiso	Morehead St.
Vanderbilt	*Mississippi
Villanova	Fordham
Virginia Tech	Rutgers
Wagner	LIU-C.W. Post
Wake Forest	Virginia
Washington	Arizona
Washington St.	Oregon
Wisconsin	Stanford
Wyoming	Air Force

[1] Little Rock, Ark.
[2] Houston, Texas
[3] East Rutherford, N.J.

THURSDAY, SEPTEMBER 26

HOME	OPPONENT
Georgia Tech	*Duke

FRIDAY, SEPTEMBER 27

HOME	OPPONENT
St. John's (N.Y.)	*Fairfield

SATURDAY, SEPTEMBER 28

HOME	OPPONENT
Air Force	Rice
Appalachian St.	Citadel
Arizona St.	*Oregon
Arkansas [1]	*Northeast La.
Boise St.	*Northwestern St.
Boston College	Navy
Boston U.	Richmond
Bowling Green	Central Mich.
Brigham Young	Southern Methodist
Bucknell	Harvard
Buffalo	*Edinboro
California	Oregon St.
Cal Poly SLO	Central Wash.
Cal St. Sacramento	*Montana
Canisius	St. Peter's
Central Conn. St.	Robert Morris
Charleston So.	Hofstra
Cheyney	Morgan St.
Cincinnati	*Miami (Ohio)
Clemson	Wake Forest
Clinch Valley	Butler
Davidson	Emory & Henry
Duquesne	Gannon
East Caro.	Central Fla.
Eastern Ky.	*Tennessee Tech
Eastern Wash.	*Portland St.
Florida	Kentucky
Florida A&M	*Howard
Florida St.	North Caro.
Fordham	Columbia
Fresno St.	*Hawaii
Hampton [2]	*Central St.
Illinois St.	Southern Ill.
Indiana	Northwestern
Iowa St.	Missouri
Jackson St.	*Mississippi Val.
James Madison	New Hampshire
Lafayette	Cornell
Lehigh	Dartmouth
Liberty	Indiana St.
LIU-C.W. Post	Monmouth (N.J.)
LSU	*New Mexico St.
Louisiana Tech	*Southwestern La.
Louisville	Southern Miss.
Maine	Delaware
Marshall	*Western Ky.
Massachusetts	Northeastern
Miami (Fla.)	Pittsburgh
Michigan	UCLA
Michigan St.	Eastern Mich.
Montana St.	Idaho St.
Morehead St.	*Ky. Wesleyan
Murray St.	*Middle Tenn. St.
Nebraska	Colorado St.
Nevada	Kent
UNLV	Wyoming
New Mexico	*Texas Christian
Norfolk St.	Delaware St.
North Texas [3]	Army
Northern Ariz.	*Cal St. Northridge
Northern Ill.	UTEP
Northern Iowa	*McNeese St.
Notre Dame	Ohio St.
Oklahoma	Tulsa
Pace	Iona
Pennsylvania	Colgate
Prairie View	Grambling
Princeton	Holy Cross
Purdue	North Caro. St.
Rhode Island	Brown
Sam Houston St.	Texas Southern
St. Mary's (Cal.)	Drake
Samford	*Alcorn St.
San Diego	*Valparaiso
Siena	Georgetown
South Caro.	Mississippi St.
South Caro. St.	Johnson Smith
Southeast Mo. St.	Austin Peay
Southern Utah	*Montana Tech
Southwest Mo. St.	*Jacksonville St.
Southwest Tex. St.	*Idaho
Stephen F. Austin	*Troy St.
Syracuse	Virginia Tech
Tenn.-Chatt.	Ga. Southern
Tenn.-Martin	Eastern Ill.
Tennessee St. [4]	Southern-B.R.
Texas A&M	Colorado
Texas Tech	*Utah St.
Toledo	*Weber St.
Towson St.	Dayton
Utah	*Kansas
Virginia	*Texas
Va. Military	Furman
Wagner	Marist

Washington St.	San Jose St.
West Va.	Maryland
Western Caro.	*East Tenn. St.
Western Mich.	*Akron
Wisconsin	Penn St.
Yale	Connecticut
Youngstown St.	*Clarion

[1] Little Rock, Ark.
[2] East Rutherford, N.J.
[3] Irving, Texas
[4] Atlanta, Ga.

THURSDAY, OCTOBER 3

HOME	OPPONENT
Tennessee [1]	*Mississippi

[1] Memphis, Tenn.

FRIDAY, OCTOBER 4

HOME	OPPONENT
Utah St.	*Brigham Young

SATURDAY, OCTOBER 5

HOME	OPPONENT
Alabama	Kentucky
Ala.-Birmingham	*Western Ky.
Alcorn St.	*Ark.-Pine Bluff
Arizona	*Washington St.
Arizona St.	*Boise St.
Arkansas	Florida
Arkansas St.	*Central Ark.
Army	Yale
Auburn	South Caro.
Bethune-Cookman	Delaware St.
Bucknell	Pennsylvania
Buffalo	Cornell
Cal St. Northridge	*Portland St.
Charleston So.	Morehead St.
Colgate	Brown
Connecticut	Villanova
Dartmouth	Fordham
Davidson	*Guilford
Delaware	Boston U.
Drake	Butler
East Tenn. St.	*Appalachian St.
Eastern Ky.	Southeast Mo. St.
Eastern Wash.	Montana St.
Evansville	Dayton
Fairfield	*St. Peter's
Florida A&M [1]	Hampton
Florida St.	*Clemson
Furman	Western Caro.
Georgetown	Marist
Georgia Tech	Virginia
Ga. Southern	Va. Military
Harvard	Lafayette
Hawaii	Colorado St.
Holy Cross	Columbia
Idaho	Cal Poly SLO
Idaho St.	*Cal St. Sacramento
Illinois	Indiana
Iona	Canisius
Iowa	Michigan St.
Jackson St.	Texas Southern
Jacksonville St.	Middle Tenn. St.
James Madison	Maine
Kansas St.	Nebraska
Kent	Akron
Langston	Prairie View
LSU	*Vanderbilt
Marshall	*Tenn.-Chatt.
Maryland	North Caro. St.
McNeese St.	*Ark.-Monticello
Memphis	*Cincinnati
Mercyhurst	Monmouth (N.J.)
Miami (Ohio)	Central Mich.
Mississippi St.	*Georgia
Montana	Southern Utah
Murray St.	Austin Peay
Navy	Duke
UNLV	Nevada
Northeast La.	*Northwestern St.
Northeastern	Richmond
Northern Ariz.	Weber St.
Northern Ill.	North Texas
Northwestern	Michigan
Ohio	Eastern Mich.
Ohio St.	Penn St.
Oklahoma	Kansas
Oregon	UCLA
Pittsburgh	Temple
Princeton	Lehigh
Purdue	Minnesota
Rhode Island	Massachusetts
Rice	*New Mexico
Robert Morris	Gannon
St. Francis (Pa.)	Wagner
St. Mary's (Cal.)	San Diego
Samford	Nicholls St.
San Diego St.	*Air Force
San Jose St.	Wyoming
Siena	Duquesne
South Caro. St.	Morgan St.
Southern-B.R.	*Mississippi Val.
Southern Cal	California
Southern Methodist	*Missouri
Southwest Mo. St.	Southern Ill.
Southwestern La.	*Houston
Syracuse	Rutgers
Tennessee St.	Lane
Tennessee Tech	Tenn.-Martin
Texas	Oklahoma St.
UTEP	*Utah
Texas A&M	Louisiana Tech
Texas Tech	*Baylor
Toledo	*Bowling Green
Towson St.	*Central Conn. St.
Troy St. [2]	*Alabama St.
Tulane	*Texas Christian
Wake Forest	North Caro.
Washington	Stanford
West Va.	Boston College
Western Ill.	Indiana St.
Western Mich.	Ball St.
William & Mary	New Hampshire
Wofford	*Presbyterian

[1] Indianapolis, Ind.
[2] Mobile, Ala.

THURSDAY, OCTOBER 10

HOME	OPPONENT
East Caro.	*Southern Miss.

FRIDAY, OCTOBER 11

HOME	OPPONENT
St. Peter's	*St. John's (N.Y.)

SATURDAY, OCTOBER 12

HOME	OPPONENT
Air Force	Navy
Alabama St. [1]	*Clark Atlanta
Appalachian St.	Furman
Arkansas [2]	*Louisiana Tech
Ball St.	Ohio
Bowling Green	Kent
Brigham Young	UNLV
Buffalo	Youngstown St.
Cal Poly SLO	St. Mary's (Cal.)
Cal St. Sacramento	*Eastern Wash.
Canisius	Siena
Central Conn. St.	Stony Brook
Central Fla.	Samford
Central Mich.	Akron
Charleston So.	Newberry
Cincinnati	*Boston College
Citadel	East Tenn. St.
Colorado	*Oklahoma St.
Connecticut	Maine
Dartmouth	Holy Cross
Davidson	Wash. & Lee
Dayton	Robert Morris
Delaware St.	Hampton
Duke	Clemson
Eastern Ill.	Western Ill.
Eastern Mich.	*Miami (Ohio)
Evansville	Drake
Florida	LSU
Florida A&M	North Caro. A&T
Fordham	Lafayette
Fresno St.	*San Jose St.
Georgetown	Iona
Georgia	Tennessee
Harvard	Cornell
Houston	*Memphis
Howard	Bethune-Cookman
Indiana	Iowa
Iowa St.	Texas A&M
Jacksonville St.	Western Ky.
James Madison	William & Mary
Kansas	Texas Tech
Kentucky	*South Caro.
Liberty	Hofstra
Marist	Fairfield
Massachusetts	Boston U.
Miami (Fla.)	Florida St.
Michigan St.	Illinois
Middle Tenn. St.	Austin Peay
Mississippi St.	*Auburn
Mississippi Val.	Grambling
Missouri	Kansas St.
Montana	Idaho St.
Montana St.	Northern Ariz.
Nebraska	Baylor
Nevada	Boise St.
New Hampshire	Lehigh
New Mexico St.	*Utah St.
Nicholls St.	*Northwestern St.
North Caro.	Maryland
North Caro. St.	Alabama
North Texas	Vanderbilt
Northeastern	Villanova
Northern Iowa	Illinois St.
Northwestern	Minnesota
Notre Dame	Washington
Ohio St.	Wisconsin
Oregon St.	Washington St.
Pennsylvania	Columbia
Penn St.	Purdue
Prairie View	Alcorn St.
Princeton	Brown
Richmond	Delaware
Rutgers	Army
St. Francis (Pa.)	Duquesne
San Diego St.	*Hawaii
Southern Cal	Arizona
Southern Ill.	Indiana St.
Southern Utah	Southwest Tex. St.
Southwestern La.	Arkansas St.
Stanford	Oregon
Stephen F. Austin	Sam Houston St.
Syracuse	Pittsburgh
Tenn.-Martin	*Murray St.
Tennessee Tech	Southeast Mo. St.
Texas [3]	Oklahoma
Texas Christian	*UTEP
Texas Southern	*Ark.-Pine Bluff
Towson St.	Colgate
Troy St.	*McNeese St.
Tulane	*Louisville
Tulsa	Colorado St.
UCLA	Arizona St.
Valparaiso	Butler
Va. Military	Marshall
Virginia Tech	Temple
Wagner	*Monmouth (N.J.)
Weber St.	Cal St. Northridge
Western Caro.	Ga. Southern
Wofford	Morehead St.
Wyoming	Western Mich.
Yale	Bucknell

[1] Mobile, Ala.
[2] Little Rock, Ark.
[3] Dallas, Texas

SATURDAY, OCTOBER 19

HOME	OPPONENT
Akron	Miami (Ohio)
Alabama	Mississippi
Ala.-Birmingham	Southwestern La.
Alcorn St.	*Texas Southern
Arizona St.	*Southern Cal
Arkansas St.	Southeast Mo. St.
Army	Tulane
Austin Peay	Tennessee Tech
Baylor	Oklahoma
Boise St.	*Utah St.
Boston College	Rutgers
Boston U.	Hofstra
Bowling Green	Ball St.
Brown	Fordham
Bucknell	Princeton
Butler	Dayton
Cal Poly SLO	Southern Utah
Cal St. Northridge	*Montana St.
Central Fla.	Northeast La.
Central Mich.	Eastern Mich.
Cincinnati	Houston
Clemson	Georgia Tech
Colorado St.	San Jose St.
Columbia	Lafayette
Connecticut	Rhode Island
Cornell	Colgate
Dartmouth	Yale
Delaware	Northeastern
Delaware St.	Florida A&M
Drake	Valparaiso
Duquesne	Georgetown
Eastern Ill.	Murray St.
Eastern Wash.	Montana
Fairfield	Canisius
Florida	Auburn
Furman	Citadel
Georgia	Vanderbilt
Ga. Southern	Appalachian St.
Grambling [1]	*Ark.-Pine Bluff
Hawaii	*UNLV
Holy Cross	Harvard
Idaho	Nevada
Indiana St.	Illinois St.
Iona	Siena
Jacksonville St.	Samford
Kansas	Colorado
Kent	Ohio
LSU	*Kentucky
Louisiana Tech	Toledo
Louisville	Northern Ill.
Maine	New Hampshire
Marist	St. John's (N.Y.)
Marshall	*Western Caro.
Maryland	Wake Forest
Massachusetts	Buffalo
Methodist	Davidson
Miami (Fla.)	East Caro.
Michigan	Indiana
Middle Tenn. St.	Eastern Ky.
Minnesota	Michigan St.
Mississippi Val.	Lane
Monmouth (N.J.)	Towson St.
Morehouse	Howard
New Mexico	*San Diego St.
Newberry	*Wofford
Nicholls St.	Stephen F. Austin
North Caro. A&T	Morgan St.
North Texas	New Mexico St.
Northern Ariz.	Cal St. Sacramento
Northern Iowa	*Southwest Mo. St.
Northwestern St.	Sam Houston St.
Notre Dame	Air Force
Oklahoma St.	Iowa St.
Oregon St.	Stanford
Pennsylvania	Lehigh
Penn St.	Iowa
Portland St.	*Weber St.
Prairie View	Alabama St.
Purdue	Ohio St.
Rice	Southern Methodist
Richmond	James Madison
St. Francis (Pa.)	Mercyhurst
San Diego	*Evansville
South Caro.	Arkansas
South Caro. St.	Bethune-Cookman
Southern-B.R.	*Jackson St.
Southern Ill.	Western Ill.
Southern Miss.	Memphis
Temple	West Va.
Tenn.-Chatt.	Va. Military
Tennessee St.	*Tenn.-Martin
Texas A&M	Kansas St.
Texas Tech	Nebraska
Troy St.	Southwest Tex. St.
Tulsa	Brigham Young
Utah	Texas Christian
Villanova	William & Mary
Virginia	North Caro. St.
Wagner	St. Peter's
Washington	UCLA
Washington St.	California
Western Ky.	*Liberty
Wisconsin	Northwestern
Wyoming	Fresno St.
Youngstown St.	*Ashland

[1] Shreveport, La.

SATURDAY, OCTOBER 26

HOME	OPPONENT
Air Force	Hawaii
Alabama A&M [1]	Alabama St.
Alcorn St.	Southern-B.R.
Appalachian St.	Marshall
Arizona	*Oregon St.
Baylor	Iowa St.
Boston College	Syracuse
Brown	Pennsylvania
Butler	San Diego
California	UCLA
UC Davis	*St. Mary's (Cal.)
Cal St. Sacramento	*Cal St. Northridge
Canisius	St. John's (N.Y.)
Central Conn. St.	Wagner
Central Mich.	Ball St.
Citadel	Ga. Southern
Colgate	Lafayette
Colorado	Texas
Colorado St.	San Diego St.
Connecticut	Hofstra
Cornell	Dartmouth
Davidson	Randolph-Macon
Dayton	Drake
Delaware	James Madison
Duke	Maryland
Duquesne	Iona
East Tenn. St.	Furman
Eastern Mich.	Kent
Evansville	Valparaiso
Florida St.	Virginia
Fordham	Georgetown
Georgia Tech	Central Fla.
Grambling	Jackson St.
Holy Cross	Bucknell
Houston	*North Caro.
Howard	North Caro. A&T
Idaho St.	Eastern Wash.
Illinois St.	Southwest Mo. St.
Indiana	Penn St.
Iowa	Ohio St.
Jacksonville St.	*Troy St.
Kansas St.	Oklahoma
Kentucky	*Georgia
Liberty	Charleston So.
LSU	*Mississippi St.
Louisiana Tech	*Ala.-Birmingham
Louisville	Cincinnati
Miami (Ohio)	Army
Michigan St.	Wisconsin
Minnesota	*Michigan
Mississippi	*Arkansas St.
Missouri	Oklahoma St.
Montana	Northern Ariz.
Montana St.	Portland St.
Morehead St.	St. Joseph's (Ind.)
Morgan St.	Delaware St.
Nebraska	Kansas
UNLV	Fresno St.
New Hampshire	Massachusetts
New Mexico St.	*Southern Utah
North Texas	Nevada
Northern Ill.	Akron
Northwestern	Illinois
Ohio	Bowling Green
Oregon	Washington
Princeton	Harvard
Rhode Island	Boston U.
Richmond	Villanova
Robert Morris	Monmouth (N.J.)
Rutgers	Temple
St. Peter's	Marist
Sam Houston St.	McNeese St.
Siena	Fairfield
South Caro. St.	Hampton
Southeast Mo. St.	Middle Tenn. St.
Southern Ill.	Northern Iowa
Southern Methodist	*New Mexico
Southwest Tex. St.	Nicholls St.
Southwestern La.	*Memphis
Stanford	Arizona St.
Stephen F. Austin	Samford
Tennessee	Alabama
Tenn.-Martin	Eastern Ky.
Tennessee St.	Austin Peay
Tennessee Tech	Eastern Ill.
UTEP	*Rice
Texas A&M	Texas Tech
Texas Christian	Brigham Young
Texas Southern	Mississippi Val.
Toledo	Western Mich.
Towson St.	St. Francis (Pa.)
Tulane	*Southern Miss.
Utah	Tulsa
Utah St.	Idaho
Vanderbilt	South Caro.
Virginia Tech	Pittsburgh
Wake Forest	Navy
Washington St.	Southern Cal
West Va.	Miami (Fla.)
Western Caro.	Tenn.-Chatt.
Western Ill.	Cal Poly SLO
Western Ky.	Indiana St.
William & Mary	Northeastern
Yale	Columbia
Youngstown St.	Northwestern St.

[1] Birmingham, Ala.

THURSDAY, OCTOBER 31

HOME	OPPONENT
Pittsburgh	*Boston College

SATURDAY, NOVEMBER 2

HOME	OPPONENT
Air Force	Colorado St.
Akron	Bowling Green
Ark.-Pine Bluff [1]	Jackson St.
Army	Lafayette
Auburn	Arkansas
Aurora	Drake
Austin Peay	Eastern Ill.
Boston U.	Connecticut
Brigham Young	UTEP
Butler	Evansville
California	Arizona
Cal Poly SLO	UC Davis
Cal St. Northridge	*Montana
Central Conn. St.	St. Francis (Pa.)
Central Fla.	Illinois St.
Charleston So.	New Haven
Clemson	Maryland
Columbia	Princeton
Cornell	Brown
Delaware St.	South Caro. St.
Duke	Virginia
Duquesne	Fairfield
East Caro.	Arkansas St.

SCHEDULES/RESULTS

Eastern Ky.	Tennessee St.
Eastern Mich.	Ball St.
Florida [2]	Georgia
Florida A&M	Morgan St.
Fordham	Holy Cross
Fresno St.	*Boise St.
Georgetown	Canisius
Ga. Southern	East Tenn. St.
Georgia Tech	*Florida St.
Hampden-Sydney	Davidson
Hampton	Liberty
Harvard	Dartmouth
Hofstra	Buffalo
Howard	Norfolk St.
Idaho	Eastern Wash.
Illinois	Iowa
Iona	St. Peter's
Iowa St.	Kansas
James Madison	Northeastern
Kent	Central Mich.
Lehigh	Bucknell
Louisville	Memphis
Marist	Towson St.
Marshall	Citadel
Massachusetts	Maine
McNeese St.	*Stephen F. Austin
Michigan	Michigan St.
Mississippi St.	Northeast La.
Mississippi Val.	Prairie View
Missouri	Colorado
Morehead St.	Quincy
Murray St.	Tennessee Tech
Navy [3]	Notre Dame
Nevada	New Mexico St.
New Hampshire	Richmond
Nicholls St.	*Southern-B.R.
North Caro.	North Caro. St.
North Caro. A&T	Bethune-Cookman
Northern Ariz.	*Idaho St.
Northern Ill.	Louisiana Tech
Ohio St.	Minnesota
Oklahoma	Nebraska
Oklahoma St.	Texas A&M
Oregon St.	Arizona St.
Pennsylvania	Yale
Penn St.	Northwestern
Portland St.	*Cal St. Sacramento
Rice	Utah
St. John's (N.Y.)	Siena
Samford	Wofford
San Diego	Whittier
San Jose St.	San Diego St.
South Caro.	Tennessee
Southeast Mo. St.	Tenn.-Martin
Southern Cal	Washington
Southern Miss.	Cincinnati
Southern Utah	St. Mary's (Cal.)
Southwest Mo. St.	Western Ill.
Southwest Tex. St.	Northwestern St.
Temple	Miami (Fla.)
Tenn.-Chatt.	Appalachian St.
Texas	Baylor
Texas Christian	UNLV
Texas Southern	Grambling
Toledo	Miami (Ohio)
Tulane	*Houston
Tulsa	New Mexico
UCLA	Stanford
Utah St.	North Texas
Valparaiso	Dayton
Vanderbilt	Ala.-Birmingham
Villanova	Rhode Island
Va. Military	Western Caro.
Virginia Tech	Southwestern La.
Wagner	Robert Morris
Weber St.	Montana St.
West Va.	Syracuse
Western Ky.	Southern Ill.
Western Mich.	Ohio
William & Mary	Delaware
Wisconsin	Purdue
Wyoming	Southern Methodist
Youngstown St.	Northern Iowa

[1] Little Rock, Ark.
[2] Jacksonville, Fla.
[3] Dublin, Ireland

THURSDAY, NOVEMBER 7

HOME	OPPONENT
San Diego St.	*Wyoming

FRIDAY, NOVEMBER 8

HOME	OPPONENT
St. John's (N.Y.)	*Georgetown

SATURDAY, NOVEMBER 9

HOME	OPPONENT
Ala.-Birmingham	Central Fla.
Arizona St.	*California
Arkansas	Mississippi
Arkansas St.	Louisiana Tech
Army	Air Force
Auburn	Northeast La.
Azusa Pacific	San Diego
Ball St.	Kent
Baylor	Texas A&M
Boise St.	North Texas
Boston College	Notre Dame
Bowling Green	Western Mich.
Brigham Young	Rice
Buffalo	New Haven
Cal St. Sacramento	*Weber St.
Charleston So.	Tusculum
Citadel	Tenn.-Chatt.
Colorado	Iowa St.
Connecticut	James Madison
Dartmouth	Columbia
Davidson	Centre
Dayton	Wofford
Delaware St.	North Caro. A&T
Drake	Wayne St. (Neb.)
East Tenn. St.	Marshall
Eastern Ky.	Murray St.
Eastern Mich.	Akron
Eastern Wash.	Northern Ariz.
Fairfield	*Iona
Florida St. [1]	Wake Forest
Fordham	Colgate
Fresno St.	*Colorado St.
Furman	Ga. Southern
Grambling	Alabama St.
Hampton	Bethune-Cookman
Harvard	Brown
Hawaii	*San Jose St.
Hofstra	Maine
Holy Cross	Lehigh
Houston	*Southern Miss.
Idaho	New Mexico St.
Idaho St.	*Cal St. Northridge
Illinois	Ohio St.
Indiana St.	Northern Iowa
Iowa	Northwestern
Jackson St.	*Central St.
Kansas	Kansas St.
Kentucky	Mississippi St.
Ky. Wesleyan	Evansville
Lafayette	Bucknell
Liberty	Livingstone
LSU	*Alabama
Marist	Canisius
McNeese St.	*Southwest Tex. St.
Memphis	Tennessee
Miami (Ohio)	Ohio
Michigan St.	Indiana
Mississippi Val.	Alcorn St.
Monmouth (N.J.)	Siena
Montana	Portland St.
Montana St.	Cal Poly SLO
Morehead St.	Western Ky.
Navy	Delaware
Nebraska	Missouri
New Hampshire	Villanova
New Mexico	Utah
Nicholls St.	*Sam Houston St.
North Caro.	Louisville
North Caro. St.	Duke
Northeastern	Boston U.
Northwestern St.	*Troy St.
Oklahoma St.	Oklahoma
Oregon	Arizona
Prairie View	Midwestern St.
Princeton	Pennsylvania
Purdue	Michigan
Rutgers	West Va.
St. Francis (Pa.)	Robert Morris
St. Joseph's (Ind.)	Butler
St. Mary's (Cal.)	Chapman
St. Peter's	Duquesne
South Caro. St.	Howard
Southeast Mo. St.	Eastern Ill.
Southern-B.R.	*Florida A&M
Southern Conn. St.	Central Conn. St.
Southwest Mo. St.	Youngstown St.
Southwestern La.	*Northern Ill.
Stanford	Southern Cal
Stephen F. Austin	Jacksonville St.
Stony Brook	Wagner
Tenn.-Martin	Middle Tenn. St.
Tennessee Tech	Tennessee St.
UTEP	*Southern Methodist
Texas Southern	Morgan St.
Texas Tech	Texas
Toledo	Central Mich.
Tulane	Syracuse
Tulsa	Texas Christian
UCLA	Washington St.
Utah St.	Nevada
Valparaiso	Aurora
Vanderbilt	Florida
Virginia	Clemson
Va. Military	Richmond
Virginia Tech	East Caro.
Washington	Oregon St.
Western Caro.	Elon
Western Ill.	Illinois St.
William & Mary	Massachusetts
Wisconsin	Minnesota
Yale	Cornell

[1] Orlando, Fla.

THURSDAY, NOVEMBER 14

HOME	OPPONENT
Maryland	*Georgia Tech

SATURDAY, NOVEMBER 16

HOME	OPPONENT
Ala.-Birmingham	Cincinnati
Alabama St.	Mississippi Val.
Arizona	UCLA
Auburn	Georgia
Austin Peay	Eastern Ky.
Ball St.	Toledo
Baylor	Missouri
Bethune-Cookman	Valparaiso
Boston College	Temple
Boston U.	New Hampshire
Bridgewater (Va.)	Davidson
Brown	Dartmouth
Bucknell	Fordham
UC Davis	*Southern Utah
Cal St. Northridge	Eastern Wash.
Canisius	Duquesne
Central Fla.	Bowling Green
Clemson	North Caro. St.
Colorado	Kansas St.
Colorado St.	Wyoming
Columbia	Cornell
Delaware	Rhode Island
East Caro.	Ohio
Evansville	Morehead St.
Florida	South Caro.
Florida A&M [1]	South Caro. St.
Florida St.	Southern Miss.
Fresno St.	Air Force
Georgetown	St. Peter's
Ga. Southern	Liberty
Hampton	Norfolk St.

Hawaii	*Brigham Young
Hofstra	Youngstown St.
Houston	*Louisville
Howard	Morgan St.
Illinois St.	Tennessee Tech
Indiana	Ohio St.
Indiana St.	Southwest Mo. St.
Iona	St. John's (N.Y.)
Iowa	Wisconsin
Iowa St.	Nebraska
Jackson St.	Prairie View
James Madison	Villanova
Kansas	Texas
Kentucky	Vanderbilt
Lafayette	Holy Cross
Lehigh	Colgate
Maine	Buffalo
Marshall	Furman
Massachusetts	Connecticut
Miami (Fla.)	Virginia Tech
Michigan	Penn St.
Middle Tenn. St.	Eastern Ill.
Minnesota	*Illinois
Mississippi	LSU
Mississippi St.	Alabama
Monmouth (N.J.)	Central Conn. St.
Montana St.	Cal St. Sacramento
Murray St.	Tennessee St.
Navy	Tulane
Nevada	Arkansas St.
UNLV	San Diego St.
New Mexico St.	Boise St.
Nicholls St.	Harding
North Caro. A&T	Grambling
North Texas	Idaho
Northeast La.	*Jacksonville St.
Northern Iowa	*Western Ill.
Northwestern	Purdue
Northwestern La.	Drake
Northwestern St.	*McNeese St.
Notre Dame	Pittsburgh
Oregon	California
Oregon St.	Northern Ill.
Pennsylvania	Harvard
Portland St.	*Idaho St.
Richmond	William & Mary
Robert Morris	LIU-C.W. Post
St. Francis (Pa.)	Bethany (W.Va.)
St. Mary's (Cal.)	Humboldt St.
Sam Houston St.	Troy St.
Samford	Tenn.-Martin
San Diego	*Dayton
Siena	Marist
Southern-B.R.	Texas Southern
Southern Ill.	Southeast Mo. St.
Southwest Tex. St.	Stephen F. Austin
Stanford	Washington St.
Syracuse	Army
Tennessee	Arkansas
Tenn.-Chatt.	East Tenn. St.
UTEP	*Tulsa
Texas A&M	Oklahoma
Texas Christian	Rice
Texas Tech	Southwestern La.
Towson St.	Wagner
Virginia	North Caro.
Va. Military	Citadel
Wake Forest	Duke
Washington	San Jose St.
Weber St.	Montana
Western Caro.	Appalachian St.
Western Mich.	Kent
Wofford	Charleston So.
Yale	Princeton

[1] Atlanta, Ga.

THURSDAY, NOVEMBER 21

HOME	OPPONENT
Ala.-Birmingham	*Charleston So.
Southern Methodist	*Texas Christian
Troy St.	*Samford

SATURDAY, NOVEMBER 23

HOME	OPPONENT
Alabama	Auburn
Alcorn St.	Jackson St.
Appalachian St.	Va. Military
Arizona	*Arizona St.
Austin Peay	Tenn.-Martin
Boise St.	Idaho
Bucknell	Colgate
California	Stanford
Cal St. Sacramento	Cal Poly SLO
Cincinnati	Northeast La.
Citadel	Wofford
Clemson	South Caro.
Columbia	Brown
Cornell	Pennsylvania
Duke	North Caro.
Eastern Ill.	Eastern Ky.
Florida A&M [1]	Bethune-Cookman
Furman	Tenn.-Chatt.
Georgetown	Holy Cross
Georgia	Mississippi
Georgia Tech	Navy
Harvard	Yale
Hofstra	Rhode Island
Howard	Delaware St.
Idaho St.	Weber St.
Illinois	Wisconsin
Kansas St.	Iowa St.
Lafayette	Lehigh
LSU	*Tulane
Maryland [2]	Florida St.
McNeese St.	*Nicholls St.
Memphis	East Caro.
Miami (Fla.)	Boston College
Middle Tenn. St.	Tennessee Tech
Minnesota	*Iowa
Mississippi St.	Arkansas
Missouri	Kansas
Montana	Montana St.
Morgan St.	Hampton
New Mexico	UTEP
North Caro. A&T [3]	South Caro. St.
North Caro. St.	Wake Forest
Northeastern	New Hampshire
Notre Dame	Rutgers
Ohio	Toledo
Ohio St.	Michigan
Oklahoma	Texas Tech
Oklahoma St.	Baylor
Oregon St.	Oregon
Penn St.	Michigan St.
Princeton	Dartmouth
Purdue	Indiana
Rice	Tulsa
Sam Houston St.	Southwest Tex. St.
San Diego St.	*Fresno St.
San Jose St.	UNLV
Stephen F. Austin	Northwestern St.
Temple	Syracuse
Tennessee	Kentucky
Tennessee St.	Southeast Mo. St.
UCLA	Southern Cal
Utah	Brigham Young
Virginia Tech	West Va.
Washington St.	Washington

[1] Tampa, Fla.
[2] Fort Lauderdale, Fla.
[3] Charlotte, N.C.

THURSDAY, NOVEMBER 28

HOME	OPPONENT
Alabama St.	Tuskegee
St. John's (N.Y.)	Stony Brook

FRIDAY, NOVEMBER 29

HOME	OPPONENT
Arkansas [1]	LSU
Nebraska	Colorado
Texas	Texas A&M
Virginia Tech	Virginia

[1] Little Rock, Ark.

SATURDAY, NOVEMBER 30

HOME	OPPONENT
East Caro. [1]	North Caro. St.
Florida St.	Florida
Georgia	Georgia Tech
Hawaii	*Wisconsin
Mississippi	*Mississippi St.
Pittsburgh	Rutgers
Southern-B.R. [2]	Grambling
Southern Cal	Notre Dame
Syracuse	Miami (Fla.)
Vanderbilt	Tennessee

[1] Charlotte, N.C.
[2] New Orleans, La.

SATURDAY, DECEMBER 7

HOME	OPPONENT
Navy [1]	Army

[1] Philadelphia, Pa.